OFFICIAL 200

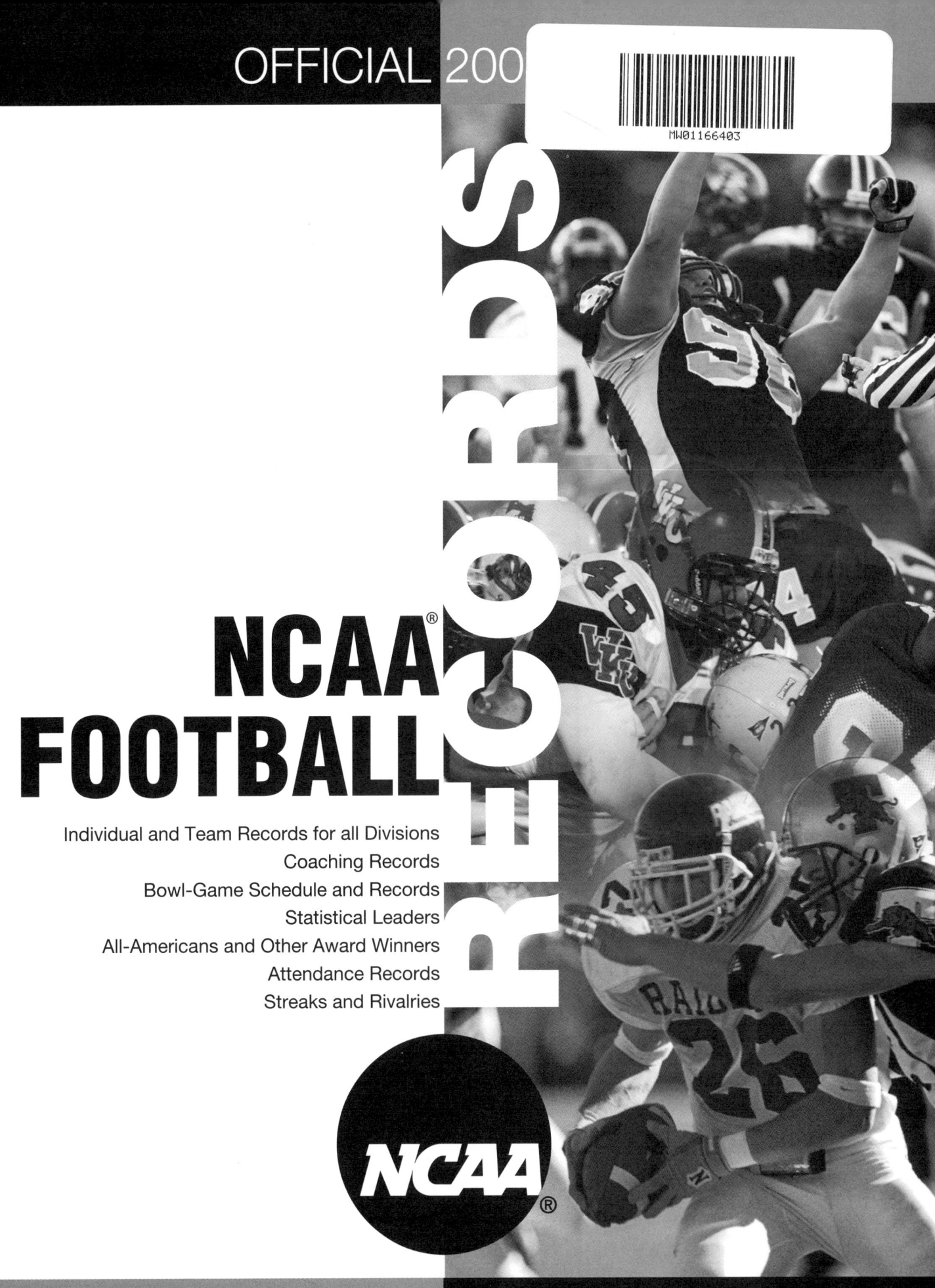

MW01166403

NCAA® FOOTBALL RECORDS

Individual and Team Records for all Divisions
Coaching Records
Bowl-Game Schedule and Records
Statistical Leaders
All-Americans and Other Award Winners
Attendance Records
Streaks and Rivalries

NCAA®

THE NATIONAL COLLEGIATE ATHLETIC ASSOCIATION
P.O. Box 6222, Indianapolis, Indiana
46206-6222
www.ncaa.org

August 2003

Compiled By:
Richard M. Campbell, *Assistant Director of Statistics.*
Sean W. Straziscar, *Assistant Director of Statistics.*

Edited By:
Scott Deitch, *Assistant Director of Communications.*

Design/Production By:
Toi Davis, *Production Designer II.*

Cover Design By:
Wayne Davis, *Graphics Manager*

Distributed to sports information directors and conference publicity directors.

Contents

Name-Change Key

Various schools have changed their name. The current school name is listed along with other names by which the schools have been referred. (Note: Not all schools in this list currently sponsor or have sponsored football.)

SCHOOL name changes

Current school name:	Changed from:
Albertson	Col. of Idaho
Alcorn St.	Alcorn A&M
Alliant Int'l	U.S. Int'l; Cal Western
Arcadia	Beaver
Ark.-Pine Bluff	Arkansas AM&N
Armstrong Atlantic	Armstrong St.
Auburn	Alabama Poly
Augusta St.	Augusta
Bemidji St.	Bemidji Teachers
Benedictine (Ill.)	Ill. Benedictine
Bradley	Bradley Tech
UC Davis	California Aggies
Cal St. Fullerton	Orange County State College; Orange St.
Cal St. Northridge	San Fernando Valley St.
Case Reserve	Case Institute of Technology
Central Okla.	Central St. (Okla.)
Charleston So.	Baptist (S.C.)
Charleston (W.Va.)	Morris Harvey
Charlotte	UNC Charlotte
Chattanooga	Tenn.-Chatt.
Cleveland St.	Fenn
Colorado St.	Colorado A&M
Columbus St.	Columbus
Concordia (Calif.)	Christ College-Irvine
Concordia (Ill.)	Concordia Teachers
Crown	St. Paul Bible
DeSales	Allentown
Detroit	Detroit Mercy; Detroit Tech
Dist. of Columbia	D.C. Teachers; Federal City
Dominican	Rosary
Drexel	Drexel Tech
Duke	Trinity (N.C.)
Eastern Mich.	Michigan Normal
Emporia St.	Kansas St. Normal
FDU-Florham	FDU-Madison
Farmington St.	Maine-Farmington
Fresno St.	Fresno Pacific
Ga. Southern	Georgia Teachers
Ill.-Chicago	Ill.-Chicago Circle
Illinois St.	Illinois St. Normal; Illinois Normal
Indiana (Pa.)	Indiana St. (Pa.)
Indianapolis	Indiana Central
Iowa	State University of Iowa
Iowa St.	Ames
James Madison	Madison
Kansas St.	Kansas Aggies
Kent St.	Kent
La Sierra	Loma Linda
Lamar	Lamar Tech
Liberty	Lynchburg Baptist; Liberty Baptist
La.-Lafayette	Southwestern La.
La.-Monroe	Northeast La.
Loyola Marymount	Loyola U. of L.A.
Lynn	College of Boca Raton
Lyon	Arkansas College
Maritime (N.Y.)	N.Y. Maritime
Martin Luther	Northwestern (Wis.)
Marycrest Int'l	Teikyo Marycrest
Md.-East. Shore	Maryland St.
Massachusetts	Massachusetts St.; Massachusetts Agriculture Col.
Mass. Liberal Arts	North Adams St.
Mass.-Dartmouth	Southeastern Mass.
Mass.-Lowell	Lowell; Lowell St.; Lowell Tech
McDaniel	Western Md.
Memphis	Memphis St.
Minn. St. Mankato	Mankato Teachers; Mankato St.
Minn. St. Moorhead	Moorhead St.; Moorhead Teachers
Mont. St.-Billings	Eastern Montana
Montana St.-Northern	Northern Montana
Murray St.	Murray Teachers
Neb.-Kearney	Kearney St.
Neb.-Omaha	Omaha
New England U.	St. Francis (Me.)
Col. of New Jersey	Trenton St.

Current school name:	Changed from:
New Jersey City	Jersey City St.
N.J. Inst. of Tech.	Newark Engineering
New Mexico St.	New Mexico A&M
New Orleans	Louisiana St. (N.O.)
North Ala.	Florence St.
N.C. Central	North Caro. College
UNC Pembroke	Pembroke St.
North Central Texas	Cooke County
North Texas	North Tex. St.
Northeastern St.	Northeastern Okla. St.
Northern Ariz.	Arizona St.-Flagstaff; Flagstaff Teachers
Northern Colo.	Colorado St. College
Northern Iowa	Iowa Teachers
Oklahoma St.	Oklahoma A&M
Old Dominion	William & Mary (Norfolk)
Pepperdine	George Pepperdine
Philadelphia U.	Philadelphia Textile
Polytechnic (N.Y.)	New York Poly; Brooklyn Poly
Rhodes	Southwestern (Tenn.)
Rice	Rice Institute
Richard Stockton	Stockton St.
Rochester Inst.	Mechanics Institute
Rowan	Glassboro St.
Southern Ind.	Indiana St.-Evansville
Southern Me.	Maine Portland-Gorham; Gorham St. (Me.)
Southern N.H.	New Hamp. Col.
Southern U.	Southern B.R.
Taylor-Ft. Wayne	Summit Christian
Tex. A&M-Commerce	East Texas St.
Tex. A&M-Kingsville	Texas A&I
Tex.-Pan American	Pan American
Towson	Towson St.
Truman	Northeast Mo. St.; Truman St.
Tulsa	Henry Kendall
Washburn	Lincoln College
Washington St.	Washington Agricultural College
West Ala.	Livingston
West Tex. A&M	West Texas St.
Western Mich.	Western State Teachers
Western N. M.	New Mexico Western
Western Ore.	Oregon Tech; Oregon College of Education
Western St.	Colo. Western; Colorado Normal
Westmar	Western Union College; Teikyo Westmar
Wichita St.	Fairmount
Widener	Pennsylvania Military College
Wm. Paterson	Paterson St.
Wis.-Eau Claire	Eau Claire Teachers
Wis.-La Crosse	La Crosse Teachers
Wis.-River Falls	River Falls Teachers
Wis.-Superior	Superior Normal; Superior St. Teachers
Xavier	St. Xavier

SCHOOLS also known as

Current school name:	Also known as:
Air Force	U.S. Air Force Academy
Apprentice School	Newport News
Army	U.S. Military Academy; West Point
Baruch	Bernard M. Baruch
Case Reserve	Case Western Reserve
CCNY	City College of New York
Coast Guard	U.S. Coast Guard Academy
GC&SU	Georgia College & State
Hawthorne	Nathaniel Hawthorne
IPFW	Indiana/Purdue-Ft. Wayne
IUPUI	Indiana/Purdue-Indianapolis
Lehman	Herbert H. Lehman
Lipscomb	David Lipscomb
Long Island	LIU-Brooklyn
LSU	Louisiana St.
Merchant Marine	King's Point; U.S. Merchant Marine Academy
MIT	Massachusetts Institute of Technology
Navy	U.S. Naval Academy
NYCCT	New York City Tech
NYIT	New York Institute of Technology; New York Tech
Rochester Inst.	RIT
Sewanee	University of the South
TCU	Texas Christian
UAB	Ala.-Birmingham
UCF	Central Fla. (was Florida Tech)
UCLA	University of California, Los Angeles
UMBC	Md.-Balt. County
UMKC	Mo.-Kansas City

Current school name:	Also known as:
UNLV	Nevada-Las Vegas (was Nevada Southern)
UTEP	Texas-El Paso (was Texas Western)
VMI	Va. Military
WPI	Worcester Poly Inst.

Division I-A Records

Individual Records

Under a three-division reorganization plan adopted by the special NCAA Convention of August 1973, teams classified major-college in football on August 1, 1973, were placed in Division I. College-division teams were divided into Division II and Division III. At the NCAA Convention of January 1978, Division I was divided into Division I-A and Division I-AA for football only. Prior to 2002, postseason games were not included in NCAA final football statistics or records. Beginning with the 2002 season, all postseason games were included in NCAA final football statistics and records.

From 1937, when official national statistics rankings began, through 1969, individual rankings were by totals. Beginning in 1970, most season individual rankings were by per-game averages. In total offense, rushing and scoring, it is yards or points per game; in receiving, catches per game and yards per game; in interceptions, catches per game; and in punt and kickoff returns, yards per return. Punting always has been by average, and all team rankings have been per-game. Beginning in 1979, passers were rated in all divisions on "efficiency rating points," which are derived from a formula that compares passers to the national averages for 14 seasons of two-platoon Division I football starting with the 1965 season. One hundred points equals the 14-year averages for all players in Division I. Those averages break down to 6.29 yards per attempt, 47.14 percent completions, 3.97 percent touchdown passes and 6.54 percent interceptions. The formula assumes that touchdowns are as good as interceptions are bad; therefore, these two figures offset each other for the average player. To determine efficiency rating points, multiply a passer's yards per attempt by 8.4, add his completion percentage, add his touchdown percentage times 3.3, then subtract his interception percentage times two.

Passers must have a minimum of 15 attempts per game to determine rating points because fewer attempts could allow a player to win the championship with fewer than 100 attempts in a season. A passer must play in at least 75 percent of his team's games to qualify for the rankings (e.g., a player on a team with a nine-game season could qualify by playing in seven games); thus, a passer with 105 attempts could qualify for the national rankings.

A pass efficiency rating comparison for each year since 1979 has been added to the passing section of all-time leaders.

All individual and team records and rankings include regular-season games only. Career records of players include only those years in which they competed in Division I-A.

Statistics in some team categories were not tabulated until the advent of the computerized statistics program in 1966. The records listed in those categories begin with the 1966 season and are so indicated.

In 1954, the regular-season schedule was limited to a maximum of 10 games, and in 1970, to a limit of 11 games, excluding postseason competition.

A player whose career includes statistics for parts of five seasons (or an active player who will play in five seasons) because he was granted an additional season of competition for reasons of hardship or a freshman redshirt are denoted by "$."

COLLEGIATE RECORDS

Individual collegiate records are determined by comparing the best records in all four divisions (I-A, I-AA, II and III) in comparable categories. Included are career records of players who played parts of their careers in different divisions (such as Dennis Shaw of San Diego State, Howard Stevens of Randolph-Macon and Louisville, and Doug Williams of Grambling). For individual collegiate career leaders, see page 262.

Total Offense

(Rushing Plus Passing)

MOST PLAYS
Quarter
41—Jason Davis, UNLV vs. Idaho, Sept. 17, 1994 (4th; 41 passes)
Half
57—Rusty LaRue, Wake Forest vs. Duke, Oct. 28, 1995 (2nd; 56 passes, 1 rush)
Game
94—Matt Vogler, TCU vs. Houston, Nov. 3, 1990 (696 yards)
Season
814—Kliff Kingsbury, Texas Tech, 2002 (4,903 yards)
2 Yrs
1,409—Kliff Kingsbury, Texas Tech, 2001-02 (8,357 yards)
3 Yrs
2,072—Kliff Kingsbury, Texas Tech, 2000-02 (11,794 yards)
Career
(4 yrs.) 2,156—Kliff Kingsbury, Texas Tech, 1999-02 (12,263 yards)

MOST PLAYS PER GAME
Season
64.0—David Klingler, Houston, 1990 (704 in 11)
2 Yrs
61.6—David Klingler, Houston, 1990-91 (1,293 in 21)
Career
50.1—Kliff Kingsbury, Texas Tech, 1999-02 (2,156 in 43)

MOST PLAYS BY A FRESHMAN
Game
80—Luke McCown, Louisiana Tech vs. Miami (Fla.), Oct. 28, 2000 (444 yards)
Season
635—Jared Lorenzen, Kentucky, 2000 (3,827 yards)
Also holds per-game record with 57.7 (635 in 11)

MOST YARDS GAINED
Quarter
347—Jason Davis, UNLV vs. Idaho, Sept. 17, 1994 (4th)
Half
510—Andre Ware, Houston vs. Southern Methodist, Oct. 21, 1989 (1st)
Game
732—David Klingler, Houston vs. Arizona St., Dec. 2, 1990 (16 rushing, 716 passing)
Season
5,221—David Klingler, Houston, 1990 (81 rushing, 5,140 passing)
2 Yrs
9,455—Ty Detmer, Brigham Young, 1989-90 (-293 rushing, 9,748 passing)
3 Yrs
13,456—Ty Detmer, Brigham Young, 1989-91 (-323 rushing, 13,779 passing)
Career
(4 yrs.) 14,665—Ty Detmer, Brigham Young, 1988-91 (-366 rushing, 15,031 passing)

MOST YARDS GAINED PER GAME
Season
474.6—David Klingler, Houston, 1990 (5,221 in 11)
2 Yrs
402.2—David Klingler, Houston, 1990-91 (8,447 in 21)
Career
382.4—Tim Rattay, Louisiana Tech, 1997-99 (12,618 in 33)

MOST YARDS GAINED, FIRST TWO SEASONS
8,808—Tim Rattay, Louisiana Tech, 1997-98
Also holds per-game record with 383.0 (8,808 in 23)

MOST SEASONS GAINING 4,000 YARDS OR MORE
3—Ty Detmer, Brigham Young, 1989-91

MOST SEASONS GAINING 3,000 YARDS OR MORE
3—Ty Detmer, Brigham Young, 1989-91; Chad Pennington, Marshall, 1997-99; Tim Rattay, Louisiana Tech, 1997-99; Kliff Kingsbury, Texas Tech, 2000-02

MOST SEASONS GAINING 2,500 YARDS OR MORE
4—Antwaan Randle El, Indiana, 1998-01
3—John Elway, Stanford, 1980-82; Doug Flutie, Boston College, 1982-84; Randall Cunningham, UNLV, 1982-84; Brian McClure, Bowling Green, 1983-85; Erik Wilhelm, Oregon St., 1986-88; Shawn Moore, Virginia, 1988-90; Ty Detmer, Brigham Young, 1989-91; Shane Matthews, Florida, 1990-92; Stoney Case, New Mexico, 1992-94; Peyton Manning, Tennessee, 1995-97; Daunte Culpepper, UCF, 1996-98; Chris Redman, Louisville, 1997-99; Drew Brees, Purdue, 1998-00; Kliff Kingsbury, Texas Tech, 2000-02; Jose Fuentes, Utah St., 2000-02

MOST YARDS GAINED BY A FRESHMAN
Game
582—David Neill, Nevada vs. New Mexico St., Oct. 10, 1998 (61 plays)
Season
3,827—Jared Lorenzen, Kentucky, 2000 (635 plays)
Per-game record—372.3, David Neill, Nevada, 1998

MOST YARDS GAINED BY A SOPHOMORE
Game
657—Brian Lindgren, Idaho vs. Middle Tenn., Oct. 6, 2001 (20 rushing, 637 passing)
Season
4,457—Timmy Chang, Hawaii, 2002 (14 games, 663 plays)
Per-game record—390.8, Scott Mitchell, Utah, 1988

MOST YARDS GAINED IN FIRST GAME OF CAREER
483—Billy Stevens, UTEP vs. North Texas, Sept. 18, 1965

MOST YARDS GAINED IN TWO, THREE AND FOUR CONSECUTIVE GAMES
2 Games
1,310—David Klingler, Houston, 1990 (578 vs. Eastern Wash., Nov. 17; 732 vs. Arizona St., Dec. 2)
3 Games
1,651—David Klingler, Houston, 1990 (341 vs. Texas, Nov. 10; 578 vs. Eastern Wash., Nov. 17; 732 vs. Arizona St., Dec. 2)
4 Games
2,276—David Klingler, Houston, 1990 (625 vs. TCU, Nov. 3; 341 vs. Texas, Nov. 10; 578 vs. Eastern Wash., Nov. 17; 732 vs. Arizona St., Dec. 2)

MOST GAMES GAINING 300 YARDS OR MORE
Season
12—Ty Detmer, Brigham Young, 1990
Career
33—Ty Detmer, Brigham Young, 1988-91

MOST CONSECUTIVE GAMES GAINING 300 YARDS OR MORE
Season
12—Ty Detmer, Brigham Young, 1990
Career
19—Ty Detmer, Brigham Young, 1989-90

MOST GAMES GAINING 400 YARDS OR MORE
Season
9—David Klingler, Houston, 1990

Career
13—Ty Detmer, Brigham Young, 1988-91

MOST CONSECUTIVE GAMES GAINING 400 YARDS OR MORE
Season
5—Ty Detmer, Brigham Young, 1990
Also holds career record with 5

MOST YARDS GAINED AGAINST ONE OPPONENT
Career
1,483—Ty Detmer, Brigham Young vs. San Diego St., 1988-91

MOST YARDS GAINED PER GAME AGAINST ONE OPPONENT
Career
(Min. 3 games) 399.0—Cody Ledbetter, New Mexico St. vs. UNLV, 1993-95 (1,197 yards)
(Min. 4 games) 370.8—Ty Detmer, Brigham Young vs. San Diego St., 1988-91 (1,483 yards)

MOST YARDS GAINED BY TWO OPPOSING PLAYERS
Game
1,321—Matt Vogler, TCU (696) & David Klingler, Houston (625), Nov. 3, 1990

GAINING 1,000 YARDS RUSHING AND 1,000 YARDS PASSING
Season
Johnny Bright (HB), Drake, 1950 (1,232 rushing, 1,168 passing); Reggie Collier (QB), Southern Miss., 1981 (1,005 rushing, 1,004 passing); Bart Weiss (QB), Air Force, 1985 (1,032 rushing, 1,449 passing); Darian Hagan (QB), Colorado, 1989 (1,004 rushing, 1,002 passing); Dee Dowis (QB), Air Force, 1989 (1,286 rushing, 1,285 passing); Brian Mitchell (QB), La.-Lafayette, 1989 (1,311 rushing, 1,966 passing); Michael Carter (QB), Hawaii, 1991 (1,092 rushing, 1,172 passing); Beau Morgan (QB), Air Force, 1995 (1,285 rushing, 1,165 passing); Beau Morgan (QB), Air Force, 1996 (1,494 rushing, 1,210 passing); Chris McCoy (QB), Navy, 1997 (1,370 rushing, 1,203 passing); Scott Frost (QB), Nebraska, 1997 (1,095 rushing, 1,237 passing); Antwaan Randle El (QB), Indiana, 2000 (1,270 rushing, 1,783 passing); Keith Boyea, Air Force, 2001 (1,216 rushing, 1,253 passing); Woodrow Dantzler (QB), Clemson, 2001 (1,004 rushing, 2,360 passing); Joshua Cribbs (QB), Kent St., 2001 (1,019 rushing, 1,516 passing) (one of only two freshmen to accomplish the feat); Eric Crouch, Nebraska, 2001 (1,115 rushing, 1,510 passing); Brad Smith, Missouri, 2002 (1,029 rushing, 2,333 passing) (one of only two freshmen to accomplish the feat); Joshua Cribbs, Kent St., 2002 (1,057 rushing, 1,014 passing); Jammal Lord, Nebraska, 2002 (1,412 rushing, 1,362 passing); Chance Harridge, Air Force, 2002 (1,229 rushing, 1,062 passing); Ell Roberson, Kansas St., 2002 (1,032 rushing, 1,580 passing)

A QUARTERBACK GAINING 2,000 YARDS PASSING AND 1,000 YARDS RUSHING
Season
Woodrow Dantzler, Clemson, 2001 (2,360 passing, 1,004 rushing); Brad Smith, Missouri, 2002 (2,333 passing, 1,029 rushing) (only freshman to accomplish the feat)

A QUARTERBACK GAINING 2,000 YARDS RUSHING AND 4,000 YARDS PASSING
Career
Prince McJunkins, Wichita St., 1979-82 (2,047 rushing, 4,544 passing); John Bond, Mississippi St., 1980-83 (2,280 rushing, 4,621 passing); Rickey Foggie, Minnesota, 1984-87 (2,038 rushing, 4,903 passing); Brian Mitchell, La.-Lafayette, 1986-89 (3,335 rushing, 5,447 passing); Major Harris, West Virginia, 1987-89 (2,030 rushing, 4,834 passing); Antwaan Randle El, Indiana, 1998-01 (3,895 rushing, 7,469 passing); Woodrow Dantzler, Clemson, 1998-01 (2,615 rushing, 5,634 passing)

A QUARTERBACK GAINING 3,000 YARDS RUSHING AND 3,000 YARDS PASSING
Career
Brian Mitchell, La.-Lafayette, 1986-89 (3,335 rushing, 5,447 passing); Beau Morgan, Air Force, 1994-96 (3,379 rushing, 3,248 passing); Antwaan Randle El, Indiana, 1998-01 (3,895 rushing, 7,469 passing)

A QUARTERBACK GAINING 3,500 YARDS RUSHING AND 7,000 YARDS PASSING
Career
Antwaan Randle El, Indiana, 1998-01 (3,895 rushing, 7,469 passing)

A QUARTERBACK GAINING 300 YARDS PASSING AND 100 YARDS RUSHING
Game
Ned James, New Mexico vs. Wyoming, Nov. 1, 1986 (118 rushing, 406 passing); Randy Welniak, Wyoming vs. Air Force, Sept. 24, 1988 (108 rushing, 359 passing); Donald Douglas, Houston vs. Southern Methodist, Oct. 19, 1991 (103 rushing, 319 passing); Shaun King, Tulane vs. Army, Nov. 14, 1998 (133 rushing, 332 passing); Michael Bishop, Kansas St. vs. Nebraska, Nov. 14, 1998 (140 rushing, 306 passing); Michael Bishop, Kansas St. vs. Texas A&M, Dec. 5, 1998 (101 rushing, 341 passing); Marques Tuiasosopo, Washington vs. Stanford, Oct. 30, 1999 (207 rushing, 302 passing); Zak Kustok, Northwestern vs. Bowling Green, Nov. 17, 2001 (111 rushing, 421 passing)

A QUARTERBACK GAINING 300 YARDS PASSING AND 200 YARDS RUSHING
Game
Marques Tuiasosopo, Washington vs. Stanford, Oct. 30, 1999 (207 rushing, 302 passing)

A QUARTERBACK GAINING 200 YARDS RUSHING AND 200 YARDS PASSING
Game
Reds Bagnell, Pennsylvania vs. Dartmouth, Oct. 14, 1950 (214 rushing, 276 passing); Steve Gage, Tulsa vs. New Mexico, Nov. 8, 1986 (212 rushing, 209 passing); Brian Mitchell, La.-Lafayette vs. Colorado St., Nov. 21, 1987 (271 rushing, 205 passing); Marques Tuiasosopo, Washington vs. Stanford, Oct. 30, 1999 (207 rushing, 302 passing); Antwaan Randle El, Indiana vs. Minnesota, Oct. 21, 2000 (210 rushing, 263 passing)

TEAMS HAVING A 3,000-YARD PASSER, 1,000-YARD RUSHER AND 1,000-YARD RECEIVER IN THE SAME YEAR
22 teams. Most recent: UCF, 2002 (Ryan Schneider [3,770 passer], Alex Haynes [1,038 rusher], Doug Gabriel [1,237 receiver] and Jimmy Fryzel [1,125 receiver]); Fresno St., 2001 (David Carr [4,308 passer], Paris Gaines [1,018 rusher], Rodney Wright [1,331 receiver] and Bernard Berrian [1,270 receiver]); Utah St., 2001 (Jose Fuentes [3,100 passer], Emmett White [1,361 rusher] and Kevin Curtis [1,531 receiver]); Louisville, 1999 (Chris Redman [3,647 passer], Frank Moreau [1,298 rusher] and Arnold Jackson [1,209 receiver]; Nevada, 1999 (David Neill [3,402 passer], Chris Lemon [1,170 rusher], and Trevor Insley [2,060 receiver]); Western Mich., 1999 (Tim Lester [3,639 passer], Robert Stanford [1,092 rusher] and Steve Neal [1,113 receiver]; Louisville, 1998 (Chris Redman [4,042 passer], Leroy Collins [1,134 rusher] and Arnold Jackson [1,165 receiver]); Western Mich., 1998 (Tim Lester [3,311 passer], Darnell Fields [1,016 rusher] and Steve Neal [1,121 receiver]); Nevada, 1998 (David Neill [3,249 passer], Chris Lemon [1,154 rusher], Geoff Noisy [1,405 receiver] and Trevor Insley [1,220 receiver]; Nevada, 1997 (John Dutton [3,526 passer], Chris Lemon [1,055 rusher], Geoff Noisy [1,184 receiver] and Trevor Insley [1,151 receiver]); Tennessee, 1997 (Peyton Manning [3,819 passer], Jamal Lewis [1,364 rusher] and Marcus Nash [1,170 receiver]); Nevada, 1995 (Mike Maxwell [3,611 passer], Kim Minor [1,052 rusher] and Alex Van Dyke [1,854 receiver]); New Mexico St., 1995 (Cody Ledbetter [3,501 passer], Denvis Manns [1,120 rusher] and Lucious Davis [1,018 receiver]); Ohio St., 1995 (Bobby Hoying [3,023 passer], Eddie George [1,826 rusher] and Terry Glenn [1,316 receiver]); San Diego St., 1995 (Billy Blanton [3,300 passer], George Jones [1,842 rusher], Will Blackwell [1,207 receiver] and Az Hakim [1,022 receiver])

(Note: UCF in 2002, Fresno St. in 2001, Nevada in 1997 and 1998, and San Diego St. in 1995, are the only teams to have two 1,000-yard receivers.)

TEAMS HAVING A 2,000-YARD RUSHER AND 2,000-YARD PASSER IN THE SAME YEAR
4—Oklahoma St., 1988 (Barry Sanders [2,628 rusher] and Mike Gundy [2,163 passer]); Colorado, 1994

(Rashaan Salaam [2,055 rusher] and Kordell Stewart [2,071 passer]); Texas, 1998 (Ricky Williams [2,124 rusher] and Major Applewhite [2,453 passer]); Penn St., 2002 (Larry Johnson [2,087 rusher] and Zach Mills [2,417 passer])

TEAMS HAVING A 2,000-YARD RUSHER, 2,000-YARD PASSER AND 1,000-YARD RECEIVER IN THE SAME YEAR
2—Oklahoma St., 1988 (Barry Sanders [2,628 rusher], Mike Gundy [2,163 passer] and Hart Lee Dykes [1,278 receiver]); Texas, 1998 (Ricky Williams [2,124 rusher], Major Applewhite [2,453 passer] and Wane McGarity [1,087 receiver])

TEAMS HAVING A 4,000-YARD PASSER AND 1,000-YARD RUSHER IN THE SAME YEAR
4—Houston, 1990 (David Klingler [5,140 passer] and Chuck Weatherspoon [1,097 rusher]); Louisville, 1998 (Chris Redman [4,042 passer] and Leroy Collins [1,134 rusher]); Houston, 1989 (Andre Ware [4,699 passer] and Chuck Weatherspoon [1,146 rusher]); Fresno St., 2001 (David Carr [4,308 passer] and Paris Gaines [1,018 rusher])

HIGHEST AVERAGE GAIN PER PLAY
Game
(Min. 37-62 plays) 14.3—Jason Martin, Louisiana Tech vs. Toledo, Oct. 19, 1996 (37 for 529)
(Min. 63 plays) 9.9—David Klingler, Houston vs. TCU, Nov. 3, 1990 (63 for 625)
Season
(Min. 3,000 yards) 9.1—Rex Grossman, Florida, 2001 (429 for 3,904)
Career
(Min. 7,500 yards) 8.2—Ty Detmer, Brigham Young, 1988-91 (1,795 for 14,665)

MOST TOUCHDOWNS RESPONSIBLE FOR (TDs Scored and Passed For)
Game
11—David Klingler, Houston vs. Eastern Wash., Nov. 17, 1990 (passed for 11)
Season
55—David Klingler, Houston, 1990 (scored 1, passed for 54)
2 Yrs
85—David Klingler, Houston, 1990-91 (scored 2, passed for 83)
3 Yrs
122—Ty Detmer, Brigham Young, 1989-91 (scored 14, passed for 108)
Career
(4 yrs) 135—Ty Detmer, Brigham Young, 1988-91 (scored 14, passed for 121)

MOST TOUCHDOWNS RESPONSIBLE FOR PER GAME
Season
5.0—David Klingler, Houston, 1990 (55 in 11)

Missouri's Brad Smith became only the second Division I-A player to throw for more than 2,000 yards and rush for more than 1,000 yards in a season, just one year after Clemson's Woodrow Dantzler accomplished the feat.

Missouri Sports Information

2 Yrs

    4.0—David Klingler, Houston, 1990-91 (85 in 21)

3 Yrs

    3.5—Tim Rattay, Louisiana Tech, 1997-99 (117 in 33)

Career

    (4 yrs) 2.9—Ty Detmer, Brigham Young, 1988-91 (135 in 46)

    Collegiate record—3.6, Dennis Shaw, San Diego St., 1968-69 (72 in 20)

MOST POINTS RESPONSIBLE FOR
(Points Scored and Passed For)

Game

    66—David Klingler, Houston vs. Eastern Wash., Nov. 17, 1990 (passed for 11 TDs)

Season

    334—David Klingler, Houston, 1990 (scored 1 TD, passed for 54 TDs, accounted for 2 two-point conversions)

2 Yrs

    514—David Klingler, Houston, 1990-91 (scored 2 TDs, passed for 83 TDs, accounted for 2 two-point conversions)

3 Yrs

    702—Tim Rattay, Louisiana Tech, 1997-99 (scored 2 TDs, passed for 115 TDs)

Career

    820—Ty Detmer, Brigham Young, 1988-91 (scored 14 TDs, passed for 121 TDs, accounted for 5 two-point conversions)

MOST POINTS RESPONSIBLE FOR PER GAME

Season

    30.4—David Klingler, Houston, 1990 (334 in 11)

2 Yrs

    22.8—Jim McMahon, Brigham Young, 1980-81 (502 in 22)

3 Yrs

    21.3—Tim Rattay, Louisiana Tech, 1997-99 (702 in 33)

Career

    (4 yrs) 17.8—Ty Detmer, Brigham Young, 1988-91 (820 in 46)

    Collegiate record—21.6, Dennis Shaw, San Diego St., 1968-69 (432 in 20)

SCORING 200 POINTS AND PASSING FOR 200 POINTS

Career

    Rick Leach, Michigan, 1975-78 (scored 204, passed for 270); Antwaan Randle El, Indiana, 1998-01 (scored 264, passed for 258)

RUSHED FOR 40 TOUCHDOWNS AND PASSED FOR 40 TOUCHDOWNS

Career

    Antwaan Randle El, Indiana, 1998-01 (44 rushing, 42 passing)

Rushing

MOST RUSHES

Quarter

    22—Alex Smith, Indiana vs. Michigan St., Nov. 11, 1995 (1st, 114 yards)

Half

    34—Tony Sands, Kansas vs. Missouri, Nov. 23, 1991 (2nd, 240 yards)

Game

    58—Tony Sands, Kansas vs. Missouri, Nov. 23, 1991 (396 yards)

Season

    403—Marcus Allen, Southern California, 1981 (2,342 yards)

2 Yrs

    757—Marcus Allen, Southern California, 1980-81 (3,905 yards)

Career

    (3 yrs.) 994—Herschel Walker, Georgia, 1980-82 (5,259 yards)

    (4 yrs.) 1,215—Steve Bartalo, Colorado St., 1983-86 (4,813 yards)

MOST RUSHES PER GAME

Season

    39.6—Ed Marinaro, Cornell, 1971 (356 in 9)

2 Yrs

    36.0—Marcus Allen, Southern California, 1980-81 (757 in 21)

Career

    34.0—Ed Marinaro, Cornell, 1969-71 (918 in 27)

MOST RUSHES BY A FRESHMAN

Game

    52—Michael Turner, Northern Ill. vs. Central Mich., Nov. 18, 2000 (281 yards)

Season

    302—Chance Kretschmer, Nevada, 2001 (1,732 yards)

MOST RUSHES PER GAME BY A FRESHMAN

Season

    29.2—Steve Bartalo, Colorado St., 1983 (292 in 10)

MOST CONSECUTIVE RUSHES BY SAME PLAYER

Game

    16—William Howard, Tennessee vs. Mississippi, Nov. 15, 1986 (during two possessions)

MOST RUSHES IN TWO CONSECUTIVE GAMES

Season

    102—Lorenzo White, Michigan St., 1985 (53 vs. Purdue, Oct. 26; 49 vs. Minnesota, Nov. 2)

MOST CONSECUTIVE RUSHES WITHOUT LOSING A FUMBLE

Season

    365—Travis Prentice, Miami (Ohio), 1998

Career

    862—Travis Prentice, Miami (Ohio), 1997-99

MOST YARDS GAINED

Quarter

    222—Corey Dillon, Washington vs. San Jose St., Nov. 16, 1996 (1st, 16 rushes)

Half

    287—Stacey Robinson, Northern Ill. vs. Fresno St., Oct. 6, 1990 (1st; 114 in first quarter, 173 in second quarter; 20 rushes); LaDainian Tomlinson, TCU vs. UTEP, Nov. 20, 1999 (2nd; 121 in third quarter, 166 in fourth quarter; 28 rushes)

Game

    406—LaDainian Tomlinson, TCU vs. UTEP, Nov. 20, 1999 (43 rushes) (59 yards in first quarter, 60 in second quarter, 121 in third quarter, 166 in fourth quarter)

Season

    2,628—Barry Sanders, Oklahoma St., 1988 (344 rushes, 11 games)

2 Yrs

    4,195—Troy Davis, Iowa St., 1995-96 (747 rushes)

Career

    (3 yrs.) 5,259—Herschel Walker, Georgia, 1980-82 (994 rushes)

    (4 yrs.) 6,397—Ron Dayne, Wisconsin, 1996-99 (1,115 rushes)

MOST YARDS GAINED PER GAME

Season

    238.9—Barry Sanders, Oklahoma St., 1988 (2,628 in 11)

2 Yrs

    190.7—Troy Davis, Iowa St., 1995-96 (4,195 in 22)

Career

    174.6—Ed Marinaro, Cornell, 1969-71 (4,715 in 27)

MOST YARDS GAINED BY A FRESHMAN

Game

    386—Marshall Faulk, San Diego St. vs. Pacific (Cal.), Sept. 14, 1991 (37 rushes)

Season

    1,863—Ron Dayne, Wisconsin, 1996 (295 rushes)

    Per-game record—158.8, Marshall Faulk, San Diego St., 1991 (1,429 in 9)

MOST YARDS GAINED BY A SOPHOMORE

Game

    351—Scott Harley, East Caro. vs. North Carolina St., Nov. 30, 1996 (42 rushes)

Season

    2,010—Troy Davis, Iowa St., 1995 (345 rushes)

    Also holds per-game record with 182.7 (2,010 in 11)

FRESHMEN GAINING 1,000 YARDS OR MORE

Season

    By 57 players (see chart after Annual Rushing Champions). Most recent: Terry Caulley, Connecticut, 2002 (1,247); Maurice Clarett, Ohio St., 2002 (1,237); DonTrell Moore, New Mexico, 2002 (1,134); Matt Milton, Nevada, 2002 (1,108); T.A. McLendon, North Carolina St., 2002 (1,101); Brad Smith, Missouri, 2002 (QB) (1,029); Chance Kretschmer, Nevada, 2001 (1,732); Anthony Davis, Wisconsin, 2001 (1,466); Joshua Cribbs, Kent St., 2001 (QB) (1,019); Avon Cobourne, West Virginia, 1999 (1,139); Derrick Nix, Southern Miss., 1998 (1,180); Ken Simonton, Oregon St., 1998 (1,028); Jamal Lewis, Tennessee, 1997 (1,364); Robert Sanford, Western Mich., 1997 (1,033); Ron Dayne, Wisconsin, 1996 (1,863); Demond Parker, Oklahoma, 1996 (1,184); Sedrick Irvin, Michigan St., 1996 (1,036)

TWO FRESHMEN, SAME TEAM, GAINING 1,000 YARDS OR MORE

Season

    Mike Smith (1,062) & Gwain Durden (1,049), Chattanooga, 1977

FIRST PLAYER TO GAIN 1,000 YARDS OR MORE

Season

    Byron "Whizzer" White, Colorado, 1937 (1,121)

    (Note: Before NCAA records began in 1937, Morley Drury of Southern California gained 1,163 yards in 1927.)

EARLIEST GAME REACHING 1,000 YARDS

Season

    5th—Ed Marinaro, Cornell, 1971 (1,026); Ricky Bell, Southern California, 1976 (1,008); Marcus Allen, Southern California, 1981 (1,136); Ernest Anderson, Oklahoma St., 1982 (1,042); Barry Sanders, Oklahoma St., 1988 (1,002); Troy Davis, Iowa St., 1995 (1,001); Troy Davis, Iowa St., 1996 (1,047); Byron Hanspard, Texas Tech, 1996 (1,112); Ricky Williams, Texas, 1998 (1,086)

EARLIEST GAME A FRESHMAN REACHED 1,000 YARDS

Season

    7th—Emmitt Smith, Florida, 1987 (1,011 vs. Temple, Oct. 17); Marshall Faulk, San Diego St., 1991 (1,157 vs. Colorado St., Nov. 9)

MOST YARDS GAINED BY A QUARTERBACK

Game

    308—Stacey Robinson, Northern Ill. vs. Fresno St., Oct. 6, 1990 (22 rushes)

Season

    1,494—Beau Morgan, Air Force, 1996 (225 rushes)

    Also holds per-game record with 135.8 (1,494 in 11)

Career

    3,895—Antwaan Randle El, Indiana, 1998-01 (857 rushes)

    Per-game record—109.1, Stacey Robinson, Northern Ill., 1988-90 (2,727 in 25)

MOST YARDS GAINED BY A FRESHMAN QUARTERBACK

Season

    1,029—Brad Smith, Missouri, 2002 (193 rushes)

LONGEST GAIN BY A QUARTERBACK

Game

    98—Mark Malone, Arizona St. vs. Utah St., Oct. 27, 1979 (TD)

MOST GAMES GAINING 100 YARDS OR MORE

Season

    11—By 14 players. Most recent: Ahman Green, Nebraska, 1997; Troy Davis, Iowa St., 1996; Wasean Tait, Toledo, 1995; Darnell Autry, Northwestern, 1995

Career

    33—Archie Griffin, Ohio St., 1972-75 (42 games); Tony Dorsett, Pittsburgh, 1973-76 (43 games)

MOST GAMES GAINING 100 YARDS OR MORE BY A FRESHMAN

Season

    10—Anthony Davis, Wisconsin, 2001

MOST CONSECUTIVE GAMES GAINING 100 YARDS OR MORE

Career

    31—Archie Griffin, Ohio St., began Sept. 15, 1973 (vs. Minnesota), ended Nov. 22, 1975 (vs. Michigan)

MOST CONSECUTIVE GAMES GAINING 100 YARDS OR MORE BY A FRESHMAN

Season

    8—Ron "Po" James, New Mexico St., 1968

MOST CONSECUTIVE GAMES GAINING 100 YARDS OR MORE BY A QUARTERBACK
Season
5—Beau Morgan, Air Force, 1995; Brian Madden, Navy, 1999

MOST GAMES GAINING 200 YARDS OR MORE
Season
8—Marcus Allen, Southern California, 1981
Career
11—Marcus Allen, Southern California, 1978-81 (in 21 games during 1980-81); Ricky Williams, Texas, 1995-98; Ron Dayne, Wisconsin, 1996-99

MOST GAMES GAINING 200 YARDS OR MORE BY A FRESHMAN
Season
4—Herschel Walker, Georgia, 1980; Ron Dayne, Wisconsin, 1996

MOST CONSECUTIVE GAMES GAINING 200 YARDS OR MORE
Season
5—Marcus Allen, Southern California, 1981 (210 vs. Tennessee, Sept. 12; 274 vs. Indiana, Sept. 19; 208 vs. Oklahoma, Sept. 26; 233 vs. Oregon St., Oct. 3; 211 vs. Arizona, Oct. 10); Barry Sanders, Oklahoma St., 1988 (320 vs. Kansas St., Oct. 29; 215 vs. Oklahoma, Nov. 5; 312 vs. Kansas, Nov. 12; 293 vs. Iowa St., Nov. 19; 332 vs. Texas Tech, Dec. 3)

MOST GAMES GAINING 300 YARDS OR MORE
Season
4—Barry Sanders, Oklahoma St., 1988
Also holds career record with 4

MOST CONSECUTIVE GAMES GAINING 300 YARDS OR MORE
Season
2—Ricky Williams, Texas, 1998 (318 vs. Rice, Sept. 26; 350 vs. Iowa St., Oct. 3)

MOST YARDS GAINED IN TWO, THREE, FOUR AND FIVE CONSECUTIVE GAMES
2 Games
668—Ricky Williams, Texas, 1998 (318 vs. Rice, Sept. 26; 350 vs. Iowa St., Oct. 3)
3 Games
937—Barry Sanders, Oklahoma St., 1988 (312 vs. Kansas, Nov. 12; 293 vs. Iowa St., Nov. 19; 332 vs. Texas Tech, Dec. 3)
4 Games
1,152—Barry Sanders, Oklahoma St., 1988 (215 vs. Oklahoma, Nov. 5; 312 vs. Kansas, Nov. 12; 293 vs. Iowa St., Nov. 19; 332 vs. Texas Tech, Dec. 3)
5 Games
1,472—Barry Sanders, Oklahoma St., 1988 (320 vs. Kansas St., Oct. 29; 215 vs. Oklahoma, Nov. 5; 312 vs. Kansas, Nov. 12; 293 vs. Iowa St., Nov. 19; 332 vs. Texas Tech, Dec. 3)

MOST SEASONS GAINING 1,500 YARDS OR MORE
Career
3—Tony Dorsett, Pittsburgh, 1973, 1975-76; Herschel Walker, Georgia, 1980-82; Travis Prentice, Miami (Ohio), 1997-99

MOST SEASONS GAINING 1,000 YARDS OR MORE
Career
4—Tony Dorsett, Pittsburgh, 1973-76; Amos Lawrence, North Carolina, 1977-80; Denvis Manns, New Mexico St., 1995-98; Ron Dayne, Wisconsin, 1996-99
Collegiate record tied by Howard Stevens, Randolph-Macon, 1968-69; Louisville, 1971-72

MOST PLAYERS REACHING 2,000 CAREER RUSHING YARDS IN THE SAME SEASON
3—Nebraska, 2000 (Cornell Buckhalter, 2,522; Dan Alexander, 2,456; Eric Crouch, 2,319)

TWO PLAYERS, SAME TEAM, EACH GAINING 1,000 YARDS OR MORE
Season
27 times. Most recent: Kansas St., 2002—Darren Sproles (1,465) & Ell Roberson (1,032); Nebraska, 2001—Dahrran Diedrick (1,299) & Eric Crouch (1,115); Nebraska, 1997—Ahman Green (1,877) & Scott Frost (1,016); Ohio, 1996—Steve Hookfin (1,125) & Kareem Wilson (1,072); Colorado St.,

1996—Calvin Branch (1,279) & Damon Washington (1,075)

TWO PLAYERS, SAME TEAM, EACH GAINING 200 YARDS OR MORE
Game
Gordon Brown, 214 (23 rushes) & Steve Gage (QB), 206 (26 rushes), Tulsa vs. Wichita St., Nov. 2, 1985; Sedrick Irvin, 238 (28 rushes) & Marc Renaud, 203 (21 rushes), Michigan St. vs. Penn St., Nov. 29, 1997

TWO OPPOSING DIVISION I-A PLAYERS EACH GAINING 200 YARDS OR MORE
Game
George Swarn, Miami (Ohio) (239) & Otis Cheathem, Western Mich. (219), Sept. 8, 1984; Barry Sanders, Oklahoma St. (215) & Mike Gaddis, Oklahoma (213), Nov. 5, 1988; Ricky Williams, Texas (249) & Michael Perry, Rice (211), Sept. 27, 1997; De'Mond Parker, Oklahoma (291) & Ricky Williams, Texas (223), Oct. 11, 1997

MOST YARDS GAINED BY TWO OPPOSING PLAYERS
Game
553—Marshall Faulk, San Diego St. (386) & Ryan Benjamin, Pacific (Cal.) (167), Sept. 14, 1991

MOST YARDS GAINED BY TWO PLAYERS, SAME TEAM
Game
476—Tony Sands (396) & Chip Hilleary (80), Kansas vs. Missouri, Nov. 23, 1991
Season
2,997—Barry Sanders (2,628) & Gerald Hudson (Sanders' backup, 369), Oklahoma St., 1988
Also hold per-game record with 272.5
Career
8,193—Eric Dickerson (4,450) & Craig James (3,743), Southern Methodist, 1979-82 (alternated at the same position during the last 36 games)

MOST YARDS GAINED IN FIRST GAME OF CAREER
273—Chris McCoy (Soph.), Navy vs. Southern Methodist, Sept. 9, 1995

MOST YARDS GAINED BY A FRESHMAN IN FIRST GAME OF CAREER
212—Greg Hill, Texas A&M vs. LSU, Sept. 14, 1991 (30 carries)

LONGEST RUSH BY A FRESHMAN IN FIRST GAME OF CAREER
98—Jerald Sowell, Tulane vs. Alabama, Sept. 4, 1993

MOST YARDS GAINED IN OPENING GAME OF SEASON
343—Tony Jeffery, TCU vs. Tulane, Sept. 13, 1986 (16 rushes)

MOST YARDS GAINED AGAINST ONE OPPONENT
Career
788—LaDainian Tomlinson, TCU vs. UTEP, 1997, 1999-00 (95 rushes)

MOST YARDS GAINED PER GAME AGAINST ONE OPPONENT
Career
(Min. 2 games) 292.0—Anthony Thompson, Indiana vs. Wisconsin, 1986, 89 (584 yards, 91 rushes)
(Min. 3 games) 262.7—LaDainian Tomlinson, TCU vs. UTEP, 1997, 1999-00 (788 yards, 95 rushes)

MOST YARDS GAINED BY TWO BROTHERS
Season
3,690—Barry Sanders, Oklahoma St. (2,628) & Byron Sanders, Northwestern (1,062), 1988

HIGHEST AVERAGE GAIN PER RUSH
Game
(Min. 8-14 rushes) 30.2—Kevin Lowe, Wyoming vs. South Dakota St., Nov. 10, 1984 (10 for 302)
(Min. 15-25 rushes) 21.4—Tony Jeffery, TCU vs. Tulane, Sept. 13, 1986 (16 for 343)
(Min. 26 rushes) 13.7—Eddie Lee Ivery, Georgia Tech vs. Air Force, Nov. 11, 1978 (26 for 356)
Season
(Min. 75-100 rushes) 11.5—Glenn Davis, Army, 1945 (82 for 944)
(Min. 101-213 rushes) 9.6—Chuck Weatherspoon, Houston, 1989 (119 for 1,146)

(Min. 214-281 rushes) 7.8—Mike Rozier, Nebraska, 1983 (275 for 2,148)
(Min. 282 rushes) 7.6—Barry Sanders, Oklahoma St., 1988 (344 for 2,628)
Career
(Min. 300-413 rushes) 8.3—Glenn Davis, Army, 1943-46 (358 for 2,957)
(Min. 414-780 rushes) 7.2—Mike Rozier, Nebraska, 1981-83 (668 for 4,780)
(Min. 781 rushes) 6.21—Ricky Williams, Texas, 1995-98 (1,011 for 6,279)

MOST TOUCHDOWNS SCORED BY RUSHING
Quarter
4—Dick Felt, Brigham Young vs. San Jose St., Nov. 8, 1952 (4th); Howard Griffith, Illinois vs. Southern Ill., Sept. 22, 1990 (3rd); Frank Moreau, Louisville vs. East Caro., Nov. 1, 1997 (2nd)
Game
8—Howard Griffith, Illinois vs. Southern Ill., Sept. 22, 1990 (5, 51, 7, 41, 5, 18, 5, 3 yards; Griffith scored three touchdowns [51, 7, 41] on consecutive carries and scored four touchdowns in the third quarter)
Season
37—Barry Sanders, Oklahoma St., 1988 (11 games)
Also holds per-game record at 3.4 (37 in 11)
Career
73—Travis Prentice, Miami (Ohio), 1996-99

MOST GAMES SCORING TWO OR MORE TOUCHDOWNS BY RUSHING
Season
11—Barry Sanders, Oklahoma St., 1988

MOST CONSECUTIVE GAMES SCORING TWO OR MORE TOUCHDOWNS BY RUSHING
Career
12—Barry Sanders, Oklahoma St. (last game of 1987, all 11 in 1988)

MOST TOUCHDOWNS SCORED BY RUSHING BY A FRESHMAN
Game
7—Marshall Faulk, San Diego St. vs. Pacific (Cal.), Sept. 14, 1991
Season
21—Marshall Faulk, San Diego St., 1991
Also holds per-game record with 2.3 (21 in 9)

MOST RUSHING TOUCHDOWNS SCORED BY A QUARTERBACK
Game
6—Dee Dowis, Air Force vs. San Diego St., Sept. 1, 1989 (55, 28, 12, 16, 60, 17 yards; 249 yards rushing on 13 carries); Craig Candeto, Navy vs.

Phil Hoffman

Craig Candeto tied the Division I-A single-game record for rushing touchdowns by a quarterback, when he crossed the goal line six times for Navy in its showdown with Army in 2002.

Army, Dec. 7, 2002 (1, 1, 42, 7, 3, 1 yards; 103 yards rushing on 18 carries)

Season

22—Chance Harridge, Air Force, 2002 (13 games)

Career

59—Eric Crouch, Nebraska, 1998-01 (43 games)

**MOST CONSECUTIVE RUSHES
FOR A TOUCHDOWN IN A GAME**

3—Howard Griffith, Illinois vs. Southern Ill., Sept. 22, 1990 (TDs of 51, 7 and 41 yards); Tiki Barber, Virginia vs. Texas, Sept. 28, 1996 (TDs of 16, 26 and 12 yards); Chris McCoy, Navy vs. Rutgers, Sept. 13, 1997 (TDs of 2, 9 and 2 yards); Aaron Greving, Iowa vs. Kent St., Sept. 1, 2001 (TDs of 14, 1 and 26 yards); Michael Robinson, Penn St. vs. Louisiana Tech, Sept. 21, 2002 (TDs of 8, 5 and 6 yards)

**MOST RUSHING TOUCHDOWNS SCORED
BY A QUARTERBACK IN TWO CONSECUTIVE
SEASONS**

38—Stacey Robinson, Northern Ill., 1989-90 (19 and 19); Eric Crouch, Nebraska, 2000-01 (20 and 18)

Passing

HIGHEST PASSING EFFICIENCY RATING POINTS
Game

(Min. 12-24 atts.) 403.4—Tim Clifford, Indiana vs. Colorado, Sept. 26, 1980 (14 attempts, 11 completions, 0 interceptions, 345 yards, 5 TD passes)

(Min. 25-49 atts.) 298.02—Marcus Arroyo, San Jose St. vs. Nevada, Nov. 10, 2001 (26 attempts, 21 completions, 0 interceptions, 476 yards, 5 TD passes)

(Min. 50 atts.) 199.2—Chris Redman, Louisville vs. East Caro., Nov. 14, 1998 (56 attempts, 44 completions, 1 interception, 592 yards, 6 TD passes)

Season

(Min. 15 atts. per game) 183.3—Shaun King, Tulane, 1998 (328 attempts, 223 completions, 6 interceptions, 3,232 yards, 36 TD passes)

Career

(Min. 325 comps.) 163.6—Danny Wuerffel, Florida, 1993-96 (1,170 attempts, 708 completions, 42 interceptions, 10,875 yards, 114 TD passes)

**HIGHEST PASSING EFFICIENCY RATING POINTS
BY A FRESHMAN**
Season

(Min. 15 atts. per game) 180.4—Michael Vick, Virginia Tech, 1999 (152 attempts, 90 completions, 5 interceptions, 1,840 yards, 12 TD passes)

MOST PASSES ATTEMPTED
Quarter

41—Jason Davis, UNLV vs. Idaho, Sept. 17, 1994 (4th, completed 28)

Half

56—Rusty LaRue, Wake Forest vs. Duke, Oct. 28, 1995 (2nd, completed 41)

Game

83—Drew Brees, Purdue vs. Wisconsin, Oct. 10, 1998 (completed 55)

Season

712—Kliff Kingsbury, Texas Tech, 2002 (14 games, completed 479)

2 Yrs

1,241—Kliff Kingsbury, Texas Tech, 2001-02 (completed 844)

3 Yrs

1,826—Kliff Kingsbury, Texas Tech, 2000-02 (completed 1,206)

Career

(4 yrs.) 1,883—Kliff Kingsbury, Texas Tech, 1999-02 (completed 1,231)

MOST PASSES ATTEMPTED PER GAME
Season

58.5—David Klingler, Houston, 1990 (643 in 11)

Career

47.0—Tim Rattay, Louisiana Tech, 1997-99 (1,552 in 33)

MOST PASSES ATTEMPTED BY A FRESHMAN
Game

72—Luke McCown, Louisiana Tech vs. Miami (Fla.), Oct. 28, 2000 (completed 42)

Season

559—Jared Lorenzen, Kentucky, 2000 (completed 321)

MOST PASSES COMPLETED
Quarter

28—Jason Davis, UNLV vs. Idaho, Sept. 17, 1994 (4th, attempted 41)

Half

41—Rusty LaRue, Wake Forest vs. Duke, Oct. 28, 1995 (2nd, attempted 56)

Game

55—Rusty LaRue, Wake Forest vs. Duke, Oct. 28, 1995 (attempted 78); Drew Brees, Purdue vs. Wisconsin, Oct. 10, 1998 (attempted 83)

Season

479—Kliff Kingsbury, Texas Tech, 2002 (14 games, attempted 712)

2 Yrs

844—Kliff Kingsbury, Texas Tech, 2001-02 (attempted 1,241)

Per-game record—34.7, Tim Couch, Kentucky, 1997-98 (763 in 22)

3 Yrs

1,206—Kliff Kingsbury, Texas Tech, 2000-02 (attempted 1,826)

Also holds per-game record with 32.6 (1,206 in 37)

Career

(4 yrs.) 1,231—Kliff Kingsbury, Texas Tech, 1999-02 (attempted 1,883)

MOST PASSES COMPLETED PER GAME
Season

36.4—Tim Couch, Kentucky, 1998 (400 in 11)

Career

30.8—Tim Rattay, Louisiana Tech, 1997-99 (1,015 in 33)

MOST PASSES COMPLETED BY A FRESHMAN
Game

47—Luke McCown, Louisiana Tech vs. Auburn, Oct. 21, 2000 (attempted 65)

Season

321—Jared Lorenzen, Kentucky, 2000 (attempted 559)

Also holds per-game record with 29.2 (321 in 11)

MOST CONSECUTIVE PASSES COMPLETED
Game

23—Tee Martin, Tennessee vs. South Carolina, Oct. 31, 1998

Season

24—Tee Martin, Tennessee, 1998 (completed last attempt vs. Alabama, Oct. 24 and first 23 vs. South Carolina, Oct. 31)

**MOST PASSES COMPLETED IN TWO, THREE AND
FOUR CONSECUTIVE GAMES**
2 Games

96—Rusty LaRue, Wake Forest, 1995 (55 vs. Duke, Oct. 28; 41 vs. Georgia Tech, Nov. 4)

3 Games

146—Rusty LaRue, Wake Forest, 1995 (55 vs. Duke, Oct. 28; 41 vs. Georgia Tech, Nov. 4; 50 vs. North Carolina St., Nov. 18)

4 Games

166—Tim Rattay, Louisiana Tech, 1999 (41 vs. Middle Tenn. St., Oct. 16; 46 vs. UCF, Oct. 23; 44 vs. Toledo, Oct. 30; 35 vs. La.-Monroe, Nov. 6)

HIGHEST PERCENTAGE OF PASSES COMPLETED
Game

(Min. 20-29 comps.) 95.8%—Tee Martin, Tennessee vs. South Carolina, Oct. 31, 1998 (23 of 24)

(Min. 30-39 comps.) 91.2%—Steve Sarkisian, Brigham Young vs. Fresno St., Nov. 25, 1995 (31 of 34)

(Min. 40 comps.) 83.1%—Kliff Kingsbury, Texas Tech vs. Texas A&M, Oct. 5, 2002 (49 of 59)

Season

(Min. 150 atts.) 73.6%—Daunte Culpepper, UCF, 1998 (296 of 402)

Career

(Min. 875-999 atts.) 66.2%—Scott Milanovich, Maryland, 1992-95 (650 of 982)

(Min. 1,000 atts.) 67.1%—Tim Couch, Kentucky, 1996-98 (795 of 1,184)

**HIGHEST PERCENTAGE OF PASSES COMPLETED
BY A FRESHMAN**
Season

(Min. 200 atts.) 66.2%—Grady Benton, Arizona St., 1992 (149 of 225)

MOST PASSES HAD INTERCEPTED
Game

9—John Reaves, Florida vs. Auburn, Nov. 1, 1969 (attempted 66)

Season

34—John Eckman, Wichita St., 1966 (attempted 458) Also holds per-game record with 3.4 (34 in 10)

Career

(3 yrs.) 68—Zeke Bratkowski, Georgia, 1951-53 (attempted 734)

(4 yrs.) 73—Mark Herrmann, Purdue, 1977-80 (attempted 1,218)

Per-game record—2.3, Steve Ramsey, North Texas, 1967-69 (67 in 29)

**LOWEST PERCENTAGE OF PASSES HAD
INTERCEPTED**
Season

(Min. 150-349 atts.) 0.0%—Matt Blundin, Virginia, 1991 (0 of 224)

(Min. 350 atts.) 0.74%—Marquel Blackwell, South Fla., 2002 (3 of 403)

Career

(Min. 600-1,049 atts.) 1.3%—Billy Volek, Fresno St., 1997-99 (12 of 934)

(Min. 1,050 atts.) 2.12%—Kliff Kingsbury, Texas Tech, 1999-02 (40 of 1,883)

**MOST PASSES ATTEMPTED WITHOUT AN
INTERCEPTION**
Game

68—David Klingler, Houston vs. Baylor, Oct. 6, 1990 (completed 35)

Entire Season

224—Matt Blundin, Virginia, 1991 (completed 135)

**MOST CONSECUTIVE PASSES ATTEMPTED
WITHOUT AN INTERCEPTION**
Season

271—Trent Dilfer, Fresno St., 1993 Also holds career record with 271

**MOST CONSECUTIVE PASSES ATTEMPTED WITH
JUST ONE INTERCEPTION**
Career

329—Damon Allen, Cal St. Fullerton, 1983-84 (during 16 games; began Oct. 8, 1983, vs. Nevada, ended Nov. 3, 1984, vs. Fresno St. Interception occurred vs. Idaho, Sept. 15, 1984)

**MOST CONSECUTIVE PASSES ATTEMPTED
WITHOUT AN INTERCEPTION AT THE START
OF A CAREER BY A FRESHMAN**

138—Mike Gundy, Oklahoma St., 1986 (during 8 games)

**MOST CONSECUTIVE PASSES ATTEMPTED
WITHOUT AN INTERCEPTION AT THE START
OF A DIVISION I-A CAREER**

202—Brad Otton, Southern California, 1994-95 (played 1993 at Division I-AA Weber St.)

MOST YARDS GAINED
Quarter

347—Jason Davis, UNLV vs. Idaho, Sept. 17, 1994 (4th)

Half

517—Andre Ware, Houston vs. Southern Methodist, Oct. 21, 1989 (1st, completed 25 of 41)

Game

716—David Klingler, Houston vs. Arizona St., Dec. 2, 1990 (completed 41 of 70)

Season

(11 games) 5,140—David Klingler, Houston, 1990 (completed 374 of 643)

(12 games) 5,188—Ty Detmer, Brigham Young, 1990 (completed 361 of 562)

2 Yrs

9,748—Ty Detmer, Brigham Young, 1989-90 (completed 626 of 974)

3 Yrs

13,779—Ty Detmer, Brigham Young, 1989-91 (completed 875 of 1,377)

Career
(4 yrs.) 15,031—Ty Detmer, Brigham Young, 1988-91 (completed 958 of 1,530)

MOST YARDS GAINED PER GAME
Season
467.3—David Klingler, Houston, 1990 (5,140 in 11)
2 Yrs
406.2—Ty Detmer, Brigham Young, 1989-90 (9,748 in 24)
Career
(3 yrs.) 386.2—Tim Rattay, Louisiana Tech, 1997-99 (12,746 in 33)
(4 yrs.) 326.8—Ty Detmer, Brigham Young, 1988-91 (15,031 in 46)

MOST YARDS GAINED BY A FRESHMAN
Game
611—David Neill, Nevada vs. New Mexico St., Oct. 10, 1998
Season
3,687—Jared Lorenzen, Kentucky, 2000
Per-game record—361.0, David Neill, Nevada, 1998 (3,249 in 9)

MOST YARDS GAINED BY A SOPHOMORE
Game
631—Scott Mitchell, Utah vs. Air Force, Oct. 15, 1988
Season
4,560—Ty Detmer, Brigham Young, 1989
Per-game record—392.9, Scott Mitchell, Utah, 1988 (4,322 in 11)

MOST SEASONS GAINING 2,000 YARDS OR MORE
Career
4—Kevin Sweeney, Fresno St., 1983-86 (2,359—3,259—2,604—2,363); Todd Santos, San Diego St., 1984-87 (2,063—2,877—2,553—3,932); Tom Hodson, LSU, 1986-89 (2,261—2,125—2,074—2,655); T. J. Rubley, Tulsa, 1987-89, 1991 (2,058—2,497—2,292—2,054); Alex Van Pelt, Pittsburgh, 1989-92 (2,527—2,427—2,796—3,163); Glenn Foley, Boston College, 1990-93 (2,189—2,225—2,231—3,397); Tim Lester, Western Mich., 1996-99 (2,189—2,160—3,311—3,639); David Garrard, East Caro., 1998-01 (2,091—2,359—2,332—2,247)

MOST YARDS GAINED IN TWO, THREE AND FOUR CONSECUTIVE GAMES
2 Games
1,288—David Klingler, Houston, 1990 (572 vs. Eastern Wash., Nov. 17; 716 vs. Arizona St., Dec. 2)
3 Games
1,798—David Klingler, Houston, 1990-91 (572 vs. Eastern Wash., Nov. 17, 1990; 716 vs. Arizona St., Dec. 2, 1990; 510 vs. Louisiana Tech, Aug. 31, 1991)
4 Games
2,150—David Klingler, Houston, 1990 (563 vs. TCU, Nov. 3; 299 vs. Texas, Nov. 10; 572 vs. Eastern Wash., Nov. 17; 716 vs. Arizona St., Dec. 2)

MOST GAMES GAINING 200 YARDS OR MORE
Season
13—Kliff Kingsbury, Texas Tech, 2002 (14 games)
Career
38—Ty Detmer, Brigham Young, 1988-91

MOST CONSECUTIVE GAMES GAINING 200 YARDS OR MORE
Season
12—Robbie Bosco, Brigham Young, 1984; Ty Detmer, Brigham Young, 1990, 1989; Chad Pennington, Marshall, 1999, 1997; Tim Rattay, Louisiana Tech, 1998; Kliff Kingsbury, Texas Tech, 2002
Career
28—Kliff Kingsbury, Texas Tech (from Oct. 10, 2000, to Nov. 16, 2002)

MOST GAMES GAINING 300 YARDS OR MORE
Season
12—Ty Detmer, Brigham Young, 1990, 1989
Career
33—Ty Detmer, Brigham Young, 1988-91

MOST CONSECUTIVE GAMES GAINING 300 YARDS OR MORE
Season
12—Ty Detmer, Brigham Young, 1990, 1989

Career
24—Ty Detmer, Brigham Young (from Sept. 2, 1989, to Dec. 1, 1990)

MOST GAMES GAINING 400 YARDS OR MORE
Season
9—David Klingler, Houston, 1990
Career
12—Ty Detmer, Brigham Young, 1988-91; Tim Rattay, Louisiana Tech, 1997-99

MOST YARDS GAINED BY TWO OPPOSING PLAYERS
Game
1,253—Matt Vogler, TCU (690) & David Klingler, Houston (563), Nov. 3, 1990

TWO PLAYERS, SAME TEAM, EACH PASSING FOR 250 YARDS OR MORE
Game
Steve Cottrell (311) & John Elway (270), Stanford vs. Arizona St., Oct. 24, 1981; Andre Ware (517) & David Klingler (254), Houston vs. Southern Methodist, Oct. 21, 1989; Jason Davis (381) & Jared Brown (254), UNLV vs. Idaho, Sept. 17, 1994

MOST YARDS GAINED IN OPENING GAME OF SEASON
590—Tim Rattay, Louisiana Tech vs. Nebraska, Aug. 29, 1998

MOST YARDS GAINED AGAINST ONE OPPONENT
Career
1,495—Ty Detmer, Brigham Young vs. New Mexico, 1988-91

MOST YARDS GAINED PER GAME AGAINST ONE OPPONENT
Career
(Min. 3 games) 410.7—Gary Schofield, Wake Forest vs. Maryland, 1981-83 (1,232 yards)
(Min. 4 games) 373.8—Ty Detmer, Brigham Young vs. New Mexico, 1988-91 (1,495 yards)

MOST YARDS GAINED PER ATTEMPT
Game
(Min. 25-39 atts.) 18.5—David Neill, Nevada vs. Idaho, Oct. 24, 1998 (26 for 480)
(Min. 40-59 atts.) 14.1—John Walsh, Brigham Young vs. Utah St., Oct. 30, 1993 (44 for 619)
(Min. 60 atts.) 10.5—Scott Mitchell, Utah vs. Air Force, Oct. 15, 1988 (60 for 631)
Season
(Min. 412 atts.) 11.1—Ty Detmer, Brigham Young, 1989 (412 for 4,560)
Career
(Min. 1,000 atts.) 9.8—Ty Detmer, Brigham Young, 1988-91 (1,530 for 15,031)

MOST YARDS GAINED PER COMPLETION
Game
(Min. 22-41 comps.) 22.9—John Walsh, Brigham Young vs. Utah St., Oct. 30, 1993 (27 for 619)
(Min. 42 comps.) 15.7—Matt Vogler, TCU vs. Houston, Nov. 3, 1990 (44 for 690)
Season
(Min. 109-204 comps.) 18.2—Doug Williams, Grambling, 1977 (181 for 3,286)
(Min. 205 comps.) 17.5—Danny Wuerffel, Florida, 1996 (207 for 3,625)
Career
(Min. 275-399 comps.) 17.3—J.J. Joe, Baylor, 1990-93 (347 for 5,995)
(Min. 400 comps.) 15.7—Shawn Moore, Virginia, 1987-90 (421 for 6,629)

MOST TOUCHDOWN PASSES
Quarter
6—David Klingler, Houston vs. Louisiana Tech, Aug. 31, 1991 (2nd)
Half
7—Dennis Shaw, San Diego St. vs. New Mexico St., Nov. 15, 1969 (1st); Terry Dean, Florida vs. New Mexico St., Sept. 3, 1994 (1st); Doug Johnson, Florida vs. Central Mich., Sept. 6, 1997 (1st)
Game
11—David Klingler, Houston vs. Eastern Wash., Nov. 17, 1990
Season
54—David Klingler, Houston, 1990 (11 games)
2 Yrs
83—David Klingler, Houston, 1990-91
Also holds per-game record with 4.0 (83 in 21)

3 Yrs
115—Tim Rattay, Louisiana Tech, 1997-99
Career
(3 yrs.) 115—Tim Rattay, Louisiana Tech, 1997-99
(4 yrs.) 121—Ty Detmer, Brigham Young, 1988-91

MOST TOUCHDOWN PASSES PER GAME
Season
4.9—David Klingler, Houston, 1990 (54 in 11)
Career
3.5—Tim Rattay, Louisiana Tech, 1997-99 (115 in 33)

HIGHEST PERCENTAGE OF PASSES FOR TOUCHDOWNS
Season
(Min. 175-374 atts.) 11.6%—Dennis Shaw, San Diego St., 1969 (39 of 335)
(Min. 375 atts.) 10.6%—Jim McMahon, Brigham Young, 1980 (47 of 445)
Career
(Min. 400-499 atts.) 9.7%—Rick Leach, Michigan, 1975-78 (45 of 462)
(Min. 500 atts.) 9.7%—Danny Wuerffel, Florida, 1993-96 (114 of 1,170)

MOST CONSECUTIVE GAMES THROWING A TOUCHDOWN PASS
Career
35—Ty Detmer, Brigham Young (from Sept. 7, 1989, to Nov. 23, 1991)

MOST CONSECUTIVE PASSES COMPLETED FOR TOUCHDOWNS
Game
6—Brooks Dawson, UTEP vs. New Mexico, Oct. 28, 1967 (first six completions of the game)

MOST TOUCHDOWN PASSES THROWN ON CONSECUTIVE PLAYS
Game
3—Jay Stuckey, UTEP vs. New Mexico St., Sept. 25, 1999 (9, 80 and 33 yards in 1:53 of playing time in second quarter)

MOST TOUCHDOWN PASSES IN FIRST GAME OF CAREER
5—John Reaves, Florida vs. Houston, Sept. 20, 1969

MOST TOUCHDOWN PASSES BY A FRESHMAN
Game
6—Bob Hoernschemeyer, Indiana vs. Nebraska, Oct. 9, 1943; Luke McCown, Louisiana Tech vs. La.-Lafayette, Oct. 14, 2000
Season
29—David Neill, Nevada, 1998

MOST TOUCHDOWN PASSES IN FRESHMAN AND SOPHOMORE SEASONS
55—Rex Grossman, Florida, 2000 (21) & 2001 (34)

MOST TOUCHDOWN PASSES BY A SOPHOMORE
39—Chad Pennington, Marshall, 1997

MOST TOUCHDOWN PASSES AT CONCLUSION OF JUNIOR SEASON
86—Ty Detmer, Brigham Young, 1988 (13), 1989 (32) & 1990 (41)

MOST TOUCHDOWN PASSES, SAME PASSER AND RECEIVER
Season
26—Tim Rattay to Troy Edwards, Louisiana Tech, 1998
Career
39—Tim Rattay to Troy Edwards, Louisiana Tech, 1997-98

MOST PASSES ATTEMPTED WITHOUT A TOUCHDOWN PASS
Season
266—Stu Rayburn, Kent St., 1984 (completed 125)

FEWEST TIMES SACKED ATTEMPTING TO PASS
Season
(Min. 300 atts.) 4—Steve Walsh, Miami (Fla.), 1988, in 390 attempts. Last 4 games of the season: Tulsa, 1 for -8 yards; LSU, 1 for -2; Arkansas, 1 for -12; Brigham Young, 1 for -9.

Receiving

MOST PASSES CAUGHT
Game

23—Randy Gatewood, UNLV vs. Idaho, Sept. 17, 1994 (363 yards)

Season

142—Manny Hazard, Houston, 1989 (1,689 yards)

Career

(2 yrs.) 227—Alex Van Dyke, Nevada, 1994-95 (3,100 yards)

(3 yrs.) 261—Howard Twilley, Tulsa, 1963-65 (3,343 yards)

(4 yrs.) 300—Arnold Jackson, Louisville, 1997-00 (3,670 yards)

MOST PASSES CAUGHT PER GAME
Season

13.4—Howard Twilley, Tulsa, 1965 (134 in 10)

Career

10.5—Manny Hazard, Houston, 1989-90 (220 in 21)

MOST PASSES CAUGHT BY TWO PLAYERS, SAME TEAM
Season

236—J.R. Tolver (128) & Kassim Osgood (108), San Diego St., 2002 (3,337 yards, 21 TDs)

Career

453—Mark Templeton (262) & Charles Lockett (191), Long Beach St., 1983-86 (4,871 yards, 30 TDs)

MOST PASSES CAUGHT IN CONSECUTIVE GAMES

38—Manny Hazard, Houston, 1989 (19 vs. TCU, Nov. 4; 19 vs. Texas, Nov. 11)

MOST CONSECUTIVE GAMES CATCHING A PASS
Career

47—Kareem Kelly, Southern California, 1999-02

MOST PASSES CAUGHT BY A TIGHT END
Game

17—Emilio Vallez, New Mexico vs. UTEP, Oct. 27, 1967 (257 yards); Jon Harvey, Northwestern vs. Michigan, Oct. 23, 1982 (208 yards)

Season

90—James Whalen, Kentucky, 1999 (1,019 yards)

Career

217—Ibn Green, Louisville, 1996-99 (2,830 yards)

MOST PASSES CAUGHT PER GAME BY A TIGHT END
Season

8.2—James Whalen, Kentucky, 1999 (90 in 11)

Career

5.4—Gordon Hudson, Brigham Young, 1980-83 (178 in 33)

MOST PASSES CAUGHT BY A RUNNING BACK
Game

18—Mark Templeton, Long Beach St. vs. Utah St., Nov. 1, 1986 (173 yards)

Season

99—Mark Templeton, Long Beach St., 1986 (688 yards)

Career

262—Mark Templeton, Long Beach St., 1983-86 (1,969 yards)

MOST PASSES CAUGHT BY A FRESHMAN
Game

18—Richard Woodley (WR), TCU vs. Texas Tech, Nov. 10, 1990 (180 yards)

Season

98—Taurean Henderson, Texas Tech, 2002 (RB) (633 yards)

Also holds per-game record with 7.0 (98 in 14)

CATCHING AT LEAST 50 PASSES AND GAINING AT LEAST 1,000 YARDS RUSHING
Season

By 10 players. Most recent: Ryan Benjamin, Pacific (Cal.), 1991 (51 catches and 1,581 yards rushing) Darrin Nelson, Stanford, holds record for most seasons at 3 (1977-78, 1981)

CATCHING AT LEAST 60 PASSES AND GAINING AT LEAST 1,000 YARDS RUSHING

Darrin Nelson, Stanford, 1981 (67 catches and 1,014 yards rushing); Brad Muster, Stanford, 1986 (61 catches and 1,053 yards rushing); Johnny Johnson, San Jose St., 1988 (61 catches and 1,219 yards rushing)

MOST YARDS GAINED
Game

405—Troy Edwards, Louisiana Tech vs. Nebraska, Aug. 29, 1998 (caught 21)

Season

2,060—Trevor Insley, Nevada, 1999 (caught 134)

Career

5,005—Trevor Insley, Nevada, 1996-99 (caught 298)

MOST YARDS GAINED PER GAME
Season

187.3—Trevor Insley, Nevada, 1999 (2,060 in 11)

Career

140.9—Alex Van Dyke, Nevada, 1994-95 (3,100 in 22)

MOST YARDS GAINED BY A TIGHT END
Game

259—Gordon Hudson, Brigham Young vs. Utah, Nov. 21, 1981 (caught 13)

Season

1,156—Chris Smith, Brigham Young, 1990 (caught 68)

Career

2,830—Ibn Green, Louisville, 1996-99 (caught 217)

MOST YARDS GAINED PER GAME BY A TIGHT END
Season

102.0—Mike Moore, Grambling, 1977 (1,122 in 11)

Career

75.3—Gordon Hudson, Brigham Young, 1980-83 (2,484 in 33)

MOST YARDS GAINED BY A FRESHMAN
Game

263—Corey Alston, Western Mich. vs. Eastern Mich., Nov. 1, 1997 (caught 9)

Season

1,265—Mike Williams, Southern California, 2002 (caught 81, 13 games)

Per-game record—101.9, Brandon Stokley, La.-Lafayette, 1995 (1,121 in 11)

MOST GAMES GAINING 100 YARDS OR MORE
Season

11—Aaron Turner, Pacific (Cal.), 1991

Also holds consecutive record with 11

Career

26—Trevor Insley, Nevada, 1996-99

Consecutive record: 11, Aaron Turner, Pacific (Cal.), 1991 (all one season) and Keyshawn Johnson, Southern California, 1994-95 (over two seasons)

MOST GAMES GAINING 200 YARDS OR MORE
Season

6—Trevor Insley, Nevada, 1999

Consecutive record: 3, Howard Twilley, Tulsa, 1965 & Trevor Insley, Nevada, 1999

MOST YARDS GAINED BY TWO PLAYERS, SAME TEAM
Game

640—Rick Eber (322) & Harry Wood (318), Tulsa vs. Idaho St., Oct. 7, 1967 (caught 33, 6 TDs)

Season

3,337—J.R. Tolver (1,785) & Kassim Osgood (1,552), San Diego St., 2002 (13 games)

TWO PLAYERS, SAME TEAM, EACH GAINING 1,000 YARDS
Season

16 times. Jason Phillips (1,444; 108 catches) & James Dixon (1,103; 102 catches), Houston, 1988; Patrick Rowe (1,392; 71 catches) & Dennis Arey (1,118; 68 catches), San Diego St., 1990; Andy Boyce (1,241; 79 catches) & Chris Smith (1,156; 68 catches), Brigham Young, 1990; Charles Johnson (1,149; 57 catches) & Michael Westbrook (1,060; 76 catches), Colorado, 1992; Bryan Reeves (1,362; 91 catches) & Michael Stephens (1,062; 80 catches), Nevada, 1993; Will Blackwell (1,207; 86 catches) & Az Hakim (1,022; 57 catches), San Diego St., 1995; E. G. Green (1,007; 60 catches) & Andre Cooper (1,002; 71 catches), Florida St., 1995; Chris Doering (1,045; 70 catches) & Ike Hilliard (1,008; 57 catches), Florida, 1995; Geoff Noisy (1,435; 98 catches) & Damond Wilkins (1,121; 114 catches), Nevada, 1996; Geoff Noisy (1,184; 86 catches) & Trevor Insley (1,151; 59 catches), Nevada, 1997; Geoff Noisy (1,405; 94 catches) & Trevor Insley (1,220; 69 catches), Nevada, 1998; Jajuan Dawson (1,051; 96 catches) & Adrian Burnette (1,095; 79 catches), Tulane, 1999; Rodney Wright (1,331; 91 catches) & Bernard Berrian (1,270; 76 catches),

Fresno St., 2001; J.R. Tolver (1,785; 128 catches) & Kassim Osgood (1,552; 108 catches), San Diego St., 2002; Doug Gabriel (1,237; 75 catches) & Jimmy Fryzel (1,126; 58 catches), UCF, 2002; Mike Williams (1,265; 81 catches) & Keary Colbert (1,029; 71 catches), Southern California, 2002

TWO PLAYERS, SAME TEAM, RANKED NO. 1 & NO. 2 IN FINAL RECEIVING RANKINGS
Season

Jason Phillips (No. 1, 9.8 catches per game) & James Dixon (No. 2, 9.3 catches per game), Houston, 1988

FOUR PLAYERS, SAME TEAM, EACH CATCHING 60 PASSES OR MORE
Season

James Jordan (81), John Simon (79), Delwyn Daigre (77) & Sean Cangelosi (62), Louisiana Tech, 1999

THREE PLAYERS, SAME TEAM, EACH CATCHING 60 PASSES OR MORE
Season

Patrick Rowe (71), Dennis Arey (68) & Jimmy Raye (62), San Diego St., 1990; Arnold Jackson (101), Ibn Green (60) & Lavell Boyd (60), Louisville, 1999

MOST 1,000-YARD RECEIVING SEASONS

3—Marc Zeno, Tulane, 1985-87 (1,137 in 1985; 1,033 in 1986; Clarkston Hines, Duke, 1987-89 (1,084 in 1987; 1,067 in 1988; 1,149 in 1989; 1,206 in 1987; Aaron Turner, Pacific (Cal.), 1990-92 (1,264 in 1990; 1,604 in 1991; 1,171 in 1992; Ryan Yarborough, Wyoming, 1991-93 (1,081 in 1991; 1,351 in 1992; 1,512 in 1993; Marcus Harris, Wyoming, 1993-96 (1,431 in 1994; 1,423 in 1995; 1,650 in 1996); Brandon Stokley, La.-Lafayette, 1995-96, 98 (1,121 in 1995; 1,160 in 1996; 1,175 in 1998); Geoff Noisy, Nevada, 1996-98 (1,435 in 1996; 1,184 in 1997; 1,405 in 1998); Trevor Insley, Nevada, 1997-99 (1,151 in 1997; 1,220 in 1998; 2,060 in 1999)

MOST RECEIVING SEASONS OVER 1,400 YARDS

3—Marcus Harris, Wyoming, 1993-96 (1,431 in 1994; 1,423 in 1995; 1,650 in 1996)

HIGHEST AVERAGE GAIN PER RECEPTION
Game

(Min. 3-4 receps.) 72.7—Terry Gallaher, East Caro. vs. Appalachian St., Sept. 13, 1975 (3 for 218; 82, 77, 59 yards)

(Min. 5-9 receps.) 52.6—Alexander Wright, Auburn vs. Pacific (Cal.), Sept. 9, 1989 (5 for 263; 78, 60, 41, 73, 11 yards)

(Min. 10 receps.) 34.9—Chuck Hughes, UTEP vs. North Texas, Sept. 18, 1965 (10 for 349)

Season

(Min. 30-49 receps.) 27.9—Elmo Wright, Houston, 1968 (43 for 1,198)

(Min. 50 receps.) 24.4—Henry Ellard, Fresno St., 1982 (62 for 1,510)

Career

(Min. 75-104 receps.) 25.7—Wesley Walker, California, 1973-76 (86 for 2,206)

(Min. 105 receps.) 22.0—Herman Moore, Virginia, 1988-90 (114 for 2,504)

HIGHEST AVERAGE GAIN PER RECEPTION BY A TIGHT END
Season

(Min. 30 receps.) 22.6—Jay Novacek, Wyoming, 1984 (33 for 745)

Career

(Min. 75 receps.) 19.2—Clay Brown, Brigham Young, 1978-80 (88 for 1,691)

MOST TOUCHDOWN PASSES CAUGHT
Game

6—Tim Delaney, San Diego St. vs. New Mexico St., Nov. 15, 1969 (16 receptions)

Season

27—Troy Edwards, Louisiana Tech, 1998 (140 receptions)

Per-game record—2.3, Tom Reynolds, San Diego St., 1969 (18 in 8); Troy Edwards, Louisiana Tech, 1998 (27 in 12)

Career

50—Troy Edwards, Louisiana Tech, 1996-98 (280 receptions)

MOST GAMES CATCHING A TOUCHDOWN PASS
Season

12—Randy Moss, Marshall, 1997

Career
27—Ryan Yarborough, Wyoming, 1990-93 (caught a total of 42 in 46 games)

MOST CONSECUTIVE GAMES CATCHING A TOUCHDOWN PASS
Season
12—Randy Moss, Marshall, 1997
Career
12—Desmond Howard, Michigan (last two games of 1990 and first 10 games of 1991); Aaron Turner, Pacific (Cal.) (last three games of 1990 and first nine games of 1991); Randy Moss, Marshall, 1997 (all in 1997)

MOST TOUCHDOWN PASSES CAUGHT BY A TIGHT END
Season
18—Dennis Smith, Utah, 1989 (73 receptions)
Career
33—Ibn Green, Louisville, 1996-99 (217 receptions)

HIGHEST PERCENTAGE OF PASSES CAUGHT FOR TOUCHDOWNS
Season
(Min. 10 TDs) 58.8%—Kevin Williams, Southern California, 1978 (10 of 17)
Career
(Min. 20 TDs) 35.3%—Kevin Williams, Southern California, 1977-80 (24 of 68)

HIGHEST AVERAGE YARDS PER TOUCHDOWN PASS
Season
(Min. 10 TDs) 56.1—Elmo Wright, Houston, 1968 (11 for 617 yards; 87, 50, 75, 2, 80, 79, 13, 67, 61, 43, 60 yards)
Career
(Min. 15 TDs) 46.5—Charles Johnson, Colorado, 1990-93 (15 for 697 yards)

MOST TOUCHDOWN PASSES CAUGHT, 50 YARDS OR MORE
Season
8—Elmo Wright, Houston, 1968 (87, 50, 75, 80, 79, 67, 61, 60 yards); Henry Ellard, Fresno St., 1982 (68, 51, 80, 61, 67, 72, 80, 72 yards)

MOST CONSECUTIVE PASSES CAUGHT FOR TOUCHDOWNS
6—Carlos Carson, LSU, 1977 (5 vs. Rice, Sept. 24; 1 vs. Florida, Oct. 1; first receptions of his career); Gerald Armstrong, Nebraska, 1992 (1 vs. Utah, Sept. 5; 1 vs. Arizona St., Sept. 26; 1 vs. Oklahoma St., Oct. 10; 1 vs. Colorado, Oct. 31; 2 vs. Kansas, Nov. 7)

MOST TOUCHDOWN PASSES CAUGHT BY A FRESHMAN
Season
14—Jabar Gaffney, Florida, 2000; Mike Williams, Southern California, 2002

MOST TOUCHDOWN PASSES CAUGHT IN FRESHMAN AND SOPHOMORE SEASONS
27—Jabar Gaffney, Florida, 2000 (14) & 2001 (13)

MOST YARDS GAINED IN A GAME WITHOUT SCORING A TOUCHDOWN
326—Nate Burleson, Nevada vs. San Jose St., Nov. 10, 2001 (12 receptions)

Punting

MOST PUNTS
Game
36—Charlie Calhoun, Texas Tech vs. Centenary (La.), Nov. 11, 1939 (1,318 yards; 20 were returned, 8 went out of bounds, 6 were downed, 1 was blocked [blocked kicks counted against the punter until 1955] and 1 went into the end zone for a touchback. Thirty-three of the punts occurred on first down during a heavy downpour in the game played at Shreveport, Louisiana)
Season
101—Jim Bailey, VMI, 1969 (3,507 yards)
Career
(3 yrs.) 276—Jim Bailey, VMI, 1969-71 (10,127 yards)

(4 yrs.) 322—Nick Harris, California, 1997-00 (13,621 yards)

HIGHEST AVERAGE PER PUNT
Game
(Min. 5-9 punts) 60.4—Lee Johnson, Brigham Young vs. Wyoming, Oct. 8, 1983 (5 for 302; 53, 44, 63, 62, 80 yards)
(Min. 10 punts) 53.6—Jim Benien, Oklahoma St. vs. Colorado, Nov. 13, 1971 (10 for 536)
Season
(Min. 36-39 punts) 50.3—Chad Kessler, LSU, 1997 (39 for 1,961)
(Min. 40-49 punts) 49.8—Reggie Roby, Iowa, 1981 (44 for 2,193)
(Min. 50-74 punts) 48.4—Todd Sauerbrun, West Virginia, 1994 (72 for 3,486)
(Min. 75 punts) 46.6—Bill Marinangel, Vanderbilt, 1996 (77 for 3,586)
Career
(Min. 150-199 punts) 46.3—Todd Sauerbrun, West Virginia, 1991-94 (167 for 7,733)
(Min. 200-249 punts) 44.7—Ray Guy, Southern Miss., 1970-72 (200 for 8,934)
(Min. 250 punts) 44.7—Shane Lechler, Texas A&M, 1996-99 (268 for 11,977)

HIGHEST AVERAGE PER PUNT BY A FRESHMAN
Season
(Min. 40 punts) 47.0—Tom Tupa, Ohio St., 1984 (41 for 1,927)

MOST YARDS ON PUNTS
Game
1,318—Charlie Calhoun, Texas Tech vs. Centenary (La.), Nov. 11, 1939 (36 punts)
Season
4,138—Johnny Pingel, Michigan St., 1938 (99 punts)
Career
13,621—Nick Harris, California, 1997-00 (322 punts)

MOST GAMES WITH A 40-YARD AVERAGE OR MORE
Career
(Min. 4 punts) 37—Shane Lechler, Texas A&M, 1996-99 (punted in 48 games)

MOST PUNTS, 50 YARDS OR MORE
Game
7—Mark Mariscal, Colorado vs. Southern California, Sept. 14, 2002 (8 punts)
Season
32—Todd Sauerbrun, West Virginia, 1994 (72 punts)
Career
(2 yrs.) 51—Marv Bateman, Utah, 1970-71 (133 punts)
(3 yrs.) 61—Russ Henderson, Virginia, 1976-78 (226 punts)
(4 yrs.) 88—Bill Smith, Mississippi, 1983-86 (254 punts)

MOST CONSECUTIVE GAMES WITH AT LEAST ONE PUNT OF 50 YARDS OR MORE
Career
32—Bill Smith, Mississippi, 1983-86

MOST PUNTS IN A CAREER WITHOUT HAVING ONE BLOCKED
300—Tony DeLeone, Kent St., 1981-84
Also holds consecutive record with 300

LONGEST PUNT
99—Pat Brady, Nevada vs. Loyola Marymount, Oct. 28, 1950

RANKING IN TOP 12 IN BOTH PUNTING AND FIELD GOALS
Steve Little, Arkansas, 1977 (No. 4 in punting, 44.3-yard average and No. 2 in field goals, 1.73 per game); Rob Keen, California, 1988 (No. 11 in punting, 42.6-yard average and No. 3 in field goals, 1.91 per game); Chris Gardocki, Clemson, 1990 (No. 4 in punting, 44.3-yard average and No. 4 in field goals, 1.73 per game), 1989 (No. 10 in punting, 42.7-yard average and No. 6 in field goals, 1.82 per game); Dan Eichloff, Kansas, 1991 (No. 12 in punting, 42.3-yard average and No. 3 in field goals, 1.64 per game); Daron Alcorn, Akron, 1992 (No. 11 in punting, 43.6-yard average and tied for No. 9 in field goals, 1.64 per game)

Interceptions

MOST PASSES INTERCEPTED
Game
5—Lee Cook, Oklahoma St. vs. Detroit, Nov. 28, 1942 (15 yards); Walt Pastuszak, Brown vs. Rhode Island, Oct. 8, 1949 (47 yards); Byron Beaver, Houston vs. Baylor, Sept. 22, 1962 (18 yards); Dan Rebsch, Miami (Ohio) vs. Western Mich., Nov. 4, 1972 (88 yards). Special note: Prior to NCAA College Division records, Dick Miller of Akron intercepted six passes vs. Baldwin-Wallace on Oct. 23, 1937.
Season
14—Al Worley, Washington, 1968 (130 yards)
Career
29—Al Brosky, Illinois, 1950-52 (356 yards)

MOST PASSES INTERCEPTED PER GAME
Season
1.4—Al Worley, Washington, 1968 (14 in 10)
Career
1.1—Al Brosky, Illinois, 1950-52 (29 in 27)

MOST PASSES INTERCEPTED BY A LINEBACKER
Game
3—Nate Kvamme, Colorado St. vs. San Jose St., Oct. 11, 1997; Aaron Humphrey, Texas vs. Rutgers, Sept. 6, 1997; Joseph Phipps, TCU vs. Oklahoma, Sept. 12, 1998; Lorenzo Ferguson, Virginia Tech vs. Clemson, Sept. 12, 1998; Dan Dawson, Rice vs. Hawaii, Oct. 21, 2000; Grant Steen, Iowa vs. Indiana, Oct. 19, 2002
Season
9—Bill Sibley, Texas A&M, 1941 (57 yards)

MOST PASSES INTERCEPTED BY A FRESHMAN
Game
4—Mario Edwards, Florida St. vs. Wake Forest, Nov. 14, 1998 (60 yards)
Season
13—George Shaw, Oregon, 1951 (136 yards)
Also holds per-game record with 1.3 (13 in 10)

MOST YARDS ON INTERCEPTION RETURNS
Game
182—Ashley Lee, Virginia Tech vs. Vanderbilt, Nov. 12, 1983 (2 interceptions)
Season
302—Charles Phillips, Southern California, 1974 (7 interceptions)
Career
501—Terrell Buckley, Florida St., 1989-91 (21 interceptions)

MOST TOUCHDOWNS SCORED ON INTERCEPTION RETURNS
Game
3—Johnny Jackson, Houston vs. Texas, Nov. 7, 1987 (31, 53, 97 yards)
Season
4—Deltha O'Neal, California, 1999 (9 interceptions)
Career
5—Jackie Walker, Tennessee, 1969-71 (11 interceptions); Ken Thomas, San Jose St., 1979-82 (14 interceptions); Deltha O'Neal, California, 1996-99 (11 interceptions)

MOST TOUCHDOWNS SCORED ON INTERCEPTION RETURNS BY A LINEBACKER
Game
2—Tom Fisher, New Mexico St. vs. Lamar, Nov. 14, 1970 (52 & 28 yards in one quarter.); Randy Neal, Virginia vs. Virginia Tech, Nov. 21, 1992 (37 & 30 yards); Patrick Brown, Kansas vs. UAB, Aug. 28, 1997 (51 & 23 yards); Nate Kvamme, Colorado St. vs. San Jose St., Oct. 11, 1997 (15 & 57 yards)
Season
2—Tom Fisher, New Mexico St., 1970; Jerry Robinson, UCLA, 1976; Randy Neal, Virginia, 1994, 1992; Mike Rose, Purdue, 1997; Patrick Brown, Kansas, 1997; Nate Kvamme, Colorado St., 1997; Chris Claiborne, Southern California, 1998; Dustin Cohen, Miami (Ohio), 1998; Dan Dawson, Rice, 2001; Spencer Havner, UCLA, 2002
Career
4—Randy Neal, Virginia, 1991-94; Dustin Cohen, Miami (Ohio), 1996-99

HIGHEST AVERAGE GAIN PER INTERCEPTION
Game

(Min. 2 ints.) 91.0—Ashley Lee, Virginia Tech vs. Vanderbilt, Nov. 12, 1983 (2 for 182)

Season

(Min. 5 ints.) 50.6—Norm Thompson, Utah, 1969 (5 for 253)

Career

(Min. 15 ints.) 26.5—Tom Pridemore, West Virginia, 1975-77 (15 for 398)

MOST CONSECUTIVE GAMES INTERCEPTING A PASS

15—Al Brosky, Illinois, began Nov. 11, 1950 (vs. Iowa), ended Oct. 18, 1952 (vs. Minnesota)

Punt Returns

MOST PUNT RETURNS
Game

20—Milton Hill, Texas Tech vs. Centenary (La.), Nov. 11, 1939 (110 yards)

Season

57—Wes Welker, Texas Tech, 2002 (752 yards, 14 games)

Per-game record—5.5, Dick Adams, Miami (Ohio), 1970 (55 in 10)

Career

153—Vai Sikahema, Brigham Young, 1980-81, 1984-85 (1,312 yards)

MOST YARDS ON PUNT RETURNS
Game

219—Golden Richards, Brigham Young vs. North Texas, Sept. 10, 1971 (5 returns)

Season

791—Lee Nalley, Vanderbilt, 1948 (43 returns)

Also holds per-game record with 79.1 (791 in 10)

Career

1,695—Lee Nalley, Vanderbilt, 1947-49 (109 returns)

HIGHEST AVERAGE GAIN PER RETURN
Game

(Min. 3-4 rets.) 59.7—Chip Hough, Air Force vs. Southern Methodist, Oct. 9, 1971 (3 for 179)

(Min. 5 rets.) 43.8—Golden Richards, Brigham Young vs. North Texas, Sept. 10, 1971 (5 for 219)

Season

(Min. 1.2 rets. per game) 25.9—Bill Blackstock, Tennessee, 1951 (12 for 311)

(Min. 1.5 rets. per game) 25.0—George Sims, Baylor, 1948 (15 for 375)

Career

(Min. 1.2 rets. per game) 23.6—Jack Mitchell, Oklahoma, 1946-48 (39 for 922)

(Min. 1.5 rets. per game) 20.5—Gene Gibson, Cincinnati, 1949-50 (37 for 760)

MOST TOUCHDOWNS SCORED ON PUNT RETURNS
Game

2—By many players. Most recent: Derek Abney, Kentucky vs. Mississippi, Nov. 2, 2002 (69 & 52 yards); DeJuan Groce, Nebraska vs. Troy St., Aug. 31, 2002 (83 & 72 yards)

Season

4—Golden Richards, Brigham Young, 1971; Cliff Branch, Colorado, 1971; James Henry, Southern Miss., 1987; Tinker Keck, Cincinnati, 1997; Quinton Spotwood, Syracuse, 1997; David Allen, Kansas St., 1998; Santana Moss, Miami (Fla.), 2000; Derek Abney, Kentucky, 2002; DeJuan Groce, Nebraska, 2002; Steve Suter, Maryland, 2002

Career

7—Jack Mitchell, Oklahoma, 1946-48 (3 in 1946, 1 in 1947, 3 in 1948); Johnny Rodgers, Nebraska, 1970-72 (2 in 1970, 3 in 1971, 2 in 1972); David Allen, Kansas St., 1997-99 (1 in 1997, 4 in 1998, 2 in 1999)

CONSECUTIVE GAMES WITH PUNT RETURN FOR A TOUCHDOWN

3—David Allen, Kansas St., 1998 (63 yards vs. Indiana St., Sept. 5; 69 yards vs. Northern Ill., Sept. 12; 93 yards vs. Texas, Sept. 19)

(Allen also returned punts for touchdowns in consecutive games in 1999 [94 yards vs. Iowa St., Sept. 25 & 74 yards vs. Texas, Oct.2])

Kickoff Returns

MOST KICKOFF RETURNS
Game

11—Trevor Cobb, Rice vs. Houston, Dec. 2, 1989 (166 yards)

Season

55—William White, Army, 2002 (1,239 yards, 11 games)

Career

123—Jeff Liggon, Tulane, 1993-96 (2,922 yards)

MOST RETURNS PER GAME
Season

5.0—William White, Army, 2002 (55 in 11)

Career

3.0—Steve Odom, Utah, 1971-73 (99 in 33)

MOST YARDS ON KICKOFF RETURNS
Game

248—Tyrone Watley, Iowa St. vs. Nebraska, Nov. 15, 1997 (10 returns)

Season

1,239—William White, Army, 2002 (55 returns, 11 games)

Career

2,922—Jeff Liggon, Tulane, 1993-96 (123 returns)

MOST YARDS RETURNED PER GAME
Season

112.7—Dwayne Owens, Oregon St., 1990 (1,014 in 9)

Career

78.2—Steve Odom, Utah, 1971-73 (2,582 in 33)

HIGHEST AVERAGE GAIN PER RETURN
Game

(Min. 3 rets.) 72.7—Anthony Davis, Southern California vs. Notre Dame, Dec. 2, 1972 (3 for 218)

Season

(Min. 1.2 rets. per game) 40.1—Paul Allen, Brigham Young, 1961 (12 for 481)

(Min. 1.5 rets. per game) 38.2—Forrest Hall, San Francisco, 1946 (15 for 573)

Career

(Min. 1.2 rets. per game) 36.2—Forrest Hall, San Francisco, 1946-47 (22 for 796)

(Min. 1.5 rets. per game) 31.0—Overton Curtis, Utah St., 1957-58 (32 for 991)

MOST TOUCHDOWNS SCORED ON KICKOFF RETURNS
Game

2—Paul Copoulos, Marquette vs. Iowa Pre-Flight, Nov. 6, 1943 (85 & 82 yards); Ron Horwath, Detroit vs. Hillsdale, Sept. 22, 1950 (96 & 96 yards); Ollie Matson, San Francisco vs. Fordham, Oct. 20, 1951 (94 & 90 yards); Anthony Davis, Southern California vs. Notre Dame, Dec. 2, 1972 (97 & 96 yards); Raghib Ismail, Notre Dame vs. Rice, Nov. 5, 1988 (87 & 83 yards); *Raghib Ismail, Notre Dame vs. Michigan, Sept. 16, 1989 (88 & 92 yards); Stacey Corley, Brigham Young vs. Air Force, Nov. 11, 1989 (99 & 85 yards); Leeland McElroy, Texas A&M vs. Rice, Oct. 23, 1993 (93 & 88 yards); Tutu Atwell, Minnesota vs. Iowa St., Sept. 13, 1997 (89 & 93 yards); Tony Lukins, New Mexico St. vs. Tulsa, Oct. 6, 2001 (83 & 100 yards)

Season

3—Forrest Hall, San Francisco, 1946; Stan Brown, Purdue, 1970; Anthony Davis, Southern California, 1974; Willie Gault, Tennessee, 1980; Terance Mathis, New Mexico, 1989; Leeland McElroy, Texas A&M, 1993.

Career

6—Anthony Davis, Southern California, 1972-74

Ismail is the only player in history to score twice in two games.

SCORING A TOUCHDOWN ON TEAM'S OPENING KICKOFF OF TWO SEASONS
Season

Barry Sanders, Oklahoma St., 1988 (100 yards vs. Miami [Ohio], Sept. 10) & 1987 (100 yards vs. Tulsa, Sept. 5)

Total Kick Returns

(Combined Punt and Kickoff Returns)

MOST KICK RETURNS
Game

20—Milton Hill, Texas Tech vs. Centenary (La.), Nov. 11, 1939 (20 punts, 110 yards)

Season

78—Steve Suter, Maryland, 2002 (56 punts, 22 kick-offs, 1,317 yards)

Career

203—Deltha O'Neal, California, 1996-99 (110 punts, 93 kickoffs, 3,455 yards)

MOST YARDS ON KICK RETURNS
Game

284—Tutu Atwell, Minnesota vs. Iowa St., Sept. 13, 1997 (59 punt returns, 225 kickoff returns)

Season

1,348—Derek Abney, Kentucky, 2002 (544 punt returns, 804 kickoff returns)

Per-game record—116.2, Dion Johnson, East Caro., 1990 (1,046 yards, with 167 on punt returns and 879 on kickoff returns in 9 games)

Career

3,455—Deltha O'Neal, California, 1996-99 (1,169 on punts & 2,286 on kickoffs)

GAINING 1,000 YARDS ON PUNT RETURNS AND 1,000 YARDS ON KICKOFF RETURNS
Career

Troy Slade, Duke, 1973-75 (1,021 & 1,757); Devon Ford, Appalachian St., 1973-76 (1,197 & 1,761); Anthony Carter, Michigan, 1979-82 (1,095 & 1,504); Willie Drewrey, West Virginia, 1981-84 (1,072 & 1,302); Tony James, Mississippi St., 1989-92 (1,332 & 1,842); Thomas Bailey, Auburn, 1991-94 (1,170 & 1,520); Tim Dwight, Iowa, 1994-97 (1,051 & 1,133); Deltha O'Neal, California, 1996-99 (1,169 & 2,286); Nick Davis, Wisconsin, 1998-01 (1,001 & 1,697)

HIGHEST AVERAGE PER KICK RETURN
(Min. 1.2 Punt Returns and 1.2 Kickoff Returns Per Game)
Season

27.2—Erroll Tucker, Utah, 1985 (40 for 1,087; 16 for 389 on punt returns, 24 for 698 on kickoff returns)

Career

22.0—Erroll Tucker, Utah, 1984-85 (79 for 1,741; 38 for 650 on punt returns, 41 for 1,091 on kickoff returns)

AVERAGING 20 YARDS EACH ON PUNT RETURNS AND KICKOFF RETURNS
(Min. 1.2 Returns Per Game Each)
Season

By 7 players. Most recent: Lee Gissendaner, North-western, 1992 (21.8 on punt returns, 15 for 327; 22.4 on kickoff returns, 17 for 381)

MOST TOUCHDOWNS SCORED ON KICK RETURNS
(Must Have at Least One Punt Return and One Kickoff Return)
Game

2—By eight players. Most recent: Derek Abney, Kentucky vs. Florida, Sept. 28, 2002 (Other players: Chad Owens, Hawaii vs. Brigham Young, Dec. 7, 2001; Kahlil Hill, Iowa vs. Western Mich., Sept. 5, 1998; Joe Rowe, Virginia vs. Central Michigan, Sept. 7, 1996; Eric Blount, North Carolina vs. William & Mary, Oct. 5, 1991; Dion Johnson, East Caro. vs. Temple, Oct. 27, 1990; Charlie Justice, North Carolina vs. Florida, Oct. 26, 1946; Ernie Steele, Washington vs. Washington St., Nov. 30, 1940)

Season

6—Derek Abney, Kentucky, 2002 (4 punt returns, 2 kickoff returns)

Career

8—Cliff Branch, Colorado, 1970-71 (6 punts, 2 kick-offs); Johnny Rodgers, Nebraska, 1970-72 (7 punts, 1 kickoff)

WINNING BOTH PUNT RETURN AND KICKOFF RETURN CHAMPIONSHIPS
Season

Erroll Tucker, Utah, 1985

Career

Ira Matthews, Wisconsin, kickoff returns (1976) and punt returns (1978); Erroll Tucker, Utah, 1985

All Runbacks

(Combined Interception Returns, Blocked Kick Returns, Fumble Returns, Punt Returns and Kickoff Returns)

SCORING MORE THAN ONE TOUCHDOWN IN AT LEAST THREE CATEGORIES
Season

Erroll Tucker, Utah, 1985 (3 interceptions, 2 punt returns, 2 kickoff returns)

SCORING AT LEAST ONE TOUCHDOWN IN AT LEAST THREE CATEGORIES
Season

Dick Harris, South Carolina, 1970; Mark Haynes, Arizona St., 1974; Scott Thomas, Air Force, 1985; Joe Crocker, Virginia, 1994; Joe Walker, Nebraska, 1998; Deltha O'Neal, California, 1999

HIGHEST AVERAGE PER RUNBACK
Season

(Min. 40 rets.) 28.3—Erroll Tucker, Utah, 1985 (46 for 1,303; 6 for 216 on interceptions, 16 for 389 on punt returns, 24 for 698 on kickoff returns)

HIGHEST AVERAGE PER RUNBACK
(At Least 7 Interceptions and Min. 1.3 Punt Returns and 1.3 Kickoff Returns Per Game)
Career

22.6—Erroll Tucker, Utah, 1984-85 (87 for 1,965; 8 for 224 on interceptions, 38 for 650 on punt returns, 41 for 1,091 on kickoff returns)

MOST TOUCHDOWNS SCORED ON RUNBACKS
Game

3—Johnny Jackson, Houston vs. Texas, Nov. 7, 1987 (3 interceptions)

MOST TOUCHDOWNS ON RUNBACKS
(Must Have at Least One Touchdown in At Least Three Categories)
Season

7—Erroll Tucker, Utah, 1985 (3 interceptions, 2 punt returns, 2 kickoff returns)

Career

9—Allen Rossum, Notre Dame, 1994-97 (3 interceptions, 3 punt returns, 3 kickoff returns)

Kicks Blocked

MOST PUNTS BLOCKED BY
Game

4—Ken Irvin, Memphis vs. Arkansas, Sept. 26, 1992; James King, Central Mich. vs. Michigan St., Sept. 8, 2001

Season

8—Jimmy Lisko, Arkansas St., 1975 (11 games); James Francis (LB), Baylor, 1989 (11 games)

MOST PAT KICKS BLOCKED BY
Season

5—Ray Farmer, Duke, 1993

Career

8—Ray Farmer, Duke, 1992-95

MOST FIELD GOAL ATTEMPTS BLOCKED BY
Quarter

2—Jerald Henry, Southern California vs. California, Oct. 22, 1994 (1st, returned first one 60 yards for touchdown); Pat Larson, Wyoming vs. Fresno St., Nov. 18, 1995 (2nd)

Game

2—Jerald Henry, Southern California vs. California, Oct. 22, 1994; Pat Larson, Wyoming vs. Fresno St., Nov. 18, 1995; Kyle Vanden Bosch, Nebraska vs. Texas A&M, Nov. 6, 2000; Antwan Peek, Cincinnati vs. Miami (Ohio), Oct. 28, 2000; Alton Moore, Auburn vs. Georgia, Nov. 10, 2001

MOST TOTAL KICKS BLOCKED BY
(Includes Punts, PAT Attempts, FG Attempts)
Game

4—Ken Irvin, Memphis vs. Arkansas, Sept. 26, 1992 (4 punts)

Career

19—James Ferebee, New Mexico St., 1978-81 (5 punts, 6 PAT attempts, 8 FG attempts)

MOST TOUCHDOWNS SCORED ON BLOCKED PUNTS
Game

2—David Langner, Auburn vs. Alabama, Dec. 2, 1972 (2nd half); Frank Staine-Pyne, Air Force vs. Hawaii, Nov. 1, 1997 (1st half)

Season

3—Joe Wessel, Florida St., 1984

All-Purpose Yards

(Yardage Gained From Rushing, Receiving and All Runbacks)

MOST PLAYS
Game

58—Tony Sands, Kansas vs. Missouri, Nov. 23, 1991 (58 rushes)

Season

432—Marcus Allen, Southern California, 1981 (403 rushes, 29 receptions)

Career

(3 yrs.) 1,034—Herschel Walker, Georgia, 1980-82 (994 rushes, 26 receptions, 14 kickoff returns)
(4 yrs.) 1,347—Steve Bartalo, Colorado St., 1983-86 (1,215 rushes, 132 receptions)

MOST YARDS GAINED
Quarter

305—Corey Dillon, Washington vs. San Jose St., Nov. 16, 1996 (1st, 222 rushing, 83 receiving)

Game

578—Emmett White, Utah St. vs. New Mexico St., Nov. 4, 2000 (322 rushing, 134 receiving, 2 punt returns, 120 kickoff returns)

Season

3,250—Barry Sanders, Oklahoma St., 1988 (2,628 rushing, 106 receiving, 95 punt returns, 421 kickoff returns; 11 games)

Career

(3 yrs.) 5,749—Herschel Walker, Georgia, 1980-82 (5,259 rushing, 243 receiving, 247 kickoff returns; 1,034 plays)
(4 yrs.) 7,206—Ricky Williams, Texas, 1995-98 (6,279 rushing, 927 receiving; 1,096 plays)

MOST YARDS GAINED PER GAME
Season

295.5—Barry Sanders, Oklahoma St., 1988 (3,250 in 11 games; 2,628 rushing, 106 receiving, 95 punt returns, 421 kickoff returns)

Career

237.8—Ryan Benjamin, Pacific (Cal.), 1990-92 (5,706 in 24 games; 3,119 rushing, 1,063 receiving, 100 punt returns, 1,424 kickoff returns)

MOST YARDS GAINED BY A FRESHMAN
Game

422—Marshall Faulk, San Diego St. vs. Pacific (Cal.), Sept. 14, 1991 (386 rushing, 11 receiving, 25 kickoff returns)

Season

2,026—Terrell Willis, Rutgers, 1993 (1,261 rushing, 61 receiving, 704 kickoff returns; 234 plays)
Per-game record—184.8, Marshall Faulk, San Diego St., 1991 (1,663 in 9)

MOST SEASONS WITH 2,000 OR MORE YARDS

2—Howard Stevens, Randolph-Macon, 1968 (2,115) & Louisville, 1972 (2,132); Napoleon McCallum, Navy, 1983 (2,385) & 1985 (2,330); Chuck Weatherspoon, Houston, 1989 (2,391) & 1990 (2,038); Sheldon Canley, San Jose St., 1989 (2,513) & 1990 (2,213); Glyn Milburn, Stanford, 1990 (2,222) & 1992 (2,121); Ryan Benjamin, Pacific (Cal.), 1991 (2,995) & 1992 (2,597); Troy Davis, Iowa St., 1995 (2,466) & 1996 (2,364); Kevin Faulk, LSU, 1996 (2,104) & 1998 (2,109); Ricky Williams, Texas, 1997 (2,043) & 1998 (2,386); Emmett White, Utah St., 2000 (2,628) & 2001 (2,014)

GAINED 1,000 YARDS RUSHING AND 1,000 YARDS RECEIVING
Career

By many players. Most recent: Levron Williams, Indiana, 1998-01 (3,095 rushing & 1,052 receiving); Emmett White, Utah St., 1998-01 (2,791 rushing & 1,044 receiving)

HIGHEST AVERAGE GAIN PER PLAY
Game

(Min. 300 yards, 25 plays) 16.8—Randy Gatewood, UNLV vs. Idaho, Sept. 17, 1994 (419 on 25)

Season

(Min. 1,500 yards, 100-124 plays) 18.5—Henry Bailey, UNLV, 1992 (1,883 on 102)
(Min. 1,500 yards, 125 plays) 17.5—Bernard Berrian, Fresno St., 2001 (2,591 on 148)

Career

(Min. 5,000 yards, 275-374 plays) 17.4—Anthony Carter, Michigan, 1979-82 (5,197 on 298)
(Min. 5,000 yards, 375 plays) 14.6—Terance Mathis, New Mexico, 1985-87, 1989 (6,691 on 457)

MOST YARDS GAINED BY TWO PLAYERS, SAME TEAM
Career

10,253—Marshall Faulk (5,595) & Darnay Scott (4,658), San Diego St., 1991-93

Scoring

MOST POINTS SCORED
(By Non-Kickers)
Game

48—Howard Griffith, Illinois vs. Southern Ill., Sept. 22, 1990 (8 TDs on runs of 5, 51, 7, 41, 5, 18, 5, 3 yards)

Game vs. Major-College Opponent

44—Marshall Faulk, San Diego St. vs. Pacific (Cal.), Sept. 14, 1991 (7 TDs, 1 two-point conversion)

Season

234—Barry Sanders, Oklahoma St., 1988 (39 TDs in 11 games)

2 Yrs

320—Ricky Williams, Texas, 1997-98 (53 TDs, 1 two-point conversion in 22 games)

3 Yrs

404—Ricky Williams, Texas, 1996-98 (67 TDs, 1 two-point conversion in 34 games)

Career

(4 yrs.) 468—Travis Prentice, Miami (Ohio), 1996-99 (78 TDs)

MOST POINTS SCORED PER GAME
Season

21.3—Barry Sanders, Oklahoma St., 1988 (234 in 11)

2 Yrs

14.5—Ricky Williams, Texas 1997-98 (320 in 22)

Career

12.1—Marshall Faulk, San Diego St., 1991-93 (376 in 31)

MOST POINTS SCORED BY A FRESHMAN
Game

44—Marshall Faulk, San Diego St. vs. Pacific (Cal.), Sept. 14, 1991 (7 TDs, 1 two-point conversion)

Season

140—Marshall Faulk, San Diego St., 1991 (23 TDs, 1 two-point conversion)
Also holds per-game record with 15.6 (140 in 9)

MOST TOUCHDOWNS SCORED
Quarter

4—Dick Felt, Brigham Young vs. San Jose St., Nov. 8, 1952 (all rushing, 4th); Howard Griffith, Illinois vs. Southern Ill., Sept. 22, 1990 (all rushing, 3rd); Eric Bieniemy, Colorado vs. Nebraska, Nov. 2, 1990 (all rushing, 4th); Corey Dillon, Washington vs. San Jose St., Nov. 16, 1996 (3 rushing, 1 receiving, 1st); Frank Moreau, Louisville vs. East Caro., Nov. 1, 1997 (all rushing, 2nd); Terry Caulley, Connecticut vs. Kent St., Nov. 9, 2002 (3 rushing, 1 receiving, 2nd)

Game

8—Howard Griffith, Illinois vs. Southern Ill., Sept. 22, 1990 (all 8 by rushing on runs of 5, 51, 7, 41, 5, 18, 5, 3 yards)

Game vs. Major-College Opponent
7—Arnold "Showboat" Boykin, Mississippi vs. Mississippi St., Dec. 1, 1951; Marshall Faulk, San Diego St. vs. Pacific (Cal.), Sept. 14, 1991

Season
39—Barry Sanders, Oklahoma St., 1988 (11 games)
Also holds per-game record with 3.5 (39 in 11)

2 Yrs
53—Ricky Williams, Texas 1997-98 (22 games)
Also holds per-game record with 2.4 (53 in 22)

3 Yrs
67—Ricky Williams, Texas, 1996-98 (34 games)

Career
(4 yrs.) 78—Travis Prentice, Miami (Ohio) (73 rushing, 5 pass receptions)

MOST TOUCHDOWNS SCORED IN TWO AND THREE CONSECUTIVE GAMES
2 Games
11—Kelvin Bryant, North Carolina, 1981 (6 vs. East Caro., Sept. 12; 5 vs. Miami [Ohio], Sept. 19; Ricky Williams, Texas, 1998 (6 vs. Rice, Sept. 26; 5 vs. Iowa St., Oct. 3)

3 Games
15—Kelvin Bryant, North Carolina, 1981 (6 vs. East Caro., Sept. 12; 5 vs. Miami [Ohio], Sept. 19; 4 vs. Boston College, Sept. 26)

MOST TOUCHDOWNS SCORED BY A FRESHMAN
Game
7—Marshall Faulk, San Diego St. vs. Pacific (Cal.), Sept. 14, 1991 (all by rushing)

Season
23—Marshall Faulk, San Diego St., 1991 (21 rushing, 2 pass receptions)
Also holds per-game record with 2.6 (23 in 9)

MOST GAMES SCORING A TOUCHDOWN
Season
14—Lee Suggs, Virginia Tech, 2002 (14 games)

Career
35—Travis Prentice, Miami (Ohio), 1996-99; Brock Forsey, Boise St., 1999-02

MOST CONSECUTIVE GAMES SCORING A TOUCHDOWN
Career
27—Lee Suggs, Virginia Tech (from Sept. 2, 2000 through Dec. 31, 2002; 57 touchdowns)

MOST GAMES SCORING TWO OR MORE TOUCHDOWNS
Season
11—Barry Sanders, Oklahoma St., 1988

Career
25—Travis Prentice, Miami (Ohio), 1996-99

MOST CONSECUTIVE GAMES SCORING TWO OR MORE TOUCHDOWNS
Season
11—Barry Sanders, Oklahoma St., 1988

Career
13—Barry Sanders, Oklahoma St. (from Nov. 14, 1987, through 1988)

MOST GAMES SCORING THREE OR MORE TOUCHDOWNS
Season
9—Barry Sanders, Oklahoma St., 1988

MOST CONSECUTIVE GAMES SCORING THREE OR MORE TOUCHDOWNS
Season
5—Paul Hewitt, San Diego St., 1987 (from Oct. 10 through Nov. 7); Barry Sanders, Oklahoma St., 1988 (from Sept. 10 through Oct. 15)

MOST TOUCHDOWNS AND POINTS SCORED BY TWO PLAYERS, SAME TEAM
Season
54 and 324—Barry Sanders (39-234) & Hart Lee Dykes (15-90), Oklahoma St., 1988

Career
97 and 585—Glenn Davis (59-354) & Doc Blanchard (38-231), Army, 1943-46
68 and 756—Brock Forsey (68-408) & Nick Calaycay (0-348), Boise St., 1999-02

PASSING FOR A TOUCHDOWN AND SCORING TOUCHDOWNS BY RUSHING AND RECEIVING
Game
By many players. Most recent: Craig Ochs, Colorado vs. Oklahoma St., Oct. 28, 2000; Eric Crouch, Nebraska vs. California, Sept. 11, 1999 (all in 2nd quarter); Antwaan Randle El, Indiana vs. Cincinnati, Sept. 26, 1998; Jacquez Green, Florida vs. Auburn, Oct. 18, 1997

PASSING FOR A TOUCHDOWN AND SCORING ON A PASS RECEPTION AND PUNT RETURN
Game
By many players. Most recent: Tim Dwight, Iowa vs. Indiana, Oct. 25, 1997

PLAYER RETURNING A BLOCKED PUNT, FUMBLE RECOVERY AND INTERCEPTION RETURN FOR A TOUCHDOWN
Season
By many players. Most recent: Tim Curry, Air Force, 1997

MOST EXTRA POINTS ATTEMPTED BY KICKING
Game
14—Terry Leiweke, Houston vs. Tulsa, Nov. 23, 1968 (13 made)

Season
71—Kurt Gunther, Brigham Young, 1980 (64 made); Bart Edmiston, Florida, 1995 (71 made); Scott Bentley, Florida St., 1995 (67 made)

Career
222—Derek Mahoney, Fresno St., 1990-93 (216 made); Kris Brown, Nebraska, 1995-98 (217 made); Nick Calaycay, Boise St., 1999-02 (213 made)

MOST EXTRA POINTS MADE BY KICKING
Game
13—Terry Leiweke, Houston vs. Tulsa, Nov. 23, 1968 (14 attempts); Derek Mahoney, Fresno St. vs. New Mexico, Oct. 5, 1991 (13 attempts)

Season
71—Bart Edmiston, Florida, 1995 (71 attempts)
Per-game record—6.1, Cary Blanchard, Oklahoma St., 1988, and Scott Bentley, Florida St., 1995 (67 in 11)

Career
217—Kris Brown, Nebraska, 1995-98 (222 attempts)
Per-game record—5.3, Bart Edmiston, Fresno St., 1993-96 (137 in 26)

BEST PERFECT RECORD OF EXTRA POINTS MADE
Season
71 of 71—Bart Edmiston, Florida, 1995

HIGHEST PERCENTAGE OF EXTRA POINTS MADE
Career
(Min. 100 atts.) 100%—Van Tiffin, Alabama, 1983-86 (135 of 135); Pete Stoyanovich, Indiana, 1985-88 (101 of 101); David Browndyke, LSU, 1986-89 (109 of 109); John Becksvoort, Tennessee, 1991-94 (161 of 161); Luke Manget, Georgia Tech, 1999-02 (160 of 160); Damon Duval, Auburn, 1999-02 (125 of 125)

MOST CONSECUTIVE EXTRA POINTS MADE
Game
13—Derek Mahoney, Fresno St. vs. New Mexico, Oct. 5, 1991 (13 attempts)

Season
71—Bart Edmiston, Florida, 1995 (71 attempts)

Career
161—John Becksvoort, Tennessee, 1991-94

MOST POINTS SCORED BY KICKING
Game
24—Mike Prindle, Western Mich. vs. Marshall, Sept. 29, 1984 (7 FGs, 3 PATs)

Season
135—Martin Gramatica, Kansas St., 1998 (22 FGs, 69 PATs)
Per-game record—11.9, Roman Anderson, Houston, 1989 (131 in 11)

Career
423—Roman Anderson, Houston, 1988-91 (70 FGs, 213 PATs)
Also holds per-game record with 9.6 (423 in 44)

HIGHEST PERCENTAGE OF EXTRA POINTS AND FIELD GOALS MADE
Season
(Min. 20 PATS and 12 FGs made) 100.0%—Marc Primanti, North Carolina St., 1996 (24 of 24 PATs, 20 of 20 FGs); Ryan White, Memphis, 1998 (22 of 22 PATs, 16 of 16 FGs)
(Min. 30 PATs and 15 FGs made) 98.3%—Chuck Nelson, Washington, 1982 (34 of 34 PATs, 25 of 26 FGs)
(Min. 40 PATs and 20 FGs made) 97.3%—Chris Jacke, UTEP, 1988 (48 of 48 PATs, 25 of 27 FGs)

Career
(Min. 100 PATs and 50 FGs made) 93.3%—John Lee, UCLA, 1982-85 (116 of 117 PATs, 79 of 92 FGs)

MOST TWO-POINT ATTEMPTS MADE
Game
6—Jim Pilot, New Mexico St. vs. Hardin-Simmons, Nov. 25, 1961 (all by running, attempted 7)

Season
6—Pat McCarthy, Holy Cross, 1960 (all by running); Jim Pilot, New Mexico St., 1961 (all by running); Howard Twilley, Tulsa, 1964 (all on pass receptions)

Career
13—Pat McCarthy, Holy Cross, 1960-62 (all by running)

MOST SUCCESSFUL TWO-POINT PASSES
Season
12—John Hangartner, Arizona St., 1958 (attempted 21)

Career
19—Pat McCarthy, Holy Cross, 1960-62 (attempted 33)

Defensive Extra Points

MOST DEFENSIVE EXTRA POINTS RETURNED
Game
2—Corey Ivy, Oklahoma vs. California, Sept. 20, 1997; Tony Holmes, Texas vs. Iowa St., Oct. 3, 1998

MOST DEFENSIVE EXTRA POINTS SCORED
Game
2—Tony Holmes, Texas vs. Iowa St., Oct. 3, 1998
Season
2—Tony Holmes, Texas, 1998

MOST DEFENSIVE EXTRA POINTS SCORED BY BOTH TEAMS
Game
2—Eric Kelly (fumbled snap return), Kentucky, and Mark Roman (blocked kick return), LSU, Oct. 17, 1998

LONGEST RETURN OF A DEFENSIVE EXTRA-POINT ATTEMPT
Game
100—Lee Ozmint (SS), Alabama vs. LSU, Nov. 11, 1989 (intercepted pass at Alabama goal line); Quintin Parker (DB), Illinois vs. Wisconsin, Oct. 28, 1989 (returned kick from Illinois goal line); Curt Newton (LB), Washington St. vs. Oregon St., Oct. 20, 1990 (intercepted pass from Washington St. goal line); William Price (CB), Kansas St. vs. Indiana St., Sept. 7, 1991 (intercepted pass three yards deep in Indiana St. end zone); Joe Crocker (CB), Virginia vs. North Carolina St., Nov. 25, 1994 (intercepted pass five yards deep in North Carolina St. end zone); Laymar Grant, Duke vs. Maryland, Oct. 26, 1996 (returned conversion pass attempt); Tony Holmes, Texas vs. Iowa St., Oct. 3, 1998 (intercepted pass); Brandon Ratcliff, New Mexico vs. UNLV, Oct. 12, 2002 (intercepted pass three yards deep in UNLV end zone)

FIRST DEFENSIVE EXTRA-POINT ATTEMPT
Thomas King (S), La.-Lafayette vs. Cal St. Fullerton, Sept. 3, 1988 (returned blocked kick 6 yards)

MOST DEFENSIVE EXTRA-POINT KICKS BLOCKED
Game
2—Nigel Codrington (DB), Rice vs. Notre Dame, Nov. 5, 1988 (1 resulted in a score)
Also holds season record with 2

Defensive Records

(Since 2000)

TOTAL TACKLES
Game
26—Brian Leigeb, Central Mich. vs. Northern Ill., Nov. 17, 2000; Doug Szymul, Northwestern vs. Navy, Sept. 21, 2002
Season
193—Lawrence Flugence, Texas Tech, 2002 (14 games)
Per-game record—15.6, Rick Sherrod, West Virginia, 2001 (156 in 10)

SOLO TACKLES
Game
19—Doug Szymul, Northwestern vs. Navy, Sept. 21, 2002
Season
135—E.J. Henderson, Maryland, 2002 (14 games)
Per-game record—10.2, Rick Sherrod, West Virginia, 2001 (102 in 10)

ASSISTED TACKLES
Game
11—Bob Sanders, Iowa vs. Indiana, Oct. 20, 2001
Season
88—David Lusky, Eastern Mich., 2002 (12 games); John Leake, Clemson, 2002 (13 games)
Per-game record—7.4, Pernell Griffin, East Caro., 2001 (81 in 11)

TACKLES FOR LOSS
Game
7.0—Chris Johnson, Kansas St. vs. Kansas, Oct. 7, 2000; Richard Seigler, Oregon St. vs. Arizona St., Oct. 20, 2001
Season
31.5—Terrell Suggs, Arizona St., 2002 (27 solo, 9 assisted in 14 games)
Per-game record—2.8, Kenny Philpot, Eastern Mich., 2001 (30.5 in 11)

PASS SACKS
Game
5.0—Wendell Bryant, Wisconsin vs. Penn St., Sept. 22, 2001
Season
24.0—Terrell Suggs, Arizona St., 2002 (23 solo, 2 assisted in 14 games)
Also holds per-game record with 1.71 (24.0 in 14)

PASSES DEFENDED
Game
8—Joselio Hanson, Texas Tech vs. Oklahoma St., Nov. 9, 2002
Season
32—Jason Goss, TCU, 2002 (24 pass breakups, 8 pass interceptions in 12 games)
Also holds per-game record with 2.67 (32 in 12)

FORCED FUMBLES
Game
3—DeLawrence Grant, Oregon St. vs. San Diego St., Sept. 23, 2000; Mason Unck, Arizona St. vs. Stanford, Sept. 28, 2002; Quintin Mikell, Boise St. vs. Hawaii, Oct. 5, 2002
Season
8—Dwight Freeney, Syracuse, 2001; Quintin Mikell, Boise St., 2002
Per-game record—0.67, Dwight Freeney, Syracuse, 2001 (8 in 12); Tom Canada, California, 2002 (6 in 9)

TOUCHDOWNS SCORED BY FUMBLE RETURN AND INTERCEPTION RETURN IN SAME GAME
2—Paul McClendon, Texas Tech vs. North Texas, Sept. 22, 2001 (six-yard fumble return and 50-yard interception return); Shawn Hackett, West Virginia vs Rutgers, Nov. 3, 2001 (50-yard interception return and 10-yard fumble return)

Fumble Returns

(Since 1992)

LONGEST FUMBLE RETURN FOR A TOUCHDOWN
100—Paul Rivers, Rutgers vs. Pittsburgh, Oct. 28, 1995; Dan Dawson, Rice vs. UNLV, Nov. 14, 1998; Kevin Thomas, UNLV vs. Baylor, Sept. 11, 1999

MOST FUMBLE RETURNS
Game
2—By many players.

MOST FUMBLE RETURNS RETURNED FOR TOUCHDOWNS
Game
2—Tyrone Carter, Minnesota vs. Syracuse, Sept. 21, 1996 (63 & 20 yards); Tony Driver, Notre Dame vs. Navy, Oct. 14, 2000 (24 & 22 yards)

Field Goals

MOST FIELD GOALS ATTEMPTED
Game
9—Mike Prindle, Western Mich. vs. Marshall, Sept. 29, 1984 (7 made)
Season
38—Jerry DePoyster, Wyoming, 1966 (13 made)
Also holds per-game record with 3.8 (38 in 10)
Career
(3 yrs.) 93—Jerry DePoyster, Wyoming, 1965-67 (36 made)
Also holds per-game record with 3.1 (93 in 30)
(4 yrs.) 105—Luis Zendejas, Arizona St., 1981-84 (78 made); Philip Doyle, Alabama, 1987-90 (78 made)
Doyle holds per-game record with 2.4 (105 in 43)

MOST FIELD GOALS MADE
Quarter
4—By 5 players. Most recent: Jose Cortez, Oregon St. vs. California, Oct. 31, 1998 (2nd)
Half
5—Dale Klein, Nebraska vs. Missouri, Oct. 19, 1985 (1st); Dat Ly, New Mexico St. vs. Kansas, Oct. 1, 1988 (1st)
Game
7—Mike Prindle, Western Mich. vs. Marshall, Sept. 29, 1984 (32, 44, 42, 23, 48, 41, 27 yards), 9 attempts; Dale Klein, Nebraska vs. Missouri, Oct. 19, 1985 (32, 22, 43, 44, 29, 43, 43 yards), 7 attempts
Season
29—John Lee, UCLA, 1984 (33 attempts)
2 Yrs
50—John Lee, UCLA, 1984-85 (57 attempts)
Career
80—Jeff Jaeger, Washington, 1983-86 (99 attempts)

MOST FIELD GOALS MADE PER GAME
Season
2.6—John Lee, UCLA, 1984 (29 in 11)
Career
1.8—John Lee, UCLA, 1982-85 (79 in 43)

BEST PERFECT RECORD OF FIELD GOALS MADE
Game
7 of 7—Dale Klein, Nebraska vs. Missouri, Oct. 19, 1985
Season
20 of 20—Marc Primanti, North Carolina St., 1996

MOST FIELD GOALS MADE BY A FRESHMAN
Game
6—*Mickey Thomas, Virginia Tech vs. Vanderbilt, Nov. 4, 1989 (6 attempts)
Season
23—Collin Mackie, South Carolina, 1987 (30 attempts)

*Conventional-style kicker.

HIGHEST PERCENTAGE OF FIELD GOALS MADE
Season
(Min. 15 atts.) 100.0%—John Lee, UCLA, 1984 (16 of 16); Marc Primanti, North Carolina St., 1996 (20 of 20); Ryan White, Memphis, 1998 (16 of 16)
Career
(Min. 45-54 atts.) 87.8%—Bobby Raymond, Florida, 1983-84 (43 of 49)
(Min. 55 atts.) 85.9%—John Lee, UCLA, 1982-85 (79 of 92)

MOST CONSECUTIVE FIELD GOALS MADE
Season
25—Chuck Nelson, Washington, 1982 (first 25, missed last attempt of season vs. Washington St., Nov. 20)

Career
30—Chuck Nelson, Washington, 1981-82 (last 5 in 1981, from vs. Southern California, Nov. 14, and first 25 in 1982, ending with last attempt vs. Washington St., Nov. 20)

MOST GAMES KICKING A FIELD GOAL
Career
40—Gary Gussman, Miami (Ohio), 1984-87 (in 44 games played)

MOST CONSECUTIVE GAMES KICKING A FIELD GOAL
19—Larry Roach, Oklahoma St., 1983-84; Gary Gussman, Miami (Ohio), 1986-87

MOST FIELD GOALS MADE, 60 YARDS OR MORE
Game
2—Tony Franklin, Texas A&M vs. Baylor, Oct. 16, 1976 (65 & 64 yards)
Season
3—Russell Erxleben, Texas, 1977 (67 vs. Rice, Oct. 1; 64 vs. Baylor, Oct. 16; 60 vs. Texas Tech, Oct. 29) (4 attempts)
Career
3—Russell Erxleben, Texas, 1975-78 (see Season Record above)

MOST FIELD GOALS ATTEMPTED, 60 YARDS OR MORE
Season
5—Tony Franklin, Texas A&M, 1976 (2 made)
Career
11—Tony Franklin, Texas A&M, 1975-78 (2 made)

MOST FIELD GOALS MADE, 50 YARDS OR MORE
Game
3—Jerry DePoyster, Wyoming vs. Utah, Oct. 8, 1966 (54, 54, 52 yards); Sergio Lopez-Chavero, Wichita St. vs. Drake, Oct. 27, 1984 (54, 54, 51 yards); Tim Douglas, Iowa vs. Illinois, Sept. 26, 1998 (51, 58, 51 yards); Dan Orner, North Carolina vs. Syracuse, Sept. 7, 2002 (52, 51, 51 yards)
Season
8—Fuad Reveiz, Tennessee, 1982 (10 attempts)
Career
20—Jason Hanson, Washington St., 1988-91 (35 attempts)

MOST FIELD GOALS ATTEMPTED, 50 YARDS OR MORE
Season
17—Jerry DePoyster, Wyoming, 1966 (5 made)
Career
38—Tony Franklin, Texas A&M, 1975-78 (16 made)

HIGHEST PERCENTAGE OF FIELD GOALS MADE, 50 YARDS OR MORE
Season
(Min. 10 atts.) 80.0%—Fuad Reveiz, Tennessee, 1982 (8 of 10)
Career
(Min. 15 atts.) 60.9%—Max Zendejas, Arizona, 1982-85 (14 of 23)

MOST FIELD GOALS MADE, 40 YARDS OR MORE
Game
5—Alan Smith, Texas A&M vs. Arkansas St., Sept. 17, 1983 (44, 45, 42, 59, 57 yards)
Season
14—Chris Jacke, UTEP, 1988 (16 attempts)
Career
39—Jason Hanson, Washington St., 1988-91 (66 attempts) (19 of 31, 40-49 yards; 20 of 35, 50 or more yards)

MOST FIELD GOALS ATTEMPTED, 40 YARDS OR MORE
Season
25—Jerry DePoyster, Wyoming, 1966 (6 made)
Career
66—Jason Hanson, Washington St., 1988-91 (39 made)

HIGHEST PERCENTAGE OF FIELD GOALS MADE, 40 YARDS OR MORE
Season
(Min. 10 made) 90.9%—John Carney, Notre Dame, 1984 (10 of 11)

Career

(Min. 20 made) 69.4%—John Lee, UCLA, 1982-85 (25 of 36)

HIGHEST PERCENTAGE OF FIELD GOALS MADE, 40-49 YARDS
Season

(Min. 10 made) 100%—John Carney, Notre Dame, 1984 (10 of 10)

Career

(Min. 15 made) 82.6%—Jeff Jaeger, Washington, 1983-86 (19 of 23)

MOST CONSECUTIVE FIELD GOALS MADE, 40-49 YARDS
Career

12—John Carney, Notre Dame, 1984-85

HIGHEST PERCENTAGE OF FIELD GOALS MADE, UNDER 40 YARDS
Season

(Min. 16 made) 100%—Paul Woodside, West Virginia, 1982 (23 of 23); Randy Pratt, California, 1983 (16 of 16); John Lee, UCLA, 1984 (16 of 16); Bobby Raymond, Florida, 1984 (18 of 18); Scott Slater, Texas A&M, 1986 (16 of 16); Philip Doyle, Alabama, 1989 (19 of 19)

Career

(Min. 30-39 made) 97.0%—Bobby Raymond, Florida, 1983-84 (32 of 33)

(Min. 40 made) 96.4%—John Lee, UCLA, 1982-85 (54 of 56)

LONGEST AVERAGE DISTANCE FIELD GOALS MADE
Game

(Min. 4 made) 49.5—Jeff Heath, East Caro. vs. Texas-Arlington, Nov. 6, 1982 (58, 53, 42, 45 yards)

Season

(Min. 10 made) 50.9—Jason Hanson, Washington St., 1991 (10 made)

Career

(Min. 25 made) 42.4—Russell Erxleben, Texas, 1975-78 (49 made)

LONGEST AVERAGE DISTANCE FIELD GOALS ATTEMPTED
Season

(Min. 20 atts.) 51.2—Jason Hanson, Washington St., 1991 (22 attempts)

Career

(Min. 40 atts.) 44.7—Russell Erxleben, Texas, 1975-78 (78 attempts)

MOST TIMES KICKING TWO OR MORE FIELD GOALS IN A GAME
Season

10—Paul Woodside, West Virginia, 1982

Career

27—Kevin Butler, Georgia, 1981-84

MOST TIMES KICKING THREE OR MORE FIELD GOALS IN A GAME
Season

6—Luis Zendejas, Arizona St., 1983; Joe Allison, Memphis, 1992

Career

13—Luis Zendejas, Arizona St., 1981-84

MOST TIMES KICKING FOUR FIELD GOALS IN A GAME
Season

4—Matt Bahr, Penn St., 1978

Career

6—John Lee, UCLA, 1982-85

LONGEST FIELD GOAL MADE

67—Russell Erxleben, Texas vs. Rice, Oct. 1, 1977; Steve Little, Arkansas vs. Texas, Oct. 15, 1977; Joe Williams, Wichita St. vs. Southern Ill., Oct. 21, 1978

LONGEST INDOOR FIELD GOAL MADE

62—Chip Lohmiller, Minnesota vs. Iowa, Nov. 22, 1986 (in Minnesota's Metrodome)

LONGEST FIELD GOAL MADE WITHOUT USE OF A KICKING TEE

65—Martin Gramatica, Kansas St., vs. Northern Ill., Sept. 12, 1998

LONGEST FIELD GOAL MADE BY A FRESHMAN

61—Kyle Bryant, Texas A&M vs. Southern Miss., Sept. 24, 1994

LONGEST FIELD GOAL MADE ON FIRST ATTEMPT OF CAREER

61—Ralf Mojsiejenko, Michigan St. vs. Illinois, Sept. 11, 1982

MOST FIELD GOALS MADE IN FIRST GAME OF CAREER

5—Joe Liljenquist, Brigham Young vs. Colorado St., Sept. 20, 1969 (6 attempts); Nathan Ritter, North Carolina St. vs. East Caro., Sept. 9, 1978 (6 attempts); Jose Oceguera, Long Beach St. vs. Kansas St., Sept. 3, 1983 (5 attempts)

MOST GAMES IN WHICH FIELD GOAL(S) PROVIDED THE WINNING MARGIN
Season

6—Henrik Mike-Mayer, Drake, 1981

Career

10—Dan Miller, Miami (Fla.), 1978-81; John Lee, UCLA, 1982-85; Jeff Ward, Texas, 1983-86

Team Records

SINGLE GAME—Offense

Total Offense

MOST PLAYS

112—Montana vs. Montana St., Nov. 1, 1952 (475 yards)

MOST PLAYS, BOTH TEAMS

196—San Diego St. (99) & North Texas (97), Dec. 4, 1971 (851 yards)

MOST PLAYS, BOTH TEAMS (OVERTIME)

198—Arkansas (106) & Mississippi (92), Nov. 3, 2001, 7 ot (988 yards)

FEWEST PLAYS

12—Texas Tech vs. Centenary (La.), Nov. 11, 1939 (10 rushes, 2 passes, -1 yard)

FEWEST PLAYS, BOTH TEAMS

33—Texas Tech (12) & Centenary (La.) (21), Nov. 11, 1939 (28 rushes, 5 passes, 30 yards)

MOST YARDS GAINED

1,021—Houston vs. Southern Methodist, Oct. 21, 1989 (250 rushing, 771 passing, 86 plays)

MOST YARDS GAINED, BOTH TEAMS

1,640—San Jose St. (849) & Nevada (791), Nov. 10, 2001 (168 plays)

FEWEST YARDS GAINED

Minus 47—Syracuse vs. Penn St., Oct. 18, 1947 (-107 rushing, gained 60 passing, 49 plays)

FEWEST YARDS GAINED, BOTH TEAMS

30—Texas Tech (-1) & Centenary (La.) (31), Nov. 11, 1939 (33 plays)

MOST YARDS GAINED BY A LOSING TEAM

791—Nevada vs. San Jose St., Nov. 10, 2001 (lost 64-45)

BOTH TEAMS GAINING 600 YARDS OR MORE

In 27 games. Most recent: San Diego St. (632) & Hawaii (610), Dec. 7, 2002 (157 plays); Hawaii (646) & Brigham Young (612), Dec. 8, 2001 (178 plays); Northwestern (624) & Bowling Green (618), Nov. 17, 2001 (183 plays); Nevada (791) & San Jose St. (849), Nov. 10, 2001 (168 plays); Idaho (760) & Middle Tenn. (685), Oct. 6, 2001 (166 plays); Nevada (653) & New Mexico St. (614), Oct. 10, 1998 (172 plays); Miami (Fla.) (689) & UCLA (670), Dec. 5, 1998 (152 plays); Tennessee (695) & Kentucky (634), Nov. 22, 1997; Kent St. (615) & UCF (612), Oct. 4, 1997 (154 plays); San Diego St. (670) & UNLV (627), Nov. 16, 1996 (166 plays); Nevada (727) & Louisiana Tech (607), Oct. 21, 1995 (180 plays); Idaho (707) & UNLV (614), Sept. 17, 1994 (181 plays); Maryland (649) & Virginia Tech (641), Sept. 25, 1993 (166 plays); Nevada (616) & Weber St. (615) Oct. 23, 1993 (180 plays)

FEWEST YARDS GAINED BY A WINNING TEAM

10—North Carolina St. vs. Virginia, Sept. 30, 1944 (won 13-0)

HIGHEST AVERAGE GAIN PER PLAY (Min. 75 Plays)

11.9—Houston vs. Southern Methodist, Oct. 21, 1989 (86 for 1,021)

MOST TOUCHDOWNS SCORED BY RUSHING AND PASSING

15—Wyoming vs. Northern Colo., Nov. 5, 1949 (9 rushing, 6 passing)

MOST TOUCHDOWNS SCORED BY RUSHING AND PASSING (OVERTIME)

16—Arkansas vs. Mississippi, Nov. 3, 2001, 7 ot (9 rushing, 7 passing)

Rushing

MOST RUSHES

99—Missouri vs. Colorado, Oct. 12, 1968 (421 yards)

MOST RUSHES, BOTH TEAMS

141—Colgate (82) & Bucknell (59), Nov. 6, 1971 (440 yards)

FEWEST RUSHES

5—Houston vs. Texas Tech, Nov. 25, 1989 (36 yards)

FEWEST RUSHES, BOTH TEAMS

28—Texas Tech (10) & Centenary (La.) (18), Nov. 11, 1939 (23 yards)

MOST YARDS GAINED

768—Oklahoma vs. Kansas St., Oct. 15, 1988 (72 rushes)

MOST YARDS GAINED, BOTH TEAMS

1,039—Lenoir-Rhyne (837) & Davidson (202), Oct. 11, 1975 (111 rushes)

MOST YARDS GAINED, BOTH TEAMS, MAJOR-COLLEGE OPPONENTS

956—Oklahoma (711) & Kansas St. (245), Oct. 23, 1971 (111 rushes)

FEWEST YARDS GAINED

Minus 109—Northern Ill. vs. Toledo, Nov. 11, 1967 (33 rushes)

FEWEST YARDS GAINED, BOTH TEAMS

Minus 24—San Jose St. (-102) & UTEP (78), Oct. 22, 1966 (75 rushes)

MOST YARDS GAINED WITHOUT LOSS

677—Nebraska vs. New Mexico St., Sept. 18, 1982 (78 rushes)

MOST YARDS GAINED BY A LOSING TEAM

545—Air Force vs. Hawaii, Nov. 24, 2001 (78 rushes, lost 50-32)

HIGHEST AVERAGE GAIN PER RUSH (Min. 50 Rushes)

11.9—Alabama vs. Virginia Tech, Oct. 27, 1973 (63 for 748)

MOST PLAYERS ON ONE TEAM EACH GAINING 100 YARDS OR MORE

4—Arizona St. vs. Arizona, Nov. 10, 1951 (Bob Tarwater 140, Harley Cooper 123, Duane Morrison 118, Buzz Walker 113); Texas vs. Southern Methodist, Nov. 1, 1969 (Jim Bertelsen 137, Steve Worster 137, James Street 121, Ted Koy 111); Alabama vs. Virginia Tech, Oct. 27, 1973 (Jimmy Taylor 142, Wilbur Jackson 138, Calvin Culliver 127, Richard Todd 102); Army vs. Montana, Nov. 17, 1984 (Doug Black 183, Nate Sassaman 155, Clarence Jones 130, Jarvis Hollingsworth 124); Nebraska vs. Baylor, Oct. 13, 2001 (Thunder Collins 165, Dahrran Diedrick 137, Eric Crouch 132, Judd Davies 119)

MOST TOUCHDOWNS SCORED BY RUSHING

12—UTEP vs. New Mexico St., Nov. 25, 1948

Passing

MOST PASSES ATTEMPTED

83—Purdue vs. Wisconsin, Oct. 10, 1998 (completed 55)

MOST PASSES ATTEMPTED, BOTH TEAMS
135—TCU (79) & Houston (56), Nov. 3, 1990 (completed 81)

FEWEST PASSES ATTEMPTED
0—By many teams. Most recent: Ohio vs. Akron, Oct. 25, 1997 (61 rushes; won 21-17)

FEWEST PASSES ATTEMPTED, BOTH TEAMS
1—Michigan St. (0) & Maryland (1), Oct. 20, 1944 (not completed)

MOST PASSES ATTEMPTED WITHOUT COMPLETION
18—West Virginia vs. Temple, Oct. 18, 1946

MOST PASSES ATTEMPTED WITHOUT INTERCEPTION
72—Houston vs. TCU, Nov. 4, 1989 (completed 47)

MOST PASSES ATTEMPTED WITHOUT INTERCEPTION, BOTH TEAMS
114—Illinois (67) & Purdue (47), Oct. 12, 1985 (completed 67)

MOST CONSECUTIVE PASSES ATTEMPTED WITHOUT A RUSHING PLAY
32—North Carolina St. vs. Duke, Nov. 11, 1989 (3rd & 4th quarters, completed 16)

MOST PASSES COMPLETED
55—Wake Forest vs. Duke, Oct. 28, 1995 (attempted 78); Purdue vs. Wisconsin, Oct. 10, 1998 (attempted 83)

MOST PASSES COMPLETED, BOTH TEAMS
81—TCU (44) & Houston (37), Nov. 3, 1990 (attempted 135)

BEST PERFECT GAME (100.0 Pct.)
12 of 12—Iowa vs. Northwestern, Nov. 9, 2002

HIGHEST PERCENTAGE OF PASSES COMPLETED
(Min. 15-24 comps.) 96.0%—Tennessee vs. South Carolina, Oct. 31, 1998 (24 of 25)
(Min. 25-34 comps.) 92.6%—UCLA vs. Washington, Oct. 29, 1983 (25 of 27)
(Min. 35 comps.) 87.0%—South Carolina vs. Mississippi St., Oct. 14, 1995 (40 of 46)

HIGHEST PERCENTAGE OF PASSES COMPLETED, BOTH TEAMS
(Min. 40 Completions)
84.6%—UCLA & Washington, Oct. 29, 1983 (44 of 52)

MOST PASSES HAD INTERCEPTED
10—Detroit vs. Oklahoma St., Nov. 28, 1942; California vs. UCLA, Oct. 21, 1978 (52 attempts)

MOST YARDS GAINED
771—Houston vs. Southern Methodist, Oct. 21, 1989 (completed 40 of 61)

MOST YARDS GAINED, BOTH TEAMS
1,253—TCU (690) & Houston (563), Nov. 3, 1990 (135 attempts)

FEWEST YARDS GAINED, BOTH TEAMS
Minus 13—North Carolina (-7 on 1 of 3 attempts) & Pennsylvania (-6 on 2 of 12 attempts), Nov. 13, 1943

MOST YARDS GAINED PER ATTEMPT
(Min. 30-39 atts.) 17.0—Nevada vs. Idaho, Oct. 24, 1998 (35 for 596)
(Min. 40 atts.) 15.9—UTEP vs. North Texas, Sept. 18, 1965 (40 for 634)

MOST YARDS GAINED PER COMPLETION
(Min. 15-24 comps.) 31.9—UTEP vs. New Mexico, Oct. 28, 1967 (16 for 510)
(Min. 25 comps.) 25.4—UTEP vs. North Texas, Sept. 18, 1965 (25 for 634)

MOST TOUCHDOWN PASSES
11—Houston vs. Eastern Wash., Nov. 17, 1990

MOST TOUCHDOWN PASSES, MAJOR-COLLEGE OPPONENTS
10—Houston vs. Southern Methodist, Oct. 21, 1989; San Diego St. vs. New Mexico St., Nov. 15, 1969

MOST TOUCHDOWN PASSES, BOTH TEAMS
14—Houston (11) & Eastern Wash. (3), Nov. 17, 1990

MOST TOUCHDOWN PASSES, BOTH TEAMS, MAJOR-COLLEGE OPPONENTS
13—San Diego St. (10) & New Mexico St. (3), Nov. 15, 1969; Hawaii (8) & Brigham Young (5), Dec. 8, 2001

Punting

MOST PUNTS
39—Texas Tech vs. Centenary (La.), Nov. 11, 1939 (1,377 yards)
38—Centenary (La.) vs. Texas Tech, Nov. 11, 1939 (1,248 yards)

MOST PUNTS, BOTH TEAMS
77—Texas Tech (39) & Centenary (La.) (38), Nov. 11, 1939 (2,625 yards) (The game was played in a heavy downpour in Shreveport, Louisiana. Forty-two punts were returned, 19 went out of bounds, 10 were downed, 1 went into the end zone for a touchback, 4 were blocked and 1 was fair caught. Sixty-seven punts [34 by Texas Tech and 33 by Centenary] occurred on first-down plays, including 22 consecutively in the third and fourth quarters. The game was a scoreless tie.)

FEWEST PUNTS
0—By many teams. Most recent: Iowa vs. Akron, Aug. 31, 2002 (won 57-21)

FEWEST PUNTS BY A LOSING TEAM
0—By many teams. Most recent: Kentucky vs. Georgia, Oct. 25, 1997 (lost 23-13)

HIGHEST AVERAGE PER PUNT
(Min. 5-9 punts) 60.4—Brigham Young vs. Wyoming, Oct. 8, 1983 (5 for 302)
(Min. 10 punts) 53.6—Oklahoma St. vs. Colorado, Nov. 13, 1971 (10 for 536)

HIGHEST AVERAGE PER PUNT, BOTH TEAMS
(Min. 10 Punts)
55.3—Brigham Young & Wyoming, Oct. 8, 1983 (11 for 608)

Punt Returns

MOST PUNT RETURNS
22—Texas Tech vs. Centenary (La.), Nov. 11, 1939 (112 yards)

MOST PUNT RETURNS, BOTH TEAMS
42—Texas Tech (22) & Centenary (La.) (20), Nov. 11, 1939 (233 yards)

MOST YARDS ON PUNT RETURNS
319—Texas A&M vs. North Texas, Sept. 21, 1946 (10 returns)

HIGHEST AVERAGE GAIN PER RETURN
(Min. 5 Returns)
44.2—Denver vs. Colorado Col., Sept. 17, 1956 (6 for 265)

MOST TOUCHDOWNS SCORED ON PUNT RETURNS
3—Wisconsin vs. Iowa, Nov. 8, 1947; Wichita St. vs. Northern St., Oct. 22, 1949; LSU vs. Mississippi, Dec. 5, 1970; Holy Cross vs. Brown, Sept. 21, 1974; Arizona St. vs. Pacific (Cal.), Nov. 15, 1975; Notre Dame vs. Pittsburgh, Nov. 16, 1996

Kickoff Returns

MOST KICKOFF RETURNS
14—Arizona St. vs. Nevada, Oct. 12, 1946 (290 yards)

MOST YARDS ON KICKOFF RETURNS
295—Cincinnati vs. Memphis, Oct. 30, 1971 (8 returns)

HIGHEST AVERAGE GAIN PER RETURN
(Min. 6 Returns)
46.2—Southern California vs. Washington St., Nov. 7, 1970 (6 for 277)

MOST TOUCHDOWNS SCORED ON KICKOFF RETURNS
2—By many teams. Most recent: New Mexico St. vs. Tulsa, Oct. 6, 2001; Minnesota vs. Iowa St., Sept.

13, 1997; Texas A&M vs. Rice, Oct. 23, 1993; Brigham Young vs. Air Force, Nov. 11, 1989; Notre Dame vs. Michigan, Sept. 16, 1989; New Mexico St. vs. Drake, Oct. 15, 1983 (consecutive returns)

TOUCHDOWNS SCORED ON BACK-TO-BACK KICKOFF RETURNS, BOTH TEAMS
2—By many teams. Most recent: Wisconsin & Northern Ill., Sept. 14, 1985

Total Kick Returns

(Combined Punt and Kickoff Returns)

MOST YARDS ON KICK RETURNS
376—Florida St. vs. Virginia Tech, Nov. 16, 1974 (9 returns)

HIGHEST AVERAGE GAIN PER RETURN
(Min. 7 Returns)
41.8—Florida St. vs. Virginia Tech, Nov. 16, 1974 (9 for 376)

Scoring

MOST POINTS SCORED
103—Wyoming vs. Northern Colo. (0), Nov. 5, 1949 (15 TDs, 13 PATs)

MOST POINTS SCORED AGAINST A MAJOR-COLLEGE OPPONENT
100—Houston vs. Tulsa (6), Nov. 23, 1968 (14 TDs, 13 PATs, 1 FG)

MOST POINTS SCORED, BOTH TEAMS (REGULATION)
128—Middle Tenn. (70) & Idaho (58), Oct. 6, 2001

MOST POINTS SCORED BY A LOSING TEAM (REGULATION)
58—Idaho vs. Middle Tenn. (70), Oct. 6, 2001

MOST POINTS, BOTH TEAMS IN A TIE GAME
104—Brigham Young (52) & San Diego St. (52), Nov. 16, 1991

MOST POINTS, BOTH TEAMS, AT THE END OF REGULATION, OVERTIME GAME
104—Akron (52) & Eastern Mich. (52), Nov. 24, 2001 (Akron won in three overtime periods, 65-62)

MOST POINTS, BOTH TEAMS, OVERTIME GAME
127—Akron (65) vs. Eastern Mich. (62), Nov. 24, 2001 (3 ot)

MOST POINTS SCORED IN ONE QUARTER
49—Houston vs. Tulsa, Nov. 23, 1968 (4th); Davidson vs. Furman, Sept. 27, 1969 (2nd); Fresno St. vs. New Mexico, Oct. 5, 1991 (2nd)

MOST POINTS SCORED IN ONE QUARTER, BOTH TEAMS
61—San Jose St. (34) vs. Hawaii (27), Nov. 6, 1999 (4th; Hawaii won, 62-41)

MOST POINTS SCORED IN ONE HALF
76—Houston vs. Tulsa, Nov. 23, 1968 (2nd)

MOST TOUCHDOWNS SCORED
15—Wyoming vs. Northern Colo., Nov. 5, 1949 (9 rushing, 6 passing)

MOST TOUCHDOWNS SCORED, BOTH TEAMS
18—Oklahoma (12) & Colorado (6), Oct. 4, 1980; Middle Tenn. (10) & Idaho (8), Oct. 6, 2001

MOST EXTRA POINTS MADE BY KICKING
13—Wyoming vs. Northern Colo., Nov. 5, 1949 (attempted 15); Houston vs. Tulsa, Nov. 23, 1968 (attempted 14); Fresno St. vs. New Mexico, Oct. 5, 1991 (attempted 13)

MOST TWO-POINT ATTEMPTS SCORED
7—Pacific (Cal.) vs. San Diego St., Nov. 22, 1958 (attempted 9)

MOST DEFENSIVE EXTRA-POINT ATTEMPTS
2—Rice vs. Notre Dame, Nov. 5, 1988 (2 kick returns; 1 scored); Northern Ill. vs. Akron, Nov. 3, 1990 (2 interception returns); Oklahoma vs. California, Sept. 20, 1997 (2 kick returns; 1 scored); Texas vs. Iowa St., Oct. 3, 1998 (2 kick returns; 2 scored)

MOST DEFENSIVE EXTRA POINTS SCORED
  2—Texas vs. Iowa St., Oct. 3, 1998 (2 kick returns)

MOST FIELD GOALS MADE
  7—Western Mich. vs. Marshall, Sept. 29, 1984
  (attempted 9); Nebraska vs. Missouri, Oct. 19, 1985
  (attempted 7)

MOST FIELD GOALS MADE, BOTH TEAMS
  9—La.-Lafayette (5) & Central Mich. (4), Sept. 9, 1989
  (attempted 11)

MOST FIELD GOALS ATTEMPTED
  9—Western Mich. vs. Marshall, Sept. 29, 1984 (made 7)

MOST FIELD GOALS ATTEMPTED, BOTH TEAMS
  12—Clemson (6) & Georgia (6), Sept. 17, 1983
  (made 6)

MOST FIELD GOALS MISSED
  7—LSU vs. Florida, Nov. 25, 1972 (attempted 8)

First Downs

MOST FIRST DOWNS
  44—Nebraska vs. Utah St., Sept. 7, 1991 (33 rush, 10
  pass, 1 penalty)

MOST FIRST DOWNS, BOTH TEAMS
  72—New Mexico (37) & San Diego St. (35), Sept. 27,
  1986

FEWEST FIRST DOWNS BY A WINNING TEAM
  0—North Carolina St. vs. Virginia, Sept. 30, 1944
  (won 13-0); Michigan vs. Ohio St., Nov. 25, 1950
  (won 9-3)

MOST FIRST DOWNS BY RUSHING
  36—Nebraska vs. New Mexico St., Sept. 18, 1982

MOST FIRST DOWNS BY PASSING
  33—Idaho vs. Middle Tenn., Oct. 6, 2001

Fumbles

MOST FUMBLES
  17—Wichita St. vs. Florida St., Sept. 20, 1969 (lost 10)

MOST FUMBLES, BOTH TEAMS
  27—Wichita St. (17) & Florida St. (10), Sept. 20,
  1969 (lost 17)

MOST FUMBLES LOST
  10—Wichita St. vs. Florida St., Sept. 20, 1969 (17
  fumbles)

MOST FUMBLES LOST, BOTH TEAMS
  17—Wichita St. (10) & Florida St. (7), Sept. 20, 1969
  (27 fumbles)

MOST FUMBLES LOST IN A QUARTER
  5—East Caro. vs. La.-Lafayette, Sept. 13, 1980 (3rd
  quarter on 5 consecutive possessions); San Diego St.
  vs. California, Sept. 18, 1982 (1st)

Penalties

MOST PENALTIES AGAINST
  24—San Jose St. vs. Fresno St., Oct. 4, 1986 (199
  yards)

MOST PENALTIES, BOTH TEAMS
  36—San Jose St. (24) & Fresno St. (12), Oct. 4, 1986
  (317 yards)

FEWEST PENALTIES, BOTH TEAMS
  0—By many teams. Most recent: Army & Navy, Dec. 6,
  1986

MOST YARDS PENALIZED
  238—Arizona St. vs. UTEP, Nov. 11, 1961 (13 penalties)

MOST YARDS PENALIZED, BOTH TEAMS
  421—Grambling (16 for 216 yards) & Texas Southern
  (17 for 205 yards), Oct. 29, 1977

Turnovers

**(Number of Times Losing the Ball on Fumbles
and Interceptions)**

MOST TURNOVERS LOST
  13—Georgia vs. Georgia Tech, Dec. 1, 1951 (5 fumbles, 8 interceptions)

MOST TURNOVERS, BOTH TEAMS
  20—Wichita St. (12) & Florida St. (8), Sept. 20, 1969
  (17 fumbles, 3 interceptions)

**MOST TOTAL PLAYS WITHOUT A TURNOVER
(Rushes, Passes, All Runbacks)**
  110—California vs. San Jose St., Oct. 5, 1968 (also
  did not fumble); Baylor vs. Rice, Nov. 13, 1976

**MOST TOTAL PLAYS WITHOUT A TURNOVER,
BOTH TEAMS**
  184—Arkansas (93) & Texas A&M (91), Nov. 2, 1968

**MOST TOTAL PLAYS WITHOUT A TURNOVER
OR A FUMBLE, BOTH TEAMS**
  158—Stanford (88) & Oregon (70), Nov. 2, 1957

MOST TURNOVERS BY A WINNING TEAM
  11—Purdue vs. Illinois, Oct. 2, 1943 (9 fumbles, 2
  interceptions; won 40-21)

**MOST PASSES HAD INTERCEPTED BY A
WINNING TEAM**
  7—Pittsburgh vs. Army, Nov. 15, 1980 (54 attempts;
  won 45-7); Florida vs. Kentucky, Sept. 11, 1993 (52
  attempts; won 24-20)

MOST FUMBLES LOST BY A WINNING TEAM
  9—Purdue vs. Illinois, Oct. 2, 1943 (10 fumbles; won
  40-21); Arizona St. vs. Utah, Oct. 14, 1972 (10 fumbles; won 59-48)

Overtimes

MOST OVERTIME PERIODS
  7—Arkansas (58) vs. Mississippi (56), Nov. 3, 2001

MOST POINTS SCORED IN OVERTIME PERIODS
  41—Arkansas (58) vs. Mississippi (56), Nov. 3, 2001
  (7 overtime periods)

**MOST POINTS SCORED IN OVERTIME PERIODS,
BOTH TEAMS**
  80—Arkansas (41) vs. Mississippi (39), Nov. 3, 2001
  (7 overtime periods; Arkansas won, 58-56)

LARGEST WINNING MARGIN IN OVERTIME
  13—Arizona St. (48) vs. Southern California (35), Oct.
  19, 1996 (2 overtime periods); Central Mich. (36) vs.
  Eastern Mich. (23), Oct. 10, 1998 (one overtime
  period)

CONSECUTIVE OVERTIME GAMES (SEASON)
  2—Southern California (41) vs. UCLA (48), Nov. 23,
  1996 & Southern California (27) vs. Notre Dame
  (20), Nov. 30, 1996; Oklahoma St. (50) vs.
  Missouri (51), Oct. 25, 1997 & Oklahoma St. (25)
  vs. Texas A&M (28), Nov. 1, 1997; Cincinnati (38)
  vs. Houston (41), Oct. 18, 1997 & Cincinnati (34)
  vs. Miami (Ohio) (31), Oct. 25, 1997; San Diego St.
  (36) vs. New Mexico (33), Oct. 17, 1998 & San
  Diego St. (21) vs. Utah (20), Oct. 24, 1998;
  Mississippi (34) vs. Vanderbilt (37), Sept. 18, 1999
  & Mississippi (24) vs. Auburn (17), Sept. 25, 1999;
  Wisconsin (28) vs. Cincinnati (25), Sept. 16, 2000
  & Wisconsin (44) vs. Northwestern (47), Sept. 23,
  2000; Oregon (56) vs. Arizona St. (55), Oct. 28,
  2000 & Oregon (27) vs. Washington St. (24), Nov.
  4, 2000; Rice (33) vs. Nevada (30), Oct. 20, 2001;
  & Rice (38) vs. Louisiana Tech (41), Oct. 27, 2001;
  New Mexico (44) vs. Utah St. (45), Oct. 19, 2002
  & New Mexico (42) vs. Utah (35), Oct. 26, 2002;
  Utah St. (45) vs. New Mexico (42), Oct. 19, 2002
  & Utah St. (48) vs. La.-Monroe (51), Oct. 26, 2002;
  Missouri (38) vs. Colorado (45), Nov. 9, 2002 &
  Missouri (33) vs. Texas A&M (27), Nov. 16, 2002

**OVERTIME GAMES WITH SAME OPPONENT IN
CONSECUTIVE YEARS**
  2—Cincinnati (34) vs. Miami (Ohio) (31), Oct. 25,
  1997 & Cincinnati (30) vs. Miami (Ohio) (23), Sept.

28, 1996; Oregon (43) vs. Fresno St. (40), Sept. 20,
1997 & Oregon (30) vs. Fresno St. (27), Aug. 31,
1996; Missouri (51) vs. Oklahoma St. (50), Oct. 25,
1997 & Missouri (35) vs. Oklahoma St. (28), Oct.
26, 1996; Arizona (41) vs. California (38), Nov.
15, 1997 & Arizona (55) vs. California (56), Nov.
2, 1996

SINGLE GAME—Defense

Total Defense

FEWEST PLAYS ALLOWED
  12—Centenary (La.) vs. Texas Tech, Nov. 11, 1939
  (10 rushes, 2 passes; -1 yard)

FEWEST YARDS ALLOWED
  Minus 47—Penn St. vs. Syracuse, Oct. 18, 1947 (-107
  rushing, 60 passing; 49 plays)

MOST YARDS ALLOWED
  1,021—Southern Methodist vs. Houston, Oct. 21,
  1989 (250 rushing, 771 passing)

Rushing Defense

FEWEST RUSHES ALLOWED
  5—Texas Tech vs. Houston, Nov. 25, 1989 (36 yards)

FEWEST RUSHING YARDS ALLOWED
  Minus 109—Toledo vs. Northern Ill., Nov. 11, 1967
  (33 rushes)

Pass Defense

FEWEST ATTEMPTS ALLOWED
  0—By many teams. Most recent: Colorado vs.
  Oklahoma, Nov. 15, 1986

FEWEST COMPLETIONS ALLOWED
  0—By many teams. Most recent: Brigham Young vs.
  Rice, Nov. 9, 1996 (5 attempts)

**LOWEST COMPLETION PERCENTAGE ALLOWED
(Min. 10 Attempts)**
  0.0%—North Carolina vs. Penn St., Oct. 2, 1943 (0 of
  12 attempts); Temple vs. West Virginia, Oct. 18, 1946
  (0 of 18 attempts); San Jose St. vs. Cal St. Fullerton,
  Oct. 10, 1992 (0 of 11 attempts)

FEWEST YARDS ALLOWED
  Minus 16—VMI vs. Richmond, Oct. 5, 1957 (2 completions)

MOST PASSES INTERCEPTED BY
  11—Brown vs. Rhode Island, Oct. 8, 1949 (136
  yards)

**MOST PASSES INTERCEPTED BY AGAINST A
MAJOR-COLLEGE OPPONENT**
  10—Oklahoma St. vs. Detroit, Nov. 28, 1942; UCLA
  vs. California, Oct. 21, 1978

MOST PASSES INTERCEPTED BY A LOSING TEAM
  7—Kentucky vs. Florida, Sept. 11, 1993 (52 attempts)

MOST YARDS ON INTERCEPTION RETURNS
  240—Kentucky vs. Mississippi, Oct. 1, 1949 (6
  returns)

**MOST TOUCHDOWNS ON INTERCEPTION
RETURNS**
  4—Houston vs. Texas, Nov. 7, 1987 (198 yards; 3
  TDs in the 4th quarter)

Defensive Records

(Since 2000)

TACKLES FOR LOSS
  20—TCU vs. Nevada, Sept. 9, 2000

PASS SACKS
  15—TCU vs. Nevada, Sept. 9, 2000

PASSES DEFENDED
(Pass Interceptions and Pass Breakups)
  19—South Carolina vs. Alabama, Oct. 2, 2000
FORCED FUMBLES
  7—Virginia vs. South Carolina, Sept. 7, 2002

First Downs

FEWEST FIRST DOWNS ALLOWED
  0—By many teams. Most recent: North Carolina St. vs. Western Caro., Sept. 1, 1990

Opponent's Kicks Blocked

MOST OPPONENT'S PUNTS BLOCKED
  4—Southern Methodist vs. Texas-Arlington, Sept. 30, 1944; Michigan vs. Ohio St., Nov. 25, 1950; Memphis vs. Arkansas, Sept. 26, 1992 (10 attempts)
MOST OPPONENT'S PUNTS BLOCKED, ONE QUARTER
  3—Purdue vs. Northwestern, Nov. 11, 1989 (4 attempts)
BLOCKED OPPONENTS' FIELD GOAL, PUNT AND EXTRA-POINT KICK
  Oregon St. blocked each type of kick against Southern California, Sept. 14, 1996
MOST OPPONENT'S FIELD GOALS BLOCKED, ONE QUARTER
  2—Southern California vs. California, Oct. 22, 1994; Wyoming vs. Fresno St., Nov. 18, 1995

Turnovers Gained

(Number of Times Gaining the Ball on Fumbles and Interceptions)
MOST TURNOVERS GAINED
  13—Georgia Tech vs. Georgia, Dec. 1, 1951 (5 fumbles, 8 interceptions)
MOST CONSECUTIVE OPPONENT'S SERIES RESULTING IN TURNOVERS
  7—Florida vs. Florida St., Oct. 7, 1972 (4 fumbles lost, 3 interceptions; first seven series of the game)

Fumble Returns

(Since 1992)
MOST TOUCHDOWNS ON FUMBLE RETURNS
  2—Toledo vs. Arkansas St., Sept. 5, 1992; Arizona vs. Illinois, Sept. 18, 1993; Duke vs. Wake Forest, Oct. 22, 1994 (both occurred in 1st quarter); Iowa vs. Minnesota, Nov. 19, 1994; Minnesota vs. Syracuse, Sept. 21, 1996; Florida vs. La.-Lafayette, Aug. 31, 1996; Arizona St. vs. Washington St., Nov. 1, 1997; Mississippi St. vs. Brigham Young, Sept. 14, 2000; Notre Dame vs. Navy, Oct. 14, 2000
LONGEST RETURN OF A FUMBLE
  100—Rutgers vs. Pittsburgh, Oct. 28, 1995; Rice vs. UNLV, Nov. 14, 1998; UNLV vs. Baylor, Sept. 11, 1999

Defensive Extra Points

MOST DEFENSIVE EXTRA POINTS SCORED AGAINST
  1—By many teams. Most recent: New Mexico vs. UNLV, Oct. 12, 2002; Kansas St. vs. Southern California, Sept. 21, 2002
MOST DEFENSIVE EXTRA-POINT ATTEMPTS AGAINST
  2—Notre Dame vs. Rice, Nov. 5, 1988 (2 blocked kick returns, 1 scored); Akron vs. Northern Ill., Nov. 3, 1990 (2 interception returns); California vs. Oklahoma, Sept. 20, 1997 (2 kick returns; 1 scored); Iowa St. vs. Texas, Oct. 3, 1998 (2 kick returns; 2 scored)

MOST DEFENSIVE EXTRA POINTS SCORED BY BOTH TEAM
  2—Kentucky (fumbled snap return) vs. LSU (blocked kick return), Oct. 17, 1998

Safeties

MOST SAFETIES BY A DEFENSE
  3—Arizona St. vs. Nebraska, Sept. 21, 1996

SEASON—Offense

Total Offense

MOST YARDS GAINED PER GAME
  624.9—Houston, 1989 (6,874 in 11)
MOST YARDS GAINED
  6,939—Hawaii, 2002 (14 games)
HIGHEST AVERAGE GAIN PER PLAY
  7.9—Army, 1945 (526 for 4,164)
GAINING 300 YARDS OR MORE PER GAME RUSHING AND 200 YARDS OR MORE PER GAME PASSING
  Houston, 1968 (361.7 rushing, 200.3 passing); Arizona St., 1973 (310.2 rushing, 255.3 passing)
MOST PLAYS PER GAME
  92.4—Notre Dame, 1970 (924 in 10)
MOST TOUCHDOWNS RUSHING AND PASSING
  84—Nebraska, 1983
  Also holds per-game record at 7.0 (84 in 12)

Rushing

MOST YARDS GAINED PER GAME
  472.4—Oklahoma, 1971 (5,196 in 11)
HIGHEST AVERAGE GAIN PER RUSH
  7.6—Army, 1945 (424 for 3,238)
HIGHEST AVERAGE GAIN PER RUSH (Min. 500 Rushes)
  7.0—Nebraska, 1995 (627 for 4,398)
MOST RUSHES PER GAME
  73.9—Oklahoma, 1974 (813 in 11)
MOST TOUCHDOWNS RUSHING PER GAME
  5.5—Nebraska, 1997 (66 in 12)

Passing

MOST YARDS GAINED PER GAME
  511.3—Houston, 1989 (5,624 in 11)
MOST YARDS GAINED
  5,624—Houston, 1989 (11 games)
HIGHEST AVERAGE GAIN PER ATTEMPT (Min. 350 Attempts)
  10.9—Brigham Young, 1989 (433 for 4,732)
HIGHEST AVERAGE GAIN PER COMPLETION
  (Min. 100-174 comps.) 19.1—Houston, 1968 (105 for 2,003)
  (Min. 175-224 comps.) 18.0—Grambling, 1977 (187 for 3,360)
  (Min. 225 comps.) 17.1—Florida, 1996 (234 for 4,007)
MOST PASSES ATTEMPTED PER GAME
  63.1—Houston, 1989 (694 in 11)
MOST PASSES COMPLETED PER GAME
  39.4—Houston, 1989 (434 in 11)
HIGHEST PERCENTAGE COMPLETED (Min. 150 Attempts)
  73.5%—UCF, 1998 (302 of 411)
LOWEST PERCENTAGE HAD INTERCEPTED
  (Min. 300-399 atts.) 0.84%—Fresno St., 1999 (3 of 359)
  (Min. 400 atts.) 1.2%—Southern California, 1993 (5 of 432)

MOST TOUCHDOWN PASSES PER GAME
  5.0—Houston, 1989 (55 in 11)
MOST TOUCHDOWN PASSES
  55—Houston, 1989 (11 games)
FEWEST TOUCHDOWN PASSES
  0—By 6 teams since 1975. Most recent: Vanderbilt, 1993 (11 games, 157 attempts)
HIGHEST PASSING EFFICIENCY RATING POINTS (Min. 150 Attempts)
  184.4—Tulane, 1998 (339 attempts, 230 completions, 6 interceptions, 3,352 yards, 38 TD passes)
A TEAM WITH THE NO. 1 & NO. 2 RECEIVERS
  Houston, 1988 (Jason Phillips, No. 1, 9.82 catches per game & James Dixon, No. 2, 9.27 catches per game)
MOST 100-YARD RECEIVING GAMES IN A SEASON, ONE TEAM
  19—San Diego St., 1990 (Patrick Rowe 9, Dennis Arey 8 & Jimmy Raye 2)

Punting

MOST PUNTS PER GAME
  13.9—Tennessee, 1937 (139 in 10)
FEWEST PUNTS PER GAME
  2.0—Nevada, 1948 (18 in 9)
HIGHEST PUNTING AVERAGE
  50.6—Brigham Young, 1983 (24 for 1,215 yards)
HIGHEST PUNTING AVERAGE (Min. 40 Punts)
  47.7—North Carolina, 1999 (81 for 3,863)
HIGHEST NET PUNTING AVERAGE
  45.0—Brigham Young, 1983 (24 for 1,215 yards, 134 yards in punts returned)
HIGHEST NET PUNTING AVERAGE (Min. 40 Punts)
  44.9—San Diego St., 1996 (48 for 2,234, 77 yards in punts returned)

Punt Returns

MOST PUNT RETURNS PER GAME
  6.9—Texas A&M, 1943 (69 in 10)
FEWEST PUNT RETURNS PER GAME
  0.5—Iowa St., 1996 (5 in 11)
MOST PUNT-RETURN YARDS PER GAME
  114.5—Colgate, 1941 (916 in 8)
HIGHEST AVERAGE GAIN PER RETURN
  (Min. 15-29 rets.) 25.2—Arizona St., 1952 (18 for 454)
  (Min. 30 rets.) 22.4—Oklahoma, 1948 (43 for 963)
MOST TOUCHDOWNS SCORED ON PUNT RETURNS (Since 1966)
  7—Southern Miss., 1987 (on 46 returns)

Kickoff Returns

MOST KICKOFF RETURNS PER GAME
  7.3—Cal St. Fullerton, 1990 (80 in 11)
FEWEST KICKOFF RETURNS PER GAME
  0.7—Boston College, 1939 (7 in 10)
MOST KICKOFF-RETURN YARDS
  1,588—Pittsburgh, 1996 (66 returns)
MOST KICKOFF-RETURN YARDS PER GAME
  144.4—Pittsburgh, 1996 (1,588 in 11)
HIGHEST AVERAGE GAIN PER RETURN
  (Min. 25-34 rets.) 30.3—Florida St., 1992 (27, for 819)
  (Min. 35 rets.) 27.5—Rice, 1973 (39 for 1,074)

MOST TOUCHDOWNS SCORED ON KICKOFF RETURNS
(Since 1966)
4—Dayton, 1974 (on 44 returns)

Scoring

MOST POINTS PER GAME
56.0—Army, 1944 (504 in 9)

MOST POINTS SCORED
624—Nebraska, 1983 (12 games)

HIGHEST SCORING MARGIN
52.1—Army, 1944 (scored 504 points for 56.0 average and allowed 35 points for 3.9 average in 9 games)

MOST POINTS SCORED, TWO CONSECUTIVE GAMES
177—Houston, 1968 (77-3 vs. Idaho, Nov. 16, and 100-6 vs. Tulsa, Nov. 23)

MOST TOUCHDOWNS PER GAME
8.2—Army, 1944 (74 in 9)

MOST TOUCHDOWNS
89—Nebraska, 1983 (12 games)

MOST EXTRA POINTS MADE BY KICKING
77—Nebraska, 1983 (77 in 12, attempted 85)
Also holds per-game record at 6.4

MOST CONSECUTIVE EXTRA POINTS MADE BY KICKING
71—Florida, 1995 (attempted 71); Nebraska, 1997 (attempted 71)

MOST TWO-POINT ATTEMPTS MADE PER GAME
2.2—Rutgers, 1958 (20 in 9, attempted 31)

MOST DEFENSIVE EXTRA-POINT ATTEMPTS
3—Rice, 1988 (1 vs. La.-Lafayette, Sept. 24, blocked kick return; 2 vs. Notre Dame, Nov. 5, 2 blocked kick returns, 1 scored)

MOST DEFENSIVE EXTRA POINTS SCORED
2—Texas, 1998 (2 vs. Iowa St., Oct. 3, 2 blocked kick returns)

MOST FIELD GOALS PER GAME
2.6—UCLA, 1984 (29 in 11); Cincinnati, 2000 (29 in 11)

First Downs

MOST FIRST DOWNS PER GAME
30.9—Brigham Young, 1983 (340 in 11)

MOST RUSHING FIRST DOWNS PER GAME
21.4—Oklahoma, 1974 (235 in 11)

MOST PASSING FIRST DOWNS PER GAME
19.8—Nevada, 1995 (218 in 11)

Fumbles

MOST FUMBLES
73—Cal St. Fullerton, 1992 (lost 41)

MOST FUMBLES LOST
41—Cal St. Fullerton, 1992 (73 fumbles)

FEWEST OWN FUMBLES LOST
1—Bowling Green, 1996; Miami (Ohio), 1998

FEWEST OWN FUMBLES LOST IN TWO CONSECUTIVE SEASONS
3—Miami (Ohio), 1998-99 (1 in 1998; 2 in 1999)

MOST CONSECUTIVE FUMBLES LOST
14—Oklahoma, 1983 (during 5 games, Oct. 8-Nov. 5)

Penalties

MOST PENALTIES PER GAME
12.9—Grambling, 1977 (142 in 11, 1,476 yards)

MOST YARDS PENALIZED PER GAME
134.2—Grambling, 1977 (1,476 in 11, 142 penalties)

Turnovers (Giveaways)

(Fumbles Lost and Passes Had Intercepted)

FEWEST TURNOVERS
8—Clemson, 1940 (2 fumbles lost, 6 interceptions); Miami (Ohio), 1966 (4 fumbles lost, 4 interceptions); Notre Dame, 2000 (4 fumbles lost, 4 interceptions)

FEWEST TURNOVERS PER GAME
0.73—Notre Dame, 2000 (8 in 11 games)

MOST TURNOVERS
61—North Texas, 1971 (28 fumbles lost, 33 interceptions); Tulsa, 1976 (37 fumbles lost, 24 interceptions)

MOST TURNOVERS PER GAME
6.1—Mississippi St., 1949 (55 in 9 games; 30 fumbles lost, 25 interceptions)

SEASON—Defense

Total Defense

FEWEST YARDS ALLOWED PER GAME
69.9—Santa Clara, 1937 (559 in 8)

FEWEST RUSHING AND PASSING TOUCHDOWNS ALLOWED PER GAME
0.0—Duke, 1938; Tennessee, 1939

LOWEST AVERAGE YARDS ALLOWED PER PLAY
1.7—Texas A&M, 1939 (447 for 763)

LOWEST AVERAGE YARDS ALLOWED PER PLAY
(Min. 600-699 plays) 2.5—Nebraska, 1967 (627 for 1,576)
(Min. 700 plays) 2.7—Toledo, 1971 (734 for 1,795)

MOST YARDS ALLOWED PER GAME
553.0—Maryland, 1993 (6,083 in 11)

Rushing Defense

FEWEST YARDS ALLOWED PER GAME
17.0—Penn St., 1947 (153 in 9)

MOST YARDS LOST BY OPPONENTS PER GAME
70.1—Wyoming, 1968 (701 in 10, 458 rushes)

LOWEST AVERAGE YARDS ALLOWED PER RUSH
(Min. 240-399 rushes) 0.6—Penn St., 1947 (240 for 153)
(Min. 400-499 rushes) 1.3—North Texas, 1966 (408 for 513)
(Min. 500 rushes) 2.1—Nebraska, 1971 (500 for 1,031)

Pass Defense

FEWEST YARDS ALLOWED PER GAME
13.1—Penn St., 1938 (105 in 8)

FEWEST YARDS ALLOWED PER ATTEMPT
(Min. 200-299 atts.) 3.4—Toledo, 1970 (251 for 856)
(Min. 300 atts.) 3.8—Notre Dame, 1967 (306 for 1,158)

FEWEST YARDS ALLOWED PER COMPLETION
(Min. 100-149 comps.) 8.8—Michigan, 1997 (145 for 1,275)
(Min. 150 comps.) 9.5—Notre Dame, 1993 (263 for 2,502)

LOWEST COMPLETION PERCENTAGE ALLOWED
(Min. 150-199 atts.) 31.1%—Virginia, 1952 (50 of 161)
(Min. 200 atts.) 33.3%—Notre Dame, 1967 (102 of 306)

FEWEST TOUCHDOWNS ALLOWED BY PASSING
0—By many teams. Most recent: LSU, 1959; North Texas, 1959

LOWEST PASS EFFICIENCY DEFENSIVE RATING (Since 1990)
65.7—Kansas St., 1999 (315 attempts, 118 completions, 21 interceptions, 1,364 yards, 5 TDs)

MOST PASSES INTERCEPTED BY PER GAME
4.1—Pennsylvania, 1940 (33 in 8)

HIGHEST PERCENTAGE INTERCEPTED BY (Min. 200 Attempts)
17.9%—Army, 1944 (36 of 201)

MOST YARDS GAINED ON INTERCEPTION RETURNS
782—Tennessee, 1971 (25 interceptions)

MOST INTERCEPTION YARDS PER GAME
72.5—Texas, 1943 (580 in 8)

HIGHEST AVERAGE PER INTERCEPTION RETURN
(Min. 10-14 ints.) 36.3—Oregon St., 1959 (12 for 436)
(Min. 15 ints.) 31.3—Tennessee, 1971 (25 for 782)

MOST TOUCHDOWNS ON INTERCEPTION RETURNS
7—Tennessee, 1971 (25 interceptions; 287 pass attempts against)

Punting

MOST OPPONENT'S PUNTS BLOCKED BY
11—Arkansas St., 1975 (11 games, 95 punts against)

Punt Returns

FEWEST RETURNS ALLOWED
5—Notre Dame, 1968 (52 yards); Nebraska, 1995 (12 yards)

FEWEST YARDS ALLOWED
2—Miami (Fla.), 1989 (12 returns)

LOWEST AVERAGE YARDS ALLOWED PER PUNT RETURN
0.2—Miami (Fla.), 1989 (12 for 2 yards)

Kickoff Returns

LOWEST AVERAGE YARDS ALLOWED PER KICKOFF RETURN
8.3—Richmond, 1951 (23 for 192 yards)

Opponent's Kicks Blocked

MOST PAT KICKS BLOCKED
Season
6—Duke, 1993

Scoring

FEWEST POINTS ALLOWED PER GAME
0.0—Duke, 1938 (9 games); Tennessee, 1939 (10 games)

MOST POINTS ALLOWED
566—Eastern Mich., 2002 (12 games)

MOST POINTS ALLOWED PER GAME
50.3—La.-Lafayette, 1997 (553 in 11)

Fumbles

MOST OPPONENT'S FUMBLES RECOVERED
36—North Texas, 1972; Brigham Young, 1977

MOST TOUCHDOWNS SCORED ON FUMBLE RETURNS
7—Georgia Tech, 1998

Turnovers (Takeaways)

(Opponent's Fumbles Recovered and Passes Intercepted)

MOST OPPONENT'S TURNOVERS
57—Tennessee, 1970 (21 fumbles recovered, 36 interceptions)

MOST OPPONENT'S TURNOVERS PER GAME
5.4—Wyoming, 1950 (49 in 9); Pennsylvania, 1950 (49 in 9), UCLA; 1952 (49 in 9); UCLA, 1954 (49 in 9)

DIVISION I-A

HIGHEST MARGIN OF TURNOVERS PER GAME OVER OPPONENTS
4.0—UCLA, 1952 (36 in 9; 13 giveaways vs. 49 takeaways)
Also holds total-margin record with 36

HIGHEST MARGIN OF TURNOVERS PER GAME BY OPPONENTS
3.1—Southern Miss., 1969 (31 in 10; 45 giveaways vs. 14 takeaways)

Defensive Extra Points

MOST DEFENSIVE EXTRA-POINT ATTEMPTS AGAINST
2—La.-Lafayette, 1988 (2 kick returns, none scored); Notre Dame, 1988 (2 kick returns, 1 scored); Akron, 1990 (2 interception returns, none scored); Oklahoma, 1992 (2 kick returns, 2 scored); Oklahoma, 1997 (2 kick returns, 1 scored); Texas, 1998 (2 kick returns, 2 scored)

MOST DEFENSIVE EXTRA POINTS SCORED AGAINST
2—Oklahoma, 1992 (vs. Texas Tech, Sept. 3, and vs. Oklahoma St., Nov. 14); Texas, 1998 (vs. Iowa St., Oct. 3)

Safeties

MOST SAFETIES BY A DEFENSE
4—Wisconsin, 1951

Consecutive Records

MOST CONSECUTIVE VICTORIES
47—Oklahoma, 1953-57

MOST CONSECUTIVE GAMES WITHOUT DEFEAT
48—Oklahoma, 1953-57 (1 tie)

MOST CONSECUTIVE LOSSES
34—Northwestern, from Sept. 22, 1979, vs. Syracuse through Sept. 18, 1982, vs. Miami (Ohio) (ended with 31-6 victory over Northern Ill., Sept. 25, 1982)

MOST CONSECUTIVE GAMES WITHOUT A VICTORY ON THE ROAD
46—Northwestern (including one tie), from Nov. 23, 1974, through Oct. 30, 1982

MOST CONSECUTIVE GAMES WITHOUT A TIE (Includes Bowl Games)
345—Miami (Fla.), from Nov. 11, 1968, through 1995 season (after 1995 tiebreaker used in Division I-A)

MOST CONSECUTIVE GAMES WITHOUT BEING SHUT OUT
349—Brigham Young (current), from Oct. 3, 1975

MOST CONSECUTIVE SHUTOUTS (Regular Season)
17—Tennessee, from Nov. 5, 1938, through Oct. 12, 1940

MOST CONSECUTIVE QUARTERS OPPONENTS HELD SCORELESS (Regular Season)
71—Tennessee, from 2nd quarter vs. LSU, Oct. 29, 1938, to 2nd quarter vs. Alabama, Oct. 19, 1940

MOST CONSECUTIVE VICTORIES AT HOME
58—Miami (Fla.) (Orange Bowl), from Oct. 12, 1985, to Sept. 24, 1994 (lost to Washington, 38-20)

MOST CONSECUTIVE WINNING SEASONS (All-Time)
42—Notre Dame, 1889-32 (no teams in 1890 & 1891)

MOST CONSECUTIVE WINNING SEASONS (After 1932)
40—Nebraska, 1962-01

MOST CONSECUTIVE NON-LOSING SEASONS
49—Penn St., 1939-87 (includes two .500 seasons)

MOST CONSECUTIVE LOSING SEASONS
28—Oregon St., 1971-98

MOST CONSECUTIVE NON-WINNING SEASONS
28—Rice, 1964-91 (includes two .500 seasons)

MOST CONSECUTIVE SEASONS WINNING NINE OR MORE GAMES
33—Nebraska 1969-01

MOST CONSECUTIVE SEASONS PLAYING IN A BOWL GAME
34—Nebraska (current), from 1969

MOST CONSECUTIVE GAMES SCORING ON A PASS
62—Florida, from Oct. 1, 1992, to Oct. 4, 1997

MOST CONSECUTIVE GAMES PASSING FOR 200 YARDS OR MORE
64—Brigham Young, from Sept. 13, 1980, through Oct. 19, 1985

MOST CONSECUTIVE GAMES INTERCEPTING A PASS (Includes Bowl Games)
39—Virginia, from Nov. 6, 1993, through Nov. 29, 1996

MOST CONSECUTIVE GAMES WITHOUT POSTING A SHUTOUT
283—New Mexico St., from Sept. 21, 1974, to Sept. 29, 2001 (31-0 over La.-Monroe)

MOST CONSECUTIVE EXTRA POINTS MADE
262—Syracuse, from Nov. 18, 1978, to Sept. 9, 1989 (By the following kickers: Dave Jacobs, last PAT of 1978; Gary Anderson, 72 from 1979 through 1981; Russ Carpentieri, 17 in 1982; Don McAulay, 62 from 1983 through 1985; Tim Vesling, 71 in 1986 and 1987; Kevin Greene, 37 in 1988; John Biskup, 2 in 1989.)

MOST CONSECUTIVE STADIUM SELLOUTS
255—Nebraska (current), from 1962

Additional Records

HIGHEST-SCORING TIE GAME
52-52—Brigham Young & San Diego St., Nov. 16, 1991

MOST TIE GAMES IN A SEASON
4—Temple, 1937 (9 games); UCLA, 1939 (10 games); Central Mich., 1991 (11 games)

MOST SCORELESS TIE GAMES IN A SEASON
4—Temple, 1937 (9 games)

MOST CONSECUTIVE SCORELESS TIE GAMES
2—Georgia Tech, 1938, vs. Florida, Nov. 19 & vs. Georgia, Nov. 26; Alabama, 1954, vs. Georgia, Oct. 30 & vs. Tulane, Nov. 6

LAST TIE GAME
Nov. 25, 1995—Wisconsin 3, Illinois 3

LAST SCORELESS TIE GAME
Nov. 19, 1983—Oregon & Oregon St.

MOST POINTS OVERCOME TO WIN A GAME (Between Division I-A Teams)
31—Maryland (42) vs. Miami (Fla.) (40), Nov. 10, 1984 (trailed 31-0 with 12:35 remaining in 3rd quarter); Ohio St. (41) vs. Minnesota (37), Oct. 28, 1989 (trailed 31-0 with 4:29 remaining in 2nd quarter)
30—California (42) vs. Oregon (41), Oct. 2, 1993 (trailed 30-0 in 2nd quarter)

MOST POINTS SCORED IN FOURTH QUARTER TO WIN OR TIE A GAME
36—Brigham Young (50) vs. Washington St. (36), Sept. 15, 1990 (trailed 29-14 at start of 4th quarter)
34—Northern Ill. (48) vs. Miami (Ohio) (41), Oct. 12, 2002 (trailed 27-14 at start of 4th quarter)
29—Bowling Green (43) vs. Northwestern (42), Nov. 17, 2001 (trailed 28-14 at start of 4th quarter)
28—Utah (28) vs. Arizona (27), Nov. 4, 1972 (trailed 27-0 beginning 4th quarter); Washington St. (49) vs. Stanford (42), Oct. 20, 1984 (trailed 42-14 with 5:38 remaining in 3rd quarter and scored 35 consecutive points); Florida St. (31) vs. Florida (31), Nov. 26, 1994 (trailed 31-3 beginning 4th quarter); Middle Tenn. (39) vs. New Mexico St. (35), Oct. 27, 2001 (trailed 35-11 beginning 4th quarter)

MOST POINTS SCORED IN A BRIEF PERIOD OF TIME BY ONE TEAM
49 in 6:25 of possession time—Fresno St. (70) vs. Utah St. (21), Dec. 1, 2001 (7 TDs, 7 PATs. The longest drive lasted 1:42 during the first and second quarters)
41 in 2:55 of possession time during six drives—Nebraska (69) vs. Colorado (19), Oct. 22, 1983 (6 TDs, 5 PATs in 3rd quarter. Drives occurred during 9:10 of total playing time in the period)
41 in 4:30 of possession time during six drives—Northern Ill. (48) vs. Miami (Ohio) (41), Oct. 12, 2002 (6 TDs, 5 PATs in final two periods)
21 in 1:24 of total playing time—San Jose St. (42) vs. Fresno St. (7), Nov. 17, 1990 (3 TDs, 3 PATs in 2nd quarter; 1:17 of possession time on two drives and one intercepted pass returned for a TD)
15 in :10 of total playing time—Utah (22) vs. Air Force (21), Oct. 21, 1995 (2 TDs, 2-point conversion, 1 PAT. Drives occurred during :41 of 4th quarter)

MOST POINTS SCORED IN A BRIEF PERIOD OF TIME BY BOTH TEAMS
29 in 1:34 of possession time during four drives (4th quarter)—Hawaii (62) vs. San Jose St. (41), Nov. 6, 1999 (4 TDs, 1 PAT, two 2-point conversions). San Jose St. scores TDs on a blocked punt and pass reception (adds two 2-point conversions); Hawaii scores TDs on rush and interception return (adds PAT)
16 in 0:29 of possession time during fourth quarter—Northwestern (27) vs. Michigan St. (26), Sept. 29, 2001 (2 TDs, 1 PAT, 1 FG)

MOST IMPROVED WON-LOST RECORD
8½ games—Hawaii, 1999 (9-4-0, including a bowl win) from 1998 (0-12-0)

MOST IMPROVED WON-LOST RECORD AFTER WINLESS SEASON
8½ games—Hawaii, 1999 (9-4-0, including a bowl win) from 1998 (0-12-0)

Annual Champions, All-Time Leaders

Total Offense

CAREER YARDS PER GAME
(Minimum 5,500 yards)

Player, Team	Years	G	Plays	Yards	TDR‡	Yd. PG
Tim Rattay, Louisiana Tech	1997-99	33	1,705	12,618	117	*382.4
Chris Vargas, Nevada	1992-93	20	872	6,417	48	320.9
Ty Detmer, Brigham Young	1988-91	46	1,795	*14,665	*135	318.8
Daunte Culpepper, UCF	1996-98	33	1,468	10,344	91	313.5
Mike Perez, San Jose St.	1986-87	20	875	6,182	37	309.1
Josh Wallwork, Wyoming	1995-96	22	845	6,753	60	307.0
Doug Gaynor, Long Beach St.	1984-85	22	1,067	6,710	45	305.0
Josh Heupel, Oklahoma	1999-00	23	923	6,898	62	299.9
Tony Eason, Illinois	1981-82	22	1,016	6,589	43	299.5
Chad Pennington, Marshall	1997-99	36	1,433	10,758	104	298.9
Drew Brees, Purdue	1997-00	40	1,754	11,815	97	295.4
David Klingler, Houston	1988-91	32	1,439	9,363	93	292.6
David Neill, Nevada	1998-01	40	1,376	11,664	87	291.6
Steve Sarkisian, Brigham Young	1995-96	25	953	7,253	56	290.1
Chris Redman, Louisville	1996-99	42	1,846	12,129	87	288.8
Kliff Kingsbury, Texas Tech	1999-02	43	*2,156	12,263	99	285.2
Steve Young, Brigham Young	1981-83	31	1,177	8,817	74	284.4
Tim Couch, Kentucky	1996-98	29	1,338	8,160	78	281.4
Doug Flutie, Boston College	1981-84	42	1,558	11,317	74	269.5
Brent Snyder, Utah St.	1987-88	22	1,040	5,916	43	268.9
Scott Mitchell, Utah	1987-89	33	1,306	8,836	71	267.8
Mike Maxwell, Nevada	1993-95	27	946	7,226	66	267.6
Anthony Calvillo, Utah St.	1992-93	22	983	5,838	43	265.4
Shane Matthews, Florida	1989-92	35	1,397	9,241	82	264.0
Chris Weinke, Florida St.	1997-00	36	1,217	9,473	81	263.1
Joe Hughes, Wyoming	1992-93	23	911	6,007	49	261.2
Antwaan Randle El, Indiana	1998-01	44	1,917	11,364	86	258.3
Larry Egger, Utah	1985-86	22	903	5,651	42	256.9
Jim Plunkett, Stanford	1968-70	31	1,174	7,887	62	254.4
Stoney Case, New Mexico	1991-94	42	1,673	10,651	98	253.6
Tim Lester, Western Mich.	1996-99	44	1,747	11,081	91	251.8
Jose Fuentes, Utah St.	1999-02	36	1,327	9,064	60	251.8
Troy Kopp, Pacific (Cal.)	1989-92	40	1,595	10,037	90	250.9
Peyton Manning, Tennessee	1994-97	44	1,534	11,020	101	250.5
Randall Cunningham, UNLV	1982-84	33	1,330	8,224	67	249.2
Michael Bishop, Kansas St.	1997-98	23	804	5,715	59	248.5
Joe Hamilton, Georgia Tech	1996-99	43	1,521	10,640	83	247.4
Eric Zeier, Georgia	1991-94	44	1,560	10,841	71	246.4
Erik Wilhelm, Oregon St.	1985-88	37	1,689	9,062	55	244.9
Todd Dillon, Long Beach St.	1982-83	23	1,031	5,588	38	243.0
Bernie Kosar, Miami (Fla.)	1983-84	23	847	5,585	48	242.8
Charlie Batch, Eastern Mich.	1994-97	32	1,179	7,715	58	241.1
Alex Van Pelt, Pittsburgh	1989-92	45	1,570	10,814	58	240.3
Steve Stenstrom, Stanford	1991-94	41	1,550	9,825	75	239.6
Cade McNown, UCLA	1995-98	44	1,429	10,487	74	238.3
Jack Trudeau, Illinois	1981, 83-85	34	1,318	8,096	56	238.1
Chuck Hixson, Southern Methodist	1968-70	29	1,358	6,884	50	237.4
Zak Kustok, Northwestern	1999-01	30	1,353	7,116	64	237.2
Robbie Bosco, Brigham Young	1983-85	35	1,159	8,299	72	237.1
Dan Robinson, Hawaii	1997-99	25	1,058	5,920	45	236.8
Dan McGwire, Iowa/San Diego St.	1986-87, 89-90	32	1,067	7,557	50	236.2
Johnny Bright, Drake	1949-51	25	825	5,903	64	236.1
Kordell Stewart, Colorado	1991-94	33	1,087	7,770	48	235.5

*Record. ‡Touchdowns-responsible-for are player's TDs scored and passed for.

SEASON YARDS PER GAME

Player, Team	Year	G	Plays	Yards	TDR‡	Yd. PG
David Klingler, Houston	†1990	11	704	*5,221	*55	*474.6
Andre Ware, Houston	†1989	11	628	4,661	49	423.7
Ty Detmer, Brigham Young	1990	12	635	5,022	45	418.5
Tim Rattay, Louisiana Tech	†1998	12	602	4,840	47	403.3
Mike Maxwell, Nevada	†1995	9	443	3,623	34	402.6
Chris Redman, Louisville	1998	10	513	4,009	31	400.9
Steve Young, Brigham Young	†1983	11	531	4,346	41	395.1
Chris Vargas, Nevada	†1993	11	535	4,332	35	393.8
Scott Mitchell, Utah	†1988	11	589	4,299	29	390.8
Jim McMahon, Brigham Young	†1980	12	540	4,627	53	385.6
Tim Rattay, Louisiana Tech	†1999	10	562	3,810	35	381.0
Daunte Culpepper, UCF	1998	11	543	4,153	40	377.5
Tim Couch, Kentucky	1998	11	617	4,151	37	377.4
David Neill, Nevada	1998	9	409	3,351	31	372.3
Ty Detmer, Brigham Young	1989	12	497	4,433	38	369.4
Troy Kopp, Pacific (Cal.)	1990	9	485	3,276	32	364.0
Tim Rattay, Louisiana Tech	†1997	11	541	3,968	35	360.7
Drew Brees, Purdue	†2000	11	564	3,939	29	358.1

Player, Team	Year	G	Plays	Yards	TDR‡	Yd. PG
Byron Leftwich, Marshall	†2002	12	528	4,267	33	355.6
Rex Grossman, Florida	†2001	11	429	3,904	39	354.9
Byron Leftwich, Marshall	2001	12	534	4,224	41	352.0
Josh Wallwork, Wyoming	†1996	12	525	4,209	35	350.8
Kliff Kingsbury, Texas Tech	2002	14	*814	4,903	47	350.2
Jared Lorenzen, Kentucky	2000	11	635	3,687	24	347.9
Jim McMahon, Brigham Young	†1981	10	487	3,458	30	345.8
Joe Hamilton, Georgia Tech	1999	11	459	3,794	35	344.9
Jimmy Klingler, Houston	†1992	11	544	3,768	34	342.5
Shaun King, Tulane	1998	11	468	3,764	46	342.2
Tim Couch, Kentucky	1997	11	613	3,759	40	341.7
Chris Weinke, Florida St.	2000	12	461	4,167	34	339.2
Cody Ledbetter, New Mexico St.	1995	11	543	3,724	32	338.6
David Carr, Fresno St.	2001	13	564	4,396	48	338.2

*Record. †National champion. ‡Touchdowns-responsible-for are player's TDs scored and passed for.

CAREER YARDS

Player, Team	Years	Plays	Yards Rush	Yards Pass	Total	Avg.
Ty Detmer, Brigham Young	1988-91	1,795	-366	*15,031	*14,665	#8.17
Tim Rattay, Louisiana Tech	1997-99	1,705	-128	12,746	12,618	7.40
Kliff Kingsbury, Texas Tech	1999-02	*2,156	-166	12,429	12,263	5.69
Chris Redman, Louisville	1996-99	1,846	-412	12,541	12,129	6.57
Drew Brees, Purdue	1997-00	1,754	906	10,909	11,815	6.74
David Neill, Nevada	1998-01	1,727	761	10,903	11,664	6.75
Antwaan Randle El, Indiana	1998-01	1,917	3,895	7,469	11,364	5.93
Doug Flutie, Boston College	1981-84	1,558	738	10,579	11,317	7.26
Carson Palmer, Southern California	$1998-02	1,758	-295	11,388	11,093	6.31
Tim Lester, Western Mich.	1996-99	1,747	-218	11,299	11,081	6.34
Peyton Manning, Tennessee	1994-97	1,534	-181	11,201	11,020	7.18
Eric Zeier, Georgia	1991-94	1,560	-312	11,153	10,841	6.95
Alex Van Pelt, Pittsburgh	1989-92	1,570	-99	10,913	10,814	6.89
Chad Pennington, Marshall	1997-99	1,433	60	10,698	10,758	7.51
Stoney Case, New Mexico	1991-94	1,673	1,191	9,460	10,651	6.37
Joe Hamilton, Georgia Tech	1996-99	1,521	1,758	8,882	10,640	7.00
Todd Santos, San Diego St.	1984-87	1,722	-912	11,425	10,513	6.11
Danny Wuerffel, Florida	1993-96	1,355	-375	10,875	10,500	7.75
Cade McNown, UCLA	1995-98	1,429	479	10,008	10,487	7.34
Daunte Culpepper, UCF	1996-98	1,468	1,003	9,341	10,344	7.05
Kevin Sweeney, Fresno St.	$1982-86	1,700	-371	10,623	10,252	6.03
David Garrard, East Caro.	1998-01	1,685	1,209	9,029	10,238	6.08
Troy Kopp, Pacific (Cal.)	1989-92	1,595	-221	10,258	10,037	6.29
Bart Hendricks, Boise St.	1997-00	1,472	1,004	9,030	10,034	6.82
Donovan McNabb, Syracuse	1995-98	1,403	1,561	8,389	9,950	7.09
Steve Stenstrom, Stanford	1991-94	1,550	-706	10,531	9,825	6.34
Brian McClure, Bowling Green	1982-85	1,630	-506	10,280	9,774	6.00
Jim McMahon, Brigham Young	1977-78, 80-81	1,325	187	9,536	9,723	7.34
Glenn Foley, Boston College	1990-93	1,440	-340	10,042	9,702	6.74
¢Luke McCown, Louisiana Tech	2000-02	1,547	145	9,420	9,565	6.18
Chris Weinke, Florida St.	1997-00	1,217	-366	9,839	9,473	7.78
Shaun King, Tulane	1995-98	1,516	1,046	8,419	9,468	6.25
Terrence Jones, Tulane	1985-88	1,620	1,761	7,684	9,445	5.83
David Klingler, Houston	1988-91	1,439	-103	9,466	9,363	6.51
Shawn Jones, Georgia Tech	1989-92	1,609	855	8,441	9,296	5.78
Shane Matthews, Florida	1989-92	1,397	-46	9,287	9,241	6.61
Spence Fischer, Duke	1992-95	1,612	89	9,021	9,110	5.65
T.J. Rubley, Tulsa	1987-89, 91	1,541	-244	9,324	9,080	5.89
Brad Tayles, Western Mich.	1989-92	1,675	354	8,717	9,071	5.42
John Elway, Stanford	1979-82	1,505	-279	9,349	9,070	6.03
Jose Fuentes, Utah St.	1999-02	1,327	-104	9,168	9,064	6.83
Erik Wilhelm, Oregon St.	1985-88	1,689	-331	9,393	9,062	5.37
Ben Bennett, Duke	1980-83	1,582	-553	9,614	9,061	5.73
Chuck Long, Iowa	$1981-85	1,410	-176	9,210	9,034	6.41
Todd Ellis, South Carolina	1986-89	1,517	-497	9,519	9,022	5.95
Jason Martin, Louisiana Tech	1993-96	1,439	-127	9,066	8,939	6.21
Tom Hodson, LSU	1986-89	1,307	-177	9,115	8,938	6.84
Jake Delhomme, La.-Lafayette	1993-96	1,476	-340	9,216	8,876	6.01
Scott Mitchell, Utah	1987-89	1,306	-145	8,981	8,836	6.77
Steve Young, Brigham Young	1981-83	1,177	1,084	7,733	8,817	7.49
Brian Mitchell, La.-Lafayette	1986-89	1,521	3,335	5,447	8,782	5.77
Marvin Graves, Syracuse	1990-93	1,373	286	8,466	8,752	6.37
Jonathan Smith, Oregon St.	1998-01	1,357	-451	9,079	8,628	6.36
Jeremy Leach, New Mexico	1988-91	1,695	-762	9,382	8,620	5.09
Jake Plummer, Arizona St.	1993-96	1,375	-107	8,626	8,519	6.20
Robert Hall, Texas Tech	1990-93	1,341	581	7,908	8,489	6.33
Mark Herrmann, Purdue	1977-80	1,354	-744	9,188	8,444	6.24
Mike McCoy, Long Beach St./Utah	1991, 92-94	1,315	97	8,342	8,439	6.42
Kurt Kittner, Illinois	1998-01	1,374	168	8,206	8,374	6.09
¢Jared Lorenzen, Kentucky	2000-02	1,368	208	8,133	8,341	6.10
Robbie Bosco, Brigham Young	1983-85	1,158	-101	8,400	8,299	7.17
Woodrow Dantzler, Clemson	1998-01	1,284	2,615	5,634	8,249	6.42
Troy Taylor, California	1986-89	1,490	110	8,126	8,236	5.53
Randall Cunningham, UNLV	1982-84	1,330	204	8,020	8,224	6.18
Cody Ledbetter, New Mexico St.	1991, 93-95	1,362	727	7,480	8,207	6.03

Kliff Kingsbury of Texas Tech was involved in 2,156 total offense plays in his career, a Division I-A record, after establishing a new single-season mark of 814 in 2002. He finished third in career total offense yards with 12,263.

L. Scott Mann/Texas Tech Sports Information

			Yards			
Player, Team	Years	Plays	Rush	Pass	Total	Avg.
Wes Counts, Middle Tenn.	1998-01	1,352	165	8,007	8,172	6.04
Steve Taneyhill, South Carolina	1992-95	1,423	-392	8,555	8,163	5.74
Tim Couch, Kentucky	1996-98	1,338	-275	8,435	8,160	6.10
Ryan Huzjak, Toledo	1993-96	1,478	1,480	6,672	8,152	5.52
Steve Slayden, Duke	1984-87	1,546	125	8,004	8,129	5.26
Jack Trudeau, Illinois	1981, 83-85	1,318	-50	8,146	8,096	6.14
Mark Barsotti, Fresno St.	1988-91	1,192	768	7,321	8,089	6.79
Gene Swick, Toledo	1972-75	1,579	807	7,267	8,074	5.11
Major Applewhite, Texas	1998-01	1,182	-294	8,353	8,059	6.82
Andre Ware, Houston	1987-89	1,194	-144	8,202	8,058	6.75
James Brown, Texas	1994-97	1,196	411	7,638	8,049	6.73
Len Williams, Northwestern	1990-93	1,614	542	7,486	8,028	4.97
Billy Blanton, San Diego St.	1993-96	1,108	-151	8,165	8,014	7.23

*Record. $See page 8 for explanation. #Record for minimum of 7,500 yards. ¢Active player.

CAREER YARDS RECORD PROGRESSION
(Record Yards—Player, Team, Seasons Played)

3,481—Davey O'Brien, TCU, 1936-38; **3,882**—Paul Christman, Missouri, 1938-40; **4,602**—Frank Sinkwich, Georgia, 1940-42; **4,627**—Bob Fenimore, Oklahoma St., 1943-46; **4,871**—Charlie Justice, North Carolina, 1946-49; **5,903**—Johnny Bright, Drake, 1949-51; **6,354**—Virgil Carter, Brigham Young, 1964-66; **6,568**—Steve Ramsey, North Texas, 1967-69; **7,887**—Jim Plunkett, Stanford, 1968-70; **8,074**—Gene Swick, Toledo, 1972-75; **8,444**—Mark Herrmann, Purdue, 1977-80; **9,723**—Jim McMahon, Brigham Young, 1977-78, 1980-81; **11,317**—Doug Flutie, Boston College, 1981-84; **14,665**—Ty Detmer, Brigham Young, 1988-91.

SEASON YARDS

				Yards			
Player, Team	Year	G	Plays	Rush	Pass	Total	Avg.
David Klingler, Houston	†1990	11	704	81	5,140	*5,221	7.42
Ty Detmer, Brigham Young	1990	12	635	-106	*5,188	5,022	7.91
Kliff Kingsbury, Texas Tech	2002	14	*814	-114	5,017	4,903	6.02
Tim Rattay, Louisiana Tech	†1998	12	602	-103	4,943	4,840	8.04
Andre Ware, Houston	†1989	11	628	-38	4,699	4,661	7.42
Jim McMahon, Brigham Young	†1980	12	540	56	4,571	4,627	8.57
Ty Detmer, Brigham Young	1989	12	497	-127	4,560	4,433	8.92
Timmy Chang, Hawaii	2002	14	663	-17	4,474	4,457	6.72
David Carr, Fresno St.	2001	13	564	97	4,299	4,396	7.79
Steve Young, Brigham Young	†1983	11	531	444	3,902	4,346	8.18
Chris Vargas, Nevada	†1993	11	535	67	4,265	4,332	8.10
Scott Mitchell, Utah	†1988	11	589	-23	4,322	4,299	7.30
Cody Pickett, Washington	2002	13	698	-185	4,458	4,273	6.12
Byron Leftwich, Marshall	†2002	12	528	-1	4,268	4,267	8.08
Byron Leftwich, Marshall	2001	12	534	92	4,132	4,224	7.91
Josh Wallwork, Wyoming	†1996	12	525	119	4,090	4,209	8.02
Daunte Culpepper, UCF	1998	11	543	463	3,690	4,153	7.65
Tim Couch, Kentucky	1998	11	617	-124	4,275	4,151	6.73
Robbie Bosco, Brigham Young	1985	13	578	-132	4,273	4,141	7.16
Chris Weinke, Florida St.	2000	12	461	-97	4,167	4,070	8.83
Chris Redman, Louisville	1998	10	513	-33	4,042	4,009	7.81
Ty Detmer, Brigham Young	†1991	12	478	-30	4,031	4,001	8.37
Brandon Doman, Brigham Young	2001	13	550	456	3,542	3,998	7.27
Steve Sarkisian, Brigham Young	1996	14	486	-44	4,027	3,983	8.20
Mike McCoy, Utah	1993	12	529	109	3,860	3,969	7.50
Tim Rattay, Louisiana Tech	†1997	11	541	87	3,881	3,968	7.33
Drew Brees, Purdue	†2000	11	564	546	3,393	3,939	6.98
Robbie Bosco, Brigham Young	†1984	12	543	57	3,875	3,932	7.24
Drew Brees, Purdue	1998	12	575	168	3,753	3,921	6.82
Rex Grossman, Florida	†2001	11	429	8	3,896	3,904	@9.10
Chad Pennington, Marshall	1999	12	460	105	3,799	3,904	8.49
Brian Jones, Toledo	2002	14	508	414	3,446	3,860	7.60
Jared Lorenzen, Kentucky	2000	11	635	140	3,687	3,827	6.03
Carson Palmer, Southern California	2002	13	539	-122	3,942	3,820	7.09
Tim Rattay, Louisiana Tech	†1999	10	562	-112	3,922	3,810	6.78
Joe Hamilton, Georgia Tech	1999	11	459	734	3,060	3,794	8.27
Peyton Manning, Tennessee	1997	12	526	-30	3,819	3,789	7.20
Jimmy Klingler, Houston	†1992	11	544	-50	3,818	3,768	6.93
Shaun King, Tulane	1998	11	468	532	3,232	3,764	8.04
Dan Robinson, Hawaii	1999	12	616	-91	3,853	3,762	6.11
Tim Couch, Kentucky	1997	11	613	-125	3,884	3,759	6.13
Cody Ledbetter, New Mexico St.	1995	11	543	223	3,501	3,724	6.86
Anthony Dilweg, Duke	1988	11	539	-111	3,824	3,713	6.89
Drew Brees, Purdue	1999	11	564	181	3,531	3,712	6.58

*Record. †National champion. @ Record for minimum of 3,000 yards.

SINGLE-GAME YARDS

Yds.	Rush	Pass	Player, Team (Opponent)	Date
732	16	716	David Klingler, Houston (Arizona St.)	Dec. 2, 1990
696	6	690	Matt Vogler, TCU (Houston)	Nov. 3, 1990
657	20	637	Brian Lindgren, Idaho (Middle Tenn.)	Oct. 6, 2001
625	62	563	David Klingler, Houston (TCU)	Nov. 3, 1990
625	-6	631	Scott Mitchell, Utah (Air Force)	Oct. 15, 1988
612	-1	613	Jimmy Klingler, Houston (Rice)	Nov. 28, 1992
603	4	599	Ty Detmer, Brigham Young (San Diego St.)	Nov. 16, 1991
601	37	564	Troy Kopp, Pacific (Cal.) (New Mexico St.)	Oct. 20, 1990

Yds.	Rush	Pass	Player, Team (Opponent)	Date
599	86	513	Virgil Carter, Brigham Young (UTEP)	Nov. 5, 1966
597	-22	619	John Walsh, Brigham Young (Utah St.)	Oct. 30, 1993
594	-28	622	Jeremy Leach, New Mexico (Utah)	Nov. 11, 1989
585	-36	621	Dave Wilson, Illinois (Ohio St.)	Nov. 8, 1980
582	-29	611	David Neill, Nevada (New Mexico St.)	Oct. 10, 1998
582	11	571	Marc Wilson, Brigham Young (Utah)	Nov. 5, 1977
578	-14	592	Chris Redman, Louisville (East Caro.)	Nov. 14, 1998
578	6	572	David Klingler, Houston (Eastern Wash.)	Nov. 17, 1990
568	-22	590	Tim Rattay, Louisiana Tech (Nebraska)	Aug. 29, 1998
568	11	557	John Dutton, Nevada (Boise St.)	Nov. 8, 1997
562	25	537	Ty Detmer, Brigham Young (Washington St.)	Sept. 7, 1989
559	13	546	Cody Ledbetter, New Mexico St. (UNLV)	Nov. 18, 1995
558	15	543	Nick Rolovich, Hawaii (Brigham Young)	Dec. 8, 2001
554	9	545	Rusty LaRue, Wake Forest (North Carolina St.)	Nov. 18, 1995
552	-13	565	Jim McMahon, Brigham Young (Utah)	Nov. 21, 1981
548	12	536	Dave Telford, Fresno St. (Pacific [Cal.])	Oct. 24, 1987
543	-9	552	Mike Maxwell, Nevada (UNLV)	Oct. 28, 1995
541	-20	561	Tim Rattay, Louisiana Tech (UCF)	Oct. 23, 1999
541	6	535	Mike Maxwell, Nevada (Louisiana Tech)	Oct. 21, 1995
540	12	528	Rohan Davey, LSU (Alabama)	Nov. 3, 2001
540	-45	585	Robbie Bosco, Brigham Young (New Mexico)	Oct. 19, 1985
540	104	436	Archie Manning, Mississippi (Alabama)	Oct. 4, 1969
539	1	538	Jim McMahon, Brigham Young (Colorado St.)	Nov. 7, 1981
538	-1	539	Tim Rattay, Louisiana Tech (Boise St.)	Oct. 3, 1998
537	65	472	Anthony Calvillo, Utah St. (Brigham Young)	Oct. 30, 1993
537	-1	538	Chris Vargas, Nevada (UNLV)	Oct. 2, 1993
537	2	535	Shane Montgomery, North Carolina St. (Duke)	Nov. 11, 1989
537	-24	561	Tony Adams, Utah St. (Utah)	Nov. 11, 1972
536	58	478	Tim Schade, Minnesota (Penn St.)	Sept. 4, 1993
536	28	508	Mike Perez, San Jose St. (Pacific [Cal.])	Oct. 25, 1986

ANNUAL CHAMPIONS

					Yads		
Year	Player, Team		Class	Plays	Rush	Pass	Total
1937	Byron "Whizzer" White, Colorado		Sr.	224	1,121	475	1,596
1938	Davey O'Brien, TCU		Sr.	291	390	1,457	1,847
1939	Kenny Washington, UCLA		Sr.	259	811	559	1,370
1940	Johnny Knolla, Creighton		Sr.	298	813	607	1,420
1941	Bud Schwenk, Washington (Mo.)		Sr.	354	471	1,457	1,928
1942	Frank Sinkwich, Georgia		Sr.	341	795	1,392	2,187
1943	Bob Hoernschemeyer, Indiana		Fr.	355	515	1,133	1,648
1944	Bob Fenimore, Oklahoma St.		So.	241	897	861	1,758
1945	Bob Fenimore, Oklahoma St.		Jr.	203	1,048	593	1,641
1946	Travis Tidwell, Auburn		Fr.	339	772	943	1,715
1947	Fred Enke, Arizona		So.	329	535	1,406	1,941
1948	Stan Heath, Nevada		Sr.	233	-13	2,005	1,992
1949	Johnny Bright, Drake		So.	275	975	975	1,950
1950	Johnny Bright, Drake		Jr.	320	1,232	1,168	2,400
1951	Dick Kazmaier, Princeton		Sr.	272	861	966	1,827
1952	Ted Marchibroda, Detroit		Sr.	305	176	1,637	1,813
1953	Paul Larson, California		Jr.	262	141	1,431	1,572
1954	George Shaw, Oregon		Sr.	276	178	1,358	1,536
1955	George Welsh, Navy		Sr.	203	29	1,319	1,348
1956	John Brodie, Stanford		Sr.	295	9	1,633	1,642
1957	Bob Newman, Washington St.		Jr.	263	53	1,391	1,444
1958	Dick Bass, Pacific (Cal.)		Jr.	218	1,361	79	1,440
1959	Dick Norman, Stanford		Jr.	319	55	1,963	2,018
1960	Bill Kilmer, UCLA		Sr.	292	803	1,086	1,889
1961	Dave Hoppmann, Iowa St.		Jr.	320	920	718	1,638
1962	Terry Baker, Oregon St.		Sr.	318	538	1,738	2,276
1963	George Mira, Miami (Fla.)		Sr.	394	163	2,155	2,318
1964	Jerry Rhome, Tulsa		Sr.	470	258	2,870	3,128
1965	Bill Anderson, Tulsa		Sr.	580	-121	3,464	3,343
1966	Virgil Carter, Brigham Young		Sr.	388	363	2,182	2,545
1967	Sal Olivas, New Mexico St.		Sr.	368	-41	2,225	2,184
1968	Greg Cook, Cincinnati		Sr.	507	-62	3,272	3,210
1969	Dennis Shaw, San Diego St.		Sr.	388	12	3,185	3,197

Beginning in 1970, ranked on per-game (instead of total) yards

					Yards			
Year	Player, Team	Class	G	Plays	Rush	Pass	Total	Avg.
1970	Pat Sullivan, Auburn	Jr.	10	333	270	2,586	2,856	285.6
1971	Gary Huff, Florida St.	Jr.	11	386	-83	2,736	2,653	241.2
1972	Don Strock, Virginia Tech	Sr.	11	480	-73	3,243	3,170	288.2
1973	Jesse Freitas, San Diego St.	Sr.	11	410	-92	2,993	2,901	263.7
1974	Steve Joachim, Temple	Sr.	10	331	277	1,950	2,227	222.7
1975	Gene Swick, Toledo	Sr.	11	490	219	2,487	2,706	246.0
1976	Tommy Kramer, Rice	Sr.	11	562	-45	3,317	3,272	297.5
1977	Doug Williams, Grambling	Sr.	11	377	-57	3,286	3,229	293.5
1978	Mike Ford, Southern Methodist	So.	11	459	-50	3,007	2,957	268.8
1979	Marc Wilson, Brigham Young	Sr.	11	488	-140	3,720	3,580	325.5
1980	Jim McMahon, Brigham Young	Jr.	12	540	56	4,571	4,627	385.6
1981	Jim McMahon, Brigham Young	Sr.	10	487	-97	3,555	3,458	345.8
1982	Todd Dillon, Long Beach St.	Jr.	11	585	70	3,517	3,587	326.1
1983	Steve Young, Brigham Young	Sr.	11	531	444	3,902	4,346	395.1

Year	Player, Team	Class	G	Plays	Rush	Pass	Total	Avg.
1984	Robbie Bosco, Brigham Young	Jr.	12	543	57	3,875	3,932	327.7
1985	Jim Everett, Purdue	Sr.	11	518	-62	3,651	3,589	326.3
1986	Mike Perez, San Jose St.	Jr.	9	425	35	2,934	2,969	329.9
1987	Todd Santos, San Diego St.	Sr.	12	562	-244	3,932	3,688	307.3
1988	Scott Mitchell, Utah	So.	11	589	-23	4,322	4,299	390.8
1989	Andre Ware, Houston	Jr.	11	628	-38	4,699	4,661	423.7
1990	David Klingler, Houston	Jr.	11	*704	81	5,140	*5,221	*474.6
1991	Ty Detmer, Brigham Young	Sr.	12	478	-30	4,031	4,001	333.4
1992	Jimmy Klingler, Houston	So.	11	544	-50	3,818	3,768	342.5
1993	Chris Vargas, Nevada	Sr.	11	535	67	4,265	4,332	393.8
1994	Mike Maxwell, Nevada	Jr.	11	477	-39	3,537	3,498	318.0
1995	Mike Maxwell, Nevada	Sr.	9	443	12	3,611	3,623	402.6
1996	Josh Wallwork, Wyoming	Sr.	12	525	119	4,090	4,209	350.8
1997	Tim Rattay, Louisiana Tech	So.	11	541	87	3,881	3,968	360.7
1998	Tim Rattay, Louisiana Tech	Jr.	12	602	-103	4,943	4,840	403.3
1999	Tim Rattay, Louisiana Tech	Sr.	10	562	-112	3,922	3,810	381.0
2000	Drew Brees, Purdue	Sr.	11	564	546	3,393	3,939	358.1
2001	Rex Grossman, Florida	So.	11	429	8	3,896	3,904	354.9
2002	Byron Leftwich, Marshall	Sr.	12	528	-1	4,268	4,267	355.6

*Record.

Rushing

CAREER YARDS PER GAME
(Minimum 2,500 yards)

Player, Team	Years	G	Plays	Yards	TD	Yd. PG
Ed Marinaro, Cornell	1969-71	27	918	4,715	50	*174.6
O. J. Simpson, Southern California	1967-68	19	621	3,124	33	164.4
Herschel Walker, Georgia	1980-82	33	994	5,259	49	159.4
LeShon Johnson, Northern Ill.	1992-93	22	592	3,314	18	150.6
Ron Dayne, Wisconsin	1996-99	43	1,115	*6,397	63	148.8
Marshall Faulk, San Diego St.	1991-93	31	766	4,589	57	148.0
George Jones, San Diego St.	1995-96	19	486	2,810	34	147.9
Tony Dorsett, Pittsburgh	1973-76	43	1,074	6,082	55	141.4
Troy Davis, Iowa St.	1994-96	31	782	4,382	36	141.4
Mike Rozier, Nebraska	1981-83	35	668	4,780	50	136.6
Ricky Williams, Texas	1995-98	46	1,011	6,279	72	136.5
Howard Stevens, Louisville	1971-72	20	509	2,723	25	136.2
Jerome Persell, Western Mich.	1976-78	31	842	4,190	39	135.2
Rudy Mobley, Hardin-Simmons	1942,46	19	414	2,543	32	133.8
Alex Smith, Indiana	1994-96	27	723	3,492	11	129.3
Vaughn Dunbar, Indiana	1990-91	22	565	2,842	24	129.2
Steve Owens, Oklahoma	1967-69	30	905	3,867	56	128.9
Byron Hanspard, Texas Tech	1994-96	33	760	4,219	29	127.8
Charles White, Southern California	1976-79	44	1,023	5,598	46	127.2
Travis Prentice, Miami (Ohio)	1996-99	44	1,138	5,596	*73	127.2
Emmitt Smith, Florida	1987-89	31	700	3,928	36	126.7
Johnny Bright, Drake	1949-51	25	513	3,134	39	125.4
Woody Green, Arizona St.	1971-73	30	601	3,754	33	125.1
Archie Griffin, Ohio St.	1972-75	42	845	5,177	25	123.3
Anthony Thompson, Indiana	1986-89	41	1,089	4,965	64	121.1
Mark Kellar, Northern Ill.	1971-73	31	743	3,745	32	120.8
Paul Gipson, Houston	1966-68	23	447	2,769	25	120.4
John Cappelletti, Penn St.	‡1972-73	22	519	2,639	29	120.0
LaDainian Tomlinson, TCU	1997-00	44	907	5,263	54	119.6
Brian Pruitt, Central Mich.	1992-94	31	671	3,693	31	119.1
Ahman Green, Nebraska	1995-97	33	574	3,880	42	117.6
Steve Bartalo, Colorado St.	1983-86	41	*1,215	4,813	46	117.4
Louie Giammona, Utah St.	1973-75	30	756	3,499	21	116.6
Paul Palmer, Temple	1983-86	42	948	4,895	39	116.5
Bill Marek, Wisconsin	1972-75	32	719	3,709	44	115.9
Toraino Singleton, UTEP	1994-95	23	560	2,635	19	114.6
Darren Lewis, Texas A&M	1987-90	44	909	5,012	44	113.9
Dick Jauron, Yale	1970-72	26	515	2,947	27	113.3
Bo Jackson, Auburn	1982-85	38	650	4,303	43	113.2
Rashaan Salaam, Colorado	1992-94	27	486	3,057	33	113.2
Joe Morris, Syracuse	1978-81	38	813	4,299	25	113.1
Darnell Autry, Northwestern	1994-96	32	738	3,617	30	113.0
Eugene "Mercury" Morris, West Tex. A&M	1966-68	30	541	3,388	34	112.9

*Record. ‡Defensive back in 1971.

SEASON YARDS PER GAME

Player, Team	Year	G	Plays	Yards	TD	Yd. PG
Barry Sanders, Oklahoma St.	†1988	11	344	*2,628	*37	*238.9
Marcus Allen, Southern California	†1981	11	*403	2,342	22	212.9
Ed Marinaro, Cornell	†1971	9	356	1,881	24	209.0
Troy Davis, Iowa St.	†1996	11	402	2,185	21	198.6
LaDainian Tomlinson, TCU	†2000	11	369	2,158	22	196.2

Player, Team	Year	G	Plays	Yards	TD	Yd. PG
Ricky Williams, Texas	†1998	11	361	2,124	27	193.1
Byron Hanspard, Texas Tech	1996	11	339	2,084	13	189.5
Rashaan Salaam, Colorado	†1994	11	298	2,055	24	186.8
Troy Davis, Iowa St.	†1995	11	345	2,010	15	182.7
Charles White, Southern California	†1979	10	293	1,803	18	180.3
LeShon Johnson, Northern Ill.	†1993	11	327	1,976	12	179.6
Mike Rozier, Nebraska	†1983	12	275	2,148	29	179.0
Tony Dorsett, Pittsburgh	†1976	11	338	1,948	21	177.1
Ollie Matson, San Francisco	†1951	9	245	1,566	20	174.0
Damien Anderson, Northwestern	2000	11	293	1,914	22	174.0
Lorenzo White, Michigan St.	†1985	11	386	1,908	17	173.5
Wasean Tait, Toledo	1995	11	357	1,905	20	173.2
Ricky Williams, Texas	†1997	11	279	1,893	25	172.1
Herschel Walker, Georgia	1981	11	385	1,891	18	171.9
Brian Pruitt, Central Mich.	1994	11	292	1,890	20	171.8
O. J. Simpson, Southern California	†1968	10	355	1,709	22	170.9
Ernest Anderson, Oklahoma St.	†1982	11	353	1,877	8	170.6
Ricky Bell, Southern California	†1975	11	357	1,875	13	170.5

*Record. †National champion.

CAREER YARDS

Player, Team	Years	Plays	Yards	Avg.	Long
Ron Dayne, Wisconsin	1996-99	1,115	*6,397	5.74	80
Ricky Williams, Texas	1995-98	1,011	6,279	††6.21	87
Tony Dorsett, Pittsburgh	1973-76	1,074	6,082	5.66	73
Charles White, Southern California	1976-79	1,023	5,598	5.47	79
Travis Prentice, Miami (Ohio)	1996-99	1,138	5,596	4.92	55
LaDainian Tomlinson, TCU	1997-00	907	5,263	5.80	89
Herschel Walker, Georgia	1980-82	994	5,259	5.29	76
Archie Griffin, Ohio St.	1972-75	845	5,177	6.13	75
Darren Lewis, Texas A&M	1987-90	909	5,012	5.51	84
Anthony Thompson, Indiana	1986-89	1,089	4,965	4.56	52
George Rogers, South Carolina	1977-80	902	4,958	5.50	80
Trevor Cobb, Rice	1989-92	1,091	4,948	4.54	79
Paul Palmer, Temple	1983-86	948	4,895	5.16	78
Steve Bartalo, Colorado St.	1983-86	*1,215	4,813	3.96	39
Ken Simonton, Oregon St.	1998-01	1,005	4,802	4.78	64
Mike Rozier, Nebraska	1981-83	668	4,780	#7.16	93
Ed Marinaro, Cornell	1969-71	918	4,715	5.14	79
Denvis Manns, New Mexico St.	1995-98	889	4,692	5.28	73
Marcus Allen, Southern California	1978-81	893	4,682	5.24	45
Chester Taylor, Toledo	1998-01	803	4,659	5.80	73
Ted Brown, North Carolina St.	1975-78	860	4,602	5.35	95
Thurman Thomas, Oklahoma St.	1984-87	898	4,595	5.12	66
Marshall Faulk, San Diego St.	1991-93	766	4,589	5.99	71
Terry Miller, Oklahoma St.	1974-77	847	4,582	5.41	81
Kevin Faulk, LSU	1995-98	856	4,557	5.32	81
Darrell Thompson, Minnesota	1986-89	911	4,518	4.96	98
Lorenzo White, Michigan St.	1984-87	991	4,513	4.55	73
Damien Anderson, Northwestern	1998-01	953	4,485	4.71	73
Eric Dickerson, Southern Methodist	1979-82	790	4,450	5.63	80
Earl Campbell, Texas	1974-77	765	4,443	5.81	‡‡83
Amos Lawrence, North Carolina	1977-80	881	4,391	4.98	62
Troy Davis, Iowa St.	1994-96	782	4,382	5.60	80
Deland McCullough, Miami (Ohio)	1992-95	949	4,368	4.60	51
David Thompson, Oklahoma St.	1993-96	846	4,318	5.10	91
Autry Denson, Notre Dame	1995-98	854	4,318	5.06	74

Player, Team	Years	Plays	Yards	Avg.	Long
Bo Jackson, Auburn	1982-85	650	4,303	6.62	80
Joe Morris, Syracuse	1978-81	813	4,299	5.29	75
Reggie Taylor, Cincinnati	1983-86	876	4,242	4.48	‡‡68
Byron Hanspard, Texas Tech	1994-96	760	4,219	5.55	72
Robert Sanford, Western Mich.	1997-00	838	4,219	5.03	67
Mike Mayweather, Army	1987-90	832	4,212	5.06	52
Jerome Persell, Western Mich.	1976-78	842	4,190	4.98	86
Napoleon McCallum, Navy	$1981-85	908	4,179	4.60	60
Tico Duckett, Michigan St.	1989-92	824	4,176	5.07	88
George Swarn, Miami (Ohio)	1983-86	881	4,172	4.74	98
Errict Rhett, Florida	$1989-93	873	4,163	4.77	49
Curtis Adams, Central Mich.	1981-84	761	4,162	5.47	87
Lamont Jordan, Maryland	1997-00	807	4,147	5.14	90
Allen Pinkett, Notre Dame	1982-85	889	4,131	4.65	76
Robert Holcombe, Illinois	1994-97	943	4,105	4.35	67
Anthony Thomas, Michigan	1997-00	846	4,098	4.84	80
Robert Lavette, Georgia Tech	1981-84	914	4,066	4.45	83
James Gray, Texas Tech	1986-89	742	4,066	5.48	72
Stump Mitchell, Citadel	1977-80	756	4,062	5.37	77
Dalton Hilliard, LSU	1982-85	882	4,050	4.59	66
Napoleon Kaufman, Washington	1991-94	710	4,041	5.69	91
Charles Alexander, LSU	1975-78	855	4,035	4.72	64
Darrin Nelson, Stanford	1977-78, 80-81	703	4,033	5.74	80

*Record. $See page 8 for explanation. ‡‡Did not score. ††Record for minimum 781 carries. #Record for minimum 414 carries.

CAREER YARDS RECORD PROGRESSION
(Record Yards—Player, Team, Seasons Played)

1,961—Marshall Goldberg, Pittsburgh, 1936-38; **2,105**—Tom Harmon, Michigan, 1938-40; **2,271**—Frank Sinkwich, Georgia, 1940-42; **2,301**—Bill Daley, Minnesota, 1940-42; Michigan, 1943; **2,957**—Glenn Davis, Army, 1943-46; **3,095**—Eddie Price, Tulane, 1946-49; **3,238**—John Papit, Virginia, 1947-50; **3,381**—Art Luppino, Arizona, 1953-56; **3,388**—Eugene "Mercury" Morris, West Tex. A&M, 1966-68; **3,867**—Steve Owens, Oklahoma, 1967-69; **4,715**—Ed Marinaro, Cornell, 1969-71; **5,177**—Archie Griffin, Ohio St., 1972-75; **6,082**—Tony Dorsett, Pittsburgh, 1973-76; **6,279**—Ricky Williams, Texas, 1995-98; **6,397**—Ron Dayne, Wisconsin, 1996-99.

CAREER RUSHING TOUCHDOWNS

Player, Team	Years	G	TD
Travis Prentice, Miami (Ohio)	1996-99	44	*73
Ricky Williams, Texas	1995-98	46	72
Anthony Thompson, Indiana	1986-89	41	64
Ron Dayne, Wisconsin	1996-99	43	63
Eric Crouch, Nebraska (QB)	1998-01	43	59
Marshall Faulk, San Diego St.	1991-93	31	57
Ken Simonton, Oregon St.	1998-01	44	56
Steve Owens, Oklahoma	1967-69	30	56
Chester Taylor, Toledo	1998-01	42	55
Tony Dorsett, Pittsburgh	1973-76	43	55
LaDainian Tomlinson, TCU	1997-00	44	54
Dwone Hicks, Middle Tenn.	1999-02	44	53
Chris Lemon, Nevada	1996-99	44	52
Pete Johnson, Ohio St.	1973-76	41	51
Brock Forsey, Boise St.	1999-02	47	50
Mike Rozier, Nebraska	1982-83	35	50
Billy Sims, Oklahoma	1975, 77-79	42	50
Ed Marinaro, Cornell	1969-71	27	50
Anthony Thomas, Michigan	1997-00	44	49
Allen Pinkett, Notre Dame	1982-85	44	49
Herschel Walker, Georgia	1980-82	33	49
Ted Brown, North Carolina St.	1975-78	43	49
Skip Hicks, UCLA	$1993-97	40	48
Brian Mitchell, La.-Lafayette (QB)	1986-89	43	47
Barry Sanders, Oklahoma St.	1986-88	30	47
Eric Dickerson, Southern Methodist	1979-82	42	47
Kevin Faulk, LSU	1995-98	41	46
Steve Bartalo, Colorado St.	1983-86	41	46
Charles White, Southern California	1976-79	44	46
Bill Burnett, Arkansas	1968-70	28	46
James Gray, Texas Tech	1986-89	44	45
Keith Byars, Ohio St.	1982-85	33	45
Robert Lavette, Georgia Tech	1981-84	43	45
Marcus Allen, Southern California	1978-81	44	45
Terry Miller, Oklahoma St.	1974-77	41	45

*Record. (Note: Howard Stevens of Louisville played two years at college division Randolph-Macon, 1968-69, with 33 touchdowns and two years at Louisville, 1971-72, with 25 touchdowns, scoring a total of 58 touchdowns in four years.) $See page **8** for explanation.

SEASON YARDS

Player, Team	Year	G	Plays	Yards	Avg.
Barry Sanders, Oklahoma St.	†1988	11	344	*2,628	‡7.64
Marcus Allen, Southern California	†1981	11	*403	2,342	5.81
Troy Davis, Iowa St.	†1996	11	402	2,185	5.44
LaDainian Tomlinson, TCU	†2000	11	369	2,158	5.85
Mike Rozier, Nebraska	†1983	12	275	2,148	#7.81
Ricky Williams, Texas	†1998	11	361	2,124	5.88
Larry Johnson, Penn St.	†2002	13	271	2,087	7.70
Byron Hanspard, Texas Tech	1996	11	339	2,084	6.15
Rashaan Salaam, Colorado	†1994	11	298	2,055	6.90
Troy Davis, Iowa St.	†1995	11	345	2,010	5.83
LeShon Johnson, Northern Ill.	†1993	11	327	1,976	6.04
Tony Dorsett, Pittsburgh	†1976	11	338	1,948	5.76
Michael Turner, Northern Ill.	2002	12	338	1,915	5.67
Damien Anderson, Northwestern	2000	11	293	1,914	6.53
Lorenzo White, Michigan St.	†1985	11	386	1,908	4.94
Wasean Tait, Toledo	1995	11	357	1,905	5.34
Ricky Williams, Texas	†1997	11	279	1,893	6.78
Herschel Walker, Georgia	1981	11	385	1,891	4.91
Brian Pruitt, Central Mich.	1994	11	292	1,890	6.47
Quentin Griffin, Oklahoma	2002	14	287	1,884	6.56
Ed Marinaro, Cornell	†1971	9	356	1,881	5.28
Ernest Anderson, Oklahoma St.	†1982	11	353	1,877	5.32
Ahman Green, Nebraska	1997	12	278	1,877	6.75
Ricky Bell, Southern California	†1975	11	357	1,875	5.25
Paul Palmer, Temple	†1986	11	346	1,866	5.39
Ron Dayne, Wisconsin	1996	12	295	1,863	6.32
LaDainian Tomlinson, TCU	†1999	11	268	1,850	6.90
George Jones, San Diego St.	1995	12	305	1,842	6.04
Chris Brown, Colorado	2002	11	303	1,841	6.08
Ron Dayne, Wisconsin	1999	11	303	1,834	6.05
Eddie George, Ohio St.	1995	12	303	1,826	6.03
Charles White, Southern California	†1979	10	293	1,803	6.15
Thomas Jones, Virginia	1999	11	334	1,798	5.38
Anthony Thompson, Indiana	†1989	11	358	1,793	5.01
Obie Graves, Cal St. Fullerton	1978	12	275	1,789	6.51
Travis Prentice, Miami (Ohio)	1998	11	365	1,787	4.90
Bo Jackson, Auburn	1985	11	278	1,786	6.42
George Rogers, South Carolina	†1980	11	297	1,781	6.00
Billy Sims, Oklahoma	†1978	11	231	1,762	7.63
Charles White, Southern California	1978	12	342	1,760	5.15
Robert Newhouse, Houston	1971	11	277	1,757	6.34
Willis McGahee, Miami (Fla.)	2002	13	282	1,753	6.22
Herschel Walker, Georgia	1982	11	335	1,752	5.23
Byron Morris, Texas Tech	1993	11	298	1,752	5.88

*Record. †National champion. ‡Record for minimum 282 carries. #Record for minimum 214 carries.

SINGLE-GAME YARDS

Yds.	Player, Team (Opponent)	Date
406	LaDainian Tomlinson, TCU (UTEP)	Nov. 20, 1999
396	Tony Sands, Kansas (Missouri)	Nov. 23, 1991
386	Marshall Faulk, San Diego St. (Pacific [Cal.])	Sept. 14, 1991
378	Troy Davis, Iowa St. (Missouri)	Sept. 28, 1996
377	Robbie Mixon, Central Mich. (Eastern Mich.)	Nov. 2, 2002
377	Anthony Thompson, Indiana (Wisconsin)	Nov. 11, 1989
376	Travis Prentice, Miami (Ohio) (Akron)	Nov. 6, 1999
373	Astron Whatley, Kent St. (Eastern Mich.)	Sept. 20, 1997
357	Mike Pringle, Cal St. Fullerton (New Mexico St.)	Nov. 4, 1989
357	Rueben Mayes, Washington St. (Oregon)	Oct. 27, 1984
356	Brian Pruitt, Central Mich. (Toledo)	Nov. 5, 1994
356	Eddie Lee Ivery, Georgia Tech (Air Force)	Nov. 11, 1978
351	Scott Harley, East Caro. (North Carolina St.)	Nov. 30, 1996
350	Ricky Williams, Texas (Iowa St.)	Oct. 3, 1998
350	Eric Allen, Michigan St. (Purdue)	Oct. 30, 1971
349	Paul Palmer, Temple (East Caro.)	Oct. 11, 1986
347	Ricky Bell, Southern California (Washington St.)	Oct. 9, 1976
347	Ron Johnson, Michigan (Wisconsin)	Nov. 16, 1968
343	Tony Jeffery, TCU (Tulane)	Sept. 13, 1986
342	Roosevelt Leaks, Texas (Southern Methodist)	Nov. 3, 1973
342	Charlie Davis, Colorado (Oklahoma St.)	Nov. 13, 1971
340	Eugene "Mercury" Morris, West Tex. A&M (Montana St.)	Oct. 5, 1968
339	Ron Dayne, Wisconsin (Hawaii)	Nov. 30, 1996
332	Barry Sanders, Oklahoma St. (Texas Tech)	Dec. 3, 1988
329	John Leach, Wake Forest (Maryland)	Nov. 20, 1993
328	Derrick Fenner, North Carolina (Virginia)	Nov. 15, 1986
327	Larry Johnson, Penn St. (Indiana)	Nov. 16, 2002
327	Chance Kretschmer, Nevada (UTEP)	Nov. 24, 2001
326	George Swarn, Miami (Ohio) (Eastern Mich.)	Nov. 16, 1985
326	Fred Wendt, UTEP (New Mexico St.)	Nov. 25, 1948
325	Andre Davis, TCU (New Mexico)	Sept. 10, 1994
322	Emmett White, Utah St. (New Mexico St.)	Nov. 4, 2000
322	LeShon Johnson, Northern Ill. (Southern Ill.)	Oct. 2, 1993
322	Greg Allen, Florida St. (Western Caro.)	Oct. 31, 1981
321	David Thompson, Oklahoma St. (Baylor)	Nov. 23, 1996
321	Frank Mordica, Vanderbilt (Air Force)	Nov. 18, 1978
320	Barry Sanders, Oklahoma St. (Kansas St.)	Oct. 29, 1988
319	Devin West, Missouri (Kansas)	Sept. 12, 1998
319	Andre Herrera, Southern Ill. (Northern Ill.)	Oct. 23, 1976
319	Jim Pilot, New Mexico St. (Hardin-Simmons)	Nov. 25, 1961

Penn State's Larry Johnson rushed for 2,087 yards last year, Division I-A's seventh-highest single-season total. The Nittany Lion earned the rushing title with an average of 160.5 yards per game.

Penn State Sports Information

Yds.	Player, Team (Opponent)	Date
318	Ricky Williams, Texas (Rice)	Sept. 26, 1998
317	Rashaan Salaam, Colorado (Texas)	Oct. 1, 1994
316	Emmitt Smith, Florida (New Mexico)	Oct. 21, 1989
316	Mike Adamle, Northwestern (Wisconsin)	Oct. 18, 1969
315	Robert Holcombe, Illinois (Minnesota)	Nov. 16, 1996
314	Eddie George, Ohio St. (Illinois)	Nov. 11, 1995
314	Tavian Banks, Iowa (Tulsa)	Sept. 13, 1997
313	Tim Biakabutuka, Michigan (Ohio St.)	Nov. 25, 1995
312	Mark Brus, Tulsa (New Mexico St.)	Oct. 27, 1990
312	Barry Sanders, Oklahoma St. (Kansas)	Nov. 12, 1988
311	Dwone Hicks, Middle Tenn. (Louisiana Tech)	Oct. 7, 2000
310	Tony Alford, Colorado St. (Utah)	Oct. 28, 1989
310	Mitchell True, Pacific (Cal.) (UC Davis)	Nov. 18, 1972
309	Chris Brown, Colorado (Kansas)	Oct. 12, 2002
308	Stacey Robinson (QB), Northern Ill. (Fresno St.)	Oct. 6, 1990
307	Curtis Kuykendall, Auburn (Miami [Fla.])	Nov. 24, 1944
306	Lamont Jordan, Maryland (Virginia)	Nov. 20, 1999
306	LeShon Johnson, Northern Ill. (Iowa)	Nov. 6, 1993
305	LaDainian Tomlinson, TCU (UTEP)	Nov. 18, 2000
304	Casey McBeth, Toledo (Akron)	Oct. 22, 1994
304	Barry Sanders, Oklahoma St. (Tulsa)	Oct. 1, 1988
304	Sam Dejarnette, Southern Miss. (Florida St.)	Sept. 25, 1982
304	Bill Marek, Wisconsin (Minnesota)	Nov. 23, 1974
303	Tony Dorsett, Pittsburgh (Notre Dame)	Nov. 15, 1975
302	Troy Davis, Iowa St. (UNLV)	Sept. 23, 1995
302	Jason Davis, Louisiana Tech (La.-Lafayette)	Sept. 29, 1990
302	Kevin Lowe, Wyoming (South Dakota St.)	Nov. 10, 1984
301	Anthony Davis, Wisconsin (Minnesota)	Nov. 23, 2002
301	DeShaun Foster, UCLA (Washington)	Oct. 13, 2001
300	Joffrey Reynolds, Houston (East Caro.)	Nov. 9, 2002
300	LaDainian Tomlinson, TCU (San Jose St.)	Oct. 9, 1999
300	Marshall Faulk, San Diego St. (Hawaii)	Nov. 14, 1992

ANNUAL CHAMPIONS

Year	Player, Team	Class	Plays	Yards
1937	Byron "Whizzer" White, Colorado	Sr.	181	1,121
1938	Len Eshmont, Fordham	So.	132	831
1939	John Polanski, Wake Forest	So.	137	882
1940	Al Ghesquiere, Detroit	Sr.	146	957
1941	Frank Sinkwich, Georgia	Jr.	209	1,103
1942	Rudy Mobley, Hardin-Simmons	So.	187	1,281
1943	Creighton Miller, Notre Dame	Sr.	151	911
1944	Wayne "Red" Williams, Minnesota	Jr.	136	911

Year	Player, Team	Class	Plays	Yards
1945	Bob Fenimore, Oklahoma St.	Jr.	142	1,048
1946	Rudy Mobley, Hardin-Simmons	Sr.	227	1,262
1947	Wilton Davis, Hardin-Simmons	So.	193	1,173
1948	Fred Wendt, UTEP	Sr.	184	1,570
1949	John Dottley, Mississippi	Jr.	208	1,312
1950	Wilford White, Arizona St.	Sr.	199	1,502
1951	Ollie Matson, San Francisco	Sr.	245	1,566
1952	Howie Waugh, Tulsa	Sr.	164	1,372
1953	J.C. Caroline, Illinois	So.	194	1,256
1954	Art Luppino, Arizona	So.	179	1,359
1955	Art Luppino, Arizona	Jr.	209	1,313
1956	Jim Crawford, Wyoming	Sr.	200	1,104
1957	Leon Burton, Arizona St.	Sr.	117	1,126
1958	Dick Bass, Pacific (Cal.)	Jr.	205	1,361
1959	Pervis Atkins, New Mexico St.	Jr.	130	971
1960	Bob Gaiters, New Mexico St.	Sr.	197	1,338
1961	Jim Pilot, New Mexico St.	So.	191	1,278
1962	Jim Pilot, New Mexico St.	Jr.	208	1,247
1963	Dave Casinelli, Memphis	Sr.	219	1,016
1964	Brian Piccolo, Wake Forest	Sr.	252	1,044
1965	Mike Garrett, Southern California	Sr.	267	1,440
1966	Ray McDonald, Idaho	Sr.	259	1,329
1967	O.J. Simpson, Southern California	Jr.	266	1,415
1968	O.J. Simpson, Southern California	Sr.	355	1,709
1969	Steve Owens, Oklahoma	Sr.	358	1,523

Beginning in 1970, ranked on per-game (instead of total) yards

Year	Player, Team	Class	G	Plays	Yards	Avg.
1970	Ed Marinaro, Cornell	Jr.	9	285	1,425	158.3
1971	Ed Marinaro, Cornell	Sr.	9	356	1,881	209.0
1972	Pete VanValkenburg, Brigham Young	Sr.	10	232	1,386	138.6
1973	Mark Kellar, Northern Ill.	Sr.	11	291	1,719	156.3
1974	Louie Giammona, Utah St.	Jr.	10	329	1,534	153.4
1975	Ricky Bell, Southern California	Jr.	11	357	1,875	170.5
1976	Tony Dorsett, Pittsburgh	Sr.	11	338	1,948	177.1
1977	Earl Campbell, Texas	Sr.	11	267	1,744	158.5
1978	Billy Sims, Oklahoma	Jr.	11	231	1,762	160.2
1979	Charles White, Southern California	Sr.	10	293	1,803	180.3
1980	George Rogers, South Carolina	Sr.	11	297	1,781	161.9
1981	Marcus Allen, Southern California	Sr.	11	*403	2,342	212.9
1982	Ernest Anderson, Oklahoma St.	Jr.	11	353	1,877	170.6
1983	Mike Rozier, Nebraska	Sr.	12	275	2,148	179.0
1984	Keith Byars, Ohio St.	Jr.	11	313	1,655	150.5
1985	Lorenzo White, Michigan St.	So.	11	386	1,908	173.5
1986	Paul Palmer, Temple	Sr.	11	346	1,866	169.6
1987	Elbert "Ickey" Woods, UNLV	Sr.	11	259	1,658	150.7
1988	Barry Sanders, Oklahoma St.	Jr.	11	344	*2,628	*238.9
1989	Anthony Thompson, Indiana	Sr.	11	358	1,793	163.0
1990	Gerald Hudson, Oklahoma St.	Sr.	11	279	1,642	149.3
1991	Marshall Faulk, San Diego St.	Fr.	9	201	1,429	158.8
1992	Marshall Faulk, San Diego St.	So.	10	265	1,630	163.0
1993	LeShon Johnson, Northern Ill.	Sr.	11	327	1,976	179.6
1994	Rashaan Salaam, Colorado	Jr.	11	298	2,055	186.8
1995	Troy Davis, Iowa St.	So.	11	345	2,010	182.7
1996	Troy Davis, Iowa St.	Jr.	11	402	2,185	198.6
1997	Ricky Williams, Texas	Jr.	11	279	1,893	172.1
1998	Ricky Williams, Texas	Sr.	11	361	2,124	193.1
1999	LaDainian Tomlinson, TCU	Jr.	11	268	1,850	168.2
2000	LaDainian Tomlinson, TCU	Sr.	11	369	2,158	196.2
2001	Chance Kretschmer, Nevada	Fr.	11	302	1,732	157.5
2002	Larry Johnson, Penn St.	Sr.	13	271	2,087	160.5

*Record.

FRESHMAN 1,000-YARD RUSHERS

Player, Team	Year	Yards
Ron "Po" James, New Mexico St.	1968	1,291
Tony Dorsett, Pittsburgh	1973	1,586
James McDougald, Wake Forest	1976	1,018
Mike Harkrader, Indiana	1976	1,003
Amos Lawrence, North Carolina	1977	1,211
Darrin Nelson, Stanford	1977	1,069
Mike Smith, Chattanooga	1977	1,062
Gwain Durden, Chattanooga	1977	1,049
Allen Ross, Northern Ill.	1977	1,043
Allen Harvin, Cincinnati	1978	1,238
Joe Morris, Syracuse	1978	1,001
Ron Lear, Marshall	1979	1,162
Herschel Walker, Georgia	1980	1,616
Kerwin Bell, Kansas	1980	1,114
Joe McIntosh, North Carolina St.	1981	1,190
Steve Bartalo, Colorado St.	1983	1,113
Spencer Tillman, Oklahoma	1983	1,047
D.J. Dozier, Penn St.	1983	1,002
Eddie Johnson, Utah	1984	1,021
Darrell Thompson, Minnesota	1986	1,240
Emmitt Smith, Florida	1987	1,341
Reggie Cobb, Tennessee	1987	1,197

Player, Team	Year	Yards
Bernie Parmalee, Ball St.	1987	1,064
Curvin Richards, Pittsburgh	1988	1,228
Chuck Webb, Tennessee	1989	1,236
Robert Smith, Ohio St.	1990	1,064
Marshall Faulk, San Diego St.	1991	1,429
Greg Hill, Texas A&M	1991	1,216
David Small, Cincinnati	1991	1,004
Winslow Oliver, New Mexico	1992	1,063
Deland McCullough, Miami (Ohio)	1992	1,026
Terrell Willis, Rutgers	1993	1,261
June Henley, Kansas	1993	1,127
Marquis Williams, Arkansas St.	1993	1,060
Leon Johnson, North Carolina	1993	1,012
Alex Smith, Indiana	1994	1,475
Astron Whatley, Kent St.	1994	1,003
Denvis Manns, New Mexico St.	1995	1,120
Silas Massey, Central Mich.	1995	1,089
Ahman Green, Nebraska	1995	1,086
Ron Dayne, Wisconsin	1996	*1,863
Demond Parker, Oklahoma	1996	1,184
Sedrick Irvin, Michigan St.	1996	1,036
Jamal Lewis, Tennessee	1997	1,364
Robert Sanford, Western Mich.	1997	1,033
Derrick Nix, Southern Miss.	1998	1,180
Ken Simonton, Oregon St.	1998	1,028
Avon Cobourne, West Virginia	1999	1,139
Chance Kretschmer, Nevada	2001	1,732
Anthony Davis, Wisconsin	2001	1,466
Cedric Benson, Texas	2001	1,053
Joshua Cribbs, Kent St. (QB)	2001	1,019
Terry Caulley, Connecticut	2002	1,247
Maurice Clarett, Ohio St.	2002	1,237
DonTrell Moore, New Mexico	2002	1,134
Matt Milton, Nevada	2002	1,108
T.A. McLenson, North Carolina St.	2002	1,101
Brad Smith, Missouri (QB)	2002	1,029

*Record for freshman.

Quarterback Rushing

SEASON YARDS

Player, Team	Year	G	Plays	Yards	TD	Avg.
Beau Morgan, Air Force	1996	11	225	*1,494	18	6.64
Stacey Robinson, Northern Ill.	1989	11	223	1,443	19	6.47
Jammal Lord, Nebraska	2002	14	251	1,412	8	5.63
Chris McCoy, Navy	1997	11	246	1,370	20	5.57
Dee Dowis, Air Force	1987	12	194	1,315	10	6.78
Brian Mitchell, La.-Lafayette	1989	11	237	1,311	19	5.53
Fred Solomon, Tampa	1974	11	193	1,300	19	6.74
Dee Dowis, Air Force	1989	12	172	1,286	18	#7.48
Beau Morgan, Air Force	1995	12	229	1,285	19	5.61
Antwaan Randle El, Indiana	2000	11	218	1,270	13	5.83
Stacey Robinson, Northern Ill.	1990	11	193	1,238	19	6.41
Chance Harridge, Air Force	2002	13	252	1,229	*22	4.88
Chris McCoy, Navy	1996	11	268	1,228	16	4.58
Keith Boyea, Air Force	2001	12	230	1,216	18	5.29
Rob Perez, Air Force	1991	12	233	1,157	10	4.97

Player, Team	Year	G	Plays	Yards	TD	Avg.
Jack Mildren, Oklahoma	1971	11	193	1,140	17	5.91
Nolan Cromwell, Kansas	1975	11	218	1,124	9	5.16
Eric Crouch, Nebraska	2001	12	203	1,115	18	5.49
Scott Frost, Nebraska	1997	12	176	1,095	19	6.22
Michael Carter, Hawaii	1991	12	221	1,092	16	4.94
Tory Crawford, Army	1986	11	244	1,075	15	4.41
Kareem Wilson, Ohio	1996	12	*275	1,072	14	3.90
Joshua Cribbs, Kent St.	2002	10	137	1,057	10	*7.72
Ell Roberson, Kansas St.	2002	12	202	1,032	16	5.11
Bart Weiss, Air Force	1985	12	180	1,032	12	5.73
Brad Smith, Missouri	2002	12	193	1,029	7	5.33
Joshua Cribbs, Kent St.	2001	11	164	1,019	5	6.21
Jimmy Sidle, Auburn	1963	10	185	1,006	10	5.44
Reggie Collier, Southern Miss.	1981	11	153	1,005	12	6.57
Woodrow Dantzler, Clemson	2001	11	206	1,004	10	4.87
Darian Hagan, Colorado	1989	11	186	1,004	17	5.40
Nate Sassaman, Army	1984	11	189	1,002	7	5.30

*Record. #Record for a minimum of 150 carries.

CAREER YARDS

Player, Team	Years	G	Plays	Yards	TD	Avg.
Antwaan Randle El, Indiana	1998-01	44	857	*3,895	44	88.5
Dee Dowis, Air Force	1986-89	47	543	3,612	41	76.9
Kareem Wilson, Ohio	1995-98	45	*885	3,597	49	79.9
Eric Crouch, Nebraska	1998-01	43	648	3,434	*59	79.9
Chris McCoy, Navy	1995-97	32	682	3,401	43	106.3
Beau Morgan, Air Force	1994-96	35	594	3,379	42	96.5
Brian Mitchell, La.-Lafayette	1986-89	43	678	3,335	47	77.6
Fred Solomon, Tampa	1971-74	43	557	3,299	39	76.7
Stacey Robinson, Northern Ill.	1988-90	25	429	2,727	38	*109.1
Jamelle Holieway, Oklahoma	1985-88	38	505	2,699	30	71.0
Woodrow Dantzler, Clemson	1998-01	36	549	2,615	27	72.6
Bill Hurley, Syracuse	1975-79	46	685	2,551	19	55.5
Michael Carter, Hawaii	1990-93	46	574	2,534	39	55.1
Corby Jones, Missouri	1995-98	39	559	2,533	38	64.9
Chad Nelson, Rice	1994-97	40	466	2,415	24	60.4
Bill Deery, William & Mary	1972-74	33	443	2,401	19	72.8
Reggie Collier, Southern Miss.	1979-82	39	446	2,304	26	59.1
John Bond, Mississippi St.	1980-83	44	572	2,280	24	51.8
Tory Crawford, Army	1984-87	31	495	2,255	34	72.7
Tom Parr, Colgate	1971-73	30	435	2,221	31	74.0
Alton Grizzard, Navy	1987-90	38	599	2,174	15	57.2
Gary Wood, Cornell	1961-63	27	433	2,156	19	79.9
Roy DeWalt, Texas-Arlington	1975, 77-79	38	468	2,136	27	56.2
Steve Taylor, Nebraska	1985-88	37	431	2,125	32	57.4
Bucky Richardson, Texas A&M	1987-88, 90-91	41	370	2,095	30	51.1
¢Joshua Cribbs, Kent St.	2001-02	21	301	2,076	15	98.9
Rocky Long, New Mexico	1969-71	31	469	2,071	21	66.8
Steve Davis, Oklahoma	1973-75	33	515	2,069	33	62.7
Rick Leach, Michigan	1975-78	43	440	2,053	34	47.7
Prince McJunkins, Wichita St.	1979-82	44	613	2,047	27	46.5
Rickey Foggie, Minnesota	1984-87	42	517	2,038	24	48.5
Major Harris, West Virginia	1987-89	33	386	2,030	18	51.5
Steve Gage, Tulsa	1983-84, 86	33	522	2,029	30	61.5
Harry Gilmer, Alabama	1944-47	40	390	2,025	19	50.6
Chad Richardson, Rice	1996-99	41	493	2,024	20	49.4
Darian Hagan, Colorado	1988-91	41	489	2,007	27	49.0

*Record. ¢Active player.

Passing

SAMPLE COMPILATION OF NCAA PASSING EFFICIENCY RATING

Player	G	Att.	Cmp.	Yds.	TD	Int.
Danny Wuerffel, Florida	46	1,170	708	10,875	114	42

		Rating Points
Completion Percentage:	60.51	
Yards Per Attempted Pass:	9.29	
Percent of Passes for TDs:	9.74	
Percent of Passes Intercepted:	3.59	

ADD the first three factors:

		Rating Points
Completion Percentage:	60.51	60.51
Yards Per Attempted Pass:	9.295 times 8.4	78.08
Percent of Passes for TDs:	9.74 times 3.3	32.14
		170.73

SUBTRACT the last factor:

Percent of Passes Intercepted:	3.59 times 2	-7.18
	Round off to:	**163.6**

DIVISION I-A PASSING EFFICIENCY RATING COMPARISON
1979-00

Passing statistics in Division I-A have increased dramatically since 1979, the first year that the NCAA official national statistics used the passing efficiency formula to rank passers in all divisions. Because passers have become more proficient every year, the average passing efficiency rating (based on final regular-season trends) also has risen at a similar rate. For historical purposes, the average passing efficiency rating for the division by year is presented below to show how any individual or team might rank in a particular season.

Year	Pass Effic. Rating	Year	Pass Effic. Rating
1979	104.49	1991	117.94
1980	106.63	1992	114.50
1981	107.00	1993	122.43
1982	110.77	1994	120.59
1983	113.56	1995	120.17
1984	113.02	1996	120.24
1985	114.58	1997	122.86
1986	115.00	1998	122.97
1987	112.67	1999	120.50
1988	114.32	2000	119.66
1989	118.35	2001	123.80
1990	117.39	2002	123.00

CAREER PASSING EFFICIENCY
(Minimum 500 Completions)

Player, Team	Years	Att.	Cmp.	Int.	Pct.	Yds.	TD	Pts.
Danny Wuerffel, Florida	1993-96	1,170	708	42	.605	10,875	114	*163.6
Ty Detmer, Brigham Young	1988-91	1,530	958	65	.626	*15,031	*121	162.7
Steve Sarkisian, Brigham Young	1995-96	789	528	26	.669	7,464	53	162.0
Billy Blanton, San Diego St.	1993-96	920	588	25	.639	8,165	67	157.1
Jim McMahon, Brigham Young	1977-78, 80-81	1,060	653	34	.616	9,536	84	156.9
Chad Pennington, Marshall	1997-99	1,265	807	30	.638	10,698	100	156.2
Donovan McNabb, Syracuse	1995-98	938	548	26	.584	8,389	77	155.1
Tim Rattay, Louisiana Tech	1997-99	1,552	1,015	35	‡.654	12,746	115	154.3
Daunte Culpepper, UCF	1996-98	1,097	721	32	.657	9,341	72	153.1
David Carr, Fresno St.	1997-98, 00-01	877	551	21	.628	7,309	66	152.9
Chris Weinke, Florida St.	1997-00	1,107	650	32	.587	9,839	79	151.1
Steve Young, Brigham Young	1981-83	908	592	33	.652	7,733	56	149.8
Robbie Bosco, Brigham Young	1983-85	997	638	36	.640	8,400	66	149.4
Mike Maxwell, Nevada	1993-95	881	560	33	.636	7,256	62	148.5
Joe Hamilton, Georgia Tech	1996-99	1,020	629	39	.617	8,882	65	148.2
Chuck Long, Iowa	$1981-85	1,072	692	46	.646	9,210	64	147.8
John Walsh, Brigham Young	1991-94	973	587	35	.603	8,375	66	147.8
Peyton Manning, Tennessee	1994-97	1,381	863	33	.625	11,201	89	147.1
Rex Grossman, Florida	2000-02	1,110	677	36	.610	9,164	77	146.8
Rob Johnson, Southern California	1991-94	963	623	24	.647	7,743	52	145.1
Andre Ware, Houston	1987-89	1,074	660	28	.615	8,202	75	143.3
Steve Stenstrom, Stanford	1991-94	1,320	833	36	.631	10,531	72	142.7
Marvin Graves, Syracuse	1990-93	943	563	45	.597	8,466	48	142.4
Tim Couch, Kentucky	1996-98	1,184	795	35	.671	8,435	74	141.7
Doug Gaynor, Long Beach St.	1984-85	837	569	35	.680	6,793	35	141.6
Danny Kanell, Florida St.	1992-95	851	529	26	.622	6,372	57	141.1
Kevin Feterik, Brigham Young	1996-99	1,004	609	27	.607	8,065	53	140.2
Dan McGwire, Iowa/San Diego St.	1986-87, 89-90	973	575	30	.591	8,164	49	140.0
Bart Hendricks, Boise St.	1997-00	1,142	650	34	.569	9,030	78	139.9
Cade McNown, UCLA	1995-98	1,153	646	39	.560	10,008	61	139.6
Chris Vargas, Nevada	1992-93	806	502	34	.623	6,359	47	139.4
John Elway, Stanford	1979-82	1,246	774	39	.621	9,349	77	139.3
Mike McCoy, Long Beach St./Utah	1991, 92-94	1,069	650	26	.608	8,342	56	138.8
Wes Counts, Middle Tenn.	1998-01	1,079	706	24	.654	8,007	50	138.6

Player, Team	Years	Att.	Cmp.	Int.	Pct.	Yds.	TD	Pts.
David Klingler, Houston	1988-91	1,268	732	38	.577	9,466	91	138.1
Scott Milanovich, Maryland	1992-95	982	650	35**.662		7,301	49	138.0
Scott Mitchell, Utah	1987-89	1,165	669	38	.574	8,981	68	137.7
Shane Matthews, Florida	1989-92	1,202	722	46	.601	9,287	74	137.6
Marc Wilson, Brigham Young	1977-79	937	535	46	.571	7,637	61	137.2
Eric Zeier, Georgia	1991-94	1,402	838	37	.598	11,153	67	137.1
Randall Cunningham, UNLV	1982-84	1,029	597	29	.580	8,020	59	136.8
Major Applewhite, Texas	1998-01	1,065	611	28	.574	8,353	60	136.6
Kerwin Bell, Florida	1984-87	953	549	35	.576	7,585	56	136.5
Josh Heupel, Oklahoma	1999-00	933	590	29	.632	6.852	50	136.4
Tom Hodson, LSU	1986-89	1,163	674	41	.580	9,115	69	136.3
Rodney Peete, Southern California	1985-88	972	571	32	.587	7,640	52	135.8
Ron Powlus, Notre Dame	1994-97	969	558	27	.576	7,602	52	135.6
John Welsh, Idaho	1998-01	968	584	38	.603	7,401	55	135.5
Billy Volek, Fresno St.	1997-99	934	564	12	.604	6,385	57	135.4
Darrell Bevell, Wisconsin	1992-95	1,012	625	37	.618	7,429	58	135.0
Pat Barnes, California	1993-96	912	522	26	.572	7,047	51	134.9
Troy Kopp, Pacific (Cal.)	1989-92	1,374	798	47	.581	10,258	87	134.9
David Neill, Nevada	1998-01	1,376	763	33	.555	10,903	73	134.7
Chris Redman, Louisville	1996-99	1,679	1,031	51	.614	12,541	84	134.6
Joe Adams, Tennessee St.	1977-80	1,100	604	60	.549	8,649	81	134.4
Drew Brees, Purdue	1997-00	1,525	942	41	.618	10,909	81	134.0
Mike Gundy, Oklahoma St.	1986-89	1,037	606	37	.584	8,072	54	133.9
Todd Santos, San Diego St.	1984-87	1,484	910	57	.613	11,425	70	133.9
Tony Eason, Illinois	1981-82	856	526	29	.615	6,608	37	133.8
Jake Plummer, Arizona St.	1993-96	1,107	613	34	.554	8,626	64	133.8
Tim Lester, Western Mich.	1996-99	1,507	875	49	.581	11,299	87	133.6
Kliff Kingsbury, Texas Tech	1999-02	*1,883	*1,231	40	.654	12,429	95	133.2
Danny McCoin, Cincinnati	1984-87	899	544	26	.605	6,801	39	132.6
Rich Campbell, California	1977-80	891	574	42	.644	6,933	33	132.6
Jim Everett, Purdue	$1981-85	923	550	30	.596	7,158	40	132.5
Matt Rodgers, Iowa	1988-91	844	516	30	.611	6,308	40	132.5
Doug Flutie, Boston College	1981-84	1,270	677	54	.533	10,579	67	132.2
David Garrard, East Caro.	1998-01	1,169	666	39	.570	9,029	60	132.1
Gino Torretta, Miami (Fla.)	1989-92	991	555	24	.560	7,690	47	132.0
Robert Hall, Texas Tech	1990-93	997	548	28	.550	7,908	48	131.9
Jack Trudeau, Illinois	1981, 83-85	1,151	736	38	.639	8,146	51	131.4
Carson Palmer, Southern California	$1998-02	1,515	895	49	.591	11,388	71	131.2
Kevin Sweeney, Fresno St.	$1982-86	1,336	731	48	.547	10,623	66	130.6
Bill Musgrave, Oregon	1987-90	1,018	582	38	.572	7,631	55	130.6

(400-499 Completions)

Player, Team	Years	Att.	Cmp.	Int.	Pct.	Yds.	TD	Pts.
Vinny Testaverde, Miami (Fla.)	1982, 84-86	674	413	25	.613	6,058	48	152.9
Josh Wallwork, Wyoming	1995-96	729	449	28	.616	6,453	54	152.7
Trent Dilfer, Fresno St.	1991-93	774	461	21	.596	6,944	51	151.2
Troy Aikman, Oklahoma/UCLA	1984-85, 87-88	637	401	18	.630	5,436	40	149.7
Chuck Hartlieb, Iowa	1985-88	716	461	17	.643	6,269	34	148.9
Elvis Grbac, Michigan	1989-92	754	477	29	.633	5,859	64	148.9
Bobby Hoying, Ohio St.	1992-95	782	463	33	.592	6,751	54	146.1
Gifford Nielsen, Brigham Young	1975-77	708	415	29	.586	5,833	55	145.3
Tom Ramsey, UCLA	1979-82	691	411	33	.595	5,844	48	143.9
Shawn Moore, Virginia	1987-90	762	421	32	.552	6,629	55	143.8
George Godsey, Georgia Tech	1998-01	765	484	18	.633	6,137	41	143.6
Moses Moreno, Colorado St.	1994-97	787	457	28	.581	6,689	49	142.9
Jerry Rhome, Southern Methodist/Tulsa	1961, 63-64	713	448	23	.628	5,472	47	142.6
Thad Busby, Florida St.	1994-97	715	420	27	.587	5,916	46	141.9
Charlie Ward, Florida St.	1989, 91-93	759	474	21	.625	5,747	49	141.8
Ryan Leaf, Washington St.	1995-97	845	456	23	.540	7,102	58	141.8
Keith Smith, Arizona	1996-99	726	434	27	.598	5,972	42	140.5
Bernie Kosar, Miami (Fla.)	1983-84	743	463	29	.623	5,971	40	139.8
Craig Erickson, Miami (Fla.)	1987-90	752	420	22	.559	6,056	46	137.8
Mike Bobo, Georgia	1994-97	766	445	26	.581	6,334	38	137.1
Dave Yarema, Michigan St.	$1982-86	727	447	29	.615	5,569	41	136.5
Ryan Clement, Miami (Fla.)	1994-97	720	427	27	.593	5,730	35	134.7
Joey Harrington, Oregon	1998-01	813	445	21	.547	6,057	52	133.3
Gary Huff, Florida St.	1970-72	796	436	42	.548	6,378	52	133.1
Joe Hughes, Wyoming	1992-95	744	424	25	.570	5,841	38	133.1
Woodrow Dantzler, Clemson	1998-01	735	429	22	.584	5,634	36	132.9
Jeff Francis, Tennessee	1985-88	768	476	26	.620	5,867	31	132.7
Mike Perez, San Jose St.	1986-87	792	471	30	.595	6,194	36	132.6
Cale Gundy, Oklahoma	1990-93	751	420	31	.559	6,142	36	132.2

(325-399 Completions)

Player, Team	Years	Att.	Cmp.	Int.	Pct.	Yds.	TD	Pts.
Joe Germaine, Ohio St.	1996-98	660	399	18	.605	5,844	52	155.4
Jim Harbaugh, Michigan	1983-86	582	368	19	.632	5,215	31	149.6
Danny White, Arizona St.	1971-73	649	345	36	.532	5,932	59	148.9
Koy Detmer, Colorado	1992, 94-96	594	350	25	.589	5,390	40	148.9
Tim Gutierrez, San Diego St.	1992-94	580	357	19	.616	4,740	36	144.1
Jim Karsatos, Ohio St.	1983-86	573	330	19	.576	4,698	36	140.6
Jerry Tagge, Nebraska	1969-71	581	348	19	.599	4,704	33	140.1
Mike Fouts, Utah	1995-96	625	356	19	.570	5,107	39	140.1
Garrett Gabriel, Hawaii	1987-90	661	356	31	.539	5,631	47	139.5
Rick Mirer, Notre Dame	1989-92	698	377	23	.540	5,996	41	139.0

Player, Team	Years	Att.	Cmp.	Int.	Pct.	Yds.	TD	Pts.
Gary Sheide, Brigham Young	1973-74	594	358	31	.603	4,524	45	138.8
Dan Speltz, Cal St. Fullerton	1988-89	583	350	19	.600	4,595	33	138.4
Mike Moschetti, Colorado	1998-99	607	366	19	.603	4,797	33	138.4
Don McPherson, Syracuse	$1983-87	687	367	29	.534	5,812	46	138.1
Joe Youngblood, Central Mich.	1990-93	572	331	28	.579	4,718	35	137.6
Kerry Collins, Penn St.	1991-94	657	370	21	.563	5,304	39	137.3
Sam King, UNLV	1979-81	625	360	29	.576	5,393	30	136.6
J.J. Joe, Baylor	1990-93	665	347	28	.522	5,995	31	134.9
Jesse Freitas, Stanford/San Diego St.	1970, 72-73	547	338	33	.618	4,408	28	134.3
Jeff Blake, East Caro.	1988-91	667	360	20	.540	5,133	43	133.9

*Record. $See page 8 for explanation. **Record for minimum 875 attempts. ‡Record for minimum 1,000 attempts.

SEASON PASSING EFFICIENCY
(Minimum 15 Attempts Per Game)

Player, Team	Year	G	Att.	Cmp.	Int.	Pct.	Yds.	TD	Pts.
Shaun King, Tulane	†1998	11	328	223	6	.680	3,232	36	*183.3
Michael Vick, Virginia Tech	†1999	10	152	90	5	.592	1,840	12	180.4
Danny Wuerffel, Florida	†1995	11	325	210	10	.646	3,266	35	178.4
Jim McMahon, Brigham Young	#†1980	12	445	284	18	.638	4,571	47	176.9
Ty Detmer, Brigham Young	†1989	12	412	265	15	.643	4,560	32	175.6
Joe Hamilton, Georgia Tech	1999	11	305	203	11	.666	3,060	29	175.0
Steve Sarkisian, Brigham Young	†1996	14	404	278	12	.688	4,027	33	173.6
Trent Dilfer, Fresno St.	†1993	11	333	217	4	.652	3,276	28	173.1
Kerry Collins, Penn St.	†1994	11	264	176	7	.667	2,679	21	172.9
Jerry Rhome, Tulsa	#†1964	10	326	224	4	.687	2,870	32	172.6
Chad Pennington, Marshall	1999	12	405	275	11	.679	3,799	37	171.4
Rex Grossman, Florida	†2001	11	395	259	12	.656	3,896	34	170.8
Bart Hendricks, Boise St.	†2000	11	347	210	8	.605	3,364	35	170.6
Danny Wuerffel, Florida	1996	12	360	207	13	.575	3,625	39	170.6
Akili Smith, Oregon	1998	11	325	191	7	.588	3,307	30	170.4
Bobby Hoying, Ohio St.	1995	12	303	192	11	.634	3,023	28	170.4
Daunte Culpepper, UCF	1998	11	402	296	7	*.736	3,690	28	170.2
Billy Blanton, San Diego St.	1996	11	344	227	5	.660	3,221	29	169.6
Elvis Grbac, Michigan	†1991	11	228	152	5	.667	1,955	24	169.0
Cade McNown, UCLA	†1997	11	283	173	5	.611	2,877	22	168.6
Ty Detmer, Brigham Young	#†1991	12	403	249	12	.618	4,031	35	168.5
Steve Young, Brigham Young	#†1983	11	429	306	10	.713	3,902	33	168.5
David Carr, Fresno St.	2001	13	476	308	7	.647	4,299	42	166.7
Wes Counts, Middle Tenn.	2001	11	259	188	4	.726	2,327	17	166.6
Vinny Testaverde, Miami (Fla.)	†1986	10	276	175	9	.634	2,557	26	165.8
Brian Dowling, Yale	1968	9	160	92	10	.575	1,554	19	165.8
Tim Rattay, Louisiana Tech	1998	12	559	380	13	.680	4,943	46	164.8
Ryan Dinwiddie, Boise St.	2001	11	322	201	11	.624	3,043	29	164.7
Byron Leftwich, Marshall	2001	12	470	315	7	.670	4,132	38	164.6
Dave Barr, California	1993	11	275	187	12	.680	2,619	21	164.5
Don McPherson, Syracuse	†1987	11	229	129	11	.563	2,341	22	164.3
Dave Wilson, Ball St.	1977	11	177	115	7	.650	1,589	17	164.2
Bob Berry, Oregon	1963	10	171	101	7	.591	1,675	16	164.0
Jim Harbaugh, Michigan	†1985	11	212	139	6	.656	1,913	18	163.7
Troy Aikman, UCLA	1987	11	243	159	6	.654	2,354	16	163.6
Chris Weinke, Florida St.	2000	12	431	266	11	.617	4,167	33	163.1
Turk Schonert, Stanford	†1979	11	221	148	6	.670	1,922	19	163.0
Jeff Smoker, Michigan St.	2001	10	230	144	7	.626	2,203	18	162.8
Donovan McNabb, Syracuse	1995	11	207	128	6	.618	1,991	16	162.3
Brian Broomell, Temple	1979	11	214	120	11	.561	2,103	22	162.3
Dennis Shaw, San Diego St.	†1969	10	335	199	26	.594	3,185	39	162.2
Timm Rosenbach, Washington St.	†1988	11	302	199	10	.659	2,791	23	162.0
Rex Grossman, Florida	2000	11	212	131	7	.618	1,866	21	161.8
Davey O'Brien, TCU	¢#†1938	10	167	93	4	.557	1,457	19	161.7
Chuck Hartlieb, Iowa	1987	12	299	196	8	.656	2,855	19	161.4
Ryan Leaf, Washington St.	1997	11	375	210	10	.560	3,637	33	161.2
Darrell Bevell, Wisconsin	1993	11	256	177	10	.691	2,294	19	161.1
David Brown, Duke	1989	9	163	104	6	.638	1,479	14	161.0
Shawn Moore, Virginia	†1990	10	241	144	9	.598	2,262	21	160.7
Joe Germaine, Ohio St.	1997	12	184	119	7	.647	1,674	15	160.4
Chuck Long, Iowa	1983	10	236	144	8	.610	2,434	14	160.4
Mike Maxwell, Nevada	#1995	9	409	277	17	.677	3,611	33	160.2
Jeff Garcia, San Jose St.	1991	9	160	99	5	.619	1,519	12	160.1

*Record. †National pass-efficiency champion. #National total-offense champion. ¢Available records before 1946 do not include TD passes except for O'Brien and relatively few other passers; thus, passing efficiency points cannot be compiled for those players without TD passes.

ANNUAL PASSING EFFICIENCY LEADERS
(% Minimum 11 Attempts Per Game)

1946—Bill Mackrides, Nevada, 176.9; **1947**—Bobby Layne, Texas, 138.9; **1948**—Stan Heath, Nevada, 157.2 (#); **1949**—Bob Williams, Notre Dame, 159.1; **1950**—Claude Arnold, Oklahoma, 157.3; **1951**—Dick Kazmaier, Princeton, 155.3 (#); **1952**—Ron Morris, Tulsa, 177.4; **1953**—Bob Garrett, Stanford, 142.2; **1954**—Pete Vann, Army, 166.5; **1955**—George Welsh, Navy, 146.1 (#); **1956**—Tom Flores, Pacific (Cal.), 147.5; **1957**—Lee Grosscup, Utah, 175.5; **1958**—John Hangartner, Arizona St., 150.1; **1959**—Charley Johnson, New Mexico St., 135.7; **1960**—Eddie Wilson, Arizona, 140.8; **1961**—Ron DiGravio, Purdue, 140.1; **1962**—John Jacobs, Arizona St., 153.9; **1963**—Bob Berry, Oregon, 164.0; **1964**—Jerry Rhome, Tulsa, 172.6 (#).

(Minimum 15 Attempts Per Game)

1946—Ben Raimondi, Indiana, 117.0; **1947**—Charley Conerly, Mississippi, 125.8; **1948**—Stan Heath, Nevada, 157.2 (#); **1949**—Dick Doheny, Fordham, 153.3; **1950**—Dick Doheny, Fordham, 149.5; **1951**—Babe Parilli, Kentucky, 130.8; **1952**—Gene Rossi, Cincinnati, 149.7; **1953**—Bob Garrett, Stanford, 142.2; **1954**—Len Dawson, Purdue, 145.8; **1955**—George Welsh, Navy, 146.1 (#); **1956**—Bob Reinhart, San Jose St., 121.3; **1957**—Bob Newman, Washington St., 126.5 (#); **1958**—Randy Duncan, Iowa, 135.1; **1959**—Charley Johnson, New Mexico St., 135.7; **1960**—Charley Johnson, New Mexico St., 134.1; **1961**—Eddie Wilson, Arizona, 134.2; **1962**—Terry Baker, Oregon St., 146.5 (#); **1963**—Bob Berry, Oregon, 164.0; **1964**—Jerry Rhome, Tulsa, 172.6 (#).

(Minimum 15 Attempts Per Game)

Year	Player, Team	G	Att.	Cmp.	Int.	Pct.	Yds.	TD	Pts.
1965	Steve Sloan, Alabama	10	160	97	3	.606	1,453	10	153.8
1966	Dewey Warren, Tennessee	10	229	136	7	.594	1,716	18	142.2
1967	Bill Andrejko, Villanova	10	187	114	6	.610	1,405	13	140.6
1968	Brian Dowling, Yale	9	160	92	10	.575	1,554	19	165.8
1969	#Dennis Shaw, San Diego St.	10	335	199	26	.594	3,185	39	162.2
1970	Jerry Tagge, Nebraska	11	165	104	7	.630	1,383	12	149.0
1971	Jerry Tagge, Nebraska	12	239	143	4	.598	2,019	17	150.9
1972	John Hufnagel, Penn St.	11	216	115	8	.532	2,039	15	148.0
1973	Danny White, Arizona St.	11	265	146	12	.551	2,609	23	157.4
1974	#Steve Joachim, Temple	10	221	128	13	.579	1,950	20	150.1
1975	James Kubacki, Harvard	8	137	77	9	.562	1,273	11	147.6
1976	Steve Haynes, Louisiana Tech	10	216	120	11	.556	1,981	16	146.9
1977	Dave Wilson, Ball St.	11	177	115	7	.650	1,589	17	164.2
1978	Paul McDonald, Southern California	11	194	111	7	.572	1,667	18	152.8

(See page 43 for annual leaders beginning in 1979)

#National total-offense champion. % In many seasons during 1946-64, only a few passers threw as many as 15 passes per game; thus, a lower minimum was used.

CAREER YARDS

Player, Team	Years	Att.	Cmp.	Int.	Pct.	Yds.	TD	Long
Ty Detmer, Brigham Young	1988-91	1,530	958	65	.626	*15,031	*121	76
Tim Rattay, Louisiana Tech	1997-99	1,552	1,015	35	‡‡.654	12,746	115	94
Chris Redman, Louisville	1996-99	1,679	1,031	51	.614	12,541	84	86
Kliff Kingsbury, Texas Tech	1999-02	*1,883	*1,231	40	.654	12,429	95	75
Todd Santos, San Diego St.	1984-87	1,484	910	57	.613	11,425	70	84
Carson Palmer, Southern California	$1998-02	1,515	895	49	.591	11,388	71	93
Tim Lester, Western Mich.	1996-99	1,507	875	49	.581	11,299	87	82
Peyton Manning, Tennessee	1994-97	1,381	863	33	.625	11,201	89	80
Eric Zeier, Georgia	1991-94	1,402	838	37	.598	11,153	67	80
Alex Van Pelt, Pittsburgh	1989-92	1,463	845	59	.578	10,913	64	91
Drew Brees, Purdue	1997-00	1,525	942	41	.618	10,909	81	99
David Neill, Nevada	1998-01	1,376	763	33	.555	10,903	73	91
Danny Wuerffel, Florida	1993-96	1,170	708	42	.605	10,875	114	85
Chad Pennington, Marshall	1997-99	1,265	807	30	.638	10,698	100	92
Kevin Sweeney, Fresno St.	$1982-86	1,336	731	48	.547	10,623	66	95
Doug Flutie, Boston College	1981-84	1,270	677	54	.533	10,579	67	80
Steve Stenstrom, Stanford	1991-94	1,320	833	36	.631	10,531	72	92
Brian McClure, Bowling Green	1982-85	1,427	900	58	.631	10,280	63	90
Troy Kopp, Pacific (Cal.)	1989-92	1,374	798	47	.581	10,258	87	80
Glenn Foley, Boston College	1990-93	1,275	703	60	.551	10,042	72	78
Cade McNown, UCLA	1995-98	1,153	646	39	.560	10,008	61	88
Chris Weinke, Florida St.	1997-00	1,107	650	32	.587	9,839	79	98
Ben Bennett, Duke	1980-83	1,375	820	57	.596	9,614	55	88
Jim McMahon, Brigham Young	1977-78, 80-81	1,060	653	34	.616	9,536	84	80
Todd Ellis, South Carolina	1986-89	1,266	704	66	.556	9,519	49	97
David Klingler, Houston	1988-91	1,268	732	38	.577	9,466	91	95
Stoney Case, New Mexico	1991-94	1,237	677	39	.547	9,460	67	79
¢Luke McCown, Louisiana Tech	2000-02	1,344	817	48	.528	9,420	68	80
Erik Wilhelm, Oregon St.	1985-88	1,480	870	61	.588	9,393	52	‡74
Jeremy Leach, New Mexico	1988-91	1,432	735	62	.513	9,382	50	82
John Elway, Stanford	1979-82	1,246	774	39	.621	9,349	77	70
Daunte Culpepper, UCF	1996-98	1,097	721	32	.657	9,341	72	71
T.J. Rubley, Tulsa	1987-89, 91	1,336	682	54	.510	9,324	73	75
Shane Matthews, Florida	1989-92	1,202	722	46	.601	9,287	74	70
Jake Delhomme, La.-Lafayette	1993-96	1,246	655	57	.526	9,216	64	79
Chuck Long, Iowa	$1981-85	1,072	692	46	.646	9,210	64	89
Mark Herrmann, Purdue	1977-80	1,218	717	*73	.589	9,188	62	75
Jose Fuentes, Utah St.	1999-02	1,270	704	43	.554	9,164	60	80
Rex Grossman, Florida	2000-02	1,110	677	36	.609	9,164	77	80
Tom Hodson, LSU	1986-89	1,163	674	41	.580	9,115	69	80
Jonathan Smith, Oregon St.	1998-01	1,197	603	29	.504	9,079	52	97
Jason Martin, Louisiana Tech	1993-96	1,320	705	55	.534	9,066	64	80
Bart Hendricks, Boise St.	1997-00	1,142	650	34	.569	9,030	78	87
David Garrard, East Caro.	1998-01	1,169	666	39	.570	9,029	60	69
¢Ryan Schneider, UCF	2000-02	1,073	646	36	.602	9,027	69	83
Spence Fischer, Duke	1992-95	1,369	786	46	.574	9,021	48	80
Scott Mitchell, Utah	1987-89	1,165	669	38	.574	8,981	68	72
Joe Hamilton, Georgia Tech	1996-99	1,020	629	39	.617	8,882	65	80
Brad Tayles, Western Mich.	1989-92	1,370	663	67	.484	8,717	49	84
Joe Adams, Tennessee St.	1977-80	1,100	604	60	.549	8,649	81	71
Jake Plummer, Arizona St.	1993-96	1,107	613	34	.554	8,626	64	83
Steve Taneyhill, South Carolina	1992-95	1,209	727	37	.601	8,555	61	93
Marvin Graves, Syracuse	1990-93	943	563	45	.597	8,466	48	84
Shawn Jones, Georgia Tech	1989-92	1,217	652	50	.536	8,441	51	82

Player, Team	Years	Att.	Cmp.	Int.	Pct.	Yds.	TD	Long
Tim Couch, Kentucky	1996-98	1,184	795	35	.671	8,435	74	97
Shaun King, Tulane.............................	1995-98	1,163	646	34	.555	8,419	70	79
Robbie Bosco, Brigham Young	1983-85	997	638	36	.640	8,400	66	‡89
Donovan McNabb, Syracuse	1995-98	938	548	26	.584	8,389	77	96
John Walsh, Brigham Young	1991-94	973	587	35	.603	8,375	66	93
Major Applewhite, Texas	1998-01	1,065	611	28	.574	8,353	60	96
Mike McCoy, Long Beach St./Utah........	1991, 92-94	1,069	650	26	.608	8,342	56	87
Kurt Kittner, Illinois	1998-01	1,204	660	32	.548	8,206	64	67
Andre Ware, Houston..........................	1987-89	1,074	660	28	.615	8,202	75	87
Billy Blanton, San Diego St.	1993-96	920	588	25	.639	8,165	67	85
Dan McGwire, Iowa/San Diego St........	1986-87, 89-90	973	575	30	.591	8,164	49	71
Jack Trudeau, Illinois	1981, 83-85	1,151	736	38	.639	8,146	51	83
¢Jared Lorenzen, Kentucky	2000-02	1,178	671	33	.570	8,133	62	89
Troy Taylor, California	1986-89	1,162	683	46	.588	8,126	51	79
Mike Gundy, Oklahoma St.	1986-89	1,037	606	37	.584	8,072	54	‡84
Kevin Feterik, Brigham Young	1996-99	1,004	609	27	.607	8,065	53	83
Jeff Graham, Long Beach St.	1985-88	1,175	664	42	.565	8,063	42	85
Randall Cunningham, UNLV.................	1982-84	1,029	597	29	.580	8,020	59	69
Brian Kuklich, Wake Forest	1994-98	1,230	665	49	.541	8,017	44	76
Stan White, Auburn............................	1990-93	1,231	659	52	.535	8,016	40	78
Wes Counts, Middle Tenn.	1998-01	1,079	706	24	.654	8,007	50	79
Steve Slayden, Duke...........................	1984-87	1,204	699	53	.581	8,004	48	73

*Record. $See page 8 for explanation. ‡Did not score. ‡‡Record for minimum 1,000 attempts. ¢Active player.

CAREER YARDS RECORD PROGRESSION
(Record Yards—Player, Team, Seasons Played)

3,075—Billy Patterson, Baylor, 1936-38; **3,777**—Bud Schwenk, Washington (Mo.), 1939-41; **4,004**—Johnny Rauch, Georgia, 1945-48; **4,736**—John Ford, Hardin-Simmons, 1947-50; **4,863**—Zeke Bratkowski, Georgia, 1951-53; **5,472**—Jerry Rhome, Southern Methodist, 1961, Tulsa, 1963-64; **6,495**—Billy Stevens, UTEP, 1965-67; **7,076**—Steve Ramsey, North Texas, 1967-69; **7,544**—Jim Plunkett, Stanford, 1968-70; **7,549**—John Reaves, Florida, 1969-71; **7,818**—Jack Thompson, Washington St., 1975-78; **9,188**—Mark Herrmann, Purdue, 1977-80; **9,536**—Jim McMahon, Brigham Young, 1977-78, 1980-81; **9,614**—Ben Bennett, Duke, 1980-83; **10,579**—Doug Flutie, Boston College, 1981-84; **10,623**—Kevin Sweeney, Fresno St., $1982-86; **11,425**—Todd Santos, San Diego St., 1984-87; **15,031**—Ty Detmer, Brigham Young, 1988-91.

$See page 6 for explanation.

CAREER YARDS PER GAME
(Minimum 5,000 yards)

Player, Team	Years	G	Att.	Cmp.	Int.	Pct.	Yds.	TD	Yd.PG
Tim Rattay, Louisiana Tech..........................1997-99		33	1,552	1,015	35	.654	12,746	115	*386.2
Ty Detmer, Brigham Young 1988-91		46	1,530	958	65	.626	*15,031	*121	326.8
Chris Vargas, Nevada 1992-93		20	806	502	34	.623	6,359	47	318.0
Mike Perez, San Jose St. 1986-87		20	792	471	30	.595	6,194	36	309.7
Doug Gaynor, Long Beach St. 1984-85		22	837	569	35	.680	6,793	35	308.8
Tony Eason, Illinois 1981-82		22	856	526	29	.614	6,608	37	300.4
Steve Sarkisian, Brigham Young...................1995-96		25	789	528	26	.669	7,464	53	298.6
Chris Redman, Louisville 1996-99		42	1,679	1,031	51	.614	12,541	84	298.6
Josh Heupel, Oklahoma 1999-00		23	933	590	29	.632	6,852	50	297.9
Chad Pennington, Marshall 1997-99		36	1,265	807	30	.638	10,698	100	297.2
David Klingler, Houston..............................1988-91		32	1,268	732	38	.577	9,466	91	295.8
Josh Wallwork, Wyoming 1995-96		22	729	449	28	.616	6,453	54	293.3
Tim Couch, Kentucky 1996-98		29	1,184	795	35	.671	8,435	74	290.9
Kliff Kingsbury, Texas Tech 1999-02		43	*1,883	*1,231	40	.654	12,429	95	289.0
Daunte Culpepper, UCF 1996-98		33	1,097	721	32	.657	9,341	72	283.1
Brent Snyder, Utah St. 1987-88		22	875	472	36	.539	6,105	39	277.5
Chris Weinke, Florida St. 1997-00		36	1,107	650	32	.587	9,839	79	273.3
Drew Brees, Purdue....................................1997-00		40	1,525	942	41	.618	10,909	81	272.7
David Neill, Nevada 1998-01		40	1,376	763	33	.555	10,903	73	272.6
Mike Maxwell, Nevada 1993-95		27	881	560	33	.636	7,256	62	268.7
Shane Matthews, Florida 1989-92		35	1,202	722	46	.601	9,287	74	265.3
Rex Grossman, Florida 2000-02		35	1,110	677	36	.609	9,164	77	261.8
Larry Egger, Utah.....................................1985-86		22	799	470	31	.588	5,749	39	261.3

*Record.

CAREER TOUCHDOWN PASSES

Player, Team	Years	G	TD Passes
Ty Detmer, Brigham Young	1988-91	46	*121
Tim Rattay, Louisiana Tech	1997-99	33	115
Danny Wuerffel, Florida	1993-96	46	114
Chad Pennington, Marshall	1997-99	36	100
Kliff Kingsbury, Texas Tech	1999-02	43	95
David Klingler, Houston	1988-91	32	91
Peyton Manning, Tennessee	1994-97	44	89
Tim Lester, Western Mich.	1996-99	44	87
Troy Kopp, Pacific (Cal.)	1989-92	40	87
Chris Redman, Louisville	1996-99	42	84
Jim McMahon, Brigham Young 1977-78, 80-81		44	84
Drew Brees, Purdue	1997-00	40	81
Joe Adams, Tennessee St.	1977-80	41	81
Chris Weinke, Florida St.	1997-00	36	79
Bart Hendricks, Boise St.	1997-00	41	78
Rex Grossman, Florida	2000-02	35	77
Donovan McNabb, Syracuse	1995-98	45	77

Player, Team	Years	G	TD Passes
John Elway, Stanford	1979-82	43	77
Andre Ware, Houston	1987-89	29	75
Tim Couch, Kentucky	1996-98	29	74
Shane Matthews, Florida	1989-92	35	74
Dan Marino, Pittsburgh	1979-82	40	74
David Neill, Nevada	1998-01	40	73
T. J. Rubley, Tulsa	1987-89, 91	47	73
Daunte Culpepper, UCF	1996-98	33	72
Steve Stenstrom, Stanford	1991-94	41	72
Glenn Foley, Boston College	1990-93	44	72
Carson Palmer, Southern California	$1998-02	50	71
Shaun King, Tulane	1995-98	41	70
Todd Santos, San Diego St.	1984-87	46	70
¢Ryan Schneider, UCF	2000-02	32	69
Tom Hodson, LSU	1986-89	44	69
Steve Ramsey, North Texas	1967-69	29	69
¢Luke McCown, Louisiana Tech	2000-02	31	68
Scott Mitchell, Utah	1987-89	33	68
Billy Blanton, San Diego St.	1993-96	38	67
Stoney Case, New Mexico	1991-94	42	67
Eric Zeier, Georgia	1991-94	44	67
Doug Flutie, Boston College	1981-84	42	67
David Carr, Fresno St.	1997-98, 00-01	36	66
John Walsh, Brigham Young	1991-94	35	66
Kevin Sweeney, Fresno St.	1983-86	47	66
Robbie Bosco, Brigham Young	1983-85	35	66
Joe Hamilton, Georgia Tech	1996-99	43	65
Kurt Kittner, Illinois	1998-01	41	64
Jake Delhomme, La.-Lafayette	1993-96	44	64
Jason Martin, Louisiana Tech	1993-96	41	64
Jake Plummer, Arizona St.	1993-96	42	64
Elvis Grbac, Michigan	1989-92	41	64
Alex Van Pelt, Pittsburgh	1989-92	45	64
Chuck Long, Iowa	$1981-85	45	64

*Record. $See page 8 for explanation. ¢Active player.

SEASON YARDS

Player, Team	Year	G	Att.	Cmp.	Int.	Pct.	Yards	TD	Yds. Per Att.
Ty Detmer, Brigham Young	1990	12	562	361	28	.642	*5,188	41	9.23
David Klingler, Houston	1990	11	643	374	20	.582	5,140	*54	7.99
Kliff Kingsbury, Texas Tech	2002	14	*712	*479	13	.673	5,017	45	7.05
Tim Rattay, Louisiana Tech	1998	12	559	380	13	.680	4,943	46	8.84
Andre Ware, Houston	1989	11	578	365	15	.631	4,699	46	8.13
Jim McMahon, Brigham Young	†1980	12	445	284	18	.638	4,571	47	10.27
Ty Detmer, Brigham Young	†1989	12	412	265	15	.643	4,560	32	11.07
Timmy Chang, Hawaii	2002	14	624	349	22	.559	4,474	25	7.17
Cody Pickett, Washington	2002	12	612	365	14	.596	4,458	28	7.28
Scott Mitchell, Utah	1988	11	533	323	15	.606	4,322	29	8.11
David Carr, Fresno St.	2001	13	476	308	7	.647	4,299	42	9.03
Tim Couch, Kentucky	1998	11	553	400	15	.723	4,275	36	7.73
Robbie Bosco, Brigham Young	1985	13	511	338	24	.661	4,273	30	8.36
Byron Leftwich, Marshall	2002	12	491	331	10	.674	4,268	30	8.69
Chris Vargas, Nevada	1993	11	490	331	18	.676	4,265	34	8.70
Chris Weinke, Florida St.	2000	12	431	266	11	.617	4,167	33	9.67
Byron Leftwich, Marshall	2001	12	470	315	7	.670	4,132	38	8.79
Josh Wallwork, Wyoming	1996	12	458	286	15	.625	4,090	33	8.93
Chris Redman, Louisville	1998	10	473	309	15	.653	4,042	29	8.55
Ty Detmer, Brigham Young	1991	12	403	249	12	.618	4,031	35	10.00
Steve Sarkisian, Brigham Young	†1996	14	404	278	12	.688	4,027	33	9.97
Carson Palmer, Southern California	2002	13	489	309	10	.632	3,942	33	8.06
Todd Santos, San Diego St.	1987	12	492	306	15	.622	3,932	26	7.99
Tim Rattay, Louisiana Tech	1999	10	516	342	12	.663	3,922	35	7.60
Steve Young, Brigham Young	†1983	11	429	306	10	.713	3,902	33	9.10
Rex Grossman, Florida	†2001	11	395	259	12	.656	3,896	34	9.86
Tim Couch, Kentucky	1997	11	547	363	19	.664	3,884	37	7.10
Tim Rattay, Louisiana Tech	†1997	11	477	293	10	.614	3,881	34	8.14
Andrew Walter, Arizona St.	2002	14	483	274	15	.567	3,877	28	8.03
Robbie Bosco, Brigham Young	1984	12	458	283	11	.618	3,875	33	8.46
Mike McCoy, Utah	1993	12	430	276	10	.642	3,860	21	8.98
Dan Robinson, Hawaii	1999	12	556	288	18	.518	3,853	28	6.93
Dan McGwire, San Diego St.	1990	11	449	270	7	.601	3,833	27	8.54
Anthony Dilweg, Duke	1988	11	484	287	18	.593	3,824	24	7.90
Peyton Manning, Tennessee	1997	12	477	287	11	.602	3,819	36	8.01
Jimmy Klingler, Houston	1992	11	504	303	18	.601	3,818	32	7.58
Chad Pennington, Marshall	1999	12	405	275	11	.679	3,799	37	9.38
Sam King, UNLV	1981	12	433	255	19	.589	3,778	18	8.73
Ryan Schneider, UCF	2002	12	430	265	16	.616	3,770	31	8.77
Troy Kopp, Pacific (Cal.)	1991	12	449	275	15	.612	3,767	37	8.39
Drew Brees, Purdue	1998	12	516	336	17	.651	3,753	36	7.27
John Walsh, Brigham Young	1993	11	397	244	15	.615	3,727	28	9.39
Marc Wilson, Brigham Young	1979	12	427	250	15	.585	3,720	29	8.71
John Walsh, Brigham Young	1994	12	463	284	14	.613	3,712	29	8.02

*Record. †National pass-efficiency champion.

SEASON YARDS PER GAME

Player, Team	Year	G	Att.	Cmp.	Int.	Pct.	Yards	TD	Yd.PG
David Klingler, Houston	1990	11	643	374	20	.582	5,140	*54	*467.3
Ty Detmer, Brigham Young	1990	12	562	361	28	.642	*5,188	41	432.3
Andre Ware, Houston	1989	11	578	365	15	.631	4,699	46	427.2
Tim Rattay, Louisiana Tech	1998	12	559	380	13	.680	4,943	46	411.9
Chris Redman, Louisville	1998	10	473	309	15	.653	4,042	29	404.2
Mike Maxwell, Nevada	1995	9	409	277	17	.677	3,611	33	401.2
Scott Mitchell, Utah	1988	11	533	323	15	.606	4,322	29	392.9
Tim Rattay, Louisiana Tech	1999	10	516	342	12	.663	3,922	35	392.2
Tim Couch, Kentucky	1998	11	553	400	15	.723	4,275	36	388.6
Chris Vargas, Nevada	1993	11	490	331	18	.676	4,265	34	387.7
Jim McMahon, Brigham Young	†1980	12	445	284	18	.638	4,571	47	380.9
Ty Detmer, Brigham Young	†1989	12	412	265	15	.643	4,560	32	380.0
Troy Kopp, Pacific (Cal.)	1990	9	428	243	14	.568	3,311	31	367.9
David Neill, Nevada	1998	9	344	199	9	.578	3,249	29	361.0
Kliff Kingsbury, Texas Tech	2002	14	*712	*479	13	.673	5,017	45	358.4
Byron Leftwich, Marshall	2002	12	491	331	10	.674	4,268	30	355.7
Jim McMahon, Brigham Young	†1981	10	423	272	7	.643	3,555	30	355.5
Steve Young, Brigham Young	†1983	11	429	306	10	.713	3,902	33	354.7
Rex Grossman, Florida	†2001	11	395	259	12	.656	3,896	34	354.2
Tim Couch, Kentucky	1997	11	547	363	19	.664	3,884	37	353.1
Tim Rattay, Louisiana Tech	†1997	11	477	293	10	.614	3,881	34	352.8
Dan McGwire, San Diego St.	1990	11	449	270	7	.601	3,833	27	348.5
Anthony Dilweg, Duke	1988	11	484	287	18	.593	3,824	24	347.6
Chris Weinke, Florida St.	2000	12	431	266	11	.617	4,167	33	347.3
Jimmy Klingler, Houston	1992	11	504	303	18	.601	3,818	32	347.1
Bill Anderson, Tulsa	†1965	10	509	296	14	.582	3,464	30	346.4
Byron Leftwich, Marshall	2001	12	470	315	7	.670	4,132	38	343.6
Cody Pickett, Washington	2002	13	612	365	14	.596	4,458	28	342.9
Josh Wallwork, Wyoming	1996	12	458	286	15	.625	4,090	33	340.8

*Record. †National pass-efficiency champion.

SEASON TOUCHDOWN PASSES

Player, Team	Year	G	TD Passes
David Klingler, Houston	1990	11	*54
Jim McMahon, Brigham Young	1980	12	47
Tim Rattay, Louisiana Tech	1998	12	46
Andre Ware, Houston	1989	11	46
Kliff Kingsbury, Texas Tech	2002	14	45
David Carr, Fresno St.	2001	13	42
Ty Detmer, Brigham Young	1990	12	41
Chad Pennington, Marshall	1997	12	39
Danny Wuerffel, Florida	1996	12	39
Dennis Shaw, San Diego St.	1969	10	39
Doug Williams, Grambling	1977	11	38
Byron Leftwich, Marshall	2001	12	38
Tim Couch, Kentucky	1997	11	37
Troy Kopp, Pacific (Cal.)	1991	11	37
Chad Pennington, Marshall	1999	12	37
Peyton Manning, Tennessee	1997	12	36
Shaun King, Tulane	1998	11	36
Tim Couch, Kentucky	1998	11	36
Drew Brees, Purdue	1998	12	36
Bart Hendricks, Boise St.	2000	11	35
Danny Wuerffel, Florida	1995	11	35
Ty Detmer, Brigham Young	1991	12	35
Tim Rattay, Louisiana Tech	1999	10	35
Dan Marino, Pittsburgh	1981	11	34
Chris Vargas, Nevada	1993	11	34
Tim Rattay, Louisiana Tech	1997	11	34
Tim Lester, Western Mich.	1999	12	34
Nick Rolovich, Hawaii	2001	10	34
Rex Grossman, Florida	2001	11	34
Carson Palmer, Southern California	2002	13	33
Brandon Doman, Brigham Young	2001	13	33
Chris Weinke, Florida St.	2000	12	33
Robbie Bosco, Brigham Young	1984	12	33
Mike Maxwell, Nevada	1995	9	33
Josh Wallwork, Wyoming	1996	12	33
Steve Sarkisian, Brigham Young	1996	14	33
Ryan Leaf, Washington St.	1997	11	33
Steve Young, Brigham Young	1983	11	33
Jerry Rhome, Tulsa	1964	10	32
Ty Detmer, Brigham Young	1989	12	32
Jimmy Klingler, Houston	1992	11	32
Danny Kanell, Florida St.	1995	11	32
Jason Martin, Louisiana Tech	1996	11	32
Jose Davis, Kent St.	1997	10	32

*Record.

CAREER YARDS PER ATTEMPT
(Minimum 900 Attempts)

Player, Team	Years	Att.	Cmp.	Pct.	Yards	Yards Per Cmp.	Per Att.
Ty Detmer, Brigham Young	1988-91	1,530	958	.626	*15,031	*15.69	*9.82
Danny Wuerffel, Florida	1993-96	1,170	708	.605	10,875	15.36	9.29
Jim McMahon, Brigham Young	1977-78, 80-81	1,060	653	.616	9,536	14.60	9.00
Marvin Graves, Syracuse	1990-93	943	563	.597	8,466	15.04	8.98
Donovan McNabb, Syracuse	1995-98	938	548	.584	8,389	15.31	8.94
Chris Weinke, Florida St.	1997-00	1,107	650	.587	9,839	15.14	8.89
Billy Blanton, San Diego St.	1993-96	920	588	.639	8,165	13.89	8.88
Joe Hamilton, Georgia Tech	1996-99	1,020	629	.617	8,882	14.12	8.71
Cade McNown, UCLA	1995-98	1,153	646	.560	10,008	15.49	8.68
John Walsh, Brigham Young	1991-94	973	587	.603	8,375	14.27	8.61
Chuck Long, Iowa	$1981-85	1,072	692	.646	9,210	13.31	8.59
Steve Young, Brigham Young	1981-83	908	592	.652	7,733	13.06	8.52
Daunte Culpepper, UCF	1996-98	1,097	721	.657	9,341	12.96	8.52
Chad Pennington, Marshall	1997-99	1,265	807	.638	10,698	13.26	8.45
Robbie Bosco, Brigham Young	1983-85	997	638	.640	8,400	13.17	8.43
Dan McGwire, Iowa/San Diego St.	1986-87, 89-90	973	575	.591	8,164	14.20	8.39
Doug Flutie, Boston College	1981-84	1,270	677	.533	10,579	15.63	8.33
Tim Rattay, Louisiana Tech	1997-99	1,552	1,015	#.654	12,746	12.56	8.21
Marc Wilson, Brigham Young	1977-79	937	535	.571	7,637	14.27	8.15
Peyton Manning, Tennessee	1994-97	1,381	863	.625	11,201	12.98	8.11
Rob Johnson, Southern California	1991-94	963	623	.647	7,743	12.43	8.04
Kevin Feterik, Brigham Young	1996-99	1,004	609	.607	8,065	13.24	8.03
Steve Stenstrom, Stanford	1991-94	1,320	833	.631	10,531	12.64	7.98
Kerwin Bell, Florida	1984-87	953	549	.576	7,585	13.82	7.96
Eric Zeier, Georgia	1991-94	1,402	838	.598	11,153	13.31	7.96
Kevin Sweeney, Fresno St.	$1982-86	1,336	731	.547	10,623	14.53	7.95
Robert Hall, Texas Tech	1990-93	997	548	.550	7,908	14.43	7.93
David Neill, Nevada	1998-01	1,376	763	.555	10,903	14.29	7.92
Bart Hendricks, Boise St.	1997-00	1,142	650	.569	9,030	13.89	7.91

*Record. $See page 8 for explanation. #Record for minimum 1,000 attempts.

SINGLE-GAME YARDS

Yds.	Player, Team (Opponent)	Date
716	David Klingler, Houston (Arizona St.)	Dec. 2, 1990
690	Matt Vogler, TCU (Houston)	Nov. 3, 1990
637	Brian Lindgren, Idaho (Middle Tenn.)	Oct. 6, 2001
631	Scott Mitchell, Utah (Air Force)	Oct. 15, 1988
622	Jeremy Leach, New Mexico (Utah)	Nov. 11, 1989
621	Dave Wilson, Illinois (Ohio St.)	Nov. 8, 1980
619	John Walsh, Brigham Young (Utah St.)	Oct. 30, 1993
613	Jimmy Klingler, Houston (Rice)	Nov. 28, 1992
611	David Neill, Nevada (New Mexico St.)	Oct. 10, 1998
599	Ty Detmer, Brigham Young (San Diego St.)	Nov. 16, 1991
592	Chris Redman, Louisville (East Caro.)	Nov. 14, 1998
590	Tim Rattay, Louisiana Tech (Nebraska)	Aug. 29, 1998
585	Robbie Bosco, Brigham Young (New Mexico)	Oct. 19, 1985
572	David Klingler, Houston (Eastern Wash.)	Nov. 17, 1990
571	Marc Wilson, Brigham Young (Utah)	Nov. 5, 1977
568	David Lowery, San Diego St. (Brigham Young)	Nov. 16, 1991
565	Jim McMahon, Brigham Young (Utah)	Nov. 21, 1981
564	Troy Kopp, Pacific (Cal.) (New Mexico St.)	Oct. 20, 1990
563	David Klingler, Houston (TCU)	Nov. 3, 1990
561	Tim Rattay, Louisiana Tech (UCF)	Oct. 23, 1999
561	Tony Adams, Utah St. (Utah)	Nov. 11, 1972
560	Ty Detmer, Brigham Young (Utah St.)	Nov. 24, 1990
558	Chuck Hartlieb, Iowa (Indiana)	Oct. 29, 1988
557	John Dutton, Nevada (Boise St.)	Nov. 8, 1997
554	Greg Cook, Cincinnati (Ohio)	Nov. 16, 1968
552	Mike Maxwell, Nevada (UNLV)	Oct. 28, 1995
551	Jose Davis, Kent St. (UCF)	Oct. 4, 1997
546	Cody Ledbetter, New Mexico St. (UNLV)	Nov. 18, 1995
545	Rusty LaRue, Wake Forest (North Carolina St.)	Nov. 18, 1995
544	Eric Zeier, Georgia (Southern Miss.)	Oct. 9, 1993
543	Nick Rolovich, Hawaii (Brigham Young)	Dec. 8, 2001
542	Jason Martin, Louisiana Tech (Toledo)	Oct. 19, 1996
542	Ryan Fien, Idaho (Wyoming)	Aug. 31, 1996
539	Tim Rattay, Louisiana Tech (Boise St.)	Oct. 3, 1998
538	Chris Vargas, Nevada (UNLV)	Oct. 2, 1993
538	Jim McMahon, Brigham Young (Colorado St.)	Nov. 7, 1981
537	Ty Detmer, Brigham Young (Washington St.)	Sept. 7, 1989
536	Andrew Walter, Arizona St. (Oregon)	Oct. 19, 2002
536	Chris Weinke, Florida St. (Duke)	Oct. 14, 2000
536	Steve Sarkisian, Brigham Young (Texas A&M)	Aug. 24, 1996
536	Dave Telford, Fresno St. (Pacific [Cal.])	Oct. 24, 1987
536	Todd Santos, San Diego St. (Stanford)	Oct. 17, 1987
536	David Spriggs, New Mexico St. (Southern Ill.)	Sept. 30, 1978

SINGLE-GAME ATTEMPTS

No.	Player, Team (Opponent)	Date
83	Drew Brees, Purdue (Wisconsin)	Oct. 10, 1998
79	Matt Vogler, TCU (Houston)	Nov. 3, 1990
78	Rusty LaRue, Wake Forest (Duke)	Oct. 28, 1995

No.	Player, Team (Opponent)	Date
76	David Klingler, Houston (Southern Methodist)	Oct. 20, 1990
75	Chris Vargas, Nevada (McNeese St.)	Sept. 19, 1992
73	Jeff Handy, Missouri (Oklahoma St.)	Oct. 17, 1992
73	Troy Kopp, Pacific (Cal.) (Hawaii)	Oct. 27, 1990
73	Shane Montgomery, North Carolina St. (Duke)	Nov. 11, 1989
72	Matt Vogler, TCU (Texas Tech)	Nov. 10, 1990
72	Luke McCown, Louisiana Tech (Miami [Fla.])	Oct. 28, 2000
71	Brian Lindgren, Idaho (Middle Tenn.)	Oct. 6, 2001
71	Jimmy Klingler, Houston (Rice)	Nov. 28, 1992
71	Sandy Schwab, Northwestern (Michigan)	Oct. 23, 1982
70	Kliff Kingsbury, Texas Tech (Missouri)	Oct. 19, 2002
70	David Klingler, Houston (Texas Tech)	Nov. 30, 1991
70	David Klingler, Houston (Arizona St.)	Dec. 2, 1990
70	Dave Telford, Fresno St. (Utah St.)	Nov. 14, 1987
69	Dave Wilson, Illinois (Ohio St.)	Nov. 8, 1980
69	Chuck Hixson, Southern Methodist (Ohio St.)	Sept. 28, 1968
68	Tim Rattay, Louisiana Tech (Southern California)	Nov. 26, 1999
68	Tim Rattay, Louisiana Tech (Nebraska)	Aug. 29, 1998
68	David Klingler, Houston (Baylor)	Oct. 6, 1990
68	Jeremy Leach, New Mexico (Utah)	Nov. 11, 1989
68	Steve Smith, Stanford (Notre Dame)	Oct. 7, 1989
68	Andre Ware, Houston (Arizona St.)	Sept. 23, 1989
67	Tim Couch, Kentucky (Arkansas)	Oct. 3, 1998
67	Rusty LaRue, Wake Forest (North Carolina St.)	Nov. 18, 1995
67	Danny Kanell, Florida St. (Virginia)	Nov. 2, 1995
67	Mike Hohensee, Minnesota (Ohio St.)	Nov. 7, 1981
66	Luke McCown, Louisiana Tech (Oklahoma St.)	Aug. 31, 2002
66	Jon VanCleave, La.-Lafayette (North Texas)	Nov. 10, 2001
66	Tim Rattay, Louisiana Tech (Toledo)	Oct. 30, 1999
66	Tim Couch, Kentucky (LSU)	Nov. 1, 1997
66	Chuck Clements, Houston (Cincinnati)	Nov. 13, 1993
66	Tim Schade, Minnesota (Penn St.)	Sept. 4, 1993
66	Drew Bledsoe, Washington St. (Montana)	Sept. 5, 1992
66	Jack Trudeau, Illinois (Purdue)	Oct. 12, 1985
66	John Reaves, Florida (Auburn)	Nov. 1, 1969
65	Kliff Kingsbury, Texas Tech (Colorado)	Oct. 26, 2002
65	Marquel Blackwell, South Fla. (Pittsburgh)	Sept. 8, 2001
65	Drew Brees, Purdue (Ohio St.)	Oct. 28, 2000
65	Luke McCown, Louisiana Tech (Auburn)	Oct. 21, 2000
65	Tim Rattay, Louisiana Tech (Texas A&M)	Sept. 4, 1999
65	Peyton Manning, Tennessee (Florida)	Sept. 21, 1996
65	Rusty LaRue, Wake Forest (Georgia Tech)	Nov. 4, 1995
65	Jason Martin, Louisiana Tech (Nevada)	Oct. 21, 1995
65	Eric Zeier, Georgia (Florida)	Oct. 30, 1993
65	Jimmy Klingler, Houston (TCU)	Oct. 31, 1992
65	Scott Mitchell, Utah (UTEP)	Oct. 1, 1988
65	Mike Bates, Miami (Ohio) (Toledo)	Oct. 24, 1987
65	Craig Burnett, Wyoming (San Diego St.)	Nov. 15, 1986
65	Gary Schofield, Wake Forest (Maryland)	Oct. 16, 1982
65	Jim McMahon, Brigham Young (Colorado St.)	Nov. 7, 1981
65	Brooks Dawson, UTEP (UC Santa Barb.)	Sept. 14, 1968
65	Bill Anderson, Tulsa (Southern Ill.)	Oct. 30, 1965
65	Bill Anderson, Tulsa (Memphis)	Oct. 9, 1965

SINGLE-GAME COMPLETIONS

No.	Player, Team (Opponent)	Date
55	Drew Brees, Purdue (Wisconsin)	Oct. 10, 1998
55	Rusty LaRue, Wake Forest (Duke)	Oct. 28, 1995
50	Rusty LaRue, Wake Forest (North Carolina St.)	Nov. 18, 1995
49	Kliff Kingsbury, Texas Tech (Missouri)	Oct. 19, 2002
49	Kliff Kingsbury, Texas Tech (Texas A&M)	Oct. 5, 2002
49	Brian Lindgren, Idaho (Middle Tenn.)	Oct. 6, 2001
48	David Klingler, Houston (Southern Methodist)	Oct. 20, 1990
47	Luke McCown, Louisiana Tech (Auburn)	Oct. 21, 2000
47	Tim Couch, Kentucky (Arkansas)	Oct. 3, 1998
46	Tim Rattay, Louisiana Tech (UCF)	Oct. 23, 1999
46	Scott Milanovich, Maryland (Florida St.)	Nov. 18, 1995
46	Tim Rattay, Louisiana Tech (Nebraska)	Aug. 29, 1998
46	Jimmy Klingler, Houston (Rice)	Nov. 28, 1992
45	Tim Rattay, Louisiana Tech (Texas A&M)	Sept. 4, 1999
45	Sandy Schwab, Northwestern (Michigan)	Oct. 23, 1982
44	Kliff Kingsbury, Texas Tech (Oklahoma St.)	Nov. 10, 2001
44	Tim Rattay, Louisiana Tech (Toledo)	Oct. 30, 1999
44	Chris Redman, Louisville (East Caro.)	Nov. 14, 1998
44	Tim Couch, Kentucky (Vanderbilt)	Nov. 14, 1998
44	Matt Vogler, TCU (Houston)	Nov. 3, 1990
44	Chuck Hartlieb, Iowa (Indiana)	Oct. 29, 1988
44	Jim McMahon, Brigham Young (Colorado St.)	Nov. 7, 1981
43	Tim Rattay, Louisiana Tech (UCF)	Sept. 5, 1998
43	Jeff Handy, Missouri (Oklahoma St.)	Oct. 17, 1992
43	Chris Vargas, Nevada (McNeese St.)	Sept. 19, 1992
43	Gary Schofield, Wake Forest (Maryland)	Oct. 17, 1981
43	Dave Wilson, Illinois (Ohio St.)	Nov. 8, 1980
43	Rich Campbell, California (Florida)	Sept. 13, 1980
42	Eli Manning, Mississippi (Arkansas)	Oct, 26, 2002
42	Luke McCown, Louisiana Tech (Miami [Fla.])	Oct. 28, 2000

No.	Player, Team (Opponent)	Date
42	Kliff Kingsbury, Texas Tech (North Texas)	Sept. 9, 2000
42	Jimmy Klingler, Houston (TCU)	Oct. 31, 1992
42	Troy Kopp, Pacific (Cal.) (Hawaii)	Oct. 27, 1990
42	Andre Ware, Houston (TCU)	Nov. 4, 1989
42	Dan Speltz, Cal St. Fullerton (Utah St.)	Oct. 7, 1989
42	Robbie Bosco, Brigham Young (New Mexico)	Oct. 19, 1985
42	Bill Anderson, Tulsa (Southern Ill.)	Oct. 30, 1965
41	Matt Schaub, Virginia (Georgia Tech)	Oct. 26, 2002
41	Ben Roethlisberger, Miami (Ohio) (Northern Ill.)	Oct. 12, 2002
41	Kliff Kingsbury, Texas Tech (New Mexico)	Sept. 27, 2002
41	Kliff Kingsbury, Texas Tech (Oklahoma)	Nov. 18, 2000
41	Tim Rattay, Louisiana Tech (Middle Tenn.)	Oct. 16, 1999
41	Tim Couch, Kentucky (Georgia)	Oct. 25, 1997
41	Tim Couch, Kentucky (LSU)	Nov. 1, 1997
41	Rusty LaRue, Wake Forest (Georgia Tech)	Nov. 4, 1995
41	Mike Maxwell, Nevada (UNLV)	Oct. 28, 1995
41	Danny Kanell, Florida St. (Georgia Tech)	Oct. 21, 1995
41	David Klingler, Houston (Texas Tech)	Nov. 30, 1991
41	David Klingler, Houston (Arizona St.)	Dec. 2, 1990
41	David Klingler, Houston (Eastern Wash.)	Nov. 17, 1990
41	Jeremy Leach, New Mexico (Utah)	Nov. 11, 1989
41	Scott Mitchell, Utah (UTEP)	Oct. 1, 1988
41	Doug Gaynor, Long Beach St. (Utah St.)	Sept. 7, 1985

ANNUAL CHAMPIONS

Year	Player, Team	Class	Att.	Cmp.	Int.	Pct.	Yds.	TD
1937	Davey O'Brien, TCU	Jr.	234	94	18	.402	969	—
1938	Davey O'Brien, TCU	Sr.	167	93	4	.557	1,457	—
1939	Kay Eakin, Arkansas	Sr.	193	78	18	.404	962	—
1940	Billy Sewell, Washington St.	Sr.	174	86	17	.494	1,023	—
1941	Bud Schwenk, Washington (Mo.)	Sr.	234	114	19	.487	1,457	—
1942	Ray Evans, Kansas	Jr.	200	101	9	.505	1,117	—
1943	Johnny Cook, Georgia	Fr.	157	73	20	.465	1,007	—
1944	Paul Rickards, Pittsburgh	So.	178	84	20	.472	997	—
1945	Al Dekdebrun, Cornell	Sr.	194	90	15	.464	1,227	—
1946	Travis Tidwell, Auburn	Fr.	158	79	10	.500	943	5
1947	Charlie Conerly, Mississippi	Sr.	233	133	7	.571	1,367	18
1948	Stan Heath, Nevada	Sr.	222	126	9	.568	2,005	22
1949	Adrian Burk, Baylor	Sr.	191	110	6	.576	1,428	14
1950	Don Heinrich, Washington	Jr.	221	134	9	.606	1,846	14
1951	Don Klosterman, Loyola Marymount	Sr.	315	159	21	.505	1,843	9
1952	Don Heinrich, Washington	Sr.	270	137	17	.507	1,647	13
1953	Bob Garrett, Stanford	Sr.	205	118	10	.576	1,637	17
1954	Paul Larson, California	Sr.	195	125	8	.641	1,537	10
1955	George Welsh, Navy	Sr.	150	94	6	.627	1,319	8
1956	John Brodie, Stanford	Sr.	240	139	14	.579	1,633	12
1957	Ken Ford, Hardin-Simmons	Sr.	205	115	11	.561	1,254	14
1958	Buddy Humphrey, Baylor	Sr.	195	112	8	.574	1,316	7
1959	Dick Norman, Stanford	Jr.	263	152	12	.578	1,963	11
1960	Harold Stephens, Hardin-Simmons	Sr.	256	145	14	.566	1,254	3
1961	Chon Gallegos, San Jose St.	Sr.	197	117	13	.594	1,480	14
1962	Don Trull, Baylor	Jr.	229	125	12	.546	1,627	11
1963	Don Trull, Baylor	Sr.	308	174	12	.565	2,157	12
1964	Jerry Rhome, Tulsa	Sr.	326	224	4	.687	2,870	32
1965	Bill Anderson, Tulsa	Sr.	509	296	14	.582	3,464	30
1966	John Eckman, Wichita St.	Jr.	458	195	*34	.426	2,339	7
1967	Terry Stone, New Mexico	Jr.	336	160	19	.476	1,946	9
1968	Chuck Hixson, Southern Methodist	So.	468	265	23	.566	3,103	21
1969	John Reaves, Florida	So.	396	222	19	.561	2,896	24

Beginning in 1970, ranked on per-game (instead of total) completions

Year	Player, Team	Class	G	Att.	Cmp.	Avg.	Int.	Pct.	Yds.	TD
1970	Sonny Sixkiller, Washington	So.	10	362	186	18.6	22	.514	2,303	15
1971	Brian Sipe, San Diego St.	Sr.	11	369	196	17.8	21	.531	2,532	17
1972	Don Strock, Virginia Tech	Sr.	11	427	228	20.7	27	.534	3,243	16
1973	Jesse Freitas, San Diego St.	Sr.	11	347	227	20.6	17	.654	2,993	21
1974	Steve Bartkowski, California	Sr.	11	325	182	16.5	7	.560	2,580	12
1975	Craig Penrose, San Diego St.	Sr.	11	349	198	18.0	24	.567	2,660	15
1976	Tommy Kramer, Rice	Sr.	11	501	269	24.5	19	.537	3,317	21
1977	Guy Benjamin, Stanford	Sr.	10	330	208	20.8	15	.630	2,521	19
1978	Steve Dils, Stanford	Sr.	11	391	247	22.5	15	.632	2,943	22

Beginning in 1979, ranked on passing efficiency rating points (instead of per-game completions)

Year	Player, Team	Class	G	Att.	Cmp.	Int.	Pct.	Yds.	TD	Pts.
1979	Turk Schonert, Stanford	Sr.	11	221	148	6	.670	1,922	19	163.0
1980	Jim McMahon, Brigham Young	Jr.	12	445	284	18	.638	4,571	47	176.9
1981	Jim McMahon, Brigham Young	Sr.	10	423	272	7	.643	3,555	30	155.0
1982	Tom Ramsey, UCLA	Sr.	11	311	191	10	.614	2,824	21	153.5
1983	Steve Young, Brigham Young	Sr.	11	429	306	10	*.713	3,902	33	168.5
1984	Doug Flutie, Boston College	Sr.	11	386	233	11	.604	3,454	27	152.9
1985	Jim Harbaugh, Michigan	Jr.	11	212	139	6	.656	1,913	18	163.7
1986	Vinny Testaverde, Miami (Fla.)	Sr.	10	276	175	9	.634	2,557	26	165.8
1987	Don McPherson, Syracuse	Sr.	11	229	129	11	.563	2,341	22	164.3
1988	Timm Rosenbach, Washington St.	Jr.	11	302	199	10	.659	2,791	23	162.0
1989	Ty Detmer, Brigham Young	So.	12	412	265	15	.643	4,560	32	175.6
1990	Shawn Moore, Virginia	Sr.	10	241	144	8	.598	2,262	21	160.7

Year	Player, Team	Class	G	Att.	Cmp.	Int.	Pct.	Yds.	TD	Pts.
1991	Elvis Grbac, Michigan	Jr.	11	228	152	5	.667	1,955	24	169.0
1992	Elvis Grbac, Michigan	Sr.	9	169	112	12	.663	1,465	15	154.2
1993	Trent Dilfer, Fresno St.	Jr.	11	333	217	4	.652	3,276	28	173.1
1994	Kerry Collins, Penn St.	Sr.	11	264	176	7	.667	2,679	21	172.9
1995	Danny Wuerffel, Florida	Jr.	11	325	210	10	.646	3,266	35	178.4
1996	Steve Sarkisian, Brigham Young	Sr.	14	404	278	12	.688	4,027	33	173.6
1997	Cade McNown, UCLA	Jr.	11	283	173	5	.611	2,877	22	168.6
1998	Shaun King, Tulane	Sr.	11	328	223	6	.680	3,232	36	183.3
1999	Michael Vick, Virginia Tech	So.	10	152	90	5	.592	1,840	12	180.4
2000	Bart Hendricks, Boise St.	Sr.	11	347	210	8	.605	3,364	35	170.6
2001	Rex Grossman, Florida	So.	11	395	259	12	.656	3,896	34	170.8
2002	Brad Banks, Iowa	Sr.	13	294	170	5	.578	2,573	26	157.1

*Record.

Receiving

CAREER RECEPTIONS PER GAME
(Minimum 125 Receptions)

Player, Team	Years	G	Rec.	Yards	TD	Rec.PG
Manny Hazard, Houston	1989-90	21	220	2,635	31	*10.5
Alex Van Dyke, Nevada	1994-95	22	227	3,100	26	10.3
Howard Twilley, Tulsa	1963-65	26	261	3,343	32	10.0
Jason Phillips, Houston	1987-88	22	207	2,319	18	9.4
Troy Edwards, Louisiana Tech	1996-98	34	280	4,352	*50	8.2
Bryan Reeves, Nevada	1992-93	21	172	2,476	27	8.2
Kevin Curtis, Utah St.	2001-02	22	174	2,789	19	7.9
Nate Burleson, Nevada	2000-02	32	248	3,293	22	7.8
Siaha Burley, UCF	1997-98	22	165	2,248	15	7.5
David Williams, Illinois	1983-85	33	245	3,195	22	7.4
Geoff Noisy, Nevada	1995-98	40	295	4,249	21	7.4
James Dixon, Houston	1987-88	22	161	1,762	14	7.3
John Love, North Texas	1965-66	20	144	2,124	17	7.2
Fred Gilbert, UCLA/Houston	1989, 91-92	22	158	1,672	14	7.2
Ron Sellers, Florida St.	1966-68	30	212	3,598	23	7.1
Keyshawn Johnson, Southern California	1994-95	21	148	2,358	12	7.1
Barry Moore, North Texas	1968-69	20	140	2,183	12	7.0
Nakia Jenkins, Utah St.	1996-97	22	155	2,483	14	7.0
Arnold Jackson, Louisville	1997-00	44	*300	3,670	31	6.8
Mike Kelly, Davidson	1967-69	23	156	2,114	17	6.8
Guy Liggins, San Jose St.	1986-87	22	149	2,191	16	6.8
Trevor Insley, Nevada	1996-99	44	298	*5,005	35	6.8
Dave Petzke, Northern Ill.	1977-78	22	148	1,960	16	6.7
Loren Richey, Utah	1985-86	21	140	1,746	13	6.7
Chris Penn, Tulsa	1991, 93	22	142	2,370	17	6.5
Antonio Wilson, Idaho	1996-97	22	142	2,113	17	6.5
Brandon Stokley, La.-Lafayette	1995-98	37	241	3,702	25	6.5
J.R. Tolver, San Diego St.	1999-02	42	262	3,572	18	6.2
Tim Delaney, San Diego St.	1968-70	29	180	2,535	22	6.2
Larry Willis, Fresno St.	1983-84	23	142	2,260	14	6.2
Phil Odle, Brigham Young	1965-67	30	183	2,548	25	6.1
Randy Gatewood, UNLV	1993-94	21	128	1,832	13	6.1
Mike Mikolayunas, Davidson	1968-70	29	175	1,768	14	6.0
Terance Mathis, New Mexico	1985-87, 89	44	263	4,254	36	6.0
Aaron Turner, Pacific (Cal.)	1989-92	44	266	4,345	43	6.0
Michael Stephens, Nevada	1992-93	21	125	1,712	15	6.0
Chad Mackey, Louisiana Tech	1993-96	44	264	3,789	22	6.0

*Record.

SEASON RECEPTIONS PER GAME

Player, Team	Year	G	Rec.	Yards	TD	Rec.PG
Howard Twilley, Tulsa	†1965	10	134	1,779	16	*13.4
Manny Hazard, Houston	†1989	11	*142	1,689	22	12.9
Trevor Insley, Nevada	†1999	11	134	*2,060	13	12.2
Alex Van Dyke, Nevada	†1995	11	129	1,854	16	11.7
Troy Edwards, Louisiana Tech	†1998	12	140	1,996	*27	11.7
Nate Burleson, Nevada	†2002	12	138	1,629	12	11.5
Damond Johnson, Nevada	†1996	11	114	1,121	4	10.4
Chris Daniels, Purdue	1999	11	109	1,133	5	9.9
J.R. Tolver, San Diego St.	2002	13	128	1,785	13	9.9
Jason Phillips, Houston	†1988	11	108	1,444	15	9.8
Fred Gilbert, Houston	†1991	11	106	957	7	9.6
Jajuan Dawson, Tulane	1999	10	96	1,051	8	9.6
Howard Twilley, Tulsa	†1964	10	95	1,178	13	9.5
Jerry Hendren, Idaho	†1969	10	95	1,452	12	9.5
Chris Penn, Tulsa	†1993	11	105	1,578	12	9.5
Sherman Smith, Houston	†1992	11	103	923	6	9.4
Eugene Baker, Kent St.	†1997	11	103	1,549	18	9.4
Troy Edwards, Louisiana Tech	1997	11	102	1,707	13	9.3
James Dixon, Houston	1988	11	102	1,103	11	9.3
David Williams, Illinois	†1984	11	101	1,278	8	9.2

Player, Team	Year	G	Rec.	Yards	TD	Rec.PG
Arnold Jackson, Louisville	1999	11	101	1,209	9	9.2
Glenn Meltzer, Wichita St.	†1966	10	91	1,115	4	9.1
Kevin Curtis, Utah St.	†2001	11	100	1,531	10	9.1
Jay Miller, Brigham Young	†1973	11	100	1,181	8	9.1
Bryan Reeves, Nevada	1993	10	91	1,362	17	9.1
James Jordan, Louisiana Tech	†2000	12	109	1,003	4	9.1
Marcus Harris, Wyoming	1996	12	109	1,650	13	9.1
Dameane Douglas, California	1998	11	100	1,150	4	9.1

*Record. †National champion.

CAREER RECEPTIONS

Player, Team	Years	Rec.	Yards	Avg.	TD
Arnold Jackson, Louisville	1997-00	*300	3,670	12.2	31
Trevor Insley, Nevada	1996-99	298	*5,005	16.8	35
Geoff Noisy, Nevada	1995-98	295	4,249	14.4	21
Troy Edwards, Louisiana Tech	1996-98	280	4,352	15.5	*50
Aaron Turner, Pacific (Cal.)	1989-92	266	4,345	16.3	43
Chad Mackey, Louisiana Tech	1993-96	264	3,789	14.4	22
Terance Mathis, New Mexico	1985-87, 89	263	4,254	16.2	36
J.R. Tolver, San Diego St.	1999-02	262	3,572	13.6	18
Mark Templeton, Long Beach St. (RB)	1983-86	262	1,969	7.5	11
Howard Twilley, Tulsa	1963-65	261	3,343	12.8	32
Marcus Harris, Wyoming	1993-96	259	4,518	17.4	38
Nate Burleson, Nevada	2000-02	248	3,219	13.3	22
James Jordan, Louisiana Tech	1998-00	246	2,489	10.1	19
David Williams, Illinois	1983-85	245	3,195	13.0	22
Troy Walters, Stanford	1996-99	244	3,986	16.3	26
Brandon Stokley, La.-Lafayette	1995-98	241	3,702	15.4	25
Kendall Newson, Middle Tenn.	1998-01	238	3,074	12.9	21
Marc Zeno, Tulane	1984-87	236	3,725	15.8	25
Steve Neal, Western Mich.	1997-00	235	3,599	15.3	27
Jason Wolf, Southern Methodist	1989-92	235	2,232	9.5	17
Ryan Yarborough, Wyoming	1990-93	229	4,357	‡19.0	42
Eugene Baker, Kent St.	1995-98	229	3,513	15.3	35
Alex Van Dyke, Nevada	1994-95	227	3,100	13.7	26
Dennis Northcutt, Arizona	1996-99	223	3,252	14.5	24
DeRonnie Pitts, Stanford	1997-00	222	2,942	13.3	24
Manny Hazard, Houston	1989-90	220	2,635	12.0	31
Kevin Lockett, Kansas St.	1993-96	217	3,032	14.0	26
Ibn Green, Louisville (TE)	1996-99	217	2,830	13.0	33
¢Rashaun Woods, Oklahoma St.	2000-02	216	3,045	14.1	27
Desmond Clark, Wake Forest	1995-98	216	2,834	13.1	20
Darrin Nelson, Stanford (RB)	1977-78, 80-81	214	2,368	11.1	16
Nate Poole, Marshall	1997-00	212	2,785	13.1	18
Ron Sellers, Florida St.	1966-68	212	3,598	17.0	23
Billy McMullen, Virginia	1999-02	210	2,978	14.2	24
Craig Yeast, Kentucky	1995-98	208	2,899	13.9	28
Jason Phillips, Houston	1987-88	207	2,319	11.2	18
Peter Warrick, Florida St.	1996-99	207	3,517	17.0	32
Terrence Edwards, Georgia	1999-02	204	3,093	15.2	30
Hart Lee Dykes, Oklahoma St.	1985-88	203	3,171	15.6	29
Carl Winston, New Mexico	1990-93	202	2,972	14.7	14
Kareem Kelly, Southern California	1999-02	201	3,071	15.3	15
Justin Gage, Missouri	1999-02	200	2,704	13.5	19
Keith Edwards, Vanderbilt	1980, 82-84	200	1,757	8.8	3
Rodney Wright, Fresno St.	1999-01	198	2,843	14.4	21
Bobby Slaughter, Louisiana Tech	1987-90	198	2,544	12.9	14
Gerald Harp, Western Caro.	1977-80	197	3,305	16.8	26
Richard Buchanan, Northwestern	1987-90	197	2,474	12.6	22
Brad Muster, Stanford (FB)	1984-87	196	1,669	8.5	6
Matt Bellini, Brigham Young (RB)	1987-90	196	2,544	13.0	13
Kelly Campbell, Georgia Tech	1998-01	195	2,907	14.9	24
Anthony White, Kentucky (RB)	1996-99	194	1,520	7.8	8
Jermaine Lewis, Maryland	1992-95	193	2,932	15.2	21
Greg Primus, Colorado St.	1989-92	192	3,200	16.7	16
Charles Lockett, Long Beach St.	1983-86	191	2,902	15.1	19
Torry Holt, North Carolina St.	1995-98	191	3,379	17.7	31

Player, Team	Years	Rec.	Yards	Avg.	TD
Pete Mitchell, Boston College (TE)	1991-94	190	2,389	12.6	20
Clarkston Hines, Duke	1986-89	189	3,318	17.6	38
Lloyd Hill, Texas Tech	1990-93	189	3,059	16.2	20
Kez McCorvey, Florida St.	1991-94	189	2,660	14.1	16
Tim Stratton, Purdue (TE)	1998-01	188	1,956	10.4	15
Boo Mitchell, Vanderbilt	1985-88	188	2,964	15.8	9
Ricky Proehl, Wake Forest	1986-89	188	2,949	15.7	25
Wil Ursin, Tulane	1990-93	188	2,466	13.1	17
Brian Roberson, Fresno St.	1993-96	188	2,956	15.7	15
Monty Gilbreath, San Diego St.	1986-89	187	2,241	12.0	8
Damon Williams, UNLV	1995-98	187	2,558	13.7	9
Eric Henley, Rice	1988-91	186	2,200	11.8	16
Mick Rossley, Southern Methodist	1991-94	186	1,911	10.3	10
Johnnie Morton, Southern California	1990-93	185	2,957	16.0	21
Geroy Simon, Maryland	1993-96	185	2,059	11.1	10
Jeff Champine, Colorado St.	1980-83	184	2,811	15.3	21
Phil Odle, Brigham Young	1965-67	183	2,548	13.9	25
Wendell Davis, LSU	1984-85	183	2,708	14.8	19
Joey Kent, Tennessee	1993-96	183	2,814	15.4	25
Mark Szlachcic, Bowling Green	1989-92	182	2,507	13.8	18
Brice Hunter, Georgia	1992-95	182	2,373	13.0	19
Kelly Blackwell, TCU (TE)	1988-91	181	2,155	11.9	13
Charlie Jones, Fresno St.	1992-95	181	3,260	18.0	25
Duane Gregory, New Mexico St.	1994-97	181	2,641	14.6	14
Tim Delaney, San Diego St.	1968-70	180	2,535	14.1	22

*Record. ‡Record for minimum of 200 catches. ¢Active player.

SEASON RECEPTIONS

Player, Team	Year	G	Rec.	Yards	TD
Manny Hazard, Houston	†1989	11	*142	1,689	22
Troy Edwards, Louisiana Tech	†1998	12	140	1,996	*27
Nate Burleson, Nevada	†2002	12	138	1,629	12
Trevor Insley, Nevada	†1999	11	134	*2,060	13
Howard Twilley, Tulsa	†1965	10	134	1,779	16
Alex Van Dyke, Nevada	†1995	11	129	1,854	16
J.R. Tolver, San Diego St.	2002	13	128	1,785	13
Damond Wilkins, Nevada	†1996	11	114	1,121	4
James Jordan, Louisiana Tech	†2000	12	109	1,003	4
Chris Daniels, Purdue	1999	11	109	1,133	5
Marcus Harris, Wyoming	1996	12	109	1,650	13
Kassim Osgood, San Diego St.	2002	13	108	1,552	8
Jason Phillips, Houston	†1988	11	108	1,444	15
Rashaun Woods, Oklahoma St.	2002	13	107	1,695	17
Fred Gilbert, Houston	†1991	11	106	957	7
Chris Penn, Tulsa	†1993	11	105	1,578	12
Eugene Baker, Kent St.	†1997	11	103	1,549	18
Sherman Smith, Houston	†1992	11	103	923	6
Troy Edwards, Louisiana Tech	1997	11	102	1,707	13
James Dixon, Houston	1988	11	102	1,103	11
Arnold Jackson, Louisville	1999	11	101	1,209	9
David Williams, Illinois	†1984	11	101	1,278	8
Kevin Curtis, Utah St.	†2001	11	100	1,531	10
Kwame Cavil, Texas	1999	13	100	1,188	6
Dameane Douglas, California	1998	11	100	1,150	4
Jay Miller, Brigham Young	†1973	11	100	1,181	8
Jason Phillips, Houston	†1987	11	99	875	3
Mark Templeton, Long Beach St. (RB)	†1986	11	99	688	2
Taurean Henderson, Texas Tech (RB)	2002	14	98	633	6
Geoff Noisy, Nevada	1996	11	98	1,435	9
Alex Van Dyke, Nevada	†1994	11	98	1,246	10
Rodney Carter, Purdue	†1985	11	98	1,099	4
Keith Edwards, Vanderbilt	†1983	11	97	909	0
Jajuan Dawson, Tulane	1999	10	96	1,051	8
Jerry Hendren, Idaho	†1969	11	95	1,452	12
Howard Twilley, Tulsa	†1964	10	95	1,178	13
Reggie Williams, Washington	2002	13	94	1,454	11
Josh Reed, LSU	2001	12	94	1,740	7
Geoff Noisy, Nevada	1998	11	94	1,405	7
Richard Buchanan, Northwestern	1989	11	94	1,115	9
Bobby Wade, Arizona	2002	12	93	1,389	8
Kevin Walter, Eastern Mich.	2002	12	93	1,368	9
Justin Colbert, Hawaii	2002	14	92	1,302	8
Ricky Williams, Texas Tech (RB)	2001	11	92	617	4
Kevin Alexander, Utah St.	1995	11	92	1,400	6
Aaron Turner, Pacific (Cal.)	1991	11	92	1,604	18

*Record. †National champion.

SEASON TOUCHDOWN RECEPTIONS

Player, Team	Year	G	TD
Troy Edwards, Louisiana Tech	1998	12	*27
Randy Moss, Marshall	1997	12	25
Manny Hazard, Houston	1989	11	22
Ashley Lelie, Hawaii	2001	12	19
Desmond Howard, Michigan	1991	11	19

Player, Team	Year	G	TD
Darius Watts, Marshall	2001	12	18
Eugene Baker, Kent St.	1997	11	18
Reidel Anthony, Florida	1996	12	18
Aaron Turner, Pacific (Cal.)	1991	11	18
Dennis Smith, Utah	1989	12	18
Tom Reynolds, San Diego St.	1971	10	18
Rashaun Woods, Oklahoma St.	2002	13	17
Terry Glenn, Ohio St.	1995	11	17
Chris Doering, Florida	1995	12	17
Bryan Reeves, Nevada	1993	10	17
J.J. Stokes, UCLA	1993	11	17
Mario Bailey, Washington	1991	11	17
Clarkston Hines, Duke	1989	11	17
Torry Holt, North Carolina St.	1997	11	16
Alex Van Dyke, Nevada	1995	11	16
Ryan Yarborough, Wyoming	1993	11	16
Dan Bitson, Tulsa	1989	11	16
Howard Twilley, Tulsa	1965	10	16
Lee Mayes, UTEP	2000	11	15
Andre Cooper, Florida St.	1995	11	15
Ike Hilliard, Florida	1995	11	15
Jack Jackson, Florida	1994	12	15
Jason Phillips, Houston	1988	11	15
Henry Ellard, Fresno St.	1982	11	15

*Record.

SINGLE-GAME RECEPTIONS

Rec.	Player, Team (Opponent)	Date
23	Randy Gatewood, UNLV (Idaho)	Sept. 17, 1994
22	Jay Miller, Brigham Young (New Mexico)	Nov. 3, 1973
21	Chris Daniels, Purdue (Michigan St.)	Oct. 16, 1999
21	Troy Edwards, Louisiana Tech (Nebraska)	Aug. 29, 1998
20	Kenny Christian, Eastern Mich. (Temple)	Sept. 23, 2000
20	Rick Eber, Tulsa (Idaho St.)	Oct. 7, 1967
19	Nate Burleson, Nevada (UTEP)	Nov. 9, 2002
19	Josh Reed, LSU (Alabama)	Nov. 3, 2001
19	Manny Hazard, Houston (Texas)	Nov. 11, 1989
19	Manny Hazard, Houston (TCU)	Nov. 4, 1989
19	Ron Fair, Arizona St. (Washington St.)	Oct. 28, 1989
19	Howard Twilley, Tulsa (Colorado St.)	Nov. 27, 1965
18	J.R. Tolver, San Diego St. (Hawaii)	Dec. 7, 2002
18	Randall Lane, Purdue (Wisconsin)	Oct. 10, 1998
18	Geoff Noisy, Nevada (Oregon)	Sept. 13, 1997
18	Geoff Noisy, Nevada (Arkansas St.)	Nov. 16, 1996
18	Albert Connell, Texas A&M (Colorado)	Sept. 28, 1996
18	Alex Van Dyke, Nevada (UNLV)	Oct. 28, 1995
18	Alex Van Dyke, Nevada (Toledo)	Sept. 23, 1995
18	Richard Woodley, TCU (Texas Tech)	Nov. 10, 1990
18	Mark Templeton (RB), Long Beach St. (Utah St.)	Nov. 1, 1986
18	Howard Twilley, Tulsa (Southern Ill.)	Oct. 30, 1965
17	Trevor Insley, Nevada (Colorado St.)	Sept. 11, 1999
17	Willie Gosha, Auburn (Arkansas)	Oct. 28, 1995
17	Chad Mackey, Louisiana Tech (Nevada)	Oct. 21, 1995
17	Curtis Shearer, San Diego St. (Air Force)	Oct. 1, 1994
17	Loren Richey, Utah (UTEP)	Nov. 29, 1986
17	Keith Edwards, Vanderbilt (Georgia)	Oct. 15, 1983
17	Jon Harvey, Northwestern (Michigan)	Oct. 23, 1982
17	Don Roberts, San Diego St. (California)	Sept. 18, 1982
17	Tom Reynolds, San Diego St. (Utah St.)	Oct. 22, 1971
17	Mike Mikolayunas, Davidson (Richmond)	Oct. 11, 1969
17	Jerry Hendren, Idaho (Southern Miss.)	Oct. 4, 1969
17	Emilio Vallez, New Mexico (New Mexico St.)	Oct. 27, 1967
17	Chuck Hughes, UTEP (Arizona St.)	Oct. 30, 1965

CAREER YARDS

Player, Team	Years	Rec.	Yards	Avg.	TD
Trevor Insley, Nevada	1996-99	298	*5,005	16.8	35
Marcus Harris, Wyoming	1993-96	259	4,518	17.4	38
Ryan Yarborough, Wyoming	1990-93	229	4,357	#19.0	42
Troy Edwards, Louisiana Tech	1996-98	280	4,352	15.5	*50
Aaron Turner, Pacific (Cal.)	1989-92	266	4,345	16.3	43
Terance Mathis, New Mexico	1985-87, 89	263	4,254	16.2	36
Geoff Noisy, Nevada	1995-98	295	4,249	14.4	21
Troy Walters, Stanford	1996-99	244	3,986	16.3	26
Chad Mackey, Louisiana Tech	1993-96	264	3,789	14.4	22
Marc Zeno, Tulane	1984-87	236	3,725	15.8	25
Brandon Stokley, La.-Lafayette	1995-98	241	3,702	15.4	25
Arnold Jackson, Louisville	1997-00	*300	3,670	12.2	31
Steve Neal, Western Mich.	1997-00	235	3,599	15.3	27
Ron Sellers, Florida St.	1966-68	212	3,598	17.0	24
J.R. Tolver, San Diego St.	1999-02	262	3,572	13.6	18
Peter Warrick, Florida St.	1996-99	207	3,517	17.0	32
Eugene Baker, Kent St.	1995-98	229	3,513	15.3	35
Torry Holt, North Carolina St.	1995-98	191	3,379	17.7	31

Player, Team	Years	Rec.	Yards	Avg.	TD
Elmo Wright, Houston	1968-70	153	3,347	21.9	34
Howard Twilley, Tulsa	1963-65	261	3,343	12.8	32
Clarkston Hines, Duke	1986-89	189	3,318	17.6	38
Gerald Harp, Western Caro.	1977-80	197	3,305	16.8	26
Dan Bitson, Tulsa	1987-89, 91	163	3,300	20.2	29
Nate Burleson, Nevada	2000-02	248	3,293	13.3	22
Charlie Jones, Fresno St.	1992-95	181	3,260	18.0	25
Dennis Northcutt, Arizona	1996-99	223	3,252	14.5	24
Greg Primus, Colorado St.	1989-92	192	3,200	16.7	16
David Williams, Illinois	1983-85	245	3,195	13.0	22
Hart Lee Dykes, Oklahoma St.	1985-88	203	3,171	15.6	29
Bryan Rowley, Utah	$1989-93	177	3,143	17.8	25
Darnay Scott, San Diego St.	1991-93	178	3,139	17.6	25
Rick Beasley, Appalachian St.	1978-80	178	3,124	17.6	23
Alex Van Dyke, Nevada	1994-95	227	3,100	13.7	26
Terrence Edwards, Georgia	1999-02	204	3,093	15.2	30
Kendall Newson, Middle Tenn.	1998-01	238	3,074	12.9	21
Kareem Kelly, Southern California	1999-02	201	3,071	15.3	15
Eric Drage, Brigham Young	1990-93	162	3,065	18.9	29
Lloyd Hill, Texas Tech	1990-93	189	3,059	16.2	20
¢Rashaun Woods, Oklahoma St.	2000-02	216	3,045	14.1	27
Mike Adams, Texas	1992-93, 95-96	177	3,032	17.1	16
Kevin Lockett, Kansas St.	1993-96	217	3,032	14.0	26
Bobby Engram, Penn St.	1991, 93-95	167	3,026	18.1	31
Billy McMullen, Virginia	1999-02	210	2,978	14.2	24
Carl Winston, New Mexico	1990-93	202	2,972	14.7	14
Brian Alford, Purdue	1994-97	160	2,968	18.6	30
Boo Mitchell, Vanderbilt	1985-88	188	2,964	15.8	9
Johnnie Morton, Southern California	1990-93	185	2,957	16.0	21
Brian Roberson, Fresno St.	1993-96	188	2,956	15.7	15
Ricky Proehl, Wake Forest	1986-89	188	2,949	15.7	25
Henry Ellard, Fresno St.	1979-82	138	2,947	21.4	25
Kendal Smith, Utah St.	1985-88	169	2,943	17.4	25
DeRonnie Pitts, Stanford	1997-00	222	2,942	13.3	24
Jermaine Lewis, Maryland	1992-95	193	2,932	15.2	21
E. G. Green, Florida St.	1994-97	166	2,920	17.6	29
Kelly Campbell, Georgia Tech	1998-01	195	2,907	14.9	24
Charles Lockett, Long Beach St.	1983-86	191	2,902	15.1	19

*Record. $See page 8 for explanation. #Record for minimum 200 catches. ¢Active player.

CAREER YARDS PER GAME
(Minimum 2,200 Yards)

Player, Team	Years	G	Yards	Yd.PG
Alex Van Dyke, Nevada	1994-95	22	3,100	*140.9
Troy Edwards, Louisiana Tech	1996-98	34	4,352	128.0
Kevin Curtis, Utah St.	2001-02	22	2,789	126.8
Manny Hazard, Houston	1989-90	21	2,635	125.5
Ron Sellers, Florida St.	1966-68	30	3,598	119.9
Bryan Reeves, Nevada	1992-93	21	2,476	117.9
Trevor Insley, Nevada	1996-99	44	*5,005	113.8
Nakia Jenkins, Utah St.	1996-97	22	2,483	112.9
Keyshawn Johnson, Southern California	1994-95	21	2,358	112.3
Elmo Wright, Houston	1968-70	30	3,347	111.6
Howard Twilley, Tulsa	1963-65	30	3,343	111.4
Chris Penn, Tulsa	1991, 93	22	2,370	107.7
Goeff Noisy, Nevada	1995-98	40	4,249	106.2
Jason Phillips, Houston	1987-88	22	2,319	105.4
Nate Burleson, Nevada	2000-02	32	3,293	102.9
Siaha Burley, UCF	1997-98	22	2,248	102.2
Brandon Stokley, La.-Lafayette	1995-98	37	3,702	100.1
Aaron Turner, Pacific (Cal.)	1989-92	44	4,345	98.8
Marcus Harris, Wyoming	1993-96	46	4,518	98.2
Rick Beasley, Appalachian St.	†1977-80	32	3,124	97.6
David Williams, Illinois	1982-85	33	3,195	96.8
Terance Mathis, New Mexico	1985-87, 89	44	4,254	96.7
Troy Walters, Stanford	1996-99	42	3,986	94.9
Ryan Yarborough, Wyoming	1990-93	46	4,357	94.7
Darnay Scott, San Diego St.	1991-93	34	3,139	92.3
Edell Shepherd, San Jose St.	2000-01	24	2,207	91.9
Eugene Baker, Kent St.	1995-98	39	3,513	90.1
Lloyd Hill, Texas Tech	1990-93	34	3,059	90.0

*Record. †Played defensive back in 1977.

CAREER TOUCHDOWN RECEPTIONS

Player, Team	Years	G	TD
Troy Edwards, Louisiana Tech	1996-98	34	*50
Aaron Turner, Pacific (Cal.)	1989-92	44	43
Ryan Yarborough, Wyoming	1990-93	46	42
Marcus Harris, Wyoming	1993-96	46	38
Clarkston Hines, Duke	1986-89	44	38
Terance Mathis, New Mexico	1985-87, 89	44	36
Trevor Insley, Nevada	1996-99	44	35

Player, Team	Years	G	TD
Eugene Baker, Kent St.	1995-98	39	35
Elmo Wright, Houston	1968-70	30	34
Ibn Green, Louisville (TE)	1996-99	43	33
Peter Warrick, Florida St.	1996-99	43	32
David Boston, Ohio St.	1996-98	34	32
Steve Largent, Tulsa	1973-75	30	32
Howard Twilley, Tulsa	1963-65	30	32
Arnold Jackson, Louisville	1997-00	44	31
Torry Holt, North Carolina St.	1995-98	40	31
Chris Doering, Florida	1992-95	43	31
Lucious Davis, New Mexico St.	1992-95	42	31
Bobby Engram, Penn St.	1991, 93-95	42	31
Manny Hazard, Houston	1989-90	21	31
Terrence Edwards, Georgia	1999-02	48	30
Brian Alford, Purdue	1994-97	38	30
Sean Dawkins, California	1990-92	33	30
Desmond Howard, Michigan	1989-91	33	30
Jade Butcher, Indiana	1967-69	30	30
E.G. Green, Florida St.	1994-97	44	29
Ike Hilliard, Florida	1994-96	32	29
Jack Jackson, Florida	1992-94	34	29
Eric Drage, Brigham Young	1990-93	46	29
Dan Bitson, Tulsa	1987-89, 91	44	29
Hart Lee Dykes, Oklahoma St.	1985-88	41	29

*Record.

SEASON YARDS

Player, Team	Year	Rec.	Yards	Avg.	TD
Trevor Insley, Nevada	†1999	134	*2,060	15.4	13
Troy Edwards, Louisiana Tech	†1998	140	1,996	14.3	*27
Alex Van Dyke, Nevada	†1995	129	1,854	14.4	16
J.R. Tolver, San Diego St.	†2002	128	1,785	14.0	13
Howard Twilley, Tulsa	1965	134	1,779	13.3	16
Josh Reed, LSU	†2001	94	1,740	18.5	7
Ashley Lelie, Hawaii	2001	84	1,713	20.4	19
Troy Edwards, Louisiana Tech	†1997	102	1,707	16.7	13
Rashaun Woods, Oklahoma St.	2002	107	1,695	15.8	17
Manny Hazard, Houston	1989	*142	1,689	11.9	22
Marcus Harris, Wyoming	†1996	109	1,650	15.1	13
Randy Moss, Marshall	1997	90	1,647	18.3	25
Nate Burleson, Nevada	2002	138	1,629	11.8	12
Aaron Turner, Pacific (Cal.)	†1991	92	1,604	17.4	18
Torry Holt, North Carolina St.	1998	88	1,604	18.2	11
Chris Penn, Tulsa	†1993	105	1,578	15.0	12
Kassim Osgood, San Diego St.	2002	108	1,552	8.3	8
Eugene Baker, Kent St.	1997	103	1,549	15.0	18
Lee Evans, Wisconsin	2001	75	1,545	20.6	9
Kevin Curtis, Utah St.	2001	100	1,531	15.3	10
Chuck Hughes, UTEP	1965	80	1,519	19.0	12
Ryan Yarborough, Wyoming	1993	67	1,512	22.6	16
Henry Ellard, Fresno St.	1982	62	1,510	††24.4	15
Edell Shepherd, San Jose St.	2001	83	1,500	18.1	14
Ron Sellers, Florida St.	1968	86	1,496	17.4	12
Chad Mackey, Louisiana Tech	1996	85	1,466	17.3	10
Troy Walters, Stanford	1999	74	1,456	19.7	10
Reggie Williams, Washington	2002	94	1,454	15.5	11
Jerry Hendren, Idaho	1969	95	1,452	15.3	12
Jason Phillips, Houston	1988	108	1,444	13.4	15

*Record. †National champion. ††Record for minimum 50 catches.

SINGLE-GAME YARDS

Yds.	Player, Team (Opponent)	Date
405	Troy Edwards, Louisiana Tech (Nebraska)	Aug. 29, 1998
363	Randy Gatewood, UNLV (Idaho)	Sept. 17, 1994
349	Chuck Hughes, UTEP (North Texas)	Sept. 18, 1965
326	Nate Burleson, Nevada (San Jose St.)	Nov. 10, 2001
322	Rick Eber, Tulsa (Idaho St.)	Oct. 7, 1967
318	Harry Wood, Tulsa (Idaho St.)	Oct. 7, 1967
316	Jeff Evans, New Mexico St. (Southern Ill.)	Sept. 30, 1978
314	Alex Van Dyke, Nevada (San Jose St.)	Nov. 18, 1995
310	Chad Mackey, Louisiana Tech (Toledo)	Oct. 19, 1996
301	Chris Daniels, Purdue (Michigan St.)	Oct. 16, 1999
297	Aaron Jones, Utah St. (Boise St.)	Nov. 11, 2000
297	Brian Oliver, Ball St. (Toledo)	Oct. 9, 1993
296	J.R. Tolver, San Diego St. (Arizona St.)	Sept. 14, 2002
296	Geoffery Noisy, Nevada (Utah St.)	Nov 9 1996
293	Josh Reed, LSU (Alabama)	Nov. 23, 2001
290	Tom Reynolds, San Diego St. (Utah St.)	Oct. 22, 1971
289	Wesley Walker, California (San Jose St.)	Oct. 2, 1976
288	Mike Siani, Villanova (Xavier [Ohio])	Oct. 30, 1971
285	Ashley Lelie, Hawaii (Air Force)	Nov. 4, 2001
285	Thomas Lewis, Indiana (Penn St.)	Nov. 6, 1993
284	Don Clune, Pennsylvania (Harvard)	Oct. 30, 1971

Yds.	Player, Team (Opponent)	Date
284	Lennie Johnson, Arkansas St. (Southwest Mo. St.)	Nov. 8, 1997
283	J.R. Tolver, San Diego St. (Hawaii)	Dec. 7, 2002
283	Chris Castor, Duke (Wake Forest)	Nov. 6, 1982
283	Jeremy McDaniel, Arizona (California)	Nov. 2, 1996
283	Geoff Noisy, Nevada (New Mexico St.)	Oct. 10, 1998
282	Larry Willis, Fresno St. (Montana St.)	Nov. 17, 1984
280	Will Blackwell, San Diego St. (California)	Sept. 14, 1996

ANNUAL CHAMPIONS

Year	Player, Team	Class	Rec.	Yards	TD
1937	Jim Benton, Arkansas	Sr.	48	814	7
1938	Sam Boyd, Baylor	Sr.	32	537	—
1939	Ken Kavanaugh, LSU	Sr.	30	467	—
1940	Eddie Bryant, Virginia	So.	30	222	2
1941	Hank Stanton, Arizona	Sr.	50	820	—
1942	Bill Rogers, Texas A&M	Sr.	39	432	—
1943	Neil Armstrong, Oklahoma St.	Fr.	39	317	—
1944	Reid Moseley, Georgia	So.	32	506	—
1945	Reid Moseley, Georgia	Jr.	31	662	—
1946	Neil Armstrong, Oklahoma St.	Sr.	32	479	1
1947	Barney Poole, Mississippi	Jr.	52	513	8
1948	Johnny "Red" O'Quinn, Wake Forest	Jr.	39	605	7
1949	Art Weiner, North Carolina	Sr.	52	762	7
1950	Gordon Cooper, Denver	Jr.	46	569	8
1951	Dewey McConnell, Wyoming	Sr.	47	725	9
1952	Ed Brown, Fordham	Sr.	57	774	6
1953	John Carson, Georgia	Sr.	45	663	4
1954	Jim Hanifan, California	Sr.	44	569	7
1955	Hank Burnine, Missouri	Sr.	44	594	2
1956	Art Powell, San Jose St.	So.	40	583	5
1957	Stuart Vaughan, Utah	Sr.	53	756	5
1958	Dave Hibbert, Arizona	Jr.	61	606	4
1959	Chris Burford, Stanford	Sr.	61	756	6
1960	Hugh Campbell, Washington St.	So.	66	881	10
1961	Hugh Campbell, Washington St.	Jr.	53	723	5
1962	Vern Burke, Oregon St.	Jr.	69	1,007	10
1963	Lawrence Elkins, Baylor	Jr.	70	873	8
1964	Howard Twilley, Tulsa	Jr.	95	1,178	13
1965	Howard Twilley, Tulsa	Sr.	134	1,779	16
1966	Glenn Meltzer, Wichita St.	So.	91	1,115	5
1967	Bob Goodridge, Vanderbilt	Sr.	79	1,114	6
1968	Ron Sellers, Florida St.	Sr.	86	1,496	12
1969	Jerry Hendren, Idaho	Sr.	95	1,452	12

Beginning in 1970, ranked on per-game (instead of total) catches

Year	Player, Team	Class	G	Rec.	Avg.	Yards	TD
1970	Mike Mikolayunas, Davidson	Sr.	10	87	8.7	1,128	8
1971	Tom Reynolds, San Diego St.	Sr.	10	67	6.7	1,070	7
1972	Tom Forzani, Utah St.	Sr.	11	85	7.7	1,169	8
1973	Jay Miller, Brigham Young	So.	11	100	9.1	1,181	8
1974	Dwight McDonald, San Diego St.	Sr.	11	86	7.8	1,157	7
1975	Bob Farnham, Brown	Jr.	9	56	6.2	701	2
1976	Billy Ryckman, Louisiana Tech	Sr.	11	77	7.0	1,382	10
1977	Wayne Tolleson, Western Caro.	Sr.	11	73	6.6	1,101	7
1978	Dave Petzke, Northern Ill.	Sr.	11	91	8.3	1,217	11
1979	Rick Beasley, Appalachian St.	Jr.	11	74	6.7	1,205	12
1980	Dave Young, Purdue	Sr.	11	67	6.1	917	8
1981	Pete Harvey, North Texas	Sr.	9	57	6.3	743	3
1982	Vincent White, Stanford	Sr.	10	68	6.8	677	8
1983	Keith Edwards, Vanderbilt	Jr.	11	97	8.8	909	8
1984	David Williams, Illinois	Jr.	11	101	9.2	1,278	8
1985	Rodney Carter, Purdue	Sr.	11	98	8.9	1,099	4
1986	Mark Templeton, Long Beach St. (RB)	Sr.	11	99	9.0	688	2
1987	Jason Phillips, Houston	Jr.	11	99	9.0	875	3
1988	Jason Phillips, Houston	Sr.	11	108	9.8	1,444	15
1989	Manny Hazard, Houston	Jr.	11	*142	12.9	1,689	22

Beginning in 1990, ranked on both per-game catches and yards per game

PER-GAME CATCHES

Year	Player, Team	Class	G	Rec.	Avg.	Yards	TD
1990	Manny Hazard, Houston	Sr.	10	78	7.8	946	9
1991	Fred Gilbert, Houston	Jr.	11	106	9.6	957	7
1992	Sherman Smith, Houston	Jr.	11	103	9.4	923	6
1993	Chris Penn, Tulsa	Sr.	11	105	9.6	1,578	12
1994	Alex Van Dyke, Nevada	Jr.	11	98	8.9	1,246	10
1995	Alex Van Dyke, Nevada	Sr.	11	129	11.7	1,854	16
1996	Damond Wilkins, Nevada	Sr.	11	114	10.4	1,121	4
1997	Eugene Baker, Kent St.	Jr.	11	103	9.4	1,549	18
1998	Troy Edwards, Louisiana Tech	Sr.	12	140	11.7	1,996	*27
1999	Trevor Insley, Nevada	Sr.	11	134	12.2	*2,060	13
2000	James Jordan, Louisiana Tech	Jr.	12	109	9.1	1,003	4
2001	Kevin Curtis, Utah St.	Jr.	11	100	9.1	1,531	10
2002	Nate Burleson, Nevada	Sr.	12	138	11.5	1,629	12

J.R. Tolver topped Division I-A in 2002 in receiving yards per game with 137.3 for San Diego State. His total of 1,785 yards put him fourth on the division's single-season list.

YARDS PER GAME

Year	Player, Team	Class	G	Rec.	Yards	Avg.	TD
1990	Patrick Rowe, San Diego St.	Jr.	11	71	1,392	126.6	8
1991	Aaron Turner, Pacific (Cal.)	Jr.	11	92	1,604	145.8	18
1992	Lloyd Hill, Texas Tech	Jr.	11	76	1,261	114.6	12
1993	Chris Penn, Tulsa	Sr.	11	105	1,578	143.5	12
1994	Marcus Harris, Wyoming	So.	12	71	1,431	119.3	11
1995	Alex Van Dyke, Nevada	Sr.	11	129	1,854	168.6	16
1996	Marcus Harris, Wyoming	Sr.	12	109	1,650	137.5	13
1997	Troy Edwards, Louisiana Tech	Jr.	11	102	1,707	155.2	13
1998	Troy Edwards, Louisiana Tech	Sr.	12	140	1,996	166.3	*27
1999	Trevor Insley, Nevada	Sr.	11	134	*2,060	*187.3	13
2000	Antonio Bryant, Pittsburgh	So.	10	68	1,302	130.2	11
2001	Josh Reed, LSU	Jr.	12	94	1,740	145.0	7
2002	J.R. Tolver, San Diego St.	Sr.	13	128	1,785	137.3	13

*Record.

Scoring

CAREER POINTS PER GAME
(Minimum 225 Points)

Player, Team	Years	G	TD	Extra Pts. Scored	FG	Pts.	Pt.PG
Marshall Faulk, San Diego St.	1991-93	31	‡62	4	0	‡376	*12.1
Ed Marinaro, Cornell	1969-71	27	52	6	0	318	11.8
Bill Burnett, Arkansas	1968-70	26	49	0	0	294	11.3
Steve Owens, Oklahoma	1967-69	30	56	0	0	336	11.2
Eddie Talboom, Wyoming	1948-50	28	34	99	0	303	10.8
Travis Prentice, Miami (Ohio)	1996-99	44	*78	0	0	*468	10.6
Troy Edwards, Louisiana Tech	1996-98	34	57	2	0	344	10.1
Howard Twilley, Tulsa	1963-65	26	32	67	0	259	10.0
Tom Harmon, Michigan	1938-40	24	33	33	2	237	9.9
Ricky Williams, Texas	1995-98	46	75	2	0	452	9.8
Lee Suggs, Virginia Tech	1999-02	35	56	0	0	336	9.6
Glenn Davis, Army	1943-46	37	59	0	0	354	9.6
Johnny Bright, Drake	1949-51	25	40	0	0	240	9.6

Player, Team	Years	G	TD	Extra Pts. Scored	FG	Pts.	Pt.PG
Anthony Thompson, Indiana	1986-89	41	65	4	0	394	9.6
Roman Anderson, Houston	1988-91	44	0	213	70	423	9.6
Stacey Robinson, Northern Ill. (QB)	1988-90	25	38	6	0	234	9.4
Floyd Little, Syracuse	1964-66	30	46	2	0	278	9.3
Anthony Davis, Southern California	1972-74	33	50	2	0	302	9.2
Felix "Doc" Blanchard, Army	1944-46	25	38	3	0	231	9.2

*Record. ‡Three-year totals record.

SEASON POINTS PER GAME

Player, Team	Years	G	TD	Extra Pts. Scored	FG	Pts.	Pt.PG
Barry Sanders, Oklahoma St.	†1988	11	*39	0	0	*234	*21.3
Bobby Reynolds, Nebraska	†1950	9	22	25	0	157	17.4
Art Luppino, Arizona	†1954	10	24	22	0	166	16.6
Ed Marinaro, Cornell	†1971	9	24	4	0	148	16.4
Lydell Mitchell, Penn St.	1971	11	29	0	0	174	15.8
Troy Edwards, Louisiana Tech	†1998	12	31	2	0	188	15.7
Marshall Faulk, San Diego St.	†1991	9	23	2	0	140	15.6
Luke Staley, Brigham Young	†2001	11	28	2	0	170	15.5
Byron "Whizzer" White, Colorado	†1937	8	16	23	1	122	15.3
Lee Suggs, Virginia Tech	†2000	11	28	0	0	168	15.3
Ricky Williams, Texas	1998	11	28	0	0	168	15.3

*Record. †National champion.

CAREER POINTS
(Non-Kickers)

Player, Team	Years	TD	Extra Pts. Scored	FG	Pts.
Travis Prentice, Miami (Ohio)	1996-99	*78	0	0	*468
Ricky Williams, Texas	1995-98	75	2	0	452
Brock Forsey, Boise St.	1999-02	68	0	0	408
Anthony Thompson, Indiana	1986-89	65	4	0	394
Ron Dayne, Wisconsin	1996-99	63	0	0	378
Marshall Faulk, San Diego St.	1991-93	‡62	4	0	‡376
Eric Crouch, Nebraska (QB)	1998-01	59	20	0	374
Dwone Hicks, Middle Tenn.	1999-02	59	4	0	358
Tony Dorsett, Pittsburgh	1973-76	59	2	0	356
Glenn Davis, Army	1943-46	59	0	0	354
Ken Simonton, Oregon St.	1998-01	57	6	0	348
Troy Edwards, Louisiana Tech	1995-98	57	2	0	344
Art Luppino, Arizona	1953-56	48	49	0	337
Lee Suggs, Virginia Tech	1999-02	56	0	0	336
Chris Lemon, Nevada	1996-99	56	0	0	336
Steve Owens, Oklahoma	1967-69	56	0	0	336
Wilford White, Arizona St.	1947-50	48	27	4	327
LaDainian Tomlinson, TCU	1997-00	54	0	0	324
Skip Hicks, UCLA	$1993-97	54	0	0	324
Barry Sanders, Oklahoma St.	1986-88	54	0	0	324
Allen Pinkett, Notre Dame	1982-85	53	2	0	320
Kevin Faulk, LSU	1995-98	53	0	0	318
Pete Johnson, Ohio St.	1973-76	53	0	0	318
Ed Marinaro, Cornell	1969-71	52	6	0	318
Herschel Walker, Georgia	1980-82	52	2	0	314
James Gray, Texas Tech	1986-89	52	0	0	312
Mike Rozier, Nebraska	1981-83	52	0	0	312
Ted Brown, North Carolina St.	1975-78	51	6	0	312
Leon Johnson, North Carolina	1993-96	50	3	0	306
John Harvey, UTEP	1985-88	51	0	0	306
Eddie Talboom, Wyoming	1948-50	34	99	0	303
Shaun Alexander, Alabama	1996-99	50	2	0	302
Anthony Davis, Southern California	1972-74	50	2	0	302
Anthony Thompson, Michigan	1997-00	50	0	0	300
Dalton Hilliard, LSU	1982-85	50	0	0	300
Billy Sims, Oklahoma	$1975-79	50	0	0	300
Charles White, Southern California	1976-79	49	2	0	296
Nolan Jones, Arizona St.	1958-61	30	77	13	296
Travis Zachery, Clemson	1998-01	49	0	0	294
Warrick Dunn, Florida St.	1993-96	49	0	0	294
Steve Bartalo, Colorado St.	1983-86	49	0	0	294
Bill Burnett, Arkansas	1968-70	49	0	0	294
Keith Byars, Ohio St.	1982-85	48	0	0	288
Brian Mitchell, La.-Lafayette	1986-89	47	4	0	286
Rick Badanjek, Maryland	1982-85	46	10	0	286

*Record. $See page 8 for explanation. ‡Three-year totals record.

CAREER POINTS
(Kickers)

Player, Team	Years	PAT	PAT Att.	FG	FG Att.	Pts.
Roman Anderson, Houston	1988-91	213	217	70	101	423
Carlos Huerta, Miami (Fla.)	1988-91	178	181	73	91	397
Jason Elam, Hawaii	$1988-92	158	161	79	100	395
Derek Schmidt, Florida St.	1984-87	174	178	73	102	393
Kris Brown, Nebraska	1995-98	*217	*222	57	77	388
Shayne Graham, Virginia Tech	1996-99	167	169	68	93	371
Jeff Hall, Tennessee	1995-98	188	202	61	89	371
Jeff Chandler, Florida	$1997-01	167	180	67	80	368
Luis Zendejas, Arizona St.	1981-84	134	135	78	*105	368
Jeff Jaeger, Washington	1983-86	118	123	*80	99	358
John Lee, UCLA	1982-85	116	117	79	92	353
Max Zendejas, Arizona	1982-85	122	124	77	104	353
Kevin Butler, Georgia	1981-84	122	125	77	98	353
Derek Mahoney, Fresno St.	1990-93	216	*222	45	63	351
Martin Gramatica, Kansas St.	1994-95, 97-98	187	192	54	70	349
Nick Calaycay, Boise St.	1999-02	213	*222	45	56	348
Philip Doyle, Alabama	1987-90	105	108	78	*105	†345
Phil Dawson, Texas	1994-97	162	170	59	79	339
Andy Trakas, San Diego St.	1989-92	170	178	56	82	338
Nathan Trout, Syracuse	1996-99	187	195	49	65	334
Owen Pochman, Brigham Young	1997-00	135	139	66	91	333
John Anderson, Washington	1999-02	148	158	61	91	331
Dan Stultz, Ohio St.	1997-00	161	169	56	82	329
Travis Dorsch, Purdue	1998-01	140	149	62	87	326
Scott Bentley, Florida St.	1993-96	200	215	42	61	326
Michael Proctor, Alabama	1992-95	131	132	65	91	326
Barry Belli, Fresno St.	1984-87	116	123	70	99	326
Kyle Bryant, Texas A&M	1994-97	145	152	60	85	325
Sebastian Janikowski, Florida St.	1997-99	125	128	66	83	323
Jason Hanson, Washington St.	1988-91	136	141	62	95	322
R.D. Lashar, Oklahoma	1987-90	194	200	42	60	320
Collin Mackie, South Carolina	1987-90	112	113	69	95	319
John Becksvoort, Tennessee	1991-94	161	161	52	75	317
Josh Brown, Nebraska	1999-02	186	190	43	62	315
Cary Blanchard, Oklahoma St.	1987-90	150	151	54	73	#314
Fuad Reveiz, Tennessee	1981-84	101	103	71	95	314
Sean Fleming, Wyoming	1988-91	150	155	54	92	312
Van Tiffin, Alabama	1983-86	135	135	59	87	312
Kris Stockton, Texas	1996, 98-00	134	139	58	77	308
Jess Atkinson, Maryland	1981-84	128	131	60	82	308
Brad Selent, Western Mich.	1997-00	157	165	50	74	307
Gary Gussman, Miami (Ohio)	1984-87	102	104	68	94	306
Greg Cox, Miami (Fla.)	1984-87	162	169	47	64	303
Peter Holt, San Diego St.	1993-96	158	169	48	72	302
Dan Eichloff, Kansas	1990-93	116	119	62	87	302
Cory Wedel, Wyoming	1994-97	139	140	54	73	301

*Record. $See page 8 for explanation. †Includes one TD reception. #Includes one two-point conversion.

SEASON POINTS

Player, Team	Year	TD	Extra Pts. Scored	FG	Pts.
Barry Sanders, Oklahoma St.	†1988	*39	0	0	*234
Brock Forsey, Boise St.	†2002	32	0	0	192
Troy Edwards, Louisiana Tech	†1998	31	2	0	188
Mike Rozier, Nebraska	†1983	29	0	0	174
Lydell Mitchell, Penn St.	1971	29	0	0	174
Luke Staley, Brigham Young	†2001	28	2	0	170
Willis McGahee, Miami (Fla.)	2002	28	0	0	168
Lee Suggs, Virginia Tech	†2000	28	0	0	168
Ricky Williams, Texas	1998	28	0	0	168
Art Luppino, Arizona	†1954	24	22	0	166
Bobby Reynolds, Nebraska	†1950	22	25	0	157
Anthony Thompson, Indiana	†1989	25	4	0	154
Ricky Williams, Texas	†1997	25	2	0	152
Randy Moss, Marshall	1997	25	2	0	152
Fred Wendt, UTEP	†1948	20	32	0	152
Skip Hicks, UCLA	1997	25	0	0	150
Travis Prentice, Miami (Ohio)	1997	25	0	0	150
Pete Johnson, Ohio St.	†1975	25	0	0	150

*Record. †National champion.

SINGLE-GAME POINTS

No.	Player, Team (Opponent)	Date
48	Howard Griffith, Illinois (Southern Ill.)	Sept. 22, 1990
44	Marshall Faulk, San Diego St. (Pacific [Cal.])	Sept. 14, 1991

No.	Player, Team (Opponent)	Date
43	Jim Brown, Syracuse (Colgate)	Nov. 17, 1956
42	Arnold "Showboat" Boykin, Mississippi (Mississippi St.)	Dec. 1, 1951
42	Fred Wendt, UTEP (New Mexico St.)	Nov. 25, 1948
38	Dick Bass, Pacific, Cal. (San Diego St.)	Nov. 22, 1958
37	Jimmy Nutter, Wichita St. (Northern St.)	Oct. 22, 1949
36	Craig Candeto, Navy (Army)	Dec. 7, 2002
36	Willis McGahee, Miami (Fla.) (Virginia Tech)	Dec. 7, 2002
36	Jonathan Golden, Baylor (Samford)	Sept. 7, 2002
36	Chance Kretschmer, Nevada (UTEP)	Nov. 24, 2001
36	Chris Brown, Colorado (Nebraska)	Nov. 23, 2001
36	Levron Williams, Indiana (Michigan St.)	Nov. 10, 2001
36	Quentin Griffin, Oklahoma (Texas)	Oct. 7, 2000
36	Dwone Hicks, Middle Tenn. (Louisiana Tech)	Oct. 7, 2000
36	LaDainian Tomlinson, TCU (UTEP)	Nov. 20, 1999
36	Ricky Williams, Texas (Rice)	Sept. 26, 1998
36	Ricky Williams, Texas (New Mexico St.)	Sept. 5, 1998
36	Scott Harley, East Caro. (Ohio)	Nov. 16, 1996
36	Antowain Smith, Houston (Southern Miss.)	Nov. 9, 1996
36	Madre Hill, Arkansas (South Carolina)	Sept. 9, 1995
36	Calvin Jones, Nebraska (Kansas)	Nov. 9, 1991
36	Blake Ezor, Michigan St. (Northwestern)	Nov. 18, 1989
36	Dee Dowis, Air Force (San Diego St.)	Sept. 2, 1989
36	Kelvin Bryant, North Carolina (East Caro.)	Sept. 12, 1981
36	Andre Herrera, Southern Ill. (Northern Ill.)	Oct. 23, 1976
36	Anthony Davis, Southern California (Notre Dame)	Dec. 2, 1972
36	Tim Delaney, San Diego St. (New Mexico St.)	Nov. 15, 1969
36	Tom Francisco, Virginia Tech (VMI)	Nov. 24, 1966
36	Howard Twilley, Tulsa (Louisville)	Nov. 6, 1965
36	Pete Pedro, West Tex. A&M (UTEP)	Sept. 30, 1961
36	Tom Powers, Duke (Richmond)	Oct. 21, 1950

ANNUAL CHAMPIONS

Year	Player, Team	Class	TD	Extra Pts. Scored	FG	Pts.
1937	Byron "Whizzer" White, Colorado	Sr.	16	23	1	122
1938	Parker Hall, Mississippi	Sr.	11	7	0	73
1939	Tom Harmon, Michigan	Jr.	14	15	1	102
1940	Tom Harmon, Michigan	Sr.	16	18	1	117
1941	Bill Dudley, Virginia	Sr.	18	23	1	134
1942	Bob Steuber, Missouri	Sr.	18	13	0	121
1943	Steve Van Buren, LSU	Sr.	14	14	0	98
1944	Glenn Davis, Army	So.	20	0	0	120
1945	Felix "Doc" Blanchard, Army	Jr.	19	1	0	115
1946	Gene Roberts, Chattanooga	Sr.	18	9	0	117
1947	Lou Gambino, Maryland	Jr.	16	0	0	96
1948	Fred Wendt, UTEP	Sr.	20	32	0	152
1949	George Thomas, Oklahoma	Sr.	19	3	0	117
1950	Bobby Reynolds, Nebraska	So.	22	25	0	157
1951	Ollie Matson, San Francisco	Sr.	21	0	0	126
1952	Jackie Parker, Mississippi St.	Jr.	16	24	0	120
1953	Earl Lindley, Utah St.	Sr.	13	3	0	81
1954	Art Luppino, Arizona	So.	24	22	0	166
1955	Jim Swink, TCU	Jr.	20	5	0	125
1956	Clendon Thomas, Oklahoma	Jr.	18	0	0	108
1957	Leon Burton, Arizona St.	Jr.	16	0	0	96
1958	Dick Bass, Pacific (Cal.)	Jr.	18	8	0	116
1959	Pervis Atkins, New Mexico St.	Jr.	17	5	0	107
1960	Bob Gaiters, New Mexico St.	Sr.	23	7	0	145
1961	Jim Pilot, New Mexico St.	So.	21	12	0	138
1962	Jerry Logan, West Tex. A&M	Sr.	13	32	0	110
1963	Cosmo Iacavazzi, Princeton	Jr.	14	0	0	84
	Dave Casinelli, Memphis	Sr.	14	0	0	84
1964	Brian Piccolo, Wake Forest	Sr.	17	9	0	111
1965	Howard Twilley, Tulsa	Sr.	16	31	0	127
1966	Ken Hebert, Houston	Jr.	11	41	2	113
1967	Leroy Keyes, Purdue	Jr.	19	0	0	114
1968	Jim O'Brien, Cincinnati	Jr.	12	31	13	142
1969	Steve Owens, Oklahoma	Sr.	23	0	0	138

Beginning in 1970, ranked on per-game (instead of total) points

Year	Player, Team	Class	G	TD	Extra Pts. Scored	FG	Pts.	Avg.
1970	Brian Bream, Air Force	Jr.	10	20	0	0	120	12.0
	Gary Kosins, Dayton	Jr.	9	18	0	0	108	12.0
1971	Ed Marinaro, Cornell	Sr.	9	24	4	0	148	16.4
1972	Harold Henson, Ohio St.	So.	10	20	0	0	120	12.0
1973	Jim Jennings, Rutgers	Sr.	11	21	2	0	128	11.6
1974	Bill Marek, Wisconsin	Jr.	9	19	0	0	114	12.7
1975	Pete Johnson, Ohio St.	Jr.	11	25	0	0	150	13.6
1976	Tony Dorsett, Pittsburgh	Sr.	11	22	2	0	134	12.2
1977	Earl Campbell, Texas	Sr.	11	19	0	0	114	10.4
1978	Billy Sims, Oklahoma	Jr.	11	20	0	0	120	10.9
1979	Billy Sims, Oklahoma	Sr.	11	22	0	0	132	12.0
1980	Sammy Winder, Southern Miss.	Jr.	11	20	0	0	120	10.9

Boise State's Brock Forsey reached the end zone 32 times last year. Forsey grabbed second place in the Division I-A single-season scoring section with 192 points. He also concluded his career in the third spot in career scoring with 408 points.

Photo credit: Boise State Sports Information

Year	Player, Team	Class	G	TD	Extra Pts. Scored	FG	Pts.	Avg.
1981	Marcus Allen, Southern California	Sr.	11	23	0	0	138	12.5
1982	Greg Allen, Florida St.	So.	11	21	0	0	126	11.5
1983	Mike Rozier, Nebraska	Sr.	12	29	0	0	174	14.5
1984	Keith Byars, Ohio St.	Jr.	11	24	0	0	144	13.1
1985	Bernard White, Bowling Green	Sr.	11	19	0	0	114	10.4
1986	Steve Bartalo, Colorado St.	Sr.	11	19	0	0	114	10.4
1987	Paul Hewitt, San Diego St.	Jr.	12	24	0	0	144	12.0
1988	Barry Sanders, Oklahoma St.	Jr.	11	*39	0	0	*234	*21.3
1989	Anthony Thompson, Indiana	Sr.	11	25	4	0	154	14.0
1990	Stacey Robinson, Northern Ill. (QB)	Sr.	11	19	6	0	120	10.9
1991	Marshall Faulk, San Diego St.	Fr.	9	23	2	0	140	15.6
1992	Garrison Hearst, Georgia	Jr.	11	21	0	0	126	11.5
1993	Byron Morris, Texas Tech	Jr.	11	22	2	0	134	12.2
1994	Rashaan Salaam, Colorado	Jr.	11	24	0	0	144	13.1
1995	Eddie George, Ohio St.	Sr.	12	24	0	0	144	12.0
1996	Corey Dillon, Washington	Jr.	11	23	0	0	138	12.6
1997	Ricky Williams, Texas	Jr.	11	25	2	0	152	13.8
1998	Troy Edwards, Louisiana Tech	Sr.	12	31	2	0	188	15.7
1999	Shaun Alexander, Alabama	Sr.	11	24	0	0	144	13.1
2000	Lee Suggs, Virginia Tech	So.	11	28	0	0	168	15.3
2001	Luke Staley, Brigham Young	Jr.	11	28	2	0	170	15.5
2002	Brock Forsey, Boise St.	Sr.	13	32	0	0	192	14.8

*Record.

Interceptions

CAREER INTERCEPTIONS

Player, Team	Years	No.	Yards	Avg.
Al Brosky, Illinois	1950-52	*29	356	12.3
Martin Bayless, Bowling Green	1980-83	27	266	9.9
John Provost, Holy Cross	1972-74	27	470	17.4
Tracy Saul, Texas Tech	1989-92	25	425	17.0
Tony Thurman, Boston College	1981-84	25	221	8.8
Tom Curtis, Michigan	1967-69	25	440	17.6
Jeff Nixon, Richmond	1975-78	23	377	16.4
Bennie Blades, Miami (Fla.)	1984-87	22	355	16.1
Jim Bolding, East Caro.	1973-76	22	143	6.5
Terrell Buckley, Florida St.	1989-91	21	*501	23.9

Player, Team	Years	No.	Yards	Avg.
Chuck Cecil, Arizona	1984-87	21	241	11.5
Barry Hill, Iowa St.	1972-74	21	202	9.6
Mike Sensibaugh, Ohio St.	1968-70	21	226	10.8
Kevin Smith, Texas A&M	1988-91	20	289	14.5
Mark Collins, Cal St. Fullerton	1982-85	20	193	9.7
Anthony Young, Temple	1981-84	20	230	11.5
Chris Williams, LSU	1977-80	20	91	4.6
Charles Jefferson, McNeese St.	1975-78	20	95	4.8
Artimus Parker, Southern California	1971-73	20	268	13.4
Dave Atkinson, Brigham Young	1971-73	20	222	11.1
Jackie Wallace, Arizona	1970-72	20	250	12.5
Tom Wilson, Colgate	1964-66	20	215	10.8
Lynn Chandnois, Michigan St.	1946-49	20	410	20.5
Bobby Wilson, Mississippi	1946-49	20	369	18.5

*Record.

SEASON INTERCEPTIONS

Player, Team	Year	No.	Yards
Al Worley, Washington	†1968	*14	130
George Shaw, Oregon	†1951	13	136
Terrell Buckley, Florida St.	†1991	12	238
Cornelius Price, Houston	†1989	12	187
Bob Navarro, Eastern Mich.	†1989	12	73
Tony Thurman, Boston College	†1984	12	99
Terry Hoage, Georgia	†1982	12	51
Frank Polito, Villanova	†1971	12	261
Bill Albrecht, Washington	1951	12	140
Hank Rich, Arizona St.	†1950	12	135

*Record. †National champion.

ANNUAL CHAMPIONS

Year	Player, Team	Class	No.	Yards
1938	Elmer Tarbox, Texas Tech	Sr.	11	89
1939	Harold Van Every, Minnesota	Sr.	8	59
1940	Dick Morgan, Tulsa	Jr.	7	210
1941	Bobby Robertson, Southern California	Sr.	9	126
1942	Ray Evans, Kansas	Jr.	10	76
1943	Jay Stoves, Washington	Sr.	7	139
1944	Jim Hardy, Southern California	Sr.	8	73
1945	Jake Leicht, Oregon	So.	9	195
1946	Larry Hatch, Washington	So.	8	114
1947	John Bruce, William & Mary	Jr.	9	78
1948	Jay Van Noy, Utah St.	Jr.	8	228
1949	Bobby Wilson, Mississippi	Sr.	10	70
1950	Hank Rich, Arizona St.	Sr.	12	135
1951	George Shaw, Oregon	Fr.	13	136
1952	Cecil Ingram, Alabama	Jr.	10	163
1953	Bob Garrett, Stanford	Sr.	9	80
1954	Gary Glick, Colorado St.	Jr.	8	168
1955	Sam Wesley, Oregon St.	Jr.	7	61
1956	Jack Hill, Utah St.	Sr.	7	132
1957	Ray Toole, North Texas	Sr.	7	133
1958	Jim Norton, Idaho	Jr.	9	222
1959	Bud Whitehead, Florida St.	Jr.	6	111
1960	Bob O'Billovich, Montana	Jr.	7	71
1961	Joe Zuger, Arizona St.	Sr.	10	121
1962	Byron Beaver, Houston	Sr.	10	56
1963	Dick Kern, William & Mary	Sr.	8	116
1964	Tony Carey, Notre Dame	Jr.	8	121
1965	Bob Sullivan, Maryland	Sr.	10	61
1966	Henry King, Utah St.	Sr.	11	180
1967	Steve Haterius, West Tex. A&M	Sr.	11	90
1968	Al Worley, Washington	Sr.	*14	130
1969	Seth Miller, Arizona St.	Sr.	11	63

Beginning in 1970, ranked on per-game (instead of total) number

Year	Player, Team	Class	G	No.	Avg.	Yards
1970	Mike Sensibaugh, Ohio St.	Sr.	8	8	1.00	40
1971	Frank Polito, Villanova	So.	10	12	1.20	261
1972	Mike Townsend, Notre Dame	Jr.	10	10	1.00	39
1973	Mike Gow, Illinois	Jr.	11	10	0.91	142
1974	Mike Haynes, Arizona St.	Jr.	11	10	0.91	115
1975	Jim Bolding, East Caro.	Jr.	10	10	1.00	51
1976	Anthony Francis, Houston	Jr.	11	10	0.91	118
1977	Paul Lawler, Colgate	Sr.	9	7	0.78	53
1978	Pete Harris, Penn St.	Jr.	11	10	0.91	155
1979	Joe Callan, Ohio	Sr.	9	9	1.00	110
1980	Ronnie Lott, Southern California	Sr.	11	8	0.73	166
	Steve McNamee, William & Mary	Sr.	11	8	0.73	125
	Greg Benton, Drake	Sr.	11	8	0.73	119
	Jeff Hipp, Georgia	Sr.	11	8	0.73	104
	Mike Richardson, Arizona St.	So.	11	8	0.73	89

Year	Player, Team	Class	G	No.	Avg.	Yards
1981	Vann McElroy, Baylor	Jr.	11	8	0.73	73
	Sam Shaffer, Temple	Sr.	10	9	0.90	76
1982	Terry Hoage, Georgia	Jr.	10	12	1.20	51
1983	Martin Bayless, Bowling Green	Sr.	11	10	0.91	64
1984	Tony Thurman, Boston College	Sr.	11	12	1.09	99
1985	Chris White, Tennessee	Sr.	11	9	0.82	168
	Kevin Walker, East Caro.	Sr.	11	9	0.82	155
1986	Bennie Blades, Miami (Fla.)	Jr.	11	10	0.91	128
1987	Keith McMeans, Virginia	Fr.	10	9	0.90	35
1988	Kurt Larson, Michigan St. (LB)	Sr.	11	8	0.73	78
	Andy Logan, Kent St.	Sr.	11	8	0.73	54
1989	Cornelius Price, Houston	Jr.	11	12	1.09	187
	Bob Navarro, Eastern Mich.	Jr.	11	12	1.09	73
1990	Jerry Parks, Houston	Jr.	11	8	0.73	124
1991	Terrell Buckley, Florida St.	Jr.	12	12	1.00	238
1992	Carlton McDonald, Air Force	Sr.	11	8	0.73	109
1993	Orlanda Thomas, La.-Lafayette	Jr.	11	9	0.82	84
1994	Aaron Beasley, West Virginia	Jr.	12	10	0.83	133
1995	Willie Smith, Louisiana Tech	Jr.	10	8	0.80	65
1996	Dre' Bly, North Carolina	Fr.	11	11	1.00	141
1997	Brian Lee, Wyoming	Sr.	11	8	0.73	103
1998	Jamar Fletcher, Wisconsin	Fr.	9	6	0.67	99
1999	Deltha O'Neal, California	Sr.	11	9	0.82	280
	Deon Grant, Tennessee	Jr.	11	9	0.82	167
	Rodregis Brooks, UAB	Jr.	11	9	0.82	152
2000	Dwight Smith, Akron	Sr.	11	10	0.91	208
	Anthony Floyd, Louisville	So.	11	10	0.91	152
2001	Edward Reed, Miami (Fla.)	Sr.	11	9	0.82	206
2002	Jim Leonhard, Wisconsin	So.	14	11	0.79	115

*Record.

Defensive Records

Total Tackles

SEASON TOTAL TACKLES PER GAME

Player, Team	Year	G	Solo	Ast.	Total	Avg.
Rick Sherrod, West Virginia	†2001	10	102	54	156	*15.6
Hanik Milligan, Houston	2001	10	82	67	149	14.9
Levar Fisher, North Carolina St.	†2000	11	93	70	163	14.8
Kyle Kayden, West Virginia	2001	11	88	71	159	14.5
Jack Brewer, Minnesota	2001	11	89	66	155	14.1
Hunter Hillenmeyer, Vanderbilt	†2002	12	116	52	168	14.0
Nick Greisen, Wisconsin	2001	12	101	66	167	13.9
Pernell Griffin, East Caro.	2001	11	72	81	153	13.9
Dexter Reid, North Carolina	2002	12	107	59	166	13.8
Lawrence Flugence, Texas Tech	2002	14	124	69	*193	13.8

*Record. †National champion.

SEASON TOTAL TACKLES

Player, Team	Year	G	Solo	Ast	Total
Lawrence Flugence, Texas Tech	2002	14	124	69	*193
Tom Ward, Toledo	2002	14	107	73	180
E.J. Henderson, Maryland	2002	14	*135	40	175
John Leake, Clemson	2002	13	81	88	169
Hunter Hillenmeyer, Vanderbilt	†2002	12	116	52	168
Byron Hardmon, Florida	2002	13	104	64	168
Rod Davis, Southern Miss.	2002	13	121	46	167
Rodney Thomas, Clemson	2002	13	82	85	167
Nick Greisen, Wisconsin	2001	12	101	66	167
Dexter Reid, North Carolina	2002	12	107	59	166
Levar Fisher, North Carolina St.	†2000	11	93	70	163
Kyle Kayden, West Virginia	2001	11	88	71	159
Max Yates, Marshall	2001	12	92	67	159

*Record. †National champion.

SINGLE-GAME TOTAL TACKLES

(Since 2000)

Tackles	Player, Team (Opponent)	Date
26	Doug Szymul, Northwestern (Navy)	Sept. 21, 2002
26	Brian Leigeb, Central Mich. (Northern Ill.)	Nov. 17, 2000
25	Bob Sanders, Iowa (Indiana)	Oct. 20, 2001
24	Pernell Griffin, East Caro. (Wake Forest)	Sept. 1, 2001
23	Quincy Monk, North Carolina (Wake Forest)	Nov. 10, 2001
23	Tito Rodriquez, UCF (Arkansas)	Nov. 10, 2001
23	Chad Carson, Clemson (Wake Forest)	Oct. 27, 2001
23	Brandon Spoon, North Carolina (Maryland)	Nov. 11, 2000

Tackles	Player, Team (Opponent)	Date
22	Tom Ward, Toledo (Ball St.)	Oct. 12, 2002
22	Tom Ward, Toledo (UNLV)	Sept. 21, 2002
22	Ahmad Brooks, Texas (Colorado)	Dec. 1, 2001
22	Robert Rodriquez, UTEP (Rice)	Nov. 17, 2001
22	Nick Duffy, Northern Ill. (Ball St.)	Nov. 17, 2001
22	Grant Wiley, West Virginia (Syracuse)	Nov. 10, 2001
22	Robert Rodriquez, UTEP (Southern Methodist)	Oct. 27, 2001
22	Marcus Rogers, Kansas (Texas Tech)	Oct. 6, 2001

ANNUAL CHAMPIONS

Year	Player, Team	Class	G	Solo	Ast.	Total	Avg.
2000	Levar Fisher, North Carolina St.	Jr.	11	93	70	163	14.8
2001	Rick Sherrod, West Virginia	Sr.	10	102	54	156	*15.6
2002	Hunter Hillenmeyer, Vanderbilt	Sr.	12	116	52	168	14.0

*Record.

Solo Tackles

SEASON SOLO TACKLES PER GAME

Player, Team	Year	G	Solo	Avg.
Rick Sherrod, West Virginia	†2001	10	102	*10.2
Hunter Hillenmeyer, Vanderbilt	†2002	12	116	9.7
E.J. Henderson, Maryland	2002	14	*135	9.6
E.J. Henderson, Maryland	2001	11	104	9.5
Rod Davis, Southern Miss.	2002	13	121	9.3
Tito Rodriquez, UCF	2001	11	100	9.1
Dexter Reid, North Carolina	2002	12	107	8.9
Tito Rodriquez, UCF	2001	9	80	8.9
Lawrence Flugence, Texas Tech	2002	14	124	8.9
Sean Doyle, Missouri	2001	11	93	8.5
D.J. Walker, UTEP	2002	11	93	8.5
Levar Fisher, North Carolina St.	2000	11	93	8.5

*Record. †National champion.

SEASON TOTAL SOLO TACKLES

Player, Team	Year	G	Solo
E.J. Henderson, Maryland	2002	14	*135
Lawrence Flugence, Texas Tech	2002	14	124
Rod Davis, Southern Miss.	2002	13	121
Hunter Hillenmeyer, Vanderbilt	†2002	12	116
Dexter Reid, North Carolina	2002	12	107
Tom Ward, Toledo	2002	14	107
Byron Hardmon, Florida	2002	13	104
E.J. Henderson, Maryland	2001	11	104
David Gardner, Toledo	2002	14	103
Rick Sherrod, West Virginia	†2001	10	102
Nick Griesen, Wisconsin	2001	12	101
Tito Rodriquez, UCF	2001	11	100

*Record. †National champion.

SINGLE-GAME SOLO TACKLES

(Since 2000)

Solo	Player, Team (Opponent)	Date
19	Doug Szymul, Northwestern (Navy)	Sept. 21, 2002
18	Nick Duffy, Northern Ill. (Ball St.)	Nov. 17, 2001
18	Brian Leigeb, Central Mich. (Northern Ill.)	Nov. 17, 2000
17	Tom Ward, Toledo (UNLV)	Sept. 21, 2002
16	E.J. Henderson, Maryland (Wake Forest)	Nov. 30, 2002
16	Dexter Reid, North Carolina (Clemson)	Nov. 9, 2002
16	Quincy Monk, North Carolina (Wake Forest)	Nov. 10, 2001
15	Clyde Surrell, Colorado (Texas Tech)	Oct. 26, 2002
15	Lawrence Flugence, Texas Tech (Ohio St.)	Aug. 24, 2002
15	Rick Sherrod, West Virginia (Virginia Tech)	Oct. 6, 2001
15	Adam Archuleta, Arizona St. (UCLA)	Sept. 30, 2000
15	Chris Lepore, Navy (Boston College)	Sept. 23, 2000
15	Jason Doering, Wisconsin (Oregon)	Sept. 9, 2000

ANNUAL CHAMPIONS

Year	Player, Team	Class	G	Solo	Avg.
2001	Rick Sherrod, West Virginia	Sr.	10	102	*10.2
2002	Hunter Hillenmeyer, Vanderbilt	Sr.	12	116	9.7

*Record.

Tackles for Loss

SEASON TACKLES FOR LOSS PER GAME

Player, Team	Year	G	Solo	Ast.	Total	Avg.
Kenny Philpot, Eastern Mich.	†2001	11	26	9	30.5	*2.8
E.J. Henderson, Maryland	2001	11	26	4	28.0	2.6
Wayne Rogers, Houston	†2000	11	27	0	27.0	2.5
Bryan Knight, Pittsburgh	2000	11	26	0	26.0	2.4
Larry Foote, Michigan	2001	10	21	5	23.5	2.4
Terrell Suggs, Arizona St.	†2002	14	27	9	*31.5	2.3
LeMarcus McDonald, TCU	2001	11	23	3	24.5	2.2
Robert Thomas, UCLA	2001	11	23	3	24.5	2.2
Julius Peppers, North Carolina	2000	11	24	0	24.0	2.2
Jason Babin, Western Mich.	2002	12	25	2	26.0	2.2

*Record. †National champion.

SEASON TACKLES FOR LOSS

Player, Team	Year	G	Solo	Ast.	Total
Terrell Suggs, Arizona St.	†2002	14	27	9	*31.5
Kenny Philpot, Eastern Mich.	†2001	11	26	9	30.5
E.J. Henderson, Maryland	2001	11	26	4	28.0
Wayne Rogers, Houston	†2000	11	27	0	27.0
Jason Babin, Western Mich.	2002	12	25	2	26.0
Bryan Knight, Pittsburgh	2000	11	26	0	26.0
Dwight Freeney, Syracuse	2001	12	24	3	25.5
LaMarcus McDonald, TCU	2002	12	20	10	25.0
Chris Johnson, Kansas St.	2000	12	25	0	25.0
LeMarcus McDonald, TCU	2001	11	23	3	24.5
Robert Thomas, UCLA	2001	11	23	3	24.5

*Record. †National champion.

SINGLE-GAME TACKLES FOR LOSS

(Since 2000)

TFL	Player, Team (Opponent)	Date
7.0	Richard Seigler, Oregon St. (Arizona St.)	Oct. 20, 2001
7.0	Chris Johnson, Kansas St. (Kansas)	Oct. 7, 2000
6.5	Terrell Suggs, Arizona St. (Washington)	Oct. 26, 2002
6.0	Wendell Bryant, Wisconsin (Penn St.)	Sept. 22, 2001
6.0	Akin Ayodele, Purdue (Cincinnati)	Sept. 2, 2001
6.0	James Davis, West Virginia (East Caro.)	Nov. 18, 2000
6.0	Julius Peppers, North Carolina (Virginia)	Oct. 28, 2000
5.5	LaMarcus McDonald, TCU (Louisville)	Nov. 23, 2001
5.0	Greg Cole, Kansas (Texas A&M)	Oct. 19, 2002
5.0	Jimmy Kennedy, Penn St. (Wisconsin)	Oct. 5, 2002
5.0	Larry Tripplett, Washington (Idaho)	Sept. 22, 2002
5.0	Jason Kaufusi, Utah (Arizona)	Sept. 14, 2002
5.0	Tully Banta-Cain, California (New Mexico St.)	Sept. 7, 2002
5.0	Maurice Gordon, Texas (Colorado)	Dec. 1, 2001
5.0	James Harrison, Kent St. (Miami [Ohio])	Nov. 24, 2001
5.0	Tully Banta-Cain, California (Rutgers)	Nov. 23, 2001
5.0	Charles Grant, Georgia (Auburn)	Nov. 10, 2001
5.0	Chris Kelsay, Nebraska (Kansas)	Nov. 3, 2001
5.0	Dewayne White, Louisville (Tulane)	Nov. 3, 2001
5.0	Elton Patterson, UCF (UAB)	Oct. 6, 2001
5.0	Robert Thomas, UCLA (Ohio St.)	Sept. 22, 2001
5.0	Algie Atkinson, Kansas (Southwest Mo. St.)	Sept. 1, 2001
5.0	Matt Rayl, Kent St. (Buffalo)	Nov. 3, 2000
5.0	Elton Patterson, UCF (La.-Monroe)	Oct. 21, 2000
5.0	Cory Redding, Texas (Missouri)	Oct. 21, 2000
5.0	D.D. Lewis, Texas (Colorado)	Oct. 14, 2000
5.0	DeJuan Goulde, Toledo (Marshall)	Oct. 14, 2000
5.0	Menson Holloway, UTEP (Tulsa)	Oct. 7, 2000
5.0	Pig Prather, Mississippi St. (Brigham Young)	Sept. 14, 2000

ANNUAL CHAMPIONS

Year	Player, Team	G	Solo	Ast.	Total	Avg.
2000	Wayne Rogers, Houston	11	27	0	27.0	2.5
2001	Kenny Philpot, Eastern Mich.	11	26	9	30.5	*2.8
2002	Terrell Suggs, Arizona St.	14	27	9	*31.5	2.3

*Record.

Pass Sacks

SEASON PASS SACKS PER GAME

Player, Team	Year	G	Solo	Ast.	Total	Avg.
Terrell Suggs, Arizona St.	†2002	14	23	2	*24.0	*1.7
Dwight Freeney, Syracuse	†2001	12	17	1	17.5	1.5
Michael Josiah, Louisville	†2000	9	12	1	12.5	1.4
Dewayne White, Louisville	2001	11	15	0	15.0	1.4
Julius Peppers, North Carolina	2000	11	15	0	15.0	1.4
Osi Umenyiora, Troy St.	2002	12	16	0	16.0	1.3
Tom Canada, California	2002	9	12	0	12.0	1.3
Bryan Thomas, UAB	2001	11	14	0	14.0	1.3
Antwan Peek, Cincinnati	2001	10	12	1	12.5	1.3
Greg Gathers, Georgia Tech	2000	11	13	0	13.0	1.2
Andre Arnold, Memphis	2000	11	13	0	13.0	1.2

Player, Team	Year	G	Solo	Ast.	Total	Avg.
Jason Babin, Western Mich.	2002	12	13	2	14.0	1.2
Michael Haynes, Penn St.	2002	13	14	2	15.0	1.2

*Record. †National champion.

SEASON TOTAL PASS SACKS

Player, Team	Year	G	Solo	Ast.	Total
Terrell Suggs, Arizona St.	†2002	14	23	2	*24.0
Dwight Freeney, Syracuse	†2001	12	17	1	17.5
Osi Umenyiora, Troy St.	2002	12	16	0	16.0
Michael Haynes, Penn St.	2002	13	14	2	15.0
Dewayne White, Louisville	2001	11	15	0	15.0
Julius Peppers, North Carolina	2000	11	15	0	15.0
Jason Babin, Western Mich.	2002	12	13	2	14.0
David Pollack, Georgia	2002	14	13	2	14.0
Bryan Thomas, UAB	2001	11	14	0	14.0
Rien Long, Washington	2002	12	12	2	13.0
Tully Banta-Cain, California	2002	12	12	2	13.0
Greg Gathers, Georgia Tech	2000	11	13	0	13.0
Andre Arnold, Memphis	2000	11	13	0	13.0

*Record. †National champion.

SINGLE-GAME PASS SACKS
(Since 2000)

PS	Player, Team (Opponent)	Date
5.0	James Harrison, Kent St. (Miami [Ohio])	Nov. 24, 2001
5.0	Wendell Bryant, Wisconsin (Penn St.)	Sept. 22, 2001
4.5	Terrell Suggs, Arizona St. (Washington)	Oct. 26, 2002
4.5	Tully Banta-Cain, California (New Mexico St.)	Sept. 7, 2002
4.0	Nick Burley, Fresno St. (San Jose St.)	Nov. 23, 2002
4.0	Shurron Pierson, South Fla. (Southern Miss.)	Oct. 12, 2002
4.0	Jimmy Kennedy, Penn St. (Wisconsin)	Oct. 5, 2002
4.0	LaMarcus McDonald, TCU (Louisville)	Nov. 23, 2001
4.0	Charles Grant, Georgia (Auburn)	Nov. 10, 2001
4.0	Chris Johnson, Kansas St. (Missouri)	Nov. 18, 2000
4.0	James Davis, West Virginia (East Caro.)	Nov. 18, 2000
4.0	Julius Peppers, North Carolina (Virginia)	Oct. 28, 2000
4.0	Willie Davis, UCF (Eastern Ky.)	Oct. 14, 2000
4.0	Michael Josiah, Louisville (Grambling)	Sept. 9, 2000

ANNUAL CHAMPIONS

Year	Player, Team	G	Solo	Ast.	Total	Avg.
2000	Michael Josiah, Louisville	9	12	1	12.5	1.4
2001	Dwight Freeney, Syracuse	12	17	1	17.5	1.5
2002	Terrell Suggs, Arizona St.	14	23	2	*24.0	*1.7

*Record.

Passes Defended

SEASON PASSES DEFENDED PER GAME

Player, Team	Year	G	PBU	Int.	Total	Avg.
Jason Goss, TCU	†2002	12	24	8	*32	*2.7
Eugene Wilson, Illinois	†2001	11	23	6	29	2.6
Lynaris Elpheage, Tulane	2002	13	23	8	31	2.4
Christian Morton, Illinois	2001	11	22	4	26	2.4
Ken Lucas, Mississippi	†2000	11	20	5	25	2.3
Steve Smith, Oregon	2001	11	18	6	24	2.2
Jason Goss, TCU	2001	11	21	3	24	2.2
Fred Smoot, Mississippi St.	2000	11	19	5	24	2.2
Lawrence Richardson, Arkansas	2001	11	20	3	23	2.1
Daniel Wilturner, Baylor	2000	11	21	2	23	2.1
Edward Reed, Miami (Fla.)	2000	11	15	8	23	2.1
Quentin Jammer, Texas	2000	11	20	3	23	2.1

*Record. †National champion.

SEASON TOTAL PASSES DEFENDED

Player, Team	Year	G	PBU	Int.	Total
Jason Goss, TCU	†2002	12	24	8	*32
Lynaris Elpheage, Tulane	2002	13	23	8	31
Eugene Wilson, Illinois	†2001	11	23	6	29
Joselio Hanson, Texas Tech	2002	14	23	3	26
Christian Morton, Illinois	2001	11	22	4	26
Jim Leonhard, Wisconsin	2002	14	14	11	25
Ken Lucas, Mississippi	†2000	11	20	5	25
Roy Hopkins, Connecticut	2002	12	18	6	24
Rod Babers, Texas	2002	13	22	2	24
Corey Webster, LSU	2002	13	17	7	24
Steve Smith, Oregon	2001	11	18	6	24
Jason Goss, TCU	2001	11	21	3	24
Quentin Jammer, Texas	2001	12	22	2	24
Fred Smoot, Mississippi St.	2000	11	19	5	24

*Record. †National champion.

SINGLE-GAME PASSES DEFENDED
(Since 2000)

PD	Player, Team (Opponent)	Date
8	Joselio Hanson, Texas Tech (Oklahoma St.)	Nov. 9, 2002
7	Jason Goss, TCU (Tulane)	Nov. 9, 2002
7	Korey Banks, Mississippi St. (Memphis)	Oct. 19, 2002
7	Nashville Dyer, Kent St. (Bucknell)	Sept. 8, 2001
7	Demerist Whitfield, Northern Ill. (Illinois St.)	Sept. 9, 2000
6	Terence Newman, Kansas St. (Oklahoma)	Sept. 29, 2001
6	Bobby Jackson, Illinois (Northern Ill.)	Sept. 8, 2001
5	Dennis Weathersby, Oregon St. (California)	Oct. 26, 2002
5	Domonique Foxworth, Maryland (Georgia Tech)	Oct. 17, 2002
5	Jahmile Addae, West Virginia (Rutgers)	Oct. 12, 2002
5	Dohnel Singfield, Buffalo (Rutgers)	Sept. 7, 2002
5	David Gardner, Toledo (Eastern Mich.)	Sept. 7, 2002
5	Jim Leonhard, Wisconsin (Fresno St.)	Aug. 23, 2002
5	Rashard Walker, Auburn (LSU)	Dec. 1, 2001
5	Jehu Anderson, Toledo (Western Mich.)	Nov. 6, 2001
5	Quentin Jammer, Texas (Baylor)	Nov. 3, 2001
5	Erwin Swiney, Nebraska (Baylor)	Oct. 13, 2001
5	DeJuan Groce, Nebraska (Missouri)	Sept. 29, 2001
5	Anthony Floyd, Louisville (Tulane)	Oct. 28, 2000
5	Jamar Fletcher, Wisconsin (Iowa)	Oct. 28, 2000
5	Davin Bush, UCF (Northwestern St.)	Sept. 9, 2000
5	Jamar Fletcher, Wisconsin (Oregon)	Sept. 9, 2000

ANNUAL CHAMPIONS

Year	Player, Team	G	PBU	Int.	Total	Avg.
2000	Ken Lucas, Mississippi	11	20	5	25	2.3
2001	Eugene Wilson, Illinois	11	23	6	29	2.6
2002	Jason Goss, TCU	12	24	8	*32	*2.7

*Record.

Forced Fumbles

SEASON FORCED FUMBLES PER GAME

Player, Team	Year	G	FF	Avg.
Tom Canada, California	†2002	9	6	*0.67
Dwight Freeney, Syracuse	†2001	12	*8	*0.67
Quintin Mikell, Boise St.	2002	13	*8	0.62
Brian Lape, Western Mich.	2001	11	6	0.55
Cory Smith, North Carolina St.	2001	11	6	0.55
Ryan Claridge, UNLV	2001	11	6	0.55
Robert Thomas, UCLA	2000	11	6	0.55
Claude Harriott, Pittsburgh	2002	13	7	0.54
Michael Haynes, Penn St.	2002	13	7	0.54
Phillip Perry, San Jose St.	2002	13	7	0.54
Antwan Peek, Cincinnati	2001	10	5	0.50
Tony Hardman, UCF	†2000	10	5	0.50

*Record. †National champion.

SEASON TOTAL FORCED FUMBLES

Player, Team	Year	G	FF
Quintin Mikell, Boise St.	2002	13	*8
Dwight Freeney, Syracuse	†2001	12	*8
Claude Harriott, Pittsburgh	2002	13	7
Michael Haynes, Penn St.	2002	13	7
Phillip Perry, San Jose St.	2002	13	7
Antwan Peek, Cincinnati	2002	14	7
Tom Canada, California	†2002	9	6
Kenechi Udeze, Southern California	2002	13	6
Terrell Suggs, Arizona St.	2002	14	6
Mason Unck, Arizona St.	2002	14	6
Brian Lape, Western Mich.	2001	11	6
Cory Smith, North Carolina St.	2001	11	6
Ryan Claridge, UNLV	2001	11	6
Robert Thomas, UCLA	2000	11	6

*Record. †National champion.

SINGLE-GAME FORCED FUMBLES
(Since 2000)

FF	Player, Team (Opponent)	Date
3	Quintin Mikell, Boise St. (Hawaii)	Oct. 5, 2002
3	Mason Unck, Arizona St. (Stanford)	Sept. 28, 2002
3	DeLawrence Grant, Oregon St. (San Diego St.)	Sept. 23, 2000
2	By many players	

ANNUAL CHAMPIONS

Year	Player, Team	G	FF	Avg.
2000	Marques Anderson, UCLA	10	‡7	0.70
	Tony Hardman, UCF	10	‡7	0.70

‡Prior to 2001, the total was forced fumbles plus fumbles recovered. Beginning in 2001, FF was forced fumbles only.

Year	Player, Team	G	FF	Avg.
2001	Dwight Freeney, Syracuse	12	*8	*0.67
2002	Tom Canada, California	9	6	*0.67

Punting

CAREER AVERAGE
(Minimum 250 Punts)

Player, Team	Years	No.	Yards	Avg.	Long
Shane Lechler, Texas A&M	1996-99	268	11,977	*44.7	76
Bill Smith, Mississippi	1983-86	254	11,260	44.3	92
Jim Arnold, Vanderbilt	1979-82	277	12,171	43.9	79
Ralf Mojsiejenko, Michigan St.	1981-84	275	11,997	43.6	72
Jim Miller, Mississippi	1976-79	266	11,549	43.4	82
Russ Henderson, Virginia	1975-78	276	11,957	43.3	74
Maury Buford, Texas Tech	1978-81	293	12,670	43.2	75
Nate Cochran, Pittsburgh	1993-96	252	10,851	43.1	80
Chris Becker, TCU	1985-88	265	11,407	43.0	77
James Gargus, TCU	1981-84	255	10,862	42.6	74
Ron Keller, New Mexico	1983-86	252	10,737	42.6	77
Brian Morton, Duke	1997-00	282	12,000	42.6	80

(150-249 Punts)

Player, Team	Years	No.	Yards	Avg.	Long
Todd Sauerbrun, West Virginia	1991-94	167	7,733	*46.3	90
Reggie Roby, Iowa	1979-82	172	7,849	45.6	69
Greg Montgomery, Michigan St.	1985-87	170	7,721	45.4	86
Tom Tupa, Ohio St.	1984-87	196	8,854	45.2	75
Barry Helton, Colorado	1984-87	153	6,873	44.9	68
Aron Langley, Wyoming	1996-98	171	7,649	44.7	72
Ray Guy, Southern Miss.	1970-72	200	8,934	44.7	93
Bucky Scribner, Kansas	1980-82	217	9,670	44.6	70
Terry Daniel, Auburn	1992-94	169	7,522	44.5	71
Greg Horne, Arkansas	1983-86	180	8,002	44.5	72
Ray Criswell, Florida	1982-85	161	7,153	44.4	73
Mark Simon, Air Force	1984-86	164	7,283	44.4	64
Brian Schmitz, North Carolina	1996-99	208	9,233	44.4	72
Russell Erxleben, Texas	1975-78	214	9,467	44.2	80
Brad Maynard, Ball St.	1993-96	242	10,702	44.2	76
Chuck Ramsey, Wake Forest	1971-73	205	9,010	44.0	70
Johnny Evans, North Carolina St.	1974-77	185	8,143	44.0	81
Jimmy Colquitt, Tennessee	1981-84	201	8,816	43.9	70
John Teltschik, Texas	1982-85	217	9,496	43.8	81

*Record.

SEASON AVERAGE
(Qualifiers for Championship)

Player, Team	Year	No.	Yards	Avg.
Chad Kessler, LSU	†1997	39	1,961	*50.3
Reggie Roby, Iowa	†1981	44	2,193	49.8
Kirk Wilson, UCLA	†1956	30	1,479	49.3
Todd Sauerbrun, West Virginia	†1994	72	3,486	‡48.4
Travis Dorsch, Purdue	†2001	49	2,370	48.4
Zack Jordan, Colorado	†1950	38	1,830	48.2
Ricky Anderson, Vanderbilt	†1984	58	2,793	48.2
Marv Bateman, Utah	†1971	68	3,269	48.1
Reggie Roby, Iowa	†1982	52	2,501	48.1
Andrew Bayes, East Caro.	†1999	47	2,259	48.1
Owen Price, UTEP	†1940	30	1,440	48.0
Jack Jacobs, Oklahoma	1940	31	1,483	47.8
Brian Schmitz, North Carolina	1999	74	3,538	47.8
Bill Smith, Mississippi	1984	44	2,099	47.7
Ed Bunn, UTEP	†1992	41	1,955	47.7

*Record. †National champion. ‡Record for minimum 50 punts.

ANNUAL CHAMPIONS

Year	Player, Team	Class	No.	Yards	Avg.
1937	Johnny Pingel, Michigan St.	Jr.	49	2,101	42.9
1938	Jerry Dowd, St. Mary's (Cal.)	Sr.	62	2,711	43.7
1939	Harry Dunkle, North Carolina	So.	37	1,725	46.6
1940	Owen Price, UTEP	Jr.	30	1,440	48.0
1941	Owen Price, UTEP	Sr.	40	1,813	45.3
1942	Bobby Cifers, Tennessee	Jr.	37	1,586	42.9
1943	Harold Cox, Arkansas	Fr.	37	1,518	41.0
1944	Bob Waterfield, UCLA	Sr.	60	2,575	42.9
1945	Howard Maley, Southern Methodist	Sr.	59	2,458	41.7
1946	Johnny Galvin, Purdue	Sr.	30	1,286	42.9
1947	Leslie Palmer, North Carolina St.	Sr.	65	2,816	43.3
1948	Charlie Justice, North Carolina	Jr.	62	2,728	44.0
1949	Paul Stombaugh, Furman	Sr.	57	2,550	44.7

Matt Payne of Brigham Young boomed 51 punts for an average of 47.6 yards in 2002 to lead Division I-A.

Year	Player, Team	Class	No.	Yards	Avg.
1950	Zack Jordan, Colorado	So.	38	1,830	48.2
1951	Chuck Spaulding, Wyoming	Jr.	37	1,610	43.5
1952	Des Koch, Southern California	Jr.	47	2,043	43.5
1953	Zeke Bratkowski, Georgia (QB)	Sr.	50	2,132	42.6
1954	A.L. Terpening, New Mexico	Sr.	41	1,869	45.6
1955	Don Chandler, Florida	Sr.	22	975	44.3
1956	Kirk Wilson, UCLA	So.	30	1,479	49.3
1957	Dave Sherer, Southern Methodist	Jr.	36	1,620	45.0
1958	Bobby Walden, Georgia	So.	44	1,991	45.3
1959	John Hadl, Kansas	So.	43	1,960	45.6
1960	Dick Fitzsimmons, Denver	So.	25	1,106	44.2
1961	Joe Zuger, Arizona St.	Sr.	31	1,305	42.1
1962	Joe Don Looney, Oklahoma	Jr.	34	1,474	43.4
1963	Danny Thomas, Southern Methodist	Jr.	48	2,110	44.0
1964	Frank Lambert, Mississippi	Sr.	50	2,205	44.1
1965	Dave Lewis, Stanford	Jr.	29	1,302	44.9
1966	Ron Widby, Tennessee	Sr.	48	2,104	43.8
1967	Zenon Andrusyshyn, UCLA	So.	34	1,502	44.2
1968	Dany Pitcock, Wichita St.	Sr.	71	3,068	43.2
1969	Ed Marsh, Baylor	Jr.	68	2,965	43.6
1970	Marv Bateman, Utah	Jr.	65	2,968	45.7
1971	Marv Bateman, Utah	Sr.	68	3,269	48.1
1972	Ray Guy, Southern Miss.	Sr.	58	2,680	46.2
1973	Chuck Ramsey, Wake Forest	Sr.	87	3,896	44.8
1974	Joe Parker, Appalachian St.	So.	63	2,788	44.3
1975	Tom Skladany, Ohio St.	Jr.	36	1,682	46.7
1976	Russell Erxleben, Texas	So.	61	2,842	46.6
1977	Jim Miller, Mississippi	So.	66	3,029	45.9
1978	Maury Buford, Texas Tech	Fr.	71	3,131	44.1
1979	Clay Brown, Brigham Young	Jr.	43	1,950	45.3

Beginning in 1980, ranked on minimum 3.6 punts per game

Year	Player, Team	Class	No.	Yards	Long	Avg.
1980	Steve Cox, Arkansas	Sr.	47	2,186	86	46.5
1981	Reggie Roby, Iowa	Jr.	44	2,193	68	49.8
1982	Reggie Roby, Iowa	Sr.	52	2,501	66	48.1
1983	Jack Weil, Wyoming	Sr.	52	2,369	86	45.6
1984	Ricky Anderson, Vanderbilt	Sr.	58	2,793	82	48.2
1985	Mark Simon, Air Force	Jr.	53	2,506	71	47.3
1986	Greg Horne, Arkansas	Sr.	49	2,313	65	47.2
1987	Tom Tupa, Ohio St. (QB)	Sr.	63	2,963	72	47.0
1988	Keith English, Colorado	Sr.	51	2,297	77	45.0

Year	Player, Team	Class	No.	Yards	Long	Avg.
1989	Tom Rouen, Colorado	So.	36	1,651	63	45.8
1990	Cris Shale, Bowling Green	Sr.	66	3,087	81	46.8
1991	Mark Bounds, Texas Tech	Sr.	53	2,481	78	46.8
1992	Ed Bunn, UTEP	Sr.	41	1,955	73	47.7
1993	Chris MacInnis, Air Force	Sr.	49	2,303	74	47.0
1994	Todd Sauerbrun West Virginia	Sr.	72	3,486	90	‡48.4
1995	Brad Maynard, Ball St.	Jr.	66	3,071	67	46.5
1996	Bill Marinangel, Vanderbilt	Sr.	77	3,586	79	46.6
1997	Chad Kessler, LSU	Sr.	39	1,961	66	*50.3
1998	Joe Kristosik, UNLV	Sr.	76	3,509	69	46.2
1999	Andrew Bayes, East Caro.	Sr.	47	2,259	78	48.1
2000	Preston Gruening, Minnesota	So.	46	2,080	65	45.2
2001	Travis Dorsch, Purdue	Sr.	49	2,370	79	48.4
2002	Matt Payne, Brigham Young	So.	51	2,427	76	47.6

Record. ‡Record for minimum of 50 punts.

Punt Returns

CAREER AVERAGE
(Minimum 1.2 Returns Per Game; Minimum 30 Returns)

Player, Team	Years	No.	Yards	TD	Long	Avg.
Jack Mitchell, Oklahoma	1946-48	39	922	**7	70	*23.6
Gene Gibson, Cincinnati	1949-50	37	760	4	75	‡20.5
Eddie Macon, Pacific (Cal.)	1949-51	48	907	4	**100	18.9
Jackie Robinson, UCLA	1939-40	37	694	2	89	18.8
Bobby Dillon, Texas	1949-51	47	830	1	84	17.7
Mike Fuller, Auburn	1972-74	50	883	3	63	17.7
Bobby Newcombe, Nebraska	1997-00	48	829	3	94	17.3
James Dye, Brigham Young/Utah St.	1992-93, 95-96	61	1,046	5	90	17.2
George Hoey, Michigan	1966-68	31	529	1	60	17.1
Erroll Tucker, Utah	1984-85	38	650	3	89	17.1
Henry Pryor, Rutgers	1948-49	37	625	1	85	16.9
Jack Christiansen, Colorado St.	1948-50	37	626	2	89	16.9
Adolph Bellizeare, Pennsylvania	1972-74	33	557	3	73	16.9
Ken Hatfield, Arkansas	1962-64	70	1,135	5	95	16.2
Gene Rossides, Columbia	1945-48	53	851	3	70	16.1
Bill Hillenbrand, Indiana	1941-42	65	1,042	2	88	16.0

*Record. **Record tied. ‡Record for minimum 1.5 returns per game.*

SEASON AVERAGE
(Minimum 1.2 Returns Per Game)

Player, Team	Year	No.	Yards	Avg.
Bill Blackstock, Tennessee	1951	12	311	*25.9
George Sims, Baylor	1948	15	375	25.0
Gene Derricotte, Michigan	1947	14	347	24.8
George Hoey, Michigan	1967	12	291	24.3
Erroll Tucker, Utah	†1985	16	389	24.3
Floyd Little, Syracuse	1965	18	423	23.5

Record. †National champion. ‡Ranked for minimum 1.5 returns per game.

ANNUAL CHAMPIONS
(Ranked on Total Yards Until 1970)

Year	Player, Team	Class	No.	Yards	Avg.
1939	Bosh Pritchard, VMI	So.	42	583	13.9
1940	Junie Hovious, Mississippi	Sr.	33	498	15.1
1941	Bill Geyer, Colgate	Sr.	33	616	18.7
1942	Bill Hillenbrand, Indiana	Jr.	23	481	20.9
1943	Marion Flanagan, Texas A&M	Jr.	49	475	9.7
1944	Joe Stuart, California	Jr.	39	372	9.5
1945	Jake Leicht, Oregon	So.	28	395	14.1

Year	Player, Team	Class	No.	Yards	Avg.
1946	Harry Gilmer, Alabama	Jr.	37	436	11.8
1947	Lindy Berry, TCU	So.	42	493	11.7
1948	Lee Nalley, Vanderbilt	Jr.	43	*791	18.4
1949	Lee Nalley, Vanderbilt	Sr.	35	498	14.2
1950	Dave Waters, Wash. & Lee	Jr.	30	445	14.8
1951	Tom Murphy, Holy Cross	So.	25	533	21.3
1952	Horton Nesrsta, Rice	Jr.	44	536	12.2
1953	Paul Giel, Minnesota	Sr.	17	288	16.9
1954	Dicky Maegle, Rice	Sr.	15	293	19.5
1955	Mike Sommer, George Washington	So.	24	330	13.8
1956	Bill Stacy, Mississippi St.	Jr.	24	290	12.1
1957	Bobby Mulgado, Arizona St.	Sr.	14	267	19.1
1958	Howard Cook, Colorado	Sr.	24	242	10.1
1959	Pervis Atkins, New Mexico St.	Jr.	16	241	15.1
1960	Lance Alworth, Arkansas	Jr.	18	307	17.1
1961	Lance Alworth, Arkansas	Sr.	28	336	12.0
1962	Darrell Roberts, Utah St.	Sr.	16	333	20.8
1963	Ken Hatfield, Arkansas	Jr.	21	350	16.7
1964	Ken Hatfield, Arkansas	Sr.	31	518	16.7
1965	Nick Rassas, Notre Dame	Sr.	24	459	19.1
1966	Vic Washington, Wyoming	Jr.	34	443	13.0
1967	Mike Battle, Southern California	Jr.	47	570	12.1
1968	Roger Wehrli, Missouri	Sr.	41	478	11.7
1969	Chris Farasopoulous, Brigham Young	Jr.	35	527	15.1

Beginning in 1970, ranked on average per return (instead of total yards)‡

Year	Player, Team	Class	No.	Yards	TD	Long	Avg.
1970	Steve Holden, Arizona St.	So.	17	327	2	94	19.2
1971	Golden Richards, Brigham Young	Jr.	33	624	**4	87	18.9
1972	Randy Rhino, Georgia Tech	So.	25	441	1	96	17.6
1973	Gary Hayman, Penn St.	Sr.	23	442	1	83	19.2
1974	John Provost, Holy Cross	Sr.	13	238	2	85	18.3
1975	Donnie Ross, New Mexico St.	Sr.	21	338	1	#81	16.1
1976	Henry Jenkins, Rutgers	Sr.	30	449	0	#40	15.0
1977	Robert Woods, Grambling	Sr.	††11	279	3	72	25.4
1978	Ira Matthews, Wisconsin	Sr.	16	270	3	78	16.9
1979	Jeffrey Shockley, Tennessee St.	Sr.	27	456	1	79	16.9
1980	Scott Woerner, Georgia	Sr.	31	488	1	67	15.7
1981	Glen Young, Mississippi St.	Jr.	19	307	2	87	16.2
1982	Lionel James, Auburn	Jr.	25	394	0	#63	15.8
1983	Jim Sandusky, San Diego St.	Sr.	20	381	1	90	19.0
1984	Ricky Nattiel, Florida	So.	22	346	1	67	15.7
1985	Erroll Tucker, Utah	Sr.	16	389	2	89	24.3
1986	Rod Smith, Nebraska	Jr.	‡‡12	227	1	63	18.9
1987	Alan Grant, Stanford	Jr.	27	446	2	77	16.5
1988	Deion Sanders, Florida St.	Jr.	33	503	1	76	15.2
1989	Larry Hargrove, Ohio	Sr.	17	309	2	83	18.2
1990	Dave McCloughan, Colorado	Sr.	32	524	2	90	16.4
1991	Bo Campbell, Virginia Tech	Jr.	15	273	0	45	18.2
1992	Lee Gissendaner, Northwestern	Jr.	15	327	1	72	21.8
1993	Aaron Glenn, Texas A&M	Sr.	17	339	2	76	19.9
1994	Steve Clay, Eastern Mich.	Jr.	14	278	1	65	19.9
1995	James Dye, Brigham Young	Jr.	20	438	2	90	21.9
1996	Allen Rossum, Notre Dame	Jr.	15	344	3	83	22.9
1997	Tim Dwight, Iowa	Sr.	19	367	3	—	19.3
1998	David Allen, Kansas St.	So.	33	730	**4	93	22.1
1999	Dennis Northcutt, Arizona	Sr.	23	436	2	81	19.0
2000	Aaron Lockett, Kansas St.	Jr.	22	501	3	83	22.8
2001	Roman Hollowell, Colorado	Sr.	29	522	2	77	18.0
2002	Dan Sheldon, Northern Ill.	So.	21	477	3	90	22.7

*Record. **Record tied. #Did not score. ‡Ranked on minimum 1.5 returns per game, 1970-73; 1.2 from 1974. ††Declared champion; with three more returns (making 1.3 per game) for zero yards still would have highest average. ‡‡Declared champion; with two more returns (making 1.2 per game) for zero yards still would have highest average.*

ANNUAL PUNT RETURN LEADERS (1939-69)
BASED ON AVERAGE PER RETURN
(Minimum 1.2 Returns Per Game)

1939—Jackie Robinson, UCLA, 20.0; **1940**—Jackie Robinson, UCLA, 21.0; **1941**—Walt Slater, Tennessee, 20.4; **1942**—Billy Hillenbrand, Indiana, 20.9; **1943**—Otto Graham, Northwestern, 19.7; **1944**—Glenn Davis, Army, 18.4; **1945**—Jake Leicht, Oregon, 14.8; **1946**—Harold Griffin, Florida, 20.1; **1947**—Gene Derricotte, Michigan, 24.8; **1948**—George Sims, Baylor, ‡25.0; **1949**—Gene Evans, Wisconsin, 21.8; **1950**—Lindy Hanson, Boston U., 22.5; **1951**—Bill Blackstock, Tennessee, *25.9; **1952**—Gil Reich, Kansas, 17.2; **1953**—Bobby Lee, New Mexico, 19.4; **1954**—Dicky Maegle, Rice, 19.5; **1955**—Ron Lind, Drake, 21.1; **1956**—Ron Lind, Drake, 19.1; **1957**—Bobby Mulgado, Arizona St., 19.1; **1958**—Herb Hallas, Yale, 23.4; **1959**—Jacque MacKinnon, Colgate, 17.5; **1960**—Pat Fischer, Nebraska, 21.2; **1961**—Tom Larscheid, Utah St., 23.4; **1962**—Darrell Roberts, Utah St., 20.8; **1963**—Rickie Harris, Arizona, 17.4; **1964**—Ken Hatfield, Arkansas, 16.7; **1965**—Floyd Little, Syracuse, 23.5; **1966**—Don Bean, Houston, 20.2; **1967**—George Hoey, Michigan, 24.3; **1968**—Rob Bordley, Princeton, 20.5; **1969**—George Hannen, Davidson, 22.4.

Record. ‡Record for minimum 1.5 returns per game.

Kickoff Returns

CAREER AVERAGE
(Minimum 1.2 Returns Per Game; Minimum 30 Returns)

Player, Team	Years	No.	Yards	Avg.
Anthony Davis, Southern California	1972-74	37	1,299	*35.1
Eric Booth, Southern Miss.	1994-97	35	1,135	32.4
Overton Curtis, Utah St.	1957-58	32	991	‡31.0
Fred Montgomery, New Mexico St.	1991-92	39	1,191	30.5
Altie Taylor, Utah St.	1966-68	40	1,170	29.3
Stan Brown, Purdue	1968-70	49	1,412	28.8
Henry White, Colgate	1974-77	41	1,180	28.8
Kevin Johnson, Syracuse	1995-98	50	1,437	28.7
Pat Johnson, Oregon	1994-97	36	1,023	28.4
Ben Kelly, Colorado	1997-99	64	1,798	28.1
Paul Loughran, Temple	1970-72	40	1,123	28.1
Jim Krieg, Washington	1970-71	31	860	27.7

Record. ‡Record for minimum 1.5 returns per game.

SEASON AVERAGE
(Minimum 1.2 Returns Per Game)

Player, Team	Year	No.	Yards	Avg.
Paul Allen, Brigham Young	1961	12	481	*40.1
Tremain Mack, Miami (Fla.)	†1996	13	514	39.5
Leeland McElroy, Texas A&M	†1993	15	590	39.3
Forrest Hall, San Francisco	†1946	15	573	‡38.2
Tony Ball, Chattanooga	†1977	13	473	36.4
George Marinkov, North Carolina St.	1954	13	465	35.8
Bob Baker, Cornell	1964	11	386	35.1

Record. †National champion. ‡Record for minimum 1.5 returns per game.

ANNUAL CHAMPIONS
(Ranked on Total Yards Until 1970)

Year	Player, Team	Class	No.	Yards	Avg.
1939	Nile Kinnick, Iowa	Sr.	15	377	25.1
1940	Jack Emigh, Montana	Sr.	18	395	21.9
1941	Earl Ray, Wyoming	So.	23	496	21.6
1942	Frank Porto, California	Sr.	17	483	28.4
1943	Paul Copoulos, Marquette	So.	11	384	34.9
1944	Paul Copoulos, Marquette	Jr.	14	337	24.1
1945	Al Dekdebrun, Cornell	Sr.	14	321	22.9
1946	Forrest Hall, San Francisco	Jr.	15	573	**38.2
1947	Doak Walker, Southern Methodist	So.	10	387	38.7
1948	Bill Gregus, Wake Forest	Jr.	19	503	26.5
1949	Johnny Subda, Nevada	Sr.	18	444	24.7
1950	Chuck Hill, New Mexico	Jr.	27	729	27.0
1951	Chuck Hill, New Mexico	Sr.	17	504	29.6
1952	Curly Powell, VMI	Sr.	27	517	19.1
1953	Max McGee, Tulane	Sr.	17	371	21.8
1954	Art Luppino, Arizona	So.	20	632	31.6
1955	Sam Woolwine, VMI	Jr.	22	471	21.4
1956	Sam Woolwine, VMI	Sr.	18	503	27.9
1957	Overton Curtis, Utah St.	Jr.	23	695	30.2
1958	Sonny Randle, Virginia	Sr.	21	506	24.1
1959	Don Perkins, New Mexico	Sr.	15	520	34.7
1960	Bruce Samples, Brigham Young	Sr.	23	577	25.1
1961	Dick Mooney, Idaho	Sr.	23	494	21.5
1962	Donnie Frederick, Wake Forest	Sr.	29	660	22.8
1963	Gary Wood, Cornell	Sr.	19	618	32.5
1964	Dan Bland, Mississippi St.	Jr.	20	558	27.9
1965	Eric Crabtree, Pittsburgh	Sr.	25	636	25.4
1966	Marcus Rhoden, Mississippi St.	Sr.	26	572	22.0

Year	Player, Team	Class	No.	Yards	Avg.
1967	Joe Casas, New Mexico	Sr.	23	602	26.2
1968	Mike Adamle, Northwestern	So.	34	732	21.5
1969	Stan Brown, Purdue	Jr.	26	698	26.8

Beginning in 1970, ranked on average per return (instead of total yards)‡

Year	Player, Team	Class	No.	Yards	Avg.
1970	Stan Brown, Purdue	Sr.	19	638	33.6
1971	Paul Loughran, Temple	Jr.	15	502	33.5
1972	Larry Williams, Texas Tech	So.	16	493	30.8
1973	Steve Odom, Utah	Sr.	21	618	29.4
1974	Anthony Davis, Southern California	Sr.	††11	467	42.5
1975	John Schultz, Maryland	Sr.	13	403	31.0
1976	Ira Matthews, Wisconsin	So.	14	415	29.6
1977	Tony Ball, Chattanooga	Fr.	13	473	36.4
1978	Drew Hill, Georgia Tech	Sr.	19	570	30.0
1979	Stevie Nelson, Ball St.	Fr.	18	565	31.4
1980	Mike Fox, San Diego St.	So.	†11	361	32.8
1981	Frank Minnifield, Louisville	Jr.	11	334	30.4
1982	Carl Monroe, Utah	Sr.	14	421	30.1
1983	Henry Williams, East Caro.	Jr.	19	591	31.1
1984	Keith Henderson, Texas Tech	Fr.	13	376	28.9
1985	Erroll Tucker, Utah	Sr.	24	698	29.1
1986	Terrance Roulhac, Clemson	Sr.	17	561	33.0
1987	Barry Sanders, Oklahoma St.	So.	14	442	31.6
1988	Raghib Ismail, Notre Dame	Fr.	#12	433	36.1
1989	Tony Smith, Southern Miss.	So.	14	455	32.5
1990	Dale Carter, Tennessee	Jr.	17	507	29.8
1991	Fred Montgomery, New Mexico St.	Jr.	25	734	29.4
1992	Fred Montgomery, New Mexico St.	Sr.	14	457	32.6
1993	Leeland McElroy, Texas A&M	Fr.	15	590	39.3
1994	Eric Moulds, Mississippi St.	Jr.	†13	426	32.8
1995	Robert Tate, Cincinnati	Jr.	15	515	34.3
1996	Tremain Mack, Miami (Fla.)	Jr.	13	514	39.5
1997	Eric Booth, Southern Miss.	Sr.	22	766	34.8
1998	Broderick McGrew, North Texas	Jr.	18	587	32.6
1999	James Williams, Marshall	Sr.	15	493	32.9
2000	LaTarence Dunbar, TCU	So.	15	506	33.7
2001	Chris Massey, Oklahoma St.	Jr.	15	522	34.8
2002	Charles Pauley, San Jose St.	Sr.	31	978	31.6

**Record for minimum 1.5 returns per game. #Declared champion; with two more returns (making 1.3 per game) for zero yards still would have highest average. †Declared champion; with one more return (making 1.2 per game) for zero yards still would have highest average. ††Declared champion; with three more returns (making 1.3 per game) for zero yards still would have highest average. ‡Ranked on minimum 1.5 returns per game, 1970-73; 1.2 from 1974.*

ANNUAL KICKOFF RETURN LEADERS (1939-69)
BASED ON AVERAGE PER RETURN
(Minimum 1.2 Returns Per Game)

1939—Nile Kinnick, Iowa, 25.1; **1940**—Bill Geyer, Colgate, 27.0; **1941**—Vern Lockard, Colorado, 24.4; **1942-45**—Not compiled; **1946**—Forrest Hall, San Francisco, ‡38.2; **1947**—Skippy Minisi, Pennsylvania, 28.8; **1948**—Jerry Williams, Washington St., 29.9; **1949**—Billy Conn, Georgetown, 31.1; **1950**—Johnny Turco, Holy Cross, 27.4; **1951**—Bob Mischak, Army, 31.3; **1952**—Carroll Hardy, Colorado, 32.2; **1953**—Carl Bolt, Wash. & Lee, 27.1; **1954**—George Marinkov, North Carolina St., 35.8; **1955**—Jim Brown, Syracuse, 32.0; **1956**—Paul Hornung, Notre Dame, 31.0; **1957**—Overton Curtis, Utah St., 30.2; **1958**—Marshall Starks, Illinois, 26.3; **1959**—Don Perkins, New Mexico, 34.7; **1960**—Tom Hennessey, Holy Cross, 33.4; **1961**—Paul Allen, Brigham Young, *40.1; **1962**—Larry Coyer, Marshall, 30.2; **1963**—Gary Wood, Cornell, 32.5; **1964**—Bob Baker, Cornell, 35.1; **1965**—Tom Barrington, Ohio St., 34.3; **1966**—Frank Moore, Louisville, 27.9; **1967**—Altie Taylor, Utah St., 31.9; **1968**—Kerry Reardon, Iowa, 32.1; **1969**—Chris Farasopoulous, Brigham Young, 32.2.

Record. ‡Record for minimum 1.5 returns per game.

All-Purpose Yards

CAREER YARDS PER GAME
(Minimum 3,500 Yards)

Player, Team	Years	G	Rush	Rcv.	Int.	PR	KOR	Yds.	Yd.PG
Ryan Benjamin, Pacific (Cal.)	1990-92	24	3,119	1,063	0	100	1,424	5,706	*237.8
Sheldon Canley, San Jose St.	1988-90	25	2,513	828	0	5	1,800	5,146	205.8
Howard Stevens, Louisville	1971-72	20	2,723	389	0	401	360	3,873	193.7
O.J. Simpson, Southern California	1967-68	19	3,124	235	0	0	307	3,666	192.9
Alex Van Dyke, Nevada	1994-95	22	7	3,100	0	5	1,034	4,146	188.5
Ed Marinaro, Cornell	1969-71	27	4,715	225	0	0	0	4,940	183.0
Marshall Faulk, San Diego St.	1991-93	31	4,589	973	0	0	33	5,595	180.5
Troy Edwards, Louisiana Tech	1996-98	34	447	4,352	0	241	991	6,031	177.4
Herschel Walker, Georgia	1980-82	33	5,259	243	0	0	247	5,749	174.2
Louie Giammona, Utah St.	1973-75	30	3,499	171	0	188	1,345	5,203	173.4

*Record.

SEASON YARDS PER GAME

Player, Team	Years	Rush	Rcv.	Int.	PR	KOR	Yds.	Yd.PG
Barry Sanders, Oklahoma St.	†1988	*2,628	106	0	95	421	*3,250	*295.5
Ryan Benjamin, Pacific (Cal.)	†1991	1,581	612	0	4	798	2,995	249.6
Byron "Whizzer" White, Colorado	†1937	1,121	0	103	587	159	1,970	246.3
Mike Pringle, Cal St. Fullerton	†1989	1,727	249	0	0	714	2,690	244.6
Paul Palmer, Temple	†1986	1,866	110	0	0	657	2,633	239.4
Emmett White, Utah St.	†2000	1,322	592	0	183	531	2,628	238.9
Ryan Benjamin, Pacific (Cal.)	†1992	1,441	434	0	96	626	2,597	236.1
Marcus Allen, Southern California	†1981	2,342	217	0	0	0	2,559	232.6
Troy Edwards, Louisiana Tech	†1998	227	*1,996	0	235	326	2,784	232.0
Sheldon Canley, San Jose St.	1989	1,201	353	0	0	959	2,513	228.5
Ollie Matson, San Francisco	†1951	1,566	58	18	115	280	2,037	226.3
Troy Davis, Iowa St.	†1995	2,010	159	0	0	297	2,466	224.2
Alex Van Dyke, Nevada	1995	6	1,854	0	0	583	2,443	222.1
Art Luppino, Arizona	†1954	1,359	50	84	68	632	2,193	219.3
Chuck Weatherspoon, Houston	1989	1,146	735	0	715	95	2,391	217.4
Anthony Thompson, Indiana	1989	1,793	201	0	0	394	2,388	217.1
Ricky Williams, Texas	1998	2,124	262	0	0	0	2,386	216.9
Napoleon McCallum, Navy	†1983	1,587	166	0	272	360	2,385	216.8
Troy Davis, Iowa St.	†1996	2,185	61	0	0	118	2,364	214.9
Ed Marinaro, Cornell	†1971	1,881	51	0	0	0	1,932	214.7
Rashaan Salaam, Colorado	†1994	2,055	294	0	0	0	2,349	213.6
Howard Stevens, Louisville	†1972	1,294	221	0	337	240	2,132	213.2
Napoleon McCallum, Navy	†1985	1,327	358	0	157	488	2,330	211.8
Brian Pruitt, Central Mich.	1994	1,890	69	0	0	330	2,289	208.1
Keith Byars, Ohio St.	†1984	1,655	453	0	0	176	2,284	207.6
Mike Rozier, Nebraska	1983	2,148	106	0	0	232	2,486	207.2

*Record. †National champion.

CAREER YARDS

Player, Team	Years	Rush	Rcv.	Int.	PR	KOR	Yds.	Yd.PP
Ricky Williams, Texas	1995-98	6,279	927	0	0	0	*7,206	6.6
Napoleon McCallum, Navy	$1981-85	4,179	796	0	858	1,339	7,172	6.3
Darrin Nelson, Stanford	1977-78, 80-81	4,033	2,368	0	471	13	6,885	7.1
Kevin Faulk, LSU	1995-98	4,557	600	0	857	819	6,833	6.8
Ron Dayne, Wisconsin	1996-99	*6,397	304	0	0	0	6,701	5.8
Terance Mathis, New Mexico	1985-87, 89	329	4,254	0	115	1,993	6,691	**14.6
Tony Dorsett, Pittsburgh	1973-76	6,082	406	0	0	127	6,615	5.9
Paul Palmer, Temple	1983-86	4,895	705	0	12	997	6,609	6.1
Charles White, Southern California	1976-79	5,598	507	0	0	440	6,545	6.0
Trevor Cobb, Rice	1989-92	4,948	892	0	21	651	6,512	5.3
LaDainian Tomlinson, TCU	1997-00	5,263	236	0	0	838	6,337	6.4
Glyn Milburn, Oklahoma/Stanford	1988, 90-92	2,302	1,495	0	1,145	1,246	6,188	8.1
Travis Prentice, Miami (Ohio)	1996-99	5,596	527	0	0	0	6,123	5.1
Anthony Thompson, Indiana	1986-89	4,965	713	0	0	412	6,090	5.1
Troy Edwards, Louisiana Tech	1996-98	447	4,352	0	241	991	6,031	15.8
Archie Griffin, Ohio St.	1972-75	5,177	286	0	0	540	6,003	6.7
Ron "Po" James, New Mexico St.	1968-71	3,884	217	0	8	1,870	5,979	6.5
Eric Wilkerson, Kent St.	1985-88	3,830	506	0	0	1,638	5,974	7.0
Steve Bartalo, Colorado St.	1983-86	4,813	1,079	0	0	0	5,892	4.4
Emmett White, Utah St.	1998-01	2,791	1,044	0	669	1,368	5,872	8.0
Wilford White, Arizona St.	1947-50	3,173	892	212	798	791	5,866	9.2
Leon Johnson, North Carolina	1993-96	3,693	1,288	0	390	457	5,828	5.9
Joe Washington, Oklahoma	1972-75	3,995	253	0	807	726	5,781	7.3
Herschel Walker, Georgia	1980-82	5,259	243	0	0	247	‡5,749	5.6
George Swarn, Miami (Ohio)	1983-86	4,172	1,057	0	0	498	5,727	5.6
Chuck Weatherspoon, Houston	1987-90	3,247	1,375	0	611	482	5,715	9.7
Ryan Benjamin, Pacific (Cal.)	1990-92	3,119	1,063	0	100	1,424	‡5,706	8.8
Eric Metcalf, Texas	1985-88	2,661	1,394	0	1,076	574	5,705	6.7
Denvis Manns, New Mexico St.	1995-98	4,692	620	0	0	384	5,696	5.9
George Rogers, South Carolina	1977-80	4,958	371	0	0	339	5,668	5.9
Napoleon Kaufman, Washington	1991-94	4,041	424	0	368	825	5,658	6.7
Jamie Morris, Michigan	1984-87	3,944	703	0	0	984	5,631	6.4
Joe Morris, Syracuse	1978-81	4,299	278	0	0	1,023	5,600	6.3

Player, Team	Years	Rush	Rcv.	Int.	PR	KOR	Yds.	Yd.PP
Deoncé Whitaker, San Jose St.	1998-01	3,515	225	0	19	1,837	5,596	7.8
James Brooks, Auburn	1977-80	3,523	219	0	128	1,726	5,596	7.6
Marshall Faulk, San Diego St.	1991-93	4,589	973	0	0	33	‡5,595	6.6
Johnny Rodgers, Nebraska	1970-72	745	2,479	0	1,515	847	‡5,586	13.8

*Record. $See page 8 for explanation. ‡Three-year totals. **Record for minimum 375 plays.

SEASON YARDS

Player, Team	Year	Rush	Rcv.	Int.	PR	KOR	Yds.	Yd.PP
Barry Sanders, Oklahoma St.	†1988	*2,628	106	0	95	421	*3,250	8.3
Ryan Benjamin, Pacific (Cal.)..........................	†1991	1,581	612	0	4	798	2,995	9.6
Troy Edwards, Louisiana Tech........................	†1998	227	1,996	0	235	326	2,784	14.7
Mike Pringle, Cal St. Fullerton....................	†1989	1,727	249	0	0	714	2,690	7.6
Larry Johnson, Penn St.	†2002	2,087	349	0	0	219	2,655	8.2
Paul Palmer, Temple	†1986	1,866	110	0	0	657	2,633	6.8
Emmett White, Utah St.	†2000	1,322	592	0	183	531	2,628	7.9
Ryan Benjamin, Pacific (Cal.).....................	†1992	1,441	434	0	96	626	2,597	8.1
Bernard Berrian, Fresno St.	2001	101	1,270	0	552	668	2,591	‡17.5
Marcus Allen, Southern California..............	†1981	2,342	217	0	0	0	2,559	5.9
Sheldon Canley, San Jose St.	1989	1,201	353	0	0	959	2,513	7.4
Mike Rozier, Nebraska	1983	2,148	106	0	0	232	2,486	8.4
Troy Davis, Iowa St.	†1995	2,010	159	0	0	297	2,466	6.7
Alex Van Dyke, Nevada	1995	6	1,854	0	0	583	2,443	15.7
Chuck Weatherspoon, Houston	1989	1,146	735	0	415	95	2,391	10.7
Anthony Thompson, Indiana.....................	1989	1,793	201	0	0	394	2,388	5.8
Ricky Williams, Texas	1998	2,124	262	0	0	0	2,386	6.2
Napoleon McCallum, Navy	†1983	1,587	166	0	272	360	2,385	6.1
Troy Davis, Iowa St.	†1996	2,185	61	0	0	118	2,364	5.7
Rashaan Salaam, Colorado	†1994	2,055	294	0	0	0	2,349	7.3
Napoleon McCallum, Navy	†1985	1,327	358	0	157	488	2,330	6.3
Brian Pruitt, Central Mich.	1994	1,890	69	0	0	330	2,289	7.3
Michael Turner, Northern Ill.	2002	1,915	100	0	0	269	2,284	6.4
Keith Byars, Ohio St.	†1984	1,655	453	0	0	176	2,284	6.4
Byron Hanspard, Texas Tech..................	1996	2,084	192	0	0	0	2,276	6.4
Mewelde Moore, Tulane.........................	2001	1,421	756	0	0	82	2,259	6.8
Dennis Northcutt, Arizona	1999	200	1,422	0	436	191	2,249	16.8
Eddie George, Ohio St.	1995	1,826	399	0	0	0	2,225	6.4
Glyn Milburn, Stanford	†1990	729	632	0	267	594	2,222	8.4
Sheldon Canley, San Jose St.	1990	1,248	386	0	5	574	2,213	6.3
Vaughn Dunbar, Indiana.........................	1991	1,699	252	0	0	262	2,213	5.9
Johnny Johnson, San Jose St.	1988	1,219	668	0	0	315	2,202	7.1
Levron Williams, Indiana........................	†2001	1,401	289	0	0	511	2,201	8.5

*Record. †National champion. ‡Record for minimum 125 plays.

ALL-PURPOSE SINGLE-GAME HIGHS

Yds.	Player, Team (Opponent)	Date
578	Emmett White, Utah St. (New Mexico St.)	Nov. 4, 2000
435	Brian Pruitt, Central Mich. (Toledo)	Nov. 5, 1994
429	Moe Williams, Kentucky (South Carolina)	Sept. 23, 1995
426	LaDainian Tomlinson, TCU (UTEP)	Nov. 20, 1999
424	Troy Edwards, Louisiana Tech (Nebraska)	Aug. 29, 1998
422	Marshall Faulk, San Diego St. (Pacific [Cal.])	Sept. 14, 1991
419	Randy Gatewood, UNLV (Idaho)	Sept. 17, 1994
417	Paul Palmer, Temple (East Caro.)	Nov. 10, 1986
417	Greg Allen, Florida St. (Western Caro.)	Oct. 31, 1981
416	Anthony Thompson, Indiana (Wisconsin)..	Nov. 11, 1989
411	Travis Prentice, Miami (Ohio) (Akron)	Nov. 6, 1999
411	John Leach, Wake Forest (Maryland)	Nov. 20, 1993
402	Ryan Benjamin, Pacific (Cal.) (Utah St.)	Nov. 21, 1992
401	Chuck Hughes, UTEP (North Texas)	Sept. 18, 1965
397	Eric Allen, Michigan St. (Purdue)	Oct. 30, 1971
388	Astron Whatley, Kent St. (Eastern Mich.)	Sept. 20, 1997
388	Ryan Benjamin, Pacific (Cal.) (Cal St. Fullerton)	Oct. 5, 1991
387	Kendal Smith, Utah St. (San Jose St.)	Oct. 22, 1988
387	Ron Johnson, Michigan (Wisconsin)	Nov. 16, 1968
386	Barry Sanders, Oklahoma St. (Kansas)...	Nov. 12, 1988
379	Glyn Milburn, Stanford (California)	Nov. 17, 1990
377	Robert Kilow, Arkansas St. (Mississippi)	Sept. 11, 1999
376	Kevin Faulk, LSU (Houston)	Sept. 7, 1996
375	Hodges Mitchell, Texas (Kansas)	Nov. 11, 2000
375	Alex Van Dyke, Nevada (Toledo)	Sept. 23, 1995
375	Rueben Mayes, Washington St. (Oregon St.)	Nov. 3, 1984
374	Troy Davis, Iowa St. (Missouri)	Sept. 28, 1996
374	Tony Dorsett, Pittsburgh (Penn St.)	Nov. 22, 1975
373	Barry Sanders, Oklahoma St. (Oklahoma)..	Nov. 5, 1988
372	Peter Warrick, Florida St. (Clemson)	Sept. 20, 1997
372	Chuck Weatherspoon, Houston (Eastern Wash.)...	Nov. 17, 1990

ANNUAL CHAMPIONS

Year	Player, Team	Class	Rush	Rcv.	Int.	PR	KOR	Yds.	Yd.PG
1937	Byron "Whizzer" White, Colorado	Sr.	1,121	0	103	587	159	1,970	246.3
1938	Parker Hall, Mississippi	Sr.	698	0	128	0	594	1,420	129.1
1939	Tom Harmon, Michigan	Jr.	868	110	98	0	132	1,208	151.0
1940	Tom Harmon, Michigan	Sr.	844	0	20	244	204	1,312	164.0

Year	Player, Team	Class	Rush	Rcv.	Int.	PR	KOR	Yds.	Yd.PG
1941	Bill Dudley, Virginia	Sr.	968	60	76	481	89	1,674	186.0
1942	records not available	—	—	—	—	—	—	—	—
1943	Stan Koslowski, Holy Cross	Fr.	784	63	50	438	76	1,411	176.4
1944	Red Williams, Minnesota	Jr.	911	0	0	242	314	1,467	163.0
1945	Bob Fenimore, Oklahoma St.	Jr.	1,048	12	129	157	231	1,577	197.1
1946	Rudy Mobley, Hardin-Simmons	Sr.	1,262	13	79	273	138	1,765	176.5
1947	Wilton Davis, Hardin-Simmons	So.	1,173	79	0	295	251	1,798	179.8
1948	Lou Kusserow, Columbia	Sr.	766	463	19	130	359	1,737	193.0
1949	Johnny Papit, Virginia	Jr.	1,214	0	0	0	397	1,611	179.0
1950	Wilford White, Arizona St.	Sr.	1,502	225	0	64	274	2,065	206.5
1951	Ollie Matson, San Francisco	Sr.	1,566	58	18	115	280	2,037	226.3
1952	Billy Vessels, Oklahoma	Sr.	1,072	165	10	120	145	1,512	151.2
1953	J.C. Caroline, Illinois	So.	1,256	52	0	129	33	1,470	163.3
1954	Art Luppino, Arizona	So.	1,359	50	84	68	632	2,193	219.3
1955	Jim Swink, TCU	Jr.	1,283	111	46	64	198	1,702	170.2
	Art Luppino, Arizona	Jr.	1,313	74	0	62	253	1,702	170.2
1956	Jack Hill, Utah St.	Sr.	920	215	132	21	403	1,691	169.1
1957	Overton Curtis, Utah St.	Jr.	616	193	60	44	695	1,608	160.8
1958	Dick Bass, Pacific (Cal.)	Jr.	1,361	121	5	164	227	1,878	187.8
1959	Pervis Atkins, New Mexico St.	Jr.	971	301	23	241	264	1,800	180.0
1960	Pervis Atkins, New Mexico St.	Sr.	611	468	23	218	293	1,613	161.3
1961	Jim Pilot, New Mexico St.	So.	1,278	20	0	161	147	1,606	160.6
1962	Gary Wood, Cornell	Jr.	889	7	0	69	430	1,395	155.0
1963	Gary Wood, Cornell	Sr.	818	15	0	57	618	1,508	167.6
1964	Donny Anderson, Texas Tech	Jr.	966	396	0	28	320	1,710	171.0
1965	Floyd Little, Syracuse	Jr.	1,065	248	0	423	254	1,990	199.0
1966	Frank Quayle, Virginia	So.	727	420	0	30	439	1,616	161.6
1967	O.J. Simpson, Southern California	Jr.	1,415	109	0	0	176	1,700	188.9
1968	O.J. Simpson, Southern California	Sr.	1,709	126	0	0	131	1,966	196.6
1969	Lynn Moore, Army	Sr.	983	44	0	223	545	1,795	179.5
1970	Don McCauley, North Carolina	Sr.	1,720	235	0	0	66	2,021	183.7
1971	Ed Marinaro, Cornell	Sr.	1,881	51	0	0	0	1,932	214.7
1972	Howard Stevens, Louisville	Sr.	1,294	221	0	377	240	2,132	213.2
1973	Willard Harrell, Pacific (Cal.)	Jr.	1,319	18	0	88	352	1,777	177.7
1974	Louie Giammona, Utah St.	Jr.	1,534	79	0	16	355	1,984	198.4
1975	Louie Giammona, Utah St.	Sr.	1,454	33	0	124	434	2,045	185.9
1976	Tony Dorsett, Pittsburgh	Sr.	1,948	73	0	0	0	2,021	183.7
1977	Earl Campbell, Texas	Sr.	1,744	111	0	0	0	1,855	168.6
1978	Charles White, Southern California	Jr.	1,760	191	0	0	145	2,096	174.7
1979	Charles White, Southern California	Sr.	1,803	138	0	0	0	1,941	194.1
1980	Marcus Allen, Southern California	Jr.	1,563	231	0	0	0	1,794	179.4
1981	Marcus Allen, Southern California	Sr.	2,342	217	0	0	0	2,559	232.6
1982	Carl Monroe, Utah	Sr.	1,507	108	0	0	421	2,036	185.1
1983	Napoleon McCallum, Navy	Jr.	1,587	166	0	272	360	2,385	216.8
1984	Keith Byars, Ohio St.	Jr.	1,655	453	0	0	176	2,284	207.6
1985	Napoleon McCallum, Navy	Sr.	1,327	358	0	157	488	2,330	211.8
1986	Paul Palmer, Temple	Sr.	1,866	110	0	0	657	2,633	239.4
1987	Eric Wilkerson, Kent St.	Jr.	1,221	269	0	0	584	2,074	188.6
1988	Barry Sanders, Oklahoma St.	Jr.	*2,628	106	0	95	421	*3,250	*295.5
1989	Mike Pringle, Cal St. Fullerton	Sr.	1,727	249	0	0	714	2,690	244.6
1990	Glyn Milburn, Stanford	So.	729	632	0	267	594	2,222	202.0
1991	Ryan Benjamin, Pacific (Cal.)	Jr.	1,581	612	0	4	798	2,995	249.6
1992	Ryan Benjamin, Pacific (Cal.)	Sr.	1,441	434	0	96	626	2,597	236.1
1993	LeShon Johnson, Northern Ill.	Sr.	1,976	106	0	0	0	2,082	189.3
1994	Rashaan Salaam, Colorado	Jr.	2,055	294	0	0	0	2,349	213.6
1995	Troy Davis, Iowa St.	So.	2,010	159	0	0	297	2,466	224.2
1996	Troy Davis, Iowa St.	Jr.	2,185	61	0	0	118	2,364	214.9
1997	Troy Edwards, Louisiana Tech	Jr.	190	1,707	0	6	241	2,144	194.9
1998	Troy Edwards, Louisiana Tech	Sr.	227	1,996	0	235	326	2,784	232.0
1999	Trevor Insley, Nevada	Sr.	5	*2,060	0	111	0	2,176	197.8
2000	Emmett White, Utah St.	Jr.	1,322	592	0	183	531	2,628	238.9
2001	Levron Williams, Indiana	Sr.	1,401	289	0	0	511	2,201	200.1
2002	Larry Johnson, Penn St.	Sr.	2,087	349	0	0	219	2,655	204.2

*Record.

Field Goals

CAREER FIELD GOALS

(One-inch tees were permitted in 1949, two-inch tees were permitted in 1965, and use of tees was eliminated in 1989. The goal posts were widened from 18 feet, 6 inches to 23 feet, 4 inches in 1959 and were narrowed back to 18 feet, 6 inches in 1991. In 1993, the hash marks were moved 6 feet, 8 inches closer to the center of the field, to 60 feet from each sideline.)

Player, Team	Years	Total	Pct.	Under 40 Yds.	40 Plus	Long	‡Won
Jeff Jaeger, Washington (S)	1983-86	*80-99	.808	59-68	21-31	52	5
John Lee, UCLA (S)	1982-85	79-92	@.859	54-56	25-36	52	**10
Jason Elam, Hawaii (S)	$1988-92	79-100	.790	50-55	29-45	56	3
Philip Doyle, Alabama (S)	1987-90	78-*105	.743	57-61	21-44	53	6
Luis Zendejas, Arizona St. (S)	1981-84	78-*105	.743	53-59	25-46	55	1
Kevin Butler, Georgia (S)	1981-84	77-98	.786	50-56	27-42	60	7
Max Zendejas, Arizona (S)	1982-85	77-104	.740	47-53	30-51	57	7
Carlos Huerta, Miami (Fla.) (S)	1988-91	73-91	.802	56-60	17-31	52	3
Derek Schmidt, Florida St. (S)	1984-87	73-104	.702	44-55	29-49	54	1
Fuad Reveiz, Tennessee (S)	1981-84	71-95	.747	45-53	26-42	60	7

Player, Team	Years	Total	Pct.	Under 40 Yds.	40 Plus	Long	‡Won
Barry Belli, Fresno St. (S)	1984-87	70-99	.707	47-53	23-46	55	5
Nelson Welch, Clemson (S)	1991-94	70-100	.700	49-64	21-36	53	7
Roman Anderson, Houston (S)	1988-91	70-101	.693	*61-*72	9-29	53	3
Collin Mackie, South Carolina (S)	1987-90	69-95	.726	48-57	21-38	52	5
Shayne Graham, Virginia Tech (S)	1996-99	68-93	.731	48-57	20-36	53	5
Larry Roach, Oklahoma St. (S)	1981-84	68-101	.673	46-54	22-47	56	5
Gary Gusman, Miami (Ohio) (S)	1984-87	68-94	.723	50-57	18-37	53	2
Rusty Hanna, Toledo (S)	1989-92	68-99	.687	51-58	17-41	51	3
Jeff Chandler, Florida (S)	$1997-01	67-80	.838	46-48	21-32	54	0
Sebastian Janikowski, Florida St. (S)	1997-99	66-83	.795	46-51	20-32	56	4
Owen Pochman, Brigham Young (S)	1997-00	66-91	.725	32-38	34-53	56	3
Paul Woodside, West Virginia (S)	1981-84	65-81	.802	45-49	20-32	55	5
Michael Proctor, Alabama (S)	1992-95	65-91	.714	48-64	17-27	53	5
John Diettrich, Ball St. (S)	1983-86	63-90	.700	42-50	21-40	62	5
Jason Hanson, Washington St. (S)	1988-91	63-96	.656	24-30	*39-*66	62	4
Travis Dorsch, Purdue (S)	1998-01	62-87	.713	39-51	23-36	50	1
Kenny Stucker, Ball St. (S)	1988-91	62-87	.713	45-51	17-36	52	4
Dan Eichloff, Kansas (S)	1990-93	62-87	.713	40-50	22-37	61	5
John Anderson, Washington (S)	1999-02	61-91	.670	42-58	19-33	56	3
Jeff Hall, Tennessee (S)	1995-98	61-89	.685	43-56	18-33	53	4
David Browndyke, LSU (S)	1986-89	61-75	.813	49-53	12-22	52	3
Todd Gregoire, Wisconsin (S)	1984-87	61-81	.753	48-56	13-25	54	6
Kanon Parkman, Georgia (S)	1991, 93-95	61-85	.718	52-61	9-24	48	1
Todd Wright, Arkansas (S)	1989-92	60-79	.759	41-47	19-32	50	2
Jess Atkinson, Maryland (S)	1981-84	60-82	.732	40-48	20-34	50	5
Kyle Bryant, Texas A&M (S)	1994-97	60-85	.706	38-48	22-37	61	3
Scott Sisson, Georgia Tech (S)	1989-92	60-88	.682	45-53	15-35	51	6
Obed Ariri, Clemson (S)	1977-80	60-92	.652	47-55	13-37	57	5
Chuck Nelson, Washington (S)	1980-82	59-72	.819	47-53	12-19	51	5
Phil Dawson, Texas (S)	1994-97	59-79	.747	33-38	26-41	54	3
Van Tiffin, Alabama (S)	1983-86	59-87	.678	32-38	27-49	57	5
John Hopkins, Stanford (S)	1987-90	59-88	.670	43-50	16-38	54	4

*Record. $See page 8 for explanation. **Record tied. @Record for minimum 55 attempts. ‡Number of games in which his field goal(s) provided the winning margin. (S) Soccer-style kicker.

SEASON FIELD GOALS

Player, Team	Years	Total	Pct.	Under 40 Yds.	40 Plus	Long	‡Won
John Lee, UCLA (S)	†1984	*29-33	.879	16-16	13-17	51	5
Paul Woodside, West Virginia (S)	†1982	28-31	.903	23-23	5-8	45	2
Luis Zendejas, Arizona St. (S)	†1983	28-37	.757	19-22	9-15	52	1
Fuad Reveiz, Tennessee (S)	1982	27-31	.871	14-14	13-17	60	2
Sebastian Janikowski, Florida St. (S)	†1998	27-32	.844	17-19	10-13	53	1
Billy Bennett, Georgia (S)	2002	26-33	.788	15-18	11-15	47	2
Jonathan Ruffin, Cincinnati (S)	†2000	26-29	.897	24-26	2-3	42	4
Mike Nugent, Ohio St. (S)	2002	25-28	.893	15-16	10-12	51	0
Chuck Nelson, Washington (S)	1982	25-26	*.962	22-23	3-3	49	1
Chris Jacke, UTEP (S)	1988	25-27	.926	11-11	*14-16	52	2
John Diettrich, Ball St. (S)	†1985	25-29	.862	16-17	9-12	54	2
Nick Novak, Maryland (S)	2002	24-28	.857	16-18	8-10	51	1
Jeff Babcock, Colorado St. (S)	2002	24-32	.750	17-22	7-10	46	1
Kendall Trainor, Arkansas (S)	†1988	24-27	.889	14-15	10-12	58	4
Brad Bohn, Utah St. (S)	1998	24-28	.857	21-22	3-6	51	2
Carlos Reveiz, Tennessee (S)	1985	24-28	.857	12-14	12-14	52	2
Chris White, Illinois (S)	1984	24-28	.857	16-17	8-11	52	1
Remy Hamilton, Michigan (S)	†1994	24-29	.828	23-27	1-2	42	2
Philip Doyle, Alabama (S)	†1990	24-29	.828	16-17	8-12	47	2
Bruce Kallmeyer, Kansas (S)	1983	24-29	.828	13-14	11-15	57	1
Mike Prindle, Western Mich. (S)	1984	24-30	.800	17-20	7-10	56	1

*Record. †National champion. ‡Number of games in which his field goal(s) provided the winning margin. (S) Soccer-style kicker.

SINGLE-GAME FIELD GOALS

No.	Player, Team (Opponent)	Date
7	Dale Klein, Nebraska (Missouri)	Oct. 19, 1985
7	Mike Prindle, Western Mich. (Marshall)	Sept. 29, 1984
6	Billy Bennett, Georgia (Georgia Tech)	Nov. 24, 2001
6	Josh McGee, North Carolina (Duke)	Nov. 20, 1999
6	Cory Wedel, Wyoming (Idaho)	Aug. 31, 1996
6	Rusty Hanna, Toledo (Northern Ill.)	Nov. 21, 1992
6	Philip Doyle, Alabama (La.-Lafayette)	Oct. 6, 1990
6	Sean Fleming, Wyoming (Arkansas St.)	Sept. 15, 1990
6	Bobby Raymond, Florida (Kentucky)	Nov. 17, 1984
6	John Lee, UCLA (San Diego St.)	Sept. 8, 1984
6	Bobby Raymond, Florida (Florida St.)	Dec. 3, 1983
6	Alan Smith, Texas A&M (Arkansas St.)	Sept. 17, 1983
6	Al Del Greco, Auburn (Kentucky)	Oct. 9, 1982
6	Vince Fusco, Duke (Clemson)	Oct. 16, 1976
6	Frank Nester, West Virginia (Villanova)	Sept. 9, 1972
6	Charley Gogolak, Princeton (Rutgers)	Sept. 25, 1965

ANNUAL CHAMPIONS

(From 1959-90, goal posts were 23 feet, 4 inches; and from 1991, narrowed to 18 feet, 6 inches)

Year	Player, Team	Total	PG	Pct.	Under 40 Yds.	40 Plus	Long	‡Won
1959	Karl Holzwarth, Wisconsin (C)	7-8	0.8	.875	7-8	0-0	29	4
1960	Ed Dyas, Auburn (C)	13-18	1.3	.722	13-17	0-1	37	2
1961	Greg Mather, Navy (C)	11-15	1.1	.733	9-12	2-3	45	1
1962	Bob Jencks, Miami (Ohio) (C)	8-11	0.8	.727	7-9	1-2	52	3
	Al Woodall, Auburn (C)	8-20	0.8	.400	8-13	0-7	35	0
1963	Billy Lothridge, Georgia Tech (C)	12-16	1.2	.750	10-14	2-2	41	3
1964	Doug Moreau, LSU (C)	13-20	1.3	.650	13-20	0-0	36	0
1965	Charley Gogolak, Princeton (S)	16-23	1.8	.696	7-10	9-13	54	0
1966	Jerry DePoyster, Wyoming (C)	13-*38	1.3	.342	7-13	6-*25	54	1
1967	Gerald Warren, North Carolina St. (C)	17-22	1.7	.773	13-14	4-8	47	1
1968	Bob Jacobs, Wyoming (C)	14-29	1.4	.483	10-15	4-14	51	2
1969	Bob Jacobs, Wyoming (C)	18-27	1.8	.667	13-16	5-11	43	2

Beginning in 1970, ranked on per-game (instead of total) made

Year	Player, Team	Total	PG	Pct.	Under 40 Yds.	40 Plus	Long	‡Won
1970	Kim Braswell, Georgia (C)	13-17	1.3	.765	11-14	2-3	43	0
1971	Nick Mike-Mayer, Temple (S)	12-17	1.3	.706	8-10	4-7	48	1
1972	Nick Mike-Mayer, Temple (S)	13-20	1.4	.650	10-11	3-9	44	3
1973	Rod Garcia, Stanford (S)	18-29	1.6	.621	10-14	8-15	59	2
1974	Dave Lawson, Air Force (C)	19-31	1.7	.613	13-14	6-17	60	1
1975	Don Bitterlich, Temple (S)	21-31	1.9	.677	13-14	8-17	56	0
1976	Tony Franklin, Texas A&M (S)	17-26	1.6	.654	9-12	8-14	65	0
1977	Paul Marchese, Kent St. (S)	18-27	1.8	.667	13-15	5-12	51	2
1978	Matt Bahr, Penn St. (S)	22-27	2.0	.815	19-20	3-7	50	3
1979	Ish Ordonez, Arkansas (S)	18-22	1.6	.818	12-14	6-8	50	2
1980	Obed Ariri, Clemson (S)	23-30	2.1	.767	18-19	5-11	52	3
1981	Bruce Lahay, Arkansas (S)	19-24	1.7	.792	12-15	7-9	49	4
	Kevin Butler, Georgia (S)	19-26	1.7	.731	11-14	8-12	52	0
	Larry Roach, Oklahoma St. (S)	19-28	1.7	.679	12-14	7-14	56	3
1982	Paul Woodside, West Virginia (S)	28-31	2.6	.903	23-23	5-8	45	2
1983	Luis Zendejas, Arizona St. (S)	28-37	2.6	.757	19-22	9-15	52	1
1984	John Lee, UCLA (S)	*29-33	*2.6	.879	16-16	13-17	51	5
1985	John Diettrich, Ball St. (S)	25-29	2.3	.862	16-17	9-12	54	2
1986	Chris Kinzer, Virginia Tech (C)	22-27	2.0	.815	14-17	8-10	50	5
1987	Collin Mackie, South Carolina (S)	23-30	2.1	.767	17-21	6-9	49	0
	Derek Schmidt, Florida St. (S)	23-31	2.1	.742	16-21	7-10	53	0
1988	Kendall Trainor, Arkansas (S)	24-27	2.2	.889	14-15	10-12	58	4
1989	Philip Doyle, Alabama (S)	22-25	2.0	.880	19-19	3-6	44	2
	Gregg McCallum, Oregon (S)	22-29	2.0	.759	15-15	7-14	47	2
	Roman Anderson, Houston (S)	22-34	2.0	.647	17-20	5-14	51	0
1990	Philip Doyle, Alabama (S)	24-29	2.2	.828	16-17	8-12	47	2
1991	Doug Brien, California (S)	19-28	1.7	.679	15-20	4-8	50	2
1992	Joe Allison, Memphis (S)	23-25	2.1	.920	13-14	10-11	51	1
1993	Michael Proctor, Alabama (S)	22-29	1.8	.759	15-20	7-9	53	0
1994	Remy Hamilton, Michigan (S)	24-29	2.2	.828	23-27	1-2	42	2
1995	Michael Reeder, TCU (S)	23-25	2.1	.920	19-19	4-6	47	3
1996	Rafael Garcia, Virginia (S)	21-27	1.9	.778	16-17	5-10	46	1
1997	Brad Palazzo, Tulane (S)	23-28	2.1	.821	15-15	8-15	52	0
1998	Sebastian Janikowski, Florida St. (S)	27-32	2.3	.844	17-19	10-13	53	1
1999	Sebastian Janikowski, Florida St. (S)	23-30	2.1	.767	15-18	8-12	54	0
2000	Jonathan Ruffin, Cincinnati (S)	26-29	2.4	.897	24-26	2-3	42	4
2001	Todd Sievers, Miami (Fla.) (S)	21-26	1.9	.808	14-17	7-9	48	1
2002	Nick Browne, TCU (S)	23-30	1.9	.767	18-20	5-10	50	0

*Record. ‡Number of games in which his field goal(s) provided the winning margin. (C) Conventional kicker. (S) Soccer-style kicker.

All-Time Longest Plays

Since 1941, official maximum length of all plays fixed at 100 yards.

RUSHING

Yds.	Player, Team (Opponent)	Year
99	Eric Vann, Kansas (Oklahoma)	1997
99	Kelsey Finch, Tennessee (Florida)	1977
99	Ralph Thompson, West Tex. A&M (Wichita St.)	1970
99	Max Anderson, Arizona St. (Wyoming)	1967
99	Gale Sayers, Kansas (Nebraska)	1963
98	Jerald Sowell, Tulane (Alabama)	1993
98	Darrell Thompson, Minnesota (Michigan)	1987
98	George Swarn, Miami, Ohio (Western Mich.)	1984
98	Mark Malone, Arizona St. (Utah St.)	1979
98	Stanley Howell, Mississippi St. (Southern Miss.)	1979
98	Steve Atkins, Maryland (Clemson)	1978
98	Granville Amos, VMI (William & Mary)	1964
98	Jim Thacker, Davidson (George Washington)	1952
98	Bill Powell, California (Oregon St.)	1951
98	Al Yannelli, Bucknell (Delaware)	1946
98	Meredith Warner, Iowa St. (Iowa Pre-Flight)	1943

PASSING

Yds.	Passer-Receiver, Team (Opponent)	Year
99	Jason Johnson-Brandon Marshall, Arizona (Idaho)	2001
99	Dan Urban-Justin McCariens, Northern Ill. (Ball State)	2000
99	Drew Brees-Vinny Sutherland, Purdue (Northwestern)	1999
99	Troy DeGar-Wes Caswell, Tulsa (Oklahoma)	1996
99	John Paci-Thomas Lewis, Indiana (Penn St.)	1993
99	Gino Torretta-Horace Copeland, Miami (Fla.) (Arkansas)	1991
99	Scott Ankrom-James Maness, TCU (Rice)	1984
99	Cris Collinsworth-Derrick Gaffney, Florida (Rice)	1977
99	Terry Peel-Robert Ford, Houston (San Diego St.)	1972
99	Terry Peel-Robert Ford, Houston (Syracuse)	1970
99	Colin Clapton-Eddie Jenkins, Holy Cross (Boston U.)	1970
99	Bo Burris-Warren McVea, Houston (Washington St.)	1966
99	Fred Owens-Jack Ford, Portland (St. Mary's [Cal.])	1947
98	Derrick Vickers-Rob Turner, Central Mich. (Northern Ill.)	2001
98	Chris Weinke-Marvin Minnis, Florida St. (Clemson)	2000
98	Joe Borchard-Troy Walters, Stanford (UCLA)	2000
98	Jose Davis-Eugene Baker, Kent St. (UCF)	1997
98	Mike Neu-Brian Oliver, Ball St. (Toledo)	1993
98	Tom Dubs-Richard Hill, Ohio (Kent St.)	1991
98	Paul Oates-Sean Foster, Long Beach St. (San Diego St.)	1989

DIVISION I-A

Yds.	Passer-Receiver, Team (Opponent)	Year
98	Barry Garrison-Al Owens, New Mexico (Brigham Young)	1987
98	Kelly Donohoe-Willie Vaughn, Kansas (Colorado)	1987
98	Jeff Martin-Mark Flaker, Drake (New Mexico St.)	1976
98	Pete Woods-Joe Stewart, Missouri (Nebraska)	1976
98	Dan Hagemann-Jack Steptoe, Utah (New Mexico)	1976
98	Bruce Shaw-Pat Kenney, North Carolina St. (Penn St.)	1972
98	Jerry Rhome-Jeff Jordan, Tulsa (Wichita St.)	1963
98	Bob Dean-Norman Dawson, Cornell (Navy)	1947

INTERCEPTION RETURNS

Since 1941, 73 players have returned interceptions 100 yards. The most recent:

Yds.	Player, Team (Opponent)	Year
100	Matt Nixon, California (Baylor)	2002
100	Nathan Ray, Fresno St. (Southern Methodist)	2002
100	Emmanuel Franklin, Arizona St. (San Diego St.)	2001
100	Marcus Hudson, North Carolina St. (Duke)	2001
100	Deltha O'Neal, California (Oregon)	1999
100	Pat Dennis, La.-Monroe (Nicholls St.)	1998
100	Steve Rosga, Colorado (Oklahoma St.)	1996
100	Michael Hicks, UTEP (Brigham Young)	1996
100	Mario Smith, Kansas St. (Missouri)	1996
100	Keion Carpenter, Virginia Tech (Miami [Fla.])	1996
100	Reggie Love, North Carolina (Tulane)	1994
100	Harold Lusk, Utah (Colorado St.)	1994
100	Marlon Kerner, Ohio St. (Purdue)	1993
100	Ray Jackson, Colorado St. (UTEP)	1993
100	John Hardy, California (Wisconsin)	1990
100	Ed Givens, Army (Lafayette)	1990

PUNT RETURNS

Yds.	Player, Team (Opponent)	Year
100	Courtney Davis, Bowling Green (Kent St.)	1996
100	Eddie Kennison, LSU (Mississippi St.)	1994
100‡	Richie Luzzi, Clemson (Georgia)	1968
100‡	Don Guest, California (Washington St.)	1966
100	Jimmy Campagna, Georgia (Vanderbilt)	1952
100	Hugh McElhenny, Washington (Southern California)	1951
100	Frank Brady, Navy (Maryland)	1951
100	Bert Rechichar, Tennessee (Wash. & Lee)	1950
100	Eddie Macon, Pacific (Cal.) (Boston U.)	1950

‡Return of field goal attempt.

KICKOFF RETURNS

Since 1941, 226 players have returned kickoffs 100 yards. The most recent:

Yds.	Player, Team (Opponent)	Year
100	C.J. Jones, Iowa (Southern California)	2002
100	Greg Heaggans, Kansas (Southwest Mo. St.)	2002
100	Derek Abney, Kentucky (Florida)	2002
100	Broderick Clark, Louisville (Kentucky)	2002
100	Jason Wright, Northwestern (TCU)	2002
100	Marquis Weeks, Virginia (North Carolina)	2002
100	Tyrone Walker, Western Mich. (Eastern Mich.)	2002
100	Tavon Mason, Virginia (Georgia Tech)	2001
100	Derrick Hamilton, Clemson (Maryland)	2001
100	Shawn Terry, West Virginia (Maryland)	2001
100	Herb Haygood, Michigan St. (Iowa)	2001
100	Corey Parchman, Ball St. (Toledo)	2001
100	Tom Pace, Arizona St. (UCLA)	2001
100	Howard Jackson, UTEP (Nevada)	2001
100	Chad Owens, Hawaii (Air Force)	2001
100	Chad Owens, Hawaii (Brigham Young)	2001
100	Tony Lukins, New Mexico St. (Tulsa)	2001
100	Julius Jones, Notre Dame (Nebraska)	2000
100	Shawn Terry, West Virginia (Syracuse)	2000
100	Tim Carter, Auburn (LSU)	2000
100	LaTarence Dunbar, TCU (Southern Methodist)	2000
100	Leonard Scott, Tennessee (Georgia)	1999
100	Bo Carroll, Florida (LSU)	1999
100	Ben Kelly, Colorado (Missouri)	1999
100	Lincoln Dupree, Eastern Mich. (Northern Ill.)	1999
100	Deltha O'Neal, California (Stanford)	1999
100	Deuce McAllister, Mississippi (Arkansas)	1999
100	Paul Arnold, Washington (Air Force)	1999

PUNTS

Yds.	Player, Team (Opponent)	Year
99	Pat Brady, Nevada (Loyola Marymount)	1950
96	George O'Brien, Wisconsin (Iowa)	1952
94	John Hadl, Kansas (Oklahoma)	1959
94	Carl Knox, TCU (Oklahoma St.)	1947
94	Preston Johnson, Southern Methodist (Pittsburgh)	1940

FUMBLE RETURNS

(Since 1992)

Yds.	Player, Team (Opponent)	Year
100	Kevin Thomas, UNLV (Baylor)	1999
100	Dan Dawson, Rice (UNLV)	1998
100	Paul Rivers, Rutgers (Pittsburgh)	1995
99	David Williams, Houston (East Caro.)	1998
99	Dennis Gibbs, Idaho (Boise St.)	1997
99	Izell McGill, Mississippi St. (Memphis)	1996
98	Cornelius Pearson, Eastern Mich. (Western Mich.)	1996
97	Josh Morgan, Mississippi St. (Brigham Young)	2000
97	Chris Martin, Northwestern (Air Force)	1994
97	Mike Collins, West Virginia (Missouri)	1993
97	Ernie Lewis, East Caro. (West Virginia)	1992
96	Ben Kelly, Colorado (Kansas)	1999
96	Jeff Arneson, Illinois (Ohio St.)	1992
95	Ben Hanks, Florida (Arkansas)	1995
94	Dorian Boose, Washington St. (Colorado)	1996

FIELD GOALS

Yds.	Player, Team (Opponent)	Year
67	Joe Williams, Wichita St. (Southern Ill.)	1978
67	Steve Little, Arkansas (Texas)	1977
67	Russell Erxleben, Texas (Rice)	1977
65†	Martin Gramatica, Kansas St. (Northern Ill.)	1998
65	Tony Franklin, Texas A&M (Baylor)	1976
64	Russell Erxleben, Texas (Oklahoma)	1977
64	Tony Franklin, Texas A&M (Baylor)	1976
63	Morten Andersen, Michigan St. (Ohio St.)	1981
63	Clark Kemble, Colorado St. (Arizona)	1975
62	Terance Kitchens, Texas A&M (Southern Miss.)	1999
62	Jason Hanson, Washington St. (UNLV)	1991
62	John Diettrich, Ball St. (Ohio)	1986
62#	Chip Lohmiller, Minnesota (Iowa)	1986
62	Tom Whelihan, Missouri (Colorado)	1986
62	Dan Christopulos, Wyoming (Colorado St.)	1977
62	Iseed Khoury, North Texas (Richmond)	1977
62	Dave Lawson, Air Force (Iowa St.)	1975
61	Garret Courtney, North Texas (Idaho)	1998
61$	Kyle Bryant, Texas A&M (Southern Miss.)	1994
61	Dan Eichloff, Kansas (Ball St.)	1992
61	Mark Porter, Kansas St. (Nebraska)	1988
61	Ralf Mojsiejenko, Michigan St. (Illinois)	1982
61	Steve Little, Arkansas (Tulsa)	1976
61	Wayne Latimer, Virginia Tech (Florida St.)	1975
61	Ray Guy, Southern Miss. (Utah St.)	1972
60	Derek Schorejs, Bowling Green (Toledo)	1995
60	John Hall, Wisconsin (Minnesota)	1995
60	Joe Nedney, San Jose St. (Wyoming)	1992
60	Don Shafer, Southern California (Notre Dame)	1986
60	Steve DeLine, Colorado St. (Air Force)	1985
60	Kevin Butler, Georgia (Clemson)	1984
60	Chris Perkins, Florida (Tulane)	1984
60	Fuad Reveiz, Tennessee (Georgia Tech)	1982
60	Russell Erxleben, Texas (Texas Tech)	1977
60	Bubba Hicks, Baylor (Rice)	1975
60	Dave Lawson, Air Force (Colorado)	1974
60	Tony Di Rienzo, Oklahoma (Kansas)	1973
60	Bill McClard, Arkansas (Southern Methodist)	1970

†Longest collegiate field goal without use of a kicking tee; all kicks after 1988 season were without the use of a tee. Also longest field goal with narrower (18'6") goal posts. $Longest field goal made by a freshman. #Longest field goal made indoors.

Team Champions

Annual Offense Champions

TOTAL OFFENSE

Year	Team	Avg.
1937	Colorado	375.4
1938	Fordham	341.6
1939	Ohio St.	309.3
1940	Lafayette	368.2
1941	Duke	372.2
1942	Georgia	429.5
1943	Notre Dame	418.0
1944	Tulsa	434.7
1945	Army	462.7
1946	Notre Dame	441.3
1947	Michigan	412.7
1948	Nevada	487.0
1949	Notre Dame	434.8
1950	Arizona St.	470.4
1951	Tulsa	480.1
1952	Tulsa	466.6
1953	Cincinnati	409.5
1954	Army	448.7
1955	Oklahoma	410.7
1956	Oklahoma	481.7
1957	Arizona St.	444.9
1958	Iowa	405.9
1959	Syracuse	451.5
1960	New Mexico St.	419.6
1961	Mississippi	418.7
1962	Arizona St.	384.4
1963	Utah St.	395.3
1964	Tulsa	461.8
1965	Tulsa	427.8
1966	Houston	437.2
1967	Houston	427.9
1968	Houston	562.0
1969	San Diego St.	532.2
1970	Arizona St.	514.5
1971	Oklahoma	566.5
1972	Arizona St.	516.5
1973	Arizona St.	565.5
1974	Oklahoma	507.7
1975	California	458.5
1976	Michigan	448.1
1977	Colgate	486.1
1978	Nebraska	501.4
1979	Brigham Young	521.4
1980	Brigham Young	535.0
1981	Arizona St.	498.7
1982	Nebraska	518.6
1983	Brigham Young	584.2
1984	Brigham Young	486.5
1985	Brigham Young	500.2
1986	San Jose St.	481.4
1987	Oklahoma	499.7
1988	Utah	526.8
1989	Houston	*624.9
1990	Houston	586.8
1991	Fresno St.	541.9
1992	Houston	519.5
1993	Nevada	569.1
1994	Penn St.	520.2
1995	Nevada	569.4
1996	Nevada	527.3
1997	Nebraska	513.7
1998	Louisville	559.6
1999	Georgia Tech	509.0
2000	Florida St.	549.0
2001	Brigham Young	542.9
2002	Boise St.	501.5

*Record.

RUSHING OFFENSE

Year	Team	Avg.
1937	Colorado	310.0
1938	Fordham	297.1
1939	Wake Forest	290.3
1940	Lafayette	306.4
1941	Missouri	307.7
1942	Hardin-Simmons	307.4
1943	Notre Dame	313.7
1944	Army	298.6
1945	Army	359.8
1946	Notre Dame	340.1
1947	Detroit	319.7
1948	UTEP	378.3
1949	UTEP	333.2
1950	Arizona St.	347.0
1951	Arizona St.	334.8
1952	Tulsa	321.5
1953	Oklahoma	306.9
1954	Army	322.0
1955	Oklahoma	328.9
1956	Oklahoma	391.0
1957	Colorado	322.4
1958	Pacific (Cal.)	259.6
1959	Syracuse	313.6
1960	Utah St.	312.0
1961	New Mexico St.	299.1
1962	Ohio St.	278.9
1963	Nebraska	262.6
1964	Syracuse	251.0
1965	Nebraska	290.0
1966	Harvard	269.0
1967	Houston	270.9
1968	Houston	361.7
1969	Texas	363.0
1970	Texas	374.5
1971	Oklahoma	*472.4
1972	Oklahoma	368.8
1973	UCLA	400.3
1974	Oklahoma	438.8
1975	Arkansas St.	340.5
1976	Michigan	362.6
1977	Oklahoma	328.9
1978	Oklahoma	427.5
1979	East Caro.	368.5
1980	Nebraska	378.3
1981	Oklahoma	334.3
1982	Nebraska	394.3
1983	Nebraska	401.7
1984	Army	345.3
1985	Nebraska	374.3
1986	Oklahoma	404.7
1987	Oklahoma	428.8
1988	Nebraska	382.3
1989	Nebraska	375.3
1990	Northern Ill.	344.6
1991	Nebraska	353.2
1992	Nebraska	328.2
1993	Army	298.5
1994	Nebraska	340.0
1995	Nebraska	399.8
1996	Army	346.5
1997	Nebraska	392.6
1998	Army	293.8
1999	Navy	292.2
2000	Nebraska	349.3
2001	Nebraska	314.7
2002	Air Force	307.8

*Record.

PASSING OFFENSE

Year	Team	Avg.
1937	Arkansas	185.0
1938	TCU	164.1
1939	TCU	148.5
1940	Cornell	186.3
1941	Arizona	177.7
1942	Tulsa	233.9
1943	Brown	133.1
1944	Tulsa	206.3
1945	St. Mary's (Cal.)	161.3
1946	Nevada	198.1
1947	Michigan	173.9
1948	Nevada	255.0
1949	Fordham	183.4
1950	Southern Methodist	214.6
1951	Loyola Marymount	210.6

Year	Team	Avg.
1952	Fordham	225.8
1953	Stanford	179.5
1954	Purdue	177.3
1955	Navy	185.1
1956	Washington St.	206.8
1957	Utah	195.2
1958	Army	172.2
1959	Stanford	227.8
1960	Washington St.	185.5
1961	Wisconsin	188.4
1962	Tulsa	199.3
1963	Tulsa	244.8
1964	Tulsa	317.9
1965	Tulsa	346.4
1966	Tulsa	272.0
1967	UTEP	301.1
1968	Cincinnati	335.8
1969	San Diego St.	374.2
1970	Auburn	288.5
1971	San Diego St.	251.4
1972	Virginia Tech	304.4
1973	San Diego St.	305.0
1974	Colorado St.	261.8
1975	San Diego St.	291.3
1976	Brigham Young	307.8
1977	Brigham Young	341.6
1978	Southern Methodist	276.2
1979	Brigham Young	368.3
1980	Brigham Young	409.8
1981	Brigham Young	356.9
1982	Long Beach St.	326.8
1983	Brigham Young	381.2
1984	Brigham Young	346.2
1985	Brigham Young	354.5
1986	San Jose St.	312.5
1987	San Jose St.	338.1
1988	Utah	395.9
1989	Houston	*511.3
1990	Houston	473.9
1991	Houston	372.8
1992	Houston	407.1
1993	Nevada	397.5
1994	Georgia	338.3
1995	Nevada	416.3
1996	Wyoming	359.2
1997	Nevada	370.2
1998	Louisiana Tech	432.1
1999	Louisiana Tech	403.1
2000	Florida St.	384.0
2001	Florida	405.2
2002	Texas Tech	388.9

*Record.

SCORING OFFENSE

Year	Team	Avg.
1937	Colorado	31.0
1938	Dartmouth	28.2
1939	Utah	28.4
1940	Boston College	32.0
1941	Texas	33.8
1942	Tulsa	42.7
1943	Duke	37.2
1944	Army	*56.0
1945	Army	45.8
1946	Georgia	37.2
1947	Michigan	38.3
1948	Nevada	44.4
1949	Army	39.3
1950	Princeton	38.8
1951	Maryland	39.2
1952	Oklahoma	40.7
1953	Texas Tech	38.9
1954	UCLA	40.8
1955	Oklahoma	36.5
1956	Oklahoma	46.6
1957	Arizona St.	39.7
1958	Rutgers	33.4
1959	Syracuse	39.0
1960	New Mexico St.	37.4
1961	Utah St.	38.7

Year	Team	Avg.
1962	Wisconsin	31.7
1963	Utah St.	31.7
1964	Tulsa	38.4
1965	Arkansas	32.4
1966	Notre Dame	36.2
1967	UTEP	35.9
1968	Houston	42.5
1969	San Diego St.	46.4
1970	Texas	41.2
1971	Oklahoma	44.9
1972	Arizona St.	46.6
1973	Arizona St.	44.6
1974	Oklahoma	43.0
1975	Ohio St.	34.0
1976	Michigan	38.7
1977	Grambling	42.0
1978	Oklahoma	40.0
1979	Brigham Young	40.6
1980	Brigham Young	46.7
1981	Brigham Young	38.7
1982	Nebraska	41.1
1983	Nebraska	52.0
1984	Boston College	36.7
1985	Fresno St.	39.1
1986	Oklahoma	42.4
1987	Oklahoma	43.5
1988	Oklahoma St.	47.5
1989	Houston	53.5
1990	Houston	46.5
1991	Fresno St.	44.2
1992	Fresno St.	40.5
1993	Florida St.	43.2
1994	Penn St.	47.8
1995	Nebraska	52.4
1996	Florida	46.6
1997	Nebraska	47.1
1998	Kansas St.	48.0
1999	Virginia Tech	41.4
2000	Boise St.	44.9
2001	Brigham Young	46.8
2002	Boise St.	45.6

*Record.

Annual Defense Champions

TOTAL DEFENSE

Year	Team	Avg.
1937	Santa Clara	*69.9
1938	Alabama	77.9
1939	Texas A&M	76.3
1940	Navy	96.0
1941	Duquesne	110.6
1942	Texas	117.3
1943	Duke	121.7
1944	Virginia	96.8
1945	Alabama	109.9
1946	Notre Dame	141.7
1947	Penn St.	76.8
1948	Georgia Tech	151.3
1949	Kentucky	153.8
1950	Wake Forest	163.2
1951	Wisconsin	154.8
1952	Tennessee	166.7
1953	Cincinnati	184.3
1954	Mississippi	172.3
1955	Army	160.7
1956	Miami (Fla.)	189.4
1957	Auburn	133.0
1958	Auburn	157.5
1959	Syracuse	96.2
1960	Wyoming	149.6
1961	Alabama	132.6
1962	Mississippi	142.2
1963	Southern Miss.	131.2
1964	Auburn	164.7
1965	Southern Miss.	161.1
1966	Southern Miss.	163.7
1967	Nebraska	157.6
1968	Wyoming	206.8
1969	Toledo	209.1
1970	Toledo	185.8
1971	Toledo	179.5

Year	Team	Avg.
1972	Louisville	202.5
1973	Miami (Ohio)	177.4
1974	Notre Dame	195.2
1975	Texas A&M	183.8
1976	Rutgers	179.2
1977	Jackson St.	207.0
1978	Penn St.	203.9
1979	Yale	175.4
1980	Pittsburgh	205.5
1981	Pittsburgh	224.8
1982	Arizona St.	228.9
1983	Texas	212.0
1984	Nebraska	203.3
1985	Oklahoma	193.5
1986	Oklahoma	169.6
1987	Oklahoma	208.1
1988	Auburn	218.1
1989	Miami (Fla.)	216.5
1990	Clemson	216.9
1991	Texas A&M	222.4
1992	Alabama	194.2
1993	Mississippi	234.5
1994	Miami (Fla.)	220.9
1995	Kansas St.	250.8
1996	West Virginia	217.5
1997	Michigan	206.9
1998	Florida St.	214.8
1999	Mississippi St.	222.5
2000	TCU	245.0
2001	Texas	236.2
2002	TCU	240.3

*Record.

RUSHING DEFENSE

Year	Team	Avg.
1937	Santa Clara	25.3
1938	Oklahoma	43.3
1939	Texas A&M	41.5
1940	Texas A&M	44.3
1941	Duquesne	56.0
1942	Boston College	48.9
1943	Duke	39.4
1944	Navy	53.8
1945	Alabama	33.9
1946	Oklahoma	58.0
1947	Penn St.	*17.0
1948	Georgia Tech	74.9
1949	Oklahoma	55.6
1950	Ohio St.	64.0
1951	San Francisco	51.6
1952	Michigan St.	83.9
1953	Maryland	83.9
1954	UCLA	73.2
1955	Maryland	75.9
1956	Miami (Fla.)	106.9
1957	Auburn	67.4
1958	Auburn	79.6
1959	Syracuse	19.3
1960	Wyoming	82.4
1961	Utah St.	50.8
1962	Minnesota	52.2
1963	Mississippi	77.3
1964	Washington	61.3
1965	Michigan St.	45.6
1966	Wyoming	38.5
1967	Wyoming	42.3
1968	Arizona St.	57.0
1969	LSU	38.9
1970	LSU	52.2
1971	Michigan	63.3
1972	Louisville	82.1
1973	Miami (Ohio)	77.0
1974	Notre Dame	102.8
1975	Texas A&M	80.3
1976	Rutgers	83.9
1977	Jackson St.	67.8
1978	Penn St.	54.5
1979	Yale	75.0
1980	Pittsburgh	65.3
1981	Pittsburgh	62.4
1982	Virginia Tech	49.5
1983	Virginia Tech	69.4
1984	Oklahoma	68.8

Year	Team	Avg.
1985	UCLA	70.3
1986	Oklahoma	60.7
1987	Michigan St.	61.5
1988	Auburn	63.2
1989	Southern California	61.5
1990	Washington	66.8
1991	Clemson	53.4
1992	Alabama	55.0
1993	Arizona	30.1
1994	Virginia	63.6
1995	Virginia Tech	77.4
1996	Florida St.	59.0
1997	Florida St.	51.9
1998	Ohio St.	67.4
1999	Mississippi St.	66.9
2000	Memphis	72.7
2001	UAB	57.3
2002	TCU	64.8

*Record.

PASSING DEFENSE

Year	Team	$Avg.
1937	Harvard	31.0
1938	Penn St.	*13.1
1939	Kansas	34.1
1940	Harvard	33.3
1941	Purdue	27.1
1942	Harvard	45.4
1943	North Carolina	36.5
1944	Michigan St.	26.7
1945	Holy Cross	37.7
1946	Holy Cross	53.7
1947	North Carolina St.	39.3
1948	Northwestern	54.1
1949	Miami (Fla.)	54.7
1950	Tennessee	67.5
1951	Wash. & Lee	67.9
1952	Virginia	50.3
1953	Richmond	40.3
1954	Alabama	45.8
1955	Florida	42.0
1956	Villanova	43.8
1957	Georgia Tech	33.4
1958	Iowa St.	39.0
1959	Alabama	45.7
1960	Iowa St.	30.2
1961	Pennsylvania	56.9
1962	New Mexico	56.8
1963	UTEP	43.8
1964	Kent St.	53.6
1965	Toledo	69.8
1966	Toledo	70.4
1967	Nebraska	90.1
1968	Kent St.	107.6
1969	Dayton	90.0
1970	Toledo	77.8
1971	Texas Tech	60.1
1972	Vanderbilt	80.3
1973	Nebraska	39.9
1974	Iowa	65.7
1975	VMI	51.1
1976	Western Mich.	78.5
1977	Tennessee St.	67.9
1978	Boston College	65.1
1979	Western Caro.	77.5
1980	Kansas St.	91.4
1981	Nebraska	100.1
1982	Missouri	123.5
1983	Ohio	115.3
1984	Texas Tech	114.8
1985	Oklahoma	103.6
1986	Oklahoma	108.9
1987	Oklahoma	102.4
1988	Baylor	117.8
1989	Kansas St.	129.3
1990	Alabama	82.5
1991	Texas	77.4
1992	Western Mich.	83.2
1993	Texas A&M	75.0
1994	Miami (Fla.)	81.3
1995	Miami (Ohio)	85.5
1996	Ohio St.	81.3
1997	Michigan	75.8

Year	Team	$Avg.
1998	Florida St.	79.9
1999	Kansas St.	65.7
2000	Texas	88.0
2001	Miami (Fla.)	75.6
2002	Miami (Fla.)	83.9

*Record. $Beginning in 1990, ranked on passing-efficiency defense rating points instead of per-game yardage allowed.

SCORING DEFENSE

Year	Team	Avg.
1937	Santa Clara	1.1
1938	Duke	**0.0
1939	Tennessee	**0.0
1940	Tennessee	2.6
1941	Duquesne	2.9
1942	Tulsa	3.2
1943	Duke	3.8
1944	Army	3.9
1945	St. Mary's (Cal.)	4.0
1946	Notre Dame	2.7
1947	Penn St.	3.0
1948	Michigan	4.9
1949	Kentucky	4.8
1950	Army	4.4
1951	Wisconsin	5.9
1952	Southern California	4.7
1953	Maryland	3.1
1954	UCLA	4.4
1955	Georgia Tech	4.6
1956	Georgia Tech	3.3
1957	Auburn	2.8
1958	Oklahoma	4.9
1959	Mississippi	2.1
1960	LSU	5.0
1961	Alabama	2.2
1962	LSU	3.4
1963	Mississippi	3.7
1964	Arkansas	5.7
1965	Michigan St.	6.2
1966	Alabama	3.7
1967	Oklahoma	6.8
1968	Georgia	9.8
1969	Arkansas	7.6
1970	Dartmouth	4.7
1971	Michigan	6.4
1972	Michigan	5.2
1973	Ohio St.	4.3
1974	Michigan	6.8
1975	Alabama	6.0
1976	Michigan	7.4
	Rutgers	7.4
1977	North Carolina	7.4
1978	Ball St.	7.5
1979	Alabama	5.3
1980	Florida St.	7.7
1981	Southern Miss.	8.1
1982	Arkansas	10.5
1983	Virginia Tech	8.3
1984	Nebraska	9.5
1985	Michigan	6.8
1986	Oklahoma	6.6
1987	Oklahoma	7.5
1988	Auburn	7.2
1989	Miami (Fla.)	9.3
1990	Central Mich.	8.9
1991	Miami (Fla.)	9.1
1992	Arizona	8.9
1993	Florida St.	9.4
1994	Miami (Fla.)	10.8
1995	Northwestern	12.7
1996	North Carolina	10.0
1997	Michigan	8.9
1998	Wisconsin	10.2
1999	Virginia Tech	10.5
2000	TCU	9.6
2001	Miami (Fla.)	9.4
2002	Kansas St.	11.8

**Record tied.

Other Annual Team Champions

NET PUNTING

Year	Team	#Avg.
1937	Iowa	43.0
1938	Arkansas	41.6
1939	Auburn	43.3
1940	Auburn	42.3
1941	Clemson	42.3
1942	Tulsa	41.3
1943	Michigan	39.2
1944	UCLA	43.0
1945	Miami (Fla.)	39.9
1946	UTEP	41.2
1947	Duke	41.9
1948	North Carolina	44.0
1949	Furman	44.7
1950	Colorado	45.1
1951	Alabama	41.8
1952	Colorado	43.3
1953	Georgia	41.2
1954	New Mexico	42.6
1955	Michigan St.	41.2
1956	Colorado St.	42.2
1957	Utah St.	40.1
1958	Georgia	41.9
1959	Brigham Young	43.2
1960	Georgia	43.7
1961	Arizona St.	42.1
1962	Wyoming	42.6
1963	Southern Methodist	41.4
1964	Mississippi	44.1
1965	Arizona St.	44.0
1966	Tennessee	43.4
1967	Houston	44.4
1968	Wichita St.	43.2
1969	Georgia	43.5
1970	Utah	45.0
1971	Utah	46.7
1972	Southern Miss.	45.1
1973	Wake Forest	44.1
1974	Ohio St.	44.9
1975	Ohio St.	44.1
1976	Colorado St.	**44.4
1977	Mississippi	43.4
1978	Texas	41.7
1979	Mississippi	42.4
1980	Florida St.	42.6
1981	Michigan	43.1
1982	Vanderbilt	42.1
1983	Brigham Young	*45.0
1984	Ohio St.	44.0
1985	Colorado	43.6
1986	Michigan	43.1
1987	Ohio St.	40.7
1988	Brigham Young	42.9
1989	Colorado	43.8
1990	Pittsburgh	41.2
1991	Texas Tech	40.6
1992	Nebraska	41.7
1993	New Mexico	41.8
1994	Ball St.	42.2
1995	Ball St.	41.3
1996	San Diego St.	44.9
1997	LSU	43.3
1998	UNLV	41.4
1999	Texas A&M	42.7
2000	Wisconsin	42.9
2001	Ohio	42.7
2002	Brigham Young	42.7

#Beginning in 1975, ranked on net punting average. *Record for net punting average. **Record for net punting average, minimum 40 punts.

PUNT RETURNS

Year	Team	Avg.
1937	—	—
1938	—	—
1939	UCLA	16.3
1940	UCLA	16.2
1941	Colgate	18.7
1942	—	—
1943	Columbia	20.9
1944	New York U.	22.0
1945	—	—
1946	Columbia	16.8
1947	Florida	19.7
1948	Oklahoma	*22.4
1949	Wichita St.	18.3
1950	Texas A&M	17.6
1951	Holy Cross	18.1
1952	Arizona St.	**25.2
1953	Kansas St.	23.8
1954	Miami (Fla.)	19.7
1955	North Carolina	22.5
1956	Cincinnati	17.7
1957	North Texas	17.5
1958	Notre Dame	17.6
1959	Wyoming	16.6
1960	Arizona	17.7
1961	Memphis	17.4
1962	West Tex. A&M	18.4
1963	Army	18.1
1964	UTEP	16.9
1965	Georgia Tech	23.0
1966	Brown	21.0
1967	Memphis	16.3
1968	Army	17.4
1969	Davidson	21.3
1970	Wichita St.	28.5
1971	Mississippi St.	20.8
1972	Georgia Tech	17.3
1973	Utah	23.4
1974	Auburn	16.6
1975	New Mexico St.	15.3
1976	Wichita St.	15.0
1977	Grambling	16.9
1978	McNeese St.	15.7
1979	Tennessee St.	16.9
1980	Georgia	16.5
1981	North Carolina St.	13.4
1982	Auburn	15.8
1983	San Diego St.	17.0
1984	Florida	13.8
1985	Utah	20.7
1986	Arizona St.	17.9
1987	Stanford	15.4
1988	Florida St.	15.5
1989	Ohio	18.2
1990	Michigan	15.6
1991	Alabama	16.9
1992	Northwestern	21.8
1993	Texas A&M	17.7
1994	Ball St.	19.9
1995	Eastern Mich.	20.8
1996	Kansas	19.5
1997	Iowa	18.2
1998	Kansas St.	21.3
1999	UAB	19.1
2000	Virginia Tech	18.2
2001	Colorado	17.4
2002	Northern Ill.	20.2

*Record for minimum 30 punt returns. **Record for minimum 15 punt returns.

KICKOFF RETURNS

Year	Team	Avg.
1937	—	—
1938	—	—
1939	Wake Forest	32.9
1940	Minnesota	36.4
1941	Tulane	32.1
1942	—	—

DIVISION I-A

Year	Team	Avg.
1943	Navy	28.8
1944	—	—
1945	—	—
1946	William & Mary	31.7
1947	Southern Methodist	31.4
1948	Wyoming	27.4
1949	Army	34.1
1950	Wyoming	29.3
1951	Marquette	25.0
1952	Wake Forest	25.1
1953	Texas Tech	23.8
1954	Arizona	26.1
1955	Southern California	25.8
1956	Georgia Tech	24.6
1957	Notre Dame	27.6
1958	Tulsa	25.8
1959	Auburn	25.8
1960	Yale	26.7
1961	Harvard	25.9
1962	Alabama	28.9
1963	Memphis	27.7
1964	Cornell	27.1
1965	Dartmouth	28.7
1966	Notre Dame	29.6
1967	Air Force	25.3
1968	Louisville	25.7
1969	Brigham Young	28.7
1970	South Carolina	26.5
1971	Miami (Fla.)	24.1
1972	Michigan	26.9
1973	Rice	*27.5
1974	Southern California	25.7
1975	Maryland	**29.5
1976	South Carolina	27.0
1977	Miami (Ohio)	24.6
1978	Utah St.	26.7
1979	Brigham Young	26.3
1980	Oklahoma	33.2
1981	Iowa	29.1
1982	Utah	25.5
1983	Tennessee	28.8
1984	Texas Tech	25.2
1985	Air Force	27.0
1986	Clemson	26.1
1987	Oklahoma St.	23.7
1988	Notre Dame	24.2
1989	Colorado	26.1
1990	Nebraska	27.8
1991	New Mexico St.	25.2

Year	Team	Avg.
1992	Florida St.	30.3
1993	Texas A&M	31.2
1994	Texas A&M	27.8
1995	New Mexico	27.1
1996	Miami (Fla.)	28.9
1997	Southern Miss.	28.2
1998	Utah	27.1
1999	TCU	27.5
2000	TCU	28.8
2001	Hawaii	30.3
2002	Iowa	25.1

*Record for minimum 35 kickoff returns. **Record for minimum 25 kickoff returns.*

TURNOVER MARGIN

Year	Team	Avg.
1992	Nebraska	1.64
1993	UCLA	1.73
1994	Clemson	1.55
1995	Toledo	2.00
1996	North Carolina	2.00
1997	Colorado St.	2.08
1998	Wisconsin	2.00
1999	Kansas St.	1.55
2000	Toledo	2.00
2001	Miami (Fla.)	*2.36
2002	South Fla.	1.91

*Record.

Defensive Single-Game Records

(Since 2000)

TACKLES FOR LOSS

TFL	Team (Opponent)	Date
20	TCU (Nevada)	Sept. 9, 2000
18	Washington (Idaho)	Sept. 22, 2002
18	Kansas (Southwest Mo. St.)	Sept. 1, 2001
18	Colorado (Missouri)	Nov. 4, 2000
17	Arizona St. (Washington)	Oct. 26, 2002
17	Toledo (Navy)	Oct. 28, 2000
17	Texas (Missouri)	Oct. 21, 2000
17	Kansas St. (Oklahoma)	Oct. 14, 2000
17	Oregon St. (San Diego St.)	Sept. 23, 2000
17	Toledo (Penn St.)	Sept. 2, 2000

PASS SACKS

Sacks	Team (Opponent)	Date
15	TCU (Nevada)	Sept. 9, 2000
14	Colorado (Missouri)	Nov. 4, 2000
13	Toledo (Penn St.)	Sept. 2, 2000
11	TCU (Louisville)	Nov. 23, 2001
10	Northern Ill. (Wisconsin)	Sept. 14, 2002
10	Maryland (Duke)	Oct. 28, 2000
10	North Carolina (Wake Forest)	Sept. 9, 2000
9	New Mexico (Wyoming)	Nov. 30, 2002
9	New Mexico (UTEP)	Sept. 1, 2001
9	Arizona St. (Arizona)	Nov. 24, 2000
9	UCF (Eastern Ky.)	Oct. 14, 2000
9	Texas (Houston)	Sept. 23, 2000

PASSES DEFENDED
(Pass Interceptions and Pass Break-ups)

PD	Team (Opponent)	Date
19	South Carolina (Alabama)	Oct. 2, 2000
17	TCU (Tulane)	Nov. 9, 2002
17	Mississippi St. (Troy St.)	Oct. 12, 2002
17	Northern Ill. (Ball St.)	Oct. 5, 2002
17	Nebraska (Iowa St.)	Oct. 7, 2000
16	West Virginia (Rutgers)	Oct. 12, 2002
15	Toledo (Eastern Mich.)	Sept. 7, 2002
15	Wisconsin (Indiana)	Nov. 11, 2000
14	Oregon St. (California)	Oct. 26, 2002
14	Auburn (LSU)	Dec. 1, 2001
14	Iowa (Penn St.)	Nov. 4, 2000

FORCED FUMBLES

FF	Team (Opponent)	Date
7	Virginia (South Carolina)	Sept. 7, 2002
6	Boston College (Navy)	Oct. 19, 2002
6	Washington (Arizona St.)	Oct. 14, 2002
6	Washington (Idaho)	Sept. 2, 2002
5	Iowa (Minnesota)	Nov. 16, 2002
5	Arizona St. (San Jose St.)	Sept. 29, 2001
5	Clemson (UCF)	Sept. 1, 2001
5	Fresno St. (Colorado)	Aug. 26, 2001
5	Georgia (New Mexico St.)	Sept. 23, 2000
4	By 19 teams	

Toughest-Schedule Annual Leaders

The NCAA's toughest-schedule program (which began in 1977) is based on what all Division I-A opponents did against other Division I-A teams when not playing the team in question. Games against non-I-A teams are deleted, and nine intradivision games are required to qualify. (Bowl games are not included.) The leaders:

Year	Team (†Record)	W	L	T	Pct.
1977	Miami (Fla.) (3-8-0)	66	42	2	.609
	Penn St. (10-1-0)	61	39	2	.608
1978	Notre Dame (8-3-0)	77	31	2	.709
	Southern California (11-1-0)	79	40	1	.663
1979	UCLA (5-6-0)	71	37	2	.655
	South Carolina (8-3-0)	69	38	2	.642
1980	Florida St. (10-1-0)	70	34	0	.673
	Miami (Fla.) (8-3-0)	64	33	1	.658
1981	Penn St. (9-2-0)	71	33	2	.679
	Temple (5-5-0)	71	33	2	.669
1982	Penn St. (10-1-0)	63	34	2	.646
	Kentucky (0-10-1)	63	34	5	.642
1983	Auburn (10-1-0)	70	31	3	.688
	UCLA (6-4-1)	68	37	5	.641
1984	Penn St. (6-5-0)	58	36	3	.613
	Georgia (7-4-0)	60	39	4	.602
1985	Notre Dame (5-6-0)	72	29	3	.707
	Alabama (8-2-1)	65	32	5	.662

				‡Opponents' Record	
Year	Team (†Record)	W	L	T	Pct.
1986	Florida (6-5-0)	64	29	3	.682
	LSU (9-2-0)	67	36	2	.648
1987	Notre Dame (8-3-0)	71	34	2	.673
	Florida St. (10-1-0)	60	29	4	.667
1988	Virginia Tech (3-8-0)	74	36	0	.673
	Arizona (7-4-0)	70	37	3	.650
1989	Notre Dame (11-1-0)	74	38	4	.655
	LSU (4-7-0)	67	41	1	.619
1990	Colorado (10-1-1)	72	42	3	.628
	Stanford (5-6-0)	67	39	4	.627
1991	South Carolina (3-6-2)	57	31	2	.644
	Florida (10-2-0)	66	37	1	.639
1992	Southern California (6-5-1)	68	38	4	.636
	Stanford (10-3-0)	73	43	4	.625
1993	LSU (5-6-0)	67	38	5	.632
	Purdue (1-10-0)	66	38	3	.631
1994	Michigan (8-4-0)	67	38	6	.631
	Oklahoma (6-6-0)	66	39	4	.624
1995	Notre Dame (9-3-0)	67	37	5	.638
	Illinois (5-5-1)	69	40	2	.631
1996	Florida (12-1)	70	41	0	.631
	UCLA (5-6)	66	41	0	.617
1997	Colorado (5-6)	76	37	0	.673
	Auburn (10-3)	80	39	0	.672

†Not including bowl games. ‡When not playing the team listed.

Top 10 Toughest-Schedule Leaders for 1998-02

1998

	Team	$Opp. Record	Pct.
1.	Auburn	74-34	.685
2.	Missouri	66-36	.647
3.	Florida St.	74-43	.632
4.	Southern California	76-46	.623
5.	LSU	65-41	.613
6.	Baylor	68-43	.613
7.	Washington	69-44	.611
8.	Alabama	67-43	.609
9.	Texas A&M	79-51	.608
10.	Michigan St.	73-49	.598

1999

	Team	$Opp. Record	Pct.
1.	Alabama	80-38	.678
2.	Auburn	62-36	.633
3.	Notre Dame	74-46	.617
4.	South Carolina	66-43	.606
5.	Florida St.	65-43	.602
6.	Miami (Fla.)	66-44	.600
7.	Ohio St.	70-47	.598
8.	Michigan	67-45	.598

Team	$Opp. Record	Pct.
9. Penn St.	72-49	.595
10. Temple	63-44	.589
Clemson	63-44	.589

2000

Team	$Opp. Record	Pct.
1. Florida	79-42	.653
2. Florida St.	78-44	.639
3. Miami (Fla.)	65-37	.637
4. Colorado	69-44	.611
5. Kansas	64-41	.610
6. Virginia Tech	67-43	.609
West Virginia	67-43	.609
8. Stanford	71-47	.601

Team	$Opp. Record	Pct.
9. Iowa	75-50	.600
10. Alabama	66-45	.595
UCLA	66-45	.595

2001

Team	$Opp. Record	Pct.
1. California	73-39	.652
2. Colorado	79-45	.637
3. Kansas	66-38	.635
4. Kansas St.	72-42	.632
5. Mississippi St.	65-38	.631
6. Tennessee	76-45	.628
7. Arkansas	64-38	.627
8. Oklahoma St.	64-39	.621
9. Florida St.	70-43	.619
Wisconsin	70-43	.619

2002

Team	$Opp. Record	Pct.
1. Southern California	107-58	.649
2. Iowa St.	107-62	.633
3. Texas Tech	108-66	.621
4. Arkansas	104-64	.619
5. Florida	97-60	.618
6. Stanford	87-54	.617
7. Florida St.	112-70	.615
8. Miami (Fla.)	91-57	.615
9. Wisconsin	108-68	.614
10. Alabama	98-62	.613

$When not playing the team listed.

Annual Most-Improved Teams

Year	Team	$Games Improved	From		To		Coach
1937	California	4½	1936	6-5-0	1937	*10-0-1	Stub Allison
	Syracuse	4½	1936	1-7-0	1937	5-2-1	#Ossie Solem
1938	TCU	5½	1937	4-4-2	1938	*11-0-0	Dutch Meyer
1939	Texas A&M	5½	1938	4-4-1	1939	*11-0-0	Homer Norton
1940	Stanford	8	1939	1-7-1	1940	*10-0-0	#Clark Shaughnessy
1941	Vanderbilt	4½	1940	3-6-1	1941	8-2-0	Red Sanders
1942	Utah St.	5½	1941	0-8-0	1942	6-3-1	Dick Romney
1943	Purdue	8	1942	1-8-0	1943	9-0-0	Elmer Burnham
1944	Ohio St.	6	1943	3-6-0	1944	9-0-0	#Carroll Widdoes
1945	Miami (Fla.)	7	1944	1-7-1	1945	*9-1-1	Jack Harding
1946	Illinois	5	1945	2-6-1	1946	*8-2-0	Ray Eliot
	Kentucky	5	1945	2-8-0	1946	7-3-0	#Paul "Bear" Bryant
1947	California	6½	1946	2-7-0	1947	9-1-0	#Lynn "Pappy" Waldorf
1948	Clemson	6	1947	4-5-0	1948	*11-0-0	Frank Howard
1949	Tulsa	5	1948	0-9-1	1949	5-4-1	J. O. Brothers
1950	Brigham Young	5	1949	0-11-0	1950	4-5-1	Chick Atkinson
	Texas A&M	5	1949	1-8-1	1950	*7-4-0	Harry Stiteler
1951	Georgia Tech	6	1950	5-6-0	1951	*11-0-1	Bobby Dodd
1952	Alabama	4½	1951	5-6-0	1952	*10-2-0	Harold "Red" Drew
1953	Texas Tech	7	1952	3-7-1	1953	*11-1-0	DeWitt Weaver
1954	Denver	5	1953	3-5-2	1954	9-1-0	Bob Blackman
1955	Texas A&M	6½	1954	1-9-0	1955	7-2-1	Paul "Bear" Bryant
1956	Iowa	5	1955	3-5-1	1956	*9-1-0	Forest Evashevski
1957	Notre Dame	5	1956	2-8-0	1957	7-3-0	Terry Brennan
	Texas	5	1956	1-9-0	1957	†6-4-1	#Darrell Royal
1958	Air Force	6	1957	3-6-1	1958	‡9-0-1	#Ben Martin
1959	Washington	6½	1958	3-7-0	1959	*10-1-0	Jim Owens
1960	Minnesota	5½	1959	2-7-0	1960	†8-2-0	Murray Warmath
	North Carolina St.	5½	1959	1-9-0	1960	6-3-1	Earle Edwards
1961	Villanova	6	1960	2-8-0	1961	*8-2-0	Alex Bell
1962	Southern California	6	1961	4-5-1	1962	*11-0-0	John McKay
1963	Illinois	6	1962	2-7-0	1963	*8-1-1	Pete Elliott
1964	Notre Dame	6½	1963	2-7-0	1964	9-1-0	#Ara Parseghian
1965	UTEP	6½	1964	0-8-2	1965	*8-3-0	#Bobby Dobbs
1966	Dayton	6½	1965	1-8-1	1966	8-2-0	John McVay
1967	Indiana	7	1966	1-8-1	1967	†9-2-0	John Pont
1968	Arkansas	5	1967	4-5-1	1968	*10-1-0	Frank Broyles
1969	UCLA	5½	1968	3-7-0	1969	8-1-1	Tommy Prothro
1970	Tulsa	5	1969	1-9-0	1970	6-4-0	#Claude Gibson
1971	Army	5	1970	1-9-1	1971	6-4-0	Tom Cahill
	Georgia	5	1970	5-5-0	1971	*11-1-0	Vince Dooley
1972	Pacific (Cal.)	5	1971	3-8-0	1972	8-3-0	Chester Caddas
	Southern California	5	1971	6-4-1	1972	*12-0-0	John McKay
	UCLA	5	1971	2-7-1	1972	8-3-0	Pepper Rodgers
1973	Pittsburgh	5	1972	1-10-0	1973	†6-5-1	#Johnny Majors
1974	Baylor	5½	1973	2-9-0	1974	†8-4-0	Grant Teaff
1975	Arizona St.	5	1974	7-5-0	1975	*12-0-0	Frank Kush
1976	Houston	7	1975	2-8-0	1976	*10-2-0	Bill Yeoman
1977	Miami (Ohio)	7	1976	3-8-0	1977	10-1-0	Dick Crum
1978	Tulsa	6	1977	3-8-0	1978	9-2-0	John Cooper
1979	Wake Forest	6½	1978	1-10-0	1979	†8-4-0	John Mackovic
1980	Florida	7	1979	0-10-1	1980	*8-4-0	Charley Pell
1981	Clemson	5½	1980	6-5-0	1981	*12-0-0	Danny Ford
1982	La.-Lafayette	6	1981	1-9-1	1982	7-3-1	Sam Robertson
	New Mexico	6	1981	4-7-1	1982	10-1-0	Joe Morrison
1983	Kentucky	5½	1982	0-10-1	1983	†6-5-1	Jerry Claiborne
	Memphis	5½	1982	1-10-0	1983	6-4-1	Rex Dockery
1984	Army	6	1983	2-9-0	1984	*8-3-1	Jim Young
1985	Colorado	5½	1984	1-10-0	1985	†7-5-0	Bill McCartney
	Fresno St.	5½	1984	6-6-0	1985	*11-0-1	Jim Sweeney
1986	San Jose St.	7	1985	2-8-1	1986	*10-2-0	Claude Gilbert

Year	Team	$Games Improved	From		To		Coach
1987	Syracuse	6	1986	5-6-0	1987	‡11-0-1	Dick MacPherson
1988	Washington St.	5	1987	3-7-1	1988	*9-3-0	Dennis Erickson
	West Virginia	5	1987	6-6-0	1988	†11-1-0	Don Nehlen
1989	Tennessee	5½	1988	5-6-0	1989	*11-1-0	Johnny Majors
1990	Temple	6	1989	1-10-0	1990	7-4-0	Jerry Berndt
1991	Tulsa	6½	1990	3-8-0	1991	*10-2-0	Dave Rader
1992	Hawaii	6	1991	4-7-1	1992	*11-2-0	Bob Wagner
1993	La.-Lafayette	6	1992	2-9-0	1993	8-3-0	Nelson Stokley
	Virginia Tech	6	1992	2-8-1	1993	*9-3-0	Frank Beamer
1994	Colorado St.	4½	1993	5-6-0	1994	†10-2-0	Sonny Lubick
	Duke	4½	1993	3-8-0	1994	†8-4-0	#Fred Goldsmith
	East Caro.	4½	1993	2-9-0	1994	†7-5-0	Steve Logan
1995	Northwestern	6	1994	3-7-1	1995	†10-2-0	Gary Barnett
1996	Brigham Young	5	1995	7-4-0	1996	*14-1-0	LaVell Edwards
1997	Western Mich.	6	1996	2-9-0	1997	8-3-0	Gary Darnell
1998	Louisville	5½	1997	1-10-0	1998	7-5-0	#John L. Smith
	TCU	5½	1997	1-10-0	1998	7-5-0	#Dennis Franchione
1999	Hawaii	8½	1998	0-12-0	1999	*9-4-0	#June Jones
2000	South Carolina	7½	1999	0-11-0	2000	*8-4-0	Lou Holtz
2001	Bowling Green	6	2000	2-9-0	2001	8-3-0	#Urban Meyer
	Colorado	6	2000	3-8-0	2001	†10-3-0	Gary Barnett
	Hawaii	6	2000	3-9-0	2001	9-3-0	June Jones
2002	Ohio St.	6	2001	7-5-0	2002	*14-0-0	Jim Tressel

$To determine games improved, add the difference in victories between the two seasons to the difference in losses, then divide by two; ties not counted. Bowl victory (*), loss (†), tie (‡) included in record. #First year as head coach at that college.

All-Time Most-Improved Teams

Games	Team (Year)	Games	Team (Year)
8½	Hawaii (1999)	7	Miami (Fla.) (1945)
8	Purdue (1943)	6½	Tulsa (1991)
8	Stanford (1940)	6½	Wake Forest (1979)
7½	South Carolina (2000)	6½	Toledo (1967)
7	San Jose St. (1986)	6½	Dayton (1966)
7	Florida (1980)	6½	UTEP (1965)
7	Miami (Ohio) (1977)	6½	Notre Dame (1964)
7	Houston (1976)	6½	Washington (1959)
7	Indiana (1967)	6½	Texas A&M (1955)
7	Texas Tech (1953)	6½	California (1947)

2002 Most-Improved Teams

College (Coach)	2001	2002	$Games Improved
Ohio St. (Jim Tressel)	7-5	14-0	6
California (Jeff Tedford)	1-10	7-5	5½
West Virginia (Rich Rodriquez)	3-8	9-4	5
Houston (Dana Dimel)	0-11	5-7	4½
Kansas St. (Bill Snyder)	6-6	11-2	4½
Kentucky (Guy Morriss)	2-9	7-5	4½
Southern California (Pete Carroll)	6-6	11-2	4½
Tulane (Chris Scelfo)	3-9	8-5	4½
Georgia (Mark Richt)	8-4	13-1	4
Notre Dame (Tyrone Willingham)	5-6	10-3	4
TCU (Gary Patterson)	6-6	10-2	4

$To determine games improved, add the difference in victories between the two seasons to the difference in losses, then divide by two. Includes bowl games.

All-Time Team Won-Lost Records

BY PERCENTAGE

Includes records as senior college only. Bowl and playoff games are included, and each tie game is computed as half won and half lost. Teams listed with years in parentheses indicates reclassification within the past 15 years. The year in parentheses is the first year of Division I-A membership. Note: Tiebreaker rule began with 1996 season.

Team	Yrs.	Won	Lost	Tied	Pct.	Total Games
Notre Dame	114	791	250	42	.750	1083
Michigan	123	823	269	36	.746	1128
Alabama	108	754	284	43	.717	1081
Oklahoma	108	725	282	53	.709	1060
Texas	110	766	306	33	.708	1105
Ohio St.	113	745	292	53	.708	1090
Nebraska	113	771	308	40	.707	1119
Tennessee	106	726	300	52	.698	1078
Penn St.	116	753	322	41	.693	1116
Southern California	110	695	296	54	.691	1045
Florida St.	56	409	194	17	.673	620
Boise St. (1996)	35	271	134	2	.668	407
South Fla. (2000)	6	44	22	0	.667	66
Washington	113	632	347	50	.638	1029
Georgia	109	662	367	54	.636	1083
Miami (Ohio)	114	611	342	44	.635	997
Miami (Fla.)	76	496	283	19	.633	798
LSU	109	636	368	47	.627	1051
Auburn	110	626	374	47	.620	1047
Arizona St.	90	502	303	24	.620	829
Colorado	113	630	384	36	.617	1050
Florida	96	582	354	40	.617	976
Central Mich.	102	519	317	36	.616	872
Army	113	622	393	51	.607	1066
Texas A&M	108	623	396	48	.606	1067
UCLA	84	499	323	37	.602	859
Syracuse	113	652	422	49	.602	1123
Michigan St.	106	572	382	44	.595	998
Arkansas	109	610	409	40	.595	1059
Southern Miss.	86	483	326	26	.594	835
Fresno St.	81	491	331	29	.594	851
Bowling Green	84	439	292	52	.594	783
Georgia Tech	110	616	415	43	.594	1074
Middle Tenn. (1999)	86	479	325	28	.593	832
Virginia Tech	109	597	405	46	.592	1048
Clemson	107	585	404	45	.588	1034
Arizona	98	517	360	33	.586	910
West Virginia	110	615	428	45	.586	1088
Minnesota	119	599	419	43	.585	1061
North Carolina	112	611	439	54	.578	1104
Stanford	96	529	381	49	.577	959
Pittsburgh	113	612	443	42	.577	1097
Boston College	104	553	401	36	.577	990
Louisiana Tech (1989)	99	505	366	37	.577	908
San Diego St.	80	447	330	32	.572	809
Mississippi	108	573	425	35	.572	1033
Utah	109	535	401	31	.569	967
Troy St. (2002)	72	392	297	15	.567	704
Western Mich.	97	469	355	24	.567	848
Brigham Young	78	447	345	26	.562	818
Hawaii	87	457	354	26	.562	837
Tulsa	98	500	394	27	.558	921
California	107	562	448	51	.554	1061
Wisconsin	113	549	439	53	.553	1041
Texas Tech	78	449	366	32	.549	847
Air Force	47	283	234	13	.546	530
Toledo	82	420	351	24	.543	795
Navy	122	581	491	57	.540	1129
UAB (1996)	12	69	59	3	.538	131
Purdue	115	529	453	48	.537	1030

Team	Yrs.	Won	Lost	Tied	Pct.	Total Games
Illinois	112	541	464	50	.536	1055
Oregon	107	509	438	46	.536	993
Ball St.	78	366	316	32	.535	714
North Texas (1995)	87	441	384	33	.533	858
UCF (1996)	24	138	121	1	.533	260
Nevada (1992)	92	439	385	32	.532	856
Virginia	113	569	501	48	.530	1118
Maryland	110	556	490	42	.530	1088
Missouri	112	549	485	52	.529	1086
East Caro.	67	344	312	12	.524	668
Duke	90	436	400	31	.521	867
Houston	57	313	288	15	.520	616
San Jose St.	84	415	383	38	.519	836
Northern Ill.	101	453	418	51	.519	922
Iowa	114	519	483	39	.517	1041
Utah St.	105	456	426	31	.516	913
Marshall (1997)	99	479	452	44	.514	975
Baylor	100	499	472	43	.513	1014
Vanderbilt	113	529	501	50	.513	1080
Akron	102	448	426	36	.512	910
Kentucky	112	528	509	44	.509	1081
North Carolina St.	111	494	480	55	.507	1029
Washington St.	106	457	447	45	.505	949
Kansas	113	519	512	58	.503	1089
TCU	106	499	492	56	.503	1047
UNLV	35	195	193	4	.503	392
Southern Methodist	86	423	422	54	.501	899
South Carolina	109	490	492	44	.499	1026
Rutgers	133	553	559	42	.497	1154
Ohio	107	459	469	48	.495	976
Louisville	84	385	395	17	.494	797
Mississippi St.	103	462	479	39	.491	980
Wyoming	106	447	463	28	.491	938
Cincinnati	115	489	512	51	.489	1052
Arkansas St. (1992)	88	377	395	37	.489	809
La.-Lafayette	95	435	457	32	.488	924
Memphis	87	391	411	32	.488	834
Oklahoma St.	101	455	484	48	.485	987
Colorado St.	104	436	466	33	.484	935
Connecticut (2002)	104	421	462	38	.478	921
Eastern Mich.	110	401	446	46	.475	893
Tulane	109	463	516	38	.474	1017
Oregon St.	106	438	498	50	.470	986
Iowa St.	111	457	527	46	.466	1030
New Mexico	104	410	477	31	.464	918
Idaho (1996)	105	410	479	25	.462	914
Temple	104	390	468	52	.457	910
New Mexico St.	107	397	495	32	.447	924
Rice	91	397	495	32	.447	924
La.-Monroe (1994)	52	236	303	8	.439	547
Buffalo (1999)	89	310	404	29	.437	743
Indiana	115	415	555	44	.431	1014
Kansas St.	107	415	560	42	.429	1017
Northwestern	115	428	579	44	.428	1051
UTEP	85	322	470	30	.410	822
Wake Forest	101	363	553	23	.399	939
Kent St.	80	277	438	28	.392	743

ALPHABETICAL LISTING

Team	Yrs.	Won	Lost	Tied	Pct.	Total Games
Air Force	47	283	234	13	.546	530
Akron	102	448	426	36	.512	910
Alabama	108	754	284	43	.717	1081
UAB (1996)	12	69	59	3	.538	131
Arizona	98	517	360	33	.586	910
Arizona St.	90	502	303	24	.620	829
Arkansas	109	610	409	40	.595	1059
Arkansas St. (1992)	88	377	395	37	.489	809
Army	113	622	393	51	.607	1066
Auburn	110	626	374	47	.620	1047
Ball St.	78	366	316	32	.535	714
Baylor	100	499	472	43	.513	1014
Boise St. (1996)	35	271	134	2	.668	407
Boston College	104	553	401	36	.577	990
Bowling Green	84	439	292	52	.594	783
Brigham Young	78	447	345	26	.562	818
Buffalo (1999)	89	310	404	29	.437	743
California	107	562	448	51	.554	1061
UCF (1996)	24	138	121	1	.533	260
Central Mich.	102	519	317	36	.616	872
Cincinnati	115	489	512	51	.489	1052
Clemson	107	585	404	45	.588	1034
Colorado	113	630	384	36	.617	1050

Team	Yrs.	Won	Lost	Tied	Pct.	Total Games
Colorado St.	104	436	466	33	.484	935
Connecticut (2002)	104	421	462	38	.478	921
Duke	90	436	400	31	.521	867
East Caro.	67	344	312	12	.524	668
Eastern Mich.	110	401	446	46	.475	893
Florida	96	582	354	40	.617	976
Florida St.	56	409	194	17	.673	620
Fresno St.	81	491	331	29	.594	851
Georgia	109	662	367	54	.636	1083
Georgia Tech	110	616	415	43	.594	1074
Hawaii	87	457	354	26	.562	837
Houston	57	313	288	15	.520	616
Idaho (1996)	105	410	479	25	.462	914
Illinois	112	541	464	50	.536	1055
Indiana	115	415	555	44	.431	1014
Iowa	114	519	483	39	.517	1041
Iowa St.	111	457	527	46	.466	1030
Kansas	113	519	512	58	.503	1089
Kansas St.	107	415	560	42	.429	1017
Kent St.	80	277	438	28	.392	743
Kentucky	112	528	509	44	.509	1081
La.-Lafayette	95	435	457	32	.488	924
La.-Monroe (1994)	52	236	303	8	.439	547
LSU	109	636	368	47	.627	1051
Louisiana Tech (1989)	99	505	366	37	.577	908
Louisville	84	385	395	17	.494	797
Marshall (1997)	99	479	452	44	.514	975
Maryland	110	556	490	42	.530	1088
Memphis	87	391	411	32	.488	834
Miami (Fla.)	76	496	283	19	.633	798
Miami (Ohio)	114	611	342	44	.635	997
Michigan	123	823	269	36	.746	1128
Michigan St.	106	572	382	44	.595	998
Middle Tenn. (1999)	86	479	325	28	.593	832
Minnesota	119	599	419	43	.585	1061
Mississippi	108	573	425	35	.572	1033
Mississippi St.	103	462	479	39	.491	980
Missouri	112	549	485	52	.529	1086
Navy	122	581	491	57	.540	1129
Nebraska	113	771	308	40	.707	1119
UNLV	35	195	193	4	.503	392
Nevada (1992)	92	439	385	32	.532	856
New Mexico	104	410	477	31	.464	918
New Mexico St.	107	397	495	32	.447	924
North Carolina	112	611	439	54	.578	1104
North Carolina St.	111	494	480	55	.507	1029
North Texas (1995)	87	441	384	33	.533	858
Northern Ill.	101	453	418	51	.519	922
Northwestern	115	428	579	44	.428	1051
Notre Dame	114	791	250	42	.750	1083
Ohio	107	459	469	48	.495	976
Ohio St.	113	745	292	53	.708	1090
Oklahoma	108	725	282	53	.709	1060
Oklahoma St.	101	455	484	48	.485	987
Oregon	107	509	438	46	.536	993
Oregon St.	106	438	498	50	.470	986
Penn St.	116	753	322	41	.693	1116
Pittsburgh	113	612	443	42	.577	1097
Purdue	115	529	453	48	.537	1030
Rice	91	397	495	32	.447	924
Rutgers	133	553	559	42	.497	1154
San Diego St.	80	447	330	32	.572	809
San Jose St.	84	415	383	38	.519	836
South Carolina	109	490	492	44	.499	1026
South Fla. (2000)	6	44	22	0	.667	66
Southern California	110	695	296	54	.691	1045
Southern Methodist	86	423	422	54	.501	899
Southern Miss.	86	483	326	26	.594	835
Stanford	96	529	381	49	.577	959
Syracuse	113	652	422	49	.602	1123
Temple	104	390	468	52	.457	910
Tennessee	106	726	300	52	.698	1078
Texas	110	766	306	33	.708	1105
Texas A&M	108	623	396	48	.606	1067
TCU	106	499	492	56	.503	1047
UTEP	85	322	470	30	.410	822
Texas Tech	78	449	366	32	.549	847
Toledo	82	420	351	24	.543	795
Troy St. (2002)	72	392	297	15	.567	704
Tulane	109	463	516	38	.474	1017
Tulsa	98	500	394	27	.558	921
UCLA	84	499	323	37	.602	859

Team	Yrs.	Won	Lost	Tied	Pct.	Total Games
Utah	109	535	401	31	.569	967
Utah St.	105	456	426	31	.516	913
Vanderbilt	113	529	501	50	.513	1080
Virginia	113	569	501	48	.530	1118
Virginia Tech	109	597	405	46	.592	1048
Wake Forest	101	363	553	23	.399	939
Washington	113	632	347	50	.638	1029
Washington St.	106	457	447	45	.505	949
West Virginia	110	615	428	45	.586	1088
Western Mich.	97	469	355	24	.567	848
Wisconsin	113	549	439	53	.553	1041
Wyoming	106	447	463	28	.491	938

BY VICTORIES

Team	Yrs.	Won	Lost	Tied	Pct.	Total Games
Michigan	123	823	269	36	.746	1128
Notre Dame	114	791	250	42	.750	1083
Nebraska	113	771	308	40	.707	1119
Texas	110	766	306	33	.708	1105
Alabama	108	754	284	43	.717	1081
Penn St.	116	753	322	41	.693	1116
Ohio St.	113	745	292	53	.708	1090
Tennessee	106	726	300	52	.698	1078
Oklahoma	108	725	282	53	.709	1060
Southern California	110	695	296	54	.691	1045
Georgia	109	662	367	54	.636	1083
Syracuse	113	652	422	49	.602	1123
LSU	109	636	368	47	.627	1051
Washington	113	632	347	50	.638	1029
Colorado	113	630	384	36	.617	1050
Auburn	110	626	374	47	.620	1047
Texas A&M	108	623	396	48	.606	1067
Army	113	622	393	51	.607	1066
Georgia Tech	110	616	415	43	.594	1074
West Virginia	110	615	428	45	.586	1088
Pittsburgh	113	612	443	42	.577	1097
Miami (Ohio)	114	611	342	44	.635	997
North Carolina	112	611	439	54	.578	1104
Arkansas	109	610	409	40	.595	1059
Minnesota	119	599	419	43	.585	1061
Virginia Tech	109	597	405	46	.592	1048
Clemson	107	585	404	45	.588	1034
Florida	96	582	354	40	.617	976
Navy	122	581	491	57	.540	1129
Mississippi	108	573	425	35	.572	1033
Michigan St.	106	572	382	44	.595	998
Virginia	113	569	501	48	.530	1118
California	107	562	448	51	.554	1061
Maryland	110	556	490	42	.530	1088
Boston College	104	553	401	36	.577	990
Rutgers	133	553	559	42	.497	1154
Missouri	112	549	485	52	.529	1086
Wisconsin	113	549	439	53	.553	1041
Illinois	112	541	464	50	.536	1055
Utah	109	535	401	31	.569	967
Purdue	115	529	453	48	.537	1030
Stanford	96	529	381	49	.577	959
Vanderbilt	113	529	501	50	.513	1080
Kentucky	112	528	509	44	.509	1081
Central Mich.	102	519	317	36	.616	872
Iowa	114	519	483	39	.517	1041
Kansas	113	519	512	58	.503	1089
Arizona	98	517	360	33	.586	910
Oregon	107	509	438	46	.536	993
Louisiana Tech (1989)	99	505	366	37	.577	908
Arizona St.	90	502	303	24	.620	829
Tulsa	98	500	394	27	.558	921
Baylor	100	499	472	43	.513	1014
TCU	106	499	492	56	.503	1047
UCLA	84	499	323	37	.602	859
Miami (Fla.)	76	496	283	19	.633	798
North Carolina St.	111	494	480	55	.507	1029
Fresno St.	81	491	331	29	.594	851
South Carolina	109	490	492	44	.499	1026
Cincinnati	115	489	512	51	.489	1052
Southern Miss.	86	483	326	26	.594	835
Marshall (1997)	99	479	452	44	.514	975
Middle Tenn. (1999)	86	479	325	28	.593	832
Western Mich.	97	469	355	24	.567	848
Tulane	109	463	516	38	.474	1017
Mississippi St.	103	462	479	39	.491	980
Ohio	107	459	469	48	.495	976
Hawaii	87	457	354	26	.562	837
Iowa St.	111	457	527	46	.466	1030
Washington St.	106	457	447	45	.505	949
Utah St.	105	456	426	31	.516	913
Oklahoma St.	101	455	484	48	.485	987
Northern Ill.	101	453	418	51	.519	922
Texas Tech	78	449	366	32	.549	847
Akron	102	448	426	36	.512	910
Brigham Young	78	447	345	26	.562	818
San Diego St.	80	447	330	32	.572	809
Wyoming	106	447	463	28	.491	938
North Texas (1995)	87	441	384	33	.533	858
Bowling Green	84	439	292	52	.594	783
Nevada (1992)	92	439	385	32	.532	856
Oregon St.	106	438	498	50	.470	986
Colorado St.	104	436	466	33	.484	935
Duke	90	436	400	31	.521	867
La.-Lafayette	95	435	457	32	.488	924
Northwestern	115	428	579	44	.428	1051
Southern Methodist	86	423	422	54	.501	899
Connecticut (2002)	104	421	462	38	.478	921
Toledo	82	420	351	24	.543	795
Indiana	115	415	555	44	.431	1014
Kansas St.	107	415	560	42	.429	1017
San Jose St.	84	415	383	38	.519	836
Idaho (1996)	105	410	479	25	.462	914
New Mexico	104	410	477	31	.464	918
Florida St.	56	409	194	17	.673	620
Eastern Mich.	110	401	446	46	.475	893
New Mexico St.	107	397	495	32	.447	924
Rice	91	397	495	32	.447	924
Troy St. (2002)	72	392	297	15	.567	704
Memphis	87	391	411	32	.488	834
Temple	104	390	468	52	.457	910
Louisville	84	385	395	17	.494	797
Arkansas St. (1992)	88	377	395	37	.489	809
Ball St.	78	366	316	32	.535	714
Wake Forest	101	363	553	23	.399	939
East Caro.	67	344	312	12	.524	668
UTEP	85	322	470	30	.410	822
Houston	57	313	288	15	.520	616
Buffalo (1999)	89	310	404	29	.437	743
Air Force	47	283	234	13	.546	530
Kent St.	80	277	438	28	.392	743
Boise St. (1996)	35	271	134	2	.668	407
La.-Monroe (1994)	52	236	303	8	.439	547
UNLV	35	195	193	4	.503	392
UCF (1996)	24	138	121	1	.533	260
UAB (1996)	12	69	59	3	.538	131
South Fla. (2000)	6	44	22	0	.667	665

Records in the 2000s

(2000-01-02, Including Bowls)

BY PERCENTAGE

Team	2000 W	L	2001 W	L	2002 W	L	Total W	L	Pct.
Miami (Fla.)	11	1	12	0	12	1	35	2	.946
Oklahoma	13	0	11	2	12	2	36	4	.900
Texas	9	3	11	2	11	2	31	7	.816
Boise St.	10	2	8	4	12	1	30	7	.811
Toledo	10	1	10	2	9	5	29	8	.784
Virginia Tech	11	1	8	3	10	4	29	8	.784
Marshall	8	5	11	2	11	2	30	9	.769
Georgia	8	4	8	4	13	1	29	9	.763
Ohio St.	8	4	7	5	14	0	29	9	.763
Oregon	10	2	11	1	7	6	28	9	.757
Florida	10	3	10	2	8	5	28	10	.737
Michigan	9	3	8	4	10	3	27	10	.730
South Fla.	7	4	8	3	9	2	24	9	.727
TCU	10	2	6	6	10	2	26	10	.722
Florida St.	11	2	8	4	9	5	28	11	.718
Kansas St.	11	3	6	6	11	2	28	11	.718
Nebraska	10	2	11	2	7	7	28	11	.718
Colorado St.	10	2	7	5	10	4	27	11	.711
Louisville	9	3	11	2	7	6	27	11	.711
Tennessee	8	4	11	2	8	5	27	11	.711
Maryland	5	6	10	2	11	3	26	11	.703
Washington	11	1	8	4	7	6	26	11	.703
LSU	8	4	10	3	8	5	26	12	.684
North Carolina St.	8	4	7	5	11	3	26	12	.684
Fresno St.	7	5	11	3	9	5	27	13	.675
Notre Dame	9	3	5	6	10	3	24	12	.667
Oregon St.	11	1	5	6	8	5	24	12	.667
Washington St.	4	7	10	2	10	3	24	12	.667
Auburn	9	4	7	5	9	4	25	13	.658
Boston College	7	5	8	4	9	4	24	13	.649
Georgia Tech	9	3	8	5	7	6	24	14	.632
Air Force	9	3	6	6	8	5	23	14	.622
Clemson	9	3	7	5	7	6	23	14	.622
Pittsburgh	7	5	7	5	9	4	23	14	.622
South Carolina	8	4	9	3	5	7	22	14	.611
Brigham Young	6	6	12	2	5	7	23	15	.605
Iowa St.	9	3	7	5	7	7	23	15	.605
Southern California	5	7	6	6	11	2	22	15	.595
Texas Tech	7	6	7	5	9	5	23	16	.590
UCF	7	4	6	5	7	5	20	14	.588
Northern Ill.	6	5	6	5	8	4	20	14	.588
Mississippi	7	5	7	4	7	6	21	15	.583
Southern Miss.	8	4	6	5	7	6	21	15	.583
Texas A&M	7	5	8	4	6	6	21	15	.583
UCLA	6	6	7	4	8	5	21	15	.583
Arkansas	6	6	7	5	9	5	22	16	.579
Colorado	3	8	10	3	9	5	22	16	.579
Hawaii	3	9	9	3	10	4	22	16	.579
Illinois	5	6	10	2	5	7	20	15	.571
Miami (Ohio)	6	5	7	5	7	5	20	15	.571
Troy St.	9	3	7	4	4	8	20	15	.571
Iowa	3	9	7	5	11	2	21	16	.568
Purdue	8	4	6	6	7	6	21	16	.568
Wisconsin	9	4	5	7	8	6	22	17	.564
Bowling Green	2	9	8	3	9	3	19	15	.559
Alabama	3	8	7	5	10	3	20	16	.556
Syracuse	6	5	10	3	4	8	20	16	.556
Cincinnati	7	5	7	5	7	7	21	17	.553
UAB	7	4	6	5	5	7	18	16	.529
Middle Tenn.	6	5	8	3	4	8	18	16	.529
Penn St.	5	7	5	6	9	4	19	17	.528
West Virginia	7	5	3	8	9	4	19	17	.528
Virginia	6	6	5	7	9	5	20	18	.526
Western Mich.	9	3	5	6	4	8	18	17	.514
East Caro.	8	4	6	6	4	8	18	18	.500
Minnesota	6	6	4	7	8	5	18	18	.500
Utah	4	7	8	4	5	6	17	17	.500
Arizona St.	6	6	4	7	8	6	18	19	.486
New Mexico	5	7	6	5	7	7	18	19	.486
UNLV	8	5	4	7	5	7	17	19	.472
North Carolina	6	5	8	5	3	9	17	19	.472
Tulane	6	5	3	9	8	5	17	19	.472
Ball St.	5	6	5	6	6	6	16	18	.471
Stanford	5	6	9	3	2	9	16	18	.471
Michigan St.	5	6	7	5	4	8	16	19	.457
North Texas	3	8	5	7	8	5	16	20	.444
Rice	3	8	8	4	4	7	15	19	.441

Team	2000 W	L	2001 W	L	2002 W	L	Total W	L	Pct.
San Jose St.	7	5	3	9	6	7	16	21	.432
New Mexico St.	3	8	5	7	7	5	15	20	.429
Northwestern	8	4	4	7	3	9	15	20	.429
Oklahoma St.	3	8	4	7	8	5	15	20	.429
Wake Forest	2	9	6	5	7	6	15	20	.429
Akron	6	5	4	7	4	8	14	20	.412
Arizona	5	6	5	6	4	8	14	20	.412
Mississippi St.	8	4	3	8	3	9	14	21	.400
Utah St.	5	6	4	7	4	7	13	20	.394
Louisiana Tech	3	9	7	5	4	8	14	22	.389
Memphis	4	7	5	6	3	9	12	22	.353
Missouri	3	8	4	7	5	7	12	22	.353
Ohio	7	4	1	10	4	8	12	22	.353
Temple	4	7	4	7	4	8	12	22	.353
UTEP	8	4	2	9	2	10	12	23	.343
California	3	8	1	10	7	5	11	23	.324
Connecticut	3	8	2	9	6	6	11	23	.324
Indiana	3	8	5	6	3	9	11	23	.324
Kentucky	2	9	2	9	7	5	11	23	.324
Kent St.	1	10	6	5	3	9	10	24	.294
Nevada	2	10	3	8	5	7	10	25	.286
San Diego St.	3	8	3	8	4	9	10	25	.286
Southern Methodist	3	9	4	7	3	9	10	25	.286
Central Mich.	2	9	3	8	4	8	9	25	.265
Kansas	4	7	3	8	2	10	9	25	.265
Arkansas St.	1	10	2	9	6	7	9	26	.257
Baylor	2	9	3	8	3	9	8	26	.235
Eastern Mich.	3	8	2	9	3	9	8	26	.235
Houston	3	8	0	11	5	7	8	26	.235
Idaho	5	6	1	10	2	10	8	26	.235
La.-Lafayette	1	10	3	8	3	9	7	27	.206
Vanderbilt	3	8	2	9	2	10	7	27	.206
Tulsa	5	7	1	10	1	11	7	28	.200
Buffalo	2	9	3	8	1	11	6	28	.176
La.-Monroe	1	10	2	9	3	9	6	28	.176
Rutgers	3	8	2	9	1	11	6	28	.176
Army	1	10	3	8	1	11	5	29	.147
Wyoming	1	10	2	9	2	10	5	29	.147
Navy	1	10	0	10	2	10	3	30	.091
Duke	0	11	0	11	2	10	2	32	.059

BY VICTORIES

Team	Wins	Team	Wins
Oklahoma	36	Colorado	22
Miami (Fla.)	35	Hawaii	22
Texas	31	South Carolina	22
Boise St.	30	Southern California	22
Marshall	30	Wisconsin	22
Toledo	29	Cincinnati	21
Virginia Tech	29	Iowa	21
Georgia	29	Mississippi	21
Ohio St.	29	Purdue	21
Florida	28	Southern Miss.	21
Florida St.	28	Texas A&M	21
Kansas St.	28	UCLA	21
Nebraska	28	Alabama	20
Oregon	28	UCF	20
Colorado St.	27	Illinois	20
Fresno St.	27	Miami (Ohio)	20
Louisville	27	Northern Ill.	20
Michigan	27	Syracuse	20
Tennessee	27	Troy St.	20
LSU	26	Virginia	20
Maryland	26	Bowling Green	19
North Carolina St.	26	Penn St.	19
TCU	26	West Virginia	19
Washington	26	UAB	18
Auburn	25	Arizona St.	18
Boston College	24	East Caro.	18
Georgia Tech	24	Middle Tenn.	18
Notre Dame	24	Minnesota	18
Oregon St.	24	New Mexico	18
South Fla.	24	Western Mich.	18
Washington St.	24	UNLV	17
Air Force	23	North Carolina	17
Brigham Young	23	Tulane	17
Clemson	23	Utah	17
Iowa St.	23	Ball St.	16
Pittsburgh	23	Michigan St.	16
Texas Tech	23	North Texas	16
Arkansas	22		

Team	Wins
San Jose St.	16
Stanford	16
New Mexico St.	15
Northwestern	15
Oklahoma St.	15
Rice	15
Wake Forest	15
Akron	14
Arizona	14
Louisiana Tech	14
Mississippi St.	14
Utah St.	13
Memphis	12
Missouri	12
Ohio	12
Temple	12
UTEP	12
California	11
Connecticut	11
Indiana	11
Kentucky	11

Team	Wins
Kent St.	10
Nevada	10
San Diego St.	10
Southern Methodist	10
Arkansas St.	9
Central Mich.	9
Kansas	9
Baylor	8
Eastern Mich.	8
Houston	8
Idaho	8
La.-Lafayette	7
Tulsa	7
Vanderbilt	7
Buffalo	6
La.-Monroe	6
Rutgers	6
Army	5
Wyoming	5
Navy	3
Duke	2

Team	W-L-T	*Pct.
UNLV	33-79-0	.295
Northern Ill.	32-78-0	.291
Buffalo	30-77-0	.280
Oregon St.	29-81-1	.266
Arkansas St.	28-80-2	.264

Team	W-L-T	*Pct.
Iowa St.	27-80-3	.259
UTEP	28-84-2	.254
Temple	22-88-0	.200
Kent St.	15-94-1	.141

*Ties counted as half won and half lost.

BY VICTORIES

Team	Wins
Marshall	114
Florida St.	109
Nebraska	108
Florida	102
Tennessee	99
Penn St.	97
Texas A&M	94
Michigan	93
Miami (Fla.)	92
Ohio St.	91
Colorado	87
Kansas St.	87
Brigham Young	86
Notre Dame	84
Alabama	83
Syracuse	82
Washington	82
Nevada	80
Air Force	78
North Carolina	78
Virginia	78
Idaho	77
Virginia Tech	77
Colorado St.	74
Texas	74
Auburn	72
Georgia	72
Toledo	72
Arizona	71
Utah	71
Oregon	70
Wyoming	70
Clemson	69
UCLA	69
Wisconsin	69
Fresno St.	68
Middle Tenn.	68
Southern California	68
Boise St.	67
UCF	67
East Caro.	67
Mississippi	67
Southern Miss.	67
Georgia Tech	66
North Carolina St.	66
Miami (Ohio)	65
West Virginia	65
Western Mich.	65
Mississippi St.	64
Arizona St.	62
Iowa	62
Michigan St.	62
San Diego St.	62
Texas Tech	62
Bowling Green	61
Louisiana Tech	61
Oklahoma	61
Stanford	60

Team	Wins
Louisville	59
La.-Monroe	58
Boston College	57
Kansas	56
Arkansas	55
California	55
Central Mich.	54
LSU	54
Washington St.	53
Ball St.	52
Rice	52
UAB	51
TCU	51
Army	50
Illinois	50
Baylor	49
Hawaii	49
Utah St.	48
Indiana	47
Purdue	47
Memphis	45
New Mexico	45
Kentucky	44
San Jose St.	44
Cincinnati	43
Missouri	43
Navy	43
Northwestern	43
Houston	42
South Carolina	42
Oklahoma St.	41
Akron	40
Minnesota	40
North Texas	40
Tulsa	40
La.-Lafayette	39
Maryland	38
Tulane	38
Wake Forest	38
Pittsburgh	37
Rutgers	37
Eastern Mich.	35
Ohio	34
Vanderbilt	34
Duke	33
UNLV	33
New Mexico St.	33
Northern Ill.	32
Southern Methodist	31
Buffalo	30
Oregon St.	29
Arkansas St.	28
UTEP	28
Iowa St.	27
Temple	22
Kent St.	15

Records in the 1990s

(1990-91-92-93-94-95-96-97-98-99, Including Bowls and Playoffs; Tie-breaker Began 1996)

BY PERCENTAGE

Team	W-L-T	*Pct.
Florida St.	109-13-1	.890
Nebraska	108-16-1	.868
Marshall	114-25-0	.820
Florida	102-22-1	.820
Tennessee	99-22-2	.813
Penn St.	97-26-0	.789
Michigan	93-26-3	.775
Miami (Fla.)	92-27-0	.773
Texas A&M	94-28-2	.766
Ohio St.	91-29-3	.752
Colorado	87-29-4	.742
Kansas St.	87-30-1	.742
Notre Dame	84-35-2	.702
Washington	82-35-1	.699
Syracuse	82-35-3	.695
Brigham Young	86-39-2	.685
Alabama	83-40-0	.675
Nevada	80-39-0	.672
North Carolina	78-39-1	.665
Virginia Tech	77-39-1	.662
Virginia	78-40-1	.660
Idaho	77-41-0	.653
Toledo	72-38-3	.650
Air Force	78-44-0	.639
Auburn	72-40-3	.639
Georgia	72-43-1	.625
Texas	74-44-2	.625
Colorado St.	74-46-0	.617
Miami (Ohio)	65-40-5	.614
Utah	71-46-0	.607
Arizona	71-46-1	.606
Wisconsin	69-45-4	.602
UCLA	69-46-0	.600
Wyoming	70-47-1	.597
Middle Tenn.	68-46-1	.596
Western Mich.	65-44-2	.595
Clemson	69-47-1	.594
Oregon	70-48-0	.593
UCF	67-46-0	.593
Southern Miss.	67-46-1	.592
East Caro.	67-47-0	.588
Mississippi	67-48-0	.583
Southern California	68-49-4	.579
Fresno St.	68-50-2	.575
Georgia Tech	66-49-1	.573
West Virginia	65-49-2	.569
Bowling Green	61-46-4	.568
North Carolina St.	66-51-1	.564
Mississippi St.	64-50-2	.560
Boise St.	67-53-0	.558
Louisiana Tech	61-48-3	.558
Arizona St.	62-51-0	.549
Oklahoma	61-51-3	.543

Team	W-L-T	*Pct.
San Diego St.	62-52-2	.543
UAB	51-43-2	.542
Texas Tech	62-53-0	.539
Iowa	62-53-2	.538
Michigan St.	62-53-2	.538
Stanford	60-54-2	.526
Louisville	59-54-1	.522
La.-Monroe	58-56-1	.509
Central Mich.	54-53-5	.504
Boston College	57-57-2	.500
Kansas	56-57-1	.496
Arkansas	55-58-2	.487
California	55-59-1	.483
LSU	54-58-1	.482
Rice	52-57-1	.477
Ball St.	52-58-2	.473
Washington St.	53-61-0	.465
TCU	51-61-1	.456
Army	50-60-1	.455
Illinois	50-63-2	.443
Baylor	49-63-1	.438
Utah St.	48-63-1	.433
Purdue	47-64-3	.425
Indiana	47-64-2	.425
Memphis	45-64-1	.414
Hawaii	49-71-2	.410
San Jose St.	44-66-2	.402
Missouri	43-67-3	.394
Cincinnati	43-67-1	.392
South Carolina	42-66-3	.392
Kentucky	44-69-0	.389
New Mexico	45-71-0	.388
Navy	43-69-0	.384
Houston	42-68-1	.383
Northwestern	43-70-1	.382
Oklahoma St.	41-68-3	.379
Akron	40-68-2	.373
North Texas	40-69-2	.369
Tulsa	40-70-1	.365
La.-Lafayette	39-70-1	.359
Minnesota	40-72-0	.357
Maryland	38-72-1	.347
Rutgers	37-72-1	.341
Tulane	38-74-0	.339
Wake Forest	38-74-0	.339
Pittsburgh	37-74-1	.335
Eastern Mich.	35-74-1	.323
Ohio	34-74-3	.320
Vanderbilt	34-76-0	.309
Duke	33-77-1	.302
New Mexico St.	33-77-0	.300
Southern Methodist	31-76-3	.295

Winningest Teams by Decade

(By Percentage; Bowls and Playoffs Included, Unless Noted)

1980-89

Rank	Team	W-L-T	Pct.†	Rank	Team	W-L-T	Pct.†
1.	Nebraska	103-20-0	.837	11.	Alabama	85-32-2	.723
2.	Miami (Fla.)	98-20-0	.831		Arkansas	85-32-2	.723
3.	Brigham Young	102-26-0	.797	13.	UCLA	81-30-6	.718
4.	Oklahoma	91-25-2	.780	14.	Washington	83-33-1	.714
5.	Clemson	86-25-4	.765	15.	Fresno St.	80-34-1	.700
6.	Penn St.	89-27-2	.763	16.	Ohio St.	82-35-2	.697
7.	Georgia	88-27-4	.756	17.	Southern Methodist	63-28-1	.690

Rank	Team	W-L-T	Pct.†	Rank	Team	W-L-T	Pct.†
8.	Florida St.	87-28-3	.750	18.	Southern California	78-35-3	.685
	Michigan	89-29-2	.750	19.	Florida	76-37-3	.668
10.	Auburn	86-31-1	.733	20.	Arizona St.	73-36-4	.664

1970-79

Rank	Team	W-L-T	Pct.†	Rank	Team	W-L-T	Pct.†
1.	Oklahoma	102-13-3	.877	11.	Arizona St.	90-28-0	.763
2.	Alabama	103-16-1	.863	12.	Yale@	67-21-2	.756
3.	Michigan	96-16-3	.848	13.	San Diego St.	82-26-2	.755
4.	Tennessee St.	85-17-2	.827	14.	Miami (Ohio)	80-26-2	.750
5.	Nebraska	98-20-4	.820	15.	Central Mich.	80-27-3	.741
6.	Penn St.	96-22-0	.814	16.	Arkansas	79-31-5	.709
7.	Ohio St.	91-20-3	.811	17.	Houston	80-33-2	.704
8.	Notre Dame	91-22-0	.805	18.	Louisiana Tech	77-34-2	.690
9.	Southern California	93-21-5	.803	19.	McNeese St.@	75-33-4	.688
10.	Texas	88-26-1	.770	20.	Dartmouth@	60-27-3	.683

1960-69

(By Percentage; Bowls and Playoffs Not Included)

Rank	Team	W-L-T	Pct.†	Rank	Team	W-L-T	Pct.†
1.	Alabama	85-12-3	.865	5.	Bowling Green	71-22-2	.758
2.	Texas	80-18-2	.810	6.	Dartmouth@	68-22-0	.750
3.	Arkansas	80-19-1	.805		Ohio St.	67-21-2	.756
4.	Mississippi	72-20-6	.765	8.	Missouri	72-22-6	.750
	Southern California	73-23-4	.750	10.	Penn St.	73-26-0	.737

Rank	Team	W-L-T	Pct.†	Rank	Team	W-L-T	Pct.†
11.	Memphis	70-25-1	.734	17.	Utah St.	68-29-3	.695
12.	Arizona St.	72-26-1	.732	18.	Purdue	64-28-3	.689
13.	LSU	70-25-5	.725	19.	Syracuse	68-31-0	.687
	Nebraska	72-27-1	.725	20.	Florida	66-30-4	.680
15.	Wyoming	69-26-4	.717		Miami (Ohio)	66-30-4	.680
16.	Princeton@	64-26-0	.711		Tennessee	65-29-6	.680

1950-59

Rank	Team	W-L-T	Pct.†	Rank	Team	W-L-T	Pct.†
1.	Oklahoma	93-10-2	.895	11.	Syracuse	62-29-2	.677
2.	Mississippi	80-21-5	.778	12.	Army	58-27-5	.672
3.	Michigan St.	70-21-1	.766	13.	Cincinnati	64-30-7	.668
4.	Princeton@	67-22-1	.750	14.	Notre Dame	64-31-4	.667
5.	Georgia Tech	79-26-6	.739	15.	Clemson	64-32-5	.658
6.	UCLA	68-26-3	.716	16.	Wisconsin	57-28-7	.658
7.	Ohio St.	63-24-5	.712	17.	Colorado	62-33-6	.644
8.	Tennessee	71-31-4	.692	18.	Duke	62-33-7	.642
9.	Penn St.	62-28-4	.681	19.	Navy	55-30-8	.634
10.	Maryland	67-31-3	.678	20.	Yale@	54-30-6	.633

†Ties computed as half won and half lost. @Now a member of Division I-AA.

Records in the Last Five Years

(1997-98-99-2000-02; Including Bowls)

BY PERCENTAGE

Team	1998 W	L	1999 W	L	2000 W	L	2001 W	L	2002 W	L	Total W	L	Pct.
Miami (Fla.)	9	3	9	4	11	1	12	0	12	1	53	9	.855
Marshall	12	1	13	0	8	5	11	2	11	2	55	10	.846
Virginia Tech	9	3	11	1	11	1	8	3	10	4	49	12	.803
Florida St.	11	2	12	0	11	2	8	4	9	5	51	13	.797
Kansas St.	11	2	11	1	11	3	6	6	11	2	50	14	.781
Tennessee	13	0	9	3	8	4	11	2	8	5	49	14	.778
Texas	9	3	9	5	9	3	11	2	11	2	49	15	.766
Oklahoma	5	6	7	5	13	0	11	2	12	2	48	15	.762
Michigan	10	3	10	2	9	3	8	4	10	3	47	15	.758
Boise St.	6	5	10	3	10	2	8	4	12	1	46	15	.754
Nebraska	9	4	12	1	10	2	11	2	7	7	49	16	.754
Florida	10	2	9	4	10	3	10	2	8	5	47	16	.746
Georgia	9	3	8	4	8	4	8	4	13	1	46	16	.742
Ohio St.	11	1	6	6	8	4	7	5	14	0	46	16	.742
Oregon	8	4	9	3	10	2	11	1	7	6	45	16	.738
South Fla.	8	3	7	4	7	4	8	3	9	2	39	16	.709
Toledo	7	5	6	5	10	1	10	2	9	5	42	18	.700
Colorado St.	8	4	8	4	10	2	7	5	10	4	43	19	.694
TCU	7	5	8	4	10	2	6	6	10	2	41	19	.683
Wisconsin	11	1	10	2	9	4	5	7	8	6	43	20	.683
Georgia Tech	10	2	8	4	9	3	8	5	7	6	42	20	.677
Air Force	12	1	6	5	9	3	6	6	8	5	41	20	.672
Louisville	7	5	7	5	9	3	11	2	7	6	41	21	.661
Troy St.	8	4	11	2	9	3	7	4	4	8	39	21	.650
Miami (Ohio)	10	1	7	4	6	5	7	5	7	5	37	20	.649
Texas A&M	11	3	8	4	7	5	8	4	6	6	40	22	.645
Washington	6	6	7	5	11	1	8	4	7	6	39	22	.639
Notre Dame	9	3	5	7	9	3	5	6	10	3	38	22	.633
Arkansas	9	3	8	4	6	6	7	5	9	5	39	23	.629
North Carolina St.	7	5	6	6	8	4	7	5	11	3	39	23	.629
Brigham Young	9	5	8	4	6	6	12	2	5	7	40	24	.625
Fresno St.	5	6	8	5	7	5	11	3	9	5	40	24	.625
Penn St.	9	3	10	3	5	7	5	6	9	4	38	23	.623
Southern Miss.	7	5	9	3	8	4	6	5	7	6	37	23	.617
Oregon St.	5	6	7	5	11	1	5	6	8	5	36	23	.610
Alabama	7	5	10	3	3	8	7	5	10	3	37	24	.607
Boston College	4	7	8	4	7	5	8	4	9	4	36	24	.600
Mississippi	7	5	8	4	7	5	7	4	7	6	36	24	.600
Colorado	8	4	7	5	3	8	10	3	9	5	37	25	.597
Purdue	9	4	7	5	8	4	6	6	7	6	37	25	.597
UCLA	10	2	4	7	6	6	7	4	8	5	35	24	.593
UCF	9	2	4	7	7	4	6	5	7	5	33	23	.589
Syracuse	8	4	7	5	6	5	10	3	4	8	35	25	.583
Southern California	8	5	6	6	5	7	6	6	11	2	36	26	.581
Texas Tech	7	5	6	6	7	6	7	5	9	5	36	26	.581
Virginia	9	3	7	5	6	6	5	7	9	5	36	26	.581
Utah	7	4	9	3	4	7	8	4	5	6	33	24	.579

Team	1998 W	L	1999 W	L	2000 W	L	2001 W	L	2002 W	L	Total W	L	Pct.
Maryland	3	8	5	6	5	6	10	2	11	3	34	25	.576
East Caro.	6	5	9	3	8	4	6	6	4	8	33	26	.559
Western Mich.	7	4	7	5	9	3	5	6	4	8	32	26	.552
Auburn	3	8	5	6	9	4	7	5	9	4	33	27	.550
LSU	4	7	3	8	8	4	10	3	8	5	33	27	.550
Arizona	12	1	6	6	5	6	5	6	4	8	32	27	.542
Michigan St.	6	6	10	2	5	6	7	5	4	8	32	27	.542
Tulane	12	0	3	8	6	5	3	9	8	5	32	27	.542
Illinois	3	8	8	4	5	6	10	2	5	7	31	27	.534
Clemson	3	8	6	6	9	3	7	5	7	6	32	28	.533
Mississippi St.	8	5	10	2	8	4	3	8	3	9	32	28	.533
Minnesota	5	6	8	4	6	6	4	7	8	5	31	28	.525
West Virginia	8	4	4	7	7	5	3	8	9	4	31	28	.525
Bowling Green	5	6	5	6	2	9	8	3	9	3	29	27	.518
Pittsburgh	2	9	5	6	7	5	7	5	9	4	30	29	.508
Washington St.	3	8	3	9	4	7	10	2	10	3	30	29	.508
Iowa St.	3	8	4	7	9	3	7	5	7	7	30	30	.500
Hawaii	0	12	9	4	3	9	9	3	10	4	31	32	.492
Arizona St.	5	6	6	6	6	6	4	7	8	6	29	31	.483
UAB	4	7	5	6	7	4	6	5	5	7	27	29	.482
Northern Ill.	2	9	5	6	6	5	6	5	8	4	27	29	.482
Louisiana Tech	6	6	8	3	3	9	7	5	4	8	28	31	.475
Stanford	3	8	8	4	5	6	9	3	2	9	27	30	.474
Middle Tenn.	5	5	5	6	8	3	4	8	4	7	26	29	.473
North Carolina	7	5	3	8	6	5	8	5	3	9	27	32	.458
Akron	4	7	5	6	6	5	4	7	6	6	25	31	.446
Rice	5	6	5	6	3	8	8	4	4	7	25	31	.446
Oklahoma St.	5	6	5	6	3	8	4	7	8	5	25	32	.439
Cincinnati	2	9	3	8	7	5	7	5	7	7	26	34	.433
Connecticut	10	3	4	7	3	8	2	9	6	6	25	33	.431
Wake Forest	3	8	7	5	2	9	6	5	7	6	25	33	.431
Iowa	3	8	1	10	3	8	7	5	11	2	25	34	.424
Idaho	9	3	7	4	5	6	1	10	2	10	24	33	.421
Missouri	8	4	4	7	3	8	4	7	5	7	24	33	.421
New Mexico St.	3	8	6	5	3	8	5	7	7	5	24	33	.421
New Mexico	3	9	4	7	5	7	6	5	7	5	25	35	.417
Kentucky	7	5	6	6	2	9	2	9	7	5	24	34	.414
South Carolina	1	10	0	11	8	4	9	3	5	7	23	35	.397
Ohio	5	6	5	6	7	4	1	10	4	8	22	34	.393
San Jose St.	4	8	3	7	7	5	3	9	6	7	23	36	.390
Utah St.	3	8	4	7	5	6	4	7	4	7	20	35	.364
North Texas	3	8	2	9	3	8	5	7	8	5	21	37	.362
Northwestern	3	9	3	8	8	4	4	7	3	9	21	37	.362
California	5	6	4	7	3	8	1	10	7	5	20	36	.357
Wyoming	8	3	7	4	1	10	2	9	2	10	20	36	.357
UNLV	0	11	3	8	8	5	4	7	5	7	20	38	.345

Team	1998 W L	1999 W L	2000 W L	2001 W L	2002 W L	Total W L Pct.
UTEP	3 8	5 7	8 4	2 9	2 10	20 38 .345
Central Mich.	6 5	4 7	2 9	3 8	4 8	19 37 .339
Indiana	4 7	4 7	3 8	5 6	3 9	19 37 .339
Memphis	2 9	5 6	4 7	5 6	3 9	19 37 .339
Nevada	6 5	3 8	2 10	3 8	5 7	19 38 .333
Southern Methodist	5 7	4 6	3 9	4 7	3 9	19 38 .333
Houston	3 8	7 4	3 8	0 11	5 7	18 38 .321
Kansas	4 7	5 7	4 7	3 8	2 10	18 39 .316
Ball St.	1 10	0 11	5 6	5 6	6 6	17 39 .304
Arkansas St.	4 8	4 7	1 10	2 9	6 7	17 41 .293
La.-Monroe	5 6	5 6	1 10	2 9	3 9	16 40 .286
Temple	2 9	2 9	4 7	4 7	4 8	16 40 .286

Team	1998 W L	1999 W L	2000 W L	2001 W L	2002 W L	Total W L Pct.
Eastern Mich.	3 8	4 7	3 8	2 9	3 9	15 41 .268
Vanderbilt	2 9	5 6	3 8	2 10	2 10	14 42 .250
Tulsa	4 7	2 9	5 7	1 10	1 11	13 44 .228
Kent St.	0 11	2 9	1 10	6 5	3 9	12 44 .214
Rutgers	5 6	1 10	3 8	2 9	1 11	12 44 .214
Army	3 8	3 8	1 10	3 8	1 11	11 45 .196
Baylor	2 9	1 10	2 9	3 8	3 9	11 45 .196
La.-Lafayette	2 9	2 9	1 10	3 8	3 9	11 45 .196
Navy	3 8	5 7	1 10	0 10	2 10	11 45 .196
Buffalo	4 7	0 11	2 9	3 8	1 11	10 46 .179
Duke	4 7	3 8	0 11	0 11	2 10	9 47 .161

BY VICTORIES

Team	Wins
Marshall	55
Miami (Fla.)	53
Florida St.	51
Kansas St.	50
Nebraska	49
Tennessee	49
Texas	49
Virginia Tech	49
Oklahoma	48
Florida	47
Michigan	47
Boise St.	46
Georgia	46
Ohio St.	46
Oregon	45
Colorado St.	43
Wisconsin	43
Georgia Tech	42
Toledo	42
Air Force	41
Louisville	41
TCU	41
Brigham Young	40
Fresno St.	40
Texas A&M	40
Arkansas	39
North Carolina St.	39
South Fla.	39
Troy St.	39
Washington	39

Team	Wins
Notre Dame	38
Penn St.	38
Alabama	37
Colorado	37
Miami (Ohio)	37
Purdue	37
Southern Miss.	37
Boston College	36
Mississippi	36
Oregon St.	36
Southern California	36
Texas Tech	36
Virginia	36
Syracuse	35
UCLA	35
Maryland	34
Auburn	33
UCF	33
East Caro.	33
LSU	33
Utah	33
Arizona	32
Clemson	32
Michigan St.	32
Mississippi St.	32
Tulane	32
Western Mich.	32
Hawaii	31
Illinois	31
Minnesota	31

Team	Wins
West Virginia	31
Iowa St.	30
Pittsburgh	30
Washington St.	30
Arizona St.	29
Bowling Green	29
Louisiana Tech	28
UAB	27
North Carolina	27
Northern Ill.	27
Stanford	27
Cincinnati	26
Middle Tenn.	26
Akron	25
Connecticut	25
Iowa	25
New Mexico	25
Oklahoma St.	25
Rice	25
Wake Forest	25
Idaho	24
Kentucky	24
Missouri	24
New Mexico St.	24
San Jose St.	23
South Carolina	23
Ohio	22
San Diego St.	22
North Texas	21

Team	Wins
Northwestern	21
California	20
UNLV	20
UTEP	20
Utah St.	20
Wyoming	20
Central Mich.	19
Indiana	19
Memphis	19
Nevada	19
Southern Methodist	19
Houston	18
Kansas	18
Arkansas St.	17
Ball St.	17
La.-Monroe	16
Temple	16
Eastern Mich.	15
Vanderbilt	14
Tulsa	13
Kent St.	12
Rutgers	12
Army	11
Baylor	11
La.-Lafayette	11
Navy	11
Buffalo	10
Duke	9

National Poll Rankings

National Champion Major Selectors (1869 to Present)

The criteria for being included in this historical list of poll selectors is that the poll be national in scope, either through distribution in newspaper, television, radio and/or computer online. The list also includes former selectors, who were instrumental in the sport of college football, as well as selectors presently among the Bowl Championship Series (BCS) selectors.

Selector	Selection Format	Active Seasons First	Active Seasons Last	Active Seasons Total	Predated Seasons	Total Rankings
Frank Dickinson	Math	1926	1940	15	1924-25	17
Deke Houlgate	Math	1927	1958	32	1885-1926	72
Dunkel	Math	1929	2002	74		74
William Boand	Math	1930	1960	31	1919-29	42
Paul Williamson	Math	1932	1963	32		32
Parke Davis	Research	1933	1933	1	1869-1932	65
Edward Litkenhous	Math	1934	1984	51		51
Richard Poling	Math	1935	1984	50	1924-34	61
Associated Press*	Poll	1936	2002	67		67
Helms Athletic Foundation	Poll	1941	1982	42	1883-1940	100
Harry DeVold	Math	1945	2001	57	1939-44	63
United Press International	Poll	1950	1995	44		44
International News Service	Poll	1952	1957	6		6
Football Writers Association	Poll	1954	2002	49		49
Football News	Poll	1958	2002	45		45
National Football Foundation	Poll	1959	2002	40		40
Herman Matthews*	Math	1966	2002	37		37
David Rothman (FACT)*	Math	1968	2001	34		34
Richard Billingsley*	Math	1970	2002	33	1869-70, 1872-1969	133
Sporting News	Poll	1975	2002	28		28
Jeff Sagarin*	Math	1978	2002	25	1938, 56-77	48

Selector	Selection Format	Active Seasons			Predated Seasons	Total Rankings
		First	Last	Total		
New York Times*	Math	1979	2002	24		24
College Football Researchers Association	Poll	1982	1992	11	1919-81	75
USA Today/CNN	Poll	1982	1996	15		15
Steve Eck	Math	1987	2002	16		16
UPI/National Football Foundation	Poll	1991	1992	2		2
Wes Colley Matrix*	Math	1992	2002	11		11
Peter Wolfe*	Math	1992	2002	11		11
USA Today/National Football Foundation	Poll	1993	1994	2		2
Kenneth Massey*	Math	1995	2002	8		8
USA Today/ESPN*	Poll	1997	2001	5		5
Jeff Anderson/Chris Hester (Seattle Times)*	Math	1997	2002	6		6

*Poll utilized in Bowl Championship Series Rankings for 2002.

POLL SYSTEMS HISTORY

Anderson/Hester (1997-present), a mathematical rating system developed by Jeff Anderson and Chris Hester. Published weekly in The Seattle Times since 1993. Member of 2002 BCS.

Associated Press (1936-present), the first major nationwide poll for ranking college football teams was voted on by sportswriters and broadcasters. It continues to this day and is probably the most well-known and widely circulated among all of history's polls. The Associated Press annual national champions were awarded the Williams Trophy and the Reverend J. Hugh O'Donnell Trophy. In 1947, Notre Dame retired the Williams Trophy (named after Henry L. Williams, Minnesota coach, and sponsored by the M Club of Minnesota). In 1956, Oklahoma retired the O'Donnell Trophy (named for Notre Dame's president and sponsored by Notre Dame alumni). Beginning with the 1957 season, the award was known as the AP Trophy, and since 1983, has been known as the Paul "Bear" Bryant Trophy. Member of 2002 BCS.

Billingsley Report (1970-present), a mathematically based power rating system developed by Richard Billingsley of Nashville, Tennessee. His work is published annually as the Billingsley Report through his own company, the College Football Research Center. In 1996, he finished his three-year research project ranking the national champions from 1869-95. The research is located on the World Wide Web at www.CFRC.com. Predated national champions from 1869-1970. Member of 2002 BCS.

Boand System (1930-60), known as the Azzi Ratem System developed by William Boand of Tucson, Arizona. He moved to Chicago in 1932. Appeared in many newspapers as well as Illustrated Football Annual (1932-42) and weekly in Football News (1942-44, 1951-60). Predated national champions from 1919-29.

College Football Researchers Association (1982-92), founded by Anthony Cusher of Reeder, North Dakota, and Robert Kirlin of Spokane, Washington. Announced its champion in its monthly bulletin and No. 1 team determined by top-10 vote of membership on a point system. Predated national champions from 1919-81, conducted on a poll by Harry Carson Frye.

Colley (1992-present), a mathematically based power rating developed by Wes Colley of Virginia. His work is published in the Atlanta Journal-Constitution. Colley is a graduate of Princeton University with a doctorate in astrophysical sciences. Member of 2002 BCS.

DeVold System (1945-present), a mathematical rating system developed by Harry DeVold from Minneapolis, Minnesota, a former football player at Cornell. He eventually settled in the Detroit, Michigan, area and worked in the real estate business. The ratings have appeared in The Football News since 1962. Predated national champions from 1939-44.

Dickinson System (1926-40), a mathematical point system devised by Frank Dickinson, a professor of economics at Illinois. The annual Dickinson ratings were emblematic of the national championship and the basis for awarding the Rissman National Trophy and the Knute K. Rockne Intercollegiate Memorial Trophy. Notre Dame gained permanent possession of the Rissman Trophy (named for Jack F. Rissman, a Chicago clothing manufacturer) after its third victory in 1930. Minnesota retired the Rockne Trophy (named in honor of the famous Notre Dame coach) after winning it for a third time in 1940.

Dunkel System (1929-present), a power index system devised by Dick Dunkel, Sr., Founder/Owner (1929-75); by Dick Dunkel Jr., Owner (1975-2002); by Bob Dunkel, Co-Owner (2002-present), Richard H. Dunkel, Jr., Co-Owner (2002-present) and John Duck, Executive Producer, of the Daytona (Fla.) Beach News-Journal.

Eck Ratings System (1987-present), a mathematical point system developed by Steve Eck, an aerospace worker with a master's degree from UCLA. The factors in the poll are game outcome, strength of opponent and location of game.

Football News (1958-present), weekly poll of its staff writers has named a national champion since 1958.

Football Writers Association of America (1954-present), the No. 1 team of the year is determined by a five-person panel representing the nation's football writers. The national championship team named receives the Grantland Rice Award.

Helms Athletic Foundation (1941-82), originally known by this name from 1936-69 and established by the founding sponsor, Paul H. Helms, Los Angeles sportsman and philanthropist. After Helms' death in 1957, United Savings & Loan Association became its benefactor during 1970-72. A merger of United Savings and Citizen Savings was completed in 1973, and the Athletic Foundation became known as Citizens Savings Athletic Foundation. In 1982, First Interstate Bank assumed sponsorship for its final rankings. In 1941, Bill Schroeder, managing director of the Helms Athletic Foundation, retroactively selected the national football champions for the period beginning in 1883 (the first year of a scoring system) through 1940. Thereafter, Schroeder, who died in 1988, then chose, with the assistance of a Hall Board, the annual national champion after the bowl games.

Houlgate System (1927-58), a mathematical rating system developed by Deke Houlgate of Los Angeles, California. His ratings were syndicated in newspapers and published in Illustrated Football and the Football Thesaurus (1946-58).

International News Service (1952-57), a poll conducted for six years by members of the International News Service (INS) before merger with United Press in 1958.

Litkenhous (1934-84), a difference-by-score formula developed by Edward E. Litkenhous, a professor of chemical engineering at Vanderbilt, and his brother, Frank.

Massey College Football Ratings (1995-present), a mathematical rating system developed by Kenneth Massey, a graduate student at Virginia Tech in mathematics. His ratings account for homefield advantage. Member of 2002 BCS.

Matthews Grid Ratings (1966-present), a mathematical rating system developed by college mathematics professor Herman Matthews of Middlesboro, Kentucky. Has appeared in Scripps-Howard newspapers and The Football News.

National Football Foundation (1959-present), the National Football Foundation and Hall of Fame named its first national champion in 1959. Headquartered in Larchmont, New York, the present National Football Foundation was established in 1947 to promote amateur athletics in America. The national champion was awarded the MacArthur Bowl from 1959-90. In 1991 and 1992, the NFF/HOF joined with UPI to award the MacArthur Bowl, and in 1993, the NFF/HOF joined with USA Today to award the MacArthur Bowl.

New York Times (1979-present), a mathematical poll that combines the voting of a panel of sportswriters. Member of 2002 BCS.

Parke Davis (1933), a noted college football historian and former Princeton lineman, Parke H. Davis went back and named the championship teams from 1869 through the 1932 season. He also named a national champion at the conclusion of the 1933 season. Interestingly, the years 1869-75 were identified by Davis as the Pioneer Period; the years 1876-93 were called the Period of the American Intercollegiate Football Association, and the years 1894-1933 were referred to as the Period of Rules Committees and Conferences. He also coached at Wisconsin, Amherst and Lafayette.

Poling System (1935-84), a mathematical rating system for college football teams developed by Richard Poling from Mansfield, Ohio, a former football player at Ohio Wesleyan. Poling's football ratings were published annually in the Football Review Supplement and in various newspapers. Predated national champions from 1924-34.

Rothman (FACT) (1968-2002), a computerized mathematical ranking system developed by David Rothman of Hawthorne, California. FACT is the Foundation for the Analysis of Competitions and Tournaments, which began selecting a national champion in 1968. Rothman is a semiretired defense and aerospace statistician and was cochair of the Committee on Statistics in Sports and Competition of the American Statistical Association in the 1970s.

Sagarin Ratings (1978-present), a mathematical rating system developed by Jeff Sagarin of Bloomington, Indiana, a 1970 MIT mathematics graduate. Runs annually in USA Today newspaper. Predated national champions from 1938 and 1956-1977. Member of 2002 BCS.

Sporting News (1975-present), voted on annually by the staff of this St. Louis-based nationally circulated sports publication.

United Press International (1950-90, 1993-95), in 1950, the United Press news service began its poll of football coaches (replaced as coaches' poll after 1990 season). When the United Press merged with the International News Service in 1958, it became known as United Press International. The weekly UPI rankings were featured in newspapers and on radio and television nationwide. UPI and the National Football Foundation formed a coalition for 1991 and 1992 to name the MacArthur Bowl national champion. Returned to single poll in 1994-95.

USA Today/Cable News Network and ESPN (1982-1996;1997-present), introduced a weekly poll of sportswriters in 1982 and ranked the top 25 teams in the nation with a point system. The poll results were featured in USA Today, a national newspaper, and on the Cable News Network, a national cable television network. Took over as the coaches' poll in 1991. USA Today also formed a coalition with the National Football Foundation in 1993 to name the MacArthur Bowl national champion. Combined with ESPN in 1997 to distribute the coaches' poll nationally. Member of 2002 BCS.

Williamson System (1932-63), a power rating system chosen by Paul Williamson of New Orleans, Louisiana, a geologist and member of the Sugar Bowl committee.

Wolfe (1992-present), a mathematically based power rating matrix developed by Peter Wolfe and Ross Baker. Member of 2002 BCS.

Thanks from the NCAA Statistics Service to Robert A. Rosiek of Dearborn, Michigan, who researched much of the former polls' history, and to Tex Noel of Bedford, Indiana, who provided information about Parke H. Davis

National Poll Champions

Over the last 132 years, there have been nearly 30 selectors of national champions using polls, historical research and mathematical rating systems. Beginning in 1936, The Associated Press began the best-known and most widely circulated poll of sportswriters and broadcasters. Before 1936, national champions were determined by historical research and retroactive ratings and polls.

*Note: * indicates selectors that chose multiple schools. The national champion was selected before bowl games as follows: AP (1936-64 and 1966-67); UP-UPI (1950-73); FWAA (1954); NFF-HOF (1959-70). In all other latter-day polls, champions were selected after bowl games.*

1869
Princeton: Billingsley, National Championship Foundation, Parke Davis*
Rutgers: Parke Davis*

1870
Princeton: Billingsley, National Championship Foundation, Parke Davis

1871
No national champions selected.

1872
Princeton: Billingsley, National Championship Foundation, Parke Davis*
Yale: Parke Davis*

1873
Princeton: Billingsley, National Championship Foundation, Parke Davis

1874
Harvard: Parke Davis*
Princeton: Billingsley, Parke Davis*
Yale: National Championship Foundation, Parke Davis*

1875
Colgate: Parke Davis*
Harvard: National Championship Foundation, Parke Davis*
Princeton: Billingsley, Parke Davis*

1876
Yale: Billingsley, National Championship Foundation, Parke Davis

1877
Princeton: Parke Davis*
Yale: Billingsley, National Championship Foundation, Parke Davis*

1878
Princeton: Billingsley, National Championship Foundation, Parke Davis

1879
Princeton: Billingsley, National Championship Foundation, Parke Davis*
Yale: Parke Davis*

1880
Princeton: National Championship Foundation*, Parke Davis*
Yale: Billingsley, National Championship Foundation*, Parke Davis*

1881
Princeton: Billingsley, Parke Davis*
Yale: National Championship Foundation, Parke Davis*

1882
Yale: Billingsley, National Championship Foundation, Parke Davis

1883
Yale: Billingsley, Helms, National Championship Foundation, Parke Davis

1884
Princeton: Parke Davis*
Yale: Billingsley, Helms, National Championship Foundation, Parke Davis*

1885
Princeton: Billingsley, Helms, Houlgate, National Championship Foundation, Parke Davis

1886
Princeton: Parke Davis*
Yale: Billingsley, Helms, National Championship Foundation, Parke Davis*

1887
Yale: Billingsley, Helms, Houlgate, National Championship Foundation, Parke Davis

1888
Yale: Billingsley, Helms, Houlgate, National Championship Foundation, Parke Davis

1889
Princeton: Billingsley, Helms, Houlgate, National Championship Foundation, Parke Davis

1890
Harvard: Billingsley, Helms, Houlgate, National Championship Foundation, Parke Davis

1891
Yale: Billingsley, Helms, Houlgate, National Championship Foundation, Parke Davis

1892
Yale: Billingsley, Helms, Houlgate, National Championship Foundation, Parke Davis

1893
Princeton: Billingsley, Helms, Houlgate, National Championship Foundation
Yale: Parke Davis

1894
Pennsylvania: Parke Davis*
Princeton: Houlgate
Yale: Billingsley, Helms, National Championship Foundation, Parke Davis*

1895
Pennsylvania: Billingsley, Helms, Houlgate, National Championship Foundation, Parke Davis*
Yale: Parke Davis*

1896
Lafayette: National Championship Foundation*, Parke Davis*
Princeton: Billingsley, Helms, Houlgate, National Championship Foundation*, Parke Davis*

1897
Pennsylvania: Billingsley, Helms, Houlgate, National Championship Foundation, Parke Davis*
Yale: Parke Davis*

1898
Harvard: Billingsley, Helms, Houlgate, National Championship Foundation
Princeton: Parke Davis

1899
Harvard: Billingsley, Helms, Houlgate, National Championship Foundation
Princeton: Parke Davis

1900
Yale: Billingsley, Helms, Houlgate, National Championship Foundation, Parke Davis

1901
Harvard: Billingsley
Michigan: Helms, Houlgate, National Championship Foundation
Yale: Parke Davis

1902
Michigan: Billingsley, Helms, Houlgate, National Championship Foundation, Parke Davis*
Yale: Parke Davis*

1903
Michigan: Billingsley, National Championship Foundation*
Princeton: Helms, Houlgate, National Championship Foundation*, Parke Davis

1904
Michigan: Billingsley, National Championship Foundation*
Pennsylvania: Helms, Houlgate, National Championship Foundation*, Parke Davis

190
Chicago: Billingsley, Helms, Houlgate, National Championship Foundation
Yale: Parke Davis

1906
Princeton: Helms, National Championship Foundation
Vanderbilt: Billingsley
Yale: Parke Davis

1907
Pennsylvania: Billingsley
Yale: Helms, Houlgate, National Championship Foundation, Parke Davis

1908
LSU: National Championship Foundation*
Pennsylvania: Billingsley, Helms, Houlgate, National Championship Foundation*, Parke Davis

1909
Yale: Billingsley, Helms, Houlgate, National Championship Foundation, Parke Davis

1910
Harvard: Helms, Houlgate, National Championship Foundation*
Michigan: Billingsley
Pittsburgh: National Championship Foundation*

1911
Penn St.: National Championship Foundation*
Princeton: Helms, Houlgate, National Championship Foundation*, Parke Davis
Vanderbilt: Billingsley

1912
Harvard: Billingsley, Helms, Houlgate, National Championship Foundation*, Parke Davis
Penn St.: National Championship Foundation*

1913
Auburn: Billingsley
Chicago: Parke Davis*
Harvard: Helms, Houlgate, National Championship Foundation, Parke Davis*

1914
Army: Helms, Houlgate, National Championship Foundation, Parke Davis*
Illinois: Billingsley, Parke Davis*

1915
Cornell: Helms, Houlgate, National Championship Foundation, Parke Davis*
Nebraska: Billingsley
Pittsburgh: Parke Davis*

1916
Army: Parke Davis*
Pittsburgh: Billingsley, Helms, Houlgate, National Championship Foundation, Parke Davis*

1917
Georgia Tech: Billingsley, Helms, Houlgate, National Championship Foundation

1918
Michigan: Billingsley, National Championship Foundation*
Pittsburgh: Helms, Houlgate, National Championship Foundation*

1919
Harvard: Football Research*, Helms, Houlgate, National Championship Foundation*, Parke Davis*
Illinois: Billingsley, Boand, Football Research*, Parke Davis*
Notre Dame: National Championship Foundation*, Parke Davis*
Texas A&M: National Championship Foundation*

1920
California: Billingsley, Football Research, Helms, Houlgate, National Championship Foundation

Harvard: Board*
Notre Dame: Parke Davis*
Princeton: Board*, Parke Davis*

1921
California: Board*, Football Research
Cornell: Helms, Houlgate, National Championship Foundation, Parke Davis*
Iowa: Billingsley, Parke Davis*
Lafayette: Board*, Parke Davis*
Wash. & Jeff.: Board*

1922
California: Houlgate, National Championship Foundation*
Cornell: Helms, Parke Davis*
Iowa: Billingsley
Princeton: Board, Football Research, National Championship Foundation*, Parke Davis*

1923
California: Houlgate
Illinois: Board, Football Research, Helms, National Championship Foundation*, Parke Davis
Michigan: Billingsley, National Championship Foundation*

1924
Notre Dame: Billingsley, Board, Dickinson, Football Research, Helms, Houlgate, National Championship Foundation, Poling
Pennsylvania: Parke Davis

1925
Alabama: Billingsley, Board, Football Research, Helms, Houlgate, National Championship Foundation, Poling
Dartmouth: Dickinson, Parke Davis

1926
Alabama: Billingsley, Football Research, Helms*, National Championship Foundation*, Poling
Lafayette: Parke Davis
Navy: Board, Houlgate
Stanford: Dickinson, Helms*, National Championship Foundation*

1927
Georgia: Board, Poling
Illinois: Billingsley, Dickinson, Helms, National Championship Foundation, Parke Davis
Notre Dame: Houlgate
Yale: Football Research

1928
Detroit: Parke Davis*
Georgia Tech: Billingsley, Board, Football Research, Helms, Houlgate, National Championship Foundation, Parke Davis*, Poling
Southern California: Dickinson

1929
Notre Dame: Billingsley, Board, Dickinson, Dunkel, Football Research, Helms, National Championship Foundation, Poling
Pittsburgh: Parke Davis
Southern California: Houlgate

1930
Alabama: Football Research, Parke Davis*
Notre Dame: Billingsley, Board, Dickinson, Dunkel, Helms, Houlgate, National Championship Foundation, Parke Davis*, Poling

1931
Pittsburgh: Parke Davis*
Purdue: Parke Davis*
Southern California: Billingsley, Board, Dickinson, Dunkel, Helms, Houlgate, Football Research, National Championship Foundation, Poling, Williamson

1932
Colgate: Parke Davis*
Michigan: Dickinson, Parke Davis*
Southern California: Billingsley, Board, Dunkel, Football Research, Helms, Houlgate, National Championship Foundation, Parke Davis*, Poling, Williamson

1933
Michigan: Billingsley, Board, Dickinson, Helms, Houlgate, Football Research, National Championship

Foundation, Parke Davis*, Poling
Ohio St.: Dunkel
Princeton: Parke Davis*
Southern California: Williamson

1934
Alabama: Dunkel, Houlgate, Poling, Williamson
Minnesota: Billingsley, Board, Dickinson, Football Research, Helms, Litkenhous, National Championship Foundation

1935
LSU: Williamson*
Minnesota: Billingsley, Board, Football Research, Helms, Litkenhous, National Championship Foundation, Poling
Princeton: Dunkel
Southern Methodist: Dickinson, Houlgate
TCU: Williamson*

1936
LSU: Williamson
Minnesota: AP, Billingsley, Dickinson, Dunkel, Helms, Litkenhous, National Championship Foundation, Poling
Pittsburgh: Board, Football Research, Houlgate

1937
California: Dunkel, Helms
Pittsburgh: AP, Billingsley, Board, Dickinson, Football Research, Houlgate, Litkenhous, National Championship Foundation, Poling, Williamson

1938
Notre Dame: Dickinson
Tennessee: Billingsley, Board, Dunkel, Football Research, Houlgate, Litkenhous, Poling, Sagarin
TCU: AP, Helms, National Championship Foundation, Williamson

1939
Cornell: Billingsley, Litkenhous
Southern California: Dickinson
Texas A&M: AP, Board, DeVold, Dunkel, Football Research, Helms, Houlgate, National Championship Foundation, Poling, Williamson

1940
Minnesota: AP, Berryman, Billingsley, Board, DeVold, Dickinson, Football Research, Houlgate, Litkenhous, National Championship Foundation
Stanford: Helms, Poling
Tennessee: Dunkel, Williamson

1941
Alabama: Houlgate
Minnesota: AP, Billingsley, Board, DeVold, Dunkel, Football Research, Helms, Litkenhous, National Championship Foundation, Poling
Texas: Berryman, Williamson

1942
Georgia: Berryman, DeVold, Houlgate, Litkenhous, Poling, Williamson
Ohio St.: AP, Billingsley, Board, Dunkel, Football Research, National Championship Foundation
Wisconsin: Helms

1943
Notre Dame: AP, Berryman, Billingsley, Board, DeVold, Dunkel, Football Research, Helms, Houlgate, Litkenhous, National Championship Foundation, Poling, Williamson

1944
Army: AP, Berryman, Billingsley, Board, DeVold, Dunkel, Football Research, Helms, Houlgate, Litkenhous, National Championship Foundation*, Poling, Sagarin, Williamson
Ohio St.: National Championship Foundation*

1945
Alabama: National Championship Foundation*
Army: AP, Berryman, Billingsley, Board, DeVold, Dunkel, Football Research, Helms, Houlgate, Litkenhous, National Championship Foundation*, Poling, Sagarin, Williamson

1946
Army: Board*, Football Research, Helms*, Houlgate, Poling*
Georgia: Williamson
Notre Dame: AP, Berryman, Billingsley, Board*,

DeVold, Dunkel, Helms*, Litkenhous, National Championship Foundation, Poling*, Sagarin

1947
Michigan: Berryman, Billingsley, Board, DeVold, Dunkel, Football Research, Helms*, Houlgate, Litkenhous, National Championship Foundation, Poling, Sagarin
Notre Dame: AP, Helms*, Williamson

1948
Michigan: AP, Berryman, Billingsley, Board, DeVold, Dunkel, Football Research, Helms, Houlgate, Litkenhous, National Championship Foundation, Poling, Sagarin, Williamson

1949
Notre Dame: AP, Berryman, Billingsley, Board, DeVold, Dunkel, Helms, Houlgate, Litkenhous, National Championship Foundation, Poling, Sagarin, Williamson
Oklahoma: Football Research

1950
Kentucky: Sagarin
Oklahoma: AP, Berryman, Helms, Litkenhous, UPI, Williamson
Princeton: Board, Poling
Tennessee: Billingsley, DeVold, Dunkel, Football Research, National Championship Foundation

1951
Georgia Tech: Berryman, Board*
Illinois: Board*
Maryland: DeVold, Dunkel, Football Research, National Championship Foundation, Sagarin
Michigan St.: Billingsley, Helms, Poling
Tennessee: AP, Litkenhous, UPI, Williamson

1952
Georgia Tech: Berryman, INS, Poling
Michigan St.: AP, Billingsley, Board, DeVold, Dunkel, Football Research, Helms, Litkenhous, National Championship Foundation, Sagarin, UPI, Williamson

1953
Maryland: AP, INS, UPI
Notre Dame: Billingsley, Board, DeVold, Dunkel, Helms, Litkenhous, National Championship Foundation, Poling, Sagarin, Williamson
Oklahoma: Berryman, Football Research

1954
Ohio St.: AP, Berryman, Board, DeVold, Football Research*, Helms*, INS, National Championship Foundation*, Poling, Sagarin, Williamson
UCLA: Billingsley, Dunkel, Football Research*, FW, Helms*, Litkenhous, National Championship Foundation*, UPI

1955
Michigan St.: Board
Oklahoma: AP, Berryman, Billingsley, DeVold, Dunkel, Football Research, FW, Helms, INS, Litkenhous, National Championship Foundation, Poling, Sagarin, UPI, Williamson

1956
Georgia Tech: Berryman
Iowa: Football Research
Oklahoma: AP, Billingsley, Board, DeVold, Dunkel, FW, Helms, INS, Litkenhous, National Championship Foundation, Sagarin, UPI, Williamson
Tennessee: Sagarin

1957
Auburn: AP, Football Research, Helms, National Championship Foundation, Poling, Williamson
Michigan St.: Billingsley, Dunkel, Sagarin
Ohio St.: Board, DeVold, FW, INS, Litkenhous, UPI
Oklahoma: Berryman

1958
Iowa: FW
LSU: AP, Berryman, Billingsley, Board, DeVold, Dunkel, FB News, Football Research, Helms, Litkenhous, National Championship Foundation, Poling, Sagarin, UPI, Williamson

1959
Mississippi: Berryman, Billingsley, Dunkel, Sagarin

Syracuse: AP, Boand, DeVold, FB News, Football Research, FW, Helms, Litkenhous, National Championship Foundation, NFF, Poling, UPI, Williamson

1960
Iowa: Berryman, Boand, Litkenhous, Sagarin
Minnesota: AP, FB News, NFF, UPI
Mississippi: Billingsley, DeVold, Dunkel, Football Research, FW, National Championship Foundation, Williamson
Missouri: Poling
Washington: Helms

1961
Alabama: AP, Berryman, Billingsley, DeVold, Dunkel, FB News, Football Research, Helms, Litkenhous, National Championship Foundation, NFF, Sagarin, UPI, Williamson
Ohio St.: FW, Poling

1962
Alabama: Billingsley
LSU: Berryman*
Southern California: AP, Berryman*, DeVold, Dunkel, FB News, Football Research, FW, Helms, National Championship Foundation, NFF, Poling, Sagarin, UPI, Williamson
Mississippi: Litkenhous

1963
Texas: AP, Berryman, Billingsley, DeVold, Dunkel, FB News, Football Research, FW, Helms, Litkenhous, National Championship Foundation, NFF, Poling, Sagarin, UPI, Williamson

1964
Alabama: AP, Berryman, Litkenhous, UPI
Arkansas: Billingsley, Football Research, FW, Helms, National Championship Foundation, Poling
Michigan: Dunkel
Notre Dame: DeVold, FB News, NFF, Sagarin

1965
Alabama: AP, Billingsley, Football Research, FW*, National Championship Foundation
Michigan St.: Berryman, DeVold, Dunkel, FB News, FW*, Helms, Litkenhous, NFF, Poling, UPI

1966
Alabama: Berryman
Michigan St.: Football Research, Helms*, NFF*, Poling*
Notre Dame: AP, Billingsley, DeVold, Dunkel, FB News, FW, Helms*, Litkenhous, Matthews, National Championship Foundation, NFF*, Poling*, Sagarin, UPI

1967
Notre Dame: Dunkel
Oklahoma: Poling
Southern California: AP, Berryman, Billingsley, DeVold, FB News, Football Research, FW, Helms, Matthews, National Championship Foundation, NFF, Sagarin, UPI
Tennessee: Litkenhous

1968
Georgia: Litkenhous
Ohio St.: AP, Berryman, Billingsley, Dunkel, FACT, FB News, Football Research, FW, Helms, National Championship Foundation, NFF, Poling, UPI
Texas: DeVold, Matthews, Sagarin

1969
Ohio St.: Matthews
Penn St.: FACT*
Texas: AP, Berryman, Billingsley, DeVold, Dunkel, FACT*, FB News, Football Research, FW, Helms, Litkenhous, National Championship Foundation, NFF, Poling, Sagarin, UPI

1970
Arizona St.: Poling
Nebraska: AP, Billingsley, DeVold, Dunkel, FACT*, FB News, Football Research, FW, Helms, National Championship Foundation
Notre Dame: FACT*, Matthews
Ohio St.: NFF*
Texas: Berryman, FACT*, Litkenhous, NFF*, Sagarin, UPI

1971
Nebraska: AP, Berryman, Billingsley, DeVold, Dunkel, FACT, FB News, Football Research, FW, Helms, Litkenhous, Matthews, National Championship Foundation, NFF, Poling, Sagarin, UPI

1972
Southern California: AP, Berryman, Billingsley, DeVold, Dunkel, FACT, FB News, Football Research, FW, Helms, Litkenhous, Matthews, National Championship Foundation, NFF, Poling, Sagarin, UPI

1973
Alabama: Berryman, UPI
Michigan: National Championship Foundation*, Poling*
Notre Dame: AP, FB News, FW, Helms, National Championship Foundation*, NFF
Ohio St.: FACT, National Championship Foundation*, Poling*
Oklahoma: Billingsley, DeVold, Dunkel, Football Research, Sagarin

1974
Ohio St.: Matthews
Oklahoma: AP, Berryman, Billingsley, DeVold, Dunkel, FACT, FB News, Football Research, Helms*, Litkenhous, National Championship Foundation*, Poling, Sagarin
Southern California: FW, Helms*, National Championship Foundation*, NFF, UPI

1975
Alabama: Matthews*
Arizona St.: National Championship Foundation*, Sporting News
Ohio St.: Berryman, FACT*, Helms*, Matthews*, Poling
Oklahoma: AP, Billingsley, DeVold, Dunkel, FACT*, FB News, Football Research, FW, Helms*, National Championship Foundation*, NFF, Sagarin, UPI

1976
Pittsburgh: AP, FACT, FB News, FW, Helms, National Championship Foundation, NFF, Poling, Sagarin, Sporting News, UPI
Southern California: Berryman, Billingsley, DeVold, Dunkel, Football Research, Matthews

1977
Alabama: Football Research*
Arkansas: FACT*
Notre Dame: AP, Billingsley, DeVold, Dunkel, FACT*, FB News, Football Research*, FW, Helms, Matthews, National Championship Foundation, NFF, Poling, Sagarin, Sporting News, UPI
Texas: Berryman, FACT*

1978
Alabama: AP, FACT*, Football Research, FW, Helms*, National Championship Foundation*, NFF
Oklahoma: Billingsley, DeVold, Dunkel, FACT*, Helms*, Litkenhous, Matthews, Poling, Sagarin
Southern California: Berryman, FACT*, FB News, Helms*, National Championship Foundation*, Sporting News, UPI

1979
Alabama: AP, Berryman, Billingsley, DeVold, Dunkel, FACT, FB News, FW, Helms, Matthews, National Championship Foundation, NFF, NY Times, Poling, Sagarin, Sporting News, UPI
Southern California: Football Research

1980
Florida St.: FACT*
Georgia: AP, Berryman, FACT*, FB News, FW, Helms, National Championship Foundation, NFF, Poling, Sporting News, UPI
Nebraska: FACT*, Sagarin
Oklahoma: Billingsley, Dunkel, Matthews
Pittsburgh: DeVold, FACT*, Football Research, NY Times

1981
Clemson: AP, Berryman, Billingsley, DeVold, FACT, FB News, Football Research, FW, Helms, Litkenhous, Matthews, National Championship Foundation*, NFF, NY Times, Poling, Sagarin, Sporting News, UPI
Nebraska: National Championship Foundation*
Penn St.: Dunkel
Pittsburgh: National Championship Foundation*
Texas: National Championship Foundation*

Southern Methodist: National Championship Foundation*

1982
Nebraska: Berryman
Penn St.: AP, Billingsley, DeVold, Dunkel, FACT, FB News, Football Research, FW, Helms*, Litkenhous, Matthews, National Championship Foundation, NFF, NY Times, Poling, Sagarin, Sporting News, UPI, USA/CNN
Southern Methodist: Helms*

1983
Auburn: FACT*, Football Research, NY Times
Miami (Fla.): AP, Billingsley, Dunkel, FB News, FW, National Championship Foundation, NFF, Sporting News, UPI, USA/CNN
Nebraska: Berryman, DeVold, FACT*, Litkenhous, Matthews, Poling, Sagarin

1984
Brigham Young: AP, Football Research, FW, National Championship Foundation*, NFF, Poling, UPI, USA/CNN
Florida: Billingsley, DeVold, Dunkel, FACT, Matthews, NY Times, Sagarin, Sporting News
Nebraska: Litkenhous
Washington: Berryman, FB News, National Championship Foundation*

1985
Michigan: Matthews, Sagarin
Oklahoma: AP, Berryman, Billingsley, DeVold, Dunkel, FACT, FB News, Football Research, FW, National Championship Foundation, NFF, NY Times, Sporting News, UPI, USA/CNN

1986
Miami (Fla.): FACT*
Oklahoma: Berryman, DeVold, Dunkel, Football Research, NY Times, Sagarin
Penn St.: AP, Billingsley, FACT*, FB News, FW, Matthews, National Championship Foundation, NFF, Sporting News, UPI, USA/CNN

1987
Florida St.: Berryman, Sagarin
Miami (Fla.): AP, Billingsley, DeVold, Dunkel, Eck, FACT, FB News, Football Research, FW, Matthews, National Championship Foundation, NFF, NY Times, Sporting News, UPI, USA/CNN

1988
Miami (Fla.): Berryman
Notre Dame: AP, Billingsley, DeVold, Dunkel, Eck, FACT, FB News, Football Research, FW, Matthews, National Championship Foundation, NFF, NY Times, Sagarin, Sporting News, UPI, USA/CNN

1989
Miami (Fla.): AP, Billingsley, DeVold, Dunkel, FACT*, FB News, Football Research, FW, Matthews, National Championship Foundation, NFF, NY Times, Sporting News, UPI, USA/CNN
Notre Dame: Berryman, Eck, FACT*, Sagarin

1990
Colorado: AP, Berryman, DeVold, FACT*, FB News, Football Research, FW, Matthews, National Championship Foundation*, NFF, Sporting News, USA/CNN
Georgia Tech: Dunkel, FACT*, National Championship Foundation*, UPI
Miami (Fla.): Billingsley, Eck, FACT*, NY Times, Sagarin
Washington: FACT*

1991
Miami (Fla.): AP, Eck, Football Research, National Championship Foundation*, NY Times, Sporting News
Washington: Berryman, Billingsley, DeVold, Dunkel, FACT, FB News, FW, Matthews, National Championship Foundation*, Sagarin, UPI/NFF, USA/CNN

1992
Alabama: AP, Berryman, Billingsley, DeVold, Dunkel, Eck, FACT, FB News, Football Research, FW, Matthews, National Championship Foundation, NY Times, Sporting News, UPI/NFF, USA/CNN
Florida St.: Sagarin

1993
Auburn: National Championship Foundation*
Florida St.: AP, Berryman, Billingsley, DeVold, Dunkel, Eck, FACT, FB News, FW, National Championship Foundation*, NY Times, Sagarin, Sporting News, UPI, USA/CNN, USA/NFF
Nebraska: National Championship Foundation*
Notre Dame: Matthews, National Championship Foundation*

1994
Florida St.: Dunkel
Nebraska: Alderson, AP, Berryman, Billingsley, FACT*, FB News, FW, National Championship Foundation*, Sporting News, UPI, USA/CNN, USA/NFF
Penn St.: DeVold, Eck, FACT*, Matthews, National Championship Foundation*, NY Times, Sagarin

1995
Nebraska: Alderson, AP, Berryman, Billingsley, DeVold, Dunkel, Eck, FACT, FB News, FW, Matthews, National Championship Foundation, NFF, NY Times, Sagarin, Sporting News, UPI, USA/CNN

1996
Florida: AP, Berryman, Billingsley, Eck, FACT, FB News, FW, NFF, Sagarin, Sporting News, USA/CNN, NY Times, National Championship Foundation, Dunkel, Matthews, DeVold
Florida St.: Alderson

1997
Michigan: AP, FB News, FW, National Championship Foundation*, NFF, Sporting News
Nebraska: Alderson, Berryman, Billingsley, DeVold, Dunkel, Eck, FACT, Matthews, National Championship Foundation*, NY Times, Sagarin, Seattle Times, USA/ESPN

1998
Ohio St.: Sagarin
Tennessee: Alderson, AP, Berryman, Billingsley, DeVold, Dunkel, Eck, FACT, FB News, FW, Matthews, National Championship Foundation, NFF, NY Times, Seattle Times, Sporting News, USA/ESPN

1999
Florida St.: AP, Berryman, Billingsley, DeVold, Dunkel, Eck, FACT, FB News, FW, Massey, Matthews, National Championship Foundation, NFF, NY Times, Sagarin, Seattle Times, Sporting News, USA/ESPN

2000
Oklahoma: AP, Berryman, Billingsley, DeVold, Dunkel, Eck, FACT, FB News, FW, Massey, Matthews, National Championship Foundation, NFF, Sagarin, Seattle Times, Sporting News, USA/ESPN
Miami (Fla.): NY Times

2001
Miami (Fla.): AP, Berryman, Billingsley, Colley, DeVold, Dunkel, Eck, FACT, FB News, FW, Massey, Matthews, NFF, NY Times, Sagarin, Seattle Times, Sporting News, USA/ESPN, Wolfe

2002
Ohio St.: AP, Berryman, Billingsley, Colley, DeVold, Eck, FACT, FB News, FW, Massey, NFF, NY Times, Seattle Times, Sporting News, USA/ESPN, Wolfe
Southern California: Dunkel, Matthews, Sagarin

(Legend of Present Major Selectors: Associated Press (AP) from 1936-present; Football Writers Association of America (FW) from 1954-present; National Football Foundation and Hall of Fame (NFF) from 1959-90 and 1995 to present; USA Today/Cable News Network (USA/CNN) from 1982-96; USA Today/ESPN (USA/ESPN) from 1997-present; USA Today/National Football Foundation and Hall of Fame (USA/NFF) from 1993-94 to present. The Associated Press has been the designated media poll since 1936. United Press International served as the coaches' poll from 1950 to 1991 when it was taken over by USA Today/Cable News Network and in 1997 became USA Today/ESPN. In 1991-92, the No. 1 team in the final UPI/NFF ratings received the MacArthur Bowl as the national champion by the NFF. In 1993-94 and again in 1996, the No. 1 team in the USA Today/NFF final poll received the MacArthur Bowl.)

Major Selectors Since 1936

ASSOCIATED PRESS

Year	Team	Record	Year	Team	Record	Year	Team	Record	Year	Team	Record
1936	Minnesota	7-1-0	1953	Maryland	10-1-0	1970	Nebraska	11-0-1	1987	Miami (Fla.)	12-0-0
1937	Pittsburgh	9-0-1	1954	Ohio St.	10-0-0	1971	Nebraska	13-0-0	1988	Notre Dame	12-0-0
1938	TCU	11-0-0	1955	Oklahoma	11-0-0	1972	Southern California	12-0-0	1989	Miami (Fla.)	11-1-0
1939	Texas A&M	11-0-0	1956	Oklahoma	10-0-0	1973	Notre Dame	11-0-0	1990	Colorado	11-1-1
1940	Minnesota	8-0-0	1957	Auburn	10-0-0	1974	Oklahoma	11-0-0	1991	Miami (Fla.)	12-0-0
1941	Minnesota	8-0-0	1958	LSU	11-0-0	1975	Oklahoma	11-1-0	1992	Alabama	13-0-0
1942	Ohio St.	9-1-0	1959	Syracuse	11-0-0	1976	Pittsburgh	12-0-0	1993	Florida St.	12-1-0
1943	Notre Dame	9-1-0	1960	Minnesota	8-2-0	1977	Notre Dame	11-1-0	1994	Nebraska	13-0-0
1944	Army	9-0-0	1961	Alabama	11-0-0	1978	Alabama	12-1-0	1995	Nebraska	12-0-0
1945	Army	9-0-0	1962	Southern California	11-0-0	1979	Alabama	12-0-0	1996	Florida	12-1-0
1946	Notre Dame	8-0-1	1963	Texas	11-0-0	1980	Georgia	12-0-0	1997	Michigan	12-0-0
1947	Notre Dame	9-0-0	1964	Alabama	10-1-0	1981	Clemson	12-0-0	1998	Tennessee	13-0-0
1948	Michigan	9-0-0	1965	Alabama	9-1-1	1982	Penn St.	11-1-0	1999	Florida St.	12-0-0
1949	Notre Dame	10-0-0	1966	Notre Dame	9-0-1	1983	Miami (Fla.)	11-1-0	2000	Oklahoma	13-0-0
1950	Oklahoma	10-1-0	1967	Southern California	10-1-0	1984	Brigham Young	13-0-0	2001	Miami (Fla.)	12-0-0
1951	Tennessee	10-0-0	1968	Ohio St.	10-0-0	1985	Oklahoma	11-1-0	2002	Ohio St.	14-0-0
1952	Michigan St.	9-0-0	1969	Texas	11-0-0	1986	Penn St.	12-0-0			

NATIONAL FOOTBALL FOUNDATION AND COLLEGE FOOTBALL HALL OF FAME
(MacArthur Bowl)

Year	Team	Record	Year	Team	Record	Year	Team	Record	Year	Team	Record
1959	Syracuse	11-0-0	1970	Ohio St. 10-1-0/Texas	10-1-0	1981	Clemson	12-0-0	1992	Alabama (UPI/NFF)	13-0-0
1960	Minnesota	8-2-0	1971	Nebraska	13-0-0	1982	Penn St.	11-1-0	1993	Florida St. (USA/NFF)	12-1-0
1961	Alabama	11-0-0	1972	Southern California	12-0-0	1983	Miami (Fla.)	11-1-0	1994	Nebraska (USA/NFF)	13-0-0
1962	Southern California	11-0-0	1973	Notre Dame	11-0-0	1984	Brigham Young	13-0-0	1995	Nebraska (USA/NFF)	12-0-0
1963	Texas	11-0-0	1974	Southern California	10-1-1	1985	Oklahoma	11-1-0	1996	Florida (USA/NFF)	12-1-0
1964	Notre Dame	9-1-0	1975	Oklahoma	11-1-0	1986	Penn St.	12-0-0	1997	Michigan	12-0-0
1965	Michigan St.	10-1-0	1976	Pittsburgh	12-0-0	1987	Miami (Fla.)	12-0-0	1998	Tennessee	13-0-0
1966	Michigan St. 9-0-1/Notre Dame	9-0-1	1977	Notre Dame	11-1-0	1988	Notre Dame	12-0-0	1999	Florida St.	12-0-0
1967	Southern California	10-1-0	1978	Alabama	11-1-0	1989	Miami (Fla.)	11-1-0	2000	Oklahoma	13-0-0
1968	Ohio St.	10-0-0	1979	Alabama	12-0-0	1990	Colorado	11-1-1	2001	Miami (Fla.)	12-0-0
1969	Texas	11-0-0	1980	Georgia	12-0-0	1991	Wash. (UPI/NFF)	12-0-0	2002	Ohio St.	14-0-0

DIVISION I-A

UNITED PRESS

Year	Team	Record	Year	Team	Record	Year	Team	Record	Year	Team	Record
1950	Oklahoma	10-1-0	1962	Southern California	11-0-0	1974	Southern California	10-1-1	1985	Oklahoma	11-1-0
1951	Tennessee	10-0-0	1963	Texas	11-0-0				1986	Penn St.	12-0-0
1952	Michigan St.	9-0-0	1964	Alabama	10-1-0	1975	Oklahoma	11-1-0	1987	Miami (Fla.)	12-0-0
1953	Maryland	10-1-0				1976	Pittsburgh	12-0-0	1988	Notre Dame	12-0-0
1954	UCLA	9-0-0	1965	Michigan St.	10-1-0	1977	Notre Dame	11-1-0	1989	Miami (Fla.)	11-1-0
			1966	Notre Dame	9-0-1	1978	Southern California	12-1-0			
1955	Oklahoma	11-0-0	1967	Southern California	10-1-0	1979	Alabama	12-0-0	1990	Georgia Tech	11-0-1
1956	Oklahoma	10-0-0	1968	Ohio St.	10-0-0				1991	Washington	12-0-0
1957	Ohio St.	9-1-0	1969	Texas	11-0-0	1980	Georgia	12-0-0	1992	Alabama	13-0-0
1958	LSU	11-0-0				1981	Clemson	12-0-0	1993	Florida St.	12-1-0
1959	Syracuse	11-0-0	1970	Texas	10-1-0	1982	Penn St.	11-1-0	1994	Nebraska	13-0-0
			1971	Nebraska	13-0-0	1983	Miami (Fla.)	11-1-0			
1960	Minnesota	8-2-0	1972	Southern California	12-0-0	1984	Brigham Young	13-0-0	1995	Nebraska	12-0-0
1961	Alabama	11-0-0	1973	Alabama	11-1-0						

FOOTBALL WRITERS'

Year	Team	Record	Year	Team	Record	Year	Team	Record	Year	Team	Record
1954	UCLA	9-0-0	1966	Notre Dame	9-0-1	1979	Alabama	12-0-0	1992	Alabama	13-0-0
1955	Oklahoma	11-0-0	1967	Southern California	10-1-0	1980	Georgia	12-0-0	1993	Florida St.	12-1-0
1956	Oklahoma	10-0-0				1981	Clemson	12-0-0	1994	Nebraska	13-0-0
1957	Ohio St.	9-1-0	1968	Ohio St.	10-0-0	1982	Penn St.	11-1-0	1995	Nebraska	12-0-0
1958	Iowa	8-1-1	1969	Texas	11-0-0				1996	Florida	12-1-0
			1970	Nebraska	11-0-1	1983	Miami (Fla.)	11-1-0	1997	Michigan	12-0-0
1959	Syracuse	11-0-0	1971	Nebraska	13-0-0	1984	Brigham Young	13-0-0			
1960	Mississippi	10-0-1	1972	Southern California	12-0-0	1985	Oklahoma	11-1-0	1998	Tennessee	13-0-0
1961	Ohio St.	8-0-1				1986	Penn St.	12-0-0	1999	Florida St.	12-0-0
1962	Southern California	11-0-0	1973	Notre Dame	11-0-0	1987	Miami (Fla.)	12-0-0	2000	Oklahoma	13-0-0
1963	Texas	11-0-0	1974	Southern California	10-1-1				2001	Miami (Fla.)	12-0-0
			1975	Oklahoma	11-1-0	1988	Notre Dame	12-0-0	2002	Ohio St.	14-0-0
1964	Arkansas	11-0-0	1976	Pittsburgh	12-0-0	1989	Miami (Fla.)	11-1-0			
1965	Alabama	9-1-1/	1977	Notre Dame	11-1-0	1990	Colorado	11-1-1			
	Michigan St.	10-1-0	1978	Alabama	11-1-0	1991	Washington	12-0-0			

USA TODAY/ESPN

Year	Team	Record	Year	Team	Record	Year	Team	Record	Year	Team	Record
1982	Penn St.	11-1-0	1988	Notre Dame (CNN)	12-0-0	1994	Nebraska (CNN)	13-0-0	2000	Oklahoma (ESPN)	13-0-0
1983	Miami (Fla.) (CNN)	11-1-0	1989	Miami (Fla.) (CNN)	11-1-0	1995	Nebraska (CNN)	12-0-0	2001	Miami (Fla.) (ESPN)	12-0-0
1984	Brigham Young (CNN)	13-0-0	1990	Colorado (CNN)	11-1-1	1996	Florida (CNN)	12-1-0	2002	Ohio St. (ESPN)	14-0-0
1985	Oklahoma (CNN)	11-1-0	1991	Washington (CNN)	12-0-0	1997	Nebraska (ESPN)	13-0-0			
1986	Penn St. (CNN)	12-0-0	1992	Alabama (CNN)	13-0-0	1998	Tennessee (ESPN)	13-0-0			
1987	Miami (Fla.) (CNN)	12-0-0	1993	Florida St. (CNN)	12-1-0	1999	Florida St. (ESPN)	12-0-0			

National Poll Champions in Bowl Games

Year	Team	Coach (Years†)	Record	Bowl (Result)
1900	Yale	Malcolm McBride	12-0-0	None
1901	Michigan	Fielding Yost	11-0-0	Rose (beat Stanford, 49-0)
	Harvard	William Reid	12-0-0	None
1902	Michigan	Fielding Yost	11-0-0	None
	Yale	Joseph Swan	11-0-1	None
1903	Princeton	Art Hillebrand	11-0-0	None
1904	Pennsylvania	Carl Williams	12-0-0	None
1905	Chicago	Amos Alonzo Stagg	11-0-0	None
	Yale	J. E. Owsley	10-0-0	None
1906	Princeton	Bill Roper	9-0-1	None
	Yale	Foster Rockwell	9-0-1	None
1907	Yale	William Knox	9-0-1	None
1908	Pennsylvania	Sol Metzer	11-0-1	None
	Harvard	Percy Haughton	9-0-1	None
1909	Yale	Howard Jones	10-0-0	None
1910	Harvard	Percy Haughton	8-0-1	None
1911	Princeton	Bill Roper	8-0-2	None
1912	Harvard	Percy Haughton	9-0-0	None
1913	Harvard	Percy Haughton	9-0-0	None
1914	Army	Charley Daly	9-0-0	None
	Harvard	Percy Haughton	7-0-2	None
1915	Cornell	Al Sharpe	9-0-0	None
1916	Pittsburgh	Glenn "Pop" Warner	8-0-0	None
1917	Georgia Tech	John Heisman	9-0-0	None
1918	Pittsburgh	Glenn "Pop" Warner	4-1-0	None
1919	Harvard	Robert Fisher	9-0-1	Rose (beat Oregon, 7-6)
	Penn St.	Hugo Bezdek	7-1-0	None
1920	California	Andy Smith	9-0-0	Rose (beat Ohio St., 28-0)
	Princeton	Bill Roper	6-0-1	None
1921	Cornell	Gil Dobie	8-0-0	None
	Penn St.	Hugo Bezdek	8-0-2	None
1922	Cornell	Gil Dobie	8-0-0	None

Consensus National Champions

SINCE 1950

AP — Associated Press
UPI — United Press International
FWAA — Football Writers Association of America
NFF — National Football Foundation/College Football Hall of Fame
USA/CNN — USA Today/CNN
USA/ESPN — USA Today/ESPN

Year	Champion (Selectors)
1950	Oklahoma (AP, UPI)
1951	Tennessee (AP, UPI)
1952	Michigan St. (AP, UPI)
1953	Maryland (AP, UPI)
1954	UCLA (FWAA, UPI)
	Ohio St. (AP
1955	Oklahoma (AP, FWAA, UPI)
1956	Oklahoma (AP, FWAA, UPI)
1957	Ohio St. (FWAA, UPI)
	Auburn (AP)
1958	LSU (AP, UPI)
	Iowa (FWAA)
1959	Syracuse (AP, FWAA, NFF, UPI)
1960	Minnesota (AP, NFF, UPI)
	Mississippi (FWAA)
1961	Alabama (AP, NFF, UPI)
	Ohio St. (FWAA)
1962	Southern California (AP, FWAA, NFF, UPI)
1963	Texas (AP, FWAA, NFF, UPI)
1964	Alabama (AP, UPI)
	Arkansas (FWAA)
	Notre Dame (NFF)
1965	Michigan St. (FWAA, NFF, UPI)
	Alabama (AP, FWAA)

Year	Team	Coach (Years†)	Record	Bowl (Result)
	Princeton	Bill Roper	8-0-0	None
1923	Illinois	Robert Zuppke	8-0-0	None
1924	Notre Dame	Knute Rockne	10-0-0	Rose (beat Stanford, 27-10)
1925	Alabama	Wallace Wade	10-0-0	Rose (beat Washington, 20-19)
	Dartmouth	Jesse Hawley	8-0-0	None
1926	Alabama	Wallace Wade	9-0-1	Rose (tied Stanford, 7-7)
	Stanford	Glenn "Pop" Warner	10-0-1	Rose (tied Alabama, 7-7)
1927	Illinois	Robert Zuppke	7-0-1	None
1928	Georgia Tech	Bill Alexander	10-0-0	Rose (beat California, 8-7)
	Southern California	Howard Jones	9-0-1	None
1929	Notre Dame	Knute Rockne	9-0-0	None
1930	Notre Dame	Knute Rockne	10-0-0	None
1931	Southern California	Howard Jones	10-1-0	Rose (beat Tulane, 21-12)
1932	Michigan	Harry Kipke	8-0-0	None
	Southern California	Howard Jones	10-0-0	Rose (beat Pittsburgh, 35-0)
1933	Michigan	Harry Kipke	7-0-1	None
1934	Minnesota	Bernie Bierman	8-0-0	None
1935	Minnesota	Bernie Bierman	8-0-0	None
	Southern Methodist	Matty Bell	12-1-0	Rose (lost to Stanford, 7-0)
1936	Minnesota	Bernie Bierman (5-15)	7-1-0	None
1937	Pittsburgh	Jock Sutherland (13-18)	9-0-1	None
1938	TCU	Dutch Meyer (5-5)	11-0-0	Sugar (beat Carnegie Mellon, 15-7)
1939	Texas A&M	Homer Norton (6-16)	11-0-0	Sugar (beat Tulane, 14-13)
1940	Minnesota	Bernie Bierman (9-19)	8-0-0	None
1941	Minnesota	Bernie Bierman (10-20)	8-0-0	None
1942	Ohio St.	Paul Brown (2-2)	9-1-0	None
1943	Notre Dame	Frank Leahy (3-5)	9-1-0	None
1944	Army	Earl "Red" Blaik (4-11)	9-0-0	None
1945	Army	Earl "Red" Blaik (5-12)	9-0-0	None
1946	Notre Dame	Frank Leahy (4-6)	8-0-1	None
1947	Notre Dame	Frank Leahy (5-7)	9-0-0	None
1948	Michigan	Bennie Oosterbaan (1-1)	9-0-0	None
1949	Notre Dame	Frank Leahy (7-9)	10-0-0	None
1950	Oklahoma	Bud Wilkinson (4-4)	10-1-0	Sugar (lost to Kentucky, 13-7)
1951	Tennessee	Robert Neyland (20-20)	10-1-0	Sugar (lost to Maryland, 28-13)
1952	Michigan St.	Clarence "Biggie" Munn (6-9)	9-0-0	None
1953	Maryland	Jim Tatum (7-9)	10-1-0	Orange (lost to Oklahoma, 7-0)
1954	Ohio St.	Woody Hayes (4-9)	10-0-0	Rose (beat Southern California, 20-7)
	UCLA	Red Sanders (6-12)	9-0-0	None
1955	Oklahoma	Bud Wilkinson (9-9)	11-0-0	Orange (beat Maryland, 20-6)
1956	Oklahoma	Bud Wilkinson (10-10)	10-0-0	None
1957	Auburn	Ralph "Shug" Jordan (7-7)	10-0-0	None
	Ohio St.	Woody Hayes (7-12)	9-1-0	Rose (beat Oregon, 10-7)
1958	LSU	Paul Dietzel (4-4)	11-0-0	Sugar (beat Clemson, 7-0)
	Iowa	Forest Evashevski (5-8)	8-1-1	Rose (beat California, 38-12)
1959	Syracuse	Ben Schwartzwalder (11-14)	11-0-0	Cotton (beat Texas, 23-14)
1960	Minnesota	Murray Warmath (7-9)	8-2-0	Rose (lost to Washington, 17-7)
	Mississippi	Johnny Vaught (14-14)	10-0-1	Sugar (beat Rice, 14-6)
1961	Alabama	Paul "Bear" Bryant (4-17)	11-0-0	Sugar (beat Arkansas, 10-3)
	Ohio St.	Woody Hayes (11-16)	8-0-1	None
1962	Southern California	John McKay (3-3)	11-0-0	Rose (beat Wisconsin, 42-37)
1963	Texas	Darrell Royal (7-10)	11-0-0	Cotton (beat Navy, 28-6)
1964	Alabama	Paul "Bear" Bryant (7-20)	10-1-0	Orange (lost to Texas, 21-17)
	Arkansas	Frank Broyles (3-4)	11-0-0	Cotton (beat Nebraska, 10-7)
	Notre Dame	Ara Parseghian (1-14)	9-1-0	None
1965	Alabama	Paul "Bear" Bryant (8-21)	9-1-1	Orange (beat Nebraska, 39-28)
	Michigan St.	Duffy Daugherty (12-12)	10-1-0	Rose (lost to UCLA, 14-12)
1966	Michigan St.	Duffy Daugherty (13-13)	9-0-1	None
	Notre Dame	Ara Parseghian (3-17)	9-0-1	None
1967	Southern California	John McKay (8-8)	10-1-0	Rose (beat Indiana, 14-3)
1968	Ohio St.	Woody Hayes (18-23)	10-0-0	Rose (beat Southern California, 27-16)
1969	Texas	Darrell Royal (13-16)	11-0-0	Cotton (beat Notre Dame, 21-17)
1970	Nebraska	Bob Devaney (9-14)	11-0-1	Orange (beat LSU, 17-12)
	Ohio St.	Woody Hayes (20-25)	9-1-0	Rose (lost to Stanford, 27-17)
	Texas	Darrell Royal (14-17)	10-1-0	Cotton (lost to Notre Dame, 24-11)
1971	Nebraska	Bob Devaney (10-15)	13-0-0	Orange (beat Alabama, 38-6)
1972	Southern California	John McKay (13-13)	12-0-0	Rose (beat Ohio St., 42-17)
1973	Alabama	Paul "Bear" Bryant (16-29)	11-1-0	Sugar (lost to Notre Dame, 24-23)
	Notre Dame	Ara Parseghian (10-23)	11-0-0	Sugar (beat Alabama, 24-23)
1974	Oklahoma	Barry Switzer (2-2)	11-0-0	None
	Southern California	John McKay (15-15)	10-1-1	Rose (beat Ohio St., 18-17)
1975	Oklahoma	Barry Switzer (3-3)	11-1-0	Orange (beat Michigan, 14-6)
1976	Pittsburgh	Johnny Majors (4-9)	12-0-0	Sugar (beat Georgia, 27-3)
1977	Notre Dame	Dan Devine (3-19)	11-1-0	Cotton (beat Texas, 38-10)
1978	Alabama	Paul "Bear" Bryant (21-34)	11-1-0	Sugar (beat Penn St., 14-7)
	Southern California	John Robinson (3-3)	12-1-0	Rose (beat Michigan, 17-10)
1979	Alabama	Paul "Bear" Bryant (22-35)	12-0-0	Sugar (beat Arkansas, 24-9)
1980	Georgia	Vince Dooley (17-17)	12-0-0	Sugar (beat Notre Dame, 17-10)
1981	Clemson	Danny Ford (4-4#)	12-0-0	Orange (beat Nebraska, 22-15)
1982	Penn St.	Joe Paterno (17-17)	11-1-0	Sugar (beat Georgia, 27-23)
1983	Miami (Fla.)	Howard Schnellenberger (5-5)	11-1-0	Orange (beat Nebraska, 31-30)
1984	Brigham Young	LaVell Edwards (13-13)	13-0-0	Holiday (beat Michigan, 24-17)
1985	Oklahoma	Barry Switzer (13-13)	11-1-0	Orange (beat Penn St., 25-10)

Year	Champion (Selectors)
1966	Notre Dame (AP, FWAA, NFF, UPI)
	Michigan St. (NFF)
1967	Southern California (AP, FWAA, NFF, UPI)
1968	Ohio St. (AP, FWAA, NFF, UPI)
1969	Texas (AP, FWAA, NFF, UPI)
1970	Nebraska (AP, FWAA)
	Texas (NFF, UPI)
	Ohio St. (NFF)
1971	Nebraska (AP, FWAA, NFF, UPI)
1972	Southern California (AP, FWAA, NFF, UPI)
1973	Notre Dame (AP, FWAA, NFF)
	Alabama (UPI)
1974	Southern California (FWAA, NFF, UPI)
	Oklahoma (AP)
1975	Oklahoma (AP, FWAA, NFF, UPI)
1976	Pittsburgh (AP, FWAA, NFF, UPI)
1977	Notre Dame (AP, FWAA, NFF, UPI)
1978	Alabama (AP, FWAA, NFF)
	Southern California (UPI)
1979	Alabama (AP, FWAA, NFF, UPI)
1980	Georgia (AP, FWAA, NFF, UPI)
1981	Clemson (AP, FWAA, NFF, UPI)
1982	Penn St. (AP, FWAA, NFF, UPI, USA/CNN)
1983	Miami (Fla.) (AP, FWAA, NFF, UPI, USA/CNN)
1984	Brigham Young (AP, FWAA, NFF, UPI, USA/CNN)
1985	Oklahoma (AP, FWAA, NFF, UPI, USA/CNN)
1986	Penn St. (AP, FWAA, NFF, UPI, USA/CNN)
1987	Miami (Fla.) (AP, FWAA, NFF, UPI, USA/CNN)
1988	Notre Dame (AP, FWAA, NFF, UPI, USA/CNN)
1989	Miami (Fla.) (AP, FWAA, NFF, UPI, USA/CNN)
1990	Colorado (AP, FWAA, NFF, USA/CNN)
	Georgia Tech (UPI)
1991	Washington (FWAA, NFF, USA/CNN, UPI)
	Miami (Fla.) (AP)
1992	Alabama (AP, FWAA, NFF, USA/CNN, UPI)
1993	Florida St. (AP, FWAA, NFF, USA/CNN, UPI)
1994	Nebraska (AP, FWAA, NFF, USA/CNN, UPI)
1995	Nebraska (AP, FWAA, NFF, USA/CNN, UPI)
1996	Florida (AP, FWAA, NFF, USA/CNN)
1997	Michigan (AP, FWAA, NFF)
	Nebraska (USA/ESPN)
1998	Tennessee (AP, FWAA, NFF, USA/ESPN)
1999	Florida St. (AP, FWAA, NFF, USA/ESPN)
2000	Oklahoma (AP, FWAA, NFF, USA/ESPN)
2001	Miami (Fla.) (AP, FWAA, NFF, USA/ESPN)
2002	Ohio St. (AP, FWAA, NFF, USA/ESPN)

Year	Team	Coach (Years†)	Record	Bowl (Result)
1986	Penn St.	Joe Paterno (21-21)	12-0-0	Fiesta (beat Miami [Fla.], 14-10)
1987	Miami (Fla.)	Jimmy Johnson (3-9)	12-0-0	Orange (beat Oklahoma, 20-14)
1988	Notre Dame	Lou Holtz (3-19)	12-0-0	Fiesta (beat West Virginia, 34-21)
1989	Miami (Fla.)	Dennis Erickson (1-8)	11-1-0	Sugar (beat Alabama, 33-25)
1990	Colorado	Bill McCartney (9-9)	11-1-1	Orange (beat Notre Dame, 10-9)
	Georgia Tech	Bobby Ross (4-14)	11-0-1	Fla. Citrus (beat Nebraska, 45-21)
1991	Miami (Fla.)	Dennis Erickson (3-10)	12-0-0	Orange (beat Nebraska, 22-0)
	Washington	Don James (17-21)	12-0-0	Rose (beat Michigan, 34-14)
1992	Alabama	Gene Stallings (3-10)	13-0-0	Sugar (beat Miami [Fla.], 34-13)
1993	Florida St.	Bobby Bowden (18-28)	12-1-0	Orange (beat Nebraska, 18-16)
1994	Nebraska	Tom Osborne (22-22)	13-0-0	Orange (beat Miami [Fla.], 24-17)
1995	Nebraska	Tom Osborne (23-23)	12-0-0	Fiesta (beat Florida, 62-24)
1996	Florida	Steve Spurrier (7-10)	12-1-0	Sugar (beat Florida St., 52-20)
1997	Michigan	Lloyd Carr (3-3)	12-0-0	Rose (beat Washington St., 21-16)
	Nebraska	Tom Osborne (25-25)	13-0-0	Orange (beat Tennessee, 42-17)
1998*	Tennessee	Phillip Fulmer (7-7)	13-0-0	Fiesta (beat Florida St., 23-16)
1999	Florida St.	Bobby Bowden (25-35)	12-0-0	Sugar (beat Virginia Tech, 46-29)
2000	Oklahoma	Bob Stoops (2-2)	13-0-0	Orange (beat Florida St., 13-2)
2001	Miami (Fla.)	Larry Coker (1-1)	12-0-0	Rose (beat Nebraska, 37-14)
2002	Ohio St.	Jim Tressel (2-17)	14-0-0	Fiesta (beat Miami [Fla.] 31-24 [2ot])

†Years head coach at that college and total years at four-year colleges. #Includes last game of 1978 season. *First year of BCS ranking system.

Associated Press Weekly Poll Leaders

The weekly dates are for Monday or Tuesday, the most frequent release dates of the poll, except when the final poll was taken after early January bowl games. A team's record includes its last game before the weekly poll. A new weekly leader's rank the previous week is indicated in parentheses after its record. Final poll leaders (annual champions) are in bold face. (Note: Only 10 teams were ranked in the weekly polls during 1962, 1963, 1964, 1965, 1966 and 1967; 20 were ranked in all other seasons until 1989, when 25 were ranked.)

1936
10-20	Minnesota	(3-0-0)
10-27	Minnesota	(4-0-0)
11-3	Northwestern	(5-0-0) (3)
11-10	Northwestern	(6-0-0)
11-17	Northwestern	(7-0-0)
11-24	Minnesota	(7-1-0) (2)
12-1	**Minnesota**	**(7-1-0)**

1937
10-20	California	(5-0-0)
10-27	California	(6-0-0)
11-2	California	(7-0-0)
11-9	Pittsburgh	(6-0-1) (3)
11-16	Pittsburgh	(7-0-1)
11-23	Pittsburgh	(8-0-1)
11-30	**Pittsburgh**	**(9-0-1)**

1938
10-18	Pittsburgh	(4-0-0)
10-25	Pittsburgh	(5-0-0)
11-1	Pittsburgh	(6-0-0)
11-8	TCU	(7-0-0) (2)
11-15	Notre Dame	(7-0-0) (2)
11-22	Notre Dame	(8-0-0)
11-29	Notre Dame	(8-0-0)
12-6	**TCU**	**(10-0-0) (2)**

1939
10-17	Pittsburgh	(3-0-0)
10-24	Tennessee	(4-0-0) (5)
10-31	Tennessee	(5-0-0)
11-7	Tennessee	(6-0-0)
11-14	Tennessee	(7-0-0)
11-21	Texas A&M	(9-0-0) (2)
11-28 (tie)	Texas A&M	(9-0-0)
(tie)	Southern California	(6-0-1) (4)
12-5	Texas A&M	(10-0-0)
12-12	**Texas A&M**	**(10-0-0)**

1940
10-15	Cornell	(2-0-0)
10-22	Cornell	(3-0-0)
10-29	Cornell	(4-0-0)
11-5	Cornell	(5-0-0)
11-12	Minnesota	(6-0-0) (2)
11-19	Minnesota	(7-0-0)
11-26	Minnesota	(8-0-0)
12-3	**Minnesota**	**(8-0-0)**

1941
10-14	Minnesota	(2-0-0)
10-21	Minnesota	(3-0-0)
10-28 (tie)	Minnesota	(4-0-0)
(tie)	Texas	(5-0-0) (2)
11-4	Texas	(6-0-0)
11-11	Minnesota	(6-0-0) (2)
11-18	Minnesota	(7-0-0)
11-25	Minnesota	(8-0-0)
12-2	**Minnesota**	**(8-0-0)**

1942
10-13	Ohio St.	(3-0-0)
10-20	Ohio St.	(4-0-0)
10-27	Ohio St.	(5-0-0)
11-3	Georgia	(7-0-0) (2)
11-10	Georgia	(8-0-0)
11-17	Georgia	(9-0-0)
11-24	Boston College	(8-0-0) (3)
12-1	**Ohio St.**	**(9-1-0) (3)**

1943
10-5	Notre Dame	(2-0-0)
10-12	Notre Dame	(3-0-0)
10-19	Notre Dame	(4-0-0)
10-26	Notre Dame	(5-0-0)
11-2	Notre Dame	(6-0-0)
11-9	Notre Dame	(7-0-0)
11-16	Notre Dame	(8-0-0)
11-23	Notre Dame	(9-0-0)
11-30	**Notre Dame**	**(9-1-0)**

1944
10-10	Notre Dame	(2-0-0)
10-17	Notre Dame	(3-0-0)
10-24	Notre Dame	(4-0-0)
10-31	Army	(5-0-0) (2)
11-7	Army	(6-0-0)
11-14	Army	(7-0-0)
11-21	Army	(8-0-0)
11-28	Army	(8-0-0)
12-5	**Army**	**(9-0-0)**

1945
10-9	Army	(2-0-0)
10-16	Army	(3-0-0)
10-23	Army	(4-0-0)
10-30	Army	(5-0-0)
11-6	Army	(6-0-0)
11-13	Army	(7-0-0)
11-20	Army	(8-0-0)
11-27	Army	(8-0-0)
12-4	**Army**	**(9-0-0)**

1946
10-8	Texas	(3-0-0)
10-15	Army	(4-0-0) (2)
10-22	Army	(5-0-0)
10-29	Army	(6-0-0)
11-5	Army	(7-0-0)
11-12	Army	(7-0-1)
11-19	Army	(8-0-1)
11-26	Army	(8-0-1)
12-3	**Notre Dame**	**(8-0-1) (2)**

1947*
10-7	Notre Dame	(1-0-0)
10-14	Michigan	(3-0-0) (2)
10-21	Michigan	(4-0-0)
10-28	Notre Dame	(4-0-0) (2)
11-4	Notre Dame	(5-0-0)
11-11	Notre Dame	(6-0-0)
11-18	Michigan	(8-0-0) (2)
11-25	Notre Dame	(8-0-0) (2)
12-2	Notre Dame	(8-0-0)
12-9	**Notre Dame**	**(9-0-0)**

1948
10-5	Notre Dame	(2-0-0)
10-12	North Carolina	(3-0-0) (3)
10-19	Michigan	(4-0-0) (4)
10-26	Michigan	(5-0-0)
11-2	Notre Dame	(6-0-0) (2)
11-9	Michigan	(7-0-0) (2)
11-16	Michigan	(8-0-0)
11-23	Michigan	(9-0-0)
11-30	**Michigan**	**(9-0-0)**

1949
10-4	Michigan	(2-0-0)
10-11	Notre Dame	(3-0-0) (2)
10-18	Notre Dame	(4-0-0)
10-25	Notre Dame	(4-0-0)
11-1	Notre Dame	(5-0-0)
11-8	Notre Dame	(6-0-0)
11-15	Notre Dame	(7-0-0)
11-22	Notre Dame	(8-0-0)
11-29	**Notre Dame**	**(9-0-0)**

1950
10-3	Notre Dame	(1-0-0)
10-10	Army	(2-0-0) (4)
10-17	Army	(3-0-0)
10-24	Southern Methodist	(5-0-0) (3)
10-31	Southern Methodist	(5-0-0)
11-7	Army	(6-0-0) (2)
11-14	Ohio St.	(6-1-0) (2)
11-21	Oklahoma	(8-0-0) (2)
11-28	**Oklahoma**	**(9-0-0)**

1951
10-2	Michigan St.	(2-0-0)
10-9	Michigan St.	(3-0-0)
10-16	California	(4-0-0) (2)
10-23	Tennessee	(4-0-0) (2)
10-30	Tennessee	(5-0-0)
11-6	Tennessee	(6-0-0)
11-13	Michigan St.	(7-0-0)(5)

Date	Team	Record
11-20	Tennessee	(8-0-0) (2)
11-27	Tennessee	(9-0-0)
12-4	**Tennessee**	**(10-0-0)**

1952

Date	Team	Record
9-30	Michigan St.	(1-0-0)
10-7	Wisconsin	(2-0-0) (8)
10-14	Michigan St.	(3-0-0)(2)
10-21	Michigan St.	(4-0-0)
10-28	Michigan St.	(5-0-0)
11-4	Michigan St.	(6-0-0)
11-11	Michigan St.	(7-0-0)
11-18	Michigan St.	(8-0-0)
11-25	Michigan St.	(9-0-0)
12-1	**Michigan St.**	**(9-0-0)**

1953

Date	Team	Record
9-29	Notre Dame	(1-0-0)
10-6	Notre Dame	(2-0-0)
10-13	Notre Dame	(2-0-0)
10-20	Notre Dame	(3-0-0)
10-27	Notre Dame	(4-0-0)
11-3	Notre Dame	(5-0-0)
11-10	Notre Dame	(6-0-0)
11-17	Notre Dame	(7-0-0)
11-24	Maryland	(10-0-0) (2)
12-1	**Maryland**	**(10-0-0)**

1954

Date	Team	Record
9-21	Oklahoma	(1-0-0)
9-28	Notre Dame	(1-0-0) (2)
10-5	Oklahoma	(2-0-0) (2)
10-12	Oklahoma	(3-0-0)
10-19	Oklahoma	(4-0-0)
10-26	Ohio St.	(5-0-0) (4)
11-2	UCLA	(7-0-0) (2)
11-9	UCLA	(8-0-0)
11-16	Ohio St.	(8-0-0) (2)
11-23	Ohio St.	(9-0-0)
11-30	**Ohio St.**	**(9-0-0)**

1955

Date	Team	Record
9-20	UCLA	(1-0-0)
9-27	Maryland	(2-0-0) (5)
10-4	Maryland	(3-0-0)
10-11	Michigan	(3-0-0) (2)
10-18	Michigan	(4-0-0)
10-25	Maryland	(6-0-0) (2)
11-1	Maryland	(7-0-0)
11-8	Oklahoma	(7-0-0) (2)
11-15	Oklahoma	(8-0-0)
11-22	Oklahoma	(9-0-0)
11-29	**Oklahoma**	**(10-0-0)**

1956

Date	Team	Record
9-25	Oklahoma	(0-0-0)
10-2	Oklahoma	(1-0-0)
10-9	Oklahoma	(2-0-0)
10-16	Oklahoma	(3-0-0)
10-23	Michigan St.	(4-0-0) (2)
10-30	Oklahoma	(5-0-0) (2)
11-6	Oklahoma	(6-0-0)
11-13	Tennessee	(7-0-0) (3)
11-20	Oklahoma	(8-0-0) (2)
11-27	Oklahoma	(9-0-0)
12-4	**Oklahoma**	**(10-0-0)**

1957

Date	Team	Record
9-24	Oklahoma	(1-0-0)
10-1	Oklahoma	(1-0-0)
10-8	Oklahoma	(2-0-0)
10-15	Michigan St.	(3-0-0) (2)
10-22	Oklahoma	(4-0-0) (2)
10-29	Texas A&M	(6-0-0) (2)
11-5	Texas A&M	(7-0-0)
11-12	Texas A&M	(8-0-0)
11-19	Michigan St.	(7-1-0)(4)
11-26	Auburn	(9-0-0) (2)
12-3	**Auburn**	**(10-0-0)**

1958

Date	Team	Record
9-23	Ohio St.	(0-0-0)
9-30	Oklahoma	(1-0-0) (2)
10-7	Auburn	(2-0-0) (2)
10-14	Army	(3-0-0) (3)
10-21	Army	(4-0-0)
10-28	LSU	(6-0-0) (2)
11-4	LSU	(7-0-0)
11-11	LSU	(8-0-0)
11-18	LSU	(9-0-0)

Date	Team	Record
11-25	LSU	(10-0-0)
12-2	**LSU**	**(10-0-0)**

1959

Date	Team	Record
9-22	LSU	(1-0-0)
9-29	LSU	(2-0-0)
10-6	LSU	(3-0-0)
10-13	LSU	(4-0-0)
10-20	LSU	(5-0-0)
10-27	LSU	(6-0-0)
11-3	LSU	(7-0-0)
11-10	Syracuse	(7-0-0) (4)
11-17	Syracuse	(8-0-0)
11-24	Syracuse	(9-0-0)
12-1	Syracuse	(9-0-0)
12-8	**Syracuse**	**(10-0-0)**

1960

Date	Team	Record
9-20	Mississippi	(1-0-0)
9-27	Mississippi	(2-0-0)
10-4	Syracuse	(2-0-0) (2)
10-11	Mississippi	(4-0-0) (2)
10-18	Iowa	(4-0-0) (2)
10-25	Iowa	(5-0-0)
11-1	Iowa	(6-0-0)
11-8	Minnesota	(7-0-0) (3)
11-15	Missouri	(9-0-0) (2)
11-22	Minnesota	(8-1-0) (4)
11-29	**Minnesota**	**(8-1-0)**

1961

Date	Team	Record
9-26	Iowa	(0-0-0)
10-3	Iowa	(1-0-0)
10-10	Mississippi	(3-0-0) (2)
10-17	Michigan St.	(3-0-0) (5)
10-24	Michigan St.	(4-0-0)
10-31	Michigan St.	(5-0-0)
11-7	Texas	(7-0-0) (3)
11-14	Texas	(8-0-0)
11-21	Alabama	(9-0-0) (2)
11-28	Alabama	(9-0-0)
12-5	**Alabama**	**(10-0-0)**

1962

Date	Team	Record
9-25	Alabama	(1-0-0)
10-2	Ohio St.	(1-0-0) (2)
10-9	Alabama	(3-0-0) (2)
10-16	Texas	(4-0-0) (2)
10-23	Texas	(5-0-0)
10-30	Northwestern	(5-0-0) (3)
11-6	Northwestern	(6-0-0)
11-13	Alabama	(8-0-0) (3)
11-20	Southern California	(8-0-0) (2)
11-27	Southern California	(9-0-0)
12-4	**Southern California**	**(10-0-0)**

1963

Date	Team	Record
9-24	Southern California	(1-0-0)
10-1	Oklahoma	(1-0-0) (3)
10-8	Oklahoma	(2-0-0)
10-15	Texas	(4-0-0) (3)
10-22	Texas	(5-0-0)
10-29	Texas	(6-0-0)
11-5	Texas	(7-0-0)
11-12	Texas	(8-0-0)
11-19	Texas	(9-0-0)
11-26	Texas	(9-0-0)
12-3	Texas	(10-0-0)
12-10	**Texas**	**(10-0-0)**

1964

Date	Team	Record
9-29	Texas	(2-0-0)
10-6	Texas	(3-0-0)
10-13	Texas	(4-0-0)
10-20	Ohio St.	(4-0-0)(2)
10-27	Ohio St.	(5-0-0)
11-3	Notre Dame	(6-0-0)(2)
11-10	Notre Dame	(7-0-0)
11-17	Notre Dame	(8-0-0)
11-24	Notre Dame	(9-0-0)
12-1	**Alabama**	**(10-0-0) (2)**

1965

Date	Team	Record
9-21	Notre Dame	(1-0-0)
9-28	Texas	(2-0-0) (3)
10-5	Texas	(3-0-0)
10-12	Texas	(4-0-0)
10-19	Arkansas	(5-0-0) (3)
10-26	Michigan St.	(6-0-0) (2)
11-2	Michigan St.	(7-0-0)
11-9	Michigan St.	(8-0-0)

Date	Team	Record
11-16	Michigan St.	(9-0-0)
11-23	Michigan St.	(10-0-0)
11-30	Michigan St.	(10-0-0)
1-4	**Alabama**	**(9-1-1) (4)**

1966

Date	Team	Record
9-20	Michigan St.	(1-0-0)
9-27	Michigan St.	(2-0-0)
10-4	Michigan St.	(3-0-0)
10-11	Michigan St.	(4-0-0)
10-18	Notre Dame	(4-0-0) (2)
10-25	Notre Dame	(5-0-0)
11-1	Notre Dame	(6-0-0)
11-8	Notre Dame	(7-0-0)
11-15	Notre Dame	(8-0-0)
11-22	Notre Dame	(8-0-1)
11-29	Notre Dame	(9-0-1)
12-5	**Notre Dame**	**(9-0-1)**

1967

Date	Team	Record
9-19	Notre Dame	(0-0-0)
9-26	Notre Dame	(1-0-0)
10-3	Southern California	(3-0-0) (2)
10-10	Southern California	(4-0-0)
10-17	Southern California	(5-0-0)
10-24	Southern California	(6-0-0)
10-31	Southern California	(7-0-0)
11-7	Southern California	(8-0-0)
11-14	UCLA	(7-0-1) (2)
11-21	Southern California	(9-1-0) (4)
11-28	**Southern California**	**(9-1-0)**

1968

Date	Team	Record
9-17	Purdue	(0-0-0)
9-24	Purdue	(1-0-0)
10-1	Purdue	(2-0-0)
10-8	Purdue	(3-0-0)
10-15	Southern California	(4-0-0) (2)
10-22	Southern California	(5-0-0)
10-29	Southern California	(5-0-0)
11-5	Southern California	(6-0-0)
11-12	Southern California	(7-0-0)
11-19	Southern California	(8-0-0)
11-26	Ohio St.	(9-0-0) (2)
12-2	Ohio St.	(9-0-0)
12-9	**Ohio St.**	**(10-0-0)**

1969

Date	Team	Record
9-23	Ohio St.	(0-0-0)
9-30	Ohio St.	(1-0-0)
10-7	Ohio St.	(2-0-0)
10-14	Ohio St.	(3-0-0)
10-21	Ohio St.	(4-0-0)
10-28	Ohio St.	(5-0-0)
11-4	Ohio St.	(6-0-0)
11-11	Ohio St.	(7-0-0)
11-18	Ohio St.	(8-0-0)
11-25	Texas	(8-0-0) (2)
12-2	Texas	(9-0-0)
12-9	Texas	(10-0-0)
1-4	**Texas**	**(11-0-0)**

1970

Date	Team	Record
9-15	Ohio St.	(0-0-0)
9-22	Ohio St.	(0-0-0)
9-29	Ohio St.	(1-0-0)
10-6	Ohio St.	(2-0-0)
10-13	Ohio St.	(3-0-0)
10-20	Ohio St.	(4-0-0)
10-27	Texas	(5-0-0) (2)
11-3	Texas	(6-0-0)
11-10	Texas	(7-0-0)
11-17	Texas	(8-0-0)
11-24	Texas	(8-0-0)
12-1	Texas	(9-0-0)
12-8	Texas	(10-0-0)
1-6	**Nebraska**	**(11-0-1) (3)**

1971

Date	Team	Record
9-14	Nebraska	(1-0-0)
9-21	Nebraska	(2-0-0)
9-28	Nebraska	(3-0-0)
10-5	Nebraska	(4-0-0)
10-12	Nebraska	(5-0-0)
10-19	Nebraska	(6-0-0)
10-26	Nebraska	(7-0-0)
11-2	Nebraska	(8-0-0)
11-9	Nebraska	(9-0-0)
11-16	Nebraska	(10-0-0)
11-23	Nebraska	(10-0-0)

Date	Team	Record
11-30	Nebraska	(11-0-0)
12-7	Nebraska	(12-0-0)
1-4	**Nebraska**	**(13-0-0)**

1972
Date	Team	Record
9-12	Southern California	(1-0-0)
9-19	Southern California	(2-0-0)
9-26	Southern California	(3-0-0)
10-3	Southern California	(4-0-0)
10-10	Southern California	(5-0-0)
10-17	Southern California	(6-0-0)
10-24	Southern California	(7-0-0)
10-31	Southern California	(8-0-0)
11-7	Southern California	(9-0-0)
11-14	Southern California	(9-0-0)
11-21	Southern California	(10-0-0)
11-28	Southern California	(10-0-0)
12-5	Southern California	(11-0-0)
1-3	**Southern California**	**(12-0-0)**

1973
Date	Team	Record
9-11	Southern California	(0-0-0)
9-18	Southern California	(1-0-0)
9-25	Southern California	(2-0-0)
10-2	Ohio St.	(2-0-0) (3)
10-9	Ohio St.	(3-0-0)
10-16	Ohio St.	(4-0-0)
10-23	Ohio St.	(5-0-0)
10-30	Ohio St.	(6-0-0)
11-6	Ohio St.	(7-0-0)
11-13	Ohio St.	(8-0-0)
11-20	Ohio St.	(9-0-0)
11-27	Alabama	(10-0-0) (2)
12-4	Alabama	(11-0-0)
1-3	**Notre Dame**	**(11-0-0) (3)**

1974
Date	Team	Record
9-10	Oklahoma	(0-0-0)
9-17	Notre Dame	(1-0-0) (2)
9-24	Ohio St.	(2-0-0) (2)
10-1	Ohio St.	(3-0-0)
10-8	Ohio St.	(4-0-0)
10-15	Ohio St.	(5-0-0)
10-22	Ohio St.	(6-0-0)
10-29	Ohio St.	(7-0-0)
11-5	Ohio St.	(8-0-0)
11-12	Oklahoma	(8-0-0) (2)
11-19	Oklahoma	(9-0-0)
11-26	Oklahoma	(10-0-0)
12-3	Oklahoma	(11-0-0)
1-3	**Oklahoma**	**(11-0-0)**

1975
Date	Team	Record
9-9	Oklahoma	(0-0-0)
9-16	Oklahoma	(1-0-0)
9-23	Oklahoma	(2-0-0)
9-30	Oklahoma	(3-0-0)
10-7	Ohio St.	(4-0-0) (2)
10-14	Ohio St.	(5-0-0)
10-21	Ohio St.	(6-0-0)
10-28	Ohio St.	(7-0-0)
11-4	Ohio St.	(8-0-0)
11-11	Ohio St.	(9-0-0)
11-18	Ohio St.	(10-0-0)
11-25	Ohio St.	(11-0-0)
12-2	Ohio St.	(11-0-0)
1-3	**Oklahoma**	**(11-1-0) (3)**

1976
Date	Team	Record
9-14	Michigan	(1-0-0)
9-21	Michigan	(2-0-0)
9-28	Michigan	(3-0-0)
10-5	Michigan	(4-0-0)
10-12	Michigan	(5-0-0)
10-19	Michigan	(6-0-0)
10-26	Michigan	(7-0-0)
11-2	Michigan	(8-0-0)
11-9	Pittsburgh	(9-0-0) (2)
11-16	Pittsburgh	(10-0-0)
11-23	Pittsburgh	(10-0-0)
11-30	Pittsburgh	(11-0-0)
1-5	**Pittsburgh**	**(12-0-0)**

1977
Date	Team	Record
9-13	Michigan	(1-0-0)
9-20	Michigan	(2-0-0)
9-27	Oklahoma	(3-0-0) (3)
10-4	Southern California	(4-0-0) (2)
10-11	Michigan	(5-0-0) (3)
10-18	Michigan	(6-0-0)
10-25	Texas	(6-0-0) (2)
11-1	Texas	(7-0-0)
11-8	Texas	(8-0-0)
11-15	Texas	(9-0-0)
11-22	Texas	(10-0-0)
11-29	Texas	(11-0-0)
1-4	**Notre Dame**	**(11-1-0) (5)**

1978
Date	Team	Record
9-12	Alabama	(1-0-0)
9-19	Alabama	(2-0-0)
9-26	Oklahoma	(3-0-0) (tie 3)
10-3	Oklahoma	(4-0-0)
10-10	Oklahoma	(5-0-0)
10-17	Oklahoma	(6-0-0)
10-24	Oklahoma	(7-0-0)
10-31	Oklahoma	(8-0-0)
11-7	Oklahoma	(9-0-0)
11-14	Penn St.	(10-0-0) (2)
11-21	Penn St.	(10-0-0)
11-28	Penn St.	(11-0-0)
12-5	Penn St.	(11-0-0)
1-4	**Alabama**	**(11-1-0) (2)**

1979
Date	Team	Record
9-11	Southern California	(1-0-0)
9-18	Southern California	(2-0-0)
9-25	Southern California	(3-0-0)
10-2	Southern California	(4-0-0)
10-9	Southern California	(5-0-0)
10-16	Alabama	(5-0-0) (2)
10-23	Alabama	(6-0-0)
10-30	Alabama	(7-0-0)
11-6	Alabama	(8-0-0)
11-13	Alabama	(9-0-0)
11-20	Alabama	(10-0-0)
11-27	Alabama	(10-0-0)
12-4	Ohio St.	(11-0-0) (3)
1-3	**Alabama**	**(12-0-0) (2)**

1980
Date	Team	Record
9-9	Ohio St.	(0-0-0)
9-16	Alabama	(1-0-0) (2)
9-23	Alabama	(2-0-0)
9-30	Alabama	(3-0-0)
10-7	Alabama	(4-0-0)
10-14	Alabama	(5-0-0)
10-21	Alabama	(6-0-0)
10-28	Alabama	(7-0-0)
11-4	Notre Dame	(7-0-0) (3)
11-11	Georgia	(9-0-0) (2)
11-18	Georgia	(10-0-0)
11-25	Georgia	(10-0-0)
12-2	Georgia	(11-0-0)
12-9	Georgia	(11-0-0)
1-4	**Georgia**	**(12-0-0)**

1981
Date	Team	Record
9-8	Michigan	(0-0-0)
9-15	Notre Dame	(1-0-0) (4)
9-22	Southern California	(2-0-0) (2)
9-29	Southern California	(3-0-0)
10-6	Southern California	(4-0-0)
10-13	Texas	(4-0-0) (3)
10-20	Penn St.	(5-0-0) (2)
10-27	Penn St.	(6-0-0)
11-3	Pittsburgh	(7-0-0) (2)
11-10	Pittsburgh	(8-0-0)
11-17	Pittsburgh	(9-0-0)
11-24	Pittsburgh	(10-0-0)
12-1	Clemson	(11-0-0) (2)
1-3	**Clemson**	**(12-0-0)**

1982
Date	Team	Record
9-7	Pittsburgh	(0-0-0)
9-14	Washington	(1-0-0) (2)
9-21	Washington	(2-0-0)
9-28	Washington	(3-0-0)
10-5	Washington	(4-0-0)
10-12	Washington	(5-0-0)
10-19	Washington	(6-0-0)
10-26	Pittsburgh	(6-0-0) (2)
11-2	Pittsburgh	(7-0-0)
11-9	Georgia	(9-0-0) (3)
11-16	Georgia	(10-0-0)
11-23	Georgia	(10-0-0)
11-30	Georgia	(11-0-0)
12-7	Georgia	(11-0-0)
1-3	**Penn St.**	**(11-1-0) (2)**

1983
Date	Team	Record
9-6	Nebraska	(1-0-0)
9-13	Nebraska	(2-0-0)
9-20	Nebraska	(3-0-0)
9-27	Nebraska	(4-0-0)
10-4	Nebraska	(5-0-0)
10-11	Nebraska	(6-0-0)
10-18	Nebraska	(7-0-0)
10-25	Nebraska	(8-0-0)
11-1	Nebraska	(9-0-0)
11-8	Nebraska	(10-0-0)
11-15	Nebraska	(11-0-0)
11-22	Nebraska	(11-0-0)
11-29	Nebraska	(12-0-0)
12-6	Nebraska	(12-0-0)
1-3	**Miami (Fla.)**	**(11-1-0) (5)**

1984
Date	Team	Record
9-4	Miami (Fla.)	(2-0-0)
9-11	Nebraska	(1-0-0) (2)
9-18	Nebraska	(2-0-0)
9-25	Nebraska	(3-0-0)
10-2	Texas	(2-0-0) (2)
10-9	Texas	(3-0-0)
10-16	Washington	(6-0-0) (2)
10-23	Washington	(7-0-0)
10-30	Washington	(8-0-0)
11-6	Washington	(9-0-0)
11-13	Nebraska	(9-1-0) (2)
11-20	Brigham Young	(11-0-0) (3)
11-27	Brigham Young	(12-0-0)
12-4	Brigham Young	(12-0-0)
1-3	**Brigham Young**	**(13-0-0)**

1985
Date	Team	Record
9-3	Oklahoma	(0-0-0)
9-10	Auburn	(1-0-0) (2)
9-17	Auburn	(2-0-0)
9-24	Auburn	(2-0-0)
10-1	Iowa	(3-0-0) (3)
10-8	Iowa	(4-0-0)
10-15	Iowa	(5-0-0)
10-22	Iowa	(6-0-0)
10-29	Iowa	(7-0-0)
11-5	Florida	(7-0-1) (2)
11-12	Penn St.	(9-0-0) (2)
11-19	Penn St.	(10-0-0)
11-26	Penn St.	(11-0-0)
12-3	Penn St.	(11-0-0)
1-3	**Oklahoma**	**(11-1-0) (4)**

1986
Date	Team	Record
9-9	Oklahoma	(1-0-0)
9-16	Oklahoma	(1-0-0)
9-23	Oklahoma	(2-0-0)
9-30	Miami (Fla.)	(4-0-0) (2)
10-7	Miami (Fla.)	(5-0-0)
10-14	Miami (Fla.)	(6-0-0)
10-21	Miami (Fla.)	(7-0-0)
10-28	Miami (Fla.)	(7-0-0)
11-4	Miami (Fla.)	(8-0-0)
11-11	Miami (Fla.)	(9-0-0)
11-18	Miami (Fla.)	(10-0-0)
11-25	Miami (Fla.)	(10-0-0)
12-2	Miami (Fla.)	(11-0-0)
1-4	**Penn St.**	**(12-0-0) (2)**

1987
Date	Team	Record
9-8	Oklahoma	(1-0-0)
9-15	Oklahoma	(2-0-0)
9-22	Oklahoma	(2-0-0)
9-29	Oklahoma	(3-0-0)
10-6	Oklahoma	(4-0-0)
10-13	Oklahoma	(5-0-0)
10-20	Oklahoma	(6-0-0)
10-27	Oklahoma	(7-0-0)
11-3	Oklahoma	(8-0-0)
11-10	Oklahoma	(9-0-0)
11-17	Nebraska	(9-0-0) (2)
11-24	Oklahoma	(11-0-0) (2)
12-1	Oklahoma	(11-0-0)
12-8	Oklahoma	(11-0-0)
1-3	**Miami (Fla.)**	**(12-0-0) (2)**

1988
Date	Team	Record
9-6	Miami (Fla.)	(1-0-0)
9-13	Miami (Fla.)	(1-0-0)
9-20	Miami (Fla.)	(2-0-0)
9-27	Miami (Fla.)	(3-0-0)
10-4	Miami (Fla.)	(4-0-0)
10-11	Miami (Fla.)	(4-0-0)
10-18	UCLA	(6-0-0) (2)
10-25	UCLA	(7-0-0)
11-1	Notre Dame	(8-0-0) (2)
11-8	Notre Dame	(9-0-0)

Date	Team	Record
11-15	Notre Dame	(9-0-0)
11-22	Notre Dame	(10-0-0)
11-29	Notre Dame	(11-0-0)
12-6	Notre Dame	(11-0-0)
1-3	**Notre Dame**	**(12-0-0)**

1989

Date	Team	Record
9-5	Notre Dame	(1-0-0)
9-12	Notre Dame	(1-0-0)
9-19	Notre Dame	(2-0-0)
9-26	Notre Dame	(3-0-0)
10-3	Notre Dame	(4-0-0)
10-10	Notre Dame	(5-0-0)
10-17	Notre Dame	(6-0-0)
10-24	Notre Dame	(7-0-0)
10-31	Notre Dame	(8-0-0)
11-7	Notre Dame	(9-0-0)
11-14	Notre Dame	(10-0-0)
11-21	Notre Dame	(11-0-0)
11-28	Colorado	(11-0-0) (2)
12-5	Colorado	(11-0-0)
1-2	**Miami (Fla.)**	**(11-1-0) (2)**

1990

Date	Team	Record
9-4	Miami (Fla.)	(0-0-0)
9-11	Notre Dame	(0-0-0) (2)
9-18	Notre Dame	(1-0-0)
9-25	Notre Dame	(2-0-0)
10-2	Notre Dame	(3-0-0)
10-9	Michigan	(3-1-0) (3)
10-16	Virginia	(6-0-0) (2)
10-23	Virginia	(7-0-0)
10-30	Virginia	(7-0-0)
11-6	Notre Dame	(7-1-0) (2)
11-13	Notre Dame	(8-1-0)
11-20	Colorado	(10-1-1) (2)
11-27	Colorado	(10-1-1)
12-4	Colorado	(10-1-1)
1-2	**Colorado**	**(11-1-1)**

1991

Date	Team	Record
9-3	Florida St.	(1-0-0)
9-10	Florida St.	(2-0-0)
9-17	Florida St.	(3-0-0)
9-23	Florida St.	(3-0-0)
9-30	Florida St.	(4-0-0)
10-7	Florida St.	(5-0-0)
10-14	Florida St.	(6-0-0)
10-21	Florida St.	(7-0-0)
10-28	Florida St.	(8-0-0)
11-4	Florida St.	(9-0-0)
11-11	Florida St.	(10-0-0)
11-18	Miami (Fla.)	(9-0-0) (2)
11-25	Miami (Fla.)	(10-0-0)
12-2	Miami (Fla.)	(11-0-0)
1-2	**Miami (Fla.)**	**(12-0-0)**

1992

Date	Team	Record
9-8	Miami (Fla.)	(1-0-0)
9-15	Miami (Fla.)	(1-0-0)
9-22	Miami (Fla.)	(2-0-0)
9-29	Washington	(3-0-0) (2)
10-6	Washington	(4-0-0)
10-13	Washington	(5-0-0)
10-20	Miami (Fla.)†	(6-0-0) (2)
10-27	Miami (Fla.)	(7-0-0)
11-3	Washington	(8-0-0) (2)
11-10	Miami (Fla.)	(8-0-0) (2)
11-17	Miami (Fla.)	(9-0-0)
11-24	Miami (Fla.)	(10-0-0)
12-1	Miami (Fla.)	(11-0-0)
12-8	Miami (Fla.)	(11-0-0)
1-2	**Alabama**	**(13-0-0) (2)**

1993

Date	Team	Record
8-31	Florida St.	(1-0-0)
9-7	Florida St.	(2-0-0)
9-14	Florida St.	(3-0-0)
9-21	Florida St.	(4-0-0)
9-28	Florida St.	(4-0-0)
10-5	Florida St.	(5-0-0)
10-12	Florida St.	(6-0-0)
10-19	Florida St.	(7-0-0)
10-26	Florida St.	(7-0-0)
11-2	Florida St.	(8-0-0)
11-9	Florida St.	(9-0-0)
11-16	Notre Dame	(10-0-0) (2)
11-23	Florida St.	(10-1-0) (2)
11-30	Florida St.	(11-1-0)
12-7	Florida St.	(11-1-0)
1-3	**Florida St.**	**(12-1-0)**

1994

Date	Team	Record
8-31	Florida	(0-0-0)
9-6	Nebraska	(1-0-0) (2)
9-13	Florida	(2-0-0) (2)
9-20	Florida	(3-0-0)
9-27	Florida	(3-0-0)
10-4	Florida	(4-0-0)
10-11	Florida	(5-0-0)
10-18	Penn St.	(6-0-0) (3)
10-25	Penn St.	(6-0-0)
11-1	Nebraska	(9-0-0) (3)
11-8	Nebraska	(10-0-0)
11-15	Nebraska	(11-0-0)
11-22	Nebraska	(11-0-0)
11-29	Nebraska	(12-0-0)
12-6	Nebraska	(12-0-0)
1-3	**Nebraska**	**(13-0-0)**

1995

Date	Team	Record
8-29	Florida St.	(0-0-0)
9-5	Florida St.	(1-0-0)
9-12	Florida St.	(2-0-0)
9-19	Florida St.	(3-0-0)
9-26	Florida St.	(4-0-0)
10-3	Florida St.	(4-0-0)
10-10	Florida St.	(5-0-0)
10-17	Florida St.	(6-0-0)
10-24	Florida St.	(7-0-0)
10-31	Nebraska	(8-0-0) (2)
11-7	Nebraska	(9-0-0)
11-14	Nebraska	(10-0-0)
11-21	Nebraska	(10-0-0)
11-28	Nebraska	(11-0-0)
12-5	Nebraska	(11-0-0)
1-3	**Nebraska**	**(12-0-0)**

1996

Date	Team	Record
8-26	Nebraska	(0-0-0)
9-2	Nebraska	(0-0-0)
9-9	Nebraska	(1-0-0)
9-16	Nebraska	(1-0-0)
9-23	Florida	(3-0-0) (4)
9-30	Florida	(4-0-0)
10-7	Florida	(5-0-0)
10-14	Florida	(6-0-0)
10-21	Florida	(7-0-0)
10-28	Florida	(7-0-0)
11-4	Florida	(8-0-0)
11-11	Florida	(9-0-0)
11-18	Florida	(10-0-0)
11-25	Florida	(10-0-0)
12-2	Florida St.	(11-0-0) (2)
12-9	Florida St.	(11-0-0)
1-3	**Florida**	**(12-1-0)**

1997

Date	Team	Record
8-25	Penn St.	(0-0-0)
9-2	Penn St.	(0-0-0)
9-8	Penn St.	(1-0-0)
9-15	Penn St.	(2-0-0)
9-22	Florida	(3-0-0) (3)
9-29	Florida	(4-0-0)
10-6	Florida	(5-0-0)
10-13	Penn St.	(5-0-0) (2)
10-20	Nebraska	(6-0-0) (2)
10-27	Nebraska	(7-0-0)
11-3	Nebraska	(8-0-0)
11-10	Michigan	(9-0-0) (4)
11-17	Michigan	(10-0-0)
11-24	Michigan	(11-0-0)
12-1	Michigan	(11-0-0)
12-8	Michigan	(11-0-0)
1-3	**Michigan**	**(12-0-0)**

1998

Date	Team	Record
9-7	Ohio St.	(1-0-0)
9-14	Ohio St.	(2-0-0)
9-21	Ohio St.	(3-0-0)
9-28	Ohio St.	(3-0-0)
10-5	Ohio St.	(4-0-0)
10-12	Ohio St.	(5-0-0)
10-19	Ohio St.	(6-0-0)
10-26	Ohio St.	(7-0-0)
11-2	Ohio St.	(8-0-0)
11-9	Tennessee	(8-0-0) (2)
11-16	Tennessee	(9-0-0)
11-23	Tennessee	(10-0-0)
11-30	Tennessee	(11-0-0)
12-7	Tennessee	(12-0-0)
1-5	**Tennessee**	**(13-0-0)**

1999

Date	Team	Record
8-30	Florida St.	(1-0-0)
9-6	Florida St.	(1-0-0)
9-13	Florida St.	(2-0-0)
9-20	Florida St.	(3-0-0)
9-27	Florida St.	(4-0-0)
10-4	Florida St.	(5-0-0)
10-11	Florida St.	(6-0-0)
10-18	Florida St.	(7-0-0)
10-25	Florida St.	(8-0-0)
11-1	Florida St.	(9-0-0)
11-8	Florida St.	(9-0-0)
11-15	Florida St.	(10-0-0)
11-22	Florida St.	(11-0-0)
11-29	Florida St.	(11-0-0)
12-6	Florida St.	(11-0-0)
1-5	**Florida St.**	**(12-0-0)**

2000

Date	Team	Record
8-28	Nebraska	(0-0-0)
9-4	Nebraska	(1-0-0)
9-11	Nebraska	(2-0-0)
9-18	Nebraska	(2-0-0)
9-25	Nebraska	(3-0-0)
10-2	Nebraska	(4-0-0)
10-9	Nebraska	(5-0-0)
10-16	Nebraska	(6-0-0)
10-23	Nebraska	(7-0-0)
10-30	Oklahoma	(7-0-0)
11-6	Oklahoma	(8-0-0)
11-13	Oklahoma	(9-0-0)
11-20	Oklahoma	(10-0-0)
11-27	Oklahoma	(11-0-0)
12-4	Oklahoma	(12-0-0)
1-5	**Oklahoma**	**(13-0-0)**

2001

Date	Team	Record
8-27	Florida	(0-0-0)
9-2	Florida	(1-0-0)
9-9	Miami (Fla.)	(2-0-0)
9-23	Miami (Fla.)	(2-0-0)
9-30	Miami (Fla.)	(3-0-0)
10-7	Florida	(4-0-0)
10-14	Miami (Fla.)	(5-0-0)
10-21	Miami (Fla.)	(6-0-0)
10-28	Miami (Fla.)	(7-0-0)
11-4	Miami (Fla.)	(7-0-0)
11-11	Miami (Fla.)	(8-0-0)
11-18	Miami (Fla.)	(9-0-0)
11-24	Miami (Fla.)	(10-0-0)
12-2	Miami (Fla.)	(11-0-0)
12-8	Miami (Fla.)	(11-0-0)
1-4	**Miami (Fla.)**	**(12-0-0)**

2002

Date	Team	Record
8-26	Miami (Fla.)	(0-0-0)
9-2	Miami (Fla.)	(1-0-0)
9-9	Miami (Fla.)	(2-0-0)
9-16	Miami (Fla.)	(3-0-0)
9-23	Miami (Fla.)	(4-0-0)
9-30	Miami (Fla.)	(4-0-0)
10-7	Miami (Fla.)	(5-0-0)
10-14	Miami (Fla.)	(6-0-0)
10-21	Miami (Fla.)	(6-0-0)
10-28	Miami (Fla.)	(7-0-0)
11-4	Oklahoma	(8-0-0) (2)
11-11	Miami (Fla.)	(9-0-0) (2)
11-18	Miami (Fla.)	(9-0-0)
11-25	Miami (Fla.)	(10-0-0)
12-2	Miami (Fla.)	(11-0-0)
12-9	Miami (Fla.)	(12-0-0)
1-3	**Ohio St.**	**(14-0-0) (2)**

*On January 6, 1948, in a special postseason poll after the Rose Bowl, The Associated Press voted Michigan No. 1 and Notre Dame No. 2. However, the postseason poll did not supersede the final regular-season poll of December 9, 1947. †Miami (Fla.) and Washington actually tied for first place in The Associated Press poll for the first time in 51 years, but Miami (Fla.) had one more first-place vote, 31-30, than Washington.

DIVISION I-A

2002 Associated Press Week-By-Week Polls

	Pre	S2	S9	S16	S23	S30	O7	O14	O21	O28	N4	N11	N18	N25	D2	D9	J3
Miami (Fla.)	1	1	1	1	1	1	1	1	1	1	2	1	1	1	1	1	2
Oklahoma	2	2	2	2	2	3	2	2	2	2	1	4	4	3	8	8	5
Texas	3	3	3	3	3	2	3	8	7	7	4	4	11	10	9	9	6
Tennessee	4	4	4	4	11	10	10	16	16	25	NR	NR	NR	NR	NR	NR	NR
Florida St.	5	5	5	5	4	11	9	12	11	18	17	15	14	23	16	16	21
Florida	6	6	12	10	7	6	16	NR	NR	NR	23	20	19	15	23	22	NR
Colorado	7	17	18	NR	NR	NR	NR	23	21	13	18	17	16	13	12	14	20
Georgia	8	10	9	8	8	7	6	5	5	5	7	7	6	5	4	4	NR
Nebraska	9	9	8	18	20	NR	NR	NR	NR	NR	NR	NR	NR	NR	NR	NR	NR
Ohio St.	10	8	6	6	6	5	5	4	4	6	3	2	2	2	2	2	1
Washington	11	14	14	13	13	12	22	22	NR	NR	NR	NR	NR	NR	NR	NR	NR
Washington St.	12	11	10	16	16	17	12	10	9	8	5	3	3	9	7	7	10
Michigan	13	7	7	14	14	14	13	11	8	15	13	12	12	12	13	12	9
LSU	14	24	25	24	22	21	18	14	10	17	16	14	21	18	NR	NR	NR
Oregon	15	13	13	9	9	8	7	6	14	19	15	23	NR	NR	NR	NR	NR
Virginia Tech	16	12	11	7	5	4	4	3	3	3	8	13	13	22	18	21	18
Louisville	17	NR	NR	NR	NR	NR	NR	NR	NR	NR	NR	NR	NR	NR	NR	NR	NR
Michigan St.	18	15	15	NR	NR	NR	NR	NR	NR	NR	NR	NR	NR	NR	NR	NR	NR
Marshall	19	16	16	NR	NR	NR	NR	NR	NR	NR	NR	NR	NR	NR	NR	NR	24
Southern California	20	18	17	11	18	18	20	19	15	11	10	8	7	6	5	5	4
Maryland	21	NR	NR	NR	NR	NR	NR	NR	NR	NR	NR	19	18	25	21	20	13
South Carolina	22	22	NR	NR	NR	NR	NR	NR	NR	NR	NR	NR	NR	NR	NR	NR	NR
Texas A&M	23	20	21	19	24	23	NR	NR	NR	NR	NR	NR	NR	NR	NR	NR	NR
Penn St.	24	NR	NR	15	12	20	15	20	18	20	19	16	15	11	10	10	16
North Carolina St.	25	21	19	17	17	16	14	13	12	10	14	22	NR	21	17	17	12
Colorado St.	NR	19	24	NR	25	25	NR	NR	NR	24	24	21	20	16	24	23	NR
Notre Dame	NR	23	20	12	10	9	8	7	6	4	9	9	8	7	11	11	17
Wisconsin	NR	25	22	22	21	19	23	NR	NR	NR	NR	NR	NR	NR	NR	NR	NR
UCLA	NR	NR	23	20	NR	NR	NR	NR	NR	NR	NR	NR	25	NR	NR	NR	NR
Iowa St.	NR	NR	NR	21	19	15	11	9	17	22	21	NR	NR	NR	NR	NR	NR
California	NR	NR	NR	23	NR	NR	NR	NR	NR	NR	NR	NR	NR	NR	NR	NR	NR
Kansas St.	NR	NR	NR	25	15	13	19	17	20	14	12	11	10	8	6	6	7
Oregon St.	NR	NR	NR	NR	23	NR	NR	NR	NR	NR	NR	NR	NR	NR	NR	NR	NR
Alabama	NR	NR	NR	NR	NR	22	NR	24	19	12	11	10	9	14	14	13	11
Iowa	NR	NR	NR	NR	NR	24	17	15	13	9	6	6	5	4	3	3	8
Air Force	NR	NR	NR	NR	NR	NR	21	18	22	NR	NR	NR	NR	NR	NR	NR	NR
Auburn	NR	NR	NR	NR	NR	NR	24	NR	NR	NR	NR	24	NR	20	20	19	14
Mississippi	NR	NR	NR	NR	NR	NR	25	21	NR	NR	NR	NR	NR	NR	NR	NR	NR
Bowling Green	NR	NR	NR	NR	NR	NR	NR	25	24	21	20	NR	NR	NR	NR	NR	NR
Arizona St.	NR	NR	NR	NR	NR	NR	NR	NR	23	16	25	NR	NR	NR	NR	NR	NR
Minnesota	NR	NR	NR	NR	NR	NR	NR	NR	25	23	NR	NR	NR	NR	NR	NR	NR
Pittsburgh	NR	NR	NR	NR	NR	NR	NR	NR	NR	NR	22	18	17	17	25	24	19
TCU	NR	NR	NR	NR	NR	NR	NR	NR	NR	NR	NR	25	22	NR	NR	NR	23
Boise St.	NR	NR	NR	NR	NR	NR	NR	NR	NR	NR	NR	NR	23	19	19	18	15
Texas Tech	NR	NR	NR	NR	NR	NR	NR	NR	NR	NR	NR	NR	24	NR	NR	NR	NR
West Virginia	NR	NR	NR	NR	NR	NR	NR	NR	NR	NR	NR	NR	NR	24	15	15	25
Arkansas	NR	NR	NR	NR	NR	NR	NR	NR	NR	NR	NR	NR	NR	NR	22	25	NR
Virginia	NR	NR	NR	NR	NR	NR	NR	NR	NR	NR	NR	NR	NR	NR	NR	NR	22

No. 1 vs. No. 2

The No. 1 and No. 2 teams in The Associated Press poll (begun in 1936) have faced each other 34 times (20 in regular-season games and 14 in bowl games). The No. 1 team has won 20, with two games ending in ties.

Date	Score	Stadium (Site)
10-9-43	No. 1 Notre Dame 35, No. 2 Michigan 12	Michigan Stadium (Ann Arbor)
11-20-43	No. 1 Notre Dame 14, No. 2 Iowa Pre-Flight 13	Notre Dame (South Bend)
12-2-44	No. 1 Army 23, No. 2 Navy 7	Municipal (Baltimore)
11-10-45	No. 1 Army 48, No. 2 Notre Dame 0	Yankee (New York)
12-1-45	No. 1 Army 32, No. 2 Navy 13	Municipal (Philadelphia)
11-9-46	No. 1 Army 0, No. 2 Notre Dame 0 (tie)	Yankee (New York)
1-1-63	No. 1 Southern California 42, No. 2 Wisconsin 37 (Rose Bowl)	Rose Bowl (Pasadena)
10-12-63	No. 2 Texas 28, No. 1 Oklahoma 7	Cotton Bowl (Dallas)
1-1-64	No. 1 Texas 28, No. 2 Navy 6 (Cotton Bowl)	Cotton Bowl (Dallas)
11-19-66	No. 1 Notre Dame 10, No. 2 Michigan St. 10 (tie)	Spartan (East Lansing)
9-28-68	No. 1 Purdue 37, No. 2 Notre Dame 22	Notre Dame (South Bend)
1-1-69	No. 1 Ohio St. 27, No. 2 Southern California 16 (Rose Bowl)	Rose Bowl (Pasadena)
12-6-69	No. 1 Texas 15, No. 2 Arkansas 14	Razorback (Fayetteville)
11-25-71	No. 1 Nebraska 35, No. 2 Oklahoma 31	Owen Field (Norman)
1-1-72	No. 1 Nebraska 38, No. 2 Alabama 6 (Orange Bowl)	Orange Bowl (Miami)
1-1-79	No. 2 Alabama 14, No. 1 Penn St. 7 (Sugar Bowl)	Sugar Bowl (New Orleans)
9-26-81	No. 1 Southern California 28, No. 2 Oklahoma 24	Coliseum (Los Angeles)
1-1-83	No. 2 Penn St. 27, No. 1 Georgia 23 (Sugar Bowl)	Sugar Bowl (New Orleans)
10-19-85	No. 1 Iowa 12, No. 2 Michigan 10	Kinnick (Iowa City)
9-27-86	No. 2 Miami (Fla.) 28, No. 1 Oklahoma 16	Orange Bowl (Miami)
1-2-87	No. 2 Penn St. 14, No. 1 Miami (Fla.) 10 (Fiesta Bowl)	Sun Devil (Tempe)
11-21-87	No. 2 Oklahoma 17, No. 1 Nebraska 7	Memorial (Lincoln)
1-1-88	No. 2 Miami (Fla.) 20, No. 1 Oklahoma 14 (Orange Bowl)	Orange Bowl (Miami)

Date	Score	Stadium (Site)
11-26-88	No. 1 Notre Dame 27, No. 2 Southern California 10	Coliseum (Los Angeles)
9-16-89	No. 1 Notre Dame 24, No. 2 Michigan 19	Michigan (Ann Arbor)
11-16-91	No. 2 Miami (Fla.) 17, No. 1 Florida St. 16	Doak Campbell (Tallahassee)
1-1-93	No. 2 Alabama 34, No. 1 Miami (Fla.) 13 (Sugar Bowl)	Superdome (New Orleans)
11-13-93	No. 2 Notre Dame 31, No. 1 Florida St. 24	Notre Dame (South Bend)
1-1-94	No. 1 Florida St. 18, No. 2 Nebraska 16 (Orange Bowl)	Orange Bowl (Miami)
1-2-96	No. 1 Nebraska 62, No. 2 Florida 24 (Fiesta Bowl)	Sun Devil (Tempe)
11-30-96	No. 2 Florida St. 24, No. 1 Florida 21	Doak Campbell (Tallahassee)
1-4-99	No. 1 Tennessee 23, No. 2 Florida St. 16 (Fiesta Bowl)	Sun Devil (Tempe)
1-4-00	No. 1 Florida St. 46, No. 2 Virginia Tech 29	Superdome (New Orleans)
1-3-03	No. 2 Ohio St. 31, No. 1 Miami (Fla.) 24 (2ot) (Fiesta Bowl)	Sun Devil (Tempe)

Games in Which a No. 1-Ranked Team Was Defeated or Tied

Listed here are 116 games in which the No. 1-ranked team in The Associated Press poll was defeated or tied. An asterisk (*) indicates the home team, an (N) a neutral site. In parentheses after the winning or tying team is its rank in the previous week's poll (NR indicates it was not ranked), its won-lost record entering the game and its score. The defeated or tied No. 1-ranked team follows with its score, and in parentheses is its rank in the poll the following week. Before 1965, the polls were final before bowl games. (Note: Only 10 teams were ranked in the weekly polls during 1962, 1963, 1964, 1965, 1966 and 1967; 20 teams all other seasons until 1989, when 25 teams were ranked.)

10-31-36	*Northwestern (3, 4-0-0) 6, Minnesota 0 (2)
11-21-36	*Notre Dame (11, 5-2-0) 26, Northwestern 6 (7)
10-30-37	(Tie) Washington (NR, 3-2-1) 0, *California 0 (2)
10-29-38	Carnegie Mellon (T19, 4-1-0) 20, *Pittsburgh 10 (3)
12-2-38	*Southern California (8, 7-2-0) 13, Notre Dame 0 (5)
10-14-39	Duquesne (NR, 3-0-0) 21, *Pittsburgh 13 (18)
11-8-41	(Tie) Baylor (NR, 3-4-0) 7, *Texas 7 (2)
10-31-42	*Wisconsin (6, 5-0-1) 17, Ohio St. 7 (6)
11-21-42	(N) Auburn (NR, 4-4-1) 27, Georgia 13 (5)
11-28-42	Holy Cross (NR, 4-4-1) 55, *Boston College 12 (8)
11-27-43	*Great Lakes NTS (NR, 9-2-0) 19, Notre Dame 14 (1)
11-9-46	(Tie) (N) Notre Dame (2, 5-0-0) 0, Army 0 (1)
10-8-49	Army (7, 2-0-0) 21, *Michigan 7 (7)
10-7-50	Purdue (NR, 0-1-0) 28, *Notre Dame 14 (10)
11-4-50	*Texas (7, 4-1-0) 23, Southern Methodist 20 (7)
11-18-50	*Illinois (10, 6-1-0) 14, Ohio St. 7 (8)
1-1-51	(Sugar Bowl) Kentucky (7, 10-1-0) 13, Oklahoma 7 (1)
10-20-51	Southern California (11, 4-1-0) 21, *California 14 (9)
1-1-52	(Sugar Bowl) Maryland (3, 9-0-0) 28, Tennessee 13 (1)
10-11-52	*Ohio St. (NR, 1-1-0) 23, Wisconsin 14 (12)
11-21-53	(Tie) Iowa (20, 5-3-0) 14, *Notre Dame 14 (2)
1-1-54	(Orange Bowl) Oklahoma (4, 8-1-1) 7, Maryland 0 (1)
10-2-54	Purdue (19, 1-0-0) 27, *Notre Dame 14 (8)
9-24-55	*Maryland (5, 1-0-0) 7, UCLA 0 (7)
10-27-56	*Illinois (NR, 1-3-0) 20, Michigan St. 13 (4)
10-19-57	Purdue (NR, 0-3-0) 20, *Michigan St. 13 (8)
11-16-57	*Rice (20, 4-3-0) 7, Texas A&M 6 (4)
10-25-58	(Tie) *Pittsburgh (NR, 4-1-0) 14, Army 14 (3)
11-7-59	*Tennessee (13, 4-1-1) 14, LSU 13 (3)
11-5-60	*Minnesota (3, 6-0-0) 27, Iowa 10 (5)
11-12-60	Purdue (NR, 2-4-1) 23, *Minnesota 14 (4)
11-19-60	Kansas (NR, 6-2-1) 23, *Missouri 7 (5)
1-1-61	(Rose Bowl) Washington (6, 9-1-0) 17, Minnesota 7 (1)
11-4-61	*Minnesota (NR, 4-1-0) 13, Michigan St. 0 (6)
11-18-61	TCU (NR, 2-4-1) 6, *Texas 0 (5)
10-6-62	*UCLA (NR, 0-0-0) 9, Ohio St. 7 (10)
10-27-62	(Tie) *Rice (NR, 0-3-1) 14, Texas 14 (5)
11-10-62	*Wisconsin (8, 5-1-0) 37, Northwestern 6 (9)
11-17-62	*Georgia Tech (NR, 5-2-1) 7, Alabama 6 (6)
9-28-63	Oklahoma (3, 1-0-0) 17, *Southern California 12 (8)
10-12-63	(N) Texas (2, 3-0-0) 28, Oklahoma 7 (6)
10-17-64	Arkansas (8, 4-0-0) 14, *Texas 13 (6)
11-28-64	*Southern California (NR, 6-3-0) 20, Notre Dame 17 (3)
1-1-65	(Orange Bowl) Texas (5, 9-1-0) 21, Alabama 17 (1)
9-25-65	*Purdue (6, 1-0-0) 25, Notre Dame 21 (8)
10-16-65	*Arkansas (3, 4-0-0) 27, Texas 24 (5)
1-1-66	(Rose Bowl) UCLA (5, 7-2-1) 14, Michigan St. 12 (2)
11-19-66	(Tie) *Michigan St. (2, 9-0-0) 10, Notre Dame 10 (1)
9-30-67	*Purdue (10, 1-0-0) 28, Notre Dame 21 (6)
11-11-67	*Oregon St. (NR, 5-2-1) 3, Southern California 0 (4)
11-18-67	*Southern California (4, 8-1-0) 21, UCLA 20 (4)
10-12-68	*Ohio St. (4, 2-0-0) 13, Purdue 0 (5)
11-22-69	*Michigan (12, 7-2-0) 24, Ohio St. 12 (4)

1-1-71	(Cotton Bowl) Notre Dame (6, 8-1-1) 24, Texas 11 (3)
9-29-73	(Tie) Oklahoma (8, 1-0-0) 7, *Southern California 7 (4)
11-24-73	(Tie) *Michigan (4, 10-0-0) 10, Ohio St. 10 (3)
12-31-73	(Sugar Bowl) Notre Dame (3, 10-0-0) 24, Alabama 23 (4)
11-9-74	*Michigan St. (NR, 4-3-1) 16, Ohio St. 13 (4)
1-1-76	(Rose Bowl) UCLA (11, 8-2-1) 23, Ohio St. 10 (4)
11-6-76	*Purdue (NR, 3-5-0) 16, Michigan 14 (4)
10-8-77	Alabama (T7, 3-1-0) 21, *Southern California 20 (6)
10-22-77	*Minnesota (NR, 4-2-0) 16, Michigan 0 (6)
1-2-78	(Cotton Bowl) Notre Dame (5, 10-1-0) 38, Texas 10 (4)
9-23-78	(N) Southern California (7, 2-0-0) 24, Alabama 14 (3)
11-11-78	*Nebraska (4, 8-1-0) 17, Oklahoma 14 (4)
1-1-79	(Sugar Bowl) Alabama (2, 10-1-0) 14, Penn St. 7 (4)
10-13-79	(Tie) Stanford (NR, 3-2-0) 21, *Southern California 21 (4)
1-1-80	(Rose Bowl) Southern California (3, 10-0-1) 17, Ohio St. 16 (4)
11-1-80	(N) Mississippi St. (NR, 6-2-0) 6, Alabama 3 (6)
11-8-80	(Tie) *Georgia Tech (NR, 1-7-0) 3, Notre Dame 3 (6)
9-12-81	*Wisconsin (NR, 0-0-0) 21, Michigan 14 (11)
9-19-81	*Michigan (11, 0-1-0) 25, Notre Dame 7 (13)
10-10-81	Arizona (NR, 2-2-0) 13, *Southern California 10 (7)
10-17-81	*Arkansas (NR, 4-1-0) 42, Texas 11 (4)
10-31-81	*Miami (Fla.) (NR, 4-2-0) 17, Penn St. 14 (5)
11-28-81	Penn St. (11, 8-2-0) 48, *Pittsburgh 14 (10)
11-6-82	Notre Dame (NR, 5-1-1) 31, *Pittsburgh 16 (8)
1-1-83	(Sugar Bowl) Penn St. (2, 10-1-0) 27, Georgia 23 (4)
1-2-84	(Orange Bowl) Miami (Fla.) (5, 10-1-0) 31, Nebraska 30 (4)
9-8-84	*Michigan (14, 0-0-0) 22, Miami (Fla.) 14 (3)
9-29-84	*Syracuse (NR, 2-1-0) 17, Nebraska 9 (8)
10-13-84	(N) (Tie) Oklahoma (3, 4-0-0) 15, Texas 15 (3)
11-10-84	*Southern California (12, 7-1-0) 16, Washington 7 (5)
11-17-84	Oklahoma (6, 7-1-1) 17, *Nebraska 7 (7)
9-28-85	*Tennessee (NR, 0-0-1) 38, Auburn 20 (14)
11-2-85	*Ohio St. (7, 6-1-0) 22, Iowa 13 (6)
11-9-85	(N) Georgia (17, 6-1-1) 24, Florida 3 (11)
1-1-86	(Orange Bowl) Oklahoma (4, 9-1-0) 25, Penn St. 10 (3)
9-27-86	*Miami (Fla.) (2, 3-0-0) 28, Oklahoma 16 (2)
1-2-87	(Fiesta Bowl) Penn St. (2, 11-0-0) 14, Miami (Fla.) 10 (2)
11-21-87	Oklahoma (2, 11-0-0) 17, *Nebraska 7 (5)
1-1-88	(Orange Bowl) Miami (Fla.) (2, 11-1-0) 20, Oklahoma 14 (3)
10-15-88	*Notre Dame (4, 5-0-0) 31, Miami (Fla.) 30 (4)
10-29-88	Washington St. (NR, 4-3-0) 34, *UCLA 30 (6)
11-25-89	*Miami (Fla.) (7, 9-1-0) 27, Notre Dame 10 (5)
1-1-90	(Orange Bowl) Notre Dame (4, 11-1-0) 21, Colorado 6 (4)
9-8-90	*Brigham Young (16, 1-0-0) 28, Miami (Fla.) 21 (10)
10-6-90	Stanford (NR, 1-3-0) 36, *Notre Dame 31 (8)
10-13-90	Michigan (NR, 1-2-1) 28, *Michigan 27 (10)
11-3-90	Georgia Tech (16, 6-0-1) 41, *Virginia 38 (11)
11-17-90	Penn St. (18, 7-2-0) 24, *Notre Dame 21 (7)
11-16-91	Miami (Fla.) (2, 8-0-0) 17, *Florida St. 16 (3)
11-7-92	*Arizona (12, 5-2-1) 16, Washington 3 (6)
1-1-93	(Sugar Bowl) Alabama (2, 12-0-0) 34, Miami (Fla.) 13 (3)
11-13-93	*Notre Dame (2, 9-0-0) 31, Florida St. 24 (2)
11-20-93	Boston College (17, 7-2-0) 41, *Notre Dame 39 (4)
10-15-94	Auburn (6, 6-0-0) 36, *Florida 33 (5)
9-21-96	*Arizona St. (17, 2-0-0) 19, Nebraska 0 (8)
11-30-96	*Florida St. (2, 10-0-0) 24, Florida 21 (4)
1-2-97	(Sugar Bowl) Florida (3, 11-1-0) 52, Florida St. 20 (3)
10-11-97	*LSU (14, 4-1-0) 28, Florida 21 (7)
11-7-98	Michigan St. (NR, 4-4) 28, *Ohio St. 24 (7)
10-28-00	*Oklahoma (3, 6-0) 31, Nebraska 14 (5)
10-13-01	*Auburn (NR, 4-1) 23, Florida 20 (7)
11-9-02	*Texas A&M (NR, 5-4) 30, Oklahoma 26 (4)
1-3-03	(Fiesta Bowl) Ohio St. (2, 13-0) 31, Miami (Fla.) 24 (2ot) (2)

Associated Press Preseason No. 1 Teams

(The No. 1-ranked team in the annual Associated Press preseason college football poll. The preseason poll started in 1950.)

Year	Team+	Year	Team+	Year	Team+	Year	Team+
1950	Notre Dame	1963	Southern California	1977	Oklahoma	1990	Miami (Fla.)
1951	Tennessee+	1964	Mississippi	1978	Alabama+	1991	Florida St.
1952	Michigan St.+			1979	Southern California	1992	Miami (Fla.)
1953	Notre Dame	1965	Nebraska			1993	Florida St.+
1954	Notre Dame	1966	Alabama	1980	Ohio St.	1994	Florida
		1967	Notre Dame	1981	Michigan		
1955	UCLA	1968	Purdue	1982	Pittsburgh	1995	Florida St.
1956	Oklahoma+	1969	Ohio St.	1983	Nebraska	1996	Nebraska
1957	Oklahoma			1984	Auburn	1997	Penn St.
1958	Ohio St.	1970	Ohio St.			1998	Ohio St.
1959	LSU	1971	Notre Dame	1985	Oklahoma+	1999	Florida St.+
		1972	Nebraska	1986	Oklahoma		
1960	Syracuse	1973	Southern California	1987	Oklahoma	2000	Nebraska
1961	Iowa	1974	Oklahoma+	1988	Florida St.	2001	Florida
1962	Ohio St.			1989	Michigan	2002	Miami (Fla.)
		1975	Oklahoma+				
		1976	Nebraska				

+Indicated eventual national champion.

Associated Press (Writers and Broadcasters) Final Polls

1936
Team
1. Minnesota
2. LSU
3. Pittsburgh
4. Alabama
5. Washington
6. Santa Clara
7. Northwestern
8. Notre Dame
9. Nebraska
10. Pennsylvania
11. Duke
12. Yale
13. Dartmouth
14. Duquesne
15. Fordham
16. TCU
17. Tennessee
18. Arkansas
    Navy
20. Marquette

1937
Team
1. Pittsburgh
2. California
3. Fordham
4. Alabama
5. Minnesota
6. Villanova
7. Dartmouth
8. LSU
9. Notre Dame
    Santa Clara
11. Nebraska
12. Yale
13. Ohio St.
14. Holy Cross
    Arkansas
16. TCU
17. Colorado
18. Rice
19. North Carolina
20. Duke

1938
Team
1. TCU
2. Tennessee
3. Duke
4. Oklahoma
5. Notre Dame
6. Carnegie Mellon
7. Southern California
8. Pittsburgh
9. Holy Cross
10. Minnesota
11. Texas Tech
12. Cornell
13. Alabama
14. California
15. Fordham
16. Michigan
17. Northwestern
18. Villanova
19. Tulane
20. Dartmouth

1939
Team
1. Texas A&M
2. Tennessee
3. Southern California
4. Cornell
5. Tulane
6. Missouri
7. UCLA
8. Duke
9. Iowa
10. Duquesne
11. Boston College
12. Clemson
13. Notre Dame
14. Santa Clara
15. Ohio St.
16. Georgia Tech
17. Fordham
18. Nebraska
19. Oklahoma
20. Michigan

1940
Team
1. Minnesota
2. Stanford
3. Michigan
4. Tennessee
5. Boston College
6. Texas A&M
7. Nebraska
8. Northwestern
9. Mississippi St.
10. Washington
11. Santa Clara
12. Fordham
13. Georgetown
14. Pennsylvania
15. Cornell
16. Southern Methodist
17. Hardin-Simmons
18. Duke
19. Lafayette

1941
Team
1. Minnesota
2. Duke
3. Notre Dame
4. Texas
5. Michigan
6. Fordham
7. Missouri
8. Duquesne
9. Texas A&M
10. Navy
11. Northwestern
12. Oregon St.
13. Ohio St.
14. Georgia
15. Pennsylvania
16. Mississippi St.
17. Missouri
18. Tennessee
19. Washington St.
20. Alabama

1942
Team
1. Ohio St.
2. Georgia
3. Wisconsin
4. Tulsa
5. Georgia Tech
6. Notre Dame
7. Tennessee
8. Boston College
9. Michigan
10. Alabama
11. Texas
12. Stanford
13. UCLA
14. William & Mary
15. Santa Clara
16. Auburn
17. Washington St.
18. Mississippi St.
19. Minnesota
    Holy Cross
    Penn St.

1943
Team
1. Notre Dame
2. Iowa Pre-Flight
3. Michigan
4. Navy
5. Purdue
6. Great Lakes
7. Duke
8. Del Monte P-F
9. Northwestern
10. March Field
11. Army
12. Washington
13. Georgia Tech
14. Texas
15. Tulsa
16. Dartmouth
17. Bainbridge NTS
18. Colorado Col.
19. Pacific (Cal.)
20. Pennsylvania

1944
Team
1. Army
2. Ohio St.
3. Randolph Field
4. Navy
5. Bainbridge NTS
6. Iowa Pre-Flight
7. Southern California
8. Michigan
9. Notre Dame
10. March Field
11. Duke
12. Tennessee
13. Georgia Tech
    Norman Pre-Flight
15. Illinois
16. El Toro Marines
17. Great Lakes
18. Fort Pierce
19. St. Mary's Pre-Flight
20. Second Air Force

1945
Team
1. Army
2. Alabama
3. Navy
4. Indiana
5. Oklahoma St.
6. Michigan
7. St. Mary's (Cal.)
8. Pennsylvania
9. Notre Dame
10. Texas
11. Southern California
12. Ohio St.
13. Duke
14. Tennessee
15. LSU
16. Holy Cross
17. Tulsa
18. Georgia
19. Wake Forest
20. Columbia

1946
Team
1. Notre Dame
2. Army
3. Georgia
4. UCLA
5. Illinois
6. Michigan
7. Tennessee
8. LSU
9. North Carolina
10. Rice
11. Georgia Tech
12. Yale
13. Pennsylvania
14. Oklahoma
15. Texas
16. Arkansas
17. Tulsa
18. North Carolina St.
19. Delaware
20. Indiana

*1947
Team
1. Notre Dame
2. Michigan
3. Southern Methodist
4. Penn St.
5. Texas
6. Alabama
7. Pennsylvania
8. Southern California
9. North Carolina
10. Georgia Tech
11. Army
12. Kansas
13. Mississippi
14. William & Mary
15. California
16. Oklahoma
17. North Carolina St.
18. Rice
19. Duke
20. Columbia

1948
Team
1. Michigan
2. Notre Dame
3. North Carolina
4. California
5. Oklahoma
6. Army
7. Northwestern
8. Georgia
9. Oregon
10. Southern Methodist
11. Clemson
12. Vanderbilt
13. Tulane
14. Michigan St.
15. Mississippi
16. Minnesota
17. William & Mary
18. Penn St.
19. Cornell
20. Wake Forest

1949
Team
1. Notre Dame
2. Oklahoma
3. California
4. Army
5. Rice
6. Ohio St.
7. Michigan
8. Minnesota
9. LSU
10. Pacific (Cal.)
11. Kentucky
12. Cornell
13. Villanova
14. Maryland
15. Santa Clara
16. North Carolina
17. Tennessee
18. Princeton
19. Michigan St.
20. Missouri
 Baylor

1950
Team
1. Oklahoma
2. Army
3. Texas
4. Tennessee
5. California
6. Princeton
7. Kentucky
8. Michigan St.
9. Michigan
10. Clemson
11. Washington
12. Wyoming
13. Illinois
14. Ohio St.
15. Miami (Fla.)
16. Alabama
17. Nebraska
18. Wash. & Lee
19. Tulsa
20. Tulane

1951
Team
1. Tennessee
2. Michigan St.
3. Maryland
4. Illinois
5. Georgia Tech
6. Princeton
7. Stanford
8. Wisconsin
9. Baylor
10. Oklahoma
11. TCU
12. California
13. Virginia
14. San Francisco
15. Kentucky
16. Boston U.
17. UCLA
18. Washington St.
19. Holy Cross
20. Clemson

1952
Team
1. Michigan St.
2. Georgia Tech
3. Notre Dame
4. Oklahoma
5. Southern California
6. UCLA
7. Mississippi
8. Tennessee
9. Alabama
10. Texas
11. Wisconsin
12. Tulsa
13. Maryland
14. Syracuse
15. Florida
16. Duke
17. Ohio St.
18. Purdue
19. Princeton
20. Kentucky

1953
Team
1. Maryland
2. Notre Dame
3. Michigan St.
4. Oklahoma
5. UCLA
6. Rice
7. Illinois
8. Georgia Tech
9. Iowa
10. West Virginia
11. Texas
12. Texas Tech
13. Alabama
14. Army
15. Wisconsin
16. Kentucky
17. Auburn
18. Duke
19. Stanford
20. Michigan

1954
Team
1. Ohio St.
2. UCLA
3. Oklahoma
4. Notre Dame
5. Navy
6. Mississippi
7. Army
8. Maryland
9. Wisconsin
10. Arkansas
11. Miami (Fla.)
12. West Virginia
13. Auburn
14. Duke
15. Michigan
16. Virginia Tech
17. Southern California
18. Baylor
19. Rice
20. Penn St.

1955
Team
1. Oklahoma
2. Michigan St.
3. Maryland
4. UCLA
5. Ohio St.
6. TCU
7. Georgia Tech
8. Auburn
9. Notre Dame
10. Mississippi
11. Pittsburgh
12. Michigan
13. Southern California
14. Miami (Fla.)
15. Miami (Ohio)
16. Stanford
17. Texas A&M
18. Navy
19. West Virginia
20. Army

1956
Team
1. Oklahoma
2. Tennessee
3. Iowa
4. Georgia Tech
5. Texas A&M
6. Miami (Fla.)
7. Michigan
8. Syracuse
9. Michigan St.
10. Oregon St.
11. Baylor
12. Minnesota
13. Pittsburgh
14. TCU
15. Ohio St.
16. Navy
17. George Washington
18. Southern California
19. Clemson
20. Colorado

1957
Team
1. Auburn
2. Ohio St.
3. Michigan St.
4. Oklahoma
5. Navy
6. Iowa
7. Mississippi
8. Rice
9. Texas A&M
10. Notre Dame
11. Texas
12. Arizona St.
13. Tennessee
14. Mississippi St.
15. North Carolina St.
16. Duke
17. Florida
18. Army
19. Wisconsin
20. VMI

1958
Team
1. LSU
2. Iowa
3. Army
4. Auburn
5. Oklahoma
6. Air Force
7. Wisconsin
8. Ohio St.
9. Syracuse
10. TCU
11. Mississippi
12. Clemson
13. Purdue
14. Florida
15. South Carolina
16. California
17. Notre Dame
18. Southern Methodist
19. Oklahoma St.
20. Rutgers

1959
Team
1. Syracuse
2. Mississippi
3. LSU
4. Texas
5. Georgia
6. Wisconsin
7. TCU
8. Washington
9. Arkansas
10. Alabama
11. Clemson
12. Penn St.
13. Illinois
14. Southern California
15. Oklahoma
16. Wyoming
17. Notre Dame
18. Missouri
19. Florida
20. Pittsburgh

1960
Team
1. Minnesota
2. Mississippi
3. Iowa
4. Navy
5. Missouri
6. Washington
7. Arkansas
8. Ohio St.
9. Alabama
10. Duke
11. Kansas
12. Baylor
13. Auburn
14. Yale
15. Michigan St.
16. Penn St.
17. New Mexico St.
18. Florida
19. Syracuse
 Purdue

1961
Team
1. Alabama
2. Ohio St.
3. Texas
4. LSU
5. Mississippi
6. Minnesota
7. Colorado
8. Michigan St.
9. Arkansas
10. Utah St.
11. Missouri
12. Purdue
13. Georgia Tech
14. Syracuse
15. Rutgers
16. UCLA
17. Rice
 Penn St.
 Arizona
20. Duke

1962
Team
1. Southern California
2. Wisconsin
3. Mississippi
4. Texas
5. Alabama
6. Arkansas
7. LSU
8. Oklahoma
9. Penn St.
10. Minnesota
Only 10 ranked

1963
Team
1. Texas
2. Navy
3. Illinois
4. Pittsburgh
5. Auburn
6. Nebraska
7. Mississippi
8. Alabama
9. Oklahoma
10. Michigan St.
Only 10 ranked

1964
Team
1. Alabama
2. Arkansas
3. Notre Dame
4. Michigan
5. Texas
6. Nebraska
7. LSU
8. Oregon St.
9. Ohio St.
10. Southern California
Only 10 ranked

1965
Team
1. Alabama
2. Michigan St.
3. Arkansas
4. UCLA
5. Nebraska
6. Missouri
7. Tennessee
8. LSU
9. Notre Dame
10. Southern California
Only 10 ranked

1966
Team
1. Notre Dame
2. Michigan St.
3. Alabama
4. Georgia
5. UCLA
6. Nebraska
7. Purdue
8. Georgia Tech
9. Miami (Fla.)
10. Southern Methodist
Only 10 ranked

1967
Team
1. Southern California
2. Tennessee
3. Oklahoma
4. Indiana
5. Notre Dame
6. Wyoming
7. Oregon St.
8. Alabama
9. Purdue
10. Penn St.
Only 10 ranked

1968
Team
1. Ohio St.
2. Penn St.
3. Texas
4. Southern California
5. Notre Dame
6. Arkansas
7. Kansas
8. Georgia
9. Missouri
10. Purdue
11. Oklahoma
12. Michigan
13. Tennessee
14. Southern Methodist
15. Oregon St.
16. Auburn
17. Alabama
18. Houston
19. LSU
20. Ohio

1969
Team
1. Texas
2. Penn St.
3. Southern California
4. Ohio St.
5. Notre Dame
6. Missouri
7. Arkansas
8. Mississippi
9. Michigan
10. LSU
11. Nebraska
12. Houston
13. UCLA
14. Florida
15. Tennessee
16. Colorado
17. West Virginia
18. Purdue
19. Stanford
20. Auburn

1970
Team
1. Nebraska
2. Notre Dame
3. Texas
4. Tennessee
5. Ohio St.
6. Arizona St.
7. LSU
8. Stanford
9. Michigan
10. Auburn
11. Arkansas
12. Toledo
13. Georgia Tech
14. Dartmouth
15. Southern California
16. Air Force
17. Tulane
18. Penn St.
19. Houston
20. Oklahoma
    Mississippi

1971
Team
1. Nebraska
2. Oklahoma
3. Colorado
4. Alabama
5. Penn St.
6. Michigan
7. Georgia
8. Arizona St.
9. Tennessee
10. Stanford
11. LSU
12. Auburn
13. Notre Dame
14. Toledo
15. Mississippi
16. Arkansas
17. Houston
18. Texas
19. Washington
20. Southern California

1972
Team
1. Southern California
2. Oklahoma
3. Texas
4. Nebraska
5. Auburn
6. Michigan
7. Alabama
8. Tennessee
9. Ohio St.
10. Penn St.
11. LSU
12. North Carolina
13. Arizona St.
14. Notre Dame
15. UCLA
16. Colorado
17. North Carolina St.
18. Louisville
19. Washington St.
20. Georgia Tech

1973
Team
1. Notre Dame
2. Ohio St.
3. Oklahoma
4. Alabama
5. Penn St.
6. Michigan
7. Southern California
8. Arizona St.
   Houston
11. Texas Tech
12. UCLA
13. LSU
14. Texas
15. Miami (Ohio)
16. North Carolina St.
17. Missouri
18. Kansas
19. Tennessee
20. Maryland
    Tulane

1974
Team
1. Oklahoma
2. Southern California
3. Michigan
4. Ohio St.
5. Alabama
6. Notre Dame
7. Penn St.
8. Auburn
9. Nebraska
10. Miami (Ohio)
11. North Carolina St.
12. Michigan St.
13. Maryland
14. Baylor
15. Florida
16. Texas A&M
17. Mississippi St.
    Texas
19. Houston
20. Tennessee

1975
Team
1. Oklahoma
2. Arizona St.
3. Alabama
4. Ohio St.
5. UCLA
6. Texas
7. Arkansas
8. Michigan
9. Nebraska
10. Penn St.
11. Texas A&M
12. Miami (Ohio)
13. Maryland
14. California
15. Pittsburgh
16. Colorado
17. Southern California
18. Arizona
19. Georgia
20. West Virginia

1976
Team
1. Pittsburgh
2. Southern California
3. Michigan
4. Houston
5. Oklahoma
6. Ohio St.
7. Texas A&M
8. Maryland
9. Nebraska
10. Georgia
11. Alabama
12. Notre Dame
13. Texas Tech
14. Oklahoma St.
15. UCLA
16. Colorado
17. Rutgers
18. Kentucky
19. Iowa St.
20. Mississippi St.

1977
Team
1. Notre Dame
2. Alabama
3. Arkansas
4. Texas
5. Penn St.
6. Kentucky
7. Oklahoma
8. Pittsburgh
9. Michigan
10. Washington
11. Ohio St.
12. Nebraska
13. Southern California
14. Florida St.
15. Stanford
16. San Diego St.
17. North Carolina
18. Arizona St.
19. Clemson
20. Brigham Young

1978
Team
1. Alabama
2. Southern California
3. Oklahoma
4. Penn St.
5. Michigan
6. Clemson
7. Notre Dame
8. Nebraska
9. Texas
10. Houston
11. Arkansas
12. Michigan St.
13. Purdue
14. UCLA
15. Missouri
16. Georgia
17. Stanford
18. North Carolina St.
19. Texas A&M
20. Maryland

1979
Team
1. Alabama
2. Southern California
3. Oklahoma
4. Ohio St.
5. Houston
6. Florida St.
7. Pittsburgh
8. Arkansas
9. Nebraska
10. Purdue
11. Washington
12. Texas
13. Brigham Young
14. Baylor
15. North Carolina
16. Auburn
17. Temple
18. Michigan
19. Indiana
20. Penn St.

1980
Team
1. Georgia
2. Pittsburgh
3. Oklahoma
4. Michigan
5. Florida St.
6. Alabama
7. Nebraska
8. Penn St.
9. Notre Dame
10. North Carolina
11. Southern California
12. Brigham Young
13. UCLA
14. Baylor
15. Ohio St.
16. Washington
17. Purdue
18. Miami (Fla.)
19. Mississippi St.
20. Southern Methodist

1981
Team
1. Clemson
2. Texas
3. Penn St.
4. Pittsburgh
5. Southern Methodist
6. Georgia
7. Alabama
8. Miami (Fla.)
9. North Carolina
10. Washington
11. Nebraska
12. Michigan
13. Brigham Young
14. Southern California
15. Ohio St.
16. Arizona St.
17. West Virginia
18. Iowa
19. Missouri
20. Oklahoma

1982
Team
1. Penn St.
2. Southern Methodist
3. Nebraska
4. Georgia
5. UCLA
6. Arizona St.
7. Washington
8. Clemson
9. Arkansas
10. Pittsburgh
11. LSU
12. Ohio St.
13. Florida St.
14. Auburn
15. Southern California
16. Oklahoma
17. Texas
18. North Carolina
19. West Virginia
20. Maryland

1983
Team
1. Miami (Fla.)
2. Nebraska
3. Auburn
4. Georgia
5. Texas
6. Florida
7. Brigham Young
8. Michigan
9. Ohio St.
10. Illinois
11. Clemson
12. Southern Methodist
13. Air Force
14. Iowa
15. Alabama
16. West Virginia
17. UCLA
18. Pittsburgh
19. Boston College
20. East Caro.

1984
Team
1. Brigham Young
2. Washington
3. Florida
4. Nebraska
5. Boston College
6. Oklahoma
7. Oklahoma St.
8. Southern Methodist
9. UCLA
10. Southern California
11. South Carolina
12. Maryland
13. Ohio St.
14. Auburn
15. LSU
16. Iowa
17. Florida St.
18. Miami (Fla.)
19. Kentucky
20. Virginia

1985
Team
1. Oklahoma
2. Michigan
3. Penn St.
4. Tennessee
5. Florida
6. Texas A&M
7. UCLA
8. Air Force
9. Miami (Fla.)
10. Iowa
11. Nebraska
12. Arkansas
13. Alabama
14. Ohio St.
15. Florida St.
16. Brigham Young
17. Baylor
18. Maryland
19. Georgia Tech
20. LSU

1986
Team
1. Penn St.
2. Miami (Fla.)
3. Oklahoma
4. Arizona St.
5. Nebraska
6. Auburn
7. Ohio St.
8. Michigan
9. Alabama
10. LSU
11. Arizona
12. Baylor
13. Texas A&M
14. UCLA
15. Arkansas
16. Iowa
17. Clemson
18. Washington
19. Boston College
20. Virginia Tech

1987
Team
1. Miami (Fla.)
2. Florida St.
3. Oklahoma
4. Syracuse
5. LSU
6. Nebraska
7. Auburn
8. Michigan St.
9. UCLA
10. Texas A&M
11. Oklahoma St.
12. Clemson
13. Georgia
14. Tennessee
15. South Carolina
16. Iowa
17. Notre Dame
18. Southern California
19. Michigan
20. Arizona St.

1988
Team
1. Notre Dame
2. Miami (Fla.)
3. Florida St.
4. Michigan
5. West Virginia
6. UCLA
7. Southern California
8. Auburn
9. Clemson
10. Nebraska
11. Oklahoma St.
12. Arkansas
13. Syracuse
14. Oklahoma
15. Georgia
16. Washington St.
17. Alabama
18. Houston
19. LSU
20. Indiana

†1989
Team
1. Miami (Fla.)
2. Notre Dame
3. Florida St.
4. Colorado
5. Tennessee
6. Auburn
7. Michigan
8. Southern California
9. Alabama
10. Illinois
11. Nebraska
12. Clemson
13. Arkansas
14. Houston
15. Penn St.
16. Michigan St.
17. Pittsburgh
18. Virginia
19. Texas Tech
20. Texas A&M
21. West Virginia
22. Brigham Young
23. Washington
24. Ohio St.
25. Arizona

1990
Team
1. Colorado
2. Georgia Tech
3. Miami (Fla.)
4. Florida St.
5. Washington
6. Notre Dame
7. Michigan
8. Tennessee
9. Clemson
10. Houston
11. Penn St.
12. Texas
13. Florida
14. Louisville
15. Texas A&M
16. Michigan St.
17. Oklahoma
18. Iowa
19. Auburn
20. Southern California
21. Mississippi
22. Brigham Young
23. Virginia
24. Nebraska
25. Illinois

1991
Team
1. Miami (Fla.)
2. Washington
3. Penn St.
4. Florida St.
5. Alabama
6. Michigan
7. Florida
8. California
9. East Caro.
10. Iowa
11. Syracuse
12. Texas A&M
13. Notre Dame
14. Tennessee
15. Nebraska
16. Oklahoma
17. Georgia
18. Clemson
19. UCLA
20. Colorado
21. Tulsa
22. Stanford
23. Brigham Young
24. North Carolina St.
25. Air Force

1992
Team
1. Alabama
2. Florida St.
3. Miami (Fla.)
4. Notre Dame
5. Michigan
6. Syracuse
7. Texas A&M
8. Georgia
9. Stanford
10. Florida
11. Washington
12. Tennessee
13. Colorado
14. Nebraska
15. Washington St.
16. Mississippi
17. North Carolina St.
18. Ohio St.
19. North Carolina
20. Hawaii
21. Boston College
22. Kansas
23. Mississippi St.
24. Fresno St.
25. Wake Forest

1993
Team
1. Florida St.
2. Notre Dame
3. Nebraska
4. Auburn
5. Florida
6. Wisconsin
7. West Virginia
8. Penn St.
9. Texas A&M
10. Arizona
11. Ohio St.
12. Tennessee
13. Boston College
14. Alabama
15. Miami (Fla.)
16. Colorado
17. Oklahoma
18. UCLA
19. North Carolina
20. Kansas St.
21. Michigan
22. Virginia Tech
23. Clemson
24. Louisville
25. California

1994
Team
1. Nebraska
2. Penn St.
3. Colorado
4. Florida St.
5. Alabama
6. Miami (Fla.)
7. Florida
8. Texas A&M
9. Auburn
10. Utah
11. Oregon
12. Michigan
13. Southern California
14. Ohio St.
15. Virginia
16. Colorado St.
17. North Carolina St.
18. Brigham Young
19. Kansas St.
20. Arizona
21. Washington St.
22. Tennessee
23. Boston College
24. Mississippi St.
25. Texas

1995
Team
1. Nebraska
2. Florida
3. Tennessee
4. Florida St.
5. Colorado
6. Ohio St.
7. Kansas St.
8. Northwestern
9. Kansas
10. Virginia Tech
11. Notre Dame
12. Southern California
13. Penn St.
14. Texas
15. Texas A&M
16. Virginia
17. Michigan
18. Oregon
19. Syracuse
20. Miami (Fla.)
21. Alabama
22. Auburn
23. Texas Tech
24. Toledo
25. Iowa

1996
Team (Record)
1. Florida (12-1)
2. Ohio St. (11-1)
3. Florida St.(11-1)
4. Arizona St. (11-1)
5. Brigham Young (14-1)
6. Nebraska (11-2)
7. Penn St. (11-2)
8. Colorado (10-2)
9. Tennessee (10-2)
10. North Carolina (10-2)
11. Alabama (10-3)
12. LSU (10-2)
13. Virginia Tech (10-2)
14. Miami (Fla.) (9-3)
15. Northwestern (9-3)
16. Washington (9-3)
17. Kansas St. (9-3)
18. Iowa (9-3)
19. Notre Dame (8-3)
20. Michigan (8-4)
21. Syracuse (9-3)
22. Wyoming (10-2)
23. Texas (8-5)
24. Auburn (8-4)
25. Army (10-2)

1997
Team (Record)
1. Michigan (12-0)
2. Nebraska (13-0)
3. Florida St. (11-1)
4. Florida (10-2)
5. UCLA (10-2)
6. North Carolina (11-1)
7. Tennessee (11-2)
8. Kansas St. (11-1)
9. Washington St. (10-2)
10. Georgia (10-2)
11. Auburn (10-3)
12. Ohio St. (10-3)
13. LSU (9-3)
14. Arizona St. (9-3)
15. Purdue (9-3)
16. Penn St. (9-3)
17. Colorado St. (11-2)
18. Washington (8-4)
19. Southern Miss. (9-3)
20. Texas A&M (9-4)
21. Syracuse (9-4)
22. Mississippi (8-4)
23. Missouri (7-5)
24. Oklahoma St. (8-4)
25. Georgia Tech (7-5)

1998
Team (Record)
1. Tennessee (13-0)
2. Ohio St. (11-1)
3. Florida St. (11-2)
4. Arizona (12-1)
5. Florida (10-2)
6. Wisconsin (11-1)
7. Tulane (12-0)
8. UCLA (10-2)
9. Georgia Tech (10-2)
10. Kansas St. (11-2)
11. Texas A&M (11-3)
12. Michigan (10-3)
13. Air Force (12-1)
14. Georgia (9-3)
15. Texas (9-3)
16. Arkansas (9-3)
17. Penn St. (9-3)
18. Virginia (9-3)
19. Nebraska (9-4)
20. Miami (Fla.) (9-3)
21. Missouri (8-4)
22. Notre Dame (9-3)
23. Virginia Tech (9-3)
24. Purdue (9-4)
25. Syracuse (8-4)

1999
Team (Record)
1. Florida St. (12-0)
2. Virginia Tech (11-1)
3. Nebraska (12-1)
4. Wisconsin (10-2)
5. Michigan (10-2)
6. Kansas St. (11-1)
7. Michigan St. (10-2)
8. Alabama (10-3)
9. Tennessee (9-3)
10. Marshall (13-0)
11. Penn St. (10-3)
12. Florida (9-4)
13. Mississippi St. (10-2)
14. Southern Miss. (9-3)
15. Miami (Fla.) (9-4)
16. Georgia (8-4)
17. Arkansas (8-4)
18. Minnesota (8-4)
19. Oregon (9-3)
20. Georgia Tech (8-4)
21. Texas (9-5)
22. Mississippi (8-4)
23. Texas A&M (8-4)
24. Illinois (8-4)
25. Purdue (7-5)

2000
Team (Record)
1. Oklahoma (13-0)
2. Miami (Fla.) (11-1)
3. Washington (11-1)
4. Oregon St. (11-1)
5. Florida St. (11-2)
6. Virginia Tech (11-1)
7. Oregon (10-2)
8. Nebraska (10-2)
9. Kansas St. (11-3)
10. Florida (10-3)
11. Michigan (9-3)
12. Texas (9-3)
13. Purdue (8-4)
14. Colorado St. (10-2)
15. Notre Dame (9-3)
16. Clemson (9-3)
17. Georgia Tech (9-3)
18. Auburn (9-4)
19. South Carolina (8-4)
20. Georgia (8-4)
21. TCU (10-2)
22. LSU (8-4)
23. Wisconsin (9-4)
24. Mississippi St. (8-4)
25. Iowa St. (9-3)

2001

Team (Record)
1. Miami (Fla.) (12-0)
2. Oregon (11-1)
3. Florida (10-2)
4. Tennessee (11-2)
5. Texas (11-2)
6. Oklahoma (11-2)
7. LSU (10-3)
8. Nebraska (11-2)
9. Colorado (10-3)
10. Washington St. (10-2)
11. Maryland (10-2)
12. Illinois (10-2)
13. South Carolina (9-3)
14. Syracuse (10-3)
15. Florida St. (8-4)
16. Stanford (9-3)
17. Louisville (11-2)
18. Virginia Tech (8-4)
19. Washington (8-4)
20. Michigan (8-4)
21. Boston College (8-4)
22. Georgia (8-4)
23. Toledo (10-2)
24. Georgia Tech (8-5)
25. Brigham Young (12-2)

2002

Team (Record)
1. Ohio St. (14-0)
2. Miami (Fla.) (12-1)
3. Georgia (13-1)
4. Southern California (11-2)
5. Oklahoma (12-2)
6. Texas (11-2)
7. Kansas St. (11-2)
8. Iowa (11-2)
9. Michigan (10-3)
10. Washington St. (10-3)
11. Alabama (10-3)
12. North Carolina St. (11-3)
13. Maryland (11-3)
14. Auburn (9-4)
15. Boise St. (12-1)
16. Penn St. (9-4)
17. Notre Dame (10-3)
18. Virginia Tech (10-4)
19. Pittsburgh (9-4)
20. Colorado (9-5)
21. Florida St. (9-5)
22. Virginia (9-5)
23. TCU (10-2)
24. Marshall (11-2)
25. West Virginia (9-4)

*On January 6, 1948, in a special postseason poll after the Rose Bowl, the Associated Press voted Michigan No. 1 and Notre Dame No. 2. However, the postseason poll did not supersede the final regular-season poll of December 6, 1947. †Beginning in 1989 season, AP selected top 25 teams instead of 20.

United Press International Final Polls

United Press (UP), 1950-57; United Press International (UPI) from 1958-95 after merger with International News Service (INS). Served as the coaches' poll until 1991, when it was taken over by USA Today/Cable News Network (CNN)/ESPN poll.

1950

Team
1. Oklahoma
2. Texas
3. Tennessee
4. California
5. Army
6. Michigan
7. Kentucky
8. Princeton
9. Michigan St.
10. Ohio St.
11. Illinois
12. Clemson
13. Miami (Fla.)
14. Wyoming
15. Washington
    Baylor
17. Alabama
18. Wash. & Lee
19. Navy
20. Nebraska
    Wisconsin
    Cornell

1951

Team
1. Tennessee
2. Michigan St.
3. Illinois
4. Maryland
5. Georgia Tech
6. Princeton
7. Stanford
8. Wisconsin
9. Baylor
10. TCU
11. Oklahoma
12. California
13. Notre Dame
14. San Francisco
    Purdue
    Washington St.
17. Holy Cross
    UCLA
    Kentucky
20. Kansas

1952

Team
1. Michigan St.
2. Georgia Tech
3. Notre Dame
4. Oklahoma
    Southern California
6. UCLA
7. Mississippi
8. Tennessee
9. Alabama
10. Wisconsin
11. Texas
12. Purdue
13. Maryland
14. Princeton
15. Ohio St.
    Pittsburgh
17. Navy
18. Duke
19. Houston
    Kentucky

1953

Team
1. Maryland
2. Notre Dame
3. Michigan St.
4. UCLA
5. Oklahoma
6. Rice
7. Illinois
8. Texas
9. Georgia Tech
10. Iowa
11. Alabama
12. Texas Tech
13. West Virginia
14. Wisconsin
15. Kentucky
16. Army
17. Stanford
18. Duke
19. Michigan
20. Ohio St.

1954

Team
1. UCLA
2. Ohio St.
3. Oklahoma
4. Notre Dame
5. Navy
6. Mississippi
7. Army
8. Arkansas
9. Miami (Fla.)
10. Wisconsin
11. Southern California
    Maryland
    Georgia Tech
14. Duke
15. Michigan
16. Penn St.
17. Southern Methodist
18. Denver
19. Rice
20. Minnesota

1955

Team
1. Oklahoma
2. Michigan St.
3. Maryland
4. UCLA
5. Ohio St.
6. TCU
7. Georgia Tech
8. Auburn
9. Mississippi
10. Notre Dame
11. Pittsburgh
12. Southern California
13. Michigan
14. Texas A&M
15. Army
16. Duke
17. West Virginia
18. Miami (Fla.)
19. Iowa
20. Navy
    Stanford
    Miami (Ohio)

1956

Team
1. Oklahoma
2. Tennessee
3. Iowa
4. Georgia Tech
5. Texas A&M
6. Miami (Fla.)
7. Michigan
8. Syracuse
9. Minnesota
10. Michigan St.
11. Baylor
12. Pittsburgh
13. Oregon St.
14. TCU
15. Southern California
16. Wyoming
17. Yale
18. Colorado
19. Navy
20. Duke

1957

Team
1. Ohio St.
2. Auburn
3. Michigan St.
4. Oklahoma
5. Iowa
6. Navy
7. Rice
8. Mississippi
9. Notre Dame
10. Texas A&M
11. Texas
12. Arizona St.
13. Army
14. Duke
    Wisconsin
16. Tennessee
17. Oregon
18. Clemson
    UCLA
20. North Carolina St.

1958

Team
1. LSU
2. Iowa
3. Army
4. Auburn
5. Oklahoma
6. Wisconsin
7. Ohio St.
8. Air Force
9. TCU
10. Syracuse
11. Purdue
12. Mississippi
13. Clemson
14. Notre Dame
15. Florida
16. California
17. Northwestern
18. Southern Methodist
(Only 18 teams received votes)

1959

Team
1. Syracuse
2. Mississippi
3. LSU
4. Texas
5. Georgia
6. Wisconsin
7. Washington
8. TCU
9. Arkansas
10. Penn St.
11. Clemson
12. Illinois
13. Alabama
    Southern California
15. Auburn
16. Michigan St.
17. Oklahoma
18. Notre Dame
19. Pittsburgh
    Missouri
    Florida

1960

Team
1. Minnesota
2. Iowa
3. Mississippi
4. Missouri
5. Wisconsin
6. Navy
7. Arkansas
8. Ohio St.
9. Kansas
10. Alabama
11. Duke
    Baylor
    Michigan St.
14. Auburn
15. Purdue
16. Florida
17. Texas
18. Yale
19. New Mexico St.
    Tennessee

1961

Team
1. Alabama
2. Ohio St.
3. LSU
4. Texas
5. Mississippi
6. Minnesota
7. Colorado
8. Arkansas
9. Michigan St.
10. Utah St.
11. Purdue
    Missouri
13. Georgia Tech
14. Duke
15. Kansas
16. Syracuse
17. Wyoming
18. Wisconsin
19. Miami (Fla.)
    Penn St.

1962
Team
1. Southern California
2. Wisconsin
3. Mississippi
4. Texas
5. Alabama
6. Arkansas
7. Oklahoma
8. LSU
9. Penn St.
10. Minnesota
11. Georgia Tech
12. Missouri
13. Ohio St.
14. Duke
    Washington
16. Northwestern
    Oregon St.
18. Arizona St.
    Illinois
    Miami (Fla.)

1963
Team
1. Texas
2. Navy
3. Pittsburgh
4. Illinois
5. Nebraska
6. Auburn
7. Mississippi
8. Oklahoma
9. Alabama
10. Michigan St.
11. Mississippi St.
12. Syracuse
13. Arizona St.
14. Memphis
15. Washington
16. Penn St.
    Southern California
    Missouri
19. North Carolina
20. Baylor

1964
Team
1. Alabama
2. Arkansas
3. Notre Dame
4. Michigan
5. Texas
6. Nebraska
7. LSU
8. Oregon St.
9. Ohio St.
10. Southern California
11. Florida St.
12. Syracuse
13. Princeton
14. Penn St.
    Utah
16. Illinois
    New Mexico
18. Tulsa
    Missouri
20. Mississippi
    Michigan St.

1965
Team
1. Michigan St.
2. Arkansas
3. Nebraska
4. Alabama
5. UCLA
6. Missouri
7. Tennessee
8. Notre Dame
9. Southern California
10. Texas Tech
11. Ohio St.
12. Florida
13. Purdue
14. LSU
15. Georgia
16. Tulsa
17. Mississippi
18. Kentucky
19. Syracuse
20. Colorado

1966
Team
1. Notre Dame
2. Michigan St.
3. Alabama
4. Georgia
5. UCLA
6. Purdue
7. Nebraska
8. Georgia Tech
9. Southern Methodist
10. Miami (Fla.)
11. Florida
12. Mississippi
13. Arkansas
14. Tennessee
15. Wyoming
16. Syracuse
17. Houston
18. Southern California
19. Oregon St.
20. Virginia Tech

1967
Team
1. Southern California
2. Tennessee
3. Oklahoma
4. Notre Dame
5. Wyoming
6. Indiana
7. Alabama
8. Oregon St.
9. Purdue
10. UCLA
11. Penn St.
12. Syracuse
13. Colorado
14. Minnesota
15. Florida St.
16. Miami (Fla.)
17. North Carolina St.
18. Georgia
19. Houston
20. Arizona St.

1968
Team
1. Ohio St.
2. Southern California
3. Penn St.
4. Georgia
5. Texas
6. Kansas
7. Tennessee
8. Notre Dame
9. Arkansas
10. Oklahoma
11. Purdue
12. Alabama
13. Oregon St.
14. Florida St.
15. Michigan
16. Southern Methodist
17. Missouri
18. Ohio
    Minnesota
20. Houston
    Stanford

1969
Team
1. Texas
2. Penn St.
3. Arkansas
4. Southern California
5. Ohio St.
6. Missouri
7. LSU
8. Michigan
9. Notre Dame
10. UCLA
11. Tennessee
12. Nebraska
13. Mississippi
14. Stanford
15. Auburn
16. Houston
17. Florida
18. Purdue
    San Diego St.
    West Virginia

1970
Team
1. Texas
2. Ohio St.
3. Nebraska
4. Tennessee
5. Notre Dame
6. LSU
7. Michigan
8. Arizona St.
9. Auburn
10. Stanford
11. Air Force
12. Arkansas
13. Houston
    Dartmouth
15. Oklahoma
16. Colorado
17. Georgia Tech
    Toledo
19. Penn St.
    Southern California

1971
Team
1. Nebraska
2. Alabama
3. Oklahoma
4. Michigan
5. Auburn
6. Arizona St.
7. Colorado
8. Georgia
9. Tennessee
10. LSU
11. Penn St.
12. Texas
13. Toledo
14. Houston
15. Notre Dame
16. Stanford
17. Iowa St.
18. North Carolina
19. Florida St.
20. Arkansas
    Mississippi

1972
Team
1. Southern California
2. Oklahoma
3. Ohio St.
4. Alabama
5. Texas
6. Michigan
7. Auburn
8. Penn St.
9. Nebraska
10. LSU
11. Tennessee
12. Notre Dame
13. Arizona St.
14. Colorado
    North Carolina
16. Louisville
17. UCLA
    Washington St.
19. Utah St.
20. San Diego St.

1973
Team
1. Alabama
2. Oklahoma
3. Ohio St.
4. Notre Dame
5. Penn St.
6. Michigan
7. Southern California
8. Texas
9. UCLA
10. Arizona St.
11. Nebraska
    Texas Tech
13. Houston
14. LSU
15. Kansas
    Tulane
17. Miami (Ohio)
18. Maryland
19. San Diego St.
    Florida

*1974
Team
1. Southern California
2. Alabama
3. Ohio St.
4. Notre Dame
5. Michigan
6. Auburn
7. Penn St.
8. Nebraska
9. North Carolina St.
10. Miami (Ohio)
11. Houston
12. Florida
13. Maryland
14. Baylor
15. Texas A&M
    Tennessee
17. Mississippi St.
18. Michigan St.
19. Tulsa

1975
Team
1. Oklahoma
2. Arizona St.
3. Alabama
4. Ohio St.
5. UCLA
6. Arkansas
7. Texas
8. Michigan
9. Nebraska
10. Penn St.
11. Maryland
12. Texas A&M
13. Arizona
    Pittsburgh
15. California
16. Miami (Ohio)
17. Notre Dame
    West Virginia
19. Georgia
    Southern California

1976
Team
1. Pittsburgh
2. Southern California
3. Michigan
4. Houston
5. Ohio St.
6. Oklahoma
7. Nebraska
8. Texas A&M
9. Alabama
10. Georgia
11. Maryland
12. Notre Dame
13. Texas Tech
14. Oklahoma St.
15. UCLA
16. Colorado
17. Rutgers
18. Iowa St.
19. Baylor
    Kentucky

1977
Team
1. Notre Dame
2. Alabama
3. Arkansas
4. Penn St.
5. Texas
6. Oklahoma
7. Pittsburgh
8. Michigan
9. Washington
10. Nebraska
11. Florida St.
12. Ohio St.
    Southern California
14. North Carolina
15. Stanford
16. North Texas
    Brigham Young
18. Arizona St.
19. San Diego St.
    North Carolina St.

1978
Team
1. Southern California
2. Alabama
3. Oklahoma
4. Penn St.
5. Michigan
6. Notre Dame
7. Clemson
8. Nebraska
9. Texas
10. Arkansas
11. Houston
12. UCLA
13. Purdue
14. Missouri
15. Georgia
16. Stanford
17. Navy
18. Texas A&M
19. Arizona St.
    North Carolina St.

1979
Team
1. Alabama
2. Southern California
3. Oklahoma
4. Ohio St.
5. Houston
6. Pittsburgh
7. Nebraska
8. Florida St.
9. Arkansas
10. Purdue
11. Washington
12. Brigham Young
13. Texas
14. North Carolina
15. Baylor
16. Indiana
17. Temple
18. Penn St.
19. Michigan
20. Missouri

1980

Team
1. Georgia
2. Pittsburgh
3. Oklahoma
4. Michigan
5. Florida St.
6. Alabama
7. Nebraska
8. Penn St.
9. North Carolina
10. Notre Dame
11. Brigham Young
12. Southern California
13. Baylor
14. UCLA
15. Ohio St.
16. Purdue
17. Washington
18. Miami (Fla.)
19. Florida
20. Southern Methodist

1981

Team
1. Clemson
2. Pittsburgh
3. Penn St.
4. Texas
5. Georgia
6. Alabama
7. Washington
8. North Carolina
9. Nebraska
10. Michigan
11. Brigham Young
12. Ohio St.
13. Southern California
14. Oklahoma
15. Iowa
16. Arkansas
17. Mississippi St.
18. West Virginia
19. Southern Miss.
20. Missouri

1982

Team
1. Penn St.
2. Southern Methodist
3. Nebraska
4. Georgia
5. UCLA
6. Arizona St.
7. Washington
8. Arkansas
9. Pittsburgh
10. Florida St.
11. LSU
12. Ohio St.
13. North Carolina
14. Auburn
15. Michigan
16. Oklahoma
17. Alabama
18. Texas
19. West Virginia
20. Maryland

1983

Team
1. Miami (Fla.)
2. Nebraska
3. Auburn
4. Georgia
5. Texas
6. Florida
7. Brigham Young
8. Ohio St.
9. Michigan
10. Illinois
11. Southern Methodist
12. Alabama
13. UCLA
14. Iowa
15. Air Force
16. West Virginia
17. Penn St.
18. Oklahoma St.
19. Pittsburgh
20. Boston College

1984

Team
1. Brigham Young
2. Washington
3. Nebraska
4. Boston College
5. Oklahoma St.
6. Oklahoma
7. Florida
8. Southern Methodist
9. Southern California
10. UCLA
11. Maryland
12. Ohio St.
13. South Carolina
14. Auburn
15. Iowa
16. LSU
17. Virginia
18. West Virginia
19. Kentucky
    Florida St.

1985

Team
1. Oklahoma
2. Michigan
3. Penn St.
4. Tennessee
5. Air Force
6. UCLA
7. Texas A&M
8. Miami (Fla.)
9. Iowa
10. Nebraska
11. Ohio St.
12. Arkansas
13. Florida St.
14. Alabama
15. Baylor
16. Fresno St.
17. Brigham Young
18. Georgia Tech
19. Maryland
20. LSU

1986

Team
1. Penn St.
2. Miami (Fla.)
3. Oklahoma
4. Nebraska
5. Arizona St.
6. Ohio St.
7. Michigan
8. Auburn
9. Alabama
10. Arizona
11. LSU
12. Texas A&M
13. Baylor
14. UCLA
15. Iowa
16. Arkansas
17. Washington
18. Boston College
19. Clemson
20. Florida St.

1987

Team
1. Miami (Fla.)
2. Florida St.
3. Oklahoma
4. Syracuse
5. LSU
6. Nebraska
7. Auburn
8. Michigan St.
9. Texas A&M
10. Clemson
11. UCLA
12. Oklahoma St.
13. Tennessee
14. Georgia
15. South Carolina
16. Iowa
17. Southern California
18. Michigan
19. Texas
20. Indiana

1988

Team
1. Notre Dame
2. Miami (Fla.)
3. Florida St.
4. Michigan
5. West Virginia
6. UCLA
7. Auburn
8. Clemson
9. Southern California
10. Nebraska
11. Oklahoma St.
12. Syracuse
13. Arkansas
14. Oklahoma
15. Georgia
16. Washington St.
17. North Carolina St.
    Alabama
19. Indiana
20. Wyoming

1989

Team
1. Miami (Fla.)
2. Florida St.
3. Notre Dame
4. Colorado
5. Tennessee
6. Auburn
7. Alabama
8. Michigan
9. Southern California
10. Illinois
11. Clemson
12. Nebraska
13. Arkansas
14. Penn St.
15. Virginia
16. Texas Tech
    Michigan St.
18. Brigham Young
19. Pittsburgh
20. Washington

#1990

Team
1. Georgia Tech
2. Colorado
3. Miami (Fla.)
4. Florida St.
5. Washington
6. Notre Dame
7. Tennessee
8. Michigan
9. Clemson
10. Penn St.
11. Texas
12. Louisville
13. Texas A&M
14. Michigan St.
15. Virginia
16. Iowa
17. Brigham Young
    Nebraska
19. Auburn
20. San Jose St.
21. Syracuse
22. Southern California
23. Mississippi
24. Illinois
25. Virginia Tech

¢1991

Team
1. Washington
2. Miami (Fla.)
3. Penn St.
4. Florida St.
5. Alabama
6. Michigan
7. Florida
8. California
9. East Caro.
10. Iowa
11. Syracuse
12. Notre Dame
13. Texas A&M
14. Tennessee
15. Nebraska
16. Oklahoma
17. Clemson
18. Colorado
19. UCLA
20. Georgia
21. Tulsa
22. Stanford
23. North Carolina St.
24. Brigham Young
25. Ohio St.

1992

Team
1. Alabama
2. Florida St.
3. Miami (Fla.)
4. Notre Dame
5. Michigan
6. Syracuse
7. Texas A&M
8. Georgia
9. Stanford
10. Florida
11. Washington
12. Tennessee
13. Colorado
14. Nebraska
15. Washington St.
16. Mississippi
17. North Carolina St.
18. North Carolina
19. Ohio St.
20. Hawaii
21. Boston College
22. Kansas
23. Fresno St.
24. Penn St.
25. Mississippi St.

1993

Team
1. Florida St.
2. Notre Dame
3. Nebraska
4. Florida
5. Wisconsin
6. Texas A&M
7. Penn St.
8. West Virginia
9. Ohio St.
10. Arizona
11. Boston College
12. Tennessee
13. Alabama
14. Miami (Fla.)
15. Oklahoma
16. Colorado
17. UCLA
18. Kansas St.
19. Michigan
20. North Carolina
21. Virginia Tech
22. Louisville
23. Clemson
24. California
25. Southern California

1994

Team
1. Nebraska
2. Penn St.
3. Colorado
4. Florida St.
5. Alabama
6. Miami (Fla.)
7. Florida
8. Utah
9. Michigan
10. Ohio St.
11. Oregon
12. Brigham Young
13. Southern California
14. Colorado St.
15. Virginia
16. Kansas St.
17. North Carolina St.
18. Tennessee
19. Washington St.
20. Arizona
21. North Carolina
22. Boston College
23. Texas
24. Virginia Tech
25. Mississippi St.

1995

Team
1. Nebraska
2. Florida
3. Tennessee
4. Colorado
5. Florida St.
6. Ohio St.
7. Kansas St.
8. Northwestern
9. Virginia Tech
10. Kansas
11. Southern California
12. Penn St.
13. Notre Dame
14. Texas A&M
15. Texas
16. Virginia
17. Syracuse
18. Oregon
19. Michigan
20. Texas Tech
21. Auburn
22. Toledo
23. Iowa
24. East Caro.
25. LSU

Beginning in 1974, by agreement with the American Football Coaches Association, teams on probation by the NCAA were ineligible for ranking and national championship consideration by the UPI Board of Coaches. #Beginning in 1990 season, UPI selected top 25 teams instead of 20. ¢In 1991-92, the No. 1 team in the final UPI/NFF poll received the MacArthur Bowl, awarded by the NFF since 1959 to recognize its national champion. Beginning in 1993, the No. 1 team in the USA Today/Hall of Fame poll was awarded the MacArthur Bowl. The National Football Foundation and Hall of Fame MacArthur Bowl national champions before 1991 are listed in national polls section.

USA Today/ESPN (Coaches) Weekly Poll Leaders

1992
9-8	Miami (Fla.)	(1-0-0)
9-15	Miami (Fla.)	(1-0-0)
9-22	Miami (Fla.)	(2-0-0)
9-29	Washington	(3-0-0) (2)
10-6	Washington	(4-0-0)
10-13	Miami (Fla.)	(5-0-0) (2)
10-20	Miami (Fla.)	(6-0-0)
10-27	Miami (Fla.)	(7-0-0)
11-3	Miami (Fla.)	(8-0-0)
11-10	Miami (Fla.)	(8-0-0)
11-17	Miami (Fla.)	(9-0-0)
11-24	Miami (Fla.)	(10-0-0)
12-1	Miami (Fla.)	(11-0-0)
12-8	Miami (Fla.)	(11-0-0)
1-2	**Alabama**	**(13-0-0) (2)**

1993
8-31	Florida St.	(1-0-0)
9-7	Florida St.	(2-0-0)
9-14	Florida St.	(3-0-0)
9-21	Florida St.	(4-0-0)
9-28	Florida St.	(4-0-0)
10-5	Florida St.	(5-0-0)
10-12	Florida St.	(6-0-0)
10-19	Florida St.	(7-0-0)
10-26	Florida St.	(7-0-0)
11-2	Florida St.	(8-0-0)
11-9	Florida St.	(9-0-0)
11-16	Notre Dame	(10-0-0) (2)
11-23	Nebraska	(10-0-0) (2)
11-30	Nebraska	(11-0-0)
12-7	Nebraska	(11-0-0)
1-3	**Florida St.**	**(12-1-0) (3)**

1994
9-6	Nebraska	(1-0-0)
9-13	Nebraska	(2-0-0)
9-20	Nebraska	(3-0-0)
9-27	Nebraska	(4-0-0)
10-4	Florida	(4-0-0) (2)
10-11	Florida	(5-0-0)
10-18	Penn St.	(6-0-0) (3)
10-25	Penn St.	(6-0-0)
11-1	Penn St.	(7-0-0)
11-8	Nebraska	(10-0-0) (2)
11-15	Nebraska	(11-0-0)
11-22	Nebraska	(11-0-0)
11-29	Nebraska	(12-0-0)
12-6	Nebraska	(12-0-0)
1-3	**Nebraska**	**(13-0-0)**

1995
9-5	Florida St.	(1-0-0)
9-12	Florida St.	(2-0-0)
9-19	Florida St.	(3-0-0)
9-26	Florida St.	(4-0-0)
10-3	Florida St.	(4-0-0)
10-10	Florida St.	(5-0-0)
10-17	Florida St.	(6-0-0)
10-24	Florida St.	(7-0-0)
10-31	Nebraska	(8-0-0) (2)
11-7	Nebraska	(9-0-0)
11-14	Nebraska	(10-0-0)

11-21	Nebraska	(10-0-0)
11-28	Nebraska	(11-0-0)
12-5	Nebraska	(11-0-0)
1-3	**Nebraska**	**(12-0-0)**

1996
9-2	Nebraska	(0-0-0)
9-9	Nebraska	(1-0-0)
9-16	Nebraska	(1-0-0)
9-23	Florida	(3-0-0) (4)
9-30	Florida	(4-0-0)
10-7	Florida	(5-0-0)
10-14	Florida	(6-0-0)
10-21	Florida	(7-0-0)
10-28	Florida	(7-0-0)
11-4	Florida	(8-0-0)
11-11	Florida	(9-0-0)
11-18	Florida	(10-0-0)
11-25	Florida	(10-0-0)
12-2	Florida St.	(11-0-0) (2)
12-9	Florida St.	(11-0-0)
1-3	**Florida**	**(12-1-0)**

1997
9-2	Florida	(1-0-0)
9-8	Florida	(2-0-0)
9-15	Florida	(2-0-0)
9-22	Florida	(3-0-0)
9-29	Florida	(4-0-0)
10-6	Florida	(5-0-0)
10-13	Penn St.	(5-0-0) (2)
10-20	Nebraska	(6-0-0) (2)
10-27	Nebraska	(7-0-0)
11-3	Nebraska	(8-0-0)
11-10	Florida St.	(9-0-0) (2)
11-17	Florida St.	(10-0-0)
11-24	Michigan	(11-0-0) (2)
12-1	Michigan	(11-0-0)
12-8	Michigan	(11-0-0)
1-3	**Nebraska**	**(13-0-0) (2)**

1998
9-7	Ohio St.	(1-0-0)
9-14	Ohio St.	(2-0-0)
9-21	Ohio St.	(3-0-0)
9-28	Ohio St.	(3-0-0)
10-5	Ohio St.	(4-0-0)
10-12	Ohio St.	(5-0-0)
10-19	Ohio St.	(6-0-0)
10-26	Ohio St.	(7-0-0)
11-2	Ohio St.	(8-0-0)
11-9	Tennessee (8-0-0) (3) & Kansas St.	(9-0-0) (2)
11-16	Kansas St.	(10-0-0)
11-23	Kansas St.	(11-0-0)
11-30	Kansas St.	(11-0-0)
12-7	Tennessee	(12-0-0) (2)
1-5	**Tennessee**	**(13-0-0**

1999
8-30	Florida St.	(1-0-0)
9-6	Florida St.	(1-0-0)
9-13	Florida St.	(2-0-0)
9-20	Florida St.	(3-0-0)
9-27	Florida St.	(4-0-0)
10-4	Florida St.	(5-0-0)

10-11	Florida St.	(6-0-0)
10-18	Florida St.	(7-0-0)
10-25	Florida St.	(8-0-0)
11-1	Florida St.	(9-0-0)
11-8	Florida St.	(9-0-0)
11-15	Florida St.	(10-0-0)
11-22	Florida St.	(11-0-0)
11-29	Florida St.	(11-0-0)
12-6	Florida St.	(11-0-0)
1-5	**Florida St.**	**(12-0-0)**

2000
8-28	Nebraska	(0-0-0)
9-4	Nebraska	(1-0-0)
9-11	Nebraska	(2-0-0)
9-18	Nebraska	(2-0-0)
9-25	Nebraska	(3-0-0)
10-2	Nebraska	(4-0-0)
10-9	Nebraska	(5-0-0)
10-16	Nebraska	(6-0-0)
10-23	Nebraska	(7-0-0)
10-30	Oklahoma	(7-0-0)
11-6	Oklahoma	(8-0-0)
11-13	Oklahoma	(9-0-0)
11-20	Oklahoma	(10-0-0)
11-27	Oklahoma	(11-0-0)
12-4	Oklahoma	(12-0-0)
1-5	**Oklahoma**	**(13-0-0)**

2001
8-27	Florida	(0-0-0)
9-2	Florida	(1-0-0)
9-9	Miami (Fla.)	(2-0-0)
9-23	Miami (Fla.)	(2-0-0)
9-30	Miami (Fla.)	(3-0-0)
10-7	Florida	(4-0-0)
10-14	Miami (Fla.)	(5-0-0)
10-21	Miami (Fla.)	(6-0-0)
10-28	Miami (Fla.)	(7-0-0)
11-4	Miami (Fla.)	(7-0-0)
11-11	Nebraska	(8-0-0)
11-18	Miami (Fla.)	(9-0-0)
11-24	Miami (Fla.)	(10-0-0)
12-2	Miami (Fla.)	(11-0-0)
12-8	Miami (Fla.)	(11-0-0)
1-4	**Miami (Fla.)**	**(12-0-0)**

2002
8-26	Miami (Fla.)	(0-0-0)
9-2	Miami (Fla.)	(1-0-0)
9-9	Miami (Fla.)	(2-0-0)
9-16	Miami (Fla.)	(3-0-0)
9-23	Miami (Fla.)	(4-0-0)
9-30	Miami (Fla.)	(4-0-0)
10-7	Miami (Fla.)	(5-0-0)
10-14	Miami (Fla.)	(6-0-0)
10-21	Miami (Fla.)	(6-0-0)
10-28	Miami (Fla.)	(7-0-0)
11-4	Oklahoma	(8-0-0) (2)
11-11	Miami (Fla.)	(9-0-0) (2)
11-18	Miami (Fla.)	(9-0-0)
11-25	Miami (Fla.)	(10-0-0)
12-2	Miami (Fla.)	(11-0-0)
12-9	Miami (Fla.)	(12-0-0)
1-4	**Ohio St.**	**(14-0-0) (2)**

2002 USA Today/ESPN Week-by-Week Polls

Team	Pre	S2	S9	S16	S23	S30	O7	O14	O21	O28	N4	N11	N18	N25	D2	D9	J4
Miami (Fla.)	1	1	1	1	1	1	1	1	1	1	1	1	1	1	1	1	2
Texas	2	2	2	2	2	2	8	7	7	4	3	11	10	8	9	7	7
Oklahoma	3	3	3	3	3	3	3	2	2	2	6	5	4	9	8		
Tennessee	4	4	4	4	11	10	9	18	15	NR	NR	NR	NR	NR	NR	NR	NR
Florida St.	5	5	5	5	4	11	12	14	13	20	18	15	14	22	18	16	23
Colorado	6	17	19	NR	NR	NR	NR	25	20	12	21	18	17	15	12	14	21
Florida	7	6	13	10	9	8	16	24	23	22	14	13	11	20	20	24	
Nebraska	8	8	7	19	19	NR	NR	NR	NR	NR	NR	NR	NR	NR	NR	NR	NR
Washington	9	14	14	13	13	12	18	17	NR	NR	NR	NR	NR	NR	NR	NR	NR
Michigan	10	7	6	14	14	13	10	9	8	13	11	10	9	14	11	11	9
Ohio St.	11	9	8	6	6	5	5	4	4	4	3	2	2	2	2	2	1
Georgia	12	11	10	8	7	6	6	5	5	5	8	7	6	5	4	4	3
Washington St.	13	12	11	18	18	17	13	11	11	9	5	4	3	9	7	7	10

DIVISION I-A

Team	Pre	S2	S9	S16	S23	S30	O7	O14	O21	O28	N4	N11	N18	N25	D2	D9	J4
LSU	14	23	22	20	20	19	15	12	10	15	14	12	20	17	25	25	NR
Oregon	15	13	12	9	8	7	7	6	12	16	15	22	NR	NR	NR	NR	NR
Virginia Tech	16	10	9	7	5	4	4	3	3	3	7	13	12	19	14	19	14
Michigan St.	17	15	15	NR	NR	NR	NR	NR	NR	NR	NR	NR	NR	NR	NR	NR	NR
Louisville	18	NR	NR	NR	NR	NR	NR	NR	NR	NR	NR	NR	NR	NR	NR	NR	NR
Southern California	19	16	16	11	22	20	24	20	16	11	9	8	7	6	5	5	4
Maryland	20	NR	NR	NR	NR	NR	NR	NR	NR	NR	25	19	18	23	19	18	13
South Carolina	21	19	NR	NR	NR	NR	NR	NR	NR	NR	NR	NR	NR	NR	NR	NR	NR
Marshall	22	18	17	NR	NR	NR	NR	NR	NR	25	NR	NR	NR	NR	NR	24	19
Penn St.	23	25	25	15	12	21	17	21	17	21	19	16	16	12	10	10	15
North Carolina St.	24	22	20	16	15	14	11	10	9	8	13	20	NR	20	17	17	11
Wisconsin	25	21	18	17	16	15	22	NR	NR	NR	NR	NR	NR	NR	NR	NR	NR
Colorado St.	NR	20	NR	25	23	22	NR	NR	NR	24	20	17	15	13	21	21	NR
Notre Dame	NR	24	21	12	10	9	8	7	6	6	10	9	8	7	13	12	17
Texas A&M	NR	NR	23	21	NR	23	NR	NR	NR	NR	NR	NR	NR	NR	NR	NR	NR
Brigham Young	NR	NR	24	NR	NR	NR	NR	NR	NR	NR	NR	NR	NR	NR	NR	NR	NR
UCLA	NR	NR	NR	22	NR	NR	25	NR	NR	NR	NR	NR	24	NR	NR	NR	NR
Kansas St.	NR	NR	NR	23	17	16	23	19	21	14	12	11	10	8	6	6	6
Iowa St.	NR	NR	NR	24	21	18	14	13	18	23	22	NR	NR	NR	NR	NR	NR
Oregon St.	NR	NR	NR	NR	24	NR	NR	NR	NR	NR	NR	NR	NR	NR	NR	NR	NR
Auburn	NR	NR	NR	NR	25	24	21	NR	NR	NR	NR	NR	NR	25	23	22	16
Air Force	NR	NR	NR	NR	NR	25	19	15	19	NR	NR	NR	NR	NR	NR	NR	NR
Iowa	NR	NR	NR	NR	NR	NR	20	16	14	10	6	5	4	3	3	3	8
Mississippi	NR	NR	NR	NR	NR	NR	NR	22	NR	NR	NR	NR	NR	NR	NR	NR	NR
Bowling Green	NR	NR	NR	NR	NR	NR	NR	23	22	18	16	25	NR	NR	NR	NR	NR
Minnesota	NR	NR	NR	NR	NR	NR	NR	NR	24	19	NR	NR	NR	NR	NR	NR	NR
Arizona St.	NR	NR	NR	NR	NR	NR	NR	NR	25	17	24	NR	NR	NR	NR	NR	NR
Pittsburgh	NR	NR	NR	NR	NR	NR	NR	NR	NR	NR	23	21	19	18	24	23	18
Boise St.	NR	NR	NR	NR	NR	NR	NR	NR	NR	NR	23	21	16	15	15	12
TCU	NR	NR	NR	NR	NR	NR	NR	NR	NR	NR	NR	24	22	NR	NR	NR	22
Texas Tech	NR	NR	NR	NR	NR	NR	NR	NR	NR	NR	NR	NR	23	NR	NR	NR	NR
Hawaii	NR	NR	NR	NR	NR	NR	NR	NR	NR	NR	NR	NR	25	24	NR	NR	NR
West Virginia	NR	NR	NR	NR	NR	NR	NR	NR	NR	NR	NR	NR	NR	21	16	13	20
Arkansas	NR	NR	NR	NR	NR	NR	NR	NR	NR	NR	NR	NR	NR	NR	22	NR	NR
Virginia	NR	NR	NR	NR	NR	NR	NR	NR	NR	NR	NR	NR	NR	NR	NR	NR	25

USA Today/ESPN Final Polls (Coaches)

Took over as coaches poll in 1991. (Cable News Network, 1982-96; ESPN 1997-present)

1982
Team
1. Penn St.
2. Southern Methodist
3. Nebraska
4. Georgia
5. UCLA
6. Arizona St.
7. Pittsburgh
8. Arkansas
9. Clemson
10. Washington
11. LSU
12. Florida St.
13. Ohio St.
14. Southern California
15. Oklahoma
16. Auburn
17. West Virginia
18. Maryland
19. North Carolina
20. Texas
21. Michigan
22. Alabama
23. Tulsa
24. Iowa
25. Florida

1983
Team
1. Miami (Fla.)
2. Auburn
3. Nebraska
4. Georgia
5. Texas
6. Brigham Young
7. Michigan
8. Ohio St.
9. Florida
10. Clemson
11. Illinois
12. Southern Methodist
13. Alabama
14. Air Force
15. West Virginia
16. Iowa
17. Tennessee
18. UCLA
19. Pittsburgh
20. Penn St.
21. Oklahoma
22. Boston College
23. Oklahoma St.
24. Maryland
25. East Caro.

1984
Team
1. Brigham Young
2. Washington
3. Florida
4. Nebraska
5. Oklahoma
6. Boston College
7. Oklahoma St.
8. Southern Methodist
9. Maryland
10. South Carolina
11. Southern California
12. UCLA
13. LSU
14. Ohio St.
15. Auburn
16. Miami (Fla.)
17. Florida St.
18. Virginia
19. Kentucky
20. Iowa
21. West Virginia
22. Army
23. Georgia
24. Air Force
25. Notre Dame

1985
Team
1. Oklahoma
2. Penn St.
3. Michigan
4. Tennessee
5. Florida
6. Miami (Fla.)
7. Air Force
8. Texas A&M
9. UCLA
10. Iowa
11. Nebraska
12. Alabama
13. Ohio St.
14. Florida St.
15. Arkansas
16. Brigham Young
17. Maryland
18. Georgia Tech
19. Baylor
20. Auburn
21. LSU
22. Army
23. Fresno St.
24. Georgia
25. Oklahoma St.

1986
Team
1. Penn St.
2. Miami (Fla.)
3. Oklahoma
4. Nebraska
5. Arizona St.
6. Ohio St.
7. Auburn
8. Michigan
9. Alabama
10. LSU
11. Arizona
12. Texas A&M
13. UCLA
14. Baylor
15. Boston College
16. Iowa
17. Arkansas
18. Clemson
19. Washington
20. Virginia Tech
21. Florida St.
22. Stanford
23. Georgia
24. North Carolina St.
25. San Diego St.

1987
Team
1. Miami (Fla.)
2. Florida St.
3. Oklahoma
4. Syracuse
5. Nebraska
6. LSU
7. Auburn
8. Michigan St.
9. Texas A&M
10. UCLA
11. Clemson
12. Oklahoma St.
13. Georgia
14. Tennessee
15. Iowa
16. Notre Dame
17. Southern California
18. South Carolina
19. Michigan
20. Texas
21. Pittsburgh
22. Indiana
23. Penn St.
24. Ohio St.
25. Alabama

1988
Team
1. Notre Dame
2. Miami (Fla.)
3. Florida St.
4. UCLA
5. Michigan
6. West Virginia
7. Southern California
8. Nebraska
9. Auburn
10. Clemson
11. Oklahoma St.
12. Syracuse
13. Oklahoma
14. Arkansas
15. Washington St.
16. Georgia
17. Alabama
18. North Carolina St.
19. Houston
20. Indiana
21. Wyoming
22. LSU
23. Colorado
24. Southern Miss.
25. Brigham Young

1989
Team
1. Miami (Fla.)
2. Notre Dame
3. Florida St.
4. Colorado
5. Tennessee
6. Auburn
7. Southern California
8. Michigan
9. Alabama
10. Illinois
11. Nebraska
12. Clemson
13. Arkansas
14. Houston
15. Penn St.
16. Virginia
17. Michigan St.
18. Texas Tech
19. Pittsburgh
20. Texas A&M
21. West Virginia
22. Brigham Young
23. Syracuse
24. Ohio St.
25. Washington

1990
Team
1. Colorado
2. Georgia Tech
3. Miami (Fla.)
4. Florida St.
5. Washington
6. Notre Dame
7. Tennessee
8. Michigan
9. Clemson
10. Texas
11. Penn St.
12. Houston
13. Florida
14. Louisville
15. Michigan St.
16. Texas A&M
17. Oklahoma
18. Iowa
19. Auburn
20. Brigham Young
21. Mississippi
22. Southern California
23. Nebraska
24. Illinois
25. Virginia

1991
Team
1. Washington
2. Miami (Fla.)
3. Penn St.
4. Florida St.
5. Alabama
6. Michigan
7. California
8. Florida
9. East Caro.
10. Iowa
11. Syracuse
12. Notre Dame
13. Texas A&M
14. Oklahoma
15. Tennessee
16. Nebraska
17. Clemson
18. UCLA
19. Georgia
20. Colorado
21. Tulsa
22. Stanford
23. Brigham Young
24. Air Force
25. North Carolina St.

1992
Team
1. Alabama
2. Florida St.
3. Miami (Fla.)
4. Notre Dame
5. Michigan
6. Texas A&M
7. Syracuse
8. Georgia
9. Stanford
10. Washington
11. Florida
12. Tennessee
13. Colorado
14. Nebraska
15. North Carolina St.
16. Mississippi
17. Washington St.
18. North Carolina
19. Ohio St.
20. Hawaii
21. Boston College
22. Fresno St.
23. Kansas
24. Penn St.
25. Wake Forest

1993
Team
1. Florida St.
2. Notre Dame
3. Nebraska
4. Florida
5. Wisconsin
6. West Virginia
7. Penn St.
8. Texas A&M
9. Arizona
10. Ohio St.
11. Tennessee
12. Boston College
13. Alabama
14. Oklahoma
15. Miami (Fla.)
16. Colorado
17. UCLA
18. Kansas St.
19. Michigan
20. Virginia Tech
21. North Carolina
22. Clemson
23. Louisville
24. California
25. Southern California

1994
Team
1. Nebraska
2. Penn St.
3. Colorado
4. Alabama
5. Florida St.
6. Miami (Fla.)
7. Florida
8. Utah
9. Ohio St.
10. Brigham Young
11. Oregon
12. Michigan
13. Virginia
14. Colorado St.
15. Southern California
16. Kansas St.
17. North Carolina St.
18. Tennessee
19. Washington St.
20. Arizona
21. North Carolina
22. Boston College
23. Texas
24. Virginia Tech
25. Mississippi St.

1995
Team
1. Nebraska
2. Tennessee
3. Florida
4. Colorado
5. Florida St.
6. Kansas St.
7. Northwestern
8. Ohio St.
9. Virginia Tech
10. Kansas
11. Southern California
12. Penn St.
13. Notre Dame
14. Texas
15. Texas A&M
16. Syracuse
17. Virginia
18. Oregon
19. Michigan
20. Texas Tech
21. Auburn
22. Iowa
23. East Caro.
24. Toledo
25. LSU

1996
Team (Record)
1. Florida (12-1)
2. Ohio St. (11-1)
3. Florida St. (11-1)
4. Arizona St. (11-1)
5. Brigham Young (14-1)
6. Nebraska (11-2)
7. Penn St. (11-2)
8. Colorado (10-2)
9. Tennessee (10-2)
10. North Carolina (10-2)
11. Alabama (10-3)
12. Virginia Tech (10-2)
13. LSU (10-2)
14. Miami (Fla.) (9-3)
15. Washington (9-3)
16. Northwestern (9-3)
17. Kansas St. (9-3)
18. Iowa (9-3)
19. Syracuse (9-3)
20. Michigan (8-4)
21. Notre Dame (8-3)
22. Wyoming (10-2)
23. Texas (8-5)
24. Army (10-2)
25. Auburn (8-4)

1997
Team (Record)
1. Nebraska (13-0)
2. Michigan (12-0)
3. Florida St. (11-1)
4. North Carolina (11-1)
5. UCLA (10-2)
6. Florida (10-2)
7. Kansas St. (11-1)
8. Tennessee (11-2)
9. Washington St. (10-2)
10. Georgia (10-2)
11. Auburn (10-3)
12. Ohio St. (10-3)
13. LSU (9-3)
14. Arizona St. (9-3)
15. Purdue (9-3)
16. Colorado St. (11-2)
17. Penn St. (9-3)
18. Washington (8-4)
19. Southern Miss. (9-3)
20. Syracuse (9-4)
21. Texas A&M (9-4)
22. Mississippi (8-4)
23. Missouri (7-5)
24. Oklahoma St. (8-4)
25. Air Force (10-3)

1998
Team (Record)
1. Tennessee (13-0)
2. Ohio St. (11-1)
3. Florida St. (11-2)
4. Arizona (12-1)
5. Wisconsin (11-1)
6. Florida (10-2)
7. Tulane (12-0)
8. UCLA (10-2)
9. Kansas St. (11-2)
10. Air Force (12-1)
11. Georgia Tech (10-2)
12. Michigan (10-3)
13. Texas A&M (11-3)
14. Georgia (9-3)
15. Penn St. (9-3)
16. Texas (9-3)
17. Arkansas (9-3)
18. Virginia (9-3)
19. Virginia Tech (9-3)
20. Nebraska (9-4)
21. Miami (Fla.) (9-3)
22. Notre Dame (9-3)
23. Purdue (9-4)
24. Syracuse (8-4)
25. Missouri (8-4)

1999
Team (Record)
1. Florida St. (12-0)
2. Nebraska (12-1)
3. Virginia Tech (11-1)
4. Wisconsin (10-2)
5. Michigan (10-2)
6. Kansas St. (11-1)
7. Michigan St. (10-2)
8. Alabama (10-3)
9. Tennessee (9-3)
10. Marshall (13-0)
11. Penn St. (10-3)
12. Mississippi St. (10-2)
13. Southern Miss. (9-3)
14. Florida (9-4)
15. Miami (Fla.) (9-4)
16. Georgia (8-4)
17. Minnesota (8-4)
18. Oregon (9-3)
19. Arkansas (8-4)
20. Texas A&M (8-4)
21. Georgia Tech (8-4)
22. Mississippi (8-4)
23. Texas (9-5)
24. Stanford (8-4)
25. Illinois (8-4)

2000
Team (Record)
1. Oklahoma (13-0)
2. Miami (Fla.) (11-1)
3. Washington (11-1)
4. Florida St. (11-2)
5. Oregon St. (11-1)
6. Virginia Tech (11-1)
7. Nebraska (10-2)
8. Kansas St. (11-3)
9. Oregon (10-2)
10. Michigan (9-3)
11. Florida (10-3)
12. Texas (9-3)
13. Purdue (8-4)
14. Clemson (9-3)
15. Colorado St. (10-2)
16. Notre Dame (9-3)
17. Georgia (8-4)
18. TCU (10-2)
19. Georgia Tech (9-3)
20. Auburn (9-4)
21. South Carolina (8-4)
22. Mississippi St. (8-4)
23. Iowa St. (9-3)
24. Wisconsin (9-4)
25. Tennessee (8-4)

2001
Team (Record)
1. Miami (Fla.) (12-0)
2. Oregon (11-1)
3. Florida (10-2)
4. Tennessee (11-2)
5. Texas (11-2)
6. Oklahoma (11-2)
7. Nebraska (11-2)
8. LSU (10-3)
9. Colorado (10-3)
10. Maryland (10-2)
11. Washington St. (10-2)
12. Illinois (10-2)
13. South Carolina (9-3)
14. Syracuse (10-3)
15. Florida St. (8-4)
16. Louisville (11-2)
17. Stanford (9-3)
18. Virginia Tech (8-4)
19. Washington (8-4)
20. Michigan (8-4)
21. Marshall (11-2)
22. Toledo (10-2)
23. Boston College (8-4)
24. Brigham Young (12-2)
25. Georgia (8-4)

2002
Team (Record)
1. Ohio St. (14-0)
2. Miami (Fla.) (12-1)
3. Georgia (13-1)
4. Southern California (11-2)
5. Oklahoma (12-2)
6. Kansas St. (11-2)
7. Texas (11-2)
8. Iowa (11-2)
9. Michigan (10-3)
10. Washington St. (10-3)
11. North Carolina St. (11-3)
12. Boise St. (12-1)
13. Maryland (11-3)
14. Virginia Tech (10-4)
15. Penn St. (9-4)
16. Auburn (9-4)
17. Notre Dame (10-3)
18. Pittsburgh (9-4)
19. Marshall (11-2)
20. West Virginia (9-4)
21. Colorado (9-5)
22. TCU (10-2)
23. Florida St. (9-5)
24. Florida (8-5)
25. Virginia (9-5)

BOWL COALITION, ALLIANCE AND BOWL CHAMPIONSHIP SERIES HISTORY

BOWL COALITION

The history of the College Football Bowl Coalition began in 1992 and lasted for three years through the 1994 season. The Bowl Coalition featured four games – the Orange, Sugar, Cotton and Fiesta Bowls – with conference champions locked into the Orange (Big Eight), Sugar (Southeastern) and Cotton (Southwest) Bowls and the Fiesta Bowl pairing two at-large teams.

The Fiesta Bowl had the ability to select one Coalition-eligible team, that was not a conference champion, before the national selection date. The original Coalition also involved champions from the Big East and Atlantic Coast Conferences, as well as Notre Dame.

Selections were made on the basis of how the champions of the Big Eight, Southeastern and Southwest Conferences finished in the final regular-season poll, which was a combination of the Associated Press and CNN/USA Today rankings. Al selections were made by the Coalition as a group on the first Sunday in December following the final weekend of the regular season.

All teams had to have at least six wins against Division I-A opponents and Notre Dame was guaranteed a spot with seven wins and could still qualify with six wins given mutual agreement between the bowls.

There were 56 Division I-A members that were members of the original Coalition, which also included original involvement with the Gator and Hancock Bowls. The remainder of the bowls remained in place, many with predetermined conference tieins. A second layer of bowls eventually was identified and came to be known as the Tier Two bowls.

BOWL COALITION (1992-94)

1992 SEASON

SUGAR BOWL
Alabama 34, Miami (Fla.) 13

(Had first selection, but had automatic matchup between SEC champion Alabama, which was ranked No. 2 in final regular-season AP poll, against Big East champion Miami (Florida), which was ranked No. 1.)

COTTON BOWL
Notre Dame 28, Texas A&M 3

(Has second selection based on SWC champion Texas A&M being ranked No. 4 at end of regular season and chose at-large selection Notre Dame.)

ORANGE BOWL
Florida St. 27, Nebraska 14

(Had third selection based on Big Eight champion Nebraska being ranked No. 11 at end of regular season and chose ACC champion Florida State.)

FIESTA BOWL
Syracuse 26, Colorado 22

(Had fourth selection and chose at-large selection Syracuse and at-large selection Colorado.)

1993 SEASON

ORANGE BOWL
Florida St. 18, Nebraska 14

(Had first selection, but had automatic matchup between Big Eight champion Nebraska, which was ranked No. 1 in final regular-season coalition poll, against ACC champion Florida State, which was ranked No. 2.)

SUGAR BOWL
Florida 41, West Virginia 7

(Had second selection based on Big East champion West Virginia being ranked No. 3 at end of regular season and chose SEC champion Florida.)

COTTON BOWL
Notre Dame 24, Texas A&M 21

(Had third selection based on SWC champion Texas A&M being ranked No. 7 at end of regular season and chose at-large selection Notre Dame.)

FIESTA BOWL
Arizona 29, Miami (Fla.) 0

(Had fourth selection and chose at-large selection Miami (Florida) and also picked at-large Arizona.)

1994 SEASON

ORANGE BOWL
Nebraska 24, Miami (Fla.) 17

(Had first selection based on Big Eight champion Nebraska being ranked No. 1 at end of regular season in coalition poll and chose Big East champion Miami [Florida].)

SUGAR BOWL
Florida St. 23, Florida 17

(Had second selection based on SEC champion Florida being ranked No. 5 and chose ACC champion Florida State.)

COTTON BOWL
Southern California 55, Texas Tech 14

(Had third selection based on SWC champion Texas Tech being unranked and chose at-large Southern California.)

FIESTA BOWL
Colorado 41, Notre Dame 24

(Had fourth selection and chose at-large Notre Dame and at-large Colorado.)

BOWL ALLIANCE

The Bowl Alliance lasted three seasons, 1995 through 1997, and involved three games – the Fiesta, Orange and Sugar Bowls. A predetermined rotation created a situation in which each year a different bowl had the first two choices, while a second bowl chose third and fifth and the third bowl chose fourth and sixth.

Conferences that were a part of the Alliance were the Big 12, Atlantic Coast, Big East and Southeastern, leaving two at-large slots.

The most noteworthy change from the Coalition to the Alliance was the elimination of the conference tie-ins which had been in existence for years. The goal was to provide the best opportunity to match the top two teams and provide the greatest flexibility in creating the postseason matchups between Alliance partners.

In 1995, the first season of the Alliance, there was only one at-large position since the merger of the Big Eight and Southwest Conferences into the Big 12 had not yet taken place, providing five guaranteed conference champions that season.

Notre Dame was guaranteed the at-large slot in 1995 by finishing in the top ten of either the Associated Press or CNN/USA Today poll.

BOWL ALLIANCE (1995-97)

1995 SEASON

FIESTA BOWL
Nebraska 62, Florida 24

(Had first and second selections and picked Big Eight champion Nebraska, which was ranked No. 1 in the regular-season AP poll, against SEC champion Florida, which was ranked No. 2. This pick was required through mandatory No. 1 vs. No. 2 matchup rules.)

ORANGE BOWL
Florida St. 31, Notre Dame 26

(Had third and fifth selections and picked ACC champion Florida State against at-large Notre Dame.)

SUGAR BOWL
Virginia Tech 28, Texas 10

(Had fourth and sixth selections and picked Big East champion Virginia Tech against SWC champion Texas.)

1996 SEASON

SUGAR BOWL
Florida 52, Florida St. 20

(Had first and second selections and picked SEC champion Florida and ACC champion Florida State.)

FIESTA BOWL
Penn State 38, Texas 15

(Had third and fifth selections and picked at-large Penn State and Big 12 champion Texas.)

ORANGE BOWL
Nebraska 41, Virginia Tech 21

(Had fourth and sixth selections and picked at-large selection Nebraska and Big East champion Virginia Tech.)

1997 SEASON

ORANGE BOWL
Nebraska 42, Tennessee 17

(Had first and second selections and picked Big 12 champion Nebraska and SEC champion Tennessee.)

SUGAR BOWL
Florida St. 31, Ohio St. 14

(Had third and fifth selections and picked ACC champion Florida State and at-large Ohio State.)

FIESTA BOWL
Kansas St. 35, Syracuse 18

(Had fourth and sixth selections and picked at-large Kansas State and Big East champion Syracuse.)

BOWL CHAMPIONSHIP SERIES

The Bowl Championship Series (BCS) was launched in 1998 to match the No. 1 and No. 2 teams in the BCS rankings in a bowl game to determine a national champion in the absence of NCAA-sponsored playoffs. The No.1 vs. No. 2 game rotates between the Fiesta, Orange, Rose and Sugar Bowls.

Top-ranked Tennessee beat Florida State, 23-16, in the Fiesta Bowl to cap the first BCS year. Florida State returned to the title game again in 1999, this time appearing in the Sugar Bowl as the No. 1 team. The Seminoles upended Virginia Tech, 46-29.

In 2000, it was the Orange Bowl's turn to host the final game, and Florida State kept its streak of appearances alive. However, Oklahoma's defense ruled the evening as the Sooners won, 13-2.

In 2001, Miami (Florida) was the only unbeaten team in Division I-A through the regular season and earned the top spot in the BCS rankings. Nebraska edged Colorado for the second spot and joined the Hurricanes in the Rose Bowl. Miami exploded for 34 unanswered points in the first half on its way to a 37-14 triumph.

Last year, Miami (Florida) again topped the BCS regular-season standings with a 2.93 mark and Ohio State was second at 3.97. However, the Buckeyes captured the No. 1 vs. No. 2 victory in the Fiesta Bowl, 31-24 in two overtimes, to take the national title.

NOTE: The NCAA football certification subcommittee has not enacted, adopted or otherwise approved of the process described below. The NCAA has no role in the selection of the institutions that participate in postseason bowl games and does not sponsor a Division I-A football championship.

2002 FINAL
BOWL CHAMPIONSHIP SERIES RANKINGS

	Poll Avg.	Comp. Avg.	Sked Rank	Loss Record	Subtotal	Quality Win	Total
1. Miami (Fla.)	1	1.17	0.76	0	2.93		2.93
2. Ohio St.	2	1.67	0.80	0	4.47	-0.5	3.97
3. Georgia	4	3.17	0.20	1	8.37		8.37
4. Southern Cal	5	3.67	0.04	2	10.71	-0.2	10.51
5. Iowa	3	4.83	1.96	1	10.79		10.79
6. Washington St.	7	7.00	0.84	2	16.84	-0.7	16.14
7. Oklahoma	8	6.33	0.56	2	16.89	-0.1	16.79
8. Kansas St.	6	10.67	2.16	2	20.83	-0.7	20.13
9. Notre Dame	11.5	6.83	0.60	2	20.93		20.93
10. Texas	9	9.50	0.88	2	21.38	-0.3	21.08
11. Michigan	11.5	9.33	0.08	3	23.91		23.91
12. Penn St.	10	13.33	0.64	3	26.97		26.97
13. Colorado	14	15.17	0.40	4	33.57	-0.3	33.27
14. Florida St.	16	13.83	0.12	4	33.95		33.95
15. West Virginia	14	17.33	1.64	3	35.97		35.97

EXPLANATION

Poll Average - Average of the AP Media Poll and USA Today/ESPN Coaches Poll. Others receiving votes calculated in order received.

Computer Average - Average of Anderson & Hester, Richard Billingsley, Colley Matrix, Kenneth Massey, New York Times, Jeff Sagarin's USA Today, and the Peter Wolfe rankings. The lowest (worst) computer ranking will be disregarded.

Schedule Rank - Rank of schedule strength compared to other Division I-A teams of actual games played divided by 25. This component is calculated by determining the cumulative won/loss records of the team's opponent (66 2/3 percent) and the cumulative won/loss records of the team's opponents' opponents (33 1/3 percent).

Losses - One point for each loss during the season.

Subtotal – The values from the four factors described above are added.

Quality Win Component - The quality win component will reward to varying degrees teams that defeat opponents ranked among the top 10 in the weekly standings. The bonus point scale will range from a high of 1.0 points for a win over the top ranked team to a low of 0.1 for a victory over the 10th-ranked BCS team. The BCS Standings at the end of the season will determine final quality win points. If a team registers a victory over a team more than once during the regular season, quality points will be awarded just once. Quality win points are based on the standings determined by the subtotal. The final standings are reconfigured to reflect the quality win point deduction.

Total – The value of the quality win component is subtracted from the subtotal.

Notes: 1. Teams on NCAA probation (i.e., not eligible for postseason competition) are not listed in the BCS standings. Teams with victories over teams on probation will receive appropriate quality win points. 2. The Tostitos Fiesta Bowl on January 3, 2003, was the host of the BCS national championship game and determined which team was presented the National Football Foundation and College Hall of Fame's MacArthur Trophy, awarded to college football's national champion since 1959.

BCS RESULTS FOR 2002-03:
Fiesta Bowl—Ohio St. 31, Miami (Fla.) 24 (2 ot)
Orange Bowl—Southern California 38, Iowa 17
Sugar Bowl—Georgia 26, Florida St. 13
Rose Bowl—Oklahoma 34, Washington St. 14

2001 SEASON
FINAL BCS RANKINGS

Rk	Team	AP	USA Today/ ESPN	Poll Avg.	And. & Hester	AJC Colley	Bill.	Massey	Roth.	Sagar.	Scripps-How.	Wolfe	Comp. Avg.	Sched. Strength	Sched. Rank	Losses	Subtotal	Quality Win	Total
1.	Miami (Fla.)	1	1	1.0	1	1	1	1	1	1	1	1	1.00	18	0.72	0	2.72	-0.1	2.62
2.	Nebraska	4	4	4.0	2	2	2	3	2	3	2	2	2.17	14	0.56	1	7.73	-0.5	7.23
3.	Colorado	3	3	3.0	4	5	4	4	5	5	5	3	4.50	2	0.08	2	9.58	-2.3	7.28
4.	Oregon	2	2	2.0	3	3	3	2	8	7	6	7	4.83	31	1.24	1	9.07	-0.4	8.67
5.	Florida	5	5	5.0	9	8	7	8	4	2	3	5	5.83	19	0.76	2	13.59	-0.5	13.09
6.	Tennessee	8	8	8.0	5	4	8	6	7	8	7	4	6.17	3	0.12	2	16.29	-1.6	14.69
7.	Texas	9	9	9.0	8	9	10	9	3	4	4	6	6.67	33	1.32	2	18.99	-1.2	17.79
8.	Illinois	7	7	7.0	7	6	6	12	13	12	10	12	9.83	37	1.48	1	19.31	0.0	19.31
9.	Stanford	11	11	11.0	6	7	11	5	9	9	8	8	7.83	22	0.88	2	21.71	-1.3	20.41
10.	Maryland	6	6	6.0	14	10	5	10	11	11	14	11	11.17	78	3.12	1	21.29	0.0	21.29
11.	Oklahoma	10	10	10.0	10	11	9	13	6	6	9	9	9.00	36	1.44	2	22.44	-0.9	21.54
12.	Washington St.	13	13	13.0	12	12	12	7	10	10	11	10	10.83	42	1.68	2	27.51	-0.6	26.91
13.	LSU	12	12	12.0	11	13	14	14	12	18	13	14	13.33	10	0.40	3	28.73	-1.0	27.73
14.	South Carolina	14	14	14.0	20	19	19	17	17	23	23	17	19.17	40	1.60	3	37.77	0.0	37.77
15.	Washington	21	20	20.5	13	15	15	11	16	25	17	13	14.83	21	0.84	3	39.17	-1.0	38.17

Key: AP (Associated Press poll); USA/ESPN (USA Today/ESPN coaches poll); Poll Avg. (Average of two polls); Bill (Richard Billingsley); Dunk (Dunkel Index); Mass (Kenneth Massey); NYT (New York Times); Roth (David Rothman); SAG (Jeff Sagarin); SH (Scripps-Howard); ST (Seattle Times); Comp Avg. (Computer Services Average); SSch (Schedule Strength); SRk (Schedule Rank); L (Losses).

EXPLANATION

Poll Average - Average of the AP Media Poll and USA Today/ESPN Coaches Poll. Others receiving votes calculated in order received.

Computer Average - Average of Anderson & Hester (And. & Hester), Atlanta Journal-Constitution Colley Matrix (AJC Colley), Richard Billingsley (Bill.), Kenneth Massey (Massey), David Rothman (Roth.), Jeff Sagar's USA Today (Sagar.), Matthews/Scripps-Howard (Scripps-How.), and the Peter Wolfe (Wolfe) rankings. The computer component will be determined by averaging six rankings. The highest and the lowest will be disregarded.

Schedule Rank - Rank of schedule strength compared to other Division I-A teams of actual games played divided by 25. This component is calculated by determining the cumulative won/loss records of the team's opponent (66 2/3 percent) and the cumulative won/loss records of the team's opponents' opponents (33 1/3 percent).

Losses - One point for each loss during the season.

Subtotal – The values from the four factors described above are added.

Quality Win Component - The quality win component will reward to varying degrees teams that defeat opponents ranked among the top 15 in the weekly standings. The bonus point scale will range from a high of 1.5 points for a win over the top ranked team to a low of 0.1 for a victory over the 15th-ranked BCS team. The BCS Standings at the end of the season will determine final quality win points. If a team registers a victory over a team more than once during the regular season, quality points will be awarded just once. Quality win points are based on the standings determined by the subtotal. The final standings are reconfigured to reflect the quality win point deduction.

Total – The value of the quality win component is subtracted from the subtotal.

BCS RESULTS
Rose Bowl—Miami (Fla.) 37, Nebraska 14
Fiesta Bowl—Oregon 38, Colorado 16
Orange Bowl—Florida 56, Maryland 23
Sugar Bowl—LSU 47, Illinois 34

2000 SEASON
FINAL BCS RANKINGS

Rk	Team	AP	USA/ ESPN	Poll Avg.	Bill	Dunk	MASS	NYT	Roth	SAG	SH	ST	Comp. Avg.	SSch	SRk	L	TOTAL
1.	Oklahoma	1	1	1.0	1	3	2	3	1	3	2	1	1.86	11	0.44	0	3.30
2.	Florida St.	3	3	3.0	2	1	1	1	2	1	1	3	1.29	2	0.08	1	5.37
3.	Miami (Fla.)	2	2	2.0	3	2	3	2	3	2	3	4	2.57	3	0.12	1	5.69
4.	Washington	4	4	4.0	10	11	5	5	4	8	4	2	5.43	6	0.24	1	10.67
5.	Virginia Tech	5	6	5.5	5	5	4	4	7	5	7	6	5.14	14	0.56	1	12.20
6.	Oregon St.	6	5	5.5	7	9	8	8	5	7	5	5	6.50	42	1.68	1	14.68
7.	Florida	7	7	7.0	4	4	7	6	9	6	6	7	5.71	1	0.04	2	14.75
8.	Nebraska	8	9	8.5	6	13	6	10	6	4	8	9	7.00	18	0.72	2	18.22
9.	Kansas St.	9	11	10.0	8	12	11	12	8	9	11	12	10.14	29	1.16	3	24.30
10.	Oregon	11	8	9.5	12	17	14	15	11	14	9	8	11.86	24	0.96	2	24.32
11.	Notre Dame	10	10	10.0	14	15	15	8	12	16	10	10	12.07	25	1.00	2	25.07
12.	Texas	12	12	12.0	11	6	9	11	10	10	12	15	9.86	84	3.36	2	27.22
13.	Georgia Tech	17	15	16.0	9	8	10	7	14	11	13	11	9.86	44	1.76	2	29.62
14.	TCU	16	13	14.5	16	7	12	20	15	12	14	20	13.71	95	3.80	1	33.01
15.	Clemson	13	16	14.5	13	21	13	19	13	15	15	13	14.43	56	2.24	2	33.17

Key: AP (Associated Press poll); USA/ESPN (USA Today/ESPN coaches poll); Poll Avg. (Average of two polls); Bill (Richard Billingsley); Dunk (Dunkel Index); Mass (Kenneth Massey); NYT (New York Times); Roth (David Rothman); SAG (Jeff Sagarin); SH (Scripps-Howard); ST (Seattle Times); Comp Avg. (Computer Services Average); SSch (Schedule Strength); SRk (Schedule Rank); L (Losses).

BCS RESULTS
Orange Bowl—Oklahoma 13, Florida St. 2
Sugar Bowl—Miami (Fla.) 37, Florida 20
Fiesta Bowl—Oregon St. 41, Notre Dame 9
Rose Bowl—Washington 34, Purdue 34

1999 SEASON
FINAL BCS RANKINGS

Team	Total Score
1. Florida St.	2.24
2. Virginia Tech	6.12
3. Nebraska	7.42
4. Alabama	12.11
5. Tennessee	13.71
6. Kansas St.	15.23
7. Wisconsin	16.71
8. Michigan	18.08
9. Michigan St.	19.11
10. Florida	23.06
11. Penn St.	28.75
12. Marshall	31.15
13. Minnesota	33.61
14. Texas A&M	34.76
15. Texas	34.81

BCS RESULTS

SUGAR BOWL
Florida St. 46, Virginia Tech 29
(Had first and second selections and picked ACC champion Florida State and Big East champion Virginia Tech)

FIESTA BOWL
Nebraska 31, Tennessee 21
(Had third and fifth selections and selected Big 12 champion Nebraska and SEC Tennessee)

ORANGE BOWL
Michigan 35, Alabama 34 (ot)
(Had fourth and sixth selections and selected Big Ten Michigan and SEC champion Alabama)

ROSE BOWL
Wisconsin 17, Stanford 9
(Selected Big Ten champion Wisconsin and Pacific-10 champion Stanford)

1998 SEASON
FINAL BCS RANKINGS

Team	Total Score
1. Tennessee	3.47
2. Florida St.	4.91
3. Kansas St.	9.96
4. Ohio St.	10.37
5. UCLA	10.90
6. Texas A&M	15.70
7. Arizona	16.49
8. Florida	19.95
9. Wisconsin	21.61
10. Tulane	26.67
11. Nebraska	29.06
12. Virginia	32.22
13. Arkansas	32.28
14. Georgia Tech	32.76
15. Syracuse	34.80

BCS RESULTS

FIESTA BOWL
Tennessee 23, Florida St. 16

(Had first and second selections and picked SEC champion Tennessee and ACC champion Florida State)

SUGAR BOWL
Ohio St. 24, Texas A&M 14

(Had third and fifth selections and picked Big Ten Ohio State and Big 12 champion Texas A&M)

ORANGE BOWL
Florida 31, Syracuse 10

(Had fourth and sixth selections and chose SEC Florida and Big East champion Syracuse)

ROSE BOWL
Wisconsin 38, UCLA 31

(Selected Big Ten Wisconsin and Pacific-10 champion UCLA)

Undefeated, Untied Teams

(Regular-Season Games Only)

Minimum of five games played against opponents above the high-school level. Subsequent bowl win is indicated by (†), loss (‡) and tie ($). Unscored-on teams are indicated by (•).

(Note: Following are undefeated, untied teams in regular-season games not included with major colleges at the time—Centre, 1919 & 1921; Lafayette, 1921, 1926 & 1937; Wash. & Jeff., 1921; Marquette, 1923; Louisville, 1925; Centenary (La.), 1927; Memphis, 1938; San Jose St., 1939; Hardin-Simmons, 1940; Arizona, 1945; Pacific [Cal.], 1949; Fresno St., 1961; and San Diego St., 1966.)

Year	College	Wins
1878	Princeton	6
1882	Yale	8
1883	Yale	8
1885	Princeton	9
1887	Yale	9
1888	Yale	•13
1889	Princeton	10
1890	Harvard	11
1891	Yale	•13
1892	Minnesota	5
	Purdue	8
	Yale	•13
1893	Minnesota	6
	Princeton	11
1894	Pennsylvania	12
	VMI	5
	Yale	16
1895	Pennsylvania	14
1896	LSU	6
1897	Pennsylvania	15
1898	Harvard	11
	Kentucky	•7
	Michigan	10
	North Carolina	9
1899	Kansas	10
	Sewanee	12
1900	Clemson	6
	Texas	6
	Tulane	•5
	Yale	12
1901	Harvard	12
	Michigan	†•10
	Wisconsin	9
1902	Arizona	•5
	California	8
	Michigan	11
	Nebraska	•9
1903	Nebraska	10
	Princeton	11
1904	Auburn	5
	Michigan	10
	Minnesota	13
	Pennsylvania	12
	Pittsburgh	10
	Vanderbilt	9
1905	Chicago	10
	Stanford	8
	Yale	10
1906	New Mexico St.	5
	Washington St.	•6
	Wisconsin	5
1907	Oregon St.	•6
1908	Kansas	9
	LSU	10
1909	Arkansas	7
	Colorado	•6
	Washington	7
	Yale	•10
1910	Colorado	6
	Illinois	•7
	Pittsburgh	•9
	Washington	6
1911	Colorado	6
	Oklahoma	8
	Utah St.	•5
	Washington	7
1912	Harvard	9
	Notre Dame	7
	Penn St.	8
	Washington	6
	Wisconsin	7
1913	Auburn	8
	Chicago	7
	Harvard	9
	Michigan St.	7

Year	College	Wins
1914	Nebraska	8
	Notre Dame	7
	Washington	7
	Army	9
	Illinois	7
	Tennessee	9
	Texas	8
	Wash. & Lee	9
1915	Colorado St.	7
	Columbia	5
	Cornell	9
	Nebraska	8
	Oklahoma	10
	Pittsburgh	8
	Washington	7
	Washington St.	†6
1916	Army	9
	Ohio St.	7
	Pittsburgh	8
	Tulsa	10
1917	Denver	9
	Georgia Tech	9
	Pittsburgh	9
	Texas A&M	•8
	Washington St.	6
1918	Michigan	5
	Oklahoma	6
	Texas	9
	Virginia Tech	7
	Washington (Mo.)	6
1919	Notre Dame	9
	Texas A&M	•10
1920	Boston College	8
	California	†8
	Notre Dame	9
	Ohio St.	‡7
	Southern California	6
	Texas	9
	VMI	9
1921	California	$9
	Cornell	8
	Iowa	7
1922	California	9
	Cornell	8
	Drake	7
	Iowa	7
	Princeton	8
	Tulsa	7
1923	Colorado	9
	Cornell	8
	Illinois	8
	Michigan	8
	Southern Methodist	9
	Yale	8
1924	Notre Dame	†9
1925	Alabama	†9
	Dartmouth	8
1926	Alabama	$9
	Stanford	$10
	Utah	7
1927	(None)	
1928	Boston College	9
	Detroit	9
	Georgia Tech	†9
1929	Notre Dame	9
	Pittsburgh	‡9
	Purdue	8
	Tulane	9
	Utah	7
1930	Alabama	†9
	Notre Dame	10
	Utah	8
	Washington St.	‡9
1931	Tulane	‡11
1932	Colgate	•9
	Michigan	8
	Southern California	†9
1933	Princeton	9
1934	Alabama	†9
	Minnesota	8
1935	Minnesota	8
	Princeton	9
	Southern Methodist	‡12
1936	(None)	
1937	Alabama	‡9
	Colorado	‡8
	Santa Clara	†8
1938	Duke	‡•9
	Georgetown	8
	Oklahoma	‡10

Year	College	Wins
	Tennessee	†10
	TCU	†10
	Texas Tech	‡10
1939	Cornell	8
	Tennessee	‡•10
	Texas A&M	†10
1940	Boston College	†10
	Lafayette	9
	Minnesota	8
	Stanford	†9
	Tennessee	‡10
1941	Duke	‡9
	Duquesne	8
	Minnesota	8
1942	Tulsa	‡10
1943	Purdue	9
1944	Army	9
	Ohio St.	9
1945	Alabama	†9
	Army	9
	Oklahoma St.	†8
1946	Georgia	†10
	Hardin-Simmons	†10
	UCLA	‡10
1947	Michigan	†9
	Notre Dame	9
	Penn St.	$9
1948	California	‡10
	Clemson	†10
	Michigan	9
1949	Army	9
	California	‡10
	Notre Dame	10
	Oklahoma	†10
1950	Oklahoma	‡10
	Princeton	9
	Wyoming	†9
1951	Maryland	†9
	Michigan St.	9
	Princeton	9
	San Francisco	9
	Tennessee	‡10
1952	Georgia Tech	†11
	Michigan St.	9
1953	Maryland	‡10
1954	Ohio St.	†9
	Oklahoma	10
	UCLA	9
1955	Maryland	‡10
	Oklahoma	†10
1956	Oklahoma	10
	Tennessee	‡10
	Wyoming	10
1957	Arizona St.	10
	Auburn	10
1958	LSU	†10
1959	Syracuse	†10
1960	New Mexico St.	†10
	Yale	9
1961	Alabama	†10
	Rutgers	9
1962	Dartmouth	9
	Mississippi	†9
	Southern California	†10
1963	Texas	†10
1964	Alabama	‡10
	Arkansas	†10
	Princeton	9
1965	Arkansas	‡10
	Dartmouth	9
	Michigan St.	‡10
	Nebraska	‡10
1966	Alabama	†10
1967	Wyoming	‡10
1968	Ohio	‡10
	Ohio St.	†9
	Penn St.	†10
1969	Penn St.	†10
	San Diego St.	†10
	Texas	†10
	Toledo	†10
1970	Arizona St.	†10
	Dartmouth	9
	Ohio St.	‡9
	Texas	†10
	Toledo	†11
1971	Alabama	‡11
	Michigan	‡11
	Nebraska	†12
	Toledo	†11

Year	College	Wins	Year	College	Wins	Year	College	Wins
1972	Southern California	†11	1980	Georgia	†11		Texas A&M	‡12
1973	Alabama	‡11	1981	Clemson	†11	1993	Auburn	11
	Miami (Ohio)	†10	1982	Georgia	†11		Nebraska	‡11
	Notre Dame	†10	1983	Nebraska	‡12		West Virginia	‡11
	Penn St.	†11		Texas	‡11	1994	Nebraska	†12
1974	Alabama	‡11	1984	Brigham Young	†12		Penn St.	†11
	Oklahoma	11	1985	Bowling Green	‡11	1995	Florida	‡12
1975	Arizona St.	†11		Penn St.	‡11		Nebraska	†11
	Arkansas St.	11	1986	Miami (Fla.)	‡11	1996	Arizona St.	‡11
	Ohio St.	‡11		Penn St.	‡11		Florida St.	‡11
1976	Maryland	‡11	1987	Miami (Fla.)	†11	1997	Michigan	†12
	Pittsburgh	†11		Oklahoma	‡11		Nebraska	†13
	Rutgers	11		Syracuse	$11	1998	Tennessee	†12
1977	Texas	‡11	1988	Notre Dame	‡11		Tulane	†11
1978	Penn St.	‡11		West Virginia	‡11	1999	Florida St.	†11
1979	Alabama	†11	1989	Colorado	‡11		Marshall	†12
	Brigham Young	‡11	1990	(None)		2000	Oklahoma	†13
	Florida St.	†11	1991	Miami (Fla.)	†11	2001	Miami (Fla.)	†12
	McNeese St.	‡11		Washington	†11	2002	Miami (Fla.)	‡12
	Ohio St.	‡11	1992	Alabama	†12		Ohio St.	†13
				Miami (Fla.)	‡11			

The Spoilers

(From 1937 Season)

Following is a list of the spoilers of major-college teams that lost their perfect (undefeated, untied) record in their **final** game of the season, including a bowl game (in parentheses). Confrontations of two undefeated, untied teams at the time are in bold face. An asterisk (*) indicates the home team in a regular-season game, a dagger (†) indicates a neutral site.

Date	Spoiler	Victim	Score
1-1-38	California	Alabama (Rose)	13-0
1-1-38	Rice	Colorado (Cotton)	28-14
12-3-38	*Southern California	Notre Dame	13-0
1-2-39	Southern California	Duke (Rose)	7-3
1-2-39	**Tennessee**	**Oklahoma (Orange)**	17-0
1-2-39	St. Mary's (Cal.)	Texas Tech (Cotton)	20-13
12-2-39	*Duquesne	Detroit	tie 10-10
1-1-40	Southern California	Tennessee (Rose)	14-0
1-1-41	**Boston College**	**Tennessee (Sugar)**	19-13
1-1-42	Oregon St.	Duke (Rose)	20-16
11-27-43	*Great Lakes	Notre Dame	19-14
1-1-44	Southern California	Washington (Rose)	29-0
11-25-44	*Virginia	Yale	tie 6-6
1-1-47	Illinois	UCLA (Rose)	45-14
1-1-48	Southern Methodist	Penn St. (Cotton)	tie 13-13
11-27-48	†Navy	Army	tie 21-21
12-2-48	*Southern California	Notre Dame	tie 14-14
1-1-49	Northwestern	California (Rose)	20-14
1-2-50	Ohio St.	California (Rose)	17-14
12-2-50	†Navy	Army	14-2
1-1-51	Kentucky	Oklahoma (Sugar)	13-7
1-1-52	**Maryland**	**Tennessee (Sugar)**	28-13
11-22-52	Southern California	*UCLA	14-12
1-1-54	Oklahoma	Maryland (Orange)	7-0
1-2-56	**Oklahoma**	**Maryland (Orange)**	20-6
1-1-57	Baylor	Tennessee (Sugar)	13-7
11-28-64	*Southern California	Notre Dame	20-17
1-1-65	Texas	Alabama (Orange)	21-17
11-20-65	Dartmouth	*Princeton	28-14
1-1-66	UCLA	Michigan St. (Rose)	14-12
1-1-66	Alabama	Nebraska (Orange)	39-28
1-1-66	LSU	Arkansas (Cotton)	14-7
11-19-66	**Notre Dame**	*Michigan St.	tie 10-10
1-1-68	LSU	Wyoming (Sugar)	20-13
11-23-68	*Harvard	Yale	tie 29-29
12-27-68	Richmond	Ohio (Tangerine)	49-42
11-22-69	*Michigan	Ohio St.	24-12
11-22-69	*Princeton	Dartmouth	35-7
11-21-70	*Ohio St.	Michigan	20-9
1-1-71	Stanford	Ohio St. (Rose)	27-17
1-1-71	Notre Dame	Texas (Cotton)	24-11
1-1-72	Stanford	Michigan (Rose)	13-12
1-1-72	**Nebraska**	**Alabama (Orange)**	38-6
11-25-72	*Ohio St.	Michigan	14-11
11-24-73	**Ohio St.**	*Michigan	tie 10-10
12-31-73	**Notre Dame**	**Alabama (Sugar)**	24-23
11-23-74	*Ohio St.	Michigan	12-10
11-23-74	*Harvard	Yale	21-16
1-1-75	Notre Dame	Alabama (Orange)	13-11
1-1-76	UCLA	Ohio St. (Rose)	23-10
1-1-77	Houston	Maryland (Cotton)	30-21

Date	Spoiler	Victim	Score
11-19-77	*Delaware	Colgate	21-3
11-2-78	Notre Dame	Texas (Cotton)	38-10
1-1-79	Alabama	Penn St. (Sugar)	14-7
11-17-79	Harvard	*Yale	22-7
12-15-79	Syracuse	McNeese St. (Independence)	31-7
12-21-79	Indiana	Brigham Young (Holiday)	38-37
1-1-80	Southern California	Ohio St. (Rose)	17-16
1-1-80	Oklahoma	Florida St. (Orange)	24-7
1-1-83	Penn St.	Georgia (Sugar)	27-23
1-2-84	Georgia	Texas (Cotton)	10-9
1-2-84	Miami (Fla.)	Nebraska (Orange)	31-30
12-14-85	Fresno St.	Bowling Green (California)	51-7
1-1-86	Oklahoma	Penn St. (Orange)	25-10
1-2-87	**Penn St.**	**Miami (Fla.) (Fiesta)**	14-10
1-1-88	Auburn	Syracuse (Sugar)	tie 16-16
1-1-88	**Miami (Fla.)**	**Oklahoma (Orange)**	20-14
1-2-89	**Notre Dame**	**West Virginia (Fiesta)**	34-21
1-1-90	Notre Dame	Colorado (Orange)	21-6
1-1-93	Notre Dame	Texas A&M (Cotton)	28-3
1-1-93	**Alabama**	**Miami (Fla.) (Sugar)**	34-13
1-1-94	Florida St.	Nebraska (Orange)	18-16
1-1-94	Florida	West Virginia (Sugar)	41-7
1-2-96	**Nebraska**	**Florida (Fiesta)**	62-24
1-1-97	Ohio St.	Arizona St. (Rose)	20-17
1-2-97	Florida	Florida St. (Sugar)	52-20
1-4-00	Florida St.	Virginia Tech (Sugar)	46-29
1-3-03	**Ohio St.**	**Miami (Fla.) (Fiesta)**	31-24 (2 ot)

Streaks and Rivalries

Longest Winning Streaks

(Includes Bowl Games)

Wins	Team	Years	Ended by	Score
47	Oklahoma	1953-57	Notre Dame	7-0
39	Washington	1908-14	Oregon St.	0-0
37	Yale	1890-93	Princeton	6-0
37	Yale	1887-89	Princeton	10-0
35	Toledo	1969-71	Tampa	21-0
34	Miami (Fla.)	2000-03	Ohio St.	*31-24 (2ot)
34	Pennsylvania	1894-96	Lafayette	6-4
31	Oklahoma	1948-50	Kentucky	*13-7
31	Pittsburgh	1914-18	Cleveland Naval Reserve	10-9
31	Pennsylvania	1896-98	Harvard	10-0
30	Texas	1968-70	Notre Dame	*24-11
29	Miami (Fla.)	1990-93	Alabama	*34-13
29	Michigan	1901-03	Minnesota	6-6
28	Alabama	1991-93	Tennessee	17-17
28	Alabama	1978-80	Mississippi St.	6-3
28	Oklahoma	1973-75	Kansas	23-3
28	Michigan St.	1950-53	Purdue	6-0
26	Nebraska	1994-96	Arizona St.	19-0
26	Cornell	1921-24	Williams	14-7
26	Michigan	1903-05	Chicago	2-0

Wins	Team	Years	Ended by	Score
25	Brigham Young	1983-85	UCLA	27-24
25	San Diego St.	1965-67	Utah St.	31-25
25	Michigan	1946-49	Army	21-7
25	Army	1944-46	Notre Dame	0-0
25	Southern California	1931-33	Oregon St.	0-0
24	Princeton	1949-52	Pennsylvania	13-7
24	Minnesota	1903-05	Wisconsin	16-12
24	Nebraska	1901-04	Colorado	6-0
24	Yale	1894-95	Boston AC	0-0
24	Harvard	1890-91	Yale	10-0
24	Yale	1882-84	Princeton	0-0
23	Alabama	1991-92	#	
23	Notre Dame	1988-89	Miami (Fla.)	27-10
23	Nebraska	1970-71	UCLA	20-17
23	Penn St.	1968-70	Colorado	41-13
23	Tennessee	1937-39	Southern California	*14-0
23	Harvard	1901-02	Yale	23-0
22	Washington	1990-92	Arizona	16-3
22	Nebraska	1982-83	Miami (Fla.)	*31-30
22	Ohio St.	1967-69	Michigan	24-12
22	Arkansas	1963-65	LSU	*14-7
22	Harvard	1912-14	Penn St.	13-13
22	Yale	1904-06	Princeton	0-0
21	Arizona St.	1969-71	Oregon St.	24-18
21	San Diego St.	1968-70	Long Beach St.	27-11
21	Notre Dame	1946-48	Southern California	14-14
21	Minnesota	1933-36	Northwestern	6-0
21	Colorado	1908-12	Colorado St.	21-0
21	Pennsylvania	1903-05	Lafayette	6-6
21	Yale	1900-01	Army	5-5
21	Harvard	1898-99	Yale	0-0
20	UCLA	1997-98	Miami (Fla.)	49-45
20	Penn St.	1993-95	Wisconsin	17-9
20	Auburn	1993-94	Georgia	23-23
20	Oklahoma	1986-87	Miami (Fla.)	*20-14
20	Tennessee	1950-51	Maryland	*28-13
20	Texas A&M	1938-40	Texas	7-0
20	Notre Dame	1929-31	Northwestern	0-0
20	Alabama	1924-26	Stanford	*7-7
20	Iowa	1920-23	Illinois	9-6
20	Notre Dame	1919-21	Iowa	10-7

*Streak ended in bowl game. #Eight victories and one tie in 1993 forfeited by action of the NCAA Committee on Infractions.

No.	Wins	Ties	Team	Years	Ended by	Score
28	28	0	Alabama	1978-80	Mississippi St.	6-3
28	28	0	Michigan St.	1950-53	Purdue	6-0
28	26	2	Southern California	1978-80	Washington	20-10
28	26	2	Army	1947-50	Navy	14-2
28	26	2	Tennessee	1930-33	Duke	10-2
28	24	4	Minnesota	1933-36	Northwestern	6-0
27	26	1	Southern California	1931-33	Stanford	13-7
27	24	3	Notre Dame	1910-14	Yale	28-0

Longest Home Winning Streaks

(Includes Bowl Games)

Wins	Team	Years	Ended by	Score
58	Miami (Fla.)	1985-94	Washington	38-20
57	Alabama	1963-82	Southern Miss.	38-29
56	Harvard	1890-95	Boston AA	0-0
50	Michigan	1901-07	Pennsylvania	6-0
47	Nebraska	1991-98	Texas	20-16
44	Washington	1908-17	Oregon St.	0-0
42	Texas	1968-76	Houston	30-0
40	Notre Dame	1907-18	Great Lakes	7-7
38	Notre Dame	1919-27	Minnesota	7-7
37	Yale	1904-08	Brown	10-10
37	Yale	1900-03	Princeton	11-6
37	Florida St.	1992-01	Miami (Fla.)	49-27
33	Nebraska	1901-06	Iowa St.	14-2
33	Harvard	1900-03	Amherst	5-0
33	Marshall	1995-00	Western Mich.	30-10
31	Texas A&M	1990-95	Texas	16-6
31	Yale	1890-93	Princeton	6-0
30	Florida	1994-99	Alabama	40-39 (ot)
30	Auburn	1952-61	Kentucky	14-12
30	Tennessee	1928-33	Alabama	12-6
29	Yale	1885-89	Princeton	10-0
28	Michigan	1969-73	Ohio St.	0-0
28	Notre Dame	1942-50	Purdue	28-14
27	Vanderbilt	1903-07	Michigan	8-0
26	Nebraska	1998-02	Texas	27-24
26	Utah	1928-34	Oregon	8-7
26	California	1919-23	Nevada	0-0
25	Ohio St.	1972-76	Missouri	22-21
25	Oklahoma	1947-53	Notre Dame	28-21
25	Wisconsin	1900-03	Chicago	15-6
24	Georgia	1980-83	Auburn	13-7
24	Georgia Tech	1916-19	Wash. & Lee	3-0
24	Virginia	1899-04	Navy	5-0
23	Kansas St.	1996-01	Colorado	16-6
23	Florida	1990-93	Florida St.	33-21
23	Nebraska	1969-72	Oklahoma	17-14
23	Tulane	1929-32	Vanderbilt	6-6
23	Michigan St.	1904-08	Michigan	0-0
23	Michigan	1897-00	Ohio St.	0-0
23	Harvard	1887-89	Princeton	41-15
22	Tennessee	1996-00	Florida	27-23
22	Wyoming	1965-70	Air Force	41-17
22	Navy	1953-64	Syracuse	14-6
22	Minnesota	1933-37	Notre Dame	7-6
22	LSU	1907-12	Mississippi	10-7
22	Notre Dame	1901-05	Wabash	5-0
21	Nebraska	1981-84	Oklahoma	17-7
21	Arizona St.	1969-71	Air Force	39-31
21	Mississippi	1952-60	LSU	6-6
21	Oklahoma	1953-57	Notre Dame	7-0
21	Miami (Ohio)	1942-48	Xavier (Ohio)	27-19
21	North Carolina	1893-00	Virginia Tech	0-0
20	Fresno St.	1987-90	Utah St.	24-24
20	Rutgers	1974-78	Colgate	14-9
20	Nebraska	1963-67	Colorado	21-16
20	Mississippi St.	1939-45	Mississippi	7-6
20	Missouri	1938-43	Oklahoma	20-13
20	Southern California	1927-29	California	15-7
20	Southern California	1919-23	California	13-7
20	Iowa	1918-23	Illinois	9-6
20	Harvard	1912-14	Penn St.	13-13

Longest Unbeaten Streaks

(Includes Bowl Games; May Include Ties)

No.	Wins	Ties	Team	Years	Ended by	Score
63	59	4	Washington	1907-17	California	27-0
56	55	1	Michigan	1901-05	Chicago	2-0
50	46	4	California	1920-25	Olympic Club	15-0
48	47	1	Oklahoma	1953-57	Notre Dame	7-0
48	47	1	Yale	1885-89	Princeton	10-0
47	42	5	Yale	1879-85	Princeton	6-5
44	42	2	Yale	1894-96	Princeton	24-6
42	39	3	Yale	1904-08	Harvard	4-0
39	37	2	Notre Dame	1946-50	Purdue	28-14
37	37	0	Yale	1890-93	Princeton	6-0
37	36	1	Oklahoma	1972-75	Kansas	23-3
35	35	0	Toledo	1969-71	Tampa	21-0
35	34	1	Minnesota	1903-05	Wisconsin	16-12
34	34	0	Miami (Fla.)	2000-03	Ohio St.	31-24 (2ot)
34	34	0	Pennsylvania	1894-96	Lafayette	6-4
34	33	1	Nebraska	1912-16	Kansas	7-3
34	32	2	Princeton	1884-87	Harvard	12-0
34	29	5	Princeton	1877-82	Harvard	1-0
33	31	2	Georgia Tech	1914-18	Pittsburgh	32-0
33	30	3	Tennessee	1926-30	Alabama	18-6
33	30	3	Harvard	1911-15	Cornell	10-0
32	31	1	Nebraska	1969-71	UCLA	20-17
32	31	1	Harvard	1898-00	Yale	28-0
32	30	2	Army	1944-47	Columbia	21-20
31	31	0	Oklahoma	1948-50	Kentucky	13-7
31	31	0	Pittsburgh	1914-18	Cleveland Naval	10-9
31	31	0	Pennsylvania	1896-98	Harvard	10-0
31	30	1	Penn St.	1967-70	Colorado	41-13
31	30	1	San Diego St.	1967-70	Long Beach St.	27-11
31	29	2	Georgia Tech	1950-53	Notre Dame	27-14
30	30	0	Texas	1968-70	Notre Dame	24-11
30	28	2	Pennsylvania	1903-06	Swarthmore	4-0
30	25	5	Penn St.	1919-22	Navy	14-0
29	29	0	Miami (Fla.)	1990-93	Alabama	34-13

Longest Losing Streaks

Losses	Team	Years	Ended with	Score
34	Northwestern	1979-82	Northern Ill.	31-6
28	Virginia	1958-61	William & Mary	21-6
28	Kansas St.	1945-48	Arkansas St.	37-6
27	New Mexico St.	1988-90	Cal St. Fullerton	43-9
27	Eastern Mich.	1980-82	Kent St.	9-7

Losses	Team	Years	Ended with	Score
26	Colorado St.	1960-63	Pacific (Cal.)	20-0
23	Duke	1999-02	East Caro.	23-16
23	Northern Ill.	1996-98	Central Mich.	16-6
21	Ball St.	1998-00	Miami (Ohio)	15-10
21	South Carolina	1998-00	New Mexico St.	31-0
21	Kent St.	1981-83	Eastern Mich.	37-13
21	New Mexico	1967-69	Kansas	16-7
20	TCU	1974-75	Rice	28-21
20	Florida St.	1972-74	Miami (Fla.)	21-14
19	Hawaii	1997-99	Eastern Ill.	31-27
18	Illinois	1996-98	Middle Tenn.	48-20
18	Rice	1987-89	Southern Methodist	35-6
18	Wisconsin	1967-69	Iowa	23-17
18	Wake Forest	1962-63	South Carolina	20-19
18	Kansas St.	1961-62	Brigham Young	24-7
17	Tulsa	2000-02	UTEP	20-0
17	Kent St.	1992-94	Akron	32-16
17	Kent St.	1989-90	Ohio	44-15
17	Memphis	1981-82	Arkansas St.	12-0
17	Kansas St.	1964-66	Kansas	3-3
17	Tulane	1961-63	South Carolina	20-7
17	Alabama	1954-56	Mississippi St.	13-12
17	Kansas	1953-55	Washington St.	13-0
16	UNLV	1997-98	North Texas	26-3
16	Kansas St.	1987-89	North Texas	20-17
16	Indiana	1983-85	Louisville	41-28
16	Vanderbilt	1961-62	Tulane	20-0
16	Iowa St.	1929-30	Simpson	6-0

Most Consecutive Non-Losing Seasons

(All-Time and Current) (.500 percentage and above)

No.	School	Years
49	Penn St.	1939-87
42	Notre Dame	1889-32#
41	Nebraska	1962-02*
40	Texas	1893-32
38	Alabama	1911-50†
35	Michigan	1968-02*
29	Oklahoma	1966-94
29	Texas	1957-85
29	Boston College	1916-44
28	Virginia	1888-15
27	Brigham Young	1974-01
27	Michigan	1892-18
26	Florida St.	1977-02*
26	Washington	1977-02*
26	Virginia Tech	1894-19
23	Florida	1980-02*
23	Syracuse	1913-35
23	Ohio St.	1899-21
21	Ohio St.	1967-87
21	Southern California	1962-82
21	Wyoming	1949-69
21	Northern Ill.	1929-49
21	Vanderbilt	1915-35
20	Texas A&M	1983-02*
19	Marshall	1984-02*
19	Wisconsin	1891-09
18	Ohio St.	1925-42
18	Nebraska	1920-37
17	Miami (Fla.)	1980-96
17	San Diego St.	1961-77
17	Miami (Ohio)	1943-59
17	Tennessee	1936-53¢
16	LSU	1958-73
16	Texas A&M	1914-29
16	Purdue	1889-05
15	Syracuse	1987-01
15	Miami (Ohio)	1961-75
15	Bowling Green	1955-69
15	Texas	1939-53
15	Utah	1928-42
15	Southern California	1919-33
15	Georgia Tech	1908-22
14	Tennessee	1989-02*
14	Virginia	1987-00
14	Purdue	1926-39
14	Kentucky	1903-16
14	Virginia Tech	1901-14
13	Arkansas	1977-89
13	Central Mich.	1973-85
13	Georgia	1964-76

No.	School	Years
13	Missouri	1957-69
13	Purdue	1957-69
13	Wyoming	1949-61
13	Navy	1889-01
12	Notre Dame	1987-98
12	Colorado	1985-96
12	Georgia	1978-89
12	Tennessee	1965-76
12	Auburn	1953-64
12	Colorado	1950-61
12	Western Mich.	1941-52
12	Ohio St.	1928-39
12	Tulane	1928-39
12	TCU	1925-36
12	West Virginia	1914-26@

*Current streak. #No teams in 1890 and 1891. †No teams in 1918 and 1943. @No team in 1918. ¢No team in 1943.

Most-Played Rivalries

(Ongoing Unless Indicated)

Games	Opponents (Series leader listed first)	Rivalry Record	First Game
112	Minnesota-Wisconsin	58-46-8	1890
111	Missouri-Kansas	52-50-9	1891
109	Nebraska-Kansas	85-21-3	1892
109	Texas-Texas A&M	70-34-5	1894
107	Miami (Ohio)-Cincinnati	57-43-7	1888
107	North Carolina-Virginia	*56-47-4	1892
106	Auburn-Georgia	51-47-8	1892
106	Oregon-Oregon St.	53-43-10	1894
105	Purdue-Indiana	64-35-6	1891
105	Stanford-California	54-40-11	1892
103	Army-Navy	49-47-7	1890
103	%Baylor-TCU	49-47-7	1899
102	Utah-Utah St.	70-28-4	1892
100	Clemson-South Carolina	60-36-4	1896
100	Kansas-Kansas St.	61-34-5	1902
99	North Carolina-Wake Forest	65-31-2	1888
99	Mississippi-Mississippi St.	56-37-6	1901
98	Tennessee-Kentucky	66-23-9	1893
98	Michigan-Ohio St.	56-37-6	1897
97	Georgia-Georgia Tech	54-38-5	1893
97	Nebraska-Iowa St.	80-15-2	1896
97	Texas-Oklahoma	55-37-5	1900
97	^Oklahoma-Kansas	63-28-6	1903
97	Oklahoma-Oklahoma St.	74-16-7	1904
96	Illinois-Northwestern	51-40-5	1892
96	Nebraska-Missouri	61-32-3	1892
96	Tennessee-Vanderbilt	65-26-5	1892
96	&Penn St.-Pittsburgh	50-42-4	1893
96	North Carolina St.-Wake Forest	59-31-6	1895
96	@Washington-Oregon	57-33-5	1900
95	Pittsburgh-West Virginia	58-34-3	1895
95	Michigan-Michigan St.	62-28-5	1898
95	Washington-Washington St.	*62-27-6	1900
94	LSU-Tulane	*65-22-7	1893
93	New Mexico-New Mexico St.	60-28-5	1894
90	#Auburn-Georgia Tech	47-39-4	1892
90	&Connecticut-Rhode Island	48-34-8	1897

*Disputed series record: Tulane claims 23-61-7 record; LSU and Tulane have not met since 1996. Virginia claims North Carolina leads the series 54-64-4, based on a forfeited game in 1956. #Have not met since 1989. %Have not met since 1995. @Did not meet in 2001. &Have not met since 2000. ^Did not meet in 2002.

Additional Records

Longest Uninterrupted Series (Must have played every year)

97 games—Kansas-Nebraska (from 1906)
96 games—Kansas-Oklahoma (1903-97)
96 games—Minnesota-Wisconsin (from 1907)
94 games—Clemson-South Carolina (from 1909)
93 games—Wake Forest-North Carolina St. (from 1910)
92 games—Kansas-Kansas St. (from 1911)
91 games—North Carolina-Virginia (from 1910)*
89 games—Illinois-Ohio St. (from 1914)
88 games—Texas-Texas A&M (from 1915)
87 games—Mississippi-Mississippi St. (from 1915)**
85 games—Michigan-Ohio St. (from 1918)
84 games—Kansas-Missouri (from 1919)
84 games—Missouri-Iowa St. (from 1919)
83 games—Indiana-Purdue (from 1920)
83 games—Tennessee-Kentucky (from 1919)**

83 games—Auburn-Georgia (from 1919)**
81 games—Missouri-Nebraska (from 1922)
81 games—Nebraska-Kansas St. (from 1922)
81 games—North Carolina-Duke (from 1922)
78 games—Georgia-Georgia Tech (from 1925)

77 games—Nebraska-Iowa St. (from 1926)
77 games—Missouri-Oklahoma (1919-95)
77 games—Tulane-LSU (1919-94)
76 games—Southern Methodist-Texas A&M (1920-95)
76 games—Navy-Notre Dame (from 1927)

74 games—Michigan-Illinois (1924-97)
73 games—Rice-TCU (1928-00)
72 games—Southern Methodist-Texas (1924-95)

*Neither school fielded a team in 1917-18 due to World War I. **Neither school fielded a team in 1943 due to World War II.*

Most Consecutive Wins Over a Major Opponent in an Uninterrupted Series (Must have played in consecutive years)
39—Notre Dame over Navy, 1964-02 (current)
34—Nebraska over Kansas, 1969-02 (current)
32—Oklahoma over Kansas St., 1937-68
29—Nebraska over Kansas St., 1969-97
28—Texas over Rice, 1966-93

26—Syracuse over Hobart, 1906-31
25—Penn St. over West Virginia, 1959-83
24—Nebraska over Missouri, 1979-02 (current)
22—Nebraska over Oklahoma St. 1974-95
22—Arkansas over TCU, 1959-80

22—Alabama over Mississippi St., 1958-79
20—Tennessee over Vanderbilt, 1983-02 (current)
20—Purdue over Iowa, 1961-80
18—Tennessee over Kentucky, 1985-02 (current)
18—UCLA over California, 1972-89

17—Virginia over Wake Forest, 1984-00
17—New Mexico over UTEP, 1970-86

17—Arizona St. over UTEP, 1957-73
17—LSU over Tulane, 1956-72
16—Michigan over Illinois, 1967-82
16—North Carolina over Wake Forest, 1908-23
15—Iowa over Iowa St., 1983-97
15—Southern Methodist over TCU, 1972-86

Most Consecutive Wins Over a Major Opponent in a Nonconsecutive Series (Did not play in consecutive years)
29—Clemson over Virginia, 1955-90 (over 36-year period)
26—Southern California over Oregon St., 1968-99 (32-year period)
24—Nebraska over Oklahoma St., 1974-99 (26-year period)
21—Ohio St. over Northwestern, 1972-98 (27-year period)
19—Washington over California, 1977-01 (25-year period)

19—Michigan over Northwestern, 1966-92 (27-year period)
19—Vanderbilt over Mississippi, 1894-38 (45-year period)
17—Tulsa over Drake, 1939-85 (47-year period)
17—Mississippi over Memphis, 1921-62 (42-year period)
17—North Carolina over Wake Forest, 1893-23 (29-year period)

Most Consecutive Wins Over a Major Opponent in a Series (Must have played every year)
39—Notre Dame over Navy, 1964-02 (66-9-1 in rivalry)
34—Nebraska over Kansas, 1969-02 (85-21-3 in rivalry)
24—Nebraska over Missouri, 1979-02 (61-32-3 in rivalry)
20—Tennessee over Vanderbilt, 1983-02 (65-26-5 in rivalry)
18—Tennessee over Kentucky, 1985-02 (66-23-9 in rivalry)

17—Virginia over Wake Forest, 1984-00 (28-11-0 in rivalry)
16—Colorado over Iowa St., 1984-99 (42-11-1 in rivalry)
14—Iowa over Iowa St., 1983-96 (32-12-0 in rivalry)
13—Florida over Kentucky, 1987-99 (33-17-0 in rivalry)
13—San Diego St. over New Mexico, 1984-96 (18-5-0 in rivalry)

Most Consecutive Games Without a Loss Against a Major Opponent
39—Notre Dame over Navy, 1964-02 (0 ties) (current)
34—Nebraska over Kansas, 1969-02 (current)
34—Oklahoma over Kansas St., 1935-68 (1 tie)

Cliffhangers

Regular-season Division I-A games won on the final play (since 1971, when first recorded). The extra point is listed when it provided the margin of victory after the winning touchdown on the game's final play. Overtime games are not included but follow Cliffhangers.

Date	Opponents, Score	Game-Winning Play
9-25-71	Marshall 15, Xavier (Ohio) 13	Terry Gardner 13 pass from Reggie Oliver
10-9-71	California 30, Oregon St. 27	Steve Sweeney 7 pass from Jay Cruze
10-23-71	Washington St. 24, Stanford 23	Don Sweet 27 FG
11-6-71	Kentucky 14, Vanderbilt 7	Darryl Bishop 43 interception return
11-4-72	LSU 17, Mississippi 16	Brad Davis 10 pass from Bert Jones (Rusty Jackson kick)
11-18-72	California 24, Stanford 21	Steve Sweeney 7 pass from Vince Ferragamo
9-15-73	Lamar 21, Howard Payne 17	Larry Spears 14 pass from Jabo Leonard
9-22-73	Hawaii 13, Fresno St. 10	Reinhold Stuprich 29 FG
11-17-73	New Mexico 23, Wyoming 21	Bob Berg 43 FG
11-23-74	Stanford 22, California 20	Mike Langford 50 FG
9-20-75	Indiana St. 23, Southern Ill. 21	Dave Vandercook 50 FG
10-18-75	Cal St. Fullerton 32, UC Riverside 31	John Choukair 52 FG
11-1-75	Yale 16, Dartmouth 14	Randy Carter 46 FG
11-8-75	West Virginia 17, Pittsburgh 14	Bill McKenzie 38 FG
11-8-75	Stanford 13, Southern California 10	Mike Langford 37 FG
11-15-75	North Carolina 17, Tulane 15	Tom Biddle 40 FG
11-6-76	Eastern Mich. 30, Central Mich. 27	Ken Dudal 38 FG
9-30-78	Virginia Tech 22, William & Mary 19	Ron Zollicoffer 50 pass from David Lamie
10-21-78	Arkansas St. 6, McNeese St. 3	Doug Dobbs 42 FG
11-9-78	San Jose St. 33, Pacific (Cal.) 31	Rick Parma 5 pass from Ed Luther
10-6-79	Stanford 27, UCLA 24	Ken Naber 56 FG
10-20-79	UNLV 43, Utah 41	Todd Peterson 49 FG
10-27-79	Michigan 27, Indiana 21	Anthony Carter 45 pass from John Wangler
11-10-79	Penn St. 9, North Carolina St. 7	Herb Menhardt 54 FG
11-17-79	Air Force 30, Vanderbilt 29	Andy Bark 14 pass from Dave Ziebart
11-24-79	Arizona 27, Arizona St. 24	Brett Weber 27 FG
9-13-80	Southern California 20, Tennessee 17	Eric Hipp 47 FG
9-13-80	Illinois 20, Michigan St. 17	Mike Bass 38 FG
9-20-80	Notre Dame 29, Michigan 27	Harry Oliver 51 FG
9-27-80	Tulane 26, Mississippi 24	Vince Manalla 29 FG
10-18-80	Connecticut 18, Holy Cross 17	Ken Miller 4 pass from Ken Sweitzer (Keith Hugger pass from Sweitzer)
10-18-80	Washington 27, Stanford 24	Chuck Nelson 25 FG
11-1-80	Tulane 24, Kentucky 22	Vince Manalla 22 FG
11-15-80	Florida 17, Kentucky 15	Brian Clark 34 FG

Date	Opponents, Score	Game-Winning Play
10-16-82	Arizona 16, Notre Dame 13	Max Zendejas 48 FG
10-23-82	Illinois 29, Wisconsin 28	Mike Bass 46 FG
11-20-82	California 25, Stanford 20	57 (5 laterals) kickoff return involving, in order: Kevin Moen, Richard Rodgers, Dwight Garner, Rodgers, Mariet Ford and Moen
10-8-83	Iowa St. 38, Kansas 35	Marc Bachrodt 47 FG
10-29-83	Bowling Green 15, Central Mich. 14	Stan Hunter 8 pass from Brian McClure
11-5-83	Baylor 24, Arkansas 21	Marty Jimmerson 24 FG
11-12-83	Pacific (Cal.) 30, San Jose St. 26	Ron Woods 85 pass from Mike Pitz
11-12-83	Miami (Fla.) 17, Florida St. 16	Jeff Davis 19 FG
11-26-83	Arizona 17, Arizona St. 15	Max Zendejas 45 FG
9-8-84	La.-Lafayette 17, Louisiana Tech 16	Patrick Broussard 21 FG
9-15-84	Syracuse 13, Northwestern 12	Jim Tait 2 pass from Todd Norley (Don McAulay kick)
10-13-84	UCLA 27, Washington St. 24	John Lee 47 FG
11-17-84	La.-Lafayette 18, Tulsa 17	Patrick Broussard 45 FG
11-17-84	Temple 19, West Virginia 17	Jim Cooper 36 FG
11-23-84	Boston College 47, Miami (Fla.) 45	Gerard Phelan 48 pass from Doug Flutie
9-14-85	Clemson 20, Virginia Tech 17	David Treadwell 36 FG
9-14-85	Oregon St. 23, California 20	Jim Nielsen 20 FG
9-14-85	Utah 29, Hawaii 27	Andre Guardi 19 FG
9-21-85	New Mexico St. 22, UTEP 20	Andy Weiler 32 FG
10-5-85	Mississippi St. 31, Memphis 28	Artie Cosby 54 FG
10-5-85	Illinois 31, Ohio St. 28	Chris White 38 FG
10-12-85	Tulsa 37, Long Beach St. 35	Jason Staurovsky 46 FG
10-19-85	Northwestern 17, Wisconsin 14	John Duvic 42 FG
10-19-85	Iowa 12, Michigan 10	Rob Houghtlin 29 FG
10-19-85	Utah 39, San Diego St. 37	Andre Guardi 42 FG
11-30-85	Alabama 25, Auburn 23	Van Tiffin 52 FG
9-13-86	Oregon 32, Colorado 30	Matt MacLeod 35 FG
9-13-86	Wyoming 23, Pacific (Cal.) 20	Greg Worker 38 FG
9-20-86	Clemson 31, Georgia 28	David Treadwell 46 FG
9-20-86	Southern California 17, Baylor 14	Don Shafer 32 FG
10-18-86	Michigan 20, Iowa 17	Mike Gillette 34 FG
10-25-86	Syracuse 27, Temple 24	Tim Vesling 32 FG
11-1-86	North Carolina St. 23, South Carolina 22	Danny Peebles 33 pass from Erik Kramer
11-1-86	North Carolina 32, Maryland 30	Lee Gliarmis 28 FG
11-8-86	Southern Miss. 23, East Caro. 21	Rex Banks 31 FG
11-15-86	Minnesota 20, Michigan 17	Chip Lohmiller 30 FG
11-29-86	Notre Dame 38, Southern California 37	John Carney 19 FG
9-12-87	Youngstown St. 20, Bowling Green 17	John Dowling 36 FG
9-19-87	Utah 31, Wisconsin 28	Scott Lieber 39 FG
10-10-87	Marshall 34, Louisville 31	Keith Baxter 31 pass from Tony Petersen
10-17-87	Texas 16, Arkansas 14	Tony Jones 18 pass from Bret Stafford
11-12-88	New Mexico 24, Colorado St. 23	Tony Jones 28 pass from Jeremy Leach
9-16-89	Southern Methodist 31, Connecticut 30	Mike Bowen 4 pass from Mike Romo
9-30-89	Kansas St. 20, North Texas 17	Frank Hernandez 12 pass from Carl Straw
10-7-89	Florida 16, LSU 13	Arden Czyzewski 41 FG
10-14-89	Southern Miss. 16, Louisville 10	Darryl Tillman 79 pass from Brett Favre
10-28-89	Virginia 16, Louisville 15	Jake McInerney 37 FG
11-4-89	Toledo 19, Western Mich. 18	Romauldo Brown 9 pass from Kevin Meger
11-4-89	Northern Ill. 23, La.-Lafayette 20	Stacey Robinson 7 run
9-8-90	Utah 35, Minnesota 29	Lavon Edwards 91 run of blocked FG
9-29-90	North Carolina St. 12, North Carolina 9	Damon Hartman 56 FG
10-6-90	Colorado 33, Missouri 31	Charles S. Johnson 1 run
10-20-90	Alabama 9, Tennessee 6	Philip Doyle 47 FG
11-3-90	Southern Miss. 14, La.-Lafayette 13	Michael Welch 11 pass from Brett Favre (Jim Taylor kick)
11-10-90	Ohio St. 27, Iowa 26	Bobby Olive 3 pass from Greg Frey
11-17-90	Stanford 27, California 25	John Hopkins 39 FG
11-24-90	Michigan 16, Ohio St. 13	J. D. Carlson 37 FG
9-7-91	Central Mich. 27, La.-Lafayette 24	L. J. Muddy 2 pass from Jeff Bender
9-21-91	California 23, Arizona 21	Doug Brien 33 FG
9-21-91	Georgia Tech 24, Virginia 21	Scott Sisson 33 FG
9-21-91	Louisiana Tech 17, Eastern Mich. 14	Chris Bonoil 54 FG
10-12-91	Ball St. 10, Eastern Mich. 8	Kenny Stucker 41 FG
11-2-91	Kentucky 20, Cincinnati 17	Doug Pelphrey 53 FG
11-2-91	Tulsa 13, Southern Miss. 10	Eric Lange 24 FG
9-5-92	Louisiana Tech 10, Baylor 9	Chris Bonoil 30 FG
9-19-92	Miami (Ohio) 17, Cincinnati 14	Chad Seitz 21 FG
9-19-92	Southern Miss. 16, Louisiana Tech 13	Johnny Lomoro 46 FG
10-3-92	Texas A&M 19, Texas Tech 17	Terry Venetoulias 21 FG
10-3-92	Georgia Tech 16, North Carolina St. 13	Scott Sisson 29 FG
10-3-92	San Jose St. 26, Wyoming 24	Joe Nedney 60 FG
10-24-92	Maryland 27, Duke 25	Marcus Badgett 38 pass from John Kaleo
10-31-92	Rutgers 50, Virginia Tech 49	Chris Brantley 15 pass from Bryan Fortay
11-14-92	UCLA 9, Oregon 6	Louis Perez 40 FG
10-2-93	Tulane 27, Navy 25	Bart Baldwin 43 FG
10-9-93	Ball St. 31, Toledo 30	Eric McCray 6 pass from Mike Neu (Matt Swart kick)
10-9-93	North Carolina St. 36, Texas Tech 34	Gary Downs 11 pass from Robert Hinton
10-16-93	Arizona 27, Stanford 24	Steve McLaughlin 27 FG
10-30-93	Missouri 37, Iowa St. 34	Kyle Pooler 40 FG
11-20-93	Maryland 33, Wake Forest 32	Russ Weaver 8 pass from Scott Milanovich (John Milligan kick)
11-20-93	Boston College 41, Notre Dame 39	David Gordon 41 FG
11-20-93	Arkansas St. 23, Nevada 21	Reginald Murphy 30 pass from Johnny Covington
9-10-94	Tulane 15, Rice 13	Bart Baldwin 47 FG
9-10-94	San Diego St. 22, California 20	Peter Holt 32 FG

Date	Opponents, Score	Game-Winning Play
9-24-94	Colorado 27, Michigan 26	Michael Westbrook 64 pass from Kordell Stewart
10-22-94	Central Mich. 32, Miami (Ohio) 30	Terrance McMillan 19 pass from Erik Timpf
10-22-94	Army 25, Citadel 24	Kurt Heiss 24 FG
11-19-94	Eastern Mich. 40, Toledo 37	Ontario Pryor 16 pass from Charlie Batch
9-16-95	Miami (Ohio) 30, Northwestern 28	Chad Seitz 20 FG
8-26-95	Michigan 18, Virginia 17	Mercury Hayes 15 pass from Scott Dreisbach
9-9-95	Kansas St. 23, Cincinnati 21	Kevin Lockett 22 pass from Matt Miller
10-21-95	Texas 17, Virginia 16	Phil Dawson 50 FG
10-28-95	East Caro. 36, Southern Miss. 34	Chad Holcomb 29 FG
8-31-96	Boston College 24, Hawaii 21	John Matich 42 FG
9-7-96	Arizona St. 45, Washington 42	Robert Nycz 38 FG
9-7-96	Air Force 20, Notre Dame 17	Dallas Thompson 27 FG
9-21-96	Notre Dame 27, Texas 24	Jim Sanson 39 FG
9-21-96	Navy 19, Southern Methodist 17	Tom Vanderhorst 38 FG
10-12-96	Louisville 23, Tulane 20	David Akers 39 FG
9-13-97	Toledo 38, Eastern Mich. 35	Chris Merrick 24 FG
9-27-97	Colorado 20, Wyoming 19	Jeremy Aldrich 18 FG
9-5-98	Tennessee 34, Syracuse 33	Jeff Hall 27 FG
9-5-98	Minnesota 17, Arkansas St. 14	Adam Bailey 17 FG
9-19-98	Marshall 24, South Carolina 21	Billy Malashevich 37 FG
9-19-98	Stanford 37, North Carolina 34	Kevin Miller 20 FG
10-17-98	Kentucky 39, LSU 36	Seth Hanson 33 FG
11-14-98	Akron 24, Eastern Mich. 21	Zac Derr 26 FG
11-14-98	Syracuse 28, Virginia Tech 26	Stephen Brominski 13 pass from Donovan McNabb
11-22-98	Toledo 17, Central Mich. 14	Todd France 29 FG
9-11-99	UNLV 27, Baylor 24	Kevin Thomas 100 fumble return
9-25-99	Western Mich. 24, Northern Ill. 21	Brad Selent 37 FG
9-25-99	Arizona 30, Washington St. 24	Bobby Wade 42 pass from Keith Smith
10-30-99	Texas 44, Iowa St. 41	Kris Stockton 18 FG
11-6-99	Minnesota 24, Penn St. 23	Dan Nystrom 32 FG
11-6-99	Virginia Tech 22, West Virginia 20	Shayne Graham 44 FG
11-27-99	Stanford 40, Notre Dame 37	Mike Biselli 22 FG
9-16-00	Notre Dame 23, Purdue 21	Nick Setta 38 FG
9-16-00	Arizona St. 13, Colorado St. 10	Mike Barth 41 FG
10-28-00	Northwestern 41, Minnesota 35	Sam Simmons 45 pass from Zak Kustok
11-24-00	Nebraska 34, Colorado 32	Josh Brown 29 FG
8-30-01	Akron 31, Ohio 29	Zac Derr 38 FG
9-29-01	Northwestern 27, Michigan St. 26	David Wasielewski 47 FG
10-6-01	Washington 27, Southern California 24	John Anderson 32 FG
10-13-01	Miami (Ohio) 30, Akron 27	Eddie Tillitz 70 pass from Ben Roethlisberger
10-27-01	Washington 33, Arizona St. 31	John Anderson 30 FG
11-9-02	LSU 33, Kentucky 30	Devery Henderson 75 pass from Marcus Randall

"CARDIAC SEASONS"

(From 1937; Won-Lost Record in Parentheses)

Games Decided by Two Points or Less
6—Kansas, 1973 (3-2-1): Tennessee 27-28, Nebraska 9-10, Iowa St. 22-20, Oklahoma St. 10-10, Colorado 17-15, Missouri 14-13 (season record: 7-3-1)
5—Illinois, 1992 (2-2-1): Minnesota 17-18, Ohio St. 18-16, Northwestern 26-27, Wisconsin 13-12, Michigan 22-22 (season record: 6-4-1)
5—Columbia, 1971 (4-1-0): Princeton 22-20, Harvard 19-21, Yale 15-14, Rutgers 17-16, Dartmouth 31-29 (season record: 6-3-0)
5—Missouri, 1957 (2-2-1): Vanderbilt 7-7, Southern Methodist 7-6, Nebraska 14-13, Kansas St. 21-23, Kansas 7-9 (season record: 5-4-1)

Games Decided by Three Points or Less
7—Bowling Green, 1980 (2-5-0): Ohio 20-21, Ball St. 24-21, Western Mich. 17-14, Kentucky 20-21, Long Beach St. 21-23, Eastern Mich. 16-18, Richmond 17-20 (season record: 4-7-0)
7—Columbia, 1971 (4-3-0): Lafayette 0-3, Princeton 22-20, Harvard 19-21, Yale 15-14, Rutgers 17-16, Cornell 21-24, Dartmouth 31-29 (season record: 6-3-0)
6—Illinois, 1992 (3-2-1): Minnesota 17-18, Ohio St. 18-16, Northwestern 26-27, Wisconsin 13-12, Purdue 20-17, Michigan 22-22 (season record: 6-4-1)
6—Central Mich., 1991 (2-0-4): Ohio 17-17, La.-Lafayette 27-24, Akron 31-29, Toledo 16-16, Miami (Ohio) 10-10, Eastern Mich. 14-14 (season record: 6-1-4)
6—Kansas, 1973 (3-2-1): Tennessee 27-28, Nebraska 9-10, Iowa St. 22-20, Oklahoma St. 10-10, Colorado 17-15, Missouri 14-13 (season record: 7-3-1)
6—Air Force, 1967 (2-2-2): Oklahoma St. 0-0, California 12-14, North Carolina 10-8, Tulane 13-10, Colorado St. 17-17, Army 7-10 (season record: 2-6-2)
6—Missouri, 1957 (3-2-1): Vanderbilt 7-7, Southern Methodist 7-6, Nebraska 14-13, Colorado 9-6, Kansas St. 21-23, Kansas 7-9 (season record: 5-4-1)

2002 DIVISION I-A OVERTIME GAMES

Date	Winner's Conference	Score (Loser's Conference)	Number of OT Periods	Regulation Score
Aug. 29	Mid-American	Northern Ill. 42, Wake Forest (Atlantic Coast) 41	1OT	35-35
Sept. 2	Conference USA	Cincinnati 36, TCU (Conference USA) 29	1OT	29-29
Sept. 7	Mountain West	Air Force 38, New Mexico (Mountain West) 31	1OT	31-31
Sept. 21	Atlantic Coast	North Carolina St. 51, Texas Tech (Big 12) 48	1OT	45-45
Sept. 26	Conference USA	Louisville 26, Florida St. (Atlantic Coast) 20	1OT	20-20
Sept. 28	Big Ten	Iowa 42, Penn St. (Big Ten) 35	1OT	35-35
Sept. 28	Mid-American	Ball St. 24, Connecticut (Independent) 21	1OT	21-21
Sept. 28	Mid-American	Eastern Mich. 48, Southern Ill. (Division I-AA) 45	2OT	35-35
Sept. 28	Southeastern	Auburn 37, Syracuse (Big East) 34	3OT	24-24
Oct. 5	Southeastern	Tennessee 41, Arkansas (Southeastern) 38	6OT	17-17
Oct. 5	Big 12	Texas Tech 48, Texas A&M (Big 12) 47	1OT	41-41
Oct. 5	Pacific-10	Washington St. 30, Southern Cal. (Pacific-10) 27	1OT	27-27
Oct. 12	Big Ten	Michigan 27, Penn St. (Big Ten) 24	1OT	21-21
Oct. 12	Big Ten	Illinois 38, Purdue (Big Ten) 31	1OT	31-31
Oct. 19	Southeastern	Florida 30, Auburn (Southeastern) 23	1OT	23-23
Oct. 19	Mid-American	Bowling Green 48, Western Mich. (Mid-American) 45	1OT	42-42
Oct. 19	Independent	Utah St. 45, New Mexico (Mountain West) 44	1OT	38-38
Oct. 26	Big East	Pittsburgh 19, Boston College (Big East) 16	1OT	16-16
Oct. 26	Sun Belt	La.-Monroe 51, Utah St. (Independent) 48	2OT	38-38
Oct. 26	Mountain West	New Mexico 42, Utah (Mountain West) 35	2OT	28-28
Nov. 2	Mountain West	UNLV 49, Wyoming (Mountain West) 48	2OT	42-42
Nov. 9	Big East	Syracuse 50, Virginia Tech (Big East) 42	3OT	35-35
Nov. 9	Big 12	Colorado 42, Missouri (Big 12) 35	1OT	35-35
Nov. 9	Conference USA	East Caro. 54, Houston (Conference USA) 48	3OT	34-34
Nov. 14	Conference USA	Louisville 20, Southern Miss. (Conference USA) 17	2OT	17-17
Nov. 16	Independent	Utah St. 19, Troy St. (Independent) 16	1OT	16-16
Nov. 16	Big Ten	Ohio St. 23, Illinois (Big Ten) 16	1OT	16-16
Nov. 16	Big 12	Missouri 33, Texas A&M (Big 12) 27	2OT	24-24
Nov. 23	Pacific-10	Washington 29, Washington St. (Pacific-10) 26	3OT	20-20
Dec. 28	Big Ten	Wisconsin 31, Colorado (Big 12) 28 (Alamo Bowl)	1OT	28-28
Jan. 3	Big Ten	Ohio State 31, Miami (Fla.) (Big East) 24 (Fiesta Bowl)	2OT	17-17

Notes: 31 games (19 with one extra period, 7 with two extra periods, 4 with three extra periods, 1 with six extra periods) – average of 1.65 extra periods

All-Time Division I-A Won-Lost Records in Overtime Games 1996-02

Team	1996	1997	1998	1999	2000	2001	2002	Overall W-L
Air Force	2-0	1-0	—	—	0-1	—	1-0	4-1
Akron	—	—	—	—	—	1-0	—	1-0
Alabama	—	0-1	1-0	1-1	—	—	—	2-2
UAB	—	—	0-1	1-0	0-1	—	—	1-2
Arizona	0-1	1-1	—	—	1-0	—	—	2-2
Arizona St.	1-0	—	1-0	—	1-2	—	—	3-2
Arkansas	1-0	—	—	—	1-0	1-0	0-1	3-1
Arkansas St.	—	—	1-0	0-1	0-2	—	—	1-3
Army	—	—	—	1-0	—	—	—	1-0
Auburn	0-1	—	—	0-1	1-0	1-0	1-1	3-3
Ball St.	1-0	1-0	—	—	—	—	1-0	3-0
Baylor	0-1	—	—	0-1	—	1-0	—	1-2
Boise St.	—	1-0	0-1	—	—	—	—	1-1
Boston College	—	0-1	—	1-0	—	—	0-1	1-2
Bowling Green	0-1	—	—	1-0	—	—	1-0	2-1
Brigham Young	1-0	1-0	—	—	1-0	—	—	3-0
Buffalo	—	—	—	—	1-0	—	—	1-0
California	2-0	0-1	—	—	1-1	—	—	3-2
UCF	—	0-1	—	0-1	—	—	—	0-2
Central Mich.	—	0-1	1-0	—	0-1	—	—	1-2
Cincinnati	1-0	1-1	—	0-1	1-1	—	1-0	4-3
Clemson	—	1-0	—	—	—	1-0	—	2-0
Colorado	—	—	—	1-1	—	—	1-1	2-2
Colorado St.	—	—	—	—	—	0-1	—	0-1
Connecticut	*	*	*	*	*	*	0-1	0-1
Duke	—	0-1	0-1	1-2	—	—	—	1-4
East Caro.	—	—	—	—	—	0-1	1-0	1-1
Eastern Mich.	—	—	0-1	0-1	—	0-1	1-0	1-3
Florida	—	—	0-1	0-1	—	—	1-0	1-2
Florida St.	—	—	—	—	—	—	0-1	0-1
Fresno St.	0-2	0-1	—	2-1	—	1-0	—	3-4
Georgia	1-0	—	—	1-1	0-1	—	—	2-2
Georgia Tech	—	—	—	2-0	0-1	0-2	—	2-3
Hawaii	—	0-1	—	1-0	—	1-0	—	2-1
Houston	2-0	1-0	—	—	1-1	—	0-1	4-2

Team	1996	1997	1998	1999	2000	2001	2002	Overall W-L
Idaho	—	0-1	1-0	1-0	1-0	0-1	—	3-2
Illinois	1-0	—	—	0-1	—	—	1-1	2-2
Indiana	0-1	—	0-1	1-0	—	—	—	1-2
Iowa	—	—	—	—	1-0	—	1-0	2-0
Iowa St.	0-1	—	—	—	—	—	—	0-1
Kansas	—	—	1-0	—	—	1-0	—	2-0
Kansas St.	—	—	0-1	—	—	—	—	0-1
Kent St.	—	—	—	—	1-1	—	—	1-1
Kentucky	—	1-0	—	—	0-1	—	—	1-1
La.-Lafayette	—	0-2	—	—	0-1	—	—	0-3
La.-Monroe	1-0	2-0	—	—	—	—	1-0	4-0
LSU	—	—	0-1	—	2-0	—	—	2-1
Louisiana Tech	—	—	—	—	0-1	1-1	—	1-2
Louisville	—	—	—	0-1	1-0	—	2-0	3-1
Marshall	—	—	—	—	—	1-0	—	1-0
Maryland	—	—	—	1-0	1-0	—	—	2-0
Memphis	—	—	—	0-2	—	—	—	0-2
Miami (Fla.)	—	1-0	0-1	—	—	—	0-1	1-2
Miami (Ohio)	0-1	0-1	—	—	—	—	—	0-2
Michigan	—	—	—	1-0	—	—	1-0	2-0
Michigan St.	—	—	1-0	—	—	—	—	1-0
Middle Tenn.	—	—	—	—	1-0	—	—	1-0
Minnesota	—	—	—	0-1	—	0-1	—	0-2
Mississippi	—	1-0	2-1	1-1	1-0	0-1	—	5-3
Mississippi St.	0-1	—	—	—	1-2	—	—	1-3
Missouri	2-0	1-1	—	0-1	—	1-0	1-1	5-3
Nebraska	—	1-0	—	1-0	1-0	—	—	3-0
Nevada	—	—	—	—	—	0-1	—	0-1
UNLV	—	0-2	0-1	—	0-1	—	1-0	1-4
New Mexico	—	—	1-1	—	—	0-1	1-2	2-4
New Mexico St.	—	0-1	0-2	—	1-1	—	—	1-4
North Carolina	—	—	1-0	0-1	—	—	—	1-1
North Carolina St.	—	1-0	0-1	1-0	2-1	—	1-0	5-2
Northern Ill.	—	—	—	—	—	—	1-0	1-0
Northwestern	—	—	1-0	1-0	—	—	—	2-0
Notre Dame	0-2	—	—	—	1-1	—	—	1-3
Ohio	0-1	—	—	—	—	—	—	0-1
Ohio St.	—	—	—	—	—	—	2-0	2-0
Oklahoma	1-0	—	—	—	—	—	—	1-0

Team	1996	1997	1998	1999	2000	2001	2002	Overall W-L
Oklahoma St.	1-1	0-2	—	—	—	0-1	—	1-4
Oregon	1-1	1-0	0-2	1-0	2-0	—	—	5-3
Oregon St.	0-1	—	1-0	—	—	0-1	—	1-2
Penn St.	—	—	—	—	0-1	—	0-2	0-3
Pittsburgh	0-1	2-0	—	—	0-1	—	1-0	3-2
Purdue	—	—	—	0-1	1-0	1-0	0-1	2-2
Rice	—	—	1-0	—	1-0	1-1	—	3-1
Rutgers	—	0-1	—	1-0	0-1	—	—	1-2
San Diego St.	—	1-1	2-0	—	—	—	—	3-1
San Jose St.	—	1-0	—	—	—	—	—	1-0
Southern California	1-2	—	—	0-1	1-0	1-0	0-1	3-4
Southern Methodist	—	0-1	0-2	—	—	0-1	—	0-4
Southern Miss.	0-1	—	—	1-0	—	0-1	—	1-2
Stanford	1-0	—	0-1	—	1-0	—	—	2-1
Syracuse	—	0-1	—	0-1	1-0	—	1-1	2-3
Tennessee	—	—	1-0	—	0-1	—	1-0	2-1
Texas	0-1	—	—	—	—	—	—	0-1
Texas A&M	—	1-0	1-0	—	0-1	—	0-2	2-3
TCU	—	—	1-0	0-1	—	0-1	0-1	1-3
UTEP	—	—	0-1	0-1	—	—	—	0-2
Texas Tech	—	—	—	—	—	0-1	1-1	1-2
Toledo	1-0	—	—	—	—	—	—	1-0
Troy St.	*	*	*	*	*	*	0-1	0-1
UCLA	1-0	—	1-0	1-0	0-1	—	—	3-1
Utah	—	—	1-1	—	—	0-1	—	1-2
Utah St.	—	—	1-1	—	—	1-0	2-1	3-2
Vanderbilt	—	—	1-1	—	—	—	—	1-1
Virginia	—	—	—	0-1	0-1	—	—	0-2
Virginia Tech	—	—	1-0	1-0	—	—	0-1	2-1
Wake Forest	—	—	—	—	—	—	0-1	0-1

Team	1996	1997	1998	1999	2000	2001	2002	Overall W-L
Washington	1-0	—	—	0-1	—	—	1-0	2-1
Washington St.	0-1	1-0	—	—	0-3	—	1-1	2-5
West Virginia	—	0-1	—	—	1-0	—	—	1-1
Western Mich.	1-1	—	—	1-0	—	—	0-1	2-2
Wisconsin	—	—	—	1-0	1-2	—	1-0	3-2
Wyoming	1-1	—	1-0	—	—	—	0-1	2-2
I-AA, II Opponents	0-2	2-0	—	—	—	2-1	0-1	4-4
Totals	**26-26**	**25-25**	**24-24**	**26-26**	**36-36**	**18-18**	**31-31**	**186-186**

*Not a Division I-A member at the time.

BY CONFERENCE

Conference	1996	1997	1998	1999	2000	2001	2002	Overall W-L
Atlantic Coast	—	2-1	1-2	3-4	3-3	2-2	1-2	12-14
Big East	0-1	3-4	1-2	2-1	2-2	—	2-4	10-14
Big Ten	1-1	—	1-1	4-3	4-3	1-1	6-4	17-13
Big 12	4-4	3-3	2-1	2-3	1-1	3-2	3-5	18-19
Big West	—	1-2	3-4	1-1	2-3	—	—	7-10
Conference USA	3-1	2-1	—	2-2	4-5	0-2	4-3	15-14
Mid-American	3-4	1-2	1-0	2-1	2-2	2-1	4-1	15-11
Mountain West	—	—	—	—	1-2	0-2	3-4	4-8
Pacific-10	8-6	3-2	3-3	2-2	7-7	1-1	2-2	26-23
Southeastern	2-2	2-1	5-4	5-5	6-5	2-1	3-2	25-20
Sun Belt	—	—	—	—	—	0-1	1-0	1-1
Western Athletic	4-3	4-6	7-6	3-3	1-0	5-4	—	24-22
I-A Independents	1-2	2-3	0-1	0-1	2-3	—	2-3	7-13
I-AA, II Opponents	0-2	2-0	—	—	1-0	2-1	0-1	5-4
Totals	**26-26**	**25-25**	**24-24**	**26-26**	**36-36**	**18-18**	**31-31**	**186-186**

Division I-A Stadiums

LISTED ALPHABETICALLY BY SCHOOL

School	Stadium	Conference	Year Built	Cap.	Surface* (Year)
Air Force	Falcon	Mountain West	1962	52,480	Grass
Akron	^Rubber Bowl	Mid-American-E	1940	35,202	AstroTurf (94)
Alabama	Bryant-Denny	Southeastern-W	1929	83,818	PAT (S91)
UAB	^Legion Field	Conference USA	1927	83,091	Grass (S95)
Arizona	Arizona	Pacific-10	1928	57,803	Grass
Arizona St.	Sun Devil	Pacific-10	1959	73,656	Grass
Arkansas	Razorback	Southeastern-W	1938	72,000	Grass (S95)
Arkansas St.	Indian	Sun Belt	1974	33,410	Grass
Army	Michie	Conference USA	1924	39,929	AstroTurf (92)
Auburn	Jordan-Hare	Southeastern-W	1939	86,063	Grass
Ball St.	Ball State	Mid-American-W	1967	22,500	Grass
Baylor	Floyd Casey	Big 12-S	1950	50,000	SportGrass (S98)
Boise St.	Bronco	Western Athletic	1970	30,000	Blue AstroTurf
Boston College	Alumni	Big East	1957	44,500	AstroTurf (97)
Bowling Green	Doyt Perry	Mid-American-E	1966	30,599	Grass
Brigham Young	LaVell Edwards	Mountain West	1964	65,000	FieldTurf (01)
Buffalo	UB Stadium	Mid-American-E	1993	30,000	Grass
California	Memorial	Pacific-10	1923	75,662	Grass (S95)
UCF	^Florida Citrus	Independent	1936	70,188	Grass
Central Mich.	Kelly-Shorts	Mid-American-W	1972	30,199	AstroTurf (97)
Cincinnati	Nippert	Conference USA	1916	35,000	FieldTurf (00)
Clemson	Memorial	Atlantic Coast	1942	81,473	Grass
Colorado	Folsom	Big 12-N	1924	50,942	Grass (S99)
Colorado St.	Hughes	Mountain West	1968	30,000	Grass
Connecticut	Rentschler Field	Independent	2003	40,000	Grass
Duke	Wallace Wade	Atlantic Coast	1929	33,941	Grass
East Caro.	Dowdy-Ficklen	Conference USA	1963	43,000	Grass (83)
Eastern Mich.	Rynearson	Mid-American-W	1969	30,200	AstroTurf (98)
Florida	Florida Field	Southeastern-E	1929	83,000	Grass (S90)
Florida St.	Doak S. Campbell	Atlantic Coast	1950	80,000	PAT (88)
Fresno St.	Bulldog	Western Athletic	1980	41,031	Grass
Georgia	Sanford	Southeastern-E	1929	86,520	Grass
Georgia Tech	Bobby Dodd/Grant Field	Atlantic Coast	1913	46,000	FieldTurf (01)
Hawaii	^Aloha	Western Athletic	1975	50,000	FieldTurf (01)
Houston	Robertson	Conference USA	1942	22,000	Grass
Idaho	#Kibbie Dome	Sun Belt	1975	16,000	AstroTurf
Idaho	^Clarence D. Martin	Sun Belt	1972	37,600	FieldTurf (00)
Illinois	Memorial	Big Ten	1923	69,249	AstroPlay (01)
Indiana	Memorial	Big Ten	1960	52,354	AstroPlay (S98)
Iowa	Kinnick	Big Ten	1929	70,397	PAT (97)
Iowa St.	Cyclone-Jack Trice	Big 12-N	1975	43,000	Grass (S96)
Kansas	Memorial	Big 12-N	1921	50,250	AstroPlay (00)
Kansas St.	K S U-Wagner Field	Big 12-N	1968	51,000	FieldTurf (02)
Kent St.	Dix	Mid-American-E	1969	30,520	AstroTurf (S97)

School	Stadium	Conference	Year Built	Cap.	Surface* (Year)
Kentucky	Commonwealth	Southeastern-E	1973	67,530	Grass
La.-Lafayette	Cajun Field	Sun Belt	1971	31,000	Grass
La.-Monroe	Malone	Sun Belt	1978	30,427	Grass
Louisiana Tech	Joe Aillet	Western Athletic	1968	30,600	Grass
Louisville	Papa John's Cardinal	Conference USA	1998	42,000	SportGrass (98)
LSU	Tiger	Southeastern-W	1924	91,600	Grass
Marshall	Marshall University	Mid-American-E	1991	38,019	PolyTurf
Maryland	Byrd	Atlantic Coast	1950	48,055	FieldTurf (01)
Memphis	^Liberty Bowl	Conference USA	1965	62,380	Grass (87)
Miami (Fla.)	^Orange Bowl	Big East	1935	72,319	PAT (94)
Miami (Ohio)	Fred C. Yager	Mid-American-E	1983	30,012	Grass
Michigan	Michigan	Big Ten	1927	107,501	FieldTurf (03)
Michigan St.	Spartan	Big Ten	1957	72,027	Grass (02)
Middle Tenn.	Floyd/Jones Field	Sun Belt	1998	31,000	AstroTurf
Minnesota	^#Metrodome	Big Ten	1982	63,669	AstroTurf-8
Mississippi	Vaught-Hemingway	Southeastern-W	1941	60,580	Grass
Mississippi St.	Davis Wade at Scott Field	Southeastern-W	1914	55,082	PAT (86)
Missouri	Memorial/Faurot Field	Big 12-N	1926	68,349	FieldTurf (S03)
Navy	Navy-Marine Corps Mem.	Independent	1959	30,000	Grass
Nebraska	Memorial/Osborne Field	Big 12-N	1923	73,918	FieldTurf (99)
UNLV	^Sam Boyd	Mountain West	1971	36,800	Grass (S99)
Nevada	Mackay	Western Athletic	1967	31,545	FieldTurf (S00)
New Mexico	University	Mountain West	1960	37,370	Grass
New Mexico St.	Aggie Memorial	Sun Belt	1978	30,343	Grass
North Carolina	Kenan Memorial	Atlantic Coast	1927	60,000	Grass
North Carolina St.	^Carter-Finley	Atlantic Coast	1966	51,500	Grass
North Texas	Fouts Field	Sun Belt	1952	30,500	All-Pro Turf
Northern Ill.	Huskie	Mid-American-W	1965	31,000	FieldTurf (01)
Northwestern	Ryan Field	Big Ten	1926	47,129	Grass (S97)
Notre Dame	Notre Dame	Independent	1930	80,795	Grass
Ohio	Peden	Mid-American-E	1929	24,000	FieldTurf (S02)
Ohio St.	Ohio	Big Ten	1922	101,568	PAT (90)
Oklahoma	Memorial	Big 12-S	1923	72,765	Grass (S94)
Oklahoma St.	Lewis	Big 12-S	1920	50,614	AstroTurf (87)
Oregon	Autzen	Pacific-10	1967	41,698	FieldTurf (02)
Oregon St.	Reser	Pacific-10	1953	35,362	FieldTurf (01)
Penn St.	Beaver	Big Ten	1960	106,537	Grass
Pittsburgh	Heinz Field	Big East	2001	65,000	Grass
Purdue	Ross-Ade	Big Ten	1924	62,500	PAT (75)
Rice	Rice	Western Athletic	1950	70,000	AstroTurf-12 (97)
Rutgers	Rutgers	Big East	1994	41,500	Grass
San Diego St.	^Qualcomm	Mountain West	1967	51,000	FieldTurf (03)
San Jose St.	Spartan	Western Athletic	1933	31,218	Grass
South Carolina	Williams-Brice	Southeastern-E	1934	80,250	Grass
South Fla.	^Raymond James	Independent	1998	41,441	Grass
Southern California	^L.A. Memorial Coliseum	Pacific-10	1923	92,000	Grass
Southern Methodist	Gerald J. Ford	Western Athletic	2000	32,000	Grass
Southern Miss.	Roberts	Conference USA	1976	33,000	Grass
Stanford	Stanford	Pacific-10	1921	85,500	Grass
Syracuse	#Carrier Dome	Big East	1980	49,550	AstroTurf
Temple	Veterans	Big East	1971	66,592	Astro-Turf-8
Tennessee	Neyland	Southeastern-E	1921	104,079	Grass (S94)
Texas	Royal-Memorial	Big 12-S	1924	80,082	PAT (S99)
Texas A&M	Kyle Field	Big 12-S	1925	82,600	Grass (S96)
TCU	Amon G. Carter	Conference USA	1929	44,008	Grass (S92)
UTEP	^Sun Bowl	Western Athletic	1963	52,000	AstroTurf (97)
Texas Tech	Jones	Big 12-S	1947	50,500	AstroTurf-8 (88)
Toledo	Glass Bowl	Mid-American-W	1937	26,248	NexTurf (01)
Troy St.	Memorial	Independent	1950	17,500	Grass
Tulane	^#Superdome	Conference USA	1975	69,767	AstroTurf (95)
Tulsa	Skelly	Western Athletic	1930	40,385	FieldTurf (00)
UCLA	^Rose Bowl	Pacific-10	1922	95,000	Grass
Utah	Rice-Eccles	Mountain West	1927	45,634	FieldTurf (S02)
Utah St.	E. L. Romney	Independent	1968	30,257	Grass
Vanderbilt	Vanderbilt	Southeastern-E	1981	41,600	Grass (S99)
Virginia	Scott/Harrison Field	Atlantic Coast	1931	61,500	PAT (S95)
Virginia Tech	Lane	Big East	1965	65,115	Grass
Wake Forest	Groves	Atlantic Coast	1968	31,500	Grass
Washington	Husky	Pacific-10	1920	72,500	FieldTurf (00)
Washington St.	Clarence D. Martin	Pacific-10	1972	37,600	FieldTurf (00)
West Virginia	Mountaineer Field	Big East	1980	63,500	AstroTurf-12 (97)
Western Mich.	Waldo	Mid-American-W	1939	30,200	NexTurf (01)
Wisconsin	Camp Randall	Big Ten	1917	76,634	AstroTurf (98)
Wyoming	War Memorial	Mountain West	1950	33,500	Grass

^Not located on campus. #Indoor facility.

STADIUMS LISTED BY CAPACITY (TOP 30)

School	Stadium	Surface* (Year)	Capacity
Michigan	Michigan	FieldTurf (03)	107,501
Penn St.	Beaver	Grass	106,537
Tennessee	Neyland	Grass (S94)	104,079

School	Stadium	Surface* (Year)	Capacity
Ohio St.	Ohio	101,568	PAT (90)
UCLA	^Rose Bowl	95,000	Grass
Southern California	^L.A. Memorial Coliseum	92,000	Grass
LSU	Tiger	91,600	Grass
Georgia	Sanford	86,520	Grass
Auburn	Jordan-Hare	86,063	Grass
Stanford	Stanford	85,500	Grass
Alabama	Bryant-Denny	83,818	PAT (S91)
UAB	^Legion Field	83,091	Grass (S95)
Florida	Florida Field	83,000	Grass (S90)
Texas A&M	Kyle Field	82,600	Grass (S96)
Clemson	Memorial	81,473	Grass
Notre Dame	Notre Dame	80,795	Grass
South Carolina	Williams-Brice	80,250	Grass
Texas	Royal-Memorial	80,082	PAT (S99)
Florida St.	Doak S. Campbell	80,000	PAT (88)
Wisconsin	Camp Randall	76,634	AstroTurf (98)
California	Memorial	75,662	Grass (S95)
Nebraska	Memorial/Osborne Field	73,918	FieldTurf (99)
Arizona St.	Sun Devil	73,656	Grass
Oklahoma	Memorial	72,765	Grass (S94)
Washington	Husky	72,500	FieldTurf (00)
Miami (Fla.)	^Orange Bowl	72,319	PAT (S77)
Michigan St.	Spartan	72,027	Grass (02)
Arkansas	Razorback	72,000	Grass (S95)
Iowa	Kinnick	70,397	PAT (S89)
UCF	^Florida Citrus Bowl	70,188	Grass

^Not located on campus.

Surface Notes: *This column indicates the type of surface (either artificial or natural grass) present this year in the stadium. The brand name of the artificial turf, if known, is listed as well as the year the last installation occurred. The "S" preceding the year indicates that the school has switched either from natural grass to artificial turf or vice-versa. Legend: Turf—Any of several types of artificial turfs (name brands include AstroTurf, All-Pro, Omni-Turf, SuperTurf, FieldTurf, etc.); Grass—Natural grass surface; PAT—Prescription Athletic Turf (a "natural-artificial" surface featuring a network of pipes connected to pumps capable of sucking water from the natural turf or watering it. The pipes

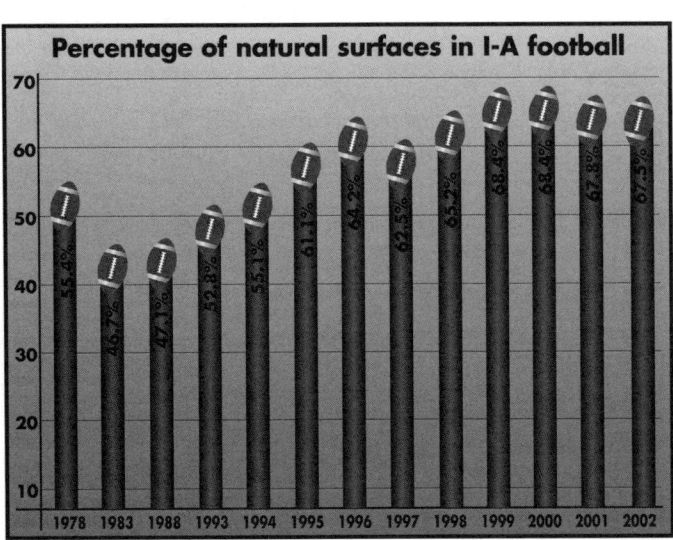

are located 18 inches from the surface and covered with a mixture of sand and filler. The turf also is lined with heating coils to keep it from freezing in temperatures below 32 degrees). SportGrass—Combines natural grass with a below-the-surface system of synthetic elements. FieldTurf—Hybrid fibers made from a polyethlyene blend, treated and tufted into a unique porous surface. The infill is made from graded silica sand and ground rubber, and provides a non-compactible, resilient, natural earth feel.

Division I-A Stadium Facts: Houston and Tulsa claim to be the first college football teams to play in an indoor stadium (the Astrodome on September 11, 1965). But actually, Utah and West Virginia met December 19, 1964, in the Liberty Bowl in the Atlantic City Convention Hall. Technically, the Astrodome was the first indoor stadium built specially for football and baseball. The first major-college football game ever played on artificial turf was between Houston and Washington State on September 23, 1966.

Major-College Statistics Trends†

(Average Per Game, One Team)

Year	Rushing					Passing			Total Offense			Scoring		
	Plays	Yds.	Avg.	Att.	Cmp.	Pct.	Yds.	Av. Att.	Plays	Yds.	Avg.	TD	FG	Pts.
1937	–	133.8	–	13.0	5.0	.381	64.5	4.96	–	198.4	–	–	–	10.1
1938	40.8	140.1	3.43	14.0	5.2	.371	70.1	5.01	54.8	210.2	3.85	1.75	0.06	11.8
1939	40.8	135.9	3.33	13.8	5.2	.374	66.4	4.81	54.6	202.3	3.70	1.66	0.09	11.4
1940	41.9	140.5	3.35	14.8	5.8	.386	77.8	5.26	56.7	218.5	3.85	1.97	0.08	13.3
1941	42.2	141.2	3.35	15.0	5.9	.392	80.7	5.38	57.2	221.8	3.88	2.03	0.06	13.8
1946	42.3	152.4	3.60	15.5	6.1	.389	88.2	5.69	57.8	240.7	4.16	2.39	0.04	16.1
1947	42.3	158.7	3.75	15.3	6.3	.414	90.3	5.91	57.6	248.8	4.32	2.37	0.04	15.9
1948	43.7	162.2	3.71	15.9	6.7	.423	94.6	5.95	59.5	256.5	4.31	2.52	0.05	17.1
1949	47.2	180.6	3.83	17.7	7.6	.431	110.4	6.24	64.9	290.7	4.48	2.86	0.04	19.4
1950	47.0	180.2	3.83	17.5	7.7	.438	108.5	6.19	64.5	288.6	4.47	2.79	0.04	18.9
1951	48.6	182.5	3.76	18.9	8.4	.446	113.7	6.02	67.5	296.1	4.39	2.86	0.05	19.4
1952	48.3	176.4	3.65	18.4	8.1	.441	111.9	6.09	66.7	288.2	4.32	2.68	0.07	18.4
1953	45.1	176.6	3.92	15.2	6.5	.428	91.7	6.03	60.3	268.2	4.45	2.54	0.05	17.1
1954	45.5	184.1	*4.05	14.9	6.5	.437	91.1	6.14	60.3	225.1	4.56	2.59	0.05	17.4
1955	46.1	176.7	3.83	13.6	5.9	.435	84.7	6.24	59.6	261.3	4.38	2.37	0.05	16.1
1956	49.2	193.1	3.93	14.1	6.2	.437	85.9	6.09	63.3	279.0	4.41	2.45	0.05	16.5
1957	49.3	177.5	3.60	14.4	6.4	.444	85.5	5.94	63.6	263.0	4.14	2.31	0.06	15.6
1958	47.1	170.7	3.62	16.1	7.4	.458	97.7	6.06	63.2	268.4	4.24	2.31	0.09	16.0
1959	46.2	166.0	3.59	16.5	7.5	.451	98.5	5.96	62.7	264.5	4.21	2.25	0.17	15.9
1960	45.3	169.9	3.75	15.8	7.2	.454	93.6	5.94	61.1	263.4	4.31	2.19	0.19	15.6
1961	45.6	166.7	3.66	15.9	7.2	.448	94.7	5.95	61.5	261.4	4.25	2.23	0.23	16.0
1962	45.3	164.0	3.63	17.2	8.0	.463	105.0	6.10	62.5	269.0	4.31	2.30	0.21	16.4
1963	44.1	160.0	3.63	17.6	8.1	.461	105.3	5.98	61.7	265.3	4.30	2.19	0.27	15.8
1964	43.7	149.7	3.43	17.9	8.5	.472	110.0	6.14	61.6	259.6	4.21	2.07	0.29	15.1
1965	45.1	149.4	3.31	20.8	9.7	.464	123.2	5.93	65.9	272.5	4.14	2.26	0.42	16.7
1966	44.3	148.7	3.36	22.0	10.3	.470	133.2	6.07	66.2	281.8	4.26	2.35	0.42	17.5
1967	47.3	154.7	3.27	22.9	10.7	.467	139.8	6.10	70.2	294.5	4.19	2.48	0.46	18.4
1968	49.7	170.8	3.44	25.4	12.1	.474	157.7	6.22	*75.1	328.5	4.38	2.89	0.46	21.2
1969	49.5	171.8	3.47	25.5	12.0	.471	157.1	6.17	74.9	328.9	4.39	2.90	0.54	21.6
1970	49.3	175.7	3.57	25.0	11.7	.467	152.7	6.12	74.2	328.3	4.42	2.83	0.57	21.3
1971	49.7	182.2	3.67	21.7	10.1	.463	132.3	6.10	71.3	314.5	4.41	2.69	0.54	20.2
1972	49.8	184.5	3.70	22.0	10.2	.462	136.9	6.24	71.8	321.4	4.48	2.71	0.61	20.6
1973	50.1	192.8	3.85	20.4	9.6	.472	130.9	6.41	70.5	323.6	4.59	2.75	0.65	21.0
1974	51.8	201.8	3.89	18.8	8.9	.474	122.3	6.50	70.7	324.1	4.59	2.64	0.63	20.2

DIVISION I-A

Year	Rushing Plays	Rushing Yds.	Avg.	Att.	Cmp.	Passing Pct.	Passing Yds.	Av. Att.	Total Offense Plays	Total Offense Yds.	Avg.	Scoring TD	Scoring FG	Pts.
1975	*51.9	*204.5	3.94	18.4	8.7	.473	119.6	6.52	70.3	324.1	4.61	2.57	0.74	20.1
1976	51.4	198.8	3.87	19.1	9.1	.474	123.5	6.49	70.4	322.2	4.58	2.57	0.75	20.0
1977	51.3	194.6	3.80	20.2	9.8	.483	134.5	6.67	71.5	329.1	4.61	2.67	0.73	20.8
1978	50.9	192.6	3.79	21.2	10.3	.486	138.9	6.55	72.1	331.5	4.60	2.64	0.76	20.8
1979	49.1	187.9	3.83	21.6	10.6	.491	139.3	6.47	70.6	327.2	4.63	2.55	0.77	20.0
1980	47.7	178.3	3.74	23.3	11.6	.500	151.9	6.52	71.0	330.2	4.65	2.61	0.81	20.5
1981	46.3	169.4	3.66	25.3	12.7	.502	164.7	6.51	71.6	334.1	4.67	2.57	0.87	20.5
1982	45.1	169.3	3.75	27.6	14.5	.522	182.4	6.61	72.7	351.7	4.84	2.71	1.02	21.9
1983	44.6	169.5	3.80	27.0	14.4	.536	182.8	6.79	71.6	352.3	4.92	2.73	1.06	22.1
1984	44.7	168.1	3.76	26.8	14.1	.527	181.1	6.77	71.5	349.2	4.89	2.66	1.15	22.1
1985	44.6	169.2	3.80	27.3	14.7	.537	186.1	6.82	71.8	355.3	4.95	2.74	1.09	22.4
1986	44.2	167.9	3.80	27.2	14.6	.537	185.1	6.81	71.4	353.0	4.95	2.80	1.07	22.7
1987	44.4	174.2	3.92	27.1	14.2	.526	183.6	6.78	71.5	357.8	5.01	2.83	1.13	23.1
1988	44.0	174.6	3.97	27.1	14.3	.529	185.8	6.87	71.1	360.3	5.07	2.91	*1.16	23.8
1989	42.7	166.4	3.90	28.5	15.4	.540	200.9	7.05	71.2	367.3	5.16	2.97	1.13	24.1
1990	43.1	167.7	3.90	28.3	15.1	.534	197.2	6.96	71.4	364.8	5.11	3.04	1.08	24.4
1991	43.3	169.7	3.91	27.2	14.6	.535	189.6	6.98	70.5	359.4	5.10	2.95	0.89	23.1
1992	42.7	165.6	3.89	28.1	14.9	.530	190.5	6.77	70.8	356.1	5.03	2.84	1.04	22.9
1993	41.8	166.3	3.98	28.7	15.9	.551	204.9	7.13	70.5	371.2	5.27	3.09	0.97	24.4
1994	41.8	166.8	3.99	28.5	15.6	.547	198.3	6.96	70.3	365.1	5.19	3.11	0.99	24.6
1995	41.5	167.3	4.03	29.7	16.3	.547	205.5	6.92	71.2	372.8	5.24	3.21	0.93	25.1
1996	41.5	164.4	3.97	28.9	15.4	.533	202.0	6.99	70.4	366.3	5.21	3.26	0.94	25.5
1997	40.2	158.7	3.94	29.2	15.8	.543	207.6	7.12	69.4	366.3	5.28	3.25	0.97	25.5
1998	40.7	158.6	3.89	29.1	15.7	.540	209.5	*7.19	69.9	368.1	5.27	3.20	1.05	25.5
1999	39.8	152.8	3.83	30.6	16.7	.544	212.5	6.94	70.4	365.3	5.18	3.23	1.05	25.6
2000	39.5	154.0	3.90	31.5	17.0	.541	216.2	6.88	71.0	370.2	5.22	3.33	1.01	26.2
2001	39.8	158.9	3.99	*31.6	*17.6	*.556	*222.7	7.04	71.4	*381.6	*5.34	*3.47	1.01	27.2
2002	39.5	158.3	4.01	31.1	17.3	.554	217.5	6.98	70.6	375.8	5.32	3.46	1.07	*27.3

*Record. †Records not compiled in 1942-45 except for Scoring Points Per Game: 1942 (15.7); 1943 (15.7); 1944 (16.3); 1945 (16.1).

Additional Major-College Statistics Trends†

Rules changes and statistics changes affecting trends: PUNTING—Beginning in 1965, 20 yards not deducted from a punt into the end zone for a touchback. INTERCEPTIONS—Interception yards not compiled, 1958-65. KICKOFF RETURNS—During 1937-45, if a kickoff went out of bounds, the receiving team put the ball in play on its 35-yard line instead of a second kickoff; in 1984 (rescinded in 1985), a 30-yard-line touchback for kickoffs crossing the goal line in flight and first touching the ground out of the end zone; in 1986, kickoffs from the 35-yard line. PUNT RETURNS—In 1967, interior linemen restricted from leaving until the ball is kicked.

(Average Per Game, One Team)

Year	Punting No.	Punting Avg.	Net Avg.	Interceptions No.	Interceptions Avg. Ret.	Interceptions Yds.	Punt Returns No.	Punt Returns Avg. Ret.	Punt Returns Yds.	Kickoff Returns No.	Kickoff Returns Avg. Ret.	Kickoff Returns Yds.	Pct. Ret'd
1937	9.2	36.3	–	1.68	–	–	–	–	–	–	–	–	–
1938	9.3	37.2	–	1.70	9.19	15.8	–	–	–	–	–	–	–
1939	*9.4	36.7	–	1.67	9.84	16.5	*4.42	9.40	41.6	2.14	19.3	41.3	.764
1940	9.1	36.6	–	1.79	10.05	18.0	4.21	10.58	44.5	2.32	20.4	47.5	.753
1941	8.9	36.1	–	*1.81	11.28	20.4	4.27	11.10	*47.4	2.41	20.2	48.6	.768
1946	7.3	36.7	–	1.75	11.79	20.6	3.70	11.32	41.9	3.01	18.9	56.9	.870
1947	6.7	36.4	30.3	1.61	11.93	19.2	3.47	11.73	40.7	3.04	18.9	57.3	.884
1948	6.3	36.3	30.2	1.60	12.59	20.2	3.09	*12.16	37.6	3.17	18.5	58.6	.873
1949	6.3	36.6	30.3	1.69	13.23	*22.3	3.21	12.13	38.9	3.51	17.9	62.8	.885
1950	6.0	36.3	30.8	1.61	11.99	19.3	3.04	10.72	32.6	3.46	16.6	57.4	.889
1951	6.4	35.9	30.7	1.67	12.00	20.1	3.10	10.58	32.8	3.53	17.0	59.9	.884
1952	6.3	36.4	31.6	1.60	11.60	18.5	3.07	9.95	30.5	3.45	17.6	60.7	.908
1953	5.2	34.9	29.7	1.37	12.12	16.6	2.57	10.66	27.4	3.27	17.8	58.2	.903
1954	4.9	34.9	29.4	1.36	12.48	16.6	2.42	11.16	27.0	3.32	18.4	61.0	*.910
1955	4.9	34.9	29.8	1.26	12.96	16.8	2.39	10.54	25.2	3.09	18.5	57.2	.892
1956	5.0	35.1	30.1	1.29	12.86	16.6	2.49	10.07	25.1	3.19	18.0	57.4	.906
1957	5.3	34.8	30.2	1.26	11.95	15.0	2.53	9.57	24.2	3.05	18.7	57.1	.897
1958	5.6	35.4	30.9	1.33	–	–	2.57	9.70	24.9	3.02	18.9	57.0	.880
1959	5.5	35.9	31.5	1.33	–	–	2.67	9.06	24.2	3.09	18.7	57.8	.892
1960	5.1	36.0	31.4	1.24	–	–	2.39	9.73	23.3	3.05	18.8	57.3	.890
1961	5.2	35.5	35.5	1.22	–	–	2.43	9.44	22.9	3.06	18.3	56.1	.873
1962	5.2	35.7	35.7	1.25	–	–	2.36	9.66	22.8	3.10	19.6	60.7	.876
1963	5.2	36.3	32.5	1.19	–	–	2.34	9.71	22.7	3.08	20.1	61.9	.880
1964	5.3	36.4	32.5	1.20	–	–	2.33	8.99	20.9	2.93	19.6	57.3	.862
1965	5.9	38.5	38.5	1.42	–	–	2.73	9.99	27.3	3.15	18.8	59.3	.849
1966	5.9	37.5	33.5	1.50	12.07	18.1	2.63	8.82	23.2	3.24	18.7	60.8	.849
1967	6.5	36.8	31.6	1.52	11.39	17.3	3.42	9.92	33.9	3.31	18.7	61.7	.831
1968	6.7	37.4	33.3	1.61	11.51	18.6	3.01	8.95	26.9	3.64	19.1	69.6	.829
1969	6.6	37.5	33.4	1.70	11.07	18.8	3.00	9.00	27.0	3.67	18.9	69.4	.818
1970	6.3	37.4	37.4	1.66	11.65	19.4	2.89	9.28	26.9	3.69	19.0	70.1	.828
1971	6.2	37.6	33.4	1.49	11.75	17.5	2.89	9.04	26.2	3.57	19.2	68.6	.834
1972	6.1	37.2	33.4	1.54	11.54	17.7	2.72	8.61	23.4	3.50	19.0	66.4	.803
1973	5.8	37.8	34.1	1.36	11.30	15.4	2.52	8.65	21.8	3.54	19.6	69.2	.797
1974	5.6	37.3	34.2	1.23	11.30	13.9	2.40	7.92	19.0	3.38	19.1	64.3	.784
1975	5.4	38.1	35.0	1.21	11.26	13.6	2.39	7.19	17.2	3.20	19.3	61.7	.733
1976	5.7	38.0	35.1	1.23	11.44	14.0	2.42	6.83	16.5	3.14	18.3	57.4	.722
1977	5.8	38.0	35.0	1.26	11.05	13.9	2.45	7.10	17.3	3.16	18.4	58.1	.711
1978	6.0	38.0	34.9	1.34	10.83	14.5	2.51	7.39	18.6	3.18	18.7	59.6	.665
1979	5.8	37.7	34.8	1.31	10.66	14.0	2.38	7.09	16.9	3.02	18.8	56.9	.637
1980	5.8	38.3	35.4	1.37	10.85	14.9	2.44	7.01	17.1	2.91	19.0	55.1	.651
1981	6.0	38.9	35.9	1.38	10.22	14.1	2.45	7.22	17.7	2.86	18.8	53.9	.636
1982	5.9	39.8	*36.5	1.39	10.70	14.9	2.40	8.00	19.2	2.69	19.3	51.9	.561
1983	5.5	39.5	35.9	1.37	10.43	14.3	2.47	7.95	19.7	2.65	19.2	50.8	.549
1984	5.6	39.7	36.3	1.31	10.07	13.2	2.47	7.61	18.8	3.03	18.6	56.2	.621

Year	Punting No.	Avg.	Net Avg.	Interceptions No.	Avg. Ret.	Yds.	Punt Returns No.	Avg. Ret.	Yds.	Kickoff Returns No.	Avg. Ret.	Yds.	Pct. Ret'd
1985	5.5	39.6	36.1	1.30	10.47	13.6	2.45	7.92	19.4	2.94	19.4	57.0	.603
1986	5.4	39.2	35.4	1.30	10.99	14.3	2.51	8.23	20.7	3.78	19.8	74.6	.770
1987	5.4	38.6	34.7	1.32	10.82	14.3	2.48	8.31	20.6	3.89	19.1	74.5	.780
1988	5.2	38.4	34.7	1.24	11.17	14.0	2.39	7.96	19.1	*3.97	19.4	77.1	.778
1989	5.2	38.5	34.3	1.28	10.75	13.8	2.36	8.46	20.0	3.92	19.7	*77.2	.776
1990	5.3	38.6	34.3	1.23	11.40	14.0	2.45	9.33	22.9	3.79	19.4	74.5	.738
1991	5.3	38.4	34.3	1.18	11.30	13.3	2.50	8.74	21.9	3.43	19.4	66.6	.741
1992	5.6	39.0	34.9	1.20	11.00	13.2	2.63	9.04	23.8	3.30	20.1	66.4	.732
1993	5.2	38.8	35.1	1.14	11.00	12.5	2.28	8.28	18.9	3.43	20.0	68.7	.679
1994	5.3	39.2	35.3	1.10	12.10	13.3	2.38	8.64	20.5	3.50	20.0	69.8	.714
1995	5.3	38.7	34.9	1.12	11.67	13.1	2.23	8.98	20.0	3.57	19.5	69.7	.848
1996	5.5	40.0	35.8	1.04	12.83	13.4	2.39	9.56	22.8	3.34	20.4	68.0	.783
1997	5.4	*40.5	36.2	1.05	12.45	13.0	2.47	9.49	23.4	3.47	20.3	70.5	.816
1998	5.5	39.8	35.5	1.05	12.80	13.4	2.53	9.45	23.9	3.52	20.6	72.4	.837
1999	5.6	39.8	35.3	1.12	13.00	14.5	2.61	9.61	25.1	3.36	20.3	68.2	.901
2000	5.6	39.0	34.2	1.12	*13.55	15.2	2.64	10.15	26.8	3.49	19.6	68.6	.807
2001	5.3	39.8	35.0	1.12	12.66	14.2	2.59	9.84	25.4	3.43	*20.7	71.0	.769
2002	5.2	39.5	34.2	1.10	12.61	13.8	2.73	10.59	28.9	3.47	20.2	70.4	.774

*Record. †Records not compiled in 1942-45.

Field Goal Trends (1938-68)

Year	Made	Year	Made	Year	Made	Atts.	Pct.
1938	47	1951	53	1961	277		
1939	80	1952	83	1962	261		
1940	84	1953	50	1963	314		
1941	59	1954	48	1964	368		
1942-45	*	1955	57	1965	484	1,035	.468
1946	44	1956	53	1966	522	1,125	.464
1947	38	1957	64	1967	555	1,266	.438
1948	53	1958	103	1968	566	1,287	.440
1949	46	1959	†199				
1950	46	1960	224				

*Records not compiled. †Goal posts widened from 18 feet, 6 inches to 23 feet, 4 inches in 1959.

Field Goal Trends (From 1969)

(Includes Field Goal Attempts by Divisions I-AA, II and III Opponents)

Year	Made	Totals Atts.	Pct.	16-39	Pct.	16-49	Pct.	40-49	Pct.	50-59	Pct.	60 Plus
1969	669	1,402	.477	538-872	.617	654-1,267	.516	116-395	.294	15-135	.111	0-8
1970	754	1,548	.487	614-990	.620	740-1,380	.536	126-390	.323	14-168	.083	1-9
1971	780	1,625	.480	607-1,022	.594	760-1,466	.518	153-444	.345	20-159	.126	0-11
1972	876	1,828	.479	705-1,150	.613	855-1,641	.521	150-491	.305	21-187	.112	1-12
1973	958	1,920	.499	728-1,139	.639	914-1,670	.547	186-531	.350	44-250	.176	1-21
1974	947	1,905	.497	706-1,096	.644	906-1,655	.547	200-559	.358	41-250	.164	1-17
1975	1,164	2,237	.520	849-1,255	.676	1,088-1,896	.574	239-641	.373	76-341	.223	4-32
1976	1,187	2,330	.509	854-1,301	.656	1,131-1,997	.566	277-696	.398	56-333	.168	3-24
1977	1,238	2,514	.492	882-1,315	.671	1,160-2,088	.556	278-773	.360	78-426	.183	6-40
1978	1,229	2,113	.582	938-1,361	.689	1,193-1,982	.602	255-621	.411	36-131	.275	1-4

Year	Made	Totals Atts.	Pct.	Under 20		20-29		30-39		40-49		50-59		60 Plus	
1979	1,241	2,129	.583	34-43	.791	455-601	.757	425-706	.602	286-600	.477	41-173	.237	0-6	.000
1980	1,245	2,128	.585	31-39	.795	408-529	.771	452-696	.649	317-682	.465	37-175	.211	0-7	.000
1981	1,368	2,254	.607	42-48	.875	471-598	.788	468-731	.631	335-698	.480	58-169	.343	1-10	.100
1982	1,224	1,915	.639	31-34	.912	384-475	.808	415-597	.695	319-604	.528	73-190	.384	2-15	.133
1983	1,329	2,025	.656	34-37	.919	417-508	.821	477-636	.750	329-628	.524	72-201	.358	0-15	.000
1984	1,442	2,112	.683	44-49	.898	450-532	.846	503-681	.739	363-630	.576	80-206	.388	2-14	.143
1985	1,360	2,106	.646	40-47	.851	416-511	.814	478-657	.728	341-647	.527	84-227	.370	1-17	.059
1986	1,326	2,034	.652	45-48	.938	445-525	.848	448-641	.699	340-629	.541	44-182	.242	4-9	.444
1987	1,381	2,058	.671	45-48	.938	484-559	.866	469-638	.735	311-604	.515	72-200	.360	0-9	.000
1988	1,421	2,110	.673	33-35	.943	487-573	.850	495-664	.745	337-610	.552	68-217	.313	1-11	.091
1989#	1,389	2,006	*.692	50-53	.943	497-565	.880	471-655	.719	319-573	.557	52-154	.338	0-6	.000
1990	1,348	2,011	.670	39-42	.929	477-546	.874	454-626	.725	319-625	.510	59-167	.353	0-5	.000
1991$	1,092	1,831	.596	31-32	.969	395-519	.761	366-612	.598	254-531	.478	45-132	.341	1-5	.200
1992	1,288	1,986	.649	32-38	.842	464-569	.815	447-673	.664	294-577	.510	49-126	.389	2-3	.667
1993§	1,182	1,832	.645	23-25	.920	490-599	.818	407-617	.660	224-488	.459	38-98	.388	0-5	.000
1994	1,220	1,877	.650	39-40	.975	458-528	.867	419-626	.669	263-547	.481	40-128	.313	1-8	.125
1995	1,150	1,759	.654	32-32	1.000	468-549	.852	373-587	.635	244-489	.499	31-100	.310	2-2	1.000
1996	1,207	1,899	.636	28-29	.966	431-509	.847	422-632	.668	277-581	.477	49-147	.333	0-1	.000
1997	1,255	1,895	.662	47-48	.979	445-524	.849	446-659	.677	272-540	.504	45-122	.369	0-2	.000
1998	1,376	2,075	.663	50-60	.833	475-563	.844	466-681	.684	336-622	.540	48-144	.333	1-5	.200
1999	1,387	2,074	.669	36-38	.947	499-608	.821	480-671	.715	321-611	.525	50-142	.352	1-4	.250
2000	1,285	1,906	.674	29-32	.906	442-517	.855	469-667	.703	297-539	.551	48-149	.322	0-2	.000
2001	1,302	1,941	.671	34-37	.919	459-530	.866	458-655	.699	306-572	.535	45-143	.315	0-4	.000
2002	1,580	2,355	.671	55-63	.873	541-637	.849	546-789	.692	389-717	.543	49-143	.343	0-6	.000

*Record. #First year after kicking tee became illegal. $First year after goal-post width narrowed back to 18'6" from 23'4". §First year after hash marks narrowed to 60 feet from each sideline.

DIVISION I-A

Field Goal Trends by Soccer-Style and Conventional Kickers

(Division I-A Kickers Only)
(Pete Gogolak of Cornell was documented as the first soccer-style kicker in college football history. The Hungarian-born kicker played at Cornell from 1961 through 1963. He set a national major-college record of 44 consecutive extra-point conversions and finished 54 of 55 for his career. His younger brother, Charley, also a soccer-styler, kicked at Princeton from 1963 through 1965.)

SOCCER-STYLE

Year	†No.	Made	Atts.	Pct.	16-39	Pct.	16-49	Pct.	40-49	Pct.	50-59	Pct.	60 Plus
1975	70	528	1,012	.522	370-540	.685	479-816	.587	109-276	.395	49-196	.250	1-17
1976	84	517	1,019	.507	350-517	.677	477-831	.574	127-314	.404	40-188	.213	3-16
1977	96	665	1,317	.505	450-649	.693	615-1,047	.587	165-398	.415	50-270	.185	2-27
1978	98	731	1,244	.588	540-768	.703	703-1,148	.612	163-380	.429	28-96	.292	1-3

Year	†No.	Made	Atts.	Pct.	Under 20	20-29	30-39	40-49	50-59	60 Plus
1979	116	839	1,413	.594	23-28	288-380	282-455	214-419	32-126	0-5
1980	121	988	1,657	.596	26-32	327-416	342-522	261-540	32-147	0-5
1981	138	1,108	1,787	.620	32-36	377-476	376-576	279-551	43-142	1-6
1982	105	1,026	1,548	.663	26-27	317-375	346-482	273-495	62-156	2-13
1983	110	1,139	1,724	.661	29-31	345-416	403-541	294-543	68-179	0-14
1984	127	1,316	1,898	*.694	43-47	414-480	438-589	341-572	78-197	2-13
1985	133	1,198	1,838	.652	35-41	369-452	415-578	306-560	72-191	1-16
1986	128	1,201	1,829	.657	37-40	398-467	410-575	313-576	39-162	4-9
1987	122	1,275	1,892	.674	40-43	458-523	424-574	290-566	63-177	0-9
1988	140	1,317	1,947	.676	31-33	445-521	468-630	311-562	61-201	1-11
1989	138	1,313	1,897	.692	49-52	462-526	441-612	310-551	51-150	0-6
1990	135	1,282	1,890	.678	36-38	450-515	432-589	308-590	56-154	0-4
1991	132	1,048	1,763	.594	30-31	381-500	349-589	243-512	44-130	1-1
1992	135	1,244	1,926	.646	31-37	447-554	429-647	288-561	47-124	2-3
1993	132	1,153	1,776	.649	23-25	475-578	398-600	219-475	38-93	0-5
1994	138	1,203	1,856	.648	38-39	452-522	410-617	263-543	39-127	1-8
1995	148	1,150	1,759	.654	32-32	468-549	373-587	244-489	31-100	2-2
1996	149	1,207	1,899	.636	28-29	431-509	422-632	277-581	49-147	0-1
1997	146	1,255	1,895	.662	47-48	445-524	446-659	272-540	45-122	0-2
1998	149	1,376	2,075	.663	50-60	475-563	466-681	336-622	48-144	1-5
1999	153	1,387	2,074	.669	36-38	499-608	480-671	321-611	50-142	1-4
2000	147	1,285	1,906	.674	29-32	442-517	469-667	297-539	48-149	0-2
2001	151	1,302	1,941	.671	34-37	459-530	458-655	306-572	45-143	0-4
2002	159	1,580	2,355	.671	55-63	541-637	546-789	389-717	49-143	0-6

CONVENTIONAL

Year	†No.	Made	Atts.	Pct.	16-39	Pct.	16-49	Pct.	40-49	Pct.	50-59	Pct.	60 Plus
1975	116	564	1,085	.520	427-640	.667	541-959	.564	114-319	.357	23-126	.183	3-13
1976	101	608	1,192	.510	460-720	.639	594-1,065	.558	134-345	.388	14-127	.110	0-7
1977	98	513	1,054	.487	384-586	.655	487-916	.532	103-330	.312	26-138	.188	4-14
1978	86	440	761	.578	352-516	.682	434-729	.595	82-213	.385	6-32	.188	0-0

Year	†No.	Made	Atts.	Pct.	Under 20	20-29	30-39	40-49	50-59	60 Plus
1979	70	333	585	.569	10-14	140-185	111-198	63-150	9-37	0-1
1980	62	258	471	.548	5-7	81-113	110-174	56-142	6-33	0-2
1981	50	195	367	.531	8-9	70-97	69-126	41-112	7-22	0-1
1982	25	103	195	.528	3-4	36-50	34-62	25-59	5-18	0-2
1983	23	112	181	.619	4-5	40-55	46-58	22-50	0-12	0-1
1984	10	44	76	.579	0-1	17-26	20-33	7-15	0-1	0-0
1985	12	81	138	.587	3-4	22-29	29-40	19-44	8-20	0-1
1986	8	58	89	.652	4-4	21-28	17-27	14-24	2-6	0-0
1987	4	35	50	.700	4-4	10-14	14-16	6-9	1-7	0-0
1988	5	26	40	.650	0-0	17-21	5-7	4-10	0-2	0-0
1989	2	37	47	.787	1-1	19-20	12-16	5-9	0-1	0-0
1990	2	23	38	.605	1-1	8-10	8-9	4-13	2-5	0-0
1991	2	16	24	.667	0-0	5-9	6-7	5-7	0-1	0-0
1992	1	12	18	.667	0-0	5-6	6-8	1-4	0-0	0-0
1993	1	6	11	.545	0-0	4-5	2-3	0-3	0-0	0-0
1994	1	17	21	*.810	1-1	6-6	9-9	0-4	1-1	0-0
1995	0	0	0	.000	0-0	0-0	0-0	0-0	0-0	0-0
1996	0	0	0	.000	0-0	0-0	0-0	0-0	0-0	0-0
1997	0	0	0	.000	0-0	0-0	0-0	0-0	0-0	0-0
1998	0	0	0	.000	0-0	0-0	0-0	0-0	0-0	0-0
1999	0	0	0	.000	0-0	0-0	0-0	0-0	0-0	0-0
2000	0	0	0	.000	0-0	0-0	0-0	0-0	0-0	0-0
2001	0	0	0	.000	0-0	0-0	0-0	0-0	0-0	0-0
2002	0	0	0	.000	0-0	0-0	0-0	0-0	0-0	0-0

*Record. †Number of kickers attempting at least one field goal.

Average Yardage of Field Goals

(Division I-A Kickers Only)

Year	Soccer-Style Made	Missed	Total	Conventional Made	Missed	Total	Nation Made	Missed	Total
1975	35.1	43.2	39.0	33.1	41.3	37.0	34.1	42.2	37.9
1976	35.0	43.1	39.0	33.2	40.7	36.9	34.0	41.8	37.9
1977	34.7	44.3	39.5	33.3	41.9	37.7	34.1	43.2	38.7
1978	34.0	39.9	36.4	31.9	38.3	34.6	33.2	39.3	35.7
1979	33.7	39.9	36.2	31.9	38.0	34.5	33.2	39.3	35.7
1980	34.0	40.7	36.7	33.4	39.6	36.2	33.8	40.4	36.6
1981	33.9	40.1	36.2	33.2	38.6	35.7	33.8	39.8	36.1
1982	34.8	41.8	37.2	34.0	39.8	36.7	34.7	41.5	37.1
1983	34.7	42.1	37.2	32.3	40.5	35.5	34.5	41.9	37.0
1984	34.4	41.8	36.7	32.3	34.9	33.4	34.3	41.5	36.5
1985	34.5	41.3	36.8	35.4	41.7	38.0	34.5	41.3	36.9
1986	33.9	41.6	36.6	32.5	38.6	34.7	33.9	41.4	36.5
1987	33.5	41.8	36.2	32.3	41.4	35.1	33.5	41.8	36.2
1988	33.9	41.7	36.4	30.0	37.6	32.7	32.0	39.3	34.4
1989	33.5	41.2	35.9	30.5	39.6	32.4	33.4	41.2	35.8
1990	33.4	41.3	36.0	33.4	42.0	36.7	33.4	41.3	36.0
1991	33.2	40.7	35.8	28.6	31.9	40.7	35.9	40.4	36.1
1992	34.1	41.2	36.7	30.1	37.8	32.7	37.2	41.3	37.8
1993	32.4	38.9	34.7	26.8	38.0	31.9	32.3	38.9	34.6
1994	32.9	40.6	35.6	31.4	45.5	34.0	32.9	40.7	35.6
1995	32.4	40.1	35.0	—	—	—	32.4	40.1	35.0
1996	33.4	40.5	36.0	—	—	—	33.4	40.5	36.0
1997	33.2	40.1	35.5	—	—	—	33.2	40.1	35.5
1998	33.4	40.6	36.1	—	—	—	33.4	40.6	36.1
1999	34.0	40.9	36.8	—	—	—	34.0	40.9	36.8
2000	33.8	40.3	36.2	—	—	—	33.8	40.3	36.2
2001	34.1	40.2	36.4	—	—	—	34.1	40.2	36.4
2002	34.9	40.5	36.6	—	—	—	34.9	40.5	36.6

Division I-A Extra-Point Trends

(From Start of Two-Point Attempts)

Year	Games	Percent of Total Tries Kick	2-Pt.	Kick Attempts Atts.	Made	Pct.	Two-Point Attempts Atts.	Made	Pct.
1958	578	#.486	*.514	1,295	889	.686	*1,371	*613	.447
1959	578	.598	.402	1,552	1,170	.754	1,045	421	.403
1960	596	.701	.299	1,849	1,448	.783	790	345	.437
1961	574	.723	.277	1,842	1,473	.800	706	312	.442
1962	602	.724	.276	1,987	1,549	.780	757	341	.450
1963	605	.776	.224	2,057	1,659	.807	595	256	.430
1964	613	.814	.186	2,053	1,704	.830	469	189	.403
1965	619	.881	.119	2,460	2,083	.847	331	134	.405
1966	626	.861	.139	2,530	2,167	.857	410	165	.402
1967	611	.869	.131	2,629	2,252	.857	397	160	.403
1968	615	.871	.129	3,090	2,629	.851	456	181	.397
1969	621	.880	.120	3,168	2,781	.878	432	170	.394
1970	667	.862	.138	3,255	2,875	.883	522	246	*.471
1971	726	.889	.111	3,466	3,081	.889	433	173	.400
1972	720	.872	.128	3,390	3,018	.890	497	219	.441
1973	741	.893	.107	3,637	3,258	.896	435	180	.414
1974	749	.885	.115	3,490	3,146	.901	455	211	.464
1975	785	.891	109	3,598	3,266	.908	440	171	.389
1976	796	.877	.123	3,579	3,241	.906	502	203	.404
1977	849	.891	.109	4,041	3,668	.908	495	209	.422
1978	816	.884	.116	3,808	3,490	.916	498	208	.418
1979	811	.897	.103	3,702	3,418	.923	424	176	.415
1980	810	.895	.105	3,785	3,480	.919	442	170	.384
1981	788	.901	.099	3,655	3,387	.927	403	172	.427
1982	599	.901	.099	2,920	2,761	.946	320	120	.375
1983	631	.896	.104	3,080	2,886	.937	356	151	.424
1984	626	.889	.111	2,962	2,789	.942	370	173	.468
1985	623	.899	.101	3,068	2,911	.949	345	121	#.351
1986	619	.905	.095	3,132	2,999	.958	330	131	.397
1987	615	.892	.108	3,094	2,935	.949	375	163	.435
1988	616	.899	.101	3,215	3,074	.956	363	156	.430
1989	614	.888	.112	3,233	3,090	.956	409	179	.438
1990	623	.911	.089	3,429	3,291	*.960	335	138	.412
1991	617	.906	.094	3,279	3,016	.920	342	128	.374
1992	619	.899	.101	3,156	2,967	.940	353	159	.450
1993	613	.912	.088	3,455	3,251	.941	333	143	.429
1994	617	.897	.103	3,433	3,207	.934	395	163	.413
1995	622	.902	.098	3,594	3,354	.933	389	173	.445
1996	644	.923	.077	3,862	3,630	.940	322	144	.447
1997	646	.913	.087	3,828	3,572	.933	367	155	.422
1998	652	.919	.081	3,826	3,590	.938	339	146	.431
1999	663	.926	.074	3,957	3,725	.941	315	128	.406
2000	638	*.934	#.066	3,955	3,701	.936	#278	#114	.410
2001	645	.923	.077	4,125	3,897	.945	342	138	.404
2002	740	.930	.070	*4,744	*4,452	.938	359	156	.435

*Record high. #Record low.

Division I-A Extra-Point Kick Attempts (1938-57)

Year	Pct. Made	Year	Pct. Made	Year	Pct. Made	Year	Pct. Made
1938	.608	1946	.657	1951	.711	1956	.666
1939	.625	1947	.657	1952	.744	1957	.653
1940	.607	1948	.708	1953	.650		
1941	.638	1949	.738	1954	.656		
1942-45	*	1950	.713	1955	.669		

*Not compiled.

Division I-A Defensive Extra-Point Trends

In 1988, the NCAA Football Rules Committee adopted a rule that gave defensive teams an opportunity to score two points on point-after-touchdown tries. The two points were awarded for returning an interception or advancing a blocked kick for a touchdown on point-after tries.

Year	Games	Kick Ret./TDs	Int. Ret./TDs	Total Ret./TDs
1988	616	8/2	6/0	14/2
1989	614	12/3	9/2	21/5
1990	623	9/3	5/2	14/5
1991	617	9/3	10/3	19/6
1992	619	8/5	1/0	9/5
1993	613	5/2	6/1	11/3
1994	617	4/0	8/3	12/3
1995	622	12/5	5/3	17/8
1996	644	9/4	7/3	16/7
1997	646	13/3	6/1	19/4
1998	652	11/4	7/4	18/8
1999	663	8/2	3/0	11/2
2000	638	10/3	5/2	15/5
2001	645	11/4	7/3	18/7
2002	740	19/4	6/3	25/7
Totals	9,569	148/47	91/30	239/77

Division I-A Fumble-Recovery Returns

In 1990, the NCAA Football Rules Committee adopted a rule that gave the defense an opportunity to advance fumbles that occur beyond the neutral zone (or line of scrimmage). In 1992, the rule was changed to allow defenses to advance any fumble regardless of position behind or beyond the line of scrimmage. Here are the number of fumble recoveries by division that were advanced, and the number that resulted in a score.

Year	Games	Fumble Rec./TDs
1990	623	51/17
1991	617	60/16
1992	619	126/34
1993	613	117/24
1994	617	131/43
1995	622	148/49
1996	644	195/86
1997	646	206/76
1998	652	136/73
1999	663	150/84
2000	638	166/75
2001	645	152/78
2002	740	177/84
Totals	8,339	1,815/739

Major-College Tie Games

The record for most tie games in a single week is six—on October 27, 1962; September 28, 1963; and October 9, 1982.

Note: Tiebreaker procedures added for 1996 season.

Year	No.	Games	Pct.	Scoreless
1954	15	551	2.72	2
1955	22	536	4.10	1
1956	28	558	5.02	2
1957*	24	570	4.21	4
1958*	19	578	3.29	2
1959	13	578	2.25	4
1960	23	596	3.86	4
1961	11	574	1.92	1
1962	20	602	3.32	2
1963	25	605	4.13	4
1964	19	613	3.10	2
1965	19	619	3.07	4
1966	13	626	2.08	0
1967	14	611	2.29	1
1968	17	615	2.76	1
1969	9	621	1.45	0
1970	7	667	1.05	0
1971	12	726	1.65	1
1972	14	720	1.94	1
1973	18	741	2.43	2
1974	18	749	2.40	0
1975	16	785	2.04	0
1976	13	796	1.63	1
1977	16	849	1.88	1
1978	16	816	1.96	1
1979	17	811	2.10	1
1980	12	810	1.48	0
1981	17	788	2.16	0
1982	14	599	2.34	0
1983	13	631	2.06	†1
1984	15	626	2.40	0
1985	13	623	2.09	0
1986	10	619	1.62	0
1987	13	615	2.11	0
1988	12	616	1.95	0
1989	15	614	2.44	0
1990	15	623	2.41	0
1991	14	617	2.27	0
1992	13	619	2.10	0
1993	11	613	1.79	0
1994	13	617	2.11	0
1995	9	622	1.45	0

*First year of two-point conversion rule. †Last scoreless tie game: Nov. 19, 1983, Oregon vs. Oregon St.

Highest-Scoring Tie Games

(Home Team Listed First; Both Teams Classified Major-College or Division I-A at Time)

Note: Tiebreaker procedures added for 1996 season.

Score	Date	Opponents
52-52	11-16-91	San Diego St.-Brigham Young
48-48	9-8-79	San Jose St.-Utah St.
43-43	11-12-88	Duke-North Carolina St.
41-41	9-10-94	Northwestern-Stanford
41-41	9-23-89	San Diego St.-Cal St. Fullerton
40-40	11-8-75	Idaho-Weber St.
39-39	11-7-82	Texas Tech-TCU
37-37	9-23-67	*Alabama-Florida St.
36-36	9-30-72	Georgia Tech-Rice
35-35	9-23-95	Michigan St.-Purdue
35-35	11-16-91	San Jose St.-Hawaii
35-35	12-9-89	Hawaii-Air Force
35-35	9-23-89	Colorado St.-Eastern Mich.
35-35	10-7-78	Ohio St.-Southern Methodist
35-35	10-19-74	Idaho-Montana
35-35	10-9-71	New Mexico-New Mexico St.
35-35	9-27-69	Minnesota-Ohio
35-35	9-21-68	Washington-Rice
35-35	11-18-67	Navy-Vanderbilt
35-35	12-11-48	†Pacific (Cal.)—Hardin-Simmons
34-34	10-6-90	Iowa St.-Kansas
33-33	10-1-83	California-Arizona
33-33	9-24-49	TCU-Oklahoma St.
33-33	10-31-31	Yale-Dartmouth

*At Birmingham. †Grape Bowl, Lodi, Calif.

Home-Field Records

(Includes Host Teams at Neutral-Site Games)

Year	Games	Home Team Won	Lost	Tied	Pct.
1966	626	365	248	13	.594
1967	611	333	264	14	.557
1968	615	348	250	17	.580
1969	621	366	246	9	.596
1970	667	399	261	7	.603
1971	726	416	298	12	.581
1972	720	441	265	14	.622
1973	741	439	284	18	.605
1974	749	457	274	18	.622
1975	785	434	335	16	.563
1976	796	463	320	13	.590
1977	849	501	332	16	.600
1978	816	482	318	16	.601
1979	811	460	334	17	.578
1980	809	471	327	12	.589
1981	788	457	314	17	.591
1982	599	368	217	14	.626
1983	631	364	254	13	.587
1984	626	371	240	15	.605
1985	623	371	239	13	.606
1986	619	363	246	10	.595
1987	615	387	215	13	*.640
1988	616	370	234	12	.610
1989	614	365	234	15	.607
1990	623	373	235	15	.611
1991	617	362	241	14	.598
1992	619	388	218	13	.637
1993	613	375	227	11	.621
1994	617	357	247	13	.589
1995	622	354	259	9	.576
1996	644	389	255	0	.604
1997	646	392	254	0	.607
1998	652	399	253	0	.612
1999	663	403	260	0	.608
2000	638	391	247	0	.613
2001	645	401	244	0	.622
2002	734	456	278	0	.621

* Record.

I-A Members Since 1978

The following list shows years of active membership for current and former Division I-A football-playing institutions. The lists are from 1978, the year Division I was divided into I-A and I-AA.

Active Members

Air Force	1978-present
Akron	1987-present
Alabama	1978-present
UAB	1996-present
Arizona	1978-present
Arizona St.	1978-present
Arkansas	1978-present
Arkansas St.	1978-81, 92-present
Army	1978-present
Auburn	1978-present
Ball St.	1978-81, 83-present
Baylor	1978-present
Boise St.	1996-present
Boston College	1978-present
Bowling Green	1978-81, 83-present
Brigham Young	1978-present
Buffalo	2002-present
California	1978-present
UCF	1996-present
Central Mich.	1978-present

Active Members

Cincinnati	1978-81, 83-present
Clemson	1978-present
Colorado	1978-present
Colorado St.	1978-present
Connecticut	2002-present
Duke	1978-present
East Caro.	1978-present
Eastern Mich.	1978-81, 83-present
Florida	1978-present
Florida St.	1978-present
Fresno St.	1978-present
Georgia	1978-present
Georgia Tech	1978-present
Hawaii	1978-present
Houston	1978-present
Idaho	1997-present
Illinois	1978-present
Indiana	1978-present
Iowa	1978-present
Iowa St.	1978-present
Kansas	1978-present
Kansas St.	1978-present

Active Members

Kent St.	1978-81, 83-present
Kentucky	1978-present
La.-Lafayette	1978-present
La.-Monroe	1978-81, 94-present
LSU	1978-present
Louisiana Tech	1978-81, 89-present
Louisville	1978-present
Marshall	1978-81, 98-present
Maryland	1978-present
Memphis	1978-present
Miami (Fla.)	1978-present
Miami (Ohio)	1978-81, 83-present
Michigan	1978-present
Michigan St.	1978-present
Middle Tenn.	1999-present
Minnesota	1978-present
Mississippi	1978-present
Mississippi St.	1978-present
Missouri	1978-present
Navy	1978-present
Nebraska	1978-present
UNLV	1978-present
Nevada	1992-present
New Mexico	1978-present
New Mexico St.	1978-present
North Carolina	1978-present

Active Members

North Carolina St.	1978-present
North Texas	1978-81, 95-present
Northern Ill.	1978-81, 83-present
Northwestern	1978-present
Notre Dame	1978-present
Ohio	1978-81, 83-present
Ohio St.	1978-present
Oklahoma	1978-present
Oklahoma St.	1978-present
Oregon	1978-present
Oregon St.	1978-present
Penn St.	1978-present
Pittsburgh	1978-present
Purdue	1978-present
Rice	1978-present
Rutgers	1978-present
San Diego St.	1978-present
San Jose St.	1978-present
South Carolina	1978-present
South Fla.	2001-present
Southern Calif.	1978-present
Southern Methodist	1978-86, 89-present
Southern Miss.	1978-present
Stanford	1978-present
Syracuse	1978-present

Active Members

Temple	1978-present
Tennessee	1978-present
Texas	1978-present
Texas A&M	1978-present
TCU	1978-present
UTEP	1978-present
Texas Tech	1978-present
Toledo	1978-present
Troy St.	2002-present
Tulane	1978-present
Tulsa	1978-present
UCLA	1978-present
Utah	1978-present
Utah St.	1978-present
Vanderbilt	1978-present
Virginia	1978-present
Virginia Tech	1978-present
Wake Forest	1978-present
Washington	1978-present
Washington St.	1978-present
West Virginia	1978-present
Western Mich.	1978-81, 83-present
Wisconsin	1978-present
Wyoming	1978-present

Former Members

Appalachian St.	1978-81
Brown	1978-81
Cal St. Fullerton	1978-92
Chattanooga	1978-81
Citadel	1978-81
Colgate	1978-81
Columbia	1978-81

Former Members

Cornell	1978-81
Dartmouth	1978-81
Drake	1978-80
East Tenn. St.	1978-81
Furman	1978-81
Harvard	1978-81
Holy Cross	1978-81
Illinois St.	1978-81
Indiana St.	1978-81
Lamar	1978-81
Long Beach St.	1978-91
McNeese St.	1978-81
Pacific (Cal.)	1978-95
Pennsylvania	1978-81
Princeton	1978-81
Richmond	1978-81
Southern Ill.	1978-81
Tennessee St.	1978-80
Texas-Arlington	1978-81
Villanova	1978-80
VMI	1978-81
West Tex. A&M	1978-80
Western Caro.	1978-81
Wichita St.	1978-86
William & Mary	1978-81
Yale	1978-81

College Football Rules Changes

The Ball

1869—Round, rubber Association ball.
1875—Egg-shaped, leather-covered Rugby ball.
1896—Prolate spheroid, without specific measurements.
1912—28-28 1/2 inches around ends, 22 1/2-23 inches around middle, weight 14-15 ounces.
1929—28-28 1/2 inches around ends, 22-22 1/2 inches around middle, weight 14-15 ounces.
1934—28-28 1/2 inches around ends, 21 1/4-21 1/2 inches around middle, weight 14-15 ounces.
1941—For night games, a white ball or other colored ball with two black stripes around the ball may be used at the discretion of the referee.
1952—Ball may be inclined no more than 45 degrees by snapper.
1956—Rubber-covered ball permitted.
1973—Teams allowed to use ball of their choice while in possession.
1978—Ball may not be altered, and new or nearly new balls added.
1982—10 7/8 to 11 7/16 inches long, 20 3/4 to 21 1/4 inches around middle, and 27 3/4 to 28 1/2 inches long-axis circumference.
1993—Rubber or composition ball ruled illegal.

The Field

1869—120 yards by 75 yards; uprights 24 feet apart.
1871—166 2/3 yards by 100 yards.
1872—133 1/3 yards by 83 1/3 yards.
1873—Uprights 25 feet apart.
1876—110 yards by 53 1/3 yards. Uprights 18 1/2 feet apart; crossbar 10 feet high.
1882—Field marked with transverse lines every five yards. This distance to be gained in three downs to retain possession.
1912—Field 120 yards by 53 1/3 yards, including two 10-yard end zones.
1927—Goal posts moved back 10 yards, to end line.
1957—Team area at 35-yard lines.
1959—Uprights widened to 23 feet, 4 inches apart.
1966—Pylons placed in corners of end zone and at goal lines mandatory in 1974.
1991—Uprights moved back to 18 feet, 6 inches apart.
1993—Hash marks moved six feet, eight inches closer to center of field to 60 feet from each sideline (40 feet apart).

Scoring

1869—All goals count 1 each.
1883—Safety 1, touchdown 4, goal after TD 4, goal from field 5.
1884—Safety 2, touchdown 4, goal from field 5.
1897—Touchdown 4, field goal 5, touchdown failing goal 5, safety 2.
1902—Teams change goals after every try at goal following a touchdown, after every goal from the field and also at the beginning of the half.
1904—Goal from field 4.
1909—Goal from field 3.
1912—Touchdown 4.
1921—Ball put in play at 30-yard line after a safety, 20-yard line after a touchback.
1922—Try-for-point by scrimmage play from 5-yard line.
1924—Try-for-point by scrimmage play from 3-yard line.
1927—Goal posts placed on end lines.
1929—Try-for-point by scrimmage play from 2-yard line.
1958—One-point & two-point conversion (from 3-yard line). One-point safety added.
1974—Ball must go between the uprights for a successful field goal, over the uprights previously scored.
1976—Forfeit score changed from 1-0 to score at time of forfeit if the offended team is ahead at time of forfeit.
1984—Try may be eliminated at end of game if both captains agree.
1995—Try at end of game mandatory unless team behind in score leaves field.

Scoring Values

1882—Touchdown 2 points; field goal 5 points; extra points 4 points
1883-87—Touchdown 4 points; field goal 5 points; extra points 4 points
1888-97—Touchdown 4 points; field goal 5 points; extra points 2 points
1898-1903—Touchdown 5 points; field goal 5 points; extra points 1 point
1904-08—Touchdown 5 points; field goal 4 points; extra points 1 point
1909-11—Touchdown 5 points; field goal 3 points; extra points 1 point
1912-57—Touchdown 6 points; field goal 3 points; extra points 1 point
1958-present—Touchdown 6 points; field goal 3 points; extra points 1 point/kick, 2 points/run or pass.
1988-present—Extra points 2 points/defense.

Note: Safety worth 1 point from 1882-1883, 2 points in all seasons since 1884.

Players

1869—Each team consisted of 25 players.
1873—Each team consisted of 20 players.
1876—Each team consisted of 15 players.
1880—Each team consisted of 11 players.
1895—Only one man in motion forward before the snap. No more than three players behind the line. One player permitted in motion toward own goal line.
1910—Seven players required on line.
1911—Illegal to conceal ball beneath a player's clothing.
1947—All players urged to be numbered in a uniform manner. Ends to wear numbers in the 80s; tackles, 70s; guards, 60s; centers, 50s; and backs, 10-49.
1966—Mandatory numbering of five players on the line 50-79.
1970—All players numbered 1-99.

Equipment

1894—No one wearing projecting nails or iron plates on his shoes, or any metal substance upon his person, is allowed to play. No greasy or sticky substance shall be used on the person of players.
1903—If head protectors are worn, there can be no sole leather or other hard or unyielding substances in their construction. Leather cleats on shoes allowed.
1908—First documented jersey numbers used by Washington & Jefferson.
1915—Numbers added to jerseys.
1927—Rubber cleats allowed, but under no conditions are cleats to be dangerously sharp.
1930—No player shall wear equipment that endangers players. The committee forbids the use of head protectors or jerseys that are so similar in color to the ball that they give the wearer an unfair and unsportsmanlike advantage over the opponent. Stripes may be used to break up the solid colors.
1933—Head protectors or helmets recommended to be worn by all players.
1937—All players must wear minimum 6-inch Arabic numerals on the front and minimum 8-inch Arabic numerals on the back of jerseys.
1939—All players must wear helmets.
1946—All players must wear minimum 8-inch Arabic numerals on front (changed from 6 inches) and minimum 10-inch Arabic numerals on back of jerseys (changed from 8 inches), of a single color which must be in sharp contrast with the color of the jerseys.
1948—One-inch kicking tees permitted.
1951—Any circular or ring cleat prohibited unless it has rounded edges and a wall at least 3/16-inch thick. Face masks added to helmet. Must be made of non-breakable, molded plastic with rounded edges.
1962—All players recommended to wear properly fitted mouth protectors.

1965—Two-inch kicking tees permitted.
1966—Players prohibited from wearing equipment with electronic, mechanical or other signal devices for the purpose of communicating with any source.
1968—Metal face masks having surfaces with material as resilient as rubber are allowed.
1970—Shoe cleats more than one-half inch in length (changed from three-quarters inch) prohibited.
1972—All players must wear mouth protectors, beginning with 1973 season.
1973—All players shall wear head protectors with a secured chin strap.
1974—All players shall wear shoulder pads.
1976—All players shall wear hip pads and thigh guards.
1979—Beginning in 1981, one team shall wear white jerseys.
1982—Tearaway jersey eliminated by charging a timeout.
1983—Mandatory white jersey for visiting teams.
1986—Therapeutic or preventive knee braces must be worn under the pants.
1989—Kicking tees eliminated for field goals and extra-point attempts.
1991—Rib and back pad covering mandatory.
1994—Standards established to limit glove stickiness. Jerseys that extend below the top of the pants must be tucked into the pants.
1995—Home team may wear white jerseys if both teams agree before the season.
1996—Cleats limited to one-half inch in length (see 1970). Violators disqualified for remainder of game and entire next game. Rule a dead ball when a ball carrier's helmet comes completely off, with the ball belonging to runner's team at that spot. Jerseys must extend to top of pants and must be tucked in if longer.
1997—Require all players on the same team to wear white or team-colored socks of the same design and length. Leg coverings, such as tights, if worn, must be in team colors and of a uniform design for all players on the same team.
1998—All eye shields, if worn, must be clear (transparent) and made from molded and rigid material. NCAA member institutions can, in the case of a death or catastrophic injury or illness, memorialize a player or person with a patch or decal not greater than 1 1/2 inches in diameter that displays the number, name or initials of the individual on the uniform or helmet.
1999—Visible bandanas are ruled an illegal uniform attachment.
2000—A maximum of two defensive players are allowed to wear 4-inch by 12-inch white towels without markings attached to the front belt.

Substitutions

1876—Fifteen players to a team and few if any substitutions.
1882—Replacements for disqualified or injured players.
1897—Substitutions may enter the game any time at discretion of captains.
1922—Players withdrawn during the first half may be returned during the second half. A player withdrawn in the second half may not return.
1941—A player may substitute any time but may not be withdrawn or the outgoing player returned to the game until one play had intervened. Platoon football made possible.
1948—Unlimited substitution on change of team possession.
1953—Two-platoon abolished and players allowed to enter the game only once in each quarter.
1954-64—Changes each year toward more liberalized substitution rule and platoon football.
1965—Platoon football returns. Unlimited substitutions between periods, after a score or try.
1974—Substitutes must be in for one play and replaced players out for one play.
1993—Players who are bleeding or whose uniforms are saturated with blood must come out of the game until their return has been approved by medical personnel.
2000—Offensive teams, while in the process of substitution or simulated substitution, are now prohibited from pushing quickly to the line of scrimmage

and snapping the ball with the obvious attempt to create a defensive disadvantage.

Passing Game

1906—One forward pass legalized behind the line if made five yards right or left of center. Ball went to opponents if it failed to touch a player of either side before touching the ground. Either team could recover a pass touched by an opponent. One pass each scrimmage down.

1910—Pass interference does not apply 20 yards beyond the line of scrimmage. Passer must be five yards behind the line of scrimmage. One forward pass permitted during each down.

1914—Roughing the passer added.

1923—Handing the ball forward is an illegal forward pass and receivers going out of bounds and returning prohibited.

1934—Three changes encourage use of pass. (1) First forward pass in series of downs can be incomplete in the end zone without loss of ball except on fourth down. (2) Circumference of ball reduced, making it easier to throw. (3) Five-yard penalty for more than one incomplete pass in same series of downs eliminated.

1941—Fourth-down forward pass incomplete in end zone no longer a touchback. Ball goes to opponent at spot where put in play.

1945—Forward pass may be thrown from anywhere behind the line, encouraging use of modern T formation.

1949—Intentional grounding of a pass shall result in a loss of down and a five-yard penalty from the spot of the foul.

1966—Compulsory numbering system makes only players numbered other than 50-79 eligible forward-pass receivers.

1976—Offensive blocking changed to provide half extension of arms to assist pass blocking.

1980—Retreat blocking added with full arm extension to assist pass blocking, and illegal use of hands reduced to five yards.

1982—Pass interference only on a catchable forward pass. Forward pass intentionally grounded to conserve time permitted.

1983—First down added to roughing the passer.

1985—Retreat block deleted and open hands and extended arms permitted anywhere on the field.

1990—Pass thrown immediately to the ground to conserve time legal.

1994—Ball must be catchable for offensive player to be charged with pass interference.

1996—Principle of "reasonable opportunity to catch the pass" applied to intentional grounding situations.

1998—A backward pass can be recovered and advanced by the defense.

1999—Intentional grounding of a pass shall result in a loss of down at the spot of the foul.

2000—Allowing a passer, who is five yards or more toward the sideline from the original position of the ball at the snap, to throw the ball so that it lands beyond the neutral zone to avoid loss of yardage without penalty.

General Changes

1876—Holding and carrying the ball permitted.

1880—Eleven players on a side and a scrimmage line established.

1882—Downs and yards to gain enter the rules.

1883—Scoring system established.

1906—Forward passes permitted. Ten yards for first down.

1920—Clipping defined.

1922—Try-for-point introduced. Ball brought out five yards from goal line for scrimmage, allowing try for extra point by place kick, drop kick, run or forward pass.

1925—Kickoff returned to 40-yard line. Clipping made a violation, with penalty of 25 yards.

1927—One-second pause imposed on shift. Thirty seconds allowed for putting ball in play. Huddle limited to 15 seconds. To encourage use of lateral pass, missed backward pass other than from center declared dead ball when it hits the ground and cannot be recovered by opponents.

1929—All fumbles ruled dead at point of recovery.

1932—Most far-reaching changes in nearly a quarter of a century set up safeguards against hazards of game. (1) Ball declared dead when any portion of player in possession, except his hands or feet, touches ground. (2) Use of flying block and flying tackle barred under penalty of five yards. (3) Players on defense forbidden to strike opponents on head, neck or face. (4) Hard and dangerous equipment must be covered with padding.

1941—Legal to hand ball forward behind the neutral zone.

1949—Blockers required to keep hands against their chest.

1951—Fair catch restored.

1952—Penalty for striking with forearm, elbow or locked hands, or for flagrantly rough play or unsportsmanlike conduct, changed from 15 yards to mandatory suspension.

1957—Penalty for grabbing face mask.

1959—Distance penalties limited to one-half distance to offending team's goal line.

1967—Coaching from sideline permitted.

1970—Eleven-game schedule permitted.

1971—Crack-back block (blocking below waist) illegal.

1972—Freshman eligibility restored.

1977—Clock started on snap after a penalty.

1978—Unsuccessful field goal returned to the previous spot.

1983—Offensive encroachment changed...no offensive player permitted in or beyond the neutral zone after snapper touches ball.

1984—Defensive pass interference penalty changed from spot of foul to 15 yards from previous spot.

1985—One or both feet on ground required for blocking below waist foul.

1986—Kickoff from the 35-yard line.

1988—Defensive team allowed to score two points on return of blocked extra-point kick attempt or interception of extra-point pass attempt.

1990—Defense allowed to advance fumbles that occur beyond the neutral zone.

1991—Width between goal-post uprights reduced from 23 feet, 4 inches to 18 feet, 6 inches. Kickoffs out of bounds allow receiving team to elect to take ball 30 yards beyond yard line where kickoff occurred. Holding behind the neutral zone penalized 10 yards from the spot of the foul.

1992—Defense allowed to advance fumbles regardless of where they occur. Changes ruling of 1990 fumble advancement.

1993—Guard-around or "fumblerooski" play ruled illegal.

1994—Players involved in a fight after half time disqualified for first half of next game; substitutes and coaches who participate in a fight in their team area or leave the team area to join a fight disqualified for entire next game; squad members and coaches involved in a fight during half time disqualified for first half of next game.

1995—Defense penalized five yards for entering neutral zone before snap and causing offensive player

to react immediately. Players prohibited from removing helmets on the field. Players disqualified after second unsportsmanlike-conduct foul in one game. Fight suspensions allowed to carry over to next season.

1996—NCAA tiebreaker system to be used in all games tied after four periods.

1997—In overtime tiebreaker system, require a team that scores a touchdown to attempt a two-point conversion in the third overtime period. Approved a rule requiring a game to be declared a tie if it is in overtime but cannot be finished due to weather, darkness or other conditions. Chop block redefined to be penalized if "obviously delayed" and added restrictions to the "crack-back" block to make it illegal up to five yards beyond line of scrimmage regardless of position of the ball. Officials prompted to enforce mouthpiece rule, charging a timeout to offending team if clock is stopped and player does not have mouthpiece in place. To prevent opponents from leveling punt returners with unnecessarily vicious hits, the penalty was increased from five to 15 yards.

1998—For the first time in history, a backward pass can be recovered and advanced by the defense. It is now consistent with the application of the rules similar to how the defense is allowed to advance a fumble.

1999—Holding behind the neutral zone will be penalized 10 yards from the previous line of scrimmage. Dead-ball fouls by both teams which are part of continuing action or of a retaliatory nature and reported at the same time will be canceled and the penalties disregarded. However, any disqualified player must leave the game. Teams may not break the huddle with 12 or more players.

2000—An illegal block shall now include any high-low, low-high or low-low combination block by any two offensive players beyond the neutral zone regardless of simultaneous contact by both. Also, blocking below the waist by offensive players ("crack-back block") now includes not only wide receivers or players in motion but any player in motion in any direction at the snap and the area is expanded to included the neutral zone and 10 yards beyond. Also, prohibiting a defensive player(s) aligned in a stationary position within one yard of the line of scrimmage from making quick or abrupt actions that are not part of normal player movement in an obvious attempt to cause an offensive player(s) to foul.

2001—A charged team timeout can be 30 seconds in duration if so desired by the team calling the timeout. Most penalties for offensive-team fouls that occur behind the neutral zone will be enforced from the previous spot.

2002—The penalty for interference with the opportunity to catch a kick, when no contact is involved, increased from five to 10 yards. Yardage enforcement of flagrant personal fouls during possession by the defensive team may carry from one extra period to the next.

2003—The game clock on all kickoffs will start when the ball is legally touched in the field of play. The two-yard restricted area around a player positioned to catch a free or scrimmage kick is deleted. Offensive linemen at the snap positioned more than seven yards in any direction from the middle lineman of the offensive formation are prohibited from blocking below the waist toward the original position of the ball in or behind the neutral zone and within 10 yards beyond the neutral zone. Backs at the snap positioned outside the normal tackle position in either direction toward a sideline, or in motion at the snap, are prohibited from blocking below the waist toward the original position of the ball in or behind the neutral zone and within 10 yards beyond the neutral zone.

Division I-AA Records

Individual Records

Total Offense

(Rushing Plus Passing)

MOST PLAYS
Quarter
33—Mickey Fein, Maine vs. Connecticut, Oct. 11, 1997 (4th)
Half
59—Joe Walland, Yale vs. Harvard, Nov. 20, 1999 (2nd)
Game
89—Thomas Leonard, Mississippi Val. vs. Texas Southern, Oct. 25, 1986 (440 yards)
Season
680—Bruce Eugene, Grambling, 2002 (5,018 yards)
Career
2,116—Marcus Brady, Cal St. Northridge, 1998-01 (13,095 yards)

MOST PLAYS PER GAME
Season
59.0—Steve McNair, Alcorn St., 1994 (649 in 11)
Career
49.5—Tom Proudian, Iona, 1993-95 (1,337 in 27)

MOST PLAYS BY A FRESHMAN
Game
81—Kevin Glenn, Illinois St. vs. Western Ill., Nov. 8, 1997 (470 yards)
Season
507—Marcus Brady, Cal St. Northridge, 1998 (2,942 yards)
Per-game record—48.9, James Lopusznick, Fairfield, 1996 (440 in 9)

MOST YARDS GAINED
Quarter
278—Willie Totten, Mississippi Val. vs. Kentucky St., Sept. 1, 1984 (2nd)
Half
404—Todd Hammel, Stephen F. Austin vs. La.-Monroe, Nov. 11, 1989 (1st)
Game
668—Robert Kent, Jackson St. vs. Alabama St., Oct. 6, 2001 (595 passing, 73 rushing)
Season
5,799—Steve McNair, Alcorn St., 1994 (4,863 passing, 936 rushing)
2 Yrs
9,629—Steve McNair, Alcorn St., 1993-94 (8,060 passing, 1,569 rushing)
3 Yrs
13,686—Steve McNair, Alcorn St., 1992-94 (11,601 passing, 2,085 rushing)
Career
(4 yrs.) 16,823—Steve McNair, Alcorn St., 1991-94 (14,496 passing, 2,327 rushing)

MOST YARDS GAINED PER GAME
Season
527.2—Steve McNair, Alcorn St., 1994 (5,799 in 11)
Career
400.5—Steve McNair, Alcorn St., 1991-94 (16,823 in 42)

MOST SEASONS GAINING 3,000 YARDS OR MORE
4—Steve McNair, Alcorn St., 1991-94

MOST YARDS GAINED BY A FRESHMAN
Game
536—Brad Otton, Weber St. vs. Northern Ariz., Nov. 6, 1993 (48 plays)
Season
3,336—Travis Brown, Northern Ariz., 1996
Per-game record—313.7, Steve McNair, Alcorn St., 1991 (3,137 in 10)

MOST YARDS GAINED IN TWO, THREE AND FOUR CONSECUTIVE GAMES
2 Games
1,280—Steve McNair, Alcorn St., 1994 (633 vs. Grambling, Sept. 3; 647 vs. Chattanooga, Sept. 10)
3 Games
1,859—Steve McNair, Alcorn St., 1994 (649 vs. Samford, Oct. 29; 624 vs. Mississippi Val., Nov. 5; 586 vs. Troy St., Nov. 12)
4 Games
2,423—Steve McNair, Alcorn St., 1994 (649 vs. Samford, Oct. 29; 624 vs. Mississippi Val., Nov. 5; 586 vs. Troy St., Nov. 12; 564 vs. Jackson St., Nov. 19)

MOST GAMES GAINING 300 YARDS OR MORE
Season
11—Steve McNair, Alcorn St., 1994
Career
32—Steve McNair, Alcorn St., 1991-94

MOST CONSECUTIVE GAMES GAINING 300 YARDS OR MORE
Season
11—Steve McNair, Alcorn St., 1994
Career
13—Neil Lomax, Portland St., 1979-80; Willie Totten, Mississippi Val., 1984-85; Steve McNair, Alcorn St., 1992-93

MOST GAMES GAINING 400 YARDS OR MORE
Season
9—Steve McNair, Alcorn St., 1994
Career
15—Steve McNair, Alcorn St., 1991-94

MOST CONSECUTIVE GAMES GAINING 400 YARDS OR MORE
5—Willie Totten, Mississippi Val., 1984; Steve McNair, Alcorn St., 1994

MOST GAMES GAINING 500 YARDS OR MORE
Season
6—Steve McNair, Alcorn St., 1994
Career
9—Steve McNair, Alcorn St., 1991-94

MOST YARDS GAINED AGAINST ONE OPPONENT
Career
1,772—Steve McNair, Alcorn St. vs. Jackson St., 1991-94
Also holds per-game record with 443.0 (1,772 in 4)

GAINING 1,000 YARDS RUSHING AND 1,000 YARDS PASSING
Season
Tracy Ham (QB), Ga. Southern, 1986 (1,048 rushing, 1,772 passing); Alcede Surtain (QB), Alabama St., 1995 (1,024 rushing, 1,224 passing); David Dinkins (QB), Morehead St., 1998 (1,169 rushing, 1,812 passing); Greg Hill (QB), Ga. Southern, 1998 (1,061 rushing, 1,193 passing); Greg Hill (QB), Ga. Southern, 1999 (1,084 rushing, 1,262 passing); David Dinkins (QB), Morehead St., 2000 (1,405 rushing, 1,704 passing)); Chaz Williams (QB), Ga. Southern, 2002 (1,422 rushing, 1,022 passing); Allen Suber (QB), Bethune-Cookman, 2002 (1,035 rushing, 1,307 passing)

GAINING 1,000 YARDS RUSHING AND 2,000 YARDS PASSING
Season
David Dinkins, Morehead St., 1999 (1,138 rushing, 2,011 passing)

GAINING 1,000 YARDS RUSHING AND 1,000 YARDS RECEIVING
Season
Brian Westbrook (TB), Villanova, 1998 (1,046 rushing, 1,144 receiving) (first NCAA player to accomplish this feat)

GAINING 2,000 YARDS RUSHING AND 4,000 YARDS PASSING
Career
Tracy Ham (QB), Ga. Southern, 1984-86 (2,506 rushing, 4,871 passing); Bill Vergantino (QB), Delaware, 1989-92 (2,287 rushing, 6,177 passing); Steve McNair (QB), Alcorn St., 1991-94 (2,327 rushing, 14,496 passing); Ryan Vena (QB), Colgate, 1996-99 (2,008 rushing, 7,427 passing); David Dinkins (QB), Morehead St., 1997-00 (3,765 rushing, 5,572 passing); Travis Wilson (QB), Wofford, 1998-01 (2,488 rushing, 4,067 passing)

GAINING 3,000 YARDS RUSHING AND 3,000 YARDS PASSING
Career
Willie Taggart (QB), Western Ky., 1995-98 (3,957 rushing, 3,029 passing); Greg Hill (QB), Ga. Southern, 1996-99 (3,309 rushing, 3,369 passing); David Dinkins (QB), Morehead St., 1997-00 (3,765 rushing, 5,572 passing)

GAINING 3,000 YARDS RUSHING AND 5,000 YARDS PASSING
Career
David Dinkins (QB), Morehead St., 1997-00 (3,765 rushing, 5,572 passing)

HIGHEST AVERAGE GAIN PER PLAY
Game
(Min. 39-49 plays) 12.4—John Whitcomb, UAB vs. Prairie View, Nov. 19, 1994 (43 for 533)
(Min. 50-59 plays) 11.4—Steve McNair, Alcorn St. vs. Chattanooga, Sept. 10, 1994 (57 for 647)
(Min. 60 plays) 9.7—Steve McNair, Alcorn St. vs. Grambling, Sept. 3, 1994 (65 for 633)
Season
(Min. 2,500-3,299 yards) 9.6—Frank Baur, Lafayette, 1988 (285 for 2,727)
(Min. 3,300 yards) 8.9—Steve McNair, Alcorn St., 1994 (649 for 5,799)
Career
(Min. 4,000 yards) 8.2—Steve McNair, Alcorn St., 1991-94 (2,055 for 16,823)

MOST TOUCHDOWNS RESPONSIBLE FOR
(TDs Scored and Passed For)
Game
9—Neil Lomax, Portland St. vs. Delaware St., Nov. 8, 1980 (passed for 8, scored 1); Willie Totten, Mississippi Val. vs. Prairie View, Oct. 27, 1984 (passed for 8, scored 1) & vs. Kentucky St., Sept. 1, 1984 (passed for 9)
Season
61—Willie Totten, Mississippi Val., 1984 (passed for 56, scored 5)
Also holds per-game record with 6.1 (61 in 10)
Career
157—Willie Totten, Mississippi Val., 1982-85 (passed for 139, scored 18)
Also holds per-game record with 3.9 (157 in 40)

MOST POINTS RESPONSIBLE FOR
(Points Scored and Passed For)
Game
56—Willie Totten, Mississippi Val. vs. Kentucky St., Sept. 1, 1984 (passed for 9 TDs and 1 two-point conversion)
Season
368—Willie Totten, Mississippi Val., 1984 (passed for 56 TDs, scored 5 TDs and passed for 1 two-point conversion)
Also holds per-game record with 36.8 (368 in 10)
Career
946—Willie Totten, Mississippi Val., 1982-85 (passed for 139 TDs, scored 18 TDs and passed for 1 two-point conversion)
Also holds per-game record with 23.7 (946 in 40)

Rushing

MOST RUSHES
Quarter
20—Arnold Mickens, Butler vs. Dayton, Oct. 15, 1994 (4th)
Half
32—David Clark, Dartmouth vs. Pennsylvania, Nov. 18, 1989 (2nd); Arnold Mickens, Butler vs. Valparaiso, Oct. 8, 1994 (1st)
Game
56—Arnold Mickens, Butler vs. Valparaiso, Oct. 8, 1994 (295 yards)
Season
409—Arnold Mickens, Butler, 1994 (2,255 yards)
Career
1,124—Charles Roberts, Sacramento St., 1997-00 (6,553 yards)

MOST RUSHES PER GAME
Season
40.9—Arnold Mickens, Butler, 1994 (409 in 10)
Career
38.2—Arnold Mickens, Butler, 1994-95 (763 in 20)

MOST RUSHES IN TWO CONSECUTIVE GAMES
110—Arnold Mickens, Butler, 1994 (56 vs. Valparaiso, Oct. 8; 54 vs. Dayton, Oct. 15)

MOST CONSECUTIVE CARRIES BY SAME PLAYER
Game
26—Arnold Mickens, Butler vs. Valparaiso, Oct. 8, 1994 (during 6 series)

MOST YARDS GAINED
Quarter
194—Otto Kelly, Nevada vs. Idaho, Nov. 12, 1983 (3rd, 8 rushes)
Half
272—Tony Vinson, Towson vs. Morgan St., Nov. 20, 1993 (1st, 26 rushes)
Game
437—Maurice Hicks, N.C. A&T vs. Morgan St., Oct. 6, 2001 (34 rushes)
Season
2,260—Charles Roberts, Sacramento St., 1998 (386 rushes)
Career
6,559—Adrian Peterson, Ga. Southern, 1998-01 (996 rushes)

MOST YARDS GAINED PER GAME
Season
225.5—Arnold Mickens, Butler, 1994 (2,255 in 10)
Career
(2 yrs.) 190.7—Arnold Mickens, Butler, 1994-95 (3,813 in 20)
(3 yrs.) 164.5—Adrian Peterson, Ga. Southern, 1998-00 (5,100 in 31)
(4 yrs.) 156.2—Adrian Peterson, Ga. Southern, 1998-01 (6,559 in 42)

MOST YARDS GAINED BY A FRESHMAN
Game
393—Ryan Fuqua, Portland St. vs. Eastern Wash., Nov. 10, 2001 (45 rushes)
Season
1,932—Adrian Peterson, Ga. Southern, 1998 (257 rushes)
Also holds per-game record with 175.6 (1,932 in 11)

MOST YARDS GAINED BY A QUARTERBACK
Game
309—Eddie Thompson, Western Ky. vs. Southern Ill., Oct. 31, 1992 (28 rushes)
Season
1,602—Matt Cannon, Southern Utah, 2000 (218 rushes)
Per-game record—156.1, David Dinkins, Morehead St., 2000 (1,405 in 9)
Career
4,852—Matt Cannon, Southern Utah, 1997-00 (674 rushes)
Also played as a slotback in 1997 and those statistics are not included

MOST GAMES GAINING 100 YARDS OR MORE
Season
11—Frank Hawkins, Nevada, 1980; Rich Lemon, Bucknell, 1994; Charles Roberts, Sacramento St., 1998; Adrian Peterson, Ga. Southern, 1998-99
Career
40—Adrian Peterson, Ga. Southern, 1998-01 (42 games)

MOST CONSECUTIVE GAMES GAINING 100 YARDS OR MORE
Season
11—Frank Hawkins, Nevada, 1980; Rich Lemon, Bucknell, 1994; Charles Roberts, Sacramento St., 1998; Adrian Peterson, Ga. Southern, 1998-99
Career
36—Adrian Peterson, Ga. Southern, 1998-01

MOST GAMES GAINING 100 YARDS OR MORE BY A FRESHMAN
11—Adrian Peterson, Ga. Southern, 1998

MOST GAMES GAINING 200 YARDS OR MORE
Season
8—Arnold Mickens, Butler, 1994

Career
13—Charles Roberts, Sacramento St., 1997-00

MOST CONSECUTIVE GAMES GAINING 200 YARDS OR MORE
Season
8—Arnold Mickens, Butler, 1994

MOST YARDS GAINED IN TWO, THREE AND FOUR CONSECUTIVE GAMES
2 Games
691—Tony Vinson, Towson, 1993 (364 vs. Bucknell, Nov. 13; 327 vs. Morgan St., Nov. 20)
3 Games
906—Ryan Fuqua, Portland St., 2001 (393 vs. Eastern Wash., Nov. 10; 270 vs. Cal St. Northridge, Nov. 17; 243 vs. Sacramento St., Nov. 24)
4 Games
1,109—Arnold Mickens, Butler, 1994 (233 vs. Georgetown [Ky.], Sept. 17; 288 vs. Wis.-Stevens Point, Sept. 24; 293 vs. Drake, Oct. 1; 295 vs. Valparaiso, Oct. 8)

MOST SEASONS GAINING 1,000 YARDS OR MORE
Career
4—Jerry Azumah, New Hampshire, 1995-98; Adrian Peterson, Ga. Southern, 1998-01

TWO PLAYERS, SAME TEAM, EACH GAINING 1,000 YARDS OR MORE
Jackson St., 1978—Perry Harrington (1,105) & Jeffrey Moore (1,094); Nevada, 1983—Otto Kelly (1,090) & Tony Corley (1,006); Eastern Ky., 1985—James Crawford (1,282) & Elroy Harris (1,134); Eastern Ky., 1986—Elroy Harris (1,152) & James Crawford (1,070); Citadel, 1988—Adrian Johnson (1,091) & Gene Brown (1,006); William & Mary, 1990—Robert Green (1,185) & Tyrone Shelton (1,020); Yale, 1991—Chris Kouri (1,101) & Nick Crawford (1,024); La.-Monroe, 1992—Greg Robinson (1,011) & Roosevelt Potts (1,004); Eastern Ky., 1993—Mike Penman (1,139) & Leon Brown (1,046); South Carolina St., 1994—Michael Hicks (1,368) & Marvin Marshall (1,201); Massachusetts, 1995—Frank Alessio (1,276) & Rene Ingoglia (1,178); Southern Utah, 1996—Brook Madsen (1,405) & Joe Dupaix (1,246); Colgate, 1997—Ed Weiss (1,069) & Daymon Smith (1,012); Cal Poly, 1997—Antonio Warren (1,151) & Craig Young (1,038); Southern Utah, 1997—Brook Madsen (1,214) & Matt Cannon (1,024); Ga. Southern, 1998—Adrian Peterson (1,932) & Greg Hill (1,061); Texas Southern, 1998—D.J. Bradley (1,219) & Thomas Sieh (1,202); Southern Utah, 1999—Matt Cannon (1,310) & Brook Madsen (1,046); Ga. Southern, 1999—Adrian Peterson (1,807) & Greg Hill (1,084); Ga. Southern, 2002—Chaz Williams (1,422) & Jermaine Austin (1,416)

MOST YARDS GAINED BY TWO PLAYERS, SAME TEAM
Game
473—Jovan Griffith (262) & Jesse Chatman (211), Eastern Wash. vs. Cal St. Northridge, Sept. 25, 1999
Season
2,993—Adrian Peterson, (1,932) & Greg Hill (1,061), Ga. Southern, 1998

EARLIEST GAME GAINING 1,000 YARDS OR MORE
Season
5th—Arnold Mickens, Butler, 1994 (1,106); Charles Roberts, Sacramento St., 1999 (1,018)

MOST YARDS GAINED IN OPENING GAME OF SEASON
304—Tony Citizen, McNeese St. vs. Prairie View, Sept. 6, 1986 (30 rushes)

MOST YARDS GAINED IN FIRST GAME OF CAREER
304—Tony Citizen, McNeese St. vs. Prairie View, Sept. 6, 1986 (30 rushes)

HIGHEST AVERAGE GAIN PER RUSH
Game
(Min. 15-19 rushes) 19.1—Gene Brown, Citadel vs. VMI, Nov. 12, 1988 (15 for 286)
(Min. 20 rushes) 17.3—Russell Davis, Idaho vs. Portland St., Oct. 3, 1981 (20 for 345)

Georgia Southern's Chaz Williams established a new Division I-AA season mark in 2002 for rushing touchdowns by a quarterback with 27.

Season
(Min. 150-199 rushes) 8.7—Tim Hall, Robert Morris, 1994 (154 for 1,336)
(Min. 200 rushes) 7.6—Ryan Fuqua, Portland St., 2001 (210 for 1,586)
Career
(Min. 350-599 rushes) 7.4—Tim Hall, Robert Morris, 1994-95 (393 for 2,908)
(Min. 600 rushes) 7.3—Matt Cannon, Southern Utah, 1997-00 (757 for 5,489)

MOST TOUCHDOWNS SCORED BY RUSHING
Game
7—Archie Amerson, Northern Ariz. vs. Weber St., Oct. 5, 1996
Season
28—Adrian Peterson, Ga. Southern, 1999
Career
84—Adrian Peterson, Ga. Southern, 1998-01

MOST TOUCHDOWNS SCORED PER GAME BY RUSHING
Season
2.5—Adrian Peterson, Ga. Southern, 1999 (28 in 11)
Career
2.0—Adrian Peterson, Ga. Southern, 1998-01 (84 in 42)

MOST TOUCHDOWNS SCORED BY RUSHING BY A QUARTERBACK
Season
27—Chaz Williams, Ga. Southern, 2002
Career
64—Matt Cannon, Southern Utah, 1997-00
Per-game record—1.7, David Dinkins, Morehead St., 1997-00 (63 in 37)

LONGEST PLAY
99—Hubert Owens, Mississippi Val. vs. Ark.-Pine Bluff, Sept. 20, 1980; Pedro Bacon, Western Ky. vs. West Ala., Sept. 13, 1986 (only rush of the game); Phillip Collins, Southwest Mo. St. vs. Western Ill., Sept. 16, 1989; Jim Varick, Monmouth vs. Sacred Heart, Oct. 29, 1994; Jermaine Creighton, St. John's (N.Y.) vs. Siena, Nov. 2, 1996

Passing

HIGHEST PASSING EFFICIENCY RATING POINTS
Game
(Min. 15-24 atts.) 389.9—Mark Washington, Jackson St. vs. Alcorn St., Nov. 20, 1999 (17 attempts, 16 completions, 0 interceptions, 363 yards, 6 TD passes)
(Min. 25-44 atts.) 287.2—Doug Turner, Morehead St. vs. Miles, Oct. 18, 1997 (26 attempts, 20 completions, 0 interceptions, 415 yards, 6 TD passes)

DIVISION I-AA

(Min. 45 atts.) 220.8—Todd Hammel, Stephen F. Austin vs. La.-Monroe, Nov. 11, 1989 (45 attempts, 31 completions, 3 interceptions, 571 yards, 8 TD passes)

Season

(Min. 15 atts. per game) 204.6—Shawn Knight, William & Mary, 1993 (177 attempts, 125 completions, 4 interceptions, 2,055 yards, 22 TD passes)

Career

(Min. 300-399 comps.) 170.8—Shawn Knight, William & Mary, 1991-94 (558 attempts, 367 completions, 15 interceptions, 5,527 yards, 46 TD passes)

(Min. 400 comps.) 166.3—Dave Dickenson, Montana, 1992-95 (1,208 attempts, 813 completions, 26 interceptions, 11,080 yards, 96 TD passes)

MOST PASSES ATTEMPTED

Quarter

33—Joe Walland, Yale vs. Harvard, Nov. 20, 1999 (3rd, completed 20)

Half

51—Joe Walland, Yale vs. Harvard, Nov. 20, 1999 (2nd, completed 33)

Game

77—Neil Lomax, Portland St. vs. Northern Colo., Oct. 20, 1979 (completed 44)

Season

578—Brett Gordon, Villanova, 2002 (completed 385)
Per-game record—52.5, Joe Lee, Towson, 1999 (577 in 11)

Career

1,680—Steve McNair, Alcorn St., 1991-94 (completed 927); Marcus Brady, Cal St. Northridge, 1998-01 (completed 1,039)
Per-game record—42.9, Stan Greene, Boston U., 1989-90 (944 in 22)

MOST PASSES ATTEMPTED BY A FRESHMAN

Game

66—Chris Swartz, Morehead St. vs. Tennessee Tech, Oct. 17, 1987 (completed 35); Kevin Glenn, Illinois St. vs. Western Ill., Nov. 8, 1997 (completed 41)

Season

411—Travis Brown, Northern Ariz., 1996 (completed 223)
Per-game record—37.8, Jason Whitmer, Idaho St., 1987 (340 in 9)

MOST PASSES COMPLETED

Quarter

20—Joe Walland, Yale vs. Harvard, Nov. 20, 1999 (3rd, attempted 33)

Half

33—Joe Walland, Yale vs. Harvard, Nov. 20, 1999 (2nd, attempted 51)

Game

48—Clayton Millis, Cal St. Northridge vs. St. Mary's (Cal.), Nov. 11, 1995 (attempted 65)

Season

385—Brett Gordon, Villanova, 2002 (attempted 578)
Per-game record—32.4, Willie Totten, Mississippi Val., 1984 (324 in 10)

Career

1,039—Marcus Brady, Cal St. Northridge, 1998-01 (attempted 1,680)
Per-game record—26.5, Chris Sanders, Chattanooga, 1999-00 (584 in 22)

MOST PASSES COMPLETED BY A FRESHMAN

Game

42—Travis Brown, Northern Ariz. vs. Montana, Oct. 26, 1996 (attempted 65)

Season

255—Marcus Brady, Cal St. Northridge, 1998 (attempted 376)
Also holds per-game record with 23.2 (255 in 11)

MOST PASSES COMPLETED IN FRESHMAN AND SOPHOMORE SEASONS

555—Marcus Brady, Cal St. Northridge, 1998-99 (attempted 860)

MOST CONSECUTIVE PASSES COMPLETED

Game

20—Austin Moherman, Southwest Mo. St. vs. Indiana St., Oct. 7, 2000; Kyle Slager, Brown vs. Rhode Island, Oct. 5, 2002

MOST CONSECUTIVE PASSES COMPLETED TO START GAME

20—Austin Moherman, Southwest Mo. St. vs. Indiana St., Oct. 7, 2000; Kyle Slager, Brown vs. Rhode Island, Oct. 5, 2002

MOST CONSECUTIVE PASSES COMPLETED TO START FIRST GAME AS A FRESHMAN

12—Daunte Culpepper, UCF vs. Eastern Ky., Aug. 31, 1995

HIGHEST PERCENTAGE OF PASSES COMPLETED

Game

(Min. 20-29 comps.) 95.7%—Butch Mosby, Murray St. vs. Tenn.-Martin, Oct. 2, 1993 (22 of 23)

(Min. 30 comps.) 85.0%—Marcus Brady, Cal St. Northridge vs. Southwest Mo. St., Nov. 14, 1998 (34 of 40)

Season

(Min. 200 atts.) 70.6%—Giovanni Carmazzi, Hofstra, 1997 (288 of 408)

Career

(Min. 750 atts.) 67.3%—Dave Dickenson, Montana, 1992-95 (813 of 1,208)

MOST PASSES HAD INTERCEPTED

Game

7—Mick Spoon, Idaho St. vs. Montana, Oct. 21, 1978 (attempted 35); Charles Hebert, Southeastern La. vs. Northwestern St., Nov. 12, 1983 (23 attempts); Carlton Jenkins, Mississippi Val. vs. Prairie View, Oct. 31, 1987 (34 attempts); Dan Crowley, Towson vs. Maine, Nov. 16, 1991 (53 attempts)

Season

29—Willie Totten, Mississippi Val., 1985 (492 attempts)
Also holds per-game record with 2.6 (29 in 11)

Career

75—Willie Totten, Mississippi Val., 1982-85
Per-game record—2.0, John Witkowski, Columbia, 1981-83 (60 in 30)

LOWEST PERCENTAGE OF PASSES HAD INTERCEPTED

Season

(Min. 175-324 atts.) 0.36%—Eric Rasmussen, San Diego, 2002 (1 of 279)

(Min. 325 atts.) 0.84%—Jimmy Blanchard, Portland St., 1999 (3 of 355)

Career

(Min. 750 atts.) 1.65%—Joe Walland, Yale, 1997-99 (13 of 787)

MOST PASSES ATTEMPTED WITHOUT INTERCEPTION

Regulation Game

68—Tony Petersen, Marshall vs. Western Caro., Nov. 14, 1987 (completed 34)

Overtime Game

69—Chris Boden, Villanova vs. Connecticut, Oct. 16, 1999 (completed 43) (3 ot)

Entire Season

150—Ryan Fitzpatrick, Harvard, 2002 (completed 94)

MOST CONSECUTIVE PASSES ATTEMPTED WITHOUT INTERCEPTION

Season

342—Jimmy Blanchard, Portland St., 1999 (in 11 games, from Sept. 4 through Nov. 13)

Career

342—Jimmy Blanchard, Portland St., began Sept. 4, 1999, ended Nov. 13, 1999

MOST YARDS GAINED

Quarter

284—Sam Clemons, Western Ill. vs. Indiana St., Nov. 17, 2001 (2nd)

Half

383—Michael Payton, Marshall vs. VMI, Nov. 16, 1991 (1st)

Game

624—Jamie Martin, Weber St. vs. Idaho St., Nov. 23, 1991

Season

4,863—Steve McNair, Alcorn St., 1994

Career

14,496—Steve McNair, Alcorn St., 1991-94

MOST YARDS GAINED PER GAME

Season

455.7—Willie Totten, Mississippi Val., 1984 (4,557 in 10)

Career

350.0—Neil Lomax, Portland St., 1978-80 (11,550 in 33)

MOST YARDS GAINED BY A FRESHMAN

Game

540—Brad Otton, Weber St. vs. Northern Ariz., Nov. 6, 1993

Season

3,398—Travis Brown, Northern Ariz., 1996
Also holds per-game record with 308.9 (3,398 in 11)

MOST YARDS GAINED IN FRESHMAN AND SOPHOMORE SEASONS

6,793—Travis Brown, Northern Ariz., 1996-97

MOST YARDS GAINED IN TWO, THREE AND FOUR CONSECUTIVE GAMES

2 Games

1,150—Steve McNair, Alcorn St., 1994 (587 vs. Samford, Oct. 29; 563 vs. Mississippi Val., Nov. 5)

3 Games

1,626—Steve McNair, Alcorn St., 1994 (587 vs. Samford, Oct. 29; 563 vs. Mississippi Val., Nov. 5; 476 vs. Troy St., Nov. 12)

4 Games

2,159—Steve McNair, Alcorn St., 1994 (587 vs. Samford, Oct. 29; 563 vs. Mississippi Val., Nov. 5; 476 vs. Troy St., Nov. 12; 533 vs. Jackson St., Nov. 19)

MOST GAMES GAINING 200 YARDS OR MORE

Season

11—By 16 players. Most recent: Chris Sanders, Chattanooga, 2000; Chris Sanders, Chattanooga, 1999; Joe Lee, Towson, 1999; Steve McNair, Alcorn St., 1994; Chris Hakel, William & Mary, 1991; Jamie Martin, Weber St., 1991

Career

41—Steve McNair, Alcorn St., 1991-94 (42 games)

MOST CONSECUTIVE GAMES GAINING 200 YARDS OR MORE

Season

11—By 13 players. Most recent: Chris Sanders, Chattanooga, 2000; Chris Sanders, Chattanooga, 1999; Steve McNair, Alcorn St., 1994; Chris Hakel, William & Mary, 1991; Jamie Martin, Weber St., 1991

Career

28—Steve McNair, Alcorn St., 1991-93; Neil Lomax, Portland St., 1978-80

MOST GAMES GAINING 300 YARDS OR MORE

Season

10—Willie Totten, Mississippi Val., 1984; John Friesz, Idaho, 1989; Steve McNair, Alcorn St., 1994

Career

28—Neil Lomax, Portland St., 1978-80

MOST CONSECUTIVE GAMES GAINING 300 YARDS OR MORE

Season

10—Willie Totten, Mississippi Val., 1984; John Friesz, Idaho, 1989

Career

13—Neil Lomax, Portland St., 1979-80

MOST YARDS GAINED AGAINST ONE OPPONENT

Career

1,675—Willie Totten, Mississippi Val. vs. Prairie View, 1982-85
Also holds per-game record with 418.8 (1,675 in 4)

MOST YARDS PER ATTEMPT

Game

(Min. 30-44 atts.) 16.1—Gilbert Renfroe, Tennessee St. vs. Dist. Columbia, Nov. 5, 1983 (30 for 484)

(Min. 45 atts.) 12.7—Todd Hammel, Stephen F. Austin vs. La.-Monroe, Nov. 11, 1989 (45 for 571)

Season

(Min. 250-324 atts.) 10.3—Mike Smith, Northern Iowa, 1986 (303 for 3,125)

(Min. 325 atts.) 9.88—Rocky Butler, Hofstra, 2001 (335 for 3,311)

Career

(Min. 500-999 atts.) 9.5—Jay Johnson, Northern Iowa, 1989-92 (744 for 7,049)

(Min. 1,000 atts.) 9.2—Dave Dickenson, Montana, 1992-95 (1,208 for 11,080)

MOST YARDS GAINED PER COMPLETION
Game
(Min. 15-19 comps.) 28.5—Kendrick Nord, Grambling vs. Alcorn St., Sept. 3, 1994 (17 for 485)
(Min. 20 comps.) 24.2—Matt Nagy, Delaware vs. Connecticut, Nov. 7, 1998 (23 for 556)
Season
(Min. 200 comps.) 16.7—Bruce Eugene, Grambling, 2002 (269 for 4,483)
Career
(Min. 350-399 comps.) 17.8—Jay Johnson, Northern Iowa, 1989-92 (397 for 7,049)
(Min. 400 comps.) 16.0—Shane Stafford, Connecticut, 1995-98 (522 for 8,368)

MOST TOUCHDOWN PASSES
Quarter
7—Neil Lomax, Portland St. vs. Delaware St., Nov. 8, 1980 (1st)
Half
7—Neil Lomax, Portland St. vs. Delaware St., Nov. 8, 1980 (1st)
Game
9—Willie Totten, Mississippi Val. vs. Kentucky St., Sept. 1, 1984
Season
56—Willie Totten, Mississippi Val., 1984
Also holds per-game record with 5.6 (56 in 10)
Career
139—Willie Totten, Mississippi Val., 1982-85
Also holds per-game record with 3.5 (139 in 40)

MOST TOUCHDOWN PASSES BY A FRESHMAN
Season
25—Marcus Brady, Cal St. Northridge, 1998

MOST CONSECUTIVE GAMES THROWING A TOUCHDOWN PASS
Career
36—Steve McNair, Alcorn St., 1991-94

MOST TOUCHDOWN PASSES, SAME PASSER AND RECEIVER
Season
27—Willie Totten to Jerry Rice, Mississippi Val., 1984
Career
47—Willie Totten to Jerry Rice, Mississippi Val., 1982-84

HIGHEST PERCENTAGE OF PASSES FOR TOUCHDOWNS
Season
(Min. 200-299 atts.) 12.5%—Ted White, Howard, 1996 (36 of 289)
(Min. 300 atts.) 10.9%—Doug Nussmeier, Idaho, 1993 (33 of 304)
Career
(Min. 500-749 atts.) 8.5%—Mike Williams, Grambling, 1977-80 (44 of 520)
(Min. 750 atts.) 8.2%—Tony Zimmerman, Duquesne, 1998-00 (73 of 889)

Receiving

MOST PASSES CAUGHT
Game
24—Jerry Rice, Mississippi Val. vs. Southern U., Oct. 1, 1983 (219 yards); Chas Gessner, Brown vs. Rhode Island, Oct. 5, 2002 (206 yards)
Season
120—Stephen Campbell, Brown, 2000 (1,332 yards)
Also holds per-game record with 12.0 (120 in 10)
Career
317—Jacquay Nunnally, Florida A&M, 1997-00 (4,239 yards)
Per-game record—7.3, Jerry Rice, Mississippi Val., 1981-84 (301 in 41)

MOST PASSES CAUGHT BY A TIGHT END
Game
18—Brian Forster, Rhode Island vs. Brown, Sept. 28, 1985 (327 yards)
Season
120—Stephen Campbell, Brown, 2000 (1,332 yards)
Also holds per-game record with 12.0 (120 in 10)
Career
245—Brian Forster, Rhode Island, 1983-85, 1987 (3,410 yards)

MOST PASSES CAUGHT BY A RUNNING BACK
Game
21—David Pandt, Montana St. vs. Eastern Wash., Sept. 21, 1985 (169 yards)
Season
89—Brian Westbrook, Villanova, 1998 (1,144 yards)
2 Yrs
135—Gordie Lockbaum, Holy Cross, 1986-87 (2,012 yards)
Also holds per-game record with 6.1 (135 in 22)
Career
188—Jason Corle, Towson, 1996-99 (1,725 yards)

MOST PASSES CAUGHT BY A FRESHMAN
Game
15—Emerson Foster, Rhode Island vs. Northeastern, Nov. 9, 1985 (205 yards); Drew Amerson, Cal St. Northridge vs. Weber St., Oct. 30, 1999 (147 yards)
Season
71—Drew Amerson, Cal St. Northridge, 1999 (897 yards)

MOST PASSES CAUGHT BY TWO PLAYERS, SAME TEAM
Season
183—Jerry Rice (103 for 1,682 yards and 27 TDs) & Joe Thomas (80 for 1,119 yards and 11 TDs), Mississippi Val., 1984
Career
420—Darrell Colbert (217 for 3,177 yards and 33 TDs) & Donald Narcisse (203 for 2,429 yards and 26 TDs), Texas Southern, 1983-86

MOST YARDS GAINED
Game
376—Kassim Osgood, Cal Poly vs. Northern Iowa, Nov. 4, 2000 (caught 17)
Season
1,712—Eddie Conti, Delaware, 1998 (caught 91)
Career
4,693—Jerry Rice, Mississippi Val., 1981-84 (caught 301)

MOST YARDS GAINED PER GAME
Season
168.2—Jerry Rice, Mississippi Val., 1984 (1,682 in 10)
Career
(Min. 2,000-2,999 yds.) 116.9—Derrick Ingram, UAB, 1993-94 (2,572 in 22)
(Min. 3,000 yds.) 114.5—Jerry Rice, Mississippi Val., 1981-84 (4,693 in 41)

MOST YARDS GAINED BY A TIGHT END
Game
327—Brian Forster, Rhode Island vs. Brown, Sept. 28, 1985 (caught 18)
Season
1,617—Brian Forster, Rhode Island, 1985 (caught 115)
Also holds per-game record with 161.7 (1,617 in 10)
Career
3,410—Brian Forster, Rhode Island, 1983-85, 1987 (caught 245)

MOST YARDS GAINED BY A RUNNING BACK
Game
228—T.J. Stallings, Morgan St. vs. N.C. A&T, Oct. 6, 2001 (caught 8)
Season
1,152—Gordie Lockbaum, Holy Cross, 1987 (caught 78)
Also holds per-game record with 104.7 (1,152 in 11)

MOST YARDS GAINED BY A FRESHMAN
Game
284—Jacquay Nunnally, Florida A&M vs. N.C. A&T, Oct. 11, 1997 (caught 13)
Season
1,073—Randy Moss, Marshall, 1996 (55 catches)

MOST YARDS GAINED BY TWO PLAYERS, SAME TEAM
Season
2,801—Jerry Rice (1,682, 103 caught and 27 TDs) & Joe Thomas (1,119, 80 caught and 11 TDs), Mississippi Val., 1984
Career
5,806—Roy Banks (3,177, 184 caught and 38 TDs) & Cal Pierce (2,629, 163 caught and 13 TDs), Eastern Ill., 1983-86

HIGHEST AVERAGE GAIN PER RECEPTION
Game
(Min. 5-9 receps.) 44.6—John Taylor, Delaware St. vs. St. Paul's, Sept. 21, 1985 (5 for 223)
(Min. 10 receps.) 29.0—Jason Cristino, Lehigh vs. Lafayette, Nov. 21, 1992 (11 for 319)
Season
(Min. 35-59 receps.) 28.9—Mikhael Ricks, Stephen F. Austin, 1997 (47 for 1,358)
(Min. 60 receps.) 20.7—Golden Tate, Tennessee St., 1983 (63 for 1,307)
Career
(Min. 90-124 receps.) 24.3—John Taylor, Delaware St., 1982-85 (100 for 2,426)
(Min. 125 receps.) 22.0—Dedric Ward, Northern Iowa, 1993-96 (176 for 3,876)

MOST GAMES GAINING 100 YARDS OR MORE
Career
23—Jerry Rice, Mississippi Val., 1981-84 (41 games)

MOST TOUCHDOWN PASSES CAUGHT
Game
6—Cos DeMatteo, Chattanooga vs. Mississippi Val., Sept. 16, 2000 (9 total catches for 203 yards)
Season
27—Jerry Rice, Mississippi Val., 1984
Career
50—Jerry Rice, Mississippi Val., 1981-84

MOST TOUCHDOWN PASSES CAUGHT BY A FRESHMAN
Season
19—Randy Moss, Marshall, 1996

MOST TOUCHDOWN PASSES CAUGHT PER GAME
Season
2.7—Jerry Rice, Mississippi Val., 1984 (27 in 10)
Career
1.2—Jerry Rice, Mississippi Val., 1981-84 (50 in 41)

MOST GAMES CATCHING A TOUCHDOWN PASS
Season
11—Randy Moss, Marshall, 1996
Also holds consecutive record with 11, 1996
Career
26—Jerry Rice, Mississippi Val., 1981-84
Also holds consecutive record with 17, 1983-84

Punting

MOST PUNTS
Game
16—Matt Stover, Louisiana Tech vs. La.-Monroe, Nov. 18, 1988 (567 yards)
Season
98—Barry Hickingbotham, Louisiana Tech, 1987 (3,821 yards)
Career
301—Barry Bowman, Louisiana Tech, 1983-86 (11,441 yards)

HIGHEST AVERAGE PER PUNT
Game
(5-9 punts) 61.5—Eddie Johnson, Idaho St. vs. Cal Poly, Nov. 16, 2002 (6 for 369)
(Min. 10 punts) 52.2—Stuart Dodds, Montana St. vs. Northern Ariz., Oct. 20, 1979 (10 for 522)
Season
(Min. 60 punts) 48.2—Mark Gould, Northern Ariz., 2002 (62 for 2,987)
Career
(Min. 150 punts) 44.4—Pumpy Tudors, Chattanooga, 1989-91 (181 for 8,041)

LONGEST PUNT
93—Tyler Grogan, Northeastern vs. Villanova, Sept. 8, 2001

Interceptions

MOST PASSES INTERCEPTED
Game
5—Karl Johnson, Jackson St. vs. Grambling, Oct. 23, 1982 (29 yards); Michael Richardson, Northwestern St. vs. Southeastern La., Nov. 12, 1983 (128 yards); Mark Cordes, Eastern Wash. vs. Boise St., Sept. 6, 1986 (48 yards)

DIVISION I-AA

Season
14—Rashean Mathis, Bethune-Cookman, 2002 (455 yards)
Per-game record—1.2, Dean Cain, Princeton, 1987 (12 in 10)
Career
31—Rashean Mathis, Bethune-Cookman, 1999-02 (682 yards)
Per-game record—0.73, Dean Cain, Princeton, 1985-87 (22 in 30)

MOST YARDS ON INTERCEPTION RETURNS
Game
216—Keiron Bigby, Brown vs. Yale, Sept. 29, 1984 (3 interceptions) (first career game)
Season
455—Rashean Mathis, Bethune-Cookman, 2002 (14 interceptions)
Career
682—Rashean Mathis, Bethune-Cookman, 1999-02 (31 interceptions)

MOST TOUCHDOWNS SCORED ON INTERCEPTION RETURNS
Game
2—By 16 players. Most recent: Weston Borba, St. Mary's (Cal.) vs. Cal Poly, Oct. 19, 2002; Mark Kasmer, Dayton vs. St. Francis (Pa.), Sept. 7, 2002; Corey Oaks, Robert Morris vs. Buffalo St., Sept. 7, 2002
Season
4—Robert Turner, Jackson St., 1990 (9 interceptions, 212 yards); Joseph Vaughn, Cal St. Northridge, 1994 (9 interceptions, 265 yards); William Hampton, Murray St., 1995 (8 interceptions, 280 yards)
Career
6—William Hampton, Murray St., 1993-96 (20 interceptions)

HIGHEST AVERAGE GAIN PER INTERCEPTION
Game
(Min. 3 ints.) 72.0—Keiron Bigby, Brown vs. Yale, Sept. 29, 1984 (3 for 216)
Season
(Min. 3 ints.) 72.0—Keiron Bigby, Brown, 1984 (3 for 216)
Career
(Min. 12 ints.) 25.8—Zack Bronson, McNeese St., 1993-96 (16 for 413)

Punt Returns

MOST PUNT RETURNS
Game
11—Peter Athans, Sacred Heart vs. Siena, Nov. 9, 2002 (98 yards)
Season
55—Tommy Houk, Murray St., 1980 (442 yards)
Also holds per-game record with 5.0 (55 in 11)
Career
123—Chuck Calhoun, Southwest Mo. St., 1990-93 (978 yards)
Per-game record—3.8, Tommy Houk, Murray St., 1979-80 (84 in 22)

MOST YARDS ON PUNT RETURNS
Game
216—Willie Ware, Mississippi Val. vs. Washburn, Sept. 15, 1984 (7 returns); Gary Harrell, Howard vs. Morgan St., Nov. 3, 1990 (7 returns); Ricky Pearsall, Northern Ariz. vs. Western N.M., Aug. 29, 1996 (5 returns)
Season
662—Dan McGrath, Fordham, 2002 (48 returns)
Per-game record—54.7, Joe Rosato, Duquesne, 1996 (547 in 10)
Career
1,488—Delvin Joyce, James Madison, 1997-00 (104 returns)

HIGHEST AVERAGE GAIN PER RETURN
Game
(Min. 5 rets.) 43.2—Ricky Pearsall, Northern Ariz. vs. Western N.M., Aug. 29, 1996 (5 for 216)
Season
(Min. 1.2 rets. per game) 26.5—Curtis DeLoatch, N.C. A&T, 2001 (20 for 530)

Career
(Min. 1.2 rets. per game) 16.4—Willie Ware, Mississippi Val., 1982-85 (61 for 1,003)

MOST TOUCHDOWNS SCORED ON PUNT RETURNS
Game
3—Aaron Fix, Canisius vs. Siena, Sept. 24, 1994 (5 returns); Zuriel Smith, Hampton vs. Virginia St., Sept. 22, 2001 (3 returns)
Season
5—Curtis DeLoatch, N.C. A&T, 2001 (20 returns)
Career
7—Kenny Shedd, Northern Iowa, 1989-92

LONGEST PUNT RETURN
98—Barney Bussey, South Carolina St. vs. Johnson Smith, Oct. 10, 1981; Willie Ware, Mississippi Val. vs. Bishop, Sept. 21, 1985

MOST CONSECUTIVE GAMES RETURNING PUNT FOR TOUCHDOWN
3—Troy Jones, McNeese St., 1989 (vs. Mississippi Col., Sept. 2; vs. Samford, Sept. 9; vs. La.-Monroe, Sept. 16)

Kickoff Returns

MOST KICKOFF RETURNS
Game
10—Merril Hoge, Idaho St. vs. Weber St., Oct. 25, 1986 (179 yards); Ryan Steen, Cal Poly vs. Eastern Wash., Sept. 10, 1994 (203 yards)
Season
50—David Primus, Samford, 1989 (1,411 yards)
Also holds per-game record with 4.5 (50 in 11)
Career
118—Clarence Alexander, Mississippi Val., 1986-89 (2,439 yards)
Per-game record—3.0, Lorenza Rivers, Tennessee Tech, 1985, 1987 (62 in 21)

MOST YARDS ON KICKOFF RETURNS
Game
326—Bashir Levingston, Eastern Wash. vs. Sacramento St., Oct. 31, 1998 (5 returns)
Season
1,411—David Primus, Samford, 1989 (50 returns)
Also holds per-game record with 128.3 (1,411 in 11)
Career
2,535—Carlos Frank, Citadel, 1996-99 (108 returns)
Also holds per-game record with 63.4 (2,535 in 40)

HIGHEST AVERAGE GAIN PER RETURN
Game
(Min. 5 rets.) 65.2—Bashir Levingston, Eastern Wash. vs. Sacramento St., Oct. 31, 1998 (5 for 326)
Season
(Min. 1.2 rets. per game) 37.3—David Fraterrigo, Canisius, 1993 (13 for 485)
Career
(Min. 1.2 Returns Per Game)
(Min. 45 rets.) 30.0—Lamont Brightful, Eastern Wash., 1998-01 (65 for 1,949)

MOST TOUCHDOWNS SCORED ON KICKOFF RETURNS
Game
3—Bashir Levingston, Eastern Wash. vs. Sacramento St., Oct. 31, 1998
Season
4—Ryan Zimpleman, Butler, 1998
Career
5—Kerry Hayes, Western Caro., 1991-94; Ryan Zimpleman, Butler, 1997-99; Lamont Brightful, Eastern Wash., 1998-01

Total Kick Returns

(Combined Punt and Kickoff Returns)

MOST KICK RETURNS
Game
12—Craig Hodge, Tennessee St. vs. Morgan St., Oct. 24, 1987 (8 punts, 4 kickoffs; 319 yards)

Season
64—Joe Markus, Connecticut, 1981 (34 punts, 30 kickoffs; 939 yards)
Career
199—Herman Hunter, Tennessee St., 1981-84 (103 punts, 96 kickoffs; 3,232 yards)

MOST YARDS ON KICK RETURNS
Game
349—Bashir Levingston, Eastern Wash. vs. Sacramento St., Oct. 31, 1998 (8 returns, 23 on punt returns, 326 on kickoff returns)
Season
1,469—David Primus, Samford, 1989 (1,411 on kickoffs, 58 on punts)
Also holds per-game record with 133.5 (1,469 in 11)
Career
3,318—Delvin Joyce, James Madison, 1997-00 (1,488 on punts, 1,830 on kickoffs)
Also holds per-game record with 85.1 (3,318 in 39)

GAINING 1,000 YARDS ON PUNT RETURNS AND 1,000 YARDS ON KICKOFF RETURNS
Career
Joe Markus, Connecticut, 1979-82 (1,012 on punts and 1,185 on kickoffs); Kenny Shedd, Northern Iowa, 1989-92 (1,081 on punts and 1,359 on kickoffs); Joe Rosato, Duquesne, 1994-97 (1,036 on punts and 1,661 on kickoffs); Delvin Joyce, James Madison, 1997-00 (1,488 on punts and 1,830 on kickoffs)

HIGHEST AVERAGE PER KICK RETURN
Game
(Min. 6 rets.) 44.7—Jay Jones, James Madison vs. Richmond, Oct. 19, 1996 (6 for 268)
Season
(Min. 40 rets.) 26.7—David Primus, Samford, 1989 (55 for 1,469)
Career
(Min. 60 rets.) 26.4—Lamont Brightful, Eastern Wash., 1998-01 (80 for 2,115)

MOST TOUCHDOWNS SCORED ON KICK RETURNS
Game
3—Aaron Fix, Canisius vs. Siena, Sept. 24, 1994 (3 punt returns); Bashir Levingston, Eastern Wash. vs. Sacramento St., Oct. 31, 1998 (3 kickoffs); Zuriel Smith, Hampton vs. Virginia St., Sept. 22, 2001 (3 punt returns)
Season
6—Bashir Levingston, Eastern Wash., 1998 (3 punt returns and 3 kickoff returns)
Career
7—Willie Ware, Mississippi Val., 1982-85 (5 punts and 2 kickoffs); Kenny Shedd, Northern Iowa, 1989-92 (7 punts); Kerry Hayes, Western Caro., 1991-94 (2 punts and 5 kickoffs); Joe Rosato, Duquesne, 1994-97 (4 punts and 3 kickoffs)

All-Purpose Yards

(Yardage Gained From Rushing, Receiving and All Runbacks; Must Have One Attempt From at Least Two Categories)

MOST PLAYS
Game
54—Ron Darby, Marshall vs. Western Caro., Nov. 12, 1988 (47 rushes, 4 receptions, 3 kickoff returns; 329 yards)
(Note: 56—Arnold Mickens, Butler vs. Valparaiso, Oct. 8, 1994; all rushes)
Season
411—Arnold Mickens, Butler, 1994 (409 rushes, 2 receptions; 2,262 yards)
Career
1,178—Charles Roberts, Sacramento St., 1997-00 (1,124 rushes, 44 receptions, 1 punt return, 9 kickoff returns; 7,112 yards)

MOST YARDS GAINED
Game
467—Joey Stockton, Western Ky. vs. Austin Peay, Sept. 16, 1995 (29 rushing, 276 receiving, 18 punt returns, 144 kickoff returns; 14 plays)
Season
3,026—Brian Westbrook, Villanova, 1998 (1,046 rushing, 1,144 receiving, 192 punt returns, 644 kickoff returns; 329 plays)
Also holds per-game record with 275.1 (3,026 in 11)

Career
9,512—Brian Westbrook, Villanova, 1997-98, 00-01 (4,298 rushing, 2,528 receiving, 343 punt returns, 2,289 kickoff returns; 1,022 plays)
Also holds per-game record with 216.2 (9,512 in 44)

MOST YARDS GAINED BY A FRESHMAN
Game
437—Ryan Fuqua, Portland St. vs. Eastern Wash., Nov. 10, 2001 (393 rushing, 44 kickoff returns)
Season
2,014—David Wright, Indiana St., 1992 (1,313 rushing, 108 receiving, 593 kickoff returns; 254 plays)

HIGHEST AVERAGE GAIN PER PLAY
Game
(Min. 20 plays) 20.6—Herman Hunter, Tennessee St. vs. Mississippi Val., Nov. 13, 1982 (453 on 22)
Season
(Min. 1,000 yards, 100 plays) 19.7—Otis Washington, Western Caro., 1988 (2,086 on 106)
Career
(Min. 4,000 yards, 350 plays) 15.7—Sean Morey, Brown, 1995-98 (5,726 on 364)

GAINING 1,000 YARDS RUSHING AND 1,000 YARDS RECEIVING
Season
Brian Westbrook, Villanova, 1998 (1,046 rushing, 1,144 receiving)

Scoring

MOST POINTS SCORED
Game
42—Archie Amerson, Northern Ariz. vs. Weber St., Oct. 5, 1996 (7 TDs); Jessie Burton, McNeese St. vs. Southern Utah, Sept. 19, 1998 (7 TDs)
Season
176—Brian Westbrook, Villanova, 2001 (29 TDs, 2 PATs)
Career
544—Brian Westbrook, Villanova, 1997-98, 00-01 (89 TDs, 10 PATs)

MOST POINTS SCORED PER GAME
Season
16.2—Jerry Rice, Mississippi Val., 1984 (162 in 10)
Career
(Min. 200-299 pts.) 11.7—Aaron Stecker, Western Ill., 1997-98 (234 in 20)
(Min. 300 pts.) 12.5—Adrian Peterson, Ga. Southern, 1998-01 (524 in 42)

MOST TOUCHDOWNS SCORED
Game
7—Archie Amerson, Northern Ariz. vs. Weber St., Oct. 5, 1996; Jessie Burton, McNeese St. vs. Southern Utah, Sept. 19, 1998
Season
29—Adrian Peterson, Ga. Southern, 1999; Brian Westbrook, Villanova, 2001
Career
89—Brian Westbrook, Villanova, 1997-98, 00-01

MOST TOUCHDOWNS SCORED PER GAME
Season
2.7—Jerry Rice, Mississippi Val., 1984 (27 in 10)
Career
(Min. 30 games) 2.07—Adrian Peterson, Ga. Southern, 1998-01 (87 in 42)

MOST TOUCHDOWNS SCORED BY A FRESHMAN
Season
26—Adrian Peterson, Ga. Southern, 1998
Also holds per-game record with 2.4 (26 in 11)

PASSING FOR A TOUCHDOWN AND SCORING TOUCHDOWNS BY RUSHING, RECEIVING AND PUNT RETURN
WR Sean Beckton, UCF, threw a 33-yard touchdown pass, rushed for an 11-yard touchdown, caught a 17-yard touchdown pass and returned a punt 60 yards for a touchdown vs. Texas Southern, Nov. 17, 1990

MOST EXTRA POINTS ATTEMPTED BY KICKING
Game
15—John Kincheloe, Portland St. vs. Delaware St., Nov. 8, 1980 (15 made)
Season
74—John Kincheloe, Portland St., 1980 (70 made)
Per-game record—7.2, Jonathan Stokes, Mississippi Val., 1984 (72 in 10)
Career
194—Gilad Landau, Grambling, 1991-94 (181 made)

MOST EXTRA POINTS MADE BY KICKING
Game
15—John Kincheloe, Portland St. vs. Delaware St., Nov. 8, 1980 (15 attempts)
Season
70—John Kincheloe, Portland St., 1980 (74 attempts)
Per-game record—6.8, Jonathan Stokes, Mississippi Val., 1984 (68 in 10)
Career
181—Gilad Landau, Grambling, 1991-94 (194 attempts)
Per-game record—4.8, Tim Openlander, Marshall, 1994-96 (159 in 33)

BEST PERFECT RECORD OF EXTRA POINTS MADE
Season
68 of 68—Mike Hollis, Idaho, 1993

HIGHEST PERCENTAGE OF EXTRA POINTS MADE
Season
(Min. 50 atts.) 100.0—Billy Hayes, Sam Houston St., 1987 (50 of 50); Jim Hodson, Lafayette, 1988 (51 of 51); Mike Hollis, Idaho, 1993 (68 of 68); Chris Dill, Murray St., 1995 (56 of 56); Tim Openlander, Marshall, 1996 (58 of 58); Chris Snyder, Montana, 2002 (50 of 50)
Career
(Min. 100-119 atts.) 100%—Anders Larsson, Montana St., 1985-88 (101 of 101)
(Min. 120 atts.) 99.2%—Brian Mitchell, Marshall/Northern Iowa, 1987, 1989-91 (130 of 131)

MOST CONSECUTIVE EXTRA POINTS MADE
Game
15—John Kincheloe, Portland St. vs. Delaware St., Nov. 8, 1980
Season
68—Mike Hollis, Idaho, 1993
Career
121—Brian Mitchell, Marshall/Northern Iowa, 1987, 1989-91

MOST POINTS SCORED BY KICKING
Game
24—Goran Lingmerth, Northern Ariz. vs. Idaho, Oct. 25, 1986 (8 FGs)
Season
116—Justin Langan, Western Ill., 2002 (20 of 27 FGs, 56 of 58 PATs)
Career
385—Marty Zendejas, Nevada, 1984-87 (72 FGs, 169 PATs)

MOST POINTS SCORED BY KICKING PER GAME
Season
10.1—Rob Hart, Murray St., 1996 (112 in 11)
Career
9.1—Tony Zendejas, Nevada, 1981-83 (300 in 33)

MOST TWO-POINT ATTEMPTS
Season
11—Brent Woods, Princeton, 1982; Jamie Martin, Weber St., 1990

MOST SUCCESSFUL TWO-POINT PASSES
Game
3—Brent Woods, Princeton vs. Lafayette, Nov. 6, 1982 (attempted 3)
Season
7—Jamie Martin, Weber St., 1992 (attempted 7)
Career
15—Jamie Martin, Weber St., 1989-92 (attempted 28)

Defensive Extra Points

MOST DEFENSIVE EXTRA-POINT RETURNS
Game
2—Joe Lee Johnson, Western Ky. vs. Indiana St., Nov. 10, 1990 (both kick returns, scored on neither)

MOST DEFENSIVE EXTRA POINTS SCORED
Game
1—By many players

Robert Mathis (55) of Alabama A&M bolted into the Division I-AA records last year in single-season pass sacks (20), single-season forced fumbles (10) and tackles for loss per game (2.8).

Season
2—Jackie Kellogg, Eastern Wash. vs. Weber St., Oct. 6, 1990 (90-yard interception return) & vs. Portland St., Oct. 27, 1990 (94-yard interception return)

LONGEST RETURN OF A DEFENSIVE EXTRA POINT
100—Morgan Ryan (DB), Montana St. vs. Sam Houston St., Sept. 7, 1991 (interception return); Rich Kinsman (DB), William & Mary vs. Lehigh, Nov. 14, 1992

FIRST DEFENSIVE EXTRA-POINT ATTEMPTS
Mike Rogers (DB), Davidson vs. Lehigh, Sept. 10, 1988 (30-yard interception return); Dave Benna (LB), Towson vs. Northeastern, Sept. 10, 1988 (35-yard interception return)

Defensive Records

(Since 2000)

TOTAL TACKLES
Game
26—Boomer Grigsby, Illinois St. vs. Youngstown St., Nov. 7, 2002
Season
192—Josh Cain, Chattanooga, 2002
Per-game record—16.3, Boomer Grigsby, Illinois St., 2002 (179 in 11)

SOLO TACKLES
Game
18—Nick Ricks, Eastern Ill. vs. Eastern Ky., Oct. 12, 2002
Season
113—Josh Cain, Chattanooga, 2002
Per-game record—9.8, Boomer Grigsby, Illinois St., 2002 (108 in 11)

ASSISTED TACKLES
Game
12—Chris Carey, Columbia vs. Harvard, Nov. 3, 2001; Boomer Grigsby, Illinois St. vs. Youngstown St., Nov. 9, 2002
Season
95—P.J. Jones, Southwest Mo. St., 2001
Also holds per-game record with 8.4 (95 in 11)

TACKLES FOR LOSS
Game
7.0—Greg Pitts, Southwest Tex. St. vs. Texas Southern, Sept. 21, 2002
Season
31.0—Sherrod Coates, Western Ky., 2002
Per-game record—2.8, Robert Mathis, Alabama A&M, 2002 (30.5 in 11)

PASS SACKS
Game
4.0—Galen Scott, Illinois St. vs. Indiana St., Oct. 14,

2000; Valdamar Brower, Massachusetts vs. Maine, Oct. 14, 2000; C.J. Carroll, Southwest Tex. St. vs. Sam Houston St., Nov. 22, 2000; Valdamar Brower, Massachusetts vs. American Int'l, Sept. 14, 2002

Season
20.0—Robert Mathis, Alabama A&M, 2002
Per-game record—1.89, Andrew Hollingsworth, Towson, 2000 (17 in 9)

PASSES DEFENDED
Game
6—Sam Young, Illinois St. vs. Youngstown St., Oct. 7, 2000; James Young, Ga. Southern vs. Bethune-Cookman, Nov. 30, 2002

Season
27—Bobby Sippio, Western Ky., 2000
Also holds per-game record with 2.7 (27 in 10)

FORCED FUMBLES
Game
3—Sterling Rogers, Southwest Tex. St. vs. Portland St., Oct. 6, 2001

Season
10—Robert Mathis, Alabama A&M, 2002
Also holds per-game record with 0.91 (10 in 11)

Opponent's Kicks Blocked

MOST OPPONENT'S TOTAL KICKS BLOCKED BY (Includes Punts, PAT Attempts, FG Attempts)
Game
3—Adrian Hardy, Northwestern St. vs. Arkansas St., Oct. 3, 1992 (2 PATs, 1 FG); Ben Duhon, McNeese St. vs. Ark.-Monticello, 1998 (3 punts); Michael Adams, Stephen F. Austin vs. Central Okla., Aug. 31, 2000 (2 punts, 1 PAT); Brandon Tinson, Colgate vs. Towson, Sept. 30, 2000 (3 punts)

Season
6—Murphy Edwards, Nicholls St., 1998 (4 PATs, 2 FGs); Ryan Crawford, Davidson, 2000 (4 punts, 2 FGs); Mark Weivoda, Idaho St., 2001 (4 PATs, 2 FGs)

Career
12—Trey Woods, Sam Houston St., 1992-95 (8 punts, 2 PATs, 2 FGs)

Field Goals

MOST FIELD GOALS ATTEMPTED
Game
8—Goran Lingmerth, Northern Ariz. vs. Idaho, Oct. 25, 1986 (made 8)

Season
33—Tony Zendejas, Nevada, 1982 (made 26); David Ettinger, Hofstra, 1995 (made 22)

Career
102—Kirk Roach, Western Caro., 1984-87 (made 71)

MOST FIELD GOALS MADE
Quarter
4—Tony Zendejas, Nevada vs. Northern Ariz., Oct. 16, 1982 (4th); Ryan Weeks, Tennessee Tech vs. Chattanooga, Sept. 9, 1989 (3rd)

Half
5—Dean Biasucci, Western Caro. vs. Mars Hill, Sept. 18, 1982 (1st); Tony Zendejas, Nevada vs. Northern Ariz., Oct. 16, 1982 (2nd); Ryan Weeks, Tennessee Tech vs. Chattanooga, Sept. 9, 1989 (2nd)

Game
8—Goran Lingmerth, Northern Ariz. vs. Idaho, Oct. 25, 1986 (39, 18, 20, 33, 46, 27, 22, 35 yards; by quarters—1, 3, 2, 2), 8 attempts

Season
26—Tony Zendejas, Nevada, 1982 (33 attempts); Brian Mitchell, Northern Iowa, 1990 (27 attempts)
Also share per-game record with 2.4 (26 in 11)

Career
72—Marty Zendejas, Nevada, 1984-87 (90 attempts)
Per-game record—2.1, Tony Zendejas, Nevada, 1981-83 (70 in 33)

HIGHEST PERCENTAGE OF FIELD GOALS MADE
Season
(Min. 20 atts.) 96.3%—Brian Mitchell, Northern Iowa, 1990 (26 of 27)

Career
(Min. 50 atts.) 82.0%—Juan Toro, Florida A&M, 1995-98 (41 of 50)

BEST PERFECT RECORD OF FIELD GOALS MADE
Season
100.0%—John Coursey, James Madison, 1995 (14 of 14)

MOST CONSECUTIVE FIELD GOALS MADE
Game
8—Goran Lingmerth, Northern Ariz. vs. Idaho, Oct. 25, 1986

Season
21—Brian Mitchell, Northern Iowa, 1990

Career
26—Brian Mitchell, Northern Iowa, 1990-91

MOST CONSECUTIVE GAMES KICKING A FIELD GOAL
Career
33—Tony Zendejas, Nevada, 1981-83 (at least one in every game played)

MOST FIELD GOALS MADE, 50 YARDS OR MORE
Game
3—Jesse Garcia, La.-Monroe vs. McNeese St., Oct. 29, 1983 (52, 56, 53 yards); Terry Belden, Northern Ariz. vs. Cal St. Northridge, Sept. 18, 1993 (60, 50, 54 yards)

Season
7—Jesse Garcia, La.-Monroe, 1983 (12 attempts); Kirk Roach, Western Caro., 1987 (12 attempts)

Career
11—Kirk Roach, Western Caro., 1984-87 (26 attempts); Pete Garces, Idaho St., 1998-99 (16 attempts)

HIGHEST PERCENTAGE OF FIELD GOALS MADE, 50 YARDS OR MORE
Season
(Min. 5 atts.) 100.0%—Wayne Boyer, Southwest Mo. St., 1996 (5 of 5)

Career
(Min. 10 atts.) 90.9%—Tim Foley, Ga. Southern, 1984-87 (10 of 11)

MOST FIELD GOALS MADE, 40 YARDS OR MORE
Season
12—Marty Zendejas, Nevada, 1985 (15 attempts)

Career
30—Marty Zendejas, Nevada, 1984-87 (45 attempts)

HIGHEST PERCENTAGE OF FIELD GOALS MADE, 40 YARDS OR MORE
Season
(Min. 8 made) 100.0%—Tim Foley, Ga. Southern, 1985 (8 of 8)

Career
(Min. 15 made) 72.0%—Tim Foley, Ga. Southern, 1984-87 (18 of 25)

HIGHEST PERCENTAGE OF FIELD GOALS MADE, 40-49 YARDS
Season
(Min. 8 made) 90.0%—Marty Zendejas, Nevada, 1985 (9 of 10)

Career
(Min. 12 made) 72.0%—Tony Zendejas, Nevada, 1981-83 (18 of 25)

HIGHEST PERCENTAGE OF FIELD GOALS MADE, UNDER 40 YARDS
Season
(Min. 15 made) 100.0%—Matt Stover, Louisiana Tech, 1986 (15 of 15); Kirk Roach, Western Caro., 1986 (17 of 17); Brian Mitchell, Northern Iowa, 1990 (23 of 23)

Career
(Min. 25 made) 93.3%—Marty Zendejas, Nevada, 1984-87 (42 of 45)

MOST TIMES KICKING TWO OR MORE FIELD GOALS IN A GAME
Season
10—Brian Mitchell, Northern Iowa, 1991

Career
25—Kirk Roach, Western Caro., 1984-87

MOST TIMES KICKING THREE OR MORE FIELD GOALS IN A GAME
Season
7—Brian Mitchell, Northern Iowa, 1991

Career
11—Brian Mitchell, Marshall/Northern Iowa, 1987, 1989-91

MOST CONSECUTIVE QUARTERS KICKING A FIELD GOAL
Season
7—Scott Roper, Arkansas St., 1986 (last 3 vs. McNeese St., Oct. 25; all 4 vs. North Texas, Nov. 1)

LONGEST AVERAGE DISTANCE FIELD GOALS MADE
Game
(Min. 3 made) 54.7—Terry Belden, Northern Ariz. vs. Sacramento St., Sept. 18, 1993 (60, 50, 54 yards)

Season
(Min. 14 made) 45.0—Jesse Garcia, La.-Monroe, 1983 (15 made)

Career
(Min. 35 made) 37.5—Roger Ruzek, Weber St., 1979-82 (46 made)

LONGEST AVERAGE DISTANCE FIELD GOALS ATTEMPTED
Game
(Min. 4 atts.) 55.5—Pete Garces, Idaho St. vs. Sacramento St., Nov. 7, 1998 (made 53, 54; missed 54, 61)

Season
(Min. 20 atts.) 45.9—Jesse Garcia, La.-Monroe, 1983 (26 attempts)

Career
(Min. 60 atts.) 40.5—Kirk Roach, Western Caro., 1984-87 (102 attempts)

LONGEST FIELD GOAL MADE
63—Scott Roper, Arkansas St. vs. North Texas, Nov. 7, 1987; Tim Foley, Ga. Southern vs. James Madison, Nov. 7, 1987; Bill Gramatica, South Fla. vs. Austin Peay, Nov. 18, 2000

LONGEST FIELD GOAL MADE BY A FRESHMAN
60—David Cool, Ga. Southern vs. James Madison, Nov. 5, 1988

MOST FIELD GOALS MADE BY A FRESHMAN
Game
5—Mike Powers, Colgate vs. Army, Sept. 10, 1983 (6 attempts); Marty Zendejas, Nevada vs. Idaho St., Nov. 17, 1984 (5 attempts); Chuck Rawlinson, Stephen F. Austin vs. Prairie View, Sept. 10, 1988 (5 attempts); Juan Vasques, Florida A&M vs. Morgan St., Sept. 9, 2000 (5 attempts)

Season
22—Marty Zendejas, Nevada, 1984 (27 attempts)

MOST FIELD GOALS MADE IN FIRST GAME OF CAREER
5—Mike Powers, Colgate vs. Army, Sept. 10, 1983 (6 attempts)

MOST GAMES IN WHICH FIELD GOAL(S) PROVIDED WINNING MARGIN
Career
11—John Dowling, Youngstown St., 1984-87

LONGEST RETURN OF A MISSED FIELD GOAL
89—Pat Bayers, Western Ill. vs. Youngstown St., Nov. 6, 1982 (TD)

Team Records

SINGLE GAME—Offense

Total Offense

MOST PLAYS
115—Buffalo vs. Connecticut, Oct. 4, 1997 (437 yards)

MOST PLAYS, BOTH TEAMS
196—Villanova (113) & Connecticut (83), Oct. 7, 1989 (904 yards)

MOST YARDS GAINED
876—Weber St. vs. Idaho St., Nov. 23, 1991 (252 rushing, 624 passing)

MOST YARDS GAINED, BOTH TEAMS
1,418—Howard (740) & Bethune-Cookman (678), Sept. 19, 1987 (161 plays)

MOST YARDS GAINED BY A LOSING TEAM
756—Alcorn St. vs. Grambling, Sept. 3, 1994 (lost 62-56)

FEWEST YARDS GAINED BY A WINNING TEAM
31—Middle Tenn. vs. Murray St., Oct. 17, 1981 (won 14-9)

HIGHEST AVERAGE GAIN PER PLAY
(Min. 55 Plays)
12.7—Marshall vs. VMI, Nov. 16, 1991 (62 for 789)

MOST TOUCHDOWNS SCORED BY RUSHING AND PASSING
14—Portland St. vs. Delaware St., Nov. 8, 1980 (10 passing, 4 rushing)

Rushing

MOST RUSHES
90—VMI vs. East Tenn. St., Nov. 17, 1990 (311 yards)

MOST RUSHES, BOTH TEAMS
127—Western Ky. (73) & Elon (54), Oct. 24, 1998 (718 yards)

FEWEST RUSHES
11—Mississippi Val. vs. Kentucky St., Sept. 1, 1984 (17 yards); Western Ill. vs. Northern Iowa, Oct. 24, 1987 (-11 yards)

MOST YARDS GAINED
681—Southwest Mo. St. vs. Mo. Southern St., Sept. 10, 1988 (83 rushes)

MOST YARDS GAINED, BOTH TEAMS
781—Dayton (462) & Morehead St. (319), Sept. 23, 2000 (109 rushes)

MOST YARDS GAINED BY A LOSING TEAM
448—Western Ky. vs. Southern Ill., Nov. 4, 1995 (lost 30-28)
(Note: Western Ky. rushed for 469 yards vs. Division I-A Louisville on Oct. 31, 1998, but lost, 63-34)

HIGHEST AVERAGE GAIN PER RUSH
(Min. 45 Rushes)
11.22—Southwest Mo. St. vs. Truman, Oct. 5, 1985 (45 for 505)
(Note: Ga. Southern rushed for 591 yards in 53 carries vs. Western Caro. on Oct. 9, 1999, for an 11.15 average)

MOST TOUCHDOWNS SCORED BY RUSHING
10—Arkansas St. vs. Tex. A&M-Commerce, Sept. 26, 1987

Passing

MOST PASSES ATTEMPTED
78—Towson vs. Lehigh, Oct. 30, 1999 (completed 47 for 567 yards)

MOST PASSES ATTEMPTED, BOTH TEAMS
122—Idaho (62) & Idaho St. (60), Sept. 24, 1983 (completed 48 for 639 yards)

FEWEST PASSES ATTEMPTED
1—By many teams. Most recent: Northeastern vs. Towson, Sept. 9, 1989 (completed 1)

FEWEST PASSES ATTEMPTED, BOTH TEAMS
11—Memphis (3) & Arkansas St. (8), Nov. 27, 1982 (completed 6); N.C. A&T (5) & Western Ky. (6), Nov. 19, 1988 (completed 2); Citadel (3) & Ga. Southern (8), Nov. 19, 1994 (completed 6)

MOST PASSES ATTEMPTED WITHOUT INTERCEPTION
72—Marshall vs. Western Caro., Nov. 14, 1987 (completed 35)

MOST PASSES COMPLETED
50—Mississippi Val. vs. Southern U., Sept. 29, 1984 (attempted 70 for 633 yards); Mississippi Val. vs. Prairie View, Oct. 27, 1984 (attempted 66 for 642 yards)

MOST PASSES COMPLETED, BOTH TEAMS I-AA
77—La.-Monroe (46) & Stephen F. Austin (31), Nov. 11, 1989 (attempted 116 for 1,190 yards)

MOST PASSES COMPLETED, BOTH TEAMS
80—Hofstra (50) & Fordham (30), Oct. 19, 1991 (attempted 120 for 987 yards)

FEWEST PASSES COMPLETED
0—By many teams. Most recent: Monmouth vs. Towson, Oct. 27, 2001

FEWEST PASSES COMPLETED, BOTH TEAMS
2—N.C. A&T (0) & Western Ky. (2), Nov. 19, 1988 (attempted 11)

HIGHEST PERCENTAGE COMPLETED
(Min. 30-44 atts.) 85.4%—Cal St. Northridge vs. Southwest Mo. St., Nov. 14, 1998 (35 of 41)
(Min. 45 atts.) 79.2%—Montana vs. Weber St., Oct. 7, 1995 (38 of 48)

LOWEST PERCENTAGE COMPLETED
(Min. 20 Attempts)
9.5%—Florida A&M vs. Central St., Oct. 11, 1986 (2 of 21)

MOST PASSES HAD INTERCEPTED
10—Mississippi Val. vs. Grambling, Oct. 17, 1987 (47 attempts); Boise St. vs. Montana, Oct. 28, 1989 (55 attempts)

MOST YARDS GAINED
699—Mississippi Val. vs. Kentucky St., Sept. 1, 1984

MOST YARDS GAINED, BOTH TEAMS
1,190—La.-Monroe (619) & Stephen F. Austin (571), Nov. 11, 1989

MOST YARDS GAINED PER ATTEMPT
(Min. 25 Attempts)
20.1—Delaware vs. Connecticut, Nov. 7, 1998 (29 for 584)

MOST YARDS GAINED PER COMPLETION
(Min. 10-24 comps.) 33.0—Jackson St. vs. Southern U., Oct. 13, 1990 (14 for 462)
(Min. 25 comps.) 22.9—Marshall vs. VMI, Nov. 16, 1991 (28 for 642)

MOST TOUCHDOWN PASSES
11—Mississippi Val. vs. Kentucky St., Sept. 1, 1984

MOST TOUCHDOWN PASSES, BOTH TEAMS
14—Mississippi Val. (8) & Texas Southern (6), Oct. 26, 1985

Punting

MOST PUNTS
16—Louisiana Tech vs. La.-Monroe, Nov. 19, 1988 (567 yards)

MOST PUNTS, BOTH TEAMS
26—Hofstra (14) vs. Buffalo (12), Nov. 2, 1996

HIGHEST AVERAGE PER PUNT
(5-9 punts) 61.5—Idaho St. vs. Cal Poly, Nov. 16, 2002 (6 for 369)

(Min. 10 punts) 52.2—Montana St. vs. Northern Ariz., Oct. 20, 1979 (10 for 522)

FEWEST PUNTS
0—By many teams. Most recent: Ga. Southern vs. Johnson Smith, Sept. 9, 2000; Ga. Southern vs. Chattanooga, Sept. 25, 1999

FEWEST PUNTS, BOTH TEAMS
0—Ga. Southern & James Madison, Nov. 15, 1986

MOST OPPONENT'S PUNTS BLOCKED BY
4—Montana vs. Montana St., Oct. 31, 1987 (13 punts); Middle Tenn. vs. Mississippi Val., Oct. 8, 1988 (7 punts)

Punt Returns

MOST PUNT RETURNS
12—Northern Iowa vs. Youngstown St., Oct. 20, 1984 (83 yards)

MOST YARDS ON PUNT RETURNS
322—Northern Ariz. vs. Western N.M., Aug. 29, 1996 (10 returns)

HIGHEST AVERAGE GAIN PER RETURN
(Min. 6 Returns)
32.2—Northern Ariz. vs. Western N.M., Aug. 29, 1996 (10 for 322, 2 TDs)

MOST TOUCHDOWNS SCORED ON PUNT RETURNS
3—Canisius vs. Siena, Sept. 24, 1994; Northern Ariz. vs. Western N.M., Aug. 29, 1996

Kickoff Returns

MOST KICKOFF RETURNS
15—Delaware St. vs. Portland St., Nov. 8, 1980 (209 yards)

MOST YARDS ON KICKOFF RETURNS
326—Eastern Wash. vs. Sacramento St., Oct. 31, 1998 (5 returns)

HIGHEST AVERAGE GAIN PER RETURN
(Min. 3-5 rets.) 65.2—Eastern Wash. vs. Sacramento St., Oct. 31, 1998 (5 for 326)
(Min. 6 rets.) 46.3—Western Caro. vs. VMI, Oct. 10, 1992 (6 for 278)

MOST TOUCHDOWNS SCORED ON KICKOFF RETURNS
3—Eastern Wash. vs. Sacramento St., Oct. 31, 1998

Total Kick Returns

(Combined Punt and Kickoff Returns)

MOST YARDS ON KICK RETURNS
349—Eastern Wash. vs. Sacramento St., Oct. 31, 1998 (23 punt returns, 326 kickoff returns)

HIGHEST AVERAGE GAIN PER RETURN
(Min. 6 Returns)
46.8—Connecticut vs. Yale, Sept. 24, 1983 (6 for 281)

MOST TOUCHDOWNS SCORED ON TOTAL KICK RETURNS
5—Hampton vs. Virginia St., Sept. 22, 2001 (3 punt returns, 2 kickoff returns)

Scoring

MOST POINTS SCORED
105—Portland St. vs. Delaware St., Nov. 8, 1980 (15 TDs, 15 PATs)

MOST POINTS SCORED, BOTH TEAMS
125—Sacramento St. (64) & Cal St. Northridge (61), Nov. 4, 2000 (18 TDs, 11 PATs, 3 2-pt. extra points)

DIVISION I-AA

MOST POINTS SCORED BY A LOSING TEAM
61—Cal St. Northridge vs. Sacramento St. (64), Nov. 4, 2000

MOST POINTS SCORED EACH QUARTER
1st: 49—Portland St. vs. Delaware St., Nov. 8, 1980
2nd: 50—Alabama St. vs. Prairie View, Oct. 26, 1991
3rd: 35—Portland St. vs. Delaware St., Nov. 8, 1980; La.-Monroe vs. Arkansas St., Nov. 6, 1993
4th: 39—Montana vs. South Dakota St., Sept. 4, 1993

MOST POINTS SCORED EACH HALF
1st: 73—Montana St. vs. Eastern Ore., Sept. 14, 1985
2nd: 56—Brown vs. Columbia, Nov. 19, 1994

MOST TOUCHDOWNS SCORED
15—Portland St. vs. Delaware St., Nov. 8, 1980

MOST POINTS SCORED IN FOURTH QUARTER, BOTH TEAMS
58—Brown (30) vs. Pennsylvania (28), Oct. 10, 1998

MOST TOUCHDOWNS SCORED, BOTH TEAMS
17—Furman (9) & Davidson (8), Nov. 3, 1979; Weber St. (9) & Eastern Wash. (8), Sept. 28, 1991; Grambling (9) & Alcorn St. (8), Sept. 3, 1994

MOST EXTRA POINTS MADE BY KICKING
15—Portland St. vs. Delaware St., Nov. 8, 1980 (15 attempts)

MOST TWO-POINT ATTEMPTS MADE
5—Weber St. vs. Eastern Wash., Oct. 6, 1990 (5 passes attempted)

MOST FIELD GOALS MADE
8—Northern Ariz. vs. Idaho, Oct. 25, 1986 (8 attempts)

MOST FIELD GOALS ATTEMPTED
8—Northern Ariz. vs. Idaho, Oct. 25, 1986 (made 8)

MOST FIELD GOALS MADE, BOTH TEAMS
9—Nevada (5) & Northern Ariz. (4), Oct. 9, 1982 (12 attempts); Nevada (5) & Weber St. (4), Nov. 6, 1982 (11 attempts, 3 ot)

MOST SAFETIES SCORED
3—Alabama St. vs. Albany St. (Ga.), Oct. 15, 1988

MOST DEFENSIVE EXTRA POINTS SCORED
2—VMI vs. Davidson, Nov. 4, 1989 (Jeff Barnes, 95-yard interception return, and Wayne Purcell, 90-yard interception return); Duquesne vs. Fairfield, Nov. 3, 2001 (Leigh Bodden, 88-yard fumble return on two-point attempt, and Armar Watson, blocked extra point return)

MOST DEFENSIVE EXTRA-POINT ATTEMPTS
2—VMI vs. Davidson, Nov. 4, 1989 (2 interception returns); Western Ky. vs. Indiana St., Nov. 10, 1990 (2 interception returns); Duquesne vs. Fairfield, Nov. 3, 2001

First Downs

MOST FIRST DOWNS
46—Weber St. vs. Idaho St., Nov. 23, 1991 (12 rushing, 31 passing, 3 penalty)

MOST FIRST DOWNS, BOTH TEAMS
72—Bethune-Cookman (40) & Howard (32), Sept. 19, 1987

MOST FIRST DOWNS BY RUSHING
31—Ga. Southern vs. Glenville St., Nov. 12, 1994

MOST FIRST DOWNS BY PASSING
32—Montana vs. Weber St., Sept. 25, 1999

MOST FIRST DOWNS BY PENALTY
11—Towson vs. Liberty, Oct. 21, 1990

Fumbles

MOST FUMBLES
16—Delaware St. vs. Portland St., Nov. 8, 1980 (lost 6)

MOST FUMBLES, BOTH TEAMS
21—N.C. A&T (15) & Lane (6), Nov. 11, 1995 (lost 12)

MOST FUMBLES LOST
9—N.C. A&T vs. Lane, Nov. 11, 1995 (15 fumbles)

MOST FUMBLES LOST, BOTH TEAMS
12—Virginia St. (7) & Howard (5), Oct. 13, 1979 (16 fumbles); Austin Peay (8) & Mars Hill (4), Nov. 17, 1979 (18 fumbles); N.C. A&T (9) & Lane (3), Nov. 11, 1995 (21 fumbles)

Penalties

MOST PENALTIES AGAINST
23—Idaho vs. Idaho St., Oct. 10, 1992 (204 yards)

MOST PENALTIES, BOTH TEAMS
39—In four games. Most recent: Jackson St. (22) & Grambling (17), Oct. 24, 1987 (370 yards)

MOST YARDS PENALIZED
260—Southern U. vs. Howard, Nov. 4, 1978 (22 penalties)

MOST YARDS PENALIZED, BOTH TEAMS
423—Southern U. (260) & Howard (163), Nov. 4, 1978 (37 penalties)

Turnovers

(Passes Had Intercepted and Fumbles Lost)

MOST TURNOVERS
12—Texas Southern vs. Lamar, Sept. 6, 1980 (4 interceptions, 8 fumbles lost)

MOST TURNOVERS, BOTH TEAMS
15—Bucknell (8) & Hofstra (7), Sept. 8, 1990 (10 interceptions, 5 fumbles lost); Stephen F. Austin (8) & Nicholls St. (7), Sept. 22, 1990 (8 interceptions, 7 fumbles lost)

Overtimes

MOST OVERTIME PERIODS
6—Rhode Island (58) vs. Maine (55), Sept. 18, 1982; Villanova (41) vs. Connecticut (35), Oct. 7, 1989; Florida A&M (59) vs. Hampton (58), Oct. 5, 1996

MOST POINTS SCORED IN OVERTIME PERIODS
39—Florida A&M (59) vs. Hampton (58), Oct. 5, 1996 (6 overtime periods)

MOST POINTS SCORED IN OVERTIME PERIODS, BOTH TEAMS
77—Florida A&M (39) vs. Hampton (38), Oct. 5, 1996 (6 overtime periods; Florida A&M won, 59-58)

LARGEST WINNING MARGIN IN OVERTIME
13—Nicholls St. (49) vs. Southwest Tex. St. (36), Oct. 26, 1996 (5 overtime periods)

MOST CONSECUTIVE OVERTIME GAMES PLAYED
2—Maine, 1982 (Rhode Island 58, Maine 55, 6 ot, Sept. 18; and Boston U. 48, Maine 45, 4 ot, Sept. 25); Connecticut, 1989 (Villanova 41, Connecticut 35, 6 ot, Oct. 7; and Connecticut 39, Massachusetts 33, Oct. 14); Montana, 1991 (Nevada 35, Montana 28, 2 ot, Nov. 9; and Montana 35, Idaho 34, Nov. 16); Tennessee Tech, 1998 (Tennessee Tech 31, Tenn.-Martin 24, Oct. 17 and Tennessee Tech 31, Eastern Ky. 29, 3 ot, Oct. 24)

SINGLE GAME—Defense

Total Defense

FEWEST PLAYS ALLOWED
31—Howard vs. Dist. Columbia, Sept. 2, 1989 (32 yards)

FEWEST YARDS ALLOWED
Minus 12—Eastern Ill. vs. Kentucky St., Nov. 13, 1982 (-67 rushing, 55 passing)

Rushing Defense

FEWEST RUSHES ALLOWED
9—Mississippi Val. vs. Alcorn St., Nov. 6, 1999 (4 yards)

FEWEST RUSHING YARDS ALLOWED
Minus 90—Sacred Heart vs. Iona, Nov. 16, 2002 (42 rushes)

Pass Defense

FEWEST ATTEMPTS ALLOWED
1—By six teams. Most recent: Western Caro. vs. Wofford, Oct. 17, 1998

FEWEST COMPLETIONS ALLOWED
0—By many teams. Most recent: Western Caro. vs. Wofford, Oct. 17, 1998 (1 attempt); South Fla. vs. Cumberland, Nov. 8, 1997 (4 attempts)

LOWEST COMPLETION PERCENTAGE ALLOWED (Min. 30 Attempts)
11.8%—Southern U. vs. Nicholls St., Oct. 11, 1980 (4 of 34)

FEWEST YARDS ALLOWED
Minus 2—Florida A&M vs. Albany St. (Ga.), Oct. 16, 1982

MOST PASSES INTERCEPTED BY
10—Grambling vs. Mississippi Val., Oct. 17, 1987 (47 attempts); Montana vs. Boise St., Oct. 28, 1989 (55 attempts)

MOST TIMES OPPONENT TACKLED FOR LOSS ATTEMPTING TO PASS
14—Duquesne vs. Iona, Oct. 31, 1998 (92 yards)

MOST INTERCEPTIONS RETURNED FOR TOUCHDOWNS
3—Chattanooga vs. La.-Lafayette, Sept. 17, 1983 (4 for 122 yards); Montana vs. Eastern Wash., Nov. 12, 1983 (4 for 134 yards); Delaware St. vs. Akron, Oct. 17, 1987 (5 for 124 yards); Canisius vs. Siena, Sept. 16, 1995 (6 for 120 yards); Nicholls St. vs. Southwest Tex. St., Oct. 26, 1996 (4 for 166 yards); Jacksonville vs. Davidson, Sept. 8, 2001 (5 for 143 yards)

Opponent's Kicks Blocked

MOST OPPONENT'S PUNTS BLOCKED
4—Montana vs. Montana St., Oct. 31, 1987 (13 punts); Middle Tenn. vs. Mississippi Val., Oct. 8, 1988 (7 punts)

MOST OPPONENT'S TOTAL KICKS BLOCKED (Includes punts, field goals, PATs)
4—Montana vs. Montana St., Oct. 31, 1987 (all punts); Middle Tenn. vs. Mississippi Val., Oct. 8, 1988 (all punts); Colgate vs. Towson, Sept. 30, 2000 (3 punts, 1 PAT)

Fumble Returns

(Since 1992)

MOST FUMBLES RETURNED FOR TOUCHDOWNS
2—Marshall vs. VMI, Oct. 9, 1993; Idaho vs. Weber St., Nov. 12, 1994; Southwest Tex. St. vs. Nicholls St., Oct. 7, 2000; Harvard vs. Northeastern, Oct. 6, 2001

Safeties

MOST SAFETIES BY A DEFENSE
2—By several teams. Most recent: Duquesne vs. St. Francis (Pa.), Sept. 12, 1998

SEASON—Offense

Total Offense

MOST YARDS GAINED PER GAME
640.1—Mississippi Val., 1984 (6,401 in 10)

HIGHEST AVERAGE GAIN PER PLAY
7.8—Alcorn St., 1994 (848 for 6,577)

MOST PLAYS PER GAME

89.6—Weber St., 1991 (986 in 11)

MOST TOUCHDOWNS BY RUSHING AND PASSING PER GAME
8.4—Mississippi Val., 1984 (84 in 10)

Rushing

MOST YARDS GAINED PER GAME
419.0—Ga. Southern, 1999 (4,609 in 11)

HIGHEST AVERAGE GAIN PER RUSH
7.0—Ga. Southern, 1999 (654 for 4,609)

MOST RUSHES PER GAME
69.8—Northeastern, 1986 (698 in 10)

MOST TOUCHDOWNS BY RUSHING PER GAME
5.5—Ga. Southern, 1999 (61 in 11)

Passing

MOST YARDS GAINED PER GAME
496.8—Mississippi Val., 1984 (4,968 in 10)

HIGHEST AVERAGE GAIN PER ATTEMPT
(Min. 250-399 atts.) 10.7—Northern Iowa, 1996 (252 for 2,700)
(Min. 400 atts.) 9.3—Montana, 1999 (438 for 4,070)

HIGHEST AVERAGE GAIN PER COMPLETION
(Min. 125-199 comps.) 19.3—Jackson St., 1990 (156 for 3,006)
(Min. 200 comps.) 16.9—Grambling, 2002 (277 for 4,689)

MOST PASSES ATTEMPTED PER GAME
55.8—Mississippi Val., 1984 (558 in 10)

MOST PASSES COMPLETED PER GAME
35.1—Mississippi Val., 1984 (351 in 10)

HIGHEST PERCENTAGE COMPLETED
(Min. 200-449 atts.) 70.6%—Hofstra, 1997 (293 of 415)
(Min. 450 atts.) 67.2%—Montana, 1995 (336 of 500)

LOWEST PERCENTAGE HAD INTERCEPTED
(Min. 200-399 atts.) 0.78%—Portland St., 1999 (3 of 383)
(Min. 400 atts.) 1.2%—Lamar, 1988 (5 of 411)

MOST CONSECUTIVE PASSES ATTEMPTED WITHOUT AN INTERCEPTION
275—Lamar, 1988 (during 8 games, Sept. 3 to Oct. 29)

MOST TOUCHDOWN PASSES PER GAME
6.4—Mississippi Val., 1984 (64 in 10)

HIGHEST PASSING EFFICIENCY RATING POINTS
190.6—William & Mary, 1993 (232 attempts, 161 completions, 4 interceptions, 2,499 yards, 24 TDs)

Punting

MOST PUNTS PER GAME
9.6—Louisiana Tech, 1987 (106 in 11)

FEWEST PUNTS PER GAME
2.1—Ga. Southern, 1999 (23 in 11)

HIGHEST PUNTING AVERAGE
47.0—Appalachian St., 1991 (64 for 3,009)

HIGHEST NET PUNTING AVERAGE
(Min. 38-45 atts.) 44.5—Marshall, 1996 (38 for 1,739; 47 yards returned)
(Min. 46 atts.) 44.3—Idaho St., 2001 (49 for 2,270; 98 yards returned)

MOST PUNTS HAD BLOCKED
8—Western Ky., 1982

Punt Returns

MOST PUNT RETURNS PER GAME
5.4—Murray St., 1980 (59 in 11)

FEWEST PUNT RETURNS PER GAME
0.45—Tenn.-Martin, 2000 (5 in 11)

MOST PUNT-RETURN YARDS PER GAME
64.8—Duquesne, 1996 (648 in 10)

HIGHEST AVERAGE GAIN PER PUNT RETURN
(Min. 20-29 rets.) 23.0—N.C. A&T, 2001 (25 for 576)
(Min. 30 rets.) 18.1—Mississippi Val., 1985 (31 for 561)

MOST TOUCHDOWNS SCORED ON PUNT RETURNS
7—N.C. A&T, 2001 (25 returns)

Kickoff Returns

MOST KICKOFF RETURNS PER GAME
7.7—Morehead St., 1994 (85 in 11; 1,582 yards)

FEWEST KICKOFF RETURNS PER GAME
1.2—McNeese St., 1997 (13 in 11)

MOST KICKOFF-RETURN YARDS PER GAME
143.8—Morehead St., 1994 (1,582 in 11; 85 returns)

HIGHEST AVERAGE GAIN PER KICKOFF RETURN (Min. 20 Returns)
29.5—Eastern Ky., 1986 (34 for 1,022)

Combined Returns

(Interceptions, Punt Returns, Fumble Returns and Kickoff Returns)

MOST TOUCHDOWNS SCORED
9—Delaware St., 1987 (5 interceptions, 3 punt returns, 1 kickoff return)

Scoring

MOST POINTS PER GAME
60.9—Mississippi Val., 1984 (609 in 10)

MOST TOUCHDOWNS PER GAME
8.7—Mississippi Val., 1984 (87 in 10)

MOST EXTRA POINTS MADE BY KICKING PER GAME
7.7—Mississippi Val., 1984 (77 in 10)

MOST CONSECUTIVE EXTRA POINTS MADE BY KICKING
56—Murray St., 1995

MOST TWO-POINT ATTEMPTS MADE
9—Weber St., 1992 (11 attempts)

MOST DEFENSIVE EXTRA-POINT ATTEMPTS
2—VMI, 1989; Eastern Wash., 1990; Western Ky., 1990

MOST DEFENSIVE EXTRA POINTS SCORED
2—VMI, 1989 (2 interception returns); Eastern Wash., 1990 (2 interception returns)

MOST FIELD GOALS MADE PER GAME
2.4—Nevada, 1982 (26 in 11); Northern Iowa, 1990 (26 in 11)

MOST SAFETIES SCORED
5—Jackson St., 1986

First Downs

MOST FIRST DOWNS PER GAME
31.7—Mississippi Val., 1984 (317 in 10)

MOST RUSHING FIRST DOWNS PER GAME
18.6—Ga. Southern, 1999 (205 in 11)

MOST PASSING FIRST DOWNS PER GAME
21.4—Mississippi Val., 1984 (214 in 10)

MOST FIRST DOWNS BY PENALTY PER GAME
3.7—Alabama St., 1984 (41 in 11; 109 penalties by opponents); Texas Southern, 1987 (41 in 11; 134 penalties by opponents)

Fumbles

MOST FUMBLES PER GAME
5.3—Prairie View, 1984 (58 in 11)

MOST FUMBLES LOST PER GAME
3.1—Idaho, 1978 (31 in 10); Delaware St., 1980 (31 in 10)

FEWEST OWN FUMBLES LOST
1—Yale, 1999 (5 fumbles)

Penalties

MOST PENALTIES
152—Alabama St., 2001

MOST PENALTIES PER GAME
13.7—Grambling, 1984 (151 in 11; 1,206 yards)

MOST YARDS PENALIZED PER GAME
125.5—Tennessee St., 1982 (1,255 in 10; 132 penalties)

Turnovers

FEWEST TURNOVERS LOST
9—Hofstra, 1995 (6 fumbles, 3 interceptions); Yale, 1999 (1 fumble, 8 interceptions); Harvard, 2001 (3 fumbles, 6 interceptions)

MOST TURNOVERS LOST
59—Texas Southern, 1980 (27 fumbles, 32 interceptions)

HIGHEST TURNOVER MARGIN PER GAME OVER OPPONENTS
3.18—St. Peter's, 2001 (47 gained, 12 lost; 11 games)

SEASON—Defense

Total Defense

FEWEST YARDS ALLOWED PER GAME
149.9—Florida A&M, 1978 (1,649 in 11)

FEWEST RUSHING AND PASSING TOUCHDOWNS ALLOWED PER GAME
0.7—Western Mich., 1982 (8 in 11)

LOWEST AVERAGE YARDS ALLOWED PER PLAY
2.4—South Carolina St., 1978 (719 for 1,736)

Rushing Defense

FEWEST YARDS ALLOWED PER GAME
39.7—Alabama A&M, 2000 (476 in 12)

LOWEST AVERAGE YARDS ALLOWED PER RUSH
1.3—Marist, 1997 (319 for 404)

FEWEST RUSHING TOUCHDOWNS ALLOWED PER GAME
0.3—Florida A&M, 1978 (3 in 11)

Pass Defense

FEWEST YARDS ALLOWED PER GAME
59.9—Bethune-Cookman, 1981 (659 in 11)

FEWEST YARDS ALLOWED PER ATTEMPT (Min. 200 Attempts)
4.0—Middle Tenn., 1988 (251 for 999)

FEWEST YARDS ALLOWED PER COMPLETION (Min. 100 Completions)
9.1—Middle Tenn., 1988 (110 for 999)

LOWEST COMPLETION PERCENTAGE ALLOWED
(Min. 200-299 atts.) 32.3%—Alcorn St., 1979 (76 of 235)
(Min. 300 atts.) 34.2%—Tennessee St., 1986 (107 of 313)

FEWEST TOUCHDOWNS ALLOWED BY PASSING
1—Nevada, 1978; Middle Tenn., 1990; Pennsylvania, 1994

LOWEST PASSING EFFICIENCY DEFENSE RATING (Since 1990)
61.0—Sacred Heart, 2002 (252 attempts, 87 completions, 19 interceptions, 1,019 yards, 4 TDs)

MOST PASSES INTERCEPTED BY, PER GAME
3.2—Florida A&M, 1981 (35 in 11)

HIGHEST PERCENTAGE INTERCEPTED BY
13.4%—Florida A&M, 1981 (35 of 262)

MOST YARDS GAINED ON INTERCEPTIONS
689—N.C. A&T, 2001 (20 interceptions)

MOST YARDS GAINED PER GAME ON INTERCEPTIONS
62.6—N.C. A&T, 2001 (689 in 11)

HIGHEST AVERAGE PER INTERCEPTION RETURN (Min. 15 Returns)
34.5—N.C. A&T, 2001 (20 for 689)

MOST TOUCHDOWNS ON INTERCEPTION RETURNS
7—Jackson St., 1985; Northeastern, 1996

Opponents' Kicks Blocked

MOST OPPONENTS' TOTAL KICKS BLOCKED (Includes punts, field goals, PATs)
13—Davidson, 1999 (6 punts, 4 field goals, 3 PATs)

Punting

MOST OPPONENTS' PUNTS BLOCKED BY
9—Middle Tenn., 1988 (73 punts)

Punt Returns

LOWEST AVERAGE YARDS ALLOWED PER PUNT RETURN
1.0—Yale, 1988 (24 for 23)

FEWEST RETURNS ALLOWED
7—Furman, 1984 (11 games, 8 yards); Cal Poly, 1997 (11 games, 108 yards)

Kickoff Returns

LOWEST AVERAGE YARDS ALLOWED PER KICKOFF RETURN
10.6—Southern Utah, 1996 (33 for 350)

Scoring

FEWEST POINTS ALLOWED PER GAME
6.5—South Carolina St., 1978 (72 in 11)

Fumbles

MOST OPPONENTS' FUMBLES RECOVERED
29—Western Ky., 1982 (43 fumbles)

Fumble Returns

(Since 1992)

MOST FUMBLES RETURNED FOR TOUCHDOWNS
3—Southwest Tex. St., 2000 (2 vs. Nicholls St., Oct. 7 & 1 vs. Northwestern St., Oct. 31)

Turnovers

MOST OPPONENTS' TURNOVERS PER GAME
4.9—Canisius, 1996 (44 in 9)

Additional Records

MOST CONSECUTIVE VICTORIES
24—Pennsylvania, from Nov. 14, 1992, through Sept. 30, 1995 (ended Oct. 7, 1995, with 24-14 loss to Columbia)

MOST CONSECUTIVE HOME VICTORIES
39—Ga. Southern, from Sept. 27, 1997 through Dec. 15, 2001 (includes 11 Division I-AA playoff games)

MOST CONSECUTIVE LOSSES
80—Prairie View, from Nov. 4, 1989, until Sept. 26, 1998

MOST CONSECUTIVE GAMES WITHOUT A WIN
80—Prairie View, from Nov. 4, 1989, until Sept. 26, 1998

MOST CONSECUTIVE GAMES WITHOUT BEING SHUT OUT
297—Dayton, from Oct. 23, 1976, through present (Note: Dayton has been a I-AA member since 1993. Boise State had a 193-game streak from Sept. 21, 1968, through Nov. 10, 1984)

MOST SHUTOUTS IN A SEASON
5—South Carolina St., 1978

MOST CONSECUTIVE QUARTERS HOLDING OPPONENTS SCORELESS
15—Robert Morris, 1996

MOST CONSECUTIVE GAMES WITHOUT A TIE
343—Richmond, from Nov. 2, 1963, to Oct. 14, 1995 (ended Oct. 21, 1995, with 3-3 tie with Fordham)

LAST TIE GAME
Nov. 18, 1995—Dartmouth 10, Princeton 10

LAST SCORELESS-TIE GAME
Oct. 26, 1985—McNeese St. & North Texas

MOST CONSECUTIVE PASSES ATTEMPTED WITHOUT AN INTERCEPTION
370—Portland St. (in 11 games from Sept 4, 1999, to Nov. 13, 1999)

MOST POINTS OVERCOME IN SECOND HALF TO WIN A GAME
35—Nevada (55) vs. Weber St. (49), Nov. 2, 1991 (trailed 49-14 with 12:16 remaining in 3rd quarter)
32—Morehead St. (36) vs. Wichita St. (35), Sept. 20, 1986 (trailed 35-3 with 9:03 remaining in 3rd quarter)
31—Montana (52) vs. South Dakota St. (48), Sept. 4, 1993 (trailed 38-7 with 8:12 remaining in 3rd quarter)

MOST POINTS OVERCOME IN FOURTH QUARTER TO WIN A GAME
28—Delaware St. (38) vs. Liberty (37), Oct. 6, 1990 (trailed 37-9 with 13:00 remaining in 4th quarter)

MOST POINTS SCORED IN FOURTH QUARTER TO WIN A GAME
39—Montana (52) vs. South Dakota St. (48), Sept. 4, 1993 (trailed 38-13 to begin 4th quarter)
33—Southwest Mo. St. (40) vs. Illinois St. (28), Oct. 9, 1993 (trailed 21-7 with 11:30 remaining in 4th quarter)

MOST CONSECUTIVE EXTRA-POINT KICKS MADE
134—Boise St. (began Oct. 27, 1984; ended Nov. 12, 1988)

MOST CONSECUTIVE WINNING SEASONS
27—Grambling (1960-86)

MOST IMPROVED WON-LOST RECORD
9 1/2 games—Montana St., 1984 (12-2-0, including 3 Division I-AA playoff games) from 1983 (1-10-0)

Annual Champions, All-Time Leaders

Total Offense

CAREER YARDS PER GAME
(Minimum 5,500 Yards)

Player, Team	Years	G	Plays	Yards	TDR‡	Yd. PG
Steve McNair, Alcorn St.	1991-94	42	2,055	*16,823	152	*400.5
Neil Lomax, Portland St.	1978-80	33	1,680	11,647	100	352.9
Aaron Flowers, Cal St. Northridge	1996-97	20	944	6,754	60	337.7
Chris Sanders, Chattanooga	1999-00	22	1,044	7,247	52	329.4
Dave Dickenson, Montana	1992-95	35	1,539	11,523	116	329.2
Willie Totten, Mississippi Val.	1982-85	40	1,812	13,007	*157	325.2
Drew Miller, Montana	1999-00	18	708	5,628	47	312.7
Tom Ehrhardt, Rhode Island	1984-85	21	1,010	6,492	66	309.1
Doug Nussmeier, Idaho	1990-93	39	1,556	12,054	109	309.1
Oteman Sampson, Florida A&M	1996-97	22	906	6,751	57	306.9
Marcus Brady, Cal St. Northridge	1998-01	43	*2,116	13,095	123	304.5
Jamie Martin, Weber St.	1989-92	41	1,838	12,287	93	299.7
Tom Proudian, Iona	1993-95	27	1,337	7,939	61	294.0
Robert Dougherty, Boston U.	1993-94	21	918	6,135	56	292.1
Stan Greene, Boston U.	1989-90	22	1,167	6,408	49	291.3
John Friesz, Idaho	1986-89	35	1,459	10,187	79	291.1
Travis Brown, Northern Ariz.	1996-99	41	1,732	11,267	95	274.8
Grady Bennett, Montana	1988-90	31	1,389	8,304	69	267.9
Sean Payton, Eastern Ill.	1983-86	39	1,690	10,298	91	264.1
James Perry, Brown	1996-99	35	1,408	9,225	75	263.6
Giovanni Carmazzi, Hofstra	1996-99	40	1,564	10,416	103	260.4
Brian Ah Yat, Montana	1995-98	36	1,365	9,319	98	258.9
John Witkowski, Columbia	1981-83	30	1,330	7,748	58	258.3
John Whitcomb, UAB	1993-94	22	800	5,683	43	258.3
Ken Hobart, Idaho	1980-83	44	1,847	11,127	105	252.9
David Dinkins, Morehead St.	1997-00	37	1,260	9,337	114	252.4
Tony Hilde, Boise St.	1993-95	29	1,175	7,284	64	251.2
Gavin Hoffman, Pennsylvania	1999-01	29	1,161	7,188	56	247.9
Jeff Wiley, Holy Cross	1985-88	40	1,428	9,877	76	246.9
Doug Butler, Princeton	1983-85	29	1,137	7,157	52	246.8
Tom Ciaccio, Holy Cross	1988-91	37	1,283	9,066	87	245.0
Greg Wyatt, Northern Ariz.	1986-89	42	1,753	10,277	75	244.7
Jeff Lewis, Northern Ariz.	1992-95	40	1,654	9,769	82	244.2
Jay Fiedler, Dartmouth	1991-93	30	1,063	7,249	73	241.6
Chris Boden, Villanova	1996-99	39	1,514	9,369	94	240.2
Chris Hakel, William & Mary	1988-91	28	915	6,458	56	239.2
Bob Jean, New Hampshire	1985-88	32	1,287	7,621	59	238.2
Ryan Vena, Colgate	1996-99	40	1,404	9,435	94	235.9
Ted White, Howard	1995-98	41	1,377	9,669	98	235.8
Michael Proctor, Murray St.	1986-89	43	1,577	9,886	66	230.0

*Record. ‡Touchdowns-responsible-for are player's TDs scored and passed for.

SEASON YARDS PER GAME

Player, Team	Year	G	Plays	Yards	TDR‡	Yd. PG
Steve McNair, Alcorn St.	†1994	11	649	*5,799	53	*527.2
Willie Totten, Mississippi Val.	†1984	10	564	4,572	*61	457.2
Steve McNair, Alcorn St.	†1992	10	519	4,057	39	405.7
Jamie Martin, Weber St.	†1991	11	591	4,337	37	394.3
Bruce Eugene, Grambling	†2002	13	*680	5,018	43	386.0
Dave Dickenson, Montana	†1995	11	544	4,209	41	382.6
Neil Lomax, Portland St.	†1980	11	550	4,157	42	377.9
Joe Lee, Towson	†1999	11	608	4,031	22	366.5
Marcus Brady, Cal St. Northridge	†2001	10	532	3,632	40	363.2
Dave Dickenson, Montana	†1993	11	530	3,978	46	361.6
Neil Lomax, Portland St.	†1979	11	611	3,966	31	360.5
John Friesz, Idaho	†1989	11	464	3,853	31	350.3
Steve McNair, Alcorn St.	1993	11	493	3,830	30	348.2
Aaron Flowers, Cal St. Northridge	†1997	9	456	3,132	26	348.0
Todd Hammel, Stephen F. Austin	1989	11	487	3,822	38	347.5
Tom Ehrhardt, Rhode Island	†1985	10	529	3,460	35	346.0
Ken Hobart, Idaho	†1983	11	578	3,800	37	345.5
David Dinkins, Morehead St.	†2000	9	408	3,109	38	345.4
Dave Dickenson, Montana	1994	9	431	3,108	27	345.3
Robert Kent, Jackson St.	2001	11	584	3,785	40	344.1
Rocky Butler, Hofstra	2001	11	450	3,764	40	342.2
Dave Stireman, Weber St.	1985	11	502	3,759	33	341.7
Chris Sanders, Chattanooga	2000	11	520	3,756	24	341.5
Brian Ah Yat, Montana	†1996	11	501	3,744	45	340.4
Willie Totten, Mississippi Val.	1985	11	561	3,742	43	340.2
Jeff Wiley, Holy Cross	†1987	11	445	3,722	34	338.4
Jamie Martin, Weber St.	†1990	11	508	3,713	25	337.6
Giovanni Carmazzi, Hofstra	1997	11	524	3,707	36	337.0
Sean Payton, Eastern Ill.	1984	11	584	3,661	31	332.8

Player, Team	Year	G	Plays	Yards	TDR‡	Yd. PG
Tod Mayfield, West Tex. A&M	1985	10	526	3,328	21	332.8
Ira Vandever, Drake	2002	11	488	3,654	32	332.2
Tom Proudian, Iona	1993	10	521	3,322	30	332.2

*Record. †National champion. ‡Touchdowns-responsible-for are player's TDs scored and passed for.

CAREER YARDS

Player, Team	Years	Plays	Yards	Avg.
Steve McNair, Alcorn St.	1991-94	2,055	*16,823	*8.19
Marcus Brady, Cal St. Northridge	1998-01	*2,116	13,095	6.19
Willie Totten, Mississippi Val.	1982-85	1,812	13,007	7.18
Jamie Martin, Weber St.	1989-92	1,838	12,287	6.68
Doug Nussmeier, Idaho	1990-93	1,556	12,054	7.75
Neil Lomax, Portland St.	1978-80	1,680	11,647	6.93
Dave Dickenson, Montana	1992-95	1,539	11,523	7.49
Travis Brown, Northern Ariz.	1996-99	1,732	11,267	6.51
Ken Hobart, Idaho	1980-83	1,847	11,127	6.02
Giovanni Carmazzi, Hofstra	1996-99	1,564	10,416	6.66
Sean Payton, Eastern Ill.	1983-86	1,690	10,298	6.09
Greg Wyatt, Northern Ariz.	1986-89	1,753	10,277	5.86
John Friesz, Idaho	1986-89	1,459	10,187	6.98
Michael Proctor, Murray St.	1986-89	1,577	9,886	6.27
Jeff Wiley, Holy Cross	1985-88	1,428	9,877	6.92
Jeff Lewis, Northern Ariz.	1992-95	1,654	9,769	5.91
Ted White, Howard	1995-98	1,377	9,669	7.02
Ryan Vena, Colgate	1996-99	1,404	9,435	6.72
Chris Boden, Villanova	1996-99	1,514	9,369	6.19
David Dinkins, Morehead St.	1997-00	1,260	9,337	7.41
Brian Ah Yat, Montana	1995-98	1,365	9,319	6.83
Matt DeGennaro, Connecticut	1987-90	1,619	9,269	5.73
Phil Stambaugh, Lehigh	1996-99	1,430	9,245	6.47
James Perry, Brown	1996-99	1,408	9,225	6.55
Ryan Helming, Northern Iowa	1997-00	1,249	9,215	7.38
Tom Ciaccio, Holy Cross	1988-91	1,283	9,066	7.07
Eric Beavers, Nevada	1983-86	1,307	9,025	6.91
Matt Cannon, Southern Utah	1997-00	1,198	9,020	7.53
Marty Horn, Lehigh	1982-85	1,612	8,956	5.56
Kirk Schulz, Villanova	1986-89	1,534	8,900	5.80
Darin Hinshaw, UCF	1991-94	1,266	8,841	6.98
Robbie Justino, Liberty	1989-92	1,469	8,803	5.99
Dan Crowley, Towson	1991-94	1,263	8,797	6.97
Mitch Maher, North Texas	1991-94	1,417	8,735	6.16
Todd Wells, East Tenn. St.	1997-00	1,303	8,711	6.69
Chris Swartz, Morehead St.	1987-90	1,559	8,648	5.55
Frank Baur, Lafayette	1985, 87-89	1,312	8,579	6.54
Steve Calabria, Colgate	1981-84	1,342	8,532	6.36
Jimmy Blanchard, Portland St.	1997-00	1,188	8,517	7.17
Mike Buck, Maine	1986-89	1,288	8,457	6.57
Jason Whitmer, Idaho St.	1987-90	1,618	8,449	5.22
Scott Davis, North Texas	1987-90	1,548	8,436	5.45
Grady Bennett, Montana	1988-90	1,389	8,304	5.98
Bill Vergantino, Delaware	1989-92	1,459	8,225	5.64
Shane Stafford, Connecticut	1995-98	1,127	8,193	7.27
Stan Yagiello, William & Mary	$1981-85	1,492	8,168	5.47
Mike Smith, Northern Iowa	1984-87	1,163	8,145	7.00

*Record. $See Page 8 for explanation.

SEASON YARDS

Player, Team	Year	G	Plays	Yards	Avg.
Steve McNair, Alcorn St.	†1994	11	649	*5,799	*8.94
Bruce Eugene, Grambling	†2002	13	*680	5,018	7.38
Willie Totten, Mississippi Val.	†1984	10	564	4,572	8.11
Jamie Martin, Weber St.	†1991	11	591	4,337	7.34
Dave Dickenson, Montana	†1995	11	544	4,209	7.74
Neil Lomax, Portland St.	†1980	11	550	4,157	7.56
Brett Gordon, Villanova	2002	15	665	4,155	6.25
Steve McNair, Alcorn St.	†1992	10	519	4,057	7.82
Joe Lee, Towson	†1999	11	608	4,031	6.63
Dave Dickenson, Montana	†1993	11	530	3,978	7.51
Neil Lomax, Portland St.	†1979	11	611	3,966	6.49
John Friesz, Idaho	†1989	11	464	3,853	8.30
Steve McNair, Alcorn St.	1993	11	493	3,830	7.77
Todd Hammel, Stephen F. Austin	1989	11	487	3,822	7.85
Ken Hobart, Idaho	†1983	11	578	3,800	6.57
Robert Kent, Jackson St.	2001	11	584	3,785	6.48
Rocky Butler, Hofstra	2001	11	450	3,764	8.36
Dave Stireman, Weber St.	1985	11	502	3,759	7.49
Chris Sanders, Chattanooga	2000	11	520	3,756	7.22
Brian Ah Yat, Montana	†1996	11	501	3,744	7.47
Willie Totten, Mississippi Val.	1985	11	561	3,742	6.67
Jeff Wiley, Holy Cross	†1987	11	445	3,722	8.36
Jamie Martin, Weber St.	†1990	11	508	3,713	7.31
Giovanni Carmazzi, Hofstra	1997	11	524	3,707	7.07
Darnell Kennedy, Alabama St.	2001	12	444	3,669	8.26

Villanova Sports Information

Villanova's Brett Gordon finished the 2002 campaign with 4,155 total offense yards to claim seventh place on the Division I-AA single-season list.

Player, Team	Year	G	Plays	Yards	Avg.
Sean Payton, Eastern Ill.	1984	11	584	3,661	6.27
Ira Vandever, Drake	2002	11	488	3,654	7.49
Todd Brunner, Lehigh	1989	11	504	3,639	7.22
Marcus Brady, Cal St. Northridge	†2001	10	532	3,632	6.83
Oteman Sampson, Florida A&M	1997	11	492	3,625	7.37
Aaron Flowers, Cal St. Northridge	†1996	11	488	3,622	7.42
Patrick Bonner, Florida A&M	†1998	11	488	3,568	7.31
Robert Kent, Jackson St.	2002	11	513	3,565	6.95
David Macchi, Valparaiso	2002	11	522	3,549	6.80
Scott Semptimphelter, Lehigh	1993	11	515	3,528	6.85
Neil Lomax, Portland St.	†1978	11	519	3,524	6.79

*Record. †National champion.

SINGLE-GAME YARDS

Yds.	Player, Team (Opponent)	Date
668	Robert Kent, Jackson St. (Alabama St.)	Oct. 6, 2001
649	Steve McNair, Alcorn St. (Southern U.)	Oct. 22, 1994
647	Steve McNair, Alcorn St. (Chattanooga)	Sept. 10, 1994
643	Jamie Martin, Weber St. (Idaho St.)	Nov. 23, 1991
633	Steve McNair, Alcorn St. (Grambling)	Sept. 3, 1994
624	Steve McNair, Alcorn St. (Samford)	Oct. 29, 1994
621	Willie Totten, Mississippi Val. (Prairie View)	Oct. 27, 1984
614	Bryan Martin, Weber St. (Cal Poly)	Sept. 23, 1995
604	Steve McNair, Alcorn St. (Jackson St.)	Nov. 21, 1992
598	Robert Kent, Jackson St. (N.C. A&T)	Sept. 7, 2002
595	Doug Pederson, La.-Monroe (Stephen F. Austin)	Nov. 11, 1989
587	Vern Harris, Idaho St. (Montana)	Oct. 12, 1985
586	Steve McNair, Alcorn St. (Troy St.)	Nov. 12, 1994
574	Dave Dickenson, Montana (Idaho)	Oct. 21, 1995
570	Steve McNair, Alcorn St. (Texas Southern)	Sept. 11, 1993
569	Jimmy Blanchard, Portland St. (Montana)	Oct. 2, 1999
566	Tom Ehrhardt, Rhode Island (Connecticut)	Nov. 16, 1985
566	Brian Ah Yat, Montana (Eastern Wash.)	Oct. 19, 1996
564	Steve McNair, Alcorn St. (Jackson St.)	Nov. 19, 1994
563	Joe Lee, Towson (Lehigh)	Oct. 30, 1999
562	Bruce Eugene, Grambling (Texas Southern)	Nov. 2, 2002
562	Todd Hammel, Stephen F. Austin (La.-Monroe)	Nov. 11, 1989
561	Willie Totten, Mississippi Val. (Southern U.)	Sept. 29, 1984
559	Bruce Eugene, Grambling (Morris Brown)	Nov. 16, 2002
555	Bobby Townsend, Howard (Morgan St.)	Nov. 13, 1999
551	David Dinkins, Morehead St. (Butler)	Sept. 9, 2000
549	Steve McNair, Alcorn St. (Jacksonville St.)	Oct. 31, 1992
549	Brian Ah Yat, Montana (Northern Ariz.)	Oct. 26, 1996

Yds.	Player, Team (Opponent)	Date
548	Ryan Helming, Northern Iowa (Western Ill.)	Nov. 13, 1999
547	Tod Mayfield, West Tex. A&M (New Mexico St.)	Nov. 16, 1985
546	Seth Burford, Cal Poly (Northern Iowa)	Nov. 4, 2000
546	Dave Stireman, Weber St. (Montana)	Nov. 2, 1985
543	Ken Hobart, Idaho (Southern Colo.)	Sept. 10, 1983

ANNUAL CHAMPIONS

Year	Player, Team	Class	G	Plays	Yards	Avg.
1978	Neil Lomax, Portland St.	So.	11	519	3,524	320.4
1979	Neil Lomax, Portland St.	Jr.	11	611	3,966	360.5
1980	Neil Lomax, Portland St.	Sr.	11	550	4,157	377.9
1981	Mike Machurek, Idaho St.	Sr.	9	363	2,645	293.9
1982	Brent Woods, Princeton	Sr.	10	577	3,079	307.9
1983	Ken Hobart, Idaho	Sr.	11	578	3,800	345.5
1984	Willie Totten, Mississippi Val.	Jr.	10	564	4,572	457.2
1985	Tom Ehrhardt, Rhode Island	Sr.	10	529	3,460	346.0
1986	Brent Pease, Montana	Sr.	10	499	3,094	309.4
1987	Jeff Wiley, Holy Cross	Jr.	11	445	3,722	338.4
1988	John Friesz, Idaho	Jr.	10	424	2,751	275.1
1989	John Friesz, Idaho	Sr.	11	464	3,853	350.3
1990	Jamie Martin, Weber St.	So.	11	508	3,713	337.6
1991	Jamie Martin, Weber St.	Jr.	11	591	4,337	394.3
1992	Steve McNair, Alcorn St.	So.	10	519	4,057	405.7
1993	Dave Dickenson, Montana	So.	11	530	3,978	361.6
1994	Steve McNair, Alcorn St.	Sr.	11	649	*5,799	*527.2
1995	Dave Dickenson, Montana	Sr.	11	544	4,209	382.6
1996	Brian Ah Yat, Montana	So.	11	501	3,744	340.4
1997	Aaron Flowers, Cal St. Northridge	Sr.	9	456	3,132	348.0
1998	Patrick Bonner, Florida A&M	Sr.	11	488	3,568	324.4
1999	Joe Lee, Towson	Sr.	11	608	4,031	366.5
2000	David Dinkins, Morehead St.	Sr.	9	408	3,109	345.4
2001	Marcus Brady, Cal St. Northridge	Sr.	10	532	3,632	363.2
2002	Bruce Eugene, Grambling	So.	13	*680	5,018	386.0

*Record.

Rushing

CAREER YARDS PER GAME
(Minimum 2,500 Yards)

Player, Team	Years	G	Plays	Yards	TD	Yd. PG
Arnold Mickens, Butler	1994-95	20	763	3,813	29	*190.7
Adrian Peterson, Ga. Southern	1998-01	42	996	*6,559	*84	156.2
Aaron Stecker, Western Ill.	1997-98	20	550	3,081	36	154.1
Tim Hall, Robert Morris	1994-95	19	393	2,908	27	153.1
Jerry Azumah, New Hampshire	1995-98	41	1,044	6,193	60	151.0
Reggie Greene, Siena	1994-97	36	890	5,415	45	150.4
Charles Roberts, Sacramento St.	1997-00	44	*1,124	6,553	56	148.9
Charles Dunn, Portland St.	1998-00	33	872	4,831	46	146.4
Archie Amerson, Northern Ariz.	1995-96	22	526	3,196	37	145.3
Keith Elias, Princeton	1991-93	30	736	4,208	49	140.3
Jesse Chatman, Eastern Wash.	1999-01	31	627	4,173	48	134.6
Mike Clark, Akron	1984-86	32	804	4,257	24	133.0
Corey Holmes, Mississippi Val.	1999-00	22	526	2,897	21	131.7
Rick Sarille, Wagner	$1995-99	41	965	5,290	50	129.0
Charles Tharp, Western Ill.	1999-00	22	520	2,834	29	128.8
Michael Hicks, South Carolina St.	1993-95	32	701	4,093	51	127.9
Louis Ivory, Furman	1998-01	42	847	5,353	53	127.5
Marcel Shipp, Massachusetts	1997-00	43	1,042	5,383	49	125.2
Matt Cannon (QB), Southern Utah	1997-00	44	757	5,489	69	124.8
Rich Erenberg, Colgate	1982-83	21	464	2,618	22	124.7
Kenny Gamble, Colgate	1984-87	42	963	5,220	55	124.3
Frank Hawkins, Nevada	1977-80	43	945	5,333	39	124.0
Curtis Keaton, James Madison	1998-99	22	513	2,723	29	123.8
Elroy Harris, Eastern Ky.	1985, 87-88	31	648	3,829	47	123.5
Chad Levitt, Cornell	1993-96	38	922	4,657	44	122.6
Thomas Haskins, VMI	1993-96	44	899	5,355	50	121.7
Gill Fenerty, Holy Cross	1983-85	30	622	3,618	26	120.6
Markus Thomas, Eastern Ky.	1989-92	43	784	5,149	51	119.7
Destry Wright, Jackson St.	1997-99	34	726	4,049	30	119.1
Marquette Smith, UCF	1994-95	22	467	2,569	19	116.8
Erik Marsh, Lafayette	1991-94	42	1,027	4,834	35	115.1
Sherriden May, Idaho	1992-94	33	689	3,748	50	113.6
Jason Grove, Drake	1995-98	37	853	4,182	42	113.0
Rene Ingoglia, Massachusetts	1992-95	41	905	4,623	54	112.8
Rabih Abdullah, Lehigh	1994-97	33	672	3,696	33	112.0
Willie High, Eastern Ill.	1992-95	38	913	4,231	37	111.3
Rich Lemon, Bucknell	1993-96	43	994	4,742	35	110.3
Derrick Harmon, Cornell	1981-83	28	545	3,074	26	109.8
Ralph Saldiveri, Iona	1997-00	41	986	4,488	36	109.5
Paul Lewis, Boston U.	1982-84	37	878	3,995	50	108.0
Eric Gant, Grambling	1990-93	34	617	3,667	32	107.9

Player, Team	Years	G	Plays	Yards	TD	Yd. PG
Derrick Franklin, Indiana St.	1989-91	30	710	3,231	23	107.7
Charvez Foger, Nevada	1985-88	42	864	4,484	52	106.8
Claude Mathis, Southwest Tex. St.	1994-97	44	882	4,691	45	106.6
James Crawford, Eastern Ky.	1985-87	32	661	3,404	22	106.4
Eion Hu, Harvard	1994-96	29	714	3,073	26	106.0
Bryan Keys, Pennsylvania	1987-89	30	609	3,137	34	104.6
Yohance Humphrey, Montana	1998-01	39	746	4,070	43	104.4
Judd Garrett, Princeton	1987-89	30	687	3,109	32	103.6

*Record. $See Page 8 for explanation.

SEASON YARDS PER GAME

Player, Team	Year	G	Plays	Yards	TD	Yd. PG
Arnold Mickens, Butler	†1994	10	*409	2,255	18	*225.5
Charles Roberts, Sacramento St.	†1998	11	386	*2,260	19	205.5
Tony Vinson, Towson	†1993	10	293	2,016	23	201.6
Jerry Azumah, New Hampshire	1998	11	342	2,195	22	199.6
Reggie Greene, Siena	†1997	9	256	1,778	18	197.6
Reggie Greene, Siena	†1996	9	280	1,719	12	191.0
Jesse Chatman, Eastern Wash.	†2001	11	285	2,096	24	190.6
Charles Roberts, Sacramento St.	†1999	11	303	2,082	22	189.3
Archie Amerson, Northern Ariz.	1996	11	333	2,079	25	189.0
Louis Ivory, Furman	†2000	11	286	2,079	16	189.0
Aaron Stecker, Western Ill.	1997	11	298	1,957	24	177.9
Marcel Shipp, Massachusetts	1998	11	319	1,949	13	177.2
Adrian Peterson, Ga. Southern	1998	11	257	1,932	25	175.6
Keith Elias, Princeton	1993	10	305	1,731	19	173.1
Gene Lake, Delaware St.	†1984	10	238	1,722	20	172.2
Karlton Carpenter, Southern Ill.	1998	11	323	1,892	16	172.0
Rich Erenberg, Colgate	†1983	11	302	1,883	20	171.2
Sean Bennett, Evansville	1997	10	235	1,668	16	166.8
Kenny Gamble, Colgate	†1986	11	307	1,816	21	165.1
Kenny Bynum, South Carolina St.	1996	10	236	1,649	14	164.9
J.J. Allen, Marist	1998	10	279	1,646	21	164.6
Adrian Peterson, Ga. Southern	1999	11	248	1,807	*28	164.3
Charles Dunn, Portland St.	2000	11	302	1,792	21	162.9
Mike Clark, Akron	1986	11	245	1,786	8	162.4
Reggie Greene, Siena	†1995	9	273	1,461	11	162.3
Randall Joseph, Colgate	1999	9	193	1,446	15	160.7
Derrick Cullors, Murray St.	1995	11	269	1,765	16	160.5
L.J. McKanas, Northeastern	2001	11	342	1,756	14	159.6
Chad Levitt, Cornell	1996	9	267	1,435	13	159.4
Keith Elias, Princeton	†1992	10	245	1,575	18	157.5
Tim Hall, Robert Morris	1995	10	239	1,572	16	157.2
Frank Hawkins, Nevada	†1980	11	307	1,719	9	156.3
David Dinkins, Morehead St.	2000	9	190	1,405	21	156.1
Arnold Mickens, Butler	1995	10	354	1,558	11	155.8
Brad Baxter, Alabama St.	1986	11	302	1,705	13	155.0
Thomas Haskins, VMI	1996	11	287	1,704	15	154.9
Elroy Harris, Eastern Ky.	1988	10	277	1,543	21	154.3
Corey Holmes, Mississippi Val.	1999	11	331	1,692	11	153.8
Richard Johnson, Butler	1993	10	322	1,535	10	153.5

*Record. †National champion.

CAREER YARDS

Player, Team	Years	Plays	Yards	Avg.	Long
Adrian Peterson, Ga. Southern	1998-01	996	*6,559	6.59	91
Charles Roberts, Sacramento St.	1997-00	*1,124	6,553	5.83	70
Jerry Azumah, New Hampshire	1995-98	1,044	6,193	5.93	96
Matt Cannon, Southern Utah (QB)	1997-00	757	5,489	‡7.25	93
Reggie Greene, Siena	1994-97	890	5,415	6.08	82
Marcel Shipp, Massachusetts	1997-00	1,042	5,383	5.17	82
Thomas Haskins, VMI	1993-96	899	5,355	5.96	80
Louis Ivory, Furman	1998-01	847	5,353	6.32	88
Frank Hawkins, Nevada	1977-80	945	5,333	5.64	50
Rick Sarille, Wagner	$1995-99	965	5,290	5.48	80
Kenny Gamble, Colgate	1984-87	963	5,220	5.42	91
Markus Thomas, Eastern Ky.	1989-92	784	5,149	6.57	90
Erik Marsh, Lafayette	1991-94	1,027	4,834	4.71	62
Charles Dunn, Portland St.	1998-00	872	4,831	5.54	67
Rich Lemon, Bucknell	1993-96	994	4,742	4.77	83
Claude Mathis, Southwest Tex. St.	1994-97	882	4,691	5.32	79
Chad Levitt, Cornell	1993-96	922	4,657	5.05	88
Rene Ingoglia, Massachusetts	1992-95	905	4,623	5.11	84
Chris Parker, Marshall	1992-95	780	4,571	5.86	89
Ralph Saldiveri, Iona	1997-00	986	4,488	4.55	91
Cedric Minter, Boise St.	1977-80	752	4,475	5.95	77
John Settle, Appalachian St.	1983-86	891	4,409	4.95	88
Jermaine Creighton, St. John's (N.Y.)	1994-97	948	4,271	4.51	99
Donte Small, Duquesne	1998-01	843	4,260	5.05	68
Mike Clark, Akron	1984-86	804	4,257	5.29	†65
Willie High, Eastern Ill.	1992-95	913	4,231	4.63	55
Keith Elias, Princeton	1991-93	736	4,208	5.72	69
Jason Grove, Drake	1995-98	853	4,182	4.90	50
David Wright, Indiana St.	1992-95	784	4,181	5.33	75

Player, Team	Years	Plays	Yards	Avg.	Long
Jesse Chatman, Eastern Wash.	1999-01	627	4,173	6.66	67
Warren Marshall, James Madison	$1982-86	737	4,168	5.66	59
Carl Tremble, Furman	1989-92	696	4,149	5.96	65
Harvey Reed, Howard	1984-87	635	4,142	6.52	85
Brandon Walker, East Tenn. St.	1996-99	776	4,095	5.28	62
Michael Hicks, South Carolina St.	1993-95	701	4,093	5.84	82
Yohance Humphrey, Montana	1998-01	746	4,070	5.46	72
Destry Wright, Jackson St.	1997-99	726	4,049	5.58	68
Paul Lewis, Boston U.	1981-84	878	3,995	4.55	80
Willie Taggart, Western Ky. (QB)	1995-98	684	3,957	5.79	74
Daryl Brown, Delaware	1991-94	678	3,932	5.80	71
Joe Ross, Ga. Southern	1987-90	687	3,876	5.64	75
Garry Pearson, Massachusetts	1979-82	808	3,859	4.78	71
Montrell Coley, Hampton	1997-00	694	3,838	5.53	89
Elroy Harris, Eastern Ky.	1985, 87-88	648	3,829	5.91	64
Lorenzo Bouier, Maine	1979-82	879	3,827	4.35	77
Lewis Tillman, Jackson St.	$1984-88	779	3,824	4.91	39
Joe Campbell, Middle Tenn.	1988-91	638	3,823	5.99	81
Carl Smith, Maine	1988-91	759	3,815	5.03	89
Arnold Mickens, Butler	1994-95	763	3,813	5.00	70
Damon Scott, Appalachian St.	1993-96	745	3,800	5.10	49

*Record. †Did not score. $See Page 8 for explanation. ‡Record for minimum 600 carries.

CAREER RUSHING TOUCHDOWNS

Player, Team	Years	G	TDs
Adrian Peterson, Ga. Southern	1998-01	42	*84
Matt Cannon, Southern Utah (QB)	1997-00	44	69
David Dinkins, Morehead St. (QB)	1997-00	37	63
Jerry Azumah, New Hampshire	1995-98	41	60
Charles Roberts, Sacramento St.	1997-00	44	56
Kenny Gamble, Colgate	1984-87	42	55
Rene Ingoglia, Massachusetts	1992-95	41	54
Louis Ivory, Furman	1998-01	42	53
Charvez Foger, Nevada	1985-88	42	52
Michael Hicks, South Carolina St.	1993-95	32	51
Markus Thomas, Eastern Ky.	1989-92	43	51
Rick Sarille, Wagner	$1995-99	41	50
Thomas Haskins, VMI	1993-96	44	50
Sherriden May, Idaho	1992-94	33	50
Paul Lewis, Boston U.	1981-84	37	50
Marcel Shipp, Massachusetts	1997-00	43	49
Montrell Coley, Hampton	1997-00	44	49
Greg Hill, Ga. Southern (QB)	1996-99	43	49
Chris Parker, Marshall	1992-95	45	49
Keith Elias, Princeton	1991-93	30	49
Jesse Chatman, Eastern Wash.	1999-01	31	48
Elroy Harris, Eastern Ky.	1985, 87-88	31	47
Harvey Reed, Howard	1984-87	41	47

*Record. (Note: Anthony Russo of St. John's [N.Y.] scored 16 TDs in 1993 at I-AA level but had 57 total touchdowns during 1990-94.) $See Page 8 for explanation.

SEASON YARDS

Player, Team	Year	G	Plays	Yards	Avg.
Charles Roberts, Sacramento St.	†1998	11	386	*2,260	5.85
Arnold Mickens, Butler	†1994	10	*409	2,255	5.51
Jerry Azumah, New Hampshire	1998	11	342	2,195	6.42
Jesse Chatman, Eastern Wash.	†2001	11	285	2,096	7.35
Charles Roberts, Sacramento St.	†1999	11	303	2,082	6.87
Louis Ivory, Furman	†2000	11	286	2,079	7.27
Archie Amerson, Northern Ariz.	1996	11	333	2,079	6.24
Tony Vinson, Towson	†1993	10	293	2,016	6.89
Aaron Stecker, Western Ill.	1997	11	298	1,957	6.57
Marcel Shipp, Massachusetts	1998	11	319	1,949	6.11
Adrian Peterson, Ga. Southern	1998	11	257	1,932	7.52
Karlton Carpenter, Southern Ill.	1998	11	323	1,892	5.86
Rich Erenberg, Colgate	†1983	11	302	1,883	6.24
Kenny Gamble, Colgate	†1986	11	307	1,816	5.92
Adrian Peterson, Ga. Southern	1999	11	248	1,807	7.29
Charles Dunn, Portland St.	2000	11	302	1,792	5.93
Mike Clark, Akron	1986	11	245	1,786	‡7.29
Reggie Greene, Siena	†1997	9	256	1,778	6.95
Derrick Cullors, Murray St.	1995	11	269	1,765	6.56
L.J. McKanas, Northeastern	2001	11	342	1,756	5.13
Keith Elias, Princeton	1993	10	305	1,731	5.68
Gene Lake, Delaware St.	†1984	10	238	1,722	7.24
Frank Hawkins, Nevada	†1980	11	307	1,719	5.60
Reggie Greene, Siena	†1996	9	280	1,719	6.14
Brad Baxter, Alabama St.	1986	11	302	1,705	5.65
Thomas Haskins, VMI	1996	11	287	1,704	5.94
Corey Holmes, Mississippi Val.	1999	11	331	1,692	5.11
Jay Bailey, Austin Peay	†2002	12	319	1,687	5.29
Frank Hawkins, Nevada	†1979	11	293	1,683	5.74
Carl Smith, Maine	†1989	11	305	1,680	5.51
Sean Bennett, Evansville	1997	10	235	1,668	7.10

Player, Team	Year	G	Plays	Yards	Avg.
Brad Hoover, Western Caro.	1998	11	331	1,663	5.02
John Settle, Appalachian St.	1986	11	317	1,661	5.24
Curtis Keaton, James Madison	1999	11	290	1,659	5.72
Yohance Humphrey, Montana	2001	12	303	1,658	5.47
Kenny Bynum, South Carolina St.	1996	10	236	1,649	6.99
J.J. Allen, Marist	1998	10	279	1,646	5.90
Destry Wright, Jackson St.	1999	12	296	1,643	5.55
Garry Pearson, Massachusetts	†1982	11	312	1,631	5.23
Morgan Welch, Weber St.	1998	11	305	1,629	5.34
Charles Roberts, Sacramento St.	2000	11	296	1,624	5.49
Lorenzo Bouier, Maine	1980	11	349	1,622	4.65
Markus Thomas, Eastern Ky.	1989	11	232	1,620	6.98

*Record. †National champion. ‡Record for minimum of 200 carries.

SINGLE-GAME YARDS

Yds.	Player, Team (Opponent)	Date
437	Maurice Hicks, N.C. A&T (Morgan St.)	Oct. 6, 2001
409	Charles Roberts, Sacramento St. (Idaho St.)	Nov. 6, 1999
393	Ryan Fuqua, Portland St. (Eastern Wash.)	Nov. 10, 2001
379	Reggie Greene, Siena (St. John's [N.Y.])	Nov. 2, 1996
364	Tony Vinson, Towson (Bucknell)	Nov. 13, 1993
353	Maurice Hicks, N.C. A&T (South Carolina St.)	Nov. 18, 2000
346	William Arnold, Jackson St. (Texas Southern)	Nov. 6, 1993
345	Russell Davis, Idaho (Portland St.)	Oct. 3, 1981
337	Frank Alessio, Massachusetts (Boston U.)	Nov. 11, 1995
337	Gill Fenerty, Holy Cross (Columbia)	Oct. 29, 1983
336	Gene Lake, Delaware St. (Liberty)	Nov. 10, 1984
329	Jerry Azumah, New Hampshire (Hofstra)	Nov. 7, 1998
327	Tony Vinson, Towson (Morgan St.)	Nov. 20, 1993
324	Charles Dunn, Portland St. (Hofstra)	Oct. 7, 2000
324	John Campbell, Wagner (Jacksonville)	Nov. 14, 1998
324	Robert Vaughn, Alabama St. (Tuskegee)	Nov. 24, 1994
323	Matt Johnson, Harvard (Brown)	Nov. 9, 1991
317	Josh Rue, Duquesne (Canisius)	Nov. 17, 2001
316	J.J. Allen, Marist (St. Francis [Pa.])	Oct. 31, 1998
315	Angelo Todd, Norfolk St. (Delaware St.)	Sept. 19, 1998
313	Sean Bennett, Evansville (San Diego)	Oct. 19, 1996
313	Rene Ingoglia, Massachusetts (Rhode Island)	Oct. 1, 1994
312	Muhammad Abdulqaadir, Southern Ill. (Eastern Mich.)	Sept. 28, 2002
312	Surkano Edwards, Samford (Tenn.-Martin)	Nov. 14, 1992
310	Claude Mathis, Southwest Tex. St. (Stephen F. Austin)	Nov. 16, 1996
309	Eddie Thompson, Western Ky. (Southern Ill.)	Oct. 29, 1992
308	J.R. Taylor, Eastern Ill. (Fla. Atlantic)	Nov. 16, 2002
308	Claude Mathis, Southwest Tex. St. (Jacksonville St.)	Nov. 15, 1997
307	Kenny Bynum, South Carolina St. (N.C. A&T)	Nov. 23, 1996
305	Lawrence Worthington, Liberty (Charleston So.)	Nov. 19, 1994
305	Lucius Floyd, Nevada (Montana St.)	Sept. 27, 1986
304	Tony Citizen, McNeese St. (Prairie View)	Sept. 6, 1986
302	Marvin Royal, Sacred Heart (Iona)	Oct. 28, 2000
302	Lorenzo Bouier, Maine (Northeastern)	Nov. 1, 1980
301	Louis Ivory, Furman (Ga. Southern)	Nov. 4, 2000
301	Jovan Rhodes, Marist (Siena)	Nov. 12, 1994
300	Jerry Azumah, New Hampshire (Boston U.)	Nov. 15, 1997
300	Markus Thomas, Eastern Ky. (Marshall)	Oct. 21, 1989

ANNUAL CHAMPIONS

Year	Player, Team	Class	G	Plays	Yards	Avg.
1978	Frank Hawkins, Nevada	So.	10	259	1,445	144.5
1979	Frank Hawkins, Nevada	Jr.	11	293	1,683	153.0
1980	Frank Hawkins, Nevada	Sr.	11	307	1,719	156.3
1981	Gregg Drew, Boston U.	Jr.	10	309	1,257	125.7
1982	Garry Pearson, Massachusetts	Sr.	11	312	1,631	148.3
1983	Rich Erenberg, Colgate	Sr.	11	302	1,883	171.2
1984	Gene Lake, Delaware St.	Jr.	10	238	1,722	172.2
1985	Burton Murchison, Lamar	So.	11	265	1,547	140.6
1986	Kenny Gamble, Colgate	Jr.	11	307	1,816	165.1
1987	Harvey Reed, Howard	Sr.	10	211	1,512	151.2
1988	Elroy Harris, Eastern Ky.	Jr.	10	277	1,543	154.3
1989	Carl Smith, Maine	So.	11	305	1,680	152.7
1990	Walter Dean, Grambling	Sr.	11	221	1,401	127.4
1991	Al Rosier, Dartmouth	Sr.	10	258	1,432	143.2
1992	Keith Elias, Princeton	Jr.	10	245	1,575	157.5
1993	Tony Vinson, Towson	Sr.	10	293	2,016	201.6
1994	Arnold Mickens, Butler	Jr.	10	*409	2,255	*225.5
1995	Reggie Greene, Siena	So.	9	273	1,461	162.3
1996	Reggie Greene, Siena	Jr.	9	280	1,719	191.0

Year	Player, Team	Class	G	Plays	Yards	Avg.
1997	Reggie Greene, Siena	Sr.	9	256	1,778	197.6
1998	Charles Roberts, Sacramento St.	So.	11	386	*2,260	205.5
1999	Charles Roberts, Sacramento St.	Jr.	11	303	2,082	189.3
2000	Louis Ivory, Furman	Jr.	11	286	2,079	189.0
2001	Jesse Chatman, Eastern Wash.	Sr.	11	285	2,096	190.6
2002	Jay Bailey, Austin Peay	Sr.	12	319	1,687	140.6

*Record.

Quarterback Rushing

CAREER YARDS
(Since 1978)

Player, Team	Years	G	Plays	Yards	TD	Yd. PG
#Matt Cannon, Southern Utah	1997-00	44	674	*4,852	*64	*110.3
Willie Taggart, Western Ky.	1995-98	41	684	3,957	46	96.5
David Dinkins, Morehead St.	1997-00	37	553	3,765	63	101.8
Jack Douglas, Citadel	1989-92	44	*832	3,674	48	83.5
Greg Hill, Ga. Southern	1996-99	41	575	3,309	49	80.7
Tracy Ham, Ga. Southern	1984-86	33	511	2,506	32	75.9
Travis Wilson, Wofford	1998-01	44	550	2,488	18	56.5
Tony Scales, VMI	1989-92	44	561	2,475	19	56.3
Eddie Thompson, Western Ky.	1991-93	27	387	2,349	19	87.0
Steve McNair, Alcorn St.	1991-94	42	375	2,327	33	55.4
Eriq Williams, James Madison	1989-92	43	642	2,321	32	54.0
Raymond Gross, Ga. Southern	1987-90	42	695	2,290	20	54.5
Bill Vergantino, Delaware	1989-92	44	656	2,287	34	52.0
Dwane Brown, Arkansas St.	1984-87	42	595	2,192	33	52.2
Roy Johnson, Arkansas St.	1988-91	43	558	2,182	22	50.7
DeAndre Smith, Southwest Mo. St.	1987-90	42	558	2,140	36	50.9
Ryan Vena, Colgate	1996-99	40	585	2,008	33	50.2
Ken Hobart, Idaho	1980-83	44	628	1,827	26	41.5
Darin Kehler, Yale	1987-90	28	402	1,643	13	58.7

*Record. #Does not include statistics as a slotback in 1997.

SEASON YARDS
(Since 1978)

Player, Team	Year	G	Plays	Yards	TD	Avg.
Matt Cannon, Southern Utah	2000	11	218	*1,602	22	7.35
Matt Cannon, Southern Utah	1998	11	199	1,533	14	7.80
Chaz Williams, Ga. Southern	2002	14	*290	1,422	*27	4.90
David Dinkins, Morehead St.	2000	9	190	1,405	21	7.39
Willie Taggart, Western Ky.	1998	11	210	1,313	15	6.25
Matt Cannon, Southern Utah	1999	11	203	1,310	23	6.45
Joe Dupaix, Southern Utah	1996	11	271	1,246	12	4.60
Willie Taggart, Western Ky.	1997	10	152	1,217	15	*8.01
Marvin Marshall, South Carolina St.	1994	11	160	1,201	10	7.51
David Dinkins, Morehead St.	1998	11	147	1,169	20	7.95
Jack Douglas, Citadel	1991	11	266	1,152	13	4.33
David Dinkins, Morehead St.	1999	10	200	1,138	20	5.69
Tony Scales, VMI	1991	11	185	1,105	8	5.97
Pa'tel Troutman, Bethune-Cookman	1999	11	220	1,089	9	4.95
Greg Hill, Ga. Southern	1999	11	152	1,084	16	7.13
Greg Hill, Ga. Southern	1998	11	202	1,061	16	5.25
Pa'tel Troutman, Bethune-Cookman	1998	11	183	1,054	15	5.76
Tracy Ham, Ga. Southern	1986	11	207	1,048	18	5.06
Allen Suber, Bethune-Cookman	2002	12	158	1,035	15	6.55
Sheraton Fox, Indiana St.	1999	11	228	1,034	8	4.54
Matt Cannon, Southern Utah	1997	11	137	1,024	10	7.47
Alcede Surtain, Alabama St.	1995	11	178	1,024	21	5.75
Nick Crawford, Yale	1991	10	210	1,024	8	4.98
Gene Brown, Citadel	1988	9	152	1,006	13	6.62
Willie Taggart, Western Ky.	1996	10	167	997	8	5.97
Kharon Brown, Hofstra	1995	11	151	977	7	6.47
Gus Papanikolas, St. Mary's (Cal.)	2000	11	194	966	8	4.98
Corey Thomas, Nicholls St.	1994	11	158	962	8	6.09
Travis Wilson, Wofford	1999	11	173	936	10	5.41
Steve McNair, Alcorn St.	1994	11	119	936	9	7.87
Jack Douglas, Citadel	1992	11	178	926	13	5.20
Roy Johnson, Arkansas St.	1989	11	193	925	6	4.79
Darin Kehler, Yale	1989	10	210	903	6	4.30

*Record.

Passing

CAREER PASSING EFFICIENCY
(Minimum 300 Completions)

Player, Team	Years	Att.	Cmp.	Int.	Pct.	Yards	TD	Pts.
Shawn Knight, William & Mary	1991-94	558	367	15	.658	5,527	46	*170.8
Dave Dickenson, Montana	1992-95	1,208	813	26	*.673	11,080	96	166.3
Drew Miller, Montana	1999-00	654	430	14	.657	5,900	46	160.5
Doug Nussmeier, Idaho	1990-93	1,225	746	32	.609	10,824	91	154.4
Mark Washington, Jackson St.	1996-99	724	384	24	.530	6,561	68	153.5
Mike Simpson, Eastern Ill.	1996-97	493	331	15	.671	3,901	32	148.9
Jay Johnson, Northern Iowa	1989-92	744	397	25	.534	7,049	51	148.9
Matt Nagy, Delaware	1997-00	771	433	32	.562	7,220	52	148.8
Ryan Vena, Colgate	1996-99	819	482	46	.589	7,427	61	148.4
Mike Cook, William & Mary	1995-98	804	495	21	.616	6,644	55	148.3
Michael Payton, Marshall	1989-92	876	542	32	.619	7,530	57	148.2
Bryan Martin, Weber St.	1992-95	606	365	14	.602	5,211	37	148.0
Aaron Flowers, Cal St. Northridge	1996-97	819	502	21	.613	6,766	54	147.3
Willie Totten, Mississippi Val.	1982-85	1,555	907	*75	.583	12,711	*139	146.8
Kenneth Biggles, Tennessee St.	1981-84	701	397	28	.566	5,933	57	146.6
Shane Stafford, Connecticut	1995-98	951	522	29	.549	8,368	67	146.0
Oteman Sampson, Florida A&M	1996-97	686	387	26	.564	6,104	46	145.7
Brian Ah Yat, Montana	1995-98	1,190	735	39	.618	9,315	89	145.6
Giovanni Carmazzi, Hofstra	1996-99	1,187	764	32	.644	9,371	71	145.0
Jimmy Blanchard, Portland St.	1997-00	1,038	618	19	.595	8,455	63	144.3
Ted White, Howard	1995-98	1,163	635	34	.546	9,611	92	144.3
Steve McNair, Alcorn St.	1991-94	*1,680	927	58	.552	*14,496	119	144.1
Mike Smith, Northern Iowa	1984-87	943	557	43	.591	8,219	58	143.5
Neil Rose, Harvard	$1998-02	729	455	23	.624	5,949	41	143.2
Braniff Bonaventure, Furman	1993-96	672	413	17	.615	5,361	39	142.6
Tom Ciaccio, Holy Cross	1988-91	1,073	658	46	.613	8,603	72	142.2
Jim Zaccheo, Nevada	1987-88	554	326	27	.588	4,750	35	142.0
Todd Donnan, Marshall	1991-94	712	425	25	.597	5,566	51	142.0
Mike Cherry, Murray St.	1995-96	526	305	24	.580	4,490	34	141.9
Eric Beavers, Nevada	1983-86	1,094	646	37	.591	8,626	77	141.8
Scott Semptimphelter, Lehigh	1990-93	823	493	27	.599	6,668	50	141.5
John Whitcomb, UAB	1993-94	738	448	28	.607	6,043	43	141.1
Harry Leons, Eastern Wash.	1995-97	523	307	23	.587	4,363	33	140.8
Jason Garrett, Princeton	1987-88	550	368	10	.669	4,274	20	140.6
Marcus Brady, Cal St. Northridge	1998-01	*1,680	*1,039	47	.618	12,479	109	140.6
Phil Stambaugh, Lehigh	1996-99	1,284	816	43	.636	9,669	78	140.2
Neil Lomax, Portland St.	1978-80	1,425	836	50	.587	11,550	88	140.1
Chris Boden, Villanova	1996-99	1,338	818	30	.611	9,538	93	139.5
Jamie Martin, Weber St.	1989-92	1,544	934	56	.605	12,207	87	138.2
Darin Hinshaw, UCF	1991-94	1,113	614	52	.552	9,000	82	138.1
Gavin Hoffman, Pennsylvania	1999-01	1,004	651	32	.648	7,542	50	138.0
Ricky Jones, Alabama St.	1988-91	644	324	30	.503	5,472	49	137.5
Jeff Carlson, Weber St.	1984, 86-88	723	384	33	.531	6,147	47	136.9
Tony Zimmerman, Duquesne	1998-00	889	443	41	.498	7,313	73	136.8
Chris Hakel, William & Mary	1988-91	812	489	26	.602	6,447	40	136.7
Jeff Wiley, Holy Cross	1985-88	1,208	723	63	.599	9,698	71	136.3
Robert Dougherty, Boston U.	1993-94	705	405	26	.574	5,608	41	136.1
Eriq Williams, James Madison	1989-92	617	326	35	.528	5,356	40	135.8
Chad Barnhardt, South Fla.	1997-98	519	300	16	.578	4,138	27	135.8
Rob Compson, Montana St.	1995-98	901	516	27	.573	6,838	55	135.2
Tom Ehrhardt, Rhode Island	1984-85	919	526	35	.572	6,722	66	134.8
Tony Hilde, Boise St.	1993-95	842	459	23	.545	6,634	49	134.4
Jeff Lewis, Northern Ariz.	1992-95	1,316	785	24	.597	9,655	67	134.4
Todd Bankhead, Massachusetts	1998-99	731	438	29	.599	5,502	42	134.2
Tom Kirchoff, Lafayette	1989-92	878	510	36	.581	6,721	53	134.1
Dan Sabella, Monmouth	1994-97	868	500	17	.576	6,229	52	133.7
Doug Baughman, Idaho St.	2001-02	748	443	24	.592	5,574	41	133.5
Mike Buck, Maine	1986-89	1,134	637	41	.562	8,721	68	133.4
Frankie DeBusk, Furman	1987-90	634	333	29	.525	5,414	35	133.3
Frank Novak, Lafayette	1981-83	834	478	36	.573	6,378	51	133.1
Robbie Justino, Liberty	1989-92	1,267	769	51	.607	9,548	64	132.6
Rick Worman, Eastern Wash.	1984-85	672	381	23	.567	5,004	41	132.5
Glenn Kempa, Lehigh	1989-91	901	520	27	.577	6,722	49	132.3
Juston Wood, Portland St.	2000-02	724	414	20	.572	5,463	37	131.9
Jay Walker, Howard	1991-93	718	377	23	.525	5,671	42	131.8
James Ritchey, Stephen F. Austin	1992-95	613	325	25	.530	4,766	40	131.7
Gilbert Renfroe, Tennessee St.	1982-85	721	370	23	.513	5,556	48	131.6
James Perry, Brown	1996-99	1,310	790	48	.603	9,293	74	131.2
Tracy Ham, Ga. Southern	1984-86	568	301	31	.530	4,881	29	131.1

*Record. $See Page 8 for explanation.

SEASON PASSING EFFICIENCY
(Minimum 15 Attempts Per Game)

Player, Team	Year	G	Att.	Cmp.	Int.	Pct.	Yards	TD	Pts.
Shawn Knight, William & Mary	†1993	10	177	125	4	.706	2,055	22	*204.6
Michael Payton, Marshall	†1991	9	216	143	5	.622	2,333	19	181.3
Alli Abrew, Cal Poly	†1997	11	191	130	4	.681	1,961	17	179.5
Tony Romo, Eastern Ill.	†2001	10	207	138	6	.667	2,068	21	178.3

Player, Team	Year	G	Att.	Cmp.	Int.	Pct.	Yards	TD	Pts.
Doug Turner, Morehead St.	1997	10	290	190	6	.655	2,869	29	177.5
Ted White, Howard	†1996	11	289	174	10	.602	2,814	36	176.2
Doug Nussmeier, Idaho	1993	11	304	185	5	.609	2,960	33	175.2
Brian Kadel, Dayton	†1995	11	183	115	6	.628	1,880	18	175.0
Chris Boden, Villanova	1997	11	345	231	4	.670	3,079	36	174.0
Kelvin Simmons, Troy St.	1993	11	224	143	6	.638	2,144	23	172.8
Rocky Butler, Hofstra	2001	11	335	206	4	.615	3,311	30	171.7
Frank Baur, Lafayette	†1988	10	256	164	11	.641	2,621	23	171.1
Bobby Lamb, Furman	†1985	11	181	106	6	.586	1,856	18	170.9
Harry Leons, Eastern Wash.	1997	10	257	159	5	.619	2,588	21	169.5
Steven Beard, Northern Iowa	1996	11	238	140	9	.588	2,526	21	169.5
Jay Fiedler, Dartmouth	†1992	10	273	175	13	.641	2,748	25	169.4
Dave Dickenson, Montana	1995	11	455	309	9	.679	4,176	38	168.6
Drew Miller, Montana	†1999	10	368	240	8	.652	3,461	32	168.6
Terrance Ley, Southern U.	†2000	11	233	139	6	.597	2,249	23	168.2
Mike Smith, Northern Iowa	†1986	11	303	190	16	.627	3,125	27	168.2
Dave Dickenson, Montana	1993	11	390	262	9	.672	3.640	32	168.0
Simon Fuentes, Eastern Ky.	1997	11	189	116	2	.614	1,932	13	167.8
Jim Blanchard, Portland St.	†1998	9	169	112	1	.663	1,512	14	167.6
Willie Totten, Mississippi Val.	†1983	9	279	174	9	.624	2,566	29	167.5
Lonnie Galloway, Western Caro.	1992	11	211	128	12	.607	2,181	20	167.4
Brant Hall, Lehigh	2001	8	176	106	3	.602	1,684	16	167.2
Leo Hamlett, Delaware	1995	11	174	95	6	.546	1,849	15	165.4
Eriq Williams, James Madison	1991	11	192	107	7	.557	1,914	19	164.8
Dave Dickenson, Montana	†1994	9	336	229	6	.682	3,053	24	164.5
Eric Rasmussen, San Diego	†2002	10	279	170	1	.609	2,473	25	164.2
Willie Totten, Mississippi Val.	†1984	10	518	*324	22	.626	4,557	*56	163.6
Jeff Wiley, Holy Cross	†1987	11	400	265	17	.663	3,677	34	163.0
Todd Hammel, Stephen F. Austin	†1989	11	401	238	13	.594	3,914	34	162.8
Mike Williams, Grambling	†1980	11	239	127	5	.531	2,116	28	162.0

*Record. †National champion.

CAREER YARDS

Player, Team	Years	Att.	Cmp.	Int.	Pct.	Yards	TD
Steve McNair, Alcorn St.	1991-94	*1,680	927	58	.552	*14,496	119
Willie Totten, Mississippi Val.	1982-85	1,555	907	*75	.583	12,711	*139
Marcus Brady, Cal St. Northridge	1998-01	*1,680	*1,039	47	.618	12,479	109
Jamie Martin, Weber St.	1989-92	1,544	934	56	.605	12,207	87
Neil Lomax, Portland St.	1978-80	1,425	836	50	.587	11,550	88
Travis Brown, Northern Ariz.	1996-99	1,577	888	42	.563	11,400	86
Dave Dickenson, Montana	1992-95	1,208	813	26	*.673	11,080	96
Doug Nussmeier, Idaho	1990-93	1,225	746	32	.609	10,824	91
John Friesz, Idaho	1986-89	1,350	801	40	.593	10,697	77
Greg Wyatt, Northern Ariz.	1986-89	1,510	926	49	.613	10,697	70
Sean Payton, Eastern Ill.	1983-86	1,408	756	55	.537	10,655	75
Jeff Wiley, Holy Cross	1985-88	1,208	723	63	.599	9,698	71
Phil Stambaugh, Lehigh	1996-99	1,284	816	43	.636	9,669	78
Jeff Lewis, Northern Ariz.	1992-95	1,316	785	24	.597	9,655	67
Ted White, Howard	1995-98	1,163	635	34	.546	9,611	92
Robbie Justino, Liberty	1989-92	1,267	769	51	.607	9,548	64
Chris Boden, Villanova	1996-99	1,338	818	30	.611	9,538	93
Giovanni Carmazzi, Hofstra	1996-99	1,187	764	32	.644	9,371	71
Brian Ah Yat, Montana	1995-98	1,190	735	39	.618	9,315	89
Kirk Schulz, Villanova	1986-89	1,297	774	70	.597	9,305	70
Ken Hobart, Idaho	1980-83	1,219	629	42	.516	9,300	79
James Perry, Brown	1996-99	1,309	789	48	.603	9,294	74
Matt DeGennaro, Connecticut	1987-90	1,319	803	49	.609	9,288	73
Marty Horn, Lehigh	1982-85	1,390	744	64	.535	9,120	62
Ryan Helming, Northern Iowa	1997-00	1,093	662	29	.606	9,089	77
Jason Whitmer, Idaho St.	1987-90	1,349	721	53	.534	9,081	55
Chris Swartz, Morehead St.	1987-90	1,408	774	47	.550	9,027	56
Darin Hinshaw, UCF	1991-94	1,114	614	52	.551	9,000	82
Dan Crowley, Towson	1991-94	1,170	617	54	.527	8,900	81
Michael Proctor, Murray St.	1986-89	1,148	578	45	.503	8,682	52
Eric Beavers, Nevada	1983-86	1,094	646	37	.590	8,626	77
Tom Ciaccio, Holy Cross	1988-91	1,073	658	46	.613	8,603	72
Steve Calabria, Colgate	1981-84	1,143	626	68	.548	8,555	54
Mike Buck, Maine	1986-89	1,102	619	39	.562	8,491	67
Jimmy Blanchard, Portland St.	1997-00	1,038	618	19	.595	8,455	63
Jeff Cesarone, Western Ky.	1984-87	1,339	714	39	.533	8,404	45
Frank Baur, Lafayette	1985, 87-89	1,103	636	46	.577	8,399	62
Shane Stafford, Connecticut	1995-98	951	522	29	.549	8,368	67
Mitch Maher, North Texas	1991-94	1,100	610	47	.555	8,252	66
Stan Yagiello, William & Mary	$1981-85	1,247	737	36	.591	8,249	51
Mike Smith, Northern Iowa	1984-87	943	557	43	.591	8,219	58
Kelly Bradley, Montana St.	1983-86	1,238	714	45	.577	8,152	60
Jim Lopusznick, Fairfield	1996-99	1,227	657	59	.535	8,092	83
Tom Proudian, Iona	1993-95	1,134	656	48	.578	8,088	58
Bob Bleier, Richmond	1983-86	1,169	672	56	.575	8,057	54
Chris Goetz, Towson	1987-90	1,172	648	51	.553	7,882	42
Mickey Fein, Maine	1995-98	1,203	644	43	.535	7,856	66
Paul Singer, Western Ill.	1985-88	1,171	646	43	.552	7,850	61
John Witkowski, Columbia	1981-84	1,176	613	60	.521	7,849	56
Greg Ryan, East Tenn. St.	1993-96	1,148	694	49	.605	7,826	56
Grady Bennett, Montana	1987-90	1,097	641	42	.584	7,778	55
Todd Wells, East Tenn. St.	1997-00	955	538	37	.564	7,755	45

Player, Team	Years	Att.	Cmp.	Int.	Pct.	Yards	TD
Bernard Hawk, Bethune-Cookman	1982-85	1,120	554	51	.495	7,737	56
Bob Jean, New Hampshire	1985-88	1,126	567	49	.504	7,704	51

*Record. $See Page 8 for explanation.

CAREER YARDS PER GAME
(Minimum 5,000 Yards)

Player, Team	Years	G	Att.	Cmp.	Yards	TD	Yd. PG
Neil Lomax, Portland St.	1978-80	33	1,425	836	11,550	88	*350.0
Steve McNair, Alcorn St.	1991-94	42	*1,680	927	*14,496	119	345.1
Aaron Flowers, Cal St. Northridge	1996-97	20	819	502	6,766	54	338.3
Chris Sanders, Chattanooga	1999-00	22	953	584	7,230	49	328.6
Drew Miller, Montana	1999-00	18	654	430	5,900	46	327.8
Willie Totten, Mississippi Val.	1982-85	40	1,555	907	12,711	*139	317.8
Dave Dickenson, Montana	1992-95	35	1,208	813	11,080	96	316.6
John Friesz, Idaho	1986-89	35	1,350	801	10,697	77	305.6
James Perry, Brown	1996-99	31	1,309	789	9,294	74	299.8
Tom Proudian, Iona	1993-95	27	1,134	656	8,088	58	299.6
Jamie Martin, Weber St.	1989-92	41	1,544	934	12,207	87	297.7
Marcus Brady, Cal St. Northridge	1998-01	43	*1,680	*1,039	12,479	109	290.2
Sean Payton, Eastern Ill.	1983-86	37	1,408	756	10,655	75	288.0
Travis Brown, Northern Ariz.	1996-99	41	1,577	888	11,400	86	278.0
Doug Nussmeier, Idaho	1990-93	39	1,225	746	10,824	91	277.5
Oteman Sampson, Florida A&M	1996-97	22	686	387	6,104	46	277.5
Robert Dougherty, Boston U.	1993-94	21	705	405	5,608	41	267.0
Gavin Hoffman, Pennsylvania	1999-01	29	1,004	651	7,542	50	260.0
Brian Ah Yat, Montana	1995-98	36	1,190	735	9,315	89	258.8
Scott Semptimphelter, Lehigh	1990-93	26	823	493	6,668	50	256.5
Greg Wyatt, Northern Ariz.	1986-89	42	1,510	926	10,697	70	254.7

*Record.

CAREER TOUCHDOWN PASSES

Player, Team	Years	G	TD Passes
Willie Totten, Mississippi Val.	1982-85	40	*139
Steve McNair, Alcorn St.	1991-94	42	119
Marcus Brady, Cal St. Northridge	1998-01	43	109
Dave Dickenson, Montana	1992-95	35	96
Chris Boden, Villanova	1996-99	39	93
Ted White, Howard	1995-98	41	92
Doug Nussmeier, Idaho	1990-93	39	91
Brian Ah Yat, Montana	1995-98	36	89
Neil Lomax, Portland St.	1978-80	33	88
Jamie Martin, Weber St.	1989-92	41	87
Travis Brown, Northern Ariz.	1996-99	41	86
Jim Lopusznick, Fairfield	1996-99	39	83
Darin Hinshaw, UCF	1991-94	40	82
Dan Crowley, Towson	1991-94	40	81
Ken Hobart, Idaho	1980-83	44	79
Phil Stambaugh, Lehigh	1996-99	44	78
Eric Beavers, Nevada	1983-86	40	77
John Friesz, Idaho	1986-89	35	77
Ryan Helming, Northern Iowa	1997-00	44	77
Sean Payton, Eastern Ill.	1983-86	39	75
James Perry, Brown	1996-99	31	74
Matt DeGennaro, Connecticut	1987-90	43	73
Tony Zimmerman, Duquesne	1998-00	33	73
Tom Ciaccio, Holy Cross	1988-91	37	72
Jeff Wiley, Holy Cross	1985-88	41	71
Giovanni Carmazzi, Hofstra	1996-99	40	71
Kirk Schulz, Villanova	1986-89	42	70
Greg Wyatt, Northern Ariz.	1986-89	42	70

*Record.

SEASON YARDS

Player, Team	Year	G	Att.	Cmp.	Int.	Pct.	Yards	TD
Steve McNair, Alcorn St.	1994	11	530	304	17	.574	*4,863	44
Willie Totten, Mississippi Val.	†1984	10	518	324	22	.626	4,557	*56
Bruce Eugene, Grambling	2002	13	543	269	16	.495	4,483	43
Brett Gordon, Villanova	2002	15	*578	*385	14	.666	4,305	36
Dave Dickenson, Montana	1995	11	455	309	9	.679	4,176	38
Joe Lee, Towson	1999	11	577	322	13	.558	4,168	22
Jamie Martin, Weber St.	1991	11	500	310	17	.620	4,125	35
Neil Lomax, Portland St.	1980	11	473	296	12	.626	4,094	37
John Friesz, Idaho	1989	11	425	260	8	.612	4,041	31
Neil Lomax, Portland St.	1979	11	516	299	16	.579	3,950	26
Todd Hammel, Stephen F. Austin	†1989	11	401	238	13	.594	3,914	34
Sean Payton, Eastern Ill.	1984	11	473	270	15	.571	3,843	28
Jamie Martin, Weber St.	1990	11	428	256	15	.598	3,700	23
Willie Totten, Mississippi Val.	1985	11	492	295	*29	.600	3,698	39
Chris Sanders, Chattanooga	2000	11	463	287	17	.620	3,691	22
Jeff Wiley, Holy Cross	†1987	11	400	265	17	.663	3,677	34
John Friesz, Idaho	1987	11	502	311	14	.620	3,677	28
Dave Dickenson, Montana	1993	11	390	262	9	.672	3,640	32
Ken Hobart, Idaho	1983	11	477	268	19	.562	3,618	32
Robert Kent, Jackson St.	2001	11	453	245	21	.541	3,615	31
Brian Ah Yat, Montana	1996	11	432	265	16	.613	3,615	42

Player, Team	Year	G	Att.	Cmp.	Int.	Pct.	Yards	TD
Glenn Kempa, Lehigh	1991	11	474	286	15	.603	3,565	31
Giovanni Carmazzi, Hofstra	1997	11	408	288	8	.706	3,554	27
Tom Ehrhardt, Rhode Island	1985	10	497	283	19	.569	3,542	35
Steve McNair, Alcorn St.	1992	10	427	231	11	.541	3,541	29
Aaron Flowers, Cal St. Northridge	1996	11	415	247	11	.595	3,540	30
Chris Sanders, Chattanooga	1999	11	490	297	14	.606	3,539	27
Tony Petersen, Marshall	1987	11	466	251	25	.539	3,529	22
Todd Brunner, Lehigh	1989	11	450	273	19	.607	3,516	26
Kelly Bradley, Montana St.	1984	11	499	289	20	.579	3,508	30
Neil Lomax, Portland St.	†1978	11	436	241	22	.553	3,506	25

*Record. †National pass-efficiency champion.

SEASON YARDS PER GAME

Player, Team	Year	G	Att.	Cmp.	Int.	Pct.	Yards	TD	Yd.PG
Willie Totten, Mississippi Val.	†1984	10	518	324	22	.626	4,557	*56	*455.7
Steve McNair, Alcorn St.	1994	11	530	304	17	.574	*4,863	44	442.1
Dave Dickenson, Montana	1995	11	455	309	9	.679	4,176	38	379.6
Joe Lee, Towson	1999	11	577	322	13	.558	4,168	22	378.9
Jamie Martin, Weber St.	1991	11	500	310	17	.620	4,125	35	375.0
Neil Lomax, Portland St.	1980	11	473	296	12	.626	4,094	37	372.2
John Friesz, Idaho	1989	11	425	260	8	.612	4,041	31	367.4
Neil Lomax, Portland St.	1979	11	516	299	16	.579	3,950	26	359.1
Aaron Flowers, Cal St. Northridge	1997	9	404	255	10	.631	3,226	24	358.4
Todd Hammel, Stephen F. Austin	†1989	11	401	238	13	.594	3,914	34	355.8
Tom Ehrhardt, Rhode Island	1985	10	497	283	19	.569	3,542	35	354.2
Steve McNair, Alcorn St.	1992	10	427	231	11	.541	3,541	29	354.1
Sean Payton, Eastern Ill.	1984	11	473	270	15	.571	3,843	28	349.4
Drew Miller, Montana	1999	10	368	240	8	.652	3,461	32	346.1
Bruce Eugene, Grambling	2002	13	543	269	16	.495	4,483	43	344.8
Dave Dickenson, Montana	†1994	9	336	229	6	.682	3,053	24	339.2
Tom Proudian, Iona	1993	10	440	262	13	.595	3,368	29	336.8
Jamie Martin, Weber St.	1990	11	428	256	15	.598	3,700	23	336.4
Willie Totten, Mississippi Val.	1985	11	492	295	*29	.600	3,698	39	336.2

*Record. †National pass-efficiency champion.

SEASON TOUCHDOWN PASSES

Player, Team	Year	G	TD Passes
Willie Totten, Mississippi Val.	1984	10	*56
Steve McNair, Alcorn St.	1994	11	44
Bruce Eugene, Grambling	2002	13	43
Brian Ah Yat, Montana	1996	11	42
Willie Totten, Mississippi Val.	1985	11	39
Dave Dickenson, Montana	1995	11	38
Patrick Bonner, Florida A&M	1998	11	37
Neil Lomax, Portland St.	1980	11	37
Brett Gordon, Villanova	2002	15	36
Chris Boden, Villanova	1997	11	36
Ted White, Howard	1996	11	36
Jamie Martin, Weber St.	1991	11	35
Tom Ehrhardt, Rhode Island	1985	10	35
Tony Romo, Eastern Ill.	2002	12	34
Marcus Brady, Cal St. Northridge	2001	10	34
Todd Hammel, Stephen F. Austin	1989	11	34
Jeff Wiley, Holy Cross	1987	11	34
Darnell Kennedy, Alabama St.	2001	12	33
Darnell Kennedy, Alabama St.	2000	11	33
Doug Nussmeier, Idaho	1993	11	33
Ira Vandever, Drake	2002	11	32
Rahsaan Matthews, Delaware St.	2000	11	32
Drew Miller, Montana	1999	10	32
Dave Dickenson, Montana	1993	11	32
Doug Hudson, Nicholls St.	1986	11	32
Ken Hobart, Idaho	1983	11	32
Robert Kent, Jackson St.	2002	11	31
Robert Kent, Jackson St.	2001	11	31
Ryan Helming, Northern Iowa	1999	11	31
Travis Brown, Northern Ariz.	1999	11	31
Ted White, Howard	1998	11	31
Chris Boden, Villanova	1998	11	31
Glenn Kempa, Lehigh	1991	11	31
John Friesz, Idaho	1989	11	31
Josh Blankenship, Eastern Wash.	2002	11	30
Rocky Butler, Hofstra	2001	11	30
Eric Webber, Brown	2000	10	30
Ryan Helming, Northern Iowa	2000	11	30
Lionel Hayes, Grambling	1999	11	30
Mike Stadler, San Diego	1997	11	30
Aaron Flowers, Cal St. Northridge	1996	11	30
Scott Semptimphelter, Lehigh	1993	11	30
Brent Pease, Montana	1986	11	30
Kelly Bradley, Montana St.	1984	11	30

*Record.

SINGLE-GAME YARDS

Yds.	Player, Team (Opponent)	Date
624	Jamie Martin, Weber St. (Idaho St.)	Nov. 23, 1991
619	Doug Pederson, La.-Monroe (Stephen F. Austin)	Nov. 11, 1989
599	Willie Totten, Mississippi Val. (Prairie View)	Oct. 27, 1984
595	Robert Kent, Jackson St. (Alabama St.)	Oct. 6, 2001
589	Vern Harris, Idaho St. (Montana)	Oct. 12, 1985
587	Steve McNair, Alcorn St. (Southern U.)	Oct. 22, 1994
571	Todd Hammel, Stephen F. Austin (La.-Monroe)	Nov. 11, 1989
567	Joe Lee, Towson (Lehigh)	Oct. 30, 1999
566	Tom Ehrhardt, Rhode Island (Connecticut)	Nov. 16, 1985
566	Seth Burford, Cal Poly (Northern Iowa)	Nov. 4, 2000
563	Steve McNair, Alcorn St. (Samford)	Oct. 29, 1994
560	Brian Ah Yat, Montana (Eastern Wash.)	Oct. 19, 1996
558	Dave Dickenson, Montana (Idaho)	Oct. 21, 1995
556	Matt Nagy, Delaware (Connecticut)	Nov. 7, 1998
553	Willie Totten, Mississippi Val. (Southern U.)	Sept. 29, 1984
553	Justin Fuente, Murray St. (Southern Ill.)	Sept. 11, 1999
553	Kevin McCarthy, Idaho St. (Southern Utah)	Oct. 23, 1999
551	Lejominick Washington, Morgan St. (N.C. A&T)	Oct. 6, 2001
550	Jimmy Blanchard, Portland St. (Montana)	Oct. 2, 1999
547	Jamie Martin, Weber St. (Montana St.)	Sept. 26, 1992
545	Willie Totten, Mississippi Val. (Grambling)	Oct. 13, 1984
541	Ryan Helming, Northern Iowa (Western Ill.)	Nov. 13, 1999
540	Robert Kent, Jackson St. (N.C. A&T)	Sept. 7, 2002
540	Brad Otten, Weber St. (Northern Ariz.)	Nov. 6, 1993
539	John Whitcomb, UAB (Prairie View)	Nov. 19, 1994
537	Tod Mayfield, West Tex. A&M (New Mexico St.)	Nov. 16, 1985
536	Willie Totten, Mississippi Val. (Kentucky St.)	Sept. 1, 1984
534	Todd Hammel, Stephen F. Austin (Sam Houston St.)	Nov. 4, 1989
534	Steve McNair, Alcorn St. (Grambling)	Sept. 3, 1994
533	Steve McNair, Alcorn St. (Jackson St.)	Nov. 19, 1994

SINGLE-GAME ATTEMPTS

No.	Player, Team (Opponent)	Date
77	Neil Lomax, Portland St. (Northern Colo.)	Oct. 20, 1979
76	Joe Lee, Towson (Lehigh)	Oct. 30, 1999
74	Paul Peterson, Idaho St. (Nevada)	Oct. 1, 1983
72	Dave Dickenson, Montana (Idaho)	Oct. 21, 1995
72	Val Troiani, Towson (St. Mary's [Cal.])	Nov. 4, 2000
71	Doug Pederson, La.-Monroe (Stephen F. Austin)	Nov. 11, 1989
71	Bobby Townsend, Howard (Morgan St.)	Nov. 13, 1999
70	Greg Farland, Rhode Island (Boston U.)	Oct. 18, 1986
70	Joe Lee, Towson (Dayton)	Nov. 6, 1999
69	Chris Boden, Villanova (Connecticut)	Oct. 16, 1999
69	Ryan Helming, Northern Iowa (Western Ill.)	Nov. 13, 1999
69	Aaron Flowers, Cal St. Northridge (Sacramento St.)	Oct. 25, 1997
69	Steve McNair, Alcorn St. (Jacksonville St.)	Oct. 31, 1992
68	Tony Petersen, Marshall (Western Caro.)	Nov. 14, 1987
68	Kevin McCarthy, Idaho St. (Southern Utah)	Oct. 23, 1999
67	Todd Wenrich, Bucknell (Fordham)	Oct. 27, 2001
67	Joe Walland, Yale (Harvard)	Nov. 20, 1999
67	Tom Proudian, Iona (Siena)	Oct. 1, 1994
67	Michael Payton, Marshall (Western Caro.)	Oct. 31, 1992
67	Vern Harris, Idaho St. (Montana)	Oct. 12, 1985
67	Rick Worman, Eastern Wash. (Nevada)	Oct. 12, 1985
67	Tod Mayfield, West Tex. A&M (Indiana St.)	Oct. 5, 1985
67	Tom Ehrhardt, Rhode Island (Brown)	Sept. 28, 1985

SINGLE-GAME COMPLETIONS

No.	Player, Team (Opponent)	Date
48	Clayton Millis, Cal St. Northridge (St. Mary's [Cal.])	Nov. 11, 1995
47	Jamie Martin, Weber St. (Idaho St.)	Nov. 23, 1991
47	Joe Lee, Towson (Lehigh)	Oct. 30, 1999
46	Doug Pederson, La.-Monroe (Stephen F. Austin)	Nov. 11, 1989
46	Willie Totten, Mississippi Val. (Southern U.)	Sept. 29, 1984
45	Willie Totten, Mississippi Val. (Prairie View)	Oct. 27, 1984
44	Kyle Slager, Brown (Rhode Island)	Oct. 5, 2002
44	Neil Lomax, Portland St. (Northern Colo.)	Oct. 20, 1979
43	Chris Boden, Villanova (Connecticut)	Oct. 16, 1999
43	Aaron Flowers, Cal St. Northridge (Sacramento St.)	Oct. 25, 1997
43	Dave Dickenson, Montana (Idaho)	Oct. 21, 1995
42	Joe Walland, Yale (Harvard)	Nov. 20, 1999
42	James Perry, Brown (Princeton)	Oct. 9, 1999
42	Travis Brown, Northern Ariz. (Montana)	Oct. 26, 1996
42	Tod Mayfield, West Tex. A&M (Indiana St.)	Oct. 5, 1985
42	Kelly Bradley, Montana St. (Eastern Wash.)	Sept. 21, 1985
42	Rusty Hill, North Texas (Tulsa)	Nov. 20, 1982

ANNUAL CHAMPIONS

Year	Player, Team	Class	G	Att.	Cmp.	Avg.	Int.	Pct.	Yds.	TD
1978	Neil Lomax, Portland St.	So.	11	436	241	21.9	22	.553	3,506	25

Beginning in 1979, ranked on passing efficiency rating points (instead of per-game completions)

Year	Player, Team	Class	G	Att.	Cmp.	Int.	Pct.	Yds.	TD	Pts.
1979	Joe Aliotti, Boise St.	Jr.	11	219	144	7	.658	1,870	19	159.7
1980	Mike Williams, Grambling	Sr.	11	239	127	5	.531	2,116	28	162.0
1981	Mike Machurek, Idaho St.	Sr.	9	313	188	11	.601	2,752	22	150.1
1982	Frank Novak, Lafayette	Jr.	10	257	154	12	.599	2,257	20	150.0
1983	Willie Totten, Mississippi Val.	So.	9	279	174	9	.624	2,566	29	167.5
1984	Willie Totten, Mississippi Val.	Jr.	10	518	324	22	.626	4,557	*56	163.6
1985	Bobby Lamb, Furman	Sr.	11	181	106	6	.586	1,856	18	170.9
1986	Mike Smith, Northern Iowa	Jr.	11	303	190	16	.627	3,125	27	168.2
1987	Jeff Wiley, Holy Cross	Jr.	11	400	265	17	.663	3,677	34	163.0
1988	Frank Baur, Lafayette	Jr.	10	256	164	11	.641	2,621	23	171.1
1989	Todd Hammel, Stephen F. Austin	Sr.	11	401	238	13	.594	3,914	34	162.8
1990	Connell Maynor, N.C. A&T	Jr.	11	191	123	10	.644	1,699	16	156.3
1991	Michael Payton, Marshall	Jr.	9	216	143	5	.662	2,333	19	181.3
1992	Jay Fiedler, Dartmouth	Jr.	10	273	175	13	.641	2,748	25	169.4
1993	Shawn Knight, William & Mary	Jr.	10	177	125	4	.706	2,055	22	*204.6
1994	Dave Dickenson, Montana	Jr.	9	336	229	6	.682	3,053	24	164.5
1995	Brian Kadel, Dayton	Sr.	11	183	115	6	.628	1,880	18	175.0
1996	Ted White, Howard	So.	11	289	174	10	.602	2,814	36	176.2
1997	Alli Abrew, Cal Poly	Sr.	11	191	130	4	.681	1,961	17	179.5
1998	Jim Blanchard, Portland St.	So.	9	169	112	1	.663	1,512	14	167.6
1999	Drew Miller, Montana	Jr.	10	368	240	8	.652	3,461	32	168.6
2000	Terrance Ley, Southern U.	Jr.	11	233	139	6	.597	2,249	23	168.2
2001	Tony Romo, Eastern Ill.	Jr.	10	207	138	6	.667	2,068	21	178.3
2002	Eric Rasmussen, San Diego	Jr.	10	279	170	1	.609	2,473	25	164.2

*Record.

Receiving

CAREER RECEPTIONS PER GAME
(Minimum 125 Receptions)

Player, Team	Years	G	Rec.	Yards	TD	Rec. PG
Stephen Campbell, Brown	1997-00	40	305	3,555	31	*7.6
Chas Gessner, Brown	1999-02	39	292	3,408	36	7.5
Jerry Rice, Mississippi Val.	1981-84	41	301	*4,693	*50	7.3
Mike Furrey, Northern Iowa	1997-99	33	242	3,544	27	7.3
Drew Amerson, Cal St. Northridge	1999-01	33	239	3,190	20	7.2
Derrick Ingram, UAB	1993-94	22	159	2,572	21	7.2
Jacquay Nunnally, Florida A&M	1997-00	44	*317	4,239	38	7.2
Jeff Johnson, East Tenn. St.	1993-94	20	142	1,772	19	7.1
Miles Macik, Pennsylvania	1993-95	29	200	2,364	26	6.9
Kevin Guthrie, Princeton	1981-83	28	193	2,645	16	6.9
Eric Yarber, Idaho	1984-85	19	129	1,920	17	6.8
Joe Douglass, Montana	1995-96	22	145	2,301	25	6.6
Rob Milanese, Pennsylvania	1999-02	39	259	3,405	21	6.6
Brian Forster, Rhode Island (TE)	1983-85, 87	38	245	3,410	31	6.5
Kasey Dunn, Idaho	1988-91	42	268	3,847	25	6.4
Carl Morris, Harvard	1999-02	39	245	3,488	28	6.3
Sean Morey, Brown	1995-98	40	251	3,850	39	6.3
Gordie Lockbaum, Holy Cross (RB)	‡1986-87	22	135	2,012	17	6.1
Derek Graham, Princeton	1981, 83-84	29	176	2,819	19	6.1
Stuart Gaussoin, Portland St.	1978-80	23	135	1,909	14	5.9
Don Lewis, Columbia	1981-83	30	176	2,207	11	5.9
Mike Barber, Marshall	1985-88	36	209	3,520	20	5.8
Rennie Benn, Lehigh	1982-85	41	237	3,662	44	5.8
Daren Altieri, Boston U.	1987-90	39	225	2,518	15	5.8

*Record. ‡Defensive back in 1984-85.

SEASON RECEPTIONS PER GAME

Player, Team	Year	G	Rec.	Yards	TD	Rec. PG
Stephen Campbell, Brown	†2000	10	*120	1,332	11	*12.0
Brian Forster, Rhode Island (TE)	†1985	10	115	1,617	12	11.5
Chas Gessner, Brown	†2002	10	114	1,166	11	11.4
Jerry Rice, Mississippi Val.	†1984	10	103	1,682	*27	10.3
Jerry Rice, Mississippi Val.	†1983	10	102	1,450	14	10.2
Stuart Gaussoin, Portland St.	†1979	9	90	1,132	8	10.0
Drew Amerson, Cal St. Northridge	†2001	10	97	1,244	5	9.7
Chas Gessner, Brown	2001	9	83	1,182	12	9.2
Carl Morris, Harvard	2002	10	90	1,288	8	9.0
Eric Krawczyk, Cornell	†1997	10	89	1,042	11	8.9
Murle Sango, Villanova	†1999	11	98	1,064	10	8.9
Stephen Campbell, Brown	1999	10	89	1,107	11	8.9

Player, Team	Year	G	Rec.	Yards	TD	Rec. PG
Kevin Guthrie, Princeton	1983	10	88	1,259	9	8.8
Eric Johnson, Yale	2000	10	87	1,017	14	8.7
David Romines, Cal St. Northridge	†1996	10	87	1,300	12	8.7
Jacquay Nunnally, Florida A&M	2000	11	95	1,082	9	8.6
Rob Milanese, Pennsylvania	2002	10	85	1,112	8	8.5
Jacquay Nunnally, Florida A&M	†1998	11	93	1,316	12	8.5
Alfred Pupunu, Weber St. (TE)	†1991	11	93	1,204	12	8.5
Aryvia Holmes, Samford	2002	10	84	1,158	9	8.4
Derek Graham, Princeton	1983	10	84	1,363	11	8.4
Don Lewis, Columbia	†1982	10	84	1,000	6	8.4
Peter Macon, Weber St.	†1989	11	92	1,047	6	8.4
Jay Barnard, Dartmouth	2002	10	83	899	8	8.3
Sean Morey, Brown	1998	10	83	1,023	10	8.3
Eddie Conti, Delaware	1998	11	91	*1,712	10	8.3
Marvin Walker, North Texas	1982	11	91	934	11	8.3

*Record. †National champion.

CAREER RECEPTIONS

Player, Team	Years	Rec.	Yards	Avg.	TD
Jacquay Nunnally, Florida A&M	1997-00	*317	4,239	13.4	38
Stephen Campbell, Brown	1997-00	305	3,555	11.7	31
Jerry Rice, Mississippi Val.	1981-84	301	*4,693	15.6	*50
Chas Gessner, Brown	1999-02	292	3,408	11.7	36
Kasey Dunn, Idaho	1988-91	268	3,847	14.4	25
Rob Milanese, Pennsylvania	1999-02	259	3,405	13.1	21
Sean Morey, Brown	1995-98	251	3,850	15.3	39
Eddie Berlin, Northern Iowa	1997-00	249	3,735	15.0	34
Carl Morris, Harvard	1999-02	245	3,488	14.2	28
Brian Forster, Rhode Island (TE)	1983-85, 87	245	3,410	13.9	31
Mike Furrey, Northern Iowa	1997-99	242	3,544	14.6	27
Drew Amerson, Cal St. Northridge	1999-01	239	3,190	13.3	20
Mark Didio, Connecticut	1988-91	239	3,535	14.8	21
Rennie Benn, Lehigh	1982-85	237	3,662	15.5	44
Daren Altieri, Boston U.	1987-90	225	2,518	11.2	15
Orshawante Bryant, Portland St.	1997-00	223	3,449	15.5	25
Jamal White, Towson	1998-00, 02	219	3,156	14.4	21
Brian Westbrook, Villanova	1997-98, 00-01	217	2,582	11.9	30
Darrell Colbert, Texas Southern	1983-86	217	3,177	14.6	33
Deron Braswell, Lehigh	1995-98	217	3,292	15.2	24
David Rhodes, UCF	1991-94	213	3,618	17.0	29
Corey Hill, Colgate	1995-98	212	3,434	16.2	34
Eric Wise, Fairfield	1996-99	211	2,139	10.1	20
Robert Wilson, Florida A&M	1993-96	209	2,949	14.1	24
Mike Barber, Marshall	1985-88	209	3,520	16.8	20
Cornell Craig, Southern Ill.	1996-99	207	3,550	17.1	37
Trevor Shaw, Weber St.	1989-90, 92-93	206	2,383	11.6	17

Player, Team	Years	Rec.	Yards	Avg.	TD
William Brooks, Boston U.	1982-85	204	3,154	15.5	26
Donald Narcisse, Texas Southern..........	1983-86	203	2,429	12.0	26
Alex Davis, Connecticut	1989-92	202	2,567	12.7	24
Shawn Collins, Northern Ariz.	1985-88	201	2,764	13.8	24
Miles Macik, Pennsylvania	1993-95	200	2,364	11.8	26
Leland Melvin, Richmond	1982-85	198	2,669	13.5	16
Mike Wilson, Boise St.	1990-93	196	3,017	15.4	13
Aaron Arnold, Cal St. Northridge	1996-99	195	2,660	13.6	26
$Javarus Dudley, Fordham	2000-02	194	2,758	14.2	20
Blake Tuffli, St. Mary's (Cal.)	1993-96	194	2,990	15.4	25
Curtis Olds, New Hampshire...............	1985-88	193	3,028	15.7	23
Kevin Guthrie, Princeton	1981-83	193	2,645	13.7	16
Raul Pacheco, Montana	1995-98	192	2,527	13.2	21
Dylan Ching, San Diego	1996-99	189	3,111	16.5	32
Matt Wells, Montana........................	1992-95	189	2,733	14.5	19
Sergio Hebra, Maine	1984-87	189	2,612	13.8	17
Jason Corle, Towson (RB)	1996-99	188	1,725	9.2	14
John Perry, New Hampshire	1989-92	186	2,798	15.0	19
Glenn Antrum, Connecticut.................	1985-88	186	2,552	13.7	14
Joe Thomas, Mississippi Val.	1982-85	186	2,816	15.1	36
Gary Harrell, Howard........................	1990-93	184	2,619	14.2	19
Roy Banks, Eastern Ill.	1983-86	184	3,177	17.3	38
Eric Johnson, Yale............................	1997-00	182	2,154	11.8	23
Merril Hoge, Idaho St. (RB)	1983-86	182	1,734	9.5	13
Eddie Conti, Delaware	1994-98	181	3,496	19.3	28
George Delaney, Colgate	1988-91	181	2,938	16.2	25
Sylvester Morris, Jackson St.	1996-99	180	3,324	18.5	34
Robert Brady, Villanova	1986-89	180	2,725	15.1	28

*Record. $Active player.

SEASON RECEPTIONS

Player, Team	Year	G	Rec.	Yards	TD
Stephen Campbell, Brown ....†2000		10	*120	1,332	11
Brian Forster, Rhode Island (TE) ....†1985		10	115	1,617	12
Chas Gessner, Brown ....†2002		10	114	1,166	11
Jerry Rice, Mississippi Val. ....†1984		10	103	1,682	*27
Jerry Rice, Mississippi Val. ....†1983		10	102	1,450	14
Murle Sango, Villanova.......................................†1999		11	98	1,064	10
Drew Amerson, Cal St. Northridge........................†2001		10	97	1,244	5
Jacquay Nunnally, Florida A&M 2000		11	95	1,082	9
Jacquay Nunnally, Florida A&M ....†1998		11	93	1,316	12
Alfred Pupunu, Weber St. (TE) ....†1991		11	93	1,204	12
Tramon Douglas, Grambling.................................. 2002		12	92	1,704	18
Peter Macon, Weber St. ....†1989		11	92	1,047	6
Eddie Conti, Delaware 1998		11	91	*1,712	10
Marvin Walker, North Texas 1982		11	91	934	11
Carl Morris, Harvard 2002		10	90	1,288	8
Stuart Gaussoin, Portland St. ....†1979		9	90	1,132	8
Stephen Campbell, Brown 1999		10	89	1,107	11
Brian Westbrook, Villanova 1998		11	89	1,144	15
Eric Krawczyk, Cornell ....†1997		10	89	1,042	11
Dave Cecchini, Lehigh ....†1993		11	88	1,318	16
Rameck Wright, Maine 1997		11	88	1,176	7
Mark Didio, Connecticut 1991		11	88	1,354	8
Kasey Dunn, Idaho...†1990		11	88	1,164	7
Donald Narcisse, Texas Southern ....†1986		11	88	1,074	15
Kevin Guthrie, Princeton 1983		10	88	1,259	9
Willie Ponder, Southeast Mo. St. 2002		12	87	1,453	15
Eric Johnson, Yale.. 2000		10	87	1,017	14
David Romines, Cal St. Northridge ....†1996		10	87	1,300	12
Richmond Flowers, Chattanooga 2000		11	86	1,035	2
Mike Furrey, Northern Iowa 1998		11	86	1,074	10
Rob Milanese, Pennsylvania 2002		10	85	1,112	8
Kasey Dunn, Idaho.. 1991		11	85	1,263	6
Aryvia Holmes, Samford..................................... 2002		10	84	1,158	9
T.C. Taylor, Jackson St. 2001		11	84	1,234	11
Elijah Thurman, Howard 1999		11	84	1,366	9
Derek Graham, Princeton 1983		10	84	1,363	11
Don Lewis, Columbia ....†1982		10	84	1,000	6

*Record. †National champion.

SEASON TOUCHDOWN RECEPTIONS

Player, Team	Year	G	TD
Jerry Rice, Mississippi Val. 1984		10	*27
Randy Moss, Marshall 1996		11	19
Tramon Douglas, Grambling 2002		12	18
Joe Douglass, Montana..1996		11	18
Jonathon Cooper, Sam Houston St. 2001		11	17
Sylvester Morris, Jackson St. 1995		11	17
Brian Finneran, Villanova..1997		11	17
Mark Carrier, Nicholls St. 1986		11	17
Dameon Reilly, Rhode Island 1985		11	17
Joe Thomas, Mississippi Val. 1985		11	17

Brown Sports Information

Chas Gessner of Brown capped his career in 2002 with 114 receptions in 10 games. Both the number of catches and his 11.4 receptions per game placed him third on the Division I-AA lists. He tied the division single-game record with 24 receptions against Rhode Island October 5, 2002.

Player, Team	Year	G	TD
Roy Banks, Eastern Ill. 1984		11	17
Reggie Harris, Duquesne 2000		11	16
Eddie Berlin, Northern Iowa 2000		11	16
Drew O'Connor, Maine 1998		11	16
Wayne Chrebet, Hofstra 1994		10	16
Dave Cecchini, Lehigh 1993		11	16
Willie Ponder, Southeast Mo. St. 2002		12	15
Kahmal Roy, Hofstra 2001		11	15
Michael Hayes, Southern U. 2000		11	15
Cornell Craig, Southern Ill. 1999		11	15
Scotty Anderson, Grambling 1999		11	15
Dave Klemic, Northeastern 1998		11	15
Brian Westbrook, Villanova 1998		11	15
Tarig Qaiyam, Florida A&M 1998		11	15
Sean Morey, Brown 1997		10	15
Donald Narcisse, Texas Southern 1986		11	15
Rennie Benn, Lehigh 1983		11	15
Jeremy Conley, Duquesne 2002		12	14
Etu Molden, Montana 2001		12	14
Gharun Hester, Georgetown 2000		11	14
Kassim Osgood, Cal Poly 2000		11	14
Eric Johnson, Yale 2000		10	14
Terrance Tillman, Murray St. 1999		11	14
Jimmy Moore, Massachusetts...1998		11	14
Macey Brooks, James Madison 1996		11	14
Dedric Ward, Northern Iowa 1996		11	14
Rennie Benn, Lehigh 1985		11	14
Jerry Rice, Mississippi Val. 1983		10	14
Bill Reggio, Columbia 1982		10	14

*Record.

SINGLE-GAME RECEPTIONS

No.	Player, Team (Opponent)	Date
24	Chas Gessner, Brown (Rhode Island)..Oct. 5, 2002
24	Jerry Rice, Mississippi Val. (Southern U.) ....Oct. 1, 1983
22	Marvin Walker, North Texas (Tulsa)..Nov. 20, 1982
21	Carl Morris, Harvard (Dartmouth) ....Nov. 2, 2002
21	David Pandt, Montana St. (Eastern Wash.) ....Sept. 21, 1985
21	Eric Johnson, Yale (Harvard)..Nov. 20, 1999
20	Tim Hilton, Cal St. Northridge (St. Mary's [Cal.]) ....Nov. 11, 1995
19	Chas Gessner, Brown (Rhode Island)..Sept. 29, 2001
19	Stephen Campbell, Brown (Rhode Island) ....Sept. 30, 2000

DIVISION I-AA

No.	Player, Team (Opponent)	Date
18	Stephen Campbell, Brown (Pennsylvania)	Oct. 28, 2000
18	Jeremy Nunamaker, St. Francis (Pa.) (Sacred Heart)	Oct. 2, 1999
18	David Romines, Cal St. Northridge (UC Davis)	Sept. 14, 1996
18	Jerome Williams, Morehead St. (Eastern Ky.)	Nov. 18, 1989
18	Brian Forster, Rhode Island (Brown)	Sept. 28, 1985
17	Kassim Osgood, Cal Poly (Northern Iowa)	Nov. 4, 2000
17	Damien Roomets, Dartmouth (New Hampshire)	Sept. 23, 2000
17	Damon Hodge, Alabama St. (Alabama A&M)	Oct. 31, 1998
17	Rameek Wright, Maine (Buffalo)	Nov. 16, 1996
17	Elliot Miller, St. Francis (Pa.) (Central Conn. St.)	Oct. 2, 1993
17	Lifford Jackson, Louisiana Tech (Kansas St.)	Oct. 1, 1988
17	Brian Forster, Rhode Island (Lehigh)	Oct. 12, 1985
17	Jerry Rice, Mississippi Val. (Southern U.)	Sept. 29, 1984
17	Jerry Rice, Mississippi Val. (Kentucky St.)	Sept. 1, 1984

CAREER YARDS

Player, Team	Years	Rec.	Yards	Avg.	TD
Jerry Rice, Mississippi Val.	1981-84	301	*4,693	15.6	*50
Jacquay Nunnally, Florida A&M	1997-00	*317	4,239	13.4	38
Dedric Ward, Northern Iowa	1993-96	176	3,876	22.0	41
Sean Morey, Brown	1995-98	251	3,850	15.3	39
Kasey Dunn, Idaho	1988-91	268	3,847	14.4	25
Eddie Berlin, Northern Iowa	1997-00	249	3,735	15.0	34
Rennie Benn, Lehigh	1982-85	237	3,662	15.5	44
David Rhodes, UCF	1991-94	213	3,618	17.0	29
Stephen Campbell, Brown	1997-00	305	3,555	11.7	31
Correll Craig, Southern Ill.	1996-99	207	3,550	17.1	37
Mike Furrey, Northern Iowa	1997-99	242	3,544	14.6	27
Mark Didio, Connecticut	1988-91	239	3,535	14.8	21
Mike Barber, Marshall	1985-88	209	3,520	16.8	20
Eddie Conti, Delaware	1994-98	291	3,496	19.3	28
Carl Morris, Harvard	1999-02	245	3,488	14.2	28
Orshawante Bryant, Portland St.	1997-00	223	3,449	15.5	25
Corey Hill, Colgate	1995-98	212	3,434	16.2	34
Brian Forster, Rhode Island (TE)	1983-85, 87	245	3,410	13.9	31
Chas Gessner, Brown	1999-02	292	3,408	11.7	36
Sylvester Morris, Jackson St.	1996-99	180	3,324	18.5	34
Deron Braswell, Lehigh	1995-98	217	3,292	15.2	28
Drew Amerson, Cal St. Northridge	1999-01	239	3,190	13.3	20
Tracy Singleton, Howard	1979-82	159	3,187	20.0	16
Courtney Batts, Delaware	1994-97	153	3,181	20.8	26
Roy Banks, Eastern Ill.	1983-86	184	3,177	17.3	38
Darrell Colbert, Texas Southern	1983-86	217	3,177	14.6	33
Jamal White, Towson	1998-00, 02	219	3,156	14.4	21
William Brooks, Boston U.	1982-85	204	3,154	15.5	26

*Record.

CAREER YARDS PER GAME
(Minimum 2,000 Yards)

Player, Team	Years	G	Yards	Yds. PG
Derrick Ingram, UAB	1993-94	22	2,572	*116.9
Jerry Rice, Mississippi Val.	1981-84	41	*4,693	114.5
Mike Furrey, Northern Iowa	1997-99	33	3,544	107.4
Joe Douglass, Montana	1995-96	22	2,301	104.6
Eddie Conti, Delaware	1994-98	35	3,496	99.9
Derek Graham, Princeton	1981, 83-84	29	2,819	97.2
Drew Amerson, Cal St. Northridge	1999-01	33	3,190	96.7
Jacquay Nunnally, Florida A&M	1997-00	44	4,239	96.3
Sean Morey, Brown	1995-98	40	3,850	96.3
Kevin Guthrie, Princeton	1981-83	28	2,645	94.5
Tracy Singleton, Howard	1979-82	34	3,187	93.7
David Rhodes, UCF	1991-94	39	3,618	92.8
Kasey Dunn, Idaho	1988-91	42	3,847	91.6
Gordie Lockbaum, Holy Cross	‡1986-87	22	2,012	91.5
Bryan Calder, Nevada	1984-86	28	2,559	91.4
Mike Barber, Marshall	1985-88	36	3,520	90.3
Dedric Ward, Northern Iowa	1993-96	43	3,876	90.1
Brian Forster, Rhode Island	1983-85, 87	38	3,410	89.7

*Record. ‡Defensive back in 1984-85.

CAREER TOUCHDOWN RECEPTIONS

Player, Team	Years	G	TD
Jerry Rice, Mississippi Val.	1981-84	41	*50
Rennie Benn, Lehigh	1982-85	41	44
Dedric Ward, Northern Iowa	1993-96	43	41
Gharun Hester, Georgetown	1997-00	36	39
Sean Morey, Brown	1995-98	40	39
Jacquay Nunnally, Florida A&M	1997-00	44	38
Roy Banks, Eastern Ill.	1983-86	38	38
Mike Jones, Tennessee St.	1979-82	42	38
Cornell Craig, Southern Ill.	1996-99	44	37

Player, Team	Years	G	TD
Chas Gessner, Brown	1999-02	39	36
Joe Thomas, Mississippi Val.	1982-85	41	36
Dameon Reilly, Rhode Island	1983-85	32	35
Reggie Harris, Duquesne	1997-00	39	34
Eddie Berlin, Northern Iowa	1997-00	44	34
Sylvester Morris, Jackson St.	1996-99	45	34
Corey Hill, Colgate	1995-98	43	34
Darrell Colbert, Texas Southern	1983-86	43	33
John Taylor, Delaware St.	1982-85	43	33
Dylan Ching, San Diego	1996-99	41	32
Trumaine Johnson, Grambling	1979-82	44	32
Stephen Campbell, Brown	1997-00	40	31
Brian Forster, Rhode Island	1983-85, 87	38	31
Brian Westbrook, Villanova	1997-98, 00-01	44	30
David Rhodes, UCF	1991-94	39	29
Tom Stenglein, Colgate	1983-85	32	29

*Record.

SEASON YARDS

Player, Team	Year	Rec.	Yards	Avg.	TD
Eddie Conti, Delaware	†1998	91	*1,712	18.8	10
Tramon Douglas, Grambling	†2002	92	1,704	18.5	18
Jerry Rice, Mississippi Val.	1984	103	1,682	16.3	*27
Brian Forster, Rhode Island	1985	115	1,617	14.1	12
Joe Douglass, Montana	1996	82	1,469	17.9	18
Derrick Ingram, UAB	1994	83	1,457	17.6	13
Willie Ponder, Southeast Mo. St.	2002	87	1,453	16.7	15
Jerry Rice, Mississippi Val.	1983	102	1,450	14.2	14
Sean Morey, Brown	†1997	73	1,427	19.6	15
Cornell Craig, Southern Ill.	†1999	77	1,419	18.4	15
B.J. Adigun, East Tenn. St.	1997	68	1,389	20.4	12
Kassim Osgood, Cal Poly	2000	83	1,377	16.6	14
Elijah Thurmon, Howard	1999	84	1,366	16.3	9
Derek Graham, Princeton	1983	84	1,363	16.2	11
Mikhael Ricks, Stephen F. Austin	1997	47	1,358	28.9	11
Mark Didio, Connecticut	†1991	88	1,354	15.4	8
Gerald Foster, Duquesne	1999	72	1,340	18.6	10
Stephen Campbell, Brown	†2000	*120	1,332	11.1	11
Michael Hayes, Southern U.	2000	80	1,328	16.6	15
Jamal White, Towson	1999	82	1,322	16.1	8
Dave Cecchini, Lehigh	†1993	88	1,318	15.0	16
Jacquay Nunnally, Florida A&M	1998	93	1,316	14.2	12
Golden Tate, Tennessee St.	1983	63	1,307	20.7	13

*Record. †National champion.

SINGLE-GAME YARDS

Yds.	Player, Team (Opponent)	Date
376	Kassim Osgood, Cal Poly (Northern Iowa)	Nov. 4, 2000
370	Michael Lerch, Princeton (Brown)	Oct. 12, 1991
354	Eddie Conti, Delaware (Connecticut)	Nov. 7, 1998
330	Nate Singleton, Grambling (Virginia Union)	Sept. 14, 1991
327	Brian Forster, Rhode Island (Brown)	Sept. 28, 1985
319	Jason Cristino, Lehigh (Lafayette)	Nov. 21, 1992
316	Marcus Hinton, Alcorn St. (Chattanooga)	Sept. 10, 1994
299	Brian Forster, Rhode Island (Lehigh)	Oct. 12, 1985
299	Treamelle Taylor, Nevada (Montana)	Oct. 14, 1989
294	Jerry Rice, Mississippi Val. (Kentucky St.)	Sept. 1, 1984
289	Derrick Ingram, UAB (Prairie View)	Nov. 19, 1994
286	Frisman Jackson, Western Ill. (Indiana St.)	Nov. 17, 2001
286	Mike Furrey, Northern Iowa (Western Ill.)	Nov. 13, 1999
285	Jerry Rice, Mississippi Val. (Jackson St.)	Sept. 22, 1984
284	Jacquay Nunnally, Florida A&M (N.C. A&T)	Oct. 11, 1997
280	Rondel Menendez, Eastern Ky. (Eastern Ill.)	Nov. 22, 1997
279	Joe Douglass, Montana (Eastern Wash.)	Oct. 19, 1996
279	Jerry Rice, Mississippi Val. (Southern U.)	Oct. 1, 1983
276	Joey Stockton, Western Ky. (Austin Peay)	Sept. 16, 1995
276	Terry Charles, Portland St. (Montana)	Oct. 2, 1999
274	Corey Hill, Colgate (Navy)	Oct. 17, 1998

ANNUAL CHAMPIONS

Year	Player, Team	Class	G	Rec.	Avg.	Yards	TD
1978	Dan Ross, Northeastern	Sr.	11	68	6.2	988	7
1979	Stuart Gaussoin, Portland St.	Jr.	9	90	10.0	1,132	8
1980	Kenny Johnson, Portland St.	So.	11	72	6.5	1,011	11
1981	Ken Harvey, Northern Iowa	Sr.	11	78	7.1	1,161	15
1982	Don Lewis, Columbia	Jr.	10	84	8.4	1,000	6
1983	Jerry Rice, Mississippi Val.	Jr.	10	102	10.2	1,450	14
1984	Jerry Rice, Mississippi Val.	Sr.	10	103	10.3	1,682	*27
1985	Brian Forster, Rhode Island (TE)	Jr.	10	115	11.5	1,617	12
1986	Donald Narcisse, Texas Southern	Sr.	11	88	8.0	1,074	15
1987	Mike Barber, Marshall	Jr.	11	78	7.1	1,237	7
	Gordie Lockbaum, Holy Cross (RB)	Sr.	11	78	7.1	1,152	9

Year	Player, Team	Class	G	Rec.	Avg.	Yards	TD
1988	Glenn Antrum, Connecticut...............	Sr.	11	77	7.0	1,130	7
1989	Peter Macon, Weber St.	Sr.	11	92	8.4	1,047	6

Beginning in 1990, ranked on both per-game catches and yards per game

PER-GAME RECEPTIONS

Year	Player, Team	Class	G	Rec.	Avg.	Yards	TD
1990	Kasey Dunn, Idaho	Jr.	11	88	8.0	1,164	7
1991	Alfred Pupunu, Weber St. (TE)	Sr.	11	93	8.5	1,204	12
1992	Glenn Krupa, Southeast Mo. St.	Sr.	11	77	7.0	773	4
1993	Dave Cecchini, Lehigh	Sr.	11	88	8.0	1,318	16
1994	Jeff Johnson, East Tenn. St.	Sr.	9	73	8.1	857	8
1995	Ed Mantie, Boston U.	Sr.	11	81	7.4	943	1
1996	David Romines, Cal St. Northridge	Sr.	10	87	8.7	1,300	12
1997	Eric Krawczyk, Cornell	Sr.	10	89	8.9	1,042	11
1998	Jacquay Nunnally, Florida A&M...........	So.	11	93	8.5	1,316	12
1999	Murle Sango, Villanova	So.	11	98	8.9	1,064	10
2000	Stephen Campbell, Brown	Sr.	10	*120	*12.0	1,332	11
2001	Drew Amerson, Cal St. Northridge	Jr.	10	97	9.7	1,244	5
2002	Chas Gessner, Brown	Sr.	10	114	11.4	1,166	11

YARDS PER GAME

Year	Player, Team	Class	G	Rec.	Avg.	Yards	TD
1990	Kasey Dunn, Idaho	Jr.	11	88	105.8	1,164	7
1991	Mark Didio, Connecticut	Sr.	11	88	123.1	1,354	8
1992	Jason Cristino, Lehigh	Sr.	11	65	116.5	1,282	9
1993	Dave Cecchini, Lehigh	Sr.	11	88	119.8	1,318	16
1994	Mark Orlando, Towson	Sr.	9	55	135.9	1,223	12
1995	Dedric Ward, Northern Iowa	Jr.	10	44	116.4	1,164	12
1996	Joe Douglass, Montana.........................	Sr.	11	82	133.6	1,469	18
1997	Sean Morey, Brown	Jr.	10	73	142.7	1,427	15
1998	Eddie Conti, Delaware	Sr.	11	91	*155.6	*1,712	10
1999	Cornell Craig, Southern Ill.	Sr.	11	77	129.0	1,419	15
2000	Stephen Campbell, Brown	Sr.	10	*120	133.2	1,332	11
2001	Chas Gessner, Brown	Jr.	9	83	131.3	1,182	12
2002	Tramon Douglas, Grambling	Jr.	12	92	142.0	1,704	18

*Record.

Scoring

CAREER POINTS PER GAME
(Minimum 225 Points)

Player, Team	Years	G	TD	Extra Pts. Scored	FG	Pts.	Pt. PG
Adrian Peterson, Ga. Southern...	1998-01	42	87	2	0	524	*12.5
Brian Westbrook, Villanova	1997-98, 00-01	44	*89	10	0	*544	12.4
Aaron Stecker, Western Ill.	1997-98	20	39	0	0	234	11.7
Keith Elias, Princeton	1991-93	30	52	8	0	320	10.7
Jesse Chatman, Eastern Wash....	1999-01	31	53	4	0	322	10.4
David Dinkins, Morehead St.	1997-00	37	63	6	0	384	10.4
Archie Amerson, Northern Ariz.	1995-96	22	38	0	0	228	10.4
Jerry Azumah, New Hampshire..	1995-98	41	69	4	0	418	10.2
Michael Hicks, South Carolina St..	1993-95	32	52	4	0	316	9.9
Matt Cannon, Southern Utah........	1997-00	44	69	6	0	420	9.5
Elroy Harris, Eastern Ky.	1985, 87-88	31	47	6	0	288	9.3
Charles Dunn, Portland St.	1998-00	33	51	0	0	306	9.3
Joel Sigel, Portland St.	1978-80	30	46	2	0	278	9.3
Tony Zendejas, Nevada.............	1981-83	33	0	90	70	300	9.1
Gerald Harris, Ga. Southern......	1984-86	31	45	2	0	272	8.8
Marty Zendejas, Nevada...........	1984-87	44	0	169	*72	385	8.8
Charvez Foger, Nevada...........	1985-88	42	60	2	0	362	8.6
Paul Lewis, Boston U.	1981-84	37	51	2	0	308	8.3
Sherriden May, Idaho	1991-94	44	61	0	0	366	8.3
Judd Garrett, Princeton	1987-89	30	41	2	0	248	8.3
Andre Garron, New Hampshire	1982-85	30	41	0	0	246	8.2
Kenny Gamble, Colgate	1984-87	42	57	0	0	342	8.1
Rene Ingoglia, Massachusetts....	1992-95	41	55	2	0	332	8.1
Reggie Greene, Siena	1994-97	36	48	2	0	290	8.1
Rick Sarille, Wagner	$1995-99	41	55	4	0	334	8.1
Charles Roberts, Sacramento St.	1997-00	44	57	10	0	352	8.0
Barry Bourassa, New Hampshire	1989-92	39	51	0	0	306	7.8
Tim Openlander, Marshall	1994-96	33	0	159	32	255	7.7
Dave Ettinger, Hofstra	1994-97	43	0	140	62	326	7.6
Louis Ivory, Furman	1998-01	42	53	0	0	318	7.5
Marcel Shipp, Massachusetts	1997-00	43	54	0	0	324	7.5
Chad Levitt, Cornell.................	1993-96	39	48	4	0	292	7.5
Markus Thomas, Eastern Ky.	1989-92	43	53	4	0	322	7.5
Kris Heppner, Montana	1997-99	33	0	138	36	246	7.5
Yohance Humphrey, Montana....	1998-01	39	48	2	0	290	7.4
Montrell Coley, Hampton...........	1997-00	44	53	8	0	326	7.4

Player, Team	Years	G	TD	Extra Pts. Scored	FG	Pts.	Pt. PG
Jerry Rice, Mississippi Val.	1981-84	41	50	2	0	302	7.4
Brian Mitchell, Marshall/ Northern Iowa	1987, 89-91	44	0	130	64	322	7.3
Stan House, Central Conn. St. ...	1994-97	40	48	2	0	290	7.3
Scott Shields, Weber St.	1995-98	44	2	109	67	322	7.3
Ronald Jean, Lehigh	1997-99	33	40	0	0	240	7.3
Harvey Reed, Howard...............	1984-87	41	48	6	0	294	7.2
Jason Corle, Towson	1996-99	39	47	0	0	282	7.2
Greg Hill, Ga. Southern	1996-99	41	49	0	0	294	7.2

*Record. $See Page 8 for explanation.

SEASON POINTS PER GAME

Player, Team	Year	G	TD	Extra Pts. Scored	FG	Pts.	Pt. PG
Jerry Rice, Mississippi Val.	†1984	10	27	0	0	162	*16.2
Brian Westbrook, Villanova...................	†2001	11	*29	2	0	*176	16.0
Adrian Peterson, Ga. Southern	†1999	11	*29	0	0	174	15.8
Jesse Chatman, Eastern Wash.	2001	11	28	4	0	172	15.6
Montrell Coley, Hampton	†2000	11	28	4	0	172	15.6
Geoff Mitchell, Weber St.	†1991	11	28	2	0	170	15.5
Brian Westbrook, Villanova	†1998	11	26	4	0	160	14.6
Tony Vinson, Towson	†1993	10	24	0	0	144	14.4
David Dinkins, Morehead St.	2000	9	21	2	0	128	14.2
Ronald Jean, Lehigh	1999	11	26	0	0	156	14.2
Adrian Peterson, Ga. Southern	1998	11	26	0	0	156	14.2
Archie Amerson, Northern Ariz.	†1996	11	26	0	0	156	14.2
Aaron Stecker, Western Ill.	†1997	11	25	0	0	150	13.6
Sherriden May, Idaho	†1992	11	25	0	0	150	13.6
Chris Reed, Monmouth	1998	10	22	0	0	132	13.2
Keith Elias, Princeton	1993	10	21	4	0	130	13.0
Elroy Harris, Eastern Ky.	†1988	10	21	2	0	128	12.8
Jerry Azumah, New Hampshire	1998	11	23	2	0	140	12.7
Jessie Burton, McNeese St.	1998	9	19	0	0	114	12.7
Charles Roberts, Sacramento St.	1999	11	22	6	0	138	12.6
Matt Cannon, Southern Utah	1999	11	23	0	0	138	12.6
J.J. Allen, Marist	1998	10	21	0	0	126	12.6
Sean Sanders, Weber St.	†1987	10	21	0	0	126	12.6
Brian Westbrook, Villanova	2000	11	22	4	0	136	12.4
Rich Erenberg, Colgate	†1983	11	21	10	0	136	12.4
David Dinkins, Morehead St.	1999	10	20	2	0	122	12.2
Reggie Greene, Siena...........................	1997	9	18	2	0	110	12.2
Sean Bennett, Evansville	1997	10	20	2	0	122	12.2
Harvey Reed, Howard	1987	10	20	2	0	122	12.2
Paul Lewis, Boston U.	1983	10	20	2	0	122	12.2
T.J. Stallings, Morgan St.	†2002	12	23	6	0	144	12.0
Dale Jennings, Butler...........................	†2002	10	20	0	0	120	12.0
J.R. Taylor, Eastern Ill.	2001	10	20	0	0	120	12.0
P.J. Mays, Youngstown St.	2001	11	22	0	0	132	12.0
Matt Cannon, Southern Utah	2000	11	22	0	0	132	12.0
Stan House, Central Conn. St.	1996	10	20	0	0	120	12.0
Alcede Surtain, Alabama St.	†1995	11	21	6	0	132	12.0
Tim Hall, Robert Morris	†1995	10	20	0	0	120	12.0
Michael Hicks, South Carolina St.	†1994	11	22	0	0	132	12.0
Sherriden May, Idaho	1993	11	22	0	0	132	12.0
Gordie Lockbaum, Holy Cross	1987	11	22	0	0	132	12.0
Gordie Lockbaum, Holy Cross	†1986	11	22	0	0	132	12.0
Gene Lake, Delaware St.	1984	10	20	0	0	120	12.0
Sean Bennett, Evansville	1996	10	19	4	0	118	11.8
Ernest Thompson, Ga. Southern	1988	10	19	2	0	116	11.6
Chaz Williams, Ga. Southern...............	2002	14	27	0	0	162	11.6
Gary Jones, Albany (N.Y.)	2002	12	23	0	0	138	11.5
Charles Dunn, Portland St.	2000	11	21	0	0	126	11.5
Marcel Shipp, Massachusetts...............	1999	11	21	0	0	126	11.5
Jerry Azumah, New Hampshire	1996	11	21	0	0	126	11.5
Barry Bourassa, New Hampshire	1991	11	21	0	0	126	11.5
Kenny Gamble, Colgate.......................	1986	11	21	0	0	126	11.5

*Record. †National champion.

CAREER POINTS
(Non-Kickers)

Player, Team	Years	TD	Extra Pts. Scored	Pts.
Brian Westbrook, Villanova	1997-98, 00-01	*89	10	*544
Adrian Peterson, Ga. Southern	1998-01	87	2	524
Matt Cannon (QB) Southern Utah	1997-00	69	6	420
Jerry Azumah, New Hampshire	1995-98	69	4	418
David Dinkins, Morehead St.	1997-00	63	6	384
Sherriden May, Idaho	1991-94	61	0	366

Player, Team	Years	TD	Extra Pts. Scored	Pts.
Charvez Foger, Nevada	1985-88	60	2	362
Charles Roberts, Sacramento St.	1997-00	57	10	352
Kenny Gamble, Colgate	1984-87	57	0	342
Rick Sarille, Wagner	$1995-99	55	4	334
Rene Ingoglia, Massachusetts	1992-95	55	2	332
Montrell Coley, Hampton	1997-00	53	8	326
Marcel Shipp, Massachusetts	1997-00	54	0	324
Jesse Chatman, Eastern Wash.	1999-01	53	4	322
Markus Thomas, Eastern Ky.	1989-92	53	4	322
Keith Elias, Princeton	1991-93	52	8	320
Louis Ivory, Furman	1998-01	53	0	318
Michael Hicks, South Carolina St.	1993-95	52	4	316
Chris Parker, Marshall	1992-95	52	2	314
Thomas Haskins, VMI	1993-96	50	8	308
Paul Lewis, Boston U.	1981-84	51	2	308
Charles Dunn, Portland St.	1998-00	51	0	306
Barry Bourassa, New Hampshire	1989-92	51	0	306
Erick Torain, Lehigh	1987-90	50	6	306
Jerry Rice, Mississippi Val.	1981-84	50	2	302
Greg Hill, Ga. Southern (QB)	1996-99	49	0	294
Claude Mathis, Southwest Tex. St.	1994-97	49	0	294
Harvey Reed, Howard	1984-87	48	6	294
Adrian Brown, Youngstown St.	1996-99	48	4	292
Chad Levitt, Cornell	1993-96	48	4	292
Reggie Greene, Siena	1994-97	48	2	290
Stan House, Central Conn. St.	1994-97	48	2	290
Jack Douglas, Citadel (QB)	1989-92	48	0	288
Elroy Harris, Eastern Ky.	1985, 87-88	47	6	288
Jason Corle, Towson	1996-99	47	0	282
Willie Taggart, Western Ky. (QB)	1995-98	46	2	278
Joel Sigel, Portland St.	1978-80	46	2	278
Joe Campbell, Middle Tenn.	1988-91	45	2	272
Gerald Harris, Ga. Southern	1984-86	45	2	272
P.J. Mays, Youngstown St.	2000-02	45	0	270
Carl Tremble, Furman	1989-92	45	0	270
Norm Ford, New Hampshire	1986-89	45	0	270
John Settle, Appalachian St.	1983-86	44	4	268
Ernest Thompson, Ga. Southern	1985, 87-89	44	2	266
Rennie Benn, Lehigh	1982-85	44	2	266
Joe Segreti, Holy Cross	1987-90	44	0	264
Gordie Lockbaum, Holy Cross	1984-87	44	0	264
Frank Hawkins, Nevada	1977-80	44	0	264

*Record. $See Page 8 for explanation.

CAREER POINTS
(Kickers)

Player, Team	Years	PAT	PAT Att.	FG	FG Att.	Pts.
Marty Zendejas, Nevada	1984-87	169	175	*72	90	*385
Dave Ettinger, Hofstra	1994-97	140	155	62	93	326
Scott Shields, Weber St.	1995-98	109	118	67	90	#322
Brian Mitchell, Marshall/ Northern Iowa	1987, 89-91	130	131	64	81	322
Thayne Doyle, Idaho	1988-91	160	174	49	75	307
Jose Larios, McNeese St.	1992-95	133	136	57	89	304
Kirk Roach, Western Caro.	1984-87	89	91	71	*102	302
Tim Foley, Ga. Southern	1984-87	151	156	50	62	301
Dewey Klein, Marshall	1988-91	156	165	48	66	300
Tony Zendejas, Nevada	1981-83	90	96	70	86	300
Jeff Wilkins, Youngstown St.	1990-93	134	136	50	73	286
Garth Petrilli, Middle Tenn.	1991-94	166	170	38	60	280
Steve Christie, William & Mary	1986-89	108	116	57	83	279
Franco Grilla, UCF	1989-92	141	147	45	69	278
Gilad Landau, Grambling	1991-94	*181	*194	32	50	277
Shonz LaFrenz, McNeese St.	1996-99	120	128	52	78	276
Mike Black, Boise St.	1988-91	122	127	51	75	275
Juan Toro, Florida A&M	1995-98	151	169	41	50	274
Kirk Duce, Montana	1988-91	131	141	47	78	272
Todd Kurz, Illinois St.	1993-96	89	94	59	87	266
Jeff Poisel, Western Ky.	1996-99	170	180	31	53	263
Paul Hickert, Murray St.	1984-87	116	121	49	79	263
Dean Biasucci, Western Caro.	1980-83	101	106	54	80	263
Andy Larson, Montana	1993-96	177	188	28	45	261
Kelly Potter, Middle Tenn.	1981-84	105	109	52	78	261
Steve Largent, Eastern Ill.	1992-95	122	126	46	73	260
Lawrence Tynes, Troy St.	1997-00	123	127	45	62	258
Brian Shallcross, William & Mary	1994-97	117	131	47	73	258
Billy Hayes, Sam Houston St.	1985-88	117	120	47	71	258
Michael O'Neal, Samford	1989-92	142	152	38	60	256
Tim Openlander, Marshall	1994-96	159	162	32	42	255
Jason McLaughlin, Lafayette	1991-94	131	138	41	74	254
Jim Hodson, Lafayette	1987-90	134	140	40	66	254

Player, Team	Years	PAT	PAT Att.	FG	FG Att.	Pts.
Dave Parkinson, Delaware St.	1985-88	134	143	40	77	254
Chuck Rawlinson, Stephen F. Austin	1988-91	106	110	49	69	253
Paul Politi, Illinois St.	1983-86	101	103	50	78	251
Wayne Boyer, Southwest Mo. St.	1993-96	100	104	49	71	247
Kris Heppner, Montana	1997-99	138	149	36	58	246
Teddy Garcia, La.-Monroe	1984-87	78	81	56	88	246

*Record. #Includes 2 TDs.

SEASON POINTS

Player, Team	Year	TD	Extra Pts. Scored	FG	Pts.
Brian Westbrook, Villanova	†2001	*29	2	0	*176
Adrian Peterson, Ga. Southern	†1999	*29	0	0	174
Jesse Chatman, Eastern Wash.	2001	28	4	0	172
Montrell Coley, Hampton	†2000	28	4	0	172
Geoff Mitchell, Weber St.	†1991	28	2	0	170
Chaz Williams, Ga. Southern	2002	27	0	0	162
Jerry Rice, Mississippi Val.	†1984	27	0	0	162
Brian Westbrook, Villanova	†1998	26	4	0	160
Ronald Jean, Lehigh	1999	26	0	0	156
Adrian Peterson, Ga. Southern	1998	26	0	0	156
Archie Amerson, Northern Ariz.	†1996	26	0	0	156
Aaron Stecker, Western Ill.	†1997	25	0	0	150
Sherriden May, Idaho	†1992	25	0	0	150
T.J. Stallings, Morgan St.	†2002	23	6	0	144
Tony Vinson, Towson	†1993	24	0	0	144
Jerry Azumah, New Hampshire	1998	23	2	0	140
Gary Jones, Albany (N.Y.)	2002	23	0	0	138
Charles Roberts, Sacramento St.	1999	22	6	0	138
Matt Cannon, Southern Utah	1999	23	0	0	138
Brian Westbrook, Villanova	2000	22	4	0	136
Rich Erenberg, Colgate	†1983	21	10	0	136
P.J. Mays, Youngstown St.	2001	22	0	0	132
Matt Cannon, Southern Utah	2000	22	0	0	132
Chris Reed, Monmouth	1998	22	0	0	132
Alcede Surtain, Alabama St.	†1995	21	6	0	132
Michael Hicks, South Carolina St.	†1994	22	0	0	132
Sherriden May, Idaho	1993	22	0	0	132
Gordie Lockbaum, Holy Cross	1987	22	0	0	132
Gordie Lockbaum, Holy Cross	†1986	22	0	0	132
Keith Elias, Princeton	1993	21	4	0	130
David Dinkins, Morehead St.	2000	21	2	0	128
Elroy Harris, Eastern Ky.	†1988	21	2	0	128
Charles Dunn, Portland St.	2000	21	0	0	126
Marcel Shipp, Massachusetts	1999	21	0	0	126
J.J. Allen, Marist	1998	21	0	0	126
Jerry Azumah, New Hampshire	1996	21	0	0	126
Barry Bourassa, New Hampshire	1991	21	0	0	126
Sean Sanders, Weber St.	†1987	21	0	0	126
Kenny Gamble, Colgate	1986	21	0	0	126
David Dinkins, Morehead St.	1999	20	2	0	122
Charles Roberts, Sacramento St.	1998	20	2	0	122
David Dinkins, Morehead St.	1998	20	2	0	122
Sean Bennett, Evansville	1997	20	2	0	122
Harvey Reed, Howard	1987	20	2	0	122
Paul Lewis, Boston U.	1983	20	2	0	122

*Record. †National champion.

ANNUAL CHAMPIONS

Year	Player, Team	Class	G	TD	Extra Pts. Scored	FG	Pts.	Avg.
1978	Frank Hawkins, Nevada	So.	10	17	0	0	102	10.2
1979	Joel Sigel, Portland St.	Jr.	10	16	0	0	96	9.6
1980	Ken Jenkins, Bucknell	Jr.	10	16	0	0	96	9.6
1981	Paris Wicks, Youngstown St.	Jr.	11	17	2	0	104	9.5
1982	Paul Lewis, Boston U.	So.	10	18	0	0	108	10.8
1983	Rich Erenberg, Colgate	Sr.	11	21	10	0	136	12.4
1984	Jerry Rice, Mississippi Val.	Sr.	10	27	0	0	162	*16.2
1985	Charvez Foger, Nevada	Fr.	10	18	0	0	108	10.8
1986	Gordie Lockbaum, Holy Cross	Jr.	11	22	0	0	132	12.0
1987	Sean Sanders, Weber St.	Sr.	10	21	0	0	126	12.6
1988	Elroy Harris, Eastern Ky.	Jr.	10	21	2	0	128	12.8
1989	Carl Smith, Maine	So.	11	20	0	0	120	10.9
1990	Barry Bourassa, New Hampshire	So.	9	16	0	0	96	10.7
1991	Geoff Mitchell, Weber St.	Sr.	11	28	2	0	170	15.5
1992	Sherriden May, Idaho	So.	11	25	0	0	150	13.6
1993	Tony Vinson, Towson	Sr.	10	24	0	0	144	14.4
1994	Michael Hicks, South Carolina St.	Jr.	11	22	0	0	132	12.0
1995	Alcede Surtain, Alabama St.	Sr.	11	21	6	0	132	12.0
	Tim Hall, Robert Morris	Sr.	10	20	0	0	120	12.0

Year	Player, Team	Class	G	TD	Extra Pts. Scored	FG	Pts.	Avg.
1996	Archie Amerson, Northern Ariz. ..	Sr.	11	26	0	0	156	14.2
1997	Aaron Stecker, Western Ill.	Jr.	11	25	0	0	150	13.6
1998	Brian Westbrook, Villanova	So.	11	26	4	0	160	14.6
1999	Adrian Peterson, Ga. Southern.....	So.	11	*29	0	0	174	15.8
2000	Montrell Coley, Hampton.............	Sr.	11	28	4	0	172	15.6
2001	Brian Westbrook, Villanova	Sr.	11	*29	2	0	*176	16.0
2002	T.J. Stallings, Morgan St.	Sr.	12	23	6	0	144	12.0
	Dale Jennings, Butler	Sr.	10	20	0	0	120	12.0

*Record.

Interceptions

CAREER INTERCEPTIONS

Player, Team	Years	No.	Yards	Avg.
Rashean Mathis, Bethune-Cookman 1999-02	*31	*682	22.0
Dave Murphy, Holy Cross 1986-89	28	309	11.0
Cedric Walker, Stephen F. Austin 1990-93	25	230	9.2
Issiac Holt, Alcorn St. 1981-84	24	319	13.3
Bill McGovern, Holy Cross..............................1981-84	24	168	7.0
Darren Sharper, William & Mary 1993-96	24	488	20.3
Scott Shields, Weber St. 1995-98	23	278	12.1
Adrion Smith, Southwest Mo. St. 1990-93	23	219	9.5
William Carroll, Florida A&M..........................1989-92	23	328	14.3
Kevin Smith, Rhode Island 1987-90	23	287	12.5
Mike Prior, Illinois St. 1981-84	23	211	9.2
Robert Taylor, Tennessee Tech 1993-96	22	267	12.1
Chris Helon, Boston U. 1991-94	22	110	5.0
Morgan Ryan, Montana St. 1990-93	22	245	11.1
Dave Roberts, Youngstown St. 1989-92	22	131	6.0
Frank Robinson, Boise St. 1988-91	22	203	9.2
Derrick Harris, East Tenn. St. 1986-89	22	453	20.6
Dean Cain, Princeton 1985-87	22	203	9.2
Steve Dogmanits, Fairfield 1997-00	21	231	11.0
Paul Serie, Siena 1995-98	21	107	5.1
Derek Carter, Maine 1994-97	21	301	14.3
Brian Randall, Delaware St. 1990-93	21	367	17.4
Kevin Dent, Jackson St. 1985-88	21	280	13.3
Mark Seals, Boston U. 1985-88	21	169	8.0
Jeff Smith, Illinois St. 1985-88	21	152	7.2
Chris Demarest, Northeastern 1984-87	21	255	12.1
Greg Greely, Nicholls St. 1981-84	21	218	10.4
George Floyd, Eastern Ky. 1978-81	21	318	15.1
Eric Kenesie, Valparaiso 1996-99	20	183	9.2
William Hampton, Murray St. 1993-96	20	409	20.5
Rick Harris, East Tenn. St. 1986-88	20	452	22.6
Mark Kelso, William & Mary 1981-84	20	171	8.6
Leslie Frazier, Alcorn St. 1977-80	20	269	13.5
Brian Dunn, Robert Morris 1994-97	19	201	10.6
Bob Jordan, New Hampshire............................1990-93	19	96	5.1
Ricky Thomas, South Carolina St. 1988-91	19	374	19.7
Dwayne Harper, South Carolina St. 1984-87	19	163	8.6
Joe Burton, Delaware St. 1983-86	19	248	13.1
Michael Richardson, Northwestern St. 1981-84	19	344	18.1
Mike Genetti, Northeastern 1980-83	19	296	15.6
George Schmitt, Delaware................................1980-82	19	280	14.7

*Record.

SEASON INTERCEPTIONS

Player, Team	Year	No.	Yards
Rashean Mathis, Bethune-Cookman.................................†2002	*14	*455
Dean Cain, Princeton...†1987	12	98
Jon Ambrose, St. Peter's...†2001	11	222
Steve Dogmanits, Fairfield..†2000	11	113
Rashean Mathis, Bethune-Cookman................................. 2000	11	157
Aeneas Williams, Southern U. ....‡1990	11	173
Claude Pettaway, Maine..‡1990	11	161
Bill McGovern, Holy Cross..†1984	11	102
Everson Walls, Grambling..†1980	11	145
Anthony Young, Jackson St..†1978	11	108
Darren Sharper, William & Mary...................................... 1996	10	228
Scott Shields, Weber St. 1996	10	101
Chris Helon, Boston U. ....†1993	10	42
Cedric Walker, Stephen F. Austin..................................... 1990	10	11
Chris Demarest, Northeastern... 1987	10	129
Kevin Dent, Jackson St. ....‡1986	10	192
Eric Thompson, New Hampshire......................................‡1986	10	94

Bethune-Cookman's Rashean Mathis grabbed 14 interceptions last year to establish a new Division I-AA record. It also enabled him to set the division's career mark with 31. Mathis also holds the records for interception return yards in a season (455 in 2002) and a career (682).

Player, Team	Year	No.	Yards
Anthony Anderson, Grambling ....‡1986	10	37
Mike Armentrout, Southwest Mo. St. ....†1983	10	42
George Schmitt, Delaware...†1982	10	186
Mike Genetti, Northeastern...†1981	10	144
Bob Mahr, Lafayette... 1981	10	48
Neale Henderson, Southern U. ....†1979	10	151

*Record. †National champion. ‡National championship shared.

ANNUAL CHAMPIONS
(Ranked on Per-Game Average)

Year	Player, Team	Class	G	No.	Avg.	Yards
1978	Anthony Young, Jackson St.	Sr.	11	11	1.00	108
1979	Neale Henderson, Southern U.	Sr.	11	10	0.91	151
1980	Everson Walls, Grambling............................	Sr.	11	11	1.00	145
1981	Mike Genetti, Northeastern..........................	So.	10	10	1.00	144
1982	George Schmitt, Delaware............................	Sr.	11	10	0.91	186
1983	Mike Armentrout, Southwest Mo. St.	Jr.	11	10	0.91	42
1984	Bill McGovern, Holy Cross	Sr.	11	11	1.00	102
1985	Mike Cassidy, Rhode Island	Sr.	10	9	0.90	169
	George Duarte, Northern Ariz.	Jr.	10	9	0.90	150
1986	Kevin Dent, Jackson St.	So.	11	10	0.91	192
	Eric Thompson, New Hampshire..................	Sr.	11	10	0.91	94
	Anthony Anderson, Grambling	Sr.	11	10	0.91	37
1987	Dean Cain, Princeton	Sr.	10	12	*1.20	98
1988	Kevin Smith, Rhode Island	So.	10	9	0.90	94
1989	Mike Babb, Weber St.	Sr.	11	9	0.82	90
1990	Aeneas Williams, Southern U.	Sr.	11	11	1.00	173
	Claude Pettaway, Maine...............................	Sr.	11	11	1.00	161
1991	Warren McIntire, Delaware	Jr.	11	9	0.82	208
1992	Dave Roberts, Youngstown St.	Sr.	11	9	0.82	39
1993	Chris Helon, Boston U.	Jr.	11	10	0.91	42
1994	Joseph Vaughn, Cal St. Northridge	Sr.	10	9	0.90	265
	Brian Clark, Hofstra	Jr.	10	9	0.90	56
1995	Picasso Nelson, Jackson St.	Sr.	9	8	0.89	101
1996	Shane Hurd, Canisius...................................	Jr.	7	7	1.00	198
1997	Roderic Parson, Brown	Sr.	8	8	1.00	93
1998	Ken Krapf, St. John's (N.Y.)	Jr.	11	9	0.82	144
	Eric Kenesie, Valparaiso	Jr.	11	9	0.82	88
1999	Ryan Crawford, Davidson	Jr.	11	8	0.73	63
2000	Steve Dogmanits, Fairfield	Sr.	10	11	1.10	113
2001	Jon Ambrose, St. Peter's	Jr.	11	11	1.00	222
2002	Rashean Mathis, Bethune-Cookman..............	Sr.	13	*14	1.08	*455

*Record.

DIVISION I-AA

Total Tackles

SEASON TOTAL TACKLES PER GAME

Player, Team	Year	G	Solo	Ast.	Total	Avg.
Boomer Grigsby, Illinois St.	†2002	11	108	71	179	*16.3
Josh Cain, Chattanooga	2002	12	*113	79	*192	16.0
Edgerton Hartwell, Western Ill.	†2000	11	107	62	169	15.4
Tim Johnson, Youngstown St.	2000	11	83	80	163	14.8
P.J. Jones, Southwest Mo. St.	†2001	11	66	95	161	14.6
Derrick Lloyd, James Madison	2001	11	94	63	157	14.3
Dietrich Lapsley, Indiana St.	2002	12	103	68	171	14.3
Aden Smith, Stony Brook	2002	10	57	83	140	14.0
Bobby Rosenberg, St. John's (N.Y.)	2002	10	80	60	140	14.0
Melvin Wisham, Western Ky.	2000	11	92	58	150	13.6

*Record. †National champion.

SEASON TOTAL TACKLES

Player, Team	Year	G	Solo	Ast.	Total
Josh Cain, Chattanooga	2002	12	*113	79	*192
Boomer Grigsby, Illinois St.	†2002	11	108	71	179
Dietrich Lapsley, Indiana St.	2002	12	103	68	171
Edgerton Hartwell, Western Ill.	†2000	11	107	62	169
Tim Johnson, Youngstown St.	2000	11	83	80	163
P.J. Jones, Southwest Mo. St.	†2001	11	66	95	161
Chuck Thompson, Western Ky.	2002	15	93	66	159
Derrick Lloyd, James Madison	2001	11	94	63	157
Cornell Middlebrook, Western Ill.	2002	13	101	53	154
Melvin Wisham, Western Ky.	2000	11	92	58	150

*Record. †National champion.

SINGLE-GAME TOTAL TACKLES
(Since 2000)

Tackles	Player, Team (Opponent)	Date
26	Boomer Grigsby, Illinois St. (Youngstown St.)	Nov. 9, 2002
25	Nick Ricks, Eastern Ill. (Eastern Ky.)	Oct. 12, 2002
25	Tim Johnson, Youngstown St. (Hofstra)	Nov. 4, 2000
23	Matt McFadden, Weber St. (Idaho St.)	Oct. 27, 2001
22	Dietrich Lapsley, Indiana St. (Southwest Mo. St.)	Oct. 12, 2002
22	Liam Ezekiel, Northeastern (Delaware)	Oct. 5, 2002
22	Adam Vogt, Northern Iowa (Youngstown St.)	Oct. 14, 2000
19	Chris Carey, Columbia (Harvard)	Nov. 3, 2001
19	Dan Mulhern, Delaware (New Hampshire)	Nov. 4, 2000
19	Pete Mazza, Yale (Brown)	Nov. 4, 2000
19	Kole Ayi, Massachusetts (New Hampshire)	Oct. 28, 2000

ANNUAL CHAMPIONS

Year	Player, Team	Class	G	Solo	Ast.	Total	Avg.
2000	Edgerton Hartwell, Western Ill.	Sr.	11	107	62	169	15.4
2001	P.J. Jones, Southwest Mo. St.	Sr.	11	66	95	161	14.6
2002	Boomer Grigsby, Illinois St.	So.	11	108	71	179	*16.3

*Record.

Solo Tackles

SEASON SOLO TACKLES PER GAME

Player, Team	Year	G	Solo	Avg.
Boomer Grigsby, Illinois St.	†2002	11	108	*9.82
Edgerton Hartwell, Western Ill.	2000	11	107	9.73
Josh Cain, Chattanooga	2002	12	*113	9.42
Derick Pack, James Madison	2000	11	97	8.82
Dietrich Lapsley, Indiana St.	2002	12	103	8.58
Derrick Lloyd, James Madison	†2001	11	94	8.55
Nick Ricks, Eastern Ill.	2001	10	85	8.50
Melvin Wisham, Western Ky.	2000	11	92	8.36
Nick Ricks, Eastern Ill.	2002	12	98	8.17

*Record. †National champion.

SEASON TOTAL SOLO TACKLES

Player, Team	Year	G	Solo
Josh Cain, Chattanooga	2002	12	*113
Boomer Grigsby, Illinois St.	†2002	11	108
Edgerton Hartwell, Western Ill.	2000	11	107
Dietrich Lapsley, Indiana St.	2002	12	103
Cornell Middlebrook, Western Ill.	2002	13	101
Nick Ricks, Eastern Ill.	2002	12	98
Jeremy Cain, Massachusetts	2002	12	97
Lee Russell, Western Ill.	2002	13	97
Derick Pack, James Madison	2000	11	97
Derrick Lloyd, James Madison	†2001	11	94

*Record. †National champion.

SINGLE-GAME SOLO TACKLES
(Since 2000)

Solo	Player, Team (Opponent)	Date
18	Nick Ricks, Eastern Ill. (Eastern Ky.)	Oct. 12, 2002
15	Matt McFadden, Weber St. (Idaho St.)	Oct. 27, 2001
14	Boomer Grigsby, Illinois St. (Youngstown St.)	Nov. 9, 2002
14	Dietrich Lapsley, Indiana St. (Western Ky.)	Oct. 26, 2002
14	Anton McKenzie, Massachusetts (Villanova)	Oct. 19, 2002
14	Aden Smith, Stony Brook (Monmouth)	Oct. 12, 2002
14	Chris Stimmel, Northern Iowa (Ball St.)	Sept. 22, 2001
13	Mike Adams, Delaware (Villanova)	Nov. 17, 2001
12	James Burchett, Ga. Southern (Wofford)	Sept. 21, 2002
11	Barton Simmons, Yale (Dartmouth)	Oct. 7, 2001
10	Brad Fradenberg, Fordham (Towson)	Nov. 10, 2001

ANNUAL CHAMPIONS

Year	Player, Team	Class	G	Solo	Avg.
2001	Derrick Lloyd, James Madison	Sr.	11	94	8.55
2002	Boomer Grigsby, Illinois St.	So.	11	108	*9.82

*Record.

Tackles for Loss

SEASON TACKLES FOR LOSS PER GAME

Player, Team	Year	G	Solo	Ast.	Total	Avg.
Robert Mathis, Alabama A&M	†2002	11	30	1	30.5	*2.77
Odain Mitchell, Sacred Heart	2002	10	20	11	25.5	2.55
Joseph Crear, Mississippi Val.	2002	11	27	2	28.0	2.55
Leonard Mack, Texas Southern	2002	11	25	5	27.5	2.50
Jamal Naji, Norfolk St.	2002	11	23	8	27.0	2.45
Andy Petek, Montana	†2000	11	27	0	27.0	2.45
D.J. Bleisath, Tennessee Tech.	†2001	10	24	0	24.0	2.40
Isaac Hilton, Hampton	2002	12	27	3	28.5	2.38
Steve Watson, Southwest Mo. St.	2002	9	21	0	21.0	2.33
Michale Spicer, Western Caro.	2002	11	24	2	25.0	2.27
Jonathan Friend, Illinois St.	2002	11	25	0	25.0	2.27

*Record. †National champion.

SEASON TACKLES FOR LOSS

Player, Team	Year	G	Solo	Ast.	Total
Sherrod Coates, Western Ky.	2002	15	31	0	*31.0
Robert Mathis, Alabama A&M	†2002	11	30	1	30.5
Isaac Hilton, Hampton	2002	12	27	3	28.5
Joseph Crear, Mississippi Val.	2002	11	27	2	28.0
Leonard Mack, Texas Southern	2002	11	25	5	27.5
Jamal Naji, Norfolk St.	2002	11	23	8	27.0
Anthony Jones, Wofford	2002	12	26	2	27.0
Andy Petek, Montana	†2000	11	27	0	27.0
Steve Baggs, Bethune-Cookman	2002	13	25	2	26.0
Odain Mitchell, Sacred Heart	2002	10	20	11	25.5

*Record. †National champion.

SINGLE-GAME TACKLES FOR LOSS
(Since 2000)

TFL	Player, Team (Opponent)	Date
7.0	Greg Pitts, Southwest Tex. St. (Texas Southern)	Sept. 21, 2002
6.0	Valdamar Brower, Massachusetts (Rhode Island)	Nov. 17, 2001
6.0	Eric Allen, Tennessee Tech (Eastern Ill.)	Nov. 11, 2000
5.0	Kyle Mitchell, Indiana St. (Illinois St.)	Nov. 16, 2002
5.0	Kyle Mitchell, Indiana St. (Western Mich.)	Aug. 29, 2002
5.0	Phil Tolliver, Stony Brook (St. John's [N.Y.])	Sept. 21, 2001
4.0	Luke Mraz, Yale (Brown)	Nov. 9, 2002
4.0	Eric Hadley, Ga. Southern (East Tenn. St.)	Nov. 2, 2002
4.0	Eric McIntire, Ga. Southern (East Tenn. St.)	Nov. 2, 2002
4.0	Steve Lhotak, Pennsylvania (Brown)	Nov. 2, 2002
4.0	DeShawn Jude, Ga. Southern (VMI)	Oct. 5, 2002
4.0	Nick Fazzie, Delaware (Richmond)	Nov. 10, 2001
4.0	Carlos Dallis, Northern Iowa (Youngstown St.)	Sept. 29, 2001
4.0	C.J. Carroll, Southwest Tex. St. (Sam Houston St.)	Nov. 22, 2000
4.0	Galen Scott, Illinois St. (Indiana St.)	Oct. 14, 2000

ANNUAL CHAMPIONS

Year	Player, Team	G	Solo	Ast.	Total	Avg.
2000	Andy Petek, Montana	11	27	0	27.0	2.45
2001	D.J. Bleisath, Tennessee Tech	10	24	0	24.0	2.40
2002	Robert Mathis, Alabama A&M	11	30	1	30.5	*2.77

*Record.

Pass Sacks

SEASON PASS SACKS PER GAME

Player, Team	Year	G	Solo	Ast.	Total	Avg.
Andrew Hollingsworth, Towson	†2000	9	16	2	17.0	*1.89
Robert Mathis, Alabama A&M	†2002	11	19	2	*20.0	1.82
Andy Petek, Montana	2000	11	19	0	19.0	1.73
Odain Mitchell, Sacred Heart	2002	10	13	6	16.0	1.60
Joseph Crear, Mississippi Val.	2002	11	13	3	14.5	1.32
Mike Foster, Drake	2000	10	13	0	13.0	1.30
Renauld Williams, Hofstra	2002	12	15	0	15.0	1.25
Anthony Jones, Wofford	2002	12	13	3	14.5	1.21
Marc Laborsky, Harvard	†2001	9	9	2	10.0	1.11
Jamal Naji, Norfolk St.	2002	11	12	0	12.0	1.09

*Record. †National champion.

SEASON TOTAL PASS SACKS

Player, Team	Year	G	Solo	Ast.	Total
Robert Mathis, Alabama A&M	†2002	11	19	2	*20.0
Andy Petek, Montana	2000	11	19	0	19.0
Andrew Hollingsworth, Towson	†2000	9	16	2	17.0
Odain Mitchell, Sacred Heart	2002	10	13	6	16.0
Renauld Williams, Hofstra	2002	12	15	0	15.0
Joseph Crear, Mississippi Val.	2002	11	13	3	14.5
Anthony Jones, Wofford	2002	12	13	3	14.5
Tim Bush, Montana	2002	13	11	4	13.0
Sherrod Coates, Western Ky.	2002	15	13	0	13.0
Mike Foster, Drake	2000	10	13	0	13.0

*Record. †National champion.

SINGLE-GAME PASS SACKS

(Since 2000)

PS	Player, Team (Opponent)	Date
4.0	Valdamar Brower, Massachusetts (American Int'l)	Sept. 14, 2002
4.0	C.J. Carroll, Southwest Tex. St. (Sam Houston St.)	Nov. 22, 2000
4.0	Valdamar Brower, Massachusetts (Maine)	Oct. 14, 2000
4.0	Galen Scott, Illinois St. (Indiana St.)	Oct. 14, 2000
3.0	Mark Patterson, Yale (Harvard)	Nov. 23, 2002
3.0	Matt Mitchell, Northern Iowa (Cal Poly)	Nov. 17, 2002
3.0	David Bamiro, Stony Brook (St. John's [N.Y.])	Sept. 21, 2001
3.0	Colby Khuns, Fordham (Fairfield)	Sept. 8, 2001
3.0	Matt Mitchell, Northern Iowa (Wayne St. [Mich.])	Aug. 30, 2001
3.0	R.D. Kern, Harvard (Holy Cross)	Sept. 16, 2000
2.5	Eric Hadley, Ga. Southern (East Tenn. St.)	Nov. 2, 2002

ANNUAL CHAMPIONS

Year	Player, Team	G	Solo	Ast.	Total	Avg.
2000	Andrew Hollingsworth, Towson	9	16	2	17.0	*1.89
2001	Marc Laborsky, Harvard	9	9	2	10.0	1.11
2002	Robert Mathis, Alabama A&M	11	19	2	*20.0	1.82

*Record.

Passes Defended

SEASON PASSES DEFENDED PER GAME

Player, Team	Year	G	PBU	Int.	Total	Avg.
Bobby Sippio, Western Ky.	†2000	10	18	9	*27	*2.70
Santino Hall, Texas Southern	†2001	10	20	6	26	2.60
Brandon Phillips, Morehead St.	2001	11	21	5	26	2.36
Leigh Bodden, Duquesne	2000	11	17	9	26	2.36
Brandon Phillips, Morehead St.	†2002	10	18	5	23	2.30
Jon Ambrose, St. Peter's	2001	11	15	10	25	2.27
Harry Sutton, Iona	2000	11	24	1	25	2.27
Yeremiah Bell, Eastern Ky.	2001	10	16	6	22	2.20
Brian Sawyer, Hampton	2002	12	23	3	26	2.17
Steve Dogmanits, Fairfield	2000	10	10	11	21	2.10
Don Milligan, Fairfield	2000	10	12	9	21	2.10

*Record. †National champion.

SEASON TOTAL PASSES DEFENDED

Player, Team	Year	G	PBU	Int.	Total
Bobby Sippio, Western Ky.	†2000	10	18	9	*27
Brian Sawyer, Hampton	2002	12	23	3	26
Santino Hall, Texas Southern	†2001	10	20	6	26
Brandon Phillips, Morehead St.	2001	11	21	5	26
Leigh Bodden, Duquesne	2000	11	17	9	26
Jon Ambrose, St. Peter's	2001	11	15	10	25
Harry Sutton, Iona	2000	11	24	1	25

Player, Team	Year	G	PBU	Int.	Total
Brandon Phillips, Morehead St.	†2002	10	18	5	23
Gary Johnson, Villanova	2001	11	21	2	23
Scott Cunningham, Tennessee St.	2002	12	19	3	22
Antwan Hill, Alabama St.	2002	12	12	10	22
Yeremiah Bell, Eastern Ky.	2001	10	16	6	22
LeVar Greene, Youngstown St.	2001	11	15	7	22

SINGLE-GAME PASSES DEFENDED

(Since 2000)

PD	Player, Team (Opponent)	Date
6	James Young, Ga. Southern (Bethune-Cookman)	Nov. 30, 2002
6	Sam Young, Illinois St. (Youngstown St.)	Oct. 7, 2000
5	Sidney Haugabrook, Delaware (Northeastern)	Sept. 29, 2001
4	Justin Sandy, Northern Iowa (Southwest Mo. St.)	Nov. 16, 2002
4	Mitchell Fitzhugh, Portland St. (Weber St.)	Oct. 12, 2001
4	Jeremy Robinson, Massachusetts (New Haven)	Sept. 23, 2000
3	By many players	

ANNUAL CHAMPIONS

Year	Player, Team	G	PBU	Int.	Total	Avg.
2000	Bobby Sippio, Western Ky.	10	18	9	*27	*2.70
2001	Santino Hall, Texas Southern	10	20	6	26	2.60
2002	Brandon Phillips, Morehead St.	10	18	5	23	2.30

*Record.

Forced Fumbles

SEASON FORCED FUMBLES PER GAME

Player, Team	Year	G	FF	Avg.
Robert Mathis, Alabama A&M	†2002	11	*10	*0.91
Nick Ricks, Eastern Ill.	2002	12	7	0.58
Andy Petek, Montana	†2000	11	6	0.55
Lee Basinger, Wofford	2002	12	6	0.50
Raleigh Robinson, Davidson	2002	10	5	0.50
Eugene Boyd, Illinois St.	2002	11	5	0.45
Steve Boyer, Richmond	2002	11	5	0.45
Quinten Swain, Fla. Atlantic	2002	11	5	0.45
Jeran Crawford, St. Peter's	†2001	11	5	0.45
Jamison Young, Villanova	†2001	11	5	0.45
C.J. Carroll, Southwest Tex. St.	†2000	11	5	0.45
Franco Madafari, Duquesne	2000	11	5	0.45

*Record. †National champion.

SEASON TOTAL FORCED FUMBLES

Player, Team	Year	G	FF
Robert Mathis, Alabama A&M	†2002	11	*10
Nick Ricks, Eastern Ill.	2002	12	7
Lee Basinger, Wofford	2002	12	6
Andy Petek, Montana	†2000	11	6
Raleigh Robinson, Davidson	2002	10	5
Eugene Boyd, Illinois St.	2002	11	5
Steve Boyer, Richmond	2002	11	5
Quinten Swain, Fla. Atlantic	2002	11	5
Jeran Crawford, St. Peter's	†2001	11	5
Jamison Young, Villanova	†2001	11	5
Chad Dewberry, Eastern Ky.	2002	12	5
Zac Prewitt, Morehead St.	2002	12	5
Vince Huntsberger, Montana	2001	12	5
C.J. Carroll, Southwest Tex. St.	†2000	11	5
Franco Madafari, Duquesne	†2000	11	5

*Record. †National champion.

SINGLE-GAME FORCED FUMBLES

(Since 2000)

FF	Player, Team (Opponent)	Date
3	Sterling Rogers, Southwest Tex. St. (Portland St.)	Oct. 6, 2001
2	Tolo Tuitele, Portland St. (Montana St.)	Nov. 16, 2002
2	Carl Kearney, Ga. Southern (Furman)	Nov. 9, 2002
2	Matt Jenkins, Portland St. (Sacramento St.)	Oct. 19, 2002
2	Benny Sapp, Northern Iowa (Youngstown St.)	Oct. 19, 2002
2	Steve Costello, Massachusetts (Richmond)	Oct. 5, 2002
2	Jarvis Phillips, Northern Iowa (Western Ky.)	Oct. 5, 2002
2	Travis Belden, Pennsylvania (Lehigh)	Sept. 28, 2002
2	Matt McFadden, Weber St. (Idaho St.)	Oct. 27, 2001
2	Jason Boehlke, Northern Iowa (Ball St.)	Sept. 22, 2001
2	Compton Webster, Massachusetts (New Hampshire)	Oct. 28, 2000

DIVISION I-AA

ANNUAL CHAMPIONS

Year	Player, Team	G	FF	Avg.
2000	Tommy Swindell, Jacksonville	11	‡9	0.82
	C.J. Carroll, Southwest Tex. St.	11	‡9	0.82
	Andy Petek, Montana	11	‡9	0.82

‡Prior to 2001, the total was forced fumbles plus fumbles recovered. Beginning in 2001, FF was forced fumbles only.

2001	Jeran Crawford, St. Peter's	11	5	0.45
	Jamison Young, Villanova	11	5	0.45
2002	Robert Mathis, Alabama A&M	11	*10	*0.91

Punting

CAREER AVERAGE
(Minimum 150 Punts)

Player, Team	Years	No.	Yards	Long	Avg.
Pumpy Tudors, Chattanooga	1989-91	181	8,041	79	*44.4
Case de Bruijn, Idaho St.	1978-81	256	11,184	76	43.7
Mike Scifres, Western Ill.	1999-02	203	8,842	89	43.6
Terry Belden, Northern Ariz.	1990-93	225	9,760	76	43.4
Chad Stanley, Stephen F. Austin	1996-98	178	7,709	79	43.3
George Cimadevilla, East Tenn. St.	1983-86	225	9,676	72	43.0
Harold Alexander, Appalachian St.	1989-92	259	11,100	78	42.9
Ken Hinsley, Western Caro.	1995-98	199	8,512	85	42.8
Brad Costello, Boston U.	1995-97	193	8,206	73	42.5
John Christopher, Morehead St.	1979-82	298	12,633	62	42.4
Matthew Peot, Montana St.	1997-99	155	6,578	61	42.4
Colin Godfrey, Tennessee St.	1989-92	213	9,012	69	42.3
Bret Wright, Southeastern La.	1981-83	165	6,963	66	42.2
Jeff Kaiser, Idaho St.	1982-84	156	6,571	88	42.1
Greg Davis, Citadel	1983-86	263	11,076	81	42.1
Mark Royals, Appalachian St.	1983-85	223	9,372	67	42.0

*Record.

SEASON AVERAGE
(Qualifiers for Championship)

Player, Team	Year	No.	Yards	Avg.
Mark Gould, Northern Ariz.	†2002	62	2,987	*48.2
Mike Scifres, Western Ill.	2002	53	2,545	48.0
Brent Barth, VMI	2002	64	3,032	47.4
Harold Alexander, Appalachian St.	†1991	64	3,009	47.0
Chad Stanley, Stephen F. Austin	†1998	58	2,703	46.6
Eddie Johnson, Idaho St.	†2001	49	2,270	46.3

Mark Gould boomed 62 punts for an average of 48.2 yards a year ago to break the Division I-AA record for Northern Arizona.

Northern Arizona Sports Information

Player, Team	Year	No.	Yards	Avg.
Eddie Johnson, Idaho St.	2002	51	2,357	46.2
Terry Belden, Northern Ariz.	†1993	59	2,712	46.0
Case de Bruijn, Idaho St.	†1981	42	1,928	45.9
Colin Godfrey, Tennessee St.	†1990	57	2,614	45.9
Barry Cantrell, Fordham	†1997	65	2,980	45.9
Matthew Peot, Montana St.	†1999	48	2,195	45.7
Stuart Dodds, Montana St.	†1979	59	2,689	45.6
Pumpy Tudors, Chattanooga	1991	53	2,414	45.5
Matt Bushart, Southern U.	1998	50	2,260	45.2
Mark Gagliano, Southern Ill.	†1996	54	2,432	45.0
Paul Asbury, Southwest Tex. St.	1990	39	1,749	44.8
Brian Bivens, Murray St.	1999	43	1,926	44.8
Tom Sugg, Idaho	1991	53	2,371	44.7
Chad Stanley, Stephen F. Austin	1997	62	2,771	44.7
Mike Rice, Montana	†1985	62	2,771	44.7
Case de Bruijn, Idaho St.	1979	73	3,261	44.7
George Cimadevilla, East Tenn. St.	1985	66	2,948	44.7
Greg Davis, Citadel	†1986	61	2,723	44.6
Pumpy Tudors, Chattanooga	1990	63	2,810	44.6
Pat Velarde, Marshall	†1983	64	2,852	44.6
Ken Hinsley, Western Caro.	1998	57	2,536	44.5
Bart Bradley, Sam Houston St.	1986	44	1,957	44.5
Harold Alexander, Appalachian St.	†1992	55	2,445	44.5
Curtis Moody, Texas Southern	1985	64	2,844	44.4
Mike Leach, William & Mary	1998	45	1,997	44.4
Terry Belden, Northern Ariz.	1991	43	1,908	44.4
Brad Costello, Boston U.	1997	73	3,239	44.4
Terry Belden, Northern Ariz.	1992	59	2,614	44.3
Bret Wright, Southeastern La.	1983	66	2,923	44.3
George Cimadevilla, East Tenn. St.	1986	65	2,876	44.2
Ryan Klaus, Sam Houston St.	1998	72	3,182	44.2
David Beckford, Alabama St.	†2000	48	2,121	44.2
Ken Hinsley, Western Caro.	1997	46	2,032	44.2
Steve Thorns, Sacramento St.	1997	66	2,907	44.1
Matt Evans, Princeton	1998	54	2,377	44.0

*Record. †National champion.

ANNUAL CHAMPIONS

Year	Player, Team	Class	No.	Yards	Avg.
1978	Nick Pavich, Nevada	So.	47	1,939	41.3
1979	Stuart Dodds, Montana St.	Sr.	59	2,689	45.6
1980	Case de Bruijn, Idaho St.	Jr.	67	2,945	44.0
1981	Case de Bruijn, Idaho St.	Sr.	42	1,928	45.9
1982	John Christopher, Morehead St.	Sr.	93	4,084	43.9
1983	Pat Velarde, Marshall	Sr.	64	2,852	44.6
1984	Steve Kornegay, Western Caro.	Jr.	49	2,127	43.4
1985	Mike Rice, Montana	Jr.	62	2,771	44.7
1986	Greg Davis, Citadel	Sr.	61	2,723	44.6
1987	Eric Stein, Eastern Wash.	Sr.	74	3,193	43.2
1988	Mike McCabe, Illinois St.	Sr.	69	3,042	44.1
1989	Pumpy Tudors, Chattanooga	So.	65	2,817	43.3
1990	Colin Godfrey, Tennessee St.	So.	57	2,614	45.9
1991	Harold Alexander, Appalachian St.	Jr.	64	3,009	47.0
1992	Harold Alexander, Appalachian St.	Sr.	55	2,445	44.5
1993	Terry Belden, Northern Ariz.	Sr.	59	2,712	46.0
1994	Scott Holmes, Samford	Jr.	49	2,099	42.8
1995	Kevin O'Leary, Northern Ariz.	Sr.	44	1,881	42.8
1996	Mark Gagliano, Southern Ill.	Sr.	54	2,432	45.0
1997	Barry Cantrell, Fordham	Sr.	65	2,980	45.9
1998	Chad Stanley, Stephen F. Austin	Sr.	58	2,703	46.6
1999	Matthew Peot, Montana St.	Jr.	48	2,195	45.7
2000	David Beckford, Alabama St.	So.	48	2,121	44.2
2001	Eddie Johnson, Idaho St.	Jr.	49	2,270	46.3
2002	Mark Gould, Northern Ariz.	Jr.	62	2,987	*48.2

*Record.

Punt Returns

CAREER AVERAGE
(Minimum 1.2 Returns Per Game; Minimum 30 Returns)

Player, Team	Years	No.	Yards	Avg.
Willie Ware, Mississippi Val.	1982-85	61	1,003	*16.4
Buck Phillips, Western Ill.	1994-95	40	656	16.4
Tim Egerton, Delaware St.	1986-89	59	951	16.1
Mark Orlando, Towson	1991-94	41	644	15.7
Joseph Jefferson, Western Ky.	1998-01	53	809	15.3
John Armstrong, Richmond	1984-85	31	449	14.5
Darrick Brown, Maine	1995-98	56	807	14.4
Joey Jamison, Texas Southern	1997-99	88	1,269	14.4
Delvin Joyce, James Madison	1997-00	104	*1,488	14.3
Ricky Pearsall, Northern Ariz.	1994-97	39	546	14.0

Player, Team	Years	No.	Yards	Avg.
Undre Williams, Florida A&M	1995-97	31	429	13.8
Kenny Shedd, Northern Iowa	1989-92	79	1,081	13.7
Chris Berry, Morehead St.	1994-97	37	505	13.7
DeRonn Finley, Idaho St.	1998,00	46	639	13.6
Dejuan Alfonzo, Indiana St.	1997-99	40	539	13.5
Dione Tyler, Southeast Mo. St.	1994-95	39	523	13.4
Reggie Barlow, Alabama St.	1992-95	49	645	13.2
Joe Fuller, Northern Iowa	1982-85	69	888	12.9
Eric Yarber, Idaho	1984-85	32	406	12.7
Troy Brown, Marshall	1991-92	36	455	12.6
Steve Hadley, Fairfield	1997-00	50	630	12.6
Trumaine Johnson, Grambling	1979-82	53	662	12.5
Kerry Hayes, Western Caro.	1991-94	70	876	12.5
Goree White, Alcorn St.	1993-96	70	902	12.5
Tony Merriwether, North Texas	1982-83	41	507	12.4
Lamont Webb, Sacramento St.	1997-00	31	384	12.4
Eric Alden, Idaho St.	1992-93	31	383	12.4
Kevin Eiben, Bucknell	1997-00	51	626	12.3
Thaylen Armstead, Grambling	1989-91	44	540	12.3

*Record.

SEASON AVERAGE

(Minimum 1.2 Returns Per Game and Qualifiers for Championship)

Player, Team	Year	No.	Yards	Avg.
Curtis DeLoatch, N.C. A&T	†2001	20	530	*26.5
Terrence McGee, Northwestern St.	†2000	18	427	23.7
Tim Egerton, Delaware St.	†1988	16	368	23.0
Ryan Priest, Lafayette	†1982	12	271	22.6
Craig Hodge, Tennessee St.	†1987	19	398	21.0
Chris Berry, Morehead St.	†1997	13	273	21.0
Reggie Barlow, Alabama St.	†1995	12	249	20.8
Bashir Levingston, Eastern Wash.	†1998	16	333	20.8
John Armstrong, Richmond	†1985	19	391	20.6
KaRon Coleman, Stephen F. Austin	†1999	17	348	20.5
Mark Orlando, Towson	†1994	19	377	19.8
Willie Ware, Mississippi Val.	†1984	19	374	19.7
Buck Phillips, Western Ill.	1994	24	464	19.3
Junior Adams, Montana St.	2001	20	381	19.1
Zuriel Smith, Hampton	†2002	27	500	18.5
Mark Hurt, Alabama St.	1988	10	185	18.5
Howard Huckaby, Florida A&M	1988	26	478	18.4
Ashley Ambrose, Mississippi Val.	†1991	28	514	18.4
Quincy Miller, South Carolina St.	†1992	17	311	18.3
Barney Bussey, South Carolina St.	†1981	14	255	18.2
Willie Ware, Mississippi Val.	1985	31	561	18.1
Chris Darrington, Weber St.	†1986	16	290	18.1
Kerry Lawyer, Boise St.	1992	18	325	18.1
Ryan Jones, Dayton	2001	23	415	18.0
Drew Haddad, Buffalo	1998	23	410	17.8
Zuriel Smith, Hampton	2001	29	514	17.7
Kenny Shedd, Northern Iowa	1992	27	477	17.7
Claude Mathis, Southwest Tex.	1995	20	352	17.6
Clarence Alexander, Mississippi Val.	1986	22	380	17.3
Henry Richard, La.-Monroe	†1989	15	258	17.2
Joseph Jefferson, Western Ky.	2001	22	377	17.1
Ray Marshall, St. Peter's	†1993	10	171	17.1
Rich Musinski, William & Mary	2001	17	290	17.1
Delvin Joyce, James Madison	1997	17	289	17.0

*Record. †National champion.

ANNUAL CHAMPIONS

Year	Player, Team	Class	No.	Yards	Avg.
1978	Ray Smith, Northern Ariz.	Sr.	13	181	13.9
1979	Joseph Markus, Connecticut	Fr.	17	219	12.9
1980	Trumaine Johnson, Grambling	So.	††13	226	17.4
1981	Barney Bussey, South Carolina St.	So.	14	255	18.2
1982	Ryan Priest, Lafayette	Fr.	12	271	22.6
1983	Joe Fuller, Northern Iowa	So.	22	344	15.6
1984	Willie Ware, Mississippi Val.	Jr.	19	374	19.7
1985	John Armstrong, Richmond	Sr.	19	391	20.6
1986	Chris Darrington, Weber St.	Sr.	16	290	18.1
1987	Craig Hodge, Tennessee St.	Sr.	19	398	21.0
1988	Tim Egerton, Delaware St.	Jr.	16	368	23.0
1989	Henry Richard, La.-Monroe	Jr.	15	258	17.2
1990	Gary Harrell, Howard	Fr.	26	417	16.0
1991	Ashley Ambrose, Mississippi Val.	Sr.	28	514	18.4
1992	Quincy Miller, South Carolina St.	Jr.	17	311	18.3
1993	Ray Marshall, St. Peter's	Jr.	10	171	17.1
1994	Mark Orlando, Towson	Sr.	19	377	19.8
1995	Reggie Barlow, Alabama St.	Sr.	12	249	20.8
1996	Ricky Pearsall, Northern Ariz.	Jr.	29	490	16.9
1997	Chris Berry, Morehead St.	Sr.	13	273	21.0
1998	Bashir Levingston, Eastern Wash.	Sr.	16	333	20.8
1999	KaRon Coleman, Stephen F. Austin	Sr.	17	348	20.5

Year	Player, Team	Class	No.	Yards	Avg.
2000	Terrence McGee, Northwestern St.	So.	18	427	23.7
2001	Curtis DeLoatch, N.C. A&T	So.	20	530	*26.5
2002	Zuriel Smith, Hampton	Sr.	27	500	18.5

*Record. ††Declared champion; with one more return (making 1.3 per game) for zero yards, still would have highest average.

Kickoff Returns

CAREER AVERAGE

(Minimum 1.2 Returns Per Game; Minimum 30 Returns)

Player, Team	Years	No.	Yards	Avg.
Lamont Brightful, Eastern Wash.	1998-01	65	1,949	*30.0
Troy Brown, Marshall	1991-92	32	950	29.7
Charles Swann, Indiana St.	1989-91	45	1,319	29.3
Craig Richardson, Eastern Wash.	1983-86	71	2,021	28.5
Ramondo North, N.C. A&T	1998-00	48	1,356	28.3
Kenyatta Sparks, Southern U.	1992-95	39	1,100	28.2
Kerry Hayes, Western Caro.	1991-94	73	2,058	28.2
Daryl Holcombe, Eastern Ill.	1986-89	49	1,379	28.1
Dwight Robinson, James Madison	1990-93	51	1,434	28.1
Curtis Chappell, Howard	1984-87	42	1,177	28.0
Leon Brown, Eastern Ky.	1990-93	44	1,230	28.0
Josh Cole, Furman	1993-96	65	1,808	27.8
Tyree Talton, Northern Iowa	1995-98	72	1,999	27.8
Joe Rosato, Duquesne	1994-97	60	1,661	27.7
Marcus Durgin, Samford	1990-93	44	1,218	27.7
Cornelius Turner, Mississippi Val.	1992-94	50	1,379	27.6
Anthony Taylor, Northern Iowa	1992-95	30	821	27.4
Jerry Parrish, Eastern Ky.	1978-81	61	1,668	27.3
Tony James, Eastern Ky.	1982-84	57	1,552	27.2
Ricky Ellis, St. Mary's (Cal.)	1994-96	31	836	27.0
Frank Selto, Idaho St.	1986-87	30	803	26.8
Chris Hickman, La.-Monroe	1991-92	30	798	26.6
Chris Pollard, Dartmouth	1986-88	52	1,376	26.5
Tyrone Butterfield, Tennessee St.	1997-98	44	1,164	26.5
John Jarvis, Howard	1986-88	39	1,031	26.4
Ronald Scott, Southern U.	1982-85	38	1,003	26.4
Vernon Williams, Eastern Wash.	1986-88	40	1,052	26.3
Rob Tesch, Montana St.	1989-92	50	1,317	26.3
Rick Sarille, Wagner	$1995-99	64	1,682	26.3
Steve Ortman, Pennsylvania	1982-84	31	808	26.1
John Armstrong, Richmond	1984-85	32	826	25.8
Renard Coleman, Montana	1985-88	57	1,465	25.7
Michael Haynes, Northern Ariz.	1986-87	36	925	25.7
Jeb Dougherty, San Diego	1993-96	62	1,589	25.6
Kevin Gainer, Bethune-Cookman	1988-90	42	1,070	25.5
Mareno Philyaw, Troy St.	1996-99	32	816	25.5
Archie Herring, Youngstown St.	1987-90	79	2,005	25.4
Joey Jamison, Texas Southern	1997-99	50	1,266	25.3
Kenny Shedd, Northern Iowa	1989-92	54	1,359	25.2
Brian Westbrook, Villanova	1997-98, 00-01	91	2,289	25.2
Damon Boddie, Montana	1993-94	49	1,232	25.1
Orshawante Bryant, Portland St.	1997-00	72	1,806	25.1
Jerry Azumah, New Hampshire	1995-98	41	1,025	25.0
Joey Stockton, Western Ky.	1994-97	87	2,175	25.0

*Record. $See Page 8 for explanation.

SEASON AVERAGE

(Minimum 1.2 Returns Per Game and Qualifiers for Championship)

Player, Team	Year	No.	Yards	Avg.
David Fraterrigo, Canisius	†1993	13	485	*37.3
Brian Bratton, Furman	†2001	14	521	37.2
Kerry Hayes, Western Caro.	1993	16	584	36.5
Cordell Roane, Richmond	†1999	13	470	36.2
Ryan Zimpleman, Butler	†1998	28	972	34.7
Craig Richardson, Eastern Wash.	†1984	21	729	34.7
Randy Moss, Marshall	†1996	14	484	34.6
Avion Black, Tennessee St.	1999	23	786	34.2
Lamont Brightful, Eastern Wash.	1999	26	882	33.9
Errin Hatwood, St. John's (N.Y.)	†1994	12	401	33.4
Marcus Durgin, Samford	†1992	15	499	33.3
Richard Holland, VMI	†2000	19	628	33.1
Rory Lee, Western Ill.	1993	16	527	32.9
Corey Alexander, Texas Southern	†2002	19	615	32.4
Cortland Finnegan, Samford	2002	23	741	32.2
Lamont Brightful, Eastern Wash.	2000	15	483	32.2
Dave Meggett, Towson	†1988	13	418	32.2
Josh Cole, Furman	†1995	17	546	32.1
Charles Swann, Indiana St.	†1990	20	642	32.1
Tyree Talton, Northern Iowa	1996	22	703	32.0

DIVISION I-AA

Player, Team	Year	No.	Yards	Avg.
Archie Herring, Youngstown St.	1990	18	575	31.9
Dwight Robinson, James Madison	1994	16	510	31.9
Davlin Mullen, Western Ky.	†1982	18	574	31.9
Todd Cleveland, UCF	1994	15	476	31.7
Naylon Albritton, South Carolina St.	1993	15	475	31.7
Jermine Sharp, Southern U.	1995	16	504	31.5
Andy Swafford, Troy St.	†1997	14	440	31.4
Ozzie Young, Valparaiso	1994	17	533	31.4
Danny Copeland, Eastern Ky.	†1986	26	812	31.2
Chris Chappell, Howard	1986	17	528	31.1
Chuck Nwokocha, Harvard	2000	11	341	31.0
Thomas Haskins, VMI	1994	15	464	30.9
Toby Moeves, Morehead St.	2001	17	522	30.7
Dave Loehle, New Hampshire	†1978	15	460	30.7
Paul Ashby, Alabama St.	†1991	17	520	30.6

*Record. †National champion.

ANNUAL CHAMPIONS

Year	Player, Team	Class	No.	Yards	Avg.
1978	Dave Loehle, New Hampshire	Jr.	15	460	30.7
1979	Garry Pearson, Massachusetts	Fr.	12	348	29.0
1980	Danny Thomas, N.C. A&T	Fr.	15	381	25.4
1981	Jerry Parrish, Eastern Ky.	Sr.	18	534	29.7

Year	Player, Team	Class	No.	Yards	Avg.
1982	Davlin Mullen, Western Ky.	Sr.	18	574	31.9
1983	Tony James, Eastern Ky.	Jr.	17	511	30.1
1984	Craig Richardson, Eastern Wash.	So.	21	729	34.7
1985	Rodney Payne, Murray St.	Fr.	16	464	29.0
1986	Danny Copeland, Eastern Ky.	Jr.	26	812	31.2
1987	Howard Huckaby, Florida A&M	So.	20	602	30.1
1988	Dave Meggett, Towson	Sr.	13	418	32.2
1989	Scott Thomas, Liberty	Fr.	13	373	28.7
1990	Charles Swann, Indiana St.	Jr.	20	642	32.1
1991	Paul Ashby, Alabama St.	Jr.	17	520	30.6
1992	Marcus Durgin, Samford	Jr.	15	499	33.3
1993	David Fraterrigo, Canisius	Sr.	13	485	*37.3
1994	Errin Hatwood, St. John's (N.Y.)	Sr.	12	401	33.4
1995	Josh Cole, Furman	Jr.	17	546	32.1
1996	Randy Moss, Marshall	Fr.	14	484	34.6
1997	Andy Swafford, Troy St.	Sr.	14	440	31.4
1998	Ryan Zimpleman, Butler	So.	28	972	34.7
1999	Cordell Roane, Richmond	Fr.	13	470	36.2
2000	Richard Holland, VMI	Sr.	19	628	33.1
2001	Brian Bratton, Furman	Fr.	14	521	37.2
2002	Corey Alexander, Texas Southern	So.	19	615	32.4

*Record.

All-Purpose Yards

CAREER YARDS PER GAME
(Minimum 3,200 Yards)

Player, Team	Years	G	Rush	Rcv.	Int.	PR	KOR	Yds.	Yd. PG
Brian Westbrook, Villanova	1997-98, 00-01	44	4,298	2,582	0	343	2,289	*9,512	*216.2
Jerry Azumah, New Hampshire	1995-98	41	6,193	1,153	0	5	1,025	8,376	204.3
Arnold Mickens, Butler	1994-95	20	3,813	47	0	0	87	3,947	197.4
Tim Hall, Robert Morris	1994-95	19	2,908	793	0	0	0	3,701	194.8
Reggie Greene, Siena	1994-97	36	5,415	274	0	53	1,217	6,959	193.3
Dave Meggett, Towson	1987-88	18	1,658	788	0	212	745	3,403	189.1
Archie Amerson, Northern Ariz.	1995-96	22	3,196	484	0	0	382	4,062	184.6
Kenny Gamble, Colgate	1984-8/	42	5,220	536	0	104	1,763	7,623	181.5
Rick Sarille, Wagner	$1995-99	41	5,290	365	0	0	1,682	7,337	179.0
Aaron Stecker, Western Ill.	1997-98	20	3,081	427	0	0	0	3,508	175.4
Rich Erenberg, Colgate	1982-83	21	2,618	423	0	268	315	3,624	172.6
Claude Mathis, Southwest Tex. St.	1994-97	44	4,691	744	0	635	1,353	7,423	168.7
Thomas Haskins, VMI	1993-96	44	5,355	179	0	216	1,661	7,411	168.4
Ozzie Young, Valparaiso	1993-95	29	1,576	1,123	0	418	1,728	4,845	167.1
Fine Unga, Weber St.	1987-88	22	2,298	391	0	7	967	3,663	166.5
Adrian Peterson, Ga. Southern	1998-01	42	*6,559	225	0	0	0	6,784	161.5
Charles Dunn, Portland St.	1998-00	33	4,831	489	0	0	0	5,320	161.2
Gill Fenerty, Holy Cross	1983-85	30	3,618	477	0	1	731	4,827	160.9
Keith Elias, Princeton	1991-93	30	4,208	508	0	0	25	4,741	158.0
Don Wilkerson, Southwest Tex. St.	1993-94	22	2,356	255	0	83	757	3,451	156.9
Marcel Shipp, Massachusetts	1997-00	43	5,383	932	0	0	392	6,707	156.0
Kito Lockwood, Wagner	1993-95	25	2,576	891	0	0	420	3,887	155.5
Tyrone Butterfield, Tennessee St.	1997-98	22	12	2,182	0	44	1,164	3,402	154.6
Jesse Chatman, Eastern Wash.	1999-01	31	4,173	614	0	0	4	4,791	154.5
Barry Bourassa, New Hampshire	1989-92	39	2,960	1,307	0	306	1,370	5,943	152.4
Charles Tharp, Western Ill.	1999-00	22	2,834	454	0	23	0	3,311	150.5
Judd Garrett, Princeton	1987-89	30	3,109	1,385	0	0	10	4,510	150.3
Treamelle Taylor, Nevada	1987-90	22	0	1,926	0	662	687	3,275	148.9
Troy Brown, Marshall	1991-92	22	138	1,716	0	455	950	3,259	148.1
Andre Garron, New Hampshire	1982-85	30	2,901	809	0	8	651	4,369	145.6
Carl Boyd, Northern Iowa	1983, 85-87	34	2,735	1,987	0	0	183	4,905	144.3
Sean Morey, Brown	1995-98	40	131	3,850	0	9	1,736	5,726	143.2
Donte Small, Duquesne	1998-01	42	4,260	306	0	0	1,426	5,992	142.7
Delvin Joyce, James Madison	1997-00	39	1,261	959	0	*1,488	1,830	5,538	142.0
Merril Hoge, Idaho St.	1983-86	39	2,713	1,734	0	1	1,005	5,453	139.8
Rich Lemon, Bucknell	1993-96	43	4,742	961	0	99	150	5,952	138.4
Jason Corle, Towson	1996-99	39	3,601	1,725	0	26	30	5,382	138.0
Pete Mandley, Northern Ariz.	1979-80, 82-83	43	436	2,598	11	901	1,979	5,925	137.8
Erik Marsh, Lafayette	1991-94	42	4,834	383	0	76	490	5,783	137.7
Joey Stockton, Western Ky.	1994-97	36	248	1,878	0	627	2,175	4,928	136.9
Kerry Hayes, Western Caro.	1991-94	41	75	2,594	0	876	2,058	5,603	136.7
Destry Wright, Jackson St.	1997-99	34	4,049	323	0	121	148	4,641	136.5
Frank Hawkins, Nevada	1977-80	43	5,333	519	0	0	0	5,852	136.1
Derrick Harmon, Cornell	1981-83	28	3,074	679	0	5	42	3,800	135.7
Dorron Hunter, Morehead St.	1977-80	38	1,336	1,320	0	510	1,970	5,136	135.2

*Record. $See Page 8 for explanation.

SEASON YARDS PER GAME

Player, Team	Year	Rush	Rcv.	Int.	PR	KOR	Yds.	Yd. PG
Brian Westbrook, Villanova	†1998	1,046	1,144	0	192	644	*3,026	*275.1
Brian Westbrook, Villanova	†2000	1,220	724	0	0	1,048	2,992	272.0
Brian Westbrook, Villanova	†2001	1,603	658	0	122	440	2,823	256.6
Jerry Azumah, New Hampshire	1998	2,195	218	0	5	308	2,726	247.8
Reggie Greene, Siena	†1996	1,719	50	0	0	337	2,106	234.0
Jesse Chatman, Eastern Wash.	2001	2,096	424	0	0	0	2,520	229.1
Arnold Mickens, Butler	†1994	2,255	7	0	0	0	2,262	226.2
Reggie Greene, Siena	†1997	1,719	50	0	0	158	2,009	223.2
Charles Roberts, Sacramento St.	1998	*2,260	79	0	0	91	2,430	220.9
Archie Amerson, Northern Ariz.	1996	2,079	262	0	0	88	2,429	220.8
Kenny Gamble, Colgate	†1986	1,816	178	0	40	391	2,425	220.5
Reggie Greene, Siena	†1995	1,461	77	0	53	363	1,954	217.1
Stephan Lewis, New Hampshire	2001	1,390	527	0	0	471	2,388	217.1
Johnnie Gray, Weber St.	2001	1,571	446	0	0	369	2,386	216.9
Eddie Conti, Delaware	1998	-2	*1,712	0	156	502	2,368	215.3
Marcel Shipp, Massachusetts	1998	1,949	288	0	0	100	2,337	212.5
Michael Clemons, William & Mary	1986	1,065	516	0	330	423	2,334	212.2
Rick Sarille, Wagner	†1999	1,373	226	0	0	475	2,074	207.4
Tony Vinson, Towson	†1993	2,016	57	0	0	0	2,073	207.3
Derrick Cullors, Murray St.	1995	1,765	312	0	0	201	2,278	207.1
Clarence Matthews, Northwestern St.	1995	1,384	194	0	145	554	2,277	207.0
Claude Mathis, Southwest Tex. St.	1995	1,286	315	0	352	308	2,261	205.6
Anthony Jordan, Samford	1994	924	400	0	169	767	2,260	205.5
Sean Bennett, Evansville	1997	1,668	260	0	81	34	2,043	204.3
Aaron Stecker, Western Ill.	1997	1,957	288	0	0	0	2,245	204.1
Rich Erenberg, Colgate	†1983	1,883	214	0	126	18	2,241	203.7
Stephan Lewis, New Hampshire	†2002	1,152	419	0	13	645	2,229	202.6
Kenny Bynum, South Carolina St.	1996	1,649	118	0	1	255	2,023	202.3
Jerry Azumah, New Hampshire	1997	1,572	297	0	0	351	2,220	201.8
Charles Roberts, Sacramento St.	1999	2,082	108	0	12	0	2,202	200.2

*Record. †National champion.

CAREER YARDS

Player, Team	Years	Rush	Rcv.	Int.	PR	KOR	Yds.	Yd. PP
Brian Westbrook, Villanova	1997-98, 00-01	4,298	2,528	0	343	2,289	*9,512	9.3
Jerry Azumah, New Hampshire	1995-98	6,193	1,153	0	5	1,025	8,376	7.4
Kenny Gamble, Colgate	1984-87	5,220	536	0	104	1,763	7,623	7.0
Claude Mathis, Southwest Tex. St.	1994-97	4,691	744	0	635	1,353	7,423	7.0
Thomas Haskins, VMI	1993-96	5,355	179	0	216	1,661	7,411	7.2
Rick Sarille, Wagner	$1995-99	5,290	365	0	0	1,682	7,337	6.9
Charles Roberts, Sacramento St.	1997-00	6,553	382	0	12	165	7,112	6.0
Reggie Greene, Siena	1994-97	5,415	274	0	53	1,217	6,959	7.1
Adrian Peterson, Ga. Southern	1998-01	*6,559	225	0	0	0	6,784	6.7
Marcel Shipp, Massachusetts	1997-00	5,383	932	0	0	392	6,707	5.7
Donte Small, Duquesne	1998-01	4,260	306	0	0	1,426	5,992	6.4
Rich Lemon, Bucknell	1993-96	4,742	961	0	99	150	5,952	5.2
Barry Bourassa, New Hampshire	1989-92	2,960	1,307	0	306	1,370	5,943	7.5
Pete Mandley, Northern Ariz.	1979-80, 82-83	436	2,598	11	901	1,979	5,925	14.8
Frank Hawkins, Nevada	1977-80	5,333	519	0	0	0	5,852	5.8
Erik Marsh, Lafayette	1991-94	4,834	383	0	76	490	5,783	5.2
Matt Cannon, Southern Utah	1997-00	5,489	236	0	0	17	5,742	7.5
Eddie Conti, Delaware	1994-98	-7	3,496	0	802	1,446	5,737	17.1
Sean Morey, Brown	1995-98	131	3,850	0	9	1,736	5,726	15.7
Kerry Hayes, Western Caro.	1991-94	5	2,594	0	876	2,058	5,603	*19.1
Jamie Jones, Eastern Ill.	1988-91	3,466	816	0	66	1,235	5,583	6.2
Chris Parker, Marshall	1992-95	4,571	838	0	0	133	5,542	6.5
Delvin Joyce, James Madison	1997-00	1,261	959	0	*1,488	1,830	5,538	9.3
Sherriden May, Idaho	1991-94	3,748	926	0	153	646	5,473	6.9
Louis Ivory, Furman	1998-01	5,353	112	0	0	0	5,465	6.3
Merril Hoge, Idaho St.	1983-86	2,713	1,734	0	1	1,005	5,453	6.6
Orshawante Bryant, Portland St.	1997-00	173	3,449	0	0	1,806	5,428	16.2
Herman Hunter, Tennessee St.	1981-84	1,049	1,129	0	974	2,258	5,410	10.5
Jason Corle, Towson	1996-99	3,601	1,725	0	26	30	5,382	5.5
David Wright, Indiana St.	1992-95	4,181	255	0	0	904	5,340	6.2
Charles Dunn, Portland St.	1998-00	4,831	489	0	0	0	5,320	5.8
Cedric Minter, Boise St.	1977-80	4,475	525	0	49	267	5,316	6.5
Charvez Foger, Nevada	1985-88	4,484	821	0	0	0	5,305	5.7
Garry Pearson, Massachusetts	1979-82	3,859	466	0	0	952	5,277	5.9
John Settle, Appalachian St.	1983-86	4,409	526	0	0	319	5,254	5.3
Joe Rosato, Duquesne	1994-97	80	2,360	0	1,036	1,661	5,137	15.6
Dorron Hunter, Morehead St.	1977-80	1,336	1,320	0	510	1,970	5,136	9.6

*Record. $See Page 8 for explanation.

SEASON YARDS

Player, Team	Year	Rush	Rcv.	Int.	PR	KOR	Yds.	Yd. PP
Brian Westbrook, Villanova	†1998	1,046	1,144	0	192	644	*3,026	9.2
Brian Westbrook, Villanova	†2000	1,220	724	0	0	1,048	2,992	10.8
Brian Westbrook, Villanova	†2001	1,603	658	0	122	440	2,823	8.5
Jerry Azumah, New Hampshire	1998	2,195	218	0	5	308	2,726	7.3
Jesse Chatman, Eastern Wash.	2001	2,096	424	0	0	0	2,520	7.8
Charles Roberts, Sacramento St.	1998	*2,260	79	0	0	91	2,430	6.1
Archie Amerson, Northern Ariz.	1996	2,079	262	0	0	88	2,429	6.9

DIVISION I-AA

Player, Team	Year	Rush	Rcv.	Int.	PR	KOR	Yds.	Yd. PP
Kenny Gamble, Colgate	†1986	1,816	178	0	40	391	2,425	7.1
Stephan Lewis, New Hampshire	2001	1,390	527	0	0	471	2,388	7.4
Johnnie Gray, Weber St.	2001	1,571	446	0	0	369	2,386	6.5
Eddie Conti, Delaware	1998	-2	*1,712	0	156	502	2,368	18.2
Marcel Shipp, Massachusetts	1998	1,949	288	0	0	100	2,337	6.6
Michael Clemons, William & Mary	1986	1,065	516	0	330	423	2,334	6.7
Derrick Cullors, Murray St.	1995	1,765	312	0	0	201	2,278	7.6
Clarence Matthews, Northwestern St.	1995	1,384	194	0	145	554	2,277	7.7
Andre Raymond, Eastern Ill.	2002	612	672	0	112	872	2,268	9.3
Arnold Mickens, Butler	†1994	2,255	7	0	0	0	2,262	5.5
Claude Mathis, Southwest Tex. St.	1995	1,286	315	0	352	308	2,261	7.3
Anthony Jordan, Samford	1994	924	400	0	169	767	2,260	10.8
Aaron Stecker, Western Ill.	1997	1,957	288	0	0	0	2,245	6.9
Rich Erenberg, Colgate	†1983	1,883	214	0	126	18	2,241	6.7
Stephan Lewis, New Hampshire	†2002	1,152	419	0	13	645	2,229	7.1
Jerry Azumah, New Hampshire	1997	1,572	297	0	0	351	2,220	7.2
Charles Roberts, Sacramento St.	1999	2,082	108	0	12	0	2,202	6.9

*Record. †National champion.

ALL-PURPOSE SINGLE-GAME HIGHS

Yds.	Player, Team (Opponent)	Date
467	Joey Stockton, Western Ky. (Austin Peay)	Sept. 16, 1995
463	Michael Lerch, Princeton (Brown)	Oct. 12, 1991
458	Brian Westbrook, Villanova (Delaware)	Nov. 18, 2000
453	Herman Hunter, Tennessee St. (Mississippi Val.)	Nov. 13, 1982
447	Maurice Hicks, N.C. A&T (Morgan St.)	Oct. 6, 2001
437	Ryan Fuqua, Portland St. (Eastern Wash.)	Nov. 10, 2001
428	Brian Westbrook, Villanova (Pittsburgh)	Sept. 5, 1998
420	Reggie Greene, Siena (St. John's [N.Y.])	Nov. 2, 1996
409	Josh Rue, Duquesne (Canisius)	Nov. 17, 2001
409	Charles Roberts, Sacramento St. (Idaho St.)	Nov. 6, 1999
405	Brian Westbrook, Villanova (James Madison)	Oct. 6, 2001
401	Eddie Conti, Delaware (Northeastern)	Oct. 3, 1998
401	Eddie Conti, Delaware (Connecticut)	Nov. 7, 1998
395	Scott Oliaro, Cornell (Yale)	Nov. 3, 1990
386	Brian Westbrook, Villanova (Hofstra)	Nov. 10, 2001
386	Gill Fenerty, Holy Cross (Columbia)	Oct. 29, 1983
378	Joe Delaney, Northwestern St. (Nicholls St.)	Oct. 28, 1978
376	Kassim Osgood, Cal Poly (Northern Iowa)	Nov. 4, 2000
373	Aaron Stecker, Western Ill. (Southern Ill.)	Nov. 1, 1997
373	William Arnold, Jackson St. (Texas Southern)	Nov. 6, 1993
372	Gary Harrell, Howard (Morgan St.)	Nov. 3, 1990
372	Treamelle Taylor, Nevada (Montana)	Oct. 14, 1989
370	Ronald Jean, Lehigh (Bucknell)	Nov. 13, 1999
369	Flip Johnson, McNeese St. (La.-Lafayette)	Nov. 15, 1986
367	Chris Darrington, Weber St. (Idaho St.)	Oct. 25, 1986
365	Erwin Matthews, Richmond (Delaware)	Sept. 26, 1987
364	Stephan Lewis, New Hampshire (Massachusetts)	Oct. 13, 2001
361	Patrick Robinson, Tennessee St. (Jackson St.)	Sept. 12, 1992
358	Claude Mathis, Southwest Tex. St. (Eastern Wash.)	Sept. 7, 1995
357	Tony Vinson, Towson (Bucknell)	Nov. 13, 1993
353	Maurice Hicks, N.C. A&T (South Carolina St.)	Nov. 18, 2000
353	Bashir Levingston, Eastern Wash. (Sacramento St.)	Oct. 31, 1998
352	Jason Anderson, Eastern Wash. (Montana)	Sept. 17, 1994
352	Andre Garron, New Hampshire (Lehigh)	Oct. 15, 1983
351	Charlie Adams, Hofstra (William & Mary)	Oct. 6, 2001

ANNUAL CHAMPIONS

Year	Player, Team	Class	Rush	Rcv.	Int.	PR	KOR	Yds.	Yd. PG
1978	Frank Hawkins, Nevada	So.	1,445	211	0	0	0	1,656	165.6
1979	Frank Hawkins, Nevada	Jr.	1,683	123	0	0	0	1,806	164.2
1980	Ken Jenkins, Bucknell	Jr.	1,270	293	0	65	256	1,884	188.4
1981	Garry Pearson, Massachusetts	Jr.	1,026	105	0	0	450	1,581	175.7
1982	Pete Mandley, Northern Ariz.	Jr.	36	1,067	0	344	532	1,979	179.9
1983	Rich Erenberg, Colgate	Sr.	1,883	214	0	126	18	2,241	203.7
1984	Gene Lake, Delaware St.	Jr.	1,722	37	0	0	0	1,759	175.9
1985	Gill Fenerty, Holy Cross	Sr.	1,368	187	0	1	414	1,970	197.0
1986	Kenny Gamble, Colgate	Jr.	1,816	178	0	40	391	2,425	220.5
1987	Dave Meggett, Towson	Jr.	814	572	0	78	327	1,791	199.0
1988	Otis Washington, Western Caro.	Sr.	66	907	0	0	1,113	2,086	189.6
1989	Dominic Corr, Eastern Wash.	Sr.	796	52	0	0	807	1,655	183.9
1990	Barry Bourassa, New Hampshire	So.	957	276	0	133	368	1,734	192.7
1991	Barry Bourassa, New Hampshire	Jr.	1,130	426	0	0	596	2,152	195.6
1992	David Wright, Indiana St.	Fr.	1,313	108	0	0	593	2,014	183.1
1993	Tony Vinson, Towson	Sr.	2,016	57	0	0	0	2,073	207.3
1994	Arnold Mickens, Butler	Jr.	2,255	7	0	0	0	2,262	226.2
1995	Reggie Greene, Siena	So.	1,461	77	0	53	363	1,954	217.1
1996	Reggie Greene, Siena	Jr.	1,719	50	0	0	337	2,106	234.0
1997	Reggie Greene, Siena	Sr.	1,778	73	0	0	158	2,009	223.2
1998	Brian Westbrook, Villanova	So.	1,046	1,144	0	192	644	*3,026	*275.1
1999	Rick Sarille, Wagner	Sr.	1,373	226	0	0	475	2,074	207.4
2000	Brian Westbrook, Villanova	Jr.	1,220	724	0	0	1,048	2,992	272.0
2001	Brian Westbrook, Villanova	Sr.	1,603	658	0	122	440	2,823	256.6
2002	Stephan Lewis, New Hampshire	Sr.	1,152	419	0	13	645	2,229	202.6

*Record.

Field Goals

CAREER FIELD GOALS

Player, Team	Years	Total	Pct.	Under 40 Yds.	40 Plus	Long
Marty Zendejas, Nevada (S)	1984-87	*72-90	.800	42-45	30-45	54
Kirk Roach, Western Caro. (S)	1984-87	71-*102	.696	45-49	26-53	57
Tony Zendejas, Nevada (S)	1981-83	70-86	*.814	45-49	25-37	58
Scott Shields, Weber St. (S)	1995-98	67-90	.744	48-55	19-35	55
Brian Mitchell, Marshall/Northern Iowa (S)	1987, 89-91	64-81	.790	48-55	16-26	57
Dave Ettinger, Hofstra (S)	1994-97	62-93	.667	37-48	24-45	54
Todd Kurz, Illinois St. (S)	1993-96	59-87	.678	40-53	19-34	51
Jose Larios, McNeese St. (S)	1992-95	57-89	.640	47-57	10-32	47
Steve Christie, William & Mary (S)	1986-89	57-83	.686	39-49	18-34	53
Teddy Garcia, La.-Monroe (S)	1984-87	56-88	.636	35-43	21-45	55
Bjorn Nittmo, Appalachian St. (S)	1985-88	55-74	.743	35-40	20-34	54
Shonz LaFrenz, McNeese St. (S)	1996-99	52-78	.667	44-65	8-13	46
Kelly Potter, Middle Tenn. (S)	1981-84	52-78	.667	37-49	15-29	57
Paul McFadden, Youngstown St. (S)	1980-83	52-90	.578	28-42	24-48	54
Mike Black, Boise St. (S)	1988-91	51-75	.680	35-43	16-32	48
Jeff Wilkins, Youngstown St. (S)	1990-93	50-73	.685	33-38	17-35	54
Tim Foley, Ga. Southern (S)	1984-87	50-62	.806	32-37	18-25	**63
Paul Politi, Illinois St. (S)	1983-86	50-78	.641	34-48	16-30	50
Wayne Boyer, Southwest Mo. St. (S)	1993-96	49-71	.690	36-45	13-26	57
Chuck Rawlinson, Stephen F. Austin (S)	1988-91	49-69	.710	34-43	15-26	58
Thayne Doyle, Idaho (S)	1988-91	49-75	.653	35-51	14-24	52
Matt Stover, Louisiana Tech (S)	1986-88	49-68	.721	29-34	20-34	57
Scott Roper, Texas-Arlington/Arkansas St. (S)	1985, 86-87	49-75	.653	35-43	14-32	**63
Paul Hickert, Murray St. (S)	1984-87	49-79	.620	34-48	15-31	62
Dewey Klein, Marshall (S)	1988-91	48-66	.727	37-47	11-19	54
John Dowling, Youngstown St. (S)	1984-87	48-76	.632	36-44	12-32	49
Brian Shallcross, William & Mary (S)	1994-97	47-73	.644	41-54	6-19	49
Kirk Duce, Montana (S)	1988-91	47-78	.603	37-51	10-27	51
Billy Hayes, Sam Houston St. (S)	1985-88	47-71	.662	37-55	10-16	54
Steve Largent, Eastern Ill. (S)	1992-95	46-73	.630	30-38	16-35	53
Roger Ruzek, Weber St. (S)	1979-82	46-78	.590	28-37	18-41	51

*Record. **Record tied. (S)Soccer-style kicker.

SEASON FIELD GOALS

Player, Team	Year	Total	Pct.	Under 40 Yds.	40 Plus	Long
Tony Zendejas, Nevada (S)	†1982	**26-**33	.788	18-20	8-13	52
Brian Mitchell, Northern Iowa (S)	†1990	**26-27	*.963	23-23	3-4	45
MacKenzie Hoambrecker, Northern Iowa (S)	†2002	25-28	.893	17-19	8-9	59
Wayne Boyer, Southwest Mo. St. (S)	†1996	25-30	.833	16-18	9-12	57
George Benyola, Louisiana Tech (S)	†1985	24-31	.774	15-18	9-13	53
Kirk Roach, Western Caro. (S)	†1986	24-28	.857	17-17	7-11	52
Tony Zendejas, Nevada (S)	†1983	23-29	.793	14-15	9-14	58
Goran Lingmerth, Northern Ariz. (S)	1986	23-29	.793	16-19	7-10	55
Matt Vick, Chattanooga (S)	†2000	22-26	.846	17-19	5-7	42
Marty Zendejas, Nevada (S)	†1984	22-27	.815	12-13	10-14	52
Mike Dodd, Boise St. (S)	†1992	22-31	.710	16-21	6-10	50
Jose Larios, McNeese St. (S)	†1993	22-28	.786	19-21	3-7	47
David Ettinger, Hofstra (S)	†1995	22-**33	.667	17-22	5-11	54
Rob Hart, Murray St. (S)	1996	22-27	.815	18-20	4-7	52
Tony Zendejas, Nevada (S)	†1981	21-24	.875	13-14	8-10	55
Scott Roper, Arkansas St. (S)	1986	21-28	.750	15-17	6-11	50
Matt Stover, Louisiana Tech (S)	1986	21-25	.840	15-15	6-10	53
Kevin McKelvie, Nevada (S)	1990	21-24	.875	16-17	5-7	52
Travis Brawner, Southwest Mo. St. (S)	†1997	21-28	.750	15-17	6-11	52
Justin Langan, Western Ill. (S)	2002	20-27	.741	13-14	7-13	53
Billy Cundiff, Drake (S)	2000	20-27	.741	12-14	8-13	62
Teddy Garcia, La.-Monroe (S)	1987	20-28	.714	10-11	10-17	55
Steve Christie, William & Mary (S)	†1989	20-29	.690	16-17	4-12	53
Darren Goodman, Idaho St. (S)	1990	20-28	.714	12-14	8-14	53

*Record. **Record tied. †National champion. (S) Soccer-style kicker.

Northern Iowa's MacKenzie Hoambrecker made 25 field goals in 2002, just one shy of the Division I-AA record.

DIVISION I-AA

ANNUAL CHAMPIONS
(Ranked on Per-Game Average)

Year	Player, Team	Total	PG	Pct.
1978	Tom Sarette, Boise St. (S)	12-20	1.2	.600
1979	Wilfredo Rosales, Alcorn St. (S)	13-20	1.3	.650
	Sandro Vitiello, Massachusetts (S)	13-22	1.3	.591
1980	Scott Norwood, James Madison (S)	15-21	1.5	.714
1981	Tony Zendejas, Nevada (S)	21-24	1.9	.875
1982	Tony Zendejas, Nevada (S)	**26-**33	**2.4	.788
1983	Tony Zendejas, Nevada (S)	23-29	2.1	.793
1984	Marty Zendejas, Nevada (S)	22-27	2.0	.815
1985	George Benyola, Louisiana Tech (S)	24-31	2.2	.774
1986	Kirk Roach, Western Caro. (S)	24-28	2.2	.857
1987	Micky Penaflor, Northern Ariz. (S)	19-27	1.9	.704
1988	Chris Lutz, Princeton (S)	19-24	1.9	.792
1989	Steve Christie, William & Mary (S)	20-29	1.8	.690
1990	Brian Mitchell, Northern Iowa (S)	**26-27	**2.4	*.963
1991	Brian Mitchell, Northern Iowa (S)	19-24	1.7	.792
1992	Mike Dodd, Boise St. (S)	22-31	2.0	.710
1993	Jose Larios, McNeese St. (S)	22-28	2.0	.786
1994	Andy Glockner, Pennsylvania (S)	14-20	1.6	.700
1995	David Ettinger, Hofstra (S)	22-**33	2.0	.667
1996	Wayne Boyer, Southwest Mo. St. (S)	25-30	2.3	.833
1997	Travis Brawner, Southwest Mo. St. (S)	21-28	1.9	.750
1998	Mike Goldstein, Northern Ariz. (S)	16-23	1.5	.696
	Scott Shields, Weber St. (S)	16-23	1.5	.696
	Bill Gramatica, South Fla. (S)	16-24	1.5	.667
	Chad Johnson, Hofstra (S)	16-27	1.5	.593
	Joe Lopez, Western Ill. (S)	16-28	1.5	.571
1999	Brett Sterba, William & Mary (S)	18-23	1.6	.783
2000	Matt Vick, Chattanooga (S)	22-26	2.0	.846
2001	Brian Morgan, Grambling (S)	18-25	1.64	.720
2002	MacKenzie Hoambrecker, Northern Iowa (S).	25-28	2.3	.893

*Record. **Record tied. (S) Soccer-style kicker.*

All-Time Longest Plays

(Since 1978 for Division I-AA records)
Since 1941, official maximum length of all plays fixed at 100 yards for every division.

RUSHING

Yds.	Player, Team (Opponent)	Year
99	Jermaine Creighton, St. John's (N.Y.) (Siena)	1996
99	Jim Varick, Monmouth (Sacred Heart)	1994
99	Phillip Collins, Southwest Mo. St. (Western Ill.)	1989
99	Pedro Bacon, Western Ky. (West Ala.)	1986
99	Hubert Owens, Mississippi Val. (Ark.-Pine Bluff)	1980
98	Jon Underhill, Jacksonville (Greensboro)	1998
98	Johnny Gordon, Nevada (Montana St.)	1984
97	Pat Williams, Delaware (West Chester)	1995
97	Norman Bradford, Grambling (Prairie View)	1992
97	David Clark, Dartmouth (Harvard)	1989
97	David Clark, Dartmouth (Princeton)	1988
96	Jerry Azumah, New Hampshire (Connecticut)	1996
96	Jim Pizano, Massachusetts (Rhode Island)	1996
96	Kelvin Anderson, Southeast Mo. St. (Murray St.)	1992
96	Andre Lockhart, Chattanooga (East Tenn. St.)	1986
95	Corey Hill, Colgate (Brown)	1996
95	Brett Chappell, Western Caro. (Elon)	1995
95	Tim Hall, Robert Morris (Gannon)	1994
95	Jeff Sawulski, Siena (Iona)	1993
95	Jerry Ellison, Chattanooga (Boise St.)	1992
95	John McNiff, Cornell (Columbia)	1990
95	Joe Sparksman, James Madison (William & Mary)	1990
94	Kenny Bynum, South Carolina St. (Delaware St.)	1996
94	Mark Vigil, Idaho (Simon Fraser)	1980

PASSING

Yds.	Passer-Receiver, Team (Opponent)	Year
99	Jimmy Blanchard-Terry Charles, Portland St. (Eastern Wash.)	1999
99	Michael Moore-Otis Covington, Morgan St. (Florida A&M)	1995
99	Todd Bennett-Jason Anderson, Eastern Wash. (Montana)	1994
99	Aaron Garcia-Greg Ochoa, Sacramento St. (Cal Poly)	1993
99	Todd Donnan-Troy Brown, Marshall (East Tenn. St.)	1991
99	Antoine Ezell-Tyrone Davis, Florida A&M (Bethune-Cookman)	1991
99	Jay Johnson-Kenny Shedd, Northern Iowa (Oklahoma St.)	1990
99	John Bonds-Hendricks Johnson, Northern Ariz. (Boise St.)	1990
99	Scott Stoker-Victor Robinson, Northwestern St. (La.-Monroe)	1989
98	Ben Anderson-Courtney Freeman, Liberty (Charleston So.)	1996
98	Derek Jensen-Jason Cannon, Southwest Mo. St. (Eastern Ill.)	1995
98	Jonathan Quinn-Dee Mostiller, Middle Tenn. (Tennessee Tech)	1995
98	Antoine Ezell-Tim Daniel, Florida A&M (Delaware St.)	1991
98	John Friesz-Lee Allen, Idaho (Northern Ariz.)	1989
98	Fred Gatlin-Treamelle Taylor, Nevada (Montana)	1989
98	Steve Monaco-Emerson Foster, Rhode Island (Holy Cross)	1988
98	Frank Baur-Maurice Caldwell, Lafayette (Columbia)	1988

Yds.	Passer-Receiver, Team (Opponent)	Year
98	David Gabianelli-Craig Morton, Dartmouth (Columbia)	1986
98	Joe Pizzo-Bryan Calder, Nevada (Eastern Wash.)	1984
98	Bobby Hebert-Randy Liles, Northwestern St. (Southeastern La.)	1980
97	Brad Smith-Sullivan Beard, Nicholls St. (Jacksonville St.)	1999
97	Peyton Jones-Mikhael Ricks, Stephen F. Austin (Troy St.)	1997
97	Lester Anderson-Kevin Glenn, Illinois St. (Ball St.)	1993
97	Nate Harrison-Brian Thomas, Southern U. (Dist. Columbia)	1989
97	Jerome Baker-John Taylor, Delaware St. (St. Paul's)	1985
97	John McKenzie-Chris Burkett, Jackson St. (Mississippi Val.)	1983
96	Chris Berg-Dedric Ward, Northern Iowa (Western Ill.)	1995
96	Damon Williams-Ryan Blakely, Alabama St. (Texas Southern)	1994
96	Greg Wyatt-Shawn Collins, Northern Ariz. (Montana St.)	1988
96	Rick Fahnestock-Albert Brown, Western Ill. (Northern Iowa)	1986
96	Jeff Cesarone-Keith Paskett, Western Ky. (Akron)	1985
96	Mike Williams-Trumaine Johnson, Grambling (Jackson St.)	1980

INTERCEPTION RETURNS

Yds.	Player, Team (Opponent)	Year
100	Ricardo Walker, Delaware (Villanova)	2000
100	Jacori Rufus, Idaho St. (Southern Utah)	1998
100	Sean Gorius, Dayton (Morehead St.)	1997
100	Tehran Hunter, Massachusetts (Buffalo)	1997
100	Derek Grier, Marshall (East Tenn.)	1991
100	Ricky Fields, Samford (Concord [W.Va.])	1990
100	Warren Smith, Stephen F. Austin (Nicholls St.)	1990
100	Rob Pouliot, Montana St. (Boise St.)	1988
100	Rick Harris, East Tenn. St. (Davidson)	1986
100	Bruce Alexander, Stephen F. Austin (Lamar)	1986
100	Guy Carbone, Rhode Island (Lafayette)	1985
100	Moses Aimable, Northern Iowa (Western Ill.)	1985
100	Kervin Fontenette, Southeastern La. (Nicholls St.)	1985
100	Jim Anderson, Princeton (Cornell)	1984
100	Keiron Bigby, Brown (Yale)	1984
100	Vencie Glenn, Indiana St. (Wayne St. [Mich.])	1984
100	George Floyd, Eastern Ky. (Youngstown St.)	1980

PUNT RETURNS

Yds.	Player, Team (Opponent)	Year
98	Willie Ware, Mississippi Val. (Bishop)	1985
98	Barney Bussey, South Carolina St. (Johnson Smith)	1981
96	Carl Williams, Texas Southern (Grambling)	1981
95	Joseph Jefferson, Western Ky. (Illinois St.)	2001
95	Clarence Weathers, Delaware St. (Salisbury)	1980
94	Drew Haddad, Buffalo (Cornell)	1998
94	Brad Friedman, Towson (St. Francis [Pa.])	1996
93	Andrew McFadden, Liberty (Delaware St.)	1995
93	Patrick Plott, Jacksonville St. (Southwest Mo. St.)	1995
93	Joe Fuller, Northern Iowa (Wis.-Whitewater)	1984

KICKOFF RETURNS

Fifty-three players have returned kickoffs 100 yards. The most recent:

Yds.	Player, Team (Opponent)	Year
100	Art Smith, Northeastern (Villanova)	2002
100	James McCowan, Weber St. (Eastern Ore.)	2002
100	James Leverett, Davidson (Randolph-Macon)	2001
100	R J Harvey, New Hampshire (Maine)	2001
100	Terry Tharps, Western Ill. (Sam Houston St.)	2001
100	Brian Bratton, Furman (Appalachian St.)	2001
100	Brian Bratton, Furman (Wofford)	2001
100	Lamont Brightful, Eastern Wash. (Montana)	2000
100	Kunle Williams, Pennsylvania (Princeton)	1999
100	Joey Hamilton, Jacksonville St. (Samford)	1999
100	Lamont Brightful, Eastern Wash. (Central Wash.)	1999
100	Darriel Ruffin, Tenn.-Martin (Murray St.)	1997
100	Corey Joyner, Ga. Southern (East Tenn. St.)	1997
100	Clemente Sainten, Weber St. (Western St.)	1996
100	Robert Davis, Fordham (Brown)	1996
100	Joey Stockton, Western Ky. (Southern Ill.)	1996
100	Goree White, Alcorn St. (Ark.-Pine Bluff)	1995
100	Joe Rosato, Duquesne (Robert Morris)	1995
100	Chris Watson, Eastern Ill. (Northern Iowa)	1995

PUNTS

Yds.	Player, Team (Opponent)	Year
93	Tyler Grogan, Northeastern (Villanova)	2001
91	Bart Helsley, North Texas (La.-Monroe)	1990
89	Mike Scifres, Western Ill. (Southwest Mo. St.)	2000
89	Jim Carriere, Connecticut (Maine)	1987
88	Jeff Kaiser, Idaho St. (UTEP)	1983
87	John Starnes, North Texas (Texas-Arlington)	1983
86	Andy Dorsey, Tennessee Tech (Eastern Ill.)	1998
85	Troy LeFever, Youngstown St. (Northern Iowa)	2000
85	Ken Hinsley, Western Caro. (Chattanooga)	1998
85	Don Alonzo, Nicholls St. (Northwestern St.)	1985
84	Billy Smith, Chattanooga (Appalachian St.)	1988
83	Jason Harkins, Appalachian St. (Citadel)	1986

Yds.	Player, Team (Opponent)	Year
82	Dan Frantz, Portland St. (Montana)	2000
82	Scott White, Delaware (Maine)	1996
82	Scott Shields, Weber St. (Cal St. Northridge)	1996
82	Tim Healy, Delaware (Boston U.)	1987
82	John Howell, Chattanooga (Vanderbilt)	1982

FUMBLE RETURNS

Yds.	Player, Team (Opponent)	Year
90	Cornell Middlebrook, Western Ill. (Northern Iowa)	2002
82	Brendan Dete, Davidson (Newberry)	2002

FIELD GOALS

Yds.	Player, Team (Opponent)	Year
63	Bill Gramatica, South Fla. (Austin Peay)	2000
63	Scott Roper, Arkansas St. (North Texas)	1987
63	Tim Foley, Ga. Southern (James Madison)	1987
62	Billy Cundiff, Drake (San Diego)	2000
62	Paul Hickert, Murray St. (Eastern Ky.)	1986
60	Pete Garces, Idaho St. (Cal St. Northridge)	1998
60	David Cool, Ga. Southern (James Madison)	1988
60	Terry Belden, Northern Ariz. (Cal St. Northridge)	1993
59	MacKenzie Hoambrecker, Northern Iowa (Southwest Mo. St.)	2002
58	Rich Emke, Eastern Ill. (Northern Iowa)	1986
58	Tony Zendejas, Nevada (Boise St.)	1983

Team Champions

Annual Offense Champions

TOTAL OFFENSE

Year	Team	Avg.
1978	Portland St.	477.4
1979	Portland St.	460.7
1980	Portland St.	504.3
1981	Idaho	438.8
1982	Drake	444.8
1983	Idaho	479.5
1984	Mississippi Val.	*640.1
1985	Weber St.	516.1
1986	Nevada	492.0
1987	Holy Cross	552.2
1988	Lehigh	485.6
1989	Idaho	495.9
1990	William & Mary	498.7
1991	Weber St.	581.4
1992	Alcorn St.	502.9
1993	Idaho	532.0
1994	Alcorn St.	597.9
1995	Montana	512.5
1996	Northern Ariz.	522.8
1997	Eastern Wash.	505.6
1998	Florida A&M	535.7
1999	Ga. Southern	551.7
2000	Morehead St.	523.9
2001	Eastern Wash.	514.5
2002	Jackson St.	485.5

*Record.

RUSHING OFFENSE

Year	Team	Avg.
1978	Jackson St.	314.5
1979	Jackson St.	288.4
1980	N.C. A&T	322.1
1981	Idaho	266.3
1982	Delaware	258.4
1983	Furman	287.1
1984	Delaware St.	377.3
1985	Southwest Mo. St.	298.7
1986	Northeastern	336.0
1987	Howard	381.6
1988	Eastern Ky.	303.0
1989	Ga. Southern	329.2
1990	Delaware St.	298.7
1991	VMI	316.9
1992	Citadel	345.5
1993	Western Ky.	300.1
1994	Citadel	382.0
1995	Massachusetts	302.5
1996	Southern Utah	330.8
1997	Western Ky.	366.0

Year	Team	Avg.
1998	Southern Utah	386.0
1999	Ga. Southern	*419.0
2000	Southern Utah	394.2
2001	Ga. Southern	323.6
2002	Ga. Southern	386.2

*Record.

PASSING OFFENSE

Year	Team	Avg.
1978	Portland St.	367.1
1979	Portland St.	368.9
1980	Portland St.	434.9
1981	Idaho St.	325.7
1982	West Tex. A&M	313.7
1983	Idaho	336.1
1984	Mississippi Val.	*496.8
1985	Rhode Island	384.3
1986	Eastern Ill.	326.1
1987	Holy Cross	358.4
1988	Lehigh	330.1
1989	Idaho	374.3
1990	Weber St.	342.2
1991	Weber St.	389.1
1992	Alcorn St.	360.5
1993	Montana	359.0
1994	Alcorn St.	442.3
1995	Montana	408.2
1996	Montana	339.6
1997	Cal. St. Northridge	358.1
1998	Florida A&M	400.6
1999	Towson	381.2
2000	Pennsylvania	342.7
2001	Jackson St.	344.4
2002	Grambling	360.7

*Record.

SCORING OFFENSE

Year	Team	Avg.
1978	Nevada	35.6
1979	Portland St.	34.3
1980	Portland St.	49.2
1981	Delaware	34.1
1982	Delaware	34.1
1983	Mississippi Val.	39.2
1984	Mississippi Val.	*60.9
1985	Mississippi Val.	41.5
1986	Nevada	39.4
1987	Holy Cross	46.5
1988	Lafayette	38.2
1989	Grambling	37.1
1990	Jackson St.	38.0
1991	Nevada	45.1
1992	Marshall	42.4
1993	Idaho	47.5

Year	Team	Avg.
1994	Alcorn St.	45.7
1995	Montana	42.5
1996	Northern Ariz.	43.2
1997	Morehead St.	41.9
1998	Florida A&M	49.6
1999	Ga. Southern	50.0
2000	Morehead St.	41.6
2001	Eastern Wash.	41.9
2002	Grambling	38.9

*Record.

Annual Defense Champions

TOTAL DEFENSE

Year	Team	Avg.
1978	Florida A&M	*149.9
1979	Alcorn St.	166.3
1980	Massachusetts	193.5
1981	South Carolina St.	204.0
1982	South Carolina St.	191.4
1983	Grambling	206.0
1984	Tennessee St.	187.0
1985	Arkansas St.	258.8
1986	Tennessee St.	178.5
1987	Southern U.	202.8
1988	Alcorn St.	215.4
1989	Howard	220.0
1990	Middle Tenn.	244.8
1991	South Carolina St.	208.9
1992	South Carolina St.	250.9
1993	McNeese St.	249.5
1994	Pennsylvania	218.9
1995	Georgetown	216.4
1996	Georgetown	218.2
1997	Marist	213.6
1998	Fairfield	213.8
1999	St. John's (N.Y.)	199.7
2000	Monmouth	232.1
2001	St. Peter's	157.7
2002	Duquesne	188.0

*Record.

RUSHING DEFENSE

Year	Team	Avg.
1978	Florida A&M	48.6
1979	Alcorn St.	56.7
1980	South Carolina St.	61.8
1981	South Carolina St.	60.8
1982	South Carolina St.	59.4
1983	Jackson St.	79.2
1984	Grambling	44.5
1985	Jackson St.	63.0

Year	Team	Avg.
1986	Eastern Ky.	62.8
1987	Southern U.	64.5
1988	Stephen F. Austin	83.5
1989	Montana	70.2
1990	Delaware St.	77.2
1991	Boise St.	84.4
1992	Villanova	77.8
1993	Wagner	87.0
1994	Idaho	65.3
1995	McNeese St.	60.9
1996	Georgetown	53.2
1997	Marist	40.4
1998	Fairfield	61.7
1999	Jackson St.	67.8
2000	Alabama A&M	*39.7
2001	Pennsylvania	58.4
2002	Pennsylvania	55.8

*Record.

PASSING DEFENSE

Year	Team	$Avg.
1978	Southern U.	85.6
1979	Mississippi Val.	64.2
1980	Howard	93.8
1981	Bethune-Cookman	*59.9
1982	Northeastern	98.8
1983	Louisiana Tech	111.4
1984	Louisiana Tech	105.5
1985	Dartmouth	110.3
1986	Bethune-Cookman	99.8
1987	Alcorn St.	101.3
1988	Middle Tenn.	90.8
1989	Chattanooga	104.4
1990	Middle Tenn.	78.83
1991	South Carolina St.	70.01
1992	Middle Tenn.	76.93
1993	Georgetown	76.92
1994	Pennsylvania	*63.15
1995	Canisius	69.13
1996	Canisius	71.99
1997	McNeese St.	79.05
1998	Davidson	74.64
1999	Robert Morris	80.80
2000	Bethune-Cookman	76.39
2001	St. Peter's	63.26
2002	Sacred Heart	61.03

*Record. $Beginning in 1990, ranked on passing-efficiency defense rating points instead of per-game yardage allowed.

SCORING DEFENSE

Year	Team	Avg.
1978	South Carolina St.	*6.5
1979	Lehigh	7.2
1980	Murray St.	9.1
1981	Jackson St.	9.4
1982	Western Mich.	7.1
1983	Grambling	8.6
1984	Northwestern St.	9.0
1985	Appalachian St.	9.9
1986	Tennessee St.	8.3
1987	Holy Cross	10.0
1988	Furman	9.7
1989	Howard	10.5
1990	Middle Tenn.	9.2
1991	Villanova	12.0
1992	Citadel	13.0
1993	Marshall	11.2
1994	Pennsylvania	7.6
1995	McNeese St.	8.9

Year	Team	Avg.
1996	Duquesne	10.1
1997	McNeese St.	10.5
1998	Western Ill.	9.4
1999	St. John's (N.Y.)	12.9
2000	Western Ky.	11.6
2001	St. Peter's	8.2
2002	Duquesne	9.6

*Record.

Other Annual Team Champions

NET PUNTING

Year	Team	Avg.
1992	Stephen F. Austin	38.2
1993	Northern Ariz.	40.1
1994	Marshall	42.9
1995	Eastern Ky.	40.4
1996	Marshall	44.5
1997	James Madison	40.5
1998	Western Ill.	41.5
	Western Caro.	41.5
1999	Southwest Mo. St.	40.0
2000	Idaho St.	39.2
2001	Idaho St.	44.3
2002	Idaho St.	42.7

PUNT RETURNS

Year	Team	Avg.
1992	South Carolina St.	17.9
1993	Montana	14.6
1994	Towson	19.5
1995	Southwest Tex. St.	19.3
1996	Northern Ariz.	16.6
1997	Morehead St.	19.4
1998	Buffalo	17.8
1999	Stephen F. Austin	19.1
2000	Northwestern St.	19.4
2001	N.C. A&T	23.0
2002	Hampton	17.8

KICKOFF RETURNS

Year	Team	Avg.
1992	Pennsylvania	25.0
1993	Western Caro.	26.8
1994	Youngstown St.	27.3
1995	Southern U.	27.0
1996	Monmouth	27.2
1997	Furman	27.1
1998	Butler	28.8
1999	Tennessee St.	27.9
2000	Weber St.	25.2
2001	Hampton	28.2
2002	Portland St.	25.2

TURNOVER MARGIN

Year	Team	Avg.
1992	Howard	1.64
	Youngstown St.	1.64
1993	St. John's (N.Y.)	1.91
1994	Robert Morris	1.89
1995	Princeton	2.20
1996	Canisius	2.44
1997	Texas Southern	1.91
1998	Yale	1.70

Year	Team	Avg.
1999	Grambling	1.45
	Valparaiso	1.45
2000	Western Ky.	2.73
2001	St. Peter's	3.18
2002	Dayton	1.92

Defensive Team Single-Game Records

(Since 2000)

TACKLES FOR LOSS

TFL	Team (Opponent)	Date
22	Illinois St. (Western Ill.)	Nov. 4, 2000
19	Pennsylvania (Brown)	Nov. 2, 2002
19	Massachusetts (American Int'l)	Sept. 14, 2002
19	Fla. Atlantic (Bethune-Cookman)	Sept. 7, 2002
17	Stony Brook (St. John's [N.Y.])	Sept. 21, 2002
16.5	Ga. Southern (East Tenn. St.)	Nov. 2, 2002
14	Delaware (William & Mary)	Sept. 28, 2002
11	Indiana St. (Western Mich.)	Aug. 29, 2002
10	Fordham (Fairfield)	Sept. 28, 2002
9	Columbia (Yale)	Oct. 27, 2001

PASS SACKS

Sacks	Team (Opponent)	Date
12	Illinois St. (Western Ill.)	Nov. 4, 2000
11	Massachusetts (American Int'l)	Sept. 14, 2002
11	Fla. Atlantic (Bethune-Cookman)	Sept. 7, 2002
8.5	Ga. Southern (East Tenn. St.)	Nov. 2, 2002
8	Pennsylvania (Brown)	Nov. 2, 2002
7	Fordham (Fairfield)	Sept. 28, 2002
6	Delaware (William & Mary)	Oct. 20, 2001
6	Harvard (Cornell)	Oct. 13, 2001
5	Portland St. (Cal St. Northridge)	Nov. 17, 2001
4	Indiana St. (Illinois St.)	Nov. 16, 2002
4	Indiana St. (Western Mich.)	Aug. 29, 2002

PASSES DEFENDED
(Pass Interceptions and Pass Break-ups)

PD	Team (Opponent)	Date
17	Pennsylvania (Lafayette)	Sept. 21, 2002
14	Massachusetts (Maine)	Oct. 12, 2002
10	Ga. Southern (Maine)	Dec. 7, 2002
10	Ga. Southern (Bethune-Cookman)	Nov. 30, 2002
10	Ga. Southern (Citadel)	Oct. 26, 2002
10	Delaware (West Chester)	Sept. 21, 2002
10	Delaware (New Hampshire)	Nov. 4, 2000
9	Illinois St. (Western Ill.)	Nov. 4, 2000
8	Columbia (Bucknell)	Sept. 22, 2001
7	Fordham (Fairfield)	Sept. 28, 2002
6	Fla. Atlantic (South Fla.)	Aug. 29, 2002

FORCED FUMBLES

FF	Team (Opponent)	Date
6	Fla. Atlantic (Troy St.)	Oct. 26, 2002
6	Delaware (Citadel)	Sept. 9, 2002
6	Delaware (Ga. Southern)	Dec. 9, 2000
5	Illinois St. (Southwest Mo. St.)	Oct. 5, 2002
4	Massachusetts (Richmond)	Oct. 5, 2002
4	Massachusetts (Rhode Island)	Nov. 17, 2001
4	Masschusetts (Northeastern)	Nov. 3, 2001
3	Pennsylvania (Columbia)	Oct. 19, 2002
3	Pennsylvania (Lehigh)	Sept. 28, 2002

Toughest-Schedule Annual Leaders

The Division I-AA toughest-schedule program, which began in 1982, is based on what all Division I-AA opponents did against other Division I-AA and Division I-A teams when *not* playing the team in question. Games against non-I-AA and I-A teams are deleted. (Playoff or postseason were included for the first time in 2002.) The top two leaders by year:

Year	Team (Record†)	¢Opponents' Record			
		W	L	T	Pct.
1982	Massachusetts (5-6-0)	50	30	1	.623
	Lehigh (4-6-0)	44	31	0	.587
1983	Florida A&M (7-4-0)	42	23	3	.640
	Grambling (8-1-2)	49	31	0	.613
1984	North Texas (2-9-0)	55	35	2	.609
	VMI (1-9-0)	53	37	2	.587
1985	South Carolina St. (5-6-0)	43	20	1	.680
	Lehigh (5-6-0)	47	33	1	.586
1986	James Madison (5-5-1)	46	28	1	.620
	Bucknell (3-7-0)	43	27	0	.614
1987	Ga. Southern (8-3-0)	47	31	0	.603
	Northeastern (6-5-0)	50	37	0	.575
1988	Northwestern St. (9-2-0)	54	36	2	.598
	Ga. Southern (9-2-0)	43	31	1	.580
1989	Liberty (7-3-0)	39	22	2	.635
	Western Caro. (3-7-1)	46	34	2	.573
1990	Ga. Southern (8-3-0)	53	25	1	.677
	Western Ky. (2-8-0)	55	36	1	.603
1991	Bucknell (1-9-0)	53	29	1	.645
	William & Mary (5-6-0)	62	43	0	.590
1992	VMI (3-8-0)	46	36	0	.561
	Harvard (3-7-0)	51	40	0	.560
1993	Samford (5-6-0)	55	26	0	.679
	Delaware St. (6-5-0)	44	30	0	.595
1994	Montana (9-2-0)	46	30	1	.604
	McNeese St. (9-2-0)	44	29	5	.596
1995	Western Ky. (2-8-0)	59	32	0	.648
	Nicholls St. (0-11-0)	61	38	0	.616
1996	Indiana St. (6-5)	50	32	0	.610
	Towson (6-4)	42	29	0	.592
1997	Lehigh (4-7)	65	39	0	.625
	William & Mary (7-4)	65	42	0	.607

Year	Team (Record†)	¢Opponents' Record			
		W	L	T	Pct.
1998	Connecticut (9-2)	66	41	0	.617
	New Hampshire (4-7)	54	40	0	.596
1999	Elon (9-2)	50	26	0	.658
	Cal Poly (3-8)	52	32	0	.619
2000	Elon (7-4)	59	31	0	.656
	Indiana St. (1-10)	62	38	0	.620
2001	Elon (2-9)	63	36	0	.636
	Nicholls St. (3-8)	55	34	0	.618
2002	McNeese St. (13-2)	104	45	0	.698
	Western Ky. (12-3)	98	49	0	.667

†Not including playoff or postseason games. ¢When not playing the team listed.

Top 10 Toughest-Schedule Leaders for 1998-02

1998

Team	¢Opp. Record	Pct.
1. Connecticut	66-41	.617
2. New Hampshire	59-40	.596
3. Fordham	63-44	.589
4. Rhode Island	62-45	.579
5. Massachusetts	61-45	.575
6. Delaware	55-41	.573
7. Florida A&M	56-42	.571
8. Wofford	59-45	.567
9. Holy Cross	60-47	.561
10. Citadel	58-46	.558

1999

Team	¢Opp. Record	Pct.
1. Elon	50-26	.658
2. Cal Poly	52-32	.619
3. Dartmouth	57-36	.613
Columbia	57-36	.613
5. Holy Cross	63-41	.606
6. Jackson St.	60-40	.600
7. Florida A&M	60-41	.594
8. South Fla.	55-39	.585
9. Alabama St.	52-37	.584
10. James Madison	62-45	.579

2000

Team	¢Opp. Record	Pct.
1. Elon	59-31	.656
2. Indiana St.	62-38	.620
3. Hofstra	67-43	.609
4. Bucknell	64-44	.593
5. Tennessee St.	65-45	.591
Troy St.	65-45	.591
7. Fordham	62-44	.585
8. Sam Houston St.	46-33	.582
9. Southern Ill.	58-42	.580
10. Richmond	52-38	.578

2001

Team	¢Opp. Record	Pct.
1. Elon	63-36	.636
2. Nicholls St.	55-34	.618
3. St. Francis (Pa.)	53-34	.609
4. Lafayette	52-37	.584
5. Canisius	51-37	.580
Jacksonville St.	51-37	.580
7. Cornell	43-32	.573
Princeton	43-32	.573
9. VMI	61-46	.570
10. Liberty	39-30	.565

2002

Team	¢Opp. Record	Pct.
1. McNeese St.	104-45	.698
2. Western Ky.	98-49	.667
3. Villanova	103-54	.656
4. Sam Houston St.	61-38	.616
5. Montana St.	66-43	.606
6. Southern Ill.	63-43	.594
Southwest Mo. St.	63-43	.594
8. Florida Int'l	70-48	.593
9. Indiana St.	59-41	.590
10. Ga. Southern	98-70	.583

¢When not playing the team listed.

DIVISION I-AA

Annual Most-Improved Teams

Year	Team	$Games Improved	From		To		Coach
1978	Western Ky.	6½	1977	1-8-1	1978	8-2-0	Jimmy Feix
1979	Murray St.	5	1978	4-7-0	1979	*9-2-1	Mike Gottfried
1980	Idaho St.	6	1979	0-11-0	1980	6-5-0	#Dave Kragthorpe
1981	Lafayette	5½	1980	3-7-0	1981	9-2-0	#Bill Russo
1982	Pennsylvania	6	1981	1-9-0	1982	7-3-0	Jerry Berndt
1983	North Texas	5½	1982	2-9-0	1983	*8-4-0	Corky Nelson
	Southern Ill.	5½	1982	6-5-0	1983	*13-1-0	Rey Dempsey
1984	Montana St.	9½	1983	1-10-0	1984	*12-2-0	Dave Arnold
1985	Appalachian St.	4	1984	4-7-0	1985	8-3-0	Sparky Woods
	Massachusetts	4	1984	3-8-0	1985	7-4-0	Bob Stull
	West Tex. A&M	4	1984	3-8-0	1985	6-3-1	#Bill Kelly
1986	Morehead St.	6	1985	1-10-0	1986	7-4-0	Bill Baldridge
1987	Weber St.	6	1986	3-8-0	1987	*10-3-0	Mike Price
1988	Stephen F. Austin	5½	1987	3-7-1	1988	*10-3-0	Jim Hess
1989	Yale	4½	1988	3-6-1	1989	8-2-0	Carmen Cozza
1990	Nevada	4	1989	7-4-0	1990	*13-2-0	Chris Ault
	N.C. A&T	4	1989	5-6-0	1990	9-2-0	Bill Hayes
1991	Alcorn St.	5	1990	2-7-0	1991	7-2-1	#Cardell Jones
	Austin Peay	5	1990	0-11-0	1991	5-6-0	#Roy Gregory
	Princeton	5	1990	3-7-0	1991	8-2-0	Steve Tosches
	Southern Ill.	5	1990	2-9-0	1991	7-4-0	Bob Smith
1992	Howard	5	1991	2-9-0	1992	7-4-0	Steve Wilson
	Pennsylvania	5	1991	2-8-0	1992	7-3-0	#Al Bagnoli
	Richmond	5	1991	2-9-0	1992	7-4-0	Jim Marshall
	Tennessee Tech	5	1991	2-9-0	1992	7-4-0	Jim Ragland
	Western Caro.	5	1991	2-9-0	1992	7-4-0	Steve Hodgin

Year	Team	$Games Improved		From		To	Coach
1993	Boston U.	8	1992	3-8-0	1993	*12-1-0	Dan Allen
1994	Boise St.	8	1993	3-8-0	1994	*13-2-0	Pokey Allen
1995	Murray St.	5½	1994	5-6-0	1995	*11-1-0	Houston Nutt
1996	Nicholls St.	7½	1995	0-11	1996	*8-4	Darren Barbier
1997	McNeese St.	8	1996	3-8	1997	*13-2	Bobby Keasler
1998	Massachusetts	8	1997	2-9	1998	*12-3	#Mark Whipple
1999	Stephen F. Austin	5	1998	3-8	1999	8-3	#Mike Santiago
2000	Sacred Heart	8	1999	2-9	2000	10-1	#Jim Fleming
2001	Alcorn St.	6	2000	0-11	2001	6-5	Johnny Thomas
	St. Peter's	6	2000	4-7	2001	10-1	Rob Stern
2002	Mississippi Val.	5	2001	0-11	2002	5-6	#Willie Totten

*$To determine games improved, add the difference in victories between the two seasons to the difference in losses, then divide by two; ties not counted. *I-AA playoff included. #First year as head coach at that college.*

ALL-TIME MOST-IMPROVED TEAMS

Games   **Team (Year)**
9½ ....Montana St. (1984)
8 ....Sacred Heart (2000)
8 ....Massachusetts (1998)
8 ....McNeese St. (1997)
8 ....Boise St. (1994)
8 ....Boston U. (1993)
7½ ....Nicholls St. (1996)
7 ....Lehigh (1998)
6½ ....Western Ky. (1978)
6 ....Alcorn St. (2001)
6 ....St. Peter's (2001)
6 ....Jacksonville St. (1998)
6 ....Colgate (1996)
6 ....Weber St. (1987)
6 ....Morehead St. (1986)
6 ....Pennsylvania (1982)
6 ....Idaho St. (1980)
5½ ....Davidson (1998)
5½ ....Illinois St. (1998)
5½ ....Fairfield (1997)
5½ ....Murray St. (1995)
5½ ....Southern U. (1993)
5½ ....Stephen F. Austin (1988)
5½ ....East Tenn. St. (1986)
5½ ....Holy Cross (1986)
5½ ....Yale (1984)
5½ ....North Texas (1983)
5½ ....Southern Ill. (1983)
5½ ....Lafayette (1981)

2002 MOST-IMPROVED TEAMS
(Includes Playoff Games)

Team (Coach)	2001	2002	$Games Improved
Mississippi Val. (Willie Totten)	0-11	5-6	5
Massachusetts (Mark Whipple)	3-8	8-4	4½
Morgan St. (Stanley Mitchell)	2-9	7-5	4½
Stony Brook (Sam Kornhauser)	3-6	8-2	4½
VMI (Cal McCombs)	1-10	6-6	4½
Western Ill. (Don Patterson)	5-5	11-2	4½
Wofford (Mike Ayers)	4-7	9-3	4½
Howard (Ray Petty)	2-9	6-5	4
Idaho St. (Larry Lewis)	4-7	8-3	4
Illinois St. (Denver Johnson)	2-9	6-5	4
Lafayette (Frank Tavani)	2-8	7-5	4
Nicholls St. (Darryl Daye)	3-8	7-4	4
Northeastern (Don Brown)	5-6	10-3	4

$To determine games improved, add the difference in victories between the two seasons to the difference in losses, then divide by two.

All-Time Team Won-Lost Records

BY PERCENTAGE (TOP 25)

Team	Yrs.	Won	Lost	Tied	Pct.	Total Games
Ga. Southern	21	211	65	1	.764	277
Yale	130	815	311	55	.713	1181
Grambling	60	451	180	15	.710	646
Florida A&M	70	497	200	18	.708	715
Gardner-Webb	3	21	9	0	.700	30

Team	Yrs.	Won	Lost	Tied	Pct.	Total Games
Tennessee St.	75	471	205	30	@.688	706
Robert Morris	9	61	28	1	.683	90
Princeton	133	749	334	50	.683	1133
Harvard	128	750	362	50	.667	1162
Jackson St.	57	376	199	13	.651	588
Eastern Ky.	79	486	276	27	.633	789
Pennsylvania	126	758	433	42	.632	1233
Southern U.	81	488	280	25	.631	793
Fordham	104	706	402	53	.631	1161
Dayton	95	554	324	26	.627	904
Hofstra	62	371	221	11	.624	603
McNeese St.	52	347	207	14	.623	568
Dartmouth	121	630	373	46	.622	1049
Appalachian St.	73	465	279	29	.620	773
Albany (N.Y.)	30	185	115	0	.617	300
Fairfield	7	44	28	0	.611	72
South Carolina St.	75	414	259	27	.611	700
Youngstown St.	62	376	242	17	.606	635
Western Ky.	84	471	305	31	.603	807
Delaware	111	583	379	44	.601	1006

Includes records as senior college only. Bowl and playoff games are included, and each tie game is computed as half won and half lost. Note: Tiebreaker rule began with 1996 season.

@Tennessee State's participation in the 1981 and 1982 Division I-AA championships (1-2 record) voided.

ALPHABETICAL LISTING

Team	Yrs.	Won	Lost	Tied	Pct.	Total Games
Alabama A&M	65	306	275	26	.526	607
Alabama St.	97	400	390	43	.506	833
Albany (N.Y.)	30	185	115	0	.617	300
Alcorn St.	79	384	277	39	.576	700
Appalachian St.	73	465	279	29	.620	773
Ark.-Pine Bluff	71	305	344	42	.472	691
Austin Peay	66	243	407	16	.377	666
Bethune-Cookman	64	350	239	22	.591	611
Brown	117	530	510	40	.509	1080
Bucknell	117	531	486	51	.521	1068
Butler	113	511	367	35	.579	913
Cal Poly	62	327	269	9	.548	605
Canisius	57	228	234	24	.494	486
Central Conn. St.	64	238	290	22	.453	550
Charleston So.	12	33	93	0	.262	126
Chattanooga	95	453	433	33	.511	919
Citadel	95	422	465	32	.477	919
Colgate	112	537	418	50	.559	1005
Columbia	112	346	560	43	.387	949
Cornell	115	591	423	34	.580	1048
Dartmouth	121	630	373	46	.622	1049
Davidson	105	379	505	45	.432	929
Dayton	95	554	324	26	.627	904
Delaware	111	583	379	44	.601	1006
Delaware St.	57	251	294	8	.461	553
Drake	109	506	452	29	.527	987
Duquesne	55	267	218	18	.549	503
East Tenn. St.	79	337	391	27	.464	755
Eastern Ill.	102	421	438	44	.491	903
Eastern Ky.	79	486	276	27	.633	789
Eastern Wash.	92	411	342	23	.544	776
Elon	81	433	342	18	.557	793
Fairfield	7	44	28	0	.611	72
Fla. Atlantic	2	6	15	0	.286	21
Florida A&M	70	497	200	18	.708	715

Team	Yrs.	Won	Lost	Tied	Pct.	Total Games
Florida Int'l.	1	5	6	0	.455	11
Fordham	104	706	402	53	.631	1161
Furman	89	502	377	37	.568	916
Ga. Southern	21	211	65	1	.764	277
Gardner-Webb	3	21	9	0	.700	30
Georgetown	91	446	303	31	.592	780
Grambling	60	451	180	15	.710	646
Hampton	101	468	349	34	.570	851
Harvard	128	750	362	50	.667	1162
Hofstra	62	371	221	11	.624	603
Holy Cross	107	552	429	55	.559	1036
Howard	106	439	358	42	.548	839
Idaho St.	98	420	392	20	.517	832
Illinois St.	103	400	462	65	.467	927
Indiana St.	86	332	393	20	.459	745
Iona	25	103	142	3	.421	248
Jackson St.	57	376	199	13	.651	588
Jacksonville	5	18	31	0	.367	49
Jacksonville St.	70	364	279	27	.563	670
James Madison	30	174	152	3	.533	329
La Salle	6	20	37	0	.351	57
Lafayette	121	599	512	39	.538	1150
Lehigh	119	584	530	45	.523	1159
Liberty	30	145	161	4	.474	310
Maine	111	447	416	38	.517	901
Marist	25	108	124	3	.466	235
Massachusetts	120	486	489	51	.499	1026
McNeese St.	52	347	207	14	.623	568
Mississippi Val.	50	197	273	11	.421	481
Monmouth	9	47	42	0	.528	89
Montana	103	450	445	26	.503	921
Montana St.	99	388	415	34	.484	837
Morehead St.	73	271	378	22	.420	671
Morgan St.	82	376	324	30	.536	730
Morris Brown	77	337	342	37	.497	716
Murray St.	78	416	324	34	.559	774
New Hampshire	106	448	399	54	.527	901
Nicholls St.	31	143	196	4	.423	343
Norfolk St.	42	202	204	7	.498	413
N.C. A&T	79	405	316	39	.559	760
Northeastern	67	261	314	17	.455	592
Northern Ariz.	78	352	352	22	#.500	726
Northern Iowa	104	536	353	47	.598	936
Northwestern St.	94	458	362	33	.556	853
Pennsylvania	126	758	433	42	.632	1233
Portland St.	56	278	284	10	.495	572
Prairie View	76	335	394	31	.461	760
Princeton	133	749	334	50	.683	1133
Rhode Island	102	350	476	41	.427	867
Richmond	119	435	567	53	.437	1055
Robert Morris	9	61	28	1	.683	90
Sacramento St.	49	217	275	8	.442	500
Sacred Heart	12	50	68	0	.424	118
Sam Houston St.	86	362	358	47	.503	767
Samford	87	396	396	34	.500	826
San Diego	35	163	163	8	.500	334
Savannah St.	3	5	24	0	.172	29
Siena	15	32	107	0	.230	139
South Carolina St.	75	414	259	27	.611	700
Southeast Mo. St.	90	383	398	37	.491	818
Southern Ill.	87	339	446	33	.435	818
Southern U.	81	488	280	25	.631	793
Southern Utah	40	191	201	6	.487	398
Southwest Mo. St.	91	406	395	40	.507	841
Southwest Tex. St.	88	433	349	27	.552	809
St. Francis (Pa.)	54	154	280	13	.359	447
St. John's (N.Y.)	34	176	143	7	.551	326
St. Mary's (Cal.)	74	366	274	20	.570	660
St. Peter's	31	74	187	1	.284	262
Stephen F. Austin	76	321	414	30	%.439	765
Stony Brook	20	91	96	2	.487	189
Tenn.-Martin	46	186	288	5	.394	479
Tennessee St.	75	471	205	30	@.688	706
Tennessee Tech	81	354	403	31	.469	788
Texas Southern	57	274	293	27	.484	594
Towson	34	192	155	4	.553	351
Valparaiso	82	332	380	24	.467	736
Villanova	105	508	410	41	.551	959
VMI	112	437	561	43	.440	1041
Wagner	72	330	274	17	.545	621
Weber St.	41	209	224	3	.483	436
Western Caro.	69	289	378	23	.436	690
Western Ill.	99	445	365	37	.547	847
Western Ky.	84	471	305	31	.603	807
William & Mary	107	488	477	37	.505	1002
Wofford	94	409	439	36	.483	884
Yale	130	815	311	55	.713	1181
Youngstown St.	62	376	242	17	.606	635

Also includes any participation in major bowl games. Ties computed as half won and half lost. #Northern Arizona's participation in the 1999 Division I-AA championship (0-1 record) voided. %Stephen F. Austin's participation in the 1989 Division I-AA championship (3-1 record) voided. @Tennessee State's participation in the 1981 and 1982 Division I-AA championships (1-2 record) voided.

BY VICTORIES

Team	Wins
Yale	815
Pennsylvania	758
Harvard	750
Princeton	749
Fordham	706
Dartmouth	630
Lafayette	599
Cornell	591
Lehigh	584
Delaware	583
Dayton	554
Holy Cross	552
Colgate	537
Northern Iowa	536
Bucknell	531
Brown	530
Butler	511
Villanova	508
Drake	506
Furman	502
Florida A&M	497
Southern U.	488
William & Mary	488
Eastern Ky.	486
Massachusetts	486
Tennessee St.	471
Western Ky.	471
Hampton	468
Appalachian St.	465
Northwestern St.	458
Chattanooga	453
Grambling	451
Montana	450
New Hampshire	448
Maine	447
Georgetown	446
Western Ill.	445
Howard	439
VMI	437
Richmond	435
Elon	433
Southwest Tex. St.	433
Citadel	422
Eastern Ill.	421
Idaho St.	420
Murray St.	416
South Carolina St.	414
Eastern Wash.	411
Wofford	409
Southwest Mo. St.	406
N.C. A&T	405
Alabama St.	400
Illinois St.	400
Samford	396
Montana St.	388
Alcorn St.	384
Southeast Mo. St.	383
Davidson	379
Jackson St.	376
Morgan St.	376
Youngstown St.	376
Hofstra	371
St. Mary's (Cal.)	366
Jacksonville St.	364
Sam Houston St.	362
Tennessee Tech	354
Northern Ariz.	352
Bethune-Cookman	350
Rhode Island	350
McNeese St.	347
Columbia	346
Southern Ill.	339
East Tenn. St.	337
Morris Brown	337
Prairie View	335
Indiana St.	332
Valparaiso	332
Wagner	330
Cal Poly	327
Stephen F. Austin	321
Alabama A&M	306
Ark.-Pine Bluff	305
Western Caro.	289
Portland St.	278
Texas Southern	274
Morehead St.	271
Duquesne	267
Northeastern	261
Delaware St.	251
Austin Peay	243
Central Conn. St.	238
Canisius	228
Sacramento St.	217
Ga. Southern	211
Weber St.	209
Norfolk St.	202
Mississippi Val.	197
Towson	192
Southern Utah	191
Tenn.-Martin	186
Albany (N.Y.)	185
St. John's (N.Y.)	176
James Madison	174
San Diego	163
St. Francis (Pa.)	154
Liberty	145
Nicholls St.	143
Marist	108
Iona	103
Stony Brook	91
St. Peter's	74
Robert Morris	61
Sacred Heart	50
Monmouth	47
Fairfield	44
Charleston So.	33
Siena	32
Gardner-Webb	21
La Salle	20
Jacksonville	18
Fla. Atlantic	6
Florida Int'l	5
Savannah St.	5

DIVISION I-AA

Records in the 2000s

(2000-01-02, Playoffs Included)

BY PERCENTAGE

Team	2000 W	L	2001 W	L	2002 W	L	Total W	L	Pct.
Sacred Heart	10	1	10	0	7	3	27	4	.871
Montana	13	2	15	1	11	3	39	6	.867
Grambling	10	2	10	1	11	2	31	5	.861
Dayton	8	3	10	1	11	1	29	5	.853
Duquesne	10	1	8	3	11	1	29	5	.853
Lehigh	12	1	11	1	8	4	31	6	.838
Ga. Southern	13	2	12	2	11	3	36	7	.837
Pennsylvania	7	3	8	1	9	1	24	5	.828
Western Ky.	11	3	8	4	12	3	31	9	.775
Bethune-Cookman	9	2	6	4	11	2	26	8	.765
Davidson	10	0	5	4	7	3	22	7	.759
Furman	9	3	12	3	8	4	29	10	.744
McNeese St.	8	4	8	4	13	2	29	10	.744
Harvard	5	5	9	0	7	3	21	8	.724
Eastern Ill.	8	4	9	2	8	4	25	10	.714
Western Ill.	9	3	5	5	11	2	25	10	.714
Youngstown St.	9	3	8	3	7	4	24	10	.706
Gardner-Webb	6	4	6	4	9	1	21	9	.700
Colgate	7	4	7	3	9	3	23	10	.697
Appalachian St.	10	4	9	4	8	4	27	12	.692
Morehead St.	6	3	6	4	9	3	21	10	.677
Maine	5	6	9	3	11	3	25	12	.676
Eastern Ky.	6	5	8	2	8	4	22	11	.667
Florida A&M	9	3	7	4	7	5	23	12	.657
Robert Morris	10	0	6	3	3	7	19	10	.655
Hofstra	9	4	9	3	6	6	24	13	.649
Villanova	5	6	8	3	11	4	24	13	.649
Northern Iowa	7	4	11	3	5	6	23	13	.639
Northwestern St.	6	5	8	4	9	4	23	13	.639
Jackson St.	7	4	7	4	7	4	21	12	.636
Hampton	7	4	7	4	7	5	21	13	.618
Portland St.	8	4	7	4	6	5	21	13	.618
Delaware	12	2	4	6	6	6	22	14	.611
Albany (N.Y.)	5	6	7	3	8	4	20	13	.606
St. Peter's	4	7	10	1	6	5	20	13	.606
Tennessee Tech	8	3	7	3	5	7	20	13	.606
Sam Houston St.	7	4	10	3	4	7	21	14	.600
N.C. A&T	8	3	8	3	4	8	20	14	.588
Wofford	7	4	4	7	9	3	20	14	.588
Fairfield	8	2	5	5	5	6	#18	13	.581
Alabama A&M	7	5	4	5	8	4	19	14	.576
Eastern Wash.	6	5	7	4	6	5	19	14	.576
Alabama St.	6	5	8	4	6	6	20	15	.571
Fordham	3	8	7	4	10	3	20	15	.571
Southern U.	6	5	7	4	6	6	19	15	.559
William & Mary	5	6	8	4	6	5	19	15	.559
Yale	7	3	3	6	6	4	16	13	.552
Drake	7	4	5	5	5	5	17	14	.548
Idaho St.	6	5	4	7	8	3	18	15	.545
Stephen F. Austin	6	5	6	5	6	5	18	15	.545
Northeastern	4	7	5	6	10	3	19	16	.543
Marist	6	4	3	6	7	4	16	14	.533
Massachusetts	7	4	3	8	8	4	18	16	.529
St. Mary's (Cal.)	6	5	6	5	6	6	18	16	.529
Brown	7	3	6	3	2	8	15	14	.517
San Diego	4	6	6	3	5	5	15	14	.517
Wagner	6	5	3	6	7	4	16	15	.516
Murray St.	6	5	4	6	7	5	17	16	.515
Northern Ariz.	3	8	8	4	6	5	17	17	.500
Towson	7	4	3	7	6	5	16	16	.500
Richmond	10	3	3	8	4	7	17	18	.486
Western Caro.	4	7	7	4	5	6	16	17	.485
Delaware St.	7	4	5	6	4	8	16	18	.471
East Tenn. St.	6	5	6	5	4	8	16	18	.471
South Carolina St.	3	8	6	5	7	5	16	18	.471
Texas Southern	8	3	3	7	4	7	15	17	.469
Florida Int'l	—	—	—	—	5	6	5	6	.455
Holy Cross	7	4	4	6	4	8	15	18	.455
Illinois St.	7	4	2	9	6	5	15	18	.455
Southwest Mo. St.	5	6	6	5	4	7	15	18	.455
Southwest Tex. St.	7	4	4	7	4	7	15	18	.455
Monmouth	5	6	7	3	2	8	14	17	.452
Stony Brook	2	8	3	6	8	2	13	16	.448
Southeast Mo. St.	3	8	4	7	8	4	15	19	.441
Bucknell	6	5	6	4	2	9	14	18	.438
Jacksonville St.	4	6	5	6	5	6	14	18	.438

Team	2000 W	L	2001 W	L	2002 W	L	Total W	L	Pct.
La Salle	6	4	5	4	2	9	13	17	.433
Iona	4	7	4	5	5	6	13	18	.419
Princeton	3	7	3	6	6	4	12	17	.414
Charleston So.	5	6	5	6	4	8	14	20	.412
Rhode Island	3	8	8	3	3	9	14	20	.412
Sacramento St.	7	4	2	9	5	7	14	20	.412
Georgetown	5	6	3	7	5	6	13	19	.406
Samford	4	7	5	5	4	7	13	19	.406
Ark.-Pine Bluff	6	5	4	7	3	8	13	20	.394
Elon	7	4	2	9	4	7	13	20	.394
New Hampshire	6	5	4	7	3	8	13	20	.394
Norfolk St.	3	8	5	6	5	6	13	20	.394
Weber St.	7	4	3	8	3	8	13	20	.394
James Madison	6	5	2	9	5	7	13	21	.382
Tennessee St.	3	8	8	3	2	10	13	21	.382
Cornell	5	5	2	7	4	6	11	18	.379
Butler	2	8	5	5	4	6	11	19	.367
Central Conn. St.	4	6	2	7	5	6	11	19	.367
Alcorn St.	0	11	6	5	6	5	12	21	.364
Austin Peay	2	9	3	7	7	5	12	21	.364
Cal Poly	3	8	6	5	3	8	12	21	.364
Jacksonville	3	8	5	5	3	7	11	20	.355
Montana St.	0	11	5	6	7	6	12	23	.343
Howard	3	8	2	9	6	5	11	22	.333
Lafayette	2	9	2	8	7	5	11	22	.333
Nicholls St.	1	10	3	8	7	4	11	22	.333
Valparaiso	7	4	3	8	1	10	11	22	.333
Morris Brown	4	6	5	6	1	11	10	23	.303
Southern Utah	7	4	2	9	1	10	10	23	.303
Chattanooga	5	6	3	8	2	10	10	24	.294
Morgan St.	1	10	2	9	7	5	10	24	.294
Fla. Atlantic	—	—	4	6	2	9	6	15	.286
Indiana St.	1	10	3	8	5	7	9	25	.265
Southern Ill.	4	7	1	10	4	8	9	25	.265
VMI	2	9	1	10	6	6	9	25	.265
St. John's (N.Y.)	5	6	1	9	2	8	#8	23	.258
Citadel	2	9	3	7	3	9	8	25	.242
Liberty	3	8	3	8	2	9	8	25	.242
Columbia	3	7	3	7	1	9	7	23	.233
Mississippi Val.	2	9	0	11	5	6	7	26	.212
Dartmouth	2	8	1	8	3	7	6	23	.207
Savannah St.	2	8	2	7	1	9	5	24	.172
Siena	1	9	1	8	3	7	5	24	.172
Prairie View	1	10	3	7	1	10	5	27	.156
Tenn.-Martin	2	9	1	10	2	10	5	29	.147
Canisius	0	10	1	9	2	9	#3	28	.097
St. Francis (Pa.)	0	11	0	10	2	8	2	29	.065

#Dropped football following 2002 season.

BY VICTORIES

Team	Wins
Montana	39
Ga. Southern	36
Grambling	31
Lehigh	31
Western Ky.	31
Dayton	29
Duquesne	29
Furman	29
McNeese St.	29
Appalachian St.	27
Sacred Heart	27
Bethune-Cookman	26
Eastern Ill.	25
Maine	25
Western Ill.	25
Hofstra	24
Pennsylvania	24
Villanova	24
Youngstown St.	24
Colgate	23
Florida A&M	23
Northern Iowa	23
Northwestern St.	23
Davidson	22
Delaware	22
Eastern Ky.	22
Gardner-Webb	21
Hampton	21
Harvard	21
Jackson St.	21

Team	Wins
Morehead St.	21
Portland St.	21
Sam Houston St.	21
Alabama St.	20
Albany (N.Y.)	20
Fordham	20
N.C. A&T	20
St. Peter's	20
Tennessee Tech	20
Wofford	20
Alabama A&M	19
Eastern Wash.	19
Northeastern	19
Robert Morris	19
Southern U.	19
William & Mary	19
Fairfield	#18
Idaho St.	18
Massachusetts	18
St. Mary's (Cal.)	18
Stephen F. Austin	18
Drake	17
Murray St.	17
Northern Ariz.	17
Richmond	17
Delaware St.	16
East Tenn. St.	16
Marist	16
South Carolina St.	16
Towson	16
Wagner	16
Western Caro.	16

Team	Wins
Yale	16
Brown	15
Holy Cross	15
Illinois St.	15
San Diego	15
Southeast Mo. St.	15
Southwest Mo. St.	15
Southwest Tex. St.	15
Texas Southern	15
Bucknell	14
Charleston So.	14
Jacksonville St.	14
Monmouth	14
Rhode Island	14
Sacramento St.	14
Ark.-Pine Bluff	13
Elon	13
Georgetown	13
Iona	13
James Madison	13
La Salle	13
New Hampshire	13
Norfolk St.	13
Samford	13
Stony Brook	13
Tennessee St.	13
Weber St.	13
Alcorn St.	12
Austin Peay	12
Cal Poly	12
Montana St.	12
Princeton	12

Team	Wins
Butler	11
Central Conn. St.	11
Cornell	11
Howard	11
Jacksonville	11
Lafayette	11
Nicholls St.	11
Valparaiso	11
Chattanooga	10
Morgan St.	10
Morris Brown	10
Southern Utah	10
Indiana St.	9
Southern Ill.	9
VMI	9
Citadel	8
Liberty	8
St. John's (N.Y.)	#8
Columbia	7
Mississippi Val.	7
Dartmouth	6
Fla. Atlantic	6
Florida Int'l	5
Prairie View	5
Savannah St.	5
Siena	5
Tenn.-Martin	5
Canisius	#3
St. Francis (Pa.)	2

#Dropped football following 2002 season.

Team	W-L-T	*Pct.
Bucknell	57-52-0	.523
Murray St.	59-54-0	.522
Alabama St.	55-51-4	.518
Connecticut	57-54-0	.514
Jacksonville St.	58-55-1	.513
Eastern Ill.	57-55-1	.509
Stony Brook	50-49-2	.505
Alcorn St.	52-52-3	.500
Davidson	49-49-1	.500
Western Ky.	54-54-0	.500
Illinois St.	55-57-2	.491
Towson	51-53-0	.490
Citadel	55-58-0	.487
Tennessee St.	54-58-0	.482
Alabama A&M	52-57-1	.477
Sam Houston St.	51-56-3	.477
Tennessee Tech	51-58-0	.468
Norfolk St.	48-55-1	.466
Colgate	52-60-1	.465
Cal St. Northridge	49-57-0	.462
Brown	46-54-0	.460
Delaware St.	50-59-0	.459
Yale	45-55-0	.450
East Tenn. St.	50-62-0	.446
Lafayette	47-59-3	.445
Harvard	43-56-1	.435
Sacramento St.	45-59-1	.433
Iona	42-56-1	.429
Richmond	47-63-1	.428
Montana St.	47-63-0	.427
Texas Southern	46-62-1	.427
Valparaiso	43-59-1	.422
Chattanooga	46-64-0	.418

Team	W-L-T	*Pct.
Indiana St.	46-64-0	.418
Morehead St.	44-62-0	.415
Bethune-Cookman	44-64-0	.407
Holy Cross	44-65-1	.405
Mississippi Val.	40-62-3	.395
Western Caro.	43-66-0	.394
Maine	43-67-0	.391
Jacksonville	7-11-0	.389
Southern U.	38-63-1	.377
Southeast Mo. St.	40-70-0	.364
Northeastern	39-70-1	.359
Morgan St.	20-37-0	.351
Canisius	34-64-1	.348
Columbia	33-65-2	.340
Southern Ill.	37-73-0	.336
Idaho St.	36-73-1	.332
Central Conn. St.	31-66-1	.321
Nicholls St.	35-75-1	.320
Rhode Island	34-75-0	.312
St. Francis (Pa.)	29-70-1	.295
Tenn.-Martin	31-79-0	.282
Sacred Heart	23-64-0	.264
La Salle	7-20-0	.259
Southwest Tex. St.	23-68-0	.253
Siena	22-69-0	.242
St. Peter's	21-70-0	.231
Austin Peay	24-85-0	.220
Charleston So.	19-73-0	.207
VMI	22-88-0	.200
Fordham	20-85-1	.193
Prairie View	3-93-0	.031

Ties counted as half won and half lost.

Records in the 1990s

(1990-91-92-93-94-95-96-97-98-99, Playoffs Included; tiebreaker began in 1996)

BY PERCENTAGE

Team	W-L-T	*Pct.
Dayton	92-17-0	.844
Youngstown St.	103-30-2	.770
Montana	93-32-0	.744
Hofstra	81-29-2	.732
Troy St.	87-32-1	.729
Delaware	88-33-1	.725
Northern Iowa	89-34-0	.724
Ga. Southern	92-36-0	.719
Eastern Ky.	85-35-0	.708
Robert Morris	42-18-1	.697
N.C. A&T	79-35-0	.693
Drake	70-31-2	.689
Hampton	78-36-1	.683
McNeese St.	84-39-2	.680
William & Mary	78-37-0	.678
Jackson St.	76-37-1	.671
Appalachian St.	79-40-0	.664
Florida A&M	79-40-0	.664
Ark.-Pine Bluff	56-31-0	.644
Dartmouth	62-35-3	.635
Fairfield	26-15-0	.634
Georgetown	63-37-0	.630
Southern Utah	66-39-0	.629
Pennsylvania	62-37-0	.626
Lehigh	70-42-1	.624
Wagner	63-38-0	.624
St. John's (N.Y.)	65-40-0	.619
Marist	61-38-2	.614
Samford	69-43-2	.614

Team	W-L-T	*Pct.
Western Ill.	71-45-1	.611
Albany (N.Y.)	62-40-0	.608
South Fla.	20-13-0	.606
Villanova	69-46-0	.600
Portland St.	70-47-0	.598
New Hampshire	65-45-2	.589
Massachusetts	67-47-1	.587
South Carolina St.	64-45-0	.587
Princeton	58-41-1	.585
Duquesne	59-42-1	.583
Howard	65-47-0	.580
Furman	66-48-1	.578
San Diego	57-42-1	.575
Southwest Mo. St.	57-43-1	.569
Monmouth	33-25-0	.569
Elon	61-47-0	.565
James Madison	65-51-0	.560
Grambling	62-50-0	.554
Northern Ariz.	62-50-0	.554
Northwestern St.	63-51-0	.553
Cornell	55-45-0	.550
Eastern Wash.	61-51-0	.545
Liberty	60-50-0	.545
St. Mary's (Cal.)	54-46-1	.540
Wofford	59-51-1	.536
Cal Poly	57-50-1	.532
Weber St.	59-52-0	.532
Stephen F. Austin	58-52-3	.527
Butler	53-48-1	.525

BY VICTORIES

(Minimum 55 victories; Playoffs Included)

Team	Wins
Youngstown St.	103
Montana	93
Dayton	92
Ga. Southern	92
Northern Iowa	89
Delaware	88
Troy St.	87
Eastern Ky.	85
McNeese St.	84
Hofstra	81
Appalachian St.	79
Florida A&M	79
N.C. A&T	79
Hampton	78
William & Mary	78
Jackson St.	76
Western Ill.	71
Drake	70
Lehigh	70
Portland St.	70
Samford	69
Villanova	69
Massachusetts	67
Furman	66
Southern Utah	66
Howard	65
James Madison	65
New Hampshire	65
St. John's (N.Y.)	65
South Carolina St.	64

Team	Wins
Georgetown	63
Northwestern St.	63
Wagner	63
Albany (N.Y.)	62
Dartmouth	62
Grambling	62
Northern Ariz.	62
Pennsylvania	62
Eastern Wash.	61
Elon	61
Marist	61
Liberty	60
Duquesne	59
Murray St.	59
Weber St.	59
Wofford	59
Jacksonville St.	58
Princeton	58
Stephen F. Austin	58
Bucknell	57
Cal Poly	57
Connecticut	57
Eastern Ill.	57
San Diego	57
Southwest Mo. St.	57
Ark.-Pine Bluff	56
Alabama St.	55
Citadel	55
Cornell	55
Illinois St.	55

DIVISION I-AA

Records in the Last Five Years

(1998-99-2000-01-02; Playoffs Included)

BY PERCENTAGE

Team	1998 W L	1999 W L	2000 W L	2001 W L	2002 W L	Total W L Pct.
Ga. Southern	14 1	13 2	13 2	12 2	11 3	63 10 .863
Lehigh	12 1	10 2	12 1	11 1	8 4	53 9 .855
Montana	8 4	9 3	13 2	15 1	11 3	56 13 .812
Duquesne	8 3	8 3	10 1	8 3	11 1	45 11 .804
Davidson	8 2	8 3	10 0	5 4	7 3	38 12 .760
Dayton	6 4	6 4	8 3	10 1	11 1	41 13 .759
Pennsylvania	8 2	5 5	7 3	8 1	9 1	37 12 .755
Grambling	5 6	7 4	10 2	10 1	11 2	43 15 .741
Bethune-Cookman	8 3	7 4	9 2	6 4	11 2	41 15 .732
Appalachian St.	10 3	9 3	10 4	9 4	8 4	46 18 .719
Colgate	8 4	10 2	7 4	7 3	9 3	41 16 .719
Western Ill.	11 3	7 4	9 3	5 5	11 2	43 17 .717
Florida A&M	11 2	10 4	9 3	7 4	7 5	44 18 .710
McNeese St.	9 3	6 5	8 4	8 4	13 2	44 18 .710
Western Ky.	7 4	6 5	11 2	8 4	12 3	44 18 .710
Hofstra	8 3	11 2	9 4	9 3	6 6	43 18 .705
Youngstown St.	6 5	12 3	9 3	8 3	7 4	42 18 .700
Albany (N.Y.)	10 1	7 2	5 6	7 3	8 4	37 16 .698
Furman	5 6	9 3	9 3	12 3	8 4	43 19 .694
Fairfield	9 2	9 2	8 2	5 5	5 6	#36 17 .679
Morehead St.	9 2	5 5	6 3	6 4	9 3	35 17 .673
N.C. A&T	8 3	11 2	8 3	8 3	4 8	39 19 .672
Jackson St.	7 4	9 3	7 4	7 4	7 4	37 19 .661
Southern U.	9 3	11 2	6 5	7 4	6 6	39 20 .661
Hampton	9 3	8 4	7 4	7 4	7 5	38 20 .655
Northern Iowa	7 4	8 3	7 4	11 3	5 6	38 20 .655
Gardner-Webb	6 5	7 4	6 4	6 4	9 1	34 18 .654
Eastern Ky.	6 5	7 4	6 5	8 2	8 4	35 20 .636
Brown	7 3	9 1	7 3	6 3	2 8	31 18 .633
Robert Morris	4 6	8 2	10 0	6 3	3 7	31 18 .633
Yale	6 4	9 1	7 3	3 6	6 4	31 18 .633
Massachusetts	12 3	9 4	7 4	3 8	8 4	39 23 .629
Villanova	6 5	7 4	5 6	8 3	11 4	37 22 .627
Northwestern St.	11 3	4 7	6 5	8 4	9 4	38 23 .623
Delaware	7 4	7 4	12 2	4 6	6 6	36 22 .621
Harvard	4 6	5 5	5 5	9 0	7 3	30 19 .612
Portland St.	5 6	8 3	8 4	7 4	6 5	34 22 .607
Drake	7 3	7 4	7 4	5 5	5 5	31 21 .596
Sacred Heart	2 8	2 9	10 1	10 0	7 3	31 21 .596
Maine	6 5	4 7	5 6	9 3	11 3	35 24 .593
Illinois St.	8 4	11 3	7 4	2 9	6 5	34 25 .576
Georgetown	9 2	9 2	5 6	3 7	5 6	31 23 .574
William & Mary	7 4	6 5	5 6	8 4	6 5	32 24 .571
Eastern Ill.	6 5	2 10	8 4	9 2	8 4	33 25 .569
Marist	7 3	6 5	6 4	3 6	7 4	29 22 .569
Tennessee St.	9 3	11 1	3 8	8 3	2 10	33 25 .569
Eastern Wash.	5 6	7 4	6 5	7 4	6 5	31 24 .564
Murray St.	7 4	7 4	6 5	4 6	7 5	31 24 .564
Wagner	7 3	5 5	6 5	3 6	7 4	28 23 .549
Alabama A&M	5 6	6 5	7 5	4 5	8 4	30 25 .545
Northern Ariz.	6 5	8 4	3 8	8 4	6 5	31 26 .544
Tennessee Tech	4 7	5 5	8 3	7 3	5 7	29 25 .537
Wofford	4 7	6 5	7 4	4 7	9 3	30 26 .536
Richmond	9 3	5 6	10 3	3 8	4 7	31 27 .534
Stephen F. Austin	3 8	8 3	6 5	6 5	6 5	29 26 .527
Sam Houston St.	3 8	6 5	7 4	10 3	4 7	30 27 .526
Towson	5 6	7 4	7 4	3 7	6 5	28 26 .519
Bucknell	6 5	7 4	6 5	6 4	2 9	27 27 .500
Texas Southern	6 5	6 5	8 3	3 7	4 7	27 27 .500
Ark.-Pine Bluff	8 3	6 5	6 5	4 7	3 8	27 28 .491
Elon	5 6	9 2	7 4	2 9	4 7	27 28 .491
Samford	6 5	7 4	4 7	5 5	4 7	26 28 .481
Alabama St.	5 6	2 9	6 5	8 4	6 6	27 30 .474
East Tenn. St.	4 7	6 5	6 5	6 5	4 8	26 30 .464
Northeastern	5 6	2 9	4 7	5 6	10 3	26 31 .456
Florida Int'l	— —	— —	— —	— —	5 6	5 6 .455
South Carolina St.	5 6	4 6	3 8	6 5	7 5	25 30 .455
Southwest Mo. St.	5 6	5 6	5 6	6 5	4 7	25 30 .455
Valparaiso	5 6	9 2	7 4	3 8	1 10	25 30 .455
Western Caro.	6 5	3 8	4 7	7 4	5 6	25 30 .455
Cornell	4 6	7 3	5 5	2 7	4 6	22 27 .449
San Diego	2 8	5 5	4 6	6 3	5 5	22 27 .449
Sacramento St.	5 6	6 5	7 4	2 9	5 7	25 31 .446
Idaho St.	3 8	3 8	6 5	4 7	8 3	24 31 .436
Iona	4 6	5 5	4 7	4 5	5 6	22 29 .431
Stony Brook	3 7	5 5	2 8	3 6	8 2	21 28 .429
Jacksonville St.	7 4	2 9	4 6	5 6	5 6	23 31 .426
Fordham	4 7	0 11	3 8	7 4	10 3	24 33 .421
James Madison	3 8	8 4	6 5	2 9	5 7	24 33 .421
Howard	7 4	5 6	3 8	2 9	6 5	23 32 .418
Southern Utah	5 6	8 3	7 4	2 9	1 10	23 32 .418
Monmouth	5 5	2 8	5 6	7 3	2 8	21 30 .412
Princeton	5 5	5 3	7 3	3 6	6 4	20 29 .408
Butler	4 6	5 5	2 8	5 5	4 6	20 30 .400
New Hampshire	4 7	5 6	6 5	4 7	3 8	22 33 .400
Southwest Tex. St.	4 7	3 8	7 4	4 7	4 7	22 33 .400
St. Mary's (Cal.)	2 8	2 9	6 5	6 5	6 6	22 33 .400
Weber St.	6 5	3 8	7 4	3 8	3 8	22 33 .400
La Salle	2 6	4 6	6 4	5 4	2 9	19 29 .396
St. John's (N.Y.)	6 5	7 4	5 6	1 9	2 8	#21 32 .396
St. Peter's	0 10	1 10	4 7	10 1	6 5	21 33 .389
Montana St.	7 4	3 8	0 11	5 6	7 6	22 35 .386
Charleston So.	3 8	4 6	5 6	5 6	4 8	21 34 .382
Central Conn. St.	4 6	4 6	4 6	2 7	5 6	19 31 .380
Southeast Mo. St.	3 8	3 8	3 8	4 7	8 4	21 35 .375
Alcorn St.	5 6	3 7	0 11	6 5	6 5	20 34 .370
Jacksonville	4 5	3 6	3 8	5 5	3 7	18 31 .367
Holy Cross	2 9	3 8	7 4	4 6	4 8	20 35 .364
Chattanooga	5 6	5 6	5 6	3 8	2 10	20 36 .357
Delaware St.	0 11	4 7	7 4	5 6	4 8	20 36 .357
Austin Peay	4 7	3 8	2 9	3 7	7 5	19 36 .345
Morris Brown	3 8	6 5	4 6	5 6	1 11	19 36 .345
Savannah St.	7 4	5 6	2 8	2 7	1 9	17 34 .333
Cal Poly	3 8	3 8	3 8	6 5	3 8	18 37 .327
Lafayette	3 8	4 7	2 9	2 8	7 5	18 37 .327
Rhode Island	3 8	1 10	3 8	8 3	3 9	18 38 .321
Liberty	5 6	4 7	3 8	3 8	2 9	17 38 .309
Norfolk St.	2 9	2 9	3 8	5 6	5 6	17 38 .309
Indiana St.	5 6	3 8	1 10	3 8	5 7	17 39 .304
Southern Ill.	3 8	5 6	4 7	1 10	4 8	17 39 .304
Nicholls St.	4 7	1 10	1 10	3 8	7 4	16 39 .291
Fla. Atlantic	— —	— —	— —	4 6	2 9	6 15 .286
Columbia	4 6	3 7	3 7	3 7	1 9	14 36 .280
Citadel	5 6	2 9	2 9	3 7	3 9	15 40 .273
Morgan St.	1 10	2 8	1 10	2 9	7 5	13 42 .236
Siena	3 6	3 7	1 9	1 8	3 7	11 37 .229
Dartmouth	2 8	2 8	2 8	1 8	3 7	10 39 .204
Mississippi Val.	1 10	3 8	2 9	0 11	5 6	11 44 .200
VMI	1 10	1 10	2 9	1 10	6 6	11 45 .196
Prairie View	1 10	2 8	1 10	3 7	1 10	8 45 .151
Canisius	3 7	1 10	0 10	1 9	2 9	#7 45 .135
Tenn.-Martin	0 11	1 10	2 9	1 10	2 10	6 50 .107
St. Francis (Pa.)	0 10	2 9	0 11	0 10	2 8	4 48 .077

#Dropped football following 2002 season.

BY VICTORIES

(Playoffs Included)

Team	Wins
Ga. Southern	63
Montana	56
Lehigh	53
Appalachian St.	46
Duquesne	45
Florida A&M	44
McNeese St.	44
Western Ky.	44
Furman	43
Grambling	43
Hofstra	43
Western Ill.	43
Youngstown St.	42
Bethune-Cookman	41
Colgate	41
Dayton	41
Massachusetts	39
N.C. A&T	39
Southern U.	39
Davidson	38
Hampton	38
Northern Iowa	38
Northwestern St.	38
Albany (N.Y.)	37
Jackson St.	37
Pennsylvania	37
Villanova	37
Delaware	36
Fairfield	#36

Team	Wins
Eastern Ky.	35
Maine	35
Morehead St.	35
Gardner-Webb	34
Illinois St.	34
Portland St.	34
Eastern Ill.	33
Tennessee St.	33
William & Mary	32
Brown	31
Drake	31
Eastern Wash.	31
Georgetown	31
Murray St.	31
Northern Ariz.	31
Richmond	31
Robert Morris	31
Sacred Heart	31
Yale	31
Alabama A&M	30
Harvard	30
Sam Houston St.	30
Wofford	30
Marist	29
Stephen F. Austin	29
Tennessee Tech	29
Towson	28
Wagner	28
Alabama St.	27
Ark.-Pine Bluff	27
Bucknell	27
Elon	27

Team	Wins
Texas Southern	27
East Tenn. St.	26
Northeastern	26
Samford	26
Sacramento St.	25
South Carolina St.	25
Southwest Mo. St.	25
Valparaiso	25
Western Caro.	25
Fordham	24
Idaho St.	24
James Madison	24
Howard	23
Jacksonville St.	23
Southern Utah	23
Cornell	22
Iona	22
Montana St.	22
New Hampshire	22
St. Mary's (Cal.)	22
San Diego	22
Southwest Tex. St.	22
Weber St.	22
Charleston So.	21
Monmouth	21
St. John's (N.Y.)	#21
St. Peter's	21
Southeast Mo. St.	21
Stony Brook	21
Alcorn St.	20
Butler	20
Chattanooga	20

Team	Wins
Delaware St.	20
Holy Cross	20
Princeton	20
Austin Peay	19
Central Conn. St.	19
La Salle	19
Morris Brown	19
Cal Poly	18
Jacksonville	18
Lafayette	18
Rhode Island	18
Indiana St.	17
Liberty	17
Norfolk St.	17
Savannah St.	17
Southern Ill.	17
Nicholls St.	16
Citadel	15
Columbia	14
Morgan St.	13
Mississippi Val.	11
Siena	11
VMI	11
Dartmouth	10
Prairie View	8
Canisius	#7
Fla. Atlantic	6
Tenn.-Martin	6
Florida Int'l	5
St. Francis (Pa.)	4

#Dropped football following 2002 season.

Records in the 1980s

(Playoffs Included)

BY PERCENTAGE

Team	W-L-T	Pct.†	Team	W-L-T	Pct.†
Eastern Ky.	88-24-2	.781	Delaware	68-36-0	.654
Furman	83-23-4	.773	Middle Tenn.	65-36-0	.644
Ga. Southern	68-22-1	*.753	Boise St.	66-38-0	.635
Jackson St.	71-25-5	.728	Southwest Tex. St.	66-39-0	.629
Grambling	68-30-3	.688	Murray St.	61-36-2	.626
Nevada	71-35-1	.668	Northern Iowa	64-38-2	.625
Holy Cross	67-33-2	.667	Towson	60-36-2	.622
Tennessee St.	64-32-4	.660	Alcorn St.	56-34-0	.622
Eastern Ill.	70-36-1	.659	La.-Monroe	64-39-0	.621
Idaho	69-36-0	.657	South Carolina St.	55-34-1	.617

†Ties counted as half won and half lost. *Includes two nonvarsity seasons and five varsity seasons; varsity record, 55-14-0 for .797.

National Poll Rankings

Final Poll Leaders

(Released before division championship playoffs prior to 2001 and released after the championship playoffs beginning with 2001. Both the Sports Network and USA Today/ESPN polls select final poll leaders following the playoffs.)

Year	Team, Record*	Coach	Record in Championship†
1978	Nevada (10-0-0)	Chris Ault	0-1 Lost in semifinals
1979	Grambling (8-2-0)	Eddie Robinson	Did not compete
1980	Lehigh (9-0-2)	John Whitehead	0-1 Lost in semifinals
1981	Eastern Ky. (9-1-0)	Roy Kidd	2-1 Lost in championship
1982	Eastern Ky. (10-0-0)	Roy Kidd	3-0 Champion
1983	Southern Ill. (10-1-0)	Rey Dempsey	3-0 Champion
1984	Alcorn St. (9-0-0)	Marino Casem	0-1 Lost in quarterfinals
1985	Middle Tenn. (11-0-0)	James Donnelly	0-1 Lost in quarterfinals
1986	Nevada (11-0-0)	Chris Ault	2-1 Lost in semifinals
1987	Holy Cross (11-0-0)	Mark Duffner	Did not compete
1988	Idaho (9-1-0)	Keith Gilbertson	2-1 Lost in semifinals
1989	Ga. Southern (11-0-0)	Erk Russell	4-0 Champion
1990	Middle Tenn. (10-1-0)	James Donnelly	1-1 Lost in quarterfinals
1991	Nevada (11-0-0)	Chris Ault	1-1 Lost in quarterfinals
1992	(tie) Citadel (10-1-0)	Charlie Taaffe	1-1 Lost in quarterfinals
	La.-Monroe (9-2-0)	Dave Roberts	1-1 Lost in quarterfinals
1993	Troy St. (10-0-1)	Larry Blakeney	2-1 Lost in semifinals
1994	Youngstown St. (10-0-1)	Jim Tressel	4-0 Champion
1995	McNeese St. (11-0-0)	Bobby Keasler	2-1 Lost in semifinals
1996	Marshall (11-0)	Bob Pruett	4-0 Champion
1997	Villanova (11-0)	Andy Talley	1-1 Lost in quarterfinals
1998	Ga. Southern (11-0)	Paul Johnson	3-1 Lost in championship
1999	Tennessee St. (11-0)	L.C. Cole	0-1 Lost in first round
2000	Montana (10-1)	Joe Glenn	3-1 Lost in championship
2001	Montana (11-1)	Joe Glenn	4-0 Champion
2002	Western Ky. (12-3)	Jack Harbaugh	4-0 Champion

*Final poll record; in some cases, a team had one or two games remaining before the championship playoffs. †Number of teams in the championship: 4 (1978-80); 8 (1981); 12 (1982-85); 16 (1986-present).

DIVISION I-AA

Final Regular-Season Polls

1978
(NCAA)
Team
1. Nevada
2. Jackson St.
3. Florida A&M
4. Massachusetts
5. Western Ky.
6. South Carolina St.
7. Northern Ariz.
   Montana St.
   Eastern Ky.
   Lehigh
   Rhode Island

1979
(NCAA)
Team
1. Grambling
2. Murray St.
3. Eastern Ky.
   Lehigh
5. Nevada
6. Alcorn St.
7. Boston U.
8. Jackson St.
9. Montana St.
10. Northern Ariz.
    Southern U.

1980
(NCAA)
Team
1. Lehigh
2. Grambling
3. Eastern Ky.
4. South Carolina St.
5. Western Ky.
6. Delaware
7. Boise St.
8. Northwestern St.
9. Boston U.
10. Connecticut
    Massachusetts
    Murray St.

1981
(NCAA)
Team
1. Eastern Ky.
2. Idaho St.
3. South Carolina St.
4. Jackson St.
5. Boise St.
6. Tennessee St.
7. Delaware
8. Lafayette
9. Murray St.
10. New Hampshire

1982
(NCAA)
Team
1. Eastern Ky.
2. Louisiana Tech
3. Delaware
4. Tennessee St.
5. Eastern Ill.
6. Furman
7. South Carolina St.
8. Jackson St.
9. Colgate
10. Grambling
11. Idaho
12. Northern Ill.
13. Holy Cross
14. Bowling Green
15. Boise St.
16. Western Mich.
17. Chattanooga
18. Northwestern St.
19. Montana
20. Lafayette

1983
(NCAA)
Team
1. Southern Ill.
2. Furman
3. Holy Cross
4. North Texas
5. Indiana St.
6. Eastern Ill.
7. Colgate
8. Eastern Ky.
9. Western Caro.
10. Grambling
11. Nevada
12. Idaho St.
13. Boston U.
    La.-Monroe
15. Jackson St.
16. Middle Tenn.
17. Tennessee St.
18. South Carolina St.
19. Mississippi Val.
20. New Hampshire

1984
(NCAA)
Team
1. Alcorn St.
2. Montana St.
   Rhode Island
4. Boston U.
5. Indiana St.
6. Middle Tenn.
   Mississippi Val.
8. Eastern Ky.
9. Louisiana Tech
10. Arkansas St.
11. New Hampshire
12. Richmond
13. Murray St.
14. Western Caro.
15. Holy Cross
16. Furman
17. Chattanooga
18. Northern Iowa
19. Delaware
20. McNeese St.

1985
(NCAA)
Team
1. Middle Tenn.
2. Furman
   Nevada
4. Northern Iowa
5. Idaho
6. Arkansas St.
7. Rhode Island
8. Grambling
9. Ga. Southern
10. Akron
11. Eastern Wash.
12. Appalachian St.
    Delaware St.
14. Louisiana Tech
15. Jackson St.
16. William & Mary
17. Murray St.
18. Richmond
19. Eastern Ky.
20. Alcorn St.

1986
(NCAA)
Team
1. Nevada
2. Arkansas St.
3. Eastern Ill.
4. Ga. Southern
5. Holy Cross
6. Appalachian St.
7. Pennsylvania
8. William & Mary
9. Jackson St.
10. Eastern Ky.
11. Sam Houston St.
12. Nicholls St.
13. Delaware
14. Tennessee St.
15. Furman
16. Idaho
17. Southern Ill.
18. Murray St.
19. Connecticut
20. N.C. A&T

1987
(NCAA)
Team
1. Holy Cross
2. Appalachian St.
3. La.-Monroe
4. Northern Iowa
5. Idaho
6. Ga. Southern
7. Eastern Ky.
8. James Madison
9. Jackson St.
10. Weber St.
11. Western Ky.
12. Arkansas St.
13. Maine
14. Marshall
15. Youngstown St.
16. North Texas
17. Richmond
18. Howard
19. Sam Houston St.
20. Delaware St.

1988
(NCAA)
Team
1. Stephen F. Austin
2. Idaho
3. Ga. Southern
4. Western Ill.
5. Furman
6. Jackson St.
7. Marshall
8. Eastern Ky.
9. Citadel
10. Northwestern St.
11. Massachusetts
12. North Texas
13. Boise St.
14. Florida A&M
    Pennsylvania
16. Western Ky.
17. Connecticut
18. Grambling
19. Montana
20. New Hampshire

1989
(NCAA)
Team
1. Ga. Southern
2. Furman
3. Stephen F. Austin
4. Holy Cross
   Idaho
6. Montana
7. Appalachian St.
8. Maine
9. Southwest Mo. St.
10. Middle Tenn.
    William & Mary
12. Eastern Ky.
13. Grambling
14. Youngstown St.
15. Eastern Ill.
16. Villanova
17. Jackson St.
18. Connecticut
19. Nevada
20. Northern Iowa

1990
(NCAA)
Team
1. Middle Tenn.
2. Youngstown St.
3. Ga. Southern
4. Nevada
5. Eastern Ky.
6. Southwest Mo. St.
7. William & Mary
8. Holy Cross
9. Massachusetts
10. Boise St.
11. Northern Iowa
12. Furman
13. Idaho
14. La.-Monroe
15. Citadel
16. Jackson St.
17. Dartmouth
18. UCF
19. New Hampshire
    N.C. A&T

1991
(NCAA)
Team
1. Nevada
2. Eastern Ky.
3. Holy Cross
4. Northern Iowa
5. Alabama St.
6. Delaware
7. Villanova
8. Marshall
9. Middle Tenn.
10. Samford
11. New Hampshire
12. Sam Houston St.
13. Youngstown St.
14. Western Ill.
15. Weber St.
16. James Madison
17. Appalachian St.
18. La.-Monroe
19. McNeese St.
20. Citadel
    Furman

1992
(NCAA)
Team
1. Citadel
   La.-Monroe
3. Northern Iowa
4. Middle Tenn.
5. Idaho
6. Marshall
7. Youngstown St.
8. Delaware
9. Samford
10. Villanova
11. McNeese St.
12. Eastern Ky.
13. William & Mary
14. Eastern Wash.
15. Florida A&M
16. Appalachian St.
17. N.C. A&T
18. Alcorn St.
19. Liberty
20. Western Ill.

1993
(Sports Network)
Team
1. Troy St.
2. Ga. Southern
3. Montana
4. La.-Monroe
5. McNeese St.
6. Boston U.
7. Youngstown St.
8. Howard
9. Marshall
10. William & Mary
11. Idaho
12. UCF
13. Northern Iowa
14. Stephen F. Austin
15. Southern U.
16. Pennsylvania
17. Eastern Ky.
18. Delaware
19. Western Ky.
20. Eastern Wash.
21. N.C. A&T
22. Tennessee Tech
23. Alcorn St.
24. Towson
25. Massachusetts

1994
(Sports Network)
Team
1. Youngstown St.
2. Marshall
3. Boise St.
4. Eastern Ky.
5. McNeese St.
6. Idaho
7. Grambling
8. Montana
9. Boston U.
10. Troy St.
11. Northern Iowa
12. New Hampshire
13. James Madison
14. Pennsylvania
15. Alcorn St.
16. Middle Tenn.
17. Appalachian St.
18. North Texas
19. William & Mary
20. UCF
21. Stephen F. Austin
22. South Carolina St.
23. Hofstra
24. Western Ill.
25. Northern Ariz.

1995
(Sports Network)
Team
1. McNeese St.
2. Appalachian St.
3. Troy St.
4. Murray St.
5. Stephen F. Austin
6. Marshall
7. Delaware
8. Montana
9. Hofstra
10. Eastern Ky.
11. Southern U.
12. Eastern Ill.
13. James Madison
14. Jackson St.
15. Ga. Southern
16. Florida A&M
17. Idaho
18. Northern Iowa
19. William & Mary
20. Richmond
21. Boise St.
22. Northern Ariz.
23. Connecticut
24. Indiana St.
25. Middle Tenn.

1996
(Sports Network)

Team
1. Marshall
2. Montana
3. Northern Iowa
4. Murray St.
5. Troy St.
6. Northern Ariz.
7. William & Mary
8. Jackson St.
(tie) East Tenn. St.
10. Western Ill.
11. Delaware
12. Florida A&M
13. Furman
14. Villanova
15. Youngstown St.
16. Eastern Ill.
17. Dartmouth
18. New Hampshire
19. Nicholls St.
20. Howard
21. Southwest Mo. St.
22. Stephen F. Austin
23. James Madison
24. Dayton
25. Appalachian St.

1997
(Sports Network)

Team
1. Villanova
2. Western Ill.
3. Delaware
4. Eastern Wash.
5. Western Ky.
6. McNeese St.
7. Hampton
8. Ga. Southern
9. Youngstown St.
10. Florida A&M
11. Montana
12. Southern U.
13. Jackson St.
14. Hofstra
15. Eastern Ky.
16. Cal Poly
17. Northwestern St.
18. Stephen F. Austin
19. South Carolina St.
20. Liberty
21. Eastern Ill.
22. Appalachian St.
23. Dayton
24. Northeastern
25. Colgate

1997
(USA Today/ESPN)

Team
1. Youngstown St.
2. McNeese St.
3. Delaware
4. Eastern Wash.
5. Villanova
6. Western Ill.
7. Western Ky.
8. Ga. Southern
9. Montana
10. Hampton
11. Southern U.
12. Florida A&M
13. Jackson St.
14. Northwestern St.
15. Eastern Ky.
16. Hofstra
17. Cal Poly
18. Stephen F. Austin
19. Liberty
20. South Carolina St.
21. Colgate
22. Eastern Ill.
23. Appalachian St.
24. Northeastern
25. Dayton

1998
(USA Today/ESPN)
(After Playoffs)

Team
1. Massachusetts
2. Ga. Southern
3. Northwestern St.
4. Western Ill.
5. Florida A&M
6. Appalachian St.
7. Connecticut
8. McNeese St.
9. Richmond
10. Hampton
11. Troy St.
12. Lehigh
13. Tennessee St.
14. Montana
15. Illinois St.
16. Southern U.
17. South Fla.
18. Hofstra
19. William & Mary
20. Murray St.
21. Colgate
22. Western Ky.
23. Bethune-Cookman
24. Delaware
25. Montana St.

1998
(Sports Network)

Team
1. Ga. Southern
2. Northwestern St.
3. Florida A&M
4. Western Ill.
5. Richmond
6. McNeese St.
7. Appalachian St.
8. Connecticut
9. Hampton
10. Tennessee St.
11. Troy St.
12. Massachusetts
13. Lehigh
14. Montana
15. Southern U.
16. William & Mary
17. Western Ky.
18. Hofstra
19. South Fla.
20. Bethune-Cookman
21. Illinois St.
22. Delaware
23. Murray St.
24. Montana St.
25. Northern Iowa

1999
(USA Today/ESPN)

Team (Record)
1. Tennessee St. (11-0)
2. Ga. Southern (9-2)
3. Appalachian St. (8-2)
4. Hofstra (10-1)
5. Illinois St. (9-2)
6. Troy St. (10-1)
7. Montana (9-2)
8. Furman (9-2)
9. Youngstown St. (9-2)
10. Southern U. (9-1)
11. Massachusetts (8-3)
12. James Madison (8-3)
13. Lehigh (10-1)
14. Jackson St. (9-2)
15. Florida A&M (8-3)
16. N.C. A&T (10-1)
17. Northern Iowa (8-3)
18. Colgate (10-1)
19. Northern Ariz. (8-3)
20. Elon (9-2)
21. Portland St. (8-3)
22. Stephen F. Austin (8-3)
23. South Fla. (7-4)
24. Southern Utah (8-3)
25. Villanova (7-4)

1999
(Sports Network)
(After Playoffs)

Team (Record)
1. Ga. Southern (13-2)
2. Youngstown St. (12-3)
3. Illinois St. (11-3)
4. Florida A&M (10-4)
5. Hofstra (11-2)
6. Troy St. (11-2)
7. Massachusetts (9-4)
8. Montana (9-3)
9. Appalachian St. (9-3)
(tie) N.C. A&T (11-2)
11. Tennessee St. (11-1)
12. Furman (9-3)
13. James Madison (8-4)
14. Lehigh (10-2)
15. Northern Iowa (8-3)
16. Northern Ariz. (8-4)
17. Southern U. (11-2)
18. Colgate (10-2)
19. Jackson St. (9-3)
20. Portland St. (8-3)
21. Elon (9-2)
22. Stephen F. Austin (8-3)
23. South Fla. (7-4)
24. Villanova (7-4)
25. Brown (9-1)

2000
(USA Today/ESPN)

Team (Record)
1. Montana (9-1)
2. Delaware (9-1)
3. Troy St. (8-2)
4. Ga. Southern (9-2)
5. Furman (8-2)
6. Western Ill. (8-2)
7. Western Ky. (9-1)
8. Richmond (8-2)
9. Youngstown St. (8-2)
10. Appalachian St. (7-3)
11. Lehigh (10-0)
12. Hofstra (7-3)
13. Grambling (9-1)
14. Florida A&M (8-2)
15. Portland St. (7-3)
16. McNeese St. (7-3)
17. Bethune-Cookman (9-1)
18. Northern Iowa (6-3)
19. Weber St. (7-4)
20. N.C. A&T (7-3)
21. Sam Houston St. (7-3)
22. Eastern Ill. (7-3)
23. James Madison (6-4)
24. Tennessee Tech (7-3)
25. Northwestern St. (6-4)

2000
(Sports Network)
(After Playoffs)

Team (Record)
1. Ga. Southern (13-2)
2. Montana (13-2)
3. Delaware (12-2)
4. Appalachian St. (10-4)
5. Western Ky. (11-2)
6. Richmond (10-3)
7. Hofstra (9-4)
8. Lehigh (12-1)
9. Troy St. (9-3)
10. Furman (9-3)
11. Youngstown St. (9-3)
12. Western Ill. (9-3)
13. Grambling (10-2)
14. Florida A&M (9-3)
15. Portland St. (8-4)
16. McNeese St. (8-4)
17. Eastern Ill. (8-4)
18. Weber St. (7-4)
19. Northern Iowa (7-4)
20. Bethune-Cookman (9-2)
21. N.C. A&T (8-3)
22. Tennessee Tech (8-3)
23. Wofford (7-4)
24. Illinois St. (7-4)
25. Southwest Tex. St. (7-4)

2001
(USA Today/ESPN)
(After Playoffs)

Team (Record)
1. Montana (15-1)
2. Furman (12-3)
3. Ga. Southern (12-2)
4. Northern Iowa (11-3)
5. Lehigh (11-1)
6. Appalachian St. (9-4)
7. Hofstra (9-3)
8. Sam Houston St. (10-3)
9. Eastern Ill. (9-2)
10. Western Ky. (8-4)
11. Grambling (10-1)
12. Maine (9-3)
13. McNeese St. (8-4)
14. Northwestern St. (8-4)
15. Northern Ariz. (8-4)
16. Youngstown St. (8-3)
17. William & Mary (8-4)
18. Eastern Ky. (8-2)
19. Villanova (8-3)
20. Rhode Island (8-3)
21. Harvard (9-0)
22. Florida A&M (7-4)
23. Tennessee Tech (7-3)
24. Pennsylvania (8-1)
25. Portland St. (7-4)

2001
(Sports Network)
(After Playoffs)

Team (Record)
1. Montana (15-1)
2. Furman (12-3)
3. Ga. Southern (12-2)
4. Northern Iowa (11-3)
5. Lehigh (11-1)
6. Appalachian St. (9-4)
7. Sam Houston St. (10-3)
8. Grambling (10-1)
9. Eastern Ill. (9-2)
10. Maine (9-3)
11. Hofstra (9-3)
12. Western Ky. (8-4)
13. McNeese St. (8-4)
14. Northwestern St. (8-4)
15. Youngstown St. (8-3)
16. Northern Ariz. (8-4)
17. William & Mary (8-4)
18. Eastern Ky. (8-2)
19. Harvard (9-0)
20. Villanova (8-3)
21. Rhode Island (8-3)
22. Florida A&M (7-4)
23. Tennessee Tech (7-3)
24. Pennsylvania (8-1)
25. Tennessee St. (8-3)

2002
(USA Today/ESPN)
(After Playoffs)

Team (Record)
1. Western Ky. (12-3)
2. McNeese St. (13-2)
3. Ga. Southern (11-3)
4. Villanova (11-4)
5. Western Ill. (11-2)
6. Maine (11-3)
(tie) Montana (11-3)
8. Grambling (11-2)
9. Furman (8-4)
10. Northeastern (10-3)
11. Wofford (9-3)
12. Bethune-Cookman (11-2)
(tie) Eastern Ill. (8-4)
14. Appalachian St. (8-4)
15. Fordham (10-3)
16. Northwestern St. (9-4)
17. Idaho St. (8-3)
(tie) Pennsylvania (9-1)
19. Montana St. (7-6)
20. Eastern Ky. (8-4)
21. Nicholls St. (7-4)
22. Murray St. (7-5)
23. Southeast Mo. St. (8-4)
24. Gardner-Webb (9-1)
25. Colgate (9-3)

2002
(Sports Network)
(After Playoffs)

Team (Record)
1. Western Ky. (12-3)
2. McNeese St. (13-2)
3. Ga. Southern (11-3)
4. Villanova (11-4)
5. Western Ill. (11-2)
6. Maine (11-3)
7. Montana (11-3)
8. Grambling (11-2)
9. Furman (8-4)
10. Appalachian St. (8-4)
11. Northeastern (10-3)
12. Fordham (10-3)
13. Eastern Ill. (8-4)
14. Wofford (9-3)
15. Bethune-Cookman (11-2)
16. Northwestern St. (9-4)
17. Pennsylvania (9-1)
18. Idaho St. (8-3)
19. Montana St. (7-6)
20. Murray St. (7-5)
21. Eastern Ky. (8-4)
22. Gardner-Webb (9-1)
23. Nicholls St. (7-4)
24. Southeast Mo. St. (8-4)
25. Colgate (9-3)

DIVISION I-AA

Undefeated, Untied Teams

Regular-season games only, from 1978. Subsequent loss in Division I-AA championship is indicated by (††).

Year	Team	Wins	Year	Team	Wins
1978	Nevada	††11		Howard	††11
1979	(None)			Pennsylvania	10
1980	(None)		1994	Pennsylvania	9
1981	(None)		1995	Appalachian St.	††11
1982	*Eastern Ky.	10		McNeese St.	††11
1983	(None)			Murray St.	††11
1984	Tennessee St.	11		Troy St.	††11
	Alcorn St.	††9	1996	Dartmouth	10
1985	Middle Tenn.	††11		Dayton	11
1986	Nevada	††11		*Marshall	11
	Pennsylvania	10		Montana	††11
1987	Holy Cross	11	1997	Villanova	††11
1988	(None)		1998	Ga. Southern	††11
1989	*Ga. Southern	11		Lehigh	††11
1990	Youngstown St.	††11	1999	(None)	
1991	Holy Cross	11	2000	Davidson	10
	Nevada	††11		Robert Morris	10
1992	(None)		2001	Sacred Heart	10
1993	Boston U.	††11		Harvard	9
			2002	(None)	

*Won Division I-AA championship.

The Spoilers

(From 1978 Season)

Following is a list of the spoilers of Division I-AA teams that lost their perfect (undefeated, untied) record in their **season-ending** game, including the Division I-AA championship playoffs. An asterisk (*) indicates a championship playoff game and a dagger (†) indicates the home team in a regular-season game.

Date	Spoiler	Victim	Score
12-9-78	*Massachusetts	Nevada	44-21
11-15-80	†Grambling	South Carolina St.	26-3
11-22-80	†Murray St.	Western Ky.	49-0
12-1-84	*Louisiana Tech	Alcorn St.	44-21
12-7-85	*Ga. Southern	Middle Tenn.	28-21
11-22-86	Boston College	†Holy Cross	56-26
12-19-86	*Ga. Southern	Nevada	48-38
11-19-88	*Cornell	Pennsylvania	19-6
11-24-90	*UCF	Youngstown St.	20-17
12-7-91	*Youngstown St.	Nevada	30-28
11-27-93	*Marshall	Howard	28-14
12-4-93	*Idaho	Boston U.	21-14
11-25-95	*Ga. Southern	Troy St.	24-21
11-25-95	*Northern Iowa	Murray St.	35-34
12-2-95	*Stephen F. Austin	Appalachian St.	27-17
12-9-95	*Marshall	McNeese St.	25-13
11-23-96	Robert Morris	Duquesne	28-26
12-21-96	*Marshall	Montana	49-29
11-22-97	†Colgate	Bucknell	48-14
12-6-97	*Youngstown St.	Villanova	37-34
12-5-98	*Massachusetts	Lehigh	27-21
12-19-98	*Massachusetts	Ga. Southern	55-43
11-27-99	*N.C. A&T	Tennessee St.	24-10
12-2-00	*Delaware	Lehigh	47-22
12-8-01	*Furman	Lehigh	34-17

Streaks and Rivalries

Because Division I-AA began in 1978, only those streaks from the period (1978-present) are listed. Only schools that have been I-AA members for five years are eligible for inclusion.

Longest Winning Streaks

(From 1978; Includes Playoff Games)

Wins	Team	Year(s)	Ended by	Score
24	Montana	2001-02	Eastern Wash.	21-30
24	Pennsylvania	1992-95	Columbia	14-24
21	Montana	1995-96	Marshall	29-49
20	Dayton	1996-97	Cal Poly	24-44
20	Holy Cross	1990-92	Army	7-17
19	Duquesne	1995-96	Robert Morris	26-28
18	Davidson	1999-01	Jacksonville	3-45
18	Eastern Ky.	1982-83	Western Ky.	10-10
17	Robert Morris	1999-00	Buffalo	27-33

Wins	Team	Year(s)	Ended by	Score
16	Ga. Southern	1989-90	Middle Tenn.	13-16
15	Dartmouth	1996-97	Lehigh	26-46
15	Marshall	1996	Moved to Division I-A	
14	Ga. Southern	1998	Massachusetts	43-55
14	Youngstown St.	1994	Kent St.	14-17
14	Delaware	1979-80	Lehigh	20-27
13	Montana	2000	Ga. Southern	25-27
13	Fairfield	1998-99	Holy Cross	23-24
13	Lehigh	1997-98	Massachusetts	21-27
13	McNeese St.	1995	Marshall	13-25
13	Holy Cross	1988-89	Army	9-45
13	Nevada	1986	Ga. Southern	38-48
13	Tennessee St.	1983-85	Western Ky.	17-22
13	Eastern Ill.	1978-79	Western Ill.	7-10
12	Harvard	2001-02	Lehigh	35-36
12	Sacred Heart	2000-02	Marist	27-38
12	Lehigh	2000	Delaware	22-47
12	Bucknell	1996-97	Colgate	14-48
12	Appalachian St.	1995	Stephen F. Austin	17-27
12	Nevada	1989-90	Boise St.	14-30
12	Furman	1989	Stephen F. Austin	19-21
12	Holy Cross	1987-88	Army	3-23
12	Southern Ill.	1982-83	Wichita St.	6-28
12	Florida A&M	1978-79	Tennessee St.	3-20

Longest Unbeaten Streaks

(From 1978; Includes Playoff Games and Ties)

No.	Wins	Ties	Team	Year(s)	Ended by
24	24	0	Montana	2001-02	Eastern Wash.
24	24	0	Pennsylvania	1992-95	Columbia
22	21	1	Dartmouth	1995-97	Lehigh
21	21	0	Montana	1995-96	Marshall
20	20	0	Dayton	1996-97	Cal Poly
20	20	0	Holy Cross	1990-92	Army
20	19	1	Youngstown St.	1993-94	Kent
19	19	0	Duquesne	1995-96	Robert Morris
19	18	1	Eastern Ky.	1982-83	Murray St.
18	18	0	Davidson	1999-01	Jacksonville
17	17	0	Robert Morris	1999-00	Buffalo
17	16	1	Alabama St.	1990-92	Alcorn St.
17	16	1	Grambling	1977-78	Florida A&M
16	16	0	Ga. Southern	1989-90	Middle Tenn.
15	15	0	Marshall	1996	Moved to Division I-A
15	14	1	Delaware	1994-95	Navy
14	14	0	Ga. Southern	1998	Massachusetts
13	13	0	Montana	2000	Ga. Southern
13	13	0	Fairfield	1998-99	Holy Cross
13	13	0	Lehigh	1997-98	Massachusetts
13	13	0	McNeese St.	1995	Marshall
13	13	0	Holy Cross	1988-89	Army
13	13	0	Nevada	1986	Ga. Southern
13	13	0	Tennessee St.	1983-85	Western Ky.
13	13	0	Eastern Ill.	1978-79	Western Ill.
13	12	1	Mississippi Val.	1983-84	Alcorn St.
13	12	1	Eastern Ill.	1981-82	Tennessee St.
12	12	0	Harvard	2001-02	Lehigh
12	12	0	Sacred Heart	2000-02	Marist
12	12	0	Lehigh	2000	Delaware
12	12	0	Bucknell	1996-97	Colgate
12	12	0	Appalachian St.	1995	Stephen F. Austin
12	12	0	Nevada	1989-90	Boise St.
12	12	0	Furman	1989	Stephen F. Austin
12	12	0	Holy Cross	1987-88	Army
12	12	0	Southern Ill.	1982-83	Wichita St.
12	12	0	Florida A&M	1978-79	Tennessee St.
12	11	1	Tennessee St.	1985-86	Alabama St.
12	11	1	Tennessee St.	1981-83	Jackson St.
11	11	0	Tennessee St.	1999	N.C. A&T
11	11	0	Florida A&M	1998	Western Ill.
11	11	0	Murray St.	1996	Troy St.
11	11	0	Pennsylvania	1985-87	Cornell
10	9	1	Stephen F. Austin	1989	Ga. Southern
10	9	1	Holy Cross	1983	Boston College
10	9	1	Jackson St.	1980	Grambling

Longest Home Winning Streaks

(From 1978; Includes Playoff Games)

Wins	Team	Years	Ended by
39	Ga. Southern	1997-01	Furman
38	Ga. Southern	1985-90	Eastern Ky.
34	Eastern Ky.	1978-84	Western Ky.
31	Middle Tenn.	1987-94	Eastern Ky.

Wins	Team	Years	Ended by
30	Montana	1994-97	Eastern Wash.
25	Montana	2000-02	Current
25	Northern Iowa	1989-92	Youngstown St.
23	Northern Iowa	1983-87	Montana
22	Nevada	1989-91	Youngstown St.
20	Arkansas St.	1984-87	Northwestern St.
16	Pennsylvania	1992-95	Princeton
16	Southwest Tex. St.	1981-83	Central St.
16	Citadel	1980-82	East Tenn. St.
15	Pennsylvania	2000-02	Current
15	Davidson	1999-02	Morehead St.
15	Holy Cross	1987-89	Massachusetts
14	Duquesne	1999-01	Dayton
14	Delaware	1994-97	Villanova
14	William & Mary	1991-94	Massachusetts
13	Youngstown St.	1992-93	Stephen F. Austin
13	William & Mary	1988-91	Delaware
13	Idaho	1987-89	Eastern Ill.
13	Sam Houston St.	1986-88	Stephen F. Austin
13	Delaware St.	1983-86	Northeastern
12	Rhode Island	1984-85	Towson
12	Eastern Ill.	1981-83	Indiana St.

Longest Losing Streaks

(From 1978; Can Include Playoff Games)

Losses	Team	Years	Ended Against
80	Prairie View	1989-98	Langston
44	Columbia	1983-88	Princeton
30	St. Francis (Pa.)	1999-02	La Salle
24	Canisius	1999-01	Siena
19	Delaware St.	1997-99	Norfolk St.
19	Charleston So.	1993-95	Morehead St.
19	Idaho St.	1978-80	Portland St.
18	Davidson	1985-87	Wofford
17	Tennessee Tech	1984-85	Morehead St.
16	Colgate	1994-96	Brown
16	Siena	1994-96	Iona
16	Middle Tenn.	1978-79	Tennessee Tech
14	St. Francis (Pa.)	1998-99	Sacred Heart
14	St. Peter's	1997-99	Canisius
14	Nicholls St.	1994-96	Jacksonville St.
14	Fordham	1993-95	Marist
13	Davidson	1987-88	Millsaps
12	Valparaiso	2001-02	Lindenwood
12	Mississippi Val.	2001-02	Delta St.
12	Tenn.-Martin	1998-99	Lambuth
12	St. Francis (Pa.)	1994-96	Waynesburg
12	Fordham	1991-92	Bucknell
12	UCF	1981-82	Elizabeth City St.

Most-Played Rivalries

(Ongoing Unless Indicated)

Games	Opponents (Series leader listed first)	Rivalry Record	First Game
138	Lafayette-Lehigh	72-61-5	1884
125	Yale-Princeton	67-48-10	1873
119	Yale-Harvard	64-47-8	1875
112	William & Mary-Richmond	57-50-5	1898
109	Pennsylvania-Cornell	62-42-5	1893
107	Yale-Brown	74-28-5	1880
106	Harvard-Dartmouth	58-43-5	1882
104	Western Ill.-Illinois St.	44-37-5	1904
102	Harvard-Brown	72-28-2	1893
102	Montana-Montana St.	64-33-5	1897
95	Princeton-Harvard	49-39-7	1877
94	Princeton-Pennsylvania	60-33-1	1876
90	Cornell-Columbia	57-30-3	1889
90	#Illinois St.-Eastern Ill.	44-37-9	1901
90	Maine-New Hampshire	42-40-8	1903
90	$@Connecticut-Rhode Island	48-34-8	1897
85	Cornell-Colgate	47-35-3	1896

#Did not play in 2001. $Have not played since 2000. @Connecticut moved to Division I-A in 2002.

Additional Rivalry Records

LONGEST UNINTERRUPTED SERIES
(Must have played every year; current unless indicated)
113 games—Lafayette-Lehigh (from 1897)$
109 games—Cornell-Pennsylvania (from 1893)
84 games—Cornell-Dartmouth (from 1919)
77 games—Dartmouth-Yale (from 1926)
71 games—Brown-Yale (from 1932)

70 games—Dartmouth-Princeton (from 1933)
61 games—Columbia-Dartmouth (from 1942)
60 games—Columbia-Yale (from 1943)
59 games—Richmond-William & Mary (from 1944)
59 games—VMI-William & Mary (from 1944)

58 games—Brown-Harvard (from 1945)
58 games—Bucknell-Lafayette (from 1945)
58 games—Harvard-Yale (from 1945)
58 games—Princeton-Yale (from 1945)
57 games—Harvard-Princeton (from 1946)

57 games—Massachusetts-Rhode Island (from 1946)
57 games—Sam Houston St.-Southwest Tex. St. (from 1946)
57 games—Southwest Tex. St.-Stephen F. Austin (from 1946)
57 games—Montana-Montana St. (from 1946)

$Played twice in 1897-1901 and 1943-44.

MOST CONSECUTIVE WINS OVER AN OPPONENT IN AN UNINTERRUPTED SERIES
(Must have played in consecutive years)
26—Grambling over Prairie View, 1977-02 (current)
22—Eastern Ky. over Tennessee Tech, 1976-97
20—Eastern Ky. over Austin Peay, 1978-97
18—Western Ill. over Southern Ill., 1984-01
18—Eastern Ky. over Morehead St., 1972-89

18—Southeast Mo. St. over Lincoln (Mo.), 1972-89
17—Princeton over Columbia, 1954-70
16—Montana over Montana St., 1986-01
16—Harvard over Columbia, 1979-94
16—Middle Tenn. over Morehead St., 1951-66

15—Delaware over West Chester, 1968-82
15—Dartmouth over Brown, 1960-74
15—Evansville over Ky. Wesleyan, 1983-97
14—Appalachian St. over East Tenn. St., 1982-95
14—Yale over Princeton, 1967-80

14—Marshall over VMI, 1983-96
14—Dartmouth over Columbia, 1984-97
13—Duquesne over St. Francis (Pa.), 1977-89
13—Massachusetts over Northeastern, 1984-96
12—Idaho over Boise St., 1982-93

12—Cornell over Columbia, 1977-88
11—Wofford over Newberry, 1960-70
11—Tennessee Tech over Morehead St., 1951-61
11—William & Mary over Richmond, 1944-54
11—Davidson over Elon, 1921-31

MOST CONSECUTIVE WINS OVER AN OPPONENT IN A SERIES
(Did not have to play in consecutive years)
46—Yale over Wesleyan (Conn.), 1875-1913
30—Harvard over Williams, 1883-1920
23—Harvard over Bates, 1899-1944
23—Brown over Rhode Island, 1909-34
21—Grambling over Mississippi Val., 1957-77

16—Montana over Montana St., 1986-01
16—Massachusetts over Northeastern, 1984-01
16—Harvard over Columbia, 1979-94
16—Yale over Connecticut, 1948-64
16—Davidson over Elon, 1921-48

14—Delaware over Massachusetts, 1958-89
12—Idaho over Ricks College, 1919-33
12—Yale over Pennsylvania, 1879-92

MOST CONSECUTIVE CURRENT WINS OVER AN OPPONENT IN AN UNINTERRUPTED SERIES
(Must have played in consecutive years)
26—Grambling over Prairie View, 1977-02
18—Western Ill. over Southern Ill., 1984-01
16—Montana over Montana St., 1996-01

DIVISION I-AA

Cliffhangers

Regular-season Division I-AA games won on the final play in regulation time. The extra point is listed when it provided the margin of victory after the winning touchdown on the game's final play.

Date	Opponents, Score	Game-Winning Play
10-21-78	Western Ky. 17, Eastern Ky. 16	Kevin McGrath 25 FG
9-8-79	Northern Ariz. 22, Portland St. 21	Ken Fraser 15 pass from Brian Potter (Mike Jenkins pass from Potter)
11-15-80	Morris Brown 19, Bethune-Cookman 18	Ray Mills 1 run (Carlton Johnson kick)
9-26-81	Abilene Christian 41, Northwestern St. 38	David Russell 17 pass from Loyal Proffitt
10-10-81	C.W. Post 37, James Madison 36	Tom DeBona 10 pass from Tom Ehrhardt
11-13-82	Pennsylvania 23, Harvard 21	Dave Shulman 27 FG
10-1-83	Connecticut 9, New Hampshire 7	Larry Corn 7 run
9-8-84	La.-Lafayette 17, Louisiana Tech 16	Patrick Broussard 21 FG
9-15-84	Lehigh 10, Connecticut 7	Dave Melick 45 FG
9-15-84	William & Mary 23, Delaware 21	Jeff Sanders 18 pass from Stan Yagiello
10-13-84	Lafayette 20, Connecticut 13	Ryan Priest 2 run
10-20-84	UCF 28, Illinois St. 24	Jeff Farmer 30 punt return
10-27-84	Western Ky. 33, Morehead St. 31	Arnold Grier 50 pass from Jeff Cesarone
9-7-85	UCF 39, Bethune-Cookman 37	Ed O'Brien 55 FG
10-26-85	VMI 39, William & Mary 38	Al Comer 3 run (James Wright run)
8-30-86	Texas Southern 38, Prairie View 35	Don Espinoza 23 FG
9-20-86	Delaware 33, West Chester 31	Fred Singleton 3 run
10-4-86	Northwestern St. 17, La.-Monroe 14	Keith Hodnett 27 FG
10-11-86	Eastern Ill. 31, Northern Iowa 30	Rich Ehmke 58 FG
9-12-87	Youngstown St. 20, Bowling Green 17	John Dowling 36 FG
10-3-87	La.-Monroe 33, Northwestern St. 31	Jackie Harris 48 pass from Stan Humphries
10-10-87	Marshall 34, Louisville 31	Keith Baxter 31 pass from Tony Petersen
10-17-87	Princeton 16, Lehigh 15	Rob Goodwin 38 FG
11-12-87	South Carolina St. 15, Grambling 13	William Wrighten 23 FG
9-24-88	Holy Cross 30, Princeton 26	70 kickoff return; Tim Donovan 55 on lateral from Darin Cromwell (15)
10-15-88	Weber St. 37, Nevada 31	Todd Beightol 57 pass from Jeff Carlson
10-29-88	Nicholls St. 13, Southwest Tex. St. 10	Jim Windham 33 FG
9-2-89	Alabama St. 16, Troy St. 13	Reggie Brown 28 pass from Antonius Smith
9-16-89	Western Caro. 26, Chattanooga 20	Terrell Wagner 68 interception return
9-23-89	Northwestern St. 18, McNeese St. 17	Chris Hamler 25 FG
10-14-89	East Tenn. St. 24, Chattanooga 23	George Searcy 1 run
9-29-90	Southwest Tex. St. 33, Nicholls St. 30	Robbie Roberson 32 FG
10-6-90	Grambling 27, Alabama A&M 20	Dexter Butcher 28 pass from Shawn Burras
11-2-91	Grambling 30, Texas Southern 27	Gilad Landau 37 FG
9-19-92	Eastern Ky. 26, La.-Monroe 21	Sean Little recovered fumble in end zone
10-10-92	Appalachian St. 27, James Madison 21	Craig Styron 44 pass from D.J. Campbell
11-14-92	Towson 33, Northeastern 32	Mark Orlando 10 pass from Dan Crowley
9-4-93	Delaware St. 31, Fayetteville St. 28	Jon Jensen 17 FG
9-11-93	Connecticut 24, New Hampshire 23	Wilbur Gilliard 14 run (Nick Sosik kick)
10-16-93	Howard 44, Towson 41	Germaine Kohn 9 pass from Jay Walker
10-7-95	Valparaiso 44, Butler 42	Cameron Hatten 27 FG
10-14-95	Montana 24, Northern Ariz. 21	Andy Larson 29 FG
10-14-95	Connecticut 31, Maine 30	David DeArmas 38 FG
10-28-95	Northern Iowa 19, Southwest Mo. St. 17	Matt Waller 39 FG
10-28-95	William & Mary 18, Villanova 15	Brian Shallcross 49 FG
9-7-96	Valparaiso 23, Hope 22	Cameron Hatten 37 FG
9-21-96	Charleston So. 17, West Virginia St. 14	Clint Kelly 20 FG
11-2-96	Butler 33, Evansville 31	Shawn Wood 32 FG
11-2-96	Wagner 38, Robert Morris 35	Carl Franke 41 FG
11-9-96	Murray St. 17, Eastern Ky. 14	Rob Hart 36 FG
9-6-97	Butler 10, Howard Payne 9	Jeremy Harkin 26 pass from Eli Stoddard (Shawn Wood kick)
9-13-97	Southern U. 36, Ark.-Pine Bluff 33	Chris Diaz 23 FG
9-20-97	Dayton 16, Robert Morris 13	Ryan Hulme 18 FG
10-4-97	Southwest Mo. St. 36, Southern Ill. 35	Travis Brawner 32 FG
11-8-97	Cal Poly 20, Montana St. 19	Alan Beilke 50 FG
11-15-97	James Madison 39, Rhode Island 37	Lindsay Fleshman 3 pass from Greg Maddox
11-22-97	Montana 27, Montana St. 25	Kris Heppner 37 FG
9-19-98	South Fla. 24, Liberty 21	Bill Gramatica 44 FG
9-19-98	Yale 30, Brown 28	Jake Borden 27 pass from Joe Walland (run failed)
10-2-99	Robert Morris 23, Wagner 21	J.T. Kirk 14 pass from Steve Tryon
11-6-99	Ga. Southern 41, Furman 38	Chris Chambers 28 FG
10-21-00	Sacramento St. 25, Eastern Wash. 22	Jimmie Sanchez 23 FG
11-4-00	Holy Cross 10, Bucknell 9	Ryan Rolfert 39 FG
11-18-00	Western Ill. 44, Northern Iowa 41	Mike Scifres 56 FG
9-22-01	Grambling 30, Portland St. 29	Randy Hymes 2 run (Brian Morgan kick)
9-29-01	Portland St. 33, Northern Ariz. 30	Mike Cajal-Willis 27 FG
9-29-01	Montana 29, Eastern Wash. 26	Etu Molden 20 pass from John Edwards
10-6-01	East Tenn. St. 23, Citadel 21	Con Chellis 41 FG
10-5-02	Southern Ill. 54, Western Ill. 52	Brandon Robinson 6 pass from Joel Sambursky
11-02-02	Portland St. 27, Idaho St. 24	Mike Cajal-Willis 20 FG

Mike Cajal-Willis won one game for Portland State in both 2001 and 2002 with last-play field goals.

Troy Wayrynen

Regular-Season Overtime Games Prior to 1996

In 1981, the NCAA Football Rules Committee approved an overtime tiebreaker system to decide a tie game for the purpose of determining a conference champion. The following conferences used the tiebreaker system to decide conference-only tie games. (Beginning in 1996, all college football games used the tiebreaker if the score was tied after four periods.) In an overtime period, one end of the field is used and each team gets an offensive possession beginning at the 25-yard line. Each team shall have possession until it has scored, failed to gain a first down or lost possession. The team scoring the greater number of points after completion of both possessions is declared the winner. The periods continue until a winner is determined.

NUMBER OF DIVISION I-AA OVERTIME GAMES SINCE 1981

1981	2	1987	6	1992	2	*1997	23
1982	4	1988	6	1993	4	*1998	25
1983	0	1989	2	1994	6	*1999	21
1984	4	1990	6	1995	8	*2000	24
1985	2	1991	5	*1996	23	*2001	18
1986	4					*2002	26

*All games tied at end of four periods use tiebreaker system.

BIG SKY CONFERENCE

Date	Opponents, Score	No. OTs	Score, Reg.
10-31-81	‡Weber St. 24, Northern Ariz. 23	1	17-17
11-21-81	‡Idaho St. 33, Weber St. 30	3	23-23
10-2-82	‡Montana St. 30, Idaho St. 27	3	17-17
11-6-82	Nevada 46, ‡Weber St. 43	3	30-30
10-13-84	‡Montana St. 44, Nevada 41	4	21-21
9-17-88	Boise St. 24, ‡Northern Ariz. 21	2	14-14
10-15-88	‡Montana 33, Northern Ariz. 26	2	26-26
9-15-90	‡Weber St. 45, Idaho St. 38	2	31-31
9-29-90	‡Nevada 31, Idaho 28	1	28-28
11-3-90	Eastern Wash. 33, ‡Idaho St. 26	1	26-26
11-10-90	Montana St. 28, ‡Eastern Wash. 25	1	25-25
10-26-91	Eastern Wash. 34, ‡Idaho 31	2	24-24
11-16-91	Montana 35, ‡Idaho 34	1	28-28
10-29-94	‡Eastern Wash. 34, Montana St. 31	3	31-31

GATEWAY CONFERENCE

Date	Opponents, Score	No. OTs	Score, Reg.
9-24-94	Western Ill. 31, ‡Southwest Mo. St. 24	1	24-24
9-30-95	Illinois St. 20, ‡Southwest Mo. St. 17	1	17-17
10-14-95	‡Southern Ill. 33, Southwest Mo. St. 30	1	30-30

MID-EASTERN ATHLETIC CONFERENCE

Date	Opponents, Score	No. OTs	Score, Reg.
11-1-86	‡N.C. A&T 30, Bethune-Cookman 24	1	24-24
10-22-93	Howard 41, ‡N.C. A&T 35	1	35-35
11-20-93	‡South Carolina St. 58, N.C. A&T 52	1	52-52

OHIO VALLEY CONFERENCE

Date	Opponents, Score	No. OTs	Score, Reg.
10-13-84	Youngstown St. 17, ‡Austin Peay 13	1	10-10
11-3-84	‡Murray St. 20, Austin Peay 13	2	10-10
10-19-85	‡Middle Tenn. 31, Murray St. 24	2	17-17
11-2-85	‡Middle Tenn. 28, Youngstown St. 21	2	14-14
10-4-86	‡Austin Peay 7, Middle Tenn. 0	1	0-0
10-10-87	‡Austin Peay 20, Morehead 13	1	13-13
11-7-87	‡Youngstown St. 20, Murray St. 13	1	13-13
10-1-88	Tennessee Tech 16, ‡Murray St. 13	1	10-10
10-29-88	Eastern Ky. 31, ‡Murray St. 24	1	24-24
11-18-89	Eastern Ky. 38, ‡Morehead St. 31	3	24-24
11-10-90	‡Tennessee Tech 20, Austin Peay 14	1	14-14
11-17-90	Murray St. 31, ‡Austin Peay 24	3	24-24
11-7-92	‡Eastern Ky. 21, Murray St. 18	1	18-18
10-2-93	Murray St. 28, ‡Tenn.-Martin 21	1	21-21
11-20-93	Tenn.-Martin 39, ‡Austin Peay 33	2	26-26

PATRIOT LEAGUE

Date	Opponents, Score	No. OTs	Score, Reg.
11-11-95	Bucknell 21, ‡Colgate 14	1	14-14
11-11-95	‡Lafayette 24, Fordham 21	2	21-21
11-18-95	‡Lehigh 37, Lafayette 30	2	30-30

SOUTHERN CONFERENCE

Date	Opponents, Score	No. OTs	Score, Reg.
10-19-91	Appalachian St. 26, Furman 23	3	20-20
11-2-91	Marshall 27, Western Caro. 24	3	20-20
11-21-92	VMI 37, Chattanooga 34	1	34-34
11-19-94	VMI 26, Appalachian St. 23	1	20-20

YANKEE CONFERENCE

Date	Opponents, Score	No. OTs	Score, Reg.
9-18-82	Rhode Island 58, ‡Maine 55	6	21-21
9-25-82	‡Boston U. 48, Maine 45	4	24-24
10-27-84	Maine 13, ‡Connecticut 10	1	10-10
9-13-86	New Hampshire 28, ‡Delaware 21	1	21-21
11-15-86	‡Connecticut 21, Rhode Island 14	1	14-14
9-19-87	‡Richmond 52, Massachusetts 51	4	28-28
9-19-87	New Hampshire 27, ‡Boston U. 20	3	17-17
10-31-87	Maine 59, ‡Delaware 56	2	49-49
11-21-87	‡Delaware 17, Boston U. 10	1	10-10
9-24-88	Villanova 31, ‡Boston U. 24	1	24-24
10-8-88	‡Richmond 23, New Hampshire 17	1	17-17
10-7-89	‡Villanova 41, Connecticut 35	6	21-21
11-16-91	Boston U. 29, ‡Connecticut 26	2	23-23
9-11-93	‡Connecticut 24, New Hampshire 23	1	17-17
10-16-93	Maine 26, ‡Rhode Island 23	2	17-17
9-17-94	Delaware 38, ‡Villanova 31	1	31-31
11-19-94	Northeastern 9, ‡James Madison 6	1	6-6
9-23-95	James Madison 28, ‡Villanova 27	1	21-21
10-7-95	‡Richmond 26, Northeastern 23	1	23-23
11-4-95	‡Maine 24, Massachusetts 21	1	21-21
11-19-94	New Hampshire 52, ‡Boston U. 51	2	45-45

‡Home team.

DIVISION I-AA

2002 Division I-AA Overtime Games

Date	Winner's Conference	Score (Loser's Conf.)	Number of OT Periods	Regulation Score
Aug. 29	Ohio Valley	Southeast Mo. St. 42, Ark.-Monticello (Division II) 41	2OT	35-35
Aug. 29	Independent	Samford 24, North Ala. (Division II) 21	2OT	21-21
Sept. 7	Metro Atlantic	St. John's (N.Y.) 17, Canisius (MAAC) 14	1OT	14-14
Sept. 7	SWAC	Ark.-Pine Bluff 36, Mississippi Val. (SWAC) 30	2OT	30-30
Sept. 14	Big Sky	Portland St. 23, N.C. A&T (MEAC) 20	1OT	17-17
Sept. 14	Independent	St. Mary's (Cal.) 23, Bucknell (Patriot) 22	2OT	16-16
Sept. 21	Atlantic-10	James Madison 24, Hofstra (Atlantic-10) 21	2OT	21-21
Sept. 28	Gateway	Indiana St. 34, Murray St. (Ohio Valley) 31	2OT	24-24
Sept. 28	Gateway	Northern Iowa 29, Cal Poly (Independent) 26	3OT	20-20
Sept. 28	SIAC (Div. II)	Kentucky St. 47, Ark.-Pine Bluff (SWAC) 44	4OT	35-35
Oct. 5	Patriot	Colgate 13, Bucknell (Patriot) 10	1OT	10-10
Oct. 5	Ivy	Cornell 34, Towson (Patriot) 31	2OT	24-24
Oct. 5	Southern	Wofford 27, Chattanooga (Southern) 21	2OT	21-21
Oct. 12	Gateway	Indiana St. 23, Southwest Mo. St. (Gateway) 20	1OT	17-17
Oct. 12	Pioneer	Drake 49, Albany (N.Y.) (Northeast) 42	2OT	35-35
Oct. 19	Atlantic-10	Rhode Island 17, Delaware (Atlantic-10) 14	2OT	14-14
Oct. 26	Ivy	Cornell 10, Brown (Ivy) 7	2OT	7-7
Oct. 26	MEAC	Morgan St. 35, Delaware St. (MEAC) 28	1OT	28-28
Oct. 26	MEAC	South Carolina St. 47, Hampton (MEAC) 41	2OT	34-34
Nov. 2	MEAC	Morgan St. 42, Morris Brown (Independent) 41	1OT	34-34
Nov. 2	Patriot	Lehigh 26, Fordham (Patriot) 23	2OT	23-23

Date	Winner's Conference	Score (Loser's Conf.)	Number of OT Periods	Regulation Score
Nov. 2	Ivy	Princeton 32, Cornell 25 (Ivy) 25	2OT	25-25
Nov. 2	Northeast	Sacred Heart 10, Wagner (Northeast) 7	1OT	7-7
Nov. 2	Ohio Valley	Eastern Ky. 35, Liberty (Big South) 28	2OT	28-28
Nov. 16	Northeast	St. Francis (Pa.) 14, Robert Morris (Northeast) 7	1OT	7-7
Nov. 16	SWAC	Mississippi Val. 13, Alabama St. (SWAC) 10	1OT	7-7

Note: 26 games (9 with one extra period, 15 with two extra periods, 1 with three extra periods, 1 with four extra periods) –average of 1.77 extra periods

Division I-AA Stadiums

LISTED ALPHABETICALLY BY SCHOOL

School	Stadium	Conference	Year Built	Cap.	Surface*
Alabama A&M	Louis Crews	SWAC-E	1996	21,000	Grass
Alabama St.	^Cramton	SWAC-E	1922	24,600	Grass
Albany (N.Y.)	University Field	Northeast	1967	10,000	Grass
Alcorn St.	Jack Spinks	SWAC-E	1992	25,000	Grass
Appalachian St.	Kidd Brewer	Southern	1962	16,650	AstroTurf
Ark.-Pine Bluff	Pumphrey	SWAC-W	1951	6,000	Grass
Austin Peay	Governors	Pioneer-S	1946	10,000	Stadia Turf
Bethune-Cookman	Municipal	MEAC	NA	10,000	Grass
Brown	Brown	Ivy	1925	20,000	Grass
Bucknell	Christy Mathewson	Patriot	1924	13,100	Grass
Butler	Butler Bowl	Pioneer-N	1927	19,000	Grass
Cal Poly	Mustang	Independent	1935	8,500	Grass
Central Conn. St.	Arute Field	Northeast	1969	5,000	Grass
Charleston So.	CSU	Big South	1970	3,000	Grass
Chattanooga	^Finley	Southern	1997	20,000	Grass
Citadel	Johnson Hagood	Southern	1948	22,500	Grass
Coastal Caro.	CCU	Big South	2003	8,200	Grass
Colgate	Andy Kerr	Patriot	1937	10,221	Grass
Columbia	Lawrence A. Wien	Ivy	1984	17,000	Grass
Cornell	Schoellkopf	Ivy	1915	27,000	All-Pro Turf
Dartmouth	Memorial Field	Ivy	1923	20,416	Grass
Davidson	Richardson	Pioneer-S	1924	4,000	Grass
Dayton	Welcome	Pioneer-N	1949	11,000	AstroTurf
Delaware	Delaware	Atlantic 10	1952	22,000	Grass
Delaware St.	Alumni Field	MEAC	1957	5,000	Grass
Drake	Drake	Pioneer-N	1925	18,000	Grass
Duquesne	Arthur J. Rooney Field	MAAC	1993	4,500	AstroTurf
East Tenn. St.	#Memorial	Southern	1977	12,000	AstroTurf
Eastern Ill.	O'Brien	Ohio Valley	1970	10,000	Grass
Eastern Ky.	Roy Kidd	Ohio Valley	1969	20,000	Grass
Eastern Wash.	Woodward	Big Sky	1967	6,000	Grass
Elon	Rhodes	Big South	2001	8,250	Grass
Florida A&M	Bragg Memorial	MEAC	1957	25,500	Grass
Fla. Atlantic	Pro Player	Independent	1987	75,540	PAT
Fordham	Jack Coffey Field	Patriot	1930	7,000	Grass
Furman	Paladin	Southern	1981	16,000	Grass
Gardner-Webb	Ernest W. Spangler	Big South	NA	5,000	Grass
Georgetown	Kehoe Field	Patriot	NA	2,400	AstroTurf
Ga. Southern	Paulson	Southern	1984	18,000	PAT
Grambling	Robinson	SWAC-W	1983	19,600	Grass
Hampton	Armstrong	MEAC	1928	17,000	Grass
Harvard	Harvard	Ivy	1903	30,898	Grass
Hofstra	James M. Shuart	Atlantic 10	1963	15,000	AstroTurf
Holy Cross	Fitton Field	Patriot	1924	23,500	Grass
Howard	Greene	MEAC	1986	8,890	AstroTurf
Idaho St.	#Holt Arena	Big Sky	1970	12,000	AstroTurf
Illinois St.	Hancock	Gateway	1967	15,000	AstroTurf
Indiana St.	Memorial	Gateway	1970	12,764	All-Pro Turf
Iona	Mazzella Field	MAAC	1989	1,200	AstroTurf
Jackson St.	^Mississippi Memorial	SWAC-E	1949	62,512	Grass
Jacksonville	Milne Field	Pioneer-S	1998	4,500	Grass
Jacksonville St.	Paul Snow	Southland	1947	15,000	Grass
James Madison	Bridgeforth	Atlantic 10	1974	12,500	AstroTurf
La Salle	McCarthy	MAAC	1936	7,500	Grass
Lafayette	Fisher Field	Patriot	1926	13,750	Grass
Lehigh	Goodman	Patriot	1988	16,000	Grass
Liberty	Williams	Big South	1989	12,000	OmniTurf
Maine	Alumni	Atlantic 10	1942	10,000	Grass
Marist	Leonidoff Field	MAAC	1972	2,500	Grass
Massachusetts	Warren McGuirk	Atlantic 10	1965	17,000	Grass
McNeese St.	Cowboy	Southland	1965	17,500	Grass
Mississippi Val.	Magnolia	SWAC-E	1958	10,500	Grass
Monmouth	Kessler Field	Northeast	1993	4,600	Grass
Montana	Washington-Grizzly	Big Sky	1986	18,845	Grass
Montana St.	Reno H. Sales	Big Sky	1973	15,197	Grass
Morehead St.	Jayne	Pioneer-S	1964	10,000	OmniTurf
Morgan St.	Hughes	MEAC	1934	10,000	Grass

School	Stadium	Conference	Year Built	Cap.	Surface*
Morris Brown	A.F. Herndon	Independent	1996	15,000	Grass
Murray St.	Stewart	Ohio Valley	1973	16,800	AstroTurf
New Hampshire	Cowell	Atlantic 10	1936	9,571	Grass
Nicholls St.	John L. Guidry	Southland	1972	12,800	Grass
Norfolk St.	Price	MEAC	1997	27,700	Grass
N.C. A&T	Aggie	MEAC	1981	21,000	Grass
Northeastern	E.S. Parsons	Atlantic 10	1933	7,000	AstroTurf
Northern Ariz.	#Walkup Skydome	Big Sky	1977	15,300	AstroTurf
Northern Iowa	#U.N.I.-Dome	Gateway	1976	16,324	AstroTurf
Northwestern St.	Turpin	Southland	1976	15,971	AstroTurf
Pennsylvania	Franklin Field	Ivy	1895	53,000	AstroTurf
Portland St.	^PGE Park	Big Sky	1928	23,000	NexTurf
Prairie View	Blackshear	SWAC-W	1960	6,000	Grass
Princeton	Princeton	Ivy	1998	30,000	Grass
Rhode Island	Meade	Atlantic 10	1928	8,000	Grass
Richmond	Richmond	Atlantic 10	1929	21,319	SuperTurf
Robert Morris	Moon	Northeast	1950	7,000	Grass
Sacramento St.	Hornet Field	Big Sky	1964	21,418	Grass
Sacred Heart	Campus Field	Northeast	1993	3,500	AstroTurf
St. Francis (Pa.)	Pine Bowl	Northeast	1979	1,500	Grass
St. Mary's (Cal.)	St. Mary's	Independent	1973	5,000	Grass
St. Peter's	Cochrane	MAAC	1990	4,000	AstroTurf
Sam Houston St.	Bowers	Southland	1986	14,000	All-Pro Turf
Samford	Seibert	Independent	1960	6,700	Grass
San Diego	USD Torero	Pioneer-N	1955	4,000	Grass
Siena	Heritage Park	MAAC	NA	5,500	Grass
South Carolina St.	Dawson Bulldog	MEAC	1955	22,000	Grass
Southeast Mo. St.	Houck	Ohio Valley	1930	10,000	Grass
Southeastern La.	Strawberry	Independent	1936	7,400	Sprinturf
Southern Ill.	McAndrew	Gateway	1975	17,324	OmniTurf
Southern U.	A.W. Mumford	SWAC-W	1928	24,000	Grass
Southern Utah	Col. of Southern Utah	Independent	1967	6,500	Grass
Southwest Mo. St.	Plaster Field	Gateway	1941	16,300	FieldTurf
Southwest Tex. St.	Bobcat	Southland	1981	15,218	Grass
Stephen F. Austin	Homer Bryce	Southland	1973	14,575	AstroTurf-12
Stony Brook	Seawolves Field	Northeast	1978	2,000	Grass
Tenn.-Martin	Skyhawk	Ohio Valley	1964	7,500	Grass
Tennessee St.	W.J. Hale	Ohio Valley	1953	16,000	Grass
Tennessee Tech	Tucker	Ohio Valley	1966	16,500	Stadia Turf
Texas Southern	^Robertson	SWAC-W	1965	22,000	Grass
Towson	Johnny Unitas	Patriot	1978	11,000	Turf
Valparaiso	Brown Field	Pioneer-N	1947	5,000	Grass
Villanova	Villanova	Atlantic 10	1927	12,000	AstroTurf
VMI	Alumni Field	Southern	1962	10,000	Grass
Wagner	Fischer Memorial Field	Northeast	1967	5,000	Grass
Weber St.	Elizabeth Dee Shaw Stewart	Big Sky	1966	17,500	Grass
Western Caro.	E. J. Whitmire	Southern	1974	12,000	AstroTurf
Western Ill.	Hanson Field	Gateway	1948	15,168	Grass
Western Ky.	L. T. Smith	Gateway	1968	17,500	Grass
William & Mary	Walter Zable	Atlantic 10	1935	15,000	Grass
Wofford	Gibbs	Southern	1996	13,000	Grass
Yale	Yale Bowl	Ivy	1914	64,269	Grass
Youngstown St.	Arnold D. Stambaugh	Gateway	1982	20,360	Sprinturf

^Not located on campus. #Indoor facility.

STADIUMS LISTED BY CAPACITY (TOP 32)

School	Stadium	Capacity	Surface*
Fla. Atlantic	Pro Player	75,540	PAT
Yale	Yale Bowl	64,269	Grass
Jackson St.	^Mississippi Memorial	62,512	Grass
Pennsylvania	Franklin Field	53,000	AstroTurf
Harvard	Harvard	30,898	Grass
Princeton	Princeton	30,000	Grass
Norfolk St.	Price	27,700	Grass
Cornell	Schoellkopf	27,000	All-Pro Turf
Florida A&M	Bragg Memorial	25,500	Grass
Alcorn St.	Jack Spinks	25,000	Grass
Alabama St.	^Cramton	24,600	Grass
Southern U.	A.W. Mumford	24,000	Grass
Holy Cross	Fitton Field	23,500	Grass
Portland St.	^PGE Park	23,000	NexTurf
Citadel	Johnson Hagood	22,500	Grass
Delaware	Delaware	22,000	Grass
South Carolina St.	Dawson Bulldog	22,000	Grass
Texas Southern	^Robertson	22,000	Grass
Sacramento St.	Hornet Field	21,418	Grass
Richmond	Richmond	21,319	SuperTurf
Alabama A&M	Louis Crews	21,000	Grass
N.C. A&T	Aggie	21,000	Grass
Dartmouth	Memorial Field	20,416	Grass
Youngstown St.	Arnold D. Stambaugh	20,360	Sprinturf
Brown	Brown	20,000	Grass
Chattanooga	^Finley	20,000	Grass
Eastern Ky.	Roy Kidd	20,000	Grass
Grambling	Robinson	19,600	Grass
Butler	Butler Bowl	19,000	Grass
Montana	Washington-Grizzly	18,845	Grass
Drake	Drake	18,000	Grass
Ga. Southern	Paulson	18,000	PAT

^Not located on campus.

Surface Notes: *This column indicates the type of surface (either artificial or natural grass) present this year in the stadium. The brand name of the artificial turf, if known, is listed. Legend: Turf—Any of several types of artificial turfs (name brands include AstroTurf, All-Pro, Omni-Turf, SuperTurf, Sprinturf, etc.); Grass—Natural grass surface; PAT—Prescription Athletic Turf (a "natural-artificial" surface featuring a network of pipes connected to pumps capable of sucking water from the natural turf or watering it. The pipes are located 18 inches from the surface and covered with a mixture of sand and filler. The turf also is lined with heating coils to keep it from freezing in temperatures below 32 degrees).

DIVISION I-AA

Division I-AA Statistics Trends

(Average Per Game, One Team)

Year	Rushing			Passing					Total Offense			Scoring		
	Plays	Yds.	Avg.	Att.	Cmp.	Pct.	Yds.	Av. Att.	Plays	Yds.	Avg.	TD	FG	Pts.
1978	*48.4	*171.8	3.55	20.7	9.5	46.2	129.3	6.24	69.1	301.1	4.36	2.60	0.52	19.5
1979	47.1	164.7	3.50	20.5	9.2	45.0	125.2	6.13	67.5	289.9	4.30	2.40	0.62	18.5
1980	45.2	164.8	3.65	22.4	10.4	46.5	144.4	6.45	67.6	309.2	4.58	2.58	0.59	19.6
1981	44.3	155.0	3.50	24.9	11.9	47.7	161.5	6.49	69.1	316.4	4.58	2.71	0.69	20.9
1982	44.4	156.6	3.53	26.1	12.8	48.9	166.0	6.35	70.5	322.6	4.57	2.62	0.80	20.5
1983	43.9	155.2	3.54	26.2	13.0	49.4	167.3	6.38	70.1	322.4	4.60	2.69	0.79	21.1
1984	42.9	152.6	3.56	27.9	14.0	50.0	181.0	6.49	70.7	333.5	4.72	2.80	0.80	21.8
1985	42.4	157.6	3.72	*28.9	14.6	50.4	187.3	6.49	*71.2	344.9	4.84	2.84	0.81	22.1
1986	42.4	157.9	3.72	28.3	14.1	49.7	186.4	6.60	70.7	344.3	4.87	2.90	0.86	22.7
1987	43.1	158.6	3.68	27.1	13.6	50.1	175.6	6.48	70.2	334.2	4.76	2.78	0.91	22.0
1988	43.2	161.3	3.74	26.5	13.3	50.2	172.7	6.53	69.6	334.0	4.80	2.80	*0.92	22.1
1989	42.5	160.2	3.77	27.7	14.2	51.3	186.0	6.71	70.2	346.2	4.93	2.72	0.75	22.8
1990	42.7	161.5	3.79	27.8	14.1	50.6	187.0	6.73	70.5	348.5	4.95	2.98	0.84	23.2
1991	43.2	170.6	3.95	26.9	14.0	51.9	184.7	6.87	70.1	355.3	5.07	3.19	0.67	24.1
1992	43.0	171.4	3.99	26.0	13.5	51.7	179.4	6.89	69.0	350.8	5.08	3.16	0.68	23.9
1993	42.4	168.3	3.97	27.0	14.0	51.8	186.4	6.90	69.4	354.7	5.11	3.20	0.70	24.2
1994	41.6	164.1	3.95	27.5	14.3	51.9	188.1	6.85	69.0	352.1	5.10	3.18	0.70	24.1
1995	42.0	165.1	3.94	27.1	13.9	51.3	177.7	6.57	69.0	342.8	4.97	3.06	0.68	23.2
1996	42.0	162.0	3.86	26.9	13.7	51.1	177.6	6.62	68.8	339.6	4.94	3.05	0.72	23.2
1997	40.2	153.2	3.81	27.8	14.3	51.3	185.2	6.67	68.0	338.4	4.98	3.06	0.72	23.3
1998	40.8	162.7	3.98	27.2	14.3	52.6	187.8	*6.91	68.0	350.5	5.15	3.26	0.71	24.7
1999	40.8	162.9	*4.02	28.8	*15.1	52.5	*197.1	6.83	69.4	*360.0	*5.19	*3.45	0.71	*25.9
2000	41.2	164.9	4.00	27.8	14.5	52.3	191.1	6.88	69.0	356.0	5.16	3.40	0.75	25.8
2001	40.6	160.4	3.95	28.1	14.8	52.6	193.7	6.89	68.7	354.1	5.15	3.34	0.72	25.3
2002	41.0	155.6	3.80	27.5	14.5	*52.7	187.5	6.81	68.5	343.1	5.01	3.19	0.75	24.3

*Record.

Additional Division I-AA Statistics Trends

(Average Per Game, One Team)

Year	Punting		Net	Interceptions		Avg.	Punt Returns		Avg.	Kickoff Returns		Avg.
	No.	Avg.	Avg.	No.	Avg. Ret.	Yds.	No.	Avg. Ret.	Yds.	No.	Avg. Ret.	Yds.
1978	*6.1	36.5	33.6	1.42	11.92	17.0	2.39	7.49	17.9	3.23	18.4	59.2
1979	6.0	36.5	33.4	1.44	11.39	16.4	2.41	7.46	18.0	3.06	18.4	56.2
1980	5.8	37.0	33.7	1.37	10.06	13.8	2.44	7.94	19.4	3.09	17.4	53.7
1981	5.9	37.2	33.9	*1.60	10.63	*17.0	2.50	7.77	19.4	3.27	18.4	60.1
1982	6.0	37.1	34.0	1.50	10.15	15.2	2.44	7.63	18.6	3.08	19.0	58.4
1983	6.0	37.3	34.1	1.52	9.99	15.1	2.59	7.58	19.6	3.06	18.6	56.9
1984	5.8	37.3	33.9	1.53	10.40	15.9	2.55	7.84	20.0	3.23	18.6	60.0
1985	5.7	37.6	*34.2	1.51	10.56	16.0	2.55	7.52	19.2	3.20	18.1	57.9
1986	5.6	37.6	34.0	1.51	10.90	16.4	2.55	7.92	20.2	*4.02	19.4	*77.9
1987	5.6	36.8	33.4	1.40	10.57	14.9	2.48	7.51	18.7	3.96	19.0	74.6
1988	5.5	36.3	32.8	1.34	10.61	14.2	2.40	7.96	19.2	3.95	18.8	74.3
1989	5.5	36.1	32.8	1.31	10.40	13.7	2.32	7.93	18.4	3.96	18.9	74.7
1990	5.4	36.7	32.7	1.38	11.94	16.5	2.49	8.46	21.0	4.02	18.9	75.9
1991	5.3	36.6	32.6	1.35	10.81	14.6	2.46	8.57	21.1	3.84	19.1	73.4
1992	5.3	36.6	32.2	1.21	10.24	12.3	2.53	9.35	23.6	3.82	19.5	74.4
1993	5.2	36.0	32.3	1.23	10.79	13.2	2.35	8.26	19.5	3.72	19.3	71.7
1994	5.2	36.3	32.1	1.27	10.94	13.8	2.38	9.20	21.9	3.83	*19.9	76.0
1995	5.4	35.8	32.0	1.16	12.20	14.1	2.36	8.57	20.2	3.73	18.6	69.4
1996	5.5	36.6	32.8	1.22	12.25	15.0	2.44	8.54	20.9	3.60	19.0	68.4
1997	5.6	37.3	33.3	1.18	12.32	14.5	2.53	8.90	22.5	3.60	19.1	68.8
1998	5.3	*37.6	33.3	1.12	12.33	13.8	2.54	8.98	22.8	3.90	19.5	75.9
1999	5.4	37.2	32.8	1.18	*12.55	14.8	2.46	9.40	23.1	3.91	19.1	74.7
2000	5.3	36.5	32.2	1.19	12.25	14.6	2.49	9.20	22.9	3.94	19.3	76.0
2001	5.4	36.5	32.1	1.16	12.45	14.4	2.45	*9.82	24.0	3.96	19.2	75.9
2002	5.5	36.7	32.2	1.11	12.10	13.4	*2.63	9.38	*24.7	3.85	19.3	74.4

*Record.

Rules changes and statistics changes affecting trends: PUNTING–Beginning in 1965, 20 yards not deducted from a punt into the end zone for a touchback. INTERCEPTIONS–Interceptions yards not compiled, 1958-65. KICKOFF RETURNS–During 1937-45, if a kickoff went out of bounds, the receiving team put the ball in play on its 35-yard line instead of a second kickoff; in 1984 (rescinded in 1985), a 30-yard-line touchback for kickoffs crossing the goal line in flight and first touching the ground out of the end zone; in 1986, kickoffs from the 35-yard line. PUNT RETURNS–In 1967, interior linemen restricted from leaving until the ball is kicked.

Division I-AA Defensive Extra-Point Trends

Year	Games	Kick Ret./TD	Int. Ret./TD	Total Ret./TD
1988	553	4/1	7/1	11/2
1989	554	11/4	4/2	15/6
1990	548	7/3	4/2	11/5
1991	560	12/3	9/2	21/5
1992	553	9/5	8/5	17/10
1993	725	11/5	19/3	30/8
1994	733	4/1	5/1	9/2
1995	736	9/2	9/4	18/6
1996	723	8/3	3/0	11/3
1997	723	11/1	7/5	18/6
1998	733	18/4	8/2	26/6
1999	742	19/5	6/2	25/7
2000	#662	13/4	5/1	18/5
2001	#644	15/6	4/2	19/8
2002	#701	18/7	6/2	24/9
Totals	**9,890**	**169/54**	**104/34**	**273/88**

#Does not include games against non-major teams.

Division I-AA Fumble-Recovery Returns

Year	Games	Fumble Rec./TDs
1990	548	34/16
1991	560	42/13
1992	553	96/42
1993	725	86/25
1994	733	99/23
1995	736	164/58
1996	723	169/63
1997	723	149/63
1998	733	121/66
1999	742	136/68
2000	662	118/51
2001	644	122/59
2002	701	127/64
Total	**8,783**	**1,463/611**

Classification History

SINCE 1978

The following lists show years of active membership for current and former Division I-AA football-playing institutions. The lists are from 1978, the year that Division I was divided into I-A and I-AA.

ACTIVE MEMBERS (120)

Alabama A&M ... 1999-current
Alabama St. ... 1992-current
Albany (N.Y.) ... 1999-current
Alcorn St. ... 1978-current
Appalachian St. ... 1992-current
Ark.-Pine Bluff ... 1998-current
Austin Peay ... 1978-current
Bethune-Cookman ... 1980-current
Brown ... 1982-current
Bucknell ... 1978-current
Butler ... 1993-current
Cal Poly ... 1994-current
Central Conn. St. ... 1993-current
Charleston So. ... 1993-current
Chattanooga ... 1982-current
Citadel ... 1982-current
Coastal Caro. ... 2003
Colgate ... 1982-current
Columbia ... 1982-current
Cornell ... 1982-current
Dartmouth ... 1982-current
Davidson ... 1978-90, 93-current
Dayton ... 1993-current
Delaware ... 1980-current
Delaware St. ... 1978, 80-current
Drake ... 1992-85, 93-current
Duquesne ... 1993-current
East Tenn. St. ... 1982-current
Eastern Ill. ... 1981-current
Eastern Ky. ... 1978-current
Eastern Wash. ... 1984-current
Elon ... 1999-current
Florida A&M ... 1979-current
Fla. Atlantic ... 2001-current
Fordham ... 1989-current
Furman ... 1982-current
Gardner-Webb ... 2002-current
Georgetown ... 1993-current
Ga. Southern ... 1984-current
Grambling ... 1978-current
Hampton ... 1997-current
Harvard ... 1982-current
Hofstra ... 1993-current
Holy Cross ... 1982-current
Howard ... 1978, 80-current
Idaho St. ... 1978-current
Illinois St. ... 1982-current
Indiana St. ... 1982-current
Iona ... 1993-current
Jackson St. ... 1978-current
Jacksonville ... 1998-current

Jacksonville St. ... 1997-current
James Madison ... 1980-current
La Salle ... 1997-current
Lafayette ... 1978-current
Lehigh ... 1978-current
Liberty ... 1989-current
Maine ... 1978-current
Marist ... 1993-current
Massachusetts ... 1978-current
McNeese St. ... 1982-current
Mississippi Val. ... 1980-current
Monmouth ... 1994-current
Montana ... 1978-current
Montana St. ... 1978-current
Morehead St. ... 1978-current
Morgan St. ... 1986-current
Morris Brown ... 2001-current
Murray St. ... 1978-current
New Hampshire ... 1978-current
Nicholls St. ... 1980-current
Norfolk St. ... 1997-current
N.C. A&T ... 1978, 80-current
Northeastern ... 1978-current
Northern Ariz. ... 1978-current
Northern Iowa ... 1981-current
Northwestern St. ... 1978-current
Pennsylvania ... 1982-current
Portland St. ... 1978-80, 98-current
Prairie View ... 1990-89, 92-current
Princeton ... 1982-current
Rhode Island ... 1978-current
Richmond ... 1982-current
Robert Morris ... 1998-current
St. Francis (Pa.) ... 1993-current
St. Mary's (Cal.) ... 1993-current
St. Peter's ... 1993-current
Sacramento St. ... 1993-current
Sacred Heart ... 1999-current
Samford ... 1989-current
Sam Houston St. ... 1986-current
San Diego ... 1993-current
Siena ... 1993-current
South Carolina St. ... 1978, 80-current
Southeast Mo. St. ... 1990-current
Southeastern La. ... 1980-85; 2003
Southern Ill. ... 1982-current
Southern U. ... 1978-current
Southern Utah ... 1993-current
Southwest Mo. St. ... 1982-current
Southwest Tex. St. ... 1984-current
Stephen F. Austin ... 1986-current
Stony Brook ... 1999-current

Tenn.-Martin ... 1992-current
Tennessee St. ... 1981-current
Tennessee Tech ... 1978-current
Texas Southern ... 1978-current
Towson ... 1987-current
Valparaiso ... 1993-current
Villanova ... 1987-current
VMI ... 1982-current
Wagner ... 1993-current
Weber St. ... 1978-current
Western Caro. ... 1982-current
Western Ill. ... 1981-current
Western Ky. ... 1978-current
William & Mary ... 1982-current
Wofford ... 1997-current
Yale ... 1982-current
Youngstown St. ... 1981-current

FORMER MEMBERS

UAB ... 1993-95
Akron ... 1980-86
Arkansas St. ... 1982-91
Ball St. ... 1982
Boise St. ... 1978-98
Boston U. ... 1978-97
Bowling Green ... 1982
Buffalo ... 1993-98
Cal St. Northridge ... 1993-01
Canisius ... 1993-02
UCF ... 1990-95
Connecticut ... 1978-01
Eastern Mich. ... 1982
Evansville ... 1993-97
Fairfield ... 1997-02
Idaho ... 1978-96
Kent St. ... 1982
Lamar ... 1982-89
La.-Monroe ... 1982-93
Louisiana Tech ... 1982-88
Marshall ... 1982-96
Middle Tenn. ... 1978-98
Nevada ... 1978-91
North Texas ... 1982-94
Northern Ill. ... 1982
Ohio ... 1982
St. John's (N.Y.) ... 1993-02
South Fla. ... 1997-00
Tex.-Arlington ... 1982-85
Troy St. ... 1993-01
West Tex. A&M ... 1982-85

Black College National Champions

Sheridan Poll

Selected by the Pittsburgh Courier, 1920-1980, and compiled by Collie Nicholson, former Grambling sports information director; William Nunn Jr., Pittsburgh Courier sports editor; and Eric "Ric" Roberts, Pittsburgh Courier sports writer and noted black college sports historian. Selected from 1981 by the Sheridan Broadcasting Network. Records include post-season games.

Year	Team	Won	Lost	Tied	Coach
1920	Howard	7	0	0	Edward Morrison
	Talladega	5	0	1	Jubie Bragg
1921	Talladega	6	0	1	Jubie Bragg
	Wiley	7	0	1	Jason Grant
1922	Hampton	6	1	0	Gideon Smith
1923	Virginia Union	6	0	1	Harold Martin
1924	Tuskegee	9	0	1	Cleve Abbott
	Wiley	8	0	1	Fred Long
1925	Tuskegee	8	0	1	Cleve Abbott
	Howard	6	0	2	Louis Watson
1926	Tuskegee	10	0	0	Cleve Abbott
	Howard	7	0	0	Louis Watson
1927	Tuskegee	9	0	1	Cleve Abbott
	Bluefield St.	8	0	1	Harry Jefferson
1928	Bluefield St.	8	0	1	Harry Jefferson
	Wiley	8	0	1	Fred Long
1929	Tuskegee	10	0	0	Cleve Abbott
1930	Tuskegee	11	0	1	Cleve Abbott
1931	Wilberforce	9	0	0	Harry Graves
1932	Wiley	9	0	0	Fred Long
1933	Morgan St.	9	0	0	Edward Hurt
1934	Kentucky St.	9	0	0	Henry Kean
1935	Texas College	9	0	0	Arnett Mumford
1936	West Virginia St.	8	0	0	Adolph Hamblin
	Virginia St.	7	0	2	Harry Jefferson
1937	Morgan St.	7	0	0	Edward Hurt
1938	Florida A&M	8	0	0	Bill Bell
1939	Langston	9	0	0	Felton "Zip" Gayles
1940	Morris Brown	9	1	0	Artis Graves
1941	Morris Brown	8	1	0	William Nicks
1942	Florida A&M	9	0	0	Bill Bell
1943	Morgan St.	5	0	0	Edward Hurt
1944	Morgan St.	6	1	0	Edward Hurt
1945	Wiley	10	0	0	Fred Long
1946	Tennessee St.	10	1	0	Henry Kean
	Morgan St.	8	0	0	Edward Hurt
1947	Tennessee St.	10	0	0	Henry Kean
	Shaw	10	0	0	Brutus Wilson
1948	Southern U.	12	0	0	Arnett Mumford
1949	Southern U.	10	0	1	Arnett Mumford
	Morgan St.	8	0	0	Edward Hurt
1950	Southern U.	10	0	1	Arnett Mumford
	Florida A&M	8	1	1	Alonzo "Jake" Gaither
1951	Morris Brown	10	1	0	Edward "Ox" Clemons
1952	Florida A&M	8	2	0	Alonzo "Jake" Gaither
	Texas Southern	10	0	1	Alexander Durley
	Lincoln (Mo.)	8	0	1	Dwight Reed
	Virginia St.	8	1	0	Sylvester "Sal" Hall
1953	Prairie View	12	0	0	William Nicks
1954	Tennessee St.	10	1	0	Henry Kean
	Southern U.	10	1	0	Arnett Mumford
	Florida A&M	8	1	0	Alonzo "Jake" Gaither
	Prairie View	10	1	0	William Nicks
1955	Grambling	10	0	0	Eddie Robinson
1956	Tennessee St.	10	0	0	Howard Gentry
1957	Florida A&M	9	0	0	Alonzo "Jake" Gaither
1958	Prairie View	10	0	1	William Nicks
1959	Florida A&M	10	0	0	Alonzo "Jake" Gaither
1960	Southern U.	9	1	0	Arnett Mumford
1961	Florida A&M	10	0	0	Alonzo "Jake" Gaither
1962	Jackson St.	10	1	0	John Merritt
1963	Prairie View	10	1	0	William Nicks
1964	Prairie View	9	0	0	William Nicks
1965	Tennessee St.	9	0	1	John Merritt
1966	Tennessee St.	10	0	0	John Merritt
1967	Morgan St.	8	0	0	Earl Banks
	Grambling	9	1	0	Eddie Robinson
1968	Alcorn St.	9	1	0	Marino Casem
	N.C. A&T	8	1	0	Hornsby Howell
1969	Alcorn St.	8	0	1	Marino Casem
1970	Tennessee St.	11	0	0	John Merritt
1971	Tennessee St.	9	1	0	John Merritt
1972	Grambling	11	2	0	Eddie Robinson

Year	Team	Won	Lost	Tied	Coach
1973	Tennessee St.	10	0	0	John Merritt
1974	Grambling	11	1	0	Eddie Robinson
	Alcorn St.	9	2	0	Marino Casem
1975	Grambling	10	2	0	Eddie Robinson
1976	South Carolina St.	10	1	0	Willie Jeffries
1977	South Carolina St.	9	1	1	Willie Jeffries
	Grambling	10	1	0	Eddie Robinson
	Florida A&M	11	0	0	Rudy Hubbard
1978	Florida A&M	12	1	0	Rudy Hubbard
1979	Tennessee St.	8	3	0	John Merritt
1980	Grambling	10	2	0	Eddie Robinson
1981	South Carolina St.	10	3	0	Bill Davis
1982	* Tennessee St.	9	0	1	John Merritt
1983	Grambling	8	1	2	Eddie Robinson
1984	Alcorn St.	9	1	0	Marino Casem
1985	Jackson St.	8	3	0	W. C. Gorden
1986	Central St.	10	1	1	Billy Joe
1987	Central St.	10	1	1	Billy Joe
1988	Central St.	11	2	0	Billy Joe
1989	Central St.	10	2	0	Billy Joe
1990	# Central St.	11	1	0	Billy Joe
1991	Alabama St.	11	0	1	Houston Markham
1992	Grambling	10	2	0	Eddie Robinson
1993	Southern U.	11	1	0	Pete Richardson
1994	Hampton	10	1	0	Joe Taylor
1995	Southern U.	11	1	0	Pete Richardson
1996	Jackson St.	10	2	0	James Carson
1997	Southern U.	11	1	0	Pete Richardson
1998	Florida A&M	11	2	0	Billy Joe
1999	N.C. A&T	11	2	0	Bill Hayes
2000	Tuskegee	12	0	0	Rick Comegy
2001	Grambling	10	1	0	Doug Williams
2002	Grambling	11	2	0	Doug Williams

*Tennessee State's participation in the 1982 Division I-AA championship (1-1 record) voided. #NAIA Division I national champion.

American Sports Wire

Selected by American Sports Wire and compiled by Dick Simpson, Executive Director. Selected from 1990 by the American Sports Wire, P.O. Box 802031, Santa Clarita, Calif. 91380-2031. Record includes postseason games.

Year	Team	Won	Lost	Tied	Coach
1990	N.C. A&T	9	2	0	Bill Hayes
1991	Alabama St.	11	0	1	Houston Markham
1992	Grambling	10	2	0	Eddie Robinson
1993	Southern U.	11	1	0	Pete Richardson
1994	Hampton	10	1	0	Joe Taylor
1995	Southern U.	11	1	0	Pete Richardson
1996	Jackson St.	10	2	0	James Carson
1997	Southern U.	11	1	0	Pete Richardson
1998	Florida A&M	11	2	0	Billy Joe
1999	N.C. A&T	11	2	0	Bill Hayes
2000	Grambling	10	2	0	Doug Williams
2001	Grambling	10	1	0	Doug Williams
2002	Grambling	11	2	0	Doug Williams

Heritage Bowl

The first bowl game matching historically black schools in Division I-AA. The champion of the Southwestern Athletic Conference meets the champion of the Mid-Eastern Athletic Conference.

Date	Score (Attendance)	Site
12-21-91	Alabama St. 36, N.C. A&T 13 (7,724)	Miami, Fla.
1-2-93	Grambling 45, Florida A&M 15 (11,273)	Tallahassee, Fla.
1-1-94	Southern U. 11, South Carolina St. 0 (36,128)	Atlanta, Ga.
12-30-94	South Carolina St. 31, Grambling 27 (22,179)	Atlanta, Ga.
12-29-95	Southern U. 30, Florida A&M 25 (25,164)	Atlanta, Ga.
12-31-96	Howard 27, Southern U. 24 (18,126)	Atlanta, Ga.
12-27-97	Southern U. 34, South Carolina St. 28 (32,629)	Atlanta, Ga.
12-26-98	Southern U. 28, Bethune-Cookman 2 (32, 955)	Atlanta, Ga.
12-18-99	Hampton 24, Southern U. 3 (29,561)	Atlanta, Ga.

All-Time Black College Football Team

(Selected by the Sheridan Broadcasting Network in 1993)

OFFENSE

QB	Doug Williams	Grambling
RB	Walter Payton	Jackson St.
RB	Tank Younger	Grambling
WR	Jerry Rice	Mississippi Val.
WR	John Stallworth	Alabama A&M
WR	Charlie Joiner	Grambling
OL	Art Shell	Md.-East. Shore

OFFENSE

OL	Rayfield Wright	Fort Valley St.
OL	Jackie Slater	Jackson St.
OL	Larry Little	Bethune-Cookman
OL	Ernie Barnes	N.C. Central

DEFENSE

DL	Willie Davis	Grambling
DL	Ed "Too Tall" Jones	Tennessee St.
DL	Deacon Jones	South Carolina St.

DEFENSE

DL	L. C. Greenwood	Ark.-Pine Bluff
LB	Robert Brazile	Jackson St.
LB	Harry Carson	South Carolina St.
LB	Willie Lanier	Morgan St.
DB	Mel Blount	Southern U.
DB	Lem Barney	Jackson St.
DB	Donnie Shell	South Carolina St.
DB	Everson Walls	Grambling

DIVISION I-AA

Division II Records

Individual Records

Official national statistics for all nonmajor four-year colleges began in 1946 with a limited post-season survey. In 1948, the service was expanded to include weekly individual and team statistics rankings in all categories except interceptions, field goals, punt returns and kickoff returns; these categories were added to official individual rankings and records in 1970. In 1992, statistics compilations for individual all-purpose yards and team net punting, punt returns, kickoff returns and turnover margin were begun.

From 1946, individual rankings were by totals. Beginning in 1970, most season individual rankings were by per-game averages. In total offense, receiving yards, all-purpose yards, rushing and scoring, yards or points per game determine rankings; in receiving and interceptions, catches per game; in punt and kickoff returns, yards per return; and in field goals, number made per game. Punting always has been by average, and all team rankings have been per game.

Beginning in 1979, passers were ranked in all divisions on efficiency rating points, and team pass defense rankings changed to the same rating system in 1990 (see page 6 for explanation).

Before 1967, rankings and records included all four-year colleges that reported their statistics to the NCAA. Beginning with the 1967 season, rankings and records included only members of the NCAA.

In 1973, College Division teams were divided into Division II and Division III under a three-division reorganization plan adopted by the special NCAA Convention on August 1, 1973. Career records of players include only those years in which they competed in Division II.

Prior to 2002, postseason games were not included in NCAA final football statistics or records. Beginning with the 2002 season, all postseason games were included in NCAA final football statistics and records.

Collegiate records for all NCAA divisions can be determined by comparing records for all four divisions.

All individual and team statistics rankings include regular-season games only.

Total Offense

(Rushing Plus Passing)

MOST PLAYS
Game
88—Jarrod DeGeorgia, Wayne St. (Neb.) vs. Drake, Nov. 9, 1996 (594 yards)
Season
639—Andrew Webb, Fort Lewis, 2001 (3,288 yards)
Per-game record—59.9, Matt Kisell, Mercyhurst, 1999 (599 in 10)
Career
2,045—Earl Harvey, N.C. Central, 1985-88 (10,667 yards)
Also holds per-game record with 49.9 (2,045 in 41)

MOST PLAYS BY A FRESHMAN
Season
538—Earl Harvey, N. C. Central, 1985 (3,008 yards)
Also holds per-game record with 53.8

MOST YARDS GAINED
Game
660—Andrew Webb, Fort Lewis vs. Mesa St., Nov. 16, 2002 (22 rushing, 638 passing)
Season
4,301—Wilkie Perez, Glenville St., 1997 (112 rushing, 4,189 passing)
Per-game record—411.0, Grady Benton, West Tex. A&M, 1994 (3,699 in 9)
Career
11,881—Curt Anes, Grand Valley St., 1999-02 (1,300 rushing, 10,581 passing)
Per-game record—323.9, Grady Benton, West Tex. A&M, 1994-95 (5,831 in 18)

MOST SEASONS GAINING 3,000 YARDS OR MORE
2—Pat Brennan, Franklin, 1983 (3,239) & 1984 (3,248); Chris Hatcher, Valdosta St., 1993 (3,532) & 1994 (3,512); Lance Funderburk, Valdosta St., 1995 (3,549) & 1996 (3,676); Curt Anes, Grand Valley St., 2001 (3,621) & 2002 (3,692)

MOST SEASONS GAINING 2,500 YARDS OR MORE
3—Jim Lindsey, Abilene Christian, 1968 (2,740), 1969 (2,646) & 1970 (2,654); Thad Trujillo, Fort Lewis, 1992 (3,047), 1993 (2,784) & 1994 (2,535); Bob McLaughlin, Lock Haven, 1993 (2,928), 1994 (2,996) & 1995 (3,092); Justin Coleman, Neb.-Kearney, 1997 (2,601), 1999 (2,966) & 2000 (2,542); Eric DeGraff, Augustana (S.D.), 1998 (2,512), 1999 (2,525) & 2000 (3,424); J. T. O'Sullivan, UC Davis, 1999 (2,608), 2000 (2,945) & 2001 (3,167); Eric Howe, Truman, 1999 (2,937), 2000 (2,892) & 2001 (2,855); Todd Cunningham, Presbyterian, 1999 (2,832), 2000 (2,618) & 2001 (3,959)

GAINING 1,000 YARDS RUSHING AND 1,000 YARDS PASSING
Season
Ed Thompson, Neb.-Omaha, 1997 (1,075 rushing, 1,164 passing) & 1998 (1,191 rushing, 1,027 passing); Kwanzi Watts, Neb.-Omaha, 1999 (1,119 rushing, 1,324 passing); Neal Philpot, Pittsburg St., 2001 (1,004 rushing, 1,219 passing); Josh Chapman, Mo. Southern St., 2001 (1,025 rushing, 1,623 passing); Josh Chapman, Mo. Southern St., 2002 (1,010 rushing, 2,398 passing); Darmel Whitfield, Gannon, 2002 (1,032 rushing, 1,770 passing)

GAINING 2,000 YARDS RUSHING AND 4,000 YARDS PASSING
Career
Brad Cornelson, Mo. Southern St., 1995-98 (2,273 rushing, 4,398 passing); Josh Chapman, Mo. Southern St., 1999-02 (3,233 rushing, 5,568 passing)

GAINING 2,500 YARDS RUSHING AND 3,000 YARDS PASSING
Career
Jeff Bentrim, North Dakota St., 1983-86 (2,946 rushing, 3,453 passing); Josh Chapman, Mo. Southern St., 1999-02 (3,233 rushing, 5,568 passing)

GAINING 1,000 YARDS RUSHING AND 10,000 YARDS PASSING
Career
Curt Anes, Grand Valley St., 1999-02 (1,300 rushing, 10,581 passing)

MOST YARDS GAINED BY A FRESHMAN
Game
563—Chris Reil, Henderson St. vs. Arkansas Tech, Oct. 28, 2000
Season
3,008—Earl Harvey, N. C. Central, 1985 (538 plays)
Per-game record—318.1, Shawn Dupris, Southwest St., 1993 (2,863 in 9)

MOST GAMES GAINING 300 YARDS OR MORE
Season
8—Chris Hegg, Truman, 1985; Andrew Webb, Fort Lewis, 2002

Career
16—Thad Trujillo, Fort Lewis, 1991-94

HIGHEST AVERAGE GAIN PER PLAY
Season
(Min. 350 plays) 10.1—Curt Anes, Grand Valley St., 2001 (360 for 3,621)
Career
(Min. 950 plays) 8.9—J.T. O'Sullivan, UC Davis, 1998-01 (987 for 8,743)

MOST TOUCHDOWNS RESPONSIBLE FOR
(TDs Scored and Passed For)
Game
10—Bruce Swanson, North Park vs. North Central, Oct. 12, 1968 (passed for 10)
Also holds Most Points Responsible For record with 60
Season
55—Dusty Bonner, Valdosta St., 2000 (passed for 54, rushed for 1)
Also holds Most Points Responsible For record with 330
Career
130—Curt Anes, Grand Valley St., 1999-02 (rushed for 16, passed for 114)
Also holds Most Points Responsible For record with 780

Rushing

MOST RUSHES
Game
62—Nelson Edmonds, Northern Mich. vs. Wayne St. (Mich.), Oct. 26, 1991 (291 yards)
Season
385—Joe Gough, Wayne St. (Mich.), 1994 (1,593 yards)
Per-game record—38.6, Mark Perkins, Hobart, 1968 (309 in 8)
Career
1,131—Josh Ranek, South Dakota St., $1997-01 (6,794 yards)
Per-game record—29.8, Bernie Peeters, Luther, 1968-71 (1,072 in 36)

$See Page 8 for explanation.

MOST CONSECUTIVE RUSHES BY SAME PLAYER
Game
21—Roger Graham, New Haven vs. Knoxville, Oct. 29, 1994 (during six possessions)

MOST RUSHES BY A QUARTERBACK
Career
730—Shawn Graves, Wofford, 1989-92

MOST YARDS GAINED
Quarter
149—Marques Glaze, Bloomsburg vs. East Stroudsburg, Oct. 13, 2001 (10 carries in 1st quarter)
Half
229—Alvon Brown, Kentucky St. vs. Ky. Wesleyan, Sept. 16, 2000
Game
405—Alvon Brown, Kentucky St. vs. Ky. Wesleyan, Sept. 16, 2000 (38 rushes)
Season
2,653—Kavin Gailliard, American Int'l, 1999 (320 rushes)
Per-game record—222.0, Anthony Gray, Western N.M., 1997 (277 rushes)
Career
6,958—Brian Shay, Emporia St., 1995-98 (1,007 rushes)
Per-game record—183.4, Anthony Gray, Western N.M., 1997-98 (3,484 in 19)

MOST YARDS GAINED BY A FRESHMAN
Game
380—Garrion Corbin, Tiffin vs. Quincy, Nov. 16, 2002 (44 rushes)
Season
2,011—Johnny Bailey, Tex. A&M-Kingsville, 1986 (271 rushes)
Also holds per-game record with 182.8 (2,011 in 11)

MOST YARDS GAINED IN FIRST GAME OF CAREER
238—Johnny Bailey, Tex. A&M-Kingsville vs. Texas Southern, Sept. 6, 1986

MOST YARDS GAINED AGAINST ONE OPPONENT
Career
1,010—Brian Shay, Emporia St. vs. Washburn, 1995-98 (112 rushes)

MOST YARDS GAINED BY TWO PLAYERS, SAME TEAM
Game
514—Thelbert Withers (333) & Derrick Ray (181), N.M. Highlands vs. Fort Lewis, Oct. 17, 1992
Season
3,526—Johnny Bailey (2,011) & Heath Sherman (1,515), Tex. A&M-Kingsville, 1986
Also hold per-game record with 320.5 (3,526 in 11)
Career
8,594—Johnny Bailey (5,051) & Heath Sherman (3,543), Tex. A&M-Kingsville, 1986-88 (1,317 rushes)

TWO PLAYERS, SAME TEAM, EACH GAINING 200 YARDS OR MORE
Game
Five times. Most recent: Thad Variance (204) & Pat Norris (203), N.M. Highlands vs. Colorado Mines, Oct. 10, 1998

TWO PLAYERS, SAME TEAM, EACH GAINING 1,000 YARDS OR MORE
Season
18 times. Most recent: Ian Smart (1,162) & Rick Haering (1,037), C. W. Post, 2000; Terrance Wilson (1,039) & Aamir Dew (1,002), Indiana (Pa.), 1999; Kwanzi Watts (1,119) & Adam Wright (1,056), Neb.-Omaha, 1999; Dorrian Glenn (1,067) & Stan Kennedy (1,021), Slippery Rock, 1999

MOST GAMES GAINING 100 YARDS OR MORE
Season
12—Ian Smart, C.W. Post, 2001
Career
34—Damian Beane, Shepherd, 1996-99 (38 games)

MOST GAMES GAINING 100 YARDS OR MORE BY A FRESHMAN
Season
11—Johnny Bailey, Tex. A&M-Kingsville, 1986

MOST CONSECUTIVE GAMES GAINING 100 YARDS OR MORE
Season
12—Ian Smart, C.W. Post, 2001
Career
25—Roger Graham, New Haven, 1992-94

MOST CONSECUTIVE GAMES GAINING 100 YARDS OR MORE BY A FRESHMAN
Season
11—Johnny Bailey, Tex. A&M-Kingsville, 1986

MOST GAMES GAINING 200 YARDS OR MORE
Season
10—Kavin Gailliard, American Int'l, 1999
Career
15—Brian Shay, Emporia St., 1995-98 (44 games)

MOST GAMES GAINING 200 YARDS OR MORE BY A FRESHMAN
Season
5—Johnny Bailey, Tex. A&M-Kingsville, 1986

MOST CONSECUTIVE GAMES GAINING 200 YARDS OR MORE
Season
8—Kavin Gailliard, American Int'l, 1999

MOST GAMES GAINING 300 YARDS OR MORE
Season
4—Anthony Gray, Western N.M., 1997

MOST YARDS GAINED BY A QUARTERBACK
Game
323—Shawn Graves, Wofford vs. Lenoir-Rhyne, Sept. 15, 1990 (23 rushes)

1,483—Shawn Graves, Wofford, 1989 (241 rushes)

Career
5,128—Shawn Graves, Wofford, 1989-92 (730 rushes)

MOST SEASONS GAINING 1,000 YARDS OR MORE
Career
4—Johnny Bailey, Tex. A&M-Kingsville, 1986-89; Jeremy Monroe, Michigan Tech, 1990-93; Jarrett Anderson, Truman, 1993-96; Damian Beane, Shepherd, 1996-99

HIGHEST AVERAGE GAIN PER RUSH
Game
(Min. 20 rushes) 17.5—Don Polkinghorne, Washington (Mo.) vs. Wash. & Lee, Nov. 23, 1957 (21 for 367)
Season
(Min. 140 rushes) 10.5—Billy Johnson, Widener, 1972 (148 for 1,556)
(Min. 200 rushes) 8.6—Roger Graham, New Haven, 1992 (200 for 1,717)
(Min. 250 rushes) 8.3—Kavin Gailliard, American Int'l, 1999 (320 for 2,653)
Career
(Min. 500 rushes) 8.5—Bill Rhodes, Western St., 1953-56 (506 for 4,294)
(Min. 750 rushes) 7.58—Ian Smart, C.W. Post, 1999-02 (877 for 6,647)

MOST RUSHING TOUCHDOWNS SCORED
Game
8—Junior Wolf, Okla. Panhandle vs. St. Mary (Kan.), Nov. 8, 1958
Season
33—Ian Smart, C. W. Post, 2001
Career
94—Ian Smart, C.W. Post, 1999-02
Also holds per-game record with 2.1 (94 in 45)

MOST RUSHING TOUCHDOWNS SCORED BY A FRESHMAN
Season
24—Shawn Graves, Wofford, 1989
Also holds per-game record with 2.2 (24 in 11)

MOST RUSHING TOUCHDOWNS SCORED BY A QUARTERBACK
Season
24—Shawn Graves, Wofford, 1989
Per-game record—2.3, Jeff Bentrim, North Dakota St., 1986 (23 in 10)
Career
72—Shawn Graves, Wofford, 1989-92
Per-game record—1.8, Jeff Bentrim, North Dakota St., 1983-86 (64 in 35)

MOST RUSHING TOUCHDOWNS SCORED BY TWO PLAYERS, SAME TEAM
Season
41—Heath Sherman (23) & Johnny Bailey (18), Tex. A&M-Kingsville, 1986; Roger Graham (22) & A. J. Livingston (19), New Haven, 1992
Per-game record—4.1, Roger Graham & A. J. Livingston, New Haven, 1992 (41 in 10)
Career
106—Heath Sherman (55) & Johnny Bailey (51), Tex. A&M-Kingsville, 1985-88

LONGEST PLAY
99 yards—21 times. Most recent: Ronaie Maye, Carson-Newman vs. Lenoir-Rhyne, Oct. 30, 1999

Passing

HIGHEST PASSING EFFICIENCY RATING POINTS
Season
(Min. 15 atts. per game) 210.1—Boyd Crawford, Col. of Idaho, 1953 (120 attempts, 72 completions, 6 interceptions, 1,462 yards, 21 TD passes)
(Min. 100 comps.) 221.6—Curt Anes, Grand Valley St., 2001 (271 attempts, 189 completions, 3 interceptions, 3,086 yards, 48 TD passes)
(Min. 200 comps.) 196.5—Dusty Bonner, Valdosta St., 2001 (319 attempts, 231 completions, 8 interceptions, 3,214 yards, 43 TD passes)
Career
(Min. 375 comps.) 190.8—Dusty Bonner, Valdosta St., 2000-01 (754 attempts, 548 completions, 14 interceptions, 7,121 yards, 97 TD passes)

(Min. 750 comps.) 153.1—Chris Hatcher, Valdosta St., 1991-94 (1,451 attempts, 1,001 completions, 38 interceptions, 10,878 yards, 116 TD passes)

MOST PASSES ATTEMPTED
Game
76—Jarrod DeGeorgia, Wayne St. (Neb.) vs. Drake, Nov. 9, 1996 (completed 56)
Season
544—Lance Funderburk, Valdosta St., 1995 (completed 356)
Per-game record—50.5, Marty Washington, West Ala., 1993 (404 in 8)
Career
1,719—Bob McLaughlin, Lock Haven, 1992-95 (completed 910)
Per-game record—46.2, Tim Von Dulm, Portland St., 1969-70 (924 in 20)

MOST PASSES COMPLETED
Game
56—Jarrod DeGeorgia, Wayne St. (Neb.) vs. Drake, Nov. 9, 1996 (attempted 76)
Season
356—Lance Funderburk, Valdosta St., 1995 (attempted 544)
Also holds per-game record with 32.4 (356 in 11)
Career
1,001—Chris Hatcher, Valdosta St., 1991-94 (attempted 1,451)
Also holds per-game record with 25.7 (1,001 in 39)

MOST PASSES COMPLETED BY A FRESHMAN
Game
41—Neil Lomax, Portland St. vs. Montana St., Nov. 19, 1977 (attempted 59)

MOST CONSECUTIVE PASSES COMPLETED
Game
20—Rod Bockwoldt, Weber St. vs. South Dakota St., Nov. 6, 1976; Chris Hatcher, Valdosta St. vs. New Haven, Oct. 8, 1994; Todd Cunningham, Presbyterian vs. Wingate, Oct. 30, 1999
Season
23—Mike Ganey, Allegheny, 1967 (completed last 16 attempts vs. Carnegie Mellon, Oct. 9, and first 7 vs. Oberlin, Oct. 16)

HIGHEST PERCENTAGE OF PASSES COMPLETED
Game
(Min. 20 comps.) 90.9%—Rod Bockwoldt, Weber St. vs. South Dakota St., Nov. 6, 1976 (20 of 22)
(Min. 35 comps.) 88.6%—Chris Hatcher, Valdosta St. vs. New Haven, Oct. 8, 1994 (39 of 44)
Season
(Min. 225 atts.) 74.7%—Chris Hatcher, Valdosta St., 1994 (321 of 430)
Career
(Min. 500 atts.) 72.7%—Dusty Bonner, Valdosta St., 2000-01 (548 of 754)
(Min. 1,000 atts.) 69.0%—Chris Hatcher, Valdosta St., 1991-94 (1,001 of 1,451)

MOST PASSES HAD INTERCEPTED
Game
9—Henry Schafer, Johns Hopkins vs. Haverford, Oct. 16, 1965; Pat Brennan, Franklin vs. Saginaw Valley, Sept. 24, 1983
Season
32—Joe Stetser, Cal St. Chico, 1967 (attempted 464)
Career
88—Bob McLaughlin, Lock Haven, 1992-95 (attempted 1,719)

LOWEST PERCENTAGE OF PASSES HAD INTERCEPTED
Season
(Min. 200 atts.) 0.4%—James Weir, New Haven, 1993 (1 of 266)
(Min. 300 atts.) 1.0%—Jesse Showerda, New Haven, 1996 (3 of 300)
Career
(Min. 500 atts.) 2.1%—Jeff Fox, Grand Valley St., 1995-98 (22 of 1,031)

MOST PASSES ATTEMPTED WITHOUT INTERCEPTION
Game
70—Tim Von Dulm, Portland St. vs. Eastern Wash., Nov. 21, 1970

Season
113—Jeff Allen, New Hampshire, 1975

MOST CONSECUTIVE PASSES ATTEMPTED WITHOUT INTERCEPTION
280—Jesse Showerda, New Haven, during 10 games from Sept. 7 to Nov. 16, 1996

MOST YARDS GAINED
Game
642—Wilkie Perez, Glenville St. vs. Concord, Oct. 25, 1997
Season
4,189—Wilkie Perez, Glenville St., 1997
Per-game record—393.4, Grady Benton, West Tex. A&M, 1994 (3,541 in 9)
Career
11,213—Justin Coleman, Neb.-Kearney, 1997-00
Per-game record—323.7, Dusty Bonner, Valdosta St., 2000-01 (7,121 in 22)

MOST YARDS GAINED BY A FRESHMAN
Game
579—Chris Reil, Henderson St. vs. Arkansas Tech, Oct. 28, 2000
Season
3,190—Earl Harvey, N.C. Central, 1985

MOST GAMES GAINING 200 YARDS OR MORE
Season
12—Curt Anes, Grand Valley St., 2002
Career
33—Todd Cunningham, Presbyterian, 1998-01

MOST CONSECUTIVE GAMES GAINING 200 YARDS OR MORE
Career
28—Chris Hatcher, Valdosta St., 1992-94 (last 6 in 1992, all 11 in 1993 and 1994)

MOST GAMES GAINING 300 YARDS OR MORE
Season
10—Brett Salisbury, Wayne St. (Neb.), 1993
Career
16—Chris Hatcher, Valdosta St., 1991-94; Justin Coleman, Neb.-Kearney, 1997-00

Grand Valley State's David Kircus caught touchdown passes in 24 consecutive games in 2001 and 2002 to set a Division II record. He also holds the division's single-season (35 in 2002) and career (76) marks for touchdown receptions.

MOST CONSECUTIVE GAMES GAINING 300 YARDS OR MORE
Season
10—Brett Salisbury, Wayne St. (Neb.), 1993

MOST YARDS GAINED PER ATTEMPT
Season
(Min. 300 atts.) 11.3—Jayson Merrill, Western St., 1991 (309 for 3,484)
Career
(Min. 500 atts.) 10.6—John Charles, Portland St., 1991-92 (510 for 5,389)
(Min. 700 atts.) 9.4—Justin Coleman, Neb.-Kearney, 1997-00 (1,193 for 11,213)

MOST YARDS GAINED PER COMPLETION
Season
(Min. 125 comps.) 18.8—J.T. O'Sullivan, UC Davis, 2000 (141 for 2,648)
(Min. 175 comps.) 17.9—Damian Poalucci, East Stroudsburg, 1996 (214 for 3,831)
Career
(Min. 300 comps.) 17.8—Jayson Merrill, Western St., 1990-91 (328 for 5,830)
(Min. 600 comps.) 15.9—Justin Coleman, Neb.-Kearney, 1997-00 (706 for 11,213)

MOST TOUCHDOWN PASSES
Quarter
5—Kevin Russell, Calif. (Pa.) vs. Frostburg St., Nov. 5, 1983 (2nd quarter); Dusty Bonner, Valdosta St. vs. Ouachita Baptist, Nov. 4, 2000 (2nd quarter)
Game
10—Bruce Swanson, North Park vs. North Central, Oct. 12, 1968
Season
54—Dusty Bonner, Valdosta St., 2000
Also holds per-game record with 4.9 (54 in 11)
Career
116—Chris Hatcher, Valdosta St., 1991-94
Also holds per-game record with 3.0 (116 in 39)

MOST TOUCHDOWN PASSES BY A FRESHMAN
Game
6—Earl Harvey, N.C. Central vs. Johnson Smith, Nov. 9, 1985; Todd Cunningham, Presbyterian vs. Newberry, Nov. 14, 1998; Chris Reil, Henderson St. vs. Arkansas Tech, Oct. 28, 2000; Tom Guy, American Int'l vs. Bryant, Nov. 4, 2000 (includes overtime); Marc Eddy, Bentley vs. American Int'l, Sept. 21, 2001
Season
32—Marc Eddy, Bentley, 2001

HIGHEST PERCENTAGE OF PASSES FOR TOUCHDOWNS
Season
(Min. 150 atts.) 17.7%—Curt Anes, Grand Valley St., 2001 (48 of 271)
(Min. 300 atts.) 12.4%—Dusty Bonner, Valdosta St., 2000 (54 of 435)
Career
(Min. 500 atts.) 12.2%—Al Niemela, West Chester, 1985-88 (73 of 600)

MOST CONSECUTIVE GAMES THROWING A TOUCHDOWN PASS
Career
25—J.T. O'Sullivan, UC Davis, 1998-01 (last 6 games of 1999, 9 in 2000, all 10 in 2001)

MOST GAMES WITH THREE OR MORE TOUCHDOWN PASSES
Season
10—Curt Anes, Grand Valley St., 2002
Career
20—Curt Anes, Grand Valley St., 1999-02

MOST GAMES WITH FIVE OR MORE TOUCHDOWN PASSES
Season
7—Curt Anes, Grand Valley St., 2002
Career
12—Curt Anes, Grand Valley St., 1999-02

MOST GAMES THROWING A TOUCHDOWN PASS
Career
41—John Craven, Gardner-Webb, 1991-94 (played in 43)

LONGEST COMPLETION
99 yards—22 times. Most recent: Tom Guy to Keith Lessner, American Int'l vs. St. Anselm, Sept. 15, 2001

Receiving

MOST PASSES CAUGHT
Game
23—Barry Wagner, Alabama A&M vs. Clark Atlanta, Nov. 4, 1989 (370 yards); Chris George, Glenville St. vs. West Va. Wesleyan, Oct. 15, 1994 (303 yards)
Season
119—Brad Bailey, West Tex. A&M, 1994 (1,552 yards)
Per-game record—11.7, Chris George, Glenville St., 1993 (117 in 10)
Career
323—Clarence Coleman, Ferris St., 1998-01 (4,983 yards)
Per-game record—11.5, Chris George, Glenville St., 1993-94 (230 in 20)

MOST CONSECUTIVE GAMES CATCHING A PASS
Career
44—Mitch Allner, Morningside, 1996-99 (all 44 played)

MOST PASSES CAUGHT BY A TIGHT END
Game
15—Eight times. Most recent: Kory Wright, Concord vs. Fairmont St., Oct. 27, 2001 (193 yards)
Season
87—Kory Wright, Concord, 2001 (1,007 yards)
Career
199—Barry Naone, Portland St., 1985-88 (2,237 yards)

MOST PASSES CAUGHT BY A RUNNING BACK
Season
94—Billy Joe Masters, Evansville, 1987 (960 yards)
Also holds per-game record with 9.4 (94 in 10)
Career
200—Mark Steinmeyer, Kutztown, 1988-91 (2,118 yards)
Per-game record—5.4, Mark Marana, Northern Mich., 1979-80 (107 in 20)

MOST PASSES CAUGHT BY A FRESHMAN
Season
94—Jarett Vito, Emporia St., 1995 (932 yards)

MOST PASSES CAUGHT BY TWO PLAYERS, SAME TEAM
Career
399—Jon Spinosa (218) & Bryan McGinty (181), Lock Haven, 1993-95 (4,615 yards)

MOST YARDS GAINED
Game
401—Kevin Ingram, West Chester, vs. Clarion, Oct. 31, 1998 (caught 13)
Season
1,876—Chris George, Glenville St., 1993 (caught 117)
Also holds per-game record with 187.6 (1,876 in 10)
Career
4,983—Clarence Coleman, Ferris St., 1998-01 (caught 323)
Per-game record—160.8, Chris George, Glenville St., 1993-94 (3,215 in 20)

MOST YARDS GAINED BY A TIGHT END
Game
290—Bob Tucker, Bloomsburg vs. Susquehanna, Oct. 7, 1967 (caught 15)
Season
1,325—Bob Tucker, Bloomsburg, 1967 (caught 77)
Career
2,494—Dan Anderson, Northwest Mo. St., 1982-85 (caught 186)

MOST YARDS GAINED BY A RUNNING BACK
Game
209—Don Lenhard, Bucknell vs. Delaware, Nov. 19, 1966 (caught 11)
Season
1,202—Larry Bales, Emory & Henry, 1968 (caught 62)
Also holds per-game record with 120.2 (1,202 in 10)

Career
2,118—Mark Steinmeyer, Kutztown, 1988-91 (caught 200)

MOST YARDS GAINED BY A FRESHMAN
Season
1,313—Dallas Mall, Bentley, 2001 (caught 69)

MOST YARDS GAINED BY TWO PLAYERS, SAME TEAM
Career
6,528—Robert Clark (4,231) & Robert Green (2,297), N.C. Central, 1983-86 (caught 363)

HIGHEST AVERAGE GAIN PER RECEPTION
Season
(Min. 30 receps.) 32.5—Tyrone Johnson, Western St., 1991 (32 for 1,039)
(Min. 40 receps.) 27.6—Chris Harkness, Ashland, 1987 (41 for 1,131)
(Min. 55 receps.) 24.0—Rod Smith, Mo. Southern St., 1991 (60 for 1,439)
Career
(Min. 135 receps.) 22.8—Tyrone Johnson, Western St., 1990-93 (163 for 3,717)
(Min. 180 receps.) 20.1—Robert Clark, N.C. Central, 1983-86 (210 for 4,231)

HIGHEST AVERAGE GAIN PER RECEPTION BY A RUNNING BACK
Season
(Min. 40 receps.) 19.4—Larry Bales, Emory & Henry, 1968 (62 for 1,202)
Career
(Min. 80 receps.) 18.1—John Smith, Boise St., 1972-75 (89 for 1,608)

MOST TOUCHDOWN PASSES CAUGHT
Quarter
4—Chris Perry, Adams St. vs. Mesa St., Nov. 4, 1995 (2nd quarter)
Game
8—Paul Zaeske, North Park vs. North Central, Oct. 12, 1968 (caught 11)
Season
35—David Kircus, Grand Valley St., 2002 (caught 77) Also holds per-game record with 2.8 in 2001 (28 in 10)
Career
76—David Kircus, Grand Valley St., 1999-02 (caught 222) Also holds per-game record with 1.8 (76 in 43)

MOST TOUCHDOWN PASSES CAUGHT BY A TIGHT END
Game
5—Alex Preuss, Grand Valley St. vs. Winona St., Sept. 17, 1988; Mike Palomino, Portland St. vs. Cal Poly, Nov. 16, 1991
Season
13—Bob Tucker, Bloomsburg, 1967

MOST TOUCHDOWN PASSES CAUGHT BY A RUNNING BACK
Season
12—Larry Bales, Emory & Henry, 1968
Career
24—John Smith, Boise St., 1972-75

MOST TOUCHDOWN PASSES CAUGHT BY A FRESHMAN
Season
24—Dallas Mall, Bentley, 2001 (caught 69)

HIGHEST PERCENTAGE OF PASSES CAUGHT FOR TOUCHDOWNS
Season
(Min. 10 TDs) 68.8%—Jim Callahan, Temple, 1966 (11 of 16)
Career
(Min. 20 TDs) 34.2%—David Kircus, Grand Valley St., 1999-02 (76 of 222)

MOST CONSECUTIVE PASSES CAUGHT FOR TOUCHDOWNS
Game
5—Jim Callahan, Temple vs. Bucknell, Oct. 8, 1966
Season
10—Jim Callahan, Temple, 1966 (first 5 games of career)

MOST CONSECUTIVE GAMES CATCHING A TOUCHDOWN PASS
Career
24—David Kircus, Grand Valley St., Aug. 30, 2001 to Dec. 14, 2002

MOST GAMES CATCHING A TOUCHDOWN PASS
Career
32—David Kircus, Grand Valley St., 1999-02 (in 43 games)

LONGEST RECEPTION
99 yards—22 times. Most recent: Keith Lessner from Tom Guy, American Int'l vs. St. Anselm, Sept. 15, 2001

Punting

MOST PUNTS
Game
32—Jan Jones, Sam Houston St. vs. Tex. A&M-Commerce, Nov. 2, 1946 (1,203 yards)
Season
98—John Tassi, Lincoln (Mo.), 1981 (3,163 yards)
Career
328—Dan Brown, Nicholls St., 1976-79 (12,883 yards)

HIGHEST AVERAGE PER PUNT
Game
(Min. 5 punts) 57.5—Tim Baer, Colorado Mines vs. Fort Lewis, Oct. 25, 1986 (8 for 460)
Season
(Min. 20 punts) 49.1—Steve Ecker, Shippensburg, 1965 (32 for 1,570)
(Min. 40 punts) 46.3—Mark Bounds, West Tex. A&M, 1990 (69 for 3,198)
Career
(Min. 100 punts) 44.3—Jason Van Dyke, Adams St., 1995-98 (242 for 10,720)

LONGEST PUNT
97 yards—Earl Hurst, Emporia St. vs. Central Mo. St., Oct. 3, 1964

Interceptions

(From 1970)

MOST PASSES INTERCEPTED
Quarter
3—Mike McDonald, La.-Lafayette vs. Lamar, Oct. 24, 1970 (4th; 25 yards); Anthony Devine, Millersville vs. Cheyney, Oct. 13, 1990 (3rd; 90 yards); Nate Neuhaus, Neb.-Kearney vs. Wayne St. (Neb.), Oct. 25, 1997 (3rd)
Half
4—Nate Neuhaus, Neb.-Kearney vs. Wayne St. (Neb.), Oct. 25, 1997 (2nd)
Game
5—Five times. Most recent: Gary Evans, Truman vs. Mo.-Rolla, Oct. 18, 1975
Season
14—Five times. Most recent: Luther Howard, Delaware St., 1972 (99 yards); Eugene Hunter, Fort Valley St., 1972 (211 yards)
Per-game record—1.6, Tom Rezzuti, Northeastern, 1971 (14 in 9); Eugene Hunter, Fort Valley St., 1972 (14 in 9); Luther Howard, Delaware St., 1972 (14 in 9)
Career
37—Tom Collins, Indianapolis, 1982-85 (390 yards)

MOST CONSECUTIVE GAMES INTERCEPTING A PASS
Career
8—Darin Nix, Mo.-Rolla, 1993-94

MOST YARDS ON INTERCEPTION RETURNS
Game
191—Demons Bryan, Saginaw Valley vs. Ferris St., Sept. 15, 2001 (2 interceptions)
Season
300—Mike Brim, Virginia Union, 1986 (8 interceptions)

Career
504—Anthony Leonard, Virginia Union, 1973-76 (17 interceptions)

HIGHEST AVERAGE GAIN PER INTERCEPTION
Season
(Min. 6 ints.) 44.7—Ray Cannon, Bowie St., 1997 (6 for 268)
Career
(Min. 10 ints.) 37.4—Greg Anderson, Montana, 1974-76 (11 for 411)
(Min. 15 ints.) 29.6—Anthony Leonard, Virginia Union, 1973-76 (17 for 504)

MOST TOUCHDOWNS SCORED ON INTERCEPTIONS
Season
4—Clay Blalack, Tenn.-Martin, 1976 (8 interceptions)

LONGEST INTERCEPTION RETURN
100 yards—Many times: Brian Holshek, Pace vs. Assumption, Oct. 26, 2002

Punt Returns

(From 1970)

MOST PUNT RETURNS
Game
12—David Nelson, Ferris St. vs. Northern Mich., Oct. 2, 1993 (240 yards)
Season
61—Armin Anderson, UC Davis, 1984 (516 yards)
Career
153—Armin Anderson, UC Davis, 1983-85 (1,207 yards)

MOST YARDS ON PUNT RETURNS
Game
265—Billy Johnson, Widener vs. St. John's (N.Y.), Sept. 23, 1972 (4 returns)
Season
612—Erik Totten, Western Wash., 2000 (39 returns)
Career
1,494—Clarence Coleman, Ferris St., 1998-01 (103 returns)

HIGHEST AVERAGE GAIN PER RETURN
Game
(Min. 4 rets.) 66.3—Billy Johnson, Widener vs. St. John's (N.Y.), Sept. 23, 1972 (4 for 265)
Season
(Min. 1.2 rets. per game) 34.1—Billy Johnson, Widener, 1972 (15 for 511)
Career
(Min. 1.2 rets. per game) 26.2—Billy Johnson, Widener, 1971-72 (29 for 759)

MOST OPPONENT'S PUNTS BLOCKED
Season
6—Tim Bowie, Northern Colo., 1995

MOST TOUCHDOWNS SCORED ON PUNT RETURNS
Game
3—Bobby Ahu, Hawaii vs. Linfield, Nov. 15, 1969; Billy Johnson, Widener vs. St. John's (N.Y.), Sept. 23, 1972; Virgil Seay, Troy St. vs. West Ala., Sept. 29, 1979
Season
5—James Rooths, Shepherd, 1998
Career
10—James Rooths, Shepherd, 1997-00 (59 returns, 1,223 yards)

LONGEST PUNT RETURN
100 yards—Many times. Most recent: Randy Ladson, Fayetteville St. vs. St. Paul's, Sept. 19, 1987

Kickoff Returns

(From 1970)

MOST KICKOFF RETURNS
Game
12—Johnny Cox, Fort Lewis vs. Mesa St., Nov. 3, 1990

DIVISION II

Season
48—Matt Kacanda, East Stroudsburg, 1999 (1,210 yards)
Career
116—Johnny Cox, Fort Lewis, 1990-93 (2,476 yards)

MOST YARDS ON KICKOFF RETURNS
Game
276—Tom Dufresne, Hamline vs. Minn. Duluth, Sept. 30, 1972 (7 returns); Matt Pericolosi, Central Conn. St. vs. Hofstra, Sept. 14, 1991 (6 returns)
Season
1,210—Matt Kacanda, East Stroudsburg, 1999 (48 returns)
Career
2,630—Dave Ludy, Winona St., 1991-94 (89 returns)

HIGHEST AVERAGE GAIN PER RETURN
Game
(Min. 3 rets.) 71.7—Clarence Martin, Cal Poly vs. Cal Poly Pomona, Nov. 20, 1982 (3 for 215)
Season
(Min. 1.2 rets. per game) 39.9—D.J. Flick, Slippery Rock, 2000 (14 for 558)
Career
(Min. 1.2 rets. per game) 34.0—Glen Printers, Southern Colo., 1973-74 (25 for 851)

MOST TOUCHDOWNS SCORED ON KICKOFF RETURNS
Game
2—Five times. Most recent: Jason Hollman, UC Davis vs. Cal St. Northridge, Oct. 13, 2001
Season
3—Eight times. Most recent: Billy Cook, Grand Valley St., 1998
Career
8—Dave Ludy, Winona St., 1991-94

LONGEST KICKOFF RETURN
100 yards—Many times. Most recent: Jason Douglas, Truman vs. Pittsburg St., Nov. 2, 2002

Total Kick Returns

(Combined Punt and Kickoff Returns)

MOST KICK RETURNS
Season
65—Clarence Coleman, Ferris St., 2001 (36 punts, 29 kickoffs, 1,233 yards)

MOST KICK-RETURN YARDS
Career
3,296—Damon Thompson, Virginia St., 1997-00 (1,153 on punt returns, 2,143 on kickoff returns, 202 returns)

MOST TOUCHDOWNS
Career
10—Anthony Leonard, Virginia Union, 1973-76 (6 punt returns, 4 kickoff returns); James Rooths, Shepherd, 1997-00 (all punt returns); Kevin Nickerson, Central Mo. St., 1998-01 (8 punt returns, 2 kickoff returns)

MOST CONSECUTIVE TOUCHDOWNS ON KICK RETURNS
Game
3—Bootsie Washington, Shepherd vs. West Va. Tech, Oct. 18, 1997 (89-yard kickoff return, 60-yard punt return, 59-yard punt return)

All Runbacks

(Combined Interceptions, Punt Returns and Kickoff Returns)

MOST TOUCHDOWNS
Season
6—Anthony Leonard, Virginia Union, 1974 (2 interceptions, 2 punt returns, 2 kickoff returns); Terry Guess, Gardner-Webb, 1994 (3 punt returns, 3 kickoff returns); Bootsie Washington, Shepherd, 1997 (1 interception, 4 punt returns, 1 kickoff return)
Career
13—Anthony Leonard, Virginia Union, 1973-76 (3 interceptions, 6 punt returns, 4 kickoff returns); James Rooths, Shepherd, 1997-00 (10 punt returns, 2 interception returns, 1 blocked field goal return)

LONGEST RETURN OF A MISSED FIELD GOAL
100—Kalvin Simmons, Clark Atlanta vs. Morris Brown, Sept. 5, 1987 (actually from 6 yards in end zone); Josh Pierce, Newberry vs. Wingate, Oct. 14, 2000 (actually from 5 yards in end zone)

Kicks Blocked

MOST TOTAL KICKS BLOCKED BY
Season
9—Clinton Washington, West Ala., 1997
Career
22—Clinton Washington, West Ala., 1996-99

All-Purpose Yards

(Yardage Gained From Rushing, Receiving and All Runbacks)

MOST PLAYS
Season
415—Steve Roberts, Butler, 1989 (325 rushes, 49 receptions, 21 punt returns, 20 kickoff returns; 2,669 yards)
Career
1,215—Josh Ranek, South Dakota St., $1997-01 (1,131 rushes, 72 receptions, 12 kickoff returns; 7,946 yards)

$See Page 8 for explanation.

MOST YARDS GAINED
Game
525—Andre Johnson, Ferris St. vs. Clarion, Sept. 16, 1989 (19 rushing, 235 receiving, 10 punt returns, 261 kickoff returns; 17 plays)
Season
3,064—Kavin Gailliard, American Int'l, 1999 (2,653 rushing, 289 receiving, 122 kickoff returns)
Per-game record—266.9, Steve Roberts, Butler, 1989 (2,669 in 10)
Career
9,301—Brian Shay, Emporia St., 1995-98 (6,958 rushing, 1,032 receiving, 104 punt returns, 1,207 kickoff returns)
Per-game record—234.0, Chris George, Glenville St., 1993-94 (4,679 in 20)

MOST YARDS GAINED BY A FRESHMAN
Season
2,425—Johnny Bailey, Tex. A&M-Kingsville, 1986 (2,011 rushing, 54 receiving, 20 punt returns, 340 kickoff returns; 296 plays)
Also holds per-game record with 220.5 (2,425 in 11)

MOST YARDS GAINED BY TWO PLAYERS, SAME TEAM
Season
4,112—Brian Shay (2,738) & Chet Pobolish (1,374), Emporia St., 1996
Also hold per-game record with 373.8 (4,112 in 11)

HIGHEST AVERAGE GAIN PER PLAY
Game
(Min. 15 plays) 30.9—Andre Johnson, Ferris St. vs. Clarion, Sept. 16, 1989 (17 for 525)
Season
(Min. 150 plays, 1,500 yards) 12.9—Billy Johnson, Widener, 1972 (175 for 2,265)
Career
(Min. 300 plays, 4,000 yards) 15.2—Chris George, Glenville St., 1993-94 (307 for 4,679)

Scoring

MOST POINTS SCORED
Game
48—Junior Wolf, Okla. Panhandle vs. St. Mary (Kan.), Nov. 8, 1958 (8 TDs); Paul Zaeske, North Park vs. North Central, Oct. 12, 1968 (8 TDs)
Season
212—David Kircus, Grand Valley St., 2002 (35 TDs, 2 PATs)
Per-game record—21.0, Carl Herakovich, Rose-Hulman, 1958 (168 in 8)
Career
570—Ian Smart, C.W. Post, 1999-02 (95 TDs)

Per-game record—13.4, Ole Gunderson, St. Olaf, 1969-71 (362 in 27)

MOST POINTS SCORED BY A FRESHMAN
Season
144—Shawn Graves, Wofford, 1989 (24 TDs); Dallas Mall, Bentley, 2001 (24 TDs)
Graves holds per-game record with 13.1 (144 in 11)

MOST POINTS SCORED BY A QUARTERBACK
Season
144—Shawn Graves, Wofford, 1989 (24 TDs)
Per-game record—13.8, Jeff Bentrim, North Dakota St., 1986 (138 in 10)
Career
438—Shawn Graves, Wofford, 1989-92
Per-game record—11.0, Jeff Bentrim, North Dakota St., 1983-86 (386 in 35)

MOST POINTS SCORED BY TWO PLAYERS, SAME TEAM
Season
356—David Kircus (212) & Reginald Spearmon (144), Grand Valley St., 2002
Career
752—David Kircus (464) & Reginald Spearmon (288), Grand Valley St., 1999-02

MOST TOUCHDOWNS SCORED
Game
8—Junior Wolf, Okla. Panhandle vs. St. Mary (Kan.), Nov. 8, 1958 (all by rushing); Paul Zaeske, North Park vs. North Central, Oct. 12, 1968 (all on pass receptions)
Season
35—David Kircus, Grand Valley St., 2002
Per-game record—3.1, Carl Herakovich, Rose-Hulman, 1958 (25 in 8)
Career
95—Ian Smart, C.W. Post, 1999-02
Per-game record—2.2, Ole Gunderson, St. Olaf, 1969-71 (60 in 27)

MOST TOUCHDOWNS SCORED BY A FRESHMAN
Season
24—Shawn Graves, Wofford, 1989; Dallas Mall, Bentley, 2001
Graves holds per-game record with 2.2 (24 in 11)

MOST TOUCHDOWNS SCORED BY A QUARTERBACK
Season
24—Shawn Graves, Wofford, 1989
Per-game record—2.3, Jeff Bentrim, North Dakota St., 1986 (23 in 10)
Career
72—Shawn Graves, Wofford, 1989-92
Per-game record—1.8, Jeff Bentrim, North Dakota St., 1983-86 (64 in 35)

MOST TOUCHDOWNS SCORED BY TWO PLAYERS, SAME TEAM
Season
59—David Kircus (35) & Reginald Spearmon (24), Grand Valley St., 2002
Career
125—David Kircus (77) & Reginald Spearmon (48), Grand Valley St., 1999-02

MOST CONSECUTIVE GAMES SCORING A TOUCHDOWN
Career
24—David Kircus, Grand Valley St., 1999-02

MOST EXTRA POINTS MADE BY KICKING
Game
14—Matt Johnson, Connecticut vs. Newport Naval Training, Oct. 22, 1949 (attempted 17); Art Anderson, North Park vs. North Central, Oct. 12, 1968 (attempted 15)
Season
75—Kevin Sonntag, Grand Valley St., 2001 (attempted 82)
Career
203—David Purnell, Northwest Mo. St., 1996-99 (attempted 215)

MOST EXTRA POINTS ATTEMPTED BY KICKING
Game
17—Matt Johnson, Connecticut vs. Newport Naval Training, Oct. 22, 1949 (made 14)

Season
82—Kevin Sonntag, Grand Valley St., 2001 (made 75)
Career
215—David Purnell, Northwest Mo. St., 1996-99 (made 203)

HIGHEST PERCENTAGE OF EXTRA POINTS MADE BY KICKING
Season
(Best perfect season) 100.0%—David Purnell, Northwest Mo. St., 1999 (56 of 56)
Career
(Min. 90 atts.) 98.9%—Mark DeMoss, Liberty, 1980-83 (92 of 93)
(Min. 150 atts.) 97.8%—Aaron Pederson, North Dakota St., 1998-01 (178 of 182)

MOST CONSECUTIVE EXTRA POINTS MADE BY KICKING
Season
56—David Purnell, Northwest Mo. St., 1999 (entire season)
Career
117—Aaron Pederson, North Dakota St. (from Nov. 14, 1998, to Sept. 22, 2001)

MOST POINTS SCORED BY KICKING
Game
20—Clarence Joseph, Central St. vs. Kentucky St., Oct. 16, 1982 (5 FGs, 5 PATs)
Season
104—Dave Hendrix, Grand Valley St., 2002 (10 FGs, 74 PATs)
Per-game record—9.6, Jason Williams, Southern Ark., 1998 (96 in 10)
Career
326—David Purnell, Northwest Mo. St., 1996-99 (41 FGs, 203 PATs)
Per-game record (min. 145 pts.)—8.3, Dave Austinson, Truman, 1981-82 (149 in 18)
Per-game record (min. 200 pts.)—7.8, David Purnell, Northwest Mo. St., 1996-99 (326 in 42)

Defensive Extra Points

MOST DEFENSIVE EXTRA POINTS SCORED
Game and Season
1—Many times

LONGEST DEFENSIVE EXTRA POINT BLOCKED-KICK RETURN
99—Robert Fair (DB), Carson-Newman vs. Mars Hill, Oct. 15, 1994 (scored)

LONGEST DEFENSIVE EXTRA POINT FUMBLE RETURN
90—Kyle Hinshaw (LB), Elon vs. Catawba, Oct. 25, 1997

LONGEST DEFENSIVE EXTRA POINT INTERCEPTION RETURN
100—Morice Mabry (DB), UC Davis vs. St. Mary's (Cal.), Sept. 28, 1991; Brian Muldrow (CB), St. Francis (Ill.) vs. Northwood, Oct. 8, 1994; Jonathan Mitchell (DB), Central Ark. vs. Delta St., Sept. 27, 1997; Deniel Anglin, Fairmont St. vs. Concord, Nov. 4, 2000; Courtney Williams, Southwestern Okla. St. vs. Panhandle St., Oct. 20, 2001

FIRST DEFENSIVE EXTRA POINT SCORED
Herman Rice (DB), Springfield vs. Worcester Tech, Sept. 9, 1988 (80-yard blocked kick return)

Defensive Records

TOTAL TACKLES
Season
151—Deric Sieck, Winona St., 2002
Per-game record—15.7, Jason Ocean, Livingstone, 2001 (141 in 9)

SOLO TACKLES
Season
92—Chris Angel, Western Ore., 2000
Per-game record—8.5, Dan Holland, Mansfield, 2002 (85 in 10)

ASSISTED TACKLES
Season
105—Brian Holliday, Fayetteville St., 2002
Per-game record—10.1, Jason Ocean, Livingstone, 2001 (91 in 9)

TACKLES FOR LOSS
Season
37—Charlie Cook, C.W. Post, 2001
Also holds per-game record with 3.1 (37 in 12)

PASS SACKS
Season
20.5—Charlie Cook, C.W. Post, 2001
Also holds per-game record with 1.7 (20.5 in 12)

PASSES DEFENDED
Season
32—Anthony Cooks, Fairmont St., 2001
Also holds per-game record with 3.6 (32 in 9)

FORCED FUMBLES
Season
7—Bryan Eakin, Neb.-Kearney, 2001; Al Sullivan, Midwestern St., 2002
Eakin holds per-game record with 0.7 (7 in 10)

Fumble Returns

LONGEST FUMBLE RETURN
100—Sam Durst, Gardner-Webb vs. West Virginia St., Sept. 19, 1998

Field Goals

MOST FIELD GOALS MADE
Game
6—Steve Huff, Central Mo. St. vs. Southeast Mo. St., Nov. 2, 1985 (37, 45, 37, 24, 32, 27 yards; 6 attempts); Austin Wellock, Ashland vs. Wayne St. (Mich.), Oct. 5, 2002 (28, 35, 32, 37, 31, 23 yards)
Season
20—Six times. Most recent: Henrik Juul-Nielsen, Neb.-Kearney, 2002 (24 attempts)
Per-game record—2.0, Jason Williams, Southern Ark., 1998 (20 in 10)
Career
64—Mike Wood, Southeast Mo. St., 1974-77 (109 attempts)
Also holds per-game record with 1.5 (64 in 44)

MOST CONSECUTIVE FIELD GOALS MADE
Career
17—Greg Payne, Catawba (from Oct. 5, 1996, to Sept. 20, 1997; ended with missed FG vs. Charleston So., Sept. 27, 1997)

MOST FIELD GOALS ATTEMPTED
Game
7—Jim Turcotte, Mississippi Col. vs. Troy St., Oct. 3, 1981 (made 2)
Season
35—Mike Wood, Southeast Mo. St., 1977 (made 16)
Per-game record—3.3, Skipper Butler, Texas-Arlington, 1968 (33 in 10)
Career
109—Mike Wood, Southeast Mo. St., 1974-77 (made 64)
Per-game record—2.7, Jaime Nunez, Weber St., 1969-71 (83 in 3)

HIGHEST PERCENTAGE OF FIELD GOALS MADE
Season
(Min. 15 atts.) 88.2%—Kurt Seibel, South Dakota, 1983 (15 of 17); Howie Guarini, Shippensburg, 1990 (15 of 17)
(Min. 20 atts.) 86.4%—Dennis Hochman, Sonoma St., 1986 (19 of 22)
Career
(Min. 35 made) 80.0%—Bill May, Clarion, 1977-80 (48 of 60)

LONGEST FIELD GOAL
67 yards—Tom Odle, Fort Hays St. vs. Washburn, Nov. 5, 1988

Team Records

Single Game—Offense

Total Offense

MOST YARDS GAINED
910—Hanover vs. Franklin, Oct. 30, 1948 (426 rushing, 484 passing; 75 plays)

MOST YARDS GAINED, BOTH TEAMS
1,328—Northwood (688) vs. Saginaw Valley (640), Oct. 24, 1998

MOST PLAYS
117—Tex. A&M-Kingsville vs. Angelo St., Oct. 30, 1982 (96 rushes, 21 passes; 546 yards)

HIGHEST AVERAGE GAIN PER PLAY
12.1—Hanover vs. Franklin, Oct. 30, 1948 (75 for 910)

MOST TOUCHDOWNS SCORED BY RUSHING AND PASSING
15—North Park vs. North Central, Oct. 12, 1968 (4 by rushing, 11 by passing)

MOST TOUCHDOWNS SCORED BY RUSHING AND PASSING, BOTH TEAMS
20—North Park (15) & North Central (5), Oct. 12, 1968

MOST YARDS GAINED BY A LOSING TEAM
749—Fort Lewis vs. Mesa St., Nov. 16, 2002 (lost 58-55)

Rushing

MOST YARDS GAINED
719—Coe vs. Beloit, Oct. 16, 1971 (73 rushes)

MOST RUSHES
97—Hobart vs. Union (N.Y.), Oct. 23, 1971 (444 yards)

HIGHEST AVERAGE GAIN PER RUSH (Min. 50 Rushes)
11.2—Wofford vs. Charleston So., Nov. 12, 1994 (53 for 595)

MOST TOUCHDOWNS SCORED BY RUSHING
12—Coe vs. Beloit, Oct. 16, 1971

MOST PLAYERS, ONE TEAM, EACH GAINING 100 YARDS OR MORE
5—South Dakota vs. St. Cloud St., Nov. 1, 1986 (James Hambrick 125, Darryl Colvin 123, Tony Higgins 118, Dave Elle 109, Joe Longueville [QB] 106; team gained 581)

Passing

MOST PASSES ATTEMPTED
85—West Tex. A&M vs. Eastern N.M., Nov. 5, 1994 (completed 47)

MOST PASSES ATTEMPTED, BOTH TEAMS
131—Presbyterian (70) & Tusculum (61), Nov. 3, 2001 (completed 82)

MOST PASSES COMPLETED
56—Wayne St. (Neb.) vs. Drake, Nov. 9, 1996 (attempted 76)

MOST PASSES COMPLETED, BOTH TEAMS
82—Presbyterian (50) & Tusculum (32), Nov. 3, 2001 (attempted 131)

MOST PASSES HAD INTERCEPTED
11—Hamline vs. Concordia-M'head, Nov. 5, 1955; Rhode Island vs. Brown, Oct. 8, 1949

MOST PASSES ATTEMPTED WITHOUT INTERCEPTION
63—Hamline vs. St. John's (Minn.), Oct. 8, 1955 (completed 34)

HIGHEST PERCENTAGE OF PASSES COMPLETED (Min. 20 Attempts)
90.9%—Northwestern St. vs. La.-Lafayette, Nov. 12, 1966 (20 of 22)

MOST YARDS GAINED
678—Portland St. vs. Mont. St.-Billings, Nov. 20, 1976

MOST YARDS GAINED, BOTH TEAMS
1,065—Western N.M. (614) & West Tex. A&M (451), Oct. 8, 1994

MOST TOUCHDOWN PASSES
11—North Park vs. North Central, Oct. 12, 1968

MOST TOUCHDOWN PASSES, BOTH TEAMS
14—North Park (11) & North Central (3), Oct. 12, 1968

Punting

MOST PUNTS
32—Sam Houston St. vs. Tex. A&M-Commerce, Nov. 2, 1946 (1,203 yards)

MOST PUNTS, BOTH TEAMS
63—Sam Houston St. (32) & Tex. A&M-Commerce (31), Nov. 2, 1946

HIGHEST AVERAGE PER PUNT (Min. 5 Punts)
57.5—Colorado Mines vs. Fort Lewis, Oct. 21, 1989 (8 for 460)

Punt Returns

MOST YARDS ON PUNT RETURNS
265—Widener vs. St. John's (N.Y.), Sept. 23, 1972 (4 returns)

MOST TOUCHDOWNS SCORED ON PUNT RETURNS
3—Hawaii vs. Linfield, Nov. 15, 1969; Widener vs. St. John's (N.Y.), Sept. 23, 1972; Troy St. vs. West Ala., Sept. 29, 1979

Scoring

MOST POINTS SCORED
125—Connecticut vs. Newport Naval Training, Oct. 22, 1949

MOST POINTS SCORED AGAINST A COLLEGE OPPONENT
106—Fort Valley St. vs. Knoxville, Oct. 11, 1969 (14 TDs, 2 PATs, 9 two-point conversions, 1 safety)

MOST POINTS SCORED BY A LOSING TEAM
66—Western N.M. vs. Fort Lewis (67), Nov. 2, 2002 (2 ot)
Note: Record for regulation game—60, New Haven vs. Southern Conn. St. (64), Oct. 25, 1991

MOST POINTS SCORED, BOTH TEAMS
136—North Park (104) & North Central (32), Oct. 12, 1968

MOST POINTS SCORED IN TWO CONSECUTIVE GAMES
172—Tuskegee, 1966 (93-0 vs. Morehouse, Oct. 14; 79-0 vs. Lane, Oct. 22)

MOST POINTS SCORED IN THREE CONSECUTIVE GAMES
190—Grand Valley St., 2001 (63 vs. Ashland, Sept. 22; 64 vs. Northern Mich., Sept. 29; 63 vs. Ferris St., Oct. 6)

MOST POINTS SCORED IN FOUR CONSECUTIVE GAMES
253—Grand Valley St., 2001 (63 vs. Ashland, Sept. 22; 64 vs. Northern Mich., Sept. 29; 63 vs. Ferris St., Oct. 6; 63 vs. Indianapolis, Oct. 13)

MOST POINTS SCORED IN FIVE CONSECUTIVE GAMES
312—Grand Valley St., 2001 (63 vs. Ashland, Sept. 22; 64 vs. Northern Mich., Sept. 29; 63 vs. Ferris St., Oct. 6; 63 vs. Indianapolis, Oct. 13; 59 vs. Mercyhurst, Oct. 20)

MOST POINTS OVERCOME TO WIN A GAME
28—Ferris St. (46) vs. Saginaw Valley (42), Nov. 11, 1995 (trailed 28-0 with 11:17 remaining in 2nd quarter)

MOST POINTS SCORED IN A BRIEF PERIOD OF TIME
21 in 1:20—Winona St. vs. Bemidji St., Oct. 15, 1994 (turned 14-0 game into 35-0 in 1st quarter)

MOST TOUCHDOWNS SCORED
17—Connecticut vs. Newport Naval Training, Oct. 22, 1949

MOST TOUCHDOWNS SCORED AGAINST A COLLEGE OPPONENT
15—Iowa Wesleyan vs. William Penn, Oct. 31, 1953; Alcorn St. vs. Paul Quinn, Sept. 9, 1967; North Park vs. North Central, Oct. 12, 1968

MOST SAFETIES SCORED
3—Fort Valley St. vs. Miles, Oct. 16, 1993

MOST POINTS AFTER TOUCHDOWN MADE BY KICKING
14—Connecticut vs. Newport Naval Training, Oct. 22, 1949 (attempted 17); North Park vs. North Central, Oct. 12, 1968 (attempted 15)

MOST TWO-POINT ATTEMPTS
11—Fort Valley St. vs. Knoxville, Oct. 11, 1969 (made 9)

MOST TWO-POINT ATTEMPTS MADE
9—Fort Valley St. vs. Knoxville, Oct. 11, 1969 (attempted 11)

MOST FIELD GOALS MADE
6—Central Mo. St. vs. Southeast Mo. St., Nov. 2, 1985 (6 attempts); Ashland vs. Wayne St. (Mich.), Oct. 5, 2002 (6 attempts)

MOST DEFENSIVE EXTRA POINTS SCORED
1—By many teams

MOST DEFENSIVE EXTRA-POINT OPPORTUNITIES
2—North Dakota St. vs. Augustana (S.D.), Sept. 24, 1988 (2 interceptions; none scored); Mo. Southern St. vs. Central Mo. St., Sept. 28, 1996 (2 interceptions; none scored)

First Downs

MOST TOTAL FIRST DOWNS
56—Concord vs. Fairmont St., Oct. 27, 2001

MOST FIRST DOWNS BY PENALTY
14—La Verne vs. Northern Ariz., Oct. 11, 1958

MOST TOTAL FIRST DOWNS, BOTH TEAMS
74—Fort Lewis (40) & Western N.M. (34), Nov. 2, 2002 (2 ot)
Note: Record for regulation game—66, Ferris St. (33) & Northwood (33), Oct. 26, 1985; North Dakota (36) & Tex. A&M-Kingsville (30), Sept. 13, 1986

Penalties

MOST PENALTIES
28—Northern Ariz. vs. La Verne, Oct. 11, 1958 (155 yards)

MOST PENALTIES, BOTH TEAMS
42—N.C. Central (23) & St. Paul's (19), Sept. 13, 1986 (453 yards)

MOST YARDS PENALIZED
293—Cal Poly vs. Portland St., Oct. 31, 1981 (26 penalties)

MOST YARDS PENALIZED, BOTH TEAMS
453—N.C. Central (256) & St. Paul's (197), Sept. 13, 1986 (42 penalties)

Fumbles

MOST FUMBLES
16—Carthage vs. North Park, Nov. 14, 1970 (lost 7)

Overtimes

MOST OVERTIME PERIODS
6—Adams St. (55) vs. Neb.-Kearney (48), Sept. 19, 1998

SINGLE GAME—Defense

Total Defense

FEWEST TOTAL OFFENSE PLAYS ALLOWED
29—North Park vs. Concordia (Ill.), Sept. 26, 1964

FEWEST TOTAL OFFENSE YARDS ALLOWED
Minus 69—Fort Valley St. vs. Miles, Oct. 16, 1993 (39 plays)

FEWEST RUSHES ALLOWED
7—Indianapolis vs. Valparaiso, Oct. 30, 1982 (-57 yards)

FEWEST RUSHING YARDS ALLOWED
Minus 95—San Diego St. vs. U.S. Int'l, Nov. 27, 1965 (35 plays)

FEWEST PASS COMPLETIONS ALLOWED
0—By many teams. Most recent: Westminster (Pa.) vs. Thiel, Oct. 14, 2000 (attempted 10)

FEWEST PASSING YARDS ALLOWED
Minus 19—Ashland vs. Heidelberg, Sept. 25, 1948 (completed 4)

Punting

MOST OPPONENT'S PUNTS BLOCKED
5—Southeastern La. vs. Troy St., Oct. 7, 1978 (holds record for most consecutive punts blocked with 4); Winston-Salem vs. N.C. Central, Oct. 4, 1986

MOST TOUCHDOWNS SCORED ON BLOCKED PUNT RETURNS
2—Northern Colo. vs. Western St., Sept. 7, 1996; Fairmont St. vs. West Va. Tech, Oct. 12, 1996

Field-Goal Blocks

MOST OPPONENT'S FIELD GOALS BLOCKED
4—Minn. Duluth vs. Winona St., Nov. 4, 2000 (three on successive plays and all four in the 4th quarter)

Interceptions

MOST PASSES INTERCEPTED BY
11—St. Cloud St. vs. Bemidji St., Oct. 31, 1970 (45 attempts); Concordia-M'head vs. Hamline, Nov. 5, 1955 (37 attempts)

MOST TOUCHDOWNS ON INTERCEPTION RETURNS
3—By many teams. Most recent: Bloomsburg vs. East Stroudsburg, Oct. 31, 1998

SEASON—Offense

Total Offense

MOST YARDS GAINED
6,841—Grand Valley St., 2002 (1,032 plays, 14 games)
Per-game record—624.1, Hanover, 1948 (4,993 in 8)

HIGHEST AVERAGE GAIN PER PLAY
(Min. 500 plays) 9.2—Hanover, 1948 (543 for 4,993)
(Min. 800 plays) 6.9—American Int'l, 1998 (805 for 5,562)

MOST PLAYS PER GAME
88.7—Cal St. Chico, 1967 (887 in 10)

Rushing

MOST YARDS GAINED
4,503—Carson-Newman, 2002 (636 rushes, 13 games)
Per-game record—404.8, Col. of Emporia, 1954 (3,643 in 9)

HIGHEST AVERAGE GAIN PER RUSH
(Min. 300 rushes) 8.4—Hanover, 1948 (382 for 3,203)
(Min. 600 rushes) 7.1—Carson-Newman, 2002 (636 for 4,503)

MOST RUSHES PER GAME
78.9—Okla. Panhandle, 1963 (789 in 10)

Passing

MOST YARDS GAINED
5,000—West Tex. A&M, 1994 (363 completions, 11 games)
Also holds per-game record with 454.5 (5,000 in 11)

HIGHEST AVERAGE GAIN PER ATTEMPT (Min. 175 Attempts)
11.5—Grand Valley St., 2001 (291 for 3,346)

HIGHEST AVERAGE GAIN PER COMPLETION
(Min. 100 comps.) 19.4—Calif. (Pa.), 1966 (116 for 2,255)
(Min. 200 comps.) 18.0—East Stroudsburg, 1996 (224 for 4,041)

MOST PASSES ATTEMPTED
623—Emporia St., 1995 (completed 322)
Also holds per-game record with 56.6 (623 in 11)

MOST PASSES COMPLETED
373—Valdosta St., 1995 (attempted 570)
Also holds per-game record with 33.9 (373 in 11)

FEWEST PASSES COMPLETED PER GAME
0.4—Hobart, 1971 (4 in 9)

HIGHEST PERCENTAGE COMPLETED (Min. 200 Attempts)
72.0%—Valdosta St., 2000 (337 of 468)

LOWEST PERCENTAGE OF PASSES HAD INTERCEPTED (Min. 275 Attempts)
0.7%—New Haven, 1993 (2 of 296)

MOST TOUCHDOWN PASSES PER GAME
5.1—Grand Valley St., 2001 (51 in 10)

HIGHEST PASSING EFFICIENCY RATING POINTS
(Min. 200 atts.) 222.5—Grand Valley St., 2001 (291 attempts, 204 completions, 3 interceptions, 3,346 yards, 51 TDs)
(Min. 300 atts.) 182.4—Valdosta St., 2000 (468 attempts, 337 completions, 7 interceptions, 4,157 yards, 55 TDs)

Punting

MOST PUNTS PER GAME
10.0—Wash. & Lee, 1968 (90 in 9)

FEWEST PUNTS PER GAME
1.8—Emporia St., 1997 (20 in 11)

HIGHEST PUNTING AVERAGE
48.0—Adams St., 1966 (36 for 1,728)

Punt Returns

MOST PUNT RETURNS
64—UC Davis, 1984 (557 yards)

MOST TOUCHDOWNS SCORED ON PUNT RETURNS
6—Northern Colo., 1996 (52 returns); Shepherd, 1998 (33 returns)

Kickoff Returns

MOST KICKOFF RETURNS
78—Ark.-Monticello, 1998 (1,634 yards)

Scoring

MOST POINTS PER GAME
58.4—Grand Valley St., 2001 (584 in 10)

MOST TOUCHDOWNS PER GAME
8.2—Grand Valley St., 2001 (82 in 10)

MOST CONSECUTIVE EXTRA POINTS MADE BY KICKING
56—Northwest Mo. St., 1999 (entire season)

MOST CONSECUTIVE FIELD GOALS MADE
13—UC Davis, 1976

MOST TWO-POINT ATTEMPTS PER GAME
6.8—Florida A&M, 1961 (61 in 9, made 32)

MOST TWO-POINT ATTEMPTS MADE PER GAME
3.6—Florida A&M, 1961 (32 in 9, attempted 61)

MOST FIELD GOALS MADE
20—Six times. Most recent: Neb.-Kearney, 2002 (attempted 24)

MOST DEFENSIVE EXTRA POINTS SCORED
2—UC Davis, 1991 (1 blocked kick return, 1 interception); Wingate, 1997 (2 blocked kick returns)

MOST DEFENSIVE EXTRA-POINT OPPORTUNITIES
3—Northern Colo., 1988 (2 blocked kick returns, 1 interception; none scored); Central Okla., 1989 (2 blocked kick returns, 1 interception; one scored); UC Davis, 1991 (2 interceptions, 1 blocked kick return; two scored)

Penalties

MOST PENALTIES AGAINST
146—Gardner-Webb, 1992 (1,344 yards); Portland St., 1994 (1,340 yards)
Per-game record—14.6, Portland St., 1994 (146 in 10)

MOST YARDS PENALIZED
1,356—Hampton, 1977 (124 penalties, 11 games)

Turnovers (Giveaways)

(From 1985)

FEWEST TURNOVERS
8—Lenoir-Rhyne, 1994 (4 interceptions, 4 fumbles lost)
Also holds per-game record with 0.8 (8 in 10)

MOST TURNOVERS
61—Cheyney, 1990 (36 interceptions, 25 fumbles lost)
Per-game record—5.8, Livingstone, 1986 (58 in 10)

FEWEST FUMBLES LOST
2—Michigan Tech, 1995 (9 fumbles); Western St., 1998 (11 fumbles)

SEASON—Defense

Total Defense

FEWEST YARDS ALLOWED PER GAME
44.4—John Carroll, 1962 (311 in 7)

LOWEST AVERAGE YARDS ALLOWED PER PLAY
(Min. 300 plays) 1.0—John Carroll, 1962 (310 for 311 yards)
(Min. 600 plays) 1.8—Alcorn St., 1976 (603 for 1,089)

Rushing Defense

FEWEST YARDS ALLOWED PER GAME
Minus 16.7—Tennessee St., 1967 (-150 in 9)

DIVISION II

LOWEST AVERAGE YARDS ALLOWED PER RUSH
(Min. 250 rushes) Minus 0.5—Tennessee St., 1967 (296 for -150 yards)
(Min. 400 rushes) 1.3—Luther, 1971 (414 for 518)

Pass Defense

FEWEST YARDS ALLOWED PER GAME
10.1—Ashland, 1948 (91 in 9)

FEWEST YARDS ALLOWED PER ATTEMPT
(Min. 200 atts.) 3.1—Virginia St., 1971 (205 for 630)
(Min. 300 atts.) 3.2—Southwest Mo. St., 1966 (315 for 996)

FEWEST YARDS ALLOWED PER COMPLETION
(Min. 100 comps.) 8.8—Long Beach St., 1965 (144 for 1,264)

LOWEST COMPLETION PERCENTAGE ALLOWED
(Min. 250 atts.) 24.1%—Southwest Mo. St., 1966 (76 of 315)

MOST PASSES INTERCEPTED PER GAME
3.9—Delaware, 1946 (35 in 9); Whitworth, 1959 (35 in 9)

FEWEST PASSES INTERCEPTED
(Min. 150 atts.) 1—Gettysburg, 1972 (175 attempts; 0 yards returned)

HIGHEST PERCENTAGE INTERCEPTED
(Min. 150 atts.) 21.7%—Stephen F. Austin, 1949 (35 of 161)
(Min. 275 atts.) 11.8%—Mo.-Rolla, 1978 (35 of 297)

MOST TOUCHDOWNS ON INTERCEPTION RETURNS
7—Virginia Union, 1986 (31 interceptions); Fort Valley St., 1991 (15 interceptions); Gardner-Webb, 1992 (35 interceptions)

LOWEST PASSING EFFICIENCY RATING ALLOWED
(Min. 250 atts.) 41.7—Fort Valley St., 1985 (allowed 283 attempts, 90 completions, 1,039 yards, 2 TDs and intercepted 33)

Blocked Kicks

MOST BLOCKED KICKS
27—Winston-Salem, 1986 (16 punts, 7 field goal attempts, 4 PAT kicks)

Scoring

FEWEST POINTS ALLOWED PER GAME
0.0—Albany St. (Ga.), 1960 (0 in 9 games)

MOST POINTS ALLOWED PER GAME
64.5—Rose-Hulman, 1961 (516 in 8)

Turnovers (Takeaways)

(From 1985)

HIGHEST TURNOVER MARGIN PER GAME
2.7—Hillsdale, 1993 (plus 30 in 11; 11 giveaways vs. 41 takeaways)

MOST TAKEAWAYS
56—Gardner-Webb, 1992 (35 interceptions, 21 fumble recoveries)
Also holds per-game record with 5.1 (56 in 11)

Additional Records

MOST CONSECUTIVE VICTORIES
34—Hillsdale (from Oct. 2, 1954, to Nov. 16, 1957; ended with 27-26 loss to Pittsburg St., Dec. 21, 1957)

MOST CONSECUTIVE VICTORIES OVER DIVISION II OPPONENTS
40—North Ala. (from Sept. 4, 1993, to Dec. 9, 1995; ended with 17-10 loss to Albany St. [Ga.], Aug. 31, 1996)

MOST CONSECUTIVE HOME VICTORIES
31—Indiana (Pa.) (from Nov. 22, 1986, to Oct. 17, 1992; ended with 35-33 loss to Towson, Oct. 31, 1992)

MOST CONSECUTIVE GAMES UNBEATEN
54—Morgan St. (from Nov. 5, 1931, to Nov. 18, 1938; ended with 15-0 loss to Virginia St., Nov. 30, 1938)

MOST CONSECUTIVE VICTORIES OVER ONE OPPONENT
40—West Chester vs. Millersville (from Nov. 18, 1922, to Oct. 5, 1974; ended with 17-12 loss Oct. 4, 1975)

MOST CONSECUTIVE VICTORIES OVER ONE OPPONENT IN AN UNINTERRUPTED SERIES (Must have played in consecutive years)
27—Minn. Duluth vs. Wis.-Superior (from Sept. 8, 1962, to Sept. 2, 1989; Wis.-Superior dropped football program during the 1992 season)

25—UC Davis vs. San Fran. St. (from Sept. 26, 1970, to Nov. 12, 1994; San Fran. St. dropped football program after 1994 season)

MOST CONSECUTIVE GAMES WITHOUT BEING SHUT OUT
227—Pittsburg St. (from Nov. 13, 1982 to Nov. 17, 2001; ended with 38-0 loss to North Dakota, Nov. 24, 2001)

MOST CONSECUTIVE WINNING SEASONS
33—UC Davis (from 1970-current)

MOST CONSECUTIVE NON-LOSING SEASONS
33—West Chester (from 1940-74; ended with 4-5-0 record in 1975); UC Davis (from 1970-current)

MOST CONSECUTIVE LOSSES
44—Minn.Morris (from Nov. 14, 1998 to present, last victory was 25-22 over Mayville St. [N.D.])
39—St. Paul's (from Oct. 23, 1948, to Oct. 24, 1953; ended with 7-6 win over Delaware St., Oct. 31, 1953); Cheyney (from Sept. 3, 1994, to Oct. 24, 1998; ended with 40-13 win over Mansfield, Oct. 31, 1998)

MOST CONSECUTIVE GAMES WITHOUT A VICTORY
49—Paine (1954-61, includes 1 tie)

MOST CONSECUTIVE GAMES WITHOUT A TIE
329—West Chester (from Oct. 26, 1945, to Oct. 31, 1980; ended with 24-24 tie vs. Cheyney, Nov. 8, 1980)

MOST TIE GAMES IN A SEASON
5—Wofford, 1948 (Sept. 25 to Oct. 23, consecutive)

HIGHEST-SCORING TIE GAME
54-54—Norfolk St. vs. Winston-Salem, Oct. 9, 1993

MOST CONSECUTIVE QUARTERS WITHOUT YIELDING A RUSHING TOUCHDOWN
51—Butler (from Sept. 25, 1982, to Oct. 15, 1983)

MOST CONSECUTIVE POINT-AFTER-TOUCHDOWN KICKS MADE
123—Liberty (from 1976 to Sept. 10, 1983; ended with missed PAT vs. Saginaw Valley, Sept. 10, 1983)

MOST IMPROVED WON-LOST RECORD
11 games—Northern Mich., 1975 (13-1, including three Division II playoff victories, from 0-10 in 1974)

Annual Champions, All-Time Leaders

Total Offense

CAREER YARDS PER GAME
(Minimum 5,000 Yards)

Player, Team	Years	G	Plays	Yards	Yd. PG
Grady Benton, West Tex. A&M	1994-95	18	844	5,831	*323.9
Wilkie Perez, Glenville St.	1997-98	17	702	5,447	320.4
Dusty Bonner, Valdosta St.	2000-01	22	837	7,016	318.9
Marty Washington, West Ala.	1992-93	17	773	5,212	306.6
J.T. O'Sullivan, UC Davis	1998-01	29	987	8,743	301.5
Todd Cunningham, Presbyterian	1998-01	39	1,635	11,578	296.9
Scott Otis, Glenville St.	1994-95	20	755	5,911	295.6
Jarrod DeGeorgia, Wayne St. (Neb.)	1995-96	18	753	5,145	285.8
Jayson Merrill, Western St.	1990-91	20	641	5,619	281.0
Jermaine Whitaker, N.M. Highlands	1992-94	31	1,374	8,650	279.0
Chris Petersen, UC Davis	1985-86	20	735	5,532	276.6
Tim Von Dulm, Portland St.	1969-70	20	989	5,501	275.1
Vernon Buck, Wingate	1991-94	41	1,761	11,227	273.8
Chris Hatcher, Valdosta St.	1991-94	39	1,557	10,588	271.5
Chris Hegg, Truman	1984-85	20	930	5,418	270.9
Pat Graham, Augustana (S.D.)	1995-96	21	948	5,672	270.1
June Jones, Portland St.	1975-76	21	760	5,590	266.2
Curt Anes, Grand Valley St.	1999-02	45	1,527	*11,881	264.1
Jeff Fox, Grand Valley St.	1995-98	34	1,341	8,941	263.0
Troy Mott, Wayne St. (Neb.)	1991-92	20	943	5,212	260.6
Earl Harvey, N.C. Central	1985-88	41	*2,045	10,667	260.2
Justin Coleman, Neb.-Kearney	1997-00	41	1,411	10,644	259.6
Jim Zorn, Cal Poly Pomona	1973-74	21	946	5,364	255.4
Bryan Harman, Fairmont St.	1998-01	38	1,471	9,638	253.6
Drew Folmar, Millersville	1997-00	40	1,537	10,105	252.6
Steve Wray, Franklin	1979, 81-82	26	1,178	6,564	252.5
Bob McLaughlin, Lock Haven	1992-95	44	2,007	11,041	250.9
Thad Trujillo, Fort Lewis	1991-94	41	1,787	10,209	249.0
Lance Funderburk, Valdosta St.	1993-96	30	1,126	7,469	249.0
Matt McCarthy, Ferris St.	1996-99	32	1,188	7,942	248.2
Rob Tomlinson, Cal St. Chico	1988-91	40	1,656	9,921	248.0
Caleb Slover, Tusculum	2000-01	21	930	5,135	244.5
Matt Kissell, Mercyhurst	1996-99	29	1,286	7,087	244.4

*Record.

SEASON YARDS PER GAME

Player, Team	Year	G	Plays	Yards	Yd. PG
Grady Benton, West Tex. A&M	†1994	9	505	3,699	*411.0
Perry Klein, C.W. Post	†1993	10	499	4,052	405.2

Player, Team	Year	G	Plays	Yards	Yd. PG
Marty Washington, West Ala.	1993	8	453	3,146	393.3
Wilkie Perez, Glenville St.	†1997	11	509	*4,301	391.0
Damian Poalucci, East Stroudsburg	†1996	10	505	3,883	388.3
Andrew Webb, Fort Lewis	†2002	11	613	4,245	385.9
Brett Salisbury, Wayne St. (Neb.)	1993	10	424	3,732	373.2
Curt Anes, Grand Valley St.	†2001	10	360	3,621	362.1
Todd Cunningham, Presbyterian	2001	11	607	3,959	359.9
Jed Drenning, Glenville St.	1993	10	473	3,593	359.3
Alfred Montez, Western N.M.	1994	6	244	2,130	355.0
Rob Tomlinson, Cal St. Chico	†1989	10	534	3,525	352.5
Dusty Bonner, Valdosta St.	†2000	11	475	3,795	345.0
Chris Hegg, Truman	†1985	11	*594	3,782	343.8
Bryan Harman, Fairmont St.	2000	10	534	3,427	342.7
Jarrod DeGeorgia, Wayne St. (Neb.)	1996	10	495	3,416	341.6
Rod Smith, Glenville St.	1996	10	472	3,410	341.0
Bob Toledo, San Fran. St.	†1967	10	409	3,407	340.7
Jayson Merrill, Western St.	†1991	10	337	3,400	340.0
John Charles, Portland St.	†1992	8	303	2,708	338.5
Bryan Harman, Fairmont St.	2001	9	452	3,021	335.7
Lance Funderburk, Valdosta St.	1996	11	490	3,676	334.2
Aaron Sparrow, Norfolk St.	†1995	10	464	3,300	330.0
J.T. O'Sullivan, UC Davis	2000	9	275	2,945	327.2
George Bork, Northern Ill.	†1963	9	413	2,945	327.2
Richard Strasser, San Fran. St.	1985	10	536	3,259	325.9
Pat Brennan, Franklin	†1984	10	583	3,248	324.8

*Record. †National champion.

CAREER YARDS

Player, Team	Years	Plays	Yards
Curt Anes, Grand Valley St.	1999-02	1,527	*11,881
Todd Cunningham, Presbyterian	1998-01	1,635	11,578
Vernon Buck, Wingate	1991-94	1,761	11,227
Bob McLaughlin, Lock Haven	1992-95	2,007	11,041
Earl Harvey, N.C. Central	1985-88	*2,045	10,667
Justin Coleman, Neb.-Kearney	1997-00	1,411	10,644
Chris Hatcher, Valdosta St.	1991-94	1,557	10,588
Thad Trujillo, Fort Lewis	1991-94	1,787	10,209
Eric DeGraff, Augustana (S.D.)	1997-00	1,643	10,128
Drew Folmar, Millersville	1997-00	1,537	10,105
Ricky Fritz, Minn. Duluth	$1998-02	1,464	9,926
Rob Tomlinson, Cal St. Chico	1988-91	1,656	9,921
Kasey Waterman, Mo. Western St.	1998-01	1,449	9,874
John Hebgen, Minn. St. Mankato	1993-96	1,545	9,772
Mike Mitros, West Chester	1996-99	1,716	9,714
Bryan Harman, Fairmont St.	1998-01	1,471	9,638
Jarrod Fergason, Fairmont St.	$1993-97	1,583	9,638
John Craven, Gardner-Webb	1991-94	1,666	9,630
Sam Mannery, Calif. (Pa.)	1987-90	1,669	9,125
Trevor Moon, Chadron St.	1995-98	1,395	9,044
Eric Howe, Truman	1998-01	1,375	9,040
Andy Breault, Kutztown	1989-92	1,459	8,975
Jeff Fox, Grand Valley St.	1995-98	1,341	8,941
Antonio Hawkins, Virginia St.	1997-00	1,392	8,871
Josh Chapman, Mo. Southern St.	1999-02	1,509	8,801
J.T. O'Sullivan, UC Davis	1998-01	987	8,743
Jermaine Whitaker, N.M. Highlands	1992-94	1,374	8,650
Damian Poalucci, East Stroudsburg	1994-97	1,365	8,569
Dave MacDonald, West Chester	1991-94	1,257	8,453
Mike Lazo, Concord	1995-98	1,222	8,390
Jim Lindsey, Abilene Christian	1967-70	1,510	8,385
Dave Walter, Michigan Tech	1983-86	1,660	8,345
Maurice Heard, Tuskegee	1988-91	1,289	8,321
Aaron Sparrow, Norfolk St.	1992-95	1,345	8,301
Jack Hull, Grand Valley St.	1988-91	1,196	8,221
Ted Larkin, Bentley	1997-00	1,351	8,150
Kevin McCarn, Ark.-Monticello	1997-00	1,435	8,134
Dave DenBraber, Ferris St.	1984-87	1,522	8,115
Tracy Kendall, Alabama A&M	1988-91	1,480	8,112

*Record. $See Page 8 for explanation.

SEASON YARDS

Player, Team	Year	G	Plays	Yards
Wilkie Perez, Glenville St.	†1997	11	509	*4,301
Andrew Webb, Fort Lewis	†2002	11	613	4,245
Perry Klein, C.W. Post	†1993	10	499	4,052
Todd Cunningham, Presbyterian	2001	11	607	3,959
Damian Poalucci, East Stroudsburg	†1996	10	505	3,883
Curt Anes, Grand Valley St.	2002	14	457	3,821
Dusty Bonner, Valdosta St.	†2000	11	475	3,795
Chris Hegg, Truman	†1985	11	594	3,782
Brett Salisbury, Wayne St. (Neb.)	1993	10	424	3,732
Grady Benton, West Tex. A&M	†1994	9	505	3,699
Lance Funderburk, Valdosta St.	1996	11	490	3,676

Curt Anes of Grand Valley State became Division II's career leader in total offense late in the 2002 season. Anes finished with a combined rushing and passing total of 11,881 yards.

Player, Team	Year	G	Plays	Yards
Curt Anes, Grand Valley St.	†2001	10	360	3,621
Jed Drenning, Glenville St.	1993	10	473	3,593
Lance Funderburk, Valdosta St.	1995	11	581	3,549
Jamie Pass, Minn. St. Mankato	1993	11	543	3,537
Tod Mayfield, West Tex. A&M	†1986	11	555	3,533
Chris Hatcher, Valdosta St.	1993	11	495	3,532
Rob Tomlinson, Cal St. Chico	†1989	10	534	3,525
Chris Hatcher, Valdosta St.	1994	11	452	3,512
Ted Larkin, Bentley	†1999	11	545	3,490
Mike Mitros, West Chester	†1998	11	537	3,478
Jeff Fox, Grand Valley St.	1998	11	481	3,472
June Jones, Portland St.	†1976	11	465	3,463
Dusty Burk, Truman	2002	11	551	3,441

*Record. †National champion.

SINGLE-GAME YARDS

Yds.	Player, Team (Opponent)	Date
660	Andrew Webb, Fort Lewis (Mesa St.)	Nov. 16, 2002
651	Wilkie Perez, Glenville St. (Concord)	Oct. 25, 1997
631	Jayce Goree, Glenville St. (Concord)	Oct. 24, 1998
623	Perry Klein, C.W. Post (Salisbury)	Nov. 6, 1993
614	Alfred Montez, Western N.M. (West Tex. A&M)	Oct. 8, 1994
610	Andrew Webb, Fort Lewis (Western N.M.)	Nov. 2, 2002
597	Damian Poalucci, East Stroudsburg (Mansfield)	Nov. 2, 1996
594	Jarrod DeGeorgia, Wayne St. (Neb.) (Drake)	Nov. 9, 1996
591	Marty Washington, West Ala. (Nicholls St.)	Sept. 11, 1993
584	Tracy Kendall, Alabama A&M (Clark Atlanta)	Nov. 4, 1989
580	Grady Benton, West Tex. A&M (Howard Payne)	Sept. 17, 1994
575	Scott Otis, Glenville St. (West Va. Wesleyan)	Oct. 15, 1994
573	Pat Graham, Augustana (S.D.) (Minn. St. Mankato)	Oct. 28, 1995
571	John Charles, Portland St. (Cal Poly)	Nov. 16, 1991
569	Bob McLaughlin, Lock Haven (Calif. [Pa.])	Oct. 29, 1994
563	Chris Reil, Henderson St. (Arkansas Tech)	Oct. 28, 2000
562	Bob Toledo, San Fran. St. (Cal St. Hayward)	Oct. 21, 1967
560	Todd Cunningham, Presbyterian (West Ga.)	Sept. 1, 2001
555	Bryan Harman, Fairmont St. (Concord)	Nov. 4, 2000
555	A.J. Vaughn, Wayne St. (Mich.) (Wis.-Milwaukee)	Sept. 30, 1967

ANNUAL CHAMPIONS

Year	Player, Team	Class	Plays	Yards
1946	Buster Dixon, Abilene Christian	Sr.	170	960
1947	Jim Peterson, Hanover	So.	108	1,449
1948	Jim Peterson, Hanover	Jr.	130	1,589
1949	Connie Callahan, Morningside	Sr.	311	2,006
1950	Bob Heimerdinger, Northern Ill.	Jr.	286	1,782
1951	Bob Heimerdinger, Northern Ill.	Sr.	292	1,775
1952	Don Gottlob, Sam Houston St.	Sr.	303	2,470
1953	Ralph Capitani, Northern Iowa	Jr.	317	1,755
1954	Bill Engelhardt, Neb.-Omaha	So.	243	1,645
1955	Jim Stehlin, Brandeis	Sr.	222	1,455
1956	Dick Jamieson, Bradley	So.	240	1,925
1957	Stan Jackson, Cal Poly Pomona	Jr.	301	2,145
1958	Stan Jackson, Cal Poly Pomona	Sr.	334	2,478
1959	Gary Campbell, Whittier	Sr.	309	2,383
1960	Charles Miller, Austin	Sr.	287	1,966
1961	Denny Spurlock, Whitworth	Sr.	224	1,684
1962	George Bork, Northern Ill.	Jr.	397	2,398

Year	Player, Team	Class	Plays	Yards
1963	George Bork, Northern Ill.	Sr.	413	2,945
1964	Jerry Bishop, Austin	Jr.	332	2,152
1965	Ron Christian, Northern Ill.	Sr.	377	2,307
1966	Joe Stetser, Cal St. Chico	Jr.	406	2,382
1967	Bob Toledo, San Fran. St.	Sr.	409	3,407
1968	Terry Bradshaw, Louisiana Tech	Jr.	426	2,987
1969	Tim Von Dulm, Portland St.	Jr.	462	2,736

Beginning in 1970, ranked on per-game (instead of total) yards

Year	Player, Team	Class	G	Plays	Yards	Avg.
1970	Jim Lindsey, Abilene Christian	Sr.	9	440	2,654	294.9
1971	Randy Mattingly, Evansville	Jr.	9	402	2,234	248.2
1972	Bob Biggs, UC Davis	Sr.	9	381	2,356	261.8
1973	Jim Zorn, Cal Poly Pomona	Jr.	11	499	3,000	272.7
1974	Jim McMillan, Boise St.	Sr.	10	403	3,101	310.1
1975	Lynn Hieber, Indiana (Pa.)	Sr.	10	402	2,503	250.3
1976	June Jones, Portland St.	Sr.	11	465	3,463	314.8
1977	Steve Mariucci, Northern Mich.	Sr.	8	270	1,780	222.5
1978	Charlie Thompson, Western St.	Jr.	9	304	2,138	237.6
1979	Phil Kessel, Northern Mich.	Jr.	9	368	2,164	240.4
1980	Curt Strasheim, Southwest St.	Jr.	10	501	2,565	256.5
1981	Steve Wray, Franklin	Jr.	10	488	2,726	272.6
1982	Steve Wray, Franklin	Sr.	8	382	2,114	264.3
1983	Pat Brennan, Franklin	Jr.	10	524	3,239	323.9
1984	Pat Brennan, Franklin	Sr.	10	583	3,248	324.8
1985	Chris Hegg, Truman	Sr.	11	*594	3,782	343.8
1986	Tod Mayfield, West Tex. A&M	Sr.	11	555	3,533	312.2
1987	Randy Hobson, Evansville	Sr.	10	457	2,964	296.4
1988	Mark Sedinger, Northern Colo.	Sr.	10	413	2,828	282.8
1989	Rob Tomlinson, Cal St. Chico	So.	10	534	3,525	352.5
1990	Andy Breault, Kutztown	Jr.	11	562	3,173	288.5
1991	Jayson Merrill, Western St.	Sr.	10	337	3,400	340.0
1992	John Charles, Portland St.	Sr.	8	303	2,708	338.5
1993	Perry Klein, C.W. Post	Sr.	10	499	4,052	405.2
1994	Grady Benton, West Tex. A&M	Jr.	9	505	3,699	*411.0
1995	Aaron Sparrow, Norfolk St.	Sr.	10	464	3,300	330.0
1996	Damian Poalucci, East Stroudsburg	Jr.	10	505	3,883	388.3
1997	Wilkie Perez, Glenville St.	Jr.	11	509	*4,301	391.0
1998	Mike Mitros, West Chester	Jr.	11	537	3,478	316.2
1999	Ted Larkin, Bentley	Jr.	11	545	3,490	317.3
2000	Dusty Bonner, Valdosta St.	Jr.	11	475	3,795	345.0
2001	Curt Anes, Grand Valley St.	Jr.	10	360	3,621	362.1
2002	Andrew Webb, Fort Lewis	Jr.	11	613	4,245	385.9

*Record.

Rushing

CAREER YARDS PER GAME
(Minimum 2,500 Yards)

Player, Team	Years	G	Plays	Yards	Yd. PG
Anthony Gray, Western N.M.	1997-98	19	503	3,484	*183.4
Damian Beane, Shepherd	1996-99	38	1,065	6,346	167.0
Johnny Bailey, Tex. A&M-Kingsville	1986-89	39	885	6,320	162.1
Tyrone Morgan, Northern St.	1998-00	30	830	4,816	160.5
Brian Shay, Emporia St.	1995-98	44	1,007	*6,958	158.1
Josh Ranek, South Dakota St.	$1997-01	44	*1,131	6,794	154.4
Fred Lane, Lane	1994-96	29	700	4,433	152.9
Kavin Gailliard, American Int'l	1996-99	43	950	6,523	151.7
Ole Gunderson, St. Olaf	1969-71	27	639	4,060	150.4
Richard Huntley, Winston-Salem	1992-95	42	932	6,286	149.7
Roger Graham, New Haven	1991-94	40	821	5,953	148.8
Ian Smart, C.W. Post	1999-02	45	877	6,647	147.7
Brad Hustad, Luther	1957-59	27	655	3,943	146.0
Rashaan Dumas, Southern Conn. St.	1996-99	37	977	5,396	145.8
Jarrett Anderson, Truman	1993-96	43	979	6,166	143.4
Quincy Tillmon, Emporia St.	1990-92, 94	29	790	4,141	142.8
Joe Iacone, West Chester	1960-62	27	565	3,767	139.5
Leonard Davis, Lenoir-Rhyne	$1990-94	35	839	4,853	138.7
Phillip Moore, North Dakota	1995-98	40	1,060	5,467	136.7
Don Aleksiewicz, Hobart	1969-72	34	819	4,525	133.1
Jim VanWagner, Michigan Tech	1973-76	36	958	4,788	133.0
Steve Roberts, Butler	1986-89	35	1,026	4,623	132.1

*Record. $See Page 8 for explanation.

SEASON YARDS PER GAME

Player, Team	Year	G	Plays	Yards	TD	Yd. PG
Anthony Gray, Western N.M.	†1997	10	277	2,220	12	*222.0
Kavin Gailliard, American Int'l	†1999	12	320	*2,653	32	221.1
Ian Smart, C.W. Post	†2001	12	308	2,536	*33	211.3
Brian Shay, Emporia St.	†1998	11	293	2,265	29	205.9
Irv Sigler, Bloomsburg	1997	10	299	2,038	20	203.8
Jarrett Anderson, Truman	†1996	11	321	2,140	27	194.5

Player, Team	Year	G	Plays	Yards	TD	Yd. PG
Brian Shay, Emporia St.	1996	11	342	2,103	18	191.2
Richard Huntley, Winston-Salem	†1995	10	273	1,889	16	188.9
Josh Ranek, South Dakota St.	1999	11	329	2,055	25	186.8
Fred Lane, Lane	1995	10	273	1,833	19	183.3
Johnny Bailey, Tex. A&M-Kingsville	†1986	11	271	2,011	18	182.8
Bob White, Western N.M.	†1951	9	202	1,643	20	182.6
Kevin Mitchell, Saginaw Valley	†1989	8	236	1,460	6	182.5
Rashaan Dumas, Southern Conn. St.	1996	9	291	1,639	18	182.1
Don Aleksiewicz, Hobart	†1971	9	276	1,616	19	179.6
Kavin Gailliard, American Int'l	1998	11	269	1,971	23	179.2
Jim Holder, Okla. Panhandle	†1963	10	275	1,775	9	177.5
Damian Beane, Shepherd	1998	10	299	1,775	17	177.5
Phillip Moore, North Dakota	1997	10	293	1,771	14	177.1
Wilmont Perry, Livingstone	1997	10	195	1,770	20	177.0
Jim Baier, Wis.-River Falls	†1966	9	240	1,587	17	176.3

*Record. †National champion.

CAREER YARDS

Player, Team	Years	Plays	Yards	Avg.
Brian Shay, Emporia St.	1995-98	1,007	*6,958	6.91
Josh Ranek, South Dakota St.	$1997-01	*1,131	6,794	6.01
Ian Smart, C.W. Post	1999-02	877	6,647	+7.58
Kavin Gailliard, American Int'l	1996-99	950	6,523	6.87
Damian Beane, Shepherd	1996-99	1,065	6,346	5.96
Johnny Bailey, Tex. A&M-Kingsville	1986-89	885	6,320	7.14
Richard Huntley, Winston-Salem	1992-95	932	6,286	6.74
Jarrett Anderson, Truman	1993-96	979	6,166	6.30
Roger Graham, New Haven	1991-94	821	5,953	7.25
Wesley Cates, Calif. (Pa.)	1998-01	937	5,647	6.03
Phillip Moore, North Dakota	1995-98	1,060	5,467	5.16
Rashaan Dumas, Southern Conn. St.	1996-99	977	5,396	5.52
Antonio Leroy, Albany St. (Ga.)	1993-96	973	5,152	5.29
Shawn Graves, Wofford	1989-92	730	5,128	7.02
Chris Cobb, Eastern Ill.	1976-79	930	5,042	5.42
Irv Sigler, Bloomsburg	1994-97	820	5,034	6.14
Andre Braxton, Virginia Union	1997-00	859	4,989	5.81
Harry Jackson, St. Cloud St.	1986-89	915	4,889	5.34
Leonard Davis, Lenoir-Rhyne	$1990-94	839	4,853	5.78
Jerry Linton, Okla. Panhandle	1959-62	648	4,839	7.47
Tyrone Morgan, Northern St.	1998-00	830	4,816	5.80
Jim VanWagner, Michigan Tech	1973-76	958	4,788	5.00
Jeremy Monroe, Michigan Tech	1990-93	666	4,661	7.00
Heath Sherman, Tex. A&M-Kingsville	1985-88	804	4,654	5.79
Steve Roberts, Butler	1986-89	1,026	4,623	4.51
Randy Martin, St. Cloud St.	1993-96	814	4,618	5.67
Eddie Acosta, Bemidji St.	1999-02	741	4,534	6.12
Don Aleksiewicz, Hobart	1969-72	819	4,525	5.53
Dale Mills, Truman	1957-60	751	4,502	5.99
Scott Schulte, Hillsdale	1990-93	879	4,495	5.11
Leo Lewis, Lincoln (Mo.)	1951-54	623	4,458	7.16

*Record. +Record for minimum 750 rushes. $See page 8 for explanation.

SEASON YARDS

Player, Team	Year	G	Plays	Yards	Avg.
Kavin Gailliard, American Int'l	†1999	12	320	*2,653	‡8.29
Ian Smart, C.W. Post	†2001	12	308	2,536	8.23
Brian Shay, Emporia St.	†1998	11	293	2,265	7.73
Anthony Gray, Western N.M.	†1997	10	277	2,220	8.01
Jarrett Anderson, Truman	†1996	11	321	2,140	6.67
Brian Shay, Emporia St.	1996	11	342	2,103	6.15
Josh Ranek, South Dakota St.	1999	11	329	2,055	6.25
Irv Sigler, Bloomsburg	1997	10	299	2,038	6.82
Ian Smart, C.W. Post	†2002	12	287	2,023	7.05
Johnny Bailey, Tex. A&M-Kingsville	†1986	11	271	2,011	7.42
Kavin Gailliard, American Int'l	1998	11	269	1,971	7.33
Wesley Cates, Calif. (Pa.)	1999	11	298	1,935	6.49
Brian Shay, Emporia St.	1997	11	269	1,912	7.11
Richard Huntley, Winston-Salem	†1995	10	273	1,889	6.92
Josh Ranek, South Dakota St.	1998	11	302	1,881	6.23
Ronald Moore, Pittsburg St.	1992	11	239	1,864	7.80
Tyrone Morgan, Northern St.	1998	11	318	1,838	5.78
Fred Lane, Lane	1995	10	273	1,833	6.71
Zed Robinson, Southern Utah	1991	11	254	1,828	7.20
Richard Huntley, Winston-Salem	1994	11	251	1,815	7.23
Jamel White, South Dakota	1999	11	316	1,807	5.72
Josh Ranek, South Dakota St.	2001	11	312	1,804	5.78

*Record. †National champion. ‡Record for minimum 250 rushes.

SINGLE-GAME YARDS

Yds.	Player, Team (Opponent)	Date
405	Alvon Brown, Kentucky St. (Ky. Wesleyan)	Sept. 16, 2000
403	Rob Davidson, Fairmont St. (Concord)	Nov. 14, 1998

Yds.	Player, Team (Opponent)	Date
382	Kelly Ellis, Northern Iowa (Western Ill.)	Oct. 13, 1979
380	Garrion Corbin, Tiffin (Quincy)	Nov. 16, 2002
378	Jason Broom, Fort Hays St. (Okla. Panhandle)	Oct. 6, 2001
373	Dallas Garber, Marietta (Wash. & Jeff.)	Nov. 7, 1959
370	Jim Hissam, Marietta (Bethany [W.Va.])	Nov. 15, 1958
370	Jim Baier, Wis.-River Falls (Wis.-Stevens Point)	Nov. 5, 1966
367	Don Polkinghorne, Washington (Mo.) (Wash. & Lee)	Nov. 23, 1957
363	Richie Weaver, Widener (Moravian)	Oct. 17, 1970
361	Richard Huntley, Winston-Salem (Virginia Union)	Nov. 5, 1994
361	Brian Shay, Emporia St. (Washburn)	Oct. 5, 1996
359	Anthony Gray, Western N.M. (Hardin-Simmons)	Oct. 4, 1997
356	Ole Gunderson, St. Olaf (Monmouth [Ill.])	Oct. 11, 1969
350	Ricke Stonewall, Millersville (New Haven)	Nov. 13, 1982
349	Alvon Brown, Kentucky St. (Morris Brown)	Nov. 7, 1998
348	Carlton Booe, Northeastern St. (Southeastern Okla.)	Oct. 31, 1998
347	Kavin Gailliard, American Int'l (Bryant)	Nov. 6, 1999

ANNUAL CHAMPIONS

Year	Player, Team	Class	Plays	Yards
1946	V.T. Smith, Abilene Christian	So.	99	733
1947	John Williams, Jacksonville St.	Jr.	150	931
1948	Hank Treesh, Hanover	Jr.	100	1,383
1949	Odie Posey, Southern U.	Jr.	121	1,399
1950	Meriel Michelson, Eastern Wash.	Sr.	180	1,234
1951	Bob White, Western N.M.	Jr.	202	1,643
1952	Al Conway, William Jewell	Sr.	134	1,325
1953	Elroy Payne, McMurry	So.	183	1,274
1954	Lem Harkey, Col. of Emporia	Sr.	121	1,146
1955	Gene Scott, Centre	Sr.	107	1,138
1956	Bill Rhodes, Western St.	Sr.	130	1,200
1957	Brad Hustad, Luther	So.	219	1,401
1958	Dale Mills, Truman	So.	186	1,358
1959	Dale Mills, Truman	Jr.	248	1,385
1960	Joe Iacone, West Chester	So.	199	1,438
1961	Bobby Lisa, St. Mary (Kan.)	Jr.	156	1,082
1962	Jerry Linton, Okla. Panhandle	Sr.	272	1,483
1963	Jim Holder, Okla. Panhandle	Sr.	275	1,775
1964	Jim Allison, San Diego St.	Sr.	174	1,186
1965	Allen Smith, Findlay	Jr.	207	1,240
1966	Jim Baier, Wis.-River Falls	Sr.	240	1,587

Year	Player, Team		Class	Plays	Yards
1967	Dickie Moore, Western Ky.		Jr.	208	1,444
1968	Howard Stevens, Randolph-Macon		Fr.	191	1,468
1969	Leon Burns, Long Beach St.		Jr.	350	1,659

Beginning in 1970, ranked on per-game (instead of total) yards

Year	Player, Team	Class	G	Plays	Yards	Avg.
1970	Dave Kiarsis, Trinity (Conn.)	Sr.	8	201	1,374	171.8
1971	Don Aleksiewicz, Hobart	Jr.	9	276	1,616	179.6
1972	Billy Johnson, Widener	So.	9	148	1,556	172.9
1973	Mike Thomas, UNLV	Jr.	11	274	1,741	158.3
1974	Jim VanWagner, Michigan Tech	So.	9	246	1,453	161.4
1975	Jim VanWagner, Michigan Tech	Jr.	9	289	1,331	147.9
1976	Ted McKnight, Minn.-Duluth	Sr.	10	220	1,482	148.2
1977	Bill Burnham, New Hampshire	Sr.	10	281	1,422	142.2
1978	Mike Harris, Truman	Sr.	11	329	1,598	145.3
1979	Chris Cobb, Eastern Ill.	Sr.	11	293	1,609	146.3
1980	Louis Jackson, Cal Poly	Sr.	10	287	1,424	142.4
1981	Rick Porter, Slippery Rock	Sr.	9	208	1,179	131.0
1982	Ricke Stonewall, Millersville	So.	10	191	1,387	138.7
1983	Mark Corbin, Central St.	So.	10	208	1,502	150.2
1984	Charles Sanders, Slippery Rock	Jr.	10	269	1,280	128.0
1985	Dan Sonnek, South Dakota St.	So.	11	303	1,518	138.0
1986	Johnny Bailey, Tex. A&M-Kingsville	Fr.	11	271	2,011	182.8
1987	Johnny Bailey, Tex. A&M-Kingsville	So.	10	217	1,598	159.8
1988	Johnny Bailey, Tex. A&M-Kingsville	Jr.	10	229	1,442	144.2
1989	Kevin Mitchell, Saginaw Valley	Jr.	8	236	1,460	182.5
1990	David Jones, Chadron St.	Sr.	10	225	1,570	157.0
1991	Quincy Tillmon, Emporia St.	So.	9	259	1,544	171.6
1992	Roger Graham, New Haven	So.	10	200	1,717	171.7
1993	Keith Higdon, Cheyney	Sr.	10	330	1,742	174.2
1994	Leonard Davis, Lenoir-Rhyne	Sr.	9	216	1,559	173.2
1995	Richard Huntley, Winston-Salem	Sr.	10	273	1,889	188.9
1996	Jarrett Anderson, Truman	Sr.	11	321	2,140	194.5
1997	Anthony Gray, Western N.M.	Jr.	10	277	2,220	*222.0
1998	Brian Shay, Emporia St.	Sr.	11	293	2,265	205.9
1999	Kavin Gailliard, American Int'l	Sr.	12	320	*2,653	221.1
2000	Dalevon Smith, Shepherd	Sr.	9	229	1,495	166.1
2001	Ian Smart, C.W. Post	Jr.	12	308	2,536	211.3
2002	Ian Smart, C.W. Post	Sr.	12	287	2,023	168.6

*Record.

Passing

CAREER PASSING EFFICIENCY
(Minimum 375 Completions)

Player, Team	Years	Att.	Cmp.	Int.	Pct.	Yards	TD	Pts.
Dusty Bonner, Valdosta St.	2000-01	754	548	14	*.727	7,121	97	*190.8
J.T. O'Sullivan, UC Davis	1998-01	808	510	32	.631	8,143	72	169.3
Wilkie Perez, Glenville St.	1997-98	567	376	17	.663	5,240	50	167.0
Corte McGuffey, Northern Colo.	1996-99	768	484	23	.630	6,975	75	165.6
Curt Anes, Grand Valley St.	1999-02	1,186	741	27	.625	10,581	114	164.6
Chris Petersen, UC Davis	1985-86	553	385	13	.696	4,988	39	164.0
Justin Coleman, Neb.-Kearney	1997-00	1,193	706	42	.592	*11,213	99	158.5
Rick Hebert, American Int'l	1996-99	699	423	16	.605	5,990	55	153.9
Chris Hatcher, Valdosta St.	1991-94	1,451	*1,001	38	‡.690	10,878	*116	+153.1
Jim McMillan, Boise St.	1971-74	640	382	29	.597	5,508	58	152.8
Brian Eyerman, Indiana (Pa.)	1999-02	837	467	32	.558	7,409	76	152.5
Chris Greisen, Northwest Mo. St.	1995-98	653	379	22	.580	5,741	51	150.9
Jack Hull, Grand Valley St.	1988-91	835	485	22	.581	7,120	64	149.7
Scott Otis, Glenville St.	1994-95	693	421	21	.608	5,563	56	148.8
Jesse Showerda, New Haven	1993-96	675	402	15	.596	5,175	57	147.4
Grady Benton, West Tex. A&M	1994-95	686	421	22	.614	5,618	49	147.3
Todd Cunningham, Presbyterian	1998-01	1,376	834	47	.606	10,937	111	147.2
Drew Folmar, Millersville	1997-00	1,241	760	34	.612	9,903	91	147.0
Bruce Upstill, Col. of Emporia	1960-63	769	438	36	.570	6,935	48	144.0
Jarrod DeGeorgia, Wayne St. (Neb.)	1995-96	645	428	18	.664	5,161	31	143.9
Eric Miller, Bloomsburg	1997-00	915	527	37	.576	7,474	70	143.4
Jeff Fox, Grand Valley St.	1995-98	1,031	626	22	.607	8,197	62	143.1

Player, Team	Years	Att.	Cmp.	Int.	Pct.	Yards	TD	Pts.
Chris Gicking, Shippensburg	1998-00	778	404	20	.519	6,365	65	143.1
Lance Funderburk, Valdosta St.	1993-96	1,054	689	23	.654	7,698	64	142.4
George Bork, Northern Ill.	1960-63	902	577	33	.640	6,782	60	141.8
June Jones, Portland St.	1975-76	658	375	34	.570	5,798	41	141.2
Steve Mariucci, Northern Mich.	1974-77	678	380	33	.561	6,022	41	140.9
Scott Barry, UC Davis	1982-84	588	377	16	.641	4,421	33	140.4
Kevin Daft, UC Davis	1995-98	805	459	23	.570	6,197	54	138.1
Matt Cook, Mo. Southern St.	$1989-93	816	411	29	.504	6,715	63	137.9
Aaron Sparrow, Norfolk St.	1992-95	1,117	615	38	.551	8,758	79	137.5
Chris Crawford, Portland St.	1985-88	954	588	35	.616	7,543	48	137.3
Trevor Spradley, Southwest Baptist	1990-92	712	441	27	.619	5,881	29	137.2
Kasey Waterman, Mo. Western St.	1998-01	1,273	714	57	.561	9,846	95	136.7
Matt McCarthy, Ferris St.	1996-99	1,077	620	26	.576	8,174	64	136.1
Dan Miles, Southern Ore.	1964-67	871	577	56	.662	6,531	52	136.1

*Record. ‡Record for minimum 1,000 attempts. +Record for minimum 750 completions. $See Page 8 for explanation.

SEASON PASSING EFFICIENCY
(Minimum 15 Attempts Per Game)

Player, Team	Year	G	Att.	Cmp.	Int.	Pct.	Yards	TD	Pts.
Curt Anes, Grand Valley St.	†2001	10	271	189	3	.697	3,086	48	+*221.6
Boyd Crawford, Col. of Idaho	†1953	8	120	72	6	.600	1,462	21	210.1
Dusty Bonner, Valdosta St.	2001	11	319	231	8	.724	3,214	43	‡196.5
J.T. O'Sullivan, UC Davis	†2000	9	226	141	7	.623	2,648	25	191.1
Chuck Green, Wittenberg	†1963	9	182	114	8	.626	2,181	19	189.0
Jayson Merrill, Western St.	†1991	10	309	195	11	.631	3,484	35	188.1
Rick Hebert, American Int'l	†1999	12	234	166	4	.709	2,351	25	187.2
Dusty Bonner, Valdosta St.	2000	11	435	317	6	.728	3,907	*54	186.5
Jim Feely, Johns Hopkins	†1967	7	110	69	5	.627	1,264	12	186.2
John Charles, Portland St.	1991	11	247	147	7	.595	2,619	32	185.7
Steve Smith, Western St.	†1992	10	271	180	5	.664	2,719	30	183.5
Jim Peterson, Hanover	†1948	8	125	81	12	.648	1,571	12	182.9
John Wristen, Southern Colo.	†1982	8	121	68	2	.562	1,358	13	182.6
Travis Miles, Northwest Mo. St.	2000	11	248	155	7	.625	2,723	25	182.4
John Charles, Portland St.	1992	8	263	179	7	.681	2,770	24	181.3
Richard Basil, Savannah St.	†1989	9	211	120	7	.569	2,148	29	181.1
Chris Hatcher, Valdosta St.	†1994	11	430	321	9	*.747	3,591	50	179.0
Wilkie Perez, Glenville St.	†1997	11	425	280	12	.658	*4,189	45	178.0
Curt Anes, Grand Valley St.	†2002	14	414	278	6	.671	3,692	47	176.6
Jim Cahoon, Ripon	†1964	8	127	74	7	.583	1,206	19	176.4
Ken Suhl, New Haven	1992	10	239	148	5	.619	2,336	26	175.7
Brian Eyerman, Indiana (Pa.)	2002	12	290	173	7	.597	2,724	36	174.7
Corte McGuffey, Northern Colo.	1999	11	296	189	11	.639	2,893	31	173.0
Tony Aliucci, Indiana (Pa.)	†1990	10	181	111	10	.613	1,801	21	172.2
James Weir, New Haven	†1993	10	266	161	1	.605	2,336	31	172.0
Shawn Behr, Fort Hays St.	†1995	11	318	191	6	.600	3,158	31	171.9
Brian Stallworth, Central Ark.	2001	11	272	177	7	.651	2,544	27	171.3

*Record. †National champion. +Record for minimum 100 completions. ‡Record for minimum 200 completions.

CAREER YARDS PER GAME
(Minimum 4,500 Yards)

Player, Team	Years	G	Att.	Cmp.	Int.	Pct.	Yards	TD	Avg.
Dusty Bonner, Valdosta St.	2000-01	22	754	548	14	*.727	7,121	97	*323.7
Grady Benton, West Tex. A&M	1994-95	18	686	421	22	.614	5,618	49	312.1
Wilkie Perez, Glenville St.	1997-98	17	567	376	17	.663	5,240	50	308.2
Tim Von Dulm, Portland St.	1969-70	20	924	500	41	.541	5,967	51	298.4
Marty Washington, West Ala.	1992-93	17	690	379	25	.549	5,018	40	295.2
Jayson Merrill, Western St.	1990-91	20	580	328	25	.566	5,830	56	291.5
Jarrod DeGeorgia, Wayne St. (Neb.)	1995-96	18	645	428	18	.664	5,161	31	286.7
John Charles, Portland St.	1991-92	19	510	326	14	.639	5,389	56	283.6
J.T. O'Sullivan, UC Davis	1998-01	29	808	510	32	.631	8,143	72	280.8
Todd Cunningham, Presbyterian	1998-01	39	1,376	834	47	.606	10,937	111	280.4
Chris Hatcher, Valdosta St.	1991-94	39	1,451	*1,001	38	‡.690	10,878	*116	278.9
Scott Otis, Glenville St.	1994-95	20	693	421	21	.608	5,563	56	278.2
June Jones, Portland St.	1975-76	21	658	375	34	.570	5,798	41	276.1
Jermaine Whitaker, N.M. Highlands	1992-94	31	1,150	625	45	.543	8,532	71	275.2
Justin Coleman, Neb.-Kearney	1997-00	41	1,193	706	42	.592	*11,213	99	273.5
Steve Wray, Franklin	1979, 81-82	26	1,070	511	40	.478	7,019	56	270.0
Pat Graham, Augustana (S.D.)	1995-96	21	820	469	26	.572	5,636	43	268.4
Earl Harvey, N.C. Central	1985-88	40	1,442	690	81	.479	10,621	86	265.5
Chris Hegg, Truman	1984-85	20	771	410	32	.532	5,306	44	265.3
Brad Norris, Adams St.	1998-99	20	653	327	18	.501	5,171	44	258.6
Pat Brennan, Franklin	1981-84	30	1,123	535	62	.476	7,717	53	257.2
Jay McLucas, New Haven	1989-90	20	699	370	30	.529	5,139	37	257.0
Lance Funderburk, Valdosta St.	1993-96	30	1,054	689	23	.654	7,698	64	256.6
Matt McCarthy, Ferris St.	1996-99	32	1,077	620	26	.576	8,174	64	255.4
Troy Mott, Wayne St. (Neb.)	1991-92	20	757	437	37	.577	5,003	25	250.2
Chris Petersen, UC Davis	1985-86	20	553	385	13	.696	4,988	39	249.4
Rich Ingold, Indiana (Pa.)	1983-85	26	852	499	36	.586	6,454	49	248.2
Matt McCarthy, Ferris St.	1996-98	22	720	410	19	.569	5,453	33	247.9
Drew Folmar, Millersville	1997-00	40	1,241	760	34	.612	9,903	91	247.6
Antonio Hawkins, Virginia St.	1997-00	38	1,212	651	56	.537	9,217	68	242.6
Jeff Phillips, Central Mo. St.	1986-88	26	892	496	54	.556	6,294	46	242.1

*Record. ‡Record for minimum 1,000 attempts.

SEASON YARDS PER GAME

Player, Team	Year	G	Att.	Cmp.	Int.	Pct.	Yards	TD	Avg.
Grady Benton, West Tex. A&M	1994	9	409	258	13	.631	3,541	30	*393.4
Damian Poalucci, East Stroudsburg	1996	10	393	214	13	.545	3,831	40	383.1
Marty Washington, West Ala.	1993	8	404	221	13	.547	3,062	26	382.8
Wilkie Perez, Glenville St.	†1997	11	425	280	12	.658	*4,189	45	380.8
Perry Klein, C.W. Post	1993	10	407	248	18	.609	3,757	38	375.7
Andrew Webb, Fort Lewis	2002	11	529	317	13	.599	4,109	37	373.5
Brett Salisbury, Wayne St. (Neb.)	1993	10	395	276	14	.699	3,729	29	372.9
Alfred Montez, Western N.M.	1994	6	231	133	7	.576	2,182	18	363.7
Dusty Bonner, Valdosta St.	2000	11	435	317	6	.728	3,907	*54	355.2
Bob Toledo, San Fran. St.	1967	10	396	211	24	.533	3,513	45	351.3
Todd Cunningham, Presbyterian	2001	11	531	335	14	.631	3,860	36	350.9
Pat Brennan, Franklin	1983	10	458	226	30	.493	3,491	25	349.1
Jayson Merrill, Western St.	†1991	10	309	195	11	.631	3,484	35	348.4
John Charles, Portland St.	1992	8	263	179	7	.681	2,770	24	346.3
Rod Smith, Glenville St.	1996	10	409	249	14	.609	3,455	29	345.5
Aaron Sparrow, Norfolk St.	1995	10	409	238	14	.581	3,434	32	343.4
George Bork, Northern Ill.	†1963	9	374	244	12	.652	3,077	32	341.9
Chris Hegg, Truman	†1985	11	503	284	20	.565	3,741	32	340.1
Lance Funderburk, Valdosta St.	1996	11	459	300	10	.654	3,732	35	339.3
Jed Drenning, Glenville St.	1993	10	390	244	12	.626	3,391	25	339.1
Jarrod DeGeorgia, Wayne St. (Neb.)	1996	10	420	286	12	.681	3,388	19	338.8
Lance Funderburk, Valdosta St.	1995	11	*544	*356	12	.654	3,706	26	336.9
Pat Brennan, Franklin	1984	10	502	238	20	.474	3,340	18	334.0

*Record. †National pass-efficiency champion.

CAREER YARDS

Player, Team	Years	Att.	Cmp.	Int.	Pct.	Yards	TD
Justin Coleman, Neb.-Kearney	1997-00	1,193	706	42	.592	*11,213	99
Todd Cunningham, Presbyterian	1998-01	1,376	834	47	.606	10,937	111
Chris Hatcher, Valdosta St.	1991-94	1,451	*1,001	38	‡.690	10,878	*116
Bob McLaughlin, Lock Haven	1992-95	*1,719	910	*88	.529	10,640	60
Earl Harvey, N.C. Central	1985-88	1,442	690	81	.479	10,621	86
Curt Anes, Grand Valley St.	1999-02	1,186	741	27	.625	10,581	114
John Craven, Gardner-Webb	1991-94	1,535	828	82	.539	9,934	80
Drew Folmar, Millersville	1997-00	1,241	760	34	.612	9,903	91
Vernon Buck, Wingate	1991-94	1,393	728	61	.523	9,884	72
Thad Trujillo, Fort Lewis	1991-94	1,455	760	57	.522	9,873	78
Jarrod Furgason, Fairmont St.	$1993-97	1,392	798	44	.573	9,856	101
Kasey Waterman, Mo. Western St.	1998-01	1,273	714	57	.561	9,846	95
Mike Mitros, West Chester	1996-99	1,402	819	48	.584	9,834	94
Eric DeGraff, Augustana (S.D.)	1997-00	1,360	813	51	.598	9,503	69
Rob Tomlinson, Cal St. Chico	1988-91	1,328	748	43	.563	9,434	52
John Hebgen, Minn. St. Mankato	1993-96	1,268	727	38	.573	9,410	71
Trevor Moon, Chadron St.	1995-98	1,241	635	36	.512	9,333	63
Antonio Hawkins, Virginia St.	1997-00	1,212	651	56	.537	9,217	68
Eric Howe, Truman	1998-01	1,203	687	51	.571	9,097	70
Andy Breault, Kutztown	1989-92	1,259	733	63	.582	9,096	86
Aaron Sparrow, Norfolk St.	1992-95	1,117	615	38	.551	8,758	79
Ricky Fritz, Minn. Duluth	$1998-02	1,090	547	53	.502	8,711	90
Sam Mannery, Calif. (Pa.)	1987-90	1,283	649	68	.506	8,680	64
Damian Poalucci, East Stroudsburg	1994-97	1,067	583	47	.546	8,654	69
Bryan Harman, Fairmont St.	1998-01	1,154	685	46	.594	8,580	64
Dave DenBraber, Ferris St.	1984-87	1,254	661	45	.527	8,536	52
Jermaine Whitaker, N.M. Highlands	1992-94	1,150	625	45	.543	8,532	71
Jim Lindsey, Abilene Christian	1967-70	1,237	642	69	.519	8,521	61
Dave MacDonald, West Chester	1991-94	1,123	604	46	.538	8,449	82
Maurice Heard, Tuskegee	1988-91	1,134	556	54	.490	8,434	87

*Record. ‡Record for minimum 1,000 attempts. $See Page 8 for explanation.

SEASON YARDS

Player, Team	Year	G	Att.	Cmp.	Int.	Pct.	Yards	TD
Wilkie Perez, Glenville St.	†1997	11	425	280	12	.658	*4,189	45
Andrew Webb, Fort Lewis	2002	11	529	317	13	.599	4,109	37
Dusty Bonner, Valdosta St.	2000	11	435	317	6	.728	3,907	*54
Todd Cunningham, Presbyterian	2001	11	531	335	14	.631	3,860	36
Damian Poalucci, East Stroudsburg	1996	10	393	214	13	.545	3,831	40
Buster Faulkner, Valdosta St.	2002	15	502	326	17	.649	3,821	41
Perry Klein, C.W. Post	1993	10	407	248	18	.609	3,757	38
Chris Hegg, Truman	1985	11	503	284	20	.565	3,741	32
Lance Funderburk, Valdosta St.	1996	11	459	300	10	.654	3,732	35
Brett Salisbury, Wayne St. (Neb.)	1993	10	395	276	14	.699	3,729	29
Lance Funderburk, Valdosta St.	1995	11	*544	*356	12	.654	3,706	26
Curt Anes, Grand Valley St.	†2002	14	414	278	6	.671	3,692	47
Tod Mayfield, West Tex. A&M	1986	11	515	317	20	.616	3,664	31
Chris Hatcher, Valdosta St.	1993	11	471	335	11	.711	3,651	37
Chris Hatcher, Valdosta St.	†1994	11	430	321	9	*.747	3,591	50
John McMenamin, Northwest Mo. St.	2002	13	491	296	12	.603	3,583	28
Grady Benton, West Tex. A&M	1994	9	409	258	13	.631	3,541	30
June Jones, Portland St.	†1976	11	423	238	24	.563	3,518	25
Bob Toledo, San Fran. St.	1967	10	396	211	24	.533	3,513	45
Pat Brennan, Franklin	1983	10	458	226	30	.493	3,491	25

Valdosta State's Buster Faulkner threw for 3,821 yards last year, the sixth-best single-season total in Division II history.

Jamie Schwaberow/NCAA Photos

DIVISION II

Player, Team	Year	G	Att.	Cmp.	Int.	Pct.	Yards	TD
Jayson Merrill, Western St.	†1991	10	309	195	11	.631	3,484	35
Rod Smith, Glenville St.	1996	10	409	249	14	.609	3,455	29

*Record. †National pass-efficiency champion.

CAREER TOUCHDOWN PASSES

Player, Team	Years	Att.	Cmp.	Int.	Pct.	Yds.	TD
Chris Hatcher, Valdosta St.	1991-94	1,451	*1,001	38	‡.690	10,878	*116
Curt Anes, Grand Valley St.	1999-02	1,186	741	27	.625	10,581	114
Todd Cunningham, Presbyterian	1998-01	1,376	834	47	.606	10,937	111
Jarrod Furgason, Fairmont St.	$1993-97	1,392	798	44	.573	9,856	101
Justin Coleman, Neb.-Kearney	1997-00	1,193	706	42	.592	*11,213	99
Dusty Bonner, Valdosta St.	2000-01	754	548	14	*.727	7,121	97
Kasey Waterman, Mo. Western St.	1998-01	1,273	714	57	.561	9,846	95
Mike Mitros, West Chester	1996-99	1,402	819	48	.584	9,834	94
Drew Folmar, Millersville	1997-00	1,241	760	34	.612	9,903	91
Ricky Fritz, Minn. Duluth	$1998-02	1,090	547	53	.502	8,711	90
Maurice Heard, Tuskegee	1988-91	1,134	556	54	.490	8,434	87
Earl Harvey, N.C. Central	1985-88	1,442	690	82	.479	10,621	86
Andy Breault, Kutztown	1989-92	1,259	733	63	.582	9,086	86
Rex Lamberti, Abilene Christian	1984-86, 93	1,133	595	44	.525	7,934	84
Dave MacDonald, West Chester	1991-94	1,123	604	46	.538	8,449	82
John Craven, Gardner-Webb	1991-94	1,535	828	82	.539	9,934	80

*Record. ‡Record for minimum 1,000 attempts. $See Page 8 for explanation.

SEASON TOUCHDOWN PASSES

Player, Team	Year	Att.	Cmp.	Int.	Pct.	Yds.	TD
Dusty Bonner, Valdosta St.	2000	435	317	6	.728	3,907	*54
Chris Hatcher, Valdosta St.	†1994	430	321	9	*.747	3,591	50
Curt Anes, Grand Valley St.	†2001	271	189	3	.697	3,086	48
Curt Anes, Grand Valley St.	†2002	414	278	6	.671	3,692	47
Wilkie Perez, Glenville St.	†1997	425	280	12	.658	*4,189	45
Bob Toledo, San Fran. St.	1967	396	211	24	.533	3,513	45
Dusty Bonner, Valdosta St.	2001	319	231	8	.724	3,214	43
Buster Faulkner, Valdosta St.	2002	502	326	17	.649	3,821	41
Damian Poalucci, East Stroudsburg	1996	393	214	13	.545	3,831	40
Perry Klein, C.W. Post	1993	407	248	18	.609	3,757	38
Andrew Webb, Fort Lewis	2002	529	317	13	.599	4,109	37
Keith Heckendorf, St. Cloud St.	2002	349	203	12	.582	2,817	37
Chris Hatcher, Valdosta St.	1993	471	335	11	.711	3,651	37
Andy Breault, Kutztown	1991	360	225	20	.625	2,927	37
Brian Eyerman, Indiana (Pa.)	2002	290	173	7	.597	2,724	36
Todd Cunningham, Presbyterian	2001	531	335	14	.631	3,860	36
Lance Funderburk, Valdosta St.	1996	459	300	10	.654	3,732	35
Jarrod Furgason, Fairmont St.	1995	349	222	8	.636	2,696	35
Dave MacDonald, West Chester	1994	458	251	18	.548	3,308	35
Jason Merrill, Western St.	1991	309	195	11	.631	3,484	35

*Record. †National pass-efficiency champion.

SINGLE-GAME YARDS

Yds.	Player, Team (Opponent)	Date
642	Wilkie Perez, Glenville St. (Concord)	Oct. 25, 1997
638	Andrew Webb, Fort Lewis (Mesa St.)	Nov. 16, 2002
616	Damian Poalucci, East Stroudsburg (Mansfield)	Nov. 2, 1996
614	Alfred Montez, Western N.M. (West Tex. A&M)	Oct. 8, 1994
614	Perry Klein, C.W. Post (Salisbury)	Nov. 6, 1993
613	Jayce Goree, Glenville St. (Concord)	Oct. 24, 1998
599	Jarrod DeGeorgia, Wayne St. (Neb.) (Drake)	Nov. 9, 1996
592	John Charles, Portland St. (Cal Poly)	Nov. 16, 1991
579	Chris Reil, Henderson St. (Arkansas Tech)	Oct. 28, 2000
568	Scott Otis, Glenville St. (West Va. Wesleyan)	Oct. 15, 1994
568	Bob Toledo, San Fran. St. (Cal St. Hayward)	Oct. 21, 1967
564	Pat Graham, Augustana (S.D.) (Minn. St. Mankato)	Oct. 28, 1995
560	Andrew Webb, Fort Lewis (Western N.M.)	Nov. 2, 2002
551	Jamie Sander, N.M. Highlands (Neb.-Kearney)	Nov. 9, 1996
550	Earl Harvey, N.C. Central (Jackson St.)	Aug. 30, 1986
549	Matt LaTour, Northern Mich. (Ashland)	Nov. 5, 1994
542	Todd Cunningham, Presbyterian (Tusculum)	Nov. 3, 2001
541	Arnold Marcha, West Tex. A&M (Okla. Panhandle)	Nov. 12, 1994
539	Maurice Heard, Tuskegee (Alabama A&M)	Nov. 10, 1990

SINGLE-GAME ATTEMPTS

No.	Player, Team (Opponent)	Date
76	Jarrod DeGeorgia, Wayne St. (Neb.) (Drake)	Nov. 9, 1996
74	Jamie Sander, N.M. Highlands (Neb.-Kearney)	Nov. 9, 1996
74	Jermaine Whitaker, N.M. Highlands (Western St.)	Nov. 5, 1994
72	Kurt Otto, North Dakota (Tex. A&M-Kingsville)	Sept. 13, 1986
72	Kaipo Spencer, Santa Clara (Portland St.)	Oct. 11, 1975
72	Joe Stetser, Cal St. Chico (Oregon Tech)	Sept. 23, 1967
71	Mac McArdle, Mercyhurst (Michigan Tech)	Sept. 9, 2000
71	Pat Brennan, Franklin (Ashland)	Nov. 3, 1984

SINGLE-GAME COMPLETIONS

No.	Player, Team (Opponent)	Date
56	Jarrod DeGeorgia, Wayne St. (Neb.) (Drake)	Nov. 9, 1996
50	Todd Cunningham, Presbyterian (Tusculum)	Nov. 3, 2001
45	Andrew Webb, Fort Lewis (Neb.-Kearney)	Oct. 12, 2001
45	Chris Hatcher, Valdosta St. (Mississippi Col.)	Oct. 23, 1993
45	Chris Hatcher, Valdosta St. (West Ga.)	Oct. 16, 1993
44	Wilkie Perez, Glenville St. (Concord)	Oct. 25, 1997
44	Tom Bonds, Cal Lutheran (St. Mary's [Cal.])	Nov. 22, 1986
43	Dusty Bonner, Valdosta St. (Delta St.)	Oct. 7, 2000
43	George Bork, Northern Ill. (Central Mich.)	Nov. 9, 1963
42	Luke Cullins, Harding (Central Okla.)	Oct. 16, 1999
42	Lance Funderburk, Valdosta St. (West Ga.)	Nov. 11, 1995
42	Jermaine Whitaker, N.M. Highlands (Western St.)	Nov. 5, 1994
42	Marty Washington, West Ala. (Jacksonville St.)	Nov. 7, 1992
42	Chris Teal, West Ga. (Valdosta St.)	Oct. 19, 1991
42	Tim Von Dulm, Portland St. (Eastern Wash.)	Nov. 21, 1970

ANNUAL CHAMPIONS

Year	Player, Team	Class	Att.	Cmp.	Int.	Pct.	Yds.	TD
1946	Hank Caver, Presbyterian	Sr.	128	59	13	.461	790	7
1947	James Batchelor, Tex. A&M-Commerce	Sr.	184	94	10	.511	1,114	9
1948	Sam Gary, Swarthmore	Jr.	153	93	11	.608	1,218	16
1949	Sam McGowan, New Mexico St.	Sr.	219	112	22	.511	1,712	12
1950	Andy MacDonald, Central Mich.	Jr.	200	109	12	.545	1,577	15
1951	Andy MacDonald, Central Mich.	Sr.	183	114	7	.623	1,560	12
1952	Wes Bair, Illinois St.	So.	242	135	18	.558	1,375	14
1953	Pence Dacus, Southwest Tex. St.	Sr.	207	113	10	.546	1,654	11
1954	Tommy Egan, Brandeis	Sr.	144	87	8	.604	1,050	11
1955	Jerry Foley, Hamline	Fr.	167	87	8	.521	1,034	6
1956	James Stehlin, Brandeis	Sr.	206	116	11	.563	1,155	6
1957	Jay Roelen, Pepperdine	Sr.	214	106	16	.495	1,428	13
1958	Stan Jackson, Cal Poly Pomona	Sr.	256	123	14	.480	1,994	16
1959	Gary Campbell, Whittier	Sr.	183	111	4	.607	1,717	12
1960	Denny Spurlock, Whitworth	Jr.	257	135	16	.525	1,892	14
1961	Tom Gryzwinski, Defiance	Jr.	258	127	17	.492	1,684	14
1962	George Bork, Northern Ill.	Jr.	356	232	11	.652	2,506	22
1963	George Bork, Northern Ill.	Sr.	374	244	12	.652	3,077	32
1964	Jerry Bishop, Austin	Jr.	300	182	16	.607	2,246	17
1965	Bob Caress, Bradley	Sr.	393	210	21	.534	2,167	24
1966	Paul Krause, Dubuque	Sr.	318	179	22	.563	2,210	16
1967	Joe Stetser, Cal St. Chico	Sr.	464	220	*32	.474	2,446	14
1968	Jim Lindsey, Abilene Christian	So.	396	204	19	.515	2,717	18
1969	Tim Von Dulm, Portland St.	Jr.	434	241	18	.555	2,926	26

Beginning in 1970, ranked on per-game (instead of total) completions

Year	Player, Team	Class	G	Att.	Cmp.	Avg.	Int.	Pct.	Yds.	TD
1970	Tim Von Dulm, Portland St.	Sr.	10	490	259	25.9	23	.529	3,041	25
1971	Bob Baron, Rensselaer	Sr.	9	302	168	18.7	13	.556	2,105	15
1972	Bob Biggs, UC Davis	Sr.	9	327	186	20.7	16	.569	2,291	15
1973	Kim McQuilken, Lehigh	Sr.	11	326	196	17.8	13	.601	2,603	19
1974	Jim McMillan, Boise St.	Sr.	10	313	192	19.2	15	.613	2,900	13
1975	Dan Hayes, UC Riverside	Sr.	10	316	171	17.1	20	.541	2,215	21
1976	June Jones, Portland St.	Sr.	11	423	238	21.6	24	.563	3,518	25
1977	Ed Schultz, Minn. St. Moorhead	Sr.	10	304	187	18.7	16	.615	1,943	21
1978	Jeff Knapple, Northern Colo.	Sr.	10	349	178	17.8	21	.510	2,191	16

Beginning in 1979, ranked on passing efficiency rating points (instead of per-game completions)

Year	Player, Team	Class	G	Att.	Cmp.	Int.	Pct.	Yds.	TD	Pts.
1979	Dave Alfaro, Santa Clara	Jr.	9	168	110	9	.655	1,721	13	166.3
1980	Willie Tullis, Troy St.	Sr.	10	203	108	8	.532	1,880	15	147.5
1981	Steve Michuta, Grand Valley St.	Sr.	8	173	114	11	.659	1,702	17	168.3
1982	John Wristen, Southern Colo.	Jr.	8	121	68	2	.562	1,358	13	182.6
1983	Kevin Parker, Fort Valley St.	Jr.	9	168	87	8	.518	1,539	18	154.6
1984	Brian Quinn, Northwest Mo. St.	Sr.	10	178	96	2	.539	1,561	14	151.3
1985	Chris Petersen, UC Davis	Jr.	10	242	167	6	.690	2,366	17	169.4
1986	Chris Petersen, UC Davis	Sr.	10	311	218	7	.701	2,622	22	159.7
1987	Dave Biondo, Ashland	Jr.	10	177	95	11	.537	1,828	14	154.1
1988	Al Niemela, West Chester	Sr.	10	217	138	9	.636	1,932	21	162.0
1989	Richard Basil, Savannah St.	Sr.	9	211	120	7	.569	2,148	29	181.1
1990	Tony Aliucci, Indiana (Pa.)	Jr.	10	181	111	10	.613	1,801	21	172.2
1991	Jayson Merrill, Western St.	Sr.	10	309	195	11	.631	3,484	35	188.1
1992	Steve Smith, Western St.	Sr.	10	271	180	5	.664	2,719	30	183.5
1993	James Weir, New Haven	Jr.	10	266	161	1	.605	2,336	31	172.0
1994	Chris Hatcher, Valdosta St.	Sr.	11	430	321	9	*.747	3,591	50	179.0
1995	Shawn Behr, Fort Hays St.	Sr.	11	318	191	6	.600	3,158	31	171.9
1996	Jesse Showerda, New Haven	Sr.	10	300	180	3	.600	2,625	31	165.6
1997	Wilkie Perez, Glenville St.	Jr.	11	425	280	12	.658	*4,189	45	178.0
1998	Sleepie Tollie, Northwood	Fr.	10	148	80	7	.540	1,862	18	††190.4
1999	Rick Hebert, American Int'l	Sr.	12	234	166	4	.709	2,351	25	187.2
2000	J.T. O'Sullivan, UC Davis	Jr.	9	226	141	7	.623	2,648	25	191.1
2001	Curt Anes, Grand Valley St.	Jr.	10	271	189	3	.697	3,086	48	*221.6
2002	Curt Anes, Grand Valley St.	Sr.	14	414	278	6	.671	3,692	47	176.6

*Record. ††Declared champion; with two more pass attempts (Making 15 per game), both interceptions, still would have the highest efficiency rating (185.2).

DIVISION II

ANNUAL PASSING EFFICIENCY LEADERS BEFORE 1979
(Minimum 11 Attempts Per Game)

1948—Jim Peterson, Hanover, 182.9; **1949**—John Ford, Hardin-Simmons, 179.6; **1950**—Edward Ludorf, Trinity (Conn.), 167.8; **1951**—Vic Lesch, Western Ill., 182.4; **1952**—Jim Gray, Tex. A&M-Commerce, 205.5; **1953**—Boyd Crawford, Col. of Idaho, *210.1; **1954**—Bill Englehardt, Neb.-Omaha, 170.7; **1955**—Robert Alexander, Trinity (Conn.), 208.7; **1956**—John Costello, Widener, 169.8; **1957**—Doug Maison, Hillsdale, 200.0; **1958**—Kurt Duecker, Ripon, 161.7; **1959**—Fred Whitmire, Humboldt St., 188.7; **1960**—Larry Cline, Otterbein, 195.2.

(Minimum 15 Attempts Per Game)

Year	Player, Team	G	Att.	Cmp.	Int.	Pct.	Yds.	TD	Pts.
1961	Denny Spurlock, Whitworth	10	189	115	16	.608	1,708	26	165.2
1962	Roy Curry, Jackson St.	10	194	104	8	.536	1,862	15	151.5
1963	Chuck Green, Wittenberg	9	182	114	8	.626	2,181	19	189.0
1964	Jim Cahoon, Ripon	8	127	74	7	.583	1,206	19	176.4
1965	Ed Buzzell, Ottawa	9	238	118	5	.496	2,170	31	165.0
1966	Jim Alcorn, Clarion	9	199	107	4	.538	1,714	24	161.9
1967	Jim Feely, Johns Hopkins	7	110	69	5	.627	1,264	12	186.2
1968	Larry Green, Doane	9	182	97	7	.533	1,592	22	159.0
1969	George Kaplan, Northern Colo.	9	155	92	5	.594	1,396	16	162.6
1970	Gary Wichard, C.W. Post	9	186	100	5	.538	1,527	12	138.6
1971	Peter Mackey, Middlebury	8	180	101	4	.561	1,597	19	161.0
1972	David Hamilton, Fort Valley St.	9	180	99	9	.550	1,571	24	162.3
1973	Jim McMillan, Boise St.	11	179	110	5	.615	1,525	17	158.8
1974	Jim McMillan, Boise St.	10	313	192	15	.613	2,900	33	164.4
1975	Joe Sterrett, Lehigh	11	228	135	13	.592	2,114	22	157.5
1976	Mike Makings, Western St.	10	179	90	6	.503	1,617	14	145.3
1977	Mike Rieker, Lehigh	11	230	137	14	.596	2,431	23	169.2
1978	Mike Moroski, UC Davis	10	205	119	9	.580	1,689	17	145.9

*Record.

Receiving

CAREER RECEPTIONS PER GAME
(Minimum 125 Receptions)

Player, Team	Years	G	Rec.	Yards	TD	Rec. PG
Chris George, Glenville St.	1993-94	20	230	3,215	30	*11.5
Ed Bell, Idaho St.	1968-69	19	163	2,608	30	8.6
Byron Chamberlain, Wayne St. (Neb.)	1993-94	19	161	1,941	14	8.3
Carlos Ferralls, Glenville St.	1994-97	32	262	3,835	43	8.2
Clarence Coleman, Ferris St.	1998-01	42	*323	*4,983	42	7.7
Jerry Hendren, Idaho	1967-69	30	230	3,435	27	7.7
Gary Garrison, San Diego St.	1964-65	20	148	2,188	26	7.4
Brad Bailey, West Tex. A&M	1992-94	30	221	2,677	22	7.4
Chris Myers, Kenyon	1967-70	35	253	3,897	33	7.2

*Record.

SEASON RECEPTIONS PER GAME

Player, Team	Year	G	Rec.	Yards	TD	Rec. PG
Chris George, Glenville St.	†1993	10	117	*1,876	15	*11.7
Chris George, Glenville St.	†1994	10	113	1,339	15	11.3
Brad Bailey, West Tex. A&M	1994	11	*119	1,552	16	10.8
Kevin Ingram, West Chester	†1998	11	115	1,673	21	10.5
Carlos Ferralls, Glenville St.	†1996	8	81	965	6	10.1
Bruce Cerone, Emporia St.	1968	9	91	1,479	15	10.1
Mike Healey, Valparaiso	†1985	10	101	1,279	11	10.1
Sean Pender, Valdosta St.	†1995	11	111	983	2	10.1
Jamal Allen, Fort Lewis	†2001	11	106	1,086	7	9.6
Barry Wagner, Alabama A&M	†1989	11	106	1,812	17	9.6
Ed Bell, Idaho St.	†1969	10	96	1,522	20	9.6
Jerry Hendren, Idaho	1968	9	86	1,457	14	9.6
Dick Hewins, Drake	†1968	10	95	1,316	13	9.5
Matt Holmlund, Augustana (S.D.)	†2000	11	104	1,365	16	9.5
Carlos Ferralls, Glenville St.	†1997	10	94	1,566	19	9.4
Jarett Vito, Emporia St.	1995	10	+94	932	7	9.4
Billy Joe Masters, Evansville	†1987	10	‡94	‡960	4	‡9.4
Joe Dittrich, Southwest St.	†1980	9	83	974	7	9.2
Mark DeBrito, Bentley	†1999	11	101	1,637	19	9.2
Manley Sarnowsky, Drake	†1966	10	92	1,114	7	9.2

*Record. †National champion. +Record for a freshman. ‡Record for a running back.

CAREER RECEPTIONS

Player, Team	Years	Rec.	Yards	TD
Clarence Coleman, Ferris St.	1998-01	*323	*4,983	42
Andrew Blakely, Truman	1999-02	300	3,458	22
Matt Holmlund, Augustana (S.D.)	1998-01	282	3,522	35
Damien Hoffman, Minn.-Morris	1997-00	273	3,128	21
Damon Thompson, Virginia St.	1997-00	268	4,387	37
Carlos Ferralls, Glenville St.	1994-97	262	3,835	43
Jon Spinosa, Lock Haven	1992-95	261	2,710	12
Chris Myers, Kenyon	1967-70	253	3,897	33
Bruce Cerone, Yankton/Emporia St.	1965-66, 68-69	241	4,354	49
Sean Scott, Millersville	1997-00	240	3,293	27
James Roe, Norfolk St.	1992-95	239	4,468	46
Mark DeBrito, Bentley	1996-99	238	3,711	41
Bryan McGinty, Lock Haven	1993-96	238	3,100	18
Kevin Ingram, West Chester	1995-96, 98-99	235	3,159	45
"Red" Roberts, Austin Peay	1967-70	232	3,005	31
Chris George, Glenville St.	1993-94	230	3,215	30
Jerry Hendren, Idaho	1967-69	230	3,435	27
Mike Lelko, Bloomsburg	1997-00	229	3,151	34
Mike Healey, Valparaiso	1982-85	228	3,212	26
Jarett Vito, Emporia St.	1995-98	226	2,608	25
William Mackall, Tenn.-Martin	1985-88	224	2,488	16
David Kircus, Grand Valley St.	1999-02	222	4,124	*76
Mike McFetridge, Millersville	1995-98	221	2,778	27
Brad Bailey, West Tex. A&M	1992-94	221	2,677	22
Johnny Cox, Fort Lewis	1990-93	220	3,611	33
Tywan Mitchell, Minn. St. Mankato	1995-98	216	3,342	30
Greg Hopkins, Slippery Rock	1991-94	215	3,382	28
Robert Clark, N.C. Central	1983-86	210	4,231	38
Neal Mozdzierz, Ferris St.	1996-99	206	2,563	22
Terry Fredenberg, Wis.-Milwaukee	1965-68	206	2,789	24
Dan Bogar, Valparaiso	1981-84	204	2,816	26

*Record.

SEASON RECEPTIONS

Player, Team	Year	G	Rec.	Yards	TD
Brad Bailey, West Tex. A&M	1994	11	*119	1,552	16
Chris George, Glenville St.	†1993	10	117	*1,876	15
Kevin Ingram, West Chester	†1998	11	115	1,673	21
Chris George, Glenville St.	†1994	10	113	1,339	15
Sean Pender, Valdosta St.	†1995	11	111	983	2
Jamal Allen, Fort Lewis	†2001	11	106	1,086	7
Barry Wagner, Alabama A&M	†1989	11	106	1,812	17
Matt Holmlund, Augustana (S.D.)	†2000	11	104	1,365	16
Mark DeBrito, Bentley	†1999	11	101	1,637	19
Mike Healey, Valparaiso	†1985	10	101	1,279	11
Terrance Banks, Grand Valley St.	2002	14	98	1,170	6
Clarence Coleman, Ferris St.	2000	11	97	1,519	15
Andrew Blakely, Truman	†2002	11	96	965	6
Gerald Gales, West Ala.	†2002	11	96	994	4
Ed Bell, Idaho St.	†1969	10	96	1,522	20
D.J. Humphries, Presbyterian	2001	11	95	1,340	14
Dick Hewins, Drake	†1968	10	95	1,316	13

Player, Team	Year	G	Rec.	Yards	TD
Clarence Coleman, Ferris St.	2001	11	94	1,346	12
Carlos Ferralls, Glenville St.	†1997	10	94	1,566	19
Jarett Vito, Emporia St.	1995	10	+94	932	7
Billy Joe Masters, Evansville	†1987	10	‡94	‡960	4
Stan Carraway, West Tex. A&M	†1986	11	94	1,175	9
Chad Luttrull, Henderson St.	2000	11	92	1,505	14
Manley Sarnowsky, Drake	†1966	10	92	1,114	7
Rus Bailey, N.M. Highlands	1993	10	91	1,192	12
Bruce Cerone, Emporia St.	1968	9	91	1,479	15
Damon Thompson, Virginia St.	1999	10	90	1,517	10

*Record. †National champion. +Record for a freshman. ‡Record for a running back.

SINGLE-GAME RECEPTIONS

No.	Player, Team (Opponent)	Date
23	Chris George, Glenville St. (West Va. Wesleyan)	Oct. 15, 1994
23	Barry Wagner, Alabama A&M (Clark Atlanta)	Nov. 4, 1989
21	Kevin Swayne, Wayne St. (Neb.) (Drake)	Nov. 9, 1996
21	Jarett Vito, Emporia St. (Truman)	Nov. 4, 1995
20	Sean Pender, Valdosta St. (Mississippi Col.)	Nov. 4, 1995
20	Keylie Martin, N.M. Highlands (Western St.)	Nov. 5, 1994
20	"Red" Roberts, Austin Peay (Murray St.)	Nov. 8, 1969
19	Preston Cunningham, Southwest St. (Mo. Western St.)	Sept. 3, 1994
19	Matt Carman, West Ala. (Jacksonville St.)	Nov. 7, 1992
19	Aaron Marsh, Eastern Ky. (Northwood)	Oct. 14, 1967
19	Donnie Pruitt, Emory & Henry (Carson-Newman)	Sept. 23, 1967
19	George LaPorte, Union (N.Y.) (Rensselaer)	Oct. 16, 1965

CAREER YARDS PER GAME

(Minimum 2,200 yards)

Player, Team	Years	G	Rec.	Yards	Avg.
Chris George, Glenville St.	1993-94	20	230	3,215	*160.8
Ed Bell, Idaho St.	1968-69	19	163	2,608	137.3
Bruce Cerone, Yankton/Emporia St.	1965-66, 68-69	36	241	4,354	120.9
Carlos Ferralls, Glenville St.	1994-97	32	262	3,835	119.8
Clarence Coleman, Ferris St.	1998-01	42	*323	*4,983	118.6
Damon Thompson, Virginia St.	1997-00	38	268	4,387	115.4
Jerry Hendren, Idaho	1967-69	30	230	3,435	114.5
Chris Myers, Kenyon	1967-70	35	253	3,897	111.3
James Roe, Norfolk St.	1992-95	41	239	4,468	109.0

*Record.

SEASON YARDS PER GAME

Player, Team	Year	G	Rec.	Yards	Avg.
Chris George, Glenville St.	†1993	10	117	*1,876	*187.6
Chris Perry, Adams St.	†1995	10	88	1,719	171.9
Barry Wagner, Alabama A&M	†1989	11	106	1,812	164.7
Bruce Cerone, Emporia St.	1968	9	91	1,479	164.3
Jerry Hendren, Idaho	†1969	9	86	1,457	161.9
Carlos Ferralls, Glenville St.	†1997	10	94	1,566	156.6
Ed Bell, Idaho St.	†1969	10	96	1,522	152.2
Kevin Ingram, West Chester	†1998	11	115	1,673	152.1
Damon Thompson, Virginia St.	†1999	10	90	1,517	151.7
Pierre Brown, Wayne St. (Mich.)	†2000	10	66	1,492	149.2
Mark DeBrito, Bentley	1999	11	101	1,637	148.8
James Roe, Norfolk St.	†1994	10	77	1,454	145.4
Dan Fulton, Neb.-Omaha	1976	11	67	1,581	143.7
Brad Bailey, West Tex. A&M	1994	11	*119	1,552	141.1

*Record. †National champion.

CAREER YARDS

Player, Team	Years	Rec.	Yards	Avg.	TD
Clarence Coleman, Ferris St.	1998-01	*323	*4,983	15.4	42
James Roe, Norfolk St.	1992-95	239	4,468	18.7	46
Damon Thompson, Virginia St.	1997-00	268	4,387	16.4	37
Bruce Cerone, Yankton/Emporia St.	1965-66, 68-69	241	4,354	18.1	49
Robert Clark, N.C. Central	1983-86	210	4,231	‡20.1	38
David Kircus, Grand Valley St.	1999-02	222	4,142	18.7	*76
Chris Myers, Kenyon	1967-70	253	3,897	15.4	33
Carlos Ferralls, Glenville St.	1994-97	262	3,835	14.6	43
Shannon Sharpe, Savannah St.	1986-89	192	3,744	19.5	40
Tyrone Johnson, Western St.	1990-93	163	3,717	*22.8	35
Mark DeBrito, Bentley	1996-99	238	3,711	15.6	41
Jeff Tiefenthaler, South Dakota St.	1983-86	173	3,621	20.9	31
Willie Richardson, Jackson St.	1959-62	166	3,616	21.8	36
Johnny Cox, Fort Lewis	1990-93	220	3,611	16.4	33

*Record. ‡Record for minimum 180 catches.

SEASON YARDS

Player, Team	Year	Rec.	Yards	Avg.	TD
Chris George, Glenville St.	†1993	117	*1,876	16.0	15
Barry Wagner, Alabama A&M	1989	106	1,812	17.1	17
Chris Perry, Adams St.	†1995	88	1,719	19.5	21

Player, Team	Year	Rec.	Yards	Avg.	TD
Kevin Ingram, West Chester	†1998	115	1,673	14.5	21
Mark DeBrito, Bentley	1999	101	1,637	16.2	19
Dan Fulton, Neb.-Omaha	1976	67	1,581	23.6	16
Carlos Ferralls, Glenville St.	†1997	94	1,566	16.6	19
Brad Bailey, West Tex. A&M	1994	*119	1,552	13.0	16
Jeff Tiefenthaler, South Dakota St.	1986	73	1,534	21.0	11
Ed Bell, Idaho St.	1969	96	1,522	15.9	20
Clarence Coleman, Ferris St.	2000	97	1,519	15.7	15
Damon Thompson, Virginia St.	†1999	90	1,517	16.9	10
Chad Luttrull, Henderson St.	2000	92	1,505	16.4	14
Rodney Robinson, Gardner-Webb	†1992	89	1,496	16.8	16
Pierre Brown, Wayne St. (Mich.)	†2000	66	1,492	22.6	17
Bruce Cerone, Emporia St.	1968	91	1,479	16.3	15
Dee Dee Carter, Central Okla.	†2001	76	1,469	19.3	8
Jerry Hendren, Idaho	1968	86	1,457	16.9	14

*Record. †National champion.

SINGLE-GAME YARDS

No.	Player, Team (Opponent)	Date
401	Kevin Ingram, West Chester (Clarion)	Oct. 31, 1998
370	Barry Wagner, Alabama A&M (Clark Atlanta)	Nov. 4, 1989
363	Tom Nettles, San Diego St. (Southern Miss.)	Nov. 9, 1968
354	Robert Clark, N.C. Central (Jackson St.)	Aug. 30, 1986
352	Chad Luttrull, Henderson St. (Arkansas Tech)	Oct. 28, 2000
325	Paul Zaeske, North Park (North Central)	Oct. 12, 1968
319	Kyle Henderson, West Ala. (Valdosta St.)	Oct. 26, 2002
317	Dan Fulton, Neb.-Omaha (South Dakota)	Sept. 4, 1976
310	Mike Collodi, Colorado Mines (Westminster [Utah])	Oct. 3, 1970

CAREER TOUCHDOWN RECEPTIONS

Player, Team	Years	G	TD
David Kircus, Grand Valley St.	1999-02	43	*76
Bruce Cerone, Yankton/Emporia St.	1965-66, 68-69	36	49
James Roe, Norfolk St.	1992-95	41	46
Kevin Ingram, West Chester	1995-96, 98-99	39	45
Ben Nelson, St. Cloud St.	1999-02	41	43
Carlos Ferralls, Glenville St.	1994-97	35	43
Clarence Coleman, Ferris St.	1998-01	42	42
Sedrick Robinson, Ky. Wesleyan	1993-96	38	42
Mark DeBrito, Bentley	1996-99	39	41
Shannon Sharpe, Savannah St.	1986-89	42	40
Brian Dolph, Saginaw Valley	1997-00	39	39
Robert Clark, N.C. Central	1983-86	40	38
Tony Willis, New Haven	1990-93	40	38
Pierre Brown, Wayne St. (Mich.)	1998-01	37	37
Damon Thompson, Virginia St.	1997-00	38	37
Willie Richardson, Jackson St.	1959-62	38	36

*Record.

SEASON TOUCHDOWN RECEPTIONS

Player, Team	Year	G	TD
David Kircus, Grand Valley St.	2002	14	*35
David Kircus, Grand Valley St.	2001	10	28
Dallas Mall, Bentley	2001	12	24
Ben Nelson, St. Cloud St.	2002	11	23
Kevin Ingram, West Chester	1998	11	21
Chris Perry, Adams St.	1995	10	21
Brian Dolph, Saginaw Valley	2000	11	20
Ed Bell, Idaho St.	1969	10	20
Tim Battaglia, Minn. Duluth	2002	12	19
Mark DeBrito, Bentley	1999	11	19
Carlos Ferralls, Glenville St.	1997	10	19
Stanley Flanders, Valdosta St.	1994	11	19
Chris Brewer, Fort Lewis	2002	11	18
Jai Hill, Indiana (Pa.)	1990	10	18
Jamar Nailor, N.M. Highlands	1996	10	18
Wayne Thomas, Miles	1996	10	18
Brian Penecale, West Chester	1997	11	18
Pierre Brown, Wayne St. (Mich.)	2000	10	17
James Roe, Norfolk St.	1997	10	17
Robert Williams, Valdosta St.	1997	11	17
Barry Wagner, Alabama A&M	1989	11	17

*Record.

ANNUAL CHAMPIONS

Year	Player, Team	Class	Rec.	Yards	TD
1946	Hugh Taylor, Oklahoma City	Jr.	23	457	8
1947	Bill Klein, Hanover	So.	52	648	12
1948	Bill Klein, Hanover	Jr.	43	812	6
1949	Cliff Coggin, Southern Miss.	Sr.	53	1,087	9
1950	Jack Bighead, Pepperdine	Jr.	38	551	6
1951	Jim Stefoff, Kalamazoo	Jr.	45	680	5

DIVISION II

Year	Player, Team	Class	Rec.	Yards	TD
1952	Jim McKinzie, Northern Ill.	Sr.	44	703	6
1953	Dick Beetsch, Northern Iowa	So.	54	837	9
1954	R.C. Owens, Col. of Idaho	Sr.	48	905	7
1955	Dick Donlin, Hamline	Sr.	41	480	2
1956	Tom Rychlec, American Int'l	Sr.	40	353	3
1957	Tom Whitaker, Nevada	Jr.	40	527	4
1958	Bruce Shenk, West Chester	Sr.	39	580	9
1959	Fred Tunnicliffe, UC Santa Barb.	So.	48	1,087	11
1960	Ken Gregory, Whittier	Sr.	74	1,018	4
1961	Marty Baumhower, Defiance	Jr.	57	708	4
1962	Hugh Rohrschneider, Northern Ill.	Jr.	76	795	5
1963	Hugh Rohrschneider, Northern Ill.	Sr.	75	1,036	14
1964	Steve Gilliatt, Parsons	So.	81	984	12
1965	George LaPorte, Union (N.Y.)	Sr.	74	724	5
1966	Manley Sarnowsky, Drake	Sr.	92	1,114	7
1967	Harvey Tanner, Murray St.	Jr.	88	1,019	3
1968	Dick Hewins, Drake	Sr.	95	1,316	13
1969	Ed Bell, Idaho St.	Sr.	96	1,522	20

Beginning in 1970, ranked on per-game (instead of total) catches.

Year	Player, Team	Class	G	Rec.	Avg.	Yards	TD
1970	Steve Mahaffey, Wash. & Lee	Sr.	9	74	8.2	897	2
1971	Kalle Kontson, Rensselaer	Sr.	9	69	7.7	1,031	7
1972	Freddie Scott, Amherst	Jr.	8	66	8.3	936	12
1973	Ron Gustafson, North Dakota	Jr.	10	67	6.7	1,210	10
1974	Andy Sanchez, Cal Poly Pomona	Sr.	10	62	6.2	903	0
1975	Butch Johnson, UC Riverside	Sr.	8	67	8.4	1,027	8
1976	Bo Darden, Shaw	So.	9	57	6.3	863	4
1977	Jeff Tesch, Minn. St. Moorhead	Sr.	10	67	6.7	760	9
1978	Mike Chrobot, Butler	Sr.	10	55	5.5	628	5
	Tom Ferguson, Cal St. Hayward	Jr.	10	55	5.5	698	6
	Mark McDaniel, Northern Colo.	Sr.	10	55	5.5	761	6
1979	Robbie Ray, Franklin	Sr.	10	63	6.3	987	3
1980	Joe Dittrich, Southwest St.	Sr.	9	83	9.2	974	7
1981	Paul Choudek, Southwest St.	Sr.	10	70	7.0	747	5
1982	Jay Barnett, Evansville	Sr.	10	81	8.1	1,181	12
1983	Perry Kemp, Calif. (Pa.)	Sr.	10	74	7.4	1,101	9
1984	Dan Bogar, Valparaiso	Sr.	10	73	7.3	861	11
1985	Mike Healey, Valparaiso	Sr.	10	101	10.1	1,279	11
1986	Stan Carraway, West Tex. A&M	Sr.	11	94	8.5	1,175	9
1987	Billy Joe Masters, Evansville	Sr.	10	‡94	‡9.4	‡960	4
1988	Todd Smith, Morningside	Sr.	11	86	7.8	1,006	8
1989	Barry Wagner, Alabama A&M	Sr.	11	106	9.6	1,812	17

Beginning in 1990, ranked on both per-game catches and yards per game.

PER-GAME RECEPTIONS

Year	Player, Team	Class	G	Rec.	Avg.	Yards	TD
1990	Mark Steinmeyer, Kutztown	Jr.	11	86	7.8	940	5
1991	Jesse Lopez, Cal St. Hayward	Sr.	10	86	8.6	861	4
1992	Randy Bartosh, Southwest Baptist	Sr.	8	65	8.1	860	2
1993	Chris George, Glenville St.	Jr.	10	117	*11.7	*1,876	15
1994	Chris George, Glenville St.	Sr.	10	113	11.3	1,339	15
1995	Sean Pender, Valdosta St.	Jr.	11	111	10.1	983	2
1996	Carlos Ferralls, Glenville St.	Jr.	8	81	10.1	965	6
1997	Carlos Ferralls, Glenville St.	Sr.	10	94	9.4	1,566	19
1998	Kevin Ingram, West Chester	Jr.	11	115	10.5	1,673	21
1999	Mark DeBrito, Bentley	Sr.	11	101	9.2	1,637	19
2000	Matt Holmlund, Augustana (S.D.)	Jr.	11	104	9.5	1,365	16
2001	Jamal Allen, Fort Lewis	Jr.	11	106	9.6	1,086	7
2002	Andrew Blakely, Truman	Sr.	11	96	8.7	965	6
	Gerald Gales, West Ala.	Jr.	11	96	8.7	994	4

YARDS PER GAME

Year	Player, Team	Class	G	Rec.	Yards	Avg.	TD
1990	Ernest Priester, Edinboro	Sr.	8	45	1,060	132.5	14
1991	Rod Smith, Mo. Southern St.	Jr.	11	60	1,439	130.8	15
1992	Rodney Robinson, Gardner-Webb	Sr.	11	89	1,496	136.0	16
1993	Chris George, Glenville St.	Jr.	10	117	*1,876	*187.6	15
1994	James Roe, Norfolk St.	Jr.	10	77	1,454	145.4	17
1995	Chris Perry, Adams St.	Sr.	10	88	1,719	171.9	21
1996	Ron Lelko, Bloomsburg	Jr.	11	87	1,455	132.3	15
1997	Carlos Ferralls, Glenville St.	Sr.	10	94	1,566	156.6	19
1998	Kevin Ingram, West Chester	Jr.	11	115	1,673	152.1	21
1999	Damon Thompson, Virginia St.	Jr.	10	90	1,517	151.7	10
2000	Pierre Brown, Wayne St. (Mich.)	Jr.	10	66	1,492	149.2	17
2001	Dee Dee Carter, Central Okla.	So.	11	76	1,469	133.6	8
2002	Chris Brewer, Fort Lewis	So.	11	85	1,274	115.8	18

*Record. ‡Record for a running back.

Scoring

CAREER POINTS PER GAME
(Minimum 225 Points)

Player, Team	Years	G	TD	Extra Pts. Scored	FG	Pts.	Pt. PG
Ole Gunderson, St. Olaf	1969-71	27	60	2	0	362	*13.4
Leon Burns, Long Beach St.	1969-70	22	47	2	0	284	12.9
Ian Smart, C.W. Post	1999-02	45	*95	0	0	*570	12.7
Brian Shay, Emporia St.	1995-98	44	88	16	0	544	12.4
Billy Johnson, Widener	1971-72	19	39	0	0	234	12.3
Tyrone Morgan, Northern St.	1998-00	30	59	0	0	354	11.8
Rashaan Dumas, Southern Conn. St.	1996-99	37	72	0	0	432	11.7
Dale Mills, Truman	1957-60	36	64	23	0	407	11.3
Kavin Gailliard, American Int'l	1996-99	43	78	8	0	476	11.1
Walter Payton, Jackson St.	1971-74	42	66	53	5	464	11.0
Jeff Bentrim, North Dakota St.	1983-86	35	64	2	0	386	11.0
Steve Roberts, Butler	1986-89	35	63	8	0	386	11.0
Shawn Graves, Wofford	1989-92	40	72	6	0	438	11.0
Johnny Bailey, Tex. A&M-Kingsville	1986-89	39	70	6	0	426	10.9
David Kircus, Grand Valley St.	1999-02	43	77	2	0	464	10.8
Garney Henley, Huron	1956-59	37	63	16	0	394	10.6
Roger Graham, New Haven	1991-94	40	70	4	0	424	10.6

*Record.

SEASON POINTS PER GAME

Player, Team	Year	G	TD	Extra Pts. Scored	FG	Pts.	Pt. PG
Carl Herakovich, Rose-Hulman	†1958	8	25	18	0	168	*21.0
Jim Switzer, Col. of Emporia	†1963	9	28	0	0	168	18.7
Billy Johnson, Widener	†1972	9	27	0	0	162	18.0
Brian Shay, Emporia St.	†1997	11	32	6	0	198	18.0
Carl Garrett, N.M. Highlands	†1966	9	26	2	0	158	17.6
Kavin Gailliard, Amerian Int'l	†1999	12	34	2	0	206	17.2
David Kircus, Grand Valley St.	†2001	10	28	0	0	168	16.8
Ted Scown, Sul Ross St.	†1948	10	28	0	0	168	16.8
Travis Walch, Winona St.	1997	11	30	2	0	182	16.5
Ian Smart, C.W. Post	2001	12	33	0	0	198	16.5
Andre Braxton, Virginia Union	†2000	11	27	14	0	176	16.0
Larry Ras, Michigan Tech	†1971	9	24	0	0	144	16.0
Brian Shay, Emporia St.	†1998	11	29	2	0	176	16.0

*Record. †National champion.

CAREER POINTS

Player, Team	Years	TD	Extra Pts. Scored	FG	Pts.
Ian Smart, C.W. Post	1999-02	*95	0	0	*570
Brian Shay, Emporia St.	1995-98	88	16	0	544
Kavin Gailliard, American Int'l	1996-99	78	8	0	476
David Kircus, Grand Valley St.	1999-02	77	2	0	464
Walter Payton, Jackson St.	1971-74	66	53	5	464
Jarrett Anderson, Truman	1993-96	73	2	0	440
Shawn Graves, Wofford	1989-92	72	6	0	438
Rashaan Dumas, Southern Conn. St.	1996-99	72	0	0	432
Josh Ranek, South Dakota St.	$1997-01	69	12	0	426
Johnny Bailey, Tex. A&M-Kingsville	1986-89	70	6	0	426
Roger Graham, New Haven	1991-94	70	4	0	424
Andre Braxton, Virginia Union	1997-00	62	36	0	408
Dale Mills, Truman	1957-60	64	23	0	407
Jeremy Monroe, Michigan Tech	1990-93	67	0	0	402
Garney Henley, Huron	1956-59	63	16	0	394
Wesley Cates, Calif. (Pa.)	1998-01	64	2	0	386
Jeff Bentrim, North Dakota St.	1983-86	64	2	0	386
Steve Roberts, Butler	1986-89	63	8	0	386
Leo Lewis, Lincoln (Mo.)	1951-54	64	0	0	384
Bob Miller, Emory & Henry	1948-51	63	1	0	379
Heath Sherman, Tex. A&M-Kingsville	1985-88	63	0	0	378
Antonio Leroy, Albany St. (Ga.)	1993-96	62	6	0	378
Damian Beane, Shepherd	1996-99	60	10	0	370
Tank Younger, Grambling	1945-48	60	9	0	369
Richard Huntley, Winston-Salem	1992-95	60	8	0	368
Bill Cooper, Muskingum	1957-60	54	37	1	364
Ole Gunderson, St. Olaf	1969-71	60	2	0	362
Eddie Acosta, Bemidji St.	1999-02	59	6	0	360
Mike Joseph, Fairmont St.	1994-97	57	14	0	356

*Record. $See Page 8 for explanation.

SEASON POINTS

Player, Team	Year	TD	Extra Pts. Scored	FG	Pts.
David Kircus, Grand Valley St.	†2002	*35	2	0	*212
Kavin Gailliard, American Int'l	†1999	34	2	0	206
Ian Smart, C.W. Post	2001	33	0	0	198
Brian Shay, Emporia St.	†1997	32	6	0	198
Travis Walch, Winona St.	1997	30	2	0	182
Ian Smart, C.W. Post	2002	30	0	0	180
Terry Metcalf, Long Beach St.	1971	29	4	0	178
Andre Braxton, Virginia Union	†2000	27	14	0	176
Brian Shay, Emporia St.	†1998	29	2	0	176
Josh Ranek, South Dakota St.	1999	28	2	0	170
David Kircus, Grand Valley St.	†2001	28	0	0	168
Jarrett Anderson, Truman	†1996	28	0	0	168
Jim Switzer, Col. of Emporia	†1963	28	0	0	168
Carl Herakovich, Rose-Hulman	†1958	25	18	0	168
Ted Scown, Sul Ross St.	†1948	28	0	0	168
Ronald Moore, Pittsburg St.	1992	27	4	0	166
Leon Burns, Long Beach St.	†1969	27	2	0	164
Mike Deutsch, North Dakota	1972	27	0	0	162
Billy Johnson, Widener	†1972	27	0	0	162

*Record. †National champion.

ANNUAL CHAMPIONS

Year	Player, Team	Class	TD	Extra Pts. Scored	FG	Pts.
1946	Joe Carter, Florida N&I	So.	21	26	0	152
1947	Darwin Horn, Pepperdine	Jr.	19	1	0	115
	Chuck Schoenherr, Wheaton (Ill.)	So.	19	1	0	115
1948	Ted Scown, Sul Ross St.	So.	28	0	0	168
1949	Sylvester Polk, Md.-East. Shore	Jr.	19	15	0	129
1950	Carl Taseff, John Carroll	Sr.	23	0	0	138
1951	Paul Yackey, Heidelberg	Jr.	22	0	0	132
1952	Al Conway, William Jewell	Sr.	22	1	0	133
1953	Leo Lewis, Lincoln (Mo.)	Jr.	22	0	0	132
1954	Jim Podoley, Central Mich.	Jr.	18	1	0	109
	Dick Nyers, Indianapolis	Sr.	16	13	0	109
1955	Nate Clark, Hillsdale	Jr.	24	0	0	144
1956	Larry Houdek, Kan. Wesleyan	Sr.	19	0	0	114
1957	Lenny Lyles, Louisville	Sr.	21	6	0	132
1958	Carl Herakovich, Rose-Hulman	Sr.	25	18	0	168
1959	Garney Henley, Huron	Sr.	22	9	0	141
1960	Bill Cooper, Muskingum	Sr.	23	14	0	152
1961	John Murio, Whitworth	Jr.	15	33	2	129
1962	Mike Goings, Bluffton	So.	22	0	0	132
1963	Jim Switzer, Col. of Emporia	Sr.	28	0	0	168
1964	Henry Dyer, Grambling	Jr.	17	2	0	104
	Dunn Marteen, Cal St. Los Angeles	Sr.	11	38	0	104
1965	Allen Smith, Findlay	Jr.	24	2	0	146
1966	Carl Garrett, N.M. Highlands	So.	26	2	0	158
1967	Bert Nye, West Chester	Jr.	19	13	0	127
1968	Howard Stevens, Randolph-Macon	Fr.	23	4	0	142
1969	Leon Burns, Long Beach St.	Jr.	27	2	0	164

Beginning in 1970, ranked on per-game (instead of total) points

Year	Player, Team	Class	G	TD	Extra Pts. Scored	FG	Pts.	Avg.
1970	Mike DiBlasi, Mount Union	Sr.	9	22	0	0	132	14.7
1971	Larry Ras, Michigan Tech	Sr.	9	24	0	0	144	16.0
1972	Billy Johnson, Widener	Jr.	9	27	0	0	162	18.0
1973	Walter Payton, Jackson St.	Jr.	11	24	13	1	160	14.5
1974	Walter Payton, Jackson St.	Sr.	10	19	6	1	123	12.3
1975	Dale Kasowski, North Dakota	Sr.	7	16	4	0	100	14.3
1976	Ted McKnight, Minn. Duluth	Sr.	10	24	0	0	144	14.4
1977	Bill Burnham, New Hampshire	Sr.	10	22	0	0	132	13.2
1978	Marschell Brunfield, Youngstown St.	Sr.	9	14	0	0	84	9.3
	Charlie Thompson, Western St.	Sr.	9	14	0	0	84	9.3
1979	Robby Robson, Youngstown St.	Jr.	10	20	0	0	120	12.0
1980	Amory Bodin, Minn. Duluth	Sr.	10	19	2	0	116	11.6
1981	George Works, Northern Mich.	Jr.	10	21	0	0	126	12.6
1982	George Works, Northern Mich.	Sr.	10	23	0	0	138	13.8
1983	Clarence Johnson, North Ala.	Jr.	10	16	0	0	96	9.6
1984	Jeff Bentrim, North Dakota St.	So.	9	14	0	0	84	9.3
1985	Jeff Bentrim, North Dakota St.	Jr.	8	18	2	0	110	††13.8
1986	Jeff Bentrim, North Dakota St.	Sr.	10	23	0	0	138	13.8
1987	Johnny Bailey, Tex. A&M-Kingsville	So.	10	20	0	0	120	12.0
1988	Steve Roberts, Butler	Jr.	10	23	4	0	142	14.2
1989	Jimmy Allen, St. Joseph's (Ind.)	Jr.	10	23	0	0	138	13.8
1990	Ernest Priester, Edinboro	Sr.	8	16	0	0	96	12.0

Year	Player, Team	Class	G	TD	Extra Pts. Scored	FG	Pts.	Avg.
1991	Quincy Tillmon, Emporia St.	So.	9	19	0	0	114	12.7
1992	David McCartney, Chadron St.	Jr.	10	25	4	0	154	15.4
1993	Roger Graham, New Haven	Jr.	10	23	0	0	138	13.8
1994	Leonard Davis, Lenoir-Rhyne	Sr.	9	19	0	0	114	12.7
1995	Antonio Leroy, Albany St. (Ga.)	Jr.	11	24	0	0	144	13.1
1996	Jarrett Anderson, Truman	Sr.	11	28	0	0	168	15.3
1997	Brian Shay, Emporia St.	Jr.	11	32	6	0	198	18.0
1998	Brian Shay, Emporia St.	Sr.	11	29	2	0	176	16.0
1999	Kavin Gailliard, American Int'l	Sr.	12	34	2	0	206	17.2
2000	Andre Braxton, Virginia Union	Sr.	11	27	14	0	176	16.0
2001	David Kircus, Grand Valley St.	Jr.	10	28	0	0	168	16.8
2002	David Kircus, Grand Valley St.	Sr.	14	*35	2	0	*212	15.1

*Record. ††Declared champion; with one more game (to meet 75 percent of games played minimum) for zero points, still would have highest per-game average (12.2).

Interceptions

CAREER INTERCEPTIONS

Player, Team	Years	No.	Yards	Avg.
Tom Collins, Indianapolis	1982-85	*37	390	10.5
Dean Diaz, Humboldt St.	1980-83	31	328	10.6
Bill Grantham, Mo.-Rolla	1977-80	29	263	9.1
Jason Johnson, Shepherd	1991-94	28	321	11.5
Tony Woods, Bloomsburg	1982-85	26	105	4.0
Buster West, Gust. Adolphus	1967-70	26	192	7.4
Nate Gruber, Winona St.	1991-94	25	275	11.0
Gary Rubeling, Towson	1980-83	25	122	4.9
Greg Mercier, Ripon	1968-70	25	243	9.7

*Record.

SEASON INTERCEPTIONS

Player, Team	Year	No.	Yards
Eugene Hunter, Fort Valley St.	†1972	**14	211
Luther Howard, Delaware St.	†1972	**14	99
Tom Rezzuti, Northeastern	†1971	**14	153
Jim Blackwell, Southern U.	†1970	**14	196
Carl Ray Harris, Fresno St.	1970	**14	98

**Record tied. †National champion.

ANNUAL CHAMPIONS

Year	Player, Team	Class	G	No.	Avg.	Yards
1970	Jim Blackwell, Southern U.	Sr.	11	**14	1.27	196
1971	Tom Rezzuti, Northeastern	Jr.	9	**14	**1.56	153
1972	Eugene Hunter, Fort Valley St.	So.	9	**14	**1.56	211
	Luther Howard, Delaware St.	Sr.	9	**14	**1.56	99
1973	Mike Pierce, Northern Colo.	Sr.	7	7	1.00	158
	James Smith, Shaw	So.	8	8	1.00	94
1974	Terry Rusin, Wayne St. (Mich.)	Fr.	10	10	1.00	62
1975	Jim Poettgen, Cal Poly Pomona	Jr.	11	12	1.09	156
1976	Johnny Tucker, Tennessee Tech	Sr.	11	10	0.91	74
1977	Mike Ellis, Norfolk St.	So.	11	12	1.09	257
	Cornelius Washington, Winston-Salem	Sr.	11	12	1.09	128
1978	Bill Grantham, Mo.-Rolla	So.	11	11	1.00	109
1979	Jeff Huffman, Michigan Tech	Sr.	10	11	1.10	97
1980	Mike Lush, East Stroudsburg	Sr.	10	12	1.20	208
1981	Bobby Futrell, Elizabeth City St.	So.	9	11	1.22	159
1982	Greg Maack, Central Mo. St.	Sr.	10	11	1.10	192
1983	Matt Didio, Wayne St. (Mich.)	Sr.	10	13	1.30	131
1984	Bob Jahelka, C.W. Post	Sr.	8	9	1.13	83
1985	Duvval Callaway, Fort Valley St.	Sr.	11	10	0.91	175
	Tony Woods, Bloomsburg	Sr.	11	10	0.91	10
1986	Doug Smart, Winona St.	Jr.	8	10	1.25	56
1987	Mike Petrich, Minn. Duluth	Jr.	11	9	0.82	151
1988	Pete Jaros, Augustana (S.D.)	Jr.	11	13	1.18	120
1989	Jacque DeMatteo, Clarion	Jr.	8	6	0.75	21
1990	Eric Turner, Tex. A&M-Commerce	So.	11	10	0.91	105
1991	Jeff Fickes, Shippensburg	Sr.	11	12	1.09	154
1992	Pat Williams, Tex. A&M-Commerce	Sr.	11	13	1.18	145
1993	Troy Crissman, Ky. Wesleyan	So.	10	9	0.90	39
1994	Keith Hawkins, Humboldt St.	Sr.	10	11	1.10	159
	Elton Rhoades, Central Okla.	Sr.	10	11	1.10	126
1995	Chenelle Jones, Western N.M.	Sr.	8	7	0.88	61
1996	Britt Henderson, Savannah St.	Sr.	11	12	1.09	180
1997	Jamey Hutchinson, Winona St.	Jr.	11	11	1.00	125
	Tim Bednarski, Mercyhurst	Jr.	9	9	1.00	59
1998	Jermel Johnson, Fayetteville St.	Sr.	10	9	0.90	95
1999	Tommie Dawson, Virginia Union	Jr.	8	8	1.00	79
2000	Tim Mustapha, Hillsdale	Jr.	11	11	1.00	78
2001	Gregg Albano, Bentley	Jr.	12	12	1.00	156
	Jason Patterson, Central Wash.	Sr.	11	11	1.00	86

Nicholas Murray of Johnson Smith pulled down 10 interceptions in 10 games last year to lead Division II with an average of 1.0 per contest.

Year	Player, Team	Class	G	No.	Avg.	Yards
	Ralph Hunter, Virginia Union	Sr.	10	10	1.00	25
	Joey Flora, Indiana (Pa.)	Sr.	8	8	1.00	75
2002	Nicholas Murray, Johnson Smith	Jr.	10	10	1.00	97

**Record tied.

Total Tackles

SEASON TOTAL TACKLES PER GAME

Player, Team	Year	G	Solo	Ast.	Total	Avg.
Jason Ocean, Livingstone	†2001	9	50	91	141	*15.7
Dan Holland, Mansfield	†2002	10	85	56	141	14.1
Danielle Rollins, Ark.-Monticello	†2000	9	57	66	123	13.7
Brian Holliday, Fayetteville St.	2001	9	46	74	120	13.3
Demarkes Dogan, Wingate	2001	10	49	80	129	12.9
Justin Valentine, West Virginia St.	2002	11	52	89	141	12.8
Chris Angel, Western Ore.	2000	11	*92	48	140	12.7
Rob North, Hillsdale	2002	11	66	73	139	12.6
Deric Sieck, Winona St.	2002	12	88	63	*151	12.6
John Grant, Morehouse	2002	10	80	45	125	12.5
Brian Holliday, Fayetteville St.	2002	12	45	105	150	12.5
Nick Childers, Indianapolis	2001	11	67	70	137	12.5

*Record. †National champion.

SEASON TOTAL TACKLES

Player, Team	Year	G	Solo	Ast.	Total
Deric Sieck, Winona St.	2002	12	88	63	*151
Brian Holliday, Fayetteville St.	2002	12	45	105	150
Dan Holland, Mansfield	†2002	10	85	56	141
Justin Valentine, West Virginia St.	2002	11	52	89	141
Jason Ocean, Livingstone	†2001	9	50	91	141
Chris Angel, Western Ore.	2000	11	*92	48	140
Rob North, Hillsdale	2002	11	66	73	139
Nick Childers, Indianapolis	2001	11	67	70	137
Adam Wheatley, Saginaw Valley	2001	11	90	42	132
Eric Walker, Mo. Western St.	2000	11	66	66	132

*Record. †National champion.

SINGLE-GAME TOTAL TACKLES
(Since 2000)

Tackles	Player, Team (Opponent)	Date
30	Shaun Maloney, Minn.-Morris (Minn. St. Moorhead)	Oct. 27, 2001
25	Alan Slaughter, Tusculum (Lenoir-Rhyne)	Sept. 30, 2000
22	Jake Tietje, Winona St. (Wis.-Stevens Point)	Nov. 11, 2000
21	Dave Morrill, Western Ore. (Carson-Newman)	Sept. 12, 2000
20	Brian Holliday, Fayetteville St. (Virginia St.)	Oct. 19, 2002
20	Matt Nicholson, St. Cloud St. (North Dakota St.)	Nov. 10, 2001
20	Jace Pavlovich, Fort Hays St. (Western St.)	Oct. 27, 2001
20	James Tindell, Indiana (Pa.) (Clarion)	Oct. 27, 2001
20	Mick Peterson, St. Cloud St. (Morningside)	Oct. 21, 2000
20	Chris Volz, Indianapolis (Northern Mich.)	Sept. 9, 2000
20	Walter Robinson, Indianapolis (Northern Mich.)	Sept. 9, 2000

ANNUAL CHAMPIONS

Year	Player, Team	Class	G	Solo	Ast.	Total	Avg.
2000	Danielle Rollins, Ark.-Monticello	Sr.	9	57	66	123	13.7
2001	Jason Ocean, Livingstone	So.	9	50	91	141	*15.7
2002	Dan Holland, Mansfield	Jr.	10	85	56	141	14.1

*Record.

Solo Tackles

SEASON SOLO TACKLES PER GAME

Player, Team	Year	G	Solo	Avg.
Dan Holland, Mansfield	†2002	10	85	*8.5
Chris Angel, Western Ore.	2000	11	*92	8.4
Adam Wheatley, Saginaw Valley	†2001	11	90	8.2
Dan Holland, Mansfield	2000	10	81	8.1
John Grant, Morehouse	2002	10	80	8.0
Josh Ison, Fairmont St.	2002	10	75	7.5
Deleon Burch, Morehouse	2001	9	67	7.4
Deric Sieck, Winona St.	2002	12	88	7.3
Steve Sheeler, Stonehill	2001	9	66	7.3
Bobby Petras, Tiffin	2002	10	71	7.1
Derrik Metz, Lock Haven	2002	11	78	7.1
Matt Baltzer, Hillsdale	2001	11	78	7.1

*Record. †National champion.

SEASON TOTAL SOLO TACKLES

Player, Team	Year	G	Solo
Chris Angel, Western Ore.	2000	11	*92
Adam Wheatley, Saginaw Valley	†2001	11	90
Deric Sieck, Winona St.	2002	12	88
Dan Holland, Mansfield	†2002	10	85
Dan Holland, Mansfield	2000	11	81
John Grant, Morehouse	2002	10	80
Derrik Metz, Lock Haven	2002	11	78
Matt Baltzer, Hillsdale	2001	11	78
Kevin Nagle, East Stroudsburg	2000	11	76

*Record. †National champion.

SINGLE-GAME SOLO TACKLES
(Since 2000)

Solo	Player, Team (Opponent)	Date
14	Garrett Padgett, Tiffin (Geneva)	Nov. 9, 2002
14	Darren Shaughnessy, Stonehill (Bryant)	Oct. 26, 2001
14	Walter Robinson, Indianapolis (Northern Mich.)	Sept. 9, 2000
13	Deric Sieck, Winona St. (South Dakota)	Aug. 30, 2001
12	Jace Pavlovich, Fort Hays St. (Western St.)	Oct. 27, 2001
12	Garrett Patty, Mercyhurst (Hillsdale)	Oct. 27, 2001
12	Derek Kent, Truman (Washburn)	Oct. 6, 2001
11	Tommy Edwards, Arkansas Tech (Delta St.)	Oct. 12, 2002
11	Matthew Tosi, Winston-Salem (Fayetteville St.)	Oct. 5, 2002
11	Darrell Lewis, Lincoln (Mo.) (Clark-Atlanta)	Sept. 7, 2002
11	Said Perez, Harding (Delta St.)	Nov. 30, 2000
11	Russell Rothar, Presbyterian (Catawba)	Sept. 23, 2000
11	Elton Sells, Western Ore. (Mesa St.)	Sept. 5, 2000

ANNUAL CHAMPIONS

Year	Player, Team	Class	G	Solo	Avg.
2001	Adam Wheatley, Saginaw Valley	Sr.	11	90	8.2
2002	Dan Holland, Mansfield	Jr.	10	85	*8.5

*Record.

Johnson Smith Sports Information

Tackles for Loss

SEASON TACKLES FOR LOSS PER GAME

Player, Team	Year	G	Solo	Ast	Total	Avg.
Charlie Cook, C.W. Post	†2001	12	36	2	*37.0	*3.1
Jason Ocean, Livingstone	†2002	10	23	14	30.0	3.0
William Yarocki, C.W. Post	2000	10	25	0	25.0	2.5
George Allen, Gannon	2002	9	22	0	22.0	2.4
Lance Flagg, St. Anselm	2002	10	22	4	24.0	2.4
Joe Spuhler, Wayne St. (Mich.)	2001	10	24	0	24.0	2.4
Ricky Leung Wai, Concord	2000	11	26	0	26.0	2.4

Record. †National champion.

SEASON TACKLES FOR LOSS

Player, Team	Year	G	Solo	Ast	Total
Charlie Cook, C.W. Post	†2001	12	36	2	*37.0
Jason Ocean, Livingstone	†2002	10	23	14	30.0
Dewayne Smith, Valdosta St.	2002	15	25	8	29.0
Shawn Morgan, Fayetteville St.	2002	12	20	16	28.0
Ricky Leung Wai, Concord	2000	11	26	0	26.0
Anthony Koon, Fort Valley St.	2002	11	25	0	25.0
William Yarocki, C.W. Post	†2000	10	25	0	25.0
Jimmy Barnett, Tarleton St.	2001	11	25	0	25.0
Tom Quinn, Assumption	2000	11	25	0	25.0
Davon Deveaux, West Va. Tech	2000	11	25	0	25.0

Record. †National champion.

SINGLE-GAME TACKLES FOR LOSS
(Since 2000)

TFL	Player, Team (Opponent)	Date
6.0	Dave Armstrong, Bloomsburg (Indiana [Pa.])	Sept. 7, 2002
6.0	Joe Spuhler, Wayne St. (Mich.) (Indianapolis)	Oct. 27, 2001
6.0	Davin Thompson, Winona St. (Minn. Duluth)	Nov. 4, 2000
5.0	Tommy Edwards, Arkansas Tech (Delta St.)	Oct. 12, 2002
5.0	Jeff Jackson, Indiana (Pa.) (Edinboro)	Oct. 20, 2001
5.0	Casey Seyfert, Fort Hays St. (Mesa St.)	Oct. 13, 2001
5.0	Luke Larson, Quincy (Westminster [Mo.])	Oct. 6, 2001
5.0	Roger Wilson, Indiana (Pa.) (Millersville)	Nov. 11, 2000
5.0	Said Perez, Harding (Arkansas Tech)	Sept. 16, 2000
4.5	Tayt Tolman, Western Ore. (Mesa St.)	Aug. 31, 2002

ANNUAL CHAMPIONS

Year	Player, Team	G	Solo	Ast	Total	Avg.
2000	William Yarocki, C.W. Post	10	25	0	25.0	2.5
2001	Charlie Cook, C.W. Post	12	36	2	*37.0	*3.1
2002	Jason Ocean, Livingstone	10	23	14	30.0	3.0

Record.

Pass Sacks

SEASON PASS SACKS PER GAME

Player, Team	Year	G	Solo	Ast	Total	Avg.
Charlie Cook, C.W. Post	†2001	12	20	1	*20.5	*1.7
Todd DeVree, Hillsdale	†2000	11	16	0	16.0	1.5
Tony Roberson, Michigan Tech	2001	10	13	2	14.0	1.4
Bill Teerlinck, Chadron St.	†2002	10	11	3	12.5	1.3
Bill Kavanaugh, Bentley	2002	11	9	9	13.5	1.2
Ted Krautmann, Bentley	2002	11	11	5	13.5	1.2
T.J. Bingham, Ouachita Baptist	2001	10	11	2	12.0	1.2
Jacques Cesaire, Southern Conn. St.	2001	10	12	0	12.0	1.2
Brad Lindamood, Lenoir-Rhyne	2001	10	11	2	12.0	1.2
Kyle Sowell, West Va. Tech	2000	10	12	0	12.0	1.2
William Yarocki, C.W. Post	2000	10	12	0	12.0	1.2
Buddy Bossiere, N.M. Highlands	2001	11	12	2	13.0	1.2
Dwayne Brown, New Haven	2001	9	10	1	10.5	1.2
Shawn Frye, New Haven	2001	9	10	1	10.5	1.2

Record. †National champion.

SEASON TOTAL PASS SACKS

Player, Team	Year	G	Solo	Ast	Total
Charlie Cook, C.W. Post	†2001	12	20	1	*20.5
Todd DeVree, Hillsdale	†2000	11	16	0	16.0
Tony Roberson, Michigan Tech	2001	10	13	2	14.0
Bill Kavanaugh, Bentley	2002	11	9	9	13.5
Ted Krautmann, Bentley	2002	11	11	5	13.5
Buddy Bossiere, N.M. Highlands	2001	11	12	2	13.0
Bill Teerlinck, Chadron St.	†2002	10	11	3	12.5
Damian Walker, Bowie St.	2002	11	12	1	12.5

Record. †National champion.

SINGLE-GAME PASS SACKS
(Since 2000)

PS	Player, Team (Opponent)	Date
5.0	Luke Larson, Quincy (Westminster [Mo.])	Oct. 6, 2001
4.0	Shawn Morgan, Fayetteville St. (Johnson Smith)	Oct. 26, 2002
4.0	Eric Schmidt, North Dakota (New Haven)	Sept. 21, 2001
3.5	Elias Shehadeh, Pace (Assumption)	Oct. 26, 2002
3.0	Many players tied	

ANNUAL CHAMPIONS

Year	Player, Team	G	Solo	Ast	Total	Avg.
2000	Todd DeVree, Hillsdale	11	16	0	16.0	1.5
2001	Charlie Cook, C.W. Post	12	20	1	*20.5	*1.7
2002	Bill Teerlinck, Chadron St.	10	11	3	12.5	1.3

Record.

Passes Defended

SEASON PASSES DEFENDED PER GAME

Player, Team	Year	G	PBU	Int.	Total	Avg.
Anthony Cooks, Fairmont St.	†2001	9	28	4	*32	*3.6
Jason Patterson, Central Wash.	2001	11	19	11	30	2.7
Stephon Kelly, Winston-Salem	2001	11	20	8	28	2.6
James Bracey, Mesa St.	†2000	9	16	5	21	2.3
Todd Geter, Newberry	2001	11	15	10	25	2.3
DeRen Ellis, Ferris St.	2000	11	17	8	25	2.3
Jerald Brown, Glenville St.	2001	9	14	6	20	2.3
Kevin Brown, South Dakota St.	†2002	10	19	3	22	2.2
Ben Nauman, Augustana (S.D.)	2001	10	13	9	22	2.2
Brady Cunningham, West Va. Wesleyan	2001	8	14	3	17	2.1
Craig Neuhaus, Neb.-Kearney	2001	10	13	8	21	2.1

Record. †National champion.

SEASON TOTAL PASSES DEFENDED

Player, Team	Year	G	PBU	Int.	Total
Anthony Cooks, Fairmont St.	†2001	9	28	4	*32
Jason Patterson, Central Wash.	2001	11	19	11	30
Stephon Kelly, Winston-Salem	2001	11	20	8	28
Todd Geter, Newberry	2001	11	15	10	25
DeRen Ellis, Ferris St.	2000	11	17	8	25
Gregg Albano, Bentley	2001	12	12	12	24
Kevin Brown, South Dakota St.	†2002	10	19	3	22
Ben Nauman, Augustana (S.D.)	2001	10	13	9	22
Roosevelt Williams, Tuskegee	2000	11	18	4	22

Record. †National champion.

SINGLE-GAME PASSES DEFENDED
(Since 2000)

PD	Player, Team (Opponent)	Date
5	Johnny Groves, Indianapolis (Ferris St.)	Nov. 16, 2002
5	Jesse Lewis, Bryant (Mass.-Lowell)	Oct. 26, 2002
5	Kairi Cooper, Indiana (Pa.) (Shippensburg)	Nov. 13, 2001
5	Joey Flora, Indiana (Pa.) (Findlay)	Sept. 1, 2001
5	Rob Keefe, Mercyhurst (Hillsdale)	Oct. 27, 2000
4	Grant Newton, Colorado Mines (Adams St.)	Nov. 19, 2002
4	Daniel Leger, Colorado Mines (Western N.M.)	Sept. 21, 2002
4	Ricardo Colclough, Tusculum (North Greenville)	Aug. 29, 2002
4	Rashaad Cooper, Harding (Ouachita Baptist)	Nov. 10, 2001
4	Tracon Adler, Adams St. (Fort Lewis)	Nov. 10, 2001
4	Ben Capers, Presbyterian (Tusculum)	Nov. 3, 2001
4	Tracon Adler, Adams St. (Northern Colo.)	Sept. 8, 2001
4	Rod Gambrell, Presbyterian (Wingate)	Oct. 21, 2000
4	Rashaun Strickland, Tusculum (West Va. Tech)	Aug. 26, 2000

ANNUAL CHAMPIONS

Year	Player, Team	G	PBU	Int.	Total	Avg.
2000	James Bracey, Mesa St.	9	16	5	21	2.3
2001	Anthony Cooks, Fairmont St.	9	28	4	*32	*3.6
2002	Kevin Brown, South Dakota St.	10	19	3	22	2.2

Record.

Forced Fumbles

SEASON FORCED FUMBLES PER GAME

Player, Team	Year	G	FF	Avg.
Bryan Eakin, Neb.-Kearney	†2001	10	7	*0.70
Courtney Johnson, Fairmont St.	2001	9	6	0.67
Al Sullivan, Midwestern St.	†2002	11	7	0.64

DIVISION II

Player, Team	Year	G	FF	Avg.
Michael Hicks, West Virginia St.	2002	10	6	0.60
Davon Deveaux, West Va. Tech	2001	10	6	0.60
James Ward, St. Anselm	2002	10	5	0.50
James Williamson, Angelo St.	2002	10	5	0.50
Sam Davis, Angelo St.	2001	10	5	0.50
Tony Roberson, Southern Conn. St.	2001	10	5	0.50
John Henao, Southern Conn. St.	2001	8	4	0.50
Jay O'Neal, Indiana (Pa.)	2000	10	5	0.50
Lamont Buch, Fairmont St.	2000	10	5	0.50

*Record. †National champion.

TOTAL FORCED FUMBLES

Player, Team	Year	G	FF
Al Sullivan, Midwestern St.	†2002	11	*7
Bryan Eakin, Neb.-Kearney	†2001	10	*7
Michael Hicks, West Virginia St.	2002	10	6
Nick Davis, Tex. A&M-Kingsville	2002	13	6
Courtney Johnson, Fairmont St.	2001	9	6
Davon Deveaux, West Va. Tech	2001	10	6
James Ward. St. Anselm	2002	10	5
James Williamson, Angelo St.	2002	10	5
Charles Alston, Bowie St.	2002	11	5
Jason Crason, Northern St.	2002	11	5
Adam Skinner, Minn. Duluth	2002	12	5
Sam Davis, Angelo St.	2001	10	5
Tony Roberson, Michigan Tech	2001	10	5
Jim Stewart, Hillsdale	2001	11	5
Todd DeVree, Hillsdale	†2000	11	5
Jay O'Neal, Indiana (Pa.)	2000	10	5
Lamont Bush, Fairmont St.	2000	10	5

*Record. †National champion.

SINGLE-GAME FORCED FUMBLES
(Since 2000)

FF	Player, Team (Opponent)	Date
3	Roger Williams, Indiana (Pa.) (Millersville)	Nov. 11, 2000
2	Marco Cole, Harding (Delta St.)	Nov. 2, 2002
2	Aaron Nettles, West Ala. (Stillman)	Sept. 7, 2002
2	Ja'thi Green, Lincoln (Mo.) (Stillman)	Nov. 10, 2001
2	Grant Webb, Quincy (Butler)	Nov. 3, 2001
2	Derek Kent, Truman (Pittsburg St.)	Oct. 27, 2001
2	Lamar Watson, Adams St. (Fort Hays St.)	Sept. 15, 2001
2	Curt Cira, Truman (Southwest Baptist)	Sept. 16, 2000
2	Chris Volz, Indianapolis (St. Joseph's [Ind.])	Sept. 2, 2000

ANNUAL CHAMPIONS

Year	Player, Team	G	FF	Avg.
2000	Dennis Gregory, Mo.-Rolla	11	‡9	0.8
	Todd DeVree, Hillsdale	11	‡9	0.8

‡Prior to 2001, the total was forced fumbles plus fumbles recovered. Beginning in 2001, FF was forced fumbles only.

2001	Bryan Eakin, Neb.-Kearney	10	*7	*0.70
2002	Al Sullivan, Midwestern St.	11	*7	0.64

*Record.

Punting

CAREER AVERAGE
(Minimum 100 Punts)

Player, Team	Years	No.	Yards	Avg.
Jason Van Dyke, Adams St.	1995-98	242	10,720	*44.30
Tim Baer, Colorado Mines	1986-89	235	10,406	44.28
Brian Moorman, Pittsburg St.	1995-98	157	6,903	44.0
Jeff Guy, Western St.	1983-85	113	4,967	44.0
Russ Pilcher, Carroll (Mont.)	1964-66	124	5,424	43.7
Russell Gonzales, Morris Brown	1976-77	111	4,833	43.5
Gerald Circo, Cal St. Chico	1964-65	103	4,470	43.4
Trent Morgan, Cal St. Northridge	1987-88	128	5,531	43.2
Bryan Wagner, Cal St. Northridge	1981-84	203	8,762	43.2
Tom Kolesar, Nevada	1973-74	140	6,032	43.1
Jimmy Morris, Angelo St.	1991-92	101	4,326	42.8
Don Geist, Northern Colo.	1981-84	263	11,247	42.8
Jan Chapman, San Diego	1958-60	106	4,533	42.8
Warner Robertson, Md.-East. Shore	1968-70	131	5,578	42.6

*Record.

SEASON AVERAGE
(Qualifiers for Championship)

Player, Team	Year	No.	Yards	Avg.
Steve Ecker, Shippensburg	†1965	32	1,570	*49.1
Don Cockroft, Adams St.	†1966	36	1,728	48.0
Jack Patterson, William Jewell	1965	29	1,377	47.5
Art Calandrelli, Canisius	†1949	25	1,177	47.1
Grover Perkins, Southern U.	†1961	22	1,034	47.0
Erskine Valrie, Alabama A&M	1966	36	1,673	46.5
Mark Bounds, West Tex. A&M	†1990	69	3,198	+46.3
Bruce Swanson, North Park	†1967	53	2,455	46.3
Jason Van Dyke, Adams St.	†1998	59	2,727	46.2
Lyle Johnston, Weber St.	1965	29	1,340	46.2

*Record. †National champion. +Record for minimum 40 punts.

ANNUAL CHAMPIONS

Year	Player, Team	Class	No.	Yards	Avg.
1948	Arthur Teixeira, Central Mich.	Sr.	42	1,867	44.5
1949	Art Calandrelli, Canisius	Jr.	25	1,177	47.1
1950	Flavian Weidekamp, Butler	Sr.	41	1,762	43.0
1951	Curtiss Harris, Savannah St.	Sr.	42	1,854	44.1
1952	Virgil Stan, Western St.	Sr.	37	1,622	43.8
1953	Bill Bradshaw, Bowling Green	Jr.	50	2,199	44.0
1954	Bill Bradshaw, Bowling Green	Sr.	28	1,228	43.9
1955	Don Baker, North Texas	Sr.	30	1,349	45.0
1956	Marion Zody, Ashland	Jr.	34	1,475	43.4
1957	Lawson Persley, Mississippi Val.	Sr.	36	1,659	46.1
1958	Tom Lewis, Lake Forest	Jr.	24	1,089	45.4
1959	Buck Grover, Salem Int'l	Fr.	27	1,203	44.6
1960	Joe Roy, N.M. Highlands	So.	40	1,744	43.6
1961	Grover Perkins, Southern U.	Fr.	22	1,034	47.0
1962	Ron Crouse, Catawba	Jr.	37	1,653	44.7
1963	Steve Bailey, Kentucky St.	Sr.	39	1,747	44.8
1964	Russ Pilcher, Carroll (Mont.)	So.	34	1,545	45.4
1965	Steve Ecker, Shippensburg	Sr.	32	1,570	*49.1
1966	Don Cockroft, Adams St.	Sr.	36	1,728	48.0
1967	Bruce Swanson, North Park	Jr.	53	2,455	46.3
1968	Warner Robertson, Md.-East. Shore	Fr.	61	2,699	44.2
1969	Warner Robertson, Md.-East. Shore	So.	37	1,629	44.0
1970	John Bonner, Chattanooga	Sr.	73	3,243	44.4
1971	Ken Gamble, Fayetteville St.	Sr.	47	2,092	44.5
1972	Raymond Key, Jackson St.	Jr.	44	1,883	42.8
1973	Jerry Pope, Louisiana Tech	Fr.	48	2,064	43.0
1974	Mike Shawen, Middle Tenn.	Sr.	62	2,720	43.9
1975	Mike Wood, Southeast Mo. St.	Jr.	40	1,729	43.2
1976	Russell Gonzales, Morris Brown	So.	54	2,474	45.8
1977	Jeff Gossett, Eastern Ill.	Jr.	62	2,668	43.0
1978	Bill Moats, South Dakota	Sr.	77	3,377	43.9
1979	Bob Fletcher, Truman	Sr.	79	3,409	43.2
1980	Sean Landeta, Towson	So.	47	2,038	43.4
1981	Gregg Lowery, Jacksonville St.	Jr.	64	2,787	43.5
1982	Don Geist, Northern Colo.	So.	66	2,966	44.4
1983	Jeff Guy, Western St.	So.	39	1,734	44.5
1984	Jeff Guy, Western St.	Jr.	46	2,012	43.7
1985	Jeff Williams, Slippery Rock	Sr.	46	1,977	43.0
1986	Tim Baer, Colorado Mines	Fr.	62	2,797	45.1
1987	Jeff McComb, Southern Utah	Sr.	42	1,863	44.4
1988	Tim Baer, Colorado Mines	Jr.	65	2,880	43.9
1989	Tim Baer, Colorado Mines	Sr.	55	2,382	43.3
1990	Mark Bounds, West Tex. A&M	Jr.	69	3,198	+46.3
1991	Doug O'Neill, Cal Poly	Sr.	42	1,895	45.1
1992	Jimmy Morris, Angelo St.	So.	45	2,001	44.5
1993	Chris Carter, Henderson St.	Sr.	53	2,305	43.5
1994	Pat Hogelin, Colorado Mines	Sr.	48	2,167	45.1
1995	Jon Mason, West Tex. A&M	Sr.	54	2,459	45.5
1996	Tom O'Brien, South Dakota St.	So.	60	2,671	44.5
1997	Brian Moorman, Pittsburg St.	Jr.	36	1,657	46.0
1998	Jason Van Dyke, Adams St.	Sr.	59	2,727	46.2
1999	Nathan White, Fairmont St.	So.	43	1,930	44.9
2000	Adam Ryan, Fort Hays St.	Sr.	69	2,981	43.2
2001	Adam Hostetter, East Stroudsburg	Sr.	54	2,397	44.4
2002	Michael Koenen, Western Wash.	So.	43	1,910	44.4

*Record. +Record for minimum 40 punts.

Punt Returns

CAREER AVERAGE
(Minimum 1.2 Returns Per Game)

Player, Team	Years	No.	Yards	Avg.
Billy Johnson, Widener	1971-72	29	759	*26.2
James Rooths, Shepherd	1997-00	59	1,223	20.7

Player, Team	Years	No.	Yards	Avg.
Bootsie Washington, Shepherd	1996-97	26	512	19.7
Chuck Goehl, Monmouth (Ill.)	1970-72	48	911	19.0
Robbie Martin, Cal Poly	1978-80	69	1,168	16.9
Tony Miles, Northwest Mo. St.	1997-00	82	1,302	15.9
Roscoe Word, Jackson St.	1970-73	35	554	15.8
Darryl Skinner, Hampton	1983-86	53	835	15.8
Alfonso Pugh, Truman	1999-02	49	721	14.7
Clarence Coleman, Ferris St.	1998-01	103	*1,494	14.5
Michael Fields, Mississippi Col.	1984-85	50	695	13.9

*Record.

SEASON AVERAGE
(Minimum 1.2 Returns Per Game)

Player, Team	Year	No.	Yards	Avg.
Billy Johnson, Widener	†1972	15	511	*34.1
William Williams, Livingstone	†1976	16	453	28.3
Terry Egerdahl, Minn. Duluth	†1975	13	360	27.7
Rodney Woodruff, Arkansas Tech	†2000	12	305	25.4
Ennis Thomas, Bishop	†1971	18	450	25.0
Chuck Goehl, Monmouth (Ill.)	1972	17	416	24.5
Doug Grant, Savannah St.	†1992	15	366	24.4
James Rooths, Shepherd	†1999	15	366	24.4
Bootsie Washington, Shepherd	†1997	19	461	24.3

*Record. †National champion.

ANNUAL CHAMPIONS

Year	Player, Team	Class	No.	Yards	Avg.
1970	Kevin Downs, Benedictine (Ill.)	Jr.	11	255	23.2
1971	Ennis Thomas, Bishop	So.	18	450	25.0
1972	Billy Johnson, Widener	Jr.	15	511	*34.1
1973	Roscoe Word, Jackson St.	Sr.	19	316	16.6
1974	Greg Anderson, Montana	So.	13	263	20.2
1975	Terry Egerdahl, Minn. Duluth	Sr.	13	360	27.7
1976	William Williams, Livingstone	So.	16	453	28.3
1977	Armando Olivieri, New York Tech	So.	14	270	19.3
1978	Dwight Walker, Nicholls St.	Fr.	16	284	17.8
1979	Ricky Eberhart, Morris Brown	Fr.	18	401	22.3
1980	Ron Bagby, Puget Sound	So.	16	242	15.1
1981	Ron Trammell, Tex. A&M-Commerce	Jr.	29	467	16.1
1982	Darrell Green, Tex. A&M-Kingsville	Sr.	19	392	20.6
1983	Steve Carter, Albany St. (Ga.)	Sr.	27	511	18.9
1984	Michael Fields, Mississippi Col.	Jr.	23	487	21.2
1985	Darryl Skinner, Hampton	Jr.	19	426	22.4
1986	Ben Frazier, Cheyney	So.	14	246	17.6
1987	Ronald Day, Savannah St.	Sr.	12	229	19.1
1988	Donnie Morris, Norfolk St.	Jr.	12	283	23.6
1989	Dennis Mailhot, East Stroudsburg	Jr.	16	284	17.8
1990	Ron West, Pittsburg St.	Jr.	23	388	16.9
1991	Doug Grant, Savannah St.	So.	19	331	17.4
1992	Doug Grant, Savannah St.	Jr.	15	366	24.4
1993	Jerry Garrett, Wayne St. (Neb.)	Jr.	26	498	19.2
1994	Terry Guess, Gardner-Webb	So.	16	312	19.5
1995	Kevin Cannon, Millersville	Sr.	16	277	17.3
1996	Sean Smith, Bloomsburg	Sr.	25	481	19.2
1997	Bootsie Washington, Shepherd	Sr.	19	461	24.3
1998	James Rooths, Shepherd	So.	21	451	21.5
1999	James Rooths, Shepherd	Jr.	15	366	24.4
2000	Rodney Woodruff, Arkansas Tech	Jr.	12	305	25.4
2001	Dexter Daniels, Southeastern Okla.	Jr.	12	235	19.6
2002	Kevin Curtin, Winona St.	Jr.	19	430	22.6

*Record.

Kickoff Returns

CAREER AVERAGE
(Minimum 1.2 Returns Per Game)

Player, Team	Years	No.	Yards	Avg.
Glen Printers, Southern Colo.	1973-74	25	851	*34.0
Karl Evans, Mo. Southern St.	1991-92	32	959	30.0
Kevin Cannon, Millersville	1992-95	67	1,999	29.8
Dave Ludy, Winona St.	1991-94	89	*2,630	29.6
Doug Parrish, San Fran. St.	1990	35	1,002	28.6
Clarence Chapman, Eastern Mich.	1973-75	45	1,278	28.4

Player, Team	Years	No.	Yards	Avg.
Greg Wilson, East Tenn. St.	1975-77	34	952	28.0
Bernie Rose, North Ala.	1974-76	62	1,681	27.1
Roscoe Word, Jackson St.	1970-73	74	1,980	26.8
Ketric Barnes, New Haven	1997-00	60	1,603	26.7

*Record.

SEASON AVERAGE
(Minimum 1.2 Returns Per Game)

Player, Team	Year	No.	Yards	Avg.
D.J. Flick, Slippery Rock	†2000	14	558	*39.9
LaVon Reis, Western St.	†1993	14	552	39.4
Danny Lee, Jacksonville St.	†1992	12	473	39.4
Fran DeFalco, Assumption	1993	12	461	38.4
Brian Sump, Colorado Mines	†2001	21	780	37.1
Kendall James, Carson-Newman	1993	15	549	36.6
Roscoe Word, Jackson St.	†1973	18	650	36.1
Steve Levenseller, Puget Sound	†1978	17	610	35.9
Winston Horshaw, Shippensburg	†1991	15	536	35.7
Boobie Thornton, Midwestern St.	†1997	12	426	35.5
Anthony Rivera, Western St.	1991	18	635	35.3
Dave Ludy, Winona St.	1992	25	881	35.2
R.J. Abercrombie, Calif. (Pa.)	†2002	14	493	35.2
Mike Scullin, Baldwin-Wallace	†1970	14	492	35.1
Billy Cook, Grand Valley St.	†1998	17	597	35.1
Rufus Smith, Eastern N.M.	†1985	11	386	35.1
Rebert Mack, West Tex. A&M	†1996	14	489	34.9
Daray Sims, Abilene Christian	2002	15	520	34.7
Jason Holleman, UC Davis	2001	12	412	34.3
Brian Polk, Slippery Rock	†1999	15	513	34.2
Norman Miller, Tex. A&M-Kingsville	1995	12	405	33.8
Greg Anderson, Montana	†1974	10	335	33.5
Jeremiah Pope, C.W. Post	2000	13	431	33.2
Cash Langeness, Minn. Duluth	2000	21	695	33.1
Kevin Cannon, Millersville	1995	14	463	33.1
Kevin McDevitt, Butler	†1975	12	395	32.9

*Record. †National champion.

ANNUAL CHAMPIONS

Year	Player, Team	Class	No.	Yards	Avg.
1970	Mike Scullin, Baldwin-Wallace	So.	14	492	35.1
1971	Joe Brockmeyer, McDaniel	Jr.	16	500	31.3
1972	Rick Murphy, Indiana St.	Jr.	22	707	32.1
1973	Roscoe Word, Jackson St.	Sr.	18	650	36.1
1974	Greg Anderson, Montana	So.	10	335	33.5
1975	Kevin McDevitt, Butler	Jr.	12	395	32.9
1976	Henry Vereen, UNLV	So.	20	628	31.4
1977	Dickie Johnson, Southern Colo.	Jr.	13	385	29.6
1978	Steve Levenseller, Puget Sound	Sr.	17	610	35.9
1979	Otha Hill, Central St.	Sr.	18	526	29.2
1980	Charlie Taylor, Southeast Mo. St.	Sr.	13	396	30.5
1981	Willie Canady, Fort Valley St.	Jr.	13	415	31.9
1982	Clarence Martin, Cal Poly	So.	11	360	32.7
1983	David Anthony, Southern Ore.	Jr.	14	436	31.1
1984	Larry Winters, St. Paul's	Sr.	20	644	32.2
1985	Rufus Smith, Eastern N.M.	Fr.	11	386	35.1
1986	John Barron, Butler	So.	21	653	31.1
1987	Albert Fann, Cal St. Northridge	Fr.	16	468	29.3
1988	Pierre Fils, New Haven	So.	12	378	31.5
1989	Dennis Mailhot, East Stroudsburg	Jr.	11	359	32.6
1990	Alfred Banks, West Ala.	Sr.	17	529	31.1
1991	Winston Horshaw, Shippensburg	Jr.	15	536	35.7
1992	Danny Lee, Jacksonville St.	Sr.	12	473	39.4
1993	LaVon Reis, Western St.	Sr.	14	552	39.4
1994	Darell Whitaker, Eastern N.M.	Sr.	20	642	32.1
1995	Melvin German, Southwest St.	Sr.	9	413	††45.9
1996	Rebert Mack, West Tex. A&M	Jr.	14	489	34.9
1997	Boobie Thornton, Midwestern St.	Fr.	12	426	35.5
1998	Billy Cook, Grand Valley St.	Sr.	17	597	35.1
1999	Brian Polk, Slippery Rock	Sr.	15	513	34.2
2000	D.J. Flick, Slippery Rock	Jr.	14	558	*39.9
2001	Brian Sump, Colorado Mines	Jr.	21	780	37.1
2002	R.J. Abercrombie, Calif. (Pa.)	Jr.	14	493	35.2

*Record. ††Declared champion; with two more returns (to make 1.2 per game minimum) for zero yards, still would have highest average (37.5).

All-Purpose Yards

CAREER YARDS PER GAME
(Minimum 3,500 Yards)

Player, Team	Years	G	Rush	Rcv.	Int.	PR	KOR	Yds.	Yd. PG
Chris George, Glenville St.	1993-94	20	23	3,215	0	391	1,050	4,679	*234.0
Brian Shay, Emporia St.	1995-98	44	*6,958	1,032	0	104	1,207	*9,301	211.4
Damon Thompson, Virginia St.	1997-00	38	303	4,387	0	1,153	2,143	7,986	210.2
Anthony Gray, Western N.M.	1997-98	19	3,484	499	0	0	8	3,991	210.1
Kavin Gailliard, American Int'l	1996-99	43	6,523	1,049	0	472	814	8,858	206.0
Howard Stevens, Randolph-Macon	1968-69	18	2,574	349	0	380	388	3,691	205.1
Johnny Bailey, Tex. A&M-Kingsville	1986-89	39	6,320	452	0	20	1,011	7,803	200.1
Clarence Coleman, Ferris St.	1998-01	42	49	*4,983	0	*1,494	1,483	8,009	190.7
Steve Roberts, Butler	1986-89	35	4,623	1,201	0	272	578	6,674	190.7
Tyrone Morgan, Northern St.	1998-00	30	4,816	79	0	0	748	5,643	188.1
Billy Johnson, Widener	1971-72	19	2,241	242	43	759	251	3,536	186.1

*Record.

SEASON YARDS PER GAME

Player, Team	Year	G	Rush	Rcv.	Int.	PR	KOR	Yds.	Yd. PG
Steve Roberts, Butler	1989	10	1,450	532	0	272	415	2,669	*266.9
Bobby Felix, Western N.M.	†1994	8	439	853	0	150	667	2,109	263.6
Chris George, Glenville St.	†1993	10	23	*1,876	0	157	562	2,618	261.8
Brian Shay, Emporia St.	†1998	11	2,265	165	0	0	389	2,819	256.3
Kavin Gailliard, American Int'l	†1999	12	*2,653	289	0	0	122	*3,064	255.3
Damon Thompson, Virginia St.	1998	10	127	1,330	0	292	770	2,519	251.9
Billy Johnson, Widener	1972	9	1,556	40	43	511	115	2,265	251.7
Brian Shay, Emporia St.	†1996	11	2,103	247	0	48	340	2,738	248.9
Damon Thompson, Virginia St.	1999	10	88	1,517	0	410	465	2,480	248.0
Brian Shay, Emporia St.	†1997	11	1,912	277	0	56	478	2,723	247.5
Clarence Coleman, Ferris St.	†2001	11	39	1,346	0	572	661	2,618	238.0
Josh Ranek, South Dakota St.	2001	11	1,804	509	0	0	295	2,608	237.1
Kavin Gailliard, American Int'l	1998	11	1,971	270	0	151	196	2,588	235.3
Roger Graham, New Haven	1993	10	1,687	116	0	0	516	2,319	231.9
Anthony Gray, Western N.M.	1997	10	2,220	78	0	0	0	2,298	229.8
Larry Jackson, Edinboro	1994	10	1,660	237	0	0	387	2,284	228.4
Ian Smart, C.W. Post	2001	12	2,536	135	0	0	0	2,671	222.6
Jamel White, South Dakota	1999	11	1,807	640	0	0	0	2,447	222.5
Damon Thompson, Virginia St.	†2000	9	55	1,103	0	273	563	1,994	221.6
Johnny Bailey, Tex. A&M-Kingsville	1986	11	2,011	54	0	20	340	2,425	220.5

*Record. †National champion.

CAREER YARDS

Player, Team	Years	Rush	Rcv.	Int.	PR	KOR	Yds.
Brian Shay, Emporia St.	1995-98	*6,958	1,032	0	104	1,207	*9,301
Kavin Gailliard, American Int'l	1996-99	6,523	1,049	0	472	814	8,858
Clarence Coleman, Ferris St.	1998-01	49	*4,983	0	*1,494	1,483	8,009
Damon Thompson, Virginia St.	1997-00	303	4,387	0	1,153	2,143	7,986
Josh Ranek, South Dakota St.	$1997-01	6,794	857	0	0	295	7,946
Johnny Bailey, Tex. A&M-Kingsville	1986-89	6,320	452	0	20	1,011	7,803
Ian Smart, C.W. Post	1999-02	6,647	293	0	33	383	7,356
Roger Graham, New Haven	1991-94	5,953	393	0	0	870	7,216
Dave Ludy, Winona St.	1991-94	3,501	906	0	34	*2,630	7,071
Albert Fann, Cal St. Northridge	1987-90	4,090	803	0	0	2,141	7,032
Curtis Delgardo, Portland St.	$1986-90	4,178	1,258	0	318	1,188	6,942
Jarrett Anderson, Truman	1993-96	6,166	633	0	0	127	6,926
Damian Beane, Shepherd	1996-99	6,346	416	0	0	0	6,762
Johnny Cox, Fort Lewis	1990-93	112	3,611	0	495	2,476	6,694
Steve Roberts, Butler	1986-89	4,623	1,201	0	272	578	6,674
Richard Huntley, Winston-Salem	1992-95	6,286	333	0	0	0	6,619
Mike Smith, Neb.-Kearney	1994-97	348	2,975	0	932	2,255	6,510
Wesley Cates, Calif. (Pa.)	1998-01	5,647	307	0	19	174	6,147
Chris Cobb, Eastern Ill.	1976-79	5,042	520	0	37	478	6,077
Don Aleksiewicz, Hobart	1969-72	4,525	470	0	320	748	6,063

*Record. $See Page 8 for explanation.

SEASON YARDS

Player, Team	Year	Rush	Rcv.	Int.	PR	KOR	Yds.
Kavin Gailliard, American Int'l	†1999	*2,653	289	0	0	122	*3,064
Brian Shay, Emporia St.	†1998	2,265	165	0	0	389	2,819
Brian Shay, Emporia St.	†1996	2,103	247	0	48	340	2,738
Brian Shay, Emporia St.	†1997	1,912	277	0	56	478	2,723
Ian Smart, C.W. Post	2001	2,536	135	0	0	0	2,671
Steve Roberts, Butler	1989	1,450	532	0	272	415	2,669
Clarence Coleman, Ferris St.	†2001	39	1,346	0	572	661	2,618
Chris George, Glenville St.	†1993	23	*1,876	0	157	562	2,618
Josh Ranek, South Dakota St.	2001	1,804	509	0	0	295	2,608
Kavin Gailliard, American Int'l	1998	1,971	270	0	151	196	2,588
Damon Thompson, Virginia St.	1998	127	1,330	0	292	770	2,519
Damon Thompson, Virginia St.	1999	88	1,517	0	410	465	2,480
Jamel White, South Dakota	1999	1,807	640	0	0	0	2,447
Johnny Bailey, Tex. A&M-Kingsville	1986	2,011	54	0	20	340	2,425
Rick Wegher, South Dakota St.	1984	1,317	264	0	0	824	2,405

Player, Team	Year	Rush	Rcv.	Int.	PR	KOR	Yds.
Steve Papin, Portland St.	†1995	1,619	525	0	1	252	2,397
Ronald Moore, Pittsburg St.	1992	1,864	141	0	0	388	2,393
Roger Graham, New Haven	1993	1,687	116	0	0	516	2,319
Josh Ranek, South Dakota St.	1999	2,055	258	0	0	0	2,313
Jarrett Anderson, Truman	1996	2,140	167	0	0	0	2,307

*Record. †National champion.

ANNUAL CHAMPIONS

Year	Player, Team	Cl.	G	Rush	Rcv.	Int.	PR	KOR	Yds.	Yd. PG
1992	Johnny Cox, Fort Lewis	Jr.	10	95	1,331	0	80	679	2,185	218.5
1993	Chris George, Glenville St.	Jr.	10	23	*1,876	0	157	562	2,618	261.8
1994	Bobby Felix, Western N.M.	Jr.	8	439	853	0	150	667	2,109	263.6
1995	Steve Papin, Portland St.	Sr.	11	1,619	525	0	1	252	2,397	217.9
1996	Brian Shay, Emporia St.	So.	11	2,103	247	0	48	340	2,738	248.9
1997	Brian Shay, Emporia St.	Jr.	11	1,912	277	0	56	478	2,723	247.5
1998	Brian Shay, Emporia St.	Sr.	11	2,265	165	0	0	389	2,819	256.3
1999	Kavin Gailliard, American Int'l.	Sr.	12	*2,653	289	0	0	122	*3,064	255.3
2000	Damon Thompson, Virginia St.	Sr.	9	55	1,103	0	273	563	1,994	221.6
2001	Clarence Coleman, Ferris St.	Sr.	11	39	1,346	0	572	661	2,618	238.0
2002	Kevin Clive, Hillsdale	Sr.	11	1,350	208	0	0	535	2,093	190.3

Field Goals

CAREER FIELD GOALS

Player, Team	Years	Made	Atts.	Pct.
Mike Wood, Southeast Mo. St. (S)	1974-77	*64	*109	.587
Cameron Peterka, North Dakota (S)	1998-01	58	80	.725
Pat Beaty, North Dakota (S)	1985-88	52	82	.634
Ed O'Brien, UCF (S)	1984-87	50	77	.649
Bob Gilbreath, Eastern N.M. (S)	1986-89	50	77	.649
Shane Meyer, Central Mo. St. (S)	1995-98	49	77	.636
Billy Watkins, Tex. A&M-Commerce (S)	1990-93	49	84	.583
Bill May, Clarion (C)	1977-80	48	60	*.800
Ed Detwiler, East Stroudsburg (S)	1989-92	48	87	.552
Steve Huff, Central Mo. St. (C)	1982-85	47	80	.588
Phil Brandt, Central Mo. St. (S)	1987-90	46	66	.697
Scott Doyle, Chadron St. (S)	1992-95	46	69	.667
Howie Guarini, Shippensburg (S)	1988-91	45	62	.726
Eric Myers, West Va. Wesleyan (S)	1993-96	45	67	.672
Mike Schauer, Northern Colo.	1996-99	45	70	.643
Ed Hotz, Southeast Mo. St. (S)	1978-81	45	77	.584
James Knowles, North Ala. (C)	1982-85	45	77	.584
Kurt Seibel, South Dakota (C)	1980-83	44	62	.710
Jason Monday, Lenoir-Rhyne (S)	1989-92	44	64	.688
Matt Pifer, Ashland (S)	1998-01	44	73	.603
Pat Bolton, Montana St. (C)	1972-75	44	76	.579
Skipper Butler, Texas-Arlington (C)	1966-69	44	101	.436

*Record. (C) Conventional kicker. (S) Soccer-style kicker.

SEASON FIELD GOALS

Player, Team	Years	Made	Atts.	Pct.
Henrik Juul-Nielsen, Neb.-Kearney (S)	†2002	**20	24	.833
Jason Williams, Southern Ark. (S)	†1998	**20	24	.833
Pat Beaty, North Dakota (S)	†1988	**20	26	.769
Raul De la Flor, Humboldt St. (S)	†1993	**20	26	.769
Cameron Peterka, North Dakota (S)	†2001	**20	29	.690
Tom Jurich, Northern Ariz. (C)	†1977	**20	29	.690
Dennis Hochman, Sonoma St. (S)	†1986	19	22	+.864
Cory Solberg, North Dakota (S)	†1989	19	27	.704
Paul Czerniak, Tusculum (S)	†2000	19	29	.655
Jaime Nunez, Weber St. (S)	†1971	19	32	.594
Jon Ruff, Indiana (Pa.) (S)	†1995	18	22	.818
Shane Meyer, Central Mo. St. (S)	†1997	18	25	.720
Bernard Henderson, Albany St. (Ga.) (S)	†1985	18	26	.692
Milan Smado, Southeastern Okla. (S)	†1999	17	19	.895
Adam Hicks, South Dakota (S)	2000	17	22	.773
Ki Tok Chu, Tenn.-Martin (S)	1988	17	22	.773
Jack McTyre, Valdosta St. (S)	1990	17	23	.739
Dino Beligrinis, Winston-Salem (S)	1988	17	23	.739
Cameron Peterka, North Dakota (S)	2000	17	24	.708
J.W. Boren, Tarleton St. (S)	2002	17	25	.680
Ed O'Brien, UCF (S)	†1987	17	26	.654
David Dell, Tex. A&M-Commerce (S)	1995	17	26	.654
Mike Swim, Northern Colo. (S)	2002	17	28	.607
Mike Wood, Southeast Mo. St. (S)	1976	17	33	.515

**Record tied. +Record for minimum 20 attempts. (C) Conventional kicker. (S) Soccer-style kicker.

Henrik Juul-Nielsen of Nebraska-Kearney joined a tie for most field goals in a season in Division II, when he made 20 in 2002.

Nebraska-Kearney Sports Information

ANNUAL CHAMPIONS

Year	Player, Team	Class	Made	Atts.	Pct.	PG
1970	Chris Guerrieri, Alfred (S)	Sr.	11	21	.524	1.38
1971	Jaime Nunez, Weber St. (S)	Sr.	19	32	.594	1.90
1972	Randy Walker, Northwestern St. (C)	Jr.	13	19	.684	1.30
1973	Reinhold Struprich, Hawaii (S)	Jr.	15	23	.652	1.36
1974	Mike Wood, Southeast Mo. St. (S)	Fr.	16	23	.696	1.45
1975	Wolfgang Taylor, Western St. (S)	Sr.	14	21	.667	1.56
1976	Rolf Benirschke, UC Davis (S)	Sr.	14	19	.737	1.56
1977	Tom Jurich, Northern Ariz. (C)	Sr.	**20	29	.690	1.81
1978	Frank Friedman, Cal St. Northridge (S)	Jr.	15	22	.682	1.50
1979	Bill May, Clarion (C)	Jr.	16	21	.762	1.60
1980	Nelson McMurain, North Ala. (S)	Jr.	14	22	.636	1.40
	Sean Landeta, Towson (S)	So.	14	28	.500	1.40
1981	Russ Meier, South Dakota St. (S)	Fr.	16	21	.762	1.60
1982	Joey Malone, Alabama A&M (C)	Jr.	15	21	.714	1.36
	Rick Ruszkiewicz, Edinboro (S)	Sr.	15	24	.625	1.36
1983	Mike Thomas, Angelo St. (S)	Sr.	16	22	.727	1.45
1984	Terry Godfrey, South Dakota (S)	Jr.	16	26	.615	1.60
1985	Bernard Henderson, Albany St. (Ga.) (S)	Sr.	18	26	.692	1.64
1986	Dennis Hochman, Sonoma St. (S)	Sr.	19	22+.864		1.90
1987	Ed O'Brien, UCF (S)	Sr.	17	26	.654	1.70
1988	Pat Beaty, North Dakota (S)	Sr.	**20	26	.769	1.82
1989	Cory Solberg, North Dakota (S)	Jr.	19	27	.704	1.73
1990	Jack McTyre, Valdosta St. (S)	Sr.	17	23	.739	1.70
1991	Billy Watkins, Tex. A&M-Commerce (S)	So.	15	24	.625	1.36
1992	Mike Estrella, St. Mary's (Cal.) (S)	Jr.	15	27	.556	1.67

DIVISION II

Year	Player, Team	Class	Made	Atts.	Pct.	PG
1993	Raul De la Flor, Humboldt St. (S)	Sr.	**20	26	.769	1.82
1994	Matt Seagreaves, East Stroudsburg (S)	So.	15	26	.577	1.50
1995	Jon Ruff, Indiana (Pa.) (S)	Sr.	18	23	.783	1.64
1996	Juan Gomez-Tagle, North Dakota (S)	Sr.	15	20	.750	1.50
1997	Shane Meyer, Central Mo. St. (S)	Jr.	18	25	.720	1.64
1998	Jason Williams, Southern Ark. (S)	So.	**20	24	.833	*2.00
1999	Milan Smado, Southeastern Okla. (S)	So.	17	19	.895	1.55
2000	Paul Czerniak, Tusculum (S)	Jr.	19	29	.655	1.73
2001	Cameron Peterka, North Dakota (S)	Sr.	**20	29	.690	1.82
2002	Henrik Juul-Nielsen, Neb.-Kearney (S)	Sr.	**20	24	.833	1.82

*Record. +Record for minimum 20 attempts. (C) Conventional kicker. (S) Soccer-style kicker.

All-Time Longest Plays

Since 1941, official maximum length of all plays fixed at 100 yards.

RUSHING

Rushing plays have covered 99 yards 21 times. The most recent:

Yds.	Player, Team (Opponent)	Year
99	Ronaie Maye, Carson-Newman (Lenoir-Rhyne)	1999
99	Thelbert Withers, N.M. Highlands (Fort Lewis)	1992
99	Lester Frye, Edinboro (Calif. [Pa.])	1991
99	Kelvin Minefee, Southern Utah (Mesa St.)	1988
99	Fred Deutsch, Springfield (Wagner)	1977
99	Sammy Croom, San Diego (Azusa Pacific)	1972
99	John Stenger, Swarthmore (Widener)	1970
99	Jed Knuttila, Hamline (St. Thomas [Minn.])	1968
99	Dave Lanoha, Colorado Col. (Texas Lutheran)	1967
99	Tom Pabst, UC Riverside (Caltech)	1965

PASSING

Pass plays have resulted in 99-yard completions 24 times. The most recent:

Yds.	Passer-Receiver, Team (Opponent)	Year
99	Nate Jackson-Jonny Chan, Colorado Mines (South Dakota Tech)	2002
99	Maurice Hill-James Johnson, Bowie St. (St. Augustine's)	2002

Yds.	Passer-Receiver, Team (Opponent)	Year
99	Tom Guy-Keith Lessner, American Int'l (St. Anselm)	2001
99	Justin Coleman-Mike Smith, Neb.-Kearney (Wayne St. [Neb.])	1997
99	Antonio Hawkins-Jovelle Tillman, Virginia St. (Fayetteville St.)	1997
99	Matt Morris-Casey Cowan, Tex. A&M-Commerce (Midwestern St.)	1997
99	Rod Smith-Scott Hammond, Glenville St. (Concord)	1996
99	Ken Collums-Jerome Davis, Central Ark. (Delta St.)	1994
99	Greg Younger-Marty Walsh, Hillsdale (St. Francis [Ill.])	1994
99	Ray Morrow-Jeff Williamson, Cal St. Hayward (Redlands)	1993
99	Bob McLaughlin-Eric Muldowney, Lock Haven (Mansfield)	1993
99	Rob Rayl-John Unger, Valparaiso (Hillsdale)	1992
99	Bret Comp-Ken Kopetchny, East Stroudsburg (Mansfield)	1990

PUNTS

Yds.	Player, Team (Opponent)	Year
97	Earl Hurst, Emporia St. (Central Mo. St.)	1964
96	Alex Campbell, Morris Brown (Clark Atlanta)	1994
96	Gary Frens, Hope (Olivet)	1966
96	Jim Jarrett, North Dakota (South Dakota)	1957
93	Elliot Mills, Carleton (Monmouth [Ill.])	1970
93	Kaspar Fitins, Taylor (Georgetown [Ky.])	1966
93	Leeroy Sweeney, Pomona-Pitzer (UC Riverside)	1960

FIELD GOALS

Yds.	Player, Team (Opponent)	Year
67	Tom Odle, Fort Hays St. (Washburn)	1988
63	Joe Duren, Arkansas St. (McNeese St.)	1974
62	Doc Proctor, Ferris St. (Michigan Tech)	1999
62	Mike Flater, Colorado Mines (Western St.)	1973
61	Duane Christian, Cameron (Southwestern Okla.)	1976
61	Mike Wood, Southeast Mo. St. (Lincoln [Mo.])	1975
61	Bill Shear, Cortland St. (Hobart)	1966
60	Mike Panasuk, Ferris St. (St. Joseph's [Ind.])	1990
60	Ed Beaulac, Sonoma St. (St. Mary's [Cal.])	1989
60	Roger McCoy, Grand Valley St. (Grand Rapids)	1976
60	Skipper Butler, Texas-Arlington (Tex. A&M-Commerce)	1968

Since 1941, many players have returned interceptions, punts and kickoffs 100 yards.

Team Champions

Annual Offense Champions

TOTAL OFFENSE

Year	Team	Avg.
1948	Hanover	*624.1
1949	Pacific (Cal.)	505.3
1950	West Tex. A&M	465.3
1951	Western Ill.	473.6
1952	Sam Houston St.	448.2
1953	Col. of Idaho	476.3
1954	Col. of Emporia	469.7
1955	Centre	431.0
1956	Florida A&M	475.0
1957	Denison	430.8
1958	Missouri Valley	449.6
1959	Whittier	461.3
1960	Muskingum	456.4
1961	Florida A&M	413.6
1962	Baker	438.4
1963	Col. of Emporia	517.1
1964	San Diego St.	422.6
1965	Long Beach St.	439.5
1966	Weber St.	460.1
1967	San Fran. St.	490.0
1968	Louisiana Tech	459.1
1969	Delaware	488.9
1970	Grambling	457.7
1971	Delaware	515.6
1972	Hobart	457.3
1973	Boise St.	466.5
1974	Boise St.	516.9
1975	Portland St.	472.4
1976	Portland St.	497.5
1977	Portland St.	506.7
1978	Western St.	487.0
1979	Delaware	450.5
1980	Southwest Tex. St.	423.0
1981	Southwest Tex. St.	482.3
1982	Northern Mich.	450.4

Year	Team	Avg.
1983	Central St.	491.1
1984	North Dakota St.	455.3
1985	Truman	471.4
1986	Tex. A&M-Kingsville	542.6
1987	Tex. A&M-Kingsville	486.4
1988	Sacramento St.	486.0
1989	Grand Valley St.	480.8
1990	Chadron St.	479.6
1991	Western St.	549.8
1992	New Haven	587.7
1993	Wayne St. (Neb.)	581.5
1994	West Tex. A&M	571.3
1995	Portland St.	472.0
1996	East Stroudsburg	509.1
1997	Emporia St.	531.5
1998	American Int'l	505.6
1999	Ferris St.	534.5
2000	Valdosta St.	502.4
2001	Grand Valley St.	600.8
2002	Carson-Newman	497.8

*Record.

RUSHING OFFENSE

Year	Team	Avg.
1948	Hanover	400.4
1949	Southern U.	382.9
1950	St. Lawrence	356.1
1951	Western N.M.	379.2
1952	William Jewell	345.0
1953	McPherson	375.9
1954	Col. of Emporia	*404.8
1955	Centre	373.4
1956	Tufts	359.9
1957	Denison	372.1
1958	Huron	353.3
1959	Bemidji St.	326.6
1960	Muskingum	355.2
1961	Huron	313.1
1962	Northern St.	355.3

Year	Team	Avg.
1963	Luther	356.0
1964	Cal St. Los Angeles	325.9
1965	Huron	303.3
1966	Neb.-Kearney	370.1
1967	North Dakota St.	299.6
1968	Delaware	315.8
1969	St. Olaf	369.1
1970	Delaware	385.9
1971	Delaware	371.2
1972	Hobart	380.7
1973	Bethune-Cookman	308.8
1974	Central Mich.	324.6
1975	North Dakota	344.4
1976	Montana St.	287.5
1977	South Carolina St.	321.5
1978	Western St.	320.2
1979	Mississippi Col.	314.5
1980	Minn. Duluth	307.3
1981	Millersville	322.9
1982	Mississippi Col.	297.5
1983	Jamestown	297.7
1984	North Dakota St.	334.7
1985	Saginaw Valley	300.4
1986	Tex. A&M-Kingsville	395.2
1987	Tex. A&M-Kingsville	330.5
1988	North Dakota St.	373.1
1989	Wofford	373.7
1990	North Dakota St.	364.2
1991	Wofford	347.9
1992	Pittsburg St.	353.8
1993	North Ala.	371.5
1994	Minn. St. Moorhead	375.0
1995	Pittsburg St.	318.8
1996	North Dakota St.	325.9
1997	Saginaw Valley	334.8
1998	Saginaw Valley	385.5
1999	Neb.-Omaha	335.2
2000	Carson-Newman	335.7

TEAM CHAMPIONS—ANNUAL OFFENSE CHAMPIONS

Year	Team	Avg.
2001	Gannon	312.9
2002	Carson-Newman	346.4

*Record.

PASSING OFFENSE

Year	Team	Avg.
1948	Hanover	223.8
1949	Baldwin-Wallace	196.9
1950	Northern Ill.	187.0
1951	Central Mich.	213.8
1952	Sam Houston St.	263.0
1953	Southern Conn. St.	193.5
1954	Northern Iowa	206.1
1955	Hamline	210.7
1956	Widener	207.7
1957	Cal Poly Pomona	236.0
1958	Cal Poly Pomona	217.6
1959	Whittier	199.3
1960	Whitworth	213.6
1961	Cal Poly Pomona	244.1
1962	Northern Ill.	285.6
1963	Northern Ill.	349.3
1964	Parsons	301.3
1965	Southern Ore. St.	268.9
1966	San Diego St.	268.1
1967	San Fran. St.	387.0
1968	Louisiana Tech	316.4
1969	Portland St.	308.6
1970	Portland St.	313.8
1971	C.W. Post	262.5
1972	Maryville (Tenn.)	277.8
1973	Lehigh	275.0
1974	Boise St.	334.5
1975	Portland St.	361.7
1976	Portland St.	404.1
1977	Portland St.	378.5
1978	Northern Mich.	242.3
1979	Northern Mich.	284.2
1980	Northern Mich.	269.6
1981	Franklin	306.5
1982	Evansville	313.0
1983	Franklin	358.0
1984	Franklin	334.0
1985	Truman	345.1
1986	West Tex. A&M.	345.5
1987	Evansville	306.6
1988	UCF	292.2
1989	Cal St. Chico	328.8
1990	New Haven	335.4
1991	Western St.	357.4
1992	Gardner-Webb	367.8
1993	C.W. Post	409.0
1994	West Tex. A&M.	*454.5
1995	Norfolk St.	367.4
1996	East Stroudsburg	404.1
1997	Glenville St.	381.9
1998	West Chester	313.8
1999	Neb.-Kearney	338.6
2000	Valdosta St.	377.9
2001	Central Ark.	373.8
2002	Fort Lewis	373.5

*Record.

SCORING OFFENSE

Year	Team	Avg.
1948	Sul Ross St.	43.1
1949	Pacific (Cal.)	50.0
1950	West Tex. A&M	37.2
1951	Western Ill.	42.1
1952	Tex. A&M-Commerce	49.6
1953	Col. of Idaho	42.4
1954	Col. of Emporia	43.2
1955	Central Mich.	36.3
1956	Florida A&M	45.9
1957	Denison	38.6
1958	West Chester	51.4
1959	Florida A&M	42.6
1960	Florida A&M	52.8
1961	Florida A&M	54.7
1962	Florida A&M	42.0
1963	Col. of Emporia	42.4
1964	San Diego St.	42.3
1965	Ottawa	43.2
1966	N.M. Highlands	48.1
1967	Waynesburg	53.7
1968	Doane	52.9
1969	St. Olaf	45.2
1970	Wittenberg	40.0
1971	Michigan Tech	42.4
1972	Fort Valley St.	45.0
1973	Western Ky.	37.7
1974	Boise St.	44.6
1975	Bethune-Cookman	37.9
1976	Northern Mich.	43.0
1977	South Carolina St.	38.4
1978	Western St.	45.2
1979	Delaware	35.5
1980	Minn. Duluth	35.4
1981	Southwest Tex. St.	37.5
1982	Truman	40.0
1983	Central St.	43.6
1984	North Dakota St.	39.0
1985	UC Davis	37.6
1986	Tex. A&M-Kingsville	43.1
1987	UCF	34.5
	West Chester	34.5
1988	North Dakota St.	39.6
	Tex. A&M-Kingsville	39.6
1989	Grand Valley St.	44.5
1990	Indiana (Pa.)	44.2
1991	Western St.	46.1
1992	New Haven	50.5
1993	New Haven	54.7
1994	Hampton	46.4
1995	Tex. A&M-Kingsville	40.1
1996	Clarion	43.5
1997	New Haven	43.3
1998	Northwest Mo. St.	46.4
1999	Ferris St.	47.3
2000	Northwest Mo. St.	48.8
2001	Grand Valley St.	*58.4
2002	Grand Valley St.	46.7

*Record.

Annual Defense Champions

TOTAL DEFENSE

Year	Team	Avg.
1948	Morgan St.	104.4
1949	Southern Conn. St.	95.6
1950	Southern Conn. St.	93.6
1951	Southern Conn. St.	84.3
1952	West Chester	128.4
1953	Shippensburg	81.9
1954	Geneva	106.3
1955	Col. of Emporia	102.0
1956	Tennessee St.	118.9
1957	West Chester	90.2
1958	Rose-Hulman	95.8
1959	Md.-East. Shore	75.3
1960	Md.-East. Shore	104.8
1961	Florida A&M	85.3
1962	John Carroll	*44.4
1963	West Chester	100.8
1964	Morgan St.	126.4
1965	Morgan St.	91.5
1966	Tennessee St.	85.7
1967	Tennessee St.	61.6
1968	Alcorn St.	103.4
1969	Livingstone	148.5
1970	Delaware St.	103.5
1971	Hampden-Sydney	115.6
1972	Wis.-Whitewater	143.8
1973	Livingstone	114.9
1974	Livingstone	120.5
1975	South Carolina St.	100.6
1976	Alcorn St.	108.9
1977	Virginia Union	160.3
1978	East Stroudsburg	153.8
1979	Virginia Union	138.2
1980	Concordia-M'head	191.7
1981	Fort Valley St.	148.3
1982	Jamestown	187.9
1983	Virginia Union	143.7
1984	Virginia St.	180.6
1985	Fort Valley St.	162.2
1986	Virginia Union	163.5
1987	Alabama A&M	167.1
1988	Alabama A&M	175.8
1989	Winston-Salem	185.7
1990	Sonoma St.	218.5
1991	Ashland	195.5
1992	Ashland	211.5
1993	Bentley	188.3
1994	Bentley	195.5
1995	Kentucky St.	205.1
1996	Stonehill	194.0
1997	Livingstone	171.5
1998	Savannah St.	166.3
1999	Northeastern St.	180.6
2000	C.W. Post	195.5
2001	N.C. Central	187.2
2002	C.W. Post	215.5

*Record.

RUSHING DEFENSE

Year	Team	Avg.
1948	Morgan St.	44.8
1949	Hanover	43.5
1950	Lewis & Clark	50.3
1951	Southern Conn. St.	17.1
1952	Tex. A&M-Commerce	48.5
1953	Shippensburg	53.6
1954	Tennessee St.	29.2
1955	Muskingum	52.5
1956	Hillsdale	51.1
1957	West Chester	27.9
1958	Ithaca	48.4
1959	Md.-East. Shore	36.3
1960	West Chester	41.4
1961	Florida A&M	20.1
1962	John Carroll	-1.0
1963	St. John's (Minn.)	12.9
1964	Fort Valley St.	39.7
1965	Morgan St.	15.0
1966	Tennessee St.	13.9
1967	Tennessee St.	*-16.7
1968	Alcorn St.	-8.8
1969	Merchant Marine	16.2
1970	Delaware St.	-4.9
1971	Northern Colo.	27.5
1972	Alcorn St.	49.8
1973	Alcorn St.	45.9
1974	Livingstone	53.0
1975	Alcorn St.	15.9
1976	Alcorn St.	32.5
1977	Virginia Union	63.6
1978	East Stroudsburg	52.2
1979	Virginia Union	41.0
1980	Mo.-Rolla	34.6
1981	Fort Valley St.	46.9
1982	Butler	71.1
1983	Butler	38.2
1984	Norfolk St.	53.8
1985	Norfolk St.	50.9
1986	Central St.	44.5
1987	West Chester	67.2
1988	Cal Poly	56.4
1989	Tex. A&M-Kingsville	60.7
1990	Sonoma St.	58.3
1991	Sonoma St.	63.6
1992	Ashland	64.4
1993	Albany St. (Ga.)	59.1
1994	Hampton	66.0
1995	North Ala.	56.8
1996	Livingstone	66.9
1997	Livingstone	52.8
1998	Savannah St.	48.8
1999	Catawba	53.4
2000	C.W. Post	42.0
2001	C.W. Post	17.6
2002	C.W. Post	43.8

*Record.

PASSING DEFENSE

Year	Team	$Avg.
1948	Ashland	*10.1
1949	Wilmington (Ohio)	39.8
1950	Vermont	34.4
1951	Alfred	52.0
1952	Cortland St.	45.9
1953	Shippensburg	28.3
1954	St. Augustine's	26.5
1955	Ithaca	15.5
1956	West Va. Tech	29.1
1957	Lake Forest	25.0
1958	Coast Guard	25.4

DIVISION II

Year	Team	Avg.
1959	Huron	21.9
1960	Susquehanna	27.3
1961	Westminster (Utah)	24.8
1962	Principia	27.8
1963	Western Caro.	39.3
1964	Mont. St.-Billings	44.1
1965	Minot St.	44.5
1966	Manchester	54.7
1967	Mount Union	61.4
1968	Bridgeport	47.6
1969	Wabash	72.0
1970	Hampden-Sydney	62.9
1971	Western Ky.	57.7
1972	Howard	48.8
1973	East Stroudsburg	37.6
1974	Tennessee St.	52.6
1975	N.C. Central	60.2
1976	Morris Brown	60.8
1977	Delaware St.	64.3
1978	Concordia-M'head	55.8
1979	Kentucky St.	62.3
1980	Norfolk St.	71.5
1981	Bowie St.	75.7
1982	Elizabeth City St.	49.0
1983	Elizabeth City St.	65.0
1984	Virginia St.	80.4
1985	Fort Valley St.	94.5
1986	Virginia Union	84.7
1987	Alabama A&M	72.5
1988	Alabama A&M	84.3
1989	Mo. Southern St.	93.0
1990	Angelo St.	65.4
1991	Carson-Newman	64.9
1992	Tex. A&M-Commerce	61.8
1993	Alabama A&M	71.5
1994	Bentley	55.6
1995	Savannah St.	72.4
1996	N.C. Central	62.1
1997	Kentucky St.	64.4
1998	Central Okla.	72.3
1999	Northeastern St.	59.2
2000	Northeastern St.	70.4
2001	Bowie St.	70.8
2002	Tuskegee	82.0

*Record. $Beginning in 1990, based on pass efficiency ranking instead of yards per game.

SCORING DEFENSE

Year	Team	Avg.
1959	Huron	2.1
1960	Albany St. (Ga.)	*0.0
1961	Florida A&M	2.8
1962	John Carroll	2.9
1963	Massachusetts	1.3
1964	Central (Iowa)	4.8
1965	St. John's (Minn.)	2.2
1966	Morgan St.	3.6
1967	Waynesburg	4.3
1968	Central Conn. St.	4.4
1969	Carthage	6.0
1970	Hampden-Sydney	2.8
1971	Hampden-Sydney	3.4
1972	Ashland	5.6
1973	Virginia Union	3.8
1974	Minn.-Duluth	5.5
1975	South Carolina St.	2.9
1976	South Carolina St.	3.4
1977	Minn. Duluth	7.8
1978	La.-Lafayette	7.1
1979	Virginia Union	6.1
1980	Minn. Duluth	7.6
1981	Minn. St. Moorhead	5.0
1982	Jamestown	5.9
1983	Towson	5.8
1984	Cal Poly	9.0
1985	Fort Valley St.	6.3
1986	North Dakota St.	6.8
1987	Tuskegee	9.1
1988	Alabama A&M	7.5
1989	Jacksonville St.	7.0
1990	Cal Poly	11.3
1991	Butler	7.1
1992	Ferris St.	10.5
1993	Albany St. (Ga.)	8.7

Year	Team	Avg.
1994	Bentley	6.0
1995	North Ala.	10.6
1996	Carson-Newman	10.7
1997	Albany St. (Ga.)	7.3
1998	Central Okla.	7.7
1999	Pittsburg St.	9.5
2000	Catawba	8.3
2001	Catawba	10.9
2002	Morehouse	11.2

*Record.

Other Annual Team Champions

NET PUNTING

Year	Team	Avg.
1992	Fort Lewis	37.9
1993	North Ala.	39.5
1994	Colorado Mines	42.9
1995	New Haven	38.7
1996	Adams St.	40.2
1997	North Ala.	39.5
1998	Adams St.	41.8
1999	Fairmont St.	40.1
2000	Carson-Newman	39.8
2001	South Dakota St.	40.8
2002	Central Wash.	41.1

PUNT RETURNS

Year	Team	Avg.
1992	Savannah St.	21.2
1993	Wayne St. (Neb.)	19.1
1994	Adams St.	16.7
1995	Elizabeth City St.	23.1
1996	Angelo St.	14.7
1997	Gardner-Webb	19.8
1998	Morehouse	19.5
1999	Northwest Mo. St.	18.0
2000	Tuskegee	21.6
2001	West Liberty St.	17.6
2002	Winona St.	19.9

KICKOFF RETURNS

Year	Team	Avg.
1992	Jacksonville St.	34.0
1993	Adams St.	27.5
1994	Western N.M.	31.8
1995	Millersville	26.0
1996	Northern Colo.	27.5
1997	Carson-Newman	30.4
1998	Central Okla.	28.9
1999	Northeastern St.	28.4
2000	Western Wash.	27.1
2001	Chadron St.	27.0
2002	Truman	26.1

TURNOVER MARGIN

Year	Team	Avg.
1992	Hillsdale	2.2
1993	Hillsdale	2.7
1994	Lenoir-Rhyne	2.6
1995	Central Okla.	2.6
1996	Central Okla.	2.3
1997	North Dakota St.	2.0
1998	Presbyterian	2.3
1999	American Int'l	*2.8
2000	American Int'l	2.3
2001	Virginia Union	2.2
2002	Southwestern Okla.	1.6

MOST IMPROVED

Year	Team	From	To	Imp.
1996	St. Joseph's (Ind.)	1-9	9-2	7½
1997	Carson-Newman	2-9	8-3	6
1998	Fort Valley St.	5-6	11-2	5
1999	Mars Hill	1-10	7-4	6
2000	Delta St.	6-4	14-1	5½
	Morehouse	2-8	8-3	5½
	Valdosta St.	4-7	10-2	5½
	Westminster (Pa.)	3-8	8-2	5½
2001	Central Ark.	3-8	9-3	5½
2002	Central Wash.	4-7	11-1	6½

*Record.

Defensive Team Single-Game Records

(Since 2000)

TACKLES FOR LOSS

TFL	Team (Opponent)	Date
25	Adams St. (Okla. Panhandle)	Oct. 13, 2001
22	Fayetteville St. (Elizabeth City St.)	Sept. 14, 2002
22	Gannon (Edinboro)	Aug. 31, 2002
22	Bemidji St. (Minn.-Morris)	Oct. 28, 2000
20	Winona St. (Minn. Duluth)	Nov. 4, 2000
20	Winona St. (Minn.-Crookston)	Oct. 7, 2000
19	Fort Hays St. (Chadron St.)	Nov. 10, 2001
19	Indianapolis (Mercyhurst)	Sept. 30, 2000
18	Presbyterian (Tusculum)	Nov. 4, 2001
17	Quincy (Culver-Stockton)	Oct. 20, 2001

PASS SACKS

Sacks	Team (Opponent)	Date
14	North Dakota (New Haven)	Sept. 21, 2001
11	Gannon (Alma)	Oct. 6, 2001
10	Quincy (Westminster [Mo.])	Oct. 6, 2001
9	Harding (Mo.-Rolla)	Aug. 31, 2002
8	Fort Hays St. (Colorado Mines)	Oct. 5, 2002
8	Merrimack (American Int'l)	Oct. 5, 2002
8	Fayetteville St. (Elizabeth City St.)	Sept. 14, 2002
8	Bloomsburg (Millersville)	Oct. 27, 2001
8	Tusculum (Morehead St.)	Aug. 30, 2001
8	Winona St. (Minn.-Crookston)	Oct. 7, 2000

PASSES DEFENDED
(Pass Interceptions and Pass Break-ups)

PDs	Team (Opponent)	Date
18	Winona St. (Concordia-St. Paul)	Oct. 27, 2001
15	Mercyhurst (Ferris St.)	Oct. 14, 2000
13	Bryant (Mass.-Lowell)	Oct. 26, 2002
13	Lincoln (Mo.) (Langston)	Oct. 20, 2001
13	Indianapolis (Findlay)	Oct. 7, 2000
12	Truman (Mo. Western St.)	Nov. 16, 2002
12	Northwest Mo. St. (Truman)	Oct. 26, 2002
12	Fort Hays St. (Fort Lewis)	Sept. 30, 2002
12	West Ala. (Belhaven)	Aug. 31, 2002
12	Adams St. (Fort Lewis)	Nov. 10, 2001
12	Presbyterian (Tusculum)	Nov. 3, 2001
12	Harding (West Ga.)	Oct. 27, 2001

FORCED FUMBLES

FF	Team (Opponent)	Date
5	Harding (Central Ark.)	Oct. 7, 2000
5	Harding (Tarleton St.)	Sept. 2, 2000
4	Indianapolis (Ashland)	Nov. 2, 2002
4	Winona St. (Concordia-St. Paul)	Nov. 2, 2002
4	Gannon (Robert Morris)	Oct. 26, 2002
4	Indianapolis (Northwood)	Oct. 12, 2002
4	Indiana (Pa.) (Clarion)	Oct. 5, 2002
4	West Ala. (Belhaven)	Aug. 31, 2002
4	Mercyhurst (Findlay)	Nov. 3, 2001
4	Presbyterian (Lenoir-Rhyne)	Oct. 27, 2001
4	Adams St. (Fort Hays St.)	Sept. 15, 2001
4	Fort Hays St. (Colorado Mines)	Sept. 23, 2000
4	Truman (Southwest Baptist)	Sept. 16, 2000

2002 Most-Improved Teams

Team	2001 W-L	2002 W-L	$Games Improved
Central Wash.	4-7	11-1	6½
Findlay	3-8	9-2	6
St. Cloud St.	4-7	9-2	5
Harding	4-6	9-2	4½
Carson-Newman	6-3	12-1	4
Henderson St.	1-10	5-6	4
Northwest Mo. St.	7-4	12-1	4
Southeastern Okla.	3-7	7-3	4
West Ala.	1-10	5-6	4
Abilene Christian	3-8	6-4	3½
Northern Colo.	7-4	12-2	3½
Virginia St.	3-6	7-3	3½

$To determine games improved, add the difference in victories between the two seasons to the difference in losses, then divide by two. Includes postseason games.

All-Time Team Won-Lost Records

Includes records as a senior college only, minimum 20 seasons of competition since 1937. Postseason games are included, and each tie game is computed as half won and half lost.

BY PERCENTAGE (TOP 26)

School	Yrs.	Won	Lost	Tied	Pct.	Total Games
Tex. A&M-Kingsville	74	518	229	16	.689	763
West Chester	74	470	215	17	.682	702
Grand Valley St.	32	226	110	3	.671	339
Indiana (Pa.)	73	436	222	23	.657	681
Pittsburg St.	95	569	299	48	.647	916
Carson-Newman	79	486	261	30	.645	777
Valdosta St.	21	148	83	3	.639	234
Central Okla.	97	548	303	47	.636	898
Neb.-Kearney	79	449	255	27	.633	731
C.W. Post	46	277	168	5	.621	450
Tuskegee	107	550	327	50	.620	927
North Dakota St.	106	552	333	34	.619	919
Minn. Duluth	70	373	226	24	.618	623
Truman	95	500	313	34	.610	847
North Dakota	106	535	337	30	.610	902
Lincoln (Mo.)	27	146	93	6	.608	245
Northern St.	97	486	308	32	.608	826
Fort Valley St.	57	327	208	21	.607	556
Virginia St.	91	464	293	48	.606	805
Angelo St.	39	248	160	7	.606	415
Arkansas Tech	88	472	303	41	.604	816
Virginia Union	102	475	305	47	.603	827
East Stroudsburg	75	386	258	19	.597	663
Hillsdale	110	536	356	46	.596	938
North Ala.	54	325	223	16	.590	564
Slippery Rock	75	390	267	28	.590	685

BY VICTORIES (TOP 25)

School	Yrs.	Won	Lost	Tied	Pct.	Total Games
Pittsburg St.	95	569	299	48	.647	916
North Dakota St.	106	552	333	34	.619	919
Tuskegee	107	550	327	50	.620	927
Central Okla.	97	548	303	47	.636	898
Hillsdale	110	536	356	46	.596	938
North Dakota	106	535	337	30	.610	902
Tex. A&M-Kingsville	74	518	229	16	.689	763
Truman	95	500	313	34	.610	847
Carson-Newman	79	486	261	30	.645	777
Northern St.	97	486	308	32	.608	826
South Dakota St.	105	478	394	38	.546	910
Virginia Union	102	475	305	47	.603	827
Arkansas Tech	88	472	303	41	.604	816
West Chester	74	470	215	17	.682	702
Virginia St.	91	464	293	48	.606	805
Central Ark.	91	458	326	42	.580	826
South Dakota	107	457	441	34	.509	932
Washburn	111	450	510	40	.470	1000
Neb.-Kearney	79	449	255	27	.633	731
Tex. A&M-Commerce	85	444	347	31	.559	822
Presbyterian	90	440	401	35	.522	876
UC Davis	84	437	318	33	.576	788
Indiana (Pa.)	73	436	222	23	.657	681
Central Mo. St.	106	435	456	51	.489	942
Emporia St.	105	429	452	44	.488	925

ALPHABETICAL LISTING
(No Minimum Seasons of Competition)

School	Yrs.	Won	Lost	Tied	Pct.	Total Games
Abilene Christian	81	400	349	32	.533	781
Adams St.	68	289	291	17	.498	597
Albany St. (Ga.)	57	289	235	21	.550	545
American Int'l	66	287	278	20	.508	585
Angelo St.	39	248	160	7	.606	415
Ark.-Monticello	85	323	404	25	.446	752
Arkansas Tech	88	472	303	41	.604	816
Ashland	80	378	312	29	.546	719
Assumption	15	44	99	1	.309	144
Augustana (S.D.)	82	327	385	14	.460	726
Bemidji St.	77	262	367	23	.419	652
Bentley	15	108	40	1	.728	149

School	Yrs.	Won	Lost	Tied	Pct.	Total Games
Bloomsburg	75	329	303	21	.520	653
Bowie St.	31	110	185	6	.375	301
Bryant	4	18	21	0	.462	39
C.W. Post	46	277	168	5	.621	450
UC Davis	84	437	318	33	.576	788
Calif. (Pa.)	73	272	336	19	.449	627
Carson-Newman	79	486	261	30	.645	777
Catawba	83	424	367	26	.535	817
Central Ark.	91	458	326	42	.580	826
Central Mo. St.	106	435	456	51	.489	942
Central Okla.	97	548	303	47	.636	898
Central Wash.	84	394	275	23	.586	692
Chadron St.	88	415	311	15	.570	741
Cheyney	49	86	358	5	.197	449
Clarion	74	347	279	17	.553	643
Clark Atlanta	64	204	323	23	.392	550
Colorado Mines	113	339	496	32	.409	867
Concord	80	337	346	27	.494	710
Concordia-St. Paul	1	9	2	0	.818	11
Delta St.	73	348	334	23	.510	705
East Central	90	409	403	38	.504	850
East Stroudsburg	75	386	258	19	.597	663
Eastern N.M.	59	303	276	15	.523	594
Edinboro	74	282	324	24	.467	630
Elizabeth City St.	61	250	291	18	.463	559
Emporia St.	105	429	452	44	.488	925
Fairmont St.	89	392	319	44	.548	755
Fayetteville St.	57	198	312	26	.394	536
Ferris St.	74	291	321	34	.477	646
Findlay	98	410	331	25	.552	766
Fort Hays St.	81	367	385	49	.489	801
Fort Lewis	40	127	253	3	.336	383
Fort Valley St.	57	327	208	21	.607	556
Gannon	16	71	78	2	.477	151
Glenville St.	90	295	356	37	.456	688
Grand Valley St.	32	226	110	3	.671	339
Harding	49	226	235	16	.491	477
Henderson St.	95	396	386	44	.506	826
Hillsdale	110	536	356	46	.596	938
Humboldt St.	75	331	314	20	.513	665
Indiana (Pa.)	73	436	222	23	.657	681
Indianapolis	65	281	302	23	.483	606
Johnson Smith	75	292	354	34	.454	680
Kentucky St.	74	314	382	26	.453	722
Ky. Wesleyan	42	129	193	16	.405	338
Kutztown	72	253	340	21	.429	614
Lane	79	209	387	26	.357	622
Lenoir-Rhyne	83	411	364	34	.529	809
Lincoln (Mo.)	27	146	93	6	.608	245
Livingstone	54	216	276	15	.441	507
Lock Haven	74	268	390	25	.411	683
Mansfield	73	219	379	30	.373	628
Mars Hill	39	181	204	10	.471	395
Mass.-Lowell	23	89	131	2	.405	222
Mercyhurst	22	106	99	4	.517	209
Merrimack	7	34	33	0	.507	67
Mesa St.	27	159	125	5	.559	289
Michigan Tech	80	285	293	17	.493	595
Midwestern St.	26	121	142	6	.461	269
Miles	33	80	218	7	.274	305
Millersville	71	329	268	21	.549	618
Minn.-Crookston	6	27	35	0	.435	62
Minn. Duluth	70	373	226	24	.618	623
Minn.-Morris	41	168	226	10	.428	404
Minn. St. Mankato	77	334	326	27	.506	687
Minn. St. Moorhead	85	374	321	31	.537	726
Mo.-Rolla	97	349	469	36	.430	854
Mo. Southern St.	35	185	165	7	.528	357
Mo. Western St.	33	167	173	9	.491	349
Morehouse	103	362	394	49	.480	805
Neb.-Kearney	79	449	255	27	.633	731
Neb.-Omaha	86	380	359	30	.514	769
New Haven	30	170	127	5	.571	302
N.M. Highlands	76	275	345	27	.446	647
Newberry	89	333	489	33	.409	855
North Ala.	54	325	223	16	.590	564
N.C. Central	72	362	289	24	.554	675
North Dakota	106	535	337	30	.610	902
North Dakota St.	106	552	333	34	.619	919
Northeastern St.	80	400	309	30	.560	739
Northern Colo.	90	394	352	24	.527	770
Northern Mich.	89	382	287	26	.568	695
Northern St.	97	486	308	32	.608	826

School	Yrs.	Won	Lost	Tied	Pct.	Total Games
Northwest Mo. St.	85	395	370	32	.516	797
Northwood	41	174	199	8	.467	381
Okla. Panhandle	79	278	444	25	.389	747
Ouachita Baptist	96	422	379	42	.526	843
Pace	25	96	141	2	.406	239
Pittsburg St.	95	569	299	48	.647	916
Presbyterian	90	440	401	35	.522	876
Quincy	16	63	90	1	.412	154
Saginaw Valley	28	167	127	3	.567	297
St. Anselm	34	106	93	11	.531	210
St. Cloud St.	81	358	310	23	.535	691
St. Joseph's (Ind.)	83	267	347	24	.437	638
Shepherd	79	359	289	26	.552	674
Shippensburg	73	355	298	21	.542	674
Slippery Rock	75	390	267	28	.590	685
South Dakota	107	457	441	34	.509	932
South Dakota St.	105	478	394	38	.546	910
Southeastern Okla.	91	381	401	44	.488	826
Southern Ark.	83	378	315	27	.544	720
Southern Conn. St.	55	299	210	11	.586	520
Southwest Baptist	20	58	142	2	.292	202
Southwest St.	35	133	217	5	.382	355
Southwestern Okla.	93	412	382	37	.518	831
Stonehill	15	64	73	3	.468	140
Tarleton St.	42	185	239	3	.437	427
Tex. A&M-Commerce	85	444	347	31	.559	822
Tex. A&M-Kingsville	73	518	229	16	.689	763
Tiffin	2	5	16	0	.238	21
Truman	95	500	313	34	.610	847
Tusculum	53	126	226	24	.367	376
Tuskegee	107	550	327	50	.620	927
Valdosta St.	21	148	83	3	.639	234
Virginia St.	91	464	293	48	.606	805
Virginia Union	102	475	305	47	.603	827
Washburn	111	450	510	40	.470	1000
Wayne St. (Mich.)	85	292	404	29	.423	725
Wayne St. (Neb.)	87	342	391	40	.468	773
West Ala.	60	232	337	15	.410	584
West Chester	74	470	215	17	.682	702
West Ga.	24	134	119	0	.530	253
West Liberty St.	76	372	302	35	.549	709
West Tex. A&M	91	397	443	22	.473	862
West Virginia St.	79	285	367	40	.441	692
West Va. Tech	83	281	386	35	.425	702
West Va. Wesleyan	97	361	430	30	.458	821
Western N.M.	66	242	319	15	.433	576
Western Ore.	77	350	286	17	.549	653
Western St.	80	347	340	14	.505	701
Western Wash.	86	346	330	32	.511	708
Wingate	17	71	105	0	.403	176
Winona St.	100	305	413	25	.427	743
Winston-Salem	59	313	242	22	.562	577

School	Won	Lost	Pct.
Central Wash.	20	13	.606
Truman	20	13	.606
Augustana (S.D.)	19	13	.594
Fayetteville St.	19	13	.594
Mars Hill	19	13	.594
Central Ark.	20	14	.588
Emporia St.	19	14	.576
Shippensburg	19	14	.576
Virginia St.	16	12	.571
Harding	18	14	.563
Northeastern St.	18	14	.563
Fairmont St.	16	13	.552
Southern Ark.	17	14	.548
Southwestern Okla.	17	14	.548
Clarion	18	15	.545
Merrimack	16	14	.533
St. Anselm	16	14	.533
Ferris St.	17	15	.531
Kutztown	17	15	.531
South Dakota St.	17	15	.531
Calif. (Pa.)	16	16	.500
Colorado Mines	16	16	.500
Western Ore.	15	15	.500
Northern Mich.	16	17	.485
West Va. Tech	16	17	.485
Western St.	16	17	.485
Albany St. (Ga.)	15	16	.484
Bowie St.	15	16	.484
New Haven	14	15	.483
Ark.-Monticello	15	17	.469
East Central	15	17	.469
Angelo St.	14	16	.467
Indianapolis	15	18	.455
Gannon	13	16	.448
N.C. Central	13	16	.448
Edinboro	14	18	.438
Findlay	14	18	.438
Miles	14	18	.438
St. Cloud St.	14	18	.438
Tex. A&M-Commerce	14	18	.438
Bryant	13	17	.433
Michigan Tech	13	17	.433
Ashland	14	19	.424
Northern St.	14	19	.424
Glenville St.	13	18	.419
Central Okla.	13	19	.406
Fort Hays St.	13	19	.406
South Dakota	13	19	.406
West Va. Wesleyan	12	18	.400
Millersville	12	19	.387

School	Won	Lost	Pct.
Minn. St. Moorhead	12	19	.387
West Chester	12	19	.387
Lincoln (Mo.)	11	18	.379
Pace	11	18	.379
Southeastern Okla.	11	19	.367
Lenoir-Rhyne	11	20	.355
North Ala.	11	20	.355
Minn.-Crookston	11	21	.344
Mo. Southern St.	11	21	.344
Minn. St. Mankato	11	22	.333
Ouachita Baptist	10	20	.333
Southwest Baptist	11	22	.333
Southwest St.	11	22	.333
Washburn	11	22	.333
Abilene Christian	10	21	.323
Wayne St. (Mich.)	10	21	.323
Adams St.	10	22	.313
Kentucky St.	10	22	.313
Lane	10	22	.313
West Virginia St.	10	22	.313
Hillsdale	10	23	.303
Lock Haven	10	23	.303
Wingate	10	23	.303
Wayne St. (Neb.)	9	23	.281
Humboldt St.	9	24	.273
Newberry	9	24	.273
West Ala.	9	24	.273
Mercyhurst	8	23	.258
St. Joseph's (Ind.)	8	23	.258
Stonehill	8	24	.250
Assumption	8	25	.242
Fort Lewis	8	25	.242
Johnson Smith	7	22	.241
Western N.M.	7	22	.241
Clark Atlanta	7	24	.226
Quincy	7	24	.226
N.M. Highlands	7	25	.219
Henderson St.	7	26	.212
West Tex. A&M	7	26	.212
Livingstone	6	23	.207
Mansfield	6	24	.200
Tiffin	2	8	.200
Ky. Wesleyan	6	25	.194
Mass.-Lowell	6	25	.194
Concord	6	26	.188
Elizabeth City St.	5	24	.172
Mo.-Rolla	4	29	.121
Okla. Panhandle	3	29	.094
Cheyney	2	29	.065
Minn.-Morris	0	33	.000

Records in the 2000s

(2000-01-02, Included Playoffs)

BY PERCENTAGE

School	Won	Lost	Pct.
Tuskegee	31	2	.939
Valdosta St.	36	4	.900
C.W. Post	30	4	.882
Grand Valley St.	34	5	.872
Catawba	30	6	.833
Northwest Mo. St.	30	6	.833
Concordia-St. Paul	9	2	.818
UC Davis	31	7	.816
Carson-Newman	26	6	.813
Chadron St.	26	6	.813
Bloomsburg	29	7	.806
Indiana (Pa.)	27	7	.794
Minn. Duluth	27	7	.794
Saginaw Valley	29	8	.784
Pittsburg St.	28	8	.778
Neb.-Kearney	24	7	.774
Central Mo. St.	26	8	.765
Winona St.	26	8	.765
Shepherd	22	8	.733
North Dakota	27	10	.730
Presbyterian	23	9	.719
Neb.-Omaha	25	10	.714
Tarleton St.	25	10	.714

School	Won	Lost	Pct.
Virginia Union	22	9	.710
Bentley	24	10	.706
Delta St.	25	11	.694
Morehouse	22	10	.688
Tusculum	22	10	.688
East Stroudsburg	21	10	.677
Western Wash.	21	10	.677
American Int'l	22	11	.667
Bemidji St.	22	11	.667
Fort Valley St.	22	11	.667
Mo. Western St.	22	11	.667
Tex. A&M-Kingsville	23	12	.657
Midwestern St.	21	11	.656
Slippery Rock	21	11	.656
Winston-Salem	21	11	.656
Eastern N.M.	20	11	.645
Northern Colo.	23	13	.639
Mesa St.	22	13	.629
Northwood	20	12	.625
North Dakota St.	21	13	.618
West Ga.	21	13	.618
Arkansas Tech	19	12	.613
Southern Conn. St.	19	12	.613
West Liberty St.	19	12	.613

BY VICTORIES

School	Wins
Valdosta St.	36
Grand Valley St.	34
Tuskegee	31
UC Davis	31
C.W. Post	30
Catawba	30
Northwest Mo. St.	30
Bloomsburg	29
Saginaw Valley	29
Pittsburg St.	28
Indiana (Pa.)	27
Minn. Duluth	27
North Dakota	27
Carson-Newman	26
Central Mo. St.	26
Chadron St.	26
Winona St.	26
Delta St.	25
Neb.-Omaha	25
Tarleton St.	25
Bentley	24
Neb.-Kearney	24
Northern Colo.	23
Presbyterian	23
Tex. A&M-Kingsville	23
American Int'l	22
Bemidji St.	22
Fort Valley St.	22
Mesa St.	22

School	Wins
Mo. Western St.	22
Morehouse	22
Shepherd	22
Tusculum	22
Virginia Union	22
East Stroudsburg	21
Midwestern St.	21
North Dakota St.	21
Slippery Rock	21
West Ga.	21
Western Wash.	21
Winston-Salem	21
Central Ark.	20
Central Wash.	20
Eastern N.M.	20
Northwood	20
Truman	20
Arkansas Tech	19
Augustana (S.D.)	19
Emporia St.	19
Fayetteville St.	19
Mars Hill	19
Shippensburg	19
Southern Conn. St.	19
West Liberty St.	19
Clarion	19
Harding	18
Northeastern St.	18
Ferris St.	17

School	Wins
Kutztown	17
South Dakota St.	17
Southern Ark.	17
Southwestern Okla.	17
Calif. (Pa.)	16
Colorado Mines	16
Fairmont St.	16
Merrimack	16
Northern Mich.	16
St. Anselm	16
Virginia St.	16
West Va. Tech	16
Western St.	16
Albany St. (Ga.)	15
Ark.-Monticello	15
Bowie St.	15
East Central	15
Indianapolis	15
Western Ore.	15
Angelo St.	14
Ashland	14
Edinboro	14
Findlay	14
Miles	14
New Haven	14
Northern St.	14
St. Cloud St.	14
Tex. A&M-Commerce	14
Bryant	13
Central Okla.	13
Fort Hays St.	13
Gannon	13
Glenville St.	13
Michigan Tech	13
N.C. Central	13
South Dakota	13
Millersville	12
Minn. St. Moorhead	12
West Chester	12
West Va. Wesleyan	12
Lenoir-Rhyne	11
Lincoln (Mo.)	11
Minn.-Crookston	11
Minn. St. Mankato	11
Mo. Southern St.	11

School	Wins
North Ala.	11
Pace	11
Southeastern Okla.	11
Southwest Baptist	11
Southwest St.	11
Washburn	11
Abilene Christian	10
Adams St.	10
Hillsdale	10
Kentucky St.	10
Lane	10
Lock Haven	10
Ouachita Baptist	10
Wayne St. (Mich.)	10
West Virginia St.	10
Wingate	10
Concordia-St. Paul	9
Humboldt St.	9
Newberry	9
Wayne St. (Neb.)	9
West Ala.	9
Assumption	8
Fort Lewis	8
Mercyhurst	8
St. Joseph's (Ind.)	8
Stonehill	8
Clark Atlanta	7
Henderson St.	7
Johnson Smith	7
N.M. Highlands	7
Quincy	7
West Tex. A&M	7
Western N.M.	7
Concord	6
Ky. Wesleyan	6
Livingstone	6
Mansfield	6
Mass.-Lowell	6
Elizabeth City St.	5
Tiffin	5
Mo.-Rolla	4
Okla. Panhandle	3
Cheyney	2
Minn.-Morris	0

School	Years*	Won	Lost	Tied	Pct.
#Butler	3	22	9	1	.703
#Southeast Mo. St.	1	7	3	0	.700
Central Wash.	2	15	7	0	.682
#Hampton	5	38	18	1	.675
#Jacksonville St.	5	40	19	1	.675
#Wofford	5	36	20	1	.640
#Sacramento St.	3	19	11	0	.633
#Troy St.	3	20	12	0	.625

*Years of NCAA Division II active membership. #No longer Division II member. Records include postseason.

BY VICTORIES

School	Years*	Won	Lost	Tied	Pct.
Pittsburg St.	10	103	18	2	.846
Indiana (Pa.)	10	94	26	1	.781
Northern Colo.	10	92	31	0	.748
Carson-Newman	9	91	18	1	.832
North Dakota St.	10	88	27	0	.765
North Ala.	10	87	31	1	.735
Tex. A&M-Kingsville	10	85	34	0	.714
UC Davis	10	81	31	2	.719
North Dakota	10	81	27	1	.748
Grand Valley St.	10	80	31	2	.717
Albany St. (Ga.)	10	79	30	1	.723
New Haven	10	79	31	1	.716
Ferris St.	10	78	34	3	.691
Chadron St.	10	77	31	1	.711
Slippery Rock	10	77	35	1	.686
Northwest Mo. St.	10	74	47	1	.611
Millersville	10	73	28	2	.718
Central Okla.	10	72	35	1	.671
Western St.	10	72	36	1	.665
Shepherd	10	71	34	1	.675
Ashland	10	68	37	1	.646
Angelo St.	10	66	36	2	.644
Saginaw Valley	10	66	40	0	.623
Truman	10	66	44	0	.600
West Chester	10	66	41	1	.616
West Ga.	10	66	43	0	.606
Valdosta St.	10	66	43	2	.604

*Years of NCAA Division II active membership. Records include postseason.

Winningest Teams of the 1990s

BY PERCENTAGE
Minimum seven years in Division II

School	Years*	Won	Lost	Tied	Pct.
Pittsburg St.	10	103	18	2	.846
Carson-Newman	9	91	18	1	.832
Indiana (Pa.)	10	94	26	1	.781
Bentley	7	56	17	0	.767
North Dakota St.	10	88	27	0	.765
Northern Colo.	10	92	31	0	.748
North Dakota	10	81	27	1	.748
North Ala.	10	87	31	1	.735
Albany St. (Ga.)	10	79	30	1	.723
UC Davis	10	81	31	2	.719
Millersville	10	73	28	2	.718
Grand Valley St.	10	80	31	2	.717
New Haven	10	79	31	1	.716
Tex. A&M-Kingsville	10	85	34	0	.714
Chadron St.	10	77	31	1	.711
C. W. Post	7	50	22	0	.694
Ferris St.	10	78	34	3	.691
Slippery Rock	10	77	35	1	.686
Shepherd	10	71	34	1	.675
Central Okla.	10	72	35	1	.671
Glenville St.	7	52	26	0	.667
Western St.	10	72	36	1	.665
Ashland	10	68	37	1	.646
Angelo St.	10	66	36	2	.644
Saginaw Valley	10	66	40	0	.623

Fewer than seven years in Division II and still active

School	Years*	Won	Lost	Tied	Pct.
Southern Ark.	3	25	6	0	.806
Northeastern St.	2	18	6	0	.750
#Albany (N.Y.)	4	31	12	0	.721

Records in the Last Five Years

(1998-99-2000-01-02; Playoffs Included)

BY PERCENTAGE

School	Won	Lost	Pct.
Northwest Mo. St.	59	7	.894
Tuskegee	50	7	.877
C.W. Post	46	8	.852
Carson-Newman	51	9	.850
UC Davis	51	11	.823
Concordia-St. Paul	9	2	.818
Catawba	47	12	.797
Grand Valley St.	48	13	.787
Indiana (Pa.)	46	13	.780
Chadron St.	42	12	.778
Pittsburg St.	45	13	.776
Shepherd	41	12	.774
Winona St.	42	14	.750
North Dakota	44	15	.746
Fort Valley St.	43	15	.741
Slippery Rock	43	15	.741
Central Mo. St.	41	15	.732
Virginia Union	38	14	.731
Northern Colo.	45	17	.726
Valdosta St.	45	17	.726
Saginaw Valley	42	16	.724
Bloomsburg	41	17	.707
Neb.-Omaha	41	17	.707
Neb.-Kearney	36	15	.706
Presbyterian	38	16	.704
American Int'l	39	17	.696
Delta St.	39	18	.684
West Ga.	39	18	.684
Eastern N.M.	36	17	.679
Northwood	35	17	.673
Bemidji St.	36	18	.667
Southern Conn. St.	34	17	.667
North Dakota St.	37	19	.661

School	Won	Lost	Pct.
Bentley	36	19	.655
Western Wash.	34	18	.654
Tex. A&M-Kingsville	39	21	.650
Southern Ark.	33	18	.647
Northeastern St.	36	20	.643
Winston-Salem	34	19	.642
Arkansas Tech	33	20	.623
Mo. Western St.	34	21	.618
Shippensburg	34	21	.618
Minn. Duluth	34	22	.607
Emporia St.	33	22	.600
Albany St. (Ga.)	31	21	.596
Fairmont St.	29	20	.592
Central Okla.	33	23	.589
Central Wash.	31	22	.585
Mesa St.	33	24	.579
Tarleton St.	33	24	.579
South Dakota St.	31	23	.574
West Liberty St.	29	22	.569
Harding	30	23	.566
Northern St.	31	24	.564
Indianapolis	30	24	.556
Ferris St.	29	24	.547
Millersville	29	24	.547
Truman	30	25	.545
Central Ark.	29	25	.537
Tusculum	29	25	.537
Bowie St.	26	23	.531
Merrimack	26	23	.531
Angelo St.	27	24	.529
Ashland	28	25	.528
Virginia St.	25	23	.521
Augustana (S.D.)	28	26	.519

School	Won	Lost	Pct.
East Stroudsburg	27	25	.519
Northern Mich.	28	26	.519
West Chester	27	25	.519
Western St.	28	26	.519
St. Anselm	20	19	.513
Kutztown	26	26	.500
Mars Hill	27	27	.500
Midwestern St.	27	27	.500
New Haven	24	25	.490
Western Ore.	24	25	.490
Fayetteville St.	25	28	.472
Calif. (Pa.)	25	29	.463
Bryant	18	21	.462
North Ala.	24	28	.462
Michigan Tech	23	27	.460
Glenville St.	24	29	.453
Morehouse	24	29	.453
Southeastern Okla.	23	28	.451
N.C. Central	22	27	.449
Clarion	24	30	.444
Pace	21	27	.438
Southwestern Okla.	22	29	.431
Minn. St. Moorhead	22	30	.423
N.M. Highlands	22	32	.407
Miles	21	31	.404
Edinboro	21	33	.389
Fort Hays St.	21	33	.389
Tex. A&M-Commerce	21	33	.389
Colorado Mines	20	32	.385
East Central	20	32	.385
Minn.-Crookston	20	32	.385
Hillsdale	21	34	.382
Washburn	21	34	.382
Findlay	16	26	.381
Lincoln (Mo.)	11	18	.379
Kentucky St.	20	34	.370
St. Cloud St.	20	34	.370
South Dakota	20	34	.370
Southwest St.	20	34	.370
Minn. St. Mankato	20	35	.364
Newberry	20	35	.364
West Va. Wesleyan	18	32	.360
Mo. Southern St.	19	34	.358
St. Joseph's (Ind.)	19	34	.358
Abilene Christian	18	33	.353
Mercyhurst	18	33	.353
Ark.-Monticello	19	35	.352
Gannon	17	32	.347
Adams St.	18	34	.346
Lenoir-Rhyne	18	35	.340
West Virginia St.	18	35	.340
Livingstone	17	34	.333
West Tex. A&M	18	37	.327
Wingate	18	37	.327
Ouachita Baptist	16	34	.320
West Va. Tech	17	38	.309
Lane	16	36	.308
Johnson Smith	15	35	.300
Humboldt St.	16	38	.296

School	Won	Lost	Pct.
Ky. Wesleyan	15	36	.294
Lock Haven	16	39	.291
Southwest Baptist	16	39	.291
Concord	15	39	.278
Western N.M.	13	34	.277
Quincy	14	38	.269
Clark Atlanta	13	38	.255
Wayne St. (Neb.)	13	41	.241
West Ala.	13	41	.241
Wayne St. (Mich.)	12	41	.226
Assumption	11	40	.216
Mass.-Lowell	11	40	.216
Henderson St.	11	44	.200
Tiffin	2	8	.200
Stonehill	10	42	.192
Fort Lewis	10	44	.185
Elizabeth City St.	8	43	.157
Mansfield	7	44	.137
Okla. Panhandle	4	37	.098
Cheyney	4	49	.075
Mo.-Rolla	4	51	.073
Minn.-Morris	1	53	.019

BY VICTORIES

School	Wins
Northwest Mo. St.	59
UC Davis	51
Carson-Newman	51
Tuskegee	50
Grand Valley St.	48
Catawba	47
C.W. Post	46
Indiana (Pa.)	46
Northern Colo.	45
Pittsburg St.	45
Valdosta St.	45
North Dakota	44
Fort Valley St.	43
Slippery Rock	43
Chadron St.	42
Saginaw Valley	42
Winona St.	42
Bloomsburg	41
Central Mo. St.	41
Neb.-Omaha	41
Shepherd	41
American Int'l	39
Delta St.	39
Tex. A&M-Kingsville	39
West Ga.	39
Presbyterian	38
Virginia Union	38
North Dakota St.	37
Bemidji St.	36
Bentley	36
Eastern N.M.	36
Neb.-Kearney	36
Northeastern St.	36

School	Wins
Northwood	35
Minn. Duluth	34
Mo. Western St.	34
Shippensburg	34
Southern Conn. St.	34
Western Wash.	34
Winston-Salem	34
Arkansas Tech	33
Central Okla.	33
Emporia St.	33
Mesa St.	33
Southern Ark.	33
Tarleton St.	33
Albany St. (Ga.)	31
Central Wash.	31
Northern St.	31
South Dakota St.	31
Harding	30
Indianapolis	30
Truman	30
Central Ark.	29
Fairmont St.	29
Ferris St.	29
Millersville	29
Tusculum	29
West Liberty St.	29
Ashland	28
Augustana (S.D.)	28
Northern Mich.	28
Western St.	28
Angelo St.	27
East Stroudsburg	27
Mars Hill	27
Midwestern St.	27
West Chester	27
Bowie St.	26
Kutztown	26
Merrimack	26
Calif. (Pa.)	25
Fayetteville St.	25
Virginia St.	25
Clarion	24
Glenville St.	24
Morehouse	24
New Haven	24
North Ala.	24
Western Ore.	24
Michigan Tech	23
Southeastern Okla.	23
Minn. St. Moorhead	22
N.M. Highlands	22
N.C. Central	22
Southwestern Okla.	22
Edinboro	21
Fort Hays St.	21
Hillsdale	21
Miles	21

School	Wins
Pace	21
Tex. A&M-Commerce	21
Washburn	21
Colorado Mines	20
East Central	20
Kentucky St.	20
Minn.-Crookston	20
Minn. St. Mankato	20
Newberry	20
St. Anselm	20
St. Cloud St.	20
South Dakota	20
Southwest St.	20
Ark.-Monticello	19
Mo. Southern St.	19
St. Joseph's (Ind.)	19
Abilene Christian	18
Adams St.	18
Bryant	18
Lenoir-Rhyne	18
Mercyhurst	18
West Tex. A&M	18
West Virginia St.	18
West Va. Wesleyan	18
Wingate	18
Gannon	17
Livingstone	17
West Va. Tech	17
Findlay	16
Humboldt St.	16
Lane	16
Lock Haven	16
Ouachita Baptist	16
Southwest Baptist	16
Concord	15
Johnson Smith	15
Ky. Wesleyan	15
Quincy	14
Clark Atlanta	13
Wayne St. (Neb.)	13
West Ala.	13
Western N.M.	13
Wayne St. (Mich.)	12
Assumption	11
Henderson St.	11
Lincoln (Mo.)	11
Mass.-Lowell	11
Fort Lewis	10
Stonehill	10
Concordia-St. Paul	9
Elizabeth City St.	8
Mansfield	7
Cheyney	4
Mo.-Rolla	4
Okla. Panhandle	4
Tiffin	2
Minn.-Morris	1

National Poll Rankings

Wire Service National Champions

(1958-74)
(For what was then known as College Division teams. Selections by United Press International from 1958 and Associated Press from 1960.)

Year	Team	Coach	Record*
1958	Southern Miss.	Thad "Pie" Vann	9-0-0
1959	Bowling Green	Doyt Perry	9-0-0
1960	Ohio	Bill Hess	10-0-0
1961	Pittsburg St.	Carnie Smith	9-0-0
1962	Southern Miss. (UPI)	Thad "Pie" Vann	9-1-0
	Florida A&M (AP)	Jake Gaither	9-0-0
1963	Delaware (UPI)	Dave Nelson	8-0-0
	Northern Ill. (AP)	Howard Fletcher	9-0-0
1964	Cal St. Los Angeles (UPI)	Homer Beatty	9-0-0
	Wittenberg (AP)	Bill Edwards	8-0-0
1965	North Dakota. St.	Darrell Mudra	10-0-0
1966	San Diego St.	Don Coryell	10-0-0
1967	San Diego St.	Don Coryell	9-1-0
1968	San Diego St. (UPI)	Don Coryell	9-0-1
	North Dakota St. (AP)	Ron Erhardt	9-0-0
1969	North Dakota St.	Ron Erhardt	9-0-0
1970	Arkansas St.	Bennie Ellender	10-0-0
1971	Delaware	"Tubby" Raymond	9-1-0
1972	Delaware	"Tubby" Raymond	10-0-0
1973	Tennessee St.	John Merritt	10-0-0
1974	Louisiana Tech (UPI)	Maxie Lambright	10-0-0
	Central Mich. (AP)	Roy Kramer	9-1-0

Regular season.

Final Poll Leaders

(Released Before division championship playoffs until 2002. Beginning in 2002, the final poll leaders were released after the championship playoffs.)

Year	Team (Record*)	Coach	Record in Championship†
1975	North Dakota (9-0)	Jerry Olson	0-1 Lost in first round
1976	Northern Mich. (10-0)	Gil Krueger	1-1 Lost in semifinals
1977	North Dakota St. (8-1-1)	Jim Wacker	1-1 Lost in semifinals
1978	Winston-Salem (10-0)	Bill Hayes	Did not compete
1979	Delaware (9-1)	"Tubby" Raymond	3-0 Champion
1980	Eastern Ill. (8-2)	Darrell Mudra	2-1 Runner-up
1981	Southwest Tex. St. (9-0)	Jim Wacker	3-0 Champion
1982	Southwest Tex. St. (11-0)	Jim Wacker	3-0 Champion
1983	UC Davis (9-0)	Jim Sochor	1-1 Lost in semifinals
1984	North Dakota St. (9-1)	Don Morton	2-1 Runner-up
1985	UC Davis (9-1)	Jim Sochor	0-1 Lost in first round
1986	North Dakota St. (10-0)	Earle Solomonson	3-0 Champion
1987	Tex. A&M-Kingsville (9-1)	Ron Harms	Did not compete
1988	North Dakota St. (10-0)	Rocky Hager	4-0 Champion
1989	Tex. A&M-Kingsville (10-0)	Ron Harms	0-1 Lost in first round
1990	North Dakota St. (10-0)	Rocky Hager	4-0 Champion
1991	Indiana (Pa.) (10-0)	Frank Cignetti	2-1 Lost in semifinals
1992	Pittsburg St. (11-0)	Chuck Broyles	3-1 Runner-up
1993	North Ala. (10-0)	Bobby Wallace	4-0 Champion
1994	North Ala. (8-1)	Bobby Wallace	4-0 Champion
1995	North Ala. (9-0)	Bobby Wallace	4-0 Champion
1996	Tex. A&M-Kingsville (7-2)	Ron Harms	0-1 Lost in first round
1997	Carson-Newman (9-0)	Ken Sparks	2-1 Lost in semifinals
1998	Central Okla. (10-0)	Gary Howard	1-1 Lost in quarterfinals
1999	Carson-Newman (10-0)	Ken Sparks	3-1 Runner-up
2000	Northwest Mo. St. (10-0)	Mel Tjeerdsma	0-1 Lost in first round
2001	Valdosta St. (11-0)	Chris Hatcher	1-1 Lost in quarterfinals
2002	Grand Valley St. (14-0)	Brian Kelly	4-0 Champion

Final poll record; in some cases, a team had one game remaining before the championship playoffs. Beginning in 2002, the final record reflects the results of the championship playoffs. †Number of teams in the championship: 8 (1975-87); 16 (1988-present).

Weekly Poll Leaders

Poll conducted by the NCAA Division II Football Committee through 1999. The American Football Coaches Association supplied weekly poll beginning in 2000. Information for 1982-96 researched and submitted by Jeff Hodges, SID, University of North Alabama. Information on missing weekly polls should be submitted to NCAA Statistics Service.

1982
9-30 .... Southwest Tex. St.
Final .... Southwest Tex. St.

1983
9-26 .... Southwest Tex. St.
10-10 .... Southwest Tex. St.
10-24 .... Mississippi Col.
10-31 .... UC Davis
11-7 .... UC Davis
Final .... UC Davis

1984
9-17 .... Troy St.
9-24 .... Central St.
10-8 .... Central St.
10-15 .... Central St.
10-29 .... North Dakota St.
Final .... North Dakota St.

1985
9-23 .... South Dakota
9-30 .... South Dakota
10-14 .... South Dakota
10-21 .... Central St.
10-28 .... Central St.
11-11 .... UC Davis
11-18 .... UC Davis
Final .... UC Davis

1986
9-15 .... North Dakota St.
9-22 .... North Dakota St.
9-29 .... North Dakota St.
10-6 .... North Dakota St.
10-13 .... North Dakota St.
10-20 .... North Dakota St.
10-27 .... North Dakota St.
11-3 .... North Dakota St.
11-10 .... North Dakota St.
Final .... North Dakota St.

1987
9-15 .... South Dakota
9-29 .... South Dakota
10-5 .... South Dakota
10-19 .... Northern Mich.
10-26 .... Northern Mich.
11-8 .... Tex. A&M-Kingsville
Final .... Tex. A&M-Kingsville

1988
Pre .... Troy St.
9-12 .... Troy St.
9-19 .... North Dakota St.
9-26 .... North Dakota St.
10-3 .... North Dakota St.
10-10 .... North Dakota St.
10-17 .... North Dakota St.
10-24 .... North Dakota St.
10-31 .... North Dakota St.
Final .... North Dakota St.

1989
Pre .... North Dakota St.
9-11 .... North Dakota St.
9-18 .... North Dakota St.
9-25 .... North Dakota St.
10-2 .... North Dakota St.
10-9 .... North Dakota St.
10-16 .... North Dakota St.
10-23 .... Tex. A&M-Kingsville
10-30 .... Tex. A&M-Kingsville
11-6 .... Tex. A&M-Kingsville

1990
9-17 .... North Dakota St.
9-24 .... North Dakota St.
10-1 .... North Dakota St.
10-8 .... North Dakota St.
10-15 .... North Dakota St.
10-22 .... North Dakota St.
10-29 .... North Dakota St.
Final .... North Dakota St.

1991
Pre .... North Dakota St.
9-16 .... Indiana (Pa.)
9-23 .... Indiana (Pa.)
9-30 .... Indiana (Pa.)
10-7 .... Indiana (Pa.)
10-14 .... Indiana (Pa.)
10-21 .... Indiana (Pa.)
10-28 .... Indiana (Pa.)
11-4 .... Indiana (Pa.)
Final .... Indiana (Pa.)

1992
Pre .... Pittsburg St.
9-14 .... Pittsburg St.
9-21 .... Pittsburg St.
9-28 .... Pittsburg St.
10-5 .... Pittsburg St.
10-12 .... Pittsburg St.
10-19 .... Pittsburg St.
10-26 .... Pittsburg St.
11-2 .... Pittsburg St.
Final .... Pittsburg St.

1993
Pre .... North Dakota St.
9-20 .... North Dakota St.
9-27 .... North Dakota St.
10-4 .... North Dakota St.
10-11 .... North Ala.
10-18 .... North Ala.
10-25 .... North Ala.
11-1 .... North Ala.
11-8 .... North Ala.
Final .... North Ala.

1994
Pre .... North Ala.
9-12 .... North Ala.
9-19 .... North Ala.
9-26 .... North Ala.
10-3 .... North Ala.
10-10 .... North Ala.
10-17 .... North Ala.
10-24 .... North Ala.
10-31 .... North Ala.
Final .... North Ala.

1995
Pre .... North Ala.
9-11 .... North Ala.
9-18 .... North Ala.
9-25 .... North Ala.

DIVISION II

10-2 ....North Ala.	10-6 ....Carson-Newman	10-18 ....Carson-Newman	10-2 ....Delta St.
10-9 ....North Ala.	10-13 ....Carson-Newman	10-25 ....Carson-Newman	10-9 ....Valdosta St.
10-16 ....North Ala.	10-20 ....Carson-Newman	11-1 ....Carson-Newman	10-16 ....Valdosta St.
10-23 ....North Ala.	10-27 ....Carson-Newman	Final ....Carson-Newman	10-23 ....Valdosta St.
10-30 ....North Ala.	11-3 ....Carson-Newman		10-30 ....Valdosta St.
Final ....North Ala.	11-10 ....Carson-Newman	**2000**	11-6 ....Valdosta St.
	Final ....Carson-Newman	Pre ....Northwest Mo. St.	11-13 ....Valdosta St.
1996		9-5 ....Northwest Mo. St.	Final ....North Dakota
Pre ....North Ala.	**1998**	9-12 ....Northwest Mo. St.	
9-9 ....Ferris St.	Pre ....Northern Colo.	9-19 ....Northwest Mo. St.	**2002**
9-16 ....Ferris St.	9-21 ....Northern Colo.	9-26 ....Northwest Mo. St.	Pre ....Grand Valley St.
9-23 ....North Dakota St.	9-28 ....Northern Colo.	10-3 ....Northwest Mo. St.	9-3 ....Grand Valley St.
9-30 ....Carson-Newman	10-5 ....Northern Colo.	10-10 ....Northwest Mo. St.	9-10 ....Grand Valley St.
10-7 ....Indiana (Pa.)	10-12 ....Northern Colo.	10-17 ....Northwest Mo. St.	9-17 ....Grand Valley St.
10-14 ....Indiana (Pa.)	10-19 ....Northern Colo.	10-24 ....Northwest Mo. St.	9-24 ....Grand Valley St.
10-21 ....Valdosta St.	10-26 ....Central Okla.	10-31 ....Northwest Mo. St.	10-1 ....Grand Valley St.
10-28 ....Valdosta St.	11-2 ....Central Okla.	11-7 ....Northwest Mo. St.	10-8 ....Grand Valley St.
11-4 ....Tex. A&M-Kingsville	Final ....Central Okla.	Final ....Delta St.	10-15 ....Grand Valley St.
Final ....Tex. A&M-Kingsville			10-22 ....Grand Valley St.
	1999	**2001**	10-29 ....Grand Valley St.
1997	Pre ....Northwest Mo. St.	Pre ....Delta St.	11-5 ....Grand Valley St.
9-8 ....Northern Colo.	9-20 ....Carson-Newman	9-4 ....Delta St.	11-12 ....Grand Valley St.
9-15 ....Carson-Newman	9-27 ....Carson-Newman	9-11 ....Delta St.	11-19 ....Grand Valley St.
9-22 ....Carson-Newman	10-4 ....Carson-Newman	9-18 ....Delta St.	Final ....Grand Valley St.
9-29 ....Carson-Newman	10-11 ....Carson-Newman	9-25 ....Delta St.	

Undefeated, Untied Teams

(Regular-Season Games Only)

In 1948, official national statistics rankings began to include all nonmajor four-year colleges. Until the 1967 season, rankings and records included all four-year colleges that reported their statistics to the NCAA. Beginning with the 1967 season, statistics (and won-lost records) included only members of the NCAA.

Since 1981, conference playoff games have been included in a team's regular-season statistics and won-lost record (previously, such games were considered postseason contests).

The regular-season list includes games in which a home team served as a predetermined, preseason host of a "bowl game" regardless of its record and games scheduled before the season, thus eliminating postseason designation for the Orange Blossom Classic, annually hosted by Florida A&M, and the Prairie View Bowl, annually hosted by Prairie View, for example.

Figures are regular-season wins only. A subsequent postseason win(s) is indicated by (*), a loss by (†) and a tie by (‡).

Year	College	Wins
1948	Alma	8
	Bloomsburg	9
	Denison	8
	Heidelberg	9
	Michigan Tech	7
	Missouri Valley	†‡9
	Occidental	*8
	Southern U.	*11
	Sul Ross St.	‡10
	Wesleyan (Conn.)	8
1949	Ball St.	8
	Emory & Henry	*†10
	Gannon	8
	Hanover	†8
	Lewis	8
	Md.-East. Shore	8
	Morgan St.	8
	Pacific (Cal.)	11
	St. Ambrose	8
	St. Vincent	*9
	Trinity (Conn.)	8
	Wayne St. (Neb.)	9
	Wofford	11

Year	College	Wins
1950	Abilene Christian	*10
	Canterbury	8
	Florida St.	8
	Frank. & Marsh.	9
	Lehigh	9
	Lewis & Clark	*8
	Md.-East. Shore	8
	Mission House	6
	New Hampshire	8
	St. Lawrence	8
	St. Norbert	7
	Thiel	7
	Valparaiso	†9
	West Liberty St.	*8
	Wis.-La Crosse	*9
	Wis.-Whitewater	6
1951	Bloomsburg	8
	Bucknell	9
	Col. of Emporia	8
	Ill. Wesleyan	8
	Lawrence	7
	McDaniel	8
	Northern Ill.	9
	Principia	6
	St. Michael's	6
	South Dakota Tech	8
	Susquehanna	6
	Col. of New Jersey	6
	Valparaiso	9
1952	Beloit	8
	Clarion	*8
	Tex. A&M-Commerce	*10
	Fairmont St.	6
	Idaho St.	8
	Lenoir-Rhyne	†8
	Northeastern St.	†9
	Peru St.	10
	Rochester	8
	St. Norbert	6
	Shippensburg	7
	West Chester	7
1953	Cal Poly	9
	Col. of Emporia	8
	Col. of Idaho	†8
	Defiance	8
	Tex. A&M-Commerce	‡8
	Florida A&M	10
	Indianapolis	8
	Iowa Wesleyan	†9
	Juniata	7
	Northern St.	8
	Martin Luther	6
	Peru St.	8
	Prairie View	10
	St. Olaf	8

Year	College	Wins
	Shippensburg	8
	Westminster (Pa.)	8
	Wis.-La Crosse	‡9
	Wis.-Platteville	6
1954	Ashland	7
	Carleton	8
	Central Conn. St.	6
	Col. of Emporia	†9
	Delta St.	8
	Hastings	*8
	Hobart	8
	Juniata	8
	Luther	9
	Miles	8
	Neb.-Omaha	*9
	Martin Luther	6
	Pomona-Pitzer	8
	Principia	7
	Southeastern La.	9
	Tennessee St.	†10
	Trinity (Conn.)	7
	Trinity (Tex.)	9
	Whitworth	8
	Widener	9
	WPI	6
1955	Alfred	8
	Centre	8
	Coe	8
	Col. of Emporia	9
	Drexel	8
	Grambling	10
	Heidelberg	9
	Hillsdale	9
	Juniata	‡8
	Md.-East. Shore	9
	Miami (Ohio)	9
	Muskingum	8
	Northern St.	†9
	Parsons	8
	Shepherd	8
	Southeast Mo. St.	9
	Trinity (Conn.)	7
	Whitworth	9
	Wis.-Stevens Point	8
1956	Alfred	7
	Central Mich.	9
	Hillsdale	9
	Lenoir-Rhyne	10
	Milton	6
	Montana St.	‡9
	Neb.-Kearney	9
	Redlands	9
	St. Thomas (Minn.)	8
	Sam Houston St.	*9
	Southern Conn. St.	9

Year	College	Wins
	Tennessee St.	10
	Westminster (Pa.)	8
1957	Elon	6
	Fairmont St.	7
	Florida A&M	9
	Hillsdale	†9
	Hobart	6
	Idaho St.	9
	Jamestown	7
	Juniata	7
	Lock Haven	8
	Middle Tenn.	10
	Pittsburg St.	*10
	Ripon	8
	St. Norbert	8
	West Chester	9
1958	Calif. (Pa.)	8
	Chadron St.	8
	Gust. Adolphus	†8
	Missouri Valley	†8
	Neb.-Kearney	9
	Northeastern St.	**9
	Northern Ariz.	*†10
	Rochester	8
	Rose-Hulman	8
	St. Benedict's	†10
	Sewanee	8
	Southern Miss.	9
	Wheaton (Ill.)	8
1959	Bowling Green	9
	Butler	8
	Coe	9
	Fairmont St.	9
	Florida A&M	10
	Hofstra	9
	John Carroll	7
	Lenoir-Rhyne	*†9
	San Fran. St.	10
	Western Ill.	9
1960	Albright	9
	Arkansas Tech	†10
	Humboldt St.	*†10
	Langston	9
	Lenoir-Rhyne	*‡10
	Montclair St.	8
	Muskingum	9
	Northern Iowa	†9
	Ohio	10
	Ottawa	9
	Wagner	9
	West Chester	9
	Whitworth	9
	Willamette	8
1961	Albion	8
	Baldwin-Wallace	9
	Butler	9
	Central Okla.	9
	Florida A&M	10
	Fresno St.	*9
	Linfield	*†10
	Mayville St.	8
	Millikin	8
	Northern St.	9
	Ottawa	9
	Pittsburg St.	**9
	Wash. & Lee	9
	Wheaton (Ill.)	8
	Whittier	†9
1962	Carthage	8
	Central Okla.	**9
	Col. of Emporia	†10
	Earlham	8
	East Stroudsburg	†8
	John Carroll	7
	Kalamazoo	8
	Lenoir-Rhyne	*†10
	Northern St.	†9
	Parsons	9
	St. John's (Minn.)	9
	Susquehanna	9
	Wittenberg	9
1963	Alabama A&M	8
	Central Wash.	9
	Coast Guard	†8
	Col. of Emporia	10
	Delaware	8
	John Carroll	7
	Lewis & Clark	8

Year	College	Wins
	Luther	9
	McNeese St.	8
	Neb.-Kearney	†9
	Northeastern	†8
	Northeastern St.	*10
	Northern Ill.	*9
	Prairie View	*†9
	Ripon	8
	St. John's (Minn.)	**8
	Sewanee	8
	Southwest Mo. St.	†9
	Southwest Tex. St.	10
	Wis.-Eau Claire	7
1964	Albion	8
	Amherst	8
	Cal St. Los Angeles	9
	Concordia-M'head	*†9
	Frank. & Marsh.	8
	Montclair St.	7
	Prairie View	9
	Wagner	10
	Western St.	†9
	Westminster (Pa.)	8
	Wittenberg	8
1965	Ball St.	‡9
	East Stroudsburg	*9
	Fairmont St.	†8
	Georgetown (Ky.)	9
	Ill. Wesleyan	8
	Ithaca	8
	Middle Tenn.	10
	Morgan St.	9
	North Dakota St.	*10
	Northern Ill.	†9
	Ottawa	9
	St. John's (Minn.)	**9
	Springfield	9
	Sul Ross St.	†10
	Tennessee St.	‡9
1966	Central (Iowa)	†9
	Clarion	*9
	Defiance	9
	Morgan St.	*8
	Muskingum	†9
	Northwestern St.	9
	San Diego St.	*10
	Tennessee St.	*9
	Waynesburg	**9
	Wilkes	8
	Wis.-Whitewater	*†9

Beginning in 1967, NCAA members only.

Year	College	Wins
1967	Alma	8
	Central (Iowa)	9
	Doane	‡8
	Lawrence	8
	Morgan St.	8
	North Dakota St.	†9
	Northern Mich.	†9
	Wagner	9
	West Chester	*†9
	Wilkes	8
1968	Alma	8
	Doane	*9
	East Stroudsburg	‡8
	Indiana (Pa.)	†9
	North Dakota St.	*9
	Randolph-Macon	9
1969	Albion	8
	Carthage	9
	Defiance	9
	Doane	8
	Montana	†10
	North Dakota St.	*9
	Northern Colo.	10
	Wesleyan (Conn.)	8
	Wittenberg	*9
1970	Arkansas St.	*10
	Jacksonville St.	10
	Montana	†10
	St. Olaf	9
	Tennessee St.	*10
	Westminster (Pa.)	**8
	Wittenberg#	9
1971	Alfred	8
	Hampden-Sydney	†10
	Westminster (Pa.)	†‡8
1972	Ashland	11

Year	College	Wins
	Bridgeport	*10
	Delaware	10
	Doane	†10
	Frank. & Marsh.	9
	Heidelberg	**9
	Louisiana Tech	*11
	Middlebury	8
	Monmouth (Ill.)	9
1973	Tennessee St.	10
	Western Ky.	**†10
1974	Louisiana Tech	*†10
	Michigan Tech	9
	UNLV	*†11
1975	East Stroudsburg	*9
	North Dakota	†9
1976	East Stroudsburg	‡9
1977	UC Davis	*†10
	Florida A&M	11
	Winston-Salem	†11
1978	Western	*†9
	Winston-Salem	*†10
1979	(None)	
1980	Minn. Duluth	10
	Mo.-Rolla	10
1981	Northern Mich.	*†10
	Shippensburg	*†11
	Virginia Union	†11
1982	UC Davis	**†10
	North Dakota St.	*†11
	Southwest Tex. St.	***†11
1983	UC Davis	**†10
	Central St.	**†10
1984	(None)	
1985	Bloomsburg	*†11
1986	UC Davis	*†10
	North Dakota St.	***†10
	Virginia Union	†11
1987	(None)	
1988	North Dakota St.	****†10
	St. Mary's (Cal.)	10
1989	Grand Valley St.	***†11
	Jacksonville St.	***†10
	Pittsburg St.	*†11
	Tex. A&M-Kingsville	†10
1990	North Dakota St.	****†10
	Pittsburg St.	**†10
1991	Carson-Newman	**†10
	Indiana (Pa.)	**†10
	Jacksonville St.	***†9
1992	New Haven	**†10
	Pittsburg St.	***†10
1993	Albany St. (Ga.)	†11
	Bentley	10
	Hampton	*†11
	Indiana (Pa.)	***†10
	New Haven	*†10
	North Ala.	****†10
	Quincy	9
1994	Bentley	*10
	Ferris St.	*†10
	Pittsburg St.	†10
1995	Ferris St.	**†10
	North Ala.	****10
1996	(None)	
1997	Albany St. (Ga.)	*†10
	Carson-Newman	**†9
	Livingstone##	10
	Northwest Mo. St.	*†10
1998	Central Okla.	*†11
	Northwest Mo. St.	****†11
1999	Carson-Newman	**†10
2000	UC Davis	**†10
	Catawba	*†10
	Northwest Mo. St.	†11
	Tuskegee	11
2001	Chadron St.	*†10
	Grand Valley St.	***†10
	Valdosta St.	*†11
2002	C.W. Post	†11
	Carson-Newman	†11
	Central Wash.	†11
	Grand Valley St.	****†10
	Minn. Duluth	†11
	Northwest Mo. St.	*†11
	Valdosta St.	***†11

#Later forfeited all games. ## Later forfeited two games.

DIVISION II

The Spoilers

Compiled since 1973, when the three-division reorganization plan was adopted by the special NCAA Convention. Following is a list of the spoilers of Division II teams that lost their perfect (undefeated, untied) record in their season-ending game, including the Division II championship playoffs. An asterisk (*) indicates an NCAA championship playoff game, a pound sign (#) indicates an NAIA championship playoff game, a dagger (†) indicates the home team in a regular-season game, and (@) indicates a neutral-site game. A game involving two undefeated, untied teams is in **bold** face.

Date	Spoiler	Victim	Score
12-15-73	* Louisiana Tech	Western Ky.	34-0
11-30-74	* Louisiana Tech	Western Caro.	10-7
11-15-75	† C.W. Post	American Int'l	21-0
11-15-75	Eastern N.M.	† Northern Colo.	16-14
11-29-75	* West Ala.	North Dakota	34-14
11-20-76	† Shippensburg	East Stroudsburg	tie 14-14
12-3-77	‡ South Carolina St.	Winston-Salem	10-7
12-3-77	* Lehigh	UC Davis	39-30
12-2-78	* Delaware	Winston-Salem	41-0
11-28-81	* Shippensburg	Virginia Union	40-27
12-5-81	* North Dakota St.	Shippensburg	18-6
12-5-81	* Southwest Tex. St.	Northern Mich.	62-0
12-4-82	* UC Davis	North Dakota St.	19-14
12-11-82	* **Southwest Tex. St.**	**UC Davis**	34-9
12-3-83	* North Dakota St.	UC Davis	26-17
12-10-83	* North Dakota St.	Central St.	41-21
12-7-85	* North Ala.	Bloomsburg	34-0
11-15-86	West Chester	† Millersville	7-3
11-29-86	* Troy St.	Virginia Union	31-7
11-29-86	* South Dakota	UC Davis	26-23
12-10-88	# Adams St.	Pittsburg St.	13-10
11-18-89	* Mississippi Col.	Tex. A&M-Kingsville	34-19
11-18-89	* Indiana (Pa.)	Grand Valley St.	34-24
11-25-89	* Angelo St.	Pittsburg St.	24-21
12-9-89	* Mississippi Col.	Jacksonville St.	3-0
12-1-90	* **North Dakota St.**	**Pittsburg St.**	39-29
11-23-91	# Western St.	Carson-Newman	38-21
12-7-91	* **Jacksonville St.**	**Indiana (Pa.)**	27-20
12-14-91	* Pittsburg St.	Jacksonville St.	23-6
11-14-92	@Minn. St. Moorhead	Michigan Tech	36-35
12-5-92	* Jacksonville St.	New Haven	46-35
12-12-92	* Jacksonville St.	Pittsburg St.	17-13
11-13-93	@Minn. Duluth	Wayne St. (Neb.)	29-28
11-20-93	* **Hampton**	**Albany St. (Ga.)**	33-7
11-27-93	* **Indiana (Pa.)**	**New Haven**	38-35
11-27-93	* **North Ala.**	**Hampton**	45-20
12-11-93	* **North Ala.**	**Indiana (Pa.)**	41-34
11-19-94	* North Dakota St.	Pittsburg St.	(3 ot) 18-12
11-26-94	* Indiana (Pa.)	Ferris St.	21-17
12-2-95	* **North Ala.**	**Ferris St.**	45-7
11-29-97	* **Carson-Newman**	**Albany St. (Ga.)**	23-22
11-29-97	* Northern Colo.	Northwest Mo. St.	35-28
12-6-97	* Northern Colo.	Carson-Newman	30-29
11-28-98	* Tex. A&M-Kingsville	Central Okla.	(ot) 24-21
12-11-99	@* Northwest Mo. St.	Carson-Newman	(4 ot) 58-52
11-18-00	* North Dakota St.	Northwest Mo. St.	31-17
11-25-00	* Delta St.	Catawba	20-14
12-2-00	* Bloomsburg	UC Davis	58-48
11-17-01	* Tarleton St.	Chadron St.	28-24
11-24-01	* Catawba	Valdosta St.	(ot) 37-34
12-8-01	@*North Dakota	Grand Valley St.	17-14
11-23-02	* **Northwest Mo. St.**	**Minn. Duluth**	45-41
11-23-02	* **Grand Valley St.**	**C.W. Post**	62-13
11-23-02	* UC Davis	Central Wash.	24-6
11-30-02	* **Valdosta St.**	**Carson-Newman**	31-28
11-30-02	* Northern Colo.	Northwest Mo. St.	23-12
12-14-02	* **Grand Valley St.**	**Valdosta St.**	31-24

‡Gold Bowl.

Streaks and Rivalries

Longest Winning Streaks

(From 1931; Includes Postseason Games)

Wins	Team	Years
34	Hillsdale	1954-57
32	Wilkes	1965-69
31	Morgan St.	1965-68
31	Missouri Valley	1946-48
30	Bentley	1993-95
29	Tex. A&M-Commerce	1951-53
27	Truman	1931-35
25	Pittsburg St.	1991-92
25	San Diego St.	1965-67
25	Peru St.	1951-54
25	Md.-East. Shore	1948-51
24	Northwest Mo. St.	1999-00
24	North Dakota St.	1964-66
24	Wesleyan (Conn.)	1945-48

Longest Unbeaten Streaks

(From 1931; Includes Postseason Games)

No.	Wins	Ties	Team	Years
54	47	7	Morgan St.	1931-38
38	36	2	Doane	1965-70
37	35	2	Southern U.	1947-51
35	34	1	North Dakota St.	1968-71
34	34	0	Hillsdale	1954-57
32	32	0	Wilkes	1965-69
31	31	0	Morgan St.	1965-68
31	31	0	Missouri Valley	1946-48
31	29	2	St. Ambrose	1935-38
30	30	0	Bentley	1993-95
30	29	1	Wittenberg	1961-65
30	29	1	Tex. A&M-Commerce	1951-53
28	27	1	Wesleyan (Conn.)	†1942-48
28	27	1	Case Reserve	1934-37
27	26	1	Pittsburg St.	1991-92
27	26	1	Juniata	1956-59
27	27	0	Truman	1931-35

†Did not field teams in 1943-44.

Most-Played Rivalries

Games	Opponents (Series leader listed first)	Series Record	First Game
109	North Dakota-North Dakota St.	61-45-3	1894
103	South Dakota-South Dakota St.	50-46-7	1889
99	Emporia St.-Washburn	50-43-6	1899
91	South Dakota-Morningside#	57-29-5	1898
91	Tuskegee-Morehouse	57-26-8	1902
91	Presbyterian-Newberry	55-31-5	1913
89	North Dakota St.-South Dakota St.	48-36-5	1903
88	Colorado Mines-Colorado Col.#	46-37-5	1889
86	Truman-Central Mo. St.	51-30-5	1905
83	Virginia Union-Hampton#	41-39-3	1906
83	Pittsburg St.-Emporia St.	50-31-2	1915
82	Catawba-Lenoir-Rhyne	41-37-4	1907
82	Truman-Northwest Mo. St.	54-24-4	1908
81	Arkansas Tech-Central Ark.	40-38-3	1911

#Have not met since 2000.

Trophy Games

Following is a list of the current Division II football trophy games. The games are listed alphabetically by the trophy-object name. The date refers to the season the trophy was first exchanged and is not necessarily the start of competition between the participants. All games involving a Division II team are listed.

Trophy	Date	Colleges
Axe Bowl	1975	Northwood-Saginaw Valley
Backyard Bowl	1987	Cheyney-West Chester
Battle Axe	1948	Bemidji St.-Minn. St. Moorhead
Battle of the Ravine	1976	Henderson St.-Ouachita Baptist
Bishop's	1987	Lenoir-Rhyne—Newberry
Bronze Derby	1946	Newberry-Presbyterian
Chennault Cup	1990	Tex. A&M-Commerce—Tex. A&M-Kingsville
Eagle-Rock	1980	Chadron St.-Black Hills St.
East Meets West	1987	Chadron St.-Peru St.
Elm City	1983	New Haven-Southern Conn. St.
Field Cup	1983	Ky. Wesleyan-Evansville
Governor's	1979	Southern Conn. St.-Central Conn. St.
Governor's Trophy	2000	Arkansas Tech-Central Ark.
Great Valley	1998	Shepherd-Shippensburg
Heritage Bell	1979	Delta St.-Mississippi Col.
John Wesley	1984	Ky. Wesleyan-Union (Ky.)
Miner's Bowl	1986	Mo. Southern St.-Pittsburg St.
Nickel	1938	North Dakota-North Dakota St.

Trophy	Date	Colleges
Old Hickory Stick	1931	Northwest Mo. St.-Truman
Old Settler's Musket	1975	Adams St.-Fort Lewis
President's Cup	1998	Central Okla.-Northeastern St.
Sitting Bull	1953	North Dakota-South Dakota
Springfield Mayor's	1941	American Int'l-Springfield
Textile	1960	Clark Atlanta-Fort Valley St.
Top Dog	1971	Indianapolis-Butler
Traveling	1976	Ashland-Hillsdale
Traveling	1997	Harding-Ouachita Baptist
Traveling Training Kit	1978	Minn. St. Mankato–St. Cloud St.
Victory Carriage	1960	UC Davis-Sacramento St.
Wagon Wheel	1986	Eastern N.M.-West Tex. A&M
Wooden Shoes	1977	Grand Valley St.-Wayne St. (Mich.)

Cliffhangers

Regular-season games won by Division II teams on the final play of the game (from 1973). The extra point is listed when it provided the margin of victory after the winning touchdown. Does not count overtime games.

Date	Opponents, Score	Game-Winning Play
9-22-73	South Dakota 9, North Dakota St. 7	Kelly Higgins 5 pass from Mark Jenkins
11-23-74	Arkansas St. 22, McNeese St. 20	Joe Duren 56 FG
10-11-75	Indiana (Pa.) 16, Westminster (Pa.) 14	Tom Alper 37 FG
9-25-76	Portland St. 50, Montana 49	Dave Stief 2 pass from June Jones
10-30-76	South Dakota St. 16, Northern Iowa 13	Monte Mosiman 53 pass from Dick Weikert
10-27-77	Albany (N.Y.) 42, Maine 39	Larry Leibowitz 19 FG
10-6-79	Indiana (Pa.) 31, Shippensburg 24	Jeff Heath 4 run
10-20-79	North Dakota 23, South Dakota 22	Tom Biolo 6 run
9-6-80	Ferris St. 20, St. Joseph's (Ind.) 15	Greg Washington 17 pass from (holder) John Gibson (after bad snap on 34 FG attempt)
11-15-80	Morris Brown 19, Bethune-Cookman 18	Ray Mills 1 run (Carlton Jackson kick)
11-15-80	Tuskegee 23, Alabama A&M 21	Korda Joseph 45 FG
9-26-81	Abilene Christian 41, Northwestern St. 38	David Russell 17 pass from Loyal Proffitt
9-26-81	Cal St. Chico 10, Santa Clara 7	Mike Sullivan 46 FG
10-10-81	C.W. Post 37, James Madison 36	Tom DeBona 10 pass from Tom Ehrhardt (Ehrhardt run)
10-9-82	Grand Valley St. 38, Ferris St. 35	Randy Spangler 20 FG
11-6-82	South Dakota 30, Augustana (S.D.) 28	Kurt Seibel 47 FG
9-17-83	Central Mo. St. 13, Sam Houston St. 10	Steve Huff 27 FG
9-22-84	Clarion 16, Shippensburg 13	Eric Fairbanks 26 FG
9-29-84	Angelo St. 18, Eastern N.M. 17	Ned Cox 3 run
10-13-84	UC Davis 16, Cal St. Chico 13	Ray Sullivan 48 FG
10-13-84	Northwest Mo. St. 35, Central Mo. St. 34	Pat Johnson 20 FG
11-3-84	Bloomsburg 34, West Chester 31	Curtis Still 50 pass from Jay Dedea
9-7-85	UCF 39, Bethune-Cookman 37	Ed O'Brien 55 FG
10-12-85	South Dakota 40, Morningside 38	Scott Jones 2 run
9-13-86	Michigan Tech 34, St. Norbert 30	Jim Wallace 41 pass from Dave Walter
10-18-86	Indianapolis 25, Evansville 24	Ken Bruce 18 FG
10-24-87	Indianapolis 27, Evansville 24	Doug Sabotin 2 pass from Tom Crowell
11-7-87	Central Mo. St. 35, Truman 33	Phil Brandt 25 FG
9-3-88	Alabama A&M 17, North Ala. 16	Edmond Allen 30 FG
9-17-88	Michigan Tech 17, Hope 14	Pete Weiss 22 FG
9-17-89	Morehouse 22, Fort Valley St. 21	David Boone 18 pass from Jimmie Davis
11-11-89	East Stroudsburg 22, Central Conn. St. 19	Frank Magolon 4 pass from Tom Taylor
10-13-90	East Stroudsburg 23, Bloomsburg 21	Ken Kopetchny 3 pass from Bret Comp
11-10-90	Southern Conn. St. 12, Central Conn. St. 10	Paul Boulanger 48 FG
9-21-91	West Ala. 22, Albany St. (Ga.) 21	Matt Carman 24 pass from Deon Timmons (Anthony Armstrong kick)
10-26-91	Central Mo. St. 38, Truman 37	Chris Pyatt 45 FG
10-26-91	Eastern N.M. 17, Tex. A&M-Commerce 14	Jodie Peterson 35 FG
10-9-93	Delta St. 20, Henderson St. 19	Greg Walker 3 run (Stephen Coker kick)
11-6-93	Henderson St. 46, West Ala. 44	Craig Moses 44 FG
9-24-94	Mo.-Rolla 15, Emporia St. 14	Jason Politte 1 run
9-24-94	St. Cloud St. 18, North Dakota 17	Todd Bouman 1 run
9-16-95	West Va. Wesleyan 16, Kutztown 14	Eric Myers 42 FG
9-30-95	Michigan Tech 37, Saginaw Valley 35	Matt Johnson 46 FG
11-23-96	Northwest Mo. St. 22, Neb.-Omaha 21	Jesse Haynes 17 pass from Greg Teale
9-6-97	Bemidji St. 25, St. John's (Minn.) 21	Ty Houglum 47 pass from Pat O'Connor
11-8-97	Harding 31, Ouachita Baptist 28	Jeremy Thompson 34 FG
10-10-98	Slippery Rock 27, Indiana (Pa.) 21	D.J. Flick 52 pass from Randy McKavish
9-18-99	Central Okla. 37, Angelo St. 34	Evan Luttrell 41 FG
11-11-00	Adams St. 20, Fort Lewis 17	Anthony May 37 FG
11-11-00	Grand Valley St. 31, Hillsdale 29	Kevin Sonntag 35 FG
9-15-01	Fort Lewis 23, Western St. 20	Steve Berglund 34 FG
10-6-01	Truman 27, Washburn 26	Austin Lepper 46 FG
9-28-02	Central Okla. 19, Tex. A&M-Commerce 16	Josh Billings 1 pass from Erick Johnson
10-5-02	Southwestern Okla. 24, Central Okla. 21	Scott Poole 40 FG

DIVISION II

2002 Division II Overtime Games

Date	Winner's Conference	Score (Loser's Conf.)	Number of OT Periods	Regulation Score
Aug. 29	Ohio Valley (Div. I-AA)	Southeast Mo. St. 42, Ark.-Monticello (Gulf South) 41	2OT	35-35
Aug. 29	NAIA	Morningside 24, Wayne St. (Neb.) (Northern Sun) 21	2OT	14-14
Aug. 29	MIAA	Mo. Western St. 31, Winona St. (Northern Sun) 30	1OT	24-24
Aug. 29	Independent (Div. I-AA)	Samford 24, North Ala. (Gulf South) 21	2OT	21-21
Sept. 1	CIAA	N.C. Central 33, N.C. A&T (MEAC/Div. I-AA) 30	1OT	27-27
Sept. 7	NAIA	Pikeville 23, Concord (WVIAC) 20	1OT	17-17
Sept. 7	Independent	St. Joseph's (Ind.) 28, St. Francis (NAIA) 27	1OT	21-21
Sept. 14	North Central	Augustana (S.D.) 29, Southwest St. (Northern Sun) 23	1OT	23-23
Sept. 14	Northeast-10	Pace 20, Stonehill (Northeast-10) 14	1OT	14-14
Sept. 14	SIAC	Tuskegee 7, Benedict (SIAC) 0	1OT	0-0
Sept. 14	WVIAC	Concord 32, Union (Ky.) (NAIA) 29	1OT	29-29
Sept. 21	GLIAC	Michigan Tech 32, Indianapolis (GLIAC) 24	3OT	24-24
Sept. 28	SIAC	Kentucky St. 47, Ark.-Pine Bluff (SWAC/Div. I-AA) 44	4OT	35-35
Oct. 5	CIAA	Fayetteville St. 30, Winston-Salem (CIAA) 26	4OT	7-7
Oct. 5	North Central	Northern Colo. 30, Neb.-Omaha (North Central) 23	2OT	20-20
Oct. 5	North Central	South Dakota 40, North Dakota St. (North Central) 37	4OT	20-20
Oct. 5	Independent	New Haven 37, Tiffin (Independent) 34	1OT	31-31
Oct. 12	GLIAC	Ferris St. 21, Michigan Tech (GLIAC) 14	1OT	14-14
Oct. 12	North Central	Northern Colo. 27, St. Cloud St. (North Central) 24	1OT	24-24
Oct. 12	North Central	South Dakota 16, Augustana (S.D.) (North Central) 10	2OT	3-3
Oct. 12	Rocky Mountain	Chadron St. 31, Mesa St. (Rocky Mountain) 30	1OT	24-24
Oct. 19	GLIAC	Ferris St. 19, Mercyhurst (GLIAC) 13	1OT	13-13
Oct. 19	SIAC	Miles 34, Lane (SIAC) 32	3OT	Not Available
Oct. 19	North Central	Augustana (S.D.) 39, South Dakota St. (North Central) 33	3OT	27-27
Oct. 19	Great Northwest	Central Wash. 35, Western Wash. (Great Northwest) 28	1OT	28-28
Oct. 26	GLIAC	Northern Mich. 49, Wayne St. (Mich.) (GLIAC) 46	1OT	43-43
Oct. 26	Gulf South	Southern Ark. 50, Ouachita Baptist (Gulf South) 47	4OT	31-31
Oct. 26	Lone Star	Northeastern St. 29, Tarleton St. (Lone Star) 28	1OT	22-22
Oct. 26	MIAA	Mo. Western St. 34, Washburn (MIAA) 28	2OT	21-21
Oct. 26	Northern Sun	Bemidji St. 35, Minn. St. Moorhead (Northern Sun) 28	2OT	28-28
Oct. 26	South Atlantic	Mars Hill 30, Wingate (South Atlantic) 24	2OT	24-24
Oct. 26	SIAC	Morehouse 19, Lane (SIAC) 16	1OT	Not Available
Nov. 2	Rocky Mountain	Fort Lewis 67, Western N.M. (Independent) 66	2OT	59-59
Nov. 9	Great Northwest	Western Wash. 20, Western Ore. (Great Northwest) 17	3OT	17-17
Nov. 9	Northeast-10	American Int'l 40, Bryant (Northeast-10) 33	2OT	26-26
Nov. 9	PSAC	Indiana (Pa.) 34, Slippery Rock (PSAC) 28	1OT	28-28
Nov. 16	MIAA	Central Mo. St. 23, Pittsburg St. (MIAA) 20	1OT	17-17
Nov. 30	Lone Star	Tex. A&M-Kingsville 27, UC Davis (Independent) 20	1OT	20-20
Dec. 7	MIAA	Emporia St. 34, Winona St. (Northern Sun) 27	1OT	27-27

Notes: 39 games (21 with one extra period, 10 with two extra periods, 4 with three extra periods, 4 with four periods)—average of 1.77 extra periods

Stadiums

LISTED ALPHABETICALLY BY SCHOOL

Team	Stadium	Year Built	Capacity	Surface
Abilene Christian	Shotwell	1959	15,000	Grass
Adams St.	Rex Field	1949	2,800	Grass
Albany St. (Ga.)	Mills Memorial	1957	11,000	Grass
American Int'l	John Homer Miller	1964	5,000	Grass
Angelo St.	San Angelo	1962	17,500	Grass
Ark.-Monticello	Cotton Boll	NA	5,000	Grass
Arkansas Tech	Buerkle	NA	6,000	Grass
Ashland	Community	1963	5,700	Grass
Assumption	Rocheleau Field	1961	1,200	Grass
Augustana (S.D.)	Howard Wood	1957	10,000	Grass
Bemidji St.	Chet Anderson	1937	4,000	Grass
Bentley	Bentley College	1990	1,500	Grass
Bloomsburg	Robert B. Redman	1974	5,000	Grass
Bowie St.	Bulldog	1992	6,000	Grass
Bryant	Bulldog	1999	4,400	Grass
C.W. Post	Hickox Field	1966	5,000	Grass
UC Davis	Toomey Field	1949	10,111	Grass
Calif. (Pa.)	Adamson	1970	5,000	Grass
Carson-Newman	Burke-Tarr	1966	5,000	Grass
Catawba	Shuford Field	1926	4,000	Grass
Central Ark.	Estes	1939	8,500	Grass
Central Mo. St.	Audrey J. Walton	1995	10,000	Grass
Central Okla.	Wantland	1965	10,000	Grass
Central Wash.	Tomlinson	NA	4,000	Grass
Chadron St.	Elliott Field	1930	2,500	Grass
Cheyney	O'Shield-Stevenson	NA	3,500	Grass
Clarion	Memorial Field	1965	5,000	Grass
Clark Atlanta	Georgia Dome#	1992	71,000	AstroTurf
Colorado Mines	Brooks Field	1922	5,000	Grass
Concord	Callahan	NA	5,000	Grass
Delta St.	Travis Parker Field	1970	8,000	Grass
East Central	Norris Field	NA	5,000	Grass
East Stroudsburg	Eiler-Martin	1969	6,000	Grass
Eastern N.M.	Greyhound	1969	5,200	Grass
Edinboro	Sox-Harrison	1965	5,000	Grass
Elizabeth City St.	Roebuck	NA	6,500	Grass
Emporia St.	Welch	1937	7,000	Grass
Fairmont St.	Durall-Rosier Field	1929	6,000	Grass
Fayetteville St.	Jeralds Athletic Complex	1993	6,100	Grass
Ferris St.	Top Taggart Field	1957	6,200	AstroTurf
Findlay	Donnell	NA	7,500	Grass
Fort Hays St.	Lewis Field	1936	5,862	Stadia-Turf
Fort Lewis	Ray Dennison Memorial	1958	4,000	Grass
Fort Valley St.	Wildcat	1957	7,500	Grass
Gannon	University Field	2001	2,500	AstroPlay
Glenville St.	Pioneer	1977	5,000	Grass
Grand Valley St.	Arend D. Lubbers	1979	4,146	PAT
Harding	First Security	1959	5,000	Grass
Henderson St.	Carpenter-Haygood	1968	9,600	Grass
Hillsdale	Frank Waters	1982	8,500	PAT
Humboldt St.	Redwood Bowl	1946	7,000	Grass
Indiana (Pa.)	George P. Miller	1962	6,500	AstroTurf
Indianapolis	Key	1971	5,500	Grass
Johnson Smith	The Bullpen	1990	7,500	Grass
Kentucky St.	Alumni Field	1978	6,000	Grass
Ky. Wesleyan	Apollo	1989	3,000	Grass
Kutztown	University Field	1987	5,600	Grass

Team	Stadium	Year Built	Capacity	Surface
Lane	Rothrock	1930	3,500	Grass
Lenoir-Rhyne	Moretz	1923	8,500	Grass
Lincoln (Mo.)	Dwight T. Reed	1970	5,600	Grass
Livingstone	Alumni	NA	5,500	Grass
Lock Haven	Hubert Jack	NA	3,000	Turf
Mansfield	Van Norman Field	NA	3,000	Grass
Mars Hill	Meares	1965	5,000	Grass
Mass.-Lowell	Cawley Memorial	1934	7,000	Grass
Mercyhurst	Tullio Field	NA	2,000	Grass
Merrimack	Merrimack	NA	2,000	Grass
Mesa St.	Stocker	1949	8,000	Grass
Michigan Tech	Sherman Field	1954	3,000	Grass
Midwestern St.	Memorial	NA	14,500	Turf
Miles	Alumni	NA	3,400	Grass
Millersville	Biemesderfer	1970	6,500	Grass
Minn.-Crookston	UMC Field	NA	2,000	Grass
Minn. Duluth	Griggs Field	1966	4,000	AstroTurf
Minn.-Morris	UMM Field	NA	5,000	Grass
Minn. St. Mankato	Blakeslee	1962	7,500	Grass
Minn. St. Moorhead	Alex Nemzek	1960	5,000	Grass
Mo.-Rolla	Jackling Field	1967	8,000	Grass
Mo. Southern St.	Fred G. Hughes	1975	7,000	Turf
Mo. Western St.	Spratt	1979	6,000	Grass
Morehouse	B. T. Harvey	1983	9,850	Grass
Neb.-Kearney	Foster Field	1929	6,500	Grass
Neb.-Omaha	Al F. Caniglia Field	1949	9,500	AstroTurf
New Haven	Robert B. Dodds	NA	3,500	Grass
N.M. Highlands	Perkins	1941	5,000	Grass
Newberry	Setzler Field	1930	4,000	Grass
North Ala.	Braly Municipal	1940	14,215	PAT
N.C. Central	O'Kelly-Riddick	1975	11,500	Grass
North Dakota	Alerus Center#	2001	13,500	AstroTurf Magic
North Dakota St.	FargoDome#	1992	18,700	AstroTurf
Northeastern St.	Gable Field	NA	12,000	Grass
Northern Colo.	Nottingham Field	1995	7,000	Grass
Northern Mich.	Superior Dome#	1991	8,000	Turf
Northern St.	Swisher	1975	6,000	Grass
Northwest Mo. St.	Rickenbrode	1917	7,500	Grass
Northwood	Louis Juillerat	1964	2,500	Grass
Okla. Panhandle	Carl Wooten	NA	5,000	Grass
Ouachita Baptist	A.U. Williams	NA	5,200	Grass
Pace	Finnerty Field	NA	1,500	Grass
Pittsburg St.	Carnie Smith	1924	8,343	Grass
Presbyterian	Bailey Memorial	NA	5,000	Grass
Quincy	QU	1938	2,500	Grass
Saginaw Valley	Harvey R. Wickes	1975	4,028	PAT
St. Anselm	Grappone	1999	4,500	Grass
St. Cloud St.	Selke Field	1937	4,000	Grass
St. Joseph's (Ind.)	Alumni Field	1947	4,000	Grass
Shepherd	Ram	1959	5,000	Grass
Shippensburg	Grove	1972	7,700	Grass
Slippery Rock	N. Kerr Thompson	1974	10,000	Grass
South Dakota	DakotaDome#	1979	10,000	Monsanto
South Dakota St.	Coughlin-Alumni	1962	16,000	Grass
Southeastern Okla.	Paul Laird Field	NA	9,000	Grass
Southern Ark.	Wilkins	1949	6,000	Grass
Southern Conn. St.	Jess Dow Field	1988	6,000	Balsam/AstroPlay
Southwest Baptist	Plaster	1986	2,500	Grass
Southwest St.	Mattke Field	1971	5,000	Grass
Southwestern Okla.	Milam	NA	4,000	Grass
Stonehill	Chieftain	1980	2,000	Grass
Tarleton St.	Memorial	1976	5,284	Grass
Tex. A&M-Commerce	Memorial	1950	10,000	Grass
Tex. A&M-Kingsville	Javelina	1950	15,000	Grass
Texas Lutheran	Matador	1959	9,500	Grass
Tiffin	Frost-Kalnow	NA	8,000	Turf
Truman	Stokes	1930	4,000	Grass
Tusculum	Pioneer Field	1991	3,500	Grass
Tuskegee	Alumni Bowl	1925	10,000	Grass
Valdosta St.	Cleveland Field	1922	11,500	Grass
Virginia St.	Rogers	1950	13,500	Grass
Virginia Union	Hovey Field	NA	10,000	Grass
Washburn	Moore Bowl	1928	7,200	Grass
Wayne St. (Mich.)	Wayne State	1968	6,000	Grass
Wayne St. (Neb.)	Memorial	1931	3,500	Grass
West Ala.	Tiger	1952	7,000	Grass
West Chester	Farrell	1970	7,500	Grass
West Ga.	Grisham	1966	6,500	Grass
West Liberty St.	Russek Field	1960	4,000	Grass
West Tex. A&M	Kimbrough	1959	20,000	Grass
West Virginia St.	Lakin Field	1964	5,000	Grass
West Va. Tech	Martin Field	NA	2,500	Turf
West Va. Wesleyan	Cebe Ross Field	1957	3,500	Grass
Western N.M.	Silver Sports Complex	1969	2,000	Grass
Western Ore.	McArthur Field	1982	2,500	Grass
Western St.	Mountaineer Bowl	1950	4,000	Grass
Western Wash.	Bellingham Civic	NA	4,500	Grass
Westminster (Pa.)	Harold Burry	1950	4,500	Grass
Wingate	Irwin Belk	NA	3,000	Grass
Winona St.	Maxwell Field	NA	3,500	Turf
Winston-Salem	Bowman-Gray	1940	18,000	Grass

LISTED BY CAPACITY (TOP 25)

Team	Stadium	Year Built	Capacity	Surface
Clark Atlanta	Georgia Dome#	1992	71,000	AstroTurf
West Tex. A&M	Kimbrough	1959	20,000	Grass
North Dakota St.	FargoDome#	1992	18,700	AstroTurf
Winston-Salem	Bowman-Gray	1940	18,000	Grass
Angelo St.	San Angelo	1962	17,500	Grass
South Dakota St.	Coughlin-Alumni	1962	16,000	Grass
Abilene Christian	Shotwell	1959	15,000	Grass
Tex. A&M-Kingsville	Javelina	1950	15,000	Grass
Midwestern St.	Memorial	NA	14,500	Turf
North Ala.	Braly	1940	14,215	PAT
North Dakota	Alerus Center#	2001	13,500	AstroTurf Magic
Virginia St.	Rogers	1950	13,500	Grass
Northeastern St.	Gable Field	NA	12,000	Grass
N.C. Central	O'Kelly-Riddick	1975	11,500	Grass
Valdosta St.	Cleveland Field	1922	11,500	Grass
Albany St. (Ga.)	Mills Memorial	1957	11,000	Grass
UC Davis	Toomey Field	1949	10,111	Grass
Augustana (S.D.)	Howard Wood	1957	10,000	Grass
Central Mo. St.	Audrey J. Walton	1995	10,000	Grass
Central Okla.	Wantland	1965	10,000	Grass
Slippery Rock	N. Kerr Thompson	1974	10,000	Grass
South Dakota	DakotaDome#	1979	10,000	Monsanto
Tex. A&M-Commerce	Memorial	1950	10,000	Grass
Tuskegee	Alumni Bowl	1925	10,000	Grass
Virginia Union	Hovey Field	NA	10,000	Grass

#Indoor facility. PAT=Prescription Athletic Turf.

DIVISION II

Statistics Trends

For valid comparisons from 1973, when College Division teams were divided into Division II and Division III.

(Average Per Game, Per Team)

Year	Rushing Plays	Rushing Yds.	Rushing Avg.	Passing Att.	Passing Cmp.	Passing Pct.	Passing Yds.	Av. Att.	Total Offense Plays	Total Offense Yds.	Total Offense Avg.	Scoring TD	Scoring FG	Scoring Pts.
1973	47.6	169.6	3.57	20.0	8.8	.442	121.5	6.08	67.6	291.1	4.31	2.53	0.42	18.2
1974	47.6	156.3	3.29	19.5	8.7	.445	122.4	6.28	67.1	278.7	4.16	2.55	0.43	19.0
1975	47.3	168.6	3.56	19.5	8.7	.448	120.6	6.21	66.8	289.2	4.33	2.49	0.45	18.6
1976	47.4	165.7	3.50	19.9	9.1	.457	125.9	6.32	67.3	291.6	4.34	2.52	0.47	18.7
1977	*48.4	173.8	3.59	20.3	9.2	.453	126.2	6.21	68.7	300.0	4.37	2.58	0.46	19.1
1978	48.0	169.3	3.52	20.6	9.2	.448	124.3	6.05	68.6	293.6	4.29	2.56	0.49	19.3
1979	45.8	154.7	3.38	21.0	9.5	.450	125.8	6.00	66.8	280.5	4.20	2.37	0.52	17.9
1980	45.3	153.8	3.40	22.4	10.4	.463	137.6	6.16	67.7	291.4	4.31	2.51	0.52	18.9
1981	44.6	146.6	3.29	24.0	11.0	.457	145.9	6.09	68.6	292.5	4.27	2.48	0.54	18.7
1982	43.3	144.1	3.32	26.1	12.3	.469	161.0	6.17	69.4	305.1	4.40	2.63	0.62	19.8
1983	43.2	145.4	3.37	26.1	12.5	.479	164.5	6.31	69.3	309.9	4.48	2.64	0.62	19.6
1984	41.9	142.2	3.39	26.0	12.5	.481	164.8	6.33	67.9	307.0	4.52	2.63	0.62	19.4
1985	41.7	144.0	3.46	27.4	13.2	.483	170.6	6.23	69.1	314.6	4.56	2.73	0.65	20.9
1986	41.8	148.9	3.56	26.9	13.0	.484	168.4	6.27	68.7	317.3	4.62	2.89	0.64	22.0
1987	42.8	151.9	3.55	24.6	11.9	.483	155.5	6.31	67.4	307.4	4.56	2.65	0.64	20.2
1988	43.9	159.4	3.64	24.6	11.9	.484	159.8	6.49	68.5	319.2	4.66	2.92	0.65	22.1
1989	43.7	166.0	3.80	25.1	12.2	.485	161.5	6.45	68.8	327.5	4.77	2.97	0.62	22.6
1990	43.7	168.3	3.86	26.4	12.8	.485	173.3	6.57	70.1	341.6	4.88	3.10	0.65	23.4
1991	43.7	167.8	3.84	26.4	12.8	.484	172.4	6.54	70.1	340.2	4.86	3.05	*0.66	23.2
1992	44.1	167.6	3.80	25.6	12.4	.484	171.4	6.70	69.7	339.0	4.87	3.01	0.65	23.1
1993	42.7	167.3	3.92	27.4	13.6	.495	180.2	6.11	70.1	347.5	4.96	3.28	0.53	24.0
1994	42.6	*174.5	*4.10	26.3	13.2	.503	178.0	6.79	68.9	*352.5	5.13	3.42	0.54	25.1
1995	41.6	164.0	3.95	26.8	13.4	.501	176.9	6.61	68.4	340.9	4.99	3.22	0.56	23.7
1996	41.9	161.5	3.86	26.0	12.9	.495	173.1	6.65	67.9	334.6	4.93	3.15	0.58	23.4
1997	42.2	167.6	3.97	25.0	12.2	.489	166.3	6.66	67.2	333.9	4.97	3.24	0.58	24.0
1998	41.6	165.9	3.98	25.7	12.8	.499	174.9	*6.81	67.3	340.8	5.06	3.27	0.65	24.5
1999	41.3	165.2	4.00	26.1	13.3	.511	176.8	6.77	67.4	342.1	5.08	3.29	0.61	24.5
2000	43.6	158.6	3.64	27.4	13.8	.505	183.7	6.71	*70.9	342.3	4.83	3.32	0.58	24.7
2001	40.6	163.0	4.04	*28.3	14.6	.514	192.4	6.79	68.9	345.4	*5.18	*3.59	0.63	*26.6
2002	38.9	151.0	3.88	*28.3	*14.7	*.520	*192.7	*6.81	67.2	343.7	5.11	3.32	0.64	24.8

*Record.

Additional Statistics Trends

(Average Per Game, Per Team)

Year	Teams†	Games	Punting No.	Punting Avg.	PAT Kick Attempts Pct. Made	PAT Kick Attempts Pct. of Total Tries	Two-Point Attempts Pct. Made	Two-Point Attempts Pct. of Total Tries	Field Goals Pct. Made
1973	131	1,326	5.8	36.0	.833	.876	.419	.124	.439
1974	136	1,388	5.7	*36.8	.830	.859	.432	.141	.472
1975	126	1,282	5.5	36.3	.837	.874	.464	.126	.476
1976	122	1,244	5.8	36.2	.841	.878	.419	.122	.461
1977	124	1,267	5.9	36.1	.832	.874	.436	.126	.442
1978	91	921	6.0	35.9	.830	.880	.452	.120	.519
1979	99	1,016	6.1	35.2	.854	.861	.459	.139	.543
1980	103	1,040	5.9	35.6	.852	.864	.438	.136	.512
1981	113	1,138	*6.1	35.6	.856	.861	.440	.139	.531
1982	118	1,196	6.1	36.4	.862	.877	.431	.123	.560
1983	115	1,175	6.0	36.1	.866	.847	.428	.153	.564
1984	112	1,150	5.9	36.4	.876	.875	.448	.125	.567
1985	107	1,098	5.8	35.9	*.905	.864	.414	.136	.549
1986	109	1,124	5.6	36.5	.870	.865	.466	.135	*.576
1987	105	1,100	5.7	35.7	.857	.865	.435	.135	.547
1988	111	1,114	5.6	35.6	.886	.868	.399	.132	.555
1989	106	1,084	5.5	36.7	.873	.845	.376	.155	.567
1990	105	1,065	5.7	35.7	.876	.885	.474	.115	.568
1991	114	1,150	5.5	36.1	.882	.880	.426	.120	.572
1992	115	1,145	5.5	35.9	.888	.870	.442	.130	.575
1993	136	1,354	5.3	35.2	.839	.853	.438	.147	.528
1994	128	1,325	5.1	36.0	.850	.840	.439	.160	.559
1995	131	1,362	5.3	34.9	.835	.837	.473	*.163	.552
1996	137	1,434	5.5	35.6	.837	.846	.473	.154	.560
1997	129	1,357	5.4	36.2	.841	.879	.425	.121	.561
1998	134	1,412	5.4	36.7	.862	.877	.387	.123	.575
1999	147	1,550	5.4	36.4	.859	.883	.419	.117	.571
2000	136	1,279	5.4	36.1	.875	.895	.457	.105	.563
2001	132	1,365	5.4	36.3	.858	*.916	*.511	.084	.563
2002	146	1,584	5.1	36.0	.863	.900	.432	.099	.557

*Record. †Teams reporting statistics, not the total number of teams in the division.

Classification History (1973-03)

The following lists show years of active membership for current and former Division II football-playing institutions. Provisional members also are shown, along with the year in which they will become active members.

ACTIVE MEMBERS (151)

Abilene Christian	1981-current
Adams St.	1983, 90-current
Albany St. (Ga.)	1976-current
American Int'l	1974-current
Angelo St.	1981-current
Ark.-Monticello	1997-current
Arkansas Tech	1997-current
Ashland	1980-current
Assumption	1993-current
Augustana (S.D.)	1973-current
Bemidji St.	1979-current
Benedict	2002-current
Bentley	1993-current
Bloomsburg	1980-current
Bowie St.	1980-current
Bryant	1999-current
C.W. Post	1973, 78-84, 93-current
UC Davis	1973-current
Calif. (Pa.)	1973-current
Carson-Newman	1991-current
Catawba	1991-current
Central Ark.	1992-current
Central Mo. St.	1973-current
Central Okla.	1976-78, 88-current
Central Wash.	1973-75, 82-83, 98-current
Chadron St.	1990-current
Charleston (W.Va.)	2003
Cheyney	1980-current
Clarion	1973-current
Clark Atlanta	1980-current
Colorado Mines	1974-current
Concord	1993-current
Concordia-St. Paul	2002-current
Delta St.	1973-current
East Central	1998-current
East Stroudsburg	1973-current
Eastern N.M.	1985-current
Edinboro	1973-current
Elizabeth City St.	1973-current
Emporia St.	1990-current
Fairmont St.	1978-79, 93-current
Fayetteville St.	1973-current
Ferris St.	1977-current
Findlay	2000-current
Fort Hays St.	1988-current
Fort Lewis	1973-84, 90-current
Fort Valley St.	1981-current
Gannon	1993-current
Glenville St.	1993-current
Grand Valley St.	1976-current
Harding	1997-current
Henderson St.	1992-current
Hillsdale	1976-78, 84-current
Humboldt St.	1973, 80-current
Indiana (Pa.)	1973-current
Indianapolis	1976-current
Johnson Smith	1973-current
Kentucky St.	1973-current
Ky. Wesleyan	1993-current
Kutztown	1980-current
Lane	1993-current
Lenoir-Rhyne	1989-current
Lincoln (Mo.)	2001-current
Livingstone	1973-current
Lock Haven	1980-current
Mansfield	1980-current
Mars Hill	1991-current
Mass.-Lowell	1993-current
Mercyhurst	1993-current
Merrimack	1996-current
Mesa St.	1982-83, 90-current
Michigan Tech	1973-current
Midwestern St.	1997-current
Miles	1988-current
Millersville	1980-current
Minn.-Crookston	2001-current

Minn. Duluth	1973-current
Minn.-Morris	1993-current
Minn. St. Mankato	1973-76, 78-current
Minn. St. Moorhead	1973-82, 93-current
Mo.-Rolla	1973-current
Mo. Southern St.	1988-current
Mo. Western St.	1988-current
Morehouse	1981-current
Neb.-Kearney	1988-current
Neb.-Omaha	1973-current
New Haven	1975-76, 81-current
N.M. Highlands	1982-84, 91-current
Newberry	1990-current
North Ala.	1973-current
N.C. Central	1973-current
North Dakota	1973-current
North Dakota St.	1973-current
North Greenville	2003
Northeastern St.	1998-current
Northern Colo.	1973-current
Northern Mich.	1973-current
Northern St.	1980-81, 93-current
Northwest Mo. St.	1973-current
Northwood	1981-87, 92-current
Okla. Panhandle	1999-current
Ouachita Baptist	1997-current
Pace	1993-current
Pittsburg St.	1988-current
Presbyterian	1991-current
Quincy	1993-94, 96-current
Saginaw Valley	1981-current
St. Anselm	1999-current
St. Cloud St.	1973-current
St. Joseph's (Ind.)	1979-current
Shepherd	1990-current
Shippensburg	1976-current
Slippery Rock	1979-current
South Dakota	1973-current
South Dakota St.	1973-current
Southeastern Okla.	1998-current
Southern Ark.	1997-current
Southern Conn. St.	1973-current
Southwest Baptist	1986-current
Southwest St.	1978-83, 93-current
Southwestern Okla.	1998-current
Stonehill	1993-current
Tarleton St.	1994-current
Tex. A&M-Commerce	1981-current
Tex. A&M-Kingsville	1980-current
Tiffin	2002-current
Truman	1973-current
Tusculum	1998-current
Tuskegee	1973-current
Valdosta St.	1982-current
Va.-Wise	2003
Virginia St.	1973-current
Virginia Union	1973-current
Washburn	1988-current
Wayne St. (Mich.)	1973-current
Wayne St. (Neb.)	1988-current
West Ala.	1974-current
West Chester	1973-current
West Ga.	1983-current
West Liberty St.	1991-current
West Tex. A&M	1986-90, 92-current
West Virginia St.	1997-current
West Va. Tech	1993-current
West Va. Wesleyan	1973-80, 93-current
Western N.M.	1983, 94-current
Western Ore.	2001-current
Western St.	1973-78, 82-85, 90-current
Western Wash.	1998-current
Wingate	1991-current
Winona St.	1978-current
Winston-Salem	1973-current

PROVISIONAL MEMBERS (0)*

FORMER MEMBERS (133)

Akron	1973-79
Alabama A&M	1973-98
Alabama St.	1973-81
Albany (N.Y.)	1995-98
Alcorn St.	1973-76
Ark.-Pine Bluff	1973-82
Arkansas St.	1973-74
Austin Peay	1973-77
Ball St.	1973-74
Bethune-Cookman	1973-79
Boise St.	1973-77
Boston U.	1973-77
Bucknell	1973-77
Butler	1973-92
UC Riverside	1973-75
UC Santa Barb.	1991
Cal Lutheran	1985-90
Cal Poly	1973-93
Cal Poly Pomona	1973-82
Cal St. Chico	1978-96
Cal St. Fullerton	1973-74
Cal St. Hayward	1973-93
Cal St. Los Angeles	1973-77
Cal St. Northridge	1973-92
Cameron	1988-92
Central Conn. St.	1973-92
UCF	1982-89
Central Mich.	1973-74
Central St.	1973-87
Chattanooga	1973-76
Connecticut	1973-77
Davidson	1977
Delaware	1973-79
Dist. Columbia	1973-75
East Tenn. St.	1973-77
Eastern Ill.	1973-80
Eastern Ky.	1973-77
Eastern Mich.	1973-75
Eastern Wash.	1978-83
Elon	1991-98
Evansville	1978-88
Florida A&M	1973-77
Franklin	1979-85
Gardner-Webb	1991-01
Georgetown (Ky.)	1980-82
Grambling	1973-76
Hampton	1973-94
Hardin-Simmons	1993
Howard	1973-77
Howard Payne	1981-86
Idaho St.	1973-77
Illinois St.	1973-75
Indiana St.	1973-75
Jackson St.	1973-76
Jacksonville St.	1973-94
James Madison	1974-76
Jamestown	1982-83
Knoxville	1989
Lafayette	1973-77
Lehigh	1973-77
Liberty	1981-87
La.-Monroe	1973-74
Louisiana Tech	1973-74
Maine	1973-77
Md.-East. Shore	1973-79
Massachusetts	1973-77
McNeese St.	1973-74
Merchant Marine	1978-81
Middle Tenn.	1973-77
Mississippi Col.	1973-96
Mississippi Val.	1973-79
Montana	1973-77
Montana St.	1973-77
Morehead St.	1973-77

DIVISION II

Morgan St.	1973-85
Morningside	1973-00
Morris Brown	1973-00
Murray St.	1973-77
Nevada	1973-77
UNLV	1973-77
New Hampshire	1973-77
NYIT	1974-83
Nicholls St.	1973-79
Norfolk St.	1973-96
N.C. A&T	1973-77
Northeastern	1973-77
Northern Ariz.	1973-77
Northern Iowa	1973-80
Northwestern St.	1973-75
Portland St.	1973-77, 81-97
Prairie View	1973-79
Puget Sound	1973-88
Rhode Island	1973-77
Sacramento St.	1973-92
St. Francis (Ill.)	1993-98

St. Mary's (Cal.)	1981-92
St. Paul's	1973-87
Sam Houston St.	1981-85
San Fran. St.	1979-94
Santa Clara	1973-92
Sacred Heart	1993-98
Savannah St.	1981-00
Sonoma St.	1984-96
South Carolina St.	1973-77
Southeast Mo. St.	1973-90
Southeastern La.	1973-79
Southern U.	1973-76
Southern Ore.	1981-83
Southern Utah	1982-92
Southwest Mo. St.	1973-81
Southwest Tex. St.	1978-83
Springfield	1973-94
Stephen F. Austin	1981-85
Stony Brook	1995-98
Tenn.-Martin	1973-91
Tennessee St.	1973-76
Tennessee Tech	1973-77

Texas Lutheran	1983, 98-02
Texas Southern	1973-76
Towson	1980-86
Troy St.	1973-92
Valparaiso	1979-92
Vermont	1973-74
Weber St.	1973-77
Western Caro.	1973-76
Western Ill.	1973-80
Western Ky.	1973-77
Westminster (Pa.)	1998-02
Wis.-Milwaukee	1973-74
Wis.-La Crosse	1975
Wis.-Oshkosh	1973-74
Wofford	1988-94
Youngstown St.	1973-80

* Provisional members are not active members of the Association and are not eligible for NCAA statistics, records and championship play. The end of the four-year provisional status and first season of active membership in Division II football is listed to the right of the school name.

Division III Records

Individual Records

Division III football records are based on the performances of Division III teams since the three-division reorganization plan was adopted by the special NCAA Convention in August 1973.

Total Offense

(Rushing Plus Passing)

MOST PLAYS
Quarter
37—Justin Peery, Westminster (Mo.) vs. MacMurray, Nov. 14, 1998 (4th)
Half
59—Justin Peery, Westminster (Mo.) vs. Bethel (Tenn.), Nov. 8, 1997 (2nd); Mike Wallace, Ohio Wesleyan vs. Denison, Oct. 3, 1981 (2nd)
Game
98—Justin Peery, Westminster (Mo.) vs. MacMurray, Nov. 14, 1998 (21 rushes, 77 passes; 628 yards)
Season
662—Steve Slowke, Alma, 2001 (3,630 yards)
Also holds per-game record with 66.2 (662 in 10)
Career
2,007—Kirk Baumgartner, Wis.-Stevens Point, 1986-89 (12,767 yards)
Per-game record—51.3, Justin Peery, Westminster (Mo.), 1996-99 (2,001 in 39)

MOST PLAYS BY A FRESHMAN
Season
571—Greg Troutman, Juniata, 2001 (3,122 yards)
Also holds per-game record with 57.1 (571 in 10)

MOST YARDS GAINED
Half
517—Justin Peery, Westminster (Mo.) vs. Bethel (Tenn.), Nov. 8, 1997 (497 passing, 20 rushing)
Game
723—Zamir Amin, Menlo vs. Cal Lutheran, Oct. 7, 2000 (731 passing, -8 rushing)
Season
4,651—Justin Peery, Westminster (Mo.), 1998 (150 rushing, 4,501 passing)
Also holds per-game record with 465.1 (4,651 in 10)
Career
13,645—Justin Peery, Westminster (Mo.), 1996-99 (383 rushing, 13,262 passing)
Also holds per-game record with 349.9 (13,645 in 39)

MOST YARDS GAINED BY A FRESHMAN
Season
3,122—Greg Troutman, Juniata, 2001 (571 plays)
Also holds per-game record with 312.2 (3,122 in 10)

MOST GAMES GAINING 300 YARDS OR MORE
Season
9—Justin Peery, Westminster (Mo.), 1999; Kyle Krober, Greenville, 2000
Career
26—Kirk Baumgartner, Wis.-Stevens Point, 1986-89

MOST CONSECUTIVE GAMES GAINING 300 YARDS OR MORE
Season
8—Danny Ragsdale, Redlands, 1999

GAINING 4,000 YARDS RUSHING AND 2,000 YARDS PASSING
Career
Chris Spriggs, Denison, 1983-86 (4,248 rushing & 2,799 passing)
Also holds record for yards gained by a running back with 7,047

GAINING 3,000 YARDS RUSHING AND 3,000 YARDS PASSING
Career
Clay Sampson (TB), Denison, 1977-80 (3,726 rushing & 3,194 passing)

HIGHEST AVERAGE GAIN PER PLAY
Season
(Min. 2,500 yards) 12.4—Adam Ryan, Wilmington (Ohio), 1999 (280 for 3,478)

Career
(Min. 6,000 yards) 8.4—Bill Borchert, Mount Union, 1994-97 (1,274 for 10,639)

MOST TOUCHDOWNS RESPONSIBLE FOR
(TDs Scored and Passed For)
Career
166—Justin Peery, Westminster (Mo.), 1996-99 (148 passing, 18 rushing)
Also holds per-game record with 4.3 (166 in 39)

Rushing

MOST RUSHES
Game
58—Bill Kaiser, Wabash vs. DePauw, Nov. 9, 1985 (211 yards)
Season
384—Dan Pugh, Mount Union, 2002 (2,300 yards)
Per-game record—38.0, Mike Birosak, Dickinson, 1989 (380 in 10)
Career
1,190—Steve Tardif, Maine Maritime, 1996-99 (6,093 yards)
Per-game record—32.7, Chris Sizemore, Bridgewater (Va.), 1972-74 (851 in 26)

MOST RUSHES BY A QUARTERBACK
Season
242—Juan Quesada, Elmhurst, 2001 (812 yards)
Per-game record—25.7, Jeff Saueressig, Wis.-River Falls, 1988 (231 in 9)

MOST CONSECUTIVE RUSHES BY THE SAME PLAYER
Game
46—Dan Walsh, Montclair St. vs. Ramapo, Sept. 30, 1989 (during 13 possessions)
Season
51—Dan Walsh, Montclair St., 1989 (Sept. 23 to Sept. 30)

MOST YARDS GAINED
Half
310—Leroy Horn, Montclair St. vs. New Jersey City, Nov. 9, 1985 (21 rushes)
Game
441—Dante Brown, Marietta vs. Baldwin-Wallace, Oct. 5, 1996
Season
2,385—Dante Brown, Marietta, 1996 (314 rushes)
Also holds per-game record with 238.5 (2,385 in 10)
Career
7,353—R.J. Bowers, Grove City, 1997-00 (1,188 rushes)
Also holds per-game record with 183.8 (7,353 in 40)

MOST YARDS GAINED BY A FRESHMAN
Season
1,380—Fredrick Nanhed, Cal Lutheran, 1995 (242 rushes)
Also holds per-game record with 153.3 (1,380 in 9)

MOST RUSHING YARDS GAINED BY A QUARTERBACK
Game
235—Mark Cota, Wis.-River Falls vs. Minn.-Morris, Sept. 13, 1986 (27 rushes)
Season
1,345—Kevin Cahill, Springfield, 1999 (243 rushes)
Also holds per-game record with 134.5 (1,345 in 10)
Career
3,315—Eric Hyten, Rose-Hulman, 1996-99 (796 rushes)

LONGEST GAIN BY A QUARTERBACK
Game
98 yards—Jon Hinds, Principia vs. Illinois Col., Sept. 20, 1986 (TD)

MOST GAMES GAINING 100 YARDS OR MORE
Career
35—R.J. Bowers, Grove City, 1997-00 (40 games)

MOST CONSECUTIVE GAMES GAINING 100 YARDS OR MORE
Career
32—R.J. Bowers, Grove City, Oct. 4, 1997-Oct. 14, 2000

MOST CONSECUTIVE GAMES GAINING 100 YARDS OR MORE BY A QUARTERBACK
Season
5—Eric Hyten, Rose-Hulman, 1996

MOST GAMES GAINING 200 YARDS OR MORE
Season
8—Ricky Gales, Simpson, 1989 (consecutive)
Career
16—R.J. Bowers, Grove City, 1997-00 (40 games)

MOST SEASONS GAINING 1,000 YARDS OR MORE
Career
4—Rich Kowalski, Hobart, 1972-75; Joe Dudek, Plymouth St., 1982-85; Jim Romagna, Loras, 1989-92; Steve Dixon, Beloit, 1990-93; Carey Bender, Coe, 1991-94; Steve Tardif, Maine Maritime, 1996-99

TWO PLAYERS, SAME TEAM, EACH GAINING 1,000 YARDS OR MORE
Season
By 11 teams. Most recent: Grove City, 1997—Doug Steiner (RB) 1,490 & R.J. Bowers (RB) 1,239

MOST YARDS GAINED RUSHING BY TWO PLAYERS, SAME TEAM
Game
519—Carey Bender (417) & Jason Whitaker (102), Coe vs. Grinnell, Oct. 9, 1993
Season
2,738—Dante Brown (RB) 2,385 & Aaron Conte (QB) 353, Marietta, 1996 (10 games)

HIGHEST AVERAGE GAIN PER RUSH
Game
(Min. 15 rushes) 19.4—Oliver Jordan, Emory & Henry vs. Greensboro, Oct. 3, 1998 (16 for 310)
(Min. 24 rushes) 15.9—Pete Baranek, Carthage vs. North Central, Oct. 5, 1985 (24 for 382)
Season
(Min. 140 rushes) 8.9—Billy Johnson, Widener, 1973 (168 for 1,494)
(Min. 200 rushes) 7.9—Jamie Lee, MacMurray, 1997 (207 for 1,639)
(Min. 250 rushes) 7.6—Carey Bender, Coe, 1994 (295 for 2,243)
Career
(Min. 500 rushes) 7.1—Joe Dudek, Plymouth St., 1982-85 (785 for 5,570)

MOST TOUCHDOWNS SCORED BY RUSHING
Game
8—Carey Bender, Coe vs. Beloit, Nov. 12, 1994
Season
35—Dan Pugh, Mount Union, 2002 (14 games)
Per-game record—3.4, R.J. Bowers, Grove City, 1998 (34 in 10)
Career
91—R.J. Bowers, Grove City, 1997-00
Also holds per-game record with 2.3 (91 in 40)

MOST RUSHING TOUCHDOWNS SCORED BY A QUARTERBACK
Season
18—Kevin Cahill, Springfield, 1999
Also holds per-game record with 1.8 (18 in 10)

Passing

HIGHEST PASSING EFFICIENCY RATING POINTS
Season
(Min. 15 atts. per game) 225.0—Mike Simpson, Eureka, 1994 (158 attempts, 116 completions, 5 interceptions, 1,988 yards, 25 TDs)
(Min. 25 atts. per game) 216.7—Bill Borchert, Mount Union, 1997 (272 attempts, 190 completions, 1 interception, 2,933 yards, 47 TDs)

Career
(Min. 650 comps.) 194.2—Bill Borchert, Mount Union, 1994-97 (1,009 attempts, 671 completions, 17 interceptions, 10,201 yards, 141 TDs)

MOST PASSES ATTEMPTED
Quarter
31—Mike Wallace, Ohio Wesleyan vs. Denison, Oct. 3, 1981 (4th)
Half
57—Mike Wallace, Ohio Wesleyan vs. Denison, Oct. 3, 1981 (2nd); Justin Peery, Westminster (Mo.) vs. Bethel (Tenn.), Nov. 8, 1997 (2nd)
Game
81—Jordan Poznick, Principia vs. Blackburn, Oct. 10, 1992 (completed 48)
Season
527—Kirk Baumgartner, Wis.-Stevens Point, 1988 (completed 276)
Per-game record—56.4, Jordan Poznick, Principia, 1992 (451 in 8)
Career
1,696—Kirk Baumgartner, Wis.-Stevens Point, 1986-89 (completed 883)
Per-game record—42.8, Justin Peery, Westminster (Mo.), 1996-99 (1,669 in 39)

MOST PASSES ATTEMPTED BY A FRESHMAN
Season
464—Greg Troutman, Juniata, 2001 (completed 228)
Per-game record—50.3, Mark Novara, Lakeland, 1994 (453 in 9)

MOST PASSES COMPLETED
Quarter
21—Rob Bristow, Pomona-Pitzer vs. Whittier, Oct. 19, 1985 (4th)
Half
36—Mike Wallace, Ohio Wesleyan vs. Denison, Oct. 3, 1981 (2nd)
Game
51—Scott Kello, Sul Ross St. vs. Howard Payne, Oct. 5, 2002 (attempted 80)
Season
329—Justin Peery, Westminster (Mo.), 1999 (attempted 498)
Also holds per-game record with 32.9 (329 in 10)
Career
1,012—Justin Peery, Westminster (Mo.), 1996-99 (attempted 1,669)
Also holds per-game record with 25.9 (1,012 in 39)

MOST PASSES COMPLETED BY A FRESHMAN
Season
228—Greg Troutman, Juniata, 2001 (attempted 464)
Per-game record—25.2, Mark Novara, Lakeland, 1994 (227 in 9)

HIGHEST PERCENTAGE OF PASSES COMPLETED
Game
(Min. 20 comps.) 91.3%—Chris Esterley, St. Thomas (Minn.) vs. St. Olaf, Sept. 23, 1995 (21 of 23)
(Min. 35 comps.) 83.3%—Scott Driggers, Colorado Col. vs. Neb. Wesleyan, Sept. 10, 1983 (35 of 42)
Season
(Min. 250 atts.) 72.9%—Jim Ballard, Mount Union, 1993 (229 of 314)
Career
(Min. 750 atts.) 66.5%—Bill Borchert, Mount Union, 1994-97 (671 of 1,009)

MOST CONSECUTIVE PASSES COMPLETED
Game
17—William Snyder, Carnegie Mellon vs. Wooster, Oct. 20, 1990
Season
27—Jordan Neal, Hardin-Simmons, 2001 (6 vs. Louisiana Col., Sept. 29; 3 vs. Mississippi Col., Oct. 6; 9 vs. East Tex. Baptist, Oct. 27; 9 vs. McMurry, Nov. 10)

MOST CONSECUTIVE PASSES COMPLETED BY TWO PLAYERS, SAME TEAM
Game
20—Kevin Keefe (16) & David Skarupa (4), Baldwin-Wallace vs. Moravian, Sept. 10, 1994

MOST PASSES HAD INTERCEPTED
Game
8—Kevin Karwath, Canisius vs. Liberty, Nov. 19, 1979; Dennis Bogacz, Wis.-Oshkosh vs. Wis.-Stevens Point, Oct. 29, 1988; Jim Higgins, Brockport St. vs. Buffalo St., Sept. 29, 1990; Jason Clark, Ohio Northern vs. John Carroll, Nov. 9, 1991
Season
43—Steve Hendry, Wis.-Superior, 1982 (attempted 480)
Also holds per-game record with 3.9 (43 in 11)
Career
117—Steve Hendry, Wis.-Superior, 1980-83 (attempted 1,343)
Per-game record—3.2, Willie Martinez, Oberlin, 1973-74 (58 in 18)

LOWEST PERCENTAGE OF PASSES HAD INTERCEPTED
Season
(Min. 150 atts.) 0.4%—Bill Borchert, Mount Union, 1997 (1 of 272)
Career
(Min. 600 atts.) 1.7%—Bill Borchert, Mount Union, 1994-97 (17 of 1,009)

MOST PASSES ATTEMPTED WITHOUT INTERCEPTION
Game
77—Justin Peery, Westminster (Mo.) vs. MacMurray, Nov. 14, 1998 (completed 50)
Season
124—Tim Tenhet, Sewanee, 1982

MOST CONSECUTIVE PASSES ATTEMPTED WITHOUT AN INTERCEPTION
Season
221—Bill Borchert, Mount Union, 1997 (during 8 games; began Sept. 27 vs. Otterbein, ended Nov. 15 vs. Hiram)

MOST YARDS GAINED
Half
497—Justin Peery, Westminster (Mo.) vs. Bethel (Tenn.), Nov. 8, 1997 (2nd)
Game
731—Zamir Amin, Menlo vs. Cal Lutheran, Oct. 7, 2000
Season
4,501—Justin Peery, Westminster (Mo.), 1998
Also holds per-game record with 450.1 (4,501 in 10)
Career
13,262—Justin Peery, Westminster (Mo.), 1996-99
Also holds per-game record with 340.1 (13,262 in 39)

MOST YARDS GAINED BY A FRESHMAN
Season
2,799—Greg Troutman, Juniata, 2001 (10 games)
Per-game record—286.2, Mark Novara, Lakeland, 1994 (2,576 in 9)

MOST GAMES PASSING FOR 200 YARDS OR MORE
Season
13—Roy Hampton, Trinity (Tex.), 2002
Career
32—Kirk Baumgartner, Wis.-Stevens Point, 1986-89; Justin Peery, Westminster (Mo.), 1996-99

MOST CONSECUTIVE GAMES PASSING FOR 200 YARDS OR MORE
Season
13—Roy Hampton, Trinity (Tex.), 2002
Career
27—Keith Bishop, Ill. Wesleyan/Wheaton (Ill.), 1981, 1983-85

MOST GAMES PASSING FOR 300 YARDS OR MORE
Season
9—Kirk Baumgartner, Wis.-Stevens Point, 1989; Justin Peery, Westminster (Mo.), 1999
Career
24—Kirk Baumgartner, Wis.-Stevens Point, 1986-89

MOST CONSECUTIVE GAMES PASSING FOR 300 YARDS OR MORE
Season
9—Kirk Baumgartner, Wis.-Stevens Point, 1989 (began Sept. 9 vs. St. Norbert, through Nov. 4 vs. Wis.-Superior)

Scott Kello of Sul Ross State upped the Division III record for single-game completions to 51 on October 5, 2002, against Howard Payne.

Career
13—Kirk Baumgartner, Wis.-Stevens Point, 1988-89 (began Oct. 22, 1988, vs. Wis.-Stout, through Nov. 4, 1989, vs. Wis.-Superior)

MOST YARDS GAINED BY TWO OPPOSING PLAYERS
Game
1,020—Josh Wakefield, Alma (569) & Travis McMahen, Franklin (451), Sept. 25, 1999 (completed 60 of 109)

MOST YARDS GAINED PER ATTEMPT
Season
(Min. 175 atts.) 12.9—Willie Seiler, St. John's (Minn.), 1993 (205 for 2,648)
(Min. 275 atts.) 11.3—Troy Dougherty, Grinnell, 1998 (293 for 3,310)
Career
(Min. 950 atts.) 10.1—Bill Borchert, Mount Union, 1994-97 (1,009 for 10,201)

MOST YARDS GAINED PER COMPLETION
Season
(Min. 100 comps.) 19.7—David Parker, Bishop, 1981 (114 for 2,242)
(Min. 200 comps.) 16.1—John Furmaniak, Eureka, 1995 (210 for 3,372)
Career
(Min. 300 comps.) 18.3—David Parker, Bishop, 1981-84 (378 for 6,934)
(Min. 425 comps.) 15.2—Bill Borchert, Mount Union, 1994-97 (671 for 10,201)

MOST TOUCHDOWN PASSES
Quarter
5—David Sullivan, Williams vs. Hamilton, Oct. 30, 1993 (2nd)
Game
9—Joe Zarlinga, Ohio Northern vs. Capital, Nov. 14, 1998
Season
54—Justin Peery, Westminster (Mo.), 1999
Also holds per-game record with 5.4 (54 in 10)
Career
148—Justin Peery, Westminster (Mo.), 1996-99
Also holds per-game record with 3.8 (148 in 39)

HIGHEST PERCENTAGE OF PASSES ATTEMPTED FOR TOUCHDOWNS
Season
(Min. 200 atts.) 17.3%—Bill Borchert, Mount Union, 1997 (47 of 272)
(Min. 300 atts.) 11.8%—Jim Ballard, Mount Union, 1993 (37 of 314)
Career
(Min. 800 atts.) 14.0%—Bill Borchert, Mount Union, 1994-97 (141 of 1,009)

Sul Ross State Sports Information

MOST TOUCHDOWN PASSES BY A FRESHMAN
Season
26—Bill Borchert, Mount Union, 1994
Also holds per-game record with 2.6 (26 in 10)

MOST CONSECUTIVE GAMES THROWING A TOUCHDOWN PASS
Career
40—Bill Borchert, Mount Union (from Sept. 10, 1994, through Nov. 15, 1997)

Receiving

MOST PASSES CAUGHT
Game
23—Sean Munroe, Mass.-Boston vs. Mass. Maritime, Oct. 10, 1992 (332 yards)
Season
136—Scott Pingel, Westminster (Mo.), 1999 (1,648 yards)
Also holds per-game record with 13.6 (136 in 10)
Career
436—Scott Pingel, Westminster (Mo.), 1996-99 (6,108 yards)
Also holds per-game record with 11.2 (436 in 39)

MOST PASSES CAUGHT BY A TIGHT END
Game
17—Matt Surette, WPI vs. Springfield, Oct. 25, 1997
Season
75—Ryan Davis, St. Thomas (Minn.), 1994 (1,164 yards); Matt Surette, WPI, 1997 (1,287 yards)
Career
185—Hanz Hoag, Evansville, 1991-93 (2,173 yards)

MOST PASSES CAUGHT BY A RUNNING BACK
Game
17—Tim Mowery, Wis.-Superior vs. Wis.-Stevens Point, Oct. 17, 1981 (154 yards); Theo Blanco, Wis.-Stevens Point vs. Wis.-Oshkosh, Oct. 31, 1987 (271 yards); Greg Siebers, Wis.-Platteville vs. Wis.-La Crosse, Oct. 6, 2001 (99 yards)
Season
106—Theo Blanco, Wis.-Stevens Point, 1987 (1,616 yards)
Career
169—Mike Christman, Wis.-Stevens Point, 1983-86 (2,190 yards)

MOST PASSES CAUGHT BY A FRESHMAN
Season
92—Darryl DeShields, Greenville, 1999 (1,515 yards)

MOST PASSES CAUGHT BY TWO PLAYERS, SAME TEAM
Season
203—Scott Pingel (WR) 130 & Logan Stanley (TE) 73, Westminster (Mo.), 1998 (3,168 yards, 33 TDs)

Hartwick's Ryan Soule concluded his career last year in a tie for the Division III lead in kickoffs returned for touchdowns with six.

Hartwick Sports Information

MOST PASSES CAUGHT BY THREE PLAYERS, SAME TEAM
Season
270—Scott Pingel (WR) 130, Logan Stanley (TE) 73 & John Squires (WR) 67, Westminster (Mo.), 1998 (3,996 yards, 33 TDs; team totals: 319 receps., 4,501 yards, 51 TDs)

MOST CONSECUTIVE GAMES CATCHING A PASS
Career
40—Brandon Good, Wooster, 1995-98

MOST YARDS GAINED
Game
418—Lewis Howes, Principia vs. Martin Luther, Oct. 12, 2002 (caught 18)
Season
2,157—Scott Pingel, Westminster (Mo.), 1998 (caught 130)
Also holds per-game record with 215.7 (2,157 in 10)
Career
6,108—Scott Pingel, Westminster (Mo.), 1996-99 (caught 436)
Also holds per-game record with 156.6 (6,108 in 39)

MOST YARDS GAINED BY A TIGHT END
Game
362—Matt Surette, WPI vs. Springfield, Oct. 25, 1997 (caught 17)
Season
1,290—Don Moehling, Wis.-Stevens Point, 1988 (caught 72)
Career
2,663—Don Moehling, Wis.-Stevens Point, 1986-89 (caught 152)

MOST YARDS GAINED BY A RUNNING BACK
Game
271—Theo Blanco, Wis.-Stevens Point vs. Wis.-Oshkosh, Oct. 31, 1987 (caught 17)
Season
1,616—Theo Blanco, Wis.-Stevens Point, 1987 (caught 106)
Career
2,190—Mike Christman, Wis.-Stevens Point, 1983-86 (caught 169)

MOST YARDS GAINED BY TWO PLAYERS, SAME TEAM
Season
3,168—Scott Pingel (WR) 2,157 & Logan Stanley (TE) 1,011, Westminster (Mo.), 1998 (caught 203, 33 TDs)

HIGHEST AVERAGE GAIN PER RECEPTION
Game
(Min. 3 receps.) 68.3—Paul Jaeckel, Elmhurst vs. Ill. Wesleyan, Oct. 8, 1983 (3 for 205)
(Min. 5 receps.) 56.8—Tom Casperson, Col. of New Jersey vs. Ramapo, Nov. 15, 1980 (5 for 284)
Season
(Min. 35 receps.) 26.9—Marty Redlawsk, Concordia (Ill.), 1985 (38 for 1,022)
(Min. 50 receps.) 23.5—Evan Elkington, WPI, 1989 (52 for 1,220)
Career
(Min. 125 receps.) 22.9—Kirk Aikens, Hartwick, 1995-98 (127 for 2,902)

HIGHEST AVERAGE GAIN PER RECEPTION BY A RUNNING BACK
Season
(Min. 50 receps.) 17.5—Barry Rose, Wis.-Stevens Point, 1989 (67 for 1,171)

MOST TOUCHDOWN PASSES CAUGHT
Game
7—Matt Perceval, Wesleyan (Conn.) vs. Middlebury, Sept. 26, 1998
Season
26—Scott Pingel, Westminster (Mo.), 1998
Also holds per-game record with 2.6 (26 in 10)
Career
75—Scott Pingel, Westminster (Mo.), 1996-99 (caught 436)
Also holds per-game record with 1.9 (75 in 39)

MOST TOUCHDOWN PASSES CAUGHT BY A FRESHMAN
Season
15—Mark Bartosic, Susquehanna, 2000

HIGHEST PERCENTAGE OF PASSES CAUGHT FOR TOUCHDOWNS
Season
(Min. 12 TDs) 55.6%—Kirk Aikens, Hartwick, 1998 (20 of 36)
Career
(Min. 20 TDs) 33.9%—Kirk Aikens, Hartwick, 1995-98 (43 of 127)

MOST CONSECUTIVE PASSES CAUGHT FOR TOUCHDOWNS
9—Keith Gilliam, Randolph-Macon, 1984 (during four games)

Punting

MOST PUNTS
Game
17—Jerry Williams, Frostburg St. vs. Salisbury, Sept. 30, 1978
Season
106—Bob Blake, Wis.-Superior, 1977 (3,404 yards)
Per-game record—11.0, Mark Roedelbronn, FDU-Madison, 1990 (99 in 9)
Career
263—Chris Gardner, Loras, 1987-90 (9,394 yards)

HIGHEST AVERAGE PER PUNT
Season
(Min. 40 punts) 45.5—Justin Shively, Anderson (Ind.), 1997 (55 for 2,502)
Career
(Min. 100 punts) 43.4—Jeff Shea, Cal Lutheran, 1994-97 (183 for 7,939)

Punt Returns

MOST PUNT RETURNS
Game
10—Ellis Wangelin, Wis.-River Falls vs. Wis.-Platteville, Oct. 12, 1985 (87 yards)
Season
48—Rick Bealer, Lycoming, 1989 (492 yards)
Career
134—Marvin Deal, McDaniel, 1996-99 (1,480 yards)

MOST YARDS ON PUNT RETURNS
Game
212—Melvin Dillard, Ferrum vs. Newport News App., Oct. 13, 1990 (6 returns)
Season
688—Melvin Dillard, Ferrum, 1990 (25 returns)
Career
1,550—Joshua Carter, Muhlenberg, 1998-01 (133 returns)

HIGHEST AVERAGE GAIN PER RETURN
Season
(Min. 1.2 rets. per game) 31.2—Chuck Downey, Stony Brook, 1986 (17 for 530)
Career
(Min. 1.2 rets. per game) 22.9—Keith Winston, Knoxville, 1986-87 (30 for 686)
(Min. 50 rets.) 20.3—Chuck Downey, Stony Brook, 1984-87 (59 for 1,198)

MOST TOUCHDOWNS SCORED ON PUNT RETURNS
Game
2—By 11 players. Most recent: Jason Hunt, Trinity (Tex.) vs. Rhodes, Nov. 2, 2002 (66 & 90 yards)
Season
5—Chris McKinney, Guilford, 2001 (21 returns)
Career
7—Chuck Downey, Stony Brook, 1984-87 (59 returns)

Kickoff Returns

MOST KICKOFF RETURNS
Game
11—Mason Tootell, Swarthmore vs. Johns Hopkins, Sept. 19, 1997 (197 yards)
Season
48—Mason Tootell, Swarthmore, 1997 (944 yards)
Career
104—Simeon Henderson, Elmhurst, 1991-94 (2,063 yards)

MOST YARDS ON KICKOFF RETURNS
Game
279—Chuck Downey, Stony Brook vs. Col. of New Jersey, Oct. 5, 1984 (7 returns)
Season
981—Joshua Carter, Muhlenberg, 1999 (28 returns)
Career
2,189—Joshua Carter, Muhlenberg, 1998-01 (75 returns)

HIGHEST AVERAGE GAIN PER RETURN
Game
(Min. 3 rets.) 68.0—Victor Johnson, Elmhurst vs. Wheaton (Ill.), Sept. 15, 1979 (3 for 204)
Season
(Min. 1.2 rets. per game) 42.2—Brandon Steinheim, Wesley, 1994 (10 for 422)
Career
(Min. 1.2 rets. per game) 34.9—David Ziegler, John Carroll, 1996-99 (30 for 1,047)

MOST TOUCHDOWNS SCORED ON KICKOFF RETURNS
Game
2—By many players. Most recent: Jabori Jackson, East Tex. Baptist vs. Texas Lutheran, Oct. 20, 2001
Season
4—Byron Womack, Iona, 1989
Career
6—Byron Womack, Iona, 1988-91; Ryan Soule, Hartwick, 1999-02

Total Kick Returns
(Combined Punt and Kickoff Returns)

MOST YARDS ON KICK RETURNS
Game
354—Chuck Downey, Stony Brook vs. Col. of New Jersey, Oct. 5, 1984 (7 kickoff returns for 279 yards, 1 punt return for 75 yards)
Career
3,739—Joshua Carter, Muhlenberg, 1998-01 (133 punt returns for 1,550 yards; 75 kickoff returns for 2,189 yards)

GAINING 1,000 YARDS ON PUNT RETURNS AND 1,000 YARDS ON KICKOFF RETURNS
Career
Chuck Downey, Stony Brook, 1984-87 (1,198 on punt returns, 1,281 on kickoff returns); LaVant King, Ohio Northern, 1991, 93-95 (1,074 on punt returns, 1,298 on kickoff returns); Charles Warren, Dickinson, 1993-96 (1,239 on punt returns, 1,021 on kickoff returns); David Ziegler, John Carroll, 1996-99 (1,063 on punt returns, 1,047 on kickoff returns); Marvin Deal, McDaniel, 1996-99 (1,480 on punt returns, 1,104 on kickoff returns); Joshua Carter, Muhlenberg, 1998-01 (1,550 on punt returns, 2,189 on kickoff returns)

MOST TOUCHDOWNS ON KICK RETURNS
Game
3—Chuck Downey, Stony Brook vs. Col. of New Jersey, Oct. 5, 1984 (2 kickoff returns, 98 & 95 yards; 1 punt return, 75 yards)
Season
5—Chuck Downey, Stony Brook, 1986 (4 punt returns, 1 kickoff return); Chris Warren, Ferrum, 1989 (4 punt returns, 1 kickoff return); Charles Jordan, Occidental, 1993 (2 punt returns, 3 kickoff returns); Chris McKinney, Guilford, 2001 (5 punt returns)
Career
10—Chuck Downey, Stony Brook, 1984-87 (7 punt returns, 3 kickoff returns)

HIGHEST AVERAGE PER KICK RETURN
(Min. 1.2 Returns Per Game Each)
Career
23.6—Chuck Downey, Stony Brook, 1984-87 (59 for 1,198 on punt returns, 46 for 1,281 on kickoff returns)

AVERAGING 20 YARDS EACH ON PUNT RETURNS AND KICKOFF RETURNS
(Min. 1.2 Returns Per Game Each)
Career
Chuck Downey, Stony Brook, 1984-87 (20.3 on punt returns, 59 for 1,198; 27.8 on kickoff returns, 46 for 1,281)

All Runbacks
(Combined Interceptions, Punt Returns and Kickoff Returns)

MOST TOUCHDOWNS ON INTERCEPTIONS, PUNT RETURNS AND KICKOFF RETURNS
Game
3—Mike Schmitz, Monmouth (Ill.) vs. Olivet Nazarene, Sept. 30, 1978 (1 interception return, 2 punt returns); Chuck Downey, Stony Brook vs. Col. of New Jersey, Oct. 5, 1984 (2 kickoff returns, 98 & 95 yards; 1 punt return, 75 yards)
Season
6—Chuck Downey, Stony Brook, 1986 (1 interception return, 4 punt returns, 1 kickoff return)
Career
11—Chuck Downey, Stony Brook, 1984-87 (1 interception return, 7 punt returns, 3 kickoff returns)

Kicks Blocked

MOST PUNTS BLOCKED BY
Game
3—Jim Perryman, Millikin vs. Carroll (Wis.), Nov. 1, 1980; Scott Lunsford, Maryville (Tenn.) vs. Rhodes, Sept. 26, 1998; Andy Waddle, Wittenberg vs. Urbana, Sept. 1, 2000
Season
9—Jim Perryman, Millikin, 1980
Career
13—Frank Lyle, Millsaps, 1979-82
Note: Daryl Hobson, Benedictine (Ill.) DB, blocked 9 punts during 17 games in 1987-88.

MOST TOTAL KICKS BLOCKED BY
(Includes Punts, PAT Attempts, FG Attempts)
Game
4—Bob Paulus, Rhodes vs. Washington (Mo.), Sept. 29, 2001 (3 FG and 1 PAT)

All-Purpose Yards
(Yardage Gained From Rushing, Receiving and All Runbacks)

MOST PLAYS
Season
429—Dan Pugh, Mount Union, 2002 (384 rushes, 32 receptions, 13 kickoff returns)
Career
1,313—Steve Tardif, Maine Maritime, 1996-99 (1,190 rushing, 58 receptions, 1 interception, 10 punt returns, 55 kickoff returns)

MOST YARDS GAINED
Game
527—Paul Smith, Gettysburg vs. Muhlenberg, Oct. 23, 1999 (390 rushing, 137 receiving)
Season
3,189—Dan Pugh, Mount Union, 2002 (2,300 rushing, 382 receiving, 507 kickoff returns)
Per-game record—297.3, Dante Brown, Marietta, 1996 (2,973 in 10)
Career
9,253—R.J. Bowers, Grove City, 1997-00 (7,353 rushing, 397 receiving, 50 punt returns, 1,453 kickoff returns)
Also holds per-game record with 231.3 (9,253 in 40)

HIGHEST AVERAGE GAIN PER PLAY
Season
(Min. 1,500 yards, 125 plays) 16.9—Matt Eisenberg, Juniata, 1999 (2,113 in 125)
Career
(Min. 4,000 yards, 300 plays) 16.0—Chris Wiesehan, Wabash, 1990-93 (4,825 in 301)

Scoring

MOST POINTS SCORED
Game
48—Carey Bender, Coe vs. Beloit, Nov. 12, 1994
Season
248—Dan Pugh, Mount Union, 2002 (41 TDs & 2 PATs)

Per-game record—20.8, James Regan, Pomona-Pitzer, 1997 (166 in 8)
Career
562—R.J. Bowers, Grove City, 1997-00 (92 TDs & 10 PATs)
Per-game record—14.4, Ricky Gales, Simpson, 1988-89 (274 in 19)

TWO PLAYERS, SAME TEAM, EACH SCORING 100 POINTS OR MORE
Season
10 times. Most recent: Dan Pugh (248) & Chad Teague (105), Mount Union, 2002; Blake Elliott (162) & Kent Crowley (126), St. John's (Minn.), 2002; Todd Canion (121) & Jerheme Urban (114), Trinity (Tex.), 2002

MOST TOUCHDOWNS SCORED
Season
41—Dan Pugh, Mount Union, 2002 (14 games)
Per-game record—3.4, R.J. Bowers, Grove City, 1998 (34 in 10)
Career
92—R.J. Bowers, Grove City, 1997-00
Also holds per-game record with 2.3 (92 in 40)

MOST GAMES SCORING A TOUCHDOWN
Career
36—Carey Bender, Coe, 1991-94 (39 games); R.J. Bowers, Grove City, 1997-00 (40 games)

MOST CONSECUTIVE GAMES SCORING A TOUCHDOWN
Career
25—Chuck Moore, Mount Union (Oct. 10, 1998 to Nov. 4, 2000)

MOST GAMES SCORING TWO OR MORE TOUCHDOWNS
Career
24—Joe Dudek, Plymouth St., 1982-85 (41 games); R.J. Bowers, Grove City, 1997-00 (40 games)

MOST EXTRA POINTS ATTEMPTED BY KICKING
Game
14—Kurt Christenson, Concordia-M'head vs. Macalester, Sept. 24, 1977 (made 13)
Season
87—Todd Canion, Trinity (Tex.), 2002 (made 82)
Career
194—Tim Mercer, Ferrum, 1987-90 (made 183)

MOST EXTRA POINTS MADE BY KICKING
Game
13—Kurt Christenson, Concordia-M'head vs. Macalester, Sept. 24, 1977 (attempted 14)
Season
82—Todd Canion, Trinity (Tex.), 2002 (attempted 87)
Career
183—Tim Mercer, Ferrum, 1987-90 (attempted 194)

HIGHEST PERCENTAGE OF EXTRA POINTS MADE
(Best Perfect Season)
100.0%—Mike Duvic, Dayton, 1989 (46 of 46)

HIGHEST PERCENTAGE OF EXTRA POINTS MADE
Career
(Min. 80 atts.) 100.0%—Mike Farrell, Adrian, 1983-85 (84 of 84)
(Min. 100 atts.) 98.5%—Rims Roof, Coe, 1982-85 (135 of 137)

MOST CONSECUTIVE EXTRA POINTS MADE BY KICKING
Game
13—Kurt Christenson, Concordia-M'head vs. Macalester, Sept. 24, 1977
Career
102—Rims Roof, Coe (from Sept. 24, 1983, through Nov. 9, 1985)

MOST POINTS SCORED BY KICKING
Game
20—Jim Hever, Rhodes vs. Millsaps, Sept. 22, 1984 (6 FGs, 2 PATs)
Season
121—Todd Canion, Trinity (Tex.), 2002 (13 FGs, 82 PATs)
Per-game record—10.2, Ken Edelman, Mount Union, 1990 (102 in 10)
Career
274—Ken Edelman, Mount Union, 1987-90 (52 FGs, 118 PATs)

DIVISION III

Also holds per-game record with 6.9 (274 in 40)

MOST SUCCESSFUL TWO-POINT PASS ATTEMPTS
Game
4—Dave Geissler, Wis.-Stevens Point vs. Wis.-La Crosse, Sept. 21, 1985 (all in 4th quarter); Rob Bristow, Pomona-Pitzer vs. Whittier, Oct. 19, 1985 (all in 4th quarter)

Season
10—Justin Peery, Westminster (Mo.), 1997 (14 attempts)

Career
25—Justin Peery, Westminster (Mo.), 1996-99 (44 attempts)
Note: Rob Bristow, Pomona-Pitzer, 1983-86, holds record for highest percentage of successful two-point pass attempts (best perfect record) at 9 of 9.

MOST TWO-POINT PASSES CAUGHT
Season
8—Scott Pingel, Westminster (Mo.), 1997
Career
17—Scott Pingel, Westminster (Mo.), 1996-99

Field Goals

MOST FIELD GOALS MADE
Game
6—Jim Hever, Rhodes vs. Millsaps, Sept. 22, 1984 (30, 24, 42, 44, 46, 30 yards; attempted 8)

Season
20—Ken Edelman, Mount Union, 1990 (attempted 27)
Also holds per-game record with 2.0 (20 in 10)

Career
52—Ken Edelman, Mount Union, 1987-90 (attempted 71)
Also holds per-game record (Min. 30) with 1.3 (52 in 40)

MOST FIELD GOALS ATTEMPTED
Game
8—Jim Hever, Rhodes vs. Millsaps, Sept. 22, 1984 (made 6)
Season
29—Scott Ryerson, UCF, 1981 (made 18)
Career
75—Carlos Martinez, Buena Vista, 1998-01 (made 48)

HIGHEST PERCENTAGE OF FIELD GOALS MADE
Season
(Min. 15 atts.) 93.8%—Steve Graeca, John Carroll, 1988 (15 of 16)
Career
(Min. 50 atts.) *77.6%—Mike Duvic, Dayton, 1986-89 (38 of 49)

Declared champion; with one more attempt (making 50), failed, still would have highest percentage (76.0).

LONGEST FIELD GOAL MADE
62—Dom Antonini, Rowan vs. Salisbury, Sept. 18, 1976

MOST FIELD GOALS ATTEMPTED WITHOUT SUCCESS
Season
11—Scott Perry, Moravian, 1986

Defensive Records

TOTAL TACKLES
Game
27—Casey McConnell, Kenyon vs. Centre, Sept. 7, 2002
Season
178—Robert Gunn, Earlham, 2000
Also holds per-game record with 17.8 (178 in 10)

SOLO TACKLES
Game
17—Casey McConnell, Kenyon vs. Centre, Sept. 7, 2002
Season
106—Robert Gunn, Earlham, 2000
Also holds per-game record with 10.6 (106 in 10)

ASSISTED TACKLES
Season
98—Greg Chrony, Maranatha Baptist, 2000
Also holds per-game record with 10.9 (98 in 9)

TACKLES FOR LOSS
Game
8.0—Brenden Givan, Stillman vs. Pikeville, Sept. 1, 2001
Season
38.5—Steve Wilson, King's (Pa.), 2001 (37 solo, 3 assisted)
Also holds per-game record with 3.9 (38.5 in 10)

PASS SACKS
Game
5.0—J.J. Zearley, Wartburg vs. Loras, Oct. 5, 2002
Season
24.0—Russ Watson, Worcester St., 2000
Also holds per-game record with 2.7 (24.0 in 9)

MOST PASSES DEFENDED
Game
10—James Patrick, Stillman vs. Edward Waters, Nov. 2, 2002 (5 pass breakups, 5 interceptions)
Season
36—Jarrod Pence, Moravian, 2001 (31 pass breakups, 5 interceptions)
Also holds per-game record with 3.6 (36 in 10)

FORCED FUMBLES
Season
8—Tony Pate, Concordia (Ill.), 2000
Also holds per-game record with 0.9 (8 in 9)

FUMBLES (FUMBLE RECOVERIES AND FORCED FUMBLES)
Season
11—Tony Pate, Concordia (Ill.), 2000
Also holds per-game record with 1.2 (11 in 9)

MOST PASSES INTERCEPTED
Game
5—By 11 players. Most recent: James Patrick, Stillman vs. Edward Waters, Nov. 2, 2002
Season
15—Mark Dorner, Juniata, 1987 (202 yards); Ben Matthews, Bethel (Minn.), 2000 (134 yards)
Also hold per-game record with 1.5 (15 in 10)
Career
29—Ralph Gebhardt, Rochester, 1973-75 (384 yards)

MOST CONSECUTIVE GAMES INTERCEPTING A PASS
Season
9—Brent Sands, Cornell College, 1992
Also holds career record with 9

MOST YARDS ON INTERCEPTION RETURNS
Game
164—Rick Conner, McDaniel vs. Dickinson, Oct. 15, 1983 (89-yard interception and 75-yard lateral after an interception)
Season
358—Rod Pesek, Whittier, 1987 (10 interceptions)
Career
443—Mark Dorner, Juniata, 1984-87 (26 interceptions)

HIGHEST AVERAGE GAIN PER INTERCEPTION
Season
(Min. 7 ints.) 38.4—Randy Ames, Hope, 1996 (7 for 269)
Career
(Min. 20 ints.) 20.4—Todd Schoelzel, Wis.-Oshkosh, 1985-88 (22 for 448)

MOST TOUCHDOWNS SCORED ON INTERCEPTIONS
Game
3—By many players
Season
3—By many players. Most recent: Mike Linhardt, Westminster (Mo.), 2002 (7 interceptions); Seth Berghoff, Pacific Lutheran, 2001 (4 interceptions)

MOST DEFENSIVE EXTRA POINTS SCORED
Game
2—Shontez Jones, Greenville vs. MacMurray, Sept. 30, 2000
Season
2—Dan Fichter, Brockport St., 1990 (2 blocked kick returns); Shontez Jones, Greenville, 2000 (2 blocked kick returns)

LONGEST DEFENSIVE EXTRA POINT BLOCKED KICK RETURN
97—Keith Mottram (CB), Colorado Col. vs. Austin, Oct. 10, 1992 (scored)

LONGEST DEFENSIVE EXTRA POINT INTERCEPTION
100—By many players. Most recent: Mike Ortiz (DB), FDU-Florham vs. Widener, Sept. 11, 1999

FIRST DEFENSIVE EXTRA POINT SCORED
Steve Nieves (DB), St. John's (N.Y.) vs. Iona, Sept. 10, 1988 (83-yard blocked kick return)

Team Records

SINGLE GAME—Offense

Total Offense

MOST PLAYS
112—Gust. Adolphus vs. Bethel (Minn.), Nov. 2, 1985 (47 rushes, 65 passes; 493 yards)

MOST PLAYS, BOTH TEAMS
214—Gust. Adolphus (112) & Bethel (Minn.) (102), Nov. 2, 1985 (71 rushes, 143 passes; 930 yards)

MOST YARDS GAINED
823—Westminster (Mo.) vs. Principia, Oct. 17, 1998 (176 rushing, 647 passing)

MOST YARDS GAINED, BOTH TEAMS
1,395—Occidental (753) & Claremont-M-S (642), Oct. 30, 1993 (136 plays)

MOST TOUCHDOWNS SCORED BY RUSHING AND PASSING
14—Concordia-M'head vs. Macalester, Sept. 24, 1977 (12 rushing, 2 passing)

Rushing

MOST RUSHES
92—Wis.-River Falls vs. Wis.-Platteville, Oct. 21, 1989 (464 yards)

MOST YARDS GAINED
642—Wis.-River Falls vs. Wis.-Superior, Oct. 14, 1989 (88 rushes)

MOST TOUCHDOWNS SCORED BY RUSHING
12—Concordia-M'head vs. Macalester, Sept. 24, 1977

Passing

MOST PASSES ATTEMPTED
81—Principia vs. Blackburn, Oct. 10, 1992 (completed 48)

MOST PASSES ATTEMPTED, BOTH TEAMS
143—Bethel (Minn.) (78) & Gust. Adolphus (65), Nov. 2, 1985 (completed 65)

MOST PASSES ATTEMPTED WITHOUT AN INTERCEPTION
77—Westminster (Mo.) vs. MacMurray, Nov. 14, 1998 (completed 50)

MOST PASSES COMPLETED
50—Hofstra vs. Fordham, Oct. 19, 1991 (attempted 69); Westminster (Mo.) vs. MacMurray, Nov. 14, 1998 (attempted 77)

MOST PASSES COMPLETED, BOTH TEAMS
72—Wis.-Superior (41) & Wis.-Stevens Point (31), Oct. 17, 1981 (attempted 131)

HIGHEST PERCENTAGE OF PASSES COMPLETED (Min. 35 Attempts)
78.9%—Wheaton (Ill.) vs. North Park, Oct. 8, 1983 (30 of 38)

MOST YARDS GAINED
731—Menlo vs. Cal Lutheran, Oct. 7, 2000

MOST YARDS GAINED, BOTH TEAMS
1,100—St. Thomas (Minn.) (602) & Bethel (Minn.) (498), Nov. 13, 1993 (attempted 113, completed 69)

MOST TOUCHDOWN PASSES
9—Westminster (Mo.) vs. Principia, Oct. 17, 1998; Ohio Northern vs. Capital, Nov. 14, 1998

MOST TOUCHDOWN PASSES, BOTH TEAMS
12—St. Thomas (Minn.) (6) & Bethel (Minn.) (6), Nov. 13, 1993

Punt Returns

MOST TOUCHDOWNS SCORED ON PUNT RETURNS
3—Emory & Henry vs. Tenn. Wesleyan, Sept. 27, 1986

Kickoff Returns

MOST YARDS ON KICKOFF RETURNS
302—MacMurray vs. Greenville, Sept. 4, 1999

Scoring

MOST POINTS SCORED
97—Concordia-M'head vs. Macalester, Sept. 24, 1977

MOST POINTS SCORED, BOTH TEAMS
123—Westminster (Mo.) (62) vs. Greenville (61), Sept. 19, 1998; Susquehanna (62) vs. Juniata (61), Oct. 24, 1998

MOST POINTS SCORED BY A LOSING TEAM
61—Greenville vs. Westminster (Mo.), Sept. 19, 1998; Juniata vs. Susquehanna, Oct. 24, 1998

MOST POINTS OVERCOME TO WIN A GAME
33—Wis.-Platteville vs. Wis.-Eau Claire, Nov. 8, 1980 (trailed 33-0 with 7:00 left in 2nd quarter; won 52-43); Salisbury vs. Randolph-Macon, Sept. 15, 1984 (trailed 33-0 with 14:18 left in 2nd quarter; won 34-33); Lakeland vs. Concordia (Wis.), Oct. 11, 1997 (trailed 33-0 with 7:53 left in 3rd quarter; won 41-33)

MOST POINTS SCORED IN A BRIEF PERIOD OF TIME
21 in 33 seconds—Mount Union vs. Defiance, Sept. 14, 1996 (turned 13-3 game into 34-3 in 2nd quarter, won 62-10)
32 in 4:04—Wis.-Stevens Point vs. Wis.-La Crosse, Sept. 21, 1985 (trailed 27-3 and 35-11 in 4th quarter; ended in 35-35 tie)

MOST POINTS SCORED IN FIRST VARSITY GAME
63—Bentley vs. Brooklyn (26), Sept. 24, 1988

MOST TOUCHDOWNS SCORED
14—Concordia-M'head vs. Macalester, Sept. 24, 1977

MOST PLAYERS SCORING TOUCHDOWNS
10—Johns Hopkins vs. Swarthmore, Sept. 19, 1997

MOST EXTRA POINTS MADE BY KICKING
13—Concordia-M'head vs. Macalester, Sept. 24, 1977 (attempted 14)

MOST FIELD GOALS MADE
6—Rhodes vs. Millsaps, Sept. 22, 1984 (attempted 8)

MOST FIELD GOALS ATTEMPTED
8—Rhodes vs. Millsaps, Sept. 22, 1984 (made 6)

MOST DEFENSIVE EXTRA-POINT RETURNS SCORED
1—By many teams

MOST DEFENSIVE EXTRA-POINT OPPORTUNITIES
2—Buffalo St. vs. Brockport St., Oct. 1, 1988 (1 interception & 1 kick return; none scored); Wis.-Platteville vs. Wis.-Oshkosh, Oct. 15, 1988 (2 interceptions; none scored); Wis.-River Falls vs. Wis.-La Crosse, Nov. 11, 1989 (2 kick returns; 1 scored); Frank. & Marsh. vs. Johns Hopkins, Nov. 7, 1992 (1 interception & 1 kick return; none scored)

Turnovers

(Most Times Losing the Ball on Interceptions and Fumbles)

MOST TURNOVERS
13—Albany (N.Y.) vs. Rochester Inst., Oct. 1, 1977; Mercyhurst vs. Buffalo St., Oct. 23, 1982 (1 interception, 12 fumbles); St. Olaf vs. St. Thomas (Minn.), Oct. 12, 1985 (10 interceptions, 3 fumbles)

MOST TURNOVERS, BOTH TEAMS
24—Albany (N.Y.) (13) & Rochester Inst. (11), Oct. 1, 1977

First Downs

MOST TOTAL FIRST DOWNS
40—Upper Iowa vs. Loras, Nov. 7, 1992 (19 rushing, 17 passing, 4 by penalty)

Penalties

MOST PENALTIES AGAINST
25—Norwich vs. Coast Guard, Sept. 29, 1985 (192 yards)

SINGLE GAME—Defense

Total Defense

FEWEST YARDS ALLOWED
Minus 52—Worcester St. vs. Maine Maritime, Sept. 28, 1996 (-71 rushing, 19 passing)

Rushing Defense

FEWEST RUSHES ALLOWED
9—Wis.-La Crosse vs. Huron, Sept. 21, 1996 (-63 yards)

FEWEST YARDS ALLOWED
Minus 112—Coast Guard vs. Wesleyan (Conn.), Oct. 7, 1989 (23 plays)

Pass Defense

FEWEST ATTEMPTS ALLOWED
0—By many teams. Most recent: Concordia-M'head vs. Macalester, Oct. 12, 1991

FEWEST COMPLETIONS ALLOWED
0—By many teams. Most recent: Hartwick vs. Rensselaer, Oct. 26, 1996 (8 attempts)

FEWEST YARDS ALLOWED
Minus 6—Central (Iowa) vs. Simpson, Oct. 19, 1985 (1 completion); Wittenberg vs. Hiram, Oct. 27, 2001

MOST PASSES INTERCEPTED BY
10—St. Thomas (Minn.) vs. St. Olaf, Oct. 12, 1985 (91 yards; 50 attempts)

MOST PLAYERS INTERCEPTING A PASS
8—Samford vs. Anderson (S.C.), Oct. 11, 1986 (8 interceptions in the game)

MOST TOUCHDOWNS ON INTERCEPTION RETURNS
4—Millikin vs. Ill. Wesleyan, Nov. 6, 1999

Defensive Records

MOST TACKLES FOR LOSS (SINCE 2000)
18—Cortland St. vs. Wm. Paterson, Oct. 21, 2000; Montclair St. vs. New Jersey City, Nov. 4, 2000; Alma vs. Hanover, Sept. 29, 2001; Rose-Hulman vs. Earlham, Sept. 7, 2002; Illinois Col. vs. Lake Forest, Oct. 19, 2002

MOST PASS SACKS (Since 2000)
12—Stillman vs. Pikeville, Sept. 1, 2001

MOST PASSES DEFENDED (Since 2000)
21—Stillman vs. Edward Waters, Nov. 2, 2002 (13 pass breakups, 8 interceptions)

MOST FORCED FUMBLES
8—Simpson vs. William Penn, Nov. 11, 2000

Punts Blocked By

MOST OPPONENT'S PUNTS BLOCKED BY
4—Benedictine (Ill.) vs. Olivet Nazarene, Oct. 22, & vs. Aurora, Oct. 29, 1988 (consecutive games, resulting in 4 TDs and 1 safety). Blocked 9 punts in three consecutive games, vs. MacMurray, Oct. 15, Olivet Nazarene and Aurora, resulting in 4 TDs and 2 safeties

First Downs

FEWEST FIRST DOWNS ALLOWED
0—Case Reserve vs. Wooster, Sept. 21, 1985

SEASON—Offense

Total Offense

MOST YARDS GAINED PER GAME
561.2—Westminster (Mo.), 1998 (5,612 in 10)

MOST YARDS GAINED
7,766—Trinity (Tex.), 2002 (15 games)

HIGHEST AVERAGE GAIN PER PLAY
8.1—Ferrum, 1990 (534 for 4,350)

MOST PLAYS PER GAME
85.6—Hampden-Sydney, 1978 (856 in 10)

MOST TOUCHDOWNS SCORED PER GAME BY RUSHING AND PASSING
8.4—St. John's (Minn.), 1993 (84 in 10; 44 rushing, 40 passing)

Rushing

MOST YARDS GAINED PER GAME
434.7—Ferrum, 1990 (3,912 in 9)

MOST YARDS GAINED
4,275—Springfield, 2000 (10 games)

HIGHEST AVERAGE GAIN PER RUSH
8.3—Ferrum, 1990 (470 for 3,912)

MOST RUSHES PER GAME
71.4—Wis.-River Falls, 1988 (714 in 10)

DIVISION III

MOST TOUCHDOWNS SCORED PER GAME BY RUSHING
  5.4—Ferrum, 1990 (49 in 9)

Passing

MOST YARDS GAINED PER GAME
  488.8—Westminster (Mo.), 1998 (4,888 in 10)

FEWEST YARDS GAINED PER GAME
  18.4—Wis.-River Falls, 1983 (184 in 10)

HIGHEST AVERAGE GAIN PER ATTEMPT
  (Min. 250 atts.) 11.1—Grinnell, 1998 (301 for 3,354)
  (Min. 350 atts.) 9.5—Case Reserve, 2002 (391 for 3,706)
  (Min. 450 atts.) 9.5—Menlo, 2000 (479 for 4,529)

HIGHEST AVERAGE GAIN PER COMPLETION (Min. 200 Completions)
  16.5—Grinnell, 1998 (203 for 3,354)

MOST PASSES ATTEMPTED PER GAME
  59.9—Sul Ross St., 2002 (599 in 10)

FEWEST PASSES ATTEMPTED PER GAME
  4.0—Wis.-River Falls, 1988 (40 in 10)

MOST PASSES COMPLETED PER GAME
  35.8—Sul Ross St., 2002 (358 in 10)

FEWEST PASSES COMPLETED PER GAME
  1.3—Wis.-River Falls, 1983 (13 in 10)

HIGHEST PERCENTAGE COMPLETED (Min. 200 Attempts)
  70.7%—Mount Union, 1993 (244 of 345)

LOWEST PERCENTAGE OF PASSES HAD INTERCEPTED (Min. 150 Attempts)
  0.7%—San Diego, 1990 (1 of 153)

MOST TOUCHDOWN PASSES PER GAME
  5.7—Westminster (Mo.), 1998 (57 in 10)

HIGHEST PASSING EFFICIENCY RATING POINTS
  (Min. 15 atts. per game) 211.3—Eureka, 1994 (205 attempts, 142 completions, 8 interceptions, 2,478 yards, 30 TDs)
  (Min. 300 atts.) 202.8—Mount Union, 1997 (311 attempts, 212 completions, 3 interceptions, 3,171 yards, 48 TDs)

Punting

MOST PUNTS PER GAME
  11.0—FDU-Madison, 1990 (99 in 9)

FEWEST PUNTS PER GAME
  2.1—Mount Union, 2002 (29 in 14)

HIGHEST PUNTING AVERAGE
  45.3—Ohio Northern, 1999 (43 for 1,950)

Scoring

MOST POINTS PER GAME
  61.5—St. John's (Minn.), 1993 (615 in 10)

MOST TOUCHDOWNS PER GAME
  8.9—St. John's (Minn.), 1993 (89 in 10)

BEST PERFECT RECORD ON EXTRA POINTS MADE BY KICKING
  49 of 49—Dayton, 1989

MOST TWO-POINT ATTEMPTS PER GAME
  2.8—Martin Luther, 1990 (17 in 6)

MOST FIELD GOALS MADE PER GAME
  2.0—Mount Union, 1990 (20 in 10)

HIGHEST SCORING MARGIN
  51.8—St. John's (Minn.), 1993 (averaged 61.5 and allowed 9.7 in 10 games)

MOST TOUCHDOWNS ON BLOCKED PUNT RETURNS
  5—Widener, 1990

MOST SAFETIES
  4—Wis.-Stevens Point, 1990; Westfield St., 1992; Central (Iowa), 1992; Alfred, 1992; Upper Iowa, 1995

MOST DEFENSIVE EXTRA-POINT RETURNS SCORED
  2—Brockport St., 1990; Eureka, 1991; Springfield, 1998; Greenville, 2000; Wis.-River Falls, 2000

MOST DEFENSIVE EXTRA POINT BLOCKED KICK RETURNS
  3—Brockport St., 1990 (2 scored); Ohio Wesleyan, 1991 (none scored); Assumption, 1992 (1 scored)

MOST DEFENSIVE EXTRA POINT INTERCEPTIONS
  2—Wis.-Platteville, 1988 (none scored); Swarthmore, 1989 (1 scored)

Penalties

MOST PENALTIES PER GAME
  13.3—Kean, 1990 (133 in 10, 1,155 yards)

MOST YARDS PENALIZED PER GAME
  121.9—Hofstra, 1991 (1,219 in 10, 124 penalties)

Turnovers (Giveaways)

(Passes Had Intercepted and Fumbles Lost, From 1985)

FEWEST TURNOVERS
  6—Mount Union, 1995 (4 interceptions, 2 fumbles lost); McDaniel, 1999 (4 interceptions, 2 fumbles lost)
  Also share per-game record with 0.6 (6 in 10)

MOST TURNOVERS
  52—William Penn, 1985 (19 interceptions, 33 fumbles lost)
  Also holds per-game record with 5.2 (52 in 10)

SEASON—Defense

Total Defense

FEWEST YARDS ALLOWED PER GAME
  94.0—Knoxville, 1977 (940 in 10)

LOWEST AVERAGE YARDS ALLOWED PER PLAY
  (Min. 500 plays) 1.8—Bowie St., 1978 (576 for 1,011)
  (Min. 650 plays) 2.0—Plymouth St., 1987 (733 for 1,488)

FEWEST RUSHING AND PASSING TOUCHDOWNS ALLOWED PER GAME
  0.3—Montclair St., 1984 (3 in 10)

Rushing Defense

FEWEST YARDS ALLOWED PER GAME
  Minus 2.3—Knoxville, 1977 (-23 in 10 games)

LOWEST AVERAGE YARDS ALLOWED PER RUSH
  (Min. 275 rushes) Minus 0.1—Knoxville, 1977 (333 for -23)
  (Min. 400 rushes) 1.0—Lycoming, 1976 (400 for 399)

FEWEST TOUCHDOWNS ALLOWED BY RUSHING
  0—New Haven, 1978 (9 games); Union (N.Y.), 1983 (9 games)

Pass Defense

FEWEST YARDS ALLOWED PER GAME
  48.5—Mass. Maritime, 1976 (388 in 8)

FEWEST YARDS ALLOWED PER ATTEMPT
  (Min. 150 atts.) 2.9—Plymouth St., 1982 (170 for 488)
  (Min. 225 atts.) 3.3—Plymouth St., 1987 (281 for 919)

FEWEST YARDS ALLOWED PER COMPLETION (Min. 100 Completions)
  8.6—Baldwin-Wallace, 1990 (151 for 1,305)

LOWEST COMPLETION PERCENTAGE ALLOWED
  (Min. 150 atts.) 24.3%—Doane, 1973 (41 of 169)
  (Min. 250 atts.) 31.3%—Hobart, 2000 (79 of 252)

HIGHEST PERCENTAGE INTERCEPTED BY (Min. 200 Attempts)
  15.2%—Rose-Hulman, 1977 (32 of 210)

MOST PASSES INTERCEPTED BY
  35—Plymouth St., 1987 (12 games, 281 attempts against, 348 yards returned)
  Per-game record—3.4, Montclair St., 1981 (34 in 10)

FEWEST PASSES INTERCEPTED BY (Min. 125 Attempts)
  1—Bates, 1987 (134 attempts against in 8 games, 0 yards returned)

MOST YARDS ON INTERCEPTION RETURNS
  576—Emory & Henry, 1987 (31 interceptions)

MOST TOUCHDOWNS SCORED ON INTERCEPTIONS
  6—Augustana (Ill.), 1987 (23 interceptions, 229 passes against); Coe, 1992 (22 interceptions, 272 passes against)

FEWEST TOUCHDOWN PASSES ALLOWED
  0—By many teams. Most recent: Amherst, 2001 (8 games); Johns Hopkins, 2001 (9 games)

LOWEST PASSING EFFICIENCY RATING POINTS ALLOWED OPPONENTS
  (Min. 150 atts.) 27.8—Plymouth St., 1982 (allowed 170 attempts, 53 completions, 488 yards, 1 TD & intercepted 25 passes)
  (Min. 275 atts.) 43.1—Plymouth St., 1987 (allowed 281 attempts, 94 completions, 919 yards, 6 TDs & intercepted 35 passes)

Punting

MOST PUNTS BLOCKED BY
  11—Benedictine (Ill.) 1987 (78 punts against in 10 games). Blocked 17 punts in 18 games during 1987-88, resulting in 5 TDs and 3 safeties

Scoring

FEWEST POINTS ALLOWED PER GAME
  3.4—Millsaps, 1980 (31 in 9)

FEWEST TOUCHDOWNS ALLOWED
  4—Millsaps, 1980 (9 games); Baldwin-Wallace, 1981 (10 games); Bentley, 1990 (8 games)

MOST SHUTOUTS
  6—Plymouth St., 1982 (consecutive); Cortland St., 1989

MOST CONSECUTIVE SHUTOUTS
  6—Plymouth St., 1982

MOST POINTS ALLOWED PER GAME
  59.1—Macalester, 1977 (532 in 9; 76 TDs, 64 PATs, 4 FGs)

MOST DEFENSIVE EXTRA-POINT ATTEMPTS BY OPPONENTS
  5—Norwich, 1992 (4 blocked kick returns, 1 interception; none scored)

Turnovers (Takeaways)

(Opponent's Passes Intercepted and Fumbles Recovered, From 1985)

HIGHEST MARGIN OF TURNOVERS PER GAME OVER OPPONENTS
  2.9—Macalester, 1986 (29 in 10; 29 giveaways vs. 58 takeaways)

MOST TAKEAWAYS
58—Macalester, 1986 (28 interceptions, 30 fumbles gained)
Also holds per-game record with 5.8 (58 in 10)

Additional Records

MOST CONSECUTIVE VICTORIES
54—Mount Union (from Sept. 14, 1996, to Dec. 4, 1999)

MOST CONSECUTIVE REGULAR-SEASON VICTORIES
84—Mount Union (from Oct. 22, 1994, to present)

MOST CONSECUTIVE GAMES WITHOUT DEFEAT
60—Augustana (Ill.), (from Sept. 17, 1983, through Nov. 22, 1987; ended with 38-36 loss to Dayton, Nov. 29, 1987, in Division III playoffs and included one tie)

MOST CONSECUTIVE REGULAR-SEASON GAMES WITHOUT DEFEAT
84—Mount Union (from Oct. 22, 1994, to present)

MOST CONSECUTIVE WINNING SEASONS
42—Central (Iowa) (from 1961 to present)

MOST CONSECUTIVE GAMES WITHOUT BEING SHUT OUT
254—Mount Union (from Nov. 7, 1981, to present)

MOST CONSECUTIVE LOSSES
50—Macalester (from Oct. 5, 1974, to Nov. 10, 1979; ended with 17-14 win over Mount Senario, Sept. 6, 1980)

MOST CONSECUTIVE GAMES WITHOUT A TIE
371—Widener (from Oct. 29, 1949, to Nov. 11, 1989; ended with 14-14 tie against Gettysburg, Sept. 8, 1990)

HIGHEST-SCORING TIE GAME
50-50—Catholic vs. Randolph-Macon, Sept. 16, 1995

LAST SCORELESS GAME
Nov. 18, 1995—Amherst vs. Williams

MOST CONSECUTIVE GAMES SCORING A TOUCHDOWN BY PASSING
105—Mount Union (from Oct. 5, 1991, to Oct. 27, 2001)

MOST CONSECUTIVE QUARTERS WITHOUT YIELDING A TOUCHDOWN BY RUSHING
61—Union (N.Y.) (in 16 games from Oct. 23, 1982, to Sept. 29, 1984); Augustana (Ill.) (in 16 games from Sept. 27, 1986, to Nov. 7, 1987; 77 including four 1986 Division III playoff games)

MOST CONSECUTIVE QUARTERS WITHOUT YIELDING A TOUCHDOWN BY PASSING
44—Swarthmore (from Oct. 31, 1981, to Nov. 13, 1982)

MOST IMPROVED WON-LOST RECORD (Including Postseason Games)
7 1/2 games—Wis.-Stout, 2000 (10-1) from 1999 (2-8)

Annual Champions, All-Time Leaders

Total Offense

CAREER YARDS PER GAME
(Minimum 5,000 Yards)

Player, Team	Years	G	Plays	Yards	Yd. PG
Justin Peery, Westminster (Mo.)	1996-99	39	2,001	*13,645	*349.9
Terry Peebles, Hanover	1992-95	23	1,140	7,672	333.6
Eric Bruns, Hanover	1999-00	20	995	6,512	325.6
Adam Ryan, Wilmington (Ohio)	1998-01	33	1,520	10,314	312.5
Kirk Baumgartner, Wis.-Stevens Point	1986-89	41	*2,007	12,767	311.4
Zamir Amin, Menlo	1999-01	26	1,015	7,836	301.4
Willie Reyna, La Verne	1991-92	17	551	4,996	293.9
Keith Bishop, Ill. Wesleyan/Wheaton (Ill.)	1981, 83-85	31	1,467	9,052	292.0
Mark Novara, Lakeland	1994-97	38	1,653	10,801	284.2
Jordan Poznick, Principia	1990-93	32	1,757	8,983	280.7
Troy Dougherty, Grinnell	1994, 97-99	37	1,520	10,314	278.8
John Rooney, Ill. Wesleyan	1982-84	27	1,260	7,393	273.8
Sean Hoolihan, Wis.-Eau Claire	1996-98	28	972	7,650	273.2
Tim Peterson, Wis.-Stout	1986-89	36	1,558	9,701	269.5
Gregg McDonald, Kalamazoo	1994-96	27	1,155	7,273	269.4
Tom Arth, John Carroll	1999-02	39	1,557	10,493	269.1
Bill Borchert, Mount Union	1994-97	40	1,274	10,639	266.0
Jim Ballard, Wilmington (Ohio)/Mount Union	1990, 91-93	40	1,328	10,545	263.6
Kevin Ricca, Catholic	1994-97	38	1,533	9,982	262.7
Robert Farra, Claremont-M-S	1978-79	16	690	4,179	261.2
Chris Ings, Wabash	1992-95	37	1,532	9,608	259.7
Jack Ramirez, Pomona-Pitzer	1994-97	34	1,328	8,721	256.5
Eric Noble, Wilmington (Ohio)	1992-95	38	1,513	9,731	256.0
Kyle Krober, Greenville	1998-01	40	1,603	10,239	256.0
Brian Partlow, Randolph-Macon	1997-99	20	882	5,111	255.6

*Record.

SEASON YARDS PER GAME

Player, Team	Year	G	Plays	Yards	Yd. PG
Justin Peery, Westminster (Mo.)	†1998	10	*645	*4,651	*465.1
Justin Peery, Westminster (Mo.)	†1999	10	599	4,419	441.9
Danny Ragsdale, Redlands	1999	9	464	3,855	428.3
Zamir Amin, Menlo	†2000	10	511	4,231	423.1
Terry Peebles, Hanover	†1995	10	572	3,981	398.1
Kyle Krober, Greenville	2000	10	468	3,676	367.6
Steve Slowke, Alma	†2001	10	662	3,630	363.0
Adam King, Howard Payne	†2002	10	505	3,613	361.3
Keith Bishop, Wheaton (Ill.)	†1983	9	421	3,193	354.8
Kirk Baumgartner, Wis.-Stevens Point	†1989	10	530	3,540	354.0
Bill Nietzke, Alma	†1996	9	468	3,185	353.9
John Furmaniak, Eureka	1995	10	414	3,503	350.3

Player, Team	Year	G	Plays	Yards	Yd. PG
Tom Stetzer, Wis.-Platteville	2002	9	553	3,136	348.4
Adam Ryan, Wilmington (Ohio)	1999	10	280	3,478	347.8
Chris Stormer, Hanover	1998	10	507	3,470	347.0
Gregg McDonald, Kalamazoo	1996	9	415	3,101	344.6
Kirk Baumgartner, Wis.-Stevens Point	†1988	11	604	3,790	344.5
Terry Peebles, Hanover	†1994	10	520	3,441	344.1
Jordan Poznick, Principia	†1992	8	519	2,747	343.4
Adam Ryan, Wilmington (Ohio)	2000	10	532	3,415	341.5
Eric Noble, Wilmington (Ohio)	1994	9	460	3,072	341.3
Brian Partlow, Randolph-Macon	1999	10	566	3,400	340.0
Chad Johnson, Pacific Lutheran	2000	9	345	3,052	339.1
Jordan Poznick, Principia	†1993	8	488	2,705	338.1
Chris Czernek, Cal Lutheran	2001	9	463	3,040	337.8

*Record. †National champion.

CAREER YARDS

Player, Team	Years	Plays	Yards
Justin Peery, Westminster (Mo.)	1996-99	2,001	*13,645
Kirk Baumgartner, Wis.-Stevens Point	1986-89	*2,007	12,767
Mark Novara, Lakeland	1994-97	1,653	10,801
Bill Borchert, Mount Union	1994-97	1,274	10,639
Jim Ballard, Wilmington (Ohio)/Mount Union	1990, 91-93	1,328	10,545
Tom Arth, John Carroll	1999-02	1,557	10,493
Adam Ryan, Wilmington (Ohio)	1998-01	1,520	10,314
Troy Dougherty, Grinnell	1994, 97-99	1,520	10,314
Kyle Krober, Greenville	1998-01	1,603	10,239
Kevin Ricca, Catholic	1994-97	1,533	9,982
Brian Dawson, Wash. & Jeff.	1999-02	1,390	9,954
Eric Noble, Wilmington (Ohio)	1992-95	1,513	9,731
Tim Peterson, Wis.-Stout	1986-89	1,558	9,701
Chris Ings, Wabash	1992-95	1,532	9,608
Matt D'Orazio, Otterbein	1996-99	1,625	9,364
Roy Hampton, Trinity (Tex.)	$1998-02	1,096	9,359
Keith Bishop, Ill. Wesleyan/Wheaton (Ill.)	1981, 83-85	1,467	9,052
Brian Tomalak, Wis.-Oshkosh	1994-98	1,313	9,022
Dave Geissler, Wis.-Stevens Point	1982-85	1,695	8,990
Jordan Poznick, Principia	1990-93	1,757	8,983
Mike Burton, Trinity (Tex.)	1996-99	1,250	8,883
Dennis Bogacz, Wis.-Oshkosh/Wis.-Whitewater	1988-89, 90-91	1,394	8,850
John Clark, Wis.-Eau Claire	1987-90	1,354	8,838
Mike Warker, Widener/Rowan	1999-02	1,133	8,743
Jack Ramirez, Pomona-Pitzer	1994-97	1,328	8,721

*Record. $See Page 8 for explanation.

SEASON YARDS

Player, Team	Year	G	Plays	Yards
Justin Peery, Westminster (Mo.)	†1998	10	*645	*4,651
Justin Peery, Westminster (Mo.)	†1999	10	599	4,419
Roy Hampton, Trinity (Tex.)	2002	10	464	4,418
Zamir Amin, Menlo	†2000	10	511	4,231
Terry Peebles, Hanover	†1995	10	572	3,981
Danny Ragsdale, Redlands	1999	9	464	3,855
Kirk Baumgartner, Wis.-Stevens Point	†1988	11	604	3,790

Player, Team	Year	G	Plays	Yards
Kirk Baumgartner, Wis.-Stevens Point	1987	11	561	3,712
Kyle Krober, Greenville	2000	10	468	3,676
Steve Slowke, Alma	†2001	10	662	3,630
Adam King, Howard Payne	†2002	10	505	3,613
Kirk Baumgartner, Wis.-Stevens Point	†1989	10	530	3,540
John Furmaniak, Eureka	1995	10	414	3,503
Adam Ryan, Wilmington (Ohio)	1999	10	280	3,478
Chris Stormer, Hanover	1998	10	507	3,470
Terry Peebles, Hanover	†1994	10	520	3,441
Adam Ryan, Wilmington (Ohio)	2000	10	532	3,415
Brian Partlow, Randolph-Macon	1999	10	566	3,400
Jim Ballard, Mount Union	1993	10	372	3,371
Troy Dougherty, Grinnell	1998	10	375	3,296
Tom Stetzer, Wis.-Platteville	2001	10	585	3,284
Eric Bruns, Hanover	2000	10	507	3,260
Eric Bruns, Hanover	1999	10	488	3,252
Mark Novara, Lakeland	†1996	10	454	3,250
Tim Peterson, Wis.-Stout	1989	10	614	3,244

Record. †National champion.

SINGLE-GAME YARDS

Yds.	Player, Team (Opponent)	Date
723	Zamir Amin, Menlo (Cal Lutheran)	Oct. 7, 2000
630	Justin Peery, Westminster (Mo.) (Colorado Col.)	Oct. 30, 1999
628	Justin Peery, Westminster (Mo.) (MacMurray)	Nov. 14, 1998
617	Justin Peery, Westminster (Mo.) (Principia)	Oct. 17, 1998
596	John Love, North Park (Elmhurst)	Oct. 13, 1990
590	Tom Stallings, St. Thomas (Minn.) (Bethel [Minn.])	Nov. 13, 1993
590	Danny Ragsdale, Redlands (Azusa Pacific)	Sept. 25, 1999
588	Danny Ragsdale, Redlands (Cal Lutheran)	Nov. 13, 1999
584	Dustin Proctor, Hardin-Simmons (Howard Payne)	Oct. 12, 2002
580	Joe Montrella, Juniata (Widener)	Nov. 13, 1999
577	Eric Noble, Wilmington (Ohio) (Urbana)	Nov. 5, 1994
567	Jim Newland, Heidelberg (Ohio Northern)	Nov. 12, 1994
564	Tim Lynch, Hofstra (Fordham)	Oct. 19, 1991
563	Justin Peery, Westminster (Mo.) (Greenville)	Sept. 19, 1998
562	Chris Smith, Menlo (Occidental)	Sept. 22, 2001
555	Bill Nietzke, Alma (Hope)	Oct. 26, 1996
549	Danny Ragsdale, Redlands (Chapman)	Oct. 9, 1999
547	Josh Wakefield, Alma (Franklin)	Sept. 25, 1999
545	Terry Peebles, Hanover (Franklin)	Nov. 12, 1994
541	Michael Kornblau, Greenville (Blackburn)	Oct. 9, 1999

ANNUAL CHAMPIONS

Year	Player, Team	Class	G	Plays	Yards	Avg.
1973	Bob Dulich, San Diego	Jr.	11	340	2,543	231.2
1974	Larry Cenotto, Pomona-Pitzer	Sr.	9	436	2,127	236.3
1975	Ricky Haygood, Millsaps	Jr.	9	332	2,176	241.8
1976	Rollie Wiebers, Buena Vista	So.	9	353	2,198	244.2
1977	Tom Hamilton, Occidental	Sr.	9	358	2,050	227.8
1978	Robert Farra, Claremont-M-S	Jr.	9	427	2,685	298.3
1979	Clay Sampson, Denison	Jr.	9	412	2,255	250.6
1980	Jeff Beer, Bethany (W.Va.)	Sr.	9	372	2,331	259.0
1981	Brion Demski, Wis.-Stevens Point	Sr.	10	503	2,895	289.5
1982	Dave McCarrell, Wheaton (Ill.)	Sr.	9	387	2,503	278.1
1983	Keith Bishop, Wheaton (Ill.)	So.	9	421	3,193	354.8
1984	Keith Bishop, Wheaton (Ill.)	Jr.	9	479	2,777	308.6
1985	Keith Bishop, Wheaton (Ill.)	Sr.	9	521	2,951	327.9
1986	Larry Barretta, Lycoming	Sr.	10	453	2,875	287.5
1987	Todde Greenough, Willamette	Jr.	9	436	2,567	285.2
1988	Kirk Baumgartner, Wis.-Stevens Point	Jr.	11	604	3,790	344.5
1989	Kirk Baumgartner, Wis.-Stevens Point	Sr.	10	530	3,540	354.0
1990	Rhory Moss, Hofstra	Jr.	9	372	2,775	308.3
1991	Willie Reyna, La Verne	Jr.	8	220	2,633	329.1
1992	Jordan Poznick, Principia	Jr.	8	519	2,747	343.4
1993	Jordan Poznick, Principia	Sr.	8	488	2,705	338.1
1994	Terry Peebles, Hanover	Jr.	10	520	3,441	344.1
1995	Terry Peebles, Hanover	Sr.	10	572	3,981	398.1
1996	Bill Nietzke, Alma	Sr.	9	468	3,185	353.9
1997	Matt Bunyan, Wis.-Stout	Jr.	10	422	3,216	321.6
1998	Justin Peery, Westminster (Mo.)	Jr.	10	*645	*4,651	*465.1
1999	Justin Peery, Westminster (Mo.)	Sr.	10	599	4,419	441.9
2000	Zamir Amin, Menlo	Sr.	10	511	4,231	423.1
2001	Steve Slowke, Alma	Jr.	10	662	3,630	363.0
2002	Adam King, Howard Payne	So.	10	505	3,613	361.3

*Record.

Rushing

CAREER YARDS PER GAME
(Minimum 2,200 Yards)

Player, Team	Years	G	Plays	Yards	Yd. PG
R.J. Bowers, Grove City	1997-00	40	1,188	*7,353	*183.8
Ricky Gales, Simpson	1988-89	19	530	3,326	175.1
Rob Marchitello, Maine Maritime	1993-95	26	879	4,300	165.4
Kelvin Gladney, Millsaps	1993-94	19	510	3,085	162.4
Carey Bender, Coe	1991-94	39	926	6,125	157.1
Brad Olson, Lawrence	1994-97	34	792	5,325	156.6
Steve Tardif, Maine Maritime	1996-99	39	*1,190	6,093	156.2
Kirk Matthieu, Maine Maritime	$1989-93	33	964	5,107	154.8
Terry Underwood, Wagner	1985-88	33	742	5,010	151.8
D'Andra Freeman, Fitchburg St.	1997-99	27	789	3,957	146.6
Anthony Russo, St. John's (N.Y.)	1990-92	30	841	4,276	142.5
Joe Dudek, Plymouth St.	1982-85	41	785	5,570	135.9
Kenneth Sasu, Marietta	1997-00	35	875	4,727	135.1
Jason Brader, Muhlenberg	1997-98	20	548	2,684	134.2
Mark Kacmarynski, Central (Iowa)	$1992-96	41	854	5,434	132.5
Rich Kowalski, Hobart	1973-75	27	762	3,574	132.4
Eric Frees, McDaniel	1988-91	40	1,059	5,281	132.0
Rick Etienne, Franklin	1994-96	30	676	3,952	131.7
Casey Donaldson, Wittenberg	1997-00	39	836	5,112	131.1
Paul Smith, Gettysburg	1996-99	40	881	5,205	130.1
Tim Barrett, John Carroll	1973-74	19	457	2,469	129.9
Heath Butler, Martin Luther	1990-93	31	767	4,000	129.0
Scott Reppert, Lawrence	1979-82	33	757	4,211	127.6
Dan McGovern, Rensselaer	1994-97	28	665	3,572	127.6

*Record. $See Page 8 for explanation.

SEASON YARDS PER GAME

Player, Team	Year	G	Plays	Yards	TD	Yd. PG
Dante Brown, Marietta	†1996	10	314	*2,385	25	*238.5
R.J. Bowers, Grove City	†1998	10	329	2,283	*34	228.3
Carey Bender, Coe	†1994	10	295	2,243	29	224.3
R.J. Bowers, Grove City	†1999	10	344	2,098	25	209.8
Jamie Lee, MacMurray	†1997	8	207	1,639	11	204.9
Ricky Gales, Simpson	†1989	10	297	2,035	26	203.5
Terry Underwood, Wagner	†1988	9	245	1,809	21	201.0
Kenneth Sasu, Marietta	1999	9	332	1,770	15	196.7
Brad Olson, Lawrence	†1995	9	242	1,760	16	195.6
Kirk Matthieu, Maine Maritime	†1992	9	327	1,733	16	192.6
Kelvin Gladney, Millsaps	1994	10	307	1,882	19	188.2
Brandon Steinheim, Wesley	1996	9	319	1,684	20	187.1
D'Andra Freeman, Fitchburg St.	1999	10	365	1,871	14	187.1
Krishaun Gilmore, Rensselaer	1998	9	228	1,670	22	185.6
Jon Warga, Wittenberg	†1990	10	254	1,836	15	183.6
Jamie Lee, MacMurray	1998	10	252	1,818	25	181.8
Anthony Jones, La Verne	1995	8	200	1,453	19	181.6
Hank Wineman, Albion	†1991	9	307	1,629	14	181.0
Eric Grey, Hamilton	1991	8	217	1,439	13	179.9
Mike Birosak, Dickinson	1989	10	*380	1,798	18	179.8
Guy Leman, Simpson	1998	10	333	1,788	31	178.8
Shane Davis, Loras	1997	10	267	1,774	14	177.4
Rob Marchitello, Maine Maritime	1995	8	292	1,413	19	176.6
Chris Babirad, Wash. & Jeff.	1992	9	243	1,589	22	176.6
Shearrod Duncan, Ursinus	†2001	10	306	1,747	19	174.7

*Record. †National champion.

CAREER YARDS

Player, Team	Years	Plays	Yards	Avg.
R.J. Bowers, Grove City	1997-00	1,188	*7,353	6.19
Carey Bender, Coe	1991-94	926	6,125	6.61
Steve Tardif, Maine Maritime	1996-99	*1,190	6,093	5.12
Joe Dudek, Plymouth St.	1982-85	785	5,570	‡7.10
Mark Kacmarynski, Central (Iowa)	$1992-96	854	5,434	6.36
Brad Olson, Lawrence	1994-97	792	5,325	6.72
Eric Frees, McDaniel	1988-91	1,059	5,281	4.99
Paul Smith, Gettysburg	1996-99	881	5,205	5.91
Casey Donaldson, Wittenberg	1997-00	836	5,112	6.11
Kirk Matthieu, Maine Maritime	$1989-93	964	5,107	5.30
Terry Underwood, Wagner	1985-88	742	5,010	6.75
Steve Dixon, Beloit	1990-93	986	4,792	4.86
Shane Davis, Loras	1994-97	694	4,738	6.83
Kenneth Sasu, Marietta	1997-00	875	4,727	5.40
Mike Birosak, Dickinson	1986-89	1,112	4,662	4.19

Player, Team	Years	Plays	Yards	Avg.
Jamie Lee, MacMurray	1994-95, 97-98	742	4,586	6.18
Will Castleberry, Thomas More	1997-00	944	4,546	4.82
Dante Brown, Marietta	1994-97	712	4,512	6.34
Jim Romagna, Loras	1989-92	983	4,493	4.57
Steve Ballinger, MacMurray	1999-02	721	4,456	6.18
Chris Babirad, Wash. & Jeff.	1989-92	683	4,419	6.47
Petie Davis, Wesley	1991-94	741	4,414	5.96
Mike Hankins, Wilkes	1996-99	874	4,399	5.03
Tim Lightfoot, Westfield St.	1992-95	876	4,380	5.00
Seto Berry, Bridgewater St.	1997-00	703	4,359	6.20

*Record. $See Page 8 for explanation. ‡Record for minimum 500 carries.

SEASON YARDS

Player, Team	Year	G	Plays	Yards	Avg.
Dante Brown, Marietta	†1996	10	314	*2,385	7.60
Dan Pugh, Mount Union	†2002	14	*384	2,300	5.99
R.J. Bowers, Grove City	†1998	10	329	2,283	6.94
Carey Bender, Coe	†1994	10	295	2,243	7.60
R.J. Bowers, Grove City	†1999	10	344	2,098	6.10
Ricky Gales, Simpson	†1989	10	297	2,035	6.85
Kelvin Gladney, Millsaps	1994	10	307	1,882	6.13
D'Andra Freeman, Fitchburg St.	1999	10	365	1,871	5.13
David McNeal, Merchant Marine	2002	11	338	1,860	5.50
Jon Warga, Wittenberg	†1990	10	254	1,836	7.23
Jamie Lee, MacMurray	1998	10	252	1,818	7.21
Terry Underwood, Wagner	†1988	9	245	1,809	6.75
Mike Birosak, Dickinson	1989	10	380	1,798	4.73
Guy Leman, Simpson	1998	10	333	1,788	5.37
Shane Davis, Loras	1997	10	267	1,774	6.64
Kenneth Sasu, Marietta	1999	9	332	1,770	5.33
Brad Olson, Lawrence	†1995	9	242	1,760	7.27
Shearrod Duncan, Ursinus	†2001	10	306	1,747	5.71
Damon Saxon, King's (Pa.)	†2000	10	281	1,744	6.21
Mark Kacmarynski, Central (Iowa)	1994	10	236	1,741	7.38
Will Castleberry, Thomas More	2000	10	324	1,736	5.36
R.J. Bowers, Grove City	2000	10	352	1,733	4.92
Kirk Matthieu, Maine Maritime	†1992	9	327	1,733	5.30
Richard Jackson, King's (Pa.)	2002	12	369	1,731	4.69
Steve Ballinger, MacMurray	2000	10	232	1,731	7.46

*Record. †National champion.

SINGLE-GAME YARDS

Yds.	Player, Team (Opponent)	Date
441	Dante Brown, Marietta (Baldwin-Wallace)	Oct. 5, 1996
436	A.J. Pittorino, Hartwick (Waynesburg)	Nov. 2, 1996
417	Carey Bender, Coe (Grinnell)	Oct. 9, 1993
413	Dante Brown, Marietta (Heidelberg)	Nov. 9, 1996
390	Paul Smith, Gettysburg (Muhlenberg)	Oct. 23, 1999
382	Pete Baranek, Carthage (North Central)	Oct. 5, 1985

Yds.	Player, Team (Opponent)	Date
382	Shane Davis, Loras (Dubuque)	Nov. 8, 1997
363	Terry Underwood, Wagner (Hofstra)	Oct. 15, 1988
361	Guy Leman, Simpson (Luther)	Nov. 14, 1998
354	Terry Underwood, Wagner (Western Conn. St.)	Oct. 3, 1986
352	Steve Tardif, Maine Maritime (Westfield St.)	Nov. 16, 1996
348	Carey Bender, Coe (Beloit)	Nov. 12, 1994
347	Chuck Wotkowicz, Johns Hopkins (Georgetown)	Oct. 22, 1993
343	Marcus Howard, Rockford (Principia)	Oct. 14, 2000
342	Dave Bednarek, Wis.-River Falls (Wis.-Stevens Point)	Oct. 29, 1983
342	Trevor Shannon, Wartburg (Loras)	Oct. 5, 1996
337	Eric Hamilton, Concordia (Wis.)(Concordia [Ill.])	Oct. 30, 1999
337	Kirk Matthieu, Maine Maritime (Curry)	Oct. 27, 1990
337	Ted Helsel, St. Francis (Pa.) (Gallaudet)	Nov. 3, 1979
335	Luke Bundgaard, Wis.-Stout (Wis.-Platteville)	Oct. 21, 2000
335	Paul Smith, Gettysburg (St. Lawrence)	Oct. 30, 1999

ANNUAL CHAMPIONS

Year	Player, Team	Class	G	Plays	Yards	Avg.
1973	Billy Johnson, Widener	Sr.	9	168	1,494	166.0
1974	Tim Barrett, John Carroll	Sr.	9	256	1,409	156.6
1975	Ron Baker, Monmouth (Ill.)	Sr.	8	200	1,116	139.5
1976	Chuck Evans, Ferris St.	Jr.	10	224	1,509	150.9
1977	Don Taylor, Central (Iowa)	Sr.	9	267	1,329	147.7
1978	Dino Hall, Rowan	Sr.	10	239	1,330	133.0
1979	Clay Sampson, Denison	Jr.	9	323	1,517	168.6
1980	Scott Reppert, Lawrence	So.	8	223	1,223	152.9
1981	Scott Reppert, Lawrence	Jr.	9	250	1,410	156.7
1982	Scott Reppert, Lawrence	Sr.	8	254	1,323	165.4
1983	John Franco, Wagner	Sr.	8	175	1,166	145.8
1984	Gary Errico, Mass.-Lowell	Sr.	9	165	1,404	156.0
1985	Bruce Montella, Chicago	Sr.	9	265	1,372	152.4
1986	Sandy Rogers, Emory & Henry	Sr.	11	231	1,730	157.3
1987	Chris Dabrow, Claremont-M-S	Sr.	9	265	1,486	165.1
1988	Terry Underwood, Wagner	Sr.	9	245	1,809	201.0
1989	Ricky Gales, Simpson	Sr.	10	297	2,035	203.5
1990	Jon Warga, Wittenberg	Sr.	10	254	1,836	183.6
1991	Hank Wineman, Albion	Sr.	9	307	1,629	181.0
1992	Kirk Matthieu, Maine Maritime	Jr.	9	327	1,733	192.6
1993	Carey Bender, Coe	Jr.	10	261	1,718	171.8
1994	Carey Bender, Coe	Sr.	10	295	2,243	224.3
1995	Brad Olson, Lawrence	So.	9	242	1,760	195.6
1996	Dante Brown, Marietta	Jr.	10	314	*2,385	*238.5
1997	Jamie Lee, MacMurray	Sr.	8	207	1,639	204.9
1998	R.J. Bowers, Grove City	So.	10	329	2,283	228.3
1999	R.J. Bowers, Grove City	Jr.	10	344	2,098	209.8
2000	Damon Saxon, King's (Pa.)	Sr.	10	281	1,744	174.4
2001	Shearrod Duncan, Ursinus	Sr.	10	306	1,747	174.7
2002	Aaron Stepka, Colby	So.	8	293	1,370	171.3

*Record.

Passing

CAREER PASSING EFFICIENCY

(Minimum 325 Completions)

Player, Team	Years	Att.	Cmp.	Int.	Pct.	Yards	TD	Pts.
Bill Borchert, Mount Union	1994-97	1,009	671	17	.665	10,201	141	*194.2
Rob Adamson, Mount Union	1998-99, 2001-02	582	369	17	.634	6,151	60	180.4
Gary Smeck, Mount Union	1997-00	752	504	15	‡.670	7,764	83	186.2
Roy Hampton, Trinity (Tex.)	$1998-02	942	600	26	.637	8,869	94	170.2
Kurt Ramler, St. John's (Minn.)	1994-96	722	420	16	.582	6,475	75	163.4
Matt Wheeler, Wartburg	1996-99	595	362	21	.608	5,390	59	162.6
Danny Ragsdale, Redlands	1997-99	610	386	17	.633	5,560	51	161.9
Tom Linnemann, St. John's (Minn.)	1998-00	552	337	23	.611	4,578	65	161.2
Zamir Amin, Menlo	1999-01	905	566	29	.625	7,982	83	160.5
Kyle Adamson, Allegheny	1995-97	608	388	18	.638	5,506	48	160.0
Craig Kusick, Wis.-La Crosse	1993-95	537	327	14	.609	4,767	48	159.8
Jim Ballard, Wilmington (Ohio)/Mount Union	1990, 91-93	1,199	743	41	.620	10,379	115	159.5
Troy Dougherty, Grinnell	1994, 97-99	1,192	734	33	.616	10,140	109	157.7
Jason Baer, Wash. & Jeff.	1993-96	671	406	24	.605	5,632	66	156.3
Matt LeFever, Western Conn. St.	1997-00	636	363	21	.571	5,762	57	156.1
Brian Dawson, Wash. & Jeff.	1999-02	1,132	670	45	.592	10,257	94	154.8
Chad Johnson, Pacific Lutheran	1998-00	699	433	20	.619	6,292	48	154.5
Joel Parrett, Bluffton	1996-99	633	412	28	.651	5,684	43	154.1
Joe Blake, Simpson	1987-90	672	399	15	.594	6,183	43	153.3

DIVISION III

Tom Arth of John Carroll is fifth in Division III career passing yards with 10,345.

Player, Team	Years	Att.	Cmp.	Int.	Pct.	Yards	TD	Pts.
Mike Burton, Trinity (Tex.)	1996-99	1,067	631	29	.591	9,008	92	153.1
Sean Hoolihan, Wis.-Eau Claire	1996-98	686	413	23	.602	6,301	46	152.8
Willie Reyna, La Verne	1991-92	542	346	19	.638	4,712	37	152.4
Mike Warker, Widener/Rowan	1999-02	914	482	38	.527	8,540	79	151.4
Greg Lister, Rowan	1994-97	773	454	29	.587	6,553	66	150.6
Justin Peery, Westminster (Mo.)	1996-99	1,669	*1,012	57	.606	*13,262	*148	149.8
Geoff Hemlinger, Baldwin-Wallace	1995-98	592	348	14	.588	4,936	46	149.7

Record. $See Page 8 for explanation. ‡Record for minimum 750 attempts.

SEASON PASSING EFFICIENCY
(Minimum 15 Attempts Per Game)

Player, Team	Year	G	Att.	Cmp.	Int.	Pct.	Yards	TD	Pts.
Mike Simpson, Eureka	†1994	10	158	116	5	.734	1,988	25	*225.0
Willie Seiler, St. John's (Minn.)	†1993	10	205	141	6	.687	2,648	33	224.6
Dustin Proctor, Hardin-Simmons	†2001	9	178	116	3	.652	2,194	28	217.2
Bill Borchert, Mount Union	†1997	10	272	190	1	.698	2,933	*47	‡216.7
Bill Borchert, Mount Union	†1996	10	240	165	6	.687	2,655	38	208.9
Gary Smeck, Mount Union	†1999	10	199	131	3	.658	2,274	30	208.6
Matt LeFever, Western Conn. St.	1999	10	158	95	7	.601	1,874	25	203.1
Brian Dawson, Wash. & Jeff.	†2000	10	227	149	6	.656	2,675	29	201.5
Troy Dougherty, Grinnell	†1998	10	293	198	5	.675	3,310	36	199.6
Bill Borchert, Mount Union	†1995	10	225	160	4	.711	2,270	30	196.3
Jim Ballard, Mount Union	1993	10	314	229	11	*.729	3,304	37	193.2
Jason Baer, Wash. & Jeff.	1995	8	146	95	3	.650	1,536	19	192.3
Greg Lister, Rowan	1997	9	162	111	4	.685	1,688	20	191.9
Gary Smeck, Mount Union	2000	10	266	184	3	.691	2,773	30	191.7
Ty Grovesteen, Wis.-Whitewater	1998	9	180	103	5	.572	2,074	22	188.8
Kurt Ramler, St. John's (Minn.)	1994	9	154	93	4	.603	1,560	22	187.4
Roy Hampton, Trinity (Tex.)	2001	9	251	168	7	.669	2,465	33	187.2
Mike Bajakian, Williams	1994	8	141	92	1	.652	1,382	17	186.0
Roy Hampton, Trinity (Tex.)	†2002	14	397	260	6	.655	4,095	43	184.9
Kevin Ricca, Catholic	1997	10	306	208	6	.679	2,990	35	183.9
Rob Adamson, Mount Union	2002	11	231	139	9	.602	2,424	30	183.4
Mitch Sanders, Bridgeport	1973	10	151	84	7	.556	1,551	23	182.9
Pat Mayew, St. John's (Minn.)	†1991	9	247	154	4	.623	2,408	30	181.0
Matt LeFever, Western Conn. St.	2000	10	171	110	4	.643	1,792	17	180.5
Chad Johnson, Pacific Lutheran	2000	9	274	185	6	.675	2,839	24	179.1

Record. †National champion. ‡Record for minimum 25 attempts per game.

CAREER YARDS

Player, Team	Years	Att.	Cmp.	Int.	Pct.	Yards	TD
Justin Peery, Westminster (Mo.)	1996-99	1,669	*1,012	57	.606	*13,262	*148
Kirk Baumgartner, Wis.-Stevens Point	1986-89	*1,696	883	57	.521	13,028	110
Mark Novara, Lakeland	1994-97	1,586	882	63	.556	11,101	100
Jim Ballard, Wilmington (Ohio)/Mount Union	1990, 91-93	1,199	743	41	.620	10,379	115
Tom Arth, John Carroll	1999-02	1,258	741	25	.589	10,345	89
Brian Dawson, Wash. & Jeff.	1999-02	1,132	670	45	.592	10,257	94
Bill Borchert, Mount Union	1994-97	1,009	671	17	.665	10,201	141
Troy Dougherty, Grinnell	1994, 97-99	1,192	734	33	.616	10,140	109
Adam Ryan, Wilmington (Ohio)	1998-01	1,223	693	43	.567	10,095	88
Bryan Snyder, Albright	1994-97	1,294	763	49	.590	9,865	92
Keith Bishop, Ill. Wesleyan/Wheaton (Ill.)	1981, 83-85	1,311	772	65	.589	9,579	71
Dennis Bogacz, Wis.-Oshkosh/Wis.-Whitewater	1988-89, 90-91	1,275	654	59	.513	9,536	66
Dave Geissler, Wis.-Stevens Point	1982-85	1,346	789	57	.586	9,518	65
Kevin Ricca, Catholic	1994-97	1,190	713	56	.643	9,469	89
Eric Noble, Wilmington (Ohio)	1992-95	1,264	682	62	.540	9,260	62
John Clark, Wis.-Eau Claire	1987-90	1,119	645	42	.576	9,196	63
Kyle Krober, Greenville	1998-01	1,288	722	45	.561	9,150	60
Mike Burton, Trinity (Tex.)	1996-99	1,067	631	29	.591	9,008	92
Brian Tomalak, Wis.-Oshkosh	1994-98	1,129	607	32	.538	8,983	83
Tim Peterson, Wis.-Stout	1986-89	1,185	653	62	.551	8,881	59
Roy Hampton, Trinity (Tex.)	$1998-02	942	600	26	.637	8,869	94
Matt D'Orazio, Otterbein	1996-99	1,224	680	35	.556	8,770	73
Mike Warker, Widener/Rowan	1999-02	914	482	38	.527	8,540	79
Jordan Poznick, Principia	1990-93	1,480	765	68	.517	8,485	55
Matt Bunyan, Wis.-Stout	1995-98	1,119	624	36	.558	8,462	85

Record. $See Page 8 for explanation.

CAREER YARDS PER GAME
(Minimum 4,500 yards)

Player, Team	Years	G	Att.	Cmp.	Int.	Pct.	Yards	TD	Avg.
Justin Peery, Westminster (Mo.)	1996-99	39	1,669	*1,012	57	.606	*13,262	*148	*340.1
Kirk Baumgartner, Wis.-Stevens Point	1986-89	41	*1,696	883	57	.521	13,028	110	317.8
Eric Bruns, Hanover	1999-00	20	842	541	30	.643	6,295	57	314.8
Keith Bishop, Ill. Wesleyan/Wheaton (Ill.)	1981, 83-85	31	1,311	772	65	.589	9,579	71	309.0
Zamir Amin, Menlo	1999-01	26	905	566	29	.625	7,982	83	307.0
Adam Ryan, Wilmington (Ohio)	1998-01	33	1,223	693	43	.567	10,095	88	305.9
Mark Novara, Lakeland	1994-97	38	1,586	882	63	.556	11,101	100	292.1
Bryan Snyder, Albright	1994-97	35	1,294	763	49	.590	9,865	92	281.9
Willie Reyna, La Verne	1991-92	17	542	346	19	.638	4,712	37	277.2
Gregg McDonald, Kalamazoo	1994-96	27	1,019	593	41	.582	7,339	50	271.8
Troy Dougherty, Grinnell	1994, 97-98	29	894	554	22	.620	7,817	80	269.6

Washington & Jefferson's Brian Dawson finished his playing days one spot behind Arth on the passing yards rankings with 10,257.

Player, Team	Years	G	Att.	Cmp.	Int.	Pct.	Yards	TD	Avg.
Tom Arth, John Carroll	1999-02	39	1,258	741	25	.589	10,345	89	265.3
Jordan Poznick, Principia	1990-93	32	1,480	765	68	.517	8,485	55	265.2
Jim Ballard, Wilmington (Ohio)/ Mount Union	1990, 91-93	40	1,199	743	41	.620	10,379	115	259.5
Travis McMahen, Franklin	1997-99	26	962	530	32	.551	6,737	59	259.1
Brian Partlow, Randolph-Macon	1997-99	20	786	421	29	.536	5,179	46	259.0
Bill Borchert, Mount Union	1994-97	40	1,009	671	17	.665	10,201	141	255.0
Curt Musser, Linfield	1999-00	18	534	304	13	.569	4,569	39	253.8
Chris Stormer, Hanover	1995-98	27	950	619	29	.652	6,814	58	252.4
Dennis Bogacz, Wis.-Oshkosh/ Wis.-Whitewater	1988-89, 90-91	38	1,275	654	59	.513	9,536	66	250.9
Gary Smeck, Mount Union	1997-00	31	752	504	15	‡.670	7,764	83	250.5
Brian Dawson, Wash. & Jeff.	1999-02	41	1,132	670	45	.592	10,257	94	250.2
Brian Tomalak, Wis.-Oshkosh	1994-98	36	1,129	607	32	.538	8,983	83	249.5
Tim Peterson, Wis.-Stout	1986-89	36	1,185	653	62	.551	8,881	59	246.7
Braxton Shaver, McMurry	1997-99	29	1,026	560	33	.546	7,147	84	246.4

*Record. ‡Record for minimum 750 attempts.

CAREER TOUCHDOWN PASSES

Player, Team	Years	G	TD
Justin Peery, Westminster (Mo.)	1996-99	39	*148
Bill Borchert, Mount Union	1994-97	40	141
Jim Ballard, Wilmington (Ohio)/Mount Union	1990, 91-93	40	115
Kirk Baumgartner, Wis.-Stevens Point	1986-89	41	110
Troy Dougherty, Grinnell	1994, 97-99	37	109
Mark Novara, Lakeland	1994-97	38	100
Matt Jozokos, Plymouth St.	1987-90	40	95
Roy Hampton, Trinity (Tex.)	$1998-02	37	94
Brian Dawson, Wash. & Jeff.	1999-02	41	94
Bryan Snyder, Albright	1994-97	35	92
Mike Burton, Trinity (Tex.)	1996-99	39	92
Tom Arth, John Carroll	1999-02	39	89
Kevin Ricca, Catholic	1994-97	34	89
Adam Ryan, Wilmington (Ohio)	1998-01	33	88
Matt Bunyan, Wis.-Stout	1995-98	36	85
Braxton Shaver, McMurry	1997-99	29	84
Zamir Amin, Menlo	1999-01	26	83
Gary Smeck, Mount Union	1997-00	31	83
Brian Tomalak, Wis.-Oshkosh	1994-98	36	83
Gary Collier, Emory & Henry	1984-87	41	80
Mike Warker, Widener/Rowan	1999-02	37	79
Terry Peebles, Hanover	1992-95	23	79

*Record. $See Page 8 for explanation.

SEASON YARDS

Player, Team	Year	G	Att.	Cmp.	Int.	Pct.	Yards	TD
Justin Peery, Westminster (Mo.)	1998	10	526	319	21	.606	*4,501	51
Zamir Amin, Menlo	2000	10	458	309	17	.674	4,320	43
Roy Hampton, Trinity (Tex.)	2002	14	397	260	6	.655	4,095	43
Justin Peery, Westminster (Mo.)	1999	10	498	*329	15	.660	4,092	*54
Kirk Baumgartner, Wis.-Stevens Point	1988	11	*527	276	16	.524	3,828	25
Kirk Baumgartner, Wis.-Stevens Point	1987	11	466	243	22	.521	3,755	31
Kirk Baumgartner, Wis.-Stevens Point	1989	10	455	247	9	.542	3,692	39
Danny Ragsdale, Redlands	1999	9	380	247	7	.650	3,639	33
Travis McMahen, Franklin	1999	10	486	264	15	.543	3,554	28
Terry Peebles, Hanover	1995	10	488	283	10	.579	3,521	39
Adam Ryan, Wilmington (Ohio)	2000	10	429	259	14	.603	3,455	23
Mark Novara, Lakeland	1996	10	410	258	12	.629	3,405	40
John Furmaniak, Eureka	1995	10	361	210	11	.581	3,372	34
Adam Ryan, Wilmington (Ohio)	1999	10	372	212	10	.569	3,343	34
Troy Dougherty, Grinnell	1998	10	293	198	5	.675	3,310	36
Greg Neuendorf, Denison	2001	10	430	230	15	.535	3,306	30
Jim Ballard, Mount Union	1993	10	314	229	11	*.729	3,304	37
Keith Bishop, Wheaton (Ill.)	1983	9	375	236	19	.629	3,274	24
Eli Grant, Case Reserve	2002	10	345	220	7	.638	3,265	33
Chris Stormer, Hanover	1998	10	424	286	8	.674	3,265	31
Kyle Krober, Greenville	2000	10	402	246	12	.611	3,264	24
Eric Bruns, Hanover	2000	10	445	285	16	.640	3,231	27
Matt Bunyan, Wis.-Stout	1997	10	399	223	12	.558	3,221	33
Matt Bunyan, Wis.-Stout	1998	10	389	227	9	.583	3,220	38
Tom Stallings, St. Thomas (Minn.)	1993	10	395	219	20	.554	3,210	22

*Record.

SEASON YARDS PER GAME

Player, Team	Year	G	Att.	Cmp.	Int.	Pct.	Yards	TD	Avg.
Justin Peery, Westminster (Mo.)	1998	10	526	319	21	.606	*4,501	51	*450.1
Zamir Amin, Menlo	2000	10	458	309	17	.674	4,320	43	432.0
Justin Peery, Westminster (Mo.)	1999	10	498	*329	15	.660	4,092	*54	409.2
Danny Ragsdale, Redlands	1999	9	380	247	7	.650	3,639	33	404.3
Kirk Baumgartner, Wis.-Stevens Point	1989	10	455	247	9	.543	3,692	39	369.2
Keith Bishop, Wheaton (Ill.)	1983	9	375	236	19	.629	3,274	24	363.8
Travis McMahen, Franklin	1999	10	486	264	15	.543	3,554	28	355.4
Bill Nietzke, Alma	1996	9	440	248	21	.563	3,197	28	355.2

Player, Team	Year	G	Att.	Cmp.	Int.	Pct.	Yards	TD	Avg.
Keith Bishop, Wheaton (Ill.)	1985	9	457	262	22	.573	3,171	25	352.3
Terry Peebles, Hanover	1995	10	488	283	10	.579	3,521	39	352.1
Kirk Baumgartner, Wis.-Stevens Point	1988	11	*527	276	16	.524	3,828	25	348.0
Adam Ryan, Wilmington (Ohio)	2000	10	429	259	14	.603	3,455	23	345.5
Gregg McDonald, Kalamazoo	1996	9	367	237	10	.645	3,089	23	343.2
Kirk Baumgartner, Wis.-Stevens Point	1987	11	466	243	22	.521	3,755	31	341.4
Mark Novara, Lakeland	1996	10	410	258	12	.629	3,405	40	340.5
Eric Noble, Wilmington (Ohio)	1994	9	398	221	17	.555	3,058	22	339.8
John Furmaniak, Eureka	1995	10	361	210	11	.581	3,372	34	337.2
Adam Ryan, Wilmington (Ohio)	1999	10	372	212	10	.569	3,343	34	334.3
Jason Visconti, Wesley	2001	9	350	222	10	.634	3,002	36	333.6
Steve Austin, Mass.-Boston	1992	9	396	181	25	.457	2,991	29	332.3
Chris Stormer, Hanover	1997	8	352	235	14	.667	2,654	20	331.8
Troy Dougherty, Grinnell	1998	10	293	198	5	.675	3,310	36	331.0
Greg Neuendorf, Denison	2001	10	430	230	15	.535	3,306	30	330.6
Jim Ballard, Mount Union	1993	10	314	229	11	*.729	3,304	37	330.4
Keith Bishop, Wheaton (Ill.)	1984	9	440	259	21	.589	2,968	21	329.8

*Record.

SEASON TOUCHDOWN PASSES

Player, Team	Year	G	TD
Justin Peery, Westminster (Mo.)	1999	10	*54
Justin Peery, Westminster (Mo.)	1998	10	51
Bill Borchert, Mount Union	1997	10	47
Roy Hampton, Trinity (Tex.)	2002	14	43
Zamir Amin, Menlo	2000	10	43
Mark Novara, Lakeland	1996	10	40
Terry Peebles, Hanover	1995	10	39
Kirk Baumgartner, Wis.-Stevens Point	1989	10	39
Bryan Snyder, Albright	1996	10	39
Matt Bunyan, Wis.-Stout	1998	10	38
Bill Borchert, Mount Union	1996	10	38
Tony Racioppi, Rowan	2001	9	37
Terry Peebles, Hanover	1994	10	37
Jim Ballard, Mount Union	1993	10	37
Daniel Pincelli, Hartwick	2002	10	36
Jason Visconti, Wesley	2001	9	36
Tom Linnemann, St. John's (Minn.)	2000	10	36
Matt D'Orazio, Otterbein	1999	10	36
Troy Dougherty, Grinnell	1998	10	36
Jake Knott, Wabash	2002	13	35
Kevin Ricca, Catholic	1997	10	35

*Record.

SINGLE-GAME YARDS

Yds.	Player, Team (Opponent)	Date
731	Zamir Amin, Menlo (Cal Lutheran)	Oct. 7, 2000
619	Justin Peery, Westminster (Mo.) (MacMurray)	Nov. 24, 1998
618	Justin Peery, Westminster (Mo.) (Principia)	Oct. 17, 1998
602	Danny Ragsdale, Redlands (Azusa Pacific)	Sept. 25, 1999
602	Tom Stallings, St. Thomas (Minn.) (Bethel [Minn.])	Nov. 13, 1993
589	Joe Montrella, Juniata (Widener)	Nov. 13, 1999
585	Tim Lynch, Hofstra (Fordham)	Oct. 19, 1991
575	Eric Noble, Wilmington (Ohio) (Urbana)	Nov. 5, 1994
574	Zamir Amin, Menlo (Linfield)	Sept. 9, 2000
569	Josh Wakefield, Alma (Franklin)	Sept. 25, 1999
563	Justin Peery, Westminster (Mo.) (Greenville)	Sept. 19, 1998
551	Justin Peery, Westminster (Mo.) (Colorado Col.)	Oct. 30, 1999
548	Danny Ragsdale, Redlands (Claremont-M-S)	Oct. 30, 1999
546	Danny Ragsdale, Redlands (Cal Lutheran)	Nov. 13, 1999
546	Bill Nietzke, Alma (Hope)	Oct. 26, 1996
543	Michael Kornblau, Greenville (Blackburn)	Oct. 9, 1999
533	Payton Parrett, Mississippi Col. (McMurry)	Sept. 29, 2001
533	John Love, North Park (Elmhurst)	Oct. 13, 1990
532	Bob Monroe, Knox (Cornell College)	Oct. 11, 1986
529	Justin Peery, Westminster (Mo.) (Bethel [Tenn.])	Nov. 7, 1998

SINGLE-GAME ATTEMPTS

Att.	Player, Team (Opponent)	Date
81	Jordan Poznick, Principia (Blackburn)	Oct. 10, 1992
80	Scott Kello, Sul Ross St. (Howard Payne)	Oct. 5, 2002
79	Mike Wallace, Ohio Wesleyan (Denison)	Oct. 3, 1981
78	Shawn Wheeler, Capital (Ohio Northern)	Nov. 13, 1999
73	Tom Stetzer, Wis.-Platteville (Olivet Nazarene)	Sept. 7, 2002
72	Scott Kello, Sul Ross St. (Louisiana Col.)	Sept. 21, 2002
72	Bob Lockhart, Millikin (Franklin)	Nov. 12, 1977

SINGLE-GAME COMPLETIONS

Cmp.	Player, Team (Opponent)	Date
51	Scott Kello, Sul Ross St. (Howard Payne)	Oct. 5, 2002
50	Justin Peery, Westminster (Mo.) (MacMurray)	Nov. 14, 1998
50	Tim Lynch, Hofstra (Fordham)	Oct. 19, 1991
48	Jordan Poznick, Principia (Blackburn)	Oct. 10, 1992
47	Mike Wallace, Ohio Wesleyan (Denison)	Oct. 3, 1981

Cmp.	Player, Team (Opponent)	Date
45	Scott Kello, Sul Ross St. (Texas Lutheran)	Nov. 16, 2002
44	Scott Kello, Sul Ross St. (Louisiana Col.)	Sept. 21, 2002
44	Chris Stormer, Hanover (Franklin)	Nov. 14, 1998
43	Chris Czernek, Cal Lutheran (Menlo)	Nov. 6, 1999
43	Bill Nietzke, Alma (Hope)	Oct. 26, 1996
43	Bill Nietzke, Alma (Olivet Nazarene)	Sept. 21, 1996
43	Terry Peebles, Hanover (Franklin)	Nov. 12, 1994
42	Tom Arth, John Carroll (Ohio Northern)	Oct. 21, 2000
42	Mark Novara, Lakeland (Concordia [Wis.])	Oct. 15, 1994
42	Tim Lynch, Hofstra (Towson)	Nov. 2, 1991
42	Keith Bishop, Wheaton (Ill.) (Millikin)	Sept. 14, 1985
41	Joel Steele, Anderson (Ind.) (Capital)	Sept. 7, 2002
41	Tom Stetzer, Wis.-Platteville (Wis.-Eau Claire)	Oct. 20, 2001
41	Tom Stetzer, Wis.-Platteville (Wis.-La Crosse)	Oct. 6, 2001
41	Jason Lee, DePauw (Hope)	Sept. 16, 2000
41	Justin Peery, Westminster (Mo.) (Colorado Col.)	Oct. 30, 1999
41	Troy Dougherty, Grinnell (Lawrence)	Oct. 1, 1994
41	Michael Doto, Hofstra (Central Conn. St.)	Sept. 14, 1991
41	Todd Monken, Knox (Cornell College)	Oct. 8, 1988

ANNUAL CHAMPIONS

Year	Player, Team	Class	G	Att.	Cmp.	Avg.	Int.	Pct.	Yds.	TD
1973	Pat Clements, Kenyon	Jr.	9	239	133	14.8	17	.556	1,738	12
1974	Larry Cenotto, Pomona-Pitzer	Sr.	9	294	147	16.3	23	.500	2,024	15
1975	Ron Miller, Elmhurst	Sr.	8	205	118	14.8	15	.576	1,398	7
1976	Tom Hamilton, Occidental	Jr.	8	235	131	16.4	10	.557	1,988	10
1977	Tom Hamilton, Occidental	Sr.	9	323	171	19.0	17	.529	2,132	13
1978	Robert Farra, Claremont-M-S	Jr.	9	359	196	21.8	15	.546	2,770	20

Beginning in 1979, ranked on passing efficiency rating points, minimum 15 attempts per game (instead of per-game completions)

Year	Player, Team	Class	G	Att.	Cmp.	Int.	Pct.	Yds.	TD	Pts.
1979	David Broecker, Wabash	Fr.	9	145	81	9	.559	1,311	13	149.0
1980	George Muller, Hofstra	Sr.	10	189	115	14	.608	1,983	15	160.4
1981	Larry Atwater, Coe	Sr.	9	172	92	10	.535	1,615	15	147.2
1982	Mike Bennett, Cornell College	Sr.	9	154	83	8	.539	1,436	17	158.3
1983	Joe Shield, Trinity (Conn.)	Jr.	8	238	135	13	.567	2,185	19	149.1
1984	Cody Dearing, Randolph-Macon	Sr.	10	226	125	12	.553	2,139	27	163.4
1985	Robb Disbennett, Salisbury	Sr.	10	153	94	6	.614	1,462	16	168.4
1986	Gary Collier, Emory & Henry	Jr.	11	171	88	6	.514	1,509	21	158.9
1987	Jimbo Fisher, Samford	Sr.	10	252	139	5	.551	2,394	34	175.4
1988	Steve Flynn, Central (Iowa)	Jr.	8	133	82	6	.616	1,190	10	152.5
1989	Joe Blake, Simpson	††Jr.	10	144	93	3	.645	1,705	19	203.3
1990	Dan Sharley, Dayton	†††Sr.	10	149	95	2	.637	1,377	12	165.1
1991	Pat Mayew, St. John's (Minn.)	Sr.	9	247	154	4	.623	2,408	30	181.0
1992	Steve Keller, Dayton	Sr.	10	153	99	5	.647	1,350	17	168.9
1993	Willie Seiler, St. John's (Minn.)	Sr.	10	205	141	6	.687	2,648	33	224.6
1994	Mike Simpson, Eureka	So.	10	158	116	5	.734	1,988	25	*225.0
1995	Bill Borchert, Mount Union	So.	10	225	160	4	.711	2,270	30	196.3
1996	Bill Borchert, Mount Union	Jr.	10	240	165	6	.687	2,655	38	208.9
1997	Bill Borchert, Mount Union	Sr.	10	272	190	1	.698	2,933	47	216.7
1998	Troy Dougherty, Grinnell	Jr.	10	293	198	5	.675	3,310	36	199.6
1999	Gary Smeck, Mount Union	Jr.	10	199	131	3	.658	2,274	30	208.6
2000	Brian Dawson, Wash. & Jeff.	So.	10	227	149	6	.656	2,675	29	201.5
2001	Dustin Proctor, Hardin-Simmons	Jr.	9	178	116	3	.652	2,194	28	217.2
2002	Roy Hampton, Trinity (Tex.)	Sr.	14	397	260	6	.655	4,095	43	184.9

*Record. ††Declared champion; with six more pass attempts (making 15 per game), all interceptions, still would have highest efficiency rating (187.3). †††Declared champion; with one more attempt (making 15 per game), an interception, still would have highest efficiency rating (162.8).

ANNUAL PASSING EFFICIENCY LEADERS BEFORE 1979

(Minimum 15 Attempts Per Game)

Year	Player, Team	G	Att.	Cmp.	Int.	Pct.	Yds.	TD	Pts.
1973	Mitch Sanders, Bridgeport	10	151	84	7	.556	1,551	23	182.9
1974	Tom McGuire, Benedictine (Ill.)	10	221	142	16	.643	2,206	16	157.5
1975	Jim Morrow, Wash. & Jeff.	9	137	82	7	.599	1,283	11	154.8
1976	Aaron Van Dyke, Cornell College	9	154	91	12	.591	1,611	14	161.4
1977	Matt Winslow, Middlebury	8	130	79	5	.608	919	17	155.6
1978	Matt Dillon, Cornell College	9	166	98	7	.590	1,567	16	161.7

Receiving

CAREER RECEPTIONS PER GAME

(Minimum 120 Receptions)

Player, Team	Years	G	Rec.	Yards	TD	Rec.PG
Scott Pingel, Westminster (Mo.)	1996-99	39	*436	*6,108	*75	*11.2
Nate Jackson, Menlo	1999-01	29	261	3,976	43	9.0
Matt Newton, Principia	1990-93	33	287	3,646	32	8.7
Darryl DeShields, Greenville	1999-01	29	248	4,051	39	8.6
Todd Bloom, Hardin-Simmons	1995-97	28	233	2,621	14	8.3
Jeff Clay, Catholic	1994-97	36	269	4,101	44	7.5
Bill Stromberg, Johns Hopkins	1978-81	36	258	3,776	39	7.2
Scott Hvistendahl, Augsburg	1995-98	40	285	4,697	40	7.1
Tarrik Wilson, Hanover	1996-99	34	240	2,897	30	7.1
Tim McNamara, Trinity (Conn.)	1981-84	21	146	2,313	19	7.0

Player, Team	Years	G	Rec.	Yards	TD	Rec.PG
Ron Severance, Otterbein	1989-91	30	207	2,378	17	6.9
Mark Brock, Maranatha Baptist	1999-00	18	124	2,048	20	6.9
Chuck Braun, Wis.-Stevens Point	1980-81	18	124	1,914	19	6.9
Michael Becker, Randolph-Macon	1997-00	40	273	3,683	19	6.8
Jim Jorden, Wheaton (Ill.)	1982-85	33	225	3,022	22	6.8
Ryan Ditze, Albright	1993-96	33	224	3,169	29	6.8
Mike Groll, Defiance	1996-99	34	231	2,812	20	6.8
Matt Plummer, Dubuque	1996-99	40	271	4,049	42	6.8
Mike Feuerstahler, Martin Luther	1998-01	33	218	2,728	17	6.6
Mike Whitehouse, St. Norbert	1986-89	35	230	3,480	37	6.6
Adam Marino, Mount Union	1998-00	30	197	3,436	40	6.6
Eric Nemec, Albright	1995-98	39	256	3,300	35	6.6
Kurt Barth, Eureka	1994-97	39	256	4,311	51	6.6
Joe Rettler, Ripon	1997-99	29	189	3,100	27	6.5
Dan Daley, Pomona-Pitzer	1985-88	35	227	2,598	10	6.5
Rich Johnson, Pace	1985-87	29	188	2,614	8	6.5

*Record.

SEASON RECEPTIONS PER GAME

Player, Team	Year	G	Rec.	Yards	TD	Rec.PG
Scott Pingel, Westminster (Mo.)	†1999	10	*136	1,648	24	*13.6
Scott Pingel, Westminster (Mo.)	†1998	10	130	*2,157	*26	13.0
Matt Newton, Principia	†1992	8	98	1,487	14	12.3
Matt Newton, Principia	†1993	8	96	1,080	11	12.0
Jeff Clay, Catholic	†1997	10	112	1,625	20	11.2
Scott Hvistendahl, Augsburg	1998	10	112	1,860	15	11.2
Ben Fox, Hanover	†1995	9	95	1,087	15	10.6
Sean Munroe, Mass.-Boston	1992	9	95	1,693	17	10.6
Nate Jackson, Menlo	†2001	10	105	1,520	17	10.5
Scott Faessler, Framingham St.	†1990	9	92	916	5	10.2
Nate Jackson, Menlo	†2000	10	101	1,515	16	10.1
Scott Pingel, Westminster (Mo.)	1997	10	98	1,420	17	9.8
Luis Uresti, Sul Ross St.	†2002	9	87	1,082	4	9.7
Mike Funk, Wabash	†1989	9	87	1,169	12	9.7
Jim Jorden, Wheaton (Ill.)	†1985	9	87	1,011	8	9.7
Theo Blanco, Wis.-Stevens Point	1987	11	106	1,616	8	9.6
Todd Bloom, Hardin-Simmons	†1996	10	96	1,019	6	9.6
Eric Nemec, Albright	1997	9	86	1,147	15	9.6
Sean Eaton, Randolph-Macon	1999	10	95	1,289	15	9.5
Jason Tincher, Wilmington (Ohio)	†1994	9	85	1,298	9	9.4
Mike Groll, Defiance	1999	9	84	1,010	11	9.3
Rick Fry, Occidental	†1976	8	74	1,214	8	9.3
Tarrik Wilson, Hanover	1999	9	83	974	7	9.2
Darryl DeShields, Greenville	1999	10	92	1,515	12	9.2
Brandy Spoerl, Carroll (Wis.)	2001	9	83	1,196	11	9.2
Mike Cook, Claremont-M-S	1995	9	83	993	7	9.2
Ron Severance, Otterbein	1990	10	92	1,049	8	9.2

*Record. †National champion.

CAREER RECEPTIONS

Player, Team	Years	Rec.	Yards	TD
Scott Pingel, Westminster (Mo.)	1996-99	*436	*6,108	*75
Matt Newton, Principia	1990-93	287	3,646	32
Scott Hvistendahl, Augsburg	1995-98	285	4,696	40
Michael Becker, Randolph-Macon	1997-00	273	3,683	19
Matt Plummer, Dubuque	1996-99	271	4,049	42
Jeff Clay, Catholic	1994-97	269	4,101	44
Nate Jackson, Menlo	1999-01	261	3,976	43
Bill Stromberg, Johns Hopkins	1978-81	258	3,776	39
Eric Nemec, Albright	1995-98	256	3,300	35
Kurt Barth, Eureka	1994-97	256	4,311	51
Darryl DeShields, Greenville	1999-01	248	4,051	39
Ryan Short, Wabash	1999-02	243	2,773	45
Tarrik Wilson, Hanover	1996-99	240	2,897	30
Jonathon Cain, Wilmington (Ohio)	1998-01	236	3,945	40
Todd Bloom, Hardin-Simmons	1995-97	233	2,621	14
Dale Amos, Frank. & Marsh.	1986-89	233	3,846	35
Scott Fredrickson, Wis.-Stout	1986-89	233	3,390	23
Mike Groll, Defiance	1996-99	231	2,812	20
Mike Whitehouse, St. Norbert	1986-89	230	3,480	37
Mike Funk, Wabash	1985, 87-89	228	2,858	33
Dan Daley, Pomona-Pitzer	1985-88	227	2,598	10
Jim Jorden, Wheaton (Ill.)	1982-85	225	3,022	22
Brandon Good, Wooster	1995-98	224	2,838	30
Ryan Ditze, Albright	1993-96	224	3,169	29
Chris Bisaillon, Ill. Wesleyan	1989-92	223	3,670	55
Theo Blanco, Wis.-Stevens Point	1985-88	223	3,139	18

*Record.

SEASON RECEPTIONS

Player, Team	Year	G	Rec.	Yards	TD
Scott Pingel, Westminster (Mo.)	†1999	10	*136	1,648	24
Scott Pingel, Westminster (Mo.)	†1998	10	130	*2,157	*26

Player, Team	Year	G	Rec.	Yards	TD
Blake Elliott, St. John's (Minn.)	2002	14	120	1,484	22
Scott Hvistendahl, Augsburg	1998	10	112	1,860	15
Jeff Clay, Catholic	†1997	10	112	1,625	20
Theo Blanco, Wis.-Stevens Point	1987	11	106	1,616	8
Nate Jackson, Menlo	†2001	10	105	1,520	17
Nate Jackson, Menlo	†2000	10	101	1,515	16
Scott Pingel, Westminster (Mo.)	1997	10	98	1,420	17
Matt Newton, Principia	†1992	8	98	1,487	14
Todd Bloom, Hardin-Simmons	†1996	10	96	1,019	6
Matt Newton, Principia	†1993	8	96	1,080	11
Jason Hunt, Trinity (Tex.)	2002	15	95	1,348	8
Sean Eaton, Randolph-Macon	1999	10	95	1,289	15
Ben Fox, Hanover	†1995	9	95	1,087	15
Sean Munroe, Mass.-Boston	1992	9	95	1,693	17
Darryl DeShields, Greenville	1999	10	92	1,515	12
Ron Severance, Otterbein	1990	10	92	1,049	8
Scott Faessler, Framingham St.	†1990	9	92	916	5
Mark Boehms, Alma	2002	11	91	1,116	11
Darryl DeShields, Greenville	2000	10	90	1,444	15
Steve Wilkerson, Catholic	1994	10	90	1,457	13
John Stephens, DePauw	2001	10	88	991	6
Jay Agan, Hanover	2000	10	88	1,056	9
Luis Uresti, Sul Ross St.	†2002	9	87	1,082	4
Jeffrey Jourdan, Hanover	2002	11	87	1,133	14
Vince Annel, Knox	1999	10	87	1,062	6
Mike Hunter, Catholic	1998	10	87	1,279	12
Greg Lehrer, Heidelberg	1993	10	87	1,202	8
Mike Funk, Wabash	†1989	9	87	1,169	12
Ted Taggart, Kenyon	1989	10	87	1,004	7
Jim Jorden, Wheaton (Ill.)	†1985	9	87	1,011	8

*Record. †National champion.

SEASON TOUCHDOWN RECEPTIONS

Player, Team	Year	G	TD
Scott Pingel, Westminster (Mo.)	1998	10	*26
Scott Pingel, Westminster (Mo.)	1999	10	24
Blake Elliott, St. John's (Minn.)	2002	14	22
David Snider, Grinnell	1998	10	21
Ryan Soule, Hartwick	2002	10	20
Ryan Johnson, Hartwick	2001	10	20
Steve Vagades, Ohio Northern	1998	10	20
Kirk Aikens, Hartwick	1998	10	20
Jeff Clay, Catholic	1997	10	20
John Aromando, Col. of New Jersey	1983	10	20
Ryan Silvis, Wash. & Jeff.	2000	10	19
Matt Eisenberg, Juniata	1999	10	19
Adam Marino, Mount Union	1999	10	19
Ben Streby, Otterbein	1999	10	19
Michael Coleman, Widener	2000	10	18
Chad Hustead, Redlands	1999	9	18
Ryan Hinske, Wis.-Oshkosh	1997	10	18
Kurt Barth, Eureka	1995	10	18
Nate Jackson, Menlo	2001	10	17
Scott Pingel, Westminster (Mo.)	1997	10	17
Junior Lord, Guilford	1997	9	17
Jeremy Loretz, St. John's (Minn.)	1994	10	17
Sean Munroe, Mass.-Boston	1992	9	17
Chris Bisaillon, Ill. Wesleyan	1991	9	17
Tom Neagle, Knox	2002	10	16
Steve Tenhagen, Wis.-Whitewater	2001	10	16
Nate Jackson, Menlo	2000	10	16
Jon May, Wis.-Oshkosh	1998	10	16
Matt Surette, WPI	1997	10	16
Wesley Bell, Upper Iowa	1996	10	16
Jeff Clay, Catholic	1996	10	16
Ryan Ditze, Albright	1996	10	16
Evan Elkington, WPI	1989	10	16

*Record.

SINGLE-GAME RECEPTIONS

No.	Player, Team (Opponent)	Date
23	Sean Munroe, Mass.-Boston (Mass. Maritime)	Oct. 10, 1992
20	Scott Pingel, Westminster (Mo.) (Colorado Col.)	Oct. 30, 1999
20	Todd Bloom, Hardin-Simmons (Mississippi Col.)	Oct. 12, 1996
20	Kurt Barth, Eureka (Concordia [Wis.])	Sept. 28, 1996
20	Rich Johnson, Pace (Fordham)	Nov. 7, 1987
20	Pete Thompson, Carroll (Wis.) (Augustana [Ill.])	Nov. 4, 1978
19	Luis Uresti, Sul Ross St. (Louisiana Col.)	Sept. 21, 2002
18	Lewis Howes, Principia (Martin Luther)	Oct. 12, 2002
18	Nate Jackson, Menlo (Azusa Pacific)	Oct. 28, 2000
18	Darryl DeShields, Greenville (Lakeland)	Oct. 2, 1999
18	Scott Hvistendahl, Augsburg (Concordia-M'head)	Nov. 13, 1998
18	Scott Pingel, Westminster (Mo.) (Greenville)	Sept. 19, 1998
18	Richard Wemer, Grinnell (Beloit)	Nov. 20, 1997
18	Adam Herbst, St. John's (Minn.) (St. Thomas [Minn.])	Nov. 7, 1997
18	Jeff Clay, Catholic (Albright)	Nov. 16, 1996

No.	Player, Team (Opponent)	Date
18	Matt Plummer, Dubuque (Buena Vista)	Oct. 12, 1996
18	Craig Antonio, Waynesburg (Bethany [W.Va.])	Oct. 16, 1993
18	Ed Sullivan, Catholic (Carnegie Mellon)	Nov. 7, 1992

CAREER YARDS

Player, Team	Years	Rec.	Yards	Avg.	TD
Scott Pingel, Westminster (Mo.)	1996-99	*436	*6,108	14.0	*75
Scott Hvistendahl, Augsburg	1995-98	285	4,696	16.5	40
Kurt Barth, Eureka	1994-97	256	4,311	16.8	51
Jeff Clay, Catholic	1994-97	269	4,101	15.2	44
Darryl DeShields, Greenville	1999-01	248	4,051	16.3	39
Matt Plummer, Dubuque	1996-99	271	4,049	14.9	42
Nate Jackson, Menlo	1999-01	261	3,976	15.2	43
Jonathon Cain, Wilmington (Ohio)	1998-01	236	3,945	16.7	40
Dale Amos, Frank. & Marsh.	1986-89	233	3,846	16.5	35
Bill Stromberg, Johns Hopkins	1978-81	258	3,776	14.6	39
Jim Bradford, Carleton	1988-91	212	3,719	17.5	32
Chris Bisaillon, Ill. Wesleyan	1989-92	223	3,670	16.5	55
Michael Becker, Randolph-Macon	1997-00	273	3,683	13.5	19
Matt Newton, Principia	1990-93	287	3,646	12.7	32
Mike Gundersdorf, Wilkes	1993-96	205	3,603	17.6	34
Jim Jones, Widener	1999-01	170	3,523	20.7	30
Matt Eisenberg, Juniata	1997-00	203	3,505	17.3	38
Mike Whitehouse, St. Norbert	1986-89	230	3,480	15.1	37
Adam Marino, Mount Union	1998-00	197	3,436	17.4	40
Derek Baker, Buffalo St.	1997-00	154	3,421	22.2	26
#Mark Bartosic, Susquehanna	2000-02	197	3,420	17.4	42
Scott Fredrickson, Wis.-Stout	1986-89	233	3,390	14.5	23
Eric Nemec, Albright	1995-98	256	3,300	12.9	35
R.J. Hoppe, Carroll (Wis.)	1993-96	152	3,295	21.7	49
Michael Coleman, Widener	1998-01	139	3,254	*23.4	44
Ryan Johnson, Hartwick	1998-01	160	3,212	20.1	41

*Record. #Active player.

CAREER YARDS PER GAME
(Minimum 2,200 Yards)

Player, Team	Years	G	Yards	Yd. PG
Scott Pingel, Westminster (Mo.)	1996-99	39	*6,108	*156.6
Darryl DeShields, Greenville	1999-01	29	4,051	139.7
Nate Jackson, Menlo	1999-01	29	3,976	137.1
Jim Jones, Widener	1999-01	30	3,523	117.4
Scott Hvistendahl, Augsburg	1995-98	40	4,696	117.4
Adam Marino, Mount Union	1998-00	30	3,436	114.5
Jeff Clay, Catholic	1994-97	36	4,101	113.9
Kurt Barth, Eureka	1994-97	39	4,311	110.5
Matt Newton, Principia	1990-93	33	3,646	110.5
Tim McNamara, Trinity (Conn.)	1981-84	21	2,313	110.1
Joe Rettler, Ripon	1997-99	29	3,100	106.9
Bill Stromberg, Johns Hopkins	1978-81	36	3,776	104.9
Chris Bisaillon, Ill. Wesleyan	1989-92	36	3,670	101.9
Matt Plummer, Dubuque	1996-99	40	4,049	101.2
Steve Vagedes, Ohio Northern	1997-99	30	3,036	101.2
Jonathon Cain, Wilmington (Ohio)	1998-01	39	3,945	101.2

*Record.

CAREER TOUCHDOWN RECEPTIONS

Player, Team	Years	G	TD
Scott Pingel, Westminster (Mo.)	1996-99	39	*75
Chris Bisaillon, Ill. Wesleyan	1989-92	36	55
Kurt Barth, Eureka	1994-97	39	51
R.J. Hoppe, Carroll (Wis.)	1993-96	37	49
Ryan Short, Wabash	1999-02	41	45
Michael Coleman, Widener	1998-01	40	44
Jeff Clay, Catholic	1994-97	36	44
#Blake Elliott, St. John's (Minn.)	2000-02	33	43
Nate Jackson, Menlo	1999-01	29	43
Steve Vagedes, Ohio Northern	1995, 97-99	40	43
Kirk Aikens, Hartwick	1995-98	38	43
Mark Loeffler, Wheaton (Ill.)	1993-96	38	43
Bill Schultz, Ripon	1993-96	38	43
#Mark Bartosic, Susquehanna	2000-02	30	42
Matt Plummer, Dubuque	1996-99	40	42
Dan Ryan, DePauw	1999-02	38	41
Ryan Johnson, Hartwick	1998-01	38	41
Jonathon Cain, Wilmington (Ohio)	1998-01	39	40
Adam Marino, Mount Union	1998-00	30	40
Scott Hvistendahl, Augsburg	1995-98	40	40
Richard Wemer, Grinnell	1995-98	38	40
Adam Herbst, St. John's (Minn.)	1995-98	39	40

*Record. #Active player.

Principia's Lewis Howes compiled 418 receiving yards against Martin Luther October 12, 2002, to establish a new Division III record.

SEASON YARDS

Player, Team	Year	Rec.	Yards	Avg.	TD
Scott Pingel, Westminster (Mo.)	1998	130	*2,157	16.6	*26
Scott Hvistendahl, Augsburg	1998	112	1,860	16.6	15
Sean Munroe, Mass.-Boston	†1992	95	1,693	17.8	17
Scott Pingel, Westminster (Mo.)	†1999	*136	1,648	12.1	24
Jeff Clay, Catholic	†1997	112	1,625	14.5	20
Theo Blanco, Wis.-Stevens Point	1987	106	1,616	15.2	8
Ryan Soule, Hartwick	†2002	76	1,550	20.4	20
Matt Eisenberg, Juniata	1999	76	1,547	20.4	19
Nate Jackson, Menlo	†2001	105	1,520	14.5	17
Nate Jackson, Menlo	†2000	101	1,515	15.0	16
Darryl DeShields, Greenville	1999	92	1,515	16.5	12
Matt Newton, Principia	1992	98	1,487	15.2	14
Blake Elliott, St. John's (Minn.)	2002	120	1,484	12.4	22
Jim Myers, Kenyon	1974	82	1,483	18.1	12
Jeff Clay, Catholic	†1996	81	1,460	18.0	16
Jonathon Cain, Wilmington (Ohio)	2000	85	1,459	17.2	15
Steve Wilkerson, Catholic	†1994	90	1,457	16.2	13
Adam Marino, Mount Union	1999	73	1,456	19.9	19
Darryl DeShields, Greenville	2000	90	1,444	16.0	15
Jim Jones, Widener	2000	62	1,439	23.2	14
Scott Pingel, Westminster (Mo.)	1997	98	1,420	14.5	17
David Snider, Grinnell	1998	63	1,383	22.0	21
Beau Almodobar, Norwich	1984	71	1,375	19.4	10
Todd Fry, Wash. & Jeff.	2001	77	1,362	17.7	13
Jason Hunt, Trinity (Tex.)	2002	95	1,348	14.2	8

*Record. †National champion.

SINGLE-GAME YARDS

Yds.	Player, Team (Opponent)	Date
418	Lewis Howes, Principia (Martin Luther)	Oct. 12, 2002
397	Matt Eisenberg, Juniata (Widener)	Nov. 13, 1999
395	Scott Pingel, Westminster (Mo.) (Bethel [Tenn.])	Nov. 7, 1998
364	Jeff Clay, Catholic (Albright)	Nov. 16, 1996
362	Matt Surette, WPI (Springfield)	Oct. 25, 1997
332	Ryan Pifer, Heidelberg (Marietta)	Nov. 8, 1997
332	Sean Munroe, Mass.-Boston (Mass. Maritime)	Oct. 10, 1992
314	Matt Eisenberg, Juniata (Albright)	Oct. 2, 1999
310	Jace Metzner, Ohio Northern (John Carroll)	Oct. 20, 2001
310	Jeff Clay, Catholic (LaSalle)	Oct. 11, 1997
309	Dale Amos, Frank. & Marsh. (McDaniel)	Oct. 24, 1987
306	Scott Pingel, Westminster (Mo.) (Greenville)	Sept. 19, 1998
303	Chuck Braun, Wis.-Stevens Point (Wis.-Superior)	Oct. 17, 1981
303	Rick Fry, Occidental (Claremont-M-S)	Oct. 30, 1976
301	Jeremy Snyder, Whittier (Occidental)	Nov. 15, 1997
301	Greg Holmes, Carroll (Wis.) (North Central)	Nov. 7, 1981
297	Adam Marino, Mount Union (Ohio Northern)	Sept. 25, 1999
296	Tim Jordain, Rensselaer (St. Lawrence)	Nov. 7, 1998
296	Joe Richards, Johns Hopkins (Georgetown)	Oct. 26, 1991
296	Vince Hull, Minn.-Morris (Bemidji St.)	Oct. 10, 1981

David Russell of Linfield racked up 180 points last year, placing him in a tie for fifth on the Division III single-season scoring list.

ANNUAL CHAMPIONS

RECEPTIONS PER GAME

Year	Player, Team	Class	G	Rec.	Avg.	Yards	TD
1973	Ron Duckett, Trinity (Conn.)	Sr.	8	57	7.1	834	7
1974	Jim Myers, Kenyon	Sr.	9	82	9.1	1,483	12
1975	C.J. DeWitt, Bridgewater (Va.)	Sr.	9	64	7.1	836	2
1976	Rick Fry, Occidental	Jr.	8	74	9.3	1,214	8
1977	Rick Fry, Occidental	Sr.	9	82	9.1	1,222	5
1978	Pat McNamara, Trinity (Conn.)	Jr.	8	67	8.4	1,024	11
1979	Theodore Anderson, Fisk	Jr.	7	49	7.0	699	2
1980	Bill Stromberg, Johns Hopkins	Jr.	9	66	7.3	907	11
1981	Bill Stromberg, Johns Hopkins	Sr.	9	78	8.7	924	10
1982	Jim Gustafson, St. Thomas (Minn.)	Jr.	10	72	7.2	990	5
1983	Ed Brady, Ill. Wesleyan	Jr.	9	80	8.9	873	7
1984	Tim McNamara, Trinity (Conn.)	Sr.	8	67	8.4	1,004	10
1985	Jim Jorden, Wheaton (Ill.)	Sr.	9	87	9.7	1,011	8
1986	John Tucci, Amherst	Sr	8	70	8.8	1,025	8
1987	Chris Vogel, Knox	So.	9	78	8.7	1,326	15
1988	Theo Blanco, Wis.-Stevens Point	Sr.	10	80	8.0	1,009	7
1989	Mike Funk, Wabash	Sr.	9	87	9.7	1,169	12
1990	Scott Faessler, Framingham St.	So.	9	92	10.2	916	5
1991	Ron Severance, Otterbein	Sr.	10	85	8.5	929	4
1992	Matt Newton, Principia	Jr.	8	98	12.3	1,487	14
1993	Matt Newton, Principia	Sr.	8	96	12.0	1,080	11
1994	Jason Tincher, Wilmington (Ohio)	Sr.	9	85	9.4	1,298	9
1995	Ben Fox, Hanover	Sr.	9	95	10.6	1,087	15
1996	Todd Bloom, Hardin-Simmons	Jr.	9	96	9.6	1,019	6
1997	Jeff Clay, Catholic	Sr.	10	112	11.2	1,625	20
1998	Scott Pingel, Westminster (Mo.)	Jr.	10	130	13.0	*2,157	*26
1999	Scott Pingel, Westminster (Mo.)	Sr.	10	*136	*13.6	1,648	24
2000	Nate Jackson, Menlo	Jr.	10	101	10.1	1,515	16
2001	Nate Jackson, Menlo	Sr.	10	105	10.5	1,520	17
2002	Luis Uresti, Sul Ross St.	Sr.	9	87	9.7	1,082	4

YARDS PER GAME

Year	Player, Team	Class	G	Rec.	Yards	TD	Avg.
1990	Ray Shelley, Juniata	Sr.	10	54	1,147	12	114.7
1991	Rodd Patten, Framingham St.	So.	8	49	956	13	119.5
1992	Sean Munroe, Mass.-Boston	Sr.	9	95	1,693	17	188.1
1993	Rob Lokerson, Muhlenberg	Jr.	9	76	1,275	6	141.7
1994	Steve Wilkerson, Catholic	Sr.	10	90	1,457	13	145.7
1995	Kurt Barth, Eureka	So.	10	68	1,337	18	133.7
1996	Jeff Clay, Catholic	Jr.	9	81	1,460	16	162.2
1997	Jeff Clay, Catholic	Sr.	10	112	1,625	20	162.5
1998	Scott Pingel, Westminster (Mo.)	Jr.	10	130	*2,157	*26	*215.7
1999	Scott Pingel, Westminster (Mo.)	Sr.	10	*136	1,648	24	164.8
2000	Nate Jackson, Menlo	Jr.	10	101	1,515	16	151.5
2001	Nate Jackson, Menlo	Sr.	10	105	1,520	17	152.0
2002	Ryan Soule, Hartwick	Sr.	10	76	1,550	20	155.0

*Record.

Scoring

CAREER POINTS PER GAME
(Minimum 225 Points)

Player, Team	Years	G	TD	Extra Pts. Scored	FG	Pts.	Pt. PG
Ricky Gales, Simpson	1988-89	19	44	10	0	274	*14.4
R.J. Bowers, Grove City	1997-00	40	*92	10	0	*562	14.1
Cory Christensen, Simpson	1996-97	19	44	0	0	264	13.9
Rob Marchitello, Maine Maritime	1993-95	26	59	4	0	358	13.8
Carey Bender, Coe	1991-94	39	86	12	0	528	13.5
Trevor Shannon, Wartburg	1995-98	39	79	10	0	484	12.4
Scott Pingel, Westminster (Mo.)	1996-99	39	75	34	0	484	12.4
Jim Regan, Pomona-Pitzer	1995-98	30	37	93	15	360	12.0
Chad Hoiska, Wis.-Eau Claire	1995-97	30	58	2	0	350	11.7
Joe Dudek, Plymouth St.	1982-85	41	79	0	0	474	11.6
Chuck Moore, Mount Union	1998-01	40	73	0	0	438	11.0
Dan Pugh, Mount Union	1999-02	41	73	2	0	440	10.7
Chris Babirad, Wash. & Jeff.	1989-92	35	62	2	0	374	10.7
Terry Underwood, Wagner	1985-88	33	58	0	0	348	10.5
Chris Bisaillon, Ill. Wesleyan	1989-92	36	61	12	0	378	10.5
Stanley Drayton, Allegheny	1989-92	32	56	0	0	336	10.5
Greg Novarro, Bentley	1990-92	24	42	0	0	252	10.5
Casey Donaldson, Wittenberg	1997-00	39	68	0	0	408	10.5
Shane Ream, Allegheny	1998-01	37	64	0	0	384	10.3
Mark Kacmarynski, Central (Iowa)	$1992-96	41	70	2	0	422	10.3
Ryan Kolpin, Coe	1987-90	28	48	0	0	288	10.3
Anthony Rice, La Verne	1994-96	27	46	0	0	276	10.2
Andrew Notarfrancesco, Catholic	1996-99	39	65	8	0	398	10.2
Jamal Robertson, Ohio Northern	1997-00	34	56	2	0	338	9.9
Nate Jackson, Menlo	1999-01	29	43	26	1	287	9.9
Kevin Cahill, Springfield	1997-00	28	44	12	0	276	9.9

*Record. $See Page 8 for explanation.

SEASON POINTS PER GAME

Player, Team	Year	G	TD	Extra Pts. Scored	FG	Pts.	Pt. PG
James Regan, Pomona-Pitzer	†1997	8	21	34	2	166	*20.8
R.J. Bowers, Grove City	†1998	10	34	2	0	206	20.6
Guy Leman, Simpson	1998	10	33	0	0	198	19.8
Carey Bender, Coe	†1994	10	32	2	0	194	19.4
Shane Ream, Allegheny	†2000	10	30	0	0	180	18.0
Dan Pugh, Mount Union	†2002	14	*41	2	0	*248	17.7
Chad Hoiska, Wis.-Eau Claire	1997	10	29	2	0	176	17.6
Jim Mormino, Allegheny	1997	10	29	0	0	174	17.4
Doug Steiner, Grove City	1997	10	29	0	0	174	17.4
Rob Marchitello, Maine Maritime	1994	9	25	4	0	154	17.1
Stanley Drayton, Allegheny	†1991	10	28	0	0	168	16.8
Dante Brown, Marietta	†1996	10	27	4	0	166	16.6
Ricky Gales, Simpson	†1989	10	26	10	0	166	16.6
Matt Malmberg, St. John's (Minn.)	†1993	10	27	2	0	164	16.4
David Russell, Linfield	2002	11	30	0	0	180	16.4
Scott Pingel, Westminster (Mo.)	1998	10	26	6	0	162	16.2
Trevor Shannon, Wartburg	1998	10	26	6	0	162	16.2
Jamie Lee, MacMurray	1998	10	26	4	0	160	16.0
Chris Babirad, Wash. & Jeff.	†1992	9	24	0	0	144	16.0
Trent Nauholz, Simpson	†1992	8	21	2	0	128	16.0
R.J. Bowers, Grove City	†1999	10	25	4	0	154	15.4
Krishaun Gilmore, Rensselaer	1998	9	23	0	0	138	15.3
Billy Johnson, Widener	†1973	9	23	0	0	138	15.3
Cory Christensen, Simpson	1997	10	25	0	0	150	15.0
Greg Novarro, Bentley	1992	10	25	0	0	150	15.0
Bruce Naszimento, New Jersey City	1973	10	25	0	0	150	15.0

*Record. †National champion.

CAREER POINTS

Player, Team	Years	TD	Extra Pts. Scored	FG	Pts.
R.J. Bowers, Grove City	1997-00	*92	10	0	*562
Carey Bender, Coe	1991-94	86	12	0	528
Scott Pingel, Westminster (Mo.)	1996-99	75	34	0	484
Trevor Shannon, Wartburg	1995-98	79	10	0	484
Joe Dudek, Plymouth St.	1982-85	79	0	0	474
Dan Pugh, Mount Union	1999-02	73	2	0	440
Chuck Moore, Mount Union	1998-01	73	0	0	438
Mark Kacmarynski, Central (Iowa)	$1992-96	70	2	0	422
Casey Donaldson, Wittenberg	1997-00	68	0	0	408
Andrew Notarfrancesco, Catholic	1996-99	65	8	0	398

Player, Team	Years	TD	Extra Pts. Scored	FG	Pts.
Shane Ream, Allegheny	1998-01	64	0	0	384
Chris Bisaillon, Ill. Wesleyan	1989-92	61	12	0	378
Chris Babirad, Wash. & Jeff.	1989-92	62	2	0	374
Paul Smith, Gettysburg	1996-99	60	2	0	362
Jim Regan, Pomona-Pitzer	1995-98	37	93	15	360
Rob Marchitello, Maine Maritime	1993-95	59	4	0	358
Chad Hoiska, Wis.-Eau Claire	1995-97	58	2	0	350
Terry Underwood, Wagner	1985-88	58	0	0	348
Jim Romagna, Loras	1989-92	57	2	0	344
#Matt Bernardo, Muhlenberg	2000-02	57	0	0	342
Jamal Robertson, Ohio Northern	1997-00	56	2	0	338
Jason Wooley, WPI	1990-93	55	8	0	338
R.J. Hoppe, Carroll (Wis.)	1993-96	54	12	0	336
Stanley Drayton, Allegheny	1989-92	56	0	0	336
Scott Tumilty, Augustana (Ill.)	1992-95	55	0	0	330
Cary Osborn, Wis.-Eau Claire	1987-90	55	0	0	330

*Record. $See Page 8 for explanation. #Active player.

SEASON POINTS

Player, Team	Year	TD	Extra Pts. Scored	FG	Pts.
Dan Pugh, Mount Union	†2002	*41	2	0	*248
R.J. Bowers, Grove City	†1998	34	2	0	206
Guy Leman, Simpson	1998	33	0	0	198
Carey Bender, Coe	†1994	32	2	0	194
David Russell, Linfield	2002	30	0	0	180
Shane Ream, Allegheny	†2000	30	0	0	180
Chad Hoiska, Wis.-Eau Claire	1997	29	2	0	176
Fredrick Jackson, Coe	2002	29	0	0	174
Jim Mormino, Allegheny	1997	29	0	0	174
Doug Steiner, Grove City	1997	29	0	0	174
Stanley Drayton, Allegheny	†1991	28	0	0	168
James Regan, Pomona-Pitzer	†1997	21	34	2	166
Dante Brown, Marietta	†1996	27	4	0	166
Ricky Gales, Simpson	†1989	26	10	0	166
Matt Malmberg, St. John's (Minn.)	†1993	27	2	0	164
Scott Pingel, Westminster (Mo.)	1998	26	6	0	162
Trevor Shannon, Wartburg	1998	26	6	0	162
Jamie Lee, MacMurray	1998	26	4	0	160
Greg Wood, Worcester St.	2002	26	2	0	158
R.J. Bowers, Grove City	†1999	25	4	0	154
Rob Marchitello, Maine Maritime	1994	25	4	0	154
Cory Christensen, Simpson	1997	25	0	0	150
Greg Novarro, Bentley	1992	25	0	0	150
Joe Dudek, Plymouth St.	1985	25	0	0	150
Bruce Naszimento, New Jersey City	1973	25	0	0	150

* Record. †National champion.

ANNUAL CHAMPIONS

Year	Player, Team	Class	G	TD	Extra Pts. Scored	FG	Pts.	Avg.
1973	Billy Johnson, Widener	Sr.	9	23	0	0	138	15.3
1974	Joe Thompson, Augustana (Ill.)	So.	9	17	0	0	102	11.3
1975	Ron Baker, Monmouth (Ill.)	Sr.	8	15	2	0	92	11.5
1976	Chris Hipsley, Cornell College	So.	9	14	42	2	132	14.7
1977	Chip Zawoiski, Widener	Sr.	9	18	0	0	108	12.0
1978	Roger Andrachik, Baldwin-Wallace	Sr.	8	16	0	0	96	12.0
1979	Jay Wessler, Illinois Col.	Jr.	8	16	4	0	100	12.5
1980	Daryl Johnson, Wabash	Jr.	9	20	0	0	120	13.3
1981	Scott Reppert, Lawrence	Jr.	9	15	0	0	90	10.0
	Daryl Johnson, Wabash	Sr.	9	15	0	0	90	10.0
1982	Rick Bell, St. John's (Minn.)	Sr.	9	21	2	0	128	14.2
1983	John Aromando, Col. of New Jersey	Jr.	10	20	0	0	120	12.0
1984	Joe Dudek, Plymouth St.	Jr.	10	21	0	0	126	12.6
1985	Kevin Weaver, Wash. & Lee	Jr.	8	17	8	0	110	13.8
1986	Jim Korfonta, Hamilton	Sr.	8	16	0	0	96	12.0
	Russ Kring, Mount Union	Jr.	10	20	0	0	120	12.0
1987	Michael Waithe, Curry	Sr.	8	19	0	0	114	14.3
1988	Terry Underwood, Wagner	Sr.	9	21	0	0	126	14.0
1989	Ricky Gales, Simpson	Sr.	10	26	10	0	166	16.6
1990	Scott Barnyak, Carnegie Mellon	Sr.	10	22	6	0	138	13.8
	Ryan Kolpin, Coe	Sr.	10	23	0	0	138	13.8
1991	Stanley Drayton, Allegheny	Jr.	10	28	0	0	168	16.8
1992	Chris Babirad, Wash. & Jeff.	Jr.	9	24	0	0	144	16.0
	Trent Nauholz, Simpson	Jr.	8	21	2	0	128	16.0
1993	Matt Malmberg, St. John's (Minn.)	Jr.	10	27	2	0	164	16.4
1994	Carey Bender, Coe	Sr.	10	32	2	0	194	19.4
1995	Anthony Jones, La Verne	Sr.	8	19	4	0	118	14.8
1996	Dante Brown, Marietta	Jr.	10	27	4	0	166	16.6
1997	James Regan, Pomona-Pitzer	Jr.	8	21	34	2	166	*20.8

Year	Player, Team	Class	G	TD	Extra Pts. Scored	FG	Pts.	Avg.
1998	R.J. Bowers, Grove City	So.	10	34	2	0	206	20.6
1999	R.J. Bowers, Grove City	Jr.	10	25	4	0	154	15.4
2000	Shane Ream, Allegheny	Jr.	10	30	0	0	180	18.0
2001	Chuck Moore, Mount Union	Sr.	10	24	0	0	144	14.4
2002	Dan Pugh, Mount Union	Sr.	14	*41	2	0	*248	17.7

*Record.

Defensive Records

Interceptions

CAREER INTERCEPTIONS

Player, Team	Years	No.	Yards	Avg.
Ralph Gebhardt, Rochester	1973-75	*29	384	13.2
Brian Fetterolf, Aurora	1986-89	28	390	13.9
Rick Bealer, Lycoming	1987-90	28	279	10.0
Andrew Ostrand, Carroll (Wis.)	1990-93	27	258	9.6
Tim Lennon, Curry	1986-89	27	190	7.0
Mike Hintz, Wis.-Platteville	1983-86	27	183	6.8
Scott Stanitous, Moravian	1985-88	27	178	6.6
Mark Dorner, Juniata	1984-87	26	*443	17.0
Cory Mabry, Susquehanna	1988-91	26	400	15.4
Jeff Hughes, Ripon	1975-78	26	333	12.8
Jon Dunham, Denison	1996-99	25	333	13.3
Neal Guggemos, St. Thomas (Minn.)	1982-85	25	377	15.1
Dave Adams, Carleton	1984-87	25	327	13.1
Will Hill, Bishop	1983-86	25	261	10.4
Tom Devine, Juniata	1979-82	25	248	9.9
Gary Ellis, Rose-Hulman	1974-77	25	226	9.1

*Record.

SEASON INTERCEPTIONS

Player, Team	Year	No.	Yards
Ben Matthews, Bethel (Minn.)	†2000	*15	134
Mark Dorner, Juniata	†1987	*15	202
Jeff Thomas, Redlands	†2002	13	127
Nate Kok, Ripon	2000	13	254
Steve Nappo, Buffalo	†1986	13	155
Antonio Moore, Widener	†1994	13	116
Chris McMahon, Catholic	†1984	13	105
Ralph Gebhardt, Rochester	†1973	13	105
David Simpson, Alma	2002	12	134
Brian Barr, Gettysburg	†1985	12	144
John Bernard, Buffalo	†1983	12	143
Mick McConkey, Neb. Wesleyan	†1982	12	111
Chris Butts, Worcester St.	†1992	12	109
Tom Devine, Juniata	†1981	12	91

*Record. †National champion.

ANNUAL CHAMPIONS
(Ranked on Average Per Game)

Year	Player, Team	Class	G	No.	Avg.	Yards
1973	Ralph Gebhardt, Rochester	So.	9	13	1.44	105
1974	Kevin Birkholz, Carleton	Jr.	9	11	1.22	137
1975	Mark Persichetti, Wash. & Jeff.	So.	9	10	1.11	97
1976	Gary Jantzer, Southern Ore. St.	Sr.	9	10	1.11	63
1977	Greg Jones, FDU-Florham	So.	9	10	1.11	106
	Mike Jones, Norwich	So.	9	10	1.11	98
1978	Don Sutton, San Fran. St.	Fr.	8	10	1.25	43
1979	Greg Holland, Simpson	Fr.	9	11	1.22	150
1980	Tim White, Lawrence	Sr.	8	10	1.25	131
1981	Tom Devine, Juniata	Sr.	9	12	1.33	91
1982	Mick McConkey, Neb. Wesleyan	Sr.	9	12	1.33	111
1983	John Bernard, Buffalo	Sr.	10	12	1.20	143
1984	Chris McMahon, Catholic	Sr.	9	13	1.44	140
1985	Kim McManis, Lane	Sr.	9	11	1.22	165
1986	Steve Nappo, Buffalo	Sr.	11	13	1.18	155
1987	Mark Dorner, Juniata	Sr.	10	*15	*1.50	202
1988	Tim Lennon, Curry	Jr.	9	11	1.22	86
1989	Ron Davies, Coast Guard	So.	9	11	1.22	90
1990	Craig Garritano, FDU-Florham	Jr.	9	10	1.11	158
	Brad Bohn, Neb. Wesleyan	So.	9	10	1.11	90
	Frank Greer, Sewanee	So.	9	10	1.11	67
	Harold Krebs, Merchant Marine	Sr.	9	10	1.11	19
1991	Murray Meadows, Millsaps	Sr.	9	11	1.22	46
1992	Chris Butts, Worcester St.	Jr.	9	12	1.33	109
1993	Ricky Webb, Emory & Henry	Sr.	8	8	1.00	56
1994	Antonio Moore, Widener	So.	10	13	1.30	116

Year	Player, Team	Class	G	No.	Avg.	Yards
1995	Mike Susi, Lebanon Valley	Sr.	8	8	1.00	153
	LeMonde Zachary, St. Lawrence	Fr.	7	7	1.00	109
1996	Peter Hinkle, Ursinus	So.	10	11	1.10	247
1997	Joel Feuerstahler, Martin Luther	Sr.	9	10	1.10	222
1998	Mike Cotton, Mass.-Dartmouth	Jr.	10	11	1.10	206
1999	Steve Cella, Trinity (Conn.)	Jr.	8	9	1.10	106
	Eric Newsome, Hobart	Jr.	8	9	1.10	148
2000	Ben Matthews, Bethel (Minn.)	Sr.	10	*15	*1.50	134
2001	Kip Daniels, Aurora	Sr.	9	9	1.00	76
	Dino Rossi, Chapman	Sr.	9	9	1.00	117
2002	Jeff Thomas, Redlands	Sr.	10	13	1.30	127

*Record.

Total Tackles

SEASON TACKLES PER GAME

Player, Team	Year	G	Solo	Ast	Total	Avg.
Robert Gunn, Earlham	†2000	10	106	72	*178	*17.8
Donnie Hohman, Chapman	†2002	10	77	95	172	17.2
Robert Aguilar, Greenville	2000	10	101	61	162	16.2
Lance Ramer, Rochester	2000	10	87	69	156	15.6
Kelvin Hutcheson, Averett	†2001	8	56	68	124	15.5
Casey McConnell, Kenyon	2001	10	86	65	151	15.1
Omar Rimlawi, Buffalo St.	2000	10	67	84	151	15.1
Greg Chrony, Maranatha Baptist	2000	9	37	98	135	15.0

* Record. †National champion.

SEASON TOTAL TACKLES

Player, Team	Year	G	Solo	Ast	Total
Robert Gunn, Earlham	†2000	10	106	72	*178
Donnie Hohman, Chapman	†2002	10	77	95	172
Robert Aguilar, Greenville	2000	10	101	61	162
Lance Ramer, Rochester	2000	10	87	69	156
Casey McConnell, Kenyon	2001	10	86	65	151
Omar Rimlawi, Buffalo St.	2000	10	67	84	151
Chris Cubero, John Carroll	2002	14	77	72	149
Chet Knake, Cornell College	2002	10	60	88	148
Ron Swearingin, Capital	2001	10	71	73	144
Casey McConnell, Kenyon	2002	10	78	65	143
Scott O'Reilly, Carleton	2001	10	84	59	143
Noland Urband, Neb. Wesleyan	2000	10	72	70	142
Tyler Freeburg, Simpson	2001	10	65	75	140

* Record. †National champion.

Steve Wilson of King's (Pennsylvania) broke his own Division III single-season record for tackles for loss with 39 last year. In 2001, he compiled 38½.

SINGLE-GAME TOTAL TACKLES

(SINCE 2000)

Tackles	Player, Team (Opponent)	Date
27	Casey McConnell, Kenyon (Centre)	Sept. 7, 2002
24	Tom Pouliot, FDU-Florham (King's [Pa.])	Nov. 4, 2000
20	Tyler Freeburg, Simpson (Luther)	Oct. 13, 2001
20	Dion Mueller, Wesleyan (Conn.) (Tufts)	Sept. 22, 2001
20	Tyler Freeburg, Simpson (Buena Vista)	Sept. 15, 2001
20	Chris Kelliher, Plymouth St. (Springfield)	Oct. 14, 2000
19	Matt Campbell, Johns Hopkins (Muhlenberg)	Oct. 19, 2002
19	Justin Oertle, Monmouth (Ill.) (Beloit)	Sept. 28, 2002
19	Brad Beyer, St. John's (Minn.) (St. Thomas [Minn.])	Sept. 29, 2001
19	Jason Robinson, Monmouth (Ill.) (Beloit)	Sept. 23, 2001

ANNUAL CHAMPIONS

Year	Player, Team	Class	G	Solo	Ast	Total	Avg.
2000	Robert Gunn, Earlham	Jr.	10	106	72	*178	*17.8
2001	Kelvin Hutcheson, Averett	So.	8	56	68	124	15.5
2002	Donnie Hohman, Chapman	Sr.	10	77	95	172	17.2

* Record.

Solo Tackles

SEASON SOLO TACKLES PER GAME

Player, Team	Year	G	Solo	Avg.
Robert Gunn, Earlham	2000	10	*106	*10.6
Robert Aguilar, Greenville	2000	10	101	10.1
Brenden Givan, Stillman	2000	9	84	9.3
Seth Duerr, Wooster	2000	10	93	9.3
Mike Davis, Heidelberg	†2002	10	92	9.2
Mike Hanna, Olivet	2002	9	81	9.0
Lance Ramer, Rochester	2000	10	87	8.7
Ron Swearingin, Capital	2000	10	87	8.7
Casey McConnell, Kenyon	†2001	10	86	8.6
Quincy Francis, Wesleyan (Conn.)	2002	8	68	8.5
Troy Sosnovik, Susquehanna	2001	10	85	8.5
Mike Dempsey, Beloit	2000	10	85	8.5

* Record. †National champion.

SEASON SOLO TACKLES

Player, Team	Year	G	Solo
Robert Gunn, Earlham	2000	10	*106
Robert Aguilar, Greenville	2000	10	101
Seth Duerr, Wooster	2000	10	93
Mike Davis, Heidelberg	†2002	10	92
Jason Leshikar, Trinity (Tex.)	2002	15	87
Lance Ramer, Rochester	2000	10	87
Ron Swearingin, Capital	2000	10	87
Casey McConnell, Kenyon	†2001	10	86
Troy Sosnovik, Susquehanna	2001	10	85
Mike Dempsey, Beloit	2000	10	85

* Record. †National champion.

SINGLE-GAME SOLO TACKLES

(SINCE 2000)

Solo	Player, Team (Opponent)	Date
17	Casey McConnell, Kenyon (Centre)	Sept. 7, 2002
16	Tyler Freeburg, Simpson (Wis.-Oshkosh)	Sept. 8, 2001
15	Nick Anzalone, Concordia (Ill.) (Aurora)	Oct. 12, 2002
15	Dion Mueller, Wesleyan (Conn.) (Tufts)	Sept. 22, 2001
15	Troy Sosnovik, Susquehanna (Delaware Valley)	Sept. 22, 2001
14	Tim Boothroyd, Plymouth St. (Coast Guard)	Nov. 2, 2002
13	Austin Bonnema, Central (Iowa) (Simpson)	Oct. 6, 2001
13	Bill Deaett, Bridgewater St. (Salve Regina)	Nov. 11, 2000
12	Sean Ross, Waynesburg (Westminster [Pa.])	Nov. 16, 2002
12	Josh Bullock, Redlands (Linfield)	Sept. 14, 2002
12	Mike Toscano, Western Conn. St. (Plymouth St.)	Sept. 30, 2000

ANNUAL CHAMPIONS

Year	Player, Team	Class	G	Solo	Avg.
2001	Casey McConnell, Kenyon	Fr.	10	86	8.6
2002	Mike Davis, Heidelberg	Jr.	10	92	9.2

Tackles for Loss

SEASON TACKLES FOR LOSS PER GAME

Player, Team	Year	G	Solo	Ast	Total	Avg.
Steve Wilson, King's (Pa.)	†2001	10	37	3	38.5	*3.9
Russ Watson, Worcester St.	†2000	9	32	0	32.0	3.6
Robert Aguilar, Greenville	2000	10	35	0	35.0	3.5

Player, Team	Year	G	Solo	Ast	Total	Avg.
Quincy Malloy, Methodist	2001	10	34	0	34.0	3.4
Patrick Ryan, Benedictine (Ill.)	†2002	10	33	0	33.0	3.3
Steve Wilson, King's (Pa.)	2002	12	38	2	*39.0	3.3
Brenden Givan, Stillman	2001	9	29	0	29.0	3.2
Brenden Givan, Stillman	2000	9	25	7	28.5	3.2
Adam Frantz, Lebanon Valley	2001	10	31	0	31.0	3.1
Jeff Heinzl, Ill. Wesleyan	2000	10	31	0	31.0	3.1
Brian Robitaille, Curry	2002	10	30	1	30.5	3.1
Mark Seagraves, Lycoming	2000	9	24	7	27.5	3.1
Russell Beditt, Albright	2000	10	24	13	30.5	3.1

* Record. †National champion.

SEASON TACKLES FOR LOSS

Player, Team	Year	G	Solo	Ast	Total
Steve Wilson, King's (Pa.)	2002	12	38	2	*39.0
Steve Wilson, King's (Pa.)	†2001	10	37	3	38.5
Robert Aguilar, Greenville	2000	10	35	0	35.0
Quincy Malloy, Methodist	2001	10	34	0	34.0
Patrick Ryan, Benedictine (Ill.)	†2002	10	33	0	33.0
Russ Watson, Worcester St.	†2000	9	32	0	32.0
Adam Frantz, Lebanon Valley	2001	10	31	0	31.0
Jeff Heinzl, Ill. Wesleyan	2000	10	31	0	31.0
Brian Robitaille, Curry	2002	10	30	1	30.5
Russell Beditt, Albright	2000	10	24	13	30.5

* Record. †National champion.

SINGLE-GAME TACKLES FOR LOSS

(SINCE 2000)

TFL	Player, Team (Opponent)	Date
8.0	Brenden Givan, Stillman (Pikeville)	Sept. 1, 2001
7.0	Jon Foss, Bethel (Minn.) (Gust. Adolphus)	Sept. 22, 2001
6.0	John Longo, Cortland St. (Kean)	Sept. 21, 2002
6.0	David Hahm, Wis. Lutheran (Rockford)	Sept. 30, 2000
5.5	Troy Sosnovik, Susquehanna (Delaware Valley)	Sept. 22, 2001
5.0	Chet Hanson, Concordia (Ill.) (Benedictine [Ill.])	Nov. 2, 2002
5.0	Willie Thompson, Illinois Col. (Lake Forest)	Oct. 19, 2002
5.0	Michael Doleman, Shenandoah (Chris. Newport)	Oct. 5, 2002
5.0	Matt Lerner, Monmouth (Ill.) (Beloit)	Sept. 28, 2002
5.0	Casey Carlson, Pacific Lutheran (Chapman)	Sept. 21, 2002
5.0	George Hewan, Shenandoah (Methodist)	Nov. 10, 2001
5.0	Preston Meyer, Mary Hardin-Baylor (Louisiana Col.)	Oct. 6, 2001
5.0	Jeremy Hood, St. John's (Minn.) (St. Olaf)	Sept. 15, 2001
5.0	Justin Snyder, Central (Iowa) (William Penn)	Oct. 21, 2000

ANNUAL CHAMPIONS

Year	Player, Team	Class	G	Solo	Ast	Total	Avg.
2000	Russ Watson, Worcester St.	Jr.	9	32	0	32.0	3.6
2001	Steve Wilson, King's (Pa.)	Sr.	10	37	3	38.5	*3.9
2002	Patrick Ryan, Benedictine (Ill.)	So.	10	33	0	33.0	3.3

* Record.

Pass Sacks

SEASON PASS SACKS PER GAME

Player, Team	Year	G	Solo	Ast	Total	Avg.
Russ Watson, Worcester St.	†2000	9	24	0	*24.0	*2.7
Steve Wilson, King's (Pa.)	†2001	10	18	3	19.5	2.0
Josh Stinehour, Union (N.Y.)	2001	10	18	2	19.0	1.9
Michael Gardner, Benedictine (Ill.)	2000	10	19	0	19.0	1.9
Brenden Givan, Stillman	2000	9	16	2	17.0	1.9
Mark Seagraves, Lycoming	2000	9	17	0	17.0	1.9
Edith Forestal, Defiance	2000	10	18	0	18.0	1.8
Lance Ramer, Rochester	2000	10	17	2	18.0	1.8
David Seal, Redlands	2000	8	14	0	14.0	1.8
Patrick Ryan, Benedictine (Ill.)	2000	10	17	0	17.0	1.7

* Record. †National champion.

SEASON TOTAL PASS SACKS

Player, Team	Year	G	Solo	Ast	Total
Russ Watson, Worcester St.	†2000	9	24	0	*24.0
Steve Wilson, King's (Pa.)	†2001	10	18	3	19.5
Josh Stinehour, Union (N.Y.)	2001	10	18	2	19.0
Michael Gardner, Benedictine (Ill.)	2000	10	19	0	19.0
Edith Forestal, Defiance	2000	10	18	0	18.0
Lance Ramer, Rochester	2000	10	17	2	18.0
Steve Wilson, King's (Pa.)	2002	12	15	4	17.0
Patrick Ryan, Benedictine (Ill.)	2001	10	17	0	17.0
Brenden Givan, Stillman	2000	9	16	2	17.0
Mark Seagraves, Lycoming	2000	9	17	0	17.0

* Record. †National champion.

SINGLE-GAME PASS SACKS

(SINCE 2000)

PS	Player, Team (Opponent)	Date
5.0	J.J. Zearley, Wartburg (Loras)	Oct. 5, 2002
4.0	Michael Sykes, Col. of New Jersey (Brockport St.)	Nov. 9, 2002
4.0	Matt Scaravaglione, Col. of New Jersey (New Jersey City)	Oct. 26, 2002
4.0	Angelo Letizia, Cortland St. (Buffalo St.)	Sept. 28, 2002
4.0	Brenden Givan, Stillman (Allen)	Sept. 21, 2002
4.0	Tyler Freeburg, Simpson (Loras)	Oct. 21, 2000
3.5	Jeremy Hood, St. John's (Minn.) (St. Olaf)	Sept. 15, 2001

ANNUAL CHAMPIONS

Year	Player, Team	Class	G	Solo	Ast	Total	Avg.
2000	Russ Watson, Worcester St.	Jr.	9	24	0	*24.0	*2.7
2001	Steve Wilson, King's (Pa.)	Sr.	10	18	3	19.5	2.0
2002	Jon Foss, Bethel (Minn.)	Sr.	10	15	2	16.0	1.6

* Record.

Passes Defended

SEASON PASSES DEFENDED PER GAME

Player, Team	Year	G	PBU	Int.	Total	Avg.
Jarrod Pence, Moravian	†2001	10	31	5	*36	*3.60
Kip Daniels, Aurora	2001	9	23	9	32	3.56
Johnny Kelly, Williams	2001	8	23	4	27	3.4
Kennard Davis, Thiel	2001	10	23	9	32	3.2
Chris Spiegel, Benedictine (Ill.)	2001	10	25	7	32	3.2
James Patrick, Stillman	†2002	10	20	11	31	3.1
B.J. Harvey, Illinois Col.	2001	10	25	6	31	3.1
Evan Zupancic, Tufts	†2000	8	18	6	24	3.0
Ki Yoon, Franklin	2001	10	23	4	27	2.7
David Thompson, Earlham	2000	10	21	6	27	2.7
Eric Moe, Wis.-Stout	2001	9	16	8	24	2.7

* Record. †National champion.

SEASON TOTAL PASSES DEFENDED

Player, Team	Year	G	PBU	Int.	Total
Jarrod Pence, Moravian	†2001	10	31	5	*36
Kip Daniels, Aurora	2001	9	23	9	32
Kennard Davis, Thiel	2001	10	23	9	32
Chris Spiegel, Benedictine (Ill.)	2001	10	25	7	32
James Patrick, Stillman	†2002	10	20	11	31
B.J. Harvey, Illinois Col.	2001	10	25	6	31
Johnny Kelly, Williams	2001	8	23	4	27
Ki Yoon, Franklin	2001	10	23	4	27
David Thompson, Earlham	2000	10	21	6	27
Kory Schramm, Hartwick	2000	10	19	7	26

* Record. †National champion.

SINGLE-GAME PASSES DEFENDED

(SINCE 2000)

PD	Player, Team (Opponent)	Date
10	James Patrick, Stillman (Edward Waters)	Nov. 2, 2002
7	Kyle Westphal, Simpson (Washington [Mo.])	Sept. 7, 2002
7	Derrick Brantley, Wesleyan (Conn.) (Colby)	Oct. 6, 2001
6	Lorenzo Morgan, Mary Hardin-Baylor (Howard Payne)	Oct. 19, 2002
6	Adam Friedman, Hamline (Augsburg)	Oct. 27, 2001
6	Ron Broking, Montclair St. (Rowan)	Nov. 11, 2000
5	Mike Brunner, Susquehanna (Juniata)	Oct. 26, 2002
5	Greg Lowder, Illinois Col. (Carroll [Wis.])	Sept. 21, 2002

ANNUAL CHAMPIONS

Year	Player, Team	Class	G	PBU	Int.	Total	Avg.
2000	Evan Zupancic, Tufts	So.	8	18	6	24	3.0
2001	Jarrod Pence, Moravian	Jr.	10	31	5	*36	*3.6
2002	James Patrick, Stillman	Jr.	10	20	11	31	3.1

* Record.

Forced Fumbles

SEASON FORCED FUMBLES PER GAME

Player, Team	Year	G	FF	Avg.
Tony Pate, Concordia (Ill.)	†2000	9	*8	*0.89
Erik Tinsley, Concordia (Ill.)	2000	9	6	0.67
Greg Boucher, Western Conn. St.	†2001	8	5	0.63
Jacob Freeman, Hardin-Simmons	2000	10	6	0.60
Brian Chaplain, Plymouth St.	2001	9	5	0.56
Jeremiah Janssen, St. Norbert	2001	9	5	0.56

Player, Team	Year	G	FF	Avg.
Brian Cook, Johns Hopkins	†2002	10	5	0.50
Casey McConnell, Kenyon	†2002	10	5	0.50
Chad Berndt, Earlham	2001	10	5	0.50
Marc Blevins, Rensselaer	2001	8	4	0.50
Adam Cappotelli, St. John Fisher	2001	10	5	0.50
Matt Scaravaglione, Col. of New Jersey	2001	10	5	0.50
Josh Stanton, Wabash	2001	10	5	0.50

*Record. †National champion.

SEASON TOTAL FORCED FUMBLES

Player, Team	Year	G	FF
Tony Pate, Concordia (Ill.)	†2000	9	*8
Erik Tinsley, Concordia (Ill.)	2000	9	6
Jacob Freeman, Hardin-Simmons	2000	10	6
Brian Cook, Johns Hopkins	†2002	10	5
Casey McConnell, Kenyon	†2002	10	5
Greg Boucher, Western Conn. St.	†2001	8	5
Brian Chaplain, Plymouth St.	2001	9	5
Jeremiah Janssen, St. Norbert	2001	9	5
Chad Berndt, Earlham	2001	10	5
Adam Cappotelli, St. John Fisher	2001	10	5
Matt Scaravaglione, Col. of New Jersey	2001	10	5
Josh Stanton, Wabash	2001	10	5

*Record. †National champion.

SINGLE-GAME FORCED FUMBLES

(Since 2000)

FF	Player, Team (Opponent)	Date
3	Joe Sollitt, Concordia (Ill.) (Benedictine [Ill.])	Nov. 2, 2002
3	Greg Boucher, Western Conn. St. (Mount Ida)	Sept. 8, 2001
2	By many players	

ANNUAL CHAMPIONS

Year	Player, Team	Class	G	FF	Avg.
2000	Tony Pate, Concordia (Ill.)	So.	9	‡11	1.22

‡Prior to 2001, the total was forced fumbles plus fumbles recovered. Beginning in 2001, FF was forced fumbles only.

2001	Greg Boucher, Western Conn. St.	Sr.	8	5	0.63
2002	Brian Cook, Johns Hopkins	Fr.	10	5	0.50
	Casey McConnell, Kenyon	So.	10	5	0.50

Punting

CAREER AVERAGE

(Minimum 100 Punts)

Player, Team	Years	No.	Yards	Avg.
Jeff Shea, Cal Lutheran	1994-97	183	7,939	*43.4
Phil Barry, St. John's (Minn.)	1996-99	126	5,327	42.3
Mike Manson, Benedictine (Ill.)	1975-78	120	5,056	42.1
Dan Osborn, Occidental	1981-83	157	6,528	41.6
Jim Allshouse, Adrian	1973-75	163	6,718	41.2
Thomas Murray, Catholic	1983-84	122	5,028	41.2
Ryan Haley, John Carroll	1991-94	151	6,208	41.1
Brad Abraham, Wis.-Platteville	1998-01	168	6,883	41.0
Mario Acosta, Chapman	1994-96, 98	164	6,695	40.8
Scott Lanz, Bethany (W.Va.)	1975-78	235	9,592	40.8
Mitch Holloway, Millsaps	1992-93	105	4,283	40.8
Richard Harr, Ferrum	1996-99	219	8,914	40.7

*Record.

SEASON AVERAGE

(Qualifiers for Championship)

Player, Team	Year	No.	Yards	Avg.
Steve Vagedes, Ohio Northern	†1999	37	1,708	*46.2
Justin Shively, Anderson (Ind.)	†1997	55	2,502	45.5
Jeff Shea, Cal Lutheran	†1996	53	2,402	45.3
Jeff Shea, Cal Lutheran	†1995	43	1,933	45.0
Mario Acosta, Chapman	1996	34	1,528	44.9
Bob Burwell, Rose-Hulman	†1978	61	2,740	44.9
Charles McPherson, Clark Atlanta	1978	50	2,237	44.7
Dan Osborn, Occidental	†1982	55	2,454	44.6
Jeff Shea, Cal Lutheran	1997	43	1,910	44.4
Phil Barry, St. John's (Minn.)	1999	49	2,176	44.4
Mike Manson, Benedictine (Ill.)	†1976	36	1,587	44.1
Linc Welles, Bloomsburg	†1973	39	1,708	43.8
Matt George, Chapman	1997	38	1,663	43.8
Scott Verhalen, East Tex. Baptist	†2001	56	2,449	43.7
Kirk Seufert, Rhodes	†1983	44	1,921	43.7
Kelvin Albert, Knoxville	†1987	30	1,308	43.6

*Record. †National champion.

ANNUAL CHAMPIONS

Year	Player, Team	Class	No.	Yards	Avg.
1973	Linc Welles, Bloomsburg	Sr.	39	1,708	43.8
1974	Sylvester Cunningham, Fort Valley St.	So.	40	1,703	42.6
1975	Larry Hersh, Shepherd	Jr.	58	2,519	43.4
1976	Mike Manson, Benedictine (Ill.)	So.	36	1,587	44.1
1977	Scott Lanz, Bethany (W.Va.)	Jr.	78	3,349	42.9
1978	Bob Burwell, Rose-Hulman	Sr.	61	2,740	44.9
1979	Jay Lenstrom, Neb. Wesleyan	Sr.	64	2,641	41.3
1980	Duane Harrison, Bridgewater (Va.)	Sr.	43	1,792	41.7
1981	Dan Paro, Denison	Jr.	54	2,223	41.2
1982	Dan Osborn, Occidental	Jr.	55	2,454	44.6
1983	Kirk Seufert, Rhodes	Jr.	44	1,921	43.7
1984	Thomas Murray, Catholic	Sr.	59	2,550	43.2
1985	Dave Lewis, Muhlenberg	So.	55	2,290	41.6
	Mike Matzen, Coe	Sr.	55	2,290	41.6
1986	Darren Estes, Millsaps	Jr.	45	1,940	43.1
1987	Kelvin Albert, Knoxville	So.	30	1,308	43.6
1988	Bobby Graves, Sewanee	So.	57	2,445	42.9
1989	Paul Becker, Kenyon	Sr.	57	2,307	40.5
1990	Bill Nolan, Carroll (Wis.)	Sr.	33	1,322	40.1
1991	Jeff Stolte, Chicago	So.	54	2,295	42.5
1992	Robert Ray, San Diego	So.	44	1,860	42.3
1993	Mitch Holloway, Millsaps	Sr.	45	1,910	42.4
1994	Ryan Haley, John Carroll	Sr.	54	2,311	42.8
1995	Jeff Shea, Cal Lutheran	So.	43	1,933	45.0
1996	Jeff Shea, Cal Lutheran	Jr.	53	2,402	45.3
1997	Justin Shively, Anderson (Ind.)	Sr.	55	2,502	45.5
1998	Chris Morehouse, Albright	Jr.	52	2,247	43.2
1999	Steve Vagedes, Ohio Northern	Sr.	37	1,708	*46.2
2000	Wilson Hillman, Mississippi Col.	Sr.	62	2,671	43.1
2001	Scott Verhalen, East Tex. Baptist	So.	56	2,449	43.7
2002	Scott Verhalen, East Tex. Baptist	Jr.	39	1,687	43.3

*Record.

Punt Returns

CAREER AVERAGE

(Minimum 1.2 Returns Per Game)

Player, Team	Years	No.	Yards	Avg.
Keith Winston, Knoxville	1986-87	30	686	*22.9
Robert Middlebrook, Knoxville	1984-85	21	473	22.5
Kevin Doherty, Mass. Maritime	1976-78, 80	45	939	20.9
Chuck Downey, Stony Brook	1984-87	59	1,198	+20.3
Mike Askew, Kean	1980-81	28	555	19.8
Willie Canady, Fort Valley St.	1979-82	41	772	18.8

*Record. +Record for minimum 50 returns.

SEASON AVERAGE

(Minimum 1.2 Returns Per Game)

Player, Team	Year	No.	Yards	Avg.
Chuck Downey, Stony Brook	†1986	17	530	*31.2
Kevin Doherty, Mass. Maritime	†1976	11	332	30.2
Robert Middlebrook, Knoxville	†1984	9	260	28.9
Joe Troise, Kean	†1974	12	342	28.5
Melvin Dillard, Ferrum	†1990	25	*688	27.5
Elliot Turner, Greenville	†2000	14	385	27.5
Chris McKinney, Guilford	†2001	20	533	26.7
Eric Green, Benedictine (Ill.)	†1993	13	346	26.6
Brad Guettel, Carroll (Wis.)	2001	10	243	24.3
Chris Warren, Ferrum	†1989	18	421	23.4
Matt Buddenhagen, Ithaca	†1998	29	667	23.0
Kevin Doherty, Mass. Maritime	1978	11	246	22.4

*Record. †National champion.

ANNUAL CHAMPIONS

Year	Player, Team	Class	No.	Yards	‡Avg.
1973	Al Shepherd, Monmouth (Ill.)	Sr.	18	347	19.3
1974	Joe Troise, Kean	Fr.	12	342	28.5
1975	Mitch Brown, St. Lawrence	So.	25	430	17.2
1976	Kevin Doherty, Mass. Maritime	Fr.	11	332	30.2
1977	Charles Watkins, Knoxville	Sr.	15	278	18.5
1978	Dennis Robinson, Wesleyan (Conn.)	Sr.	††9	263	29.2
1979	Steve Moffett, Maryville (Tenn.)	Jr.	19	357	18.8
1980	Mike Askew, Kean	Jr.	16	304	19.0
1981	Mike Askew, Kean	Sr.	12	251	20.9
1982	Tom Southall, Colorado Col.	So.	13	281	21.6
1983	Edmond Donald, Millsaps	Jr.	15	320	21.3
1984	Robert Middlebrook, Knoxville	So.	9	260	28.9
1985	Dan Schone, Illinois Col.	Fr.	11	231	21.0
1986	Chuck Downey, Stony Brook	Jr.	17	530	*31.2
1987	Keith Winston, Knoxville	Sr.	16	343	21.4

Year	Player, Team	Class	No.	Yards	‡Avg.
1988	Dennis Tarr, Framingham St.	Jr.	9	178	19.8
1989	Chris Warren, Ferrum	Sr.	18	421	23.4
1990	Melvin Dillard, Ferrum	Sr.	25	*688	27.5
1991	Jordan Nixon, Augustana (Ill.)	Sr.	27	473	17.5
1992	Vic Moncato, FDU-Florham	So.	†††10	243	24.3
1993	Eric Green, Benedictine (Ill.)	Sr.	13	346	26.6
1994	Ariel Bell, Frostburg St.	Sr.	19	329	17.3
1995	Jim Wallace, Ripon	Jr.	17	305	17.9
1996	Tyrone Brown, Howard Payne	Sr.	21	415	19.8
1997	Seth Wallace, Coe	Fr.	††††10	301	30.1
1998	Matt Buddenhagen, Ithaca	Sr.	29	667	23.0
1999	Jake Wolter, Wis.-Whitewater	Jr.	12	230	19.2
2000	Elliot Turner, Greenville	Jr.	14	385	27.5
2001	Chris McKinney, Guilford	Jr.	20	533	26.7
2002	Chad Strehlo, Hamline	Sr.	11	192	17.5

*Record. ‡Ranked on minimum of 1.5 returns per game in 1973; 1.2 from 1974. ††Declared champion; with one more return (making 1.25 per game) for zero yards, still would have highest average (26.3). †††Declared champion; with one more return (making 1.22 per game) for zero yards, still would have highest average (22.1). ††††Declared champion; with one more return (making 1.22 per game) for zero yards, still would have highest average (27.4).

Kickoff Returns

CAREER AVERAGE
(Minimum 1.2 Returns Per Game)

Player, Team	Years	No.	Yards	Avg.
David Ziegler, John Carroll	1996-99	30	1,047	$34.9
Daryl Brown, Tufts	1974-76	38	1,111	29.2
Joshua Carter, Muhlenberg	1998-01	75	*2,189	29.2
Darnell Rubin, Chapman	1994, 96	17	485	28.5
Mike Askew, Kean	1980-81	33	938	28.4
Chuck Downey, Stony Brook	1984-87	46	1,281	27.8
R.J. Hoppe, Carroll (Wis.)	1993-96	59	1,632	27.7
Ryan Reynolds, Thomas More	1991-94	49	1,311	26.8
Jeff Dillingham, Kalamazoo	1996-99	59	1,560	26.4
LaVant King, Ohio Northern	1991, 93-95	50	1,298	26.0
Scott Reppert, Lawrence	1979-82	44	1,134	25.8
Lamont Rhim, Buffalo St.	1994-96	47	1,210	25.7
Jerome Porter, Kean	1996-98	51	1,286	25.2
Rick Rosenfeld, McDaniel	1973-76	69	1,732	25.1

*Record. $Declared record; with 5 more returns (making 35), for zero yards, still would have highest average (29.9).

SEASON AVERAGE
(Minimum 1.2 Returns Per Game)

Player, Team	Year	No.	Yards	Avg.
Brandon Steinheim, Wesley	†1994	10	422	*42.2
Jason Martin, Coe	†1992	11	438	39.8
Tony Hill, Salisbury	†1998	14	549	39.2
Nate Kirtman, Pomona-Pitzer	†1990	14	515	36.8
Tom Myers, Coe	†1983	11	401	36.5
Ron Scott, Occidental	1983	10	363	36.3
Alan Hill, DePauw	1980	12	434	36.2

Player, Team	Year	No.	Yards	Avg.
Trevor Shannon, Wartburg	1996	14	501	35.8
David Ziegler, John Carroll	†1999	11	393	35.7
Al White, Wm. Paterson	1990	12	427	35.6
Byron Womack, Iona	†1989	15	531	35.4
Derrick Brooms, Chicago	†1995	12	422	35.2
Joshua Carter, Muhlenberg	1999	28	*981	35.0
Darnell Marshall, Carroll (Wis.)	1989	17	586	34.5
Andy Traetow, Gust. Adolphus	†2000	17	584	34.4
Daryl Brown, Tufts	†1976	11	377	34.3
Rich Jinnette, Methodist	1992	15	514	34.3
Jeff Higgins, Ithaca	1995	12	407	33.9
Oscar Ford, Chapman	1995	11	373	33.9
Kenny Bohman, Whittier	2000	10	339	33.9
Sean Healy, Coe	1989	11	372	33.8
Anthony Drakeford, Ferrum	†1987	15	507	33.8
Ryan Reynolds, Thomas More	1992	14	473	33.8
Pete Gordon, Heidelberg	2000	11	371	33.7
Glenn Koch, Tufts	†1986	14	472	33.7

*Record. †National champion.

ANNUAL CHAMPIONS

Year	Player, Team	Class	No.	Yards	‡Avg.
1973	Greg Montgomery, Wis.-Whitewater	So.	17	518	30.5
1974	Tom Oleksa, Muhlenberg	Sr.	15	467	31.1
1975	Jeff Levant, Beloit	Jr.	15	434	28.9
1976	Daryl Brown, Tufts	Sr.	11	377	34.3
1977	Charlie Black, Marietta	Jr.	14	465	33.2
1978	Russ Atchison, Centre	So.	11	284	25.8
1979	Jim Iannone, Rochester	Jr.	13	411	31.6
1980	Mike Askew, Kean	So.	††10	415	41.5
1981	Gene Cote, Wesleyan (Conn.)	Sr.	16	521	32.6
1982	Jim Hachey, Bridgewater St.	Jr.	16	477	29.8
1983	Tom Myers, Coe	So.	11	401	36.5
1984	Mike Doetsch, Trinity (Conn.)	Jr.	13	434	33.4
1985	Gary Newsom, Lane	So.	10	319	31.9
1986	Glenn Koch, Tufts	Sr.	14	472	33.7
1987	Anthony Drakeford, Ferrum	Sr.	15	507	33.8
1988	Harold Owens, Wis.-La Crosse	Jr.	10	508	29.9
1989	Byron Womack, Iona	Sr.	15	531	35.4
1990	Nate Kirtman, Pomona-Pitzer	Jr.	14	515	36.8
1991	Tom Reason, Albion	So.	13	423	32.5
1992	Jason Martin, Coe	So.	11	438	39.8
1993	Eric Green, Benedictine (Ill.)	Sr.	19	628	33.1
1994	Brandon Steinheim, Wesley	Fr.	10	422	*42.2
1995	Derrick Brooms, Chicago	Sr.	12	422	35.2
1996	Trevor Shannon, Wartburg	So.	14	501	35.8
1997	Qasim Ward, Mass.-Boston	Fr.	10	314	31.4
1998	Tony Hill, Salisbury	Sr.	14	549	39.2
1999	David Ziegler, John Carroll	Sr.	11	393	35.7
2000	Andy Traetow, Gust. Adolphus	So.	17	584	34.4
2001	Kevin Gniadek, Worcester St.	Jr.	15	469	31.3
2002	Roger Snyder, Wash. & Jeff.	Sr.	19	616	32.4

*Record. ‡Ranked on minimum of 1.5 returns per game in 1973; 1.2 from 1974. ††Declared champion; with one more return (making 1.2 per game) for zero yards, still would have highest average (37.7).

All-Purpose Yards

CAREER YARDS PER GAME
(Minimum 3,500 Yards)

Player, Team	Years	G	Rush	Rcv.	Int.	PR	KOR	Yds.	Yd. PG
R.J. Bowers, Grove City	1997-00	40	*7,353	397	0	50	1,453	*9,253	*231.3
Paul Smith, Gettysburg	1996-99	40	5,205	758	0	959	2,182	9,104	227.6
Kirk Matthieu, Maine Maritime	$1989-93	33	5,107	315	0	254	1,279	6,955	210.8
Carey Bender, Coe	1991-94	39	6,125	1,751	0	7	87	7,970	204.4
Steve Tardif, Maine Maritime	1996-99	39	6,093	643	8	65	1,151	7,960	204.1
Gary Trettel, St. Thomas (Minn.)	1988-90	29	3,483	834	0	0	1,407	5,724	197.4

*Record. $See Page 8 for explanation.

SEASON YARDS PER GAME

Player, Team	Year	G	Rush	Rcv.	Int.	PR	KOR	Yds.	Yd. PG
Dante Brown, Marietta	†1996	10	*2,385	174	0	46	368	*2,973	*297.3
R.J. Bowers, Grove City	†1998	10	2,283	51	0	4	538	2,876	287.6
Paul Smith, Gettysburg	†1999	10	1,546	301	0	255	615	2,717	271.7
Carey Bender, Coe	†1994	10	2,243	319	0	7	87	2,656	265.6
Kenneth Sasu, Marietta	1999	9	1,770	82	0	0	374	2,226	247.3
Steve Tardif, Maine Maritime	1999	9	1,567	149	8	0	479	2,203	244.8
Paul Smith, Gettysburg	1998	10	1,515	178	0	191	554	2,438	243.8
Kirk Matthieu, Maine Maritime	†1992	9	1,733	91	0	56	308	2,188	243.1
Guy Leman, Simpson	1998	10	1,788	210	0	0	408	2,406	240.6

Player, Team	Year	G	Rush	Rcv.	Int.	PR	KOR	Yds.	Yd. PG
Ray Neosh, Coe	1996	9	1,472	273	0	0	403	2,148	238.7
Ricky Gales, Simpson	1989	10	2,035	102	0	0	248	2,385	238.5
R.J. Bowers, Grove City	1999	10	2,098	34	0	0	240	2,372	237.2
Paul Smith, Gettysburg	†1997	10	1.256	102	0	199	805	2,362	236.2
Gary Trettel, St. Thomas (Minn.)	1989	10	1,502	337	0	0	496	2,335	233.5
Kirk Matthieu, Maine Maritime	1990	9	1,428	77	0	99	495	2,099	233.2
Gary Trettel, St. Thomas (Minn.)	1990	10	1,620	388	0	0	319	2,327	232.7
Carey Bender, Coe	†1993	10	1,718	601	0	0	0	2,319	231.9

*Record. †National champion.

CAREER YARDS

Player, Team	Years	Rush	Rcv.	Int.	PR	KOR	Yds.
R.J. Bowers, Grove City	1997-00	*7,353	397	0	50	1,453	*9,253
Paul Smith, Gettysburg	1996-99	5,205	758	0	959	2,182	9,104
Carey Bender, Coe	1991-94	6,125	1,751	0	7	87	7,970
Steve Tardif, Maine Maritime	1996-99	6,093	643	8	65	1,151	7,960
Kirk Matthieu, Maine Maritime	$1989-93	5,107	315	0	254	1,279	6,955
Eric Frees, McDaniel	1988-91	5,281	392	0	47	1,158	6,878
Joshua Carter, Muhlenberg	1998-01	170	2,733	0	*1,550	*2,189	6,642
Joe Dudek, Plymouth St.	1982-85	5,570	348	0	0	243	6,509
Richard Wemer, Grinnell	1995-98	1,016	3,133	7	674	1,657	6,487
Trevor Shannon, Wartburg	1995-98	4,292	1,037	0	0	964	6,293
Dante Brown, Marietta	1994-97	4,512	425	0	202	1,040	6,179
Scott Pingel, Westminster (Mo.)	1996-99	5	*6,108	0	0	0	6,113
Adam Henry, Carleton	1990-93	3,482	601	0	186	1,839	6,108
Kenneth Sasu, Marietta	1997-00	4,727	217	0	0	1,139	6,083
Brad Olson, Lawrence	1994-97	5,325	590	0	14	145	6,074
Mark Kacmarnyski, Central (Iowa)	$1992-96	5,434	211	0	45	364	6,054
Gary Trettel, St. Thomas (Minn.)	1988-90	3,724	853	0	0	1,467	6,044

*Record. $See Page 8 for explanation.

SEASON YARDS

Player, Team	Year	Rush	Rcv.	Int.	PR	KOR	Yds.
Dan Pugh, Mount Union	†2002	2,300	382	0	0	507	*3,189
Dante Brown, Marietta	†1996	*2,385	174	0	46	368	2,973
R. J. Bowers, Grove City	†1998	2,283	51	0	4	538	2,876
Paul Smith, Gettysburg	†1999	1,546	301	0	255	615	2,717
Carey Bender, Coe	†1994	2,243	319	0	7	87	2,656
Fredrick Jackson, Coe	2002	1,702	234	0	260	346	2,542
Blake Elliott, St. John's (Minn.)	2002	72	1,484	0	385	520	2,461
Paul Smith, Gettysburg	1998	1,515	178	0	191	554	2,438
Theo Blanco, Wis.-Stevens Point	1987	454	1,616	0	245	103	2,418
Guy Leman, Simpson	1998	1,788	210	0	0	408	2,406
Ricky Gales, Simpson	1989	2,035	102	0	0	248	2,385
R.J. Bowers, Grove City	1999	2,098	34	0	0	240	2,372
Paul Smith, Gettysburg	†1997	1,256	102	0	199	805	2,362
Gary Trettel, St. Thomas (Minn.)	1989	1,502	337	0	0	496	2,335
Gary Trettel, St. Thomas (Minn.)	1990	1,620	388	0	0	319	2,327

*Record. †National champion.

ANNUAL CHAMPIONS

Year	Player, Team	Class	Rush	Rcv.	Int.	PR	KOR	Yds.	Yd. PG
1992	Kirk Matthieu, Maine Maritime	Jr.	1,733	91	0	56	308	2,188	243.1
1993	Carey Bender, Coe	Jr.	1,718	601	0	0	0	2,319	231.9
1994	Carey Bender, Coe	Sr.	2,243	319	0	7	87	2,656	265.6
1995	Brad Olson, Lawrence	So.	1,760	279	0	0	0	2,039	226.6
1996	Dante Brown, Marietta	Jr.	*2,385	174	0	46	368	2,973	*297.3
1997	Paul Smith, Gettysburg	So.	1,256	102	0	199	805	2,362	236.2
1998	R.J. Bowers, Grove City	So.	2,283	51	0	4	538	2,876	287.6
1999	Paul Smith, Gettysburg	Sr.	1,546	301	0	255	615	2,717	271.7
2000	Jamal Robertson, Ohio Northern	Sr.	1,664	300	0	0	344	2,308	230.8
2001	Chris Sullivan, Wash. & Lee	Jr.	1,189	268	16	204	347	2,024	202.4
2002	Dan Pugh, Mount Union	Sr.	2,300	382	0	0	507	*3,189	227.8

*Record.

Field Goals

CAREER FIELD GOALS

Player, Team	Years	Made	Atts.	Pct.
Ken Edelman, Mount Union (S)	1987-90	*52	71	.732
Carlos Martinez, Buena Vista (S)	1998-01	48	*75	.640
Ted Swan, Colorado Col. (S)	1973-76	43	57	.754
Jim Hever, Rhodes (S)	1982-85	42	66	.636
Manny Matsakis, Capital (C)	1980-83	40	66	.606
Doug Hart, Grove City (S)	1985-88	40	71	.563
Mike Duvic, Dayton (S)	1986-89	38	49	$.776
Jeff Reitz, Lawrence (C)	1974-77	37	60	.617

Player, Team	Years	Made	Atts.	Pct.
Dan Deneher, Montclair St. (S)	1978-79, 81-82	37	65	.569
Jim Flynn, Gettysburg (S)	1982-85	37	68	.544

*Record. $Declared record; with one more attempt (making 50), failed, still would have highest percentage (.760). (C) Conventional kicker. (S) Soccer-style kicker.

SEASON FIELD GOALS

Player, Team	Year	Made	Atts.	Pct.
Ken Edelman, Mount Union (S)	†1990	*20	27	.741
Scott Ryerson, UCF (S)	†1981	18	*29	.621
Carlos Martinez, Buena Vista (S)	†2000	17	24	.708
Christopher Reed, Muhlenberg (S)	2002	16	21	.762
George Merrill, Albright (S)	†2001	16	26	.615
Dennis Unger, Albright (S)	†1995	16	20	.800

Player, Team	Year	Made	Atts.	Pct.
Ben Lambert, Washington (Mo.) (S)	†2002	15	21	.714
Sean Lipscomb, Redlands (S)	2000	15	25	.600
Haakon Nelson, St. Olaf (S)	†1999	15	20	.750
Steve Graeca, John Carroll (S)	†1988	15	16	*.938
Ken Edelman, Mount Union (S)	1988	15	17	.882
Gary Potter, Hamline (C)	†1984	15	21	.714
Jeff Reitz, Lawrence (C)	†1975	15	26	.577

*Record. †National champion. (C) Conventional kicker. (S) Soccer-style kicker.

ANNUAL CHAMPIONS

Year	Player, Team	Class	Made	Atts.	Pct.	PG
1973	Chuck Smeltz, Susquehanna (C)	Jr.	10	14	.714	1.11
1974	Ted Swan, Colorado Col. (S)	So.	13	15	.867	1.44
1975	Jeff Reitz, Lawrence (C)	So.	15	26	.577	1.67
1976	Mark Sniegocki, Bethany (W.Va.) (C)	So.	11	14	.786	1.22
1977	Bob Unruh, Wheaton (Ill.) (S)	Jr.	11	14	.786	1.22
1978	Craig Walker, McDaniel (C)	So.	13	24	.542	1.44
1979	Jeff Holter, Concordia-M'head (S)	Jr.	12	15	.800	1.33
1980	Jeff Holter, Concordia-M'head (S)	Sr.	13	19	.684	1.30
1981	Scott Ryerson, UCF (S)	So.	18	*29	.621	1.80
1982	Manny Matsakis, Capital (C)	Jr.	13	20	.650	1.44
1983	Mike Farrell, Adrian (S)	So.	12	21	.571	1.33
1984	Gary Potter, Hamline (C)	Jr.	15	21	.714	1.50
1985	Joe Bevelhimer, Wabash (C)	Sr.	14	22	.636	1.40
	Jim Hever, Rhodes (S)	Sr.	14	23	.609	1.40
1986	Tim Dewberry, Occidental (C)	Sr.	13	21	.619	1.44
1987	Doug Dickason, John Carroll (S)	Sr.	13	21	.619	1.44
1988	Steve Graeca, John Carroll (S)	Fr.	15	16	*.938	1.67
1989	Dave Bergmann, San Diego (S)	So.	14	18	.778	1.56
	Rich Egal, Merchant Marine (S)	Fr.	14	22	.636	1.56
1990	Ken Edelman, Mount Union (S)	Sr.	*20	27	.741	*2.00
1991	Greg Harrison, Union (N.Y.) (S)	So.	12	16	.750	1.33
1992	Todd Holthaus, Rose-Hulman (S)	Jr.	13	19	.684	1.30
1993	Steve Milne, Brockport St. (S)	Sr.	13	16	.813	1.30
1994	Chris Kondik, Baldwin-Wallace (S)	Fr.	13	17	.765	1.30
1995	Dennis Unger, Albright (S)	So.	16	20	.800	1.60
1996	Roger Egbert, Union (N.Y.) (S)	Sr.	11	15	.733	1.22
1997	Ryan Boutwell, Gust. Adolphus (S)	Jr.	13	18	.722	1.30
1998	David Vitatoe, John Carroll (S)	Jr.	13	16	.813	1.30
	Michael Padgett, Bridgewater (Va.) (S)	Sr.	13	23	.565	1.30
1999	Ryan Geisler, Cal Lutheran (S)	Jr.	14	18	.778	1.56
2000	Carlos Martinez, Buena Vista (S)	Jr.	17	24	.708	1.70
2001	George Merrill, Albright (S)	Sr.	16	26	.615	1.60
2002	Ben Lambert, Washington (Mo.) (S)	So.	15	21	.714	1.50

*Record. (C) Conventional kicker. (S) Soccer-style kicker.

All-Time Longest Plays

Since 1941, official maximum length of all plays fixed at 100 yards.

RUSHING

Yds.	Player, Team (Opponent)	Year
99	Derek Garrod, Ohio Northern (Wilmington [Ohio])	2002
99	Reggie Boyce, Salisbury (Chowan)	2000
99	Bill Casey, Mass.-Dartmouth (Norwich)	1995
99	Kelly Wilkinson, Principia (Trinity Bible)	1995
99	Derrick Johnson, Kenyon (Denison)	1994
99	Arnie Boigner, Ohio Northern (Muskingum)	1992
99	Reese Wilson, MacMurray (Eureka)	1986
99	Don Patria, Rensselaer (Mass.-Lowell)	1981
99	Kevin Doherty, Mass. Maritime (New Haven)	1980
99	Sam Halliston, Albany (N.Y.) (Norwich)	1977

PASSING

Yds.	Passer-Receiver, Team (Opponent)	Year
99	Clay Groefsema-Shawn Watson, Redlands (Whittier)	2001
99	Dan Pincelli-John Nowak, Hartwick (Union [N.Y.])	1999
99	Greg Kaiser-Mark Warder, St. Thomas (Minn.) (Augsburg)	1998
99	Brian Partlow-Sean Eaton, Randolph-Macon (Catholic)	1998
99	Tim Vinyard-L.C. Lewis, Coe (Loras)	1998
99	Dave Johnson-Kevin McGuirl, Kean (Lycoming)	1998
99	Eric Block-R.J. Hoppe, Carroll (Wis.) (Lake Forest)	1996
99	Mike Schultz-R.J. Hoppe, Carroll (Wis.) (Ripon)	1995
99	Mike Magistrelli-Jason Martin, Coe (Quincy)	1994
99	Jim Connolley-Duane Martin, Wesley (FDU-Florham)	1993
99	Marc Klausner-Eric Frink, Pace (Hobart)	1992

Yds.	Passer-Receiver, Team (Opponent)	Year
99	Carlos Nazario-Ray Marshall, St. Peter's (Georgetown)	1991
99	Mike Jones-Warren Tweedy, Frostburg St. (Waynesburg)	1990
99	Chris Etzler-Andy Nowlin, Bluffton (Urbana)	1990
99	John Clark-Pete Balistrieri, Wis.-Eau Claire (Minn. Duluth)	1989
99	Kelly Sandidge-Mark Green, Centre (Sewanee)	1988
99	Mike Francis-John Winter, Carleton (Trinity [Tex.])	1983
99	Rich Boling-Lewis Borsellino, DePauw (Valparaiso)	1976
99	John Wicinski-Donnell Lipford, John Carroll (Allegheny)	1975
99	Jack Berry-Mercer West, Wash. & Lee (Hampden-Sydney)	1974
99	Gary Shope-Rick Rudolph, Juniata (Moravian)	1973

INTERCEPTION RETURNS

Thirty-two players have returned interceptions 100 yards. The most recent:

Yds.	Player, Team (Opponent)	Year
100	Kevin Wingo, Maryville (Tenn.) (Centre)	2000
100	Jeremy Jones, Mississippi Col. (Austin)	1999
100	Duane Manson, Wesley (Stonehill)	1998
100	Michael Turner, Chicago (Rose-Hulman)	1998
100	Brian McConnell, Kenyon (Oberlin)	1998
100	Terrance Oliver, Delaware Valley (Lebanon Valley)	1997
100	Randy Ames, Hope (Adrian)	1996
100	Dan Gilson, Curry (Stonehill)	1995
100	Tony Hinkle, Rose-Hulman (Millsaps)	1995
100	Mike Gerhart, Susquehanna (Moravian)	1994
100	Bruce Pritchett, Kean (Widener)	1994
100	Adam Smith, Heidelberg (Capital)	1994
100	Jason Pass, Hamline (St. John's [Minn.])	1994
100	Guy Nardulli, Elmhurst (North Central)	1994

PUNT RETURNS

Yds.	Player, Team (Opponent)	Year
99	Robert Middlebrook, Knoxville (Miles)	1985
98	Mark Griggs, Wooster (Oberlin)	1980
98	Ron Mabry, Emory & Henry (Maryville [Tenn.])	1973
97	Rob Allard, Nichols (Curry)	1991
97	Leon Kornegaey, Carthage (Millikin)	1985
96	Marvin Robbins, Salisbury (Wesley)	1987
96	Gary Martin, Muskingum (Wooster)	1976
95	Tyrone Croom, Susquehanna (Delaware Valley)	1993
95	Brian Sarver, William Penn (Dubuque)	1992
95	Stan Thompson, Knoxville (Livingstone)	1982

KICKOFF RETURNS

Forty-eight players have returned kickoffs 100 yards. The most recent:

Yds.	Player, Team (Opponent)	Year
100	Gino Gosciaco, Menlo (La Verne)	2001
100	Joel Robnett, Whitworth (Chapman)	2000
100	Paul Sage, Colorado Col. (Pomona-Pitzer)	1999
100	Greg Ortberg, Dubuque (Upper Iowa)	1999
100	Michael Kirtman, Pomona-Pitzer (Colorado Col.)	1999
100	Scott Meinerz, Concordia (Ill.) (Principia)	1998
100	Lamar Wilson, Buffalo St. (Rochester)	1998
100	Jeff Rogers, Albright (Wm. Paterson)	1998
100	Eric Green, Benedictine (Ill.) (Carthage)	1992

PUNTS

Yds.	Player, Team (Opponent)	Year
90	Sean Lipscomb, Redlands (Pomona-Pitzer)	2002
90	Dan Heeren, Coe (Lawrence)	1974
88	Steve Vagedes, Ohio Northern (Capital)	1999
86	David Anastasi, Buffalo (John Carroll)	1989
86	Dana Loucks, Buffalo (Frostburg St.)	1987
86	John Pavlik, Wabash (Centre)	1978
85	Jeff Shea, Cal Lutheran (Azusa Pacific)	1996
84	Todd Whitehurst, Menlo (Cal Lutheran)	1997
84	Rob Sarvis, Norwich (Western Conn. St.)	1995
84	Jason Berg, Mass. Maritime (Fitchburg St.)	1989

FIELD GOALS

Yds.	Player, Team (Opponent)	Year
62	Dom Antonini, Rowan (Salisbury)	1976
60	Rick Brands, Alma (Franklin)	1998
59	Chris Gustafson, Carroll (Wis.) (North Park)	1985
59	Hartmut Strecker, Dayton (Iowa St.)	1977
57	Scott Fritz, Wartburg (Simpson)	1982
57	Kevin Shea, St. Mary's (Cal.) (Oregon Tech)	1976

DIVISION III

Team Champions

Annual Offense Champions

TOTAL OFFENSE

Year	Team	Avg.
1973	San Diego	441.0
1974	Ithaca	487.9
1975	Frank. & Marsh.	439.4
1976	St. John's (Minn.)	451.8
1977	St. John's (Minn.)	437.5
1978	Lawrence	432.6
1979	Norwich	465.2
1980	Widener	459.0
1981	Middlebury	446.5
1982	West Ga.	470.6
1983	Elmhurst	483.3
1984	Alma	465.1
1985	St. Thomas (Minn.)	446.9
1986	Mount Union	452.8
1987	Samford	523.1
1988	Wagner	465.9
1989	Simpson	514.0
1990	Hofstra	505.7
1991	St. John's (Minn.)	503.8
1992	Mount Union	463.7
1993	St. John's (Minn.)	549.7
1994	Allegheny	543.8
1995	Mount Union	495.8
1996	Albion	538.0
1997	Simpson	*565.3
1998	Westminster (Mo.)	561.2
1999	Mount Union	559.5
2000	Mount Union	530.0
2001	Rowan	526.8
2002	Trinity (Tex.)	517.7

*Record.

RUSHING OFFENSE

Year	Team	Avg.
1973	Widener	361.7
1974	Albany (N.Y.)	361.6
1975	Widener	345.8
1976	St. John's (Minn.)	348.9
1977	St. John's (Minn.)	315.3
1978	Ithaca	320.1
1979	Norwich	383.1
1980	Widener	317.5
1981	Augustana (Ill.)	313.6
1982	West Ga.	319.6
1983	Augustana (Ill.)	345.7
1984	Augustana (Ill.)	338.4
1985	Denison	351.0
1986	Wis.-River Falls	361.4
1987	Augustana (Ill.)	369.1
1988	Tufts	369.0
1989	Wis.-River Falls	388.5
1990	Ferrum	*434.7
1991	Ferrum	361.4
1992	Wis.-River Falls	315.6
1993	Chicago	324.8
1994	Wis.-River Falls	336.5
1995	Lawrence	344.0
1996	Springfield	351.2
1997	Wis.-River Falls	365.6
1998	Wis.-River Falls	393.9
1999	Springfield	375.3
2000	Springfield	427.5
2001	Augustana (Ill.)	389.4
2002	Springfield	356.7

*Record.

PASSING OFFENSE

Year	Team	Avg.
1973	San Diego	231.7
1974	Benedictine (Ill.)	255.4
1975	St. Norbert	227.7
1976	Occidental	255.4
1977	Southwestern	257.8
1978	Claremont-M-S	331.7

Year	Team	Avg.
1979	Claremont-M-S	250.1
1980	Occidental	255.9
1981	Wis.-Stevens Point	288.9
1982	Wheaton (Ill.)	308.7
1983	Wheaton (Ill.)	380.4
1984	Wheaton (Ill.)	351.6
1985	Wheaton (Ill.)	371.6
1986	Pace	286.9
1987	Wis.-Stout	314.6
1988	Wis.-Stevens Point	356.7
1989	Wis.-Stevens Point	380.4
1990	Hofstra	342.2
1991	St. John's (Minn.)	302.8
1992	Mass.-Boston	337.0
1993	Mount Union	352.8
1994	Hanover	351.3
1995	Hanover	362.8
1996	Alma	368.3
1997	Lakeland	357.3
1998	Westminster (Mo.)	488.8
1999	Redlands	421.8
2000	Menlo	*530.0
2001	Wis.-Platteville	358.8
2002	Case Reserve	370.6

*Record.

SCORING OFFENSE

Year	Team	Avg.
1973	San Diego	40.1
1974	Frank. & Marsh.	45.1
1975	Frank. & Marsh.	38.2
1976	St. John's (Minn.)	42.5
1977	Lawrence	38.2
1978	Georgetown	36.5
1979	Wittenberg	39.7
1980	Widener	43.3
1981	Lawrence	35.3
1982	West Ga.	42.1
1983	Elmhurst	38.1
1984	Hope	40.3
1985	Salisbury	39.5
1986	Dayton	40.8
1987	Samford	51.7
1988	Central (Iowa)	37.6
1989	Ferrum	46.7
1990	Ferrum	47.3
1991	Union (N.Y.)	46.1
1992	Coe	46.4
1993	St. John's (Minn.)	*61.5
1994	St. John's (Minn.)	47.1
1995	Chapman	47.2
1996	Albion	50.8
1997	Mount Union	54.5
1998	MacMurray	48.2
1999	Mount Union	53.4
2000	Mount Union	49.1
2001	Rowan	50.6
2002	Mount Union	46.7

*Record.

Annual Defense Champions

TOTAL DEFENSE

Year	Team	Avg.
1973	Doane	144.3
1974	Alfred	153.6
1975	Lycoming	133.1
1976	Albion	129.9
1977	Knoxville	*94.0
1978	Bowie St.	112.3
1979	Catholic	116.9
1980	Maine Maritime	127.2
1981	Millsaps	147.6
1982	Plymouth St.	122.2
1983	Lycoming	154.5
1984	Swarthmore	159.2
1985	Augustana (Ill.)	149.1
1986	Augustana (Ill.)	136.2
1987	Plymouth St.	135.3

Year	Team	Avg.
1988	Plymouth St.	143.6
1989	Frostburg St.	119.7
1990	Bentley	139.8
1991	Wash. & Jeff.	143.0
1992	Bentley	184.5
1993	Wash. & Jeff.	142.4
1994	Wash. & Jeff.	165.3
1995	Mass. Maritime	161.2
1996	Worcester St.	125.8
1997	Salve Regina	146.0
1998	St. John's (Minn.)	182.6
1999	Washington (Mo.)	192.1
2000	Ferrum	165.5
2001	Westfield St.	188.0
2002	Westfield St.	175.6

*Record.

RUSHING DEFENSE

Year	Team	Avg.
1973	Oregon Col.	61.2
1974	Millersville	57.2
1975	Cal Lutheran	62.4
1976	Lycoming	44.3
1977	Knoxville	*-2.3
1978	McDaniel	43.4
1979	Catholic	46.4
1980	Maine Maritime	3.2
1981	Augustana (Ill.)	30.7
1982	Lycoming	34.2
1983	DePauw	41.6
1984	Swarthmore	40.0
1985	Augustana (Ill.)	35.1
1986	Dayton	13.5
1987	Lycoming	35.4
1988	Worcester St.	43.9
1989	Frostburg St.	49.7
1990	Ohio Wesleyan	18.9
1991	Wash. & Jeff.	64.6
1992	Bridgewater St.	43.2
1993	Wash. & Jeff.	19.1
1994	Wash. & Jeff.	23.7
1995	Marietta	46.2
1996	Worcester St.	20.3
1997	Mount Union	48.6
1998	Widener	31.4
1999	Rowan	35.9
2000	Chicago	44.2
2001	Mary Hardin-Baylor	31.8
2002	Wis.-Stout	50.0

*Record.

PASSING DEFENSE

Year	Team	$Avg.
1973	Nichols	53.0
1974	Findlay	49.2
1975	Wash. & Jeff.	56.0
1976	Mass. Maritime	*48.5
1977	Hofstra	49.4
1978	Bowie St.	64.7
1979	Wagner	59.5
1980	Williams	63.8
1981	Plymouth St.	66.9
1982	Plymouth St.	48.8
1983	Muhlenberg	76.4
1984	Bridgewater St.	68.7
1985	Bridgewater St.	77.3
1986	Knoxville	83.2
1987	New Jersey City	67.0
1988	Colorado Col.	78.9
1989	Frostburg St.	70.0
1990	Bentley	47.4
1991	Wash. & Jeff.	50.3
1992	St. Peter's	51.7
1993	Worcester St.	50.0
1994	Worcester St.	69.2
1995	Union (N.Y.)	54.6
1996	Worcester St.	50.6
1997	Salve Regina	57.3
1998	Wittenberg	64.7
1999	Union (N.Y.)	69.7

Year	Team	$Avg.
2000	Hobart	48.5
2001	Johns Hopkins	64.2
2002	Brockport St.	71.4

*Record. $Beginning in 1990, ranked on passing efficiency defense rating points instead of per-game yardage allowed.

SCORING DEFENSE

Year	Team	Avg.
1973	Fisk	6.4
	Slippery Rock	6.4
1974	Central (Iowa)	6.9
	Rhodes	6.9
1975	Millsaps	5.0
1976	Albion	5.4
1977	Central (Iowa)	5.0
1978	Minn.-Morris	5.9
1979	Carnegie Mellon	4.9
1980	Millsaps	*3.4
1981	Baldwin-Wallace	3.9
1982	West Ga.	4.6
1983	Carnegie Mellon	5.3
1984	Union (N.Y.)	4.6
1985	Augustana (Ill.)	4.7
1986	Augustana (Ill.)	5.1
1987	Plymouth St.	6.2
1988	Plymouth St.	6.5
1989	Millikin	4.8
1990	Bentley	4.5
1991	Mass.-Lowell	5.4
1992	Dayton	6.7
1993	Wash. & Jeff.	6.1
1994	Trinity (Tex.)	6.2
1995	Wash. & Jeff.	5.6
	Williams	5.6
1996	Amherst	8.4
1997	Mount Union	5.6
1998	Wittenberg	5.3
1999	Lycoming	6.0

Year	Team	Avg.
2000	Brockport St.	5.5
2001	Amherst	6.1
2002	Brockport St.	9.4

*Record.

Other Annual Team Champions

NET PUNTING

Year	Team	Avg.
1992	San Diego	39.2
1993	Benedictine (Ill.)	38.9
1994	Redlands	37.9
1995	Hardin-Simmons	37.9
1996	Cal Lutheran	39.0
1997	John Carroll	40.7
1998	Chapman	39.8
1999	Ohio Northern	41.3
2000	Redlands	40.6
2001	Central (Iowa)	38.0
2002	East Tex. Baptist	38.6

PUNT RETURNS

Year	Team	Avg.
1992	Occidental	18.7
1993	Curry	17.9
	Wheaton (Ill.)	17.9
1994	Frostburg St.	15.2
1995	Ohio Northern	16.5
1996	Howard Payne	17.4
1997	Juniata	18.4
1998	Ithaca	22.5
1999	Westminster (Mo.)	20.1
2000	Greenville	16.7
2001	Guilford	24.5
2002	Whittier	20.3

KICKOFF RETURNS

Year	Team	Avg.
1992	Thomas More	27.7
1993	St. John's (Minn.)	28.9
1994	Buffalo St.	26.8
1995	Howard Payne	29.5
1996	Trinity (Conn.)	30.1
1997	McDaniel	29.2
1998	John Carroll	29.5
1999	Muhlenberg	28.7
2000	McDaniel	26.4
2001	Mount Union	26.5
2002	Wabash	27.5

TURNOVER MARGIN

Year	Team	Avg.
1992	Illinois Col.	2.44
1993	Trinity (Conn.)	2.87
1994	Dickinson	2.70
1995	Thomas More	2.80
1996	DePauw	2.50
1997	Rennselaer	2.22
1998	McDaniel	2.30
	Wartburg	2.30
1999	Rennselaer	2.44
2000	Bethel (Minn.)	2.80
2001	Western Conn. St.	2.63
2002	Mass.-Dartmouth	2.67

MOST IMPROVED

Year	Team	Imp.
1996	DePauw	6
1997	Grove City	6½
1998	Curry	6
1999	Ursinus	6
2000	Wis.-Stout	7½
2001	Westfield St.	6
2002	Westminster (Mo.)	5½

2002 Most-Improved Teams

Team (Coach)	2002	2001	$Games Improved
Westminster (Mo.) (John Welty)	7-2	2-8	5½
Mt. St. Joseph (Rod Huber)	5-5	0-10	5
Hanover (Wayne Perry)	10-1	5-5	4½
Lake Forest (Chad Eisele)	9-2	4-6	4½
Olivet (Kevin Bozeman)	5-4	1-9	4½
Salisbury (Sherman Wood)	9-2	4-6	4½
Adrian (Jim Lyall)	6-4	2-8	4
Macalester (Dennis Czech)	5-5	1-9	4
Maranatha Baptist (Terry Price)	6-3	2-7	4
Wooster (Mike Schmitz)	8-2	4-6	4

$To determine games improved, add the difference in victories between the two seasons to the difference in losses, then divide by two. Includes postseason.

All-Time Most-Improved Leaders

Team (Coach)	Year	W-L	Pvs.	$Games Improved
Wis.-Stout (Ed Meierkort)	2000	10-1-0	2-8-0	7½
Catholic (Tom Clark)	1994	8-2-0	1-9-0	7
Susquehanna (Rocky Rees)	1986	11-1-0	3-7-0	7
Maryville (Tenn.) (Jim Jordan)	1976	7-2-0	0-9-0	7

$To determine games improved, add the difference in victories between the two seasons to the difference in losses, then divide by two. Includes postseason.

DIVISION III

All-Time Team Won-Lost Records

Won-lost-tied record includes postseason games

BY PERCENTAGE (TOP 25)

(Minimum 20 seasons of competition)

Team	Yrs.	Won	Lost	Tied	Pct.
St. John's (Minn.)	92	496	213	24	.693
Wis.-La Crosse	78	481	205	40	.690
Plymouth St.	33	213	101	7	.675
Ithaca	70	384	197	11	.658
Wittenberg	109	636	324	32	.657
Linfield	88	451	239	30	.647
Pacific Lutheran	74	414	222	33	.644
Augustana (Ill.)	90	472	256	28	.643
Central (Iowa)	94	500	283	26	.634
Concordia (Wis.)	23	135	78	3	.632
Wis.-Whitewater	78	408	235	21	.630
Baldwin-Wallace	98	496	286	30	.629
Montclair St.	72	371	218	20	.626
Williams	117	571	333	47	.625
Concordia-M'head	83	425	251	38	.622
Wash. & Jeff.	111	596	359	40	.619
Widener	122	596	363	38	.617
Millikin	97	488	300	28	.615
Lycoming	53	288	180	11	.613
Gust. Adolphus	87	428	274	21	.607
Albion	116	531	338	43	.606
Cal Lutheran	41	237	153	7	.606
St. Thomas (Minn.)	97	475	303	32	.606
Hardin-Simmons	66	349	223	35	.604
Rowan	43	250	163	8	.603

BY VICTORIES (TOP 25)

(Minimum 20 seasons of competition)

Team	Yrs.	Won	Lost	Tied	Pct.
Wittenberg	109	636	324	32	.657
Wash. & Jeff.	111	596	359	40	.619
Widener	122	596	363	38	.617
Mount Union	106	577	381	38	.598
Williams	117	571	333	47	.625
Amherst	123	547	385	54	.582
Wabash	116	543	358	59	.596
Frank. & Marsh.	115	538	422	47	.558
Albion	116	531	338	43	.606
Ohio Wesleyan	112	520	428	44	.546
Coe	110	502	345	38	.589
Centre	110	501	372	37	.571
Central (Iowa)	94	500	283	26	.634
Gettysburg	110	498	444	42	.527
St. John's (Minn.)	92	496	213	24	.693
Baldwin-Wallace	98	496	286	30	.629
Millikin	97	488	300	28	.615
Denison	113	484	420	57	.533
DePauw	115	482	440	41	.522
Wis.-La Crosse	78	481	205	40	.690
Ill. Wesleyan	111	480	345	41	.578
McDaniel	108	479	394	48	.546
Trinity (Conn.)	118	477	337	42	.582
St. Thomas (Minn.)	97	475	303	32	.606
Augustana (Ill.)	90	472	256	28	.643

ALPHABETICAL

(No minimum seasons of competition)

Team	Yrs.	Won	Lost	Tied	Pct.
Adrian	100	324	417	18	.439
Albion	116	531	338	43	.606
Albright	90	364	411	22	.471
Alfred	104	406	336	45	.545
Allegheny	108	444	373	44	.541
Alma	106	440	359	27	.549
Amherst	123	547	385	54	.582
Anderson (Ind.)	56	249	250	12	.499
Augsburg	71	182	394	18	.322
Augustana (Ill.)	90	472	256	28	.643
Aurora	17	91	60	3	.601
Austin	106	405	429	39	.486
Averett	3	5	23	0	.179
Baldwin-Wallace	98	496	286	30	.629
Bates	107	289	463	46	.391
Beloit	112	388	457	47	.461

Team	Yrs.	Won	Lost	Tied	Pct.
Benedictine (Ill.)	81	268	327	24	.452
Bethany (W.Va.)	102	316	479	34	.402
Bethel (Minn.)	50	186	261	8	.418
Blackburn	14	28	98	0	.222
Bluffton	80	267	363	23	.427
Bowdoin	109	360	438	44	.454
Bridgewater St.	43	197	177	6	.526
Bridgewater (Va.)	58	164	318	11	.344
Brockport St.	56	179	279	14	.394
Buena Vista	98	385	362	28	.515
Buffalo St.	22	109	103	0	.514
Cal Lutheran	41	237	153	7	.606
Capital	79	302	330	27	.479
Carleton	108	431	371	25	.536
Carnegie Mellon	93	446	325	29	.576
Carroll (Wis.)	99	392	314	38	.552
Carthage	106	386	381	42	.503
Case Reserve	33	121	184	4	.398
Catholic	57	246	230	13	.516
Central (Iowa)	94	500	283	26	.634
Centre	110	501	372	37	.571
Chapman	19	55	87	7	.393
Chicago	83	368	335	33	.522
Chowan	10	46	91	1	.337
Chris. Newport	2	11	9	0	.550
Claremont-M-S	45	150	242	5	.384
Coast Guard	79	270	368	19	.425
Coe	110	502	345	38	.589
Colby	109	321	435	33	.428
Colorado Col.	117	447	429	35	.510
Concordia (Ill.)	64	175	323	19	.357
Concordia-M'head	83	425	251	38	.622
Concordia (Wis.)	23	135	78	3	.632
Cornell College	112	472	383	33	.550
Cortland St.	76	326	274	27	.542
Curry	38	136	192	6	.416
Defiance	80	320	341	20	.485
Delaware Valley	55	197	273	10	.421
Denison	113	484	420	57	.533
DePauw	115	482	440	41	.522
Dickinson	114	432	490	55	.470
Dubuque	80	271	380	25	.419
Earlham	112	336	502	23	.404
Eastern Ore.	70	198	384	14	.344
Elmhurst	83	250	417	24	.379
Emory & Henry	87	466	347	19	.572
Eureka	69	168	366	26	.323
FDU-Florham	29	75	186	1	.288
Ferrum	18	108	74	1	.593
Fitchburg St.	19	35	136	1	.206
Framingham St.	29	91	169	2	.351
Franklin	102	367	448	31	.452
Frank. & Marsh.	115	538	422	47	.558
Frostburg St.	42	204	189	8	.519
Gallaudet	96	204	437	19	.324
Gettysburg	110	498	444	42	.527
Greensboro	6	20	39	0	.339
Grinnell	112	376	493	33	.435
Grove City	108	425	431	60	.497
Guilford	97	264	514	26	.345
Gust. Adolphus	87	428	274	21	.607
Hamilton	109	340	433	47	.443
Hamline	111	386	398	30	.493
Hampden-Sydney	108	444	414	38	.517
Hanover	110	415	366	29	.530
Hardin-Simmons	66	349	223	35	.604
Hartwick	31	105	139	11	.433
Heidelberg	107	416	446	41	.483
Hiram	104	252	530	32	.329
Hobart	109	401	440	40	.478
Hope	93	371	292	38	.556
Howard Payne	97	438	389	41	.528
Illinois Col.	106	365	433	36	.459
Ill. Wesleyan	111	480	345	41	.578
Ithaca	70	384	197	11	.658
John Carroll	80	395	274	37	.586
Johns Hopkins	118	404	447	57	.476
Juniata	80	335	317	22	.513
Kalamazoo	108	365	426	41	.463
Kean	31	111	180	9	.385
Kenyon	113	321	535	47	.382
King's (Pa.)	28	83	142	8	.373
Knox	109	380	475	43	.447
La Verne	77	299	329	18	.477

Team	Yrs.	Won	Lost	Tied	Pct.
Lake Forest	110	370	424	55	.468
Lakeland	67	270	266	13	.504
Lawrence	109	464	358	29	.562
Lebanon Valley	102	352	486	36	.423
Lewis & Clark	57	239	242	13	.497
Linfield	88	451	239	30	.647
Loras	74	322	265	30	.546
Luther	89	378	334	21	.530
Lycoming	53	288	180	11	.613
Macalester	100	240	485	29	.338
MacMurray	18	97	79	1	.551
Maine Maritime	57	232	223	9	.510
Manchester	77	235	389	20	.380
Maranatha Baptist	43	120	157	5	.434
Marietta	108	374	484	36	.439
Martin Luther	104	334	334	31	.500
Maryville (Tenn.)	105	399	444	35	.474
Mass.-Dartmouth	15	85	60	0	.586
MIT	15	48	77	1	.385
Mass. Maritime	30	147	125	1	.540
McDaniel	108	479	394	48	.546
McMurry	77	312	392	35	.446
Menlo	17	69	87	2	.443
Merchant Marine	58	260	262	13	.498
Methodist	14	56	84	0	.400
Middlebury	106	365	370	42	.497
Millikin	97	488	300	28	.615
Millsaps	80	335	324	36	.508
Mississippi Col.	90	429	339	37	.556
Monmouth (Ill.)	110	442	437	39	.503
Montclair St.	72	371	218	20	.626
Moravian	69	302	280	21	.518
Mt. St. Joseph	13	41	86	1	.324
Mount Union	106	577	381	38	.598
Muhlenberg	103	420	454	41	.481
Muskingum	108	472	381	39	.551
Neb. Wesleyan	94	417	371	42	.528
Col. of New Jersey	78	301	290	32	.509
New Jersey City	35	111	215	3	.342
Nichols	44	180	179	6	.501
North Central	98	343	398	36	.465
North Park	44	90	303	7	.234
Norwich	104	312	455	31	.410
Oberlin	112	357	524	39	.409
Occidental	101	414	365	26	.530
Ohio Northern	104	416	417	35	.499
Ohio Wesleyan	112	520	428	44	.546
Olivet	102	282	478	33	.376
Otterbein	113	362	536	43	.408
Pacific Lutheran	74	414	222	33	.644
Plymouth St.	33	213	101	7	.675
Pomona-Pitzer	105	365	391	31	.484
Principia	69	192	331	16	.371
Puget Sound	94	375	348	36	.518
Randolph-Macon	115	436	415	57	.512
Redlands	93	422	366	28	.534
Rensselaer	113	342	494	46	.414
Rhodes	91	330	354	38	.483
Ripon	109	463	315	46	.590
Rochester	114	451	435	38	.509
Rose-Hulman	107	357	473	29	.433
Rowan	43	250	163	8	.603
St. John Fisher	15	45	96	0	.319
St. John's (Minn.)	92	496	213	24	.693
St. Lawrence	108	346	419	29	.454
St. Norbert	69	325	254	20	.559
St. Olaf	85	378	310	20	.548
St. Thomas (Minn.)	97	475	303	32	.606
Salisbury	31	158	139	4	.532
Salve Regina	10	65	26	0	.714
Sewanee	108	450	410	39	.522
Simpson	97	411	439	37	.484
Springfield	109	469	403	55	.536
Susquehanna	104	387	419	38	.481
Thiel	98	306	426	36	.422
Thomas More	13	95	37	0	.720
Trinity (Conn.)	118	477	337	42	.582
Trinity (Tex.)	98	402	416	49	.492
Tufts	121	462	464	47	.499
Union (N.Y.)	115	455	403	62	.528
Upper Iowa	100	315	407	25	.438
Ursinus	110	346	522	52	.404
Wabash	116	543	358	59	.596
Wartburg	67	307	270	12	.531

Team	Yrs.	Won	Lost	Tied	Pct.
Washington (Mo.)	105	436	420	28	.509
Wash. & Jeff.	111	596	359	40	.619
Wash. & Lee	109	424	467	39	.477
Waynesburg	99	377	355	37	.514
Wesley	17	94	70	1	.573
Wesleyan (Conn.)	120	470	452	42	.509
Western Conn. St.	31	126	170	3	.426
Western New Eng.	22	70	123	1	.363
Westfield St.	21	98	104	1	.485
Westminster (Mo.)	40	143	126	17	.530
Wheaton (Ill.)	90	395	317	29	.553
Whittier	93	427	348	36	.549
Whitworth	88	276	357	19	.438
Widener	122	596	363	38	.617
Wilkes	57	235	258	8	.477
Willamette	104	433	351	38	.550
Wm. Paterson	31	112	191	4	.371
Williams	117	571	333	47	.625
Wilmington (Ohio)	70	281	305	14	.480
Wis.-Eau Claire	84	329	332	34	.498
Wis.-La Crosse	78	481	205	40	.690
Wis.-Oshkosh	76	244	354	30	.412
Wis.-Platteville	94	314	345	31	.478
Wis.-River Falls	77	378	251	32	.596
Wis.-Stevens Point	103	416	335	43	.551
Wis.-Stout	83	245	416	33	.377
Wis.-Whitewater	78	408	235	21	.630
Wittenberg	109	636	324	32	.657
Wooster	104	451	388	41	.536
Worcester St.	18	107	67	0	.615
WPI	113	279	446	30	.389

Winningest Teams of the 2000s

(2000-01-02)

BY PERCENTAGE (TOP 26)

School	Yrs.	Won	Lost	Pct.
Mount Union	3	42	0	1.000
Bridgewater (Va.)	3	33	4	.892
Mary Hardin-Baylor	3	27	4	.871
St. Norbert	3	27	4	.871
Wittenberg	3	33	5	.868
Linfield	3	26	4	.867
Widener	3	32	5	.865
Central (Iowa)	3	29	5	.853
Hardin-Simmons	3	28	5	.848
Rowan	3	28	5	.848
Trinity (Tex.)	3	33	6	.846
Thomas More	3	27	5	.844
Wartburg	3	27	5	.844
Worcester St.	3	26	5	.839
St. John's (Minn.)	3	36	7	.837
Amherst	3	20	4	.833
Williams	3	20	4	.833
Wash. & Jeff.	3	29	6	.829
Brockport St.	3	27	6	.818
Western Conn. St.	3	25	6	.806
Ripon	3	24	6	.800
McDaniel	3	27	7	.794
Wabash	3	26	7	.788
Lycoming	3	21	6	.778
Augustana (Ill.)	3	24	7	.774
Millikin	3	24	7	.774

BY VICTORIES (TOP 30)

School	Yrs.	Won	Lost	Pct.
Mount Union	3	42	0	1.000
St. John's (Minn.)	3	36	7	.837
Bridgewater (Va.)	3	33	4	.892
Trinity (Tex.)	3	33	6	.846
Wittenberg	3	33	5	.868
Widener	3	32	5	.865
Central (Iowa)	3	29	5	.853
Wash. & Jeff.	3	29	6	.829
Hardin-Simmons	3	28	5	.848
Rowan	3	28	5	.848
Brockport St.	3	27	6	.818

School	Yrs.	Won	Lost	Pct.
Mary Hardin-Baylor	3	27	4	.871
McDaniel	3	27	7	.794
St. Norbert	3	27	4	.871
Thomas More	3	27	5	.844
Wartburg	3	27	5	.844
John Carroll	3	26	8	.765
Linfield	3	26	4	.867
Muhlenberg	3	26	8	.765
Wabash	3	26	7	.788
Worcester St.	3	26	5	.839
Ithaca	3	25	8	.758
Western Conn. St.	3	25	6	.806
Augustana (Ill.)	3	24	7	.774
Bethel (Minn.)	3	24	8	.750
King's (Pa.)	3	24	10	.706
MacMurray	3	24	8	.750
Millikin	3	24	7	.774
Ripon	3	24	6	.800
Wheaton (Ill.)	3	24	8	.750

Winningest Teams of the 1990s

Won-lost-tied record includes postseason games

BY PERCENTAGE (TOP 25)

(Minimum seven seasons as Division III member)

School	Yrs.	Won	Lost	Tied	Pct.
Mount Union	10	120	7	1	.941
Williams	10	70	8	2	.888
Central (Iowa)	10	91	15	0	.858
Allegheny	10	93	16	1	.850
Albion	10	83	14	2	.848
St. John's (Minn.)	10	97	17	1	.848
Salve Regina	7	53	10	0	.841
Wittenberg	10	86	17	1	.832
Lycoming	10	91	19	1	.824
Wis.-La Crosse	10	93	20	1	.820
Union (N.Y.)	10	80	18	0	.816
Rowan	10	99	23	1	.809
Wash. & Jeff.	10	89	21	0	.809
Emory & Henry	10	81	22	0	.786
Wartburg	10	81	23	0	.779
Ill. Wesleyan	10	72	21	1	.771
Carnegie Mellon	10	77	23	0	.770
John Carroll	10	76	22	4	.765
Baldwin-Wallace	10	76	24	1	.757
Augustana (Ill.)	10	71	23	0	.755
Buffalo St.	10	78	26	0	.750
Hanover	8	62	21	0	.747
Coe	10	73	25	0	.745
Dickinson	10	75	25	2	.745
Ithaca	10	79	27	0	.745

BY VICTORIES (TOP 28)

School	Yrs.	Won	Lost	Tied	Pct.
Mount Union	10	120	7	1	.941
Rowan	10	99	23	1	.809
St. John's (Minn.)	10	97	17	1	.848
Allegheny	10	93	16	1	.850
Wis.-La Crosse	10	93	20	1	.820
Central (Iowa)	10	91	15	0	.858
Lycoming	10	91	19	1	.824
Wash. & Jeff.	10	89	21	0	.809
Wittenberg	10	86	17	1	.832
Albion	10	83	14	2	.848
Emory & Henry	10	81	22	0	.786
Wartburg	10	81	23	0	.779
Union (N.Y.)	10	80	18	0	.816
Ithaca	10	79	27	0	.745
Buffalo St.	10	78	26	0	.750
Carnegie Mellon	10	77	23	0	.770
Baldwin-Wallace	10	76	24	1	.757
Frostburg St.	10	76	26	2	.740
John Carroll	10	76	22	4	.765
Simpson	10	76	27	1	.736
Dickinson	10	75	25	2	.745
Coe	10	73	25	0	.745
Ill. Wesleyan	10	72	21	1	.771
Wis.-Whitewater	10	72	28	0	.720

School	Yrs.	Won	Lost	Tied	Pct.
Augustana (Ill.)	10	71	23	0	.755
Hardin-Simmons	10	71	27	0	.724
Plymouth St.	10	71	29	2	.706
Wesley	10	71	30	1	.701

National Poll Rankings

Final Poll Leaders

(Released Before Division Championship Playoffs)

Year	Team (Record*)	Coach	Record in Championship†
1975	Ithaca (8-0-0)	Jim Butterfield	2-1 Runner-up
1976	St. John's (Minn.) (7-0-1)	John Gagliardi	3-0 Champion
1977	Wittenberg (8-0-0)	Dave Maurer	Did not compete
1978	Minn.-Morris (9-0-0)	Al Molde	1-1 Lost in semifinals
1979	Wittenberg (8-0-0)	Dave Maurer	2-1 Runner-up
1980	Ithaca (10-0-0)	Jim Butterfield	2-1 Runner-up
1981	Widener (9-0-0)	Bill Manlove	3-0 Champion
1982	Baldwin-Wallace (10-0-0)	Bob Packard	0-1 Lost in first round
1983	Augustana (Ill.) (9-0-0)	Bob Reade	3-0 Champion
1984	Augustana (Ill.) (9-0-0)	Bob Reade	3-0 Champion
1985	Augustana (Ill.) (9-0-0)	Bob Reade	4-0 Champion
1986	Dayton (10-0-0)	Mike Kelly	0-1 Lost in first round
1987	Augustana (Ill.) (9-0-0)	Bob Reade	1-1 Lost in quarterfinals
1988	**East Region**		
	Cortland St. (9-0-0)	Dennis Kayser	1-1 Lost in quarterfinals
	North Region		
	Dayton (9-1-0)	Mike Kelly	0-1 Lost in first round
	South Region		
	Ferrum (9-0-0)	Hank Norton	2-1 Lost in semifinals
	West Region		
	Central (Iowa) (8-0-0)	Ron Schipper	3-1 Runner-up
1989	**East Region**		
	Union (N.Y.) (9-0-0)	Al Bagnoli	3-1 Runner-up
	North Region		
	Dayton (8-0-1)	Mike Kelly	4-0 Champion
	South Region		
	Rhodes (7-0-0)	Mike Clary	Did not compete
	West Region		
	Central (Iowa) (8-0-0)	Ron Schipper	1-1 Lost in quarterfinals
1990	**East Region**		
	Hofstra (9-0-0)	Joe Gardi	2-1 Lost in semifinals
	North Region		
	Dayton (9-0-0)	Mike Kelly	1-1 Lost in quarterfinals
	South Region		
	Ferrum (8-0-0)	Hank Norton	0-1 Lost in first round
	West Region		
	Wis.-Whitewater (9-0-0)	Bob Berezowitz	0-1 Lost in first round
1991	**East Region**		
	Ithaca (7-1-0)	Jim Butterfield	4-0 Champion
	North Region		
	Allegheny (10-0-0)	Ken O'Keefe	1-1 Lost in quarterfinals
	South Region		
	Lycoming (8-0-0)	Frank Girardi	1-1 Lost in quarterfinals
	West Region		
	St. John's (Minn.) (9-0-0)	John Gagliardi	2-1 Lost in semifinals
1992	**East Region**		
	Rowan (9-0-0)	John Bunting	2-1 Lost in semifinals
	North Region		
	Dayton (9-0-0)	Mike Kelly	0-1 Lost in first round
	South Region		
	Wash. & Jeff. (8-0-0)	John Luckhardt	3-1 Runner-up
	West Region		
	Central (Iowa) (9-0-0)	Ron Schipper	1-1 Lost in quarterfinals
1993	**East Region**		
	Rowan (7-1-0)	K. C. Keeler	3-1 Runner-up
	North Region		
	Mount Union (9-0-0)	Larry Kehres	4-0 Champion
	South Region		
	Wash. & Jeff. (8-0-0)	John Luckhardt	2-1 Lost in semifinals
	West Region		
	Wis.-La Crosse (9-0-0)	Roger Harring	1-1 Lost in quarterfinals
1994	**East Region**		
	Plymouth St. (9-0-0)	Don Brown	1-1 Lost in quarterfinals
	North Region		
	Allegheny (9-0-0)	Ken O'Keefe	0-1 Lost in first round
	South Region		
	Dickinson (9-0-0)	Darwin Breaux	0-1 Lost in first round
	West Region		
	Central (Iowa) (9-0-0)	Ron Schipper	0-1 Lost in first round
1995	**East Region**		
	Buffalo St. (8-1-0)	Jerry Boyes	0-1 Lost in first round

Year	Team (Record*)	Coach	Record in Championship†
	North Region		
	Mount Union (9-0-0)	Larry Kehres	2-1 Lost in semifinals
	South Region		
	Wash. & Jeff. (7-0-0)	John Luckhardt	2-1 Lost in semifinals
	West Region		
	Wis.-La Crosse (9-0-0)	Roger Harring	4-0 Champion
1996	**East Region**		
	Buffalo St. (7-1)	Jerry Boyes	0-1 Lost in first round
	North Region		
	Mount Union (9-0)	Larry Kehres	4-0 Champion
	South Region		
	Lycoming (8-0)	Frank Girardi	2-1 Lost in semifinals
	West Region		
	Wis.-La Crosse (9-0)	Roger Harring	2-1 Lost in semifinals
1997	**East Region**		
	Rowan (8-0)	K.C. Keeler	2-1 Lost in semifinals
	North Region		
	Mount Union (9-0)	Larry Kehres	4-0 Champion
	South Region		
	Lycoming (8-0)	Frank Girardi	3-1 Runner-up

Year	Team (Record*)	Coach	Record in Championship†
	West Region		
	Wis.-Whitewater (9-0)	Bob Berezowitz	0-1 Lost in first round
1998	**East Region**		
	Springfield (9-0)	Mike DeLong	0-1 Lost in first round
	North Region		
	Mount Union (10-0)	Larry Kehres	4-0 Champion
	South Region		
	Lycoming (8-0)	Frank Girardi	1-1 Lost in quarterfinals
	West Region		
	Central (Iowa) (9-0)	Rich Kacmarynski	0-1 Lost in first round
1999	Mount Union (10-0)	Larry Kehres	2-1 Lost in semifinals
2000	Mount Union (10-0)	Larry Kehres	4-0 Champion
2001	Mount Union (10-0)	Larry Kehres	4-0 Champion
2002	Mount Union (10-0)	Larry Kehres	4-0 Champion

*Final poll record. †Number of teams in the championship: 8 (1975-84); 16 (1985-98); 28 (1999-02).
Poll conducted by the NCAA Division III Football Committee through 1998. The American Football Coaches Association supplied poll beginning in 1999.

Undefeated, Untied Teams

(Regular-Season Games Only)

Following is a list of undefeated and untied teams since 1973, when College Division teams were divided into Division II and Division III under a three-division reorganization plan adopted by the special NCAA Convention in August 1973. Since 1981, conference playoff games have been included in a team's won-lost record (previously, such games were considered postseason contests). Figures indicate the regular-season wins (minimum seven games against four-year varsity opponents). A subsequent postseason win(s) in the Division III championship or a conference playoff game (before 1981) is indicated by (*), a loss by (†) and a tie by (‡).

Year	College	Wins
1973	Fisk	9
	Wittenberg	***9
1974	Albany (N.Y.)	9
	Central (Iowa)	**9
	Frank. & Marsh.	9
	Ithaca	*†9
	Towson	10
1975	Cal Lutheran	*†9
	Ithaca	**†8
	Widener	*†9
	Wittenberg	†***9
1976	Albion	9
1977	Central (Iowa)	†9
	Cornell College	†8
	Wittenberg	†9
1978	Baldwin-Wallace	‡***8
	Illinois Col.	9
	Minn.-Morris	*†10
	Wittenberg	‡***8
1979	Carnegie Mellon	*†9
	Dubuque	†9
	Jamestown	7
	Tufts	8
	Widener	*†9
	Wittenberg	***†8
1980	Adrian	9
	Baldwin-Wallace	†9
	Bethany (W.Va.)	†9
	Dayton	***11
	Ithaca	**†10
	Millsaps	9
	Widener	*†10
1981	Alfred	†10
	Augustana (Ill.)	†9

Year	College	Wins
	Lawrence	*†9
	West Ga.	†9
	Widener	***10
1982	Augustana (Ill.)	**†9
	Baldwin-Wallace	†10
	Plymouth St.	10
	St. John's (Minn.)	9
	St. Lawrence	*†9
	Wabash	10
	West Ga.	***9
1983	Augustana (Ill.)	***9
	Carnegie Mellon	†9
	Hofstra	†10
	WPI	8
1984	Amherst	8
	Augustana (Ill.)	***9
	Case Reserve	9
	Central (Iowa)	**†9
	Dayton	†10
	Hope	9
	Occidental	†10
	Plymouth St.	†10
1985	Augustana (Ill.)	****9
	Carnegie Mellon	†8
	Central (Iowa)	**†9
	Denison	†10
	Lycoming	†10
	Mount Union	*†10
	Union (N.Y.)	†9
1986	Central (Iowa)	*†10
	Dayton	†10
	Ithaca	**†9
	Mount Union	*†10
	Salisbury	***†10
	Susquehanna	*†10
	Union (N.Y.)	†9
1987	Augustana (Ill.)	*†9
	Gust. Adolphus	†10
	Wash. & Jeff.	*†9
1988	Cortland St.	*†10
	Ferrum	***†9
1989	Central (Iowa)	*†9
	Millikin	*†9
	Union (N.Y.)	***†10
	Williams	8
1990	Carnegie Mellon	†10
	Dayton	*†10
	Hofstra	**†10
	Lycoming	***†9
	Mount Union	†10
	Wash. & Jeff.	*†9
	Williams	8
	Wis.-Whitewater	†10
1991	Allegheny	*†10

Year	College	Wins
	Baldwin-Wallace	†10
	Dayton	***†10
	Dickinson	†10
	Eureka	†10
	Lycoming	*†9
	Mass.-Lowell	†10
	St. John's (Minn.)	**†9
	Simpson	†10
	Thomas More	10
	Union (N.Y.)	*†9
1992	Aurora	†9
	Central (Iowa)	*†9
	Cornell College	10
	Dayton	†10
	Emory & Henry	*†10
	Ill. Wesleyan	*†9
	Mount Union	**†10
	Rowan	**†10
1993	Albion	*†9
	Anderson (Ind.)	†10
	Coe	†10
	Mount Union	****†10
	St. John's (Minn.)	**†10
	Trinity (Conn.)	8
	Union (N.Y.)	†9
	Wash. & Jeff.	**†9
	Wilkes	†10
	Wis.-La Crosse	**†10
1994	Albion	****9
	Allegheny	†10
	Central (Iowa)	†10
	Dickinson	†10
	La Verne	†9
	Plymouth St.	*†9
	Trinity (Tex.)	†10
	Williams	8
1995	Central (Iowa)	†10
	Hanover	†10
	La Verne	9
	Mount Union	**†10
	Plymouth St.	†9
	Thomas More	10
	Wash. & Jeff.	**†8
	Wheaton (Ill.)	*†9
	Wis.-La Crosse	****†10
	Wittenberg	†10
1996	Albion	†9
	Allegheny	†10
	Ill. Wesleyan	*†9
	Lycoming	**†9
	Mount Union	****†10
	St. John's (Minn.)	*†10
	Salve Regina	9
	Simpson	†10

DIVISION III

Year	College	Wins	Year	College	Wins	Year	College	Wins
	Worcester St.	†10		Williams	8		Wittenberg	**†10
1997	Catholic	†10	1999	Bridgewater St.	†10	2001	Bridgewater (Va.)	***†9
	Hanover	†10		Hanover	†10		Mount Union	****†10
	Lakeland	10		Hardin-Simmons	**†10		Rensselaer	†8
	Lycoming	***†9		Lycoming	†9		Thomas More	*†10
	McDaniel	†10		McDaniel	*†10		Wash. & Jeff.	*†10
	Mount Union	****†10		Mount Union	**†10		Westfield St.	†10
	Rowan	**†9		Rensselaer	†9		Widener	**†10
	Simpson	**†10		Trinity (Tex.)	**†10		Williams	8
	Trinity (Tex.)	*†9		Wartburg	†10	2002	Bridgewater (Va.)	*†10
	Wis.-Whitewater	†9		Western Conn. St.	†10		Hanover	†10
1998	Catholic	†10		Wittenberg	*†10		Linfield	*†9
	Central (Iowa)	†10	2000	Bethel (Minn.)	†10		MacMurray	†10
	Emory & Henry	10		Brockport St.	†8		Mary Hardin-Baylor	†10
	Grinnell	10		Central (Iowa)	**†10		Mass.-Dartmouth	†10
	Lycoming	*†9		Hardin-Simmons	***†10		Mount Union	****†10
	McDaniel	†10		Linfield	†9		Rowan	†10
	Mount Union	****†10		Mount Union	****†10		Trinity (Tex.)	****†10
	St. John's (Minn.)	*†10		St. Norbert	†10		Wabash	**†10
	Trinity (Tex.)	**†10		Wis.-Stout	†10			

The Spoilers

(Since 1973, when the three-division reorganization plan was adopted by the special NCAA Convention, creating Divisions II and III.)

Following is a list of the spoilers of Division III teams that lost their perfect (undefeated, untied) record in their **season-ending** game, including the Division III championship playoffs. An asterisk (*) indicates a Division III championship playoff game and a dagger (†) indicates the home team in a regular-season game or a conference playoff. A game involving two undefeated, untied teams is in **bold face**.

Date	Spoiler	Victim	Score
11-17-73	† Williams	Amherst	30-14
12-7-74	* Central (Iowa)	Ithaca	10-8
11-8-75	Cornell College	† Lawrence	17-16
11-22-75	* **Ithaca**	**Widener**	23-14
12-6-75	* Wittenberg	Ithaca	28-0
11-12-77	Norwich	† Middlebury	34-20
11-12-77	Ripon	† Cornell College	10-7
11-19-77	† Baldwin-Wallace	Wittenberg	14-7
11-19-77	* Widener	Central (Iowa)	19-0
11-25-78	* Wittenberg	Minn.-Morris	35-14
11-17-79	* Ithaca	Dubuque	27-7
11-17-79	‡ Findlay	Jamestown	41-15
11-24-79	* **Wittenberg**	**Widener**	17-14
11-24-79	* Ithaca	Carnegie Mellon	15-6
12-1-79	* Ithaca	Wittenberg	28-0
11-8-80	DePauw	† Wabash	tie 22-22
11-22-80	* **Widener**	**Bethany (W.Va.)**	43-12
11-22-80	* Dayton	Baldwin-Wallace	34-0
11-29-80	* Dayton	Widener	28-24
12-6-80	#* Dayton	Ithaca	63-0
11-14-81	† DePauw	Wabash	21-14
11-14-81	† St. Mary's (Cal.)	San Diego	31-14
11-21-81	* Widener	West Ga.	10-3
11-21-81	* Dayton	Augustana (Ill.)	19-7
11-21-81	* Montclair St.	Alfred	13-12
11-28-81	* Dayton	Lawrence	38-0
11-13-82	† Widener	Swarthmore	24-7
11-20-82	‡ Northwestern (Iowa)	St. John's (Minn.)	33-28
11-20-82	* **Augustana (Ill.)**	**Baldwin-Wallace**	28-22
11-27-82	* **Augustana (Ill.)**	**St. Lawrence**	14-0
12-4-82	* **West Ga.**	**Augustana (Ill.)**	14-0
11-19-83	* Salisbury	Carnegie Mellon	16-14
11-19-83	* Union (N.Y.)	Hofstra	51-19
11-10-84	St. John's (N.Y.)	† Hofstra	19-16
11-10-84	† St. Olaf	Hamline	tie 7-7
11-17-84	* Union (N.Y.)	Plymouth St.	26-14
11-17-84	* Central (Iowa)	Occidental	23-22
11-17-84	* Augustana (Ill.)	Dayton	14-13
12-8-84	* **Augustana (Ill.)**	**Central (Iowa)**	21-12
11-23-85	* Gettysburg	Lycoming	14-10
11-23-85	* **Mount Union**	**Denison**	35-3
11-23-85	* Salisbury	Carnegie Mellon	35-22
11-23-85	* Ithaca	Union (N.Y.)	13-12
11-30-85	* **Augustana (Ill.)**	**Mount Union**	21-14
12-7-85	* **Augustana (Ill.)**	**Central (Iowa)**	14-7
11-15-86	† Lawrence	Coe	14-10
11-22-86	* **Mount Union**	**Dayton**	42-36
11-22-86	* **Ithaca**	**Union (N.Y.)**	(ot) 24-17
11-29-86	* Concordia-M'head	Central (Iowa)	17-14
11-29-86	* **Salisbury**	**Susquehanna**	31-17

Date	Spoiler	Victim	Score
11-29-86	* **Augustana (Ill.)**	**Mount Union**	16-7
12-6-86	* Salisbury	Ithaca	44-40
12-13-86	* Augustana (Ill.)	Salisbury	31-3
11-11-87	St. Norbert	† Monmouth (Ill.)	20-15
11-21-87	* St. John's (Minn.)	Gust. Adolphus	7-3
11-28-87	* Emory & Henry	Wash. & Jeff.	23-16
11-28-87	$* Dayton	Augustana (Ill.)	38-36
11-12-88	† St. Norbert	Monmouth (Ill.)	12-0
11-19-88	Coast Guard	† Plymouth St.	28-19
11-26-88	* Ithaca	Cortland St.	24-17
12-3-88	* Ithaca	Ferrum	62-28
11-11-89	† Baldwin-Wallace	John Carroll	25-19
11-11-89	† **Bridgewater St.**	**Mass.-Lowell**	14-10
11-11-89	† Centre	Rhodes	13-10
11-18-89	† Alfred	Bridgewater St.	30-27
11-25-89	* St. John's (Minn.)	Central (Iowa)	27-24
11-25-89	* Dayton	Millikin	28-16
12-9-89	* Dayton	Union (N.Y.)	17-7
11-10-90	Col. of New Jersey	† Ramapo	9-0
11-10-90	† Waynesburg	Frostburg St.	28-18
11-17-90	* Allegheny	Mount Union	26-15
11-17-90	* **Lycoming**	**Carnegie Mellon**	17-7
11-17-90	* St. Thomas (Minn.)	Wis.-Whitewater	24-23
11-24-90	* Allegheny	Dayton	31-23
11-24-90	* **Lycoming**	**Wash. & Jeff.**	24-0
12-1-90	* Lycoming	Hofstra	20-10
12-8-90	* Allegheny	Lycoming	(ot) 21-14
11-9-91	† Coe	Beloit	26-10
11-23-91	* **Union (N.Y.)**	**Mass.-Lowell**	55-16
11-23-91	* **Dayton**	**Baldwin-Wallace**	27-10
11-30-91	* **Dayton**	**Allegheny**	(ot) 28-25
11-30-91	* Ithaca	Union (N.Y.)	35-23
11-30-91	* Susquehanna	Lycoming	31-24
12-7-91	* **Dayton**	**St. John's (Minn.)**	19-7
12-14-91	* Ithaca	Dayton	34-20
11-7-92	Cornell College	† Coe	37-20
11-7-92	Union (N.Y.)	† Rochester	14-10
11-21-92	* **Ill. Wesleyan**	**Aurora**	21-12
11-21-92	* **Mount Union**	**Dayton**	27-10
11-28-92	* **Mount Union**	**Ill. Wesleyan**	49-27
11-28-92	* Wash. & Jeff.	Emory & Henry	51-15
11-28-92	* Wis.-La Crosse	Central (Iowa)	34-9
12-5-92	* Wash. & Jeff.	Rowan	18-13
12-5-92	* Wis.-La Crosse	Mount Union	29-24
10-30-93	Mount Senario	† Martin Luther	21-20
11-13-93	Hastings	† Colorado Col.	22-21
11-20-93	* **Albion**	**Anderson (Ind.)**	41-21
11-20-93	* **St. John's (Minn.)**	**Coe**	32-14
11-20-93	* Frostburg St.	Wilkes	26-25
11-20-93	* Wm. Paterson	Union (N.Y.)	17-7
11-27-93	* **Mount Union**	**Albion**	30-16
11-27-93	* **St. John's (Minn.)**	**Wis.-La Crosse**	47-25
12-5-93	* **Mount Union**	**St. John's (Minn.)**	56-8
12-5-93	* Rowan	Wash. & Jeff.	23-16
11-12-94	John Carroll	† Baldwin-Wallace	9-0
11-19-94	* Mount Union	Allegheny	28-19
11-19-94	* Wartburg	Central (Iowa)	22-21
11-19-94	* St. John's (Minn.)	La Verne	51-12
11-19-94	* Widener	Dickinson	14-0
11-19-94	* Wash. & Jeff.	Trinity (Tex.)	28-0

Date	Spoiler	Victim	Score
11-26-94	* Ithaca	Plymouth St.	22-7
11-11-95	Amherst	† Williams	0-0
11-18-95	* **Mount Union**	**Hanover**	52-18
11-18-95	* **Wheaton (Ill.)**	**Wittenberg**	63-41
11-18-95	* Wis.-River Falls	Central (Iowa)	10-7
11-18-95	* Union (N.Y.)	Plymouth St.	24-7
11-25-95	* **Mount Union**	**Wheaton (Ill.)**	40-14
12-2-95	* **Wis.-La Crosse**	**Mount Union**	20-17
12-2-95	* Rowan	Wash. & Jeff.	28-15
11-9-96	Williams	† Amherst	19-13
11-23-96	Ithaca	Worcester St.	27-21
11-23-96	* **Mount Union**	**Allegheny**	31-26
11-23-96	* **Ill. Wesleyan**	**Albion**	23-20
11-23-96	* **St. John's (Minn.)**	**Simpson**	21-18
11-30-96	* **Mount Union**	**Ill. Wesleyan**	49-14
11-30-96	* Wis.-La Crosse	St. John's (Minn.)	37-30
12-7-96	* Rowan	Lycoming	33-14
11-1-97	† Cornell College	Coe	28-21
11-8-97	† Williams	Amherst	48-46
11-15-97	† **Catholic**	**Albright**	44-22
11-22-97	* John Carroll	Hanover	30-20
11-22-97	* **Simpson**	**Wis.-Whitewater**	34-31
11-22-97	* **Lycoming**	**McDaniel**	27-13
11-22-97	* **Trinity (Tex.)**	**Catholic**	44-33
11-29-97	* **Lycoming**	**Trinity (Tex.)**	46-26
12-6-97	* **Mount Union**	**Simpson**	54-7
12-6-97	* **Lycoming**	**Rowan**	28-20
12-13-97	* **Mount Union**	**Lycoming**	61-12
11-14-98	DePauw	† Wabash	42-7
11-14-98	MacMurray	† Westminster (Mo.)	52-51
11-21-98	* **Lycoming**	**Catholic**	49-14
11-21-98	* Wis.-Eau Claire	Central (Iowa)	28-21
11-21-98	* **Trinity (Tex.)**	**McDaniel**	30-20
11-28-98	* **Trinity (Tex.)**	**Lycoming**	37-21
11-28-98	* Wis.-Eau Claire	St. John's (Minn.)	10-7
11-28-98	* **Mount Union**	**Wittenberg**	21-19
12-5-98	* **Mount Union**	**Trinity (Tex.)**	34-29
11-13-99	Montclair St.	† Rowan	28-24
11-20-99	* Ohio Northern	Hanover	56-14
11-20-99	* Rowan	Rensselaer	29-10
11-20-99	* Ursinus	Bridgewater St.	43-38
11-20-99	* Wash. & Jeff.	Lycoming	14-7
11-27-99	* Ohio Northern	Wittenberg	58-24
11-27-99	* Montclair St.	Western Conn. St.	32-24
11-27-99	* Pacific Lutheran	Wartburg	49-14
11-27-99	* **Trinity (Tex.)**	**McDaniel**	20-16
12-4-99	* **Trinity (Tex.)**	**Hardin-Simmons**	40-33
12-11-99	* Rowan	Mount Union	(ot) 24-17
12-11-99	* Pacific Lutheran	Trinity (Tex.)	49-28
11-11-00	† Ill. Wesleyan	Millikin	10-8
11-18-00	* **Central (Iowa)**	**St. Norbert**	29-14
11-18-00	* Pacific Lutheran	Bethel (Minn.)	41-13
11-18-00	* St. John's (Minn.)	Wis.-Stout	26-19
11-25-00	* Springfield	Brockport St.	13-6
11-25-00	* **Central (Iowa)**	**Linfield**	(ot) 20-17
12-2-00	* St. John's (Minn.)	Central (Iowa)	21-18
12-2-00	* **Mount Union**	**Wittenberg**	32-15
12-9-00	* St. John's (Minn.)	Hardin-Simmons	38-14
11-10-01	† **Williams**	**Amherst**	(ot) 23-20
11-17-01	* Western Conn. St.	Westfield St.	8-7
11-24-01	* Wittenberg	Thomas More	41-0
11-24-01	* Ithaca	Rensselaer	27-10
11-24-01	* **Widener**	**Wash. & Jeff.**	46-30
12-1-01	* **Bridgewater (Va.)**	**Widener**	57-32
12-15-01	* **Mount Union**	**Bridgewater (Va.)**	30-27
11-23-02	* Muhlenberg	Mass.-Dartmouth	56-6
11-23-02	* Wittenberg	Hanover	34-33
11-23-02	* **Wabash**	**MacMurray**	42-7
11-23-02	* **Trinity (Tex.)**	**Mary Hardin-Baylor**	48-38
11-30-02	* Brockport St.	Rowan	15-12
12-7-02	* **Mount Union**	**Wabash**	45-16
12-7-02	* St. John's (Minn.)	Linfield	21-14
12-7-02	* **Trinity (Tex.)**	**Bridgewater (Va.)**	38-32
12-21-02	* **Mount Union**	**Trinity (Tex.)**	48-7

‡*NAIA championship playoff game. #Defeated three consecutive perfect-record teams in the Division III championship playoffs. $Ended Augustana's (Illinois) 60-game undefeated streak.*

Streaks and Rivalries

Longest Winning Streaks

(Minimum Two Seasons in Division III; Includes Postseason Games)

Wins	Team	Years
54	Mount Union	1996-99
42	Mount Union	2000-Current
37	Augustana (Ill.)	1983-85
24	Allegheny	1990-91
23	Wis.-La Crosse	1995-96
23	Williams	1988-91
22	Dayton	1989-90
22	Augustana (Ill.)	1986-87
21	Dayton	1979-81
20	Plymouth St.	1987-88
19	Mount Union	1993-94
19	Wis.-La Crosse	1992-93
19	Plymouth St.	1981-82
18	Lawrence	1980-81
18	Ithaca	1979-80

Longest Unbeaten Streaks

(Minimum Two Seasons in Division III; Includes Postseason Games)

No.	Wins	Ties	Team	Years
60	59	1	Augustana (Ill.)	1983-87
54	54	0	Mount Union	1996-99
42	42	0	Mount Union	2000-Current
25	24	1	Dayton	1989-90
24	24	0	Allegheny	1990-91
24	23	1	Wis.-La Crosse	1992-93
24	23	1	Wabash	1979-81
23	23	0	Wis.-La Crosse	1995-96
23	23	0	Williams	1988-91
22	21	1	Dayton	1979-81
21	20	1	Baldwin-Wallace	1977-79
20	20	0	Plymouth St.	1987-88
20	18	2	St. John's (Minn.)	1975-76

Longest Division III Series

Games	Opponents (Series leader listed first)	Series Record	First Game
117	Williams-Amherst	65-47-5	1881
116	Albion-Kalamazoo	78-34-4	1896
114	Bowdoin-Colby	62-43-9	1892
113	Monmouth (Ill.)-Knox	53-50-10	1891
112	Coe-Cornell College	56-52-4	1891
109	DePauw-Wabash	50-50-9	1890
108	Williams-Wesleyan (Conn.)	66-37-5	1881
108	Amherst-Wesleyan (Conn.)	58-41-9	1882
108	Hampden-Sydney—Randolph-Macon	53-44-11	1893
105	Bowdoin-Bates	60-38-7	1889
105	Colby-Bates	56-41-8	1893
104	Occidental—Pomona-Pitzer	55-46-3	1895
103	Hamline-Macalester	58-41-4	1887
102	Wesleyan (Conn.)-Trinity (Conn.)	52-49-1	1885
102	Ripon-Lawrence	48-47-7	1893

Trophy Games

Following is a list of the current Division III football trophy games. The games are listed alphabetically by the trophy-object name. The date refers to the season the trophy was first exchanged and is not necessarily the start of the competition between the participants.

Trophy	Date	Colleges
Academic Bowl	1986	Carnegie Mellon-Case Reserve
Admiral's Cup	1980	Maine Maritime-Mass. Maritime
Baird Bros. Golden Stringer	1984	Case Reserve-Wooster
Bell	1931	Franklin-Hanover
Bill Edwards Trophy	1989	Case Reserve-Wittenberg

DIVISION III

Trophy	Date	Colleges	Trophy	Date	Colleges
Bridge Bowl	1990	Mt. St. Joseph-Thomas More	Old Tin Cup	1954	Gettysburg-Muhlenberg
Bronze Turkey	1929	Knox-Monmouth (Ill.)	Old Water Bucket	1989	Maranatha Baptist-Martin Luther
CBB	1966	Bates, Bowdoin, Colby			
Conestoga Wagon	1963	Dickinson-Frank. & Marsh.	Paint Bucket	1965	Hamline-Macalester
Cortaca Jug	1959	Cortland St.-Ithaca	Pella Corporation Classic	1988	Central (Iowa)-William Penn
			President's Cup	1971	Case Reserve-John Carroll
Cranberry Bowl	1979	Bridgewater St.-Mass. Maritime	President's Cup	1982	Western New Eng.-Westfield St.
Doehling-Heselton Helmet	1988	Lawrence-Ripon	Regents Cup	1999	Frostburg St.-Salisbury
Drum	1940	Occidental—Pomona-Pitzer			
Dutchman's Shoes	1950	Rensselaer-Union (N.Y.)	Rhine River Cup	1992	Heidelberg-Otterbein
Edumund Orgill	1954	Rhodes-Sewanee	Secretary's Cup	1981	Coast Guard-Merchant Marine
			Shoes	1946	Occidental-Whittier
Founder's	1987	Chicago-Washington (Mo.)	Shot Glass	1938	Coast Guard-Rensselaer
Goat	1931	Carleton-St. Olaf	Soup Bowl	1997	Guilford-Greensboro
John Wesley	1984	Ky. Wesleyan-Union (Ky.)			
Keystone Cup	1981	Delaware Valley-Widener	Steve Dean Memorial	1976	Catholic-Georgetown
Little Brass Bell	1947	North Central-Wheaton (Ill.)	Totem Pole	1950	Pacific Lutheran-Puget Sound
			Transit	1980	Rensselaer-WPI
Little Brown Bucket	1938	Dickinson-Gettysburg	Victory Bell	1946	Loras-St. Thomas (Minn.)
Little Three	1971	Amherst, Wesleyan (Conn.), Williams	Victory Bell	1949	Upper Iowa-Wartburg
Mercer County Cup	1984	Grove City-Thiel			
Monon Bell	1932	DePauw-Wabash	Wadsworth	1977	Middlebury-Norwich
Mug	1931	Coast Guard-Norwich	Wagon Wheel	1949	Lewis & Clark-Willamette
			Wilford Moore Trophy	1997	Hardin-Simmons—McMurry
Old Goal Post	1953	Juniata-Susquehanna	Wilson Brothers Cup	1986	Hamline-St. Thomas (Minn.)
Old Musket	1964	Carroll (Wis.)-Carthage	Wooden Shoes	1946	Hope-Kalamazoo
Old Rocking Chair	1980	Hamilton-Middlebury			

Cliffhangers

Regular-season games won by Division III teams on the final play of the game in regulation time (from 1973). The extra point is listed when it provided the margin of victory after the winning touchdown.

Date	Opponents, Score	Game-Winning Play
9-22-73	Hofstra 21, Seton Hall 20	Tom Calder 15 pass from Steve Zimmer (Jim Hogan kick)
9-18-76	Ohio Wesleyan 23, DePauw 20	Tom Scurfield 48 pass from Bob Mauck
10-27-77	Albany (N.Y.) 42, Maine 39	Larry Leibowitz 19 FG
9-22-79	Augustana (Ill.) 19, Carthage 18	John Stockton 14 pass from Mark Schick
10-6-79	Carleton 17, Lake Forest 14	Tim Schoonmaker 46 FG
11-10-79	Dayton 24, St. Norbert 22	Jim Fullenkamp 21 FG
9-13-80	Cornell College 14, Lawrence 13	John Bryant 8 pass from Matt Dillon (Keith Koehler kick)
9-27-80	Muhlenberg 41, Johns Hopkins 38	Mickey Mottola 1 run
10-25-80	Mass.-Lowell 15, Marist 13	Ed Kulis 3 run
10-17-81	Carleton 22, Ripon 21	John Winter 23 pass from Billy Ford (Dave Grein kick)
10-2-82	Frostburg St. 10, Mercyhurst 7	Mike Lippold 34 FG
11-6-82	Williams 27, Wesleyan (Conn.) 24	Marc Hummon 33 pass from Robert Connolly
10-7-83	Johns Hopkins 19, Ursinus 17	John Tucker 10 pass from Mark Campbell
10-8-83	Susquehanna 17, Widener 14	Todd McCarthy 20 FG
10-29-83	Frank. & Marsh. 16, Swarthmore 15	Billy McLean 51 pass from Niall Rosenzweig
9-24-84	Muhlenberg 3, Frank. & Marsh. 0	Tom Mulroy 26 FG
9-14-85	Principia 26, Illinois Col. 22	Dan Sellers 48 pass from Jon Hinds
10-26-85	Buffalo 13, Brockport St. 11	Dan Friedman 37 FG
11-9-85	Frank. & Marsh. 29, Johns Hopkins 28	Brad Ramsey 1 run (Ken Scalet pass from John Travagline)
9-18-86	Beloit 16, Lakeland 13	Sean Saturnio 38 pass from Ed Limon
9-20-86	Susquehanna 43, Lycoming 42	Rob Sochovka 40 pass from Todd Coolidge (Randy Pozsar kick)
10-18-86	Ill. Wesleyan 25, Elmhurst 23	Dave Anderson 11 pass from Doug Moews
9-5-87	Wash. & Jeff. 17, Ohio Wesleyan 16	John Ivory 28 FG
9-26-87	Gust. Adolphus 19, Macalester 17	Dave Fuecker 8 pass from Dean Kraus
10-3-87	Wis.-Whitewater 10, Wis.-Platteville 7	Dave Emond 25 FG
10-24-87	Geneva 9, St. Francis (Pa.) 7	John Moores 19 FG
10-1-88	Canisius 17, Rochester 14	Jim Ehrig 34 FG
10-1-88	Cortland St. 24, Western Conn. St. 21	Ted Nagengast 35 FG
10-8-88	UC Santa Barb. 20, Sonoma St. 18	Harry Konstantinopoulos 52 FG
10-8-88	Hamilton 13, Bowdoin 10	Nate O'Steen 19 FG
11-5-88	Colby 20, Middlebury 18	Eric Aulenback 1 run
11-12-88	Wis.-River Falls 24, Wis.-Stout 23	Andy Feil 45 FG
10-7-89	Moravian 13, Juniata 10	Mike Howey 75 pass from Rob Light
10-21-89	Western New Eng. 17, Bentley 14	Leo Coughlin 17 FG
10-21-89	Thiel 19, Carnegie Mellon 14	Bill Barber 4 pass from Jeff Sorenson
9-8-90	Emory & Henry 22, Wash. & Lee 21	Todd Woodall 26 pass from Pat Walker
9-15-90	Otterbein 20, Capital 17	Korey Brown 39 FG
10-27-90	Hamline 26, Gust. Adolphus 24	Mike Sunnarborg 2 pass from Bob Hackney
11-10-90	Colby 23, Bowdoin 20	Paul Baisley 10 pass from Bob Ward
9-7-91	Central (Iowa) 26, Gust. Adolphus 25	Brian Krob 1 pass from Shad Flynn
9-13-91	St. John's (N.Y.) 30, Iona 27	John Ledwith 42 FG
10-5-91	Trinity (Conn.) 30, Williams 27	John Mullaney 5 pass from James Lane
10-26-91	DePauw 12, Anderson (Ind.) 7	Steve Broderick 65 pass from Brian Goodman
9-19-92	Lake Forest 9, North Park 7	Dave Mills 2 pass from Jim DeLisa
10-17-92	Elmhurst 30, North Central 28	Eric Ekstrom 2 pass from Jack Lamb
10-16-93	Union (N.Y.) 16, Rensselaer 13	Greg Harrison 38 FG
10-16-93	North Central 24, Elmhurst 22	Bryce Cann 35 FG
10-23-93	Stony Brook 21, Merchant Marine 20	Brian Hughes 44 FG
10-30-93	Thomas More 24, Defiance 18	Greg Stofko 6 blocked field goal return
9-10-94	Colorado Col. 16, Buena Vista 14	Josh Vitt 4 run
9-8-95	FDU-Florham 20, Johns Hopkins 17	Jason Herrick 37 FG
10-12-96	Defiance 20, Mt. St. Joseph 19	Randy Weldman 40 pass from Jeff Edred

Date	Opponents, Score	Game-Winning Play
9-13-97	Adrian 10, Heidelberg 7	Mike Hirvela 24 FG
10-25-97	Carthage 22, Millikin 17	Kris Norton 45 pass from Eric Corbett
11-15-97	WPI 9, Plymouth St. 7	Matt Surette 2 pass from John Riccio
9-12-98	Elmhurst 12, Ripon 10	Brendon Lyons 5 pass from Rasand Hall
9-19-98	Wis.-Oshkosh 41, Menlo 38	David Gaulke 31 FG
10-10-98	Baldwin-Wallace 38, Ohio Northern 35	Brian Hegnauer 44 FG
9-18-99	Springfield 41, Merchant Marine 35	Rob Dickson 6 blocked field goal return
10-2-99	Western Conn. St. 12, Plymouth St. 9	Adam Kennett 29 FG
10-7-00	Worcester St. 33, Mass. Maritime 31	Pat Arnold 21 pass from Cean Oksanish
9-15-01	Bluffton 23, Thiel 20	Adam Burgess 42 FG
11-11-01	Wabash 27, DePauw 21	Kurt Casper 52 pass from Jake Knott
11-2-02	Waynesburg 24, Frostburg St. 21	Brian Cence 35 FG

Overtime Games

In 1981, the NCAA Football Rules Committee approved an overtime tiebreaker system to decide a tie game for the purpose of determining a conference champion in regular-season play. In 1996, the tiebreaker became mandatory in all games tied after four periods.

2002 Division III Overtime Games

Date	Winner's Conference	Score (Loser's Conf.)	Number of OT Periods	Regulation Score
Sept. 7	Old Dominion	Randolph-Macon 17, Chowan (Dixie) 14	1OT	14-14
Sept. 7	Wisconsin	Wis.-Eau Claire 28, St. John's (Minn.) (Minnesota) 21	1OT	21-21
Sept. 7	Upper Midwest	Westminster (Mo.) 41, Maryville (Tenn.) (Independent) 38	1OT	35-35
Sept. 14	New Jersey	Col. of New Jersey 41, Cortland St. (New Jersey) 38	1OT	35-35
Sept. 14	NAIA	Azusa Pacific 44, Pacific Lutheran (Northwest) 42	3OT	29-29
Sept. 14	University Athletic	Carnegie Mellon 9, Grove City (Presidents') 6	1OT	3-3
Sept. 14	Centennial	Johns Hopkins 21, Wash. & Lee (Old Dominion) 14	1OT	14-14
Sept. 21	Northwest	Linfield 42, Southern Ore. (NAIA) 35	2OT	28-28
Sept. 21	Illinois & Wisconsin	Ill. Wesleyan 31, Washington (Mo.) (University Athletic) 24	1OT	24-24
Sept. 28	Illini-Badger	Benedictine (Ill.) 27, Greenville (Illini-Badger) 21	1OT	21-21
Sept. 28	Independent	Brockport St. 31, Frostburg St. (Atlantic Central) 25	3OT	25-25
Sept. 28	Middle Atlantic	Widener 27, Moravian (Middle Atlantic) 20	1OT	20-20
Oct. 5	New England	Salve Regina 20, Western New Eng. (New England) 14	1OT	14-14
Oct. 5	Southern Collegiate	Rhodes 34, Washington (Mo.) (University Athletic) 27	1OT	27-27
Oct. 5	Middle Atlantic	Widener 20, Lycoming (Middle Atlantic) 14	1OT	14-14
Oct. 5	Wisconsin	Wis.-Platteville 34, Wis.-Stout (Wisconsin) 31	1OT	28-28
Oct. 5	Illini-Badger	Eureka 22, Greenville (Illini-Badger) 16	1OT	16-16
Oct. 12	Middle Atlantic	FDU-Florham 34, Lycoming (Middle Atlantic) 28	1OT	28-28
Oct. 12	North Coast	Wabash 46, Wittenberg (North Coast) 43	1OT	43-43
Oct. 12	Northwest	Whitworth 44, Willamette (Northwest) 31	1OT	31-31
Oct. 12	Southern California	Redlands 42, Occidental (Southern California) 35	2OT	28-28
Oct. 12	Wisconsin	Wis.-La Crosse 35, Wis.-Platteville (Wisconsin) 28	1OT	28-28
Oct. 19	Old Dominion	Catholic 41, Frostburg St. (Atlantic Central) 35	1OT	35-35
Oct. 19	Dixie	Greensboro 24, Shenandoah (Dixie) 21	1OT	21-21
Oct. 19	Southern Collegiate	Rose-Hulman 35, Millsaps (Southern Collegiate) 28	1OT	28-28
Oct. 26	Freedom Football	Merchant Marine 20, Western Conn. St. (Freedom) 17	1OT	17-17
Oct. 26	Iowa	Upper Iowa 35, Cornell College (Iowa) 28	2OT	28-28
Oct. 26	New England Small College	Amherst 27, Tufts (New England Small College) 24	1OT	24-24
Oct. 26	Upstate Collegiate	Hobart 25, Alfred (Empire 8) 19	2OT	19-19
Oct. 26	Wisconsin	Wis.-Whitewater 23, Wis.-La Crosse (Wisconsin) 20	1OT	20-20
Nov. 2	Middle Atlantic	Lebanon Valley 33, Delaware Valley (Middle Atlantic) 26	1OT	26-26
Nov. 9	Illinois & Wisconsin	Augustana (Ill.) 34, Carthage (Illinois & Wisconsin) 28	1OT	28-28
Nov. 9	Southern California	Cal Lutheran 6, Occidental (Southern California) 0	2OT	0-0
Nov. 9	Wisconsin	Wis.-Stevens Point 34, Wis.-Platteville (Wisconsin) 28	1OT	28-28
Nov. 9	Independent	Menlo 32, Pacific Lutheran (Northwest) 29	1OT	29-29
Nov. 16	Middle Atlantic	Delaware Valley 35, FDU-Florham (Middle Atlantic) 29	4OT	14-14
Dec. 7	Ohio Athletic	John Carroll 16, Brockport St. (Independent) 10	1OT	10-10

Notes: 37 games (29 with one extra period, 5 with two extra periods, 2 with three extra periods, 1 with four extra periods) – average of 1.32 extra periods

Regular-Season Overtime Games

In 1981, the NCAA Football Rules Committee approved an overtime tiebreaker system to decide a tie game for the purpose of determining a conference champion in regular-season play. In 1996, the tiebreaker became mandatory in all games tied after four periods. The following conferences used the tiebreaker system from 1981 through 1995 to decide conference-only tie games. The number of overtimes is indicated in parentheses.

EASTERN COLLEGIATE FOOTBALL CONFERENCE

Date	Opponents, Score
10-28-95	Western New Eng. 6, Nichols 0 (4 ot)

IOWA INTERCOLLEGIATE ATHLETIC CONFERENCE

Date	Opponents, Score
9-26-81	William Penn 24, Wartburg 21 (1 ot)
9-25-82	Dubuque 16, Buena Vista 13 (1 ot)
10-2-82	Luther 25, Dubuque 22 (1 ot)
10-30-82	Wartburg 27, Dubuque 24 (3 ot)
10-4-86	Luther 28, Wartburg 21 (1 ot)
9-26-87	William Penn 19, Upper Iowa 13 (2 ot)
11-7-87	William Penn 17, Loras 10 (1 ot)
10-10-92	Simpson 20, Loras 14 (1 ot)
11-14-92	Luther 17, Buena Vista 10 (1 ot)

DIVISION III

MIDWEST CONFERENCE

Date	Opponents, Score
10-25-86	Lake Forest 30, Chicago 23 (1 ot)
10-26-86	Lawrence 7, Beloit 0 (1 ot)
9-30-89	Illinois Col. 26, Ripon 20 (3 ot)
10-27-90	Beloit 16, St. Norbert 10 (1 ot)
11-2-91	Monmouth (Ill.) 13, Knox 7 (1 ot)
10-29-94	Monmouth (Ill.) 26, Grinnell 20 (1 ot)
10-14-95	Beloit 20, Carroll (Wis.) 14 (1 ot)

NEW ENGLAND FOOTBALL CONFERENCE
(From 1987)

Date	Opponents, Score
10-31-87	Nichols 21, Mass.-Lowell 20 (1 ot)
9-17-88	Mass.-Lowell 22, Worcester St. 19 (2 ot)
9-30-89	Worcester St. 23, Mass.-Dartmouth 20 (1 ot)
10-27-89	Westfield St. 3, Mass.-Dartmouth 0 (3 ot)
10-28-89	Worcester St. 27, Nichols 20 (1 ot)
11-7-92	Mass.-Dartmouth 21, Westfield St. 14 (3 ot)
9-25-93	Mass. Maritime 28, Mass.-Dartmouth 21 (1 ot)
11-5-94	Mass.-Dartmouth 21, Westfield St. 14 (1 ot)

SOUTHERN CALIFORNIA INTERCOLLEGIATE ATHLETIC CONFERENCE

Date	Opponents, Score
10-18-86	La Verne 53, Occidental 52 (1 ot)
9-26-87	Claremont-M-S 33, Occidental 30 (1 ot)
10-27-90	Occidental 47, Claremont-M-S 41 (1 ot)
10-17-92	Cal Lutheran 17, Occidental 14 (1 ot)
10-30-93	Redlands 23, Cal Lutheran 17 (2 ot)

NUMBER OF DIVISION III OVERTIME GAMES BY YEAR

Year		Year	
1981	1	1992	4
1982	3	1993	2
1983	0	1994	2
1984	0	1995	2
1985	0	1996	20
1986	4	1997	32
1987	4	1998	23
1988	1	1999	16
1989	4	2000	7
1990	2	2001	15
1991	1	2002	37

Stadiums

STADIUMS LISTED ALPHABETICALLY BY SCHOOL

School	Stadium	Year Built	Capacity	Surface
Adrian	Maple	1960	5,000	Grass
Albion	Sprankle-Sprandel	1976	5,010	Grass
Albright	Eugene L. Shirk	1925	7,000	Grass
Alfred	Merrill Field	1926	5,000	Turf
Allegheny	Robertson Field	1948	5,000	Grass
Alma	Bahlke Field	1986	4,000	Turf
Amherst	Pratt Field	1891	8,000	Grass
Anderson (Ind.)	Macholtz	NA	4,200	Grass
Augsburg	Anderson-Nelson Field	1984	2,000	AstroTurf
Augustana (Ill.)	Ericson Field	1938	3,200	Grass
Aurora	Aurora Field	NA	1,500	Grass
Austin	Jerry Apple	2000	2,500	Grass
Averett	Hawkins Bradley	2000	5,000	Grass
Baldwin-Wallace	George Finnie	1971	8,100	StadiaTurf
Bates	Garcelon Field	1900	3,000	Grass
Beloit	Strong	1934	3,500	Grass
Benedictine (Ill.)	Alumni	1951	3,000	Grass
Bethany (W.Va.)	Bethany Field	1938	1,000	Grass
Bethel (Minn.)	Armstrong Stadium	1996	3,000	Grass
Blackburn	Blackburn College	NA	1,500	Grass
Bluffton	Salzman	1993	3,000	Grass
Bowdoin	Whittier Field	NA	9,000	Grass
Bridgewater St.	Swenson Field	1974	3,000	Grass
Bridgewater (Va.)	Jopson Field	1971	3,000	Grass
Brockport St.	Special Olympics	1979	10,000	Grass
Buena Vista	J. Leslie Rollins	1980	3,500	Grass
Buffalo St.	Coyer Field	NA	3,000	Grass
Cal Lutheran	Mt. Clef	1962	2,000	Grass
Capital	Bernlohr	1928	2,500	Grass
Carleton	Laird	1926	7,500	Grass
Carnegie Mellon	Gesling	1990	3,500	Omni-Turf
Carroll (Wis.)	Van Male Field	1976	4,200	Grass

School	Stadium	Year Built	Capacity	Surface
Carthage	Art Keller Field	1965	3,100	Grass
Case Reserve	E.L. Finningan Field	1968	3,000	Grass
Catholic	Cardinal Field	1985	3,500	Grass
Central (Iowa)	A.N. Kuyper	1977	5,000	Grass
Centre	Farris	1925	2,500	Grass
Chapman	Ernie Chapman	NA	3,000	Grass
Chicago	Stagg Field	1969	1,500	Grass
Chowan	James G. Garrison	NA	3,500	Grass
Chris. Newport	Christopher Newport	2001	3,200	Grass
Claremont-M-S	Zinda Field	1955	3,000	Grass
Coast Guard	Cadet Memorial Field	1932	4,500	Grass
Coe	Clark Field	1989	2,200	Grass
Colby	Seaverns	1948	5,000	Grass
Colorado Col.	Washburn Field	1898	2,000	Grass
Concordia (Ill.)	Concordia	NA	1,500	Field Turf
Concordia (Wis.)	Century	NA	2,500	Grass
Concordia-M'head	Jake Christiansen	NA	7,500	Grass
Cornell College	Ash Park Field	1922	2,500	Grass
Cortland St.	Cortland Stadium Complex	2002	6,500	SprinTurf
Curry	D. Forbes Will Field	NA	1,500	Grass
Defiance	Justin F. Coressel	1994	4,000	Grass
Delaware Valley	James Work Memorial	1978	4,500	Grass
Denison	Deeds Field	1922	5,000	Grass
DePauw	Blackstock	1941	4,000	Grass
Dickinson	Biddle Field	1909	2,577	Grass
Dubuque	Chalmers Field	1942	2,800	PAT
Earlham	M.O. Ross Field	1975	1,500	Grass
East Tex. Baptist	Ornelas	2000	2,950	Grass
Eastern Ore.	Community	NA	3,000	Grass
Elmhurst	Langhorst Field	1920	2,500	Grass
Emory & Henry	Fullerton Field	NA	5,500	Grass
Eureka	McKinzie	1913	3,000	Grass
FDU-Florham	Robert T. Shields	1973	4,000	Grass
Ferrum	W. B. Adams	1970	5,500	Grass
Fitchburg St.	Robert Elliot	1984	1,200	Grass
Framingham St.	Maple Street Field	NA	1,500	Grass
Franklin	Goodell Field	1889	2,000	Grass
Frank. & Marsh.	Sponaugle-Williamson Field	1920	4,000	Grass
Frostburg St.	Bobcat	1974	4,000	Grass
Gettysburg	Musselman	1965	6,176	Grass
Greensboro	Jamieson	NA	10,000	Grass
Greenville	Francis Field	NA	2,000	NA
Grinnell	Rosenbloom Field	1911	1,750	Grass
Grove City	Thorn Field	1981	3,500	Grass
Guilford	Armfield Athletic Center	1960	3,500	Grass
Gust. Adolphus	Hollingsworth Field	1929	4,500	Grass
Hamilton	Steuben Field	NA	2,500	Grass
Hamline	Norton	1921	2,000	Grass
Hampden-Sydney	Hundley	1964	2,400	Grass
Hanover	L.S. Ayers Field	1973	4,000	Grass
Hardin-Simmons	Shelton	1993	4,000	Grass
Hartwick	All-Weather Field	1985	1,200	AstroTurf
Heidelberg	Frost-Kalnow	1941	7,500	Grass
Hiram	Charles Henry Field	1958	3,000	Grass
Hobart	Boswell Field	1975	4,500	Grass
Hope	Holland Municipal	1979	5,322	Grass
Howard Payne	Gordon Wood	NA	7,600	Grass
Illinois Col.	England Field	1960	2,500	Grass
Ill. Wesleyan	Ill. Wesleyan	1893	3,500	Grass
Ithaca	Jim Butterfield	1958	5,000	Grass
John Carroll	Don Shula	2002	6,000	Turf
Johns Hopkins	Homewood Field	1906	8,000	Turf
Juniata	Chuck Knox	1988	3,000	Grass
Kalamazoo	Angell Field	1946	3,000	Grass
Kean	Zweidinger Field	NA	2,200	Grass
Kenyon	McBride Field	1962	2,500	Grass
King's (Pa.)	Monarch Field	NA	3,000	Grass
Knox	Knox Bowl	1968	6,000	Grass
La Verne	Ortmayer	1991	1,500	Grass
Lake Forest	Farwell Field	NA	2,000	Grass
Lakeland	John Taylor Field	1958	1,500	Grass
Lawrence	Banta Bowl	1965	5,255	Grass
Lebanon Valley	Arnold Field	1969	2,500	Grass
Lewis & Clark	Griswold	NA	3,700	Turf
Linfield	Maxwell Field	1922	4,000	Grass
Loras	Rock Bowl	1945	3,000	Grass
Luther	Carlson	1966	5,000	Grass
Lycoming	Person Field	1962	2,500	Grass
Macalester	Macalester	1965	4,000	Grass
MacMurray	MacMurray Field	1984	5,000	Grass
Maine Maritime	Ritchie	1965	3,500	Turf
Manchester	Burt Memorial	NA	4,500	Grass

School	Stadium	Year Built	Capacity	Surface
Maranatha Baptist	Maranatha	NA	3,000	Grass
Marietta	Don Drumm Field	1935	7,000	Grass
Martin Luther	MLC Bowl	NA	1,500	Grass
Mary Hardin-Baylor	Tiger Field	1996	7,000	Grass
Maryville (Tenn.)	Thornton-Honaker Field	1951	2,500	Grass
Mass.-Dartmouth	University	NA	1,850	Grass
MIT	Henry G. Steinbrenner	1980	1,600	Grass
Mass. Maritime	Edward Ellis Field	1972	3,000	Grass
McDaniel	Scott S. Bair	1981	4,000	Grass
McMurry	Indian	1937	4,500	Grass
Menlo	Conner Field	1972	1,000	Grass
Merchant Marine	Captain Tomb Field	1945	5,840	Grass
Methodist	Monarch Field	1989	1,500	Grass
Middlebury	Alumni	1991	3,500	Grass
Millikin	Frank M. Lindsay Field	1987	4,000	Grass
Millsaps	Alumni Field	NA	4,000	Grass
Mississippi Col.	Robinson-Hale	1985	8,500	Grass
Monmouth (Ill.)	Bobby Woll Memorial Field	1981	3,000	Grass
Montclair St.	Sprague Field	1934	6,000	AstroTurf
Moravian	Steel Field	1932	2,200	Grass
Mt. St. Joseph	Elder High School	NA	4,000	Grass
Mount Union	Mount Union	1915	5,700	Grass
Muhlenberg	Scotty Wood Stadium	1998	3,000	AstroTurf
Muskingum	McConagha	1925	5,000	Grass
Neb. Wesleyan	Abel	1986	2,000	Grass
Col. of New Jersey	Lions	1984	5,000	AstroTurf
New Jersey City	Thomas M. Gerrity Ath. Complex	1986	3,000	Grass
Nichols	Bison Bowl	1961	3,000	Grass
North Central	Kroehler Field	NA	3,000	Grass
North Park	Hedstrand Field	1955	2,500	Grass
Norwich	Sabine Field	1921	5,000	Grass
Oberlin	Dill Field	1925	3,500	Grass
Occidental	Patterson Field	1900	4,000	Grass
Ohio Northern	Ada War Memorial	1948	4,000	Grass
Ohio Wesleyan	Selby	1929	9,600	Grass
Olivet	Griswold Field	1972	3,500	Grass
Otterbein	Memorial	1946	4,000	Grass
Pacific Lutheran	Sparks Stadium	1985	4,500	Turf
Plymouth St.	Currier Memorial Field	1970	1,000	Grass
Pomona-Pitzer	Merritt Field	1991	2,000	Grass
Principia	Clark Field	1937	1,000	Grass
Puget Sound	Baker	1964	6,000	Grass
Randolph-Macon	Day Field	1953	5,000	Grass
Redlands	Ted Runner	1968	7,000	Grass
Rensselaer	86 Field	1912	3,000	Grass
Rhodes	Fargason Field	1964	5,000	Grass
Ripon	Ingalls Field	1888	2,500	Grass
Rochester	Edwin Fauver	1930	5,000	All-Pro Turf
Rose-Hulman	Phil Brown Field	NA	2,500	Grass
Rowan	John Page	1969	5,000	Grass
St. John Fisher	Growney Stadium	1999	2,100	AstroTurf
St. John's (Minn.)	Clemens	1908	5,500	Grass
St. Lawrence	Weeks Field	1906	3,000	Grass
St. Norbert	Minahan	1937	3,100	Grass
St. Olaf	Manitou Field	1930	5,000	Grass
St. Thomas (Minn.)	O'Shaughnessy	1948	5,025	Grass
Salisbury	Sea Gull	1980	2,500	Grass
Salve Regina	Toppa	NA	2,500	Grass
Sewanee	McGee Field	1935	1,500	Grass
Shenandoah	Shentel	2001	2,500	Grass
Simpson	Bill Buxton	1990	5,000	AstroPlay
Springfield	Benedum Field	1971	2,500	All-Pro Plus
Stillman	Stillman	1999	9,000	Grass
Sul Ross St.	Jackson Field	NA	2,500	Grass
Susquehanna	Amos Alonzo Stagg Field	1892	4,600	Grass
Thiel	Stewart Field	1954	5,000	Grass
Thomas More	Thomas More Stadium	1999	3,000	Grass
Trinity (Conn.)	Dan Jessee Field	1900	6,500	Grass
Trinity (Tex.)	E.M. Stevens	1972	3,500	Grass
Tufts	Ellis Oval	1923	6,000	Grass
Union (N.Y.)	Frank Bailey Field	1981	2,000	AstroTurf
Upper Iowa	Eischeid	1993	3,500	Grass
Ursinus	Patterson Field	1923	2,500	Grass
Wabash	Little Giant	1967	4,200	Grass
Wartburg	Walston-Hoover	2002	4,000	FieldTurf
Washington (Mo.)	Francis Field	1904	4,000	Grass

School	Stadium	Year Built	Capacity	Surface
Wash. & Jeff.	Cameron	1958	4,500	FieldTurf
Wash. & Lee	Wilson Field	1930	7,000	Grass
Waynesburg	Wiley Stadium	1999	4,000	Grass
Wesley	Wolverine	1989	2,000	Grass
Wesleyan (Conn.)	Andrus Field	1881	5,000	Grass
Western Conn. St.	Midtown Campus Field	NA	2,500	Turf
Western New Eng.	WNEC	NA	1,500	Grass
Westfield St.	Alumni Field	1982	4,800	AstroTurf
Westminster (Mo.)	Priest Field	1906	1,500	Grass
Wheaton (Ill.)	McCully Field	1956	7,000	Grass
Whittier	Memorial	NA	7,000	Grass
Whitworth	Pine Bowl	NA	2,200	Grass
Widener	Leslie C. Quick Jr.	1994	4,000	Grass
Wilkes	Ralston Field	1965	4,000	Grass
Willamette	McCulloch	1950	2,400	Grass
Wm. Paterson	Wrightman	NA	2,000	Grass
Williams	Weston Field	1875	10,000	Grass
Wilmington (Ohio)	Williams	1983	3,250	Grass
Wis.-Eau Claire	Carson Park	NA	6,500	Grass
Wis.-La Crosse	Veterans Memorial	1924	4,349	Grass
Wis.-Oshkosh	Titan	1970	9,800	Grass
Wis.-Platteville	Ralph E. Davis Pioneer	1972	10,000	Grass
Wis.-River Falls	Ramer Field	1966	4,800	Grass
Wis.-Stevens Point	Goerke Field	1932	4,000	Grass
Wis.-Stout	Nelson Field	1936	5,000	Grass
Wis.-Whitewater	Forrest Perkins	1970	11,000	Grass
Wittenberg	Edwards-Maurer	1995	2,400	StadiaTurf
Wooster	John P. Papp	1991	4,500	Grass
Worcester St.	John Coughlin Memorial	1976	2,500	AstroTurf
WPI	Alumni Field	1916	2,800	Omni-Turf

STADIUMS LISTED BY CAPACITY (TOP 35)

School	Stadium	Surface*	Capacity
Wis.-Whitewater	Forrest Perkins	Grass	11,000
Brockport St.	Special Olympics	Grass	10,000
Greensboro	Jamieson	Grass	10,000
Williams	Weston Field	Grass	10,000
Wis.-Platteville	Ralph E. Davis Pioneer	Grass	10,000
Wis.-Oshkosh	Titan	Grass	9,800
Ohio Wesleyan	Selby	Grass	9,600
Bowdoin	Whittier Field	Grass	9,000
Stillman	Stillman	Grass	9,000
Mississippi Col.	Robinson-Hale	Grass	8,500
Baldwin-Wallace	George Finnie	StadiaTurf	8,100
Amherst	Pratt Field	Grass	8,000
Johns Hopkins	Homewood Field	Turf	8,000
Wesleyan (Conn.)	Andrus Field	Grass	8,000
Howard Payne	Gordon Wood	Grass	7,600
Carleton	Laird	Grass	7,500
Concordia-M'head	Jake Christiansen	Grass	7,500
Heidelberg	Frost-Kalnow	Grass	7,500
Albright	Eugene L. Shirk	Grass	7,000
Marietta	Don Drumm Field	Grass	7,000
Mary Hardin-Baylor	Tiger Field	Grass	7,000
Redlands	Ted Runner	Grass	7,000
Wash. & Lee	Wilson Field	Grass	7,000
Wheaton (Ill.)	McCully Field	Grass	7,000
Whittier	Memorial	Grass	7,000
Thomas More	Lockland	Grass	6,500
Trinity (Conn.)	Dan Jessee Field	Grass	6,500
Wis.-Eau Claire	Carson Park	Grass	6,500
Gettysburg	Musselman	Grass	6,176
Knox	Knox Bowl	Grass	6,000
Montclair St.	Sprague Field	AstroTurf	6,000
Puget Sound	Baker	Grass	6,000
Tufts	Ellis Oval	Grass	6,000
Merchant Marine	Captain Tomb Field	Grass	5,840
Mount Union	Mount Union	Grass	5,700

Surface Notes: *This column indicates the type of surface (either artificial or natural grass) present this year in the stadium. The brand name of the artificial turf, if known, is listed. Legend: Turf—Any of several types of artificial turfs (name brands include AstroTurf, All-Pro, Omni-Turf, SuperTurf, etc.); Grass—Natural grass surface; PAT—Prescription Athletic Turf (a "natural-artificial" surface featuring a network of pipes connected to pumps capable of sucking water from the natural turf or watering it. The pipes are located 18 inches from the surface and covered with a mixture of sand and filler. The turf also is lined with heating coils to keep it from freezing in temperatures below 32 degrees).

DIVISION III

Statistics Trends

(Average Per Game, One Team)

	Rushing					Passing				Total Off.				Scoring			Punting	
Year	Plays	Yds.	Avg.	Att.	Cmp.	Pct.	Yds.	Avg. Att.	Plays	Yds.	Avg.	TD	FG	Pts.	No.	Avg.
1995	42.8	159.9	3.74	25.5	12.5	49.1	159.3	6.24	68.3	319.2	4.67	3.01	0.41	21.	5.6	33.3
1996	42.8	166.9	3.90	25.9	12.8	49.4	167.8	6.48	68.7	334.7	4.87	3.21	0.43	23.3	5.4	34.3
1997	41.8	159.1	3.81	26.6	13.2	49.7	175.3	6.58	68.4	334.4	4.89	3.26	0.43	23.6	5.5	35.0
1998	41.6	159.8	3.84	26.9	13.6	50.5	181.4	6.75	68.5	341.2	4.98	3.37	0.46	24.5	5.4	35.0
1999	41.0	155.0	3.78	28.9	14.6	50.5	191.8	6.64	69.9	346.8	4.96	3.36	0.47	24.4	5.6	34.9
2000	41.0	154.1	3.76	28.2	14.2	50.5	185.2	6.57	69.2	339.3	4.90	3.27	0.51	24.0	5.6	34.4
2001	41.1	156.8	3.82	29.0	14.7	50.7	191.4	6.61	70.0	348.3	4.97	3.42	0.48	24.8	5.6	34.0
2002	40.7	153.6	3.78	28.3	14.5	51.2	185.3	6.54	69.0	338.9	4.91	3.32	0.48	24.2	5.3	34.2

Additional Statistics Trends

		Avg.	PAT Kick Attempts	Pct. of	Two-Point Attempts	Pct. of	Pct. of Field Goals
Year	Teams	Games	Pct. Made	Total Tries	Pct. Made	Total Tries	Made
1995	187	9.48	.818	.854	.456	.146	.533
1996	197	9.52	.850	.862	.483	.138	.528
1997	199	9.43	.824	.859	.476	.141	.542
1998	198	9.63	.854	.867	.461	.133	.544
1999	206	9.65	.838	.877	.419	.123	.557
2000	203	9.69	.825	.871	.421	.129	.565
2001	192	9.54	.842	.890	.442	.110	.549
2002	222	10.03	.845	.885	.418	.115	.551

Classification History

The following lists show years of active membership for current and former Division III football-playing institutions. Provisional members also are shown along with the year in which they will become active members.

ACTIVE MEMBERS (227)

Adrian 1973-current
Albion...........................1973-current
Albright.........................1973-current
Alfred 1973-current
Allegheny.......................1973-current
Alma 1973-current
Amherst.........................1973-current
Anderson (Ind.) 1992-current
Augsburg 1982-current
Augustana (Ill.)...............1973-current
Aurora 1988-current
Austin...............1973-77, 97-current
Averett..........................2000-current
Baldwin-Wallace.............1973-current
Bates 1973-current
Beloit 1973-current
Benedictine (Ill.) 1973-current
Bethany (W.Va.) 1973-current
Bethel (Minn.) 1983-current
Blackburn 1990-current
Bluffton 1990, 92-current
Bowdoin 1973-current
Bridgewater St. 1973-current
Bridgewater (Va.).............1973-current
Brockport St. 1973-current
Buena Vista 1976-current
Buffalo St. 1981-current
Cal Lutheran 1975-77, 91-current
Capital..........................1973-current
Carleton 1973-current
Carnegie-Mellon 1973-current
Carroll (Wis.)..................1976-current
Carthage 1976-current
Case Reserve..................1973-current
Catholic 1978-current
Central (Iowa)................1973-current
Centre...........................1973-current
Chapman 1994-current
Chicago 1973-current
Chowan 1997-current
Chris. Newport 2001-current
Claremont-M-S.................1973-current
Coast Guard...................1973-current
Coe 1973-current
Colby 1973-current
Colorado Col. 1973-current

Concordia (Ill.) 1973-75, 81-current
Concordia-M'head 1977-current
Concordia (Wis.) 1997-current
Cornell College................1973-current
Cortland St. 1973-current
Curry 1973-current
Defiance 1973-75, 91-current
Delaware Valley 1973-current
Denison.........................1973-current
DePauw 1973-current
Dickinson 1973-current
Dubuque 1976-current
Earlham 1982-current
East Tex. Baptist.............2001-current
Eastern Ore. 1999-current
Elmhurst.........................1973-current
Emory & Henry 1973-current
Eureka 1978-current
FDU-Florham 1973-current
Ferrum 1985-current
Fitchburg St. 1984-current
Framingham St. 1973-current
Franklin 1992-current
Frank. & Marsh. 1973-current
Frostburg St. 1977-current
Gallaudet..1973-79,86-94, 2001-current
Gettysburg......................1973-current
Greensboro 1997-current
Greenville......................1997-current
Grinnell.........................1973-current
Grove City 1973-current
Guilford 1990-current
Gust. Adolphus 1973-current
Hamilton 1973-current
Hamline 1973-current
Hampden-Sydney 1973-current
Hanover.........................1973-current
Hardin-Simmons 1990-92, 94-current
Hartwick 1992-current
Heidelberg......................1973-current
Hiram 1973-current
Hobart 1973-current
Hope 1973-current
Howard Payne 1994-current
Illinois Col. 1978-current
Ill. Wesleyan 1978-current

Ithaca 1973-current
John Carroll 1973-current
Johns Hopkins.................1973-current
Juniata 1973-current
Kalamazoo......................1973-current
Kean.............................1973-current
Kenyon 1973-current
King's (Pa.)....................1994-current
Knox 1973-current
La Verne 1982-current
Lake Forest 1973-current
Lakeland 1994-current
Lawrence........................1973-current
Lebanon Valley 1973-current
Lewis & Clark 1998-current
Linfield 1998-current
Loras............................1986-current
Louisiana Col. 2003
Luther............................1973-current
Lycoming........................1973-current
Macalester 1973-current
MacMurray 1984-current
Maine Maritime 1973-current
Manchester......................1992-current
Maranatha Baptist...........1999-current
Marietta 1973-current
Martin Luther 1991-current
Mary Hardin-Baylor.........2000-current
Maryville (Tenn.) 1973-current
Mass.-Dartmouth 1988-current
MIT 1988-current
Mass. Maritime 1973-current
McDaniel........................1973-current
McMurry 1997-current
Menlo 1986-current
Merchant Marine...1973-77, 82-current
Methodist 1989-current
Middlebury......................1973-current
Millikin 1976-current
Millsaps 1973-current
Mississippi Col. 1997-current
Monmouth (Ill.).................1973-current
Montclair St. 1973-current
Moravian 1973-current
Mount Ida 2002-current
Mt. St. Joseph 1998-current

Mount Union...................1973-current
Muhlenberg 1973-current
Muskingum 1973-current
Neb. Wesleyan 1973-current
Col. of New Jersey..........1973-current
Nichols 1973-current
North Central 1973-current
North Park......................1973-current
Norwich..........................1973-current
Oberlin 1973-current
Occidental 1973-current
Ohio Northern 1973-current
Ohio Wesleyan 1973-current
Olivet............................1973-current
Otterbein........................1973-current
Pacific Lutheran 1998-current
Plymouth St. 1973-current
Pomona-Pitzer 1973-current
Principia.........................1973-current
Puget Sound 1999-current
Randolph-Macon 1973-current
Redlands 1973-78, 82-current
Rensselaer 1973-current
Rhodes 1984-current
Ripon 1973-current
Rochester 1973-current
Rockford.........................2000-current
Rose-Hulman 1973-current
Rowan 1973-current
St. John Fisher.................1988-current
St. John's (Minn.)............1973-current
St. Lawrence 1973-current
St. Norbert 1973-current
St. Olaf 1973-current
St. Thomas (Minn.) 1973-current
Salisbury........................1973-current
Salve Regina 1993-current
Sewanee 1973-current
Shenandoah 2000-current
Simpson 1973-current
Springfield......................1995-current
Stillman 1999-current
Sul Ross St. 1997-current
Susquehanna 1973-current
Texas Lutheran 2002-current
Thiel 1973-current

Thomas More	1990-current
Trinity (Conn.)	1973-current
Trinity (Tex.)	1973-current
Tufts	1973-current
Union (N.Y.)	1973-current
Upper Iowa	1976-current
Ursinus	1973-current
Utica	2001-current
Wabash	1973-current
Wartburg	1973-current
Washington (Mo.)	1973-current
Wash. & Jeff.	1973-current
Wash. & Lee	1973-current
Waynesburg	1990-current
Wesley	1986-current
Wesleyan (Conn.)	1973-current
Western Conn. St.	1977-current
Western New Eng.	1981-current
Westfield St.	1982-current
Westminster (Mo.)	1997-current
Westminster (Pa.)	2002-current
Wheaton (Ill.)	1973-current
Whittier	1973-current
Whitworth	1998-current
Widener	1973-current
Wilkes	1973-current
Willamette	1998-current
Wm. Paterson	1973-current
Williams	1973-current
Wilmington (Ohio)	1977-80, 90-current
Wis.-Eau Claire	1986-current
Wis.-La Crosse	1983-current
Wis.-Oshkosh	1975-current
Wis.-Platteville	1980-current
Wis.-River Falls	1977, 82-current
Wis.-Stevens Point	1980-current
Wis.-Stout	1980-current
Wis.-Whitewater	1973-77, 80-current

Wis. Lutheran	1999-current
Wittenberg	1973-current
Wooster	1973-current
Worcester St.	1985-current
WPI	1973-current

PROVISIONAL MEMBER (0)*

FORMER MEMBERS

UAB	1991-92
Albany (N.Y.)	1973-94
Albany St. (Ga.)	1973-75
American Int'l	1973
Ashland	1973-79
Assumption	1988-92
Bentley	1988-92
Bloomsburg	1973-79
Bowie St.	1973-79
Bridgeport	1973
Brooklyn	1978-91
Buffalo	1978-92
C.W. Post	1975-77, 84, 89-92
UC Santa Barb.	1986-90
Cal St. Chico	1973-77
Caltech	1973-77
Cameron	1973
Canisius	1975-92
UCF	1980-81
Charleston So.	1991-92
Cheyney	1973-79
Clark Atlanta	1973-79
Colorado Mines	1973
Davidson	1990-92
Dayton	1976-92
Delaware St.	1973-77
Dist. Columbia	1978
Drake	1987-92
Duquesne	1979-92

Evansville	1973-77, 89-92
Ferris St.	1975-76
Fisk	1973-83
Fordham	1973-88
Fort Valley St.	1973-80
Gannon	1989-92
Georgetown	1973-92
Hillsdale	1975
Hofstra	1973-92
Humboldt St.	1975-79
Ill.-Chicago	1973
Iona	1978-92
James Madison	1977-79
Ky. Wesleyan	1983-92
Knoxville	1973-88
Kutztown	1973-79
Lane	1973-87
Livingston	1973
Lock Haven	1973-79
Mansfield	1973-79
Marist	1978-92
Maritime (N.Y.)	1985, 88
Mass.-Boston	1988-00
Mass.-Lowell	1981-92
Mercyhurst	1982-92
Merrimack	1989
Miles	1973-87
Millersville	1973-79
Minn.-Morris	1978-84
Minn. St. Mankato	1977
Morehouse	1973-80
New Haven	1973, 77-80
New Jersey City	1973-02
NYIT	1973
Oswego St.	1976
Pace	1978-92
Plattsburg St.	1973-78
Quincy	1987-92

Ramapo	1981-92
Rochester Inst.	1973-77
Sacred Heart	1991-92
St. Francis (Pa.)	1978-92
St. John's (N.Y.)	1978-92
St. Joseph's (Ind.)	1973-78
St. Mary's (Cal.)	1973-80
St. Peter's	1973-92
Samford	1985-88
San Diego	1973-92
San Fran. St.	1973-78
Savannah St.	1973-80
Seton Hall	1973-76, 78-80
Shepherd	1973-75
Shippensburg	1973-75
Siena	1988-92
Slippery Rock	1973-78
Sonoma St.	1980-83
Stonehill	1989-92
Stony Brook	1983-94
Swarthmore	1973-00
Tarleton St.	1977
Towson	1973-79
Upsala	1973-96
Valparaiso	1973-78
Villanova	1985-86
Wagner	1973-92
West Ga.	1981-82
William Penn	1976-00
Winona St.	1975
Wis.-Superior	1973-92

Provisional members are not active members of the Association and, thus are not eligible for NCAA statistics, records and championship play. The end of the provisional status and first season of active membership in Division III football is listed to the right of the school name.

DIVISION III

Individual
Collegiate
Records

Individual Collegiate Records

Individual collegiate records are determined by comparing the best records in all four divisions (I-A, I-AA, II and III) in comparable categories. Prior to 2002, postseason games were not included in NCAA final football statistics or records. Beginning with the 2002 season, all postseason games were included in NCAA final football statistics and records. Included are career records of players who played in two divisions (e.g., Dennis Shaw of San Diego St., Howard Stevens of Randolph-Macon and Louisville, and Tom Ehrhardt of C.W. Post and Rhode Island). Players who played seasons other than in the NCAA will have statistics only including NCAA seasons.

Total Offense

CAREER YARDS PER GAME

(Minimum 5,500 Yards)

Player, Team (Division[s])	Years	G	Plays	Yards	TDR‡	Yd. PG
Steve McNair, Alcorn St. (I-AA)	1991-94	42	2,055	*16,823	152	*400.5
Tim Rattay, Louisiana Tech (I-A)	1997-99	33	1,705	12,618	117	382.4
Justin Peery, Westminster (Mo.) (III)	1996-99	39	2,001	13,645	*166	349.9
Aaron Flowers, Cal St. Northridge (I-AA)	1996-97	20	944	6,754	60	337.7
Terry Peebles, Hanover (III)	1992-95	23	1,140	7,672	89	333.6
Dave Dickenson, Montana (I-AA)	1992-95	35	1,539	11,523	116	329.2
Eric Bruns, Hanover (III)	1999-00	20	995	6,512	44	325.6
Willie Totten, Mississippi Val. (I-AA)	1982-85	40	1,812	13,007	157	325.2
Grady Benton, West Tex. A&M (II)	1994-95	18	844	5,831	55	323.9
Ty Detmer, Brigham Young (I-A)	1988-91	46	1,795	14,665	135	318.8
Neil Lomax, Portland St. (II; I-AA)	1977; 78-80	42	1,901	13,345	120	317.7
Drew Miller, Montana (I-AA)	1999-00	18	708	5,628	47	312.7
Adam Ryan, Wilmington (Ohio) (III)	1998-01	33	1,520	10,314	47	312.5
Kirk Baumgartner, Wis.-Stevens Point (III)	1986-89	41	2,007	12,767	110	311.4
Mike Perez, San Jose St. (I-A)	1986-87	20	875	6,182	37	309.1
Doug Nussmeier, Idaho (I-AA)	1990-93	39	1,556	12,054	109	309.1
Josh Wallwork, Wyoming (I-A)	1995-96	22	845	6,753	60	307.0
Oteman Sampson, Florida A&M (I-AA)	1996-97	22	906	6,751	57	306.9
Doug Gaynor, Long Beach St. (I-A)	1984-85	22	1,067	6,710	45	305.0
Tod Mayfield, West Tex. A&M (I-AA; II)	1984-85; 86	24	1,165	7,316	58	304.8
Marcus Brady, Cal St. Northridge (I-AA)	1998-01	43	2,116	13,095	123	304.5
J.T. O'Sullivan, UC Davis (II)	1998-01	29	987	8,743	78	301.5
Zamir Amin, Menlo (III)	1999-01	26	1,015	7,836	87	301.4
Jamie Martin, Weber St. (I-AA)	1989-92	41	1,838	12,287	93	299.7
Tony Eason, Illinois (I-A)	1981-82	22	1,016	6,589	43	299.5
Todd Cunningham, Presbyterian (II)	1998-01	39	1,635	11,578	121	296.9
Scott Otis, Glenville St. (II)	1994-95	20	755	5,911	66	295.6
Drew Brees, Purdue (I-A)	1997-00	40	1,754	11,815	97	295.4
Tom Proudian, Iona (I-AA)	1993-95	27	1,337	7,939	61	294.0
Robert Dougherty, Boston U. (I-AA)	1993-94	21	918	6,135	56	292.1
Keith Bishop, Ill. Wesleyan/Wheaton (Ill.) (III)	1981, 83-85	31	1,467	9,052	77	292.0
David Neill, Nevada (I-A)	1998-01	40	1,376	11,664	87	291.6
David Klingler, Houston (I-A)	1988-91	32	1,431	9,327	93	291.5
Stan Greene, Boston U. (I-AA)	1989-90	22	1,167	6,408	49	291.3
John Friesz, Idaho (I-AA)	1986-89	35	1,459	10,187	79	291.1
Steve Sarkisian, Brigham Young (I-A)	1995-96	25	953	7,253	56	290.1
Chris Redman, Louisville (I-A)	1996-99	42	1,846	12,129	87	288.8
Kliff Kingsbury, Texas Tech (I-A)	1999-02	43	*2,156	12,263	99	285.2
Steve Young, Brigham Young (I-A)	1981-83	31	1,177	8,817	74	284.4
Mark Novara, Lakeland (III)	1994-97	38	1,653	10,801	112	284.2
Daunte Culpepper, UCF (I-AA; I-A)	1995-98	44	1,847	12,432	108	282.5
Tim Couch, Kentucky (I-A)	1996-98	29	1,338	8,160	78	281.4
Jayson Merrill, Western St. (II)	1990-91	20	641	5,619	57	281.0
Jordan Poznick, Principia (III)	1990-93	32	1,757	8,983	71	280.7

*Record. ‡Touchdowns-responsible-for are player's TDs scored and passed for.

SEASON YARDS PER GAME

Player, Team (Division)	Year	G	Plays	Yards	TDR‡	Yd. PG
Steve McNair, Alcorn St. (I-AA)	†1994	11	649	*5,799	53	*527.2
David Klingler, Houston (I-A)	†1990	11	704	5,221	55	474.6
Justin Peery, Westminster (Mo.) (III)	†1998	10	645	4,651	57	465.1
Willie Totten, Mississippi Val. (I-AA)	†1984	10	564	4,572	*61	457.2
Justin Peery, Westminster (Mo.) (III)	†1999	10	599	4,419	60	441.9
Danny Ragsdale, Redlands (III)	1999	9	464	3,855	35	428.3
Andre Ware, Houston (I-A)	†1989	11	628	4,661	49	423.7
Zamir Amin, Menlo (III)	†2000	10	511	4,231	43	423.1
Ty Detmer, Brigham Young (I-A)	1990	12	635	5,022	45	418.5
Grady Benton, West Tex. A&M (II)	†1994	9	505	3,699	35	411.0
Steve McNair, Alcorn St. (I-AA)	†1992	10	519	4,057	39	405.7
Perry Klein, C.W. Post (II)	†1993	10	499	4,052	41	405.2
Tim Rattay, Louisiana Tech (I-A)	†1998	12	602	4,840	47	403.3
Mike Maxwell, Nevada (I-A)	†1995	9	443	3,623	34	402.6
Chris Redman, Louisville (I-A)	1998	10	513	4,009	31	400.9
Terry Peebles, Hanover (III)	†1995	10	572	3,981	43	398.1
Steve Young, Brigham Young (I-A)	†1983	11	531	4,346	41	395.1

Player, Team (Division)	Year	G	Plays	Yards	TDR‡	Yd. PG
Jamie Martin, Weber St. (I-AA)	†1991	11	591	4,337	37	394.3
Chris Vargas, Nevada (I-A)	†1993	11	535	4,332	35	393.8
Marty Washington, West Ala. (II)	1993	8	453	3,146	29	393.8
Wilkie Perez, Glenville St. (II)	†1997	11	509	4,301	45	391.0
Scott Mitchell, Utah (I-A)	†1988	11	589	4,299	29	390.8
Damian Poalucci, East Stroudsburg (II)	†1996	10	505	3,883	41	388.3
Bruce Eugene, Grambling (I-AA)	2002	13	680	5,018	43	386.0
Andrew Webb, Fort Lewis (II)	†2002	11	613	4,245	42	385.9
Jim McMahon, Brigham Young (I-A)	†1980	12	540	4,627	53	385.6
Dave Dickenson, Montana (I-AA)	†1995	11	544	4,209	41	382.6
Tim Rattay, Louisiana Tech (I-A)	†1999	10	562	3,810	35	381.0
Neil Lomax, Portland St. (I-AA)	†1980	11	550	4,157	42	377.9
Daunte Culpepper, UCF (I-A)	1998	11	543	4,153	40	377.5
Tim Couch, Kentucky (I-A)	1998	11	617	4,151	37	377.4
Brett Salisbury, Wayne St. (Neb.) (II)	1993	10	424	3,732	32	373.2
David Neill, Nevada (I-A)	1998	9	409	3,351	31	372.3
Ty Detmer, Brigham Young (I-A)	1989	12	497	4,433	38	369.4
Kyle Krober, Greenville (III)	2000	10	468	3,676	28	376.6
Joe Lee, Towson (I-AA)	†1999	11	608	4,031	22	366.5
Troy Kopp, Pacific (Cal.) (I-A)	1990	9	485	3,276	32	364.0
Marcus Brady, Cal St. Northridge (I-AA)	†2001	10	532	3,632	40	363.2
Steve Slowke, Alma (III)	†2001	10	662	3,630	34	363.0
Curt Anes, Grand Valley St. (II)	†2001	10	360	3,621	55	362.1
Dave Dickenson, Montana (I-AA)	†1993	11	530	3,978	46	361.6
Adam King, Howard Payne (III)	†2002	10	505	3,613	31	361.3
Tim Rattay, Louisiana Tech (I-A)	†1997	11	541	3,968	35	360.7
Neil Lomax, Portland St. (I-AA)	†1979	11	611	3,966	31	360.5
Todd Cunningham, Presbyterian (II)	2001	11	607	3,959	40	359.9
Jed Drenning, Glenville St. (II)	1993	10	473	3,593	32	359.3
Drew Brees, Purdue (I-A)	†2000	11	564	3,939	29	358.1
Byron Leftwich, Marshall (I-A)	†2002	12	528	4,267	33	355.6
Alfred Montez, Western N.M. (II)	1994	6	244	2,130	18	355.0
Rex Grossman, Florida (I-A)	†2001	11	429	3,904	39	354.9
Keith Bishop, Wheaton (III.)	†1983	9	421	3,193	24	354.8
Kirk Baumgartner, Wis.-Stevens Point (III)	†1989	10	530	3,540	39	354.0
Bill Nietzke, Alma (III)	†1996	9	468	3,185	29	353.9
Rob Tomlinson, Cal St. Chico (II)	†1989	10	534	3,525	26	352.5
Byron Leftwich, Marshall (I-A)	2001	12	534	4,224	41	352.0
Josh Wallwork, Wyoming (I-A)	†1996	12	525	4,209	35	350.8
John Furmaniak, Eureka (III)	1995	10	414	3,503	35	350.3
John Friesz, Idaho (I-AA)	†1989	11	464	3,853	31	350.3

*Record. †National total-offense champion. ‡Touchdowns-responsible-for are player's TDs scored and passed for.

CAREER YARDS

Player, Team (Division[s])	Years	Plays	Yards	Avg.
Steve McNair, Alcorn St. (I-AA)	1991-94	2,055	*16,823	8.19
Ty Detmer, Brigham Young (I-A)	1988-91	1,795	14,665	8.17
Justin Peery, Westminster (Mo.) (III)	1996-99	2,001	13,645	6.82
Neil Lomax, Portland St. (II; I-AA)	1977; 78-80	1,901	13,345	7.02
Marcus Brady, Cal St. Northridge (I-AA)	1998-01	2,116	13,095	6.19
Willie Totten, Mississippi Val. (I-AA)	1982-85	1,812	13,007	7.18
Kirk Baumgartner, Wis.-Stevens Point (III)	1986-89	2,007	12,767	6.36
Tim Rattay, Louisiana Tech (I-A)	1997-99	1,705	12,618	7.40
Daunte Culpepper, UCF (I-AA; I-A)	1995-98	1,847	12,432	6.73
Chad Pennington, Marshall (I-AA, I-A)	1995, 97-99	1,719	12,313	7.16
Jamie Martin, Weber St. (I-AA)	1989-92	1,838	12,287	6.68
Kliff Kingsbury, Texas Tech (I-A)	1999-02	*2,156	12,263	5.69
Chris Redman, Louisville (I-A)	1996-99	1,846	12,129	6.57
Doug Nussmeier, Idaho (I-AA)	1990-93	1,556	12,054	7.75
Curt Anes, Grand Valley St. (II)	1999-02	1,527	11,881	7.78
Drew Brees, Purdue (I-A)	1997-00	1,754	11,815	6.74
David Neill, Nevada (I-A)	1998-01	1,727	11,664	6.75
Todd Cunningham, Presbyterian (II)	1998-01	1,635	11,578	7.08
Dave Dickenson, Montana (I-AA)	1992-95	1,539	11,523	7.49
Antwaan Randle El, Indiana (I-A)	1998-01	1,917	11,364	5.93
Doug Flutie, Boston College (I-A)	1981-84	1,558	11,317	7.26
Travis Brown, Northern Ariz. (I-AA)	1996-99	1,732	11,267	6.51
Vernon Buck, Wingate (II)	1991-94	1,761	11,227	6.38
Ken Hobart, Idaho (I-AA)	1980-83	1,847	11,127	6.02
Carson Palmer, Southern California (I-A)	$1998-02	1,785	11,093	6.31
Tim Lester, Western Mich. (I-A)	1996-99	1,747	11,081	6.34
Bob McLaughlin, Lock Haven (II)	1992-95	2,007	11,041	5.50
Peyton Manning, Tennessee (I-A)	1994-97	1,534	11,020	7.18
Eric Zeier, Georgia (I-A)	1991-94	1,560	10,841	6.95
Alex Van Pelt, Pittsburgh (I-A)	1989-92	1,570	10,814	6.89
Mark Novara, Lakeland (III)	1994-97	1,653	10,801	6.53
Earl Harvey, N.C. Central (II)	1985-88	2,045	10,667	5.22
Stoney Case, New Mexico (I-A)	1991-94	1,673	10,651	6.37

Player, Team (Division[s])	Years	Plays	Yards	Avg.
Justin Coleman, Neb.-Kearney (II)	1997-00	1,411	10,644	7.54
Joe Hamilton, Georgia Tech (I-A)	1996-99	1,758	10,640	7.00
Bill Borchert, Mount Union (III)	1994-97	1,274	10,639	*8.35
Chris Hatcher, Valdosta St. (II)	1991-94	1,557	10,588	6.80
Jim Ballard, Wilmington (Ohio)/ Mount Union (III)	1990, 91-93	1,328	10,545	7.94
Todd Santos, San Diego St. (I-A)	1984-87	1,722	10,513	6.11
Danny Wuerffel, Florida (I-A)	1993-96	1,355	10,500	7.75
Tom Arth, John Carroll (III)	1999-02	1,557	10,493	6.74
Cade McNown, UCLA (I-A)	1995-98	1,429	10,487	7.34
Giovanni Carmazzi, Hofstra (I-AA)	1996-99	1,564	10,416	6.66
Adam Ryan, Wilmington (Ohio) (III)	1998-01	1,520	10,314	6.79
Troy Dougherty, Grinnell (III)	1994, 97-99	1,520	10,314	6.79
Sean Payton, Eastern Ill. (I-AA)	1983-86	1,690	10,298	6.09
Greg Wyatt, Northern Ariz. (I-AA)	1986-89	1,753	10,277	5.86
Dusty Bonner, Kentucky (I-A); Valdosta St. (II)	1997,99-01	1,429	10,253	7.17
Kevin Sweeney, Fresno St. (I-A)	$1982-86	1,700	10,252	6.03
Kyle Krober, Greenville (III)	1998-01	1,603	10,239	6.39
David Garrard, East Caro. (I-A)	1998-01	1,685	10,238	6.08
Thad Trujillo, Fort Lewis (II)	1991-94	1,787	10,209	5.71
John Friesz, Idaho (I-AA)	1986-89	1,459	10,187	6.98
Eric DeGraff, Augustana (S.D.) (II)	1997-00	1,643	10,128	6.16
Drew Folmar, Millersville (II)	1997-00	1,537	10,105	6.57
Troy Kopp, Pacific (Cal.) (I-A)	1989-92	1,595	10,037	6.29
Bart Hendricks, Boise St. (I-A)	1997-00	1,472	10,034	6.82
Kevin Ricca, Catholic (III)	1994-97	1,533	9,982	6.51
Brian Dawson, Wash. & Jeff. (III)	1999-02	1,390	9,954	7.16
Donovan McNabb, Syracuse (I-A)	1995-98	1,403	9,950	7.09
Ricky Fritz, Minn. Duluth (II)	$1998-02	1,464	9,926	6.78
Rob Tomlinson, Cal St. Chico (II)	1988-91	1,656	9,921	5.99
Michael Proctor, Murray St. (I-AA)	1986-89	1,577	9,886	6.27
Jeff Wiley, Holy Cross (I-AA)	1985-88	1,428	9,877	6.92
Kasey Waterman, Mo. Western St. (II)	1998-01	1,449	9,874	6.81
Tom Ehrhardt, C.W. Post (II); Rhode Island (I-AA)	1981-82; 84-85	1,674	9,793	5.85

Player, Team (Division[s])	Years	Plays	Yards	Avg.
Brian McClure, Bowling Green (I-A)	1982-85	1,630	9,774	6.00
John Hebgen, Minn. St. Mankato (II)	1993-96	1,545	9,772	6.32
Jeff Lewis, Northern Ariz. (I-AA)	1992-95	1,654	9,769	5.91
Eric Noble, Wilmington (Ohio) (III)	1992-95	1,513	9,731	6.43
Jim McMahon, Brigham Young (I-A)	1977-78, 80-81	1,325	9,723	7.34
Mike Mitros, West Chester (II)	1996-99	1,716	9,714	5.66
Glenn Foley, Boston College (I-A)	1990-93	1,440	9,702	6.74
Tim Peterson, Wis.-Stout (III)	1986-89	1,558	9,701	6.23
Ted White, Howard (I-AA)	1995-98	1,377	9,669	7.02
Bryan Harman, Fairmont St. (II)	1998-01	1,471	9,638	6.55
Jarrod Furgason, Fairmont St. (II)	$1993-97	1,583	9,638	6.09
John Craven, Gardner-Webb (II)	1991-94	1,666	9,630	5.78
Chris Ings, Wabash (III)	1992-95	1,532	9,608	6.27

*Record. $See Page 8 for explanation.

SEASON YARDS

Player, Team (Division)	Year	G	Plays	Yards	Avg.
Steve McNair, Alcorn St. (I-AA)	†1994	11	649	*5,799	8.94
David Klingler, Houston (I-A)	†1990	11	704	5,221	7.42
Ty Detmer, Brigham Young (I-A)	1990	12	635	5,022	7.91
Bruce Eugene, Grambling (I-AA)	2002	13	680	5,018	7.38
Kliff Kingsbury, Texas Tech (I-A)	2002	14	*814	4,903	6.02
Tim Rattay, Louisiana Tech (I-A)	†1998	12	602	4,840	8.04
Andre Ware, Houston (I-A)	†1989	11	628	4,661	7.42
Justin Peery, Westminster (Mo.) (III)	†1998	10	645	4,651	6.58
Jim McMahon, Brigham Young (I-A)	†1980	12	540	4,627	8.57
Willie Totten, Mississippi Val. (I-AA)	†1984	10	564	4,572	8.11
Timmy Chang, Hawaii (I-A)	2002	14	663	4,457	6.72
Ty Detmer, Brigham Young (I-A)	1989	12	497	4,433	8.92
Justin Peery, Westminster (Mo.) (III)	†1999	10	599	4,419	7.38
Roy Hampton, Trinity (Tex.) (III)	2002	14	464	4,418	@9.52
David Carr, Fresno St. (I-A)	2001	13	564	4,396	7.79
Steve Young, Brigham Young (I-A)	†1983	11	531	4,346	8.18
Jamie Martin, Weber St. (I-AA)	†1991	11	591	4,337	7.34
Chris Vargas, Nevada (I-A)	†1993	11	535	4,332	8.10
Wilkie Perez, Glenville St. (II)	†1997	11	509	4,301	8.45
Scott Mitchell, Utah (I-A)	†1988	11	589	4,299	7.30
Cody Pickett, Washington (I-A)	2002	13	698	4,273	6.12
Byron Leftwich, Marshall (I-A)	†2002	12	528	4,267	8.08
Andrew Webb, Fort Lewis (II)	†2002	11	613	4,245	6.92
Zamir Amin, Menlo (III)	†2000	10	511	4,231	8.28
Byron Leftwich, Marshall (I-A)	2001	12	534	4,224	7.91
Dave Dickenson, Montana (I-AA)	†1995	11	544	4,209	7.74
Josh Wallwork, Wyoming (I-A)	†1996	12	525	4,209	8.02
Neil Lomax, Portland St. (I-AA)	†1980	11	550	4,157	7.56
Brett Gordon, Villanova (I-AA)	2002	15	665	4,155	6.25
Daunte Culpepper, UCF (I-A)	1998	11	543	4,153	7.65
Tim Couch, Kentucky (I-A)	1998	11	617	4,151	6.73
Robbie Bosco, Brigham Young (I-A)	1985	13	578	4,141	7.16
Chris Weinke, Florida St. (I-A)	2000	12	461	4,070	8.83
Steve McNair, Alcorn St. (I-AA)	†1992	10	519	4,057	7.82
Perry Klein, C.W. Post (II)	†1993	10	499	4,052	8.12
Joe Leo, Towson (I-AA)	†1999	11	608	4,031	6.63
Chris Redman, Louisville (I-A)	1998	10	513	4,009	7.81
Ty Detmer, Brigham Young (I-A)	†1991	12	478	4,001	8.37
Brandon Doman, Brigham Young (I-A)	2001	13	550	3,998	7.27
Steve Sarkisian, Brigham Young (I-A)	1996	14	486	3,983	8.20
Terry Peebles, Hanover (III)	†1995	10	572	3,981	6.96
Dave Dickenson, Montana (I-AA)	†1993	11	530	3,978	7.51
Tim Rattay, Louisiana Tech (I-A)	†1997	11	541	3,968	7.33
Neil Lomax, Portland St. (I-AA)	†1979	11	611	3,966	6.49
Todd Cunningham, Presbyterian (II)	2001	11	607	3,959	6.52
Drew Brees, Purdue (I-A)	†2000	11	564	3,939	6.98
Robbie Bosco, Brigham Young (I-A)	†1984	12	543	3,932	7.24
Drew Brees, Purdue (I-A)	1998	12	575	3,921	6.82
Rex Grossman, Florida (I-A)	†2001	11	429	3,904	9.10
Chad Pennington, Marshall (I-A)	1999	12	460	3,904	8.49
Damian Poalucci, East Stroudsburg (II)	†1996	10	505	3,883	7.69
Brian Jones, Toledo (I-A)	2002	14	508	3,860	7.60
Mike McCoy, Utah (I-A)	1993	12	529	3,860	7.50
Danny Ragsdale, Redlands (III)	1999	9	464	3,855	8.31
John Friesz, Idaho (I-AA)	†1989	11	464	3,853	8.30
Steve McNair, Alcorn St. (I-AA)	1993	11	493	3,830	7.77
Jared Lorenzen, Kentucky (I-A)	2000	11	635	3,827	6.03
Todd Hammel, Stephen F. Austin (I-AA)	1989	11	487	3,822	7.85
Curt Anes, Grand Valley St. (II)	2002	14	457	3,821	8.36
Carson Palmer, Southern California (I-A)	2002	13	539	3,820	7.09
Tim Rattay, Louisiana Tech (I-A)	†1999	10	562	3,810	6.78
Ken Hobart, Idaho (I-AA)	1983	11	578	3,800	6.57
Dusty Bonner, Valdosta St. (II)	†2000	11	475	3,795	7.99
Joe Hamilton, Georgia Tech (I-A)	1999	11	459	3,794	8.27
Kirk Baumgartner, Wis.-Stevens Point (III)	†1988	11	604	3,790	6.27

Player, Team (Division)	Year	G	Plays	Yards	Avg.
Peyton Manning, Tennessee (I-A)	1997	12	526	3,789	7.20
Robert Kent, Jackson St. (I-AA)	2001	11	584	3,785	6.48
Chris Hegg, Truman (II)	†1985	11	594	3,782	6.37
Jimmy Klingler, Houston (I-A)	†1992	11	544	3,768	6.93
Rocky Butler, Hofstra (I-AA)	2001	11	450	3,764	8.36
Shaun King, Tulane (I-A)	1998	11	468	3,764	8.04
Dan Robinson, Hawaii (I-A)	1999	12	616	3,762	6.11
Dave Stireman, Weber St. (I-AA)	1985	11	502	3,759	7.49
Tim Couch, Kentucky (I-A)	1997	11	613	3,759	6.13
Chris Sanders, Chattanooga (I-AA)	2000	11	520	3,756	7.22

*Record. †National total-offense champion. @ Record for minimum 3,000 yards.

SINGLE-GAME YARDS

Yds.	Div.	Player, Team (Opponent)	Date
732	I-A	David Klingler, Houston (Arizona St.)	Dec. 2, 1990
723	III	Zamir Amin, Menlo (Cal Lutheran)	Oct. 7, 2000
696	I-A	Matt Vogler, TCU (Houston)	Nov. 3, 1990
668	I-AA	Robert Kent, Jackson St. (Alabama St.)	Oct. 6, 2001
660	II	Andrew Webb, Fort Lewis (Mesa St.)	Nov. 16, 2002
657	I-A	Brian Lindgren, Idaho (Middle Tenn.)	Oct. 6, 2001
651	II	Wilkie Perez, Glenville St. (Concord)	Oct. 25, 1997
649	I-AA	Steve McNair, Alcorn St. (Southern U.)	Oct. 22, 1994
647	I-AA	Steve McNair, Alcorn St. (Chattanooga)	Sept. 10, 1994
643	I-AA	Jamie Martin, Weber St. (Idaho St.)	Nov. 23, 1991
633	I-AA	Steve McNair, Alcorn St. (Grambling)	Sept. 3, 1994
631	II	Jayce Goree, Glenville St. (Concord)	Oct. 24, 1998
630	III	Justin Peery, Westminster (Mo.) (Colorado Col.)	Oct. 30, 1999
628	III	Justin Peery, Westminster (Mo.) (MacMurray)	Nov. 14, 1998
625	I-A	David Klingler, Houston (TCU)	Nov. 3, 1990
625	I-A	Scott Mitchell, Utah (Air Force)	Oct. 15, 1988
624	I-AA	Steve McNair, Alcorn St. (Samford)	Oct. 29, 1994
623	II	Perry Klein, C.W. Post (Salisbury)	Nov. 6, 1993
621	I-AA	Willie Totten, Mississippi Val. (Prairie View)	Oct. 27, 1984
617	III	Justin Peery, Westminster (Mo.) (Principia)	Oct. 17, 1998
614	I-AA	Bryan Martin, Weber St. (Cal Poly)	Sept. 23, 1995
614	II	Alfred Montez, Western N.M. (West Tex. A&M)	Oct. 8, 1994
612	I-A	Jimmy Klingler, Houston (Rice)	Nov. 28, 1992
610	II	Andrew Webb, Fort Lewis (Western N.M.)	Nov. 2, 2002
604	I-AA	Steve McNair, Alcorn St. (Jackson St.)	Nov. 21, 1992
603	I-A	Ty Detmer, Brigham Young (San Diego St.)	Nov. 16, 1991
601	I-A	Troy Kopp, Pacific (Cal.) (New Mexico St.)	Oct. 20, 1990
599	I-A	Virgil Carter, Brigham Young (UTEP)	Nov. 5, 1966
598	I-AA	Robert Kent, Jackson St. (N.C. A&T)	Sept. 7, 2002
597	II	Damian Poalucci, East Stroudsburg (Mansfield)	Nov. 2, 1996
597	I-A	John Walsh, Brigham Young (Utah St.)	Oct. 30, 1993
596	III	John Love, North Park (Elmhurst)	Oct. 13, 1990
595	I-AA	Doug Pederson, La.-Monroe (Stephen F. Austin)	Nov. 11, 1989
594	II	Jarrod DeGeorgia, Wayne St. (Neb.) (Drake)	Nov. 9, 1996
594	I-A	Jeremy Leach, New Mexico (Utah)	Nov. 11, 1989
591	II	Marty Washington, West Ala. (Nicholls St.)	Sept. 11, 1993
590	III	Danny Ragsdale, Redlands (Azusa Pacific)	Sept. 25, 1999
590	III	Tom Stallings, St. Thomas (Minn.) (Bethel [Minn.])	Nov. 13, 1993
588	III	Danny Ragsdale, Redlands (Cal Lutheran)	Nov. 13, 1999
587	I-AA	Vern Harris, Idaho St. (Montana)	Oct. 12, 1985
586	I-AA	Steve McNair, Alcorn St. (Troy St.)	Nov. 12, 1994
585	I-A	Dave Wilson, Illinois (Ohio St.)	Nov. 8, 1980

Rushing

CAREER YARDS PER GAME

(Minimum 2,500 Yards)

Player, Team (Division[s])	Years	G	Plays	Yards	TD	Yd. PG
Arnold Mickens, Butler (I-AA)	1994-95	20	763	3,813	29	*190.7
R.J. Bowers, Grove City (III)	1997-00	40	1,188	*7,353	91	183.8
Anthony Gray, Western N.M. (II)	1997-98	19	503	3,484	19	183.4
Ed Marinaro, Cornell (I-A)	1969-71	27	918	4,715	50	174.6
Damian Beane, Shepherd (II)	1996-99	38	1,065	6,346	58	167.0
Rob Marchitello, Maine Maritime (III)	1993-95	26	879	4,300	59	165.4
O.J. Simpson, Southern California (I-A)	1967-68	19	621	3,214	33	164.4
Kelvin Gladney, Millsaps (III)	1993-94	19	510	3,085	36	162.4
Johnny Bailey, Tex. A&M-Kingsville (II)	1986-89	39	885	6,320	66	162.1
Tyrone Morgan, Northern St. (II)	1998-00	30	830	4,816	56	160.5
Herschel Walker, Georgia (I-A)	1980-82	33	994	5,259	49	159.4
Brian Shay, Emporia St. (II)	1995-98	44	1,007	6,958	83	158.1
Carey Bender, Coe (III)	1991-94	39	926	6,125	71	157.1
Brad Olson, Lawrence (III)	1994-97	34	792	5,325	44	156.6
Steve Tardif, Maine Maritime (III)	1996-99	39	1,190	6,093	50	156.2
Adrian Peterson, Ga. Southern (I-AA)	1998-01	42	996	6,559	84	156.2
Kirk Matthieu, Maine Maritime (III)	$1989-93	33	964	5,107	41	154.8
Josh Ranek, South Dakota St. (II)	$1997-01	44	1,131	6,794	62	154.4
Aaron Stecker, Western Ill. (I-AA)	1997-98	20	550	3,081	36	154.1

Player, Team (Division[s])	Years	G	Plays	Yards	TD	Yd. PG
Tim Hall, Robert Morris (I-AA)	1994-95	19	393	2,908	27	153.1
Fred Lane, Lane (II)	1994-96	29	700	4,433	41	152.9
Terry Underwood, Wagner (III)	1985-88	33	742	5,010	52	151.8
Kavin Gailliard, American Int'l (II)	1996-99	43	950	6,523	69	151.7
Jerry Azumah, New Hampshire (I-AA)	1995-98	41	1,044	6,193	60	151.0
LeShon Johnson, Northern Ill. (I-A)	1992-93	22	592	3,314	18	150.6
Reggie Greene, Siena (I-AA)	1994-97	36	890	5,415	45	150.4
Ole Gunderson, St. Olaf (II)	1969-71	27	639	4,060	56	150.4
Richard Huntley, Winston-Salem (II)	1992-95	42	932	6,286	57	149.7
Charles Roberts, Sacramento St. (I-AA)	1997-00	44	1,124	6,553	56	148.9
Roger Graham, New Haven (II)	1991-94	40	821	5,953	66	148.8
Ron Dayne, Wisconsin (I-A)	1996-99	43	1,115	6,397	63	148.8
Marshall Faulk, San Diego St. (I-A)	1991-93	31	766	4,589	57	148.0
George Jones, San Diego St. (I-A)	1995-96	19	486	2,810	34	147.9
Ian Smart, C.W. Post (II)	1999-02	45	877	6,647	*94	147.7
D'Andra Freeman, Fitchburg St. (III)	1997-99	27	789	3,957	29	146.6
Brad Hustad, Luther (II)	1957-59	27	655	3,943	25	146.0
Rashaan Dumas, Southern Conn. St. (II)	1996-99	37	977	5,396	71	145.8
Archie Amerson, Northern Ariz. (I-AA)	1995-96	22	526	3,196	37	145.3
Jarrett Anderson, Truman (II)	1993-96	43	979	6,166	69	143.4
Quincy Tillmon, Emporia St. (II)	1990-92, 94	29	790	4,141	37	142.8
Anthony Russo, St. John's (N.Y.) (III)	1990-93	41	1,152	5,834	57	142.3
Tony Dorsett, Pittsburgh (I-A)	1973-76	43	1,074	6,082	55	141.4
Troy Davis, Iowa St. (I-A)	1994-96	31	782	4,382	36	141.4
Keith Elias, Princeton (I-AA)	1991-93	30	736	4,208	49	140.3

*Record. $See Page 8 for explanation.

SEASON YARDS PER GAME

Player, Team (Division)	Year	G	Plays	Yards	TD	Yd. PG
Barry Sanders, Oklahoma St. (I-A)	†1988	11	344	2,628	*37	*238.9
Dante Brown, Marietta (III)	†1996	10	314	2,385	25	238.5
R.J. Bowers, Grove City (III)	†1998	10	329	2,283	34	228.3
Arnold Mickens, Butler (I-AA)	†1994	10	*409	2,255	18	225.5
Carey Bender, Coe (III)	†1994	10	295	2,243	29	224.3
Anthony Gray, Western N.M. (II)	†1997	10	277	2,220	12	222.0
Kavin Gailliard, American Int'l (II)	†1999	12	320	*2,653	32	221.1
Marcus Allen, Southern California (I-A)	†1981	11	403	2,342	22	212.9
Ian Smart, C.W. Post (II)	†2001	12	308	2,536	33	211.3
R.J. Bowers, Grove City (III)	†1999	10	344	2,098	25	209.8
Ed Marinaro, Cornell (I-A)	†1971	9	356	1,881	24	209.0
Brian Shay, Emporia St. (II)	†1998	11	293	2,265	29	205.9
Charles Roberts, Sacramento St. (I-AA)	1998	11	386	2,260	19	205.5
Irv Sigler, Bloomsburg (II)	1997	10	299	2,038	20	203.8
Ricky Gales, Simpson (III)	†1989	10	297	2,035	26	203.5
Tony Vinson, Towson (I-AA)	†1993	10	293	2,016	23	201.6
Terry Underwood, Wagner (III)	†1988	9	245	1,809	21	201.0
Jerry Azumah, New Hampshire (I-AA)	1998	11	342	2,195	22	199.6
Troy Davis, Iowa St. (I-A)	†1996	11	402	2,185	21	198.6
Reggie Greene, Siena (I-AA)	†1997	9	256	1,778	18	197.6
Kenneth Sasu, Marietta (III)	1999	9	332	1,770	15	196.7
LaDainian Tomlinson, TCU (I-A)	†2000	11	369	2,158	22	196.2
Brad Olson, Lawrence (III)	†1995	9	242	1,760	16	195.6
Jarrett Anderson, Truman (II)	†1996	11	321	2,140	27	194.5
Ricky Williams, Texas (I-A)	†1998	11	361	2,124	27	193.1
Kirk Matthieu, Maine Maritime (III)	†1992	9	327	1,733	16	192.6
Brian Shay, Emporia St. (II)	1996	11	342	2,103	18	191.2
Reggie Greene, Siena (I-AA)	†1996	9	280	1,719	12	191.0
Jesse Chatman, Eastern Wash. (I-AA)	†2001	11	285	2,096	24	190.6
Byron Hanspard, Texas Tech (I-A)	1996	11	339	2,084	13	189.5
Charles Roberts, Sacramento St. (I-AA)	1999	11	303	2,082	22	189.3
Louis Ivory, Furman (I-AA)	†2000	11	286	2,079	16	189.0
Archie Amerson, Northern Ariz. (I-AA)	1996	11	333	2,079	25	189.0
Richard Huntley, Winston-Salem (II)	†1995	10	273	1,889	16	188.9
Kelvin Gladney, Millsaps (III)	1994	10	307	1,882	19	188.2
Brandon Steinheim, Wesley (III)	1996	9	319	1,684	20	187.1
D'Andra Freeman, Fitchburg St. (III)	1999	10	365	1,871	14	187.1
Rashaan Salaam, Colorado (I-A)	†1994	11	298	2,055	24	186.8
Josh Ranek, South Dakota St. (II)	1999	11	329	2,055	25	186.8
Krishaun Gilmore, Rensselaer (III)	1998	9	228	1,670	22	185.6
Jon Warga, Wittenberg (III)	†1990	10	254	1,836	15	183.6
Fred Lane, Lane (II)	1995	10	273	1,833	19	183.3
Johnny Bailey, Tex. A&M-Kingsville (II)	†1986	11	271	2,011	18	182.8
Troy Davis, Iowa St. (I-A)	†1995	11	345	2,010	15	182.7
Bob White, Western N.M. (II)	†1951	9	202	1,643	20	182.6
Kevin Mitchell, Saginaw Valley (II)	1989	8	236	1,460	6	182.5
Rashaan Dumas, Southern Conn. St. (II)	1996	9	291	1,639	18	182.1
Jamie Lee, MacMurray (III)	1998	10	252	1,818	25	181.8
Anthony Jones, La Verne (III)	1995	8	200	1,453	19	181.6
Hank Wineman, Albion (III)	†1991	9	307	1,629	14	181.0
Charles White, Southern California (I-A)	†1979	10	293	1,803	18	180.3

*Record. †National champion.

CAREER YARDS

Player, Team (Division[s])	Years	Plays	Yards	Avg.
R.J. Bowers, Grove City (III)	1997-00	1,188	*7,353	6.19
Brian Shay, Emporia St. (II)	1995-98	1,007	6,958	6.91
Josh Ranek, South Dakota St. (II)	$1997-01	1,131	6,794	6.01
Ian Smart, C.W. Post (II)	1999-02	877	6,647	++7.58
Adrian Peterson, Ga. Southern (I-AA)	1998-01	996	6,559	6.59
Charles Roberts, Sacramento St. (I-AA)	1997-00	1,124	6,553	5.83
Kavin Gailliard, American Int'l (II)	1996-99	950	6,523	6.87
Ron Dayne, Wisconsin (I-A)	1996-99	1,115	6,397	5.74
Damian Beane, Shepherd (II)	1996-99	1,065	6,346	5.96
Johnny Bailey, Tex. A&M-Kingsville (II)	1986-89	885	6,320	7.14
Richard Huntley, Winston-Salem (II)	1992-95	932	6,286	6.74
Ricky Williams, Texas (I-A)	1995-98	1,011	6,279	6.21
Jerry Azumah, New Hampshire (I-AA)	1995-98	1,044	6,193	5.93
Jarrett Anderson, Truman (II)	1993-96	979	6,166	6.30
Carey Bender, Coe (III)	1991-94	926	6,125	6.61
Steve Tardif, Maine Maritime (III)	1996-99	1,190	6,093	5.12
Tony Dorsett, Pittsburgh (I-A)	1973-76	1,074	6,082	5.66
Charles Dunn, Portland St. (II;I-AA)	1997; 98-00	1,098	6,007	5.47
Roger Graham, New Haven (II)	1991-94	821	5,953	7.25
Anthony Russo, St. John's (N.Y.) (III)	1990-93	1,152	5,834	5.06
Wesley Cates, Calif. (Pa.) (II)	1998-01	937	5,647	6.03
Charles White, Southern California (I-A)	1976-79	1,023	5,598	5.47
Travis Prentice, Miami (Ohio) (I-A)	1996-99	1,138	5,596	4.92
Joe Dudek, Plymouth St. (III)	1982-85	785	5,570	7.10
Matt Cannon, Southern Utah (QB) (I-AA)	1997-00	757	5,489	7.25
Phillip Moore, North Dakota (II)	1995-98	1,060	5,467	5.16
Mark Kacmarynski, Central (Iowa) (III)	$1992-96	854	5,434	6.36
Reggie Greene, Siena (I-AA)	1994-97	890	5,415	6.08
Rashaan Dumas, Southern Conn. St. (II)	1996-99	977	5,396	5.52
Marcel Shipp, Massachusetts (I-AA)	1997-00	1,042	5,383	5.17
Thomas Haskins, VMI (I-AA)	1993-96	899	5,355	5.96
Louis Ivory, Furman (I-AA)	1998-01	847	5,353	6.32
Frank Hawkins, Nevada (I-A)	1977-80	945	5,333	5.64
Howard Stevens, Randolph-Macon (II); Louisville (I-A)	1968-69; 71-72	891	5,297	5.95
Rick Sarille, Wagner (I-AA)	$1995-99	965	5,290	5.48
Eric Frees, McDaniel (III)	1988-91	1,059	5,281	4.99
LaDainian Tomlinson, TCU (I-A)	1997-00	907	5,263	5.80
Herschel Walker, Georgia (I-A)	1980-82	994	5,259	5.29
Kenny Gamble, Colgate (I-AA)	1984-87	963	5,220	5.42
Paul Smith, Gettysburg (III)	1996-99	881	5,205	5.91
Archie Griffin, Ohio St. (I-A)	1972-75	845	5,177	6.13
Antonio Leroy, Albany St. (Ga.) (II)	1993-96	973	5,152	5.29
Markus Thomas, Eastern Ky. (I-AA)	1989-92	784	5,149	6.57
Shawn Graves, Wofford (QB) (II)	1989-92	730	5,128	7.02
Casey Donaldson, Wittenberg (III)	1997-00	836	5,112	6.11
Kirk Matthieu, Maine Maritime (III)	$1989-93	964	5,107	5.30
Chris Cobb, Eastern Ill. (II)	1976-79	930	5,042	5.42
Irv Sigler, Bloomsburg (II)	1994-97	820	5,034	6.14

Mount Union's Dan Pugh (31) became just the sixth NCAA player to run for at least 2,300 yards in a season in 2002. He also set all-divisions records for touchdowns (41) and points scored (248) last year.

Andres Alonzo/NCAA Photos

Player, Team (Division[s])	Years	Plays	Yards	Avg.
Darren Lewis, Texas A&M (I-A)	1987-90	909	5,012	5.51
Terry Underwood, Wagner (III)	1985-88	742	5,010	6.75
Andre Braxton, Virginia Union (II)	1997-00	859	4,989	5.81
Anthony Thompson, Indiana (I-A)	1986-89	1,089	4,965	4.56
George Rogers, South Carolina (I-A)	1977-80	902	4,958	5.50
Trevor Cobb, Rice (I-A)	1989-92	1,091	4,948	4.54
Paul Palmer, Temple (I-A)	1983-86	948	4,895	5.16
Harry Jackson, St. Cloud St. (II)	1986-89	915	4,890	5.34
Leonard Davis, Lenoir-Rhyne (II)	$1990-94	839	4,853	5.78
Jerry Linton, Okla. Panhandle (II)	1959-62	648	4,839	7.47
Erik Marsh, Lafayette (I-AA)	1991-94	1,027	4,834	4.71
Tyrone Morgan, Northern St. (II)	1998-00	830	4,816	5.80

*Record. ++Record for minimum 600 carries. $See Page 8 for explanation.

SEASON YARDS

Player, Team (Division)	Year	G	Plays	Yards	Avg.
Kavin Gailliard, American Int'l (II)	†1999	12	320	*2,653	††8.29
Barry Sanders, Oklahoma St. (I-A)	†1988	11	344	2,628	7.64
Ian Smart, C.W. Post (II)	†2001	12	308	2,536	8.23
Dante Brown, Marietta (III)	†1996	10	314	2,385	7.60
Marcus Allen, Southern California (I-A)	†1981	11	403	2,342	5.81
Dan Pugh, Mount Union (III)	†2002	14	384	2,300	5.99
R.J. Bowers, Grove City (III)	†1998	10	329	2,283	6.94
Brian Shay, Emporia St. (II)	†1998	11	293	2,265	7.73
Charles Roberts, Sacramento St. (I-AA)	†1998	11	386	2,260	5.85
Arnold Mickens, Butler (I-AA)	†1994	10	*409	2,255	5.51
Carey Bender, Coe (III)	†1994	10	295	2,243	7.60
Anthony Gray, Western N.M. (II)	†1997	10	277	2,220	8.01
Jerry Azumah, New Hampshire (I-AA)	1998	11	342	2,195	6.42
Troy Davis, Iowa St. (I-A)	†1996	11	402	2,185	5.44
LaDainian Tomlinson, TCU (I-A)	†2000	11	369	2,158	5.85
Mike Rozier, Nebraska (I-A)	†1983	12	275	2,148	7.81
Jarrett Anderson, Truman (II)	†1996	11	321	2,140	6.67
Ricky Williams, Texas (I-A)	†1998	11	361	2,124	5.88
Brian Shay, Emporia St. (II)	1996	11	342	2,103	6.15
R.J. Bowers, Grove City (III)	†1999	10	344	2,098	6.10
Jesse Chatman, Eastern Wash. (I-AA)	†2001	11	285	2,096	7.35
Larry Johnson, Penn St. (I-A)	†2002	13	271	2,087	7.70
Byron Hanspard, Texas Tech (I-A)	1996	11	339	2,084	6.15
Charles Roberts, Sacramento St. (I-AA)	†1999	11	303	2,082	6.87
Louis Ivory, Furman (I-AA)	†2000	11	286	2,079	7.27
Archie Amerson, Northern Ariz. (I-AA)	1996	11	333	2,079	6.24
Rashaan Salaam, Colorado (I-A)	†1994	11	298	2,055	6.90
Josh Ranek, South Dakota St. (II)	1999	11	329	2,055	6.25
Irv Sigler, Bloomsburg (II)	1997	10	299	2,038	6.82
Ricky Gales, Simpson (III)	†1989	10	297	2,035	6.85
Ian Smart, C.W. Post (II)	†2002	12	287	2,023	7.05
Tony Vinson, Towson (I-AA)	†1993	10	293	2,016	6.89
Johnny Bailey, Tex. A&M-Kingsville (II)	†1986	11	271	2,011	7.42
Troy Davis, Iowa St. (I-A)	†1995	11	345	2,010	5.83
LeShon Johnson, Northern Ill. (I-A)	†1993	11	327	1,976	6.04
Kavin Gailliard, American Int'l (II)	1998	11	269	1,971	7.33
Aaron Stecker, Western Ill. (I-AA)	1997	11	298	1,957	6.57
Marcel Shipp, Massachusetts (I-AA)	1998	11	319	1,949	6.11
Tony Dorsett, Pittsburgh (I-A)	†1976	11	338	1,948	5.76
Wesley Cates, Calif. (Pa.) (II)	1999	11	298	1,935	6.49
Adrian Peterson, Ga. Southern (I-AA)	1998	11	257	1,932	7.52
Michael Turner, Northern Ill. (I-A)	2002	12	338	1,915	5.67
Damien Anderson, Northwestern (I-A)	2000	11	293	1,914	6.53
Brian Shay, Emporia St. (II)	1997	11	269	1,912	7.11
Lorenzo White, Michigan St. (I-A)	†1985	11	386	1,908	4.94
Wasean Tait, Toledo (I-A)	1995	11	357	1,905	5.34
Ricky Williams, Texas (I-A)	†1997	11	279	1,893	6.78
Karlton Carpenter, Southern Ill. (I-AA)	1998	11	323	1,892	5.86
Herschel Walker, Georgia (I-A)	†1981	11	385	1,891	4.91
Brian Pruitt, Central Mich. (I-A)	1994	11	292	1,890	6.47

Player, Team (Division)	Year	G	Plays	Yards	Avg.
Richard Huntley, Winston-Salem (II)	†1995	10	273	1,889	6.92
Quentin Griffin, Oklahoma (I-A)	2002	14	287	1,884	6.56
Rich Erenberg, Colgate (I-AA)	†1983	11	302	1,883	6.24
Kelvin Gladney, Millsaps (III)	1994	10	307	1,882	6.13
Ed Marinaro, Cornell (I-A)	†1971	9	356	1,881	5.28
Josh Ranek, South Dakota St. (II)	1998	11	302	1,881	6.23
Ernest Anderson, Oklahoma St. (I-A)	†1982	11	353	1,877	5.32
Ahman Green, Nebraska (I-A)	1997	12	278	1,877	6.75
Ricky Bell, Southern California (I-A)	†1975	11	357	1,875	5.25
D'Andra Freeman, Fitchburg St. (III)	1999	10	365	1,871	5.13
Paul Palmer, Temple (I-A)	†1986	11	346	1,866	5.39
Ronald Moore, Pittsburg St. (II)	1992	11	239	1,864	7.80
Ron Dayne, Wisconsin (I-A)	1996	12	295	1,863	6.32
David McNeal, Merchant Marine (III)	2002	11	338	1,860	5.50
LaDainian Tomlinson, TCU (I-A)	†1999	11	268	1,850	6.90

*Record. †National champion. ††Record for minimum 214 carries.

SINGLE-GAME YARDS

Yds.	Div.	Player, Team (Opponent)	Date
441	III	Dante Brown, Marietta (Baldwin-Wallace)	Oct. 5, 1996
437	I-AA	Maurice Hicks, N.C. A&T (Morgan St.)	Oct. 6, 2001
436	III	A.J. Pittorino, Hartwick (Waynesburg)	Nov. 2, 1996
417	III	Carey Bender, Coe (Grinnell)	Oct. 9, 1993
413	III	Dante Brown, Marietta (Heidelberg)	Nov. 9, 1996
409	I-AA	Charles Roberts, Sacramento St. (Idaho St.)	Nov. 6, 1999
406	I-A	LaDainian Tomlinson, TCU (UTEP)	Nov. 20, 1999
405	II	Alvon Brown, Kentucky St. (Ky. Wesleyan)	Sept. 16, 2000
403	II	Rob Davidson, Fairmont St. (Concord)	Nov. 14, 1998
396	I-A	Tony Sands, Kansas (Missouri)	Nov. 23, 1991
393	I-AA	Ryan Fuqua, Portland St. (Eastern Wash.)	Nov. 10, 2001
390	III	Paul Smith, Gettysburg (Muhlenberg)	Oct. 23, 1999
386	I-A	Marshall Faulk, San Diego St. (Pacific [Cal.])	Sept. 14, 1991
382	III	Shane Davis, Loras (Dubuque)	Nov. 8, 1997
382	III	Pete Baranek, Carthage (North Central)	Oct. 5, 1985
382	II	Kelly Ellis, Northern Iowa (Western Ill.)	Oct. 13, 1979
380	II	Garrion Corbin, Tiffin (Quincy)	Nov. 16, 2002
379	I-AA	Reggie Greene, Siena (St. John's [N.Y.])	Nov. 2, 1996
378	II	Jason Broom, Fort Hays St. (Okla. Panhandle)	Oct. 6, 2001
378	I-A	Troy Davis, Iowa St. (Missouri)	Sept. 28, 1996
377	I-A	Robbie Mixon, Central Mich. (Eastern Mich.)	Nov. 2, 2002
377	I-A	Anthony Thompson, Indiana (Wisconsin)	Nov. 11, 1989
376	I-A	Travis Prentice, Miami (Ohio) (Akron)	Nov. 6, 1999
373	I-A	Astron Whatley, Kent St. (Eastern Mich.)	Sept. 20, 1997
373	II	Dallas Garber, Marietta (Wash. & Jeff.)	Nov. 7, 1959
370	II	Jim Baier, Wis.-River Falls (Wis.-Stevens Point)	Nov. 5, 1966
370	II	Jim Hissam, Marietta (Bethany [W.Va.])	Nov. 15, 1958
367	II	Don Polkinghorne, Washington (Mo.) (Wash. & Lee)	Nov. 23, 1957
364	I-AA	Tony Vinson, Towson (Bucknell)	Nov. 13, 1993
363	III	Terry Underwood, Wagner (Hofstra)	Oct. 15, 1988
363	II	Richie Weaver, Widener (Moravian)	Oct. 17, 1970
361	III	Guy Leman, Simpson (Luther)	Nov. 14, 1998
361	II	Brian Shay, Emporia St. (Washburn)	Oct. 5, 1996
361	II	Richard Huntley, Winston-Salem (Virginia Union)	Nov. 5, 1994
359	II	Anthony Gray, Western N.M. (Hardin-Simmons)	Oct. 4, 1997
357	I-A	Mike Pringle, Cal St. Fullerton (New Mexico St.)	Nov. 4, 1989
357	I-A	Rueben Mayes, Washington St. (Oregon)	Oct. 27, 1984
356	I-A	Brian Pruitt, Central Mich. (Toledo)	Nov. 5, 1994
356	I-A	Eddie Lee Ivery, Georgia Tech (Air Force)	Nov. 11, 1978
356	II	Ole Gunderson, St. Olaf (Monmouth [Ill.])	Oct. 11, 1969
354	III	Terry Underwood, Wagner (Western Conn. St.)	Oct. 3, 1986
353	I-AA	Maurice Hicks, N.C. A&T (South Carolina St.)	Nov. 18, 2000
352	III	Steve Tardif, Maine Maritime (Westfield St.)	Nov. 16, 1996
351	I-A	Scott Harley, East Caro. (North Carolina St.)	Nov. 30, 1996
350	II	Ricke Stonewall, Millersville (New Haven)	Nov. 13, 1982
350	I-A	Eric Allen, Michigan St. (Purdue)	Oct. 30, 1971

Passing

CAREER PASSING EFFICIENCY

(Minimum 475 Completions)

Player, Team (Division[s])	Years	Att.	Cmp.	Int.	Pct.	Yds.	TD	Pts.
Bill Borchert, Mount Union (III)	1994-97	1,009	671	17	.665	10,201	141	*194.2
Gary Smeck, Mount Union (III)	1997-00	752	504	15	.670	7,764	83	186.2
Roy Hampton, Trinity (Tex.) (III)	$1998-02	942	600	26	.637	8,869	94	170.2
Dusty Bonner, Kentucky (I-A); Valdosta St. (II)	1997,99-01	1,233	861	27	.698	10,501	123	169.9
J.T. O'Sullivan, UC Davis (II)	1998-01	808	510	32	.631	8,143	72	169.3
Dave Dickenson, Montana (I-AA)	1992-95	1,208	813	26	.673	11,080	96	166.3
Corte McGuffey, Northern Colo. (II)	1996-99	768	484	23	.630	6,975	75	165.6
Curt Anes, Grand Valley St. (II)	1999-02	1,186	741	27	.625	10,581	114	164.6
Danny Wuerffel, Florida (I-A)	1993-96	1,170	708	42	.605	10,875	114	163.6
Chad Johnson, Pacific Lutheran (III)	1998-00	699	491	20	.702	6,292	48	162.8
Ty Detmer, Brigham Young (I-A)	1988-91	1,530	958	65	.626	*15,031	121	162.7
Steve Sarkisian, Brigham Young (I-A)	1995-96	789	528	26	.669	7,464	53	162.0
Zamir Amin, Menlo (III)	1999-01	905	566	29	.625	7,982	83	160.5
Mike Simpson, Eureka (III)/ Eastern Ill. (I-AA)	1993-94, 96-97	724	481	25	.664	6,402	58	160.3
Jim Ballard, Wilmington (Ohio)/ Mount Union (III)	1990, 91-93	1,199	743	41	.620	10,379	115	159.5
Justin Coleman, Neb.-Kearney (II)	1997-00	1,193	706	42	.592	11,213	99	158.5
Troy Dougherty, Grinnell (III)	1994, 97-99	1,192	734	33	.616	10,140	109	157.7
Billy Blanton, San Diego St. (I-A)	1993-96	920	588	25	.639	8,165	67	157.1
Jim McMahon, Brigham Young (I-A)	1977-78, 80-81	1,060	653	34	.616	9,536	84	156.9
Donovan McNabb, Syracuse (I-A)	1995-98	938	548	26	.584	8,389	77	155.1
Brian Dawson, Wash. & Jeff. (III)	1999-02	1,132	670	45	.592	10,257	94	154.8
Doug Nussmeier, Idaho (I-AA)	1990-93	1,225	746	32	.609	10,824	91	154.4
Tim Rattay, Louisiana Tech (I-A)	1997-99	1,552	1,015	35	.654	12,746	115	154.3
Chris Hatcher, Valdosta St. (II)	1991-94	1,451	1,001	38	.690	10,878	116	153.1
Mike Burton, Trinity (Tex.) (III)	1996-99	1,067	631	29	.591	9,008	92	153.1
David Carr, Fresno St. (I-A)	1997-98, 00-01	877	551	21	.628	7,309	66	152.9
Mike Warker, Widener/Rowan (III)	1999-02	914	482	38	.527	8,540	79	151.4
Chad Pennington, Marshall (I-AA; I-A)	1995, 97-99	1,501	947	39	.631	12,348	110	151.2
Chris Weinke, Florida St. (I-A)	1997-00	1,107	650	32	.587	9,839	79	151.1
Steve Young, Brigham Young (I-A)	1981-83	908	592	33	.652	7,733	56	149.8
Justin Peery, Westminster (Mo.) (III)	1996-99	1,669	1,012	57	.606	13,262	*148	149.8
Jack Hull, Grand Valley St. (II)	1988-91	835	485	22	.581	7,120	64	149.7
Robbie Bosco, Brigham Young (I-A)	1983-85	997	638	36	.640	8,400	66	149.4
Elvis Grbac, Michigan (I-A)	1989-92	754	477	29	.633	5,859	64	148.9
Mike Maxwell, Nevada (I-A)	1993-95	881	560	33	.636	7,256	62	148.5
Ryan Vena, Colgate (I-AA)	1996-99	819	482	46	.589	7,427	61	148.4
Mike Cook, William & Mary (I-AA)	1995-98	804	495	21	.616	6,644	55	148.3
Michael Payton, Marshall (I-AA)	1989-92	876	542	32	.619	7,530	57	148.2
Joe Hamilton, Georgia Tech (I-A)	1996-99	1,020	629	39	.617	8,882	65	148.2
Chuck Long, Iowa (I-A)	$1981-85	1,072	692	46	.646	9,210	64	147.8
John Walsh, Brigham Young (I-A)	1991-94	973	587	35	.603	8,375	66	147.8
Aaron Flowers, Cal St. Northridge (I-AA)	1996-97	819	502	21	.613	6,766	54	147.3
Todd Cunningham, Presbyterian (II)	1998-01	1,376	834	47	.606	10,937	111	147.2
Peyton Manning, Tennessee (I-A)	1994-97	1,381	863	33	.625	11,201	89	147.1
Drew Folmar, Millersville (II)	1997-00	1,241	760	34	.612	9,903	91	147.0
Rex Grossman, Florida (I-A)	2000-02	1,110	677	36	.610	9,164	77	146.8
Willie Totten, Mississippi Val. (I-AA)	1982-85	1,555	907	75	.583	12,711	139	146.8
Daunte Culpepper, UCF (I-AA; I-A)	1995-98	1,391	889	42	.639	11,412	84	146.7
John Koz, Baldwin-Wallace (III)	1990-93	981	609	28	.621	7,724	71	146.4
Shane Stafford, Connecticut (I-AA)	1995-98	951	522	29	.549	8,368	67	146.0
Brian Ah Yat, Montana (I-AA)	1995-98	1,190	735	39	.618	9,315	89	145.6
Rob Johnson, Southern California (I-A)	1991-94	963	623	24	.647	7,743	52	145.1
Giovanni Carmazzi, Hofstra (I-AA)	1996-99	1,187	764	32	.644	9,371	71	145.0
Ron Sermarini, McDaniel (III)	1996-99	970	617	20	.636	7,197	68	144.9
Greg Kaiser, St. Thomas (Minn.) (III)	1996-99	810	498	23	.615	6,439	54	144.6
Jimmy Blanchard, Portland St. (I-AA)	1997-00	1,038	618	19	.595	8,455	63	144.3
Ted White, Howard (I-AA)	1995-98	1,163	635	34	.546	9,611	92	144.3
Steve McNair, Alcorn St. (I-AA)	1991-94	1,680	929	58	.553	14,496	119	144.3
George Godsey, Georgia Tech (I-A)	1998-01	765	484	18	.633	6,137	41	143.6
Mike Smith, Northern Iowa (I-AA)	1984-87	943	557	43	.591	8,219	58	143.5
Eric Miller, Bloomsburg (II)	1997-00	915	527	37	.576	7,474	70	143.4
Jeff Fox, Grand Valley St. (II)	1995-98	1,031	626	22	.607	8,197	62	143.1
Steve Stenstrom, Stanford (I-A)	1991-94	1,320	833	36	.631	10,531	72	142.7
Neil Lomax, Portland St. (II; I-AA)	1977, 78-80	1,606	938	55	.584	13,220	106	142.5
Lance Funderburk, Valdosta St. (II)	1993-96	1,054	689	23	.654	7,698	64	142.4
Marvin Graves, Syracuse (I-A)	1990-93	943	563	45	.597	8,466	48	142.4
Tom Ciaccio, Holy Cross (I-AA)	1988-91	1,073	658	46	.613	8,603	72	142.2
Kevin Ricca, Catholic (III)	1994-97	1,109	713	56	.643	9,469	89	142.0
Chris Esterley, St. Thomas (Minn.) (III)	1993-96	1,012	615	30	.608	7,709	71	142.0
George Bork, Northern Ill. (II)	1960-63	902	577	33	.640	6,782	60	141.8
Eric Beavers, Nevada (I-AA)	1983-86	1,094	646	37	.591	8,626	77	141.8
Tim Couch, Kentucky (I-A)	1996-98	1,184	795	35	.671	8,435	74	141.7
Doug Gaynor, Long Beach St. (I-A)	1984-85	837	569	35	.680	6,793	35	141.6
Scott Semptimphelter, Lehigh (I-AA)	1990-93	823	493	27	.599	6,668	50	141.5
Ed Hesson, Rowan (III)	1990-93	895	504	26	.563	7,053	67	141.2
Danny Kanell, Florida St. (I-A)	1992-95	851	529	26	.622	6,372	57	141.1

*Record. $See Page 8 for explanation.

CAREER PASSING EFFICIENCY

(Minimum 375-474 Completions)

Player, Team (Division)	Years	Att.	Cmp.	Int.	Pct.	Yds.	TD	Pts.
Chris Petersen, UC Davis (II)	1985-86	553	385	13	*.696	4,988	39	164.0
Kurt Ramler, St. John's (Minn.) (III)	1994-96	722	420	16	.582	6,475	75	163.4
Danny Ragsdale, Redlands (III)	1997-99	610	386	17	.633	5,560	51	161.9
Drew Miller, Montana (I-AA)	1999-00	654	430	14	.657	5,900	46	160.5
Kyle Adamson, Allegheny (III)	1995-97	608	388	18	.638	5,506	48	160.0
Jason Baer, Wash. & Jeff. (III)	1993-96	671	406	24	.605	5,632	66	156.3
Joe Germaine, Ohio St. (I-A)	1996-98	660	399	18	.605	5,844	52	155.4
Chad Johnson, Pacific Lutheran (III)	1998-00	699	433	20	.619	6,292	48	154.5
Joel Parrett, Bluffton (III)	1996-99	633	412	28	.651	5,684	43	154.1
Rick Hebert, American Int'l (II)	1996-99	699	423	16	.605	5,990	55	153.9
Mark Washington, Jackson St. (I-AA)	1996-99	724	384	24	.530	6,561	68	153.5
Joe Blake, Simpson (III)	1987-90	672	399	15	.594	6,183	43	153.3
Vinny Testaverde, Miami (Fla.) (I-A)	1982, 84-86	674	413	25	.613	6,058	48	152.9
Jim McMillan, Boise St. (II)	1971-74	640	382	29	.597	5,508	58	152.8
Sean Hoolihan, Wis.-Eau Claire (III)	1996-98	686	413	23	.602	6,301	46	152.8
Josh Wallwork, Wyoming (I-A)	1995-96	729	449	28	.616	6,453	54	152.7
Brian Eyerman, Indiana (Pa.) (II)	1999-02	837	467	32	.558	7,409	76	152.5
Trent Dilfer, Fresno St. (I-A)	1991-93	774	461	21	.596	6,944	51	151.2
Chris Greisen, Northwest Mo. St. (II)	1995-98	653	379	22	.580	5,741	51	150.9
Greg Lister, Rowan (III)	1994-97	773	454	29	.587	6,553	66	150.6
Troy Aikman, Oklahoma/UCLA (I-A)	1984-85, 87-88	637	401	18	.630	5,436	40	149.7
Chuck Hartlieb, Iowa (I-A)	1985-88	716	461	17	.643	6,269	34	148.9
Jay Johnson, Northern Iowa (I-AA)	1989-92	744	397	25	.534	7,049	51	148.9
Matt Nagy, Delaware (I-AA)	1997-00	771	433	32	.562	7,200	52	148.8
Scott Otis, Glenville St. (II)	1994-95	693	421	21	.608	5,563	56	148.8
Gary Collier, Emory & Henry (III)	1984-87	738	386	33	.523	6,103	80	148.6
Jesse Showerda, New Haven (II)	1993-96	675	402	15	.596	5,175	57	147.4
Grady Benton, West Tex. A&M (II)	1994-95	686	421	22	.614	5,618	49	147.3
Kenneth Biggles, Tennessee St. (I-AA)	1981-84	701	397	28	.566	5,933	57	146.6
Bobby Hoying, Ohio St. (I-A)	1992-95	782	463	33	.592	6,751	54	146.1
Oteman Sampson, Florida A&M (I-AA)	1996-97	686	387	26	.564	6,104	46	145.7
Gifford Nielsen, Brigham Young (I-A)	1975-77	708	415	29	.586	5,833	55	145.3
Bruce Upstill, Col. of Emporia (II)	1960-63	769	438	36	.570	6,935	48	144.0
Tom Ramsey, UCLA (I-A)	1979-82	691	411	33	.595	5,844	48	143.9
Jarrod DeGeorgia, Wayne St. (Neb.) (II)	1995-96	645	428	18	.664	5,161	31	143.9
Shawn Moore, Virginia (I-A)	1987-90	762	421	32	.552	6,629	55	143.8
Jeff Brown, Wheaton (Ill.) (III)	1992-95	767	441	30	.575	6,219	60	143.6
Neil Rose, Harvard (I-AA)	$1998-02	729	455	23	.624	5,949	41	143.2
Chris Gicking, Shippensburg (II)	1998-00	778	404	20	.519	6,365	65	143.1
Moses Moreno, Colorado St. (I-A)	1994-97	787	457	28	.581	6,689	49	142.9
Jerry Rhome, Southern Methodist/Tulsa (I-A)	1961, 63-64	713	448	23	.628	5,472	47	142.6
Braniff Bonaventure, Furman (I-AA)	1993-96	672	413	17	.615	5,361	39	142.6
Lon Erickson, Ill. Wesleyan (III)	1993-96	786	461	24	.587	6,108	58	142.2
Todd Donnan, Marshall (I-AA)	1991-94	712	425	25	.597	5,566	51	142.0

*Record. $See Page 8 for explanation.

SEASON PASSING EFFICIENCY

(Minimum 30 Attempts Per Game)

Player, Team (Division)	Year	G	Att.	Cmp.	Int.	Pct.	Yds.	TD	Pts.
Jim Ballard, Mount Union (III)	1993	10	314	229	11	.729	3,304	37	*193.2
Jayson Merrill, Western St. (II)	†1991	10	309	195	11	.631	3,484	35	188.1
Dusty Bonner, Valdosta St. (II)	2000	11	435	317	6	.728	3,907	54	186.5
Kevin Ricca, Catholic (III)	1997	10	306	208	6	.679	2,990	35	183.9
John Charles, Portland St. (II)	1992	8	263	179	7	.681	2,770	24	181.3
Chad Johnson, Pacific Lutheran (III)	2000	9	274	185	6	.675	2,839	24	179.1
Chris Hatcher, Valdosta St. (II)	†1994	11	430	321	9	*.747	3,591	50	179.0
Wilkie Perez, Glenville St. (II)	†1997	11	425	280	12	.658	4,189	45	178.0
Jim McMahon, Brigham Young (I-A)	†1980	12	445	284	18	.638	4,571	47	176.9
Ty Detmer, Brigham Young (I-A)	†1989	12	412	265	15	.643	4,560	32	175.6
Chris Boden, Villanova (I-AA)	1997	11	345	231	4	.670	3,079	36	174.0
Trent Dilfer, Fresno St. (I-A)	†1993	11	333	217	4	.652	3,276	28	173.1
Jerry Rhome, Tulsa (I-A)	†1964	10	326	224	4	.687	2,870	32	172.6
Rocky Butler, Hofstra (I-AA)	2001	11	335	206	4	.615	3,311	30	171.7
Rex Grossman, Florida (I-A)	†2001	11	395	259	12	.656	3,896	34	170.8
Danny Wuerffel, Florida (I-A)	1996	12	360	207	13	.575	3,625	39	170.6
Bart Hendricks, Boise St. (I-A)	†2000	11	347	210	8	.605	3,364	35	170.6
Daunte Culpepper, UCF (I-A)	1998	11	402	296	7	.736	3,690	28	170.2
Billy Blanton, San Diego St. (I-A)	1996	11	344	227	5	.660	3,221	29	169.6
Dave Dickenson, Montana (I-AA)	1995	11	455	309	9	.679	4,176	38	168.6
Drew Miller, Montana (I-AA)	†1999	10	368	240	8	.652	3,461	32	168.6
Ty Detmer, Brigham Young (I-A)	1991	12	403	249	12	.618	4,031	35	168.5
Steve Young, Brigham Young (I-A)	†1983	11	429	306	10	.713	3,902	33	168.5
Willie Totten, Mississippi Val. (I-AA)	†1983	9	279	174	9	.624	2,566	29	167.5
David Carr, Fresno St. (I-A)	2001	13	476	308	7	.647	4,299	42	166.7
Byron Leftwich, Marshall (I-A)	2001	12	470	315	7	.670	4.132	38	164.6
Dave Dickenson, Montana (I-AA)	†1994	9	336	229	6	.682	3,053	24	164.5
Jim McMillan, Boise St. (II)	†1974	10	313	192	15	.613	2,900	33	164.4
Willie Totten, Mississippi Val. (I-AA)	†1984	10	518	324	22	.626	4,557	*56	163.6
Chris Weinke, Florida St. (I-A)	2000	12	431	266	11	.617	4,167	33	163.1
Jeff Wiley, Holy Cross (I-AA)	†1987	11	400	265	17	.663	3,677	34	163.0

Player, Team (Division)	Year	G	Att.	Cmp.	Int.	Pct.	Yds.	TD	Pts.
Todd Hammel, Stephen F. Austin (I-AA)	†1989	11	401	238	13	.594	3,914	34	162.8
Dennis Shaw, San Diego St. (I-A)	†1969	10	335	199	26	.594	3,185	39	162.2
Giovanni Carmazzi, Hofstra (I-AA)	1997	11	408	288	8	.706	3,554	27	161.7
John Friesz, Idaho (I-AA)	1989	11	425	260	8	.612	4,041	31	161.4
Willie Reyna, La Verne (III)	1991	8	267	170	6	.636	2,543	16	158.8

*Record. †National pass-efficiency champion.

SEASON PASSING EFFICIENCY

(Minimum 15 Attempts Per Game)

Player, Team (Division)	Year	G	Att.	Cmp.	Int.	Pct.	Yds.	TD	Pts.
Mike Simpson, Eureka (III)	†1994	10	158	116	5	.734	1,988	25	*225.0
Willie Seiler, St. John's (Minn.) (III)	†1993	10	205	141	6	.687	2,648	33	224.6
Curt Anes, Grand Valley St. (II)	†2001	10	271	189	3	.697	3,086	48	221.6
Dustin Proctor, Hardin-Simmons (III)	†2001	9	178	116	3	.652	2,194	28	217.2
Bill Borchert, Mount Union (III)	†1997	10	272	190	1	.698	2,933	47	216.7
Boyd Crawford, Col. of Idaho (II)	†1953	8	120	72	6	.600	1,462	21	210.1
Bill Borchert, Mount Union (III)	†1996	10	240	165	6	.687	2,655	38	208.9
Gary Smeck, Mount Union (III)	†1999	10	199	131	3	.658	2,274	30	208.6
Shawn Knight, William & Mary (I-AA)	†1993	10	177	125	4	.706	2,055	22	204.6
Matt LeFever, Western Conn. St. (III)	1999	10	158	95	7	.601	1,874	25	203.1
Brian Dawson, Wash. & Jeff. (III)	†2000	10	227	149	6	.656	2,675	29	201.5
Troy Dougherty, Grinnell (III)	†1998	10	293	198	5	.675	3,310	36	199.6
Dusty Bonner, Valdosta St. (II)	2001	11	319	231	8	.724	3,214	43	196.5
Bill Borchert, Mount Union (III)	†1995	10	225	160	4	.711	2,270	30	196.3
Jason Baer, Wash. & Jeff. (III)	1995	8	146	95	3	.650	1,536	19	192.3
Greg Lister, Rowan (III)	1997	9	162	111	4	.685	1,688	20	191.9
Gary Smeck, Mount Union (III)	2000	10	266	184	3	.691	2,773	30	191.7
J.T. O'Sullivan, UC Davis (II)	†2000	9	226	141	7	.623	2,648	25	191.1
Chuck Green, Wittenberg (II)	†1963	9	182	114	8	.626	2,181	19	189.0
Ty Grovesteen, Wis.-Whitewater (III)	1998	9	180	103	5	.572	2,074	22	188.8
Kurt Ramler, St. John's (Minn.) (III)	1994	9	154	93	4	.603	1,560	22	187.4
Roy Hampton, Trinity (Tex.) (III)	2001	9	251	168	7	.669	2,465	33	187.2
Rick Hebert, American Int'l (II)	†1999	12	234	166	4	.709	2,351	25	187.2
Jim Feeley, Johns Hopkins (II)	†1967	7	110	69	5	.627	1,264	12	186.2
Mike Bajakian, Williams (III)	1994	8	141	92	1	.652	1,382	17	186.0
John Charles, Portland St. (II)	1991	11	247	147	7	.595	2,619	32	185.7
Roy Hampton, Trinity (Tex.) (III)	†2002	14	397	260	6	.655	4,095	43	184.9
Steve Smith, Western St. (II)	†1992	10	271	180	5	.664	2,719	30	183.5
Rob Adamson, Mount Union (III)	2002	11	231	139	9	.602	2,424	30	183.4
Shaun King, Tulane (I-A)	†1998	11	328	223	6	.680	3,232	36	183.3
Mitch Sanders, Bridgeport (III)	†1973	10	151	84	7	.556	1,551	23	182.9
Jim Peterson, Hanover (II)	†1948	8	125	81	12	.648	1,571	12	182.9
John Wristen, Southern Colo. (II)	†1982	8	121	68	2	.562	1,358	13	182.6
Travis Miles, Northwest Mo. St. (II)	2000	11	248	155	7	.625	2,723	25	182.4
Michael Payton, Marshall (I-AA)	†1991	9	216	143	5	.622	2,333	19	181.3
Richard Basil, Savannah St. (II)	†1989	9	211	120	7	.568	2,148	29	181.1
Pat Mayew, St. John's (Minn.) (III)	†1991	9	247	154	4	.623	2,408	30	181.0
Matt LeFever, Western Conn. St. (III)	2000	10	171	110	4	.643	1,792	17	180.5
Michael Vick, Virginia Tech (I-A)	†1999	10	152	90	5	.592	1,840	12	180.4
Alli Abrew, Cal Poly (I-AA)	†1997	11	191	130	4	.681	1,961	17	179.5
Danny Wuerffel, Florida (I-A)	†1995	11	325	210	10	.646	3,266	35	178.4
Tony Romo, Eastern Ill. (I-AA)	†2001	10	207	138	6	.667	2,068	21	178.3
Doug Turner, Morehead St. (I-AA)	1997	10	290	190	6	.655	2,869	29	177.5
Guy Simons, Coe (III)	1993	10	185	110	9	.594	1,979	21	177.1
Curt Anes, Grand Valley St. (II)	†2002	14	414	278	6	.671	3,692	47	176.6
Jim Cahoon, Ripon (II)	†1964	8	127	74	7	.583	1,206	19	176.4
Ted White, Howard (I-AA)	†1996	11	289	174	10	.602	2,814	36	176.2
Rob Adamson, Mount Union (III)	2001	10	216	137	6	.634	2,252	20	176.0
Kyle Adamson, Allegheny (III)	1996	10	182	119	3	.653	1,761	18	176.0
Ken Suhl, New Haven (II)	1992	10	239	148	5	.619	2,336	26	175.7
Jimbo Fisher, Samford (III)	†1987	10	252	139	5	.551	2,394	34	175.4
Doug Nussmeier, Idaho (I-AA)	1993	11	304	185	5	.609	2,960	33	175.2
Joe Hamilton, Georgia Tech (I-A)	1999	11	305	203	11	.666	3,060	29	175.0
Brian Kadel, Dayton (I-AA)	†1995	11	183	115	6	.628	1,880	18	175.0
Gary Collier, Emory & Henry (III)	1987	11	249	152	10	.610	2,317	33	174.8
Brian Eyerman, Indiana (Pa.) (II)	2002	12	290	173	7	.597	2,724	36	174.7
Paul Bell, Allegheny (III)	1994	10	215	142	2	.660	2,137	17	173.8

*Record. †National pass-efficiency champion.

CAREER YARDS

Player, Team (Division[s])	Years	Att.	Cmp.	Int.	Pct.	Yds.	TD
Ty Detmer, Brigham Young (I-A)	1988-91	1,530	958	65	.626	*15,031	121
Steve McNair, Alcorn St. (I-AA)	1991-94	1,680	929	58	.553	14,496	119
Justin Peery, Westminster (Mo.) (III)	1996-99	1,669	1,012	57	.606	13,262	*148
Neil Lomax, Portland St. (II; I-AA)	1977, 78-80	1,606	938	55	.584	13,220	106
Kirk Baumgartner, Wis.-Stevens Point (III)	1986-89	1,696	883	57	.521	13,028	110
Tim Rattay, Louisiana Tech (I-A)	1997-99	1,552	1,015	35	.654	12,746	115
Willie Totten, Mississippi Val. (I-AA)	1982-85	1,555	907	75	.583	12,711	139
Chris Redman, Louisville (I-A)	1996-99	1,679	1,031	51	.614	12,541	84
Marcus Brady, Cal St. Northridge (I-AA)	1998-01	1,680	1,039	47	.618	12,479	109
Kliff Kingsbury, Texas Tech (I-A)	1999-02	*1,883	*1,231	40	.654	12,429	95
Chad Pennington, Marshall (I-AA; I-A)	1995, 97-99	1,501	947	39	.631	12,348	110

Player, Team (Division[s])	Years	Att.	Cmp.	Int.	Pct.	Yds.	TD
Jamie Martin, Weber St. (I-AA)	1989-92	1,544	934	56	.605	12,207	87
Todd Santos, San Diego St. (I-A)	1984-87	1,484	910	57	.613	11,425	70
Daunte Culpepper, UCF (I-AA; I-A)	1995-98	1,391	889	42	.639	11,412	84
Travis Brown, Northern Ariz. (I-AA)	1996-99	1,577	888	42	.563	11,400	86
Carson Palmer, Southern California (I-A)	$1998-02	1,515	895	49	.591	11,388	71
Tim Lester, Western Mich. (I-A)	1996-99	1,507	875	49	.581	11,299	87
Justin Coleman, Neb.-Kearney (II)	1997-00	1,193	706	42	.592	11,213	99
Peyton Manning, Tennessee (I-A)	1994-97	1,381	863	33	.625	11,201	89
Eric Zeier, Georgia (I-A)	1991-94	1,402	838	37	.598	11,153	67
Mark Novara, Lakeland (III)	1994-97	1,586	882	63	.556	11,101	100
Dave Dickenson, Montana (I-AA)	1992-95	1,208	813	26	.673	11,080	96
Todd Cunningham, Presbyterian (II)	1998-01	1,376	834	47	.606	10,937	111
Alex Van Pelt, Pittsburgh (I-A)	1989-92	1,463	845	59	.578	10,913	64
Drew Brees, Purdue (I-A)	1997-00	1,525	942	41	.618	10,909	81
David Neill, Nevada (I-A)	1998-01	1,376	763	33	.555	10,903	73
Chris Hatcher, Valdosta St. (II)	1991-94	1,451	1,001	38	.690	10,878	116
Danny Wuerffel, Florida (I-A)	1993-96	1,170	708	42	.605	10,875	114
Doug Nussmeier, Idaho (I-AA)	1990-93	1,225	746	32	.609	10,824	91
John Friesz, Idaho (I-AA)	1986-89	1,350	801	40	.593	10,697	77
Greg Wyatt, Northern Ariz. (I-AA)	1986-89	1,510	926	49	.613	10,697	70
Sean Payton, Eastern Ill. (I-AA)	1983-86	1,408	756	55	.537	10,655	75
Bob McLaughlin, Lock Haven (II)	1992-95	1,719	910	*88	.529	10,640	60
Kevin Sweeney, Fresno St. (I-A)	$1982-86	1,336	731	48	.547	10,623	66
Earl Harvey, N.C. Central (II)	1985-88	1,442	690	81	.479	10,621	86
Curt Anes, Grand Valley St. (II)	1999-02	1,186	741	27	.625	10,581	114
Doug Flutie, Boston College (I-A)	1981-84	1,270	677	54	.533	10,579	67
Dusty Bonner, Kentucky (I-A); Valdosta St. (II)	1997, 99-01	1,233	861	27	.698	10,501	123
Jim Ballard, Wilmington (Ohio)/Mount Union (III)	1990, 91-93	1,199	743	41	.620	10,379	115
Tom Arth, John Carroll (III)	1999-02	1,258	741	25	.589	10,345	89
Tom Ehrhardt, C. W. Post (II); Rhode Island (I-AA)	1981-82, 84-85	1,489	833	63	.559	10,325	92
Brian McClure, Bowling Green (I-A)	1982-85	1,427	900	58	.631	10,280	63
Troy Kopp, Pacific (Cal.) (I-A)	1989-92	1,374	798	47	.581	10,258	87
Brian Dawson, Wash. & Jeff. (III)	1999-02	1,132	670	45	.592	10,257	94
Bill Borchert, Mount Union (III)	1994-97	1,009	671	17	.665	10,201	141
Troy Dougherty, Grinnell (III)	1994, 97-99	1,192	734	33	.616	10,140	109
Adam Ryan, Wilmington (Ohio) (III)	1998-01	1,223	693	43	.567	10,095	88
Glenn Foley, Boston College (I-A)	1990-93	1,275	703	60	.551	10,042	72
Cade McNown, UCLA (I-A)	1995-98	1,153	646	39	.560	10,008	61
John Craven, Gardner-Webb (II)	1991-94	1,535	828	82	.539	9,934	80
Drew Folmar, Millersville (II)	1997-00	1,241	760	34	.612	9,903	91
Vernon Buck, Wingate (II)	1991-94	1,393	728	61	.523	9,884	72
Thad Trujillo, Fort Lewis (II)	1991-94	1,455	760	57	.522	9,873	78
Bryan Snyder, Albright (III)	1994-97	1,294	763	49	.590	9,865	92
Jarrod Furgason, Fairmont St. (II)	$1993-97	1,392	798	44	.573	9,856	101
Kasey Waterman, Mo. Western St. (II)	1998-01	1,273	714	57	.561	9,846	95
Chris Weinke, Florida St. (I-A)	1997-00	1,107	650	32	.587	9,839	79
Mike Mitros, West Chester (II)	1996-99	1,402	819	48	.584	9,834	94

*Record. $See Page 8 for explanation.

CAREER YARDS PER GAME

(Minimum 5,000 Yards)

Player, Team (Division[s])	Years	G	Att.	Cmp.	Int.	Pct.	Yds.	TD	Yd. PG
Tim Rattay, Louisiana Tech (I-A)	1997-99	33	1,552	1,015	35	.654	12,746	115	*386.2
Steve McNair, Alcorn St. (I-AA)	1991-94	42	1,680	929	58	.553	14,496	119	345.1
Justin Peery, Westminster (Mo.) (III)	1996-99	39	1,669	1,012	57	.606	13,262	*148	340.1
Aaron Flowers, Cal St. Northridge (I-AA)	1996-97	20	819	502	21	.613	6,766	54	338.3
Drew Miller, Montana (I-AA)	1999-00	18	654	430	14	.657	5,900	46	327.8
Ty Detmer, Brigham Young (I-A)	1988-91	46	1,530	958	65	.626	*15,031	121	326.8
Willie Totten, Mississippi Val. (I-AA)	1982-85	40	1,555	907	75	.583	12,711	139	317.8
Kirk Baumgartner, Wis.-Stevens Point (III)	1986-89	41	1,696	883	57	.521	13,028	110	317.8
Dave Dickenson, Montana (I-AA)	1992-95	35	1,208	813	26	.673	11,080	96	316.6
Eric Bruns, Hanover (III)	1999-00	20	842	541	30	.643	6,295	57	314.8
Neil Lomax, Portland St. (II; I-AA)	1977; 78-80	42	1,606	938	55	.584	13,220	106	314.8
Grady Benton, West Tex. A&M (II)	1994-95	18	686	421	22	.614	5,618	49	312.1
Mike Perez, San Jose St. (I-A)	1986-87	20	792	471	30	.595	6,194	36	309.7
Keith Bishop, Ill. Wes./Wheaton (Ill.) (III)	1981, 83-85	31	1,311	772	65	.589	9,579	71	309.0
Doug Gaynor, Long Beach St. (I-A)	1984-85	22	837	569	35	.680	6,793	35	308.8
Zamir Amin, Menlo (III)	1999-01	26	905	566	29	.625	7,982	83	307.0
Adam Ryan, Wilmington (Ohio) (III)	1998-01	33	1,223	693	43	.567	10,095	88	305.9
John Friesz, Idaho (I-AA)	1986-89	35	1,350	801	40	.593	10,697	77	305.6
Tony Eason, Illinois (I-A)	1981-82	22	856	526	29	.615	6,608	37	300.4

*Record.

CAREER TOUCHDOWN PASSES

Player, Team (Division[s])	Years	Att.	Cmp.	Int.	Pct.	Yds.	TD
Justin Peery, Westminster (Mo.) (III)	1996-99	1,669	1,012	57	.606	13,262	*148
Bill Borchert, Mount Union (III)	1994-97	1,009	671	17	.665	10,201	141
Willie Totten, Mississippi Val. (I-AA)	1982-85	1,555	907	75	.583	12,711	139
Dusty Bonner, Kentucky (I-A); Valdosta St. (II)	1997, 99-01	1,233	861	27	.698	10,501	123
Ty Detmer, Brigham Young (I-A)	1988-91	1,530	958	65	.626	*15,031	121
Steve McNair, Alcorn St. (I-AA)	1991-94	1,680	929	58	.553	14,496	119
Chris Hatcher, Valdosta St. (II)	1991-94	1,451	1,001	38	.690	10,878	116

Player, Team (Division[s])	Years	Att.	Cmp.	Int.	Pct.	Yds.	TD
Jim Ballard, Wilmington (Ohio)/Mount Union (III)	1990, 91-93	1,199	743	41	.620	10,379	115
Tim Rattay, Louisiana Tech (I-A)	1997-99	1,552	1,015	35	.654	12,746	115
Curt Anes, Grand Valley St. (II)	1999-02	1,186	741	27	.625	10,581	114
Danny Wuerffel, Florida (I-A)	1993-96	1,170	708	42	.605	10,875	114
Todd Cunningham, Presbyterian (II)	1998-01	1,376	834	47	.606	10,937	111
Kirk Baumgartner, Wis.-Stevens Point (III)	1986-89	1,696	883	57	.521	13,028	110
Chad Pennington, Marshall (I-AA; I-A)	1995, 97-99	1,501	947	39	.631	12,348	110
Marcus Brady, Cal St. Northridge (I-AA)	1998-01	1,680	1,039	47	.618	12,479	109
Troy Dougherty, Grinnell (III)	1994, 97-99	1,192	734	33	.616	10,140	109
Neil Lomax, Portland St. (II; I-AA)	1977; 78-80	1,606	938	55	.584	13,220	106
Jarrod Furgason, Fairmont St. (II)	$1993-97	1,392	798	44	.573	9,856	101
Mark Novara, Lakeland (III)	1994-97	1,586	882	63	.556	11,101	100
Justin Coleman, Neb.-Kearney (II)	1997-00	1,193	706	42	.592	11,213	99
Dave Dickenson, Montana (I-AA)	1992-95	1,208	813	26	.673	11,080	96
Kliff Kingsbury, Texas Tech (I-A)	1999-02	*1,883	*1,231	40	.654	12,429	95
Kasey Waterman, Mo. Western St. (II)	1998-01	1,273	714	57	.561	9,846	95
Matt Jozokos, Plymouth St. (III)	1987-90	1,003	527	39	.525	7,658	95
Roy Hampton, Trinity (Tex.) (III)	$1998-02	942	600	26	.637	8,869	94
Brian Dawson, Wash. & Jeff. (III)	1999-02	1,132	670	45	.592	10,257	94
Mike Mitros, West Chester (II)	1996-99	1,402	819	48	.584	9,834	94
Doug Williams, Grambling (II; I-A)	1974-76; 77	1,009	484	52	.480	8,411	93
Chris Boden, Villanova (I-AA)	1996-99	1,338	818	30	.611	9,538	93
Mike Burton, Trinity (Tex.) (III)	1996-99	1,067	631	29	.591	9,008	92
Ted White, Howard (I-AA)	1995-98	1,163	635	34	.546	9,611	92
Bryan Snyder, Albright (III)	1994-97	1,294	763	49	.590	9,865	92
Tom Ehrhardt, C.W. Post (II); Rhode Island (I-AA)	1981-82; 84-85	1,489	833	63	.559	10,325	92
Drew Folmar, Millersville (II)	1997-00	1,241	760	34	.612	9,903	91
Doug Nussmeier, Idaho (I-AA)	1990-93	1,225	746	32	.609	10,824	91
David Klingler, Houston (I-A)	1988-91	1,261	726	38	.576	9,430	91
Ricky Fritz, Minn. Duluth (II)	$1998-02	1,090	547	53	.502	8,711	90
Tom Arth, John Carroll (III)	1999-02	1,258	741	25	.589	10,345	89
Brian Ah Yat, Montana (I-AA)	1995-98	1,190	735	39	.618	9,315	89
Peyton Manning, Tennessee (I-A)	1994-97	1,381	863	33	.625	11,201	89
Kevin Ricca, Catholic (III)	1994-97	1,190	713	56	.643	9,469	89
Adam Ryan, Wilmington (Ohio) (III)	1998-01	1,223	693	43	.567	10,095	88
Maurice Heard, Tuskegee (II)	1988-91	1,134	556	54	.490	8,434	87
Tim Lester, Western Mich. (I-A)	1996-99	1,507	875	49	.581	11,299	87
Troy Kopp, Pacific (Cal.) (I-A)	1989-92	1,374	798	47	.581	10,258	87
Jamie Martin, Weber St. (I-AA)	1989-92	1,544	934	56	.605	12,207	87
Travis Brown, Northern Ariz. (I-AA)	1996-99	1,577	888	42	.563	11,400	86
Andy Breault, Kutztown (II)	1989-92	1,259	733	63	.582	9,086	86
Earl Harvey, N.C. Central (II)	1985-88	1,442	690	81	.479	10,621	86
Matt Bunyan, Wis.-Stout (III)	1995-98	1,119	624	36	.558	8,462	85

*Record. $See Page 8 for explanation.

SEASON YARDS

Player, Team (Division)	Year	G	Att.	Cmp.	Int.	Pct.	Yds.	TD
Ty Detmer, Brigham Young (I-A)	†1990	12	562	361	28	.642	*5,188	41
David Klingler, Houston (I-A)	1990	11	643	374	20	.582	5,140	54
Kliff Kingsbury, Texas Tech (I-A)	2002	14	*712	*479	13	.673	5,017	45
Tim Rattay, Louisiana Tech (I-A)	1998	12	559	380	13	.680	4,943	46
Steve McNair, Alcorn St. (I-AA)	1994	11	530	304	17	.574	4,863	44
Andre Ware, Houston (I-A)	†1989	11	578	365	15	.631	4,699	46
Jim McMahon, Brigham Young (I-A)	†1980	12	445	284	18	.638	4,571	47
Ty Detmer, Brigham Young (I-A)	1989	12	412	265	15	.643	4,560	32
Willie Totten, Mississippi Val. (I-AA)	†1984	10	518	324	22	.626	4,557	*56
Justin Peery, Westminster (Mo.) (III)	1998	10	526	319	21	.606	4,501	51
Bruce Eugene, Grambling (I-AA)	2002	13	543	269	16	.495	4,483	43
Timmy Chang, Hawaii (I-A)	2002	14	624	349	22	.559	4,474	25
Cody Pickett, Washington (I-A)	2002	13	612	365	14	.596	4,458	28
Scott Mitchell, Utah (I-A)	1988	11	533	323	15	.606	4,322	29
Zamir Amin, Menlo (III)	2000	10	458	309	17	.674	4,320	43
Brett Gordon, Villanova (I-AA)	2002	15	578	385	14	.666	4,305	36
David Carr, Fresno St. (I-A)	2001	13	476	308	7	.647	4,299	42
Tim Couch, Kentucky (I-A)	1998	11	553	400	15	.723	4,275	36
Byron Leftwich, Marshall (I-A)	2002	12	491	331	10	.674	4,268	30
Chris Vargas, Nevada (I-A)	1993	11	490	331	18	.676	4,265	34
Robbie Bosco, Brigham Young (I-A)	1985	13	511	338	24	.661	4,257	30
Wilkie Perez, Glenville St. (II)	†1997	11	425	280	12	.658	4,189	45
Dave Dickenson, Montana (I-AA)	1995	11	455	309	9	.679	4,176	38
Joe Lee, Towson (I-AA)	1999	11	577	322	13	.558	4,168	22
Chris Weinke, Florida St. (I-A)	2000	12	431	266	11	.617	4,167	33
Byron Leftwich, Marshall (I-A)	2001	12	470	315	7	.670	4,132	38
Jamie Martin, Weber St. (I-AA)	1991	11	500	310	17	.620	4,125	35
Andrew Webb, Fort Lewis (II)	2002	11	529	317	13	.599	4,109	37
Roy Hampton, Trinity (Tex.) (III)	†2002	14	397	260	6	.655	4,095	43
Neil Lomax, Portland St. (I-AA)	1980	11	473	296	12	.626	4,094	37
Justin Peery, Westminster (Mo.) (III)	1999	10	498	329	15	.660	4,092	54
Josh Wallwork, Wyoming (I-A)	1996	12	458	286	15	.625	4,090	33
Chris Redman, Louisville (I-A)	1998	10	473	309	15	.653	4,042	29
John Friesz, Idaho (I-AA)	†1989	11	425	260	8	.612	4,041	31
Ty Detmer, Brigham Young (I-A)	1991	12	403	249	12	.618	4,031	35
Steve Sarkisian, Brigham Young (I-A)	†1996	14	404	278	12	.688	4,027	33

Player, Team (Division)	Year	G	Att.	Cmp.	Int.	Pct.	Yds.	TD
Neil Lomax, Portland St. (I-AA)	1979	11	516	299	16	.579	3,950	26
Carson Palmer, Southern California (I-A)	2002	13	489	309	10	.632	3,942	33
Todd Santos, San Diego St. (I-A)	1987	12	492	306	15	.622	3,932	26
Tim Rattay, Louisiana Tech (I-A)	1999	10	516	342	12	.663	3,922	35
Todd Hammel, Stephen F. Austin (I-AA)	1989	11	401	238	13	.594	3,914	34
Dusty Bonner, Valdosta St. (II)	2000	11	435	317	6	.728	3,907	54
Steve Young, Brigham Young (I-A)	†1983	11	429	306	10	.713	3,902	33
Rex Grossman, Florida (I-A)	†2001	11	395	259	12	.656	3,896	34
Tim Couch, Kentucky (I-A)	1997	11	547	363	19	.664	3,884	37
Tim Rattay, Louisiana Tech (I-A)	1997	11	477	293	10	.614	3,881	34
Andrew Walter, Arizona St. (I-A)	2002	14	483	274	15	.567	3,877	28
Robbie Bosco, Brigham Young (I-A)	1984	12	458	283	11	.618	3,875	33
Todd Cunningham, Presbyterian (II)	2001	11	531	335	14	.631	3,860	36
Mike McCoy, Utah (I-A)	1993	12	430	276	10	.642	3,860	21
Dan Robinson, Hawaii (I-A)	1999	12	556	288	18	.518	3,853	28
Sean Payton, Eastern Ill. (I-AA)	1984	11	473	270	15	.571	3,843	28
Dan McGwire, San Diego St. (I-A)	1990	11	449	270	7	.601	3,833	27
Damian Poalucci, East Stroudsburg (II)	1996	11	393	214	13	.545	3,831	40
Kirk Baumgartner, Wis.-Stevens Point (III)	1988	11	527	276	16	.524	3,828	25
Anthony Dilweg, Duke (I-A)	1988	11	484	287	18	.593	3,824	24
Buster Faulkner, Valdosta St. (II)	2002	15	502	326	17	.649	3,821	41
Peyton Manning, Tennessee (I-A)	1997	12	477	287	11	.602	3,819	36
Jimmy Klingler, Houston (I-A)	1992	11	504	303	18	.601	3,818	32

*Record. †National pass-efficiency champion.

SEASON YARDS PER GAME

Player, Team (Division)	Year	G	Att.	Cmp.	Int.	Pct.	Yds.	TD	Yd. PG
David Klingler, Houston (I-A)	1990	11	643	374	20	.582	5,140	54	*467.3
Willie Totten, Mississippi Val. (I-AA)	1984	10	518	324	22	.626	4,557	*56	455.7
Justin Peery, Westminster (Mo.) (III)	1998	10	526	319	21	.606	4,501	51	450.1
Steve McNair, Alcorn St. (I-AA)	1994	11	530	304	17	.574	4,863	44	442.1
Ty Detmer, Brigham Young (I-A)	1990	12	562	361	28	.642	*5,188	41	432.3
Zamir Amin, Menlo (III)	2000	10	458	309	17	.674	4,320	43	432.0
Andre Ware, Houston (I-A)	1989	11	578	365	15	.631	4,699	46	427.2
Tim Rattay, Louisiana Tech (I-A)	1998	12	559	380	13	.680	4,943	46	411.9
Justin Peery, Westminster (Mo.) (III)	1999	10	498	329	15	.660	4,092	54	409.2
Danny Ragsdale, Redlands (III)	1999	9	380	247	7	.650	3,639	33	404.3
Chris Redman, Louisville (I-A)	1998	10	473	309	15	.653	4,042	29	404.2
Mike Maxwell, Nevada (I-A)	1995	9	409	277	17	.677	3,611	33	401.2
Grady Benton, West Tex. A&M (II)	1994	9	409	258	13	.631	3,541	30	393.4
Scott Mitchell, Utah (I-A)	1988	11	533	323	15	.606	4,322	29	392.9
Tim Rattay, Louisiana Tech (I-A)	1999	10	516	342	12	.663	3,922	35	392.2
Tim Couch, Kentucky (I-A)	1998	11	553	400	15	.723	4,275	36	388.6
Chris Vargas, Nevada (I-A)	1993	11	490	331	18	.676	4,265	34	387.7
Damian Poalucci, East Stroudsburg (II)	1996	11	393	214	13	.545	3,831	40	383.1
Marty Washington, West Ala. (II)	1993	8	404	221	13	.547	3,062	26	382.8
Jim McMahon, Brigham Young (I-A)	1980	12	445	284	18	.638	4,571	47	380.9
Wilkie Perez, Glenville St. (II)	1997	11	425	280	12	.658	4,189	45	380.8
Ty Detmer, Brigham Young (I-A)	1989	12	412	265	15	.643	4,560	32	380.0

*Record.

SEASON TOUCHDOWN PASSES

Player, Team (Division)	Year	Att.	Cmp.	Int.	Pct.	Yds.	TD
Willie Totten, Mississippi Val. (I-AA)	1984	518	324	22	.626	4,557	*56
Dusty Bonner, Valdosta St. (II)	2000	435	317	6	.728	3,907	54
Justin Peery, Westminster (Mo.) (III)	1999	498	329	15	.660	4,092	54
David Klingler, Houston (I-A)	1990	643	374	20	.582	5,140	54
Justin Peery, Westminster (Mo.) (III)	1998	526	319	21	.606	4,501	51
Chris Hatcher, Valdosta St. (II)	†1994	430	321	9	*.747	3,591	50
Curt Anes, Grand Valley St. (II)	†2001	271	189	3	.697	3,086	48
Curt Anes, Grand Valley St. (II)	†2002	414	278	6	.671	3,692	47
Bill Borchert, Mount Union (III)	†1997	272	190	1	.698	2,933	47
Jim McMahon, Brigham Young (I-A)	1980	445	284	18	.638	4,571	47
Tim Rattay, Louisiana Tech (I-A)	1998	559	380	13	.680	4,943	46
Andre Ware, Houston (I-A)	1989	578	365	15	.631	4,699	46
Kliff Kingsbury, Texas Tech (I-A)	2002	*712	*479	13	.673	5,017	45
Wilkie Perez, Glenville St. (II)	†1997	425	280	12	.658	4,189	45
Bob Toledo, San Fran. St. (II)	1967	396	211	24	.533	3,513	45
Steve McNair, Alcorn St. (I-AA)	1994	530	304	17	.574	4,863	44
Bruce Eugene, Grambling (I-AA)	2002	543	269	16	.495	4,483	43
Roy Hampton, Trinity (Tex.) (III)	†2002	397	260	6	.655	4,095	43
Dusty Bonner, Valdosta St. (II)	2001	319	231	8	.724	3,214	43
Zamir Amin, Menlo (III)	2000	458	309	17	.674	4,320	43
David Carr, Fresno St. (I-A)	2001	476	308	7	.647	4,299	42
Brian Ah Yat, Montana (I-AA)	1996	432	265	16	.613	3,615	42
Buster Faulkner, Valdosta St. (II)	2002	502	326	17	.649	3,821	41
Ty Detmer, Brigham Young (I-A)	1990	562	361	28	.642	*5,188	41

Player, Team (Division)	Year	Att.	Cmp.	Int.	Pct.	Yds.	TD
Damian Poalucci, East Stroudsburg (II)	1996	393	214	13	.545	3,831	40
Mark Novara, Lakeland (III)	1996	410	258	12	.629	3,405	40
Chad Pennington, Marshall (I-A)	1997	428	253	12	.591	3,480	39
Danny Wuerffel, Florida (I-A)	1996	360	207	13	.575	3,625	39
Terry Peebles, Hanover (III)	1995	488	283	10	.579	3,521	39
Kirk Baumgartner, Wis.-Stevens Point (III)	1989	455	247	9	.542	3,692	39
Willie Totten, Mississippi Val. (I-AA)	1985	492	295	29	.600	3,698	39
Dennis Shaw, San Diego St. (I-A)	1969	335	199	26	.594	3,185	39
Byron Leftwich, Marshall (I-A)	2001	470	315	7	.670	4,132	38
Matt Bunyan, Wis.-Stout (III)	1998	389	227	9	.583	3,220	38
Bryan Snyder, Albright (III)	1996	358	223	9	.622	2,983	38
Bill Borchert, Mount Union (III)	†1996	240	165	6	.687	2,655	38
Dave Dickenson, Montana (I-AA)	1995	455	309	9	.679	4,176	38
Perry Klein, C.W. Post (II)	1993	407	248	18	.609	3,757	38
Doug Williams, Grambling (I-A)	1977	352	181	18	.514	3,286	38

*Record. †National pass-efficiency champion.

SINGLE-GAME YARDS

Yds.	Div.	Player, Team (Opponent)	Date
731	III	Zamir Amin, Menlo (Cal Lutheran)	Oct. 7, 2000
716	I-A	David Klingler, Houston (Arizona St.)	Dec. 2, 1990
690	I-A	Matt Vogler, TCU (Houston)	Nov. 3, 1990
642	II	Wilkie Perez, Glenville St. (Concord)	Oct. 25, 1997
638	II	Andrew Webb, Fort Lewis (Mesa St.)	Nov. 16, 2002
637	I-A	Brian Lindgren, Idaho (Middle Tenn.)	Oct. 6, 2001

Yds.	Div.	Player, Team (Opponent)	Date
631	I-A	Scott Mitchell, Utah (Air Force)	Oct. 15, 1988
624	I-AA	Jamie Martin, Weber St. (Idaho St.)	Nov. 23, 1991
622	I-A	Jeremy Leach, New Mexico (Utah)	Nov. 11, 1989
621	I-A	Dave Wilson, Illinois (Ohio St.)	Nov. 8, 1980
619	III	Justin Peery, Westminster (Mo.) (MacMurray)	Nov. 14, 1998
619	I-A	John Walsh, Brigham Young (Utah St.)	Oct. 30, 1993
619	I-AA	Doug Pederson, La.-Monroe (Stephen F. Austin)	Nov. 11, 1989
618	III	Justin Peery, Westminster (Mo.) (Principia)	Oct. 17, 1998
616	II	Damian Poalucci, East Stroudsburg (Mansfield)	Nov. 2, 1996
614	II	Alfred Montez, Western N.M. (West Tex. A&M)	Oct. 8, 1994
614	II	Perry Klein, C.W. Post (Salisbury)	Nov. 6, 1993
613	II	Jayce Goree, Glenville St. (Concord)	Oct. 24, 1998
613	I-A	Jimmy Klingler, Houston (Rice)	Nov. 28, 1992
611	I-A	David Neill, Nevada (New Mexico St.)	Oct. 10, 1998
602	III	Danny Ragsdale, Redlands (Azusa Pacific)	Sept. 25, 1999
602	III	Tom Stallings, St. Thomas (Minn.) (Bethel [Minn.])	Nov. 13, 1993
599	II	Jarrod DeGeorgia, Wayne St. (Neb.) (Drake)	Nov. 9, 1996
599	I-A	Ty Detmer, Brigham Young (San Diego St.)	Nov. 16, 1991
599	I-AA	Willie Totten, Mississippi Val. (Prairie View)	Oct. 27, 1984
595	III	Robert Kent, Jackson St. (Alabama St.)	Oct. 6, 2001
592	I-A	Chris Redman, Louisville (East Caro.)	Nov. 14, 1998
592	II	John Charles, Portland St. (Cal Poly)	Nov. 16, 1991
590	I-A	Tim Rattay, Louisiana Tech (Nebraska)	Aug. 29, 1998
589	III	Joe Montrella, Juniata (Widener)	Nov. 13, 1999
589	I-AA	Vern Harris, Idaho St. (Montana)	Oct. 12, 1985
587	I-AA	Steve McNair, Alcorn St. (Southern U.)	Oct. 22, 1994
585	III	Tim Lynch, Hofstra (Fordham)	Oct. 19, 1991
585	I-A	Robbie Bosco, Brigham Young (New Mexico)	Oct. 19, 1985
579	II	Chris Reil, Henderson St. (Arkansas Tech)	Oct. 28, 2000
575	III	Eric Noble, Wilmington (Ohio) (Urbana)	Nov. 5, 1994
574	III	Zamir Amin, Menlo (Linfield)	Sept. 9, 2000
572	I-A	David Klingler, Houston (Eastern Wash.)	Nov. 17, 1990
571	I-AA	Todd Hammel, Stephen F. Austin (La.-Monroe)	Nov. 11, 1989
571	I-A	Marc Wilson, Brigham Young (Utah)	Nov. 5, 1977

SINGLE-GAME ATTEMPTS

Atts.	Div.	Player, Team (Opponent)	Date
83	I-A	Drew Brees, Purdue (Wisconsin)	Oct. 10, 1998
81	III	Jordan Poznick, Principia (Blackburn)	Oct. 10, 1992
80	III	Scott Kello, Sul Ross St. (Howard Payne)	Oct. 5, 2002
79	I-A	Matt Vogler, TCU (Houston)	Nov. 3, 1990
79	III	Mike Wallace, Ohio Wesleyan (Denison)	Oct. 3, 1981
78	III	Shawn Wheeler, Capital (Ohio Northern)	Nov. 13, 1999
78	I-A	Rusty LaRue, Wake Forest (Duke)	Oct. 28, 1995
77	III	Justin Peery, Westminster (Mo.) (MacMurray)	Nov. 14, 1998
77	I-AA	Neil Lomax, Portland St. (Northern Colo.)	Oct. 20, 1979
76	I-AA	Joe Lee, Towson (Lehigh)	Oct. 30, 1999
76	II	Jarrod DeGeorgia, Wayne St. (Neb.) (Drake)	Nov. 9, 1996
76	I-A	David Klingler, Houston (Southern Methodist)	Oct. 20, 1990
75	I-A	Chris Vargas, Nevada (McNeese St.)	Sept. 19, 1992
74	II	Jamie Sander, N.M. Highlands (Neb.-Kearney)	Nov. 9, 1996
74	II	Jermaine Whitaker, N.M. Highlands (Western St.)	Nov. 5, 1994
74	I-AA	Paul Peterson, Idaho St. (Nevada)	Oct. 1, 1983
73	III	Tom Stetzer, Wis.-Platteville (Olivet Nazarene)	Sept. 7, 2002
73	I-A	Jeff Handy, Missouri (Oklahoma St.)	Oct. 17, 1992
73	I-A	Troy Kopp, Pacific (Cal.) (Hawaii)	Oct. 27, 1990
73	I-A	Shane Montgomery, North Carolina St. (Duke)	Nov. 11, 1989
72	III	Scott Kello, Sul Ross St. (Louisiana Col.)	Sept. 21, 2002
72	I-A	Luke McCown, Louisiana Tech (Miami [Fla.])	Oct. 28, 2000
72	I-AA	Val Troiani, Towson (St. Mary's [Cal.])	Nov. 4, 2000
72	I-AA	Dave Dickenson, Montana (Idaho)	Oct. 21, 1995
72	I-A	Matt Vogler, TCU (Texas Tech)	Nov. 10, 1990
72	II	Kurt Otto, North Dakota (Tex. A&M-Kingsville)	Sept. 13, 1986
72	III	Bob Lockhart, Millikin (Franklin)	Nov. 12, 1977
72	II	Kaipo Spencer, Santa Clara (Portland St.)	Oct. 11, 1975
72	II	Joe Stetser, Cal St. Chico (Oregon Tech)	Sept. 23, 1967

SINGLE-GAME COMPLETIONS

Cmp.	Div.	Player, Team (Opponent)	Date
56	II	Jarrod DeGeorgia, Wayne St. (Neb.) (Drake)	Nov. 9, 1996
55	I-A	Drew Brees, Purdue (Wisconsin)	Oct. 10, 1998
55	I-A	Rusty LaRue, Wake Forest (Duke)	Oct. 28, 1995
51	III	Scott Kello, Sul Ross St. (Howard Payne)	Oct. 5, 2002
50	II	Todd Cunningham, Presbyterian (Tusculum)	Nov. 3, 2001
50	III	Justin Peery, Westminster (Mo.) (MacMurray)	Nov. 14, 1998
50	I-A	Rusty LaRue, Wake Forest (North Carolina St.)	Nov. 18, 1995
50	III	Tim Lynch, Hofstra (Fordham)	Oct. 19, 1991
49	I-A	Kliff Kingsbury, Texas Tech (Missouri)	Oct. 19, 2002
49	I-A	Kliff Kingsbury, Texas Tech (Texas A&M)	Oct. 5, 2002
49	I-A	Brian Lindgren, Idaho (Middle Tenn.)	Oct. 6, 2001
48	I-AA	Clayton Millis, Cal St. Northridge (St. Mary's [Cal.])	Nov. 11, 1995
48	III	Jordan Poznick, Principia (Blackburn)	Oct. 10, 1992
48	I-A	David Klingler, Houston (Southern Methodist)	Oct. 20, 1990
47	I-A	Luke McCown, Louisiana Tech (Auburn)	Oct. 21, 2000

Cmp.	Div.	Player, Team (Opponent)	Date
47	I-AA	Joe Lee, Towson (Lehigh)	Oct. 30, 1999
47	I-A	Tim Couch, Kentucky (Arkansas)	Oct. 3, 1998
47	I-AA	Jamie Martin, Weber St. (Idaho St.)	Nov. 23, 1991
47	III	Mike Wallace, Ohio Wesleyan (Denison)	Oct. 3, 1981
46	I-A	Tim Rattay, Louisiana Tech (UCF)	Oct. 23, 1999
46	I-A	Tim Rattay, Louisiana Tech (Nebraska)	Aug. 29, 1998
46	I-A	Scott Milanovich, Maryland (Florida St.)	Nov. 18, 1995
46	I-A	Jimmy Klingler, Houston (Rice)	Nov. 28, 1992
46	I-AA	Doug Pederson, La.-Monroe (Stephen F. Austin)	Nov. 11, 1989
46	I-AA	Willie Totten, Mississippi Val. (Southern U.)	Sept. 29, 1984
45	III	Scott Kello, Sul Ross St. (Texas Lutheran)	Nov. 16, 2002
45	II	Andrew Webb, Fort Lewis (Neb.-Kearney)	Oct. 12, 2001
45	I-A	Tim Rattay, Louisiana Tech (Texas A&M)	Sept. 4, 1999
45	II	Chris Hatcher, Valdosta St. (Mississippi Col.)	Oct. 23, 1993
45	II	Chris Hatcher, Valdosta St. (West Ga.)	Oct. 16, 1993
45	I-AA	Willie Totten, Mississippi Val. (Prairie View)	Oct. 27, 1984
45	I-A	Sandy Schwab, Northwestern (Michigan)	Oct. 23, 1982
44	I-AA	Kyle Slager, Brown (Rhode Island)	Oct. 5, 2002
44	III	Scott Kello, Sul Ross St. (Louisiana Col.)	Sept. 21, 2002
44	I-A	Kliff Kingsbury, Texas Tech (Oklahoma St.)	Nov. 10, 2001
44	I-A	Tim Rattay, Louisiana Tech (Toledo)	Oct. 30, 1999
44	III	Chris Stormer, Hanover (Franklin)	Nov. 14, 1998
44	I-A	Chris Redman, Louisville (East Caro.)	Nov. 14, 1998
44	I-A	Tim Couch, Kentucky (Vanderbilt)	Nov. 14, 1998
44	II	Wilkie Perez, Glenville St. (Concord)	Oct. 25, 1997
44	I-A	Matt Vogler, TCU (Houston)	Nov. 3, 1990
44	I-A	Chuck Hartlieb, Iowa (Indiana)	Oct. 29, 1988
44	II	Tom Bonds, Cal Lutheran (St. Mary's [Cal.])	Nov. 22, 1986
44	III	Jim McMahon, Brigham Young (Colorado St.)	Nov. 7, 1981
44	I-AA	Neil Lomax, Portland St. (Northern Colo.)	Oct. 20, 1979

Receiving

CAREER RECEPTIONS

Player, Team (Division)	Years	Rec.	Yards	Avg.	TD
Scott Pingel, Westminster (Mo.) (III)	1996-99	*436	*6,108	14.0	*75
Clarence Coleman, Ferris St. (II)	1998-01	323	4,983	15.4	42
Jacquay Nunnally, Florida A&M (I-AA)	1997-00	317	4,239	13.4	38
Stephen Campbell, Brown (I-AA)	1997-00	305	3,555	11.7	31
Jerry Rice, Mississippi Val. (I-AA)	1981-84	301	4,693	15.6	50
Andrew Blakely, Truman (II)	1999-02	300	3,458	11.5	22
Arnold Jackson, Louisville (I-A)	1997-00	300	3,670	12.2	31
Trevor Insley, Nevada (I-A)	1996-99	298	5,005	16.8	35
Geoff Noisy, Nevada (I-A)	1995-98	295	4,249	14.4	21
Chas Gessner, Brown (I-AA)	1999-02	292	3,408	11.7	36
Matt Newton, Principia (III)	1990-93	287	3,646	12.7	32
Scott Hvistendahl, Augsburg (III)	1995-98	285	4,696	16.5	40
Matt Holmlund, Augustana (S.D.) (II)	1998-01	282	3,522	12.5	35
Carlos Ferralls, Glenville St. (II)	1994-97	282	4,091	14.5	53
Troy Edwards, Louisiana Tech (I-A)	1996-98	280	4,352	15.5	50
Michael Becker, Randolph-Macon (III)	1997-00	273	3,683	13.5	19
Damien Hoffman, Minn.-Morris (II)	1997-00	273	3,128	11.5	21
Matt Plummer, Dubuque (III)	1996-99	271	4,049	14.9	42
Jeff Clay, Catholic (III)	1994-97	269	4,101	15.2	44
Damon Thompson, Virginia St. (II)	1997-00	268	4,387	16.4	37
Kasey Dunn, Idaho (I-AA)	1988-91	268	3,847	14.4	25
Aaron Turner, Pacific (Cal.) (I-A)	1989-92	266	4,345	16.3	43
Chad Mackey, Louisiana Tech (I-A)	1993-96	264	3,789	14.4	22

Andrew Blakely of Truman joined only six other NCAA receivers in reaching the lofty plateau of at least 300 catches in a career.

Truman Sports Information

Player, Team (Division)	Years	Rec.	Yards	Avg.	TD
Terance Mathis, New Mexico (I-A)	1985-87, 89	263	4,254	16.2	36
J.R. Tolver, San Diego St. (I-A)	1999-02	262	3,572	13.6	18
Mark Templeton, Long Beach St. (I-A) (RB)	1983-86	¢262	1,969	7.5	11
Nate Jackson, Menlo (III)	1999-01	261	3,976	15.2	43
Jon Spinosa, Lock Haven (II)	1992-95	261	2,710	10.4	12
Howard Twilley, Tulsa (I-A)	1963-65	261	3,343	12.8	32
Rob Milanese, Pennsylvania (I-AA)	1999-02	259	3,405	13.1	21
Marcus Harris, Wyoming (I-A)	1993-96	259	4,518	17.4	38
Bill Stromberg, Johns Hopkins (III)	1978-81	258	3,776	14.6	39
Eric Nemec, Albright (III)	1995-98	256	3,300	12.9	35
Kurt Barth, Eureka (III)	1994-97	256	4,311	16.8	51
Chris Myers, Kenyon (III)	1967-70	253	3,897	15.4	33
Sean Morey, Brown (I-AA)	1995-98	251	3,850	15.3	39
Eddie Berlin, Northern Iowa (I-AA)	1997-00	249	3,735	15.0	34
Nate Burleson, Nevada (I-A)	2000-02	248	3,219	13.3	22
Darryl DeShields, Greenville (III)	1999-01	248	4,051	16.3	39
Drew Amerson, Cal St. Northridge (I-AA)/ Troy St. (I-A)	1999-01; 02	246	3,264	13.3	20
James Jordan, Louisiana Tech (I-A)	1998-00	246	2,489	10.1	19
Carl Morris, Harvard (I-AA)	1999-02	245	3,488	14.2	28
Brian Forster, Rhode Island (I-AA) (TE)	1983-85, 87	#245	#3,410	13.9	31
David Williams, Illinois (I-A)	1983-85	245	3,195	13.0	22
Troy Walters, Stanford (I-A)	1996-99	244	3,986	16.3	26
Ryan Short, Wabash (III)	1999-02	243	2,773	11.4	45
Mike Furrey, Northern Iowa (I-AA)	1997-99	242	3,544	14.6	27
Brandon Stokley, La.-Lafayette (I-A)	1995-98	241	3,702	15.4	25
Bruce Cerone, Yankton/Emporia St. (II)	1965-66, 68-69	241	4,354	18.1	49
Sean Scott, Millersville (II)	1997-00	240	3,293	13.7	27
James Roe, Norfolk St. (II)	1992-95	239	4,468	18.7	46
Mark Didio, Connecticut (I-AA)	1988-91	239	3,535	14.8	21
Kendall Newson, Middle Tenn. (I-A)	1998-01	238	3,074	12.9	21
Mark DeBrito, Bentley (II)	1996-99	238	3,711	15.6	41
Bryan McGinty, Lock Haven (II)	1993-96	238	3,100	13.0	18
Rennie Benn, Lehigh (I-AA)	1982-85	237	3,662	15.5	44
Jonathon Cain, Wilmington (Ohio) (III)	1998-01	236	3,945	16.7	40
Marc Zeno, Tulane (I-A)	1984-87	236	3,725	15.8	25
Steve Neal, Western Mich. (I-A)	1997-00	235	3,599	15.3	27
Kevin Ingram, West Chester (II)	1995-96, 98-99	235	3,159	13.4	45
Jason Wolf, Southern Methodist (I-A)	1989-00	235	2,232	9.5	17

*Record. ¢Record for a running back. #Record for a tight end.

CAREER RECEPTIONS PER GAME

(Minimum 125 Receptions)

Player, Team (Division[s])	Years	G	Rec.	Yards	TD	Rec. PG
Chris George, Glenville St. (II)	1993-94	20	230	3,215	30	*11.5
Scott Pingel, Westminster (Mo.) (III)	1996-99	39	*436	*6,108	75	11.2
Manny Hazard, Houston (I-A)	1989-90	21	220	2,635	31	10.5
Alex Van Dyke, Nevada (I-A)	1994-95	22	227	3,100	26	10.3
Howard Twilley, Tulsa (I-A)	1963-65	26	261	3,343	32	10.0
Jason Phillips, Houston (I-A)	1987-88	22	207	2,319	18	9.4
Nate Jackson, Menlo (III)	1999-01	29	261	3,976	43	9.0
Matt Newton, Principia (III)	1990-93	33	287	3,646	32	8.7
Ed Bell, Idaho St. (II)	1968-69	19	163	2,608	30	8.6
Darryl DeShields, Greenville (III)	1999-01	29	248	4,051	39	8.6
Byron Chamberlain, Wayne St. (Neb.) (II)	1993-94	19	161	1,941	14	8.5
Todd Bloom, Hardin-Simmons (III)	1995-97	28	233	2,621	14	8.3
Troy Edwards, Louisiana Tech (I-A)	1996-98	34	280	4,352	50	8.2
Carlos Ferralls, Glenville St. (II)	1994-97	35	282	4,091	53	8.1
Kevin Curtis, Utah St. (I-A)	2001-02	22	174	2,789	19	7.9
Nate Burleson, Nevada (I-A)	2000-02	32	248	3,293	22	7.8
Clarence Coleman, Ferris St. (II)	1998-01	42	323	4,982	42	7.7
Jerry Hendren, Idaho (II)	1967-69	30	230	3,435	27	7.7
Stephen Campbell, Brown (I-AA)	1997-00	40	305	3,555	31	7.6
Bryan Reeves, Nevada (I-AA; I-A)	1991; 92-93	31	234	3,407	32	7.6
Siaha Burley, UCF (I-A)	1997-98	22	165	2,248	15	7.5
Chas Gessner, Brown (I-AA)	1999-02	39	292	3,408	36	7.5
Jeff Clay, Catholic (III)	1994-97	36	269	4,101	44	7.5
Geoff Noisy, Nevada (I-A)	1995-98	40	295	4,249	21	7.4
David Williams, Illinois (I-A)	1983-85	33	245	3,195	22	7.4
Gary Garrison, San Diego St. (II)	1964-65	20	148	2,188	26	7.4
Brad Bailey, West Tex. A&M (II)	1992-94	30	221	2,677	22	7.4
Jerry Rice, Mississippi Val. (I-AA)	1981-84	41	301	4,693	50	7.3
James Dixon, Houston (I-A)	1987-88	22	161	1,762	14	7.3
Mike Furrey, Northern Iowa (I-AA)	1997-99	33	242	3,544	27	7.3

*Record.

CAREER TOUCHDOWN RECEPTIONS

Player, Team (Division[s])	Years	G	TD
David Kircus, Grand Valley St. (II)	1999-02	43	*76
Scott Pingel, Westminster (Mo.) (III)	1996-99	39	75
Chris Bisaillon, Ill. Wesleyan (III)	1989-92	36	55
Kurt Barth, Eureka (III)	1994-97	39	51

Player, Team (Division[s])	Years	G	TD
Troy Edwards, Louisiana Tech (I-A)	1996-98	34	50
Jerry Rice, Mississippi Val. (I-AA)	1981-84	41	50
Bruce Cerone, Yankton/Emporia St. (II)	1965-66, 68-69	36	49
R.J. Hoppe, Carroll (Wis.) (III)	1993-96	37	49
James Roe, Norfolk St. (II)	1992-95	41	46
Ryan Short, Wabash (III)	1999-02	41	45
Kevin Ingram, West Chester (II)	1995-96, 98-99	39	45
Michael Coleman, Widener (II)	1998-01	40	44
Randy Moss, Marshall (I-AA; I-A)	1996-97	23	44
Jeff Clay, Catholic (III)	1994-97	36	44
Rennie Benn, Lehigh (I-AA)	1982-85	41	44
Ben Nelson, St. Cloud St. (II)	1999-02	41	43
¢Blake Elliott, St. John's (Minn.) (III)	2000-02	33	43
Nate Jackson, Menlo (III)	1999-01	29	43
Steve Vagedes, Ohio Northern (III)	1995, 97-99	40	43
Bill Schultz, Ripon (III)	1993-96	38	43
Aaron Turner, Pacific (Cal.) (I-A)	1989-92	44	43
Carlos Ferralls, Glenville St. (II)	1994-97	35	43
Mark Loeffler, Wheaton (Ill.) (III)	1993-96	38	43
¢Mark Bartosic, Susquehanna (III)	2000-02	30	42
Clarence Coleman, Ferris St. (II)	1998-01	42	42
Matt Plummer, Dubuque (III)	1996-99	40	42
Sedrick Robinson, Ky. Wesleyan (II)	1993-96	38	42
Ryan Yarborough, Wyoming (I-A)	1990-93	46	42
Dan Ryan, DePauw (III)	1999-02	38	41
Ryan Johnson, Hartwick (III)	1998-01	38	41
Mark DeBrito, Bentley (II)	1996-99	39	41
Dedric Ward, Northern Iowa (I-AA)	1993-96	43	41
Jonathon Cain, Wilmington (Ohio) (III)	1998-01	39	40
Adam Marino, Mount Union (III)	1998-00	30	40
Richard Wemer, Grinnell (III)	1995-98	38	40
Scott Hvistendahl, Augsburg (III)	1995-98	40	40
Shannon Sharpe, Savannah St. (II)	1986-89	42	40

*Record. ¢Active player.

SEASON RECEPTIONS

Player, Team (Division)	Year	G	Rec.	Yards	TD
Manny Hazard, Houston (I-A)	†1989	11	*142	1,689	22
Troy Edwards, Louisiana Tech (I-A)	†1998	12	140	1,996	27
Nate Burleson, Nevada (I-A)	†2002	12	138	1,629	12
Scott Pingel, Westminster (Mo.) (III)	†1999	10	136	1,648	24
Trevor Insley, Nevada (I-A)	†1999	11	134	2,060	13
Howard Twilley, Tulsa (I-A)	†1965	10	134	1,779	16
Scott Pingel, Westminster (Mo.) (III)	†1998	10	130	*2,157	26
Alex Van Dyke, Nevada (I-A)	†1995	11	129	1,854	16
J.R. Tolver, San Diego St. (I-A)	2002	13	128	1,785	13
Stephen Campbell, Brown (I-AA)	†2000	10	120	1,332	11
Brad Bailey, West Tex. A&M (II)	1994	11	119	1,552	16
Chris George, Glenville St. (II)	†1993	10	117	1,876	15
Kevin Ingram, West Chester (II)	†1998	11	115	1,673	21
Brian Forster, Rhode Island (I-AA) (TE)	†1985	10	115	1,617	12
Chas Gessner, Brown (I-AA)	†2002	11	114	1,166	11
Damond Wilkins, Nevada (I-A)	†1996	11	114	1,121	4
Chris George, Glenville St. (II)	†1994	10	113	1,339	15
Scott Hvistendahl, Augsburg (III)	1998	10	112	1,860	15
Jeff Clay, Catholic (III)	†1997	10	112	1,625	20
Sean Pender, Valdosta St. (II)	†1995	11	111	983	2
James Jordan, Louisiana Tech (I-A)	†2000	12	109	1,003	4
Chris Daniels, Purdue (I-A)	1999	11	109	1,133	5
Marcus Harris, Wyoming (I-A)	1996	12	109	1,650	13
Kassim Osgood, San Diego St. (I-A)	2002	13	108	1,552	8
Rashaun Woods, Oklahoma St. (I-A)	2002	13	107	1,695	17
Jamal Allen, Fort Lewis (II)	†2001	11	106	1,086	7
Fred Gilbert, Houston (I-A)	1991	11	106	957	7
Barry Wagner, Alabama A&M (II)	†1989	11	106	1,812	17
Theo Blanco, Wis.-Stevens Point (III) (RB)	1987	11	#106	#1,616	8
Nate Jackson, Menlo (III)	†2001	10	105	1,520	17
Chris Penn, Tulsa (I-A)	1993	11	105	1,578	12
Matt Holmlund, Augustana (S.D.) (II)	†2000	11	104	1,365	16
Eugene Baker, Kent St. (I-A)	1997	11	103	1,549	18
Sherman Smith, Houston (I-A)	1992	11	103	923	6
Jerry Rice, Mississippi Val. (I-AA)	†1984	10	103	1,682	27
Troy Edwards, Louisiana Tech (I-A)	1997	11	102	1,707	13
James Dixon, Houston (I-A)	1988	11	102	1,103	11
Jerry Rice, Mississippi Val. (I-AA)	†1983	10	102	1,450	14
Nate Jackson, Menlo (III)	†2000	10	101	1,515	16
Mark DeBrito, Bentley (II)	†1999	11	101	1,637	19
Arnold Jackson, Louisville (I-A)	1999	11	101	1,209	9
Mike Healey, Valparaiso (II)	†1985	10	101	1,279	11
David Williams, Illinois (I-A)	1984	11	101	1,278	8
Kevin Curtis, Utah St. (I-A)	†2001	11	100	1,531	10
Kwame Cavil, Texas (I-A)	1999	13	100	1,188	6
Dameane Douglas, California (I-A)	1998	11	100	1,150	4
Jay Miller, Brigham Young (I-A)	†1973	11	100	1,181	8

*Record. †National champion. #Record for a running back.

SEASON RECEPTIONS PER GAME

Player, Team (Division)	Year	G	Rec.	Yards	TD	Rec. PG
Scott Pingel, Westminster (Mo.) (III)	†1999	10	136	1,648	24	*13.6
Howard Twilley, Tulsa (I-A)	†1965	10	134	1,779	16	13.4
Scott Pingel, Westminster (Mo.) (III)	†1998	10	130	*2,157	26	13.0
Manny Hazard, Houston (I-A)	†1989	11	*142	1,689	22	12.9
Matt Newton, Principia (III)	†1992	8	98	1,487	14	12.3
Trevor Insley, Nevada (I-A)	†1999	11	134	2,060	13	12.2
Matt Newton, Principia (III)	†1993	8	96	1,080	11	12.0
Stephen Campbell, Brown (I-AA)	†2000	10	120	1,332	11	12.0
Nate Burleson, Nevada (I-A)	†2002	12	138	1,629	12	11.8
Alex Van Dyke, Nevada (I-A)	†1995	11	129	1,854	16	11.7
Chris George, Glenville St. (II)	†1993	10	117	1,876	15	11.7
Troy Edwards, Louisiana Tech (I-A)	†1998	12	140	1,996	27	11.7
Brian Forster, Rhode Island (I-AA) (TE)	†1985	10	115	1,617	12	11.5
Chas Gessner, Brown (I-AA)	†2002	10	114	1,166	11	11.4
Chris George, Glenville St. (II)	†1994	10	113	1,339	15	11.3
Scott Hvistendahl, Augsburg (III)	1998	10	112	1,860	15	11.2
Jeff Clay, Catholic (III)	†1997	10	112	1,625	20	11.2
Brad Bailey, West Tex. A&M (II)	1994	11	119	1,552	16	10.8
Ben Fox, Hanover (III)	†1995	9	95	1,087	15	10.6
Sean Munroe, Mass.-Boston (III)	1992	9	95	1,693	17	10.6
Nate Jackson, Menlo (III)	†2001	10	105	1,520	17	10.5
Kevin Ingram, West Chester (II)	†1998	11	115	1,673	21	10.5
Damond Wilkins, Nevada (I-A)	†1996	11	114	1,121	4	10.4
Jerry Rice, Mississippi Val. (I-AA)	†1984	10	103	1,682	27	10.3
Scott Faessler, Framingham St. (III)	†1990	9	92	916	5	10.2
Jerry Rice, Mississippi Val. (I-AA)	†1983	10	102	1,450	14	10.2
Bruce Cerone, Emporia St. (II)	1968	9	91	1,479	15	10.1
Nate Jackson, Menlo (III)	†2000	10	101	1,515	16	10.1
Mike Healy, Valparaiso (II)	†1985	10	101	1,279	11	10.1
Sean Pender, Valdosta St. (II)	†1995	11	111	983	2	10.1
Carlos Ferralls, Glenville St. (II)	†1996	8	81	965	6	10.1
Stuart Gaussoin, Portland St. (I-AA)	†1979	9	90	1,132	8	10.0

*Record. †National champion.

SINGLE-GAME RECEPTIONS

No.	Div.	Player, Team (Opponent)	Date
24	I-AA	Chas Gessner, Brown (Rhode Island)	Oct. 5, 2002
24	I-AA	Jerry Rice, Mississippi Val. (Southern U.)	Oct. 1, 1983
23	II	Chris George, Glenville St. (West Va. Wesleyan)	Oct. 15, 1994
23	I-A	Randy Gatewood, UNLV (Idaho)	Sept. 17, 1994
23	III	Sean Munroe, Mass.-Boston (Mass. Maritime)	Oct. 10, 1992
23	II	Barry Wagner, Alabama A&M (Clark Atlanta)	Nov. 4, 1989
22	I-AA	Marvin Walker, North Texas (Tulsa)	Nov. 20, 1982
22	I-A	Jay Miller, Brigham Young (New Mexico)	Nov. 3, 1973
21	I-AA	Carl Morris, Harvard (Dartmouth)	Nov. 2, 2002
21	I-A	Chris Daniels, Purdue (Michigan St.)	Oct. 16, 1999
21	I-AA	Eric Johnson, Yale (Harvard)	Nov. 20, 1999
21	I-A	Troy Edwards, Louisiana Tech (Nebraska)	Aug. 29, 1998
21	II	Kevin Swayne, Wayne St. (Neb.) (Drake)	Nov. 9, 1996
21	II	Jarett Vito, Emporia St. (Truman)	Nov. 4, 1995
21#	I-AA	David Pandt, Montana St. (Eastern Wash.)	Sept. 21, 1985
20	I-A	Kenny Christian, Eastern Mich. (Temple)	Sept. 23, 2000
20	III	Scott Pingel, Westminster (Mo.) (Colorado Col.)	Oct. 30, 1999
20	III	Todd Bloom, Hardin-Simmons (Mississippi Col.)	Oct. 12, 1996
20	III	Kurt Barth, Eureka (Concordia [Wis.])	Sept. 28, 1996
20	I-AA	Tim Hilton, Cal St. Northridge (St. Mary's [Cal.])	Nov. 11, 1995
20	II	Sean Pender, Valdosta St. (Mississippi Col.)	Nov. 4, 1995
20	II	Keylie Martin, N.M. Highlands (Western St.)	Nov. 5, 1994
20	III	Rich Johnson, Pace (Fordham)	Nov. 7, 1987
20	III	Pete Thompson, Carroll (Wis.) (Augustana [Ill.])	Nov. 4, 1978
20	II	Harold "Red" Roberts, Austin Peay (Murray St.)	Nov. 8, 1969
20	I-A	Rick Eber, Tulsa (Idaho St.)	Oct. 7, 1967

#Record for a running back.

CAREER YARDS

Player, Team (Division)	Years	Rec.	Yards	Avg.	TD
Scott Pingel, Westminster (Mo.) (III)	1996-99	*436	*6,108	14.0	75
Trevor Insley, Nevada (I-A)	1996-99	298	5,005	16.8	35
Clarence Coleman, Ferris St. (II)	1998-01	323	4,983	15.4	42
Scott Hvistendahl, Augsburg (III)	1995-98	285	4,696	16.5	40
Jerry Rice, Mississippi Val. (I-AA)	1981-84	301	4,693	15.6	50
Marcus Harris, Wyoming (I-A)	1993-96	259	4,518	17.4	38
James Roe, Norfolk St. (II)	1992-95	239	4,468	18.7	46
Damon Thompson, Virginia St. (II)	1997-00	268	4,387	16.4	37
Ryan Yarborough, Wyoming (I-A)	1990-93	229	4,357	19.0	42
Bruce Cerone, Yankton/Emporia St. (II)	1965-66, 68-69	241	4,354	18.1	49
Troy Edwards, Louisiana Tech (I-A)	1996-98	280	4,352	15.5	50
Aaron Turner, Pacific (Cal.) (I-A)	1989-92	266	4,345	16.3	43
Kurt Barth, Eureka (III)	1994-97	256	4,311	16.8	51
Terance Mathis, New Mexico (I-A)	1985-87, 89	263	4,254	16.2	36
Geoff Noisy, Nevada (I-A)	1995-98	295	4,249	14.4	21
Jacquay Nunnally, Florida A&M (I-AA)	1997-00	317	4,239	13.4	38

Player, Team (Division)	Years	Rec.	Yards	Avg.	TD
Robert Clark, N.C. Central (II)	1983-86	210	4,231	‡20.1	38
David Kircus, Grand Valley St. (II)	1999-02	222	4,142	18.7	*76
Jeff Clay, Catholic (III)	1994-97	269	4,101	15.2	44
Carlos Ferralls, Glenville St. (II)	1994-97	282	4,091	14.5	53
Darryl DeShields, Greenville (III)	1999-01	248	4,051	16.3	39
Matt Plummer, Dubuque (III)	1996-99	271	4,049	14.9	42
Troy Walters, Stanford (I-A)	1996-99	244	3,986	16.3	26
Nate Jackson, Menlo (III)	1999-01	261	3,976	15.2	43
Jonathon Cain, Wilmington (Ohio) (III)	1998-01	236	3,945	16.7	40
Chris Myers, Kenyon (II)	1967-70	253	3,897	15.4	33
Dedric Ward, Northern Iowa (I-AA)	1993-96	176	3,876	22.0	41
Sean Morey, Brown (I-AA)	1995-98	251	3,850	15.3	39
Kasey Dunn, Idaho (I-AA)	1988-91	268	3,847	14.4	25
Dale Amos, Frank. & Marsh. (III)	1986-89	233	3,846	16.5	35
Chad Mackey, Louisiana Tech (I-A)	1993-96	264	3,789	14.4	22
Bill Stromberg, Johns Hopkins (III)	1978-81	258	3,776	14.6	39
Shannon Sharpe, Savannah St. (II)	1986-89	192	3,744	19.5	40
Eddie Berlin, Northern Iowa (I-AA)	1997-00	249	3,735	15.0	34
Marc Zeno, Tulane (I-A)	1984-87	236	3,725	15.8	25
Jim Bradford, Carleton (III)	1988-91	212	3,719	17.5	32
Tyrone Johnson, Western St. (II)	1990-93	163	3,717	22.8	35
Mark DeBrito, Bentley (II)	1996-99	238	3,711	15.6	41
Brandon Stokley, La.-Lafayette (I-A)	1995-98	241	3,702	15.4	25
Michael Becker, Randolph-Macon (III)	1997-00	273	3,683	13.5	19
Arnold Jackson, Louisville (I-A)	1997-00	300	3,670	12.2	31
Chris Bisaillon, Ill. Wesleyan (III)	1989-92	223	3,670	16.5	55
Rennie Benn, Lehigh (I-AA)	1982-85	237	3,662	15.5	44
Matt Newton, Principia (III)	1990-93	287	3,646	12.7	32
Jeff Tiefenthaler, South Dakota St. (II)	1983-86	173	3,621	20.9	31
David Rhodes, UCF (I-AA)	1991-94	213	3,618	17.0	29
Willie Richardson, Jackson St. (II)	1959-62	166	3,616	21.8	36
Johnny Cox, Fort Lewis (II)	1990-93	220	3,611	16.4	33
Mike Gundersdorf, Wilkes (III)	1993-96	205	3,603	17.6	34

*Record. ‡Record for minimum 180 catches.

CAREER YARDS PER GAME

(Minimum 2,200 Yards)

Player, Team (Division[s])	Years	G	Yards	Yd. PG
Chris George, Glenville St. (II)	1993-94	20	3,215	*160.8
Scott Pingel, Westminster (Mo.) (III)	1996-99	39	*6,108	156.6
Alex Van Dyke, Nevada (I-A)	1994-95	22	3,100	140.9
Darryl DeShields, Greenville (III)	1999-01	29	4,051	139.7
Ed Bell, Idaho St. (II)	1968-69	19	2,608	137.3
Nate Jackson, Menlo (III)	1999-01	29	3,976	137.1
Troy Edwards, Louisiana Tech (I-A)	1996-98	34	4,352	128.0
Kevin Curtis, Utah St. (I-A)	2001-02	22	2,789	126.8
Manny Hazard, Houston (I-A)	1989-90	21	2,635	125.5
Bruce Cerone, Yankton/Emporia St. (II)	1965-66, 68-69	36	4,354	120.9
Ron Sellers, Florida St. (I-A)	1966-68	30	3,598	119.9
Clarence Coleman, Ferris St. (II)	1998-01	42	4,983	118.6
Randy Moss, Marshall (I-AA; I-A)	1996-97	23	2,720	118.3
Jim Jones, Widener (III)	1999-01	30	3,523	117.4
Scott Hvistendahl, Augsburg (III)	1995-98	40	4,696	117.4
Derrick Ingram, UAB (I-AA)	1993-94	22	2,572	116.9
Carlos Ferralls, Glenville St. (II)	1994-97	35	4,091	116.9
Damon Thompson, Virginia St. (II)	1997-00	38	4,387	115.4
Adam Marino, Mount Union (III)	1998-00	30	3,436	114.5
Jerry Rice, Mississippi Val. (I-AA)	1981-84	41	4,693	114.5
Jerry Hendren, Idaho (II)	1967-69	30	3,435	114.5
Jeff Clay, Catholic (III)	1994-97	36	4,101	113.9
Trevor Insley, Nevada (I-A)	1996-99	44	5,005	113.8
Nakia Jenkins, Utah St. (I-A)	1996-97	22	2,483	112.9
Elmo Wright, Houston (I-A)	1968-70	30	3,347	111.6
Howard Twilley, Tulsa (I-A)	1963-65	30	3,343	111.4
Chris Myers, Kenyon (II)	1967-70	35	3,897	111.3
Kurt Barth, Eureka (III)	1994-97	39	4,311	110.5
Matt Newton, Principia (III)	1990-93	33	3,646	110.5
Tim McNamara, Trinity (Conn.) (III)	1981-84	21	2,313	110.1
Bryan Reeves, Nevada (I-AA; I-A)	1991; 92-93	31	3,407	109.9
James Roe, Norfolk St. (II)	1992-95	41	4,468	109.0
Chris Penn, Tulsa (I-A)	1991, 93	22	2,370	107.7
Mike Furrey, Northern Iowa (I-AA)	1997-99	33	3,544	107.4
Joe Rettler, Ripon (III)	1997-99	29	3,100	106.9
Geoff Noisy, Nevada (I-A)	1995-98	40	4,249	106.2
Jason Phillips, Houston (I-A)	1987-88	22	2,319	105.4

*Record.

SEASON YARDS

Player, Team (Division)	Year	Rec.	Yards	Avg.	TD
Scott Pingel, Westminster (Mo.) (III)	†1998	130	*2,157	16.6	26
Trevor Insley, Nevada (I-A)	†1999	134	2,060	15.4	13
Troy Edwards, Louisiana Tech (I-A)	†1998	140	1,996	14.3	27
Chris George, Glenville St. (II)	†1993	117	1,876	16.0	15

Player, Team (Division)	Year	Rec.	Yards	Avg.	TD
Scott Hvistendahl, Augsburg (III)	1998	112	1,860	16.6	15
Alex Van Dyke, Nevada (I-A)	†1995	129	1,854	14.4	16
Barry Wagner, Alabama A&M (II)	†1989	106	1,812	17.1	17
J.R. Tolver, San Diego St. (I-A)	†2002	128	1,785	14.0	13
Howard Twilley, Tulsa (I-A)	†1965	134	1,779	13.3	16
Josh Reed, LSU (I-A)	†2001	94	1,740	18.5	7
Chris Perry, Adams St. (II)	†1995	88	1,719	19.5	21
Ashley Lelie, Hawaii (I-A)	2001	84	1,713	20.4	19
Eddie Conti, Delaware (I-AA)	†1998	91	1,712	18.8	10
Troy Edwards, Louisiana Tech (I-A)	†1997	102	1,707	16.7	13
Tramon Douglas, Grambling (I-AA)	†2002	92	1,704	18.5	18
Rashaun Woods, Oklahoma St. (I-A)	2002	107	1,695	15.8	17
Sean Munroe, Mass.-Boston (III)	†1992	95	1,693	17.8	17
Manny Hazard, Houston (I-A)	†1989	*142	1,689	11.9	22
Jerry Rice, Mississippi Val. (I-AA)	†1984	103	1,682	16.3	27
Kevin Ingram, West Chester (II)	†1998	115	1,673	14.5	21
Marcus Harris, Wyoming (I-A)	†1996	109	1,650	15.1	13
Scott Pingel, Westminster (Mo.) (III)	†1999	136	1,648	12.1	24
Randy Moss, Marshall (I-A)	1997	90	1,647	18.3	25
Mark DeBrito, Bentley (II)	1999	101	1,637	16.2	19
Nate Burleson, Nevada (I-A)	2002	138	1,629	11.8	12
Jeff Clay, Catholic (III)	†1997	112	1,625	14.5	25
Brian Forster, Rhode Island (I-AA) (TE)	†1985	115	1,617	14.1	12
Theo Blanco, Wis.-Stevens Point (III) (RB)	1987	#106	#1,616	15.2	8
Aaron Turner, Pacific (Cal.) (I-A)	†1991	92	1,604	17.4	18
Torry Holt, North Carolina St. (I-A)	1998	88	1,604	18.2	11

*Record. †National champion. #Record for a running back.

SEASON YARDS PER GAME

Player, Team (Division)	Year	G	Rec.	Yards	Yd. PG
Scott Pingel, Westminster (Mo.) (III)	†1998	10	130	*2,157	*215.7
Sean Munroe, Mass.-Boston (III)	†1992	9	95	1,693	188.1
Chris George, Glenville St. (II)	†1993	10	117	1,876	187.6
Trevor Insley, Nevada (I-A)	†1999	11	134	2,060	187.3
Scott Hvistendahl, Augsburg (III)	1998	10	112	1,860	186.0
Matt Newton, Principia (III)	†1992	8	98	1,487	185.9
Howard Twilley, Tulsa (I-A)	†1965	10	134	1,779	177.9
Chris Perry, Adams St. (II)	†1995	10	88	1,719	171.9
Alex Van Dyke, Nevada (I-A)	†1995	11	129	1,854	168.5
Jerry Rice, Mississippi Val. (I-AA)	†1984	10	103	1,682	168.2
Troy Edwards, Louisiana Tech (I-A)	†1998	12	140	1,996	166.3
Scott Pingel, Westminster (Mo.) (III)	†1999	10	136	1,648	164.8
Barry Wagner, Alabama A&M (II)	†1989	11	106	1,812	164.7
Bruce Cerone, Emporia St. (II)	†1968	9	91	1,479	164.3
Jeff Clay, Catholic (III)	†1997	10	112	1,625	162.5
Jeff Clay, Catholic (III)	†1996	9	81	1,460	162.2
Brian Forster, Rhode Island (I-AA)	†1985	10	115	1,617	161.7

*Record. †National champion.

SEASON TOUCHDOWN RECEPTIONS

Player, Team (Division)	Year	G	TD
David Kircus, Grand Valley St. (II)	2002	14	*35
David Kircus, Grand Valley St. (II)	2001	10	28
Troy Edwards, Louisiana Tech (I-A)	1998	12	27
Jerry Rice, Mississippi Val. (I-AA)	1984	10	27
Scott Pingel, Westminster (Mo.) (III)	1998	10	26
Randy Moss, Marshall (I-A)	1997	12	25
Dallas Mall, Bentley (II)	2001	12	24
Scott Pingel, Westminster (Mo.) (III)	1999	10	24
Ben Nelson, St. Cloud St. (II)	2002	11	23
Blake Elliott, St. John's (Minn.) (III)	2002	14	22
Manny Hazard, Houston (I-A)	1989	11	22
David Snider, Grinnell (III)	1998	10	21
Chris Perry, Adams St. (II)	1995	10	21
Ryan Soule, Hartwick (III)	2002	10	20
Ryan Johnson, Hartwick (III)	2001	10	20
Brian Dolph, Saginaw Valley (II)	2000	11	20
Kirk Aikens, Hartwick (III)	1998	10	20
Steve Vagades, Ohio Northern (III)	1998	10	20
Jeff Clay, Catholic (III)	1997	10	20
John Aromando, Col. of New Jersey (III)	1983	10	20
Ed Bell, Idaho St. (II)	1969	10	20
Tim Battaglia, Minn. Duluth (II)	2002	12	19
Ashley Lelie, Hawaii (I-A)	2001	11	19
Ryan Silvis, Wash. & Jeff. (III)	2000	10	19
Mark DeBrito, Bentley (II)	1999	11	19
Matt Eisenberg, Juniata (III)	1999	10	19
Adam Marino, Mount Union (III)	1999	10	19
Ben Streby, Otterbein (III)	1999	10	19
Jerry Hampton, Rhodes (III)	1997	9	19
Carlos Ferralls, Glenville St. (II)	1997	10	19
Randy Moss, Marshall (I-AA)	1996	11	19
Stanley Flanders, Valdosta St. (II)	1994	11	19

Player, Team (Division)	Year	G	TD
Desmond Howard, Michigan (I-A)	1991	11	19
Tramon Douglas, Grambling (I-AA)	2002	12	18
Chris Brewer, Fort Lewis (II)	2002	11	18
Darius Watts, Marshall (I-A)	2001	12	18
Michael Coleman, Widener (III)	2000	10	18
Jai Hill, Indiana (Pa.) (II)	2000	10	18
Chad Hustead, Redlands (III)	1999	9	18
Eugene Baker, Kent St. (I-A)	1997	11	18
Ryan Hinske, Wis.-Oshkosh (III)	1997	10	18
Joe Douglass, Montana (I-AA)	1996	11	18
Jamar Nailor, N.M. Highlands (II)	1996	10	18
Wayne Thomas, Miles (III)	1996	10	18
Kurt Barth, Eureka (III)	1995	10	18
Brian Penecale, West Chester (II)	1994	11	18
Aaron Turner, Pacific (Cal.) (I-A)	1991	11	18
Dennis Smith, Utah (I-A)	1989	12	18
Tom Reynolds, San Diego St. (I-A)	1971	10	18

*Record.

SINGLE-GAME YARDS

Yds.	Div.	Player, Team (Opponent)	Date
418	III	Lewis Howes, Principia (Martin Luther)	Oct. 12, 2002
405	I-A	Troy Edwards, Louisiana Tech (Nebraska)	Aug. 29, 1998
401	II	Kevin Ingram, West Chester (Clarion)	Oct. 31, 1998
397	III	Matt Eisenberg, Juniata (Widener)	Nov. 13, 1999
395	III	Scott Pingel, Westminster (Mo.) (Bethel [Tenn.])	Nov. 7, 1998
376	I-AA	Kassim Osgood, Cal Poly (Northern Iowa)	Nov. 4, 2000
370	I-AA	Michael Lerch, Princeton (Brown)	Oct. 12, 1991
370	II	Barry Wagner, Alabama A&M (Clark Atlanta)	Nov. 4, 1989
364	III	Jeff Clay, Catholic (Albright)	Nov. 16, 1996
363	I-A	Randy Gatewood, UNLV (Idaho)	Sept. 17, 1994
363	II	Tom Nettles, San Diego St. (Southern Miss.)	Nov. 9, 1968
362	III	Matt Surette, WPI (Springfield)	Oct. 25, 1997
354	I-AA	Eddie Conti, Delaware (Connecticut)	Nov. 7, 1998
354	II	Robert Clark, N.C. Central (Jackson St.)	Aug. 30, 1986
352	II	Chad Luttrell, Henderson St. (Arkansas Tech)	Oct. 28, 2000
349	I-A	Chuck Hughes, UTEP (North Texas)	Sept. 18, 1965
332	III	Ryan Pifer, Heidelberg (Marietta)	Nov. 8, 1997
332	III	Sean Munroe, Mass.-Boston (Mass. Maritime)	Oct. 10, 1992
330	I-AA	Nate Singleton, Grambling (Virginia Union)	Sept. 14, 1991
327@	I-AA	Brian Forster, Rhode Island (Brown)	Sept. 28, 1985
326	I-A	Nate Burleson, Nevada (San Jose St.)	Nov. 10, 2001
325	II	Paul Zaeske, North Park (North Central)	Oct. 12, 1968
322	I-A	Rick Eber, Tulsa (Idaho St.)	Oct. 7, 1967
319	II	Kyle Henderson, West Ala. (Valdosta St.)	Oct. 26, 2002
319	I-AA	Jason Cristino, Lehigh (Lafayette)	Nov. 21, 1992
318	I-A	Harry Wood, Tulsa (Idaho St.)	Oct. 7, 1967
317	II	Dan Fulton, Neb.-Omaha (South Dakota)	Sept. 4, 1976
316	I-AA	Marcus Hinton, Alcorn St. (Chattanooga)	Sept. 10, 1994
316	I-A	Jeff Evans, New Mexico St. (Southern Ill.)	Sept. 30, 1978
314	III	Matt Eisenberg, Juniata (Albright)	Oct. 2, 1999
314	I-A	Alex Van Dyke, Nevada (San Jose St.)	Nov. 18, 1995
310	III	Jace Metzner, Ohio Northern (John Carroll)	Oct. 20, 2001
310	III	Jeff Clay, Catholic (La Salle)	Oct. 11, 1997
310	I-A	Chad Mackey, Louisiana Tech (Toledo)	Oct. 19, 1996
310	II	Mike Collodi, Colorado Mines (Westminster [Utah])	Oct. 3, 1970

@Record for a tight end.

Defensive Records

Interceptions

CAREER INTERCEPTIONS

Player, Team (Division[s])	Years	No.	Yards	Avg.
Tom Collins, Indianapolis (II)	1982-85	*37	390	10.5
Ralph Gebhardt, Rochester (II; III)	1972; 73-75	34	406	11.9
Dean Diaz, Humboldt St. (II)	1980-83	31	328	10.6
Bill Grantham, Mo.-Rolla (II)	1977-80	29	263	9.1
Eugene Hunter, Fort Valley St. (II; III)	1972; 73-74	29	479	16.5
Al Brosky, Illinois (I-A)	1950-52	29	356	12.3
Jason Johnson, Shepherd (II)	1991-94	28	321	11.5
Rick Bealer, Lycoming (III)	1987-90	28	279	10.0
Brian Fetterolf, Aurora (III)	1986-89	28	390	13.9
Dave Murphy, Holy Cross (I-AA)	1986-89	28	309	11.0
Andrew Ostrand, Carroll (Wis.) (III)	1990-93	27	258	9.6
Tim Lennon, Curry (III)	1986-89	27	190	7.0
Scott Stanitous, Moravian (III)	1985-88	27	178	6.6
Mike Hintz, Wis.-Platteville (III)	1983-86	27	183	6.8
Martin Bayless, Bowling Green (I-A)	1980-83	27	266	9.9

Player, Team (Division[s])	Years	No.	Yards	Avg.
John Provost, Holy Cross (I-A)	1972-74	27	470	17.4
Cory Mabry, Susquehanna (III)	1988-91	26	400	15.4
Mark Dorner, Juniata (III)	1984-87	26	443	17.0
Tony Woods, Bloomsburg (II)	1982-85	26	105	4.0
Jeff Hughes, Ripon (III)	1975-78	26	333	12.8
Buster West, Gust. Adolphus (II)	1967-70	26	192	7.4

*Record.

SEASON INTERCEPTIONS

Player, Team (Division)	Year	No.	Yards
Ben Matthews, Bethel (Minn.) (III)	†2000	*15	134
Mark Dorner, Juniata (III)	†1987	*15	202
Rashean Mathis, Bethune-Cookman (I-AA)	†2002	14	*455
Eugene Hunter, Fort Valley St. (II)	†1972	14	211
Luther Howard, Delaware St. (II)	†1972	14	99
Tom Rezzuti, Northeastern (II)	†1971	14	153
Jim Blackwell, Southern U. (II)	†1970	14	196
Carl Ray Harris, Fresno St. (II)	†1970	14	98
Al Worley, Washington (I-A)	†1968	14	130

*Record. †National champion.

Total Tackles

(Since 2000)

SEASON TOTAL TACKLES PER GAME

Player, Team (Division)	Year	G	Solo	Ast	Total	Avg.
Robert Gunn, Earlham (III)	†2000	10	106	72	178	*17.8
Donnie Hohman, Chapman (III)	†2002	10	77	95	172	17.2
Boomer Grigsby, Illinois St. (I-AA)	†2002	11	108	71	179	16.3
Robert Aguilar, Greenville (III)	2000	10	101	61	162	16.2
Josh Cain, Chattanooga (I-AA)	2002	12	113	79	192	16.0
Jason Ocean, Livingstone (II)	†2001	9	50	91	141	15.7
Rick Sherrod, West Virginia (I-A)	†2001	10	102	54	156	15.6
Lance Ramer, Rochester (III)	2000	10	87	69	156	15.6
Kelvin Hutcheson, Averett (III)	†2001	8	56	68	124	15.5
Edgerton Hartwell, Western Ill. (I-AA)	†2000	11	107	62	169	15.4

*Record. †National champion.

SEASON TOTAL TACKLES

Player, Team (Division)	Year	G	Solo	Ast	Total
Lawrence Flugence, Texas Tech (I-A)	2002	14	124	69	*193
Josh Cain, Chattanooga (I-AA)	2002	12	113	79	192
Tom Ward, Toledo (I-A)	2002	14	107	73	180
Boomer Grigsby, Illinois St. (I-AA)	†2002	11	108	71	179
Robert Gunn, Earlham (III)	†2000	10	106	72	178
E.J. Henderson, Maryland (I-A)	2002	14	*135	40	175
Donnie Hohman, Chapman (III)	†2002	10	77	95	172
Dietrich Lapsley, Indiana St. (I-AA)	2002	12	103	68	171
John Leake, Clemson (I-A)	2002	13	81	88	169
Edgerton Hartwell, Western Ill. (I-AA)	†2000	11	107	62	169

*Record. †National champion.

SINGLE-GAME TOTAL TACKLES

Tkls.	Div.	Player, Team (Opponent)	Date
30	II	Shaun Maloney, Minn.-Morris (Minn. St. Moorhead)	Oct. 27, 2001
27	III	Casey McConnell, Kenyon (Centre)	Sept. 7, 2002
26	I-AA	Boomer Grigsby, Illinois St. (Youngstown St.)	Nov. 9, 2002
26	I-A	Doug Szymul, Northwestern (Navy)	Sept. 21, 2002
26	I-A	Brian Leigeb, Central Mich. (Northern Ill.)	Nov. 17, 2000
25	I-AA	Nick Ricks, Eastern Ill. (Eastern Ky.)	Oct. 12, 2002
25	I-A	Bob Sanders, Iowa (Indiana)	Oct. 20, 2001
25	I-AA	Tim Johnson, Youngstown St. (Hofstra)	Nov. 4, 2000
25	II	Alan Slaughter, Tusculum (Lenoir-Rhyne)	Sept. 30, 2000
24	I-A	Pernell Griffin, East Caro. (Wake Forest)	Sept. 1, 2001
24	III	Tom Pouliot, FDU-Florham (King's [Pa.])	Nov. 4, 2000

Solo Tackles

SEASON SOLO TACKLES PER GAME

Player, Team (Division)	Year	G	Solo	Avg.
Robert Gunn, Earlham (III)	†2000	10	106	*10.6
Rick Sherrod, West Virginia (I-A)	†2001	10	102	10.2
Robert Aguilar, Greenville (III)	2000	10	101	10.1
Boomer Grigsby, Illinois St. (I-AA)	†2002	11	108	9.82
Edgerton Hartwell, Western Ill. (I-AA)	†2000	11	107	9.73
Hunter Hillenmeyer, Vanderbilt (I-A)	†2002	12	116	9.67
E.J. Henderson, Maryland (I-A)	2002	14	*135	9.64
E.J. Henderson, Maryland (I-A)	2001	11	104	9.45

Player, Team (Division)	Year	G	Solo	Avg.
Josh Cain, Chattanooga (I-AA)	2002	12	113	9.42
Brenden Givan, Stillman (III)	2000	9	84	9.33

*Record. †National champion.

SEASON TOTAL SOLO TACKLES

Player, Team (Division)	Year	G	Solo
E.J. Henderson, Maryland (I-A)	2002	14	*135
Lawrence Flugence, Texas Tech (I-A)	2002	14	124
Rod Davis, Southern Miss. (I-A)	2002	13	121
Hunter Hillenmeyer, Vanderbilt (I-A)	†2002	12	116
Josh Cain, Chattanooga (I-AA)	2002	12	113
Boomer Grigsby, Illinois St. (I-AA)	†2002	11	108
Dexter Reid, North Carolina (I-A)	2002	12	107
Tom Ward, Toledo (I-A)	2002	14	107
Edgerton Hartwell, Western Ill. (I-AA)	†2000	11	107
Robert Gunn, Earlham (III)	†2000	10	106

*Record. †National champion.

SINGLE-GAME SOLO TACKLES

Solo	Div	Player, Team (Opponent)	Date
19	I-A	Doug Szymul, Northwestern (Navy)	Sept. 21, 2002
18	I-AA	Nick Ricks, Eastern Ill. (Eastern Ky.)	Oct. 12, 2002
18	I-AA	Nick Duffy, Northern Ill. (Ball St.)	Nov. 17, 2001
18	I-A	Brian Leigeb, Central Mich. (Northern Ill.)	Nov. 17, 2000
17	I-A	Tom Ward, Toledo (UNLV)	Sept. 21, 2002
17	III	Casey McConnell, Kenyon (Centre)	Sept. 7, 2002
16	I-A	E.J. Henderson, Maryland (Wake Forest)	Nov. 30, 2002
16	I-A	Dexter Reid, North Carolina (Clemson)	Nov. 9, 2002
16	I-A	Quincy Monk, North Carolina (Wake Forest)	Nov. 10, 2001
16	III	Tyler Freeburg, Simpson (Wis.-Oshkosh)	Sept. 8, 2001

Tackles for Loss

SEASON TACKLES FOR LOSS PER GAME

Player, Team (Division)	Year	G	Solo	Ast	Total	Avg.
Steve Wilson, King's (Pa.) (III)	†2001	10	37	3	38.5	3.85
Russ Watson, Worcester St. (III)	†2000	9	32	0	32.0	3.56
Robert Aguilar, Greenville (III)	2000	10	35	0	35.0	3.50
Quincy Malloy, Methodist (III)	2001	10	34	0	34.0	3.40
Patrick Ryan, Benedictine (Ill.) (III)	†2002	10	33	0	33.0	3.30
Steve Wilson, King's (Pa.) (III)	2002	12	38	2	*39.0	3.25
Brenden Givan, Stillman (III)	2001	9	29	0	29.0	3.22
Brenden Givan, Stillman (III)	2000	9	25	7	28.5	3.17
Adam Frantz, Lebanon Valley (III)	2001	10	31	0	31.0	3.10
Jeff Heinz, Ill. Wesleyan (III)	2000	10	31	0	31.0	3.10

*Record. †National champion.

SEASON TOTAL TACKLES FOR LOSS

Player, Team (Division)	Year	G	Solo	Ast	Total
Steve Wilson, King's (Pa.) (III)	†2002	12	38	2	*39.0
Steve Wilson, King's (Pa.) (III)	†2001	10	37	3	38.5
Charlie Cook, C.W. Post (II)	†2001	12	36	2	37.0
Robert Aguilar, Greenville (III)	2000	10	35	0	35.0
Quincy Malloy, Methodist (III)	2001	10	34	0	34.0
Patrick Ryan, Benedictine (Ill.) (III)	†2002	10	33	0	33.0
Russ Watson, Worcester St. (III)	†2000	9	32	0	32.0
Terrell Suggs, Arizona St. (I-A)	†2002	14	27	9	31.5
Sherrod Coates, Western Ky. (I-AA)	2002	15	31	0	31.0
Adam Frantz, Lebanon Valley (III)	2001	10	31	0	31.0
Jeff Heinz, Ill. Wesleyan (III)	2000	10	31	0	31.0

*Record. †National champion.

SINGLE-GAME TACKLES FOR LOSS

TFL	Div.	Player, Team (Opponent)	Date
8.0	III	Brenden Givan, Stillman (Pikeville)	Sept. 1, 2001
7.0	I-AA	Greg Pitts, Southwest Tex. St. (Texas Southern)	Sept. 21, 2002
7.0	I-A	Richard Seigler, Oregon St. (Arizona St.)	Oct. 20, 2001
7.0	III	Jon Foss, Bethel (Minn.) (Gust. Adolphus)	Sept. 22, 2001
7.0	I-A	Chris Johnson, Kansas St. (Kansas)	Oct. 7, 2000
6.5	I-A	Terrell Suggs, Arizona St. (Washington)	Oct. 26, 2002
6.0	III	John Longo, Cortland St. (Kean)	Sept. 21, 2002
6.0	II	Dave Armstrong, Bloomsburg (Indiana [Pa.])	Sept. 7, 2002
6.0	I-AA	Valdamar Brower, Massachusetts (Rhode Island)	Nov. 17, 2001
6.0	II	Joe Spuhler, Wayne St. (Mich.) (Indianapolis)	Oct. 27, 2001
6.0	I-A	Wendell Bryant, Wisconsin (Penn St.)	Sept. 22, 2001
6.0	I-A	Akin Ayodele, Purdue (Cincinnati)	Sept. 2, 2001
6.0	I-AA	Eric Allen, Tennessee Tech (Eastern Ill.)	Nov. 21, 2000
6.0	I-A	James Davis, West Virginia (East Caro.)	Nov. 18, 2000
6.0	II	Davin Thompson, Winona St. (Minn. Duluth)	Nov. 4, 2000
6.0	I-A	Julius Peppers, North Carolina (Virginia)	Oct. 28, 2000
6.0	III	David Hahm, Wis. Lutheran (Rockford)	Sept. 30, 2000

Pass Sacks

SEASON PASS SACKS PER GAME

Player, Team (Division)	Year	G	Solo	Ast	Total	Avg.
Russ Watson, Worcester St. (III)	†2000	9	24	0	*24.0	*2.67
Steve Wilson, King's (Pa.) (III)	†2001	10	18	3	19.5	1.95
Josh Stinehour, Union (N.Y.) (III)	2001	10	18	2	19.0	1.90
Michael Gardner, Benedictine (III.) (III)	2000	10	19	0	19.0	1.90
Andrew Hollingsworth, Towson (I-AA)	†2000	9	16	2	17.0	1.89
Brenden Givan, Stillman (III)	2000	9	16	2	17.0	1.89
Mark Seagraves, Lycoming (III)	2000	9	17	0	17.0	1.89
Robert Mathis, Alabama A&M (I-AA)	†2002	11	19	2	20.0	1.82
Edith Forestal, Defiance (III)	2000	10	18	1	18.0	1.80
Lance Ramer, Rochester (III)	2000	10	17	2	18.0	1.80

*Record. †National champion.

SEASON TOTAL PASS SACKS

Player, Team (Division)	Year	G	Solo	Ast	Total
Terrell Suggs, Arizona St. (I-A)	†2002	14	23	2	*24.0
Russ Watson, Worcester St. (III)	†2000	9	24	0	*24.0
Charlie Cook, C.W. Post (II)	†2001	12	20	1	20.5
Robert Mathis, Alabama A&M (I-AA)	†2002	11	19	2	20.0
Steve Wilson, King's (Pa.) (III)	†2001	10	18	3	19.5
Josh Stinehour, Union (N.Y.) (III)	2001	10	18	2	19.0
Andy Petek, Montana (I-AA)	2000	11	19	0	19.0
Michael Gardner, Benedictine (III.) (III)	2000	10	19	0	19.0
Edith Forestal, Defiance (III)	2000	10	18	0	18.0
Lance Ramer, Rochester (III)	2000	10	17	2	18.0

*Record. †National champion.

SINGLE-GAME PASS SACKS

PS	Div.	Player, Team (Opponent)	Date
5.0	I-A	James Harrison, Kent St. (Miami [Ohio])	Nov. 24, 2001
5.0	II	Luke Larson, Quincy (Westminster [Mo.])	Oct. 6, 2001
5.0	I-A	Wendell Bryant, Wisconsin (Penn St.)	Sept. 22, 2001
4.5	I-A	Terrell Suggs, Arizona St. (Washington)	Oct. 26, 2002
4.5	I-A	Tully Banta-Cain, California (New Mexico St.)	Sept. 7, 2002
4.0	By 21 players, all divisions		

Passes Defended

SEASON PASSES DEFENDED PER GAME

Player, Team (Division)	Year	G	PBU	Int	Total	Avg.
Jarrod Pence, Moravian (III)	†2001	10	31	5	*36	3.60
Anthony Cooks, Fairmont St. (II)	†2001	9	28	4	32	3.56
Kip Daniels, Aurora (III)	2001	9	23	9	32	3.56
Johnny Kelly, Williams (III)	2001	8	23	4	27	3.38
Kennard Davis, Thiel (III)	2001	10	23	9	32	3.20
Chris Speigel, Benedictine (III.) (III)	2001	10	25	7	32	3.20
James Patrick, Stillman (III)	†2002	10	20	11	31	3.10
B.J. Harvey, Illinois Col. (III)	2001	10	25	6	31	3.10
Evan Zupancic, Tufts (III)	†2000	8	18	6	24	3.00

*Record. †National champion.

SEASON TOTAL PASSES DEFENDED

Player, Team (Division)	Year	G	PBU	Int	Total
Jarrod Pence, Moravian (III)	†2001	10	31	5	*36
Jason Goss, TCU (I-A)	†2002	12	24	8	32
Anthony Cooks, Fairmont St. (II)	†2001	9	28	4	32
Kip Daniels, Aurora (III)	2001	9	23	9	32
Kennard Davis, Thiel (III)	2001	10	23	9	32
Chris Speigel, Benedictine (III.) (III)	2001	10	25	7	32
Lynaris Elpheage, Tulane (I-A)	2002	13	23	8	31
James Patrick, Stillman (III)	†2002	10	20	11	31
B.J. Harvey, Illinois Col. (III)	2001	10	25	6	31
Jason Patterson, Central Wash. (II)	2001	11	19	11	30

*Record. †National champion.

SINGLE-GAME PASSES DEFENDED

PD	Div.	Player, Team (Opponent)	Date
10	III	James Patrick, Stillman (Edward Waters)	Nov. 2, 2002
8	I-A	Joselio Hanson, Texas Tech (Oklahoma St.)	Nov. 9, 2002
7	I-A	Jason Goss, TCU (Tulane)	Nov. 9, 2002
7	I-A	Korey Banks, Mississippi St. (Memphis)	Oct. 19, 2002
7	III	Kyle Westphal, Simpson (Washington [Mo.])	Sept. 7, 2002
7	III	Derrick Brantley, Wesleyan (Conn.) (Colby)	Oct. 6, 2001
7	I-A	Nashville Dyer, Kent St. (Bucknell)	Sept. 8, 2001
7	I-A	Demerist Whitfield, Northern III. (Illinois St.)	Sept. 9, 2000

Forced Fumbles

SEASON FORCED FUMBLES PER GAME

Player, Team (Division)	Year	G	FF	Avg.
Robert Mathis, Alabama A&M (I-AA)	†2002	11	*10	*0.91
Tony Pate, Concordia (III.) (III)	†2000	9	8	0.89
Bryan Eakin, Neb.-Kearney (II)	†2001	10	7	0.70
Tom Canada, California (I-A)	†2002	9	6	0.67
Courtney Johnson, Fairmont St. (II)	2001	9	6	0.67
Dwight Freeney, Syracuse (I-A)	†2001	12	8	0.67
Erik Tinsley, Concordia (III.) (III)	2000	9	6	0.67
Al Sullivan, Midwestern St. (II)	†2002	11	7	0.64
Greg Boucher, Western Conn. St. (III)	†2001	8	5	0.63
Quintin Mikell, Boise St. (I-A)	2002	13	8	0.62

*Record. †National champion.

SEASON TOTAL FORCED FUMBLES

Player, Team (Division)	Year	G	FF
Robert Mathis, Alabama A&M (I-AA)	†2002	11	*10
Quintin Mikell, Boise St. (I-A)	2002	13	8
Tony Pate, Concordia (III.) (III)	†2000	9	8
Dwight Freeney, Syracuse (I-A)	†2001	12	8
Al Sullivan, Midwestern St. (II)	†2002	11	7
Nick Ricks, Eastern III. (I-AA)	2002	12	7
Claude Harriott, Pittsburgh (I-A)	2002	13	7
Michael Haynes, Penn St. (I-A)	2002	13	7
Phillip Perry, San Jose St. (I-A)	2002	13	7
Antwan Peek, Cincinnati (I-A)	2002	14	7
Bryan Eakin, Neb.-Kearney (II)	†2001	10	7

*Record. †National champion.

SINGLE-GAME FORCED FUMBLES

FF	Div.	Player, Team (Opponent)	Date
3	III	Joe Sollitt, Concordia (III.) (Benedictine [III.])	Nov. 2, 2002
3	I-A	Quintin Mikell, Boise St. (Hawaii)	Oct. 5, 2002
3	I-A	Mason Unck, Arizona St. (Stanford)	Sept. 28, 2002
3	I-AA	Sterling Rogers, Southwest Tex. St. (Portland St.)	Oct. 6, 2001
3	III	Greg Boucher, Western Conn. St. (Mount Ida)	Sept. 8, 2001
3	II	Roger Williams, Indiana (Pa.) (Millersville)	Nov. 11, 2000
3	I-A	DeLawrence Grant, Oregon St. (San Diego St.)	Sept. 23, 2000

Punt Returns

CAREER AVERAGE

(Minimum 1.2 Returns Per Game; Minimum 30 Returns)

Player, Team (Division[s])	Years	No.	Yards	Avg.
Billy Johnson, Widener (II; III)	1971-72; 73	40	989	*24.7
Jack Mitchell, Oklahoma (I-A)	1946-48	39	922	23.6
Keith Winston, Knoxville (II)	1986-87	30	686	22.9
Kevin Doherty, Mass. Maritime (III)	1976-78, 80	45	939	20.9
James Rooths, Shepherd (II)	1997-00	59	1,223	**20.7
Chuck Downey, Stony Brook (III)	1984-87	59	1,198	20.3
Chuck Goehl, Monmouth (III.) (II)	1970-72	48	911	19.0
Eddie Macon, Pacific (Cal.) (I-A)	1949-51	48	907	18.9
Jackie Robinson, UCLA (I-A)	1939-40	37	694	18.8
Willie Canady, Fort Valley St. (III)	1979-82	41	772	18.8

*Record. **Record for minimum 50 returns.

SEASON AVERAGE

(Minimum 1.2 Returns Per Game and Qualifiers for Championship)

Player, Team (Division)	Year	No.	Yards	Avg.
Billy Johnson, Widener (II)	†1972	15	511	*34.1
Chuck Downey, Stony Brook (III)	†1986	17	530	31.2
Kevin Doherty, Mass. Maritime (III)	†1976	11	332	30.2
Dennis Robinson, Wesleyan (Conn.) (III)	†1978	9	263	29.2
Robert Middlebrook, Knoxville (III)	†1984	9	260	28.9
Joe Troise, Kean (III)	†1974	12	342	28.5
William Williams, Livingstone (II)	†1976	16	453	28.3
Terry Egerdahl, Minn. Duluth (II)	†1975	13	360	27.7
Melvin Dillard, Ferrum (III)	†1990	25	688	27.5
Elliot Turner, Greenville (III)	†2000	14	385	27.5
Chris McKinney, Guilford (III)	†2001	20	533	26.7
Eric Green, Benedictine (III)	†1993	13	346	26.6
Curtis DeLoatch, N.C. A&T (I-AA)	†2001	20	530	26.5
Bill Blackstock, Tennessee (I-A)	1951	12	311	25.9
Rodney Woodruff, Arkansas Tech (II)	†2000	12	305	25.4
George Sims, Baylor (I-A)	1948	15	375	25.0
Ennis Thomas, Bishop (II)	†1971	18	450	25.0

*Record. †National champion.

Kickoff Returns

CAREER AVERAGE

(Minimum 1.2 Returns Per Game; Minimum 30 Returns)

Player, Team (Division)	Years	No.	Yards	Avg.
Anthony Davis, Southern California (I-A)	1972-74	37	1,299	*35.1
Eric Booth, Southern Miss. (I-A)	1994	35	1,135	32.4
Overton Curtis, Utah St. (I-A)	1957-58	32	991	31.0
Fred Montgomery, New Mexico St. (I-A)	1991-92	39	1,191	30.5
Lamont Brightful, Eastern Wash. (I-AA)	1998-01	65	1,949	30.0
Karl Evans, Mo. Southern St. (II)	1991-92	32	959	30.0
Kevin Cannon, Millersville (II)	1992-95	67	1,999	29.8
Troy Brown, Marshall (I-AA)	1991-92	32	950	29.7
Dave Ludy, Winona St. (II)	1991-94	89	2,630	29.6
Charles Swann, Indiana St. (I-AA)	1989-91	45	1,319	29.3
Altie Taylor, Utah St. (I-A)	1966-68	40	1,170	29.3
Daryl Brown, Tufts (III)	1974-76	38	1,111	29.2
Joshua Carter, Muhlenberg (III)	1998-01	75	2,189	29.2
Stan Brown, Purdue (I-A)	1968-70	49	1,412	28.8
Henry White, Colgate (I-A)	1974-77	41	1,180	28.8
Kevin Johnson, Syracuse (I-A)	1995-98	50	1,437	28.7
Doug Parrish, San Fran. St. (II)	1990	35	1,002	28.6
Craig Richardson, Eastern Wash. (I-AA)	1983-86	71	2,021	28.5

*Record.

SEASON AVERAGE

(Minimum 1.2 Returns Per Game and Qualifiers for Championship)

Player, Team (Division)	Year	No.	Yards	Avg.
Brandon Steinheim, Wesley (III)	†1994	10	422	*42.2
Paul Allen, Brigham Young (I-A)	1961	12	481	40.1
D.J. Flick, Slippery Rock (II)	†2000	14	558	39.9
Jason Martin, Coe (III)	†1992	11	438	39.8
Tremain Mack, Miami (Fla.) (I-A)	†1996	13	514	39.5
LaVon Reis, Western St. (II)	†1993	14	552	39.4
Danny Lee, Jacksonville St. (II)	†1992	12	473	39.4
Leeland McElroy, Texas A&M (I-A)	†1993	15	590	39.3
Tony Hill, Salisbury (III)	†1998	14	549	39.2
Fran DeFalco, Assumption (II)	1993	12	461	38.4
Forrest Hall, San Francisco (I-A)	1946	15	573	@38.2
David Fraterrigo, Canisius (I-AA)	†1993	13	485	37.3
Brian Bratton, Furman (I-AA)	†2001	14	521	37.2
Brian Sump, Colorado Mines (III)	†2001	21	780	37.1
Nate Kirtman, Pomona-Pitzer (III)	†1990	14	515	36.8
Kendall James, Carson-Newman (II)	1993	15	549	36.6
Kerry Hayes, Western Caro. (I-AA)	1993	16	584	36.5
Tom Myers, Coe (III)	†1983	11	401	36.5
Tony Ball, Chattanooga (I-AA)	†1977	13	473	36.4
Ron Scott, Occidental (III)	1983	10	363	36.3
Alan Hill, DePauw (III)	1980	12	434	36.2
Cordell Roane, Richmond (I-AA)	†1999	13	470	36.2
Roscoe Word, Jackson St. (II)	†1973	18	650	36.1
Steve Levenseller, Puget Sound (II)	†1978	17	610	35.9
Trevor Shannon, Wartburg (III)	†1996	14	501	35.8
George Marinkov, North Carolina St. (I-A)	1954	13	465	35.8

*Record. †National champion. @ Record for minimum 1.5 returns per game.

Field Goals

(One-inch tees were permitted in 1949, two-inch tees were permitted in 1965, and use of tees was eliminated before the 1989 season. The goal posts were widened from 18 feet, 6 inches to 23 feet, 4 inches in 1959 and were narrowed back to 18 feet, 6 inches before the 1991 season. The hash marks were moved six feet, eight inches closer to the center of the field to 60 feet from each sideline in 1993.)

CAREER FIELD GOALS

Player, Team (Division)	Years	FGM	FGA	Pct.
Jeff Jaeger, Washington (S) (I-A)	1983-86	*80	99	.808
John Lee, UCLA (S) (I-A)	1982-85	79	92	*.859
Philip Doyle, Alabama (S) (I-A)	1987-90	78	*105	.743
Luis Zendejas, Arizona St. (S) (I-A)	1981-84	78	*105	.743
Max Zendejas, Arizona (S) (I-A)	1982-85	77	104	.740
Kevin Butler, Georgia (S) (I-A)	1981-84	77	98	.786
Carlos Huerta, Miami (Fla.) (S) (I-A)	1988-91	73	91	.802
Derek Schmidt, Florida St. (S) (I-A)	1984-87	73	104	.702
Marty Zendejas, Nevada (S) (I-AA)	1984-87	72	90	.800
Kirk Roach, Western Caro. (S) (I-AA)	1984-87	71	102	.696
Fuad Reveiz, Tennessee (S) (I-A)	1981-84	71	95	.747
Roman Anderson, Houston (S) (I-A)	1988-91	70	101	.693
Barry Belli, Fresno St. (S) (I-A)	1984-87	70	99	.707
Tony Zendejas, Nevada (S) (I-AA)	1981-83	70	86	.814
Collin Mackie, South Carolina (S) (I-A)	1987-90	69	95	.726

Player, Team (Division)	Years	FGM	FGA	Pct.
Shayne Graham, Virginia Tech (S) (I-A)	1996-99	68	93	.731
Gary Gussman, Miami (Ohio) (S) (I-A)	1984-87	68	94	.723
Larry Roach, Oklahoma St. (S) (I-A)	1981-84	68	101	.673
Jeff Chandler, Florida (S) (I-A)	1998-01	67	80	.838
Scott Shields, Weber St. (S) (I-AA)	1995-98	67	90	.744

*Record. (S) Soccer-style kicker.

SEASON FIELD GOALS

Player, Team (Division)	Year	FGM	FGA	Pct.
John Lee, UCLA (S) (I-A)	1984	*29	33	.879
Luis Zendejas, Arizona St. (S) (I-A)	1983	28	37	.757
Paul Woodside, West Virginia (S) (I-A)	1982	28	31	.903
Sebastian Janikowski, Florida St. (S) (I-A)	1998	27	32	.844
Fuad Reveiz, Tennessee (S) (I-A)	1982	27	31	.871
Billy Bennett, Georgia (S) (I-A)	2002	26	33	.788
Jonathan Ruffin, Cincinnati (S) (I-A)	2000	26	29	.897
Brian Mitchell, Northern Iowa (S) (I-AA)	1990	26	27	*.963
Tony Zendejas, Nevada (S) (I-AA)	1982	26	33	.788
Mike Nugent, Ohio St. (S) (I-A)	2002	25	28	.893
MacKenzie Hoambrecker, Northern Iowa (S) (I-AA)	2002	25	28	.893
Wayne Boyer, Southwest Mo. St. (S) (I-AA)	1996	25	30	.833
Chris Jacke, UTEP (S) (I-A)	1988	25	27	.926
John Diettrich, Ball St. (S) (I-A)	1985	25	29	.862
Chuck Nelson, Washington (S) (I-A)	1982	25	26	.962
Nick Novak, Maryland (S) (I-A)	2002	24	28	.857
Jeff Babcock, Colorado St. (S) (I-A)	2002	24	32	.750
Brad Bohn, Utah St. (S) (I-A)	1998	24	28	.857
Remy Hamilton, Michigan (S) (I-A)	1994	24	29	.828
Philip Doyle, Alabama (S) (I-A)	1990	24	29	.828
Kendall Trainor, Arkansas (S) (I-A)	1988	24	27	.889
Kirk Roach, Western Caro. (S) (I-AA)	1986	24	28	.857
Carlos Reveiz, Tennessee (S) (I-A)	1985	24	28	.857
George Benyola, Louisiana Tech (S) (I-AA)	1985	24	31	.774
Chris White, Illinois (S) (I-A)	1984	24	28	.857
Mike Prindle, Western Mich. (S) (I-A)	1984	24	30	.800
Bruce Kallmeyer, Kansas (S) (I-A)	1983	24	29	.828

*Record. (S) Soccer-style kicker. (Record for attempts is 38)

LONGEST FIELD GOALS

Yds.	Div.	Player, Team (Opponent)	Year
67	II	Tom Odle, Fort Hays St. (Washburn)	1988
67	I-A	Joe Williams, Wichita St. (Southern Ill.)	1978
67	I-A	Russell Erxleben, Texas (Rice)	1977
67	I-A	Steve Little, Arkansas (Texas)	1977
65*	I-A	Martin Gramatica, Kansas St. (Northern Ill.)	1998
65	I-A	Tony Franklin, Texas A&M (Baylor)	1976
64	I-A	Russell Erxleben, Texas (Oklahoma)	1977
64	I-A	Tony Franklin, Texas A&M (Baylor)	1976
63	I-AA	Bill Gramatica, South Fla. (Austin Peay)	2000
63	I-AA	Tim Foley, Ga. Southern (James Madison)	1987
63	I-AA	Scott Roper, Arkansas St. (North Texas)	1987
63	I-A	Morten Andersen, Michigan St. (Ohio St.)	1981
63	I-A	Clark Kemble, Colorado St. (Arizona)	1975
63	II	Joe Duren, Arkansas St. (McNeese St.)	1974
62	I-AA	Billy Cundiff, Drake (San Diego)	2000
62	I-A	Terance Kitchens, Texas A&M (Southern Miss.)	1999
62	II	Doc Proctor, Ferris St. (Michigan Tech)	1999
62	I-A	Jason Hanson, Washington St. (UNLV)	1991
62	I-A	John Diettrich, Ball St. (Ohio)	1986
62	I-A	Paul Hickert, Murray St. (Eastern Ky.)	1986
62#	I-A	Chip Lohmiller, Minnesota (Iowa)	1986
62	I-A	Tom Whelihan, Missouri (Colorado)	1986
62	I-A	Dan Christopulos, Wyoming (Colorado St.)	1977
62	I-A	Iseed Khoury, North Texas (Richmond)	1977
62	III	Dom Antonini, Rowan (Salisbury)	1976
62	I-A	Dave Lawson, Air Force (Iowa St.)	1975
62	II	Mike Flater, Colorado Mines (Western St.)	1973

*Longest collegiate field goal without use of a tee and also longest collegiate field goal with narrower goal posts (18 feet, 6 inches). #Longest field goal made indoors.

Special Reference: Ove Johannson, Abilene Christian (not an NCAA-member college at the time), kicked a 69-yard field goal against East Texas State, Oct. 16, 1976, the longest collegiate field goal.

Punting

CAREER PUNTING AVERAGE

(Minimum 150 Punts)

Player, Team (Division)	Years	No.	Yards	Avg.
Todd Sauerbrun, West Virginia (I-A)	1991-94	167	7,733	*46.3
Reggie Roby, Iowa (I-A)	1979-82	172	7,849	45.6
Greg Montgomery, Michigan St. (I-A)	1985-87	170	7,721	45.4
Tom Tupa, Ohio St. (I-A)	1984-87	196	8,854	45.2

Player, Team (Division)	Years	No.	Yards	Avg.
Barry Helton, Colorado (I-A)	1984-87	153	6,873	44.9
Aron Langley, Wyoming (I-A)	1996-98	171	7,649	44.7
Shane Lechler, Texas A&M (I-A)	1996-99	268	11,977	44.7
Ray Guy, Southern Miss. (I-A)	1970-72	200	8,934	44.7
Bucky Scribner, Kansas (I-A)	1980-82	217	9,670	44.6
Terry Daniel, Auburn (I-A)	1992-94	169	7,522	44.5
Greg Horne, Arkansas (I-A)	1983-86	180	8,002	44.5
Ray Criswell, Florida (I-A)	1982-85	161	7,153	44.4
Pumpy Tudors, Chattanooga (I-AA)	1988-91	181	8,041	44.4
Mark Simon, Air Force (I-A)	1984-86	164	7,283	44.4
Brian Schmitz, North Carolina (I-A)	1996-99	208	9,233	44.4
Bill Smith, Mississippi (I-A)	1983-86	254	11,260	44.3
Jason Van Dyke, Adams St. (II)	1995-98	242	10,720	44.3
Tim Baer, Colorado Mines (II)	1986-89	235	10,406	44.3
Russell Erxleben, Texas (I-A)	1975-78	214	9,467	44.2
Brad Maynard, Ball St. (I-A)	1993-96	242	10,702	44.2
Mark Simon, Air Force (I-A)	1984-86	156	6,898	44.2
Johnny Evans, North Carolina St. (I-A)	1974-77	185	8,143	44.0
Brian Moorman, Pittsburg St. (II)	1995-98	157	6,903	44.0
Chuck Ramsey, Wake Forest (I-A)	1971-73	205	9,010	44.0

*Record.

SEASON PUNTING AVERAGE

(Qualifiers for Championship)

Player, Team (Division)	Year	No.	Yards	Avg.
Chad Kessler, LSU (I-A)	†1997	39	1,961	*50.3
Reggie Roby, Iowa (I-A)	†1981	44	2,193	49.8
Kirk Wilson, UCLA (I-A)	†1956	30	1,479	49.3
Steve Ecker, Shippensburg (II)	†1965	32	1,570	49.1
Todd Sauerbrun, West Virginia (I-A)	†1994	72	3,486	48.4
Travis Dorsch, Purdue (I-A)	†2001	49	2,370	48.4

Player, Team (Division)	Year	No.	Yards	Avg.
Mark Gould, Northern Ariz. (I-AA)	†2002	62	2,987	48.2
Zack Jordan, Colorado (I-A)	†1950	38	1,830	48.2
Ricky Anderson, Vanderbilt (I-A)	†1984	58	2,793	48.2
Reggie Roby, Iowa (I-A)	†1982	52	2,501	48.1
Marv Bateman, Utah (I-A)	†1971	68	3,269	48.1
Andrew Bayes, East Caro. (I-A)	†1999	47	2,259	48.1
Mike Scifres, Western Ill. (I-AA)	2002	53	2,545	48.0
Don Cockroft, Adams St. (II)	†1966	36	1,728	48.0
Owen Price, UTEP (I-A)	†1940	30	1,440	48.0
Jack Jacobs, Oklahoma (I-A)	1940	31	1,483	47.8
Brian Schmitz, North Carolina (I-A)	1999	74	3,538	47.8
Bill Smith, Mississippi (I-A)	1984	44	2,099	47.7

*Record. †National champion.

LONGEST PUNTS

Yds.	Div.	Player, Team (Opponent)	Year
99	I-A	Pat Brady, Nevada (Loyola Marymount)	1950
97	II	Earl Hurst, Emporia St. (Central Mo. St.)	1964
96	II	Alex Campbell, Morris Brown (Clark Atlanta)	1994
96	II	Gary Frens, Hope (Olivet)	1966
96	II	Jim Jarrett, North Dakota (South Dakota)	1957
96	I-A	George O'Brien, Wisconsin (Iowa)	1952
94	I-A	John Hadl, Kansas (Oklahoma)	1959
94	I-A	Carl Knox, TCU (Oklahoma St.)	1947
94	I-A	Preston Johnson, Southern Methodist (Pittsburgh)	1940
93	I-AA	Tyler Grogan, Northeastern (Villanova)	2001
93	I-A	Ray Guy, Southern Miss. (Mississippi)	1972
93	II	Elliot Mills, Carleton (Monmouth [Ill.])	1970
93	II	Kasper Fitins, Taylor (Georgetown [Ky.])	1966
93	II	Leeroy Sweeney, Pomona-Pitzer (UC Riverside)	1960
93	I-A	Bob Handke, Drake (Wichita St.)	1949

All-Purpose Yards

CAREER YARDS

Player, Team (Division[s])	Years	Rush	Rcv.	Int.	PR	KO	Yds.
Brian Westbrook, Villanova (I-AA)	1997-98, 00-01	4,298	2,528	0	343	2,289	*9,512
Brian Shay, Emporia St. (II)	1995-98	6,958	1,032	0	104	1,207	9,301
R.J. Bowers, Grove City (III)	1997-00	*7,353	397	0	50	1,453	9,253
Paul Smith, Gettysburg (III)	1996-99	5,205	758	0	959	2,182	9,104
Kavin Gailliard, American Int'l (II)	1996-99	6,523	1,049	0	472	814	8,858
Jerry Azumah, New Hampshire (I-AA)	1995-98	6,193	1,153	0	5	1,025	8,376
Clarence Coleman, Ferris St. (II)	1998-01	49	4,983	0	1,494	1,483	8,009
Damon Thompson, Virginia St. (II)	1997-00	303	4,387	0	1,153	2,143	7,986
Carey Bender, Coe (III)	1991-94	6,125	1,751	0	7	87	7,970
Steve Tardif, Maine Maritime (III)	1996-99	6,093	643	8	65	1,151	7,960
Josh Ranek, South Dakota St. (II)	$1997-01	6,794	857	0	0	295	7,946
Johnny Bailey, Tex. A&M-Kingsville (II)	1986-89	6,320	452	0	20	1,011	7,803
Kenny Gamble, Colgate (I-AA)	1984-87	5,220	536	0	104	1,763	7,623
Howard Stevens, Randolph-Macon (II); Louisville (I-A)	1968-69; 71-72	5,297	738	0	781	748	7,564
Claude Mathis, Southwest Tex. St. (I-AA)	1994-97	4,691	744	0	635	1,353	7,423
Thomas Haskins, VMI (I-AA)	1993-96	5,355	179	0	216	1,661	7,411
Ian Smart, C.W. Post (II)	1999-02	6,647	293	0	33	383	7,356
Rick Sarille, Wagner (I-AA)	$1995-99	5,290	365	0	0	1,682	7,337
Roger Graham, New Haven (II)	1991-94	5,953	393	0	0	870	7,216
Ricky Williams, Texas (I-A)	1995-98	6,279	927	0	0	0	7,206
Napoleon McCallum, Navy (I-A)	$1981-85	4,179	796	0	858	1,339	7,172
Charles Roberts, Sacramento St. (I-AA)	1997-00	6,553	382	0	12	165	7,112
Dave Ludy, Winona St. (II)	1991-94	3,501	906	0	34	2,630	7,071
Albert Fann, Cal St. Northridge (II)	1987-90	4,090	803	0	0	2,141	7,032
Reggie Greene, Siena (I-AA)	1994-97	5,415	274	0	53	1,217	6,959
Kirk Matthieu, Maine Maritime (III)	$1989-93	5,107	315	0	254	1,279	6,955
Curtis Delgardo, Portland St. (II)	$1986-90	4,178	1,258	0	318	1,188	6,942
Jarrett Anderson, Truman (II)	1993-96	6,166	633	0	0	127	6,926
Darrin Nelson, Stanford (I-A)	1977-78, 80-81	4,033	2,368	0	471	13	6,885
Eric Frees, McDaniel (III)	1988-91	5,281	392	0	47	1,158	6,878
Kevin Faulk, LSU (I-A)	1995-98	4,557	600	0	857	819	6,833
Adrian Peterson, Ga. Southern (I-AA)	1998-01	6,559	225	0	0	0	6,784
Damian Beane, Shepherd (II)	1996-99	6,346	416	0	0	0	6,762
Marcel Shipp, Massachusetts (I-AA)	1997-00	5,383	932	0	0	392	6,707
Ron Dayne, Wisconsin (I-A)	1996-99	6,397	304	0	0	0	6,701
Johnny Cox, Fort Lewis (II)	1990-93	112	3,611	0	495	2,476	6,694
Steve Roberts, Butler (II)	1986-89	4,623	1,201	0	272	578	6,674
Anthony Russo, St. John's (N.Y.) (III; I-AA)	1990-92; 93	5,834	405	0	25	379	6,643
Joshua Carter, Muhlenberg (III)	1998-01	170	2,733	0	1,550	2,189	6,642

Player, Team (Division[s])	Years	Rush	Rcv.	Int.	PR	KO	Yds.
Charles Dunn, Portland St. (II; I-AA)	1997; 98-00	6,007	626	0	0	0	6,633
Richard Huntley, Winston-Salem (II)	1992-95	6,286	333	0	0	0	6,619
Tony Dorsett, Pittsburgh (I-A)	1973-76	6,082	406	0	0	127	6,615
Paul Palmer, Temple (I-A)	1983-86	4,895	705	0	0	997	6,609
Charles White, Southern California (I-A)	1976-79	5,598	507	0	0	440	6,545
Trevor Cobb, Rice (I-A)	1989-92	4,948	892	0	21	651	6,512
Mike Smith, Neb.-Kearney (II)	1994-97	348	2,975	0	932	2,255	6,510
Joe Dudek, Plymouth St. (III)	1982-85	5,570	348	0	0	243	6,509
Richard Wemer, Grinnell (III)	1995-98	1,016	3,133	7	674	1,657	6,487
LaDainian Tomlinson, TCU (I-A)	1997-00	5,263	236	0	0	838	6,337
Glyn Milburn, Oklahoma/Stanford (I-A)	1988, 90-92	2,302	1,495	0	1,145	1,246	6,188
Dante Brown, Marietta (III)	1994-97	4,512	425	0	202	1,040	6,179
Wesley Cates, Calif. (Pa.) (II)	1998-01	5,647	307	0	19	174	6,147
Travis Prentice, Miami (Ohio) (I-A)	1996-99	5,596	527	0	0	0	6,123
Adam Henry, Carleton (III)	1990-93	3,482	601	0	186	1,839	6,108

*Record. $See Page 8 for explanation.

CAREER YARDS PER GAME

(Minimum 3,500 Yards)

Player, Team (Division[s])	Years	G	Rush	Rcv.	Int.	PR	KO	Yds.	Yd. PG
Ryan Benjamin, Pacific (Cal.) (I-A)	1990-92	24	3,119	1,063	0	100	1,424	5,706	*237.8
Chris George, Glenville St. (II)	1993-94	20	23	3,215	0	391	1,050	4,679	234.0
R.J. Bowers, Grove City (III)	1997-00	40	*7,353	397	0	50	1,453	9,253	231.3
Paul Smith, Gettysburg (III)	1996-99	40	5,205	758	0	959	2,182	9,104	227.6
Brian Westbrook, Villanova (I-AA)	1997-98, 00-01	44	4,298	2,582	0	343	2,289	*9,512	216.2
Brian Shay, Emporia St. (II)	1995-98	44	6,958	1,032	0	104	1,207	9,301	211.4
Kirk Matthieu, Maine Maritime (III)	$1989-93	33	5,107	315	0	254	1,279	6,955	210.8
Damon Thompson, Virginia St. (II)	1997-00	38	303	4,387	0	1,153	2,143	7,986	210.2
Anthony Gray, Western N.M. (II)	1997-98	19	3,484	499	0	0	8	3,991	210.1
Kavin Gailliard, American Int'l (II)	1996-99	43	6,523	1,049	0	472	814	8,858	206.0
Sheldon Canley, San Jose St. (I-A)	1988-90	25	2,513	828	0	5	1,800	5,146	205.8
Carey Bender, Coe (III)	1991-94	39	6,125	1,751	0	7	87	7,970	204.4
Jerry Azumah, New Hampshire (I-AA)	1995-98	41	6,193	1,153	0	5	1,025	8,376	204.3
Steve Tardif, Maine Maritime (III)	1996-99	39	6,093	643	8	65	1,151	7,960	204.1
Johnny Bailey, Tex. A&M-Kingsville (II)	1986-89	39	6,320	452	0	20	1,011	7,803	200.1
Howard Stevens, Randolph-Macon (II); Louisville (I-A)	1968-69; 71-72	38	5,297	738	0	781	748	7,564	199.1
Gary Trettel, St. Thomas (Minn.) (III)	1988-90	29	3,483	834	0	0	1,407	5,724	197.4
Arnold Mickens, Butler (I-AA)	1994-95	22	3,813	47	0	0	87	3,947	197.4
Tim Hall, Robert Morris (I-AA)	1994-95	19	2,908	793	0	0	0	3,701	194.8
Reggie Greene, Siena (I-AA)	1994-97	36	5,415	274	0	53	1,217	6,959	193.3
Billy Johnson, Widener (II; III)	1971-72; 73	28	3,737	27	0	43	989	5,404	193.0
O.J. Simpson, Southern California (I-A)	1967-68	19	3,124	235	0	0	307	3,666	192.9
Clarence Coleman, Ferris St. (II)	1998-01	42	49	4,983	0	1,494	1,483	8,009	190.7
Steve Roberts, Butler (II)	1986-89	35	4,623	1,201	0	272	578	6,674	190.7

*Record. $See Page 8 for explanation.

SEASON YARDS

Player, Team (Division)	Year	Rush	Rcv.	Int.	PR	KO	Yds.
Barry Sanders, Oklahoma St. (I-A)	†1988	2,628	106	0	95	421	*3,250
Kavin Gailliard, American Int'l (II)	†1999	*2,653	289	0	0	122	3,064
Brian Westbrook, Villanova (I-AA)	†1998	1,046	1,144	0	192	644	3,026
Ryan Benjamin, Pacific (Cal.) (I-A)	†1991	1,581	612	0	4	798	2,995
Brian Westbrook, Villanova (I-AA)	†2000	1,220	724	0	0	1,048	2,992
Dante Brown, Marietta (III)	†1996	2,385	174	0	46	368	2,973
R.J. Bowers, Grove City (III)	†1998	2,283	51	0	4	538	2,876
Brian Westbrook, Villanova (I-AA)	†2001	1,603	658	0	122	440	2,823
Brian Shay, Emporia St. (II)	†1998	2,265	165	0	0	389	2,819
Troy Edwards, Louisiana Tech (I-A)	†1998	227	1,996	0	235	326	2,784
Brian Shay, Emporia St. (II)	†1996	2,103	247	0	48	340	2,738
Jerry Azumah, New Hampshire (I-AA)	1998	2,195	218	0	5	308	2,726
Brian Shay, Emporia St. (II)	†1997	1,912	277	0	56	478	2,723
Paul Smith, Gettysburg (III)	†1999	1,546	301	0	255	615	2,717
Mike Pringle, Cal St. Fullerton (I-A)	†1989	1,727	249	0	0	714	2,690
Ian Smart, C. W. Post (II)	2001	2,536	135	0	0	0	2,671
Steve Roberts, Butler (II)	†1989	1,450	532	0	272	415	2,669
Carey Bender, Coe (III)	†1994	2,243	319	0	7	87	2,656
Larry Johnson, Penn St. (I-A)	†2002	2,087	349	0	0	219	2,655
Paul Palmer, Temple (I-A)	†1986	1,866	110	0	0	657	2,633
Emmett White, Utah St. (I-A)	†2000	1,322	592	0	183	531	2,628
Clarence Coleman, Ferris St. (II)	†2001	39	1,346	0	572	661	2,618
Chris George, Glenville St. (II)	†1993	23	1,876	0	157	562	2,618
Josh Ranek, South Dakota St. (II)	2001	1,804	509	0	0	295	2,608
Ryan Benjamin, Pacific (Cal.) (I-A)	†1992	1,441	434	0	96	626	2,597
Bernard Berrian, Fresno St. (I-A)	2001	101	1,270	0	552	668	2,591
Kavin Gailliard, American Int'l (II)	1998	1,971	270	0	151	196	2,588
Marcus Allen, Southern California (I-A)	†1981	2,342	217	0	0	0	2,559
Jesse Chatman, Eastern Wash. (I-AA)	2001	2,096	424	0	0	0	2,520
Damon Thompson, Virginia St. (II)	1998	127	1,330	0	292	770	2,519
Sheldon Canley, San Jose St. (I-A)	1989	1,201	353	0	0	959	2,513
Mike Rozier, Nebraska (I-A)	1983	2,148	106	0	0	232	2,486
Damon Thompson, Virginia St. (II)	1999	88	1,517	0	410	465	2,480
Troy Davis, Iowa St. (I-A)	†1995	2,010	159	0	0	297	2,466
Jamel White, South Dakota (II)	1999	1,807	640	0	0	0	2,447
Alex Van Dyke, Nevada (I-A)	1995	6	1,854	0	0	583	2,443

All-purpose yardage is the combined net yards gained by rushing, receiving, interception (and fumble) returns, punt returns, kickoff returns and runbacks of field goal attempts. All-purpose yardage does not include forward passing yardage.

Total offense is the total of net gain rushing and net gain forward passing. Receiving and runback yards are not included in total offense.

Player, Team (Division)	Year	Rush	Rcv.	Int.	PR	KO	Yds.
Paul Smith, Gettysburg (III)	1998	1,515	178	0	191	554	2,438
Charles Roberts, Sacramento St. (I-AA)	1998	2,260	79	0	0	91	2,430
Archie Amerson, Northern Ariz. (I-AA)	1996	2,079	262	0	0	88	2,429
Johnny Bailey, Tex. A&M-Kingsville (II)	†1986	2,011	54	0	20	340	2,425
Kenny Gamble, Colgate (I-AA)	†1986	1,816	198	0	40	391	2,425
Theo Blanco, Wis.-Stevens Point (III)	1987	454	1,616	0	245	103	2,418
Guy Leman, Simpson (III)	1998	1,788	210	0	0	408	2,406
Rick Wegher, South Dakota St. (II)	1984	1,317	264	0	0	824	2,405

*Record. †National champion.

SEASON YARDS PER GAME

Player, Team (Division)	Year	G	Rush	Rcv.	Int.	PR	KO	Yds.	Yd.PG
Dante Brown, Marietta (III)	†1996	10	2,385	174	0	46	368	2,973	*297.3
Barry Sanders, Oklahoma St. (I-A)	†1988	11	2,628	106	0	0	95	*3,250	295.5
R.J. Bowers, Grove City (III)	†1998	10	2,283	51	0	4	538	2,876	287.6
Brian Westbrook, Villanova (I-AA)	†1998	11	1,046	1,144	0	192	644	3,026	275.1
Brian Westbrook, Villanova (I-AA)	†2000	11	1,220	724	0	0	1,048	2,992	272.0
Paul Smith, Gettysburg (III)	†1999	10	1,546	301	0	255	615	2,717	271.7
Steve Roberts, Butler (II)	†1989	10	1,450	532	0	272	415	2,669	266.9
Carey Bender, Coe (III)	†1994	10	2,243	319	0	7	87	2,656	265.6
Bobby Felix, Western N.M. (II)	†1994	8	439	853	0	150	667	2,109	263.6
Chris George, Glenville St. (II)	†1993	10	23	1,876	0	157	562	2,618	261.8
Brian Westbrook, Villanova (I-AA)	†2001	11	1,603	658	0	122	440	2,823	256.6
Brian Shay, Emporia St. (II)	†1998	11	2,265	165	0	0	389	2,819	256.3
Kavin Gailliard, American Int'l (II)	†1999	12	*2,653	289	0	0	122	3,064	255.3
Damon Thompson, Virginia St. (II)	1998	10	127	1,330	0	292	770	2,519	251.9
Billy Johnson, Widener (II)	1972	9	1,556	40	43	511	115	2,265	251.7
Ryan Benjamin, Pacific (Cal.) (I-A)	†1991	12	1,581	612	0	4	798	2,995	249.6
Brian Shay, Emporia St. (II)	†1996	11	2,103	247	0	48	340	2,738	248.9
Damon Thompson, Virginia St. (II)	1999	10	88	1,517	0	410	465	2,480	248.0
Jerry Azumah, New Hampshire (I-AA)	1998	11	2,195	218	0	5	308	2,726	247.8
Brian Shay, Emporia St. (II)	†1997	11	1,912	277	0	56	478	2,723	247.5
Kenneth Sasu, Marietta (III)	1999	9	1,770	82	0	0	374	2,226	247.3
Byron "Whizzer" White, Colorado (I-A)	†1937	8	1,121	0	103	587	159	1,970	246.3
Steve Tardif, Maine Maritime (III)	1999	9	1,567	149	8	0	479	2,203	244.8
Mike Pringle, Cal St. Fullerton (I-A)	†1989	11	1,727	249	0	0	714	2,690	244.4
Paul Smith, Gettysburg (III)	1998	10	1,515	178	0	191	554	2,438	243.8
Kirk Matthieu, Maine Maritime (III)	†1992	9	1,733	91	0	56	308	2,188	243.1
Guy Leman, Simpson (III)	1998	10	1,788	210	0	0	408	2,406	240.6
Paul Palmer, Temple (I-A)	†1986	11	1,866	110	0	0	657	2,633	239.4
Emmett White, Utah St. (I-A)	†2000	11	1,322	592	0	183	531	2,628	238.9
Ray Neosh, Coe (III)	1996	9	1,472	273	0	0	403	2,148	238.7
Ricky Gales, Simpson (III)	†1989	10	2,035	102	0	0	248	2,385	238.5
Clarence Coleman, Ferris St. (II)	†2001	11	39	1,346	0	572	661	2,618	238.0
R.J. Bowers, Grove City (III)	1999	10	2,098	34	0	0	240	2,372	237.2
Josh Ranek, South Dakota St. (II)	2001	11	1,804	509	0	0	295	2,608	237.1
Paul Smith, Gettysburg (III)	†1997	10	1,256	102	0	199	805	2,362	236.2
Ryan Benjamin, Pacific (Cal.) (I-A)	†1992	11	1,441	434	0	96	626	2,597	236.1
Kavin Gailliard, American Int'l (II)	1998	11	1,971	270	0	151	196	2,588	235.3
Reggie Greene, Siena (I-AA)	†1996	9	1,719	50	0	0	337	2,106	234.0

*Record. †National champion.

C.W. Post's Ian Smart assumed the title of NCAA football career scoring leader last year, as he finished with 570 points. Smart also is fourth across all divisions in career rushing yards with 6,647.

Scoring

CAREER POINTS

Player, Team (Division[s])	Years	TD	Extra Pts. Scored	FG	Pts.
Ian Smart, C.W. Post (II)	1999-02	*95	0	0	*570
R.J. Bowers, Grove City (III)	1997-00	92	10	0	562
Brian Westbrook, Villanova (I-AA)	1997-98, 00-01	89	10	0	544
Brian Shay, Emporia St. (II)	1995-98	88	16	0	544
Carey Bender, Coe (III)	1991-94	86	12	0	528
Adrian Peterson, Ga. Southern (I-AA)	1998-01	87	2	0	524
Scott Pingel, Westminster (Mo.) (III)	1996-99	75	34	0	484
Trevor Shannon, Wartburg (III)	1995-98	79	10	0	484
Kavin Gailliard, American Int'l (II)	1996-99	78	8	0	476
Joe Dudek, Plymouth St. (III)	1982-85	79	0	0	474
Travis Prentice, Miami (Ohio) (I-A)	1996-99	78	0	0	468
David Kircus, Grand Valley St. (II)	1999-02	77	2	0	464
Walter Payton, Jackson St. (II)	1971-74	66	53	5	464
Ricky Williams, Texas (I-A)	1995-98	75	2	0	452
Dan Pugh, Mount Union (III)	1999-02	73	2	0	440
Jarrett Anderson, Truman (II)	1993-96	73	2	0	440
Chuck Moore, Mount Union (III)	1998-01	73	0	0	438
Shawn Graves, Wofford (QB) (II)	1989-92	72	3	0	438
Rashaan Dumas, Southern Conn. St. (II)	1996-99	72	0	0	432
Josh Ranek, South Dakota St. (II)	$1997-01	69	12	0	426
Johnny Bailey, Tex. A&M-Kingsville (II)	1986-89	70	3	0	426
Roger Graham, New Haven (II)	1991-94	70	2	0	424

Player, Team (Division[s])	Years	TD	Extra Pts. Scored	FG	Pts.
Roman Anderson, Houston (I-A)	1988-91	0	213	70	423
Mark Kacmarynski, Central (Iowa) (III)	$1992-96	70	2	0	422
Matt Cannon, Southern Utah (I-AA)	1997-00	69	3	0	420
Jerry Azumah, New Hampshire (I-AA)	1995-98	69	4	0	418
Howard Stevens, Randolph-Macon (II); Louisville (I-A)	1968-69; 71-72	69	4	0	418
Brock Forsey, Boise St. (I-A)	1999-02	68	0	0	408
Casey Donaldson, Wittenberg (III)	1997-00	68	0	0	408
Andre Braxton, Virginia Union (II)	1997-00	62	36	0	408
Dale Mills, Truman (II)	1957-60	64	23	0	407
Jeremy Monroe, Michigan Tech (II)	1990-93	67	0	0	402
Andrew Notarfrancesco, Catholic (III)	1996-99	65	8	0	398
Carlos Huerta, Miami (Fla.) (I-A)	1988-91	0	178	73	397
Jason Elam, Hawaii (I-A)	$1988-92	0	158	79	395
Anthony Thompson, Indiana (I-A)	1986-89	65	4	0	394
Garney Henley, Huron (II)	1956-59	63	16	0	394
Derek Schmidt, Florida St. (I-A)	1984-87	0	174	73	393
Kris Brown, Nebraska (I-A)	1995-98	0	217	57	388
Wesley Cates, Calif. (Pa.)	1998-01	64	2	0	386
Steve Roberts, Butler (II)	1986-89	63	4	0	386
Jeff Bentrim, North Dakota St. (QB) (II)	1983-86	64	2	0	386
Marty Zendejas, Nevada (I-AA)	1984-87	0	169	72	385
Shane Ream, Allegheny (III)	1998-01	64	0	0	384
David Dinkins, Morehead St. (I-AA)	1997-00	63	3	0	384
Leo Lewis, Lincoln (Mo.) (II)	1951-54	64	0	0	384
Ron Dayne, Wisconsin (I-A)	1996-99	63	0	0	378
Chris Bisaillon, Ill. Wesleyan (III)	1989-92	61	12	0	378
Heath Sherman, Tex. A&M-Kingsville (II)	1985-88	63	0	0	378
Marshall Faulk, San Diego St. (I-A)	1991-93	62	4	0	376
Eric Crouch, Nebraska (I-A)	1998-01	59	20	0	374
Chris Babirad, Wash. & Jeff. (III)	1989-92	62	2	0	374
Billy Johnson, Widener (II; III)	1971-72; 73	62	0	0	372
Shayne Graham, Virginia Tech (I-A)	1996-99	0	167	68	371
Jeff Hall, Tennessee (I-A)	1995-98	0	188	61	371

*Record. $See Page 8 for explanation.

CAREER POINTS PER GAME

(Minimum 225 Points)

Player, Team (Division[s])	Years	G	TD	Extra Pts. Scored	FG	Pts.	Pt.PG
R.J. Bowers, Grove City (III)	1997-00	40	92	10	0	562	*14.1
Cory Christensen, Simpson (III)	1996-97	19	44	0	0	264	13.9
Rob Marchitello, Maine Maritime (III)	1993-95	26	59	4	0	358	13.8
Carey Bender, Coe (III)	1991-94	39	86	12	0	528	13.5
Ole Gunderson, St. Olaf (II)	1969-71	27	60	2	0	362	13.4
Billy Johnson, Widener (II; III)	1971-72; 73	28	62	0	0	372	13.3
Leon Burns, Long Beach St. (II)	1969-70	22	47	2	0	284	12.9
Ian Smart, C.W. Post (II)	1999-02	45	*95	0	0	*570	12.6
Adrian Peterson, Ga. Southern (I-AA)	1998-01	42	87	2	0	524	12.5
Trevor Shannon, Wartburg (III)	1995-98	39	79	10	0	484	12.4
Brian Westbrook, Villanova (I-AA)	1997-98, 00-01	44	89	10	0	544	12.4
Brian Shay, Emporia St. (II)	1995-98	44	88	16	0	544	12.4
Scott Pingel, Westminster (Mo.) (III)	1996-99	39	75	34	0	484	12.4
Marshall Faulk, San Diego St. (I-A)	1991-93	31	62	4	0	376	12.1
Jim Regan, Pomona-Pitzer (III)	1995-98	30	37	93	15	360	12.0
Tyrone Morgan, Northern St. (II)	1998-00	30	59	0	0	354	11.8
Ed Marinaro, Cornell (I-A)	1969-71	27	52	6	0	318	11.8
Aaron Stecker, Western Ill. (I-AA)	1997-98	20	39	0	0	234	11.7
Rashaan Dumas, Southern Conn. St. (II)	1996-99	37	72	0	0	432	11.7
Chad Hoiska, Wis.-Eau Claire (III)	1995-97	30	58	2	0	350	11.7
Joe Dudek, Plymouth St. (III)	1982-85	41	79	0	0	474	11.6
Bill Burnett, Arkansas (I-A)	1968-70	26	49	0	0	294	11.3
Dale Mills, Truman (II)	1957-60	36	64	23	0	407	11.3
Steve Owens, Oklahoma (I-A)	1967-69	30	56	0	0	336	11.2
Kavin Gailliard, American Int'l (II)	1996-99	43	78	8	0	476	11.1
Walter Payton, Jackson St. (II)	1971-74	42	66	53	5	464	11.0
Steve Roberts, Butler (II)	1986-89	35	63	4	0	386	11.0
Jeff Bentrim, North Dakota St. (II)	1983-86	35	64	2	0	386	11.0
Chuck Moore, Mount Union (III)	1998-01	40	73	0	0	438	11.0
Shawn Graves, Wofford (II)	1989-92	40	72	3	0	438	11.0
Johnny Bailey, Tex. A&M-Kingsville	1986-89	39	70	3	0	426	10.9
Eddie Talboom, Wyoming (I-A)	1948-50	28	34	99	0	303	10.8
David Kircus, Grand Valley St. (II)	1999-02	43	77	2	0	464	10.8
Dan Pugh, Mount Union (III)	1999-02	41	73	2	0	440	10.7
Chris Babirad, Wash. & Jeff. (III)	1989-92	35	62	2	0	374	10.7
Keith Elias, Princeton (I-AA)	1991-93	30	52	8	0	320	10.7

*Record.

SEASON POINTS

Player, Team (Division)	Year	TD	Extra Pts. Scored	FG	Pts.
Dan Pugh, Mount Union (III)	†2002	*41	2	0	*248
Barry Sanders, Oklahoma St. (I-A)	†1988	39	0	0	234
David Kircus, Grand Valley St. (II)	†2002	35	2	0	212
Kavin Gailliard, American Int'l (II)	†1999	34	2	0	206
R.J. Bowers, Grove City (III)	†1998	34	2	0	206
Ian Smart, C.W. Post (II)	2001	33	0	0	198
Brian Shay, Emporia St. (II)	†1997	32	6	0	198
Guy Leman, Simpson (III)	1998	33	0	0	198
Carey Bender, Coe (III)	†1994	32	2	0	194
Brock Forsey, Boise St. (I-A)	†2002	32	0	0	192
Troy Edwards, Louisiana Tech (I-A)	†1998	31	2	0	188
Travis Walch, Winona St. (II)	1997	30	2	0	182
Ian Smart, C.W. Post (II)	2002	30	0	0	180
David Russell, Linfield (III)	2002	30	0	0	180
Shane Ream, Allegheny (III)	†2000	30	0	0	180
Terry Metcalf, Long Beach St. (II)	1971	29	4	0	178
Brian Westbrook, Villanova (I-AA)	†2001	29	2	0	176
Andre Braxton, Virginia Union (II)	†2000	27	14	0	176
Brian Shay, Emporia St. (II)	†1998	29	2	0	176
Chad Hoiska, Wis.-Eau Claire (III)	1997	29	2	0	176
Fredrick Jackson, Coe (III)	2002	29	0	0	174
Adrian Peterson, Ga. Southern (I-AA)	†1999	29	0	0	174
Jim Mormino, Allegheny (III)	1997	29	0	0	174
Doug Steiner, Grove City (III)	1997	29	0	0	174
Mike Rozier, Nebraska (I-A)	†1983	29	0	0	174
Lydell Mitchell, Penn St. (I-A)	1971	29	0	0	174
Jesse Chatman, Eastern Wash. (I-AA)	2001	28	4	0	172
Montrell Coley, Hampton (I-AA)	†2000	28	2	0	172
Luke Staley, Brigham Young (I-A)	†2001	28	2	0	170
Josh Ranek, South Dakota St. (II)	1999	28	2	0	170
Geoff Mitchell, Weber St. (I-AA)	†1991	28	2	0	170
Willis McGahee, Miami (Fla.) (I-A)	2002	28	0	0	168
David Kircus, Grand Valley St. (II)	†2001	28	0	0	168
Lee Suggs, Virginia Tech (I-A)	†2000	28	0	0	168
Ricky Williams, Texas (I-A)	1998	28	0	0	168
Jarrett Anderson, Truman (II)	†1996	28	0	0	168
Stanley Drayton, Allegheny (III)	†1991	28	0	0	168
Jim Switzer, Col. of Emporia (II)	†1963	28	0	0	168
Carl Herakovich, Rose-Hulman (II)	†1958	25	18	0	168
Ted Scown, Sul Ross St. (II)	†1948	28	0	0	168
James Regan, Pomona-Pitzer (III)	†1997	21	34	2	166
Dante Brown, Marietta (III)	†1996	27	4	0	166
Ronald Moore, Pittsburg St. (II)	1992	27	4	0	166
Ricky Gales, Simpson (III)	1989	26	10	0	166
Art Luppino, Arizona (I-A)	†1954	24	22	0	166
Matt Malmberg, St. John's (Minn.) (III)	†1993	27	2	0	164
Leon Burns, Long Beach St. (II)	†1969	27	2	0	164
Chaz Williams, Ga. Southern (I-AA)	2002	27	0	0	162
Scott Pingel, Westminster (Mo.) (III)	1998	26	6	0	162
Trevor Shannon, Wartburg (III)	1998	26	6	0	162
Jerry Rice, Mississippi Val. (I-AA)	†1984	27	0	0	162
Mike Deutsch, North Dakota (II)	1972	27	0	0	162
Billy Johnson, Widener (II)	†1972	27	0	0	162

*Record. †National champion.

SEASON POINTS PER GAME

Player, Team (Division)	Year	G	TD	Extra Pts. Scored	FG	Pts.	Pt.PG
Barry Sanders, Oklahoma St. (I-A)	†1988	11	39	0	0	234	*21.3
Carl Herakovich, Rose-Hulman (II)	†1958	8	25	18	0	168	21.0
James Regan, Pomona-Pitzer (III)	†1997	8	21	34	2	166	20.8
R.J. Bowers, Grove City (III)	†1998	10	34	2	0	206	20.6
Guy Leman, Simpson (III)	1998	10	33	0	0	198	19.8
Carey Bender, Coe (III)	†1994	10	32	2	0	194	19.4
Jim Switzer, Col. of Emporia (II)	†1963	9	28	0	0	168	18.7
Shane Ream, Allegheny (III)	†2000	10	30	0	0	180	18.0
Brian Shay, Emporia St. (II)	†1997	11	32	6	0	198	18.0
Billy Johnson, Widener (II)	†1972	9	27	0	0	162	18.0
Dan Pugh, Mount Union (III)	†2002	14	*41	2	0	*248	17.7
Chad Hoiska, Wis.-Eau Claire (III)	1997	10	29	2	0	176	17.6
Carl Garrett, N.M. Highlands (II)	†1966	9	26	2	0	158	17.6
Jim Mormino, Allegheny (III)	1997	10	29	0	0	174	17.4
Doug Steiner, Grove City (III)	1997	10	29	0	0	174	17.4
Bobby Reynolds, Nebraska (I-A)	†1950	9	22	25	0	157	17.4
Kavin Gailliard, American Int'l (II)	†1999	12	34	2	0	206	17.2
Rob Marchitello, Maine Maritime (III)	1994	9	25	4	0	154	17.1
David Kircus, Grand Valley St. (II)	†2001	10	28	0	0	168	16.8

Player, Team (Division)	Year	G	TD	Extra Pts. Scored	FG	Pts.	Pt.PG
Stanley Drayton, Allegheny (III)	†1991	10	28	0	0	168	16.8
Ted Scown, Sul Ross St. (II)	†1948	10	28	0	0	168	16.8
Dante Brown, Marietta (III)	†1996	10	27	4	0	166	16.6
Ricky Gales, Simpson (III)	†1989	10	26	10	0	166	16.6
Art Luppino, Arizona (I-A)	†1954	10	24	22	0	166	16.6
Travis Walch, Winona St. (II)	1997	11	30	2	0	182	16.5
Ian Smart, C.W. Post (II)	2001	12	33	0	0	198	16.5
Ed Marinaro, Cornell (I-A)	†1971	9	24	4	0	148	16.4
Matt Malmberg, St. John's (Minn.) (III)	†1993	10	27	2	0	164	16.4
David Russell, Linfield (III)	2002	11	30	0	0	180	16.4
Scott Pingel, Westminster (Mo.) (III)	1998	10	26	6	0	162	16.2
Jerry Rice, Mississippi Val. (I-AA)	†1984	10	27	0	0	162	16.2
Trevor Shannon, Wartburg (III)	1998	10	26	6	0	162	16.2
Brian Westbrook, Villanova (I-AA)	†2001	11	29	2	0	176	16.0
Andre Braxton, Virginia Union (II)	†2000	11	27	14	0	176	16.0
Jamie Lee, MacMurray (III)	1998	10	26	4	0	160	16.0
Brian Shay, Emporia St. (II)	†1998	11	29	2	0	176	16.0
Chris Babirad, Wash. & Jeff. (III)	†1992	9	24	0	0	144	16.0
Larry Ras, Michigan Tech (II)	†1971	9	24	0	0	144	16.0
Trent Nauholz, Simpson (III)	†1992	8	21	2	0	128	16.0

Player, Team (Division)	Year	G	TD	Extra Pts. Scored	FG	Pts.	Pt.PG
Adrian Peterson, Ga. Southern (I-AA)	†1999	11	29	0	0	174	15.8
Lydell Mitchell, Penn St. (I-A)	1971	11	29	0	0	174	15.8
Troy Edwards, Louisiana Tech (I-A)	†1998	12	31	2	0	188	15.7
Jesse Chatman, Eastern Wash. (I-AA)	2001	11	28	4	0	172	15.6
Montrell Coley, Hampton (I-AA)	†2000	11	28	2	0	172	15.6
Marshall Faulk, San Diego St. (I-A)	†1991	9	23	2	0	140	15.6

*Record. †National champion.

SINGLE-GAME POINTS

Pts.	Div.	Player, Team (Opponent)	Date
48	III	Carey Bender, Coe (Beloit)	Nov. 12, 1994
48	I-A	Howard Griffith, Illinois (Southern Ill.)	Sept. 22, 1990
48	II	Paul Zaeske, North Park (North Central)	Oct. 12, 1968
48	II	Junior Wolf, Okla. Panhandle (St. Mary [Kan.])	Nov. 8, 1958
44	I-A	Marshall Faulk, San Diego St. (Pacific [Cal.])	Sept. 14, 1991
43	I-A	Jim Brown, Syracuse (Colgate)	Nov. 17, 1956
42	I-A	Arnold "Showboat" Boykin, Mississippi (Mississippi St.)	Dec. 1, 1951
42	I-A	Fred Wendt, UTEP (New Mexico St.)	Nov. 25, 1948

Award Winners

Consensus All-America Selections, 1889-2002

In 1950, the National Collegiate Athletic Bureau (the NCAA's service bureau) compiled the first official comprehensive roster of all-time all-Americans. The compilation of the all-American roster was supervised by a panel of analysts working in large part with the historical records contained in the files of the Dr. Baker Football Information Service.

The roster consists of only those players who were first-team selections on one or more of the all-America teams that were selected for the national audience and received nationwide circulation. Not included are the thousands of players who received mention on all-America second or third teams, nor the numerous others who were selected by newspapers or agencies with circulations that were not primarily national and with viewpoints, therefore, that were not normally nationwide in scope.

The following chart indicates, by year (in left column), which national media and organizations selected all-America teams. The headings at the top of each column refer to the selector (see legend after chart)

All-America Selectors

Year	AA	AP	C	CNN	COL	CP	FBW	FC	FN	FW	INS	L	LIB	M	N	NA	NEA	SN	UP	UPI	W	WCF
1889	-	-	-	.	.	-	-	.	-	-	.	-	.	.	-	-	.	.	-	-	√	.
1890	-	-	-	.	.	-	-	.	-	-	.	-	.	.	-	-	.	.	-	-	√	.
1891	-	-	-	.	.	-	-	.	-	-	.	-	.	.	-	-	.	.	-	-	√	.
1892	-	-	-	.	.	-	-	.	-	-	.	-	.	.	-	-	.	.	-	-	√	.
1893	-	-	-	.	.	-	-	.	-	-	.	-	.	.	-	-	.	.	-	-	√	.
1894	-	-	-	.	.	-	-	.	-	-	.	-	.	.	-	-	.	.	-	-	√	.
1895	-	-	-	.	.	-	-	.	-	-	.	-	.	.	-	-	.	.	-	-	√	.
1896	-	-	-	.	.	-	-	.	-	-	.	-	.	.	-	-	.	.	-	-	√	.
1897	-	-	-	.	.	-	-	.	-	-	.	-	.	.	-	-	.	.	-	-	√	.
1898	-	-	√	.	.	-	-	.	-	-	.	-	.	.	-	-	.	.	-	-	√	.
1899	-	-	√	.	.	-	-	.	-	-	.	-	.	.	-	-	.	.	-	-	√	.
1900	-	-	√	.	.	-	-	.	-	-	.	-	.	.	-	-	.	.	-	-	√	.
1901	-	-	√	.	.	-	-	.	-	-	.	-	.	.	-	-	.	.	-	-	√	.
1902	-	-	√	.	.	-	-	.	-	-	.	-	.	.	-	-	.	.	-	-	√	.
1903	-	-	√	.	.	-	-	.	-	-	.	-	.	.	-	-	.	.	-	-	√	.
1904	-	-	√	.	.	-	-	.	-	-	.	-	.	.	-	-	.	.	-	-	√	.
1905	-	-	√	.	.	-	-	.	-	-	.	-	.	.	-	-	.	.	-	-	√	.
1906	-	-	√	.	.	-	-	.	-	-	.	-	.	.	-	-	.	.	-	-	√	.
1907	-	-	√	.	.	-	-	.	-	-	.	-	.	.	-	-	.	.	-	-	√	.
1908	-	-	√	.	.	-	-	.	-	-	.	-	.	.	-	-	.	.	-	-	√	.
1909	-	-	√	.	.	-	-	.	-	-	.	-	.	.	-	-	.	.	-	-	-	.
1910	-	-	√	.	.	-	-	.	-	-	.	-	.	.	-	-	.	.	-	-	-	.
1911	-	-	√	.	.	-	-	.	-	-	.	-	.	.	-	-	.	.	-	-	-	.
1912	-	-	√	.	.	-	-	.	-	-	.	-	.	.	-	-	.	.	-	-	-	.
1913	-	-	√	.	.	-	-	.	-	-	√	-	.	.	-	-	.	.	-	-	-	.
1914	-	-	√	.	.	-	-	.	-	-	√	-	.	.	-	-	.	.	-	-	-	.
1915	-	-	√	.	.	-	-	.	-	-	√	-	.	.	-	-	.	.	-	-	-	.
1916	-	-	√	.	.	-	-	.	-	-	√	-	.	.	-	-	.	.	-	-	-	.
1917	-	-	(*)	.	.	-	-	.	-	-	√	-	.	√	-	-	√	.	-	-	-	.
1918	-	-	-	.	.	-	-	.	-	-	√	-	.	√	-	-	.	.	-	-	-	.
1919	-	-	√	.	.	-	-	.	-	-	.	-	√	.	-	-	.	.	-	-	-	.
1920	-	-	√	.	.	-	√	.	-	-	√	-	√	.	-	-	.	.	-	-	-	.
1921	-	-	√	.	.	-	-	.	-	-	.	-	.	.	-	-	.	.	-	-	-	.
1922	-	-	√	.	.	-	-	.	-	-	.	-	.	.	-	-	.	.	-	-	-	.
1923	-	-	√	.	.	-	√	.	-	-	.	-	.	.	-	-	.	.	-	-	-	.
1924	√	-	√	.	.	-	√	.	-	-	√	√	.	.	-	-	√	.	-	-	-	.
1925	√	√	-	.	√	-	√	.	-	-	√	√	.	.	-	-	√	.	√	-	-	.
1926	√	√	-	.	√	-	-	.	-	-	√	-	.	.	-	-	√	.	√	-	-	.
1927	√	√	-	.	√	-	-	.	-	-	√	-	.	.	-	√	√	.	√	-	-	.
1928	√	√	-	.	√	-	-	.	-	-	√	-	.	.	-	√	√	.	√	-	-	.
1929	√	√	-	.	√	-	-	.	-	-	√	-	.	.	-	√	√	.	√	-	-	.
1930	√	√	-	.	√	-	-	.	-	-	√	-	.	.	-	√	√	.	√	-	-	.
1931	√	√	-	.	√	-	-	.	-	-	√	-	√	.	-	√	√	.	√	-	-	.
1932	√	√	-	.	√	-	-	.	-	-	√	-	√	.	-	√	√	.	√	-	-	.
1933	√	√	-	.	√	-	-	.	-	-	√	-	.	.	-	√	√	.	√	-	-	.
1934	√	√	-	.	-	-	-	.	-	-	√	-	.	.	-	√	√	√	√	-	-	.
1935	√	√	-	.	-	-	-	.	-	-	√	-	.	.	-	√	√	√	√	-	-	.
1936	√	√	-	.	-	-	-	.	-	-	√	-	.	.	-	√	√	√	√	-	-	.
1937	√	√	-	.	-	-	-	.	-	-	√	-	.	.	√	√	√	√	√	-	-	.
1938	√	√	-	.	-	-	-	.	-	-	√	-	.	.	√	√	√	√	√	-	-	.
1939	√	√	-	.	-	-	-	.	-	-	√	-	.	√	√	√	√	-	√	-	-	.
1940	√	√	-	.	-	-	-	.	-	-	√	-	.	√	√	√	√	-	√	-	-	.
1941	√	√	-	.	√	-	-	.	-	-	√	-	.	√	√	√	√	-	√	-	-	.
1942	√	√	-	.	√	-	-	.	-	-	√	√	.	√	√	√	√	-	√	-	-	.
1943	√	√	-	.	√	-	-	√	-	-	√	-	.	.	-	-	√	-	√	-	-	.
1944	√	√	-	.	√	-	-	√	√	-	√	-	.	.	-	-	√	-	√	-	-	.
1945	√	√	-	.	√	-	-	.	√	√	√	√	.	.	-	-	√	-	√	-	-	.
1946	√	√	-	.	√	-	-	.	√	√	√	(†)	.	.	-	-	√	-	√	-	-	.
1947	-	√	-	.	√	-	-	.	√	-	√	-	.	.	-	-	√	-	√	-	-	.
1948	-	√	-	.	(§)	-	-	.	√	√	(#)√	-	.	.	-	-	√	-	√	-	-	.
1949	√	√	-	.	-	-	-	.	√	-	√	-	.	.	-	-	√	-	√	-	-	.
1950	√	√	-	.	-	-	-	.	√	-	√	-	.	.	-	-	√	√	√	-	-	.
1951	√	√	√	.	-	-	-	.	√	-	√	-	.	.	-	-	√	-	√	-	-	.
1952	√	√	√	.	-	-	√	.	-	√	√	-	.	.	-	-	-	√	√	√	√	.
1953	√	√	√	.	-	-	√	.	-	√	√	-	.	.	-	-	-	√	√	√	√	.

	AA	AP	C	CNN	COL	CP	FBW	FC	FN	FW	INS	L	LIB	M	N	NA	NEA	SN	UP	UPI	W	WCF
1954	√	√	-	-	-	-	-	√	-	√	√	-	-	-	-	-	√	√	√	-	-	-
1955	√	√	-	-	-	-	-	√	-	√	√	-	-	-	-	-	√	√	√	-	-	-
1956	-	√	-	-	-	-	-	√	-	√	√	-	-	-	-	-	√	√	√	-	-	-
1957	-	√	-	-	-	-	-	√	-	√	√	-	-	-	-	-	√	√	√	-	-	-
1958	-	√	-	-	-	-	-	√	-	√	-	-	-	-	-	-	√	√	-	√	-	-
1959	-	√	-	-	-	-	-	√	-	√	-	-	-	-	-	-	√	√	-	√	-	-
1960	-	√	-	-	-	-	-	√	-	√	-	-	-	-	-	-	√	√	-	√	-	-
1961	-	√	-	-	-	-	-	√	-	√	-	-	-	-	-	-	√	√	-	√	-	-
1962	-	√	-	-	-	-	-	√	-	√	-	-	-	-	-	-	√	√	-	√	-	-
1963	-	√	-	-	-	√	-	√	-	√	-	-	-	-	-	-	√	√	-	√	-	-
1964	-	√	-	-	√	-	-	√	-	√	-	-	-	-	-	-	√	-	-	√	-	-
1965	-	√	-	-	√	-	-	√	-	√	-	-	-	-	-	-	√	-	-	√	-	-
1966	-	√	-	-	√	-	-	√	-	√	-	-	-	-	-	-	√	-	-	√	-	-
1967	-	√	-	-	√	-	-	√	-	√	-	-	-	-	-	-	√	-	-	√	-	-
1968	-	√	-	-	√	-	-	√	-	√	-	-	-	-	-	-	√	-	-	√	-	-
1969	-	√	-	-	√	-	-	√	-	√	-	-	-	-	-	-	√	-	-	√	-	-
1970	-	√	-	-	√	-	-	√	-	√	-	-	-	-	-	-	√	-	-	√	-	-
1971	-	√	-	-	-	-	-	√	-	√	-	-	-	-	-	-	√	-	-	√	-	-
1972	-	√	-	-	-	-	-	√	-	√	-	-	-	-	-	-	√	-	-	√	-	√
1973	-	√	-	-	-	-	-	√	-	√	-	-	-	-	-	-	√	-	-	√	-	√
1974	-	√	-	-	-	-	-	√	-	√	-	-	-	-	-	-	-	-	-	√	-	√
1975	-	√	-	-	-	-	-	√	-	√	-	-	-	-	-	-	-	-	-	√	-	-
1976	-	√	-	-	-	-	-	√	-	√	-	-	-	-	-	-	-	-	-	√	-	-
1977	-	√	-	-	-	-	-	√	-	√	-	-	-	-	-	-	-	-	-	√	-	-
1978	-	√	-	-	-	-	-	√	-	√	-	-	-	-	-	-	-	-	-	√	-	-
1979	-	√	-	-	-	-	-	√	-	√	-	-	-	-	-	-	-	-	-	√	-	-
1980	-	√	-	-	-	-	-	√	-	√	-	-	-	-	-	-	-	-	-	√	-	-
1981	-	√	-	-	-	-	-	√	-	√	-	-	-	-	-	-	-	-	-	√	-	-
1982	-	√	-	-	-	-	-	√	-	√	-	-	-	-	-	-	-	-	-	√	-	-
1983	-	√	-	-	-	-	-	√	-	√	-	-	-	-	-	-	-	-	-	√	-	√
1984	-	√	-	-	-	-	-	√	-	√	-	-	-	-	-	-	-	-	-	√	-	-
1985	-	√	-	-	-	-	-	√	-	√	-	-	-	-	-	-	-	-	-	√	-	-
1986	-	√	-	-	-	-	-	√	-	√	-	-	-	-	-	-	-	-	-	√	-	-
1987	-	√	-	-	-	-	-	√	-	√	-	-	-	-	-	-	-	-	-	√	-	-
1988	-	√	-	-	-	-	-	√	-	√	-	-	-	-	-	-	-	-	-	√	-	-
1989	-	√	-	-	-	-	-	√	-	√	-	-	-	-	-	-	-	-	-	√	-	-
1990	-	√	-	-	-	-	-	√	-	√	-	-	-	-	-	-	-	-	-	√	-	-
1991	-	√	-	-	-	-	-	√	-	√	-	-	-	-	-	-	-	-	-	√	-	-
1992	-	√	-	-	-	-	-	√	-	√	-	-	-	-	-	-	-	-	-	√	-	-
1993	-	√	-	-	-	-	-	√	√	√	-	-	-	-	-	-	√	-	-	√	-	-
1994	-	√	-	-	-	-	-	√	√	√	-	-	-	-	-	-	-	-	-	√	-	-
1995	-	√	-	-	-	-	-	√	√	√	-	-	-	-	-	-	-	-	-	-	-	√
1996	-	√	-	-	-	-	-	√	√	√	-	-	-	-	-	-	-	-	-	-	-	√
1997	-	√	-	-	-	-	-	√	√	√	-	-	-	-	-	-	-	-	-	-	-	√
1998	-	√	-	-	-	-	-	√	√	√	-	-	-	-	-	-	-	-	-	-	-	√
1999	-	√	-	-	-	-	-	√	√	√	-	-	-	-	-	-	-	√	-	-	-	√
2000	-	√	-	-	-	-	-	√	√	√	-	-	-	-	-	-	-	√	-	-	-	√
2001	-	√	-	√	-	-	-	√	√	√	-	-	-	-	-	-	-	√	-	-	-	√
2002	-	√	-	-	-	-	-	√	√	√	-	-	-	-	-	-	-	√	-	-	-	√

*In 1917, Walter Camp selected an all-Service, all-America team composed of military personnel. †During 1946-70, Look Magazine published the Football Writers Association of America's selections, listed under FW. §During 1948-56, Collier's Magazine published the American Football Coaches Association's selections, listed under FC. #International News Service was the first to select offensive and defensive teams.

LEGEND FOR SELECTORS

AA—All-America Board
AP—Associated Press
C—Walter Camp (published in Harper's Weekly, 1897; in Collier's Magazine, 1898-1924)
CNN—Cable News Network-Sports Illustrated.com
COL—Collier's Magazine (selections by Grantland Rice, 1925-47; published American Football Coaches Association teams, 1948-56, listed under FC)
CP—Central Press
FBW—Football World Magazine
FC—American Football Coaches Association (published in Saturday Evening Post Magazine, 1945-47; in Collier's Magazine, 1948-56; sponsored by General Mills in 1957-59 and by Eastman Kodak from 1960-93)
FN—Football News
FW—Football Writers Association of America (published in Look Magazine, 1946-70)
INS—International News Service (merged with United Press in 1958 to form UPI)
L—Look Magazine (published Football Writers Association of America teams, 1946-70, listed under FW)
LIB—Liberty Magazine
M—Frank Menke Syndicate
N—Newsweek
NA—North American Newspaper Alliance
NEA—Newspaper Enterprise Association
SN—Sporting News
UP—United Press (merged with International News Service in 1958 to form UPI)
UPI—United Press International
W—Caspar Whitney (published in The Week's Sport in association with Walter Camp, 1889-90; published in Harper's Weekly, 1891-96, and in Outing Magazine, which he owned, 1898-1908; Walter Camp substituted for Whitney, who was on a world sports tour, and selected Harper's Weekly's team for 1897)
WCF—Walter Camp Foundation

AWARD WINNERS

All-America Selections

Listed on the following pages are the consensus all-Americans (i.e., the players who were accorded a majority of votes at their positions by the selectors). Included are the selections of 1889-97, 1909-12 and 1921-22 when there was only one selector.

1889
E—Amos Alonzo Stagg, Yale; Arthur Cumnock, Harvard; T—Hector Cowan, Princeton; Charles Gill, Yale; G—Pudge Heffelfinger, Yale; John Cranston, Harvard; C—William George, Princeton; B—Edgar Allan Poe, Princeton; Roscoe Channing, Princeton; Knowlton Ames, Princeton; James Lee, Harvard.

1890
E—Frank Hallowell, Harvard; Ralph Warren, Princeton; T—Marshall Newell, Harvard; William Rhodes, Yale; G—Pudge Heffelfinger, Yale; Jesse Riggs, Princeton; C—John Cranston, Harvard; B—Thomas McClung, Yale; Sheppard Homans, Princeton; Dudley Dean, Harvard; John Corbett, Harvard.

1891
E—Frank Hinkey, Yale; John Hartwell, Yale; T—Wallace Winter, Yale; Marshall Newell, Harvard; G—Pudge Heffelfinger, Yale; Jesse Riggs, Princeton; C—John Adams, Pennsylvania; B—Philip King, Princeton; Everett Lake, Harvard; Thomas McClung, Yale; Sheppard Homans, Princeton.

1892
E—Frank Hinkey, Yale; Frank Hallowell, Harvard; T—Marshall Newell, Harvard; A. Hamilton Wallis, Yale; G—Arthur Wheeler, Princeton; Bertram Waters, Harvard; C—William Lewis, Harvard; B—Charles Brewer, Harvard; Vance McCormick, Yale; Philip King, Princeton; Harry Thayer, Pennsylvania.

1893
E—Frank Hinkey, Yale; Thomas Trenchard, Princeton; T—Langdon Lea, Princeton; Marshall Newell, Harvard; G—Arthur Wheeler, Princeton; William Hickok, Yale; C—William Lewis, Harvard; B—Philip King, Princeton; Charles Brewer, Harvard; Franklin Morse, Princeton; Frank Butterworth, Yale.

1894
E—Frank Hinkey, Yale; Charles Gelbert, Pennsylvania; T—Bertram Waters, Harvard; Langdon Lea, Princeton; G—Arthur Wheeler, Princeton; William Hickok, Yale; C—Philip Stillman, Yale; B—George Adee, Yale; Arthur Knipe, Pennsylvania; George Brooke, Pennsylvania; Frank Butterworth, Yale.

1895
E—Norman Cabot, Harvard; Charles Gelbert, Pennsylvania; T—Langdon Lea, Princeton; Fred Murphy, Yale; G—Charles Wharton, Pennsylvania; Dudley Riggs, Princeton; C—Alfred Bull, Pennsylvania; B—Clinton Wyckoff, Cornell; Samuel Thorne, Yale; Charles Brewer, Harvard; George Brooke, Pennsylvania.

1896
E—Norman Cabot, Harvard; Charles Gelbert, Pennsylvania; T—William Church, Princeton; Fred Murphy, Yale; G—Charles Wharton, Pennsylvania; Wylie Woodruff, Pennsylvania; C—Robert Gailey, Princeton; B—Clarence Fincke, Yale; Edgar Wrightington, Harvard; Addison Kelly, Princeton; John Baird, Princeton.

1897
E—Garrett Cochran, Princeton; John Hall, Yale; T—Burr Chamberlain, Yale; John Outland, Pennsylvania; G—T. Truxton Hare, Pennsylvania; Gordon Brown, Yale; C—Alan Doucette, Harvard; B—Charles DeSaulles, Yale; Benjamin Dibblee, Harvard; Addison Kelly, Princeton; John Minds, Pennsylvania.

1898
E—Lew Palmer, Princeton; John Hallowell, Harvard; T—Arthur Hillebrand, Princeton; Burr Chamberlain, Yale; G—T. Truxton Hare, Pennsylvania; Gordon Brown, Yale; Walter Boal, Harvard; C—Pete Overfield, Pennsylvania; William Cunningham, Michigan; B—Charles Daly, Harvard; Benjamin Dibblee, Harvard; John Outland, Pennsylvania; Clarence Herschberger, Chicago; Malcolm McBride, Yale; Charles Romeyn, Army.

1899
E—David Campbell, Harvard; Arthur Poe, Princeton; T—Arthur Hillebrand, Princeton; George Stillman, Yale; G—T. Truxton Hare, Pennsylvania; Gordon Brown, Yale; C—Pete Overfield, Pennsylvania; B—Charles Daly, Harvard; Josiah McCracken, Pennsylvania; Malcolm McBride, Yale; Isaac Seneca, Carlisle; Albert Sharpe, Yale; Howard Reiter, Princeton.

1900
E—John Hallowell, Harvard; David Campbell, Harvard; William Smith, Army; T—George Stillman, Yale; James Bloomer, Yale; G—Gordon Brown, Yale; T. Truxton Hare, Pennsylvania; C—Herman Olcott, Yale; Walter Bachman, Lafayette; B—Bill Morley, Columbia; George Chadwick, Yale; Perry Hale, Yale; William Fincke, Yale; Charles Daly, Harvard; Raymond Starbuck, Cornell.

1901
E—David Campbell, Harvard; Ralph Davis, Princeton; Edward Bowditch, Harvard; Neil Snow, Michigan; T—Oliver Cutts, Harvard; Paul Bunker, Army; Crawford Blagden, Harvard; G—William Warner, Cornell; William Lee, Harvard; Charles Barnard, Harvard; Sanford Hunt, Cornell; C—Henry Holt, Yale; Walter Bachman, Lafayette; B—Robert Kernan, Harvard; Charles Daly, Army; Thomas Graydon, Harvard; Harold Weekes, Columbia; Bill Morley, Columbia.

1902
E—Thomas Shevlin, Yale; Edward Bowditch, Harvard; T—Ralph Kinney, Yale; James Hogan, Yale; Paul Bunker, Army; G—Edgar Glass, Yale; John DeWitt, Princeton; William Warner, Cornell; C—Henry Holt, Yale; Robert Boyers, Army; B—Foster Rockwell, Yale; George Chadwick, Yale; Thomas Graydon, Harvard; Thomas Barry, Brown.

1903
E—Howard Henry, Princeton; Charles Rafferty, Yale; T—Daniel Knowlton, Harvard; James Hogan, Yale; Fred Schacht, Minnesota; G—John DeWitt, Princeton; Andrew Marshall, Harvard; James Bloomer, Yale; C—Henry Hooper, Dartmouth; B—Willie Heston, Michigan; J. Dana Kafer, Princeton; James Johnson, Carlisle; Richard Smith, Columbia; Myron Witham, Dartmouth; W. Ledyard Mitchell, Yale.

1904
E—Thomas Shevlin, Yale; Fred Speik, Chicago; T—James Hogan, Yale; James Cooney, Princeton; G—Frank Piekarski, Pennsylvania; Joseph Gilman, Dartmouth; Ralph Kinney, Yale; C—Arthur Tipton, Army; B—Daniel Hurley, Harvard; Walter Eckersall, Chicago; Vincent Stevenson, Pennsylvania; Willie Heston, Michigan; Andrew Smith, Pennsylvania; Foster Rockwell, Yale; Henry Torney, Army.

1905
E—Thomas Shevlin, Yale; Ralph Glaze, Dartmouth; Mark Catlin, Chicago; T—Otis Lamson, Pennsylvania; Beaton Squires, Harvard; Karl Brill, Harvard; G—Roswell Tripp, Yale; Francis Burr, Harvard; C—Robert Torrey, Pennsylvania; B—Walter Eckersall, Chicago; Howard Roome, Yale; John Hubbard, Amherst; James McCormick, Princeton; Guy Hutchinson, Yale; Daniel Hurley, Harvard; Henry Torney, Army.

1906
E—Robert Forbes, Yale; L. Casper Wister, Princeton; T—L. Horatio Biglow, Yale; James Cooney, Princeton; Charles Osborne, Harvard; G—Francis Burr, Harvard; Elmer Thompson, Cornell; August Ziegler, Pennsylvania; C—William Dunn, Penn St.; William Newman, Cornell; B—Walter Eckersall, Chicago; Hugh Knox, Yale; Edward Dillon, Princeton; John Mayhew, Brown; William Hollenback, Pennsylvania; Paul Veeder, Yale.

1907
E—Bill Dague, Navy; Clarence Alcott, Yale; Albert Exendine, Carlisle; L. Casper Wister, Princeton; T—Dexter Draper, Pennsylvania; L. Horatio Biglow, Yale; G—August Ziegler, Pennsylvania; William Erwin, Army; C—Adolph Schulz, Michigan; Patrick Grant, Harvard; B—John Wendell, Harvard; Thomas A. D. Jones, Yale; Edwin Harlan, Princeton; James McCormick, Princeton; Edward Coy, Yale; Peter Hauser, Carlisle.

1908
E—Hunter Scarlett, Pennsylvania; George Schildmiller, Dartmouth; T—Hamilton Fish, Harvard; Frank Horr, Syracuse; Percy Northcroft, Navy; G—Clark Tobin, Dartmouth; William Goebel, Yale; Hamlin Andrus, Yale; Bernard O'Rourke, Cornell; C—Charles Nourse, Harvard; B—Edward Coy, Yale; Frederick Tibbott, Princeton; William Hollenback, Pennsylvania; Walter Steffen, Chicago; Ed Lange, Navy; Hamilton Corbett, Harvard.

1909
E—Adrian Regnier, Brown; John Kilpatrick, Yale; T—Hamilton Fish, Harvard; Henry Hobbs, Yale; G—Albert Benbrook, Michigan; Hamlin Andrus, Yale; C—Carroll Cooney, Yale; B—Edward Coy, Yale; John McGovern, Minnesota; Stephen Philbin, Yale; Wayland Minot, Harvard.

1910
E—John Kilpatrick, Yale; Stanfield Wells, Michigan; T—Robert McKay, Harvard; James Walker, Minnesota; G—Robert Fisher, Harvard; Albert Benbrook, Michigan; C—Ernest Cozens, Pennsylvania; B—E. LeRoy Mercer, Pennsylvania; Percy Wendell, Harvard; Earl Sprackling, Brown; Talbot Pendleton, Princeton.

1911
E—Douglass Bomeisler, Yale; Sanford White, Princeton; T—Edward Hart, Princeton; Leland Devore, Army; G—Robert Fisher, Harvard; Joseph Duff, Princeton; C—Henry Ketcham, Yale; B—Jim Thorpe, Carlisle; Percy Wendell, Harvard; Arthur Howe, Yale; Jack Dalton, Navy.

1912
E—Samuel Felton, Harvard; Douglass Bomeisler, Yale; T—Wesley Englehorn, Dartmouth; Robert Butler, Wisconsin; G—Stanley Pennock, Harvard; John Logan, Princeton; C—Henry Ketcham, Yale; B—Charles Brickley, Harvard; Jim Thorpe, Carlisle; George Crowther, Brown; E. LeRoy Mercer, Pennsylvania.

1913
E—Robert Hogsett, Dartmouth; Louis Merrillat, Army; T—Harold Ballin, Princeton; Nelson Talbott, Yale; Miller Pontius, Michigan; Harvey Hitchcock, Harvard; G—John Brown, Navy; Stanley Pennock, Harvard; Ray Keeler, Wisconsin; C—Paul Des Jardien, Chicago; B—Charles Brickley, Harvard; Edward Mahan, Harvard; Jim Craig, Michigan; Ellery Huntington, Colgate; Gus Dorais, Notre Dame.

1914
E—Huntington Hardwick, Harvard; John O'Hearn, Cornell; Perry Graves, Illinois; T—Harold Ballin, Princeton; Walter Trumbull, Harvard; G—Stanley Pennock, Harvard; Ralph Chapman, Illinois; Clarence Spears, Dartmouth; C—John McEwan, Army; B—John Maulbetsch, Michigan; Edward Mahan, Harvard; Charles Barrett, Cornell; John Spiegel, Wash. & Jeff.; Harry LeGore, Yale.

1915
E—Murray Shelton, Cornell; Guy Chamberlin, Nebraska; T—Joseph Gilman, Harvard; Howard Buck, Wisconsin; G—Clarence Spears, Dartmouth; Harold White, Syracuse; C—Robert Peck, Pittsburgh; B—Charles Barrett, Cornell; Edward Mahan, Harvard; Richard King, Harvard; Bart Macomber, Illinois; Eugene Mayer, Virginia; Neno Jerry DaPrato, Michigan St.

1916
E—Bert Baston, Minnesota; James Herron, Pittsburgh; T—Clarence Horning, Colgate; D. Belford West, Colgate; G—Clinton Black, Yale; Harrie Dadmun, Harvard; Frank Hogg, Princeton; C—Robert Peck, Pittsburgh; B—Elmer Oliphant, Army; Oscar Anderson, Colgate; Fritz Pollard, Brown; Charles Harley, Ohio St.

1917
E—Charles Bolen, Ohio St.; Paul Robeson, Rutgers; Henry Miller, Pennsylvania; T—Alfred Cobb, Syracuse; George Hauser, Minnesota; G—Dale Seis, Pittsburgh; John Sutherland, Pittsburgh; Eugene Neely, Dartmouth; C—Frank Rydzewski, Notre Dame; B—Elmer Oliphant, Army; Ben Boynton, Williams; Everett Strupper, Georgia Tech; Charles Harley, Ohio St.

1918
E—Paul Robeson, Rutgers; Bill Fincher, Georgia Tech; T—Wilbur Henry, Wash. & Jeff.; Leonard Hilty, Pittsburgh; Lou Usher, Syracuse; Joe Guyon, Georgia Tech; G—Joe Alexander, Syracuse; Lyman Perry, Navy; C—Ashel Day, Georgia Tech; John Depler, Illinois; B—Frank Murrey, Princeton; Tom Davies, Pittsburgh; Wolcott Roberts, Navy; George McLaren, Pittsburgh.

1919

E—Bob Higgins, Penn St.; Henry Miller, Pennsylvania; Lester Belding, Iowa; T—Wilbur Henry, Wash. & Jeff.; D. Belford West, Colgate; G—Joe Alexander, Syracuse; Adolph Youngstrom, Dartmouth; C—James Weaver, Centre; Charles Carpenter, Wisconsin; B—Charles Harley, Ohio St.; Ira Rodgers, West Virginia; Edward Casey, Harvard; Bo McMillin, Centre; Ben Boynton, Williams.

1920

E—Luke Urban, Boston College; Charles Carney, Illinois; Bill Fincher, Georgia Tech; T—Stan Keck, Princeton; Ralph Scott, Wisconsin; G—Tim Callahan, Yale; Tom Woods, Harvard; Iolas Huffman, Ohio St.; C—Herb Stein, Pittsburgh; B—George Gipp, Notre Dame; Donold Lourie, Princeton; Gaylord Stinchcomb, Ohio St.; Charles Way, Penn St.

1921

E—Brick Muller, California; Eddie Anderson, Notre Dame; T—Dan McMillan, California; Iolas Huffman, Ohio St.; G—Frank Schwab, Lafayette; John Brown, Harvard; Stan Keck, Princeton; C—Herb Stein, Pittsburgh; B—Aubrey Devine, Iowa; Glenn Killinger, Penn St.; Bo McMillin, Centre; Malcolm Aldrich, Yale; Edgar Kaw, Cornell.

1922

E—Brick Muller, California; Wendell Taylor, Navy; T—C. Herbert Treat, Princeton; John Thurman, Pennsylvania; G—Frank Schwab, Lafayette; Charles Hubbard, Harvard; C—Ed Garbisch, Army; B—Harry Kipke, Michigan; Gordon Locke, Iowa; John Thomas, Chicago; Edgar Kaw, Cornell.

1923

E—Pete McRae, Syracuse; Ray Ecklund, Minnesota; Lynn Bomar, Vanderbilt; T—Century Milstead, Yale; Marty Below, Wisconsin; G—Charles Hubbard, Harvard; James McMillen, Illinois; C—Jack Blott, Michigan; B—George Pfann, Cornell; Red Grange, Illinois; William Mallory, Yale; Harry Wilson, Penn St.

Beginning in 1924, unanimous selections are indicated by (*).

1924

E—Jim Lawson, Stanford, 5-11, 190, Long Beach, Calif.; (tie) E—Dick Luman, Yale, 6-1, 176, Pinedale, Wyo.; Henry Wakefield, Vanderbilt, 5-10, 160, Petersburg, Tenn.; T—Ed McGinley, Pennsylvania, 5-11, 185, Swarthmore, Pa.; T—Ed Weir, Nebraska, 6-1, 194, Superior, Neb.; G—Joe Pondelik, Chicago, 5-11, 215, Cicero, Ill.; G—Carl Diehl, Dartmouth, 6-1, 205, Chicago, Ill.; C—Edwin Horrell, California, 5-11, 185, Pasadena, Calif.; B—*Red Grange, Illinois, 5-10, 170, Wheaton, Ill.; B—Harry Stuhldreher, Notre Dame, 5-7, 151, Massillon, Ohio; B—Jimmy Crowley, Notre Dame, 5-11, 162, Green Bay, Wis.; B—Elmer Layden, Notre Dame, 6-0, 162, Davenport, Iowa.

1925

E—Bennie Oosterbaan, Michigan, 6-0, 180, Muskegon, Mich.; E—George Tully, Dartmouth, 5-10, 175, Orange, N.J.; T—*Ed Weir, Nebraska, 6-1, 194, Superior, Neb.; T—Ralph Chase, Pittsburgh, 6-3, 202, Easton, Pa.; G—Carl Diehl, Dartmouth, 6-1, 205, Chicago, Ill.; G—Ed Hess, Ohio St., 6-1, 190, Cincinnati, Ohio; C—Ed McMillan, Princeton, 6-0, 208, Pittsburgh, Pa.; B—*Andy Oberlander, Dartmouth, 6-0, 197, Everett, Mass.; B—Red Grange, Illinois, 5-10, 170, Wheaton, Ill.; B—Ernie Nevers, Stanford, 6-0, 200, Superior, Wis.; (tie) B—Benny Friedman, Michigan, 5-8, 170, Cleveland, Ohio; George Wilson, Washington, 5-11, 190, Everett, Wash.

1926

E—Bennie Oosterbaan, Michigan, 6-0, 186, Muskegon, Mich.; E—Vic Hanson, Syracuse, 5-10, 174, Syracuse, N.Y.; T—*Frank Wickhorst, Navy, 6-0, 218, Oak Park, Ill.; T—Bud Sprague, Army, 6-2, 210, Dallas, Texas; G—Harry Connaughton, Georgetown, 6-2, 275, Philadelphia, Pa.; G—Bernie Shively, Illinois, 6-4, 208, Oliver, Ill.; C—Bud Boeringer, Notre Dame, 6-1, 186, St. Paul, Minn.; B—Benny Friedman, Michigan, 5-8, 172, Cleveland, Ohio; B—Mort Kaer, Southern California, 5-11, 167, Red Bluff, Calif.; B—Ralph Baker, Northwestern, 5-10, 172, Rockford, Ill.; B—Herb Joesting, Minnesota, 6-1, 192, Owatonna, Minn.

1927

E—*Bennie Oosterbaan, Michigan, 6-0, 186, Muskegon, Mich.; E—Tom Nash, Georgia, 6-3, 200, Washington, Ga.; T—Jesse Hibbs, Southern California, 5-11, 185, Glendale, Calif.; T—Ed Hake, Pennsylvania, 6-0, 190, Philadelphia, Pa.; G—Bill Webster, Yale, 6-0, 200, Shelton, Conn.; G—John Smith, Notre Dame, 5-9, 164, Hartford, Conn.; (tie) C—Larry Bettencourt, St. Mary's (Cal.), 5-10, 187, Centerville, Calif.; John Charlesworth, Yale, 5-11, 198, North Adams, Mass.; B—*Gibby Welch, Pittsburgh, 5-11, 170, Parkersburg, W. Va.; B—Morley Drury, Southern California, 6-0, 185, Long Beach, Calif.; B—Red Cagle, Army, 5-9, 167, Merryville, La.; B—Herb Joesting, Minnesota, 6-1, 192, Owatonna, Minn.

1928

E—Irv Phillips, California, 6-1, 188, Salinas, Calif.; E—Wes Fesler, Ohio St., 6-0, 173, Youngstown, Ohio; T—Otto Pommerening, Michigan, 6-0, 178, Ann Arbor, Mich.; T—Mike Getto, Pittsburgh, 6-2, 198, Jeannette, Pa.; G—Seraphim Post, Stanford, 6-0, 190, Berkeley, Calif.; (tie) G—Don Robesky, Stanford, 5-11, 198, Bakersfield, Calif.; Edward Burke, Navy, 6-0, 180, Larksville, Pa.; C—Pete Pund, Georgia Tech, 6-0, 195, Augusta, Ga.; B—*Red Cagle, Army, 5-9, 167, Merryville, La.; B—Paul Scull, Pennsylvania, 5-8, 187, Bala, Pa.; (tie) B—Ken Strong, New York U., 6-0, 201, West Haven, Conn.; Howard Harpster, Carnegie Mellon, 6-1, 160, Akron, Ohio; B—Charles Carroll, Washington, 6-0, 190, Seattle, Wash.

1929

E—*Joe Donchess, Pittsburgh, 6-0, 175, Youngstown, Ohio; E—Wes Fesler, Ohio St., 6-0, 183, Youngstown, Ohio; T—Bronko Nagurski, Minnesota, 6-2, 217, International Falls, Minn.; T—Elmer Sleight, Purdue, 6-2, 193, Morris, Ill.; G—Jack Cannon, Notre Dame, 5-11, 193, Columbus, Ohio; G—Ray Montgomery, Pittsburgh, 6-1, 188, Wheeling, W.Va.; C—Ben Ticknor, Harvard, 6-2, 193, New York, N.Y.; B—*Frank Carideo, Notre Dame, 5-7, 175, Mount Vernon, N.Y.; B—Ralph Welch, Purdue, 6-1, 189, Whitesboro, Texas; B—Red Cagle, Army, 5-9, 167, Merryville, La.; B—Gene McEver, Tennessee, 5-10, 185, Bristol, Va.

1930

E—*Wes Fesler, Ohio St., 6-0, 185, Youngstown, Ohio; E—Frank Baker, Northwestern, 6-2, 175, Cedar Rapids, Iowa; T—*Fred Sington, Alabama, 6-2, 215, Birmingham, Ala.; T—Milo Lubratovich, Wisconsin, 6-2, 216, Duluth, Minn.; G—Ted Beckett, California, 6-1, 190, Oroville, Calif.; G—Barton Koch, Baylor, 5-10, 195, Temple, Texas; C—*Ben Ticknor, Harvard, 6-2, 193, New York, N.Y.; B—*Frank Carideo, Notre Dame, 5-7, 175, Mount Vernon, N.Y.; B—Marchy Schwartz, Notre Dame, 5-11, 172, Bay St. Louis, Miss.; B—Erny Pinckert, Southern California, 6-0, 189, San Bernardino, Calif.; B—Leonard Macaluso, Colgate, 6-2, 210, East Aurora, N.Y.

1931

E—*Jerry Dalrymple, Tulane, 5-10, 175, Arkadelphia, Ark.; E—Vernon Smith, Georgia, 6-2, 190, Macon, Ga.; T—Jesse Quatse, Pittsburgh, 5-8, 198, Greensburg, Pa.; (tie) T—Jack Riley, Northwestern, 6-2, 218, Wilmette, Ill.; Dallas Marvil, Northwestern, 6-3, 227, Laurel, Del.; G—Biggie Munn, Minnesota, 5-10, 217, Minneapolis, Minn.; G—John Baker, Southern California, 5-10, 185, Kingsburg, Calif.; C—Tommy Yarr, Notre Dame, 5-11, 197, Chimacum, Wash.; B—Gus Shaver, Southern California, 5-11, 185, Covina, Calif.; B—Marchy Schwartz, Notre Dame, 5-11, 178, Bay St. Louis, Miss.; B—Pug Rentner, Northwestern, 6-1, 185, Joliet, Ill.; B—Barry Wood, Harvard, 6-1, 173, Milton, Mass.

1932

E—*Paul Moss, Purdue, 6-2, 185, Terre Haute, Ind.; E—Joe Skladany, Pittsburgh, 5-10, 185, Larksville, Pa.; T—*Joe Kurth, Notre Dame, 6-2, 204, Madison, Wis.; T—*Ernie Smith, Southern California, 6-2, 215, Los Angeles, Calif.; G—Milt Summerfelt, Army, 6-0, 181, Benton Harbor, Mich.; G—Bill Corbus, Stanford, 5-11, 188, Vallejo, Calif.; C—Pete Gracey, Vanderbilt, 6-0, 188, Franklin, Tenn.; B—*Harry Newman, Michigan, 5-7, 175, Detroit, Mich.; B—*Warren Heller, Pittsburgh, 6-0, 170, Steelton, Pa.; B—Don Zimmerman, Tulane, 5-10, 190, Lake Charles, La.; B—Jimmy Hitchcock, Auburn, 5-11, 172, Union Springs, Ala.

1933

E—Joe Skladany, Pittsburgh, 5-10, 190, Larksville, Pa.; E—Paul Geisler, Centenary (La.), 6-2, 189, Berwick, La.; T—Fred Crawford, Duke, 6-2, 195, Waynesville, N.C.; T—Francis Wistert, Michigan, 6-3, 212, Chicago, Ill.; G—Bill Corbus, Stanford, 5-11, 195, Vallejo, Calif.; G—Aaron Rosenberg, Southern California, 6-0, 210, Los Angeles, Calif.; C—*Chuck Bernard, Michigan, 6-2, 215, Benton Harbor, Mich.; B—*Cotton Warburton, Southern California, 5-7, 147, San Diego, Calif.; B—George Sauer, Nebraska, 6-2, 195, Lincoln, Neb.; B—Beattie Feathers, Tennessee, 5-10, 180, Bristol, Va.; B—Duane Purvis, Purdue, 6-1, 190, Mattoon, Ill.

1934

E—Don Hutson, Alabama, 6-1, 185, Pine Bluff, Ark.; E—Frank Larson, Minnesota, 6-3, 190, Duluth, Minn.; T—Bill Lee, Alabama, 6-2, 225, Eutaw, Ala.; T—Bob Reynolds, Stanford, 6-4, 220, Okmulgee, Okla.; G—Chuck Hartwig, Pittsburgh, 6-0, 190, Benwood, W.Va.; G—Bill Bevan, Minnesota, 5-11, 194, St. Paul, Minn.; (tie) C—Jack Robinson, Notre Dame, 6-3, 195, Huntington, N.Y.; Darrell Lester, TCU, 6-4, 218, Jacksboro, Texas; George Shotwell, Pittsburgh; B—Bobby Grayson, Stanford, 5-11, 186, Portland, Ore.; B—Pug Lund, Minnesota, 5-11, 185, Rice Lake, Wis.; B—Dixie Howell, Alabama, 5-10, 164, Hartford, Ala.; B—Fred Borries, Navy, 6-0, 175, Louisville, Ky.

1935

E—Wayne Millner, Notre Dame, 6-0, 184, Salem, Mass.; (tie) E—James Moscrip, Stanford, 6-0, 186, Adena, Ohio; Gaynell Tinsley, LSU, 6-0, 188, Homer, La.; T—Ed Widseth, Minnesota, 6-2, 220, McIntosh, Minn.; T—Larry Lutz, California, 6-0, 201, Santa Ana, Calif.; G—John Weller, Princeton, 6-0, 195, Wynnewood, Pa.; (tie) G—Sidney Wagner, Michigan St., 5-11, 186, Lansing, Mich.; J. C. Wetsel, Southern Methodist, 5-10, 185, Dallas, Texas; (tie) C—Gomer Jones, Ohio St., 5-8, 210, Cleveland, Ohio; Darrell Lester, TCU, 6-4, 218, Jacksboro, Texas; B—*Jay Berwanger, Chicago, 6-0, 195, Dubuque, Iowa; B—*Bobby Grayson, Stanford, 5-11, 190, Portland, Ore.; B—Bobby Wilson, Southern Methodist, 5-10, 147, Corsicana, Texas; B—Riley Smith, Alabama, 6-1, 195, Columbus, Miss.

1936

E—*Larry Kelley, Yale, 6-1, 190, Williamsport, Pa.; E—*Gaynell Tinsley, LSU, 6-0, 196, Homer, La.; T—*Ed Widseth, Minnesota, 6-2, 220, McIntosh, Minn.; T—Averell Daniell, Pittsburgh, 6-3, 200, Mt. Lebanon, Pa.; G—Steve Reid, Northwestern, 5-9, 192, Chicago, Ill.; G—Max Starcevich, Washington, 5-10, 198, Duluth, Minn.; (tie) C—Alex Wojciechowicz, Fordham, 6-0, 192, South River, N.J.; Mike Basrak, Duquesne, 6-1, 210, Bellaire, Ohio; B—Sammy Baugh, TCU, 6-2, 180, Sweetwater, Texas; B—Ace Parker, Duke, 5-11, 175, Portsmouth, Va.; B—Ray Buivid, Marquette, 6-1, 193, Port Washington, Wis.; B—Sam Francis, Nebraska, 6-1, 207, Oberlin, Kan.

1937

E—Chuck Sweeney, Notre Dame, 6-0, 190, Bloomington, Ill.; E—Andy Bershak, North Carolina, 6-0, 190, Clairton, Pa.; T—Ed Franco, Fordham, 5-8, 196, Jersey City, N.J.; T—Tony Matisi, Pittsburgh, 6-0, 224, Endicott, N.Y.; G—Joe Routt, Texas A&M, 6-0, 193, Chappel Hill, Texas; G—Leroy Monsky, Alabama, 6-0, 198, Montgomery, Ala.; C—Alex Wojciechowicz, Fordham, 6-0, 196, South River, N.J.; B—*Clint Frank, Yale, 5-10, 190, Evanston, Ill.; B—Marshall Goldberg, Pittsburgh, 5-11, 185, Elkins, W.Va.; B—Byron "Whizzer" White, Colorado, 6-1, 185, Wellington, Colo.; B—Sam Chapman, California, 6-0, 190, Tiburon, Calif.

1938

E—Waddy Young, Oklahoma, 6-2, 203, Ponca City, Okla.; (tie) E—Brud Holland, Cornell, 6-1, 205, Auburn, N.Y.; Bowden Wyatt, Tennessee, 6-1, 190, Kingston, Tenn.; T—*Ed Beinor, Notre Dame, 6-2, 207, Harvey, Ill.; T—Alvord Wolff, Santa Clara, 6-2, 220, San Francisco, Calif.; G—*Ralph Heikkinen, Michigan, 5-10, 185, Ramsey, Mich.; G—Ed Bock, Iowa St., 6-0, 202, Fort Dodge, Iowa; C—Ki Aldrich, TCU, 5-11, 195, Temple, Texas; B—*Davey O'Brien, TCU, 5-7, 150, Dallas, Texas; B—*Marshall Goldberg, Pittsburgh, 6-0, 190, Elkins, W.Va.; B—Bob MacLeod, Dartmouth, 6-0, 190, Glen Ellyn, Ill.; B—Vic Bottari, California, 5-9, 182, Vallejo, Calif.

1939

E—Esco Sarkkinen, Ohio St., 6-0, 192, Fairport Harbor, Ohio; E—Ken Kavanaugh, LSU, 6-3, 203, Little Rock, Ark.; T—Nick Drahos, Cornell, 6-3, 200, Cedarhurst, N.Y.; T—Harley McCollum, Tulane, 6-4, 235, Wagoner, Okla.; G—*Harry Smith, Southern California, 5-11, 218, Ontario, Calif.; G—Ed Molinski, Tennessee, 5-10, 190, Massillon, Ohio; C—John Schiechl, Santa Clara, 6-2, 220, San Francisco, Calif.; B—Nile Kinnick, Iowa, 5-8, 167, Omaha, Neb.; B—Tom Harmon, Michigan, 6-0,

195, Gary, Ind.; B—John Kimbrough, Texas A&M, 6-2, 210, Haskell, Texas; B—George Cafego, Tennessee, 6-0, 174, Scarbro, W.Va.

1940
E—Gene Goodreault, Boston College, 5-10, 184, Haverhill, Mass.; E—Dave Rankin, Purdue, 6-1, 190, Warsaw, Ind.; T—Nick Drahos, Cornell, 6-3, 212, Cedarhurst, N.Y.; (tie) T—Alf Bauman, Northwestern, 6-1, 210, Chicago, Ill.; Urban Odson, Minnesota, 6-3, 247, Clark, S.D.; G—*Bob Suffridge, Tennessee, 6-0, 190, Knoxville, Tenn.; G—Marshall Robnett, Texas A&M, 6-1, 205, Klondike, Texas; C—Rudy Mucha, Washington, 6-2, 210, Chicago, Ill.; B—*Tom Harmon, Michigan, 6-0, 195, Gary, Ind.; B—*John Kimbrough, Texas A&M, 6-2, 221, Haskell, Texas; B—Frank Albert, Stanford, 5-9, 170, Glendale, Calif.; B—George Franck, Minnesota, 6-0, 175, Davenport, Iowa.

1941
E—Holt Rast, Alabama, 6-1, 185, Birmingham, Ala.; E—Bob Dove, Notre Dame, 6-2, 195, Youngstown, Ohio; T—Dick Wildung, Minnesota, 6-0, 210, Luverne, Minn.; T—Ernie Blandin, Tulane, 6-3, 245, Keighley, Kan.; G—*Endicott Peabody, Harvard, 6-0, 181, Syracuse, N.Y.; G—Ray Frankowski, Washington, 5-10, 210, Hammond, Ind.; C—Darold Jenkins, Missouri, 6-0, 195, Higginsville, Mo.; B—Bob Westfall, Michigan, 5-8, 190, Ann Arbor, Mich.; B—Bruce Smith, Minnesota, 6-0, 193, Faribault, Minn.; B—Frank Albert, Stanford, 5-9, 173, Glendale, Calif.; (tie) B—Bill Dudley, Virginia, 5-10, 175, Bluefield, Va.; Frank Sinkwich, Georgia, 5-8, 180, Youngstown, Ohio.

1942
E—*Dave Schreiner, Wisconsin, 6-2, 198, Lancaster, Wis.; E—Bob Dove, Notre Dame, 6-2, 195, Youngstown, Ohio; T—Dick Wildung, Minnesota, 6-0, 215, Luverne, Minn.; T—Albert Wistert, Michigan, 6-2, 205, Chicago, Ill.; G—Chuck Taylor, Stanford, 5-11, 200, San Jose, Calif.; (tie) G—Harvey Hardy, Georgia Tech, 5-10, 185, Thomaston, Ga.; Julie Franks, Michigan, 6-0, 187, Hamtramck, Mich.; C—Joe Domnanovich, Alabama, 6-1, 200, South Bend, Ind.; B—*Frank Sinkwich, Georgia, 5-8, 185, Youngstown, Ohio; B—Paul Governali, Columbia, 5-11, 186, New York, N.Y.; B—Mike Holovak, Boston College, 6-2, 214, Lansford, Pa.; B—Billy Hillenbrand, Indiana, 6-0, 195, Evansville, Ind.

1943
E—Ralph Heywood, Southern California, 6-2, 195, Huntington Park, Calif.; E—John Yonakor, Notre Dame, 6-4, 220, Dorchester, Mass.; T—Jim White, Notre Dame, 6-2, 210, Edgewater, N.J.; T—Don Whitmire, Navy, 5-11, 215, Decatur, Ala.; G—Alex Agase, Purdue, 5-10, 190, Evanston, Ill.; G—Pat Filley, Notre Dame, 5-8, 175, South Bend, Ind.; C—*Casimir Myslinski, Army, 5-11, 186, Steubenville, Ohio; B—*Bill Daley, Michigan, 6-2, 206, St. Cloud, Minn.; B—Angelo Bertelli, Notre Dame, 6-1, 173, West Springfield, Mass.; B—Creighton Miller, Notre Dame, 6-0, 185, Wilmington, Del.; B—Bob Odell, Pennsylvania, 5-11, 182, Sioux City, Iowa.

1944
E—Phil Tinsley, Georgia Tech, 6-1, 188, Bessemer, Ala.; (tie) E—Paul Walker, Yale, 6-3, 203, Oak Park, Ill.; Jack Dugger, Ohio St., 6-3, 210, Canton, Ohio; T—*Don Whitmire, Navy, 5-11, 215, Decatur, Ala.; T—John Ferraro, Southern California, 6-3, 235, Maywood, Calif.; G—Bill Hackett, Ohio St., 5-9, 191, London, Ohio; G—Ben Chase, Navy, 6-1, 195, San Diego, Calif.; C—John Tavener, Indiana, 6-0, 220, Granville, Ohio; B—*Les Horvath, Ohio St., 5-10, 167, Parma, Ohio; B—Glenn Davis, Army, 5-9, 170, Claremont, Calif.; B—Doc Blanchard, Army, 6-0, 205, Bishopville, S.C.; B—Bob Jenkins, Navy, 6-1, 195, Talladega, Ala.

1945
E—Dick Duden, Navy, 6-2, 203, New York, N.Y.; (tie) E—Hubert Bechtol, Texas, 6-2, 190, Lubbock, Texas; Bob Ravensberg, Indiana, 6-1, 180, Bellevue, Ky.; Max Morris, Northwestern, 6-2, 195, West Frankfort, Ill.; T—Tex Coulter, Army, 6-3, 220, Fort Worth, Texas; T—George Savitsky, Pennsylvania, 6-3, 250, Camden, N.J.; G—*Warren Amling, Ohio St., 6-0, 197, Pana, Ill.; G—John Green, Army, 5-11, 190, Shelbyville, Ky.; C—Vaughn Mancha, Alabama, 6-0, 235, Birmingham, Ala.; B—*Glenn Davis, Army, 5-9, 170, Claremont, Calif.; B—*Doc Blanchard, Army, 6-0, 205, Bishopville, S.C.; B—*Herman Wedemeyer, St. Mary's (Cal.), 5-10, 173, Honolulu, Hawaii; B—Bob Fenimore, Oklahoma St., 6-2, 188, Woodward, Okla.

1946
E—*Burr Baldwin, UCLA, 6-1, 196, Bakersfield, Calif.; (tie) E—Hubert Bechtol, Texas, 6-2, 201, Lubbock, Texas; Hank Foldberg, Army, 6-1, 200, Dallas, Texas; T—George Connor, Notre Dame, 6-3, 225, Chicago, Ill.; (tie) T—Warren Amling, Ohio St., 6-0, 197, Pana, Ill.; Dick Huffman, Tennessee, 6-2, 230, Charleston, W.Va.; G—Alex Agase, Illinois, 5-10, 191, Evanston, Ill.; G—Weldon Humble, Rice, 6-1, 214, San Antonio, Texas; C—Paul Duke, Georgia Tech, 6-1, 210, Atlanta, Ga.; B—*John Lujack, Notre Dame, 6-0, 180, Connellsville, Pa.; B—*Charley Trippi, Georgia, 5-11, 185, Pittston, Pa.; B—*Glenn Davis, Army, 5-9, 170, Claremont, Calif.; B—*Doc Blanchard, Army, 6-0, 205, Bishopville, S.C.

1947
E—Paul Cleary, Southern California, 6-1, 195, Santa Ana, Calif.; E—Bill Swiacki, Columbia, 6-2, 198, Southbridge, Mass.; T—Bob Davis, Georgia Tech, 6-4, 220, Columbus, Ga.; T—George Connor, Notre Dame, 6-3, 225, Chicago, Ill.; G—Joe Steffy, Army, 5-11, 190, Chattanooga, Tenn.; G—Bill Fischer, Notre Dame, 6-2, 230, Chicago, Ill.; C—Chuck Bednarik, Pennsylvania, 6-3, 220, Bethlehem, Pa.; B—*John Lujack, Notre Dame, 6-0, 180, Connellsville, Pa.; B—*Bob Chappuis, Michigan, 6-0, 180, Toledo, Ohio; B—Doak Walker, Southern Methodist, 5-11, 170, Dallas, Texas; (tie) B—Charley Conerly, Mississippi, 6-0, 184, Clarksdale, Miss.; Bobby Layne, Texas, 6-0, 191, Dallas, Texas.

1948
E—Dick Rifenburg, Michigan, 6-3, 197, Saginaw, Mich.; E—Leon Hart, Notre Dame, 6-4, 225, Turtle Creek, Pa.; T—Leo Nomellini, Minnesota, 6-2, 248, Chicago, Ill.; T—Alvin Wistert, Michigan, 6-3, 218, Chicago, Ill.; G—Buddy Burris, Oklahoma, 5-11, 214, Muskogee, Okla.; G—Bill Fischer, Notre Dame, 6-2, 233, Chicago, Ill.; C—Chuck Bednarik, Pennsylvania, 6-3, 220, Bethlehem, Pa.; B—*Doak Walker, Southern Methodist, 5-11, 168, Dallas, Texas; B—Charlie Justice, North Carolina, 5-10, 165, Asheville, N.C.; B—Jackie Jensen, California, 5-11, 195, Oakland, Calif.; (tie) B—Emil Sitko, Notre Dame, 5-8, 180, Fort Wayne, Ind.; Clyde Scott, Arkansas, 6-0, 175, Smackover, Ark.

1949
E—*Leon Hart, Notre Dame, 6-5, 260, Turtle Creek, Pa.; E—James Williams, Rice, 6-0, 197, Waco, Texas; T—Leo Nomellini, Minnesota, 6-2, 255, Chicago, Ill.; T—Alvin Wistert, Michigan, 6-3, 223, Chicago, Ill.; G—*Rod Franz, California, 6-1, 198, San Francisco, Calif.; G—Ed Bagdon, Michigan St., 5-10, 200, Dearborn, Mich.; C—*Clayton Tonnemaker, Minnesota, 6-3, 240, Minneapolis, Minn.; B—*Emil Sitko, Notre Dame, 5-8, 180, Fort Wayne, Ind.; B—Doak Walker, Southern Methodist, 5-11, 170, Dallas, Texas; B—Arnold Galiffa, Army, 6-2, 190, Donora, Pa.; B—Bob Williams, Notre Dame, 6-1, 180, Baltimore, Md.

1950
E—*Dan Foldberg, Army, 6-1, 185, Dallas, Texas; E—Bill McColl, Stanford, 6-4, 225, San Diego, Calif.; T—Bob Gain, Kentucky, 6-3, 230, Weirton, W.Va.; T—Jim Weatherall, Oklahoma, 6-4, 220, White Deer, Texas; G—Bud McFadin, Texas, 6-3, 225, Iraan, Texas; G—Les Richter, California, 6-2, 220, Fresno, Calif.; C—Jerry Groom, Notre Dame, 6-3, 215, Des Moines, Iowa; B—*Vic Janowicz, Ohio St., 5-9, 189, Elyria, Ohio; B—Kyle Rote, Southern Methodist, 6-0, 190, San Antonio, Texas; B—Babe Parilli, Kentucky, 6-1, 183, Rochester, Pa.; B—Leon Heath, Oklahoma, 6-1, 195, Hollis, Okla.

1951
E—*Bill McColl, Stanford, 6-4, 225, San Diego, Calif.; E—Bob Carey, Michigan St., 6-5, 215, Charlevoix, Mich.; T—*Don Coleman, Michigan St., 5-10, 185, Flint, Mich.; T—*Jim Weatherall, Oklahoma, 6-4, 230, White Deer, Texas; G—*Bob Ward, Maryland, 5-10, 185, Elizabeth, N.J.; G—Les Richter, California, 6-2, 230, Fresno, Calif.; C—Dick Hightower, Southern Methodist, 6-1, 215, Tyler, Texas; B—*Dick Kazmaier, Princeton, 5-11, 171, Maumee, Ohio; B—*Hank Lauricella, Tennessee, 5-10, 169, New Orleans, La.; B—Babe Parilli, Kentucky, 6-1, 188, Rochester, Pa.; B—Johnny Karras, Illinois, 5-11, 171, Argo, Ill.

1952
E—Frank McPhee, Princeton, 6-3, 203, Youngstown, Ohio; E—Bernie Flowers, Purdue, 6-1, 189, Erie, Pa.; T—Dick Modzelewski, Maryland, 6-0, 235, West Natrona, Pa.; T—Hal Miller, Georgia Tech, 6-4, 235, Kingsport, Tenn.; G—John Michels, Tennessee, 5-10, 195, Philadelphia, Pa.; G—Elmer Wilhoite, Southern California, 6-2, 216, Winton, Calif.; C—Donn Moomaw, UCLA, 6-4, 220, Santa Ana, Calif.; B—*Jack Scarbath, Maryland, 6-1, 190, Baltimore, Md.; B—*Johnny Lattner, Notre Dame, 6-1, 190, Chicago, Ill.; B—Billy Vessels, Oklahoma, 6-0, 185, Cleveland, Okla.; B—Jim Sears, Southern California, 5-9, 167, Inglewood, Calif.

1953
E—Don Dohoney, Michigan St., 6-1, 193, Ann Arbor, Mich.; E—Carlton Massey, Texas, 6-4, 210, Rockwall, Texas; T—*Stan Jones, Maryland, 6-0, 235, Lemoyne, Pa.; T—Art Hunter, Notre Dame, 6-2, 226, Akron, Ohio; G—J. D. Roberts, Oklahoma, 5-10, 210, Dallas, Texas; G—Crawford Mims, Mississippi, 5-10, 200, Greenwood, Miss.; C—Larry Morris, Georgia Tech, 6-0, 205, Decatur, Ga.; B—*Johnny Lattner, Notre Dame, 6-1, 190, Chicago, Ill.; B—*Paul Giel, Minnesota, 5-11, 185, Winona, Minn.; B—Paul Cameron, UCLA, 6-0, 185, Burbank, Calif.; B—J. C. Caroline, Illinois, 6-0, 184, Columbia, S.C.

1954
E—Max Boydston, Oklahoma, 6-2, 207, Muskogee, Okla.; E—Ron Beagle, Navy, 6-0, 185, Covington, Ky.; T—Jack Ellena, UCLA, 6-3, 214, Susanville, Calif.; T—Sid Fournet, LSU, 5-11, 225, Baton Rouge, La.; G—*Bud Brooks, Arkansas, 5-11, 200, Wynne, Ark.; G—Calvin Jones, Iowa, 6-0, 200, Steubenville, Ohio; C—Kurt Burris, Oklahoma, 6-1, 209, Muskogee, Okla.; B—*Ralph Guglielmi, Notre Dame, 6-0, 185, Columbus, Ohio; B—*Howard Cassady, Ohio St., 5-10, 177, Columbus, Ohio; B—*Alan Ameche, Wisconsin, 6-0, 215, Kenosha, Wis.; B—Dicky Maegle, Rice, 6-0, 175, Taylor, Texas.

1955
E—*Ron Beagle, Navy, 6-0, 186, Covington, Ky.; E—Ron Kramer, Michigan, 6-3, 218, East Detroit, Mich.; T—Norman Masters, Michigan St., 6-2, 225, Detroit, Mich.; T—Bruce Bosley, West Virginia, 6-2, 225, Green Bank, W.Va.; G—Bo Bolinger, Oklahoma, 5-10, 206, Muskogee, Okla.; (tie) G—Calvin Jones, Iowa, 6-0, 220, Steubenville, Ohio; Hardiman Cureton, UCLA, 6-0, 213, Duarte, Calif.; C—*Bob Pellegrini, Maryland, 6-2, 225, Yatesboro, Pa.; B—*Howard Cassady, Ohio St., 5-10, 172, Columbus, Ohio; B—*Jim Swink, TCU, 6-1, 180, Rusk, Texas; B—Earl Morrall, Michigan St., 6-1, 180, Muskegon, Mich.; B—Paul Hornung, Notre Dame, 6-2, 205, Louisville, Ky.

1956
E—*Joe Walton, Pittsburgh, 5-11, 205, Beaver Falls, Pa.; E—*Ron Kramer, Michigan, 6-3, 220, East Detroit, Mich.; T—John Witte, Oregon St., 6-2, 232, Klamath Falls, Ore.; T—Lou Michaels, Kentucky, 6-2, 229, Swoyersville, Pa.; G—*Jim Parker, Ohio St., 6-2, 251, Toledo, Ohio; G—*Bill Glass, Baylor, 6-4, 220, Corpus Christi, Texas; C—*Jerry Tubbs, Oklahoma, 6-2, 205, Breckenridge, Texas; B—*Jim Brown, Syracuse, 6-2, 212, Manhasset, N.Y.; B—*John Majors, Tennessee, 5-10, 162, Huntland, Tenn.; B—Tommy McDonald, Oklahoma, 5-9, 169, Albuquerque, N.M.; B—John Brodie, Stanford, 6-1, 190, Oakland, Calif.

1957
E—*Jimmy Phillips, Auburn, 6-2, 205, Alexander City, Ala.; E—Dick Wallen, UCLA, 6-0, 185, Alhambra, Calif.; T—Lou Michaels, Kentucky, 6-2, 235, Swoyersville, Pa.; T—Alex Karras, Iowa, 6-2, 233, Gary, Ind.; G—Bill Krisher, Oklahoma, 6-1, 213, Midwest City, Okla.; G—Al Ecuyer, Notre Dame, 5-10, 190, New Orleans, La.; C—Dan Currie, Michigan St., 6-3, 225, Detroit, Mich.; B—*John David Crow, Texas A&M, 6-2, 214, Springhill, La.; B—Walt Kowalczyk, Michigan St., 6-0, 205, Westfield, Mass.; B—Bob Anderson, Army, 6-2, 200, Cocoa, Fla.; B—Clendon Thomas, Oklahoma, 6-2, 188, Oklahoma City, Okla.

1958
E—Buddy Dial, Rice, 6-1, 185, Magnolia, Texas; E—Sam Williams, Michigan St., 6-5, 225, Dansville, Mich.; T—Ted Bates, Oregon St., 6-2, 215, Los Angeles, Calif.; T—Brock Strom, Air Force, 6-0, 217, Ironwood, Mich.; G—John Guzik, Pittsburgh, 6-3, 223, Lawrence, Pa.; (tie) G—Zeke Smith, Auburn, 6-2, 210, Uniontown, Ala.; George Deiderich, Vanderbilt, 6-1, 198, Toronto, Ohio; C—Bob Harrison, Oklahoma, 6-2, 206, Stamford, Texas; B—*Randy Duncan, Iowa, 6-0, 180, Des Moines, Iowa; B—*Pete Dawkins, Army, 6-1, 197, Royal Oak, Mich.; B—*Billy Cannon, LSU, 6-1, 200, Baton Rouge, La.; B—Bob White, Ohio St., 6-2, 212, Covington, Ky.

1959

E—Bill Carpenter, Army, 6-2, 210, Springfield, Pa.; E—Monty Stickles, Notre Dame, 6-4, 225, Poughkeepsie, N.Y.; T—*Dan Lanphear, Wisconsin, 6-2, 214, Madison, Wis.; T—Don Floyd, TCU, 6-3, 215, Midlothian, Texas; G—*Roger Davis, Syracuse, 6-2, 228, Solon, Ohio; G—Bill Burrell, Illinois, 6-0, 210, Chebanse, Ill.; C—Maxie Baughan, Georgia Tech, 6-1, 212, Bessemer, Ala.; B—Richie Lucas, Penn St., 6-1, 185, Glassport, Pa.; B—Billy Cannon, LSU, 6-1, 208, Baton Rouge, La.; B—Charlie Flowers, Mississippi, 6-0, 198, Marianna, Ark.; B—Ron Burton, Northwestern, 5-9, 185, Springfield, Ohio.

1960

E—*Mike Ditka, Pittsburgh, 6-3, 215, Aliquippa, Pa.; E—*Danny LaRose, Missouri, 6-4, 220, Crystal City, Mo.; T—*Bob Lilly, TCU, 6-5, 250, Throckmorton, Texas; T—Ken Rice, Auburn, 6-3, 250, Bainbridge, Ga.; G—*Tom Brown, Minnesota, 6-0, 225, Minneapolis, Minn.; G—Joe Romig, Colorado, 5-10, 197, Lakewood, Colo.; C—E. J. Holub, Texas Tech, 6-4, 215, Lubbock, Texas; B—*Jake Gibbs, Mississippi, 6-0, 185, Grenada, Miss.; B—*Joe Bellino, Navy, 5-9, 181, Winchester, Mass.; B—*Bob Ferguson, Ohio St., 6-0, 217, Troy, Ohio; B—Ernie Davis, Syracuse, 6-2, 205, Elmira, N.Y.

1961

E—Gary Collins, Maryland, 6-3, 205, Williamstown, Pa.; E—Bill Miller, Miami (Fla.), 6-0, 188, McKeesport, Pa.; T—*Billy Neighbors, Alabama, 5-11, 229, Tuscaloosa, Ala.; T—Merlin Olsen, Utah St., 6-5, 265, Logan, Utah; G—*Roy Winston, LSU, 6-1, 225, Baton Rouge, La.; G—Joe Romig, Colorado, 5-10, 199, Lakewood, Colo.; C—Alex Kroll, Rutgers, 6-2, 228, Leechburg, Pa.; B—*Ernie Davis, Syracuse, 6-2, 210, Elmira, N.Y.; B—*Bob Ferguson, Ohio St., 6-0, 217, Troy, Ohio; B—*Jimmy Saxton, Texas, 5-11, 160, Palestine, Texas; B—Sandy Stephens, Minnesota, 6-0, 215, Uniontown, Pa.

1962

E—Hal Bedsole, Southern California, 6-5, 225, Northridge, Calif.; E—Pat Richter, Wisconsin, 6-5, 229, Madison, Wis.; T—*Bobby Bell, Minnesota, 6-4, 214, Shelby, N.C.; T—Jim Dunaway, Mississippi, 6-4, 260, Columbia, Miss.; G—*Johnny Treadwell, Texas, 6-1, 194, Austin, Texas; G—Jack Cvercko, Northwestern, 6-0, 230, Campbell, Ohio; C—*Lee Roy Jordan, Alabama, 6-2, 207, Monroeville, Ala.; B—*Terry Baker, Oregon St., 6-3, 191, Portland, Ore.; B—*Jerry Stovall, LSU, 6-2, 195, West Monroe, La.; B—Mel Renfro, Oregon, 5-11, 190, Portland, Ore.; B—George Saimes, Michigan St., 5-10, 186, Canton, Ohio.

1963

E—Vern Burke, Oregon St., 6-4, 195, Bakersfield, Calif.; E—Lawrence Elkins, Baylor, 6-1, 187, Brownwood, Texas; T—*Scott Appleton, Texas, 6-3, 235, Brady, Texas; T—Carl Eller, Minnesota, 6-6, 241, Winston-Salem, N.C.; G—*Bob Brown, Nebraska, 6-5, 259, Cleveland, Ohio; G—Rick Redman, Washington, 5-11, 210, Seattle, Wash.; C—*Dick Butkus, Illinois, 6-3, 234, Chicago, Ill.; B—*Roger Staubach, Navy, 6-2, 190, Cincinnati, Ohio; B—Sherman Lewis, Michigan St., 5-8, 154, Louisville, Ky.; B—Jim Grisham, Oklahoma, 6-2, 205, Olney, Texas; (tie) B—Gale Sayers, Kansas, 6-0, 196, Omaha, Neb.; Paul Martha, Pittsburgh, 6-1, 180, Wilkinsburg, Pa.

1964

E—Jack Snow, Notre Dame, 6-2, 210, Long Beach, Calif.; E—Fred Biletnikoff, Florida St., 6-1, 186, Erie, Pa.; T—*Larry Kramer, Nebraska, 6-2, 240, Austin, Minn.; T—Ralph Neely, Oklahoma, 6-5, 243, Farmington, N.M.; G—Rick Redman, Washington, 5-11, 215, Seattle, Wash.; G—Glenn Ressler, Penn St., 6-2, 230, Dornsife, Pa.; C—Dick Butkus, Illinois, 6-3, 237, Chicago, Ill.; B—John Huarte, Notre Dame, 6-0, 180, Anaheim, Calif.; B—Gale Sayers, Kansas, 6-0, 194, Omaha, Neb.; B—Lawrence Elkins, Baylor, 6-1, 187, Brownwood, Texas; B—Tucker Frederickson, Auburn, 6-2, 210, Hollywood, Fla.

Beginning in 1965, offense and defense selected.

1965

Offense E—*Howard Twilley, Tulsa, 5-10, 180, Galena Park, Texas; E—Freeman White, Nebraska, 6-5, 220, Detroit, Mich.; T—Sam Ball, Kentucky, 6-4, 241, Henderson, Ky.; T—Glen Ray Hines, Arkansas, 6-5, 235, El Dorado, Ark.; G—*Dick Arrington, Notre Dame, 5-11, 232, Erie, Pa.; G—Stas Maliszewski, Princeton, 6-1, 215, Davenport, Iowa; C—Paul Crane, Alabama, 6-2, 188, Prichard, Ala.; B—*Mike Garrett, Southern California, 5-9, 185, Los Angeles, Calif.; B—*Jim Grabowski, Illinois, 6-2, 211, Chicago, Ill.; B—Bob Griese, Purdue, 6-1, 185, Evansville, Ind.; B—Donny Anderson, Texas Tech, 6-3, 210, Stinnett, Texas.

Defense E—Aaron Brown, Minnesota, 6-4, 230, Port Arthur, Texas; E—Bubba Smith, Michigan St., 6-7, 268, Beaumont, Texas; T—Walt Barnes, Nebraska, 6-3, 235, Chicago, Ill.; T—Loyd Phillips, Arkansas, 6-3, 221, Longview, Texas; T—Bill Yearby, Michigan, 6-3, 222, Detroit, Mich.; LB—Carl McAdams, Oklahoma, 6-3, 215, White Deer, Texas; LB—Tommy Nobis, Texas, 6-2, 230, San Antonio, Texas; LB—Frank Emanuel, Tennessee, 6-3, 228, Newport News, Va.; B—George Webster, Michigan St., 6-4, 204, Anderson, S.C.; B—Johnny Roland, Missouri, 6-2, 198, Corpus Christi, Texas; B—Nick Rassas, Notre Dame, 6-0, 185, Winnetka, Ill.

1966

Offense E—*Jack Clancy, Michigan, 6-1, 192, Detroit, Mich.; E—Ray Perkins, Alabama, 6-0, 184, Petal, Miss.; T—*Cecil Dowdy, Alabama, 6-0, 206, Cherokee, Ala.; T—Ron Yary, Southern California, 6-6, 265, Bellflower, Calif.; G—Tom Regner, Notre Dame, 6-1, 245, Kenosha, Wis.; G—LaVerne Allers, Nebraska, 6-0, 209, Davenport, Iowa; C—Jim Breland, Georgia Tech, 6-2, 223, Blacksburg, Va.; B—*Steve Spurrier, Florida, 6-2, 203, Johnson City, Tenn.; B—*Nick Eddy, Notre Dame, 6-0, 195, Lafayette, Calif.; B—Mel Farr, UCLA, 6-2, 208, Beaumont, Texas; B—Clint Jones, Michigan St., 6-0, 206, Cleveland, Ohio.

Defense E—*Bubba Smith, Michigan St., 6-7, 283, Beaumont, Texas; E—Alan Page, Notre Dame, 6-5, 238, Canton, Ohio; T—*Loyd Phillips, Arkansas, 6-3, 230, Longview, Texas; T—Tom Greenlee, Washington, 6-0, 195, Seattle, Wash.; MG—Wayne Meylan, Nebraska, 6-0, 239, Bay City, Mich.; MG—John LaGrone, Southern Methodist, 5-10, 232, Borger, Texas; LB—*Jim Lynch, Notre Dame, 6-1, 225, Lima, Ohio; LB—Paul Naumoff, Tennessee, 6-1, 209, Columbus, Ohio; B—*George Webster, Michigan St., 6-4, 218, Anderson, S.C.; B—Tom Beier, Miami (Fla.), 5-11, 197, Fremont, Ohio; B—Nate Shaw, Southern California, 6-2, 205, San Diego, Calif.

1967

Offense E—Dennis Homan, Alabama, 6-0, 182, Muscle Shoals, Ala.; E—Ron Sellers, Florida St., 6-4, 187, Jacksonville, Fla.; T—*Ron Yary, Southern California, 6-6, 245, Bellflower, Calif.; T—Ed Chandler, Georgia, 6-2, 222, Cedartown, Ga.; G—Harry Olszewski, Clemson, 5-11, 237, Baltimore, Md.; G—Rich Stotter, Houston, 5-11, 225, Shaker Heights, Ohio; C—*Bob Johnson, Tennessee, 6-4, 232, Cleveland, Tenn.; B—Gary Beban, UCLA, 6-0, 191, Redwood City, Calif.; B—*Leroy Keyes, Purdue, 6-3, 199, Newport News, Va.; B—*O. J. Simpson, Southern California, 6-2, 205, San Francisco, Calif.; B—*Larry Csonka, Syracuse, 6-3, 230, Stow, Ohio.

Defense E—*Ted Hendricks, Miami (Fla.), 6-8, 222, Miami Springs, Fla.; E—Tim Rossovich, Southern California, 6-5, 235, Mountain View, Calif.; T—Dennis Byrd, North Carolina St., 6-4, 250, Lincolnton, N.C.; MG—*Granville Liggins, Oklahoma, 5-11, 216, Tulsa, Okla.; MG—Wayne Meylan, Nebraska, 6-0, 231, Bay City, Mich.; LB—Adrian Young, Southern California, 6-1, 210, La Puente, Calif.; LB—Don Manning, UCLA, 6-2, 204, Culver City, Calif.; B—Tom Schoen, Notre Dame, 5-11, 178, Euclid, Ohio; B—Frank Loria, Virginia Tech, 5-9, 174, Clarksburg, W.Va.; B—Bobby Johns, Alabama, 6-1, 180, Birmingham, Ala.; B—Dick Anderson, Colorado, 6-2, 204, Boulder, Colo.

1968

Offense E—*Ted Kwalick, Penn St., 6-4, 230, McKees Rocks, Pa.; E—Jerry LeVias, Southern Methodist, 5-10, 170, Beaumont, Texas; T—*Dave Foley, Ohio St., 6-5, 246, Cincinnati, Ohio; T—George Kunz, Notre Dame, 6-5, 240, Arcadia, Calif.; G—*Charles Rosenfelder, Tennessee, 6-1, 220, Humboldt, Tenn.; (tie) G—Jim Barnes, Arkansas, 6-4, 227, Pine Bluff, Ark.; Mike Montler, Colorado, 6-4, 235, Columbus, Ohio; C—*John Didion, Oregon St., 6-4, 242, Woodland, Calif.; B—*O. J. Simpson, Southern California, 6-2, 205, San Francisco, Calif.; B—*Leroy Keyes, Purdue, 6-3, 205, Newport News, Va.; B—Terry Hanratty, Notre Dame, 6-1, 200, Butler, Pa.; B—Chris Gilbert, Texas, 5-11, 176, Spring, Texas.

Defense E—*Ted Hendricks, Miami (Fla.), 6-8, 222, Miami Springs, Fla.; E—John Zook, Kansas, 6-4, 230, Larned, Kan.; T—Bill Stanfill, Georgia, 6-5, 245, Cairo, Ga.; T—Joe Greene, North Texas, 6-4, 274, Temple, Texas; MG—Ed White, California, 6-3, 245, Palm Desert, Calif.; MG—Chuck Kyle, Purdue, 6-1, 225, Fort Thomas, Ky.; LB—Steve Kiner, Tennessee, 6-1, 205, Tampa, Fla.; LB—Dennis Onkotz, Penn St., 6-2, 205, Northampton, Pa.; B—Jake Scott, Georgia, 6-1, 188, Arlington, Va.; B—Roger Wehrli, Missouri, 6-0, 184, King City, Mo.; B—Al Worley, Washington, 6-0, 175, Wenatchee, Wash.

1969

Offense E—Jim Mandich, Michigan, 6-3, 222, Solon, Ohio; (tie) E—Walker Gillette, Richmond, 6-5, 200, Capron, Va.; Carlos Alvarez, Florida, 5-11, 180, Miami, Fla.; T—Bob McKay, Texas, 6-6, 245, Crane, Texas; T—John Ward, Oklahoma St., 6-5, 248, Tulsa, Okla.; G—Chip Kell, Tennessee, 6-0, 255, Decatur, Ga.; G—Bill Bridges, Houston, 6-2, 230, Carrollton, Texas; C—Rodney Brand, Arkansas, 6-2, 218, Newport, Ark.; B—*Mike Phipps, Purdue, 6-3, 206, Columbus, Ind.; B—*Steve Owens, Oklahoma, 6-2, 215, Miami, Okla.; B—Jim Otis, Ohio St., 6-0, 214, Celina, Ohio; B—Bob Anderson, Colorado, 6-0, 208, Boulder, Colo.

Defense E—Jim Gunn, Southern California, 6-1, 210, San Diego, Calif.; E—Phil Olsen, Utah St., 6-5, 255, Logan, Utah; T—*Mike Reid, Penn St., 6-3, 240, Altoona, Pa.; T—*Mike McCoy, Notre Dame, 6-5, 274, Erie, Pa.; MG—Jim Stillwagon, Ohio St., 6-0, 216, Mount Vernon, Ohio; LB—*Steve Kiner, Tennessee, 6-1, 215, Tampa, Fla.; LB—Dennis Onkotz, Penn St., 6-2, 212, Northampton, Pa.; LB—Mike Ballou, UCLA, 6-3, 230, Los Angeles, Calif.; B—Jack Tatum, Ohio St., 6-0, 204, Passaic, N.J.; B—Buddy McClinton, Auburn, 5-11, 190, Montgomery, Ala.; B—Tom Curtis, Michigan, 6-1, 190, Aurora, Ohio.

1970

Offense E—Tom Gatewood, Notre Dame, 6-2, 208, Baltimore, Md.; E—Ernie Jennings, Air Force, 6-0, 172, Kansas City, Mo.; E—Elmo Wright, Houston, 6-0, 195, Brazoria, Texas; T—Dan Dierdorf, Michigan, 6-4, 250, Canton, Ohio; (tie) T—Bobby Wuensch, Texas, 6-3, 230, Houston, Texas; Bob Newton, Nebraska, 6-4, 248, LaMirada, Calif.; G—*Chip Kell, Tennessee, 6-0, 240, Decatur, Ga.; G—Larry DiNardo, Notre Dame, 6-1, 235, New York, N.Y.; C—Don Popplewell, Colorado, 6-2, 240, Raytown, Mo.; QB—Jim Plunkett, Stanford, 6-3, 204, San Jose, Calif.; RB—Steve Worster, Texas, 6-0, 210, Bridge City, Texas; RB—Don McCauley, North Carolina, 6-0, 211, Garden City, N.Y.

Defense E—Bill Atessis, Texas, 6-3, 255, Houston, Texas; E—Charlie Weaver, Southern California, 6-2, 214, Richmond, Calif.; T—Rock Perdoni, Georgia Tech, 5-11, 236, Wellesley, Mass.; T—Dick Bumpas, Arkansas, 6-1, 225, Fort Smith, Ark.; MG—*Jim Stillwagon, Ohio St., 6-0, 220, Mount Vernon, Ohio; LB—Jack Ham, Penn St., 6-3, 212, Johnstown, Pa.; LB—Mike Anderson, LSU, 6-3, 225, Baton Rouge, La.; B—*Jack Tatum, Ohio St., 6-0, 208, Passaic, N.J.; B—Larry Willingham, Auburn, 6-1, 185, Birmingham, Ala.; B—Dave Elmendorf, Texas A&M, 6-1, 190, Houston, Texas; B—Tommy Casanova, LSU, 6-1, 191, Crowley, La.

1971

Offense E—*Terry Beasley, Auburn, 5-11, 184, Montgomery, Ala.; E—Johnny Rodgers, Nebraska, 5-10, 171, Omaha, Neb.; T—*Jerry Sisemore, Texas, 6-4, 255, Plainview, Texas; T—Dave Joyner, Penn St., 6-0, 235, State College, Pa.; G—*Royce Smith, Georgia, 6-3, 240, Savannah, Ga.; G—Reggie McKenzie, Michigan, 6-4, 232, Highland Park, Mich.; C—Tom Brahaney, Oklahoma, 6-2, 231, Midland, Texas; QB—*Pat Sullivan, Auburn, 6-0, 191, Birmingham, Ala.; RB—*Ed Marinaro, Cornell, 6-3, 210, New Milford, N.J.; RB—*Greg Pruitt, Oklahoma, 5-9, 176, Houston, Texas; RB—Johnny Musso, Alabama, 5-11, 194, Birmingham, Ala.

Defense E—*Walt Patulski, Notre Dame, 6-5, 235, Liverpool, N.Y.; E—Willie Harper, Nebraska, 6-3, 207, Toledo, Ohio; T—Larry Jacobson, Nebraska, 6-6, 250, Sioux Falls, S.D.; T—Mel Long, Toledo, 6-1, 230, Toledo, Ohio; T—Sherman White, California, 6-5, 250, Portsmouth, N.H.; LB—*Mike Taylor, Michigan, 6-2, 224, Detroit, Mich.; LB—Jeff Siemon, Stanford, 6-2, 225, Bakersfield, Calif.; B—*Bobby Majors, Tennessee, 6-1, 197, Sewanee, Tenn.; B—Clarence Ellis, Notre Dame, 6-0, 178, Grand Rapids, Mich.; B—Ernie Jackson, Duke, 5-10, 170, Hopkins, S.C.; B—Tommy Casanova, LSU, 6-2, 195, Crowley, La.

1972

Offense WR—*Johnny Rodgers, Nebraska, 5-9, 173, Omaha, Neb.; TE—*Charles Young, Southern California, 6-4, 228, Fresno, Calif.; T—*Jerry Sisemore, Texas, 6-4, 260, Plainview, Texas; T—Paul Seymour, Michigan, 6-5, 250, Berkley, Mich.; G—*John Hannah, Alabama, 6-3, 282, Albertville, Ala.; G—Ron Rusnak, North Carolina, 6-1, 223, Prince George, Va.; C—Tom Brahaney, Oklahoma, 6-2, 227, Midland, Texas; QB—Bert Jones, LSU, 6-3, 205, Ruston, La.; RB—*Greg Pruitt, Oklahoma, 5-9, 177, Houston, Texas; RB—Otis Armstrong, Purdue, 5-11, 197, Chicago, Ill.; RB—Woody Green, Arizona St., 6-1, 190, Portland, Ore.

Defense E—Willie Harper, Nebraska, 6-2, 207, Toledo, Ohio; E—Bruce Bannon, Penn St., 6-3, 224, Rockaway, N.J.; T—*Greg Marx, Notre Dame, 6-5, 265, Redford, Mich.; T—Dave Butz, Purdue, 6-7, 279, Park Ridge, Ill.; MG—*Rich Glover, Nebraska, 6-1, 234, Jersey City, N.J.; LB—Randy Gradishar, Ohio St., 6-3, 232, Champion, Ohio; LB—John Skorupan, Penn St., 6-2, 208, Beaver, Pa.; B—*Brad VanPelt, Michigan St., 6-5, 221, Owosso, Mich.; B—Cullen Bryant, Colorado, 6-2, 215, Colorado Springs, Colo.; B—Robert Popelka, Southern Methodist, 6-1, 190, Temple, Texas; B—Randy Logan, Michigan, 6-2, 192, Detroit, Mich.

1973

Offense WR—Lynn Swann, Southern California, 6-0, 180, Foster City, Calif.; TE—Dave Casper, Notre Dame, 6-3, 252, Chilton, Wis.; T—*John Hicks, Ohio St., 6-3, 258, Cleveland, Ohio; T—Booker Brown, Southern California, 6-3, 270, Santa Barbara, Calif.; G—Buddy Brown, Alabama, 6-2, 242, Tallahassee, Fla.; G—Bill Yoest, North Carolina St., 6-0, 235, Pittsburgh, Pa.; C—Bill Wyman, Texas, 6-2, 235, Spring, Texas; QB—Dave Jaynes, Kansas, 6-2, 212, Bonner Springs, Kan.; RB—*John Cappelletti, Penn St., 6-1, 206, Upper Darby, Pa.; RB—Roosevelt Leaks, Texas, 5-11, 209, Brenham, Texas; RB—Woody Green, Arizona St., 6-1, 202, Portland, Ore.; RB—Kermit Johnson, UCLA, 6-0, 185, Los Angeles, Calif.

Defense L—*John Dutton, Nebraska, 6-7, 248, Rapid City, S.D.; L—Dave Gallagher, Michigan, 6-4, 245, Piqua, Ohio; L—*Lucious Selmon, Oklahoma, 5-11, 236, Eufaula, Okla.; L—Tony Cristiani, Miami (Fla.), 5-10, 215, Brandon, Fla.; LB—*Randy Gradishar, Ohio St., 6-3, 236, Champion, Ohio; LB—Rod Shoate, Oklahoma, 6-1, 214, Spiro, Okla.; LB—Richard Wood, Southern California, 6-2, 217, Elizabeth, N.J.; B—Mike Townsend, Notre Dame, 6-3, 183, Hamilton, Ohio; B—Artimus Parker, Southern California, 6-3, 215, Sacramento, Calif.; B—Dave Brown, Michigan, 6-1, 188, Akron, Ohio; B—Randy Rhino, Georgia Tech, 5-10, 179, Charlotte, N.C.

1974

Offense WR—Pete Demmerle, Notre Dame, 6-1, 190, New Canaan, Conn.; TE—Bennie Cunningham, Clemson, 6-5, 252, Seneca, S.C.; T—Kurt Schumacher, Ohio St., 6-4, 250, Lorain, Ohio; T—Marvin Crenshaw, Nebraska, 6-6, 240, Toledo, Ohio; G—Ken Huff, North Carolina, 6-4, 261, Coronado, Calif.; G—John Roush, Oklahoma, 6-0, 252, Arvada, Colo.; G—Gerry DiNardo, Notre Dame, 6-1, 237, New York, N.Y.; C—Steve Myers, Ohio St., 6-2, 244, Kent, Ohio; QB—Steve Bartkowski, California, 6-4, 215, Santa Clara, Calif.; RB—*Archie Griffin, Ohio St., 5-9, 184, Columbus, Ohio; RB—*Joe Washington, Oklahoma, 5-10, 178, Port Arthur, Texas; RB—*Anthony Davis, Southern California, 5-9, 183, San Fernando, Calif.

Defense L—*Randy White, Maryland, 6-4, 238, Wilmington, Del.; L—Mike Hartenstine, Penn St., 6-4, 233, Bethlehem, Pa.; L—Pat Donovan, Stanford, 6-5, 240, Helena, Mont.; L—Jimmy Webb, Mississippi St., 6-5, 245, Florence, Miss.; L—Leroy Cook, Alabama, 6-4, 205, Abbeville, Ala.; MG—Louie Kelcher, Southern Methodist, 6-5, 275, Beaumont, Texas; MG—Rubin Carter, Miami (Fla.), 6-3, 260, Ft. Lauderdale, Fla.; LB—*Rod Shoate, Oklahoma, 6-1, 213, Spiro, Okla.; LB—Richard Wood, Southern California, 6-2, 213, Elizabeth, N.J.; LB—Ken Bernich, Auburn, 6-2, 240, Gretna, La.; LB—Woodrow Lowe, Alabama, 6-0, 211, Phenix City, Ala.; B—*Dave Brown, Michigan, 6-1, 188, Akron, Ohio; B—Pat Thomas, Texas A&M, 5-9, 180, Plano, Texas; B—John Provost, Holy Cross, 5-10, 180, Quincy, Mass.

1975

Offense E—Steve Rivera, California, 6-0, 185, Wilmington, Calif.; E—Larry Seivers, Tennessee, 6-4, 198, Clinton, Tenn.; T—Bob Simmons, Texas, 6-5, 245, Temple, Texas; T—Dennis Lick, Wisconsin, 6-3, 262, Chicago, Ill.; G—Randy Johnson, Georgia, 6-2, 250, Rome, Ga.; G—Ted Smith, Ohio St., 6-1, 242, Gibsonburg, Ohio; C—*Rik Bonness, Nebraska, 6-4, 223, Bellevue, Neb.; QB—John Sciarra, UCLA, 5-10, 178, Alhambra, Calif.; RB—*Archie Griffin, Ohio St., 5-9, 182, Columbus, Ohio; RB—*Ricky Bell, Southern California, 6-2, 215, Los Angeles, Calif.; RB—Chuck Muncie, California, 6-3, 220, Uniontown, Pa.

Defense E—*Leroy Cook, Alabama, 6-4, 205, Abbeville, Ala.; E—Jimbo Elrod, Oklahoma, 6-0, 210, Tulsa, Okla.; T—*Lee Roy Selmon, Oklahoma, 6-2, 256, Eufaula, Okla.; T—*Steve Niehaus, Notre Dame, 6-5, 260, Cincinnati, Ohio; MG—Dewey Selmon, Oklahoma, 6-1, 257, Eufaula, Okla.; LB—*Ed Simonini, Texas A&M, 6-0, 215, Las Vegas, Nev.; LB—Greg Buttle, Penn St., 6-3, 220, Linwood, N.J.; LB—Sammy Green, Florida, 6-2, 228, Ft. Meade, Fla.; B—*Chet Moeller, Navy, 6-0, 189, Kettering, Ohio; B—Tim Fox, Ohio St., 6-0, 186, Canton, Ohio; B—Pat Thomas, Texas A&M, 5-10, 180, Plano, Texas.

1976

Offense SE—Larry Seivers, Tennessee, 6-4, 200, Clinton, Tenn.; TE—Ken MacAfee, Notre Dame, 6-4, 251, Brockton, Mass.; T—Mike Vaughan, Oklahoma, 6-5, 275, Ada, Okla.; T—Chris Ward, Ohio St., 6-4, 274, Dayton, Ohio; G—Joel Parrish, Georgia, 6-3, 232, Douglas, Ga.; G—Mark Donahue, Michigan, 6-3, 245, Oak Lawn, Ill.; C—Derrel Gofourth, Oklahoma St., 6-2, 250, Parsons, Kan.; QB—Tommy Kramer, Rice, 6-2, 190, San Antonio, Texas; RB—*Tony Dorsett, Pittsburgh, 5-11, 192, Aliquippa, Pa.; RB—*Ricky Bell, Southern California, 6-2, 218, Los Angeles, Calif.; RB—Rob Lytle, Michigan, 6-1, 195, Fremont, Ohio; PK—Tony Franklin, Texas A&M, 5-10, 170, Fort Worth, Texas.

Defense E—*Ross Browner, Notre Dame, 6-3, 248, Warren, Ohio; E—Bob Brudzinski, Ohio St., 6-4, 228, Fremont, Ohio; T—Wilson Whitley, Houston, 6-3, 268, Brenham, Texas; T—Gary Jeter, Southern California, 6-5, 255, Cleveland, Ohio; T—Joe Campbell, Maryland, 6-6, 255, Wilmington, Del.; MG—Al Romano, Pittsburgh, 6-3, 230, Solvay, N.Y.; LB—*Robert Jackson, Texas A&M, 6-2, 228, Houston, Texas; LB—Jerry Robinson, UCLA, 6-3, 208, Santa Rosa, Calif.; B—*Bill Armstrong, Wake Forest, 6-4, 205, Randolph, N.J.; B—Gary Green, Baylor, 5-11, 182, San Antonio, Texas; B—Dennis Thurman, Southern California, 5-11, 170, Santa Monica, Calif.; B—Dave Butterfield, Nebraska, 5-10, 182, Kersey, Colo.

1977

Offense WR—John Jefferson, Arizona St., 6-1, 184, Dallas, Texas; WR—Ozzie Newsome, Alabama, 6-4, 210, Leighton, Ala.; TE—*Ken MacAfee, Notre Dame, 6-4, 250, Brockton, Mass.; T—*Chris Ward, Ohio St., 6-4, 272, Dayton, Ohio; T—Dan Irons, Texas Tech, 6-7, 260, Lubbock, Texas; G—*Mark Donahue, Michigan, 6-3, 245, Oak Lawn, Ill.; G—Leotis Harris, Arkansas, 6-1, 254, Little Rock, Ark.; C—Tom Brzoza, Pittsburgh, 6-3, 240, New Castle, Pa.; QB—Guy Benjamin, Stanford, 6-4, 202, Sepulveda, Calif.; RB—*Earl Campbell, Texas, 6-1, 220, Tyler, Texas; RB—*Terry Miller, Oklahoma St., 6-0, 196, Colorado Springs, Colo.; RB—Charles Alexander, LSU, 6-1, 215, Galveston, Texas; K—Steve Little, Arkansas, 6-0, 179, Overland Park, Kan.

Defense L—*Ross Browner, Notre Dame, 6-3, 247, Warren, Ohio; L—*Art Still, Kentucky, 6-8, 247, Camden, N.J.; L—*Brad Shearer, Texas, 6-4, 255, Austin, Texas; L—Randy Holloway, Pittsburgh, 6-6, 228, Sharon, Pa.; L—Dee Hardison, North Carolina, 6-4, 252, Newton Grove, N.C.; LB—*Jerry Robinson, UCLA, 6-3, 208, Santa Rosa, Calif.; LB—Tom Cousineau, Ohio St., 6-3, 228, Fairview Park, Ohio; LB—Gary Spani, Kansas St., 6-2, 222, Manhattan, Kan.; B—*Dennis Thurman, Southern California, 5-11, 173, Santa Monica, Calif.; B—*Zac Henderson, Oklahoma, 6-1, 184, Burkburnett, Texas; B—Luther Bradley, Notre Dame, 6-2, 204, Muncie, Ind.; B—Bob Jury, Pittsburgh, 6-0, 190, Library, Pa.

1978

Offense WR—Emanuel Tolbert, Southern Methodist, 5-10, 180, Little Rock, Ark.; TE—Kellen Winslow, Missouri, 6-6, 235, East St. Louis, Ill.; T—*Keith Dorney, Penn St., 6-5, 257, Allentown, Pa.; T—Kelvin Clark, Nebraska, 6-4, 275, Odessa, Texas; G—*Pat Howell, Southern California, 6-6, 255, Fresno, Calif.; G—*Greg Roberts, Oklahoma, 6-3, 238, Nacogdoches, Texas; C—Dave Huffman, Notre Dame, 6-5, 245, Dallas, Texas; C—Jim Ritcher, North Carolina St., 6-3, 242, Hinckley, Ohio; QB—*Chuck Fusina, Penn St., 6-1, 195, McKees Rocks, Pa.; RB—*Billy Sims, Oklahoma, 6-0, 205, Hooks, Texas; RB—*Charles White, Southern California, 5-11, 183, San Fernando, Calif.; RB—Ted Brown, North Carolina St., 5-10, 195, High Point, N.C.; RB—Charles Alexander, LSU, 6-1, 214, Galveston, Texas.

Defense L—*Al Harris, Arizona St., 6-5, 240, Wheeler AFB, Hawaii; L—*Bruce Clark, Penn St., 6-3, 246, New Castle, Pa.; L—Hugh Green, Pittsburgh, 6-2, 215, Natchez, Miss.; L—Mike Bell, Colorado St., 6-5, 265, Wichita, Kan.; L—Marty Lyons, Alabama, 6-6, 250, St. Petersburg, Fla.; LB—*Bob Golic, Notre Dame, 6-3, 244, Willowick, Ohio; LB—*Jerry Robinson, UCLA, 6-3, 209, Santa Rosa, Calif.; LB—Tom Cousineau, Ohio St., 6-3, 227, Fairview Park, Ohio; B—*Johnnie Johnson, Texas, 6-2, 183, LaGrange, Texas; B—Kenny Easley, UCLA, 6-2, 202, Chesapeake, Va.; B—Jeff Nixon, Richmond, 6-4, 195, Glendale, Ariz.

1979

Offense WR—Ken Margerum, Stanford, 6-1, 175, Fountain Valley, Calif.; TE—*Junior Miller, Nebraska, 6-4, 222, Midland, Texas; T—*Greg Kolenda, Arkansas, 6-1, 258, Kansas City, Kan.; T—Jim Bunch, Alabama, 6-2, 240, Mechanicsville, Va.; G—*Brad Budde, Southern California, 6-5, 253, Kansas City, Mo.; G—Ken Fritz, Ohio St., 6-3, 238, Ironton, Ohio; C—*Jim Ritcher, North Carolina St., 6-3, 245, Hinckley, Ohio; QB—*Marc Wilson, Brigham Young, 6-5, 204, Seattle, Wash.; RB—*Charles White, Southern California, 6-0, 185, San Fernando, Calif.; RB—*Billy Sims, Oklahoma, 6-0, 205, Hooks, Texas; RB—Vagas Ferguson, Notre Dame, 6-1, 194, Richmond, Ind.; PK—Dale Castro, Maryland, 6-1, 170, Shady Side, Md.

Defense L—*Hugh Green, Pittsburgh, 6-2, 220, Natchez, Miss.; L—*Steve McMichael, Texas, 6-2, 250, Freer, Texas; L—Bruce Clark, Penn St., 6-3, 255, New Castle, Pa.; L—Jim Stuckey, Clemson, 6-5, 241, Cayce, S.C.; MG—Ron Simmons, Florida St., 6-1, 235, Warner Robins, Ga.; LB—*George Cumby, Oklahoma, 6-0, 205, Tyler, Texas; LB—Ron Simpkins, Michigan, 6-2, 220, Detroit, Mich.; LB—Mike Singletary, Baylor, 6-1, 224, Houston, Texas; B—*Kenny Easley, UCLA, 6-3, 204, Chesapeake, Va.; B—*Johnnie Johnson, Texas, 6-2, 190, LaGrange, Texas; B—Roland James, Tennessee, 6-2, 182, Jamestown, Ohio; P—Jim Miller, Mississippi, 5-11, 183, Ripley, Miss.

1980

Offense WR—*Ken Margerum, Stanford, 6-1, 175, Fountain Valley, Calif.; TE—*Dave Young, Purdue, 6-6, 242, Akron, Ohio; L—*Mark May, Pittsburgh, 6-6, 282, Oneonta, N.Y.; L—Keith Van Horne, Southern California, 6-7, 265, Fullerton, Calif.; L—Nick Eyre, Brigham Young, 6-5, 276, Las Vegas, Nev.; L—Louis Oubre, Oklahoma, 6-4, 262, New Orleans, La.; L—Randy Schleusener, Nebraska, 6-7, 242, Rapid City, S.D.; C—*John Scully, Notre Dame, 6-5, 255, Huntington, N.Y.; QB—*Mark Herrmann, Purdue, 6-4, 187, Carmel, Ind.; RB—*George Rogers, South Carolina, 6-2, 220, Duluth, Ga.; RB—*Herschel Walker, Georgia, 6-2, 220, Wrightsville, Ga.; RB—Jarvis Redwine, Nebraska, 5-11, 204, Inglewood, Calif.

Defense L—*Hugh Green, Pittsburgh, 6-2, 222, Natchez, Miss.; L—*E. J. Junior, Alabama, 6-3, 227, Nashville, Tenn.; L—Kenneth Sims, Texas, 6-6, 265, Groesbeck, Texas; L—Leonard Mitchell, Houston, 6-7, 270, Houston, Texas; MG—Ron Simmons, Florida St., 6-1, 230, Warner Robins, Ga.; LB—*Mike Singletary, Baylor, 6-1, 232, Houston, Texas; LB—*Lawrence Taylor, North Carolina, 6-3, 237, Williamsburg, Va.; LB—David Little, Florida, 6-1, 228, Miami, Fla.; LB—Bob Crable, Notre Dame, 6-3, 222, Cincinnati, Ohio; B—*Kenny Easley, UCLA, 6-3, 206, Chesapeake, Va.; B—*Ronnie Lott, Southern California, 6-2, 200, Rialto, Calif.; B—John Simmons, Southern Methodist, 5-11, 188, Little Rock, Ark.

1981

Offense WR—*Anthony Carter, Michigan, 5-11, 161, Riviera Beach, Fla.; TE—*Tim Wrightman, UCLA, 6-3, 237, San Pedro, Calif.; L—*Sean Farrell, Penn St., 6-3, 266, Westhampton Beach, N.Y.; L—Roy Foster, Southern California, 6-4, 265, Overland Park, Kan.; L—Terry Crouch, Oklahoma, 6-1, 275, Dallas, Texas; L—Ed Muransky, Michigan, 6-7, 275, Youngstown, Ohio; L—Terry Tausch, Texas, 6-4, 265, New Braunfels, Texas; L—Kurt Becker, Michigan, 6-6, 260, Aurora, Ill.; C—*Dave Rimington, Nebraska, 6-3, 275, Omaha, Neb.; QB—*Jim McMahon, Brigham Young, 6-0, 185, Roy, Utah; RB—*Marcus Allen, Southern California, 6-2, 202, San Diego, Calif.; RB—*Herschel Walker, Georgia, 6-2, 222, Wrightsville, Ga.

Defense L—*Billy Ray Smith, Arkansas, 6-4, 228, Plano, Texas; L—*Kenneth Sims, Texas, 6-6, 265, Groesbeck, Texas; L—Andre Tippett, Iowa, 6-4, 235, Newark, N.J.; L—Tim Krumrie, Wisconsin, 6-3, 237, Mondovi, Wis.; LB—Bob Crable, Notre Dame, 6-3, 225, Cincinnati, Ohio; LB—Jeff Davis, Clemson, 6-0, 223, Greensboro, N.C.; LB—Sal Sunseri, Pittsburgh, 6-0, 220, Pittsburgh, Pa.; DB—Tommy Wilcox, Alabama, 5-11, 187, Harahan, La.; DB—Mike Richardson, Arizona St., 6-1, 192, Compton, Calif.; DB—Terry Kinard, Clemson, 6-1, 183, Sumter, S.C.; DB—Fred Marion, Miami (Fla.), 6-3, 194, Gainesville, Fla.; P—Reggie Roby, Iowa, 6-3, 215, Waterloo, Iowa.

1982

Offense WR—*Anthony Carter, Michigan, 5-11, 161, Riviera Beach, Fla.; TE—*Gordon Hudson, Brigham Young, 6-4, 224, Salt Lake City, Utah; L—*Don Mosebar, Southern California, 6-7, 270, Visalia, Calif.; L—*Steve Korte, Arkansas, 6-2, 270, Littleton, Colo.; L—Jimbo Covert, Pittsburgh, 6-5, 279, Conway, Pa.; L—Bruce Matthews, Southern California, 6-5, 265, Arcadia, Calif.; C—*Dave Rimington, Nebraska, 6-3, 290, Omaha, Neb.; QB—*John Elway, Stanford, 6-4, 202, Northridge, Calif.; RB—*Herschel Walker, Georgia, 6-2, 222, Wrightsville, Ga.; RB—*Eric Dickerson, Southern Methodist, 6-2, 215, Sealy, Texas; RB—Mike Rozier, Nebraska, 5-11, 210, Camden, N.J.; PK—*Chuck Nelson, Washington, 5-11, 178, Everett, Wash.

Defense L—*Billy Ray Smith, Arkansas, 6-3, 228, Plano, Texas; L—Vernon Maxwell, Arizona St., 6-2, 225, Carson, Calif.; L—Mike Pitts, Alabama, 6-5, 255, Baltimore, Md.; L—Wilber Marshall, Florida, 6-1, 230, Titusville, Fla.; L—Gabriel Rivera, Texas Tech, 6-3, 270, San Antonio, Texas; L—Rick Bryan, Oklahoma, 6-4, 260, Coweta, Okla.; MG—George Achica, Southern California, 6-5, 260, San Jose, Calif.; LB—*Darryl Talley, West Virginia, 6-4, 210, East Cleveland, Ohio; LB—Ricky Hunley, Arizona, 6-1, 230, Petersburg, Va.; LB—Marcus Marek, Ohio St., 6-2, 224, Masury, Ohio; DB—*Terry Kinard, Clemson, 6-1, 189, Sumter, S.C.; DB—Mike Richardson, Arizona St., 6-0, 190, Compton, Calif.; DB—Terry Hoage, Georgia, 6-3, 196, Huntsville, Texas; P—*Jim Arnold, Vanderbilt, 6-3, 205, Dalton, Ga.

1983

Offense WR—*Irving Fryar, Nebraska, 6-0, 200, Mount Holly, N.J.; TE—*Gordon Hudson, Brigham Young, 6-4, 231, Salt Lake City, Utah; L—*Bill Fralic, Pittsburgh, 6-5, 270, Penn Hills, Pa.; L—Terry Long, East Carolina, 6-0, 280, Columbia, S.C.; L—Dean Steinkuhler, Nebraska, 6-3, 270, Burr, Neb.; L—Doug Dawson, Texas, 6-3, 263, Houston, Texas; C—Tony Slaton, Southern California, 6-4, 260, Merced, Calif.; QB—*Steve Young, Brigham Young, 6-1, 198, Greenwich, Conn.; RB—*Mike Rozier, Nebraska, 5-11, 210, Camden, N.J.; RB—Bo Jackson, Auburn, 6-1, 222, Bessemer, Ala.; RB—Greg Allen, Florida St., 6-0, 200, Milton, Fla.; RB—Napoleon McCallum, Navy, 6-2, 208, Milford, Ohio; PK—Luis Zendejas, Arizona St., 5-9, 186, Chino, Calif.

Defense L—*Rick Bryan, Oklahoma, 6-4, 260, Coweta, Okla.; L—*Reggie White, Tennessee, 6-5, 264, Chattanooga, Tenn.; L—William Perry, Clemson, 6-3, 320, Aiken, S.C.; L—William Fuller, North Carolina, 6-4, 250, Chesapeake, Va.; LB—*Ricky Hunley, Arizona, 6-2, 230, Petersburg, Va.; LB—Wilber Marshall, Florida, 6-1, 230, Titusville, Fla.; LB—Ron Rivera, California, 6-3, 225, Monterey, Calif.; LB—Jeff Leiding, Texas, 6-4, 240, Tulsa, Okla.; DB—*Russell Carter, Southern Methodist, 6-3, 193, Ardmore, Pa.; DB—Jerry Gray, Texas, 6-1, 183, Lubbock, Texas; DB—Terry Hoage, Georgia, 6-3, 196, Huntsville, Texas; DB—Don Rogers, UCLA, 6-2, 208, Sacramento, Calif.; P—Jack Weil, Wyoming, 5-11, 171, Northglenn, Colo.

1984

Offense WR—*David Williams, Illinois, 6-3, 195, Los Angeles, Calif.; WR—Eddie Brown, Miami (Fla.), 6-0, 185, Miami, Fla.; TE—Jay Novacek, Wyoming, 6-4, 211, Gothenburg, Neb.; T—*Bill Fralic, Pittsburgh, 6-5, 285, Penn Hills, Pa.; T—Lomas Brown, Florida, 6-5, 277, Miami, Fla.; G—Del Wilkes, South Carolina, 6-3, 255, Columbia, S.C.; G—Jim Lachey, Ohio St., 6-6, 274, St. Henry, Ohio; G—Bill Mayo, Tennessee, 6-3, 280, Dalton, Ga.; C—*Mark Traynowicz, Nebraska, 6-6, 265, Bellevue, Neb.; QB—*Doug Flutie, Boston College, 5-9, 177, Natick, Mass.; RB—*Keith Byars, Ohio St., 6-2, 233, Dayton, Ohio; RB—*Kenneth Davis, TCU, 5-11, 205, Temple, Texas; RB—Rueben Mayes, Washington St., 6-0, 200, North Battleford, Saskatchewan, Canada; PK—Kevin Butler, Georgia, 6-1, 190, Stone Mountain, Ga.

Defense DL—Bruce Smith, Virginia Tech, 6-4, 275, Norfolk, Va.; DL—Tony Degrate, Texas, 6-4, 280, Snyder, Texas; DL—Ron Holmes, Washington, 6-4, 255, Lacey, Wash.; DL—Tony Casillas, Oklahoma, 6-3, 272, Tulsa, Okla.; LB—Gregg Carr, Auburn, 6-2, 215, Birmingham, Ala.; LB—Jack Del Rio, Southern California, 6-4, 235, Hayward, Calif.; LB—Larry Station, Iowa, 5-11, 233, Omaha, Neb.; DB—*Jerry Gray, Texas, 6-1, 183, Lubbock, Texas; DB—Tony Thurman, Boston College, 6-0, 179, Lynn, Mass.; DB—Jeff Sanchez, Georgia, 6-0, 183, Yorba Linda, Calif.; DB—David Fulcher, Arizona St., 6-3, 220, Los Angeles, Calif.; DB—Rod Brown, Oklahoma St., 6-3, 188, Gainesville, Texas; P—*Ricky Anderson, Vanderbilt, 6-2, 190, St. Petersburg, Fla.

1985

Offense WR—*David Williams, Illinois, 6-3, 195, Los Angeles, Calif.; WR—Tim McGee, Tennessee, 5-10, 181, Cleveland, Ohio; TE—Willie Smith, Miami (Fla.), 6-2, 230, Jacksonville, Fla.; L—*Jim Dombrowski, Virginia, 6-5, 290, Williamsville, N.Y.; L—Jeff Bregel, Southern California, 6-4, 280, Granada Hills, Calif.; L—Brian Jozwiak, West Virginia, 6-6, 290, Catonsville, Md.; L—John Rienstra, Temple, 6-4, 280, Colorado Springs, Colo.; L—J. D. Maarleveld, Maryland, 6-5, 300, Rutherford, N.J.; L—Jamie Dukes, Florida St., 6-0, 272, Orlando, Fla.; C—Pete Anderson, Georgia, 6-3, 264, Glen Ridge, N.J.; QB—*Chuck Long, Iowa, 6-4, 213, Wheaton, Ill.; RB—*Bo Jackson, Auburn, 6-1, 222, Bessemer, Ala.; RB—*Lorenzo White, Michigan St., 5-11, 205, Fort Lauderdale, Fla.; RB—Thurman Thomas, Oklahoma St., 5-11, 186, Missouri City, Texas; RB—Reggie Dupard, Southern Methodist, 6-0, 201, New Orleans, La.; RB—Napoleon McCallum, Navy, 6-2, 214, Milford, Ohio; PK—*John Lee, UCLA, 5-11, 187, Downey, Calif.

Defense L—*Tim Green, Syracuse, 6-2, 246, Liverpool, N.Y.; L—*Leslie O'Neal, Oklahoma St., 6-3, 245, Little Rock, Ark.; L—Tony Casillas, Oklahoma, 6-3, 280, Tulsa, Okla.; L—Mike Ruth, Boston College, 6-2, 250, Norristown, Pa.; L—Mike Hammerstein, Michigan, 6-4, 240, Wapakoneta, Ohio; LB—*Brian Bosworth, Oklahoma, 6-2, 234, Irving, Texas; LB—*Larry Station, Iowa, 5-11, 227, Omaha, Neb.; LB—Johnny Holland, Texas A&M, 6-2, 219, Hempstead, Texas; DB—David Fulcher, Arizona St., 6-3, 228, Los Angeles, Calif.; DB—Brad Cochran, Michigan, 6-3, 219, Royal Oak, Mich.; DB—Scott Thomas, Air Force, 6-0, 185, San Antonio, Texas; P—Barry Helton, Colorado, 6-3, 195, Simla, Colo.

1986

Offense WR—Cris Carter, Ohio St., 6-3, 194, Middletown, Ohio; TE—*Keith Jackson, Oklahoma, 6-3, 241, Little Rock, Ark.; L—Jeff Bregel, Southern California, 6-4, 280, Granada Hills, Calif.; L—Randy Dixon, Pittsburgh, 6-4, 286, Clewiston, Fla.; L—Danny Villa, Arizona St., 6-5, 284, Nogales, Ariz.; L—John Clay, Missouri, 6-5, 285, St. Louis, Mo.; C—*Ben Tamburello, Auburn, 6-3, 268, Birmingham, Ala.; QB—*Vinny Testaverde, Miami (Fla.), 6-5, 218, Elmont, N.Y.; RB—*Brent Fullwood, Auburn, 5-11, 209, St. Cloud, Fla.; RB—*Paul Palmer, Temple, 5-10, 180, Potomac, Md.; RB—Terrence Flagler, Clemson, 6-1, 200, Fernandina Beach, Fla.; RB—Brad Muster, Stanford, 6-3, 226, Novato, Calif.; RB—D. J. Dozier, Penn St., 6-1, 204, Virginia Beach, Va.; PK—Jeff Jaeger, Washington, 5-11, 191, Kent, Wash.

Defense L—*Jerome Brown, Miami (Fla.), 6-2, 285, Brooksville, Fla.; L—*Danny Noonan, Nebraska, 6-4, 280, Lincoln, Neb.; L—Tony Woods, Pittsburgh, 6-4, 240, Newark, N.J.; L—Jason Buck, Brigham Young, 6-6, 270, St. Anthony, Idaho; L—Reggie Rogers, Washington, 6-6, 260, Sacramento, Calif.; LB—*Cornelius Bennett, Alabama, 6-4, 235, Birmingham, Ala.; LB—Shane Conlan, Penn St., 6-3, 225, Frewsburg, N.Y.; LB—Brian Bosworth, Oklahoma, 6-2, 240, Irving, Texas; LB—Chris Spielman, Ohio St., 6-2, 227, Massillon, Ohio; DB—*Thomas Everett, Baylor, 5-9, 180, Daingerfield, Texas; DB—Tim McDonald, Southern California, 6-3, 205, Fresno, Calif.; DB—Bennie Blades, Miami (Fla.), 6-0, 207, Ft. Lauderdale, Fla.; DB—Rod Woodson, Purdue, 6-0, 195, Fort Wayne, Ind.; DB—Garland Rivers, Michigan, 6-1, 187, Canton, Ohio; P—Barry Helton, Colorado, 6-4, 200, Simla, Colo.

1987

Offense WR—*Tim Brown, Notre Dame, 6-0, 195, Dallas, Texas; WR—Wendell Davis, LSU, 6-0, 186, Shreveport, La.; TE—*Keith Jackson, Oklahoma, 6-3, 248, Little Rock, Ark.; L—*Mark Hutson, Oklahoma, 6-4, 282, Fort Smith, Ark.; L—Dave Cadigan, Southern California, 6-5, 280, Newport Beach, Calif.; L—John Elliott, Michigan, 6-7, 306, Lake Ronkonkoma, N.Y.; L—Randall McDaniel, Arizona St., 6-5, 261, Avondale, Ariz.; C—*Nacho Albergamo, LSU, 6-2, 257, Marrera, La.; QB—*Don McPherson, Syracuse, 6-0, 182, West Hempstead, N.Y.; RB—Lorenzo White, Michigan St., 5-11, 211, Fort Lauderdale, Fla.; RB—Craig Heyward, Pittsburgh, 6-0, 260, Passaic, N.J.; PK—David Treadwell, Clemson, 6-1, 165, Jacksonville, Fla.

Defense L—*Daniel Stubbs, Miami (Fla.), 6-4, 250, Red Bank, N.J.; L—*Chad Hennings, Air Force, 6-5, 260, Elboron, Iowa; L—Tracy Rocker, Auburn, 6-3, 258, Atlanta, Ga.; L—Ted Gregory, Syracuse, 6-1, 260, East Islip, N.Y.; L—John Roper, Texas A&M, 6-2, 215, Houston, Texas; LB—*Chris Spielman, Ohio St., 6-2, 236, Massillon, Ohio; LB—Aundray Bruce, Auburn, 6-6, 236, Montgomery, Ala.; LB—Dante Jones, Oklahoma, 6-2, 235, Dallas, Texas; DB—*Bennie Blades, Miami (Fla.), 6-0, 215, Fort Lauderdale, Fla.; DB—*Deion Sanders, Florida St., 6-0, 192, Fort Myers, Fla.; DB—Rickey Dixon, Oklahoma, 5-10, 184, Dallas, Texas; DB—Chuck Cecil, Arizona, 6-0, 185, Red Bluff, Calif.; P—*Tom Tupa, Ohio St., 6-5, 215, Brecksville, Ohio.

1988

Offense WR—Jason Phillips, Houston, 5-9, 175, Houston, Texas; WR—Hart Lee Dykes, Oklahoma St., 6-4, 220, Bay City, Texas; TE—Marv Cook, Iowa, 6-4, 243, West Branch, Iowa; L—*Tony Mandarich, Michigan St., 6-6, 315, Oakville, Ontario, Canada; L—*Anthony Phillips, Oklahoma, 6-3, 286, Tulsa, Okla.; L—Mike Utley, Washington St., 6-6, 302, Seattle, Wash.; L—Mark Stepnoski, Pittsburgh, 6-3, 265, Erie, Pa.; C—Jake Young, Nebraska, 6-5, 260, Midland, Texas; C—John Vitale, Michigan, 6-1, 273, Detroit, Mich.; QB—Steve Walsh, Miami (Fla.), 6-3, 195, St. Paul, Minn.; QB—Troy Aikman, UCLA, 6-4, 217, Henryetta, Okla.; RB—*Barry Sanders, Oklahoma St., 5-8, 197, Wichita, Kan.; RB—Anthony Thompson, Indiana, 6-0, 205, Terre Haute, Ind.; RB—Tim Worley, Georgia, 6-2, 216, Lumberton, N.C.; PK—Kendall Trainor, Arkansas, 6-2, 205, Fredonia, Kan.

Defense L—*Mark Messner, Michigan, 6-3, 244, Hartland, Mich.; L—*Tracy Rocker, Auburn, 6-3, 278, Atlanta, Ga.; L—Wayne Martin, Arkansas, 6-5, 263, Cherry Valley, Ark.; L—Frank Stams, Notre Dame, 6-4, 237, Akron, Ohio; L—Bill Hawkins, Miami (Fla.), 6-6, 260, Hollywood, Fla.; LB—*Derrick Thomas, Alabama, 6-4, 230, Miami, Fla.; LB—*Broderick Thomas, Nebraska, 6-3, 235, Houston, Texas; LB—Michael Stonebreaker, Notre Dame, 6-1, 228, River Ridge, La.; DB—*Deion Sanders, Florida St., 6-0, 195, Fort Myers, Fla.; DB—Donnell Woolford, Clemson, 5-10, 195, Fayetteville, N.C.; DB—Louis Oliver, Florida, 6-2, 222, Bell Glade, Fla.; DB—Darryl Henley, UCLA, 5-10, 165, Ontario, Calif.; P—Keith English, Colorado, 6-3, 215, Greeley, Colo.

1989

Offense WR—*Clarkston Hines, Duke, 6-1, 170, Chapel Hill, N.C.; WR—Terance Mathis, New Mexico, 5-9, 167, Stone Mountain, Ga.; TE—Mike Busch, Iowa St., 6-5, 252, Donahue, Iowa; L—Jim Mabry, Arkansas, 6-4, 262, Memphis, Tenn.; L—Bob Kula, Michigan St., 6-4, 282, West Bloomfield, Mich.; L—Mohammed Elewonibi, Brigham Young, 6-5, 290, Kamloops, British Columbia, Canada; L—Joe Garten, Colorado, 6-3, 280, Placentia, Calif.; L—*Eric Still, Tennessee, 6-3, 283, Germantown, Tenn.; C—Jake Young, Nebraska, 6-4, 270, Midland, Texas; QB—Andre Ware, Houston, 6-2, 205, Dickinson, Texas; RB—*Anthony Thompson, Indiana, 6-0, 209, Terre Haute, Ind.; RB—*Emmitt Smith, Florida, 5-10, 201, Pensacola, Fla.; PK—*Jason Hanson, Washington St., 6-0, 164, Spokane, Wash.

Defense L—Chris Zorich, Notre Dame, 6-1, 268, Chicago, Ill.; L—Greg Mark, Miami (Fla.), 6-4, 255, Pennsauken, N.J.; L—Tim Ryan, Southern California, 6-5, 260, San Jose, Calif.; L—*Moe Gardner, Illinois, 6-2, 250, Indianapolis, Ind.; LB—*Percy Snow, Michigan St., 6-3, 240, Canton, Ohio; LB—*Keith McCants, Alabama, 6-5, 256, Mobile, Ala.; LB—Alfred Williams, Colorado, 6-6, 230, Houston, Texas; DB—*Todd Lyght, Notre Dame, 6-1, 181, Flint, Mich.; DB—*Mark Carrier, Southern California, 6-1, 185, Long Beach, Calif.; DB—*Tripp Welborne, Michigan, 6-1, 193, Greensboro, N.C.; DB—LeRoy Butler, Florida St., 6-0, 194, Jacksonville, Fla.; P—Tom Rouen, Colorado, 6-3, 220, Littleton, Colo.

1990

Offense WR—*Raghib Ismail, Notre Dame, 5-10, 175, Wilkes-Barre, Pa.; WR—Herman Moore, Virginia, 6-5, 197, Danville, Va.; TE—*Chris Smith, Brigham Young, 6-4, 230, La Canada, Calif.; OL—*Antone Davis, Tennessee, 6-4, 310, Fort Valley, Ga.; OL—*Joe Garten, Colorado, 6-3, 280, Placentia, Calif.; OL—*Ed King, Auburn, 6-4, 284, Phenix City, Ala.; OL—Stacy Long, Clemson, 6-2, 275, Griffin, Ga.; C—John Flannery, Syracuse, 6-4, 301, Pottsville, Pa.; QB—Ty Detmer, Brigham Young, 6-0, 175, San Antonio, Texas; RB—*Eric Bieniemy, Colorado, 5-7, 195, West Covina, Calif.; RB—Darren Lewis, Texas A&M, 6-0, 220, Dallas, Texas; PK—*Philip Doyle, Alabama, 6-1, 190, Birmingham, Ala.

Defense DL—*Russell Maryland, Miami (Fla.), 6-2, 273, Chicago, Ill.; DL—*Chris Zorich, Notre Dame, 6-1, 266, Chicago, Ill.; DL—Moe Gardner, Illinois, 6-2, 258, Indianapolis, Ind.; DL—David Rocker, Auburn, 6-4, 264, Atlanta, Ga.; LB—*Alfred Williams, Colorado, 6-6, 236, Houston, Texas; LB—*Michael Stonebreaker, Notre Dame, 6-1, 228, River Ridge, La.; LB—Maurice Crum, Miami (Fla.), 6-0, 222, Tampa, Fla.; DB—*Tripp Welborne, Michigan, 6-1, 201, Greensboro, N.C.; DB—*Darryll Lewis, Arizona, 5-9, 186, West Covina, Calif.; DB—*Ken Swilling, Georgia Tech, 6-3, 230, Toccoa, Ga.; DB—Todd Lyght, Notre Dame, 6-1, 184, Flint, Mich.; P—Brian Greenfield, Pittsburgh, 6-1, 210, Sherman Oaks, Calif.

1991

Offense WR—*Desmond Howard, Michigan, 5-9, 176, Cleveland, Ohio; WR—Mario Bailey, Washington, 5-9, 167, Seattle, Wash.; TE—Kelly Blackwell, TCU, 6-2, 242, Fort Worth, Texas; OL—*Greg Skrepenak, Michigan, 6-8, 322, Wilkes-Barre, Pa.; OL—Bob Whitfield, Stanford, 6-7, 300, Carson, Calif.; OL—Jeb Flesch, Clemson, 6-3, 266, Morrow, Ga.; (tie) OL—Jerry Ostroski, Tulsa, 6-4, 305, Collegeville, Pa.; Mirko Jurkovic, Notre Dame, 6-4, 289, Calumet City, Ill.; C—*Jay Leeuwenburg, Colorado, 6-3, 265, Kirkwood, Mo.; QB—Ty Detmer, Brigham Young, 6-0, 175, San Antonio, Texas; RB—*Vaughn Dunbar, Indiana, 6-0, 207, Fort Wayne, Ind.; (tie) RB—Trevor Cobb, Rice, 5-9, 180, Houston, Texas; Russell White, California, 6-0, 210, Van Nuys, Calif.; PK—Carlos Huerta, Miami (Fla.), 5-9, 186, Miami, Fla.

Defense DL—*Steve Emtman, Washington, 6-4, 280, Cheney, Wash.; DL—*Santana Dotson, Baylor, 6-5, 264, Houston, Texas; DL—Brad Culpepper, Florida, 6-2, 263, Tallahassee, Fla.; DL—Leroy Smith, Iowa, 6-2, 214, Sicklerville, N.J.; LB—*Robert Jones, East Carolina, 6-3, 234, Blackstone, Va.; LB—Marvin Jones, Florida St., 6-2, 220, Miami, Fla.; LB—Levon Kirkland, Clemson, 6-2, 245, Lamar, S.C.; DB—*Terrell Buckley, Florida St., 5-10, 175, Pascagoula, Miss.; DB—Dale Carter, Tennessee, 6-2, 182, Oxford, Ga.; DB—Kevin Smith, Texas A&M, 6-0, 180, Orange, Texas; DB—Darryl Williams, Miami (Fla.), 6-2, 190, Miami, Fla.; P—*Mark Bounds, Texas Tech, 5-11, 185, Stamford, Texas.

1992

Offense WR—O. J. McDuffie, Penn St., 5-11, 185, Warrensville Heights, Ohio; WR—Sean Dawkins, California, 6-4, 205, Sunnyvale, Calif.; TE—*Chris Gedney, Syracuse, 6-5, 256, Liverpool, N.Y.; OL—*Lincoln Kennedy, Washington, 6-7, 325, San Diego, Calif.; OL—*Will Shields, Nebraska, 6-1, 305, Lawton, Okla.; OL—Aaron Taylor, Notre Dame, 6-4, 294, Concord, Calif.; (tie) OL—Willie Roaf, Louisiana Tech, 6-5, 300, Pine Bluff, Ark.; Everett Lindsay, Mississippi, 6-5, 290, Raleigh, N.C.; C—Mike Compton, West Virginia, 6-7, 289, Richlands, Va.; QB—*Gino Torretta, Miami (Fla.), 6-3, 205, Pinole, Calif.; RB—*Marshall Faulk, San Diego St., 5-10, 200, New Orleans, La.; RB—*Garrison Hearst, Georgia, 5-11, 202, Lincolnton, Ga.; PK—Joe Allison, Memphis, 6-0, 184, Atlanta, Ga.

Defense DL—Eric Curry, Alabama, 6-6, 265, Thomasville, Ga.; DL—John Copeland, Alabama, 6-3, 261, Lanett, Ala.; DL—Chris Slade, Virginia, 6-5, 235, Tabb, Va.; DL—Rob Waldrop, Arizona, 6-2, 265, Phoenix, Ariz.; LB—*Marcus Buckley, Texas A&M, 6-4, 230, Fort Worth, Texas; LB—*Marvin Jones, Florida St., 6-2, 235, Miami, Fla.; LB—Micheal Barrow, Miami (Fla.), 6-2, 230, Homestead, Fla.; DB—*Carlton McDonald, Air Force, 6-0, 185, Jacksonville, Fla.; DB—Carlton Gray, UCLA, 6-0, 194, Cincinnati, Ohio; DB—Deon Figures, Colorado, 6-1, 195, Compton, Calif.; DB—Ryan McNeil, Miami (Fla.), 6-2, 185, Fort Pierce, Fla.; P—Sean Snyder, Kansas St., 6-1, 190, Greenville, Texas.

1993

Offense WR—*J. J. Stokes, UCLA, 6-5, 214, San Diego, Calif.; WR—Johnnie Morton, Southern California, 6-0, 190, Torrance, Calif.; OL—Mark Dixon, Virginia, 6-4, 283, Jamestown, N.C.; OL—Stacy Seegars, Clemson, 6-4, 320, Kershaw, S.C.; OL—*Aaron Taylor, Notre Dame, 6-4, 299, Concord, Calif.; OL—Wayne Gandy, Auburn, 6-5, 275, Haines City, Fla.; C—*Jim Pyne, Virginia Tech, 6-2, 280, Milford, Mass.; QB—*Charlie Ward, Florida St., 6-2, 190, Thomasville, Ga.; RB—*Marshall Faulk, San Diego St., 5-10, 200, New Orleans, La.; RB—*LeShon Johnson, Northern Ill., 6-0, 201, Haskell, Okla.; PK—Bjorn Merten, UCLA, 6-0, 203, Centreville, Va.; KR—David Palmer, Alabama, 5-9, 170, Birmingham, Ala.

Defense DL—*Rob Waldrop, Arizona, 6-2, 275, Phoenix, Ariz.; DL—Dan Wilkinson, Ohio St., 6-5, 300, Dayton, Ohio; DL—Sam Adams, Texas A&M, 6-4, 269, Cypress, Texas; LB—*Trev Alberts, Nebraska, 6-4, 240, Cedar Falls, Iowa; LB—*Derrick Brooks, Florida St., 6-1, 225, Pensacola, Fla.; LB—Jamir Miller, UCLA, 6-4, 233, El Cerrito, Calif.; DB—*Antonio Langham, Alabama, 6-1, 170, Town Creek, Ala.; DB—Aaron Glenn, Texas A&M, 5-10, 182, Aldine, Texas; DB—Jeff Burris, Notre Dame, 6-0, 204, Rock Hill, S.C.; DB—Corey Sawyer, Florida St., 5-11, 171, Key West, Fla.; P—Terry Daniel, Auburn, 6-1, 226, Valley, Ala.

1994

Offense WR—Jack Jackson, Florida, 5-9, 171, Moss Point, Miss.; WR—Michael Westbrook, Colorado, 6-4, 210, Detroit, Mich.; TE—Pete Mitchell, Boston College, 6-2, 238, Bloomfield Hills, Mich.; OL—*Zach Wiegert, Nebraska, 6-5, 300, Fremont, Neb.; OL—Tony Boselli, Southern California, 6-8, 305, Boulder, Colo.; OL—Korey Stringer, Ohio St., 6-5, 315, Warren, Ohio; OL—Brenden Stai, Nebraska, 6-4, 300, Yorba Linda, Calif.; C—Cory Raymer, Wisconsin, 6-4, 290, Fond du Lac, Wis.; QB—Kerry Collins, Penn St., 6-5, 235, West Lawn, Pa.; RB—*Rashaan Salaam, Colorado, 6-1, 210, San Diego, Calif.; RB—*Ki-Jana Carter, Penn St., 5-10, 212, Westerville, Ohio; PK—Steve McLaughlin, Arizona, 6-1, 175, Tucson, Ariz.; KR—Leeland McElroy, Texas A&M, 5-11, 200, Beaumont, Texas.

Defense DL—*Warren Sapp, Miami (Fla.), 6-3, 284, Plymouth, Fla.; DL—Tedy Bruschi, Arizona, 6-1, 255, Roseville, Calif.; DL—Luther Elliss, Utah, 6-6, 288, Mancos, Colo.; DL Kevin Carter, Florida, 6-6, 265, Tallahassee, Fla.; LB—*Dana Howard, Illinois, 6-0, 235, East St. Louis, Ill.; LB—Ed Stewart, Nebraska, 6-1, 215, Chicago, Ill.; LB—Derrick Brooks, Florida St., 6-1, 226, Pensacola, Fla.; DB—Clifton Abraham, Florida St., 5-9, 185, Dallas, Texas; DB—Bobby Taylor, Notre Dame, 6-3, 201, Longview, Texas; DB—Chris Hudson, Colorado, 5-11, 195, Houston, Texas; DB—Brian Robinson, Auburn, 6-3, 194, Fort Lauderdale, Fla.; DB—Tony Bouie, Arizona, 5-10, 183, New Orleans, La.; P—*Todd Sauerbrun, West Virginia, 6-0, 205, Setauket, N.Y.

1995

Offense WR—Terry Glenn, Ohio St., 5-11, 185, Columbus, Ohio; WR—*Keyshawn Johnson, Southern California, 6-4, 210, Los Angeles, Calif.; TE—*Marco Battaglia, Rutgers, 6-3, 240, Queens, N.Y.; OL—*Jonathan Ogden, UCLA, 6-8, 310, Washington, D.C.; OL—*Jason Odom, Florida, 6-5, 291, Bartow, Fla.; OL—*Orlando Pace, Ohio St., 6-6, 320, Sandusky, Ohio; OL—Jeff Hartings, Penn St., 6-3, 278, St. Henry, Ohio; (tie) C—Clay Shiver, Florida St., 6-2, 285, Tifton, Ga.; Bryan Stoltenberg, Colorado, 6-2, 280, Sugarland, Texas; QB—Tommie Frazier, Nebraska, 6-2, 205, Bradenton, Fla.; RB—*Eddie George, Ohio St., 6-3, 230, Philadelphia, Pa.; RB—Troy Davis, Iowa St., 5-8, 182, Miami, Fla.; PK—Michael Reeder, TCU, 6-0, 160, Sulphur, La.

Defense DL—*Tedy Bruschi, Arizona, 6-1, 253, Roseville, Calif.; DL—Cornell Brown, Virginia Tech, 6-2, 240, Lynchburg, Va.; DL—Marcus Jones, North Carolina, 6-6, 270, Jacksonville, N.C.; DL—Tony Brackens, Texas, 6-4, 250, Fairfield, Texas; LB—*Zach Thomas, Texas Tech, 6-0, 232, Pampa, Texas; LB—Kevin Hardy, Illinois, 6-4, 243, Evansville, Ind.; LB—Pat Fitzgerald, Northwestern, 6-4, 228, Orland Park, Ill.; DB—Chris Canty, Kansas St., 5-10, 190, Voorhees, N.J.; DB—*Lawyer Milloy, Washington, 6-2, 200, Tacoma, Wash.; DB—Aaron Beasley, West Virginia, 6-0, 190, Pottstown, Pa.; DB—Greg Myers, Colorado St., 6-2, 191, Windsor, Colo.; P—Brad Maynard, Ball St., 6-1, 175, Atlanta, Ind.

1996

Offense WR—Marcus Harris, Wyoming, 6-2, 216, Senior, Minneapolis, Minn.; (tie) WR—Ike Hilliard, Florida, 5-11, 182, Junior, Patterson, La.; Reidel Anthony, Florida, 6-0, 181, Junior, South Bay, Fla.; TE—Tony Gonzalez, California, 6-6, 235, Junior, Huntington Beach, Calif.; OL—*Orlando Pace, Ohio St., 6-6, 330, Junior, Sandusky, Ohio; OL—Juan Roque, Arizona St., 6-8, 319, Senior, Ontario, Calif.; OL—Chris Naeole, Colorado, 6-4, 310, Senior, Kaaava, Hawaii; OL—Dan Neil, Texas, 6-2, 283, Senior, Cypress Creek, Texas; OL—Benji Olson, Washington, 6-4, 310, Sophomore, Port Orchard, Wash.; C—Aaron Taylor, Nebraska, 6-1, 305, Junior, Wichita Falls, Texas; QB—Danny Wuerffel, Florida, 6-2, 209, Senior, Fort Walton Beach, Fla.; RB—*Byron Hanspard, Texas Tech, 6-0, 193, Junior, DeSoto, Texas; RB—Troy Davis, Iowa St., 5-8, 185, Junior, Miami, Fla.; PK—Marc Primanti, North Carolina St., 5-7, 171, Senior, Thorndale, Pa.

Defense DL—Grant Wistrom, Nebraska, 6-5, 250, Junior, Webb City, Mo.; DL—Peter Boulware, Florida St., 6-5, 255, Junior, Columbia, S.C.; DL—Reinard Wilson, Florida St., 6-2, 255, Senior, Lake City, Fla.; (tie) DL—Derrick Rodgers, Arizona St., 6-2, 220, Junior, Cordova, Tenn.; Mike Vrabel, Ohio St., 6-4, 260, Senior, Akron, Ohio; LB—#Canute Curtis, West Virginia, 6-2, 250, Senior, Amityville, N.Y.; LB—Pat Fitzgerald, Northwestern, 6-2, 243, Senior, Orland Park, Ill.; LB—Matt Russell, Colorado, 6-2, 245, Senior, Fairview Heights, Ill.; LB—Jarrett Irons, Michigan, 6-2, 234, Senior, The Woodlands, Texas; DB—*Chris Canty, Kansas St., 5-10, 190, Junior, Voorhees, N.J.; DB—*Kevin Jackson, Alabama, 6-2, 206, Senior, Dothan, Ala.; DB—Dre' Bly, North Carolina, 5-10, 180, Freshman, Chesapeake, Va.; DB—Shawn Springs, Ohio St., 6-0, 188, Junior, Silver Spring, Md.; P—Brad Maynard, Ball St., 6-1, 176, Senior, Atlanta, Ind.

1997

Offense WR—*Randy Moss, Marshall, 6-5, 210, Sophomore, Rand, W.Va.; WR—Jacquez Green, Florida, 5-9, 168, Junior, Ft. Valley, Ga.; TE—Alonzo Mayes, Oklahoma St., 6-6, 265, Senior, Oklahoma City, Okla.; OL—*Aaron Taylor, Nebraska, 6-1, 305, Senior, Wichita Falls, Texas; OL—Alan Faneca, LSU, 6-5, 310, Junior, Rosenberg, Texas; OL—Kyle Turley, San Diego St., 6-6, 305, Senior, Moreno Valley, Calif.; OL—Chad Overhauser, UCLA, 6-6, 304, Senior, Sacramento, Calif.; C—Olin Kreutz, Washington, 6-4, 290, Junior, Honolulu, Hawaii; QB—Peyton Manning, Tennessee, 6-5, 222, Senior, New Orleans, La.; RB—*Ricky Williams, Texas, 6-0, 220, Junior, San Diego, Calif.; RB—Curtis Enis, Penn St., 6-1, 233, Junior, Union City, Ohio; PK—Martin Gramatica, Kansas St., 5-9, 170, Junior, Buenos Aires, Argentina; KR—Tim Dwight, Iowa, 5-9, 185, Senior, Iowa City, Iowa.

Defense DL—Grant Wistrom, Nebraska, 6-5, 255, Senior, Webb City, Mo.; DL—Andre Wadsworth, Florida St., 6-4, 282, Senior, Miami, Fla.; DL—Greg Ellis, North Carolina, 6-6, 265, Senior, Wendell, N.C.; DL—Jason Peter, Nebraska, 6-5, 285, Senior, Locust, N.J.; LB—Andy Katzenmoyer, Ohio St., 6-4, 260, Sophomore, Westerville, Ohio; LB—Sam Cowart, Florida St., 6-3, 239, Senior, Jacksonville, Fla.; LB—Anthony Simmons, Clemson, 6-1, 225, Junior, Spartanburg, S.C.; LB—Brian Simmons, North Carolina, 6-4, 230, Senior, New Bern, N.C.; DB—*Charles Woodson, Michigan, 6-1, 198, Junior, Fremont, Ohio; DB—Dre' Bly, North Carolina, 5-10, 185, Sophomore, Chesapeake, Va.; DB—Fred Weary, Florida, 5-10, 180, Senior, Jacksonville, Fla.; DB—Brian Lee, Wyoming, 6-2, 200, Senior, Arvada, Colo.; P—Chad Kessler, LSU, 6-1, 197, Senior, Longwood, Fla.

1998

Offense WR—Torry Holt, North Carolina St., 6-2, 188, Senior, Gibsonville, N.C. (Eastern Guilford HS); WR—Peter Warrick, Florida St., 6-0, 190, Junior, Bradenton, Fla. (Southeast HS); WR —Troy Edwards, Louisiana Tech, 5-10, 195, Senior, Shreveport, La. (Huntington HS); TE—*Rufus French, Mississippi, 6-4, 245, Junior, Amory, Miss. (Amory HS); OL—Kris Farris, UCLA, 6-9, 310, Junior, Mission Viejo, Calif. (Santa Margarita HS); OL—Aaron Gibson, Wisconsin, 6-7, 372, Senior, Indianapolis, Ind. (Decatur Central HS); OL—Matt Stinchcomb, Georgia, 6-6, 291, Senior, Lilburn, Ga. (Lilburn HS); OL—Rob Murphy, Ohio St., 6-5, 300, Junior, Cincinnati, Ohio (Moeller HS); C—Craig Page, Georgia Tech, 6-3, 288, Senior, Jupiter, Fla. (Jupiter HS); (tie) QB—Cade McNown, UCLA, 6-1, 214, Senior, West Linn, Ore. (West Linn HS); Michael Bishop, Kansas St., 6-1, 205,

Senior, Willis, Texas (Willis HS); Tim Couch, Kentucky, 6-5, 225, Junior, Hyden, Ky. (Leslie County HS); RB—*Ricky Williams, Texas, 6-0, 225, Senior, San Diego, Calif. (Patrick Henry HS); RB—Mike Cloud, Boston College, 5-11, 201, Senior, Portsmouth, R.I. (Portsmouth HS); PK—Sebastian Janikowski, Florida St., 6-2, 255, Sophomore, Daytona Beach, Fla. (Seabreeze HS); KR—David Allen, Kansas St., 5-9, 185, Sophomore, Liberty, Mo. (Liberty HS).

Defense DL—*Tom Burke, Wisconsin, 6-4, 249, Senior, Poplar, Wis. (Northwestern HS); DL—Montae Reagor, Texas Tech, 6-2, 254, Senior, Waxahachie, Texas (Waxahachie HS); DL—Jared DeVries, Iowa, 6-4, 284, Senior, Aplington, Iowa (Aplington-Parkersburg HS); LB—*Chris Claiborne, Southern California, 6-3, 250, Junior, Riverside, Calif. (North HS); LB—*Dat Nguyen, Texas A&M, 6-0, 216, Senior, Rockport, Texas (Rockport-Fulton HS); LB—Jeff Kelly, Kansas St., 6-0, 250, Senior, LaGrange, Texas (LaGrange HS); LB—Al Wilson, Tennessee, 6-0, 226, Senior, Jackson, Tenn. (Central Merry HS); DB—*Chris McAlister, Arizona, 6-2, 185, Senior, Pasadena, Calif. (Pasadena HS); DB—*Antoine Winfield, Ohio St., 5-9, 180, Senior, Akron, Ohio (Garfield HS); DB—Champ Bailey, Georgia, 6-1, 186, Junior, Folkston, Ga. (Folkston HS); DB—Anthony Poindexter, Virginia, 6-1, 220, Senior, Forest, Va. (Jefferson Forest HS); P—Joe Kristosik, UNLV, 6-3, 220, Junior, Las Vegas, Nev. (Bishop Gorman HS).

1999

Offense WR—Troy Walters, Stanford, 5-8, 170, Senior, College Station, Texas (A&M Consolidated HS); WR—*Peter Warrick, Florida St., 6-0, 195, Senior, Bradenton, Fla. (Southeast HS); TE—James Whalen, Kentucky, 6-4, 231, Senior, Portland, Ore. (LaSalle HS); OL—*Chris McIntosh, Wisconsin, 6-7, 310, Senior, Pewaukee, Wis. (Pewaukee HS); OL—*Chris Samuels, Alabama, 6-6, 291, Senior, Mobile, Ala. (Shaw HS); OL—Cosey Coleman, Tennessee, 6-5, 315, Junior, Clarkston, Ga. (Southwest DeKalb HS); OL—Jason Whitaker, Florida St., 6-5, 300, Senior, Panama City, Fla. (Moseley HS); C—Ben Hamilton, Minnesota, 6-5, 271, Junior, Plymouth, Minn. (Wayzata HS); C—Rob Riti, Missouri, 6-3, 289, Senior, Florissant, Mo. (Hazelwood West HS); QB—Joe Hamilton, Georgia Tech, 5-10, 189, Senior, Alvin, S.C. (Macedonia HS); RB—*Ron Dayne, Wisconsin, 5-10, 254, Senior, Berlin, N.J. (Overbrook HS); RB—Thomas Jones, Virginia, 5-10, 205, Senior, Big Stone Gap, Va. (Powell Valley HS); PK—*Sebastian Janikowski, Florida St., 6-2, 255, Junior, Daytona Beach, Fla. (Seabreeze HS); AP—Dennis Northcutt, Arizona, 5-11, 178, Senior, Los Angeles, Calif. (Dorsey HS).

Defense DL—*Courtney Brown, Penn St., 6-5, 270, Senior, Alvin, S.C. (Macedonia HS); DL—*Corey Moore, Virginia Tech, 6-0, 225, Senior, Brownsville, Tenn. (Haywood HS); DL—Corey Simon, Florida St., 6-4, 275, Senior, Pompano Beach, Fla. (Ely HS); LB—*LaVar Arrington, Penn St., 6-3, 242, Junior, Pittsburgh, Pa. (North Hills HS); LB—Mark Simoneau, Kansas St., 6-0, 240, Senior, Smith Center, Kan. (Smith Center HS); LB—Brandon Short, Penn St., 6-3, 252, Senior, McKeesport, Pa. (McKeesport HS); DB—Tyrone Carter, Minnesota, 5-9, 184, Senior, Pompano Beach, Fla. (Ely HS); DB—Brian Urlacher, New Mexico, 6-4, 240, Senior, Lovington, N.M. (Lovington HS); DB—Ralph Brown, Nebraska, 5-10, 180, Senior, Hacienda Heights, Calif. (Bishop Amat HS); DB—Deon Grant, Tennessee, 6-3, 205, Junior, Augusta, Ga. (Josey HS); DB—Deltha O'Neal, California, 5-11, 195, Senior, Milpitas, Calif. (Milpitas HS); P—Andrew Bayes, East Caro., 6-3, 200, Senior, Hyattsville, Md. (DeMatha HS).

2000

Offense WR—Marvin Minnis, Florida St., 6-1, 185, Senior, Miami, Fla. (Northwestern HS); (tie) WR—Antonio Bryant, Pittsburgh, 6-2, 185, Sophomore, Miami, Fla. (Northwestern HS); Fred Mitchell, UCLA, 6-0, 188, Junior, Lakeland, Fla. (Kathleen HS); TE—*Brian Natkin, UTEP, 6-4, 245, Senior, San Antonio,

Texas (Churchill HS); OL—*Steve Hutchinson, Michigan, 6-5, 299, Senior, Coral Springs, Fla. (Coral Springs HS); OL—Ben Hamilton, Minnesota, 6-5, 285, Senior, Plymouth, Minn. (Wayzata HS); OL—Chris Brown, Georgia Tech, 6-6, 315, Senior, Augusta, Ga. (Butler HS); OL—Leonard Davis, Texas, 6-6, 365, Senior, Wortham, Texas (Wortham HS); C—Dominic Raiola, Nebraska, 6-2, 300, Junior, Honolulu, Hawaii (St. Louis HS); QB—Josh Heupel, Oklahoma, 6-2, 214, Senior, Aberdeen, S.D. (Central HS); RB—*LaDainian Tomlinson, TCU, 5-11, 220, Senior, Waco, Texas (University HS); RB—Damien Anderson, Northwestern, 5-11, 202, Junior, Wilmington, Ill. (Wilmington HS); PK—Jonathan Ruffin, Cincinnati, 5-10, 184, Sophomore, Metairie, La. (Ridgewood Prep HS); AP—Santana Moss, Miami (Fla.), 5-10, 180, Senior, Miami, Fla. (Carol City HS).

Defense DL—*Jamal Reynolds, Florida St., 6-4, 254, Senior, Aiken, S.C. (Aiken HS); DL—*Andre Carter, California, 6-5, 265, Senior, San Jose, Calif. (Oak Grove HS); DL—Casey Hampton, Texas, 6-1, 310, Senior, Galveston, Texas (Ball HS); DL—John Henderson, Tennessee, 6-7, 290, Junior, Nashville, Tenn. (Pearl Cohn HS); LB—*Dan Morgan, Miami (Fla.), 6-3, 245, Senior, Coral Springs, Fla. (Taravella HS); LB—Rocky Calmus, Oklahoma, 6-3, 240, Junior, Jenks, Okla. (Jenks HS); LB—Keith Adams, Clemson, 5-11, 220, Junior, College Park, Ga. (Westlake HS); DB—Dwight Smith, Akron, 5-11, 205, Senior, Detroit, Mich. (Central HS); DB—Jamar Fletcher, Wisconsin, 5-10, 175, Junior, St. Louis, Mo. (Hazelwood East HS); DB—Fred Smoot, Mississippi St., 6-1, 179, Senior, Jackson, Miss. (Provine HS); (tie) DB—Tay Cody, Florida St., 5-11, 180, Senior, Blakely, Ga. (Early County HS); Edward Reed, Miami (Fla.), 6-0, 190, Junior, St. Rose, La. (Destrehan HS); J. T. Thatcher, Oklahoma, 6-0, 225, Senior, Norman, Okla. (Norman HS); P—Nick Harris, California, 6-3, 225, Senior, Avondale, Ariz. (Westview HS).

2001

Offense WR—*Jabar Gaffney, Florida, 6-1, 197, Sophomore, Jacksonville, Fla. (Raines HS); WR—Josh Reed, LSU, 5-11, 205, Junior, Rayne, La. (Rayne HS); TE—Dan Graham, Colorado, 6-3, 245, Senior, Denver, Colo. (Thomas Jefferson HS); OL—*Bryant McKinnie, Miami (Fla.), 6-9, 335, Senior, Woodbury, N. J. (Woodbury HS); OL—Toniu Fonoti, Nebraska, 6-4, 340, Junior, Hauula, Hawaii (Kahuku HS); (tie) OL—Andre Gurode, Colorado, 6-4, 320, Senior, Houston, Tex. (North Shore HS); Mike Williams, Texas, 6-6, 339, Senior, The Colony, Tex. (The Colony HS); Mike Pearson, Florida, 6-7, 300, Junior, Seffner, Fla. (Armwood HS); Terrence Metcalf, Mississippi, 6-4, 315, Senior, Clarksdale, Miss. (Clarksdale HS); C—LeCharles Bentley, Ohio St., 6-2, 300, Senior, Cleveland, Ohio (St. Ignatius HS); QB—Rex Grossman, Florida, 6-1, 223, Sophomore, Bloomington, Ind. (Bloomington South HS); RB—Luke Staley, Brigham Young, 6-2, 225, Junior, Tualatin, Ore. (Tualatin HS); RB—William Green, Boston College, 6-1, 217, Junior, Atlantic City, N. J. (Holy Spirit HS); PK—Damon Duval, Auburn, 6-1, 186, Junior, Chattanooga, Tenn. (Central HS).

Defense DL—Alex Brown, Florida, 6-4, 254, Senior, White Springs, Fla. (Hamilton County HS); DL—*Dwight Freeney, Syracuse, 6-1, 250, Senior, Bloomfield, Conn. (Bloomfield HS); DL—John Henderson, Tennessee, 6-7, 290, Senior, Nashville, Tenn. (Pearl Cohn HS); DL—*Julius Peppers, North Carolina, 6-6, 285, Junior, Bailey, N.C. (Southern Nash HS); LB—Rocky Calmus, Oklahoma, 6-3, 235, Senior, Jenks, Okla. (Jenks HS); LB—Robert Thomas, UCLA, 6-2, 237, Senior, Imperial, Cal. (Imperial HS); LB—E. J. Henderson, Maryland, 6-2, 238, Junior, Aberdeen, Md. (Aberdeen HS); DB—*Quentin Jammer, Texas, 6-1, 200, Senior, Angleton, Tex. (Angleton HS); DB—*Edward Reed, Miami (Fla.), 6-0, 198, Senior, St. Rose, La. (Destrehan HS); DB—*Roy Williams, Oklahoma, 6-0, 215, Junior, Union City, Cal. (James Logan HS); P—Travis Dorsch, Purdue, 6-6, 222, Junior, Bozeman, Mont. (Bozeman HS).

2002

The 26-man NCAA Consensus All-America Football Team features 14 players on offense and 12 on defense. The players listed had the majority of votes competing against players at that position only. Three first-team votes were considered the minimum number required of the five teams, except in case of ties at those positions. The only tie was at wide receiver, where two players tied with two votes each, both were listed. Seven players were unanimous choices by all five teams used in the consensus chart — Associated Press, Football Writers Association of America, American Football Coaches Association, Walter Camp Foundation and The Sporting News.

Offense WR—*Charles Rogers, Michigan St., 6-4, 205, Junior, Saginaw, Mich. (Saginaw HS); (tie) WR—Reggie Williams, Washington, 6-4, 200, Sophomore, Tacoma, Wash. (Lakes HS); WR—Rashaun Woods, Oklahoma St., 6-2, 187, Junior, Oklahoma City, Okla. (Millwood HS); TE—*Dallas Clark, Iowa, 6-4, 244, Junior, Livermore, Iowa (Twin River Valley HS); OL—Shawn Andrews, Arkansas, 6-5, 345, Sophomore, Camden, Ark. (Fairview HS); OL—Eric Steinbach, Iowa, 6-7, 284, Senior, Lockport, Ill. (Providence Catholic HS); OL—Derrick Dockery, Texas, 6-6, 345, Senior, Garland, Texas (Lakeview Centennial HS); OL—Jordan Gross, Utah, 6-5, 306, Senior, Fruitland, Idaho (Fruitland HS); C—Brett Romberg, Miami (Fla.), 6-3, 290, Senior, Windsor, Ontario, Canada (Belle River HS); QB—Carson Palmer, Southern California, 6-5, 225, Senior, Laguna Niguel, Calif. (Santa Margarita HS); RB—*Larry Johnson, Penn St., 6-2, 222, Senior, State College, Pa. (State College Area HS); RB—Willis McGahee, Miami (Fla.), 6-1, 224, Sophomore, Miami, Fla. (Central HS); PK—Mike Nugent, Ohio St., 5-10, 170, Sophomore, Centerville, Ohio (Centerville HS); AP/KR—Derek Abney, Kentucky, 5-10, 175, Junior, Mosinee, Wis. (Everest HS).

Defense DL—*Terrell Suggs, Arizona St., 6-3, 251, Junior, Chandler, Ariz. (Hamilton HS); DL—David Pollack, Georgia, 6-2, 275, Sophomore, Snellville, Ga. (Shiloh HS); DL—Rien Long, Washington St., 6-6, 287, Junior, Anacortes, Wash. (Anacortes HS); DL—Tommie Harris, Oklahoma, 6-3, 280, Sophomore, Killeen, Texas (Ellison HS); **LB—E. J. Henderson, Maryland, 6-2, 250, Senior, Aberdeen, Md. (Aberdeen HS)**; LB—Teddy Lehman, Oklahoma, 6-2, 244, Junior, Fort Gibson, Okla. (Fort Gibson HS); LB—Matt Wilhelm, Ohio St., 6-5, 245, Senior, Lorain, Ohio (Elyria Catholic HS); DB—*Mike Doss, Ohio St., 5-11, 204, Senior, Canton, Ohio (McKinley HS); DB—*Terence Newman, Kansas St., 5-11, 185, Senior, Salina, Kan. (Central HS); DB—*Shane Walton, Notre Dame, 5-11, 185, Senior, San Diego, Calif. (Bishops School HS); DB—Troy Polamalu, Southern California, 5-10, 215, Senior, Tenmile, Ore. (Douglas HS); P—Mark Mariscal, Colorado, 6-2, 200, Senior, Tallahassee, Fla. (Lincoln HS).
*—Indicates unanimous selection. **Boldface indicates consensus repeater from 2001.**
Consensus Team Class Makeup: 13 seniors, 7 juniors and 6 sophomores.

Other First-Team Votes from the Five Consensus Teams
Offense
QB Ken Dorsey, Miami (Fla.) (2* votes); QB Brad Banks, Iowa (1*); RB Chris Brown, Colorado (1); WR Nate Burleson, Nevada (1); C Jeff Faine, Notre Dame (1); OL Brett Williams, Florida St. (1); OL Bruce Nelson, Iowa (1); OL Derrick Roche, Washington St. (1); Jon Stinchcomb, Georgia (1); OL Wayne Lucier, Colorado (1); PK Nate Kaeding, Iowa (2); AP/KR DeJuan Groce, Nebraska (1).
Defense
DL Jimmy Kennedy, Penn St. (2); DL Calvin Pace, Wake Forest (1); DL Cory Redding, Texas (1); DL Michael Haynes, Penn St. (1); DL Jerome McDougle, Miami (Fla.) (1); LB Boss Bailey, Georgia (2); LB Bradie James, LSU (2); DB Terrence Holt, North Carolina St. (1); DB Brandon Everage, Oklahoma (1); P Andy Groom, Ohio St. (1).

*Tied for Walter Camp vote at QB.

Consensus All-Americans by College

Beginning in 1924, unanimous selections are indicated by (*).

AIR FORCE
58— Brock Strom, T
70— Ernie Jennings, E
85— Scott Thomas, DB
87— *Chad Hennings, DL
92— *Carlton McDonald, DB

AKRON
2000—Dwight Smith, DB

ALABAMA
30— *Fred Sington, T
34— Don Hutson, E
        Bill Lee, T
        Dixie Howell, B
35— Riley Smith, B
37— Leroy Monsky, G
41— Holt Rast, E
42— Joe Domnanovich, C
45— Vaughn Mancha, C
61— *Billy Neighbors, T
62— *Lee Roy Jordan, C
65— Paul Crane, C
66— Ray Perkins, E
        *Cecil Dowdy, T
67— Dennis Homan, E
        Bobby Johns, DB
71— Johnny Musso, B
72— *John Hannah, G
73— Buddy Brown, G
74— Leroy Cook, DL
        Woodrow Lowe, LB
75— *Leroy Cook, DE
77— Ozzie Newsome, WR
78— Marty Lyons, DL
79— Jim Bunch, T
80— E. J. Junior, DL
81— Tommy Wilcox, DB
82— Mike Pitts, DL
86— *Cornelius Bennett, LB
88— *Derrick Thomas, LB
89— *Keith McCants, LB
90— *Philip Doyle, PK
92— John Copeland, DL
        Eric Curry, DL
93— David Palmer, KR
        *Antonio Langham, DB
96— *Kevin Jackson, DB
99— *Chris Samuels, OL

AMHERST
05— John Hubbard, B

ARIZONA
82— Ricky Hunley, LB
83— *Ricky Hunley, LB
87— Chuck Cecil, DB
90— *Darryll Lewis, DB
92— Rob Waldrop, DL
93— *Rob Waldrop, DL
94— Steve McLaughlin, PK
        Tedy Bruschi, DL
        Tony Bouie, DB
95— *Tedy Bruschi, DL
98— *Chris McAlister, DB
99— Dennis Northcutt, AP

ARIZONA ST.
72— Woody Green, B
73— Woody Green, B
77— John Jefferson, WR
78— *Al Harris, DL
81— Mike Richardson, DB
82— Mike Richardson, DB
        Vernon Maxwell, DL
83— Luis Zendejas, PK
84— David Fulcher, DB
85— David Fulcher, DB
86— Danny Villa, OL
87— Randall McDaniel, OL
96— Juan Roque, OL
        Derrick Rodgers, DL
2002—*Terrell Suggs, DL

ARKANSAS
48— Clyde Scott, B
54— *Bud Brooks, G

65— Glen Ray Hines, T
        Loyd Phillips, DT
66— *Loyd Phillips, DT
68— Jim Barnes, G
69— Rodney Brand, C
70— Dick Bumpas, DT
77— Leotis Harris, G
        Steve Little, K
79— *Greg Kolenda, T
81— *Billy Ray Smith, DL
82— *Billy Ray Smith, DL
        *Steve Korte, OL
88— Kendall Trainor, PK
        Wayne Martin, DL
89— Jim Mabry, OL
2002—Shawn Andrews, OL

ARMY
1898— Charles Romeyn, B
00— William Smith, E
01— Paul Bunker, T
        Charles Daly, B
02— Paul Bunker, T-B
        Robert Boyers, C
04— Arthur Tipton, C
        Henry Torney, B
05— Henry Torney, B
07— William Erwin, G
11— Leland Devore, T
13— Louis Merillat, E
14— John McEwan, C
16— Elmer Oliphant, B
17— Elmer Oliphant, B
22— Ed Garbisch, C
26— Bud Sprague, T
27— Red Cagle, B
28— *Red Cagle, B
29— Red Cagle, B
32— Milt Summerfelt, G
43— *Casimir Myslinski, C
44— Glenn Davis, B
        Doc Blanchard, B
45— Tex Coulter, T
        John Green, G
        *Glenn Davis, B
        *Doc Blanchard, B
46— Hank Foldberg, E
        *Glenn Davis, B
        *Doc Blanchard, B
47— Joe Steffy, G
49— Arnold Galiffa, B
50— *Dan Foldberg, E
57— Bob Anderson, B
58— *Pete Dawkins, B
59— Bill Carpenter, E

AUBURN
32— Jimmy Hitchcock, B
57— *Jimmy Phillips, E
58— Zeke Smith, G
60— Ken Rice, T
64— Tucker Frederickson, B
69— Buddy McClinton, DB
70— Larry Willingham, DB
71— *Pat Sullivan, QB
        *Terry Beasley, E
74— Ken Bernich, LB
83— Bo Jackson, RB
84— Gregg Carr, LB
85— *Bo Jackson, RB
86— *Ben Tamburello, C
        *Brent Fullwood, RB
87— Tracy Rocker, DL
        Aundray Bruce, LB
88— *Tracy Rocker, DL
90— *Ed King, OL
        David Rocker, DL
93— Wayne Gandy, OL
        Terry Daniel, P
94— Brian Robinson, DB
2001— Damon Duval, PK

BALL ST.
95— Brad Maynard, P
96— Brad Maynard, P

BAYLOR
30— Barton Koch, G
56— *Bill Glass, G
63— Lawrence Elkins, E
64— Lawrence Elkins, B
76— Gary Green, DB
79— Mike Singletary, LB
80— *Mike Singletary, LB

86— *Thomas Everett, DB
91— *Santana Dotson, DL

BOSTON COLLEGE
20— Luke Urban, E
40— Gene Goodreault, E
42— Mike Holovak, B
84— *Doug Flutie, QB
        Tony Thurman, DB
85— Mike Ruth, DL
94— Pete Mitchell, TE
98— Mike Cloud, RB
2001— William Green, RB

BRIGHAM YOUNG
79— *Marc Wilson, QB
80— Nick Eyre, OL
81— *Jim McMahon, QB
82— *Gordon Hudson, TE
83— *Gordon Hudson, TE
        *Steve Young, QB
86— Jason Buck, DL
89— Mohammed Elewonibi, OL
90— *Ty Detmer, QB
        *Chris Smith, TE
91— Ty Detmer, QB
2001— Luke Staley, RB

BROWN
02— Thomas Barry, B
06— John Mayhew, B
09— Adrian Regnier, E
10— Earl Sprackling, B
12— George Crowther, B
16— Fritz Pollard, B

CALIFORNIA
21— Brick Muller, E
        Dan McMillan, T
22— Brick Muller, E
24— Edwin Horrell, C
28— Irv Phillips, E
30— Ted Beckett, G
35— Larry Lutz, T
37— Sam Chapman, B
38— Vic Bottari, B
48— Jackie Jensen, B
49— *Rod Franz, G
50— Les Richter, G
51— Les Richter, G
68— Ed White, MG
71— Sherman White, DT
74— Steve Bartkowski, QB
75— Chuck Muncie, RB
        Steve Rivera, E
83— Ron Rivera, LB
91— Russell White, RB
92— Sean Dawkins, WR
96— Tony Gonzalez, TE
99— Deltha O'Neal, DB
2000—*Andre Carter, DL
        Nick Harris, P

CARLISLE
1899— Isaac Seneca, B
03— James Johnson, B
07— Albert Exendine, E
        Peter Hauser, B
11— Jim Thorpe, B
12— Jim Thorpe, B

CARNEGIE MELLON
28— Howard Harpster, B

CENTENARY (LA.)
33— Paul Geisler, E

CENTRE
19— James Weaver, C
        Bo McMillin, B
21— Bo McMillin, B

CHICAGO
1898— Clarence Herschberger, B
04— Fred Speik, E
        Walter Eckersall, B
05— Mark Catlin, E
        Walter Eckersall, B
06— Walter Eckersall, B
08— Walter Steffen, B
13— Paul Des Jardien, C
22— John Thomas, B
24— Joe Pondelik, G
35— *Jay Berwanger, B

CINCINNATI
2000—Jonathan Ruffin, PK

CLEMSON
67— Harry Olszewski, G
74— Bennie Cunningham, TE
79— Jim Stuckey, DL
81— Jeff Davis, LB
        Terry Kinard, DB
82— *Terry Kinard, DB
83— William Perry, DL
86— Terrence Flagler, RB
87— David Treadwell, PK
88— Donnell Woolford, DB
90— Stacy Long, OL
91— Jeb Flesch, OL
        Levon Kirkland, LB
93— Stacy Seegars, OL
97— Anthony Simmons, LB
2000— Keith Adams, LB

COLGATE
13— Ellery Huntington, B
16— Clarence Horning, T
        D. Belford West, T
        Oscar Anderson, B
19— D. Belford West, T
30— Leonard Macaluso, B

COLORADO
37— Byron White, B
60— Joe Romig, G
61— Joe Romig, G
67— Dick Anderson, DB
68— Mike Montler, G
69— Bob Anderson, B
70— Don Popplewell, C
72— Cullen Bryant, DB
85— Barry Helton, P
86— Barry Helton, P
88— Keith English, P
89— Joe Garten, OL
        Alfred Williams, LB
        Tom Rouen, P
90— *Eric Bieniemy, RB
        *Joe Garten, OL
        *Alfred Williams, LB
91— *Jay Leeuwenburg, OL
92— Deon Figures, DB
94— Michael Westbrook, WR
        *Rashaan Salaam, RB
        Chris Hudson, DB
95— Bryan Stoltenberg, C
96— Matt Russell, LB
        Chris Naeole, OL
2001— Dan Graham, TE
        Andre Gurode, OL
02— Mark Mariscal, P

COLORADO ST.
78— Mike Bell, DL
95— Greg Myers, DB

COLUMBIA
00— Bill Morley, B
01— Harold Weekes, B
        Bill Morley, B
03— Richard Smith, B
42— Paul Governali, B
47— Bill Swiacki, E

CORNELL
1895— Clinton Wyckoff, B
00— Raymond Starbuck, B
01— William Warner, G
        Sanford Hunt, G
02— William Warner, G
06— Elmer Thompson, G
        William Newman, C
08— Bernard O'Rourke, G
14— John O'Hearn, E
        Charles Barrett, B
15— Murray Shelton, E
        Charles Barrett, B
21— Edgar Kaw, B
22— Edgar Kaw, B
23— George Pfann, B
38— Brud Holland, E
39— Nick Drahos, T
40— Nick Drahos, T
71— *Ed Marinaro, B

DARTMOUTH
03— Henry Hooper, C
        Myron Witham, B
04— Joseph Gilman, E
05— Ralph Glaze, E
08— George Schildmiller, E

Clark Tobin, G
12— Wesley Englehorn, T
13— Robert Hogsett, E
14— Clarence Spears, G
15— Clarence Spears, G
17— Eugene Neely, G
19— Adolph Youngstrom, G
24— Carl Diehl, G
25— Carl Diehl, G
George Tully, E
*Andy Oberlander, B
38— Bob MacLeod, B

DUKE
33— Fred Crawford, T
36— Ace Parker, B
71— Ernie Jackson, DB
89— *Clarkston Hines, WR

DUQUESNE
36— Mike Basrak, C

EAST CARO.
83— Terry Long, OL
91— *Robert Jones, LB
99— Andrew Bayes, P

FLORIDA
66— *Steve Spurrier, B
69— Carlos Alvarez, E
75— Sammy Green, LB
80— David Little, LB
82— Wilber Marshall, DL
83— Wilber Marshall, LB
84— Lomas Brown, OT
88— Louis Oliver, DB
89— *Emmitt Smith, RB
91— Brad Culpepper, DL
94— Jack Jackson, WR
Kevin Carter, DL
95— *Jason Odom, OL
96— Danny Wuerffel, QB
Ike Hilliard, WR
Reidel Anthony, WR
97— Jacquez Green, WR
Fred Weary, DB
2001—*Jabar Gaffney, WR
Mike Pearson, OL
Rex Grossman, QB
Alex Brown, DL

FLORIDA ST.
64— Fred Biletnikoff, E
67— Ron Sellers, E
79— Ron Simmons, MG
80— Ron Simmons, MG
83— Greg Allen, RB
85— Jamie Dukes, OL
87— *Deion Sanders, DB
88— *Deion Sanders, DB
89— LeRoy Butler, DB
91— *Terrell Buckley, DB
Marvin Jones, LB
92— *Marvin Jones, LB
93— *Charlie Ward, QB
*Derrick Brooks, LB
Corey Sawyer, DB
94— Derrick Brooks, LB
Clifton Abraham, DB
95— Clay Shiver, C
96— Peter Boulware, DL
Reinard Wilson, DL
97— Andre Wadsworth, DL
Sam Cowart, LB
98— Peter Warrick, WR
Sebastian Janikowski, PK
99— *Sebastian Janikowski, PK
*Peter Warrick, WR
Jason Whitaker, OL
Corey Simon, DL
2000— Marvin Minnis, WR
*Jamal Reynolds, DL
Tay Cody, DB

FORDHAM
36— Alex Wojciechowicz, C
37— Ed Franco, T
Alex Wojciechowicz, C

GEORGETOWN
26— Harry Connaughton, G

GEORGIA
27— Tom Nash, E
31— Vernon Smith, E
41— Frank Sinkwich, B

42— *Frank Sinkwich, B
46— *Charley Trippi, B
67— Ed Chandler, T
68— Bill Stanfill, DT
Jake Scott, DB
71— *Royce Smith, G
75— Randy Johnson, G
76— Joel Parrish, G
80— *Herschel Walker, RB
81— *Herschel Walker, RB
82— *Herschel Walker, RB
Terry Hoage, DB
83— Terry Hoage, DB
84— Kevin Butler, PK
Jeff Sanchez, DB
85— Pete Anderson, C
88— Tim Worley, RB
92— *Garrison Hearst, RB
98— Champ Bailey, DB
Matt Stinchcomb, OL
2002—David Pollack, DL

GEORGIA TECH
17— Everett Strupper, B
18— Bill Fincher, E
Joe Guyon, T
Ashel Day, C
20— Bill Fincher, E
28— Pete Pund, C
42— Harvey Hardy, G
44— Phil Tinsley, E
46— Paul Duke, C
47— Bob Davis, T
52— Hal Miller, T
53— Larry Morris, C
59— Maxie Baughan, C
66— Jim Breland, C
70— Rock Perdoni, DT
73— Randy Rhino, DB
90— *Ken Swilling, DB
98— Craig Page, C
99— Joe Hamilton, QB
2000— Chris Brown, OL

HARVARD
1889— Arthur Cumnock, E
John Cranston, G
James Lee, B
1890— Frank Hallowell, E
Marshall Newell, T
John Cranston, C
Dudley Dean, B
John Corbett, B
1891— Marshall Newell, T
Everett Lake, B
1892— Frank Hallowell, E
Marshall Newell, T
Bertram Waters, G
William Lewis, C
Charles Brewer, B
1893— Marshall Newell, T
William Lewis, C
Charles Brewer, B
1894— Bertram Waters, T
1895— Norman Cabot, E
Charles Brewer, B
1896— Norman Cabot, E
Edgar Wrightington, B
1897— Alan Doucette, C
Benjamin Dibblee, B
1898— John Hallowell, E
Walter Boal, G
Charles Daly, B
Benjamin Dibblee, B
1899— David Campbell, E
Charles Daly, B
1900— John Hallowell, E
David Campbell, E
Charles Daly, B
01— David Campbell, E
Edward Bowditch, E
Oliver Cutts, T
Crawford Blagden, T
William Lee, G
Charles Barnard, G
Robert Kernan, B
Thomas Graydon, B
02— Edward Bowditch, E
Thomas Graydon, B
03— Daniel Knowlton, T
Andrew Marshall, G
04— Daniel Hurley, B
05— Beaton Squires, T
Karl Brill, T
Francis Burr, G

Daniel Hurley, B
06— Charles Osborne, T
Francis Burr, G
07— Patrick Grant, C
John Wendell, B
08— Hamilton Fish, T
Charles Nourse, C
Hamilton Corbett, B
09— Hamilton Fish, T
Wayland Minot, B
10— Robert McKay, T
Robert Fisher, G
Percy Wendell, B
11— Robert Fisher, G
Percy Wendell, B
12— Samuel Felton, E
Stanley Pennock, G
Charles Brickley, B
13— Harvey Hitchcock, T
Stanley Pennock, G
Charles Brickley, B
Edward Mahan, B
14— Huntington Hardwick, E
Walter Trumbull, T
Stanley Pennock, G
Edward Mahan, B
15— Joseph Gilman, T
Edward Mahan, B
Richard King, B
16— Harrie Dadmun, G
19— Edward Casey, B
20— Tom Woods, G
21— John Brown, G
22— Charles Hubbard, G
23— Charles Hubbard, G
29— Ben Ticknor, C
30— *Ben Ticknor, C
31— Barry Wood, B
41— *Endicott Peabody, G

HOLY CROSS
74— John Provost, DB

HOUSTON
67— Rich Stotter, G
69— Bill Bridges, G
70— Elmo Wright, E
76— Wilson Whitley, DT
80— Leonard Mitchell, DL
88— Jason Phillips, WR
89— Andre Ware, QB

ILLINOIS
14— Perry Graves, E
Ralph Chapman, G
15— Bart Macomber, B
18— John Depler, C
20— Charles Carney, E
23— James McMillen, G
Red Grange, B
24— *Red Grange, B
25— *Red Grange, B
26— Bernie Shively, G
46— Alex Agase, G
51— Johnny Karras, B
53— J. C. Caroline, B
59— Bill Burrell, G
63— *Dick Butkus, C
64— *Dick Butkus, C
65— *Jim Grabowski, B
84— *David Williams, WR
85— *David Williams, WR
89— *Moe Gardner, DL
90— Moe Gardner, DL
94— *Dana Howard, LB
95— Kevin Hardy, LB

INDIANA
42— Billy Hillenbrand, B
44— John Tavener, C
45— Bob Ravensberg, E
88— Anthony Thompson, RB
89— *Anthony Thompson, RB
91— *Vaughn Dunbar, RB

IOWA
19— Lester Belding, E
21— Aubrey Devine, B
22— Gordon Locke, B
39— Nile Kinnick, B
54— Calvin Jones, G
55— Calvin Jones, G
57— Alex Karras, T
58— *Randy Duncan, B
81— Andre Tippett, DL

Reggie Roby, P
84— Larry Station, LB
85— *Chuck Long, QB
*Larry Station, LB
88— Marv Cook, TE
91— Leroy Smith, DL
97— Tim Dwight, KR
98— Jared DeVries, DL
2002—*Dallas Clark, TE
Eric Steinbach, OL

IOWA ST.
38— Ed Bock, G
89— Mike Busch, TE
95— Troy Davis, RB
96— Troy Davis, RB

KANSAS
63— Gale Sayers, B
64— Gale Sayers, B
68— John Zook, DE
73— David Jaynes, QB

KANSAS ST.
77— Gary Spani, LB
92— Sean Snyder, P
95— Chris Canty, DB
96— *Chris Canty, DB
97— Martin Gramatica, PK
98— Jeff Kelly, LB
Michael Bishop, QB
David Allen, KR
99— Mark Simoneau, LB
2002—*Terence Newman, DB

KENTUCKY
50— Bob Gain, T
Babe Parilli, B
51— Babe Parilli, B
56— Lou Michaels, T
57— Lou Michaels, T
65— Sam Ball, T
77— *Art Still, DL
98— Tim Couch, QB
99— James Whalen, TE
2002—Derek Abney, AP/KR

LAFAYETTE
00— Walter Bachman, C
01— Walter Bachman, C
21— Frank Schwab, G
22— Frank Schwab, G

LSU
35— Gaynell Tinsley, E
36— *Gaynell Tinsley, E
39— Ken Kavanaugh, E
54— Sid Fournet, T
58— *Billy Cannon, B
59— *Billy Cannon, B
61— *Roy Winston, G
62— *Jerry Stovall, B
70— Mike Anderson, LB
Tommy Casanova, DB
71— Tommy Casanova, DB
72— Bert Jones, QB
77— Charles Alexander, RB
78— Charles Alexander, RB
87— Wendell Davis, WR
*Nacho Albergamo, C
97— Alan Faneca, OL
Chad Kessler, P
2001— Josh Reed, WR

LOUISIANA TECH
92— Willie Roaf, OL
98— Troy Edwards, WR

MARQUETTE
36— Ray Buivid, B

MARSHALL
97— *Randy Moss, WR

MARYLAND
51— *Bob Ward, G
52— Dick Modzelewski, T
*Jack Scarbath, B
53— *Stan Jones, T
55— *Bob Pellegrini, C
61— Gary Collins, E
74— *Randy White, DL
76— Joe Campbell, DT
79— Dale Castro, PK
85— J.D. Maarleveld, OL
2001— E.J. Henderson, LB
02— E.J. Henderson, LB

MEMPHIS
92— Joe Allison, PK

MIAMI (FLA.)
61— Bill Miller, E
66— Tom Beier, DB
67— *Ted Hendricks, DE
68— *Ted Hendricks, DE
73— Tony Cristiani, DL
74— Rubin Carter, MG
81— Fred Marion, DB
84— Eddie Brown, WR
85— Willie Smith, TE
86— *Vinny Testaverde, QB
       *Jerome Brown, DL
       Bennie Blades, DB
87— *Daniel Stubbs, DL
       *Bennie Blades, DB
88— Steve Walsh, QB
       Bill Hawkins, DL
89— Greg Mark, DL
90— Maurice Crum, LB
       *Russell Maryland, DL
91— Carlos Huerta, PK
       Darryl Williams, DB
92— *Gino Torretta, QB
       Micheal Barrow, LB
       Ryan McNeil, DB
94— *Warren Sapp, DL
2000— Santana Moss, AP
       *Dan Morgan, LB
       Edward Reed, DB
01— *Bryant McKinnie, OL
       *Edward Reed, DB
02— Willis McGahee, RB
       Brett Romberg, C

MICHIGAN
1898— William Cunningham, C
01— Neil Snow, E
03— Willie Heston, B
04— Willie Heston, B
07— Adolph Schulz, C
09— Albert Benbrook, G
10— Stanfield Wells, E
       Albert Benbrook, G
13— Miller Pontius, T
       Jim Craig, B
14— John Maulbetsch, B
22— Harry Kipke, B
23— Jack Blott, C
25— Bennie Oosterbaan, E
       Benny Friedman, B
26— Bennie Oosterbaan, E
       Benny Friedman, B
27— *Bennie Oosterbaan, E
28— Otto Pommerening, T
32— *Harry Newman, B
33— Francis Wistert, T
       *Chuck Bernard, C
38— *Ralph Heikkinen, G
39— Tom Harmon, B
40— *Tom Harmon, B
41— Bob Westfall, B
42— Albert Wistert, T
       Julie Franks, G
43— *Bill Daley, B
47— *Bob Chappuis, B
48— Dick Rifenburg, E
       Alvin Wistert, T
49— Alvin Wistert, T
55— Ron Kramer, E
56— *Ron Kramer, E
65— Bill Yearby, DT
66— *Jack Clancy, E
69— *Jim Mandich, E
       Tom Curtis, DB
70— Dan Dierdorf, T
71— Reggie McKenzie, G
       *Mike Taylor, LB
72— Paul Seymour, T
       Randy Logan, DB
73— Dave Gallagher, DL
       Dave Brown, DB
74— *Dave Brown, DB
76— Rob Lytle, RB
       Mark Donahue, G
77— *Mark Donahue, G
79— Ron Simpkins, LB
81— *Anthony Carter, WR
       Ed Muransky, OL
       Kurt Becker, G
82— *Anthony Carter, WR

85— Mike Hammerstein, DL
       Brad Cochran, DB
86— Garland Rivers, DB
87— John Elliott, OL
88— John Vitale, C
       *Mark Messner, DL
89— *Tripp Welborne, DB
90— *Tripp Welborne, DB
91— *Desmond Howard, WR
       *Greg Skrepenak, OL
96— Jarrett Irons, LB
97— *Charles Woodson, DB
2000— *Steve Hutchinson, OL

MICHIGAN ST.
15— Neno Jerry DaPrato, B
35— Sidney Wagner, G
49— Ed Bagdon, G
51— Bob Carey, E
       *Don Coleman, T
53— Don Dohoney, E
55— Norman Masters, T
       Earl Morrall, B
57— Dan Currie, C
       Walt Kowalczyk, B
58— Sam Williams, E
62— George Saimes, B
63— Sherman Lewis, B
65— Bubba Smith, DE
       *George Webster, DB
66— Clint Jones, B
       *Bubba Smith, DE
       *George Webster, DB
72— *Brad VanPelt, DB
85— *Lorenzo White, RB
87— Lorenzo White, RB
88— Tony Mandarich, OL
89— *Percy Snow, LB
       Bob Kula, OL
2002— *Charles Rogers, WR

MINNESOTA
03— Fred Schacht, T
09— John McGovern, B
10— James Walker, T
16— Bert Baston, E
17— George Hauser, T
23— Ray Ecklund, E
26— Herb Joesting, B
27— Herb Joesting, B
29— Bronko Nagurski, T
31— Biggie Munn, G
34— Frank Larson, E
       Bill Bevan, G
       Pug Lund, B
35— Ed Widseth, T
36— *Ed Widseth, T
40— Urban Odson, T
       George Franck, B
41— Dick Wildung, T
       Bruce Smith, B
42— Dick Wildung, T
48— Leo Nomellini, T
49— Leo Nomellini, T
       *Clayton Tonnemaker, C
53— *Paul Giel, B
60— *Tom Brown, G
61— Sandy Stephens, B
62— *Bobby Bell, T
63— Carl Eller, T
65— Aaron Brown, DE
99— Tyrone Carter, DB
       Ben Hamilton, C
2000— Ben Hamilton, OL

MISSISSIPPI
47— Charley Conerly, B
53— Crawford Mims, G
59— Charlie Flowers, B
60— *Jake Gibbs, B
62— Jim Dunaway, T
79— Jim Miller, P
92— Everett Lindsay, OL
98— *Rufus French, TE
2001— Terrence Metcalf, OL

MISSISSIPPI ST.
74— Jimmy Webb, DL
2000— Fred Smoot, DB

MISSOURI
41— Darold Jenkins, C
60— *Danny LaRose, E
65— Johnny Roland, DB
68— Roger Wehrli, DB

78— Kellen Winslow, TE
86— John Clay, OL
99— Rob Riti, C

NAVY
07— Bill Dague, E
08— Percy Northcroft, T
       Ed Lange, B
11— Jack Dalton, B
13— John Brown, G
18— Lyman Perry, G
       Wolcott Roberts, B
22— Wendell Taylor, T
26— *Frank Wickhorst, T
28— Edward Burke, G
34— Fred Borries, B
43— Don Whitmire, T
44— *Don Whitmire, T
       Ben Chase, G
       Bob Jenkins, B
45— Dick Duden, E
54— Ron Beagle, E
55— Ron Beagle, E
60— *Joe Bellino, B
63— *Roger Staubach, B
75— *Chet Moeller, DB
83— Napoleon McCallum, RB
85— Napoleon McCallum, RB

NEBRASKA
15— Guy Chamberlin, E
24— Ed Weir, T
25— *Ed Weir, T
33— George Sauer, B
36— Sam Francis, B
63— Bob Brown, G
64— *Larry Kramer, T
65— Freeman White, E
       Walt Barnes, DT
66— LaVerne Allers, G
       Wayne Meylan, MG
67— Wayne Meylan, MG
70— Bob Newton, T
71— Johnny Rodgers, FL
       Willie Harper, DE
       Larry Jacobson, DT
72— *Johnny Rodgers, FL
       Willie Harper, DE
       *Rich Glover, MG
73— *John Dutton, DL
74— Marvin Crenshaw, OT
75— *Rik Bonness, C
76— Dave Butterfield, DB
78— Kelvin Clark, OT
79— *Junior Miller, TE
80— Randy Schleusener, OL
       Jarvis Redwine, RB
81— *Dave Rimington, C
82— *Dave Rimington, C
       Mike Rozier, RB
83— Irving Fryar, WR
       Dean Steinkuhler, OL
       *Mike Rozier, RB
84— *Mark Traynowicz, C
86— *Danny Noonan, DL
88— Jake Young, C
       *Broderick Thomas, LB
89— Jake Young, C
92— *Will Shields, OL
93— *Trev Alberts, LB
94— *Zach Wiegert, OL
       Brenden Stai, OL
       Ed Stewart, LB
95— Tommie Frazier, QB
96— Aaron Taylor, C
       Grant Wistrom, DL
97— *Aaron Taylor, OL
       Grant Wistrom, DL
       Jason Peter, DL
99— Ralph Brown, DB
2000— Dominic Raiola, C
01— Toniu Fonoti, OL

UNLV
98— Joe Kristosik, P

NEW MEXICO
89— Terance Mathis, WR
99— Brian Urlacher, DB

NEW YORK U.
28— Ken Strong, B

NORTH CAROLINA
37— Andy Bershak, E

48— Charlie Justice, B
70— Don McCauley, B
72— Ron Rusnak, G
74— Ken Huff, G
77— Dee Hardison, DL
80— *Lawrence Taylor, LB
83— William Fuller, DL
95— Marcus Jones, DL
96— Dre' Bly, DB
97— Greg Ellis, DL
       Brian Simmons, LB
       Dre' Bly, DB
2001— *Julius Peppers, DL

NORTH CAROLINA ST.
67— Dennis Byrd, DT
73— Bill Yoest, G
78— Jim Ritcher, C
       Ted Brown, RB
79— *Jim Ritcher, C
96— Marc Primanti, PK
98— Torry Holt, WR

NORTH TEXAS
68— Joe Greene, DT

NORTHERN ILL.
93— *LeShon Johnson, RB

NORTHWESTERN
26— Ralph Baker, B
30— Frank Baker, E
31— Jack Riley, T
       Dallas Marvil, T
       Pug Rentner, B
36— Steve Reid, G
40— Alf Bauman, T
45— Max Morris, E
59— Ron Burton, B
62— Jack Cvercko, G
95— Pat Fitzgerald, LB
96— Pat Fitzgerald, LB
2000— Damien Anderson, RB

NOTRE DAME
13— Gus Dorais, B
17— Frank Rydzewski, C
20— George Gipp, B
21— Eddie Anderson, E
24— Harry Stuhldreher, B
       Jimmy Crowley, B
       Elmer Layden, B
26— Bud Boeringer, C
27— John Smith, G
29— Jack Cannon, G
       *Frank Carideo, B
30— *Frank Carideo, B
       Marchy Schwartz, B
31— Tommy Yarr, C
       Marchy Schwartz, B
32— *Joe Kurth, T
34— Jack Robinson, C
35— Wayne Millner, E
37— Chuck Sweeney, E
38— *Ed Beinor, T
41— Bob Dove, E
42— Bob Dove, E
43— John Yonakor, E
       Jim White, T
       Pat Filley, G
       Angelo Bertelli, B
       Creighton Miller, B
46— George Connor, T
       *John Lujack, B
47— George Connor, T
       Bill Fischer, G
       *John Lujack, B
48— Leon Hart, E
       Bill Fischer, G
       Emil Sitko, B
49— *Leon Hart, E
       *Emil Sitko, B
       Bob Williams, B
50— Jerry Groom, C
52— *Johnny Lattner, B
53— Art Hunter, T
       *Johnny Lattner, B
54— *Ralph Guglielmi, B
55— Paul Hornung, B
57— Al Ecuyer, G
59— Monty Stickles, E
64— Jack Snow, E
       John Huarte, B
65— *Dick Arrington, G
       Nick Rassas, B

66— Tom Regner, G
  *Nick Eddy, B
  Alan Page, DE
  *Jim Lynch, LB
67— Tom Schoen, DB
68— George Kunz, T
  Terry Hanratty, QB
69— *Mike McCoy, DT
70— Tom Gatewood, E
  Larry DiNardo, G
71— *Walt Patulski, DE
  Clarence Ellis, DB
72— *Greg Marx, DT
73— Dave Casper, TE
  Mike Townsend, DB
74— Pete Demmerle, WR
  Gerry DiNardo, G
75— *Steve Niehaus, DT
76— Ken MacAfee, TE
  *Ross Browner, DE
77— *Ken MacAfee, TE
  *Ross Browner, DL
  Luther Bradley, DB
78— Dave Huffman, C
  *Bob Golic, LB
79— Vagas Ferguson, RB
80— *John Scully, C
  Bob Crable, LB
81— Bob Crable, LB
87— *Tim Brown, WR
88— Frank Stams, DL
  Michael Stonebreaker, LB
89— *Todd Lyght, DB
  Chris Zorich, DL
90— *Raghib Ismail, WR
  Todd Lyght, DB
  *Michael Stonebreaker, LB
  *Chris Zorich, DL
91— Mirko Jurkovic, OL
92— Aaron Taylor, OL
93— *Aaron Taylor, OL
  Jeff Burris, DB
94— Bobby Taylor, DB
2002—*Shane Walton, DB

OHIO ST.
16— Charles Harley, B
17— Charles Bolen, E
  Charles Harley, B
19— Charles Harley, B
20— Iolas Huffman, G
  Gaylord Stinchcomb, B
21— Iolas Huffman, T
25— Ed Hess, G
28— Wes Fesler, E
29— Wes Fesler, E
30— *Wes Fesler, E
35— Gomer Jones, C
39— Esco Sarkkinen, E
44— Jack Dugger, E
  Bill Hackett, G
  *Les Horvath, B
45— *Warren Amling, G
46— Warren Amling, T
50— *Vic Janowicz, B
54— *Howard Cassady, B
55— *Howard Cassady, B
56— *Jim Parker, G
58— Bob White, B
60— *Bob Ferguson, B
61— *Bob Ferguson, B
68— *Dave Foley, T
69— Jim Otis, B
  Jim Stillwagon, MG
  Jack Tatum, DB
70— *Jim Stillwagon, MG
  *Jack Tatum, DB
72— Randy Gradishar, LB
73— *John Hicks, OT
  *Randy Gradishar, LB
74— Kurt Schumacher, OT
  Steve Myers, C
  *Archie Griffin, RB
75— *Archie Griffin, RB
  Ted Smith, G
  Tim Fox, DB
76— Chris Ward, T
  Bob Brudzinski, DE
77— *Chris Ward, T
  Tom Cousineau, LB
78— Tom Cousineau, LB
79— Ken Fritz, G
82— Marcus Marek, LB

84— Jim Lachey, OG
  *Keith Byars, RB
86— Cris Carter, WR
  Chris Spielman, LB
87— *Chris Spielman, LB
  *Tom Tupa, P
93— Dan Wilkinson, DL
94— Korey Stringer, OL
95— Terry Glenn, WR
  *Orlando Pace, OL
  *Eddie George, RB
96— *Orlando Pace, OL
  Mike Vrabel, DL
  Shawn Springs, DB
97— Andy Katzenmoyer, LB
98— *Antoine Winfield, DB
  Rob Murphy, OL
2001—LeCharles Bentley, C
02— Mike Nugent, PK
  *Mike Doss, DB
  Matt Wilhelm, LB

OKLAHOMA
38— Waddy Young, E
48— Buddy Burris, G
50— Jim Weatherall, T
  Leon Heath, B
51— *Jim Weatherall, T
52— Billy Vessels, B
53— J. D. Roberts, G
54— Max Boydston, E
  Kurt Burris, C
55— Bo Bolinger, G
56— *Jerry Tubbs, C
  Tommy McDonald, B
57— Bill Krisher, G
  Clendon Thomas, B
58— Bob Harrison, C
63— Jim Grisham, B
64— Ralph Neely, T
65— Carl McAdams, LB
67— *Granville Liggins, MG
69— *Steve Owens, B
71— *Greg Pruitt, B
  Tom Brahaney, C
72— *Greg Pruitt, B
  Tom Brahaney, C
73— *Lucious Selmon, DL
  Rod Shoate, LB
74— John Roush, G
  *Joe Washington, RB
  *Rod Shoate, LB
75— *Lee Roy Selmon, DT
  Dewey Selmon, MG
  Jimbo Elrod, DE
76— *Mike Vaughan, OT
77— *Zac Henderson, DB
78— *Greg Roberts, G
  *Billy Sims, RB
79— *Billy Sims, RB
  *George Cumby, LB
80— Louis Oubre, OL
81— Terry Crouch, OL
82— Rick Bryan, DL
83— *Rick Bryan, DL
84— Tony Casillas, DL
85— Tony Casillas, DL
  *Brian Bosworth, LB
86— *Keith Jackson, TE
  *Brian Bosworth, LB
87— *Keith Jackson, TE
  *Mark Hutson, OL
  Dante Jones, LB
  Rickey Dixon, DB
88— *Anthony Phillips, OL
2000— Josh Heupel, QB
  Rocky Calmus, LB
  J. T. Thatcher, DB
01— Rocky Calmus, LB
  *Roy Williams, DB
02— Tommie Harris, DL
  Teddy Lehman, LB

OKLAHOMA ST.
45— Bob Fenimore, B
69— John Ward, T
76— Derrel Gofourth, C
77— *Terry Miller, RB
84— Rod Brown, DB
85— Thurman Thomas, RB
  *Leslie O'Neal, DL
88— Hart Lee Dykes, WR
  *Barry Sanders, RB
97— Alonzo Mayes, TE
2002—Rashaun Woods, WR

OREGON
62— Mel Renfro, B

OREGON ST.
56— John Witte, T
58— Ted Bates, T
62— *Terry Baker, B
63— Vern Burke, E
68— *John Didion, C

PENNSYLVANIA
1891— John Adams, C
1892— Harry Thayer, B
1894— Charles Gelbert, E
  Arthur Knipe, B
  George Brooke, B
1895— Charles Gelbert, E
  Charles Wharton, G
  Alfred Bull, C
  George Brooke, B
1896— Charles Gelbert, E
  Charles Wharton, G
  Wylie Woodruff, G
1897— John Outland, T
  T. Truxton Hare, G
  John Minds, B
1898— T. Truxton Hare, G
  Pete Overfield, C
  John Outland, B
1899— T. Truxton Hare, G
  Pete Overfield, C
  Josiah McCracken, B
00— T. Truxton Hare, G
04— Frank Piekarski, G
  Vincent Stevenson, B
  Andrew Smith, B
05— Otis Lamson, T
  Robert Torrey, C
06— August Ziegler, G
  William Hollenback, B
07— Dexter Draper, T
  August Ziegler, G
08— Hunter Scarlett, E
  William Hollenback, B
10— Ernest Cozens, C
  E. LeRoy Mercer, B
12— E. LeRoy Mercer, B
17— Henry Miller, E
19— Henry Miller, E
22— John Thurman, T
24— Ed McGinley, T
27— Ed Hake, T
28— Paul Scull, B
43— Bob Odell, B
45— George Savitsky, T
47— Chuck Bednarik, C
48— Chuck Bednarik, C

PENN ST.
06— William Dunn, C
19— Bob Higgins, E
20— Charles Way, B
21— Glenn Killinger, B
23— Harry Wilson, B
59— Richie Lucas, B
64— Glenn Ressler, G
68— *Ted Kwalick, E
  Dennis Onkotz, LB
69— *Mike Reid, DT
  Dennis Onkotz, LB
70— Jack Ham, LB
71— Dave Joyner, T
72— Bruce Bannon, DE
  John Skorupan, LB
73— *John Cappelletti, B
74— Mike Hartenstine, DL
75— Greg Buttle, LB
78— *Keith Dorney, OT
  *Chuck Fusina, QB
  *Bruce Clark, DL
79— Bruce Clark, DL
81— *Sean Farrell, OL
86— D.J. Dozier, RB
  Shane Conlan, LB
92— O.J. McDuffie, WR
94— Kerry Collins, QB
  *Ki-Jana Carter, RB
95— Jeff Hartings, OL
97— Curtis Enis, RB
99— *LaVar Arrington, LB
  *Courtney Brown, DL
  Brandon Short, LB
2002—*Larry Johnson, RB

PITTSBURGH
15— Robert Peck, C
16— James Herron, E
  Robert Peck, C
17— Dale Seis, G
  John Sutherland, G
18— Leonard Hilty, T
  Tom Davies, B
  George McLaren, B
20— Herb Stein, C
21— Herb Stein, C
25— *Ralph Chase, T
27— *Gibby Welch, B
28— Mike Getto, T
29— *Joe Donchess, E
  Ray Montgomery, G
31— Jesse Quatse, T
32— Joe Skladany, E
  *Warren Heller, B
33— Joe Skladany, E
34— Chuck Hartwig, G
  George Shotwell, C
36— Averell Daniell, T
37— Tony Matisi, T
  Marshall Goldberg, B
38— *Marshall Goldberg, B
56— *Joe Walton, E
58— John Guzik, B
60— *Mike Ditka, E
63— Paul Martha, B
76— *Tony Dorsett, RB
  Al Romano, MG
77— Tom Brzoza, C
  Randy Holloway, DL
  Bob Jury, DB
78— Hugh Green, DL
79— *Hugh Green, DL
80— *Hugh Green, DL
  *Mark May, OL
81— Sal Sunseri, LB
82— Jimbo Covert, OL
83— *Bill Fralic, OL
84— *Bill Fralic, OT
86— Randy Dixon, OL
  Tony Woods, DL
87— Craig Heyward, RB
88— Mark Stepnoski, OL
90— Brian Greenfield, P
2000— Antonio Bryant, WR

PRINCETON
1889— Hector Cowan, T
  William George, C
  Edgar Allan Poe, B
  Roscoe Channing, B
  Knowlton Ames, B
1890— Ralph Warren, E
  Jesse Riggs, G
  Sheppard Homans, B
1891— Jesse Riggs, G
  Philip King, G
  Sheppard Homans, B
1892— Arthur Wheeler, G
  Philip King, B
1893— Thomas Trenchard, E
  Langdon Lea, T
  Arthur Wheeler, G
  Philip King, B
  Franklin Morse, B
1894— Langdon Lea, T
  Arthur Wheeler, G
1895— Langdon Lea, T
  Dudley Riggs, G
1896— William Church, T
  Robert Gailey, C
  Addison Kelly, B
  John Baird, B
1897— Garrett Cochran, E
  Addison Kelly, B
1898— Lew Palmer, E
  Arthur Hillebrand, T
1899— Arthur Hillebrand, T
  Arthur Poe, E
  Howard Reiter, B
01— Ralph Davis, E
02— John DeWitt, G
03— Howard Henry, E
  John DeWitt, G
  J. Dana Kafer, B
04— James Cooney, T
05— James McCormick, B
06— L. Casper Wister, E

James Cooney, T
Edward Dillon, B
07— L. Casper Wister, E
Edwin Harlan, B
James McCormick, B
08— Frederick Tibbott, B
10— Talbot Pendleton, B
11— Sanford White, E
Edward Hart, T
Joseph Duff, G
12— John Logan, G
13— Harold Ballin, T
14— Harold Ballin, T
16— Frank Hogg, G
18— Frank Murrey, B
20— Stan Keck, T
Donold Lourie, B
21— Stan Keck, G
22— C. Herbert Treat, T
25— Ed McMillan, C
35— John Weller, G
51— *Dick Kazmaier, B
52— Frank McPhee, E
65— Stas Maliszewski, G

PURDUE
29— Elmer Sleight, T
Ralph Welch, B
32— *Paul Moss, E
33— Duane Purvis, B
40— Dave Rankin, E
43— Alex Agase, G
52— Bernie Flowers, E
65— Bob Griese, QB
67— Leroy Keyes, B
68— Leroy Keyes, B
Chuck Kyle, MG
69— *Mike Phipps, QB
72— Otis Armstrong, B
Dave Butz, DT
80— *Dave Young, TE
*Mark Herrmann, QB
86— Rod Woodson, DB
2001— Travis Dorsch, P

RICE
46— Weldon Humble, G
49— James Williams, E
54— Dicky Maegle, B
58— Buddy Dial, E
76— Tommy Kramer, QB
91— Trevor Cobb, RB

RICHMOND
69— Walker Gillette, E
78— Jeff Nixon, DB

RUTGERS
17— Paul Robeson, E
18— Paul Robeson, E
61— Alex Kroll, C
95— *Marco Battaglia, TE

ST. MARY'S (CAL.)
27— Larry Bettencourt, C
45— *Herman Wedemeyer, B

SAN DIEGO ST.
92— *Marshall Faulk, RB
93— *Marshall Faulk, RB
97— Kyle Turley, OL

SANTA CLARA
38— Alvord Wolff, T
39— John Schiechl, C

SOUTH CAROLINA
80— *George Rogers, RB
84— Del Wilkes, OG

SOUTHERN CALIFORNIA
26— Mort Kaer, B
27— Jesse Hibbs, T
Morley Drury, B
30— Erny Pinckert, B
31— John Baker, G
Gus Shaver, B
32— *Ernie Smith, T
33— Aaron Rosenberg, G
*Cotton Warburton, B
39— *Harry Smith, G
43— Ralph Heywood, E
44— John Ferraro, T
47— Paul Cleary, E
52— Elmer Willhoite, G
Jim Sears, B

62— Hal Bedsole, E
65— *Mike Garrett, B
66— Ron Yary, T
Nate Shaw, DB
67— *Ron Yary, T
*O.J. Simpson, B
Tim Rossovich, DE
Adrian Young, LB
68— *O.J. Simpson, B
69— Jim Gunn, DE
70— Charlie Weaver, DE
72— *Charles Young, TE
73— Lynn Swann, WR
Booker Brown, OT
Richard Wood, LB
Artimus Parker, DB
74— *Anthony Davis, RB
Richard Wood, LB
75— *Ricky Bell, RB
76— *Ricky Bell, RB
Gary Jeter, DT
Dennis Thurman, DB
77— *Dennis Thurman, DB
78— *Pat Howell, G
*Charles White, RB
79— *Brad Budde, G
*Charles White, RB
80— Keith Van Horne, OL
*Ronnie Lott, DB
81— Roy Foster, OL
*Marcus Allen, RB
82— *Don Mosebar, OL
Bruce Matthews, OL
George Achica, MG
83— Tony Slaton, C
84— Jack Del Rio, LB
85— Jeff Bregel, OL
86— Jeff Bregel, OL
Tim McDonald, DB
87— Dave Cadigan, OL
89— *Mark Carrier, DB
Tim Ryan, DL
93— Johnnie Morton, WR
94— Tony Boselli, OL
95— *Keyshawn Johnson, WR
98— *Chris Claiborne, LB
2002—Carson Palmer, QB
Troy Polamalu, DB

SOUTHERN METHODIST
35— *J.C. Wetsel, G
Bobby Wilson, B
47— Doak Walker, B
48— *Doak Walker, B
49— Doak Walker, B
50— Kyle Rote, B
51— Dick Hightower, C
66— John LaGrone, MG
68— Jerry LeVias, E
72— Robert Popelka, DB
74— Louie Kelcher, G
78— Emanuel Tolbert, WR
80— John Simmons, DB
82— *Eric Dickerson, RB
83— *Russell Carter, DB
85— Reggie Dupard, RB

STANFORD
24— Jim Lawson, E
25— Ernie Nevers, B
28— Seraphim Post, G
Don Robesky, G
32— Bill Corbus, G
33— Bill Corbus, G
34— Bob Reynolds, T
Bobby Grayson, B
35— James Moscrip, E
*Bobby Grayson, B
40— Frank Albert, B
41— Frank Albert, B
42— Chuck Taylor, G
50— Bill McColl, E
51— *Bill McColl, E
56— John Brodie, QB
70— Jim Plunkett, QB
71— Jeff Siemon, LB
74— Pat Donovan, DL
77— Guy Benjamin, QB
79— Ken Margerum, WR
80— Ken Margerum, WR
82— *John Elway, QB
86— Brad Muster, RB

91— Bob Whitfield, OL
99— Troy Walters, WR
SYRACUSE
08— Frank Horr, T
15— Harold White, G
17— Alfred Cobb, T
18— Lou Usher, T
Joe Alexander, G
19— Joe Alexander, G
23— Pete McRae, E
26— Vic Hanson, E
56— *Jim Brown, B
59— *Roger Davis, G
60— Ernie Davis, B
61— *Ernie Davis, B
67— *Larry Csonka, B
85— *Tim Green, DL
87— *Don McPherson, QB
Ted Gregory, DL
90— John Flannery, C
92— *Chris Gedney, TE
2001— *Dwight Freeney, DL

TEMPLE
85— John Rienstra, OL
86— *Paul Palmer, RB

TENNESSEE
29— Gene McEver, B
33— Beattie Feathers, B
38— Bowden Wyatt, E
39— Ed Molinski, G
George Cafego, B
40— Bob Suffridge, G
46— Dick Huffman, T
51— *Hank Lauricella, B
52— John Michels, G
56— *John Majors, B
65— Frank Emanuel, LB
66— Paul Naumoff, G
67— Bob Johnson, C
68— *Charles Rosenfelder, G
Steve Kiner, LB
69— Chip Kell, G
*Steve Kiner, LB
70— *Chip Kell, G
71— *Bobby Majors, DB
75— Larry Sievers, E
76— Larry Sievers, SE
79— Roland James, DB
83— *Reggie White, DL
84— Bill Mayo, OG
85— Tim McGee, WR
89— *Eric Still, G
90— *Antone Davis, OL
91— Dale Carter, DB
97— Peyton Manning, QB
98— Al Wilson, LB
99— Cosey Coleman, OL
Deon Grant, DB
2000— John Henderson, DL
01— John Henderson, DL

TEXAS
45— Hubert Bechtol, E
46— Hubert Bechtol, E
47— Bobby Layne, B
50— Bud McFadin, G
53— Carlton Massey, E
61— *Jimmy Saxton, B
62— *Johnny Treadwell, G
63— *Scott Appleton, T
65— Tommy Nobis, LB
68— Chris Gilbert, B
69— Bob McKay, T
70— Bobby Wuensch, T
Steve Worster, B
Bill Atessis, DE
71— *Jerry Sisemore, T
72— *Jerry Sisemore, T
73— *Bill Wyman, C
Roosevelt Leaks, B
75— Bob Simmons, T
77— *Earl Campbell, RB
*Brad Shearer, DL
78— *Johnnie Johnson, DB
79— *Steve McMichael, DL
*Johnnie Johnson, DB
80— Kenneth Sims, DL
81— Terry Tausch, OL
*Kenneth Sims, DL
83— Doug Dawson, OL

Jeff Leiding, LB
Jerry Gray, DB
84— Tony Degrate, DL
*Jerry Gray, DB
95— Tony Brackens, DL
96— Dan Neil, OL
97— *Ricky Williams, RB
98— *Ricky Williams, RB
2000— Leonard Davis, OL
Casey Hampton, DL
01— Mike Williams, OL
*Quentin Jammer, DB
02— Derrick Dockery, OL

TEXAS A&M
37— Joe Routt, G
39— John Kimbrough, B
40— Marshall Robnett, G
*John Kimbrough, B
57— *John David Crow, B
70— Dave Elmendorf, DB
74— Pat Thomas, DB
75— *Ed Simonini, LB
Pat Thomas, DB
76— Tony Franklin, PK
*Robert Jackson, LB
85— Johnny Holland, LB
87— John Roper, DL
90— Darren Lewis, RB
91— Kevin Smith, DB
92— *Marcus Buckley, LB
93— Aaron Glenn, DB
Sam Adams, DL
94— Leeland McElroy, KR
98— *Dat Nguyen, LB

TCU
34— Darrell Lester, C
35— Darrell Lester, C
36— Sammy Baugh, B
38— Ki Aldrich, C
*Davey O'Brien, B
55— *Jim Swink, B
59— Don Floyd, T
60— *Bob Lilly, T
84— *Kenneth Davis, RB
91— Kelly Blackwell, TE
95— Michael Reeder, PK
2000— *LaDainian Tomlinson, RB

UTEP
2000— *Brian Natkin, TE

TEXAS TECH
60— E.J. Holub, C
65— Donny Anderson, B
77— Dan Irons, T
82— Gabriel Rivera, DL
91— *Mark Bounds, P
95— *Zach Thomas, LB
96— *Byron Hanspard, RB
98— Montae Reagor, DL

TOLEDO
71— Mel Long, DT

TULANE
31— *Jerry Dalrymple, E
32— Don Zimmerman, B
39— Harley McCollum, T
41— Ernie Blandin, T

TULSA
65— *Howard Twilley, E
91— Jerry Ostroski, OL

UCLA
46— *Burr Baldwin, E
52— Donn Moomaw, C
53— Paul Cameron, B
54— Jack Ellena, T
55— Hardiman Cureton, G
57— Dick Wallen, E
66— Mel Farr, B
67— *Gary Beban, B
Don Manning, LB
69— Mike Ballou, LB
73— Kermit Johnson, B
75— John Sciarra, QB
76— Jerry Robinson, LB
77— *Jerry Robinson, LB
78— *Jerry Robinson, LB
Kenny Easley, DB
79— *Kenny Easley, DB
80— *Kenny Easley, DB
81— *Tim Wrightman, TE

83— Don Rogers, DB
85— *John Lee, PK
88— Troy Aikman, QB
    Darryl Henley, DB
92— Carlton Gray, DB
93— *J. J. Stokes, WR
    Bjorn Merten, PK
    Jamir Miller, LB
95— *Jonathan Ogden, OL
97— Chad Overhauser, OL
98— Cade McNown, QB
    Kris Farris, OL
2000— Fred Mitchell, WR
01— Robert Thomas, LB

UTAH
94— Luther Elliss, DL
2002—Jordan Gross, OL

UTAH ST.
61— Merlin Olsen, T
69— Phil Olsen, DE

VANDERBILT
23— Lynn Bomar, E
24— Henry Wakefield, E
32— Pete Gracey, C
58— George Deiderich, G
82— *Jim Arnold, P
84— *Ricky Anderson, P

VIRGINIA
15— Eugene Mayer, B
41— Bill Dudley, B
85— *Jim Dombrowski, OL
90— Herman Moore, WR
92— Chris Slade, DL
93— Mark Dixon, OL
98— Anthony Poindexter, DB
99— Thomas Jones, RB

VIRGINIA TECH
67— Frank Loria, DB
84— Bruce Smith, DL
93— *Jim Pyne, C
95— Cornell Brown, DL
99— *Corey Moore, DL

WAKE FOREST
76— *Bill Armstrong, DB

WASH. & JEFF.
14— John Spiegel, B
18— Wilbur Henry, T
19— Wilbur Henry, T

WASHINGTON
25— George Wilson, B
28— Charles Carroll, B
36— Max Starcevich, G
40— Rudy Mucha, C
41— Ray Frankowski, G
63— Rick Redman, G
64— Rick Redman, G
66— Tom Greenlee, DT
68— Al Worley, DB
82— *Chuck Nelson, PK
84— Ron Holmes, DL
86— Jeff Jaeger, PK
    Reggie Rogers, DL
91— *Steve Emtman, DL
    Mario Bailey, WR
92— *Lincoln Kennedy, OL
95— *Lawyer Milloy, DB
96— Benji Olson, OL
97— Olin Kreutz, C
2002—Reggie Williams, WR

WASHINGTON ST.
84— Rueben Mayes, RB
88— Mike Utley, OL
89— *Jason Hanson, PK
2002—Rien Long, DL

WEST VIRGINIA
19— Ira Rodgers, B
55— Bruce Bosley, T
82— *Darryl Talley, LB
85— Brian Jozwiak, OL
92— Mike Compton, C
94— *Todd Sauerbrun, P
95— Aaron Beasley, DB
96— Canute Curtis, LB

WILLIAMS
17— Ben Boynton, B
19— Ben Boynton, B

WISCONSIN
12— Robert Butler, T
13— Ray Keeler, G
15— Howard Buck, T
19— Charles Carpenter, C
20— Ralph Scott, T
23— Marty Below, T
30— Milo Lubratovich, T
42— *Dave Schreiner, E
54— *Alan Ameche, B
59— *Dan Lanphear, T
62— Pat Richter, E
75— Dennis Lick, T
81— Tim Krumrie, DL
94— Cory Raymer, C
98— Aaron Gibson, OL
    *Tom Burke, DL
99— *Chris McIntosh, OL
    *Ron Dayne, RB
2000— Jamar Fletcher, DB

WYOMING
83— Jack Weil, P
84— Jay Novacek, TE
96— Marcus Harris, WR
97— Brian Lee, DB

YALE
1889— Amos Alonzo Stagg, E
    Charles Gill, T
    Pudge Heffelfinger, G
1890— William Rhodes, T
    Pudge Heffelfinger, G
    Thomas McClung, B
1891— Frank Hinkey, E
    John Hartwell, E
    Wallace Winter, T
    Pudge Heffelfinger, G
    Thomas McClung, B
1892— Frank Hinkey, E
    A. Hamilton Wallis, T
    Vance McCormick, B
1893— Frank Hinkey, E
    William Hickok, G
    Frank Butterworth, B
1894— Frank Hinkey, E
    William Hickok, G
    Philip Stillman, C
    George Adee, B
    Frank Butterworth, B
1895— Fred Murphy, T
    Samuel Thorne, B
1896— Fred Murphy, T
    Clarence Fincke, B
1897— John Hall, E
    Burr Chamberlin, T
    Gordon Brown, G
    Charles DeSaulles, B
1898— Burr Chamberlin, T
    Gordon Brown, G
    Malcolm McBride, B
1899— George Stillman, T
    Gordon Brown, G
    Malcolm McBride, B
    Albert Sharpe, B

00— George Stillman, T
    James Bloomer, T
    Gordon Brown, G
    Herman Olcott, C
    George Chadwick, B
    Perry Hale, B
    William Fincke, B
01— Henry Holt, C
02— Thomas Shevlin, E
    Ralph Kinney, T
    James Hogan, T
    Edgar Glass, G
    Henry Holt, C
    Foster Rockwell, B
    George Chadwick, B
03— Charles Rafferty, E
    James Hogan, T
    James Bloomer, G
    W. Ledyard Mitchell, B
04— Thomas Shevlin, E
    James Hogan, T
    Ralph Kinney, G
    Foster Rockwell, B
05— Thomas Shevlin, E
    Roswell Tripp, G
    Howard Roome, B
    Guy Hutchinson, B
06— Robert Forbes, E
    L. Horatio Biglow, T
    Hugh Knox, B
    Paul Veeder, B
07— Clarence Alcott, E
    L. Horatio Biglow, T
    Thomas A. D. Jones, B
    Edward Coy, B
08— William Goebel, G
    Hamlin Andrus, G
    Edward Coy, B
09— John Kilpatrick, E
    Henry Hobbs, T
    Hamlin Andrus, G
    Carroll Cooney, C
    Edward Coy, B
    Stephen Philbin, B
10— John Kilpatrick, E
11— Douglass Bomeisler, E
    Henry Ketcham, G
    Arthur Howe, B
12— Douglass Bomeisler, E
    Henry Ketcham, G
13— Nelson Talbott, T
14— Harry LeGore, B
16— Clinton Black, G
20— Tim Callahan, G
21— Malcolm Aldrich, B
23— Century Milstead, T
    William Mallory, B
24— Dick Luman, E
27— Bill Webster, G
    John Charlesworth, C
36— Larry Kelley, E
37— *Clint Frank, B
44— Paul Walker, E

Team Leaders in Consensus All-Americans

(Ranked on Total Number of Selections; Minimum 5 Selections)

Team	No.	Players
Yale	100	69
Notre Dame	94	78
Harvard	89	59
Michigan	68	56
Ohio St.	68	53
Princeton	65	49
Southern California	63	56
Oklahoma	59	49
Nebraska	52	43
Pittsburgh	48	41
Pennsylvania	46	32
Texas	41	36
Alabama	38	37
Army	37	28
Penn St.	34	32
Tennessee	34	25
Miami (Fla.)	32	29
UCLA	32	28
Minnesota	32	27
Florida St.	31	25
Colorado	28	24
Stanford	26	21
Michigan St.	25	22
Auburn	24	22
California	24	22
Georgia	24	20
Navy	23	20
Illinois	23	18
Florida	22	21
Georgia Tech	20	19
Washington	20	19
Texas A&M	20	18
Wisconsin	19	19
Iowa	19	17
Syracuse	19	17
Cornell	19	15
LSU	19	15
Purdue	18	17
Arkansas	18	16
Dartmouth	17	15
Clemson	16	15
Southern Methodist	16	14
Arizona St.	15	12
North Carolina	14	13
Northwestern	13	13
Maryland	12	11
TCU	12	11
Brigham Young	12	10
Arizona	12	9
Oklahoma St.	11	11
Chicago	11	9
Kansas St.	10	9
Kentucky	10	8
Boston College	9	9
Mississippi	9	9
Baylor	9	7
Texas Tech	8	8
Virginia	8	8
West Virginia	8	8
Houston	7	7
Missouri	7	7
North Carolina St.	7	6
Brown	6	6
Rice	6	6
Vanderbilt	6	6
Carlisle	6	5
Colgate	6	5
Columbia	6	5
Indiana	6	5
Air Force	5	5
Oregon St.	5	5
Virginia Tech	5	5

AWARD WINNERS

Special Awards

HEISMAN MEMORIAL TROPHY

Originally presented in 1935 as the DAC Trophy by the Downtown Athletic Club of New York City to the best college player east of the Mississippi River. In 1936, players across the country were eligible and the award was renamed the Heisman Memorial Trophy to honor former college coach and DAC athletics director John W. Heisman. The award now goes to the outstanding college football player in the United States. The bronze trophy was sculpted by Frank Eliscu, with the aid of Jim Crowley, one of Notre Dame's famed Four Horsemen. Crowley was then coach at Fordham, and some of his players posed as models for the trophy.

Year	Player (Winner Bold), School, Position	Points
1935	**Jay Berwanger,** Chicago, HB	84
	2nd—Monk Meyer, Army	29
	3rd—Bill Shakespeare, Notre Dame, HB	23
	4th—Pepper Constable, Princeton, FB	20
1936	**Larry Kelley,** Yale, E	219
	2nd—Sam Francis, Nebraska, FB	47
	3rd—Ray Buivid, Marquette, HB	43
	4th—Sammy Baugh, TCU, HB	39
1937	**Clint Frank,** Yale, HB	524
	2nd—Byron White, Colorado, HB	264
	3rd—Marshall Goldberg, Pittsburgh, HB	211
	4th—Alex Wojciechowicz, Fordham, C	85
1938	**Davey O'Brien,** TCU, QB	519
	2nd—Marshall Goldberg, Pittsburgh, HB	294
	3rd—Sid Luckman, Columbia, QB	154
	4th—Bob MacLeod, Dartmouth, HB	78
1939	**Nile Kinnick,** Iowa, HB	651
	2nd—Tom Harmon, Michigan, HB	405
	3rd—Paul Christman, Missouri, QB	391
	4th—George Cafego, Tennessee, QB	296
1940	**Tom Harmon,** Michigan, HB	1,303
	2nd—John Kimbrough, Texas A&M, FB	841
	3rd—George Franck, Minnesota, HB	102
	4th—Frankie Albert, Stanford, QB	90
1941	**Bruce Smith,** Minnesota, HB	554
	2nd—Angelo Bertelli, Notre Dame, QB	345
	3rd—Frankie Albert, Stanford, QB	336
	4th—Frank Sinkwich, Georgia, HB	249
1942	**Frank Sinkwich,** Georgia, HB	1,059
	2nd—Paul Governali, Columbia, QB	218
	3rd—Clint Castleberry, Georgia Tech, HB	99
	4th—Mike Holovak, Boston College, FB	95
1943	**Angelo Bertelli,** Notre Dame, QB	648
	2nd—Bob Odell, Pennsylvania, HB	177
	3rd—Otto Graham, Northwestern, QB	140
	4th—Creighton Miller, Notre Dame, HB	134
1944	**Les Horvath,** Ohio St., QB/HB	412
	2nd—Glenn Davis, Army, HB	287
	3rd—Doc Blanchard, Army, FB	237
	4th—Don Whitmire, Navy, T	115
1945	* **Doc Blanchard,** Army, FB	860
	2nd—Glenn Davis, Army, HB	638
	3rd—Bob Fenimore, Oklahoma St., HB	187
	4th—Herman Wedemeyer, St. Mary's (Cal.), HB	152
1946	**Glenn Davis,** Army, HB	792
	2nd—Charlie Trippi, Georgia, HB	435
	3rd—Johnny Lujack, Notre Dame, QB	379
	4th—Doc Blanchard, Army, FB	267
1947	**Johnny Lujack,** Notre Dame, QB	742
	2nd—Bob Chappuis, Michigan, HB	555
	3rd—Doak Walker, Southern Methodist, HB	196
	4th—Charlie Conerly, Mississippi, HB	186
1948	* **Doak Walker,** Southern Methodist, HB	778
	2nd—Charlie Justice, North Carolina, HB	443
	3rd—Chuck Bednarik, Pennsylvania, C	336
	4th—Jackie Jensen, California, HB	143
1949	**Leon Hart,** Notre Dame, E	995
	2nd—Charlie Justice, North Carolina, HB	272
	3rd—Doak Walker, Southern Methodist, HB	229
	4th—Arnold Galiffa, Army, QB	196

Year	Player (Winner Bold), School, Position	Points
1950	* **Vic Janowicz,** Ohio St., HB	633
	2nd—Kyle Rote, Southern Methodist, HB	280
	3rd—Reds Bagnell, Pennsylvania, HB	231
	4th—Babe Parilli, Kentucky, QB	214
1951	**Dick Kazmaier,** Princeton, HB	1,777
	2nd—Hank Lauricella, Tennessee, HB	424
	3rd—Babe Parilli, Kentucky, QB	344
	4th—Bill McColl, Stanford, E	313
1952	**Billy Vessels,** Oklahoma, HB	525
	2nd—Jack Scarbath, Maryland, QB	367
	3rd—Paul Giel, Minnesota, HB	329
	4th—Donn Moomaw, UCLA, C	257
1953	**Johnny Lattner,** Notre Dame, HB	1,850
	2nd—Paul Giel, Minnesota, HB	1,794
	3rd—Paul Cameron, UCLA, HB	444
	4th—Bernie Faloney, Maryland, QB	258
1954	**Alan Ameche,** Wisconsin, FB	1,068
	2nd—Kurt Burris, Oklahoma, C	838
	3rd—Howard Cassady, Ohio St., HB	810
	4th—Ralph Guglielmi, Notre Dame, QB	691
1955	**Howard Cassady,** Ohio St., HB	2,219
	2nd—Jim Swink, TCU, HB	742
	3rd—George Welsh, Navy, QB	383
	4th—Earl Morrall, Michigan St., QB	323
1956	**Paul Hornung,** Notre Dame, QB	1,066
	2nd—Johnny Majors, Tennessee, HB	994
	3rd—Tommy McDonald, Oklahoma, HB	973
	4th—Jerry Tubbs, Oklahoma, C	724
1957	**John David Crow,** Texas A&M, HB	1,183
	2nd—Alex Karras, Iowa, T	693
	3rd—Walt Kowalczyk, Michigan St., HB	630
	4th—Lou Michaels, Kentucky, T	330
1958	**Pete Dawkins,** Army, HB	1,394
	2nd—Randy Duncan, Iowa, QB	1,021
	3rd—Billy Cannon, LSU, HB	975
	4th—Bob White, Ohio St., HB	365
1959	**Billy Cannon,** LSU, HB	1,929
	2nd—Richie Lucas, Penn St., QB	613
	3rd—Don Meredith, Southern Meth., QB	286
	4th—Bill Burrell, Illinois, G	196
1960	**Joe Bellino,** Navy, HB	1,793
	2nd—Tom Brown, Minnesota, G	731
	3rd—Jake Gibbs, Mississippi, QB	453
	4th—Ed Dyas, Auburn, HB	319
1961	**Ernie Davis,** Syracuse, HB	824
	2nd—Bob Ferguson, Ohio St., HB	771
	3rd—Jimmy Saxton, Texas, HB	551
	4th—Sandy Stephens, Minnesota, QB	543
1962	**Terry Baker,** Oregon St., QB	707
	2nd—Jerry Stovall, LSU, HB	618
	3rd—Bobby Bell, Minnesota, T	429
	4th—Lee Roy Jordan, Alabama, C	321
1963	* **Roger Staubach,** Navy, QB	1,860
	2nd—Billy Lothridge, Georgia Tech, QB	504
	3rd—Sherman Lewis, Michigan St., HB	369
	4th—Don Trull, Baylor, QB	253
1964	**John Huarte,** Notre Dame, QB	1,026
	2nd—Jerry Rhome, Tulsa, QB	952
	3rd—Dick Butkus, Illinois, C	505
	4th—Bob Timberlake, Michigan, QB	361
1965	**Mike Garrett,** Southern California, HB	926
	2nd—Howard Twilley, Tulsa, E	528
	3rd—Jim Grabowski, Illinois, HB	481
	4th—Donny Anderson, Texas Tech, HB	408
1966	**Steve Spurrier,** Florida, QB	1,679
	2nd—Bob Griese, Purdue, QB	816
	3rd—Nick Eddy, Notre Dame, HB	456
	4th—Bob Apisa, UCLA, QB	318
1967	**Gary Beban,** UCLA, QB	1,968
	2nd—O. J. Simpson, Southern California, HB	1,722
	3rd—Leroy Keyes, Purdue, HB	1,366
	4th—Larry Csonka, Syracuse, FB	136
1968	**O. J. Simpson,** Southern California, HB	2,853
	2nd—Leroy Keyes, Purdue, HB	1,103
	3rd—Terry Hanratty, Notre Dame, QB	387
	4th—Ted Kwalik, Penn St., TE	254
1969	**Steve Owens,** Oklahoma, HB	1,488
	2nd—Mike Phipps, Purdue, QB	1,344
	3rd—Rex Kern, Ohio St., QB	856
	4th—Archie Manning, Mississippi, QB	582

Year	Player (Winner Bold), School, Position	Points
1970	**Jim Plunkett,** Stanford, QB	2,229
	2nd—Joe Theismann, Notre Dame, QB	1,410
	3rd—Archie Manning, Mississippi, QB	849
	4th—Steve Worster, Texas, RB	398
1971	**Pat Sullivan,** Auburn, QB	1,597
	2nd—Ed Marinaro, Cornell, RB	1,445
	3rd—Greg Pruitt, Oklahoma, RB	586
	4th—Johnny Musso, Alabama, RB	365
1972	**Johnny Rodgers,** Nebraska, WR	1,310
	2nd—Greg Pruitt, Oklahoma, RB	966
	3rd—Rich Glover, Nebraska, MG	652
	4th—Bert Jones, LSU, QB	351
1973	**John Cappelletti,** Penn St., RB	1,057
	2nd—John Hicks, Ohio St., OT	524
	3rd—Roosevelt Leaks, Texas, RB	482
	4th—David Jaynes, Kansas, QB	394
1974	* **Archie Griffin,** Ohio St., RB	1,920
	2nd—Anthony Davis, Southern California, RB	819
	3rd—Joe Washington, Oklahoma, RB	661
	4th—Tom Clements, Notre Dame, QB	244
1975	**Archie Griffin,** Ohio St., RB	1,800
	2nd—Chuck Muncie, California, RB	730
	3rd—Ricky Bell, Southern California, RB	708
	4th—Tony Dorsett, Pittsburgh, RB	616
1976	**Tony Dorsett,** Pittsburgh, RB	2,357
	2nd—Ricky Bell, Southern California, RB	1,346
	3rd—Rob Lytle, Michigan, RB	413
	4th—Terry Miller, Oklahoma St., RB	197
1977	**Earl Campbell,** Texas, RB	1,547
	2nd—Terry Miller, Oklahoma St., RB	812
	3rd—Ken MacAfee, Notre Dame, TE	343
	4th—Doug Williams, Grambling, QB	266
1978	* **Billy Sims,** Oklahoma, RB	827
	2nd—Chuck Fusina, Penn St., QB	750
	3rd—Rick Leach, Michigan, QB	435
	4th—Charles White, Southern California, RB	354
1979	**Charles White,** Southern California, RB	1,695
	2nd—Billy Sims, Oklahoma, RB	773
	3rd—Marc Wilson, Brigham Young, QB	589
	4th—Art Schlichter, Ohio St., QB	251
1980	**George Rogers,** South Carolina, RB	1,128
	2nd—Hugh Green, Pittsburgh, DE	861
	3rd—Herschel Walker, Georgia, RB	683
	4th—Mark Hermann, Purdue, QB	405
1981	**Marcus Allen,** Southern California, RB	1,797
	2nd—Herschel Walker, Georgia, RB	1,199
	3rd—Jim McMahon, Brigham Young, QB	706
	4th—Dan Marino, Pittsburgh, QB	256
1982	* **Herschel Walker,** Georgia, RB	1,926
	2nd—John Elway, Stanford, QB	1,231
	3rd—Eric Dickerson, Southern Meth., RB	465
	4th—Anthony Carter, Michigan, WR	142
1983	**Mike Rozier,** Nebraska, RB	1,801
	2nd—Steve Young, Brigham Young, QB	1,172
	3rd—Doug Flutie, Boston College, QB	253
	4th—Turner Gill, Nebraska, QB	190
1984	**Doug Flutie,** Boston College, QB	2,240
	2nd—Keith Byars, Ohio St., RB	1,251
	3rd—Robbie Bosco, Brigham Young, QB	443
	4th—Bernie Kosar, Miami (Fla.), QB	320
1985	**Bo Jackson,** Auburn, RB	1,509
	2nd—Chuck Long, Iowa, QB	1,464
	3rd—Robbie Bosco, Brigham Young, QB	459
	4th—Lorenzo White, Michigan St., RB	391
1986	**Vinny Testaverde,** Miami (Fla.), QB	2,213
	2nd—Paul Palmer, Temple, RB	672
	3rd—Jim Harbaugh, Michigan, QB	458
	4th—Brian Bosworth, Oklahoma, LB	395
1987	**Tim Brown,** Notre Dame, WR	1,442
	2nd—Don McPherson, Syracuse, QB	831
	3rd—Gordie Lockbaum, Holy Cross, WR/DB	657
	4th—Lorenzo White, Michigan St., RB	632
1988	* **Barry Sanders,** Oklahoma St., RB	1,878
	2nd—Rodney Peete, Southern California, QB	912
	3rd—Troy Aikman, UCLA, QB	582
	4th—Steve Walsh, Miami (Fla.), QB	341
1989	* **Andre Ware,** Houston, QB	1,073
	2nd—Anthony Thompson, Indiana, RB	1,003
	3rd—Major Harris, West Virginia, QB	709
	4th—Tony Rice, Notre Dame, QB	523

Year	Player (Winner Bold), School, Position	Points
1990	*Ty Detmer, Brigham Young, QB	1,482
	2nd—Raghib Ismail, Notre Dame, WR	1,177
	3rd—Eric Bieniemy, Colorado, RB	798
	4th—Shawn Moore, Virginia, QB	465
1991	#Desmond Howard, Michigan, WR	2,077
	2nd—Casey Weldon, Florida St., QB	503
	3rd—Ty Detmer, Brigham Young, QB	445
	4th—Steve Emtman, Washington, DT	357
1992	Gino Torretta, Miami (Fla.), QB	1,400
	2nd—Marshall Faulk, San Diego St., RB	1,080
	3rd—Garrison Hearst, Georgia, RB	982
	4th—Marvin Jones, Florida St., LB	392
1993	Charlie Ward, Florida St., QB	2,310
	2nd—Heath Shuler, Tennessee, QB	688
	3rd—David Palmer, Alabama, RB	292
	4th—Marshall Faulk, San Diego St., RB	250
1994	*Rashaan Salaam, Colorado, RB	1,743
	2nd—Ki-Jana Carter, Penn St., RB	901
	3rd—Steve McNair, Alcorn St., QB	655
	4th—Kerry Collins, Penn St., QB	639
1995	Eddie George, Ohio St., RB	1,460
	2nd—Tommie Frazier, Nebraska, QB	1,196
	3rd—Danny Wuerffel, Florida, QB	987
	4th—Darnell Autry, Northwestern, RB	535
1996	Danny Wuerffel, Florida, QB	1,363
	2nd—Troy Davis, Iowa St., RB	1,174
	3rd—Jake Plummer, Arizona St., QB	685
	4th—Orlando Pace, Ohio St., OL	599
1997	*Charles Woodson, Michigan, DB	1,815
	2nd—Peyton Manning, Tennessee, QB	1,543
	3rd—Ryan Leaf, Washington St., QB	861
	4th—Randy Moss, Marshall, WR	253
1998	Ricky Williams, Texas, RB	2,355
	2nd—Michael Bishop, Kansas St., QB	792
	3rd—Cade McNown, UCLA, QB	696
	4th—Tim Couch, Kentucky, QB	527
1999	Ron Dayne, Wisconsin, RB	2,042
	2nd—Joe Hamilton, Georgia Tech, QB	994
	3rd—Michael Vick, Virginia Tech, QB	319
	4th—Drew Brees, Purdue, QB	308
2000	Chris Weinke, Florida St., QB	1,628
	2nd—Josh Heupel, Oklahoma, QB	1,552
	3rd—Drew Brees, Purdue, QB	619
	4th—LaDainian Tomlinson, TCU, RB	566
2001	Eric Crouch, Nebraska, QB	770
	2nd—Rex Grossman, Florida, QB	708
	3rd—Ken Dorsey, Miami (Fla.), QB	638
	4th—Joey Harrington, Oregon, QB	364

*Winner as junior (all others seniors). #Had one year of eligibility remaining.

2002 Heisman Voting

(First-, second- and third-place votes, and total points; voting on a 3-2-1 basis)

	1st	2nd	3rd	Total
1. Carson Palmer, QB, Southern California	242	224	154	1,328
2. Brad Banks, QB, Iowa	199	173	152	1,095
3. Larry Johnson, RB, Penn St.	108	130	142	726
4. #Willis McGahee, RB, Miami (Fla.)	101	118	121	660
5. Ken Dorsey, QB, Miami (Fla.)	122	89	99	643
6. Byron Leftwich, QB, Marshall	22	26	34	152
7. Jason Gesser, QB, Washington St.	5	22	15	74
8. *Chris Brown, RB, Colorado	5	11	11	48
9. Kliff Kingsbury, QB, Texas Tech	6	2	11	33
10. Quentin Griffin, RB, Oklahoma	1	8	9	28

#Sophomore. *Junior. All others seniors.

Heisman Trophy Winners by Position

- Running Back - 40
- Receiver - 5
- Quarterback - 22
- Defensive back - 1

MAXWELL AWARD

First presented in 1937 to honor the nation's outstanding college football player by the Maxwell Memorial Football Club of Philadelphia. The award is named after Robert "Tiny" Maxwell, a Philadelphia native who played at the University of Chicago as a lineman near the turn of the century.

Year	Player, College, Position
1937	Clint Frank, Yale, HB
1938	Davey O'Brien, TCU, QB
1939	Nile Kinnick, Iowa, HB
1940	Tom Harmon, Michigan, HB
1941	Bill Dudley, Virginia, HB
1942	Paul Governali, Columbia, HB
1943	Bob Odell, Pennsylvania, HB
1944	Glenn Davis, Army, HB
1945	Doc Blanchard, Army, FB
1946	Charley Trippi, Georgia, HB
1947	Doak Walker, Southern Methodist, HB
1948	Chuck Bednarik, Pennsylvania, C
1949	Leon Hart, Notre Dame, E
1950	Reds Bagnell, Pennsylvania, HB
1951	Dick Kazmaier, Princeton, HB
1952	Johnny Lattner, Notre Dame, HB
1953	Johnny Lattner, Notre Dame, HB
1954	Ron Beagle, Navy, E
1955	Howard Cassady, Ohio St., HB
1956	Tommy McDonald, Oklahoma, HB
1957	Bob Reifsnyder, Navy, T
1958	Pete Dawkins, Army, HB
1959	Rich Lucas, Penn St., QB
1960	Joe Bellino, Navy, HB
1961	Bob Ferguson, Ohio St., FB
1962	Terry Baker, Oregon St., QB
1963	Roger Staubach, Navy, QB
1964	Glenn Ressler, Penn St., C
1965	Tommy Nobis, Texas, LB
1966	Jim Lynch, Notre Dame, LB
1967	Gary Beban, UCLA, QB
1968	O.J. Simpson, Southern California, RB
1969	Mike Reid, Penn St., DT
1970	Jim Plunkett, Stanford, QB
1971	Ed Marinaro, Cornell, RB
1972	Brad VanPelt, Michigan St., DB
1973	John Cappelletti, Penn St., RB
1974	Steve Joachim, Temple, QB
1975	Archie Griffin, Ohio St., RB
1976	Tony Dorsett, Pittsburgh, RB
1977	Ross Browner, Notre Dame, DE
1978	Chuck Fusina, Penn St., QB
1979	Charles White, Southern California, RB
1980	Hugh Green, Pittsburgh, DE
1981	Marcus Allen, Southern California, RB
1982	Herschel Walker, Georgia, RB
1983	Mike Rozier, Nebraska, RB
1984	Doug Flutie, Boston College, QB
1985	Chuck Long, Iowa, QB
1986	Vinny Testaverde, Miami (Fla.), QB
1987	Don McPherson, Syracuse, QB
1988	Barry Sanders, Oklahoma St., RB
1989	Anthony Thompson, Indiana, RB
1990	Ty Detmer, Brigham Young, QB
1991	Desmond Howard, Michigan, WR
1992	Gino Torretta, Miami (Fla.), QB
1993	Charlie Ward, Florida St., QB
1994	Kerry Collins, Penn St., QB
1995	Eddie George, Ohio St., RB

Carson Palmer is Southern California's fifth Heisman Trophy winner. He also received the 2002 Johnny Unitas Golden Arm Award.

Year	Player, College, Position
1996	Danny Wuerffel, Florida, QB
1997	Peyton Manning, Tennessee, QB
1998	Ricky Williams, Texas, RB
1999	Ron Dayne, Wisconsin, RB
2000	Drew Brees, Purdue, QB
2001	Ken Dorsey, Miami (Fla.), QB
2002	Larry Johnson, Penn St., RB

OUTLAND TROPHY

First presented in 1946 to honor the outstanding interior lineman in the nation by the Football Writers Association of America. The award is named for its benefactor, Dr. John H. Outland.

Year	Player, College, Position
1946	George Connor, Notre Dame, T
1947	Joe Steffy, Army, G
1948	Bill Fischer, Notre Dame, G
1949	Ed Bagdon, Michigan St., G
1950	Bob Gain, Kentucky, T
1951	Jim Weatherall, Oklahoma, T
1952	Dick Modzelewski, Maryland, T
1953	J.D. Roberts, Oklahoma, G
1954	Bill Brooks, Arkansas, G
1955	Calvin Jones, Iowa, G
1956	Jim Parker, Ohio St., G
1957	Alex Karras, Iowa, T
1958	Zeke Smith, Auburn, G
1959	Mike McGee, Duke, T
1960	Tom Brown, Minnesota, G
1961	Merlin Olsen, Utah St., T
1962	Bobby Bell, Minnesota, T
1963	Scott Appleton, Texas, T
1964	Steve DeLong, Tennessee, T
1965	Tommy Nobis, Texas, G
1966	Loyd Phillips, Arkansas, T
1967	Ron Yary, Southern California, T
1968	Bill Stanfill, Georgia, T

Iowa Sports Information

Iowa's Brad Banks joined former Hawkeye standout Chuck Long as a recipient of the Davey O'Brien National Quarterback Award.

Year	Player, College, Position
1969	Mike Reid, Penn St., DT
1970	Jim Stillwagon, Ohio St., MG
1971	Larry Jacobson, Nebraska, DT
1972	Rich Glover, Nebraska, MG
1973	John Hicks, Ohio St., OT
1974	Randy White, Maryland, DE
1975	Lee Roy Selmon, Oklahoma, DT
1976	*Ross Browner, Notre Dame, DE
1977	Brad Shearer, Texas, DT
1978	Greg Roberts, Oklahoma, G
1979	Jim Ritcher, North Carolina St., C
1980	Mark May, Pittsburgh, OT
1981	*Dave Rimington, Nebraska, C
1982	Dave Rimington, Nebraska, C
1983	Dean Steinkuhler, Nebraska, G
1984	Bruce Smith, Virginia Tech, DT
1985	Mike Ruth, Boston College, NG
1986	Jason Buck, Brigham Young, DT
1987	Chad Hennings, Air Force, DT
1988	Tracy Rocker, Auburn, DT
1989	Mohammed Elewonibi, Brigham Young, G
1990	Russell Maryland, Miami (Fla.), DT
1991	*Steve Emtman, Washington, DT
1992	Will Shields, Nebraska, G
1993	Rob Waldrop, Arizona, NG
1994	Zach Wiegert, Nebraska, OT
1995	Jonathan Ogden, UCLA, OT
1996	*Orlando Pace, Ohio St., OT
1997	Aaron Taylor, Nebraska, OG
1998	*Kris Farris, UCLA, OT
1999	Chris Samuels, Alabama, OT
2000	*John Henderson, Tennessee, DL
2001	Bryant McKinnie, Miami (Fla.), OT
2002	Rien Long, Washington St., DT

*Junior (all others seniors).

WALTER CAMP AWARD

First presented in 1967 to honor the nation's outstanding college football player by the Walter Camp Foundation in balloting by Division I-A coaches and sports information directors. The award is named after Walter Camp, one of the founders of modern American football.

Year	Player, College, Position
1967	O.J. Simpson, Southern California, RB
1968	O.J. Simpson, Southern California, RB
1969	Steve Owens, Oklahoma, RB
1970	Jim Plunkett, Stanford, QB

Year	Player, College, Position
1971	Pat Sullivan, Auburn, QB
1972	Johnny Rodgers, Nebraska, WR
1973	John Cappelletti, Penn St., RB
1974	Archie Griffin, Ohio St., RB
1975	Archie Griffin, Ohio St., RB
1976	Tony Dorsett, Pittsburgh, RB
1977	Ken MacAfee, Notre Dame, TE
1978	Billy Sims, Oklahoma, RB
1979	Charles White, Southern California, RB
1980	Hugh Green, Pittsburgh, DE
1981	Marcus Allen, Southern California, RB
1982	Herschel Walker, Georgia, RB
1983	Mike Rozier, Nebraska, RB
1984	Doug Flutie, Boston College, QB
1985	Bo Jackson, Auburn, RB
1986	Vinny Testaverde, Miami (Fla.), QB
1987	Tim Brown, Notre Dame, WR
1988	Barry Sanders, Oklahoma St., RB
1989	Andre Ware, Houston, QB
1990	Raghib Ismail, Notre Dame, RB/WR
1991	Desmond Howard, Michigan, WR
1992	Gino Torretta, Miami (Fla.), QB
1993	Charlie Ward, Florida St., QB
1994	Rashaan Salaam, Colorado, RB
1995	Eddie George, Ohio St., RB
1996	Danny Wuerffel, Florida, QB
1997	Charles Woodson, Michigan, DB
1998	Ricky Williams, Texas, RB
1999	Ron Dayne, Wisconsin, RB
2000	Josh Heupel, Oklahoma, QB
2001	Eric Crouch, Nebraska, QB
2002	Larry Johnson, Penn St., RB

VINCE LOMBARDI/ROTARY AWARD

First presented in 1970 to honor the outstanding college lineman of the year by the Rotary Club of Houston, Texas. The award is named after professional football coach Vince Lombardi, a member of the legendary "Seven Blocks of Granite" at Fordham in the 1930s.

Year	Player, College, Position
1970	Jim Stillwagon, Ohio St., MG
1971	Walt Patulski, Notre Dame, DE
1972	Rich Glover, Nebraska, MG
1973	John Hicks, Ohio St., OT
1974	Randy White, Maryland, DT
1975	Lee Roy Selmon, Oklahoma, DT
1976	Wilson Whitley, Houston, DT
1977	Ross Browner, Notre Dame, DE
1978	Bruce Clark, Penn St., DT
1979	Brad Budde, Southern California, G
1980	Hugh Green, Pittsburgh, DE
1981	Kenneth Sims, Texas, DT
1982	Dave Rimington, Nebraska, C
1983	Dean Steinkuhler, Nebraska, G
1984	Tony Degrate, Texas, DT
1985	Tony Casillas, Oklahoma, NG
1986	Cornelius Bennett, Alabama, LB
1987	Chris Spielman, Ohio St., LB
1988	Tracy Rocker, Auburn, DT
1989	Percy Snow, Michigan St., LB
1990	Chris Zorich, Notre Dame, NT
1991	Steve Emtman, Washington, DT
1992	Marvin Jones, Florida St., LB
1993	Aaron Taylor, Notre Dame, OT
1994	Warren Sapp, Miami (Fla.), DT
1995	Orlando Pace, Ohio St., OT
1996	Orlando Pace, Ohio St., OT
1997	Grant Wistrom, Nebraska, DE
1998	Dat Nguyen, Texas A&M, LB
1999	Corey Moore, Virginia Tech, DE
2000	Jamal Reynolds, Florida St., DE
2001	Julius Peppers, North Carolina, DE
2002	Terrell Suggs, Arizona St., DE

DAVEY O'BRIEN NATIONAL QUARTERBACK AWARD

First presented in 1977 as the O'Brien Memorial Trophy to the outstanding player in the Southwest. In 1981, the Davey O'Brien Educational and Charitable Trust of Fort Worth, Texas, renamed the award the Davey O'Brien National Quarterback Award, and it now honors the nation's best quarterback.

MEMORIAL TROPHY

Year	Player, College, Position
1977	Earl Campbell, Texas, RB
1978	Billy Sims, Oklahoma, RB
1979	Mike Singletary, Baylor, LB
1980	Mike Singletary, Baylor, LB

NATIONAL QB AWARD

Year	Player, College
1981	Jim McMahon, Brigham Young
1982	Todd Blackledge, Penn St.
1983	Steve Young, Brigham Young
1984	Doug Flutie, Boston College
1985	Chuck Long, Iowa
1986	Vinny Testaverde, Miami (Fla.)
1987	Don McPherson, Syracuse
1988	Troy Aikman, UCLA
1989	Andre Ware, Houston
1990	Ty Detmer, Brigham Young
1991	Ty Detmer, Brigham Young
1992	Gino Torretta, Miami (Fla.)
1993	Charlie Ward, Florida St.
1994	Kerry Collins, Penn St.
1995	Danny Wuerffel, Florida
1996	Danny Wuerffel, Florida
1997	Peyton Manning, Tennessee
1998	Michael Bishop, Kansas St.
1999	Joe Hamilton, Georgia Tech
2000	Chris Weinke, Florida St.
2001	Eric Crouch, Nebraska
2002	Brad Banks, Iowa

BUTKUS AWARD

First presented in 1985 to honor the nation's best collegiate linebacker by the Downtown Athletic Club of Orlando, Fla. The award is named after Dick Butkus, two-time consensus all-American at Illinois and six-time all-pro linebacker with the Chicago Bears.

Year	Player, College
1985	Brian Bosworth, Oklahoma
1986	Brian Bosworth, Oklahoma
1987	Paul McGowan, Florida St.
1988	Derrick Thomas, Alabama
1989	Percy Snow, Michigan St.
1990	Alfred Williams, Colorado
1991	Erick Anderson, Michigan
1992	Marvin Jones, Florida St.
1993	Trev Alberts, Nebraska
1994	Dana Howard, Illinois
1995	Kevin Hardy, Illinois
1996	Matt Russell, Colorado
1997	Andy Katzenmoyer, Ohio St.
1998	Chris Claiborne, Southern California
1999	LaVar Arrington, Penn St.
2000	Dan Morgan, Miami (Fla.)
2001	Rocky Calmus, Oklahoma
2002	E.J. Henderson, Maryland

JIM THORPE AWARD

First presented in 1986 to honor the nation's best defensive back by the Jim Thorpe Athletic Club of Oklahoma City. The award is named after Jim Thorpe, Olympic champion, two-time consensus all-American halfback at Carlisle and professional football player.

Year	Player, College
1986	Thomas Everett, Baylor
1987	Bennie Blades, Miami (Fla.)
	Rickey Dixon, Oklahoma
1988	Deion Sanders, Florida St.
1989	Mark Carrier, Southern California
1990	Darryll Lewis, Arizona
1991	Terrell Buckley, Florida St.
1992	Deon Figures, Colorado
1993	Antonio Langham, Alabama
1994	Chris Hudson, Colorado
1995	Greg Myers, Colorado St.
1996	Lawrence Wright, Florida
1997	Charles Woodson, Michigan
1998	Antoine Winfield, Ohio St.
1999	Tyrone Carter, Minnesota
2000	Jamar Fletcher, Wisconsin
2001	Roy Williams, Oklahoma
2002	Terence Newman, Kansas St.

JOHNNY UNITAS GOLDEN ARM AWARD

First presented in 1987 to honor the nation's top senior quarterback by the Kentucky Chapter of the National Football Foundation and College Football Hall of Fame, Inc. Each year, a committee composed of NFL executives, coaches, scouts and media members selects the winner based on citizenship, scholarship, leadership and athletic accomplishments. The award is named after Pro Football Hall of Fame quarterback Johnny Unitas.

Year	Player, College
1987	Don McPherson, Syracuse
1988	Rodney Peete, Southern California
1989	Tony Rice, Notre Dame
1990	Craig Erickson, Miami (Fla.)
1991	Casey Weldon, Florida St.
1992	Gino Torretta, Miami (Fla.)
1993	Charlie Ward, Florida St.
1994	Jay Barker, Alabama
1995	Tommy Frazier, Nebraska
1996	Danny Wuerffel, Florida
1997	Peyton Manning, Tennessee
1998	Cade McNown, UCLA
1999	Chris Redman, Louisville
2000	Chris Weinke, Florida St.
2001	David Carr, Fresno St.
2002	Carson Palmer, Southern California

DOAK WALKER NATIONAL RUNNING BACK AWARD

First presented in 1990 to honor the nation's best running back among Division I-A juniors or seniors who combine outstanding achievements on the field, in the classroom and in the community, by the GTE/Southern Methodist Athletic Forum in Dallas, Texas, and sponsored by Dr. Pepper, a $10,000 scholarship is donated to the recipient's university in his name. It is voted on by a 16-member panel of media and former college football standouts. The award is named after Doak Walker, Southern Methodist's three-time consensus all-American halfback and 1948 Heisman Trophy winner.

Year	Player, College
1990	Greg Lewis, Washington
1991	Trevor Cobb, Rice
1992	Garrison Hearst, Georgia
1993	Byron Morris, Texas Tech
1994	Rashaan Salaam, Colorado
1995	Eddie George, Ohio St.
1996	Byron Hanspard, Texas Tech
1997	Ricky Williams, Texas
1998	Ricky Williams, Texas
1999	Ron Dayne, Wisconsin
2000	LaDainian Tomlinson, TCU
2001	Luke Staley, Brigham Young
2002	Larry Johnson, Penn St.

LOU GROZA COLLEGIATE PLACE-KICKER AWARD

First presented in 1992 to honor the nation's top collegiate place-kicker by the Palm Beach County Sports Commission in conjunction with the Orange Bowl Committee. The award is named after Pro Football Hall of Fame kicker Lou Groza.

Year	Player, College
1992	Joe Allison, Memphis
1993	Judd Davis, Florida
1994	Steve McLaughlin, Arizona
1995	Michael Reeder, TCU
1996	Marc Primanti, North Carolina St.
1997	Martin Gramatica, Kansas St.
1998	Sebastian Janikowski, Florida St.
1999	Sebastian Janikowski, Florida St.
2000	Jonathan Ruffin, Cincinnati
2001	Seth Marler, Tulane
2002	Nate Kaeding, Iowa

BRONKO NAGURSKI AWARD

First presented in 1993 to honor the nation's top collegiate defensive player by the Football Writers Association of America and the Charlotte (N.C.) Touchdown Club. The award is named after Bronko Nagurski, consensus all-America tackle and running back at Minnesota in 1929, and a member of both the College Football Hall of Fame and Pro Football Hall of Fame.

Year	Player, College, Position
1993	Rob Waldrop, Arizona, DL
1994	Warren Sapp, Miami (Fla.), DT
1995	Pat Fitzgerald, Northwestern, LB
1996	Pat Fitzgerald, Northwestern, LB
1997	Charles Woodson, Michigan, CB
1998	Champ Bailey, Georgia, DB
1999	Corey Moore, Virginia Tech, DE
2000	Dan Morgan, Miami (Fla.), LB
2001	Roy Williams, Oklahoma, DB
2002	Terrell Suggs, Arizona St., DE

FRED BILETNIKOFF RECEIVER AWARD

First presented in 1994 to honor the nation's top collegiate pass receiver by the Quarterback Club of Tallahassee, Fla. The award is named after Fred Biletnikoff, former Florida State all-American and NFL Oakland Raider receiver, a member of both the College Football Hall of Fame and Pro Football Hall of Fame.

Year	Player, College
1994	Bobby Engram, Penn St.
1995	Terry Glenn, Ohio St.
1996	Marcus Harris, Wyoming
1997	Randy Moss, Marshall
1998	Troy Edwards, Louisiana Tech
1999	Troy Walters, Stanford
2000	Antonio Bryant, Pittsburgh
2001	Josh Reed, LSU
2002	Charles Rogers, Michigan St.

CHUCK BEDNARIK AWARD

First presented in 1995 to honor the collegiate defensive player of the year by the Maxwell Memorial Football Club of Philadelphia. The award is named after Chuck Bednarik, consensus all-America center at Pennsylvania in 1947-48 and a member of both the College Football Hall of Fame and Pro Football Hall of Fame.

Year	Player, College
1995	Pat Fitzgerald, Northwestern
1996	Pat Fitzgerald, Northwestern
1997	Charles Woodson, Michigan
1998	Dat Nguyen, Texas A&M
1999	LaVar Arrington, Penn St.
2000	Dan Morgan, Miami (Fla.)
2001	Julius Peppers, North Carolina
2002	E.J. Henderson, Maryland

MOSI TATUPU SPECIAL TEAMS PLAYER OF THE YEAR AWARD

First presented in 1997 to the top special teams player in the country by the Maui (Hawaii) Touchdown Club. The award is named after Mosi Tatupu, who played high school football in Honolulu and collegiate football at Southern California. He went on to a 14-year playing career in the NFL.

Year	Player, College
1997	Brock Olivo, Missouri
1998	Chris McAlister, Arizona
1999	Deltha O'Neal, California
2000	J.T. Thatcher, Oklahoma
2001	Kahlil Hill, Iowa
2002	Glenn Pakulak, Kentucky

RAY GUY PUNTING AWARD

First presented in 2000 to honor the nation's top collegiate punter by the Greater Augusta (Ga.) Sports Council. The winner will display leadership, self-discipline and have a significant impact on the team's success. Voted upon by a panel of sports writers, college football coaches and former punters. The award is named after Ray Guy, former punter at Southern Mississippi and NFL All-Pro punter for the Oakland Raiders.

Year	Player, College
2000	Kevin Stemke, Wisconsin
2001	Travis Dorsch, Purdue
2002	Mark Mariscal, Colorado

JOHN MACKEY TIGHT END AWARD

First presented in 2000 to honor the nation's top collegiate tight end by the Nassau County (N.Y.) Sports Commission. The award is named after John Mackey, the first tight end inducted into the Pro Football Hall of Fame.

Year	Player, College
2000	Tim Stratton, Purdue
2001	Dan Graham, Colorado
2002	Dallas Clark, Iowa

DAVE RIMINGTON CENTER TROPHY

First presented in 2000 to honor the nation's top collegiate offensive center by the Boomer Esiason Foundation. The award is named after Dave Rimington, consensus all-America center at Nebraska in 1981-82 who was inducted into the College Football Hall of Fame in 1997.

Year	Player, College
2000	Dominic Raiola, Nebraska
2001	LeCharles Bentley, Ohio St.
2002	Brett Romberg, Miami (Fla.)

TED HENDRICKS DEFENSIVE END AWARD

First presented in 2002 to honor the nation's top defensive end by the Miami (Florida) Touchdown Club. The award is named after Ted Hendricks, College Football Hall of Fame member from Miami (Florida) and a member of the Pro Football Hall of Fame.

Year	Player, College
2002	Terrell Suggs, Arizona St.

Division I-AA

WALTER PAYTON PLAYER OF THE YEAR AWARD

First presented in 1987 to honor the top Division I-AA football player by the Sports Network and voted on by Division I-AA sports information directors. The award is named after Walter Payton, former Jackson State player and the National Football League's all-time leading rusher.

Year	Player, College, Position
1987	Kenny Gamble, Colgate, RB
1988	Dave Meggett, Towson, RB
1989	John Friesz, Idaho, QB
1990	Walter Dean, Grambling, RB
1991	Jamie Martin, Weber St., QB
1992	Michael Payton, Marshall, QB
1993	Doug Nussmeier, Idaho, QB
1994	Steve McNair, Alcorn St., QB
1995	Dave Dickenson, Montana, QB
1996	Archie Amerson, Northern Ariz., RB
1997	Brian Finneran, Villanova, WR
1998	Jerry Azumah, New Hampshire, RB
1999	Adrian Peterson, Ga. Southern, RB
2000	Louis Ivory, Furman, RB
2001	Brian Westbrook, Villanova, RB
2002	Tony Romo, Eastern Ill., QB

ERNIE DAVIS AWARD

First presented in 1992 to honor a Division I-AA college football player who has overcome personal, athletic or academic adversity and performs in an exemplary manner by the American Sports Wire. The award is named after the late Ernie Davis, Syracuse halfback who won the Heisman Trophy in 1961.

Year	Player, College, Position
1992	Gilad Landau, Grambling, PK
1993	Jay Walker, Howard, QB
1994	Steve McNair, Alcorn St., QB
1995	Earl Holmes, Florida A&M, LB
1996	Jason DeCuir, Howard, PK
1997	DeMingo Graham, Hofstra, OL
1998	Chris Boden, Villanova, QB
1999	Matt Bushart, Southern U., P
2000	Charles Roberts, Cal St. Sacramento, RB
2001	Mark Leyenaar, Robert Morris, OL
2002	Kayode Mayowa, Sacred Heart, LB

BUCK BUCHANAN AWARD

First presented in 1995 to the nation's outstanding I-AA defensive player by The Sports Network. The award is named after Junious 'Buck' Buchanan, NAIA all-American defensive lineman at Grambling from 1959 through 1962 and Pro Football Hall of Fame inductee after an outstanding 13-year career.

Year	Player, College, Position
1995	Dexter Coakley, Appalachian St., LB
1996	Dexter Coakley, Appalachian St., LB
1997	Chris McNeil, N.C. A&T, DE
1998	James Milton, Western Ill., LB
1999	Al Lucas, Troy St., DT
2000	Edgerton Hartwell, Western Ill., DL
2001	Derrick Lloyd, James Madison, LB
2002	Rashean Mathis, Bethune-Cookman, DB

Division II

HARLON HILL TROPHY

First presented in 1986 to honor the best Division II player by the Harlon Hill Award Committee of Florence, Alabama. The award is named after Harlon Hill, former receiver at North Alabama and the National Football League's most valuable player for the Chicago Bears in 1955.

Year	Player, College, Position
1986	Jeff Bentrim, North Dakota St., QB
1987	Johnny Bailey, Tex. A&M-Kingsville, RB
1988	Johnny Bailey, Tex. A&M-Kingsville, RB
1989	Johnny Bailey, Tex. A&M-Kingsville, RB
1990	Chris Simdorn, North Dakota St., QB
1991	Ronnie West, Pittsburg St., WR
1992	Ronald Moore, Pittsburg St., RB
1993	Roger Graham, New Haven, RB
1994	Chris Hatcher, Valdosta St., QB
1995	Ronald McKinnon, North Ala., LB
1996	Jarrett Anderson, Truman, RB
1997	Irv Sigler, Bloomsburg, RB
1998	Brian Shay, Emporia St., RB
1999	Corte McGuffey, Northern Colo., QB
2000	Dusty Bonner, Valdosta St., QB
2001	Dusty Bonner, Valdosta St., QB
2002	Curt Anes, Grand Valley St., QB

Division III

GAGLIARDI TROPHY

First presented in 1993 to the nation's outstanding Division III player by the St. John's (Minn.) University J-Club. The award is named after John Gagliardi, St. John's head

Joe Theismann led Notre Dame to a 9-1 record in 1970, followed by a Cotton Bowl win over Texas and a second-place finish in the Heisman Trophy balloting. Theismann is one of the 2003 College Football Hall of Fame inductees.

coach for 48 seasons and one of only seven coaches in college football history to win 300 games.

Year	Player, College, Position
1993	Jim Ballard, Mount Union, QB
1994	Carey Bender, Coe, RB
1995	Chris Palmer, St. John's (Minn.), WR
1996	Lon Erickson, Ill. Wesleyan, QB
1997	Bill Borchert, Mount Union, QB
1998	Scott Hvistendahl, Augsburg, WR/P
1999	Danny Ragsdale, Redlands, QB
2000	Chad Johnson, Pacific Lutheran, QB
2001	Chuck Moore, Mount Union, RB
2002	Dan Pugh, Mount Union, RB

MELBERGER AWARD

First presented in 1993 to the nation's outstanding Division III player by the Downtown Wilkes-Barre (Pa.) Touchdown Club. The award is named after Clifford K. Melberger, captain of the 1960 Bucknell football team that won the Lambert Cup and a member of the Touchdown Club's board of directors.

Year	Player, College, Position
1993	Jim Ballard, Mount Union, QB
1994	Carey Bender, Coe, RB
1995	Craig Kusick, Wis.-La Crosse, QB
1996	Bill Borchert, Mount Union, QB
1997	Bill Borchert, Mount Union, QB
1998	Mike Burton, Trinity (Tex.), QB
1999	Scott Pingel, Westminster (Mo.), WR
2000	R.J. Bowers, Grove City, RB
2001	Chuck Moore, Mount Union, RB
2002	Dan Pincelli, Hartwick, QB

2002 COACHING AWARDS

THE HOME DEPOT COACH OF THE YEAR – Tyrone Willingham, Notre Dame (Presented by The Home Depot to the nation's top coach)
EDDIE ROBINSON COACH OF THE YEAR (FWAA) – Jim Tressel, Ohio St. (Presented by the Football Writers' Association of America)
BEAR BRYANT COACH OF THE YEAR – Jim Tressel, Ohio St. (Presented by the National Sportscasters and Sportswriters Association)
WALTER CAMP COACH OF THE YEAR – Kirk Ferentz, Iowa (Presented by the Walter Camp Foundation)
ASSOCIATED PRESS COACH OF THE YEAR – Kirk Ferentz, Iowa (Presented by The Associated Press member newspapers, TV and radio stations)
BOBBY DODD COACH OF THE YEAR – Jim Tressel, Ohio St. (Presented by the Bobby Dodd Coach of the Year Foundation, Atlanta, Georgia)
GEORGE MUNGER COACH OF THE YEAR – Tyrone Willingham, Notre Dame (Presented annually by the Maxwell Football Club. The award is named for former University of Pennsylvania coach George Munger. His devotion to ethics in athletics, and his commitment to education is the standard for which all college coaches should strive.)
AFCA/GTE COACH OF THE YEAR (Division I-A) – Jim Tressel, Ohio St. (Presented by the American Football Coaches Association)
AFCA/GTE COACH OF THE YEAR (Division I-AA) – Jack Harbaugh, Western Ky. (Presented by the American Football Coaches Association)
AFCA/GTE COACH OF THE YEAR (NCAA Division II & all NAIA) – Brian Kelly, Grand Valley St. (Presented by the American Football Coaches Association)
AFCA/GTE COACH OF THE YEAR (Division III) – Larry Kehres, Mount Union (Presented by the American Football Coaches Association)
AFCA ASSISTANT COACH OF THE YEAR (Division I-A) – Ron Aiken, Iowa, Defensive Line Coach (Presented by the American Football Coaches Association)
AFCA ASSISTANT COACH OF THE YEAR (Division I-AA) – Roy Wittke, Eastern Ill., Assistant Head Coach/Offensive Coordinator (Presented by the American Football Coaches Association)
AFCA ASSISTANT COACH OF THE YEAR (Division II) – Tony Ierulli, Shippensburg, Defensive Coordinator/Linebackers Coach (Presented by the American Football Coaches Association)
AFCA ASSISTANT COACH OF THE YEAR (Division III) – Brian Ward, Wabash, Special Teams Coordinator/Defensive Backs Coach (Presented by the American Football Coaches Association)

SCHUTT DIVISION I-A COACH OF THE YEAR – Larry Coker, Miami (Fla.) (Presented by American Football Monthly magazine)
SCHUTT DIVISION I-AA COACH OF THE YEAR – Dave Clawson, Fordham (Presented by American Football Monthly magazine)
SCHUTT DIVISION II COACH OF THE YEAR – Chris Hatcher, Valdosta St. (Presented by American Football Monthly magazine)
SCHUTT DIVISION III COACH OF THE YEAR – John Gagliardi, St. John's (Minn.) (Presented by American Football Monthly magazine)
FRANK BROYLES AWARD (Top Division I-A Assistant Coach Award) – Norm Chow, Southern California, Offensive Coordinator (Presented by Former Arkansas head coach Frank Broyles)
SPORTING NEWS SPORTSMAN OF THE YEAR –Tyrone Willingham, Notre Dame (Presented by The Sporting News)
EDDIE ROBINSON DIVISION I-AA COACH OF THE YEAR – Tommy Tate, McNeese St. (Presented by The Sports Network)
2003 AMOS ALONZO STAGG AWARD – Lavell Edwards, Brigham Young (Presented by the American Football Coaches Association)

COLLEGE FOOTBALL HALL OF FAME

Established: In 1947, by the National Football Foundation and College Hall of Fame, Inc. The first class of enshrinement of Division I or major-college players began in 1951. In 1996, the yearly classes elected were expanded to include other than Division I players. **Eligibility:** A nominated player must be out of college at least 10 years and a first-team all-America selection by a major selector during his career. For divisional (college-division) players, the player must have been a first-team selection on a recognized all-America team in Division I-AA, II and III and the NAIA. Coaches must be retired three years. The voting is done by a 12-member panel made up of athletics directors, conference and bowl officials, and media representatives.

Member players are listed with the final year they played in college, and member coaches are listed with the year they were inducted. ($) Indicates college-division member. (†) Indicates deceased members. (#) Indicates dual member of the Pro Football Hall of Fame.

2003 COLLEGE FOOTBALL HALL OF FAME CLASS

(To be inducted at the 46th annual awards dinner on December 9, 2003)

DIVISION I-A CLASS

Player, School	Pos.	Years
Ricky Bell, Southern California	RB	1973-76
Murry Bowden, Dartmouth	DB	1967-70
Tom Brown, Minnesota	G	1958-60
Jimbo Covert, Pittsburgh	OT	1980-83
Jerry LeVias, Southern Methodist	E	1965-68
Billy Neighbors, Alabama	T	1959-61
Ron Pritchard, Arizona St.	LB	1966-68
John Rauch, Georgia	QB	1945-48
Barry Sanders, Oklahoma St.	TB	1986-88
Joe Theismann, Notre Dame	QB	1968-70
Roger Wehrli, Missouri	DB	1966-68

Coach, School(s)	Years	Record
Doug Dickey, Tennessee, Florida	1964-78	104-58-6
Hayden Fry, Southern Methodist, North Texas, Iowa	1962-98	232-188-10

DIVISIONAL CLASS (DIVISIONS I-AA, II AND III, NAIA)

Player, School	Pos.	Years
Brad Calip, East Central	QB	1981-84
Dwayne Nix, Tex. A&M-Kingsville	TE	1965-68
Scott Reppert, Lawrence	RB	1979-82
Willie Richardson, Jackson St.	E	1959-62
Calvin Roberts, Gust. Adolphus	T	1949-52
Ben Stevenson, Tuskegee	RB	1924-30

Coach, School(s)	Years	Record
Marino Casem, Alabama St., Alcorn St., Southern U.	1963, 1964-85, 1987-88, 1992	160-91-8

Coach, School(s)	Years	Record
Roy Kidd, Eastern Ky.	1964-00	315-123-8
Harold "Tubby" Raymond, Delaware	1966-01	300-119-3

PLAYERS

Player, College	Year
†Earl Abell, Colgate	1915
Alex Agase, Purdue/Illinois	1946
†Harry Agganis, Boston U.	1952
Frank Albert, Stanford	1941
†Ki Aldrich, TCU	1938
†Malcolm Aldrich, Yale	1921
Marcus Allen, Southern California#	1981
†Joe Alexander, Syracuse	1920
Lance Alworth, Arkansas#	1961
†Alan Ameche, Wisconsin	1954
†Knowlton Ames, Princeton	1889
Warren Amling, Ohio St.	1946
Dick Anderson, Colorado	1967
Donny Anderson, Texas Tech	1965
†Hunk Anderson, Notre Dame	1921
Jon Arnett, Southern California	1956
Doug Atkins, Tennessee#	1952
Bob Babich, Miami (Ohio)	1968
†Everett Bacon, Wesleyan (Conn.)	1912
†Reds Bagnell, Pennsylvania	1950
Johnny Bailey, Tex. A&M-Kingsville ($)	1989
†Hobey Baker, Princeton	1913
†John Baker, Southern California	1931
†Moon Baker, Northwestern	1926
Terry Baker, Oregon St.	1962
†Harold Ballin, Princeton	1914
†Bill Banker, Tulane	1929
Vince Banonis, Detroit	1941
†Stan Barnes, California	1921
†Charles Barrett, Cornell	1915
†Bert Baston, Minnesota	1916
†Cliff Battles, West Va. Wesleyan#	1931
Sammy Baugh, TCU#	1936
Maxie Baughan, Georgia Tech	1959
†James Bausch, Wichita St./Kansas	1930
Ron Beagle, Navy	1955
Terry Beasley, Auburn	1971
Gary Beban, UCLA	1967
Hub Bechtol, Texas Tech/Texas	1946
Ray Beck, Georgia Tech	1951
†John Beckett, Oregon	1916
Chuck Bednarik, Pennsylvania#	1948
Forrest Behm, Nebraska	1940
Bobby Bell, Minnesota#	1962
Joe Bellino, Navy	1960
†Marty Below, Wisconsin	1923
†Al Benbrook, Michigan	1910
Jeff Bentrim, North Dakota St. ($)	1986
†Charlie Berry, Lafayette	1924
Angelo Bertelli, Notre Dame	1943
†Jay Berwanger, Chicago	1935
†Lawrence Bettencourt, St. Mary's (Cal.)	1927
Fred Biletnikoff, Florida St.#	1964
Doc Blanchard, Army	1946
Tony Blazine, Ill. Wesleyan ($)	1934
†Al Blozis, Georgetown	1941
Ed Bock, Iowa St.	1938
†Lynn Bomar, Vanderbilt	1924
†Douglas Bomeisler, Yale	1912
†Albie Booth, Yale	1931
George Bork, Northern Ill. ($)	1963
†Fred Borries, Navy	1934
Bruce Bosley, West Virginia	1955
Don Bosseler, Miami (Fla.)	1956
†Vic Bottari, California	1938
†Ben Boynton, Williams	1920
Terry Bradshaw, Louisiana Tech# ($)	1969
†Charles Brewer, Harvard	1895
†Johnny Bright, Drake	1951
John Brodie, Stanford	1956
†George Brooke, Swarthmore/Pennsylvania	1895
Al Brosky, Illinois	1952
Bob Brown, Nebraska	1963
George Brown, Navy/San Diego St.	1947
†Gordon Brown, Yale	1900
Jim Brown, Syracuse#	1956
†John Brown Jr., Navy	1913
†Johnny Mack Brown, Alabama	1925

Player, College	Year
†Tay Brown, Southern California	1932
Ross Browner, Notre Dame	1977
Tel Bruner, Centre ($)	1985
†Buck Buchanan, Grambling# ($)	1962
Brad Budde, Southern California	1979
†Paul Bunker, Army	1902
Chris Burford, Stanford	1959
Kurt Burris, Oklahoma	1954
Ron Burton, Northwestern	1959
Dick Butkus, Illinois#	1964
†Robert Butler, Wisconsin	1913
Kevin Butler, Georgia	1984
†George Cafego, Tennessee	1939
†Red Cagle, La.-Lafayette/Army	1929
†John Cain, Alabama	1932
Ed Cameron, Wash. & Lee	1924
†David Campbell, Harvard	1901
Earl Campbell, Texas#	1977
†Jack Cannon, Notre Dame	1929
John Cappelletti, Penn St.	1973
†Frank Carideo, Notre Dame	1930
†Charles Carney, Illinois	1921
J.C. Caroline, Illinois	1954
Bill Carpenter, Army	1959
†Hunter Carpenter, Virginia Tech/North Carolina	1905
Charles Carroll, Washington	1928
Harry Carson, South Carolina St. ($)	1975
Anthony Carter, Michigan	1982
Tommy Casanova, LSU	1971
†Edward Casey, Harvard	1919
Rod Cason, Angelo St. ($)	1971
Howard Cassady, Ohio St.	1955
†Guy Chamberlin, Neb. Wesleyan/Nebraska#	1915
Sam Chapman, California	1937
Bob Chappuis, Michigan	1947
†Paul Christman, Missouri	1940
Joe Cichy, North Dakota St. ($)	1970
†Dutch Clark, Colorado Col.#	1929
Paul Cleary, Southern California	1947
†Zora Clevenger, Indiana	1903
Jack Cloud, William & Mary	1949
†Gary Cochran, Princeton	1897
†Josh Cody, Vanderbilt	1919
Don Coleman, Michigan St.	1951
†Charlie Conerly, Mississippi	1947
†George Connor, Holy Cross/Notre Dame#	1947
Bill Cooper, Muskingum ($)	1960
†William Corbin, Yale	1888
William Corbus, Stanford	1933
†Hector Cowan, Princeton	1889
†Edward Coy, Yale	1909
Brad Crawford, Franklin ($)	1977
†Fred Crawford, Duke	1933
John David Crow, Texas A&M	1957
†Jim Crowley, Notre Dame	1924
Larry Csonka, Syracuse#	1967
Slade Cutter, Navy	1934
†Ziggie Czarobski, Notre Dame	1947
Carroll Dale, Virginia Tech	1959
†Gerald Dalrymple, Tulane	1931
†John Dalton, Navy	1911
†Charles Daly, Harvard/Army	1902
Averell Daniell, Pittsburgh	1936
†James Daniell, Ohio St.	1941
†Tom Davies, Pittsburgh	1921
†Ernie Davis, Syracuse	1961
Glenn Davis, Army	1946
Robert Davis, Georgia Tech	1947
Pete Dawkins, Army	1958
Tom Deery, Widener ($)	1981
†Joe Delaney, Northwestern St. ($)	1980
Steve DeLong, Tennessee	1964
Vern Den Herder, Central (Iowa) ($)	1970
Al DeRogatis, Duke	1948
†Paul DesJardien, Chicago	1914
†Aubrey Devine, Iowa	1921
†John DeWitt, Princeton	1903
Buddy Dial, Rice	1958
Chuck Dicus, Arkansas	1970
Don Dierdorf, Michigan#	1970
Mike Ditka, Pittsburgh#	1960
†Glenn Dobbs, Tulsa	1942
†Bobby Dodd, Tennessee	1930

Player, College	Year
Holland Donan, Princeton	1950
†Joseph Donchess, Pittsburgh	1929
Tony Dorsett, Pittsburgh#	1976
†Nathan Dougherty, Tennessee	1909
Bob Dove, Notre Dame	1942
Nick Drahos, Cornell	1940
†Paddy Driscoll, Northwestern#	1916
†Morley Drury, Southern California	1927
Fred Dryer, San Diego St. ($)	1968
Joe Dudek, Plymouth St. ($)	1985
Dick Duden, Navy	1945
Bill Dudley, Virginia#	1941
Randy Duncan, Iowa	1958
Kenny Easley, UCLA	1980
†Walter Eckersall, Chicago	1906
†Turk Edwards, Washington St.#	1931
†William Edwards, Princeton	1899
†Ray Eichenlaub, Notre Dame	1914
Steve Eisenhauer, Navy	1953
Lawrence Elkins, Baylor	1964
Bump Elliott, Michigan/Purdue	1947
Pete Elliott, Michigan	1948
Dave Elmendorf, Texas A&M	1970
John Elway, Stanford	1982
Ray Evans, Kansas	1947
†Albert Exendine, Carlisle	1907
†Nello Falaschi, Santa Clara	1936
†Tom Fears, Santa Clara/UCLA#	1947
†Beattie Feathers, Tennessee	1933
Bob Fenimore, Oklahoma St.	1946
†Doc Fenton, LSU	1909
Bob Ferguson, Ohio St.	1961
John Ferraro, Southern California	1947
†Wes Fesler, Ohio St.	1930
†Bill Fincher, Davidson/Georgia Tech	1920
Bill Fischer, Notre Dame	1948
†Hamilton Fish, Harvard	1909
†Robert Fisher, Harvard	1911
†Allen Flowers, Davidson/Georgia Tech	1920
Charlie Flowers, Mississippi	1959
George Floyd, Eastern Ky. ($)	1981
†Danny Fortmann, Colgate#	1935
Bill Fralic, Pittsburgh	1984
†Sam Francis, Nebraska	1936
George "Sonny" Franck, Minnesota	1940
†Ed Franco, Fordham	1937
†Clint Frank, Yale	1937
Rodney Franz, California	1949
Tucker Frederickson, Auburn	1964
†Benny Friedman, Michigan	1926
Roman Gabriel, North Carolina St.	1961
Bob Gain, Kentucky	1950
†Arnold Galiffa, Army	1949
Willie Galimore, Florida A&M ($)	1956
Hugh Gallarneau, Stanford	1940
Kenny Gamble, Colgate ($)	1987
†Edgar Garbisch, Wash. & Jeff./Army	1924
Mike Garrett, Southern California	1965
†Charles Gelbert, Pennsylvania	1896
†Forest Geyer, Oklahoma	1915
Jake Gibbs, Mississippi	1960
†Paul Giel, Minnesota	1953
Frank Gifford, Southern California#	1951
Chris Gilbert, Texas	1968
†Walter Gilbert, Auburn	1936
Harry Gilmer, Alabama	1947
†George Gipp, Notre Dame	1920
†Chet Gladchuk, Boston College	1940
Bill Glass, Baylor	1956
Rich Glover, Nebraska	1972
Marshall Goldberg, Pittsburgh	1938
Gene Goodreault, Boston College	1940
†Walter Gordon, California	1918
†Paul Governali, Columbia	1942
Jim Grabowski, Illinois	1965
Randy Gradishar, Ohio St.	1973
Otto Graham, Northwestern#	1943
†Red Grange, Illinois#	1925
†Bobby Grayson, Stanford	1935
Charlie Green, Wittenberg ($)	1964
Hugh Green, Pittsburgh	1980
†Jack Green, Tulane/Army	1945
Tim Green, Syracuse	1985
Joe Greene, North Texas#	1968

Player, College	Year
Bob Griese, Purdue#	1966
Archie Griffin, Ohio St.	1975
William Grinnell, Tufts ($)	1934
Jerry Groom, Notre Dame	1950
Ralph Guglielmi, Notre Dame	1954
†Merle Gulick, Toledo/Hobart	1929
†Joe Guyon, Carlisle/Georgia Tech#	1918
John Hadl, Kansas	1961
†Edwin Hale, Mississippi Col.	1921
L. Parker Hall, Mississippi	1938
Jack Ham, Penn St.#	1970
Bob Hamilton, Stanford	1935
†Tom Hamilton, Navy	1926
John Hannah, Alabama#	1972
†Vic Hanson, Syracuse	1926
†Pat Harder, Wisconsin	1942
†Tack Hardwick, Harvard	1914
†T. Truxton Hare, Pennsylvania	1900
†Chick Harley, Ohio St.	1919
†Tom Harmon, Michigan	1940
†Howard Harpster, Carnegie Mellon	1928
†Edward Hart, Princeton	1911
†Leon Hart, Notre Dame	1949
Bill Hartman, Georgia	1937
Jim Haslett, Indiana (Pa.) ($)	1978
Frank Hawkins, Nevada ($)	1980
Michael Haynes, Arizona St.#	1975
†Homer Hazel, Rutgers	1924
†Matt Hazeltine, California	1954
†Ed Healey, Holy Cross/Dartmouth#	1919
†Pudge Heffelfinger, Yale	1891
†Mel Hein, Washington St.#	1930
†Don Heinrich, Washington	1952
Ted Hendricks, Miami (Fla.)#	1968
†Wilbur Henry, Wash. & Jeff.#	1919
†Clarence Herschberger, Chicago	1898
†Robert Herwig, California	1937
†Willie Heston, San Jose St./Michigan#	1904
†Herman Hickman, Tennessee	1931
†William Hickok, Yale	1894
John Hicks, Ohio St.	1973
†Dan Hill, Duke	1938
†Art Hillebrand, Princeton	1899
†Frank Hinkey, Yale	1894
†Carl Hinkle, Vanderbilt	1937
†Clarke Hinkle, Bucknell#	1931
Elroy Hirsch, Wisconsin/Michigan#	1943
†James Hitchcock, Auburn	1932
Terry Hoage, Georgia	1983
†Frank Hoffmann, Notre Dame	1931
†James J. Hogan, Yale	1904
†Brud Holland, Cornell	1938
†Don Holleder, Army	1955
†Bill Hollenback, Pennsylvania	1908
Mike Holovak, Boston College	1942
Pierce Holt, Angelo St. ($)	1987
E.J. Holub, Texas Tech	1960
Paul Hornung, Notre Dame#	1956
†Edwin Horrell, California	1924
†Les Horvath, Ohio St.	1944
†Arthur Howe, Yale	1911
†Dixie Howell, Alabama	1934
†Cal Hubbard, Geneva/Centenary (La.)#	1926
†John Hubbard, Amherst	1906
†Pooley Hubert, Alabama	1925
Sam Huff, West Virginia#	1955
Weldon Humble, La.-Lafayette/Rice	1946
Ricky Hunley, Arizona	1983
†Joel Hunt, Texas A&M	1927
†Ellery Huntington, Colgate	1913
†Don Hutson, Alabama#	1934
Cosmo Iacovazzi, Princeton	1964
†Jonas Ingram, Navy	1906
†Cecil Isbell, Purdue	1937
†Harvey Jablonsky, Army/Washington (Mo.)	1933
Bo Jackson, Auburn	1985
Keith Jackson, Oklahoma	1987
†Vic Janowicz, Ohio St.	1951
John Jefferson, Arizona St.	1977
†Darold Jenkins, Missouri	1941
†Jackie Jensen, California	1948
†Herbert Joesting, Minnesota	1927
Billy Johnson, Widener ($)	1972
Bob Johnson, Tennessee	1967

Player, College	Year
Gary Johnson, Grambling ($)	1974
†Jimmie Johnson, Carlisle/Northwestern	1905
Ron Johnson, Michigan	1968
Brent Jones, Santa Clara ($)	1985
†Calvin Jones, Iowa	1955
†Gomer Jones, Ohio St.	1935
Stan Jones, Maryland#	1953
Lee Roy Jordan, Alabama	1962
†Frank Juhan, Sewanee	1910
Charlie Justice, North Carolina	1949
†Mort Kaer, Southern California	1926
Alex Karras, Iowa	1957
Ken Kavanaugh, LSU	1939
†Edgar Kaw, Cornell	1922
Dick Kazmaier, Princeton	1951
†Stan Keck, Princeton	1921
Larry Kelley, Yale	1936
†Wild Bill Kelly, Montana	1926
Doug Kenna, Army	1944
†George Kerr, Boston College	1940
†Henry Ketcham, Yale	1913
Leroy Keyes, Purdue	1968
†Glenn Killinger, Penn St.	1921
Billy Kilmer, UCLA	1960
†John Kilpatrick, Yale	1910
John Kimbrough, Texas A&M	1940
†Frank Kinard, Mississippi#	1937
Terry Kinard, Clemson	1982
Steve Kiner, Tennessee	1969
†Phillip King, Princeton	1893
†Nile Kinnick, Iowa	1939
†Harry Kipke, Michigan	1923
†John Kitzmiller, Oregon	1930
†Barton Koch, Baylor	1930
†Walt Koppisch, Columbia	1924
Ron Kramer, Michigan	1956
Alex Kroll, Yale/Rutgers	1961
Charlie Krueger, Texas A&M	1957
Malcolm Kutner, Texas	1941
Ted Kwalick, Penn St.	1968
†Steve Lach, Duke	1941
†Myles Lane, Dartmouth	1927
Willie Lanier, Morgan St.# ($)	1966
Johnny Lattner, Notre Dame	1953
Hank Lauricella, Tennessee	1951
†Lester Lautenschlaeger, Tulane	1925
†Elmer Layden, Notre Dame	1924
†Bobby Layne, Texas#	1947
†Langdon Lea, Princeton	1895
Eddie LeBaron, Pacific (Cal.)	1949
Jim LeClair, North Dakota ($)	1971
†James Leech, VMI	1920
†Darrell Lester, TCU	1935
D.D. Lewis, Mississippi St.	1968
Bob Lilly, TCU#	1960
†Augie Lio, Georgetown	1940
Floyd Little, Syracuse	1966
Gordie Lockbaum, Holy Cross ($)	1987
†Gordon Locke, Iowa	1922
Neil Lomax, Portland St. ($)	1980
Chuck Long, Iowa	1985
Mel Long, Toledo	1971
†Frank Loria, Virginia Tech	1967
Ronnie Lott, Southern California	1980
†Don Lourie, Princeton	1921
Richie Lucas, Penn St.	1959
†Sid Luckman, Columbia#	1938
Johnny Lujack, Notre Dame	1947
†Pug Lund, Minnesota	1934
Jim Lynch, Notre Dame	1966
Ken MacAfee, Notre Dame	1977
†Robert MacLeod, Dartmouth	1938
†Bart Macomber, Illinois	1916
Dicky Maegle, Rice	1954
†Ned Mahon, Harvard	1915
Johnny Majors, Tennessee	1956
†William Mallory, Yale	1923
Vaughn Mancha, Alabama	1947
†Gerald Mann, Southern Methodist	1927
Archie Manning, Mississippi	1970
Edgar Manske, Northwestern	1933
Ed Marinaro, Cornell	1971
Dan Marino, Pittsburgh	1982
†Vic Markov, Washington	1937

Player, College	Year
†Bobby Marshall, Minnesota	1906
Jim Martin, Notre Dame	1949
Ollie Matson, San Francisco#	1951
Ray Matthews, TCU	1927
†John Maulbetsch, Adrian/Michigan	1916
†Pete Mauthe, Penn St.	1912
†Robert Maxwell, Chicago/Swarthmore	1905
George McAfee, Duke#	1939
Napoleon McCallum, Navy	1985
Don McCauley, North Carolina	1970
†Thomas McClung, Yale	1891
Bill McColl, Stanford	1951
†Jim McCormick, Princeton	1907
Tommy McDonald, Oklahoma#	1956
†Jack McDowall, North Carolina St.	1927
Hugh McElhenny, Washington#	1951
†Gene McEver, Tennessee	1931
†John McEwan, Army	1916
Banks McFadden, Clemson	1939
Bud McFadin, Texas	1950
Mike McGee, Duke	1959
†Edward McGinley, Pennsylvania	1924
†John McGovern, Minnesota	1910
Thurman McGraw, Colorado St.	1949
Tyrone McGriff, Florida A&M ($)	1979
†Mike McKeever, Southern California	1960
Reggie McKenzie, Michigan	1971
†George McLaren, Pittsburgh	1918
Jim McMahon, Brigham Young	1981
†Dan McMillan, Southern California/California	1921
†Bo McMillin, Centre	1921
†Bob McWhorter, Georgia	1913
†Roy Mercer, Pennsylvania	1912
Don Meredith, Southern Methodist	1959
Frank Merritt, Army	1943
†Bert Metzger, Notre Dame	1930
†Wayne Meylan, Nebraska	1967
Lou Michaels, Kentucky	1957
John Michels, Tennessee	1952
Abe Mickal, LSU	1935
†Creighton Miller, Notre Dame	1943
†Don Miller, Notre Dame	1924
†Eugene Miller, Penn St.	1913
†Fred Miller, Notre Dame	1928
†Rip Miller, Notre Dame	1924
†Wayne Millner, Notre Dame	1935
†Century Milstead, Wabash/Yale	1923
†John Minds, Pennsylvania	1897
Skip Minisi, Pennsylvania/Navy	1947
Dick Modzelewski, Maryland	1952
†Alex Moffat, Princeton	1883
†Ed Molinski, Tennessee	1940
Cliff Montgomery, Columbia	1933
Wilbert Montgomery, Abilene Christian ($)	1976
Donn Moomaw, UCLA	1952
†William Morley, Columbia	1901
George Morris, Georgia Tech	1952
Larry Morris, Georgia Tech	1954
†Bill Morton, Dartmouth	1931
Craig Morton, California	1964
†Monk Moscrip, Stanford	1935
†Brick Muller, California	1922
Johnny Musso, Alabama	1971
†Bronko Nagurski, Minnesota#	1929
†Ernie Nevers, Stanford#	1925
†Marshall Newell, Harvard	1893
Harry Newman, Michigan	1932
Ozzie Newsome, Alabama#	1977
Gifford Nielsen, Brigham Young	1977
Tommy Nobis, Texas	1965
Leo Nomellini, Minnesota#	1949
†Andrew Oberlander, Dartmouth	1925
†Davey O'Brien, TCU	1938
Ken O'Brien, UC Davis ($)	1982
†Pat O'Dea, Wisconsin	1899
Bob Odell, Pennsylvania	1943
†Jack O'Hearn, Cornell	1914
Robin Olds, Army	1942
†Elmer Oliphant, Army/Purdue	1917
Merlin Olsen, Utah St.#	1961
Dennis Onkotz, Penn St.	1969
†Bennie Oosterbaan, Michigan	1927
Charles O'Rourke, Boston College	1940

AWARD WINNERS

Player, College	Year
†John Orsi, Colgate	1931
†Win Osgood, Cornell/Pennsylvania	1894
Bill Osmanski, Holy Cross	1938
†John Outland, Kansas/Pennsylvania	1899
†George Owen, Harvard	1922
Jim Owens, Oklahoma	1949
Steve Owens, Oklahoma	1969
Alan Page, Notre Dame#	1966
Joe Palumbo, Virginia	1951
Jack Pardee, Texas A&M	1956
Babe Parilli, Kentucky	1951
Ace Parker, Duke#	1936
Jackie Parker, Mississippi St.	1953
Jim Parker, Ohio St.#	1956
†Walter Payton, Jackson St.# ($)	1974
†Vince Pazzetti, Wesleyan/Lehigh	1912
Chub Peabody, Harvard	1941
†Robert Peck, Pittsburgh	1916
Bob Pellegrini, Maryland	1955
†Stan Pennock, Harvard	1914
George Pfann, Cornell	1923
†H.D. Phillips, Sewanee	1905
Loyd Phillips, Arkansas	1966
Pete Pihos, Indiana#	1946
†Erny Pinckert, Southern California	1931
†John Pingel, Michigan St.	1938
Jim Plunkett, Stanford	1970
†Arthur Poe, Princeton	1899
†Fritz Pollard, Brown	1916
George Poole, Mississippi/North Carolina/Army	1948
Marvin Powell, Southern California	1976
Merv Pregulman, Michigan	1943
†Eddie Price, Tulane	1949
Greg Pruitt, Oklahoma	1972
Larry Pugh, Westminster (Pa.) ($)	1964
†Peter Pund, Georgia Tech	1928
Garrard Ramsey, William & Mary	1942
Gary Reasons, Northwestern St. ($)	1983
Bill Redell, Occidental ($)	1963
Rick Redman, Washington	1964
†Claude Reeds, Oklahoma	1913
Mike Reid, Penn St.	1969
Steve Reid, Northwestern	1936
†William Reid, Harvard	1899
Bob Reifsnyder, Navy	1958
Mel Renfro, Oregon#	1963
†Pug Rentner, Northwestern	1932
Glenn Ressler, Penn St.	1969
†Bob Reynolds, Stanford	1935
†Bobby Reynolds, Nebraska	1952
Randy Rhino, Georgia Tech	1974
Jerry Rhome, Southern Methodist/Tulsa	1964
Les Richter, California	1951
Pat Richter, Wisconsin	1962
†Jack Riley, Northwestern	1931
Dave Rimington, Nebraska	1982
†Charles Rinehart, Lafayette	1897
Jim Ritcher, North Carolina St.	1979
Richard Ritchie, Tex. A&M-Kingsville ($)	1976
J.D. Roberts, Oklahoma	1953
†Paul Robeson, Rutgers	1918
Dave Robinson, Penn St.	1962
Jerry Robinson, UCLA	1978
†Ira Rodgers, West Virginia	1919
Johnny Rodgers, Nebraska	1972
†Edward Rogers, Carlisle/Minnesota	1903
George Rogers, South Carolina	1980
Johnny Roland, Missouri	1965
Joe Romig, Colorado	1961
†Aaron Rosenberg, Southern California	1933
†Kyle Rote, Southern Methodist	1950
†Joe Routt, Texas A&M	1937
†Red Salmon, Notre Dame	1903
Alex Sarkisian, Northwestern	1948
†George Sauer, Nebraska	1933
George Savitsky, Pennsylvania	1947
James Saxton, Texas	1961
Gale Sayers, Kansas#	1964
Jack Scarbath, Maryland	1952
†Hunter Scarlett, Pennsylvania	1908
Bob Schloredt, Washington	1960
Joe Schmidt, Pittsburgh#	1952
†Wear Schoonover, Arkansas	1929
†Dave Schreiner, Wisconsin	1942
†Germany Schultz, Michigan	1908

Player, College	Year
†Dutch Schwab, Lafayette	1922
†Marchy Schwartz, Notre Dame	1931
†Paul Schwegler, Washington	1931
Clyde Scott, Navy/Arkansas	1948
Freddie Scott, Amherst ($)	1973
Richard Scott, Navy	1947
Tom Scott, Virginia	1952
†Henry Seibels, Sewanee	1900
Ron Sellers, Florida St.	1968
Lee Roy Selmon, Oklahoma#	1975
Harley Sewell, Texas	1952
†Bill Shakespeare, Notre Dame	1935
Donnie Shell, South Carolina St. ($)	1973
†Murray Shelton, Cornell	1915
†Tom Shevlin, Yale	1905
†Bernie Shively, Illinois	1926
†Monk Simons, Tulane	1934
O.J. Simpson, Southern California	1968
Billy Sims, Oklahoma	1979
Mike Singletary, Baylor#	1980
Fred Sington, Alabama	1930
†Frank Sinkwich, Georgia	1942
Jerry Sisemore, Texas	1972
†Emil Sitko, Notre Dame	1949
†Joe Skladany, Pittsburgh	1933
†Duke Slater, Iowa	1921
Billy Ray Smith, Arkansas	1982
†Bruce Smith, Minnesota	1941
Bubba Smith, Michigan St.	1966
†Clipper Smith, Notre Dame	1927
†Ernie Smith, Southern California	1932
Harry Smith, Southern California	1939
Jim Ray Smith, Baylor	1954
Riley Smith, Alabama	1935
†Vernon Smith, Georgia	1931
†Neil Snow, Michigan	1901
Gary Spani, Kansas St.	1977
Al Sparlis, UCLA	1945
†Clarence Spears, Knox/Dartmouth	1915
†W.D. Spears, Vanderbilt	1927
†William Sprackling, Brown	1911
†Bud Sprague, Army/Texas	1928
Steve Spurrier, Florida	1966
Harrison Stafford, Texas	1932
†Amos Alonzo Stagg, Yale	1889
Bill Stanfill, Georgia	1968
†Max Starcevich, Washington	1936
Roger Staubach, Navy#	1964
†Walter Steffen, Chicago	1908
Joe Steffy, Tennessee/Army	1947
†Herbert Stein, Pittsburgh	1921
Bob Steuber, DePauw/Missouri	1943
†Mal Stevens, Washburn/Yale	1923
†Vincent Stevenson, Pennsylvania	1905
Jim Stillwagon, Ohio St.	1970
†Pete Stinchcomb, Ohio St.	1920
Brock Strom, Air Force	1958
†Ken Strong, New York U.#	1928
†George Strupper, Georgia Tech	1917
†Harry Stuhldreher, Notre Dame	1924
†Herb Sturhahn, Yale	1926
†Joe Stydahar, West Virginia#	1935
†Bob Suffridge, Tennessee	1940
†Steve Suhey, Penn St.	1947
Pat Sullivan, Auburn	1971
†Frank Sundstrom, Cornell	1923
Lynn Swann, Southern California#	1973
†Clarence Swanson, Nebraska	1921
†Bill Swiacki, Holy Cross/Columbia	1947
Jim Swink, TCU	1956
†Eddie Talboom, Wyoming	1950
George Taliaferro, Indiana	1948
Fran Tarkenton, Georgia#	1960
John Tavener, Indiana	1944
Bruce Taylor, Boston U. ($)	1969
†Chuck Taylor, Stanford	1942
Aurelius Thomas, Ohio St.	1957
†Joe Thompson, Geneva/Pittsburgh	1906
Lynn Thomsen, Augustana (Ill.)$	1986
†Samuel Thorne, Yale	1895
†Jim Thorpe, Carlisle#	1912
†Ben Ticknor, Harvard	1930
†John Tigert, Vanderbilt	1903
Gaynell Tinsley, LSU	1936
Eric Tipton, Duke	1938
†Clayton Tonnemaker, Minnesota	1949
†Bob Torrey, Pennsylvania	1905

Player, College	Year
Randy Trautman, Boise St. ($)	1981
†Brick Travis, Tarkio/Missouri	1920
Charley Trippi, Georgia#	1946
†Edward Tryon, Colgate	1925
Jerry Tubbs, Oklahoma	1956
Bulldog Turner, Hardin-Simmons#	1939
Howard Twilley, Tulsa	1965
†Joe Utay, Texas A&M	1907
†Norm Van Brocklin, Oregon#	1948
Brad Van Pelt, Michigan St.	1972
†Dale Van Sickel, Florida	1929
†H. Van Surdam, Wesleyan (Conn.)	1905
†Dexter Very, Penn St.	1912
†Billy Vessels, Oklahoma	1952
†Ernie Vick, Michigan	1921
†Hube Wagner, Pittsburgh	1913
†Doak Walker, Southern Methodist#	1949
Herschel Walker, Georgia	1982
†Bill Wallace, Rice	1935
†Adam Walsh, Notre Dame	1924
†Cotton Warburton, Southern California	1934
Bob Ward, Maryland	1951
†William Warner, Cornell	1902
†Kenny Washington, UCLA	1939
†Jim Weatherall, Oklahoma	1951
George Webster, Michigan St.	1966
Herman Wedemeyer, St. Mary's (Cal.)	1947
†Harold Weekes, Columbia	1902
Art Weiner, North Carolina	1949
†Ed Weir, Nebraska	1925
†Gus Welch, Carlisle	1914
†John Weller, Princeton	1935
†Percy Wendell, Harvard	1912
†Belford West, Colgate	1919
†Bob Westfall, Michigan	1941
†Babe Weyand, Army	1915
†Buck Wharton, Pennsylvania	1896
†Arthur Wheeler, Princeton	1894
†Byron White, Colorado	1937
Charles White, Southern California	1979
Danny White, Arizona St.	1973
Ed White, California	1968
Randy White, Maryland#	1974
Reggie White, Tennessee	1983
†Don Whitmire, Navy/Alabama	1944
†Frank Wickhorst, Navy	1926
Ed Widseth, Minnesota	1936
†Dick Wildung, Minnesota	1942
Bob Williams, Notre Dame	1950
Doug Williams, Grambling ($)	1977
Froggie Williams, Rice	1949
Bill Willis, Ohio St.#	1944
Bobby Wilson, Southern Methodist	1935
†George Wilson, Washington	1925
†Harry Wilson, Army/Penn St.	1927
Marc Wilson, Brigham Young	1979
Mike Wilson, Lafayette	1928
Kellen Winslow, Missouri	1978
Albert Wistert, Michigan	1942
Alvin Wistert, Boston U./Michigan	1949
†Whitey Wistert, Michigan	1933
†Alex Wojciechowicz, Fordham#	1937
†Barry Wood, Harvard	1931
†Andy Wyant, Bucknell/Chicago	1894
†Bowden Wyatt, Tennessee	1938
†Clint Wyckoff, Cornell	1895
†Tommy Yarr, Notre Dame	1931
Ron Yary, Southern California#	1967
†Lloyd Yoder, Carnegie Mellon	1926
†Buddy Young, Illinois	1946
†Harry Young, Wash. & Lee	1916
Steve Young, Brigham Young	1983
†Waddy Young, Oklahoma	1938
Jack Youngblood, Florida#	1970
Jim Youngblood, Tennessee Tech ($)	1972
Paul Younger, Grambling ($)	1948
Gust Zarnas, Ohio St.	1937

COACHES

Coach	Year
†Joe Aillet	1989
†Bill Alexander	1951
†Eddie Anderson	1971
†Ike Armstrong	1957
Chris Ault ($)	2002
†Charlie Bachman	1978
Earl Banks	1992

Coach	Year
†Harry Baujan	1990
†Matty Bell	1955
†Hugo Bezdek	1954
†Dana X. Bible	1951
†Bernie Bierman	1955
†Bob Blackman	1987
†Earl "Red" Blaik	1964
Frank Broyles	1983
Earle Bruce	2002
†Paul "Bear" Bryant	1986
Harold Burry ($)	1996
Jim Butterfield ($)	1997
†Wally Butts	1997
†Charlie Caldwell	1961
†Walter Camp	1951
†Len Casanova	1977
†Frank Cavanaugh	1954
Jerry Claiborne	1999
†Dick Colman	1990
Don Coryell ($)	1999
Carmen Cozza	2002
†Fritz Crisler	1954
†Duffy Daugherty	1984
†Bob Devaney	1981
†Dan Devine	1985
†Gil Dobie	1951
†Bobby Dodd	1993
†Michael Donahue	1951
Terry Donahue	2000
Vince Dooley	1994
†Gus Dorais	1954
†Bill Edwards	1986
†Rip Engle	1973
Forest Evashevski	2000
†Don Faurot	1961
Joseph Fusco ($)	2001
†Jake Gaither	1975
†Sid Gillman#	1989
†Ernest Godfrey	1972
Ray Graves	1990
†Andy Gustafson	1985
†Edward Hall	1951
†Jack Hardin	1980
†Richard Harlow	1954
†Harvey Harman	1981
†Jesse Harper	1971
†Percy Haughton	1951
†Woody Hayes	1983
†John W. Heisman	1954
†Robert Higgins	1954
†Paul Hoernemann ($)	1997
†Babe Hollingberry	1979
†Frank Howard	1989
Marcelino Huerta ($)	2002
†Bill Ingram	1973
Don James	1997
†Morley Jennings	1973
†Biff Jones	1954
†Howard Jones	1951
†Tad Jones	1958
†Lloyd Jordan	1978
†Ralph "Shug" Jordan	1982
†Andy Kerr	1951
Chuck Klausing ($)	1998
Frank Kush	1995
†Frank Leahy	1970
†George Little	1955
†Lou Little	1960
†Slip Madigan	1974
Fred Martinelli ($)	2002
Dave Maurer	1991
†Charlie McClendon	1986
Herb McCracken	1973
†Dan McGugin	1951
†John McKay	1988
Allyn McKeen	1991
†Tuss McLaughry	1962
†John Merritt	1994
†Dutch Meyer	1956
†Jack Mollenkopf	1988
†Bernie Moore	1954
†Scrappy Moore	1980
†Ray Morrison	1954
Darrell Mudra ($)	2000
†Arnett "Ace" Mumford ($)	2001
†George Munger	1976
†Clarence "Biggie" Munn	1959
†Bill Murray	1974
†Frank Murray	1974
†Ed "Hook" Mylin	1974
†Earle "Greasy" Neale #	1967
†Jess Neely	1971
†David Nelson	1987
†Robert Neyland	1956
Billy Nicks ($)	1999
†Homer Norton	1971
†Frank "Buck" O'Neill	1951
Tom Osborne	1998
†Bennie Owen	1951
Ara Parseghian	1980
†Doyt Perry	1988
†Jimmy Phelan	1973
†Tommy Prothro	1991
John Ralston	1992
Bob Reade ($)	1998
†E.N. Robinson	1955
Eddie Robinson ($)	1997
†Knute Rockne	1951
†Dick Romney	1954
†Bill Roper	1951
Darrell Royal	1983
Adolph Rutschman ($)	1998
†Henry "Red" Sanders	1996
†George Sanford	1971
Glenn "Bo" Schembechler	1993
Ron Schipper ($)	2000
†Francis Schmidt	1971
†Ben Schwartzwalder	1982
†Clark Shaughnessy	1968
†Buck Shaw	1972
Edgar Sherman ($)	1996
†Andy Smith	1951
†Carl Snavely	1965
Jim Sochor ($)	1999
†Amos Alonzo Stagg	1951
†Gil Steinke ($)	1996
†Jock Sutherland	1951
Barry Switzer	2001
†Jim Tatum	1984
Grant Teaff	2001
†Frank Thomas	1951
†Lee Tressel ($)	1996
†Thad "Pie" Vann	1987
Johnny Vaught	1979
†Wallace Wade	1955
†Lynn "Pappy" Waldorf	1966
†Glenn "Pop" Warner	1951
Frank "Muddy" Waters ($)	2000
†E.E. "Tad" Wieman	1956
†John Wilce	1954
†Bud Wilkinson	1969
†Henry Williams	1951
†George Woodruff	1963
†Warren Woodson	1989
†Bowden Wyatt	1997
Bill Yeoman	2001
†Fielding "Hurry Up" Yost	1951
Jim Young	1999
†Bob Zuppke	1951

†Deceased

DIVISION II NATIONAL HALL OF FAME
(at Florence, Alabama)

1999

Johnny Bailey, Tex. A&M-Kingsville, RB
Jeff Bentrim, North Dakota St., QB
Walter Payton, Jackson St., RB

2000

Harry Carson, South Carolina St., LB
Pierce Holt, Angelo St., DL

John Stallworth, Alabama A&M, WR

2001

Brent Jones, Santa Clara, TE
Greg Lloyd, Fort Valley St., LB
Ken Davis, UC Davis, QB

2002

Scott Brunner, Delaware, QB
Andre Reed, Kutztown, WR
Jessie Tuggle, Valdosta St., LB

First-Team All-Americans Below Division I-A

2002 Selectors (and division[s]): American Football Coaches Association (I-AA, II, III); Associated Press (I-AA, II, III); Football Gazette (I-AA, II, III); The Sports Network (I-AA); Daktronics (II); D2 Football.com (II); Hewlett-Packard (III); D3 Football.com (III).

Selection of Associated Press Little All-America Teams began in 1934. Early AP selectors were not bound by NCAA membership classifications; therefore, several current Division I-A teams are included in this list.

The American Football Coaches Association began selecting all-America teams below Division I-A in 1967 for two College Division classifications. Its College Division I team included NCAA Division II and National Association of Intercollegiate Athletics (NAIA) Division I players. The AFCA College Division II team included NCAA Division III and NAIA Division II players. The AFCA renamed the College Division I team to Division II, and the College Division II team to Division III, in 1996; players at NAIA institutions are no longer eligible for these teams.

The AFCA added a Division I-AA team in 1979; AP began selecting a Division I-AA team in 1982; the Sports Network added a Division I-AA team in 1994; and these players are included. In 1993, the College Sports Information Directors of America Division II team was added, selected by sports information directors from every NCAA Division II institution. In 1997, the Daktronics team for Division II was added. In 1990, the Champion USA Division III team was added, selected by a panel of 25 sports information directors and replaced by the Hewlett-Packard Division III team in 1995. In 1993, Football Gazette's team was added for Divisions I-AA, II and III. In 2002, D2 Football.com and D3 Football.com were added for Divisions II and III, respectively.

Nonmembers of the NCAA are included in this list, as are colleges that no longer play varsity football.

Players selected to a Division I-AA all-America team are indicated by (†). Current members of Division I-A are indicated by (*).

All-Americans are listed by college, year selected and position.

ABILENE CHRISTIAN (19)
48— V.T. Smith, B
51— Lester Wheeler, OT
52— Wallace Bullington, DB
65— Larry Cox, OT
69— Chip Bennett, LB
70— Jim Lindsey, QB
73— Wilbert Montgomery, RB
74— Chip Martin, DL
77— Chuck Sitton, DB
82— Grant Feasel, C
83— Mark Wilson, DB
84— Dan Remsberg, OT
87— Richard Van Druten, OT
89— John Layfield, OG
90— Dennis Brown, PK
91— Jay Jones, LB
97— Junior Filikitonga, DL
      Victor Burke, DB
2001—Brad Raphelt, P

ADAMS ST. (6)
79— Ronald Johnson, DB
84— Bill Stone, RB
87— Dave Humann, DB
95— Chris Perry, WR
97— Jason Van Dyke, P
98— Jason Van Dyke, P

AKRON* (9)
69— John Travis, OG
71— Michael Hatch, DB
76— Mark Van Horn, OG
      Steve Cockerham, LB
77— Steve Cockerham, LB
80— †Brad Reece, LB
81— †Brad Reece, LB
85— †Wayne Grant, DL
86— †Mike Clark, RB

UAB* (1)
94— †Derrick Ingram, WR

ALABAMA A&M (4)
87— Howard Ballard, OL
88— Fred Garner, OL
89— Barry Wagner, WR
2002—†Robert Mathis, DL

ALABAMA ST. (6)
90— †Eddie Robinson, LB
91— †Patrick Johnson, OL
      †Eddie Robinson, LB
2000—†David Beckford, P
01— †David Beckford, P
      †Chris Coleman, TE

ALBANY (N.Y.) (4)
92— Scott Turrin, OL
94— Scott Turrin, OL
98— Matt Caliandro, DL
2000—†J.T. Herfurth, OL

ALBANY ST. (GA.) (1)
72— Harold Little, DE

ALBION (16)
40— Walter Ptak, G
58— Tom Taylor, E
76— Steve Spencer, DL
86— Joe Felton, OG
      Mike Grant, DB
91— Hank Wineman, RB
93— Ron Dawson, OL
      Jeff Brooks, OL
94— Jeff Robinson, RB
      Martin Heyboer, C
      David Lefere, DB
95— David Lefere, DB
96— Jason Carriveau, OG
98— Pat Sloane, DL
      Jason Carriveau, OL
2000—Keith Debbaudt, PK

ALBRIGHT (7)
36— Richard Riffle, B
37— Richard Riffle, B

75— Chris Simcic, OL
95— Dennis Unger, PK
96— Ryan Ditze, WR
      Bob Maro, DB
98— Chris Morehouse, P

ALCORN ST. (14)
69— David Hadley, DB
70— Fred Carter, DT
71— Harry Gooden, LB
72— Alex Price, DT
73— Leonard Fairley, DB
74— Jerry Dismuke, OG
75— Lawrence Pillers, DE
76— Augusta Lee, RB
      Larry Warren, DT
79— †Leslie Frazier, DB
84— †Issiac Holt, DB
93— †Goree White, KR
94— †Steve McNair, QB
99— †Chad Slaughter, OL

ALFRED (7)
51— Ralph DiMicco, B
52— Ralph DiMicco, B
55— Charles Schultz, E
56— Charles Schultz, E
75— Joseph Van Cura, DE
82— Brian O'Neil, DB
92— Mark Obuszewski, DB

ALLEGHENY (22)
75— Charles Slater, OL
87— Mike Mates, OL
88— Mike Parker, OL
90— Jeff Filkovski, QB
      David LaCarte, DB
      John Marzca, C
91— Ron Bendekovic, OT
      Stanley Drayton, RB
      Tony Bifulco, DB
92— Ron Bendekovic, OT
      Stanley Drayton, RB
94— Matt Allison, OL
      Paul Bell, QB
      Marvin Farr, DB
95— Brian Adams, C
      Nick Reiser, DE
      Anson Park, OL
96— Chris Conrad, KR
      Nick Reiser, DL
      Bob Tatsch, DL
97— Jim Mormino, RB
2000—Bill Andrews, OL

ALMA (1)
2002—David Simpson, DB

AMERICAN INT'L (14)
71— Bruce Laird, RB
80— Ed Cebula, C
82— Paul Thompson, DT
85— Keith Barry, OL
86— Jon Provost, OL
87— Jon Provost, OL
88— Greg Doherty, OL
89— Lamont Cato, DB
90— George Patterson, DL
91— Gabe Mokwuah, DL
98— Ray Shuster, OL
99— Kavin Gailliard, RB
2000—Bob Parker, DB
01— Dan Porter, OL

AMHERST (5)
42— Adrian Hasse, E
72— Richard Murphy, QB
73— Fred Scott, FL
96— Alex Bernstein, DL
97— Devin Moriarty, DL

ANDERSON (IND.) (1)
97— Justin Shively, P

ANGELO ST. (14)
75— James Cross, DB
78— Jerry Aldridge, RB
      Kelvin Smith, LB
81— Clay Weishuhn, LB
82— Mike Elarms, WR
83— Mike Thomas, K
85— Henry Jackson, RB
86— Pierce Holt, DL
87— Pierce Holt, DL
88— Henry Alsbrooks, LB
92— Jimmy Morris, P

93— Anthony Hooper, DB
95— Greg Stokes, LB
2001—Dan Krager, DL

APPALACHIAN ST. (26)
48— John Caskey, E
63— Greg Van Orden, G
85— †Dino Hackett, LB
87— †Anthony Downs, DE
88— †Bjorn Nittmo, PK
89— †Derrick Graham, OL
      †Keith Collins, DB
91— †Harold Alexander, P
92— †Avery Hall, DL
      †Harold Alexander, P
94— †Chip Miller, DL
      †William Peebles, DL
      †Brad Ohrt, OL
      †Dexter Coakley, LB
      †Matt Stevens, DB
95— †Dexter Coakley, LB
      †Matt Stevens, DB
      †Chip Miller, DL
      †Scott Kadlub, C
96— †Scott Kadlub, C
      †Dexter Coakley, LB
97— †Jackie Avery, DL
99— †Corey Hall, DB
2000—†Corey Hall, DB
01— †Josh Jeffries, DL
02— †Josh Jeffries, DL

ARIZONA* (1)
41— Henry Stanton, E

ARKANSAS ST.* (17)
53— Richard Woit, B
64— Dan Summers, OG
65— Dan Summers, OG
68— Bill Bergey, LB
69— Dan Buckley, C
      Clovis Swinney, DT
70— Bill Phillips, OG
      Calvin Harrell, HB
71— Calvin Harrell, RB
      Dennis Meyer, DB
      Wayne Dorton, OG
73— Doug Lowrey, OG
84— †Carter Crawford, DL
85— †Carter Crawford, DL
86— †Randy Barnhill, OG
87— †Jim Wiseman, C
      †Charlie Fredrick, DT

ARKANSAS TECH (5)
58— Edward Meador, B
61— Powell McClellan, E
95— Piotr Styczen, PK
99— Todd Matthews, OG
2002—Tommy Edwards, DL

ASHLAND (9)
70— Len Pettigrew, LB
78— Keith Dare, DL
85— Jeff Penko, OL
86— Vince Mazza, PK
89— Douglas Powell, DB
90— Morris Furman, LB
91— Ron Greer, LB
93— Bill Royce, DL
94— Sam Hohler, DE

AUGUSTANA (ILL.) (14)
72— Willie Van, DT
73— Robert Martin, OT
83— Kurt Kapischke, OL
84— Greg King, C
86— Lynn Thomsen, DL
87— Carlton Beasley, DL
88— John Bothe, OL
90— Barry Reade, PK
91— Mike Hesler, DB
92— George Annang, DL
95— Rusty Van Wetzinga, LB
2000—Mack Hay, OG
01— J.D. Sheldon, OL
02— J.D. Sheldon, OL

AUGUSTANA (S.D.) (6)
60— John Simko, E
87— Tony Adkins, DL
88— Pete Jaros, DB
94— Bryan Schwartz, LB
2000—Matt Holmlund, WR
01— Matt Holmlund, WR

AUGSBURG (2)
97— Scott Hvistendahl, WR
98— Scott Hvistendahl, WR

AURORA (3)
99— Jeremy Benson, DL
2000—Jeremy Benson, DL
01— Kip Daniels, DB

AUSTIN (10)
37— Wallace Johnson, C
79— Price Clifford, LB
80— Chris Luper, DB
81— Larry Shillings, QB
83— Ed Holt, DL
84— Jeff Timmons, PK
87— Otis Amy, WR
88— Otis Amy, WR
90— Jeff Cordell, DB
94— Brent Badger, P

AUSTIN PEAY (10)
65— Tim Chilcutt, DB
66— John Ogles, FB
70— Harold Roberts, OE
77— Bob Bible, LB
78— Mike Betts, DB
80— Brett Williams, DE
82— Charlie Tucker, OL
92— †Richard Darden, DL
2001—†Dustin Wilson, LB
02— †Jay Bailey, RB

AZUSA PACIFIC (3)
86— Christian Okoye, RB
95— Jake Wiersma, OL
2001—Jeremiah Beery, LB

BAKER (3)
83— Chris Brown, LB
85— Kevin Alewine, RB
90— John Campbell, OL

BALDWIN-WALLACE (12)
50— Norbert Hecker, E
68— Bob Quackenbush, DT
78— Jeff Jenkins, OL
80— Dan Delfino, DE
82— Pete Primeau, DL
83— Steve Varga, K
89— Doug Halbert, DL
91— John Koz, QB
        Jim Clardy, LB
94— Chris Kondik, PK
        Phil Sahley, DL
97— Fred Saylor, DL

BALL ST.* (4)
67— Oscar Lubke, OT
68— Amos Van Pelt, HB
72— Douglas Bell, C
73— Terry Schmidt, DB

BATES (1)
81— Larry DiGammarino, WR

BELOIT (1)
95— Maurice Redd, DB

BEMIDJI ST. (1)
83— Bruce Ecklund, TE

BENEDICTINE (ILL.) (3)
72— Mike Rogowski, LB
92— Bob McMillen, TE
93— Eric Green, KR

BENEDICTINE (KAN.) (1)
36— Leo Deutsch, E

BENTLEY (2)
99— Mark DeBrito, WR
2001—Gregg Albano, DB

BETHANY (W.VA.) (2)
77— Scott Lanz, P
93— Brian Darden, PK

BETHEL (KAN.) (1)
80— David Morford, C

BETHEL (MINN.) (2)
99— Chico Rowland, OL
2000—Ben Matthews, DB

BETHUNE-COOKMAN (4)
75— Willie Lee, DE
81— Booker Reese, DE
98— † James Souder, LB
2002—†Rashean Mathis, DB

BIRMINGHAM-SOUTHERN (1)
37— Walter Riddle, T

BISHOP (1)
81— Carlton Nelson, DL

BLOOMSBURG (13)
79— Mike Morucci, RB
82— Mike Blake, TE
83— Frank Sheptock, LB
84— Frank Sheptock, LB
85— Frank Sheptock, LB
        Tony Woods, DB
91— Eric Jonassen, OL
96— Ron Lelko, WR
        Sean Smith, KR
97— Tim Baer, OL
        Irvin Sigler, RB
98— Tim Baer, OG
2000—Jeff Smith, OT

BOISE ST. *(23)
72— Al Marshall, OE
73— Don Hutt, WR
74— Jim McMillan, QB
75— John Smith, FL
77— Chris Malmgren, DT
        Terry Hutt, WR
        Harold Cotton, OT
79— †Joe Aliotti, QB
        †Doug Scott, DT
80— †Randy Trautman, DT
81— †Randy Trautman, DT
        †Rick Woods, DB
82— †John Rade, DL
        †Carl Keever, LB
84— †Carl Keever, LB
85— †Marcus Koch, DL
87— †Tom DeWitz, OG
        †Pete Kwiatkowski, DT
90— †Erik Helgeson, DL
91— †Frank Robinson, DB
92— †Michael Dodd, PK
94— †Joe O'Brien, DL
        †Rashid Gayle, DB

BOSTON U. (19)
67— Dick Farley, DB
68— Bruce Taylor, DB
69— Bruce Taylor, DB
79— †Mal Najarian, RB
        †Tom Pierzga, DL
81— †Bob Speight, OT
        †Gregg Drew, RB
82— †Mike Mastrogiacomo, OG
83— †Paul Lewis, RB
84— †Paul Lewis, RB
86— †Kevin Murphy, DT
87— †Mark Seals, DB
88— †Mark Seals, DB
89— †Daren Altieri, WR
93— †Chris Helon, DB
        †Andre Maksimov, C
94— †Andre Maksimov, C
96— †Brad Costello, P
97— †Brad Costello, P

BOWDOIN (1)
77— Steve McCabe, OL

BOWIE ST. (3)
80— Victor Jackson, CB
81— Marco Tongue, DB
2002—Charles Alston, DL

BOWLING GREEN* (2)
59— Bob Zimpfer, T
82— †Andre Young, DL

BRADLEY (1)
38— Ted Panish, B

BRANDEIS (2)
54— William McKenna, E
56— James Stehlin, B

BRIDGEPORT (1)
72— Dennis Paldin, DB

BRIDGEWATER ST. (1)
92— Erik Arthur, DL

BRIDGEWATER (VA.) (6)
75— C.J. DeWitt, SE
98— Mike Padgett, PK
2001—Michael Day, OL
        Davon Cruz, RB

02— Michael Day, OL
        Jermaine Taylor, LB

BROCKPORT ST. (6)
90— Ed Smart, TE
93— Steve Milne, PK
97— Tom Massey, DB
2000—Josh Warner, OL
01— Jason Johnson, LB
02— Mike Condello, DL

BROWN (6)
96—†Paul Choquette, TE
97—†Sean Morey, WR
        †Roderic Parson, DB
98—†Zach Burns, TE
2000—†Stephen Campbell, WR
01—†Chas Gassner, WR

BUCKNELL (13)
51— George Young, DT
60— Paul Terhes, B
64— Tom Mitchell, OE
65— Tom Mitchell, OE
74— Larry Schoenberger, LB
80— Mike McDonald, OT
90— †Mike Augsberger, DB
95— †Ed Burman, DL
96— †Brandon Little, LB
97— †Willie Hill, LB
2000—†Kevin Eiben, DB
01— †Adam Lord, DL
02— †Adam Lord, DL

BUENA VISTA (5)
72— Joe Kotval, OG
73— Joe Kotval, OG
76— Keith Kerkhoff, DL
87— Jim Higley, LB
2001—Carlos Martinez, PK

BUFFALO* (4)
84— Gerry Quinlivan, LB
87— Steve Wojciechowski, LB
95—†Pete Conley, LB
96—†Michael Chichester, DB

BUFFALO ST. (3)
93— John Mattey, OL
98— Dan Lauta, OL
99— Jon Crumley, LB

BUTLER (2)
88— Steve Roberts, RB
94—†Arnold Mickens, RB

C.W. POST (9)
71— Gary Wichard, QB
77— John Mohring, DE
78— John Mohring, DE
81— Tom DeBona, WR
89— John Levelis, DL
2000—William Yarocki, DL
01— Ian Smart, RB
02— Jon Isopo, OG
        Ian Smart, RB

UC DAVIS (19)
72— Bob Biggs, QB
        David Roberts, OT
76— Andrew Gagnon, OL
77— Chuck Fomasi, DT
78— Casey Merrill, DL
79— Jeffrey Allen, DB
82— Ken O'Brien, QB
83— Bo Eason, DB
84— Scott Barry, QB
85— Mike Wise, DL
94— Aaron Bennetts, TE
96— Josh Antstey, DE
97— Wes Terrell, TE
        Kevin Daft, QB
98— Wes Terrell, TE
99— Troy Larkin, OL
        Joe Caviglia, DB
2000—Eric Friend, PK
02— Forrest Vance, OL

UC RIVERSIDE (1)
75— Michael Johnson, SE

UC SANTA BARB. (3)
36— Douglas Oldershaw, G
37— Douglas Oldershaw, G
67— Paul Vallerga, DB

CALIF. (PA.) (3)
83— Perry Kemp, WR
2001—Wesley Cates, RB
02— R.J. Abercrombie, KR

CAL LUTHERAN (6)
72— Brian Kelley, LB
79— Mike Hagen, SE
95— Jeff Shea, P
96— Jeff Shea, P
97— Jeff Shea, P
99— Ryan Geisler, PK

CAL POLY (14)
53— Stan Sheriff, C
58— Charles Gonzales, G
66— David Edmondson, C
72— Mike Amos, DB
73— Fred Stewart, OG
78— Louis Jackson, RB
80— Louis Jackson, RB
        Robbie Martin, FL
81— Charles Daum, OL
84— Nick Frost, DB
89— Robert Morris, DL
90— Pat Moore, DL
91— Doug O'Neill, P
2000—†Kassim Osgood, WR

CAL ST. CHICO (1)
87— Chris Verhulst, TE

CAL ST. HAYWARD (4)
75— Greg Blankenship, LB
84— Ed Lively, DT
86— Fred Williams, OL
93— Jeff Williamson, TE

CAL ST. NORTHRIDGE (9)
75— Mel Wilson, DB
82— Pat Hauser, OT
83— Pat Hauser, OT
87— Kip Dukes, DB
91— Don Goodman, OL
94—†Joe Vaughn, DB
99—†Brennen Swanson, DE
2001—†Drew Amerson, WR
        †Marcus Brady, QB

CANISIUS (3)
87— Tom Doctor, LB
88— Marty Hurley, DB
94—†Aaron Fix, PR

CAPITAL (5)
74— Greg Arnold, OG
80— John Phillips, DL
        Steve Wigton, C
2001—Ron Swearingin, LB
02— Ron Swearingin, LB

CARLETON (1)
90— Jim Bradford, WR

CARNEGIE MELLON (5)
81— Ken Murawski, LB
85— Robert Butts, OL
91— Chuck Jackson, OT
93— Chad Wilson, LB
2000—Nick Zitelli, LB

CARROLL (MONT.) (6)
76— Richard Dale, DB
79— Don Diggins, DL
87— Jeff Beaudry, DB
88— Paul Petrino, QB
89— Suitoa Keleti, OL
2002—Casey Fitzsimmons, TE

CARROLL (WIS.) (3)
74— Robert Helf, TE
90— Bill Nolan, P
93— Andy Ostrand, DB

CARSON-NEWMAN (18)
78— Tank Black, FL
80— Brad Payne, S
83— Dwight Wilson, RB
90— Robert Hardy, RB
92— Darryl Gooden, LB
93— Kendall James, KR
95— Steve Mellon, DL
        Anthony Davis, LB
96— Mike Clowney, LB
97— Cedric Killings, DL
        Jacques Rumph, RS
        Jon Jon Simmons, DB
98— Ques Rumph, RS

Cedric Killings, DL
Montrae Ford, DB
99— Cedric Killings, DL
2000—Clay Clevenger, OL
02— Leonard Guyton, QB

CASE RESERVE (4)
41— Mike Yurcheshen, E
52— Al Feeny, DE
84— Fred Manley, DE
85— Mark Raiff, OL

CATAWBA (12)
34— Charles Garland, T
35— Charles Garland, T
45— Carroll Bowen, B
72— David Taylor, OT
74— Mike McDonald, LB
96— Greg Payne, PK
97— Maurice Miller, DL
98— Brian Hinson, OL
99— Brian Hinson, OL
2000—Radell Lockhart, DL
DeVonte Peterson, DL
02— Todd McComb, LB

CATHOLIC (8)
84— Chris McMahon, DB
94— Steve Wilkerson, WR
96— Matt Taylor, FB
Jeff Clay, WR
97— Jeff Clay, WR
Tony Faison, OL
99— Brian Hee, LB
2000—Dan Riely, OL

CENTRAL (IOWA) (18)
70— Vernon Den Herder, DT
74— Al Dorenkamp, LB
77— Donald Taylor, RB
84— Scott Froehle, DB
85— Rich Thomas, DL
88— Mike Stumberg, DL
89— Mike Estes, DL
Kris Reis, LB
92— Bill Maulder, LB
93— Jeff Helle, OL
94— Jeff Helle, OL
Mark Kacmarynski, RB
Rick Sanger, LB
95— Rick Sanger, LB
96— Mark Kacmarynski, RB
97— Matt Paulson, DB
98— Andrew Paulsen, DB
2000—Jeff Sanger, LB

CENTRAL ARK. (6)
80— Otis Chandler, MG
84— David Burnette, DT
91— David Henson, DL
95— Bart Reynolds, DL
96— Don Struebing, C
99— Scott Stephens, P

CENTRAL CONN. ST. (4)
74— Mike Walton, C
84— Sal Cintorino, LB
88— Doug Magazu, DL
89— Doug Magazu, DL

UCF* (4)
87— Bernard Ford, WR
Ed O'Brien, PK
93—†David Rhodes, WR
94—†Charlie Pierce, PK

CENTRAL MICH.* (4)
42— Warren Schmakel, G
59— Walter Beach, B
62— Ralph Soffredine, G
74— Rick Newsome, DL

CENTRAL MO. ST. (7)
68— Jim Urczyk, OT
85— Steve Huff, PK
88— Jeff Wright, DL
92— Bart Woods, DL
93— Bart Woods, DL
97— Shane Meyer, PK
99— Colston Weatherington, DL

CENTRAL OKLA. (11)
65— Jerome Bell, OE
87— Gary Smith, TE
94— Elton Rhoades, DB
Joe Aska, RB
96— Johnny Luter, LB

97— Dustin McNeal, OL
98— Johnny Luter, LB
John Fitzgerald, OG
Reggie Donner, RB
Brandon Carder, DB
99— Johnnie Jones, DB

CENTRAL ST. (OHIO) (9)
83— Mark Corbin, RB
84— Dave Dunham, OT
85— Mark Corbin, RB
86— Terry Morrow, RB
89— Kenneth Vines, OG
90— Eric Williams, OL
92— Marvin Coleman, DB
93— Marvin Coleman, DB
94— Hugh Douglas, DL

CENTRAL WASH. (8)
48— Robert Osgood, G
50— Jack Hawkins, G
88— Mike Estes, DL
91— Eric Lamphere, OL
2001—Jason Patterson, DB
02— Brian Potucek, WR
Rob Williams, C
Lance Gibson, DL

CENTRE (8)
55— Gene Scott, B
84— Teel Bruner, DB
85— Teel Bruner, DB
86— Jeff Leonard, OL
88— John Gohmann, DL
89— Jeff Bezold, LB
97— Montas Allen, RS
2001—Brian Britt, RS

CHADRON ST. (9)
74— Dennis Fitzgerald, DB
78— Rick Mastey, OL
90— David Jones, RB
94— Scott Doyle, PK
97— Kevin Homer, LB
99— Jess Clarke, TE
Casey Beran, DL
2001—Jeremy Eardley, LB
02— Marvin Jackson, DB

CHAPMAN (1)
98— Keith Dykes, LB

CHATTANOOGA (23)
35— Robert Klein, E
38— Robert Sutton, G
39— Jack Gregory, T
45— Thomas Stewart, T
46— Gene Roberts, B
48— Ralph Hutchinson, T
49— Vincent Sarratore, G
51— Chester LaGod, DT
52— Chester LaGod, DT
54— Richard Young, B
57— Howard Clark, E
58— John Green, B
60— Charles Long, T
64— Jerry Harris, S
66— Harry Sorrell, OG
76— Tim Collins, LB
86—†Mike Makins, DL
89—†Pumpy Tudors, P
†Junior Jackson, LB
90—†Troy Boeck, DL
†Tony Hill, DL
†Pumpy Tudors, P
2000—†Matt Vick, PK

CHICAGO (4)
91— Neal Cawi, DE
Jeff Stolte, P
93— Frank Baker, FB
95— Derrick Brooms, KR

CITADEL (11)
82— Jim Ettari, DL
84— Jim Gabrish, OL
85— Jim Gabrish, OL
86— Scott Thompson, DT
88—†Carlos Avalos, OL
90—†DeRhon Robinson, OL
92—†Corey Cash, OL
†Lester Smith, DB
94—†Levi Davis, OL
95—†Brad Keeney, DL
97—†Carlos Frank, KR

CLARION (13)
78— Jeff Langhans, OL
80— Steve Scillitani, MG
Gary McCauley, TE
81— Gary McCauley, TE
83— Elton Brown, RB
85— Chuck Duffy, OL
87— Lou Weiers, DL
93— Tim Brown, TE
95— Kim Niedbala, DB
96— Chris Martin, OL
Kim Niedbala, DB
2002—Reggie Wells, OL
Troy Bowers, DL

CLARK ATLANTA (1)
79— Curtis Smith, OL

CLINCH VALLEY (1)
95— Shonn Bell, TE

COAST GUARD (5)
90— Ron Davies, DB
91— Ron Davies, DB
97— Ed Hernaez, LB
2000—Mike Benson, RS
02— Brad Brunaugh, OL

COE (9)
74— Dan Schmidt, OG
76— Paul Wagner, OT
85— Mike Matzen, P
90— Richard Matthews, DB
93— Carey Bender, RB
Craig Chmelicek, OL
94— Carey Bender, RB
99— Zak Gordon, DB
2002—Fredrick Jackson, RB/RS

COLGATE (11)
82—†Dave Wolf, LB
83—†Rich Erenberg, RB
84—†Tom Stenglein, WR
85—†Tom Stenglein, WR
86—†Kenny Gamble, RB
87—†Kenny Gamble, RB
†Greg Manusky, LB
96—†Adam Sofran, LB
97—†Tim Girard, OL
98—†Corey Hill, WR
99—†Paul Clasby, OL

COL. OF EMPORIA (1)
51— William Chai, OG

COL. OF IDAHO (2)
53— Norman Hayes, T
54— R. C. Owens, E

COL. OF NEW JERSEY (6)
74— Eric Hamilton, C
83— John Aromando, WR
91— Chris Shaw, C
97— Jim Haines, OL
Tom Ruggia, DL
98— Tom Ruggia, DL

COLORADO COL. (4)
72— Ed Smith, DE
73— Darryl Crawford, DB
82— Ray Bridges, DL
93— Todd Mays, DL

COLORADO MINES (6)
39— Lloyd Madden, B
41— Dick Moe, T
59— Vince Tesone, B
72— Roger Cirimotich, DB
86— Tim Baer, P
94— Pat Hogelin, P

CONCORD (3)
86— Kevin Johnson, LB
92— Chris Hairston, RB
2002—Kory Wright, TE

CONCORDIA-M'HEAD (4)
77— Barry Bennett, DT
90— Mike Gindorff, DT
Shayne Lindsay, NG
95— Tim Lowry, OL

CONNECTICUT* (8)
45— Walter Trojanowski, B
73— Richard Foye, C
80—†Reggie Eccleston, WR
83—†John Dorsey, LB
88—†Glenn Antrum, WR

89—†Troy Ashley, LB
91—†Mark Didio, WR
97—†TaVarr Closs, OL

CORNELL (4)
82—†Dan Suren, TE
86—†Tom McHale, DE
93—†Chris Zingo, LB
96—†Chad Levitt, RB

CORNELL COLLEGE (2)
82— John Ward, WR
92— Brent Sands, DB

CORTLAND ST. (7)
67— Rodney Verkey, DE
89— Jim Cook, OL
90— Chris Lafferty, OG
Vinny Swanda, LB
91— Vinny Swanda, LB
96— Pat Lalley, OL
97— Brian McAvan, OL

CUMBERLAND (KY.) (4)
87— David Carmichael, DB
89— Ralph McWilliams, OL
93— Doug Binkley, DB
94— Doug Binkley, LB

DAKOTA WESLEYAN (1)
45— Robert Kirkman, T

DARTMOUTH (5)
91—†Al Rosier, RB
92—†Dennis Durkin, PK
96—†Brian Larsen, OL
97—†Zach Walz, LB
2002—†Casey Cramer, TE

DAVIDSON (2)
34— John Mackorell, B
99—†Ryan Crawford, DB

DAYTON (12)
36— Ralph Niehaus, T
78— Rick Chamberlin, LB
81— Chris Chaney, DB
84— David Kemp, LB
86— Gerry Meyer, OL
89— Mike Duvic, PK
90— Steve Harder, OL
91— Brian Olson, OG
92— Andy Pellegrino, OL
94—†Tim Duvic, PK
2001—†Eric Willman, OL
02—†Mark Kasmer, DB

DEFIANCE (1)
93— Sammy Williams, WR

DELAWARE (37)
42— Hugh Bogovich, G
46— Tony Stalloni, T
54— Don Miller, B
63— Mike Brown, B
66— Herb Slattery, OT
69— John Favero, OL
70— Conway Hayman, OG
71— Gardy Kahoe, RB
72— Joe Carbone, DE
Dennis Johnson, DT
73— Jeff Cannon, DT
74— Ed Clark, LB
Ray Sweeney, OG
75— Sam Miller, DE
76— Robert Pietuszka, DB
78— Jeff Komlo, QB
79—†Herb Beck, OG
†Scott Brunner, QB
80—†Gary Kuhlman, OT
81—†Gary Kuhlman, OL
82—†George Schmitt, DB
85—†Jeff Rosen, OL
86—†Darrell Booker, LB
87—†James Anderson, WR
88—†Mike Renna, DL
89—†Mike Renna, DL
91—†Warren McIntire, DB
92—†Matt Morrill, DL
93—†Matt Morrill, DL
94—†Daryl Brown, RB
95—†Kenny Bailey, DB
96—†Kenny Bailey, DB
97—†Brian Smith, LB
98—†Eddie Conti, WR
2000—†Jamin Elliott, WR
†Jeff Fiss, OL
†Brian McKenna, LB

DELAWARE ST. (6)
84— Gene Lake, RB
86— Joe Burton, DB
91— †Rod Milstead, OL
92— †LeRoy Thompson, DL
2000—†Darnerien McCants, TE
02— †DaShaun Morris, RS

DELTA ST. (6)
67— Leland Hughes, OG
95— Jerome Williams, DB
2000—Chris Booker, OG
       Rory Bell, DB
01—Chris Booker, OL
02—Chris Booker, OL

DENISON (5)
47— William Hart, E
48— William Wehr, C
75— Dennis Thome, DL
79— Clay Sampson, RB
86— Dan Holland, DL

DePAUW (3)
63— Richard Dean, C
96— Scott Farnham, DB
       Jay Pettigrew, TE

DETROIT TECH (1)
39— Mike Kostiuk, T

DICKINSON (4)
91— Shaughn White, DB
92— Brian Ridgway, DL
94— Jason Fox, LB
98— Jason Shoff, DL

DICKINSON ST. (2)
81— Tony Moore, DL
92— Rory Farstveet, OL

DOANE (1)
66— Fred Davis, OT

DRAKE (6)
72— Mike Samples, DT
82— Pat Dunsmore, TE
       Craig Wederquist, OT
95— †Matt Garvis, LB
99— †Mike Foster, DL
2000—†Mike Foster, DL

DREXEL (2)
55— Vincent Vidas, T
56— Vincent Vidas, T

DUBUQUE (1)
96— Matt Plummer, WR

DUQUESNE (3)
2001—†Leigh Bodden, DB
02— †Jeremy Conley, WR
       †Leigh Bodden, DB

EAST CARO.* (1)
64— Bill Cline, HB

EAST CENTRAL (2)
84— Don Wilson, C
2002—Kwame Ferguson, LB

EAST STROUDSBURG (9)
65— Barry Roach, DB
75— William Stem, DB
79— Ronald Yakavonis, DL
83— Mike Reichenbach, LB
84— Andy Baranek, QB
91— Curtis Bunch, DB
94— Steve Hynes, OL
2000—Kevin Nagle, LB
01— Adam Hostetter, P

EAST TENN. ST. (9)
53— Hal Morrison, E
68— Ron Overbay, DB
70— William Casey, DB
85— George Cimadevilla, P
86— George Cimadevilla, P
94— †Jeff Johnson, WR
96— †James Russell, DL
97— †B. J. Adigun, DB
       †Mario Hankerson, LB

EAST TEXAS BAPTIST (2)
2001—Scott Verhalen, P
02— Scott Verhalen, P

EASTERN ILL. (22)
72— Nate Anderson, RB
76— Ted Petersen, C
78— James Warring, WR

79— Chris Cobb, RB
       Pete Catan, DE
80— Pete Catan, DE
81— †Kevin Grey, DB
82— †Robert Williams, DB
       Bob Norris, OG
83— †Robert Williams, DB
       †Chris Nicholson, DT
84— †Jerry Wright, WR
86— †Roy Banks, WR
88— †John Jurkovic, DL
89— †John Jurkovic, DL
90— †Tim Lance, DB
95— †Willie High, RB
       †Tim Carver, LB
02— †Kevin Hill, OL
       †Tony Romo, QB
       †J.R. Taylor, RB
       †Nick Ricks, LB

EASTERN KY. (30)
69— Teddy Taylor, MG
74— Everett Talbert, RB
75— Junior Hardin, MG
76— Roosevelt Kelly, OL
79— †Bob McIntyre, LB
80— †George Floyd, DB
81— †George Floyd, DB
       †Kevin Greve, OG
82— †Steve Bird, WR
83— †Chris Sullivan, OL
84— †Chris Sullivan, C
85— †Joe Spadafino, OL
86— †Fred Harvey, LB
87— †Aaron Jones, DL
88— †Elroy Harris, RB
       †Jessie Small, DL
89— †Al Jacevicius, OL
90— †Kelly Blount, LB
       †Al Jacevicius, OL
91— †Carl Satterly, OL
       †Ernest Thompson, DL
92— †Markus Thomas, RB
93— †Chad Bratzke, DL
94— †James Hand, OL
95— †James Hand, OL
       †Marc Collins, P
96— †Tony McCombs, LB
98— †Tyrone Hopson, OL
2000—†Alex Bannister, WR
01— †Yeremiah Bell, DB

EASTERN MICH.* (5)
68— John Schmidt, C
69— Robert Lints, MG
70— Dave Pureifory, DT
71— Dave Pureifory, DT
73— Jim Pietrzak, OT

EASTERN N.M. (9)
81— Brad Beck, RB
83— Kevin Kott, QB
87— Earl Jones, OL
89— Murray Garrett, DL
90— Anthony Pertile, DB
94— Conrad Hamilton, DB
95— Conrad Hamilton, DB
98— Michael Walton, LB
99— Michael Walton, LB

EASTERN ORE. (1)
96— Shea Little, OL

EASTERN WASH. (16)
57— Richard Huston, C
65— Mel Stanton, HB
73— Scott Garske, TE
81— John Tighe, OL
86— Ed Simmons, OT
87— †Eric Stein, P
91— †Kevin Sargent, OL
97— †Harry Leons, QB
       †Chris Scott, DL
       †Jim Buzzard, OL
98— †Bashir Levingston, RS
99— †Lance Knaevelsrud, OL
2000—†Jeff Allen, DL
01— †Jesse Chatman, RB
       †Chris Polinder, OL
       †Lamont Brightful, RS

EDINBORO (6)
82— Rick Ruszkiewicz, K
89— Elbert Cole, RB
90— Ernest Priester, WR

93— Mike Kegarise, OL
95— Pat Schuster, DL
2002—Sean McNicholas, P

ELMHURST (1)
82— Lindsay Barich, OL

ELON (10)
50— Sal Gero, T
68— Richard McGeorge, OE
69— Richard McGeorge, OE
73— Glenn Ellis, DT
76— Ricky Locklear, DT
       Dan Bass, OL
77— Dan Bass, OL
80— Bobby Hedrick, RB
86— Ricky Sigmon, OL
2001—Scott McLain, OL

EMORY & HENRY (18)
50— Robert Miller, B
51— Robert Miller, B
56— William Earp, C
68— Sonny Wade, B
85— Keith Furr, DB
       Rob McMillen, DL
86— Sandy Rogers, RB
87— Gary Collier, QB
88— Steve Bowman, DL
89— Doug Reavis, DL
90— Billy Salyers, OL
91— Jason Grooms, DL
92— Pat Buchanan, OL
       Scott Pruner, DL
97— Jamie Harless, DL
98— Mike Kassnove, OL
99— Charles Peterson, DB
2001—Jelani Patterson, DL

EMPORIA ST. (10)
35— James Fraley, B
37— Harry Klein, E
68— Bruce Cerone, OE
69— Bruce Cerone, OE
91— Quincy Tillmon, RB
96— Brian Shay, RB
97— Brian Shay, RB
98— John Hesse, OL
       Brian Shay, RB
2002—Dontaye McCoy, DB

EUREKA (1)
95— Kurt Barth, WR

EVANSVILLE (3)
46— Robert Hawkins, T
93— †Hanz Hoag, TE
94— †Hanz Hoag, TE

FAIRFIELD (1)
2000—†Steve Dogmanits, DB

FDU-FLORHAM (4)
84— Ira Epstein, DL
86— Eric Brey, DB
87— Frank Illidge, DL
93— Vic Moncato, P

FAIRMONT ST. (4)
67— Dave Williams, DT
84— Ed Coleman, WR
88— Lou Mabin, DB
99— Nathan White, P

FAYETTEVILLE ST. (1)
90— Terrence Smith, LB

FERRIS ST. (9)
76— Charles Evans, RB
92— Monty Brown, LB
93— Ed Phillion, DL
94— Tyree Dye, RB
95— Bill Love, QB
96— Kelly Chisholm, DL
99— Doc Proctor, PK
2000—Clarence Coleman, WR
01— Clarence Coleman, WR/AP

FERRUM (9)
87— Dave Harper, LB
88— Dave Harper, LB
89— Chris Warren, RB
90— Melvin Dillard, DB/KR
91— John Sheets, OG
2000—Toné Dancy, DB
01— Tim Carter, DB

FINDLAY (5)
65— Allen Smith, HB

80— Nelson Bolden, FB
85— Dana Wright, RB
90— Tim Russ, OL
2002—Robert Campbell, RB

FLORIDA A&M (21)
61— Curtis Miranda, C
62— Robert Paremore, B
67— Major Hazelton, DB
       John Eason, OE
73— Henry Lawrence, OT
75— Frank Poole, LB
77— Tyrone McGriff, OG
78— Tyrone McGriff, OG
79— †Tyrone McGriff, OG
       †Kiser Lewis, C
80— †Gifford Ramsey, DB
83— †Ray Alexander, WR
95— †Earl Holmes, LB
96— †Jamie Nails, OL
97— †Oteman Sampson, QB
       †Juan Toro, PK
98— †Patrick Bonner, QB
       †Jacquay Nunnally, WR
       †Juan Toro, PK
       †Olrick Johnson, LB
2000—†Freddie Moore, OL

FLORIDA ST.* (1)
51— William Dawkins, OG

FORDHAM (1)
97— †Barry Cantrell, P

FORT HAYS ST. (3)
95— Lance Schwindt, TE
       Shawn Behr, QB
2000—Adam Ryan, P

FORT LEWIS (3)
89— Eric Fadness, P
92— Johnny Cox, WR
93— Johnny Cox, AP

FORT VALLEY ST. (9)
74— Fred Harris, OT
80— Willie Canady, DB
81— Willie Canady, DB
83— Tugwan Taylor, DB
92— Joseph Best, DB
93— Joseph Best, DB
94— Tyrone Poole, DB
2002 Duron Croson, RB
       Rico Cody, DB

FRANKLIN (3)
82— Joe Chester, WR
95— Michael Brouwer, DB
2001—Josh McMillin, DL

FRANK. & MARSH. (9)
35— Woodrow Sponaugle, C
38— Sam Roeder, B
40— Alex Schibanoff, T
47— William Iannicelli, E
50— Charles Cope, C
81— Vin Carioscia, OL
82— Vin Carioscia, OL
89— Dale Amos, WR
95— Steve DeLuca, LB

FRESNO ST.* (5)
39— Jack Mulkey, E
40— Jack Mulkey, E
60— Douglas Brown, G
68— Tom McCall, LB
       Erv Hunt, DB

FROSTBURG ST. (12)
80— Terry Beamer, LB
82— Steve Forsythe, WR
83— Kevin Walsh, DL
85— Bill Bagley, WR
86— Marcus Wooley, LB
88— Ken Boyd, DB
89— Ken Boyd, DB
93— Russell Williams, DB
94— Joe Holland, DL
       Ariel Bell, KR
96— Ron Wallace, DB
2002—George O'Brien II, DL

FURMAN (21)
82— †Ernest Gibson, DB
83— †Ernest Gibson, DB
84— †Rock Hurst, LB
85— †Gene Reeder, C

88— †Jeff Blankenship, LB
89— †Kelly Fletcher, DL
90— †Steve Duggan, C
    †Kevin Kendrick, LB
91— †Eric Walter, OL
92— †Kota Suttle, LB
94— †Jim Richter, PK
97— †Bryan Dailer, DL
98— †Orlando Ruff, LB
99— †John Keith, DB
2000—†Louis Ivory, RB
    †Josh Moore, OL
    †Marty Priore, OL
    †Will Bouton, LB
01— †Donnie Littlejohn, OL
    †Will Bouton, LB
02— †Trevor Kruger, OL

GALLAUDET (1)
87— Shannon Simon, OL

GARDNER-WEBB (4)
73— Richard Grissom, LB
87— Jeff Parker, PK
92— Rodney Robinson, WR
93— Gabe Wilkins, DL

GEORGETOWN (3)
73— Robert Morris, DE
74— Robert Morris, DE
91— Chris Murphy, DE

GEORGETOWN (KY.) (11)
74— Charles Pierson, DL
78— John Martinelli, OL
85— Rob McCrary, RB
87— Chris Reed, C
88— Chris Reed, OL
89— Steve Blankenbaker, DL
91— Chris Hogan, DL
92— Chris Hogan, DL
2000—Shane Pearson, LB
01— Walt DeLong, OL
02— Shan Housekeeper, LB

GA. SOUTHERN (33)
85— †Vance Pike, OL
    †Tim Foley, PK
86— †Fred Stokes, OT
    †Tracy Ham, QB
87— †Flint Matthews, LB
    †Dennis Franklin, C
    †Tim Foley, PK
88— †Dennis Franklin, C
    †Darren Alford, DL
89— †Joe Ross, RB
    †Giff Smith, DL
90— †Giff Smith, DL
91— †Rodney Oglesby, DB
92— †Alex Mash, DL
93— †Alex Mash, DL
    †Franklin Stephens, OL
94— †Franklin Stephens, OL
96— †Edward Thomas, DL
97— †Roderick Russell, FB
98— †Matt Winslette, C
    †Adrian Peterson, RB
    †Mark Williams, OL
    †Voncellies Allen, DL
    †Arkee Thompson, DB
99— †Adrian Peterson, RB
    †Mark Williams, OL
    †Voncellies Allen, DL
2000—†Adrian Peterson, RB
    †Freddy Pesqueira, DL
01— †Adrian Peterson, RB
    †Freddy Pesqueira, DL
02— †Charles Clarke, OL
    †Freddy Pesqueira, DL

GA. SOUTHWESTERN (2)
85— Roger Glover, LB
86— Roger Glover, LB

GETTYSBURG (7)
66— Joseph Egresitz, DE
83— Ray Condren, RB
84— Ray Condren, RB
85— Brian Barr, DB
94— Dwayne Marcus, FB
98— Paul Smith, RS
99— Paul Smith, RS

GLENVILLE ST. (7)
73— Scotty Hamilton, DB
83— Byron Brooks, RB

84— Mike Payne, DB
93— Chris George, WR
94— Chris George, WR
96— Carlos Ferralls, WR
97— Carlos Ferralls, WR

GONZAGA (2)
34— Ike Peterson, B
39— Tony Canadeo, B

GRAMBLING (32)
62— Junious Buchanan, T
64— Alphonse Dotson, OT
65— Willie Young, OG
    Frank Cornish, DT
69— Billy Manning, C
70— Richard Harris, DE
    Charles Roundtree, DT
71— Solomon Freelon, OG
    John Mendenhall, DE
72— Steve Dennis, DB
    Gary Johnson, DT
73— Gary Johnson, DT
    Willie Bryant, DB
74— Gary Johnson, DT
75— Sammie White, WR
    James Hunter, DB
79— †Joe Gordon, DT
    †Aldrich Allen, LB
    †Robert Salters, DB
80— †Trumaine Johnson, WR
    †Mike Barker, DT
81— †Andre Robinson, LB
82— †Trumaine Johnson, WR
83— †Robert Smith, DL
85— †James Harris, LB
90— †Walter Dean, RB
    †Jake Reed, WR
94— †Curtis Ceaser, WR
2001—†Robert Taylor, LB
02— †Tramon Douglas, WR
    †Bruce Eugene, QB
    †Terry Riley, OL

GRAND VALLEY ST. (15)
79— Ronald Essink, OL
89— Todd Tracey, DL
91— Chris Tiede, C
94— Mike Sheldon, OL
95— Diriki Mose, WR
96— Matt Potter, DE
2001—Curt Anes, QB
    David Kircus, WR
    Dale Westrick, OL
02— Curt Anes, QB
    David Kircus, WR
    Reggie Spearmon, RB
    Dale Westrick, OL
    Scott Mackey, DB
    Keyonta Marshall, DL

GRINNELL (1)
99— Jeff Pedersen, TE

GROVE CITY (5)
87— Doug Hart, PK
97— Doug Steiner, FB
98— R.J. Bowers, FB
99— R.J. Bowers, FB
2000—R.J. Bowers, FB

GUILFORD (4)
75— Steve Musulin, OT
91— Rodney Alexander, DE
94— Bryan Garland, OL
2001—Chris McKinney, KR

GUST. ADOLPHUS (8)
37— Wendell Butcher, B
50— Calvin Roberts, T
51— Haldo Norman, OE
52— Calvin Roberts, DT
54— Gene Nei, G
67— Richard Jaeger, LB
84— Kurt Ploeger, DL
97— Ryan Boutwell, PK

HAMILTON (2)
86— Joe Gilbert, OL
91— Eric Grey, RB

HAMLINE (4)
55— Dick Donlin, E
84— Kevin Graslewicz, WR
85— Ed Hitchcock, OL
89— Jon Voss, TE

HAMPDEN-SYDNEY (8)
48— Lynn Chewning, B
54— Stokeley Fulton, C
72— Michael Leidy, LB
74— Ed Kelley, DE
75— Ed Kelley, DE
77— Robert Wilson, OL
78— Tim Smith, DL
86— Jimmy Hondroulis, PK

HAMPTON (12)
84— Ike Readon, MG
85— Ike Readon, DL
93— Emerson Martin, OL
    Christopher Williams, DL
94— John Meredith, LB
95— †Hugh Hunter, DL
96— †Darrell Flythe, LB
97— †Cordell Taylor, DB
98— †Charles Preston, DL
99— †Deon Hunt, LB
2002—†Zuriel Smith, RS
    †Erik Steiner, OL

HANOVER (6)
86— Jon Pinnick, QB
88— Mike Luker, WR
95— Ben Fox, WR
    Terry Peebles, QB
97— Kevin O'Donohue, LB
99— Anthony Weigleb, OL

HARDIN-SIMMONS (9)
37— Burns McKinney, B
39— Clyde Turner, C
40— Owen Goodnight, B
42— Rudy Mobley, B
46— Rudy Mobley, B
94— Colin McCormick, WR
99— Gary Gutierrez, OL
2002—Thomas Anderson, OL
    Alex Hansen, DB

HARDING (3)
74— Barney Crawford, DL
91— Pat Gill, LB
94— Paul Simmons, LB

HARTWICK (1)
2002—Ryan Soule, WR

HARVARD (5)
82— †Mike Corbat, OL
84— †Roger Caron, OL
99— †Isaiah Kacyvenski, LB
2000—†Mike Clare, OL
02— †Carl Morris, WR

HASTINGS (2)
84— Dennis Sullivan, OL
94— Jeff Drake, DL

HAWAII* (2)
41— Nolle Smith, B
68— Tim Buchanan, LB

HENDERSON ST. (3)
90— Todd Jones, OL
93— Chris Carter, P
96— Robert Thomas, LB

HILLSDALE (11)
49— William Young, B
55— Nate Clark, B
56— Nate Clark, B
75— Mark Law, OG
81— Mike Broome, OG
82— Ron Gladnick, DE
86— Al Huge, DL
87— Al Huge, DL
88— Rodney Patterson, LB
2000—Todd DeVree, DL
    Tim Mustapha, DB

HOBART (6)
72— Don Aleksiewicz, RB
75— Rich Kowalski, RB
86— Brian Verdon, DB
93— Bill Palmer, DB
96— Nico Karagosian, TE
97— David Russell, DL

HOFSTRA (20)
83— Chuck Choinski, DL
86— Tom Salamone, P
88— Tom Salamone, DB
90— George Tischler, LB
94— †Brian Clark, DB
95— †Dave Fiore, OL

    †Dave Ettinger, PK
    †Buck Buchanan, LB
96— †Eugene McAleer, LB
97— †Dave Ettinger, PK
    †Lance Schulters, DB
99— †Giovanni Carmazzi, QB
    †Jim Magda, DL
2000—†Rocky Butler, QB
    †Doug Shanahan, DB
    †Khary Williams, DL
01— †Rocky Butler, QB
    †Kahmal Roy, WR
    †Dan Zorger, OL
    †Ryan Fletcher, DL

HOLY CROSS (14)
83— †Bruce Kozerski, OT
    †Steve Raquet, DL
84— †Bill McGovern, DB
    †Kevin Garvey, OG
85— †Gill Fenerty, RB
86— †Gordie Lockbaum, RB-DB
87— †Jeff Wiley, QB
    †Gordie Lockbaum, WR-SP
88— †Dennis Golden, OL
89— †Dave Murphy, DB
90— †Craig Callahan, LB
91— †Jerome Fuller, RB
93— †Rob Milanette, LB
95— †Tom Claro, OL

HOPE (2)
79— Craig Groendyk, OL
82— Kurt Brinks, C

HOWARD (5)
75— Ben Harris, DL
87— †Harvey Reed, RB
98— †Marques Douglas, DL
99— †Elijah Thurmon, WR
2001—†Tracy White, LB

HOWARD PAYNE (8)
61— Ray Jacobs, T
72— Robert Woods, LB
73— Robert Woods, LB
92— Scott Lichner, QB
94— Steven Seale, OL
95— Sean Witherwax, DL
97— Sedrick Medlock, DB
98— Sedrick Medlock, DB

HUMBOLDT ST. (6)
61— Drew Roberts, E
62— Drew Roberts, E
76— Michael Gooing, OL
82— David Rush, MG
83— Dean Diaz, DB
95— Randy Matyshock, TE

HURON (1)
76— John Aldridge, OL

IDAHO *(14)
83— †Ken Hobart, QB
85— †Eric Yarber, WR
88— †John Friesz, QB
89— †John Friesz, QB
    †Lee Allen, WR
90— †Kasey Dunn, WR
91— †Kasey Dunn, WR
92— †Yo Murphy, WR
    †Jeff Robinson, DL
93— †Doug Nussmeier, QB
    †Mat Groshong, C
94— †Sherriden May, RB
    †Jim Mills, OL
95— †Ryan Phillips, DL

IDAHO ST. (8)
69— Ed Bell, OE
77— Ray Allred, MG
81— †Case de Bruijn, P
    †Mike Machurek, QB
83— †Jeff Kaiser, P
84— †Steve Anderson, DL
97— †Trevor Bell, DB
2001—†Eddie Johnson, P

ILLINOIS COL. (2)
81— Joe Aiello, DL
2002—B.J. Harvey, KR

ILLINOIS ST. (11)
68— Denny Nelson, OT
85— †Jim Meyer, OL
86— †Brian Gant, LB

88— †Mike McCabe, P
93— †Todd Kurz, PK
98— †Chad Pegues, DL
    †Galen Scott, LB
99— †Damien Gregory, DL
    †Mike Rodbro, OG
    †Sam Young, DB
2002—†Boomer Grigsby, LB

ILL. WESLEYAN (9)
34— Tony Blazine, T
74— Caesar Douglas, OT
91— Chris Bisaillon, WR
92— Chris Bisaillon, WR
96— Adam Slotkus, C
    John Munch, LB
    John Munch, LB
97— John Munch, LB
98— Kevin Fahey, DB
2000—Jeff Heinzl, DL

INDIANA (PA.) (23)
75— Lynn Hieber, QB
76— Jim Haslett, DE
77— Jim Haslett, DE
78— Jim Haslett, DE
79— Terrence Skelley, OE
80— Joe Cuigari, DT
84— Gregg Brenner, WR
86— Jim Angelo, OL
87— Troy Jackson, LB
88— Dean Cottrill, LB
90— Andrew Hill, WR
91— Tony Aliucci, QB
93— Matt Dalverny, OL
    Mike Geary, PK
    Michael Mann, RB
94— Jeff Turnage, DL
95— Jon Ruff, PK
    Jeff Turnage, DL
97— Barry Threats, DB
98— Barry Threats, DB
99— Leander Jordan, OL
2000—Mike Borisenko, LB
01— Joey Flora, DB

INDIANA ST. (13)
69— Jeff Keller, DE
75— Chris Hicks, OL
    Vince Allen, RB
83— †Ed Martin, DE
84— †Wayne Davis, DB
85— †Vencie Glenn, DB
86— †Mike Simmonds, OL
93— †Shawn Moore, OL
94— †Dan Brandenburg, DL
95— †Dan Bradenburg, DL
    †Tom Allison, PK
98— †Troy Lefevra, DE
99— †DeJuan Alfonzo, DB/KR

INDIANAPOLIS (9)
83— Mark Bless, DL
84— Paul Loggan, DB
85— Tom Collins, DB
86— Dan Jester, TE
87— Thurman Montgomery, DL
91— Greg Matheis, DL
98— Ted Liette, LB
99— Josh Gentry, LB
2001—Neal Blank, DL

IOWA WESLEYAN (1)
87— Mike Wiggins, P

ITHACA (15)
72— Robert Wojnar, OT
74— David Remick, RB
75— Larry Czarnecki, DT
79— John Laper, LB
80— Bob Ferrigno, HB
84— Bill Sheerin, DL
85— Tim Torrey, LB
90— Jeff Wittman, FB
91— Jeff Wittman, FB
92— Jeff Wittman, FB
    Dave Brumfield, OL
95— Scott Connolly, DL
98— Matt Buddenhagen, KR
    Mike Sansone, LB
2000—Ron Amato, DB

JACKSON ST. (26)
62— Willie Richardson, E
69— Joe Stephens, OG
71— Jerome Barkum, OE
74— Walter Payton, RB

Robert Brazile, LB
78— Robert Hardy, DT
80— †Larry Werts, LB
81— †Mike Fields, OT
85— †Jackie Walker, LB
86— †Kevin Dent, DB
87— †Kevin Dent, DB
88— †Lewis Tillman, RB
    †Kevin Dent, DB
89— †Darion Conner, LB
90— †Robert Turner, DB
91— †Deltrich Lockridge, OL
92— †Lester Holmes, OL
95— †Picasso Nelson, DB
96— †Sean Woodson, DB
    †Grailyn Pratt, QB
    †Otha Evans, LB
97— †Toby Myles, OL
98— †Sylvester Morris, WR
99— †Tommie Head, LB
    †Sylvester Morris, WR
2002—†Elgin Andrews, LB

JACKSONVILLE ST. (10)
52— Jodie Connell, OG
66— Ray Vinson, DB
70— Jimmy Champion, C
77— Jesse Baker, DT
78— Jesse Baker, DT
82— Ed Lett, QB
86— Joe Billingsley, OT
88— Joe Billingsley, OT
95— †Darron Edwards, DB
2002—†Deon White, OL

JAMES MADISON (17)
77— Woody Bergeria, DT
78— Rick Booth, OL
85— †Charles Haley, LB
86— †Carlo Bianchini, OG
89— †Steve Bates, DL
90— †Eupton Jackson, DB
93— †David McLeod, WR
94— †Dwight Robinson, DB
95— †John Coursey, PK
    †David Bailey, C
    †Ed Perry, TE
96— †Ed Perry, TE
97— †Tony Booth, DB
99— †Curtis Keaton, RB
2000—†Chris Morant, DL
    †Derick Pack, LB
01— †Derrick Lloyd, LB

JAMESTOWN (2)
76— Brent Tischer, OL
81— Ron Hausaver, OL

JOHN CARROLL (14)
50— Carl Taseff, B
74— Tim Barrett, RB
94— Jason Goldberg, PK
    Ryan Haley, P
95— Chris Anderson, LB
96— London Fletcher, LB
    Scott O'Donnell, DL
    Chris Anderson, LB
97— London Fletcher, LB
    David Ziegler, R
98— David Vitatoe, PK
99— Tom Rini, DB
2002—Tom Arth, QB
    Chris Cubero, LB

JOHNS HOPKINS (3)
80— Bill Stromberg, WR
81— Bill Stromberg, WR
96— Jim Wilson, DL

JOHNSON SMITH (2)
82— Dan Beauford, DE
88— Ronald Capers, LB

JUNIATA (4)
54— Joe Veto, T
86— Steve Yerger, OL
87— Mark Dorner, DB
99— Matt Eisenberg, WR

KANSAS WESLEYAN (2)
35— Virgil Baker, G
56— Larry Houdek, B

KEAN (1)
87— Kevin McGuirl, TE

KENTUCKY ST. (3)
72— Wiley Epps, LB
98— Cletidus Hunt, DL
99— Ike Ihejeto, TE

KENYON (1)
74— Jim Myers, WR

KING'S (PA.) (3)
2000—Damon Saxon, RB
01— Steven Wilson, DL
02— Steven Wilson, DL

KNOX (4)
86— Rich Schiele, TE
87— Chris Vogel, WR
96— Chris Warwick, PK
98— Josh Fourdyce, DL

KNOXVILLE (1)
77— Dwight Treadwell, OL

KUTZTOWN (5)
77— Steve Head, OG
95— John Mobley, LB
97— Denauld Brown, DL
2001—Pete Mendez, DB
02— Pete Mendez, DB

LA SALLE (2)
38— George Somers, T
39— Frank Loughney, G

LA VERNE (3)
72— Dana Coleman, DT
91— Willie Reyna, QB
95— Anthony Jones, RB

LAFAYETTE (7)
79—†Rich Smith, TE
81—†Joe Skladany, LB
82—†Tony Green, DL
88—†Frank Baur, QB
92—†Edward Hudak, OL
96—†B. J. Galles, DB
97—†Dan Bengele, LB

LAKE FOREST (1)
2002—Casey Urlacher, LB

LAKELAND (1)
89— Jeff Ogiego, P

LAMAR (5)
57— Dudley Meredith, T
61— Bobby Jancik, B
67— Spergon Wynn, OG
83— †Eugene Seale, LB
85— †Burton Murchison, RB

LAMBUTH (2)
93— Jo Jo Jones, RB
94— Jo Jo Jones, RB

LANE (1)
73— Edward Taylor, DT

LANGSTON (2)
73— Thomas Henderson, DE
94— Paul Reed, DB

LAWRENCE (11)
49— Claude Radtke, E
67— Charles McKee, QB
77— Frank Bouressa, C
78— Frank Bouressa, C
80— Scott Reppert, HB
81— Scott Reppert, HB
82— Scott Reppert, RB
83— Murray McDonough, DB
86— Dan Galante, DL
95— Brad Olson, RB
97— Brad Olson, FB

LEHIGH (26)
49— Robert Numbers, C
50— Dick Doyne, B
57— Dan Nolan, B
59— Walter Meincke, T
69— Thad Jamula, OT
71— John Hill, C
73— Kim McQuilken, QB
75— Joe Sterrett, QB
77— Steve Kreider, WR
    Mike Reiker, QB
79— †Dave Melone, OL
    †Jim McCormick, QB
80— †Bruce Rarig, LB
83— †John Shigo, LB
85— †Rennie Benn, WR

90— †Keith Petzold, OL
93— †Dave Cecchini, WR
95— †Brian Klingerman, WR
    †Rabih Abdullah, RB
96— †Ben Talbott, P
98— †Nick Martucci, DL
99— †Ian Eason, LB
2000—†Brian McDonald, OL
01— †Abdul Byron, DB
    †Josh Snyder, WR
02— †Jeff Santacroce, OL

LENOIR-RHYNE (5)
52— Steve Trudnak, B
62— Richard Kemp, B
67— Eddie Joyner, OT
92— Jason Monday, PK
94— Leonard Davis, RB

LEWIS & CLARK (2)
68— Bill Bailey, DT
91— Dan Ruhl, RB

LIBERTY (6)
82— John Sanders, LB
86— Mark Mathis, DB
95— †Andrew McFadden, KR
    †Tony Dews, TE
98— †Jesse Riley, LB
2000—†Jason Wells, DL

LINCOLN (MO.) (2)
53— Leo Lewis, B
54— Leo Lewis, B

LINFIELD (12)
57— Howard Morris, G
64— Norman Musser, C
72— Bernard Peterson, OE
75— Ken Cutcher, OL
78— Paul Dombroski, DB
80— Alan Schmidlin, QB
83— Steve Lopes, OL
84— Steve Boyea, OL
94— Darrin Causey, LB
2002—Daryl Agpalsa, OL
    David Russell, B
    Ray Lions, DB

LIVINGSTONE (2)
84— Jo Jo White, RB
98— Charles Cooley, OL

LOCK HAVEN (1)
45— Robert Eyer, E

LONG BEACH ST. (4)
68— Bill Parks, OE
69— Leon Burns, FB
70— Leon Burns, RB
71— Terry Metcalf, RB

LORAS (3)
47— Robert Hanlon, B
84— James Drew, P
97— Shane Davis, RB

LOS ANGELES ST. (1)
64— Walter Johnson, OG

LOUISIANA (1)
50— Bernard Calendar, E

LA.-LAFAYETTE* (1)
69— Glenn LaFleur, LB

LA.-MONROE* (19)
67— Vic Bender, C
70— Joe Profit, RB
72— Jimmy Edwards, RB
73— Glenn Fleming, MG
74— Glenn Fleming, MG
82— †Arthur Christophe, C
    †Bruce Daigle, DB
83— †Mike Grantham, OG
84— †Mike Grantham, OG
85— †Mike Turner, DB
87— †John Clement, OT
    †Claude Brumfield, DT
88— †Cyril Crutchfield, DB
89— †Jackie Harris, E
92— †Jeff Blackshear, OL
    †Vic Zordan, OL
    †Roosevelt Potts, RB
93— †Raymond Batiste, OL
    †James Folston, DL

LOUISIANA TECH* (15)
41— Garland Gregory, G

46— Mike Reed, G
68— Terry Bradshaw, QB
69— Terry Bradshaw, QB
72— Roger Carr, WR
73— Roger Carr, FL
74— Mike Barber, TE
　　 Fred Dean, DT
82— †Matt Dunigan, QB
84— †Doug Landry, LB
　　 †Walter Johnson, DE
85— †Doug Landry, LB
86— †Walter Johnson, LB-DE
87— †Glenell Sanders, LB
88— †Glenell Sanders, LB

LOUISVILLE* (1)
57— Leonard Lyles, B

LOYOLA (ILL.) (2)
35— Billy Roy, B
37— Clay Calhoun, B

LOYOLA MARYMOUNT (1)
42— Vince Pacewic, B

LUTHER (1)
57— Bruce Hartman, T

LYCOMING (10)
83— John Whalen, OL
85— Walt Zataveski, OL
89— Rick Bealer, DB
90— Rick Bealer, DB
91— Darrin Kenney, OT
　　 Don Kinney, DL
　　 Bill Small, LB
96— Michael Downey, OL
98— Jason Marraccini, QB
99— Cameron Coleman, DL

MacMURRAY (3)
97— Jamie Lee, RB
98— Jamie Lee, RB
2001—Curtis Fisher, OL

MAINE (11)
65— John Huard, LB
66— John Huard, LB
80— †Lorenzo Bouier, RB
89— †Carl Smith, RB
　　 †Scott Hough, OL
90— †Claude Pettaway, DB
99— †Jojo Oliphant, DL
2001—†Chad Hayes, TE
　　 †Stephen Cooper, LB
　　 †Lennard Byrd, KR
02— †Stephan Cooper, LB

MAINE MARITIME (2)
92— Kirk Matthieu, RB
95— Rob Marchitello, RB

MANSFIELD (1)
2002—Dan Holland, LB

MARIETTA (1)
96— Dante Brown, RB

MARS HILL (6)
78— Alan Rice, OL
79— Steven Campbell, DB
87— Lee Marchman, LB
2000—Terrence Stokes, RB
01— David Cassell, TE
02— Khalid Abdullah, LB

MARSHALL* (29)
37— William Smith, E
40— Jackie Hunt, B
41— Jackie Hunt, B
87— †Mike Barber, WR
　　 †Sean Doctor, TE
88— †Mike Barber, WR
　　 †Sean Doctor, TE
90— †Eric Ihnat, TE
91— †Phil Ratliff, OL
92— †Michael Payton, QB
　　 †Troy Brown, WR
　　 †Phil Ratliff, OL
93— †Chris Deaton, OL
　　 †William King, LB
　　 †Roger Johnson, DB
94— †Roger Johnson, DB
　　 †William Pannell, OL
　　 †Travis Colquitt, P
95— †Chris Parker, RB
　　 †William Pannell, OL
　　 †Billy Lyon, DL

†Melvin Cunningham, DB
96—†Randy Moss, WR
　　 †Billy Lyon, DL
　　 †Aaron Ferguson, OL
　　 †B.J. Cohen, DL
　　 †Jermaine Swafford, LB
　　 †Eugene McAleer, LB
　　 †Melvin Cunningham, DB

MARTIN LUTHER (1)
97— John Feuersthaler, DB

MARY HARDIN-BAYLOR (3)
2001—Preston Meyer, LB
02— Ryan Harris, OL
　　 Preston Meyer, LB

MD.-EAST. SHORE (2)
64— John Smith, DT
68— Bill Thompson, DB

MARYVILLE (TENN.) (5)
67— Steve Dockery, DB
73— Earl McMahon, OG
77— Wayne Dunn, LB
92— Tom Smith, OL
93— Tom Smith, OL

MASSACHUSETTS (31)
52— Tony Chambers, OE
63— Paul Graham, T
64— Milt Morin, DE
67— Greg Landry, QB
71— William DeFlavio, MG
72— Steve Schubert, OE
73— Tim Berra, OE
75— Ned Deane, OL
76— Ron Harris, DB
77— Kevin Cummings, TE
　　 Bruce Kimball, OL
78— Bruce Kimball, OG
80— †Bob Manning, DB
81— †Garry Pearson, RB
82— †Garry Pearson, RB
85— †Mike Dwyer, DL
88— †John McKeown, LB
90— †Paul Mayberry, OL
92— †Don Caparotti, DB
93— †Bill Durkin, OL
94— †Breon Parker, DB
95— †Rene Ingoglia, RB
98— †Marcel Shipp, RB
　　 †Khari Samuel, LB
　　 †Kerry Taylor, TE
99— †Jeremy Robinson, DB
　　 †Kole Ayi, LB
　　 †Jerard White, DB
　　 †Sean Higgins, TE
2000—†Kole Ayi, LB
01— †Valdamar Brower, DL

MASS.-BOSTON (1)
92— Sean Munroe, WR

MASS.-DARTMOUTH (1)
98— Mike Cotton, DB

MASS. MARITIME (1)
95— Paul Diamantopoulos, DE

McDANIEL (5)
51— Victor Makovitch, DG
78— Ricci Bonaccorsy, DL
79— Ricci Bonaccorsy, DL
98— Mat Mathias, OL
2001—Jason Wingeart, DB

McMURRY (6)
49— Brad Rowland, B
50— Brad Rowland, B
58— Charles Davis, G
68— Telly Windham, DE
74— Randy Roemisch, OT
80— Rick Nolly, OL

McNEESE ST. (26)
52— Charles Kuehn, E
69— Glenn Kidder, OG
72— James Moore, TE
74— James Files, OT
82— †Leonard Smith, DB
92— †Terry Irving, LB
93— †Jose Larios, PK
　　 †Terry Irving, LB
94— †Ronald Cherry, DL
95— †Kavika Pittman, DL
　　 †Marsh Buice, DL

†Zack Bronson, DB
　　 †Vincent Landrum, LB
96—†Zack Bronson, DB
97— †Reggie Nelson, OL
　　 †Chris Fontenot, TE
　　 †Donnie Ashley, PR
98— †Reggie Nelson, OL
　　 †Charles Ayro, LB
2000—†Wes Hines, OL
　　 †Jake Morrison, DL
01— †Joe Judge, DB
02— †Jason Davis, OL
　　 †B.J. McNutt, DL
　　 †Hadley Prince, DB
　　 †Roderick Royal, LB

MEMPHIS* (1)
54— Robert Patterson, G

MENLO (2)
2000—Nate Jackson, WR
01— Nate Jackson, WR

MERCHANT MARINE (5)
52— Robert Wiechard, LB
69— Harvey Adams, DE
90— Harold Krebs, DB
97— Anthony Jacobs, OL
2002—David McNeal, RB

MESA ST. (8)
82— Dean Haugum, DT
83— Dean Haugum, DL
84— Don Holmes, DB
85— Mike Berk, OL
86— Mike Berk, OL
88— Tracy Bennett, PK
89— Jeff Russell, OT
90— Brian Johnson, LB

METHODIST (1)
97— Trayfer Monroe, DB

MIAMI (FLA.)* (2)
45— Ed Cameron, G
　　 William Levitt, C

MIAMI (OHIO)* (1)
82— †Brian Pillman, MG

MICHIGAN TECH (1)
76— Jim VanWagner, RB

MIDDLE TENN.* (12)
64— Jimbo Pearson, S
65— Keith Atchley, LB
83— †Robert Carroll, OL
84— †Kelly Potter, PK
85— †Don Griffin, DB
88— †Don Thomas, LB
90— †Joe Campbell, RB
91— †Steve McAdoo, OL
　　 †Joe Campbell, RB
92— †Steve McAdoo, OL
93— †Pat Hicks, OL
95— †Nathaniel Claybrooks, DL

MIDDLEBURY (3)
36— George Anderson, G
83— Jonathan Good, DL
2000—Andy Steele, LB

MIDLAND LUTHERAN (2)
76— Dave Marreel, DE
79— Scott Englehardt, OL

MILLERSVILLE (8)
76— Robert Parr, DB
80— Rob Riddick, RB
81— Mark Udovich, C
86— Jeff Hannis, DL
93— Scott Martin, DL
　　 Greg Faulkner, OL
95— Kevin Cannon, AP
98— Mike McFetridge, WR

MILLIKIN (2)
42— Virgil Wagner, B
92— Mike Hall, KR

MILLSAPS (12)
72— Rowan Torrey, DB
73— Michael Reams, OL
76— Rickie Haygood, QB
78— David Culpepper, LB
79— David Culpepper, LB
83— Edmond Donald, RB
85— Tommy Powell, LB
90— Sean Brewer, DL

91— Sean Brewer, DL
92— Sean Brewer, DL
93— Mitch Holloway, P
94— Kelvin Gladney, RB

MINN. DULUTH (4)
74— Mark Johnson, DB
75— Terry Egerdahl, RB
76— Ted McKnight, RB
82— Gary Birkholz, OG

MINN. ST. MANKATO (11)
73— Marty Kranz, DB
87— Duane Goldammer, OG
91— John Kelling, B
93— Jamie Pass, QB
94— Josh Nelsen, WR
95— Mark Erickson, AP
96— Tywan Mitchell, WR
　　 Greg Janacek, PK
97— Tywan Mitchell, WR
98— Tywan Mitchell, WR
2002—Andrew Tippins, DL

MINN. ST. MOORHEAD (2)
76— Rocky Gullickson, OG
84— Randy Sullivan, DB

MISSISSIPPI COL. (12)
72— Ricky Herzog, FL
79— Calvin Howard, RB
80— Bert Lyles, DE
82— Major Everett, RB
83— Wayne Frazier, OL
85— Earl Conway, DL
88— Terry Fleming, DL
89— Terry Fleming, DL
90— Fred McAfee, RB
92— Johnny Poole, OL
93— Kelly Ray, C
2000—Wilson Hillman, P

MISSISSIPPI VAL. (8)
79— †Carl White, OG
83— †Jerry Rice, WR
84— †Jerry Rice, WR
　　 †Willie Totten, QB
87— †Vincent Brown, LB
91— †Ashley Ambrose, DB
97— †Terry Houzah, LB
98— †Terry Houzah, LB

MIT (1)
97— Duane Stevens, DB

MO.-ROLLA (5)
41— Ed Kromka, T
69— Frank Winfield, OG
74— Merle Dillow, TE
80— Bill Grantham, S
93— Elvind Listerud, PK

MO. SOUTHERN ST. (3)
93— Rod Smith, WR
　　 Ron Burton, LB
95— Yancy McKnight, OL

MISSOURI VALLEY (3)
47— James Nelson, G
48— James Nelson, G
49— Herbert McKinney, T

MONMOUTH (1)
2002—†Joe Sentipal, LB

MONMOUTH (ILL.) (1)
75— Ron Baker, RB

MONTANA (32)
67— Bob Beers, LB
70— Ron Stein, DB
76— Greg Anderson, DB
79— †Jim Hard, FL
83— †Brian Salonen, TE
85— †Mike Rice, P
87— †Larry Clarkson, OL
88— †Tim Hauck, DB
89— †Kirk Scafford, OL
　　 †Tim Hauck, DB
93— †Dave Dickenson, QB
　　 †Todd Ericson, DB
94— †Scott Gragg, OL
95— †Dave Dickenson, QB
　　 †Matt Wells, WR
　　 †Mike Agee, OL
　　 †Eric Simonson, OL
96— †Joe Douglass, WR
　　 †Mike Agee, OL

†Brian Ah Yat, QB
†Jason Crebo, LB
†David Kempfert, OL
97— †Jason Crebo, LB
99— †Kelley Bryant, DL
2000—†Drew Miller, QB
†Thatcher Szalay, OL
†Andy Petek, DL
01— †Thatcher Szalay, OL
†Vince Huntsberger, DB
†Mark Spencer, P
02— †Dylan McFarland, OL
†Trey Young, DB

MONTANA ST. (13)
66— Don Hass, HB
67— Don Hass, HB
70— Gary Gustafson, LB
73— Bill Kollar, DT
75— Steve Kracher, RB
76— Lester Leininger, DL
78— Jon Borchardt, OT
81— †Larry Rubens, OL
84— †Mark Fellows, LB
†Dirk Nelson, P
93— †Sean Hill, DB
97— †Neal Smith, DL
99— †Matthew Peot, P

MONTANA TECH (3)
73— James Persons, OT
80— Steve Hossler, HB
81— Craig Opatz, OL

MONTCLAIR ST. (14)
75— Barry Giblin, DB
77— Mario Benimeo, DT
79— Tom Morton, OL
80— Sam Mills, LB
81— Terrance Porter, WR
82— Mark Casale, QB
84— Jim Rennae, OL
85— Dan Zakashefski, DL
86— Dan Zakashefski, DL
89— Paul Cioffi, LB
90— Paul Cioffi, LB
93— Jeff Bargiel, DL
95— Jeff Bargiel, DL
96— Jeff Bargiel, DL

MORAVIAN (1)
2002—Jarrod Pence, DB

MOREHEAD ST. (5)
38— John Horton, C
42— Vincent Zachem, C
69— Dave Haverdick, DT
82— †John Christopher, P
86— †Randy Poe, OG

MORGAN ST. (8)
65— Willie Lanier, LB
67— Jeff Queen, DE
70— Willie Germany, DB
72— Stan Cherry, LB
73— Eugene Simms, LB
78— Joe Fowlkes, DB
80— Mike Holston, WR
93— †Matthew Steeple, DL

MORNINGSIDE (2)
49— Connie Callahan, B
91— Jorge Diaz, PK

MOUNT UNION (36)
84— Troy Starr, LB
87— Russ Kring, RB
90— Ken Edelman, PK
Dave Lasecki, LB
92— Mike Elder, OL
Jim Ballard, QB
Chris Dattilio, LB
93— Rob Atwood, TE
Jim Ballard, QB
Ed Bubonics, WR
Mike Hallet, DL
94— Rob Rodgers, LB
95— Mike Wonderfer, OG
Matt Liggett, DL
96— Bill Borchert, QB
Joe Weimer, OL
Josh Weber, OT
Brian Wervey, LB
97— Bill Borchert, QB
Joe Weimer, OL
Vic Ricketts, G

98— Jason Hall, LB
Kris Bugara, DB
99— Tom Bauer, LB
2000—Jason Gerber, OT
Adam Marino, WR
Gary Smeck, QB
01— Chuck Moore, RB
Adam Indorf, OL
Todd Bhraden, DL
Matt Campbell, DL
Chris Kern, DB
02— Larry Kinnard, OT
Dan Pugh, RB
Matt Campbell, DE
Chris Kern, DB

MUHLENBERG (6)
46— George Bibighaus, E
47— Harold Bell, B
93— Rob Lokerson, WR
99— Joshua Carter, KR
2000—Joshua Carter, KR
02— Chris Reed, PK

MURRAY ST. (8)
37— Elmer Cochran, G
73— Don Clayton, RB
79— †Terry Love, DB
86— †Charley Wiles, OL
95— †Derrick Cullors, RB
†William Hampton, DB
96— †William Hampton, DB
2001—†Shane Andrus, PK

MUSKINGUM (5)
40— Dave Evans, T
60— Bill Cooper, B
66— Mark DeVilling, DT
75— Jeff Heacock, DB
95— Connon Thompson, DB

NEB.-KEARNEY (6)
76— Dale Mitchell Johnson, DB
78— Doug Peterson, DL
95— Matt Bruggeman, DL
97— Mike Smith, RT
2002—Henrik Juul-Nielson, PK
Mike Miller, RB

NEB.-OMAHA (14)
64— Gerald Allen, HB
68— Dan Klepper, OG
76— Dan Fulton, WR
77— Dan Fulton, OE
80— Tom Sutko, LB
82— John Walker, DT
83— Tim Carlson, LB
84— Ron Petersen, OT
86— Keith Coleman, LB
98— Chris Bober, OT
99— Chris Bober, OL
2000—Chris Cooper, DL
01— Chad Geiger, DB
02— Conor Riley, OL

NEB. WESLEYAN (4)
90— Brad Bohn, DB
91— Darren Stohlmann, TE
92— Darren Stohlmann, TE
2000—Noland Urban, LB

NEVADA* (23)
52— Neil Garrett, DB
74— Greg Grouwinkel, DB
78— James Curry, MG
Frank Hawkins, RB
79— †Frank Hawkins, RB
†Lee Fobbs, DB
80— †Frank Hawkins, RB
†Bubba Puha, DL
81— †John Ramatici, LB
†Tony Zendejas, K
82— †Tony Zendejas, K
†Charles Mann, DT
83— †Tony Zendejas, K
†Jim Werbeckes, OG
†Tony Shaw, DB
85— †Greg Rea, OL
†Marty Zendejas, PK
†Pat Hunter, DB
86— †Henry Rolling, DE-LB
88— †Bernard Ellison, DB
90— †Bernard Ellison, DB
†Treamelle Taylor, KR
91— †Matt Clafton, LB

UNLV* (3)
73— Mike Thomas, RB
74— Mike Thomas, RB
75— Joseph Ingersoll, DL

NEW HAMPSHIRE (15)
50— Ed Douglas, G
68— Al Whittman, DT
75— Kevin Martell, C
76— Bill Burnham, RB
77— Bill Burnham, RB
Grady Vigneau, OT
85— †Paul Dufault, OL
87— †John Driscoll, OL
91— †Barry Bourassa, RB
†Dwayne Sabb, LB
94— †Mike Foley, DL
97— †Jerry Azumah, RS/RB
98— †Jerry Azumah, RB
†Walter Jones, OL
2002—†Stephan Lewis, RB

NEW HAVEN (17)
85— David Haubner, OL
87— Erik Lesinski, LB
88— Rob Thompson, OL
90— Jay McLucas, QB
92— Scott Emmert, OL
Roger Graham, RB
93— Roger Graham, RB
George Byrd, DB
Tony Willis, WR
94— Roger Graham, RB
95— Scott Riggs, LB
96— Jesse Showerda, QB
97— Mario DiDino, OL
Cazzie Kosciolek, QB
2000—Steve Cedor, LB
01— Idris Price, LB
02— Phil Bogle, OL

N.M. HIGHLANDS (8)
66— Carl Garrett, HB
67— Carl Garrett, HB
68— Carl Garrett, HB
81— Jay Lewis, WR
85— Neil Windham, LB
86— Tim Salz, PK
93— Rus Bailey, WR
96— Jamar Nailor, WR

NEWBERRY (3)
40— Dominic Collangelo, B
81— Stan Stanton, DL
97— Anthony Heatley, OL

NICHOLLS ST. (8)
76— Gerald Butler, OE
77— Rusty Rebowe, LB
81— †Dwight Walker, WR
82— †Clint Conque, LB
84— †Dewayne Harrison, TE
86— †Mark Carrier, WR
94— †Darryl Pounds, DB
2002—†LeJuan Walker, RS

NICHOLS (1)
81— Ed Zywien, LB

NORFOLK ST. (5)
79— Mike Ellis, DB
89— Arthur Jimmerson, LB
94— James Roe, WR
95— James Roe, WR
Aaron Sparrow, QB

NORTH ALA. (20)
82— Don Smith, C
84— Daryl Smith, DB
85— Bruce Jones, DB
90— James Davis, LB
Mike Nord, DL
92— Harvey Summerhill, DB
93— Jeff Redcross, DL
Tyrone Rush, RB
Jeff Surbaugh, OL
Ronald McKinnon, LB
94— Jon Thompson, OL
Ronald McKinnon, LB
Marcus Keyes, DL
95— Jon Thompson, OL
Israel Raybon, DE
Ronald McKinnon, LB
Marcus Keyes, DL
96— Gerald Smith, DB

97— Reginald Ruffin, LB
Marcus Hill, DB

N.C. A&T (10)
69— Merl Code, DB
70— Melvin Holmes, OT
81— †Mike West, OL
86— †Ernest Riddick, NG
88— †Demetrius Harrison, LB
93— †Ronald Edwards, OL
95— †Jamain Stephens, OL
97— †Chris McNeil, DL
2001—†Curtis DeLoatch, RS
†Qasim Mitchell, OL

N.C. CENTRAL (5)
68— Doug Wilkerson, MG
69— Doug Wilkerson, OT
74— Charles Smith, DE
88— Earl Harvey, QB
96— Tommy Dorsey, LB

NORTH CENTRAL (1)
97— Jim Witte, OL

NORTH DAKOTA (30)
55— Steve Myhra, G
56— Steve Myhra, G
63— Neil Reuter, T
65— Dave Lince, DE
66— Roger Bonk, LB
71— Jim LeClair, LB
Dan Martinsen, DB
72— Mike Deutsch, RB
75— Bill Deutsch, RB
79— Paul Muckenhirn, TE
80— Todd Thomas, OT
81— Milson Jones, RB
89— Cory Solberg, PK
91— Shannon Burnell, RB
93— Shannon Burnell, RB
Kevin Robson, OL
94— Mike Mooney, DL
95— Dave Hillesheim, DE
96— Juan Gomez-Tagle, PK
Mark Callahan, DL
Tim Tibesar, LB
97— Phillip Moore, RB
Jim Kleinsasser, TE
98— Jim Kleinsasser, TE
Phillip Moore, RB
99— Kelly Howe, DB
2000—Cameron Peterka, PK
01— Cameron Peterka, PK
Travis O'Neel, LB
Dan Graf, AP

NORTH DAKOTA ST. (33)
34— Melvin Hanson, B
46— Cliff Rothrock, C
66— Walt Odegaard, MG
67— Jim Ferge, LB
68— Jim Ferge, DT
Paul Hatchett, B
69— Paul Hatchett, HB
Joe Cichy, DB
70— Joe Cichy, DB
74— Jerry Dahl, DE
76— Rick Budde, LB
77— Lew Curry, OL
81— Wayne Schluchter, DB
82— Cliff Carmody, OG
Steve Garske, LB
83— Mike Whetstone, OG
84— Greg Hagfors, C
86— Jeff Bentrim, QB
Jim Dick, DB
87— Mike Favor, C
88— Matt Tracy, OL
Mike Favor, C
Yorrick Byers, LB
90— Phil Hansen, DL
Chris Simdorn, QB
93— Scott Fuchs, OL
T.R. McDonald, WR
95— Brad Servais, OL
97— Sean Fredricks, OL
99— Tim Strehlow, AP
2000—Lamar Gordon, RB
01— Leif Murphy, DL
Richard Lewis, KR

NORTH PARK (2)
72— Greg Nugent, OE
90— John Love, QB

NORTH TEXAS* (6)
47— Frank Whitlow, T
51— Ray Renfro, DB
83— †Ronnie Hickman, DE
    †Rayford Cooks, DL
88— †Rex Johnson, DL
90— †Mike Davis, DL

NORTHEASTERN (4)
72— Tom Rezzuti, DB
78— Dan Ross, TE
96— †Jerome Daniels, OL
2001—†L.J. McKansas, RB

NORTHEASTERN ST. (7)
69— Manuel Britto, HB
71— Roosevelt Manning, DT
74— Kevin Goodlet, DB
82— Cedric Mack, WR
94— Ricky Ceasar, DL
2000—Rod Kelly, DL
02— Micah Lomas, OL

NORTHERN ARIZ. (20)
66— Rick Ries, LB
67— Bill Hanna, DE
68— Larry Small, OG
77— Larry Friedrichs, OL
    Tom Jurich, K
78— Jerry Lumpkin, LB
79— †Ed Judie, LB
82— †Pete Mandley, WR
83— †Pete Mandley, WR
    †James Gee, DT
86— †Goran Lingmerth, PK
89— †Darrell Jordan, LB
93— †Terry Belden, P
95— †Rayna Stewart, DB
    †Kevin O'Leary, P
    †Ben Petrucci, DL
96— †Archie Amerson, RB
    †Ricky Pearsall, PR
97— †Dan Finn, OL
2002—†Mark Gould, P

NORTHERN COLO. (23)
68— Jack O'Brien, DB
80— Todd Volkart, DT
81— Brad Wimmer, OL
82— Mark Mostek, OG
    Kevin Jelden, PK
89— Vance Lechman, DB
90— Frank Wainwright, TE
92— David Oliver, OL
93— Jeff Pease, LB
94— Jeff Pease, LB
95— Tony Ramirez, OL
    Tim Bowie, DB
96— Tony Ramirez, OL
    Delano Washington, DB
97— Aaron Smith, DL
    Dirk Johnson, DB
98— Aaron Smith, DL
    Scott Zimmerman, LB
99— Corte McGuffey, QB
    Jamie Heiner, LB
2000—Ryan Burkholder, OL
02— Anthony Dunn, DL
    Cabel Rohloff, LB

NORTHERN ILL.* (2)
62— George Bork, B
63— George Bork, B

NORTHERN IOWA (24)
52— Lou Bohnsack, C
60— George Asleson, G
61— Wendell Williams, G
64— Randy Schultz, FB
65— Randy Schultz, FB
67— Ray Pedersen, MG
75— Mike Timmermans, OT
85— Joe Fuller, DB
87— †Carl Boyd, RB
90— †Brian Mitchell, PK
91— †Brian Mitchell, PK
92— †Kenny Shedd, WR
    †William Freeney, LB
94— †Andre Allen, LB
95— †Dedric Ward, WR
96— †Dedric Ward, WR
99— †Brad Meester, C
    †Mike Furrey, WR
2000—†Eddie Berlin, WR
    †Ryan Helming, QB

    †Ryan Doak, DB
01—†MacKenzie Hoambrecker, PK
    †Adam Vogt, LB
02—†MacKenzie Hoambrecker, PK

NORTHERN MICH. (8)
75— Daniel Stencil, OL
76— Maurice Mitchell, FL
77— Joseph Stemo, DB
82— George Works, RB
87— Jerry Woods, DB
88— Jerry Woods, DB
99— Ty Hartung, P
2000—Mark Dugas, OL

NORTHERN ST. (1)
76— Larry Kolbo, DL

NORTHWEST MO. ST. (19)
39— Marion Rogers, G
84— Steve Hansley, WR
89— Jason Agee, DB
96— Matt Uhde, DL
97— Chris Greisen, QB
98— Twan Young, DB
    Aaron Crowe, LB
    Chris Greisen, QB
    Steve Coppinger, C
    Aaron Becker, DL
99— Tony Miles, AP
    David Purnell, PK
    Chad Thompson, OG
2000—Andy Erpelding, OT
    Tony Miles, AP/WR
    Aaron Becker, DL
    Brian Williams, LB
01— Seth Wand, OL
02— Seth Wand, OL

N'WESTERN (IOWA) (1)
71— Kevin Korvor, DE

NORTHWESTERN ST. (17)
66— Al Dodd, DB
80— †Warren Griffith, C
    †Joe Delaney, RB
81— †Gary Reasons, LB
82— †Gary Reasons, LB
83— †Gary Reasons, LB
84— †Arthur Berry, DT
87— †John Kulakowski, DE
91— †Andre Carron, LB
92— †Adrian Hardy, DB
    †Marcus Spears, OL
93— †Marcus Spears, OL
97— †Tony Maranto, DB
98— †Jermaine Jones, DB
99— †Mike Green, DB
2000—†Terrence McGee, PR
02— †Roy Locks, DL

NORTHWOOD (3)
73— Bill Chandler, DT
74— Bill Chandler, DT
98— Tyrone Nelson, OL

NORWICH (3)
79— Milt Williams, RB
84— Beau Almodobar, WR
85— Mike Norman, OL

OBERLIN (1)
45— James Boswell, B

OCCIDENTAL (6)
76— Rick Fry, FL
77— Rick Fry, SE
82— Dan Osborn, P
83— Ron Scott, DB
89— David Hodges, LB
90— Peter Tucker, OL

OHIO* (2)
35— Art Lewis, T
60— Dick Grecni, C

OHIO NORTHERN (8)
95— LaVant King, WR
96— Jerry Adams, DB
98— Steve Vagedes, P
99— Jamal Robertson, RB
    Kory Allen, OL
    Jeremy Presar, DB
    Steve Vagedes, P/WR
2000—Jamal Robertson, RB

OHIO WESLEYAN (8)
34— John Turley, B
51— Dale Bruce, OE
71— Steve Dutton, DE

83— Eric DiMartino, LB
90— Jeff Court, OG
    Neil Ringers, DL
91— Kevin Rucker, DL
96— Craig Anderson, LB

OKLA. PANHANDLE (2)
82— Tom Rollison, DB
83— Tom Rollison, DB

OTTERBEIN (4)
82— Jim Hoyle, K
90— Ron Severance, WR
91— Ron Severance, WR
2001—Jeff Gibbs, TE

OUACHITA BAPTIST (2)
79— Ezekiel Vaughn, LB
2001—T.J. Bingham, DL

PACIFIC (CAL.) (4)
34— Cris Kjeldsen, G
47— Eddie LeBaron, B
48— Eddie LeBaron, B
49— Eddie LeBaron, B

PACIFIC LUTHERAN (11)
40— Marv Tommervik, B
41— Marv Tommervik, B
47— Dan D'Andrea, C
52— Ron Billings, DB
65— Marvin Peterson, C
78— John Zamberlin, LB
85— Mark Foege, PK
    Tim Shannon, DL
88— Jon Kral, DL
2000—Chad Johnson, QB
02— Kyle Brown, WR

PENNSYLVANIA (9)
86— †Marty Peterson, OL
88— †John Zinser, OL
90— †Joe Valerio, OL
93— †Miles Macik, WR
94— †Pat Goodwillie, LB
95— †Miles Macik, WR
    †Tom McGarrity, DL
96— †Mitch Marrow, DL
2001—†Jeff Hatch, OL

PEPPERDINE (2)
47— Darwin Horn, B
55— Wixie Robinson, G

PERU ST. (4)
52— Robert Lade, OT
53— Robert Lade, T
81— Alvin Holder, RB
91— Tim Herman, DL

PILLSBURY (1)
85— Calvin Addison, RB

PITTSBURG ST. (27)
61— Gary Snadon, B
70— Mike Potchard, OT
78— Brian Byers, OL
88— Jesse Wall, OL
89— John Roderique, LB
90— Ron West, WR
91— Ron West, WR
92— Ronald Moore, RB
93— Doug Bullard, OL
94— Andy Sweet, LB
    Chris Brown, DB
95— Phil Schepens, OT
    B.J. McGivern, LB
    Chris Brown, DB
96— Bob Goltra, OL
97— Sean McNamara, OL
    Brian Moorman, P
98— Ben Peterson, DE
    Brian Moorman, P
99— Andrew Poling, DB
2000—Wes Baker, LB
01— Matt Howard, OL
    Earl Henry, LB
    Aaron McConnell, DL
02— Daniel Chappell, PK
    Eric Johnson, C
    Aaron McConnell, DL

PLYMOUTH ST. (8)
74— Robert Gibson, DB
82— Mark Barrows, C
83— Joe Dudek, RB
84— Joe Dudek, RB

85— Joe Dudek, RB
91— Scott Allen, LB
94— Colby Compton, LB
95— Colby Compton, LB

POMONA-PITZER (1)
74— Larry Cenotto, QB

PORTLAND ST. (18)
76— June Jones, QB
77— Dave Stief, OE
79— †Stuart Gaussoin, SE
    †Kurt Ijanoff, OT
80— †Neil Lomax, QB
84— Doug Mikolas, DL
88— Bary Naone, TE
    Chris Crawford, QB
89— Darren Del'Andrae, QB
91— James Fuller, DB
92— John Charles, QB
93— Rick Cruz, LB
94— Sam Peoples, DB
    Jesus Moreno, OT
95— Steve Papin, RB
98— †Bobby Singh, OL
2000—†Charles Dunn, RB
01— †Terry Charles, WR

PRAIRIE VIEW (2)
64— Otis Taylor, OE
70— Bivian Lee, DB

PRESBYTERIAN (10)
45— Andy Kavounis, G
46— Hank Caver, B
52— Joe Kirven, OE
68— Dan Eckstein, DB
71— Robert Norris, LB
78— Roy Walker, OL
79— Roy Walker, OL
83— Jimmie Turner, LB
2001—Todd Cunningham, QB
    D.J. Humphries, WR

PRINCETON (5)
87— †Dean Cain, DB
89— †Judd Garrett, RB
92— †Keith Elias, RB
93— †Keith Elias, RB
2001—†Taylor Northrop, PK

PRINCIPIA (1)
93— Matt Newton, WR

PUGET SOUND (9)
56— Robert Mitchell, G
63— Ralph Bauman, G
66— Joseph Peyton, OE
75— Bill Linnenkohl, LB
76— Dan Kuehl, DL
81— Bob Jackson, MG
82— Mike Bos, WR
83— Larry Smith, DB
87— Mike Oliphant, RB

RANDOLPH-MACON (9)
47— Albert Oley, G
57— Dave Young, G
79— Rick Eades, DL
80— Rick Eades, DL
84— Cody Dearing, QB
88— Aaron Boston, OL
96— Tim Armoska, DL
98— Chuck Davis, DL
99— Sean Eaton, WR

REDLANDS (4)
77— Randy Van Horn, OL
92— James Shields, DL
2002—Sean Lipscomb, P
    Jeff Thomas, DB

RENSSELAER (3)
96— Scott Cafarelli, OL
98— Krishaun Gilmore, RB
99— Chris Swartz, DB

RHODE ISLAND (9)
55— Charles Gibbons, T
82— †Richard Pelzer, OL
83— †Tony DeLuca, OL
84— †Brian Forster, TE
85— †Brian Forster, TE
    †Tom Ehrhardt, QB
90— †Kevin Smith, DB
92— †Darren Rizzi, TE
96— †Frank Ferrara, DL

RHODES (5)
36— Henry Hammond, E
38— Gaylon Smith, B
76— Conrad Bradburn, DB
85— Jim Hever, PK
88— Larry Hayes, OL

RICHMOND (6)
84— †Eddie Martin, OL
97— †Shawn Barber, LB
    †Marc Megna, DL
98— †Marc Megna, DT
    †Eric King, OL
2000—†Eric Beatty, OL

RIPON (7)
57— Peter Kasson, E
75— Dick Rehbein, C
76— Dick Rehbein, OL
79— Art Peters, TE
82— Bob Wallner, OL
95— Jim Wallace, DB
2000—Nate Kok, DB

ROANOKE (1)
38— Kenneth Moore, E

ROCHESTER (7)
51— Jack Wilson, DE
52— Donald Bardell, DG
67— Dave Ragusa, LB
75— Ralph Gebhardt, DB
90— Craig Chodak, P
92— Brian Laudadio, DL
93— Geoff Long, DL

ROCKHURST (1)
41— Joe Kiernan, T

ROCKY MOUNTAIN (1)
2001—Travis Salter, DB

ROLLINS (1)
40— Charles Lingerfelt, E

ROSE-HULMAN (2)
77— Gary Ellis, DB
92— Todd Holthaus, PK

ROWAN (12)
78— Dino Hall, RB
93— Bill Fisher, DL
95— LeRoi Jones, LB
97— Terrick Grace, DB
98— Jarryn Avery, OL
99— John Gavlick, LB
    Jarryn Avery, OL
    Cornelius White, DL
2000—Ron Gibson, DB
01— Tony Racioppi, QB
    Rob Rieck, OL
02— Gerrit Tosh, DL

SACRAMENTO ST. (8)
64— William Fuller, OT
91— Troy Mills, RB
    Jim Crouch, PK
92— Jon Kirksey, DL
98—†Charles Roberts, RB
99—†Charles Roberts, RB
    †Jon Osterhout, OL
2000—†Charles Roberts, RB

SAGINAW VALLEY (8)
81— Eugene Marve, LB
84— Joe Rice, DL
90— David Cook, DB
92— Bill Schafer, TE
97— Paul Spicer, DL
    Kent Kraatz, OT
98— Lamar King, DL
2000—Brian Dolph, WR

ST. AMBROSE (5)
40— Nick Kerasiotis, G
51— Robert Flanagan, B
58— Robert Webb, B
87— Jerry Klosterman, DL
97— Craig Shepherd, OL

ST. BONAVENTURE (2)
46— Phil Colella, B
48— Frank LoVuola, E

ST. CLOUD ST. (6)
85— Mike Lambrecht, DL
95— Randy Martin, RB
96— Randy Martin, RB

97— Mike McKinney, WR
2002—Matt Huebner, TE
    Ben Nelson, WR

ST. JOHN'S (MINN.) (18)
65— Pat Whalin, DB
79— Ernie England, MG
82— Rick Bell, RB
83— Chris Biggins, TE
91— Pat Mayew, QB
93— Burt Chamberlin, OL
    Jim Wagner, DL
94— Jim Wagner, DL
95— Chris Palmer, WR
96— Jesse Redepenning, OL
98— Brandon Novak, LB
99— Brandon Novak, LB
    Phil Barry, P
2000—Nathan Kirschner, TE
    Chris Salvato, OL
02— Blake Elliott, AP/WR
    Jeremy Hood, DL
    Cam McCambridge, LB

ST. JOHN'S (N.Y.) (1)
83— Todd Jamison, QB

ST. LAWRENCE (2)
51— Ken Spencer, LB
77— Mitch Brown, DB

ST. MARY (KAN.) (1)
86— Joe Brinson, RB

ST. MARY'S (CAL.) (7)
79— Fran McDermott, DB
80— Fran McDermott, DB
88— Jon Braff, TE
92— Mike Estrella, PK
2001—†Travis White, DL
02— †Nathan Frowsing, OL
    †Weston Borba, DB

ST. MARY'S (TEX.) (1)
36— Douglas Locke, B

ST. NORBERT (5)
57— Norm Jarock, B
64— Dave Jauquet, DE
2000—Jerimiah Janssen, DL
01— Jerimiah Janssen, LB
02— Kevin O'Malley, OL

ST. OLAF (3)
53— John Gustafson, E
78— John Nahorniak, LB
80— Jon Anderson, DL

ST. THOMAS (MINN.) (11)
45— Theodore Molitor, E
48— Jack Salscheider, B
84— Neal Guggemos, DB
85— Neal Guggemos, DB
90— Gary Trettel, RB
91— Kevin DeVore, OL
94— Ryan Davis, TE
95— Ryan Davis, TE
96— Ryan Collins, TE
97— Ryan Collins, TE
2002—Sean O'Leary, DL

SALISBURY (6)
82— Mark Lagowski, LB
84— Joe Mammano, OL
85— Robb Disbennett, QB
86— Tom Kress, DL
95— Mark Hannah, LB
2002—Beau Ridgway, OL

SAM HOUSTON ST. (6)
49— Charles Williams, E
52— Don Gottlob, B
91—†Michael Bankston, DL
2001—†Jonathon Cooper, WR
    †Keith Heinrich, TE
    †Keith Davis, DB

SAMFORD (3)
36— Norman Cooper, C
94— †Anthony Jordan, AP
2002—†Cortland Finnegan, RS

SAN DIEGO (3)
73— Bob Dulich, QB
81— Dan Herbert, DB
92— Robert Ray, P

SAN DIEGO ST.* (6)
35— John Butler, G

66— Don Horn, QB
67— Steve Duich, OT
    Haven Moses, OE
68— Fred Dryer, DE
    Lloyd Edwards, B

SAN FRANCISCO (1)
42— John Sanchez, T

SAN FRAN. ST. (7)
51— Robert Williamson, OT
60— Charles Fuller, B
67— Joe Koontz, OE
76— Forest Hancock, LB
78— Frank Duncan, DB
82— Poncho James, RB
84— Jim Jones, TE

SAN JOSE ST.* (2)
38— Lloyd Thomas, E
39— LeRoy Zimmerman, B

SANTA CLARA (8)
64— Lou Pastorini, LB
71— Ronald Sani, C
79— Jim Leonard, C
80— Brian Sullivan, K
82— Gary Hoffman, OT
83— Alex Vlahos, C
    Mike Rosselli, LB
85— Brent Jones, TE

SAVANNAH ST. (3)
79— Timothy Walker, DL
89— Shannon Sharpe, TE
96— Britt Henderson, DB

SEWANEE (9)
63— Martin Agnew, B
73— Mike Lumpkin, DE
77— Nino Austin, DB
79— John Hill, DB
80— Mallory Nimocs, TE
81— Greg Worsowicz, DB
86— Mark Kent, WR
90— Ray McGowan, DL
99— Antonio Crook, OL

SHENANDOAH (1)
2002—Gregg Anderson, DB

SHEPHERD (5)
98— James Rooths, KR
99— Damian Beane, RB
    James Rooths, KR
2000—James Rooths, DB
    Dalevon Smith, RB

SHIPPENSBURG (5)
53— Robert Adams, G
91— Jeff Fickes, DB
94— Doug Seidenstricker, DB
99— Jamie Ware, WR
2001—Chad Oberholzer, DL

SIENA (2)
95—†Reggie Greene, AP
97—†Reggie Greene, RB

SIMON FRASER (1)
90— Nick Mazzoli, WR

SIMPSON (6)
89— Ricky Gales, RB
96— Brent Parrott, DB
    Chris Whiney, OT
97— Jeremy Whalen, DL
98— Guy Leman, RB
    Clint Head, OL

SLIPPERY ROCK (8)
74— Ed O'Reilly, RB
75— Jerry Skocik, TE
76— Chris Thull, LB
77— Bob Schrantz, TE
78— Bob Schrantz, TE
85— Jeff Williams, P
97— Dave Sabolcik, DL
98— Matt Kinsinger, DL

SONOMA ST. (3)
86— Mike Henry, LB
92— Larry Allen, OL
93— Larry Allen, OL

SOUTH CAROLINA ST. (24)
67— Tyrone Caldwell, DE
71— James Evans, LB
72— Barney Chavous, DE
73— Donnie Shell, DB

75— Harry Carson, DE
76— Robert Sims, DL
77— Ricky Anderson, RB
79— †Phillip Murphy, DL
80— †Edwin Bailey, OG
81— †Anthony Reed, FB
    †Dwayne Jackson, DL
82— †Dwayne Jackson, DE
    †Anthony Reed, RB
    †Ralph Green, OT
    †John Courtney, DT
83— †Ralph Green, OT
89— †Eric Douglas, OL
91— †Robert Porcher, DE
93— †Anthony Cook, DE
94— †Anthony Cook, DL
96— †Raleigh Roundtree, OL
97— †Chartric Darby, DL
98— †Jermaine Derricott, DB
2001—†Derek Harrison, LB

SOUTH DAKOTA (12)
68— John Kohler, OT
69— John Kohler, OT
71— Gene Macken, OG
72— Gary Kipling, OG
78— Bill Moats, DB
79— Benjamin Long, LB
83— Kurt Seibel, K
86— Jerry Glinsky, C
    Todd Salat, DB
88— Doug VanderEsch, LB
97— Brent Petersen, DL
2000—Russel Burwell, DB

SOUTH DAKOTA ST. (17)
67— Darwin Gonnerman, HB
68— Darwin Gonnerman, FB
74— Lynn Boden, OT
77— Bill Matthews, DE
79— Charles Loewen, OL
84— Rick Wegher, RB
85— Jeff Tiefenthaler, WR
86— Jeff Tiefenthaler, WR
91— Kevin Tetzlaff, OL
92— Doug Miller, LB
93— Adam Timmerman, DL
94— Jake Hines, TE
    Adam Vinatieri, P
    Adam Timmerman, OL
96— Tom O'Brien, P
99— Josh Ranek, RB
2001—Josh Ranek, RB

SOUTH DAKOTA TECH (1)
73— Charles Waite, DB

SOUTH FLA.* (1)
98—†Bill Gramatica, PK

SOUTHEAST MO. ST. (5)
37— Wayne Goddard, T
94—†Doug Berg, DL
95—†Frank Russell, DB
97—†Angel Rubio, DL
2002—†Willie Ponder, WR

SOUTHEASTERN LA. (3)
70— Ronnie Hornsby, LB
83— †Bret Wright, P
85— †Willie Shepherd, DL

SOUTHERN U. (8)
70— Isiah Robertson, LB
72— James Wright, OG
73— Godwin Turk, LB
79— †Ken Times, DL
87— †Gerald Perry, OT
93— †Sean Wallace, DB
95— †Kendell Shello, DL
2000—†Michael Hayes, WR

SOUTHERN ARK. (6)
84— Greg Stuman, LB
85— Greg Stuman, LB
97— Fred Perry, LB
98— Jason Williams, PK
2001—Eddie Key, LB
02— Nik Lewis, WR

SOUTHERN CONN. ST. (11)
82— Mike Marshall, DB
83— Kevin Gray, DL
84— William Sixsmith, LB
86— Rick Atkinson, DB
91— Ron Lecointe, OL
92— Steve Lawrence, LB

94— Anthony Idone, DL
95— †Joe Andruzzi, OL
96— Joe Andruzzi, OL
2000—Damon Richardson, DB
02— Jacques Cesaire, DL

SOUTHERN ILL. (7)
70— Lionel Antoine, OE
71— Lionel Antoine, OE
83— †Donnell Daniel, DB
†Terry Taylor, DB
96— †Mark Gagliano, P
99— †Cornell Craig, WR
2002—†Mo Abdulqaadir, RB

SOUTHERN MISS.* (4)
53— Hugh Pepper, B
56— Don Owens, T
58— Robert Yencho, E
59— Hugh McInnis, E

SOUTHERN ORE. ST. (2)
75— Dennis Webber, LB
99— Griff Yates, RB

SOUTHERN UTAH (10)
79— Lane Martino, DL
87— Jeff McComb, P
89— Randy Bostic, C
90— Randy Bostic, C
95— †Micah Deckert, TE
97— †Jimmy Brimmer, LB
99— †John Uriarte, OL
†Josh Roberts, DB
2000—†Matt Cannon, QB
†Randy Clark, OL

SOUTHWEST MO. ST. (12)
66— William Stringer, OG
87— †Matt Soraghan, LB
89— †Mark Christenson, OL
90— †DeAndre Smith, QB
91— †Bill Walter, DL
93— †Adrion Smith, DB
95— †DeLaun Fowler, LB
96— †Michael Cosey, RB
†Wayne Boyer, PK
†Mike Miano, DL
97— †Travis Brawner, PK
2001—†P.J. Jones, LB

SOUTHWEST ST. (2)
87— James Ashley, WR
91— Wayne Hawkins, DE

SOUTHWEST TEX. ST. (14)
53— Pence Dacus, B
63— Jerry Cole, E
64— Jerry Cole, DB
72— Bob Daigle, C
75— Bobby Kotzur, DT
82— Tim Staskus, LB
83— Tim Staskus, LB
84— †Scott Forester, C
90— †Reggie Rivers, RB
91— †Ervin Thomas, C
94— †Don Wilkerson, RB
97— †Claude Mathis, RB
2000—†C.J. Carroll, DB
01— †Clenton Ballard, DL

SOUTHWESTERN (KAN.) (2)
82— Tom Audley, DL
84— Jackie Jenson, RB

SOUTHWESTERN OKLA. (2)
77— Louis Blanton, DB
82— Richard Lockman, LB

SPRINGFIELD (16)
68— Dick Dobbert, C
70— John Curtis, OE
76— Roy Samuelsen, MG
78— Jack Quinn, DB
79— Jack Quinn, DB
80— Steve Foster, OT
81— Jon Richardson, LB
83— Wally Case, DT
Ed Meachum, TE
85— Jim Anderson, LB
91— Fran Papasedero, DL
94— Matt Way, OL
96— Jamie McGourty, DL
98— John Cena, OL
2000—Matt Sallilia, OG
02— Greg Switaj, PK

STEPHEN F. AUSTIN (15)
51— James Terry, DE
79— Ronald Haynes, DL
85— James Noble, WR
86— †Darrell Harkless, DB
88— †Eric Lokey, LB
89— †David Whitmore, DB
93— †Cedric Walker, DB
95— †Joey Wylie, OL
†Lee Kirk, OL
†Damiyon Bell, DB
96— †Jeremiah Trotter, LB
97— †Mikhael Ricks, WR
†Jeremiah Trotter, LB
98— †Chad Stanley, P
99— †Ka Ron Coleman, PR

STILLMAN (1)
2002—James Patrick, DB

STONY BROOK (2)
87— Chuck Downey, DB
88— David Lewis, P

SUL ROSS ST. (2)
65— Tom Nelson, DE
88— Francis Jones, DB

SUSQUEHANNA (5)
51— James Hazlett, C
90— Keith Henry, DL
92— Andy Watkins, LB
96— Jeremy Ziesloft, DB
99— Antonio Nash, DB

SWARTHMORE (1)
89— Marshall Happer, OL

TAMPA (5)
65— John Perry, DB
68— Ron Brown, MG
70— Leon McQuay, RB
71— Ron Mikolajczyk, OT
Sammy Gellerstedt, MG

TENN.-MARTIN (3)
68— Julian Nunnamaker, OG
88— Emanuel McNeil, DL
91— Oscar Bunch, TE

TENNESSEE ST. (21)
67— Claude Humphrey, DT
68— Jim Marsalis, DB
69— Joe Jones, DE
70— Vernon Holland, OT
71— Cliff Brooks, DB
Joe Gilliam, QB
72— Robert Woods, OT
Waymond Bryant, LB
73— Waymond Bryant, LB
Ed Jones, DE
74— Cleveland Elam, DE
81— †Mike Jones, WR
†Malcolm Taylor, DT
82— †Walter Tate, OL
86— †Onzy Elam, LB
90— †Colin Godfrey, P
93— †Brent Alexander, DB
98— †Tyrone Butterfield, WR
99— †Lamar Carter, DL
†Avion Black, RS
†Michael Thompson, OL

TENNESSEE TECH (13)
52— Tom Fann, OT
59— Tom Hackler, E
60— Tom Hackler, E
61— David Baxter, T
69— Larry Schreiber, HB
71— Jim Youngblood, LB
72— Jim Youngblood, LB
74— Elois Grooms, DE
76— Ed Burns, OT
89— †Ryan Weeks, PK
96— †Robert Taylor, DB
2001—†Joey Bishop, OL
†D.J. Bleisath, DL

TENN. WESLEYAN (1)
92— Derrick Scott, PK

TEXAS-ARLINGTON (5)
66— Ken Ozee, DT
67— Robert Diem, OG
Robert Willbanks, S
83— †Mark Cannon, C
84— †Bruce Collie, OL

TEX. A&M-COMMERCE (20)
38— Darrell Tully, B
53— Bruno Ashley, G
58— Sam McCord, B
59— Sam McCord, B
68— Chad Brown, OT
70— William Lewis, C
72— Curtis Wester, OG
73— Autry Beamon, DB
84— Alan Veingrad, OG
88— Kim Morton, DL
90— Terry Bagsby, DL
91— Eric Turner, DB
Dwayne Phorne, OL
92— Eric Turner, DB
Pat Williams, DB
93— Fred Woods, LB
Billy Watkins, PK
95— Kevin Mathis, DB
96— Kevin Mathis, DB
99— Antonio Wilson, LB

TEX. A&M-KINGSVILLE (57)
40— Stuart Clarkson, C
41— Stuart Clarkson, C
59— Gerald Lambert, G
60— William Crafts, T
62— Douglas Harvey, C
63— Sid Blanks, B
65— Randy Johnson, QB
66— Dwayne Nix, OE
67— Dwayne Nix, OE
68— Dwayne Nix, OE
Ray Hickl, OG
70— Dwight Harrison, DB
Margarito Guerrero, MG
71— Eldridge Small, OE
Levi Johnson, DB
72— Ernest Price, DE
74— Don Hardeman, RB
75— David Hill, TE
76— Richard Ritchie, QB
Larry Grunewald, LB
77— Larry Collins, RB
John Barefield, DE
78— Billy John, OT
79— Andy Hawkins, LB
80— Don Washington, CB
81— Durwood Roquemore, DB
82— Darrell Green, DB
83— Loyd Lewis, OG
84— Neal Lattue, PK
85— Charles Smith, C
86— Johnny Bailey, RB
Moses Horn, OG
87— Johnny Bailey, RB
Moses Horn, OG
88— Rod Mounts, OL
Johnny Bailey, RB
John Randle, DL
89— Johnny Bailey, RB
90— Keithen DeGrate, OL
91— Brian Nielsen, OL
92— Earl Dotson, OL
93— Anthony Phillips, DB
Moke Simon, DL
94— Jeff Rodgers, DL
Kevin Dogins, C
95— Jermane Mayberry, OT
Jaime Martinez, OG
Kevin Dogins, C
96— Todd Perkins, OT
97— Chris Hensley, LB
98— Cedric Johnson, DB
Cliff Clemons, OL
99— Robert Garza, C
2000—Robert Garza, C
01— Kiah Johnson, LB
02— Mike Clay, DL
Nicholas Davis, DB

TEXAS LUTHERAN (3)
73— David Wehmeyer, RB
74— D.W. Rutledge, LB
75— Jerry Ellis, OL

TEXAS SOUTHERN (3)
70— Nathaniel Allen, DB
76— Freddie Dean, OL
92— †Michael Strahan, DL

TEXAS TECH* (2)
35— Herschel Ramsey, E
45— Walter Schlinkman, B

THIEL (1)
2001—Kennard Davis, DB

THOMAS MORE (5)
93— Mike Flesch, OL
96— Brent Moses, OL
97— Chris Wells, LB
98— Chris Wells, LB
2000—Will Castleberry, RB

TIFFIN (1)
93— Brian Diliberto, RB

TOLEDO* (1)
38— Dan Buckwick, G

TOWSON (13)
75— Dan Dullea, QB
76— Skip Chase, OE
77— Randy Bielski, DB
78— Ken Snoots, SE
82— Sean Landeta, P
83— Gary Rubeling, DB
84— Terry Brooks, OG
85— Stan Eisentooth, OL
86— David Haden, LB
93— †Tony Vinson, RB
94— †Mark Orlando, WR
99— †Jamal White, WR
2000—†Andrew Hollingsworth, DL

TRINITY (CONN.) (8)
35— Mickey Kobrosky, B
36— Mickey Kobrosky, B
55— Charles Sticka, B
59— Roger LeClerc, C
70— David Kiarsis, HB
78— Pat McNamara, FL
93— Eric Mudry, DB
94— Greg Schramm, DB

TRINITY (TEX.) (18)
54— Alvin Beal, B
55— Hubert Cook, C
56— Milton Robichaux, E
67— Marvin Upshaw, DT
94— James Vallerie, LB
96— John Beckwith, LB
97— Paul Morris, PK
Danny Palmer, G
98— David Coney, DL
99— David Coney, OL
Ryan Deck, LB
Mike Burton, QB
2000—John Paul Visosky, LB
01— Bill Smith, OL
02— Roy Hampton, QB
Gary Ihfe, C
Jerheme Urban, WR
Jason Leshikar, LB

TROY ST.* (23)
39— Sherrill Busby, E
73— Mark King, C
74— Mark King, C
76— Perry Griggs, OE
78— Tim Tucker, LB
80— Willie Tullis, QB
84— Mitch Geier, OG
86— Freddie Thomas, DB
87— Mike Turk, QB
Freddie Thomas, DB
94— †Bob Hall, OL
95— †Bob Hall, OL
96— †Pratt Lyons, DL
†Kerry Jenkins, OL
97— †Clifford Ivory, DB
†Andy Swafford, KR
98— †Marcus Spriggs, DL
†Cleve Roberts, OL
†Al Lucas, DT
99— †Al Lucas, DT
†Michael Moore, OT
†Anthony Rabb, DL
2000—†Lawrence Tynes, PK

TRUMAN (5)
60— Dale Mills, B
65— Richard Rhodes, OT
85— Chris Hegg, QB
93— Mike Roos, DL
96— Jarrett Anderson, RB

TUFTS (6)
34— William Grinnell, E
76— Tim Whelan, RB

78— Mark Buben, DL
79— Chris Connors, QB
80— Mike Brown, OL
86— Bob Patz, DL

TULSA* (1)
34— Rudy Prochaska, C

TUSCULUM (3)
94— Matt Schults, OL
95— Eric Claridy, RB
2002—Donald Amaker, RS

TUSKEGEE (3)
98— Che' Bryant, DB
99— Andre Dudley, DL
2002—Drayton Florence, DB

UNION (N.Y.) (11)
39— Sam Hammerstrom, B
82— Steve Bodmer, DL
83— Tim Howell, LB
84— Brian Cox, DE
85— Anthony Valente, DL
86— Rich Romer, DL
87— Rich Romer, DL
91— Greg Harrison, PK
93— Marco Lainez, LB
96— Roger Egbert, PK
2001—Joshua Stinehour, DL

UNION (TENN.) (2)
41— James Jones, B
42— James Jones, B

U.S. INT'L (2)
72— Jerry Robinson, DB
75— Steve Matson, FL

UPSALA (1)
64— Dick Giessuebel, LB

URSINUS (3)
96— Peter Hinckle, DB
2000—Eric Cowie, DB
01— Shearrod Duncan, RB

VALDOSTA ST. (13)
82— Mark Catano, OL
86— Jessie Tuggle, LB
89— Randy Fisher, WR
90— Deon Searcy, DB
93— Chris Hatcher, QB
94— Chris Hatcher, QB
96— Lance Funderburk, QB
97— Richard Freeman, DL/DE
2000—Dusty Bonner, QB
       C.J. Lofton, TE
01— Dusty Bonner, QB
       Tully Payne, C
02— C.J. Lofton, TE

VALPARAISO (6)
51— Joe Pahr, B
71— Gary Puetz, OT
72— Gary Puetz, OT
76— John Belskis, DB
85— Mike Healey, WR
99— †Eric Kenesie, DB

VILLANOVA (12)
88— †Paul Berardelli, OL
89— †Bryan Russo, OL
91— †Curtis Eller, LB
92— †Curtis Eller, LB
94— †Tyrone Frazier, LB
96— †Brian Finneran, WR
97— †Brian Finneran, WR
       †Chris Boden, QB
98— †Brian Westbrook, AP/WR
2000—†Brian Westbrook, AP/RS
01— †Eamonn Allen, OL
       †Brian Westbrook, RB/AP

VMI (4)
88— †Mark Stock, WR
95— †Thomas Haskins, RB
96— †Thomas Haskins, RB
2000—†Richard Holland, KR

VIRGINIA ST. (5)
71— Larry Brooks, DT
84— John Greene, LB
85— James Ward, B
98— Damon Thompson, AP
99— Damon Thompson, WR

VIRGINIA UNION (14)
73— Herb Scott, OG

74— Herb Scott, OG
75— Anthony Leonard, DB
77— Frank Dark, DB
79— Plummer Bullock, DE
80— William Dillon, DB
81— William Dillon, DB
82— William Dillon, DB
83— Larry Curtis, DT
88— Leroy Gause, LB
91— Paul DeBerry, DB
       Kevin Williams, LB
99— Ronald Hardge, DB
2001—Ralph Hunter, DB

WABASH (7)
76— Jimmy Parker, DB
77— David Harvey, QB
81— Pete Metzelaars, TE
88— Tim Pliske, PK
89— Mike Funk, WR
2002—Ryan Short, TE
       Nate Boulais, LB

WAGNER (10)
67— John Gloistein, OT
80— Phil Theis, OL
81— Alonzo Patterson, RB
82— Alonzo Patterson, RB
83— Selwyn Davis, OT
86— Charles Stinson, DL
87— Rich Negrin, OT
88— Terry Underwood, RB
91— Walter Lopez, PK
99— †Rick Sarille, AP

WARTBURG (4)
94— Jamey Parker, OL
       Vince Penningroth, DL
95— Vince Penningroth, DL
2001—Joel Demro, OL

WASHBURN (2)
64— Robert Hardy, DB
88— Troy Slusser, WR

WASHINGTON (MO.) (8)
72— Shelby Jordan, LB
73— Stu Watkins, OE
74— Marion Stallings, DB
88— Paul Matthews, TE
94— Matt Gomric, LB
95— Chris Nalley, DB
96— Chris Nalley, DB
99— Tim Runnalls, DL

WASH. & JEFF. (15)
84— Ed Kusko, OL
87— A. J. Pagano, RB
91— Chris Babirad, RB
       Gilbert Floyd, DB
92— Chris Babirad, RB
       Todd Pivnick, OL
       Kevin Pintar, OL
93— Jason Moore, OL
       Shawn Prendergast, LB
94— Matt Szczypinski, DL
       Mike Jones, OL
       Mike Brooder, OL
95— Mike Jones, OL
96— Dan Primrose, DL
2002—Roger Snyder, RS

WASH. & LEE (5)
76— Tony Perry, OE
81— Mike Pressler, DL
83— Glenn Kirschner, OL
86— John Packett, DL
95— Robert Hall, DL

WAYNE ST. (NEB.) (3)
84— Herve Roussel, PK
85— Ruben Mendoza, OL
95— Brad Ottis, DL

WAYNESBURG (1)
41— Nick George, G

WEBER ST. (20)
66— Ronald McCall, DE
67— Lee White, FB
       Jim Schmedding, OG
69— Carter Campbell, DE
70— Henry Reed, DE
71— David Taylor, OT
77— Dennis Duncanson, DB
78— Dennis Duncanson, DB
       Randy Jordan, WR

80— †Mike Humiston, LB
89— †Peter Macon, WR
91— †Jamie Martin, QB
       †Alfred Pupunu, WR
93— †Pat McNarney, TE
95— †Pokey Eckford, WR
96— †Scott Shields, DB
97— †Cameron Quayle, TE
       †Scott Shields, DB/AP
98— †Scott Shields, DB
2000—†Ryan Prince, TE

WESLEY (7)
91— Fran Naselli, KR
95— Brandon Steinheim, RB
96— Brandon Steinheim, RB
       Demetrius Stevenson, DL
97— Nate Casella, LB
99— Sean McCullin, OL
2001—Jason Visconti, QB

WESLEYAN (CONN.) (7)
46— Bert VanderClute, G
48— Jack Geary, T
72— Robert Heller, C
73— Robert Heller, C
76— John McVicar, DL
77— John McVicar, DL
99— Matt Perceval, WR

WEST ALA. (5)
82— Charles Martin, DT
84— Andrew Fields, WR
87— Ronnie Glanton, DL
93— Matt Carman, WR
97— John Sedely, PK

WEST CHESTER (11)
52— Charles Weber, DG
58— Richard Emerich, T
61— Joe Iacone, B
62— Joe Iacone, B
72— Tim Pierantozzi, QB
76— William Blystone, RB
87— Ralph Tamm, OL
88— Bill Hess, WR
92— Lee Woodall, DL
98— Kevin Ingram, WR
99— Kevin Ingram, WR

WEST GA. (7)
96— Byron Slack, TE
97— Corey Jarrells, DB
       Chris Williams, OT
98— Chris Williams, OL
2000—Abed Taha, OL
01— Nate Coggins, DB
02— Marquis Floyd, DB

WEST LIBERTY ST. (1)
97— Greg Dailer, WR

WEST TEX. A&M (5)
86— Stan Carraway, WR
90— Mark Bounds, P
94— Brad Bailey, WR
       Brian Hurley, OL
95— Jon Mason, P

WEST VIRGINIA* (1)
34— Tod Goodwin, E

WEST VA. TECH (3)
82— Elliott Washington, DB
86— Calvin Wallace, DL
89— Phil Hudson, WR

WEST VA. WESLEYAN (2)
36— George Mike, T
82— Jerry Free, T

WESTERN CARO. (15)
49— Arthur Byrd, G
71— Steve Williams, DT
73— Mark Ferguson, OT
74— Jerry Gaines, SE
       Steve Yates, LB
84— †Louis Cooper, DL
       †Kirk Roach, PK
       †Steve Kornegay, P
85— †Clyde Simmons, DL
86— †Alonzo Carmichael, TE
       †Kirk Roach, PK
87— †Kirk Roach, PK
93— †Kerry Hayes, KR/WR
98— †Eric Johnson, DB
       †Ken Hinsley, P

WESTERN CONN. ST. (3)
99— Greg Boucher, DL
2000—Jason Plachcinski, OT
       Greg Boucher, DL

WESTERN ILL. (28)
59— Bill Larson, B
61— Leroy Jackson, B
74— John Passananti, OT
76— Scott Levenhagen, TE
       Greg Lee, DB
77— Craig Phalen, DT
78— Bill Huskisson, DL
80— Mike Maher, TE
       Don Greco, OG
83— †Chris Gunderson, MG
84— †Chris Gunderson, T
86— †Frank Winters, C
       †Todd Auer, LB
88— †Marlin Williams, DL
93— †Rodney Harrison, DB
94— †Ross Schulte, P
97— †Aaron Stecker, RB
       †Jason Grott, OL
98— †David Watson, DE
       †David Bowens, DL
       †James Milton, LB
99— †Edgerton Hartwell, LB
2000—†Edgerton Hartwell, LB
       †Mike Scifres, P
02— †Justin Langan, PK
       †R.J. Luke, TE
       †Brian Caesar, DL
       †Mike Scifres, P

WESTERN KY. (24)
64— Dale Lindsey, LB
70— Lawrence Brame, DE
73— Mike McKoy, DB
74— John Bushong, DL
       Virgil Livers, DB
75— Rick Green, LB
77— Chip Carpenter, OL
80— †Pete Walters, OG
       †Tim Ford, DL
81— †Donnie Evans, DE
82— †Paul Gray, LB
83— †Paul Gray, LB
87— †James Edwards, DB
88— †Dean Tiebout, OL
       †Joe Arnold, RB
95— †Brian Bixler, C
97— †Patrick Goodman, OL
98— †Patrick Goodman, C
2000—†Bobby Sippio, DB
       †Melvin Wisham, LB
01— †Erik Dandy, LB
       †Mel Mitchell, DB
02— †Chris Price, OL
       †Sherrod Coates, LB

WESTERN MICH.* (1)
82— †Matt Meares, OL

WESTERN N.M. (4)
83— Jay Ogle, WR
88— Pat Maxwell, P
97— Anthony Gray, RB
98— Anthony Gray, RB

WESTERN ORE. (1)
2000—Brian Crawford, OL

WESTERN ST. (10)
56— Bill Rhodes, B
78— Bill Campbell, DB
80— Justin Cross, OT
84— Jeff Guy, P
92— Reggie Alexander, WR
94— Derren Bryan, OL
96— Ben Kern, TE
       Kurt Clay, DB
97— Shane Carwin, LB
2001—Josh Hotchkiss, LB

WESTERN WASH. (5)
51— Norman Hash, DB
79— Patrick Locker, RB
95— Orlando Steinauer, DB
2000—Erik Totten, RS
02— Michael Koenen, P

WESTMINSTER (MO.) (6)
97— Scott Pingel, WR
98— Scott Pingel, WR
       Logan Stanley, TE

Justin Peery, QB
99— Scott Pingel, WR
Justin Peery, QB

WESTMINSTER (PA.) (10)
73— Robert Pontius, DB
77— Rex Macey, FL
82— Gary DeGruttola, LB
83— Scott Higgins, DB
86— Joe Keaney, LB
88— Kevin Myers, LB
89— Joe Micchia, QB
90— Brad Tokar, RB
91— Brian DeLorenzo, DL
92— Matt Raich, LB

WHEATON (ILL.) (12)
55— Dave Burnham, B
58— Robert Bakke, T
77— Larry Wagner, LB
78— Scott Hall, QB
83— Keith Bishop, QB
95— Doug Johnston, OL
Chip Parrish, LB
96— Chip Parrish, LB
Mark Loeffler, WR
97— Chris Brown, OL
99— Chris Baughman, PK
2002—James Hoxworth, G

WHITTIER (3)
38— Myron Claxton, T
62— Richard Peter, T
77— Michael Ciacci, DB

WHITWORTH (5)
52— Pete Swanson, OG
54— Larry Paradis, T
85— Wayne Ralph, WR
86— Wayne Ralph, WR
2000—Sky Blake, DL

WIDENER (20)
72— Billy Johnson, RB
73— Billy Johnson, RB
75— John Warrington, DB
76— Al Senni, OL
77— Chip Zawoiski, RB
79— Tom Deery, DB
80— Tom Deery, DB
81— Tom Deery, DB
82— Tony Stefanoni, DL
88— Dave Duffy, DL
94— O.J. McElroy, DL
Antoine Moore, DB
95— Blaise Coleman, LB
98— Bill Nourse, DL
99— Tom Eisenhower, LB
2000—Jim Jones, WR
01— Michael Coleman, WR
Jim Jones, WR
T.J. Hess, DB
02— Ryan Killian, DL

WILKES (3)
73— Jeff Grandinetti, DT
93— Jason Feese, DL
97— J.J. Fadden, DL

WILLAMETTE (14)
34— Loren Grannis, G
35— John Oravec, B
36— Richard Weisgerber, B
46— Marvin Goodman, E
58— William Long, C
59— Marvin Cisneros, G
64— Robert Burles, DT
65— Robert Burles, DT

69— Calvin Lee, LB
75— Gary Johnson, DL
82— Richard Milroy, DB
97— Kamell Eckroth-Bernard, DB
98— Brian Greer, OL

WILLIAM & MARY (12)
83— †Mario Shaffer, OL
86— †Michael Clemons, RB
89— †Steve Christie, P
90— †Pat Crowley, DL
93— †Craig Staub, DL
95— †Darren Sharper, DB
96— †Josh Beyer, OL
†Darren Sharper, DB
97— †Ron Harrison, DB
99— †Brett Sterba, PK
2000—†Raheem Walker, DL
02— †Dwight Beard, OL

WILLIAM JEWELL (4)
52— Al Conway, B
73— John Strada, OE
81— Guy Weber, DL
83— Mark Mundel, OL

WM. PATERSON (2)
92— Craig Paskas, DB
93— Craig Paskas, DB

WILLIAM PENN (1)
72— Bruce Polen, DB

WILLIAMS (8)
51— Charles Salmon, DG
69— Jack Maitland, HB
74— John Chandler, LB
78— Greg McAleenan, DB
90— George Rogers, DL
94— Bobby Walker, LB
95— Ethan Brooks, DL
2002—Scott Farley, SpT/DB

WILMINGTON (OHIO) (4)
72— William Roll, OG
94— Jason Tincher, WR
2000—Antonio Broadnax, DB
01— Antonio Broadnax, DB

WINGATE (1)
89— Jimmy Sutton, OT

WINONA ST. (5)
92— Dave Ludy, AP
94— Dave Ludy, AP
97— Jamey Hutchinson, DB
2002—Kevin Curtin, RS
Deric Sieck, LB

WINSTON-SALEM (8)
77— Cornelius Washington, DB
78— Tim Newsome, RB
84— Danny Moore, OG
87— Barry Turner, G
95— Richard Huntley, RB
96— LaTori Workman, DL
99— Thomas Washington, DL
2001—Stephon Kelly, DB

WIS.-EAU CLAIRE (1)
81— Roger Vann, RB

WIS.-LA CROSSE (19)
52— Ted Levanhagen, LB
72— Bryon Buelow, DB
78— Joel Williams, LB
83— Jim Byrne, DL
85— Tom Newberry, OL
88— Ted Pretasky, RB
89— Terry Strouf, OL

91— Jon Lauscher, LB
92— Norris Thomas, DB
Mike Breit, LB
93— Rick Schaaf, DL
95— Craig Kusick, QB
Erik Halverson, OL
96— Erik Halverson, OL
Mike Maslowski, LB
97— Ric Mathias, DB
99— Brock Ryan, DL
2000—Jeff Kostrewa, TE
Brian Portilia, DB

WIS.-MILWAUKEE (1)
70— Pete Papara, LB

WIS.-PLATTEVILLE (2)
73— William Vander Velden, DE
86— Mike Hintz, DB

WIS.-RIVER FALLS (6)
80— Gerald Sonsalla, OG
82— Roland Hall, LB
87— Greg Corning, RB
95— Brian Izdepski, OT
99— Joe Green, DL
2000—Michael Snowberry, C

WIS.-STEVENS POINT (8)
77— Reed Giordana, QB
81— Chuck Braun, WR
92— Randy Simpson, DB
93— Jimmy Henderson, RB
94— Randy Simpson, LB
97— Clint Kriewalt, LB
98— Clint Kriewalt, LB
99— Andy Palzkill, DB

WIS.-STOUT (6)
79— Joseph Bullis, DL
2000—Jeff Hazuga, DL
Kevin McCulley, P
01— Tony Beckham, DB
02— Tyrone Rhone, DB
Jamie Spielman, LB

WIS.-SUPERIOR (3)
66— Mel Thake, DB
83— Larry Banks, MG
85— Phil Eiting, LB

WIS.-WHITEWATER (6)
75— William Barwick, OL
79— Jerry Young, WR
82— Daryl Schleim, DL
90— Reggie White, OL
96— Derrick LeVake, OL
97— Derrick LeVake, OL

WITTENBERG (28)
62— Donald Hunt, G
63— Bob Cherry, E
64— Chuck Green, QB
68— Jim Felts, DE
73— Steve Drongowski, OT
74— Arthur Thomas, LB
75— Robert Foster, LB
76— Dean Caven, DL
78— Dave Merritt, RB
79— Joe Govern, DL
80— Mike Dowds, DE
81— Bill Beach, DB
83— Bryant Lemon, DL
87— Eric Horstman, OL
88— Ken Bonner, OT
Eric Horstman, OL
90— Jon Warga, RB
92— Taver Johnson, LB
93— Taver Johnson, LB
Greg Brame, PK

95— Ron Cunningham, OT
Jimmy Watts, PK
96— Xan Smith, OL
97— Jonathan Farley, C
Kent Rafey, LB
Russ Fedyk, KR
98— Ken Pope, DB
99— Casey Donaldson, RB

WOFFORD (14)
42— Aubrey Faust, E
47— Ken Dubard, T
49— Elbert Hammett, T
51— Jack Beeler, G
57— Charles Bradshaw, B
61— Dan Lewis, G
70— Sterling Allen, OG
79— Keith Kinard, OL
90— David Wiley, OL
91— Tom Colter, OL
94— Brian Porzio, PK
97— †Dan Williams, OL/C
2002—†Anthony Jones, DL
†Matt Nelson, DB

WOOSTER (3)
79— Blake Moore, C
99— Seth Duerr, LB
2000—Seth Duerr, LB

WORCESTER ST. (5)
92— Chris Butts, DB
93— Chris Butts, DB
94— Brian Fitzpatrick, DB
2000—Russ Watson, DL
01— Russ Watson, DL

WPI (2)
97— Matt Surette, TE
98— Matt Surette, TE

XAVIER (OHIO) (1)
51— Tito Carinci, LB

YALE (1)
84— †John Zanieski, DL

YOUNGSTOWN ST. (28)
74— Don Calloway, DB
75— Don Calloway, DB
78— Ed McGlasson, OL
79— James Ferranti, OE
Jeff Lear, OT
80— Jeff Gergel, LB
81— †Paris Wicks, RB
82— †Paris Wicks, RB
88— †Jim Zdelar, OL
89— †Paul Soltis, LB
90— †Tony Bowens, DL
91— †Pat Danko, DL
92— †Dave Roberts, DB
93— †Drew Garber, OL
†Tamron Smith, RB
†Jeff Wilkins, PK
94— †Randy Smith, KR
†Leon Jones, LB
†Lester Weaver, DB
†Chris Sammarone, OL
95—†Leon Jones, LB
†Jermaine Hopkins, DL
97—†Matt Hogg, OL
†Harry Deligianis, DL
99—†Ian Dominelli, LB
2000—†Tim Johnson, LB
01—†Pat Crummey, OL
†LeVar Greene, DB

NCAA Postgraduate Scholarship Winners

Following are football players who are NCAA postgraduate scholarship winners, whether or not they were able to accept the grant, plus all alternates (indicated by *) who accepted grants. The program began with the 1964 season. (Those who played in 1964 are listed as 1965 winners, those who played in 1965 as 1966 winners, etc.) To qualify, student-athletes must maintain a 3.000 grade-point average (on a 4.000 scale) during their collegiate careers, perform with distinction in varsity football and behave, on and off the field, in a manner that has brought credit to the student-athlete, his institution and intercollegiate athletics.

ABILENE CHRISTIAN
71— James Lindsey
83— *Grant Feasel
85— Daniel Remsberg
86— *James Embry
       Craig Huff
90— William Clayton

ADAMS ST.
2000—Ryan Hollingshead

ADRIAN
94— Jeffrey Toner

AIR FORCE
65— Edward Fausti
67— James Hogarty
68— Kenneth Zagzebski
69— *Richard Rivers Jr.
70— Charles Longnecker
       *Alfred Wurglitz
71— Ernest Jennings
       Robert Parker Jr.
72— Darryl Haas
73— Mark Prill
75— *Joseph Debes
84— Jeffrey Kubiak
86— Derek Brown
88— Chad Hennings
89— David Hlatky
90— Steven Wilson
91— Christopher Howard
92— Ronald James
93— Scott Hufford
95— Preston McConnell
96— Bret Cillessen
97— Carlton Hendrix
99— Charles Gilliam
2000—Cale Bonds

UAB
97— John Rea
2000—Lee Carter

ALABAMA
69— Donald Sutton
72— John Musso Jr.
75— Randy Hall
80— Steadman Shealy

ALABAMA ST.
92— Edward Robinson Jr.

ALBANY (N.Y.)
88— *Thomas Higgins

ALBION
81— Joel Manby
94— Michael Montico
95— Jeffrey Shooks
96— Timothy Schafer
97— Kyle Klein
98— Neil Johnson

ALBRIGHT
67— *Paul Chaiet

ALLEGHENY
65— David Wion
92— Darren Hadlock
97— Nicholas Reiser

ALMA
67— Keith Bird Jr.
79— Todd Friesner
99— Eric Brands
2000—Dustin Armstrong

AMHERST
66— David Greenblatt
76— Geoffrey Miller
85— Raymond Nurme
96— Gregory Schneider

ANGELO ST.
99— Kyle Kirk
2002—Curry Dawson

APPALACHIAN ST.
78— Gill Beck
93— D.J. Campbell

ARIZONA
69— William Michael Moody
78— Jon Abbott
80— Jeffrey Whitton
88— Charles Cecil
97— Wayne Wyatt

ARIZONA ST.
78— John Harris
90— Mark Tingstad
97— Devin Kendall
98— Patrick Tillman

ARKANSAS
70— Terry Stewart
71— William Burnett
79— William Bradford Shoup
85— *Mark Lee

ARKANSAS ST.
72— John Meyer
77— Thomas Humphreys

ARKANSAS TECH
2001—Paul Peletz

ARMY
66— Samuel Champi Jr.
68— Bohdan Neswiacheny
69— James McCall Jr.
       Thomas Wheelock
70— Theodore Shadid Jr.
78— Curtis Downs
81— *Stanley March
86— Donald Smith
       Douglas Black
88— William Conner
90— Michael Thorson
93— Michael McElrath
95— Eric Oliver

ASHLAND
78— Daniel Bogden
88— David Biondo
90— Douglas Powell

AUBURN
66— John Cochran
69— *Roger Giffin
85— Gregg Carr
90— James Lyle IV

AUGSBURG
90— Terry Mackenthun
98— Ted Schultz

AUGUSTANA (ILL.)
69— *Jeffrey Maurus
71— Kenneth Anderson
77— Joe Thompson
86— Steven Sanders
96— Thomas King
97— Ryan Carpenter
99— Chris Meskan
2001—MacKenzie Hay
03— Todd Baldwin

AUGUSTANA (S.D.)
72— Michael Olson

75— David Zelinsky
77— James Clemens
78— Dee Donlin
       Roger Goebel
90— *David Gubbrud
91— Scott Boyens
97— Mitchell Pruett

BALL ST.
67— *John Hostrawser
73— Gregory Mack
77— Arthur Yaroch
84— Richard Chitwood
88— Ronald Duncan
90— Theodore Ashburn
93— Troy Hoffer

BATES
79— Christopher Howard

BAYLOR
65— Michael Kennedy
66— Edward Whiddon
94— John Eric Joe

BENEDICTINE (ILL.)
70— David Cyr
71— Thomas Danaher

BOISE ST.
72— Brent McIver
76— *Glenn Sparks
79— Samuel Miller
82— Kip Bedard
92— Larry Stayner
93— David Tingstad

BOSTON COLLEGE
66— *Lawrence Marzetti
67— Michael O'Neill
69— Gary Andrachik
70— Robert Bouley
78— Richard Scudellari
87— Michael Degnan

BOSTON U.
69— Suren Donabedian Jr.
81— David Bengtson

BOWDOIN
65— Steven Ingram
67— Thomas Allen

BOWIE ST.
92— Mark Fitzgerald

BOWLING GREEN
77— Richard Preston
78— Mark Miller
91— Patrick Jackson

BRIDGEPORT
70— Terry Sparker

BRIDGEWATER (VA.)
2002—Matthew Huffman

BRIGHAM YOUNG
67— Virgil Carter
76— Orrin Olsen
77— *Stephen Miller
78— Gifford Nielsen
80— Marc Wilson
82— Daniel Plater
83— Bart Oates
84— Steve Young
85— Marvin Allen
89— Charles Cutler
94— Eric Drage
97— Chad Lewis

BROWN
65— John Kelly Jr.
70— James Lukens
74— Douglas Jost
75— William Taylor
77— Scott Nelson
78— Louis Cole
79— Robert Forster
82— Travis Holcombe
95— Rene Abdalah

BUCKNELL
71— *Kenneth Donahue
74— John Dailey
75— Steve Leskinen
77— Lawrence Brunt
85— David Kucera
93— David Berardinelli

BUENA VISTA
77— Steven Trost
87— Michael Habben
94— Cary Murphy

BUFFALO ST.
87— James Dunbar

BUTLER
72— George Yearsich
78— William Ginn
85— Stephen Kollias

C.W. POST
79— John Luchsinger

CALIFORNIA
66— William Krum
67— John Schmidt
68— Robert Crittenden
70— James Calkins
71— Robert Richards
83— Harvey Salem
94— Douglas Brien

UC DAVIS
76— Daniel Carmazzi
       David Gellerman
77— Rolf Benirschke
79— Mark Markel
86— Robert Hagenau
90— *James Tomasin
92— Robert Kincade
       Michael Shepard
93— Brian Andersen
97— Mark Grieb
99— Wesley Terrell

UC RIVERSIDE
72— Tyrone Hooks
74— Gary Van Jandegian

CAL LUTHERAN
90— *Gregory Maw

CAL POLY
69— William Creighton

CALTECH
67— William Mitchell
68— John Frazzini
74— Frank Hobbs Jr.

CANISIUS
84— Thomas Schott

CAPITAL
84— *Michael Linton

CARLETON
67— Robert Paarlberg
73— Mark Williams
83— Paul Vaaler
93— Arthur Gilliland

CARNEGIE MELLON
80— Gusty Sunseri
91— Robert O'Toole
99— Jason Funke
2000—Mike Campie

CARROLL (WIS.)
77— Stephen Thompson
95— Christopher Klippel

CARSON-NEWMAN
2001—Charlie Walker Jr.

CARTHAGE
70— William Radakovitz

CASE RESERVE
89— Christopher Nutter
91— James Meek

CENTRAL (IOWA)
71— Vernon Den Herder
87— Scott Lindell
89— Eric Perry
92— Richard Kacmarynski
96— Rick Sanger

CENTRAL ARK.
96— Brian Barnett

CENTRAL MICH.
77— John Wunderlich
80— *Michael Ball
85— Kevin Egnatuk
88— Robert Stebbins
92— Jeffrey Bender

CENTRAL MO. ST.
99— Shane Meyer

CENTRAL WASH.
70— Danny Collins

CENTRE
69— Glenn Shearer
86— Casteel "Teel" Bruner II
88— *Robert Clark
90— James Ellington

CHADRON ST.
96— Corey Campbell

CHATTANOOGA
67— Harvey Ouzts
72— *Frank Webb
74— John McBrayer
76— Russell Gardner

CHEYNEY
76— Steven Anderson

CHICAGO
86— *Bruce Montella
89— Paul Haar
94— Frank Baker

CINCINNATI
71— *Earl Willson

CITADEL
74— Thomas Leitner
79— Kenneth Caldwell
84— *William West IV
97— Derek Beres

CLAREMONT-M-S
68— Craig Dodel
70— *Gregory Long
71— Stephen Endemano
73— Christopher Stecher
74— Samuel Reece

CLEMSON
65— James Bell Jr.
68— James Addison
73— Benjamin Anderson
79— Stephen Fuller

COAST GUARD
73— Rodney Leis
74— Leonard Kelly
81— Bruce Hensel
89— *Ty Rinoski
       *Jeffery Peters
90— Richard Schachner
91— John Freda

COE
67— Lynn Harris

COLBY
71— Ronald Lupton
       Frank Apantaku

COLGATE
73— Kenneth Nelson
80— Angelo Colosimo
89— Donald Charney

COLORADO
93— James Hansen

COLORADO COL.
69— Steven Ehrhart
72— Randy Bobier
75— Bruce Kolbezen
84— Herman Motz III
97— Ryan Egeland
98— Christopher Smith

COLORADO MINES
66— Stuart Bennett
67— Michael Greensburg
       Charles Kirby
75— David Chambers

COLORADO ST.
65— Russel Mowrer
76— Mark Driscoll
87— Stephan Bartalo
88— Joseph Brookhart
93— Gregory Primus
96— Gregory Myers
99— Nathaniel Kvamme

COLUMBIA
72— John Sefcik
80— Mario Biaggi Jr.

CONNECTICUT
77— *Bernard Palmer

CORNELL
68— Ronald Kipicki
72— Thomas Albright
84— Derrick Harmon

CORNELL COLLEGE
65— Steven Miller
72— David Hilmers
73— Robert Ash
79— Brian Farrell
       Thomas Zinkula
81— *Timothy Garry
83— John Ward
93— Brent Sands
94— Matthew Miller
95— Mark McDermott
99— Matthew Weiss

DARTMOUTH
66— Anthony Yezer
68— Henry Paulson Jr.
69— Randolph Wallick
71— Willie Bogan
73— Frederick Radke
74— Thomas Csatari
       *Robert Funk
77— Patrick Sullivan
89— Paul Sorensen
95— O. Josh Bloom
98— Dominic Lanza

DAVIDSON
66— Stephen Smith
71— Rick Lyon
72— Robert Norris
86— *Louis Krempel
97— John Cowan Jr.

DAYTON
73— Timothy Quinn
76— Roy Gordon III
83— *Michael Pignatiello
91— Daniel Sharley
2003—Mark Kasmer

DELAWARE
86— Brian Farrell

DELAWARE VALLEY
85— Daniel Glowatski

DELTA ST.
76— William Hood

DENISON
70— Richard Trumball
73— Steven Smiljanich
76— *Dennis Thome
78— David Holcombe
86— Brian Gearinger
88— Grant Jones
92— Jonathan Fortkamp
2000—Jon Dunhan

DePAUW
68— Bruce Montgomerie
78— Mark Frazer
81— Jay True
85— Richard Bonaccorsi
86— Anthony deNicola
92— Thomas Beaulieu
2000—Tyler Kelley

DICKINSON
66— Robert Averback
71— *John West
75— *Gerald Urich

DOANE
68— John Lothrop
70— Richard Held

DRAKE
73— Joseph Worobec

DREXEL
72— Blake Lynn Ferguson

DUBUQUE
82— Timothy Finn

DUKE
68— Robert Lasky
71— *Curt Rawley

EAST CARO.
92— Keith Arnold

EAST TENN. ST.
82— Jay Patterson

EASTERN KY.
78— Steven Frommeyer

EASTERN N.M.
66— Richard James

EASTERN WASH.
98— Steven Mattson

ELIZABETH CITY ST.
73— Darnell Johnson
80— David Nickelson

ELMHURST
80— Richard Green

EMORY & HENRY
82— Thomas Browder Jr.

EVANSVILLE
75— David Mattingly
76— Charles Uhde Jr.
79— *Neil Saunders

FERRIS ST.
79— Robert Williams
93— Monty Brown

FLORIDA
72— Carlos Alvarez
77— Darrell Carpenter
85— Garrison Rolle
87— Bret Wiechmann
90— *Cedric Smith
91— Huey Richardson
95— Michael Gilmore
97— Danny Wuerffel
99— Terrance Jackson

FLORIDA ST.
88— David Palmer
91— David Roberts
94— Kenneth Alexander
95— Derrick Brooks
98— Daryl Bush

FORDHAM
91— Eric Schweiker

FORT HAYS ST.
94— David Foster
99— Clinton Albers
2002—Casey Seyfert

FRANK. & MARSH.
69— Frank deGenova
83— *Robert Shepardson

FRESNO ST.
70— *Henry Corda
74— Dwayne Westphal
83— William Griever Jr.

FROSTBURG ST.
2000—Marty Mood

FURMAN
77— Thomas Holcomb III
82— Charles Anderson
84— Ernest Gibson
86— *David Jager
87— Stephen Squire
90— Christopher Roper
92— Paul Siffri
       Eric Von Walter
96— William Phillip Jones

GANNON
97— Patrick Rodkey

GEORGETOWN
75— James Chesley Jr.
98— Stephen Iorio
2000—Jim Gallagher

GEORGIA
68— Thomas Lawhorne Jr.
69— William Payne
71— Thomas Lyons
72— Thomas Nash Jr.
       Raleigh Mixon Robinson
78— Jeffrey Lewis
80— Jeffrey Pyburn
81— Christopher Welton
84— Terrell Hoage
88— Kim Stephens
89— Richard Tardits
99— Matthew Stinchcomb
2003—Jonathan Stinchcomb

GA. SOUTHERN
2000—Voncellies Allen

GEORGIA TECH
68— William Eastman
75— James Robinson
81— Sheldon Fox
83— Ellis Gardner
86— John Ivemeyer
2003—Daniel Dyke

GETTYSBURG
70— *Herbert Ruby III
80— Richard Swartz
2003—Clifford Mason

GRAMBLING
73— Stephen Dennis

GRINNELL
72— Edward Hirsch
80— *Derek Muehrcke
2000—Troy Dougherty

GROVE CITY
95— Stephen Sems

GUST. ADOLPHUS
74— James Goodwin
81— *David Najarian
2002—Brian Bergstrom

HAMLINE
85— Kyle Aug
91— Robert Hackney

HAMPDEN-SYDNEY
78— *Wilson Newell
80— Timothy Maxa

HARVARD
68— Alan Bersin
71— *Richard Frisbie
75— Patrick McInally
76— William Emper
81— Charles Durst
85— Brian Bergstrom
87— Scott Collins

HAWAII
68— James Roberts
73— *Don Satterlee

HIRAM
68— Sherman Riemenschneider
74— Donald Brunetti

HOLY CROSS
84— *Bruce Kozerski
89— Jeffrey Wiley
91— John Lavalette

HOPE
74— Ronald Posthuma
80— Craig Groendyk
83— Kurt Brinks
85— *Scott Jecmen
98— Brandon Graham

HOUSTON
86— Gary Schoppe
87— Robert Brezina
99— Peter deGroot

IDAHO
67— Michael Lavens
       Joseph McCollum Jr.
84— Boyce Bailey

IDAHO ST.
76— Richard Rodgers
92— Steven Boyenger

ILLINOIS
72— Robert Bucklin
73— Laurence McCarren Jr.
91— Curtis Lovelace
92— Michael Hopkins
93— John Wright

ILL. WESLEYAN
93— Christopher Bisaillon
97— Lon Erickson

INDIANA
73— Glenn Scolnik
79— David Abrams
81— Kevin Speer

INDIANA (PA.)
78— *John Mihota
84— Kenneth Moore

INDIANA ST.
86— Jeffrey Miller

INDIANAPOLIS
76— Rodney Pawlik

IONA
81— Neal Kurtti
82— *Paul Rupp

IOWA
69— Michael Miller
76— Robert Elliott
78— Rodney Sears
86— Larry Station Jr.
88— Michael Flagg
89— Charles Hartlieb
99— Matthew Reischl
        Derek Rose

IOWA ST.
70— William Bliss

JACKSON ST.
80— *Lester Walls

JACKSONVILLE ST.
79— Dewey Barker

JAMES MADISON
79— Warren Coleman
90— Mark Kiefer

JOHNS HOPKINS
73— Joseph Ouslander
74— Gunter Glocker
94— Steuart Markley
95— Michael House
99— Lawrence Gulotta

JUNIATA
72— Maurice Taylor
87— Robert Crossey

KANSAS
65— Ronald Oelschlager
69— David Morgan
72— Michael McCoy
73— John Schroll
78— Tom Fitch
87— Mark Henderson

KANSAS ST.
66— *Larry Anderson
83— James Gale
88— Matthew Garver

KENTUCKY
76— Thomas Ranieri
79— James Kovach
84— *Keith Martin
97— Michael Schellenberger

KENTUCKY ST.
68— James Jackson

KENYON
75— Patrick Clements

KNOX
88— Robert Monroe

LAFAYETTE
71— William Sprecher
76— Michael Kline
78— Victor Angeline III

LAMAR
73— *Richard Kubiak

LAWRENCE
68— Charles McKee
83— Christopher Matheus

LEBANON VALLEY
74— *Alan Shortell

LEHIGH
66— Robert Adelaar
68— Richard Miller
73— *Thomas Benfield
75— James Addonizio
76— *Robert Liptak
77— *Michael Yaszemski
80— David Melone

LONG BEACH ST.
84— Joseph Donohue

LSU
79— Robert Dugas
83— James Britt
88— Ignazio Albergamo
91— Solomon Graves
94— Chad Loup
95— Michael Blanchard
98— Chad Kessler

LA.-LAFAYETTE
71— *George Coussa

LA.-MONROE
93— Darren Rimmer
94— Robert Cobb
        Michael Young

LUTHER
67— Thomas Altemeier
78— *Mark Larson
85— Larry Bonney

MARIETTA
98— Thomas Couhig

MARYLAND
78— Jonathan Claiborne

MARYVILLE (TENN.)
67— Frank Eggers II

MIT
91— Darcy Prather
92— Rodrigo Rubiano
93— Roderick Tranum
95— Corey Foster
99— Duane Stevens
2000—Nik Kozy
03— Keith Battocchi

McDANIEL
99— Thomas Lapato
2002—Jason Wingeart

McNEESE ST.
81— Daryl Burckel
86— Ross Leger

MEMPHIS
77— *James Mincey Jr.

MERCHANT MARINE
70— Robert Lavinia
76— *John Castagna

MIAMI (FLA.)
90— Robert Chudzinski
91— Michael Sullivan

MICHIGAN
67— David Fisher
74— David Gallagher
81— *John Wangler
82— Norm Betts
84— Stefan Humphries
        Thomas Dixon
86— Clayton Miller
87— Kenneth Higgins
93— Christopher Hutchinson
94— Marc Milia
98— Brian Griese
2000—Rob Renes

MICHIGAN ST.
69— Allen Brenner
70— Donald Baird
94— Steven Wasylk

MICHIGAN TECH
72— Larry Ras
74— Bruce Trusock
75— Daniel Rhude

MIDDLE TENN.
73— *Edwin Zaunbrecher

MIDDLEBURY
79— Franklin Kettle

MIDLAND LUTHERAN
76— Thomas Hale

MILLERSVILLE
92— Thomas Burns III

MILLIKIN
90— *Charles Martin

MILLSAPS
67— Edward Weller
73— *Russell Gill
92— David Harrison Jr.
99— Thomas Ingram

MINNESOTA
69— Robert Stein
71— Barry Mayer
73— Douglas Kingsriter
78— Robert Weber
99— Parc Williams

MINN. ST. MANKATO
70— Bernard Maczuga

MINN. ST. MOORHEAD
2000—Erik Pederson

MISSISSIPPI
66— Stanley Hindman
69— Steve Hindman
81— Kenneth Toler Jr.
86— Richard Austin
87— Jeffrey Noblin
88— Daniel Hoskins
89— Charles Walls
91— Todd Sandroni

MISSISSIPPI COL.
80— Stephen Johnson
98— Joseph Fulcher
2000—Michael Brown

MISSISSIPPI ST.
69— William Nelson
73— Frank Dowsing Jr.
75— James Webb
77— William Coltharp
93— Daniel Boyd

MISSOURI
66— Thomas Lynn
67— James Whitaker
69— *Charles Weber
71— John Weisenfels
79— Christopher Garlich
82— Van Darkow
99— Jacob Stueve

MO.-ROLLA
69— Robert Nicodemus
73— Kim Colter
81— Paul Janke

MONMOUTH (ILL.)
72— Dale Brooks
90— Brent Thurness

MONTANA
75— Rock Svennungsen
79— Steven Fisher
84— Brian Salonen
91— Michael McGowan
96— David Dickenson
97— Michael Bouchee
        Blaine McElmurry
98— Josh Branen
2000—Dallas Neil
01— Matt Thuesen
02— Vincent Huntsberger

MONTANA ST.
65— Gene Carlson
68— Russell Dodge
71— Jay Groepper
77— Bert Markovich
79— Jon Borchardt
        James Mickelson
90— Derrick Isackson
92— Travis Annette
2003—Ryan Johnson

MORAVIAN
73— Daniel Joseph
94— Judson Frank

MOREHEAD ST.
92— James Appel

MORNINGSIDE
65— Larry White

MORRIS BROWN
83— Arthur Knight Jr.

MOUNT UNION
89— Paul Hrics
2000—Tom Bauer
01— Matt LaVerde
02— Charles Moore

MUHLENBERG
73— Edward Salo
76— Eric Butler
78— Mark Stull
81— Arthur Scavone
91— Michael Hoffman

MURRAY ST.
71— Matthew Haug
78— Edward McFarland
81— *Kris Robbins
90— Eric Crigler

NAVY
65— William Donnelly
69— William Newton
70— Daniel Pike
75— *Timothy Harden
76— Chester Moeller II
81— Theodore Dumbauld
2000—Terrence Anderson

NEBRASKA
70— Randall Reeves
71— *John Decker
72— Larry Jacobson
73— David Mason
74— Daniel Anderson
76— Thomas Heiser
77— Vince Ferragamo
78— Ted Harvey
79— James Pillen
80— Timothy Smith
81— Randy Schleusener
        Jeffrey Finn
82— Eric Lindquist
85— Scott Strasburger
88— Jeffrey Jamrog
89— Mark Blazek
90— Gerald Gdowski
        Jacob Young III
91— David Edeal
        Patrick Tyrance Jr.
92— Patrick Engelbert
93— Michael Stigge
94— Trev Alberts
95— Robert Zatechka
96— Aaron Graham
97— Jonathan Hesse
98— Grant Wistrom
99— Joel Makovicka
2000—Tim DeBates
        Brian Shaw
01— Kyle Vanden Bosch

NEB.-OMAHA
84— Kirk Hutton
        Clark Toner
99— Edward Thompson

NEB. WESLEYAN
97— Justin Rice
        Bren Chambers
98— Dusten Olds
        Chad Wemhoff
99— Ryan Shanesy
2003—Luke Klinker

UNLV
95— Howard McGowan

NEW HAMPSHIRE
85— Richard Leclerc

NEW MEXICO
72— Roderick Long
76— Robert Berg
79— Robert Rumbaugh
83— George Parks

NEW MEXICO ST.
76— Ralph Jackson
77— *Joseph Fox
99— David Patterson

NORTH ALA.
82— *Warren Moore

NORTH CAROLINA
75— Christopher Kupec
81— William Donnalley
83— David Drechsler
91— Kevin Donnalley

N.C. CENTRAL
91— Anthony Cooley

NORTH CAROLINA ST.
75— Justus Everett
82— *Calvin Warren Jr.

NORTH DAKOTA
79— Dale Lian
81— Douglas Moen
82— Paul Franzmeier
85— Glen Kucera
88— Kurt Otto
89— Matthew Gulseth
93— Timothy Gelinske
97— Thomas Langer
        Timothy Tibesar
2003—Kelby Klosterman

NORTH DAKOTA ST.
66— James Schindler
69— *Stephen Stephens
71— Joseph Cichy
75— Paul Cichy
84— Doug Hushka
89— Charles Stock
94— Arden Beachy
98— Sean Fredricks

NORTH TEXAS
68— Ruben Draper
77— Peter Morris

NORTHERN ARIZ.
78— Larry Friedrichs
2000—Jake Crissup

NORTHERN COLO.
76— Robert Bliss
91— Thomas Langer
2000—Corte McGuffey

NORTHERN IOWA
81— Owen Dockter

NORTHERN MICH.
73— Guy Falkenhagen
81— Phil Kessel
86— Keith Nelsen

NORTHWEST MO. ST.
82— Robert Gregory
97— Greg Teale

NORTHWESTERN
70— *Bruce Hubbard
74— Steven Craig
77— Randolph Dean
81— Charles Kern
96— Salvatore Valenzisi
Ryan Padgett
99— Barry Gardner

NORTHWESTERN ST.
95— John Dippel
2000—William Broussard
02— Grayson Tennison

NORWICH
68— Richard Starbuck
74— Matthew Hincks

NOTRE DAME
67— Frederick Schnurr
68— James Smithberger
69— George Kunz
70— Michael Oriard
71— Lawrence DiNardo
72— Thomas Gatewood
73— Gregory Marx
74— David Casper
75— Peter Demmerle
Reggie Barnett
79— Joseph Restic
81— Thomas Gibbons
82— John Krimm Jr.
86— Gregory Dingens
89— Reginald Ho
94— Timothy Ruddy

OCCIDENTAL
66— James Wanless
67— Richard Verry
69— John St. John
78— Richard Fry
80— *Timothy Bond
89— *Curtis Page
95— Davin Lundquist

OHIO
78— *Robert Weidaw
80— Mark Geisler

OHIO NORTHERN
79— Mark Palmer
82— Larry Egbert

OHIO ST.
65— Arnold Chonko
66— Donald Unverferth
67— Ray Pryor
69— David Foley
71— Rex Kern
74— Randolph Gradishar
76— Brian Baschnagel
77— William Lukens
80— James Laughlin
84— John Frank
85— David Crecelius
86— Michael Lanese
97— Greg Bellisari

OKLAHOMA
72— Larry Jack Mildren Jr.
73— Joe Wylie
81— Jay Jimerson
89— Anthony Phillips
91— Michael Sawatzky
2001—Nicholas Kempenich

OKLAHOMA ST.
83— *Doug Freeman
2003—Kyle Eaton

OLIVET
75— William Ziem

OREGON
79— *Willie Blasher Jr.
91— William Musgrave
2002—Ryan Schmid

OREGON ST.
69— William Enyart
69— *Jerry Belcher

PACIFIC (CAL.)
72— *Byron Cosgrove
78— Brian Peets
80— Bruce Filarsky

PENNSYLVANIA
68— Ben Mortensen
95— Michael Turner
98— John Bishop
99— David Rader

PENN ST.
66— Joseph Bellas
67— John Runnells III
71— Robert Holuba
72— David Joyner
73— Bruce Bannon
74— Mark Markovich
75— John Baiorunos
79— *Charles Correal
80— *Michael Guman
81— John Walsh
84— Harry Hamilton
85— Douglas Strange
87— Brian Silverling
90— Roger Thomas Duffy
94— Craig Fayak
95— Charles Pittman
2000—Travis Forney
03— Joseph Iorio

PITTSBURGH
79— Jeff Delaney
86— Robert Schilken
89— Mark Stepnoski

POMONA-PITZER
69— *Lee Piatek
77— Scott Borg
83— *Calvin Oishi
85— *Derek Watanabe
88— Edward Irick
93— Torin Cunningham

PORTLAND ST.
79— John Urness

PRINCETON
67— Charles Peters
69— Richard Sandler
70— Keith Mauney
76— Ronald Beible
81— Mark Bailey
83— Brent Woods
86— James Petrucci
87— John Hammond
97— Marc Washington Jr.
99— Alexander Sierk

PUGET SOUND
68— Stephen Doolittle
79— *Patrick O'Loughlin
83— *Anthony Threlkeld

PURDUE
70— Michael Phipps
74— Robert Hoftiezer
75— Lawrence Burton

RANDOLPH-MACON
98— Joseph Seetoo

REDLANDS
65— Robert Jones
97— Morgan Bannister

RENSSELAER
67— Robert Darnall
69— John Contento

RHODES
71— John Churchill
79— *Philip Mischke
81— Jeffrey Lane
83— *Russell Ashford
85— *John Foropoulos
89— James Augustine
2002—Christopher Huff

RICE
81— *Lamont Jefferson
91— Donald Hollas
96— James Lamy

RICHMOND
86— Leland Melvin

RIPON
65— Phillip Steans
69— Steven Thompson
80— Thomas Klofta

RUTGERS
90— Steven Tardy

ST. CLOUD ST.
90— Richard Rodgers

ST. FRANCIS (PA.)
87— Christopher Tantlinger
99— Matthew Farabaugh

ST. JOHN'S (MINN.)
92— Denis McDonough
96— Christopher Palmer

ST. JOSEPH'S (IND.)
80— Michael Bettinger

ST. NORBERT
66— Michael Ryan
88— Matthew Lang

ST. PAUL'S
80— Gerald Hicks

ST. THOMAS (MINN.)
75— Mark Dienhart
97— Christopher Esterley
2000—Greg Kaiser
03— Jacob Barkley
Andrew Hilliard

SAN DIEGO
96— Douglas Popovich
2000—Michael Stadler

SAN DIEGO ST.
99— Scott Auerbach

SANTA CLARA
72— Ronald Sani
77— Mark Tiernan
81— *David Alfaro
85— Alexis Vlahos
87— Patrick Sende

SEWANEE
65— Frank Stubblefield
66— Douglas Paschall
69— James Beene
71— John Popham IV
77— Dudley West
82— Gregory Worsowicz
Domenick Reina
83— Michael York
84— Michael Jordan
93— Jason Forrester
94— Frederick Cravens
96— Stephen Tudor
2003—Benjamin Tuck

SHIPPENSBURG
77— Anthony Winter

SIMPSON
71— Richard Clogg
74— Hugh Lickiss
90— Roger Grover
94— Chad Earwood

SLIPPERY ROCK
98— David Sabolcik Jr.
2000—Tim Kusniez

SOUTH CAROLINA
67— Steven Stanley Juk Jr.

SOUTH DAKOTA
79— Michael Schurrer
87— Todd Salat
93— Jason Seurer

SOUTH DAKOTA ST.
80— Charles Loewen

AWARD WINNERS

81— Paul Kippley
88— Daniel Sonnek
95— Jacob Hines
2002—Joshua Ranek

SOUTHEASTERN LA.
74— William Percy Jr.

SOUTHEASTERN OKLA.
2001—Joe Jones

SOUTHERN U.
70— Alden Roche

SOUTHERN CALIFORNIA
66— Charles Arrobio
69— Steven Sogge
70— Harry Khasigian
Steve Lehmer
74— Monte Doris
75— Patrick Haden
76— Kevin Bruce
78— Gary Bethel
80— Brad Budde
Paul McDonald
81— Gordon Adams
*Jeffrey Fisher
85— Duane Bickett
86— Anthony Colorito
*Matthew Koart
87— Jeffrey Bregel
90— John Jackson
96— Jeremy Hogue
97— Matthew Keneley

SOUTHERN COLO.
70— Gregory Smith
73— Collon Kennedy III

SOUTHERN METHODIST
83— *Brian O'Meara
85— *Monte Goen
87— David Adamson
93— Cary Brabham

SOUTHERN MISS.
83— Richard Thompson
84— Stephen Carmody

SOUTHERN UTAH
92— Stephen McDowell

SOUTHWEST MO. ST.
80— Richard Suchenski
Mitchel Ware
85— Michael Armentrout
2000—Travis Brawner

SOUTHWEST TEX. ST.
82— Michael Miller

STANFORD
65— *Joe Neal
66— *Terry DeSylvia
68— John Root
71— John Sande III
72— Jackie Brown
74— Randall Poltl
75— *Keith Rowen
76— Gerald Wilson
77— Duncan McColl
81— Milton McColl
84— John Bergren
85— Scott Carpenter
86— Matthew Soderlund
87— Brian Morris
88— Douglas Robison
95— Stephen Stenstrom
96— Eric Abrams
David Walker
97— Marlon Evans

STONEHILL
93— Kevin Broderick

SUSQUEHANNA
77— Gerald Huesken
82— Daniel Distasio
2001—David Wonderlick

SWARTHMORE
72— Christopher Leinberger
83— *John Walsh

SYRACUSE
78— *Robert Avery
86— Timothy Green
94— Patrick O'Neill
95— Eric Chenoweth

TEMPLE
74— Dwight Fulton

TENNESSEE
71— Donald Denbo
        Timothy Priest
77— Michael Mauck
81— Timothy Irwin
98— Peyton Manning

TENNESSEE TECH
2002—Grant Swallows

TEXAS
69— Corbin Robertson Jr.
71— Willie Zapalac Jr.
73— *Michael Bayer
74— Patrick Kelly
75— Wade Johnston
76— Robert Simmons
77— William Hamilton
97— Patrick Fitzgerald

TEXAS-ARLINGTON
69— Michael Baylor

UTEP
80— Eddie Forkerway
89— Patrick Hegarty
92— Robert Sesich

TEXAS A&M
69— Edward Hargett
71— David Elmendorf
72— Stephen Luebbehusen
88— Kip Corrington

TCU
67— John Richards
68— Eldon Gresham Jr.
73— Scott Walker
75— Terry Drennan
88— J. Clinton Hailey

TEXAS SOUTHERN
65— Leon Hardy

TEXAS TECH
65— James Ellis Jr.
68— John Scovell
75— Jeffrey Jobe
78— *Richard Arledge
85— *Bradford White
90— Thomas Mathiasmeier
2000—Jesse Cockrum

THOMAS MORE
98— Michael Bramlage Jr.

TOLEDO
82— Tad Wampfler
89— Kenneth Moyer
95— Chadd Dehn
97— Craig Dues
2002—Todd France
03— Christopher Tuminello

TOWSON
2003—Benjamin Whitacre

TRINITY (CONN.)
67— *Howard Wrzosek
68— Keith Miles

TRINITY (TEX.)
84— *Peter Broderick
95— Martin Thompson
98— Mark Byarlay
        Jack Doran
2000—Bo Edwards

TROY ST.
75— Mark King

TRUMAN
83— Roy Pettibone
99— Thomas Hernandez

TUFTS
65— Peter Smith
70— Robert Bass
79— *Don Leach
80— *James Ford
82— *Brian Gallagher
87— Robert Patz
92— Paulo Oliveira

TULSA
67— *Larry Williams

75— James Mack Lancaster II
98— Levi Gillen

TUSKEGEE
68— James Greene

UCLA
67— *Raymond Armstrong
        Dallas Grider
70— Gregory Jones
74— Steven Klosterman
76— John Sciarra
77— Jeffrey Dankworth
78— John Fowler Jr.
83— Cormac Carney
84— Richard Neuheisel
86— Michael Hartmeier
90— Richard Meyer
93— Carlton Gray
96— George Kase
99— Shawn Stuart
        Christian Sailer
2000—Danny Farmer

UNION (N.Y.)
88— Richard Romer

UTAH
81— James Baldwin
93— Steven Young
95— Jason Jones
2001—Kimball Christianson

UTAH ST.
67— Ronnie Edwards
68— Garth Hall
70— Gary Anderson
76— Randall Stockham

VALDOSTA ST.
95— Christopher Hatcher

VALPARAISO
75— *Richard Seall

VANDERBILT
73— Barrett Sutton Jr.
75— Douglas Martin
2003—Hunter Hillenmeyer

VILLANOVA
77— David Graziano
89— Richard Spugnardi

VIRGINIA
67— Frederick Jones
83— Patrick Chester
94— Thomas Burns Jr.
96— Patrick Jeffers
98— Stephen Phelan Jr.

VMI
79— Robert Bookmiller
80— Richard Craig Jones

VIRGINIA TECH
73— Thomas Carpenito
97— Brandon Semones

WABASH
74— *Mark Nicolini
81— *Melvin Gore
83— David Broecker
87— James Herrmann
92— William Padgett

WAKE FOREST
70— Joseph Dobner
74— *Daniel Stroup
76— Thomas Fehring
78— *Michael McGlamry
83— Philip Denfeld
87— Toby Cole Jr.

WARTBURG
75— Conrad Mandsager
76— James Charles Peterson
82— *Rod Feddersen
94— Koby Kreinbring
96— Vincent Penningroth

WASHINGTON
65— William Douglas
67— Michael Ryan

72— *James Krieg
73— John Brady
77— Scott Phillips
78— Blair Bush
80— Bruce Harrell
82— Mark Jerue
83— Charles Nelson
        Mark Stewart
88— David Rill
92— Edward Cunningham
97— David Janoski
2001—Marques Tuiasosopo

WASHINGTON (MO.)
94— Aaron Keen
98— Bradley Klein

WASH. & JEFF.
70— Edward Guna
82— Max Regula
91— David Conn
93— Raymond Cross Jr.
95— Michael Jones
2002—Matthew Dietz

WASH. & LEE
70— Michael Thornton
74— William Wallace Jr.
78— Jeffrey Slatcoff
79— Richard Wiles
80— *Scott Smith
81— Lonnie Nunley III
89— Michael Magoline
2003—John Melillo

WASHINGTON ST.
67— Richard Sheron
68— A. Douglas Flansburg
83— Gregory Porter
84— Patrick Lynch Jr.
85— Daniel Lynch

WAYNE ST. (MICH.)
76— Edward Skowneski Jr.
81— Phillip Emery

WEBER ST.
68— Phillip Tuckett
74— *Douglas Smith
92— David Hall
94— Deric Gurley
98— Cameron Quayle

WESLEYAN (CONN.)
67— John Dwyer
69— Stuart Blackburn
71— James Lynch
78— John McVicar
2000—Matt Perceval

WEST TEX. A&M
75— *Ben Bentley
82— Kevin Dennis

WEST VIRGINIA
74— Ade Dillion
        *Daniel Larcamp
82— Oliver Luck

WESTERN CARO.
94— Thomas Jackson III

WESTERN ILL.
89— Paul Singer

WESTERN KY.
72— Jimmy Barber
80— Charles DeLacey

WESTERN MICH.
68— Martin Barski
71— Jonathan Bull

WESTERN N.M.
68— Richard Mahoney

WESTERN ST.
98— Jason Eves

WESTMINSTER (PA.)
99— Brian Mihok

WHEATON (ILL.)
89— David Lauber

93— Bart Moseman
96— Pedro Arruza
99— Timothy Hardy

WHITTIER
76— John Getz
79— Mark Deven
87— *Timothy Younger

WIDENER
2002—Timothy Hess

WILLAMETTE
87— *Gerry Preston

WILLIAM & MARY
78— G. Kenneth Smith
80— Clarence Gaines
85— Mark Kelso

WILLIAM JEWELL
66— Charles Scrogin
70— Thomas Dunn
        John Johnston

WILLIAMS
65— Jerry Jones
72— John Murray
95— Nathan Sleeper
96— Medley Gatewood

WINONA ST.
95— Nathan Gruber

WINSTON-SALEM
84— Eddie Sauls

WISCONSIN
66— David Fronek
80— Thomas Stauss
82— *David Mohapp
83— Mathew Vanden Boom

WIS.-LA CROSSE
97— Troy Harcey

WIS.-OSHKOSH
2000—Craig Pierstorff

WIS.-PLATTEVILLE
87— Michael Hintz

WIS.-STEVENS POINT
98— Joel Hornby
2000—Andy Palzkill

WIS.-WHITEWATER
96— Scott Huwig
2002—Peter Katz

WITTENBERG
82— William Beach
98— Kent Rafey

WOOSTER
80— Edward Blake Moore
2000—Matt Mahaffey

WYOMING
74— Steven Cockreham
85— Bob Gustafson
89— Randall Welniak
96— Joseph Cummings
98— Jay Korth
        Cory Wedel

XAVIER (OHIO)
65— William Eastlake

YALE
66— *James Groninger
67— Howard Hilgendorf Jr.
69— Frederick Morris
71— Thomas Neville
72— David Bliss
75— John Burkus
77— *Stone Phillips
79— William Crowley
82— Richard Diana
91— Vincent Mooney
96— Matthew Siskosky

YOUNGSTOWN ST.
96— Mark Brungard

Academic All-America Hall of Fame

Since its inception in 1988, 39 former NCAA football players have been inducted into the GTE Academic All-America Hall of Fame. They were selected from among nominees by the College Sports Information Directors of America from past academic all-Americans of the 1950s, '60s, '70s, '80s and '90s. Following are the football selections by the year selected and each player's team, position and last year played:

1988
Pete Dawkins, Army, HB, 1958
Pat Haden, Southern California, QB, 1974
Rev. Donn Moomaw, UCLA, LB, 1953
Merlin Olsen, Utah St., T, 1961

1989
Carlos Alvarez, Florida, WR, 1971
Willie Bogan, Dartmouth, DB, 1970
Steve Bramwell, Washington, DB, 1965
Joe Romig, Colorado, G, 1961
Jim Swink, TCU, B, 1956
John Wilson, Michigan St., DB, 1952

1990
Joe Theismann, Notre Dame, QB, 1970
Howard Twilley, Tulsa, TE, 1965

1991
Terry Baker, Oregon St., QB, 1962
Joe Holland, Cornell, RB, 1978
David Joyner, Penn St., OT, 1971
Brock Strom, Air Force, T, 1958

1992
Alan Ameche, Wisconsin, RB, 1954

Stephen Eisenhauer, Navy, G, 1953
Randy Gradishar, Ohio St., LB, 1973

1993
Raymond Berry, Southern Methodist, E, 1954
Dave Casper, Notre Dame, E, 1973
Jim Grabowski, Illinois, FB, 1965

1994
Richard Mayo, Air Force, QB, 1961
Lee Roy Selmon, Oklahoma, DT, 1975

1995
Pat Richter, Wisconsin, E, 1962

1996
Wade Mitchell, Georgia Tech, QB, 1956
Bob Thomas, Notre Dame, K, 1973
Byron "Whizzer" White, Colorado, HB, 1937 (honorary selection)

1997
Todd Blackledge, Penn St., QB, 1983
Tim Foley, Purdue, DB, 1970

1998
Bernie Kosar, Miami (Fla.), QB, 1984
Jack Mildren, Oklahoma, QB, 1971
Marv Levy, Coe, RB, 1949 (honorary selection)

1999
John Fowler, UCLA, LB, 1978
Chad Hennings, Air Force, DL, 1988

2000
Oliver Luck, West Virginia, QB, 1981

2001
Cris Collingsworth, Florida, WR, 1980
John R. Hall, Vanderbilt, G, 1954

2002
Richard Balzhiser, Michigan, FB, 1955

2003
Kip Corrington, Texas A&M, DB
Chris Howard, Air Force, RB
Steve Young, Brigham Young, QB

Academic All-Americans by School

Academic all-America teams have been selected by the College Sports Information Directors of America since 1952 and sponsored by Verizon since 1985. To be eligible, student-athletes must be regular performers and have at least a 3.200 grade-point average (on a 4.000 scale) during their college careers. University division teams (I-A and I-AA) are complete in this list, but college division teams (II, III, NAIA) before 1970 are missing from CoSIDA archives, with few exceptions. Following are all known first-team selections:

ABILENE CHRISTIAN
63—Jack Griggs, LB
70—Jim Lindsey, QB
74—Greg Stirman, E
76—Bill Curbo, T
77—Bill Curbo, T
87—Bill Clayton, DL
88—Bill Clayton, DL
89—Bill Clayton, DL
90—Sean Grady, WR

ADRIAN
84—Steve Dembowski, QB
94—Jay Overmyer, DB

AIR FORCE
58—Brock Strom, T
59—Rich Mayo, B
60—Rich Mayo, B
70—Ernie Jennings, E
71—Darryl Haas, LB/K
72—Bob Homburg, DE
    Mark Prill, LB
73—Joe Debes, OT
74—Joe Debes, OT
78—Steve Hoog, WR
81—Mike France, LB
83—Jeff Kubiak, P
86—Chad Hennings, DL
87—Chad Hennings, DL
88—David Hlatky, OL
90—Chris Howard, RB
92—Grant Johnson, LB

AKRON
80—Andy Graham, PK

UAB
97—Johnny Rea, OL

ALABAMA
61—Tommy Brooker, E
    Pat Trammell, B
64—Gaylon McCollough, C
65—Steve Sloan, QB
    Dennis Homan, HB
67—Steve Davis, K

Bob Childs, LB
70—Johnny Musso, HB
71—Johnny Musso, HB
73—Randy Hall, DT
74—Randy Hall, DT
75—Danny Ridgeway, KS
79—Major Ogilvie, RB

ALABAMA A&M
89—Tracy Kendall, QB
90—Tracy Kendall, QB

ALBANY (N.Y.)
86—Thomas Higgins, OT
87—Thomas Higgins, OT
94—Andy Shein, WR
95—Rich Tallarico, OL
2000—J.T. Herfurth, OL

ALBION
82—Bruce Drogosch, LB
86—Michael Grant, DB
90—Scott Bissell, DB
93—Eric Baxmann, LB
    Jeffrey Shooks, P
94—Jeffrey Shooks, P
95—David Lefere, DB
96—David Lefere, DB

ALFRED
89—Mark Szynkowski, OL

ALLEGHENY
81—Kevin Baird, P
91—Adam Lechman, OL
    Darren Hadlock, LB

ALMA
86—Greg Luczak, TE
98—Rick Brands, PK
99—Dustin Armstrong, DB

AMERICAN INT'L
81—Todd Scyocurka, LB
99—Dan Grant, WR

ANGELO ST.
98—Kyle Kirk, LB

APPALACHIAN ST.
77—Gill Beck, C
92—D.J. Campbell, QB

ARIZONA
68—Mike Moody, OG
75—Jon Abbott, LB
76—Jon Abbott, T/LB
77—Jon Abbott, T/LB
79—Jeffrey Whitton, DL
87—Charles Cecil, DB
96—Wayne Wyatt, OL

ARIZONA ST.
66—Ken Dyer, OE
88—Mark Tingstad, LB
97—Patrick Tillman, LB

ARKANSAS
57—Gerald Nesbitt, FB
61—Lance Alworth, B
64—Ken Hatfield, B
65—Randy Stewart, C
    Jim Lindsey, HB
    Jack Brasuell, DB
68—Bob White, K
69—Bill Burnett, HB
    Terry Stewart, DB
78—Brad Shoup, DB

ARK.-MONTICELLO
85—Ray Howard, OG
88—Sean Rochelle, QB

ARKANSAS ST.
59—Larry Zabrowski, OT
61—Jim McMurray, QB

ARKANSAS TECH
90—Karl Kuhn, TE
91—Karl Kuhn, TE
2000—Robert Bayer, DL
    Paul Peletz, PK
01—Robert Bayer, DL

ARMY
55—Ralph Chesnauskas, E
57—James Kernan, C
    Pete Dawkins, HB
58—Pete Dawkins, HB
59—Don Usry, E
65—Sam Champi, DE
67—Bud Neswiacheny, DE
69—Theodore Shadid, C
89—Michael Thorson, DB
92—Mike McElrath, DB
94—Eric Oliver, LB
2001—Brandon Perdue, DL

ASHLAND
73—Mark Gulling, DB
74—Ron Brown, LB
76—Dan Bogden, E
77—Bruce Niehm, LB
81—Mark Braun, C
91—Thomas Shiban, RB

93—Jerry Spatny, DL
96—Chad DiFranco, DB

AUBURN
57—Jimmy Phillips, E
59—Jackie Burkett, C
60—Ed Dyas, B
65—Bill Cody, B
69—Buddy McClinton, DB
74—Bobby Davis, LB
75—Chuck Fletcher, DT
76—Chris Vacarella, RB
84—Gregg Carr, LB
94—Matt Hawkins, PK

AUGSBURG
81—Paul Elliott, DL
97—Ted Schultz, TE

AUGUSTANA (ILL.)
75—George Wesbey, T
80—Bill Dannehl, WR
84—Steve Sanders, OT
85—Steve Sanders, OT
95—Ryan Carpenter, OL
96—Ryan Carpenter, OL
97—Chris Meskan, OL
98—Chris Meskan, OL
2000—MacKenzie Hay, OL
01—Todd Baldwin, DB
02—Todd Baldwin, DB

AUGUSTANA (S.D.)
72—Pat McNerney, T
73—Pat McNerney, T
74—Jim Clemens, G
75—Jim Clemens, C
77—Stan Biondi, K
86—David Gubbrud, DL
87—David Gubbrud, DL
88—David Gubbrud, LB
89—David Gubbrud, LB
96—Mitchell Pruett, TE
97—Thayne Munce, OL

AUSTIN
81—Gene Branum, PK
99—Joe Fox, OL

AUSTIN PEAY
74—Gregory Johnson, G

BAKER
61—John Jacobs, B

BALDWIN-WALLACE
70—Earl Stolberg, DB
72—John Yezerski, G
78—Roger Andrachik, RB
    Greg Monda, LB
81—Chuck Krajacic, OG
88—Shawn Gorman, P
91—Tom Serdinak, P
93—Adrian Allison, DL
    David Coverdale, DL
94—David Coverdale, DL

2001—Matt Kish, OL
02— Matt Kish, OL

BALL ST.
83— Rich Chitwood, C
85— Ron Duncan, TE
86— Ron Duncan, TE
87— Ron Duncan, TE
88— Ted Ashburn, OL
  Greg Shackelford, DL
89— Ted Ashburn, OL
  David Haugh, DB
91— Troy Hoffer, DB
92— Troy Hoffer, DB
2002—Travis Barclay, OL

BATES
82— Neal Davidson, DB

BAYLOR
61— Ronnie Bull, RB
62— Don Trull, QB
63— Don Trull, QB
76— Cris Quinn, DE
89— Mike Welch, DB
90— Mike Welch, DB
96— Ty Atteberry, P

BELOIT
90— Shane Stadler, RB

BENEDICTINE (ILL.)
2002—Patrick Ryan, DL

BENTLEY
2000—Brian Holland, DB

BETHANY (KAN.)
86— Wade Gaeddert, DB

BETHANY (W.VA.)
2001—Eugene Ochap, OL

BETHEL (MINN.)
2001—Hans Bengston, DB

BLOOMSBURG
83— Dave Pepper, DL

BOISE ST.
71— Brent McIver, IL
73— Glenn Sparks, G
78— Sam Miller, DB

BOSTON COLLEGE
77— Richard Scudellari, LB
86— Michael Degnan, DL

BOSTON U.
83— Steve Shapiro, K
85— Brad Hokin, DB
93— Andre Maksimov, OL
94— Andre Maksimov, OL

BOWDOIN
84— Mike Siegel, P
93— Michael Turmelle, DB

BOWLING GREEN
75— John Boles, DE
89— Pat Jackson, LB
90— Pat Jackson, TE

BRIGHAM YOUNG
73— Steve Stratton, RB
80— Scott Phillips, RB
81— Dan Plater, WR
87— Chuck Cutler, WR
88— Chuck Cutler, WR
  Tim Clark, DL
89— Fred Whittingham, RB
90— Andy Boyce, WR
93— Eric Drage, WR
2000—Jared Lee, DB
01— Ryan Denney, DL

BROCKPORT ST.
97— Tom Massey, DB
98— Tom Massey, DB

BROWN
81— Travis Holcombe, OG
82— Dave Folsom, DB
86— Marty Edwards, C
87— John Cuozzo, C

BUCKNELL
72— Douglas Nauman, T
  John Ondrasik, DB
73— John Dailey, LB
74— Steve Leskinen, T
75— Larry Brunt, E
76— Larry Brunt, E

84— Rob Masonis, RB
  Jim Reilly, TE
86— Mike Morrow, WR
91— David Berardinelli, WR
92— David Berardinelli, WR

BUENA VISTA
99— Ben Smith, RB

BUFFALO
63— Gerry Philbin, T
84— Gerry Quinlivan, LB
85— James Dunbar, C
86— James Dunbar, C
98— Dan Poulsen, DL

BUFFALO ST.
87— Clint Morano, OT

BUTLER
84— Steve Kollias, L
98— Nick Batalis, OL
  Mike Goletz, DL
99— Mike Goletz, LB

C.W. POST
70— Art Canario, T
75— Frank Prochilo, RB
84— Bob Jahelka, DB
93— Jim Byrne, WR

CALIFORNIA
67— Bob Crittenden, DG
70— Robert Richards, OT
82— Harvey Salem, OT

UC DAVIS
72— Steve Algeo, LB
75— Dave Gellerman, LB
90— Mike Shepard, DL
98— Wes Terrell, TE

UC RIVERSIDE
71— Tyrone Hooks, HB

CAL LUTHERAN
81— John Walsh, OT

CANISIUS
82— Tom Schott, WR
83— Tom Schott, TE
86— Mike Panepinto, RB
2000—Jake Coppola, WR

CAPITAL
70— Ed Coy, E
83— Mike Linton, G
85— Kevin Sheets, WR
2002—Trevor Alexander, DL

CARLETON
92— Scott Hanks, TE

CARNEGIE MELLON
76— Rick Lackner, LB
  Dave Nackoul, E
84— Roger Roble, WR
87— Bryan Roessler, DL
  Chris Haupt, LB
89— Robert O'Toole, LB
90— Frank Bellante, RB
  Robert O'Toole, LB
94— Aaron Neal, TE
  Merle Atkinson, DL
98— Jason Funke, DB

CARROLL (WIS.)
76— Stephen Thompson, QB

CARSON-NEWMAN
61— David Dale, E
93— Chris Horton, OL
94— Chris Horton, OL
2000—Keith Akard, DL

CARTHAGE
61— Bob Halsey, B
77— Mark Phelps, QB

CASE RESERVE
75— John Kosko, T
82— Jim Donnelly, RB
83— Jim Donnelly, RB
84— Jim Donnelly, RB
88— Chris Hutter, TE
90— Michael Bissler, DB
95— Doug Finefrock, LB
96— Tom Mager, LB
  Kenyon Meadows, DL
2000—Tim Gustafason, DL

CENTRAL ARK.
2002—Landon Trusty, TE

CENTRAL (IOWA)
79— Chris Adkins, LB
85— Scott Lindrell, LB
86— Scott Lindrell, LB
91— Rich Kacmarynski, RB

CENTRAL MICH.
70— Ralph Burde, DL
74— Mike Franckowiak, QB
  John Wunderlich, T
79— Mike Ball, WR
84— John DeBoer, WR
91— Jeff Bender, QB
2001—Rob Turner, WR

CENTRAL MO. ST.
97— Shane Meyer, PK

CENTRE
84— Teel Bruner, DB
85— Teel Bruner, DB
89— Bryan Ellington, DB
91— Eric Horstmeyer, WR

CHADRON ST.
73— Jerry Sutton, LB
75— Bob Lacey, KS
79— Jerry Carder, TE
95— Corey Campbell, RB
99— Casey Beran, DL

CHAPMAN
96— Matt Hertzler, OL
97— Matt Hertzler, OL

CHEYNEY
75— Steve Anderson, G

CHICAGO
87— Paul Haar, OG
88— Paul Haar, OL
93— Frank Baker, RB

CINCINNATI
81— Kari Yli-Renko, OT
90— Kyle Stroh, DL
91— Kris Bjorson, TE
97— John Kobalka, DL

CITADEL
63— Vince Petno, E
76— Kenny Caldwell, LB
77— Kenny Caldwell, LB
78— Kenny Caldwell, LB
87— Thomas Frooman, RB
89— Thomas Frooman, RB

CLARION
96— Steve Witte, RB

CLEMSON
59— Lou Cordileone, T
78— Steve Fuller, QB
99— Kyle Young, OL
2000—Chad Carson, LB
  Kyle Young, OL
01— Chad Carson, LB
  Kyle Young, OL

COAST GUARD
70— Charles Pike, LB
71— Bruce Melnick, DB
81— Mark Butt, DB

COE
93— Marcus Adkins, DL
2000—Timothy Vinyard, QB

COLGATE
78— Angelo Colosimo, RB
79— Angelo Colosimo, RB
85— Tom Stenglein, WR
89— Jeremy Garvey, TE

COLORADO
60— Joe Romig, G
61— Joe Romig, G
67— Kirk Tracy, OG
70— Jim Cooch, DB
73— Rick Stearns, LB
74— Rick Stearns, LB
75— Steve Young, DT
87— Eric McCarty, OL
90— Jim Hansen, OL
91— Jim Hansen, OL
92— Jim Hansen, OL

96— Ryan Olson, DL
97— Ryan Olson, DL

COLORADO COL.
96— Ryan Egeland, OL
  Ryan Haygood, DL

COLORADO MINES
72— Dave Chambers, RB
83— Charles Lane, T

COLORADO ST.
55— Gary Glick, B
69— Tom French, OT
86— Steve Bartalo, RB
95— Greg Myers, DB
98— Mike Newell, OL
  Nate Kvamme, LB
2002—Eric Pauly, LB

COLUMBIA
52— Mitch Price, B
53— John Gasella, T
56— Claude Benham, B
71— John Sefcik, HB

CONCORDIA-ST. PAUL
2000—Andrew Fleischman, OL

CORNELL
77— Joseph Holland, RB
78— Joseph Holland, RB
82— Derrick Harmon, RB
83— Derrick Harmon, RB
85— Dave Van Metre, DL

CORNELL COLLEGE
72— Rob Ash, QB
  Dewey Birkhofer, S
76— Joe Lauterbach, G
  Tom Zinkula, DT
77— Tom Zinkula, DT
78— Tom Zinkula, DL
82— John Ward, WR
91— Bruce Feldmann, QB
92— Brent Sands, DB
93— Mark McDermott, DB
94— Mark McDermott, DB
95— Mike Tressel, DB
97— Matt Weiss, DL
98— Matt Weiss, DL

CULVER-STOCKTON
95— Mason Kaiser, DB

DARTMOUTH
70— Willie Bogan, DB
83— Michael Patsis, DB
87— Paul Sorensen, LB
88— Paul Sorensen, LB
90— Brad Preble, DB
91— Mike Bobo, WR
  Tom Morrow, LB
92— Russ Torres, RB
94— David Shearer, WR
  Zach Lehman, DL
97— Dominic Lanza, OL

DAYTON
71— Tim Quinn, LB
72— Tim Quinn, DT
79— Scott Terry, QB
84— Greg French, K
  David Kemp, LB
  Jeff Slayback, L
85— Greg French, K
86— Gerry Meyer, OT
91— Brett Cuthbert, DB
  Dan Rosenbaum, DB
92— Steve Lochow, DL
  Dan Rosenbaum, DB
93— Steve Lochow, DL
  Brad Mager, DB
94— David Overhoiser, RB
96— Josh Lemmon, OL
98— Jacob Jones, RB
99— Jimmy Lee, RB
2001—Mark Kasmer, LB
  Marty McNamara, DB
02— Mark Kasmer, DB

DEFIANCE
80— Jill Bailey, OT
  Mark Bockelman, TE

DELAWARE
70— Yancey Phillips, T
71— Robert Depew, DE
72— Robert Depew, DE

DELAWARE VALLEY
84—Dan Glowatski, WR

DELTA ST.
70—Hal Posey, RB
74—Billy Hood, E
　　Ricky Lewis, LB
　　Larry Miller, RB
75—Billy Hood, E
78—Terry Moody, DB
79—Charles Stavley, G

DENISON
75—Dennis Thome, LB
87—Grant Jones, DB
98—Jonathan Dunham, DB
99—Jonathan Dunham, DB

DePAUW
70—Jim Ceaser, LB
71—Jim Ceaser, LB
73—Neil Oslos, RB
80—Jay True, WR
85—Tony deNicola, QB
87—Michael Sherman, DB
90—Tom Beaulieu, DL
91—Tom Beaulieu, DL
　　Matt Nelson, LB
94—Mike Callahan, LB

DICKINSON
74—Gerald Urich, RB
79—Scott Mumma, RB

DRAKE
74—Todd Gaffney, KS
83—Tom Holt, RB

DREXEL
70—Lynn Ferguson, S

DUBUQUE
80—Tim Finn, RB

DUKE
66—Roger Hayes, DE
67—Bob Lasky, DT
70—Curt Rawley, DT
86—Mike Diminick, DB
87—Mike Diminick, DB
88—Mike Diminick, DB
89—Doug Key, DL
93—Travis Pearson, DL

EAST STROUDSBURG
84—Ernie Siegrist, TE

EAST TENN. ST.
71—Ken Oster, DB

EASTERN ILL.
95—Tim Carver, LB

EASTERN KY.
77—Steve Frommeyer, S

EASTERN N.M.
80—Tom Sager, DL
81—Tom Sager, DL

EASTERN WASH.
97—Jeff Ogden, WR
　　Steve Mattson, DL
2002—Kyler Randall, WR

ELON
73—John Rascoe, E
79—Bryan Burney, DB

EMORY & HENRY
71—Tom Wilson, LB
2000—Nathan Tuck, WR

EMPORIA ST.
79—Tom Lingg, DL
2002—Tyler Paul, RB

EVANSVILLE
74—David Mattingly, S
76—Michael Pociask, C
87—Jeffery Willman, TE
97—Sean Bennett, RB

FERRIS ST.
81—Vic Trecha, OT
92—Monty Brown, LB

FINDLAY
97—Bo Hurley, QB

FLORIDA
65—Charles Casey, E
69—Carlos Alvarez, WR

71—Carlos Alvarez, WR
76—David Posey, KS
77—Wes Chandler, RB
80—Cris Collinsworth, WR
91—Brad Culpepper, DL
93—Michael Gilmore, DB
94—Terry Dean, QB
　　Michael Gilmore, DB
95—Danny Wuerffel, QB
96—Danny Wuerffel, QB

FLORIDA A&M
90—Irvin Clark, DL

FLORIDA ST.
72—Gary Huff, QB
79—William Jones, DB
　　Phil Williams, WR
80—William Jones, DB
81—Rohn Stark, P
94—Derrick Brooks, LB
96—Daryl Bush, LB
97—Daryl Bush, LB
2000—Christopher Hope, DB
01—Christopher Hope, DB

FORDHAM
90—Eric Schweiker, OL

FORT HAYS ST.
75—Greg Custer, RB
82—Ron Johnson, P
85—Paul Nelson, DL
86—Paul Nelson, DL
89—Dean Gengler, OL
2000—Adam Ryan, P
01—Casey Seyfert, DL

FORT LEWIS
72—Dee Tennison, E

FRANK. & MARSH.
77—Joe Fry, DB
78—Joe Fry, DB
2001—Mark Rowand, P

FURMAN
76—Jeff Holcomb, T
85—Brian Jager, RB
88—Kelly Fletcher, DL
89—Kelly Fletcher, DL
　　Chris Roper, LB
91—Eric Walter, OL
99—Stuart Rentz, RB
2000—Marion Martin, LB

GANNON
2002—John Yurisinec, DB

GEORGETOWN
71—Gerry O'Dowd, HB
86—Andrew Phelan, OG

GEORGETOWN (KY.)
89—Eric Chumbley, OL
92—Bobby Wasson, PK
2001—Eddie Eviston, QB

GEORGIA
60—Francis Tarkenton, QB
65—Bob Etter, K
66—Bob Etter, K
　　Lynn Hughes, DB
68—Bill Stanfill, DT
71—Tom Nash, OT
　　Mixon Robinson, DE
77—Jeff Lewis, LB
82—Terry Hoage, DB
83—Terry Hoage, DB
92—Todd Peterson, PK
97—Matt Stinchcomb, OL
98—Matt Stinchcomb, OL
2001—Jon Stinchcomb, OL
02—Jon Stinchcomb, OL

GA. SOUTHERN
95—Rob Stockton, DB
99—Voncellies Allen, DL

GA. SOUTHWESTERN
87—Gregory Slappery, RB

GEORGIA TECH
52—Ed Gossage, T
　　Cecil Trainer, DE
　　Larry Morris, LB
55—Wade Mitchell, B
56—Allen Ecker, G

66—Jim Breland, C
　　W.J. Blaine, LB
　　Bill Eastman, DB
67—Bill Eastman, DB
80—Sheldon Fox, LB
90—Stefen Scotton, RB
99—Dan Dyke, P
2000—Dan Dyke, P
01—Dan Dyke, P
02—Dan Dyke, P

GETTYSBURG
79—Richard Swartz, LB
2002—Cliff Mason, LB

GRAMBLING
72—Floyd Harvey, RB
93—Gilad Landau, PK

GRAND VALLEY ST.
91—Mark Smith, OL
　　Todd Wood, DB

GRINNELL
71—Edward Hirsch, E
81—David Smiley, TE
98—Richard Wemer, WR

GROVE CITY
74—Pat McCoy, LB
89—Travis Croll, P

GUST. ADOLPHUS
80—Dave Najarian, DL
81—Dave Najarian, LB
98—Dan Duncan, OL
99—Dan Duncan, OL
2000—Brian Bergstrom, LB
01—Brian Bergstrom, LB

HAMLINE
73—Thomas Dufresne, E
89—Jon Voss, TE

HAMPDEN-SYDNEY
82—John Dickinson, OG
90—W.R. Jones, OL
91—David Brickhill, PK

HAMPTON
93—Tim Benson, WR

HARVARD
99—Ben Green, DB

HAWAII
97—Chris Shinnick, DB

HEIDELBERG
82—Jeff Kurtzman, DL
99—Joe Conduah, LB

HENDERSON ST.
98—Lee Daily, LB

HILLSDALE
61—James Richendollar, T
72—John Cervini, G
81—Mark Kellogg, LB
93—Jason Ahee, DB
96—Kyle Wojciechowski, OL

HOLY CROSS
83—Bruce Kozerski, T
85—Kevin Reilly, OT
87—Jeff Wiley, QB
91—Pete Dankert, DL

HOPE
73—Ronald Posthuma, T
79—Craig Groendyk, T
80—Greg Bekius, PK
82—Kurt Brinks, C
84—Scott Jecmen, DB
86—Timothy Chase, OG

HOUSTON
64—Horst Paul, E
76—Mark Mohr, DB
　　Kevin Rollwage, OT
77—Kevin Rollwage, OT

IDAHO
70—Bruce Langmeade, T

IDAHO ST.
84—Brent Koetter, DB
91—Steve Boyenger, DB
96—Trevor Bell, DB

ILLINOIS
52—Bob Lenzini, DT

64—Jim Grabowski, FB
65—Jim Grabowski, FB
66—John Wright, E
70—Jim Rucks, DE
71—Bob Bucklin, DE
80—Dan Gregus, DL
81—Dan Gregus, DL
82—Dan Gregus, DL
91—Mike Hopkins, DB
92—John Wright Jr., WR
94—Brett Larsen, P
99—Josh Whitman, TE
2000—Josh Whitman, TE

ILLINOIS COL.
80—Jay Wessler, RB
94—Warren Dodson, OL

ILLINOIS ST.
76—Tony Barnes, C
80—Jeff Hembrough, DL
89—Dan Hackman, OL
95—Keith Goodnight, RB
2000—Adam Waugh, LB
01—Adam Waugh, LB

ILL. WESLEYAN
71—Keith Ihlenfeldt, DE
80—Jim Eaton, DL
　　Rick Hanna, DL
　　Mike Watson, DB
81—Mike Watson, DB
91—Chris Bisaillon, WR
92—Chris Udovich, DL
95—Jason Richards, TE
96—Lon Erickson, QB

INDIANA
67—Harry Gonso, HB
72—Glenn Scolnik, RB
80—Kevin Speer, C
94—John Hammerstein, DL

INDIANA (PA.)
82—Kenny Moore, DB
83—Kenny Moore, DB

INDIANA ST.
71—Gary Brown, E
72—Michael Eads, E

INDIANAPOLIS
76—William Willan, E
95—Ted Munson, DL
2000—Brad Crawford, OL

IONA
80—Neal Kurtti, DL

IOWA
52—Bill Fenton, DE
53—Bill Fenton, DE
75—Bob Elliott, DB
85—Larry Station, LB
2001—Aaron Kampman, DL

IOWA ST.
52—Max Burkett, DB
82—Mark Carlson, LB
99—Dave Brcka, LB
2002—Jordan Carstens, DL

ITHACA
72—Dana Hallenbeck, LB
85—Brian Dougherty, DB
89—Peter Burns, OL

JACKSONVILLE ST.
77—Dewey Barker, E
78—Dewey Barker, TE

JAMES MADISON
78—Warren Coleman, OT

JOHN CARROLL
83—Nick D'Angelo, LB
　　Jim Sferra, DL
85—Joe Burrello, LB
86—Joe Burrello, LB

JOHNS HOPKINS
77—Charles Hauck, DT
93—Michael House, DL
94—Michael House, DL
98—Chris Baugh, OL

JUNIATA
70—Ray Grabiak, DL
71—Ray Grabiak, DE
　　Maurice Taylor, IL

KALAMAZOO
92—Sean Mullendore, LB
2001—Brant Haverdink, LB

KANSAS
64—Fred Elder, T
67—Mike Sweatman, LB
68—Dave Morgan, LB
71—Mike McCoy, C
76—Tom Fitch, S
95—Darrin Simmons, P

KANSAS ST.
74—Don Lareau, LB
77—Floyd Dorsey, OG
81—Darren Gale, DB
82—Darren Gale, DB
      Mark Hundley, RB
85—Troy Faunce, P
95—Kevin Lockett, WR
96—Kevin Lockett, WR
      Jason Johnson, OL
2000—Jon McGraw, DB
01—Jon McGraw, DB

KENT ST.
72—Mark Reiheld, DB
91—Brad Smith, RB
2001—Brian Hallett, OL

KENTUCKY
74—Tom Ranieri, LB
78—Mark Keene, C
      Jim Kovach, LB
85—Ken Pietrowiak, C
98—Jeff Zurcher, DB

KENYON
77—Robert Jennings, RB
85—Dan Waldeck, TE

LA VERNE
82—Scott Shier, OT

LAFAYETTE
70—William Sprecher, T
74—Mike Kline, DB
79—Ed Rogusky, RB
80—Ed Rogusky, RB

LAWRENCE
81—Chris Matheus, DL
      Scott Reppert, RB
82—Chris Matheus, DL

LEHIGH
90—Shon Harker, DB

LEWIS & CLARK
61—Pat Clock, G
81—Dan Jones, WR

LIBERTY
98—Jarrol Everson, DL

LONG BEACH ST.
83—Joe Donohue, LB

LORAS
84—John Coyle, DL
      Pete Kovatisis, DB
85—John Coyle, DL
91—Mark Goedken, DL
93—Travis Michaels, LB

LA.-MONROE
70—Tom Miller, KS
74—Mike Bialas, T

LSU
59—Mickey Mangham, E
60—Charles Strange, C
61—Billy Booth, T
71—Jay Michaelson, KS
73—Tyler Lafauci, OG
      Joe Winkler, DB
74—Brad Davis, RB
77—Robert Dugas, OT
84—Juan Carlos Betanzos, PK
94—Michael Blanchard, OL
97—Chad Kessler, P
2002—Rodney Reed, OL

LUTHER
83—Larry Bonney, DL
84—Larry Bonney, DL
89—Larry Anderson, RB
90—Joel Nerem, DL
91—Joel Nerem, DL
95—Karl Borge, DL

LYCOMING
74—Thomas Vanaskie, DB
85—Mike Kern, DL

MACALESTER
82—Lee Schaefer, OG

MANSFIELD
83—John Delate, DB

MARIETTA
83—Matt Wurtzbacher, DL

MARS HILL
92—Brent Taylor, DL

MARSHALL
98—Chad Pennington, QB
99—Chad Pennington, QB

MARYLAND
53—Bernie Faloney, B
75—Kim Hoover, DE
78—Joe Muffler, DL

MARYVILLE (TENN.)
99—Kevin Hedrick, DL

MASSACHUSETTS
99—Mike Wynne, OL

MASS.-LOWELL
85—Don Williams, RB

MIT
89—Anthony Lapes, WR
90—Darcy Prather, LB
91—Rodrigo Rubiano, DL
92—Roderick Tranum, WR
93—Corey Foster, OL
94—Corey Foster, OL
95—Scott Vollrath, P
96—Duane Stevens, DB
      Brad Gray, DL
97—Duane Stevens, DB
      Mike Butville, LB
      Brad Gray, DL
99—Nik Kozy, DL
      Angus Huang, DB
2000—Angus Huang, DB

McDANIEL
73—Chip Chaney, S
98—Tom Lapato, DB

McGILL
87—Bruno Pietrobon, WR

McNEESE ST.
78—Jim Downing, OT
79—Jim Downing, OT
90—David Easterling, DB
2000—Wes Hines, OL
02—Hadley Prince, DB

MEMPHIS
92—Pat Jansen, DL

MIAMI (FLA.)
59—Fran Curci, B
84—Bernie Kosar, QB
2002—Jonathan Vilma, LB
      Matt Walters, DL

MIAMI (OHIO)
73—Andy Pederzolli, DB
2000—Brian Potter, DL

MICHIGAN
52—Dick Balzhiser, B
55—Jim Orwig, T
57—Jim Orwig, T
64—Bob Timberlake, QB
66—Dave Fisher, FB
      Dick Vidmer, FB
69—Jim Mandich, OE
70—Phil Seymour, DE
71—Bruce Elliott, DB
72—Bill Hart, OG
74—Kirk Lewis, OG
75—Dan Jilek, DE
81—Norm Betts, TE
82—Stefan Humphries, OG
      Robert Thompson, LB
83—Stefan Humphries, OG
85—Clay Miller, OT
86—Kenneth Higgins, WR
99—Rob Renes, DL

MICHIGAN ST.
52—John Wilson, DB

53—Don Dohoney, E
55—Buck Nystrom, G
57—Blanche Martin, HB
65—Don Bierowicz, DT
      Don Japinga, DB
66—Pat Gallinagh, DT
68—Al Brenner, E/DB
69—Ron Saul, OG
      Rich Saul, DE
73—John Shinsky, DT
79—Alan Davis, DB
85—Dean Altobelli, DB
86—Dean Altobelli, DB
86—Shane Bullough, LB
92—Steve Wasylk, DB
93—Steve Wasylk, DB

MICHIGAN TECH
71—Larry Ras, HB
73—Bruce Trusock, C
76—Jim Van Wagner, RB
92—Kurt Coduti, QB

MIDWESTERN ST.
95—Corby Walker, LB

MILLERSVILLE
91—Tom Burns, OL

MILLIKIN
61—Gerald Domesick, B
75—Frank Stone, G
78—Charlie Sammis, K
79—Eric Stevens, WR
83—Marc Knowles, WR
84—Tom Kreller, RB
85—Cary Bottorff, LB
      Tom Kreller, RB
90—Tim Eimermann, PK

MINNESOTA
56—Bob Hobert, T
60—Frank Brixius, T
68—Bob Stein, DE
70—Barry Mayer, RB
89—Brent Herbel, P
94—Justin Conzemius, DB

MINN ST. MANKATO
74—Dan Miller, C

MINN ST. MOORHEAD
88—Brad Shamla, DL
99—Adam Vossen, DL
      Eric Pederson, LB

MISSISSIPPI
54—Harold Easterwood, C
59—Robert Khayat, T
      Charlie Flowers, B
61—Doug Elmore, B
65—Stan Hindman, G
68—Steve Hindman, HB
69—Julius Fagan, K
74—Greg Markow, DE
77—Robert Fabris, OE
      George Plasketes, DE
80—Ken Toler, WR
86—Danny Hoskins, OG
87—Danny Hoskins, OG
88—Wesley Walls, TE
89—Todd Sandroni, DB

MISSISSIPPI COL.
75—Anthony Saway, S
78—Steve Johnson, OT
79—Steve Johnson, OT
83—Wayne Frazier, C
97—Kyle Fulcher, LB

MISSISSIPPI ST.
53—Jackie Parker, B
56—Ron Bennett, E
72—Frank Dowsing, DB
73—Jimmy Webb, DE
76—Will Coltharp, DE
89—Stacy Russell, DB
2000—Scott Westerfield, PK

MISSOURI
62—Tom Hertz, G
66—Dan Schuppan, DE
      Bill Powell, DT
68—Carl Garber, MG
70—John Weisenfels, LB
72—Greg Hill, KS
81—Van Darkow, LB

93—Matt Burgess, OL
98—Jake Stueve, TE

MO.-ROLLA
72—Kim Colter, DB
80—Paul Janke, OG
86—Tom Reed, RB
87—Jim Pfeiffer, OT
88—Jim Pfeiffer, OL
91—Don Huff, DB
92—Don Huff, DB
94—Brian Gilmore, LB
95—Brian Gilmore, LB
96—Brian Gilmore, LB

MO. SOUTHERN ST.
85—Mike Testman, DB
93—Chris Tedford, OL
94—Chris Tedford, OL

MONMOUTH
2002—Justin Rosato, DB

MONMOUTH (ILL.)
83—Robb Long, QB

MONTANA
77—Steve Fisher, DE
79—Ed Cerkovnik, DB
88—Michael McGowan, LB
89—Michael McGowan, LB
90—Michael McGowan, LB
93—Dave Dickenson, QB
95—Matt Wells, WR
96—Josh Branen, RB
      Blaine McElmurry, DB
98—Justin Olsen, WR
99—Vince Huntsberger, DB
2000—Vince Huntsberger, DB
      Matt Thuesen, OL
01—Vince Huntsberger, DB

MONTANA ST.
84—Dirk Nelson, P
88—Anders Larsson, PK
96—Devlan Geddes, DL
2000—Ryan Johnson, RB
01—Ryan Johnson, RB
02—Ryan Johnson, RB
      Jon Montoya, DL

MONTCLAIR ST.
70—Bill Trimmer, DL
82—Daniel Deneher, KS

MORAVIAN
87—Jeff Pollock, WR
96—Mike Paciulli, DB

MOREHEAD ST.
74—Don Russell, KS
90—James Appel, OL
91—James Appel, OL
96—Mike Appel, OL

MORGAN ST.
96—Willie Thompson, DL

MOUNT UNION
71—Dennis Montgomery, QB
84—Rick Marabito, L
86—Scott Gindlesberger, QB
87—Paul Hrics, C
98—Darin Kershner, WR
2000—Chuck Moore, RB
01—Chuck Moore, RB
02—Matt Campbell, DL

MUHLENBERG
70—Edward Salo, G
71—Edward Salo, IL
72—Edward Salo, C
75—Keith Ordemann, LB
80—Arthur Scavone, OT
89—Joe Zeszotarski, DL
90—Mike Hoffman, DB

MURRAY ST.
76—Eddie McFarland, DB

MUSKINGUM
78—Dan Radalia, DL
79—Dan Radalia, DL

NAVY
53—Steve Eisenhauer, G
57—Tom Forrestal, QB
58—Joe Tranchini, B
69—Dan Pike, RB

80—Ted Dumbauld, LB

NEBRASKA
62—James Huge, E
63—Dennis Calridge, B
66—Marv Mueller, DB
69—Randy Reeves, DB
71—Larry Jacobson, DT
Jeff Kinney, HB
73—Frosty Anderson, E
75—Rik Bonness, C
Tom Heiser, RB
76—Vince Ferragamo, QB
Ted Harvey, DB
77—Ted Harvey, DB
78—George Andrews, DL
James Pillen, DB
79—Rod Horn, DL
Kelly Saalfeld, C
Randy Schleusener, OG
80—Jeff Finn, TE
Randy Schleusener, OG
81—Eric Lindquist, DB
David Rimington, C
Randy Theiss, OT
82—David Rimington, C
83—Scott Strasburger, DL
Rob Stuckey, DL
84—Scott Strasburger, DL
Rob Stuckey, DL
Mark Traynowicz, C
86—Dale Klein, K
Thomas Welter, OT
87—Jeffrey Jamrog, DB
Mark Blazek, DB
88—Mark Blazek, DB
John Kroeker, P
89—Gerry Gdowski, QB
Jake Young, OL
90—David Edeal, OL
Pat Tyrance, LB
Jim Wanek, OL
91—Pat Engelbert, DL
Mike Stigge, P
92—Mike Stigge, P
93—Rob Zatechka, OL
Terry Connealy, DL
Trev Alberts, LB
94—Matt Shaw, TE
Rob Zatechka, OL
Terry Connealy, DL
95—Aaron Graham, OL
96—Grant Wistrom, LB
97—Joel Mackovicka, RB
Grant Wistrom, DL
98—Joel Makovicka, RB
Chad Kelsay, DL
William Lafleur, P
99—Kyle Vanden Bosch, DL
Mike Brown, DB
2000—Kyle Vanden Bosch, DL
01—Tracey Wistrom, TE

NEB.-KEARNEY
70—John Makovicka, RB
75—Tim Brodahl, E
99—Volker Olbrich, PK

NEB.-OMAHA
82—Kirk Hutton, DB
Clark Toner, LB
83—Kirk Hutton, DB
84—Jerry Kripal, QB

NEB. WESLEYAN
87—Pat Sweeney, DB
88—Pat Sweeney, DB
Mike Surls, LB
89—Scott Shaffer, RB
Scott Shipman, DB
95—Justin Rice, DL
96—Justin Rice, DL
97—Chad Wemhoff, WR
98—Ryan Shanesy, DL
2001—Grant Leach, OL
Justin Buresh, LB

NEVADA
82—David Heppe, P
2002—Erick Streelman, TE

NEW HAMPSHIRE
52—John Driscoll, T
84—Dave Morton, OL

COL. OF NEW JERSEY
2000—Curt Monday, DB

NEW MEXICO
75—Bob Johnson, S
77—Robert Rumbaugh, DT
78—Robert Rumbaugh, DL
93—Justin Hall, OL
98—Chad Smith, DB

NEW MEXICO ST.
66—Jim Bohl, B
74—Ralph Jackson, OG
75—Ralph Jackson, OG
85—Andy Weiler, KS
92—Todd Cutler, TE
Shane Hackney, OL
Tim Mauck, LB
93—Tim Mauck, LB
96—David Patterson, WR
97—David Patterson, WR
98—David Patterson, WR

NICHOLS
89—David Kane, DB

NORTH CAROLINA
64—Ken Willard, B
85—Kevin Anthony, QB

NORTH CAROLINA ST.
60—Roman Gabriel, QB
63—Joe Scarpati, B
67—Steve Warren, OT
71—Craig John, OG
73—Justus Everett, C
Stan Fritts, RB
74—Justus Everett, C
80—Calvin Warren, P

NORTH DAKOTA
87—Kurt Otto, QB
88—Chuck Clairmont, OL
Matt Gulseth, DB
92—Tim Gelinske, WR
Mark Ewen, LB
96—Tim Tibesar, LB
2002—Mac Schneider, OL

NORTH DAKOTA ST.
71—Tomm Smail, DT
93—T.R. McDonald, WR

NORTH PARK
83—Mike Lilgegren, DB
85—Scott Love, WR
86—Todd Love, WR
87—Todd Love, WR

NORTH TEXAS
75—Pete Morris, LB
76—Pete Morris, LB

NORTHEASTERN
85—Shawn O'Malley, LB

NORTHERN ARIZ.
89—Chris Baniszewski, WR

NORTHERN COLO.
71—Charles Putnik, OG
81—Duane Hirsch, DL
Ray Sperger, DB
82—Jim Bright, RB
89—Mike Yonkovich, DL
Tom Langer, LB
90—Tom Langer, LB
98—Corte McGuffey, QB
99—Corte McGuffey, QB

NORTHERN IOWA
99—Brad Meester, OL

NORTHERN ILL.
2000—Thomas Hammock, RB
01—Thomas Hammock, RB

NORTHERN MICH.
83—Bob Stefanski, WR
2002—Ben Laarman, LB

NORTHWEST MO. ST.
81—Robert "Chip" Gregory, LB

NORTHWESTERN
56—Al Viola, G
58—Andy Cvercko, T
61—Larry Onesti, C
62—Paul Flatley, E
63—George Burman, E
70—Joe Zigulich, OG
76—Randolph Dean, E
80—Jim Ford, OT
86—Michael Baum, OT
Bob Dirkes, DL

Todd Krehbiel, DB
87—Mike Baum, OL
88—Mike Baum, OL
90—Ira Adler, PK
95—Sam Valenzisi, PK
2002—Jason Wright, RB

N'WESTERN (IOWA)
83—Mark Muilenberg, RB
92—Joel Bundt, OL

NORTHWESTERN (MINN.)
2002—Jon Peterson, DB

N'WESTERN (OKLA.)
61—Stewart Arthurs, B

NORTHWESTERN ST.
92—Guy Hedrick, RB
94—John Dippel, OL

NORWICH
70—Gary Fry, RB

NOTRE DAME
52—Joe Heap, B
53—Joe Heap, B
54—Joe Heap, B
55—Don Schaefer, B
58—Bob Wetoska, E
63—Bob Lehmann, G
66—Tom Regner, OG
Jim Lynch, LB
67—Jim Smithberger, DB
68—George Kunz, OT
69—Jim Reilly, OT
70—Tom Gatewood, E
Larry DiNardo, OG
Joe Theismann, QB
71—Greg Marx, DT
Tom Gatewood, E
72—Michael Creaney, E
Greg Marx, DT
73—David Casper, E
Gary Potempa, LB
Bob Thomas, K
74—Reggie Barnett, DB
Pete Demmerle, E
77—Ken MacAfee, E
Joe Restic, S
Dave Vinson, OG
78—Joe Restic, DB
80—Bob Burger, OG
Tom Gibbons, DB
81—John Krimm, DB
85—Greg Dingens, DL
87—Ted Gradel, PK
Vince Phelan, P
92—Tim Ruddy, OL
93—Tim Ruddy, OL

OCCIDENTAL
88—Curtis Page, DL

OHIO
71—John Rousch, HB

OHIO NORTHERN
76—Jeff McFarlin, S
79—Robert Coll, WR
86—David Myers, DL
90—Chad Hummell, OL
97—Andy Roecker, OL

OHIO ST.
52—John Borton, B
54—Dick Hilinski, T
58—Bob White, B
61—Tom Perdue, E
65—Bill Ridder, MG
66—Dave Foley, OT
68—Dave Foley, OT
Mark Stier, LB
69—Bill Urbanik, DT
71—Rick Simon, OG
73—Randy Gradishar, LB
74—Brian Baschnagel, RB
75—Brian Baschnagel, RB
76—Pete Johnson, RB
Bill Lukens, OG
77—Jeff Logan, RB
80—Marcus Marek, LB
82—John Frank, TE
Joseph Smith, OT
83—John Frank, TE
84—David Crecelius, DL
Michael Lanese, WR

85—Michael Lanese, WR
89—Joseph Staysniak, OL
92—Leonard Hartman, OL
Gregory Smith, DL
95—Greg Bellisari, LB
96—Greg Bellisari, LB
99—Ahmed Plummer, DB

OHIO WESLEYAN
70—Tony Heald, LB
Tom Liller, E
81—Ric Kinnan, WR
85—Kevin Connell, OG
94—Craig Anderson, LB
95—Craig Anderson, LB
96—Craig Anderson, LB

OKLAHOMA
52—Tom Catlin, C
54—Carl Allison, E
56—Jerry Tubbs, C
57—Doyle Jenning, T
58—Ross Coyle, E
62—Wayne Lee, C
63—Newt Burton, G
64—Newt Burton, G
66—Ron Shotts, HB
67—Ron Shotts, HB
68—Eddie Hinton, DB
70—Joe Wylie, RB
71—Jack Mildren, QB
72—Joe Wylie, RB
74—Randy Hughes, S
75—Dewey Selmon, LB
Lee Roy Selmon, DT
80—Jay Jimerson, DB
86—Brian Bosworth, LB

OKLA. PANHANDLE
76—Larry Johnson, G

OKLAHOMA ST.
54—Dale Meinert, G
72—Tom Wolf, OT
73—Doug Tarrant, LB
74—Tom Wolf, OT
77—Joe Avanzini, DE
2002—Kyle Eaton, OL

OREGON
62—Steve Barnett, T
65—Tim Casey, LB
86—Mike Preacher, P
90—Bill Musgrave, QB
2000—Ryan Schmid, OL
01—Joey Harrington, QB
Ryan Schmid, OL

OREGON ST.
62—Terry Baker, B
67—Bill Enyart, FB
68—Bill Enyart, FB
93—Chad Paulson, RB

OUACHITA BAPTIST
78—David Cowling, OG

PACIFIC (CAL.)
78—Bruce Filarsky, OG
79—Bruce Filarsky, DL

PACIFIC LUTHERAN
82—Curt Rodin, TE

PENNSYLVANIA
86—Rich Comizio, RB
99—Michael Germino, DL

PENN ST.
65—Joe Bellas, T
John Runnells, LB
66—John Runnells, LB
67—Rich Buzin, OT
69—Charlie Pittman, HB
Dennis Onkotz, LB
71—Dave Joyner, OT
72—Bruce Bannon, DE
73—Mark Markovich, OG
76—Chuck Benjamin, OT
78—Keith Dorney, OT
82—Todd Blackledge, QB
Harry Hamilton, DB
Scott Radicec, LB
83—Harry Hamilton, LB
84—Lance Hamilton, DB
Carmen Masciantonio, LB
85—Lance Hamilton, DB

86—John Shaffer, QB
94—Jeff Hartings, OL
Tony Pittman, DB
95—Jeff Hartings, OL
99—Travis Forney, PK
2002—Joe Iorio, OL

PITTSBURG ST.
72—Jay Sperry, RB
89—Brett Potts, DL
91—Mike Brockel, OL
92—Mike Brockel, OL
96—Brian Moorman, P
97—Brian Moorman, P
98—Ben Petersen, DL
2000—Chris Gab, LB
01—Caleb White, DL

PITTSBURGH
52—Dick Deitrick, DT
54—Lou Palatella, T
56—Joe Walton, E
58—John Guzik, G
76—Jeff Delaney, LB
80—Greg Meisner, DL
81—Rob Fada, OG
82—Rob Fada, OG
J.C. Pelusi, DL
88—Mark Stepnoski, OL
2002—Vince Crochunis, DL

PORTLAND ST.
72—Bill Dials, T
77—John Urness, WR
78—John Urness, WR
2000—Chris Cain, DL

PRINCETON
68—Dick Sandler, DT
76—Kevin Fox, OG
82—Kevin Guthrie, WR
83—Kevin Guthrie, WR
98—Alex Sierk, PK

PUGET SOUND
82—Buster Crook, DB

PURDUE
56—Len Dawson, QB
60—Jerry Beabout, T
65—Sal Ciampi, G
67—Jim Beirne, E
Lance Olssen, DT
68—Tim Foley, DB
69—Tim Foley, DB
Mike Phipps, QB
Bill Yanchar, DT
73—Bob Hoftiezer, DE
79—Ken Loushin, DL
80—Tim Seneff, DB
81—Tim Seneff, DB
89—Bruce Brineman, OL
2000—Drew Brees, QB
02—John Standeford, WR

RENSSELAER
95—Alic Scott, OL
96—Dan McGovern, RB
97—Chris Cochran, DL
98—Jason Kepler, OL
99—Jason Kepler, OL
2002—Flynn Cochran, WR

RHODE ISLAND
76—Richard Moser, RB
77—Richard Moser, RB

RHODES
90—Robert Heck, DL

RICE
52—Richard Chapman, DG
53—Richard Chapman, DG
54—Dicky Maegle, B
69—Steve Bradshaw, DG
79—LaMont Jefferson, LB
83—Brian Patterson, DB
95—Jay Lamy, DB

ROCHESTER
82—Bob Cordaro, LB
92—Jeremy Hurd, RB
93—Jeremy Hurd, RB
2000—Brian Kowalski, LB

ROSE-HULMAN
78—Rick Matovich, DL
79—Scott Lindner, DL

80—Scott Lindner, DL
Jim Novacek, P
83—Jack Grote, LB
84—Jack Grote, LB
88—Greg Kremer, LB
Shawn Ferron, PK
89—Shawn Ferron, PK
90—Ed Huonden, WR
92—Greg Hubbard, OL
93—Greg Hubbard, OL
2002— Jesse McQuiston, DB
Tim Swan, LB

SAGINAW VALLEY
93—Troy Hendrickson, PK

ST. CLOUD ST.
88—Rick Rodgers, DB
89—Rick Rodgers, DB

ST. FRANCIS (PA.)
93—Todd Eckenroad, WR
98—Matt Farabaugh, LB

ST. JOHN'S (MINN.)
72—Jim Kruzich, E
79—Terry Geraghty, DB
94—Chris Palmer, WR
Matthew Malmberg, RB
95—Chris Palmer, WR
97—Matt Emmerich, DB

ST. JOHN'S (N.Y.)
93—Anthony Russo, RB

ST. JOSEPH'S (IND.)
77—Mike Bettinger, DB
78—Mike Bettinger, DB
79—Mike Bettinger, DB
85—Ralph Laura, OT
88—Keith Woodason, OL
89—Jeff Fairchild, P

ST. NORBERT
86—Matthew Lang, LB
Karl Zacharias, P
87—Karl Zacharias, PK
Matthew Lang, LB
88—Mike Whitehouse, WR
89—Mike Whitehouse, WR
99—Mike Krueger, WR

ST. OLAF
61—Dave Hindermann, T

ST. THOMAS (MINN.)
73—Mark Dienhart, T
74—Mark Dienhart, T
77—Tom Kelly, OG
80—Doug Groebner, C
94—Curt Behrns, DB
2000—Jake Barkley, RB
01—Jake Barkley, RB
Andrew Hilliard, WR
02—Jake Barkley, RB
Andrew Hilliard, WR

SALVE REGINA
98—Mark DeBiasio, RB
99—Mark DeBiasio, RB

SAM HOUSTON ST.
72—Walter Anderson, KS
73—Walter Anderson, KS
93—Kevin Riley, DB

SAN DIEGO
87—Bryan Day, DB
88—Bryan Day, DB
94—Doug Popovich, DB
95—Doug Popovich, DB
96—Jeb Dougherty, DB

SAN DIEGO ST.
98—Scott Auerbach, DB

SAN JOSE ST.
75—Tim Toews, OG

SANTA CLARA
71—Ron Sani, IL
73—Alex Damascus, RB
74—Steve Lagorio, LB
75—Mark Tiernan, LB
76—Lou Marengo, KS
Mark Tiernan, LB
80—Dave Alfaro, QB

SEWANEE
2002—Ben Tuck, PK

SHIPPENSBURG
76—Tony Winter, LB
82—Dave Butler, DL
94—Joel Yohn, PK
95—Joel Yohn, PK

SIMPSON
98—Guy Leman, RB

SOUTH CAROLINA
87—Mark Fryer, OL
88—Mark Fryer, OL
91—Joe Reeves, LB

SOUTH DAKOTA
78—Scott Pollock, QB
82—Jerus Campbell, DL
83—Jeff Sime, T
87—Dan Sonnek, RB
2002—Jarrod Edelen, P

SOUTH DAKOTA ST.
74—Bob Gissler, E
75—Bill Matthews, T
77—Bill Matthews, DE
79—Tony Harris, PK
Paul Kippley, DB

SOUTHERN CALIFORNIA
52—Dick Nunis, DB
59—Mike McKeever, G
60—Mike McKeever, G
Marlin McKeever, E
65—Charles Arrobio, T
67—Steve Sogge, QB
68—Steve Sogge, QB
69—Harry Khasigian, OG
73—Pat Haden, QB
74—Pat Haden, QB
78—Rich Dimler, DL
79—Brad Budde, OG
Paul McDonald, QB
Keith Van Horne, T
84—Duane Bickett, LB
85—Matt Koart, DL
86—Jeffrey Bregel, OG
88—John Jackson, WR
89—John Jackson, WR
95—Jeremy Hogue, OL
Matt Keneley, DL
96—Matt Keneley, DL

SOUTHERN COLO.
83—Dan DeRose, LB

SOUTHERN CONN. ST.
84—Gerald Carbonaro, OL

SOUTHERN ILL.
70—Sam Finocchio, G
88—Charles Harmke, RB
91—Dwayne Summers, DL
Jon Manley, L

SOUTHERN METHODIST
52—Dave Powell, E
53—Darrell Lafitte, G
54—Raymond Berry, E
55—David Hawk, G
57—Tom Koenig, G
58—Tom Koenig, G
62—Raymond Schoenke, T
66—John LaGrone, MG
Lynn Thornhill, OG
68—Jerry LeVias, OE
72—Cleve Whitener, LB
83—Brian O'Meara, T

SOUTHERN MISS.
92—James Singleton, DL
97—Jeremy Lindley, OL

SOUTHERN ORE.
97—Ian Reid, OL

SOUTHERN UTAH
88—Jim Andrus, RB
90—Steve McDowell, P

SOUTHWEST MO. ST.
73—Kent Stringer, QB
75—Kent Stringer, QB
78—Steve Newbold, WR

SOUTHWEST ST.
88—Bruce Saugstad, DB

SOUTHWEST TEX. ST.
72—Jimmy Jowers, LB
73—Jimmy Jowers, LB

78—Mike Ferris, OG
79—Mike Ferris, G
Allen Kiesling, DL
81—Mike Miller, QB

SPRINGFIELD
71—Bruce Rupert, LB
84—Sean Flanders, DL
85—Sean Flanders, DL
2002—Ben Bristol, OL

STANFORD
70—John Sande, C
Terry Ewing, DB
75—Don Stevenson, RB
76—Don Stevenson, RB
77—Guy Benjamin, QB
78—Vince Mulroy, WR
Jim Stephens, OG
79—Pat Bowe, TE
Milt McColl, LB
Joe St. Geme, DB
81—John Bergren, DL
Darrin Nelson, RB
82—John Bergren, DL
83—John Bergren, DL
85—Matt Soderlund, LB
87—Brad Muster, RB
90—Ed McCaffrey, WR
91—Tommy Vardell, RB
94—Justin Armour, WR
99—Troy Walters, WR

SUL ROSS ST.
73—Archie Nexon, RB

SUSQUEHANNA
75—Gerry Huesken, T
76—Gerry Huesken, T
80—Dan Distasio, LB
99—Dave Wonderlick, OL
2000—Dave Wonderlick, OL
02—Mike Bowman, QB

SYRACUSE
60—Fred Mautino, E
71—Howard Goodman, LB
83—Tony Romano, LB
84—Tim Green, DL
85—Tim Green, DL
99—Mark Baniewicz, OL

TARLETON ST.
81—Ricky Bush, RB
90—Mike Loveless, OL

TENNESSEE
56—Charles Rader, T
57—Bill Johnson, G
65—Mack Gentry, DT
67—Bob Johnson, C
70—Tim Priest, DB
80—Timothy Irwin, OT
82—Mike Terry, DL
97—Peyton Manning, QB

TENN.-MARTIN
74—Randy West, E

TENNESSEE TECH
87—Andy Rittenhouse, DL
99—Wes Gallagher, OL

TEXAS
59—Maurice Doke, G
61—Johnny Treadwell, G
62—Johnny Treadwell, G
Pat Culpepper, B
63—Duke Carlisle, B
66—Gene Bledsoe, OT
67—Mike Perrin, DE
Corby Robertson, LB
68—Corby Robertson, LB
Scott Henderson, LB
69—Scott Henderson, LB
Bill Zapalac, DE
70—Scott Henderson, LB
Bill Zapalac, LB
72—Mike Bayer, S
Tommy Keel, S
Steve Oxley, T
73—Tommy Keel, S
83—Doug Dawson, G
88—Lee Brockman, DL
95—Pat Fitzgerald, TE
96—Pat Fitzgerald, TE
97—Dusty Renfro, LB

UTEP
88—Pat Hegarty, QB

TEXAS A&M
56—Jack Pardee, B
71—Steve Luebbehusen, LB
76—Kevin Monk, LB
77—Kevin Monk, LB
85—Kip Corrington, DB
86—Kip Corrington, DB
87—Kip Corrington, DB
2001—Seth McKinney, OL

TEX. A&M-COMMERCE
77—Mike Hall, OT

TEX. A&M-KINGSVILLE
72—Floyd Goodwin, T
73—Johnny Jackson, E
76—Wade Whitmer, DL
77—Joe Henke, LB
       Wade Whitmer, DL
78—Wade Whitmer, DL

TCU
52—Marshall Harris, T
55—Hugh Pitts, C
       Jim Swink, B
56—Jim Swink, B
57—John Nikkel, E
68—Jim Ray, G
72—Scott Walker, C
74—Terry Drennan, DB
80—John McClean, DL
2002—Nick Browne, PK

TEXAS TECH
72—Jeff Jobe, E
79—Maury Buford, P
83—Chuck Alexander, DB
93—Robert King, P
99—Keith Cockrum, LB
2002—Kliff Kingsbury, QB

THOMAS MORE
97—Mike Bramlage Jr., DB

TOLEDO
83—Michael Matz, DL
95—Craig Dues, LB
2001—Todd France, PK

TOWSON
2000—Adam Overbey, WR

TRINITY (CONN.)
96—Joseph DeAngelis, OL

TRINITY (TEX.)
92—Jeff Bryan, OL
97—Mark Byarlay, RB

TRUMAN
73—Tom Roberts, T
78—Keith Driscoll, LB
79—Keith Driscoll, LB
92—K. C. Conaway, P
2001—Austin Lepper, PK
       Lance Dorsey, DB

TUFTS
70—Bruce Zinsmeister, DL
81—Brian Gallagher, OG
83—Richard Guiunta, G
98—Eric Brum, DL

TULANE
71—David Hebert, DB

TULSA
64—Howard Twilley, E
65—Howard Twilley, E
74—Mack Lancaster, T
95—David Millwee, OL
96—Levi Gillen, DB
97—Levi Gillen, DB
2001—Drew McLaughlin, DL

UCLA
52—Ed Flynn, G
       Donn Moomaw, LB
53—Ira Pauly, C
54—Sam Boghosian, G
66—Ray Armstrong, E
75—John Sciarra, QB
77—John Fowler, LB
81—Cormac Carney, WR
       Tim Wrightman, TE
82—Cormac Carney, WR

85—Mike Hartmeier, OG
92—Carlton Gray, DB
95—George Kase, DL
98—Shawn Stuart, OL

UNION (N.Y.)
71—Tom Anacher, LB
73—Dave Ricks, DB
87—Richard Romer, DL
93—Greg Oswitt, OL
96—Roger Egbert, PK

URSINUS
86—Chuck Odgers, DB
87—Chuck Odgers, LB

UTAH
64—Mel Carpenter, T
71—Scott Robbins, DB
73—Steve Odom, RB
76—Dick Graham, E

UTAH ST.
61—Merlin Olsen, T
69—Gary Anderson, LB
74—Randy Stockham, DE
75—Randy Stockham, DE

VALDOSTA ST.
93—Chris Hatcher, QB
94—Chris Hatcher, QB

VANDERBILT
58—Don Donnell, C
68—Jim Burns, DB
74—Doug Martin, E
75—Damon Regen, LB
77—Greg Martin, K
83—Phil Roach, WR
2002—Hunter Hillenmeyer, LB

VILLANOVA
86—Ron Sency, RB
88—Peter Lombardi, RB
92—Tim Matas, DL

VIRGINIA
72—Tom Kennedy, OG
75—Bob Meade, DT
92—Tom Burns, LB
93—Tom Burns, LB
95—Tiki Barber, RB
96—Tiki Barber, RB
97—Stephen Phelan, DB

VMI
78—Craig Jones, PK
79—Craig Jones, PK
84—David Twillie, OL
86—Dan Young, DL
88—Anthony McIntosh, DB

VIRGINIA TECH
67—Frank Loria, DB
72—Tommy Carpenito, LB
2001—Andre Davis, WR

WABASH
70—Roscoe Fouts, DB
71—Kendrick Shelburne, DT
82—Dave Broecker, QB

WARTBURG
75—James Charles Peterson, DB
76—Randy Groth, DB
77—Neil Mandsager, LB
90—Jerrod Staack, OL
93—Koby Kreinbring, LB
94—Vince Penningroth, DL
95—Vince Penningroth, DL
99—Paul Seberger, TE
2000—Mike Trettin, OL
01—Seth Roberson, OL

WASHINGTON
55—Jim Houston, E
63—Mike Briggs, T
64—Rick Redman, G
65—Steve Bramwell, DB
79—Bruce Harrell, LB
81—Mark Jerue, LB
       Chuck Nelson, PK
82—Chuck Nelson, PK
86—David Rill, LB
87—David Rill, LB
91—Ed Cunningham, OL

WASHINGTON (MO.)
97—Brad Klein, LB

WASH. & JEFF.
92—Raymond Cross, DL
93—Michael Jones, OL
94—Michael Jones, OL

WASH. & LEE
75—John Cocklereece, DB
78—George Ballantyne, LB
92—Evans Edwards, OL
2001—Jay Thomas, TE
02—John Melillo, OL

WASHINGTON ST.
89—Jason Hanson, PK
90—Lee Tilleman, DL
       Jason Hanson, PK
91—Jason Hanson, PK

WAYNE ST. (MICH.)
71—Gary Schultz, DB
72—Walt Stasinski, DB

WAYNE ST. (NEB.)
99—Jeff Shabram, OL

WAYNESBURG
77—John Culp, RB
78—John Culp, RB
89—Andrew Barrish, OL
90—Andrew Barrish, OL
91—Karl Petrof, OL
2000—Jason Berkhimer, WR

WEBER ST.
97—Cameron Quayle, TE

WEST CHESTER
83—Eric Wentling, K
86—Gerald Desmond, K

WEST VIRGINIA
52—Paul Bischoff, E
54—Fred Wyant, B
55—Sam Huff, T
70—Kim West, K
80—Oliver Luck, QB
81—Oliver Luck, QB
83—Jeff Hostetler, QB
92—Mike Compton, OL
94—Matt Taffoni, LB
98—Eric de Groh, OL

WESTERN CARO.
75—Mike Wade, E
76—Mike Wade, LB
84—Eddie Maddox, RB

WESTERN ILL.
61—Jerry Blew, G
85—Jeff McKinney, RB
91—David Fierke, OL

WESTERN KY.
71—James Barber, LB
81—Tim Ford, DL
84—Mark Fatkin, OL
85—Mark Fatkin, OG
95—Brian Bixler, OL
2002—Brian Lowder, DB

WESTERN MICH.
70—Jon Bull, OT
94—Rich Kaiser, DL
95—Rich Kaiser, DL

WESTERN ORE.
61—Francis Tresler, C

WESTERN ST.
78—Bill Campbell, DB
88—Damon Lockhart, RB

WESTERN WASH.
2000—Erik Totten, DB

WESTMINSTER (PA.)
73—Bob Clark, G
77—Scott McLuckey, LB
93—Brian Wilson, OL
98—Brian Mihok, DL

WHEATON (ILL.)
73—Bill Hyer, E
75—Eugene Campbell, RB
76—Eugene Campbell, RB
88—Paul Sternenberg, DL
92—Bart Moseman, DB
94—Pedro Arruza, RB
95—Jeff Brown, QB
       Pedro Arruzo, RB

WHITTIER
86—Brent Kane, DL

WIDENER
98—Brendon Richards, LB
2001—T.J. Hess, DB

WILKES
70—Al Kenney, C
2000—Frank McCabe, TE
02—Mike Liberski, OL

WILLAMETTE
61—Stuart Hall

WILLIAM & MARY
74—John Gerdelman, RB
75—Ken Smith, DB
77—Ken Smith, DB
78—Robert Musculus, TE
84—Mark Kelso, DB
88—Chris Gessner, DB
90—Jeff Nielsen, LB
93—Craig Staub, DL

WM. PATERSON
92—John Trust, RB

WILMINGTON (OHIO)
99—Kevin Otte, DB

WINONA ST.
93—Nathan Gruber, DB
94—Nathan Gruber, DB
97—Travis Walch, RB
2001—Adam Lilla, WR

WISCONSIN
52—Bob Kennedy, DG
53—Alan Ameche, B
54—Alan Ameche, B
58—Jon Hobbs, B
59—Dale Hackbart, B
62—Pat Richter, E
63—Ken Bowman, C
72—Rufus Ferguson, RB
82—Kyle Borland, LB
87—Don Davey, DL
88—Don Davey, DL
89—Don Davey, DL
90—Don Davey, DL

WIS.-EAU CLAIRE
74—Mark Anderson, RB
80—Mike Zeihen, DB
2001—Mike Bestul, OL
02—Mike Bestul, OL

WIS.-LA CROSSE
95—Troy Harcey, WR
96—Troy Harcey, WR

WIS.-OSHKOSH
96—Rob Stoltz, WR
97—Ryan Hinske, WR
99—Craig Pierstoff, LB
2002—Justin Schneider, DL

WIS.-PLATTEVILLE
85—Mark Hintz, DB
       Mark Rae, P
86—Mike Hintz, QB
87—Mark Rae, P

WIS.-RIVER FALLS
91—Mike Olson, LB
95—Brian Izdepski, OT

WIS.-STEVENS POINT
97—Joel Hornby, DL

WIS.-WHITEWATER
95—Scott Hawig, OL
2000—Peter Katz, DL
01—Peter Katz, DL

WITTENBERG
80—Bill Beach, DB
81—Bill Beach, DB
82—Tom Jones, OT
88—Paul Kungl, WR
90—Victor Terebuh, DB

WOFFORD
2000—Brian Bodor, DL

WOOSTER
73—Dave Foy, LB
77—Blake Moore, C
78—Blake Moore, C
79—Blake Moore, C

80— Dale Fortner, DB
   John Weisensell, OG
99— Matt Mahaffey, P
WYOMING
65— Bob Dinges, DE
67— George Mills, OG
73— Mike Lopiccolo, OT

84— Bob Gustafson, OT
87— Patrick Arndt, OG
94— Ryan Christopherson, RB
95— Joe Cummings, DL
96— Jay Korth, OL
   Cory Wedel, PK
97— Jay Korth, OL
   Cory Wedel, PK

   Brian Lee, DB
98— Brian Brown, LB
YALE
68— Fred Morris, C
70— Tom Neville, DT
78— William Crowley, LB
81— Rich Diana, RB

   Frederick Leone, DL
89— Glover Lawrence, DL
91— Scott Wagner, DB
99— Eric Johnson, WR
YOUNGSTOWN ST.
93— John Quintana, TE
98— Anthony Pannunzio, DB

Bowl/All-Star Game Records

2003-04 Bowl Schedule

ALAMO BOWL
San Antonio, Texas, December 29, 2003, 9 p.m.
Derrick Fox, Executive Director
San Antonio Bowl Association, Inc.
100 Montana Street, Suite 3D01
San Antonio, Texas 78203-1031
www.alamobowl.com
Phone: 210/226-2695 Fax: 210/704-6399
Televising Network: ESPN
Facility: Alamodome
Capacity: 65,000
Presenting Sponsor: MasterCard
Teams: Big 10 #4 vs. Big 12 #4

AXA LIBERTY BOWL
Memphis, Tennessee, December 31, 2003, 3:30 p.m.
Steve Ehrhart, Executive Director
AXA Financial Group
3767 New Getwell Road
Memphis, Tennessee 38118
www.libertybowl.org
Phone: 901/795-7700 Fax: 901/795-7826
Televising Network: ESPN
Facility: Liberty Bowl Memorial Stadium
Capacity: 62,000
Title Sponsor: AXA Financial Group
Teams: Conference USA #1 vs. Mountain West #1

CAPITAL ONE BOWL
Orlando, Florida, January 1, 2004, 1 p.m.
Thomas P. Mickle, Executive Director
Florida Citrus Sports Association, Inc.
One Citrus Bowl Place
Orlando, Florida 32805-2451
www.fcsports.com
Phone: 407/423-2476 Fax: 407/425-8451
Televising Network: ABC
Facility: Florida Citrus Bowl
Capacity: 65,525
Title Sponsor: Capital One Financial Corporation
Teams: Southeastern #2 vs. Big Ten #2

CHICK-FIL-A PEACH BOWL
Atlanta, Georgia, January 2, 2004, 4:30 p.m.
Gary Stokan, President
Peach Bowl, Inc.
235 International Drive N.W.
Atlanta, Georgia 30303
www.peachbowl.com
Phone: 404/586-8500 Fax: 404/586-8508
Televising Network: ESPN
Facility: Georgia Dome
Capacity: 72,212
Title Sponsor: Chick-Fil-A
Teams: Southeastern #5 vs. Atlantic Coast #3

CONAGRA FOODS HAWAII BOWL
Honolulu, Hawaii, December 25, 2002, 8 p.m.
Jim Donovan, Executive Director
1357 Kapi'olani Boulevard, Suite 1450
Honolulu, Hawaii 96814-4358
www.hawaiibowl.com
Phone: 808/983-1132 Fax: 808/955-0200
Television Network: ESPN
Facility: Aloha Stadium
Capacity: 50,000
Teams: Western Athletic vs. Conference USA #4/#5

CONTINENTAL TIRE BOWL
Charlotte, North Carolina, December 27, 2003,
Time to be determined
Ken Haines, Executive Director
2815 Coliseum Centre Drive, Suite 200
Charlotte, North Carolina 28217
Phone: 704/378-4440
Television Network: ESPN or ESPN2
Facility: Ericsson Stadium
Capacity: 73,367
Title Sponsor: Continental Tires
Teams: Big East #3/#4/#5 vs. Atlantic Coast #5/#6

CRUCIAL.COM HUMANITARIAN BOWL
Boise, Idaho, January 3, 2004, Noon
Gary Beck, Executive Director
1109 Main Street
Lower Lobby, Suite B
Boise, Idaho 83702
www.humanitarianbowl.org

Phone: 208/424-1011 Fax: 208/424-1121
Televising Network: ESPN or ESPN2
Facility: Bronco Stadium
Capacity: 30,000
Title Sponsor: Crucial Technology
Teams: Western Athletic vs. At Large

DIAMOND WALNUT SAN FRANCISCO BOWL
San Francisco, California, December 31, 2003,
10:30 p.m.
Gary Cavalli, Executive Director
Pacific Bell Park
24 Willie Mays Plaza
San Francisco, CA 94107
Tel: 415/972-1812
Fax: 415/947-2925
gcavalli@sfbowl.com
www.diamondsfbowl.com
Phone: 650/851-6761 Fax: 650/851-0798
Television Network: ESPN2
Facility: Pacific Bell Park
Capacity: 48,750 (37,000 for football)
Title Sponsor: Diamond Walnut Growers, Inc.
Teams: Mountain West #3 vs. Big East #3/#4/#5

FEDEX ORANGE BOWL
Miami, Florida, January 1, 2004, 8 p.m.
Keith V. Tribble, Chief Executive Officer
Orange Bowl Committee
601 Brickell Key Drive, Suite 206
Miami, Florida 33131
www.orangebowl.org
Phone: 305/371-4600 Fax: 305/371-8565
Televising Network: ABC
Facility: Pro Player Stadium
Capacity: 72,230
Title Sponsor: Federal Express
Teams: Bowl Championship Series

FORT WORTH BOWL
Fort Worth, Texas, December 23, 2003, 7:30 p.m.
Chuck Gerber, Executive Vice President
ESPN Regional
11001 Rushmore Drive
Charlotte, North Carolina 28277
Phone: 704/973-5200 Fax: 704/973-5090
Televising Network: ESPN
Facility: Amon G. Carter Stadium; Texas Christian University
Capacity: 46,000
Title Sponsor: None
Teams: Big 12 vs. Conference USA

GAYLORD HOTELS MUSIC CITY BOWL
Nashville, Tennessee, December 31, 2003, Noon
Scott Ramsey, Executive Director
211 Commerce Street, Suite 100
Nashville, Tennessee 37201
www.musiccitybowl.com
Phone: 615/743-3130 Fax: 615/244-3540
Televising Network: ESPN
Facility: Adelphia Coliseum
Capacity: 67,000
Title Sponsor: Gaylord Entertainment Company
Teams: Big Ten #6 vs. Southeastern #6

GMAC BOWL
Mobile, Alabama, December 18, 2002, 7:30 p.m.
Jerry Silverstein, President
GMAC Bowl
1000 Hillcrest Road, Suite 115
Mobile, Alabama 36695
www.gmacbowl.com
Phone: 251/635-0011 Fax: 251/635-0014
Television Network: ESPN2
Facility: Ladd Peebles Stadium
Title Sponsors: Mobile Alabama, Inc. and GMAC Financial Services
Capacity: 40,048
Teams: Conference USA #2 vs. Mid-American #2

HOUSTON BOWL
Houston, Texas, December 30, 2003, 4:30 p.m.
Jerry Ippoliti, President/CEO

Reliant Park
8400 Kirby Drive
Houston, Texas 77054
www.houstonbowl.net
Phone: 713/799-9561 Fax: 713/799-9599
Televising Network: ESPN or ESPN2
Facility: Reliant Stadium
Capacity: 69,500
Teams: Conference USA #3 vs. Big 12 #5/#6/#7

INSIGHT BOWL
Tempe, Arizona, December 26, 2003, 8:30 p.m.
John Junker, Executive Director
Insight Bowl
120 South Ash Avenue
Tempe, Arizona 85281
Phone: 480/350-0900 Fax: 480/350-0916
Televising Network: ESPN or ESPN2
Facility: Bank One Ballpark
Capacity: 43,463
Title Sponsor: Insight Enterprises
Teams: Big East #3/#4/#5 or Notre Dame vs. Pacific 10 #4

LAS VEGAS BOWL
Las Vegas, Nevada, December 24, 2003, 7:30 p.m.
Tina Kunzer-Murphy, Executive Director
Las Vegas Convention & Visitors Authority
4505 Maryland Parkway
Box 45 0001
Las Vegas, Nevada 89154-0001
www.lvbowl.com
Phone: 702/ 895-2868 Fax: 702/ 892-7515
Televising Network: ESPN
Facility: Sam Boyd Stadium
Capacity: 40,000
Title Sponsor: None
Teams: Pacific 10 #5 vs. Mountain West #2

MAINSTAY INDEPENDENCE BOWL
Shreveport, Louisiana, December 31, 2003, 7:30 p.m.
Glen Krupica, Executive Director
Independence Bowl Foundation
700 Clyde Fant Parkway
Shreveport, Louisiana 71166
www.independencebowl.org
Phone: 318/221-0712 Fax: 318/221-7366
Televising Network: ESPN or ESPN2
Facility: Independence Stadium
Capacity: 50,000
Title Sponsor: MainStay Funds
Teams: Big 12 #5/#6/#7 vs. Southeastern #7

MAZDA TANGERINE BOWL
Orlando, Florida, December 22, 2003, 5:30 p.m.
Thomas P. Mickle, Executive Director
Florida Citrus Sports
One Citrus Bowl Place
Orlando, Florida 32805
www.fcsports.com
Phone: 407/423-2476 Fax: 407/425-8451
Televising Network: ESPN
Facility: Florida Citrus Bowl
Capacity: 65,465
Title Sponsor: Mazda North American Operations
Teams: Atlantic Coast #4 or #5 vs. Big 12 #5/#6/#7

MOTOR CITY BOWL
Pontiac, Michigan, December 26, 2003, 5 p.m.
Ken Hoffman, Executive Director
Ford Division (Ford Motor Company)
1200 Featherstone Drive
Pontiac, Michigan 48342
www.motorcitybowl.com
Phone: 248/456-1694 Fax: 248/456-1983
Televising Network: ESPN or ESPN2
Facility: Ford Field
Capacity: 65,000
Presenting Sponsors/Host: General Motors/Daimler Chrysler/Ford Motor Company
Teams: Mid-American #1 vs. Big 10 #7

NEW ORLEANS BOWL
New Orleans, Louisiana, December 16, 2003, 7 p.m.
Ron Maestri, Executive Director
New Orleans Bowl
New Orleans Center
1400 Poydras Street, Suite 918

New Orleans, Louisiana 70112
www.neworleansbowl.org
Phone: 504/525-5678 Fax: 504/529-1622
Televising Network: ESPN2
Facility: Louisiana Superdome
Capacity: 76,791
Title Sponsor: Greater New Orleans Sports Foundation
Teams: Sun Belt #1 vs. Conference USA #4/#5

NOKIA SUGAR BOWL
New Orleans, Louisiana, January 4, 2004, 8 p.m.
Paul J. Hoolahan, Executive Director
The Sugar Bowl Committee
1500 Sugar Bowl Drive
New Orleans, Louisiana 70112
www.nokiasugarbowl.org
Phone: 504/525-8573 Fax: 504/525-4867
Televising Network: ABC
Facility: Louisiana Superdome
Capacity: 76,791
Title Sponsor: Nokia Mobile Telephones
Teams: Bowl Championship Series

OUTBACK BOWL
Tampa, Florida, January 1, 2004, 11 a.m.
James P. McVay, President/CEO
Tampa Bay Bowl Association, Inc.
4511 North Himes Avenue, Suite 260
Tampa, Florida 33614
www.outbackbowl.com
Phone: 813/874-2695 Fax: 813/873-1959
Televising Network: ESPN
Facility: Raymond James Stadium
Capacity: 65,655
Title Sponsor: Outback Steakhouse, Inc.
Teams: Big Ten #3 vs. Southeastern #3/#4

PACIFIC LIFE HOLIDAY BOWL
San Diego, California, December 30, 2002, 8 p.m.
Bruce Binkowski, Executive Director
San Diego Bowl Game Association
P.O. Box 601400
San Diego, California 92160
www.holidaybowl.com
Phone: 619/283-5808 Fax: 619/281-7947
Televising Network: ESPN
Facility: Qualcomm Stadium

Capacity: 69,000
Title Sponsor: Pacific Life Insurance Company
Teams: Pacific 10 #2 vs. Big 12 #3

ROSE BOWL
Pasadena, California, January 1, 2004, 5 p.m.
John Dorger, CEO
Pasadena Tournament of Roses Association
391 South Orange Grove Boulevard
Pasadena, California 91184
www.tournamentofroses.com
Alternate Contact: Kevin Ash, CAO, Rose Bowl Game
Phone: 626/449-4100 Fax: 626/449-9786
Televising Network: ABC
Facility: Rose Bowl
Capacity: 90,000
Teams: Bowl Championship Series

SBC COTTON BOWL CLASSIC
Dallas, Texas, January 2, 2004, 2 p.m.
Rick Baker, President
Cotton Bowl Athletic Association
Physical Address:
1300 W. Mockingbird Lane, Suite 500
Dallas, Texas 75247
Mailing Address:
P.O. Box 569420
Dallas, Texas 75356
www.sbccottonbowl.com
Phone: 214/634-7525 Fax: 214/634-7764
Televising Network: Fox
Facility: Cotton Bowl Stadium
Capacity: 68,252
Title Sponsor: SBC Communications
Teams: Big 12 #2 vs. Southeastern #3/#4

SILICON VALLEY CLASSIC
San Jose, California, December 30, 2003, 10:30 p.m.
Chuck Shelton, Executive Director
Silicon Valley Football Classic, Inc.
1393 South 7th Street
San Jose, California 95112
www.bowlbythebay.com
Phone: 408/924-1468 Fax: 408/924-1163
Televising Network: ESPN2
Facility: Spartan Stadium; San Jose State University
Capacity: 30,578

Title Sponsor: None
Teams: Western Athletic vs. At Large

SUN BOWL
El Paso, Texas, December 31, 2003, 2 p.m.
Bernie Olivas, Executive Director
Sun Bowl Association
4100 Rio Bravo, Suite 303
El Paso, Texas 79902-1049
www.sunbowl.org
Phone: 915/533-4416 Fax: 915/533-0661
Televising Network: CBS
Facility: Sun Bowl Stadium
Capacity: 51,171
Title Sponsor: Wells Fargo Corporation
Teams: Big 10 #5 vs. Pacific 10 #3

TOSTITOS FIESTA BOWL
Tempe, Arizona, January 2, 2004, 8 p.m.
John Junker, President
Arizona Sports Foundation
120 South Ash Avenue
Tempe, Arizona 85281
www.tostitosfiestabowl.com
Phone: 480/350-0900 Fax: 480/350-0916
Televising Network: ABC
Facility: Sun Devil Stadium
Capacity: 73,185
Title Sponsor: Frito-Lay/Tostitos
Teams: Bowl Championship Series

TOYOTA GATOR BOWL
Jacksonville, Florida, January 1, 2004, 12:30 p.m.
Richard Catlett, President
Toyota Motor Sales/Southeast Toyota
One Gator Bowl Boulevard
Jacksonville, Florida 32202
www.gatorbowl.com
Phone: 904/798-1700 Fax: 904/632-2080
Televising Network: NBC
Facility: Alltel Stadium
Capacity: 76,9451
Title Sponsor: Toyota Motor Sales of America
Teams: Atlantic Coast #2 vs. Big East #2 or Notre Dame

2002-03 Bowl Results

Game-by-Game Summaries

NEW ORLEANS BOWL
December 17, 2002
Louisiana Superdome
New Orleans, Louisiana

Cincinnati	7	0	6	9	—	19
North Texas	3	14	7	0	—	24

Attendance: 19,024

GMAC BOWL
December 18, 2002
Ladd-Peebles Stadium
Mobile, Alabama

Marshall	7	10	7	14	—	38
Louisville	0	7	0	8	—	15

Attendance: 40,646

MAZDA TANGERINE BOWL
December 23, 2002
Florida Citrus Bowl
Orlando, Florida

Texas Tech	17	17	7	14	—	55
Clemson	0	2	7	6	—	15

Attendance: 21,689

SEGA SPORTS LAS VEGAS BOWL
December 25, 2002
Sam Boyd Stadium
Las Vegas, Nevada

New Mexico	6	0	0	7	—	13
UCLA	3	3	7	14	—	27

Attendance: 30,324

CONAGRA FOODS HAWAII BOWL
December 25, 2002
Aloha Stadium
Honolulu, Hawaii

Hawaii	7	7	0	14	—	28
Tulane	0	6	20	10	—	36

Attendance: 31,535

MOTOR CITY BOWL
December 26, 2002
Ford Field
Detroit, Michigan

Boston College	14	28	6	3	—	51
Toledo	3	15	7	0	—	25

Attendance: 51,872

INSIGHT BOWL
December 26, 2002
Bank One Ballpark
Phoenix, Arizona

Pittsburgh	7	3	14	14	—	38
Oregon St.	7	3	3	0	—	13

Attendance: 40,533

HOUSTON BOWL
December 27, 2002
Reliant Stadium
Houston, Texas

Southern Miss.	3	10	10	0	—	23
Oklahoma St.	10	10	0	13	—	33

Attendance: 44,687

MAINSTAY INDEPENDENCE BOWL
December 27, 2002
Independence Stadium
Shreveport, Louisiana

Nebraska	3	14	3	3	—	23
Mississippi	0	14	10	3	—	27

Attendance: 46,096

PACIFIC LIFE HOLIDAY BOWL
December 27, 2002
Qualcomm Stadium
San Diego, California

Kansas St.	0	14	0	20	—	34
Arizona St.	0	20	0	7	—	27

Attendance: 58,717

CONTINENTAL TIRE BOWL
December 27, 2002
Ericsson Stadium
Charlotte, North Carolina

West Virginia	10	0	6	6	— 22
Virginia	7	21	10	10	— 48

Attendance: 73,535

ALAMO BOWL PRESENTED BY MASTERCARD
December 28, 2002
Alamodome
San Antonio, Texas

Colorado	14	0	14	0	0	—28
Wisconsin	7	14	0	7	3	—31

Attendance: 50,690

GAYLORD HOTELS MUSIC CITY BOWL
December 30, 2002
Adelphia Coliseum
Nashville, Tennessee

Arkansas	7	0	0	7	— 14
Minnesota	6	6	7	10	— 29

Attendance: 39,183

SEATTLE BOWL
December 30, 2002
Seahawks Stadium
Seattle, Washington

Wake Forest	7	14	10	7	— 38
Oregon	3	7	7	0	— 17

Attendance: 38,241

CRUCIAL.COM HUMANITARIAN BOWL
December 31, 2002
Bronco Stadium
Boise, Idaho

Iowa St.	3	7	0	6	— 16
Boise St.	0	7	14	13	— 34

Attendance: 30,446

WELLS FARGO SUN BOWL
December 31, 2002
Sun Bowl
El Paso, Texas

Washington	17	0	0	7	— 24
Purdue	0	14	17	3	— 34

Attendance: 48,917

AXA LIBERTY BOWL
December 31, 2002
Liberty Bowl Stadium
Memphis, Tennessee

Colorado St.	0	0	3	0	— 3
TCU	0	7	0	10	— 17

Attendance: 55,207

SILICON VALLEY CLASSIC
December 31, 2002
Spartan Stadium
San Jose, California

Georgia Tech	7	0	14	0	— 21
Fresno St.	3	10	7	10	— 30

Attendance: 10,132

CHICK-FIL-A PEACH BOWL
December 31, 2002
Georgia Dome
Atlanta, Georgia

Tennessee	0	3	0	0	— 3
Maryland	7	10	3	10	— 30

Attendance: 68,330

DIAMOND WALNUT SAN FRANCISCO BOWL
December 31, 2002
Pacific Bell Park
San Francisco, California

Air Force	10	0	0	3	— 13
Virginia Tech	7	3	7	3	— 20

Attendance: 25,966

OUTBACK BOWL
January 1, 2003
Raymond James Stadium
Tampa, Florida

Florida	0	16	7	7	— 30
Michigan	7	14	14	3	— 38

SBC COTTON BOWL
January 1, 2003
Cotton Bowl Stadium
Dallas, Texas

LSU	10	7	0	3	— 20
Texas	7	14	7	7	— 35

Attendance: 70,817

TOYOTA GATOR BOWL
January 1, 2003
Alltel Stadium
Jacksonville, Florida

North Carolina St.	0	21	0	7	— 28
Notre Dame	3	0	3	0	— 6

Attendance: 73,491

CAPITAL ONE CITRUS BOWL
January 1, 2003
Florida Citrus Bowl
Orlando, Florida

Auburn	0	0	7	6	— 13
Penn St.	3	3	0	3	— 9

Attendance: 66,334

BOWL CHAMPIONSHIP SERIES 2002-03:
ROSE BOWL PRESENTED BY SONY
January 1, 2003
Rose Bowl
Pasadena, California

Oklahoma	3	14	3	14	— 34
Washington St.	0	0	0	14	— 14

Attendance: 86,848

NOKIA SUGAR BOWL
January 1, 2003
Louisiana Superdome
New Orleans, Louisiana

Florida St.	0	7	6	0	— 13
Georgia	3	14	6	3	— 26

Attendance: 74,269

FEDEX ORANGE BOWL
January 2, 2003
Pro Player Stadium
Miami, Florida

Iowa	10	0	0	7	— 17
Southern California	7	3	14	14	— 38

Attendance: 75,971

TOSTITOS FIESTA BOWL
January 3, 2003
Sun Devil Stadium
Tempe, Arizona

Ohio St.	0	14	3	0	7	7	—31
Miami (Fla.)	7	0	7	3	7	0	—24

Attendance: 77,502

All-Time Bowl-Game Results

Major Bowl Games

ROSE BOWL

Present Site: Pasadena, California
Stadium (Capacity): Rose Bowl (96,576)
Playing Surface: Grass
Playing Sites: Tournament Park, Pasadena (1902, 1916-22); Rose Bowl, Pasadena (1923-41); Duke Stadium, Durham, N.C. (1942); Rose Bowl (since 1943)

1-1-02—Michigan 49, Stanford 0
1-1-16—Washington St. 14, Brown 0
1-1-17—Oregon 14, Pennsylvania 0
1-1-18—Mare Island 19, Camp Lewis 7
1-1-19—Great Lakes 17, Mare Island 0
1-1-20—Harvard 7, Oregon 6
1-1-21—California 28, Ohio St. 0
1-2-22—California 0, Wash. & Jeff. 0
1-1-23—Southern California 14, Penn St. 3
1-1-24—Navy 14, Washington 14
1-1-25—Notre Dame 27, Stanford 10

1-1-26—Alabama 20, Washington 19
1-1-27—Alabama 7, Stanford 7
1-2-28—Stanford 7, Pittsburgh 6
1-1-29—Georgia Tech 8, California 7
1-1-30—Southern California 47, Pittsburgh 14
1-1-31—Alabama 24, Washington St. 0
1-1-32—Southern California 21, Tulane 12
1-2-33—Southern California 35, Pittsburgh 0
1-1-34—Columbia 7, Stanford 0
1-1-35—Alabama 29, Stanford 13
1-1-36—Stanford 7, Southern Methodist 0
1-1-37—Pittsburgh 21, Washington 0
1-1-38—California 13, Alabama 0
1-2-39—Southern California 7, Duke 3

1-1-40—Southern California 14, Tennessee 0
1-1-41—Stanford 21, Nebraska 13
1-1-42—Oregon St. 20, Duke 16 (at Durham)
1-1-43—Georgia 9, UCLA 0
1-1-44—Southern California 29, Washington 0
1-1-45—Southern California 25, Tennessee 0
1-1-46—Alabama 34, Southern California 14
1-1-47—Illinois 45, UCLA 14

1-1-48—Michigan 49, Southern California 0
1-1-49—Northwestern 20, California 14
1-2-50—Ohio St. 17, California 14
1-1-51—Michigan 14, California 6
1-1-52—Illinois 40, Stanford 7
1-1-53—Southern California 7, Wisconsin 0
1-1-54—Michigan St. 28, UCLA 20
1-1-55—Ohio St. 20, Southern California 7
1-2-56—Michigan St. 17, UCLA 14
1-1-57—Iowa 35, Oregon St. 19
1-1-58—Ohio St. 10, Oregon 7
1-1-59—Iowa 38, California 12
1-1-60—Washington 44, Wisconsin 8
1-2-61—Washington 17, Minnesota 7
1-1-62—Minnesota 21, UCLA 3
1-1-63—Southern California 42, Wisconsin 37
1-1-64—Illinois 17, Washington 7
1-1-65—Michigan 34, Oregon St. 7
1-1-66—UCLA 14, Michigan St. 12
1-2-67—Purdue 14, Southern California 13
1-1-68—Southern California 14, Indiana 3
1-1-69—Ohio St. 27, Southern California 16

1-1-70—Southern California 10, Michigan 3
1-1-71—Stanford 27, Ohio St. 17
1-1-72—Stanford 13, Michigan 12
1-1-73—Southern California 42, Ohio St. 17
1-1-74—Ohio St. 42, Southern California 21

1-1-75—Southern California 18, Ohio St. 17
1-1-76—UCLA 23, Ohio St. 10
1-1-77—Southern California 14, Michigan 6
1-2-78—Washington 27, Michigan 20
1-1-79—Southern California 17, Michigan 10

1-1-80—Southern California 17, Ohio St. 16
1-1-81—Michigan 23, Washington 6
1-1-82—Washington 28, Iowa 0
1-1-83—UCLA 24, Michigan 14
1-2-84—UCLA 45, Illinois 9

1-1-85—Southern California 20, Ohio St. 17
1-1-86—UCLA 45, Iowa 28
1-1-87—Arizona St. 22, Michigan 15
1-1-88—Michigan St. 20, Southern California 17
1-2-89—Michigan 22, Southern California 14

1-1-90—Southern California 17, Michigan 10
1-1-91—Washington 46, Iowa 34
1-1-92—Washington 34, Michigan 14
1-1-93—Michigan 38, Washington 31
1-1-94—Wisconsin 21, UCLA 16

1-2-95—Penn St. 38, Oregon 20
1-1-96—Southern California 41, Northwestern 32
1-1-97—Ohio St. 20, Arizona St. 17
1-1-98—Michigan 21, Washington St. 16
1-1-99—Wisconsin 38, UCLA 31

1-1-00—Wisconsin 17, Stanford 9
1-1-01—Washington 34, Purdue 24
1-3-02—Miami (Fla.) 37, Nebraska 14
1-1-03—Oklahoma 34, Washington St. 14

ORANGE BOWL

Present Site: Miami, Florida
Stadium (Capacity): Pro Player Stadium (72,230)
Playing Surface: Prescription Athletic Turf
Name Changes: Orange Bowl (1935-88); Federal Express Orange Bowl (since 1989)
Playing Sites: Miami Field Stadium (1935-37); Orange Bowl (1938-96); Joe Robbie Stadium, renamed Pro Player Stadium in 1996 (since 1997)

1-1-35—Bucknell 26, Miami (Fla.) 0
1-1-36—Catholic 20, Mississippi 0
1-1-37—Duquesne 13, Mississippi St. 12
1-1-38—Auburn 6, Michigan St. 0
1-2-39—Tennessee 17, Oklahoma 0

1-1-40—Georgia Tech 21, Missouri 7
1-1-41—Mississippi St. 14, Georgetown 7
1-1-42—Georgia 40, TCU 26
1-1-43—Alabama 37, Boston College 21
1-1-44—LSU 19, Texas A&M 14

1-1-45—Tulsa 26, Georgia Tech 12
1-1-46—Miami (Fla.) 13, Holy Cross 6
1-1-47—Rice 8, Tennessee 0
1-1-48—Georgia Tech 20, Kansas 14
1-1-49—Texas 41, Georgia 28

1-2-50—Santa Clara 21, Kentucky 13
1-1-51—Clemson 15, Miami (Fla.) 14
1-1-52—Georgia Tech 17, Baylor 14
1-1-53—Alabama 61, Syracuse 6
1-1-54—Oklahoma 7, Maryland 0

1-1-55—Duke 34, Nebraska 7
1-2-56—Oklahoma 20, Maryland 6
1-1-57—Colorado 27, Clemson 21
1-1-58—Oklahoma 48, Duke 21
1-1-59—Oklahoma 21, Syracuse 6

1-1-60—Georgia 14, Missouri 0
1-2-61—Missouri 21, Navy 14
1-1-62—LSU 25, Colorado 7
1-1-63—Alabama 17, Oklahoma 0
1-1-64—Nebraska 13, Auburn 7

1-1-65—Texas 21, Alabama 17
1-1-66—Alabama 39, Nebraska 28
1-2-67—Florida 27, Georgia Tech 12
1-1-68—Oklahoma 26, Tennessee 24
1-1-69—Penn St. 15, Kansas 14

1-1-70—Penn St. 10, Missouri 3
1-1-71—Nebraska 17, LSU 12
1-1-72—Nebraska 38, Alabama 6
1-1-73—Nebraska 40, Notre Dame 6
1-1-74—Penn St. 16, LSU 9

1-1-75—Notre Dame 13, Alabama 11
1-1-76—Oklahoma 14, Michigan 6
1-1-77—Ohio St. 27, Colorado 10
1-2-78—Arkansas 31, Oklahoma 6
1-1-79—Oklahoma 31, Nebraska 24

1-1-80—Oklahoma 24, Florida St. 7
1-1-81—Oklahoma 18, Florida St. 17
1-1-82—Clemson 22, Nebraska 15
1-1-83—Nebraska 21, LSU 20
1-2-84—Miami (Fla.) 31, Nebraska 30

1-1-85—Washington 28, Oklahoma 17
1-1-86—Oklahoma 25, Penn St. 10
1-1-87—Oklahoma 42, Arkansas 8
1-1-88—Miami (Fla.) 20, Oklahoma 14
1-2-89—Miami (Fla.) 23, Nebraska 3

1-1-90—Notre Dame 21, Colorado 6
1-1-91—Colorado 10, Notre Dame 9
1-1-92—Miami (Fla.) 22, Nebraska 0
1-1-93—Florida St. 27, Nebraska 14
1-1-94—Florida St. 18, Nebraska 16

1-1-95—Nebraska 24, Miami (Fla.) 17
1-1-96—Florida St. 31, Notre Dame 26
12-31-96—Nebraska 41, Virginia Tech 21
1-2-98—Nebraska 42, Tennessee 17
1-2-99—Florida 31, Syracuse 10

1-1-00—Michigan 35, Alabama 34 (ot)
1-3-01—Oklahoma 13, Florida St. 2
1-2-02—Florida 56, Maryland 23
1-2-03—Southern California 38, Iowa 17

SUGAR BOWL

Present Site: New Orleans, Louisiana
Stadium (Capacity): Louisiana Superdome (76,791)
Playing Surface: AstroTurf
Name Changes: Sugar Bowl (1935-87); USF&G Sugar Bowl (1988-95); Nokia Sugar Bowl (since 1996)
Playing Sites: Tulane Stadium, New Orleans (1935-74); Louisiana Superdome (since 1975)

1-1-35—Tulane 20, Temple 14
1-1-36—TCU 3, LSU 2
1-1-37—Santa Clara 21, LSU 14
1-1-38—Santa Clara 6, LSU 0
1-2-39—TCU 15, Carnegie Mellon 7

1-1-40—Texas A&M 14, Tulane 13
1-1-41—Boston College 19, Tennessee 13
1-1-42—Fordham 2, Missouri 0
1-1-43—Tennessee 14, Tulsa 7
1-1-44—Georgia Tech 20, Tulsa 18

1-1-45—Duke 29, Alabama 26
1-1-46—Oklahoma St. 33, St. Mary's (Cal.) 13
1-1-47—Georgia 20, North Carolina 10
1-1-48—Texas 27, Alabama 7
1-1-49—Oklahoma 14, North Carolina 6

1-2-50—Oklahoma 35, LSU 0
1-1-51—Kentucky 13, Oklahoma 7
1-1-52—Maryland 28, Tennessee 13
1-1-53—Georgia Tech 24, Mississippi 7
1-1-54—Georgia Tech 42, West Virginia 19

1-1-55—Navy 21, Mississippi 0
1-2-56—Georgia Tech 7, Pittsburgh 0
1-1-57—Baylor 13, Tennessee 7
1-1-58—Mississippi 39, Texas 7
1-1-59—LSU 7, Clemson 0

1-1-60—Mississippi 21, LSU 0
1-2-61—Mississippi 14, Rice 6
1-1-62—Alabama 10, Arkansas 3
1-1-63—Mississippi 17, Arkansas 13
1-1-64—Alabama 12, Mississippi 7

1-1-65—LSU 13, Syracuse 10
1-1-66—Missouri 20, Florida 18
1-2-67—Alabama 34, Nebraska 7
1-1-68—LSU 20, Wyoming 13
1-1-69—Arkansas 16, Georgia 2

1-1-70—Mississippi 27, Arkansas 22
1-1-71—Tennessee 34, Air Force 13
1-1-72—Oklahoma 40, Auburn 22
12-31-72—Oklahoma 14, Penn St. 0
12-31-73—Notre Dame 24, Alabama 23

12-31-74—Nebraska 13, Florida 10
12-31-75—Alabama 13, Penn St. 6
1-1-77—Pittsburgh 27, Georgia 3
1-2-78—Alabama 35, Ohio St. 6
1-1-79—Alabama 14, Penn St. 7

1-1-80—Alabama 24, Arkansas 9

1-1-81—Georgia 17, Notre Dame 10
1-1-82—Pittsburgh 24, Georgia 20
1-1-83—Penn St. 27, Georgia 23
1-2-84—Auburn 9, Michigan 7

1-1-85—Nebraska 28, LSU 10
1-1-86—Tennessee 35, Miami (Fla.) 7
1-1-87—Nebraska 30, LSU 15
1-1-88—Auburn 16, Syracuse 16
1-2-89—Florida St. 13, Auburn 7

1-1-90—Miami (Fla.) 33, Alabama 25
1-1-91—Tennessee 23, Virginia 22
1-1-92—Notre Dame 39, Florida 28
1-1-93—Alabama 34, Miami (Fla.) 13
1-1-94—Florida 41, West Virginia 7

1-2-95—Florida St. 23, Florida 17
12-31-95—Virginia Tech 28, Texas 10
1-2-97—Florida 52, Florida St. 20
1-1-98—Florida St. 31, Ohio St. 14
1-1-99—Ohio St. 24, Texas A&M 14

1-4-00—Florida St. 46, Virginia Tech 29
1-2-01—Miami (Fla.) 37, Florida 20
1-1-02—LSU 47, Illinois 34
1-1-03—Georgia 26, Florida St. 13

COTTON BOWL

Present Site: Dallas, Texas
Stadium (Capacity): Cotton Bowl (68,252)
Playing Surface: Grass
Name Changes: Cotton Bowl (1937-88, 1996); Mobil Cotton Bowl (1989-95); Southwestern Bell Cotton Bowl (1997-00); SBC Cotton Bowl Classic (since 2001)
Playing Sites: Fair Park Stadium, Dallas (1937); Cotton Bowl (since 1938)

1-1-37—TCU 16, Marquette 6
1-1-38—Rice 28, Colorado 14
1-2-39—St. Mary's (Cal.) 20, Texas Tech 13
1-1-40—Clemson 6, Boston College 3
1-1-41—Texas A&M 13, Fordham 12

1-1-42—Alabama 29, Texas A&M 21
1-1-43—Texas 14, Georgia Tech 7
1-1-44—Randolph Field 7, Texas 7
1-1-45—Oklahoma St. 34, TCU 0
1-1-46—Texas 40, Missouri 27

1-1-47—Arkansas 0, LSU 0
1-1-48—Penn St. 13, Southern Methodist 13
1-1-49—Southern Methodist 21, Oregon 13
1-2-50—Rice 27, North Carolina 13
1-1-51—Tennessee 20, Texas 14

1-1-52—Kentucky 20, TCU 7
1-1-53—Texas 16, Tennessee 0
1-1-54—Rice 28, Alabama 6
1-1-55—Georgia Tech 14, Arkansas 6
1-2-56—Mississippi 14, TCU 13

1-1-57—TCU 28, Syracuse 27
1-1-58—Navy 20, Rice 7
1-1-59—Air Force 0, TCU 0
1-1-60—Syracuse 23, Texas 14
1-2-61—Duke 7, Arkansas 6

1-1-62—Texas 12, Mississippi 7
1-1-63—LSU 13, Texas 0
1-1-64—Texas 28, Navy 6
1-1-65—Arkansas 10, Nebraska 7
1-1-66—LSU 14, Arkansas 7

12-31-66—Georgia 24, Southern Methodist 9
1-1-68—Texas A&M 20, Alabama 16
1-1-69—Texas 36, Tennessee 13
1-1-70—Texas 21, Notre Dame 17
1-1-71—Notre Dame 24, Texas 11

1-1-72—Penn St. 30, Texas 6
1-1-73—Texas 17, Alabama 13
1-1-74—Nebraska 19, Texas 3
1-1-75—Penn St. 41, Baylor 20
1-1-76—Arkansas 31, Georgia 10

1-1-77—Houston 30, Maryland 21
1-2-78—Notre Dame 38, Texas 10
1-1-79—Notre Dame 35, Houston 34
1-1-80—Houston 17, Nebraska 14
1-1-81—Alabama 30, Baylor 2

1-1-82—Texas 14, Alabama 12
1-1-83—Southern Methodist 7, Pittsburgh 3
1-2-84—Georgia 10, Texas 9
1-1-85—Boston College 45, Houston 28
1-1-86—Texas A&M 36, Auburn 16

1-1-87—Ohio St. 28, Texas A&M 12

1-1-88—Texas A&M 35, Notre Dame 10
1-2-89—UCLA 17, Arkansas 3
1-1-90—Tennessee 31, Arkansas 27
1-1-91—Miami (Fla.) 46, Texas 3

1-1-92—Florida St. 10, Texas A&M 2
1-1-93—Notre Dame 28, Texas A&M 3
1-1-94—Notre Dame 24, Texas A&M 21
1-2-95—Southern California 55, Texas Tech 14
1-1-96—Colorado 38, Oregon 6

1-1-97—Brigham Young 19, Kansas St. 15
1-1-98—UCLA 29, Texas A&M 23
1-1-99—Texas 38, Mississippi St. 11
1-1-00—Arkansas 27, Texas 6
1-1-01—Kansas St. 35, Tennessee 21

1-1-02—Oklahoma 10, Arkansas 3
1-1-03—Texas 35, LSU 20

SUN BOWL

Present Site: El Paso, Texas
Stadium (Capacity): Sun Bowl Stadium (51,270)
Playing Surface: AstroTurf
Name Changes: Sun Bowl (1936-86, 1994-95); John Hancock Sun Bowl (1987-88); John Hancock Bowl (1989-93); Norwest Bank Sun Bowl (1996); Norwest Sun Bowl (1997-99); Wells Fargo Sun Bowl (since 2000)
Playing Sites: Kidd Field, UTEP, El Paso (1936-62); Sun Bowl (since 1963)

1-1-36—Hardin-Simmons 14, New Mexico St. 14
1-1-37—Hardin-Simmons 34, UTEP 6
1-1-38—West Virginia 7, Texas Tech 6
1-2-39—Utah 26, New Mexico 0
1-1-40—Arizona St. 0, Catholic 0

1-1-41—Case Reserve 26, Arizona St. 13
1-1-42—Tulsa 6, Texas Tech 0
1-1-43—Second Air Force 13, Hardin-Simmons 7
1-1-44—Southwestern (Tex.) 7, New Mexico 0
1-1-45—Southwestern (Tex.) 35, U. of Mexico 0

1-1-46—New Mexico 34, Denver 24
1-1-47—Cincinnati 18, Virginia Tech 6
1-1-48—Miami (Ohio) 13, Texas Tech 12
1-1-49—West Virginia 21, UTEP 12
1-2-50—UTEP 33, Georgetown 20

1-1-51—West Tex. A&M 14, Cincinnati 13
1-1-52—Texas Tech 25, Pacific (Cal.) 14
1-1-53—Pacific (Cal.) 26, Southern Miss. 7
1-1-54—UTEP 37, Southern Miss. 14
1-1-55—UTEP 47, Florida St. 20

1-2-56—Wyoming 21, Texas Tech 14
1-1-57—George Washington 13, UTEP 0
1-1-58—Louisville 34, Drake 20
12-31-58—Wyoming 14, Hardin-Simmons 6
12-31-59—New Mexico St. 28, North Texas 8

12-31-60—New Mexico St. 20, Utah St. 13
12-30-61—Villanova 17, Wichita St. 9
12-31-62—West Tex. A&M 15, Ohio 14
12-31-63—Oregon 21, Southern Methodist 14
12-26-64—Georgia 7, Texas Tech 0

12-31-65—UTEP 13, TCU 12
12-24-66—Wyoming 28, Florida St. 20
12-30-67—UTEP 14, Mississippi 7
12-28-68—Auburn 34, Arizona 10
12-20-69—Nebraska 45, Georgia 6

12-19-70—Georgia Tech 17, Texas Tech 9
12-18-71—LSU 33, Iowa St. 15
12-30-72—North Carolina 32, Texas Tech 28
12-29-73—Missouri 34, Auburn 17
12-28-74—Mississippi St. 26, North Carolina 24

12-26-75—Pittsburgh 33, Kansas 19
1-2-77—Texas A&M 37, Florida 14
12-31-77—Stanford 24, LSU 14
12-23-78—Texas 42, Maryland 0
12-22-79—Washington 14, Texas 7

12-27-80—Nebraska 31, Mississippi St. 17
12-26-81—Oklahoma 40, Houston 14
12-25-82—North Carolina 26, Texas 10
12-24-83—Alabama 28, Southern Methodist 7
12-22-84—Maryland 28, Tennessee 27

12-28-85—Arizona 13, Georgia 13
12-25-86—Alabama 28, Washington 6
12-25-87—Oklahoma St. 35, West Virginia 33
12-24-88—Alabama 29, Army 28
12-30-89—Pittsburgh 31, Texas A&M 28

12-31-90—Michigan St. 17, Southern California 16
12-31-91—UCLA 6, Illinois 3

12-31-92—Baylor 20, Arizona 15
12-24-93—Oklahoma 41, Texas Tech 10
12-30-94—Texas 35, North Carolina 31

12-29-95—Iowa 38, Washington 18
12-31-96—Stanford 38, Michigan St. 0
12-31-97—Arizona St. 17, Iowa 7
12-31-98—TCU 28, Southern California 19
12-31-99—Oregon 24, Minnesota 20

12-29-00—Wisconsin 21, UCLA 20
12-31-01—Washington St. 33, Purdue 27
12-31-02—Purdue 34, Washington 24

GATOR BOWL

Present Site: Jacksonville, Florida
Stadium (Capacity): Alltel Stadium (76,976)
Playing Surface: Grass
Name Changes: Gator Bowl (1946-85, 1991); Mazda Gator Bowl (1986-90); Outback Steakhouse Gator Bowl (1992-94); Toyota Gator Bowl (since 1995)
Playing Sites: Gator Bowl (1946-93); Florida Field, Gainesville, Fla. (1994); Jacksonville Municipal Stadium, renamed Alltel Stadium in 1997 (since 1995)

1-1-46—Wake Forest 26, South Carolina 14
1-1-47—Oklahoma 34, North Carolina St. 13
1-1-48—Georgia 20, Maryland 20
1-1-49—Clemson 24, Missouri 23
1-2-50—Maryland 20, Missouri 7

1-1-51—Wyoming 20, Wash. & Lee 7
1-1-52—Miami (Fla.) 14, Clemson 0
1-1-53—Florida 14, Tulsa 13
1-1-54—Texas Tech 35, Auburn 13
12-31-54—Auburn 33, Baylor 13

12-31-55—Vanderbilt 25, Auburn 13
12-29-56—Georgia Tech 21, Pittsburgh 14
12-28-57—Tennessee 3, Texas A&M 0
12-27-58—Mississippi 7, Florida 3
1-2-60—Arkansas 14, Georgia Tech 7

12-31-60—Florida 13, Baylor 12
12-30-61—Penn St. 30, Georgia Tech 15
12-29-62—Florida 17, Penn St. 7
12-28-63—North Carolina 35, Air Force 0
1-2-65—Florida St. 36, Oklahoma 19

12-31-65—Georgia Tech 31, Texas Tech 21
12-31-66—Tennessee 18, Syracuse 12
12-30-67—Florida St. 17, Penn St. 17
12-28-68—Missouri 35, Alabama 10
12-27-69—Florida 14, Tennessee 13

1-2-71—Auburn 35, Mississippi 28
12-31-71—Georgia 7, North Carolina 3
12-30-72—Auburn 24, Colorado 3
12-29-73—Texas Tech 28, Tennessee 19
12-30-74—Auburn 27, Texas 3

12-29-75—Maryland 13, Florida 0
12-27-76—Notre Dame 20, Penn St. 9
12-30-77—Pittsburgh 34, Clemson 3
12-29-78—Clemson 17, Ohio St. 15
12-28-79—North Carolina 17, Michigan 15

12-29-80—Pittsburgh 37, South Carolina 9
12-28-81—North Carolina 31, Arkansas 27
12-30-82—Florida St. 31, West Virginia 12
12-30-83—Florida 14, Iowa 6
12-28-84—Oklahoma St. 21, South Carolina 14

12-30-85—Florida St. 34, Oklahoma St. 23
12-27-86—Clemson 27, Stanford 21
12-31-87—LSU 30, South Carolina 13
1-1-89—Georgia 34, Michigan St. 27
12-30-89—Clemson 27, West Virginia 7

1-1-91—Michigan 35, Mississippi 3
12-29-91—Oklahoma 48, Virginia 14
12-31-92—Florida 27, North Carolina St. 10
12-31-93—Alabama 24, North Carolina 10
12-30-94—Tennessee 45, Virginia Tech 23

1-1-96—Syracuse 41, Clemson 0
1-1-97—North Carolina 20, West Virginia 13
1-1-98—North Carolina 42, Virginia Tech 3
1-1-99—Georgia Tech 35, Notre Dame 28
1-1-00—Miami (Fla.) 28, Georgia Tech 13

1-1-01—Virginia Tech 41, Clemson 20
1-1-02—Florida St. 30, Virginia Tech 17
1-1-03—North Carolina St. 28, Notre Dame 6

CAPITAL ONE BOWL

Present Site: Orlando, Florida
Stadium (Capacity): Florida Citrus Bowl (70,000)
Playing Surface: Grass

Name Changes: Tangerine Bowl (1947-82); Florida Citrus Bowl (1983-93); CompUSA Florida Citrus Bowl (1994-99); OurHouse.com Florida Citrus Bowl (2000); Capital One/Florida Citrus Bowl (2001-02); Capital One Bowl (since 2003)
Playing Sites: Tangerine Bowl, Orlando (1947-72); Florida Field, Gainesville (1973); Tangerine Bowl (now Florida Citrus Bowl) (1974-82); Orlando Stadium (now Florida Citrus Bowl) (1983-85); Florida Citrus Bowl (since 1986)

1-1-47—Catawba 31, Maryville (Tenn.) 6
1-1-48—Catawba 7, Marshall 0
1-1-49—Murray St. 21, Sul Ross St. 21
1-2-50—St. Vincent 7, Emory & Henry 6
1-1-51—Charleston (W.Va.) 35, Emory & Henry 14

1-1-52—Stetson 35, Arkansas St. 20
1-1-53—Tex. A&M-Commerce 33, Tennessee Tech 21
1-1-54—Arkansas St. 7, Tex. A&M-Commerce 7
1-1-55—Neb.-Omaha 7, Eastern Ky. 6
1-2-56—Juniata 6, Missouri Valley 6

1-1-57—West Tex. A&M 20, Southern Miss. 13
1-1-58—Tex. A&M-Commerce 10, Southern Miss. 9
12-27-58—Tex. A&M-Commerce 26, Missouri Valley 7
1-1-60—Middle Tenn. 21, Presbyterian 12
12-30-60—Citadel 27, Tennessee Tech 0

12-29-61—Lamar 21, Middle Tenn. 14
12-22-62—Houston 49, Miami (Ohio) 21
12-28-63—Western Ky. 27, Coast Guard 0
12-12-64—East Caro. 14, Massachusetts 13
12-11-65—East Caro. 31, Maine 0

12-10-66—Morgan St. 14, West Chester 6
12-16-67—Tenn.-Martin 25, West Chester 8
12-27-68—Richmond 49, Ohio 42
12-26-69—Toledo 56, Davidson 33
12-28-70—Toledo 40, William & Mary 12

12-28-71—Toledo 28, Richmond 3
12-29-72—Tampa 21, Kent St. 18
12-22-73—Miami (Ohio) 16, Florida 7
12-21-74—Miami (Ohio) 21, Georgia 10
12-20-75—Miami (Ohio) 20, South Carolina 7

12-18-76—Oklahoma St. 49, Brigham Young 21
12-23-77—Florida St. 40, Texas Tech 17
12-23-78—North Carolina 30, Pittsburgh 17
12-22-79—LSU 34, Wake Forest 10
12-20-80—Florida 35, Maryland 20

12-19-81—Missouri 19, Southern Miss. 17
12-18-82—Auburn 33, Boston College 26
12-17-83—Tennessee 30, Maryland 23
12-22-84—Florida St. 17, Georgia 17
12-28-85—Ohio St. 10, Brigham Young 7

1-1-87—Auburn 16, Southern California 7
1-1-88—Clemson 35, Penn St. 10
1-2-89—Clemson 13, Oklahoma 6
1-1-90—Illinois 31, Virginia 21
1-1-91—Georgia Tech 45, Nebraska 21

1-1-92—California 37, Clemson 13
1-1-93—Georgia 21, Ohio St. 14
1-1-94—Penn St. 31, Tennessee 13
1-2-95—Alabama 24, Ohio St. 17
1-1-96—Tennessee 20, Ohio St. 14

1-1-97—Tennessee 48, Northwestern 28
1-1-98—Florida 21, Penn St. 6
1-1-99—Michigan 45, Arkansas 31
1-1-00—Michigan St. 37, Florida 34
1-1-01—Michigan 31, Auburn 28

1-1-02—Tennessee 45, Michigan 17
1-1-03—Auburn 13, Penn St. 9

Note: No classified major teams participated in games from January 1, 1947, through January 1, 1960, or in 1961 and 1963 through 1967.

LIBERTY BOWL

Present Site: Memphis, Tennessee
Stadium (Capacity): Liberty Bowl Memorial Stadium (62,338)
Playing Surface: Prescription Athletic Turf
Name Changes: Liberty Bowl (1959-92); St. Jude Liberty Bowl (1993-96); AXA Liberty Bowl (since 1997)
Playing Sites: Municipal Stadium, Philadelphia (1959-63); Convention Hall, Atlantic City, N.J. (1964); Liberty Bowl Memorial Stadium (since 1965)

12-19-59—Penn St. 7, Alabama 0
12-17-60—Penn St. 41, Oregon 12
12-16-61—Syracuse 15, Miami (Fla.) 14
12-15-62—Oregon St. 6, Villanova 0

12-21-63—Mississippi St. 16, North Carolina St. 12

12-19-64—Utah 32, West Virginia 6

12-18-65—Mississippi 13, Auburn 7

12-10-66—Miami (Fla.) 14, Virginia Tech 7

12-16-67—North Carolina St. 14, Georgia 7

12-14-68—Mississippi 34, Virginia Tech 17

12-13-69—Colorado 47, Alabama 33

12-12-70—Tulane 17, Colorado 3

12-20-71—Tennessee 14, Arkansas 13

12-18-72—Georgia Tech 31, Iowa St. 30

12-17-73—North Carolina St. 31, Kansas 18

12-16-74—Tennessee 7, Maryland 3

12-22-75—Southern California 20, Texas A&M 0

12-20-76—Alabama 36, UCLA 6

12-19-77—Nebraska 21, North Carolina 17

12-23-78—Missouri 20, LSU 15

12-22-79—Penn St. 9, Tulane 6

12-27-80—Purdue 28, Missouri 25

12-30-81—Ohio St. 31, Navy 28

12-29-82—Alabama 21, Illinois 15

12-29-83—Notre Dame 19, Boston College 18

12-27-84—Auburn 21, Arkansas 15

12-27-85—Baylor 21, LSU 7

12-29-86—Tennessee 21, Minnesota 14

12-29-87—Georgia 20, Arkansas 17

12-28-88—Indiana 34, South Carolina 10

12-28-89—Mississippi 42, Air Force 29

12-27-90—Air Force 23, Ohio St. 11

12-29-91—Air Force 38, Mississippi St. 15

12-31-92—Mississippi 13, Air Force 0

12-28-93—Louisville 18, Michigan St. 7

12-31-94—Illinois 30, East Caro. 0

12-30-95—East Caro. 19, Stanford 13

12-27-96—Syracuse 30, Houston 17

12-31-97—Southern Miss. 41, Pittsburgh 7

12-31-98—Tulane 41, Brigham Young 27

12-31-99—Southern Miss. 23, Colorado St. 17

12-29-00—Colorado St. 22, Louisville 17

12-31-01—Louisville 28, Brigham Young 10

12-31-02—TCU 17, Colorado St. 3

PEACH BOWL

Present Site: Atlanta, Georgia
Stadium (Capacity): Georgia Dome (71,228)
Name Changes: Peach Bowl (1968-96); Chick-Fil-A Peach Bowl (since 1997)
Playing Surface: AstroTurf
Playing Sites: Grant Field, Atlanta (1968-70); Atlanta/Fulton County Stadium (1971-92); Georgia Dome (since 1993)

12-30-68—LSU 31, Florida St. 27

12-30-69—West Virginia 14, South Carolina 3

12-30-70—Arizona St. 48, North Carolina 26

12-30-71—Mississippi 41, Georgia Tech 18

12-29-72—North Carolina St. 49, West Virginia 13

12-28-73—Georgia 17, Maryland 16

12-28-74—Texas Tech 6, Vanderbilt 6

12-31-75—West Virginia 13, North Carolina St. 10

12-31-76—Kentucky 21, North Carolina 0

12-31-77—North Carolina St. 24, Iowa St. 14

12-25-78—Purdue 41, Georgia Tech 21

12-31-79—Baylor 24, Clemson 18

1-2-81—Miami (Fla.) 20, Virginia Tech 10

12-31-81—West Virginia 26, Florida 6

12-31-82—Iowa 28, Tennessee 22

12-30-83—Florida St. 28, North Carolina 3

12-31-84—Virginia 27, Purdue 24

12-31-85—Army 31, Illinois 29

12-31-86—Virginia Tech 25, North Carolina 24

1-2-88—Tennessee 27, Indiana 22

12-31-88—North Carolina St. 28, Iowa 23

12-30-89—Syracuse 19, Georgia 18

12-29-90—Auburn 27, Indiana 23

1-1-92—East Caro. 37, North Carolina St. 34

1-2-93—North Carolina 21, Mississippi St. 17

12-31-93—Clemson 14, Kentucky 13

1-1-95—North Carolina St. 28, Mississippi St. 24

12-30-95—Virginia 34, Georgia 27

12-28-96—LSU 10, Clemson 7

1-2-98—Auburn 21, Clemson 17

12-31-98—Georgia 35, Virginia 33

12-30-99—Mississippi St. 17, Clemson 7

12-29-00—LSU 28, Georgia Tech 14

12-31-01—North Carolina 16, Auburn 10

12-31-02—Maryland 30, Tennessee 3

FIESTA BOWL

Present Site: Tempe, Arizona
Stadium (Capacity): Sun Devil Stadium (73,471)
Playing Surface: Grass
Name Changes: Fiesta Bowl (1971-85, 1991-92); Sunkist Fiesta Bowl (1986-90); IBM OS/2 Fiesta Bowl (1993-95); Tostitos Fiesta Bowl (since 1996)
Playing Sites: Sun Devil Stadium (since 1971)

12-27-71—Arizona St. 45, Florida St. 38

12-23-72—Arizona St. 49, Missouri 35

12-21-73—Arizona St. 28, Pittsburgh 7

12-28-74—Oklahoma St. 16, Brigham Young 6

12-26-75—Arizona St. 17, Nebraska 14

12-25-76—Oklahoma 41, Wyoming 7

12-25-77—Penn St. 42, Arizona St. 30

12-25-78—Arkansas 10, UCLA 10

12-25-79—Pittsburgh 16, Arizona 10

12-26-80—Penn St. 31, Ohio St. 19

1-1-82—Penn St. 26, Southern California 10

1-1-83—Arizona St. 32, Oklahoma 21

1-2-84—Ohio St. 28, Pittsburgh 23

1-1-85—UCLA 39, Miami (Fla.) 37

1-1-86—Michigan 27, Nebraska 23

1-2-87—Penn St. 14, Miami (Fla.) 10

1-1-88—Florida St. 31, Nebraska 28

1-2-89—Notre Dame 34, West Virginia 21

1-1-90—Florida St. 41, Nebraska 17

1-1-91—Louisville 34, Alabama 7

1-1-92—Penn St. 42, Tennessee 17

1-1-93—Syracuse 26, Colorado 22

1-1-94—Arizona 29, Miami (Fla.) 0

1-2-95—Colorado 41, Notre Dame 24

1-2-96—Nebraska 62, Florida 24

1-1-97—Penn St. 38, Texas 15

12-31-97—Kansas St. 35, Syracuse 18

1-4-99—Tennessee 23, Florida St. 16

1-2-00—Nebraska 31, Tennessee 21

1-1-01—Oregon St. 41, Notre Dame 9

1-1-02—Oregon 38, Colorado 16

1-3-03—Ohio St. 31, Miami (Fla.) 24 (2 ot)

INDEPENDENCE BOWL

Present Site: Shreveport, Louisiana
Stadium (Capacity): Independence Stadium (50,459)
Playing Surface: Grass
Name Changes: Independence Bowl (1976-89); Poulan Independence Bowl (1990); Poulan/Weed Eater Independence Bowl (1991-97); Sanford Independence Bowl (1998-00); MainStay Independence Bowl (since 2001)
Playing Sites: Independence Stadium (since 1976)

12-13-76—McNeese St. 20, Tulsa 16

12-17-77—Louisiana Tech 24, Louisville 14

12-16-78—East Caro. 35, Louisiana Tech 13

12-15-79—Syracuse 31, McNeese St. 7

12-13-80—Southern Miss. 16, McNeese St. 14

12-12-81—Texas A&M 33, Oklahoma St. 16

12-11-82—Wisconsin 14, Kansas St. 3

12-10-83—Air Force 9, Mississippi 3

12-15-84—Air Force 23, Virginia Tech 7

12-21-85—Minnesota 20, Clemson 13

12-20-86—Mississippi 20, Texas Tech 17

12-19-87—Washington 24, Tulane 12

12-23-88—Southern Miss. 38, UTEP 18

12-16-89—Oregon 27, Tulsa 24

12-15-90—Louisiana Tech 34, Maryland 34

12-29-91—Georgia 24, Arkansas 15

12-31-92—Wake Forest 39, Oregon 35

12-31-93—Virginia Tech 45, Indiana 20

12-28-94—Virginia 20, TCU 10

12-29-95—LSU 45, Michigan St. 26

12-31-96—Auburn 32, Army 29

12-28-97—LSU 27, Notre Dame 9

12-31-98—Mississippi 35, Texas Tech 18

12-31-99—Mississippi 27, Oklahoma 25

12-31-00—Mississippi St. 43, Texas A&M 41 (ot)

12-27-01—Alabama 14, Iowa St. 13

12-27-02—Mississippi 27, Nebraska 23

HOLIDAY BOWL

Present Site: San Diego, California
Stadium (Capacity): Qualcomm Stadium (68,500)
Playing Surface: Grass
Name Changes: Holiday Bowl (1978-85, 2002); Sea World Holiday Bowl (1986-90); Thrifty Car Rental Holiday Bowl (1991-94); Plymouth Holiday Bowl (1995-97); Culligan Holiday Bowl (1998-01); Pacific Life Holiday Bowl (since 2002)
Playing Sites: San Diego Jack Murphy Stadium, renamed Qualcomm Stadium in 1997 (since 1978)

12-22-78—Navy 23, Brigham Young 16

12-21-79—Indiana 38, Brigham Young 37

12-19-80—Brigham Young 46, Southern Methodist 45

12-18-81—Brigham Young 38, Washington St. 36

12-17-82—Ohio St. 47, Brigham Young 17

12-23-83—Brigham Young 21, Missouri 17

12-21-84—Brigham Young 24, Michigan 17

12-22-85—Arkansas 18, Arizona St. 17

12-30-86—Iowa 39, San Diego St. 38

12-30-87—Iowa 20, Wyoming 19

12-30-88—Oklahoma St. 62, Wyoming 14

12-29-89—Penn St. 50, Brigham Young 39

12-29-90—Texas A&M 65, Brigham Young 14

12-30-91—Brigham Young 13, Iowa 13

12-30-92—Hawaii 27, Illinois 17

12-30-93—Ohio St. 28, Brigham Young 21

12-30-94—Michigan 24, Colorado St. 14

12-29-95—Kansas St. 54, Colorado St. 21

12-30-96—Colorado 33, Washington 21

12-29-97—Colorado St. 35, Missouri 24

12-30-98—Arizona 23, Nebraska 20

12-29-99—Kansas St. 24, Washington 20

12-29-00—Oregon 35, Texas 30

12-28-01—Texas 47, Washington 43

12-27-02—Kansas St. 34, Arizona St. 27

OUTBACK BOWL

Present Site: Tampa, Florida
Stadium (Capacity): Raymond James Stadium (65,657)
Playing Surface: Grass
Name Changes: Hall of Fame Bowl (1986-95); Outback Bowl (since 1996)
Playing Sites: Tampa Stadium, renamed Houlihan's Stadium in 1997 (1986-97); Tampa Community Stadium (1998); Raymond James Stadium (since 1999)

12-23-86—Boston College 27, Georgia 24

1-2-88—Michigan 28, Alabama 24

1-2-89—Syracuse 23, LSU 10

1-1-90—Auburn 31, Ohio St. 14

1-1-91—Clemson 30, Illinois 0

1-1-92—Syracuse 24, Ohio St. 17

1-1-93—Tennessee 38, Boston College 23

1-1-94—Michigan 42, North Carolina St. 7

1-2-95—Wisconsin 34, Duke 20

1-1-96—Penn St. 43, Auburn 14

1-1-97—Alabama 17, Michigan 14

1-1-98—Georgia 33, Wisconsin 6

1-1-99—Penn St. 26, Kentucky 14

1-1-00—Georgia 28, Purdue 25 (ot)

1-1-01—South Carolina 24, Ohio St. 7

1-1-02—South Carolina 31, Ohio St. 28

1-1-03—Michigan 38, Florida 30

INSIGHT BOWL

Present Site: Tucson, Arizona
Stadium (Capacity): Bank One Ballpark (43,080)
Playing Surface: Grass
Name Changes: Copper Bowl (1989, 1996); Domino's Pizza Copper Bowl (1990-91); Weiser Lock Copper Bowl (1992-95); Insight.com Bowl (1997-01); Insight Bowl (since 2002)
Playing Sites: Arizona Stadium (since 1989-99); Bank One Ballpark (since 2000)

12-31-89—Arizona 17, North Carolina St. 10

12-31-90—California 17, Wyoming 15

12-31-91—Indiana 24, Baylor 0

12-29-92—Washington St. 31, Utah 28

12-29-93—Kansas St. 52, Wyoming 17

12-29-94—Brigham Young 31, Oklahoma 6

12-27-95—Texas Tech 55, Air Force 41

12-27-96—Wisconsin 38, Utah 10

12-27-97—Arizona 20, New Mexico 14

12-26-98—Missouri 34, West Virginia 31

12-31-99—Colorado 62, Boston College 28

12-28-00—Iowa St. 37, Pittsburgh 29

12-29-01—Syracuse 26, Kansas St. 3

12-26-02—Pittsburgh 38, Oregon St. 13

TANGERINE BOWL

Present Site: Orlando, Florida

Stadium (Capacity): Florida Citrus Bowl (70,000)
Playing Surface: Grass
Name Changes: Blockbuster Bowl (1990-93); Carquest Bowl (1994-97); Micron PC Bowl (1998); MicronPC.com Bowl (1999-00); Visit Florida Tangerine Bowl (2001); Mazda Tangerine Bowl (2002)
Note: The game was known as the Sunshine Football Classic for a short time in the 1997-98 offseason after Carquest Auto Parts dropped its sponsorship and before Micron agreed to be the title sponsor. Also, this game should not be confused with the Tangerine Bowl that became the Florida Citrus Bowl in 1982 and is now known as the Capital One Bowl.
Playing Sites: Joe Robbie Stadium, renamed Pro Player Stadium in 1996 (1990-00); Florida Citrus Bowl (since 2001)

12-28-90—Florida St. 24, Penn St. 17
12-28-91—Alabama 30, Colorado 25
1-1-93—Stanford 24, Penn St. 3
1-1-94—Boston College 31, Virginia 13
1-2-95—South Carolina 24, West Virginia 21

12-30-95—North Carolina 20, Arkansas 10
12-27-96—Miami (Fla.) 31, Virginia 21
12-29-97—Georgia Tech 35, West Virginia 30
12-29-98—Miami (Fla.) 46, North Carolina St. 23
12-30-99—Illinois 63, Virginia 21

12-28-00—North Carolina St. 38, Minnesota 30
12-20-01—Pittsburgh 34, North Carolina St. 19
12-23-02—Texas Tech 55, Clemson 15

LAS VEGAS BOWL

Present Site: Las Vegas, Nevada
Stadium (Capacity): Sam Boyd Stadium (40,000)
Playing Surface: Monsanto Turf (retractable)
Name Changes: Las Vegas Bowl (1992-98, 2000, since 2003); EA Sports Las Vegas Bowl (1999); Sega Sports Las Vegas Bowl (2001-02)
Playing Sites: Sam Boyd Stadium (since 1992)

12-18-92—Bowling Green 35, Nevada 34
12-17-93—Utah St. 42, Ball St. 33
12-15-94—UNLV 52, Central Mich. 24
12-14-95—Toledo 40, Nevada 37 (ot)
12-19-96—Nevada 18, Ball St. 15

12-20-97—Oregon 41, Air Force 13
12-19-98—North Carolina 20, San Diego St. 13
12-18-99—Utah 17, Fresno St. 16
12-21-00—UNLV 31, Arkansas 14
12-25-01—Utah 10, Southern California 6

12-25-02—UCLA 27, New Mexico 13

ALAMO BOWL

Present Site: San Antonio, Texas
Stadium (Capacity): Alamodome (65,000)
Playing Surface: AstroTurf
Name Changes: Builders Square Alamo Bowl (1993-98); Sylvania Alamo Bowl (1999-01); Alamo Bowl (since 2002)
Playing Sites: Alamodome (since 1993)

12-31-93—California 37, Iowa 3
12-31-94—Washington St. 10, Baylor 3
12-28-95—Texas A&M 22, Michigan 20
12-29-96—Iowa 27, Texas Tech 0
12-30-97—Purdue 33, Oklahoma St. 20

12-29-98—Purdue 37, Kansas St. 34
12-28-99—Penn St. 24, Texas A&M 0
12-30-00—Nebraska 66, Northwestern 17
12-29-01—Iowa 19, Texas Tech 16
12-28-02—Wisconsin 31, Colorado 28 (ot)

HUMANITARIAN BOWL

Present Site: Boise, Idaho
Stadium (Capacity): Bronco Stadium (30,000)
Playing Surface: Blue AstroTurf
Name Changes: Sports Humanitarian Bowl (1997); Humanitarian Bowl (1998); Crucial.com Humanitarian Bowl (since 1999)
Playing Sites: Bronco Stadium (since 1997)

12-29-97—Cincinnati 35, Utah St. 19
12-30-98—Idaho 42, Southern Miss. 35
12-30-99—Boise St. 34, Louisville 31
12-28-00—Boise St. 38, UTEP 23
12-31-01—Clemson 49, Louisiana Tech 24

12-31-02—Boise St. 34, Iowa St. 16

MOTOR CITY BOWL

Present Site: Detroit, Michigan
Stadium (Capacity): Ford Field (65,000)
Playing Surface: FieldTurf
Playing Sites: Pontiac Silverdome (1997-01); Ford Field (since 2002)

12-26-97—Mississippi 34, Marshall 31
12-23-98—Marshall 48, Louisville 29
12-27-99—Marshall 21, Brigham Young 3
12-27-00—Marshall 25, Cincinnati 14
12-29-01—Toledo 23, Cincinnati 16

12-26-02—Boston College 51, Toledo 25

MUSIC CITY BOWL

Present Site: Nashville, Tennessee
Stadium (Capacity): Adelphia Coliseum (67,000)
Playing Surface: Grass
Name Changes: Music City Bowl (1998, 2000-01); HomePoint.com Music City Bowl (1999); Gaylord Hotels Music City Bowl (since 2002)
Playing Sites: Vanderbilt Stadium (1998); Adelphia Coliseum (since 1999)

12-29-98—Virginia Tech 38, Alabama 7
12-29-99—Syracuse 20, Kentucky 13
12-28-00—West Virginia 49, Mississippi 38
12-28-01—Boston College 20, Georgia 16
12-30-02—Minnesota 29, Arkansas 14

GMAC BOWL

Present Site: Mobile, Alabama
Stadium (Capacity): Ladd-Peebles Stadium (40,643)
Playing Surface: Grass
Name Changes: Mobile Alabama Bowl (1999); GMAC Mobile Alabama Bowl (2000); GMAC Bowl (since 2001)
Playing Sites: Ladd-Peebles Stadium (since 1999)

12-22-99—TCU 28, East Caro. 14
12-20-00—Southern Miss. 28, TCU 21
12-19-01—Marshall 64, East Caro. 61 (2 ot)
12-18-02—Marshall 38, Louisville 15

SILICON VALLEY FOOTBALL CLASSIC

Present Site: San Jose, California
Stadium (Capacity): Spartan Stadium (31,500)
Playing Surface: Grass
Playing Sites: Spartan Stadium (since 2000)

12-31-00—Air Force 37, Fresno St. 34
12-31-01—Michigan St. 44, Fresno St. 35
12-31-02—Fresno St. 30, Georgia Tech 21

HOUSTON BOWL

Present Site: Houston, Texas
Stadium (Capacity): Reliant Astrodome (65,000)
Playing Surface: AstroTurf
Name Changes: galleryfurniture.com Bowl (2000-01); Houston Bowl (since 2002)
Playing Sites: Reliant Astrodome (since 2000)

12-27-00—East Caro. 40, Texas Tech 27
12-28-01—Texas A&M 28, TCU 9
12-27-02—Oklahoma St. 33, Southern Miss. 23

NEW ORLEANS BOWL

Present Site: New Orleans, Louisiana
Stadium (Capacity): Louisiana Superdome (76,791)
Playing Surface: AstroTurf
Playing Sites: Louisiana Superdome (since 2001)

12-18-01—Colorado St. 45, North Texas 20
12-17-02—North Texas 24, Cincinnati 19

CONAGRA FOODS HAWAII BOWL

Present Site: Honolulu, Hawaii
Stadium (Capacity): Aloha Stadium (50,000)
Playing Surface: AstroTurf
Playing Site: Aloha Stadium (since 2002)

12-25-02—Tulane 36, Hawaii 28

CONTINENTAL TIRE BOWL

Present Site: Charlotte, North Carolina
Stadium (Capacity): Ericsson Stadium (73,367)
Playing Surface: Grass
Playing Site: Ericsson Stadium (since 2002)

12-28-02—Virginia 48, West Virginia 22

DIAMOND WALNUT SAN FRANCISCO BOWL

Present Site: San Francisco, California
Stadium (Capacity): Pacific Bell Park (37,000 for football)
Playing Surface: Grass
Playing Site: Pacific Bell Park (since 2002)

12-31-02—Virginia Tech 20, Air Force 13

FORT WORTH BOWL

Present Site: Fort Worth, Texas
Stadium (Capacity): Amon G. Carter Stadium (46,000)
Playing Surface: Grass
Playing Site: Amon G. Carter Stadium (since 2003)

First game—December 23, 2003

Bowl-Game Title Sponsors

Bowl	Title Sponsor[s] (Year Began)	Bowl Name (Years)
Alamo	Builders Square (1993-98)	Builders Square Alamo (1993-98)
	Sylvania (1999-01)	Sylvania Alamo (1999-01)
	MasterCard (since 2002)	Alamo Bowl Presented By MasterCard (since 2002)
Capital One	Florida Department of Citrus (1983-02)	Florida Citrus (1983-93)
	Comp USA (1994-99)	CompUSA Florida Citrus (1994-99)
	OurHouse.com (2000)	OurHouse.com Florida Citrus (2000)
	Capital One (since 2001)	Capital One Florida Citrus (2001-02)
		Capital One (since 2003)
Continental Tire	Continental Tires (since 2002)	Continental Tire (since 2002)

Bowl	Title Sponsor[s] (Year Began)	Bowl Name (Years)
Cotton	Mobil (1989-95)	Cotton (1937-88, 1996)
	Southwestern Bell (1997-00)	Mobil Cotton (1989-95)
	SBC Communications (since 2001)	Southwestern Bell (1997-00)
		SBC Cotton Bowl Classic (since 2001)
Fiesta	Sunkist (1986-90)	Fiesta (1971-85; 1991-92)
	IBM (1993-95)	Sunkist Fiesta (1986-90)
	FritoLay/Tostitos (since 1996)	IBM OS/2 Fiesta (1993-95)
		Tostitos Fiesta (since 1996)
Fort Worth	To be named	Fort Worth (since 2003)
Gator	Mazda (1986-91)	Gator (1946-85)
	Outback Steakhouse (1992-94)	Mazda Gator (1986-91)
	Toyota (since 1995)	Outback Steakhouse Gator (1992-94)
		Toyota Gator (since 1995)

Bowl	Title Sponsor[s] (Year Began)	Bowl Name (Years)
GMAC	Mobile Alabama, Inc. (1999) GMAC Financial Services and the City of Mobile (since 2000)	Mobile Alabama (1999) GMAC Mobile Alabama (2000) GMAC (since 2001)
Hawaii	ConAgra Foods (since 2002)	ConAgra Foods Hawaii (since 2002)
Holiday	Sea World (1986-90) Thrifty Car Rental (1991-94) Plymouth (1995-97) Culligan (1998-01) Pacific Life (since 2002)	Holiday (1978-85; since 2002) Sea World Holiday (1986-90) Thrifty Car Rental Holiday (1991-94) Plymouth Holiday (1995-97) Culligan Holiday (1998-01) Pacific Life Holiday (since 2002)
Houston	Gallery Furniture (2000-01)	Galleryfurniture.com (2000-01) Houston (since 2002)
Humanitarian	Humanitarian Bowl Association (1997-98) Crucial Technology (since1999)	Sports Humanitarian (1997) Humanitarian (1998) Crucial.com Humanitarian (since 1999)
Independence	Poulan (1990-97) Sanford (1998-00) MainStay Management (since 2001)	Independence (1976-89) Poulan Independence (1990) Poulan/Weed Eater Independence (1991-97) Sanford Independence (1998-00) MainStay Independence (since 2001)
Insight	Domino's Pizza (1990-91) Weiser Lock (1992-95) Insight Enterprises (since 1997)	Copper (1989, 1996) Domino's Pizza Copper (1990-91) Weiser Lock Copper (1992-95) Insight.com (1997-01) Insight (since 2002)
Las Vegas	Las Vegas Convention & Visitor's Authority (1998, 2000-01) EA Sports (1999) Sega of America (2001-02)	Las Vegas (1992-98, 2000) EA Sports Las Vegas (1999) Sega Sports Las Vegas (2001-02) Las Vegas (since 2003)
Liberty	St. Jude (1993-96) AXA/Equitable (since 1997)	Liberty (1959-92) St. Jude Liberty (1993-96) AXA Liberty (since 1997)
Motor City	Motor City Bowl, Inc. (1997) General Motors, Daimler-Chrysler and Ford (Presenting Sponsors since 1998)	Ford Motor City (1997) Motor City (since 1998)
Music City	American General (1998) HomePoint.com (1999) Gaylord Entertainment (since 2002)	Music City (1998, 2000-01) HomePoint.com Music City (1999) Gaylord Hotels Music City (since 2002)
New Orleans	Greater New Orleans Sports Foundation (since 2001)	New Orleans (since 2001)
Orange	Federal Express (since 1989)	Orange (1935-88) Federal Express Orange (since 1989)
Outback	Outback Steakhouse (since 1996)	Hall of Fame (1986-95) Outback (since 1996)
Peach	Chick-Fil-A (since 1997)	Peach (1968-96) Chick-Fil-A Peach (since 1997)
Rose	Pasadena Tournament of Roses Association (1902, since 1916) AT&T (Presenting Sponsor, 1999-02) Sony Electronics (Presenting Sponsor since 2003)	Rose (since 1902) Rose Bowl Presented by AT&T (1999-02) Rose Bowl Presented By Sony (since 2003)
San Francisco	Diamond Walnut Growers (since 2002)	Diamond Walnut San Francisco (since 2002)
Silicon Valley	None	Silicon Valley Classic (since 2000)
Sugar	USF&G Sugar (1988-95) Nokia Mobile Telephones (since 1996)	Sugar (1935-87) USF&G Sugar (1988-95) Nokia Sugar (since 1996)
Sun	John Hancock (1987-93) Norwest Corporation (1996-98) Wells Fargo (since 1999)	Sun (1936-86, 1994-95) John Hancock Sun (1987-88) John Hancock (1989-93) Norwest Bank Sun (1996) Norwest Sun (1997-98) Wells Fargo Sun (since 1999)
Tangerine	Blockbuster Video (1990-93) Carquest Parts (1994-97) Micron PC (1998-00) Florida Tourism (2001) Mazda (since 2002)	Blockbuster (1990-93) Carquest (1994-97) Micron PC (1998) Micron PC.com (1999-00) Visit Florida Tangerine (2001) Mazda Tangerine (since 2002)

Bowl Financial Analysis, 1976-03

(Payouts are estimates.)

Year	No. Bowls	No. Teams	Total Payout	Per-Game Payout	Per-Team Payout
1976-77	11	22	$11,345,851	$515,714	$257,857
1977-78	12	24	13,323,638	1,110,303	555,152
1978-79	13	26	15,506,516	1,192,809	596,405
1979-80	13	26	17,219,624	1,324,586	662,293
1980-81	13	26	19,517,938	1,501,380	750,690
1981-82	14	28	21,791,222	1,556,516	778,258
1982-83	15	30	26,682,486	1,778,832	889,416
1983-84	15	30	32,535,788	2,169,052	1,084,256
1984-85	16	32	36,666,738	2,291,671	1,145,836
1985-86	16	32	36,995,864	2,312,242	1,156,121
1986-87	17	34	45,830,906	2,695,936	1,347,968
1987-88	17	34	48,251,516	2,838,324	1,419,162
1988-89	17	34	52,905,426	3,112,084	1,556,042
1989-90	18	36	58,208,058	3,233,781	1,616,891
1990-91	19	38	60,378,362	3,177,809	1,588,904
1991-92	18	36	63,494,554	3,527,475	1,763,738
1992-93	18	36	67,950,000	3,775,000	1,887,500
1993-94	19	38	71,006,000	3,737,158	1,868,579
1994-95	19	38	72,416,000	3,811,368	1,905,684
1995-96	18	36	101,390,000	5,632,778	2,816,389
1996-97	18	36	101,316,000	5,628,667	2,814,333
1997-98	20	40	108,750,000	5,437,500	2,718,750
1998-99	22	44	145,924,000	6,632,909	3,316,455
1999-00	23	46	146,000,000	6,373,913	3,186,957
2000-01	25	50	161,826,000	6,473,040	3,236,520
2001-02	25	50	156,900,000	6,276,000	3,138,000
2002-03	28	56	172,710,000	6,168,214	3,084,107

29 Former Major Bowl Games

(Games in which at least one team was classified major that season)

ALAMO
(San Antonio, Texas)

1-4-47—Hardin-Simmons 20, Denver 0

ALL-AMERICAN
(Called Hall of Fame Classic, 1977-85)
(Birmingham, Ala.)

12-22-77—Maryland 17, Minnesota 7
12-20-78—Texas A&M 28, Iowa St. 12
12-29-79—Missouri 24, South Carolina 14
12-27-80—Arkansas 34, Tulane 15
12-31-81—Mississippi St. 10, Kansas 0
12-31-82—Air Force 36, Vanderbilt 28
12-22-83—West Virginia 20, Kentucky 16
12-29-84—Kentucky 20, Wisconsin 19
12-31-85—Georgia Tech 17, Michigan St. 14
12-31-86—Florida St. 27, Indiana 13
12-22-87—Virginia 22, Brigham Young 16
12-29-88—Florida 14, Illinois 10
12-28-89—Texas Tech 49, Duke 21
12-28-90—North Carolina St. 31, Southern Miss. 27

BOWL/ALL-STAR RECORDS

ALOHA
(Honolulu, Hawaii)

12-25-82—Washington 21, Maryland 20
12-26-83—Penn St. 13, Washington 10
12-29-84—Southern Methodist 27, Notre Dame 20
12-28-85—Alabama 24, Southern California 3
12-27-86—Arizona 30, North Carolina 21

12-25-87—UCLA 20, Florida 16
12-25-88—Washington St. 24, Houston 22
12-25-89—Michigan St. 33, Hawaii 13
12-25-90—Syracuse 28, Arizona 0
12-25-91—Georgia Tech 18, Stanford 17

12-25-92—Kansas 23, Brigham Young 20
12-25-93—Colorado 41, Fresno St. 30
12-25-94—Boston College 12, Kansas St. 7
12-25-95—Kansas 51, UCLA 30
12-25-96—Navy 42, California 38

12-25-97—Washington 51, Michigan St. 23
12-25-98—Colorado 51, Oregon 43
12-25-99—Wake Forest 23, Arizona St. 3
12-25-00—Boston College 31, Arizona St. 17

AVIATION
(Dayton, Ohio)

12-9-61—New Mexico 28, Western Mich. 12

BACARDI
(Cuban National Sports Festival at Havana)

1-1-37—Auburn 7, Villanova 7

BLUEBONNET
(Houston, Texas)

12-19-59—Clemson 23, TCU 7
12-17-60—Alabama 3, Texas 3
12-16-61—Kansas 33, Rice 7
12-22-62—Missouri 14, Georgia Tech 10
12-21-63—Baylor 14, LSU 7

12-19-64—Tulsa 14, Mississippi 7
12-18-65—Tennessee 27, Tulsa 6
12-17-66—Texas 19, Mississippi 0
12-23-67—Colorado 31, Miami (Fla.) 21
12-31-68—Southern Methodist 28, Oklahoma 27

12-31-69—Houston 36, Auburn 7
12-31-70—Alabama 24, Oklahoma 24
12-31-71—Colorado 29, Houston 17
12-30-72—Tennessee 24, LSU 17
12-29-73—Houston 47, Tulane 7

12-23-74—Houston 31, North Carolina St. 31
12-27-75—Texas 38, Colorado 21
12-31-76—Nebraska 27, Texas Tech 24
12-31-77—Southern California 47, Texas A&M 28
12-31-78—Stanford 25, Georgia 22

12-31-79—Purdue 27, Tennessee 22
12-31-80—North Carolina 16, Texas 7
12-31-81—Michigan 33, UCLA 14
12-31-82—Arkansas 28, Florida 24
12-31-83—Oklahoma St. 24, Baylor 14

12-31-84—West Virginia 31, TCU 14
12-31-85—Air Force 24, Texas 16
12-31-86—Baylor 21, Colorado 9
12-31-87—Texas 32, Pittsburgh 27

BLUEGRASS
(Louisville, Ky.)

12-13-58—Oklahoma St. 15, Florida St. 6

CALIFORNIA
(Fresno, Calif.)

12-19-81—Toledo 27, San Jose St. 25
12-18-82—Fresno St. 29, Bowling Green 28

12-17-83—Northern Ill. 20, Cal St. Fullerton 13
12-15-84—UNLV 30, *Toledo 13
12-14-85—Fresno St. 51, Bowling Green 7
12-13-86—San Jose St. 37, Miami (Ohio) 7
12-12-87—Eastern Mich. 30, San Jose St. 27
12-10-88—Fresno St. 35, Western Mich. 30
12-9-89—Fresno St. 27, Ball St. 6
12-8-90—San Jose St. 48, Central Mich. 24

12-14-91—Bowling Green 28, Fresno St. 21
*Won by forfeit.

CAMELLIA
(Lafayette, La.)

12-30-48—Hardin-Simmons 49, Wichita St. 12

CHERRY
(Pontiac, Mich.)

12-22-84—Army 10, Michigan St. 6
12-21-85—Maryland 35, Syracuse 18

DELTA
(Memphis, Tenn.)

1-1-48—Mississippi 13, TCU 9
1-1-49—William & Mary 20, Oklahoma St. 0

DIXIE BOWL
(Birmingham, Ala.)

1-1-48—Arkansas 21, William & Mary 19
1-1-49—Baylor 20, Wake Forest 7

DIXIE CLASSIC
(Dallas, Texas)

1-2-22—Texas A&M 22, Centre 14
1-25—West Va. Wesleyan 9, Southern Methodist 7
1-1-34—Arkansas 7, Centenary (La.) 7

FORT WORTH CLASSIC
(Fort Worth, Texas)

1-1-21—Centre 63, TCU 7

FREEDOM
(Anaheim, Calif.)

12-26-84—Iowa 55, Texas 17
12-30-85—Washington 20, Colorado 17
12-30-86—UCLA 31, Brigham Young 10
12-30-87—Arizona St. 33, Air Force 28
12-29-88—Brigham Young 20, Colorado 17

12-30-89—Washington 34, Florida 7
12-29-90—Colorado St. 32, Oregon 31
12-30-91—Tulsa 28, San Diego St. 17
12-29-92—Fresno St. 24, Southern California 7
12-30-93—Southern California 28, Utah 21

12-27-94—Utah 16, Arizona 13

GARDEN STATE
(East Rutherford, N.J.)

12-16-78—Arizona St. 34, Rutgers 18
12-15-79—Temple 28, California 17
12-14-80—Houston 35, Navy 0
12-13-81—Tennessee 28, Wisconsin 21

GOTHAM
(New York, N.Y.)

12-9-61—Baylor 24, Utah St. 9
12-15-62—Nebraska 36, Miami (Fla.) 34

GREAT LAKES
(Cleveland, Ohio)

12-6-47—Kentucky 24, Villanova 14

HARBOR
(San Diego, Calif.)

1-1-47—Montana St. 13, New Mexico 13
1-1-48—Hardin-Simmons 53, San Diego St. 0
1-1-49—Villanova 27, Nevada 7

LOS ANGELES CHRISTMAS FESTIVAL
(Los Angeles, Calif.)

12-25-24—Southern California 20, Missouri 7

MERCY
(Los Angeles, Calif.)

11-23-61—Fresno St. 36, Bowling Green 6

OIL
(Houston, Texas)

1-1-46—Georgia 20, Tulsa 6
1-1-47—Georgia Tech 41, St. Mary's (Cal.) 19

PASADENA
(Called Junior Rose in 1967)
(Pasadena, Calif.)

12-2-67—West Tex. A&M 35, Cal St. Northridge 13
12-6-69—San Diego St. 28, Boston U. 7
12-19-70—Long Beach St. 24, Louisville 24
12-18-71—Memphis 28, San Jose St. 9

PRESIDENTIAL CUP
(College Park, Md.)

12-9-50—Texas A&M 40, Georgia 20

RAISIN
(Fresno, Calif.)

1-1-46—Drake 13, Fresno St. 12
1-1-47—San Jose St. 20, Utah St. 0
1-1-48—Pacific (Cal.) 26, Wichita St. 14
1-1-49—Occidental 21, Colorado St. 20
12-31-49—San Jose St. 20, Texas Tech 13

SALAD
(Phoenix, Ariz.)

1-1-48—Nevada 13, North Texas 6
1-1-49—Drake 14, Arizona 13
1-1-50—Xavier (Ohio) 33, Arizona St. 21
1-1-51—Miami (Ohio) 34, Arizona St. 21
1-1-52—Houston 26, Dayton 21

SAN DIEGO EAST-WEST CHRISTMAS CLASSIC
(San Diego, Calif.)

12-26-21—Centre 38, Arizona 0
12-25-22—West Virginia 21, Gonzaga 13

SEATTLE
(Seattle, Washington)

12-25-98—Air Force 45, Washington 25
12-29-99—Hawaii 23, Oregon St. 17
12-24-00—Georgia 37, Virginia 14
12-27-01—Georgia Tech 24, Stanford 14
12-30-02—Wake Forest 38, Oregon 17

SHRINE
(Little Rock, Ark.)

12-18-48—Hardin-Simmons 40, Ouachita Baptist 12

Other Major Postseason Games

There was a proliferation of postseason benefit games specially scheduled at the conclusion of the regular season during the Great Depression (principally in 1931) to raise money for relief of the unemployed in response to the President's Committee on Mobilization of Relief Resources and for other charitable causes.

The exact number of these games is unknown, but it is estimated that more than 100 college games were played nationwide during this period, often irrespective of the competing teams' records.

Most notable among these postseason games were the Tennessee-New York University game of 1931 and the Army-Navy contests of 1930 and 1931 (the two academies had severed athletics relations during 1928-31 and did not meet in regular-season play). All three games were played before huge crowds in New York City's Yankee Stadium.

Following is a list of the principal postseason benefit and charity games involving at least one major college. Not included (nor included in all-time team won-lost records) are several special feature, same-day double-header tournaments in 1931 in which four participating teams were paired to play halves or modified quarters.

Date	Site	Opposing Teams
12-6-30	New York	Colgate 7, New York U. 0
12-13-30	New York	Army 6, Navy 0
11-28-31	Kansas City	Temple 38, Missouri 6

Date	Site	Opposing Teams
11-28-31	Chicago	Purdue 7, Northwestern 0
11-28-31	Minneapolis	Minnesota 19, Ohio St. 7
11-28-31	Ann Arbor	Michigan 16, Wisconsin 0
11-28-31	Philadelphia	Penn St. 31, Lehigh 0
12-2-31	Chattanooga	Alabama 49, Chattanooga 0
12-3-31	Brooklyn	Manhattan 7, Rutgers 6
12-5-31	Denver	Nebraska 20, Colorado St. 7
12-5-31	Pittsburgh	Carnegie Mellon 0, Duquesne 0
12-5-31	New York	Tennessee 13, New York U. 0
12-5-31	St. Louis	St. Louis 31, Missouri 6
12-5-31	Topeka	Kansas 6, Washburn 0
12-5-31	Wichita	Kansas St. 20, Wichita St. 6
12-5-31	Columbia	Centre 9, South Carolina 7
12-5-31	Norman	Oklahoma City 6, Oklahoma 0
12-12-31	New York	Army 17, Navy 7
12-12-31	Tulsa	Oklahoma 20, Tulsa 7
1-2-33	El Paso	Southern Methodist 26, UTEP 0
12-8-34	St. Louis	Southern Methodist 7, Washington (Mo.) 0

Team-by-Team Bowl Results

All-Time Bowl-Game Records

This list includes all bowls played by a current major team, providing its opponent was classified as a major that season or it was a major team then. The list excludes games in which a home team served as a predetermined, preseason host regardless of its record and/or games scheduled before the season, thus eliminating the old Pineapple, Glass and Palm Festival. Following is the alphabetical list showing the record of each current major team in all major bowls.

Team	W	L	T
Air Force	8	8	1
Alabama	29	19	3
Arizona	5	7	1
Arizona St.	10	9	1
Arkansas	10	20	3
Army	2	2	0
Auburn	15	12	2
Ball St.	0	3	0
Baylor	8	8	0
Boise St.	3	0	0
Boston College	8	6	0
Bowling Green	2	3	0
Brigham Young	7	15	1
California	5	7	1
Central Mich.	0	2	0
Cincinnati	2	4	0
Clemson	13	13	0
Colorado	11	14	0
Colorado St.	4	5	0
Duke	3	5	0
East Caro.	4	3	0
Eastern Mich.	1	0	0
Florida	14	16	0
Florida St.	18	11	2

Team	W	L	T
Fresno St.	7	6	0
Georgia	20	15	3
Georgia Tech	20	11	0
Hawaii	2	2	0
Houston	7	6	1
Idaho	1	0	0
Illinois	6	8	0
Indiana	3	5	0
Iowa	9	8	1
Iowa St.	1	6	0
Kansas	3	5	0
Kansas St.	6	5	0
Kent St.	0	1	0
Kentucky	5	5	0
LSU	16	17	1
Louisiana Tech	1	2	1
Louisville	4	5	1
Marshall	5	1	0
Maryland	7	10	2
Memphis	1	0	0
Miami (Fla.)	15	12	0
Miami (Ohio)	5	2	0
Michigan	18	16	0

Team	W	L	T
Michigan St.	7	9	0
Minnesota	3	5	0
Mississippi	18	12	0
Mississippi St.	6	6	0
Missouri	9	12	0
Navy	4	4	0
Nebraska	20	21	0
Nevada	2	3	0
UNLV	#3	0	0
New Mexico	2	4	1
New Mexico St.	2	0	1
North Carolina	12	12	0
North Carolina St.	10	10	1
North Texas	1	3	0
Northern Ill.	1	0	0
Northwestern	1	3	0
Notre Dame	13	12	0
Ohio	0	2	0
Ohio St.	15	19	0
Oklahoma	23	12	1
Oklahoma St.	10	4	0
Oregon	7	10	0
Oregon St.	3	4	0
Penn St.	23	12	2
Pittsburgh	10	12	0
Purdue	7	4	0
Rice	4	3	0
Rutgers	0	1	0
San Diego St.	1	4	0
San Jose St.	4	3	0

Team	W	L	T
South Carolina	3	8	0
Southern California	26	15	0
Southern Methodist	4	6	1
Southern Miss.	5	6	0
Stanford	9	10	1
Syracuse	12	8	1
Temple	1	1	0
Tennessee	23	20	0
Texas	20	20	2
UTEP	5	5	0
Texas A&M	13	14	0
TCU	7	12	1
Texas Tech	6	19	1
Toledo	6	2	0
Tulane	4	6	0
Tulsa	4	7	0
UCLA	12	11	1
Utah	5	3	0
Utah St.	1	4	0
Vanderbilt	1	1	1
Virginia	5	8	0
Virginia Tech	6	10	0
Wake Forest	4	2	0
Washington	14	14	1
Washington St.	5	4	0
West Virginia	9	13	0
Western Mich.	0	2	0
Wisconsin	8	6	0
Wyoming	4	6	0
TOTALS	**788**	**788**	**42**

#Later lost game by forfeit. The following current Division I-A teams have not played in a major bowl game: Akron, UAB, Arkansas St., UCF, Connecticut, La.-Lafayette, La.-Monroe, Middle Tenn., South Fla. and Troy St.

Major Bowl Records of Non-Division I-A Teams

Boston U. 0-1-0; Brown 0-1-0; Bucknell 1-0-0; Cal St. Fullerton 0-1-0; Cal St. Northridge 0-1-0; Carnegie Mellon 0-1-0; Case Reserve 1-0-0; Catholic 1-0-1; Centenary (La.) 0-0-1; Centre 2-1-0; Citadel 1-0-0; Columbia 1-0-0; Davidson 0-1-0; Dayton 0-1-0; Denver 0-2-0; Drake 2-1-0; Duquesne 1-0-0; Fordham 1-1-0; George Washington 1-0-0; Georgetown 0-2-0; Gonzaga 0-1-0; Hardin-Simmons 5-2-1; Harvard 1-0-0; Holy Cross 0-1-0; Long Beach St. 0-0-1; Marquette 0-1-0; McNeese St. 1-2-0; Montana St. 0-0-1; Occidental 1-0-0; Ouachita Baptist 0-1-0; Pacific (Cal.) 2-1-0; Pennsylvania 0-1-0; Randolph Field 0-0-1; Richmond 1-1-0; St. Mary's (Cal.) 1-2-0; Santa Clara 3-0-0; Second Air Force 1-0-0; Southwestern (Tex.) 2-0-0; Tampa 1-0-0; Tennessee Tech 0-1-0; U. of Mexico 0-1-0; Villanova 2-2-1; Wash. & Jeff. 0-0-1; Wash. & Lee 0-1-0; West Tex. A&M 3-0-0; West Va. Wesleyan 1-0-0; Wichita St. 0-3-0; William & Mary 1-2-0; Xavier (Ohio) 1-0-0. TOTALS: 39-37-8

All-Time Bowl Appearances Leaders

(Must be classified as a major bowl game where one team was considered a major college at the time.)

Team	Appearances	Team	Appearances
Alabama	51	Texas A&M	27
Tennessee	43		
Texas	42	Clemson	26
Nebraska	41	Texas Tech	26
Southern California	41	Colorado	25
		Notre Dame	25
Georgia	38	North Carolina	24
Penn St.	37		
Oklahoma	36	UCLA	24
LSU	34	Brigham Young	23
Michigan	34	Pittsburgh	22
		West Virginia	22
Ohio St.	34	Missouri	21
Arkansas	33		
Florida St.	31	North Carolina St.	21
Georgia Tech	31	Syracuse	21
Florida	30	Arizona St.	20
		Stanford	20
Mississippi	30	Maryland	19
Auburn	29		
Washington	29	Iowa	18
Miami (Fla.)	27	Baylor	16

All-Time Bowl Victories Leaders

(Includes bowls where at least one team was classified a major college at the time.)

Team	Victories	Team	Victories
Alabama	29	Ohio St.	15
Southern California	26	Florida	14
Oklahoma	23	Washington	14
Penn St.	23	Clemson	13
Tennessee	23	Notre Dame	13
Georgia	20	Texas A&M	13
Georgia Tech	20	North Carolina	12
Nebraska	20	Syracuse	12
Texas	20	UCLA	12
Florida St.	18	Colorado	11
Michigan	18	Arizona St.	10
Mississippi	18	Arkansas	10
Auburn	15	Oklahoma St.	10
LSU	15	Missouri	9
Miami (Fla.)	15	Stanford	9

Team-by-Team Major Bowl Scores With Coach of Each Bowl Team

Listed below are the 106 I-A teams that have participated in history's 851 major bowl games (the term "major bowl" is defined above the alphabetical list of team bowl records). The teams are listed alphabetically, with each coach listed along with the bowl participated in, date played, opponent, score and team's all-time bowl-game record. Following the I-A list is a group of 49 teams that played in a major bowl game or games but are no longer classified as I-A.

School/Coach	Bowl/Date	Opponent/Score
AIR FORCE		
Ben Martin	Cotton 1-1-59	TCU 0-0
Ben Martin	Gator 12-28-63	North Carolina 0-35
Ben Martin	Sugar 1-1-71	Tennessee 13-34
Ken Hatfield	Hall of Fame 12-31-82	Vanderbilt 36-28
Ken Hatfield	Independence 12-10-83	Mississippi 9-3
Fisher DeBerry	Independence 12-15-84	Virginia Tech 23-7
Fisher DeBerry	Bluebonnet 12-31-85	Texas 24-16

School/Coach	Bowl/Date	Opponent/Score
Fisher DeBerry	Freedom 12-30-87	Arizona St. 28-33
Fisher DeBerry	Liberty 12-28-89	Mississippi 29-42
Fisher DeBerry	Liberty 12-27-90	Ohio St. 23-11
Fisher DeBerry	Liberty 12-29-91	Mississippi St. 38-15
Fisher DeBerry	Liberty 12-31-92	Mississippi 0-13
Fisher DeBerry	Copper 12-27-95	Texas Tech 41-55
Fisher DeBerry	Las Vegas 12-20-97	Oregon 13-41
Fisher DeBerry	Oahu Classic 12-25-98	Washington 45-25
Fisher DeBerry	Silicon Valley 12-31-00	Fresno St. 37-34
Fisher DeBerry	San Francisco 12-31-02	Virginia Tech 13-20
All bowls 8-8-1		
ALABAMA		
Wallace Wade	Rose 1-1-26	Washington 20-19
Wallace Wade	Rose 1-1-27	Stanford 7-7
Wallace Wade	Rose 1-1-31	Washington St. 24-0
Frank Thomas	Rose 1-1-35	Stanford 29-13
Frank Thomas	Rose 1-1-38	California 0-13
Frank Thomas	Cotton 1-1-42	Texas A&M 29-21
Frank Thomas	Orange 1-1-43	Boston College 37-21
Frank Thomas	Sugar 1-1-45	Duke 26-29
Frank Thomas	Rose 1-1-46	Southern California 34-14
Harold "Red" Drew	Sugar 1-1-48	Texas 7-27
Harold "Red" Drew	Orange 1-1-53	Syracuse 61-6
Harold "Red" Drew	Cotton 1-1-54	Rice 6-28
Paul "Bear" Bryant	Liberty 12-19-59	Penn St. 0-7
Paul "Bear" Bryant	Bluebonnet 12-17-60	Texas 3-3
Paul "Bear" Bryant	Sugar 1-1-62	Arkansas 10-3
Paul "Bear" Bryant	Orange 1-1-63	Oklahoma 17-0
Paul "Bear" Bryant	Sugar 1-1-64	Mississippi 12-7
Paul "Bear" Bryant	Orange 1-1-65	Texas 17-21
Paul "Bear" Bryant	Orange 1-1-66	Nebraska 39-28
Paul "Bear" Bryant	Sugar 1-2-67	Nebraska 34-7
Paul "Bear" Bryant	Cotton 1-1-68	Texas A&M 16-20
Paul "Bear" Bryant	Gator 12-28-68	Missouri 10-35
Paul "Bear" Bryant	Liberty 12-13-69	Colorado 33-47
Paul "Bear" Bryant	Bluebonnet 12-31-70	Oklahoma 24-24
Paul "Bear" Bryant	Orange 1-1-72	Nebraska 6-38
Paul "Bear" Bryant	Cotton 1-1-73	Texas 13-17
Paul "Bear" Bryant	Sugar 12-31-73	Notre Dame 23-24
Paul "Bear" Bryant	Orange 1-1-75	Notre Dame 11-13
Paul "Bear" Bryant	Sugar 12-31-75	Penn St. 13-6
Paul "Bear" Bryant	Liberty 12-20-76	UCLA 36-6
Paul "Bear" Bryant	Sugar 1-2-78	Ohio St. 35-6
Paul "Bear" Bryant	Sugar 1-1-79	Penn St. 14-7
Paul "Bear" Bryant	Sugar 1-1-80	Arkansas 24-9
Paul "Bear" Bryant	Cotton 1-1-81	Baylor 30-2
Paul "Bear" Bryant	Cotton 1-1-82	Texas 12-14
Paul "Bear" Bryant	Liberty 12-29-82	Illinois 21-15
Ray Perkins	Sun 12-24-83	Southern Methodist 28-7
Ray Perkins	Aloha 12-28-85	Southern California 24-3
Ray Perkins	Sun 12-25-86	Washington 28-6
Bill Curry	Hall of Fame 1-2-88	Michigan 24-28
Bill Curry	Sun 12-24-88	Army 29-28
Bill Curry	Sugar 1-1-90	Miami (Fla.) 25-33
Gene Stallings	Fiesta 1-1-91	Louisville 7-34
Gene Stallings	Blockbuster 12-28-91	Colorado 30-25
Gene Stallings	Sugar 1-1-93	Miami (Fla.) 34-13
Gene Stallings	Gator 12-31-93	North Carolina 24-10
Gene Stallings	Florida Citrus 1-2-95	Ohio St. 24-17
Gene Stallings	Outback 1-1-97	Michigan 17-14
Mike DuBose	Music City 12-29-98	Virginia Tech 7-38
Mike DuBose	Orange 1-1-00	Michigan 34-35 (ot)
Dennis Franchione	Independence 12-27-01	Iowa St. 14-13
All bowls 29-19-3		
ARIZONA		
J.F. "Pop" McKale	San Diego East-West Christmas Classic 12-26-21	Centre 0-38
Miles Casteel	Salad 1-1-49	Drake 13-14
Darrell Mudra	Sun 12-28-68	Auburn 10-34
Tony Mason	Fiesta 12-25-79	Pittsburgh 10-16
Larry Smith	Sun 12-28-85	Georgia 13-13
Larry Smith	Aloha 12-27-86	North Carolina 30-21
Dick Tomey	Copper 12-31-89	North Carolina St. 17-10
Dick Tomey	Aloha 12-25-90	Syracuse 0-28
Dick Tomey	John Hancock 12-31-92	Baylor 15-20
Dick Tomey	Fiesta 1-1-94	Miami (Fla.) 29-0
Dick Tomey	Freedom 12-27-94	Utah 13-16
Dick Tomey	Insight.com 12-27-97	New Mexico 20-14
Dick Tomey	Holiday 12-30-98	Nebraska 23-20
All bowls 5-7-1		

School/Coach	Bowl/Date	Opponent/Score
ARIZONA ST.		
Millard "Dixie" Howell	Sun 1-1-40	Catholic 0-0
Millard "Dixie" Howell	Sun 1-1-41	Case Reserve 13-26
Ed Doherty	Salad 1-1-50	Xavier (Ohio) 21-33
Ed Doherty	Salad 1-1-51	Miami (Ohio) 21-34
Frank Kush	Peach 12-30-70	North Carolina 48-26
Frank Kush	Fiesta 12-27-71	Florida St. 45-38
Frank Kush	Fiesta 12-23-72	Missouri 49-35
Frank Kush	Fiesta 12-21-73	Pittsburgh 28-7
Frank Kush	Fiesta 12-26-75	Nebraska 17-14
Frank Kush	Fiesta 12-25-77	Penn St. 30-42
Frank Kush	Garden State 12-16-78	Rutgers 34-18
Darryl Rogers	Fiesta 1-1-83	Oklahoma 32-21
John Cooper	Holiday 12-22-85	Arkansas 17-18
John Cooper	Rose 1-1-87	Michigan 22-15
John Cooper	Freedom 12-30-87	Air Force 33-28
Bruce Snyder	Rose 1-1-97	Ohio St. 17-20
Bruce Snyder	Sun 12-31-97	Iowa 17-7
Bruce Snyder	Aloha Classic 12-25-99	Wake Forest 3-23
Bruce Snyder	Aloha Classic 12-25-00	Boston College 17-31
Dirk Koetter	Holiday 12-27-02	Kansas St. 27-34
All bowls 10-9-1		
ARKANSAS		
Fred Thomsen	Dixie Classic 1-1-34	Centenary (La.) 7-7
John Barnhill	Cotton 1-1-47	LSU 0-0
John Barnhill	Dixie 1-1-48	William & Mary 21-19
Bowden Wyatt	Cotton 1-1-55	Georgia Tech 6-14
Frank Broyles	Gator 1-2-60	Georgia Tech 14-7
Frank Broyles	Cotton 1-2-61	Duke 6-7
Frank Broyles	Sugar 1-1-62	Alabama 3-10
Frank Broyles	Sugar 1-1-63	Mississippi 13-17
Frank Broyles	Cotton 1-1-65	Nebraska 10-7
Frank Broyles	Cotton 1-1-66	LSU 7-14
Frank Broyles	Sugar 1-1-69	Georgia 16-2
Frank Broyles	Sugar 1-1-70	Mississippi 22-27
Frank Broyles	Liberty 12-20-71	Tennessee 13-14
Frank Broyles	Cotton 1-1-76	Georgia 31-10
Lou Holtz	Orange 1-2-78	Oklahoma 31-6
Lou Holtz	Fiesta 12-25-78	UCLA 10-10
Lou Holtz	Sugar 1-1-80	Alabama 9-24
Lou Holtz	Hall of Fame 12-27-80	Tulane 34-15
Lou Holtz	Gator 12-28-81	North Carolina 27-31
Lou Holtz	Bluebonnet 12-31-82	Florida 28-24
Ken Hatfield	Liberty 12-27-84	Auburn 15-21
Ken Hatfield	Holiday 12-22-85	Arizona St. 18-17
Ken Hatfield	Orange 1-1-87	Oklahoma 8-42
Ken Hatfield	Liberty 12-29-87	Georgia 17-20
Ken Hatfield	Cotton 1-2-89	UCLA 3-17
Ken Hatfield	Cotton 1-1-90	Tennessee 27-31
Jack Crowe	Independence 12-29-91	Georgia 15-24
Danny Ford	Carquest 12-30-95	North Carolina 10-20
Houston Nutt	Florida Citrus 1-1-99	Michigan 31-45
Houston Nutt	Cotton 1-1-00	Texas 27-6
Houston Nutt	Las Vegas 12-21-00	UNLV 14-31
Houston Nutt	Cotton 1-1-02	Oklahoma 3-10
Houston Nutt	Music City 12-30-02	Minnesota 14-29
All bowls 10-20-3		
ARMY		
Jim Young	Cherry 12-22-84	Michigan St. 10-6
Jim Young	Peach 12-31-85	Illinois 31-29
Jim Young	Sun 12-24-88	Alabama 28-29
Bob Sutton	Independence 12-31-96	Auburn 29-32
All bowls 2-2-0		
AUBURN		
Jack Meagher	Bacardi, Cuba 1-1-37	Villanova 7-7
Jack Meagher	Orange 1-1-38	Michigan St. 6-0
Ralph "Shug" Jordan	Gator 1-1-54	Texas Tech 13-35
Ralph "Shug" Jordan	Gator 12-31-54	Baylor 33-13
Ralph "Shug" Jordan	Gator 12-31-55	Vanderbilt 13-25
Ralph "Shug" Jordan	Orange 1-1-64	Nebraska 7-13
Ralph "Shug" Jordan	Liberty 12-18-65	Mississippi 7-13
Ralph "Shug" Jordan	Sun 12-28-68	Arizona 34-10
Ralph "Shug" Jordan	Bluebonnet 12-31-69	Houston 7-36
Ralph "Shug" Jordan	Gator 1-2-71	Mississippi 35-28
Ralph "Shug" Jordan	Sugar 1-1-72	Oklahoma 22-40
Ralph "Shug" Jordan	Gator 12-30-72	Colorado 24-3
Ralph "Shug" Jordan	Sun 12-29-73	Missouri 17-34
Ralph "Shug" Jordan	Gator 12-30-74	Texas 27-3
Pat Dye	Tangerine 12-18-82	Boston College 33-26
Pat Dye	Sugar 1-1-84	Michigan 9-7
Pat Dye	Liberty 12-27-84	Arkansas 21-15
Pat Dye	Cotton 1-1-86	Texas A&M 16-36
Pat Dye	Florida Citrus 1-1-87	Southern California 16-7
Pat Dye	Sugar 1-1-88	Syracuse 16-16

School/Coach	Bowl/Date	Opponent/Score
Pat Dye	Sugar 1-2-89	Florida St. 7-13
Pat Dye	Hall of Fame 1-1-90	Ohio St. 31-24
Pat Dye	Peach 12-29-90	Indiana 27-23
Terry Bowden	Outback 1-1-96	Penn St. 14-43
Terry Bowden	Independence 12-31-96	Army 33-29
Terry Bowden	Peach 1-2-98	Clemson 21-17
Tommy Tuberville	Florida Citrus 1-1-01	Michigan 28-31
Tommy Tuberville	Peach 12-31-01	North Carolina 10-16
Tommy Tuberville	Capital One 1-1-03	Penn St. 13-9
All bowls 15-12-2		
BALL ST.		
Paul Schudel	California 12-9-89	Fresno St. 6-27
Paul Schudel	Las Vegas 12-17-93	Utah St. 33-42
Bill Lynch	Las Vegas 12-19-96	Nevada 15-18
All bowls 0-3-0		
BAYLOR		
Bob Woodruff	Dixie 1-1-49	Wake Forest 20-7
George Sauer	Orange 1-1-52	Georgia Tech 14-17
George Sauer	Gator 12-31-54	Auburn 13-33
Sam Boyd	Sugar 1-1-57	Tennessee 13-7
John Bridgers	Gator 12-31-60	Florida 12-13
John Bridgers	Gotham 12-9-61	Utah St. 24-9
John Bridgers	Bluebonnet 12-21-63	LSU 14-7
Grant Teaff	Cotton 1-1-75	Penn St. 20-41
Grant Teaff	Peach 12-31-79	Clemson 24-18
Grant Teaff	Cotton 1-1-81	Alabama 2-30
Grant Teaff	Bluebonnet 12-31-83	Oklahoma St. 14-24
Grant Teaff	Liberty 12-27-85	LSU 21-7
Grant Teaff	Bluebonnet 12-31-86	Colorado 21-9
Grant Teaff	Copper 12-31-91	Indiana 0-24
Grant Teaff	John Hancock 12-31-92	Arizona 20-15
Chuck Reedy	Alamo 12-31-94	Washington St. 3-10
All bowls 8-8-0		
BOISE ST.		
Dirk Koetter	Humanitarian 12-30-99	Louisville 34-31
Dirk Koetter	Humanitarian 12-28-00	UTEP 38-23
Dan Hawkins	Humanitarian 12-31-02	Iowa St. 34-16
All bowls 3-0-0		
BOSTON COLLEGE		
Frank Leahy	Cotton 1-1-40	Clemson 3-6
Frank Leahy	Sugar 1-1-41	Tennessee 19-13
Denny Myers	Orange 1-1-43	Alabama 21-37
Jack Bicknell	Tangerine 12-18-82	Auburn 26-33
Jack Bicknell	Liberty 12-29-83	Notre Dame 18-19
Jack Bicknell	Cotton 1-1-85	Houston 45-28
Jack Bicknell	Hall of Fame 12-23-86	Georgia 27-24
Tom Coughlin	Hall of Fame 1-1-93	Tennessee 23-38
Tom Coughlin	Carquest 1-1-94	Virginia 31-13
Dan Henning	Aloha 12-25-94	Kansas St. 12-7
Tom O'Brien	Insight.com 12-31-99	Colorado 28-62
Tom O'Brien	Aloha Classic 12-25-00	Arizona St. 31-17
Tom O'Brien	Music City 12-28-01	Georgia 20-16
Tom O'Brien	Motor City 12-26-02	Toledo 51-25
All bowls 8-6-0		
BOWLING GREEN		
Doyt Perry	Mercy 11-23-61	Fresno St. 6-36
Denny Stolz	California 12-18-82	Fresno St. 28-29
Denny Stolz	California 12-14-85	Fresno St. 7-51
Gary Blackney	California 12-14-91	Fresno St. 28-21
Gary Blackney	Las Vegas 12-18-92	Nevada 35-34
All bowls 2-3-0		
BRIGHAM YOUNG		
LaVell Edwards	Fiesta 12-28-74	Oklahoma St. 6-16
LaVell Edwards	Tangerine 12-18-76	Oklahoma St. 21-49
LaVell Edwards	Holiday 12-22-78	Navy 16-23
LaVell Edwards	Holiday 12-21-79	Indiana 37-38
LaVell Edwards	Holiday 12-19-80	Southern Methodist 46-45
LaVell Edwards	Holiday 12-18-81	Washington St. 38-36
LaVell Edwards	Holiday 12-17-82	Ohio St. 17-47
LaVell Edwards	Holiday 12-23-83	Missouri 21-17
LaVell Edwards	Holiday 12-21-84	Michigan 24-17
LaVell Edwards	Florida Citrus 12-28-85	Ohio St. 7-10
LaVell Edwards	Freedom 12-30-86	UCLA 10-31
LaVell Edwards	All-American 12-22-87	Virginia 16-22
LaVell Edwards	Freedom 12-29-88	Colorado 20-17
LaVell Edwards	Holiday 12-29-89	Penn St. 39-50
LaVell Edwards	Holiday 12-29-90	Texas A&M 14-65
LaVell Edwards	Holiday 12-30-91	Iowa 13-13
LaVell Edwards	Aloha 12-25-92	Kansas 20-23
LaVell Edwards	Holiday 12-30-93	Ohio St. 21-28
LaVell Edwards	Copper 12-29-94	Oklahoma 31-6
LaVell Edwards	Cotton 1-1-97	Kansas St. 19-15

School/Coach	Bowl/Date	Opponent/Score
LaVell Edwards	Liberty 12-31-98	Tulane 27-41
LaVell Edwards	Motor City 12-27-99	Marshall 3-21
Gary Crowton	Liberty 12-31-01	Louisville 10-28

All bowls 7-15-1

CALIFORNIA

School/Coach	Bowl/Date	Opponent/Score
Andy Smith	Rose 1-1-21	Ohio St. 28-0
Andy Smith	Rose 1-2-22	Wash. & Jeff. 0-0
Clarence "Nibs" Price	Rose 1-1-29	Georgia Tech 7-8
Leonard "Stub" Allison	Rose 1-1-38	Alabama 13-0
Lynn "Pappy" Waldorf	Rose 1-1-49	Northwestern 14-20
Lynn "Pappy" Waldorf	Rose 1-2-50	Ohio St. 14-17
Lynn "Pappy" Waldorf	Rose 1-1-51	Michigan 6-14
Pete Elliott	Rose 1-1-59	Iowa 12-38
Roger Theder	Garden State 12-15-79	Temple 17-28
Bruce Snyder	Copper 12-31-90	Wyoming 17-15
Bruce Snyder	Florida Citrus 1-1-92	Clemson 37-13
Keith Gilbertson	Alamo 12-31-93	Iowa 37-3
Steve Mariucci	Aloha 12-25-96	Navy 38-42

All bowls 5-7-1

CENTRAL MICH.

School/Coach	Bowl/Date	Opponent/Score
Herb Deromedi	California 12-8-90	San Jose St. 24-48
Dick Flynn	Las Vegas 12-15-94	UNLV 24-52

All bowls 0-2-0

CINCINNATI

School/Coach	Bowl/Date	Opponent/Score
Ray Nolting	Sun 1-1-47	Virginia Tech 18-6
Sid Gillman	Sun 1-1-51	West Tex. A&M 13-14
Rick Minter	Humanitarian 12-29-97	Utah St. 35-19
Rick Minter	Motor City 12-27-00	Marshall 14-25
Rick Minter	Motor City 12-29-01	Toledo 16-23
Rick Minter	New Orleans 12-17-02	North Texas 19-24

All bowls 2-4-0

CLEMSON

School/Coach	Bowl/Date	Opponent/Score
Jess Neely	Cotton 1-1-40	Boston College 6-3
Frank Howard	Gator 1-1-49	Missouri 24-23
Frank Howard	Orange 1-1-51	Miami (Fla.) 15-14
Frank Howard	Gator 1-1-52	Miami (Fla.) 0-14
Frank Howard	Orange 1-1-57	Colorado 21-27
Frank Howard	Sugar 1-1-59	LSU 0-7
Frank Howard	Bluebonnet 12-19-59	TCU 23-7
Charley Pell	Gator 12-30-77	Pittsburgh 3-34
Danny Ford	Gator 12-29-78	Ohio St. 17-15
Danny Ford	Peach 12-31-79	Baylor 18-24
Danny Ford	Orange 1-1-82	Nebraska 22-15
Danny Ford	Independence 12-21-85	Minnesota 13-20
Danny Ford	Gator 12-27-86	Stanford 27-21
Danny Ford	Florida Citrus 1-1-88	Penn St. 35-10
Danny Ford	Florida Citrus 1-2-89	Oklahoma 23-6
Danny Ford	Gator 12-30-89	West Virginia 27-7
Ken Hatfield	Hall of Fame 1-1-91	Illinois 30-0
Ken Hatfield	Florida Citrus 1-1-92	California 13-37
Tommy West	Peach 12-31-93	Kentucky 14-13
Tommy West	Gator 1-1-96	Syracuse 0-41
Tommy West	Peach 12-28-96	LSU 7-10
Tommy West	Peach 1-2-98	Auburn 17-21
Tommy Bowden	Peach 12-30-99	Mississippi St. 7-17
Tommy Bowden	Gator 1-1-01	Virginia Tech 20-41
Tommy Bowden	Humanitarian 12-31-01	Louisiana Tech 49-24
Tommy Bowden	Mazda Tangerine 12-23-02	Texas Tech 15-55

All bowls 13-13-0

COLORADO

School/Coach	Bowl/Date	Opponent/Score
Bernard "Bunnie" Oaks	Cotton 1-1-38	Rice 14-28
Dallas Ward	Orange 1-1-57	Clemson 27-21
Sonny Grandelius	Orange 1-1-62	LSU 7-25
Eddie Crowder	Bluebonnet 12-23-67	Miami (Fla.) 31-21
Eddie Crowder	Liberty 12-13-69	Alabama 47-33
Eddie Crowder	Liberty 12-12-70	Tulane 3-17
Eddie Crowder	Bluebonnet 12-31-71	Houston 29-17
Eddie Crowder	Gator 12-30-72	Auburn 3-24
Bill Mallory	Bluebonnet 12-27-75	Texas 21-38
Bill Mallory	Orange 1-1-77	Ohio St. 10-27
Bill McCartney	Freedom 12-30-85	Washington 17-20
Bill McCartney	Bluebonnet 12-31-86	Baylor 9-21
Bill McCartney	Freedom 12-29-88	Brigham Young 17-20
Bill McCartney	Orange 1-1-90	Notre Dame 6-21
Bill McCartney	Orange 1-1-91	Notre Dame 10-9
Bill McCartney	Blockbuster 12-28-91	Alabama 25-30
Bill McCartney	Fiesta 1-1-93	Syracuse 22-26
Bill McCartney	Aloha 12-25-93	Fresno St. 41-30
Bill McCartney	Fiesta 1-2-95	Notre Dame 41-24
Rick Neuheisel	Cotton 1-1-96	Oregon 38-6
Rick Neuheisel	Holiday 12-30-96	Washington 33-21

School/Coach	Bowl/Date	Opponent/Score
Rick Neuheisel	Aloha Classic 12-25-98	Oregon 51-43
Gary Barnett	Insight.com 12-31-99	Boston College 62-28
Gary Barnett	Fiesta 1-1-02	Oregon 16-38
Gary Barnett	Alamo 12-28-02	Wisconsin 28-31 (ot)

All bowls 11-14-0

COLORADO ST.

School/Coach	Bowl/Date	Opponent/Score
Bob Davis	Raisin 1-1-49	Occidental 20-21
Earle Bruce	Freedom 12-24-90	Oregon 32-31
Sonny Lubick	Holiday 12-30-94	Michigan 14-24
Sonny Lubick	Holiday 12-29-95	Kansas St. 21-54
Sonny Lubick	Holiday 12-29-97	Missouri 35-24
Sonny Lubick	Liberty 12-31-99	Southern Miss. 17-23
Sonny Lubick	Liberty 12-29-00	Louisville 22-17
Sonny Lubick	New Orleans 12-18-01	North Texas 45-20
Sonny Lubick	Liberty 12-31-02	TCU 3-17

All bowls 4-5-0

DUKE

School/Coach	Bowl/Date	Opponent/Score
Wallace Wade	Rose 1-2-39	Southern California 3-7
Wallace Wade	Rose 1-1-42	Oregon St. 16-20
Eddie Cameron	Sugar 1-1-45	Alabama 29-26
Bill Murray	Orange 1-1-55	Nebraska 34-7
Bill Murray	Orange 1-1-58	Oklahoma 21-48
Bill Murray	Cotton 1-2-61	Arkansas 7-6
Steve Spurrier	All-American 12-28-89	Texas Tech 21-49
Fred Goldsmith	Hall of Fame 1-2-95	Wisconsin 20-34

All bowls 3-5-0

EAST CARO.

School/Coach	Bowl/Date	Opponent/Score
Pat Dye	Independence 12-16-78	Louisiana Tech 35-13
Bill Lewis	Peach 1-1-92	North Carolina St. 37-34
Steve Logan	Liberty 12-31-94	Illinois 0-30
Steve Logan	Liberty 12-30-95	Stanford 19-13
Steve Logan	Mobile Alabama 12-22-99	TCU 14-28
Steve Logan	galleryfurniture.com 12-27-00	Texas Tech 40-27
Steve Logan	GMAC 12-19-01	Marshall 61-64 (2 ot)

All bowls 4-3-0

EASTERN MICH.

School/Coach	Bowl/Date	Opponent/Score
Jim Harkema	California 12-12-87	San Jose St. 30-27

All bowls 1-0-0

FLORIDA

School/Coach	Bowl/Date	Opponent/Score
Bob Woodruff	Gator 1-1-53	Tulsa 14-13
Bob Woodruff	Gator 12-27-58	Mississippi 3-7
Ray Graves	Gator 12-31-60	Baylor 13-12
Ray Graves	Gator 12-29-62	Penn St. 17-7
Ray Graves	Sugar 1-1-66	Missouri 18-20
Ray Graves	Orange 1-2-67	Georgia Tech 27-12
Ray Graves	Gator 12-27-69	Tennessee 14-13
Doug Dickey	Tangerine 12-22-73	Miami (Ohio) 7-16
Doug Dickey	Sugar 12-31-74	Nebraska 10-13
Doug Dickey	Gator 12-29-75	Maryland 0-13
Doug Dickey	Sun 1-2-77	Texas A&M 14-37
Charley Pell	Tangerine 12-20-80	Maryland 35-20
Charley Pell	Peach 12-31-81	West Virginia 6-26
Charley Pell	Bluebonnet 12-31-82	Arkansas 24-28
Charley Pell	Gator 12-30-83	Iowa 14-6
Galen Hall	Aloha 12-25-87	UCLA 16-20
Galen Hall	All-American 12-29-88	Illinois 14-10
Gary Darnell	Freedom 12-30-89	Washington 7-34
Steve Spurrier	Sugar 1-1-92	Notre Dame 28-39
Steve Spurrier	Gator 12-31-92	North Carolina St. 27-10
Steve Spurrier	Sugar 1-1-94	West Virginia 41-7
Steve Spurrier	Sugar 1-2-95	Florida St. 17-23
Steve Spurrier	Fiesta 1-2-96	Nebraska 24-62
Steve Spurrier	Sugar 1-2-97	Florida St. 52-20
Steve Spurrier	Florida Citrus 1-1-98	Penn St. 21-6
Steve Spurrier	Orange 1-2-99	Syracuse 31-10
Steve Spurrier	Florida Citrus 1-1-00	Michigan St. 34-37
Steve Spurrier	Sugar 1-2-01	Miami (Fla.) 20-37
Steve Spurrier	Orange 1-2-02	Maryland 56-23
Ron Zook	Outback 1-1-03	Michigan 30-38

All bowls 14-16-0

FLORIDA ST.

School/Coach	Bowl/Date	Opponent/Score
Tom Nugent	Sun 1-1-55	UTEP 20-47
Tom Nugent	Bluegrass 12-13-58	Oklahoma St. 6-15
Bill Peterson	Gator 1-2-65	Oklahoma 36-19
Bill Peterson	Sun 12-24-66	Wyoming 20-28
Bill Peterson	Gator 12-30-67	Penn St. 17-17
Bill Peterson	Peach 12-30-68	LSU 27-31
Larry Jones	Fiesta 12-27-71	Arizona St. 38-45
Bobby Bowden	Tangerine 12-23-77	Texas Tech 40-17
Bobby Bowden	Orange 1-1-80	Oklahoma 7-24
Bobby Bowden	Orange 1-1-81	Oklahoma 17-18

School/Coach	Bowl/Date	Opponent/Score
Bobby Bowden	Gator 12-30-82	West Virginia 31-12
Bobby Bowden	Peach 12-30-83	North Carolina 28-3
Bobby Bowden	Florida Citrus 12-22-84	Georgia 17-17
Bobby Bowden	Gator 12-30-85	Oklahoma St. 34-23
Bobby Bowden	All-American 12-31-86	Indiana 27-13
Bobby Bowden	Fiesta 1-1-88	Nebraska 31-28
Bobby Bowden	Sugar 1-2-89	Auburn 13-7
Bobby Bowden	Fiesta 1-1-90	Nebraska 41-17
Bobby Bowden	Blockbuster 12-28-90	Penn St. 24-17
Bobby Bowden	Cotton 1-1-92	Texas A&M 10-2
Bobby Bowden	Orange 1-1-93	Nebraska 27-14
Bobby Bowden	Orange 1-1-94	Nebraska 18-16
Bobby Bowden	Sugar 1-2-95	Florida 23-17
Bobby Bowden	Orange 1-1-96	Notre Dame 31-26
Bobby Bowden	Sugar 1-2-97	Florida 20-52
Bobby Bowden	Sugar 1-1-98	Ohio St. 31-14
Bobby Bowden	Fiesta 1-4-99	Tennessee 16-23
Bobby Bowden	Sugar 1-4-00	Virginia Tech 46-29
Bobby Bowden	Orange 1-3-01	Oklahoma 2-13
Bobby Bowden	Gator 1-1-02	Virginia Tech 30-17
Bobby Bowden	Sugar 1-1-03	Georgia 13-26

All bowls 18-11-2

FRESNO ST.

School/Coach	Bowl/Date	Opponent/Score
Alvin "Pix" Pierson	Raisin 1-1-46	Drake 12-13
Cecil Coleman	Mercy 11-23-61	Bowling Green 36-6
Jim Sweeney	California 12-18-82	Bowling Green 29-28
Jim Sweeney	California 12-14-85	Bowling Green 51-7
Jim Sweeney	California 12-10-88	Western Mich. 35-30
Jim Sweeney	California 12-9-89	Ball St. 27-6
Jim Sweeney	California 12-14-91	Bowling Green 21-28
Jim Sweeney	Freedom 12-29-92	Southern California 24-7
Jim Sweeney	Aloha 12-25-93	Colorado 30-41
Pat Hill	Las Vegas 12-18-99	Utah 16-17
Pat Hill	Silicon Valley 12-31-00	Air Force 34-37
Pat Hill	Silicon Valley 12-31-01	Michigan St. 35-44
Pat Hill	Silicon Valley 12-31-02	Georgia Tech 30-21

All bowls 7-6-0

GEORGIA

School/Coach	Bowl/Date	Opponent/Score
Wally Butts	Orange 1-1-42	TCU 40-26
Wally Butts	Rose 1-1-43	UCLA 9-0
Wally Butts	Oil 1-1-46	Tulsa 20-6
Wally Butts	Sugar 1-1-47	North Carolina 20-10
Wally Butts	Gator 1-1-48	Maryland 20-20
Wally Butts	Orange 1-1-49	Texas 28-41
Wally Butts	Presidential 12-9-50	Texas A&M 20-40
Wally Butts	Orange 1-1-60	Missouri 14-0
Vince Dooley	Sun 12-26-64	Texas Tech 7-0
Vince Dooley	Cotton 12-31-66	Southern Methodist 24-9
Vince Dooley	Liberty 12-16-67	North Carolina St. 7-14
Vince Dooley	Sugar 1-1-69	Arkansas 2-16
Vince Dooley	Sun 12-20-69	Nebraska 6-45
Vince Dooley	Gator 12-31-71	North Carolina 7-3
Vince Dooley	Peach 12-28-73	Maryland 17-16
Vince Dooley	Tangerine 12-21-74	Miami (Ohio) 10-21
Vince Dooley	Cotton 1-1-76	Arkansas 10-31
Vince Dooley	Sugar 1-1-77	Pittsburgh 3-27
Vince Dooley	Bluebonnet 12-31-78	Stanford 22-25
Vince Dooley	Sugar 1-1-81	Notre Dame 17-10
Vince Dooley	Sugar 1-1-82	Pittsburgh 20-24
Vince Dooley	Sugar 1-1-83	Penn St. 23-27
Vince Dooley	Cotton 1-2-84	Texas 10-9
Vince Dooley	Florida Citrus 12-22-84	Florida St. 17-17
Vince Dooley	Sun 12-28-85	Arizona 13-13
Vince Dooley	Hall of Fame 12-23-86	Boston College 24-27
Vince Dooley	Liberty 12-29-87	Arkansas 20-17
Vince Dooley	Gator 1-1-89	Michigan St. 34-27
Ray Goff	Peach 12-30-89	Syracuse 18-19
Ray Goff	Independence 12-29-91	Arkansas 24-15
Ray Goff	Florida Citrus 1-1-93	Ohio St. 21-14
Ray Goff	Peach 12-30-95	Virginia 27-34
Jim Donnan	Outback 1-1-98	Wisconsin 33-6
Jim Donnan	Peach 12-31-98	Virginia 35-33
Jim Donnan	Outback 1-1-00	Purdue 28-25 (ot)
Jim Donnan	Oahu Classic 12-24-00	Virginia 37-14
Mark Richt	Music City 12-28-01	Boston College 16-20
Mark Richt	Sugar 1-1-03	Florida St. 26-13

All bowls 20-15-3

GEORGIA TECH

School/Coach	Bowl/Date	Opponent/Score
Bill Alexander	Rose 1-1-29	California 8-7
Bill Alexander	Orange 1-1-40	Missouri 21-7
Bill Alexander	Cotton 1-1-43	Texas 7-14
Bill Alexander	Sugar 1-1-44	Tulsa 20-18
Bill Alexander	Orange 1-1-45	Tulsa 12-26
Bobby Dodd	Oil 1-1-47	St. Mary's (Cal.) 41-19
Bobby Dodd	Orange 1-1-48	Kansas 20-14
Bobby Dodd	Orange 1-1-52	Baylor 17-14
Bobby Dodd	Sugar 1-1-53	Mississippi 24-7
Bobby Dodd	Sugar 1-1-54	West Virginia 42-19
Bobby Dodd	Cotton 1-1-55	Arkansas 14-6
Bobby Dodd	Sugar 1-2-56	Pittsburgh 7-0
Bobby Dodd	Gator 12-29-56	Pittsburgh 21-14
Bobby Dodd	Gator 1-2-60	Arkansas 7-14
Bobby Dodd	Gator 12-30-61	Penn St. 15-30
Bobby Dodd	Bluebonnet 12-22-62	Missouri 10-14
Bobby Dodd	Gator 12-31-65	Texas Tech 31-21
Bobby Dodd	Orange 1-2-67	Florida 12-27
Bud Carson	Sun 12-19-70	Texas Tech 17-9
Bud Carson	Peach 12-30-71	Mississippi 18-41
Bill Fulcher	Liberty 12-18-72	Iowa St. 31-30
Pepper Rodgers	Peach 12-25-78	Purdue 21-41
Bill Curry	Hall of Fame 12-31-85	Michigan St. 17-14
Bobby Ross	Florida Citrus 1-1-91	Nebraska 45-21
Bobby Ross	Aloha 12-25-91	Stanford 18-17
George O'Leary	Carquest 12-29-97	West Virginia 35-30
George O'Leary	Gator 1-1-99	Notre Dame 35-28
George O'Leary	Gator 1-1-00	Miami (Fla.) 13-28
George O'Leary	Peach 12-29-00	LSU 14-28
Mac McWhorter	Seattle 12-27-01	Stanford 24-14
Chan Gailey	Silicon Valley 12-31-02	Fresno St. 21-30

All bowls 20-11-0

HAWAII

School/Coach	Bowl/Date	Opponent/Score
Bob Wagner	Aloha 12-25-89	Michigan St. 13-33
Bob Wagner	Holiday 12-30-92	Illinois 27-17
June Jones	Oahu Classic 12-25-99	Oregon St. 23-17
June Jones	Hawaii 12-25-02	Tulane 28-36

All bowls 2-2-0

HOUSTON

School/Coach	Bowl/Date	Opponent/Score
Clyde Lee	Salad 1-1-52	Dayton 26-21
Bill Yeoman	Tangerine 12-22-62	Miami (Ohio) 49-21
Bill Yeoman	Bluebonnet 12-31-69	Auburn 36-7
Bill Yeoman	Bluebonnet 12-31-71	Colorado 17-29
Bill Yeoman	Bluebonnet 12-29-73	Tulane 47-7
Bill Yeoman	Bluebonnet 12-23-74	North Carolina St. 31-31
Bill Yeoman	Cotton 1-1-77	Maryland 30-21
Bill Yeoman	Cotton 1-1-79	Notre Dame 34-35
Bill Yeoman	Cotton 1-1-80	Nebraska 17-14
Bill Yeoman	Garden State 12-14-80	Navy 35-0
Bill Yeoman	Sun 12-26-81	Oklahoma 14-40
Bill Yeoman	Cotton 1-1-85	Boston College 28-45
Jack Pardee	Aloha 12-25-88	Washington St. 22-24
Kim Helton	Liberty 12-27-96	Syracuse 17-30

All bowls 7-6-1

IDAHO

School/Coach	Bowl/Date	Opponent/Score
Chris Tormey	Humanitarian 12-30-98	Southern Miss. 42-35

All bowls 1-0-0

ILLINOIS

School/Coach	Bowl/Date	Opponent/Score
Ray Eliot	Rose 1-1-47	UCLA 45-14
Ray Eliot	Rose 1-1-52	Stanford 40-7
Pete Elliott	Rose 1-1-64	Washington 17-7
Mike White	Liberty 12-29-82	Alabama 15-21
Mike White	Rose 1-2-84	UCLA 9-45
Mike White	Peach 12-31-85	Army 29-31
John Mackovic	All-American 12-29-88	Florida 10-14
John Mackovic	Florida Citrus 1-1-90	Virginia 31-21
John Mackovic	Hall of Fame 1-1-91	Clemson 0-30
Lou Tepper	John Hancock 12-31-91	UCLA 3-6
Lou Tepper	Holiday 12-30-92	Hawaii 17-27
Lou Tepper	Liberty 12-31-94	East Caro. 30-0
Ron Turner	Micronpc.com 12-30-99	Virginia 63-21
Ron Turner	Sugar 1-1-02	LSU 34-47

All bowls 6-8-0

INDIANA

School/Coach	Bowl/Date	Opponent/Score
John Pont	Rose 1-1-68	Southern California 3-14
Lee Corso	Holiday 12-21-79	Brigham Young 38-37
Bill Mallory	All-American 12-31-86	Florida St. 13-27
Bill Mallory	Peach 1-2-88	Tennessee 22-27
Bill Mallory	Liberty 12-28-88	South Carolina 34-10
Bill Mallory	Peach 12-29-90	Auburn 23-27
Bill Mallory	Copper 12-31-91	Baylor 24-0
Bill Mallory	Independence 12-31-93	Virginia Tech 20-45

All bowls 3-5-0

IOWA

School/Coach	Bowl/Date	Opponent/Score
Forest Evashevski	Rose 1-1-57	Oregon St. 35-19
Forest Evashevski	Rose 1-1-59	California 38-12

BOWL/ALL-STAR RECORDS

School/Coach	Bowl/Date	Opponent/Score
Hayden Fry	Rose 1-1-82	Washington 0-28
Hayden Fry	Peach 12-31-82	Tennessee 28-22
Hayden Fry	Gator 12-30-83	Florida 6-14
Hayden Fry	Freedom 12-26-84	Texas 55-17
Hayden Fry	Rose 1-1-86	UCLA 28-45
Hayden Fry	Holiday 12-30-86	San Diego St. 39-38
Hayden Fry	Holiday 12-30-87	Wyoming 20-19
Hayden Fry	Peach 12-31-88	North Carolina St. 23-28
Hayden Fry	Rose 1-1-91	Washington 34-46
Hayden Fry	Holiday 12-30-91	Brigham Young 13-13
Hayden Fry	Alamo 12-31-93	California 3-37
Hayden Fry	Sun 12-29-95	Washington 38-18
Hayden Fry	Alamo 12-29-96	Texas Tech 27-0
Hayden Fry	Sun 12-31-97	Arizona St. 7-17
Kirk Ferentz	Alamo 12-29-01	Texas Tech 16-13
Kirk Ferentz	Orange 1-2-03	Southern California 17-38

All bowls 9-8-1

IOWA ST.

School/Coach	Bowl/Date	Opponent/Score
Johnny Majors	Sun 12-18-71	LSU 15-33
Johnny Majors	Liberty 12-18-72	Georgia Tech 30-31
Earle Bruce	Peach 12-31-77	North Carolina St. 14-24
Earle Bruce	Hall of Fame 12-20-78	Texas A&M 12-28
Dan McCarney	Insight.com 12-28-00	Pittsburgh 37-29
Dan McCarney	Independence 12-27-01	Alabama 13-14
Dan McCarney	Humanitarian 12-31-02	Boise St. 16-34

All bowls 1-6-0

KANSAS

School/Coach	Bowl/Date	Opponent/Score
George Sauer	Orange 1-1-48	Georgia Tech 14-20
Jack Mitchell	Bluebonnet 12-16-61	Rice 33-7
Pepper Rodgers	Orange 1-1-69	Penn St. 14-15
Don Fambrough	Liberty 12-17-73	North Carolina St. 18-31
Bud Moore	Sun 12-26-75	Pittsburgh 19-33
Don Fambrough	Hall of Fame 12-31-81	Mississippi St. 0-10
Glen Mason	Aloha 12-25-92	Brigham Young 23-20
Glen Mason	Aloha 12-25-95	UCLA 51-30

All bowls 3-5-0

KANSAS ST.

School/Coach	Bowl/Date	Opponent/Score
Jim Dickey	Independence 12-11-82	Wisconsin 3-14
Bill Snyder	Copper 12-29-93	Wyoming 52-17
Bill Snyder	Aloha 12-25-94	Boston College 7-12
Bill Snyder	Holiday 12-29-95	Colorado St. 54-21
Bill Snyder	Cotton 1-1-97	Brigham Young 15-19
Bill Snyder	Fiesta 12-31-97	Syracuse 35-18
Bill Snyder	Alamo 12-29-98	Purdue 34-37
Bill Snyder	Holiday 12-29-99	Washington 24-20
Bill Snyder	Cotton 1-1-01	Tennessee 35-21
Bill Snyder	Insight.com 12-29-01	Syracuse 3-26
Bill Snyder	Holiday 12-27-02	Arizona St. 34-27

All bowls 6-5-0

KENT ST.

School/Coach	Bowl/Date	Opponent/Score
Don James	Tangerine 12-29-72	Tampa 18-21

All bowls 0-1-0

KENTUCKY

School/Coach	Bowl/Date	Opponent/Score
Paul "Bear" Bryant	Great Lakes 12-6-47	Villanova 24-14
Paul "Bear" Bryant	Orange 1-2-50	Santa Clara 13-21
Paul "Bear" Bryant	Sugar 1-1-51	Oklahoma 13-7
Paul "Bear" Bryant	Cotton 1-1-52	TCU 20-7
Fran Curci	Peach 12-31-76	North Carolina 21-0
Jerry Claiborne	Hall of Fame 12-22-83	West Virginia 16-20
Jerry Claiborne	Hall of Fame 12-29-84	Wisconsin 20-19
Bill Curry	Peach 12-31-93	Clemson 13-14
Hal Mumme	Outback 1-1-99	Penn St. 14-26
Hal Mumme	Music City 12-29-99	Syracuse 13-20

All bowls 5-5-0

LSU

School/Coach	Bowl/Date	Opponent/Score
Bernie Moore	Sugar 1-1-36	TCU 2-3
Bernie Moore	Sugar 1-1-37	Santa Clara 14-21
Bernie Moore	Sugar 1-1-38	Santa Clara 0-6
Bernie Moore	Orange 1-1-44	Texas A&M 19-14
Bernie Moore	Cotton 1-1-47	Arkansas 0-0
Gaynell Tinsley	Sugar 1-2-50	Oklahoma 0-35
Paul Dietzel	Sugar 1-1-59	Clemson 7-0
Paul Dietzel	Sugar 1-1-60	Mississippi 0-21
Paul Dietzel	Orange 1-1-62	Colorado 25-7
Charlie McClendon	Cotton 1-1-63	Texas 13-0
Charlie McClendon	Bluebonnet 12-21-63	Baylor 7-14
Charlie McClendon	Sugar 1-1-65	Syracuse 13-10
Charlie McClendon	Cotton 1-1-66	Arkansas 14-7
Charlie McClendon	Sugar 1-1-68	Wyoming 20-13
Charlie McClendon	Peach 12-30-68	Florida St. 31-27
Charlie McClendon	Orange 1-1-71	Nebraska 12-17
Charlie McClendon	Sun 12-18-71	Iowa St. 33-15
Charlie McClendon	Bluebonnet 12-30-72	Tennessee 17-24
Charlie McClendon	Orange 1-1-74	Penn St. 9-16
Charlie McClendon	Sun 12-31-77	Stanford 14-24
Charlie McClendon	Liberty 12-23-78	Missouri 15-20
Charlie McClendon	Tangerine 12-22-79	Wake Forest 34-10
Jerry Stovall	Orange 1-1-83	Nebraska 20-21
Bill Arnsparger	Sugar 1-1-85	Nebraska 10-28
Bill Arnsparger	Liberty 12-27-85	Baylor 7-21
Bill Arnsparger	Sugar 1-1-87	Nebraska 15-30
Mike Archer	Gator 12-31-87	South Carolina 30-13
Mike Archer	Hall of Fame 1-2-89	Syracuse 10-23
Gerry DiNardo	Independence 12-29-95	Michigan St. 45-26
Gerry DiNardo	Peach 12-28-96	Clemson 10-7
Gerry DiNardo	Independence 12-28-97	Notre Dame 27-9
Nick Saban	Peach 12-29-00	Georgia Tech 28-14
Nick Saban	Sugar 1-1-02	Illinois 47-34
Nick Saban	Cotton 1-1-03	Texas 20-35

All bowls 16-17-1

LOUISIANA TECH

School/Coach	Bowl/Date	Opponent/Score
Maxie Lambright	Independence 12-17-77	Louisville 24-14
Maxie Lambright	Independence 12-16-78	East Caro. 13-35
Joe Raymond Peace	Independence 12-15-90	Maryland 34-34
Jack Bicknell III	Humanitarian 12-31-01	Clemson 24-49

All bowls 1-2-1

LOUISVILLE

School/Coach	Bowl/Date	Opponent/Score
Frank Camp	Sun 1-1-58	Drake 34-20
Lee Corso	Pasadena 12-19-70	Long Beach St. 24-24
Vince Gibson	Independence 12-17-77	Louisiana Tech 14-24
Howard Schnellenberger	Fiesta 1-1-91	Alabama 34-7
Howard Schnellenberger	Liberty 12-28-93	Michigan St. 18-7
John L. Smith	Motor City 12-23-98	Marshall 29-48
John L. Smith	Humanitarian 12-30-99	Boise St. 31-34
John L. Smith	Liberty 12-29-00	Colorado St. 17-22
John L. Smith	Liberty 12-31-01	Brigham Young 28-10
John L. Smith	GMAC 12-18-02	Marshall 15-38

All bowls 4-5-1

MARSHALL

School/Coach	Bowl/Date	Opponent/Score
Bob Pruett	Motor City 12-26-97	Mississippi 31-34
Bob Pruett	Motor City 12-23-98	Louisville 48-29
Bob Pruett	Motor City 12-27-99	Brigham Young 21-3
Bob Pruett	Motor City 12-27-00	Cincinnati 25-14
Bob Pruett	GMAC 12-19-01	East Caro. 64-61 (2 ot)
Bob Pruett	GMAC 12-18-02	Louisville 38-15

All bowls 5-1-0

MARYLAND

School/Coach	Bowl/Date	Opponent/Score
Jim Tatum	Gator 1-1-48	Georgia 20-20
Jim Tatum	Gator 1-2-50	Missouri 20-7
Jim Tatum	Sugar 1-1-52	Tennessee 28-13
Jim Tatum	Orange 1-1-54	Oklahoma 0-7
Jim Tatum	Orange 1-2-56	Oklahoma 6-20
Jerry Claiborne	Peach 12-28-73	Georgia 16-17
Jerry Claiborne	Liberty 12-16-74	Tennessee 3-7
Jerry Claiborne	Gator 12-29-75	Florida 13-0
Jerry Claiborne	Cotton 1-1-77	Houston 21-30
Jerry Claiborne	Hall of Fame 12-22-77	Minnesota 17-7
Jerry Claiborne	Sun 12-23-78	Texas 0-42
Jerry Claiborne	Tangerine 12-20-80	Florida 20-35
Bobby Ross	Aloha 12-25-82	Washington 20-21
Bobby Ross	Florida Citrus 12-17-83	Tennessee 23-30
Bobby Ross	Sun 12-22-84	Tennessee 28-27
Bobby Ross	Cherry 12-21-85	Syracuse 35-18
Joe Krivak	Independence 12-15-90	Louisiana Tech 34-34
Ralph Friedgen	Orange 1-2-02	Florida 23-56
Ralph Friedgen	Peach 12-31-02	Tennessee 30-3

All bowls 7-10-2

MEMPHIS

School/Coach	Bowl/Date	Opponent/Score
Billy Murphy	Pasadena 12-18-71	San Jose St. 28-9

All bowls 1-0-0

MIAMI (FLA.)

School/Coach	Bowl/Date	Opponent/Score
Tom McCann	Orange 1-1-35	Bucknell 0-26
Jack Harding	Orange 1-1-46	Holy Cross 13-6
Andy Gustafson	Orange 1-1-51	Clemson 14-15
Andy Gustafson	Gator 1-1-52	Clemson 14-0
Andy Gustafson	Liberty 12-16-61	Syracuse 14-15
Andy Gustafson	Gotham 12-15-62	Nebraska 34-36
Charlie Tate	Bluebonnet 12-10-66	Virginia Tech 14-7
Charlie Tate	Bluebonnet 12-31-67	Colorado 21-31
Howard Schnellenberger	Peach 1-2-81	Virginia Tech 20-10
Howard Schnellenberger	Orange 1-2-84	Nebraska 31-30
Jimmy Johnson	Fiesta 1-1-85	UCLA 37-39

School/Coach	Bowl/Date	Opponent/Score
Jimmy Johnson	Sugar 1-1-86	Tennessee 7-35
Jimmy Johnson	Fiesta 1-2-87	Penn St. 10-14
Jimmy Johnson	Orange 1-1-88	Oklahoma 20-14
Jimmy Johnson	Orange 1-2-89	Nebraska 23-3
Dennis Erickson	Sugar 1-1-90	Alabama 33-25
Dennis Erickson	Cotton 1-1-91	Texas 46-3
Dennis Erickson	Orange 1-1-92	Nebraska 22-0
Dennis Erickson	Sugar 1-1-93	Alabama 13-34
Dennis Erickson	Fiesta 1-1-94	Arizona 0-29
Dennis Erickson	Orange 1-1-95	Nebraska 17-24
Butch Davis	Carquest 12-27-96	Virginia 31-21
Butch Davis	Micron PC 12-29-98	North Carolina St. 46-23
Butch Davis	Gator 1-1-00	Georgia Tech 28-13
Butch Davis	Sugar 1-2-01	Florida 37-20
Larry Coker	Rose 1-3-02	Nebraska 37-14
Larry Coker	Fiesta 1-3-03	Ohio St. 24-31 (2 ot)

All bowls 15-12-0

MIAMI (OHIO)

School/Coach	Bowl/Date	Opponent/Score
Sid Gillman	Sun 1-1-48	Texas Tech 13-12
Woody Hayes	Salad 1-1-51	Arizona St. 34-21
John Pont	Tangerine 12-22-62	Houston 21-49
Bill Mallory	Tangerine 12-22-73	Florida 16-7
Dick Crum	Tangerine 12-21-74	Georgia 21-10
Dick Crum	Tangerine 12-20-75	South Carolina 20-7
Tim Rose	California 12-13-86	San Jose St. 7-37

All bowls 5-2-0

MICHIGAN

School/Coach	Bowl/Date	Opponent/Score
Fielding "Hurry Up" Yost	Rose 1-1-02	Stanford 49-0
H.O. "Fritz" Crisler	Rose 1-1-48	Southern California 49-0
Bennie Oosterbaan	Rose 1-1-51	California 14-6
Chalmers "Bump" Elliott	Rose 1-1-65	Oregon St. 34-7
Glenn "Bo" Schembechler	Rose 1-1-70	Southern California 3-10
Glenn "Bo" Schembechler	Rose 1-1-72	Stanford 12-13
Glenn "Bo" Schembechler	Orange 1-1-76	Oklahoma 6-14
Glenn "Bo" Schembechler	Rose 1-1-77	Southern California 6-14
Glenn "Bo" Schembechler	Rose 1-2-78	Washington 20-27
Glenn "Bo" Schembechler	Rose 1-1-79	Southern California 10-17
Glenn "Bo" Schembechler	Gator 12-28-79	North Carolina 15-17
Glenn "Bo" Schembechler	Rose 1-1-81	Washington 23-6
Glenn "Bo" Schembechler	Bluebonnet 12-31-81	UCLA 33-14
Glenn "Bo" Schembechler	Rose 1-1-83	UCLA 14-24
Glenn "Bo" Schembechler	Sugar 1-2-84	Auburn 7-9
Glenn "Bo" Schembechler	Holiday 12-21-84	Brigham Young 17-24
Glenn "Bo" Schembechler	Fiesta 1-1-86	Nebraska 27-23
Glenn "Bo" Schembechler	Rose 1-1-87	Arizona St. 15-22
Glenn "Bo" Schembechler	Hall of Fame 1-2-88	Alabama 28-24
Glenn "Bo" Schembechler	Rose 1-2-89	Southern California 22-14
Glenn "Bo" Schembechler	Rose 1-1-90	Southern California 10-17
Gary Moeller	Gator 1-1-91	Mississippi 35-3
Gary Moeller	Rose 1-1-92	Washington 14-34
Gary Moeller	Rose 1-1-93	Washington 38-31
Gary Moeller	Hall of Fame 1-1-94	North Carolina St. 42-7
Gary Moeller	Holiday 12-30-94	Colorado St. 24-14
Lloyd Carr	Alamo 12-28-95	Texas A&M 20-22
Lloyd Carr	Outback 1-1-97	Alabama 14-17
Lloyd Carr	Rose 1-1-98	Washington St. 21-16
Lloyd Carr	Florida Citrus 1-1-99	Arkansas 45-31
Lloyd Carr	Orange 1-1-00	Alabama 35-34 (ot)
Lloyd Carr	Florida Citrus 1-1-01	Auburn 31-28
Lloyd Carr	Florida Citrus 1-1-02	Tennessee 17-45
Lloyd Carr	Outback 1-1-03	Florida 38-30

All bowls 18-16-0

MICHIGAN ST.

School/Coach	Bowl/Date	Opponent/Score
Charlie Bachman	Orange 1-1-38	Auburn 0-6
Clarence "Biggie" Munn	Rose 1-1-54	UCLA 28-20
Duffy Daugherty	Rose 1-2-56	UCLA 17-14
Duffy Daugherty	Rose 1-1-66	UCLA 12-14
George Perles	Cherry 12-22-84	Army 6-10
George Perles	Hall of Fame 12-31-85	Georgia Tech 14-17
George Perles	Rose 1-1-88	Southern California 20-17
George Perles	Gator 1-1-89	Georgia 27-34
George Perles	Aloha 12-25-89	Hawaii 33-13
George Perles	John Hancock 12-31-90	Southern California 17-6
George Perles	Liberty 12-28-93	Louisville 7-18
Nick Saban	Independence 12-29-95	LSU 26-45
Nick Saban	Sun 12-31-96	Stanford 0-38
Nick Saban	Aloha 12-25-97	Washington 23-51
Bobby Williams	Florida Citrus 1-1-00	Florida 37-34
Bobby Williams	Silicon Valley 12-31-01	Fresno St. 44-35

All bowls 7-9-0

MINNESOTA

School/Coach	Bowl/Date	Opponent/Score
Murray Warmath	Rose 1-2-61	Washington 7-17
Murray Warmath	Rose 1-1-62	UCLA 21-3
Cal Stoll	Hall of Fame 12-22-77	Maryland 7-17
John Gutekunst	Independence 12-21-85	Clemson 20-13
John Gutekunst	Liberty 12-29-86	Tennessee 14-21
Glen Mason	Sun 12-31-99	Oregon 20-24
Glen Mason	Micronpc.com 12-28-00	North Carolina St. 30-38
Glen Mason	Music City 12-30-02	Arkansas 29-14

All bowls 3-5-0

MISSISSIPPI

School/Coach	Bowl/Date	Opponent/Score
Ed Walker	Orange 1-1-36	Catholic 19-20
John Vaught	Delta 1-1-48	TCU 13-9
John Vaught	Sugar 1-1-53	Georgia Tech 7-24
John Vaught	Sugar 1-1-55	Navy 0-21
John Vaught	Cotton 1-2-56	TCU 14-13
John Vaught	Sugar 1-1-58	Texas 39-7
John Vaught	Gator 12-27-58	Florida 7-3
John Vaught	Sugar 1-1-60	LSU 21-0
John Vaught	Sugar 1-2-61	Rice 14-6
John Vaught	Cotton 1-1-62	Texas 7-12
John Vaught	Sugar 1-1-63	Arkansas 17-13
John Vaught	Sugar 1-1-64	Alabama 7-12
John Vaught	Bluebonnet 12-19-64	Tulsa 7-14
John Vaught	Liberty 12-18-65	Auburn 13-7
John Vaught	Bluebonnet 12-17-66	Texas 0-19
John Vaught	Sun 12-30-67	UTEP 7-14
John Vaught	Liberty 12-14-68	Virginia Tech 34-17
John Vaught	Sugar 1-1-70	Arkansas 27-22
John Vaught	Gator 1-2-71	Auburn 28-35
Billy Kinard	Peach 12-30-71	Georgia Tech 41-18
Billy Brewer	Independence 12-10-83	Air Force 3-9
Billy Brewer	Independence 12-20-86	Texas Tech 20-17
Billy Brewer	Liberty 12-28-89	Air Force 42-29
Billy Brewer	Gator 1-1-91	Michigan 3-35
Billy Brewer	Liberty 12-31-92	Air Force 13-0
Tommy Turberville	Motor City 12-26-97	Marshall 34-31
David Cutcliffe	Independence 12-31-98	Texas St. 35-18
David Cutcliffe	Independence 12-31-99	Oklahoma 27-25
David Cutcliffe	Music City 12-28-00	West Virginia 38-49
David Cutcliffe	Independence 12-27-02	Nebraska 27-23

All bowls 18-12-0

MISSISSIPPI ST.

School/Coach	Bowl/Date	Opponent/Score
Ralph Sasse	Orange 1-1-37	Duquesne 12-13
Allyn McKeen	Orange 1-1-41	Georgetown 14-7
Paul Davis	Liberty 12-21-63	North Carolina St. 16-12
Bob Tyler	Sun 12-28-74	North Carolina 26-24
Emory Bellard	Sun 12-27-80	Nebraska 17-31
Emory Bellard	Hall of Fame 12-31-81	Kansas 10-0
Jackie Sherrill	Liberty 12-29-91	Air Force 15-38
Jackie Sherrill	Peach 1-2-93	North Carolina 17-21
Jackie Sherrill	Peach 1-1-95	North Carolina St. 24-28
Jackie Sherrill	Cotton 1-1-99	Texas 11-38
Jackie Sherrill	Peach 12-30-99	Clemson 17-7
Jackie Sherrill	Independence 12-31-00	Texas A&M 43-41 (ot)

All bowls 6-6-0

MISSOURI

School/Coach	Bowl/Date	Opponent/Score
Gwinn Henry	Los Angeles Christmas Festival 12-25-24	Southern California 7-20
Don Faurot	Orange 1-1-40	Georgia Tech 7-21
Don Faurot	Sugar 1-1-42	Fordham 0-2
Chauncey Simpson	Cotton 1-1-46	Texas 27-40
Don Faurot	Gator 1-1-49	Clemson 23-24
Don Faurot	Gator 1-2-50	Maryland 7-20
Dan Devine	Orange 1-1-60	Georgia 0-14
Dan Devine	Orange 1-2-61	Navy 21-14
Dan Devine	Bluebonnet 12-22-62	Georgia Tech 14-10
Dan Devine	Sugar 1-1-66	Florida 20-18
Dan Devine	Gator 12-28-68	Alabama 35-10
Dan Devine	Orange 1-1-70	Penn St. 3-10
Al Onofrio	Fiesta 12-23-72	Arizona St. 35-49
Al Onofrio	Sun 12-29-73	Auburn 34-17
Warren Powers	Liberty 12-23-78	LSU 20-15
Warren Powers	Hall of Fame 12-29-79	South Carolina 24-14
Warren Powers	Liberty 12-27-80	Purdue 25-28
Warren Powers	Tangerine 12-19-81	Southern Miss. 19-17
Warren Powers	Holiday 12-23-83	Brigham Young 17-21
Larry Smith	Holiday 12-29-97	Colorado St. 24-35
Larry Smith	Insight.com 12-26-98	West Virginia 34-31

All bowls 9-12-0

School/Coach	Bowl/Date	Opponent/Score
NAVY		
Bob Folwell	Rose 1-1-24	Washington 14-14
Eddie Erdelatz	Sugar 1-1-55	Mississippi 21-0
Eddie Erdelatz	Cotton 1-1-58	Rice 20-7
Wayne Hardin	Orange 1-1-61	Missouri 14-21
Wayne Hardin	Cotton 1-1-64	Texas 6-28
George Welsh	Holiday 12-22-78	Brigham Young 23-16
George Welsh	Garden State 12-14-80	Houston 0-35
George Welsh	Liberty 12-30-81	Ohio St. 28-31
Charlie Weatherbie	Aloha 12-25-96	California 42-38
All bowls 4-4-1		
NEBRASKA		
Lawrence McC. "Biff" Jones	Rose 1-1-41	Stanford 13-21
Bill Glassford	Orange 1-1-55	Duke 7-34
Bob Devaney	Gotham 12-15-62	Miami (Fla.) 36-34
Bob Devaney	Orange 1-1-64	Auburn 13-7
Bob Devaney	Cotton 1-1-65	Arkansas 7-10
Bob Devaney	Orange 1-1-66	Alabama 28-39
Bob Devaney	Sugar 1-2-67	Alabama 7-34
Bob Devaney	Sun 12-20-69	Georgia 45-6
Bob Devaney	Orange 1-1-71	LSU 17-12
Bob Devaney	Orange 1-1-72	Alabama 38-6
Bob Devaney	Orange 1-1-73	Notre Dame 40-6
Tom Osborne	Cotton 1-1-74	Texas 19-3
Tom Osborne	Sugar 12-31-74	Florida 13-10
Tom Osborne	Fiesta 12-26-75	Arizona St. 14-17
Tom Osborne	Bluebonnet 12-31-76	Texas Tech 27-24
Tom Osborne	Liberty 12-19-77	North Carolina 21-17
Tom Osborne	Orange 1-1-79	Oklahoma 24-31
Tom Osborne	Cotton 1-1-80	Houston 14-17
Tom Osborne	Sun 12-27-80	Mississippi St. 31-17
Tom Osborne	Orange 1-1-82	Clemson 15-22
Tom Osborne	Orange 1-1-83	LSU 21-20
Tom Osborne	Orange 1-2-84	Miami (Fla.) 30-31
Tom Osborne	Sugar 1-1-85	LSU 28-10
Tom Osborne	Fiesta 1-1-86	Michigan 23-27
Tom Osborne	Sugar 1-1-87	LSU 30-15
Tom Osborne	Fiesta 1-1-88	Florida St. 28-31
Tom Osborne	Orange 1-2-89	Miami (Fla.) 3-23
Tom Osborne	Fiesta 1-1-90	Florida St. 17-41
Tom Osborne	Florida Citrus 1-1-91	Georgia Tech 21-45
Tom Osborne	Orange 1-1-92	Miami (Fla.) 0-22
Tom Osborne	Orange 1-1-93	Florida St. 14-27
Tom Osborne	Orange 1-1-94	Florida St. 16-18
Tom Osborne	Orange 1-1-95	Miami (Fla.) 24-17
Tom Osborne	Fiesta 1-2-96	Florida 62-24
Tom Osborne	Orange 12-31-96	Virginia Tech 41-21
Tom Osborne	Orange 1-2-98	Tennessee 42-17
Frank Solich	Holiday 12-30-98	Arizona 20-23
Frank Solich	Fiesta 1-2-00	Tennessee 31-21
Frank Solich	Alamo 12-30-00	Northwestern 66-17
Frank Solich	Rose 1-3-02	Miami (Fla.) 14-37
Frank Solich	Independence 12-27-02	Mississippi 23-27
All bowls 20-21-0		
NEVADA		
Joe Sheeketski	Salad 1-1-48	North Texas 13-6
Joe Sheeketski	Harbor 1-1-49	Villanova 7-27
Chris Ault	Las Vegas 12-18-92	Bowling Green 34-35
Chris Ault	Las Vegas 12-14-95	Toledo 37-40 (ot)
Jeff Tisdel	Las Vegas 12-29-96	Ball St. 18-15
All bowls 2-3-0		
UNLV		
Harvey Hyde	California 12-15-84	Toledo 30-13
Jeff Horton	Las Vegas 12-15-94	Central Mich. 52-24
John Robinson	Las Vegas 12-21-00	Arkansas 31-14
All bowls 3-0-0		
NEW MEXICO		
Ted Shipkey	Sun 1-2-39	Utah 0-26
Willis Barnes	Sun 1-1-44	Southwestern (Tex.) 0-7
Willis Barnes	Sun 1-1-46	Denver 34-24
Willis Barnes	Harbor 1-1-47	Montana St. 13-13
Bill Weeks	Aviation 12-9-61	Western Mich. 28-12
Dennis Franchione	Insight.com 12-27-97	Arizona 14-20
Rocky Long	Las Vegas 12-25-02	UCLA 13-27
All bowls 2-4-1		
NEW MEXICO ST.		
Jerry Hines	Sun 1-1-36	Hardin-Simmons 14-14
Warren Woodson	Sun 12-31-59	North Texas 28-8
Warren Woodson	Sun 12-31-60	Utah St. 20-13
All bowls 2-0-1		

School/Coach	Bowl/Date	Opponent/Score
NORTH CAROLINA		
Carl Snavely	Sugar 1-1-47	Georgia 10-20
Carl Snavely	Sugar 1-1-49	Oklahoma 6-14
Carl Snavely	Cotton 1-2-50	Rice 13-27
Jim Hickey	Gator 12-28-63	Air Force 35-0
Bill Dooley	Peach 12-30-70	Arizona St. 26-48
Bill Dooley	Gator 12-31-71	Georgia 3-7
Bill Dooley	Sun 12-30-72	Texas Tech 32-28
Bill Dooley	Sun 12-28-74	Mississippi St. 24-26
Bill Dooley	Peach 12-31-76	Kentucky 0-21
Bill Dooley	Liberty 12-19-77	Nebraska 17-21
Dick Crum	Gator 12-28-79	Michigan 17-15
Dick Crum	Bluebonnet 12-31-80	Texas 16-7
Dick Crum	Gator 12-28-81	Arkansas 31-27
Dick Crum	Sun 12-25-82	Texas 26-10
Dick Crum	Peach 12-30-83	Florida St. 3-28
Dick Crum	Aloha 12-27-86	Arizona 21-30
Mack Brown	Peach 1-2-93	Mississippi St. 21-17
Mack Brown	Gator 12-31-93	Alabama 10-24
Mack Brown	Sun 12-30-94	Texas 31-35
Mack Brown	Carquest 12-30-95	Arkansas 20-10
Mack Brown	Gator 1-1-97	West Virginia 20-13
Carl Torbush	Gator 1-1-98	Virginia Tech 42-3
Carl Torbush	Las Vegas 12-19-98	San Diego St. 20-13
John Bunting	Peach 12-31-01	Auburn 16-10
All bowls 12-12-0		
NORTH CAROLINA ST.		
Beattie Feathers	Gator 1-1-47	Oklahoma 13-34
Earle Edwards	Liberty 12-21-63	Mississippi St. 12-16
Earle Edwards	Liberty 12-16-67	Georgia 14-7
Lou Holtz	Peach 12-29-72	West Virginia 49-13
Lou Holtz	Liberty 12-17-73	Kansas 31-18
Lou Holtz	Bluebonnet 12-23-74	Houston 31-31
Lou Holtz	Peach 12-31-75	West Virginia 10-13
Bo Rein	Peach 12-31-77	Iowa St. 24-14
Bo Rein	Tangerine 12-23-78	Pittsburgh 30-17
Dick Sheridan	Peach 12-31-86	Virginia Tech 24-25
Dick Sheridan	Peach 12-31-88	Iowa 28-23
Dick Sheridan	Copper 12-31-89	Arizona 10-17
Dick Sheridan	All-American 12-28-90	Southern Miss. 31-27
Dick Sheridan	Peach 1-1-92	East Caro. 34-37
Dick Sheridan	Gator 12-31-92	Florida 10-27
Mike O'Cain	Hall of Fame 1-1-94	Michigan 7-42
Mike O'Cain	Peach 1-1-95	Mississippi St. 28-24
Mike O'Cain	Micron PC 12-29-98	Miami (Fla.) 23-46
Chuck Amato	Micronpc.com 12-28-00	Minnesota 38-30
Chuck Amato	Tangerine 12-20-01	Pittsburgh 19-34
Chuck Amato	Gator 1-1-03	Notre Dame 28-6
All bowls 10-10-1		
NORTH TEXAS		
Odus Mitchell	Salad 1-1-48	Nevada 6-13
Odus Mitchell	Sun 12-31-59	New Mexico St. 8-28
Darrell Dickey	New Orleans 12-18-01	Colorado St. 20-45
Darrell Dickey	New Orleans 12-17-02	Cincinnati 24-19
All bowls 1-3-0		
NORTHERN ILL.		
Bill Mallory	California 12-17-83	Cal St. Fullerton 20-13
All bowls 1-0-0		
NORTHWESTERN		
Bob Voigts	Rose 1-1-49	California 20-14
Gary Barnett	Rose 1-1-96	Southern California 32-41
Gary Barnett	Florida Citrus 1-1-97	Tennessee 28-48
Randy Walker	Alamo 12-30-00	Nebraska 17-66
All bowls 1-3-0		
NOTRE DAME		
Knute Rockne	Rose 1-1-25	Stanford 27-10
Ara Parseghian	Cotton 1-1-70	Texas 17-21
Ara Parseghian	Cotton 1-1-71	Texas 24-11
Ara Parseghian	Orange 1-1-73	Nebraska 6-40
Ara Parseghian	Sugar 12-31-73	Alabama 24-23
Ara Parseghian	Orange 1-1-75	Alabama 13-11
Dan Devine	Gator 12-27-76	Penn St. 20-9
Dan Devine	Cotton 1-2-78	Texas 38-10
Dan Devine	Cotton 1-1-79	Houston 35-34
Dan Devine	Sugar 1-1-81	Georgia 10-17
Gerry Faust	Liberty 12-29-83	Boston College 19-18
Gerry Faust	Aloha 12-29-84	Southern Methodist 20-27
Lou Holtz	Cotton 1-1-88	Texas A&M 10-35
Lou Holtz	Fiesta 1-2-89	West Virginia 34-21
Lou Holtz	Orange 1-1-90	Colorado 21-6

School/Coach	Bowl/Date	Opponent/Score
Lou Holtz	Orange 1-1-91	Colorado 9-10
Lou Holtz	Sugar 1-1-92	Florida 39-28
Lou Holtz	Cotton 1-1-93	Texas A&M 28-3
Lou Holtz	Cotton 1-1-94	Texas A&M 24-21
Lou Holtz	Fiesta 1-2-95	Colorado 24-41
Lou Holtz	Orange 1-1-96	Florida St. 26-31
Bob Davie	Independence 12-28-97	LSU 9-27
Bob Davie	Gator 1-1-99	Georgia Tech 28-35
Bob Davie	Fiesta 1-1-01	Oregon St. 9-41
Tyrone Willingham	Gator 1-1-03	North Carolina St. 6-28

All bowls 13-12-0

OHIO

School/Coach	Bowl/Date	Opponent/Score
Bill Hess	Sun 12-31-62	West Tex. A&M 14-15
Bill Hess	Tangerine 12-27-68	Richmond 42-49

All bowls 0-2-0

OHIO ST.

School/Coach	Bowl/Date	Opponent/Score
John Wilce	Rose 1-1-21	California 0-28
Wes Fesler	Rose 1-2-50	California 17-14
Woody Hayes	Rose 1-1-55	Southern California 20-7
Woody Hayes	Rose 1-1-58	Oregon 10-7
Woody Hayes	Rose 1-1-69	Southern California 27-16
Woody Hayes	Rose 1-1-71	Stanford 17-27
Woody Hayes	Rose 1-1-73	Southern California 17-42
Woody Hayes	Rose 1-1-74	Southern California 42-21
Woody Hayes	Rose 1-1-75	Southern California 17-18
Woody Hayes	Rose 1-1-76	UCLA 10-23
Woody Hayes	Orange 1-1-77	Colorado 27-10
Woody Hayes	Sugar 1-2-78	Alabama 6-35
Woody Hayes	Gator 12-29-78	Clemson 15-17
Earle Bruce	Rose 1-1-80	Southern California 16-17
Earle Bruce	Fiesta 12-26-80	Penn St. 19-31
Earle Bruce	Liberty 12-30-81	Navy 31-28
Earle Bruce	Holiday 12-17-82	Brigham Young 47-17
Earle Bruce	Fiesta 1-2-84	Pittsburgh 28-23
Earle Bruce	Rose 1-1-85	Southern California 17-20
Earle Bruce	Florida Citrus 12-28-85	Brigham Young 10-7
Earle Bruce	Cotton 1-1-87	Texas A&M 28-12
John Cooper	Hall of Fame 1-1-90	Auburn 14-31
John Cooper	Liberty 12-27-90	Air Force 11-23
John Cooper	Hall of Fame 1-1-92	Syracuse 17-24
John Cooper	Florida Citrus 1-1-93	Georgia 14-21
John Cooper	Holiday 12-30-93	Brigham Young 28-21
John Cooper	Florida Citrus 1-2-95	Alabama 17-24
John Cooper	Florida Citrus 1-1-96	Tennessee 14-20
John Cooper	Rose 1-1-97	Arizona St. 20-17
John Cooper	Sugar 1-1-98	Florida St. 14-31
John Cooper	Sugar 1-1-99	Texas A&M 24-14
John Cooper	Outback 1-1-01	South Carolina 7-24
John Cooper	Outback 1-1-02	South Carolina 28-31
Jim Tressel	Fiesta 1-3-03	Miami (Fla.) 31-24 (2 ot)

All bowls 15-19-0

OKLAHOMA

School/Coach	Bowl/Date	Opponent/Score
Tom Stidham	Orange 1-2-39	Tennessee 0-17
Jim Tatum	Gator 1-1-47	North Carolina St. 34-13
Bud Wilkinson	Sugar 1-1-49	North Carolina 14-6
Bud Wilkinson	Sugar 1-2-50	LSU 35-0
Bud Wilkinson	Sugar 1-1-51	Kentucky 7-13
Bud Wilkinson	Orange 1-1-54	Maryland 7-0
Bud Wilkinson	Orange 1-2-56	Maryland 20-6
Bud Wilkinson	Orange 1-1-58	Duke 48-21
Bud Wilkinson	Orange 1-1-59	Syracuse 21-6
Bud Wilkinson	Orange 1-1-63	Alabama 0-17
Gomer Jones	Gator 1-2-65	Florida St. 19-36
Chuck Fairbanks	Orange 1-1-68	Tennessee 26-24
Chuck Fairbanks	Bluebonnet 12-31-68	Southern Methodist 27-28
Chuck Fairbanks	Bluebonnet 12-31-70	Alabama 24-24
Chuck Fairbanks	Sugar 1-1-72	Auburn 40-22
Chuck Fairbanks	Sugar 12-31-72	Penn St. 14-0
Barry Switzer	Orange 1-1-76	Michigan 14-6
Barry Switzer	Fiesta 12-25-76	Wyoming 41-7
Barry Switzer	Orange 1-2-78	Arkansas 6-31
Barry Switzer	Orange 1-1-79	Nebraska 31-24
Barry Switzer	Orange 1-1-80	Florida St. 24-7
Barry Switzer	Orange 1-1-81	Florida St. 18-17
Barry Switzer	Sun 12-26-81	Houston 40-14
Barry Switzer	Fiesta 1-1-83	Arizona St. 21-32
Barry Switzer	Orange 1-1-85	Washington 17-28
Barry Switzer	Orange 1-1-86	Penn St. 25-10
Barry Switzer	Orange 1-1-87	Arkansas 42-8
Barry Switzer	Orange 1-1-88	Miami (Fla.) 14-20
Barry Switzer	Florida Citrus 1-2-89	Clemson 6-13
Gary Gibbs	Gator 12-29-91	Virginia 48-14
Gary Gibbs	John Hancock 12-24-93	Texas Tech 41-10
Gary Gibbs	Copper 12-29-94	Brigham Young 6-31
Bob Stoops	Independence 12-31-99	Mississippi 25-27
Bob Stoops	Orange 1-3-01	Florida St. 13-2
Bob Stoops	Cotton 1-1-02	Arkansas 10-3
Bob Stoops	Rose 1-1-03	Washington St. 34-14

All bowls 23-12-1

OKLAHOMA ST.

School/Coach	Bowl/Date	Opponent/Score
Jim Lookabaugh	Cotton 1-1-45	TCU 34-0
Jim Lookabaugh	Sugar 1-1-46	St. Mary's (Cal.) 33-13
Jim Lookabaugh	Delta 1-1-49	William & Mary 0-20
Cliff Speegle	Bluegrass 12-13-58	Florida St. 15-6
Jim Stanley	Fiesta 12-28-74	Brigham Young 16-6
Jim Stanley	Tangerine 12-18-76	Brigham Young 49-12
Jimmy Johnson	Independence 12-12-81	Texas A&M 16-33
Jimmy Johnson	Bluebonnet 12-31-83	Baylor 24-14
Pat Jones	Gator 12-28-84	South Carolina 21-14
Pat Jones	Gator 12-30-85	Florida St. 23-34
Pat Jones	Sun 12-25-87	West Virginia 35-33
Pat Jones	Holiday 12-30-88	Wyoming 62-14
Bob Simmons	Alamo 12-30-97	Purdue 20-33
Les Miles	Houston 12-27-02	Southern Miss. 33-23

All bowls 10-4-0

OREGON

School/Coach	Bowl/Date	Opponent/Score
Hugo Bezdek	Rose 1-1-17	Pennsylvania 14-0
Charles "Shy" Huntington	Rose 1-1-20	Harvard 6-7
Jim Aiken	Cotton 1-1-49	Southern Methodist 13-21
Len Casanova	Rose 1-1-58	Ohio St. 7-10
Len Casanova	Liberty 12-17-60	Penn St. 12-41
Len Casanova	Sun 12-31-63	Southern Methodist 21-14
Rich Brooks	Independence 12-16-89	Tulsa 27-24
Rich Brooks	Freedom 12-29-90	Colorado St. 31-32
Rich Brooks	Independence 12-31-92	Wake Forest 35-39
Rich Brooks	Rose 1-2-95	Penn St. 20-38
Mike Bellotti	Cotton 1-1-96	Colorado 6-38
Mike Bellotti	Las Vegas 12-20-97	Air Force 41-13
Mike Bellotti	Aloha Classic 12-25-98	Colorado 43-51
Mike Bellotti	Sun 12-31-99	Minnesota 24-20
Mike Bellotti	Holiday 12-29-00	Texas 35-30
Mike Bellotti	Fiesta 1-1-02	Colorado 38-16
Mike Bellotti	Seattle 12-30-02	Wake Forest 17-38

All bowls 7-10-0

OREGON ST.

School/Coach	Bowl/Date	Opponent/Score
Lon Stiner	Rose 1-1-42	Duke 20-16
Tommy Prothro	Rose 1-1-57	Iowa 19-35
Tommy Prothro	Liberty 12-15-62	Villanova 6-0
Tommy Prothro	Rose 1-1-65	Michigan 7-34
Dennis Erickson	Oahu Classic 12-25-99	Hawaii 17-23
Dennis Erickson	Fiesta 1-1-01	Notre Dame 41-9
Dennis Erickson	Insight 12-26-02	Pittsburgh 13-38

All bowls 3-4-0

PENN ST.

School/Coach	Bowl/Date	Opponent/Score
Hugo Bezdek	Rose 1-1-23	Southern California 3-14
Bob Higgins	Cotton 1-1-48	Southern Methodist 13-13
Charles "Rip" Engle	Liberty 12-19-59	Alabama 7-0
Charles "Rip" Engle	Liberty 12-17-60	Oregon 41-12
Charles "Rip" Engle	Gator 12-30-61	Georgia Tech 30-15
Charles "Rip" Engle	Gator 12-29-62	Florida 7-17
Joe Paterno	Gator 12-30-67	Florida St. 17-17
Joe Paterno	Orange 1-1-69	Kansas 15-14
Joe Paterno	Orange 1-1-70	Missouri 10-3
Joe Paterno	Cotton 1-1-72	Texas 30-6
Joe Paterno	Sugar 12-31-72	Oklahoma 0-14
Joe Paterno	Orange 1-1-74	LSU 16-9
Joe Paterno	Cotton 1-1-75	Baylor 41-20
Joe Paterno	Sugar 12-31-75	Alabama 6-13
Joe Paterno	Gator 12-27-76	Notre Dame 9-20
Joe Paterno	Fiesta 12-25-77	Arizona St. 42-30
Joe Paterno	Sugar 1-1-79	Alabama 7-14
Joe Paterno	Liberty 12-22-79	Tulane 9-6
Joe Paterno	Fiesta 12-26-80	Ohio St. 31-19
Joe Paterno	Fiesta 1-1-82	Southern California 26-10
Joe Paterno	Sugar 1-1-83	Georgia 27-23
Joe Paterno	Aloha 12-26-83	Washington 13-10
Joe Paterno	Orange 1-1-86	Oklahoma 10-25
Joe Paterno	Fiesta 1-2-87	Miami (Fla.) 14-10
Joe Paterno	Florida Citrus 1-1-88	Clemson 10-35
Joe Paterno	Holiday 12-29-89	Brigham Young 50-39
Joe Paterno	Blockbuster 12-28-90	Florida St. 17-24
Joe Paterno	Fiesta 1-1-92	Tennessee 42-17
Joe Paterno	Blockbuster 1-1-93	Stanford 3-24
Joe Paterno	Florida Citrus 1-1-94	Tennessee 31-13

School/Coach	Bowl/Date	Opponent/Score
Joe Paterno	Rose 1-2-95	Oregon 38-20
Joe Paterno	Outback 1-1-96	Auburn 43-14
Joe Paterno	Fiesta 1-1-97	Texas 38-15
Joe Paterno	Flordia Citrus 1-1-98	Florida 6-21
Joe Paterno	Outback 1-1-99	Kentucky 26-14
Joe Paterno	Alamo 12-28-99	Texas A&M 24-0
Joe Paterno	Capital One 1-1-03	Auburn 9-13

All bowls 23-12-2

PITTSBURGH

School/Coach	Bowl/Date	Opponent/Score
Jock Sutherland	Rose 1-2-28	Stanford 6-7
Jock Sutherland	Rose 1-1-30	Southern California 14-47
Jock Sutherland	Rose 1-2-33	Southern California 0-35
Jock Sutherland	Rose 1-1-37	Washington 21-0
John Michelosen	Sugar 1-2-56	Georgia Tech 0-7
John Michelosen	Gator 12-29-56	Georgia Tech 14-21
Johnny Majors	Fiesta 12-21-73	Arizona St. 7-28
Johnny Majors	Sun 12-26-75	Kansas 33-19
Johnny Majors	Sugar 1-1-77	Georgia 27-3
Jackie Sherrill	Gator 12-30-77	Clemson 34-3
Jackie Sherrill	Tangerine 12-23-78	North Carolina St. 17-30
Jackie Sherrill	Fiesta 12-25-79	Arizona 16-10
Jackie Sherrill	Gator 12-29-80	South Carolina 37-9
Jackie Sherrill	Sugar 1-1-82	Georgia 24-20
Foge Fazio	Cotton 1-1-83	Southern Methodist 3-7
Foge Fazio	Fiesta 1-2-84	Ohio St. 23-28
Mike Gottfried	Bluebonnet 12-31-87	Texas 27-32
Paul Hackett	John Hancock 12-30-89	Texas A&M 31-28
Walt Harris	Liberty 12-31-97	Southern Miss. 7-41
Walt Harris	Insight.com 12-28-00	Iowa St. 29-37
Walt Harris	Tangerine 12-20-01	North Carolina St. 34-19
Walt Harris	Insight 12-26-02	Oregon St. 38-13

All bowls 10-12-0

PURDUE

School/Coach	Bowl/Date	Opponent/Score
Jack Mollenkopf	Rose 1-2-67	Southern California 14-13
Jim Young	Peach 12-25-78	Georgia Tech 41-21
Jim Young	Bluebonnet 12-31-79	Tennessee 27-22
Jim Young	Liberty 12-27-80	Missouri 28-25
Leon Burtnett	Peach 12-31-84	Virginia 24-27
Joe Tiller	Alamo 12-30-97	Oklahoma St. 33-20
Joe Tiller	Alamo 12-29-98	Kansas St. 37-34
Joe Tiller	Outback 1-1-00	Georgia 25-28 (ot)
Joe Tiller	Rose 1-1-01	Washington 24-34
Joe Tiller	Sun 12-31-01	Washington St. 27-33
Joe Tiller	Sun 12-31-02	Washington 34-24

All bowls 7-4-0

RICE

School/Coach	Bowl/Date	Opponent/Score
Jimmy Kitts	Cotton 1-1-38	Colorado 28-14
Jess Neely	Orange 1-1-47	Tennessee 8-0
Jess Neely	Cotton 1-2-50	North Carolina 27-13
Jess Neely	Cotton 1-1-54	Alabama 28-6
Jess Neely	Cotton 1-1-58	Navy 7-20
Jess Neely	Sugar 1-2-61	Mississippi 6-14
Jess Neely	Bluebonnet 12-16-61	Kansas 7-33

All bowls 4-3-0

RUTGERS

School/Coach	Bowl/Date	Opponent/Score
Frank Burns	Garden State 12-16-78	Arizona St. 18-34

All bowls 0-1-0

SAN DIEGO ST.

School/Coach	Bowl/Date	Opponent/Score
Bill Schutte	Harbor 1-1-48	Hardin-Simmons 0-53
Don Coryell	Pasadena 12-6-69	Boston U. 28-7
Denny Stolz	Holiday 12-30-86	Iowa 38-39
Al Luginbill	Freedom 12-30-91	Tulsa 17-28
Ted Tollner	Las Vegas 12-19-98	North Carolina 13-20

All bowls 1-4-0

SAN JOSE ST.

School/Coach	Bowl/Date	Opponent/Score
Bill Hubbard	Raisin 1-1-47	Utah St. 20-0
Bill Hubbard	Raisin 12-31-49	Texas Tech 20-13
Dewey King	Pasadena 12-18-71	Memphis 9-28
Jack Elway	California 12-19-81	Toledo 25-27
Claude Gilbert	California 12-31-86	Miami (Ohio) 37-7
Claude Gilbert	California 12-12-87	Eastern Mich. 27-30
Terry Shea	California 12-8-90	Central Mich. 48-24

All bowls 4-3-0

SOUTH CAROLINA

School/Coach	Bowl/Date	Opponent/Score
Johnny McMillan	Gator 1-1-46	Wake Forest 14-26
Paul Dietzel	Peach 12-30-69	West Virginia 3-14
Jim Carlen	Tangerine 12-20-75	Miami (Ohio) 7-20
Jim Carlen	Hall of Fame 12-29-79	Missouri 14-24
Jim Carlen	Gator 12-29-80	Pittsburgh 9-37
Joe Morrison	Gator 12-28-84	Oklahoma St. 14-21

School/Coach	Bowl/Date	Opponent/Score
Joe Morrison	Gator 12-31-87	LSU 13-30
Joe Morrison	Liberty 12-28-88	Indiana 10-34
Brad Scott	Carquest 1-2-95	West Virginia 24-21
Lou Holtz	Outback 1-1-01	Ohio St. 24-7
Lou Holtz	Outback 1-1-02	Ohio St. 31-28

All bowls 3-8-0

SOUTHERN CALIFORNIA

School/Coach	Bowl/Date	Opponent/Score
Elmer "Gus" Henderson	Rose 1-1-23	Penn St. 14-3
Elmer "Gus" Henderson	Los Angeles Christmas Festival 12-25-24	Missouri 20-7
Howard Jones	Rose 1-1-30	Pittsburgh 47-14
Howard Jones	Rose 1-1-32	Tulane 21-12
Howard Jones	Rose 1-2-33	Pittsburgh 35-0
Howard Jones	Rose 1-1-39	Duke 7-3
Howard Jones	Rose 1-1-40	Tennessee 14-0
Jeff Cravath	Rose 1-1-44	Washington 29-0
Jeff Cravath	Rose 1-1-45	Tennessee 25-0
Jeff Cravath	Rose 1-1-46	Alabama 14-34
Jeff Cravath	Rose 1-1-48	Michigan 0-49
Jess Hill	Rose 1-1-53	Wisconsin 7-0
Jess Hill	Rose 1-1-55	Ohio St. 7-20
John McKay	Rose 1-1-63	Wisconsin 42-37
John McKay	Rose 1-2-67	Purdue 13-14
John McKay	Rose 1-1-68	Indiana 14-3
John McKay	Rose 1-1-69	Ohio St. 16-27
John McKay	Rose 1-1-70	Michigan 10-3
John McKay	Rose 1-1-73	Ohio St. 42-17
John McKay	Rose 1-1-74	Ohio St. 21-42
John McKay	Rose 1-1-75	Ohio St. 18-17
John McKay	Liberty 12-22-75	Texas A&M 20-0
John Robinson	Rose 1-1-77	Michigan 14-6
John Robinson	Bluebonnet 12-31-77	Texas A&M 47-28
John Robinson	Rose 1-1-79	Michigan 17-10
John Robinson	Rose 1-1-80	Ohio St. 17-16
John Robinson	Fiesta 1-1-82	Penn St. 10-26
Ted Tollner	Rose 1-1-85	Ohio St. 20-17
Ted Tollner	Aloha 12-28-85	Alabama 3-24
Ted Tollner	Florida Citrus 1-1-87	Auburn 7-16
Larry Smith	Rose 1-1-88	Michigan St. 17-20
Larry Smith	Rose 1-1-89	Michigan 14-22
Larry Smith	Rose 1-1-90	Michigan 17-10
Larry Smith	John Hancock 12-31-90	Michigan St. 16-17
Larry Smith	Freedom 12-29-92	Fresno St. 7-24
John Robinson	Freedom 12-30-93	Utah 28-21
John Robinson	Cotton 1-2-95	Texas Tech 55-14
John Robinson	Rose 1-1-96	Northwestern 41-32
Paul Hackett	Sun 12-31-98	TCU 19-28
Pete Carroll	Las Vegas 12-25-01	Utah 6-10
Pete Carroll	Orange 1-2-03	Iowa 38-17

All bowls 26-15-0

SOUTHERN METHODIST

School/Coach	Bowl/Date	Opponent/Score
Ray Morrison	Dixie Classic 1-1-25	West Va. Wesleyan 7-9
Matty Bell	Rose 1-1-36	Stanford 0-7
Matty Bell	Cotton 1-1-48	Penn St. 13-13
Matty Bell	Cotton 1-1-49	Oregon 21-13
Hayden Fry	Sun 12-31-63	Oregon 14-21
Hayden Fry	Cotton 12-31-66	Georgia 9-24
Hayden Fry	Bluebonnet 12-31-68	Oklahoma 28-27
Ron Meyer	Holiday 12-19-80	Brigham Young 45-46
Bobby Collins	Cotton 1-1-83	Pittsburgh 7-3
Bobby Collins	Sun 12-24-83	Alabama 7-28
Bobby Collins	Aloha 12-29-84	Notre Dame 27-20

All bowls 4-6-1

SOUTHERN MISS.

School/Coach	Bowl/Date	Opponent/Score
Thad "Pie" Vann	Sun 1-1-53	Pacific (Cal.) 7-26
Thad "Pie" Vann	Sun 1-1-54	UTEP 14-37
Bobby Collins	Independence 12-13-80	McNeese St. 16-14
Bobby Collins	Tangerine 12-19-81	Missouri 17-19
Curley Hallman	Independence 12-23-88	UTEP 38-18
Jeff Bower	All-American 12-28-90	North Carolina St. 27-31
Jeff Bower	Liberty 12-31-97	Pittsburgh 41-7
Jeff Bower	Humanitarian 12-30-98	Idaho 35-42
Jeff Bower	Liberty 12-31-99	Colorado St. 23-17
Jeff Bower	Mobile Alabama 12-20-00	TCU 28-21
Jeff Bower	Houston 12-27-02	Oklahoma St. 23-33

All bowls 5-6-0

STANFORD

School/Coach	Bowl/Date	Opponent/Score
Charlie Fickert	Rose 1-1-02	Michigan 0-49
Glenn "Pop" Warner	Rose 1-1-25	Notre Dame 10-27
Glenn "Pop" Warner	Rose 1-1-27	Alabama 7-7
Glenn "Pop" Warner	Rose 1-2-28	Pittsburgh 7-6

School/Coach	Bowl/Date	Opponent/Score
Claude "Tiny" Thornhill	Rose 1-1-34	Columbia 0-7
Claude "Tiny" Thornhill	Rose 1-1-35	Alabama 13-29
Claude "Tiny" Thornhill	Rose 1-1-36	Southern Methodist 7-0
Clark Shaughnessy	Rose 1-1-41	Nebraska 21-13
Chuck Taylor	Rose 1-1-52	Illinois 7-40
John Ralston	Rose 1-1-71	Ohio St. 27-17
John Ralston	Rose 1-1-72	Michigan 13-12
Bill Walsh	Sun 12-31-77	LSU 24-14
Bill Walsh	Bluebonnet 12-31-78	Georgia 25-22
Jack Elway	Gator 12-27-86	Clemson 21-27
Dennis Green	Aloha 12-25-91	Georgia Tech 17-18
Bill Walsh	Blockbuster 1-1-93	Penn St. 24-3
Tyrone Willingham	Liberty 12-30-95	East Caro. 13-19
Tyrone Willingham	Sun 12-31-96	Michigan St. 38-0
Tyrone Willingham	Rose 1-1-00	Wisconsin 9-17
Tyrone Willingham	Seattle 12-27-01	Georgia Tech 14-24
All bowls 9-10-1		

SYRACUSE

School/Coach	Bowl/Date	Opponent/Score
Ben Schwartzwalder	Orange 1-1-53	Alabama 6-61
Ben Schwartzwalder	Cotton 1-1-57	TCU 27-28
Ben Schwartzwalder	Orange 1-1-59	Oklahoma 6-21
Ben Schwartzwalder	Cotton 1-1-60	Texas 23-14
Ben Schwartzwalder	Liberty 12-16-61	Miami (Fla.) 15-14
Ben Schwartzwalder	Sugar 1-1-65	LSU 10-13
Ben Schwartzwalder	Gator 12-31-66	Tennessee 12-18
Frank Maloney	Independence 12-15-79	McNeese St. 31-7
Dick MacPherson	Cherry 12-21-85	Maryland 18-35
Dick MacPherson	Sugar 1-1-88	Auburn 16-16
Dick MacPherson	Hall of Fame 1-2-89	LSU 23-10
Dick MacPherson	Peach 12-30-89	Georgia 19-18
Dick MacPherson	Aloha 12-25-90	Arizona 28-0
Paul Pasqualoni	Hall of Fame 1-1-92	Ohio St. 24-17
Paul Pasqualoni	Fiesta 1-1-93	Colorado 26-22
Paul Pasqualoni	Gator 1-1-96	Clemson 41-0
Paul Pasqualoni	Liberty 12-27-96	Houston 30-17
Paul Pasqualoni	Fiesta 12-31-97	Kansas St. 18-35
Paul Pasqualoni	Orange 1-2-99	Florida 10-31
Paul Pasqualoni	Music City 12-29-99	Kentucky 20-13
Paul Pasqualoni	Insight.com 12-29-01	Kansas St. 26-3
All bowls 12-8-1		

TEMPLE

School/Coach	Bowl/Date	Opponent/Score
Glenn "Pop" Warner	Sugar 1-1-35	Tulane 14-20
Wayne Hardin	Garden State 12-15-79	California 28-17
All bowls 1-1-0		

TENNESSEE

School/Coach	Bowl/Date	Opponent/Score
Bob Neyland	Orange 1-2-39	Oklahoma 17-0
Bob Neyland	Rose 1-1-40	Southern California 0-14
Bob Neyland	Sugar 1-1-41	Boston College 13-19
John Barnhill	Sugar 1-1-43	Tulsa 14-7
John Barnhill	Rose 1-1-45	Southern California 0-25
Bob Neyland	Orange 1-1-47	Rice 0-8
Bob Neyland	Cotton 1-1-51	Texas 20-14
Bob Neyland	Sugar 1-1-52	Maryland 13-28
Bob Neyland	Cotton 1-1-53	Texas 0-16
Bowden Wyatt	Sugar 1-1-57	Baylor 7-13
Bowden Wyatt	Gator 12-28-57	Texas A&M 3-0
Doug Dickey	Bluebonnet 12-18-65	Tulsa 27-6
Doug Dickey	Gator 12-31-66	Syracuse 18-12
Doug Dickey	Orange 1-1-68	Oklahoma 24-26
Doug Dickey	Cotton 1-1-69	Texas 13-36
Doug Dickey	Gator 12-27-69	Florida 13-14
Bill Battle	Sugar 1-1-71	Air Force 34-13
Bill Battle	Liberty 12-20-71	Arkansas 14-13
Bill Battle	Bluebonnet 12-30-72	LSU 24-17
Bill Battle	Gator 12-29-73	Texas Tech 19-28
Bill Battle	Liberty 12-16-74	Maryland 7-3
Johnny Majors	Bluebonnet 12-31-79	Purdue 22-27
Johnny Majors	Garden State 12-13-81	Wisconsin 28-21
Johnny Majors	Peach 12-31-82	Iowa 22-28
Johnny Majors	Florida Citrus 12-17-83	Maryland 30-23
Johnny Majors	Sun 12-24-84	Maryland 27-28
Johnny Majors	Sugar 1-1-86	Miami (Fla.) 35-7
Johnny Majors	Liberty 12-29-86	Minnesota 21-14
Johnny Majors	Peach 1-2-88	Indiana 27-22
Johnny Majors	Cotton 1-1-90	Arkansas 31-27
Johnny Majors	Sugar 1-1-91	Virginia 23-22
Johnny Majors	Fiesta 1-1-92	Penn St. 17-42
Phillip Fulmer	Hall of Fame 1-1-93	Boston College 38-23
Phillip Fulmer	Florida Citrus 1-1-94	Penn St. 13-31
Phillip Fulmer	Gator 12-30-94	Virginia Tech 45-23
Phillip Fulmer	Florida Citrus 1-1-96	Ohio St. 20-14
Phillip Fulmer	Florida Citrus 1-1-97	Northwestern 48-28
Phillip Fulmer	Orange 1-2-98	Nebraska 17-42
Phillip Fulmer	Fiesta 1-4-99	Florida St. 23-16
Phillip Fulmer	Fiesta 1-2-00	Nebraska 21-31
Phillip Fulmer	Cotton 1-1-01	Kansas St. 21-35
Phillip Fulmer	Florida Citrus 1-1-02	Michigan 45-17
Phillip Fulmer	Peach 12-31-02	Maryland 3-30
All bowls 23-20-0		

TEXAS

School/Coach	Bowl/Date	Opponent/Score
Dana Bible	Cotton 1-1-43	Georgia Tech 14-7
Dana Bible	Cotton 1-1-44	Randolph Field 7-7
Dana Bible	Cotton 1-1-46	Missouri 40-27
Blair Cherry	Sugar 1-1-48	Alabama 27-7
Blair Cherry	Orange 1-1-49	Georgia 41-28
Blair Cherry	Cotton 1-1-51	Tennessee 14-20
Ed Price	Cotton 1-1-53	Tennessee 16-0
Darrell Royal	Sugar 1-1-58	Mississippi 7-39
Darrell Royal	Cotton 1-1-60	Syracuse 14-23
Darrell Royal	Bluebonnet 12-17-60	Alabama 3-3
Darrell Royal	Cotton 1-1-62	Mississippi 12-7
Darrell Royal	Cotton 1-1-63	LSU 0-13
Darrell Royal	Cotton 1-1-64	Navy 28-6
Darrell Royal	Orange 1-1-65	Alabama 21-17
Darrell Royal	Bluebonnet 12-17-66	Mississippi 19-0
Darrell Royal	Cotton 1-1-69	Tennessee 36-13
Darrell Royal	Cotton 1-1-70	Notre Dame 21-17
Darrell Royal	Cotton 1-1-71	Notre Dame 11-24
Darrell Royal	Cotton 1-1-72	Penn St. 6-30
Darrell Royal	Cotton 1-1-73	Alabama 17-13
Darrell Royal	Cotton 1-1-74	Nebraska 3-19
Darrell Royal	Gator 12-30-74	Auburn 3-27
Darrell Royal	Bluebonnet 12-27-75	Colorado 38-21
Fred Akers	Cotton 1-2-78	Notre Dame 10-38
Fred Akers	Sun 12-23-78	Maryland 42-0
Fred Akers	Sun 12-22-79	Washington 7-14
Fred Akers	Bluebonnet 12-31-80	North Carolina 7-16
Fred Akers	Cotton 1-1-82	Alabama 14-12
Fred Akers	Sun 12-25-82	North Carolina 10-26
Fred Akers	Cotton 1-2-84	Georgia 9-10
Fred Akers	Freedom 12-26-84	Iowa 17-55
Fred Akers	Bluebonnet 12-31-85	Air Force 16-24
David McWilliams	Bluebonnet 12-31-87	Pittsburgh 32-27
David McWilliams	Cotton 1-1-91	Miami (Fla.) 3-46
John Mackovic	Sun 12-30-94	North Carolina 35-31
John Mackovic	Sugar 12-31-95	Virginia Tech 10-28
John Mackovic	Fiesta 1-1-97	Penn St. 15-38
Mack Brown	Cotton 1-1-99	Mississippi St. 38-11
Mack Brown	Cotton 1-1-00	Arkansas 6-27
Mack Brown	Holiday 12-29-00	Oregon 30-35
Mack Brown	Holiday 12-28-01	Washington 47-43
Mack Brown	Cotton 1-1-03	LSU 35-20
All bowls 20-20-2		

UTEP

School/Coach	Bowl/Date	Opponent/Score
Mack Saxon	Sun 1-1-37	Hardin-Simmons 6-34
Jack "Cactus Jack" Curtice	Sun 1-1-49	West Virginia 12-21
Jack "Cactus Jack" Curtice	Sun 1-2-50	Georgetown 33-20
Mike Brumbelow	Sun 1-1-54	Southern Miss. 37-14
Mike Brumbelow	Sun 1-1-55	Florida St. 47-20
Mike Brumbelow	Sun 1-1-57	George Washington 0-13
Bobby Dobbs	Sun 12-31-65	TCU 13-12
Bobby Dobbs	Sun 12-30-67	Mississippi 14-7
Bob Stull	Independence 12-23-88	Southern Miss. 18-38
Gary Nord	Humanitarian 12-28-00	Boise St. 23-38
All bowls 5-5-0		

TEXAS A&M

School/Coach	Bowl/Date	Opponent/Score
Dana Bible	Dixie Classic 1-2-22	Centre 22-14
Homer Norton	Sugar 1-1-40	Tulane 14-13
Homer Norton	Cotton 1-1-41	Fordham 13-12
Homer Norton	Cotton 1-1-42	Alabama 21-29
Homer Norton	Orange 1-1-44	LSU 14-19
Harry Stiteler	Presidential 12-9-50	Georgia 40-20
Paul "Bear" Bryant	Gator 12-28-57	Tennessee 0-3
Gene Stallings	Cotton 1-1-68	Alabama 20-16
Emory Bellard	Liberty 12-22-75	Southern California 0-20
Emory Bellard	Sun 1-2-77	Florida 37-14
Emory Bellard	Bluebonnet 12-31-77	Southern California 28-47
Tom Wilson	Hall of Fame 12-20-78	Iowa St. 28-12
Tom Wilson	Independence 12-12-81	Oklahoma St. 33-16
Jackie Sherrill	Cotton 1-1-86	Auburn 36-16
Jackie Sherrill	Cotton 1-1-87	Ohio St. 12-28
Jackie Sherrill	Cotton 1-1-88	Notre Dame 35-10
R.C. Slocum	John Hancock 12-30-89	Pittsburgh 28-31
R.C. Slocum	Holiday 12-29-90	Brigham Young 65-14
R.C. Slocum	Cotton 1-1-92	Florida St. 2-10
R.C. Slocum	Cotton 1-1-93	Notre Dame 3-28

School/Coach	Bowl/Date	Opponent/Score
R.C. Slocum	Cotton 1-1-94	Notre Dame 21-24
R.C. Slocum	Alamo 12-28-95	Michigan 22-20
R.C. Slocum	Cotton 1-1-98	UCLA 23-29
R.C. Slocum	Sugar 1-1-99	Ohio St. 14-24
R.C. Slocum	Alamo 12-28-99	Penn St. 0-24
R.C. Slocum	Independence 12-31-00	Mississippi St. 41-43 (ot)
R.C. Slocum	Galleryfurniture.com 12-28-01	TCU 28-9

All bowls 13-14-0

TCU

School/Coach	Bowl/Date	Opponent/Score
Bill Driver	Fort Worth Classic 1-1-21	Centre 7-63
Leo "Dutch" Meyer	Sugar 1-1-36	LSU 3-2
Leo "Dutch" Meyer	Cotton 1-1-37	Marquette 16-6
Leo "Dutch" Meyer	Sugar 1-2-39	Carnegie Mellon 15-7
Leo "Dutch" Meyer	Orange 1-1-42	Georgia 26-40
Leo "Dutch" Meyer	Cotton 1-1-45	Oklahoma St. 0-34
Leo "Dutch" Meyer	Delta 1-1-48	Mississippi 9-13
Leo "Dutch" Meyer	Cotton 1-1-52	Kentucky 7-20
Abe Martin	Cotton 1-2-56	Mississippi 13-14
Abe Martin	Cotton 1-1-57	Syracuse 28-27
Abe Martin	Cotton 1-1-59	Air Force 0-0
Abe Martin	Bluebonnet 12-19-59	Clemson 7-23
Abe Martin	Sun 12-31-65	UTEP 12-13
Jim Wacker	Bluebonnet 12-31-84	West Virginia 14-31
Pat Sullivan	Independence 12-28-94	Virginia 10-20
Dennis Franchione	Sun 12-31-98	Southern California 28-19
Dennis Franchione	Mobile Alabama 12-22-99	East Caro. 28-14
Gary Patterson	Mobile Alabama 12-20-00	Southern Miss. 21-28
Gary Patterson	Galleryfurniture.com 12-28-01	Texas A&M 9-28
Gary Patterson	Liberty 12-31-02	Colorado St. 17-3

All bowls 7-12-1

TEXAS TECH

School/Coach	Bowl/Date	Opponent/Score
Pete Cawthon	Sun 1-1-38	West Virginia 6-7
Pete Cawthon	Cotton 1-2-39	St. Mary's (Cal.) 13-20
Dell Morgan	Sun 1-1-42	Tulsa 0-6
Dell Morgan	Sun 1-1-48	Miami (Ohio) 12-13
Dell Morgan	Raisin 12-31-49	San Jose St. 13-20
DeWitt Weaver	Sun 1-1-52	Pacific (Cal.) 25-14
DeWitt Weaver	Gator 1-1-54	Auburn 35-13
DeWitt Weaver	Sun 1-2-56	Wyoming 14-21
J.T. King	Sun 12-26-64	Georgia 0-7
J.T. King	Gator 12-31-65	Georgia Tech 21-31
Jim Carlen	Sun 12-19-70	Georgia Tech 9-17
Jim Carlen	Sun 12-30-72	North Carolina 28-32
Jim Carlen	Gator 12-29-73	Tennessee 28-19
Jim Carlen	Peach 12-28-74	Vanderbilt 6-6
Steve Sloan	Bluebonnet 12-31-76	Nebraska 24-27
Steve Sloan	Tangerine 12-23-77	Florida St. 17-40
Spike Dykes	Independence 12-20-86	Mississippi 17-20
Spike Dykes	All-American 12-28-89	Duke 49-21
Spike Dykes	John Hancock 12-24-93	Oklahoma 10-41
Spike Dykes	Cotton 1-2-95	Southern California 14-55
Spike Dykes	Copper 12-27-95	Air Force 55-41
Spike Dykes	Alamo 12-29-96	Iowa 0-27
Spike Dykes	Independence 12-31-98	Mississippi 18-35
Mike Leach	Galleryfurniture.com 12-27-00	East Caro. 27-40
Mike Leach	Alamo 12-29-01	Iowa 13-16
Mike Leach	Mazda Tangerine 12-23-02	Clemson 55-15

All bowls 6-19-1

TOLEDO

School/Coach	Bowl/Date	Opponent/Score
Frank Lauterbur	Tangerine 12-26-69	Davidson 56-33
Frank Lauterbur	Tangerine 12-28-70	William & Mary 40-12
Jack Murphy	Tangerine 12-28-71	Richmond 28-3
Chuck Stobart	California 12-19-81	San Jose St. 27-25
Dan Simrell	California 12-15-84	UNLV 13-30
Gary Pinkel	Las Vegas 12-14-95	Nevada 40-37 (ot)
Tom Anstutz	Motor City 12-29-01	Cincinnati 23-16
Tom Anstutz	Motor City 12-26-02	Boston College 25-51

All bowls 6-2-0

TULANE

School/Coach	Bowl/Date	Opponent/Score
Bernie Bierman	Rose 1-1-32	Southern California 12-21
Ted Cox	Sugar 1-1-35	Temple 20-14
Lowell "Red" Dawson	Sugar 1-1-40	Texas A&M 13-14
Jim Pittman	Liberty 12-12-70	Colorado 17-3
Bennie Ellender	Bluebonnet 12-29-73	Houston 7-47
Larry Smith	Liberty 12-22-79	Penn St. 6-9
Vince Gibson	Hall of Fame 12-27-80	Arkansas 15-34
Mack Brown	Independence 12-19-87	Washington 12-24
Tommy Bowden	Liberty 12-31-98	Brigham Young 41-27
Chris Scelfo	Hawaii 12-25-02	Hawaii 36-28

All bowls 4-6-0

TULSA

School/Coach	Bowl/Date	Opponent/Score
Henry Frnka	Sun 1-1-42	Texas Tech 6-0
Henry Frnka	Sugar 1-1-43	Tennessee 7-14
Henry Frnka	Sugar 1-1-44	Georgia Tech 18-20
Henry Frnka	Orange 1-1-45	Georgia Tech 26-12
Henry Frnka	Oil 1-1-46	Georgia 6-20
J.O. "Buddy" Brothers	Gator 1-1-53	Florida 13-14
Glenn Dobbs	Bluebonnet 12-19-64	Mississippi 14-7
Glenn Dobbs	Bluebonnet 12-18-65	Tennessee 6-27
F.A. Dry	Independence 12-13-76	McNeese St. 16-20
Dave Rader	Independence 12-16-89	Oregon 24-27
Dave Rader	Freedom 12-30-91	San Diego St. 28-17

All bowls 4-7-0

UCLA

School/Coach	Bowl/Date	Opponent/Score
Edwin "Babe" Horrell	Rose 1-1-43	Georgia 0-9
Bert LaBrucherie	Rose 1-1-47	Illinois 14-45
Henry "Red" Sanders	Rose 1-1-54	Michigan St. 20-28
Henry "Red" Sanders	Rose 1-2-56	Michigan St. 14-17
Bill Barnes	Rose 1-1-62	Minnesota 3-21
Tommy Prothro	Rose 1-1-66	Michigan St. 14-12
Dick Vermeil	Rose 1-1-76	Ohio St. 23-10
Terry Donahue	Liberty 12-20-76	Alabama 6-36
Terry Donahue	Fiesta 12-25-78	Arkansas 10-10
Terry Donahue	Bluebonnet 12-31-81	Michigan 14-33
Terry Donahue	Rose 1-1-83	Michigan 24-14
Terry Donahue	Rose 1-2-84	Illinois 45-9
Terry Donahue	Fiesta 1-1-85	Miami (Fla.) 39-37
Terry Donahue	Rose 1-1-86	Iowa 45-28
Terry Donahue	Freedom 12-30-86	Brigham Young 31-10
Terry Donahue	Aloha 12-25-87	Florida 20-16
Terry Donahue	Cotton 1-1-89	Arkansas 17-3
Terry Donahue	John Hancock 12-31-91	Illinois 6-3
Terry Donahue	Rose 1-1-94	Wisconsin 16-21
Terry Donahue	Aloha 12-25-95	Kansas 30-51
Bob Toledo	Cotton 1-1-98	Texas A&M 29-23
Bob Toledo	Rose 1-1-99	Wisconsin 31-38
Bob Toledo	Sun 12-29-00	Wisconsin 20-21
Ed Kezirian	Las Vegas 12-25-02	New Mexico 27-13

All bowls 12-11-1

UTAH

School/Coach	Bowl/Date	Opponent/Score
Ike Armstrong	Sun 1-2-39	New Mexico 26-0
Ray Nagel	Liberty 12-19-64	West Virginia 32-6
Ron McBride	Copper 12-29-92	Washington St. 28-31
Ron McBride	Freedom 12-30-93	Southern California 21-28
Ron McBride	Freedom 12-27-94	Arizona 16-13
Ron McBride	Copper 12-27-96	Wisconsin 10-38
Ron McBride	Las Vegas 12-18-99	Fresno St. 17-16
Ron McBride	Las Vegas 12-25-01	Southern California 10-6

All bowls 5-3-0

UTAH ST.

School/Coach	Bowl/Date	Opponent/Score
E.L. "Dick" Romney	Raisin 1-1-47	San Jose St. 0-20
John Ralston	Sun 12-31-60	New Mexico St. 13-20
John Ralston	Gotham 12-9-61	Baylor 9-24
Charlie Weatherbie	Las Vegas 12-17-93	Ball St. 42-33
John L. Smith	Humanitarian 12-29-97	Cincinnati 19-35

All bowls 1-4-0

VANDERBILT

School/Coach	Bowl/Date	Opponent/Score
Art Guepe	Gator 12-31-55	Auburn 25-13
Steve Sloan	Peach 12-28-74	Texas Tech 6-6
George MacIntyre	Hall of Fame 12-31-82	Air Force 28-36

All bowls 1-1-1

VIRGINIA

School/Coach	Bowl/Date	Opponent/Score
George Welsh	Peach 12-31-84	Purdue 27-24
George Welsh	All-American 12-22-87	Brigham Young 22-16
George Welsh	Florida Citrus 1-1-90	Illinois 21-31
George Welsh	Sugar 1-1-91	Tennessee 22-23
George Welsh	Gator 12-29-91	Oklahoma 14-48
George Welsh	Carquest 1-1-94	Boston College 13-31
George Welsh	Independence 12-28-94	TCU 20-10
George Welsh	Peach 12-30-95	Georgia 34-27
George Welsh	Carquest 12-27-96	Miami (Fla.) 21-31
George Welsh	Peach 12-31-98	Georgia 33-35
George Welsh	Micronpc.com 12-30-99	Illinois 21-63
George Welsh	Oahu Classic 12-24-00	Georgia 14-37
Al Groh	Continental Tire 12-28-02	West Virginia 48-22

All bowls 5-8-0

VIRGINIA TECH

School/Coach	Bowl/Date	Opponent/Score
Jimmy Kitts	Sun 1-1-47	Cincinnati 6-18
Jerry Claiborne	Liberty 12-10-66	Miami (Fla.) 7-14
Jerry Claiborne	Liberty 12-14-68	Mississippi 17-34
Bill Dooley	Peach 1-2-81	Miami (Fla.) 10-20
Bill Dooley	Independence 12-15-84	Air Force 7-23

School/Coach	Bowl/Date	Opponent/Score
Bill Dooley	Peach 12-31-86	North Carolina St. 25-24
Frank Beamer	Independence 12-31-93	Indiana 45-20
Frank Beamer	Gator 12-30-94	Tennessee 23-45
Frank Beamer	Sugar 12-31-95	Texas 28-10
Frank Beamer	Orange 12-31-96	Nebraska 21-41
Frank Beamer	Gator 1-1-98	North Carolina 3-42
Frank Beamer	Music City 12-28-98	Alabama 38-7
Frank Beamer	Sugar 1-4-00	Florida St. 29-46
Frank Beamer	Gator 1-1-01	Clemson 41-20
Frank Beamer	Gator 1-1-02	Florida St. 17-30
Frank Beamer	San Francisco 12-31-02	Air Force 20-13

All bowls 6-10-0

WAKE FOREST

School/Coach	Bowl/Date	Opponent/Score
D.C. "Peahead" Walker	Gator 1-1-46	South Carolina 26-14
D.C. "Peahead" Walker	Dixie 1-1-49	Baylor 7-20
John Mackovic	Tangerine 12-22-79	LSU 10-34
Bill Dooley	Independence 12-31-92	Oregon 39-35
Jim Caldwell	Aloha Classic 12-25-99	Arizona St. 23-3
Jim Grobe	Seattle 12-30-02	Oregon 38-17

All bowls 4-2-0

WASHINGTON

School/Coach	Bowl/Date	Opponent/Score
Enoch Bagshaw	Rose 1-1-24	Navy 14-14
Enoch Bagshaw	Rose 1-1-26	Alabama 19-20
Jimmy Phelan	Rose 1-1-37	Pittsburgh 0-21
Ralph "Pest" Welch	Rose 1-1-44	Southern California 0-29
Jim Owens	Rose 1-1-60	Wisconsin 44-8
Jim Owens	Rose 1-2-61	Minnesota 17-7
Jim Owens	Rose 1-1-64	Illinois 7-17
Don James	Rose 1-2-78	Michigan 27-20
Don James	Sun 12-22-79	Texas 14-7
Don James	Rose 1-1-81	Michigan 6-23
Don James	Rose 1-1-82	Iowa 28-0
Don James	Aloha 12-25-82	Maryland 21-20
Don James	Aloha 12-26-83	Penn St. 10-13
Don James	Orange 1-1-85	Oklahoma 28-17
Don James	Freedom 12-30-85	Colorado 20-17
Don James	Sun 12-25-86	Alabama 6-28
Don James	Independence 12-19-87	Tulane 24-12
Don James	Freedom 12-30-89	Florida 34-7
Don James	Rose 1-1-91	Iowa 46-34
Don James	Rose 1-1-92	Michigan 34-14
Don James	Rose 1-1-93	Michigan 31-38
Jim Lambright	Sun 12-29-95	Iowa 18-38
Jim Lambright	Holiday 12-30-96	Colorado 21-33
Jim Lambright	Aloha 12-25-97	Michigan St. 51-23
Jim Lambright	Oahu Classic 12-25-98	Air Force 25-45
Rick Neuheisel	Holiday 12-29-99	Kansas St. 20-24
Rick Neuheisel	Rose 1-1-01	Purdue 34-24
Rick Neuheisel	Holiday 12-28-01	Texas 43-47
Rick Neuheisel	Sun 12-31-02	Purdue 24-34

All bowls 14-14-1

WASHINGTON ST.

School/Coach	Bowl/Date	Opponent/Score
Bill "Lone Star" Dietz	Rose 1-1-16	Brown 14-0
Orin "Babe" Hollingbery	Rose 1-1-31	Alabama 0-24
Jim Walden	Holiday 12-18-81	Brigham Young 36-38
Dennis Erickson	Aloha 12-25-88	Houston 24-22
Mike Price	Copper 12-29-92	Utah 31-28
Mike Price	Alamo 12-31-94	Baylor 10-3
Mike Price	Rose 1-1-98	Michigan 16-21
Mike Price	Sun 12-31-01	Purdue 33-27
Mike Price	Rose 1-1-03	Oklahoma 14-34

All bowls 5-4-0

WEST VIRGINIA

School/Coach	Bowl/Date	Opponent/Score
Clarence "Doc" Spears	San Diego East-West Christmas Classic 12-25-22	Gonzaga 21-13
Marshall "Little Sleepy" Glenn	Sun 1-1-38	Texas Tech 7-6
Dud DeGroot	Sun 1-1-49	UTEP 21-12
Art Lewis	Sugar 1-1-54	Georgia Tech 19-42
Gene Corum	Liberty 12-19-64	Utah 6-32
Jim Carlen	Peach 12-30-69	South Carolina 14-3
Bobby Bowden	Peach 12-29-72	North Carolina St. 13-49
Bobby Bowden	Peach 12-31-75	North Carolina St. 13-10
Don Nehlen	Peach 12-31-81	Florida 26-6
Don Nehlen	Gator 12-30-82	Florida St. 12-31
Don Nehlen	Hall of Fame 12-22-83	Kentucky 20-16
Don Nehlen	Bluebonnet 12-31-84	TCU 31-14
Don Nehlen	Sun 12-25-87	Oklahoma St. 33-35
Don Nehlen	Fiesta 1-2-89	Notre Dame 21-34
Don Nehlen	Gator 12-30-89	Clemson 7-27
Don Nehlen	Sugar 1-1-94	Florida 7-41
Don Nehlen	Carquest 1-2-95	South Carolina 21-24
Don Nehlen	Gator 1-1-97	North Carolina 13-20
Don Nehlen	Carquest 12-29-97	Georgia Tech 30-35
Don Nehlen	Insight.com 12-26-98	Missouri 31-34
Don Nehlen	Music City 12-28-00	Mississippi 49-38
Rich Rodriquez	Continental Tire 12-28-02	Virginia 22-48

All bowls 9-13-0

WESTERN MICH.

School/Coach	Bowl/Date	Opponent/Score
Merle Schlosser	Aviation 12-9-61	New Mexico 12-28
Al Molde	California 12-10-88	Fresno St. 30-35

All bowls 0-2-0

WISCONSIN

School/Coach	Bowl/Date	Opponent/Score
Ivy Williamson	Rose 1-1-53	Southern California 0-7
Milt Bruhn	Rose 1-1-60	Washington 8-44
Milt Bruhn	Rose 1-2-63	Southern California 37-42
Dave McClain	Garden State 12-13-81	Tennessee 21-28
Dave McClain	Independence 12-11-82	Kansas St. 14-3
Dave McClain	Hall of Fame 12-29-84	Kentucky 19-20
Barry Alvarez	Rose 1-1-94	UCLA 21-16
Barry Alvarez	Hall of Fame 1-2-95	Duke 34-20
Barry Alvarez	Copper 12-27-96	Utah 38-10
Barry Alvarez	Outback 1-1-98	Georgia 6-33
Barry Alvarez	Rose 1-1-99	UCLA 38-31
Barry Alvarez	Rose 1-1-00	Stanford 17-9
Barry Alvarez	Sun 12-29-00	UCLA 21-20
Barry Alvarez	Alamo 12-28-02	Colorado 31-28 (ot)

All bowls 8-6-0

WYOMING

School/Coach	Bowl/Date	Opponent/Score
Bowden Wyatt	Gator 1-1-51	Wash. & Lee 20-7
Phil Dickens	Sun 1-2-56	Texas Tech 21-14
Bob Devaney	Sun 12-31-58	Hardin-Simmons 14-6
Lloyd Eaton	Sun 12-24-66	Florida St. 28-20
Lloyd Eaton	Sugar 1-1-68	LSU 13-20
Fred Akers	Fiesta 12-25-76	Oklahoma 7-41
Paul Roach	Holiday 12-30-87	Iowa 19-20
Paul Roach	Holiday 12-30-88	Oklahoma St. 14-62
Paul Roach	Copper 12-31-90	California 15-17
Joe Tiller	Copper 12-29-93	Kansas St. 17-52

All bowls 4-6-0

Played in Major Bowl—No Longer I-A

School/Coach	Bowl/Date	Opponent/Score
BOSTON U.		
Larry Naviaux	Pasadena 12-6-69	San Diego St. 7-28
All bowls 0-1-0		
BROWN		
Ed Robinson	Rose 1-1-16	Washington St. 0-14
All bowls 0-1-0		
BUCKNELL		
Edward "Hook" Mylin	Orange 1-1-35	Miami (Fla.) 26-0
All bowls 1-0-0		
CAL ST. FULLERTON		
Gene Murphy	California 12-17-83	Northern Ill. 13-20
All bowls 0-1-0		
CAL ST. NORTHRIDGE		
Sam Winningham	Pasadena 12-2-67	West Tex. A&M 13-35
All bowls 0-1-0		
CARNEGIE MELLON		
Bill Kern	Sugar 1-2-39	TCU 7-15
All bowls 0-1-0		
CASE RESERVE		
Bill Edwards	Sun 1-1-41	Arizona St. 26-13
All bowls 1-0-0		
CATHOLIC		
Arthur "Dutch" Bergman	Orange 1-1-36	Mississippi 20-19
Arthur "Dutch" Bergman	Sun 1-1-40	Arizona St. 0-0
All bowls 1-0-1		
CENTENARY (LA.)		
Homer Norton	Dixie Classic 1-1-34	Arkansas 7-7
All bowls 0-0-1		
CENTRE		
Charley Moran	Fort Worth Classic 1-1-21	TCU 63-7
Charley Moran	San Diego East-West Christmas Classic 12-26-21	Arizona 38-0
Charley Moran	Dixie Classic 1-2-22	Texas A&M 14-22
All bowls 2-1-0		

School/Coach	Bowl/Date	Opponent/Score
CITADEL		
Eddie Teague	Tangerine 12-30-60	Tennessee Tech 27-0
All bowls 1-0-0		
COLUMBIA		
Lou Little	Rose 1-1-34	Stanford 7-0
All bowls 1-0-0		
DAVIDSON		
Homer Smith.........................	Tangerine 12-26-69	Toledo 33-56
All bowls 0-1-0		
DAYTON		
Joe Gavin..............................	Salad 1-1-52	Houston 21-26
All bowls 0-1-0		
DENVER		
Clyde "Cac" Hubbard.............	Sun 1-1-46	New Mexico 24-34
Clyde "Cac" Hubbard.............	Alamo 1-4-47	Hardin-Simmons 0-20
All bowls 0-2-0		
DRAKE		
Vee Green	Raisin 1-1-46	Fresno St. 13-12
Al Kawal	Salad 1-1-49	Arizona 14-13
Warren Gaer	Sun 1-1-58	Louisville 20-34
All bowls 2-1-0		
DUQUESNE		
John "Little Clipper" Smith........	Orange 1-1-37	Mississippi St. 13-12
All bowls 1-0-0		
FORDHAM		
Jim Crowley...........................	Cotton 1-1-41	Texas A&M 12-13
Jim Crowley...........................	Sugar 1-1-42	Missouri 2-0
All bowls 1-1-0		
GEORGE WASHINGTON		
Eugene "Bo" Sherman.............	Sun 1-1-57	UTEP 13-0
All bowls 1-0-0		
GEORGETOWN		
Jack Hagerty	Orange 1-1-41	Mississippi St. 7-14
Bob Margarita	Sun 1-2-50	UTEP 20-33
All bowls 0-2-0		
GONZAGA		
Charles "Gus" Dorais	San Diego East-West Christmas Classic 12-15-22	West Virginia 13-21
All bowls 0-1-0		
HARDIN-SIMMONS		
Frank Kimbrough	Sun 1-1-36	New Mexico St. 14-14
Frank Kimbrough	Sun 1-1-37	UTEP 34-6
Warren Woodson	Sun 1-1-43	Second Air Force 7-13
Warren Woodson	Alamo 1-4-47	Denver 20-6
Warren Woodson	Harbor 1-1-48	San Diego St. 53-0
Warren Woodson	Shrine 12-18-48	Ouachita Baptist 40-12
Warren Woodson	Camellia 12-30-48	Wichita St. 29-12
Sammy Baugh	Sun 12-31-58	Wyoming 6-14
All bowls 5-2-1		
HARVARD		
Robert Fisher..........................	Rose 1-1-20	Oregon 7-6
All bowls 1-0-0		
HOLY CROSS		
John "Ox" Da Grosa..............	Orange 1-1-46	Miami (Fla.) 6-13
All bowls 0-1-0		
LONG BEACH ST.		
Jim Stangeland	Pasadena 12-19-70	Louisville 24-24
All bowls 0-0-1		
MARQUETTE		
Frank Murray..........................	Cotton 1-1-37	TCU 6-16
All bowls 0-1-0		
McNEESE ST.		
Jack Doland	Independence 12-13-76	Tulsa 20-16
Ernie Duplechin......................	Independence 12-15-79	Syracuse 7-31
Ernie Duplechin......................	Independence 12-13-80	Southern Miss. 14-16
All bowls 1-2-0		
MONTANA ST.		
Clyde Carpenter	Harbor 1-1-47	New Mexico 13-13
All bowls 0-0-1		
OCCIDENTAL		
Roy Dennis............................	Raisin 1-1-49	Colorado St. 21-20
All bowls 1-0-0		
OUACHITA BAPTIST		
Wesley Bradshaw...................	Shrine 12-18-48	Hardin-Simmons 12-40
All bowls 0-1-0		

School/Coach	Bowl/Date	Opponent/Score
PACIFIC (CAL.)		
Larry Siemering......................	Raisin 1-1-48	Wichita St. 26-14
Ernie Jorge	Sun 1-1-52	Texas Tech 14-25
Ernie Jorge	Sun 1-1-53	Southern Miss. 26-7
All bowls 2-1-0		
PENNSYLVANIA		
Bob Folwell	Rose 1-1-17	Oregon 0-14
All bowls 0-1-0		
RANDOLPH FIELD		
Frank Tritico..........................	Cotton 1-1-44	Texas 7-7
All bowls 0-0-1		
RICHMOND		
Frank Jones	Tangerine 12-27-68	Ohio 49-42
Frank Jones	Tangerine 12-28-71	Toledo 3-28
All bowls 1-1-0		
ST. MARY'S (CAL.)		
Edward "Slip" Madigan	Cotton 1-2-39	Texas Tech 20-13
Jimmy Phelan	Sugar 1-1-46	Oklahoma St. 13-33
Jimmy Phelan	Oil 1-1-47	Georgia Tech 19-41
All bowls 1-2-0		
SANTA CLARA		
Lawrence "Buck" Shaw	Sugar 1-1-37	LSU 21-14
Lawrence "Buck" Shaw	Sugar 1-1-38	LSU 6-0
Len Casanova........................	Orange 1-2-50	Kentucky 21-13
All bowls 3-0-0		
SECOND AIR FORCE		
Red Reese	Sun 1-1-43	Hardin-Simmons 13-7
All bowls 1-0-0		
SOUTHWESTERN (TEX.)		
Randolph R. M. Medley	Sun 1-1-44	New Mexico 7-0
Randolph R. M. Medley	Sun 1-1-45	U. of Mexico 35-0
All bowls 2-0-0		
TAMPA		
Earle Bruce...........................	Tangerine 12-29-72	Kent St. 21-18
All bowls 1-0-0		
TENNESSEE TECH		
Wilburn Tucker	Tangerine 12-30-60	Citadel 0-27
All bowls 0-1-0		
U. OF MEXICO		
Bernard A. Hoban	Sun 1-1-45	Southwestern (Tex.) 0-35
All bowls 0-1-0		
VILLANOVA		
Maurice "Clipper" Smith..........	Bacardi, Cuba 1-1-37	Auburn 7-7
Jordan Olivar	Great Lakes 12-6-47	Kentucky 14-24
Jordan Olivar	Harbor 1-1-49	Nevada 27-7
Alex Bell..............................	Sun 12-30-61	Wichita St. 17-9
Alex Bell..............................	Liberty 12-15-62	Oregon St. 0-6
All bowls 2-2-1		
WASH. & JEFF.		
Earle "Greasy" Neale	Rose 1-2-22	California 0-0
All bowls 0-0-1		
WASH. & LEE		
George Barclay	Gator 1-1-51	Wyoming 7-20
All bowls 0-1-0		
WEST TEX. A&M		
Frank Kimbrough	Sun 1-1-51	Cincinnati 14-13
Joe Kerbel	Sun 12-31-62	Ohio 15-14
Joe Kerbel	Pasadena 12-2-67	Cal St. Northridge 35-13
All bowls 3-0-0		
WEST VA. WESLEYAN		
Bob Higgins	Dixie Classic 1-1-25	Southern Methodist 9-7
All bowls 1-0-0		
WICHITA ST.		
Ralph Graham	Raisin 1-1-48	Pacific (Cal.) 14-26
Jim Trimble	Camellia 12-30-48	Hardin-Simmons 12-49
Hank Foldberg	Sun 12-30-61	Villanova 9-17
All bowls 0-3-0		
WILLIAM & MARY		
Rube McCray	Dixie 1-1-48	Arkansas 19-21
Rube McCray	Delta 1-1-49	Oklahoma St. 20-0
Lou Holtz.............................	Tangerine 12-28-70	Toledo 12-40
All bowls 1-2-0		
XAVIER (OHIO)		
Ed Kluska	Salad 1-1-50	Arizona St. 33-21
All bowls 1-0-0		

Major Bowl-Game Attendance

Total Yearly Attendance

Year	No. Bowls	Total Attendance	Per/Game Average
1902	1	8,000	8,000
1916	1	7,000	7,000
1917	1	26,000	26,000
1920	1	30,000	30,000
1921	2	51,000	25,500
1922	3	57,000	19,000
1923	2	48,000	24,000
1924	1	40,000	40,000
1925	3	107,000	35,667
1926	1	50,000	50,000
1927	1	57,417	57,417
1928	1	65,000	65,000
1929	1	66,604	66,604
1930	1	72,000	72,000
1931	1	60,000	60,000
1932	1	75,562	75,562
1933	1	78,874	78,874
1934	2	47,000	23,500
1935	3	111,634	37,211
1936	4	137,042	34,261
1937	6	176,396	29,399
1938	5	202,972	40,594
1939	5	224,643	44,929
1940	5	226,478	45,296
1941	5	253,735	50,747
1942	5	215,786	43,157
1943	5	240,166	48,033
1944	5	195,203	39,041
1945	5	236,279	47,256
1946	8	308,071	38,509
1947	10	304,316	30,432
1948	12	404,772	33,731
1949	13	442,531	34,041
1950	8	384,505	48,063
1951	8	392,548	49,069
1952	7	388,588	55,513
1953	6	366,299	61,050
1954	6	359,285	59,881
1955	6	357,871	59,645
1956	6	379,723	63,287
1957	6	369,162	61,527
1958	6	385,427	64,238
1959	7	392,394	56,056
1960	8	481,814	60,227
1961	9	490,113	54,457
1962	11	509,654	46,332
1963	10	481,722	48,172
1964	8	460,720	57,590
1965	8	448,541	56,068
1966	8	482,106	60,263
1967	8	521,427	**65,178
1968	9	532,113	59,124
1969	10	585,621	58,562
1970	11	649,915	59,083
1971	11	623,072	56,643
1972	12	668,031	55,669
1973	11	668,461	60,769
1974	11	631,229	57,384
1975	11	597,079	54,280
1976	11	650,881	59,171
1977	12	660,429	55,036
1978	13	730,078	56,160
1979	15	726,064	48,404
1980	15	865,236	57,682
1981	15	856,730	57,115
1982	16	871,594	54,475
1983	16	919,193	57,450
1984	16	867,319	54,207
1985	18	977,374	54,299
1986	18	975,756	54,209
1987	18	958,933	53,274
1988	18	995,830	55,324
1989	17	937,323	55,137
1990	18	1,047,772	58,210
1991	19	1,048,306	55,174
1992	18	1,049,694	58,316
1993	18	973,570	54,087
1994	19	1,036,950	54,576
1995	19	1,064,640	56,034
1996	18	1,021,466	56,748
1997	18	985,292	54,738
1998	20	1,083,244	54,162
1999	22	1,224,414	55,655
2000	23	1,241,109	53,961
2001	25	1,291,557	51,662
2002	25	1,334,808	53,392
2003	28	*1,416,103	50,575

*Record. **Record for year with more than one game played.

Bowl-by-Bowl Attendance

(Current site and stadium capacity in parentheses. For participating teams, refer to pages 340-344.)

ROSE BOWL
(Rose Bowl, Pasadena, Calif.; Capacity: 96,576)

Date	Attendance
1-1-02	8,000
1-1-16	7,000
1-1-17	26,000
1-1-20	30,000
1-1-21	42,000
1-2-22	40,000
1-1-23	43,000
1-1-24	40,000
1-1-25	53,000
1-1-26	50,000
1-1-27	57,417
1-2-28	65,000
1-1-29	66,604
1-1-30	72,000
1-1-31	60,000
1-1-32	75,562
1-2-33	78,874
1-1-34	35,000
1-1-35	84,474
1-1-36	84,474
1-1-37	87,196
1-1-38	90,000
1-2-39	89,452
1-1-40	92,200
1-1-41	91,500
1-1-42#	56,000
1-1-43	93,000
1-1-44	68,000
1-1-45	91,000
1-1-46	93,000
1-1-47	90,000
1-1-48	93,000
1-1-49	93,000
1-2-50	100,963
1-1-51	98,939
1-1-52	96,825
1-1-53	101,500
1-1-54	101,000
1-1-55	89,191
1-2-56	100,809
1-1-57	97,126
1-1-58	98,202
1-1-59	98,297
1-1-60	100,809
1-2-61	97,314
1-1-62	98,214
1-1-63	98,698
1-1-64	96,957
1-1-65	100,423
1-1-66	100,087
1-2-67	100,807
1-1-68	102,946
1-1-69	102,063
1-1-70	103,878
1-1-71	103,839
1-1-72	103,154
1-1-73	*106,869
1-1-74	105,267
1-1-75	106,721
1-1-76	105,464
1-1-77	106,182
1-2-78	105,312
1-1-79	105,629
1-1-80	105,526
1-1-81	104,863
1-1-82	105,611
1-1-83	104,991
1-2-84	103,217
1-1-85	102,594
1-1-86	103,292
1-1-87	103,168
1-1-88	103,847
1-2-89	101,688
1-1-90	103,450
1-1-91	101,273
1-1-92	103,566
1-1-93	94,236
1-1-94	101,237
1-2-95	102,247
1-1-96	100,102
1-1-97	100,635
1-1-98	101,219
1-1-99	93,872
1-1-00	93,731
1-1-01	94,392
1-3-02	93,781
1-1-03	86,848

*Record attendance. #Game held at Duke, Durham, N.C., due to war-time West Coast restrictions.

ORANGE BOWL
(Pro Player Stadium, Miami, Fla.; Capacity: 72,230)

Date	Attendance
1-1-35	5,134
1-1-36	6,568
1-1-37	9,210
1-1-38	18,972
1-2-39	32,191
1-1-40	29,278
1-1-41	29,554
1-1-42	35,786
1-1-43	25,166
1-1-44	25,203
1-1-45	23,279
1-1-46	35,709
1-1-47	36,152
1-1-48	59,578
1-1-49	60,523
1-2-50	64,816
1-1-51	65,181
1-1-52	65,839
1-1-53	66,280

Date	Attendance
1-1-54	68,640
1-1-55	68,750
1-2-56	76,561
1-1-57	73,280
1-1-58	76,561
1-1-59	75,281
1-1-60	72,186
1-2-61	72,212
1-1-62	68,150
1-1-63	72,880
1-1-64	72,647
1-1-65	72,647
1-1-66	72,214
1-2-67	72,426
1-1-68	77,993
1-1-69	77,719
1-1-70	77,282
1-1-71	80,699
1-1-72	78,151
1-1-73	80,010
1-1-74	60,477
1-1-75	71,801
1-1-76	76,799
1-1-77	65,537
1-2-78	60,987
1-1-79	66,365
1-1-80	66,714
1-1-81	71,043
1-1-82	72,748
1-1-83	68,713
1-2-84	72,549
1-1-85	56,294
1-1-86	74,178
1-1-87	52,717
1-1-88	74,760
1-2-89	79,480
1-1-90	81,190
1-1-91	77,062
1-1-92	77,747
1-1-93	57,324
1-1-94	81,536
1-1-95	*81,753
1-1-96	72,198
12-31-96	63,297
1-2-98	74,002
1-2-99	67,919
1-1-00	70,461
1-3-01	76,835
1-2-02	73,640
1-2-03	75,971

*Record attendance.

SUGAR BOWL

(Louisiana Superdome, New Orleans, La.; Capacity: 76,791)

Date	Attendance
1-1-35	22,026
1-1-36	35,000
1-1-37	41,000
1-1-38	45,000
1-2-39	50,000
1-1-40	73,000
1-1-41	73,181
1-1-42	72,000
1-1-43	70,000
1-1-44	69,000
1-1-45	72,000
1-1-46	75,000
1-1-47	73,300
1-1-48	72,000
1-1-49	82,000
1-2-50	82,470
1-1-51	82,000
1-1-52	82,000
1-1-53	82,000
1-1-54	76,000
1-1-55	82,000
1-2-56	80,175
1-1-57	81,000
1-1-58	82,000
1-1-59	82,000
1-1-60	83,000
1-2-61	82,851
1-1-62	82,910
1-1-63	82,900
1-1-64	80,785
1-1-65	65,000
1-1-66	67,421
1-2-67	82,000
1-1-68	78,963
1-1-69	82,113
1-1-70	82,500
1-1-71	78,655
1-1-72	84,031
12-31-72	80,123
12-31-73	*85,161
12-31-74	67,890
12-31-75	75,212
1-1-77	76,117
1-2-78	76,811
1-1-79	76,824
1-1-80	77,486
1-1-81	77,895
1-1-82	77,224
1-1-83	78,124
1-2-84	77,893
1-1-85	75,608
1-1-86	77,432
1-1-87	76,234
1-1-88	75,495
1-2-89	61,934
1-1-90	77,452
1-1-91	75,132
1-1-92	76,447
1-1-93	76,789
1-1-94	75,437
1-2-95	76,224
12-31-95	70,283
1-2-97	78,344
1-1-98	67,289
1-1-99	76,503
1-4-00	79,280
1-2-01	64,407
1-1-02	77,688
1-1-03	74,269

*Record attendance.

COTTON BOWL

(Cotton Bowl, Dallas, Texas; Capacity: 68,252)

Date	Attendance
1-1-37	17,000
1-1-38	37,000
1-2-39	40,000
1-1-40	20,000
1-1-41	45,500
1-1-42	38,000
1-1-43	36,000
1-1-44	15,000
1-1-45	37,000
1-1-46	45,000
1-1-47	38,000
1-1-48	43,000
1-1-49	69,000
1-2-50	75,347
1-1-51	75,349
1-1-52	75,347
1-1-53	75,504
1-1-54	75,504
1-1-55	75,504
1-2-56	75,504
1-1-57	68,000
1-1-58	75,504
1-1-59	75,504
1-1-60	75,504
1-2-61	74,000
1-1-62	75,504
1-1-63	75,504
1-1-64	75,504
1-1-65	75,504
1-1-66	76,200
12-31-66	75,400
1-1-68	75,504
1-1-69	72,000
1-1-70	73,000
1-1-71	72,000
1-1-72	72,000
1-1-73	72,000
1-1-74	67,500
1-1-75	67,500
1-1-76	74,500
1-1-77	54,500
1-2-78	*76,601
1-1-79	32,500
1-1-80	72,032
1-1-81	74,281
1-1-82	73,243
1-1-83	60,359
1-2-84	67,891
1-1-85	56,522
1-1-86	73,137
1-1-87	74,188
1-1-88	73,006
1-2-89	74,304
1-1-90	74,358
1-1-91	73,521
1-1-92	73,728
1-1-93	71,615
1-1-94	69,855
1-2-95	70,218
1-1-96	58,214
1-1-97	71,928
1-1-98	59,215
1-1-99	72,611
1-1-00	72,723
1-1-01	63,465
1-1-02	72,955
1-1-03	70,817

*Record attendance.

SUN BOWL#

(Sun Bowl, El Paso, Texas; Capacity: 51,270)

Date	Attendance
1-1-36	11,000
1-1-37	10,000
1-1-38	12,000
1-2-39	13,000
1-1-40	12,000
1-1-41	14,000
1-1-42	14,000
1-1-43	16,000
1-1-44	18,000
1-1-45	13,000
1-1-46	15,000
1-1-47	10,000
1-1-48	18,000
1-1-49	13,000
1-2-50	15,000
1-1-51	16,000
1-1-52	17,000
1-1-53	11,000
1-1-54	9,500
1-1-55	14,000
1-2-56	14,500
1-1-57	13,500
1-1-58	12,000
12-31-58	13,000
12-31-59	14,000
12-31-60	16,000
12-30-61	15,000
12-31-62	16,000
12-31-63	26,500
12-26-64	28,500
12-31-65	27,450
12-24-66	24,381
12-30-67	34,685
12-28-68	32,307
12-20-69	29,723
12-19-70	30,512
12-18-71	33,503
12-30-72	31,312
12-29-73	30,127
12-28-74	30,131
12-26-75	33,240
1-2-77	33,252
12-31-77	31,318
12-23-78	33,122
12-22-79	33,412
12-27-80	34,723
12-26-81	33,816
12-25-82	31,359
12-24-83	41,412
12-22-84	50,126
12-28-85	*52,203
12-25-86	48,722

Date	Attendance
12-25-87	43,240
12-24-88	48,719
12-30-89	44,887
12-31-90	50,562
12-31-91	42,821
12-31-92	41,622
12-24-93	43,848
12-30-94	50,612
12-29-95	49,116
12-31-96	42,721
12-31-97	49,104
12-31-98	46,612
12-31-99	48,757
12-29-00	49,093
12-31-01	47,812
12-31-02	48,917

*Record attendance. #Named John Hancock Bowl, 1989-93.

GATOR BOWL

(Alltel Stadium, Jacksonville, Fla.; Capacity: 76,976)

Date	Attendance
1-2-46	7,362
1-1-47	10,134
1-1-48	16,666
1-1-49	32,939
1-2-50	18,409
1-1-51	19,834
1-1-52	34,577
1-1-53	30,015
1-1-54	28,641
12-31-54	28,426
12-31-55	32,174
12-29-56	36,256
12-28-57	41,160
12-27-58	41,312
1-2-60	45,104
12-31-60	50,112
12-30-61	50,202
12-29-62	50,026
12-28-63	50,018
1-2-65	50,408
12-31-65	60,127
12-31-66	60,312
12-30-67	68,019
12-28-68	68,011
12-27-69	72,248
1-2-71	71,136
12-31-71	71,208
12-30-72	71,114
12-29-73	62,109
12-30-74	63,811
12-29-75	64,012
12-27-76	67,827
12-30-77	72,289
12-29-78	72,011
12-28-79	70,407
12-29-80	72,297
12-28-81	71,009
12-30-82	80,913
12-30-83	81,293
12-28-84	82,138
12-30-85	79,417
12-27-86	80,104
12-31-87	82,119
1-1-89	76,236
12-30-89	*82,911
1-1-91	68,927
12-29-91	62,003
12-31-92	71,233
12-31-93	67,205
12-30-94†	62,200
1-1-96	45,202
1-1-97	52,103
1-1-98	54,116
1-1-99	70,791
1-1-00	43,416
1-1-01	68,741
1-1-02	72,202
1-1-03	73,491

*Record attendance. †Played at Gainesville, Fla.

LIBERTY BOWL†

(Liberty Bowl Memorial Stadium, Memphis, Tenn.; Capacity: 62,338)

Date	Attendance
12-19-59	36,211
12-17-60	16,624
12-16-61	15,712
12-15-62	17,048
12-31-63	8,309
12-19-64	6,059
12-18-65	38,607
12-10-66	39,101
12-16-67	35,045
12-14-68	46,206
12-13-69	50,042
12-12-70	44,640
12-20-71	51,410
12-18-72	50,021
12-17-73	50,011
12-16-74	51,284
12-22-75	52,129
12-20-76	52,736
12-19-77	49,456
12-23-78	53,064
12-22-79	50,021
12-27-80	53,667
12-30-81	43,216
12-29-82	54,123
12-29-83	38,229
12-27-84	50,108
12-27-85	40,186
12-29-86	51,327
12-29-87	53,249
12-28-88	39,210
12-28-89	60,128
12-27-90	13,144
12-29-91	*61,497
12-31-92	32,107
12-28-93	21,097
12-31-94	33,280
12-30-95	47,398
12-27-96	49,163
12-31-97	50,209
12-31-98	52,192
12-31-99	54,866
12-29-00	58,302
12-31-01	58,968
12-31-02	55,207

*Record attendance. †Played at Philadelphia, 1959-63; Atlantic City, 1964; Memphis, from 1965.

CAPITAL ONE BOWL#

(Florida Citrus Bowl, Orlando, Fla.; Capacity: 70,000)

Date	Attendance
12-30-60	13,000
12-22-62	7,500
12-27-68	16,114
12-26-69	16,311
12-28-70	15,164
12-28-71	16,750
12-29-72	20,062
12-22-73@	37,234
12-21-74	20,246
12-20-75	20,247
12-18-76	37,812
12-23-77	44,502
12-23-78	31,356
12-22-79	38,666
12-20-80	52,541
12-19-81	50,045
12-18-82	51,296
12-17-83	50,183
12-22-84	51,821
12-28-85	50,920
1-1-87	51,113
1-1-88	53,152
1-2-89	53,571
1-1-90	60,016
1-1-91	72,328
1-1-92	64,192
1-1-93	65,861
1-1-94	72,456
1-2-95	71,195
1-1-96	70,797

Date	Attendance
1-1-97	63,467
1-1-98	*72,940
1-1-99	63,584
1-1-00	62,011
1-1-01	66,928
1-1-02	59,693
1-1-03	66,334

*Record attendance. #Named Tangerine Bowl from 1947-82; named Florida Citrus Bowl from 1983-93; named CompUSA Florida Citrus Bowl from 1994-99; named OurHouse.com Florida Citrus Bowl (2000); named Capital One/Florida Citrus Bowl (2001-02) and named Capital One Bowl since 2003. #The first 14 games in the Tangerine Bowl, through 12-30-60, are not listed because no major teams were involved. The same is true for those games played in December 1961, 1963, 1964, 1965, 1966 and 1967. @ Played at Gainesville, Fla.

PEACH BOWL

(Georgia Dome, Atlanta, Ga.; Capacity: 71,228)

Date	Attendance
12-30-68	35,545
12-30-69	48,452
12-30-70	52,126
12-30-71	36,771
12-29-72	52,671
12-28-73	38,107
12-28-74	31,695
12-31-75	45,134
12-31-76	54,132
12-31-77	36,733
12-25-78	20,277
12-31-79	57,371
1-2-81	45,384
12-31-81	37,582
12-31-82	50,134
12-30-83	25,648
12-31-84	41,107
12-31-85	29,857
12-31-86	53,668
1-2-88	58,737
12-31-88	44,635
12-30-89	44,991
12-29-90	38,912
1-1-92	59,322
1-2-93	69,125
12-31-93	63,416
1-1-95	64,902
12-30-95	70,825
12-28-96	63,622
1-2-98	71,212
12-31-98	72,876
12-30-99	73,315
12-29-00	*73,614
12-31-01	71,827
12-31-02	68,330

*Record attendance.

FIESTA BOWL

(Sun Devil Stadium, Tempe, Ariz.; Capacity: 73,471)

Date	Attendance
12-27-71	51,089
12-23-72	51,318
12-21-73	50,878
12-28-74	50,878
12-26-75	51,396
12-25-76	48,174
12-25-77	57,727
12-25-78	55,227
12-25-79	55,347
12-26-80	66,738
1-1-82	71,053
1-1-83	70,533
1-2-84	66,484
1-1-85	60,310
1-1-86	72,454
1-2-87	73,098
1-1-88	72,112
1-2-89	74,911
1-1-90	73,953
1-1-91	69,098
1-1-92	71,133

Date	Attendance
1-1-93	70,224
1-1-94	72,260
1-2-95	73,968
1-2-96	79,864
1-1-97	65,106
12-31-97	69,367
1-4-99	*80,470
1-2-00	71,526
1-1-01	75,428
1-1-02	74,118
1-3-03	77,502

*Record attendance.

INDEPENDENCE BOWL

(Independence Stadium, Shreveport, La.; Capacity: 50,459)

Date	Attendance
12-13-76	15,542
12-17-77	18,500
12-16-78	18,200
12-15-79	27,234
12-13-80	45,000
12-12-81	47,300
12-11-82	49,503
12-10-83	41,274
12-15-84	41,000
12-21-85	42,800
12-20-86	46,369
12-19-87	41,683
12-23-88	20,242
12-16-89	30,333
12-15-90	48,325
12-29-91	46,932
12-31-92	31,337
12-31-93	33,819
12-28-94	27,242
12-29-95	48,835
12-31-96	41,366
12-28-97	*50,459
12-31-98	46,862
12-31-99	49,873
12-31-00	36.974
12-27-01	45,627
12-27-02	46,096

*Record attendance.

HOLIDAY BOWL

(Qualcomm Stadium, San Diego, Calif.; Capacity: 68,500)

Date	Attendance
12-28-78	52,500
12-21-79	52,200
12-19-80	50,214
12-18-81	52,419
12-17-82	52,533
12-23-83	51,480
12-21-84	61,243
12-22-85	42,324
12-30-86	59,473
12-30-87	61,892
12-30-88	60,718
12-29-89	61,113
12-29-90	61,441
12-30-91	60,646
12-30-92	44,457
12-30-93	52,108
12-30-94	59,453
12-29-95	51,051
12-30-96	54,749
12-29-97	50,761
12-30-98	*65,354
12-29-99	57,118
12-29-00	63,278
12-28-01	60,548
12-27-02	58,717

*Record attendance.

OUTBACK BOWL#

(Raymond James Stadium, Tampa, Fla.; Capacity: 65,657)

Date	Attendance
12-23-86	25,368
1-2-88	60,156
1-2-89	51,112

Date	Attendance
1-1-90	52,535
1-1-91	63,154
1-1-92	57,789
1-1-93	52,056
1-1-94	52,649
1-2-95	61,384
1-1-96	65,313
1-1-97	53,161
1-1-98	56,186
1-1-99	66,005
1-1-00	54,059
1-1-01	65,229
1-1-02	*66,249
1-1-03	65,101

*Record attendance. #Named Hall of Fame Bowl before 1996.

INSIGHT BOWL#

(Bank One Ballpark, Phoenix, Ariz.; Capacity: 43,080)

Date	Attendance
12-31-89	37,237
12-31-90	36,340
12-31-91	35,752
12-29-92	40,876
12-29-93	49,075
12-29-94	45,122
12-27-95	41,004
12-27-96	42,122
12-27-97	*49,385
12-26-98	36,147
12-31-99	35,762
12-28-00	41,813
12-29-01	40,028
12-26-02	40,533

*Record attendance. #Named Copper Bowl before 1997; named Insight.com Bowl from 1997-02.

TANGERINE BOWL#

(Florida Citrus Bowl, Orlando, Fla.; Capacity: 70,000)

Date	Attendance
12-28-90	*74,021
12-28-91	52,644
1-1-93	45,554
1-1-94	38,516
1-2-95	50,833
12-30-95	34,428
12-27-96	46,418
12-29-97	28,262
12-29-98	44,387
12-20-99	31,089
12-28-00	28,359
12-20-01	28,562
12-23-02	21,689

*Record attendance. #Named the Blockbuster Bowl from 1990-93; named Carquest Bowl from 1994-97; named Micron PC Bowl (1998); named MicronPC.com Bowl (1999-00); named Visit Florida Tangerine Bowl (2001) and named Mazda Tangerine Bowl since 2002.

LAS VEGAS BOWL

(Sam Boyd Stadium, Las Vegas, Nev.; Capacity: 40,000)

Date	Attendance
12-18-92	15,476
12-17-93	15,508
12-15-94	17,562
12-14-95	11,127
12-19-96	10,118
12-20-97	21,514
12-19-98	21,429
12-18-99	28,227
12-21-00	29,113
12-25-01	*30,894
12-25-02	30,324

*Record attendance.

ALAMO BOWL

(Alamodome, San Antonio, Texas; Capacity: 65,000)

Date	Attendance
12-31-93	45,716
12-31-94	44,106
12-28-95	64,597

Date	Attendance
12-29-96	55,677
12-30-97	55,552
12-29-98	60,780
12-28-99	*65,380
12-30-00	60,028
12-29-01	65,232
12-28-02	50,690

*Record attendance.

HUMANITARIAN BOWL

(Bronco Stadium, Boise, Idaho; Capacity: 30,000)

Date	Attendance
12-29-97	16,131
12-30-98	19,664
12-30-99	29,283
12-28-00	26,203
12-31-01	23,472
12-31-02	*30,446

*Record attendance.

MOTOR CITY BOWL

(Ford Field, Detroit, Mich.; Capacity: 65,000)

Date	Attendance
12-26-97	43,340
12-23-98	32,206
12-27-99	44,863
12-27-00	*52,911
12-29-01	44,164
12-26-02	51,872

*Record attendance. Played in Pontiac Silverdome, Pontiac, Mich, from 1997-01.

MUSIC CITY BOWL

(Adelphia Coliseum, Nashville, Tenn.; Capacity: 67,000)

Date	Attendance
12-29-98	#41,248
12-29-99	*59,221
12-28-00	47,119
12-28-01	46,125
12-30-02	39,183

*Record attendance. #Held at Vanderbilt Stadium.

GMAC BOWL#

(Ladd-Peebles Stadium, Mobile, Ala.; Capacity: 40,643)

Date	Attendance
12-22-99	34,200
12-20-00	40,300
12-19-01	40,139
12-18-02	*40,646

*Record attendance. #Named Mobile Alabama Bowl before 2001.

HOUSTON BOWL#

(Reliant Stadium, Houston, Texas; Capacity: 69,500)

Date	Attendance
12-27-00	33,899
12-28-01	*53,480
12-27-02	44,687

*Record attendance. #Named galleryfurniture.com Bowl before 2002. Played at Reliant Astrodome, Houston, Texas, from 2000-01.

SILICON VALLEY CLASSIC

(Spartan Stadium, San Jose, California: Capacity: 31,500)

Date	Attendance
12-31-00	26,542
12-31-01	*30,456
12-31-02	10,132

*Record attendance.

NEW ORLEANS BOWL

(New Orleans Superdome, New Orleans, La.: Capacity: 76,791)

Date	Attendance
12-18-01	*27,004
12-17-02	19,024

*Record attendance.

CONAGRA FOODS HAWAII BOWL
(Aloha Stadium, Honolulu, Hawaii; Capacity: 50,000)

Date	Attendance
12-25-02	31,535

CONTINENTAL TIRE BOWL
(Ericsson Stadium, Charlotte, North Carolina; Capacity: 73,367)

Date	Attendance
12-28-02	73,535

DIAMOND WALNUT SAN FRANCISCO BOWL
(Pacific Bell Park, San Francisco, California; Capacity: 37,000)

Date	Attendance
12-31-02	25,966

Former Major Bowl Games

(For participating teams, refer to pages 345-346.)

ALAMO
(San Antonio, Texas)

Date	Attendance
1-4-47	3,730

ALL-AMERICAN
(Birmingham, Ala.)

Date	Attendance
12-22-77	47,000
12-20-78	41,500
12-29-79	62,785
12-27-80	30,000
12-31-81	41,672
12-31-82	75,000
12-22-83	42,000
12-29-84	47,300
12-31-85	45,000
12-31-86	30,000
12-22-87	37,000
12-29-88	48,218
12-28-89	47,750
12-28-90	44,000

(Named Hall of Fame Classic until 1986 and then discontinued after 1990 game; played at Legion Field, capacity 75,952)

ALOHA CLASSIC#
(Honolulu, Hawaii)

Date	Attendance
12-25-82	30,055
12-26-83	37,212
12-29-84	41,777
12-28-85	35,183
12-27-86	26,743
12-25-87	24,839
12-25-88	35,132
12-25-89	*50,000
12-25-90	14,185
12-25-91	34,433
12-25-92	42,933
12-25-93	44,009
12-25-94	44,862
12-25-95	41,111
12-25-96	43,380
12-25-97	44,598
12-25-98	46,451
12-25-99	40,974
12-25-00	24,397

*Record attendance. #Named Aloha Bowl before 1998.

AVIATION
(Dayton, Ohio)

Date	Attendance
12-9-61	3,694

BACARDI
(Havana, Cuba)

Date	Attendance
1-1-37	12,000

BLUEBONNET
(Houston, Texas)

Date	Attendance
12-19-59	55,000
12-17-60	68,000
12-16-61	52,000
12-22-62	55,000
12-21-63	50,000
12-19-64	50,000
12-18-65	40,000
12-17-66	67,000
12-23-67	30,156
12-31-68	53,543
12-31-69	55,203
12-31-70	53,829
12-31-71	54,720
12-30-72	52,961
12-29-73	44,358
12-23-74	35,122
12-27-75	52,748
12-31-76	48,618
12-31-77	52,842
12-31-78	34,084
12-31-79	40,542
12-31-80	36,667
12-31-81	40,309
12-31-82	31,557
12-31-83	50,090
12-31-84	43,260
12-31-85	42,000
12-31-86	40,476
12-31-87	23,282

(Played at Rice Stadium 1959-67 and 1985, Astrodome 1968-84 and from 1986; Astrodome capacity 60,000)

BLUEGRASS
(Louisville, Ky.)

Date	Attendance
12-13-58	7,000

CALIFORNIA
(Fresno, Calif.)

Date	Attendance
12-19-81	15,565
12-18-82	30,000
12-17-83	20,464
12-15-84	21,741
12-14-85	32,554
12-13-86	10,743
12-12-87	24,000
12-10-88	31,272
12-9-89	31,610
12-8-90	25,431
12-14-91	34,825

CAMELLIA
(Lafayette, La.)

Date	Attendance
12-30-48	4,500

CHERRY
(Pontiac, Mich.)

Date	Attendance
12-22-84	70,332
12-21-85	51,858

DELTA
(Memphis, Tenn.)

Date	Attendance
1-1-48	28,120
1-1-49	15,069

DIXIE BOWL
(Birmingham, Ala.)

Date	Attendance
1-1-48	22,000
1-1-49	20,000

DIXIE CLASSIC
(Dallas, Texas)

Date	Attendance
1-2-22	12,000
1-1-25	7,000
1-1-34	12,000

FORT WORTH CLASSIC
(Fort Worth, Texas)

Date	Attendance
1-1-21	9,000

FREEDOM
(Anaheim, Calif.)

Date	Attendance
12-26-84	24,093
12-30-85	30,961
12-30-86	55,422
12-30-87	33,261
12-29-88	35,941
12-30-89	33,858
12-29-90	41,450
12-30-91	34,217
12-29-92	50,745
12-30-93	37,203
12-27-94	27,477

GARDEN STATE
(East Rutherford, N.J.)

Date	Attendance
12-16-78	33,402
12-15-79	55,493
12-14-80	41,417
12-13-81	38,782

GOTHAM
(New York, N.Y.)

Date	Attendance
12-9-61	15,123
12-15-62	6,166

GREAT LAKES
(Cleveland, Ohio)

Date	Attendance
12-6-47	14,908

HARBOR
(San Diego, Calif.)

Date	Attendance
1-1-47	7,000
1-1-48	12,000
1-1-49	20,000

LOS ANGELES CHRISTMAS FESTIVAL
(Los Angeles, Calif.)

Date	Attendance
12-25-24	47,000

MERCY
(Los Angeles, Calif.)

Date	Attendance
11-23-61	33,145

OIL
(Houston, Texas)

Date	Attendance
1-1-46	27,000
1-1-47	23,000

PASADENA
(Pasadena, Calif.)

Date	Attendance
12-2-67	28,802
12-6-69	41,276
12-19-70	20,472
12-18-71	15,244

PRESIDENTIAL CUP
(College Park, Md.)

Date	Attendance
12-9-50	12,245

RAISIN
(Fresno, Calif.)

Date	Attendance
1-1-46	10,000
1-1-47	13,000
1-1-48	13,000
1-1-49	10,000
12-31-49	9,000

SALAD
(Phoenix, Ariz.)

Date	Attendance
1-1-48	12,500
1-1-49	17,500

Date	Attendance
1-1-50	18,500
1-1-51	23,000
1-1-52	17,000

SAN DIEGO EAST-WEST CHRISTMAS CLASSIC
(San Diego, Calif.)

Date	Attendance
12-26-21	5,000
12-25-22	5,000

SEATTLE BOWL#
(Seattle, Wash.)

Date	Attendance
12-25-98	*46,451
12-25-99	40,974
12-24-00	24,187

Date	Attendance
12-27-01	30,144
12-30-02	38,241

*Record attendance. #Named Oahu Classic before 2001 and played at Honolulu, Hawaii. In 2001, played at Safeco Field, Seattle, Wash. In 2002, played at Seahawks Stadium, Seattle, Wash.

SHRINE
(Little Rock, Ark.)

Date	Attendance
12-18-48	5,000

Individual Records

Only official records after 1937 are included. Prior records are included if able to be substantiated. Each team's score is in parentheses after the team name. The year listed is the actual (calendar) year the game was played; the date is included if the bowl was played twice (i.e., January and December) during one calendar year. The list also includes discontinued bowls, marked with (D). Bowls are listed by the name of the bowl at the time it was played: the first Hall of Fame Bowl (1977-85) was called the All-American Bowl in 1986-90; the second Hall of Fame Bowl (1986-95) is now called the Outback Bowl and is played in Tampa, Fla.; the Sun Bowl was called the John Hancock Bowl in 1989-93, the John Hancock Sun Bowl in 1987-88, and reverted to the Sun Bowl in 1994; the Blockbuster Bowl changed its name to the Carquest Bowl in 1993, to the Micronpc.com Bowl in 1998, to the Tangerine Bowl in 2001 and to the Mazda Tangerine Bowl in 2002; and the Copper Bowl changed its name to the Insight.com Bowl in 1997 and to the Insight Bowl in 2002. The Capital One Bowl was the former and original Tangerine Bowl from 1947-82 and was known as the Florida Citrus Bowl from 1983-02. The current Mazda Tangerine Bowl is not to be confused with the Capital One Bowl, which is the former and original Tangerine Bowl. All former bowl names and sites are listed with each present bowl history. The NCAA Statistics Service thanks former staff member Steve Boda for his valuable assistance in compiling these records.

Total Offense

MOST TOTAL PLAYS
83—Kyle Orton, Purdue (27) vs. Washington St. (33) (Sun, 2001) (9 rush, 74 pass, 402 yards)

MOST TOTAL YARDS
594—Ty Detmer, Brigham Young (39) vs. Penn St. (50) (Holiday, 1989) (18 rushing yards, 576 passing yards, 67 plays)

HIGHEST AVERAGE PER PLAY
(Min. 10 Plays)
24.1—Dicky Maegle, Rice (28) vs. Alabama (6) (Cotton, 1954) (11 for 265)

MOST TOUCHDOWNS RESPONSIBLE FOR
(TDs Scored & Passed For)
6—Bobby Layne, Texas (40) vs. Missouri (27) (Cotton, 1946) (3 rush, 2 pass, 1 receiving); (D) Chuck Long, Iowa (55) vs. Texas (17) (Freedom, 1984) (6 pass)

Rushing

MOST RUSHING ATTEMPTS
46—(D) Ron Jackson, Tulsa (28) vs. San Diego St. (17) (Freedom, 1991) (211 yards)

MOST NET RUSHING YARDS
280—(D) James Gray, Texas Tech (49) vs. Duke (21) (All-American, 1989) (33 carries)

MOST NET RUSHING YARDS BY A QUARTERBACK
199—Tommie Frazier, Nebraska (62) vs. Florida (24) (Fiesta, 1996) (16 carries)

HIGHEST AVERAGE PER RUSH
(Min. 9 Carries)
24.1—Dicky Maegle, Rice (28) vs. Alabama (6) (Cotton, 1954) (11 for 265)

MOST NET RUSHING YARDS BY TWO RUSHERS, SAME TEAM, OVER 100 YARDS RUSHING EACH
373—Woody Green (202) & Brent McClanahan (171), Arizona St. (49) vs. Missouri (35) (Fiesta, 1972)

MOST RUSHING TOUCHDOWNS
5—Neil Snow, Michigan (49) vs. Stanford (0) (Rose, 1902) (touchdowns counted as five-point scores); Barry Sanders, Oklahoma St. (62) vs. Wyoming (14) (Holiday, 1988) (runs of 33, 2, 67, 1, 10 yards)

Passing

MOST PASS ATTEMPTS
74—Kyle Orton, Purdue (27) vs. Washington St. (33) (Sun, 2001) (completed 38)

MOST PASS COMPLETIONS
43—(D) Steve Clarkson, San Jose St. (25) vs. Toledo (27) (California, 1981) (attempted 62)

MOST CONSECUTIVE PASS COMPLETIONS
19—Mike Bobo, Georgia (33) vs. Wisconsin (6) (Outback, 1998)

MOST NET PASSING YARDS
576—Ty Detmer, Brigham Young (39) vs. Penn St. (50) (Holiday, 1989) (42 of 59 with 2 interceptions); Byron Leftwich, Marshall (64) vs. East Caro. (61) (2 ot) (GMAC, 2001) (41 of 70 with 2 interceptions)

MOST NET PASSING YARDS, ONE QUARTER
223—Browning Nagle, Louisville (34) vs. Alabama (7) (Fiesta, 1991) (1st quarter, 9 of 16)

MOST TOUCHDOWN PASSES THROWN
6—(D) Chuck Long, Iowa (55) vs. Texas (17) (Freedom, 1984) (29 of 39 with no interceptions) (touchdown passes of 6, 11, 33, 49, 4, 15 yards)

MOST PASSES HAD INTERCEPTED
6—Bruce Lee, Arizona (10) vs. Auburn (34) (Sun, 1968) (6 of 24)

HIGHEST COMPLETION PERCENTAGE
(Min. 10 Attempts)
.929—Mike Bobo, Georgia (33) vs. Wisconsin (6) (Outback, 1998) (26 of 28 with no interceptions)

MOST YARDS PER PASS ATTEMPT
(Min. 10 Attempts)
21.3—(D) Chris McCoy, Navy (42) vs. California (38) (Aloha, 1996) (13 for 277)

MOST YARDS PER PASS COMPLETION
(Min. 7 Completions)
30.8—(D) Chris McCoy, Navy (42) vs. California (38) (Aloha, 1996) (9 for 277)

Receiving

MOST PASS RECEPTIONS
20—Walker Gillette, Richmond (49) vs. Ohio (42) (Tangerine, 1968) (242 yards); (D) Norman Jordan, Vanderbilt (28) vs. Air Force (36) (Hall of Fame, 1982) (173 yards)

MOST PASS RECEIVING YARDS
299—Rodney Wright, Fresno St. (35) vs. Michigan St. (44) (Silicon Valley, 2001) (13 receptions)

HIGHEST AVERAGE PER CATCH
(Min. 3 Receptions)
52.3—Phil Harris, Texas (28) vs. Navy (6) (Cotton, 1964) (3 for 157); Jason Anderson, Wake Forest (38) vs. Oregon (17) (Seattle, 2002) (3 for 157)

MOST TOUCHDOWNS RECEIVING
4—(D) Bob McChesney, Hardin-Simmons (49) vs. Wichita St. (12) (Camellia, 1948) (8 catches); Fred Biletnikoff, Florida St. (36) vs. Oklahoma (19) (Gator, Jan. 2, 1965) (13 catches)

Scoring

MOST POINTS SCORED
30—Barry Sanders, Oklahoma St. (62) vs. Wyoming (14) (Holiday, 1988) (5 touchdowns); (D) Sheldon Canley, San Jose St. (48) vs. Central Mich. (24) (California, 1990) (5 touchdowns)

MOST POINTS RESPONSIBLE FOR (TDs SCORED & PASSED FOR, EXTRA POINTS, AND FGs)
40—Bobby Layne, Texas (40) vs. Missouri (27) (Cotton, 1946) (18 rushing, 12 passing, 6 receiving and 4 PATs)

MOST TOUCHDOWNS SCORED
5—Neil Snow, Michigan (49) vs. Stanford (0) (Rose, 1902) (5 rushing five-point TDs); Barry Sanders,

Oklahoma St. (62) vs. Wyoming (14) (Holiday, 1988) (5 rushing); (D) Sheldon Canley, San Jose St. (48) vs. Central Mich. (24) (California, 1990) (4 rushing, 1 receiving)

MOST TWO-POINT CONVERSIONS
2—Ernie Davis, Syracuse (23) vs. Texas (14) (Cotton, 1960) (2 receptions)

Kicking

MOST FIELD GOALS ATTEMPTED
6—Kyle Bryant, Texas A&M (22) vs. Michigan (20) (Alamo, 1995) (made 5)

MOST FIELD GOALS MADE
5—Jess Atkinson, Maryland (23) vs. Tennessee (30) (Florida Citrus, 1983) (18, 48, 31, 22, 26 yards); Arden Czyzewski, Florida (28) vs. Notre Dame (39) (Sugar, 1992) (26, 24, 36, 37, 24 yards); Tim Rogers, Mississippi St. (24) vs. North Carolina St. (28) (Peach, Jan. 1, 1995) (37, 21, 29, 36, 30 yards); Kyle Bryant, Texas A&M (22) vs. Michigan (20) (Alamo, 1995) (27, 49, 47, 31, 37 yards); Dan Nystrom, Minnesota (29) vs. Arkansas (14) (Music City, 2002) (24, 45, 21, 22, 29 yards)

MOST EXTRA-POINT KICK ATTEMPTS
9—(D) James Weaver, Centre (63) vs. TCU (7) (Fort Worth Classic, 1921) (9 made); Bobby Luna, Alabama (61) vs. Syracuse (6) (Orange, 1953) (7 made); Layne Talbot, Texas A&M (65) vs. Brigham Young (14) (Holiday, 1990) (9 made)

MOST EXTRA-POINT KICKS MADE
9—(D) James Weaver, Centre (63) vs. TCU (7) (Fort Worth Classic, 1921) (9 attempts); Layne Talbot, Texas A&M (65) vs. Brigham Young (14) (Holiday, 1990) (9 attempts)

MOST POINTS BY A KICKER
19—Kevin Miller, East Caro. (61) vs. Marshall (64) (2 ot) (GMAC, 2001) (4 FGs, 7 PATs)

Punting

MOST PUNTS
21—Everett Sweeney, Michigan (49) vs. Stanford (0) (Rose, 1902)

**HIGHEST AVERAGE PER PUNT
(Min. 5 Punts)**
53.8—Mat McBriar, Hawaii (28) vs. Tulane (36) (Hawaii, 2002) (5 for 269)

Punt Returns

MOST PUNT RETURNS
9—Paddy Driscoll, Great Lakes (17) vs. Mare Island (0) (Rose, 1919) (115 yards); Buzy Rosenberg, Georgia (7) vs. North Carolina (3) (Gator, Dec. 31, 1971) (54 yards)

MOST PUNT RETURN YARDS
136—Johnny Rodgers, Nebraska (38) vs. Alabama (6) (Orange, 1972) (6 returns)

**HIGHEST PUNT RETURN AVERAGE
(Min. 3 Returns)**
40.7—George Fleming, Washington (44) vs. Wisconsin (8) (Rose, 1960) (3 for 122)

MOST TOUCHDOWNS ON PUNT RETURNS
2—James Henry, Southern Miss. (38) vs. UTEP (18) (Independence, 1988) (65 and 45 yards)

Kickoff Returns

MOST KICKOFF RETURNS
8—Todd Howard, Michigan (17) vs. Tennessee (45) (Florida Citrus, 2002) (125 yards)

MOST KICKOFF RETURN YARDS
220—Mike Rigell, Brigham Young (27) vs. Tulane (41) (Liberty, 1998) (6 returns)

**HIGHEST KICKOFF RETURN AVERAGE
(Min. 2 Returns)**
60.5—(D) Bob Smith, Texas A&M (40) vs. Georgia (20) (Presidential Cup, 1950) (2 for 121)

MOST TOUCHDOWNS ON KICKOFF RETURNS
1—Many players tied

Interceptions

MOST INTERCEPTIONS MADE
4—(D) Manuel Aja, Arizona St. (21) vs. Xavier (Ohio) (33) (Salad, 1950); Jim Dooley, Miami (Fla.) (14) vs. Clemson (0) (Gator, 1952)

MOST INTERCEPTION RETURN YARDAGE
148—Elmer Layden, Notre Dame (27) vs. Stanford (10) (Rose, 1925) (2 interceptions)

All-Purpose Yards

(Includes All Runs From Scrimmage, Pass Receptions and All Returns)

**MOST ALL-PURPOSE PLAYS
(Must Have at Least One Reception or Return)**
47—(D) Ron Jackson, Tulsa (28) vs. San Diego St. (17) (Freedom, 1991) (46 rushes, 1 reception)

**MOST ALL-PURPOSE YARDS GAINED
(Must Have at Least One Reception or Return)**
359—Sherman Williams, Alabama (24) vs. Ohio St. (17) (Florida Citrus, 1995) (166 rushing, 155 receiving, 38 kickoff returns)

Defensive Statistics

MOST TOTAL TACKLES MADE (Includes Assists)
31—Lee Roy Jordan, Alabama (17) vs. Oklahoma (0) (Orange, 1963)

MOST SOLO TACKLES
18—Rod Smith, Notre Dame (39) vs. Florida (28) (Sugar, 1992)

MOST TACKLES FOR LOSSES
5—Jimmy Walker, Arkansas (10) vs. UCLA (10) (Fiesta, 1978); (D) Michael Jones, Colorado (17) vs. Brigham Young (20) (Freedom, 1988) (20 yards)

MOST QUARTERBACK SACKS
6—Shay Muirbrook, Brigham Young (19) vs. Kansas St. (15) (Cotton, 1997)

MOST FUMBLE RECOVERIES
2—Rod Kirby, Pittsburgh (7) vs. Arizona St. (28) (Fiesta, 1973); (D) Michael Stewart, Fresno St. (51) vs. Bowling Green (7) (California, 1985); Randall Brown, Ohio St. (17) vs. Alabama (24) (Florida Citrus, 1995)

MOST BLOCKED KICKS
2—Carlton Williams, Pittsburgh (7) vs. Arizona St. (28) (Fiesta, 1973) (2 PATs); Bracey Walker, North Carolina (21) vs. Mississippi St. (17) (Peach, Jan. 2, 1993) (2 punts)

MOST BLOCKED PUNTS
2—Bracey Walker, North Carolina (21) vs. Mississippi St. (17) (Peach, Jan. 2, 1993)

MOST PASSES BROKEN UP
5—Dyshod Carter, Kansas St. (34) vs. Purdue (37) (Alamo, 1998)

Team Records

Totals for each team in both-team records are in brackets after the team's score.

Total Offense

MOST TOTAL PLAYS
107—Purdue (27) vs. Washington St. (33) (Sun, 2001) (32 rush, 75 pass) (474 yards)

MOST TOTAL PLAYS, BOTH TEAMS
180—Marshall (64) [104] & East Caro. (61) [76] (2 ot) (GMAC, 2001) (1,141 yards)

MOST YARDS GAINED
718—Arizona St. (49) vs. Missouri (35) (Fiesta, 1972) (452 rushing, 266 passing)

MOST YARDS GAINED, BOTH TEAMS
1,143—(D) Southern California (47) [624] & Texas A&M (28) [519] (Bluebonnet, 1977) (148 plays)

HIGHEST AVERAGE GAINED PER PLAY
9.5—Louisville (34) vs. Alabama (7) (Fiesta, 1991) (60 for 571)

FEWEST PLAYS
35—Tennessee (0) vs. Texas (16) (Cotton, 1953) (29 rush, 6 pass)

FEWEST PLAYS, BOTH TEAMS
107—TCU (16) [54] & Marquette (6) [53] (Cotton, 1937)

FEWEST YARDS
Minus 21—U. of Mexico (0) vs. Southwestern (Tex.) (35) (Sun, 1945) (29 rushing, -50 passing)

FEWEST YARDS, BOTH TEAMS
260—Randolph Field (7) [150] & Texas (7) [110] (Cotton, 1944)

LOWEST AVERAGE GAINED PER PLAY
0.9—Tennessee (0) vs. Texas (16) (Cotton, 1953) (35 for 32)

Rushing

MOST RUSHING ATTEMPTS
87—Oklahoma (40) vs. Auburn (22) (Sugar, Jan. 1, 1972) (439 yards)

MOST RUSHING ATTEMPTS, BOTH TEAMS
122—Mississippi St. (26) [68] & North Carolina (24) [54] (Sun, 1974) (732 yards); (D) Southern California (47) [50] & Texas A&M (28) [72] (Bluebonnet, 1977) (864 yards)

MOST NET RUSHING YARDS
524—Nebraska (62) vs. Florida (24) (Fiesta, 1996) (68 attempts)

MOST NET RUSHING YARDS, BOTH TEAMS
864—(D) Southern California (47) [378] & Texas A&M (28) [486] (Bluebonnet, 1977) (122 attempts)

**HIGHEST RUSHING AVERAGE
(Min. 30 Attempts)**
9.3—Texas Tech (55) vs. Air Force (41) (Copper, 1995) (39 for 361)

FEWEST RUSHING ATTEMPTS
12—(D) Vanderbilt (28) vs. Air Force (36) (Hall of Fame, 1982) (35 yards)

FEWEST RUSHING ATTEMPTS, BOTH TEAMS
56—Mississippi (27) [33] & Oklahoma (25) [23] (Independence, 1999)

FEWEST RUSHING YARDS
Minus 61—(D) Kansas St. (7) vs. Boston College (12) (Aloha, 1994) (23 attempts)

FEWEST RUSHING YARDS, BOTH TEAMS
51—(D) Utah (16) [6] & Arizona (13) [45] (Freedom, 1994)

**LOWEST RUSHING AVERAGE
(Min. 20 Attempts)**
Minus 2.7—(D) Kansas St. (7) vs. Boston College (12) (Aloha, 1994) (23 for -61)

RUSHING DEFENSE, FEWEST YARDS ALLOWED
Minus 61—(D) Boston College (12) vs. Kansas St. (7) (Aloha, 1994) (23 attempts)

Passing

MOST PASS ATTEMPTS
75—Purdue (27) vs. Washington St. (33) (Sun, 2001) (38 completions, 4 interceptions, 419 yards)

MOST PASS ATTEMPTS, BOTH TEAMS
116—Purdue (27) [75] & Washington St. (33) [41] (Sun, 2001) (53 completions)

MOST PASS COMPLETIONS
43—(D) San Jose St. (25) vs. Toledo (27) (California, 1981) (63 attempts, 5 interceptions, 467 yards)

MOST PASS COMPLETIONS, BOTH TEAMS
64—Texas (47) [37] & Washington (43) [27] (Holiday, 2001) (109 attempted); Texas Tech (55) [39] & Clemson (15) [25] (Tangerine, 2002) (108 attempted)

MOST PASSING YARDS
576—Brigham Young (39) vs. Penn St. (50) (Holiday, 1989) (42 completions, 59 attempts, 2 interceptions); Marshall (64) vs. East Caro. (61) (2 ot) (GMAC, 2001) (41 completions, 70 attempts, 2 interceptions)

MOST PASSING YARDS, BOTH TEAMS
907—Michigan St. (44) [376] & Fresno St. (35) [531] (Silicon Valley, 2001) (90 attempted)

MOST PASSES HAD INTERCEPTED
8—Arizona (10) vs. Auburn (34) (Sun, 1968)

MOST PASSES HAD INTERCEPTED, BOTH TEAMS
12—Auburn (34) [4] & Arizona (10) [8] (Sun, 1968)

MOST PASSES ATTEMPTED WITHOUT AN INTERCEPTION
57—(D) Western Mich. (30) vs. Fresno St. (35) (California, 1988) (24 completions)

MOST PASSES ATTEMPTED BY BOTH TEAMS WITHOUT AN INTERCEPTION
93—Idaho (42) [41] & Southern Miss. (35) [52] (Humanitarian, 1998) (55 completions)

**HIGHEST COMPLETION PERCENTAGE
(Min. 10 Attempts)**
.929—Texas (40) vs. Missouri (27) (Cotton, 1946) (13 of 14, no interceptions, 234 yards)

**MOST YARDS PER ATTEMPT
(Min. 10 Attempts)**
21.7—Southern California (47) vs. Pittsburgh (14) (Rose, 1930) (13 for 282)

**MOST YARDS PER COMPLETION
(Min. 8 Completions)**
35.2—Southern California (47) vs. Pittsburgh (14) (Rose, 1930) (8 for 282)

FEWEST PASS ATTEMPTS
2—West Virginia (14) vs. South Carolina (3) (Peach, 1969) (1 completion); (D) Army (10) vs. Michigan St. (6) (Cherry, 1984) (1 completion); Air Force (38) vs. Mississippi St. (15) (Liberty, 1991) (1 completion)

FEWEST PASS ATTEMPTS, BOTH TEAMS
9—Fordham (2) [4] & Missouri (0) [5] (Sugar, 1942)

FEWEST PASS COMPLETIONS
0—13 teams tied (see Team Record Lists)

FEWEST PASS COMPLETIONS, BOTH TEAMS
3—Arizona St. (0) [0] & Catholic (0) [3] (Sun, 1940)

FEWEST PASSING YARDS
Minus 50—U. of Mexico (0) vs. Southwestern (Tex.) (35) (Sun, 1945) (2 completions, 9 attempts, 3 interceptions)

FEWEST PASSING YARDS, BOTH TEAMS
16—Arkansas (0) [0] & LSU (0) [16] (Cotton, 1947)

LOWEST COMPLETION PERCENTAGE
.000—13 teams tied (see Team Record Lists)

FEWEST YARDS PER PASS ATTEMPT
Minus 5.6—U. of Mexico (0) vs. Southwestern (Tex.) (35) (Sun, 1945) (9 for -50)

**FEWEST YARDS PER PASS COMPLETION
(Min. 1 Completion)**
Minus 25.0—U. of Mexico (0) vs. Southwestern (Tex.) (35) (Sun, 1945) (2 for -50)

Scoring

MOST TOUCHDOWNS
10—Nebraska (66) vs. Northwestern (17) (Alamo, 2000) (6 rush, 4 pass)

MOST TOUCHDOWNS, BOTH TEAMS
16—Marshall (64) [9] & East Caro. (61) [7] (2 ot) (GMAC, 2001)

MOST TOUCHDOWNS RUSHING
8—(D) Centre (63) vs. TCU (7) (Fort Worth Classic, 1921)

MOST TOUCHDOWNS RUSHING, BOTH TEAMS
12—Texas Tech (55) [6] & Air Force (41) [6] (Copper, 1995)

MOST TOUCHDOWNS PASSING
6—(D) Iowa (55) vs. Texas (17) (Freedom, 1984)

MOST TOUCHDOWNS PASSING, BOTH TEAMS
8—Richmond (49) [4] & Ohio (42) [4] (Tangerine, 1968); (D) Iowa (55) [6] & Texas (17) [2] (Freedom, 1984); LSU (47) [3] & Illinois (34) [5] (Sugar, 2002)

MOST FIELD GOALS MADE
5—Maryland (23) vs. Tennessee (30) (Florida Citrus, 1983) (18, 48, 31, 22, 26 yards); Florida (28) vs. Notre Dame (39) (Sugar, 1992) (26, 24, 36, 37, 24 yards); Mississippi St. (24) vs. North Carolina St. (28) (Peach, Jan. 1, 1995) (37, 21, 29, 36, 30 yards); Texas A&M (22) vs. Michigan (20) (Alamo, 1995) (27, 49, 47, 31, 37 yards)

MOST FIELD GOALS MADE, BOTH TEAMS
7—Texas A&M (22) [5] & Michigan (20) [2] (Alamo, 1995); North Carolina St. (28) [2] & Mississippi St. (24) [5] (Peach, Jan. 1, 1995); Iowa (19) [4] & Texas Tech (16) [3] (Alamo, 2001)

MOST POINTS, WINNING TEAM
66—Nebraska vs. Northwestern (17) (Alamo, 2000)

MOST POINTS, LOSING TEAM
61—East Caro. vs. Marshall (64) (2 ot) (GMAC, 2001)

MOST POINTS, BOTH TEAMS
125—Marshall (64) & East Carolina (61) (2 ot) (GMAC, 2001)

LARGEST MARGIN OF VICTORY
55—Alabama (61) vs. Syracuse (6) (Orange, 1953)

FEWEST POINTS, WINNING TEAM
2—Fordham vs. Missouri (0) (Sugar, 1942)

FEWEST POINTS, LOSING TEAM
0—By many teams

FEWEST POINTS, BOTH TEAMS
0—California (0) & Wash. & Jeff. (0) (Rose, 1922); Arizona St. (0) & Catholic (0) (Sun, 1940); Arkansas (0) & LSU (0) (Cotton, 1947); Air Force (0) & TCU (0) (Cotton, 1959)

MOST POINTS SCORED IN FIRST HALF
45—Colorado (62) vs. Boston College (28) (Insight.com, 1999)

MOST POINTS IN SECOND HALF
45—Oklahoma St. (62) vs. Wyoming (14) (Holiday, 1988)

**MOST POINTS SCORED IN SECOND HALF
(Including Overtime Periods)**
56—Marshall (64) vs. East Caro. (61) (2 ot) (GMAC, 2001) (43 in regulation plus 13 in overtime)

MOST POINTS SCORED IN FIRST HALF, BOTH TEAMS
63—(D) Navy (42) [28] & California (38) [35] (Aloha, 1996)

MOST POINTS SCORED IN SECOND HALF, BOTH TEAMS
64—Penn St. (50) [38] & Brigham Young (39) [26] (Holiday, 1989); (D) Kansas (51) [34] & UCLA (30) [30] (Aloha, 1995)

**MOST POINTS IN SECOND HALF, BOTH TEAMS
(Including Overtime Periods)**
79—Marshall (64) [56] vs. East Caro. (61) [23] (2 ot) (GMAC, 2001) (56 in regulation plus 23 in overtime)

MOST POINTS SCORED EACH QUARTER
1st: 28—Southern California (55) vs. Texas Tech (14) (Cotton, 1995)
2nd: 29—Nebraska (62) vs. Florida (24) (Fiesta, 1996)
3rd: 31—(D) Iowa (55) vs. Texas (17) (Freedom, 1984)
4th: 30—Oklahoma (40) vs. Houston (14) (Sun, 1981)

MOST POINTS SCORED EACH QUARTER, BOTH TEAMS
1st: 28—Louisiana Tech (24) [21] & Louisville (14) [7] (Independence, 1977); Indiana (38) [14] & Brigham Young (37) [14] (Holiday, 1979); Texas Tech (55) [21] & Air Force (41) [7] (Copper, 1995); Southern California (55) [28] & Texas Tech (14) [0] (Cotton, 1995)
2nd: 45—Nebraska (66) [31] & Northwestern (17) [14] (Alamo, 2000)
3rd: 35—Oklahoma St. (62) [28] & Wyoming (14) [7] (Holiday, 1988); Kansas St. (54) [21] & Colorado St. (21) [14] (Holiday, 1995)
4th: 37—Oklahoma (40) [30] & Houston (14) [7] (Sun, 1981); (D) Kansas (51) [14] & UCLA (30) [23] (Aloha, 1995)

First Downs

MOST FIRST DOWNS
36—Oklahoma (48) vs. Virginia (14) (Gator, Dec. 29, 1991) (16 rush, 18 pass, 2 penalty); Marshall (64) vs. East Caro. (61) (2 ot) (GMAC, 2001) (9 rush, 25 pass, 2 penalty)

MOST FIRST DOWNS, BOTH TEAMS
61—Penn St. (50) [26] & Brigham Young (39) [35] (Holiday, 1989)

MOST FIRST DOWNS RUSHING
26—Oklahoma (40) vs. Auburn (22) (Sugar, Jan. 1, 1972)

MOST FIRST DOWNS RUSHING, BOTH TEAMS
36—Colorado (47) [24] & Alabama (33) [12] (Liberty, 1969); Miami (Fla.) (46) [16] & Texas (3) [20] (Cotton, 1991)

MOST FIRST DOWNS PASSING
27—Brigham Young (39) vs. Penn St. (50) (Holiday, 1989)

MOST FIRST DOWNS PASSING, BOTH TEAMS
38—Penn St. (50) [11] & Brigham Young (39) [27] (Holiday, 1989)

MOST FIRST DOWNS BY PENALTY
6—Texas (3) vs. Miami (Fla.) (46) (Cotton, 1991); Florida (52) vs. Florida St. (20) (Sugar, 1997)

MOST FIRST DOWNS BY PENALTY, BOTH TEAMS
8—Miami (Fla.) (46) [2] & Texas (3) [6] (Cotton, 1991); Texas A&M (22) [4] & Michigan (20) [4] (Alamo, 1995); Florida (52) [6] & Florida St. (20) [2] (Sugar, 1997)

FEWEST FIRST DOWNS
1—Arkansas (0) vs. LSU (0) (Cotton, 1947) (1 rush); Alabama (29) vs. Texas A&M (21) (Cotton, 1942) (1 pass)

FEWEST FIRST DOWNS, BOTH TEAMS
10—Randolph Field (7) [7] & Texas (7) [3] (Cotton, 1944)

FEWEST FIRST DOWNS RUSHING
0—Alabama (29) vs. Texas A&M (21) (Cotton, 1942); Navy (6) vs. Texas (28) (Cotton, 1964); Florida (18) vs. Missouri (20) (Sugar, 1966); Southern California (19) vs. TCU (28) (Sun, 1998)

FEWEST FIRST DOWNS RUSHING, BOTH TEAMS
3—Alabama (29) [0] & Texas A&M (21) [3] (Cotton, 1942)

FEWEST FIRST DOWNS PASSING
0—By 13 teams (see Team Record Lists)

FEWEST FIRST DOWNS PASSING, BOTH TEAMS
1—Alabama (10) [0] & Arkansas (3) [1] (Sugar, 1962)

Punting

MOST PUNTS
17—Duke (3) vs. Southern California (7) (Rose, 1939)

MOST PUNTS, BOTH TEAMS
28—Santa Clara (6) [14] & LSU (0) [14] (Sugar, 1938); Rice (8) [13] & Tennessee (0) [15] (Orange, 1947)

HIGHEST PUNTING AVERAGE (Min. 5 Punts)
53.9—Southern California (7) vs. Wisconsin (0) (Rose, 1953) (8 for 431)

FEWEST PUNTS
0—Oklahoma (41) vs. Wyoming (7) (Fiesta, 1976); Oklahoma St. (62) vs. Wyoming (14) (Holiday, 1988); Illinois (63) vs. Virginia (21) (Micronpc.com, 1999)

LOWEST PUNTING AVERAGE (Min. 3 Punts)
17.0—Nevada (34) vs. Bowling Green (35) (Las Vegas, 1992) (4 for 68); Kentucky (14) vs. Penn St. (26) (Outback, 1999) (3 for 51)

MOST PUNTS BLOCKED BY ONE TEAM
2—North Carolina St. (14) vs. Georgia (7) (Liberty, 1967); North Carolina (21) vs. Mississippi St. (17) (Peach, 1992)

Punt Returns

MOST PUNT RETURNS
9—Georgia (7) vs. North Carolina (3) (Gator, Dec. 31, 1971) (6.8 average)

MOST PUNT RETURN YARDS
136—Nebraska (38) vs. Alabama (6) (Orange, 1972) (6 returns)

HIGHEST PUNT RETURN AVERAGE (Min. 3 Returns)
33.0—Kent St. (18) vs. Tampa (21) (Tangerine, 1972) (3 for 99)

Kickoff Returns

MOST KICKOFF RETURNS
10—Wyoming (14) vs. Oklahoma St. (62) (Holiday, 1988) (20.5 average); Florida (24) vs. Nebraska (62) (Fiesta, 1996) (26.8 average)

MOST KICKOFF RETURN YARDS
268—Florida (24) vs. Nebraska (62) (Fiesta, 1996) (10 returns)

HIGHEST KICKOFF RETURN AVERAGE (Min. 3 Returns)
42.5—Tennessee (27) vs. Maryland (28) (Sun, 1984) (4 for 170)

Fumbles

MOST FUMBLES
11—Mississippi (7) vs. Alabama (12) (Sugar, 1964) (lost 6)

MOST FUMBLES, BOTH TEAMS
17—Alabama (12) [6] & Mississippi (7) [11] (Sugar, 1964) (lost 9)

MOST FUMBLES LOST
6—By five teams (see Team Record Lists)

MOST FUMBLES LOST, BOTH TEAMS
9—Alabama (12) [3] & Mississippi (7) [6] (Sugar, 1964) (17 fumbles)

Penalties

MOST PENALTIES
21—Mississippi St. (17) vs. Clemson (7) (Peach, 1999) (188 yards)

MOST PENALTIES, BOTH TEAMS
29—McNeese St. (20) [13] & Tulsa (16) [16] (Independence, 1976) (205 yards); Florida (52) [15] & Florida St. (20) [14] (Sugar, 1997) (217 yards); Mississippi St. (17) [21] & Clemson (7) [8] (Peach, 1999) (270 yards)

MOST YARDS PENALIZED
202—Miami (Fla.) (46) vs. Texas (3) (Cotton, 1991) (16 penalties)

MOST YARDS PENALIZED, BOTH TEAMS
270—Miami (Fla.) (46) [202] & Texas (3) [68] (Cotton, 1991); Mississippi St. (17) [188] & Clemson (7) [82] (Peach, 1999)

FEWEST PENALTIES
0—By eight teams (see Team Record Lists)

FEWEST PENALTIES, BOTH TEAMS
3—In five games (see Team Record Lists)

FEWEST YARDS PENALIZED
0—By eight teams (see Team Record Lists)

FEWEST YARDS PENALIZED, BOTH TEAMS
10—Duquesne (13) [5] & Mississippi St. (12) [5] (Orange, 1937)

Individual Record Lists

Only official records after 1937 are included. Prior records are included if able to be substantiated. Each team's score is in parentheses after the team name. The year listed is the actual (calendar) year the game was played; the date is included if the bowl was played twice (i.e., January and December) during one calendar year. The list also includes discontinued bowls, marked with (D). Bowls are listed by the name of the bowl at the time it was played: the first Hall of Fame Bowl (1977-85) was called the All-American Bowl in 1986-90; the second Hall of Fame Bowl (1986-95) is now called the Outback Bowl and is played in Tampa, Fla.; the Sun Bowl was called the John Hancock Bowl in 1989-93, the John Hancock Sun Bowl in 1987-88, and reverted to the Sun Bowl in 1994; the Blockbuster Bowl changed its name to the Carquest Bowl in 1993, to the Micronpc.com Bowl in 1998, to the Tangerine Bowl in 2001 and to the Mazda Tangerine Bowl in 2002; and the Copper Bowl changed its name to the Insight.com Bowl in 1997 and to the Insight Bowl in 2002. The Capital One Bowl was the former and original Tangerine Bowl from 1947-82 and was known as the Florida Citrus Bowl from 1983-02. The current Mazda Tangerine Bowl is not to be confused with the Capital One Bowl, which is the former and original Tangerine Bowl.

Total Offense

MOST PLAYS
83—Kyle Orton, Purdue (27) vs. Washington St. (33) (Sun, 2001)
82—Byron Leftwich, Marshall (64) vs. East Caro. (61) (2 ot) (GMAC, 2001)
74—(D) Tony Kimbrough, Western Mich. (30) vs. Fresno St. (35) (California, 1988)
69—Drew Brees, Purdue (25) vs. Georgia (28) (ot) (Outback, 2000)
68—Hines Ward, Georgia (27) vs. Virginia (34) (Peach, Dec. 30, 1995)
67—Ty Detmer, Brigham Young (39) vs. Penn St. (50) (Holiday, 1989)
65—Shane Matthews, Florida (28) vs. Notre Dame (39) (Sugar, 1992)
65—Tony Eason, Illinois (15) vs. Alabama (21) (Liberty, 1982)
65—Buster O'Brien, Richmond (49) vs. Ohio (42) (Tangerine, 1968)
63—Luke McCown, Louisiana Tech (24) vs. Clemson (49) (Humanitarian, 2001)
63—Drew Brees, Purdue (37) vs. Kansas St. (34) (Alamo, 1998)
63—(D) Steve Clarkson, San Jose St. (25) vs. Toledo (27) (California, 1981)
62—Andrew Walter, Arizona St. (27) vs. Kansas St. (34) (Holiday, 2002)
62—Mark Young, Mississippi (20) vs. Texas Tech (17) (Independence, 1986)
62—Jack Trudeau, Illinois (29) vs. Army (31) (Peach, 1985)
62—Dennis Sproul, Arizona St. (30) vs. Penn St. (42) (Fiesta, 1977)
61—David Carr, Fresno St. (35) vs. Michigan St. (44) (Silicon Valley, 2001)
61—Jeff Blake, East Caro. (37) vs. North Carolina St. (34) (Peach, 1992)
61—Shawn Halloran, Boston College (27) vs. Georgia (24) (Hall of Fame, 1986)
61—Kim Hammond, Florida St. (17) vs. Penn St. (17) (Gator, 1967)
60—Josh Heupel, Oklahoma (25) vs. Mississippi (27) (Independence, 1999)
59—Lee Roberts, Southern Miss. (35) vs. Idaho (42) (Humanitarian, 1998)
59—Vinny Testaverde, Miami (Fla.) (10) vs. Penn St. (14) (Fiesta, 1987)
59—Jim McMahon, Brigham Young (46) vs. Southern Methodist (45) (Holiday, 1980)
58—Kliff Kingsbury, Texas Tech (16) vs. Iowa (19) (Alamo, 2001)
58—Tim Couch, Kentucky (14) vs. Penn St. (26) (Outback, 1999)
58—Terrence Jones, Tulane (12) vs. Washington (24) (Independence, 1987)
58—(D) Jerry Rhome, Tulsa (14) vs. Mississippi (7) (Bluebonnet, 1964)

MOST TOTAL YARDS
594—Ty Detmer, Brigham Young (39) vs. Penn St. (50) (Holiday, 1989) (576 pass)
566—Byron Leftwich, Marshall (64) vs. East Caro. (61) (2 ot) (GMAC, 2001) (576 pass)
508—David Carr, Fresno St. (35) vs. Michigan St. (44) (Silicon Valley, 2001) (531 pass)
486—Buster O'Brien, Richmond (49) vs. Ohio (42) (Tangerine, 1968) (447 pass)
481—(D) Chuck Long, Iowa (55) vs. Texas (17) (Freedom, 1984) (461 pass)
476—Major Applewhite, Texas (47) vs. Washington (43) (Holiday, 2001) (473 pass)
474—Trent Dilfer, Fresno St. (30) vs. Colorado (41) (Aloha, 1993) (523 pass)
469—Hines Ward, Georgia (27) vs. Virginia (34) (Peach, Dec. 30, 1995) (413 pass)
464—(D) Steve Clarkson, San Jose St. (25) vs. Toledo (27) (California, 1981) (467 pass)
457—(D) Akili Smith, Oregon (43) vs. Colorado (51) (Aloha, 1998) (456 pass)
454—John Walsh, Brigham Young (31) vs. Oklahoma (6) (Copper, 1994) (454 pass)
446—Jim McMahon, Brigham Young (46) vs. Southern Methodist (45) (Holiday, 1980) (446 pass)
446—(D) Whit Taylor, Vanderbilt (28) vs. Air Force (36) (Hall of Fame, 1982) (452 pass)
445—Chad Pennington, Marshall (48) vs. Louisville (29) (Motor City, 1998) (411 pass)

431—(D) Tony Kimbrough, Western Mich. (30) vs. Fresno St. (35) (California, 1988) (366 pass)
431—Browning Nagle, Louisville (34) vs. Alabama (7) (Fiesta, 1991) (451 pass)
427—Rohan Davey, LSU (47) vs. Illinois (34) (Sugar, 2002) (444 pass)
424—Marc Bulger, West Virginia (31) vs. Missouri (34) (Insight.com, 1998) (429 pass)
420—(D) Ralph Martini, San Jose St. (48) vs. Central Mich. (24) (California, 1990) (404 pass)
414—Peter Tom Willis, Florida St. (41) vs. Nebraska (17) (Fiesta, 1990) (422 pass)
413—Tony Eason, Illinois (15) vs. Alabama (21) (Liberty, 1982) (423 pass)
412—David Smith, Alabama (29) vs. Army (28) (John Hancock Sun, 1988) (412 pass)
410—Chuck Hartlieb, Iowa (23) vs. North Carolina St. (28) (Peach, Dec. 31, 1988) (428 pass)
408—Marc Wilson, Brigham Young (37) vs. Indiana (38) (Holiday, 1979) (380 pass)
407—Jack Trudeau, Illinois (29) vs. Army (31) (Peach, 1985) (401 pass)

HIGHEST AVERAGE PER PLAY
(Minimum 10 Plays)
24.1—Dicky Maegle, Rice (28) vs. Alabama (6) (Cotton, 1954) (11 for 265)
16.5—Chad Pennington, Marshall (48) vs. Louisville (29) (Motor City, 1998) (27 for 445)
14.1—Marcus Dupree, Oklahoma (21) vs. Arizona St. (32) (Fiesta, 1983) (17 for 239)
14.0—Bucky Richardson, Texas A&M (65) vs. Brigham Young (14) (Holiday, 1990) (23 for 322)
13.2—Kordell Stewart, Colorado (41) vs. Notre Dame (24) (Fiesta, 1995) (28 for 369)
12.2—Ger Schwedes, Syracuse (23) vs. Texas (14) (Cotton, 1960) (10 for 122)
12.0—Tony Rice, Notre Dame (34) vs. West Virginia (21) (Fiesta, 1989) (24 for 288)
11.3—Rob Johnson, Southern California (55) vs. Texas Tech (14) (Cotton, 1995) (24 for 271)
11.2—(D) Dwight Ford, Southern California (47) vs. Texas A&M (28) (Bluebonnet, 1977) (14 for 157)
11.1—Browning Nagle, Louisville (34) vs. Alabama (7) (Fiesta, 1991) (39 for 431)
10.8—Danny White, Arizona St. (49) vs. Missouri (35) (Fiesta, 1972) (27 for 291)
10.8—(D) Ralph Martini, San Jose St. (48) vs. Central Mich. (24) (California, 1990) (39 for 420)
10.8—Byron Hanspard, Texas Tech (55) vs. Air Force (41) (Copper, 1995) (24 for 260)
10.5—(D) Chuck Long, Iowa (55) vs. Texas (17) (Freedom, 1984) (46 for 481)
10.4—Frank Sinkwich, Georgia (40) vs. TCU (26) (Orange, 1942) (35 for 365)
10.3—Chuck Curtis, TCU (28) vs. Syracuse (27) (Cotton, 1957) (18 for 185)

MOST TOUCHDOWNS RESPONSIBLE FOR (TDS SCORED & PASSED FOR)
6—(D) Chuck Long, Iowa (55) vs. Texas (17) (Freedom, 1984) (6 pass)
6—Bobby Layne, Texas (40) vs. Missouri (27) (Cotton, 1946) (3 rush, 2 pass, 1 catch)
5—Byron Leftwich, Marshall (64) vs. East Caro. (61) (2 ot) (GMAC, 2001) (4 pass, 1 rush)
5—Casey Clausen, Tennessee (45) vs. Michigan (17) (Florida Citrus, 2002) (3 pass, 2 rush)
5—Michael Bishop, Kansas St. (35) vs. Syracuse (18) (Fiesta, 1997) (4 pass, 1 rush)
5—Jeff Blake, East Caro. (37) vs. North Carolina St. (34) (Peach, 1992) (4 pass, 1 rush)
5—Peter Tom Willis, Florida St. (41) vs. Nebraska (17) (Fiesta, 1990) (5 pass)
5—(D) Sheldon Canley, San Jose St. (48) vs. Central Mich. (24) (California, 1990) (4 rush, 1 pass)
5—Johnny Rodgers, Nebraska (40) vs. Notre Dame (6) (Orange, 1973) (3 rush, 1 pass, 1 catch)
5—Buster O'Brien, Richmond (49) vs. Ohio (42) (Tangerine, 1968) (4 pass, 1 rush)
5—Steve Tensi, Florida St. (36) vs. Oklahoma (19) (Gator, Jan. 2, 1965) (5 pass)
5—Neil Snow, Michigan (49) vs. Stanford (0) (Rose, 1902) (5 rush)

Rushing

MOST RUSHING ATTEMPTS
46—(D) Ron Jackson, Tulsa (28) vs. San Diego St. (17) (Freedom, 1991) (211 yards)
43—Fred Taylor, Florida (21) vs. Penn St. (6) (Florida Citrus, 1998) (234 yards)
42—Tellis Redmon, Minnesota (30) vs. North Carolina St. (38) (Micronpc.com, 2000) (246 yards)
41—(D) Blake Ezor, Michigan St. (33) vs. Hawaii (13) (Aloha, 1989) (179 yards)
39—Terrell Fletcher, Wisconsin (34) vs. Duke (20) (Hall of Fame, 1995) (241 yards)
39—Raymont Harris, Ohio St. (28) vs. Brigham Young (21) (Holiday, 1993) (235 yards)
39—Errict Rhett, Florida (27) vs. North Carolina St. (10) (Gator, 1992) (182 yards)
39—Charlie Wysocki, Maryland (20) vs. Florida (35) (Tangerine, 1980) (159 yards)
39—Charles White, Southern California (17) vs. Ohio St. (16) (Rose, 1980) (247 yards)
37—Ronnie Brown, Auburn (13) vs. Penn St. (9) (Capital One, 2003) (184 yards)
37—Rodney Davis, Fresno St. (30) vs. Georgia Tech (21) (Silicon Valley, 2002) (153 yards)
37—(D) Charles Davis, Colorado (29) vs. Houston (17) (Bluebonnet, 1971) (202 yards)
36—Cecil Sapp, Colorado St. (22) vs. Louisville (17) (Liberty, 2000) (160 yards)
36—LaDainian Tomlinson, TCU (28) vs. East Caro. (14) (Mobile Alabama, 1999) (124 yards)
36—Brent Moss, Wisconsin (21) vs. UCLA (16) (Rose, 1994) (158 yards)
36—Herschel Walker, Georgia (17) vs. Notre Dame (10) (Sugar, 1981) (150 yards)
36—Don McCauley, North Carolina (26) vs. Arizona St. (48) (Peach, 1970) (143 yards)
35—William Green, Boston College (20) vs. Georgia (16) (Music City, 2001) (149 yards)
35—Ja'Mar Toombs, Texas A&M (41) vs. Mississippi St. (43) (ot) (Independence, 2000) (193 yards)

35—Blair Thomas, Penn St. (50) vs. Brigham Young (39) (Holiday, 1989) (186 yards)
35—Lorenzo White, Michigan St. (20) vs. Southern California (17) (Rose, 1988) (113 yards)
35—(D) Robert Newhouse, Houston (17) vs. Colorado (29) (Bluebonnet, 1971) (168 yards)
35—Ed Williams, West Virginia (14) vs. South Carolina (3) (Peach, 1969) (208 yards)
35—Bob Anderson, Colorado (47) vs. Alabama (33) (Liberty, 1969) (254 yards)
34—Ron Dayne, Wisconsin (17) vs. Stanford (9) (Rose, 2000) (200 yards)
34—Mike Anderson, Utah (17) vs. Fresno St. (16) (Las Vegas, 1999) (254 yards)
34—Rondell Mealey, LSU (27) vs. Notre Dame (9) (Independence, 1997) (222 yards)
34—(D) Curtis Dickey, Texas A&M (28) vs. Iowa St. (12) (Hall of Fame, 1978) (276 yards)
34—Vic Bottari, California (13) vs. Alabama (0) (Rose, 1938) (137 yards)
34—Ernie Nevers, Stanford (10) vs. Notre Dame (27) (Rose, 1925) (114 yards)

MOST NET RUSHING YARDS
280—(D) James Gray, Texas Tech (49) vs. Duke (21) (All-American, 1989) (33 carries)
276—(D) Curtis Dickey, Texas A&M (28) vs. Iowa St. (12) (Hall of Fame, 1978) (34 carries)
266—(D) Gaston Green, UCLA (31) vs. Brigham Young (10) (Freedom, 1986) (33 carries)
265—Dicky Maegle, Rice (28) vs. Alabama (6) (Cotton, 1954) (11 carries)
260—Byron Hanspard, Texas Tech (55) vs. Air Force (41) (Copper, 1995) (24 carries)
254—Bob Anderson, Colorado (47) vs. Alabama (33) (Liberty, 1969) (35 carries)
254—Mike Anderson, Utah (17) vs. Fresno St. (16) (Las Vegas, 1999) (34 carries)
250—Chuck Webb, Tennessee (31) vs. Arkansas (27) (Cotton, 1990) (26 carries)
247—Charles White, Southern California (17) vs. Ohio St. (16) (Rose, 1980) (39 carries)
246—Tellis Redmon, Minnesota (30) vs. North Carolina St. (38) (Micronpc.com, 2000) (42 carries)
246—Ron Dayne, Wisconsin (38) vs. Utah (10) (Copper, 1996) (30 carries)
246—Ron Dayne, Wisconsin (38) vs. UCLA (31) (Rose, 1999) (27 carries)
241—Terrell Fletcher, Wisconsin (34) vs. Duke (20) (Hall of Fame, 1995) (39 carries)
240—Dan Alexander, Nebraska (66) vs. Northwestern (17) (Alamo, 2000) (20 carries)
239—Marcus Dupree, Oklahoma (21) vs. Arizona St. (32) (Fiesta, 1983) (17 carries)
235—Tyrone Wheatley, Michigan (38) vs. Washington (31) (Rose, 1993) (15 carries)
235—Raymont Harris, Ohio St. (28) vs. Brigham Young (21) (Holiday, 1993) (39 carries)
234—Jamie Morris, Michigan (28) vs. Alabama (24) (Hall of Fame, 1988) (23 carries)
234—Kevin Faulk, LSU (45) vs. Michigan St. (26) (Independence, 1995) (25 carries)
234—Fred Taylor, Florida (21) vs. Penn St. (6) (Florida Citrus, 1998) (43 carries)
227—Eric Ball, UCLA (45) vs. Iowa (28) (Rose, 1986) (22 carries)
225—Craig James, Southern Methodist (45) vs. Brigham Young (46) (Holiday, 1980) (23 carries)
222—Barry Sanders, Oklahoma St. (62) vs. Wyoming (14) (Holiday, 1988) (29 carries)
222—Rondell Mealey, LSU (27) vs. Notre Dame (9) (Independence, 1997) (34 carries)
216—Floyd Little, Syracuse (12) vs. Tennessee (18) (Gator, 1966) (29 carries)
211—(D) Ron Jackson, Tulsa (28) vs. San Diego St. (17) (Freedom, 1991) (46 carries)
208—Ed Williams, West Virginia (14) vs. South Carolina (3) (Peach, 1969) (35 carries)
206—Ahman Green, Nebraska (42) vs. Tennessee (17) (Orange, 1998) (29 carries)
205—Roland Sales, Arkansas (31) vs. Oklahoma (6) (Orange, 1978) (22 carries)
205—(D) Sammie Smith, Florida St. (27) vs. Indiana (13) (All-American, 1986) (25 carries)
203—Ricky Williams, Texas (38) vs. Mississippi St. (11) (Cotton, 1999) (30 carries)
202—(D) Charles Davis, Colorado (29) vs. Houston (17) (Bluebonnet, 1971) (37 carries)
202—Woody Green, Arizona St. (49) vs. Missouri (35) (Fiesta, 1972) (25 carries)
202—Tony Dorsett, Pittsburgh (27) vs. Georgia (3) (Sugar, 1977) (32 carries)
201—Malcolm Thomas, Syracuse (30) vs. Houston (17) (Liberty, 1996) (24 carries)
201—Cortlen Johnson, Colorado (62) vs. Boston College (28), (Insight.com, 1999) (15 carries)
200—Ron Dayne, Wisconsin (17) vs. Stanford (9) (Rose, 2000) (34 carries)

MOST NET RUSHING YARDS BY A QUARTERBACK
199—Tommie Frazier, Nebraska (62) vs. Florida (24) (Fiesta, 1996) (16 carries)
180—(D) Mike Mosley, Texas A&M (28) vs. Southern California (47) (Bluebonnet, 1977) (20 carries)
164—Eddie Phillips, Texas (11) vs. Notre Dame (24) (Cotton, 1971) (23 carries)
149—Jack Mildren, Oklahoma (40) vs. Auburn (22) (Sugar, 1972) (30 carries)
143—Kordell Stewart, Colorado (41) vs. Notre Dame (24) (Fiesta, 1995) (7 carries)
136—(D) Nate Sassaman, Army (10) vs. Michigan St. (6) (Cherry, 1984) (28 carries)
133—(D) Eddie Wolgast, Arizona (13) vs. Drake (14) (Salad, 1949) (22 carries) (listed in newspaper accounts as halfback but also attempted 15 passes in game)
132—Corby Jones, Missouri (24) vs. Colorado St. (35) (Holiday, 1997) (20 carries)
129—Rex Kern, Ohio St. (17) vs. Stanford (27) (Rose, 1971) (20 carries)
129—Beau Morgan, Air Force (41) vs. Texas Tech (55) (Copper, 1995) (22 carries)
127—J.C. Watts, Oklahoma (24) vs. Florida St. (7) (Orange, 1980) (12 carries)
119—Bucky Richardson, Texas A&M (65) vs. Brigham Young (14) (Holiday, 1990) (12 carries)
114—Eric Crouch, Nebraska (14) vs. Miami (Fla.) (37) (Rose, 2002) (22 carries)
113—Harry Gilmer, Alabama (34) vs. Southern California (14) (Rose, 1946)
109—Shaun King, Tulane (41) vs. Brigham Young (27) (Liberty, 1998) (16 carries)
107—Darrell Shepard, Oklahoma (40) vs. Houston (14) (Sun, 1981) (12 carries)
103—Major Harris, West Virginia (33) vs. Oklahoma St. (35) (John Hancock Sun, 1987)

HIGHEST AVERAGE PER RUSH
(Minimum 9 Carries)
24.1—Dicky Maegle, Rice (28) vs. Alabama (6) (Cotton, 1954) (11 for 265)
21.6—Bob Jeter, Iowa (38) vs. California (12) (Rose, 1959) (9 for 194)
15.7—Tyrone Wheatley, Michigan (38) vs. Washington (31) (Rose, 1993) (15 for 235)

14.2—(D) Gary Anderson, Arkansas (34) vs. Tulane (15) (Hall of Fame, 1980) (11 for 156)
14.1—Mike Holovak, Boston College (21) vs. Alabama (37) (Orange, 1943) (10 for 141)
14.1—Marcus Dupree, Oklahoma (21) vs. Arizona St. (32) (Fiesta, 1983) (17 for 239)
13.5—James Mungro, Syracuse (20) vs. Kentucky (13) (Music City, 1999) (12 for 162)
13.4—Cortlen Johnson, Colorado (62) vs. Boston College (28) (Insight.com, 1999) (15 for 201)
12.6—Ben Barnett, Army (28) vs. Alabama (29) (John Hancock Sun, 1988) (14 for 177)
12.6—Randy Baldwin, Mississippi (42) vs. Air Force (29) (Liberty, 1989) (14 for 177)
12.4—Tommie Frazier, Nebraska (62) vs. Florida (24) (Fiesta, 1996) (16 for 199)
12.3—Tatum Bell, Oklahoma St. (33) vs. Southern Miss. (23) (Houston, 2002) (13 for 160)
12.3—George Smith, Texas Tech (28) vs. North Carolina (32) (Sun, 1972) (14 for 172)
12.0—Dan Alexander, Nebraska (66) vs. Northwestern (17) (Alamo, 2000) (20 for 240)
11.2—Elliott Walker, Pittsburgh (33) vs. Kansas (19) (Sun, 1975) (11 for 123)
11.2—(D) Dwight Ford, Southern California (47) vs. Texas A&M (28) (Bluebonnet, 1977) (14 for 157)
10.9—Rodney Hampton, Georgia (34) vs. Michigan St. (27) (Gator, Jan. 1, 1989) (10 for 109)
10.8—Bobby Cavazos, Texas Tech (35) vs. Auburn (13) (Gator, Jan. 1, 1954) (13 for 141)
10.8—Byron Hanspard, Texas Tech (55) vs. Air Force (41) (Copper, 1995) (24 for 260)
10.6—Wali Lundy, Virginia (48) vs. West Virginia (22) (Continental Tire, 2002) (12 for 127)
10.6—J.C. Watts, Oklahoma (24) vs. Florida St. (7) (Orange, 1980) (12 for 127)
10.6—Travis Henry, Tennessee (21) vs. Kansas St. (35) (Cotton, 2001) (17 for 180)
10.5—Ray Brown, Mississippi (39) vs. Texas (7) (Sugar, 1958) (15 for 157)
10.3—Eric Ball, UCLA (45) vs. Iowa (28) (Rose, 1986) (22 for 227)
10.2—(D) Bill Tobin, Missouri (14) vs. Georgia Tech (10) (Bluebonnet, 1962) (11 for 112)
10.2—Jamie Morris, Michigan (28) vs. Alabama (24) (Hall of Fame, 1988) (23 for 234)

THREE RUSHERS, SAME TEAM, GAINING MORE THAN 100 YARDS
366—Tony Dorsett (142), Elliott Walker (123) & Robert Haygood (QB) (101), Pittsburgh (33) vs. Kansas (19) (Sun, 1975)

TWO RUSHERS, SAME TEAM, GAINING MORE THAN 100 YARDS
373—Woody Green (202) & Brent McClanahan (171), Arizona St. (49) vs. Missouri (35) (Fiesta, 1972)
365—(D) George Woodard (185) & Mike Mosley (QB) (180), Texas A&M (28) vs. Southern California (47) (Bluebonnet, 1977)
365—Bob Anderson (254) & Jim Bratten (111), Colorado (47) vs. Alabama (33) (Liberty, 1969)
364—Tommie Frazier (QB) (199) & Lawrence Phillips (165), Nebraska (62) vs. Florida (24) (Fiesta, 1996)
347—Walter Packer (183) & Terry Vitrano (164), Mississippi St. (26) vs. North Carolina (24) (Sun, 1974)
343—(D) Charles White (186) & Dwight Ford (157), Southern California (47) vs. Texas A&M (28) (Bluebonnet, 1977)
330—Floyd Little (216) & Larry Csonka (114), Syracuse (12) vs. Tennessee (18) (Gator, 1966)
297—Monroe Eley (173) & Bob Thomas (124), Arizona St. (48) vs. North Carolina (26) (Peach, 1970)
292—Kelvin Bryant (148) & Ethan Horton (144), North Carolina (31) vs. Arkansas (27) (Gator, 1981)
291—Billy Sims (164) & J.C. Watts (QB) (127), Oklahoma (24) vs. Florida St. (7) (Orange, 1980)
288—Billy Sims (181) & Darrell Shepard (QB) (107), Oklahoma (40) vs. Houston (14) (Sun, 1981)
277—Danta Johnson (148) & Beau Morgan (QB) (129), Air Force (41) vs. Texas Tech (55) (Copper, 1995)
277—Willie Heston (170) & Neil Snow (107), Michigan (49) vs. Stanford (0) (Rose, 1902)
270—Anthony Brown (167) & Major Harris (QB) (103), West Virginia (33) vs. Oklahoma St. (35) (John Hancock Sun, 1987)
257—Sedrick Shaw (135) & Tavian Banks (122), Iowa (38) vs. Washington (18) (Sun, 1995)
253—Alois Blackwell (149) & Dyral Thomas (104), Houston (30) vs. Maryland (21) (Cotton, 1977)
246—T. Robert Hopkins (125) & Leonard Brown (121), Missouri (27) vs. Texas (40) (Cotton, 1946)
240—Jon Vaughn (128) & Ricky Powers (112), Michigan (35) vs. Mississippi (3) (Gator, Jan. 1, 1991)
237—James Rouse (134) & Barry Foster (103), Arkansas (27) vs. Tennessee (31) (Cotton, 1990)
237—Raymond Bybee (127) & Thomas Reamon (110), Missouri (34) vs. Auburn (17) (Sun, 1973)
236—Corby Jones (132) & Devin West (104), Missouri (24) vs. Colorado St. (35) (Holiday, 1997)
230—Rex Kern (QB) (129) & John Brockington (101), Ohio St. (17) vs. Stanford (27) (Rose, 1971)
224—Clinton Portis (117) & James Jackson (107), Miami (Fla.) (28) vs. Georgia Tech (13) (Gator, 2000)
223—Bucky Richardson (QB) (119) & Darren Lewis (104), Texas A&M (65) vs. Brigham Young (14) (Holiday, 1990)

222—(D) Marshall Johnson (114) & Donnie McGraw (108), Houston (47) vs. Tulane (7) (Bluebonnet, 1973)
218—Travis Sims (113) & Michael Carter (105), Hawaii (27) vs. Illinois (17) (Holiday, 1992)
218—Steve Giese (111) & Bob Torrey (107), Penn St. (42) vs. Arizona St. (30) (Fiesta, 1977)
215—(D) Jeff Atkins (112) & Reggie Dupard (103), Southern Methodist (27) vs. Notre Dame (20) (Aloha, 1984)
215—Allen Pinkett (111) & Chris Smith (104), Notre Dame (19) vs. Boston College (18) (Liberty, 1983)
212—Toney Converse (103) & Shaun King (109), Tulane (41) vs. Brigham Young (27) (Liberty, 1998)
204—Johnny "Ham" Jones (104) & Johnny "Jam" Jones (100), Texas (42) vs. Maryland (0) (Sun, 1978)
201—Jerome Heavens (101) & Vagas Ferguson (100), Notre Dame (38) vs. Texas (10) (Cotton, 1978)

MOST RUSHING TOUCHDOWNS
5—Barry Sanders, Oklahoma St. (62) vs. Wyoming (14) (Holiday, 1988) (runs of 33, 2, 67, 1, 10)
5—Neil Snow, Michigan (49) vs. Stanford (0) (Rose, 1902) (five-point scores)
4—Chris Perry, Michigan (38) vs. Florida (30) (Outback, 2003) (runs of 4, 1, 7, 12)
4—Domanick Davis, LSU (47) vs. Illinois (34) (Sugar, 2002) (runs of 4, 25, 16, 4)
4—Ron Dayne, Wisconsin (38) vs. UCLA (31) (Rose, 1999) (runs of 54, 7, 10, 22)
4—Byron Hanspard, Texas Tech (55) vs. Air Force (41) (Copper, 1995) (runs of 2, 11, 2, 29)
4—Wasean Tait, Toledo (40) vs. Nevada (37) (ot) (Las Vegas, 1995) (runs of 18, 31, 26, 3)
4—(D) Ron Jackson, Tulsa (28) vs. San Diego St. (17) (Freedom, 1991) (runs of 10, 6, 3, 4)
4—(D) Sheldon Canley, San Jose St. (48) vs. Central Mich. (24) (California, 1990) (runs of 5, 22, 59, 5)
4—(D) James Gray, Texas Tech (49) vs. Duke (21) (All-American, 1989) (runs of 2, 54, 18, 32)
4—Thurman Thomas, Oklahoma St. (35) vs. West Virginia (33) (John Hancock Sun, 1987) (runs of 5, 9, 4, 4)
4—Eric Ball, UCLA (45) vs. Iowa (28) (Rose, 1986) (runs of 30, 40, 6, 32)
4—Terry Miller, Oklahoma St. (49) vs. Brigham Young (21) (Tangerine, 1976) (runs of 3, 78, 6, 1)
4—Sam Cunningham, Southern California (42) vs. Ohio St. (17) (Rose, 1973) (runs of 2, 1, 1, 1)
4—Woody Green, Arizona St. (49) vs. Missouri (35) (Fiesta, 1972) (runs of 2, 12, 17, 21)
4—Charles Cole, Toledo (56) vs. Davidson (33) (Tangerine, 1969) (runs of 1, 11, 16, 1)
4—(D) Gene Shannon, Houston (26) vs. Dayton (21) (Salad, 1952) (runs of 15, 19, 1, 10)

Passing

MOST PASS ATTEMPTS
74—Kyle Orton, Purdue (27) vs. Washington St. (33) (Sun, 2001)
70—Byron Leftwich, Marshall (64) vs. East Caro. (61) (2 ot) (GMAC, 2001)
63—(D) Trent Dilfer, Fresno St. (30) vs. Colorado (41) (Aloha, 1993)
62—(D) Steve Clarkson, San Jose St. (25) vs. Toledo (27) (California, 1981)
61—Danny O'Neil, Oregon (20) vs. Penn St. (38) (Rose, 1995)
61—(D) Sean Covey, Brigham Young (16) vs. Virginia (22) (All-American, 1987)
60—Drew Brees, Purdue (25) vs. Georgia (28) (ot) (Outback, 2000)
59—Hines Ward, Georgia (27) vs. Virginia (34) (Peach, Dec. 30, 1995)
59—Ty Detmer, Brigham Young (39) vs. Penn St. (50) (Holiday, 1989)
58—Shane Matthews, Florida (28) vs. Notre Dame (39) (Sugar, 1992)
58—Buster O'Brien, Richmond (49) vs. Ohio (42) (Tangerine, 1968)
57—Andrew Walter, Arizona St. (27) vs. Kansas St. (34) (Holiday, 2002)
57—(D) Tony Kimbrough, Western Mich. (30) vs. Fresno St. (35) (California, 1988)
56—David Carr, Fresno St. (35) vs. Michigan St. (44) (Silicon Valley, 2001)
56—Gino Torretta, Miami (Fla.) (13) vs. Alabama (34) (Sugar, 1993)
55—Major Applewhite, Texas (47) vs. Washington (43) (Holiday, 2001)
55—Jack Trudeau, Illinois (29) vs. Army (31) (Peach, 1985)
55—Tony Eason, Illinois (15) vs. Alabama (21) (Liberty, 1982)
54—Cody Pickett, Washington (43) vs. Texas (47) (Holiday, 2001)
53—Rohan Davey, LSU (47) vs. Illinois (34) (Sugar, 2002)
53—Josh Heupel, Oklahoma (25) vs. Mississippi (27) (Independence, 1999)
53—Drew Brees, Purdue (37) vs. Kansas St. (34) (Alamo, 1998)
53—(D) Tim Cowan, Washington (21) vs. Maryland (20) (Aloha, 1982)
53—Kim Hammond, Florida St. (17) vs. Penn St. (17) (Gator, 1967)
52—Luke McCown, Louisiana Tech (24) vs. Clemson (49) (Humanitarian, 2001)
52—David Smith, Alabama (29) vs. Army (28) (John Hancock Sun, 1988)
52—Shawn Halloran, Boston College (27) vs. Georgia (24) (Hall of Fame, 1986)
51—Chris Weinke, Florida St. (2) vs. Oklahoma (13) (Orange, 2001)
51—Lee Roberts, Southern Miss. (35) vs. Idaho (42) (Humanitarian, 1998)
51—Jeff Blake, East Caro. (37) vs. North Carolina St. (34) (Peach, 1992)
51—Danny McManus, Florida St. (31) vs. Nebraska (28) (Fiesta, 1988)
51—Chuck Hartlieb, Iowa (23) vs. North Carolina St. (28) (Peach, Dec. 31, 1988)
51—Craig Burnett, Wyoming (19) vs. Iowa (20) (Holiday, 1987)
51—(D) Whit Taylor, Vanderbilt (28) vs. Air Force (36) (Hall of Fame, 1982)

MOST PASS COMPLETIONS

43—(D) Steve Clarkson, San Jose St. (25) vs. Toledo (27) (California, 1981)
42—Ty Detmer, Brigham Young (39) vs. Penn St. (50) (Holiday, 1989)
41—Byron Leftwich, Marshall (64) vs. East Caro. (61) (2 ot) (GMAC, 2001)
41—Danny O'Neil, Oregon (20) vs. Penn St. (38) (Rose, 1995)
39—Josh Heupel, Oklahoma (25) vs. Mississippi (27) (Independence, 1999)
39—Buster O'Brien, Richmond (49) vs. Ohio (42) (Tangerine, 1968)
38—Kyle Orton, Purdue (27) vs. Washington St. (33) (Sun, 2001)
38—Jack Trudeau, Illinois (29) vs. Army (31) (Peach, 1985)
38—(D) Whit Taylor, Vanderbilt (28) vs. Air Force (36) (Hall of Fame, 1982)
37—Major Applewhite, Texas (47) vs. Washington (43) (Holiday, 2001)
37—(D) Trent Dilfer, Fresno St. (30) vs. Colorado (41) (Aloha, 1993)
37—(D) Sean Covey, Brigham Young (16) vs. Virginia (22) (All-American, 1987)
37—Kim Hammond, Florida St. (17) vs. Penn St. (17) (Gator, 1967)
36—Drew Brees, Purdue (25) vs. Georgia (28) (ot) (Outback, 2000)
35—David Carr, Fresno St. (35) vs. Michigan St. (44) (Silicon Valley, 2001)
35—Tony Eason, Illinois (15) vs. Alabama (21) (Liberty, 1982)
34—Tom Brady, Michigan (35) vs. Alabama (34) (ot) (Orange, 2000)
34—Marc Bulger, West Virginia (31) vs. Missouri (34) (Insight.com, 1998)
33—David Smith, Alabama (29) vs. Army (28) (John Hancock Sun, 1988)
33—(D) Tim Cowan, Washington (21) vs. Maryland (20) (Aloha, 1982)
33—Ron VanderKelen, Wisconsin (37) vs. Southern California (42) (Rose, 1963)
32—Kliff Kingsbury, Texas Tech (55) vs. Clemson (15) (Tangerine, 2002)
32—Jim McMahon, Brigham Young (46) vs. Southern Methodist (45) (Holiday, 1980)
31—Rohan Davey, LSU (47) vs. Illinois (34) (Sugar, 2002)
31—Kliff Kingsbury, Texas Tech (27) vs. East Caro. (40) (Galleryfurniture.com, 2000)
31—Hines Ward, Georgia (27) vs. Virginia (34) (Peach, Dec. 30, 1995)
31—John Walsh, Brigham Young (31) vs. Oklahoma (6) (Copper, 1994)
31—Jeff Blake, East Caro. (37) vs. North Carolina St. (34) (Peach, 1992)
31—Stan White, Auburn (27) vs. Indiana (23) (Peach, 1990)
31—Shawn Halloran, Boston College (27) vs. Georgia (24) (Hall of Fame, 1986)
31—Mark Young, Mississippi (20) vs. Texas Tech (17) (Independence, 1986)
31—Bernie Kosar, Miami (Fla.) (37) vs. UCLA (39) (Fiesta, 1985)
31—John Congemi, Pittsburgh (23) vs. Ohio St. (28) (Fiesta, 1984)
31—(D) Jeff Tedford, Fresno St. (29) vs. Bowling Green (28) (California, 1982)

MOST CONSECUTIVE PASS COMPLETIONS

19—Mike Bobo, Georgia (33) vs. Wisconsin (6) (Outback, 1998)
10—Danny Wuerffel, Florida (17) vs. Florida St. (23) (Sugar, Jan. 2, 1995)
10—Rick Neuheisel, UCLA (45) vs. Illinois (9) (Rose, 1984)
9—(D) Rob Johnson, Southern California (28) vs. Utah (21) (Freedom, 1993)
9—Bill Montgomery, Arkansas (16) vs. Georgia (2) (Sugar, 1969)
9—Glenn Dobbs, Tulsa (7) vs. Tennessee (14) (Sugar, 1943)
8—Billy Roland, Houston (49) vs. Miami (Ohio) (21) (Tangerine, 1962)
8—Bobby Layne, Texas (40) vs. Missouri (27) (Cotton, 1946)
8—Harry Gilmer, Alabama (26) vs. Duke (29) (Sugar, 1945)
7—(D) Daniel Ford, Arizona St. (33) vs. Air Force (28) (Freedom, 1987)

MOST NET PASSING YARDS
(Followed by Comp.-Att.-Int.)

576—Byron Leftwich, Marshall (64) vs. East Caro. (61) (2 ot) (GMAC, 2001) (41-70-2)
576—Ty Detmer, Brigham Young (39) vs. Penn St. (50) (Holiday, 1989) (42-59-2)
531—David Carr, Fresno St. (35) vs. Michigan St. (44) (Silicon Valley, 2001) (35-56-2)
523—(D) Trent Dilfer, Fresno St. (30) vs. Colorado (41) (Aloha, 1993) (37-63-1)
476—Drew Bledsoe, Washington St. (31) vs. Utah (28) (Copper, 1992) (30-46-1)
473—Major Applewhite, Texas (47) vs. Washington (43) (Holiday, 2001) (37-55-3)
467—(D) Steve Clarkson, San Jose St. (25) vs. Toledo (27) (California, 1981) (43-62-5)
461—(D) Chuck Long, Iowa (55) vs. Texas (17) (Freedom, 1984) (29-39-0)
456—Danny O'Neil, Oregon (20) vs. Penn St. (38) (Rose, 1995) (41-61-2)
456—(D) Akili Smith, Oregon (43) vs. Colorado (51) (Aloha, 1998) (24-46-2)
454—John Walsh, Brigham Young (31) vs. Oklahoma (6) (Copper, 1994) (31-45-0)
452—(D) Whit Taylor, Vanderbilt (28) vs. Air Force (36) (Hall of Fame, 1982) (38-51-3)
451—Browning Nagle, Louisville (34) vs. Alabama (7) (Fiesta, 1991) (20-33-1)
447—Buster O'Brien, Richmond (49) vs. Ohio (42) (Tangerine, 1968) (39-58-2)
446—Jim McMahon, Brigham Young (46) vs. Southern Methodist (45) (Holiday, 1980) (32-49-1)
444—Rohan Davey, LSU (47) vs. Illinois (34) (Sugar, 2002) (31-53-0)
429—Marc Bulger, West Virginia (31) vs. Missouri (34) (Insight.com, 1998) (34-50-1)
428—Chuck Hartlieb, Iowa (23) vs. North Carolina St. (28) (Peach, Dec. 31, 1988) (30-51-4)
423—Tony Eason, Illinois (15) vs. Alabama (21) (Liberty, 1982) (35-55-4)
422—Peter Tom Willis, Florida St. (41) vs. Nebraska (17) (Fiesta, 1990) (25-40-0)
419—Kyle Orton, Purdue (27) vs. Washington St. (33) (Sun, 2001) (38-74-4)
413—Hines Ward, Georgia (27) vs. Virginia (34) (Peach, Dec. 30, 1995) (31-59-2)
412—David Smith, Alabama (29) vs. Army (28) (John Hancock Sun, 1988) (33-52-1)
411—Chad Pennington, Marshall (48) vs. Louisville (29) (Motor City, 1998) (18-24-0)
408—Peyton Manning, Tennessee (48) vs. Northwestern (28) (Florida Citrus, 1997) (27-39-0)
404—(D) Ralph Martini, San Jose St. (48) vs. Central Mich. (24) (California, 1990) (27-36-1)
401—Ron VanderKelen, Wisconsin (37) vs. Southern California (42) (Rose, 1963) (33-48-3)
401—Jack Trudeau, Illinois (29) vs. Army (31) (Peach, 1985) (38-55-2)

MOST NET PASSING YARDS, ONE QUARTER

223—Browning Nagle, Louisville (34) vs. Alabama (7) (Fiesta, 1991) (1st, 9 of 16)
202—(D) Bret Stafford, Texas (32) vs. Pittsburgh (27) (Bluebonnet, 1987) (1st)

MOST TOUCHDOWN PASSES THROWN

6—(D) Chuck Long, Iowa (55) vs. Texas (17) (Freedom, 1984) (6, 11, 33, 49, 4, 15 yards)
5—Brad Lewis, West Virginia (49) vs. Mississippi (38) (Music City, 2000) (40,11,35,60,10 yards)
5—Peter Tom Willis, Florida St. (41) vs. Nebraska (17) (Fiesta, 1990)
5—Steve Tensi, Florida St. (36) vs. Oklahoma (19) (Gator, Jan. 2, 1965)
4—Rex Grossman, Florida (56) vs. Maryland (23) (Orange, 2002)
4—Kurt Kittner, Illinois (34) vs. LSU (47) (Sugar, 2002)
4—Joey Harrington, Oregon (38) vs. Colorado (16) (Fiesta, 2002)
4—Byron Leftwich, Marshall (64) vs. East Caro. (61) (2 ot) (GMAC, 2001)
4—Major Applewhite, Texas (47) vs. Washington (43) (Holiday, 2001)
4—David Carr, Fresno St. (35) vs. Michigan St. (44) (Silicon Valley, 2001)
4—Woody Dantzler, Clemson (49) vs. Louisiana Tech (24) (Humanitarian, 2001)
4—John Walsh, Idaho (42) vs. Southern Miss. (35) (Humanitarian, 1998)
4—Chad Pennington, Marshall (48) vs. Louisville (29) (Motor City, 1998)
4—Marc Bulger, West Virginia (31) Missouri (34) (Insight.com, 1998)
4—Michael Bishop, Kansas St. (35) vs. Syracuse (18) (Fiesta, 1997)
4—Peyton Manning, Tennessee (48) vs. Northwestern (28) (Florida Citrus, 1997)
4—Danny Kanell, Florida St. (31) vs. Notre Dame (26) (Orange, 1996)
4—Wally Richardson, Penn St. (43) vs. Auburn (14) (Outback, 1996)
4—Brian Kavanagh, Kansas St. (54) vs. Colorado St. (21) (Holiday, 1995)
4—Johnny Johnson, Illinois (30) vs. East Caro. (0) (Liberty, 1994)
4—John Walsh, Brigham Young (31) vs. Oklahoma (6) (Copper, 1994)
4—Tony Sacca, Penn St. (42) vs. Tennessee (17) (Fiesta, 1992)
4—Jeff Blake, East Caro. (37) vs. North Carolina St. (34) (Peach, 1992)
4—Elvis Grbac, Michigan (35) vs. Mississippi (3) (Gator, Jan. 1, 1991)
4—Rick Neuheisel, UCLA (45) vs. Illinois (9) (Rose, 1984)
4—Jim McMahon, Brigham Young (46) vs. Southern Methodist (45) (Holiday, 1980)
4—Mark Herrmann, Purdue (28) vs. Missouri (25) (Liberty, 1980)
4—(D) Rob Hertel, Southern California (47) vs. Texas A&M (28) (Bluebonnet, 1977)
4—Matt Cavanaugh, Pittsburgh (34) vs. Clemson (3) (Gator, 1977)
4—Gordon Slade, Davidson (33) vs. Toledo (55) (Tangerine, 1969)
4—Buster O'Brien, Richmond (49) vs. Ohio (42) (Tangerine, 1968)
4—Cleve Bryant, Ohio (42) vs. Richmond (49) (Tangerine, 1968)
4—Pete Beathard, Southern California (42) vs. Wisconsin (37) (Rose, 1963)

MOST PASSES HAD INTERCEPTED
(Followed by Comp.-Att.-Int.)

6—Bruce Lee, Arizona (10) vs. Auburn (34) (Sun, 1968) (6-24-6)
5—Wade Hill, Arkansas (15) vs. Georgia (24) (Independence, 1991) (12-31-5)
5—Kevin Murray, Texas A&M (12) vs. Ohio St. (28) (Cotton, 1987) (12-31-5)
5—Vinny Testaverde, Miami (Fla.) (10) vs. Penn St. (14) (Fiesta, 1987) (26-50-5)
5—Jeff Wickersham, LSU (10) vs. Nebraska (28) (Sugar, 1985) (20-38-5)
5—(D) Steve Clarkson, San Jose St. (25) vs. Toledo (27) (California, 1981) (43-62-5)
5—Terry McMillan, Missouri (3) vs. Penn St. (10) (Orange, 1970) (6-28-5)
5—Paul Gilbert, Georgia (6) vs. Nebraska (45) (Sun, 1969) (10-30-5)

HIGHEST COMPLETION PERCENTAGE
(Minimum 10 Attempts) (Followed by Comp.-Att.-Int.)

.929—Mike Bobo, Georgia (33) vs. Wisconsin (6) (Outback, 1998) (26-28-0)
.917—Bobby Layne, Texas (40) vs. Missouri (27) (Cotton, 1946) (11-12-0)
.900—Ken Ploen, Iowa (35) vs. Oregon St. (19) (Rose, 1957) (9-10-0)
.846—Tom Sorley, Nebraska (21) vs. North Carolina (17) (Liberty, 1977) (11-13-0)
.833—Mike Gundy, Oklahoma St. (62) vs. Wyoming (14) (Holiday, 1988) (20-24-0)
.833—Richard Todd, Alabama (13) vs. Penn St. (6) (Sugar, 1975) (10-12-0)
.818—Mark Farris, Texas A&M (41) vs. Mississippi St. (43) (ot) (Independence, 2000) (9-11-1)
.818—Bucky Richardson, Texas A&M (65) vs. Brigham Young (14) (Holiday, 1990) (9-11-0)
.806—Cale Gundy, Oklahoma (48) vs. Virginia (14) (Gator, Dec. 29, 1991) (25-31-0)
.800—Art Schlichter, Ohio St. (15) vs. Clemson (17) (Gator, 1978) (16-20-1)
.800—Jim Stevens, Georgia Tech (31) vs. Iowa St. (30) (Liberty, 1972) (12-15-0)
.800—Don Altman, Duke (7) vs. Arkansas (6) (Cotton, 1961) (12-15-0)
.800—Chuck Curtis, TCU (28) vs. Syracuse (27) (Cotton, 1957) (12-15-0)
.789—Charles Ortmann, Michigan (14) vs. California (6) (Rose, 1951) (15-19-0)
.786—Chad Hutchinson, Stanford (38) vs. Michigan St. (0) (Sun, 1996) (22-28-1)
.786—Mark Herrmann, Purdue (28) vs. Missouri (25) (Liberty, 1980) (22-28-0)

MOST YARDS PER PASS ATTEMPT
(Minimum 10 Attempts)

21.3—(D) Chris McCoy, Navy (42) vs. California (38) (Aloha, 1996) (13 for 277)
19.4—Tony Rice, Notre Dame (34) vs. West Virginia (21) (Fiesta, 1989) (11 for 213)
18.7—Frank Sinkwich, Georgia (40) vs. TCU (26) (Orange, 1942) (13 for 243)
18.5—Bucky Richardson, Texas A&M (65) vs. Brigham Young (14) (Holiday, 1990) (11 for 203)
17.3—Don Rumley, New Mexico (34) vs. Denver (24) (Sun, 1946) (12 for 207)
17.1—Chad Pennington, Marshall (48) vs. Louisville (29) (Motor City, 1998) (24 for 411)
16.7—Blane Morgan, Air Force (45) vs. Washington (25) (Oahu, 1998) (16 for 267)
16.4—(D) Rob Hertel, Southern California (47) vs. Texas A&M (28) (Bluebonnet, 1977) (15 for 246)
15.4—James Street, Texas (36) vs. Tennessee (13) (Cotton, 1969) (13 for 200)
15.4—Tee Martin, Tennessee (23) vs. Florida St. (16) (Fiesta, 1999) (11 for 278)
14.2—Danny White, Arizona St. (28) vs. Pittsburgh (7) (Fiesta, 1973) (19 for 269)
13.8—Rob Johnson, Southern California (55) vs. Texas Tech (14) (Cotton, 1995) (21 for 289)
13.8—Michael Bishop, Kansas St. (35) vs. Syracuse (18) (Fiesta, 1997) (23 for 317)

13.7—Browning Nagle, Louisville (34) vs. Alabama (7) (Fiesta, 1991) (33 for 451)
13.6—Bob Churchich, Nebraska (28) vs. Alabama (39) (Orange, 1966) (17 for 232)
13.4—Donovan McNabb, Syracuse (41) vs. Clemson (0) (Gator, 1996) (23 for 309)
13.3—Scott Covington, Miami (Fla.) (46) vs. North Carolina St. (23) (Micron PC, 1998) (24 for 320)
13.2—Bobby Layne, Texas (40) vs. Missouri (27) (Cotton, 1946) (12 for 158)

MOST YARDS PER PASS COMPLETION
(Minimum 7 Completions)
30.8—(D) Chris McCoy, Navy (42) vs. California (38) (Aloha, 1996) (9 for 277)
30.4—Duke Carlisle, Texas (28) vs. Navy (6) (Cotton, 1964) (7 for 213)
30.4—Tony Rice, Notre Dame (34) vs. West Virginia (21) (Fiesta, 1989) (7 for 213)
28.6—James Street, Texas (36) vs. Tennessee (13) (Cotton, 1969) (7 for 200)
27.2—Chris Rix, Florida St. (30) vs. Virginia Tech (17) (Gator, 2002) (12 for 326)
27.0—Frank Sinkwich, Georgia (40) vs. TCU (26) (Orange, 1942) (9 for 243)

Receiving

MOST PASS RECEPTIONS
20—(D) Norman Jordan, Vanderbilt (28) vs. Air Force (36) (Hall of Fame, 1982) (173 yards)
20—Walker Gillette, Richmond (49) vs. Ohio (42) (Tangerine, 1968) (242 yards)
18—(D) Gerald Willhite, San Jose St. (25) vs. Toledo (27) (California, 1981) (124 yards)
15—Denero Marriott, Marshall (64) vs. East Caro. (61) (2 ot) (GMAC, 2001) (234 yards)
15—(D) Stephone Paige, Fresno St. (29) vs. Bowling Green (28) (California, 1982) (246 yards)
14—Josh Reed, LSU (47) vs. Illinois (34) (Sugar, 2002) (239 yards)
14—Alex Van Dyke, Nevada (37) vs. Toledo (40) (ot) (Las Vegas, 1995) (176 yards)
14—J.J. Stokes, UCLA (16) vs. Wisconsin (21) (Rose, 1994) (176 yards)
14—Ron Sellers, Florida St. (17) vs. Penn St. (17) (Gator, 1967) (145 yards)
13—Rodney Wright, Fresno St. (35) vs. Michigan St. (44) (Silicon Valley, 2001) (299 yards)
13—Plaxico Burress, Michigan St. (37) vs. Florida (34) (Florida Citrus, 2000) (185 yards)
13—Fred Biletnikoff, Florida St. (36) vs. Oklahoma (19) (Gator, Jan. 2, 1965) (192 yards)
12—John Standeford, Purdue (27) vs. Washington St. (33) (Sun, 2001) (103 yards)
12—Tim Stratton, Purdue (27) vs. Washington St. (33) (Sun, 2001) (86 yards)
12—Chris Daniels, Purdue (25) vs. Georgia (28) (ot) (Outback, 2000) (103 yards)
12—Sherrod Gideon, Southern Miss. (35) vs. Idaho (42) (Humanitarian, 1998) (117 yards)
12—Hines Ward, Georgia (33) vs. Wisconsin (6) (Outback, 1998) (122 yards)
12—Keyshawn Johnson, Southern California (41) vs. Northwestern (32) (Rose, 1996) (216 yards)
12—Luke Fisher, East Caro. (37) vs. North Carolina St. (34) (Peach, 1992) (144 yards)
12—Chuck Dicus, Arkansas (16) vs. Georgia (2) (Sugar, 1969) (169 yards)
12—Bill Moremen, Florida St. (17) vs. Penn St. (17) (Gator, 1967) (106 yards)
11—Kellen Winslow, Miami (Fla.) (24) vs. Ohio St. (31) (2 ot) (Fiesta, 2003) (122 yards)
11—Roy Williams, Texas (47) vs. Washington (43) (Holiday, 2001) (134 yards)
11—Travis Taylor, Florida (34) vs. Michigan St. (37) (Florida Citrus, 2000) (156 yards)
11—David Boston, Ohio St. (24) vs. Texas A&M (14) (Sugar, 1999) (105 yards)
11—Shawn Foreman, West Virginia (31) vs. Missouri (34) (Insight.com, 1998) (189 yards)
11—Isaac Jones, Purdue (37) vs. Kansas St. (34) (Alamo, 1998) (98 yards)
11—Josh Wilcox, Oregon (20) vs. Penn St. (38) (Rose, 1995) (135 yards)
11—Bill Khayat, Duke (20) vs. Wisconsin (34) (Hall of Fame, 1995) (109 yards)
11—(D) Mark Szlachcic, Bowling Green (28) vs. Fresno St. (21) (California, 1991) (189 yards)
11—Ronnie Harmon, Iowa (28) vs. UCLA (45) (Rose, 1986) (102 yards)
11—David Mills, Brigham Young (24) vs. Michigan (17) (Holiday, 1984) (103 yards)
11—(D) Chip Otten, Bowling Green (28) vs. Fresno St. (29) (California, 1982) (76 yards)
11—(D) Anthony Hancock, Tennessee (28) vs. Wisconsin (21) (Garden State, 1981) (196 yards)
11—Pat Richter, Wisconsin (37) vs. Southern California (42) (Rose, 1963) (163 yards)
11—(D) James Ingram, Baylor (14) vs. LSU (7) (Bluebonnet, 1963) (163 yards)

MOST PASS RECEIVING YARDS
299—Rodney Wright, Fresno St. (35) vs. Michigan St. (44) (Silicon Valley, 2001) (13 catches)
270—Charles Rogers, Michigan St. (44) vs. Fresno St. (35) (Silicon Valley, 2001) (10 catches)
252—Andre Rison, Michigan St. (27) vs. Georgia (34) (Gator, Jan. 1, 1989) (9 catches)
246—(D) Stephone Paige, Fresno St. (29) vs. Bowling Green (28) (California, 1982) (15 catches)
242—(D) Tony Jones, Texas (32) vs. Pittsburgh (27) (Bluebonnet, 1987) (8 catches)
242—Walker Gillette, Richmond (49) vs. Ohio (42) (Tangerine, 1968) (20 catches)
239—Josh Reed, LSU (47) vs. Illinois (34) (Sugar, 2002) (14 catches)
234—Denero Marriott, Marshall (64) vs. East Caro. (61) (2 ot) (GMAC, 2001) (15 catches)
222—Keyshawn Johnson, Southern California (55) vs. Texas Tech (14) (Cotton, 1995) (8 catches)
216—Keyshawn Johnson, Southern California (41) vs. Northwestern (32) (Rose, 1996) (12 catches)
212—Phillip Bobo, Washington St. (31) vs. Utah (28) (Copper, 1992) (7 catches)
206—Darnell McDonald, Kansas St. (35) vs. Syracuse (18) (Fiesta, 1997) (7 catches)
201—(D) Bob McChesney, Hardin-Simmons (49) vs. Wichita St. (12) (Camellia, 1948) (8 catches)
199—Andre Johnson, Miami (Fla.) (37) vs. Nebraska (14) (Rose, 2002) (7 catches)
199—Peerless Price, Tennessee (23) vs. Florida St. (16) (Fiesta, 1999) (4 catches)
196—Taylor Stubblefield, Purdue (27) vs. Washington St. (33) (Sun, 2001) (9 catches)
196—(D) Anthony Hancock, Tennessee (28) vs. Wisconsin (21) (Garden State, 1981) (11 catches)
194—(D) Cory Schemm, Navy (42) vs. California (38) (Aloha, 1996) (5 catches)
192—Fred Biletnikoff, Florida St. (36) vs. Oklahoma (19) (Gator, Jan. 2, 1965) (13 catches)
189—Shawn Foreman, West Virginia (31) vs. Missouri (34) (Insight.com, 1998) (11 catches)
189—(D) Mark Szlachcic, Bowling Green (28) vs. Fresno St. (21) (California, 1991) (11 catches)
188—(D) David Miles, Brigham Young (16) vs. Virginia (22) (All-American, 1987) (10 catches)
186—Greg Hudson, Arizona St. (28) vs. Pittsburgh (7) (Fiesta, 1973) (8 catches)
185—Plaxico Burress, Michigan St. (37) vs. Florida (34) (Florida Citrus, 2000) (13 catches)
182—Rob Turner, Indiana (34) vs. South Carolina (10) (Liberty, 1988) (5 catches)
180—Freddie Mitchell, UCLA (20) vs. Wisconsin (21) (Sun, 2000) (9 catches)

HIGHEST AVERAGE PER RECEPTION
(Minimum 3 Receptions)
52.3—Jason Anderson, Wake Forest (38) vs. Oregon (17) (Seattle, 2002) (3 for 157)
52.3—Phil Harris, Texas (28) vs. Navy (6) (Cotton, 1964) (3 for 157)
49.8—Peerless Price, Tennessee (23) vs. Florida St. (16) (Fiesta, 1999) (4 for 199)
48.8—Javon Walker, Florida St. (30) vs. Virginia Tech (17) (Gator, 2002) (4 for 195)
39.7—Ike Hilliard, Florida (17) vs. Florida St. (23) (Sugar, Jan. 2, 1995) (3 for 119)
38.8—(D) Cory Schemm, Navy (42) vs. California (38) (Aloha, 1996) (5 for 194)
36.4—Rob Turner, Indiana (34) vs. South Carolina (10) (Liberty, 1988) (5 for 182)
36.3—Clarence Cannon, Boston College (31) vs. Virginia (13) (Carquest, 1994) (3 for 109)
35.5—Roy Williams, Texas (35) vs. LSU (20) (Cotton, 2003) (4 for 142)
35.5—(D) Rodney Harris, Kansas (23) vs. Brigham Young (20) (Aloha, 1992) (4 for 142)
35.3—Anthony Carter, Michigan (15) vs. North Carolina (17) (Gator, 1979) (4 for 141)
34.3—(D) Andre Alexander, Fresno St. (35) vs. Western Mich. (30) (California, 1988) (3 for 103)
34.3—Ron Beverly, Arizona St. (49) vs. Missouri (35) (Fiesta, 1972) (3 for 103)
34.0—Durell Price, UCLA (31) vs. Wisconsin (38) (Rose, 1999) (3 for 102)
34.0—Jimmy Cefalo, Penn St. (41) vs. Baylor (20) (Cotton, 1975) (3 for 102)
33.7—Justin Shull, Colorado St. (14) vs. Michigan (24) (Holiday, 1994) (3 for 101)
33.7—J.D. Hill, Arizona St. (48) vs. North Carolina (26) (Peach, 1970) (3 for 101)
33.3—Tony Buford, Indiana (34) vs. South Carolina (10) (Liberty, 1988) (3 for 100)
33.2—Melvin Bonner, Baylor (20) vs. Arizona (15) (John Hancock, 1992) (5 for 166)
33.2—Todd Dixon, Wake Forest (39) vs. Oregon (35) (Independence, 1992) (5 for 166)
33.0—Ed Hervey, Southern California (55) vs. Texas Tech (14) (Cotton, 1995) (3 for 99)
32.3—Dez White, Georgia Tech (35) vs. Notre Dame (28) (Gator, 1999) (4 for 129)
32.2—Cotton Speyrer, Texas (36) vs. Tennessee (13) (Cotton, 1969) (5 for 161)
32.0—(D) Darrin Chiaverini, Colorado (51) vs. Oregon (43) (Aloha, 1998) (3 for 96)
31.6—Andre Davis, Virginia Tech (17) vs. Florida St. (30) (Gator, 2002) (5 for 158)
31.0—Olanda Truitt, Pittsburgh (31) vs. Texas A&M (28) (John Hancock, 1989) (4 for 124)
31.0—Clay Brown, Brigham Young (46) vs. Southern Methodist (45) (Holiday, 1980) (5 for 155)

MOST TOUCHDOWNS RECEIVING
4—Fred Biletnikoff, Florida St. (36) vs. Oklahoma (19) (Gator, Jan. 2, 1965) (13 catches)
4—(D) Bob McChesney, Hardin-Simmons (49) vs. Wichita St. (12) (Camellia, 1948) (8 catches)
3—Plaxico Burress, Michigan St. (37) vs. Florida (34) (Florida Citrus, 2000) (13 catches)
3—Travis Taylor, Florida (34) vs. Michigan St. (37) (Florida Citrus, 2000) (11 catches)
3—Darnell McDonald, Kansas St. (35) vs. Syracuse (18) (Fiesta, 1997) (7 catches)
3—Ike Hilliard, Florida (52) vs. Florida St. (20) (Sugar, 1997) (7 catches)
3—Keyshawn Johnson, Southern California (55) vs. Texas Tech (14) (Cotton, 1995) (8 catches)
3—(D) Ken Ealy, Central Mich. (24) vs. San Jose St. (48) (California, 1990) (7 catches)
3—Wendell Davis, LSU (30) vs. South Carolina (13) (Gator, 1987) (9 catches)
3—(D) Anthony Allen, Washington (21) vs. Maryland (20) (Aloha, 1982) (8 catches)
3—(D) Norman Jordan, Vanderbilt (28) vs. Air Force (36) (Hall of Fame, 1982) (20 catches)
3—(D) Dwayne Dixon, Florida (24) vs. Arkansas (28) (Bluebonnet, 1982) (8 catches)
3—(D) Mervyn Fernandez, San Jose St. (25) vs. Toledo (27) (California, 1981) (9 catches)
3—Clay Brown, Brigham Young (46) vs. Southern Methodist (45) (Holiday, 1980) (5 catches)
3—Elliott Walker, Pittsburgh (34) vs. Clemson (3) (Gator, 1977) (6 catches)
3—Rhett Dawson, Florida St. (38) vs. Arizona St. (45) (Fiesta, 1971) (8 catches)
3—George Hannen, Davidson (33) vs. Toledo (56) (Tangerine, 1969)
3—Todd Snyder, Richmond (49) vs. Ohio (42) (Tangerine, 1968)

Scoring

MOST POINTS SCORED
30—(D) Sheldon Canley, San Jose St. (48) vs. Central Mich. (24) (California, 1990) (5 TDs)

BOWL/ALL-STAR RECORDS

30—Barry Sanders, Oklahoma St. (62) vs. Wyoming (14) (Holiday, 1988) (5 TDs)
28—Bobby Layne, Texas (40) vs. Missouri (27) (Cotton, 1946) (4 TDs, 4 PATs)
25—Neil Snow, Michigan (49) vs. Stanford (0) (Rose, 1902) (5 five-point TDs)
24—Chris Perry, Michigan (38) vs. Florida (30) (Outback, 2003) (4 TDs)
24—Wali Lundy, Virginia (48) vs. West Virginia (22) (Continental Tire, 2002) (4 TDs)
24—Domanick Davis, LSU (47) vs. Illinois (34) (Sugar, 2002) (4 TDs)
24—Ron Dayne, Wisconsin (38) vs. UCLA (31) (Rose, 1999) (4 TDs)
24—Byron Hanspard, Texas Tech (55) vs. Air Force (41) (Copper, 1995) (4 TDs)
24—Wasean Tait, Toledo (40) vs. Nevada (37) (ot) (Las Vegas, 1995) (4 TDs)
24—(D) Ron Jackson, Tulsa (28) vs. San Diego St. (17) (Freedom, 1991) (4 TDs)
24—(D) James Gray, Texas Tech (49) vs. Duke (21) (All-American, 1989) (4 TDs)
24—Thurman Thomas, Oklahoma St. (35) vs. West Virginia (33) (John Hancock Sun, 1987) (4 TDs)
24—Eric Ball, UCLA (45) vs. Iowa (28) (Rose, 1986) (4 TDs)
24—Terry Miller, Oklahoma St. (49) vs. Brigham Young (21) (Tangerine, 1976) (4 TDs)
24—Sam Cunningham, Southern California (42) vs. Ohio St. (17) (Rose, 1973) (4 TDs)
24—Johnny Rodgers, Nebraska (40) vs. Notre Dame (6) (Orange, 1973) (4 TDs)
24—Woody Green, Arizona St. (49) vs. Missouri (35) (Fiesta, 1972) (4 TDs)
24—Charles Cole, Toledo (56) vs. Davidson (33) (Tangerine, 1969) (4 TDs)
24—Fred Biletnikoff, Florida St. (36) vs. Oklahoma (19) (Gator, Jan. 2, 1965) (4 TDs)
24—Joe Lopasky, Houston (49) vs. Miami (Ohio) (21) (Tangerine, 1962) (4 TDs)
24—(D) Gene Shannon, Houston (26) vs. Dayton (21) (Salad, 1952) (4 TDs)
24—(D) Bob McChesney, Hardin-Simmons (49) vs. Wichita St. (12) (Camellia, 1948) (4 TDs)

MOST POINTS RESPONSIBLE FOR
(TDs Scored & Passed For, Extra Points, and FGs)
40—Bobby Layne, Texas (40) vs. Missouri (27) (Cotton, 1946) (18 rush, 12 pass, 6 receiving and 4 PATs)
36—(D) Chuck Long, Iowa (55) vs. Texas (17) (Freedom, 1984) (36 pass)
30—Byron Leftwich, Marshall (64) vs. East Caro. (61) (2 ot) (GMAC, 2001) (24 pass, 6 rush)
30—Casey Clausen, Tennessee (45) vs. Michigan (17) (Florida Citrus, 2002) (18 pass, 12 rush)
30—Michael Bishop, Kansas St. (35) vs. Syracuse (18) (Fiesta, 1997) (24 pass, 6 rush)
30—Jeff Blake, East Caro. (37) vs. North Carolina St. (34) (Peach, 1992) (24 pass, 6 rush)
30—(D) Sheldon Canley, San Jose St. (48) vs. Central Mich. (24) (California, 1990) (24 rush, 6 receiving)
30—Peter Tom Willis, Florida St. (41) vs. Nebraska (17) (Fiesta, 1990) (30 pass)
30—Barry Sanders, Oklahoma St. (62) vs. Wyoming (14) (Holiday, 1988) (30 rush)
30—Johnny Rodgers, Nebraska (40) vs. Notre Dame (6) (Orange, 1973) (18 rush, 6 pass, 6 receiving)
30—Steve Tensi, Florida St. (36) vs. Oklahoma (19) (Gator, Jan. 2, 1965) (30 pass)

MOST TOUCHDOWNS
5—(D) Sheldon Canley, San Jose St. (48) vs. Central Mich. (24) (California, 1990) (4 rush, 1 catch)
5—Barry Sanders, Oklahoma St. (62) vs. Wyoming (14) (Holiday, 1988) (5 rush)
5—Neil Snow, Michigan (49) vs. Stanford (0) (Rose, 1902) (5 rush five-point TDs)
4—Chris Perry, Michigan (38) vs. Florida (30) (Outback, 2003) (4 rush)
4—Wali Lundy, Virginia (48) vs. West Virginia (22) (Continental Tire, 2002) (2 rush, 2 catch)
4—Domanick Davis, LSU (47) vs. Illinois (34) (Sugar, 2002) (4 rush)
4—Ron Dayne, Wisconsin (38) vs. UCLA (31) (Rose, 1999) (4 rush)
4—Byron Hanspard, Texas Tech (55) vs. Air Force (41) (Copper, 1995) (4 rush)
4—Wasean Tait, Toledo (40) vs. Nevada (37) (ot) (Las Vegas, 1995) (4 rush)
4—(D) Ron Jackson, Tulsa (28) vs. San Diego St. (17) (Freedom, 1991) (4 rush)
4—(D) James Gray, Texas Tech (49) vs. Duke (21) (All-American, 1989) (4 rush)
4—Thurman Thomas, Oklahoma St. (35) vs. West Virginia (33) (John Hancock Sun, 1987) (4 rush)
4—Eric Ball, UCLA (45) vs. Iowa (28) (Rose, 1986) (4 rush)
4—Terry Miller, Oklahoma St. (49) vs. Brigham Young (21) (Tangerine, 1976) (4 rush)
4—Sam Cunningham, Southern California (42) vs. Ohio St. (17) (Rose, 1973) (4 rush)
4—Johnny Rodgers, Nebraska (40) vs. Notre Dame (6) (Orange, 1973) (3 rush, 1 catch)
4—Woody Green, Arizona St. (49) vs. Missouri (35) (Fiesta, 1972) (4 rush)
4—Charles Cole, Toledo (56) vs. Davidson (33) (Tangerine, 1969) (4 rush)
4—Fred Biletnikoff, Florida St. (36) vs. Oklahoma (19) (Gator, Jan. 2, 1965) (4 catch)
4—Joe Lopasky, Houston (49) vs. Miami (Ohio) (21) (Tangerine, 1962) (2 rush, 1 catch, 1 punt return)
4—(D) Gene Shannon, Houston (26) vs. Dayton (21) (Salad, 1952) (4 rush)
4—(D) Bob McChesney, Hardin-Simmons (49) vs. Wichita St. (12) (Camellia, 1948) (4 catch)
4—Bobby Layne, Texas (40) vs. Missouri (27) (Cotton, 1946) (3 rush, 1 catch)
4—(D) Alvin McMillin, Centre (63) vs. TCU (7) (Fort Worth Classic, 1921) (4 rush)

MOST TWO-POINT CONVERSIONS
2—Ernie Davis, Syracuse (23) vs. Texas (14) (Cotton, 1960) (2 pass receptions)

Kicking

MOST FIELD GOALS ATTEMPTED
6—Kyle Bryant, Texas A&M (22) vs. Michigan (20) (Alamo, 1995) (5 made)
5—Billy Bennett, Georgia (26) vs. Florida St. (13) (Sugar, 2003) (4 made)
5—Dan Nystrom, Minnesota (29) vs. Arkansas (14) (Music City, 2002) (5 made)
5—Nate Kaeding, Iowa (19) vs. Texas Tech (16) (Alamo, 2001) (4 made)
5—Travis Forney, Penn St. (26) vs. Kentucky (14) (Outback, 1999) (4 made)
5—Chad Holcomb, East Caro. (19) vs. Stanford (13) (Liberty, 1995) (4 made)
5—Dan Mowrey, Florida St. (23) vs. Florida (17) (Sugar, Jan. 2, 1995) (3 made)
5—Tim Rogers, Mississippi St. (24) vs. North Carolina St. (28) (Peach, Jan. 1, 1995) (5 made)
5—Scott Bentley, Florida St. (18) vs. Nebraska (16) (Orange, 1994) (4 made)
5—Arden Czyzewski, Florida (28) vs. Notre Dame (39) (Sugar, 1992) (5 made)
5—Jess Atkinson, Maryland (23) vs. Tennessee (30) (Florida Citrus, 1983) (5 made)
5—Bob White, Arkansas (16) vs. Georgia (2) (Sugar, 1969) (3 made)
5—Tim Davis, Alabama (12) vs. Mississippi (7) (Sugar, 1964) (5 made)
4—Luke Phillips, Oklahoma St. (33) vs. Southern Miss. (23) (Houston, 2002) (4 made)
4—Drew Dunning, Washington St. (33) vs. Purdue (27) (Sun, 2001) (4 made)
4—John Anderson, Washington (43) vs. Texas (47) (Holiday, 2001) (3 made)
4—Kevin Miller, East Caro. (61) vs. Marshall (64) (2 ot) (GMAC, 2001) (4 made)
4—Brett Conway, Penn St. (43) vs. Auburn (14) (Outback, 1996) (3 made)
4—Kanon Parkman, Georgia (27) vs. Virginia (34) (Peach, Dec. 30, 1995) (4 made)
4—Carlos Huerta, Miami (Fla.) (22) vs. Nebraska (0) (Orange, 1992) (3 made)
4—Greg Worker, Wyoming (19) vs. Iowa (20) (Holiday, 1987) (2 made)
4—Tim Lashar, Oklahoma (25) vs. Penn St. (10) (Orange, 1986) (4 made)
4—Kent Bostrom, Arizona St. (17) vs. Arkansas (18) (Holiday, 1985) (3 made)
4—(D) Todd Gregoire, Wisconsin (19) vs. Kentucky (20) (Hall of Fame, 1984) (4 made)
4—Bill Capece, Florida St. (17) vs. Oklahoma (18) (Orange, 1981) (1 made)
4—David Hardy, Texas A&M (33) vs. Oklahoma St. (16) (Independence, 1981) (4 made)
4—Bob Lucchesi, Missouri (19) vs. Southern Miss. (17) (Tangerine, 1981) (4 made)
4—Paul Woodside, West Virginia (26) vs. Florida (6) (Peach, Dec. 31, 1981) (4 made)
4—(D) Fuad Reveiz, Tennessee (28) vs. Wisconsin (21) (Garden State, 1981) (2 made)
4—Dale Castro, Maryland (20) vs. Florida (35) (Tangerine, 1980) (4 made)
4—Brent Johnson, Brigham Young (37) vs. Indiana (38) (Holiday, 1979) (3 made)
4—Ricky Townsend, Tennessee (19) vs. Texas Tech (28) (Gator, 1973) (2 made)
4—Paul Rogers, Nebraska (45) vs. Georgia (6) (Sun, 1969) (4 made)

MOST FIELD GOALS MADE
5—Dan Nystrom, Minnesota (29) vs. Arkansas (14) (Music City, 2002) (24, 45, 21, 22, 29 yards)
5—Kyle Bryant, Texas A&M (22) vs. Michigan (20) (Alamo, 1995) (27, 49, 47, 31, 37 yards)
5—Tim Rogers, Mississippi St. (24) vs. North Carolina St. (28) (Peach, Jan. 1, 1995) (37, 21, 29, 36, 30 yards)
5—Arden Czyzewski, Florida (28) vs. Notre Dame (39) (Sugar, 1992) (26, 24, 36, 37, 24 yards)
5—Jess Atkinson, Maryland (23) vs. Tennessee (30) (Florida Citrus, 1983) (18, 48, 31, 22, 26 yards)
4—Billy Bennett, Georgia (26) vs. Florida St. (13) (Sugar, 2003) (23, 42, 25, 35 yards)
4—Luke Phillips, Oklahoma St. (33) vs. Southern Miss. (23) (Houston, 2002) (46, 52, 29, 23 yards)
4—Drew Dunning, Washington St. (33) vs. Purdue (27) (Sun, 2001) (47, 34, 30, 37 yards)
4—Nate Kaeding, Iowa (19) vs. Texas Tech (16) (Alamo, 2001) (36, 31, 46, 47 yards)
4—Kevin Miller, East Caro. (61) vs. Marshall (64) (2 ot) (GMAC, 2001) (25, 22, 32, 37 yards)
4—Travis Forney, Penn St. (26) vs. Kentucky (14) (Outback, 1999) (43, 26, 21, 25)
4—Chad Holcomb, East Caro. (19) vs. Stanford (13) (Liberty, 1995) (46, 26, 41, 34 yards)
4—Kanon Parkman, Georgia (27) vs. Virginia (34) (Peach, Dec. 30, 1995) (36, 37, 20, 42 yards)
4—Scott Bentley, Florida St. (18) vs. Nebraska (16) (Orange, 1994) (34, 25, 39, 22 yards)
4—Tim Lashar, Oklahoma (25) vs. Penn St. (10) (Orange, 1986) (26, 31, 21, 22 yards)
4—(D) Todd Gregoire, Wisconsin (19) vs. Kentucky (20) (Hall of Fame, 1984) (40, 27, 20, 40 yards)
4—David Hardy, Texas A&M (33) vs. Oklahoma St. (16) (Independence, 1981) (33, 32, 50, 18 yards)
4—Paul Woodside, West Virginia (26) vs. Florida (6) (Peach, Dec. 31, 1981) (35, 42, 49, 24 yards)
4—Bob Lucchesi, Missouri (19) vs. Southern Miss. (17) (Tangerine, 1981) (45, 41, 30, 28 yards)
4—Dale Castro, Maryland (20) vs. Florida (35) (Tangerine, 1980) (35, 27, 27, 43 yards)
4—Paul Rogers, Nebraska (45) vs. Georgia (6) (Sun, 1969) (50, 32, 42, 37 yards, all in 1st quarter)
4—Tim Davis, Alabama (12) vs. Mississippi (7) (Sugar, 1964) (31, 46, 22, 48 yards)

MOST EXTRA-POINT KICK ATTEMPTS
9—Josh Brown, Nebraska (66) vs. Northwestern (17) (Alamo, 2000) (9 made)
9—Neil Rackers, Illinois (63) vs. Virginia (21) (Micronpc.com, 1999) (9 made)
9—Layne Talbot, Texas A&M (65) vs. Brigham Young (14) (Holiday, 1990) (9 made)
9—Bobby Luna, Alabama (61) vs. Syracuse (6) (Orange, 1953) (7 made)
9—(D) James Weaver, Centre (63) vs. TCU (7) (Fort Worth Classic, 1921) (9 made)
8—Jeff Chandler, Florida (56) vs. Maryland (23) (Orange, 2002) (8 made)
8—Jeremy Aldrich, Colorado (62) vs. Boston College (28) (Insight.com, 1999) (8 made)
8—Cary Blanchard, Oklahoma St. (62) vs. Wyoming (14) (Holiday, 1988) (8 made)
8—Ken Crots, Toledo (56) vs. Davidson (33) (Tangerine, 1969) (8 made)
7—Aaron Hunt, Clemson (49) vs. Louisiana Tech (24) (Humanitarian, 2001) (7 made)

7—Kevin Miller, East Caro. (61) vs. Marshall (64) (2 ot) (GMAC, 2001) (7 made)
7—Martin Gramatica, Kansas St. (54) vs. Colorado St. (21) (Holiday, 1995) (6 made)
7—Tony Rogers, Texas Tech (55) vs. Air Force (41) (Copper, 1995) (7 made)
7—Cole Ford, Southern California (55) vs. Texas Tech (14) (Cotton, 1995) (7 made)
7—Scott Blanton, Oklahoma (48) vs. Virginia (14) (Gator, Dec. 29, 1991) (6 made)
7—(D) Barry Belli, Fresno St. (51) vs. Bowling Green (7) (California, 1985) (7 made)
7—(D) Tom Nichol, Iowa (55) vs. Texas (17) (Freedom, 1984) (7 made)
7—Juan Cruz, Arizona St. (49) vs. Missouri (35) (Fiesta, 1972) (7 made)
7—Ron Sewell, North Carolina St. (49) vs. West Virginia (13) (Peach, 1972) (7 made)
7—Don Ekstrand, Arizona St. (48) vs. North Carolina (26) (Peach, 1970) (6 made)
7—Bill McMillan, Houston (49) vs. Miami (Ohio) (21) (Tangerine, 1962) (7 made)
7—Jesse Whittenton, UTEP (47) vs. Florida St. (20) (Sun, 1955) (5 made)
7—Jim Brieske, Michigan (49) vs. UCLA (0) (Rose, 1948) (7 made)
7—(D) Pat Bailey, Hardin-Simmons (49) vs. Wichita St. (12) (Camellia, 1948) (7 made)

MOST EXTRA-POINT KICKS MADE
9—Josh Brown, Nebraska (66) vs. Northwestern (17) (Alamo, 2000) (9 attempts)
9—Neil Rackers, Illinois (63) vs. Virginia (21) (Micronpc.com, 1999) (9 attempts)
9—Layne Talbot, Texas A&M (65) vs. Brigham Young (14) (Holiday, 1990) (9 attempts)
9—(D) James Weaver, Centre (63) vs. TCU (7) (Fort Worth Classic, 1921) (9 attempts)
8—Jeff Chandler, Florida (56) vs. Maryland (23) (Orange, 2002) (8 attempts)
8—Jeremy Aldrich, Colorado (62) vs. Boston College (28) (Insight.com, 1999)
  (8 attempts)
8—Cary Blanchard, Oklahoma St. (62) vs. Wyoming (14) (Holiday, 1988) (8 attempts)
8—Ken Crots, Toledo (56) vs. Davidson (33) (Tangerine, 1969) (8 attempts)
7—Aaron Hunt, Clemson (49) vs. Louisiana Tech (24) (Humanitarian, 2001) (7 attempts)
7—Kevin Miller, East Caro. (61) vs. Marshall (64) (2 ot) (GMAC, 2001) (7 attempts)
7—Tony Rogers, Texas Tech (55) vs. Air Force (41) (Copper, 1995) (7 attempts)
7—Cole Ford, Southern California (55) vs. Texas Tech (14) (Cotton, 1995) (7 attempts)
7—(D) Barry Belli, Fresno St. (51) vs. Bowling Green (7) (California, 1985) (7 attempts)
7—(D) Tom Nichol, Iowa (55) vs. Texas (17) (Freedom, 1984) (7 attempts)
7—Juan Cruz, Arizona St. (49) vs. Missouri (35) (Fiesta, 1972) (7 attempts)
7—Ron Sewell, North Carolina St. (49) vs. West Virginia (13) (Peach, 1972)
  (7 attempts)
7—Bill McMillan, Houston (49) vs. Miami (Ohio) (21) (Tangerine, 1962) (7 attempts)
7—Bobby Luna, Alabama (61) vs. Syracuse (6) (Orange, 1953) (9 attempts)
7—Jim Brieske, Michigan (49) vs. UCLA (0) (Rose, 1948) (7 attempts)
7—(D) Pat Bailey, Hardin-Simmons (49) vs. Wichita St. (12) (Camellia, 1948) (7 attempts)

MOST POINTS BY A KICKER
19—Kevin Miller, East Caro. (61) vs. Marshall (64) (2 ot) (GMAC, 2001) (4 FGs, 7
  PATs)
17—Dan Nystrom, Minnesota (29) vs. Arkansas (14) (Music City, 2002) (5 FGs, 2 PATs)
16—Kyle Bryant, Texas A&M (22) vs. Michigan (20) (Alamo, 1995) (5 FGs, 1 PAT)
16—Tim Rogers, Mississippi St. (24) vs. North Carolina St. (28) (Peach, Jan. 1, 1995)
  (5 FGs, 1 PAT)
16—Arden Czyzewski, Florida (28) vs. Notre Dame (39) (Sugar, 1992) (5 FGs, 1 PAT)
15—Sandro Sciortino, Boston College (51) vs. Toledo (25) (Motor City, 2002) (3 FGs,
  6 PATs)
15—Luke Phillips, Oklahoma St. (33) vs. Southern Miss. (23) (Houston, 2002) (4 FGs, 3
  PATs)
15—Drew Dunning, Washington St. (33) vs. Purdue (27) (Sun, 2001) (4 FGs, 3 PATs)
15—(D) Jeremy Aldrich, Colorado (51) vs. Oregon (43) (Aloha, 1998) (3 FGs, 6 PATs)
15—Jess Atkinson, Maryland (23) vs. Tennessee (30) (Florida Citrus, 1983) (5 FGs)
15—David Hardy, Texas A&M (33) vs. Oklahoma St. (16) (Independence, 1981)
  (4 FGs, 3 PATs)
15—Paul Rogers, Nebraska (45) vs. Georgia (6) (John Hancock, 1969) (4 FGs, 3 PATs)
14—Billy Bennett, Georgia (26) vs. Florida St. (13) (Sugar, 2003) (4 FGs, 2 PATs)
14—Jeremy Aldrich, Colorado (62) vs. Boston College (28) (Insight.com, 1999)
  (2 FGs, 8 PATs)
14—Cary Blanchard, Oklahoma St. (62) vs. Wyoming (14) (Holiday, 1988) (2 FGs, 8
  PATs)
14—Paul Woodside, West Virginia (26) vs. Florida (6) (Peach, Dec. 31, 1981)
  (4 FGs, 2 PATs)
13—Nate Kaeding, Iowa (19) vs. Texas Tech (16) (Alamo, 2001) (4 FGs, 1 PATs)
13—John Anderson, Washington (43) vs. Texas (47) (Holiday, 2001) (3 FGs, 4 PATs)
13—Chad Holcomb, East Caro. (19) vs. Stanford (13) (Liberty, 1995) (4 FGs, 1 PAT)
13—Kanon Parkman, Georgia (27) vs. Virginia (34) (Peach, Dec. 30, 1995) (4 FGs, 1
  PAT)
13—Tony Rogers, Texas Tech (55) vs. Air Force (41) (Copper, 1995) (2 FGs, 7 PATs)
13—Damon Shea, Nevada (37) vs. Toledo (40) (ot) (Las Vegas, 1995) (3 FGs, 4 PATs)
13—Cole Ford, Southern California (55) vs. Texas Tech (14) (Cotton, 1995) (2 FGs, 7
  PATs)
13—Tim Lashar, Oklahoma (25) vs. Penn. St. (10) (Orange, 1986) (4 FGs, 1 PAT)
13—John Lee, UCLA (39) vs. Miami (Fla.) (37) (Fiesta, 1985) (3 FGs, 4 PATs)
13—(D) Tom Nichol, Iowa (55) vs. Texas (17) (Freedom, 1984) (2 FGs, 7 PATs)
13—(D) Todd Gregoire, Wisconsin (19) vs. Kentucky (20) (Hall of Fame, 1984)
  (4 FGs, 1 PAT)
13—Bob Lucchesi, Missouri (19) vs. Southern Miss. (17) (Tangerine, 1981) (4 FGs, 1
  PAT)
13—Dave Johnson, Brigham Young (37) vs. Indiana (38) (Holiday, 1979) (3 FGs, 4
  PATs)
12—Nick Novak, Maryland (30) vs. Tennessee (3) (Peach, 2002) (3 FGs, 3 PATs)
12—Asen Asparuhov, Fresno St. (30) vs. Georgia Tech (21) (Silicon Valley, 2002) (3
  FGs, 3 PATs)
12—Josh Brown, Nebraska (66) vs. Northwestern (17) (Alamo, 2000) (1FG, 9 PATs)
12—Dan Nystrom, Minnesota (30) vs. North Carolina St. (38) (Micronpc.com, 2000) (3
  FGs, 3 PATs)

12—Billy Malashevich, Marshall (48) vs. Louisville (29) (Motor City, 1998) (2 FGs,
  6 PATs)
12—Scott Bentley, Florida St. (18) vs. Nebraska (16) (Orange, 1994) (4 FGs)
12—Chris Gardocki, Clemson (30) vs. Illinois (0) (Hall of Fame, 1991) (3 FGs, 3 PATs)
12—Ray Tarasi, Penn St. (50) vs. Brigham Young (39) (Holiday, 1989) (3 FGs, 3 PATs)
12—Luis Zendejas, Arizona St. (32) vs. Oklahoma (21) (Fiesta, 1983) (3 FGs, 3 PATs)
12—Dale Castro, Maryland (20) vs. Florida (35) (Tangerine, 1980) (4 FGs)
12—Nathan Ritter, North Carolina St. (30) vs. Pittsburgh (17) (Tangerine, 1978)
  (3 FGs, 3 PATs)
12—Buckey Berrey, Alabama (36) vs. UCLA (6) (Liberty, 1976) (3 FGs, 3 PATs)
12—Al Vitiello, Penn St. (30) vs. Texas (6) (Cotton, 1972) (3 FGs, 3 PATs)
12—Frank Fontes, Florida St. (38) vs. Arizona St. (45) (Fiesta, 1971) (3 FGs, 3 PATs)

Punting

MOST PUNTS
21—Everett Sweeney, Michigan (49) vs. Stanford (0) (Rose, 1902)
16—Lem Pratt, New Mexico St. (14) vs. Hardin-Simmons (14) (Sun, 1936) (38.4 average)
14—Sammy Baugh, TCU (3) vs. LSU (2) (Sugar, 1936)
13—Hugh Keeney, Rice (8) vs. Tennessee (0) (Orange, 1947)
13—N.A. Keithley, Tulsa (6) vs. Texas Tech (0) (Sun, 1942) (37.0 average)
13—Hugh McCullough, Oklahoma (0) vs. Tennessee (17) (Orange, 1939) (40.6 average)
13—Tyler, Hardin-Simmons (14) vs. New Mexico St. (14) (Sun, 1936) (45.2 average)
13—(D) Tom Murphy, Arkansas (7) vs. Centenary (La.) (7) (Dixie Classic, 1934) (44.0 average)
12—Mitch Berger, Colorado (25) vs. Alabama (30) (Blockbuster, 1991) (41.0 average)
12—Bob Parsons, Penn St. (10) vs. Missouri (3) (Orange, 1970) (42.6 average)
12—Jim Callahan, Texas Tech (0) vs. Tulsa (6) (Sun, 1942) (43.0 average)
12—Mike Palm, Penn St. (3) vs. Southern California (14) (Rose, 1923)

HIGHEST AVERAGE PER PUNT
(Minimum 5 Punts)
53.8—Mat McBriar, Hawaii (28) vs. Tulane (36) (Hawaii, 2002) (5 for 269)
52.7—Des Koch, Southern California (7) vs. Wisconsin (0) (Rose, 1953) (7 for 369)
  (adjusted to current statistical rules)
52.4—Mike Sochko, Maryland (21) vs. Houston (30) (Cotton, 1977) (5 for 262)
52.0—Nick Gallery, Iowa (27) vs. Texas Tech (0) (Alamo, 1996) (5 for 260)
51.5—Nick Pietsch, Colorado (51) vs. Oregon (43) (Aloha, 1998) (6 for 309)
51.0—Chris Clauss, Penn St. (10) vs. Clemson (35) (Florida Citrus, 1988) (5 for 255)
50.2—Jose Arroyo, Oregon (17) vs. Wake Forest (38) (Seattle, 2002) (6 for 301)
50.2—Curtis Head, Marshall (38) vs. Louisville (15) (GMAC, 2002) (6 for 301)
50.0—Dana Moore, Mississippi St. (17) vs. Nebraska (31) (Sun, 1980) (5 for 250)
49.8—Joey Biasatti, TCU (9) vs. Texas A&M (28) (Galleryfurniture.com, 2001) (6 for
  299)
49.3—Damon Duval, Auburn (10) vs. North Carolina (16) (Peach, 2001) (9 for 444)
49.3—Chris McInally, Clemson (0) vs. Syracuse (41) (Gator, 1996) (6 for 296)
49.2—(D) Mark Simon, Air Force (24) vs. Texas (16) (Bluebonnet, 1985) (11 for 541)
49.2—Allen Meacham, Arkansas (3) vs. UCLA (17) (Cotton, 1989) (6 for 295)
49.1—Adam Wulfeck, Cincinnati (16) vs. Toledo (23) (Motor City, 2001) (7 for 344)
49.0—Jim DiGuilio, Indiana (24) vs. Baylor (0) (Copper, 1991) (6 for 294)
49.0—(D) Dana Moore, Mississippi St. (10) vs. Kansas (0) (Hall of Fame, 1981) (9 for
  441)
48.8—Glenn Beard, UTEP (23) vs. Boise St. (38) (Humanitarian, 2000) (5 for 244)
48.4—Ryan Plackemeier, Wake Forest (38) vs. Oregon (17) (Seattle, 2002) (5 for 242)
48.3—Jesse Sowards, Brigham Young (3) vs. Marshall (21) (Motor City, 1999) (7 for
  338)
48.2—Dan Dyke, Georgia Tech (14) vs. LSU (28) (Peach, 2000) (5 for 241)
48.1—Robby Stevenson, Florida (52) vs. Florida St. (20) (Sugar, 1997) (7 for 337)
48.1—Brent Bartholomew, Ohio St. (14) vs. Tennessee (20) (Florida Citrus, 1996) (7 for
  337)
48.0—Dan Eichloff, Kansas (23) vs. Brigham Young (20) (Aloha, 1992) (8 for 384)

Punt Returns

MOST PUNT RETURNS
9—Buzy Rosenberg, Georgia (7) vs. North Carolina (3) (Gator, Dec. 31, 1971)
  (54 yards)
9—Paddy Driscoll, Great Lakes (17) vs. Mare Island (0) (Rose, 1919) (115 yards)
8—Thomas Lewis, Indiana (20) vs. Virginia Tech (45) (Independence, 1993) (58 yards)
7—Michael Waddell, North Carolina (16) vs. Auburn (10) (Peach, 2001) (66 yards)
7—Roderick Hood, Auburn (10) vs. North Carolina (16) (Peach, 2001) (26 yards)
7—Curtis Fagan, Oklahoma (10) vs. Arkansas (3) (Cotton, 2002) (20 yards)
6—Dale Carter, Tennessee (17) vs. Penn St. (42) (Fiesta, 1992)
6—Joey Smith, Louisville (34) vs. Alabama (7) (Fiesta, 1991) (35 yards)
6—David Palmer, Alabama (30) vs. Colorado (25) (Blockbuster, 1991) (74 yards)
6—(D) Hesh Colar, San Jose St. (48) vs. Central Mich. (24) (California, 1990)
6—David Kintigh, Miami (Fla.) (10) vs. Penn St. (14) (Fiesta, 1987) (32 yards)
6—(D) Eric Metcalf, Texas (16) vs. Air Force (24) (Bluebonnet, 1985) (49 yards)
6—Vai Sikahema, Brigham Young (7) vs. Ohio St. (10) (Florida Citrus, 1985)
6—(D) Ray Horton, Washington (21) vs. Maryland (20) (Aloha, 1982) (28 yards)
6—Bill Gribble, Washington St. (36) vs. Brigham Young (38) (Holiday, 1981) (39 yards)
6—Johnny Rodgers, Nebraska (38) vs. Alabama (6) (Orange, 1972) (136 yards)
6—Rick Sygar, Michigan (34) vs. Oregon St. (7) (Rose, 1965) (50 yards)

6—Billy Hair, Clemson (0) vs. Miami (Fla.) (14) (Gator, 1952) (73 yards)
6—Don Zimmerman, Tulane (12) vs. Southern California (21) (Rose, 1932)

MOST PUNT RETURN YARDS

136—Johnny Rodgers, Nebraska (38) vs. Alabama (6) (Orange, 1972) (6 returns)
122—George Fleming, Washington (44) vs. Wisconsin (8) (Rose, 1960) (3 returns)
122—Bobby Kellogg, Tulane (13) vs. Texas A&M (14) (Sugar, 1940) (5 returns)
115—Paddy Driscoll, Great Lakes (17) vs. Mare Island (0) (Rose, 1919) (9 returns)
110—James Henry, Southern Miss. (38) vs. UTEP (18) (Independence, 1988)
  (2 returns, touchdowns of 65 and 45 yards)
106—Kevin Baugh, Penn St. (27) vs. Georgia (23) (Sugar, 1983) (5 returns)
106—Steve Holden, Arizona St. (45) vs. Florida St. (38) (Fiesta, 1971) (3 returns)
104—Leo Daniels, Texas A&M (21) vs. Alabama (29) (Cotton, 1942) (5 returns)
103—Jon Staggers, Missouri (3) vs. Penn St. (10) (Orange, 1970)
89—Lawrence Williams, Texas Tech (28) vs. North Carolina (32) (Sun, 1972)
  (5 returns)
88—Ben Kelly, Colorado (62) vs. Boston College (28) (Insight.com, 1999) (1 return)
87—Vai Sikahema, Brigham Young (46) vs. Southern Methodist (45) (Holiday, 1980) (2
  returns)
86—Bobby Majors, Tennessee (34) vs. Air Force (13) (Sugar, 1971) (4 returns)
86—Aramis Dandoy, Southern California (7) vs. Ohio St. (20) (Rose, 1955) (1 return)
82—Marcus Wall, North Carolina (31) vs. Texas (35) (Sun, 1994) (1 return)
82—Willie Drewrey, West Virginia (12) vs. Florida St. (31) (Gator, 1982) (1 return)
80—(D) Gary Anderson, Arkansas (34) vs. Tulane (15) (Hall of Fame, 1980) (2 returns)
80—Cecil Ingram, Alabama (61) vs. Syracuse (6) (Orange, 1953) (1 return)

HIGHEST PUNT RETURN AVERAGE
(Minimum 3 Returns)

40.7—George Fleming, Washington (44) vs. Wisconsin (8) (Rose, 1960) (3 for 122)
35.3—Steve Holden, Arizona St. (45) vs. Florida St. (38) (Fiesta, 1971) (3 for 106)
24.4—Bobby Kellogg, Tulane (13) vs. Texas A&M (14) (Sugar, 1940) (5 for 122)
24.0—Shayne Wasden, Auburn (31) vs. Ohio St. (14) (Hall of Fame, 1990) (3 for 72)
22.7—Johnny Rodgers, Nebraska (38) vs. Alabama (6) (Orange, 1972) (6 for 136)
21.5—Bobby Majors, Tennessee (34) vs. Air Force (13) (Sugar, 1971) (4 for 86)
21.0—Tiki Barber, Virginia (34) vs. Georgia (27) (Peach, Dec. 30, 1995) (3 for 63)
21.0—(D) Brian Williams, Kentucky (16) vs. West Virginia (20) (Hall of Fame, 1983) (3
  for 63)
20.8—Leo Daniels, Texas A&M (21) vs. Alabama (29) (Cotton, 1942) (5 for 104)
19.5—(D) Zippy Morocco, Georgia (20) vs. Texas A&M (40) (Presidential Cup, 1950)
  (4 for 78)
19.3—Dave Liegi, Nebraska (14) vs. Houston (17) (Cotton, 1980) (3 for 58)
19.0—Gary Moss, Georgia (10) vs. Texas (9) (Cotton, 1984) (3 for 57)

Kickoff Returns

MOST KICKOFF RETURNS

8—Todd Howard, Michigan (17) vs. Tennessee (45) (Florida Citrus, 2002) (125 yards)
7—Dale Carter, Tennessee (17) vs. Penn St. (42) (Fiesta, 1992) (132 yards)
7—(D) Jeff Sydner, Hawaii (13) vs. Michigan St. (33) (Aloha, 1989) (174 yards)
7—Homer Jones, Brigham Young (37) vs. Indiana (38) (Holiday, 1979) (126 yards)
6—Koren Robinson, North Carolina St. (38) vs. Minnesota (30) (Micronpc.com, 2000)
  (151 yards)
6—Mike Rigell, Brigham Young (27) vs. Tulane (41) (Liberty, 1998) (220 yards)
6—(D) Deltha O'Neal, California (38) vs. Navy (42) (Aloha, 1996) (186 yards)
6—Dave Beazley, Northwestern (28) vs. Tennessee (48) (Florida Citrus, 1997) (137
  yards)
6—Eugene Napoleon, West Virginia (21) vs. Notre Dame (34) (Fiesta, 1989) (107
  yards)
6—Tim Brown, Notre Dame (10) vs. Texas A&M (35) (Cotton, 1988) (129 yards)
6—Leroy Thompson, Penn St. (10) vs. Clemson (35) (Florida Citrus, 1988)
6—(D) Anthony Roberson, Air Force (28) vs. Arizona St. (33) (Freedom, 1987) (109
  yards)
6—Casey Tiumalu, Brigham Young (17) vs. Ohio St. (47) (Holiday, 1982) (116 yards)
6—Brian Nelson, Texas Tech (17) vs. Florida St. (40) (Tangerine, 1977) (143 yards)
6—Wally Henry, UCLA (6) vs. Alabama (36) (Liberty, 1976)
6—Steve Williams, Alabama (6) vs. Nebraska (38) (Orange, 1972)
6—Mike Fink, Missouri (35) vs. Arizona St. (49) (Fiesta, 1972) (203 yards)

MOST KICKOFF RETURN YARDS

220—Mike Rigell, Brigham Young (27) vs. Tulane (41) (Liberty, 1998) (6 returns)
203—Mike Fink, Missouri (35) vs. Arizona St. (49) (Fiesta, 1972) (6 returns)
186—(D) Deltha O'Neal, California (38) vs. Navy (42) (Aloha, 1996) (6 returns)
178—Al Hoisch, UCLA (14) vs. Illinois (45) (Rose, 1947) (4 returns)
174—(D) Jeff Sydner, Hawaii (13) vs. Michigan St. (33) (Aloha, 1989) (7 returns)
169—C.J. Jones, Iowa (17) vs. Southern California (38) (Orange, 2003) (4 returns)
169—Jerome Thomas, Idaho (42) vs. Southern Miss. (35) (Humanitarian, 1998) (5
  returns)
166—Willie Jones, Iowa St. (30) vs. Georgia Tech (31) (Liberty, 1972) (4 returns)
154—(D) Martin Mitchell, Tulane (7) vs. Houston (47) (Bluebonnet, 1973) (5 returns)
154—Dave Lowery, Brigham Young (21) vs. Oklahoma St. (49) (Tangerine, 1976)
  (4 returns)
151—Koren Robinson, North Carolina St. (38) vs. Minnesota (30) (Micronpc.com,
  2000) (6 returns)

148—Earl Allen, Houston (28) vs. Boston College (45) (Cotton, 1985) (4 returns)
147—Carlos Snow, Ohio St. (17) vs. Syracuse (24) (Hall of Fame, 1992) (4 returns)
144—Clint Johnson, Notre Dame (39) vs. Florida (28) (Sugar, 1992) (5 returns)
143—Barry Smith, Florida St. (38) vs. Arizona St. (45) (Fiesta, 1971) (5 returns)
143—Brian Nelson, Texas Tech (17) vs. Florida St. (40) (Tangerine, 1977) (6 returns)

HIGHEST KICKOFF RETURN AVERAGE
(Minimum 2 Returns)

60.5—(D) Bob Smith, Texas A&M (40) vs. Georgia (20) (Presidential Cup, 1950)
  (2 for 121)
60.0—Jerome Pathon, Washington (21) vs. Colorado (33) (Holiday, 1996) (2 for 120)
58.0—Eddie Kennison, LSU (45) vs. Michigan St. (26) (Independence, 1995) (2 for 116)
57.5—Pete Panuska, Tennessee (27) vs. Maryland (28) (Sun, 1984) (2 for 115)
55.5—Todd Snyder, Ohio (42) vs. Richmond (49) (Tangerine, 1968) (2 for 111)
46.7—(D) Cal Beck, Utah (16) vs. Arizona (13) (Freedom, 1994) (3 for 140)
44.5—Al Hoisch, UCLA (14) vs. Illinois (45) (Rose, 1947) (4 for 178)
43.7—Larry Key, Florida St. (40) vs. Texas Tech (17) (Tangerine, 1977) (3 for 131)
43.3—Victor Ike, Texas (30) vs. Oregon (35) (Holiday, 2000) (3 for 130)
42.3—C.J. Jones, Iowa (17) vs. Southern California (38) (Orange, 2003) (4 for 169)
41.5—Willie Jones, Iowa St. (30) vs. Georgia Tech (31) (Liberty, 1972) (4 for 166)
41.0—Kevin Williams, Miami (Fla.) (46) vs. Texas (3) (Cotton, 1991) (2 for 82)
40.3—(D) Willie Gault, Tennessee (28) vs. Wisconsin (21) (Garden State, 1981)
  (3 for 121)
39.0—Damon Dunn, Stanford (13) vs. East Caro. (19) (Liberty, 1995) (3 for 117)
37.0—Earl Allen, Houston (28) vs. Boston College (45) (Cotton, 1985) (4 for 148)
36.8—Carlos Snow, Ohio St. (17) vs. Syracuse (24) (Hall of Fame, 1992) (4 for 147)
36.7—Mike Rigell, Brigham Young (27) vs. Tulane (41) (Liberty, 1998) (6 for 220)
33.8—Mike Fink, Missouri (35) vs. Arizona St. (49) (Fiesta, 1972) (6 for 203)
33.8—Demetrius Allen, Virginia (34) vs. Georgia (27) (Peach, Dec. 30, 1995)
  (4 for 135)
33.8—Jerome Thomas, Idaho (42) vs. Southern Miss. (35) (Humanitarian, 1998)
  (5 for 169)
33.2—Hudhaifa Ismaeli, Northwestern (32) vs. Southern California (41) (Rose, 1996) (5
  for 166)
33.0—Derrick Mason, Michigan St. (26) vs. LSU (45) (Independence, 1995) (4 for 132)
32.6—(D) Jim McElroy, UCLA (30) vs. Kansas (51) (Aloha, 1995) (5 for 163)
32.5—Reidel Anthony, Florida (24) vs. Nebraska (62) (Fiesta, 1996) (6 for 195)
32.0—Harry Jones, Kentucky (20) vs. TCU (7) (Cotton, 1952) (2 for 64)
32.0—Jim Brown, Syracuse (27) vs. TCU (28) (Cotton, 1957) (3 for 96)
32.0—(D) Eric Alozie, Washington (34) vs. Florida (7) (Freedom, 1989) (2 for 64)

Interceptions

MOST INTERCEPTIONS MADE

4—Jim Dooley, Miami (Fla.) (14) vs. Clemson (0) (Gator, 1952)
4—(D) Manuel Aja, Arizona St. (21) vs. Xavier (Ohio) (33) (Salad, 1950)
3—Michael Brooks, North Carolina St. (28) vs. Iowa (23) (Peach, Dec. 31, 1988)
3—Bud Hebert, Oklahoma (24) vs. Florida St. (7) (Orange, 1980)
3—Louis Campbell, Arkansas (13) vs. Tennessee (14) (Liberty, 1971)
3—Bud McClinton, Auburn (34) vs. Arizona (10) (Sun, 1968)
3—(D) Les Derrick, Texas (19) vs. Mississippi (0) (Bluebonnet, 1966)
3—(D) Tommy Luke, Mississippi (0) vs. Texas (19) (Bluebonnet, 1966)
3—Jerry Cook, Texas (12) vs. Mississippi (7) (Cotton, 1962)
3—Ray Brown, Mississippi (39) vs. Texas (7) (Sugar, 1958)
3—Bill Paulman, Stanford (7) vs. Southern Methodist (0) (Rose, 1936)
3—Shy Huntington, Oregon (14) vs. Pennsylvania (0) (Rose, 1917)

MOST INTERCEPTION RETURN YARDAGE

148—Elmer Layden, Notre Dame (27) vs. Stanford (10) (Rose, 1925) (2 interceptions)
95—Marcus Washington, Colorado (38) vs. Oregon (6) (Cotton, 1996) (1 interception)
94—David Baker, Oklahoma (48) vs. Duke (21) (Orange, 1958) (1 interception)
91—Donald Strickland, Colorado (28) vs. Wisconsin (31) (ot) (Alamo, 2002) (1 interception)
90—Norm Beal, Missouri (21) vs. Navy (14) (Orange, 1961) (1 interception)
90—Charlie Brembs, South Carolina (14) vs. Wake Forest (26) (Gator, 1946) (1 interception)
89—Al Hudson, Miami (Fla.) (13) vs. Holy Cross (6) (Orange, 1946) (1 interception)
88—Dwayne Rudd, Alabama (17) vs. Michigan (14) (Outback, 1997) (1 interception)
81—Gary Moss, Georgia (24) vs. Boston College (27) (Hall of Fame, 1986) (1 interception)
80—(D) Russ Meredith, West Virginia (21) vs. Gonzaga (13) (San Diego East-West
  Christmas Classic, 1922) (1 interception)
79—Michael Jordan, Tulane (41) vs. Brigham Young (27) (Liberty, 1998) (1 interception)
77—George Halas, Great Lakes (17) vs. Mare Island (0) (Rose, 1919) (1 interception)
75—Hugh Morrow, Alabama (26) vs. Duke (29) (Sugar, 1945) (1 interception)
73—Jason David, Washington St. (33) vs. Purdue (27) (Sun, 2001) (2 interceptions)
72—(D) Alton Montgomery, Houston (22) vs. Washington St. (24) (Aloha, 1988) (1 interception)
71—Bruce Thornton, Georgia (26) vs. Florida St. (13) (Sugar, 2003) (1 interception)
70—Robert Bailey, Mississippi (34) vs. Virginia Tech (17) (Liberty, 1968) (1 interception)
70—(D) Mel McGaha, Arkansas (21) vs. William & Mary (19) (Dixie, 1948) (1 interception)
69—Chris Carter, Texas (35) vs. North Carolina (31) (Sun, 1994) (1 interception)

69—Howard Ehler, Florida St. (36) vs. Oklahoma (19) (Gator, Jan. 2, 1965) (1 interception)

67—John Matsock, Michigan St. (28) vs. UCLA (20) (Rose, 1954) (2 interceptions)

All-Purpose Yards

(Includes All Runs From Scrimmage, Pass Receptions and All Returns)

MOST ALL-PURPOSE PLAYS
(Must Have at Least One Reception or Return)

47—Tellis Redmon, Minnesota (30) vs. North Carolina St. (38) (Micronpc.com, 2000) (42 rush, 3 receptions, 2 punt returns)

47—(D) Ron Jackson, Tulsa (28) vs. San Diego St. (17) (Freedom, 1991) (46 rush, 1 reception)

46—Errict Rhett, Florida (27) vs. North Carolina St. (10) (Gator, 1992) (39 rush, 7 receptions)

42—(D) Blake Ezor, Michigan St. (33) vs. Hawaii (13) (Aloha, 1989) (41 rush, 1 reception)

41—Terrell Fletcher, Wisconsin (34) vs. Duke (20) (Hall of Fame, 1995) (39 rush, 1 reception, 1 kickoff return)

40—LaDainian Tomlinson, TCU (28) vs. East Caro. (14) (Mobile Alabama, 1999) (36 rush, 4 receptions)

39—(D) Marshall Faulk, San Diego St. (17) vs. Tulsa (28) (Freedom, 1991) (30 rush, 9 receptions)

38—Ronnie Brown, Auburn (13) vs. Penn St. (9) (Capital One, 2003) (37 rush, 1 reception)

38—Rodney Davis, Fresno St. (30) vs. Georgia Tech (21) (Silicon Valley, 2002) (37 rush, 1 reception)

37—William Green, Boston College (20) vs. Georgia (16) (Music City, 2001) (35 rush, 2 receptions)

37—Cecil Sapp, Colorado St. (22) vs. Louisville (17) (Liberty, 2000) (36 rush, 1 reception)

37—Ja'Mar Toombs, Texas A&M (41) vs. Mississippi St. (43) (ot) (Independence, 2000) (35 rush, 2 receptions)

37—Wasean Tait, Toledo (40) vs. Nevada (37) (ot) (Las Vegas, 1995) (31 rush, 6 receptions)

37—Sherman Williams, Alabama (24) vs. Ohio St. (17) (Florida Citrus, 1995) (27 rush, 8 receptions, 2 kickoff returns)

37—O.J. Simpson, Southern California (16) vs. Ohio St. (27) (Rose, 1969) (28 rush, 8 receptions, 1 kickoff return)

36—Anthony Thomas, Michigan (31) vs. Auburn (28) (Florida Citrus, 2001) (32 rush, 4 receptions)

36—Rondell Mealey, LSU (27) vs. Notre Dame (9) (Independence, 1997) (34 rush, 2 kickoff returns)

36—Thurman Thomas, Oklahoma St. (35) vs. West Virginia (33) (John Hancock Sun, 1987) (33 rush, 6 receptions)

36—Bob Anderson, Colorado (47) vs. Alabama (33) (Liberty, 1969) (35 rush, 1 kickoff return)

35—Mike Anderson, Utah (17) vs. Fresno St. (16) (Las Vegas, 1999) (34 rush, 1 reception)

35—Ricky Williams, Texas (38) vs. Mississippi St. (11) (Cotton, 1999) (30 rush, 5 receptions)

35—Ricky Ervins, Southern California (17) vs. Michigan (10) (Rose, 1990) (30 rush, 5 receptions)

35—(D) Eric Bieniemy, Colorado (17) vs. Brigham Young (20) (Freedom, 1988) (33 rush, 2 receptions)

MOST ALL-PURPOSE YARDS GAINED
(Must Have at Least One Reception or Return)

359—Sherman Williams, Alabama (24) vs. Ohio St. (17) (Florida Citrus, 1995) (166 rush, 155 receptions, 38 kickoff returns)

318—Rodney Wright, Fresno St. (35) vs. Michigan St. (44) (Silicon Valley, 2001) (19 rush, 299 receptions)

303—(D) Bob Smith, Texas A&M (40) vs. Georgia (20) (Presidential Cup, 1950) (160 rush, 22 receptions, 121 kickoff returns)

283—Andre Coleman, Kansas St. (52) vs. Wyoming (17) (Copper, 1993) (7 rush, 144 receptions, 73 punt returns, 54 kickoff returns)

278—Byron Hanspard, Texas Tech (55) vs. Air Force (41) (Copper, 1995) (260 rush, 18 receptions)

277—Bob Anderson, Colorado (47) vs. Alabama (33) (Liberty, 1969) (254 rush, 23 kickoff returns)

276—O.J. Simpson, Southern California (16) vs. Ohio St. (27) (Rose, 1969) (171 rush, 85 receptions, 20 kickoff returns)

272—Pat Johnson, Oregon (41) vs. Air Force (13) (Las Vegas, 1997) (169 receptions, 49 punt returns, 54 kickoff returns)

270—Charles Rogers, Michigan St. (44) vs. Fresno St. (35) (Silicon Valley, 2001) (270 receptions)

269—Mike Anderson, Utah (17) vs. Fresno St. (16) (Las Vegas, 1999) (254 rush, 15 receptions)

256—Terrell Fletcher, Wisconsin (34) vs. Duke (20) (Hall of Fame, 1995) (241 rush, 8 receptions, 7 kickoff returns)

256—Rondell Mealey, LSU (27) vs. Notre Dame (9) (Independence, 1997) (222 rush, 34 kickoff returns)

248—Ricky Williams, Texas (38) vs. Mississippi St. (11) (Cotton, 1999) (203 rush, 45 receptions)

247—(D) Wilford White, Arizona St. (21) vs. Miami (Ohio) (34) (Salad, 1951) (106 rush, 87 receptions, 54 kickoff returns)

246—Ernie Jones, Indiana (22) vs. Tennessee (27) (Peach, 1988) (15 rush, 150 receptions, 81 kickoff returns)

246—Demetrius Allen, Virginia (34) vs. Georgia (27) (Peach, Dec. 30, 1995) (111 receiving, 135 kickoff returns)

244—Taylor Stubblefield, Purdue (27) vs. Washington St. (33) (Sun, 2001) (196 receptions, 48 kickoff returns)

242—Errict Rhett, Florida (27) vs. North Carolina St. (10) (Gator, 1992) (182 rush, 60 receptions)

239—Josh Reed, LSU (47) vs. Illinois (34) (Sugar, 2002) (239 receptions)

239—Tyrone Wheatley, Michigan (38) vs. Washington (31) (Rose, 1993) (235 rush, 4 receptions)

238—Wasean Tait, Toledo (40) vs. Nevada (37) (ot) (Las Vegas, 1995) (185 rush, 53 receptions)

237—Ahman Green, Nebraska (42) vs. Tennessee (17) (Orange, 1998) (206 rush, 31 receptions)

236—(D) Gary Anderson, Arkansas (34) vs. Tulane (15) (Hall of Fame, 1980) (156 rush, 80 punt returns)

234—Denero Marriott, Marshall (64) vs. East Caro. (61) (2 ot) (GMAC, 2001) (234 receptions)

230—Jamie Morris, Michigan (28) vs. Alabama (24) (Hall of Fame, 1987) (234 rush, -4 receptions)

228—Phillip Bobo, Washington St. (31) vs. Utah (28) (Copper, 1992) (16 rush, 212 receptions)

227—Marcus Wall, North Carolina (31) vs. Texas (35) (Sun, 1994) (30 rush, 82 receptions, 82 punt returns, 33 kickoff returns)

226—Andre Johnson, Miami (Fla.) (37) vs. Nebraska (14) (Rose, 2002) (199 receptions, 27 kickoff returns)

225—(D) Ron Jackson, Tulsa (28) vs. San Diego St. (17) (Freedom, 1991) (211 rush, 14 receptions)

223—Donny Anderson, Texas Tech (21) vs. Georgia Tech (31) (Gator, 1966) (85 rush, 138 receptions)

212—Troy Stradford, Boston College (45) vs. Houston (28) (Cotton, 1985) (196 rush, 16 receptions)

211—(D) Charles White, Southern California (47) vs. Texas A&M (28) (Bluebonnet, 1977) (186 rush, 25 receptions)

208—(D) Sheldon Canley, San Jose St. (48) vs. Central Mich. (24) (California, 1990) (164 rush, 44 receptions)

Defensive Statistics

MOST TOTAL TACKLES MADE
(Includes Assists)

31—Lee Roy Jordan, Alabama (17) vs. Oklahoma (0) (Orange, 1963)

22—Bubba Brown, Clemson (17) vs. Ohio St. (15) (Gator, 1978)

22—Gordy Ceresino, Stanford (24) vs. LSU (14) (Sun, Dec. 31, 1977)

20—Vada Murray, Michigan (10) vs. Southern California (17) (Rose, 1990)

20—(D) Gordy Ceresino, Stanford (25) vs. Georgia (22) (Bluebonnet, 1978)

18—Allen Stansberry, LSU (45) vs. Michigan St. (26) (Independence, 1995)

18—Ted Johnson, Colorado (41) vs. Notre Dame (24) (Fiesta, 1995)

18—Rod Smith, Notre Dame (39) vs. Florida (28) (Sugar, 1992)

18—Erick Anderson, Michigan (10) vs. Southern California (17) (Rose, 1990)

18—(D) Yepi Pauu, San Jose St. (27) vs. Eastern Mich. (30) (California, 1987)

18—Garland Rivers, Michigan (17) vs. Brigham Young (24) (Holiday, 1984)

18—(D) Terry Hubbard, Cal St. Fullerton (13) vs. Northern Ill. (20) (California, 1983)

18—(D) Don Turner, Fresno St. (29) vs. Bowling Green (28) (California, 1982)

18—Matt Millen, Penn St. (42) vs. Arizona St. (30) (Fiesta, 1977)

MOST SOLO TACKLES

18—Rod Smith, Notre Dame (39) vs. Florida (28) (Sugar, 1992)

17—Garland Rivers, Michigan (17) vs. Brigham Young (24) (Holiday, 1984)

15—Lynn Evans, Missouri (35) vs. Arizona St. (49) (Fiesta, 1972)

15—(D) Ken Norton Jr., UCLA (31) vs. Brigham Young (10) (Freedom, 1986)

15—Randy Neal, Virginia (35) vs. Boston College (31) (Carquest, 1994)

MOST TACKLES FOR LOSSES

6—LeMarcus McDonald, TCU (9) vs. Texas A&M (28) (galleryfurniture.com, 2001)

5—(D) Michael Jones, Colorado (17) vs. Brigham Young (20) (Freedom, 1988)

5—Jimmy Walker, Arkansas (10) vs. UCLA (10) (Fiesta, 1978)

4—Willie Blade, Mississippi St. (43) vs. Texas A&M (41) (ot) (Independence, 2000)

4—Eric Wilson, Michigan (31) vs. Auburn (28) (Florida Citrus, 2001)

4—Courtney Brown, Penn St. (26) vs. Kentucky (14) (Outback, 1999)

4—Sedrick Hodge, North Carolina (20) vs. San Diego St. (13) (Las Vegas, 1998)

4—Mike Pringley, North Carolina (20) vs. San Diego St. (13) (Las Vegas, 1998)

4—Chike Okeafor, Purdue (37) vs. Kansas St. (34) (Alamo, 1998)

4—Corey Terry, Tennessee (48) vs. Northwestern (28) (Florida Citrus, 1997)

4—(D) Clint Bruce, Navy (42) vs. California (38) (Aloha, 1996)

4—Montae Reagor, Texas Tech (0) vs. Iowa (27) (Alamo, 1996)

4—Reggie Garnett, Michigan St. (0) vs. Stanford (38) (Sun, 1996)

4—Matt Finkes, Ohio St. (14) vs. Tennessee (20) (Florida Citrus, 1996)

4—(D) Ken Norton Jr., UCLA (31) vs. Brigham Young (10) (Freedom, 1986)

3—Dat Nguyen, Texas A&M (14) vs. Ohio St. (24) (Sugar, 1999)

3—Cornelius Anthony, Texas A&M (14) vs. Ohio St. (24) (Sugar, 1999)

3—Eric Westmoreland, Tennessee (23) vs. Florida St. (16) (Fiesta, 1999)

3—Marc Matock, Southern California (19) vs. TCU (28) (Sun, 1998)
3—Kenny Smith, Alabama (7) vs. Virginia Tech (38) (Music City, 1998)
3—Chris Hoke, Brigham Young (27) vs. Tulane (41) (Liberty, 1998)
3—Raymone Lacey, TCU (28) vs. Southern California (19) (Sun, 1998)
3—James Hamilton, North Carolina (20) vs. West Virginia (13) (Gator, 1996)
3—Mike Vrabel, Ohio St. (14) vs. Tennessee (20) (Florida Citrus, 1996)
3—Nate Hemsley, Syracuse (41) vs. Clemson (0) (Gator, 1996)
3—Marcus Jones, North Carolina (20) vs. Arkansas (10) (Carquest, Dec. 30, 1995)
3—(D) Guy Boliaux, Wisconsin (21) vs. Tennessee (28) (Garden State, 1981)

MOST QUARTERBACK SACKS

6—Shay Muirbrook, Brigham Young (19) vs. Kansas St. (15) (Cotton, 1997)
4—Rusty Medearis, Miami (Fla.) (22) vs. Nebraska (0) (Orange, 1992)
4—Bobby Bell, Missouri (17) vs. Brigham Young (21) (Holiday, 1983)
3—Kalimba Edwards, South Carolina (24) vs. Ohio St. (7) (Outback, 2001)
3—Chike Okeafor, Purdue (37) vs. Kansas St. (34) (Alamo, 1998)
3—Andy Katzenmoyer, Ohio St. (20) vs. Arizona St. (17) (Rose, 1997)
3—Travis Ochs, Kansas St. (15) vs. Brigham Young (19) (Cotton, 1997)
3—Trevor Pryce, Clemson (7) vs. LSU (10) (Peach, 1996)
3—Jamie Sharper, Virginia (21) vs. Miami (Fla.) (31) (Carquest, 1996)
3—Mike Crawford, Nevada (18) vs. Ball St. (15) (Las Vegas, 1996)
3—Gabe Northern, LSU (45) vs. Michigan St. (26) (Independence, 1995)
3—James Gillyard, LSU (45) vs. Michigan St. (26) (Independence, 1995)
3—Dewayne Harris, Nebraska (24) vs. Miami (Fla.) (17) (Orange, 1995)
3—Trev Alberts, Nebraska (16) vs. Florida St. (18) (Orange, 1994)
3—(D) Alfred Williams, Colorado (17) vs. Brigham Young (20) (Freedom, 1988)
3—(D) Jim Wahler, UCLA (31) vs. Brigham Young (10) (Freedom, 1986)
3—James Mosley, Texas Tech (17) vs. Mississippi (20) (Independence, 1986)
3—(D) Ernie Barnes, Mississippi St. (10) vs. Kansas (0) (Hall of Fame, 1981)

FUMBLE RECOVERIES

2—Randall Brown, Ohio St. (17) vs. Alabama (24) (Florida Citrus, 1995)
2—(D) Michael Stewart, Fresno St. (51) vs. Bowling Green (7) (California, 1985)
2—Rod Kirby, Pittsburgh (7) vs. Arizona St. (28) (Fiesta, 1973)

BLOCKED KICKS

2—Bracey Walker, North Carolina (21) vs. Mississippi St. (17) (Peach, Jan. 2, 1993)
2—Carlton Williams, Pittsburgh (7) vs. Arizona St. (28) (Fiesta, 1973)

PASSES BROKEN UP

5—Dyshod Carter, Kansas St. (34) Purdue (37) (Alamo, 1998)
4—Chris Cummings, LSU (27) vs. Notre Dame (9) (Independence, 1997)
3—Sedrick Curry, Texas A&M (14) vs. Ohio St. (24) (Sugar, 1999)
3—Ahmed Plummer, Ohio St. (24) vs. Texas A&M (14) (Sugar, 1999)
3—(D) Damen Wheeler, Colorado (51) vs. Oregon (43) (Aloha, 1998)
3—Damion McIntosh, Kansas St. (34) vs. Purdue (37) (Alamo, 1998)
3—Kevin Hill, Idaho (42) vs. Southern Miss. (35) (Humanitarian, 1998)
3—Robert Williams, North Carolina (20) vs. West Virginia (13) (Gator, 1996)
3—Mark Tate, Penn St. (43) vs. Auburn (14) (Outback, 1996)
3—Kwame Ellis, Stanford (13) vs. East Caro. (19) (Liberty, 1995)
3—Mickey Dalton, Air Force (41) vs. Texas Tech (55) (Copper, 1995)
3—Barron Miles, Nebraska (24) vs. Miami (Fla.) (17) (Orange, 1995)
3—Percy Ellsworth, Virginia (20) vs. TCU (10) (Independence, 1994)
3—Sam McKiver, Virginia (20) vs. TCU (10) (Independence, 1994)
3—Tyrone Williams, Nebraska (16) vs. Florida St. (18) (Orange, 1994)
3—(D) John Herpin, Southern California (28) vs. Utah (21) (Freedom, 1993)
3—Demouy Williams, Washington (24) vs. Tulane (12) (Independence, 1987)

Team Record Lists

Only official records after 1937 are included. Prior records are included if able to be substantiated. Each team's score is in parentheses after the team name. Totals for each team in both-team records are in brackets after the team's score. The year listed is the actual (calendar) year the game was played; the date is included if the bowl was played twice (i.e., January and December) during one calendar year. The list also includes discontinued bowls, marked with (D). Bowls are listed by the name of the bowl at the time it was played: the first Hall of Fame Bowl (1977-85) was called the All-American Bowl in 1986-90; the second Hall of Fame Bowl (1986-95) is now called the Outback Bowl and is played in Tampa, Fla.; the Sun Bowl was called the John Hancock Bowl in 1989-93, the John Hancock Sun Bowl in 1987-88, and reverted to the Sun Bowl in 1994; the Blockbuster Bowl changed its name to the Carquest Bowl in 1993, to the Micronpc.com Bowl in 1998, to the Tangerine Bowl in 2001 and to the Mazda Tangerine Bowl in 2002; and the Copper Bowl changed its name to the Insight.com Bowl in 1997 and to the Insight Bowl in 2002. The Capital One Bowl was the former and original Tangerine Bowl from 1947-82 and was known as the Florida Citrus Bowl from 1983-2002. The current Mazda Tangerine Bowl is not to be confused with the Capital One Bowl, which is the former and original Tangerine Bowl.

Total Offense

MOST TOTAL PLAYS

107—Purdue (27) vs. Washington St. (33) (Sun, 2001) (474 yards)
104—Marshall (64) vs. East Caro. (61) (2 ot) (GMAC, 2001) (649 yards)
97—LSU (47) vs. Illinois (34) (Sugar, 2002) (595 yards)
96—North Carolina St. (10) vs. Arizona (17) (Copper, 1989) (310 yards)
95—LSU (20) vs. Texas (35) (Cotton, 2003) (441 yards)
95—Georgia (27) vs. Virginia (34) (Peach, Dec. 30, 1995) (525 yards)
95—Toledo (40) vs. Nevada (37) (ot) (Las Vegas, 1995) (561 yards)
95—North Carolina St. (28) vs. Iowa (23) (Peach, Dec. 31, 1988) (431 yards)
94—Arkansas (27) vs. Tennessee (31) (Cotton, 1990) (568 yards)
93—Miami (Fla.) (10) vs. Penn St. (14) (Fiesta, 1987) (445 yards)
92—Southern Miss. (35) vs. Idaho (42) (Humanitarian, 1998) (479 yards)
92—Oregon (20) vs. Penn St. (38) (Rose, 1995) (501 yards)
92—(D) Washington St. (24) vs. Houston (22) (Aloha, 1988) (460 yards)
92—(D) Western Mich. (30) vs. Fresno St. (35) (California, 1988) (503 yards)
92—(D) Purdue (27) vs. Tennessee (22) (Bluebonnet, 1979) (483 yards)
92—Arizona St. (30) vs. Penn St. (42) (Fiesta, 1977) (426 yards)
91—Florida (28) vs. Notre Dame (39) (Sugar, 1992) (511 yards)
91—Baylor (21) vs. LSU (7) (Liberty, 1985) (489 yards)
90—Clemson (7) vs. Mississippi St. (17) (Peach, 1999) (391 yards)
90—Virginia Tech (25) vs. North Carolina St. (24) (Peach, 1986) (487 yards)
90—Maryland (0) vs. Texas (42) (Sun, 1978) (248 yards)
90—Nebraska (40) vs. Notre Dame (6) (Orange, 1973) (560 yards)
90—(D) Oklahoma (27) vs. Southern Methodist (28) (Bluebonnet, 1968)
90—Richmond (49) vs. Ohio (42) (Tangerine, 1968) (556 yards)

MOST TOTAL PLAYS, BOTH TEAMS

180—Marshall (64) [104] & East Caro. (61) [76] (2 ot) (GMAC, 2001) (1,141 yards)
175—Washington St. (33) [68] & Purdue (27) [107] (Sun, 2001) (836 yards)
175—Toledo (40) [95] & Nevada (37) [80] (ot) (Las Vegas, 1995) (974 yards)
171—Auburn (34) [82] & Arizona (10) [89] (Sun, 1968) (537 yards)
169—Clemson (49) [84] & Louisiana Tech (24) [85] (Humanitarian, 2001) (998 yards)
167—Texas (47) [85] vs. Washington (43) [82] (Holiday, 2001) (1,036 yards)
167—Idaho (42) [75] & Southern Miss. (35) [92] (Humanitarian, 1998) (900 yards)
167—(D) Fresno St. (35) [75] & Western Mich. (30) [92] (California, 1988) (943 yards)
167—Arizona St. (45) [86] & Florida St. (38) [81] (Fiesta, 1971) (863 yards)
166—Colorado (47) [86] & Alabama (33) [80] (Liberty, 1969) (930 yards)
165—North Carolina St. (28) [95] & Iowa (23) [70] (Peach, Dec. 31, 1988)
165—East Caro. (35) [80] & Louisiana Tech (13) [85] (Independence, 1978) (607 yards)
165—Penn St. (42) [73] & Arizona St. (30) [92] (Fiesta, 1977) (777 yards)
164—Texas Tech (55) [79] & Clemson (15) [85] (Tangerine, 2002) (915 yards)
164—Nebraska (66) [83] & Northwestern (17) [81] (Alamo, 2000) (1,019 yards)
163—Nebraska (45) [88] & Georgia (6) [75] (Sun, 1969) (540 yards)
162—Penn St. (38) [70] & Oregon (20) [92] (Rose, 1995) (931 yards)
161—Mississippi St. (17) [71] & Clemson (7) [90] (Peach, 1999) (656 yards)
161—Ohio St. (28) [78] & Pittsburgh (23) [83] (Fiesta, 1984) (897 yards)
161—Auburn (35) [84] & Mississippi (28) [77] (Gator, Jan. 2, 1971) (1,024 yards)
160—Boise St. (34) [81] & Louisville (31) [79] (Humanitarian, 1999) (936 yards)
160—Texas (35) [76] & North Carolina (31) [84] (Sun, 1994) (903 yards)
160—Texas Tech (55) [80] & Air Force (41) [80] (Copper, 1995) (1,120 yards)
160—Mississippi (42) [78] & Air Force (29) [82] (Liberty, 1989) (1,047 yards)
159—Notre Dame (39) [68] & Florida (28) [91] (Sugar, 1992) (944 yards)
159—Notre Dame (38) [85] & Texas (10) [74] (Cotton, 1978) (690 yards)
159—Texas (42) [69] & Maryland (0) [90] (Sun, 1978) (517 yards)

MOST YARDS GAINED

718—Arizona St. (49) vs. Missouri (35) (Fiesta, 1972) (452 rush, 266 pass)
715—Michigan (35) vs. Mississippi (3) (Gator, Jan. 1, 1991) (324 rush, 391 pass)
698—Oklahoma St. (62) vs. Wyoming (14) (Holiday, 1988) (320 rush, 378 pass)
680—Texas A&M (65) vs. Brigham Young (14) (Holiday, 1989) (356 rush, 324 pass)
659—Florida (56) vs. Maryland (23) (Orange, 2002) (203 rush, 456 pass)
655—(D) Houston (47) vs. Tulane (7) (Bluebonnet, 1973) (402 rush, 253 pass)
651—Brigham Young (39) vs. Penn St. (50) (Holiday, 1989) (75 rush, 576 pass)
649—Marshall (64) vs. East Caro. (61) (2 ot) (GMAC, 2001) (73 rush, 576 pass)
646—(D) Navy (42) vs. California (38) (Aloha, 1996) (251 rush, 395 pass)
642—(D) San Jose St. (48) vs. Central Mich. (24) (California, 1990) (200 rush, 442 pass)
636—Nebraska (66) vs. Northwestern (17) (Alamo, 2000) (476 rush, 160 pass)
629—Nebraska (62) vs. Florida (24) (Fiesta, 1996) (524 rush, 105 pass)
624—(D) Southern California (47) vs. Texas A&M (28) (Bluebonnet, 1977) (378 rush, 246 pass)
618—Oklahoma (48) vs. Virginia (14) (Gator, Dec. 29, 1991) (261 rush, 357 pass)
613—Marshall (48) vs. Louisville (29) (Motor City, 1998) (202 rush, 411 pass)
611—Illinois (63) vs. Virginia (21) (Micronpc.com, 1999) (325 rush, 286 pass)
606—Texas Tech (55) vs. Air Force (41) (Copper, 1995) (361 rush, 245 pass)
596—Alabama (61) vs. Syracuse (6) (Orange, 1953) (296 rush, 300 pass)
594—Miami (Fla.) (46) vs. North Carolina St. (23) (Micron PC, 1998) (269 rush, 325 pass)
592—Texas (47) vs. Washington (43) (Holiday, 2001) (119 rush, 473 pass)
589—UNLV (52) vs. Central Mich. (24) (Las Vegas, 1994) (301 rush, 288 pass)
583—Oregon (41) vs. Air Force (13) (Las Vegas, 1997) (266 rush, 317 pass)
578—Southern California (55) vs. Texas Tech (14) (Cotton, 1995) (143 rush, 435 pass)
575—Indiana (34) vs. South Carolina (10) (Liberty, 1988) (185 rush, 390 pass)

571—Louisville (34) vs. Alabama (7) (Fiesta, 1991) (113 rush, 458 pass)
569—Florida St. (34) vs. Oklahoma St. (23) (Gator, 1985) (231 rush, 338 pass)
568—Arkansas (27) vs. Tennessee (31) (Cotton, 1990) (361 rush, 207 pass)
566—Pittsburgh (34) vs. Clemson (3) (Gator, 1977) (179 rush, 387 pass)

MOST YARDS GAINED, BOTH TEAMS

1,143—(D) Southern California (47) [624] & Texas A&M (28) [519] (Bluebonnet, 1977) (148 plays)
1,141—Marshall (64) [649] & East Caro. (61) [492] (2 ot) (GMAC, 2001) (180 plays)
1,129—Arizona St. (49) [718] & Missouri (35) [411] (Fiesta, 1972) (134 plays)
1,120—Texas Tech (55) [606] & Air Force (41) [514] (Copper, 1995) (160 plays)
1,115—Penn St. (50) [464] & Brigham Young (39) [651] (Holiday, 1989) (157 plays)
1,092—Miami (Fla.) (46) [594] & North Carolina St. (23) [498] (Micron PC, 1998) (149 plays)
1,080—(D) Navy (42) [646] & California (38) [434] (Aloha, 1996) (147 plays)
1,048—Michigan (35) [715] & Mississippi (3) [333] (Gator, Jan. 1, 1991) (153 plays)
1,047—Mississippi (42) [533] & Air Force (29) [514] (Liberty, 1989) (160 plays)
1,045—Marshall (48) [611] & Louisville (29) [432] (Motor City, 1998) (144 plays)
1,038—Tennessee (31) [470] & Arkansas (27) [568] (Cotton, 1990) (155 plays)
1,036—Texas (47) [592] vs. Washington (21) [444] (Holiday, 2001) (167 plays)
1,035—Wisconsin (38) [497] & UCLA (31) [538] (Rose, 1999) (139 plays)
1,024—Auburn (35) [559] & Mississippi (28) [465] (Gator, Jan. 2, 1971) (161 plays)
1,019—Florida (56) [659] & Maryland (23) [360] (Orange, 2002) (153 plays)
1,019—Nebraska (66) [636] & Northwestern (17) [383] (Alamo, 2000) (164 plays)
1,018—Mississippi (34) [511] & Marshall (31) [507] (Motor City, 1997) (155 plays)
1,007—(D) Toledo (27) [486] & San Jose St. (25) [521] (California, 1981) (158 plays)
998—Clemson (49) [548] vs. Louisiana Tech (24) [450] (Humanitarian, 2001) (169 plays)
991—Illinois (63) [611] & Virginia (21) [380] (Micronpc.com, 1999) (145 plays)
978—Pittsburgh (31) [530] & Texas A&M (28) [448] (John Hancock, 1989) (158 plays)
974—Toledo (40) [561] & Nevada (37) [413] (ot) (Las Vegas, 1995) (175 plays)
965—UNLV (52) [589] & Central Mich. (24) [376] (Las Vegas, 1994) (145 plays)
958—LSU (47) [595] & Illinois (34) [363] (Sugar, 2002) (154 plays)
954—Mississippi (27) [427] & Arkansas (22) [527] (Sugar, 1970)
950—Texas (40) [436] & Missouri (27) [514] (Cotton, 1946)
944—Notre Dame (39) [433] & Florida (28) [511] (Sugar, 1992) (159 plays)

HIGHEST AVERAGE GAINED PER PLAY

9.5—Louisville (34) vs. Alabama (7) (Fiesta, 1991) (60 for 571)
9.1—Miami (Fla.) (46) vs. North Carolina St. (23) (Micron PC, 1998) (65 for 594)
9.1—(D) Navy (42) vs. California (38) (Aloha, 1996) (71 for 646)
8.9—Florida (56) vs. Maryland (23) (Orange, 2002) (74 for 659)
8.9—Marshall (48) vs. Louisville (29) (Motor City, 1998) (69 for 613)
8.7—Oklahoma St. (62) vs. Wyoming (14) (Holiday, 1988) (80 for 698)
8.4—Michigan (35) vs. Mississippi (3) (Gator, Jan. 1, 1991) (85 for 715)
8.3—Texas A&M (65) vs. Brigham Young (14) (Holiday, 1990) (82 for 680)
8.3—Illinois (63) vs. Virginia (21) (Micronpc.com, 1999) (74 for 611)
8.1—Arizona St. (49) vs. Missouri (35) (Fiesta, 1972) (89 for 718)
8.0—Oregon (41) vs. Air Force (13) (Las Vegas, 1997) (73 for 583)
7.9—Brigham Young (39) vs. Penn St. (50) (Holiday, 1989) (82 for 651)
7.7—Alabama (61) vs. Syracuse (6) (Orange, 1953) (77 for 596)
7.7—(D) Vanderbilt (28) vs. Air Force (36) (Hall of Fame, 1982) (63 for 487)
7.7—Tennessee (31) vs. Arkansas (27) (Cotton, 1990) (61 for 470)
7.7—(D) Kansas (51) vs. UCLA (30) (Aloha, 1995) (71 for 548)
7.7—Nebraska (66) vs. Northwestern (17) (Alamo, 2000) (83 for 636)
7.6—Florida St. (41) vs. Nebraska (18) (Fiesta, 1990) (65 for 494)
7.6—Texas Tech (55) vs. Air Force (41) (Copper, 1995) (80 for 606)
7.6—Nebraska (62) vs. Florida (24) (Fiesta, 1996) (83 for 629)
7.5—Kansas St. (52) vs. Wyoming (17) (Copper, 1993) (71 for 536)
7.5—(D) Houston (47) vs. Tulane (7) (Bluebonnet, 1973) (87 for 655)
7.5—Iowa (38) vs. California (12) (Rose, 1959) (69 for 516)
7.5—Marshall (31) vs. Mississippi (34) (Motor City, 1997) (68 for 507)
7.4—(D) UCLA (31) vs. Brigham Young (10) (Freedom, 1986) (70 for 518)
7.3—(D) UNLV (30) vs. Toledo (13) (California, 1984) (56 for 409)
7.3—(D) San Jose St. (48) vs. Central Mich. (24) (California, 1990) (88 for 642)
7.3—UCLA (31) vs. Wisconsin (38) (Rose, 1999) (74 for 538)

FEWEST PLAYS

35—Tennessee (0) vs. Texas (16) (Cotton, 1953) (29 rush, 6 pass)
36—Arkansas (3) vs. UCLA (17) (Cotton, 1989) (22 rush, 14 pass)
37—TCU (0) vs. Oklahoma St. (34) (Cotton, 1945) (27 rush, 10 pass)
38—Iowa (3) vs. California (37) (Alamo, 1993) (21 rush, 17 pass)

FEWEST PLAYS, BOTH TEAMS

107—TCU (16) [54] & Marquette (6) [53] (Cotton, 1937)

FEWEST YARDS

-21—U. of Mexico (0) vs. Southwestern (Tex.) (35) (Sun, 1945) (29 rush, -50 pass)
23—Alabama (10) vs. Missouri (35) (Gator, 1968) (-45 rush, 68 pass)
32—Tennessee (0) vs. Texas (16) (Cotton, 1953) (-14 rush, 46 pass)
38—Miami (Fla.) (0) vs. Bucknell (26) (Orange, 1935) (20 rush, 18 pass)
41—Southern California (14) vs. Alabama (34) (Rose, 1946) (6 rush, 35 pass)
42—Arkansas (3) vs. UCLA (17) (Cotton, 1989) (21 rush, 21 pass)
48—New Mexico (0) vs. Southwestern (Tex.) (7) (Sun, 1944) (38 rush, 10 pass)
50—Arkansas (3) vs. Oklahoma (10) (Cotton, 2002) (37 rush, 13 pass)
54—Arkansas (0) vs. LSU (0) (Cotton, 1947) (54 rush, 0 pass)
57—Michigan St. (0) vs. Auburn (6) (Orange, 1938) (32 rush, 25 pass)

FEWEST YARDS, BOTH TEAMS

260—Randolph Field (7) [150] & Texas (7) [110] (Cotton, 1944)
263—LSU (19) [92] & Texas A&M (14) [171] (Orange, 1944)

Rushing

MOST RUSHING ATTEMPTS

87—Oklahoma (40) vs. Auburn (22) (Sugar, Jan. 1, 1972) (439 yards)
82—Missouri (35) vs. Alabama (10) (Gator, 1968) (402 yards)
79—West Virginia (14) vs. South Carolina (3) (Peach, 1969) (356 yards)
79—Georgia Tech (31) vs. Texas Tech (21) (Gator, Dec. 31, 1965) (364 yards)
78—(D) Houston (35) vs. Navy (0) (Garden State, 1980) (405 yards)
78—Texas (16) vs. Tennessee (0) (Cotton, 1953) (296 yards)
76—Oklahoma (14) vs. Penn St. (0) (Sugar, Dec. 31, 1972) (278 yards)
74—Oklahoma (41) vs. Wyoming (7) (Fiesta, 1976) (415 yards)
74—Michigan (12) vs. Stanford (13) (Rose, 1972) (264 yards)
74—Ohio St. (20) vs. Southern California (7) (Rose, 1955) (305 yards)
73—Syracuse (31) vs. McNeese St. (7) (Independence, 1979) (276 yards)
73—Penn St. (41) vs. Oregon (12) (Liberty, 1960) (301 yards)
72—Arkansas (27) vs. Tennessee (31) (Cotton, 1990) (361 yards)
72—North Carolina St. (28) vs. Iowa (23) (Peach, Dec. 31, 1988) (236 yards)
72—(D) Texas A&M (28) vs. Southern California (47) (Bluebonnet, 1977) (486 yards)

MOST RUSHING ATTEMPTS, BOTH TEAMS

122—(D) Southern California (47) [50] & Texas A&M (28) [72] (Bluebonnet, 1977) (864 yards)
122—Mississippi St. (26) [68] & North Carolina (24) [54] (Sun, 1974) (732 yards)
120—Pittsburgh (33) [53] & Kansas (19) [67] (Sun, 1975) (714 yards)
117—Oklahoma (14) [65] & Michigan (6) [52] (Orange, 1976) (451 yards)
117—West Virginia (14) [79] & South Carolina (3) [38] (Peach, 1969) (420 yards)
116—Oklahoma (41) [74] & Wyoming (7) [42] (Fiesta, 1976) (568 yards)
116—Colorado (47) [70] & Alabama (33) [46] (Liberty, 1969) (628 yards)
115—Southern California (7) [47] & Wisconsin (0) [68] (Rose, 1953) (259 yards)
113—Oklahoma (40) [54] & Houston (14) [59] (Sun, 1981) (566 yards)
113—(D) Houston (35) [78] & Navy (0) [35] (Garden State, 1980) (540 yards)
113—Missouri (34) [71] & Auburn (17) [42] (Sun, 1973) (408 yards)
112—Arkansas (31) [65] & Georgia (10) [47] (Cotton, 1976) (426 yards)
112—(D) Colorado (29) [62] & Houston (17) [50] (Bluebonnet, 1971) (552 yards)

MOST NET RUSHING YARDS

524—Nebraska (62) vs. Florida (24) (Fiesta, 1996) (68 attempts)
486—(D) Texas A&M (28) vs. Southern California (47) (Bluebonnet, 1977) (72 attempts)
476—Nebraska (66) vs. Northwestern (17) (Alamo, 2000) (69 attempts)
473—Colorado (47) vs. Alabama (33) (Liberty, 1969) (70 attempts)
455—Mississippi St. (26) vs. North Carolina (24) (Sun, 1974) (68 attempts)
452—Arizona St. (49) vs. Missouri (35) (Fiesta, 1972) (65 attempts)
439—Oklahoma (40) vs. Auburn (22) (Sugar, Jan. 1, 1972) (87 attempts)
434—Oklahoma (41) vs. Wyoming (7) (Fiesta, 1976) (74 attempts)
431—Air Force (41) vs. Texas Tech (55) (Copper, 1995) (67 attempts)
429—Iowa (38) vs. California (12) (Rose, 1959) (55 attempts)
423—Auburn (33) vs. Baylor (13) (Gator, Dec. 31, 1954) (48 attempts)
423—(D) UCLA (31) vs. Brigham Young (10) (Freedom, 1986) (49 attempts)
417—Oklahoma (21) vs. Arizona St. (32) (Fiesta, 1983) (63 attempts)
411—Oklahoma (24) vs. Florida St. (7) (Orange, 1980) (62 attempts)
409—Oklahoma (40) vs. Houston (14) (Sun, 1981) (54 attempts)
409—Nebraska (42) vs. Tennessee (17) (Orange, 1998) (68 attempts)
408—Missouri (27) vs. Texas (40) (Cotton, 1946)
405—(D) Houston (35) vs. Navy (0) (Garden State, 1980) (78 attempts)
402—(D) Houston (47) vs. Tulane (7) (Bluebonnet, 1973) (58 attempts)

MOST NET RUSHING YARDS, BOTH TEAMS

864—(D) Southern California (47) [378] & Texas A&M (28) [486] (Bluebonnet, 1977) (122 attempts)
792—Texas Tech (55) [361] & Air Force (41) [431] (Copper, 1995) (107 attempts)
732—Mississippi St. (26) [455] & North Carolina (24) [277] (Sun, 1974) (122 attempts)
714—Pittsburgh (33) [372] & Kansas (19) [342] (Sun, 1975) (120 attempts)
708—Nebraska (66) [476] & Northwestern (17) [232] (Alamo, 2000) (107 attempts)
701—Arizona St. (49) [453] & Missouri (35) [248] (Fiesta, 1972) (109 attempts)
681—Tennessee (31) [320] & Arkansas (27) [361] (Cotton, 1990) (110 attempts)
643—Iowa (38) [429] & California (12) [214] (Rose, 1959) (108 attempts)
628—Colorado (47) [473] & Alabama (33) [155] (Liberty, 1969) (116 attempts)
616—Oklahoma (41) [434] & Wyoming (7) [182] (Fiesta, 1976) (116 attempts)
610—Texas (40) [202] & Missouri (27) [408] (Cotton, 1946)

HIGHEST RUSHING AVERAGE
(Minimum 30 Attempts)

9.3—Texas Tech (55) vs. Air Force (41) (Copper, 1995) (39 for 361)
8.6—(D) UCLA (31) vs. Brigham Young (10) (Freedom, 1986) (49 for 423)
8.6—Michigan (38) vs. Washington (31) (Rose, 1993) (36 for 308)
8.4—Tennessee (31) vs. Arkansas (27) (Cotton, 1990) (38 for 320)
8.0—Toledo (56) vs. Davidson (33) (Tangerine, 1969) (42 for 334)
7.8—Iowa (38) vs. California (12) (Rose, 1959) (55 for 429)
7.7—Texas Tech (28) vs. North Carolina (32) (Sun, 1972) (38 for 293)
7.7—Nebraska (62) vs. Florida (24) (Fiesta, 1996) (68 for 524)
7.6—Oklahoma (42) vs. Arkansas (8) (Orange, 1987) (48 for 366)
7.6—Oklahoma (40) vs. Houston (14) (Sun, 1981) (54 for 409)
7.6—(D) Southern California (47) vs. Texas A&M (28) (Bluebonnet, 1977) (50 for 378)

7.4—Michigan (35) vs. Mississippi (3) (Gator, Jan. 1, 1991) (53 for 391)
7.2—Boston College (28) vs. Colorado (62) (Insight.com, 1999) (51 for 365)
7.1—Wisconsin (38) vs. UCLA (31) (Rose, 1999) (48 for 343)
7.1—Boston College (45) vs. Houston (28) (Cotton, 1985) (50 for 353)
7.0—Pittsburgh (33) vs. Kansas (19) (Sun, 1975) (53 for 372)
7.0—Arizona St. (49) vs. Missouri (35) (Fiesta, 1972) (65 for 453)

FEWEST RUSHING ATTEMPTS
12—(D) Vanderbilt (28) vs. Air Force (36) (Hall of Fame, 1982) (35 yards)
16—Florida (18) vs. Missouri (20) (Sugar, 1966) (-2 yards)
16—Colorado (7) vs. LSU (25) (Orange, 1962) (24 yards)
17—Florida St. (2) vs. Oklahoma (13) (Orange, 2001) (27 yards)
17—(D) Duke (21) vs. Texas Tech (49) (All-American, 1989) (67 yards)
17—Illinois (9) vs. UCLA (45) (Rose, 1984) (0 yards)
18—Brigham Young (46) vs. Southern Methodist (45) (Holiday, 1980) (-2 yards)
19—Iowa (23) vs. North Carolina St. (28) (Peach, Dec. 31, 1988) (46 yards)
19—Baylor (13) vs. Auburn (33) (Gator, Dec. 31, 1954) (108 yards)
20—Texas Tech (16) vs. Iowa (19) (Alamo, 2001) (80 yards)
20—Cincinnati (16) vs. Toledo (23) (Motor City, 2001) (13 yards)
20—Florida (20) vs. Miami (Fla.) (37) (Sugar, 2001) (140 yards)
20—Utah St. (19) vs. Cincinnati (35) (Humanitarian, 1997) (76 yards)
20—(D) San Jose St. (27) vs. Eastern Mich. (30) (California, 1987) (81 yards)
20—Tulane (6) vs. Penn St. (9) (Liberty, 1979) (-8 yards)
21—Illinois (34) vs. LSU (47) (Sugar, 2002) (61 yards)
21—Tennessee (17) vs. Nebraska (42) (Orange, 1998) (128 yards)
21—Florida (24) vs. Nebraska (62) (Fiesta, 1996) (-28 yards)
21—Iowa (3) vs. California (37) (Alamo, 1993) (20 yards)
21—Brigham Young (14) vs. Texas A&M (65) (Holiday, 1990) (-12 yards)
21—(D) Houston (22) vs. Washington St. (24) (Aloha, 1988) (68 yards)
21—Wyoming (19) vs. Iowa (20) (Holiday, 1987) (43 yards)
21—(D) San Jose St. (25) vs. Toledo (27) (California, 1981) (54 yards)

FEWEST RUSHING ATTEMPTS, BOTH TEAMS
53—Oklahoma (13) [36] & Florida St. (2) [17] (Orange, 2001)
56—Texas Tech (55) [27] & Clemson (15) [29] (Tangerine, 2002)
56—Marshall (38) [30] & Louisville (15) [26] (GMAC, 2002)
56—Mississippi (27) [33] & Oklahoma (25) [23] (Independence, 1999)
57—Iowa (20) [36] & Wyoming (19) [21] (Holiday, 1987)
58—Texas (47) [30] & Washington (43) [28] (Holiday, 2001)
59—Oregon (38) [28] & Colorado (16) [31] (Fiesta, 2002)
59—Washington St. (33) [27] & Purdue (27) [32] (Sun, 2001)
59—Hawaii (23) [24] & Oregon St. (17) [35] (Oahu Classic, 1999)
60—Michigan (35) [23] & Alabama (34) [37] (ot) (Orange, 2000)
60—Tennessee (48) [32] & Northwestern (28) [28] (Florida Citrus, 1997)
61—Marshall (21) [31] & Brigham Young (3) [30] (Motor City, 1999)
61—Arkansas (27) [36] & Texas (6) [25] (Cotton, 2000)
62—Mississippi (34) [39] & Marshall (31) [23] (Motor City, 1997)
63—Miami (Fla.) (37) [43] & Florida (20) [20] (Sugar, 2001)
63—Georgia (28) [34] & Purdue (25) [29] (ot) (Outback, 2000)
63—Auburn (21) [36] & Clemson (17) [27] (Peach, 1998)
63—(D) Southern California (28) [38] & Utah (21) [25] (Freedom, 1993)
64—North Carolina St. (28) [26] & Notre Dame (6) [38] (Gator, 2003)
64—Purdue (34) [40] & Washington (24) [24] (Sun, 2002)
64—Michigan St. (44) [42] & Fresno St. (35) [22] (Silicon Valley, 2001)
64—Iowa (19) [44] & Texas Tech (16) [20] (Alamo, 2001)
65—Florida (56) [25] & Maryland (23) [40] (Orange, 2002)
65—LSU (47) [44] & Illinois (34) [21] (Sugar, 2002)
65—Pittsburgh (34) [39] & North Carolina St. (19) [26] (Tangerine, 2001)
65—West Virginia (49) [34] & Mississippi (38) [31] (Music City, 2000)
65—Purdue (33) [28] & Oklahoma St. (20) [37] (Alamo, 1997)
66—Tulane (36) [44] & Hawaii (28) [22] (Hawaii, 2002)
66—Southern Miss. (23) [34] & Colorado St. (17) [32] (Liberty, 1999)
66—Southern California (41) [27] & Northwestern (32) [39] (Rose, 1996)
66—Brigham Young (13) [33] & Iowa (13) [33] (Holiday, 1991)
66—Miami (Fla.) (23) [28] & Nebraska (3) [38] (Orange, 1989)
66—TCU (16) [34] & Marquette (6) [32] (Cotton, 1937)
67—Mississippi St. (17) [33] & Clemson (7) [34] (Peach, 1999)
67—UCLA (6) [41] & Illinois (3) [26] (John Hancock, 1991)
67—Southern California (7) [39] & Duke (3) [28] (Rose, 1939)

FEWEST RUSHING YARDS
-61—(D) Kansas St. (7) vs. Boston College (12) (Aloha, 1994) (23 attempts)
-45—Alabama (10) vs. Missouri (35) (Gator, 1968) (29 attempts)
-30—Florida (6) vs. West Virginia (26) (Peach, Dec. 31, 1981) (34 attempts)
-28—Florida (24) vs. Nebraska (62) (Fiesta, 1996) (21 attempts)
-27—Texas (6) vs. Arkansas (27) (Cotton, 2000) (25 attempts)
-26—TCU (9) vs. Texas A&M (28) (Galleryfurniture.com, 2001) (24 attempts)
-23—Southern California (19) vs. TCU (28) (Sun, 1998) (21 attempts)
-21—Florida St. (20) vs. Wyoming (28) (Sun, 1966) (31 attempts)
-16—Brigham Young (3) vs. Marshall (21) (Motor City, 1999) (30 attempts)
-15—LSU (0) vs. Mississippi (20) (Sugar, 1960)
-14—Navy (6) vs. Texas (28) (Cotton, 1964) (29 attempts)
-14—Tennessee (0) vs. Texas (16) (Cotton, 1953) (29 attempts)
-12—Brigham Young (14) vs. Texas A&M (65) (Holiday, 1990) (21 attempts)
-12—Air Force (13) vs. Tennessee (34) (Sugar, 1971)
-11—Colorado (25) vs. Alabama (30) (Blockbuster, 1991) (30 attempts)
-8—Tulane (6) vs. Penn St. (9) (Liberty, 1979) (20 attempts)
-8—Navy (14) vs. Missouri (21) (Orange, 1961) (24 attempts)

-5—Stanford (9) vs. Wisconsin (17) (Rose, 2000) (27 attempts)
-2—Brigham Young (46) vs. Southern Methodist (45) (Holiday, 1980) (24 attempts)
-2—Florida (18) vs. Missouri (20) (Sugar, 1966) (16 attempts)

FEWEST RUSHING YARDS, BOTH TEAMS
51—(D) Utah (16) [6] & Arizona (13) [45] (Freedom, 1994)
74—Tennessee (34) [86] & Air Force (13) [-12] (Sugar, 1971)
78—Texas A&M (28) [104] & TCU (9) [-26] (galleryfurniture.com, 2001)
81—Washington St. (10) [7] & Baylor (3) [74] (Alamo, 1994)
81—Florida St. (23) [76] & Florida (17) [5] (Sugar, Jan. 2, 1995)
83—Oklahoma (13) [56] & Florida St. (2) [27] (Orange, 2001)
88—(D) Boston College (12) [149] & Kansas St. (7) [-61] (Aloha, 1994)
93—Oklahoma (10) [56] & Arkansas (8) [37] (Cotton, 2002)
118—UCLA (27) [73] & New Mexico (13) [45] (Las Vegas, 2002)
125—Pittsburgh (38) [117] & Oregon St. (13) [8] (Insight, 2002)
131—Purdue (37) [5] & Kansas St. (34) [126] (Alamo, 1998)
131—Marshall (21) [147] & Brigham Young (3) [-16] (Motor City, 1999)
132—Texas Tech (55) [91] & Clemson (15) [41] (Tangerine, 2002)
136—Washington St. (33) [81] & Purdue (27) [55] (Sun, 2001)
137—Iowa (20) [94] & Wyoming (19) [43] (Holiday, 1987)
142—Louisville (28) [58] & BYU (10) [84] (Liberty, 2001)
143—Brigham Young (31) [71] & Oklahoma (6) [72] (Copper, 1994)
144—Notre Dame (9) [17] & Oregon St. (41) [127] (Fiesta, 2001)
145—Arkansas (10) [45] & Nebraska (7) [100] (Cotton, 1965)
147—Florida St. (30) [104] & Virginia Tech (17) [43] (Gator, 2002)
147—(D) San Jose St. (37) [123] & Miami (Ohio) (7) [24] (California, 1986)

LOWEST RUSHING AVERAGE
(Minimum 20 Attempts)
-2.7—(D) Kansas St. (7) vs. Boston College (12) (Aloha, 1994) (23 for -61)
-1.6—Alabama (10) vs. Missouri (35) (Gator, 1968) (29 for -45)
-1.3—Florida (24) vs. Nebraska (62) (Fiesta, 1996) (21 for -28)
-1.1—Texas (6) vs. Arkansas (27) (Cotton, 2000) (25 for -27)
-1.1—Southern California (19) vs. TCU (28) (Sun, 1998) (21 for -23)
-0.9—Florida (6) vs. West Virginia (26) (Peach, Dec. 31, 1981) (32 for -30)
-0.7—Florida St. (20) vs. Wyoming (28) (Sun, 1966) (31 for -21)
-0.6—Brigham Young (14) vs. Texas A&M (65) (Holiday, 1990) (21 for -12)
-0.5—Brigham Young (3) vs. Marshall (21) (Motor City, 1999) (30 for -16)
-0.5—Navy (6) vs. Texas (28) (Cotton, 1964) (29 for -14)
-0.5—Tennessee (0) vs. Texas (16) (Cotton, 1953) (29 for -14)
-0.4—Colorado (25) vs. Alabama (30) (Blockbuster, 1991) (30 for -11)
-0.3—Navy (14) vs. Missouri (21) (Orange, 1961) (24 for -8)

RUSHING DEFENSE, FEWEST YARDS ALLOWED
-61—(D) Boston College (12) vs. Kansas St. (7) (Aloha, 1994) (23 attempts)
-45—Missouri (35) vs. Alabama (10) (Gator, 1968) (29 attempts)
-30—West Virginia (26) vs. Florida (6) (Peach, Dec. 31, 1981) (32 attempts)
-28—Nebraska (62) vs. Florida (24) (Fiesta, 1996) (21 attempts)
-27—Texas (6) vs. Arkansas (27) (Cotton, 2000) (25 attempts)
-23—TCU (28) vs. Southern California (19) (Sun, 1998) (21 attempts)
-21—Wyoming (28) vs. Florida St. (20) (Sun, 1966) (31 attempts)
-16—Brigham Young (3) vs. Marshall (21) (Motor City, 1999) (30 attempts)
-15—Mississippi (20) vs. LSU (0) (Sugar, 1960)
-14—Texas (28) vs. Navy (6) (Cotton, 1964) (29 attempts)
-14—Texas (16) vs. Tennessee (0) (Cotton, 1953) (29 attempts)
-12—Texas A&M (65) vs. Brigham Young (14) (Holiday, 1990) (21 attempts)
-12—Tennessee (34) vs. Air Force (13) (Sugar, 1971)
-11—Alabama (30) vs. Colorado (25) (Blockbuster, 1991) (30 attempts)
-8—Penn St. (9) vs. Tulane (6) (Liberty, 1979) (20 attempts)
-8—Missouri (21) vs. Navy (14) (Orange, 1961) (24 attempts)
-5—Stanford (9) vs. Wisconsin (17) (Rose, 2000) (27 attempts)
-2—Southern Methodist (45) vs. Brigham Young (46) (Holiday, 1980) (24 attempts)
-2—Missouri (20) vs. Florida (18) (Sugar, 1966) (16 attempts)

Passing

MOST PASS ATTEMPTS
(Followed by Comp.-Att.-Int. and Yardage)
75—Purdue (27) vs. Washington St. (33) (Sun, 2001) (38-75-4, 419 yards)
70—Marshall (64) vs. East Caro. (61) (2 ot) (GMAC, 2001) (41-70-2, 576 yards)
63—(D) Fresno St. (30) vs. Colorado (41) (Aloha, 1993) (37-63-1, 523 yards)
63—(D) San Jose St. (25) vs. Toledo (27) (California, 1981) (43-63-5, 467 yards)
61—Oregon (20) vs. Penn St. (38) (Rose, 1995) (41-61-2, 456 yards)
61—(D) Brigham Young (16) vs. Virginia (22) (All-American, 1987) (37-61-1, 394 yards)
60—Purdue (25) vs. Georgia (28) (ot) (Outback, 2000) (36-60-1, 378 yards)
59—Louisiana Tech (24) vs. Clemson (49) (Humanitarian, 2001) (401 yards)
59—Georgia (27) vs. Virginia (34) (Peach, Dec. 30, 1995) (31-59-2, 413 yards)
59—Brigham Young (39) vs. Penn St. (50) (Holiday, 1989) (42-59-2, 576 yards)
58—Fresno St. (35) vs. Michigan St. (44) (Silicon Valley, 2001) (35-58-2, 531 yards)
58—Florida (28) vs. Notre Dame (39) (Sugar, 1992) (28-58-2, 370 yards)
58—Illinois (15) vs. Alabama (21) (Liberty, 1982) (35-58-7, 423 yards)
58—Richmond (49) vs. Ohio (42) (Tangerine, 1968) (39-58-2, 447 yards)
57—Arizona St. (27) vs. Kansas St. (34) (Holiday, 2002) (28-57-1, 293 yards)
57—(D) Western Mich. (30) vs. Fresno St. (35) (California, 1988) (24-57-0, 366 yards)
56—Clemson (15) vs. Texas Tech (55) (Tangerine, 2002) (25-56-4, 319 yards)
56—Clemson (7) vs. Mississippi St. (17) (Peach, 1999) (25-56-5, 306 yards)

56—Miami (Fla.) (13) vs. Alabama (34) (Sugar, 1993) (24-56-3, 278 yards)
56—(D) Washington (21) vs. Maryland (20) (Aloha, 1982) (35-56-0, 369 yards)
55—Texas (47) vs. Washington (43) (Holiday, 2001) (37-55-3, 473 yards)
55—Illinois (29) vs. Army (31) (Peach, 1985) (38-55-2, 401 yards)
55—Florida St. (17) vs. Penn St. (17) (Gator, 1967) (38-55-4, 363 yards)
54—Washington (24) vs. Purdue (34) (Sun, 2002) (25-54-1, 272 yards)
54—Washington (43) vs. Texas (47) (Holiday, 2001) (27-54-2, 293 yards)
54—Oklahoma (25) vs. Mississippi (27) (Independence, 1999) (39-54-1, 390 yards)
54—Louisville (29) vs. Marshall (48) (Motor City, 1998) (35-54-1, 336 yards)
53—LSU (47) vs. Illinois (34) (Sugar, 2002) (31-53-0, 444 yards)
53—Purdue (37) vs. Kansas St. (34) (Alamo, 1998) (25-53-2, 230 yards)

MOST PASS ATTEMPTS, BOTH TEAMS
116—Washington St. (33) [41] & Purdue (27) [75] (Sun, 2001) (53 completed)
109—Texas (47) [55] & Washington (43) [54] (Holiday, 2001) (64 completed)
108—Texas Tech (55) [52] & Clemson (15) [56] (Tangerine, 2002) (64 completed)
94—Mississippi St. (17) [38] & Clemson (7) [56] (Peach, 1999) (42 completed)
93—Marshall (64) [70] & East Caro. (61) [23] (2 ot) (GMAC, 2001) (52 completed)
93—Georgia (28) [33] & Purdue (25) [60] (ot) (Outback, 2000) (56 completed)
93—Idaho (42) [41] & Southern Miss. (35) [52] (Humanitarian, 1998) (55 completed)
93—Mississippi (34) [48] & Marshall (31) [45] (Motor City, 1997) (52 completed)
92—Marshall (38) [44] & Louisville (15) [48] (GMAC, 2002) (43 completed)
92—Toledo (40) [41] & Nevada (37) [51] (ot) (Las Vegas, 1995) (50 completed)
92—Penn St. (38) [31] & Oregon (20) [61] (Rose, 1995) (61 completed)
92—Tennessee (34) [46] & Air Force (13) [46] (Sugar, 1971) (47 completed)
91—Purdue (34) [37] & Washington (24) [54] (Sun, 2002) (50 completed)
91—Tulane (36) [39] & Hawaii (28) [52] (Hawaii, 2002) (52 completed)
91—Florida St. (2) [52] & Oklahoma (13) [39] (Orange, 2001) (50 completed)
91—Miami (Fla.) (37) [40] & Florida (20) [51] (Sugar, 2001) (46 completed)
91—Richmond (49) [58] & Ohio (42) [33] (Tangerine, 1968) (56 completed)
90—Michigan St. (44) [32] & Fresno St. (35) [58] (Silicon Valley, 2001) (57 completed)
90—Bowling Green (35) [41] & Nevada (34) [49] (Las Vegas, 1992) (54 completed)
90—Mississippi (20) [50] & Texas Tech (17) [40] (Independence, 1986) (48 completed)
89—LSU (47) [53] & Illinois (34) [36] (Sugar, 2002) (46 completed)
89—Oregon (38) [47] & Colorado (16) [42] (Fiesta, 2002) (52 completed)
88—Florida (56) [49] & Maryland (23) [39] (Orange, 2002) (56 completed)
88—Clemson (49) [29] & Louisiana Tech (24) [59] (Humanitarian, 2001) (45 completed)
88—Washington St. (31) [48] & Utah (28) [40] (Copper, 1992) (53 completed)
88—(D) Washington (21) [56] & Maryland (20) [32] (Aloha, 1982) (54 completed)
86—Michigan St. (37) [35] & Florida (34) [51] (Florida Citrus, 2000) (46 completed)
86—Boise St. (34) [39] & Louisville (31) [47] (Humanitarian, 1999) (46 completed)
86—(D) Fresno St. (35) [29] & Western Mich. (30) [57] (California, 1988) (39 completed)
86—Iowa (20) [35] & Wyoming (19) [51] (Holiday, 1987) (49 completed)
85—North Carolina St. (28) [41] & Notre Dame (6) [44] (Gator, 2003) (48 completed)
85—Kansas St. (34) [28] & Arizona St. (27) [57] (Holiday, 2002) (39 completed)
85—Ohio St. (10) [35] & Brigham Young (7) [50] (Florida Citrus, 1985) (45 completed)
85—(D) Toledo (27) [22] & San Jose St. (25) [63] (California, 1981) (54 completed)

MOST PASS COMPLETIONS
(Followed by Comp.-Att.-Int. and Yardage)
43—(D) San Jose St. (25) vs. Toledo (27) (California, 1981) (43-63-5, 467 yards)
42—Brigham Young (39) vs. Penn St. (50) (Holiday, 1989) (42-59-2, 576 yards)
41—Marshall (64) vs. East Caro. (61) (2 ot) (GMAC, 2001) (41-70-2, 576 yards)
41—Oregon (20) vs. Penn St. (38) (Rose, 1995) (41-61-2, 456 yards)
39—Texas Tech (55) vs. Clemson (15) (Tangerine, 2002) (39-52-1, 464 yards)
39—Oklahoma (25) vs. Mississippi (27) (Independence, 1999) (39-54-1, 390 yards)
39—Richmond (49) vs. Ohio (42) (Tangerine, 1968) (39-58-2, 447 yards)
38—Purdue (27) vs. Washington St. (33) (Sun, 2001) (38-75-4, 419 yards)
38—Illinois (29) vs. Army (31) (Peach, 1985) (38-55-2, 401 yards)
38—(D) Vanderbilt (28) vs. Air Force (36) (Hall of Fame, 1982) (38-51-3, 452 yards)
38—Florida St. (17) vs. Penn St. (17) (Gator, 1967) (38-55-4, 363 yards)
37—Texas (47) vs. Washington (43) (Holiday, 2001) (37-55-3, 473 yards)
37—(D) Fresno St. (30) vs. Colorado (41) (Aloha, 1993) (37-63-1, 523 yards)
37—(D) Brigham Young (16) vs. Virginia (22) (All-American, 1987) (37-61-1, 394 yards)
36—Purdue (25) vs. Georgia (28) (ot) (Outback, 2000) (36-60-1, 378 yards)
35—Fresno St. (35) vs. Michigan St. (44) (Silicon Valley, 2001) (35-58-2, 531 yards)
35—Michigan (35) vs. Alabama (34) (ot) (Orange, 2000) (35-47-0, 369 yards)
35—Louisville (29) vs. Marshall (48) (Motor City, 1998) (35-54-1, 336 yards)
35—West Virginia (31) vs. Missouri (34) (Insight.com, 1998) (35-51-2, 452 yards)
35—Brigham Young (24) vs. Michigan (17) (Holiday, 1984) (35-49-3, 371 yards)
35—Illinois (15) vs. Alabama (21) (Liberty, 1982) (35-58-7, 423 yards)
35—(D) Washington (21) vs. Maryland (20) (Aloha, 1982) (35-56-0, 369 yards)
34—Wisconsin (37) vs. Southern California (42) (Rose, 1963) (34-49-3, 419 yards)
33—Florida (56) vs. Maryland (23) (Orange, 2002) (33-49-2, 456 yards)
33—Alabama (29) vs. Army (28) (John Hancock Sun, 1988) (33-52-1, 412 yards)

MOST PASS COMPLETIONS, BOTH TEAMS
64—Texas Tech (55) [39] & Clemson (15) [25] (Tangerine, 2002) (108 attempted)
64—Texas (47) [37] & Washington (43) [27] (Holiday, 2001) (109 attempted)
61—Penn St. (38) [20] & Oregon (20) [41] (Rose, 1995) (92 attempted)
57—Michigan St. (44) [22] & Fresno St. *(35) [35] (Silicon Valley, 2001) (90 attempted)
56—Florida (56) [33] & Maryland (23) [23] (Orange, 2002) (88 attempted)

56—Georgia (28) [20] & Purdue (25) [36] (ot) (Outback, 2000) (93 attempted)
56—Richmond (49) [39] & Ohio (42) [17] (Tangerine, 1968) (91 attempted)
55—Idaho (42) [24] & Southern Miss. (35) [31] (Humanitarian, 1998) (93 attempted)
54—Florida St. (23) [24] & Florida (17) [30] (Sugar, Jan. 2, 1995) (84 attempted)
54—Bowling Green (35) [25] & Nevada (34) [29] (Las Vegas, 1992) (90 attempted)
54—(D) Washington (21) [35] & Maryland (20) [19] (Aloha, 1982) (88 attempted)
54—(D) Toledo (27) [11] & San Jose St. (25) [43] (California, 1981) (85 attempted)
53—Washington St. (33) [15] & Purdue (27) [38] (Sun, 2001) (116 attempted)
53—Marshall (64) [41] & East Caro. (61) [11] (2 ot) (GMAC, 2001) (93 attempted)
53—Louisville (29) [35] & Marshall (48) [18] (Motor City, 1998) (78 attempted)
53—(D) Southern California (28) [30] & Utah (21) [23] (Freedom, 1993) (84 attempted)
53—Washington St. (31) [32] & Utah (28) [21] (Copper, 1992) (88 attempted)
53—Penn St. (50) [11] & Brigham Young (39) [42] (Holiday, 1989) (80 attempted)
53—(D) Fresno St. (29) [31] & Bowling Green (28) [22] (California, 1982) (82 attempted)
52—Boston College (51) [25] & Toledo (25) [27] (Motor City, 2002) (76 attempted)
52—Tulane (36) [20] & Hawaii (28) [32] (Hawaii, 2002) (91 attempted)
52—Oregon (38) [28] & Colorado (16) [24] (Fiesta, 2002) (89 attempted)
52—Mississippi (34) [29] & Marshall (31) [23] (Motor City, 1997) (93 attempted)
52—Southern California (41) [29] & Northwestern (32) [23] (Rose, 1996) (83 attempted)
50—Purdue (34) [25] & Washington (24) [25] (Sun, 2002) (91 attempted)
50—Florida St. (2) [25] & Oklahoma (13) [25] (Orange, 2001) (91 attempted)
50—Tulane (41) [23] & Brigham Young (27) [27] (Liberty, 1998) (82 attempted)
50—Toledo (40) [23] & Nevada (37) [27] (ot) (Las Vegas, 1995) (92 attempted)
50—Kansas St. (52) [19] & Wyoming (17) [31] (Copper, 1993) (79 attempted)
50—Auburn (35) [27] & Mississippi (28) [23] (Gator, Jan. 2, 1971) (83 attempted)

MOST PASSING YARDS
(Followed by Comp.-Att.-Int.)
576—Marshall (64) vs. East Caro. (61) (2 ot) (GMAC, 2001) (41-70-2)
576—Brigham Young (39) vs. Penn St. (50) (Holiday, 1989) (42-59-2)
531—Fresno St. (35) vs. Michigan St. (44) (Silicon Valley, 2001) (35-58-2)
523—(D) Fresno St. (30) vs. Colorado (41) (Aloha, 1993) (37-63-1)
492—Washington St. (31) vs. Utah (28) (Copper, 1992) (32-48-1)
485—Brigham Young (31) vs. Oklahoma (6) (Copper, 1994) (23-46-0)
473—Texas (47) vs. Washington (43) (Holiday, 2001) (37-55-3)
469—(D) Iowa (55) vs. Texas (17) (Freedom, 1984) (30-40-0)
467—(D) San Jose St. (25) vs. Toledo (27) (California, 1981) (43-63-5)
464—Texas Tech (55) vs. Clemson (15) (Tangerine, 2002) (39-52-1)
458—Louisville (34) vs. Alabama (7) (Fiesta, 1991) (21-39-3)
456—Florida (56) vs. Maryland (23) (Orange, 2002) (33-49-2)
456—Oregon (20) vs. Penn St. (38) (Rose, 1995) (41-61-2)
456—(D) Oregon (43) vs. Colorado (51) (Aloha, 1998) (24-46-2)
455—Florida St. (40) vs. Texas Tech (17) (Tangerine, 1977) (25-35-0)
452—(D) Vanderbilt (28) vs. Air Force (36) (Hall of Fame, 1982) (38-51-3)
452—West Virginia (31) vs. Missouri (34) (Insight.com, 1998) (35-51-2)
449—Florida (17) vs. Florida St. (23) (Sugar, Jan. 2, 1995) (30-43-1)
447—Richmond (49) vs. Ohio (42) (Tangerine, 1968) (39-58-2)
446—Brigham Young (46) vs. Southern Methodist (45) (Holiday, 1980) (32-49-1)
444—LSU (47) vs. Illinois (34) (Sugar, 2002) (31-53-0)
442—(D) San Jose St. (48) vs. Central Mich. (24) (California, 1990) (32-43-1)
435—Southern California (55) vs. Texas Tech (14) (Cotton, 1995) (24-35-0)
428—Iowa (23) vs. North Carolina St. (28) (Peach, Dec. 31, 1988) (30-51-4)
423—Illinois (15) vs. Alabama (21) (Liberty, 1982) (35-58-7)
422—Florida St. (41) vs. Nebraska (17) (Fiesta, 1990) (25-41-0)
419—Purdue (27) vs. Washington St. (33) (Sun, 2001) (38-75-4)
419—Wisconsin (37) vs. Southern California (42) (Rose, 1963) (34-49-3)
418—UCLA (31) vs. Wisconsin (38) (Rose, 1999) (21-36-1)
413—Georgia (27) vs. Virginia (34) (Peach, Dec. 30, 1995) (31-59-2)
412—Alabama (29) vs. Army (28) (John Hancock Sun, 1988) (33-52-1)

MOST PASSING YARDS, BOTH TEAMS
907—Michigan St. (44) [376] & Fresno St. (35) [531] (Silicon Valley, 2001) (90 attempted)
808—Washington St. (31) [492] & Utah (28) [316] (Copper, 1992) (88 attempted)
791—Penn St. (50) [215] & Brigham Young (39) [576] (Holiday, 1989) (80 attempted)
783—Texas Tech (55) [464] & Clemson (15) [319] (Tangerine, 2002) (108 attempted)
774—Florida St. (23) [325] & Florida (17) [449] (Sugar, Jan. 2, 1995) (84 attempted)
766—Texas (47) [473] & Washington (43) [293] (Holiday, 2001) (109 attempted)
747—Marshall (48) [411] & Louisville (29) [336] (Motor City, 1998) (78 attempted)
746—LSU (47) [444] & Illinois (34) [302] (Sugar, 2002) (89 attempted)
737—Marshall (64) [576] & East Caro. (61) [161] (2 ot) (GMAC, 2001) (93 attempted)
734—Florida St. (40) [455] & Texas Tech (17) [279] (Tangerine, 1977) (63 attempted)
732—(D) Toledo (27) [265] & San Jose St. (25) [467] (California, 1981) (85 attempted)
727—Southern California (41) [391] & Northwestern (32) [336] (Rose, 1996) (83 attempted)
713—Florida (56) [456] & Maryland (23) [257] (Orange, 2002) (88 attempted)
708—(D) Navy (42) [395] & California (38) [313] (Aloha, 1996) (59 attempted)
706—Mississippi (38) [388] & West Virginia (49) [318] (Music City, 2000) (72 attempted)
700—Washington St. (33) [281] & Purdue (27) [419] (Sun, 2001) (116 attempted)
677—(D) Colorado (51) [221] & Oregon (43) [456] (Aloha, 1998) (70 attempted)
676—Clemson (49) [275] & Louisiana Tech (24) [401] (Humanitarian, 2001) (88 attempted)

673—Boston College (51) [342] & Toledo (25) [331] (Motor City, 2002) (76 attempted)
672—Southern California (42) [253] & Wisconsin (37) [419] (Rose, 1963) (69 attempted)
669—Mississippi (34) [332] & Marshall (31) [337] (Motor City, 1997) (93 attempted)
662—(D) San Jose St. (48) [442] & Central Mich. (24) [220] (California, 1990) (68 attempted)
658—Penn St. (38) [202] & Oregon (20) [456] (Rose, 1995) (92 attempted)
655—Pittsburgh (29) [347] & Iowa St. (37) [308] (Insight.com, 2000) (70 attempted)
654—(D) Iowa (55) [469] & Texas (17) [185] (Freedom, 1984) (74 attempted)
653—Idaho (42) [291] & Southern Miss. (35) [362] (Humanitarian, 1998) (93 attempted)

MOST PASSES HAD INTERCEPTED
8—Arizona (10) vs. Auburn (34) (Sun, 1968)
7—Illinois (15) vs. Alabama (21) (Liberty, 1982)
7—Missouri (3) vs. Penn St. (10) (Orange, 1970)
7—Texas A&M (21) vs. Alabama (29) (Cotton, 1942)
6—Georgia Tech (21) vs. Fresno St. (30) (Silicon Valley, 2002)
6—Georgia (6) vs. Nebraska (45) (Sun, 1969)
6—TCU (26) vs. Georgia (40) (Orange, 1942)
6—Southern Methodist (0) vs. Stanford (7) (Rose, 1936)

MOST PASSES HAD INTERCEPTED, BOTH TEAMS
12—Auburn (34) [4] & Arizona (10) [8] (Sun, 1968)
10—Georgia (40) [6] & TCU (26) [4] (Orange, 1942)
9—Alabama (21) [2] & Illinois (15) [7] (Liberty, 1982)
8—Ohio St. (28) [3] & Texas A&M (12) [5] (Cotton, 1987)
8—Nebraska (28) [3] & LSU (10) [5] (Sugar, 1985)
8—Penn St. (10) [1] & Missouri (3) [7] (Orange, 1970)
8—Nebraska (45) [2] & Georgia (6) [6] (Sun, 1969)
8—Texas (12) [3] & Mississippi (7) [5] (Cotton, 1962)

MOST PASSES ATTEMPTED WITHOUT AN INTERCEPTION
(Followed by Comp.-Att.-Int. and Yardage)
57—(D) Western Mich. (30) vs. Fresno St. (35) (California, 1988) (24-57-0, 366 yards)
53—LSU (47) vs. Illinois (38) (Sugar, 2002) (31-53-0, 444 yards)
52—Southern Miss. (35) vs. Idaho (42) (Humanitarian, 1998) (31-52-0, 362 yards)
51—Nevada (37) vs. Toledo (40) (ot) (Las Vegas, 1995) (27-51-0, 330 yards)
51—Florida (34) vs. Michigan St. (37) (Florida Citrus, 2000) (25-51-0, 300 yards)

MOST PASSES ATTEMPTED BY BOTH TEAMS WITHOUT AN INTERCEPTION
(Followed by Comp.-Att.-Int. and Yardage)
93—Idaho (42) [41] & Southern Miss. (35) [52] (Humanitarian, 1998) (55-93-0, 653 yards)
90—Bowling Green (35) [49] & Nevada (34) [41] (Las Vegas, 1992) (54-90-0, 597 yards)

HIGHEST COMPLETION PERCENTAGE
(Minimum 10 Attempts) (Followed by Comp.-Att.-Int. and Yardage)
.929—Texas (40) vs. Missouri (27) (Cotton, 1946) (13-14-0, 234 yards)
.900—Mississippi (13) vs. Air Force (0) (Liberty, 1992) (9-10-0, 163 yards)
.897—Georgia (33) vs. Wisconsin (6) (Outback, 1998) (26-29-0, 267 yards)
.889—Texas A&M (65) vs. Brigham Young (14) (Holiday, 1990) (16-18-0, 324 yards)
.833—Alabama (13) vs. Penn St. (6) (Sugar, 1975) (10-12-0, 210 yards)
.828—Oklahoma St. (62) vs. Wyoming (14) (Holiday, 1988) (24-29-0, 378 yards)
.824—Nebraska (21) vs. North Carolina (17) (Liberty, 1977) (14-17-2, 161 yards)
.818—Texas A&M (41) vs. Mississippi St. (43) (ot) (Independence, 2000) (9-11-1, 133 yards)
.813—TCU (28) vs. Syracuse (27) (Cotton, 1957) (13-16-0, 202 yards)
.800—Ohio St. (15) vs. Clemson (17) (Gator, 1978) (16-20-1, 205 yards)
.800—Georgia Tech (31) vs. Iowa St. (30) (Liberty, 1972) (12-15-1, 157 yards)
.783—Virginia Tech (20) vs. Air Force (13) (San Francisco, 2002) (18-23-0, 177 yards)
.778—Tennessee (27) vs. Indiana (22) (Peach, 1988) (21-27-0, 230 yards)
.771—Tennessee (45) vs. Michigan (17) (Florida Citrus, 2002) (27-35-0, 406 yards)
.771—Washington St. (10) vs. Baylor (3) (Alamo, 1994) (27-35-0, 286 yards)
.765—Illinois (17) vs. Hawaii (27) (Holiday, 1992) (26-34-1, 248 yards)
.765—Duke (7) vs. Arkansas (6) (Cotton, 1961) (13-17-1, 93 yards)
.763—Iowa (28) vs. UCLA (45) (Rose, 1986) (29-38-1, 319 yards)
.750—Texas Tech (55) vs. Clemson (15) (Tangerine, 2002) (39-52-1, 464 yards)
.750—Colorado St. (35) vs. Missouri (24) (Holiday, 1997) (18-24-0, 206 yards)
.750—Kansas St. (54) vs. Colorado St. (21) (Holiday, 1995) (24-32-1, 324 yards)
.750—Oklahoma (48) vs. Virginia (14) (Gator, Dec. 29, 1991) (27-36-0, 357 yards)
.750—(D) Iowa (55) vs. Texas (17) (Freedom, 1984) (30-40-0, 469 yards)

MOST YARDS PER ATTEMPT
(Minimum 10 Attempts)
21.7—Southern California (47) vs. Pittsburgh (14) (Rose, 1930) (13 for 282)
18.8—(D) Navy (42) vs. California (38) (Aloha, 1996) (21 for 295)
18.0—Texas A&M (65) vs. Brigham Young (14) (Holiday, 1990) (18 for 324)
17.5—Alabama (13) vs. Penn St. (6) (Sugar, 1975) (12 for 210)
17.1—Marshall (48) vs. Louisville (29) (Motor City, 1998) (24 for 411)
16.7—Texas (40) vs. Missouri (27) (Cotton, 1946) (14 for 234)
16.7—Texas (36) vs. Tennessee (13) (Cotton, 1969) (14 for 234)
16.7—Air Force (45) vs. Washington (25) (Oahu Classic, 1998) (16 for 267)
15.1—West Virginia (49) vs. Mississippi (38) (Music City, 2000) (21 for 318)
14.0—Michigan (31) vs. Auburn (28) (Florida Citrus, 2001) (21 for 294)
13.8—Kansas St. (35) vs. Syracuse (18) (Fiesta, 1997) (23 for 317)

MOST YARDS PER COMPLETION
(Minimum 8 Completions)
35.2—Southern California (47) vs. Pittsburgh (14) (Rose, 1930) (8 for 282)
29.3—Texas (28) vs. Navy (6) (Cotton, 1964) (8 for 234)
29.3—Texas (36) vs. Tennessee (13) (Cotton, 1969) (8 for 234)

FEWEST PASS ATTEMPTS
2—Air Force (38) vs. Mississippi St. (15) (Liberty, 1991) (completed 1)
2—(D) Army (10) vs. Michigan St. (6) (Cherry, 1984) (completed 1)
2—West Virginia (14) vs. South Carolina (3) (Peach, 1969) (completed 1)
3—Air Force (23) vs. Ohio St. (11) (Liberty, 1990) (completed 1)
3—Oklahoma (31) vs. Nebraska (24) (Orange, 1979) (completed 2)
3—Georgia Tech (21) vs. Pittsburgh (14) (Gator, 1956) (completed 3)
3—Georgia Tech (7) vs. Pittsburgh (0) (Sugar, 1956) (completed 0)
3—Miami (Fla.) (14) vs. Clemson (0) (Gator, 1952) (completed 2)
3—Hardin-Simmons (7) vs. Second Air Force (13) (Sun, 1943) (completed 1)
3—Catholic (20) vs. Mississippi (19) (Orange, 1936) (completed 1)

FEWEST PASS ATTEMPTS, BOTH TEAMS
9—Fordham (2) [4] & Missouri (0) [5] (Sugar, 1942)
13—Colorado (27) [9] & Clemson (21) [4] (Orange, 1957)
14—Texas (16) [8] & Tennessee (0) [6] (Cotton, 1953)
15—Utah (26) [4] & New Mexico (0) [11] (Sun, 1939)
15—LSU (7) [11] & Clemson (0) [4] (Sugar, 1959)

FEWEST PASS COMPLETIONS
(Followed by Comp.-Att.-Int.)
0—Army (28) vs. Alabama (29) (John Hancock Sun, 1988) (0-6-1)
0—Missouri (35) vs. Alabama (10) (Gator, 1968) (0-6-2)
0—(D) Missouri (14) vs. Georgia Tech (10) (Bluebonnet, 1962) (0-7-2)
0—(D) New Mexico (28) vs. Western Mich. (12) (Aviation, 1961) (0-4-0)
0—Utah St. (13) vs. New Mexico St. (20) (Sun, 1960) (0-4-0)
0—Georgia Tech (7) vs. Pittsburgh (0) (Sugar, 1956) (0-3-1)
0—Arkansas (0) vs. LSU (0) (Cotton, 1947) (0-4-1)
0—Rice (8) vs. Tennessee (0) (Orange, 1947) (0-4-2)
0—Miami (Fla.) (13) vs. Holy Cross (6) (Orange, 1946) (0-10-3)
0—Fordham (2) vs. Missouri (0) (Sugar, 1942) (0-4-0)
0—Arizona St. (0) vs. Catholic (0) (Sun, 1940) (0-7-2)
0—Tulane (13) vs. Texas A&M (14) (Sugar, 1940) (0-4-0)
0—West Virginia (7) vs. Texas Tech (6) (Sun, 1938) (0-7-0)

FEWEST PASS COMPLETIONS, BOTH TEAMS
3—Arizona St. (0) [0] & Catholic (0) [3] (Sun, 1940)
4—Penn St. (7) [2] & Alabama (0) [2] (Liberty, 1959)
5—Oklahoma (14) [3] & Michigan (6) [2] (Orange, 1976)
5—Kentucky (21) [2] & North Carolina (0) [3] (Peach, 1976)
5—Texas (16) [2] & Tennessee (0) [3] (Cotton, 1953)
5—Arkansas (0) [0] & LSU (0) [5] (Cotton, 1947)
5—Wake Forest (26) [1] & South Carolina (14) [4] (Gator, 1946)
5—Utah (26) [1] & New Mexico (0) [4] (Sun, 1939)

FEWEST PASSING YARDS
(Followed by Comp.-Att.-Int.)
-50—U. of Mexico (0) vs. Southwestern (Tex.) (35) (Sun, 1945) (2-9-3)
-2—Oklahoma (40) vs. Houston (14) (Sun, 1981) (1-5-1)
0—Army (28) vs. Alabama (29) (John Hancock Sun, 1988) (0-6-1)
0—Missouri (35) vs. Alabama (10) (Gator, 1968) (0-6-2)
0—(D) Missouri (14) vs. Georgia Tech (10) (Bluebonnet, 1962) (0-7-2)
0—(D) New Mexico (28) vs. Western Mich. (12) (Aviation, 1961) (0-4-0)
0—Utah St. (13) vs. New Mexico St. (20) (Sun, 1960) (0-4-0)
0—Georgia Tech (7) vs. Pittsburgh (0) (Sugar, 1956) (0-3-1)
0—Arkansas (0) vs. LSU (0) (Cotton, 1947) (0-4-1)
0—Rice (8) vs. Tennessee (0) (Orange, 1947) (0-4-2)
0—Miami (Fla.) (13) vs. Holy Cross (6) (Orange, 1946) (0-10-3)
0—Fordham (2) vs. Missouri (0) (Sugar, 1942) (0-4-0)
0—Tulane (13) vs. Texas A&M (14) (Sugar, 1940) (0-4-0)
0—Arizona St. (0) vs. Catholic (0) (Sun, 1940) (0-7-2)
0—West Virginia (7) vs. Texas Tech (6) (Sun, 1938) (0-7-0)
0—California (0) vs. Wash. & Jeff. (0) (Rose, 1922)
0—Oregon (6) vs. Harvard (7) (Rose, 1920)

FEWEST PASSING YARDS, BOTH TEAMS
16—Arkansas (0) [0] & LSU (0) [16] (Cotton, 1947)
16—Arizona St. (0) [0] & Catholic (0) [16] (Sun, 1940)
21—Fordham (2) [0] & Missouri (0) [21] (Sugar, 1942)
32—Rice (8) [0] & Tennessee (0) [32] (Orange, 1947)
40—Kentucky (21) [16] & North Carolina (0) [24] (Peach, 1976)
52—Colorado (27) [25] & Clemson (21) [27] (Orange, 1957)
59—Miami (Fla.) (13) [0] & Holy Cross (6) [59] (Orange, 1946)
60—North Carolina (26) [10] & Texas (16) [50] (Sun, 1982)
68—Penn St. (7) [41] & Alabama (0) [27] (Liberty, 1959)
68—Missouri (35) [0] & Alabama (10) [68] (Gator, 1968)
74—Oklahoma (41) [23] & Wyoming (7) [51] (Fiesta, 1976)
75—Southwestern (Tex.) (7) [65] & New Mexico (0) [10] (Sun, 1944)
77—Utah (26) [18] & New Mexico (0) [59] (Sun, 1939)
78—Texas (16) [32] & Tennessee (0) [46] (Cotton, 1953)

LOWEST COMPLETION PERCENTAGE
(Followed by Comp.-Att.-Int.)
.000—Army (28) vs. Alabama (29) (John Hancock Sun, 1988) (0-6-1)
.000—Missouri (35) vs. Alabama (10) (Gator, 1968) (0-6-2)

.000—(D) Missouri (14) vs. Georgia Tech (10) (Bluebonnet, 1962) (0-7-2)
.000—(D) New Mexico (28) vs. Western Mich. (12) (Aviation, 1961) (0-4-0)
.000—Utah St. (13) vs. New Mexico St. (20) (Sun, 1960) (0-4-0)
.000—Georgia Tech (7) vs. Pittsburgh (0) (Sugar, 1956) (0-3-1)
.000—Arkansas (0) vs. LSU (0) (Cotton, 1947) (0-4-1)
.000—Rice (8) vs. Tennessee (0) (Orange, 1947) (0-4-2)
.000—Miami (Fla.) (13) vs. Holy Cross (6) (Orange, 1946) (0-10-3)
.000—Fordham (2) vs. Missouri (0) (Sugar, 1942) (0-4-0)
.000—Tulane (13) vs. Texas A&M (14) (Sugar, 1940) (0-4-0)
.000—Arizona St. (0) vs. Catholic (0) (Sun, 1940) (0-7-2)
.000—West Virginia (7) vs. Texas Tech (6) (Sun, 1938) (0-7-0)

FEWEST YARDS PER PASS ATTEMPT

-5.6—U. of Mexico (0) vs. Southwestern (Tex.) (35) (Sun, 1945) (9 for -50)
-0.4—Oklahoma (40) vs. Houston (14) (Sun, 1981) (5 for -2)
0.0—Army (28) vs. Alabama (29) (John Hancock Sun, 1988) (6 for 0)
0.0—Missouri (35) vs. Alabama (10) (Gator, 1968) (6 for 0)
0.0—(D) Missouri (14) vs. Georgia Tech (10) (Bluebonnet, 1962) (7 for 0)
0.0—(D) New Mexico (28) vs. Western Mich. (12) (Aviation, 1961) (4 for 0)
0.0—Utah St. (13) vs. New Mexico St. (20) (Sun, 1960) (4 for 0)
0.0—Georgia Tech (7) vs. Pittsburgh (0) (Sugar, 1956) (3 for 0)
0.0—Arkansas (0) vs. LSU (0) (Cotton, 1947) (4 for 0)
0.0—Rice (8) vs. Tennessee (0) (Orange, 1947) (4 for 0)
0.0—Miami (Fla.) (13) vs. Holy Cross (6) (Orange, 1946) (10 for 0)
0.0—Fordham (2) vs. Missouri (0) (Sugar, 1942) (4 for 0)
0.0—Tulane (13) vs. Texas A&M (14) (Sugar, 1940) (4 for 0)
0.0—Arizona St. (0) vs. Catholic (0) (Sun, 1940) (7 for 0)
0.0—West Virginia (7) vs. Texas Tech (6) (Sun, 1938) (7 for 0)

FEWEST YARDS PER PASS COMPLETION
(Minimum 1 completion)

-25.0—U. of Mexico (0) vs. Southwestern (Tex.) (35) (Sun, 1945) (2 for -50)
-2.0—Oklahoma (40) vs. Houston (14) (Sun, 1981) (1 for -2)
3.0—West Virginia (14) vs. South Carolina (3) (Peach, 1969) (1 for 3)
3.2—LSU (0) vs. Arkansas (0) (Cotton, 1947) (5 for 16)
3.3—New Mexico (0) vs. Southwestern (Tex.) (7) (Sun, 1944) (3 for 10)
3.3—North Carolina (26) vs. Texas (10) (Sun, 1982) (3 for 10)
4.5—Alabama (34) vs. Miami (Fla.) (13) (Sugar, 1993) (4 for 18)
4.6—Texas (14) vs. Georgia Tech (7) (Cotton, 1943) (5 for 23)
4.8—UTEP (33) vs. Georgetown (20) (Sun, 1950) (5 for 24)
5.3—Case Reserve (26) vs. Arizona St. (13) (Sun, 1941) (3 for 16)
5.3—Arkansas (3) vs. UCLA (17) (Cotton, 1989) (4 for 21)

Scoring

MOST TOUCHDOWNS

10—Nebraska (66) vs. Northwestern (17) (Alamo, 2000) (6 rush, 4 pass)
9—Marshall (64) vs. East Caro. (61) (2 ot) (GMAC, 2001) (3 rush, 4 pass, 2 interception returns)
9—Illinois (63) vs. Virginia (21) (Micronpc.com, 1999) (6 rush, 3 pass)
9—Texas A&M (65) vs. Brigham Young (14) (Holiday, 1990) (5 rush, 4 pass)
9—Alabama (61) vs. Syracuse (6) (Orange, 1953) (4 rush, 3 pass, 1 punt return, 1 interception return)
9—(D) Centre (63) vs. TCU (7) (Fort Worth Classic, 1921) (8 rush, 1 blocked punt recovery in end zone)
8—Florida (56) vs. Maryland (23) (Orange, 2002) (3 rush, 5 pass)
8—Colorado (62) vs. Boston College (28) (Insight.com, 1999) (5 rush, 2 interception return, 1 punt return)
8—Nebraska (62) vs. Florida (24) (Fiesta, 1996) (6 rush, 1 pass, 1 interception return)
8—Kansas St. (54) vs. Colorado St. (21) (Holiday, 1995) (4 rush, 4 pass)
8—Oklahoma St. (62) vs. Wyoming (14) (Holiday, 1988) (6 rush, 2 pass)
8—Toledo (56) vs. Davidson (33) (Tangerine, 1969) (4 rush, 3 pass, 1 fumble return)
7—Texas Tech (55) vs. Clemson (15) (Tangerine, 2002) (1 rush, 5 pass, 1 punt return)
7—LSU (47) vs. Illinois (34) (Sugar, 2002) (4 rush, 3 pass)
7—Clemson (49) vs. Louisiana Tech (24) (Humanitarian, 2001) (2 rush, 5 pass)
7—East Caro. (61) vs. Marshall (64) (2 ot) (GMAC, 2001) (5 rush, 1 fumble return, 1 interception return)
7—West Virginia (49) vs. Mississippi (38) (Music City, 2000) (1 rush, 5 pass, 1 kickoff return)
7—(D) Washington (51) vs. Michigan St. (23) (Aloha, 1997) (3 rush, 2 pass, 2 interception returns)
7—Texas Tech (55) vs. Air Force (41) (Copper, 1995) (6 rush, 1 pass)
7—Southern California (55) vs. Texas Tech (14) (Cotton, 1995) (1 rush, 5 pass, 1 interception return)
7—UNLV (52) vs. Central Mich. (24) (Las Vegas, 1994) (3 rush, 3 pass, 1 fumble return)
7—Kansas St. (52) vs. Wyoming (17) (Copper, 1993) (3 rush, 2 pass, 1 punt return, 1 interception return)
7—Oklahoma (48) vs. Virginia (14) (Gator, Dec. 29, 1991) (4 rush, 2 pass, 1 blocked punt return)
7—(D) Texas Tech (49) vs. Duke (21) (All-American, 1989) (6 rush, 1 pass)
7—(D) Fresno St. (51) vs. Bowling Green (7) (California, 1985) (4 rush, 3 pass)
7—(D) Iowa (55) vs. Texas (17) (Freedom, 1984) (1 rush, 6 pass)
7—(D) Houston (47) vs. Tulane (7) (Bluebonnet, 1973) (7 rush)
7—Arizona St. (49) vs. Missouri (35) (Fiesta, 1972) (5 rush, 2 pass)
7—North Carolina St. (49) vs. West Virginia (13) (Peach, 1972) (4 rush, 3 pass)

7—Arizona St. (48) vs. North Carolina (26) (Peach, 1970) (6 rush, 1 pass)
7—Houston (49) vs. Miami (Ohio) (21) (Tangerine, 1962) (4 rush, 2 pass, 1 punt return)
7—Oklahoma (48) vs. Duke (21) (Orange, 1958) (3 rush, 2 pass, 1 interception return, 1 intercepted lateral return)
7—UTEP (47) vs. Florida St. (20) (Sun, 1955) (4 rush, 3 pass)
7—Michigan (49) vs. Southern California (0) (Rose, 1948) (3 rush, 4 pass)
7—Illinois (45) vs. UCLA (14) (Rose, 1947) (5 rush, 2 interception returns)

MOST TOUCHDOWNS, BOTH TEAMS

16—Marshall (64) [9] & East Caro. (61) (2 ot) [7] (GMAC, 2001)
13—Texas Tech (55) [7] & Air Force (41) [6] (Copper, 1995)
13—Richmond (49) [7] & Ohio (42) [6] (Tangerine, 1968)
12—LSU (47) [7] & Illinois (34) [5] (Sugar, 2002)
12—Nebraska (66) [10] & Northwestern (17) [2] (Alamo, 2000)
12—Colorado (62) [8] & Boston College (28) [4] (Insight.com, 1999)
12—Illinois (63) [9] & Virginia (21) [3] (Micronpc.com, 1999)
12—(D) Colorado (51) [6] & Oregon (43) [6] (Aloha, 1998)
11—Florida (56) [8] & Maryland (23) [3] (Orange, 2002)
11—Texas (47) [6] & Washington (43) [5] (Holiday, 2001)
11—West Virginia (49) [7] & Mississippi (38) [4] (Music City, 2000)
11—Idaho (42) [6] & Southern Miss. (35) [5] (Humanitarian, 1998)
11—(D) Navy (42) [6] & California (38) [5] (Aloha, 1996)
11—Nebraska (62) [8] & Florida (24) [3] (Fiesta, 1996)
11—Kansas St. (54) [8] & Colorado St. (21) [3] (Holiday, 1995)
11—Washington (46) [6] & Iowa (34) [5] (Rose, 1991)
11—Texas A&M (65) [9] & Brigham Young (14) [2] (Holiday, 1990)
11—Penn St. (50) [6] & Brigham Young (39) [5] (Holiday, 1989)
11—Arizona St. (49) [7] & Missouri (35) [4] (Fiesta, 1971)
11—Arizona St. (48) [7] & North Carolina (26) [4] (Peach, 1970)
11—Southern California (42) [6] & Wisconsin (37) [5] (Rose, 1963)
10—Clemson (49) [7] & Louisiana Tech (24) [3] (Humanitarian, 2001)
10—Marshall (48) [6] & Louisville (29) [4] (Motor City, 1998)
10—(D) Washington (51) [7] & Michigan St. (23) [3] (Aloha, 1997)
10—UNLV (52) [7] & Central Mich. (24) [3] (Las Vegas, 1994)
10—Utah St. (42) [6] & Ball St. (33) [4] (Las Vegas, 1993)
10—East Caro. (37) [5] & North Carolina St. (34) [5] (Peach, 1992)
10—(D) Texas Tech (49) [7] & Duke (21) [3] (All-American, 1989)
10—Mississippi (42) [6] & Air Force (29) [4] (Liberty, 1989)
10—Oklahoma St. (62) [8] & Wyoming (14) [2] (Holiday, 1988)
10—Boston College (45) [6] & Houston (28) [4] (Cotton, 1985)
10—Colorado (47) [6] & Alabama (33) [4] (Liberty, 1969)
10—(D) Nebraska (36) [5] & Miami (Fla.) (34) [5] (Gotham, 1962)
10—UTEP (47) [7] & Florida St. (20) [3] (Sun, 1955)
10—Alabama (61) [9] & Syracuse (6) [1] (Orange, 1953)

MOST TOUCHDOWNS RUSHING

8—(D) Centre (63) vs. TCU (7) (Fort Worth Classic, 1921)
7—(D) Houston (47) vs. Tulane (7) (Bluebonnet, 1973)
6—Nebraska (66) vs. Northwestern (17) (Alamo, 2000)
6—Illinois (63) vs. Virginia (21) (Micronpc.com, 1999)
6—Nebraska (42) vs. Tennessee (17) (Orange, 1998)
6—(D) Navy (42) vs. California (38) (Aloha, 1996)
6—Nebraska (62) vs. Florida (24) (Fiesta, 1996)
6—Texas Tech (55) vs. Air Force (41) (Copper, 1995)
6—Air Force (41) vs. Texas Tech (55) (Copper, 1995)
6—Texas Tech (49) vs. Duke (21) (All-American, 1989)
6—Oklahoma St. (62) vs. Wyoming (14) (Holiday, 1988)
6—Oklahoma (42) vs. Arkansas (8) (Orange, 1987)
6—Ohio St. (47) vs. Brigham Young (17) (Holiday, 1982)
6—Oklahoma (49) vs. Brigham Young (21) (Tangerine, 1976)
6—Arizona St. (48) vs. North Carolina (26) (Peach, 1970)
6—Michigan (49) vs. Stanford (0) (Rose, 1902)

MOST TOUCHDOWNS RUSHING, BOTH TEAMS

12—Texas Tech (55) [6] & Air Force (41) [6] (Copper, 1995)
9—Arizona St. (48) [6] & North Carolina (26) [3] (Peach, 1970)
8—Marshall (64) [3] & East Caro. (61) [5] (2 ot) (GMAC, 2001)
8—Oklahoma St. (62) [6] & Wyoming (14) [2] (Holiday, 1988)
8—Colorado (47) [5] & Alabama (33) [3] (Liberty, 1969)
7—Nebraska (66) [6] & Northwestern (17) [1] (Alamo, 2000)
7—Illinois (63) [6] & Virginia (21) [1] (Micronpc.com, 1999)
7—(D) Navy (42) [6] & California (38) [1] (Aloha, 1996)
7—Nebraska (62) [6] & Florida (24) [1] (Fiesta, 1996)
7—Kansas St. (54) [4] & Colorado St. (21) [3] (Holiday, 1995)
7—Oklahoma (42) [6] & Arkansas (8) [1] (Orange, 1987)
7—Oklahoma (35) [4] & West Virginia (33) [3] (John Hancock Sun, 1987)
7—UCLA (45) [5] & Iowa (28) [2] (Rose, 1986)
7—Oklahoma St. (49) [6] & Brigham Young (21) [1] (Tangerine, 1976)
7—Arizona St. (49) [5] & Missouri (35) [2] (Fiesta, 1972)
7—Penn St. (41) [5] & Oregon (12) [2] (Liberty, 1960)

MOST TOUCHDOWNS PASSING

6—(D) Iowa (55) vs. Texas (17) (Freedom, 1984)
5—Texas Tech (55) vs. Clemson (15) (Tangerine, 2002)
5—Florida (56) vs. Maryland (23) (Orange, 2002)
5—Illinois (34) vs. LSU (47) (Sugar, 2002)
5—Clemson (49) vs. Louisiana Tech (24) (Humanitarian, 2001)

5—West Virginia (49) vs. Mississippi (38) (Music City, 2000)
5—Southern California (55) vs. Texas Tech (14) (Cotton, 1995)
5—Florida St. (41) vs. Nebraska (17) (Fiesta, 1990)
5—Florida St. (36) vs. Oklahoma (19) (Gator, Jan. 2, 1965)
4—Marshall (38) vs. Louisville (15) (GMAC, 2002)
4—Oregon (38) vs. Colorado (16) (Fiesta, 2002)
4—Fresno St. (35) vs. Michigan St. (44) (Silicon Valley, 2001)
4—Texas (47) vs. Washington (43) (Holiday, 2001)
4—Marshall (64) vs. East Caro. (61) (2 ot) (GMAC, 2001)
4—Nebraska (66) vs. Northwestern (17) (Alamo, 2000)
4—Purdue (25) vs. Georgia (28) (ot) (Outback, 2000)
4—Michigan (35) vs. Alabama (34) (ot) (Orange, 2000)
4—Florida St. (46) vs. Virginia Tech (29) (Sugar, 2000)
4—Marshall (48) vs. Louisville (29) (Motor City, 1998)
4—West Virginia (31) vs. Missouri (34) (Insight.com, 1998)
4—Colorado (51) vs. Oregon (43) (Aloha, 1998)
4—Kansas St. (35) vs. Syracuse (18) (Fiesta, 1997)
4—Florida St. (31) vs. Notre Dame (26) (Orange, 1996)
4—Penn St. (43) vs. Auburn (14) (Outback, 1996)
4—Kansas St. (54) vs. Colorado St. (21) (Holiday, 1995)
4—East Caro. (37) vs. North Carolina St. (34) (Peach, 1992)
4—Miami (Fla.) (46) vs. Texas (3) (Cotton, 1991)
4—Michigan (35) vs. Mississippi (3) (Gator, Jan. 1, 1991)
4—Texas A&M (65) vs. Brigham Young (14) (Holiday, 1990)
4—UCLA (45) vs. Illinois (9) (Rose, 1984)
4—Purdue (28) vs. Missouri (25) (Liberty, 1980)
4—Pittsburgh (34) vs. Clemson (3) (Gator, 1977)
4—Florida St. (40) vs. Texas Tech (17) (Tangerine, 1977)
4—Davidson (33) vs. Toledo (56) (Tangerine, 1969)
4—Richmond (49) vs. Ohio (42) (Tangerine, 1968)
4—Ohio (42) vs. Richmond (49) (Tangerine, 1968)
4—Southern California (42) vs. Wisconsin (37) (Rose, 1963)
4—Michigan (49) vs. Southern California (0) (Rose, 1948)
4—Georgia (40) vs. TCU (26) (Orange, 1942)
4—Southern California (47) vs. Pittsburgh (14) (Rose, 1930)

MOST TOUCHDOWNS PASSING, BOTH TEAMS
8— LSU (47) [3] & Illinois (34) [5] (Sugar, 2002)
8—West Virginia (49) [5] & Mississippi (38) [3] (Music City, 2000)
8—(D) Iowa (55) [6] & Texas (17) [2] (Freedom, 1984)
8—Richmond (49) [4] & Ohio (42) [4] (Tangerine, 1968)
7—Michigan St. (44) [3] & Fresno St. (35) [4] (Silicon Valley, 2001)
7—Florida St. (31) [4] & Notre Dame (26) [3] (Orange, 1996)
7—East Caro. (37) [4] & North Carolina St. (34) [3] (Peach, 1992)
7—Toledo (56) [3] & Davidson (33) [4] (Tangerine, 1969)
7—Georgia (40) [4] & TCU (26) [3] (Orange, 1942)
6—Texas Tech (55) [5] & Clemson (15) [1] (Tangerine, 2002)
6—Florida (56) [5] & Maryland (23) [1] (Orange, 2002)
6—Clemson (49) [5] & Louisiana Tech (24) [1] (Humanitarian, 2001)
6—Texas (47) [4] & Washington (43) [2] (Holiday, 2001)
6—Michigan St. (37) [3] & Florida (34) [3] (Florida Citrus, 2000)
6—Purdue (37) [3] & Kansas St. (34) [3] (Alamo, 1998)
6—Mississippi (34) [3] & Marshall (31) [3] (Motor City, 1997)
6—Southern California (55) [5] & Texas Tech (14) [1] (Cotton, 1995)
6—(D) Kansas (51) [3] & UCLA (30) [3] (Aloha, 1995)
6—Utah St. (42) [3] & Ball St. (33) [3] (Las Vegas, 1993)
6—Miami (Fla.) (33) [3] & Alabama (25) [3] (Sugar, 1990)
6—Florida St. (41) [5] & Nebraska (17) [1] (Fiesta, 1990)
6—Texas A&M (65) [4] & Brigham Young (14) [2] (Holiday, 1990)
6—Florida St. (36) [5] & Oklahoma (19) [1] (Gator, Jan. 2, 1965)
6—Southern California (42) [4] & Wisconsin (37) [2] (Rose, 1963)

MOST FIELD GOALS MADE
5—Minnesota (29) vs. Arkansas (14) (Music City, 2002) (24, 45, 21, 22, 29 yards)
5—Texas A&M (22) vs. Michigan (20) (Alamo, 1995) (27, 49, 47, 31, 37 yards)
5—Mississippi St. (24) vs. North Carolina St. (28) (Peach, Jan. 1, 1995) (37, 21, 29, 36, 30 yards)
5—Florida (28) vs. Notre Dame (39) (Sugar, 1992) (26, 24, 36, 37, 24 yards)
5—Maryland (23) vs. Tennessee (30) (Florida Citrus, 1983) (18, 48, 31, 22, 26 yards)
4—Georgia (26) vs. Florida St. (13) (Sugar, 2003) (23, 42, 25, 35 yards)
4—Oklahoma St. (33) vs. Southern Miss. (23) (Houston, 2002) (46, 52, 29, 23 yards)
4—Washington St. (33) vs. Purdue (27) (Sun, 2001) (47, 34, 30, 37 yards)
4—Iowa (19) vs. Texas Tech (16) (Alamo, 2001) (36, 31, 46, 47 yards)
4—East Caro. (61) vs. Marshall (64) (2 ot) (GMAC, 2001) (25, 22, 32, 37 yards)
4—East Caro. (19) vs. Stanford (13) (Liberty, 1995) (46, 26, 41, 34 yards)
4—Oklahoma (25) vs. Penn St. (10) (Orange, 1986) (26, 31, 21, 22 yards)
4—North Carolina (26) vs. Texas (10) (Sun, 1982) (53, 47, 24, 42 yards)
4—Texas A&M (33) vs. Oklahoma St. (16) (Independence, 1981) (33, 32, 50, 18 yards)
4—West Virginia (26) vs. Florida (6) (Peach, Dec. 31, 1981) (35, 42, 49, 24 yards)
4—Missouri (19) vs. Southern Miss. (17) (Tangerine, 1981) (45, 41, 30, 28 yards)
4—Nebraska (45) vs. Georgia (6) (Sun, 1969) (50, 32, 42, 37 yards)
4—Alabama (12) vs. Mississippi (7) (Sugar, 1964) (46, 31, 34, 48 yards)

MOST FIELD GOALS MADE, BOTH TEAMS
(At Least One Field Goal by Both Teams)
7—Iowa (19) [4] & Texas Tech (16) [3] (Alamo, 2001)

7—Texas A&M (22) [5] & Michigan (20) [2] (Alamo, 1995)
7—North Carolina St. (28) [2] & Mississippi St. (24) [5] (Peach, Jan. 1, 1995)
6—Washington St. (33) [4] & Purdue (27) [2] (Sun, 2001)
6—Toledo (23) [3] & Cincinnati (16) [3] (Motor City, 2001)
6—Notre Dame (39) [1] & Florida (28) [5] (Sugar, 1992)
6—Syracuse (16) [3] & Auburn (16) [3] (Sugar, 1988)
6—Tennessee (30) [1] & Maryland (23) [5] (Florida Citrus, 1983)
5—Ohio St. (31) [3] & Miami (Fla.) (24) [2] (2 ot) (Fiesta, 2003)
5—Texas (47) [2] & Washington (43) [3] (Holiday, 2001)
5—Marshall (64) [1] & East Caro. (61) (2 ot) [4] (GMAC, 2001)
5—LSU (27) [2] & Notre Dame (9) [3] (Independence, 1997)
5—Penn St. (50) [3] & Brigham Young (39) [2] (Holiday, 1989)
5—Oklahoma (25) [4] & Penn St. (10) [1] (Orange, 1986)
5—North Carolina (26) [4] & Texas (10) [1] (Sun, 1982)
5—Texas A&M (33) [4] & Oklahoma St. (16) [1] (Independence, 1981)
5—Missouri (19) [4] & Southern Miss. (17) [1] (Tangerine, 1981)
5—Penn St. (9) [3] & Tulane (6) [2] (Liberty, 1979)
5—Penn St. (30) [3] & Texas (6) [2] (Cotton, 1972)

MOST POINTS, WINNING TEAM
66—Nebraska vs. Northwestern (17) (Alamo, 2000)
65—Texas A&M vs. Brigham Young (14) (Holiday, 1990)
64—Marshall vs. East Caro. (61) (2 ot) (GMAC, 2001)
63—Illinois vs. Virginia (21) (Micronpc.com, 1999)
62—Colorado vs. Boston College (28) (Insight.com, 1999)
62—Nebraska vs. Florida (24) (Fiesta, 1996)
62—Oklahoma St. vs. Wyoming (14) (Holiday, 1988)
61—Alabama vs. Syracuse (6) (Orange, 1953)
56—Florida vs. Maryland (23) (Orange, 2002)
56—Toledo vs. Davidson (33) (Tangerine, 1969)
55—Texas Tech vs. Clemson (15) (Tangerine, 2002)
55—Texas Tech vs. Air Force (41) (Copper, 1995)
55—Southern California vs. Texas Tech (14) (Cotton, 1995)
55—(D) Iowa vs. Texas (17) (Freedom, 1984)
54—Kansas St. vs. Colorado St. (21) (Holiday, 1995)
52—Florida vs. Florida St. (20) (Sugar, 1997)
52—UNLV vs. Central Mich. (24) (Las Vegas, 1994)
52—Kansas St. vs. Wyoming (17) (Copper, 1993)
51—Boston College vs. Toledo (25) (Motor City, 2002)
51—(D) Colorado vs. Oregon (43) (Aloha, 1998)
51—(D) Washington vs. Michigan St. (23) (Aloha, 1997)
51—(D) Kansas vs. UCLA (30) (Aloha, 1995)
51—(D) Fresno St. vs. Bowling Green (7) (California, 1985)
50—Penn St. vs. Brigham Young (39) (Holiday, 1989)

MOST POINTS, LOSING TEAM
61—East Caro. vs. Marshall (64) (2 ot) (GMAC, 2001)
45—Southern Methodist vs. Brigham Young (46) (Holiday, 1980)
43—Washington vs. Texas (47) (Holiday, 2001)
43—(D) Oregon vs. Colorado (51) (Aloha, 1998)
42—Ohio vs. Richmond (49) (Tangerine, 1968)
41—Texas A&M vs. Mississippi St. (43) (ot) (Independence, 2000)
41—Air Force vs. Texas Tech (55) (Copper, 1995)
39—Brigham Young vs. Penn St. (50) (Holiday, 1989)
38—Mississippi vs. West Virginia (49) (Music City, 2000)
38—(D) California vs. Navy (42) (Aloha, 1996)
38—San Diego St. vs. Iowa (39) (Holiday, 1986)
38—Florida St. vs. Arizona St. (45) (Fiesta, 1971)
37—Nevada vs. Toledo (40) (ot) (Las Vegas, 1995)
37—Miami (Fla.) vs. UCLA (39) (Fiesta, 1985)
37—Brigham Young vs. Indiana (38) (Holiday, 1979)
37—Wisconsin vs. Southern California (42) (Rose, 1963)
36—Washington St. vs. Brigham Young (38) (Holiday, 1981)
43—Washington vs. Texas (47) (Holiday, 2001)
35—Fresno St. vs. Michigan St. (44) (Silicon Valley, 2001)
35—Oregon vs. Wake Forest (39) (Independence, 1992)
35—Missouri vs. Arizona St. (49) (Fiesta, 1972)
34—Illinois vs. LSU (47) (Sugar, 2002)
34—Fresno St. vs. Air Force (37) (Silicon Valley, 2000)
34—Alabama vs. Michigan (35) (ot) (Orange, 2000)
34—Florida vs. Michigan St. (37) (Florida Citrus, 2000)
34—Kansas St. vs. Purdue (37) (Alamo, 1998)
34—Nevada vs. Bowling Green (35) (Las Vegas, 1992)
34—North Carolina St. vs. East Caro. (37) (Peach, 1992)
34—Iowa vs. Washington (46) (Rose, 1991)
34—Houston vs. Notre Dame (35) (Cotton, 1979)
34—(D) Miami (Fla.) vs. Nebraska (36) (Gotham, 1962)

MOST POINTS, BOTH TEAMS
125—Marshall (64) & East Caro. (61) (2 ot) (GMAC, 2001)
96—Texas Tech (55) & Air Force (41) (Copper, 1995)
94—(D) Colorado (51) & Oregon (43) (Aloha, 1998)
91—Brigham Young (46) & Southern Methodist (45) (Holiday, 1980)
91—Richmond (49) & Ohio (42) (Tangerine, 1968)
90—Texas (47) & Washington (43) (Holiday, 2001)
90—Colorado (62) & Boston College (28) (Insight.com, 1999)
89—Penn St. (50) & Brigham Young (39) (Holiday, 1989)

89—Toledo (56) & Davidson (33) (Tangerine, 1969)
87—West Virginia (49) & Mississippi (38) (Music City, 2000)
86—Nebraska (62) & Florida (24) (Fiesta, 1996)
84—Mississippi St. (43) & Texas A&M (41) (ot) (Independence, 2000)
84—Illinois (63) & Virginia (21) (Micronpc.com, 1999)
84—Arizona St. (49) & Missouri (35) (Fiesta, 1972)
83—Nebraska (66) & Northwestern (17) (Alamo, 2000)
83—Arizona St. (45) & Florida St. (38) (Fiesta, 1971)
81—LSU (47) & Illinois (34) (Sugar, 2002)
81—(D) Kansas (51) & UCLA (30) (Aloha, 1995)
80—(D) Navy (42) & California (38) (Aloha, 1996)
80—Washington (46) & Iowa (34) (Rose, 1991)
80—Colorado (47) & Alabama (33) (Liberty, 1969)
79—Florida (56) & Maryland (23) (Orange, 2002)
79—Michigan St. (44) & Fresno St. (35) (Silicon Valley, 2001)
79—Texas A&M (65) & Brigham Young (14) (Holiday, 1990)
79—Southern California (42) & Wisconsin (37) (Rose, 1963)
77—Marshall (48) & Louisville (29) (Motor City, 1998)
77—Idaho (42) & Southern Miss. (35) (Humanitarian, 1998)
77—Toledo (40) & Nevada (37) (ot) (Las Vegas, 1995)
77—Iowa (39) & San Diego St. (38) (Holiday, 1986)
76—Boston College (51) & Toledo (25) (Motor City, 2002)
76—Michigan (45) & Arkansas (31) (Florida Citrus, 1999)
76—Tennessee (48) & Northwestern (28) (Florida Citrus, 1997)
76—UNLV (52) & Central Mich. (24) (Las Vegas, 1994)
76—Oklahoma St. (62) & Wyoming (14) (Holiday, 1988)
75—Florida St. (46) & Virginia Tech (29) (Sugar, 2000)
75—Kansas St. (54) & Colorado St. (21) (Holiday, 1995)
75—Utah St. (42) & Ball St. (33) (Las Vegas, 1993)
75—Indiana (38) & Brigham Young (37) (Holiday, 1979)
75—Houston (47) & Miami (Ohio) (28) (Tangerine, 1962)

LARGEST MARGIN OF VICTORY
55—Alabama (61) vs. Syracuse (6) (Orange, 1953)
51—Texas A&M (65) vs. Brigham Young (14) (Holiday, 1990)
49—Nebraska (66) vs. Northwestern (17) (Alamo, 2000)
48—Oklahoma St. (62) vs. Wyoming (14) (Holiday, 1988)
44—(D) Fresno St. (51) vs. Bowling Green (7) (California, 1985)
43—Miami (Fla.) (46) vs. Texas (3) (Cotton, 1991)
42—Illinois (63) vs. Virginia (21) (Micronpc.com, 1999)
42—Texas (42) vs. Maryland (0) (Sun, 1978)
41—Syracuse (41) vs. Clemson (0) (Gator, 1996)
41—Southern California (55) vs. Texas Tech (14) (Cotton, 1995)
40—Texas Tech (55) vs. Clemson (15) (Tangerine, 2002)
40—(D) Houston (47) vs. Tulane (7) (Bluebonnet, 1973)
39—North Carolina (42) vs. Virginia Tech (3) (Gator, 1998)
39—Nebraska (45) vs. Georgia (6) (Sun, 1969)
38—Stanford (38) vs. Michigan St. (0) (Sun, 1996)
38—Nebraska (62) vs. Florida (24) (Fiesta, 1996)
38—(D) Iowa (55) vs. Texas (17) (Freedom, 1984)
36—North Carolina St. (49) vs. West Virginia (13) (Peach, 1972)
35—Michigan (42) vs. North Carolina St. (7) (Hall of Fame, 1994)
35—Kansas St. (52) vs. Wyoming (17) (Copper, 1993)
35—(D) Houston (35) vs. Navy (0) (Garden State, 1980)
35—North Carolina (35) vs. Air Force (0) (Gator, 1963)
35—Oklahoma (35) vs. LSU (0) (Sugar, 1950)
35—Southwestern (Tex.) (35) vs. U. of Mexico (0) (Sun, 1945)

FEWEST POINTS, WINNING TEAM
2—Fordham vs. Missouri (0) (Sugar, 1942)
3—Tennessee vs. Texas A&M (0) (Gator, 1957)
3—TCU vs. LSU (2) (Sugar, 1936)
6—UCLA vs. Illinois (3) (John Hancock, 1991)
6—Oregon St. vs. Villanova (0) (Liberty, 1962)
6—Tulsa vs. Texas Tech (0) (Sun, 1942)
6—Clemson vs. Boston College (3) (Cotton, 1940)
6—Auburn vs. Michigan St. (0) (Orange, 1938)
6—Santa Clara vs. LSU (0) (Sugar, 1938)

FEWEST POINTS, LOSING TEAM
0—By many teams

FEWEST POINTS, BOTH TEAMS
0—Air Force (0) & TCU (0) (Cotton, 1959)
0—Arkansas (0) & LSU (0) (Cotton, 1947)
0—Arizona St. (0) & Catholic (0) (Sun, 1940)
0—California (0) & Wash. & Jeff. (0) (Rose, 1922)

MOST POINTS SCORED IN ONE HALF
45—Colorado (62) vs. Boston College (28) (Insight.com, 1999) (1st half)
45—Oklahoma St. (62) vs. Wyoming (14) (Holiday, 1988) (2nd half)
43—Marshall (64) vs. East Caro. (61) (2 ot) (GMAC, 2001) (2nd half)
42—Boston College (51) vs. Toledo (25) (Motor City, 2002) (1st half)
42—Illinois (63) vs. Virginia (21) (Micronpc.com, 1999) (1st half)
42—Toledo (56) vs. Davidson (33) (Tangerine, 1969) (1st half)
40—Alabama (61) vs. Syracuse (6) (Orange, 1953) (2nd half)
38—East Caro. (61) vs. Marshall (64) (2 ot) (GMAC, 2001) (1st half)
38—Nebraska (66) vs. Northwestern (17) (Alamo, 2000) (1st half)

38—Penn St. (50) vs. Brigham Young (39) (Holiday, 1989) (2nd half)
38—Penn St. (41) vs. Baylor (20) (Cotton, 1975) (2nd half)
38—Mississippi (41) vs. Georgia Tech (18) (Peach, 1971) (1st half)
37—Michigan St. (44) vs. Fresno St. (35) (Silicon Valley, 2001) (1st half)
37—(D) Colorado (51) vs. Oregon (43) (Aloha, 1998) (1st half)
37—Texas A&M (65) vs. Brigham Young (14) (Holiday, 1990) (1st half)
35—Clemson (49) vs. Louisiana Tech (24) (Humanitarian, 2001) (2nd half)
35—West Virginia (49) vs. Mississippi (38) (Music City, 2000) (1st half)
35—(D) California (38) vs. Navy (42) (Aloha, 1996) (1st half)
35—Nebraska (62) vs. Florida (24) (Fiesta, 1996) (1st half)
35—Tennessee (45) vs. Virginia Tech (23) (Gator, 1994) (1st half)
35—Penn St. (42) vs. Tennessee (17) (Fiesta, 1992) (2nd half)
35—Southern California (42) vs. Ohio St. (17) (Rose, 1973) (2nd half)
35—North Carolina St. (49) vs. West Virginia (13) (Peach, 1972) (2nd half)
35—Houston (49) vs. Miami (Ohio) (21) (Tangerine, 1962) (2nd half)
34—Texas Tech (55) vs. Clemson (15) (Tangerine, 2002) (1st half)
34—Miami (Fla.) (37) vs. Nebraska (14) (Rose, 2002) (1st half)
34—LSU (47) vs. Illinois (34) (Sugar, 2002) (1st half)
34—Air Force (37) vs. Fresno St. (34) (Silicon Valley, 2000) (1st half)
34—East Caro. (40) vs. Texas Tech (27) (Galleryfurniture.com, 2000) (1st half)
34—(D) Kansas (51) vs. UCLA (30) (Aloha, 1995) (2nd half)
34—Southern California (55) vs. Texas Tech (14) (Cotton, 1995) (1st half)
34—Oklahoma (48) vs. Virginia (14) (Gator, Dec. 29, 1991) (1st half)
34—Purdue (41) vs. Georgia Tech (21) (Peach, 1978) (1st half)
34—Oklahoma (48) vs. Duke (21) (Orange, 1958) (2nd half)
34—UTEP (47) vs. Florida St. (20) (Sun, 1955) (1st half)

MOST POINTS SCORED IN ONE HALF, BOTH TEAMS
64—Kansas (51) [34] & UCLA (30) [30] (Aloha, 1995) (2nd half)
64—Penn St. (50) [38] & Brigham Young (39) [26] (Holiday, 1989) (2nd half)
63—(D) Navy (42) [28] & California (38) [35] (Aloha, 1996) (1st half)
60—Boston College (51) [42] & Toledo (25) [18] (Motor City, 2002) (1st half)
58—Michigan St. (44) [37] & Fresno St. (35) [21] (Silicon Valley, 2001) (1st half)
56—Marshall (64) [43] & East Caro. (61) [13] (2 ot) (GMAC, 2001) (2nd half)
55—Nebraska (66) [38] & Northwestern (17) [17] (Alamo, 2000) (1st half)
54—Utah St. (42) [21] & Ball St. (33) [33] (Las Vegas, 1993) (2nd half)
53—Texas (47) [33] & Washington (43) [20] (Holiday, 2001) (2nd half)
52—Colorado (62) [45] & Boston College (28) [7] (Insight.com, 1999) (1st half)
52—Tennessee (48) [31] & Northwestern (28) [21] (Florida Citrus, 1997) (1st half)
52—Texas Tech (55) [24] & Air Force (41) [28] (Copper, 1995) (2nd half)
52—Oklahoma St. (62) [45] & Wyoming (14) [7] (Holiday, 1988) (2nd half)
51—(D) Colorado (51) [37] & Oregon (43) [14] (Aloha, 1998) (1st half)
51—Penn St. (41) [38] & Baylor (20) [13] (Cotton, 1975) (2nd half)
49—Clemson (49) [35] & Louisiana Tech (24) [14] (Humanitarian, 2001) (2nd half)
49—Illinois (63) [42] & Virginia (21) [7] (Micronpc.com, 1999) (1st half)
49—Idaho (42) [28] & Southern Miss. (35) [21] (Humanitarian, 1998) (1st half)
49—Brigham Young (46) [33] & Southern Methodist (45) [16] (Holiday, 1980) (2nd half)
49—(D) Houston (31) [28] & North Carolina St. (31) [21] (Bluebonnet, 1974) (2nd half)
49—Arizona St. (49) [21] & Missouri (35) [28] (Fiesta, 1972) (2nd half)
49—Arizona St. (45) [21] & Florida St. (38) [28] (Fiesta, 1971) (1st half)
49—Toledo (56) [42] & Davidson (33) [7] (Tangerine, 1969) (1st half)
49—Richmond (49) [28] & Ohio (42) [21] (Tangerine, 1968) (1st half)
48—Oklahoma (48) [34] & Duke (21) [14] (Orange, 1958) (2nd half)
47—Arizona St. (48) [21] & North Carolina (26) [26] (Peach, 1970) (1st half)
46—Marshall (64) [8] & East Caro. (61) [38] (2 ot) (GMAC, 2001) (1st half)
45—South Carolina (31) [17] & Ohio St. (28) [28] (Outback, 2002) (2nd half)
45—Boise St. (34) [21] & Louisville (31) [24] (Humanitarian, 1999) (1st half)
45—Wisconsin (38) [24] & UCLA (31) [21] (Rose, 1999) (1st half)
45—Colorado (33) [24] & Washington (21) [21] (Holiday, 1996) (1st half)
45—LSU (45) [21] & Michigan St. (26) [24] (Independence, 1995) (1st half)
45—Tennessee (45) [35] & Virginia Tech (23) [10] (Gator, 1994) (1st half)
45—Boston College (45) [31] & Houston (28) [14] (Cotton, 1985) (1st half)
45—Southern California (42) [35] & Ohio St. (17) [10] (Rose, 1973) (2nd half)

MOST POINTS SCORED IN ONE QUARTER
31—Nebraska (66) vs. Northwestern (17) (Alamo, 2000) (2nd quarter)
31—(D) Iowa (55) vs. Texas (17) (Freedom, 1984) (3rd quarter)
30—Oklahoma (40) vs. Houston (14) (Sun, 1981) (4th quarter)
29—Oregon St. (41) vs. Notre Dame (9) (Fiesta, 2001) (3rd quarter)
29—Nebraska (62) vs. Florida (24) (Fiesta, 1996) (2nd quarter)
28—Boston College (55) vs. Toledo (25) (Motor City, 2002) (2nd quarter)
28—Clemson (49) vs. Louisiana Tech (24) (Humanitarian, 2001) (3rd quarter)
28—Marshall (64) vs. East Caro. (61) (ot) (GMAC, 2001) (3rd quarter)
28—West Virginia (49) vs. Mississippi (38) (Music City, 2000) (2nd quarter)
28—Illinois (63) vs. Virginia (21) (Micronpc.com, 1999) (2nd quarter)
28—Southern California (55) vs. Texas Tech (14) (Cotton, 1995) (1st quarter)
28—Oklahoma St. (62) vs. Wyoming (14) (Holiday, 1988) (3rd quarter)
28—Missouri (34) vs. Auburn (17) (Sun, 1973) (2nd quarter)
28—Mississippi (41) vs. Georgia Tech (18) (Peach, 1971) (2nd quarter)
28—Toledo (56) vs. Davidson (33) (Tangerine, 1969) (2nd quarter)
28—Houston (49) vs. Miami (Ohio) (21) (Tangerine, 1962) (2nd quarter)
27—Miami (Fla.) (37) vs. Nebraska (14) (Rose, 2002) (2nd quarter)
27—LSU (47) vs. Illinois (34) (Sugar, 2002) (2nd quarter)
27—Texas (47) vs. Washington (43) (Holiday, 2001) (4th quarter)
27—Penn St. (43) vs. Auburn (14) (Outback, 1996) (3rd quarter)
27—Oklahoma (48) vs. Virginia (14) (Gator, Dec. 29, 1991) (2nd quarter)

27—Brigham Young (46) vs. Southern Methodist (45) (Holiday, 1980) (4th quarter)
27—Oklahoma (48) vs. Duke (21) (Orange, 1958) (4th quarter)
27—UTEP (47) vs. Florida St. (20) (Sun, 1955) (2nd quarter)
27—Illinois (40) vs. Stanford (7) (Rose, 1952) (4th quarter)
26—North Carolina (26) vs. Arizona St. (48) (Peach, 1970) (2nd quarter)
25—Louisville (34) vs. Alabama (7) (Fiesta, 1991) (1st quarter)

MOST POINTS SCORED IN ONE QUARTER, BOTH TEAMS
45—Nebraska (66) [31] & Northwestern (17) [14] (Alamo, 2000) (2nd quarter)
43—Boston College (55) [28] & Toledo (25) [15] (Motor City, 2002) (2nd quarter)
43—(D) Navy (42) [21] & California (38) [22] (Aloha, 1996) (2nd quarter)
40—Arizona St. (48) [14] & North Carolina (26) [26] (Peach, 1970) (2nd quarter)
38—Missouri (34) [28] & Auburn (17) [10] (Sun, 1973) (2nd quarter)
37—Texas (47) [14] & Washington (43) [23] (Holiday, 2001) (2nd quarter)
37—(D) Kansas (51) [14] & UCLA (30) [23] (Aloha, 1995) (4th quarter)
37—Oklahoma (40) [30] & Houston (14) [7] (Sun, 1981) (4th quarter)
35—Michigan (35) [21] & Alabama (34) [14] (Orange, 2000) (3rd quarter)
35—Marshall (48) [14] & Louisville (29) [21] (Motor City, 1998) (2nd quarter)
35—Kansas St. (54) [21] & Colorado St. (21) [14] (Holiday, 1995) (3rd quarter)
35—Oklahoma St. (62) [28] & Wyoming (14) [7] (Holiday, 1988) (3rd quarter)
35—Oklahoma St. (49) [21] & Brigham Young (21) [14] (Tangerine, 1976) (2nd quarter)
35—(D) Houston (31) [21] & North Carolina St. (31) [14] (Bluebonnet, 1974) (4th quarter)
35—Arizona St. (49) [21] & Missouri (35) [14] (Fiesta, 1972) (4th quarter)
35—Richmond (49) [21] & Ohio (42) [14] (Tangerine, 1968) (2nd quarter)
34—Kansas St. (34) [14] & Arizona St. (27) [20] (Holiday, 2002) (2nd quarter)
34—LSU (47) [27] & Illinois (34) [7] (Sugar, 2002) (2nd quarter)
34—Texas (47) [27] & Washington (43) [7] (Holiday, 2001) (4th quarter)
34—West Virginia (49) [28] & Mississippi (38) [6] (Music City, 2000) (2nd quarter)
34—(D) Colorado (51) [20] & Oregon (43) [14] (Aloha, 1998) (2nd quarter)
34—Oklahoma (48) [27] & Virginia (14) [7] (Gator, Dec. 29, 1991) (2nd quarter)
34—Penn St. (50) [21] & Brigham Young (39) [13] (Holiday, 1989) (4th quarter)
34—Brigham Young (46) [27] & Southern Methodist (45) [7] (Holiday, 1980) (4th quarter)
34—Penn St. (42) [18] & Arizona St. (30) [16] (Fiesta, 1977) (4th quarter)
34—Mississippi (41) [28] & Georgia Tech (18) [6] (Peach, 1971) (2nd quarter)
34—Oklahoma (48) [27] & Duke (21) [7] (Orange, 1958) (4th quarter)

First Downs

MOST FIRST DOWNS
36—Marshall (64) vs. East Caro. (61) (2 ot) (GMAC, 2001) (9 rush, 25 pass, 2 penalty)
36—Oklahoma (48) vs. Virginia (14) (Gator, Dec. 29, 1991) (16 rush, 18 pass, 2 penalty)
35—Michigan (35) vs. Mississippi (3) (Gator, Jan. 1, 1991) (20 rush, 14 pass, 1 penalty)
35—Brigham Young (39) vs. Penn St. (50) (Holiday, 1989) (8 rush, 27 pass, 0 penalty)
34—(D) Fresno St. (30) vs. Colorado (41) (Aloha, 1993) (4 rush, 25 pass, 5 penalty)
34—Oklahoma St. (62) vs. Wyoming (14) (Holiday, 1988) (15 rush, 17 pass, 2 penalty)
34—(D) Miami (Fla.) (34) vs. Nebraska (36) (Gotham, 1962)
33—Toledo (40) vs. Nevada (37) (ot) (Las Vegas, 1995) (19 rush, 12 pass, 2 penalty)
33—Arizona St. (49) vs. Missouri (35) (Fiesta, 1972) (22 rush, 11 pass, 0 penalty)
32—LSU (47) vs. Illinois (34) (Sugar, 2002) (7 rush, 23 pass, 2 penalty)
32—Brigham Young (24) vs. Michigan (17) (Holiday, 1984)
32—Richmond (49) vs. Ohio (42) (Tangerine, 1968) (8 rush, 24 pass, 0 penalty)
32—Wisconsin (37) vs. Southern California (42) (Rose, 1963) (7 rush, 23 pass, 2 penalty)
31—Minnesota (30) vs. North Carolina St. (38) (Micronpc.com, 2000) (20 rush, 8 pass, 3 penalty)
31—North Carolina St. (23) vs. Miami (Fla.) (46) (Micron PC, 1998) (18 rush, 10 pass, 3 penalty)
31—UCLA (16) vs. Wisconsin (21) (Rose, 1994)
31—Arkansas (27) vs. Tennessee (31) (Cotton, 1990) (21 rush, 10 pass, 0 penalty)
31—Florida St. (34) vs. Oklahoma St. (23) (Gator, 1985) (10 rush, 21 pass, 0 penalty)
31—Brigham Young (37) vs. Indiana (38) (Holiday, 1979) (9 rush, 21 pass, 1 penalty)
31—(D) Purdue (27) vs. Tennessee (22) (Bluebonnet, 1979)
31—(D) Houston (26) vs. Dayton (21) (Salad, 1952) (25 rush, 6 pass, 0 penalty)

MOST FIRST DOWNS, BOTH TEAMS
61—Penn St. (50) [26] & Brigham Young (39) [35] (Holiday, 1989)
59—Marshall (64) [36] & East Caro. (61) (2 ot) [23] (GMAC, 2001)
58—Miami (Fla.) (46) [27] & North Carolina St. (23) [31] (Micron PC, 1998)
56—Toledo (40) [33] & Nevada (37) [23] (ot) (Las Vegas, 1995)
56—Mississippi (42) [30] & Air Force (29) [26] (Liberty, 1989)
55—Michigan (35) [35] & Mississippi (3) [20] (Gator, Jan. 1, 1991)
54—Boise St. (34) [28] & Louisville (31) [26] (Humanitarian, 1999)
54—UCLA (45) [29] & Iowa (28) [25] (Rose, 1986)
54—Florida St. (34) [31] & Oklahoma St. (23) [23] (Gator, 1985)
53—Clemson (49) [28] & Louisiana Tech (24) [25] (Humanitarian, 2001)
53—Miami (Fla.) (37) [28] & Florida (20) [25] (Sugar, 2001)
53—North Carolina St. (38) [22] & Minnesota (30) [31] (Micronpc.com, 2000)
53—Marshall (48) [27] & Louisville (29) [26] (Motor City, 1998)
53—Texas Tech (55) [28] & Air Force (41) [25] (Copper, 1995)
53—Colorado (41) [19] & Fresno St. (30) [34] (Aloha, 1993)
53—Tennessee (23) [28] & Virginia (22) [25] (Sugar, 1991)
53—Colorado (47) [29] & Alabama (33) [24] (Liberty, 1969)
52—Michigan St. (37) [25] & Florida (34) [27] (Florida Citrus, 2000)

52—Georgia Tech (35) [28] & West Virginia (30) [24] (Carquest, 1997)
52—Mississippi (34) [29] & Marshall (31) [23] (Motor City, 1997)
52—Wisconsin (21) [21] & UCLA (16) [31] (Rose, 1994)
52—Notre Dame (39) [23] & Florida (28) [29] (Sugar, 1992)
52—Indiana (38) [21] & Brigham Young (37) [31] (Holiday, 1979)
51—Boston College (51) [30] & Toledo (25) [21] (Motor City, 2002)
51—Texas (47) [29] & Washington (43) [22] (Holiday, 2001)
51—Georgia (28) [21] & Purdue (25) [30] (ot) (Outback, 2000)
51—Miami (Fla.) (28) [22] & Georgia Tech (13) [29] (Gator, 2000)
51—Idaho (42) [26] & Southern Miss. (35) [25] (Humanitarian, 1998)
51—Tennessee (48) [29] & Northwestern (28) [22] (Florida Citrus, 1997)
51—Texas (35) & North Carolina (31) (Sun, 1994)
51—(D) Arkansas (28) [28] & Florida (24) [23] (Bluebonnet, 1982)
50—(D) Toledo (27) [21] & San Jose St. (25) [29] (California, 1981)
50—Texas (21) [25] & Notre Dame (17) [25] (Cotton, 1970)

MOST FIRST DOWNS RUSHING
26—Oklahoma (40) vs. Auburn (22) (Sugar, Jan. 1, 1972)
25—(D) Houston (26) vs. Dayton (21) (Salad, 1952)
24—Nebraska (66) vs. Northwestern (17) (Alamo, 2000)
24—Colorado (47) vs. Alabama (33) (Liberty, 1969)
23—Georgia Tech (31) vs. Texas Tech (21) (Gator, Dec. 31, 1965)
22—Syracuse (30) vs. Houston (17) (Liberty, 1996)
22—(D) Arkansas (28) vs. Florida (24) (Bluebonnet, 1982)
22—Oklahoma (41) vs. Wyoming (7) (Fiesta, 1976)
22—Arizona St. (49) vs. Missouri (35) (Fiesta, 1972)
21—Nebraska (62) vs. Florida (24) (Fiesta, 1996)
21—Arkansas (27) vs. Tennessee (31) (Cotton, 1990)
21—Florida St. (7) vs. Oklahoma (24) (Orange, 1980)
21—(D) Houston (35) vs. Navy (0) (Garden State, 1980)
21—Mississippi St. (26) vs. North Carolina (24) (Sun, 1974)
21—Missouri (35) vs. Alabama (10) (Gator, 1968)

MOST FIRST DOWNS RUSHING, BOTH TEAMS
36—Miami (Fla.) (46) [16] & Texas (3) [20] (Cotton, 1991)
36—Colorado (47) [24] & Alabama (33) [12] (Liberty, 1969)
32—Miami (Fla.) (46) [14] & North Carolina St. (23) [18] (Micron PC, 1998)
32—Texas Tech (55) [15] & Air Force (41) [17] (Copper, 1995)
32—Tennessee (31) [11] & Arkansas (27) [21] (Cotton, 1990)
32—Oklahoma (41) [22] & Wyoming (7) [10] (Fiesta, 1976)
32—Arizona St. (49) [22] & Missouri (35) [10] (Fiesta, 1972)
32—Texas (21) [19] & Notre Dame (17) [13] (Cotton, 1970)
31—Air Force (38) [18] & Mississippi St. (15) [13] (Liberty, 1991)

MOST FIRST DOWNS PASSING
27—Brigham Young (39) vs. Penn St. (50) (Holiday, 1989)
25—Marshall (64) vs. East Caro. (61) (2 ot) (GMAC, 2001)
25—(D) Fresno St. (30) vs. Colorado (41) (Aloha, 1993)
24—West Virginia (31) vs. Missouri (34) (Insight.com, 1998)
24—Richmond (49) vs. Ohio (42) (Tangerine, 1968)
23—LSU (47) vs. Illinois (34) (Sugar, 2002)
23—Florida (56) vs. Maryland (23) (Orange, 2002)
23—Tennessee (48) vs. Northwestern (28) (Florida Citrus, 1997)
23—(D) San Jose St. (25) vs. Toledo (27) (California, 1981)
23—Wisconsin (37) vs. Southern California (42) (Rose, 1963)
21—Southern California (41) vs. Northwestern (32) (Rose, 1996)
21—(D) Fresno St. (29) vs. Bowling Green (28) (California, 1982)
21—Brigham Young (46) vs. Southern Methodist (45) (Holiday, 1980)
21—Brigham Young (37) vs. Indiana (38) (Holiday, 1979)
20—Nevada (18) vs. Ball St. (15) (Las Vegas, 1996)
20—Mississippi (20) vs. Texas Tech (17) (Independence, 1986)
20—Brigham Young (24) vs. Michigan (17) (Holiday, 1984)
20—(D) Vanderbilt (28) vs. Air Force (36) (Hall of Fame, 1982)
19—Brigham Young (21) vs. Ohio St. (28) (Holiday, 1993)
19—(D) Oregon (31) vs. Colorado St. (32) (Freedom, 1990)
19—Florida St. (31) vs. Nebraska (28) (Fiesta, 1988)
19—Florida St. (34) vs. Oklahoma (23) (Gator, 1985)
19—Illinois (29) vs. Army (31) (Peach, 1985)

MOST FIRST DOWNS PASSING, BOTH TEAMS
38—Penn St. (50) [11] & Brigham Young (39) [27] (Holiday, 1989)
36—Tennessee (48) [23] & Northwestern (28) [13] (Florida Citrus, 1997)
35—Miami (Fla.) (37) [18] & Florida (20) [17] (Sugar, 2001)
33—Florida (56) [23] & Maryland (23) [10] (Orange, 2002)
33—Texas (43) [17] & Washington (43) [16] (Holiday, 2001)
33—Marshall (64) [25] & East Caro. (8) (61) (2 ot) (GMAC, 2001)
32—LSU (47) [23] & Illinois (34) [9] (Sugar, 2002)
32—Southern California (41) [21] & Northwestern (32) [11] (Rose, 1996)
31—Missouri (34) [7] & West Virginia (31) [24] (Insight.com, 1998)
30—Idaho (42) [15] & Southern Miss. (35) [15] (Humanitarian, 1998)
30—Georgia Tech (35) [15] & West Virginia (30) [15] (Carquest, 1997)
30—(D) Colorado (41) [5] & Fresno St. (30) [25] (Aloha, 1993)
30—(D) Fresno St. (29) [21] & Bowling Green (28) [9] (California, 1982)
30—Richmond (49) [24] & Ohio (42) [6] (Tangerine, 1968)
29—(D) Navy (42) [12] & California (38) [17] (Aloha, 1996)
29—Mississippi (42) [17] & Air Force (29) [12] (Liberty, 1989)
29—Indiana (38) [8] & Brigham Young (37) [21] (Holiday, 1979)
28—Ohio St. (28) [12] & Pittsburgh (23) [16] (Fiesta, 1984)

27—Florida St. (23) [12] & Florida (17) [15] (Sugar, Jan. 2, 1995)
27—Brigham Young (31) [18] & Oklahoma (6) [9] (Copper, 1994)
27—Arizona St. (45) [13] & Florida St. (38) [14] (Fiesta, 1971)
26—Clemson (49) [8] & Louisiana Tech (24) [18] (Humanitarian, 2001)
26—Boston College (31) [16] & Virginia (13) [10] (Carquest, 1994)
26—(D) Southern California (28) [15] & Utah (21) [11] (Freedom, 1993)
26—Brigham Young (24) [20] & Michigan (17) [6] (Holiday, 1984)
26—(D) Washington (21) [15] & Maryland (20) [11] (Aloha, 1982)
26—(D) Air Force (36) [6] & Vanderbilt (28) [20] (Hall of Fame, 1982)
25—Nevada (18) [20] & Ball St. (15) [5] (Las Vegas, 1996)
25—Wisconsin (34) [8] & Duke (20) [17] (Hall of Fame, 1995)
25—Texas (35) [9] & North Carolina (31) [16] (Sun, 1994)
25—Oklahoma St. (62) [17] & Wyoming (14) [8] (Holiday, 1988)
25—Florida St. (31) [19] & Nebraska (28) [6] (Fiesta, 1988)
25—Miami (Fla.) (31) [15] & Nebraska (30) [10] (Orange, 1984)
25—Brigham Young (46) [21] & Southern Methodist (45) [4] (Holiday, 1980)

MOST FIRST DOWNS BY PENALTY
6—Florida (52) vs. Florida St. (20) (Sugar, 1997)
6—Texas (3) vs. Miami (Fla.) (46) (Cotton, 1991)
5—Iowa (27) vs. Texas Tech (0) (Alamo, 1996)
5—(D) Arizona (13) vs. Utah (16) (Freedom, 1994)
5—(D) Fresno St. (30) vs. Colorado (41) (Aloha, 1993)
5—West Virginia (21) vs. Notre Dame (34) (Fiesta, 1989)
5—(D) Washington (34) vs. Florida (7) (Freedom, 1989)
5—(D) Western Mich. (30) vs. Fresno St. (35) (California, 1988)
5—Miami (Fla.) (7) vs. Tennessee (35) (Sugar, 1986)
5—(D) Miami (Ohio) (7) vs. San Jose St. (37) (California, 1986)
4—Texas A&M (27) vs. TCU (9) (Galleryfurniture.com, 2001)
4—Purdue (37) vs. Kansas St. (34) (Alamo, 1998)
4—(D) Oregon (43) vs. Colorado (51) (Aloha, 1998)
4—Syracuse (18) vs. Kansas St. (35) (Fiesta, 1997)
4—Northwestern (28) vs. Tennessee (48) (Florida Citrus, 1997)
4—Texas A&M (22) vs. Michigan (20) (Alamo, 1995)
4—Michigan (20) vs. Texas A&M (22) (Alamo, 1995)
4—Texas (35) vs. North Carolina (31) (Sun, 1994)
4—Alabama (25) vs. Miami (Fla.) (33) (Sugar, 1990)
4—Brigham Young (14) vs. Texas A&M (65) (Holiday, 1990)
4—Georgia (10) vs. Texas (9) (Cotton, 1984)
4—(D) Iowa (55) vs. Texas (17) (Freedom, 1984)
4—(D) Vanderbilt (28) vs. Air Force (36) (Hall of Fame, 1982)
4—Maryland (20) vs. Florida (35) (Tangerine, 1980)
4—Baylor (20) vs. Penn St. (41) (Cotton, 1975)
4—Arkansas (13) vs. Tennessee (14) (Liberty, 1971)
4—Arizona St. (45) vs. Florida St. (38) (Fiesta, 1971)
4—Alabama (33) vs. Colorado (47) (Liberty, 1969)
4—Texas A&M (21) vs. Alabama (29) (Cotton, 1942)

MOST FIRST DOWNS BY PENALTY, BOTH TEAMS
8—Florida (52) [6] & Florida St. (20) [2] (Sugar, 1997)
8—Texas A&M (22) [4] & Michigan (20) [4] (Alamo, 1995)
8—Miami (Fla.) (46) [2] & Texas (3) [6] (Cotton, 1991)
7—Iowa (27) [5] & Texas Tech (0) [2] (Alamo, 1996)
7—(D) Washington (34) [5] & Florida (7) [2] (Freedom, 1989)
7—Tennessee (35) [2] & Miami (Fla.) (7) [5] (Sugar, 1986)
6—Tennessee (48) [2] & Northwestern (28) [4] (Florida Citrus, 1997)
6—(D) Colorado (41) [1] & Fresno St. (30) [5] (Aloha, 1993)
6—Miami (Fla.) (33) [2] & Alabama (25) [4] (Sugar, 1990)
5—Texas A&M (14) & Ohio St. (24) [2] (Sugar, 1999)
5—Idaho (42) [3] & Southern Miss. (35) [2] (Humanitarian, 1998)
5—(D) Colorado (51) [1] & Oregon (43) [4] (Aloha, 1998)
5—North Carolina (20) [3] & West Virginia (13) [2] (Gator, 1996)
5—Texas (35) [4] & North Carolina (31) [1] (Sun, 1994)
5—(D) Utah (16) [0] & Arizona (13) [5] (Freedom, 1994)
5—Florida (41) [3] & West Virginia (7) [2] (Sugar, 1994)
5—Texas A&M (65) [1] & Brigham Young (14) [4] (Holiday, 1990)
5—Notre Dame (34) [0] & West Virginia (21) [5] (Fiesta, 1989)
5—Georgia (10) [4] & Texas (9) [1] (Cotton, 1984)
5—Southern Methodist (7) [3] & Pittsburgh (3) [2] (Cotton, 1983)
5—Pittsburgh (16) [3] & Arizona (10) [2] (Fiesta, 1979)
5—Penn St. (41) [1] & Baylor (20) [4] (Cotton, 1975)

FEWEST FIRST DOWNS
1—Alabama (29) vs. Texas A&M (21) (Cotton, 1942) (passing)
1—Arkansas (0) vs. LSU (0) (Cotton, 1947) (rushing)
2—Michigan St. (0) vs. Auburn (6) (Orange, 1938) (1 rushing, 1 passing)

FEWEST FIRST DOWNS, BOTH TEAMS
10—Texas (7) [3] & Randolph Field (7) [7] (Cotton, 1944)
12—LSU (19) [4] & Texas A&M (14) [8] (Orange, 1944)

FEWEST FIRST DOWNS RUSHING
0—Southern California (19) vs. TCU (28) (Sun, 1998)
0—Florida (18) vs. Missouri (20) (Sugar, 1966)
0—Navy (6) vs. Texas (28) (Cotton, 1964)
0—Alabama (29) vs. Texas A&M (21) (Cotton, 1942)

FEWEST FIRST DOWNS RUSHING, BOTH TEAMS
3—Alabama (29) [0] & Texas A&M (21) [3] (Cotton, 1942)

8—(D) Southern California (28) [4] & Utah (21) [4] (Freedom, 1993)
9—Texas (28) [9] & Navy (6) [0] (Cotton, 1964)
9—Florida St. (41) [2] & Nebraska (17) [7] (Fiesta, 1990)

FEWEST FIRST DOWNS PASSING
0—Army (28) vs. Alabama (29) (John Hancock Sun, 1988)
0—Oklahoma (40) vs. Houston (10) (Sun, 1981)
0—West Virginia (14) vs. South Carolina (3) (Peach, 1969)
0—Missouri (35) vs. Alabama (10) (Gator, 1968)
0—Virginia Tech (7) vs. Miami (Fla.) (14) (Liberty, 1966)
0—Auburn (7) vs. Mississippi (13) (Liberty, 1965)
0—Alabama (10) vs. Arkansas (3) (Sugar, 1962)
0—(D) Missouri (14) vs. Georgia Tech (10) (Bluebonnet, 1962)
0—Utah St. (13) vs. New Mexico St. (20) (Sun, 1960)
0—Arkansas (0) vs. LSU (0) (Cotton, 1947)
0—Fordham (2) vs. Missouri (0) (Sugar, 1942)
0—Arizona St. (0) vs. Catholic (0) (Sun, 1940)
0—West Virginia (7) vs. Texas Tech (6) (Sun, 1938)

FEWEST FIRST DOWNS PASSING, BOTH TEAMS
1—Alabama (10) [0] & Arkansas (3) [1] (Sugar, 1962)
4—Rice (28) [3] & Colorado (14) [1] (Cotton, 1938)
4—Texas (16) [2] & Tennessee (0) [2] (Cotton, 1953)
4—Oklahoma (41) [1] & Wyoming (7) [3] (Fiesta, 1976)

Punting

MOST PUNTS
17—Duke (3) vs. Southern California (7) (Rose, 1939)
16—Alabama (29) vs. Texas A&M (21) (Cotton, 1942)
16—New Mexico St. (14) vs. Hardin-Simmons (14) (Sun, 1936)
15—Tennessee (0) vs. Rice (8) (Orange, 1947)
14—Tulsa (7) vs. Tennessee (14) (Sugar, 1943)
14—Santa Clara (6) vs. LSU (0) (Sugar, 1938)
14—LSU (0) vs. Santa Clara (6) (Sugar, 1938)
14—TCU (3) vs. LSU (2) (Sugar, 1936)
13—Rice (8) vs. Tennessee (0) (Orange, 1947)
13—Tennessee (0) vs. Southern California (25) (Rose, 1945)
13—Oklahoma (0) vs. Tennessee (17) (Orange, 1939)
13—Catholic (20) vs. Mississippi (19) (Orange, 1936)
13—LSU (2) vs. TCU (3) (Sugar, 1936)
13—Miami (Fla.) (0) vs. Bucknell (26) (Orange, 1935)

MOST PUNTS, BOTH TEAMS
28—Santa Clara (6) [14] & LSU (0) [14] (Sugar, 1938)
28—Rice (8) [13] & Tennessee (0) [15] (Orange, 1947)
27—TCU (3) [14] & LSU (2) [13] (Sugar, 1936)
25—Tennessee (17) [12] & Oklahoma (0) [13] (Orange, 1939)
24—Catholic (20) [13] & Mississippi (19) [11] (Orange, 1936)
23—UTEP (14) [12] & Mississippi (7) [11] (Sun, 1967)
22—Auburn (6) [10] & Michigan St. (0) [12] (Orange, 1938)

HIGHEST PUNTING AVERAGE
(Minimum 5 Punts)
53.9—Southern California (7) vs. Wisconsin (0) (Rose, 1953) (8 for 431)
53.8—Hawaii (28) vs. Tulane (36) (Hawaii, 2002) (5 for 269)
52.3—Tennessee (17) vs. Nebraska (42) (Orange, 1998) (6 for 314)
52.0—Iowa (27) vs. Texas Tech (0) (Alamo, 1996) (5 for 260)
51.5—(D) Colorado (51) vs. Oregon (43) (Aloha, 1998) (6 for 309)
51.0—Penn St. (10) vs. Clemson (35) (Florida Citrus, 1988) (5 for 255)
50.2—Marshall (38) vs. Louisville (15) (GMAC, 2002) (6 for 301)
50.0—(D) Oregon (17) vs. Wake Forest (38) (Seattle, 2002) (6 for 300)
50.0—Nevada (37) vs. Toledo (40) (ot) (Las Vegas, 1995) (5 for 250)
50.0—Mississippi St. (17) vs. Nebraska (31) (Sun, 1980) (5 for 250)
49.8—TCU (9) vs. Texas A&M (28) (Galleryfurniture.com, 2001) (6 for 299)
49.3—Auburn (10) vs. North Carolina (16) (Peach, 2001) (9 for 444)
49.3—Clemson (0) vs. Syracuse (41) (Gator, 1996) (6 for 296)
49.2—(D) Air Force (24) vs. Texas (16) (Bluebonnet, 1985) (11 for 541)
49.2—Arkansas (3) vs. UCLA (17) (Cotton, 1989) (6 for 295)
49.1—Cincinnati (16) vs. Toledo (23) (Motor City, 2001) (7 for 344)
49.0—Iowa (7) vs. Arizona St. (17) (Sun, 1997) (8 for 392)
49.0—Indiana (24) vs. Baylor (0) (Copper, 1991) (6 for 294)
49.0—(D) Mississippi St. (10) vs. Kansas (0) (Hall of Fame, 1981) (9 for 441)
48.8—UTEP (23) vs. Boise St. (38) (Humanitarian, 2000) (5 for 244)
48.3—Brigham Young (3) vs. Marshall (21) (Motor City, 1999) (7 for 338)
48.2—Georgia Tech (14) vs. LSU (28) (Peach, 2000) (5 for 241)
48.1—Florida (52) vs. Florida St. (20) (Sugar, 1997) (7 for 337)
48.1—Ohio St. (14) vs. Tennessee (20) (Florida Citrus, 1996) (7 for 337)
48.0—(D) Wake Forest (38) vs. Oregon (17) (Seattle, 2002) (5 for 240)
48.0—Oklahoma (41) vs. Texas Tech (10) (John Hancock, 1993) (7 for 336)
48.0—(D) Kansas (23) vs. Brigham Young (20) (Aloha, 1992) (8 for 384)
47.9—Penn St. (42) vs. Tennessee (17) (Fiesta, 1992) (9 for 431)
47.9—Oregon St. (20) vs. Duke (16) (Rose, 1942) (7 for 335)
47.7—Ohio St. (31) vs. Miami (Fla.) (24) (2 ot) (Fiesta, 2003) (6 for 286)
47.7—Tennessee (3) vs. Maryland (30) (Peach, 2002) (6 for 286)
47.7—South Carolina (31) vs. Ohio St. (28) (Outback, 2002) (6 for 286)
47.6—Oklahoma (42) vs. Arkansas (8) (Orange, 1987) (5 for 238)

47.5—St. Mary's (Cal.) (20) vs. Texas Tech (13) (Cotton, 1939) (11 for 523)
47.4—(D) Georgia Tech (18) vs. Stanford (17) (Aloha, 1991) (7 for 332)
47.4—(D) Fresno St. (51) vs. Bowling Green (7) (California, 1985) (7 for 332)
47.4—(D) Tennessee (28) vs. Wisconsin (21) (Garden State, 1981) (5 for 237)

FEWEST PUNTS
0—Illinois (63) vs. Virginia (21) (Micronpc.com, 1999)
0—Oklahoma St. (62) vs. Wyoming (14) (Holiday, 1988)
0—Oklahoma (41) vs. Wyoming (7) (Fiesta, 1976)
1—Virginia (48) vs. West Virginia (22) (Continental Tire, 2002)
1—Boston College (51) vs. Toledo (25) (Motor City, 2002)
1—Oklahoma (25) vs. Mississippi (27) (Independence, 1999)
1—Nebraska (62) vs. Florida (24) (Fiesta, 1996)
1—Brigham Young (39) vs. Penn St. (50) (Holiday, 1989)
1—Nebraska (21) vs. LSU (20) (Orange, 1983)
1—North Carolina St. (31) vs. Kansas (18) (Liberty, 1973)
1—Utah (32) vs. West Virginia (6) (Liberty, 1964)
1—(D) Miami (Fla.) (34) vs. Nebraska (36) (Gotham, 1962)
1—Georgia Tech (42) vs. West Virginia (19) (Sugar, 1954)
1—West Virginia (19) vs. Georgia Tech (42) (Sugar, 1954)
1—Missouri (23) vs. Clemson (24) (Gator, 1949)

LOWEST PUNTING AVERAGE
(Minimum 3 Punts)
17.0—Nevada (34) vs. Bowling Green (35) (Las Vegas, 1992) (4 for 68)
17.0—Kentucky (14) vs. Penn St. (26) (Outback, 1999) (3 for 51)
19.0—Cincinnati (18) vs. Virginia Tech (6) (Sun, 1947) (6 for 114)
22.0—Mississippi St. (16) vs. North Carolina St. (12) (Liberty, 1963) (3 for 66)
23.0—Bowling Green (35) vs. Nevada (34) (Las Vegas, 1992) (5 for 115)
25.5—Houston (34) vs. Notre Dame (35) (Cotton, 1979) (10 for 255)
26.0—Air Force (37) vs. Fresno St. (34) (Silicon Valley, 2000) (3 for 78)
26.1—Michigan (14) vs. Alabama (17) (Outback, 1997) (7 for 183)
26.3—Oklahoma St. (34) vs. TCU (0) (Cotton, 1945) (6 for 158)
26.3—Rice (28) vs. Alabama (6) (Cotton, 1954) (8 for 210)
26.3—Notre Dame (35) vs. Houston (34) (Cotton, 1979) (7 for 184)

MOST PUNTS BLOCKED BY ONE TEAM
2—LSU (25) vs. Colorado (7) (Orange, 1962)
2—North Carolina St. (14) vs. Georgia (7) (Liberty, 1967)
2—North Carolina (21) vs. Mississippi St. (17) (Peach, Jan. 2, 1993)

Punt Returns

MOST PUNT RETURNS
9—Georgia (7) vs. North Carolina (3) (Gator, Dec. 31, 1971) (6.8 average)
8—Indiana (20) vs. Virginia Tech (45) (Independence, 1993) (7.3 average)
8—Tennessee (34) vs. Air Force (13) (Sugar, 1971) (10.8 average)
8—Mississippi (7) vs. UTEP (14) (Sun, 1967) (9.4 average)
8—Michigan (34) vs. Oregon (7) (Rose, 1965) (10.6 average)
7—North Carolina (16) vs. Auburn (10) (Peach, 2001) (9.4 average)
7—Auburn (10) vs. North Carolina (16) (Peach, 2001) (3.7 average)
7—Oklahoma (10) vs. Arkansas (3) (Cotton, 2002) (2.9 average)
7—Stanford (38) vs. Michigan St. (0) (Sun, 1996) (13.4 average)
7—Louisville (34) vs. Alabama (7) (Fiesta, 1991) (7.3 average)
6—UCLA (29) vs. Texas A&M (23) (Cotton, 1998) (11.0 average)
6—Florida (52) vs. Florida St. (20) (Sugar, 1997) (11.5 average)
6—Ohio St. (14) vs. Tennessee (20) (Florida Citrus, 1996) (5.0 average)
6—Tennessee (17) vs. Penn St. (42) (Fiesta, 1992) (8.2 average)
6—Clemson (30) vs. Illinois (0) (Hall of Fame, 1991)
6—(D) San Jose St. (48) vs. Central Mich. (24) (California, 1990)
6—Brigham Young (7) vs. Ohio St. (10) (Florida Citrus, 1985)
6—Texas (9) vs. Georgia (10) (Cotton, 1984) (2.5 average)
6—(D) Washington (21) vs. Maryland (20) (Aloha, 1982) (4.7 average)
6—(D) Vanderbilt (28) vs. Air Force (36) (Hall of Fame, 1982)
6—Washington St. (36) vs. Brigham Young (38) (Holiday, 1981)
6—Nebraska (38) vs. Alabama (6) (Orange, 1972) (22.7 average)
6—Miami (Fla.) (14) vs. Syracuse (15) (Liberty, 1961) (13.0 average)
6—Air Force (0) vs. TCU (0) (Cotton, 1959) (5.8 average)
6—Tulane (13) vs. Texas A&M (14) (Sugar, 1940) (21.0 average)
6—Tulane (20) vs. Temple (14) (Sugar, 1935)
6—Tulane (12) vs. Southern California (21) (Rose, 1932)

MOST PUNT RETURN YARDS
136—Nebraska (38) vs. Alabama (6) (Orange, 1972) (6 returns)
128—Oklahoma (48) vs. Duke (21) (Orange, 1958)
126—Tulane (13) vs. Texas A&M (14) (Sugar, 1940) (6 returns)
124—Washington (44) vs. Wisconsin (8) (Rose, 1960) (4 returns)
124—California (37) vs. Clemson (13) (Florida Citrus, 1992) (5 returns)
108—Southern Miss. (38) vs. UTEP (18) (Independence, 1988) (2 returns)
107—Arizona St. (45) vs. Florida St. (38) (Fiesta, 1971) (5 returns)
104—Texas A&M (21) vs. Alabama (29) (Cotton, 1942) (5 returns)
100—Virginia (34) vs. Georgia (27) (Peach, Dec. 30, 1995) (4 returns)
99—Kent St. (18) vs. Tampa (21) (Tangerine, 1972) (3 returns)
98—Brigham Young (46) vs. Southern Methodist (45) (Holiday, 1980) (3 returns)
94—Denver (24) vs. New Mexico (34) (Sun, 1946)
94—Stanford (38) vs. Michigan St. (0) (Sun, 1996) (7 returns)
93—Auburn (35) vs. Mississippi (28) (Gator, Jan. 2, 1971) (4 returns)
92—Southern California (7) vs. Ohio St. (20) (Rose, 1955) (2 returns)
89—Nebraska (28) vs. Florida St. (31) (Fiesta, 1988) (3 returns)

88—Penn St. (42) vs. Arizona St. (30) (Fiesta, 1977) (2 returns)

HIGHEST PUNT RETURN AVERAGE
(Minimum 3 Returns)
33.0—Kent St. (18) vs. Tampa (21) (Tangerine, 1972) (3 for 99)
32.7—Brigham Young (46) vs. Southern Methodist (45) (Holiday, 1980) (3 for 98)
31.0—Washington (44) vs. Wisconsin (8) (Rose, 1960) (4 for 124)
30.7—Michigan (42) vs. North Carolina St. (7) (Hall of Fame, 1994) (3 for 92)
29.7—Nebraska (28) vs. Florida St. (31) (Fiesta, 1988) (3 for 89)
27.6—Kansas St. (52) vs. Wyoming (17) (Copper, 1993) (3 for 83)
25.0—Virginia (34) vs. Georgia (27) (Peach, Dec. 30, 1995) (4 for 100)
24.8—California (37) vs. Clemson (13) (Florida Citrus, 1992) (5 for 124)
24.0—Auburn (31) vs. Ohio St. (14) (Hall of Fame, 1990) (3 for 72)
23.3—Auburn (35) vs. Mississippi (28) (Gator, Jan. 2, 1971) (4 for 93)
22.7—Nebraska (38) vs. Alabama (6) (Orange, 1972) (6 for 136)
21.4—Arizona St. (45) vs. Florida St. (38) (Fiesta, 1971) (5 for 107)
21.0—Tulane (13) vs. Texas A&M (14) (Sugar, 1940) (6 for 126)
21.0—Arkansas (6) vs. Duke (7) (Cotton, 1961) (3 for 63)
20.8—Texas A&M (21) vs. Alabama (29) (Cotton, 1942) (5 for 104)
19.5—(D) Georgia (20) vs. Texas A&M (40) (Presidential Cup, 1950) (4 for 78)
19.3—Nebraska (14) vs. Houston (17) (Cotton, 1980) (3 for 58)

Kickoff Returns

MOST KICKOFF RETURNS
10—Florida (24) vs. Nebraska (62) (Fiesta, 1996) (26.8 average)
10—Wyoming (14) vs. Oklahoma St. (62) (Holiday, 1988) (20.5 average)
9—Maryland (23) vs. Florida (56) (Orange, 2002) (13.7 average)
9—Brigham Young (14) vs. Texas A&M (65) (Holiday, 1990) (18.2 average)
8—Michigan (17) vs. Tennessee (45) (Florida Citrus, 2002) (15.6 average)
8—Washington (43) vs. Texas (47) (Holiday, 2001) (18.0 average)
8—Brigham Young (27) vs. Tulane (41) (Liberty, 1998) (31.0 average)
8—North Carolina St. (23) vs. Miami (Fla.) (46) (Micron PC, 1998) (18.3 average)
8—Virginia Tech (3) vs. North Carolina (42) (Gator, 1998) (19.4 average)
8—Florida St. (20) vs. Florida (52) (Sugar, 1997) (19.0 average)
8—Northwestern (32) vs. Southern California (41) (Rose, 1996) (28.1 average)
8—Nebraska (21) vs. Georgia Tech (45) (Florida Citrus, 1991) (23.6 average)
8—Notre Dame (10) vs. Texas A&M (35) (Cotton, 1988) (18.9 average)
8—Texas Tech (17) vs. Florida St. (40) (Tangerine, 1977)
8—UCLA (6) vs. Alabama (36) (Liberty, 1976) (17.6 average)
8—Brigham Young (21) vs. Oklahoma St. (49) (Tangerine, 1976)
8—(D) Tulane (7) vs. Houston (47) (Bluebonnet, 1973) (28.1 average)
8—Missouri (35) vs. Arizona St. (49) (Fiesta, 1972) (32.3 average)
8—Arizona St. (45) vs. Florida St. (38) (Fiesta, 1971) (16.4 average)
8—Florida St. (38) vs. Arizona St. (45) (Fiesta, 1971) (23.0 average)
8—Colorado (47) vs. Alabama (33) (Liberty, 1969) (27.8 average)
8—Ohio (42) vs. Richmond (49) (Tangerine, 1968)
8—Florida St. (20) vs. UTEP (47) (Sun, 1955)
8—UCLA (14) vs. Illinois (45) (Rose, 1947) (32.4 average)

MOST KICKOFF RETURN YARDS
268—Florida (24) vs. Nebraska (62) (Fiesta, 1996) (10 returns)
259—UCLA (14) vs. Illinois (45) (Rose, 1947) (8 returns)
258—Missouri (35) vs. Arizona St. (49) (Fiesta, 1972) (8 returns)
248—Brigham Young (27) vs. Tulane (41) (Liberty, 1998) (8 returns)
225—(D) Tulane (7) vs. Houston (47) (Bluebonnet, 1973) (8 returns)
225—Northwestern (32) vs. Southern California (41) (Rose, 1996) (8 returns)
222—Colorado (47) vs. Alabama (33) (Liberty, 1969) (8 returns)
207—(D) California (38) vs. Navy (42) (Aloha, 1996) (7 returns)
205—Wyoming (14) vs. Oklahoma (62) (Holiday, 1988) (10 returns)
204—Brigham Young (21) vs. Oklahoma St. (49) (Tangerine, 1976) (8 returns)
191—(D) Houston (22) vs. Washington St. (24) (Aloha, 1988) (5 returns)
189—Nebraska (21) vs. Georgia Tech (45) (Florida Citrus, 1991) (8 returns)
188—Stanford (13) vs. East Caro. (19) (Liberty, 1995) (6 returns)
187—Houston (28) vs. Boston College (45) (Cotton, 1985) (7 returns)
187—Idaho (42) vs. Southern Miss. (35) (Humanitarian, 1998) (6 returns)
184—Florida St. (38) vs. Arizona St. (45) (Fiesta, 1971) (8 returns)
179—Washington (21) vs. Colorado (33) (Holiday, 1996) (5 returns)
176—Missouri (34) vs. West Virginia (31) (Insight.com, 1998) (6 returns)
174—(D) Hawaii (13) vs. Michigan St. (33) (Aloha, 1989) (7 returns)
170—Tennessee (27) vs. Maryland (28) (John Hancock, 1984) (4 returns)
169—Oregon St. (19) vs. Iowa (35) (Rose, 1957) (5 returns)
164—Brigham Young (14) vs. Texas A&M (65) (Holiday, 1990) (9 returns)

HIGHEST KICKOFF RETURN AVERAGE
(Minimum 3 Returns)
42.5—Tennessee (27) vs. Maryland (28) (John Hancock, 1984) (4 for 170)
38.3—(D) Fresno St. (30) vs. Colorado (41) (Aloha, 1993) (3 for 115)
38.3—Ohio St. (28) vs. Pittsburgh (23) (Fiesta, 1984) (4 for 153)
38.2—(D) Houston (22) vs. Washington St. (24) (Aloha, 1988) (5 for 191)
37.5—LSU (45) vs. Michigan St. (26) (Independence, 1995) (4 for 150)
37.5—Notre Dame (24) vs. Alabama (23) (Sugar, 1973) (4 for 150)
36.8—Ohio St. (17) vs. Syracuse (24) (Hall of Fame, 1992) (4 for 147)
36.7—Indiana (20) vs. Virginia Tech (45) (Independence, 1993) (3 for 110)
35.8—Washington (21) vs. Colorado (33) (Holiday, 1996) (5 for 179)
33.8—Oregon St. (19) vs. Iowa (35) (Rose, 1957) (5 for 169)
32.8—Florida St. (40) vs. Texas Tech (17) (Tangerine, 1977) (4 for 131)

32.6—(D) UCLA (30) vs. Kansas (51) (Aloha, 1995) (5 for 163)
32.4—UCLA (14) vs. Illinois (45) (Rose, 1947) (8 for 259)
32.3—Missouri (35) vs. Arizona St. (49) (Fiesta, 1972) (8 for 258)
31.7—Penn St. (41) vs. Baylor (20) (Cotton, 1975) (3 for 95)
31.6—Virginia Tech (21) vs. Nebraska (41) (Orange, 1996) (3 for 95)
31.5—Kentucky (14) vs. Penn St. (26) (Outback, 1999) (4 for 126)
31.3—Penn St. (38) vs. Texas (15) (Fiesta, 1997) (4 for 125)
31.3—Stanford (13) vs. East Caro. (19) (Liberty, 1995) (6 for 188)
31.2—Idaho (42) vs. Southern Miss. (35) (Humanitarian, 1998) (6 for 187)
31.0—Brigham Young (27) vs. Tulane (41) (Liberty, 1998) (8 for 248)
29.5—(D) California (38) vs. Navy (42) (Aloha, 1996) (7 for 207)
29.4—Virginia (34) vs. Georgia (27) (Peach, Dec. 31, 1995) (5 for 147)
29.3—Missouri (34) vs. West Virginia (31) (Insight.com, 1998) (6 for 176)
29.0—Mississippi St. (17) vs. Nebraska (31) (Sun, 1980) (4 for 116)
28.1—Northwestern (32) vs. Southern California (41) (Rose, 1996) (8 for 225)
27.8—Brigham Young (21) vs. Ohio St. (28) (Holiday, 1993) (5 for 139)
27.6—Houston (17) vs. Syracuse (30) (Liberty, 1996) (5 for 138)
27.2—West Virginia (30) vs. Georgia Tech (35) (Carquest, 1997) (6 for 163)
27.0—Arizona St. (17) vs. Arkansas (18) (Holiday, 1985) (3 for 81)
26.8—Florida (24) vs. Nebraska (62) (Fiesta, 1996) (10 for 268)
26.7—Houston (28) vs. Boston College (45) (Cotton, 1985) (7 for 187)

Fumbles

MOST FUMBLES
11—Mississippi (7) vs. Alabama (12) (Sugar, 1964) (lost 6)
9—Texas (11) vs. Notre Dame (24) (Cotton, 1971) (lost 5)
8—North Carolina St. (28) vs. Iowa (23) (Peach, Dec. 31, 1988) (lost 5)
8—(D) Houston (35) vs. Navy (0) (Garden State, 1980) (lost 3)
8—Louisville (14) vs. Louisiana Tech (24) (Independence, 1977) (lost 3)
8—North Texas (8) vs. New Mexico St. (28) (Sun, 1959) (lost 6)
8—TCU (0) vs. Air Force (0) (Cotton, 1959) (lost 3)
8—Colorado (27) vs. Clemson (21) (Orange, 1957) (lost 3)
7—Georgia Tech (14) vs. LSU (28) (Peach, 2000) (lost 4)
7—(D) Florida (7) vs. Washington (34) (Freedom, 1989) (lost 3)
7—(D) Hawaii (13) vs. Michigan St. (33) (Aloha, 1989) (lost 4)
7—Toledo (27) vs. San Jose St. (25) (California, 1981) (lost 2)
7—(D) Texas A&M (28) vs. Southern California (47) (Bluebonnet, 1977) (lost 5)
7—Auburn (27) vs. Texas (3) (Gator, 1974) (lost 5)
7—Tennessee (34) vs. Air Force (13) (Sugar, 1971) (lost 4)
7—Air Force (13) vs. Tennessee (34) (Sugar, 1971) (lost 3)
7—Georgia (2) vs. Arkansas (16) (Sugar, 1969) (lost 5)
7—Alabama (0) vs. Penn St. (7) (Liberty, 1959) (lost 4)
7—Southern California (7) vs. Ohio St. (20) (Rose, 1955) (lost 3)
7—Wash. & Lee (7) vs. Wyoming (20) (Gator, 1951) (lost 2)
7—Missouri (7) vs. Maryland (20) (Gator, 1950) (lost 5)
7—(D) Georgia (20) vs. Texas A&M (40) (Presidential Cup, 1950)
7—(D) Arizona St. (21) vs. Xavier (Ohio) (33) (Salad, 1950) (lost 6)

MOST FUMBLES, BOTH TEAMS
17—Alabama (12) [6] & Mississippi (7) [11] (Sugar, 1964) (lost 9)
14—Louisiana Tech (24) [6] & Louisville (14) [8] (Independence, 1977) (lost 6)
14—Tennessee (34) [7] & Air Force (13) [7] (Sugar, 1971) (lost 7)
13—TCU (0) [8] & Air Force (0) [5] (Cotton, 1959) (lost 6)
12—North Carolina St. (28) [8] & Iowa (23) [4] (Peach, Dec. 31, 1988) (lost 8)
12—(D) Houston (35) [8] & Navy (0) [4] (Garden State, 1980) (lost 6)
12—New Mexico St. (28) [4] & North Texas (8) [8] (Sun, 1959) (lost 8)
11—(D) Toledo (27) [7] & San Jose St. (25) [4] (California, 1981) (lost 3)
11—Oklahoma (41) [6] & Wyoming (7) [5] (Fiesta, 1976)
10—LSU (28) [3] & Georgia Tech (14) [7] (Peach, 2000) (lost 5)
10—Alabama (30) [5] & Baylor (3) [5] (Cotton, 1981) (lost 5)
10—(D) Houston (31) [5] & North Carolina St. (31) [5] (Bluebonnet, 1974) (lost 4)
10—Notre Dame (24) [1] & Texas (11) [9] (Cotton, 1971) (lost 6)
10—Illinois (17) [5] & Washington (7) [5] (Rose, 1964) (lost 6)
10—Navy (20) [5] & Rice (7) [5] (Cotton, 1958) (lost 8)
10—Mississippi (7) [5] & Florida (3) [5] (Gator, 1958) (lost 5)
10—Texas (16) [5] & Tennessee (0) [5] (Cotton, 1953) (lost 6)

MOST FUMBLES LOST
6—Texas A&M (2) vs. Florida St. (10) (Cotton, 1992) (6 fumbles)
6—East Caro. (31) vs. Maine (0) (Tangerine, 1965) (6 fumbles)
6—Mississippi (7) vs. Alabama (12) (Sugar, 1964) (11 fumbles)
6—North Texas (8) vs. New Mexico St. (28) (Sun, 1959) (8 fumbles)
6—(D) Arizona St. (21) vs. Xavier (Ohio) (33) (Salad, 1950) (7 fumbles)
6—Southern Miss. (35) vs. Idaho (42) (Humanitarian, 1998) (6 fumbles)
5—UCLA (16) vs. Wisconsin (21) (Rose, 1994) (5 fumbles)
5—North Carolina St. (28) vs. Iowa (23) (Peach, Dec. 31, 1988) (8 fumbles)
5—(D) North Carolina (21) vs. Arizona (30) (Aloha, 1986) (5 fumbles)
5—(D) Bowling Green (7) vs. Fresno St. (51) (California, 1985) (6 fumbles)
5—(D) Georgia (22) vs. Stanford (25) (Bluebonnet, 1978) (6 fumbles)
5—(D) Texas A&M (28) vs. Southern California (47) (Bluebonnet, 1977) (7 fumbles)
5—Auburn (27) vs. Texas (3) (Gator, 1974) (7 fumbles)
5—Texas (11) vs. Notre Dame (24) (Cotton, 1971) (9 fumbles)
5—Georgia (2) vs. Arkansas (16) (Sugar, 1969) (7 fumbles)
5—(D) Utah St. (9) vs. Baylor (24) (Gotham, 1961) (5 fumbles)
5—Rice (7) vs. Navy (20) (Cotton, 1958) (5 fumbles)

5—Auburn (13) vs. Vanderbilt (25) (Gator, 1955) (5 fumbles)
5—Oklahoma (7) vs. Kentucky (13) (Sugar, 1951)
5—Missouri (7) vs. Maryland (20) (Gator, 1950) (7 fumbles)
5—Texas A&M (21) vs. Alabama (29) (Cotton, 1942) (6 fumbles)

MOST FUMBLES LOST, BOTH TEAMS
9—Alabama (12) [3] & Mississippi (7) [6] (Sugar, 1964) (17 fumbles)
8—Idaho (42) [3] & Southern Miss. (35) [5] (Humanitarian, 1998) (9 fumbles)
8—North Carolina St. (28) [5] & Iowa (23) [3] (Peach, Dec. 31, 1988) (12 fumbles)
8—New Mexico St. (28) [2] & North Texas (8) [6] (Sun, 1959) (12 fumbles)
8—Navy (20) [3] & Rice (7) [5] (Cotton, 1958) (10 fumbles)
7—Florida St. (10) [1] & Texas A&M (2) [6] (Cotton, 1992) (7 fumbles)
7—Texas A&M (37) [3] & Florida (14) [4] (Sun, Jan. 2, 1977) (8 fumbles)
7—Arizona St. (28) [3] & Pittsburgh (7) [4] (Fiesta, 1973) (9 fumbles)
7—Tennessee (34) [4] & Air Force (13) [3] (Sugar, 1971) (14 fumbles)
7—Michigan St. (28) [4] & UCLA (20) [3] (Rose, 1954) (8 fumbles)

Penalties

MOST PENALTIES
21—Mississippi St. (17) vs. Clemson (7) (Peach, 1999) (188 yards)
20—(D) Fresno St. (35) vs. Western Mich. (30) (California, 1988) (166 yards)
19—Oregon (41) vs. Air Force (13) (Las Vegas, 1997) (166 yards)
18—Alabama (34) vs. Michigan (35) (ot) (Orange, 2000) (132 yards)
18—Washington St. (31) vs. Utah (28) (Copper, 1992) (136 yards)
16—Miami (Fla.) (46) vs. Texas (3) (Cotton, 1991) (202 yards)
16—Tulsa (16) vs. McNeese St. (20) (Independence, 1976) (100 yards)
16—Tennessee (17) vs. Oklahoma (0) (Orange, 1939) (130 yards)
15—Utah (17) vs. Fresno St. (16) (Las Vegas, 1999) (151 yards)
15—Florida (52) vs. Florida St. (20) (Sugar, 1997) (102 yards)
15—Washington St. (10) vs. Baylor (3) (Alamo, 1994) (110 yards)
15—Illinois (30) vs. East Caro. (0) (Liberty, 1994) (164 yards)
15—Utah St. (42) vs. Ball St. (33) (Las Vegas, 1993) (150 yards)
15—Miami (Fla.) (7) vs. Tennessee (35) (Sugar, 1986) (120 yards)
15—(D) Michigan (33) vs. UCLA (14) (Bluebonnet, 1981) (148 yards)
14—Minnesota (30) vs. North Carolina St. (38) (Micronpc.com, 2000) (107 yards)
14—Purdue (25) vs. Georgia (28) (ot) (Outback, 2000) (153 yards)
14—Oregon St. (17) vs. Hawaii (23) (Oahu Classic, 1999) (138 yards)
14—Louisville (31) vs. Boise St. (34) (Humanitarian, 1999) (120 yards)
14—Kentucky (14) vs. Penn St. (26) (Outback, 1999) (103 yards)
14—Marshall (48) vs. Louisville (29) (Motor City, 1998) (123 yards)
14—Kansas St. (34) vs. Purdue (37) (Alamo, 1998) (125 yards)
14—Florida St. (20) vs. Florida (52) (Sugar, 1997) (115 yards)
14—(D) San Jose St. (37) vs. Miami (Ohio) (7) (California, 1986) (163 yards)

MOST PENALTIES, BOTH TEAMS
29—Mississippi St. (17) [21] & Clemson (7) [8] (Peach, 1999) (270 yards)
29—Florida (52) [15] & Florida St. (20) [14] (Sugar, 1997) (217 yards)
29—McNeese St. (20) [13] & Tulsa (16) [16] (Independence, 1976) (205 yards)
28—Michigan (35) [10] & Alabama (34) [18] (ot) (Orange, 2000) (247 yards)
28—(D) Fresno St. (35) [20] & Western Mich. (30) [8] (California, 1988) (231 yards)
27—Marshall (48) [14] & Louisville (29) [13] (Motor City, 1998) (232 yards)
26—Oregon (41) [19] & Air Force (13) [7] (Las Vegas, 1997) (223 yards)
26—Tennessee (35) [11] & Miami (Fla.) (7) [15] (Sugar, 1986) (245 yards)
25—Washington St. (31) [18] & Utah (28) [7] (Copper, 1992) (191 yards)
25—Tennessee (17) [16] & Oklahoma (0) [9] (Orange, 1939) (221 yards)
24—Georgia (28) [10] & Purdue (25) [14] (ot) (Outback, 2000) (208 yards)
24—Miami (Fla.) (46) [16] & Texas (3) [8] (Cotton, 1991) (270 yards)
24—(D) San Jose St. (37) [14] & Miami (Ohio) (7) [10] (California, 1986) (264 yards)
24—(D) Michigan (33) [15] & UCLA (14) [9] (Bluebonnet, 1981) (242 yards)
23—Hawaii (23) [9] & Oregon St. (17) [14] (Oahu Classic, 1999) (226 yards)
23—Kansas St. (54) [12] & Colorado St. (21) [11] (Holiday, 1995) (219 yards)
23—(D) Fresno St. (51) [12] & Bowling Green (7) [11] (California, 1985) (183 yards)
22—Penn St. (26) [8] & Kentucky (14) [14] (Outback, 1999) (161 yards)
22—(D) Eastern Mich. (30) [9] & San Jose St. (27) [13] (California, 1987) (162 yards)
21—North Carolina St. (38) [7] & Minnesota (30) [14] (Micronpc.com, 2000) (182 yards)
21—Utah (17) [15] & Fresno St. (16) [6] (Las Vegas, 1999) (210 yards)
21—Florida St. (16) [12] & Tennessee (23) [9] (Fiesta, 1999) (165 yards)
21—Purdue (37) [7] & Kansas St. (34) [14] (Alamo, 1998) (160 yards)
21—Illinois (30) [15] & East Caro. (0) [6] (Liberty, 1994) (204 yards)
21—Florida St. (18) [10] & Nebraska (16) [11] (Orange, 1994) (184 yards)
21—Ohio St. (47) [12] & Brigham Young (17) [9] (Holiday, 1982) (184 yards)
21—Oklahoma St. (16) [12] & Brigham Young (6) [9] (Fiesta, 1974) (150 yards)

MOST YARDS PENALIZED
202—Miami (Fla.) (46) vs. Texas (3) (Cotton, 1991) (16 penalties)
188—Mississippi St. (17) vs. Clemson (7) (Peach, 1999) (21 penalties)
166—Oregon (41) vs. Air Force (13) (Las Vegas, 1997) (19 penalties)
166—(D) Fresno St. (35) vs. Western Mich. (30) (California, 1988) (20 penalties)
164—Illinois (30) vs. East Caro. (0) (Liberty, 1994) (15 penalties)
163—(D) San Jose St. (37) vs. Miami (Ohio) (7) (California, 1986) (14 penalties)
153—Purdue (25) vs. Georgia (28) (ot) (Outback, 2000) (14 penalties)
151—Utah (17) vs. Fresno St. (16) (Las Vegas, 1999) (15 penalties)
150—Utah St. (42) vs. Ball St. (33) (Las Vegas, 1993) (15 penalties)
150—Oklahoma (48) vs. Duke (21) (Orange, 1958) (12 penalties)

148—(D) Michigan (33) vs. UCLA (14) (Bluebonnet, 1981) (15 penalties)
143—Miami (Fla.) (22) vs. Nebraska (0) (Orange, 1992) (12 penalties)
140—Lamar (21) vs. Middle Tenn. (14) (Tangerine, 1961) (13 penalties)
138—Oregon St. (17) vs. Hawaii (23) (Oahu Classic, 1999) (14 penalties)
136—Washington St. (31) vs. Utah (28) (Copper, 1992) (18 penalties)
135—Florida St. (41) vs. Nebraska (17) (Fiesta, 1990) (13 penalties)
132—Alabama (34) vs. Michigan (35) (ot) (Orange, 2000) (18 penalties)
130—LSU (15) vs. Nebraska (30) (Sugar, 1987) (12 penalties)
130—Tennessee (17) vs. Oklahoma (0) (Orange, 1939)

MOST YARDS PENALIZED, BOTH TEAMS
270—Mississippi St. (17) [188] & Clemson (7) [82] (Peach, 1999)
270—Miami (Fla.) (46) [202] & Texas (3) [68] (Cotton, 1991)
264—(D) San Jose St. (37) [163] & Miami (Ohio) (7) [101] (California, 1986)
247—Michigan (35) [115] & Alabama (34) [132] (ot) (Orange, 2000)
245—Tennessee (35) [125] & Miami (Fla.) (7) [120] (Sugar, 1986)
242—(D) Michigan (33) [148] & UCLA (14) [94] (Bluebonnet, 1981)
232—Marshall (48) [123] & Louisville (29) [109] (Motor City, 1998)
231—(D) Fresno St. (35) [166] & Western Mich. (30) [65] (California, 1988)
226—Hawaii (23) [88] & Oregon St. (17) [138] (Oahu Classic, 1999)
223—Oregon (41) [166] & Air Force (13) [57] (Las Vegas, 1997)
221—Tennessee (16) [130] & Oklahoma (0) [91] (Orange, 1939)
219—Kansas St. (54) [124] & Colorado St. (21) [95] (Holiday, 1995)
217—Florida (52) [102] & Florida St. (20) [115] (Sugar, 1997)
210—Utah (17) [151] & Fresno St. (16) [59] (Las Vegas, 1999)
208—Georgia (28) [55] & Purdue (25) [153] (ot) (Outback, 2000)
205—McNeese St. (20) [105] & Tulsa (16) [100] (Independence, 1976)
204—Illinois (30) [164] & East Caro. (0) [40] (Liberty, 1994)

FEWEST PENALTIES
0—Southern Methodist (7) vs. Alabama (28) (Sun, 1983)
0—Louisiana Tech (13) vs. East Caro. (35) (Independence, 1978)
0—Texas (17) vs. Alabama (13) (Cotton, 1973)
0—(D) Rice (7) vs. Kansas (33) (Bluebonnet, 1961)
0—Pittsburgh (14) vs. Georgia Tech (21) (Gator, 1956)
0—Clemson (0) vs. Miami (Fla.) (14) (Gator, 1952)
0—Texas (7) vs. Randolph Field (7) (Cotton, 1944)
0—Alabama (20) vs. Washington (19) (Rose, 1926)

FEWEST PENALTIES, BOTH TEAMS
3—Alabama (28) [3] & Southern Methodist (7) [0] (Sun, 1983)
3—Penn St. (30) [2] & Texas (6) [1] (Cotton, 1972)
3—Texas (21) [1] & Notre Dame (17) [2] (Cotton, 1970)
3—Penn St. (15) [1] & Kansas (14) [2] (Orange, 1969)
3—(D) Kansas (33) [3] & Rice (7) [0] (Bluebonnet, 1961)

FEWEST YARDS PENALIZED
0—Southern Methodist (7) vs. Alabama (28) (Sun, 1983)
0—Louisiana Tech (13) vs. East Caro. (35) (Independence, 1978)
0—Texas (17) vs. Alabama (13) (Cotton, 1973)
0—(D) Rice (7) vs. Kansas (33) (Bluebonnet, 1961)
0—Pittsburgh (14) vs. Georgia Tech (21) (Gator, 1956)
0—Clemson (0) vs. Miami (Fla.) (14) (Gator, 1952)
0—Texas (7) vs. Randolph Field (7) (Cotton, 1944)
0—Alabama (20) vs. Washington (19) (Rose, 1926)

FEWEST YARDS PENALIZED, BOTH TEAMS
10—Duquesne (13) [5] & Mississippi St. (12) [5] (Orange, 1937)
15—Texas (21) [5] & Notre Dame (17) [10] (Cotton, 1970)
15—(D) Kansas (33) [15] vs. Rice (7) [0] (Bluebonnet, 1961)

Miscellaneous Records

SCORELESS TIES#
1959—Air Force 0, TCU 0 (Cotton)
1947—Arkansas 0, LSU 0 (Cotton)
1940—Arizona St. 0, Catholic 0 (Sun)
1922—California 0, Wash. & Jeff. 0 (Rose)

TIE GAMES#
(Not Scoreless)
1991—Brigham Young 13, Iowa 13 (Holiday)
1990—Louisiana Tech 34, Maryland 34 (Independence)
1988—Auburn 16, Syracuse 16 (Sugar)
1985—Arizona 13, Georgia 13 (Sun)
1984—Florida St. 17, Georgia 17 (Florida Citrus)
1978—Arkansas 10, UCLA 10 (Fiesta)
1977—(D) Maryland 17, Minnesota 17 (Hall of Fame)
1974—Texas Tech 6, Vanderbilt 6 (Peach)
1974—(D) Houston 31, North Carolina St. 31 (Bluebonnet)
1970—(D) Alabama 24, Oklahoma 24 (Bluebonnet)
1970—(D) Long Beach St. 24, Louisville 24 (Pasadena)
1967—Florida St. 17, Penn St. 17 (Gator)
1960—(D) Alabama 3, Texas 3 (Bluebonnet)
1948—Georgia 20, Maryland 20 (Gator)
1948—Penn St. 13, Southern Methodist 13 (Cotton)
1947—(D) Montana St. 13, New Mexico 13 (Harbor)

1944—Randolph Field 7, Texas 7 (Cotton)
1937—(D) Auburn 7, Villanova 7 (Bacardi)
1936—Hardin-Simmons 14, New Mexico St. 14 (Sun)
1934—(D) Arkansas 7, Centenary (La.) 7 (Dixie Classic)
1927—Alabama 7, Stanford 7 (Rose)
1924—Navy 14, Washington 14 (Rose)

LARGEST DEFICIT OVERCOME TO WIN
30—Marshall (64) vs. East Caro. (61) (2 ot) (GMAC, 2001) (trailed 38-8 at half)
25—Georgia (28) vs. Purdue (25) (ot) (Outback, 2000) (trailed 25-0 in 2nd quarter)
24—North Carolina St. (38) vs. Minnesota (30) (Micronpc.com, 2000) (trailed 24-0 in 2nd quarter)
22—Brigham Young (46) vs. Southern Methodist (45) (Holiday, 1980) (trailed 35-13 in 3rd quarter and then trailed 45-25 with four minutes remaining in the game)
22—Notre Dame (35) vs. Houston (34) (Cotton, 1979) (trailed 34-12 in 4th quarter)
21—(D) Fresno St. (29) vs. Bowling Green (28) (California, 1982) (trailed 21-0 in 2nd quarter)
19—Texas (47) vs. Washington (43) (Holiday, 2001) (trailed 36-17 in 3rd quarter)
19—Wake Forest (39) vs. Oregon (35) (Independence, 1992) (trailed 29-10 in 3rd quarter)
14—Mississippi St. (43) vs. Texas A&M (41) (ot) (Independence, 2000) (trailed 35-21 in 4th quarter)
14—Colorado (33) vs. Washington (21) (Holiday, 1996) (trailed 14-0 with 3:10 remaining in first quarter)
14—Rice (28) vs. Colorado (14) (Cotton, 1938) (trailed 14-0 in 2nd quarter)
13—Wisconsin (21) vs. UCLA (20) (Sun, 2000) (trailed 20-7 in 3rd quarter)
13—Mississippi (14) vs. TCU (13) (Cotton, 1956) (trailed 13-0 in 2nd quarter)
11—LSU (28) vs. Georgia Tech (14) (Peach, 2000) (trailed 14-3 in 2nd quarter)
11—Michigan (27) vs. Nebraska (23) (Fiesta, 1986) (trailed 14-3 in 3rd quarter)

OVERTIME GAMES#
1995—Toledo (40) vs. Nevada (37) (Las Vegas) (1 ot)
2000—Georgia (28) vs. Purdue (25) (Outback) (1 ot); Michigan (35) vs. Alabama (34) (Orange) (1 ot)
2000—Mississippi St. (43) vs. Texas A&M (41) (Independence) (1 ot)
2001—Marshall (64) vs. East Caro. (61) (GMAC) (2 ot)
2002—Wisconsin (31) vs. Colorado (28) (Alamo) (1 ot)
2003—Ohio St. (31) vs. Miami (Fla.) (24) (Fiesta) (2 ot)

#Beginning in 1995-96, tied bowl games were allowed to use a tiebreaker system.

Longest Plays

(D) Denotes discontinued bowl. Year listed is actual year bowl was played.

LONGEST RUNS FROM SCRIMMAGE

Yds.	Player, Team (Score) vs. Opponent (Score)	Bowl, Year
99*	Terry Baker (QB), Oregon St. (6) vs. Villanova (0)	Liberty, 1962
95*#	Dicky Maegle, Rice (28) vs. Alabama (6)	Cotton, 1954
94*(D)	Dwight Ford, Southern California (47) vs. Texas A&M (28)	Bluebonnet, 1977
94*	Larry Smith, Florida (27) vs. Georgia Tech (12)	Orange, 1967
94*	Hascall Henshaw, Arizona St. (13) vs. Case Reserve (26)	Sun, 1941

*#Famous bench-tackle play; Maegle tackled on Alabama 40-yard line by Tommy Lewis, awarded touchdown. * Scored touchdown on play.*

LONGEST PASS PLAYS

Yds.	Player, Team (Score) vs. Opponent (Score)	Bowl, Year
95*	Ronnie Fletcher to Ben Hart, Oklahoma (19) vs. Florida St. (36)	Gator, Jan. 2, 1965
93*(D)	Stan Heath to Tommy Kalminir, Nevada (13) vs. North Texas (6)	Salad, 1948
91*(D)	Mark Barsotti to Stephen Shelley, Fresno St. (27) vs. Ball St. (6)	California, 1989
89*	Pete Gonzalez to Jake Hoffart, Pittsburgh (7) vs. Southern Miss. (41)	Liberty, 1997
88*	Michael Bishop to Darnell McDonald, Kansas St. (34) vs. Purdue (37)	Alamo, 1998
88*	Dave Schnell to Rob Turner, Indiana (34) vs. South Carolina (10)	Liberty, 1988
87*(D)	Mike Thomas to L. C. Stevens, North Carolina (20) vs. Arkansas (10)	Carquest, Dec. 30, 1995
87*	Drew Bledsoe to Phillip Bobo, Washington St. (31) vs. Utah (28)	Copper, 1992
87*	Randy Wright to Tim Stracka, Wisconsin (14) vs. Kansas St. (3)	Independence, 1982
87*	Ger Schwedes to Ernie Davis, Syracuse (23) vs. Texas (14)	Cotton, 1960
86*	Brad Otton to Keyshawn Johnson, Southern California (55) vs. Texas Tech (14)	Cotton, 1995

* Scored touchdown on play.

LONGEST FIELD GOALS

Yds.	Player, Team (Score) vs. Opponent (Score)	Bowl, Year
62	Tony Franklin, Texas A&M (37) vs. Florida (14)	Sun, Jan. 2, 1977

56	Greg Cox, Miami (Fla.) (20) vs. Oklahoma (14)	Orange, 1988
55(D)	Russell Erxleben, Texas (38) vs. Colorado (21)	Bluebonnet, 1975
54	Carlos Huerta, Miami (Fla.) (22) vs. Nebraska (0)	Orange, 1992
54	Quin Rodriguez, Southern California (16) vs. Michigan St. (17)	John Hancock, 1990
54	Luis Zendejas, Arizona St. (32) vs. Oklahoma (21)	Fiesta, 1983

LONGEST PUNTS

Yds.	Player, Team (Score) vs. Opponent (Score)	Bowl, Year
84$	Kyle Rote, Southern Methodist (21) vs. Oregon (13)	Cotton, 1949
82	Ike Pickle, Mississippi St. (12) vs. Duquesne (13)	Orange, 1937
80	Elmer Layden, Notre Dame (27) vs. Stanford (10)	Rose, 1925
79$	Doak Walker, Southern Methodist (21) vs. Oregon (13)	Cotton, 1949
77	Mike Sochko, Maryland (21) vs. Houston (30)	Cotton, 1977
73	Sean Reali, Syracuse (41) vs. Clemson (0)	Gator, 1996

$Quick kick.

LONGEST PUNT RETURNS

Yds.	Player, Team (Score) vs. Opponent (Score)	Bowl, Year
88*	Ben Kelly, Colorado (62) vs. Boston College (28)	Insight.com, 1999
86*	Aramis Dandoy, Southern California (7) vs. Ohio St. (20)	Rose, 1955
85*	Darran Hall, Colorado St. (35) vs. Missouri (24)	Holiday, 1997
83*	Vai Sikahema, Brigham Young (46) vs. Southern Methodist (45)	Holiday, 1980
82*	Marcus Wall, North Carolina (31) vs. Texas (35)	Sun, 1994
82	Willie Drewrey, West Virginia (12) vs. Florida St. (31)	Gator, 1982
80*(D)	Gary Anderson, Arkansas (34) vs. Tulane (15)	Hall of Fame, 1980
80*	Cecil Ingram, Alabama (61) vs. Syracuse (6)	Orange, 1953

*Scored touchdown on play.

LONGEST KICKOFF RETURNS

Yds.	Player, Team (Score) vs. Opponent (Score)	Bowl, Year
100*	C.J. Jones, Iowa (17) vs. Southern California (38)	Orange, 2003
100*(D)	Deltha O'Neal, California (38) vs. Navy (42)	Aloha, 1996
100*	Derrick Mason, Michigan St. (26) vs. LSU (45)	Independence, 1995
100*	Kirby Dar Dar, Syracuse (26) vs. Colorado (22)	Fiesta, 1993
100*	Pete Panuska, Tennessee (27) vs. Maryland (28)	Sun, 1984
100*	Dave Lowery, Brigham Young (21) vs. Oklahoma St. (49)	Tangerine, 1976
100*	Mike Fink, Missouri (35) vs. Arizona St. (49)	Fiesta, 1972
100*(D)	Bob Smith, Texas A&M (40) vs. Georgia (20)	Presidential Cup, 1950
100*!	Al Hoisch, UCLA (14) vs. Illinois (45)	Rose, 1947

*Scored touchdown on play. !Rose Bowl records carry as 103-yard return.

LONGEST INTERCEPTION RETURNS

Yds.	Player, Team (Score) vs. Opponent (Score)	Bowl, Year
95*	Marcus Washington, Colorado (38) vs. Oregon (6)	Cotton, 1996
94*	David Baker, Oklahoma (48) vs. Duke (21)	Orange, 1958
91*	Donald Strickland, Colorado (28) vs. Wisconsin (31)	Alamo, 2002
91*	Don Hoover, Ohio (14) vs. West Tex. A&M (15)	Sun, 1962
90*	Norm Beal, Missouri (21) vs. Navy (14)	Orange, 1961
90*	Charlie Brembs, South Carolina (14) vs. Wake Forest (26)	Gator, 1946
90*(D)	G. P. Jackson, TCU (7) vs. Centre (63)	Fort Worth Classic, 1921

*Scored touchdown on play.

LONGEST MISCELLANEOUS RETURNS

Yds.	Player, Team (Score) vs. Opponent (Score)	Bowl, Year
98	Greg Mather, Navy (14) vs. Missouri (21) (Int. Lat.)	Orange, 1961
89	Charlie Owens, TCU (9) vs. Texas A&M (28) (Fumble return)	galleryfurniture.com, 2001
80	Antonio Banks, Virginia Tech (45) vs. Indiana (20) (Blocked field goal return)	Independence, 1993
79	Tremain Mack, Miami (Fla.) (31) vs. Virginia (21) (Fumble return)	Carquest, 1996
75	Payton Williams, Fresno St. (16) vs. Utah (17) (Blocked field goal return)	Las Vegas, 1999
73	Dick Carpenter, Oklahoma (48) vs. Duke (21) (Int. Lat.)	Orange, 1958
70	Carlos Posey, Missouri (34) vs. West Virginia (31) (Blocked punt return)	Insight.com, 1998
65	Steve Manstedt, Nebraska (19) vs. Texas (3) (Fumble return)	Cotton, 1974

Bowl Coaching Records

All-Time Bowl Appearances

(Ranked by Most Bowl Games Coached)

Coach (Teams Taken to Bowl)	G	W-L-T	Pct.
*Joe Paterno, Penn St.	31	20-10-1	.661
Paul "Bear" Bryant, Alabama, Texas A&M, Kentucky	29	15-12-2	.552
*Bobby Bowden, West Virginia, Florida St.	26	18-7-1	.712
Tom Osborne, Nebraska	25	12-13-0	.480
*Lou Holtz, William & Mary, North Carolina St., Arkansas, Notre Dame, South Carolina	22	12-8-2	.591
LaVell Edwards, Brigham Young	22	7-14-1	.341
Vince Dooley, Georgia	20	8-10-2	.450
John Vaught, Mississippi	18	10-8-0	.556
Hayden Fry, Southern Methodist, Iowa	17	7-9-1	.441
Bo Schembechler, Michigan	17	5-12-0	.294
Johnny Majors, Iowa St., Pittsburgh, Tennessee	16	9-7-0	.563
Darrell Royal, Texas	16	8-7-1	.531
Don James, Kent St., Washington	15	10-5-0	.667
George Welsh, Navy, Virginia	15	5-10-0	.333
Bobby Dodd, Georgia Tech	13	9-4-0	.692
Terry Donahue, UCLA	13	8-4-1	.654
Barry Switzer, Oklahoma	13	8-5-0	.615
Charlie McClendon, LSU	13	7-6-0	.538
Earle Bruce, Ohio St., Colorado St.	12	7-5-0	.583
Woody Hayes, Miami (Ohio), Ohio St.	12	6-6-0	.500
Shug Jordan, Auburn	12	5-7-0	.417

*Active coach. Ties computed as half won and half lost.

All-Time Bowl Victories

Coach	Wins	Record	Coach	Wins	Record
*Joe Paterno	20	20-10-1	Barry Switzer	8	8-5-0
*Bobby Bowden	18	18-7-1	Darrell Royal	8	8-7-1
Paul "Bear" Bryant	15	15-12-2	Vince Dooley	8	8-10-2
Tom Osborne	12	12-13-0	Pat Dye	7	7-2-1
*Lou Holtz	12	12-8-2	Bob Devaney	7	7-3-0
Don James	10	10-5-0	Dan Devine	7	7-3-0
John Vaught	10	10-8-0	Earle Bruce	7	7-5-0
Bobby Dodd	9	9-4-0	Charlie McClendon	7	7-6-0
Johnny Majors	9	9-7-0	Hayden Fry	7	7-9-1
*John Robinson	8	8-1-0	LaVell Edwards	7	7-15-1
Terry Donahue	8	8-4-1			

*Active coach.

All-Time Bowl Winning Percentage

(Minimum 11 Games)

Coach, Last Team Coached	G	W-L-T	Pct.
*Bobby Bowden, Florida St.	25	18-7-1	.712
Bobby Dodd, Georgia Tech	13	9-4-0	.692
Don James, Washington	15	10-5-0	.667
*Joe Paterno, Penn St.	31	20-10-1	.661
Terry Donahue, UCLA	13	8-4-1	.654
Barry Switzer, Oklahoma	13	8-5-0	.615
*Lou Holtz, South Carolina	22	12-8-2	.591
Bill Yeoman, Houston	11	6-4-1	.591
Earle Bruce, Colorado St.	12	7-5-0	.583
*Jackie Sherrill, Mississippi St.	14	8-6-0	.571
Johnny Majors, Pittsburgh	16	9-7-0	.563
John Vaught, Mississippi	18	10-8-0	.556
Paul "Bear" Bryant, Alabama	29	15-12-2	.552
*Mack Brown, Texas	11	6-5-0	.545
*Phillip Fulmer, Tennessee	11	6-5-0	.545
Charlie McClendon, LSU	13	7-6-0	.538
Darrell Royal, Texas	16	8-7-1	.531
*Fisher DeBerry, Air Force	12	6-6-0	.500
Woody Hayes, Ohio St.	12	6-6-0	.500
Tom Osborne, Nebraska	25	12-13-0	.480

Coach, Last Team Coached	G	W-L-T	Pct.
Steve Spurrier, Florida	11	5-6-0	.455
Vince Dooley, Georgia	20	8-10-2	.450
Hayden Fry, Iowa	17	7-9-1	.441
Shug Jordan, Auburn	12	5-7-0	.417
John Cooper, Ohio St.	14	5-9-0	.357
George Welsh, Virginia	15	5-10-0	.333

*Active coach. Ties computed as half won and half lost.

All-Time Bowl Coaching History

A total of 483 coaches have head-coached in history's 851 major bowl games (the term "major bowl" is defined above the alphabetical list of team bowl records). Below is an alphabetical list of all 483 bowl coaches, with their alma mater and year, their birth date, and their game-by-game bowl records, with name and date of each bowl, opponent, final score (own score first) and opposing coach (in parentheses). A handful coached service teams or colleges never in the major category but are included because they coached against a major team in a major bowl.

Coach/School	Bowl/Date	Opponent/Score (Coach)
JIM AIKEN, 0-1-0	(Wash. & Jeff. '22)	Born 5-26-1899
Oregon	Cotton 1-1-49	Southern Methodist 12-21 (Matty Bell)
FRED AKERS, 2-8-0	(Arkansas '60)	Born 3-17-38
Wyoming	Fiesta 12-19-76	Oklahoma 7-41 (Barry Switzer)
Texas	Cotton 1-2-78	Notre Dame 10-38 (Dan Devine)
Texas	Sun 12-23-78	Maryland 42-0 (Jerry Claiborne)
Texas	Sun 12-22-79	Washington 7-14 (Don James)
Texas	Bluebonnet 12-31-80	North Carolina 7-16 (Dick Crum)
Texas	Cotton 1-1-82	Alabama 14-12 (Paul "Bear" Bryant)
Texas	Sun 12-25-82	North Carolina 10-26 (Dick Crum)
Texas	Cotton 1-2-84	Georgia 9-10 (Vince Dooley)
Texas	Freedom 12-26-84	Iowa 17-55 (Hayden Fry)
Texas	Bluebonnet 12-31-85	Air Force 16-24 (Fisher DeBerry)
BILL ALEXANDER, 3-2-0	(Georgia Tech '12)	Born 6-6-1889
Georgia Tech	Rose 1-1-29	California 8-7 (Clarence "Nibs" Price)
Georgia Tech	Orange 1-1-40	Missouri 21-7 (Don Faurot)
Georgia Tech	Cotton 1-1-43	Texas 7-14 (Dana Bible)
Georgia Tech	Sugar 1-1-44	Tulsa 20-18 (Henry Frnka)
Georgia Tech	Orange 1-1-45	Tulsa 12-26 (Henry Frnka)
LEONARD "STUB" ALLISON, 1-0-0	(Carleton '17)	Born 1892
California	Rose 1-1-38	Alabama 13-0 (Frank Thomas)
BARRY ALVAREZ, 6-1-0	(Nebraska '69)	Born 12-30-46
Wisconsin	Rose 1-1-94	UCLA 21-16 (Terry Donahue)
Wisconsin	Hall of Fame 1-2-95	Duke 34-20 (Fred Goldsmith)
Wisconsin	Copper 12-27-96	Utah 38-10 (Ron McBride)
Wisconsin	Outback 1-1-98	Georgia 6-33 (Jim Donnan)
Wisconsin	Rose 1-1-99	UCLA 38-31 (Bob Toledo)
Wisconsin	Rose 1-1-00	Stanford 17-9 (Tyrone Willingham)
Wisconsin	Sun 12-29-00	UCLA 21-20 (Bob Toledo)
Wisconsin	Alamo 12-28-02	Colorado 31-28 (ot) (Gary Barnett)
CHUCK AMATO, 2-1-0	(North Carolina St. '69)	Born 6-26-46
North Carolina St.	Micronpc.com 12-28-00	Minnesota 38-30 (Glen Mason)
North Carolina St.	Tangerine 12-20-01	Pittsburgh 19-34 (Walt Harris)
North Carolina St.	Gator 1-1-03	Notre Dame 28-6 (Tyrone Willingham)
TOM ANSTUTZ, 1-1-0	(Toledo '77)	Born 8-30-55
Toledo	Motor City 12-29-01	Cincinnati 23-16 (Rick Mintor)
Toledo	Motor City 12-26-02	Boston College 25-51 (Tom O'Brien)
MIKE ARCHER, 1-1-0	(Miami [Fla.] '75)	Born 7-26-53
LSU	Gator 12-31-87	South Carolina 30-13 (Joe Morrison)
LSU	Hall of Fame 1-2-89	Syracuse 10-23 (Dick MacPherson)
IKE ARMSTRONG, 1-0-0	(Drake '23)	Born 6-8-1895
Utah	Sun 1-2-39	New Mexico 16-0 (Ted Shipkey)
BILL ARNSPARGER, 0-3-0	(Miami [Ohio] '50)	Born 12-16-26
LSU	Sugar 1-1-85	Nebraska 10-28 (Tom Osborne)
LSU	Liberty 12-27-85	Baylor 7-21 (Grant Teaff)
LSU	Sugar 1-1-87	Nebraska 15-30 (Tom Osborne)
CHRIS AULT, 0-2-0	(Nevada '68)	Born 11-8-47
Nevada	Las Vegas 12-18-92	Bowling Green 34-35 (Gary Blackney)
Nevada	Las Vegas 12-14-95	Toledo 37-40 (ot) (Gary Pinkel)
CHARLEY BACHMAN, 0-1-0	(Notre Dame '17)	Born 12-1-92
Michigan St.	Orange 1-1-38	Auburn 0-6 (Jack Meagher)
ENOCH BAGSHAW, 0-1-1	(Washington '08)	Born 1884
Washington	Rose 1-1-24	Navy 14-14 (Bob Folwell)
Washington	Rose 1-1-26	Alabama 19-20 (Wallace Wade)
GEORGE BARCLAY, 1-0-0	(North Carolina '35)	Born 5-14-11
Wash. & Lee	Gator 1-1-51	Wyoming 7-20 (Bowden Wyatt)
BILL BARNES, 0-1-0	(Tennessee '41)	Born 10-20-17
UCLA	Rose 1-1-62	Minnesota 3-21 (Murray Warmath)
WILLIS BARNES, 1-1-1	(Nebraska)	Born 10-22-1900
New Mexico	Sun 1-1-44	Southwestern (Tex.) 0-7 (R. M. Medley)
New Mexico	Sun 1-1-46	Denver 34-24 (Clyde "Cac" Hubbard)
New Mexico	Harbor 1-1-47	Montana St. 13-13 (Clyde Carpenter)

Coach/School	Bowl/Date	Opponent/Score (Coach)
GARY BARNETT, 1-4-0	(Missouri '69)	Born 5-23-46
Northwestern	Rose 1-1-96	Southern California 32-41 (John Robinson)
Northwestern	Fla. Citrus 1-1-97	Tennessee 28-48 (Phillip Fulmer)
Colorado	Insight.com 12-31-99	Boston College 62-28 (Tom O'Brien)
Colorado	Fiesta 1-1-02	Oregon 16-38 (Mike Bellotti)
Colorado	Alamo 12-28-02	Wisconsin 28-31 (ot) (Barry Alvarez)
JOHN BARNHILL, 2-1-1	(Tennessee '28)	Born 2-21-03
Tennessee	Sugar 1-1-43	Tulsa 14-7 (Henry Frnka)
Tennessee	Rose 1-1-45	Southern California 0-25 (Jeff Cravath)
Arkansas	Cotton 1-1-47	LSU 0-0 (Bernie Moore)
Arkansas	Dixie 1-1-48	William & Mary 21-19 (Rube McCray)
BILL BATTLE, 4-1-0	(Alabama '63)	Born 12-8-41
Tennessee	Sugar 1-1-71	Air Force 34-13 (Ben Martin)
Tennessee	Liberty 12-20-71	Arkansas 14-13 (Frank Broyles)
Tennessee	Bluebonnet 12-30-72	LSU 24-17 (Charlie McClendon)
Tennessee	Gator 12-29-73	Texas Tech 19-28 (Jim Carlen)
Tennessee	Liberty 12-16-74	Maryland 7-3 (Jerry Claiborne)
SAMMY BAUGH, 0-1-0	(TCU '37)	Born 3-17-14
Hardin-Simmons	Sun 12-31-58	Wyoming 6-14 (Bob Devaney)
FRANK BEAMER, 5-5-0	(Virginia Tech '69)	Born 10-18-46
Virginia Tech	Independence 12-31-93	Indiana 45-20 (Bill Mallory)
Virginia Tech	Gator 12-30-94	Tennessee 23-45 (Phillip Fulmer)
Virginia Tech	Sugar 12-31-95	Texas 28-10 (John Mackovic)
Virginia Tech	Orange 12-31-96	Nebraska 21-41 (Tom Osborne)
Virginia Tech	Gator 1-1-98	North Carolina 3-42 (Carl Torbush)
Virginia Tech	Music City 12-29-98	Alabama 38-7 (Mike DuBose)
Virginia Tech	Sugar 1-4-00	Florida St. 29-46 (Bobby Bowden)
Virginia Tech	Gator 1-1-01	Clemson 41-20 (Tommy Bowden)
Virginia Tech	Gator 1-1-02	Florida St. 17-30 (Bobby Bowden)
Virginia Tech	San Francisco 12-31-02	Air Force 20-13 (Fisher DeBerry)
ALEX BELL, 1-1-0	(Villanova '38)	Born 8-12-15
Villanova	Sun 12-20-61	Wichita St. 17-9 (Hank Foldberg)
Villanova	Liberty 12-15-62	Oregon St. 0-6 (Tommy Prothro)
MATTY BELL, 1-1-1	(Centre '20)	Born 2-22-1899
Southern Methodist	Rose 1-1-36	Stanford 0-7 (Claude "Tiny" Thornhill)
Southern Methodist	Cotton 1-1-48	Penn St. 13-13 (Bob Higgins)
Southern Methodist	Cotton 1-1-49	Oregon 21-13 (Jim Aiken)
EMORY BELLARD, 2-3-0	(Southwest Tex. St. '49)	Born 12-17-27
Texas A&M	Liberty 12-22-75	Southern California 0-20 (John McKay)
Texas A&M	Sun 1-2-77	Florida 37-14 (Doug Dickey)
Texas A&M	Bluebonnet 12-31-77	Southern California 28-47 (John Robinson)
Mississippi St.	Sun 12-27-80	Nebraska 17-31 (Tom Osborne)
Mississippi St.	Hall of Fame 12-31-81	Kansas 10-0 (Don Fambrough)
MIKE BELLOTTI, 4-3-0	(UC Davis '73)	Born 12-21-50
Oregon	Cotton 1-1-96	Colorado 6-38 (Rick Neuheisel)
Oregon	Las Vegas 12-20-97	Air Force 41-13 (Fisher DeBerry)
Oregon	Aloha Classic 12-25-98	Colorado 43-51 (Rick Neuheisel)
Oregon	Sun 12-31-99	Minnesota 24-20 (Glen Mason)
Oregon	Holiday 12-29-00	Texas 35-30 (Mack Brown)
Oregon	Fiesta 1-1-02	Colorado 38-16 (Gary Barnett)
Oregon	Seattle 12-30-02	Wake Forest 17-38 (Jim Grobe)
ARTHUR "DUTCH" BERGMAN, 1-0-1	(Notre Dame '20)	Born 2-23-1895
Catholic	Orange 1-1-36	Mississippi 20-19 (Ed Walker)
Catholic	Sun 1-1-40	Arizona St. 0-0 (Millard "Dixie" Howell)
HUGO BEZDEK, 1-1-0	(Chicago '06)	Born 4-1-1884
Oregon	Rose 1-1-17	Pennsylvania 14-0 (Bob Folwell)
Penn St.	Rose 1-1-23	Southern California 3-14 (Elmer "Gus" Henderson)
DANA BIBLE, 3-0-1	(Carson-Newman '12)	Born 10-8-1891
Texas A&M	Dixie Classic 1-2-22	Centre 22-14 (Charley Moran)
Texas	Cotton 1-1-43	Georgia Tech 14-7 (Bill Alexander)
Texas	Cotton 1-1-44	Randolph Field 7-7 (Frank Tritico)
Texas	Cotton 1-1-46	Missouri 40-27 (Chauncey Simpson)
JACK BICKNELL, 2-2-0	(Montclair St. '60)	Born 2-20-38
Boston College	Tangerine 12-18-82	Auburn 26-33 (Pat Dye)
Boston College	Liberty 12-29-83	Notre Dame 18-19 (Gerry Faust)
Boston College	Cotton 1-1-85	Houston 45-28 (Bill Yeoman)
Boston College	Hall of Fame 12-23-86	Georgia 27-24 (Vince Dooley)
JACK BICKNELL III, 0-1-0	(Boston College '84)	Born 11-17-63
Louisiana Tech	Humanitarian 12-31-01	Clemson 24-49 (Tommy Bowden)
BERNIE BIERMAN, 0-1-0	(Minnesota '16)	Born 3-11-1894
Tulane	Rose 1-1-32	Southern California 12-21 (Howard Jones)
GARY BLACKNEY, 2-0-0	(Connecticut '67)	Born 12-10-55
Bowling Green	California 12-14-91	Fresno St. 28-21 (Jim Sweeney)
Bowling Green	Las Vegas 12-18-92	Nevada 35-34 (Chris Ault)
BOBBY BOWDEN, 18-7-1	(Samford '53)	Born 11-8-29
West Virginia	Peach 12-29-72	North Carolina St. 13-49 (Lou Holtz)
West Virginia	Peach 12-31-75	North Carolina St. 13-10 (Lou Holtz)
Florida St.	Tangerine 12-23-77	Texas Tech 40-17 (Steve Sloan)
Florida St.	Orange 1-1-80	Oklahoma 7-24 (Barry Switzer)
Florida St.	Orange 1-1-81	Oklahoma 17-18 (Barry Switzer)
Florida St.	Gator 12-30-82	West Virginia 31-12 (Don Nehlen)
Florida St.	Peach 12-30-83	North Carolina 28-3 (Dick Crum)

Coach/School	Bowl/Date	Opponent/Score (Coach)
Florida St.	Fla. Citrus 12-22-84	Georgia 17-17 (Vince Dooley)
Florida St.	Gator 12-30-85	Oklahoma St. 34-23 (Pat Jones)
Florida St.	All-American 12-31-86	Indiana 27-13 (Bill Mallory)
Florida St.	Fiesta 1-1-88	Nebraska 31-28 (Tom Osborne)
Florida St.	Sugar 1-2-89	Auburn 13-7 (Pat Dye)
Florida St.	Fiesta 1-1-90	Nebraska 41-17 (Tom Osborne)
Florida St.	Blockbuster 12-28-90	Penn St. 24-17 (Joe Paterno)
Florida St.	Cotton 1-1-92	Texas A&M 10-2 (R. C. Slocum)
Florida St.	Orange 1-1-93	Nebraska 27-14 (Tom Osborne)
Florida St.	Orange 1-1-94	Nebraska 18-16 (Tom Osborne)
Florida St.	Sugar 1-2-95	Florida 23-17 (Steve Spurrier)
Florida St.	Orange 1-1-96	Notre Dame 31-26 (Lou Holtz)
Florida St.	Sugar 1-2-97	Florida 20-52 (Steve Spurrier)
Florida St.	Sugar 1-1-98	Ohio St. 31-14 (John Cooper)
Florida St.	Fiesta 1-4-99	Tennessee 16-23 (Phillip Fulmer)
Florida St.	Sugar 1-4-00	Virginia Tech 46-29 (Frank Beamer)
Florida St.	Orange 1-3-01	Oklahoma 2-13 (Bob Stoops)
Florida St.	Gator 1-1-02	Virginia Tech 30-17 (Frank Beamer)
Florida St.	Sugar 1-1-03	Georgia 13-26 (Mark Richt)

TERRY BOWDEN, 2-1-0 (West Virginia '78) Born 2-24-56

Auburn..................	Outback 1-1-96	Penn St. 14-43 (Joe Paterno)
Auburn..................	Independence 12-31-96	Army 32-29 (Bob Sutton)
Auburn..................	Peach 1-2-98	Clemson 21-17 (Tommy West)

TOMMY BOWDEN, 2-2-0 (West Virginia '77) Born 7-10-54

Clemson..................	Peach 12-30-99	Mississippi St. 7-17 (Jackie Sherrill)
Clemson..................	Gator 1-1-01	Virginia Tech 20-41 (Frank Beamer)
Clemson..................	Humanitarian 12-31-01	Louisiana Tech 49-24 (Jack Bicknell III)
Clemson..................	Tangerine 12-23-02	Texas Tech 15-55 (Mike Leach)

JEFF BOWER, 3-3-0 (Southern Miss. '76) Born 5-28-53

Southern Miss.	All-American 12-28-90	North Carolina St. 27-31 (Dick Sheridan)
Southern Miss.	Liberty 12-31-97	Pittsburgh 41-7 (Walt Harris)
Southern Miss.	Humanitarian 12-30-98	Idaho 35-42 (Chris Tormey)
Southern Miss.	Liberty 12-31-99	Colorado St. 23-17 (Sonny Lubick)
Southern Miss.	Mobile Alabama 12-20-00	TCU 28-21 (Gary Patterson)
Southern Miss.	Houston 12-27-02	Oklahoma St. 23-33 (Les Miles)

SAM BOYD, 1-0-0 (Baylor '38) Born 8-12-15

Baylor..................	Sugar 1-1-57	Tennessee 13-7 (Bowden Wyatt)

WESLEY BRADSHAW, 0-1-0 (Baylor '23) Born 11-26-1898

Ouachita Baptist	Shrine 12-18-48	Hardin-Simmons 12-40 (Warren Woodson)

BILLY BREWER, 3-2-0 (Mississippi '61) Born 10-8-35

Mississippi............	Independence 12-10-83	Air Force 3-9 (Ken Hatfield)
Mississippi............	Independence 12-20-86	Texas Tech 20-17 (Spike Dykes)
Mississippi............	All-American 12-29-89	Air Force 42-29 (Fisher DeBerry)
Mississippi............	Gator 1-1-91	Michigan 3-35 (Gary Moeller)
Mississippi............	Liberty 12-31-92	Air Force 13-0 (Fisher DeBerry)

JOHN BRIDGERS, 2-1-0 (Auburn '47) Born 1-13-22

Baylor..................	Gator 12-31-60	Florida 12-13 (Ray Graves)
Baylor..................	Gotham 12-9-61	Utah St. 24-9 (John Ralston)
Baylor..................	Bluebonnet 12-21-63	LSU 14-7 (Charlie McClendon)

RICH BROOKS, 1-3-0 (Oregon St. '63) Born 8-20-41

Oregon..................	Independence 12-16-89	Tulsa 27-24 (Dave Rader)
Oregon..................	Freedom 12-29-90	Colorado St. 31-32 (Earle Bruce)
Oregon..................	Independence 12-31-92	Wake Forest 35-39 (Bill Dooley)
Oregon..................	Rose 1-2-95	Penn St. 20-38 (Joe Paterno)

J.O. "BUDDY" BROTHERS, 0-1-0 (Texas Tech '31) Born 5-29-09

Tulsa....................	Gator 1-1-53	Florida 13-14 (Bob Woodruff)

MACK BROWN, 6-5-0 (Florida St. '74) Born 8-27-51

Tulane..................	Independence 12-19-87	Washington 12-24 (Don James)
North Carolina	Peach 1-2-93	Mississippi St. 21-17 (Jackie Sherrill)
North Carolina	Gator 12-31-93	Alabama 10-24 (Gene Stallings)
North Carolina	Sun 12-30-94	Texas 31-35 (John Mackovic)
North Carolina	Carquest 12-30-95	Arkansas 20-10 (Danny Ford)
North Carolina	Gator 1-1-97	West Virginia 20-13 (Don Nehlen)
Texas..................	Cotton 1-1-99	Mississippi St. 38-11 (Jackie Sherrill)
Texas..................	Cotton 1-1-00	Arkansas 6-27 (Houston Nutt)
Texas..................	Holiday 12-29-00	Oregon 30-35 (Mike Bellotti)
Texas..................	Holiday 12-28-01	Washington 47-43 (Rick Neuheisel)
Texas..................	Cotton 1-1-03	LSU 35-20 (Nick Saban)

FRANK BROYLES, 4-6-0 (Georgia Tech '47) Born 12-26-24

Arkansas..............	Gator 1-2-60	Duke 6-7 (Bill Murray)
Arkansas..............	Cotton 1-2-61	Duke 6-7 (Bill Murray)
Arkansas..............	Sugar 1-1-62	Alabama 3-10 (Paul "Bear" Bryant)
Arkansas..............	Sugar 1-1-63	Mississippi 13-17 (John Vaught)
Arkansas..............	Cotton 1-1-65	Nebraska 10-7 (Bob Devaney)
Arkansas..............	Cotton 1-1-66	LSU 7-14 (Charlie McClendon)
Arkansas..............	Sugar 1-1-69	Georgia 16-2 (Vince Dooley)
Arkansas..............	Sugar 1-1-70	Mississippi 22-27 (John Vaught)
Arkansas..............	Liberty 12-20-71	Tennessee 13-14 (Bill Battle)
Arkansas..............	Cotton 1-1-76	Georgia 31-10 (Vince Dooley)

EARLE BRUCE, 7-5-0 (Ohio St. '53) Born 3-8-31

Tampa..................	Tangerine 12-29-72	Kent St. 21-18 (Don James)
Iowa St.................	Peach 12-31-77	North Carolina St. 14-24 (Bo Rein)
Iowa St.................	Hall of Fame 12-20-78	Texas A&M 12-28 (Tom Wilson)

Coach/School	Bowl/Date	Opponent/Score (Coach)
Ohio St.	Rose 1-1-80	Southern California 16-17 (John Robinson)
Ohio St.	Fiesta 12-26-80	Penn St. 19-31 (Joe Paterno)
Ohio St.	Liberty 12-30-81	Navy 31-28 (George Welsh)
Ohio St.	Holiday 12-17-82	Brigham Young 47-17 (LaVell Edwards)
Ohio St.	Fiesta 1-2-84	Pittsburgh 28-23 (Foge Fazio)
Ohio St.	Rose 1-1-85	Southern California 17-20 (Ted Tollner)
Ohio St.	Fla. Citrus 12-28-85	Brigham Young 10-7 (LaVell Edwards)
Ohio St.	Cotton 1-1-87	Texas A&M 28-12 (Jackie Sherrill)
Colorado St.	Freedom 12-29-90	Oregon 32-31 (Rich Brooks)

MILT BRUHN, 0-2-0 (Minnesota '35) Born 7-28-12

Wisconsin..............	Rose 1-1-60	Washington 8-44 (Jim Owens)
Wisconsin..............	Rose 1-2-63	Southern California 37-42 (John McKay)

MIKE BRUMBELOW, 2-1-0 (TCU '30) Born 7-13-06

UTEP....................	Sun 1-1-54	Southern Miss. 37-14 (Thad "Pie" Vann)
UTEP....................	Sun 1-1-55	Florida St. 47-20 (Tom Nugent)
UTEP....................	Sun 1-1-57	George Washington 0-13 (Eugene "Bo" Sherman)

PAUL "BEAR" BRYANT, 15-12-2 (Alabama '36) Born 9-11-13

Kentucky...............	Great Lakes 12-6-47	Villanova 24-14 (Jordan Oliver)
Kentucky...............	Orange 1-2-50	Santa Clara 13-21 (Len Casanova)
Kentucky...............	Sugar 1-1-51	Oklahoma 13-7 (Bud Wilkinson)
Kentucky...............	Cotton 1-1-52	TCU 20-7 (Leo "Dutch" Meyer)
Texas A&M............	Gator 12-28-57	Tennessee 0-3 (Bowden Wyatt)
Alabama................	Liberty 12-19-59	Penn St. 0-7 (Charles "Rip" Engle)
Alabama................	Bluebonnet 12-17-60	Texas 3-3 (Darrell Royal)
Alabama................	Sugar 1-1-62	Arkansas 10-3 (Frank Broyles)
Alabama................	Orange 1-1-63	Oklahoma 17-0 (Bud Wilkinson)
Alabama................	Sugar 1-1-64	Mississippi 12-7 (John Vaught)
Alabama................	Orange 1-1-65	Texas 17-21 (Darrell Royal)
Alabama................	Orange 1-1-66	Nebraska 39-28 (Bob Devaney)
Alabama................	Sugar 1-2-67	Nebraska 34-7 (Bob Devaney)
Alabama................	Cotton 1-1-68	Texas A&M 16-20 (Gene Stallings)
Alabama................	Gator 12-28-68	Missouri 10-35 (Dan Devine)
Alabama................	Liberty 12-13-69	Colorado 33-47 (Eddie Crowder)
Alabama................	Bluebonnet 12-31-70	Oklahoma 24-24 (Chuck Fairbanks)
Alabama................	Orange 1-1-72	Nebraska 6-38 (Bob Devaney)
Alabama................	Cotton 1-1-73	Texas 13-17 (Darrell Royal)
Alabama................	Sugar 12-31-73	Notre Dame 23-24 (Ara Parseghian)
Alabama................	Orange 1-1-75	Notre Dame 11-13 (Ara Parseghian)
Alabama................	Sugar 12-31-75	Penn St. 13-6 (Joe Paterno)
Alabama................	Liberty 12-20-76	UCLA 36-6 (Terry Donahue)
Alabama................	Sugar 1-2-78	Ohio St. 35-6 (Woody Hayes)
Alabama................	Sugar 1-1-79	Penn St. 14-7 (Joe Paterno)
Alabama................	Sugar 1-1-80	Arkansas 24-9 (Lou Holtz)
Alabama................	Cotton 1-1-81	Baylor 30-2 (Grant Teaff)
Alabama................	Cotton 1-1-82	Texas 12-14 (Fred Akers)
Alabama................	Liberty 12-29-82	Illinois 21-15 (Mike White)

JOHN BUNTING, 1-0-0 (North Carolina '72) Born 7-15-50

North Carolina........	Peach 12-31-01	Auburn 16-10 (Tommy Tuberville)

FRANK BURNS, 0-1-0 (Rutgers '49) Born 3-16-28

Rutgers.................	Garden State 12-16-78	Arizona St. 18-34 (Frank Kush)

LEON BURTNETT, 0-1-0 (Southwestern [Kan.] '65) Born 5-30-43

Purdue..................	Peach 12-31-84	Virginia 24-27 (George Welsh)

WALLY BUTTS, 5-2-1 (Mercer '28) Born 2-7-05

Georgia.................	Orange 1-1-42	TCU 40-26 (Leo "Dutch" Meyer)
Georgia.................	Rose 1-1-43	UCLA 9-0 (Edwin "Babe" Horrell)
Georgia.................	Oil 1-1-46	Tulsa 20-6 (Henry Frnka)
Georgia.................	Sugar 1-1-47	North Carolina 20-10 (Carl Snavely)
Georgia.................	Gator 1-1-48	Maryland 20-20 (Jim Tatum)
Georgia.................	Orange 1-1-49	Texas 28-41 (Blair Cherry)
Georgia.................	Presidential Cup 12-9-50	Texas A&M 20-40 (Harry Stiteler)
Georgia.................	Orange 1-1-60	Missouri 14-0 (Dan Devine)

JIM CALDWELL, 1-0-0 (Iowa '77) Born 1-16-55

Wake Forest	Aloha Classic 12-25-99	Arizona St. 23-3 (Bruce Snyder)

EDDIE CAMERON, 1-0-0 (Wash. & Lee '24) Born 4-22-02

Duke	Sugar 1-1-45	Alabama 29-26 (Frank Thomas)

FRANK CAMP, 1-0-0 (Transylvania '30) Born 12-23-05

Louisville...............	Sun 1-1-58	Drake 34-20 (Warren Gaer)

JIM CARLEN, 2-5-1 (Georgia Tech '55) Born 7-11-33

West Virginia..........	Peach 12-30-69	South Carolina 14-3 (Paul Dietzel)
Texas Tech.............	Sun 12-19-70	Georgia Tech 9-17 (Bud Carson)
Texas Tech.............	Sun 12-30-72	North Carolina 28-32 (Bill Dooley)
Texas Tech.............	Gator 12-29-73	Tennessee 28-19 (Bill Battle)
Texas Tech.............	Peach 12-28-74	Vanderbilt 6-6 (Steve Sloan)
South Carolina........	Tangerine 12-20-75	Miami (Ohio) 7-20 (Dick Crum)
South Carolina........	Hall of Fame 12-29-79	Missouri 14-24 (Warren Powers)
South Carolina........	Gator 12-29-80	Pittsburgh 8-37 (Jackie Sherrill)

CLYDE CARPENTER, 0-0-1 (Montana '32) Born 4-17-08

Montana St............	Harbor 1-1-47	New Mexico 13-13 (Willis Barnes)

LLOYD CARR, 5-3-0 (Northern Mich. '68) Born 7-30-45

Michigan...............	Alamo 12-28-95	Texas A&M 20-22 (R. C. Slocum)
Michigan...............	Outback 1-1-97	Alabama 14-17 (Gene Stallings)
Michigan...............	Rose 1-1-98	Washington St. 21-16 (Mike Price)
Michigan...............	Florida Citrus 1-1-99	Arkansas 45-31 (Houston Nutt)

Coach/School	Bowl/Date	Opponent/Score (Coach)
Michigan	Orange 1-1-00	Alabama 35-34 (ot) (Mike DuBose)
Michigan	Fla. Citrus 1-1-01	Auburn 31-28 (Tommy Tuberville)
Michigan	Fla. Citrus 1-1-02	Tennessee 17-45 (Phillip Fulmer)
Michigan	Outback 1-1-03	Florida 38-30 (Ron Zook)

PETE CARROLL, 1-1-0 (Pacific '73) Born 9-15-51

Southern California	Las Vegas 12-25-01	Utah 6-10 (Ron McBride)
Southern California	Orange 1-2-03	Iowa 38-17 (Kirk Ferentz)

BUD CARSON, 1-1-0 (North Carolina '52) Born 4-28-30

Georgia Tech	Sun 12-19-70	Texas Tech 17-9 (Jim Carlen)
Georgia Tech	Peach 12-30-71	Mississippi 18-41 (Billy Kinard)

LEN CASANOVA, 2-2-0 (Santa Clara '27) Born 6-12-05

Santa Clara	Orange 1-2-50	Kentucky 21-13 (Paul "Bear" Bryant)
Oregon	Rose 1-1-58	Ohio St. 7-10 (Woody Hayes)
Oregon	Liberty 12-17-60	Penn St. 12-41 (Charles "Rip" Engle)
Oregon	Sun 12-31-63	Southern Methodist 21-14 (Hayden Fry)

MILES CASTEEL, 0-1-0 (Kalamazoo '25) Born 12-30-1896

Arizona	Salad 1-1-49	Drake 13-14 (Al Kawal)

PETE CAWTHON, 0-2-0 (Southwestern [Tex.] '20) Born 8-24-1898

Texas Tech	Sun 1-1-38	West Virginia 6-7 (Marshall "Little Sleepy" Glenn)
Texas Tech	Cotton 1-2-39	St. Mary's (Cal.) 13-20 (Edward "Slip" Madigan)

BLAIR CHERRY, 2-1-0 (TCU '24) Born 9-7-01

Texas	Sugar 1-1-48	Alabama 27-7 (Harold "Red" Drew)
Texas	Orange 1-1-49	Georgia 41-28 (Wally Butts)
Texas	Cotton 1-1-51	Tennessee 14-20 (Bob Neyland)

JERRY CLAIBORNE, 3-8-0 (Kentucky '50) Born 8-26-28

Virginia Tech	Liberty 12-10-66	Miami (Fla.) 7-14 (Charlie Tate)
Virginia Tech	Liberty 12-14-68	Mississippi 17-34 (John Vaught)
Maryland	Peach 12-28-73	Georgia 16-17 (Vince Dooley)
Maryland	Liberty 12-16-74	Tennessee 3-7 (Bill Battle)
Maryland	Gator 12-29-75	Florida 13-0 (Doug Dickey)
Maryland	Cotton 1-1-77	Houston 21-30 (Bill Yeoman)
Maryland	Hall of Fame 12-27-77	Minnesota 17-7 (Cal Stoll)
Maryland	Sun 12-23-78	Texas 0-42 (Fred Akers)
Maryland	Tangerine 12-20-80	Florida 20-35 (Charley Pell)
Kentucky	Hall of Fame 12-22-83	West Virginia 16-20 (Don Nehlen)
Kentucky	Hall of Fame 12-29-84	Wisconsin 20-19 (Dave McClain)

LARRY COKER, 1-1-0 (Northeastern '70) Born 6-23-48

Miami (Fla.)	Rose 1-3-02	Nebraska 37-14 (Frank Solich)
Miami (Fla.)	Fiesta 1-3-02	Ohio St. 24-31 (2 ot) (Jim Tressel)

CECIL COLEMAN, 1-0-0 (Arizona St. '50) Born 4-12-26

Fresno St.	Mercy 11-23-61	Bowling Green 36-6 (Doyt Perry)

BOBBY COLLINS, 3-2-0 (Mississippi St. '55) Born 10-25-33

Southern Miss.	Independence 12-13-70	McNeese St. 16-14 (Ernie Duplechin)
Southern Miss.	Tangerine 12-19-81	Missouri 17-19 (Warren Powers)
Southern Methodist	Cotton 1-1-83	Pittsburgh 7-3 (Foge Fazio)
Southern Methodist	Sun 12-24-83	Alabama 7-28 (Ray Perkins)
Southern Methodist	Aloha 12-29-84	Notre Dame 27-20 (Gerry Faust)

JOHN COOPER, 5-9-0 (Iowa St. '62) Born 7-2-37

Arizona St.	Holiday 12-22-85	Arkansas 17-18 (Ken Hatfield)
Arizona St.	Rose 1-1-87	Michigan 22-15 (Glenn "Bo" Schembechler)
Arizona St.	Freedom 12-30-87	Air Force 33-28 (Fisher DeBerry)
Ohio St.	Hall of Fame 1-1-90	Auburn 14-31 (Pat Dye)
Ohio St.	Liberty 12-27-90	Air Force 11-23 (Fisher DeBerry)
Ohio St.	Hall of Fame 1-1-92	Syracuse 17-24 (Paul Pasqualoni)
Ohio St.	Fla. Citrus 1-1-93	Georgia 14-21 (Ray Goff)
Ohio St.	Holiday 12-30-93	Brigham Young 28-21 (LaVell Edwards)
Ohio St.	Fla. Citrus 1-2-95	Alabama 17-24 (Gene Stallings)
Ohio St.	Fla. Citrus 1-1-96	Tennessee 14-20 (Phillip Fulmer)
Ohio St.	Rose 1-1-97	Arizona St. 20-17 (Bruce Snyder)
Ohio St.	Sugar 1-1-98	Florida St. 14-31 (Bobby Bowden)
Ohio St.	Sugar 1-1-99	Texas A&M 24-14 (R.C. Slocum)
Ohio St.	Outback 1-1-01	South Carolina 7-24 (Lou Holtz)

LEE CORSO, 1-0-1 (Florida St. '57) Born 8-7-35

Louisville	Pasadena 12-19-70	Long Beach St. 24-24 (Jim Stangeland)
Indiana	Holiday 12-21-79	Brigham Young 38-37 (LaVell Edwards)

GENE CORUM, 0-1-0 (West Virginia '48) Born 5-29-21

West Virginia	Liberty 12-19-64	Utah 6-32 (Ray Nagel)

DON CORYELL, 1-0-0 (Washington '50) Born 10-17-24

San Diego St.	Pasadena 12-26-69	Boston U. 28-7 (Larry Naviaux)

TOM COUGHLIN, 1-1-0 (Syracuse '68) Born 8-31-46

Boston College	Hall of Fame 1-1-93	Tennessee 23-38 (Phillip Fulmer)
Boston College	Carquest 1-1-94	Virginia 31-13 (George Welsh)

TED COX, 1-0-0 (Minnesota '26) Born 6-30-03

Tulane	Sugar 1-1-35	Temple 20-14 (Glenn "Pop" Warner)

JEFF CRAVATH, 2-2-0 (Southern California '27) Born 2-5-05

Southern California	Rose 1-1-44	Washington 29-0 (Ralph "Pest" Welch)
Southern California	Rose 1-1-45	Tennessee 25-0 (John Barnhill)
Southern California	Rose 1-1-46	Alabama 14-34 (Frank Thomas)
Southern California	Rose 1-1-48	Michigan 0-49 (H.O. "Fritz" Crisler)

H.O. "FRITZ" CRISLER, 1-0-0 (Chicago '22) Born 1-2-1899

Michigan	Rose 1-1-48	Southern California 49-0 (Jeff Cravath)

EDDIE CROWDER, 3-2-0 (Oklahoma '55) Born 8-26-31

Colorado	Bluebonnet 12-23-67	Miami (Fla.) 31-21 (Charlie Tate)
Colorado	Liberty 12-13-69	Alabama 47-33 (Paul "Bear" Bryant)
Colorado	Liberty 12-12-70	Tulane 3-17 (Jim Pittman)
Colorado	Bluebonnet 12-31-71	Houston 29-17 (Bill Yeoman)
Colorado	Gator 12-20-72	Auburn 3-24 (Ralph "Shug" Jordan)

JACK CROWE, 0-1-0 (UAB '70) Born 4-6-48

Arkansas	Independence 12-29-91	Georgia 15-24 (Ray Goff)

JIM CROWLEY, 1-1-0 (Notre Dame '25) Born 9-10-02

Fordham	Cotton 1-1-41	Texas A&M 12-13 (Homer Norton)
Fordham	Sugar 1-1-42	Missouri 2-0 (Don Faurot)

GARY CROWTON, 0-1-0 (Brigham Young '83) Born 6-14-57

Brigham Young	Liberty 12-31-01	Louisville 10-28 (John L. Smith)

DICK CRUM, 6-2-0 (Mount Union '57) Born 4-29-34

Miami (Ohio)	Tangerine 12-21-74	Georgia 21-10 (Vince Dooley)
Miami (Ohio)	Tangerine 12-20-75	South Carolina 20-7 (Jim Carlen)
North Carolina	Gator 12-28-79	Michigan 17-15 (Glenn "Bo" Schembechler)
North Carolina	Bluebonnet 12-31-80	Texas 16-7 (Fred Akers)
North Carolina	Gator 12-28-81	Arkansas 31-27 (Lou Holtz)
North Carolina	Sun 12-25-82	Texas 26-10 (Fred Akers)
North Carolina	Peach 12-30-83	Florida St. 3-28 (Bobby Bowden)
North Carolina	Aloha 12-27-86	Arizona 21-30 (Larry Smith)

FRAN CURCI, 1-0-0 (Miami [Fla.] '60) Born 6-11-38

Kentucky	Peach 12-31-76	North Carolina 21-0 (Bill Dooley)

BILL CURRY, 2-3-0 (Georgia Tech '65) Born 10-21-42

Georgia Tech	Hall of Fame 12-31-85	Michigan St. 17-14 (George Perles)
Alabama	Hall of Fame 1-2-88	Michigan 24-28 (Glenn "Bo" Schembechler)
Alabama	Sun 12-24-88	Army 29-28 (Jim Young)
Alabama	Sugar 1-1-90	Miami (Fla.) 25-33 (Dennis Erickson)
Kentucky	Peach 12-31-93	Clemson 13-14 (Tommy West)

JACK "CACTUS JACK" CURTICE, 1-1-0 (Transylvania '30) Born 5-24-07

UTEP	Sun 1-1-49	West Virginia 12-21 (Dud DeGroot)
UTEP	Sun 1-2-50	Georgetown 33-20 (Bob Margarita)

DAVID CUTCLIFFE, 3-1-0 (Alabama '76) Born 9-16-54

Mississippi	Independence 12-31-98	Texas Tech 35-18 (Spike Dykes)
Mississippi	Independence 12-31-99	Oklahoma 27-25 (Bob Stoops)
Mississippi	Music City 12-28-00	West Virginia 38-49 (Don Nehlen)
Mississippi	Independence 12-27-02	Nebraska 27-23 (Frank Solich)

JOHN "OX" Da GROSA, 0-1-0 (Colgate '26) Born 2-7-02

Holy Cross	Orange 1-1-46	Miami (Fla.) 6-13 (Jack Harding)

GARY DARNELL, 0-1-0 (Oklahoma St. '71) Born 10-15-48

Florida	Freedom 12-29-89	Washington 7-34 (Don James)

DUFFY DAUGHERTY, 1-1-0 (Syracuse '40) Born 9-8-15

Michigan St.	Rose 1-2-56	UCLA 17-14 (Henry "Red" Sanders)
Michigan St.	Rose 1-1-66	UCLA 12-14 (Tommy Prothro)

BOB DAVIE, 0-3-0 (Youngstown St. '76) Born 9-30-54

Notre Dame	Independence 12-28-97	LSU 9-27 (Gerry DiNardo)
Notre Dame	Gator 1-1-99	Georgia Tech 28-35 (George O'Leary)
Notre Dame	Fiesta 1-1-01	Oregon St. 9-41 (Dennis Erickson)

BOB DAVIS, 0-1-0 (Utah '30) Born 2-13-08

Colorado St.	Raisin 1-1-49	Occidental 20-21 (Roy Dennis)

BUTCH DAVIS, 4-0-0 (Arkansas '74) Born 11-17-51

Miami (Fla.)	Carquest 12-27-96	Virginia 31-21 (George Welsh)
Miami (Fla.)	Micron PC 12-29-98	North Carolina St. 46-23 (Mike O'Cain)
Miami (Fla.)	Gator 1-1-00	Georgia Tech 28-13 (George O'Leary)
Miami (Fla.)	Sugar 1-2-01	Florida 37-20 (Steve Spurrier)

PAUL DAVIS, 1-0-0 (Mississippi '47) Born 2-3-22

Mississippi St.	Liberty 12-21-63	North Carolina St. 16-12 (Earle Edwards)

LOWELL "RED" DAWSON, 0-1-0 (Tulane '30) Born 12-26-06

Tulane	Sugar 1-1-40	Texas A&M 13-14 (Homer Norton)

FISHER DeBERRY, 6-6-0 (Wofford '60) Born 9-9-38

Air Force	Independence 12-15-84	Virginia Tech 23-7 (Bill Dooley)
Air Force	Bluebonnet 12-31-85	Texas 24-16 (Fred Akers)
Air Force	Freedom 12-30-87	Arizona St. 28-33 (John Cooper)
Air Force	Liberty 12-29-89	Mississippi 29-42 (Billy Brewer)
Air Force	Liberty 12-27-90	Ohio St. 23-11 (John Cooper)
Air Force	Liberty 12-29-91	Mississippi St. 38-15 (Jackie Sherrill)
Air Force	Liberty 12-31-92	Mississippi 0-13 (Billy Brewer)
Air Force	Copper 12-29-95	Texas Tech 41-55 (Spike Dykes)
Air Force	Las Vegas 12-20-97	Oregon 13-41 (Mike Bellotti)
Air Force	Oahu Classic 12-25-98	Washington 45-25 (Jim Lambright)
Air Force	Silicon Valley 12-31-00	Fresno St. 37-34 (Pat Hill)
Air Force	San Francisco 12-31-02	Virginia Tech 13-20 (Frank Beamer)

Coach/School	Bowl/Date	Opponent/Score (Coach)
DUD DeGROOT, 1-0-0 (Stanford '24) Born 11-20-1895		
West Virginia..........	Sun 1-1-49	UTEP 21-12 (Jack "Cactus Jack" Curtice)
ROY DENNIS, 1-0-0 (Occidental '33) Born 5-13-05		
Occidental..............	Raisin 1-1-49	Colorado St. 21-20 (Bob Davis)
HERB DEROMEDI, 0-1-0 (Michigan '60) Born 5-26-39		
Central Mich.	California 12-8-90	San Jose St. 24-48 (Terry Shea)
BOB DEVANEY, 7-3-0 (Alma '39) Born 4-2-15		
Wyoming	Sun 12-31-58	Hardin-Simmons 14-6 (Sammy Baugh)
Nebraska	Gotham 12-15-62	Miami (Fla.) 36-34 (Andy Gustafson)
Nebraska	Orange 1-1-64	Auburn 13-7 (Ralph "Shug" Jordan)
Nebraska	Cotton 1-1-65	Arkansas 7-10 (Frank Broyles)
Nebraska	Orange 1-1-66	Alabama 28-39 (Paul "Bear" Bryant)
Nebraska	Sugar 1-2-67	Alabama 7-34 (Paul "Bear" Bryant)
Nebraska	Sun 12-20-69	Georgia 45-6 (Vince Dooley)
Nebraska	Orange 1-1-71	LSU 17-12 (Charlie McClendon)
Nebraska	Orange 1-1-72	Alabama 38-6 (Paul "Bear" Bryant)
Nebraska	Orange 1-1-73	Notre Dame 40-6 (Ara Parseghian)
DAN DEVINE, 7-3-0 (Minn. Duluth '48) Born 12-23-24		
Missouri..................	Orange 1-1-60	Georgia 0-14 (Wally Butts)
Missouri..................	Orange 1-2-61	Navy 21-14 (Wayne Hardin)
Missouri..................	Bluebonnet 12-22-62	Georgia Tech 14-10 (Bobby Dodd)
Missouri..................	Sugar 1-1-66	Florida 20-18 (Ray Graves)
Missouri..................	Gator 12-28-68	Alabama 35-10 (Paul "Bear" Bryant)
Missouri..................	Orange 1-1-70	Penn St. 3-10 (Joe Paterno)
Notre Dame............	Gator 12-27-76	Penn St. 20-9 (Joe Paterno)
Notre Dame............	Cotton 1-2-78	Texas 38-10 (Fred Akers)
Notre Dame............	Cotton 1-1-79	Houston 35-34 (Bill Yeoman)
Notre Dame............	Sugar 1-1-81	Georgia 10-17 (Vince Dooley)
PHIL DICKENS, 1-0-0 (Tennessee '37) Born 6-29-14		
Wyoming	Sun 1-2-56	Texas Tech 21-14 (DeWitt Weaver)
DARRELL DICKEY, 1-1-0 (Kansas St. '84) Born 12-6-59		
North Texas	New Orleans 12-18-01	Colorado St. 20-45 (Sonny Lubick)
North Texas	New Orleans 12-17-02	Cincinnati 24-19 (Rick Minter)
DOUG DICKEY, 2-7-0 (Florida '54) Born 6-24-32		
Tennessee	Bluebonnet 12-18-65	Tulsa 27-6 (Glenn Dobbs)
Tennessee	Gator 12-31-66	Syracuse 18-12 (Ben Schwartzwalder)
Tennessee	Orange 1-1-68	Oklahoma 24-26 (Chuck Fairbanks)
Tennessee	Cotton 1-1-69	Texas 13-35 (Darrell Royal)
Tennessee	Gator 12-27-69	Florida 13-14 (Ray Graves)
Florida....................	Tangerine 12-22-73	Miami (Ohio) 7-16 (Bill Mallory)
Florida....................	Sugar 12-31-74	Nebraska 10-13 (Tom Osborne)
Florida....................	Gator 12-29-75	Maryland 0-13 (Jerry Claiborne)
Florida....................	Sun 1-2-77	Texas A&M 14-37 (Emory Bellard)
JIM DICKEY, 0-1-0 (Houston '56) Born 3-22-34		
Kansas St................	Independence 12-11-82	Wisconsin 3-14 (Dave McClain)
BILL "LONE STAR" DIETZ, 1-0-0 (Carlisle '12) Born 8-15-1885		
Washington St.	Rose 1-1-16	Brown 14-0 (Ed Robinson)
PAUL DIETZEL, 2-2-0 (Miami [Ohio] '48) Born 9-5-24		
LSU	Sugar 1-1-59	Clemson 7-0 (Frank Howard)
LSU	Sugar 1-1-60	Mississippi 0-21 (John Vaught)
LSU	Orange 1-1-62	Colorado 25-7 (Sonny Grandelius)
South Carolina	Peach 12-20-69	West Virginia 3-14 (Jim Carlen)
GERRY DiNARDO, 3-0-0 (Notre Dame '75) Born 11-10-52		
LSU	Independence 12-29-95	Michigan St. 45-26 (Nick Saban)
LSU	Peach 12-28-96	Clemson 10-7 (Tommy West)
LSU	Independence 12-28-97	Notre Dame 27-9 (Bob Davie)
BOBBY DOBBS, 2-0-0 (Army '46) Born 10-13-22		
UTEP	Sun 12-31-65	TCU 13-12 (Abe Martin)
UTEP	Sun 12-30-67	Mississippi 14-7 (John Vaught)
GLENN DOBBS, 1-1-0 (Tulsa '43) Born 7-12-20		
Tulsa	Bluebonnet 12-19-64	Mississippi 14-7 (John Vaught)
Tulsa	Bluebonnet 12-18-65	Tennessee 6-27 (Doug Dickey)
BOBBY DODD, 9-4-0 (Tennessee '31) Born 11-11-08		
Georgia Tech..........	Oil 1-1-47	St. Mary's (Cal.) 41-19 (Jimmy Phelan)
Georgia Tech..........	Orange 1-1-48	Kansas 20-14 (George Sauer)
Georgia Tech..........	Orange 1-1-52	Baylor 17-14 (George Sauer)
Georgia Tech..........	Sugar 1-1-53	Mississippi 24-7 (John Vaught)
Georgia Tech..........	Sugar 1-1-54	West Virginia 42-19 (Art Lewis)
Georgia Tech..........	Cotton 1-1-55	Arkansas 14-6 (Bowden Wyatt)
Georgia Tech..........	Sugar 1-2-56	Pittsburgh 7-0 (John Michelosen)
Georgia Tech..........	Gator 12-29-56	Pittsburgh 21-14 (John Michelosen)
Georgia Tech..........	Gator 1-2-60	Arkansas 7-14 (Frank Broyles)
Georgia Tech..........	Gator 12-30-61	Penn St. 15-30 (Charles "Rip" Engle)
Georgia Tech..........	Bluebonnet 12-22-62	Missouri 10-14 (Dan Devine)
Georgia Tech..........	Gator 12-31-65	Texas Tech 31-21 (J.T. King)
Georgia Tech..........	Orange 1-2-67	Florida 12-27 (Ray Graves)
ED DOHERTY, 0-2-0 (Boston College '44) Born 7-25-18		
Arizona St.	Salad 1-1-50	Xavier (Ohio) 21-33 (Ed Kluska)
Arizona St.	Salad 1-1-51	Miami (Ohio) 21-34 (Woody Hayes)
JACK DOLAND, 1-0-0 (Tulane '50) Born 3-3-28		
McNeese St.	Independence 12-13-76	Tulsa 20-16 (F.A. Dry)

Coach/School	Bowl/Date	Opponent/Score (Coach)
TERRY DONAHUE, 8-4-1 (UCLA '67) Born 6-24-44		
UCLA	Liberty 12-30-76	Alabama 6-36 (Paul "Bear" Bryant)
UCLA	Fiesta 12-25-78	Arkansas 10-10 (Lou Holtz)
UCLA	Bluebonnet 12-31-81	Michigan 14-33 (Glenn "Bo" Schembechler)
UCLA	Rose 1-1-83	Michigan 24-14 (Glenn "Bo" Schembechler)
UCLA	Rose 1-2-84	Illinois 45-9 (Mike White)
UCLA	Fiesta 1-1-85	Miami (Fla.) 39-37 (Jimmy Johnson)
UCLA	Rose 1-1-86	Iowa 45-28 (Hayden Fry)
UCLA	Freedom 12-30-86	Brigham Young 31-10 (LaVell Edwards)
UCLA	Aloha 12-25-87	Florida 20-16 (Galen Hall)
UCLA	Cotton 1-2-89	Arkansas 17-3 (Ken Hatfield)
UCLA	John Hancock 12-31-91	Illinois 6-3 (Lou Tepper)
UCLA	Rose 1-1-94	Wisconsin 16-21 (Barry Alvarez)
UCLA	Aloha 12-25-95	Kansas 30-51 (Glen Mason)
JIM DONNAN, 4-0-0 (North Carolina St. '68) Born 1-29-45		
Georgia	Outback 1-1-98	Wisconsin 33-6 (Barry Alvarez)
Georgia	Peach 12-31-98	Virginia 35-33 (George Welsh)
Georgia	Outback 1-1-00	Purdue 28-25 (ot) (Joe Tiller)
Georgia	Oahu Classic 12-24-00	Virginia 37-14 (George Welsh)
BILL DOOLEY, 3-7-0 (Mississippi St. '56) Born 5-19-34		
North Carolina........	Peach 12-30-70	Arizona St. 26-48 (Frank Kush)
North Carolina........	Gator 12-31-71	Georgia 3-7 (Vince Dooley)
North Carolina........	Sun 12-30-72	Texas Tech 32-28 (Jim Carlen)
North Carolina........	Sun 12-28-74	Mississippi St. 24-26 (Bob Tyler)
North Carolina........	Peach 12-31-76	Kentucky 0-21 (Fran Curci)
North Carolina........	Liberty 12-19-77	Nebraska 17-21 (Tom Osborne)
Virginia Tech...........	Peach 1-2-81	Miami (Fla.) 10-20 (Howard Schnellenberger)
Virginia Tech...........	Independence 12-15-84	Air Force 7-23 (Fisher DeBerry)
Virginia Tech...........	Peach 12-31-86	North Carolina St. 25-24 (Dick Sheridan)
Wake Forest	Independence 12-31-92	Oregon 39-35 (Rich Brooks)
VINCE DOOLEY, 8-10-2 (Auburn '54) Born 9-4-32		
Georgia	Sun 12-26-64	Texas Tech 7-0 (J.T. King)
Georgia	Cotton 12-31-66	Southern Methodist 24-9 (Hayden Fry)
Georgia	Liberty 12-16-67	North Carolina St. 7-14 (Earle Edwards)
Georgia	Sugar 1-1-69	Arkansas 2-16 (Frank Broyles)
Georgia	Sun 12-20-69	Nebraska 6-45 (Bob Devaney)
Georgia	Gator 12-31-71	North Carolina 7-3 (Bill Dooley)
Georgia	Peach 12-28-73	Maryland 17-16 (Jerry Claiborne)
Georgia	Tangerine 12-21-74	Miami (Ohio) 10-21 (Dick Crum)
Georgia	Cotton 1-1-76	Arkansas 10-31 (Frank Broyles)
Georgia	Sugar 1-1-77	Pittsburgh 3-27 (Johnny Majors)
Georgia	Bluebonnet 12-31-78	Stanford 22-25 (Bill Walsh)
Georgia	Sugar 1-1-81	Notre Dame 17-10 (Dan Devine)
Georgia	Sugar 1-1-82	Pittsburgh 20-24 (Jackie Sherrill)
Georgia	Sugar 1-1-83	Penn St. 23-27 (Joe Paterno)
Georgia	Cotton 1-2-84	Texas 10-9 (Fred Akers)
Georgia	Fla. Citrus 12-22-84	Florida St. 17-17 (Bobby Bowden)
Georgia	Sun 12-28-85	Arizona 13-13 (Larry Smith)
Georgia	Hall of Fame 12-23-86	Boston College 24-27 (Jack Bicknell)
Georgia	Liberty 12-29-87	Arkansas 20-17 (Ken Hatfield)
Georgia	Gator 1-1-89	Michigan St. 34-27 (George Perles)
CHARLES "GUS" DORAIS, 0-1-0 (Notre Dame '14) Born 7-21-1891		
Gonzaga.................	San Diego East-West Christmas Classic 12-25-22	West Virginia 13-21 (Clarence "Doc" Spears)
HAROLD "RED" DREW, 1-2-0 (Bates '16) Born 11-9-1894		
Alabama	Sugar 1-1-48	Texas 7-27 (Blair Cherry)
Alabama	Orange 1-1-53	Syracuse 61-6 (Ben Schwartzwalder)
Alabama	Cotton 1-1-54	Rice 6-28 (Jess Neely)
BILL DRIVER, 0-1-0 (Missouri '09) Born 11-7-1883		
TCU	Fort Worth Classic 1-1-21	Centre 7-63 (Charley Moran)
F.A. DRY, 0-1-0 (Oklahoma St. '53) Born 9-2-31		
Tulsa	Independence 12-13-76	McNeese St. 16-20 (Jack Doland)
MIKE DuBOSE, 0-2-0 (Alabama '74) Born 1-5-53		
Alabama	Music City 12-29-98	Virginia Tech 7-38 (Frank Beamer)
Alabama	Orange 1-1-00	Michigan 34-35 (ot) (Lloyd Carr)
ERNIE DUPLECHIN, 0-2-0 (Louisiana Col. '55) Born 7-19-32		
McNeese St.	Independence 12-15-79	Syracuse 7-31 (Frank Maloney)
McNeese St.	Independence 12-13-80	Southern Miss. 14-16 (Bobby Collins)
PAT DYE, 7-2-1 (Georgia '62) Born 11-6-39		
East Caro.	Independence 12-16-78	Louisiana Tech 35-13 (Maxie Lambright)
Auburn	Tangerine 12-18-82	Boston College 33-26 (Jack Bicknell)
Auburn	Sugar 1-2-84	Michigan 9-7 (Glenn "Bo" Schembechler)
Auburn	Liberty 12-27-84	Arkansas 21-15 (Ken Hatfield)
Auburn	Cotton 1-1-86	Texas A&M 16-36 (Jackie Sherrill)
Auburn	Fla. Citrus 1-1-87	Southern California 16-7 (Ted Tollner)
Auburn	Sugar 1-1-88	Syracuse 16-16 (Dick MacPherson)
Auburn	Sugar 1-2-89	Florida St. 7-13 (Bobby Bowden)
Auburn	Hall of Fame 1-1-90	Ohio St. 31-14 (John Cooper)
Auburn	Peach 12-29-90	Indiana 27-23 (Bill Mallory)

Coach/School	Bowl/Date	Opponent/Score (Coach)
SPIKE DYKES, 2-5-0 (Stephen F. Austin '59)		Born 4-15-38
Texas Tech	Independence 12-20-86	Mississippi 17-20 (Billy Brewer)
Texas Tech	All-American 12-28-89	Duke 49-21 (Steve Spurrier)
Texas Tech	John Hancock 12-24-93	Oklahoma 10-41 (Gary Gibbs)
Texas Tech	Cotton 1-2-95	Southern California 14-55 (John Robinson)
Texas Tech	Copper 12-27-95	Air Force 55-41 (Fisher DeBerry)
Texas Tech	Alamo 12-29-96	Iowa 0-27 (Hayden Fry)
Texas Tech	Independence 12-31-98	Mississippi 18-35 (David Cutcliffe)
LLOYD EATON, 1-1-0 (Black Hills St. '40)		Born 3-23-18
Wyoming	Sun 12-24-66	Florida St. 28-20 (Bill Peterson)
Wyoming	Sun 12-16-67	LSU 13-20 (Charlie McClendon)
BILL EDWARDS, 1-0-0 (Wittenberg '31)		Born 6-21-05
Case Reserve	Sun 1-1-41	Arizona St. 26-13 (Millard "Dixie" Howell)
EARLE EDWARDS, 1-1-0 (Penn St. '31)		Born 11-10-08
North Carolina St.	Liberty 12-21-63	Mississippi St. 12-16 (Paul Davis)
North Carolina St.	Liberty 12-16-67	Georgia 14-7 (Vince Dooley)
LaVELL EDWARDS, 7-14-1 (Utah St. '52)		Born 10-11-30
Brigham Young	Fiesta 12-28-74	Oklahoma St. 6-16 (Jim Stanley)
Brigham Young	Tangerine 12-18-76	Oklahoma St. 21-49 (Jim Stanley)
Brigham Young	Holiday 12-22-78	Navy 16-23 (George Welsh)
Brigham Young	Holiday 12-21-79	Indiana 37-38 (Lee Corso)
Brigham Young	Holiday 12-19-80	Southern Methodist 46-45 (Ron Meyer)
Brigham Young	Holiday 12-18-81	Washington St. 38-36 (Jim Walden)
Brigham Young	Holiday 12-17-82	Ohio St. 17-47 (Earle Bruce)
Brigham Young	Holiday 12-23-83	Missouri 21-17 (Warren Powers)
Brigham Young	Holiday 12-21-84	Michigan 24-17 (Glenn "Bo" Schembechler)
Brigham Young	Fla. Citrus 12-28-85	Ohio St. 7-10 (Earle Bruce)
Brigham Young	Freedom 12-30-86	UCLA 10-31 (Terry Donahue)
Brigham Young	All-American 12-22-87	Virginia 16-22 (George Welsh)
Brigham Young	Freedom 12-29-88	Colorado 20-17 (Bill McCartney)
Brigham Young	Holiday 12-29-89	Penn St. 39-50 (Joe Paterno)
Brigham Young	Holiday 12-29-90	Texas A&M 14-65 (R.C. Slocum)
Brigham Young	Holiday 12-30-91	Iowa 13-13 (Hayden Fry)
Brigham Young	Aloha 12-25-92	Kansas 20-23 (Glen Mason)
Brigham Young	Holiday 12-30-93	Ohio St. 21-28 (John Cooper)
Brigham Young	Copper 12-29-94	Oklahoma 31-6 (Gary Gibbs)
Brigham Young	Cotton 1-1-97	Kansas St. 19-15 (Bill Snyder)
Brigham Young	Liberty 12-31-98	Tulane 27-14 (Chris Scelfo)
Brigham Young	Motor City 12-27-99	Marshall 3-21 (Bob Pruett)
RAY ELIOT, 2-0-0 (Illinois '32)		Born 6-13-05
Illinois	Rose 1-1-47	UCLA 45-14 (Bert LaBrucherie)
Illinois	Rose 1-1-52	Stanford 40-7 (Chuck Taylor)
BENNIE ELLENDER, 0-1-0 (Tulane '48)		Born 3-2-25
Tulane	Bluebonnet 12-29-73	Houston 7-47 (Bill Yeoman)
CHALMERS "BUMP" ELLIOTT, 1-0-0 (Michigan '48)		Born 1-30-25
Michigan	Rose 1-1-65	Oregon St. 34-7 (Tommy Prothro)
PETE ELLIOTT, 1-1-0 (Michigan '49)		Born 9-29-26
California	Rose 1-1-59	Iowa 12-38 (Forest Evashevski)
Illinois	Rose 1-1-64	Washington 17-7 (Jim Owens)
JACK ELWAY, 0-2-0 (Washington St. '53)		Born 5-30-31
San Jose St.	California 12-19-81	Toledo 25-27 (Chuck Stobart)
Stanford	Gator 12-27-86	Clemson 21-27 (Danny Ford)
CHARLES "RIP" ENGLE, 3-1-0 (McDaniel '30)		Born 3-26-06
Penn St.	Liberty 12-19-53	Alabama 7-0 (Paul "Bear" Bryant)
Penn St.	Liberty 12-17-60	Oregon 41-12 (Len Casanova)
Penn St.	Gator 12-30-61	Georgia Tech 30-15 (Bobby Dodd)
Penn St.	Gator 12-29-62	Florida 7-17 (Ray Graves)
EDDIE ERDELATZ, 2-0-0 (St. Mary's [Cal.] '36)		Born 4-21-13
Navy	Sugar 1-1-55	Mississippi 21-0 (John Vaught)
Navy	Cotton 1-1-58	Rice 20-7 (Jess Neely)
DENNIS ERICKSON, 5-5-0 (Montana St. '70)		Born 3-24-47
Washington St.	Aloha 12-25-88	Houston 24-22 (Jack Pardee)
Miami (Fla.)	Sugar 1-1-90	Alabama 33-25 (Bill Curry)
Miami (Fla.)	Cotton 1-1-91	Texas 46-3 (David McWilliams)
Miami (Fla.)	Orange 1-1-92	Nebraska 22-0 (Tom Osborne)
Miami (Fla.)	Sugar 1-1-93	Alabama 13-34 (Gene Stallings)
Miami (Fla.)	Fiesta 1-1-94	Arizona 0-24 (Dick Tomey)
Miami (Fla.)	Orange 1-1-95	Nebraska 17-24 (Tom Osborne)
Oregon St.	Oahu Classic 12-25-99	Hawaii 17-23 (June Jones)
Oregon St.	Fiesta 1-1-01	Notre Dame 41-9 (Bob Davie)
Oregon St.	Insight 12-26-02	Pittsburgh 13-38 (Walt Harris)
FOREST EVASHEVSKI, 2-0-0 (Michigan '41)		Born 2-19-18
Iowa	Rose 1-1-57	Oregon St. 35-19 (Tommy Prothro)
Iowa	Rose 1-1-59	California 38-12 (Pete Elliott)
CHUCK FAIRBANKS, 3-1-1 (Michigan St. '55)		Born 6-10-33
Oklahoma	Orange 1-1-68	Tennessee 26-24 (Doug Dickey)
Oklahoma	Bluebonnet 12-31-68	Southern Methodist 27-28 (Hayden Fry)
Oklahoma	Bluebonnet 12-31-70	Alabama 24-24 (Paul "Bear" Bryant)
Oklahoma	Sugar 1-1-72	Auburn 40-22 (Ralph "Shug" Jordan)
Oklahoma	Sugar 12-31-72	Penn St. 14-0 (Joe Paterno)

Coach/School	Bowl/Date	Opponent/Score (Coach)
DON FAMBROUGH, 0-2-0 (Kansas '48)		Born 10-19-22
Kansas	Liberty 12-17-73	North Carolina St. 18-31 (Lou Holtz)
Kansas	Hall of Fame 12-31-81	Mississippi St. 0-10 (Emory Bellard)
DON FAUROT, 0-4-0 (Missouri '25)		Born 6-23-02
Missouri	Orange 1-1-40	Georgia Tech 7-21 (Bill Alexander)
Missouri	Sugar 1-1-42	Fordham 0-2 (Jim Crowley)
Missouri	Gator 1-1-49	Clemson 23-24 (Frank Howard)
Missouri	Gator 1-2-50	Maryland 7-21 (Jim Tatum)
GERRY FAUST, 1-1-0 (Dayton '58)		Born 5-21-35
Notre Dame	Liberty 12-29-83	Boston College 19-18 (Jack Bicknell)
Notre Dame	Aloha 12-29-84	Southern Methodist 20-27 (Bobby Collins)
FOGE FAZIO, 0-2-0 (Pittsburgh '60)		Born 2-28-39
Pittsburgh	Cotton 1-1-83	Southern Methodist 3-7 (Bobby Collins)
Pittsburgh	Fiesta 1-2-84	Ohio St. 23-28 (Earle Bruce)
BEATTIE FEATHERS, 0-1-0 (Tennessee '34)		Born 6-1-12
North Carolina St.	Gator 1-1-47	Oklahoma 13-34 (Jim Tatum)
KIRK FERENTZ, 1-1-0 (Connecticut '78)		Born 8-1-55
Iowa	Alamo 12-29-01	Texas Tech 19-16 (Mike Leach)
Iowa	Orange 1-2-03	Southern California 17-38 (Pete Carroll)
WES FESLER, 1-0-0 (Ohio St. '32)		Born 6-29-08
Ohio St.	Rose 1-2-50	California 17-14 (Lynn "Pappy" Waldorf)
CHARLIE FICKERT, 0-1-0 (Stanford '98)		Born 2-23-1873
Stanford	Rose 1-1-02	Michigan 0-49 (Fielding "Hurry Up" Yost)
ROBERT FISHER, 1-0-0 (Harvard '12)		Born 12-3-1888
Harvard	Rose 1-1-20	Oregon 7-6 (Charles "Shy" Huntington)
DICK FLYNN, 0-1-0 (Michigan St. '65)		Born 7-17-43
Central Mich.	Las Vegas 12-15-94	UNLV 24-52 (Jeff Horton)
HANK FOLDBERG, 0-1-0 (Army '48)		Born 3-12-23
Wichita St.	Sun 12-30-61	Villanova 9-17 (Alex Bell)
BOB FOLWELL, 0-1-1 (Pennsylvania '08)		Born 1885
Pennsylvania	Rose 1-1-17	Oregon 0-14 (Hugo Bezdek)
Navy	Rose 1-1-24	Washington 14-14 (Enoch Bagshaw)
DANNY FORD, 6-3-0 (Alabama '70)		Born 4-2-48
Clemson	Gator 12-29-78	Ohio St. 17-15 (Woody Hayes)
Clemson	Peach 12-31-79	Baylor 18-24 (Grant Teaff)
Clemson	Orange 1-1-82	Nebraska 22-15 (Tom Osborne)
Clemson	Independence 12-21-85	Minnesota 13-20 (John Gutekunst)
Clemson	Gator 12-27-86	Stanford 27-21 (Jack Elway)
Clemson	Fla. Citrus 1-1-88	Penn St. 35-10 (Joe Paterno)
Clemson	Fla. Citrus 1-2-89	Oklahoma 23-6 (Barry Switzer)
Clemson	Gator 12-30-89	West Virginia 27-7 (Don Nehlen)
Arkansas	Carquest 12-30-95	North Carolina 10-20 (Mack Brown)
DENNIS FRANCHIONE, 2-2-0 (Pittsburg St. '73)		Born 3-28-51
New Mexico	Insight.com 12-27-97	Arizona 14-20 (Dick Tomey)
TCU	Sun 12-31-98	Southern California 28-19 (Paul Hackett)
TCU	Mobile Alabama 12-22-99	East Caro. 28-14 (Steve Logan)
Alabama	Independence 12-27-01	Iowa St. 14-13 (Dan McCarney)
RALPH FRIEDGEN, 1-1-0 (Maryland '69)		Born 4-4-47
Maryland	Orange 1-2-02	Florida 23-56 (Steve Spurrier)
Maryland	Peach 12-31-02	Tennessee 30-3 (Phillip Fulmer)
HENRY FRNKA, 2-3-0 (Austin '26)		Born 3-16-03
Tulsa	Sun 1-1-42	Texas Tech 6-0 (Dell Morgan)
Tulsa	Sugar 1-1-43	Tennessee 7-14 (John Barnhill)
Tulsa	Sugar 1-1-44	Georgia Tech 18-20 (Bill Alexander)
Tulsa	Orange 1-1-45	Georgia Tech 26-12 (Bill Alexander)
Tulsa	Oil 1-1-46	Georgia 6-20 (Wally Butts)
HAYDEN FRY, 7-9-1 (Baylor '51)		Born 2-28-29
Southern Methodist	Sun 12-31-63	Oregon 13-21 (Len Casanova)
Southern Methodist	Cotton 12-31-66	Georgia 9-24 (Vince Dooley)
Southern Methodist	Bluebonnet 12-31-68	Oklahoma 28-27 (Chuck Fairbanks)
Iowa	Rose 1-1-82	Washington 0-28 (Don James)
Iowa	Peach 12-31-82	Tennessee 28-22 (Johnny Majors)
Iowa	Gator 12-30-83	Florida 6-14 (Charley Pell)
Iowa	Freedom 12-26-84	Texas 55-17 (Fred Akers)
Iowa	Rose 1-1-86	UCLA 28-45 (Terry Donahue)
Iowa	Holiday 12-30-86	San Diego St. 39-38 (Denny Stolz)
Iowa	Holiday 12-30-87	Wyoming 20-19 (Paul Roach)
Iowa	Peach 12-31-88	North Carolina St. 23-29 (Dick Sheridan)
Iowa	Rose 1-1-91	Washington 34-46 (Don James)
Iowa	Holiday 12-30-91	Brigham Young 13-13 (LaVell Edwards)
Iowa	Alamo 12-31-93	California 3-37 (Keith Gilbertson)
Iowa	Sun 12-29-95	Washington 38-18 (Jim Lambright)
Iowa	Alamo 12-29-96	Texas Tech 27-0 (Spike Dykes)
Iowa	Sun 12-31-97	Arizona St. 7-17 (Bruce Snyder)
BILL FULCHER, 1-0-0 (Georgia Tech '57)		Born 2-9-34
Georgia Tech	Liberty 12-18-72	Iowa St. 31-30 (Johnny Majors)
PHILLIP FULMER, 6-5-0 (Tennessee '72)		Born 9-1-50
Tennessee	Hall of Fame 1-1-93	Boston College 38-23 (Tom Coughlin)
Tennessee	Fla. Citrus 1-1-94	Penn St. 13-31 (Joe Paterno)

Coach/School	Bowl/Date	Opponent/Score (Coach)
Tennessee	Gator 12-30-94	Virginia Tech 45-23 (Frank Beamer)
Tennessee	Fla. Citrus 1-1-96	Ohio St. 20-14 (John Cooper)
Tennessee	Fla. Citrus 1-1-97	Northwestern 48-28 (Gary Barnett)
Tennessee	Orange 1-2-98	Nebraska 17-42 (Tom Osborne)
Tennessee	Fiesta 1-4-99	Florida St. 23-16 (Bobby Bowden)
Tennessee	Fiesta 1-2-00	Nebraska 21-31 (Frank Solich)
Tennessee	Cotton 1-1-01	Kansas St. 21-35 (Bill Snyder)
Tennessee	Fla. Citrus 1-1-02	Michigan 45-17 (Lloyd Carr)
Tennessee	Peach 12-31-02	Maryland 3-30 (Ralph Friedgen)

WARREN GAER, 0-1-0 (Drake '35) Born 2-7-12
| Drake | Sun 1-1-58 | Louisville 20-34 (Frank Camp) |

CHAN GAILEY, 0-1-0 (Florida '74) Born 1-5-52
| Georgia Tech | Silicon Valley 12-31-02 | Fresno St. 21-30 (Pat Hill) |

JOE GAVIN, 0-1-0 (Notre Dame '31) Born 3-20-08
| Dayton | Salad 1-1-52 | Houston 21-26 (Clyde Lee) |

GARY GIBBS, 2-1-0 (Oklahoma '75) Born 8-13-52
Oklahoma	Gator 12-29-91	Virginia 48-14 (George Welsh)
Oklahoma	John Hancock 12-24-93	Texas Tech 41-10 (Spike Dykes)
Oklahoma	Copper 12-29-94	Brigham Young 6-31 (LaVell Edwards)

VINCE GIBSON, 0-2-0 (Florida St. '55) Born 3-27-33
| Louisville | Independence 12-17-77 | Louisiana Tech 14-24 (Maxie Lambright) |
| Tulane | Hall of Fame 12-27-80 | Arkansas 15-34 (Lou Holtz) |

CLAUDE GILBERT, 1-1-0 (San Jose St. '59) Born 7-10-32
| San Jose St. | California 12-13-86 | Miami (Ohio) 37-7 (Tim Rose) |
| San Jose St. | California 12-12-87 | Eastern Mich. 27-30 (Jim Harkema) |

KEITH GILBERTSON, 1-0-0 (Central Wash. '71) Born 5-15-48
| California | Alamo 12-31-93 | Iowa 37-3 (Hayden Fry) |

SID GILLMAN, 1-1-0 (Ohio St. '34) Born 10-26-11
| Miami (Ohio) | Sun 1-1-48 | Texas Tech 13-12 (Dell Morgan) |
| Cincinnati | Sun 1-1-51 | West Tex. A&M 13-14 (Frank Kimbrough) |

BILL GLASSFORD, 0-1-0 (Pittsburgh '37) Born 3-8-14
| Nebraska | Orange 1-1-55 | Duke 7-34 (Bill Murray) |

MARSHALL "LITTLE SLEEPY" GLENN, 1-0-0 (West Virginia '31) Born 4-22-08
| West Virginia | Sun 1-1-38 | Texas Tech 7-6 (Pete Cawthon) |

RAY GOFF, 2-2-0 (Georgia '78) Born 7-10-55
Georgia	Peach 12-30-89	Syracuse 18-19 (Dick MacPherson)
Georgia	Independence 12-29-91	Arkansas 24-15 (Jack Crowe)
Georgia	Fla. Citrus 1-1-93	Ohio St. 21-14 (John Cooper)
Georgia	Peach 12-30-95	Virginia 27-34 (George Welsh)

FRED GOLDSMITH, 0-1-0 (Florida '67) Born 3-3-44
| Duke | Hall of Fame 1-2-95 | Wisconsin 20-34 (Barry Alvarez) |

MIKE GOTTFRIED, 0-1-0 (Morehead St. '66) Born 12-17-44
| Pittsburgh | Bluebonnet 12-31-87 | Texas 27-32 (David McWilliams) |

RALPH GRAHAM, 0-1-0 (Kansas St. '34) Born 8-16-10
| Wichita St. | Raisin 1-1-48 | Pacific (Cal.) 14-26 (Larry Siemering) |

SONNY GRANDELIUS, 0-1-0 (Michigan St. '51) Born 4-16-29
| Colorado | Orange 1-1-62 | LSU 7-25 (Paul Dietzel) |

RAY GRAVES, 4-1-0 (Tennessee '43) Born 12-31-18
Florida	Gator 12-31-60	Baylor 13-12 (John Bridgers)
Florida	Gator 12-29-62	Penn St. 17-7 (Charles "Rip" Engle)
Florida	Sugar 1-1-66	Missouri 18-20 (Dan Devine)
Florida	Orange 1-2-67	Georgia Tech 27-12 (Bobby Dodd)
Florida	Gator 12-27-69	Tennessee 14-13 (Doug Dickey)

DENNIS GREEN, 0-1-0 (Iowa '71) Born 2-17-49
| Stanford | Aloha 12-25-91 | Georgia Tech 17-18 (Bobby Ross) |

VEE GREEN, 1-0-0 (Illinois '24) Born 10-9-1900
| Drake | Raisin 1-1-46 | Fresno St. 13-12 (Alvin "Pix" Pierson) |

JIM GROBE, 1-0-0 (Virginia '75) Born 2-17-52
| Wake Forest | Seattle 12-30-02 | Oregon 38-17 (Mike Bellotti) |

AL GROH, 1-0-0 (Virginia '67) Born 7-13-44
| Virginia | Continental Tire 12-28-02 | West Virginia 48-22 (Rich Rodriguez) |

ART GUEPE, 1-0-0 (Marquette '37) Born 1-28-15
| Vanderbilt | Gator 12-31-55 | Auburn 25-13 (Ralph "Shug" Jordan) |

ANDY GUSTAFSON, 1-3-0 (Pittsburgh '26) Born 4-3-03
Miami (Fla.)	Orange 1-1-51	Clemson 14-15 (Frank Howard)
Miami (Fla.)	Gator 1-1-52	Clemson 14-0 (Frank Howard)
Miami (Fla.)	Liberty 12-16-61	Syracuse 14-15 (Ben Schwartzwalder)
Miami (Fla.)	Gotham 12-15-62	Nebraska 34-36 (Bob Devaney)

JOHN GUTEKUNST, 1-1-0 (Duke '66) Born 4-13-44
| Minnesota | Independence 12-21-85 | Clemson 20-13 (Danny Ford) |
| Minnesota | Liberty 12-29-86 | Tennessee 14-21 (Johnny Majors) |

PAUL HACKETT, 1-1-0 (UC Davis '69) Born 6-5-47
| Pittsburgh | John Hancock 12-30-89 | Texas A&M 31-28 (R.C. Slocum) |
| Southern California | Sun 12-31-98 | TCU 19-28 (Dennis Franchione) |

JACK HAGERTY, 0-1-0 (Georgetown '26) Born 7-3-03
| Georgetown | Orange 1-1-41 | Mississippi St. 7-14 (Alvin McKeen) |

GALEN HALL, 1-1-0 (Penn St. '62) Born 8-14-40
| Florida | Aloha 12-25-87 | UCLA 16-20 (Terry Donahue) |
| Florida | All-American 12-29-88 | Illinois 14-10 (John Mackovic) |

CURLEY HALLMAN, 1-0-0 (Texas A&M '70) Born 9-3-47
| Southern Miss. | Independence 12-23-88 | UTEP 38-18 (Bob Stull) |

WAYNE HARDIN, 1-2-0 (Pacific [Cal.] '50) Born 3-23-27
Navy	Orange 1-2-61	Missouri 14-21 (Dan Devine)
Navy	Cotton 1-1-64	Texas 6-28 (Darrell Royal)
Temple	Garden State 12-15-79	California 28-17 (Roger Theder)

JACK HARDING, 1-0-0 (Pittsburgh '26) Born 1-5-1898
| Miami (Fla.) | Orange 1-1-48 | Holy Cross 13-6 (John "Ox" Da Grosa) |

JIM HARKEMA, 1-0-0 (Kalamazoo '64) Born 6-25-42
| Eastern Mich. | California 12-12-87 | San Jose St. 30-27 (Claude Gilbert) |

WALT HARRIS, 2-2-0 (Pacific [Cal.] '68) Born 11-9-46
Pittsburgh	Liberty 12-31-97	Southern Miss. 7-41 (Jeff Bower)
Pittsburgh	Insight.com 12-28-00	Iowa St. 29-37 (Dan McCarney)
Pittsburgh	Tangerine 12-20-01	North Carolina St. 34-19 (Chuck Amato)
Pittsburgh	Insight 12-26-02	Oregon St. 38-13 (Dennis Erickson)

KEN HATFIELD, 4-6-0 (Arkansas '65) Born 6-8-43
Air Force	Hall of Fame 12-31-82	Vanderbilt 36-28 (George MacIntyre)
Air Force	Independence 12-10-83	Mississippi 9-3 (Billy Brewer)
Arkansas	Liberty 12-27-84	Auburn 15-21 (Pat Dye)
Arkansas	Holiday 12-22-85	Arizona St. 18-17 (John Cooper)
Arkansas	Orange 1-1-87	Oklahoma 8-42 (Barry Switzer)
Arkansas	Liberty 12-29-87	Georgia 17-20 (Vince Dooley)
Arkansas	Cotton 1-2-89	UCLA 3-17 (Terry Donahue)
Arkansas	Cotton 1-1-90	Tennessee 27-31 (Johnny Majors)
Clemson	Hall of Fame 1-1-91	Illinois 30-0 (John Mackovic)
Clemson	Fla. Citrus 1-1-92	California 13-37 (Bruce Snyder)

DAN HAWKINS, 1-0-0 (UC Davis '84) Born 11-10-60
| Boise St. | Humanitarian 12-31-02 | Iowa St. 34-16 (Dan McCarney) |

WOODY HAYES, 6-6-0 (Denison '35) Born 2-14-13
Miami (Ohio)	Salad 1-1-51	Arizona St. 34-21 (Ed Doherty)
Ohio St.	Rose 1-1-55	Southern California 20-7 (Jess Hill)
Ohio St.	Rose 1-1-58	Oregon 10-7 (Len Casanova)
Ohio St.	Rose 1-1-69	Southern California 27-16 (John McKay)
Ohio St.	Rose 1-1-71	Stanford 17-27 (John Ralston)
Ohio St.	Rose 1-1-73	Southern California 17-42 (John McKay)
Ohio St.	Rose 1-1-74	Southern California 42-21 (John McKay)
Ohio St.	Rose 1-1-75	Southern California 17-18 (John McKay)
Ohio St.	Rose 1-1-76	UCLA 10-23 (Dick Vermeil)
Ohio St.	Orange 1-1-77	Colorado 27-10 (Bill Mallory)
Ohio St.	Sugar 1-2-78	Alabama 6-35 (Paul "Bear" Bryant)
Ohio St.	Gator 12-29-78	Clemson 15-17 (Danny Ford)

KIM HELTON, 0-1-0 (Florida '70) Born 7-28-48
| Houston | Liberty 12-27-96 | Syracuse 17-30 (Paul Pasqualoni) |

ELMER "GUS" HENDERSON, 2-0-0 (Oberlin '12) Born 3-10-1889
| Southern California | Rose 1-1-23 | Penn St. 14-3 (Hugo Bezdek) |
| Southern California | L.A. Christmas Festival 12-25-24 | Missouri 20-7 (Gwinn Henry) |

DAN HENNING, 1-0-0 (William & Mary '64) Born 7-21-42
| Boston College | Aloha 12-25-94 | Kansas St. 12-7 (Bill Snyder) |

GWINN HENRY, 0-1-0 (Howard Payne '17) Born 8-5-1887
| Missouri | L.A. Christmas Festival 12-25-24 | Southern California 7-20 (Elmer "Gus" Henderson) |

BILL HESS, 0-2-0 (Ohio '47) Born 2-5-23
| Ohio | Sun 12-31-62 | West Tex. A&M 14-15 (Joe Kerbel) |
| Ohio | Tangerine 12-27-68 | Richmond 42-49 (Frank Jones) |

JIM HICKEY, 1-0-0 (William & Mary '42) Born 1-22-20
| North Carolina | Gator 12-28-63 | Air Force 35-0 (Ben Martin) |

BOB HIGGINS, 1-0-1 (Penn St. '20) Born 12-24-1893
| West Va. Wesleyan | Dixie Classic 1-1-25 | Southern Methodist 9-7 (Ray Morrison) |
| Penn St. | Cotton 1-1-48 | Southern Methodist 13-13 (Matty Bell) |

JESS HILL, 1-1-0 (Southern California '30) Born 1-20-07
| Southern California | Rose 1-1-53 | Wisconsin 7-0 (Ivy Williamson) |
| Southern California | Rose 1-1-55 | Ohio St. 7-20 (Woody Hayes) |

PAT HILL, 1-3-0 (UC Riverside '73) Born 12-17-51
Fresno St.	Las Vegas 12-18-99	Utah 16-17 (Ron McBride)
Fresno St.	Silicon Valley 12-31-00	Air Force 34-37 (Fisher DeBerry)
Fresno St.	Silicon Valley 12-31-01	Michigan St. 35-44 (Bobby Williams)
Fresno St.	Silicon Valley 12-31-02	Georgia Tech 30-21 (Chan Gailey)

JERRY HINES, 0-0-1 (New Mexico St. '26) Born 10-11-03
| New Mexico St. | Sun 1-1-36 | Hardin-Simmons 14-14 (Frank Kimbrough) |

BERNARD A. HOBAN, 0-1-0 (Dartmouth '12) Born 4-21-1890
| U. of Mexico | Sun 1-1-45 | Southwestern (Tex.) 0-35 (Randolph R.M. Medley) |

ORIN "BABE" HOLLINGBERY, 0-1-0 (No college) Born 7-15-1893
| Washington St. | Rose 1-1-31 | Alabama 0-24 (Wallace Wade) |

Coach/School	Bowl/Date	Opponent/Score (Coach)
LOU HOLTZ, 12-8-2	(Kent St. '59)	Born 1-6-37
William & Mary	Tangerine 12-28-70	Toledo 12-40 (Frank Lauterbur)
North Carolina St.	Peach 12-29-72	West Virginia 49-13 (Bobby Bowden)
North Carolina St.	Liberty 12-17-73	Kansas 31-18 (Don Fambrough)
North Carolina St.	Bluebonnet 12-23-74	Houston 31-31 (Bill Yeoman)
North Carolina St.	Peach 12-31-75	West Virginia 10-13 (Bobby Bowden)
Arkansas	Orange 1-2-78	Oklahoma 31-6 (Barry Switzer)
Arkansas	Fiesta 12-25-78	UCLA 10-10 (Terry Donahue)
Arkansas	Sugar 1-1-80	Alabama 9-24 (Paul "Bear" Bryant)
Arkansas	Hall of Fame 12-27-80	Tulane 34-15 (Vince Gibson)
Arkansas	Gator 12-28-81	North Carolina 27-31 (Dick Crum)
Arkansas	Bluebonnet 12-31-82	Florida 28-24 (Charley Pell)
Notre Dame	Cotton 1-1-88	Texas A&M 10-35 (Jackie Sherrill)
Notre Dame	Fiesta 1-2-89	West Virginia 34-21 (Don Nehlen)
Notre Dame	Orange 1-1-90	Colorado 21-6 (Bill McCartney)
Notre Dame	Orange 1-1-91	Colorado 9-10 (Bill McCartney)
Notre Dame	Sugar 1-1-92	Florida 39-28 (Steve Spurrier)
Notre Dame	Cotton 1-1-93	Texas A&M 28-3 (R.C. Slocum)
Notre Dame	Cotton 1-1-94	Texas A&M 24-21 (R.C. Slocum)
Notre Dame	Fiesta 1-2-95	Colorado 24-41 (Bill McCartney)
Notre Dame	Orange 1-1-96	Florida St. 26-31 (Bobby Bowden)
South Carolina	Outback 1-1-01	Ohio St. 24-7 (John Cooper)
South Carolina	Outback 1-1-02	Ohio St. 31-28 (Jim Tressel)
EDWIN "BABE" HORRELL, 0-1-0	(California '26)	Born 9-29-02
UCLA	Rose 1-1-43	Georgia 0-9 (Wally Butts)
JEFF HORTON, 1-0-0	(Nevada '81)	Born 7-13-57
UNLV	Las Vegas 12-15-94	Central Mich. 52-24 (Dick Flynn)
FRANK HOWARD, 3-3-0	(Alabama '31)	Born 3-25-09
Clemson	Gator 1-1-49	Missouri 24-23 (Don Faurot)
Clemson	Orange 1-1-51	Miami (Fla.) 15-14 (Andy Gustafson)
Clemson	Gator 1-1-52	Miami (Fla.) 0-14 (Andy Gustafson)
Clemson	Orange 1-1-57	Colorado 21-27 (Dallas Ward)
Clemson	Sugar 1-1-59	LSU 0-7 (Paul Dietzel)
Clemson	Bluebonnet 12-19-59	TCU 23-7 (Abe Martin)
MILLARD "DIXIE" HOWELL, 0-1-1	(Alabama '35)	Born 11-24-12
Arizona St.	Sun 1-1-40	Catholic 0-0 (Arthur "Dutch" Bergman)
Arizona St.	Sun 1-1-41	Case Reserve 13-26 (Bill Edwards)
BILL HUBBARD, 2-0-0	(Stanford '30)	Born 2-5-07
San Jose St.	Raisin 1-1-47	Utah St. 20-0 (E.L. "Dick" Romney)
San Jose St.	Raisin 12-31-49	Texas Tech 20-13 (Dell Morgan)
CLYDE "CAC" HUBBARD, 0-2-0	(Oregon St. '21)	Born 9-13-1897
Denver	Sun 1-1-46	New Mexico 24-34 (Willis Barnes)
Denver	Alamo 1-4-47	Hardin-Simmons 0-20 (Warren Woodson)
CHARLES "SHY" HUNTINGTON, 0-1-0	(Oregon)	Born 7-7-1891
Oregon	Rose 1-1-20	Harvard 6-7 (Robert Fisher)
HARVEY HYDE, 1-0-0	(Redlands '62)	Born 7-13-39
UNLV	California 12-15-84	Toledo 30-13 (Dan Simrell)
DON JAMES, 10-5-0	(Miami [Fla.] '54)	Born 12-31-32
Kent St.	Tangerine 12-29-72	Tampa 18-21 (Earle Bruce)
Washington	Rose 1-2-78	Michigan 27-20 (Glenn "Bo" Schembechler)
Washington	Sun 12-22-79	Texas 14-7 (Fred Akers)
Washington	Rose 1-1-81	Michigan 6-23 (Glenn "Bo" Schembechler)
Washington	Rose 1-1-82	Iowa 28-0 (Hayden Fry)
Washington	Aloha 12-25-82	Maryland 21-20 (Bobby Ross)
Washington	Aloha 12-26-83	Penn St. 10-13 (Joe Paterno)
Washington	Orange 1-1-85	Oklahoma 28-17 (Barry Switzer)
Washington	Freedom 12-30-85	Colorado 20-17 (Bill McCartney)
Washington	Sun 12-25-86	Alabama 6-28 (Ray Perkins)
Washington	Independence 12-18-87	Tulane 24-12 (Mack Brown)
Washington	Freedom 12-29-89	Florida 34-7 (Gary Darnell)
Washington	Rose 1-1-91	Iowa 46-34 (Hayden Fry)
Washington	Rose 1-1-92	Michigan 34-14 (Gary Moeller)
Washington	Rose 1-1-93	Michigan 31-38 (Gary Moeller)
JIMMY JOHNSON, 3-4-0	(Arkansas '65)	Born 7-16-43
Oklahoma St.	Independence 12-12-81	Texas A&M 16-33 (Tom Wilson)
Oklahoma St.	Bluebonnet 12-31-83	Baylor 24-14 (Grant Teaff)
Miami (Fla.)	Fiesta 1-1-85	UCLA 37-39 (Terry Donahue)
Miami (Fla.)	Sugar 1-1-86	Tennessee 7-35 (Johnny Majors)
Miami (Fla.)	Fiesta 1-2-87	Penn St. 10-14 (Joe Paterno)
Miami (Fla.)	Orange 1-1-88	Oklahoma 20-14 (Barry Switzer)
Miami (Fla.)	Orange 1-2-89	Nebraska 23-3 (Tom Osborne)
FRANK JONES, 1-1-0	(North Carolina '48)	Born 8-30-21
Richmond	Tangerine 12-27-68	Ohio 49-42 (Bill Hess)
Richmond	Tangerine 12-28-71	Toledo 3-28 (John Murphy)
GOMER JONES, 0-1-0	(Ohio St. '36)	Born 2-26-14
Oklahoma	Gator 1-2-65	Florida St. 19-36 (Bill Peterson)
HOWARD JONES, 5-0-0	(Yale '08)	Born 8-23-1885
Southern California	Rose 1-1-30	Pittsburgh 47-14 (Jock Sutherland)
Southern California	Rose 1-1-32	Tulane 21-12 (Bernie Bierman)
Southern California	Rose 1-2-33	Pittsburgh 35-0 (Jock Sutherland)

Coach/School	Bowl/Date	Opponent/Score (Coach)
Southern California	Rose 1-2-39	Duke 7-3 (Wallace Wade)
Southern California	Rose 1-1-40	Tennessee 14-0 (Bob Neyland)
JUNE JONES, 1-1-0	(Portland St. '77)	Born 2-14-53
Hawaii	Oahu Classic 12-25-99	Oregon St. 23-17 (Dennis Erickson)
Hawaii	Hawaii 12-25-02	Tulane 28-36 (Chris Scelfo)
LARRY JONES, 0-1-0	(LSU '54)	Born 12-18-33
Florida St.	Fiesta 12-27-71	Arizona St. 38-45 (Frank Kush)
LAWRENCE McC. "BIFF" JONES, 0-1-0	(Army '17)	Born 10-8-95
Nebraska	Rose 1-1-41	Stanford 13-21 (Clark Shaughnessy)
PAT JONES, 3-1-0	(Arkansas '69)	Born 11-4-47
Oklahoma St.	Gator 12-28-84	South Carolina 21-14 (Joe Morrison)
Oklahoma St.	Gator 12-30-85	Florida St. 23-34 (Bobby Bowden)
Oklahoma St.	Sun 12-25-87	West Virginia 35-33 (Don Nehlen)
Oklahoma St.	Holiday 12-30-88	Wyoming 62-14 (Paul Roach)
RALPH "SHUG" JORDAN, 5-7-0	(Auburn '32)	Born 9-25-10
Auburn	Gator 1-1-54	Texas Tech 13-35 (DeWitt Weaver)
Auburn	Gator 12-31-54	Baylor 33-13 (George Sauer)
Auburn	Gator 12-31-55	Vanderbilt 13-25 (Art Gueppe)
Auburn	Orange 1-1-64	Nebraska 7-13 (Bob Devaney)
Auburn	Liberty 12-18-65	Mississippi 7-13 (John Vaught)
Auburn	Sun 12-28-68	Arizona 34-10 (Darrell Mudra)
Auburn	Bluebonnet 12-31-69	Houston 7-36 (Bill Yeoman)
Auburn	Gator 1-2-71	Mississippi 35-28 (John Vaught)
Auburn	Sugar 1-1-72	Oklahoma 22-40 (Chuck Fairbanks)
Auburn	Gator 12-30-72	Colorado 24-3 (Eddie Crowder)
Auburn	Sun 12-29-73	Missouri 17-34 (Al Onofrio)
Auburn	Gator 12-30-74	Texas 27-3 (Darrell Royal)
ERNIE JORGE, 1-1-0	(St. Mary's [Cal.] '36)	Born 10-7-14
Pacific (Cal.)	Sun 1-1-52	Texas Tech 14-25 (DeWitt Weaver)
Pacific (Cal.)	Sun 1-1-53	Southern Miss. 26-7 (Thad "Pie" Vann)
AL KAWAL, 1-0-0	(Northwestern '35)	Born 7-4-12
Drake	Salad 1-1-49	Arizona 14-13 (Miles Casteel)
JOE KERBEL, 2-0-0	(Oklahoma '47)	Born 5-3-21
West Tex. A&M	Sun 12-21-62	Ohio 15-14 (Bill Hess)
West Tex. A&M	Pasadena 12-2-67	Cal St. Northridge 35-13 (Sam Winningham)
BILL KERN, 0-1-0	(Pittsburgh '28)	Born 9-2-06
Carnegie Mellon	Sugar 1-2-39	TCU 7-15 (Leo "Dutch" Meyer)
ED KEZIRIAN, 1-0-0	(UCLA '75)	Born 8-4-52
UCLA	Las Vegas 12-25-02	New Mexico 27-13 (Rocky Long)
FRANK KIMBROUGH, 2-0-1	(Hardin-Simmons '26)	Born 6-24-04
Hardin-Simmons	Sun 1-1-36	New Mexico St. 14-14 (Jerry Hines)
Hardin-Simmons	Sun 1-1-37	UTEP 34-6 (Max Saxon)
West Tex. A&M	Sun 1-1-51	Cincinnati 14-13 (Sid Gillman)
BILLY KINARD, 1-0-0	(Mississippi '56)	Born 12-16-33
Mississippi	Peach 12-30-71	Georgia Tech 41-18 (Bud Carson)
DEWEY KING, 0-1-0	(North Dakota '50)	Born 10-1-25
San Jose St.	Pasadena 12-18-71	Memphis 9-28 (Billy Murphy)
J.T. KING, 0-2-0	(Texas '38)	Born 10-22-12
Texas Tech	Sun 12-26-64	Georgia 0-7 (Vince Dooley)
Texas Tech	Gator 12-31-65	Georgia Tech 21-31 (Bobby Dodd)
JIMMY KITTS, 1-1-0	(Southern Methodist)	Born 6-14-1900
Rice	Cotton 1-1-38	Colorado 28-14 (Bernard "Bunnie" Oakes)
Virginia Tech	Sun 1-1-47	Cincinnati 6-18 (Ray Nolting)
ED KLUSKA, 1-0-0	(Xavier [Ohio] '40)	Born 5-21-18
Xavier (Ohio)	Salad 1-1-50	Arizona St. 33-21 (Ed Doherty)
DIRK KOETTER, 2-1-0	(Idaho St. '81)	Born 2-5-59
Boise St.	Humanitarian 12-30-99	Louisville 34-31 (John L. Smith)
Boise St.	Humanitarian 12-28-00	UTEP 38-23 (Gary Nord)
Arizona St.	Holiday 12-27-02	Kansas St. 27-34 (Bill Snyder)
JOE KRIVAK, 0-0-1	(Syracuse '57)	Born 3-20-35
Maryland	Independence 12-15-90	Louisiana Tech 34-34 (Joe Raymond Peace)
FRANK KUSH, 6-1-0	(Michigan St. '53)	Born 1-20-29
Arizona St.	Peach 12-30-70	North Carolina 48-26 (Bill Dooley)
Arizona St.	Fiesta 12-27-71	Florida St. 45-38 (Larry Jones)
Arizona St.	Fiesta 12-23-72	Missouri 49-35 (Al Onofrio)
Arizona St.	Fiesta 12-21-73	Pittsburgh 28-7 (Johnny Majors)
Arizona St.	Fiesta 12-25-77	Penn St. 30-42 (Joe Paterno)
Arizona St.	Garden State 12-16-78	Rutgers 34-18 (Frank Burns)
BERT LaBRUCHERIE, 0-1-0	(UCLA '29)	Born 1-19-05
UCLA	Rose 1-1-47	Illinois 14-45 (Ray Eliot)
JIM LAMBRIGHT, 1-3-0	(Washington '65)	Born 4-26-42
Washington	Sun 12-29-95	Iowa 18-38 (Hayden Fry)
Washington	Holiday 12-30-96	Colorado 21-33 (Rick Neuheisel)
Washington	Aloha 12-25-97	Michigan 51-23 (Nick Saban)
Washington	Oahu Classic 12-25-98	Air Force 25-45 (Fisher DeBerry)

Coach/School	Bowl/Date	Opponent/Score (Coach)
MAXIE LAMBRIGHT, 1-1-0 (Southern Miss. '49) Born 6-3-24		
Louisiana Tech	Independence 12-17-77	Louisville 24-14 (Vince Gibson)
Louisiana Tech	Independence 12-16-78	East Caro. 13-35 (Pat Dye)
FRANK LAUTERBUR, 2-0-0 (Mount Union '49) Born 8-8-25		
Toledo	Tangerine 12-26-69	Davidson 56-33 (Homer Smith)
Toledo	Tangerine 12-28-70	William & Mary 40-12 (Lou Holtz)
MIKE LEACH, 1-2-0 (Brigham Young '83) Born 3-9-61		
Texas Tech	Galleryfurniture.com 12-27-00	East Caro. 27-40 (Steve Logan)
Texas Tech	Alamo 12-29-01	Iowa 16-19 (Kirk Ferentz)
Texas Tech	Tangerine 12-23-02	Clemson 55-15 (Tommy Bowden)
FRANK LEAHY, 1-1-0 (Notre Dame '31) Born 8-27-08		
Boston College	Cotton 1-1-40	Clemson 3-6 (Jess Neely)
Boston College	Sugar 1-1-41	Tennessee 19-13 (Bob Neyland)
CLYDE LEE, 1-0-0 (Centenary [La.] '32) Born 2-11-08		
Houston	Salad 1-1-52	Dayton 26-21 (Joe Gavin)
ART LEWIS, 0-1-0 (Ohio '36) Born 2-18-11		
West Virginia	Sugar 1-1-54	Georgia Tech 19-42 (Bobby Dodd)
BILL LEWIS, 1-0-0 (East Stroudsburg '63) Born 8-5-41		
East Caro.	Peach 1-1-92	North Carolina St. 37-34 (Dick Sheridan)
LOU LITTLE, 1-0-0 (Pennsylvania '20) Born 12-6-1893		
Columbia	Rose 1-1-34	Stanford 7-0 (Claude "Tiny" Thornhill)
STEVE LOGAN, 2-3-0 (Tulsa '75) Born 2-3-53		
East Caro.	Liberty 12-31-94	Illinois 0-30 (Lou Tepper)
East Caro.	Liberty 12-30-95	Stanford 19-13 (Tyrone Willingham)
East Caro.	Mobile Alabama 12-22-99	TCU 14-28 (Dennis Franchione)
East Caro.	Galleryfurniture.com 12-27-00	Texas Tech 40-27 (Mike Leach)
East Caro.	GMAC 12-19-01	Marshall 61-64 (2 ot) (Bob Pruett)
ROCKY LONG, 0-1-0 (New Mexico '74) Born 1-27-50		
New Mexico	Las Vegas 12-25-02	UCLA 13-27 (Ed Kezirian)
JIM LOOKABAUGH, 2-1-0 (Oklahoma St. '25) Born 6-15-02		
Oklahoma St.	Cotton 1-1-45	TCU 34-0 (Leo "Dutch" Meyer)
Oklahoma St.	Sugar 1-1-46	St. Mary's (Cal.) 33-13 (Jimmy Phelan)
Oklahoma St.	Delta 1-1-49	William & Mary 0-20 (Rube McCray)
SONNY LUBICK, 3-4-0 (Western Mont. '60) Born 3-12-37		
Colorado St.	Holiday 12-30-94	Michigan 14-24 (Gary Moeller)
Colorado St.	Holiday 12-29-95	Kansas St. 21-54 (Bill Snyder)
Colorado St.	Holiday 12-29-97	Missouri 35-24 (Larry Smith)
Colorado St.	Liberty 12-31-99	Southern Miss. 17-23 (Jeff Bower)
Colorado St.	Liberty 12-29-00	Louisville 22-17 (John L. Smith)
Colorado St.	New Orleans 12-18-01	North Texas 45-20 (Darrell Dickey)
Colorado St.	Liberty 12-31-02	TCU 3-17 (Gary Patterson)
AL LUGINBILL, 0-1-0 (Cal Poly Pomona '67) Born 11-3-46		
San Diego St.	Freedom 12-30-91	Tulsa 17-28 (Dave Rader)
BILL LYNCH, 0-1-0 (Butler '77) Born 6-12-54		
Ball St.	Las Vegas 12-19-96	Nevada 15-18 (Jeff Tisdel)
GEORGE MacINTYRE, 0-1-0 (Miami [Fla.] '61) Born 4-30-39		
Vanderbilt	Hall of Fame 12-31-82	Air Force 28-36 (Ken Hatfield)
JOHN MACKOVIC, 2-5-0 (Wake Forest '65) Born 10-1-43		
Wake Forest	Tangerine 12-22-79	LSU 10-34 (Charlie McClendon)
Illinois	All-American 12-29-88	Florida 10-14 (Galen Hall)
Illinois	Fla. Citrus 1-1-90	Virginia 31-21 (George Welsh)
Illinois	Hall of Fame 1-1-91	Clemson 0-30 (Ken Hatfield)
Texas	Sun 12-30-94	North Carolina 35-31 (Mack Brown)
Texas	Sugar 12-31-95	Virginia Tech 10-28 (Frank Beamer)
Texas	Fiesta 1-1-97	Penn St. 15-38 (Joe Paterno)
DICK MacPHERSON, 3-1-1 (Springfield '58) Born 11-4-30		
Syracuse	Cherry 12-21-85	Maryland 18-35 (Bobby Ross)
Syracuse	Sugar 1-1-88	Auburn 16-16 (Pat Dye)
Syracuse	Hall of Fame 1-2-89	LSU 23-10 (Mike Archer)
Syracuse	Peach 12-30-89	Georgia 19-18 (Ray Goff)
Syracuse	Aloha 12-25-90	Arizona 28-0 (Dick Tomey)
EDWARD "SLIP" MADIGAN, 1-0-0 (Notre Dame '20) Born 11-18-1895		
St. Mary's (Cal.)	Cotton 1-2-39	Texas Tech 20-13 (Pete Cawthon)
JOHNNY MAJORS, 9-7-0 (Tennessee '57) Born 5-21-35		
Iowa St.	Sun 12-18-71	LSU 15-33 (Charlie McClendon)
Iowa St.	Liberty 12-18-72	Georgia Tech 30-31 (Bill Fulcher)
Pittsburgh	Fiesta 12-21-73	Arizona St. 7-28 (Frank Kush)
Pittsburgh	Sun 12-26-75	Kansas 33-19 (Bud Moore)
Pittsburgh	Sugar 1-1-77	Georgia 27-3 (Vince Dooley)
Tennessee	Bluebonnet 12-31-79	Purdue 22-27 (Jim Young)
Tennessee	Garden State 12-13-81	Wisconsin 28-21 (Dave McClain)
Tennessee	Peach 12-31-82	Iowa 22-28 (Hayden Fry)
Tennessee	Fla. Citrus 12-17-83	Maryland 30-23 (Bobby Ross)
Tennessee	Sun 12-24-84	Maryland 27-28 (Bobby Ross)
Tennessee	Sugar 1-1-86	Miami (Fla.) 35-7 (Jimmy Johnson)
Tennessee	Liberty 12-29-86	Minnesota 21-14 (John Gutekunst)
Tennessee	Peach 1-2-88	Indiana 27-22 (Bill Mallory)
Tennessee	Cotton 1-1-90	Arkansas 31-27 (Ken Hatfield)
Tennessee	Sugar 1-1-91	Virginia 23-22 (George Welsh)
Tennessee	Fiesta 1-1-92	Penn St. 17-42 (Joe Paterno)
BILL MALLORY, 4-6-0 (Miami [Ohio] '57) Born 5-30-35		
Miami (Ohio)	Tangerine 12-22-73	Florida 16-7 (Doug Dickey)
Colorado	Bluebonnet 12-27-75	Texas 21-38 (Darrell Royal)
Colorado	Orange 1-1-77	Ohio St. 10-27 (Woody Hayes)
Northern Ill.	California 12-17-83	Cal St. Fullerton 20-13 (Gene Murphy)
Indiana	All-American 12-31-86	Florida St. 13-27 (Bobby Bowden)
Indiana	Peach 1-2-88	Tennessee 22-27 (Johnny Majors)
Indiana	Liberty 12-28-88	South Carolina 34-10 (Joe Morrison)
Indiana	Peach 12-29-90	Auburn 23-27 (Pat Dye)
Indiana	Copper 12-31-91	Baylor 24-0 (Grant Teaff)
Indiana	Independence 12-31-93	Virginia Tech 20-45 (Frank Beamer)
FRANK MALONEY, 1-0-0 (Michigan '62) Born 9-26-40		
Syracuse	Independence 12-15-79	McNeese St. 31-7 (Ernie Duplechin)
BOB MARGARITA, 0-1-0 (Brown '44) Born 11-3-20		
Georgetown	Sun 1-2-50	UTEP 20-33 (Jack "Cactus Jack" Curtice)
STEVE MARIUCCI, 0-1-0 (Northern Mich. '77) Born 11-4-55		
California	Aloha 12-25-96	Navy 38-42 (Charlie Weatherbie)
ABE MARTIN, 1-3-1 (TCU '32) Born 10-8-08		
TCU	Cotton 1-2-56	Mississippi 13-14 (John Vaught)
TCU	Cotton 1-1-57	Syracuse 28-27 (Ben Schwartzwalder)
TCU	Cotton 1-1-59	Air Force 0-0 (Ben Martin)
TCU	Bluebonnet 12-19-59	Clemson 7-23 (Frank Howard)
TCU	Sun 12-31-65	UTEP 12-13 (Bobby Dobbs)
BEN MARTIN, 0-2-1 (Navy '46) Born 6-28-21		
Air Force	Cotton 1-1-59	TCU 0-0 (Abe Martin)
Air Force	Gator 12-28-63	North Carolina 0-35 (Jim Hickey)
Air Force	Sugar 1-1-71	Tennessee 13-34 (Bill Battle)
GLEN MASON, 3-1-0 (Ohio St. '72) Born 4-9-50		
Kansas	Aloha 12-25-92	Brigham Young 23-20 (LaVell Edwards)
Kansas	Aloha 12-25-95	UCLA 51-30 (Terry Donahue)
Minnesota	Sun 12-31-99	Oregon 20-24 (Mike Bellotti)
Minnesota	Music City 12-30-02	Arkansas 29-14 (Houston Nutt)
TONY MASON, 0-1-0 (Clarion '50) Born 3-2-30		
Arizona	Fiesta 12-25-79	Pittsburgh 10-16 (Jackie Sherrill)
RON McBRIDE, 3-3-0 (San Jose St. '63) Born 10-14-39		
Utah	Copper 12-29-92	Washington St. 28-31 (Mike Price)
Utah	Freedom 12-30-93	Southern California 21-28 (John Robinson)
Utah	Freedom 12-27-94	Arizona 16-13 (Dick Tomey)
Utah	Copper 12-27-96	Wisconsin 10-38 (Barry Alvarez)
Utah	Las Vegas 12-18-99	Fresno St. 17-16 (Pat Hill)
Utah	Las Vegas 12-25-01	Southern California 10-6 (Pete Carroll)
TOM McCANN, 0-1-0 (Illinois '24) Born 11-7-1898		
Miami (Fla.)	Orange 1-1-35	Bucknell 0-26 (Edward "Hook" Mylin)
DAN McCARNEY, 1-2-0 (Iowa '75) Born 7-28-53		
Iowa St.	Insight.com 12-28-00	Pittsburgh 37-29 (Walt Harris)
Iowa St.	Independence 12-27-01	Alabama 13-14 (Dennis Franchione)
Iowa St.	Humanitarian 12-31-02	Boise St. 16-34 (Dan Hawkins)
BILL McCARTNEY, 3-6-0 (Missouri '62) Born 8-22-40		
Colorado	Freedom 12-30-85	Washington 17-20 (Don James)
Colorado	Bluebonnet 12-31-86	Baylor 9-21 (Grant Teaff)
Colorado	Freedom 12-29-88	Brigham Young 17-20 (LaVell Edwards)
Colorado	Orange 1-1-90	Notre Dame 6-21 (Lou Holtz)
Colorado	Orange 1-1-91	Notre Dame 10-9 (Lou Holtz)
Colorado	Blockbuster 12-28-91	Alabama 25-30 (Gene Stallings)
Colorado	Fiesta 1-1-93	Syracuse 22-26 (Paul Pasqualoni)
Colorado	Aloha 12-25-93	Fresno St. 41-30 (Jim Sweeney)
Colorado	Fiesta 1-2-95	Notre Dame 41-24 (Lou Holtz)
DAVE McCLAIN, 1-2-0 (Bowling Green '60) Born 1-28-38		
Wisconsin	Garden State 12-13-81	Tennessee 21-28 (Johnny Majors)
Wisconsin	Independence 12-11-82	Kansas St. 14-3 (Jim Dickey)
Wisconsin	Hall of Fame 12-29-84	Kentucky 19-20 (Jerry Claiborne)
CHARLIE McCLENDON, 7-6-0 (Kentucky '50) Born 10-17-22		
LSU	Cotton 1-1-63	Texas 13-0 (Darrell Royal)
LSU	Bluebonnet 12-21-63	Baylor 7-14 (John Bridgers)
LSU	Sugar 1-1-65	Syracuse 13-10 (Ben Schwartzwalder)
LSU	Cotton 1-1-66	Arkansas 14-7 (Frank Broyles)
LSU	Sugar 1-1-68	Wyoming 20-13 (Lloyd Eaton)
LSU	Peach 12-30-68	Florida St. 31-27 (Bill Peterson)
LSU	Orange 1-1-71	Nebraska 12-17 (Bob Devaney)
LSU	Sun 12-18-71	Iowa St. 33-15 (Johnny Majors)
LSU	Bluebonnet 12-30-72	Tennessee 17-24 (Bill Battle)
LSU	Orange 1-1-74	Penn St. 9-16 (Joe Paterno)
LSU	Sun 12-31-77	Stanford 14-24 (Bill Walsh)
LSU	Liberty 12-23-78	Missouri 15-20 (Warren Powers)
LSU	Tangerine 12-22-79	Wake Forest 34-10 (John Mackovic)
RUBE McCRAY, 1-1-0 (Ky. Wesleyan '30) Born 6-13-05		
William & Mary	Dixie 1-1-48	Arkansas 19-21 (John Barnhill)
William & Mary	Delta 1-1-49	Oklahoma St. 20-0 (Jim Lookabaugh)

Coach/School	Bowl/Date	Opponent/Score (Coach)
J.F. "POP" McKALE, 0-1-0 (Albion '10)		Born 6-12-1887
Arizona	San Diego East-West Christmas Classic 12-26-21	Centre 0-38 (Charley Moran)
JOHN McKAY, 6-3-0 (Oregon St. '50)		Born 7-5-23
Southern California	Rose 1-2-63	Wisconsin 42-37 (Milt Bruhn)
Southern California	Rose 1-2-67	Purdue 13-14 (Jack Mollenkopf)
Southern California	Rose 1-1-68	Indiana 14-3 (John Pont)
Southern California	Rose 1-1-69	Ohio St. 16-27 (Woody Hayes)
Southern California	Rose 1-1-70	Michigan 10-3 (Glenn "Bo" Schembechler)
Southern California	Rose 1-1-73	Ohio St. 42-17 (Woody Hayes)
Southern California	Rose 1-1-74	Ohio St. 21-42 (Woody Hayes)
Southern California	Rose 1-1-75	Ohio St. 18-17 (Woody Hayes)
Southern California	Liberty 12-22-75	Texas A&M 20-0 (Emory Bellard)
ALLYN McKEEN, 1-0-0 (Tennessee '29)		Born 1-26-05
Mississippi St.	Orange 1-1-41	Georgetown 14-7 (Jack Hagerty)
JOHNNIE McMILLAN, 0-1-0 (South Carolina '41)		Born 1-27-19
South Carolina	Gator 1-1-46	Wake Forest 14-26 (D.C. "Peahead" Walker)
MAC McWHORTER, 1-0-0 (Georgia '73)		Born 6-17-50
Georgia Tech	Seattle 12-27-01	Stanford 24-14 (Tyrone Willingham)
DAVID McWILLIAMS, 1-1-0 (Texas '64)		Born 4-18-42
Texas	Bluebonnet 12-31-87	Pittsburgh 32-27 (Mike Gottfried)
Texas	Cotton 1-1-91	Miami (Fla.) 3-46 (Dennis Erickson)
JACK MEAGHER, 1-0-1 (Notre Dame '17)		Born 7-4-1894
Auburn	Bacardi, Cuba 1-1-37	Villanova 7-7 (Maurice "Clipper" Smith)
Auburn	Orange 1-1-38	Michigan St. 6-0 (Charlie Bachman)
RANDOLPH R.M. MEDLEY, 2-0-0 (Mo. Wesleyan '21)		Born 9-22-1898
Southwestern (Tex.)	Sun 1-1-44	New Mexico 7-0 (Willis Barnes)
Southwestern (Tex.)	Sun 1-1-45	U. of Mexico 35-0 (Bernard A. Hoban)
LEO "DUTCH" MEYER, 3-4-0 (TCU '22)		Born 1-15-1898
TCU	Sugar 1-1-36	LSU 3-2 (Bernie Moore)
TCU	Cotton 1-1-37	Marquette 16-6 (Frank Murray)
TCU	Sugar 1-2-39	Carnegie Mellon 15-7 (Bill Kern)
TCU	Orange 1-1-42	Georgia 26-40 (Wally Butts)
TCU	Cotton 1-1-45	Oklahoma St. 0-34 (Jim Lookabaugh)
TCU	Delta 1-1-48	Mississippi 9-13 (John Vaught)
TCU	Cotton 1-1-52	Kentucky 7-20 (Paul "Bear" Bryant)
RON MEYER, 0-1-0 (Purdue '63)		Born 2-17-41
Southern Methodist	Holiday 12-19-80	Brigham Young 45-46 (LaVell Edwards)
JOHN MICHELOSEN, 0-2-0 (Pittsburgh '38)		Born 2-13-16
Pittsburgh	Sugar 1-2-56	Georgia Tech 0-7 (Bobby Dodd)
Pittsburgh	Gator 12-29-56	Georgia Tech 14-21 (Bobby Dodd)
LES MILES, 1-0-0 (Michigan '76)		Born 11-10-53
Oklahoma St.	Houston 12-27-02	Southern Miss. 33-23 (Jeff Bower)
RICK MINTER, 1-3-0 (Henderson St. '77)		Born 10-4-54
Cincinnati	Humanitarian 12-29-97	Utah St. 35-19 (John L. Smith)
Cincinnati	Motor City 12-27-00	Marshall 14-25 (Bob Pruett)
Cincinnati	Motor City 12-29-01	Toledo 16-23 (Tom Anstutz)
Cincinnati	New Orleans 12-17-02	North Texas 19-24 (Darrell Dickey)
JACK MITCHELL, 1-0-0 (Oklahoma '49)		Born 12-3-24
Kansas	Bluebonnet 12-16-61	Rice 33-7 (Jess Neely)
ODUS MITCHELL, 0-2-0 (West Tex. A&M '25)		Born 6-29-1899
North Texas	Salad 1-1-48	Nevada 6-13 (Joe Sheeketski)
North Texas	Sun 12-31-59	New Mexico St. 8-28 (Warren Woodson)
GARY MOELLER, 4-1-0 (Ohio St. '63)		Born 1-26-41
Michigan	Gator 1-1-91	Mississippi 35-3 (Billy Brewer)
Michigan	Rose 1-1-92	Washington 14-34 (Don James)
Michigan	Rose 1-1-93	Washington 38-31 (Don James)
Michigan	Hall of Fame 1-1-94	North Carolina St. 42-7 (Mike O'Cain)
Michigan	Holiday 12-30-94	Colorado St. 24-14 (Sonny Lubick)
AL MOLDE, 0-1-0 (Gust. Adolphus '66)		Born 11-15-43
Western Mich.	California 12-10-88	Fresno St. 30-35 (Jim Sweeney)
JACK MOLLENKOPF, 1-0-0 (Bowling Green '31)		Born 11-24-05
Purdue	Rose 1-2-67	Southern California 14-13 (John McKay)
BERNIE MOORE, 1-3-1 (Carson-Newman '17)		Born 4-30-1895
LSU	Sugar 1-1-36	TCU 2-3 (Leo "Dutch" Meyer)
LSU	Sugar 1-1-37	Santa Clara 14-21 (Lawrence "Buck" Shaw)
LSU	Sugar 1-1-38	Santa Clara 0-6 (Lawrence "Buck" Shaw)
LSU	Orange 1-1-44	Texas A&M 19-14 (Homer Norton)
LSU	Cotton 1-1-47	Arkansas 0-0 (John Barnhill)
BUD MOORE, 0-1-0 (Alabama '61)		Born 10-16-39
Kansas	Sun 12-26-75	Pittsburgh 19-33 (Johnny Majors)
CHARLEY MORAN, 2-1-0 (Tennessee '98)		Born 2-22-1878
Centre	Fort Worth Classic 1-1-21	TCU 63-7 (Bill Driver)

Coach/School	Bowl/Date	Opponent/Score (Coach)
Centre	San Diego East-West Christmas Classic 12-26-21	Arizona 38-0 (J.F. "Pop" McKale)
Centre	Dixie Classic 1-2-22	Texas A&M 14-22 (Dana Bible)
DELL MORGAN, 0-3-0 (Austin '25)		Born 2-14-02
Texas Tech	Sun 1-1-42	Tulsa 0-6 (Henry Frnka)
Texas Tech	Sun 1-1-48	Miami (Ohio) 12-13 (Sid Gillman)
Texas Tech	Raisin 12-31-49	San Jose St. 13-20 (Bill Hubbard)
JOE MORRISON, 0-3-0 (Cincinnati '59)		Born 8-21-37
South Carolina	Gator 12-28-84	Oklahoma St. 14-21 (Pat Jones)
South Carolina	Gator 12-31-87	LSU 13-30 (Mike Archer)
South Carolina	Liberty 12-28-88	Indiana 10-34 (Bill Mallory)
RAY MORRISON, 0-1-0 (Vanderbilt '12)		Born 2-28-1885
Southern Methodist	Dixie Classic 1-1-25	West Va. Wesleyan 7-9 (Bob Higgins)
DARRELL MUDRA, 0-1-0 (Peru St. '51)		Born 1-4-29
Arizona	Sun 12-28-68	Auburn 10-34 (Ralph "Shug" Jordan)
HAL MUMME, 0-2-0 (Tarleton St. '75)		Born 3-29-52
Kentucky	Outback 1-1-99	Penn St. 14-26 (Joe Paterno)
Kentucky	Music City 12-29-99	Syracuse 13-20 (Paul Pasqualoni)
CLARENCE "BIGGIE" MUNN, 1-0-0 (Minnesota '32)		Born 9-11-08
Michigan St.	Rose 1-1-54	UCLA 28-20 (Henry "Red" Sanders)
BILLY MURPHY, 1-0-0 (Mississippi St. '47)		Born 1-13-21
Memphis	Pasadena 12-18-71	San Jose St. 28-9 (Dewey King)
GENE MURPHY, 0-1-0 (North Dakota '62)		Born 8-6-39
Cal St. Fullerton	California 12-17-83	Northern Ill. 13-20 (Bill Mallory)
JACK MURPHY, 1-0-0 (Heidelberg '54)		Born 8-6-32
Toledo	Tangerine 12-28-71	Richmond 28-3 (Frank Jones)
BILL MURRAY, 2-1-0 (Duke '31)		Born 9-9-08
Duke	Orange 1-1-55	Nebraska 34-7 (Bill Glassford)
Duke	Orange 1-1-58	Oklahoma 21-48 (Bud Wilkinson)
Duke	Cotton 1-2-61	Arkansas 7-6 (Frank Broyles)
FRANK MURRAY, 0-1-0 (Tufts '08)		Born 2-12-85
Marquette	Cotton 1-1-37	TCU 6-16 (Leo "Dutch" Meyer)
DENNY MYERS, 0-1-0 (Iowa '30)		Born 11-10-05
Boston College	Orange 1-1-43	Alabama 21-37 (Frank Thomas)
EDWARD "HOOK" MYLIN, 1-0-0 (Frank. & Marsh.)		Born 10-23-1897
Bucknell	Orange 1-1-35	Miami (Fla.) 26-0 (Tom McCann)
RAY NAGEL, 1-0-0 (UCLA '50)		Born 5-18-27
Utah	Liberty 12-19-64	West Virginia 32-6 (Gene Corum)
LARRY NAVIAUX, 0-1-0 (Nebraska '59)		Born 12-17-36
Boston U.	Pasadena 12-6-69	San Diego St. 7-28 (Don Coryell)
EARLE "GREASY" NEALE, 0-0-1 (West Va. Wesleyan '14)		Born 11-5-1891
Wash. & Jeff.	Rose 1-2-22	California 0-0 (Andy Smith)
JESS NEELY, 4-3-0 (Vanderbilt '23)		Born 1-4-1898
Clemson	Cotton 1-1-40	Boston College 6-3 (Frank Leahy)
Rice	Orange 1-1-47	Tennessee 8-0 (Bob Neyland)
Rice	Cotton 1-2-50	North Carolina 27-13 (Carl Snavely)
Rice	Cotton 1-1-54	Alabama 28-6 (Harold "Red" Drew)
Rice	Cotton 1-1-58	Navy 7-20 (Eddie Erdelatz)
Rice	Sugar 1-2-61	Mississippi 6-14 (John Vaught)
Rice	Bluebonnet 12-16-61	Kansas 7-33 (Jack Mitchell)
DON NEHLEN, 4-9-0 (Bowling Green '58)		Born 1-1-36
West Virginia	Peach 12-31-81	Florida 26-6 (Charley Pell)
West Virginia	Gator 12-30-82	Florida St. 12-31 (Bobby Bowden)
West Virginia	Hall of Fame 12-22-83	Kentucky 20-16 (Jerry Claiborne)
West Virginia	Bluebonnet 12-31-84	TCU 31-14 (Jim Wacker)
West Virginia	Sun 12-25-87	Oklahoma St. 33-35 (Pat Jones)
West Virginia	Fiesta 1-2-89	Notre Dame 21-34 (Lou Holtz)
West Virginia	Gator 12-30-89	Clemson 7-27 (Danny Ford)
West Virginia	Sugar 1-1-94	Florida 7-41 (Steve Spurrier)
West Virginia	Carquest 1-2-95	South Carolina 21-24 (Brad Scott)
West Virginia	Gator 1-1-97	North Carolina 13-20 (Mack Brown)
West Virginia	Carquest 12-29-97	Georgia Tech 30-35 (George O'Leary)
West Virginia	Insight.com 12-26-98	Missouri 31-34 (Larry Smith)
West Virginia	Music City 12-28-00	Mississippi 49-38 (David Cutcliffe)
RICK NEUHEISEL, 4-3-0 (UCLA '84)		Born 2-7-61
Colorado	Cotton 1-1-96	Oregon 38-6 (Mike Bellotti)
Colorado	Holiday 12-30-96	Washington 33-21 (Jim Lambright)
Colorado	Aloha Classic 12-25-98	Oregon 51-43 (Mike Bellotti)
Washington	Holiday 12-29-99	Kansas St. 20-24 (Bill Snyder)
Washington	Rose 1-1-01	Purdue 34-24 (Joe Tiller)
Washington	Holiday 12-28-01	Texas 43-47 (Mack Brown)
Washington	Sun 12-31-02	Purdue 34-24 (Joe Tiller)
BOB NEYLAND, 2-5-0 (Army '16)		Born 2-17-1892
Tennessee	Orange 1-2-39	Oklahoma 17-0 (Tom Stidham)
Tennessee	Rose 1-1-40	Southern California 0-14 (Howard Jones)
Tennessee	Sugar 1-1-41	Boston College 13-19 (Frank Leahy)
Tennessee	Orange 1-1-47	Rice 0-8 (Jess Neely)
Tennessee	Cotton 1-1-51	Texas 20-14 (Blair Cherry)
Tennessee	Sugar 1-1-52	Maryland 13-28 (Jim Tatum)
Tennessee	Cotton 1-1-53	Texas 0-16 (Ed Price)

Coach/School	Bowl/Date	Opponent/Score (Coach)

RAY NOLTING, 1-0-0 (Cincinnati '36) Born 11-8-13
Cincinnati .... Sun 1-1-47 — Virginia Tech 18-6 (Jimmy Kitts)

HOMER NORTON, 2-2-1 (Birmingham Southern '16) Born 12-30-1896
Centenary (La.)......... Dixie Classic 1-1-34 — Arkansas 7-7 (Fred Thomsen)
Texas A&M............... Sugar 1-1-40 — Tulane 14-13 (Lowell "Red" Dawson)
Texas A&M............... Cotton 1-1-41 — Fordham 13-12 (Jim Crowley)
Texas A&M............... Cotton 1-1-42 — Alabama 21-29 (Frank Thomas)
Texas A&M............... Orange 1-1-44 — LSU 14-19 (Bernie Moore)

TOM NUGENT, 0-2-0 (Ithaca '36) Born 2-24-16
Florida St. .... Sun 1-1-55 — UTEP 20-47 (Mike Brumbelow)
Florida St. .... Bluegrass 12-13-58 — Oklahoma St. 6-15 (Cliff Speegle)

HOUSTON NUTT, 1-4-0 (Oklahoma St. '81) Born 10-14-57
Arkansas .... Fla. Citrus 1-1-99 — Michigan 31-45 (Lloyd Carr)
Arkansas .... Cotton 1-1-00 — Texas 27-6 (Mack Brown)
Arkansas .... Las Vegas 12-21-00 — UNLV 14-31 (John Robinson)
Arkansas .... Cotton 1-1-02 — Oklahoma 3-10 (Bob Stoops)
Arkansas .... Music City 12-30-02 — Minnesota 14-29 (Glen Mason)

TOM O'BRIEN, 3-1-0 (Navy '71) Born 10-5-48
Boston College......... Insight.com 12-31-99 — Colorado 28-62 (Gary Barnett)
Boston College......... Aloha Classic 12-25-00 — Arizona St. 31-17 (Bruce Snyder)
Boston College......... Music City 12-28-01 — Georgia 20-16 (Mark Richt)
Boston College......... Motor City 12-26-02 — Toledo 51-25 (Tom Anstutz)

MIKE O'CAIN, 1-2-0 (Clemson '77) Born 7-20-54
North Carolina St. ... Hall of Fame 1-1-94 — Michigan 7-42 (Gary Moeller)
North Carolina St. ... Peach 1-1-95 — Mississippi St. 28-24 (Jackie Sherrill)
North Carolina St. ... Micron PC 12-29-98 — Miami (Fla.) 23-46 (Butch Davis)

GEORGE O'LEARY, 2-2-0 (New Hampshire '68) Born 8-17-46
Georgia Tech........... Carquest 12-29-97 — West Virginia 35-30 (Don Nehlen)
Georgia Tech........... Gator 1-1-99 — Notre Dame 35-28 (Bob Davie)
Georgia Tech........... Gator 1-1-00 — Miami (Fla.) 13-28 (Butch Davis)
Georgia Tech........... Peach 12-29-00 — LSU 14-28 (Nick Saban)

BERNARD "BUNNIE" OAKES, 0-1-0 (Illinois '24) Born 9-15-1898
Colorado .... Cotton 1-1-38 — Rice 14-28 (Jimmy Kitts)

JORDAN OLIVAR, 1-1-0 (Villanova '38) Born 1-30-15
Villanova .... Great Lakes 12-6-47 — Kentucky 14-24 (Paul "Bear" Bryant)
Villanova .... Harbor 1-1-49 — Nevada 27-7 (Joe Sheeketski)

AL ONOFRIO, 1-1-0 (Arizona St. '43) Born 3-15-21
Missouri.................. Fiesta 12-23-72 — Arizona St. 35-49 (Frank Kush)
Missouri.................. Sun 12-29-73 — Auburn 34-17 (Ralph "Shug" Jordan)

BENNIE OOSTERBAAN, 1-0-0 (Michigan '28) Born 2-24-06
Michigan .... Rose 1-1-51 — California 14-6 (Lynn "Pappy" Waldorf)

TOM OSBORNE, 12-13-0 (Hastings '59) Born 2-23-37
Nebraska .... Cotton 1-1-74 — Texas 19-3 (Darrell Royal)
Nebraska .... Sugar 12-31-74 — Florida 13-10 (Doug Dickey)
Nebraska .... Fiesta 12-26-75 — Arizona St. 14-17 (Frank Kush)
Nebraska .... Bluebonnet 12-31-76 — Texas Tech 27-24 (Steve Sloan)
Nebraska .... Liberty 12-19-77 — North Carolina 21-17 (Bill Dooley)
Nebraska .... Orange 1-1-79 — Oklahoma 24-31 (Barry Switzer)
Nebraska .... Cotton 1-1-80 — Houston 14-17 (Bill Yeoman)
Nebraska .... Sun 12-27-80 — Mississippi St. 31-17 (Emory Bellard)
Nebraska .... Orange 1-1-82 — Clemson 15-22 (Danny Ford)
Nebraska .... Orange 1-1-83 — LSU 21-20 (Jerry Stovall)
Nebraska .... Orange 1-2-84 — Miami (Fla.) 30-31 (Howard Schnellenberger)
Nebraska .... Sugar 1-1-85 — LSU 28-10 (Bill Arnsparger)
Nebraska .... Fiesta 1-1-86 — Michigan 23-27 (Glenn "Bo" Schembechler)
Nebraska .... Sugar 1-1-87 — LSU 30-15 (Bill Arnsparger)
Nebraska .... Fiesta 1-1-88 — Florida St. 28-31 (Bobby Bowden)
Nebraska .... Orange 1-2-89 — Miami (Fla.) 3-23 (Jimmy Johnson)
Nebraska .... Fiesta 1-1-90 — Florida St. 17-41 (Bobby Bowden)
Nebraska .... Fla. Citrus 1-1-91 — Georgia Tech 21-45 (Bobby Ross)
Nebraska .... Orange 1-1-92 — Miami (Fla.) 0-22 (Dennis Erickson)
Nebraska .... Orange 1-1-93 — Florida St. 14-27 (Bobby Bowden)
Nebraska .... Orange 1-1-94 — Florida St. 16-18 (Bobby Bowden)
Nebraska .... Orange 1-1-95 — Miami (Fla.) 24-17 (Dennis Erickson)
Nebraska .... Fiesta 1-2-96 — Florida 62-24 (Steve Spurrier)
Nebraska .... Orange 12-31-96 — Virginia Tech 41-21 (Frank Beamer)
Nebraska .... Orange 1-2-98 — Tennessee 42-17 (Phillip Fulmer)

JIM OWENS, 2-1-0 (Oklahoma '50) Born 3-6-27
Washington .... Rose 1-1-60 — Wisconsin 44-8 (Milt Bruhn)
Washington .... Rose 1-2-61 — Minnesota 17-7 (Murray Warmath)
Washington .... Rose 1-1-64 — Illinois 7-17 (Pete Elliott)

JACK PARDEE, 0-1-0 (Texas A&M '57) Born 4-9-36
Houston .... Aloha 12-25-88 — Washington St. 22-24 (Dennis Erickson)

ARA PARSEGHIAN, 3-2-0 (Miami [Ohio] '49) Born 5-21-23
Notre Dame............ Cotton 1-1-70 — Texas 17-21 (Darrell Royal)
Notre Dame............ Cotton 1-1-71 — Texas 24-11 (Darrell Royal)
Notre Dame............ Orange 1-1-73 — Nebraska 6-40 (Bob Devaney)
Notre Dame............ Sugar 12-31-73 — Alabama 24-23 (Paul "Bear" Bryant)
Notre Dame............ Orange 1-1-75 — Alabama 13-11 (Paul "Bear" Bryant)

PAUL PASQUALONI, 6-2-0 (Penn St. '72) Born 8-16-49
Syracuse................. Hall of Fame 1-1-92 — Ohio St. 24-17 (John Cooper)
Syracuse................. Fiesta 1-1-93 — Colorado 26-22 (Bill McCartney)
Syracuse................. Gator 1-1-96 — Clemson 41-0 (Tommy West)
Syracuse................. Liberty 12-27-96 — Houston 30-17 (Kim Helton)
Syracuse................. Fiesta 12-31-97 — Kansas St. 18-35 (Bill Snyder)
Syracuse................. Orange 1-2-99 — Florida 10-31 (Steve Spurrier)
Syracuse................. Music City 12-29-99 — Kentucky 20-13 (Hal Mumme)
Syracuse................. Insight.com 12-29-01 — Kansas St. 26-3 (Bill Snyder)

JOE PATERNO, 20-10-1 (Brown '50) Born 12-21-26
Penn St. .... Gator 12-30-67 — Florida St. 17-17 (Bill Peterson)
Penn St. .... Orange 1-1-69 — Kansas 15-14 (Pepper Rodgers)
Penn St. .... Orange 1-1-70 — Missouri 10-3 (Dan Devine)
Penn St. .... Cotton 1-1-72 — Texas 30-6 (Darrell Royal)
Penn St. .... Sugar 12-31-72 — Oklahoma 0-14 (Chuck Fairbanks)
Penn St. .... Orange 1-1-74 — LSU 16-9 (Charlie McClendon)
Penn St. .... Cotton 1-1-75 — Baylor 41-20 (Grant Teaff)
Penn St. .... Sugar 12-31-75 — Alabama 6-13 (Paul "Bear" Bryant)
Penn St. .... Gator 12-27-76 — Notre Dame 9-20 (Dan Devine)
Penn St. .... Fiesta 12-25-77 — Arizona St. 42-30 (Frank Kush)
Penn St. .... Sugar 1-1-79 — Alabama 7-14 (Paul "Bear" Bryant)
Penn St. .... Liberty 12-22-79 — Tulane 9-6 (Larry Smith)
Penn St. .... Fiesta 12-26-80 — Ohio St. 31-19 (Earle Bruce)
Penn St. .... Fiesta 1-1-82 — Southern California 26-10 (John Robinson)
Penn St. .... Sugar 1-1-83 — Georgia 27-23 (Vince Dooley)
Penn St. .... Aloha 12-26-83 — Washington 13-10 (Don James)
Penn St. .... Orange 1-1-86 — Oklahoma 10-25 (Barry Switzer)
Penn St. .... Fiesta 1-1-87 — Miami (Fla.) 14-10 (Jimmy Johnson)
Penn St. .... Fla. Citrus 1-1-88 — Clemson 10-35 (Danny Ford)
Penn St. .... Holiday 12-29-89 — Brigham Young 50-39 (LaVell Edwards)
Penn St. .... Blockbuster 12-28-90 — Florida St. 17-24 (Bobby Bowden)
Penn St. .... Fiesta 1-1-92 — Tennessee 42-17 (Johnny Majors)
Penn St. .... Blockbuster 1-1-93 — Stanford 3-24 (Bill Walsh)
Penn St. .... Fla. Citrus 1-1-94 — Tennessee 31-13 (Phillip Fulmer)
Penn St. .... Rose 1-2-95 — Oregon 38-20 (Rich Brooks)
Penn St. .... Outback 1-1-96 — Auburn 43-14 (Terry Bowden)
Penn St. .... Fiesta 1-1-97 — Texas 38-15 (John Mackovic)
Penn St. .... Alamo 12-28-99 — Texas A&M 24-0 (R.C. Slocum)
Penn St. .... Fla. Citrus 1-1-98 — Florida 6-21 (Steve Spurrier)
Penn St. .... Outback 1-1-99 — Kentucky 26-14 (Hal Mumme)
Penn St. .... Alamo 12-28-99 — Texas A&M 24-0 (R. C. Slocum)
Penn St. .... Capital One 1-1-03 — Auburn 9-13 (Tommy Tuberville)

GARY PATTERSON, 1-2-0 (Kansas St. '83) Born 2-13-60
TCU .... Mobile Alabama 12-20-00 — Southern Miss. 21-28 (Jeff Bower)
TCU .... galleryfurniture.com 12-28-01 — Texas A&M 9-28 (R.C. Slocum)
TCU .... Liberty 12-31-02 — Colorado St. 17-3 (Sonny Lubick)

JOE RAYMOND PEACE, 0-0-1 (Louisiana Tech '68) Born 6-5-45
Louisiana Tech .... Independence 12-15-90 — Maryland 34-34 (Joe Krivak)

CHARLEY PELL, 2-3-0 (Alabama '64) Born 2-27-41
Clemson .... Gator 12-30-77 — Pittsburgh 3-34 (Jackie Sherrill)
Florida.................... Tangerine 12-20-80 — Maryland 35-20 (Jerry Claiborne)
Florida.................... Peach 12-31-81 — West Virginia 6-26 (Don Nehlen)
Florida.................... Bluebonnet 12-31-82 — Arkansas 24-28 (Lou Holtz)
Florida.................... Gator 12-30-83 — Iowa 14-6 (Hayden Fry)

RAY PERKINS, 3-0-0 (Alabama '67) Born 11-6-41
Alabama .... Sun 12-24-83 — Southern Methodist 28-7 (Bobby Collins)
Alabama .... Aloha 12-28-85 — Southern California 24-3 (Ted Tollner)
Alabama .... Sun 12-26-86 — Washington 28-6 (Don James)

GEORGE PERLES, 3-4-0 (Michigan St. '60) Born 7-16-34
Michigan St. .... Cherry 12-22-84 — Army 6-10 (Jim Young)
Michigan St. .... Hall of Fame 12-31-85 — Georgia Tech 14-17 (Bill Curry)
Michigan St. .... Rose 1-1-88 — Southern California 20-17 (Larry Smith)
Michigan St. .... Gator 1-1-89 — Georgia 27-34 (Vince Dooley)
Michigan St. .... Aloha 12-25-89 — Hawaii 33-13 (Bob Wagner)
Michigan St. .... John Hancock 12-31-90 — Southern California 17-16 (Larry Smith)
Michigan St. .... Liberty 12-28-93 — Louisville 7-18 (Howard Schnellenberger)

DOYT PERRY, 0-1-0 (Bowling Green '32) Born 1-6-10
Bowling Green......... Mercy 11-23-61 — Fresno St. 6-36 (Cecil Coleman)

BILL PETERSON, 1-2-1 (Ohio Northern '46) Born 5-14-20
Florida St. .... Gator 1-2-65 — Oklahoma 36-19 (Gomer Jones)
Florida St. .... Sun 12-24-66 — Wyoming 20-28 (Lloyd Eaton)
Florida St. .... Gator 12-30-67 — Penn St. 17-17 (Joe Paterno)
Florida St. .... Peach 12-30-68 — LSU 27-31 (Charlie McClendon)

JIMMY PHELAN, 0-3-0 (Notre Dame '19) Born 12-5-1892
Washington .... Rose 1-1-37 — Pittsburgh 0-21 (Jock Sutherland)
St. Mary's (Cal.)....... Sugar 1-1-46 — Oklahoma St. 12-33 (Jim Lookabaugh)
St. Mary's (Cal.)....... Oil 1-1-47 — Georgia Tech 19-41 (Bobby Dodd)

ALVIN "PIX" PIERSON, 0-1-0 (Nevada '22) Born 7-25-1898
Fresno St. .... Raisin 1-1-46 — Drake 12-13 (Vee Green)

GARY PINKEL, 1-0-0 (Kent St. '75) Born 4-27-52
Toledo .... Las Vegas 12-14-95 — Nevada 40-37 (ot) (Chris Ault)

Coach/School	Bowl/Date	Opponent/Score (Coach)
JIM PITTMAN, 1-0-0	(Mississippi St. '50)	Born 8-28-25
Tulane	Liberty 12-12-70	Colorado 17-3 (Eddie Crowder)
JOHN PONT, 0-2-0	(Miami [Ohio] '52)	Born 11-13-27
Miami (Ohio)............	Tangerine 12-22-52	Houston 21-49 (Bill Yeoman)
Indiana...................	Rose 1-1-68	Southern California 3-14 (John McKay)
WARREN POWERS, 3-2-0	(Nebraska '63)	Born 2-19-41
Missouri.................	Liberty 12-23-78	LSU 20-15 (Charlie McClendon)
Missouri.................	Hall of Fame 12-29-79	South Carolina 24-14 (Jim Carlen)
Missouri.................	Liberty 12-27-80	Purdue 25-28 (Jim Young)
Missouri.................	Tangerine 12-19-81	Southern Miss. 19-17 (Bobby Collins)
Missouri.................	Holiday 12-23-83	Brigham Young 17-21 (LaVell Edwards)
CLARENCE "NIBS" PRICE, 0-1-0	(California '14)	Born 1889
California	Rose 1-1-29	Georgia Tech 7-8 (Bill Alexander)
ED PRICE, 1-0-0	(Texas '33)	Born 1-12-09
Texas	Cotton 1-1-53	Tennessee 16-0 (Bob Neyland)
MIKE PRICE, 3-2-0	(Puget Sound '69)	Born 4-6-46
Washington St.	Copper 12-29-92	Utah 31-28 (Ron McBride)
Washington St.	Alamo 12-31-94	Baylor 10-3 (Chuck Reedy)
Washington St.	Rose 1-1-98	Michigan 16-21 (Lloyd Carr)
Washington St.	Sun 12-31-01	Purdue 33-27 (Joe Tiller)
Washington St.	Rose 1-1-03	Oklahoma 14-34 (Bob Stoops)
TOMMY PROTHRO, 2-2-0	(Duke '42)	Born 7-20-20
Oregon St.	Rose 1-1-57	Iowa 19-35 (Forest Evashevski)
Oregon St.	Liberty 12-15-62	Villanova 6-0 (Alex Bell)
Oregon St.	Rose 1-1-65	Michigan 7-34 (Chalmers "Bump" Elliott)
UCLA	Rose 1-1-66	Michigan St. 14-12 (Duffy Daugherty)
BOB PRUETT, 5-1-0	(Marshall '65)	Born 6-30-43
Marshall	Motor City 12-26-97	Mississippi 31-34 (Tommy Tuberville)
Marshall	Motor City 12-23-98	Louisville 48-29 (John L. Smith)
Marshall	Motor City 12-27-99	Brigham Young 21-3 (LaVell Edwards)
Marshall	Motor City 12-27-00	Cincinnati 25-14 (Rick Minter)
Marshall	GMAC 12-19-01	East Caro. 64-61 (2 ot) (Steve Logan)
Marshall	GMAC 12-18-02	Louisville 38-15 (John L. Smith)
DAVE RADER, 1-1-0	(Tulsa '80)	Born 3-9-57
Tulsa	Independence 12-16-89	Oregon 24-27 (Rich Brooks)
Tulsa	Freedom 12-30-91	San Diego St. 28-17 (Al Luginbill)
JOHN RALSTON, 2-2-0	(California '54)	Born 4-25-27
Utah St.	Sun 12-31-60	New Mexico St. 13-20 (Warren Woodson)
Utah St.	Gotham 12-9-61	Baylor 9-24 (John Bridgers)
Stanford	Rose 1-1-71	Ohio St. 27-17 (Woody Hayes)
Stanford	Rose 1-1-72	Michigan 13-12 (Glenn "Bo" Schembechler)
CHUCK REEDY, 0-1-0	(Appalachian St. '71)	Born 5-31-49
Baylor	Alamo 12-31-94	Washington St. 3-10 (Mike Price)
RED REESE, 1-0-0	(Washington St. '25)	Born 3-2-1899
Second Air Force	Sun 1-1-43	Hardin-Simmons 13-7 (Warren Woodson)
BO REIN, 2-0-0	(Ohio St. '68)	Born 7-20-45
North Carolina St.....	Peach 12-31-77	Iowa St. 24-14 (Earle Bruce)
North Carolina St.....	Tangerine 12-23-78	Pittsburgh 30-17 (Jackie Sherrill)
MARK RICHT, 1-1-0	(Miami [Fla.] '82)	Born 2-18-60
Georgia	Music City 12-28-01	Boston College 16-20 (Tom O'Brien)
Georgia	Sugar 1-1-03	Florida St. 26-13 (Bobby Bowden)
PAUL ROACH, 0-3-0	(Black Hills St. '52)	Born 10-24-27
Wyoming	Holiday 12-30-87	Iowa 19-20 (Hayden Fry)
Wyoming	Holiday 12-30-88	Oklahoma St. 14-62 (Pat Jones)
Wyoming	Copper 12-31-90	California 15-17 (Bruce Snyder)
ED ROBINSON, 0-1-0	(Brown '96)	Born 10-15-73
Brown	Rose 1-1-16	Washington St. 0-14 (Bill "Lone Star" Dietz)
JOHN ROBINSON, 8-1-0	(Oregon '58)	Born 7-25-35
Southern California...	Rose 1-1-77	Michigan 14-6 (Glenn "Bo" Schembechler)
Southern California...	Bluebonnet 12-31-77	Texas A&M 47-28 (Emory Bellard)
Southern California...	Rose 1-1-79	Michigan 17-10 (Glenn "Bo" Schembechler)
Southern California...	Rose 1-1-80	Ohio St. 17-16 (Earle Bruce)
Southern California...	Fiesta 1-1-82	Penn St. 10-26 (Joe Paterno)
Southern California...	Freedom 12-30-93	Utah 28-21 (Ron McBride)
Southern California...	Cotton 1-2-95	Texas Tech 55-14 (Spike Dykes)
Southern California...	Rose 1-1-96	Northwestern 41-32 (Gary Barnett)
UNLV	Las Vegas 12-21-00	Arkansas 31-14 (Houston Nutt)
KNUTE ROCKNE, 1-0-0	(Notre Dame '14)	Born 3-4-1888
Notre Dame	Rose 1-1-25	Stanford 27-10 (Glenn "Pop" Warner)
PEPPER RODGERS, 0-2-0	(Georgia Tech '55)	Born 10-8-31
Kansas	Orange 1-1-69	Penn St. 14-15 (Joe Paterno)
Georgia Tech..........	Peach 12-25-78	Purdue 21-41 (Jim Young)
RICH RODRIGUEZ, 0-1-0	(West Virginia '86)	Born 5-24-63
West Virginia..........	Continental Tire 12-28-02	Virginia 22-48 (Al Groh)

Coach/School	Bowl/Date	Opponent/Score (Coach)
DARRYL ROGERS, 1-0-0	(Fresno St. '57)	Born 5-28-34
Arizona St.	Fiesta 1-1-83	Oklahoma 32-21 (Barry Switzer)
E.L. "DICK" ROMNEY, 0-1-0	(Utah '17)	Born 2-12-1895
Utah St.	Raisin 1-1-47	San Jose St. 0-20 (Bill Hubbard)
TIM ROSE, 0-1-0	(Xavier [Ohio] '62)	Born 10-14-41
Miami (Ohio)	California 12-13-86	San Jose St. 7-37 (Claude Gilbert)
BOBBY ROSS, 4-2-0	(VMI '59)	Born 12-23-36
Maryland................	Aloha 12-25-82	Washington 20-21 (Don James)
Maryland................	Fla. Citrus 12-17-83	Tennessee 23-30 (Johnny Majors)
Maryland................	Sun 12-22-84	Tennessee 28-27 (Johnny Majors)
Maryland................	Cherry 12-21-85	Syracuse 35-18 (Dick MacPherson)
Georgia Tech..........	Fla. Citrus 1-1-91	Nebraska 45-21 (Tom Osborne)
Georgia Tech..........	Aloha 12-25-91	Stanford 18-17 (Dennis Green)
DARRELL ROYAL, 8-7-1	(Oklahoma '50)	Born 7-6-24
Texas	Sugar 1-1-58	Mississippi 7-39 (John Vaught)
Texas	Cotton 1-1-60	Syracuse 14-23 (Ben Schwartzwalder)
Texas	Bluebonnet 12-17-60	Alabama 3-3 (Paul "Bear" Bryant)
Texas	Cotton 1-1-62	Mississippi 12-7 (John Vaught)
Texas	Cotton 1-1-63	LSU 0-13 (Charlie McClendon)
Texas	Cotton 1-1-64	Navy 28-6 (Wayne Hardin)
Texas	Orange 1-1-65	Alabama 21-17 (Paul "Bear" Bryant)
Texas	Bluebonnet 12-17-66	Mississippi 19-0 (John Vaught)
Texas	Cotton 1-1-69	Tennessee 36-13 (Doug Dickey)
Texas	Cotton 1-1-70	Notre Dame 21-17 (Ara Parseghian)
Texas	Cotton 1-1-71	Notre Dame 11-24 (Ara Parseghian)
Texas	Cotton 1-1-72	Penn St. 6-30 (Joe Paterno)
Texas	Cotton 1-1-73	Alabama 17-13 (Paul "Bear" Bryant)
Texas	Cotton 1-1-74	Nebraska 3-19 (Tom Osborne)
Texas	Gator 12-30-74	Auburn 3-27 (Ralph "Shug" Jordan)
Texas	Bluebonnet 12-27-75	Colorado 38-21 (Bill Mallory)
NICK SABAN, 2-4-0	(Kent St. '73)	Born 10-31-51
Michigan St.	Independence 12-29-95	LSU 26-45 (Gerry DiNardo)
Michigan St.	Sun 12-31-96	Stanford 0-38 (Tyrone Willingham)
Michigan St.	Aloha 12-25-97	Washington 23-51 (Jim Lambright)
LSU	Peach 12-29-00	Georgia Tech 28-14 (George O'Leary)
LSU	Sugar 1-1-02	Illinois 47-34 (Ron Turner)
LSU	Cotton 1-1-03	Texas 20-35 (Mack Brown)
HENRY "RED" SANDERS, 0-2-0	(Vanderbilt '27)	Born 3-7-05
UCLA	Rose 1-1-54	Michigan St. 20-28 (Clarence "Biggie" Munn)
UCLA	Rose 1-2-56	Michigan St. 14-17 (Duffy Daugherty)
RALPH SASSE, 0-1-0	(Army '10)	Born 7-19-89
Mississippi St.	Orange 1-1-37	Duquesne 12-13 (John Smith)
GEORGE SAUER, 0-3-0	(Nebraska '34)	Born 12-11-10
Kansas	Orange 1-1-48	Georgia Tech 14-20 (Bobby Dodd)
Baylor	Orange 1-1-52	Georgia Tech 14-17 (Bobby Dodd)
Baylor	Gator 12-31-54	Auburn 13-33 (Ralph "Shug" Jordan)
MACK SAXON, 0-1-0	(Texas)	Born 1901
UTEP	Sun 1-1-37	Hardin-Simmons 6-34 (Frank Kimbrough)
CHRIS SCELFO, 2-0-0	(La.-Monroe '85)	Born 9-30-63
Tulane	Liberty 12-31-98	Brigham Young 41-27 (LaVell Edwards)
Tulane	Hawaii 12-25-02	Hawaii 36-28 (June Jones)
GLENN "BO" SCHEMBECHLER, 5-12-0	(Miami [Ohio] '51)	Born 4-1-29
Michigan	Rose 1-1-70	Southern California 3-10 (John McKay)
Michigan	Rose 1-1-72	Stanford 12-13 (John Ralston)
Michigan	Orange 1-1-76	Oklahoma 6-14 (Barry Switzer)
Michigan	Rose 1-1-77	Southern California 6-14 (John Robinson)
Michigan	Rose 1-2-78	Washington 20-27 (Don James)
Michigan	Rose 1-1-79	Southern California 10-17 (John Robinson)
Michigan	Gator 12-28-79	North Carolina 15-17 (Dick Crum)
Michigan	Rose 1-1-81	Washington 23-6 (Don James)
Michigan	Bluebonnet 12-31-81	UCLA 33-14 (Terry Donahue)
Michigan	Rose 1-1-83	UCLA 14-24 (Terry Donahue)
Michigan	Sugar 1-2-84	Auburn 7-9 (Pat Dye)
Michigan	Holiday 12-21-84	Brigham Young 17-24 (LaVell Edwards)
Michigan	Fiesta 1-1-86	Nebraska 27-23 (Tom Osborne)
Michigan	Rose 1-1-87	Arizona St. 15-22 (John Cooper)
Michigan	Hall of Fame 1-2-88	Alabama 28-24 (Bill Curry)
Michigan	Rose 1-1-89	Southern California 22-14 (Larry Smith)
Michigan	Rose 1-1-90	Southern California 10-17 (Larry Smith)
MERLE SCHLOSSER, 0-1-0	(Illinois '50)	Born 10-14-27
Western Mich.	Aviation 12-9-61	New Mexico 12-28 (Bill Weeks)
HOWARD SCHNELLENBERGER, 4-0-0	(Kentucky '56)	Born 3-16-34
Miami (Fla.)	Peach 1-2-81	Virginia Tech 20-10 (Bill Dooley)
Miami (Fla.)	Orange 1-2-84	Nebraska 31-30 (Tom Osborne)
Louisville	Fiesta 1-1-91	Alabama 34-7 (Gene Stallings)
Louisville	Liberty 12-28-93	Michigan St. 18-7 (George Perles)
PAUL SCHUDEL, 0-2-0	(Miami [Ohio] '66)	Born 7-2-44
Ball St.	California 12-9-89	Fresno St. 6-27 (Jim Sweeney)
Ball St.	Las Vegas 12-17-93	Utah St. 33-42 (Charlie Weatherbie)
BILL SCHUTTE, 0-1-0	(Idaho '33)	Born 5-7-10
San Diego St.	Harbor 1-1-48	Hardin-Simmons 0-53 (Warren Woodson)

Coach/School	Bowl/Date	Opponent/Score (Coach)
BEN SCHWARTZWALDER, 2-5-0 (West Virginia '35) Born 6-2-09		
Syracuse	Orange 1-1-53	Alabama 6-61 (Harold "Red" Drew)
Syracuse	Cotton 1-1-57	TCU 27-28 (Abe Martin)
Syracuse	Orange 1-1-59	Oklahoma 6-21 (Bud Wilkinson)
Syracuse	Cotton 1-1-60	Texas 23-14 (Darrell Royal)
Syracuse	Liberty 12-16-61	Miami (Fla.) 15-14 (Andy Gustafson)
Syracuse	Sugar 1-1-65	LSU 10-13 (Charlie McClendon)
Syracuse	Gator 12-31-66	Tennessee 12-18 (Doug Dickey)
BRAD SCOTT, 1-0-0 (Mo.-Rolla '76) Born 9-30-54		
South Carolina	Carquest 1-2-95	West Virginia 24-21 (Don Nehlen)
CLARK SHAUGHNESSY, 1-0-0 (Minnesota '14) Born 3-6-1892		
Stanford	Rose 1-1-41	Nebraska 21-13 (Lawrence McC. "Biff" Jones)
LAWRENCE "BUCK" SHAW, 2-0-0 (Notre Dame '22) Born 3-28-99		
Santa Clara	Sugar 1-1-37	LSU 21-14 (Bernie Moore)
Santa Clara	Sugar 1-1-38	LSU 6-0 (Bernie Moore)
TERRY SHEA, 1-0-0 (Oregon '68) Born 6-12-46		
San Jose St.	California 12-8-90	Central Mich. 48-24 (Herb Deromedi)
JOE SHEEKETSKI, 1-1-0 (Notre Dame '33) Born 4-15-09		
Nevada	Salad 1-1-48	North Texas 13-6 (Odus Mitchell)
Nevada	Harbor 1-1-49	Villanova 7-27 (Jordan Olivar)
DICK SHERIDAN, 2-4-0 (South Carolina '64) Born 8-9-41		
North Carolina St.	Peach 12-31-86	Virginia Tech 24-25 (Bill Dooley)
North Carolina St.	Peach 12-31-88	Iowa 28-23 (Hayden Fry)
North Carolina St.	Copper 12-31-89	Arizona 10-17 (Dick Tomey)
North Carolina St.	All-American 12-28-90	Southern Miss. 31-27 (Jeff Bower)
North Carolina St.	Peach 1-1-92	East Caro. 34-37 (Bill Lewis)
North Carolina St.	Gator 1-1-92	Florida 10-27 (Steve Spurrier)
EUGENE "BO" SHERMAN, 1-0-0 (Henderson St. '30) Born 7-5-08		
Geo. Washington	Sun 1-1-57	UTEP 13-0 (Mike Brumbelow)
JACKIE SHERRILL, 8-6-0 (Alabama '66) Born 11-28-43		
Pittsburgh	Gator 12-30-77	Clemson 34-3 (Charley Pell)
Pittsburgh	Tangerine 12-23-78	North Carolina St. 17-30 (Bo Rein)
Pittsburgh	Fiesta 12-25-79	Arizona 16-10 (Tony Mason)
Pittsburgh	Gator 12-29-80	South Carolina 37-9 (Jim Carlen)
Pittsburgh	Sugar 1-1-82	Georgia 24-20 (Vince Dooley)
Texas A&M	Cotton 1-1-86	Auburn 36-16 (Pat Dye)
Texas A&M	Cotton 1-1-87	Ohio St. 12-28 (Earle Bruce)
Texas A&M	Cotton 1-1-88	Notre Dame 35-10 (Lou Holtz)
Mississippi St.	Liberty 12-29-91	Air Force 15-38 (Fisher DeBerry)
Mississippi St.	Peach 1-2-93	North Carolina 17-21 (Mack Brown)
Mississippi St.	Peach 1-1-95	North Carolina St. 24-28 (Mike O'Cain)
Mississippi St.	Cotton 1-1-99	Texas 11-38 (Mack Brown)
Mississippi St.	Peach 12-30-99	Clemson 17-7 (Tommy Bowden)
Mississippi St.	Independence 12-31-00	Texas A&M 43-41 (ot) (R.C. Slocum)
TED SHIPKEY, 0-1-0 (Stanford '27) Born 9-28-04		
New Mexico	Sun 1-2-39	Utah 0-28 (Ike Armstrong)
LARRY SIEMERING, 1-0-0 (San Francisco '35) Born 11-24-10		
Pacific (Cal.)	Raisin 1-1-48	Wichita St. 26-14 (Ralph Graham)
BOB SIMMONS, 0-1-0 (Bowling Green '71) Born 6-13-48		
Oklahoma St.	Alamo 12-30-97	Purdue 20-33 (Joe Tiller)
CHAUNCEY SIMPSON, 0-1-0 (Missouri '25) Born 12-21-02		
Missouri	Cotton 1-1-46	Texas 27-40 (Dana Bible)
DAN SIMRELL, 0-1-0 (Toledo '65) Born 4-9-43		
Toledo	California 12-15-84	UNLV 13-30 (Harvey Hyde)
STEVE SLOAN, 0-2-1 (Alabama '66) Born 8-19-44		
Vanderbilt	Peach 12-28-74	Texas Tech 6-6 (Jim Carlen)
Texas Tech	Bluebonnet 12-31-76	Nebraska 24-27 (Tom Osborne)
Texas Tech	Tangerine 12-23-77	Florida St. 17-40 (Bobby Bowden)
R.C. SLOCUM, 3-8-0 (McNeese St. '67) Born 11-7-44		
Texas A&M	John Hancock 12-30-89	Pittsburgh 28-31 (Paul Hackett)
Texas A&M	Holiday 12-29-90	Brigham Young 65-14 (LaVell Edwards)
Texas A&M	Cotton 1-1-92	Florida St. 2-10 (Bobby Bowden)
Texas A&M	Cotton 1-1-93	Notre Dame 3-28 (Lou Holtz)
Texas A&M	Cotton 1-1-94	Notre Dame 21-24 (Lou Holtz)
Texas A&M	Alamo 12-28-95	Michigan 22-20 (Lloyd Carr)
Texas A&M	Cotton 1-1-98	UCLA 23-29 (Bob Toledo)
Texas A&M	Sugar 1-1-99	Ohio St. 14-24 (John Cooper)
Texas A&M	Alamo 12-28-99	Penn St. 0-24 (Joe Paterno)
Texas A&M	Independence 12-31-00	Mississippi St. 41-43 (ot) (Jackie Sherrill)
Texas A&M	galleryfurniture.com 12-28-01	TCU 28-9 (Gary Patterson)
ANDY SMITH, 1-0-1 (Pennsylvania '06) Born 9-10-1883		
California	Rose 1-1-21	Ohio St. 28-0 (John Wilce)
California	Rose 1-2-22	Wash. & Jeff. 0-0 (Earle "Greasy" Neale)
HOMER SMITH, 0-1-0 (Princeton '54) Born 10-9-31		
Davidson	Tangerine 12-26-69	Toledo 33-56 (Frank Lauterbur)
JOHN L. SMITH, 1-5-0 (Weber St. '71) Born 11-5-48		
Utah St.	Humanitarian 12-29-97	Cincinnati 19-35 (Rick Minter)
Louisville	Motor City 12-23-98	Marshall 29-48 (Bob Pruett)
Louisville	Humanitarian 12-30-99	Boise St. 31-34 (Dirk Koetter)
Louisville	Liberty 12-29-00	Colorado St. 17-22 (Sonny Lubick)
Louisville	Liberty 12-31-01	Brigham Young 28-10 (Gary Crowton)
Louisville	GMAC 12-18-02	Marshall 15-38 (Bob Pruett)
JOHN "LITTLE CLIPPER" SMITH, 1-0-0 (Notre Dame '29) Born 12-12-04		
Duquesne	Orange 1-1-37	Mississippi St. 13-12 (Ralph Sasse)
LARRY SMITH, 3-6-1 (Bowling Green '62) Born 9-12-39		
Tulane	Liberty 12-22-79	Penn St. 6-9 (Joe Paterno)
Arizona	Sun 12-28-85	Georgia 13-13 (Vince Dooley)
Arizona	Aloha 12-27-86	North Carolina 30-21 (Dick Crum)
Southern California	Rose 1-1-88	Michigan St. 17-20 (George Perles)
Southern California	Rose 1-2-89	Michigan 14-22 (Glenn "Bo" Schembechler)
Southern California	Rose 1-1-90	Michigan 17-10 (Glenn "Bo" Schembechler)
Southern California	John Hancock 12-31-90	Michigan St. 16-17 (George Perles)
Southern California	Freedom 12-29-92	Fresno St. 7-24 (Jim Sweeney)
Missouri	Holiday 12-29-97	Colorado St. 24-35 (Sonny Lubick)
Missouri	Insight.com 12-26-98	West Virginia 34-31 (Don Nehlen)
MAURICE "CLIPPER" SMITH, 0-0-1 (Notre Dame '21) Born 10-15-1898		
Villanova	Bacardi, Cuba 1-1-37	Auburn 7-7 (Jack Meagher)
CARL SNAVELY, 0-3-0 (Lebanon Valley '15) Born 7-30-1894		
North Carolina	Sugar 1-1-47	Georgia 10-20 (Wally Butts)
North Carolina	Sugar 1-1-49	Oklahoma 6-14 (Bud Wilkinson)
North Carolina	Cotton 1-2-50	Rice 13-27 (Jess Neely)
BILL SNYDER, 6-4-0 (William Jewell '63) Born 10-7-41		
Kansas St.	Copper 12-29-93	Wyoming 52-17 (Joe Tiller)
Kansas St.	Aloha 12-25-94	Boston College 7-12 (Dan Henning)
Kansas St.	Holiday 12-29-95	Colorado St. 54-21 (Sonny Lubick)
Kansas St.	Cotton 1-1-97	Brigham Young 15-19 (LaVell Edwards)
Kansas St.	Fiesta 12-31-97	Syracuse 35-18 (Paul Pasqualoni)
Kansas St.	Alamo 12-29-98	Purdue 34-37 (Joe Tiller)
Kansas St.	Holiday 12-29-99	Washington 24-20 (Rick Neuheisel)
Kansas St.	Cotton 1-1-01	Tennessee 35-21 (Phillip Fulmer)
Kansas St.	Insight.com 12-29-01	Syracuse 3-26 (Paul Pasqualoni)
Kansas St.	Holiday 12-27-02	Arizona St. 34-27 (Dirk Koetter)
BRUCE SNYDER, 3-3-0 (Oregon '62) Born 3-14-40		
California	Copper 12-31-90	Wyoming 17-15 (Paul Roach)
California	Fla. Citrus 1-1-92	Clemson 37-13 (Ken Hatfield)
Arizona St.	Rose 1-1-97	Ohio St. 17-20 (John Cooper)
Arizona St.	Sun 12-31-97	Iowa 17-7 (Hayden Fry)
Arizona St.	Aloha Classic 12-25-99	Wake Forest 3-23 (Jim Caldwell)
Arizona St.	Aloha Classic 12-25-00	Boston College 17-31 (Tom O'Brien)
FRANK SOLICH, 2-3-0 (Nebraska '66) Born 9-8-44		
Nebraska	Holiday 12-30-98	Arizona 20-23 (Dick Tomey)
Nebraska	Fiesta 1-2-00	Tennessee 31-21 (Phillip Fulmer)
Nebraska	Alamo 12-30-00	Northwestern 66-17 (Randy Walker)
Nebraska	Rose 1-3-02	Miami (Fla.) 14-37 (Larry Coker)
Nebraska	Independence 12-27-02	Mississippi 23-27 (David Cutcliffe)
CLARENCE "DOC" SPEARS, 1-0-0 (Dartmouth '16) Born 7-24-1894		
West Virginia	San Diego East-West Christmas Classic 12-25-22	Gonzaga 21-13 (Charles "Gus" Dorais)
CLIFF SPEEGLE, 1-0-0 (Oklahoma '41) Born 11-4-17		
Oklahoma St.	Bluegrass 12-13-58	Florida St. 15-6 (Tom Nugent)
STEVE SPURRIER, 5-6-0 (Florida '67) Born 4-20-45		
Duke	All-American 12-28-89	Texas Tech 21-49 (Spike Dykes)
Florida	Sugar 1-1-92	Notre Dame 28-39 (Lou Holtz)
Florida	Gator 12-31-92	North Carolina St. 27-10 (Dick Sheridan)
Florida	Sugar 1-1-94	West Virginia 41-7 (Don Nehlen)
Florida	Sugar 1-2-95	Florida St. 17-23 (Bobby Bowden)
Florida	Fiesta 1-2-96	Nebraska 24-62 (Tom Osborne)
Florida	Sugar 1-2-97	Florida St. 52-20 (Bobby Bowden)
Florida	Fla. Citrus 1-1-98	Penn St. 21-6 (Joe Paterno)
Florida	Orange 1-2-99	Syracuse 31-10 (Paul Pasqualoni)
Florida	Fla. Citrus 1-1-00	Michigan St. 34-37 (Bobby Williams)
Florida	Sugar 1-2-01	Miami (Fla.) 20-37 (Butch Davis)
Florida	Orange 1-2-02	Maryland 56-23 (Ralph Friedgen)
GENE STALLINGS, 6-1-0 (Texas A&M '57) Born 3-2-35		
Texas A&M	Cotton 1-1-68	Alabama 20-16 (Paul "Bear" Bryant)
Alabama	Fiesta 1-1-91	Louisville 7-34 (Howard Schnellenberger)
Alabama	Blockbuster 12-28-91	Colorado 30-25 (Bill McCartney)
Alabama	Sugar 1-1-93	Miami (Fla.) 34-13 (Dennis Erickson)
Alabama	Gator 12-31-93	North Carolina 24-10 (Mack Brown)
Alabama	Fla. Citrus 1-2-95	Ohio St. 24-17 (John Cooper)
Alabama	Outback 1-1-97	Michigan 17-14 (Lloyd Carr)
JIM STANGELAND, 0-0-1 (Arizona St. '48) Born 12-21-21		
Long Beach St.	Pasadena 12-19-70	Louisville 24-24 (Lee Corso)
JIM STANLEY, 2-0-0 (Texas A&M '59) Born 5-22-35		
Oklahoma St.	Fiesta 12-28-74	Brigham Young 16-6 (LaVell Edwards)
Oklahoma St.	Tangerine 12-18-76	Brigham Young 49-12 (LaVell Edwards)
TOM STIDHAM, 0-1-0 (Haskell '27) Born 3-27-04		
Oklahoma	Orange 1-2-39	Tennessee 0-17 (Bob Neyland)

Coach/School	Bowl/Date	Opponent/Score (Coach)
LON STINER, 1-0-0	(Nebraska '27)	Born 6-20-03
Oregon St.	Rose 1-1-42	Duke 20-16 (Wallace Wade)
HARRY STITELER, 1-0-0	(Texas A&M '31)	Born 9-17-09
Texas A&M	Presidential Cup 12-9-50	Georgia 40-20 (Wally Butts)
CHUCK STOBART, 1-0-0	(Ohio '59)	Born 10-27-34
Toledo	California 12-19-81	San Jose St. 27-25 (Jack Elway)
CAL STOLL, 0-1-0	(Minnesota '50)	Born 12-12-23
Minnesota	Hall of Fame 12-22-77	Maryland 7-17 (Jerry Claiborne)
DENNY STOLZ, 0-3-0	(Alma '55)	Born 9-12-34
Bowling Green	California 12-18-82	Fresno St. 28-29 (Jim Sweeney)
Bowling Green	California 12-14-85	Fresno St. 7-51 (Jim Sweeney)
San Diego St.	Holiday 12-30-86	Iowa 38-39 (Hayden Fry)
BOB STOOPS, 3-1-0	(Iowa '83)	Born 9-6-60
Oklahoma	Independence 12-31-99	Mississippi 25-27 (David Cutcliffe)
Oklahoma	Orange 1-3-01	Florida St. 13-2 (Bobby Bowden)
Oklahoma	Cotton 1-1-02	Arkansas 10-3 (Houston Nutt)
Oklahoma	Rose 1-1-03	Washington St. 34-14 (Mike Price)
JERRY STOVALL, 0-1-0	(LSU '63)	Born 4-30-41
LSU	Orange 1-1-83	Nebraska 20-21 (Tom Osborne)
BOB STULL, 0-1-0	(Kansas St. '68)	Born 11-21-45
UTEP	Independence 12-23-88	Southern Miss. 18-38 (Curley Hallman)
PAT SULLIVAN, 0-1-0	(Auburn '72)	Born 1-18-50
TCU	Independence 12-28-94	Virginia 10-20 (George Welsh)
JOCK SUTHERLAND, 1-3-0	(Pittsburgh '18)	Born 3-21-1889
Pittsburgh	Rose 1-1-28	Stanford 6-7 (Glenn "Pop" Warner)
Pittsburgh	Rose 1-1-30	Southern California 14-47 (Howard Jones)
Pittsburgh	Rose 1-2-33	Southern California 0-35 (Howard Jones)
Pittsburgh	Rose 1-1-37	Washington 21-0 (Jimmy Phelan)
BOB SUTTON, 0-1-0	(Eastern Mich. '74)	Born 1-28-51
Army	Independence 12-31-96	Auburn 29-32 (Terry Bowden)
JIM SWEENEY, 5-2-0	(Portland '51)	Born 9-1-29
Fresno St.	California 12-18-82	Bowling Green 29-28 (Denny Stolz)
Fresno St.	California 12-14-85	Bowling Green 51-7 (Denny Stolz)
Fresno St.	California 12-10-88	Western Mich. 35-30 (Al Molde)
Fresno St.	California 12-9-89	Ball St. 27-8 (Paul Schudel)
Fresno St.	California 12-13-91	Bowling Green 21-28 (Gary Blackney)
Fresno St.	Freedom 12-29-92	Southern California 24-7 (Larry Smith)
Fresno St.	Aloha 12-25-93	Colorado 30-41 (Bill McCartney)
BARRY SWITZER, 8-5-0	(Arkansas '60)	Born 10-5-37
Oklahoma	Orange 1-1-76	Michigan 14-6 (Glenn "Bo" Schembechler)
Oklahoma	Fiesta 12-25-76	Wyoming 41-7 (Fred Akers)
Oklahoma	Orange 1-2-78	Arkansas 6-31 (Lou Holtz)
Oklahoma	Orange 1-1-79	Nebraska 31-24 (Tom Osborne)
Oklahoma	Orange 1-1-80	Florida St. 24-7 (Bobby Bowden)
Oklahoma	Orange 1-1-81	Florida St. 18-17 (Bobby Bowden)
Oklahoma	Sun 12-26-81	Houston 40-14 (Bill Yeoman)
Oklahoma	Fiesta 1-1-83	Arizona St. 21-32 (Darryl Rogers)
Oklahoma	Orange 1-1-85	Washington 17-28 (Don James)
Oklahoma	Orange 1-1-86	Penn St. 25-10 (Joe Paterno)
Oklahoma	Orange 1-1-87	Arkansas 42-8 (Ken Hatfield)
Oklahoma	Orange 1-1-88	Miami (Fla.) 14-20 (Jimmy Johnson)
Oklahoma	Fla. Citrus 1-2-89	Clemson 6-13 (Danny Ford)
CHARLIE TATE, 1-1-0	(Florida '42)	Born 2-20-21
Miami (Fla.)	Liberty 12-10-66	Virginia Tech 14-7 (Jerry Claiborne)
Miami (Fla.)	Bluebonnet 12-23-67	Colorado 21-31 (Eddie Crowder)
JIM TATUM, 3-2-1	(North Carolina '35)	Born 7-22-13
Oklahoma	Gator 1-1-47	North Carolina St. 34-13 (Beattie Feathers)
Maryland	Gator 1-1-48	Georgia 20-20 (Wally Butts)
Maryland	Gator 1-2-50	Missouri 20-7 (Don Faurot)
Maryland	Sugar 1-1-52	Tennessee 28-13 (Bob Neyland)
Maryland	Orange 1-1-54	Oklahoma 0-7 (Bud Wilkinson)
Maryland	Orange 1-2-56	Oklahoma 6-20 (Bud Wilkinson)
CHUCK TAYLOR, 0-1-0	(Stanford '43)	Born 1-24-20
Stanford	Rose 1-1-52	Illinois 7-40 (Ray Eliot)
GRANT TEAFF, 4-4-0	(McMurry '56)	Born 11-12-33
Baylor	Cotton 1-1-75	Penn St. 20-41 (Joe Paterno)
Baylor	Peach 12-31-79	Clemson 24-18 (Danny Ford)
Baylor	Cotton 1-1-81	Alabama 2-30 (Paul "Bear" Bryant)
Baylor	Bluebonnet 12-31-83	Oklahoma St. 14-24 (Jimmy Johnson)
Baylor	Liberty 12-27-85	LSU 21-7 (Bill Arnsparger)
Baylor	Bluebonnet 12-31-86	Colorado 21-9 (Bill McCartney)
Baylor	Copper 12-31-91	Indiana 0-24 (Bill Mallory)
Baylor	John Hancock 12-31-92	Arizona 20-15 (Dick Tomey)
EDDIE TEAGUE, 1-0-0	(North Carolina '44)	Born 12-14-21
Citadel	Tangerine 12-30-60	Tennessee Tech 27-0 (Wilburn Tucker)
LOU TEPPER, 1-2-0	(Rutgers '67)	Born 7-21-45
Illinois	John Hancock 12-31-91	UCLA 3-6 (Terry Donahue)
Illinois	Holiday 12-30-92	Hawaii 17-27 (Bob Wagner)
Illinois	Liberty 12-31-94	East Caro. 30-0 (Steve Logan)

Coach/School	Bowl/Date	Opponent/Score (Coach)
ROBERT THEDER, 0-1-0	(Western Mich. '63)	Born 9-22-39
California	Garden State 12-15-79	Temple 17-28 (Wayne Hardin)
FRANK THOMAS, 4-2-0	(Notre Dame '23)	Born 11-14-1898
Alabama	Rose 1-1-35	Stanford 29-13 (Claude "Tiny" Thornhill)
Alabama	Rose 1-1-38	California 0-13 (Leonard "Stub" Allison)
Alabama	Cotton 1-1-42	Texas A&M 29-21 (Homer Norton)
Alabama	Orange 1-1-43	Boston College 37-21 (Denny Myers)
Alabama	Sugar 1-1-45	Duke 26-29 (Eddie Cameron)
Alabama	Rose 1-1-46	Southern California 34-14 (Jeff Cravath)
FRED THOMSEN, 0-0-1	(Nebraska '25)	Born 4-25-1897
Arkansas	Dixie Classic 1-1-34	Centenary (La.) 7-7 (Homer Norton)
CLAUDE "TINY" THORNHILL, 1-2-0	(Pittsburgh '17)	Born 4-14-1893
Stanford	Rose 1-1-34	Columbia 0-7 (Lou Little)
Stanford	Rose 1-1-35	Alabama 13-29 (Frank Thomas)
Stanford	Rose 1-1-36	Southern Methodist 7-0 (Matty Bell)
JOE TILLER, 3-4-0	(Montana St. '64)	Born 12-7-42
Wyoming	Copper 12-29-93	Kansas St. 17-52 (Bill Snyder)
Purdue	Alamo 12-30-97	Oklahoma St. 33-20 (Bob Simmons)
Purdue	Alamo 12-29-98	Kansas St. 37-34 (Bill Snyder)
Purdue	Outback 1-1-00	Georgia 25-28 (ot) (Jim Donnan)
Purdue	Rose 1-1-01	Washington 24-34 (Rick Neuheisel)
Purdue	Sun 12-31-01	Washington St. 27-33 (Mike Price)
Purdue	Sun 12-31-02	Washington 34-24 (Rick Neuheisel)
GAYNELL TINSLEY, 0-1-0	(LSU '37)	Born 2-1-15
LSU	Sugar 1-2-50	Oklahoma 0-35 (Bud Wilkinson)
JEFF TISDEL, 1-0-0	(Nevada '77)	Born 1-10-56
Nevada	Las Vegas 12-19-96	Ball St. 18-15 (Bill Lynch)
BOB TOLEDO, 1-2-0	(San Francisco St. '68)	Born 3-4-46
UCLA	Cotton 1-1-98	Texas A&M 29-23 (R.C. Slocum)
UCLA	Rose 1-1-99	Wisconsin 31-38 (Barry Alvarez)
UCLA	Sun 12-29-00	Wisconsin 20-21 (Barry Alvarez)
TED TOLLNER, 1-3-0	(Cal Poly '62)	Born 5-29-40
Southern California	Rose 1-1-85	Ohio St. 20-17 (Earle Bruce)
Southern California	Aloha 12-28-85	Alabama 3-24 (Ray Perkins)
Southern California	Fla. Citrus 1-1-87	Auburn 7-16 (Pat Dye)
San Diego St.	Las Vegas 12-19-98	North Carolina 13-20 (Carl Torbush)
DICK TOMEY, 4-3-0	(DePauw '61)	Born 6-20-38
Arizona	Copper 12-30-89	North Carolina St. 17-10 (Dick Sheridan)
Arizona	Aloha 12-28-90	Syracuse 0-28 (Dick MacPherson)
Arizona	John Hancock 12-31-92	Baylor 15-20 (Grant Teaff)
Arizona	Fiesta 1-1-94	Miami (Fla.) 29-0 (Dennis Erickson)
Arizona	Freedom 12-27-94	Utah 13-16 (Ron McBride)
Arizona	Insight.com 12-27-97	New Mexico 20-14 (Dennis Franchione)
Arizona	Holiday 12-30-98	Nebraska 23-20 (Frank Solich)
CARL TORBUSH, 2-0-0	(Carson-Newman '74)	Born 10-11-51
North Carolina	Gator 1-1-98	Virginia Tech 42-3 (Frank Beamer)
North Carolina	Las Vegas 12-19-98	San Diego St. 20-13 (Ted Tollner)
CHRIS TORMEY, 1-0-0	(Idaho '78)	Born 5-1-55
Idaho	Humanitarian 12-30-98	Southern Miss. 42-35 (Jeff Bower)
JIM TRESSEL, 1-1-0	(Baldwin-Wallace '75)	Born 12-5-52
Ohio St.	Outback 1-1-02	South Carolina 28-31 (Lou Holtz)
Ohio St.	Fiesta 1-3-03	Miami (Fla.) 31-24 (2 ot) (Larry Coker)
JIM TRIMBLE, 0-1-0	(Indiana '42)	Born 5-29-18
Wichita St.	Camellia 12-30-48	Hardin-Simmons 12-49 (Warren Woodson)
FRANK TRITICO, 0-0-1	(La.-Lafayette '34)	Born 3-25-09
Randolph Field	Cotton 1-1-44	Texas 7-7 (Dana Bible)
TOMMY TUBERVILLE, 3-2-0	(Southern Ark. '76)	Born 9-18-54
Mississippi	Motor City 12-26-97	Marshall 34-31 (Bob Pruett)
Mississippi	Independence 12-31-98	Texas Tech 35-18 (Spike Dykes)
Auburn	Fla. Citrus 1-1-01	Michigan 28-31 (Lloyd Carr)
Auburn	Peach 12-31-01	North Carolina 10-16 (John Bunting)
Auburn	Capital One 1-1-03	Penn St. 13-9 (Joe Paterno)
WILBURN TUCKER, 0-1-0	(Tennessee Tech '43)	Born 8-11-20
Tennessee Tech	Tangerine 12-30-60	Citadel 0-27 (Eddie Teague)
RON TURNER, 1-1-0	(Pacific [Cal.] '77)	Born 12-5-53
Illinois	Micronpc.com 12-30-99	Virginia 63-21 (George Welsh)
Illinois	Sugar 1-1-02	LSU 34-47 (Nick Saban)
BOB TYLER, 1-0-0	(Mississippi '58)	Born 7-4-32
Mississippi St.	Sun 12-28-74	North Carolina 26-24 (Bill Dooley)
THAD "PIE" VANN, 0-2-0	(Mississippi '28)	Born 9-22-07
Southern Miss.	Sun 1-1-53	Pacific (Cal.) 7-26 (Ernie Jorge)
Southern Miss.	Sun 1-1-54	UTEP 14-37 (Mike Brumbelow)
JOHN VAUGHT, 10-8-0	(TCU '33)	Born 5-6-08
Mississippi	Delta 1-1-48	TCU 13-9 (Leo "Dutch" Meyer)
Mississippi	Sugar 1-1-53	Georgia Tech 7-24 (Bobby Dodd)
Mississippi	Sugar 1-1-55	Navy 0-21 (Eddie Erdelatz)
Mississippi	Cotton 1-2-56	TCU 14-13 (Abe Martin)
Mississippi	Sugar 1-1-58	Texas 39-7 (Darrell Royal)
Mississippi	Gator 12-27-58	Florida 7-3 (Bob Woodruff)
Mississippi	Sugar 1-1-60	LSU 21-0 (Paul Dietzel)

Coach/School	Bowl/Date	Opponent/Score (Coach)
Mississippi	Sugar 1-2-61	Rice 14-6 (Jess Neely)
Mississippi	Cotton 1-1-62	Texas 7-12 (Darrell Royal)
Mississippi	Sugar 1-1-63	Arkansas 17-13 (Frank Broyles)
Mississippi	Sugar 1-1-64	Alabama 7-12 (Paul "Bear" Bryant)
Mississippi	Bluebonnet 12-19-64	Tulsa 7-14 (Glenn Dobbs)
Mississippi	Liberty 12-18-65	Auburn 13-7 (Ralph "Shug" Jordan)
Mississippi	Bluebonnet 12-17-66	Texas 0-19 (Darrell Royal)
Mississippi	Sun 12-30-67	UTEP 7-14 (Bobby Dobbs)
Mississippi	Liberty 12-14-68	Virginia Tech 34-17 (Jerry Claiborne)
Mississippi	Sugar 1-1-70	Arkansas 27-22 (Frank Broyles)
Mississippi	Gator 1-2-71	Auburn 28-35 (Ralph "Shug" Jordan)

DICK VERMEIL, 1-0-0 (San Jose St. '58) Born 10-30-36
| UCLA | Rose 1-1-76 | Ohio St. 23-10 (Woody Hayes) |

BOB VOIGTS, 1-0-0 (Northwestern '39) Born 3-29-16
| Northwestern | Rose 1-1-49 | California 20-14 (Lynn "Pappy" Waldorf) |

JIM WACKER, 0-1-0 (Valparaiso '60) Born 4-28-37
| TCU | Bluebonnet 12-31-84 | West Virginia 14-31 (Don Nehlen) |

WALLACE WADE, 2-2-1 (Brown '17) Born 6-15-1892
Alabama	Rose 1-1-26	Washington 20-19 (Enoch Bagshaw)
Alabama	Rose 1-1-27	Stanford 7-7 (Glenn "Pop" Warner)
Alabama	Rose 1-1-31	Washington St. 24-0 (Orin "Babe" Hollingbery)
Duke	Rose 1-2-39	Southern California 3-7 (Howard Jones)
Duke	Rose 1-1-42	Oregon St. 16-20 (Lon Stiner)

BOB WAGNER, 1-1-0 (Wittenberg '69) Born 5-16-47
| Hawaii | Aloha 12-25-89 | Michigan St. 13-33 (George Perles) |
| Hawaii | Holiday 12-30-92 | Illinois 27-17 (Lou Tepper) |

JIM WALDEN, 0-1-0 (Wyoming '60) Born 4-10-38
| Washington St. | Holiday 12-18-81 | Brigham Young 36-38 (LaVell Edwards) |

LYNN "PAPPY" WALDORF, 0-3-0 (Syracuse '25) Born 10-3-02
California	Rose 1-1-49	Northwestern 14-20 (Bob Voigts)
California	Rose 1-2-50	Ohio St. 14-17 (Wes Fesler)
California	Rose 1-1-51	Michigan 6-14 (Bennie Oosterbaan)

D.C. "PEAHEAD" WALKER, 1-1-0 (Samford '22) Born 2-17-1900
| Wake Forest | Gator 1-1-46 | South Carolina 26-14 (Johnnie McMillan) |
| Wake Forest | Dixie 1-1-49 | Baylor 7-20 (Bob Woodruff) |

ED WALKER, 0-1-0 (Stanford '27) Born 3-25-01
| Mississippi | Orange 1-1-36 | Catholic 19-20 (Arthur "Dutch" Bergman) |

RANDY WALKER, 0-1-0 (Miami [Ohio] '76) Born 5-29-54
| Northwestern | Alamo 12-20-00 | Nebraska 17-66 (Frank Solich) |

BILL WALSH, 3-0-0 (San Jose St. '54) Born 11-30-31
Stanford	Sun 12-31-77	LSU 24-14 (Charlie McClendon)
Stanford	Bluebonnet 12-31-78	Georgia 25-22 (Vince Dooley)
Stanford	Blockbuster 1-1-93	Penn St. 24-3 (Joe Paterno)

DALLAS WARD, 1-0-0 (Oregon St. '27) Born 8-11-06
| Colorado | Orange 1-1-57 | Clemson 27-21 (Frank Howard) |

MURRAY WARMATH, 1-1-0 (Tennessee '35) Born 12-26-13
| Minnesota | Rose 1-2-61 | Washington 7-17 (Jim Owens) |
| Minnesota | Rose 1-1-62 | UCLA 21-3 (Bill Barnes) |

GLENN "POP" WARNER, 1-2-1 (Cornell '95) Born 4-5-1871
Stanford	Rose 1-1-25	Notre Dame 10-27 (Knute Rockne)
Stanford	Rose 1-1-27	Alabama 7-7 (Wallace Wade)
Stanford	Rose 1-2-28	Pittsburgh 7-6 (Jock Sutherland)
Temple	Sugar 1-1-35	Tulane 14-20 (Ted Cox)

CHARLIE WEATHERBIE, 2-0-0 (Oklahoma St. '77) Born 1-17-55
| Utah St. | Las Vegas 12-17-93 | Ball St. 42-33 (Paul Schudel) |
| Navy | Aloha 12-25-96 | California 42-38 (Steve Mariucci) |

DeWITT WEAVER, 2-1-0 (Tennessee '37) Born 5-11-12
Texas Tech	Sun 1-1-52	Pacific (Cal.) 25-14 (Ernie Jorge)
Texas Tech	Gator 1-1-54	Auburn 35-13 (Ralph "Shug" Jordan)
Texas Tech	Sun 1-2-56	Wyoming 14-21 (Phil Dickens)

BILL WEEKS, 1-0-0 (Iowa St. '51) Born 10-20-29
| New Mexico | Aviation 12-9-61 | Western Mich. 28-12 (Merle Schlosser) |

RALPH "PEST" WELCH, 0-1-0 (Purdue '30) Born 8-11-07
| Washington | Rose 1-1-44 | Southern California 0-29 (Jeff Cravath) |

GEORGE WELSH, 5-10-0 (Navy '56) Born 8-26-33
Navy	Holiday 12-22-78	Brigham Young 23-16 (LaVell Edwards)
Navy	Garden State 12-14-80	Houston 0-35 (Bill Yeoman)
Navy	Liberty 12-30-81	Ohio St. 28-31 (Earle Bruce)
Virginia	Peach 12-31-84	Purdue 27-24 (Leon Burtnett)
Virginia	All-American 12-22-87	Brigham Young 22-16 (LaVell Edwards)
Virginia	Fla. Citrus 1-1-90	Illinois 21-31 (John Mackovic)
Virginia	Sugar 1-1-91	Tennessee 22-23 (Johnny Majors)
Virginia	Gator 12-29-91	Oklahoma 14-48 (Gary Gibbs)
Virginia	Carquest 1-1-94	Boston College 13-31 (Tom Coughlin)
Virginia	Independence 12-28-94	TCU 20-10 (Pat Sullivan)
Virginia	Peach 12-30-95	Georgia 34-27 (Ray Goff)
Virginia	Carquest 12-27-96	Miami (Fla.) 21-31 (Butch Davis)
Virginia	Peach 12-31-98	Georgia 33-35 (Jim Donnan)
Virginia	Micronpc.com 12-30-99	Illinois 21-63 (Ron Turner)
Virginia	Oahu Classic 12-24-00	Georgia 14-37 (Jim Donnan)

TOMMY WEST, 1-3-0 (Tennessee '75) Born 7-31-54
Clemson	Peach 12-31-93	Kentucky 14-13 (Bill Curry)
Clemson	Gator 1-1-96	Syracuse 0-41 (Paul Pasqualoni)
Clemson	Peach 12-28-96	LSU 7-10 (Gerry DiNardo)
Clemson	Peach 1-2-98	Auburn 17-21 (Terry Bowden)

MIKE WHITE, 0-3-0 (California '58) Born 1-3-36
Illinois	Liberty 12-29-82	Alabama 15-21 (Paul "Bear" Bryant)
Illinois	Rose 1-2-84	UCLA 9-45 (Terry Donahue)
Illinois	Peach 12-31-85	Army 29-31 (Jim Young)

JOHN WILCE, 0-1-0 (Wisconsin '10) Born 5-12-88
| Ohio St. | Rose 1-1-21 | California 0-28 (Andy Smith) |

BUD WILKINSON, 6-2-0 (Minnesota '37) Born 4-12-16
Oklahoma	Sugar 1-1-49	North Carolina 14-6 (Carl Snavely)
Oklahoma	Sugar 1-2-50	LSU 35-0 (Gaynell Tinsley)
Oklahoma	Sugar 1-1-51	Kentucky 7-13 (Paul "Bear" Bryant)
Oklahoma	Orange 1-1-54	Maryland 7-0 (Jim Tatum)
Oklahoma	Orange 1-2-56	Maryland 20-6 (Jim Tatum)
Oklahoma	Orange 1-1-58	Duke 48-21 (Bill Murray)
Oklahoma	Orange 1-1-59	Syracuse 21-6 (Ben Schwartzwalder)
Oklahoma	Orange 1-1-63	Alabama 0-17 (Paul "Bear" Bryant)

BOBBY WILLIAMS, 2-0-0 (Purdue '82) Born 11-21-58
| Michigan St. | Fla. Citrus 1-1-00 | Florida 37-34 (Steve Spurrier) |
| Michigan St. | Silicon Valley 12-31-01 | Fresno St. 44-35 (Pat Hill) |

IVY WILLIAMSON, 0-1-0 (Michigan '33) Born 2-4-11
| Wisconsin | Rose 1-1-53 | Southern California 0-7 (Jess Hill) |

TYRONE WILLINGHAM, 1-4-0 (Michigan St. '77) Born 12-30-53
Stanford	Liberty 12-30-95	East Caro. 13-19 (Steve Logan)
Stanford	Sun 12-31-96	Michigan St. 38-0 (Nick Saban)
Stanford	Rose 1-1-00	Wisconsin 9-17 (Barry Alvarez)
Stanford	Seattle 12-27-01	Georgia Tech 14-24 (Mac McWhorter)
Notre Dame	Gator 1-1-03	North Carolina St. 6-28 (Chuck Amato)

TOM WILSON, 2-0-0 (Texas Tech '66) Born 2-24-44
| Texas A&M | Hall of Fame 12-20-78 | Iowa St. 28-12 (Earle Bruce) |
| Texas A&M | Independence 12-12-81 | Oklahoma St. 33-16 (Jimmy Johnson) |

SAM WINNINGHAM, 0-1-0 (Colorado '50) Born 10-11-26
| Cal St. Northridge | Pasadena 12-2-67 | West Tex. A&M 13-35 (Joe Kerbel) |

BOB WOODRUFF, 2-1-0 (Tennessee '39) Born 3-14-16
Baylor	Dixie 1-1-49	Wake Forest 20-7 (D.C. "Peahead" Walker)
Florida	Gator 1-1-53	Tulsa 14-13 (J.O. "Buddy" Brothers)
Florida	Gator 12-27-58	Mississippi 3-7 (John Vaught)

WARREN WOODSON, 6-1-0 (Baylor '24) Born 2-24-03
Hardin-Simmons	Sun 1-1-43	Second Air Force 7-13 (Red Reese)
Hardin-Simmons	Alamo 1-4-47	Denver 20-6 (Clyde "Cac" Hubbard)
Hardin-Simmons	Harbor 1-1-48	San Diego St. 53-0 (Bill Schutte)
Hardin-Simmons	Shrine 12-18-48	Ouachita Baptist 40-12 (Wesley Bradshaw)
Hardin-Simmons	Camellia 12-30-48	Wichita St. 49-12 (Jim Trimble)
New Mexico St.	Sun 12-31-59	North Texas 28-8 (Odus Mitchell)
New Mexico St.	Sun 12-31-60	Utah St. 20-13 (John Ralston)

BOWDEN WYATT, 2-2-0 (Tennessee '39) Born 11-3-17
Wyoming	Gator 1-1-51	Wash. & Lee 20-7 (George Barclay)
Arkansas	Cotton 1-1-55	Georgia Tech 6-14 (Bobby Dodd)
Tennessee	Sugar 1-1-57	Baylor 7-13 (Sam Boyd)
Tennessee	Gator 12-26-57	Texas A&M 3-0 (Paul "Bear" Bryant)

BILL YEOMAN, 6-4-1 (Army '50) Born 12-26-27
Houston	Tangerine 12-22-62	Miami (Ohio) 49-21 (John Pont)
Houston	Bluebonnet 12-31-69	Auburn 36-7 (Ralph "Shug" Jordan)
Houston	Bluebonnet 12-31-71	Colorado 17-29 (Eddie Crowder)
Houston	Bluebonnet 12-29-73	Tulane 47-7 (Bennie Ellender)
Houston	Bluebonnet 12-23-74	North Carolina St. 31-31 (Lou Holtz)
Houston	Cotton 1-1-77	Maryland 30-21 (Jerry Claiborne)
Houston	Cotton 1-1-79	Notre Dame 34-35 (Dan Devine)
Houston	Cotton 1-1-80	Nebraska 17-14 (Tom Osborne)
Houston	Garden State 12-14-80	Navy 35-0 (George Welsh)
Houston	Sun 12-26-81	Oklahoma 14-40 (Barry Switzer)
Houston	Cotton 1-1-85	Boston College 28-45 (Jack Bicknell)

FIELDING "HURRY UP" YOST, 1-0-0 (Lafayette '97) Born 4-30-1871
| Michigan | Rose 1-1-02 | Stanford 49-0 (Charlie Fickert) |

JIM YOUNG, 5-1-0 (Bowling Green '57) Born 4-21-35
Purdue	Peach 12-25-78	Georgia Tech 41-21 (Pepper Rodgers)
Purdue	Bluebonnet 12-31-79	Tennessee 27-22 (Johnny Majors)
Purdue	Liberty 12-27-80	Missouri 28-25 (Warren Powers)
Army	Cherry 12-22-84	Michigan St. 10-6 (George Perles)
Army	Peach 12-31-85	Illinois 31-29 (Mike White)
Army	Sun 12-24-88	Alabama 28-29 (Bill Curry)

RON ZOOK, 0-1-0 (Miami [Ohio] '76) Born 4-28-54
| Florida | Outback 1-1-03 | Michigan 30-38 (Lloyd Carr) |

Coaches Who Have Taken More Than One Team to a Bowl Game

FIVE TEAMS (1)
* Lou Holtz: William & Mary, North Carolina St., Arkansas, Notre Dame & South Carolina

FOUR TEAMS (3)
Earle Bruce: Tampa, Iowa St., Ohio St. & Colorado St.
Bill Mallory: Miami (Ohio), Colorado, Northern Ill. & Indiana
Larry Smith: Tulane, Arizona, Southern California & Missouri

THREE TEAMS (13)
* Mack Brown: Tulane, North Carolina & Texas
Bear Bryant: Kentucky, Texas A&M & Alabama
Jim Carlen: West Virginia, Texas Tech & South Carolina
Jerry Claiborne: Virginia Tech, Maryland & Kentucky
Bill Curry: Georgia Tech, Alabama & Kentucky

Bill Dooley: North Carolina, Virginia Tech & Wake Forest
Dennis Erickson: Washington St., Miami (Fla.) & Oregon St.
* Dennis Franchione: New Mexico, TCU & Alabama
* Ken Hatfield: Air Force, Arkansas & Clemson
* John Mackovic: Wake Forest, Illinois & Texas

Johnny Majors: Iowa St., Pittsburgh & Tennessee
* Jackie Sherrill: Pittsburgh, Texas A&M & Mississippi St.
Bowden Wyatt: Wyoming, Arkansas & Tennessee

TWO TEAMS (64)
Fred Akers: Wyoming & Texas
* Gary Barnett: Northwestern & Colorado
John Barnhill: Tennessee & Arkansas
Emory Bellard: Texas A&M & Mississippi St.
Hugo Bezdek: Oregon & Penn St.

Dana X. Bible: Texas A&M & Texas
* Bobby Bowden: West Virginia & Florida St.
Len Casanova: Santa Clara & Oregon
Bobby Collins: Southern Miss. & Southern Methodist
John Cooper: Arizona St. & Ohio St.

Lee Corso: Louisville & Indiana
Dick Crum: Miami (Ohio) & North Carolina
Bob Devaney: Wyoming & Nebraska
Dan Devine: Missouri & Notre Dame
Doug Dickey: Tennessee & Florida

Paul Dietzel: LSU & South Carolina
Pat Dye: East Caro. & Auburn
Pete Elliott: California & Illinois
Jack Elway: San Jose St. & Stanford
Bob Folwell: Pennsylvania & Navy

Danny Ford: Clemson & Arkansas
Hayden Fry: Southern Methodist & Iowa
Vince Gibson: Louisville & Tulane
Sid Gillman: Miami (Ohio) & Cincinnati
Paul Hackett: Pittsburgh & Southern California

Wayne Hardin: Navy & Temple
Woody Hayes: Miami (Ohio) & Ohio St.
Bob Higgins: West Va. Wesleyan & Penn St.
Don James: Kent & Washington
Jimmy Johnson: Oklahoma St. & Miami (Fla.)

Frank Kimbrough: Hardin-Simmons & West Tex. A&M
Jimmy Kitts: Rice & Virginia Tech
* Dirk Koetter: Boise St. & Arizona St.
* Glen Mason: Kansas & Minnesota
Jess Neely: Clemson & Rice

Rick Neuheisel: Colorado & Washington
Homer Norton: Centenary (La.) & Texas A&M
Charley Pell: Clemson & Florida
Jimmy Phelan: Washington & St. Mary's (Cal.)
John Pont: Miami (Ohio) & Indiana

Tommy Prothro: Oregon St. & UCLA
John Ralston: Utah St. & Stanford
* John Robinson: Southern California & UNLV
Pepper Rodgers: Kansas & Georgia Tech
Bobby Ross: Maryland & Georgia Tech

* Nick Saban: Michigan St. & LSU
George Sauer: Kansas & Baylor
Howard Schnellenberger: Miami (Fla.) & Louisville
Steve Sloan: Vanderbilt & Texas Tech
* John L. Smith: Utah St. & Louisville

Bruce Snyder: California & Arizona St.
Steve Spurrier: Duke & Florida
Gene Stallings: Texas A&M & Alabama
Denny Stolz: Bowling Green & San Diego St.
Jim Tatum: Oklahoma & Maryland

* Joe Tiller: Wyoming & Purdue
Ted Tollner: Southern California & San Diego St.
Wallace Wade: Alabama & Duke

Pop Warner: Stanford & Temple
Charlie Weatherbie: Utah St. & Navy

George Welsh: Navy & Virginia
Bob Woodruff: Baylor & Florida
Warren Woodson: Hardin-Simmons & New Mexico St.
Jim Young: Purdue & Army

*Active coach.

Coaches With the Most Years Taking One College to a Bowl Game

Coach, Team Taken	Bowls	Consecutive Years
* Joe Paterno, Penn St.	31	13 (1971-83)
Tom Osborne, Nebraska	25	25 (1973-97)
Bear Bryant, Alabama	24	24 (1959-82)
* Bobby Bowden, Florida St.	24	21 (1983-2002)
LaVell Edwards, Brigham Young	22	17 (1978-94)
Vince Dooley, Georgia	20	9 (1980-88)
John Vaught, Mississippi	18	14 (1957-70)
Bo Schembechler, Michigan	17	15 (1975-89)
Darrell Royal, Texas	16	8 (1968-75)
Don James, Washington	14	9 (1979-87)
Hayden Fry, Iowa	14	8 (1981-88)
Bobby Dodd, Georgia Tech	13	6 (1951-56)
Terry Donahue, UCLA	13	8 (1981-88)
Charlie McClendon, LSU	13	4 (1970-73)
Don Nehlen, West Virginia	13	4 (1981-84)
Barry Switzer, Oklahoma	13	8 (1975-82)
* Fisher DeBerry, Air Force	12	4 (1989-92)
Ralph Jordan, Auburn	12	7 (1968-74)
George Welsh, Virginia	12	4 (1993-96)
John Cooper, Ohio St.	11	10 (1990-99)
Woody Hayes, Ohio St.	11	7 (1972-78)
Johnny Majors, Tennessee	11	7 (1981-87)
R.C. Slocum, Texas A&M	11	5 (1989-94)
Steve Spurrier, Florida	11	11 (1992-2002)
Bill Yeoman, Houston	11	4 (1978-81)
Frank Broyles, Arkansas	10	4 (1959-62)
Fred Akers, Texas	9	9 (1977-85)
Bob Devaney, Nebraska	9	5 (1962-66)
Pat Dye, Auburn	9	9 (1982-90)
* Lou Holtz, Notre Dame	9	9 (1987-95)
Bill McCartney, Colorado	9	7 (1988-94)
John McKay, Southern California	9	4 (1966-69; 1972-75)
Earle Bruce, Ohio St.	8	8 (1979-86)
Wally Butts, Georgia	8	4 (1945-48)
Danny Ford, Clemson	8	5 (1985-89)
* John Robinson, Southern California	8	4 (1976-79)
Grant Teaff, Baylor	8	2 (1979-80; 1985-86; 1991-92)
Bud Wilkinson, Oklahoma	8	3 (1948-50)

*Active coach.

Coaches Who Have Coached In a Bowl Game and Also Coached a Team in the NCAA Basketball Tournament

Coach, School	Bowl	NCAA Tournament
Clarence "Nibs" Price, California	Rose 1-1-29	NCAA 1946
E.L. "Dick" Romney, Utah St.	Raisin 1-1-47	NCAA 1939

Conference Bowl Records

2002-03 Bowl Records by Conference

Conference (Teams in Bowls)	W-L	Pct.
Sun Belt (1)	1-0	1.000
Big Ten (7)	5-2	.714
Western Athletic (3)	2-1	.667
Big 12 (8)	5-3	.625
Big East (5)	3-2	.600
Atlantic Coast (7)	4-3	.571
Mid-American (2)	1-1	.500
Southeastern (7)	3-4	.429
Conference USA (5)	2-3	.400
Pacific-10 (7)	2-5	.286
Mountain West (3)	0-3	.000
Independent (1)	0-1	.000

All-Time Division I-A Won-Lost Records

(Through 2002-03 Bowls, Using Present Conference Alignments)

ATLANTIC COAST CONFERENCE

School	Bowls	W-L-T	Pct.	Last Appearance
Clemson	26	13-13-0	.500	2002 Tangerine
Duke	8	3-5-0	.375	1995 Hall of Fame
Florida St.	31	18-11-2	.613	2003 Sugar
Georgia Tech	31	20-11-0	.645	2002 Silicon Valley
Maryland	19	7-10-2	.421	2002 Peach
North Carolina	24	12-12-0	.500	2001 Peach
North Carolina St.	21	10-10-1	.500	2003 Gator
Virginia	13	5-8-0	.385	2002 Cont. Tire
Wake Forest	6	4-2-0	.667	2002 Seattle
Current Members	**179**	**92-82-5**	**.528**	

BIG EAST CONFERENCE

School	Bowls	W-L-T	Pct.	Last Appearance
Boston College	14	8-6-0	.571	2002 Motor City
Miami (Fla.)	27	15-12-0	.556	2003 Fiesta
Pittsburgh	22	10-12-0	.455	2002 Insight
Rutgers	1	0-1-0	.000	1978 Garden State
Syracuse	21	12-8-1	.595	2001 Insight.com
Temple	2	1-1-0	.500	1979 Garden State
Virginia Tech	16	6-10-0	.375	2002 San Francisco
West Virginia	22	9-13-0	.409	2002 Cont. Tire
Current Members	**125**	**61-63-1**	**.492**	

BIG 12 CONFERENCE

School	Bowls	W-L-T	Pct.	Last Appearance
North				
Iowa St.	7	1-6-0	.143	2002 Humanitarian
Kansas	8	3-5-0	.375	1995 Aloha
Kansas St.	11	6-5-0	.545	2002 Holiday
Missouri	20	9-11-0	.450	1998 Insight.com
Nebraska	41	20-21-0	.488	2002 Independence
South				
Baylor	16	8-8-0	.500	1994 Alamo
Oklahoma	36	23-12-1	.653	2003 Rose
Oklahoma St.	14	10-4-0	.714	2002 Houston
Texas	42	20-20-2	.500	2003 Cotton
Texas A&M	27	13-14-0	.481	2001 galleryfurniture.com
Texas Tech	26	6-19-1	.250	2002 Tangerine
Current Members	**273**	**130-139-4**	**.484**	

BIG TEN CONFERENCE

School	Bowls	W-L-T	Pct.	Last Appearance
Illinois	14	6-8-0	.429	2002 Sugar
Indiana	8	3-5-0	.375	1993 Independence
Iowa	18	9-8-1	.528	2003 Orange
Michigan	34	18-16-0	.529	2003 Outback
Michigan St.	16	7-9-0	.438	2001 Silicon Valley
Minnesota	8	3-5-0	.375	2002 Music City
Northwestern	4	1-3-0	.250	2000 Alamo
Ohio St.	34	15-19-0	.441	2003 Fiesta
Penn St.	37	23-12-2	.649	2003 Capital One
Purdue	11	7-4-0	.636	2002 Sun
Wisconsin	14	8-6-0	.571	2002 Alamo
Current Members	**198**	**100-95-3**	**.513**	

CONFERENCE USA

School	Bowls	W-L-T	Pct.	Last Appearance
UAB	0	0-0-0	.000	Has never appeared
Army	4	2-2-0	.500	1996 Independence
Cincinnati	6	2-4-0	.333	2002 New Orleans
East Caro.	7	4-3-0	.571	2001 GMAC
Houston	14	7-6-1	.536	1996 Liberty
Louisville	10	4-5-1	.450	2002 GMAC
Memphis	1	1-0-0	1.000	1971 Pasadena
Southern Miss.	11	5-6-0	.455	2002 Houston
TCU	20	7-12-1	.375	2002 Liberty
Tulane	10	4-6-0	.400	2002 Hawaii
Current Members	**83**	**36-44-3**	**.452**	

MID-AMERICAN CONFERENCE

School	Bowls	W-L-T	Pct.	Last Appearance
East				
Akron	0	0-0-0	.000	Has never appeared
Bowling Green	5	2-3-0	.400	1992 Las Vegas
Buffalo	0	0-0-0	.000	Has never appeared
Kent St.	1	0-1-0	.000	1972 Tangerine
Marshall	6	5-1-0	.833	2002 GMAC
Miami (Ohio)	7	5-2-0	.714	1986 California
Ohio	2	0-2-0	.000	1968 Tangerine

School	Bowls	W-L-T	Pct.	Last Appearance
West				
Ball St.	3	0-3-0	.000	1996 Las Vegas
Central Mich.	2	0-2-0	.000	1994 Las Vegas
Eastern Mich.	1	1-0-0	1.000	1987 California
Northern Ill.	1	1-0-0	1.000	1983 California
Toledo	8	6-2-0	.750	2002 Motor City
Western Mich.	2	0-2-0	.000	1988 California
Current Members	**38**	**20-18-0**	**.526**	

MOUNTAIN WEST CONFERENCE

School	Bowls	W-L-T	Pct.	Last Appearance
Air Force	17	8-8-1	.500	2002 San Francisco
Brigham Young	23	7-15-1	.326	2001 Liberty
Colorado St.	9	4-5-0	.444	2002 Liberty
UNLV	3	3-0-0	1.000	2000 Las Vegas
New Mexico	7	2-4-1	.357	2002 Las Vegas
San Diego St.	5	1-4-0	.200	1998 Las Vegas
Utah	8	5-3-0	.625	2001 Las Vegas
Wyoming	10	4-6-0	.400	1993 Copper
Current Members	**82**	**34-45-3**	**.433**	

PACIFIC-10 CONFERENCE

School	Bowls	W-L-T	Pct.	Last Appearance
Arizona	13	5-7-1	.423	1998 Holiday
Arizona St.	20	10-9-1	.525	2002 Holiday
California	13	5-7-1	.423	1996 Aloha
Oregon	17	7-10-0	.412	2002 Seattle
Oregon St.	7	3-4-0	.429	2002 Insight
Southern California	40	25-15-0	.625	2001 Las Vegas
Stanford	20	9-10-1	.475	2001 Seattle
UCLA	24	12-11-1	.521	2002 Las Vegas
Washington	29	14-14-1	.500	2002 Sun
Washington St.	9	5-4-0	.556	2003 Rose
Current Members	**193**	**96-91-6**	**.513**	

SOUTHEASTERN CONFERENCE

School	Bowls	W-L-T	Pct.	Last Appearance
Eastern				
Florida	30	14-16-0	.467	2003 Outback
Georgia	38	20-15-3	.566	2003 Sugar
Kentucky	10	5-5-0	.500	1999 Music City
South Carolina	11	3-8-0	.273	2002 Outback
Tennessee	43	23-20-0	.535	2002 Peach
Vanderbilt	3	1-1-1	.500	1982 Hall of Fame
Western				
Alabama	51	29-19-3	.598	2001 Independence
Arkansas	33	10-20-3	.348	2002 Music City
Auburn	29	15-12-2	.552	2003 Capital One
LSU	34	16-17-1	.485	2003 Cotton
Mississippi	30	18-12-0	.600	2002 Independence
Mississippi St.	12	6-6-0	.500	2000 Independence
Current Members	**316**	**155-148-13**	**.511**	

SUN BELT CONFERENCE

School	Bowls	W-L-T	Pct.	Last Appearance
Arkansas St.	0	0-0-0	.000	Has never appeared
Idaho	1	1-0-0	1.000	1998 Humanitarian
La.-Lafayette	0	0-0-0	.000	Has never appeared
La.-Monroe	0	0-0-0	.000	Has never appeared
Middle Tenn.	0	0-0-0	.000	Has never appeared
New Mexico St.	3	2-0-1	.833	1960 Sun
North Texas	4	1-3-0	.250	2002 New Orleans
Current Members	**8**	**4-3-1**	**.563**	

WESTERN ATHLETIC CONFERENCE

School	Bowls	W-L-T	Pct.	Last Appearance
Boise St.	3	3-0-0	1.000	2002 Humanitarian
Fresno St.	13	7-6-0	.538	2002 Silicon Valley
Hawaii	4	2-2-0	.500	2002 Hawaii
Louisiana Tech	4	1-2-1	.375	2001 Humanitarian
Nevada	5	2-3-0	.400	1996 Las Vegas
Rice	7	4-3-0	.571	1961 Bluebonnet
San Jose St.	7	4-3-0	.571	1990 California
Southern Methodist	11	4-6-1	.409	1984 Aloha
UTEP	10	5-5-0	.500	2000 Humanitarian
Tulsa	11	4-7-0	.364	1991 Freedom
Current Members	**75**	**36-37-2**	**.493**	

INDEPENDENTS

School	Bowls	W-L-T	Pct.	Last Appearance
UCF	0	0-0-0	.000	Has never appeared
Connecticut	0	0-0-0	.000	Has never appeared
Navy	9	4-4-1	.500	1996 Aloha
Notre Dame	25	13-12-0	.520	2003 Gator
South Fla.	0	0-0-0	.000	Has never appeared
Troy St.	0	0-0-0	.000	Has never appeared
Utah St.	5	1-4-0	.200	1997 Humanitarian
Current Members	**39**	**18-20-1**	**.474**	

Award Winners in Bowl Games

Most Valuable Players in Major Bowls

Bowls that are played twice in the same calendar year (i.e., January and December) are listed in chronological order.

ALAMO BOWL

Year	Player, Team, Position
1993	Dave Barr, California, quarterback (offense)
	Jerrott Willard, California, linebacker (defense)
	Larry Blue, Iowa, defensive tackle (sportsmanship award)
1994	Chad Davis, Washington St., quarterback (offense)
	Ron Childs, Washington St., linebacker (defense)
	Adrian Robinson, Baylor, defensive back (sportsmanship award)
1995	Kyle Bryant, Texas A&M, kicker (offense)
	Keith Mitchell, Texas A&M, linebacker (defense)
	Jarrett Irons, Michigan, linebacker (sportsmanship award)
1996	Sedrick Shaw, Iowa, running back (offense)
	James DeVries, Iowa, defensive lineman (defense)
	Shane Dunn, Texas Tech (sportsmanship award)
1997	Billy Dicken, Purdue, quarterback (offense)
	Adrian Beasley, Purdue, safety (defense)
	Kevin Williams, Oklahoma St., cornerback (sportsmanship award)
1998	Drew Brees, Purdue, quarterback (offense)
	Rosevelt Colvin, Purdue, defensive end (defense)
	Jarrod Cooper, Kansas St., free safety (sportsmanship award)
1999	Rashard Casey, Penn St., quarterback (offense)
	LaVar Arrington, Penn St., linebacker (defense)
2000	Dan Alexander, running back, Nebraska (offense)
	Kyle Vanden Bosch, defensive line, Nebraska (defense)
2001	Aaron Greving, running back, Iowa (offense)
	Derrick Pickens, defensive line, Iowa (defense)
2002	Brooks Bollinger, Wisconsin, quarterback (offense)
	Jeff Mack, Wisconsin, linebacker (defense)
	Zac Colvin, Colorado, wide receiver (sportsmanship award)

CAPITAL ONE BOWL
(Formerly Tangerine Bowl and Florida Citrus Bowl)

Year	Player, Team, Position
1949	Dale McDaniels, Murray St.
	Ted Scown, Sul Ross St.
1950	Don Henigan, St. Vincent
	Chick Davis, Emory & Henry
1951	Pete Anania, Charleston (W.Va.)
	Charles Hubbard, Charleston (W.Va.)
1952	Bill Johnson, Stetson
	Dave Laude, Stetson
1953	Marvin Brown, Tex. A&M-Commerce
1954	Billy Ray Norris, Tex. A&M-Commerce
	Bobby Spann, Arkansas St.
1955	Bill Englehardt, Neb.-Omaha
1956	Pat Tarquinio, Juniata
1957	Ron Mills, West Tex. A&M
1958	Garry Berry, Tex. A&M-Commerce
	Neal Hinson, Tex. A&M-Commerce
1958	Sam McCord, Tex. A&M-Commerce
1960	Bucky Pitts, Middle Tenn.
	Bob Waters, Presbyterian
	Jerry Nettles, Citadel
1961	Win Herbert, Lamar
1962	Joe Lopasky, Houston
	Billy Roland, Houston
1963	Sharon Miller, Western Ky.
1964	Bill Cline, East Caro.
	Jerry Whelchel, Massachusetts
1965	Dave Alexander, East Caro.
1966	Willie Lanier, Morgan St.
1967	Errol Hook, Tenn.-Martin
	Gordon Lambert, Tenn.-Martin
1968	Buster O'Brien, Richmond, back
	Walker Gillette, Richmond, lineman
1969	Chuck Ealy, Toledo, back
	Dan Crockett, Toledo, lineman
1970	Chuck Ealy, Toledo, back
	Vince Hubler, William & Mary, lineman

Year	Player, Team, Position
1971	Chuck Ealy, Toledo, back
	Mel Long, Toledo, lineman
1972	Freddie Solomon, Tampa, back
	Jack Lambert, Kent St., lineman
1973	Chuck Varner, Miami (Ohio), back
	Brad Cousino, Miami (Ohio), lineman
1974	Sherman Smith, Miami (Ohio), back
	Brad Cousino, Miami (Ohio), lineman (tie)
	John Roudebush, Miami (Ohio), lineman (tie)
1975	Rob Carpenter, Miami (Ohio), back
	Jeff Kelly, Miami (Ohio), lineman
1976	Terry Miller, Oklahoma St., back
	Phillip Dokes, Oklahoma St., lineman
	Most Valuable Player (1977-Present)
1977	Jimmy Jordan, Florida St., quarterback
1978	Ted Brown, North Carolina St., running back
1979	David Woodley, LSU, quarterback
1980	Cris Collinsworth, Florida, wide receiver
1981	Jeff Gaylord, Missouri, linebacker
1982	Randy Campbell, Auburn, quarterback
1983	Johnnie Jones, Tennessee, running back
1984	James Jackson, Georgia, quarterback
1985	Larry Kolic, Ohio St., middle guard
1987	Aundray Bruce, Auburn, linebacker
1988	Rodney Williams, Clemson, quarterback
1989	Terry Allen, Clemson, tailback
1990	Jeff George, Illinois, quarterback
1991	Shawn Jones, Georgia Tech, quarterback
1992	Mike Pawlawski, California, quarterback
1993	Garrison Hearst, Georgia, running back
1994	Bobby Engram, Penn St., wide receiver (overall)
	Charlie Garner, Tennessee, tailback (offense)
	Lee Rubin, Penn St., free safety (defense)
	Raymond Austin, Tennessee, strong safety (defense)
1995	Sherman Williams, Alabama, running back (overall)
	Joey Galloway, Ohio St., wide receiver (offense)
	Dameian Jeffries, Alabama, defensive end (defense)
	Matt Finkes, Ohio St., defensive end (defense)
1996	Jay Graham, Tennessee, running back (overall)
	Rickey Dudley, Ohio St., tight end (offense)
	Leonard Little, Tennessee, defensive end (defense)
	Matt Finkes, Ohio St., defensive end (defense)
1997	Peyton Manning, Tennessee, quarterback (overall)
	Brian Musso, Northwestern, wide receiver (offense)
	Tyrone Hines, Tennessee, linebacker (defense)
	Mike Nelson, Northwestern, linebacker (defense)
1998	Fred Taylor, Florida, tailback (overall)
	Fred Weary, Florida, cornerback (defense)
	Chris Eberly, Penn St., tailback (offense)
	Brandon Short, Penn St., linebacker (defense)
1999	Anthony Thomas, Michigan, running back
	Sam Sword, Michigan, linebacker (defense)
2000	Plaxico Burress, Michigan St., wide receiver (overall)
	Travis Taylor, Florida, wide receiver (offense)
	Julien Peterson, Michigan St. (defense)
	Andra Davis, Florida (defense)
2001	Anthony Thomas, Michigan, running back (overall)
	Ben Leard, Auburn, quarterback (offense)
	Javar Mills, Auburn, defensive end (defense)
	Eric Wilson, Michigan, defensive line (defense)
2002	Casey Clausen, Tennessee, quarterback (overall)
	B.J. Askew, Michigan, running back (offense)
	John Henderson, Tennessee, defensive line (defense)
	Larry Foote, Michigan, linebacker (defense)
2003	Ronnie Brown, Auburn, running back (overall)
	Michael Robinson, Penn St., quarterback (offense)
	Dontarrious Thomas, Auburn, linebacker (defense)
	Anthony Adams, Penn St., defensive tackle (defense)

CONTINENTAL TIRE BOWL

Year	Player, Team, Position
2002	Wali Lundy, Virginia, running back

COTTON BOWL

Year	Player, Team, Position
1937	Ki Aldrich, TCU, center
	Sammy Baugh, TCU, quarterback
	L.D. Meyer, TCU, end

Year	Player, Team, Position
1938	Ernie Lain, Rice, back
	Byron "Whizzer" White, Colorado, quarterback
1939	Jerry Dowd, St. Mary's (Tex.), center
	Elmer Tarbox, Texas Tech, back
1940	Banks McFadden, Clemson, back
1941	Charles Henke, Texas A&M, guard
	John Kimbrough, Texas A&M, fullback
	Chip Routt, Texas A&M, tackle
	Lou De Filippo, Fordham, center
	Joe Ungerer, Fordham, tackle
1942	Martin Ruby, Texas A&M, tackle
	Jimmy Nelson, Alabama, halfback
	Holt Rast, Alabama, end
	Don Whitmire, Alabama, tackle
1943	Jack Freeman, Texas, guard
	Roy McKay, Texas, fullback
	Stanley Mauldin, Texas, tackle
	Harvey Hardy, Georgia Tech, guard
	Jack Marshall, Georgia Tech, end
1944	Joe Parker, Texas, end
	Martin Ruby, Randolph Field, tackle
	Glenn Dobbs, Randolph Field, quarterback
1945	Neil Armstrong, Oklahoma St., end
	Bob Fenimore, Oklahoma St., back
	Ralph Foster, Oklahoma St., tackle
1946	Hub Bechtol, Texas, end
	Bobby Layne, Texas, back
	Jim Kekeris, Missouri, tackle
1947	Alton Baldwin, Arkansas, end
	Y.A. Tittle, LSU, quarterback
1948	Doak Walker, Southern Methodist, back
	Steve Suhey, Penn St., guard
1949	Kyle Rote, Southern Methodist, back
	Doak Walker, Southern Methodist, back
	Brad Ecklund, Oregon, center
	Norm Van Brocklin, Oregon, quarterback
1950	Billy Burkhalter, Rice, halfback
	Joe Watson, Rice, center
	James "Froggie" Williams, Rice, end
1951	Bud McFadin, Texas, guard
	Andy Kozar, Tennessee, fullback
	Hank Lauricella, Tennessee, halfback
	Horace "Bud" Sherrod, Tennessee, defensive end
1952	Keith Flowers, TCU, fullback
	Emery Clark, Kentucky, halfback
	Ray Correll, Kentucky, guard
	Vito "Babe" Parilli, Kentucky, quarterback
1953	Richard Ochoa, Texas, fullback
	Harley Sewell, Texas, guard
	Bob Griesbach, Tennessee, linebacker
1954	Richard Chapman, Rice, tackle
	Dan Hart, Rice, end
	Dicky Maegle, Rice, halfback
1955	Bud Brooks, Arkansas, guard
	George Humphreys, Georgia Tech, fullback
1956	Buddy Alliston, Mississippi, guard
	Eagle Day, Mississippi, quarterback
1957	Norman Hamilton, TCU, tackle
	Jim Brown, Syracuse, halfback
1958	Tom Forrestal, Navy, quarterback
	Tony Stremic, Navy, guard
1959	Jack Spikes, TCU, fullback
	Dave Phillips, Air Force, tackle
1960	Maurice Doke, Texas, guard
	Ernie Davis, Syracuse, halfback
1961	Lance Alworth, Arkansas, halfback
	Dwight Bumgarner, Duke, tackle
1962	Mike Cotten, Texas, quarterback
	Bob Moser, Texas, end
1963	Johnny Treadwell, Texas, guard
	Lynn Amedee, LSU, quarterback
1964	Scott Appleton, Texas, tackle
	Duke Carlisle, Texas, quarterback
1965	Ronnie Caveness, Arkansas, linebacker
	Fred Marshall, Arkansas, quarterback
1966	Joe Labruzzo, LSU, tailback
	David McCormick, LSU, tackle
1966	Kent Lawrence, Georgia, tailback
	George Patton, Georgia, tackle
1968	Grady Allen, Texas A&M, defensive end
	Edd Hargett, Texas A&M, quarterback
	Bill Hobbs, Texas A&M, linebacker
1969	Tom Campbell, Texas, linebacker
	Charles "Cotton" Speyrer, Texas, wide receiver
	James Street, Texas, quarterback
1970	Steve Worster, Texas, fullback
	Bob Olson, Notre Dame, linebacker

Year	Player, Team, Position
1971	Eddie Phillips, Texas, quarterback
	Clarence Ellis, Notre Dame, cornerback
1972	Bruce Bannon, Penn St., defensive end
	Lydell Mitchell, Penn St., running back
1973	Randy Braband, Texas, linebacker
	Alan Lowry, Texas, quarterback
1974	Wade Johnston, Texas, linebacker
	Tony Davis, Nebraska, tailback
1975	Ken Quesenberry, Baylor, safety
	Tom Shuman, Penn St., quarterback
1976	Ike Forte, Arkansas, running back
	Hal McAfee, Arkansas, linebacker
1977	Alois Blackwell, Houston, running back
	Mark Mohr, Houston, cornerback
1978	Vagas Ferguson, Notre Dame, running back
	Bob Golic, Notre Dame, linebacker
1979	David Hodge, Houston, linebacker
	Joe Montana, Notre Dame, quarterback
1980	Terry Elston, Houston, quarterback
	David Hodge, Houston, linebacker
1981	Warren Lyles, Alabama, nose guard
	Major Ogilvie, Alabama, running back
1982	Robert Brewer, Texas, quarterback
	Robbie Jones, Alabama, linebacker
1983	Wes Hopkins, Southern Methodist, strong safety
	Lance McIlhenny, Southern Methodist, quarterback
1984	Jeff Leiding, Texas, linebacker
	John Lastinger, Georgia, quarterback
1985	Bill Romanowski, Boston College, linebacker
	Steve Strachan, Boston College, fullback
1986	Domingo Bryant, Texas A&M, strong safety
	Bo Jackson, Auburn, tailback
1987	Chris Spielman, Ohio St., linebacker
	Roger Vick, Texas A&M, fullback
1988	Adam Bob, Texas A&M, linebacker
	Bucky Richardson, Texas A&M, quarterback
1989	LaSalle Harper, Arkansas, linebacker
	Troy Aikman, UCLA, quarterback
1990	Carl Pickens, Tennessee, free safety
	Chuck Webb, Tennessee, tailback
1991	Craig Erickson, Miami (Fla.), quarterback
	Russell Maryland, Miami (Fla.), defensive lineman
1992	Sean Jackson, Florida St., running back
	Chris Crooms, Texas A&M, safety
1993	Rick Mirer, Notre Dame, quarterback
	Devon McDonald, Notre Dame, defensive end
1994	Lee Becton, Notre Dame, running back
	Antonio Shorter, Texas A&M, linebacker
1995	Keyshawn Johnson, Southern California, wide receiver
	John Herpin, Southern California, cornerback
1996	Herchell Troutman, Colorado, running back
	Marcus Washington, Colorado, defensive back
1997	Steve Sarkisian, Brigham Young, quarterback
	Kevin Lockett, Kansas St., wide receiver
	Shay Muirbrook, Brigham Young, linebacker
1998	Cade McNown, UCLA, quarterback
	Dat Nguyen, Texas A&M, linebacker
1999	Ricky Williams, Texas, running back
	Aaron Babino, Texas, linebacker
2000	Cedric Cobbs, Arkansas, running back
	D.J. Cooper, Arkansas, linebacker
2001	Jonathan Beasley, Kansas St., quarterback
	Chris Johnson, Kansas St., defensive end
2002	Quentin Griffin, Oklahoma, running back
	Roy Williams, Oklahoma, defensive back
2003	Roy Williams, Texas, wide receiver (offense)
	Cory Redding, Texas, defensive line (defense)

FIESTA BOWL

Year	Player, Team, Position
1971	Gary Huff, Florida St., quarterback
	Junior Ah You, Arizona St., defensive end
1972	Woody Green, Arizona St., halfback
	Mike Fink, Missouri, defensive back
1973	Greg Hudson, Arizona St., split end
	Mike Haynes, Arizona St., cornerback
1974	Kenny Walker, Oklahoma St., running back
	Phillip Dokes, Oklahoma St., defensive tackle
1975	John Jefferson, Arizona St., split end
	Larry Gordon, Arizona St., linebacker
1976	Thomas Lott, Oklahoma, quarterback
	Terry Peters, Oklahoma, cornerback
1977	Matt Millen, Penn St., linebacker
	Dennis Sproul, Arizona St., quarterback (sportsmanship award)

Year	Player, Team, Position
1978	James Owens, UCLA, running back
	Jimmy Walker, Arkansas, defensive tackle
	Kenny Easley, UCLA, safety (sportsmanship award)
1979	Mark Schubert, Pittsburgh, kicker
	Dave Liggins, Arizona, safety
	Dan Fidler, Pittsburgh, offensive guard (sportsmanship award)
1980	Curt Warner, Penn St., running back
	Frank Case, Penn St., defensive end (sportsmanship award)
1982	Curt Warner, Penn St., running back
	Leo Wisniewski, Penn St., nose tackle
	George Achica, Southern California, nose guard (sportsmanship award)
1983	Marcus Dupree, Oklahoma, running back
	Jim Jeffcoat, Arizona St., defensive lineman
	Paul Ferrer, Oklahoma, center (sportsmanship award)
1984	John Congemi, Pittsburgh, quarterback
	Rowland Tatum, Ohio St., linebacker (sportsmanship award)
1985	Gaston Green, UCLA, tailback
	James Washington, UCLA, defensive back
	Bruce Fleming, Miami (Fla.), linebacker (sportsmanship award)
1986	Jamie Morris, Michigan, running back
	Mark Messner, Michigan, defensive tackle
	Mike Mallory, Michigan, linebacker (sportsmanship award)
1987	D.J. Dozier, Penn St., running back
	Shane Conlan, Penn St., linebacker
	Paul O'Connor, Miami (Fla.), offensive guard (sportsmanship award)
1988	Danny McManus, Florida St., quarterback
	Neil Smith, Nebraska, defensive lineman
	Steve Forch, Nebraska, linebacker (sportsmanship award)
1989	Tony Rice, Notre Dame, quarterback
	Frank Stams, Notre Dame, defensive end
	Chris Parker, West Virginia, defensive lineman (sportsmanship award)
1990	Peter Tom Willis, Florida St., quarterback
	Odell Haggins, Florida St., nose guard
	Jake Young, Nebraska, center (sportsmanship award)
1991	Browning Nagle, Louisville, quarterback
	Ray Buchanan, Louisville, free safety
1992	O.J. McDuffie, Penn St., wide receiver
	Reggie Givens, Penn St., outside linebacker
1993	Marvin Graves, Syracuse, quarterback
	Kevin Mitchell, Syracuse, nose guard
1994	Chuck Levy, Arizona, running back
	Tedy Bruschi, Arizona, defensive end
	Paul White, Miami (Fla.), cornerback (sportsmanship award)
1995	Kordell Stewart, Colorado, quarterback
	Shannon Clavelle, Colorado, defensive tackle
	Oliver Gibson, Notre Dame, nose guard (sportsmanship award)
1996	Tommie Frazier, Nebraska, quarterback
	Michael Booker, Nebraska, cornerback
	Danny Wuerffel, Florida, quarterback (sportsmanship award)
1997	Curtis Enis, Penn St., tailback
	Brandon Noble, Penn St., defensive tackle
	Ryan Fiebiger, Texas, center (sportsmanship award)
1998	Michael Bishop, Kansas St., quarterback
	Travis Ochs, Kansas St., linebacker
	Jason Walters, Syracuse, end (sportsmanship)
1999	Peerless Price, Tennessee, wide receiver
	Dwayne Goodrich, Tennessee, cornerback
	Ross Brannon, Florida St., offensive tackle (sportsmanship)
2000	Eric Crouch, Nebraska, quarterback
	Mike Brown, Nebraska, defensive back (defense)
2001	Jonathan Smith, Oregon St., quarterback
	Darnell Robinson, Oregon St., linebacker
2002	Joey Harrington, Oregon, quarterback
	Steve Smith, Oregon, defensive back
2003	Craig Krenzel, Ohio St., quarterback
	Mike Doss, Ohio St., defensive back

GATOR BOWL

Year	Player, Team
1946	Nick Sacrinty, Wake Forest
1947	Joe Golding, Oklahoma
1948	Lu Gambino, Maryland
1949	Bobby Gage, Clemson
1950	Bob Ward, Maryland

Year	Player, Team, Position
1951	Eddie Talboom, Wyoming
1952	Jim Dooley, Miami (Fla.)
1953	Marv Matuszak, Tulsa
	John Hall, Florida
1954	Vince Dooley, Auburn
	Bobby Cavazos, Texas Tech
1954	Billy Hooper, Baylor
	Joe Childress, Auburn
1955	Joe Childress, Auburn
	Don Orr, Vanderbilt
1956	Corny Salvaterra, Pittsburgh
	Wade Mitchell, Georgia Tech
1957	John David Crow, Texas A&M
	Bobby Gordon, Tennessee
1958	Dave Hudson, Florida
	Bobby Franklin, Mississippi
1960	Maxie Baughan, Georgia Tech
	Jim Mooty, Arkansas
1960	Bobby Ply, Baylor
	Larry Libertore, Florida
1961	Joe Auer, Georgia Tech
	Galen Hall, Penn St.
1962	Dave Robinson, Penn St.
	Tom Shannon, Florida
1963	David Sicks, Air Force
	Ken Willard, North Carolina
1965	Carl McAdams, Oklahoma
	Fred Biletnikoff, Florida St.
	Steve Tensi, Florida
1965	Donny Anderson, Texas Tech
	Lenny Snow, Georgia Tech
1966	Floyd Little, Syracuse
	Dewey Warren, Tennessee
1967	Tom Sherman, Penn St.
	Kim Hammond, Florida St.
1968	Mike Hall, Alabama
	Terry McMillan, Missouri
1969	Curt Watson, Tennessee
	Mike Kelley, Florida
1971	Archie Manning, Mississippi
	Pat Sullivan, Auburn
1971	James Webster, North Carolina
	Jimmy Poulos, Georgia
1972	Mark Cooney, Colorado
	Wade Whatley, Auburn
1973	Haskell Stanback, Tennessee
	Joe Barnes, Texas Tech
1974	Earl Campbell, Texas
	Phil Gargis, Auburn
1975	Sammy Green, Florida
	Steve Atkins, Maryland
1976	Jim Cefalo, Penn St.
	Al Hunter, Notre Dame
1977	Jerry Butler, Clemson
	Matt Cavanaugh, Pittsburgh
1978	Art Schlichter, Ohio St.
	Steve Fuller, Clemson
1979	John Wangler, Michigan
	Anthony Carter, Michigan
	Matt Kupec, North Carolina
	Amos Lawrence, North Carolina
1980	George Rogers, South Carolina
	Rick Trocano, Pittsburgh
1981	Gary Anderson, Arkansas
	Kelvin Bryant, North Carolina
	Ethan Horton, North Carolina
1982	Paul Woodside, West Virginia
	Greg Allen, Florida St.
1983	Owen Gill, Iowa
	Tony Lilly, Florida
1984	Mike Hold, South Carolina
	Thurman Thomas, Oklahoma St.
1985	Thurman Thomas, Oklahoma St.
	Chip Ferguson, Florida St.
1986	Brad Muster, Stanford
	Rodney Williams, Clemson
1987	Harold Green, South Carolina
	Wendell Davis, LSU
1989	Andre Rison, Michigan St.
	Wayne Johnson, Georgia
1989	Mike Fox, West Virginia
	Levon Kirkland, Clemson
1991	Tyrone Ashley, Mississippi
	Michigan offensive line: Tom Dohring, Matt Elliott, Steve Everitt, Dean Dingman, Greg Skrepenak
1991	Cale Gundy, Oklahoma
	Tyrone Lewis, Virginia
1992	Errict Rhett, Florida
	Reggie Lawrence, North Carolina St.
1993	Brian Burgdorf, Alabama
	Corey Holliday, North Carolina

Year	Player, Team, Position
1994	James Stewart, Tennessee
	Dwayne Thomas, Virginia Tech
1996	Donovan McNabb, Syracuse, quarterback
	Peter Ford, Clemson, cornerback
1997	Oscar Davenport, North Carolina, quarterback
	David Saunders, West Virginia, wide receiver
1998	Chris Keldorf, North Carolina, quarterback
	Al Clark, Virginia Tech, quarterback
1999	Dez White, Georgia Tech, wide receiver
	Joe Hamilton, Georgia Tech, running back
	Autry Denson, Notre Dame, running back
2000	Nate Webster, Miami (Fla.), linebacker
2001	Michael Vick, Virginia Tech, quarterback
2002	Chris Rix, Florida St., quarterback
2003	Phillip Rivers, North Carolina St., quarterback

GMAC BOWL
(Formerly Mobile Alabama Bowl)

Year	Player, Team, Position
1999	Casey Printers, TCU, quarterback
2000	LaDainian Tomlinson, TCU, running back (overall)
	LeRoy Handy, Southern Miss., wide receiver (offense)
	Leo Barnes, Southern Miss., defensive back (defense)
2001	Byron Leftwich, Marshall, quarterback
2002	Byron Leftwich, Marshall, quarterback

HAWAII BOWL

Year	Player, Team, Position
2002	Lynaris Elpheage, Tulane, cornerback

HOLIDAY BOWL

Year	Player, Team, Position
1978	Phil McConkey, Navy, wide receiver
1979	Marc Wilson, Brigham Young, quarterback
	Tim Wilbur, Indiana, cornerback
1980	Jim McMahon, Brigham Young, quarterback
	Craig James, Southern Methodist, running back
1981	Jim McMahon, Brigham Young, quarterback
	Kyle Whittingham, Brigham Young, linebacker
1982	Tim Spencer, Ohio St., running back
	Garcia Lane, Ohio St., cornerback
1983	Steve Young, Brigham Young, quarterback
	Bobby Bell, Missouri, defensive end
1984	Robbie Bosco, Brigham Young, quarterback
	Leon White, Brigham Young, linebacker
1985	Bobby Joe Edmonds, Arkansas, running back
	Greg Battle, Arizona St., linebacker
1986	Todd Santos, San Diego St., quarterback (co-offensive)
	Mark Vlasic, Iowa, quarterback (co-offensive)
	Richard Brown, San Diego St., linebacker
1987	Craig Burnett, Wyoming, quarterback
	Anthony Wright, Iowa, cornerback
1988	Barry Sanders, Oklahoma St., running back
	Sim Drain, Oklahoma St., linebacker
1989	Blair Thomas, Penn St., running back
	Ty Detmer, Brigham Young, quarterback
1990	Bucky Richardson, Texas A&M, quarterback
	William Thomas, Texas A&M, linebacker
1991	Ty Detmer, Brigham Young, quarterback
	Josh Arnold, Brigham Young, defensive back (co-defensive)
	Carlos James, Iowa, defensive back (co-defensive)
1992	Michael Carter, Hawaii, quarterback
	Junior Tagoai, Hawaii, defensive tackle
1993	John Walsh, Brigham Young, quarterback (co-offensive)
	Raymont Harris, Ohio St., running back (co-offensive)
	Lorenzo Styles, Ohio St., linebacker
1994	Todd Collins, Michigan, quarterback (co-offensive)
	Anthoney Hill, Colorado St., quarterback (co-offensive)
	Matt Dyson, Michigan, linebacker
1995	Brian Kavanagh, Kansas St., quarterback (offense)
	Mario Smith, Kansas St., defensive back (defense)
1996	Koy Detmer, Colorado, quarterback (offense)
	Nick Ziegler, Colorado, defensive end (defense)
1997	Moses Moreno, Colorado St., quarterback
	Darran Hall, Colorado St., wide receiver
1998	Keith Smith, Arizona, quarterback
	Chris McAlister, Arizona, cornerback
1999	Jonathan Beasley, Kansas St., quarterback
	Darren Howard, Kansas St., linebacker

Year	Player, Team, Position
2000	Joey Harrington, Oregon, quarterback
2001	Major Applewhite, Texas, quarterback (co-offensive)
	Willie Hurst, Washington, tailback (co-offensive)
	Derrick Johnson, Texas, linebacker (defensive)
2002	Ell Roberson, Kansas St., quarterback (offense)
	Terrell Suggs, Arizona St., defensive end (defense)

HOUSTON BOWL
(Formerly galleryfurniture.com Bowl)

Year	Player, Team, Position
2001	Byron Jones, Texas A&M, defensive back (overall)
	Joe Weber, Texas A&M, running back (offense)
2002	Rashaun Woods, Oklahoma St., wide receiver (overall/offense)

HUMANITARIAN BOWL

Year	Player, Team, Position
1997	Steve Smith, Utah St., wide receiver
	Chad Plummer, Cincinnati, quarterback
1998	Lee Roberts, Southern Miss., quarterback
	John Walsh, Idaho, quarterback
1999	Brock Forsey, Boise St., running back
	Chris Redman, Louisville, quarterback
2000	Bart Hendricks, Boise St., quarterback
	Chris Porter, UTEP, running back
2001	Woodrow Dantzler, Clemson, quarterback
2002	Bobby Hammer, Boise St., defensive lineman

INDEPENDENCE BOWL

Year	Player, Team, Position
1976	Terry McFarland, McNeese St., quarterback
	Terry Clark, Tulsa, cornerback
1977	Keith Thibodeaux, Louisiana Tech, quarterback
	Otis Wilson, Louisville, linebacker
1978	Theodore Sutton, East Caro., fullback
	Zack Valentine, East Caro., defensive end
1979	Joe Morris, Syracuse, running back
	Clay Carroll, McNeese St., defensive tackle
1980	Stephan Starring, McNeese St., quarterback
	Jerald Baylis, Southern Miss., nose guard
1981	Gary Kubiak, Texas A&M, quarterback
	Mike Green, Oklahoma St., linebacker
1982	Randy Wright, Wisconsin, quarterback
	Tim Krumrie, Wisconsin, nose guard
1983	Marty Louthan, Air Force, quarterback
	Andre Townsend, Mississippi, defensive tackle
1984	Bart Weiss, Air Force, quarterback
	Scott Thomas, Air Force, safety
1985	Rickey Foggie, Minnesota, quarterback
	Bruce Holmes, Minnesota, linebacker
1986	Mark Young, Mississippi, quarterback
	James Mosley, Texas Tech, defensive end
1987	Chris Chandler, Washington, quarterback
	David Rill, Washington, linebacker
1988	James Henry, Southern Miss., punt returner/cornerback
1989	Bill Musgrave, Oregon, quarterback
	Chris Oldham, Oregon, defensive back
1990	Mike Richardson, Louisiana Tech, running back
	Lorenzo Baker, Louisiana Tech, linebacker
1991	Andre Hastings, Georgia, flanker
	Torrey Evans, Georgia, linebacker
1992	Todd Dixon, Wake Forest, split end
1993	Maurice DeShazo, Virginia Tech, quarterback
	Antonio Banks, Virginia Tech, safety
1994	Mike Groh, Virginia, quarterback
	Mike Frederick, Virginia, defensive end
1995	Kevin Faulk, LSU, running back
	Gabe Northern, LSU, defensive end
1996	Dameyune Craig, Auburn, quarterback
	Takeo Spikes, Auburn, linebacker
	Ben Kotwica, Army, linebacker
1997	Rondell Mealey, LSU, running back
	Arnold Miller, LSU, defensive end
1998	Romaro Miller, Mississippi, quarterback
1999	Tim Strickland, Mississippi, cornerback
2000	Ja'Mar Toombs, Texas A&M, running back
	Willie Blade, Mississippi St., defensive tackle
2001	Seneca Wallace, Iowa St., quarterback
	Waine Bacon, Alabama, safety (co-defense)
	Matt Word, Iowa St., linebacker (co-defense)
2002	Eli Manning, Mississippi, quarterback (offense)
	Chris Kelsay, Nebraska, defensive end (defense)

INSIGHT BOWL
(Formerly Copper Bowl and Insight.com Bowl)

Year	Player, Team, Position
1989	Shane Montgomery, North Carolina St., quarterback
	Scott Geyer, Arizona, defensive back
1990	Mike Pawlawski, California, quarterback
	Robert Midgett, Wyoming, linebacker
1991	Vaughn Dunbar, Indiana, tailback
	Mark Hagen, Indiana, linebacker
1992	Drew Bledsoe, Washington St., quarterback (overall)
	Phillip Bobo, Washington St., wide receiver (offense)
	Kareem Leary, Utah, defensive back (defense)
1993	Andre Coleman, Kansas St., wide receiver (offense)
	Kenny McEntyre, Kansas St., cornerback (defense)
1994	John Walsh, Brigham Young, quarterback (overall)
	Jamal Willis, Brigham Young, running back (offense)
	Broderick Simpson, Oklahoma, linebacker (defense)
1995	Byron Hanspard, Texas Tech, running back (overall)
	Zebbie Lethridge, Texas Tech, quarterback (offense)
	Mickey Dalton, Air Force, cornerback (defense)
1996	Ron Dayne, Wisconsin, running back
1997	Kelvin Eafon, Arizona, running back
1998	Julian Jones, Missouri, free safety
1999	Cortlen Johnson, Colorado, running back
2000	Sage Rosenfels, Iowa St., quarterback (offense)
	Reggie Hayward, Iowa St., defensive end (defense)
2001	James Mungro, Syracuse, running back
2002	Brandon Miree, Pittsburgh, running back (offense)
	Claude Harriott, Pittsburgh, defensive lineman (defense)
	Derek Anderson, Oregon St., quarterback (sportsmanship)

LAS VEGAS BOWL

Year	Player, Team, Position
1992	Chris Vargas, Nevada, quarterback
1993	Anthony Calvillo, Utah St., quarterback
	Mike Neu, Ball St., quarterback
1994	Henry Bailey, UNLV, running back
1995	Wasean Tait, Toledo, running back
	Alex Van Dyke, Nevada, wide receiver
1996	Brad Maynard, Ball St., punter
	Mike Crawford, Nevada, linebacker
1997	Pat Johnson, Oregon, wide receiver
	Bryce Fisher, Air Force, defensive tackle
1998	Joe Tuipala, San Diego St., linebacker
	Ronald Curry, North Carolina, quarterback
1999	Mike Anderson, Utah, running back
2000	Jason Thomas, UNLV, quarterback
	Boo Williams, Arkansas, wide receiver
2001	Dameon Hunter, Utah, running back
	Troy Polamalu, Southern California, safety
2002	Craig Bragg, UCLA, wide receiver

LIBERTY BOWL

Year	Player, Team
1959	Jay Huffman, Penn St.
1960	Dick Hoak, Penn St.
1961	Ernie Davis, Syracuse
1962	Terry Baker, Oregon St.
1963	Ode Burrell, Mississippi St.
1964	Ernest Adler, Utah
1965	Tom Bryan, Auburn
1966	Jimmy Cox, Miami (Fla.)
1967	Jim Donnan, North Carolina St.
1968	Steve Hindman, Mississippi
1969	Bob Anderson, Colorado
1970	Dave Abercrombie, Tulane
1971	Joe Ferguson, Arkansas
1972	Jim Stevens, Georgia Tech
1973	Stan Fritts, North Carolina St.
1974	Randy White, Maryland
1975	Ricky Bell, Southern California
1976	Barry Krauss, Alabama
1977	Matt Kupec, North Carolina
1978	James Wilder, Missouri
1979	Roch Hontas, Tulane
1980	Mark Herrmann, Purdue
1981	Eddie Meyers, Navy
1982	Jeremiah Castille, Alabama
1983	Doug Flutie, Boston College

Year	Player, Team
1984	Bo Jackson, Auburn
1985	Cody Carlson, Baylor
1986	Jeff Francis, Tennessee
1987	Greg Thomas, Arkansas
1988	Dave Schnell, Indiana
1989	Randy Baldwin, Mississippi
1990	Rob Perez, Air Force
1991	Rob Perez, Air Force
1992	Cassius Ware, Mississippi
1993	Jeff Brohm, Louisville
1994	Johnny Johnson, Illinois
1995	Kwame Ellis, Stanford, cornerback
1996	Malcolm Thomas, Syracuse, running back
1997	Sherrod Gideon, Southern Miss., wide receiver
1998	Shaun King, Tulane, quarterback
1999	Adalius Thomas, Southern Miss., defensive end
2000	Cecil Sapp, Colorado St., running back
2001	David Ragone, Louisville, quarterback
2002	LaTarence Dunbar, TCU, wide receiver (offense)
	Jason Goss, TCU, defensive back (defense)

MOTOR CITY BOWL

Year	Player, Team, Position
1997	Deuce McCallister, Mississippi, running back
	B.J. Cohen, Marshall, defensive end
1998	Chad Pennington, Marshall, quarterback
1999	Doug Chapman, Marshall, running back
2000	Byron Leftwich, Marshall, quarterback
	Michael Owens, Marshall, roverback
2001	Chester Taylor, Toledo, running back
	David Gardner, Toledo, defensive line
2002	Brian St. Pierre, Boston College, quarterback

MUSIC CITY BOWL

Year	Player, Team, Position
1998	Corey Moore, Virginia Tech, defensive end
1999	James Mungro, Syracuse, running back
2000	Brad Lewis, West Virginia, quarterback
2001	William Green, Boston College, running back
2002	Dan Nystrom, Minnesota, place kicker

NEW ORLEANS BOWL

Year	Player, Team, Position
2001	Justin Gallimore, Colorado St., defensive back
2002	Kevin Galbreath, North Texas, running back

ORANGE BOWL

Year	Player, Team, Position
1965	Joe Namath, Alabama, quarterback
1966	Steve Sloan, Alabama, quarterback
1967	Larry Smith, Florida, tailback
1968	Bob Warmack, Oklahoma, quarterback
1969	Donnie Shanklin, Kansas, halfback
1970	Chuck Burkhart, Penn St., quarterback
	Mike Reid, Penn St., defensive tackle
1971	Jerry Tagge, Nebraska, quarterback
	Willie Harper, Nebraska, defensive end
1972	Jerry Tagge, Nebraska, quarterback
	Rich Glover, Nebraska, defensive guard
1973	Johnny Rodgers, Nebraska, wingback
	Rich Glover, Nebraska, defensive guard
1974	Tom Shuman, Penn St., quarterback
	Randy Crowder, Penn St., defensive tackle
1975	Wayne Bullock, Notre Dame, fullback
	Leroy Cook, Alabama, defensive end
1976	Steve Davis, Oklahoma, quarterback
	Lee Roy Selmon, Oklahoma, defensive tackle
1977	Rod Gerald, Ohio St., quarterback
	Tom Cousineau, Ohio St., linebacker
1978	Roland Sales, Arkansas, running back
	Reggie Freeman, Arkansas, nose guard
1979	Billy Sims, Oklahoma, running back
	Reggie Kinlaw, Oklahoma, nose guard
1980	J.C. Watts, Oklahoma, quarterback
	Bud Hebert, Oklahoma, free safety
1981	J.C. Watts, Oklahoma, quarterback
	Jarvis Coursey, Florida St., defensive end
1982	Homer Jordan, Clemson, quarterback
	Jeff Davis, Clemson, linebacker
1983	Turner Gill, Nebraska, quarterback
	Dave Rimington, Nebraska, center
1984	Bernie Kosar, Miami (Fla.), quarterback
	Jack Fernandez, Miami (Fla.), linebacker
1985	Jacque Robinson, Washington, tailback
	Ron Holmes, Washington, defensive tackle
1986	Sonny Brown, Oklahoma, defensive back
	Tim Lashar, Oklahoma, kicker

Year	Player, Team, Position
1987	Dante Jones, Oklahoma, linebacker
	Spencer Tillman, Oklahoma, halfback
1988	Bernard Clark, Miami (Fla.), linebacker
	Darrell Reed, Oklahoma, defensive end
1989	Steve Walsh, Miami (Fla.), quarterback
	Charles Fryar, Nebraska, cornerback
1990	Raghib Ismail, Notre Dame, tailback/wide receiver
	Darian Hagan, Colorado, quarterback
1991	Charles Johnson, Colorado, quarterback
	Chris Zorich, Notre Dame, nose guard
1992	Larry Jones, Miami (Fla.), running back
	Tyrone Leggett, Nebraska, cornerback
1993	Charlie Ward, Florida St., quarterback
	Corey Dixon, Nebraska, split end
1994	Tommie Frazier, Nebraska, quarterback
	Charlie Ward, Florida St., quarterback
1995	Tommie Frazier, Nebraska, quarterback
	Chris T. Jones, Miami (Fla.), cornerback
1996	Andre Cooper, Florida St., wide receiver
	Derrick Mayes, Notre Dame, wide receiver
1997	Damon Benning, Nebraska, running back
	Ken Oxendine, Virginia Tech, running back
1998	Ahman Green, Nebraska, running back
1999	Travis Taylor, Florida, wide receiver
2000	David Terrell, Michigan, wide receiver
2001	Torrance Marshall, Oklahoma, linebacker
2002	Taylor Jacobs, Florida, wide receiver
2003	Carson Palmer, Southern California, quarterback

OUTBACK BOWL
(Formerly Hall of Fame Bowl, 1986-95)

Year	Player, Team, Position
1986	Shawn Halloran, Boston College, quarterback
	James Jackson, Georgia, quarterback
1988	Jamie Morris, Michigan, tailback
	Bobby Humphrey, Alabama, tailback
1989	Robert Drummond, Syracuse, running back
1990	Reggie Slack, Auburn, quarterback
	Derek Isaman, Ohio St., linebacker
1991	DeChane Cameron, Clemson, quarterback
1992	Marvin Graves, Syracuse, quarterback
1993	Heath Shuler, Tennessee, quarterback
1994	Tyrone Wheatley, Michigan, running back
1995	Terrell Fletcher, Wisconsin, running back
1996	Bobby Engram, Penn St., wide receiver
1997	Dwayne Rudd, Alabama, linebacker
1998	Mike Bobo, Georgia, quarterback
1999	Courtney Brown, Penn St., defensive end
2000	Drew Brees, Purdue, quarterback
2001	Ryan Brewer, South Carolina, wide receiver
2002	Phil Petty, South Carolina, quarterback
2003	Chris Perry, Michigan, running back

PEACH BOWL

Year	Player, Team, Position
1968	Mike Hillman, LSU (offense)
	Buddy Millican, Florida St. (defense)
1969	Ed Williams, West Virginia (offense)
	Carl Crennel, West Virginia (defense)
1970	Monroe Eley, Arizona St. (offense)
	Junior Ah You, Arizona St. (defense)
1971	Norris Weese, Mississippi (offense)
	Crowell Armstrong, Mississippi (defense)
1972	Dave Buckey, North Carolina St. (offense)
	George Bell, North Carolina St. (defense)
1973	Louis Carter, Maryland (offense)
	Sylvester Boler, Georgia (defense)
1974	Larry Isaac, Texas Tech (offense)
	Dennis Harrison, Vanderbilt (defense)
1975	Dan Kendra, West Virginia (offense)
	Ray Marshall, West Virginia (defense)
1976	Rod Stewart, Kentucky (offense)
	Mike Martin, Kentucky (defense)
1977	Johnny Evans, North Carolina St. (offense)
	Richard Carter, North Carolina St. (defense)
1978	Mark Herrmann, Purdue (offense)
	Calvin Clark, Purdue (defense)
1979	Mike Brannan, Baylor (offense)
	Andrew Melontree, Baylor (defense)
1980	Jim Kelly, Miami (Fla.) (offense)
	Jim Burt, Miami (Fla.) (defense)
1981	Mickey Walczak, West Virginia (offense)
	Don Stemple, West Virginia (defense)
1982	Chuck Long, Iowa (offense)
	Clay Uhlenhake, Iowa (defense)
1983	Eric Thomas, Florida St. (offense)
	Alphonso Carreker, Florida St. (defense)

Year	Player, Team, Position
1984	Howard Petty, Virginia (offense)
	Ray Daly, Virginia (defense)
1985	Rob Healy, Army (offense)
	Peel Chronister, Army (defense)
1986	Erik Kramer, North Carolina St. (offense)
	Derrick Taylor, North Carolina St. (defense)
1987	Reggie Cobb, Tennessee (offense)
	Van Waiters, Indiana (defense)
1988	Shane Montgomery, North Carolina St. (offense)
	Michael Brooks, North Carolina St. (defense)
1989	Michael Owens, Syracuse (offense)
	Rodney Hampton, Georgia (offense)
	Terry Wooden, Syracuse (defense)
	Morris Lewis, Georgia (defense)
1990	Stan White, Auburn (offense)
	Vaughn Dunbar, Indiana (offense)
	Darrel Crawford, Auburn (defense)
	Mike Dumas, Indiana (defense)
1991	Jeff Blake, East Caro. (offense)
	Terry Jordan, North Carolina St. (offense)
	Robert Jones, East Caro. (defense)
	Billy Ray Haynes, North Carolina St. (defense)
1993	Natrone Means, North Carolina, running back (offense)
	Greg Plump, Mississippi St., quarterback (offense)
	Bracey Walker, North Carolina, strong safety (defense)
	Marc Woodard, Mississippi St., linebacker (defense)
1993	Emory Smith, Clemson, fullback (offense)
	Pookie Jones, Kentucky, quarterback (offense)
	Brentson Buckner, Clemson, tackle (defense)
	Zane Beehn, Kentucky, end (defense)
1995	Treymayne Stephens, North Carolina St., running back
1995	Tiki Barber, Virginia, running back (offense)
	Hines Ward, Georgia, quarterback (offense)
	Skeet Jones, Virginia, linebacker (defense)
	Whit Marshall, Georgia, linebacker (defense)
1996	Herb Tyler, LSU, quarterback (offense)
	Raymond Priester, Clemson, running back (offense)
	Anthony McFarland, LSU, defensive lineman (defense)
	Trevor Pryce, Clemson, defensive lineman (defense)
1998	Dameyune Craig, Auburn, quarterback
	Takeo Spikes, Auburn, linebacker
	Raymond Priester, Clemson, running back
	Rahim Abdullah, Clemson, linebacker
1999	Brian Wofford, Clemson, wide receiver
	Chad Carson, Clemson, linebacker
	Robert Bean, Mississippi St., cornerback
2000	Rohan Davey, LSU, quarterback
	Bradie James, LSU, linebacker
2001	Ronald Curry, North Carolina, quarterback (offense)
	Ryan Sims, North Carolina, defensive line (defense)
2002	Scott McBrien, Maryland, quarterback (offense)
	E.J. Henderson, Maryland, linebacker (defense)

ROSE BOWL

Year	Player, Team, Position
1902	Neil Snow, Michigan, fullback
1916	Carl Dietz, Washington St., fullback
1917	John Beckett, Oregon, tackle
1918	Hollis Huntington, Mare Island, fullback
1919	George Halas, Great Lakes, end
1920	Edward Casey, Harvard, halfback
1921	Harold "Brick" Muller, California, end
1922	Russell Stein, Wash. & Jeff., tackle
1923	Leo Calland, Southern California, guard
1924	Ira McKee, Navy, quarterback
1925	Elmer Layden, Notre Dame, fullback
	Ernie Nevers, Stanford, fullback
1926	Johnny Mack Brown, Alabama, halfback
	George Wilson, Washington, halfback
1927	Fred Pickhard, Alabama, tackle
1928	Clifford Hoffman, Stanford, fullback
1929	Benjamin Lom, California, halfback
1930	Russell Saunders, Southern California, quarterback
1931	John "Monk" Campbell, Alabama, quarterback
1932	Ernie Pinckert, Southern California, halfback
1933	Homer Griffith, Southern California, quarterback
1934	Cliff Montgomery, Columbia, quarterback
1935	Millard "Dixie" Howell, Alabama, halfback
1936	James "Monk" Moscrip, Stanford, end
	Keith Topping, Stanford, end
1937	William Daddio, Pittsburgh, end

Year	Player, Team, Position
1938	Victor Bottari, California, halfback
1939	Doyle Nave, Southern California, quarterback
	Alvin Krueger, Southern California, end
1940	Ambrose Schindler, Southern California, quarterback
1941	Peter Kmetovic, Stanford, halfback
1942	Donald Durdan, Oregon St., halfback
1943	Charles Trippi, Georgia, halfback
1944	Norman Verry, Southern California, guard
1945	James Hardy, Southern California, quarterback
1946	Harry Gilmer, Alabama, halfback
1947	Claude "Buddy" Young, Illinois, halfback
	Julius Rykovich, Illinois, halfback
1948	Robert Chappius, Michigan, halfback
1949	Frank Aschenbrenner, Northwestern, halfback
1950	Fred Morrison, Ohio St., fullback
1951	Donald Dufek, Michigan, fullback
1952	William Tate, Illinois, halfback
1953	Rudy Bukich, Southern California, quarterback
1954	Billy Wells, Michigan St., halfback
1955	Dave Leggett, Ohio St., quarterback
1956	Walter Kowalczyk, Michigan St., halfback
1957	Kenneth Ploen, Iowa, quarterback
1958	Jack Crabtree, Oregon, quarterback
1959	Bob Jeter, Iowa, halfback
1960	Bob Schloredt, Washington, quarterback
	George Fleming, Washington, halfback
1961	Bob Schloredt, Washington, quarterback
1962	Sandy Stephens, Minnesota, quarterback
1963	Pete Beathard, Southern California, quarterback
	Ron VanderKelen, Wisconsin, quarterback
1964	Jim Grabowski, Illinois, fullback
1965	Mel Anthony, Michigan, fullback
1966	Bob Stiles, UCLA, defensive back
1967	John Charles, Purdue, halfback
1968	O.J. Simpson, Southern California, tailback
1969	Rex Kern, Ohio St., quarterback
1970	Bob Chandler, Southern California, flanker
1971	Jim Plunkett, Stanford, quarterback
1972	Don Bunce, Stanford, quarterback
1973	Sam Cunningham, Southern California, fullback
1974	Cornelius Greene, Ohio St., quarterback
1975	Pat Haden, Southern California, quarterback
	John McKay Jr., Southern California, split end
1976	John Sciarra, UCLA, quarterback
1977	Vince Evans, Southern California, quarterback
1978	Warren Moon, Washington, quarterback
1979	Charles White, Southern California, tailback
	Rick Leach, Michigan, quarterback
1980	Charles White, Southern California, tailback
1981	Butch Woolfolk, Michigan, running back
1982	Jacque Robinson, Washington, running back
1983	Don Rogers, UCLA, free safety
	Tom Ramsey, UCLA, quarterback
1984	Rick Neuheisel, UCLA, quarterback
1985	Tim Green, Southern California, quarterback
	Jack Del Rio, Southern California, linebacker
1986	Eric Ball, UCLA, tailback
1987	Jeff Van Raaphorst, Arizona St., quarterback
1988	Percy Snow, Michigan St., linebacker
1989	Leroy Hoard, Michigan, fullback
1990	Ricky Ervins, Southern California, tailback
1991	Mark Brunell, Washington, quarterback
1992	Steve Emtman, Washington, defensive tackle
	Billy Joe Hobert, Washington, quarterback
1993	Tyrone Wheatley, Michigan, running back
1994	Brent Moss, Wisconsin, tailback
1995	Danny O'Neil, Oregon, quarterback
	Ki-Jana Carter, Penn St., running back
1996	Keyshawn Johnson, Southern California, wide receiver
1997	Joe Germaine, Ohio St., quarterback
1998	Brian Griese, Michigan, quarterback
1999	Ron Dayne, Wisconsin, running back
2000	Ron Dayne, Wisconsin, running back
2001	Marques Tuiasosopo, Washington, quarterback
2002	Ken Dorsey, Miami (Fla.), quarterback
	Andre Johnson, Miami (Fla.), wide receiver
2003	Nate Hybl, Oklahoma, quarterback

SAN FRANCISCO BOWL

Year	Player, Team, Position
2002	Bryan Randall, Virginia Tech, quarterback (offense)
	Anthony Schlegel, Air Force, linebacker (defense)

SILICON VALLEY BOWL

Year	Player, Team, Position
2001	Nick Myers, Michigan St., defensive end
	Charles Rogers, Michigan St., wide receiver
2002	Rodney Davis, Fresno St., running back

SUGAR BOWL

Miller-Digby Memorial Trophy

Year	Player, Team, Position
1948	Bobby Layne, Texas, quarterback
1949	Jack Mitchell, Oklahoma, quarterback
1950	Leon Heath, Oklahoma, fullback
1951	Walt Yowarsky, Kentucky, tackle
1952	Ed Modzelewski, Maryland, fullback
1953	Leon Hardemann, Georgia Tech, halfback
1954	"Pepper" Rodgers, Georgia Tech, quarterback
1955	Joe Gattuso, Navy, fullback
1956	Franklin Brooks, Georgia Tech, guard
1957	Del Shofner, Baylor, halfback
1958	Raymond Brown, Mississippi, quarterback
1959	Billy Cannon, LSU, halfback
1960	Bobby Franklin, Mississippi, quarterback
1961	Jake Gibbs, Mississippi, quarterback
1962	Mike Fracchia, Alabama, fullback
1963	Glynn Griffing, Mississippi, quarterback
1964	Tim Davis, Alabama, kicker
1965	Doug Moreau, LSU, flanker
1966	Steve Spurrier, Florida, quarterback
1967	Kenny Stabler, Alabama, quarterback
1968	Glenn Smith, LSU, halfback
1969	Chuck Dicus, Arkansas, flanker
1970	Archie Manning, Mississippi, quarterback
1971	Bobby Scott, Tennessee, quarterback
1972	Jack Mildren, Oklahoma, quarterback
1972	Tinker Owens, Oklahoma, flanker
1973	Tom Clements, Notre Dame, quarterback
1974	Tony Davis, Nebraska, fullback
1975	Richard Todd, Alabama, quarterback
1977	Matt Cavanaugh, Pittsburgh, quarterback
1978	Jeff Rutledge, Alabama, quarterback
1979	Barry Krauss, Alabama, linebacker
1980	Major Ogilvie, Alabama, running back
1981	Herschel Walker, Georgia, running back
1982	Dan Marino, Pittsburgh, quarterback
1983	Todd Blackledge, Penn St., quarterback
1984	Bo Jackson, Auburn, running back
1985	Craig Sundberg, Nebraska, quarterback
1986	Daryl Dickey, Tennessee, quarterback
1987	Steve Taylor, Nebraska, quarterback
1988	Don McPherson, Syracuse, quarterback
1989	Sammie Smith, Florida St., running back
1990	Craig Erickson, Miami (Fla.), quarterback
1991	Andy Kelly, Tennessee, quarterback
1992	Jerome Bettis, Notre Dame, fullback
1993	Derrick Lassic, Alabama, running back
1994	Errict Rhett, Florida, running back
1995	Warrick Dunn, Florida St., running back
1995	Bryan Still, Virginia Tech, wide receiver
1997	Danny Wuerffel, Florida, quarterback
1998	E.G. Green, Florida St., wide receiver
1999	David Boston, Ohio St., wide receiver
2000	Peter Warrick, Florida St., wide receiver
2001	Ken Dorsey, Miami (Fla.), quarterback
2002	Rohan Davey, LSU, quarterback
2003	Musa Smith, Georgia, running back

SUN BOWL

(Named John Hancock Bowl, 1989-93)

C.M. Hendricks Most Valuable Player Trophy (1954-Present)
Jimmy Rogers Jr. Most Valuable Lineman Trophy (1961-Present)
John Folmer Most Valuable Special Teams Trophy (1994)

Year	Player, Team, Position
1950	Harvey Gabriel, UTEP, halfback
1951	Bill Cross, West Tex. A&M, end
1952	Junior Arteburn, Texas Tech, quarterback
1953	Tom McCormick, Pacific (Cal.), halfback
1954	Dick Shinaut, UTEP, quarterback
1955	Jesse Whittenton, UTEP, quarterback
1956	Jim Crawford, Wyoming, halfback
1957	Claude Austin, George Washington
1958	Leonard Kucewski, Wyoming, guard
1959	Charley Johnson, New Mexico St., quarterback
1960	Charley Johnson, New Mexico St., quarterback
1961	Billy Joe, Villanova, fullback
	Richie Ross, Villanova, guard
1962	Jerry Logan, West Tex. A&M, halfback
	Don Hoovler, Ohio, guard
1963	Bob Berry, Oregon, quarterback
	John Hughes, Southern Methodist, guard
1964	Preston Ridlehuber, Georgia, quarterback
	Jim Wilson, Georgia, tackle
1965	Billy Stevens, UTEP, quarterback
	Ronny Nixon, TCU, tackle
1966	Jim Kiick, Wyoming, tailback
	Jerry Durling, Wyoming, middle guard
1967	Billy Stevens, UTEP, quarterback
	Fred Carr, UTEP, linebacker
1968	Buddy McClintock, Auburn, defensive back
	David Campbell, Auburn, tackle
1969	Paul Rogers, Nebraska, halfback
	Jerry Murtaugh, Nebraska, linebacker
1970	Rock Perdoni, Georgia Tech, defensive tackle
	Bill Flowers, Georgia Tech, linebacker
1971	Bert Jones, LSU, quarterback
	Matt Blair, Iowa St., linebacker
1972	George Smith, Texas Tech, halfback
	Ecomet Burley, Texas Tech, defensive tackle
1973	Ray Bybee, Missouri, fullback
	John Kelsey, Missouri, tight end
1974	Terry Vitrano, Mississippi St., fullback
	Jimmy Webb, Mississippi St., defensive tackle
1975	Robert Haygood, Pittsburgh, quarterback
	Al Romano, Pittsburgh, middle guard
1977	Tony Franklin, Texas A&M, kicker
	Edgar Fields, Texas A&M, defensive tackle
1977	Charles Alexander, LSU, tailback
	Gordy Ceresino, Stanford, linebacker
1978	Johnny "Ham" Jones, Texas, running back
	Dwight Jefferson, Texas, defensive end
1979	Paul Skansi, Washington, flanker
	Doug Martin, Washington, defensive tackle
1980	Jeff Quinn, Nebraska, quarterback
	Jimmy Williams, Nebraska, defensive end
1981	Darrell Shepard, Oklahoma, quarterback
	Rick Bryan, Oklahoma, defensive tackle
1982	Ethan Horton, North Carolina, tailback
	Ronnie Mullins, Texas, defensive end
1983	Walter Lewis, Alabama, quarterback
	Wes Neighbors, Alabama, center
1984	Rick Badanjek, Maryland, fullback
	Carl Zander, Tennessee, linebacker
1985	Max Zendejas, Arizona, kicker
	Peter Anderson, Georgia, center
1986	Cornelius Bennett, Alabama, defensive end
	Steve Alvord, Washington, middle guard
1987	Thurman Thomas, Oklahoma St., running back
	Darnell Warren, West Virginia, linebacker
1988	David Smith, Alabama, quarterback
	Derrick Thomas, Alabama, linebacker
1989	Alex Van Pelt, Pittsburgh, quarterback
	Anthony Williams, Texas A&M, linebacker
1990	Courtney Hawkins, Michigan St., wide receiver
	Craig Hartsuyker, Southern California, linebacker
1991	Arnold Ale, UCLA, inside linebacker
	Jimmy Rogers Jr., Illinois, lineman
1992	Melvin Bonner, Baylor, flanker
1993	Jerald Moore, Oklahoma, running back
1994	Priest Holmes, Texas, running back
	Blake Brockermeyer, Texas, offensive lineman
	Marcus Wall, North Carolina, wide receiver
1995	Sedrick Shaw, Iowa, running back
	Jared DeVries, Iowa, defensive tackle
	Brion Hurley, Iowa, kicker
1996	Troy Walters, Stanford, flanker
	Kailee Wong, Stanford, defensive end
	Chad Hutchinson, Stanford, quarterback
1997	Mike Martin, Arizona St., running back
1998	Basil Mitchell, TCU, tailback
	London Dunlap, TCU, defensive end
	Adam Abrams, Southern California, placekicker
1999	Billy Cockerham, Minnesota, quarterback
	Dyron Russ, Minnesota, tackle
	Ryan Rindels, Minnesota, punter
2000	Freddie Mitchell, UCLA, wide receiver
	Oscar Cabrera, UCLA, offensive lineman
	Michael Bennett, Wisconsin, running back
2001	Lamont Thompson, Washington St., safety
	Akin Ayodele, Purdue, defensive end
	Drew Dunning, Washington St., placekicker
2002	Kyle Orton, Purdue, quarterback
	Shaun Phillips, Purdue, defensive end
	Anthony Chambers, Purdue, wide receiver

TANGERINE BOWL

(Formerly Blockbuster Bowl, 1990-93; Carquest Bowl,1994-97; Micron PC Bowl, 1998; MicronPC.com,1999-00; Visit Florida Tangerine, 2001)

Year	Player, Team, Position
1990	Amp Lee, Florida St., running back
1991	David Palmer, Alabama, wide receiver
1992	Darrien Gordon, Stanford, cornerback
1993	Glenn Foley, Boston College, quarterback
1995	Leon Johnson, North Carolina, running back
1996	Tremain Mack, Miami (Fla.), strong safety
1997	Joe Hamilton, Georgia Tech, quarterback
1998	Scott Covington, Miami (Fla.), quarterback

Year	Player, Team, Position
1999	Kurt Kittner, Illinois, quarterback
2000	Philip Rivers, North Carolina St., quarterback
2001	Antonio Bryant, Pittsburgh, wide receiver (overall)
	Phillip Rivers, North Carolina St., quarterback (offense)
	Lewis Moore, Pittsburgh, linebacker (defense)
	Terrance Martin, North Carolina St., defensive line (defense)
	Dantonio Burnett, North Carolina St., linebacker (defense)
2002	Kliff Kingsbury, Texas Tech, quarterback (Player of Game)
	Kliff Kingsbury, Texas Tech, quarterback (MVP Offense)
	Derrick Hamilton, Clemson, wide receiver (MVP Offense)
	John Saldi, Texas Tech, linebacker (MVP Defense)
	John Leake, Clemson, linebacker (MVP Defense)

Most Valuable Players in Former Major Bowls

ALL-AMERICAN BOWL
(Birmingham, Ala.; Known as Hall of Fame Classic, 1977-85)

Year	Player, Team, Position
1977	Chuck White, Maryland, split end
	Charles Johnson, Maryland, defensive tackle
1978	Curtis Dickey, Texas A&M, running back
1979	Phil Bradley, Missouri, quarterback
1980	Gary Anderson, Arkansas, running back
	Billy Ray Smith, Arkansas, linebacker
1981	John Bond, Mississippi St., quarterback
	Johnie Cooks, Mississippi St., linebacker
1982	Whit Taylor, Vanderbilt, quarterback
	Carl Dieudonne, Air Force, defensive end
1983	Jeff Hostetler, West Virginia, quarterback
1984	Mark Logan, Kentucky, running back
	Todd Gregoire, Wisconsin, placekicker
1985	Mark Ingram, Michigan St., wide receiver
1986	Sammie Smith, Florida St., running back
1987	Scott Secules, Virginia, quarterback
1988	Emmitt Smith, Florida, running back
1989	Jerry Gray, Texas Tech, running back
1990	Brett Favre, Southern Miss., quarterback

ALOHA CLASSIC
(Honolulu, Hawaii; Named Aloha Bowl, 1982-97)

Year	Player, Team, Position
1982	Offense—Tim Cowan, Washington, quarterback
	Defense—Tony Caldwell, Washington, linebacker
1983	Offense—Danny Greene, Washington, wide receiver
	Defense—George Reynolds, Penn St., punter
1984	Offense—Jeff Atkins, Southern Methodist, running back
	Defense—Jerry Ball, Southern Methodist, nose guard
1985	Offense—Gene Jelks, Alabama, running back
	Defense—Cornelius Bennett, Alabama, linebacker
1986	Offense—Alfred Jenkins, Arizona, quarterback
	Defense—Chuck Cecil, Arizona, safety
1987*	Troy Aikman, UCLA, quarterback
	Emmitt Smith, Florida, running back
1988	David Dacus, Houston quarterback
	Victor Wood, Washington St., wide receiver
1989	Blake Ezor, Michigan St., tailback
	Chris Roscoe, Hawaii, wide receiver
1990	Todd Burden, Arizona, cornerback
	Marvin Graves, Syracuse, quarterback
1991	Tommy Vardell, Stanford, running back
	Shawn Jones, Georgia Tech, quarterback
1992	Tom Young, Brigham Young, quarterback
	Dana Stubblefield, Kansas, defensive tackle
1993	Rashaan Salaam, Colorado, tailback
	Trent Dilfer, Fresno St., quarterback
1994	David Green, Boston College, running back (offensive)
	Mike Mamula, Boston College, defensive end (defense)
	Joe Gordon, Kansas St., cornerback
1995	Mark Williams, Kansas, quarterback
	Karim Abdul-Jabbar, UCLA, running back

Year	Player, Team, Position
1996	Chris McCoy, Navy, quarterback
	Pat Barnes, California, quarterback
1997	Rashaan Shehee, Washington, running back
1998	Mike Moschetti, Colorado, quarterback
	Akili Smith, Oregon, quarterback
1999	Ben Sankey, Wake Forest, quarterback
2000	Tim Hasselbeck, Boston College, quarterback

AVIATION BOWL
(Dayton, Ohio)

Year	Player, Team, Position
1961	Bobby Santiago, New Mexico, running back
	Chuck Cummings, New Mexico, guard

BLUEBONNET BOWL
(Houston, Texas)

Year	Player, Team
1959	Lowndes Shingles, Clemson
	Bob Lilly, TCU
1960	James Saxton, Texas
	Lee Roy Jordan, Alabama
1961	Ken Coleman, Kansas
	Elvin Basham, Kansas
1962	Bill Tobin, Missouri
	Conrad Hitchler, Missouri
1963	Don Trull, Baylor
	James Ingram, Baylor
1964	Jerry Rhome, Tulsa
	Willy Townes, Tulsa
1965	Dewey Warren, Tennessee
	Frank Emanuel, Tennessee
1966	Chris Gilbert, Texas
	Fred Edwards, Texas
1967	Bob Anderson, Colorado
	Ted Hendricks, Miami (Fla.)
1968	Joe Pearce, Oklahoma
	Rufus Cormier, Southern Methodist
1969	Jim Strong, Houston
	Jerry Drones, Houston
1970	Greg Pruitt, Oklahoma
	Jeff Rouzie, Alabama
1971	Charlie Davis, Colorado
	Butch Brezina, Houston
1972	Condredge Holloway, Tennessee
	Carl Johnson, Tennessee
1973	D.C. Nobles, Houston
	Deryl McGallion, Houston
1974	John Housmann, Houston
	Mack Mitchell, Houston
1975	Earl Campbell, Texas
	Tim Campbell, Texas
1976	Chuck Malito, Nebraska
	Rodney Allison, Texas Tech
1977	Rob Hertel, Southern California
	Walt Underwood, Southern California
1978	Steve Dils, Stanford
	Gordy Ceresino, Stanford
1979	Mark Herrmann, Purdue
	Roland James, Tennessee
1980	Amos Lawrence, North Carolina
	Steve Streater, North Carolina
1981	Butch Woolfolk, Michigan
	Ben Needham, Michigan
1982	Gary Anderson, Arkansas
	Dwayne Dixon, Florida
1983	Rusty Hilger, Oklahoma St.
	Alfred Anderson, Baylor
1984	Willie Drewrey, West Virginia
1985	Pat Evans, Air Force
	James McKinney, Texas
1986	Ray Berry, Baylor
	Mark Hatcher, Colorado
1987	Tony Jones, Texas
	Zeke Gadson, Pittsburgh

BLUEGRASS BOWL
(Louisville, Ky.)

Year	Player, Team
1958	Forrest Campbell, Oklahoma St.

CALIFORNIA RAISIN BOWL
(Beginning in 1992, Mid-American Conference and Big West Conference winners met in Las Vegas Bowl)

Year	Player, Team, Position
1981	Arnold Smiley, Toledo, running back
	Marlin Russell, Toledo, linebacker

Year	Player, Team, Position
1982	Chip Otten, Bowling Green, tailback
	Jac Tomasello, Bowling Green, defensive back
1983	Lou Wicks, Northern Ill., fullback
	James Pruitt, Cal St. Fullerton, wide receiver
1984	Randall Cunningham, UNLV, quarterback
	Steve Morgan, Toledo, tailback
1985	Mike Mancini, Fresno St., punter
	Greg Meehan, Bowling Green, flanker
1986	Mike Perez, San Jose St., quarterback
	Andrew Marlatt, Miami (Ohio), defensive tackle
1987	Gary Patton, Eastern Mich., tailback
	Mike Perez, San Jose St., quarterback
1988	Darrell Rosette, Fresno St., running back
	Tony Kimbrough, Western Mich., quarterback
1989	Ron Cox, Fresno St., linebacker
	Sean Jones, Ball St., wide receiver
1990	Sheldon Canley, San Jose St., tailback
	Ken Ealy, Central Mich., wide receiver
1991	Mark Szlachcic, Bowling Green, wide receiver
	Mark Barsotti, Fresno St., quarterback

CHERRY BOWL
(Pontiac, Mich.)

Year	Player, Team
1984	Nate Sassaman, Army
1985	Stan Gelbaugh, Maryland
	Scott Shankweiler, Maryland

DELTA BOWL
(Memphis, Tenn.)

Year	Player, Team
1948	Charlie Conerly, Mississippi

FREEDOM BOWL
(Anaheim, Calif.)

Year	Player, Team, Position
1984	Chuck Long, Iowa, quarterback
	William Harris, Texas, tight end
1985	Chris Chandler, Washington, quarterback
	Barry Helton, Colorado, punter
1986	Gaston Green, UCLA, tailback
	Shane Shumway, Brigham Young, defensive back
1987	Daniel Ford, Arizona St., quarterback
	Chad Hennings, Air Force, defensive tackle
1988	Ty Detmer, Brigham Young, quarterback
	Eric Bieniemy, Colorado, halfback
1989	Cary Conklin, Washington, quarterback
	Huey Richardson, Florida, linebacker
1990	Todd Yert, Colorado St., running back
	Bill Musgrave, Oregon, quarterback
1991	Marshall Faulk, San Diego St., running back
	Ron Jackson, Tulsa, running back
1992	Lorenzo Neal, Fresno St., fullback
	Estrus Crayton, Southern California, tailback
1993	Johnnie Morton, Southern California, wide receiver
	Henry Lusk, Utah, wide receiver
1994	Tedy Bruschi, Arizona, defensive end
	Cal Beck, Utah, kick returner

GARDEN STATE BOWL
(East Rutherford, N.J.)

Year	Player, Team
1978	John Mistler, Arizona St.
1979	Mark Bright, Temple
1980	Terald Clark, Houston
1981	Steve Alatorre, Tennessee
	Anthony Hancock, Tennessee
	Randy Wright, Wisconsin

GOTHAM BOWL
(New York, N.Y.)

Year	Player, Team
1961	Don Trull, Baylor
1962	Willie Ross, Nebraska
	George Mira, Miami (Fla.)

HARBOR BOWL
(San Diego, Calif.)

Year	Player, Team
1947	Bryan Brock, New Mexico
	Bill Nelson, Montana St.

MERCY BOWL
(Los Angeles, Calif.)

Year	Player, Team
1961	Beau Carter, Fresno St.

PASADENA BOWL
(Pasadena, Calif.; called Junior Rose Bowl in 1967)

Year	Player, Team
1967	Eugene "Mercury" Morris, West Tex. A&M
	Albie Owens, West Tex. A&M
1969	John Featherstone, San Diego St.
1970	Leon Burns, Long Beach St.
	Paul Mattingly, Louisville

Year	Player, Team
1971	Tom Carlsen, Memphis
	Dornell Harris, Memphis

PRESIDENTIAL CUP
(College Park, Md.)

Year	Player, Team
1950	Bob Smith, Texas A&M
	Zippy Morocco, Georgia

SALAD BOWL
(Phoenix, Ariz.)

Year	Player, Team
1950	Bob McQuade, Xavier
	Wilford White, Arizona St.

Year	Player, Team
1951	Jim Bailey, Miami (Ohio)
1952	Gene Shannon, Houston

SEATTLE BOWL
(Seattle, Wash.)
(Formerly Oahu Classic)

Year	Player, Team Position
1998	Blane Morgan, Air Force, quarterback
1999	Avion Weaver, Hawaii, running back
2000	Terrance Edwards, Georgia, wide receiver
2001	George Godsey, Georgia Tech, quarterback
2002	James MacPherson, Wake Forest, quarterback

Heisman Trophy Winners in Bowl Games

YEAR-BY-YEAR BOWL RESULTS FOR HEISMAN WINNERS
(Includes bowl games immediately after award of Heisman Trophy)

Of the 67 winners of the 68 Heisman Trophies (Archie Griffin won twice), 43 played in bowl games after they received their prize. Of those 43 players, only 21 were on the winning team in the bowl.

Houston's Andre Ware is the only Heisman recipient to miss a bowl date since 1969. The Cougars were on probation during the 1989 season and were ineligible for selection to a bowl. Before that lapse, Oklahoma's Steve Owens in 1969 was the last Heisman awardee not to participate in a bowl game.

Only three of the first 22 Heisman Trophy winners played in bowl games after receiving the award—TCU's Davey O'Brien in 1938, Georgia's Frank Sinkwich in 1942 and Southern Methodist's Doak Walker in 1948.

Year	Heisman Winner, Team, Position	Bowl (Opponent, Result)
1935	Jay Berwanger, Chicago, HB	Did not play in bowl
1936	Larry Kelley, Yale, E	Did not play in bowl
1937	Clint Frank, Yale, HB	Did not play in bowl
1938	Davey O'Brien, TCU, QB	Sugar (Carnegie Mellon, W 15-7)
1939	Nile Kinnick, Iowa, HB	Did not play in bowl
1940	Tom Harmon, Michigan, HB	Did not play in bowl
1941	Bruce Smith, Minnesota, HB	Did not play in bowl
1942	Frank Sinkwich, Georgia, HB	Rose (UCLA, W 9-0)
1943	Angelo Bertelli, Notre Dame, QB	Did not play in bowl
1944	Les Horvath, Ohio St., QB	Did not play in bowl
1945	Doc Blanchard, Army, FB	Did not play in bowl
1946	Glenn Davis, Army, HB	Did not play in bowl
1947	Johnny Lujack, Notre Dame, QB	Did not play in bowl
1948	Doak Walker, Southern Methodist, HB	Cotton (Oregon, W 21-13)
1949	Leon Hart, Notre Dame, E	Did not play in bowl
1950	Vic Janowicz, Ohio St., HB	Did not play in bowl
1951	Dick Kazmeier, Princeton, HB	Did not play in bowl
1952	Billy Vessels, Oklahoma, HB	Did not play in bowl
1953	John Lattner, Notre Dame, HB	Did not play in bowl
1954	Alan Ameche, Wisconsin, FB	Did not play in bowl
1955	Howard Cassady, Ohio St., HB	Did not play in bowl
1956	Paul Hornung, Notre Dame, HB	Did not play in bowl
1957	John David Crow, Texas A&M, HB	Gator (Tennessee, L 3-0)
1958	Pete Dawkins, Army, HB	Did not play in bowl
1959	Billy Cannon, LSU, HB	Sugar (Mississippi, L 21-0)
1960	Joe Bellino, Navy, HB	Orange (Missouri, L 21-14)
1961	Ernie Davis, Syracuse, HB	Liberty (Miami, Fla., W 15-14)
1962	Terry Baker, Oregon St., QB	Liberty (Villanova, W 6-0)
1963	Roger Staubach, Navy, QB	Cotton (Texas, L 28-6)
1964	John Huarte, Notre Dame, QB	Did not play in bowl
1965	Mike Garrett, Southern California, HB	Did not play in bowl
1966	Steve Spurrier, Florida, QB	Orange (Georgia Tech, W 27-12)
1967	Gary Beban, UCLA, QB	Did not play in bowl
1968	O.J. Simpson, Southern California, HB	Rose (Ohio St., L 27-16)
1969	Steve Owens, Oklahoma, HB	Did not play in bowl
1970	Jim Plunkett, Stanford, QB	Rose (Ohio St., W 27-17)
1971	Pat Sullivan, Auburn, QB	Sugar (Oklahoma, L 40-22)
1972	Johnny Rodgers, Nebraska, FL	Orange (Notre Dame, W 40-6)
1973	John Cappelletti, Penn St., HB	Orange (LSU, W 16-9)
1974	Archie Griffin, Ohio St., HB	Rose (Southern California, L 18-17)
1975	Archie Griffin, Ohio St., HB	Rose (UCLA, L 23-10)
1976	Tony Dorsett, Pittsburgh, HB	Sugar (Georgia, W 27-3)

Year	Heisman Winner, Team, Position	Bowl (Opponent, Result)
1977	Earl Campbell, Texas, HB	Cotton (Notre Dame, L 38-10)
1978	Billy Sims, Oklahoma, HB	Orange (Nebraska, W 31-24)
1979	Charles White, Southern California, HB	Rose (Ohio St., W 17-16)
1980	George Rogers, South Carolina, HB	Gator (Pittsburgh, L 37-9)
1981	Marcus Allen, Southern California, HB	Fiesta (Penn St., L 26-10)
1982	Herschel Walker, Georgia, HB	Sugar (Penn St., L 27-23)
1983	Mike Rozier, Nebraska, HB	Orange (Miami, Fla., L 31-30)
1984	Doug Flutie, Boston College, QB	Cotton (Houston, W 45-28)
1985	Bo Jackson, Auburn, HB	Cotton (Texas A&M, L 36-16)
1986	Vinny Testaverde, Miami (Fla.), QB	Fiesta (Penn St., L 14-10)
1987	Tim Brown, Notre Dame, WR	Cotton (Texas A&M, L 35-10)
1988	Barry Sanders, Oklahoma St., RB	Holiday (Wyoming, W 62-14)
1989	Andre Ware, Houston, QB	Did not play in bowl
1990	Ty Detmer, Brigham Young, QB	Holiday (Texas A&M, L 65-14)
1991	Desmond Howard, Michigan, WR	Rose (Washington, L 34-14)
1992	Gino Torretta, Miami (Fla.), QB	Sugar (Alabama, L 34-13)
1993	Charlie Ward, Florida St., QB	Orange (Nebraska, W 18-16)
1994	Rashaan Salaam, Colorado, RB	Fiesta (Notre Dame, W 41-24)
1995	Eddie George, Ohio St., RB	Fla. Citrus (Tennessee, L 20-14)
1996	Danny Wuerffel, Florida, QB	Sugar (Florida St., W 52-20)
1997	Charles Woodson, Michigan, CB	Rose (Washington St., W 21-16)
1998	Ricky Williams, Texas, RB	Cotton (Mississippi St., W 38-11)
1999	Ron Dayne, Wisconsin, RB	Rose (Stanford, W 17-9)
2000	Chris Weinke, Florida St., QB	Orange (Oklahoma, L 13-2)
2001	Eric Crouch, Nebraska, QB	Rose (Miami [Fla.], L 37-14)
2002	Carson Palmer, Southern California, QB	Orange (Iowa, W 38-17)

BOWLS FOR HEISMAN WINNERS

Bowl	Heisman Winner Year	Heisman Winners
Rose	1942, 1968, 1970, 1974, 1975, 1979, 1991, 1997, 1999, 2001	10
Orange	1960, 1966, 1972, 1973, 1978, 1983, 1993, 2003	8
Sugar	1938, 1959, 1971, 1976, 1982, 1992, 1996	7
Cotton	1948, 1963, 1977, 1984, 1985, 1987, 1998	7
Fiesta	1981, 1986, 1994	3
Gator	1957, 1980	2
Holiday	1988, 1990	2
Liberty	1961, 1962	2
Fla. Citrus	1995	1

HEISMAN TROPHY WINNERS WHO WERE BOWL-GAME MVPs

Heisman Winner, Team (Year Won)	Bowl, Year Played
Doak Walker, Southern Methodist (1948)	Cotton, 1948
Doak Walker, Southern Methodist (1948)	Cotton, 1949
John David Crow, Texas A&M (1957)	Gator, 1957
Billy Cannon, LSU (1959)	Sugar, 1959
Ernie Davis, Syracuse (1961)	Cotton, 1960
Ernie Davis, Syracuse (1961)	Liberty, 1961
Terry Baker, Oregon St. (1962)	Liberty, 1962
Steve Spurrier, Florida (1966)	Sugar, 1966
O.J. Simpson, Southern California (1968)	Rose, 1968
Jim Plunkett, Stanford (1970)	Rose, 1971
Pat Sullivan, Auburn (1971)	Gator, 1971
Johnny Rodgers, Nebraska (1972)	Orange, 1973
Earl Campbell, Texas (1977)	Gator, 1973
Earl Campbell, Texas (1977)	Bluebonnet, 1975*
Billy Sims, Oklahoma (1978)	Orange, 1979
Charles White, Southern California (1979)	Rose, 1979

Heisman Winner, Team (Year Won)	Bowl, Year Played
Charles White, Southern California (1979)	Rose, 1980
George Rogers, South Carolina (1980)	Gator, 1980
Herschel Walker, Georgia (1982)	Sugar, 1981
Doug Flutie, Boston College (1984)	Liberty, 1983
Bo Jackson, Auburn (1985)	Sugar, 1984
Bo Jackson, Auburn (1985)	Liberty, 1984
Bo Jackson, Auburn (1985)	Cotton, 1986
Barry Sanders, Oklahoma St. (1988)	Holiday, 1988
Ty Detmer, Brigham Young (1990)	Freedom, 1988*
Ty Detmer, Brigham Young (1990)	Holiday, 1989
Ty Detmer, Brigham Young (1990)	Holiday, 1991
Charlie Ward, Florida St. (1993)	Orange, 1994
Danny Wuerffel, Florida (1996)	Sugar, 1997
Ricky Williams, Texas (1998)	Cotton, 1999
Ron Dayne, Wisconsin (1999)	Rose, 1999
Ron Dayne, Wisconsin (1999)	Rose, 2000
Carson Palmer, Southern California (2002)	Orange, 2003

*Discontinued bowl.

Bowls and Polls

Associated Press No. 1 Teams Defeated in Bowl Games

Date	Bowl	Teams Involved	Score	New No. 1
1-1-51	Sugar	No. 7 Kentucky beat No. 1 Oklahoma	13-7	Same
1-1-52	Sugar	No. 3 Maryland beat No. 1 Tennessee	28-13	Same
1-1-54	Orange	No. 4 Oklahoma beat No. 1 Maryland	7-0	Same
1-1-61	Rose	No. 6 Washington beat No. 1 Minnesota	17-7	Same
1-1-65	Orange	No. 5 Texas beat No. 1 Alabama	21-17	Same
1-1-71	Cotton	No. 6 Notre Dame beat No. 1 Texas	24-11	Nebraska
12-31-73	Sugar	No. 3 Notre Dame beat No. 1 Alabama	24-23	Notre Dame
1-1-76	Rose	No. 11 UCLA beat No. 1 Ohio St.	23-10	Oklahoma
1-2-78	Cotton	No. 5 Notre Dame beat No. 1 Texas	38-10	Notre Dame
1-1-79	Sugar	No. 2 Alabama beat No. 1 Penn St.	14-7	Alabama
1-1-83	Sugar	No. 2 Penn St. beat No. 1 Georgia	27-23	Penn St.
1-2-84	Orange	No. 5 Miami (Fla.) beat No. 1 Nebraska	31-30	Miami (Fla.)
1-1-86	Orange	No. 3 Oklahoma beat No. 1 Penn St.	25-10	Oklahoma
1-2-87	Fiesta	No. 2 Penn St. beat No. 1 Miami (Fla.)	14-10	Penn St.
1-1-88	Orange	No. 2 Miami (Fla.) beat No. 1 Oklahoma	20-14	Miami (Fla.)
1-1-90	Orange	No. 4 Notre Dame beat No. 1 Colorado	21-6	Miami (Fla.)
1-1-93	Sugar	No. 2 Alabama beat No. 1 Miami (Fla.)	34-13	Alabama
1-2-97	Sugar	No. 3 Florida beat No. 1 Florida St.	52-20	Florida
1-3-03	Fiesta	No. 2 Ohio St. beat No. 1 Miami (Fla.)	31-24 (2 ot)	Ohio St.

Associated Press No. 1 Vs. No. 2 in Bowl Games

Date	Bowl	Teams, Score
1-1-63	Rose	No. 1 Southern California 42, No. 2 Wisconsin 37
1-1-64	Cotton	No. 1 Texas 28, No. 2 Navy 6
1-1-69	Rose	No. 1 Ohio St. 27, No. 2 Southern California 16
1-1-72	Orange	No. 1 Nebraska 38, No. 2 Alabama 6
1-1-79	Sugar	No. 2 Alabama 14, No. 1 Penn St. 7
1-1-83	Sugar	No. 2 Penn St. 27, No. 1 Georgia 23
1-2-87	Fiesta	No. 2 Penn St. 14, No. 1 Miami (Fla.) 10
1-1-88	Orange	No. 2 Miami (Fla.) 20, No. 1 Oklahoma 14
1-1-93	Sugar*	No. 2 Alabama 34, No. 1 Miami (Fla.) 13
1-1-94	Orange*	No. 1 Florida St. 18, No. 2 Nebraska 16
1-2-96	Fiesta*	No. 1 Nebraska 62, No. 2 Florida 24
1-4-99	Fiesta#	No. 1 Tennessee 23, No. 2 Florida St. 16
1-4-00	Sugar#	No. 1 Florida St. 46, No. 2 Virginia Tech 29
1-3-03	Fiesta#	No. 2 Ohio St. 31, No. 1 Miami (Fla.) 24 (2 ot)

*Bowl alliance matched the No. 1 and No. 2 teams. #Bowl Championship Series matched the No. 1 and No. 2 teams.

Bowl Games and the National Championship

(How the bowl games determined the national champion from 1965 to present. Year listed is the football season before the bowl games.)
Note: The national champion was selected before the bowl games as follows: Associated Press (1936-64 and 1966-67); United Press International (1950-73); Football Writers Association of America (1954); and National Football Foundation and Hall of Fame (1959-70).

1965 The Associated Press (AP) selected Alabama as national champion after it defeated Nebraska, 39-28, in the Orange Bowl on January 1, 1966.

1968 AP selected Ohio State as national champion after it defeated Southern California, 27-16, in the Rose Bowl on January 1, 1969.

1969 AP selected Texas as national champion after it defeated Notre Dame, 21-17, in the Cotton Bowl on January 1, 1970.

1970 AP selected Nebraska as national champion after it defeated LSU, 17-12, in the Orange Bowl on January 1, 1971.

1971 AP selected Nebraska as national champion after it defeated Alabama, 38-6, in the Orange Bowl on January 1, 1972.

1972 AP selected Southern California as national champion after it defeated Ohio State, 42-17, in the Rose Bowl on January 1, 1973.

1973 AP selected Notre Dame as national champion after it defeated Alabama, 24-23, in the Sugar Bowl on December 31, 1973.

Beginning in 1974, all four of the national polls waited until after the bowl-game results before selecting a national champion. The following list shows how the bowl games figured in the final national championship polls for AP and UPI:

1974 First year of the agreement between the American Football Coaches Association (AFCA) and the UPI Board of Coaches to declare any teams on NCAA probation ineligible for the poll. AP—Oklahoma (11-0-0) did not participate in a bowl game because of NCAA probation. UPI—Southern California (10-1-1) defeated Ohio State, 18-17, in the Rose Bowl on January 1, 1975.

1975 AP and UPI both selected Oklahoma (11-1-0). Coach Barry Switzer's Sooners defeated Michigan, 14-6, in the Orange Bowl on January 1, 1976. Ohio State had led the top slot in the AP poll for nine consecutive weeks until a 23-10 loss to UCLA in the Rose Bowl on January 1, 1976. Oklahoma had led the AP poll for the first four weeks of the year.

1976 AP and UPI both selected Tony Dorsett-led Pittsburgh (12-0-0). Pittsburgh whipped Georgia, 27-3, in the Sugar Bowl on January 1, 1977. Pittsburgh took over the No. 1 position from Michigan in the ninth week of the season en route to an undefeated year.

1977 AP and UPI were in agreement again, picking Notre Dame as national titlist. The Irish crushed previously undefeated and top-ranked Texas, 38-10, in the Cotton Bowl on January 2, 1978. Notre Dame was the sixth team to be ranked No. 1 during the 1977 season in the AP poll.

1978 This was the last time until the 1991 season that the two polls split on a national champion, with AP selecting Alabama (11-1-0) and UPI going for Southern California (12-1-0). Alabama, ranked No. 2 in the AP poll, upset No. 1 Penn State, 14-7, in the Sugar Bowl on January 1, 1979. Alabama had been ranked No. 1 in the first two weeks of the season until a 24-14 loss to Southern California.

1979 Unbeaten Alabama (12-0-0) was the unanimous choice of both polls. Bear Bryant's Tide whipped Arkansas easily, 24-9, in the Sugar Bowl on January 1, 1980, to claim the title.

1980 Georgia made it three No. 1's in a row for the Southeastern Conference with an undefeated season (12-0-0) to take the top spot in both polls. Vince Dooley's Bulldogs downed Notre Dame, 17-10, behind freshman phenom Herschel Walker in the Sugar Bowl on January 1, 1981.

1981 Both polls selected unbeaten Clemson (12-0-0). The Tigers gave coach Danny Ford the first Clemson national football championship with a 22-15 victory over Nebraska in the Orange Bowl on January 1, 1982. Clemson did not take over the AP No. 1 slot until the next-to-last poll of the year.

1982 AP and UPI both selected Penn State (11-1-0). The Nittany Lions were No. 2 in the AP poll but knocked off No. 1 Georgia, 27-23, in the Sugar Bowl on January 1, 1983. Georgia had led the AP poll for the final five weeks of the season.

1983 AP and UPI had no choice but to select Miami (Florida) as the unanimous champion after the No. 2 Hurricanes downed No. 1 Nebraska, 31-30, in the Orange Bowl on January 2, 1984. Many observers felt this may have been the most exciting Orange Bowl ever played as the Cornhuskers failed on a two-point conversion attempt with 48 seconds remaining. Nebraska had led the AP poll since the first week of the season.

1984 Unknown and a victim of the Mountain time zone, Brigham Young (13-0-0) overcame many obstacles to ascend to No. 1 in both polls. Coach LaVell Edwards' Cougars downed Michigan, 24-17, in the Holiday Bowl on December 21, 1984. BYU took over the top spot in the AP poll with three weeks left in the season after four other teams came and went as the top-rated team.

1985 Oklahoma (11-1-0) returned as the unanimous choice of both polls. Barry Switzer's Sooners knocked off top-rated Penn State, 25-10, in the Orange Bowl on January 1, 1986, to claim the national title.

1986 Penn State (12-0-0) had to battle top-rated Miami (Florida) in the Fiesta Bowl to take the top slot in both polls. Joe Paterno's No. 2 Nittany Lions upset the Hurricanes, 14-10, on January 2, 1987, to claim the championship. Miami (Florida) had been ranked No. 1 for the final 10 weeks of the season.

1987 Miami (Florida) (12-0-0) bounced back to a similar scenario as Jimmy Johnson's Hurricanes played underdog and finished ranked first in both polls. The No. 2 Hurricanes beat No. 1-ranked Oklahoma, 20-14, in the Orange Bowl on January 1, 1988. The Sooners had been the top-rated AP team for 13 of the season's 15 polls.

1988 Notre Dame (12-0-0) finished as the top team in both polls and gave the Fiesta Bowl its second national title game in three seasons. Lou Holtz's Irish whipped West Virginia, 34-21, on January 2, 1989, to claim their eighth AP title. Notre Dame took over the top spot in the poll from UCLA in the ninth week of the season.

1989 Miami (Florida) (11-1-0) claimed its second national title in three years in both polls. The Hurricanes downed Alabama, 33-25, in the Sugar Bowl on January 1, 1990, while No. 1-ranked Colorado lost to Notre Dame, 21-6, in the Orange Bowl to clear the way. Notre Dame led the AP poll for 12 of the 15 weeks.

1990 Colorado (11-1-0) and Georgia Tech (11-0-1) split the polls for the first time since 1978 with the Buffs taking the AP vote and the Jackets the UPI. Colorado bounced back from a disappointing 1989 title march to edge Notre Dame, 10-9, in the Orange Bowl on January 1, 1991. Georgia Tech had little trouble with Nebraska, 45-21, in the Florida Citrus Bowl on January 1, 1991, to finish as Division I-A's only undefeated team.

1991 Miami (Florida) (12-0-0) and Washington (12-0-0) kept Division I-A playoff talk alive with a split in the national polls for the second consecutive year. The Hurricanes took

the AP vote, while the Huskies took both the USA Today/CNN and UPI polls. If either had stumbled in a bowl, then the other would have been a unanimous selection. However, Washington drubbed Michigan, 34-14, in the Rose Bowl, and Miami (Florida) had little trouble shutting out Nebraska, 22-0, in the Orange Bowl later that evening.

1992 No. 2 Alabama (13-0-0) turned in a magnificent performance in the Sugar Bowl by upsetting No. 1 Miami (Florida), 34-13, in a game dominated by the Crimson Tide. It marked the first year of the bowl coalition, and the bowlmeisters managed to match the top two teams for the national championship. It also marked the 17th time that a No. 1 team in the AP poll was knocked off in a bowl game since 1951. Alabama was named No. 1 in all polls after the January 1, 1993, matchup.

1993 No. 1 Florida State downed No. 2 Nebraska, 18-16, in the Orange Bowl to become a unanimous national champion. Notre Dame, winner over Texas A&M (24-21) in the Cotton Bowl, wanted to claim the title after beating the Seminoles in the regular season. But a late-season loss to Boston College cost the Irish in the polls. Florida State was No. 1 in all polls after the bowls.

1994 No. 1 Nebraska halted a seven-game bowl losing streak by posting a come-from-behind victory, 24-17, over Miami (Florida) in the Orange Bowl to cap a perfect 13-0 season with the national title. No. 2 Penn State, also undefeated at 12-0, downed Oregon, 38-20, in the Rose Bowl but had to settle for second place in the polls. Nebraska was No. 1 in all polls after the bowls.

1995 Another unanimous year for undefeated and No. 1 Nebraska. The Cornhuskers posted back-to-back national titles with a convincing 62-24 victory over No. 2 Florida in the bowl alliance's Fiesta Bowl matchup.

1996 No. 3 Florida took the national crown in all polls after meeting and beating No. 1 Florida State, 52-20, in the bowl alliance matchup in the Sugar Bowl. Just a month earlier, the Seminoles had knocked off No. 1 Florida and the Gators returned the favor. No. 2 Arizona State was defeated, 20-17, by Ohio State in the non-alliance Rose Bowl and dropped out of national championship consideration.

1997 In the last year before the bowl alliance would include the Rose Bowl, the two top-ranked teams—Michigan and Nebraska—never met for the title. Michigan, the final No. 1 in the Associated Press media poll defeated Washington State, 21-16, in the Rose Bowl while Nebraska, No. 1 in the final USA Today/ESPN coaches' poll, rolled over Tennessee, 42-17, in the Orange Bowl. Both teams were rewarded with a piece of the national title. It was the fourth time in the 1990s that the national champion was either shared or unclear.

1998 In the first year of the Bowl Championship Series (BCS), the No. 1 and No. 2 teams (Tennessee and Florida State, respectively) met for the title in the Fiesta. The BCS rankings were a compilation of the Associated Press, USA Today/ESPN, Seattle Times, New York Times, Sagarin polls and schedule strength to arrive at the top two teams. Tennessee defeated Florida State, 23-16, and was a unanimous No. 1 in all polls.

1999 In the second year of the BCS, No. 1 Florida State met No. 2 Virginia Tech in the Sugar Bowl. Florida State downed the Hokies, 46-29, to capture the title. The Seminoles, ranked No. 1 all year, went wire-to-wire in most polls for its second national prize in the 1990s.

2000 The third year of the BCS again matched the No. 1 and No. 2 teams (Oklahoma and Florida State, respectively), this time in the Orange Bowl. Oklahoma used team speed and a stingy defense to down the Seminoles, 13-2, holding Heisman Trophy winner Chirs Weinke without a touchdown. The Sooners were a unanimous pick in all polls.

2001 In the fourth year of the BCS, Miami (Florida) became the only undefeated team in the country (12-0) and claimed the mythical title by defeating Nebraska, 37-14, in the Rose Bowl. Miami was ranked No. 1 in the AP poll but Nebraska, No. 4 in the poll, was selected for the championship game over No. 2 Oregon. Heisman Trophy winner Eric Crouch was a member of the losing Cornhusker squad, while coach Larry Coker led Miami to the title in his first season as a head coach.

2002 The fifth year of the BCS ratings matched the No. 1 and No. 2 teams (Miami [Florida] and Ohio State) in the Fiesta Bowl and it turned out to be one of the most exciting college football bowls/poll championships. No. 2 Ohio State prevailed 31-24 after two overtime periods over No. 1 Miami (Florida), a team that had been ranked No. 1 since the first week of the season. Jim Tressel coached the Buckeyes to their first title since 1968 in only his second year at the helm. He also had four Division I-AA national titles at Youngstown State.

Bowl Results of Teams Ranked in The Associated Press Poll

The bowls and national polls have been perpetually linked since 1936, when The Associated Press introduced its weekly college football poll. The final AP poll was released at the end of the regular season until 1965, when bowl results were included for one year, dropped for two more and then added again in 1968 until the present. This is a list of the key bowl games as they related to the AP poll since 1936 (with pertinent references made to other polls where applicable).

(Key to polls: AP, Associated Press; UPI, United Press International; FW, Football Writers; NFF, National Football Foundation and Hall of Fame; USA/CNN, USA Today/Cable News Network; USA/NFF, USA Today/National Football Foundation and Hall of Fame; UPI/NFF, United Press International/National Football Foundation and Hall of Fame.)

1936 SUGAR—No. 6 Santa Clara beat No. 2 LSU, 21-14; ROSE—No. 3 Pittsburgh beat No. 5 Washington, 21-0; ORANGE—No. 14 Duquesne beat unranked Mississippi St., 13-12; COTTON—No. 16 TCU beat No. 20 Marquette, 16-6. (Minnesota selected No. 1 but did not play in a bowl)

1937 ROSE—No. 2 California beat No. 4 Alabama, 13-0; SUGAR—No. 9 Santa Clara beat No. 8 LSU, 6-0; COTTON—No. 18 Rice beat No. 17 Colorado, 28-14. (Pittsburgh selected No. 1 but did not play in a bowl)

1938 SUGAR—No. 1 TCU beat No. 6 Carnegie Mellon, 15-7; ORANGE—No. 2 Tennessee beat No. 4 Oklahoma, 17-0; ROSE—No. 7 Southern California beat No. 3 Duke, 7-3; COTTON—Unranked St. Mary's (Cal.) beat No. 11 Texas Tech, 20-13. (TCU selected No. 1)

1939 SUGAR—No. 1 Texas A&M beat No. 5 Tulane, 14-13; ROSE—No. 3 Southern California beat No. 2 Tennessee, 14-0; ORANGE—No. 16 Georgia Tech beat No. 6 Missouri, 21-7; COTTON—No. 12 Clemson beat No. 11 Boston College, 6-3. (Texas A&M selected No. 1)

1940 ROSE—No. 2 Stanford beat No. 7 Nebraska, 21-13; SUGAR—No. 5 Boston College beat No. 4 Tennessee, 19-13; COTTON—No. 6 Texas A&M beat No. 12 Fordham, 13-12; ORANGE—No. 9 Mississippi St. beat No. 13 Georgetown, 14-7. (Minnesota selected No. 1 but did not play in a bowl)

1941 ROSE—No. 12 Oregon St. beat No. 2 Duke, 20-16 (played at Durham, N.C., because of World War II); SUGAR—No. 6 Fordham beat No. 7 Missouri, 2-0; COTTON—No. 20 Alabama beat No. 9 Texas A&M, 29-21; ORANGE—No. 14 Georgia beat unranked TCU, 40-26. (Minnesota selected No. 1 but did not play in a bowl)

1942 ROSE—No. 2 Georgia beat No. 13 UCLA, 9-0; SUGAR—No. 7 Tennessee beat No. 4 Tulsa, 14-7; COTTON—No. 11 Texas beat No. 5 Georgia Tech, 14-7; ORANGE—No. 10 Alabama beat No. 8 Boston College, 37-21. (Ohio St. selected No. 1 but did not play in a bowl)

1943 ROSE—Unranked Southern California beat No. 12 Washington, 29-0; COTTON—No. 14 Texas tied unranked Randolph Field, 7-7; SUGAR—No. 13 Georgia Tech beat No. 15 Tulsa, 20-18. (Notre Dame selected No. 1 but did not play in a bowl)

1944 ROSE—No. 7 Southern California beat No. 12 Tennessee, 25-0; ORANGE—Unranked Tulsa beat No. 13 Georgia Tech, 26-12; No. 3 Randolph Field beat No. 20 Second Air Force, 13-6, in a battle of military powers. (Army selected No. 1 but did not play in a bowl)

1945 ROSE—No. 2 Alabama beat No. 11 Southern California, 34-14; COTTON—No. 10 Texas beat unranked Missouri, 40-27; ORANGE—Unranked Miami (Fla.) beat No. 16 Holy Cross, 13-6; SUGAR—No. 5 Oklahoma St. beat No. 7 St. Mary's (Cal.), 33-13. (Army selected No. 1 but did not play in a bowl)

1946 COTTON—No. 8 LSU tied No. 16 Arkansas, 0-0; ROSE—No. 5 Illinois beat No. 4 UCLA, 45-14; SUGAR—No. 3 Georgia beat No. 9 North Carolina, 20-10; ORANGE—No. 10 Rice beat No. 7 Tennessee, 8-0. (Notre Dame selected No. 1 but did not play in a bowl)

1947 ORANGE—No. 10 Georgia Tech beat No. 12 Kansas, 20-14; ROSE—No. 2 Michigan beat No. 8 Southern California, 49-0; SUGAR—No. 5 Alabama, 27-7; COTTON—No. 3 Southern Methodist tied No. 4 Penn St., 13-13. (Notre Dame selected No. 1 but did not play in a bowl; Michigan also declared champion in vote after Rose Bowl victory but AP kept Notre Dame as vote of record)

1948 ROSE—No. 7 Northwestern beat No. 4 California, 20-14; COTTON—No. 10 Southern Methodist beat No. 9 Oregon, 21-13; SUGAR—No. 5 Oklahoma beat No. 3 North Carolina, 14-6; ORANGE—Unranked Texas beat No. 8 Georgia, 41-28. (Michigan selected No. 1 but did not play in a bowl)

1949 ORANGE—No. 15 Santa Clara beat No. 11 Kentucky, 21-13; COTTON—No. 5 Rice beat No. 16 North Carolina, 27-13; ROSE—No. 6 Ohio St. beat No. 3 California, 17-14; SUGAR—No. 2 Oklahoma beat No. 9 LSU, 35-0. (Notre Dame selected No. 1 but did not play in a bowl)

1950 ROSE—No. 9 Michigan beat No. 5 California, 14-6; SUGAR—No. 7 Kentucky beat No. 1 Oklahoma, 13-7; ORANGE—No. 10 Clemson beat No. 15 Miami (Fla.), 15-14; COTTON—No. 4 Tennessee beat No. 3 Texas, 20-14. (Oklahoma selected No. 1 in vote before losing in Sugar Bowl)

1951 COTTON—No. 15 Kentucky beat No. 11 TCU, 20-7; ORANGE—No. 5 Georgia Tech beat No. 9 Baylor, 17-14; ROSE—No. 4 Illinois beat No. 7 Stanford, 40-7; SUGAR—No. 3 Maryland beat No. 1 Tennessee, 28-13. (Tennessee selected No. 1 in vote before losing in Sugar Bowl)

1952 ROSE—No. 5 Southern California beat No. 11 Wisconsin, 7-0; SUGAR—No. 2 Georgia Tech beat No. 7 Mississippi, 24-7; ORANGE—No. 9 Alabama beat No. 14 Syracuse, 61-6; COTTON—No. 10 Texas beat No. 8 Tennessee, 16-0. (Michigan St. selected No. 1 but did not play in a bowl)

1953 SUGAR—No. 8 Georgia Tech beat No. 10 West Virginia, 42-19; ORANGE—No. 4 Oklahoma beat No. 1 Maryland, 7-0; COTTON—No. 5 Rice beat No. 13 Alabama, 28-6; ROSE—No. 3 Michigan St. beat No. 5 UCLA, 28-20. (Maryland selected No. 1 before losing in Orange Bowl)

1954 ROSE—No. 1 Ohio St. beat No. 17 Southern California, 20-7; ORANGE—No. 14 Duke beat unranked Nebraska, 34-7; SUGAR—No. 5 Navy beat No. 6 Mississippi, 21-0; COTTON—Unranked Georgia Tech beat No. 10 Arkansas, 14-6. (Ohio St. remained No. 1 but UCLA named in UPI and FW polls)

1955 GATOR—Unranked Vanderbilt beat No. 8 Auburn, 25-13; ROSE—No. 2 Michigan St. beat No. 4 UCLA, 17-14; ORANGE—No. 1 Oklahoma beat No. 3 Maryland, 20-6; COTTON—No. 10 Mississippi beat No. 6 TCU, 14-13; SUGAR—No. 7 Georgia Tech beat No. 11 Pittsburgh, 7-0. (Oklahoma remained No. 1)

1956 SUGAR—No. 11 Baylor beat No. 2 Tennessee, 13-7; ORANGE—No. 20 Colorado beat No. 19 Clemson, 27-21; GATOR—No. 4 Georgia Tech beat No. 13 Pittsburgh, 21-14; ROSE—No. 3 Iowa beat No. 10 Oregon St., 35-19; COTTON—No. 14 TCU beat No. 8 Syracuse, 28-27. (Oklahoma selected No. 1 but did not play in a bowl)

1957 GATOR—No. 13 Tennessee beat No. 9 Texas A&M, 3-0; ROSE—No. 2 Ohio St. beat unranked Oregon, 10-7; COTTON—No. 5 Navy beat No. 8 Rice, 20-7; ORANGE—No. 4 Oklahoma beat No. 16 Duke, 48-21; SUGAR—No. 7 Mississippi beat No. 11 Texas, 39-7. (Auburn selected No. 1 but did not play in a bowl; Ohio St. selected No. 1 in both UPI and FW polls)

1958 SUGAR—No. 1 LSU beat No. 12 Clemson, 7-0; COTTON—No. 6 Air Force tied No. 10 TCU, 0-0; ROSE—No. 2 Iowa beat No. 16 California, 38-12; ORANGE—No. 5 Oklahoma beat No. 9 Syracuse, 21-6. (LSU remained No. 1 in AP and UPI but Iowa selected in FW poll)

1959 COTTON—No. 1 Syracuse beat No. 4 Texas, 23-14; ROSE—No. 8 Washington beat No. 6 Wisconsin, 44-8; ORANGE—No. 5 Georgia beat No. 18 Missouri, 14-0; SUGAR—No. 2 Mississippi beat No. 3 LSU, 21-0; BLUEBONNET—No. 11 Clemson beat No. 7 TCU, 23-7; LIBERTY—No. 12 Penn St. beat No. 10 Alabama, 7-0; GATOR—No. 9 Arkansas beat unranked Georgia Tech, 14-7. (Syracuse selected No. 1 by all four polls)

1960 ROSE—No. 6 Washington beat No. 1 Minnesota, 17-7; COTTON—No. 10 Duke beat No. 7 Arkansas, 7-6; SUGAR—No. 2 Mississippi beat unranked Rice, 14-6; ORANGE—No. 5 Missouri beat No. 4 Navy, 21-14; BLUEBONNET—No. 9 Alabama tied unranked Texas, 3-3. (Minnesota selected No. 1 by AP, UPI and NFF before losing in Rose Bowl; Mississippi named No. 1 in FW poll)

1961 COTTON—No. 3 Texas beat No. 5 Mississippi, 12-7; SUGAR—No. 1 Alabama beat No. 9 Arkansas, 10-3; ORANGE—No. 4 LSU beat No. 7 Colorado, 25-7; GOTHAM—Unranked Baylor beat No. 10 Utah St., 24-9; ROSE—No. 6 Minnesota beat No. 16 UCLA, 21-3. (Alabama selected No. 1 in AP, UPI and NFF, but Ohio St. picked by FW poll)

1962 ROSE—No. 1 Southern California beat No. 2 Wisconsin, 42-37; SUGAR—No. 3 Mississippi beat No. 6 Arkansas, 17-13; COTTON—No. 7 LSU beat No. 4 Texas, 13-0; GATOR—Unranked Florida beat No. 9 Penn St., 17-7; ORANGE—No. 5 Alabama beat No. 8 Oklahoma, 17-0. (Southern California selected No. 1 by all four polls)

1963 COTTON—No. 1 Texas beat No. 2 Navy, 28-6; ORANGE—No. 6 Nebraska beat No. 5 Auburn, 13-7; ROSE—No. 3 Illinois beat unranked Washington, 17-7; SUGAR—No. 8 Alabama beat No. 7 Mississippi, 12-7. (Texas selected No. 1 by all four polls)

1964 ORANGE—No. 5 Texas beat No. 1 Alabama, 21-17; ROSE—No. 4 Michigan beat No. 8 Oregon St., 34-7; COTTON—No. 2 Arkansas beat No. 6 Nebraska, 10-7; SUGAR—No. 7 LSU beat unranked Syracuse, 13-10. (Alabama selected No. 1 by AP and UPI before losing in the Orange Bowl, while Arkansas No. 1 in FW poll and Notre Dame No. 1 in NFF poll)

1965 *(First year final poll taken after bowl games)* ROSE—No. 5 UCLA beat No. 1 Michigan St., 14-12; COTTON—Unranked LSU beat No. 2 Arkansas, 14-7; SUGAR—No. 6 Missouri beat unranked Florida, 20-18; ORANGE—No. 4 Alabama beat No. 3 Nebraska, 39-28; BLUEBONNET—No. 7 Tennessee beat unranked Tulsa, 27-6; GATOR—Unranked Georgia Tech beat No. 10 Texas Tech, 31-21. (Alabama selected No. 1 in final poll but Michigan St. named by UPI and NFF polls and they tied in FW poll)

1966 *(Returned to final poll taken before bowls)* SUGAR—No. 3 Alabama beat No. 6 Nebraska, 34-7; ROSE—No. 7 Purdue beat unranked Southern California, 14-13; COTTON—No. 4 Georgia beat No. 10 Southern Methodist, 24-9; ORANGE—Unranked Florida beat No. 8 Georgia Tech, 27-12; LIBERTY—No. 9 Miami (Fla.) beat unranked Virginia Tech, 14-7. (Notre Dame selected No. 1 by AP, UPI and FW polls and tied with Michigan St. in NFF poll; neither team played in a bowl game and they tied in a regular-season game)

1967 ROSE—No. 1 Southern California beat No. 4 Indiana, 14-3; SUGAR—Unranked LSU beat No. 6 Wyoming, 20-13; ORANGE—No. 3 Oklahoma beat No. 2 Tennessee, 26-24; COTTON—Unranked Texas A&M beat No. 8 Alabama, 20-16; GATOR—No. 10 Penn St. tied unranked Florida St., 17-17. (Southern California selected No. 1 in all four polls)

1968 *(Returned to final poll taken after bowl games)* ROSE—No. 1 Ohio St. beat No. 2 Southern California, 27-16; SUGAR—No. 9 Arkansas beat No. 4 Georgia, 16-2; ORANGE—No. 3 Penn St. beat No. 6 Kansas, 15-14; COTTON—No. 5 Texas beat No. 8 Tennessee, 36-13; BLUEBONNET—No. 20 Southern Methodist beat No. 10 Oklahoma, 28-27; GATOR—No. 16 Missouri beat No. 12 Alabama, 35-10. (Ohio St. remained No. 1)

1969 COTTON—No. 1 Texas beat No. 9 Notre Dame, 21-17; SUGAR—No. 13 Mississippi beat No. 3 Arkansas, 27-22; ORANGE—No. 2 Penn St. beat No. 6 Missouri, 10-3; ROSE—No. 5 Southern California beat No. 7 Michigan, 10-3. (Texas remained No. 1)

1970 COTTON—No. 6 Notre Dame beat No. 1 Texas, 24-11; ROSE—No. 12 Stanford beat No. 2 Ohio St., 27-17; SUGAR—No. 3 Tennessee beat No. 11 Air Force, 34-13; ORANGE—No. 3 Nebraska beat No. 8 LSU, 17-12; PEACH—No. 9 Arizona St. beat unranked North Carolina, 48-26. (Nebraska selected No. 1 in AP and FW polls while Texas was No. 1 in UPI and tied with Ohio St. in NFF poll)

1971 ORANGE—No. 1 Nebraska beat No. 2 Alabama, 38-6; SUGAR—No. 3 Oklahoma beat No. 5 Auburn, 40-22; ROSE—No. 16 Stanford beat No. 4 Michigan, 13-12; GATOR—No. 6 Georgia beat unranked North Carolina, 7-3; COTTON—No. 10 Penn St. beat No. 12 Texas, 30-6; FIESTA—No. 8 Arizona St. beat unranked Florida St., 45-38; BLUEBONNET—No. 7 Colorado beat No. 15 Houston, 29-17. (Nebraska remained No. 1 in all four polls)

1972 ROSE—No. 1 Southern California beat No. 3 Ohio St., 42-17; COTTON—No. 7 Texas beat No. 4 Alabama, 17-13; SUGAR—No. 2 Oklahoma beat No. 5 Penn St., 14-0; ORANGE—No. 9 Nebraska beat No. 12 Notre Dame, 40-6; GATOR—No. 6 Auburn beat No. 13 Colorado, 24-3; BLUEBONNET—No. 11 Tennessee beat No. 10 LSU, 24-17. (Southern California remained No. 1 in all four polls)

1973 SUGAR—No. 3 Notre Dame beat No. 1 Alabama, 24-23; ROSE—No. 4 Ohio St. beat No. 7 Southern California, 42-21; ORANGE—No. 6 Penn St. beat No. 13 LSU, 16-9; COTTON—No. 12 Nebraska beat No. 8 Texas, 19-3; FIESTA—No. 10 Arizona St. beat unranked Pittsburgh, 28-7; BLUEBONNET—No. 14 Houston beat No. 17 Tulane, 47-7. (Notre Dame selected No. 1 in AP, FW and NFF polls, Alabama named No. 1 by UPI but No. 2 Oklahoma was on probation and could not go to a bowl game)

1974 ROSE—No. 5 Southern California beat No. 3 Ohio St., 18-17; ORANGE—No. 9 Notre Dame beat No. 2 Alabama, 13-11; GATOR—No. 6 Auburn beat No. 11 Texas,

27-3; COTTON—No. 7 Penn St. beat No. 12 Baylor, 41-20; SUGAR—No. 8 Nebraska beat No. 18 Florida, 13-10; LIBERTY—Unranked Tennessee beat No. 10 Maryland, 7-3. (Oklahoma selected No. 1 in AP poll despite being on probation and not able to participate in bowl game; Southern California named No. 1 by UPI, FW and NFF polls)

1975 ROSE—No. 11 UCLA beat No. 1 Ohio St., 23-10; ORANGE—No. 3 Oklahoma beat No. 5 Michigan, 14-6; LIBERTY—No. 17 Southern California beat No. 2 Texas A&M, 20-0; SUGAR—No. 4 Alabama beat No. 8 Penn St., 13-6; FIESTA—No. 7 Arizona St. beat No. 6 Nebraska, 17-14; COTTON—No. 18 Arkansas beat No. 12 Georgia, 31-10; BLUEBONNET—No. 9 Texas beat No. 10 Colorado, 38-21. (Oklahoma selected No. 1 in all four polls)

1976 SUGAR—No. 1 Pittsburgh beat No. 5 Georgia, 27-3; ROSE—No. 3 Southern California beat No. 2 Michigan, 14-6; COTTON—No. 6 Houston beat No. 4 Maryland, 30-21; LIBERTY—No. 16 Alabama beat No. 7 UCLA, 36-6; ORANGE—No. 11 Ohio St. beat No. 12 Colorado, 27-10; FIESTA—No. 8 Oklahoma beat unranked Wyoming, 41-7; SUN—No. 10 Texas A&M beat unranked Florida, 37-14; BLUEBONNET—No. 13 Nebraska beat No. 9 Texas Tech, 27-24. (Pittsburgh remained No. 1 in all four polls)

1977 COTTON—No. 5 Notre Dame beat No. 1 Texas, 38-10; ORANGE—No. 6 Arkansas beat No. 2 Oklahoma, 31-6; SUGAR—No. 3 Alabama beat No. 9 Ohio St., 35-6; ROSE—No. 13 Washington beat No. 4 Michigan, 27-20; FIESTA—No. 8 Penn St. beat No. 15 Arizona St., 42-30; GATOR—No. 10 Pittsburgh beat No. 11 Clemson, 34-3. (Notre Dame selected No. 1 in all four polls)

1978 SUGAR—No. 2 Alabama beat No. 1 Penn St., 14-7; ROSE—No. 3 Southern California beat No. 5 Michigan, 17-10; ORANGE—No. 4 Oklahoma beat No. 6 Nebraska, 31-24; COTTON—No. 10 Notre Dame beat No. 9 Houston, 35-34; GATOR—No. 7 Clemson beat No. 20 Ohio St., 17-15; FIESTA—No. 8 Arkansas tied No. 15 UCLA, 10-10. (Alabama selected No. 1 in AP, FW and NFF polls, while Southern California named in UPI)

1979 ROSE—No. 3 Southern California beat No. 1 Ohio St., 17-16; SUGAR—No. 2 Alabama beat No. 6 Arkansas, 24-9; ORANGE—No. 5 Oklahoma beat No. 4 Florida St., 24-7; COTTON—No. 8 Houston beat No. 7 Nebraska, 17-14; SUN—No. 13 Washington beat No. 11 Texas, 14-7; FIESTA—No. 10 Pittsburgh beat unranked Arizona, 16-10. (Alabama selected No. 1 in all four polls)

1980 SUGAR—No. 1 Georgia beat No. 7 Notre Dame, 17-10; ORANGE—No. 4 Oklahoma beat No. 2 Florida St., 18-17; ROSE—No. 5 Michigan beat No. 16 Washington, 23-6; COTTON—No. 9 Alabama beat No. 6 Baylor, 30-2; GATOR—No. 3 Pittsburgh beat No. 18 South Carolina, 37-9; SUN—No. 8 Nebraska beat No. 17 Mississippi St., 31-17; FIESTA—No. 10 Penn St. beat No. 11 Ohio St., 31-19; BLUEBONNET—No. 13 North Carolina beat unranked Texas, 16-7. (Georgia remained No. 1 in all four polls)

1981 ORANGE—No. 1 Clemson beat No. 4 Nebraska, 22-15; SUGAR—No. 10 Pittsburgh beat No. 2 Georgia, 24-20; COTTON—No. 6 Texas beat No. 3 Alabama, 14-12; GATOR—No. 11 North Carolina beat unranked Arkansas, 31-27; ROSE—No. 12 Washington beat No. 13 Iowa, 28-0; FIESTA—No. 7 Penn St. beat No. 8 Southern California, 26-10. (Clemson remained No. 1 in all four polls)

1982 SUGAR—No. 2 Penn St. beat No. 1 Georgia, 27-23; ORANGE—No. 3 Nebraska beat No. 13 LSU, 21-20; COTTON—No. 4 Southern Methodist beat No. 6 Pittsburgh, 7-3; ROSE—No. 5 UCLA beat No. 19 Michigan, 24-14; ALOHA—No. 9 Washington beat No. 14 Maryland, 21-20; FIESTA—No. 11 Arizona St. beat No. 12 Oklahoma, 32-21; BLUEBONNET—No. 14 Arkansas beat unranked Florida, 28-24. (Penn St. selected No. 1 in all four polls)

1983 ORANGE—No. 5 Miami (Fla.) beat No. 1 Nebraska, 31-30; COTTON—No. 7 Georgia beat No. 2 Texas, 10-9; SUGAR—No. 3 Auburn beat No. 8 Michigan, 9-7; ROSE—Unranked UCLA beat No. 4 Illinois, 45-9; HOLIDAY—No. 9 Brigham Young beat unranked Missouri, 21-17; GATOR—No. 11 Florida beat No. 10 Iowa, 14-6; FIESTA—No. 14 Ohio St. beat No. 15 Pittsburgh, 28-23. (Miami [Fla.], selected No. 1 in all four polls)

1984 HOLIDAY—No. 1 Brigham Young beat unranked Michigan, 24-17; ORANGE—No. 4 Washington beat No. 2 Oklahoma, 28-17; SUGAR—No. 5 Nebraska beat No. 11 LSU, 28-10; ROSE—No. 18 Southern California beat No. 6 Ohio St., 20-17; COTTON—No. 8 Boston College beat unranked Houston, 45-28; GATOR—No. 9 Oklahoma St. beat No. 7 South Carolina, 21-14; ALOHA—No. 10 Southern Methodist beat No. 17 Notre Dame, 27-20. (Brigham Young remained No. 1 in all four polls)

1985 ORANGE—No. 3 Oklahoma beat No. 1 Penn St., 25-10; SUGAR—No. 8 Tennessee beat No. 2 Miami (Fla.), 35-7; ROSE—No. 13 UCLA beat No. 4 Iowa, 45-28; COTTON—No. 11 Texas A&M beat No. 16 Auburn, 36-16; FIESTA—No. 5 Michigan beat No. 7 Nebraska, 27-23; BLUEBONNET—No. 10 Air Force beat unranked Texas, 24-16. (Oklahoma selected No. 1 in all four polls)

1986 FIESTA—No. 2 Penn St. beat No. 1 Miami (Fla.), 14-10; ORANGE—No. 3 Oklahoma beat No. 9 Arkansas, 42-8; ROSE—No. 7 Arizona St. beat No. 4 Michigan, 22-15; SUGAR—No. 6 Nebraska beat No. 5 LSU, 30-15; COTTON—No. 11 Ohio St. beat No. 8 Texas A&M, 28-12; CITRUS—No. 10 Auburn beat unranked Southern California, 16-7; SUN—No. 13 Alabama beat No. 12 Washington, 28-6. (Penn St. selected No. 1 in all four polls)

1987 ORANGE—No. 2 Miami (Fla.) beat No. 1 Oklahoma, 20-14; FIESTA—No. 3 Florida St. beat No. 5 Nebraska, 31-28; SUGAR—No. 4 Syracuse tied No. 6 Auburn, 16-16; ROSE—No. 8 Michigan St. beat No. 16 Southern California, 20-17; COTTON—No. 13 Texas A&M beat No. 12 Notre Dame, 35-10; GATOR—No. 7 LSU beat No. 9 South Carolina, 30-13; ALOHA—No. 10 UCLA beat unranked Florida, 20-16. (Miami [Fla.], selected No. 1 in all four polls)

1988 FIESTA—No. 1 Notre Dame beat No. 3 West Virginia, 34-21; ORANGE—No. 2 Miami (Fla.) beat No. 6 Nebraska, 23-3; SUGAR—No. 4 Florida St. beat No. 7 Auburn, 13-7; ROSE—No. 11 Michigan beat No. 5 Southern California, 22-14; COTTON—No. 9 UCLA beat No. 8 Arkansas, 17-3; CITRUS—No. 13 Clemson beat No. 10 Oklahoma, 13-6. (Notre Dame selected No. 1 in all four polls)

1989 ORANGE—No. 4 Notre Dame beat No. 1 Colorado, 21-6; SUGAR—No. 2 Miami (Fla.) beat No. 7 Alabama, 33-25; ROSE—No. 12 Southern California beat No. 3 Michigan, 17-10; COTTON—No. 8 Tennessee beat No. 10 Arkansas, 31-27; FIESTA—No. 5 Florida St. beat No. 6 Nebraska, 41-17; HALL OF FAME—No. 9 Auburn beat No. 21 Ohio St., 31-14; CITRUS—No. 11 Illinois beat No. 15 Virginia, 31-21. (Miami [Fla.], selected No. 1 in all four polls)

1990 ORANGE—No. 1 Colorado beat No. 5 Notre Dame, 10-9; CITRUS—No. 2 Georgia Tech beat No. 19 Nebraska, 45-21; COTTON—No. 4 Miami (Fla.) beat No. 3 Texas, 46-3; BLOCKBUSTER—No. 6 Florida St. beat No. 7 Penn St., 24-17; ROSE—No. 8 Washington beat No. 17 Iowa, 46-34; GATOR—No. 12 Michigan beat No. 15 Mississippi, 35-3; SUGAR—No. 10 Tennessee beat unranked Virginia, 23-22. (Colorado selected No. 1 in AP, FW and NFF polls, but Georgia Tech picked in UPI poll)

1991 ORANGE—No. 1 Miami (Fla.) beat No. 11 Nebraska, 22-0; ROSE—No. 2 Washington beat No. 4 Michigan, 34-14; COTTON—No. 5 Florida St. beat No. 9 Texas A&M, 10-3; BLOCKBUSTER—No. 8 Alabama beat No. 15 Colorado, 30-25; SUGAR—No. 18 Notre Dame beat No. 3 Florida, 39-28; FIESTA—No. 6 Penn St. beat No. 10 Tennessee, 42-17; CITRUS—No. 14 California beat No. 13 Clemson, 37-13; PEACH—No. 12 East Caro. beat No. 21 North Carolina St., 37-34; HOLIDAY—No. 7 Iowa tied unranked Brigham Young, 13-13. (Miami [Fla.], selected No. 1 in AP poll, while Washington named in USA/CNN, NFF and FW polls)

1992 SUGAR—No. 2 Alabama beat No. 1 Miami (Fla.), 34-13; GATOR—No. 14 Florida beat No. 12 North Carolina St., 27-10; COTTON—No. 5 Notre Dame beat No. 4 Texas A&M, 28-3; HALL OF FAME—No. 17 Tennessee beat No. 16 Boston College, 38-23; CITRUS—No. 8 Georgia beat No. 15 Ohio St., 21-14; ROSE—No. 7 Michigan beat No. 9 Washington, 38-31; ORANGE—No. 3 Florida St. beat No. 11 Nebraska, 27-14; FIESTA—No. 6 Syracuse beat No. 10 Colorado, 26-22; BLOCKBUSTER—No. 13 Stanford beat No. 21 Penn St., 24-3; PEACH—No. 19 North Carolina beat No. 24 Mississippi St., 21-17; COPPER—No. 18 Washington St. beat unranked Utah, 31-28. (Alabama selected No. 1 in all four polls)

1993 ORANGE—No. 1 Florida St. beat No. 2 Nebraska, 18-16; SUGAR—No. 8 Florida beat No. 3 West Virginia, 41-7; ROSE—No. 9 Wisconsin beat No. 14 UCLA, 21-16; COTTON—No. 4 Notre Dame beat No. 7 Texas A&M, 24-21; CARQUEST—No. 15 Boston College beat unranked Virginia, 31-13; FIESTA—No. 16 Arizona beat No. 10 Miami (Fla.), 29-0; FLORIDA CITRUS—No. 13 Penn St. beat No. 6 Tennessee, 31-13; HALL OF FAME—No. 23 Michigan beat unranked North Carolina St., 42-7; GATOR—No. 18 Alabama beat No. 12 North Carolina, 24-10; PEACH—No. 24 Clemson beat unranked Kentucky, 14-13; INDEPENDENCE—No. 22 Virginia Tech beat unranked Indiana, 45-20; HOLIDAY—No. 11 Ohio St. beat unranked Brigham Young, 28-21; COPPER—No. 20 Kansas St. beat unranked Wyoming, 52-17; LIBERTY—No. 25 Louisville beat unranked Michigan St., 18-7; ALOHA—No. 17 Colorado beat No. 25 Fresno St., 41-30; JOHN HANCOCK—No. 19 Oklahoma beat unranked Texas Tech, 41-10. (Florida St. selected in all four major polls—AP, FW, USA/CNN and USA/NFF)

1994 ORANGE—No. 1 Nebraska beat No. 3 Miami (Fla.), 24-17; ROSE—No. 2 Penn St. beat No. 12 Oregon, 38-20; FIESTA—No. 4 Colorado beat unranked Notre Dame, 41-24; SUGAR—No. 7 Florida St. beat No. 5 Florida, 23-17; FLORIDA CITRUS—No. 6 Alabama beat No. 13 Ohio St., 24-17; FREEDOM—No. 14 Utah beat No. 15 Arizona, 16-13; ALOHA—Unranked Boston College beat No. 11 Kansas St., 12-7; HOLIDAY—No. 20 Michigan beat No. 10 Colorado St., 24-14; PEACH—No. 23 North Carolina St. beat No. 16 Mississippi St., 28-24; INDEPENDENCE—No. 18 Virginia beat unranked TCU, 20-10; SUN—Unranked Texas beat No. 19 North Carolina, 35-31; GATOR—Unranked Tennessee beat No. 17 Virginia Tech, 45-23. (Nebraska selected in all four major polls—AP, UPI, USA/CNN and FW)

1995 FIESTA—No. 1 Nebraska beat No. 2 Florida, 62-24; ROSE—No. 17 Southern California beat No. 3 Northwestern, 41-32; FLORIDA CITRUS—No. 4 Tennessee beat No. 4 Ohio St., 20-14; ORANGE—No. 8 Florida St. beat No. 6 Notre Dame, 31-26; COTTON—No. 7 Colorado beat No. 12 Oregon, 38-6; SUGAR—No. 13 Virginia Tech beat No. 9 Texas, 28-10; HOLIDAY—No. 10 Kansas St. beat unranked Colorado St., 54-21; ALOHA—No. 11 Kansas beat unranked UCLA, 51-30; ALAMO—No. 19 Texas A&M beat No. 14 Michigan, 22-20; OUTBACK—No. 15 Penn St. beat No. 16 Auburn, 43-14; PEACH—No. 18 Virginia beat unranked Georgia, 34-27. (Nebraska selected in all four major polls—AP, UPI, USA/CNN and FW)

1996 SUGAR—No. 3 Florida beat No. 1 Florida St., 52-20; FIESTA—No. 7 Penn St. beat No. 20 Texas, 38-15; ROSE—No. 4 Ohio St. beat No. 2 Arizona St., 20-17; COTTON—No. 5 Brigham Young beat No. 14 Kansas St., 19-15; FLORIDA CITRUS—No. 9 Tennessee beat No. 11 Northwestern, 48-28; GATOR—No. 12 North Carolina beat No. 25 West Virginia, 20-13; OUTBACK—No. 16 Alabama beat No. 15 Michigan, 17-14; ORANGE—No. 6 Nebraska beat No. 10 Virginia Tech, 41-21; INDEPENDENCE—Unranked Auburn beat No. 24 Army, 32-29; SUN—Unranked Stanford beat unranked Michigan St., 38-0; HOLIDAY—No. 8 Colorado beat No. 13 Washington, 33-21; ALAMO—No. 21 Iowa beat unranked Texas Tech, 27-0; PEACH—No. 17 LSU beat unranked Clemson, 10-7; COPPER—Unranked Wisconsin beat unranked Utah, 38-10; CARQUEST—No. 19 Miami (Fla.) beat unranked Virginia, 31-21; LIBERTY—No. 23 Syracuse beat unranked Houston, 30-17; ALOHA—Unranked Navy beat unranked California, 42-38; LAS VEGAS—Unranked Nevada beat unranked Ball St., 18-15. (Florida selected in all four major polls—AP, USA/CNN, FW and NFF/HOF)

1997 ROSE—No. 1 Michigan beat No. 9 Washington St., 21-16; ORANGE—No. 2 Nebraska beat No. 7 Tennessee, 42-17; SUGAR—No. 3 Florida St. beat No. 12 Ohio St., 31-14; FIESTA—No. 8 Kansas St. beat No. 21 Syracuse, 35-18; COTTON—No. 5 UCLA beat No. 20 Texas A&M, 29-23; FLORIDA CITRUS—No. 4 Florida beat No. 16 Penn St., 21-6; ALAMO—No. 15 Purdue beat No. 24 Oklahoma St., 33-20; GATOR—No. 6 North Carolina beat unranked Virginia Tech, 42-3; HOLIDAY—No. 17 Colorado St. beat No. 23 Missouri, 35-24; PEACH—No. 11 Auburn beat unranked Clemson, 21-17; LAS VEGAS—Unranked Oregon beat unranked Air Force, 41-13; ALOHA—No. 18 Washington beat unranked Michigan St., 51-23; MOTOR CITY—No. 22 Mississippi beat unranked Marshall, 34-31; INSIGHT.COM—Unranked Arizona beat unranked New Mexico, 20-14; INDEPENDENCE—No. 13 LSU beat unranked Notre Dame, 27-9; CARQUEST—No. 25 Georgia Tech beat unranked West Virginia, 35-30; HUMANITARIAN—Unranked Cincinnati beat unranked Utah St., 35-19; SUN—No. 14 Arizona St. beat unranked Iowa, 17-7; LIBERTY—No. 19 Southern Miss. beat unranked Pittsburgh, 41-7; OUTBACK—No. 10 Georgia beat unranked Wisconsin, 33-6. (Michigan selected by AP [media], FW and NFF/HOF while Nebraska was picked by the USA/ESPN [coaches])

1998 FIESTA—No. 1 Tennessee beat No. 2 Florida St., 23-16; SUGAR—No. 3 Ohio St. beat No. 8 Texas A&M, 24-14; ROSE—No. 9 Wisconsin beat No. 6 UCLA, 38-31; ORANGE—No. 7 Florida beat No. 18 Syracuse, 31-10; HOLIDAY—No. 5 Arizona beat No. 14 Nebraska, 23-20; FLORIDA CITRUS—No. 15 Michigan beat No. 11 Arkansas, 45-31; GATOR—No. 12 Georgia Tech beat No. 17 Notre Dame, 35-28; COTTON—No. 20 Texas beat No. 25 Mississippi St., 38-11; PEACH—No. 19 Georgia beat No. 13 Virginia, 35-33; LIBERTY—No. 10 Tulane beat unranked Brigham Young, 41-27; OUTBACK—No. 22 Penn St. beat unranked Kentucky, 26-14; MICRON PC—No. 24 Miami (Fla.) beat unranked North Carolina St., 46-23; OAHU CLASSIC—No. 16 Air Force beat unranked Washington, 45-25; ALOHA CLASSIC—Unranked Colorado beat No. 21 Oregon, 51-43; INSIGHT.COM—No. 23 Missouri beat unranked West Virginia, 34-31; LAS VEGAS—Unranked North Carolina beat unranked San Diego St., 20-13; MOTOR CITY—Unranked Marshall beat unranked Louisville, 48-29; MUSIC CITY—Unranked Virginia Tech beat unranked Alabama, 38-7; HUMANITARIAN—Unranked Idaho beat unranked Southern Miss., 42-35; SUN—Unranked TCU beat unranked Southern California, 28-19; INDEPENDENCE—Unranked Mississippi beat unranked Texas Tech, 35-18. (Tennessee, No. 1 in the BCS poll, defeated No. 2 Florida St., 23-16, in the Fiesta Bowl and was named champion in all four major polls—AP [media], USA/ESPN [coaches], FW and NFF/HOF)

1999 SUGAR—No. 1 Florida St. beat No. 2 Virginia Tech, 46-29; FIESTA—No. 3 Nebraska beat No. 6 Tennessee, 31-21; ROSE—No. 4 Wisconsin beat No. 22 Stanford, 17-9; ORANGE—No. 8 Michigan beat No. 5 Alabama, 35-34 in overtime; HOLIDAY—No. 7 Kansas St. beat unranked Washington, 24-20; FLORIDA CITRUS—No. 9 Michigan St. beat No. 10 Florida, 37-34; MOTOR CITY—No. 11 Marshall beat unranked Brigham Young, 21-3; SUN—Unranked Oregon beat No. 12 Minnesota, 24-20; ALAMO—No. 13 Penn St. beat No. 18 Texas A&M, 24-0; COTTON—No. 24 Arkansas beat No. 14 Texas, 27-6; PEACH—No. 15 Mississippi St. beat unranked Clemson, 17-7; LIBERTY—No. 16 Southern Miss. beat unranked Colorado St., 23-17; GATOR—No. 23 Miami (Fla.) beat No. 17 Georgia Tech, 28-13; OUTBACK—No. 21 Georgia beat No. 19 Purdue, 28-25 in overtime; INSIGHT.COM—Unranked Colorado beat No. 25 Boston College, 62-28; LAS VEGAS—Unranked Utah beat unranked Fresno St., 17-16; MOBILE ALABAMA—Unranked TCU beat unranked East Caro., 28-14; ALOHA CLASSIC—Unranked Wake Forest beat unranked Arizona St., 23-3; OAHU CLASSIC—Unranked Hawaii beat unranked Oregon St., 23-17; MUSIC CITY—Unranked Syracuse beat unranked Kentucky, 20-13; HUMANITARIAN—Unranked Boise St. beat unranked Louisville, 34-31; MICRONPC.COM—Unranked Illinois beat unranked Virginia, 63-21; INDEPENDENCE—Unranked Mississippi beat unranked Oklahoma, 27-25. (BCS No. 1 Florida St. beat BCS No. 2 Virginia Tech, 46-29, in the Sugar Bowl and was selected champion in all four major polls—AP [media], USA/ESPN [coaches], FW and NFF/HOF)

2000 ORANGE—No. 1 Oklahoma beat No. 3 Florida St., 13-2; SUGAR—No. 2 Miami (Fla.) beat No. 7 Florida, 37-20; FIESTA—No. 5 Oregon St. beat No. 10 Notre Dame, 41-9; ROSE—No. 4 Washington beat No. 14 Purdue, 34-24; FLORIDA CITRUS—No. 17 Michigan beat No. 20 Auburn, 31-28; GATOR—No. 6 Virginia Tech beat No. 16 Clemson, 41-20; OUTBACK—Unranked South Carolina beat No. 19 Ohio St., 24-7; COTTON—No. 11 Kansas St. beat No. 21 Tennessee, 35-21; INDEPENDENCE–Unranked Mississippi St. beat unranked Texas A&M, 43-41, in overtime; ALAMO—No. 9 Nebraska beat No. 18 Northwestern, 66-17; HOLIDAY—No. 8 Oregon beat No. 12 Texas, 35-30; LIBERTY—No. 23 Colorado St. beat No. 22 Louisville, 22-17; PEACH—Unranked LSU beat No. 15 Georgia Tech, 28-14; OAHU CLASSIC—No. 24 Georgia beat unranked Virginia, 37-14; MOBILE ALABAMA—Unranked Southern Miss. beat No. 13 TCU, 28-21. (BCS No. 1 Oklahoma beat BCS No. 2 Florida St., 13-2, in the Orange Bowl and was selected champion in all four major polls—AP [media], USA/ESPN [coaches], FW and NFF/HOF)

2001 ROSE—No. 1 Miami (Fla.) beat No. 4 Nebraska, 37-14; FIESTA—No. 2 Oregon beat No. 3 Colorado, 38-16; ORANGE—No. 5 Florida beat No. 6 Maryland, 56-23; SUGAR—No. 12 LSU beat No. 7 Illinois, 47-34; FLORIDA CITRUS—No. 8 Tennessee beat No. 17 Michigan, 45-17; GATOR—No. 24 Florida St. beat No. 15 Virginia Tech, 30-17; OUTBACK—No. 14 South Carolina beat No. 22 Ohio St., 31-28; COTTON—No. 10 Oklahoma beat unranked Arkansas, 10-3; PEACH—Unranked North Carolina beat unranked Auburn, 16-10; LIBERTY—No. 23 Louisville beat No. 19 Brigham Young, 28-10; SILICON VALLEY—Unranked Michigan St. beat No. 20 Fresno St., 44-35; SUN—No. 13 Washington St. beat unranked Purdue, 33-27; INSIGHT.COM—No. 18 Syracuse beat unranked Kansas St., 26-3; MOTOR CITY—No. 25 Toledo beat unranked Cincinnati, 23-16; HOLIDAY—No. 9 Texas beat No. 21 Washington, 47-43; MUSIC CITY—Unranked Boston College beat No. 16 Georgia, 20-16; SEATTLE—Unranked Georgia Tech beat No. 11 Stanford, 24-14. (BCS No. 1 Miami [Fla.] beat BCS No. 2 Nebraska, 37-14, in the Rose Bowl and was selected champion in all four major polls—AP [media], USA/ESPN [coaches], FW and NFF/HOF).

2002 FIESTA—No. 2 Ohio St. beat No. 1 Miami (Fla.), 31-24 (2 ot); ORANGE—No. 5 Southern California beat No. 3 Iowa, 38-17; ROSE—No. 8 Oklahoma beat No. 7 Washington St., 34-14; SUGAR—No. 4 Georgia beat No. 16 Florida St., 26-13; CAPITAL ONE—No. 19 Auburn beat No. 10 Penn St., 13-9; GATOR—No. 17 North Carolina St. beat No. 11 Notre Dame, 28-6. (BCS No. 2 Ohio St. beat BCS No. 1 Miami [Fla.], 31-24 in two overtimes, in the Fiesta Bowl and was selected chanpion in all four major polls—AP [media], USA/ESPN [coaches], FW and NFF/HOF).

Most Consecutive Bowl-Game Victories

(Bowls do not have to be in consecutive years; year listed is calendar year in which bowl was played)

College	Victories (Years)
Florida St.	11 (1985-86-88-89-90-90-92-93-94-95-96)
Southern California	9 (1923-24-30-32-33-39-40-44-45)
UCLA	8 (1983-84-85-86-86-87-89-91)
Georgia Tech	8 (1947-48-52-53-54-55-56-56)
Syracuse	7 (1989-89-90-92-93-96-97)
Colorado	6 (1993-95-96-97-98-99)
Penn St.	6 (1994-95-96-97-98-99)
Alabama	6 (1975-76-78-79-80-81)
Nebraska	6 (1969-71-72-73-74-74)
Arizona St.	5 (1970-71-72-73-75)
Alabama	5 (1991-93-93-95-97)
Notre Dame	5 (1973-75-76-78-79)
Tennessee	5 (1986-86-88-90-91)
Penn St.	5 (1979-80-81-82-83)
Air Force	4 (1982-83-84-85)
Alabama	4 (1982-83-85-86)
North Carolina	4 (1979-80-81-82)
Michigan	4 (1902-48-51-65)
Southern California	3 (1993-95-96)
California	3 (1990-92-93)
Notre Dame	3 (1992-93-94)

Most Consecutive Seasons With Bowl-Game Victories

11 Florida St.—85 Gator, Oklahoma St. 34-23; 86 All-American, Indiana 27-13; 87 Fiesta, Nebraska 31-28; 88 Sugar, Auburn 13-7; 89 Fiesta, Nebraska 41-17; 90 Blockbuster, Penn St. 24-17; 92 Cotton, Texas A&M 10-2; 93 Orange, Nebraska 27-14; 94 Orange, Nebraska 18-16; 95 Sugar, Florida 23-17; 96 Orange, Notre Dame 31-26. Coach: Bobby Bowden.
7 UCLA—83 Rose, Michigan 24-14; 84 Rose, Illinois 45-9; 85 Fiesta, Miami (Fla.) 39-37; 86 Rose, Iowa 45-28; 86 Freedom, Brigham Young 31-10; 87 Aloha, Florida 20-16; 89 Cotton, Arkansas, 17-3. Coach: Terry Donahue.
6 Georgia Tech—52 Orange, Baylor 17-14; 53 Sugar, Mississippi 24-7; 54 Sugar, West Virginia 42-19; 55 Cotton, Arkansas 14-6; 56 Sugar, Pittsburgh 7-0; 56 Gator, Pittsburgh 21-14. Coach: Bobby Dodd.
6 Nebraska—71 Orange, LSU 17-12; 72 Orange, Alabama 38-6; 73 Orange, Notre Dame 40-6; 74 Cotton, Texas 19-3;69 Sun, Georgia 45-6; 74 Sugar, Florida 13-10; Coaches: Bob Devaney first 4 games, Tom Osborne last 2.
6 Alabama—75 Sugar, Penn St. 13-6; 76 Liberty, UCLA 36-6; 78 Sugar, Ohio St. 35 6; 79 Sugar, Penn St. 14-7; 80 Sugar, Arkansas 24-9; 81 Cotton, Baylor 30-2. Coach: Paul "Bear" Bryant.

Active Consecutive Appearances in Bowl Games

(Must have appeared in 2002-03 bowls)

Team	Appearances	Team	Appearances
Nebraska	34	Florida St.	21
Michigan	28	Tennessee	14

Undefeated, Untied Team Matchups in Bowl Games

Bowl	Date	Winner (Record Going In, Coach)	Loser (Record Going In, Coach)
Rose	1-1-21	California 28 (8-0, Andy Smith)	Ohio St. 0 (7-0, John Wilce)
Rose	1-2-22	0-0 tie: California (9-0, Andy Smith); Wash. & Jeff. (10-0, Earle "Greasy" Neale)	
Rose	1-1-27	7-7 tie: Alabama (9-0, Wallace Wade); Stanford (10-0, Glenn "Pop" Warner)	
Rose	1-1-31	Alabama 24 (9-0, Wallace Wade)	Washington St. 0 (9-0, Orin "Babe" Hollingbery)
Orange	1-2-39	Tennessee 17 (10-0, Bob Neyland)	Oklahoma 0 (10-0, Tom Stidham)
Sugar	1-1-41	Boston College 19 (10-0, Frank Leahy)	Tennessee 13 (10-0, Bob Neyland)
Sugar	1-1-52	Maryland 28 (9-0, Jim Tatum)	Tennessee 13 (10-0, Bob Neyland)
Orange	1-2-56	Oklahoma 20 (10-0, Bud Wilkinson)	Maryland 6 (10-0, Jim Tatum)
Orange	1-1-72	Nebraska 38 (12-0, Bob Devaney)	Alabama 6 (11-0, Paul "Bear" Bryant)
Sugar	12-31-73	Notre Dame 24 (10-0, Ara Parseghian)	Alabama 23 (11-0, Paul "Bear" Bryant)
Fiesta	1-2-87	Penn St. 14 (11-0, Joe Paterno)	Miami (Fla.) 10 (11-0, Jimmy Johnson)
Orange	1-1-88	Miami (Fla.) 20 (11-0, Jimmy Johnson)	Oklahoma 14 (11-0, Barry Switzer)
Fiesta	1-2-89	Notre Dame 34 (11-0, Lou Holtz)	West Virginia 21 (11-0, Don Nehlen)
Sugar	1-1-93	Alabama 34 (12-0, Gene Stallings)	Miami (Fla.) 13 (11-0, Dennis Erickson)
Fiesta	1-2-96	Nebraska 62 (11-0, Tom Osborne)	Florida 24 (12-0, Steve Spurrier)
Sugar	1-4-00	Florida St. 46 (11-0, Bobby Bowden)	Virginia Tech 29 (11-0, Frank Beamer)
Fiesta	1-3-03	Ohio St. 31 (13-0, Jim Tressel)	Miami (Fla.) 24 (2 ot) (12-0, Larry Coker)

Undefeated Team Matchups in Bowl Games

(Both teams were undefeated but one or both was tied one or more times)

Bowl	Date	Winner (Record Going In, Coach)	Loser (Record Going In, Coach)
Rose	1-1-25	Notre Dame 27 (9-0, Knute Rockne)	Stanford 10 (7-0-1, Glenn "Pop" Warner)
Rose	1-1-26	Alabama 20 (9-0, Wallace Wade)	Washington 19 (10-0-1, Enoch Bagshaw)
Rose	1-2-33	Southern California 35 (9-0, Howard Jones)	Pittsburgh 0 (8-0-2, Jock Sutherland)
Rose	1-1-35	Alabama 29 (9-0, Frank Thomas)	Stanford 13 (9-0-1, Claude "Tiny" Thornhill)
Rose	1-1-38	California 13 (9-0-1, Leonard "Stub" Allison)	Alabama 0 (9-0, Frank Thomas)
Rose	1-1-40	Southern California 14 (7-0-2, Howard Jones)	Tennessee 0 (10-0, Bob Neyland)
Sugar	1-1-40	Texas A&M 14 (10-0, Homer Norton)	Tulane 13 (8-0-1, Lowell "Red" Dawson)
Rose	1-1-45	Southern California 25 (7-0-2, Jeff Cravath)	Tennessee 0 (7-0-1, John Barnhill)
Cotton	1-1-48	13-13 tie: Penn St. (9-0, Bob Higgins); Southern Methodist (9-0-1, Matty Bell)	
Orange	1-1-51	Clemson 15 (8-0-1, Frank Howard)	Miami (Fla.) 14 (9-0-1, Andy Gustafson)
Sugar	1-1-53	Georgia Tech 24 (11-0, Bobby Dodd)	Mississippi 7 (8-0-2, John Vaught)
Rose	1-1-69	Ohio St. 27 (9-0, Woody Hayes)	Southern California 16 (9-0-1, John McKay)
Rose	1-1-80	Southern California 17 (10-0-1, John Robinson)	Ohio St. 16 (11-0, Earle Bruce)
California	12-14-85	Fresno St. 51 (10-0-1, Jim Sweeney)	Bowling Green 7 (11-0, Denny Stolz)

Bowl Rematches of Regular-Season Opponents

Date	Regular Season	Date	Bowl-Game Rematch
10-9-43	Texas A&M 28, LSU 13	1-1-44	(Orange) LSU 19, Texas A&M 14
11-22-45	South Carolina 13, Wake Forest 13	1-1-46	(Gator) Wake Forest 26, South Carolina 14
10-6-56	Iowa 14, Oregon St. 13	1-1-57	(Rose) Iowa 35, Oregon St. 19
10-31-59	LSU 7, Mississippi 3	1-1-60	(Sugar) Mississippi 21, LSU 0
9-18-65	Michigan St. 13, UCLA 3	1-1-66	(Rose) UCLA 14, Michigan St. 12
10-4-75	Ohio St. 41, UCLA 20	1-1-76	(Rose) UCLA 23, Ohio St. 10

Date	Regular Season	Date	Bowl-Game Rematch
11-11-78	Nebraska 17, Oklahoma 14	1-1-79	(Orange) Oklahoma 31, Nebraska 24
9-25-82	UCLA 31, Michigan 27	1-1-83	(Rose) UCLA 24, Michigan 14
9-7-87	Michigan St. 27, Southern California 13	1-1-88	(Rose) Michigan St. 20, Southern California 17
11-26-94	Florida 31, Florida St. 31	1-2-95	(Sugar) Florida St. 23, Florida 17
9-23-95	Toledo 49, Nevada 35	12-14-95	(Las Vegas) Toledo 40, Nevada 37 (ot)
11-30-96	Florida St. 24, Florida 21	1-2-97	(Sugar) Florida 52, Florida St. 20
11-15-97	Notre Dame 24, LSU 6	12-28-97	(Independence) LSU 27, Notre Dame 9

Bowl-Game Facts

The Bowl/Basketball Connection

Ten times in history, a football bowl winner also won the NCAA men's basketball championship during the same academic year. They are as follows:

Year	School	Bowl	Date of Bowl
1999-00	Michigan St.	Florida Citrus	1-1-00
1992-93	North Carolina	Peach	1-2-93
1988-89	Michigan	Rose	1-2-89
1981-82	North Carolina	Gator	12-28-81
1973-74	North Carolina St.	Liberty	12-17-73
1965-66	UTEP	Sun	12-31-65
1950-51	Kentucky	Sugar	1-1-51
1947-48	Kentucky	Great Lakes	12-6-47
1945-46	Oklahoma St.	Sugar	1-1-46
1944-45	Oklahoma St.	Cotton	1-1-45

One-Time Wonders

Six major-college teams have played in only one bowl game in their football history, and four of those have posted victories. The one-time bowlers (listed alphabetically) are as follows:

School	Date	Bowl	Opponent (Score)
Eastern Mich.	12-12-87	California	San Jose St. (30-27)
Idaho	12-30-98	Humanitarian	Southern Miss. (42-35)
Kent St.	12-29-72	Tangerine	Tampa (18-21)
Memphis	12-18-71	Pasadena	San Jose St. (28-9)
Northern Ill.	12-17-83	California	Cal St. Fullerton (20-13)
Rutgers	12-16-78	Garden State	Arizona St. (18-34)

Year-by-Year Bowl Facts

(A note about bowl-game dates: Traditionally, bowl games have been played on January 1, but as more bowl games joined the holiday lineup, schedule adjustments were made whereby some bowl games are now played as early as mid-December. In the interest of avoiding confusion, all years referred to in bowl records are the actual calendar year in which the bowl game was played.)

1917 Coach Hugo Bezdek led the first of three teams to the Rose Bowl from 1917 to 1923. His Oregon team beat Pennsylvania, 14-0, in 1917; his Mare Island squad defeated Camp Lewis, 19-7, in 1918; and his Penn State team lost to Southern California, 14-3, in 1923. In his 1923 trip with the Nittany Lions, Bezdek almost came to blows with Southern California coach Elmer "Gloomy Gus" Henderson because Penn State did not arrive for the game until an hour after the scheduled kickoff time. Henderson accused Bezdek of not taking the field until the hot California sun had gone down to give his winterized Easterners an advantage.

1919 George Halas (yes, "Papa Bear") was the player of the game for Great Lakes Naval Training Station in Chicago as the Sailors shut out Mare Island, 17-0, in another of the wartime Rose Bowls.

1923 The first Rose Bowl game actually played in the stadium in Pasadena saw Southern California defeat Penn State, 14-3.

1926 Johnny Mack Brown, one of Hollywood's most famous movie cowboys, also was one of college football's most exciting players at Alabama. He was selected player of the game for the Rose Bowl in the Crimson Tide's 20-19 victory over Washington.

1927 The Rose Bowl becomes the first coast-to-coast radio broadcast of a sporting event.

1929 The Rose Bowl game became one of the most famous in bowl history because of California player Roy Riegels' now-legendary wrong-way run. Early in the second quarter, with each team just changing possessions, Georgia Tech was on its own 20. Tech halfback Stumpy Thompson broke for a seven-yard run, fumbled, and Riegels picked up the ball, momentarily headed for the Tech goal, then reversed his field and started running the wrong way. Teammate Benny Lom tried to stop him and finally did on the California one-yard line, where the dazed Riegels was pounced on by a group of Tech tacklers. Lom went back to punt on the next play and the kick was blocked out of the end zone for a safety, which decided the contest, eventually won by Georgia Tech, 8-7.

1938 The first Orange Bowl played in Miami's new stadium, which seated 22,000 at the time, saw Auburn edge Michigan State, 6-0. Also, in the second annual Cotton Bowl, Colorado's do-it-all standout Byron "Whizzer" White, the Rhodes Scholar and future U.S. Supreme Court justice, passed for one score and returned a pass interception for another, but the Buffs lost to Rice, 28-14.

1941 On December 6, 1941, Hawaii defeated Willamette, 20-6, but a second Rainbows' postseason game, scheduled with San Jose State for the next week, was cancelled after the attack on Pearl Harbor.

1942 You would think a team making only one first down and gaining only 75 yards to its opponent's 309 yards could not come out of a game a 29-21 victor, but it happened in the Cotton Bowl as Alabama downed Texas A&M. The Tide intercepted seven of A&M's 42 passes and recovered five Aggie fumbles. Also, the Rose Bowl was moved for one year to Durham, N.C., because of wartime considerations that precluded large gatherings on the West Coast, and Oregon State downed Duke, 20-16.

1946 The first and only bowl game decided after time expired was the Orange Bowl when Miami (Florida) downed Holy Cross, 13-6. Time expired as Miami halfback Al Hudson returned an 89-yard intercepted pass for the deciding score.

1949 A Pacific Coast team had never been allowed to play in a major bowl other than the Rose Bowl, but the conference leadership let Oregon play in the Cotton Bowl against Southern Methodist. Doak Walker and Kyle Rote led Southern Methodist to a 20-13 victory over the Ducks and quarterback Norm Van Brocklin. John McKay, later the head coach at Southern California, also was on the Oregon roster.

1953 The Rose, Cotton, Sugar and Orange Bowls were televised nationally for the first time.

1954 Dicky Maegle of Rice may be the best-remembered bowl player, not because of his 265 yards rushing and three touchdowns vs. Alabama in 1954, but because of what happened on a 95-yard scoring run. Alabama's Tommy Lewis became infamous by coming off the bench to tackle Maegle in the Cotton Bowl, won by Rice, 28-6.

1960 In one of those pupil-vs.-teacher battles, former Georgia Tech player and assistant coach Frank Broyles led his Arkansas Razorbacks to a 14-7 Gator Bowl victory over his former coach, Bobby Dodd, and the Yellow Jackets.

1962 Oregon State quarterback Terry Baker turned in the longest run in bowl history with a 99-yard scamper to down Villanova, 6-0, in the Liberty Bowl. Baker, an outstanding athlete, became the only Heisman Trophy winner to play in an NCAA Final Four basketball game later that academic year (1963).

1964 Utah and West Virginia became the first teams to play a major bowl game indoors when they met in the Atlantic City Convention Hall. Utah won the Liberty Bowl, 32-6, beneath the bright indoor lights.

1965 The first Orange Bowl played under the lights in Miami saw Texas stun national champion Alabama and quarterback Joe Namath, 21-17.

1968 It was the student beating the teacher in the Cotton Bowl as Texas A&M head coach Gene Stallings saw his Aggies hold on for a 20-16 victory over Alabama and legendary head coach Paul "Bear" Bryant. Stallings had played (at Texas A&M) and coached (at Alabama) under Bryant. The "Bear" met Stallings at midfield after the contest and lifted the 6-foot-3 Aggie coach up in admiration. Also, the Astro-Bluebonnet Bowl (also known as the Bluebonnet Bowl) became the first bowl game to be played in a domed stadium as the Astrodome served as the site of the December 31, 1968, game between Southern Methodist (28) and Oklahoma (27).

1970 Three of the legendary Four Horsemen of Notre Dame came to Dallas to watch the Fighting Irish drop a 21-17 Cotton Bowl game to Texas. The only other time Notre Dame had played in a bowl game was the 1925 Rose Bowl, when the Four Horsemen led the Irish to a 27-10 victory over Stanford.

1971 Notre Dame snapped the second-longest winning streak going into a bowl game by halting Texas' 30-game string, 24-11, in the Cotton Bowl. In 1951, Kentucky had stopped Oklahoma's 31-game streak in the Sugar Bowl, 13-7.

1976 Archie Griffin started his fourth straight Rose Bowl for Ohio State (1973-76), totaling 412 yards on 79 carries in the four games. The Buckeyes, under legendary head coach Woody Hayes, won only the 1974 contest, but Griffin is the only player to win two Heisman Trophies (1974-75).

1989 Texas Tech's James Gray set a college bowl record with 280 yards rushing in the All-American Bowl against Duke. Brigham Young's Ty Detmer set the bowl passing mark with 576 yards versus Penn State in the Holiday Bowl.

Special Regular- and Postseason Games

Postseason Games

UNSANCTIONED OR OTHER BOWLS

The following bowl and/or postseason games were unsanctioned by the NCAA or otherwise had no team classified as major college at the time of the bowl. Most are postseason games; in many cases, complete dates and/or statistics are not available and the scores are listed only to provide a historical reference. Attendance of the game, if known, is listed in parentheses after the score.

ALL-SPORTS BOWL
(Oklahoma City, Okla.)
12-9-61—Okla. Panhandle 28, Langston 14 (8,000)
12-8-62—Neb.-Omaha 34, East Central 21 (2,500)
12-7-63—Northeastern St. 59, Slippery Rock 12
12-5-64—Sul Ross St. 21, East Central 13

ALUMINUM BOWL (NAIA Title Game)
(Little Rock, Ark.)
12-22-56—Montana St. 0, St. Joseph's (Ind.) 0

ANGEL BOWL
(Los Angeles, Calif.)
12-28-46—Florida A&M 6, Wiley 6 (12,000)

AZALEA BOWL
(Orlando, Fla.)
1-1-46—Knoxville 18, Florida Normal 0 (4,000)

AZALEA CLASSIC
(Mobile, Ala.)
12-4-71—Jackson St. 40, Alabama A&M 21
12-7-74—Bethune-Cookman 19, Langston 3 (1,000)

AZTEC BOWL
(Mexico City, Mexico)
12-50—Whittier 27, Mexico All-Stars 14
12-53—Mexico City 45, Eastern N.M. 26

BEAN BOWL
(Scottsbluff, Neb.)
11-24-49—Idaho St. 20, Chadron St. 2
11-23-50—Doane 14, Northern Colo. 6

BEAVER BOWL
(Corry, Pa.)
11-15-58—Slippery Rock 6, Edinboro 0 (3,000)

BICENTENNIAL BOWL
(Little Rock, Ark.)
11-29-75—Henderson St. 27, East Central 14 (2,000)

BICENTENNIAL BOWL
(Richmond, Va.)
12-11-76—South Carolina St. 26, Norfolk St. 10 (7,500)

BOOT HILL BOWL
(Dodge City, Kan.)
12-70—Cameron 13, N.M. Highlands 12
12-4-71—Dakota St. 23, Northwestern Okla. 20 (2,000)
12-2-72—William Penn 17, Emporia St. 14 (2,000)
12-1-73—Millikin 51, Bethany (Kan.) 7 (1,600)
11-30-74—Washburn 21, Millikin 7 (2,500)
11-22-75—Buena Vista 24, St. Mary's (Kan.) 21 (2,700)
11-20-76—Benedictine 29, Washburn 3 (3,000)
11-19-77—Mo. Western St. 35, Benedictine 30 (1,000)
11-18-78—Chadron St. 30, Baker (Kan.) 19 (3,000)
11-17-79—Pittsburg St. 43, Peru St. 14 (2,800)
11-21-80—Cameron 34, Adams St. 16

BOTANY BOWL
11-24-55—Neb.-Kearney 34, Northern St. 13

BOY'S RANCH BOWL
(Abilene, Texas)
12-13-47—Missouri Valley 20, McMurry 13 (2,500)

BURLEY BOWL
(Johnson City, Tenn.)
1-1-46—High Point 7, Milligan 7 (3,500)
11-28-46—Southeastern La. 21, Milligan 13 (7,500)
11-27-47—West Chester 20, Carson-Newman 6 (10,000)
11-25-48—West Chester 7, Appalachian St. 2 (12,000)
11-24-49—Emory & Henry 32, Hanover 0 (12,000)
11-23-50—Emory & Henry 26, Appalachian St. 6 (12,000)
11-22-51—Charleston (W.Va.) 27, Lebanon Valley 20 (9,000)
11-27-52—East Tenn. St. 34, Emory & Henry 16
11-26-53—East Tenn. St. 48, Emory & Henry 12

11-25-54—Appalachian St. 28, East Tenn. St. 13
11-24-55—East Tenn. St. 7, Appalachian St. 0
11-22-56—Memphis 32, East Tenn. St. 12

CAJUN BOWL
12-47—McNeese St. 0, Southern Ark. 0

CATTLE BOWL
(Fort Worth, Texas)
1-1-47—Ark.-Pine Bluff 7, Lane 0 (1,000)
1-1-48—Samuel Huston 7, Philander Smith 0 (800)

CEMENT BOWL
(Allentown, Pa.)
12-8-62—West Chester 46, Hofstra 12

CHARITY BOWL
(Los Angeles, Calif.)
12-25-37—Fresno St. 27, Central Ark. 26 (5,000)

CHRISTMAS BOWL
(Natchitoches, La.)
12-6-58—Northwestern St. 18, Sam Houston St. 11
12-5-59—Delta St. 19, East Central 0

CIGAR BOWL
(Tampa, Fla.)
1-1-47—Delaware 21, Rollins 7 (9,500)
1-1-48—Missouri Valley 26, West Chester 7 (10,000)
1-1-49—Missouri Valley 13, St. Thomas (Minn.) 13 (11,000)
1-2-50—Florida St. 19, Wofford 6 (14,000)
1-1-51—Wis.-La Crosse 47, Valparaiso 14 (12,000)
12-29-51—Brooke Army Medical 20, Camp LeJeune Marines 0 (7,500) (see Cigar Bowl in Service Games)
12-13-52—Tampa 21, Lenoir-Rhyne 12 (7,500)
1-1-54—Missouri Valley 12, Wis.-La Crosse 12 (5,000)
12-17-54—Tampa 21, Charleston (W.Va.) 0

CITRACADO BOWL
(see Citracado Bowl in Service Games)

COCONUT BOWL
(Miami, Fla.)
1-1-42—Florida Normal 0, Miami All-Stars 0 (9,000)
1-1-46—Bethune-Cookman 32, Albany St. (Ga.) 0 (5,000)
1-1-47—Bethune-Cookman 13, Columbia (S.C.) Sporting Club 0 (5,000)

CORN BOWL
(Bloomington, Ill.)
11-27-47—Southern Ill. 21, North Central 0 (5,500)
11-25-48—Ill. Wesleyan 6, Eastern Ill. 0 (8,500)
11-24-49—Western Ill. 13, Wheaton (Ill.) 0 (4,567)
11-23-50—Mo.-Rolla 7, Illinois St. 6 (2,500)
11-22-51—Lewis 21, William Jewell 12 (2,000)
11-26-53—Western Ill. 32, Iowa Wesleyan 0
11-24-55—Luther 24, Western Ill. 20 (3,100)

COSMOPOLITAN BOWL
(Alexandria, La.)
12-51—McNeese St. 13, Louisiana Col. 6

COTTON-TOBACCO BOWL
(Greensboro, N.C.)
1-1-46—Johnson Smith 18, Allen 6
1-1-47—Norfolk St. 0, Richmond 0 (10,000)

COWBOY BOWL
(Lawton, Okla.)
12-11-71—Howard Payne 16, Cameron 13
12-9-72—Harding 30, Langston 27

DOLL AND TOY CHARITY GAME
(Gulfport, Miss.)
12-3-37—Southern Miss. 7, Appalachian St. 0 (2,000)

EASTERN BOWL
(Allentown, Pa.)
12-14-63—East Caro. 27, Northeastern 6 (2,700)

ELKS BOWL
1-2-54—Charleston (W.Va.) 12, East Caro. 0 (4,500) (at Greenville, N.C.)
12-11-54—Newberry 20, Appalachian St. 13 (at Raleigh, N.C.)

FISH BOWL
(Corpus Christi, Texas)
11-48—Southwestern (Tex.) 7, Corpus Christi 0

FISH BOWL
(Norfolk, Va.)
12-4-48—Hampton 20, Central St. 19

FLOWER BOWL
(Jacksonville, Fla.)
1-1-42—Johnson Smith 13, Lane 0 (4,500)
1-1-43—N.C. A&T 14, Southern U. 6 (2,000)
1-1-44—Allen 33, Winston-Salem 0 (2,000)
1-1-45—Texas College 18, N.C. A&T 0 (5,000)
1-1-46—Grambling 19, Lane 6 (6,000)
1-1-47—Delaware St. 7, Florida Normal 6 (3,000)
1-1-48—Bethune-Cookman 6, Lane 0 (3,000)

FRUIT BOWL
(San Francisco, Calif.)
12-14-47—Central St. 26, Prairie View 0 (9,000)
12-5-48—Southern U. 30, San Fran. St. 0 (5,000)

GATE CITY BOWL
(Atlanta, Ga.)
12-21-74—Tuskegee 15, Norfolk St. 14 (6,252)

GLASS BOWL
(Toledo, Ohio)
12-7-46—Toledo 21, Bates 12 (12,000)
12-6-47—Toledo 20, New Hampshire 14 (13,500)
12-4-48—Toledo 27, Oklahoma City 14 (8,500)
12-3-49—Cincinnati 33, Toledo 13

GOLD BOWL
(Richmond, Va.)
12-3-77—South Carolina St. 10, Winston-Salem 7 (14,000)
12-2-78—Virginia Union 21, N.C. A&T 6 (7,500)
12-1-79—South Carolina St. 39, Norfolk St. 7 (8,000)
12-6-80—N.C. A&T 37, N.C. Central 0 (3,374)

GOLDEN ISLES BOWL
(Brunswick, Ga.)
12-1-62—McNeese St. 21, Samford 14

GRAPE BOWL
(Lodi, Calif.)
12-13-47—Pacific (Cal.) 35, Utah St. 21 (12,000)
12-11-48—Hardin-Simmons 35, Pacific (Cal.) 35 (10,000)

GREAT LAKES BOWL
(Cleveland, Ohio)
12-5-48—John Carroll 14, Canisius 13 (18,000)

GREAT SOUTHWEST BOWL
(Grand Prairie, Texas)
12-31-60—Tex. A&M-Kingsville 45, Arkansas Tech 14 (3,900)

HOLIDAY BOWL
(St. Petersburg, Fla.)
12-21-57—Pittsburg St. 27, Hillsdale 26
12-20-58—Northeastern St. 19, Northern Ariz. 13
12-19-59—Tex. A&M-Kingsville 20, Lenoir-Rhyne 7 (9,500)
12-10-60—Lenoir-Rhyne 15, Humboldt St. 14 (also served as NAIA national title game)

HOOSIER BOWL
(See Turkey Bowl)

INTERNATIONAL BOWL
12-52—Tex. A&M-Kingsville 49, Hereico Colegio Military 0

IODINE BOWL
(Charleston, S.C.)
12-3-49—Johnson Smith 20, Allen 12
12-9-50—Allen 20, Bethune-Cookman 0 (1,000)
12-1-51—Allen 33, Morris College 14 (3,000)
12-5-53—Allen 33, Paul Quinn 6

KICKAPOO BOWL
(Wichita Falls, Texas)
12-5-47—Midwestern St. 39, Central Ark. 20 (5,000)

LIONS BOWL
(Ruston, La.)
12-46—Grambling 69, Miss. Industrial 12
12-5-47—Grambling 47, Bethune-Cookman 6
12-49—Grambling 21, Texas College 18
12-2-50—Bishop 35, Grambling 0
12-1-51—Grambling 52, Bishop 0 (at Shreveport, La.)
12-6-52—Grambling 27, Alcorn St. 13 (at Monroe, La.)

LIONS BOWL
(Salisbury, N.C.)
12-13-52—Clarion 13, East Caro. 6 (3,000)

MERCY BOWL II
(Anaheim, Calif.)
12-11-71—Cal St. Fullerton 17, Fresno St. 14 (16,854)

MINERAL WATER BOWL
(Excelsior Springs, Mo.)
11-25-54—Hastings 20, Col. of Emporia 14 (4,000)
11-24-55—Missouri Valley 31, Hastings 7
11-22-56—St. Benedict's 14, Northeastern St. 13 (2,000)
11-30-57—William Jewell 33, Hastings 14 (2,000)
11-22-58—Lincoln (Mo.) 21, Emporia St. 0 (2,500)
11-28-59—Col. of Emporia 21, Austin (Tex.) 20 (3,000)
11-26-60—Hillsdale 17, Northern Iowa 6 (6,000)
11-25-61—Truman 22, Parsons 8 (8,000)
11-24-62—Adams St. 23, Northern Ill. 20
11-30-63—Northern Ill. 21, Southwest Mo. St. 14
11-28-64—North Dakota St. 14, Western St. 13 (4,500)
11-27-65—North Dakota 37, Northern Ill. 20
11-26-66—Adams St. 14, Southwest Mo. St. 8 (5,500)
11-25-67—Doane 14, William Jewell 14 (6,500)
11-30-68—Doane 10, Central Mo. St. 0 (6,000)
11-29-69—St. John's (Minn.) 21, Simpson 0 (5,000)
11-28-70—Franklin 40, Wayne St. (Neb.) 12 (2,500)
12-4-71—Bethany (Kan.) 17, Missouri Valley 14 (2,500)
11-18-72—Ottawa 27, Friends 20 (4,500)
11-73—William Jewell 20, St. Mary's (Kan.) 9
11-23-74—Midland 32, Friends 6 (1,500)
11-22-75—Mo. Western St. 44, Graceland (Ia.) 0 (3,300)

MIRZA SHRINE BOWL
(Pittsburg, Kan.)
12-1-50—Central Mo. St. 32, Pittsburg St. 21

MISSOURI-KANSAS BOWL
(Kansas City, Mo.)
12-4-48—Emporia St. 34, Southwest Mo. St. 20

MOILA SHRINE CLASSIC
(St. Joseph, Mo.)
11-24-79—Mo. Western St. 72, William Jewell 44 (1,600)
11-22-80—Truman 17, Pittsburg St. 14 (500)

NATIONAL CLASSIC
(Greensboro, N.C.)
12-4-54—N.C. Central 19, Tennessee St. 6

NEW YEAR'S CLASSIC
(Honolulu, Hawaii)
1-1-34—Santa Clara 26, Hawaii 7
1-1-35—Hawaii 14, California 0 (later called Poi Bowl)

OIL BOWL
(Houston, Texas)
1-1-44—La.-Lafayette 24, Ark.-Monticello 7 (12,000)

OLEANDER BOWL
(Galveston, Texas)
1-2-50—McMurry 19, Missouri Valley 13 (7,500)

OLYMPIAN BOWL
(see Pythian Bowl)

OPTIMIST BOWL
(Houston, Texas)
12-21-46—North Texas 14, Pacific (Cal.) 13 (5,000)

ORANGE BLOSSOM CLASSIC
(Miami, Fla.)
12-2-33—Florida A&M 9, Howard 6
12-13-34—Florida A&M 13, Virginia St. 12
12-12-35—Kentucky St. 19, Florida A&M 10
12-5-36—Prairie View 25, Florida A&M 0
12-9-37—Florida A&M 25, Hampton 20
12-8-38—Florida A&M 9, Kentucky St. 7
12-9-39—Florida A&M 42, Wiley 0
12-7-40—Central St. 0, Florida A&M 0
12-6-41—Florida A&M 15, Tuskegee 7
12-12-42—Florida A&M 12, Texas College 6
12-4-43—Hampton 39, Florida A&M 0
12-9-44—Virginia St. 19, Florida A&M 6
12-8-45—Wiley 32, Florida A&M 6
12-7-46—Lincoln (Pa.) 20, Florida A&M 0 (at Tampa)
12-6-47—Florida A&M 7, Hampton 0
12-4-48—Virginia Union 10, Florida A&M 6 (16,000)
12-10-49—N.C. A&T 20, Florida A&M 14
12-2-50—Central St. 13, Florida A&M 6
12-1-51—Florida A&M 67, N.C. Central 6
12-6-52—Florida A&M 29, Virginia St. 7
12-5-53—Prairie View 33, Florida A&M 27
12-4-54—Florida A&M 67, Md.-East. Shore 19
12-3-55—Grambling 28, Florida A&M 21
12-1-56—Tennessee St. 41, Florida A&M 39
12-14-57—Florida A&M 27, Md.-East. Shore 21
12-13-58—Prairie View 26, Florida A&M 8
12-5-59—Florida A&M 28, Prairie View 7
12-10-60—Florida A&M 40, Langston 26
12-9-61—Florida A&M 14, Jackson St. 8 (47,791)
12-8-62—Jackson St. 22, Florida A&M 6

12-14-63—Morgan St. 30, Florida A&M 7
12-5-64—Florida A&M 42, Grambling 15
12-4-65—Morgan St. 36, Florida A&M 7
12-3-66—Florida A&M 43, Alabama A&M 26
12-2-67—Grambling 28, Florida A&M 25
12-7-68—Alcorn St. 36, Florida A&M 9 (37,398)
12-6-69—Florida A&M 23, Grambling 19 (36,784) (at Tallahassee, Fla.)
12-12-70—Jacksonville St. 21, Florida A&M 7 (31,184)
12-11-71—Florida A&M 9, Kentucky St. 9 (26,161)
12-2-72—Florida A&M 41, Md.-East. Shore 21 (21,606)
12-8-73—Florida A&M 23, South Carolina St. 12 (18,996)
12-7-74—Florida A&M 17, Howard 13 (20,166)
12-6-75—Florida A&M 40, Kentucky St. 13 (27,875)
12-4-76—Florida A&M 26, Central St. 21 (18,000)
12-3-77—Florida A&M 37, Delaware St. 15 (29,493)
12-2-78—Florida A&M 31, Grambling 7

ORCHID BOWL
(Mexico City, Mexico)
1-1-42—Louisiana Col. 10, U. of Mexico 0 (8,000)
12-28-46—Mississippi Col. 43, U. of Mexico 7 (7,500)

PALM FESTIVAL
(Miami, Fla.)
1-2-33—Miami (Fla.) 7, Manhattan 0 (6,000)
1-1-34—Duquesne 33, Miami (Fla.) 7 (3,500) (forerunner to Orange Bowl)

PALMETTO SHRINE
(Columbia, S.C.)
12-10-55—Lenoir-Rhyne 14, Newberry 13 (6,000)

PAPER BOWL
(Pensacola, Fla.)
12-18-48—Jacksonville St. 19, Troy St. 0
12-16-49—Jacksonville St. 12, West Ala. 7 (3,000)
12-2-50—Pensacola Alumni Cardinals 7, Jacksonville St. 6 (3,600)

PEACH BLOSSOM CLASSIC
(Atlanta, Ga.)
12-9-39—Morris Brown 13, Virginia St. 7
12-6-40—Morris Brown 28, Kentucky St. 6 (1,500)
12-6-41—Morris Brown 7, N.C. Central 6 (6,000) (at Columbus, Ga.)
12-4-42—Morris Brown 20, Lane 0 (3,000) (at Columbus, Ga.)

PEACH BOWL
(Macon, Ga.)
12-13-46—Tenn. Wesleyan 14, Ga. Military 13 (5,000)
12-6-47—Virginia St. 48, Morris Brown 0
12-3-49—Morris Brown 33, Texas College 28 (at Atlanta, Ga.)

PEANUT BOWL
(Dothan, Ala.)
12-21-68—Ouachita Baptist 39, West Ala. 6

PEAR BOWL
(Medford, Ore.)
11-28-46—Southern Ore. St. 13, Central Wash. 8 (3,000) (at Ashland, Ore.)
11-27-47—Pacific Lutheran 27, Southern Ore. St. 21
11-25-48—Col. of Idaho 27, Southern Ore. St. 20 (2,500)
11-24-49—Pacific (Ore.) 33, UC Davis 15 (4,000)
11-23-50—Lewis & Clark 61, San Fran. St. 7 (4,000)
11-24-51—Pacific (Ore.) 25, UC Davis 7 (4,000)

PECAN BOWL
(Orangeburg, S.C.)
12-7-46—South Carolina St. 13, Johnson Smith 6
12-13-47—South Carolina St. 7, Allen 0 (3,000)

PELICAN BOWL
(New Orleans, La.)
12-2-72—Grambling 56, N.C. Central 6 (22,500) (at Durham, N.C.)
12-7-74—Grambling 28, South Carolina St. 7 (30,120)
12-27-75—Southern U. 15, South Carolina St. 12 (6,748)

PENINSULA BOWL
(Charleston, S.C.)
12-2-50—Allen 47, South Carolina St. 13 (7,500)

PHILLIPS FIELD BOWL
(Tampa, Fla.)
12-8-51—Tampa 7, Brandeis 0

PIEDMONT TOBACCO BOWL
(Fayetteville, N.C.)
12-7-46—Allen 40, Fayetteville St. 6 (900)

PINEAPPLE BOWL
(Honolulu, Hawaii)
1-1-40—Oregon St. 39, Hawaii 6 (formerly called Poi Bowl)
1-1-41—Fresno St. 3, Hawaii 0
1-1-47—Hawaii 19, Utah 16 (25,000)
1-1-48—Hawaii 33, Redlands 32 (12,000)
1-1-49—Oregon St. 47, Hawaii 27 (15,000)
1-2-50—Stanford 74, Hawaii 20
1-1-51—Hawaii 28, Denver 27
1-1-52—San Diego St. 34, Hawaii 13

POI BOWL
(Honolulu, Hawaii)
1-1-36—Southern California 38, Hawaii 6
1-2-37—Hawaii 18, Honolulu All-Stars 12
1-1-38—Washington 53, Hawaii 13 (13,500)
1-2-39—UCLA 32, Hawaii 7 (later called Pineapple Bowl)

POULTRY BOWL
(Gainesville, Ga.)
12-8-73—Stephen F. Austin 31, Gardner-Webb 10 (2,500)
12-7-74—Guilford 7, William Penn 7 (1,000) (at Greensboro, N.C.) (Guilford awarded win on 10-8 edge in first downs)

PRAIRIE VIEW BOWL
(Also called Bayou City Bowl)
(Houston, Texas)
1-1-29—Atlanta 7, Prairie View 0
1-1-30—Fisk 20, Prairie View 0
1-1-31—Tuskegee 19, Prairie View 7
1-1-32—Prairie View 27, Alabama St. 2
1-1-33—Prairie View 14, Tuskegee 0
1-1-34—Prairie View 20, Langston 7
1-1-35—Tuskegee 15, Prairie View 6
1-1-36—Wiley 7, Prairie View 6
1-1-37—Tuskegee 6, Prairie View 0 (3,000)
1-1-38—Prairie View 27, Florida A&M 14
1-2-39—Prairie View 34, Tuskegee 0
1-1-40—Prairie View 7, Xavier (La.) 6
1-1-41—Prairie View 7, Alabama St. 6
1-1-42—Kentucky St. 19, Prairie View 13
1-1-43—Langston 18, Prairie View 13
1-1-44—Prairie View 6, Wiley 0 (5,000)
1-1-45—Wiley 26, Prairie View 0 (4,000)
1-1-46—Prairie View 12, Tuskegee 0 (10,000)
1-1-47—Prairie View 14, Lincoln (Mo.) 0 (1,500) (called Houston Bowl)
1-1-48—Texas Southern 13, Prairie View 0
1-1-49—Central St. 6, Prairie View 0 (9,000)
1-2-50—Prairie View 27, Fisk 6 (4,718)
1-1-51—Prairie View 6, Bishop 0
1-1-52—Prairie View 27, Ark.-Pine Bluff 26
1-1-53—Texas Southern 13, Prairie View 12 (13,000)
1-1-54—Prairie View 33, Texas Southern 8
1-1-55—Prairie View 14, Texas Southern 12 (10,000)
1-2-56—Prairie View 59, Fisk 0 (7,500)
1-1-57—Prairie View 27, Texas Southern 6
1-1-58—Prairie View 6, Texas Southern 6 (3,500)
1-1-59—Prairie View 34, Langston 8
1-1-60—Prairie View 47, Wiley 10 (1,200)
12-31-60—Prairie View 19, Ark.-Pine Bluff 8 (1,400)
12-1-62—Prairie View 37, Central St. 16

PRETZEL BOWL
(Reading, Pa.)
11-24-51—West Chester 32, Albright 9 (7,500)

PYTHIAN BOWL
(Salisbury, N.C.)
11-26-49—Appalachian St. 21, Catawba 7
12-9-50—West Liberty St. 28, Appalachian St. 26
12-8-51—Lenoir-Rhyne 13, Calif. (Pa.) 7 (4,500)

REFRIGERATOR BOWL
(Evansville Ind.)
12-4-48—Evansville 13, Missouri Valley 7 (7,500)
12-3-49—Evansville 22, Hillsdale 7
12-2-50—Abilene Christian 13, Gust. Adolphus 7 (8,000)
12-2-51—Arkansas St. 46, Camp Breckinridge 12 (10,000)
12-7-52—Western Ky. 34, Arkansas St. 19 (9,500)
12-6-53—Sam Houston St. 14, Col. of Idaho 12 (7,500)
12-5-54—Delaware 19, Kent St. 7 (4,500)
12-4-55—Jacksonville St. 12, Rhode Island 10 (7,000)
12-1-56—Sam Houston St. 27, Middle Tenn. 13 (3,000)

RICE BOWL
(Stuggart, Ark.)
12-57—Arkansas Tech 19, Ark.-Monticello 7
12-58—Louisiana Col. 39, Arkansas Tech 12
12-2-60—East Central 25, Henderson St. 7

ROCKET BOWL
(Huntsville, Ala.)
11-19-60—Maryville (Tenn.) 19, Millsaps 0

SAN JACINTO SHRINE BOWL
(Pasadena, Texas)
12-4-76—Abilene Christian 22, Harding 12 (8,000)

SHARE BOWL
(Knoxville, Tenn.)
12-11-71—Carson-Newman 54, Fairmont St. 3 (1,200)

SHRIMP BOWL
(Galveston, Texas)
12-27-52—Sam Houston St. 41, Northeastern St. 20
(3,500)

SHRINE BOWL
(Ardmore, Okla.)
12-9-72—Southwestern Okla. 28, Angelo St. 6

SILVER BOWL
(Mexico City, Mexico)
12-20-47—Mexico All-Stars 24, Randolph Field 19
12-11-48—Pacific Fleet 33, Mexico All-Stars 26
12-17-49—Trinity (Tex.) 52, Mexico 6

SMOKY MOUNTAIN BOWL
(Bristol, Tenn.)
11-24-49—West Liberty St. 20, Western Caro. 0 (1,000)

SPACE CITY BOWL
(Huntsville, Ala.)
11-24-66—Jacksonville St. 41, Ark.-Monticello 30
12-9-67—Samford 20, Ark.-Monticello 7

STEEL BOWL
(Birmingham, Ala.)
1-1-41—Morris Brown 19, Central St. 3 (8,000)
1-1-42—Southern College All-Stars 26, Nashville Pros 13
1-1-52—Bethune-Cookman 27, Texas College 13
(1,500)

SUGAR CUP CLASSIC
(New Orleans, La.)
11-28-64—Grambling 42, Bishop 6

TEXHOMA BOWL
(Denison, Texas)
12-10-48—Ouachita Baptist 7, Southeastern Okla. 0
11-25-49—Austin (Tex.) 27, East Central 6

TEXTILE BOWL
(Spartanburg, S.C.)
11-30-74—Wofford 20, South Carolina St. 0 (3,000)

TOBACCO BOWL
(Lexington, Ky.)
12-14-46—Muhlenberg 26, St. Bonaventure 25 (3,000)

TROPICAL BOWL
12-18-51—Morris Brown 21, Alcorn St. 0
12-13-52—Bethune-Cookman 54, Albany St. (Ga.) 0
12-12-53—Virginia Union 13, Bethune-Cookman 0

TURKEY BOWL
11-28-46—Evansville 19, Northern Ill. 7 (12,000) (also
called Hoosier Bowl)

VULCAN BOWL
(Birmingham, Ala.)
1-1-42—Langston 13, Morris Brown 0 (7,000)
1-1-43—Texas College 13, Tuskegee 10 (6,000)
1-1-44—Tuskegee 12, Clark (Ga.) 7 (6,000)
1-1-45—Tennessee St. 13, Tuskegee 0 (5,000)
1-1-46—Tennessee St. 33, Texas College 6 (9,000)
1-1-47—Tennessee St. 32, Louisville Municipal 0 (4,000)
1-2-48—Central St. 27, Grambling 21 (8,000)
1-1-49—Kentucky St. 23, N.C. A&T 13 (5,000)

WEST VIRGINIA BOWL
(Clarksburg, W.Va.)
12-60—Fairmont St. 13, Salem Int'l 7
11-61—West Va. Wesleyan 12, Salem Int'l 0

WILL ROGERS BOWL
(Oklahoma City, Okla.)
1-1-47—Pepperdine 38, Neb. Wesleyan 13 (800)

YAM BOWL
(Dallas, Texas)
12-25-46—Texas Southern 64, Tuskegee 7 (5,000)
12-25-47—Southern U. 46, Fort Valley St. 0 (1,200)

SERVICE GAMES

AIRBORNE BOWL
12-15-57—101st Airborne 20, 82nd Airborne 14
12-5-59—Fort Campbell 26, Fort Bragg 7

ARAB BOWL
(Oran, Africa)
1-1-44—Army 10, Navy 7 (15,000)

ARMY ALL-STAR GAMES
8-30-42—Washington Redskins 26, Western Army All-
Stars 7 (at Los Angeles, Calif.)
9-6-42—Western Army All-Stars 16, Chicago Cardinals
10 (at Denver, Colo.)
9-9-42—Western Army All-Stars 12, Detroit Lions 0 (at
Detroit, Mich.)
9-12-42—Eastern Army All-Stars 16, New York Giants 0
(at New York, N.Y.)
9-13-42—Green Bay Packers 36, Western Army All-
Stars 21 (at Milwaukee, Wis.)
9-16-42—Eastern Army All-Stars 13, Brooklyn Dodgers
7 (at Baltimore, Md.)
9-19-42—New York Giants 10, Western Army All-Stars
7 (at New York, N.Y.)
9-20-42—Chicago Bears 14, Eastern Army All-Stars 7
(at Boston, Mass.)

ARMY PACIFIC OLYMPICS
(Osaka, Japan)
1-13-46—11th Airborne Angels 27, Clark Field 6
1-27-46—11th Airborne Angels 18, Honolulu All-Stars 0

ARMY-NAVY BENEFIT BOWL
(Tallahassee, Fla.)
12-20-52—Parris Island 49, Fort Benning 0

ATOM BOWL
(Nagasaki, Japan)
12-45—Nishahaya Tigers 14, Bertelli's Bears 13 (2,000)

BAMBINO BOWL
(Bari, Italy)
11-23-44—Technical School 13, Playboys 0 (5,000)

BAMBOO BOWL
(Manila, Philippines)
1-1-46—Clark Field Acpacs 14, Leyte Base 12 (40,000)
1-1-47—Manila Raiders 13, Scofield Barracks 6 (12,000)
12-47—Ryukgus Command Sea Horses 21, Hawaiian
Mid-Pacific Commandos 0
1-1-50—All-Navy Guam 19, Clark Air Force Base 7

BLUEBONNET BOWL
(Houston, Texas)
12-25-46—Texas Southern 49, Camp Hood 0

CHERRY BOWL
(Yokohama, Japan)
1-1-52—Camp Drake 26, Yoksuka Naval Base 12

CHIGGER BOWL
(Dutch Guiana)
1-1-45—Army Air Base Bonecrushers 6, Army Airway
Rams 0 (1,200)

CHINA BOWL
(Shanghai)
1-27-46—Navy All-Stars 12, Army All-Stars 0
1-1-47—11th Airborne 12, Army-Navy All-Stars 6
1-1-48—Marines (Guam) 45, China All-Stars 0

CIGAR BOWL
12-29-51—Brooke Army Medical 20, Camp LeJeune 0
(7,500)

CITRICADO BOWL
12-56—San Diego Marines 25, UC Santa Barb. 14

COCONUT BOWL
(New Guinea)
1-6-45—Bulldogs 18, Crimson Tide 7 (3,000)

COFFEE BOWL
(London, England)
3-19-44—United States 18, Canada 0

CONCH BOWL
(Key West, Fla.)
11-24-57—Keesler Air Force Base 27, Maxwell Air
Force Base 7
11-28-58—Keesler Air Force Base 14, Maxwell Air
Force Base 8

COSMOPOLITAN BOWL
(Alexandria, La.)
12-50—Camp Polk 26, Louisiana Col. 7
12-52—Louisiana Col. 14, Alexander Air Base 0

ELECTRONICS BOWL
(Biloxi, Miss.)
12-9-51—Keesler Air Force Base 13, Camp LeJeune 0
12-53—Eglin Air Force Base 19, Keesler Air Force Base 8
12-54—Shaw Air Force Base 20, Keesler Air Force Base
19

EUROPEAN "ORANGE BOWL"
(Heidelberg, Germany)
12-7-46—1st Division Artillery 27, 60th Infantry 13

EUROPEAN "ROSE BOWL"
(Augsburg, Germany)
12-7-46—9th Division 20, 16th Infantry 7 (3,000)

EUROPEAN "SUGAR BOWL"
(Nuremberg, Germany)
12-7-46—Grafenwohr Military 0, 39th Infantry 0

G. I. BOWL
(London, England)
11-12-44—Army G.I.'s 20, Navy Bluejackets 0 (60,000)

ICE BOWL
(Fairbanks, Alaska)
1-1-49—Ladd Air Force Base 0, University of Alaska 0
(500)
1-2-50—University of Alaska 3, Ladd Air Force Base 0
1-1-51—University of Alaska 0, Ladd Air Force Base 0
12-30-52—Ladd Air Force Base 47, University of Alaska 0

IRANIAN BOWL
(Teheran, Iran)
12-12-44—Camp Amirabad 20, Camp Khorramsahr 0
(9,000)

JUNGLE BOWL
(Southwest Pacific)
1-1-45—American All-Stars 49, Marines 0 (6,400)

LILY BOWL
(Hamilton, Bermuda)
1-3-43—Army 19, Navy 18
1-1-44—Navy 19, Army 0
1-7-45—Navy 39, Army 6 (11,000)
1-5-47—Army 7, Navy 7 (9,000)
1-1-48—Air Force 12, Navy 12
1-1-49—Navy All-Stars 25, Kindley Fliers 6

MARINE BOWL
(Pritchard Field, Southwest Pacific)
12-24-44—4th Marines 0, 29th Marines 0 (7,000)

MISSILE BOWL
(Orlando, Fla.)
12-3-60—Quantico Marines 36, Pensacola Air Force
Base 6
12-9-61—Fort Eustis 25, Quantico Marines 24
12-15-62—Fort Campbell 14, Lackland Air Force Base 10
12-14-63—Quantico Marines 13, San Diego Marines 10
12-5-64—Fort Benning 9, Fort Eustis 3

PALMETTO SHRINE
(Charleston, S.C.)
1-1-55—Fort Jackson 26, Shaw Air Force Base 21

PARC DES PRINCES BOWL
(Paris, France)
12-19-44—9th Air Force 6, 1st General Hospital 0
(20,000)

POI BOWL
(Honolulu, Hawaii)
(Pacific Ocean Areas Service Championship)
1-8-45—Navy 14, Army Air Force 0 (29,000)

POINSETTIA BOWL
(San Diego, Calif.)
12-20-52—Bolling Air Force Base 35, San Diego NTC 14
12-19-53—Fort Ord 55, Quantico Marines 19
12-19-54—Fort Sill 27, Bolling Air Force Base 6
12-17-55—Fort Ord 35, Pensacola NAS 13

POTATO BOWL
(Belfast, Ireland)
1-1-44—Galloping Gaels 0, Wolverines 0

RICE BOWL
(Tokyo, Japan)
1-1-46—11th Airborne Angels 25, 41st Division 12
(15,000)
12-46—Yokota Air Base 13, 1st AD 8 (7,000)
1-1-48—Korea All-Stars 19, Japan All-Stars 13
1-1-49—Army Ground Forces 13, Air Force 7 (20,000)
1-1-50—Air Force All-Stars 18, Army All-Stars 14
1-1-53—Camp Drake 25, Yokosuka Naval Base 6
1-1-54—Camp Fisher 19, Nagoya Air Base 13
1-1-55—Air Force 21, Marines 14
12-31-55—Air Force 33, Army 14 (40,000)
12-30-56—Army 21, Air Force 6
12-7-57—Johnson Air Base Vanguards 6, Marine Corps
Sukiran Streaks 0
12-20-58—Air Force 20, Army 0

BOWL/ALL-STAR RECORDS

RIVIERA BOWL
(Marseille, France)
1-1-45—Railway Shop Battalion Unit 37, Army All-Stars 0 (18,000)

SALAD BOWL
(Phoenix, Ariz.)
1-1-53—San Diego Navy 81, 101st Airborne 20
1-1-54—Fort Ord 67, Great Lakes 12

SATELLITE BOWL
(Cocoa, Fla.)
12-29-57—Fort Carson 12, Fort Dix 6

SHRIMP BOWL
(Galveston, Texas)
1-1-55—Fort Ord 36, Fort Hood 0
12-18-55—Fort Hood 33, Little Creek 13
12-8-56—Bolling Air Force Base 29, Fort Hood 14
12-15-57—Bolling Air Force Base 28, San Diego Marines 7
12-14-58—Eglin Air Force Base 15, Brooke Medics 7
12-13-59—Quantico Marines 90, McClellan Air Force Base 0

SHURI BOWL
12-58—Air Force 60, Marine Corps 0

SPAGHETTI BOWL
(Florence, Italy)
1-1-45—5th Army 20, 12th Air Force 0 (20,000)
1-1-53—Salzburg Army 12, Wiesbaden AFC 7 (at Leghorn, Italy)

SUKIYAKI BOWL
12-56—Air Force 29, Marines 7

TEA BOWL
(London, England)
2-13-44—Canada 16, United States 6 (30,000)
12-31-44—Air Service Command Warriors 13, 8th Air Force Shuttle Raiders 0 (12,000)

TREASURY BOWL
(New York, N.Y.)
12-16-44—Randolph Field 13, 2nd Air Force 6 (8,356)

TYPHOON BOWL
12-56—Army 13, Marines 0

VALOR BOWL
(Chattanooga, Tenn.)
12-7-57—Hamilton Air Force Base 12, Quantico Marines 6

POSTSEASON BOWL INVOLVING NON-I-A TEAMS

HERITAGE BOWL
Site: Atlanta, Ga.
Stadium (Capacity): Georgia Dome (71,228)
Name Changes: Alamo Heritage Bowl (1991); Heritage Bowl (1993-94, 96-99); Jim Walters Heritage Bowl (1995)
Playing Surface: AstroTurf
Playing Sites: Joe Robbie Stadium, Miami (1991); Bragg Memorial Stadium, Tallahassee (1993); Georgia Dome, Atlanta (1994-99)

Date	Score (Attendance)
12-21-91	Alabama St. 36, N.C. A&T 13 (7,724)
1-2-93	Grambling 45, Florida A&M 15 (11,273)
1-1-94	Southern U. 11, South Carolina St. 0 (36,128)
12-30-94	South Carolina St. 31, Grambling 27 (22,179)
12-29-95	Southern U. 30, Florida A&M 25 (25,164)
12-31-96	Howard 27, Southern U. 24 (18,126)
12-27-97	Southern U. 34, South Carolina St. 28 (32,629)
12-26-98	Southern U. 28, Bethune-Cookman 2 (32,955)
12-18-99	Hampton 24, Southern U. 3 (29,561)

NCAA-CERTIFIED ALL-STAR GAMES

EAST-WEST SHRINE CLASSIC
Present Site: San Francisco, Calif.
Stadium (Capacity): Pacific Bell Park (37,000)
Playing Surface: SportsTurf
Playing Sites: Ewing Field, San Francisco (1925); Kezar Stadium, San Francisco (1927-41); Sugar Bowl, New Orleans (1942); Kezar Stadium, San Francisco (1943-66); Candlestick Park, San Francisco (1967-68); Stanford Stadium, Palo Alto (1969); Oakland Coliseum (1971); Candlestick Park, San Francisco (1971-73); Stanford Stadium, Palo Alto (1974-00) Pacific Bell Park, San Francisco (since 2001)

Date	Score (Attendance)
12-26-25	West 7-0 (20,000)
1-1-27	West 7-3 (15,000)
12-26-27	West 16-6 (27,500)
12-29-28	East 20-0 (55,000)
1-1-30	East 19-7 (58,000)
12-27-30	West 3-0 (40,000)
1-1-32	East 6-0 (45,000)
1-2-33	West 21-13 (45,000)
1-1-34	West 12-0 (35,000)
1-1-35	West 19-13 (52,000)
1-1-36	East 19-3 (55,000)
1-1-37	East 3-0 (38,000)
1-1-38	Tie 0-0 (55,000)
1-2-39	West 14-0 (60,000)
1-1-40	West 28-11 (50,000)
1-1-41	West 20-14 (60,000)
1-3-42	Tie 6-6 (35,000)
1-1-43	East 13-12 (57,000)
1-1-44	Tie 13-13 (55,000)
1-1-45	West 13-7 (60,000)
1-1-46	Tie 7-7 (60,000)
1-1-47	West 13-9 (60,000)
1-1-48	East 40-9 (60,000)
1-1-49	East 14-12 (59,000)
12-31-49	East 28-6 (60,000)
12-30-50	West 16-7 (60,000)
12-29-51	East 15-14 (60,000)
12-27-52	East 21-20 (60,000)
1-2-54	West 31-7 (60,000)
1-1-55	East 13-12 (60,000)
12-31-55	East 29-6 (60,000)
12-29-56	West 7-6 (60,000)
12-28-57	West 27-13 (60,000)
12-27-58	East 26-14 (60,000)
1-2-60	West 21-14 (60,000)
12-31-60	East 7-0 (60,000)
12-30-61	West 21-8 (60,000)
12-29-62	East 25-19 (60,000)
12-28-63	Tie 6-6 (60,000)
1-2-65	West 11-7 (60,000)
12-31-65	West 22-7 (47,000)
12-31-66	East 45-22 (46,000)
12-30-67	East 16-14 (29,000)
12-28-68	West 18-7 (29,000)
12-27-69	West 15-0 (70,000)
1-2-71	West 17-13 (50,000)
12-31-71	West 17-13 (35,000)
12-30-72	West 9-3 (37,000)
12-29-73	East 35-7 (30,000)
12-28-74	East 16-14 (35,000)
1-3-76	West 21-14 (75,000)
1-2-77	West 30-14 (45,000)
12-31-77	West 23-3 (65,000)
1-6-79	East 56-17 (72,000)
1-5-80	West 20-10 (75,000)
1-10-81	East 21-3 (76,000)
1-9-82	West 20-13 (75,000)
1-15-83	East 26-25 (72,999)
1-7-84	East 27-19 (77,000)
1-5-85	West 21-10 (72,000)
1-11-86	East 18-7 (77,000)
1-10-87	West 24-21 (74,000)
1-16-88	West 16-13 (62,000)
1-15-89	East 24-6 (76,000)
1-21-90	West 22-21 (78,000)
1-26-91	West 24-21 (72,000)
1-19-92	West 14-6 (83,000)
1-24-93	East 31-17 (84,000)
1-15-94	West 29-28 (60,000)
1-14-95	West 30-28 (35,079)
1-13-96	West 34-18 (8,500)
1-11-97	East 17-13 (62,500)
1-10-98	West 24-7 (32,500)
1-16-99	East 20-10 (50,000)
1-15-00	East 35-21 (65,246)
1-14-01	West 20-10 (31,549)
1-12-02	West 21-13 (25,035)
1-11-03	East 20-17

Series record: West won 41, East 32, 5 ties.

BLUE-GRAY ALL-STAR CLASSIC
Present Site: Montgomery, Ala.
Stadium (Capacity): Cramton Bowl (24,600)
Playing Surface: Grass
Playing Sites: Cramton Bowl, Montgomery (since 1939)

Date	Score (Attendance)
1-2-39	Blue 7-0 (8,000)
12-30-39	Gray 33-20 (10,000)
12-28-40	Blue 14-12 (14,000)
12-27-41	Gray 16-0 (15,571)
12-26-42	Gray 24-0 (16,000)
1943	No Game
12-30-44	Gray 24-7 (16,000)
12-29-45	Blue 26-0 (20,000)
12-28-46	Gray 20-13 (22,500)
12-27-47	Gray 33-6 (22,500)
12-25-48	Blue 19-13 (15,000)
12-31-49	Gray 27-13 (21,500)
12-30-50	Gray 31-6 (21,000)
12-29-51	Gray 20-14 (22,000)
12-27-52	Gray 28-7 (22,000)
12-26-53	Gray 40-20 (18,500)
12-25-54	Blue 14-7 (18,000)
12-31-55	Gray 20-19 (19,000)
12-29-56	Blue 14-0 (21,000)
12-28-57	Gray 21-20 (16,000)
12-27-58	Blue 16-0 (16,000)
12-26-59	Blue 20-8 (20,000)
12-31-60	Blue 35-7 (18,000)
12-30-61	Gray 9-7 (18,000)
12-29-62	Blue 10-6 (20,000)
12-28-63	Gray 21-14 (20,000)
12-26-64	Blue 10-6 (16,000)
12-25-65	Gray 23-19 (18,000)
12-24-66	Blue 14-9 (18,000)
12-30-67	Blue 22-16 (23,350)
12-28-68	Gray 28-7 (18,000)
12-27-69	Tie 6-6 (21,500)
12-28-70	Gray 38-7 (23,000)
12-28-71	Gray 9-0 (24,000)
12-27-72	Gray 27-15 (20,000)
12-18-73	Blue 20-14 (21,000)
12-17-74	Blue 29-24 (12,000)
12-19-75	Blue 14-13 (10,000)
12-24-76	Gray 31-10 (16,000)
12-30-77	Blue 20-16 (5,000)
12-29-78	Gray 28-24 (18,380)
12-25-79	Blue 22-13 (18,312)
12-25-80	Blue 24-23 (25,000)
12-25-81	Blue 21-9 (19,000)
12-25-82	Gray 20-10 (21,000)
12-25-83	Gray 17-13 (2,000)
12-25-84	Gray 33-6 (24,080)
12-25-85	Blue 37-20 (18,500)
12-25-86	Blue 31-7 (18,500)
12-25-87	Gray 12-10 (20,300)
12-25-88	Blue 22-21 (20,000)
12-25-89	Gray 28-10 (16,000)
12-25-90	Blue 17-14 (17,500)
12-25-91	Gray 20-12 (21,000)
12-25-92	Gray 27-17 (20,500)
12-25-93	Gray 17-10 (18,500)
12-25-94	Blue 38-27 (23,500)
12-25-95	Blue 26-7 (18,500)
12-25-96	Blue 44-34 (17,000)
12-25-97	Gray 31-24 (25,214)
12-25-98	Gray 31-24 (17,500)
12-25-99	Tie 22-22 (15,531)
12-25-00	Gray 40-37 (18,500)
12-25-01	Blue 28-10 (18,000)
12-25-02	No game played

Series record: Gray won 33, Blue 28, 2 ties.

HULA BOWL
Present Site: Maui, Hawaii
Stadium (Capacity): War Memorial (24,000)
Playing Surface: Grass
Format: From 1947 through 1950, the College All-Stars played the Hawaii All-Stars. Beginning in 1951, the Hawaiian team was augmented by players from the National Football League. This format, however, was changed to an all-collegiate contest—first between the East and West, then between North and South (in 1963), and then back to East and West in 1974 and 1995-96. In 1994, the format went to a collection of collegiate all-stars versus a collection of Hawaiian former collegiate players. In 1997, it reverted back to North-South. Teams are broken down into players from the northern United States (team named Kai, Hawaiian for ocean) against southern United States (team named Aina, Hawaiian for land)
Playing Sites: Honolulu Stadium (1960-74); Aloha Stadium (1975-98); War Memorial (since 1999)

Date	Score (Attendance)
1-10-60	East 34-8 (23,000)

Date	Score (Attendance)
1-8-61	East 14-7 (17,017)
1-7-62	Tie 7-7 (20,598)
1-6-63	North 20-13 (20,000)
1-4-64	North 20-13 (18,177)
1-9-65	South 16-14 (22,100)
1-8-66	North 27-26 (25,000)
1-7-67	North 28-27 (23,500)
1-6-68	North 50-6 (21,000)
1-4-69	North 13-7 (23,000)
1-10-70	South 35-13 (25,000)
1-9-71	North 42-32 (23,500)
1-8-72	North 24-7 (23,000)
1-6-73	South 17-3 (23,000)
1-5-74	East 24-14 (23,000)
1-4-75	East 34-25 (22,000)
1-10-76	East 16-0 (45,458)
1-8-77	West 20-17 (45,579)
1-7-78	West 42-22 (48,197)
1-6-79	East 29-24 (49,132)
1-5-80	East 17-10 (47,096)
1-10-81	West 24-17 (39,010)
1-9-82	West 26-23 (43,002)
1-15-83	East 30-14 (39,456)
1-7-84	West 21-16 (34,216)
1-5-85	East 34-14 (30,767)
1-11-86	West 23-10 (29,564)
1-10-87	West 16-14 (17,775)
1-16-88	West 20-18 (26,737)
1-7-89	East 21-10 (25,000)
1-13-90	West 21-13 (28,742)
1-19-91	East 23-10 (21,926)
1-11-92	West 27-20 (23,112)
1-16-93	West 13-10 (25,479)
1-22-94	College All-Stars 28-15 (33,947)
1-22-95	East 20-9 (19,074)
1-21-96	East 17-10 (25,112)
1-19-97	South 26, North 13 (24,725)
1-18-98	South 20, North 19 (20,079)
1-24-99	South 34, North 14 (23,719)
12-22-99	Tie 28-28 (23,719)
1-20-01	North 31, South 23 (23,719)
2-2-02	South 45, North 28 (24,000)
2-1-03	South 32, North 24

Series records: North-South (1963-73, 97-03)—North won 9, South 8, 1 tie; East-West (1960-62, 1974-93 and 1995-96)—East won 13, West 11, 1 tie; College All-Stars vs. Hawaiian All-Stars (1994)—College All-Stars won 1, Hawaiian All-Stars 0.

SENIOR BOWL
Played at Ladd-Peebles Stadium in Mobile, Ala., since 1951 under the auspices of the National Football League. North and South teams are composed of senior players who have used all of their collegiate eligibility. In 1991, the teams switched from North and South to AFC and NFC; in 1994, the teams switched back to North and South.

Date	Score (Attendance)
1-7-50	South 22, North 13 (at Jacksonville, Fla.)
1-6-51	South 19, North 18
1-5-52	North 20, South 6
1-3-53	North 28, South 13
1-9-54	North 20, South 14
1-8-55	South 12, North 6
1-7-56	South 12, North 2
1-5-57	South 21, North 7
1-11-58	North 15, South 13
1-3-59	South 21, North 12
1-9-60	North 26, South 7 (40,119)
1-7-61	South 33, North 26
1-6-62	South 42, North 7
1-5-63	South 33, North 27
1-4-64	South 28, North 21 (37,094)
1-9-65	Tie 7-7 (40,605)
1-8-66	South 27, North 18
1-7-67	North 35, South 13
1-6-68	South 34, North 21
1-11-69	North 27, South 16
1-10-70	Tie 37-37
1-9-71	North 31, South 13 (40,646)
1-8-72	North 26, South 13 (40,646)
1-6-73	South 33, North 30 (40,646)
1-12-74	North 16, South 13 (40,646)
1-11-75	Tie 17-17 (40,646)
1-10-76	North 42, South 35 (40,646)

Date	Score (Attendance)
1-9-77	North 27, South 24 (40,646)
1-7-78	Tie 17-17 (40,646)
1-13-79	South 41, North 21 (40,100)
1-12-80	North 57, South 3 (40,646)
1-17-81	North 23, South 10 (40,102)
1-16-82	South 27, North 10 (39,410)
1-22-83	North 14, South 6 (37,511)
1-14-84	South 21, North 20 (38,254)
1-12-85	South 23, North 7 (33,500)
1-18-86	North 31, South 17 (40,646)
1-17-87	South 42, North 38
1-23-88	North 21, South 7
1-21-89	South 13, North 12 (39,742)
1-20-90	North 41, South 0 (42,400)
1-19-91	AFC 38, NFC 28 (37,500)
1-18-92	AFC 13, NFC 10 (37,100)
1-16-93	NFC 21, AFC 6 (37,124)
1-22-94	South 35, North 32 (39,200)
1-21-95	South 14, North 7 (40,007)
1-20-96	North 25, South 10 (40,700)
1-18-97	North 35, South 14 (40,646)
1-17-98	South 31, North 8 (40,820)
1-23-99	South 31, North 21 (41,000)
1-22-00	North 24, South 21 (40,646)
1-21-01	South 21, North 16 (40,646)
1-19-02	South 41, North 26 (40,646)
1-18-03	North 17, South 0 (40,646)

Series records: North-South (1950-90 and 1994 to present)—South won 25, North 22, 4 ties; AFC-NFC (1991-93)—AFC won 2, NFC 1.

ROTARY GRIDIRON CLASSIC
Present Site: Orlando, Fla.
Stadium (Capacity): Florida Citrus Bowl (70,000)
Playing Surface: Grass

Date	Score (Attendance)
1-16-99	Team Florida 17, Team USA 9 (29,725)
1-15-00	Team USA 21, Team Florida 14 (21,298)
1-13-01	Team Florida, 10 Team USA 0 (25,000)
1-19-02	Team Florida 42, Team USA 13 (20,344)
1-25-03	Team USA 20, Team Florida 17 (9,375)

DISCONTINUED ALL-STAR FOOTBALL GAMES
Many of these games were identified without complete information such as scores, teams, sites or dates. Please send any updates or additional information to: NCAA Statistics Service, P.O. Box 6222, Indianapolis, Indiana 46206-6222.

ALL-AMERICAN BOWL (1969-77)
(Tampa, Fla.)

Date	Score (Attendance)
1-4-69	North 21, South 15 (16,380)
1-3-70	South 24, North 23 (17,642)
1-10-71	North 39, South 2 (12,000)
1-9-72	North 27, South 8 (20,137)
1-7-73	North 10, South 6 (23,416)
1-6-74	North 28, South 7 (24,536)
1-5-75	South 28, North 22 (19,246)
1-10-76	North 21, South 14 (15,321)
1-2-77	North 21, South 20 (14,207)

AMERICAN COLLEGE ALL-STAR GAME (1948)
(Los Angeles, Calif.)

Date	Score
12-18-48	American All-Stars 43, Canadian All-Stars 0
12-26-48	American All-Stars 14, Hawaiian All-Stars 0

BLACK COLLEGE ALL-STAR BOWL (1979-82)

Date	Score (Location, Attendance)
1-7-79	East 25, West 20 (at New Orleans, La.)
1-5-80	West 27, East 21 (ot) (at New Orleans, La.)
1-17-81	West 19, East 10 (at Jackson, Miss.) (7,500)
1-16-82	West 7, East 0 (at Jackson, Miss.)

CAMP FOOTBALL FOUNDATION BOWL (1974)

CANADIAN-AMERICAN BOWL (1978-79)
(Tampa, Fla.)

Date	Score (Attendance)
1-8-78	U.S. All-Stars 22, Canadian All-Stars 7 (11,328)
1-6-79	U.S. All-Stars 34, Canadian All-Stars 14 (11,033)

CHALLENGE BOWL (1978-79)
(Seattle, Wash.)

Date	Score (Attendance)
1-14-78	Pacific-8 27, Big Ten 20 (20,578)
1-13-79	Pacific-10 36, Big Eight 23 (23,961)

CHICAGO COLLEGE ALL-STAR FOOTBALL GAME (1934-76)
An all-star team composed of the top senior collegiate players met the National Football League champions (1933-66) or the Super Bowl champions (1967-75) from the previous season, beginning in 1934. The only time the all-stars did not play the league champions was in 1935. All games except 1943 and 1944 were played at Soldier Field, Chicago, Ill. The 1943 and 1944 games were played at Dyche Stadium, Evanston, Ill.

Date	Score (Attendance)
8-31-34	(Tie) Chicago Bears 0-0 (79,432)
8-29-35	Chicago Bears 5, All-Stars 0 (77,450)
9-2-36	(Tie) Detroit 7-7 (76,000)
9-1-37	All-Stars 6, Green Bay 0 (84,560)
8-31-38	All-Stars 28, Washington 16 (74,250)
8-30-39	New York Giants 9, All-Stars 0 (81,456)
8-29-40	Green Bay 45, All-Stars 28 (84,567)
8-28-41	Chicago Bears 37, All-Stars 13 (98,203)
8-28-42	Chicago Bears 21, All-Stars 0 (101,100)
8-25-43	All-Stars 27, Washington 7 (48,471)
8-30-44	Chicago Bears 24, All-Stars 21 (48,769)
8-30-45	Green Bay 19, All-Stars 7 (92,753)
8-23-46	All-Stars 16, Los Angeles 0 (97,380)
8-22-47	All-Stars 16, Chicago Bears 0 (105,840)
8-20-48	Chicago Cardinals 28, All-Stars 0 (101,220)
8-12-49	Philadelphia 38, All-Stars 0 (93,780)
8-11-50	All-Stars 17, Philadelphia 7 (88,885)
8-17-51	Cleveland 33, All-Stars 0 (92,180)
8-15-52	Los Angeles 10, All-Stars 7 (88,316)
8-14-53	Detroit 24, All-Stars 10 (93,818)
8-13-54	Detroit 31, All-Stars 6 (93,470)
8-12-55	All-Stars 30, Cleveland 27 (75,000)
8-10-56	Cleveland 26, All-Stars 0 (75,000)
8-9-57	New York Giants 22, All-Stars 12 (75,000)
8-15-58	All-Stars 35, Detroit 19 (70,000)
8-14-59	Baltimore 29, All-Stars 0 (70,000)
8-12-60	Baltimore 32, All-Stars 7 (70,000)
8-4-61	Philadelphia 28, All-Stars 14 (66,000)
8-3-62	Green Bay 42, All-Stars 20 (65,000)
8-2-63	All-Stars 20, Green Bay 17 (65,000)
8-7-64	Chicago Bears 28, All-Stars 17 (65,000)
8-6-65	Cleveland 24, All-Stars 16 (68,000)
8-5-66	Green Bay 38, All-Stars 0 (72,000)
8-4-67	Green Bay 27, All-Stars 0 (70,934)
8-2-68	Green Bay 34, All-Stars 17 (69,917)
8-1-69	New York Jets 26, All-Stars 24 (74,208)
7-31-70	Kansas City 24, All-Stars 3 (69,940)
7-30-71	Baltimore 24, All-Stars 17 (52,289)
7-28-72	Dallas 20, All-Stars 7 (54,162)
7-27-73	Miami 14, All-Stars 3 (54,103)
1974	No game played
8-1-75	Pittsburgh 21, All-Stars 14 (54,103)
7-23-76	*Pittsburgh 24, All-Stars 0 (52,895)

*Game was not completed due to thunderstorms.

CHRISTIAN BOWL (1955)
(Murfreesboro, Tenn.)

Date	Score (Attendance)
12-26-55	East 21, West 10 (4,000)

COACHES ALL-AMERICAN GAME (1961-76)

at Buffalo, N.Y.

6-23-61	West 30, East 20 (12,913)
6-29-62	East 13, West 8 (22,759)
6-29-63	West 22, East 21 (20,840)
6-27-64	East 18, West 15 (21,112)
6-26-65	East 34, West 14 (25,501)

at Atlanta, Ga.

7-9-66	West 24, East 7 (38,236)
7-9-67	East 12, West 9 (29,145)
6-28-68	West 34, East 20 (21,120)
6-28-69	West 14, East 10 (17,008)

at Lubbock, Texas

6-28-70	East 34, West 27 (42,150)
6-26-71	West 33, East 28 (43,320)
6-24-72	East 42, West 20 (42,314)
6-23-73	West 20, East 6 (43,272)
6-22-74	West 36, East 6 (42,368)

Date	Score (Attendance)
6-21-75	East 23, West 21 (36,108)
6-19-76	West 35, East 17 (36,504)

COPPER BOWL (1958-60)
(Tempe, Ariz.)

Date	Score (Attendance)
12-20-58	Southwest All-Stars 22, National All-Stars 13 (12,000)
12-26-59	National All-Stars 21, Southwest All-Stars 6 (16,000)
12-31-60	National All-Stars 27, Southwest All-Stars 8 (8,000)

CRUSADE BOWL (1963)
(Baltimore, Md.)

Date	Score (Attendance)
1-6-63	East 38, West 10 (2,400)

DALLAS ALL-STAR GAME (1936-39)
(Dallas, Texas)

Date	Score
9-7-36	Southwest All-Stars 7, Chicago Bears 6
9-6-37	Southwest All-Stars 6, Chicago Bears 0
9-5-38	Southwest All-Stars 13, Washington Redskins 7
9-4-39	Green Bay Packers 31, Southwest All-Stars 20

DIXIE CLASSIC (1928-31)
(Dallas, Texas)

Date	Score (Attendance)
12-29-28	Southwest Conference 14, Small Texas Schools 6
1-1-29	Big Six Conference 14, Southwest Conference 6 (10,000)
1-1-30	Midwest 25, Southwest Conference 12 (15,000)
1-1-31	Southwest Conference 18, Midwest 0 (14,000)

EAST-WEST BLACK ALL-STAR GAME (1971)
(Houston, Texas)

Date	Score (Attendance)
12-11-71	East 19, West 10 (5,156)

EAST-WEST COLLEGE ALL-STAR GAME (1932)
(Demonstrated at Tenth Olympiad, Los Angeles, Calif.; East team composed of players from Harvard, Princeton and Yale, West team composed of players from California, Southern California and Stanford)

Date	Score (Attendance)
8-8-32	West 7, East 6 (50,000)

FREEDOM BOWL ALL-STAR CLASSIC (1984-86)
(Atlanta, Ga. and Washington, D.C.)
Southwestern Athletic Conference vs. Mid-Eastern Athletic Conference.

Date	Score (Attendance)
1-14-84	SWAC 36, MEAC 22 (16,097)
1-12-85	SWAC 14, MEAC 0 (18,352)
1-11-86	SWAC 16, MEAC 14 (10,200)
12-20-86	MEAC 12, SWAC 7 (8,962)

FREEDOM BOWL ALL-STAR CLASSIC (1990)
(Houston, Texas)

Date	Score
1-13-90	North 14, South 13

FREEDOM CLASSIC (1976)

Year	Score (Attendance)
1976	West 12, East 9 (6,654)

JAPAN BOWL
(Yokohama, Japan)

Date	Score (Attendance)
1-18-76	West 27-18 (68,000)
1-16-77	West 21-10 (58,000)
1-15-78	East 26-10 (32,500)
1-14-79	East 33-14 (55,000)
1-13-80	West 28-17 (27,000)
1-17-81	West 25-13 (30,000)
1-16-82	West 28-17 (28,000)
1-23-83	West 30-21 (30,000)
1-15-84	West 26-21 (26,000)
1-13-85	West 28-14 (30,000)
1-11-86	East 31-14 (30,000)
1-11-87	West 24-17 (30,000)
1-10-88	West 17-3 (30,000)
1-15-89	East 30-7 (29,000)
1-13-90	East 24-10 (27,000)
1-12-91	West 20-14 (30,000)
1-11-92	East 14-13 (50,000)
1-9-93	East 27-13 (46,000)

LOS ANGELES ALL-STAR GAME (1948)
(Los Angeles, Calif.)

Date	Score
1-18-48	West 34, East 20

MARTIN LUTHER KING ALL-AMERICA CLASSIC (1990-91)
(Division I-A vs. all other divisions)

Date	Score (Attendance)
1-15-90	All Div. All-Stars 35, I-A All-Stars 24 (350) (at San Jose, Calif.)
1-14-91	I-A All-Stars 21, All Div. All-Stars 14 (6,272) (at St. Petersburg, Fla.)

NEW YORK ALL-STAR GAME
(New York, N.Y.)

Date	Teams, Score
1936	New York Giants 12, All-Stars 2
1937	New York Giants 14, All-Stars 7
1938	New York Giants 6, All-Stars 0
1939	New York Giants 10, All-Stars 0
1940	All-Stars 16, New York Giants 6
1941	New York Giants 23, All-Stars 3
9-12-42	Eastern Army All-Stars 16, New York Giants 0 (see Army All-Star Games)
1947	New York Giants 21, All-Stars 0
1949	All-Stars 28, New York Giants 13

NORTH-SOUTH ALL-STAR SHRINE GAME
(1930-34, 39-48, 1948-73, 1976)

Date	Score (Attendance)
1-1-30	North 21, South 12 (20,000) (at Atlanta, Ga.) (Southern Conference All-Star Game)
12-28-30	South 7, North 0 (2,000) (at New York, N.Y.)
12-10-32	South 7, North 6 (500) (at Baltimore, Md.)
12-24-33	North 3, South 0 (5,000) (at New York, N.Y.)
1-1-34	North 7, South 0 (12,000) (at Knoxville, Tenn.) (Southeastern Conference All-Star Game)

at Birmingham, Ala.

Date	Score
1-39	North 7, South 0
12-39	South 33, North 20
12-40	North 14, South 12
12-41	South 16, North 0
12-42	South 24, North 0
1-44	South 24, North 7
1-45	North 26, South 0
1-46	South 20, North 13
1-47	South 33, North 6
1-48	North 19, South 13

at Miami, Fla.

Date	Score
12-25-48	South 24, North 14 (33,056)
12-25-49	North 20, South 14 (37,378)
12-25-50	South 14, North 9 (39,132)
12-25-51	South 35, North 7 (39,995)
12-25-52	North 21, South 21 (42,866)
12-25-53	South 20, North 0 (44,715)
12-25-54	South 20, North 17 (37,847)
12-25-55	South 20, North 7 (42,179)
12-26-56	North 17, South 7 (39,181)
12-25-57	North 23, South 20 (28,303)
12-27-58	South 49, North 20 (35,519)
12-26-59	North 27, South 17 (35,185)
12-26-60	North 41, South 14 (26,146)
12-25-61	South 35, North 16 (18,892)
12-22-62	South 15, North 14 (16,952)
12-21-63	South 23, North 14 (19,120)
12-25-64	North 37, South 30 (29,124)
12-25-65	South 21, North 14 (25,640)
12-26-66	North 27, South 14 (28,569)
12-25-67	North 24, South 0 (17,400)
12-25-68	North 3, South 0 (18,063)
12-25-69	North 31, South 10 (23,527)
12-25-70	North 28, South 7 (15,402)
12-27-71	South 7, North 6 (18,640)
12-25-72	North 17, South 10 (18,013)
12-25-73	South 27, North 6 (10,672)

at Pontiac, Mich.

Date	Score
12-17-76	South 24, North 0 (41,627)

OHIO SHRINE BOWL (1972-76)
(Columbus, Ohio)

Date	Score
12-9-72	East 20, West 7
12-1-73	East 8, West 6
12-7-74	East 27, West 6
1975	West 17, East 7
12-4-76	East 24, West 8 (played elsewhere)

OLYMPIA GOLD BOWL (1982)
(San Diego, Calif.)

Date	Score (Attendance)
1-16-82	National All-Stars 30, American All-Stars 21 (22,316)

OLYMPIC GAME (1933)
(Chicago, Ill.)

Date	Score (Attendance)
8-24-33	East 13, West 7 (50,000)

OPTIMIST ALL-AMERICA BOWL (1958-62)
(Tucson, Ariz.)

Date	Score (Attendance)
1-4-58	College All-Stars 56, Tucson Cowboys 28
1-3-59	Major-College 14, Small-College 12 (10,000)
1-2-60	Major College 53, Small-College 0 (14,500)
12-26-60	Major-College 25, Small-College 12
12-30-61	Major-College 31, Small-College 0 (14,000)
12-29-62	Small-College 14, Major-College 13

POTATO BOWL (1967)
(Bakersfield, Calif.)

Date	Score (Attendance)
12-23-67	North 23, South 7 (5,600)

ROCKY MOUNTAIN CONFERENCE-NORTH CENTRAL CONFERENCE GAME (1930)
(Elks Charity Bowl)
(Denver, Colo.)

Date	Score
1-1-30	North Central 13, Rocky Mountain 6

SALAD BOWL ALL-STAR GAME (1955)
(Phoenix, Ariz.)

Date	Score (Attendance)
1-1-55	Skyline Conference 20, Border Conference 13 (8,000)
12-31-55	Border Conference 13, Skyline Conference 10

SHERIDAN BLACK ALL-STAR GAME (1979-82)
(See Black College All-Star Bowl)

SMOKE BOWL (1941)
(Richmond, Va.)

Date	Score (Attendance)
1-1-41	Norfolk All-Stars 16, Richmond All-Stars 2 (5,000)

SOUTHWEST CHALLENGE BOWL (1963-64)
(Corpus Christi, Texas)

Date	Score (Attendance)
1-5-63	National 33, Southwest 13
1-4-64	National 66, Southwest 14 (10,200)

U.S. BOWL (1962)
(Washington, D. C.)
(Teams were composed of players selected in the recent NFL draft)

Date	Score
1-7-62	West 33, East 19

Special Regular-Season Games

REGULAR-SEASON GAMES PLAYED IN USA

EDDIE ROBINSON CLASSIC
Playing Sites: Ohio Stadium, Columbus, Ohio (1997); Memorial Stadium, Lincoln, Neb. (1998); Notre Dame Stadium, South Bend, Ind. (1999); Arrowhead Stadium, Kansas City, Mo. (2000, 2002); Camp Randall Stadium, Madison, Wis. (2001)

Date	Score (Attendance)
8-28-97	Ohio St. 24, Wyoming 10 (89,112)
8-29-98	Nebraska 56, Louisiana Tech 27 (76,021)
8-28-99	Notre Dame 48, Kansas 13 (80,012)
8-26-00	Kansas St. 27, Iowa 7 (77,148)
8-25-01	Wisconsin 26, Virginia 17 (76,740)
8-24-02	Florida St. 38, Iowa St. 31 (55,132)

BCA CLASSIC
Present Site: Kansas City, Mo.
Stadium (Capacity): Arrowhead Stadium (79,000)
Playing Surface: Grass
Sponsor: Black Coaches' Association
Playing Sites: Spartan Stadium, East Lansing, Mich. (1998); Royal-Memorial Stadium, Austin, Texas (1999);

LaVell Edwards Stadium, Provo, Utah (2001); Memorial/Osborne Stadium, Lincoln, Neb. (2002); Arrowhead Stadium, Kansas City, Mo. (2003)

Date	Score (Attendance)
8-29-98	Colorado St. 23, Michigan St. 16 (68,624)
8-28-99	North Carolina St. 23, Texas 20 (82,252)
8-27-00	Game cancelled because of weather
8-25-01	Brigham Young 70, Tulane 35 (49,008)
8-24-02	Nebraska 48, Arizona St. 10 (77,779)
8-23-03	California vs. Kansas St.

KICKOFF CLASSIC
Sponsor: National Association of Collegiate Directors of Athletics (NACDA).
Playing Site: Giants Stadium (1983-02)

Date	Score (Attendance)
8-29-83	Nebraska 44, Penn St. 6 (71,123)
8-27-84	Miami (Fla.) 20, Auburn 18 (51,131)
8-29-85	Brigham Young 28, Boston College 14 (51,227)
8-27-86	Alabama 16, Ohio St. 10 (68,296)
8-30-87	Tennessee 23, Iowa 22 (54,681)
8-27-88	Nebraska 23, Texas A&M 14 (58,172)
8-31-89	Notre Dame 36, Virginia 13 (77,323)
8-31-90	Southern California 34, Syracuse 16 (57,293)
8-28-91	Penn St. 34, Georgia Tech 22 (77,409)
8-29-92	North Carolina St. 24, Iowa 14 (46,251)
8-28-93	Florida St. 42, Kansas 0 (51,734)
8-28-94	Nebraska 31, West Virginia 0 (58,233)
8-27-95	Ohio St. 38, Boston College 6 (62,711)
8-25-96	Penn St. 24, Southern California 7 (77,716)
8-24-97	Syracuse 34, Wisconsin 0 (51,185)
8-31-98	Florida St. 23, Texas A&M 14 (59,232)
8-29-99	Miami (Fla.) 23, Ohio St. 12 (73,037)
8-27-00	Southern California 29, Penn St. 5 (78,902)
8-26-01	Georgia Tech 13, Syracuse 7 (41,517)
8-31-02	Notre Dame 22, Maryland 0 (72,903)

PIGSKIN CLASSIC
Playing Sites: Anaheim Stadium (now Edison Field), Anaheim, Calif. (1990-94); Michigan Stadium, Ann Arbor, Michigan (1995); Cougar Stadium (now LaVell Edwards Stadium), Provo, Utah (1996); Soldier Field, Chicago (1997); L. A. Memorial Coliseum, Los Angeles, Calif. (1998); Beaver Stadium, State College, Pa. (1999); Alltel Stadium, Jacksonville, Fla. (2000); Memorial/Osborne Stadium, Lincoln, Neb. (2001); Ohio Stadium, Columbus, Ohio (2002)

Date	Score (Attendance)
8-26-90	Colorado 31, Tennessee 31 (33,458)
8-29-91	Florida St. 44, Brigham Young 28 (38,363)
8-26-92	Texas A&M 10, Stanford 7 (35,240)
8-29-93	North Carolina 31, Southern California 9 (49,309)
8-29-94	Ohio St. 34, Fresno St. 10 (28,513)
8-26-95	Michigan 18, Virginia 17 (101,444)
8-24-96	Brigham Young 41, Texas A&M 37 (55,229)
8-23-97	Northwestern 24, Oklahoma 0 (36,804)
8-30-98	Southern California 27, Purdue 17 (56,623)
8-28-99	Penn St. 41, Arizona 7 (97,168)
8-26-00	Florida St. 29, Brigham Young 3 (54,260)
8-25-01	Nebraska 21, TCU 7 (77,473)
8-24-02	Ohio St. 45, Texas Tech 21 (100,037)

HISPANIC COLLEGE FUND CLASSIC
Sponsor: Transamerica
Playing Sites: Jones Stadium, Lubbock, Texas (2000); Memorial Stadium, Norman, Okla. (2001); Lane Stadium, Blacksburg, Va. (2002)

Date	Score (Attendance)
8-26-00	Texas Tech 24, New Mexico 3 (42,238)
8-25-01	Oklahoma 41, North Carolina 27 (75,423)
8-25-02	Virginia Tech 63, Arkansas St. 7 (54,016)

JIM THORPE CLASSIC
Sponsor: Jim Thorpe Association
Playing Sites: Folsom Field, Boulder, Colo. (2001); Scott/Harrison Field, Charlottesville, Va. (2002)

Date	Score (Attendance)
8-26-01	Fresno St. 24, Colorado 22 (47,762)
8-22-02	Colorado St. 35, Virginia 29 (57,120)

JOHN THOMPSON FOUNDATION CHALLENGE CLASSIC
Sponsor: John Thompson Foundation
Playing Sites: Papa John's Cardinal Stadium, Louisville, Ky. (2001); Camp Randall Stadium, Madison, Wis. (2002)

Date	Score (Attendance)
8-23-01	Louisville 45, New Mexico St. 24 (38,129)
8-23-02	Wisconsin 23, Fresno St. 21 (75,136)

BCA BOWL
Playing Site: Carter-Finley Stadium, Raleigh, N.C. (2002)

Date	Score (Attendance)
8-24-02	North Carolina St. 34, New Mexico 24 (47,018)

BIG 12 CONFERENCE CHAMPIONSHIP
Present Site: Kansas City, Mo.
Stadium (Capacity): Arrowhead Stadium (79,000)
Playing Surface: Grass
Playing Sites: Trans World Dome (now Edward Jones Dome), St. Louis, Mo. (1996; 1998); Alamodome, San Antonio, Texas (1997; 1999); Arrowhead Stadium, Kansas City, Mo. (2000, 2003); Texas Stadium, Irving, Texas (2001); Reliant Stadium, Houston, Texas (2002)

Date	Score (Attendance)
12-7-96	Texas (South Div.) 37, Nebraska (North Div.) 27 (63,109)
12-6-97	Nebraska (North Div.) 54, Texas A&M (South Div.) 15 (64,824)
12-5-98	Texas A&M (South Div.) 36, Kansas St. (North Div.) 33 (60,789)
12-4-99	Nebraska (North Div.) 22, Texas (South Div.) 6 (65,035)
12-2-00	Oklahoma (South Div.) 27, Kansas St. (North Div.) 24 (79,655)
12-1-01	Colorado (North Div.) 39, Texas (South Div.) 37 (65,675)
12-7-02	Oklahoma (South Div.) 29, Colorado (North Div.) 7 (63,332)

MID-AMERICAN CONFERENCE CHAMPIONSHIP
Present Site: Western Division winner
Stadium (Capacity): Unknown
Playing Surface: Unknown
Playing Sites: Marshall University Stadium, Huntington, W.Va. (1997-00, 02); Glass Bowl, Toledo, Ohio (2001)

Date	Score (Attendance)
12-5-97	Marshall (East Div.) 34, Toledo (West Div.) 14 (28,021)
12-4-98	Marshall (East Div.) 23, Toledo (West Div.) 17 (28,085)
12-3-99	Marshall (East Div.) 34, Western Mich. (West Div.) 30 (28,069)
12-1-00	Marshall (East Div.) 19, Western Mich. (West Div.) 14 (24,816)
11-30-01	Toledo (West Div.) 41, Marshall (East Div.) 36 (20,025)
12-07-02	Marshall (East Div.) 49, Toledo (West Div.) 45 (24,582)

SOUTHEASTERN CONFERENCE CHAMPIONSHIP
Present Site: Atlanta, Ga.
Stadium (Capacity): Georgia Dome (71,228)
Playing Surface: AstroTurf
Playing Sites: Legion Field, Birmingham, Ala. (1992-93); Georgia Dome, Atlanta (since 1994)

Date	Score (Attendance)
12-5-92	Alabama (Western Div.) 28, Florida (Eastern Div.) 21 (83,091)
12-4-93	Florida (Eastern Div.) 28, Alabama (Western Div.) 13 (76,345)
12-3-94	Florida (Eastern Div.) 24, Alabama (Western Div.) 23 (74,751)
12-2-95	Florida (Eastern Div.) 34, Arkansas (Western Div.) 3 (71,325)
12-7-96	Florida (Eastern Div.) 45, Alabama (Western Div.) 30 (74,132)
12-6-97	Tennessee (Eastern Div.) 30, Auburn (Western Div.) 29 (74,896)
12-5-98	Tennessee (Eastern Div.) 24, Mississippi St. (Western Div.) 14 (74,795)
12-4-99	Alabama (Western Div.) 34, Florida (Eastern Div.) 7 (74,309)
12-2-00	Florida (Eastern Div.) 28, Auburn (Western Div.) 6 (73,427)
12-8-01	LSU (Western Div.) 31, Tennessee (Eastern Div.) 20 (74,843)
12-7-02	Georgia (Eastern Div.) 30, Arkansas (Western Div.) 3 (75,835)

WESTERN ATHLETIC CONFERENCE CHAMPIONSHIP
Site: Las Vegas, Nev.

Stadium (Capacity): Sam Boyd (32,000)
Playing Surface: Monsanto Turf
Playing Site: Sam Boyd Stadium (1996-98)

Date	Score (Attendance)
12-7-96	Brigham Young (Mountain Div.) 28, Wyoming (Pacific Div.) 25 (41,238)
12-6-97	Colorado St. (Pacific Div.) 41, New Mexico (Mountain Div.) 13 (12,706)
12-5-98	Air Force (Pacific Div.) 20, Brigham Young (Mountain Div.) 13 (32,745)

REGULAR-SEASON GAMES PLAYED IN FOREIGN COUNTRIES

TOKYO, JAPAN
(Called Mirage Bowl 1976-85, Coca-Cola Classic from 1986. Played at Tokyo Olympic Memorial Stadium 1976-87, Tokyo Dome from 1988-93.)

Date	Score (Attendance)
9-4-76	Grambling 42, Morgan St. 16 (50,000)
12-11-77	Grambling 35, Temple 32 (50,000)
12-10-78	Temple 28, Boston College 24 (55,000)
11-24-79	Notre Dame 40, Miami (Fla.) 15 (62,574)
11-30-80	UCLA 34, Oregon St. 3 (86,000)
11-28-81	Air Force 21, San Diego St. 16 (80,000)
11-27-82	Clemson 21, Wake Forest 17 (64,700)
11-26-83	Southern Methodist 34, Houston 12 (70,000)
11-17-84	Army 45, Montana 31 (60,000)
11-30-85	Southern California 20, Oregon 6 (65,000)
11-30-86	Stanford 29, Arizona 24 (55,000)
11-28-87	California 17, Washington St. 17 (45,000)
12-3-88	Oklahoma St. 45, Texas Tech 42 (56,000)
12-4-89	Syracuse 24, Louisville 13 (50,000)
12-2-90	Houston 62, Arizona St. 45 (50,000)
11-30-91	Clemson 33, Duke 21 (50,000)
12-6-92	Nebraska 38, Kansas St. 24 (50,000)
12-5-93	Wisconsin 41, Michigan St. 20 (51,500)

MELBOURNE, AUSTRALIA

Date	Score (Attendance)
12-6-85*	Wyoming 24, UTEP 21 (22,000)
12-4-87†	Brigham Young 30, Colorado St. 26 (76,652)

*Played at V.F.L. Park. †Played at Princes Park.

YOKOHAMA, JAPAN

Date	Score (Attendance)
12-2-78	Brigham Young 28, UNLV 24 (27,500)

OSAKA, JAPAN

Date	Score (Attendance)
9-3-78	Utah St. 10, Idaho St. 0 (15,000)

HAVANA, CUBA
(Played at Almandares Park)

Date	Score (Attendance)
12-25-07	LSU 56, Havana University 0 (10,000)

DUBLIN, IRELAND
#Called Emerald Isle Classic. Played at Lansdowne Road Stadium. ¢Played at Croke Park.

Date	Score (Attendance)
11-19-88	Boston College 38, Army 24 (45,525)#
12-2-89	Pittsburgh 46, Rutgers 29 (19,800)#
11-2-96	Notre Dame 54, Navy 27 (38,651)¢

LONDON, ENGLAND

Date	Score (Attendance)
10-16-88	Richmond 20, Boston U. 17 (6,000)

MILAN, ITALY
(Played at The Arena.)

Date	Score (Attendance)
10-28-89	Villanova 28, Rhode Island 25 (5,000)

LIMERICK, IRELAND
(Wild Geese Classic. Played at Limerick Gaelic Grounds.)

Date	Score (Attendance)
11-16-91	Holy Cross 24, Fordham 19 (17,411)

FRANKFURT, GERMANY
(Played at Wald Stadium.)

Date	Score (Attendance)
9-19-92	Heidelberg 7, Otterbein 7 (4,351)

GALWAY, IRELAND
(Called Christopher Columbus Classic.)

Date	Score (Attendance)
11-29-92	Bowdoin 7, Tufts 6 (2,500)

HAMILTON, BERMUDA
(Played at Bermuda National Soccer Stadium.)

Date	Score (Attendance)
11-20-93	Georgetown 17, Wash. & Lee 14 (3,218)
11-19-94	Davidson 28, Sewanee 14 (2,000)
10-28-95	Fordham 17, Holy Cross 10 (2,436)

EXHIBITION GAMES
(Games involving an active NCAA member versus an exhibition opponent played in the United States. Not counted as a regular-season game.)

ORLANDO, FLORIDA
(Played at Citrus Bowl)

Date	Score (Attendance)
10-3-92	UCF 42, Moscow Bears 6 (5,412)

EXHIBITION GAMES PLAYED IN FOREIGN COUNTRIES
(Games involving an active NCAA member versus a team from another country. Not counted as a regular-season game.)

KYOTO, JAPAN
(Played at Nishi Kyogoku Stadium)

Date	Score (Attendance)
3-29-97	Harvard 42, Kyoto 35 (16,000)

COLLEGE FOOTBALL TROPHY GAMES

Following is a list of the current college football trophy games. The games are listed alphabetically by the trophy-object name. The date refers to the season the trophy was first exchanged and is not necessarily the start of competition between the participants. A game involving interdivision teams is listed in the higher-division classification.

DIVISION I-A

Trophy	Date	Colleges
Anniversary Award	1985	Bowling Green-Kent St.
Apple Cup	1962	Washington-Washington St.
Axe	1933	California-Stanford
Band Drum	1935	Kansas-Missouri
Battle for the Bell	1997	Marshall-Ohio
Bayou Bucket	1974	Houston-Rice
Beehive Boot	1971	Brigham Young, Utah, Utah St., Southern Utah, Weber St.
Bell	1927	Missouri-Nebraska
Bell Clapper	1931	Oklahoma-Oklahoma St.
Big Game	1979	Arizona-Arizona St.
Black Diamond Trophy	1997	Virginia Tech-West Virginia
Blue Key Victory Bell	1940	Ball St.-Indiana St.
Brass Spittoon	1950	Indiana-Michigan St.
Brass Spittoon	1981	New Mexico St.-UTEP
Bronze Boot	1968	Colorado St.-Wyoming
Cannon	1943	Illinois-Purdue
Commander in Chief's	1972	Air Force, Army, Navy
Commonwealth Cup	1996	Virginia-Virginia Tech
Cy-Hawk	1977	Iowa-Iowa St.
Floyd of Rosedale	1935	Iowa-Minnesota
Foy-O.D.K.	1948	Alabama-Auburn
Fremont Cannon	1970	Nevada-UNLV
Golden Boot	1996	LSU-Arkansas
Golden Egg	1927	Mississippi-Mississippi St.
Golden Hat	1941	Oklahoma-Texas
Governor's Cup	1969	Kansas-Kansas St.
Governor's Cup	1958	Florida-Florida St.
Governor's Cup	1983	Colorado-Colorado St.
Governor's Cup	1994	Louisville-Kentucky
Govenor's Cup	1995	Georgia-Georgia Tech
Governor's Flag*	1953	Arizona-Arizona St.
Governor's Victory Bell	1993	Minnesota-Penn St.
Illibuck	1925	Illinois-Ohio St.
Iron Bowl	1983	Alabama-Auburn
Jefferson-Epps Trophy	1995	Florida St.-Virginia
Keg of Nails	1950	Cincinnati-Louisville
Kit Carson Rifle	1938	Arizona-New Mexico
Land Grant Trophy	1993	Michigan St.-Penn St.
Little Brown Jug	1909	Michigan-Minnesota
Mayors' Cup	1998	Rice-Southern Methodist
Megaphone	1949	Michigan St.-Notre Dame
Old Oaken Bucket	1925	Indiana-Purdue
Old Wagon Wheel	1948	Brigham Young-Utah St.
Paniolo Trophy	1979	Hawaii-Wyoming
Paul Bunyan Axe	1948	Minnesota-Wisconsin
Paul Bunyan-Governor of Michigan	1953	Michigan-Michigan St.
Peace Pipe	1929	Missouri-Oklahoma
Peace Pipe	1955	Miami (Ohio)-Western Mich.
Peace Pipe	1980	Bowling Green-Toledo
Ram-Falcon	1980	Air Force-Colorado St.
Sabine Shoe	1937	Lamar-La.-Lafayette
Schwartzwalder Trophy	1993	Syracuse-West Virginia
Shillelagh	1952	Notre Dame-Southern California
Shillelagh	1958	Notre Dame-Purdue
Silver Spade/Brass Spittoon	1955	New Mexico St.-UTEP
Steel Tire	1976	Akron-Youngstown St.
Telephone	1960	Iowa St.-Missouri
Territorial Cup	1899	Arizona-Arizona St.
Textile Bowl	1981	Clemson-North Carolina St.
Tomahawk	1945	Illinois-Northwestern
Victory Bell	1942	Southern California-UCLA
Victory Bell	1948	Cincinnati-Miami (Ohio)
Victory Bell	1948	Duke-North Carolina
Wagon Wheel	1946	Akron-Kent St.
Williams Trophy	1998	Rice-Tulsa

Changed to Big Game Trophy in 1979.

DIVISION I-AA

Trophy	Date	Colleges
Battle for the Paddle	1998	Nicholls St.-Southwest Texas St.
Bill Knight	1986	Massachusetts-New Hampshire
Brice-Colwell Musket	1946	Maine-New Hampshire
Chief Caddo	1962	Northwestern St.-Stephen F. Austin
Field Cup	1983	Evansville-Ky. Wesleyan
Gem State	1978	Boise St., Idaho, Idaho St.
Governor's	1979	Central Conn. St.-Southern Conn. St.
Governor's Cup	1972	Brown-Rhode Island
Governor's Cup	1975	Dartmouth-Princeton
Governor's Cup	1984	Eastern Wash.-Idaho
Grizzly-Bobcat Painting	1984	Montana-Montana St.
Harvey—Shin-A-Ninny Totem Pole	1961	Middle Tenn.-Tennessee Tech
Little Brown Stein	1938	Idaho-Montana
Mare's	1987	Murray St.-Tenn.-Martin
Ol' Mountain Jug	1976	Appalachian St.-Western Caro.
Ol' School Bell	1988	Jacksonville St.-Troy St.
Ram—Crusader Cup	1951	Fordham-Holy Cross
Red Belt	1978	Murray St.-Western Ky.
Ron Rogerson Memorial	1988	Maine-Rhode Island
Silver Shako	1976	Citadel-VMI
Team of Game's MVP	1960	Lafayette-Lehigh
Top Dog	1971	Butler-Indianapolis
Victory Carriage	1960	UC Davis-Sacramento St.

NON-NCAA MEMBERS

Trophy	Date	Colleges
Home Stake-Gold Mine	1950	Black Hills St.-South Dak. Tech
Paint Bucket	1961	Jamestown-Valley City St.

Coaching Records

All-Division Coaching Records

Coaches With Career Winning Percentage of .800 or Better

This list includes all coaches in history with a winning percentage of at least .800 over a career of at least 10 seasons at four-year colleges (regardless of division or association). Bowl and playoff games included.

Coach (Alma Mater) (Colleges Coached, Tenure)	Years	Won	Lost	Tied	Pct.
#Larry Kehres (Mount Union '71) (Mount Union 1986—)	†17	192	17	3	.912
Knute Rockne (Notre Dame '14) (Notre Dame 1918-30)	13	105	12	5	.881
Frank Leahy (Notre Dame '31) (Boston College 1939-40; Notre Dame 1941-43, 1946-53)	13	107	13	9	.864
Bob Reade (Cornell College '54) (Augustana [Ill.] 1979-94)	†16	146	23	1	.862
#Dick Farley (Boston U. '68) (Williams 1987—)	†16	108	17	3	.855
Doyt Perry (Bowling Green '32) (Bowling Green 1955-64)	†10	77	11	5	.855
George Woodruff (Yale '89) (Pennsylvania 1892-1901; Illinois 1903; Carlisle 1905)	12	142	25	2	.846
Jake Gaither (Knoxville '27) (Florida A&M 1945-69)	†25	203	36	4	.844
Dave Maurer (Denison '54) (Wittenberg 1969-83)	†15	129	23	3	.842
Paul Hoerneman (Heidelberg '38) (Heidelberg 1946-59)	†14	102	18	4	.839
Barry Switzer (Arkansas '60) (Oklahoma 1973-88)	16	157	29	4	.837
Tom Osborne (Hastings '59) (Nebraska 1973-97)	25	255	49	3	.836
Don Coryell (Washington '50) (Whittier 1957-59; San Diego St. 1961-72)	†15	127	24	3	.834
#Mike Kelly (Manchester '70) (Dayton 1981—)	†22	206	41	1	.833
Percy Haughton (Harvard '99) (Cornell 1899-1900; Harvard 1908-16; Columbia 1923-24)	13	96	17	6	.832
Bob Neyland (Army '16) (Tennessee 1926-34, 1936-40, 1946-52)	21	173	31	12	.829
Fielding Yost (Lafayette '97) (Ohio Wesleyan 1897; Nebraska 1898; Kansas 1899; Stanford 1900; Michigan 1901-23, 1925-26)	29	196	36	12	.828

Mike Kelly won his 200th game at Dayton during the 2002 season, and moved into 14th place on the all-division winning percentage list with an .833 mark.

Dayton Sports Information

Coach (Alma Mater) (Colleges Coached, Tenure)	Years	Won	Lost	Tied	Pct.
Bud Wilkinson (Minnesota '37) (Oklahoma 1947-63)	17	145	29	4	.826
Chuck Klausing (Slippery Rock '48) (Indiana [Pa.] 1964-69; Carnegie Mellon 1976-85)	†16	123	26	2	.821
Vernon McCain (Langston '31) (Md.-East. Shore 1948-63)	†16	102	21	5	.816
Jock Sutherland (Pittsburgh '18) (Lafayette 1919-23; Pittsburgh 1924-38)	20	144	28	14	.812
#Ken Sparks (Carson-Newman '68) (Carson-Newman 1980—)	†23	223	52	2	.809
Ron Schipper (Hope '52) (Central [Iowa] 1961-96)	†36	287	67	3	.808
Bob Devaney (Alma '39) (Wyoming 1957-61; Nebraska 1962-72)	16	136	30	7	.806
Biggie Munn (Minnesota '32) (Albright 1935-36; Syracuse 1946; Michigan St. 1947-53)	10	71	16	3	.805
#Phillip Fulmer (Tennessee '72) (Tennessee 1992—)	11	103	25	0	.805
Sid Gillman (Ohio St. '34) (Miami [Ohio] 1944-47; Cincinnati 1949-54)	†10	81	19	2	.804

†*Zero to nine years in Division I-A.* #*Active coach.*

Coaches With 200 or More Career Victories

This list includes all coaches who have won at least 200 games at four-year colleges (regardless of classification or association). Bowl and playoff games included.

Coach (Alma Mater) (Colleges Coached, Tenure)	Years	Won	Lost	Tied	Pct.
Eddie Robinson (Leland '41) (Grambling 1941-42, 1945-97)	†55	408	165	15	.707
#John Gagliardi (Colorado Col. '49) (Carroll [Mont.] 1949-52; St. John's [Minn.] 1953—)	†54	400	114	11	.772
#Joe Paterno (Brown '50) (Penn St. 1966—)	37	336	100	3	.769
#Bobby Bowden (Samford '53) (Samford 1959-62; West Virginia 1970-75; Florida St. 1976—)	37	332	96	4	.773
Bear Bryant (Alabama '36) (Maryland 1945; Kentucky 1946-53; Texas A&M 1954-57; Alabama 1958-82)	38	323	85	17	.780
Pop Warner (Cornell '95) (Georgia 1895-96; Cornell 1897-98; Carlisle 1899-1903; Cornell 1904-06; Carlisle 1907-14; Pittsburgh 1915-23; Stanford 1924-32; Temple 1933-38)	44	319	106	32	.733
Roy Kidd (Eastern Ky. '54) (Eastern Ky. 1964-02)	†39	315	123	8	.715
Amos Alonzo Stagg (Yale '88) (Springfield 1890-91; Chicago 1892-1932; Pacific [Cal.] 1933-46)	57	314	199	35	.605
Tubby Raymond (Michigan '50) (Delaware 1966-01)	†36	300	119	3	.714
#Frosty Westering (Neb.-Omaha '52) (Parsons 1962-63; Albert Lea 1966-71; Pacific Lutheran 1972—)	†38	299	93	7	.758
Ron Schipper (Hope '52) (Central [Iowa] 1961-96)	†36	287	67	3	.808
Roger Harring (Wis.-La Crosse '58) (Wis.-La Crosse 1969-99)	†31	261	75	7	.771
LaVell Edwards (Utah St. '52) (Brigham Young 1972-00)	29	257	101	3	.716
Tom Osborne (Hastings '59) (Nebraska 1973-97)	25	255	49	3	.836
Jim Malosky (Minnesota '51) (Minn.-Duluth 1958-97)	†40	255	125	13	.665
Woody Hayes (Denison '35) (Denison 1946-48; Miami [Ohio] 1949-50; Ohio St. 1951-78)	33	238	72	10	.759
#Lou Holtz (Kent St. '59) (William & Mary 1969-71; North Carolina St. 1972-75; Arkansas 1977-83; Minnesota 1984-85; Notre Dame 1986-96; South Carolina 1999—)	31	238	120	7	.662
Bo Schembechler (Miami [Ohio] '51) (Miami [Ohio] 1963-68; Michigan 1969-89)	27	234	65	8	.775
Arnett Mumford (Wilberforce '24) (Jarvis 1924-26; Bishop 1927-29; Texas College 1931-35; Southern U. 1936-42, 1944-61)	†36	233	85	23	.717
††John Merritt (Kentucky St. '50) (Jackson St. 1953-62; Tennessee St. 1963-83)	†31	232	65	11	.771
#Frank Girardi (West Chester '61) (Lycoming 1972—)	†31	232	72	5	.759
Hayden Fry (Baylor '51) (Southern Methodist 1962-72; North Texas 1973-78; Iowa 1979-98)	37	232	178	10	.564

Coach (Alma Mater) (Colleges Coached, Tenure)	Years	Won	Lost	Tied	Pct.
#Billy Joe (Villanova '63) .... (Cheyney 1972-78; Central St. [Ohio] 1981-93; Florida A&M 1994—)	†29	228	94	4	.706
Fred Long (Millikin '18)........................... (Paul Quinn 1921-22; Wiley 1923-47; Prairie View 1948; Texas College 1949-55; Wiley 1956-65)	†45	227	151	31	.593
#Ken Sparks (Carson-Newman '68) .... (Carson-Newman 1980—)	†23	223	52	2	.809
Gene Carpenter (Huron '63)...................... (Adams St. 1968; Millersville 1970-00)	†32	220	90	6	.706
@Ron Harms (Valparaiso '59)..................... (Concordia [Neb.] 1964-69; Adams St. 1970-73; Tex. A&M-Kingsville 1979-99)	†31	219	112	4	.660
Jim Christopherson (Concordia-M'head '60).............. (Concordia-M'head 1969-00)	†32	217	102	7	.676
Fred Martinelli (Otterbein '51)................... (Ashland 1959-93)	†35	217	119	12	.641
Bill Manlove (Temple '58) .... (Widener 1969-91; Delaware Valley 1992-95; La Salle 1997-01)	†32	212	110	1	.658
Jess Neely (Vanderbilt '24) .... (Southwestern [Tenn.] 1924-27; Clemson 1931-39; Rice 1940-66)	40	207	176	19	.539
#Mike Kelly (Manchester '70) .... (Dayton 1981—)	†22	206	41	1	.833
Jim Butterfield (Maine '53) .... (Ithaca 1967-93)	†27	206	71	1	.743
#Willard Bailey (Norfolk St. '61)................. (Norfolk St. 1985-91; Virginia Union 1971-83, 95—)	†30	205	105	8	.657
#Ron Randleman (William Penn '64)............. (William Penn 1969-75; Pittsburg St. 1976-81; Sam Houston St. 1982—)	†34	205	155	6	.568
Jake Gaither (Knoxville '27) .... (Florida A&M 1945-69)	†25	203	36	4	.844
Warren Woodson (Baylor '24) .... (Conway St. 1935-40; Hardin-Simmons 1941-42, 1946-51; Arizona 1952-56; New Mexico St. 1958- 67; Trinity [Tex.] 1972-73)	31	203	95	14	.673
Don Nehlen (Bowling Green '58).................. (Bowling Green 1968-76; West Virginia 1980-00)	30	202	128	8	.609
Vince Dooley (Auburn '54) .... (Georgia 1964-88)	25	201	77	10	.715
Eddie Anderson (Notre Dame '22) .... (Loras 1922-24; DePaul 1925-31; Holy Cross 1933- 38; Iowa 1939-42, 1946-49; Holy Cross 1950-64)	39	201	128	15	.606
Darrell Mudra (Peru St. '51)....................... (Adams St. 1959-62; North Dakota St. 1963-65; Arizona 1967-68; Western Ill. 1969-73; Florida St. 1974-75; Eastern Ill. 1978-82; Northern Iowa 1983-87)	†26	200	81	4	.709
Jim Sweeney (Portland '51)........................ (Montana St. 1963-67; Washington St. 1968-75; Fresno St. 1976-96)	32	200	154	4	.564

#Active coach. †Zero to nine years in Division I-A. ††Tennessee State's participation in the 1981 and 1982 Division I-AA championships (1-2 record) vacated by action of the NCAA Committee on Infractions. @Texas A&M-Kingsville's participation in the 1996, 1997 and 1998 Division II championships (2-3 record) was vacated by action of the NCAA Committee on Infractions.

Matchups of Coaches Each With 200 Victories

Date	Coaches, Teams (Victories Going In)	Winner (Score)
11-11-61	Arnett Mumford, Southern U. (232) Fred Long, Wiley (215)	Wiley (21-19)
1-1-78 Sugar Bowl	Bear Bryant, Alabama (272) Woody Hayes, Ohio St. (231)	Alabama (35-6)
10-11-80	Eddie Robinson, Grambling (284) John Merritt, Tennessee St. (200)	Grambling (52-27)
10-10-81	Eddie Robinson, Grambling (294) John Merritt, Tennessee St. (209)	Tennessee St. (14-10)
10-9-82	Eddie Robinson, Grambling (301) John Merritt, Tennessee St. (218)	Tennessee St. (22-8)
10-8-83	Eddie Robinson, Grambling (308) John Merritt, Tennessee St. (228)	Tie (7-7)
11-28-87	John Gagliardi, St. John's (Minn.) (251) Ron Schipper, Central (Iowa) (202)	Central (Iowa) (13-3)
11-25-89	John Gagliardi, St. John's (Minn.) (268) Ron Schipper, Central (Iowa) (224)	St. John's (Minn.) (27-24)
12-28-90 Blockbuster Bowl	Joe Paterno, Penn St. (229) Bobby Bowden, Florida St. (204)	Florida St. (24-17)
11-27-93	John Gagliardi, St. John's (Minn.) (305) Roger Harring, Wis.-La Crosse (210)	St. John's (Minn.) (47-25)
1-1-94	Bobby Bowden, Florida St. (238)	Florida St. (18-16)

Date	Coaches, Teams (Victories Going In)	Winner (Score)
Orange Bowl 9-17-94	Tom Osborne, Nebraska (206) Joe Paterno, Penn St. (258)	Penn St. (61-21)
10-21-95	Hayden Fry, Iowa (202) Joe Paterno, Penn St. (273) Hayden Fry, Iowa (210)	Penn St. (41-27)
1-1-96 Orange Bowl	Bobby Bowden, Florida St. (258) Lou Holtz, Notre Dame (208)	Florida St. (31-26)
10-19-96	Joe Paterno, Penn St. (284) Hayden Fry, Iowa (217)	Iowa (21-20)
11-17-96	Jim Malosky, Minn.-Duluth (250) Roger Harring, Wis.-La Crosse (241)	Minn.-Duluth (17-3)
11-30-96	John Gagliardi, St. John's (Minn.) (336) Roger Harring, Wis.-La Crosse (242)	Wis.-La Crosse (37-30)
12-4-99	John Gagliardi, St. John's (Minn.) (364) Frosty Westering, Pacific Lutheran (274)	Pacific Lutheran (19-9)
8-26-00	Bobby Bowden, Florida St. (304) LaVell Edwards, Brigham Young (251)	Florida St. (29-3)
11-25-00	John Gagliardi, St. John's (Minn.) (374) Frosty Westering, Pacific Lutheran (286)	St. John's (Minn.) (28-21) (ot)
12-1-01	John Gagliardi, St. John's (Minn.) (387) Frosty Westering, Pacific Lutheran (294)	St. John's (Minn.) (31-6)

Coaches With 200 or More Victories at One College

(Bowl and Playoff Games Included)

Coach (College, Tenure)	Years	Won	Lost	Tied	Pct.
Eddie Robinson, Grambling (1941-42, 45-97)	†55	408	165	15	.707
#John Gagliardi, St. John's (Minn.) (1953-)...............	†50	375	108	10	.771
#Joe Paterno, Penn St. (1966-)	37	336	100	3	.769
Roy Kidd, Eastern Ky. (1964-02)......................	†39	315	123	8	.715
Tubby Raymond, Delaware (1966-01)..................	†36	300	119	3	.714
Ron Schipper, Central (Iowa) (1961-96)...............	†36	287	67	3	.808
Roger Harring, Wis.-La Crosse (1969-99)	†31	261	75	7	.771
#Bobby Bowden, Florida St. (1976-)	27	259	64	4	.798
LaVell Edwards, Brigham Young (1972-00)	29	257	101	3	.716
Tom Osborne, Nebraska (1973-97)	25	255	49	3	.836
#Frosty Westering, Pacific Lutheran (1972-)	†31	255	67	4	.788
Jim Malosky, Minn.-Duluth (1958-97)	†40	255	125	13	.665
Amos Alonzo Stagg, Chicago (1892-32)...............	41	244	111	27	.674
Bear Bryant, Alabama (1958-82).....................	25	232	46	9	.824
#Frank Girardi, Lycoming (1972-)	†31	232	72	5	.759
#Ken Sparks, Carson-Newman (1980-)	†23	223	52	2	.809
Fred Martinelli, Ashland (1959-93)	†35	217	119	12	.641
#Mike Kelly, Dayton (1981-)	†22	206	41	1	.833
Jim Butterfield, Ithaca (1967-93)	†27	206	71	1	.743
Woody Hayes, Ohio St. (1951-78)	28	205	61	10	.761
Jake Gaither, Florida A&M (1945-69)	†25	203	36	4	.844
Vince Dooley, Georgia (1964-88)...................	25	201	77	10	.715

†Zero to nine years in Division I-A. #Active coach.

Division I-A Coaching Records

Winningest Active Division I-A Coaches

(Minimum five years as Division I-A head coach; record at four-year colleges only.)

BY PERCENTAGE

Coach, College	Years	Won	Lost	Tied	†Pct.	Postseason W-L-T
Bob Pruett, Marshall	7	80	13	0	.86022	9-1-0
Phillip Fulmer, Tennessee	11	103	25	0	.80469	6-5-0
Bobby Bowden, Florida St.	37	332	96	4	.77315	18-7-1
Joe Paterno, Penn St.	37	336	100	3	.76879	20-10-1
Lloyd Carr, Michigan	8	76	23	0	.76768	5-3-0
Frank Solich, Nebraska	5	49	16	0	.75385	2-3-0
Bill Snyder, Kansas St.	14	116	51	1	.69345	6-4-0
Dennis Franchione, Texas A&M......	20	155	73	2	.67826	5-2-0
Paul Pasqualoni, Syracuse	17	129	64	1	.66753	6-2-0
John Robinson, UNLV	16	124	62	4	.66316	8-1-0
Tommy Bowden, Clemson.............	6	47	24	0	.66197	1-3-0
Lou Holtz, South Carolina	31	238	120	7	.66164	12-8-2
Sonny Lubick, Colorado St.	14	105	57	0	.64815	3-4-0
John L. Smith, Michigan St.	14	110	60	0	.64706	4-10-0
Nick Saban, LSU	9	69	38	1	.64352	2-4-0
Fisher DeBerry, Air Force	19	149	83	1	.64163	6-6-0
Frank Beamer, Virginia Tech	22	159	92	4	.63137	5-5-0
Dirk Koetter, Arizona St.	5	38	23	0	.62295	2-1-0
Mike Bellotti, Oregon	13	88	54	2	.61806	4-3-0

Coach, College	Years	Won	Lost	Tied	†Pct.	Postseason W-L-T
Houston Nutt, Arkansas	10	74	46	0	.61667	2-6-0
Jackie Sherrill, Mississippi St.	25	178	110	4	.61644	8-6-0
Gary Pinkel, Missouri	12	82	51	3	.61397	1-0-0
David Cutcliffe, Mississippi	5	30	19	0	.61224	3-1-0
Pat Hill, Fresno St.	6	46	30	0	.60526	1-3-0
Mack Brown, Texas	19	135	89	1	.60222	6-5-0
Barry Alvarez, Wisconsin	13	92	61	4	.59873	7-1-0
Joe Tiller, Purdue	12	85	58	1	.59375	3-4-0
Tommy Tuberville, Auburn	8	55	39	0	.58511	2-2-0
Tyrone Willingham, Notre Dame	8	54	39	1	.57979	1-4-0
Ken Hatfield, Rice	24	159	115	4	.57914	4-6-0
Jeff Bower, Southern Miss.	13	80	58	1	.57914	3-3-0
Mike Kruczek, UCF	5	33	24	0	.57895	0-0-0
Tom O'Brien, Boston College	6	40	31	0	.56338	3-1-0
Bobby Wallace, Temple	15	98	76	1	.56286	13-3-0
Randy Walker, Northwestern	13	77	63	5	.54828	0-1-0
John Mackovic, Arizona	15	94	78	3	.54571	2-5-0
Jim Grobe, Wake Forest	8	46	44	1	.51099	1-0-0
Gary Barnett, Colorado	13	73	76	2	.49007	2-3-0
Gerry DiNardo, Indiana	10	55	58	1	.48684	3-0-0
Glen Mason, Minnesota	17	93	101	1	.47949	3-2-0
Ron Turner, Illinois	7	38	42	0	.47500	1-1-0
Chris Tormey, Nevada	8	43	48	0	.47253	1-1-0
Tommy West, Memphis	9	43	50	0	.46237	1-3-0
Rick Minter, Cincinnati	9	48	56	1	.46190	1-3-0
Rich Brooks, Kentucky	18	91	109	4	.45588	1-3-0
Walt Harris, Pittsburgh	9	47	59	0	.44340	2-2-0
Chris Scelfo, Tulane	5	21	27	0	.43750	2-0-0
Al Groh, Virginia	8	40	52	0	.43478	1-0-0

Coach, College	Years	Won	Lost	Tied	†Pct.	Postseason W-L-T
Gary Darnell, Western Mich.	10	46	62	0	.42593	0-1-0
Rocky Long, New Mexico	5	25	35	0	.41667	0-1-0
Dan McCarney, Iowa St.	8	36	57	0	.38710	1-2-0
Tony Samuel, New Mexico St.	6	26	42	0	.38235	0-0-0
Watson Brown, UAB	18	74	124	1	.37437	0-0-0
Lee Owens, Akron	8	33	56	0	.37079	0-0-0
Darrell Dickey, North Texas	5	21	37	0	.36207	1-1-0
Joe Novak, Northern Ill.	7	28	50	0	.35897	0-0-0
Dean Pees, Kent St.	5	12	44	0	.21429	0-0-0

Less than five years as Division I-A head coach (school followed by years in Division I-A, must have at least five years at four-year college, includes record at all four-year colleges):

Coach, College	Years	Won	Lost	Tied	†Pct.	Postseason W-L-T
Dan Hawkins, Boise St. (2)	7	60	16	1	.78571	0-0-0
Paul Johnson, Navy (1)	6	64	19	0	.77108	14-3-0
Jim Tressel, Ohio St. (2)	17	156	62	2	.71364	24-7-0
Jim Leavitt, South Fla. (2)	6	44	22	0	.66667	0-0-0
John Bunting, North Carolina (1)	7	49	28	0	.63636	1-0-0
Mick Dennehy, Utah St. (3)	9	62	45	0	.57944	0-0-0
Bobby Johnson, Vanderbilt (1)	9	62	46	0	.57407	4-4-0
Steve Roberts, Arkansas St. (1)	9	54	41	1	.56771	0-0-0
Jim Hofher, Buffalo (2)	10	48	55	0	.46602	0-0-0
Kirk Ferentz, Iowa (4)	7	33	47	0	.41250	1-0-0
Buddy Teevens, Stanford (1)	13	46	78	1	.37200	0-0-0
Todd Berry, Army (3)	7	29	53	0	.35366	2-1-0
Larry Blakeney, Troy St. (1)	12	102	42	1	.00000	5-7-0
Rich Rodriguez, West Virginia (2)	10	59	56	2	.00000	0-1-0

†Ties computed as half won and half lost. *Includes bowl and playoff games.

BY VICTORIES

(Minimum five years as Division I-A head coach)

Coach, College	*Wins	Coach, College	*Wins	Coach, College	*Wins	Coach, College	*Wins
Joe Paterno, Penn St.	336	Bobby Wallace, Temple	98	Nick Saban, LSU	69	Tom O'Brien, Boston College	40
Bobby Bowden, Florida St.	332	John Mackovic, Arizona	94	Gerry DiNardo, Indiana	55	Dirk Koetter, Arizona St.	38
Lou Holtz, South Carolina	238	Glen Mason, Minnesota	93	Tommy Tuberville, Auburn	55	Ron Turner, Illinois	38
Jackie Sherrill, Mississippi St.	178	Barry Alvarez, Wisconsin	92	Tyrone Willingham, Notre Dame	54	Dan McCarney, Iowa St.	36
Frank Beamer, Virginia Tech	159	Rich Brooks, Kentucky	91	Frank Solich, Nebraska	49	Mike Kruczek, UCF	33
Ken Hatfield, Rice	159	Mike Bellotti, Oregon	88	Rick Minter, Cincinnati	48	Lee Owens, Akron	33
Dennis Franchione, Texas A&M	155	Joe Tiller, Purdue	85	Tommy Bowden, Clemson	47	David Cutcliffe, Mississippi	30
Fisher DeBerry, Air Force	149	Gary Pinkel, Missouri	82	Walt Harris, Pittsburgh	47	Joe Novak, Northern Ill.	28
Mack Brown, Texas	135	Jeff Bower, Southern Miss.	80	Gary Darnell, Western Mich.	46	Tony Samuel, New Mexico St.	26
Paul Pasqualoni, Syracuse	129	Bob Pruett, Marshall	80	Jim Grobe, Wake Forest	46	Rocky Long, New Mexico	25
John Robinson, UNLV	124	Randy Walker, Northwestern	77	Pat Hill, Fresno St.	46	Darrell Dickey, North Texas	21
Bill Snyder, Kansas St.	116	Lloyd Carr, Michigan	76	Chris Tormey, Nevada	43	Chris Scelfo, Tulane	21
John L. Smith, Michigan St.	110	Watson Brown, UAB	74	Tommy West, Memphis	43	Dean Pees, Kent St.	12
Sonny Lubick, Colorado St.	105	Houston Nutt, Arkansas	74	Al Groh, Virginia	40		
Phillip Fulmer, Tennessee	103	Gary Barnett, Colorado	73				

*Includes bowls and playoff games.

Winningest All-Time Division I-A Coaches

Minimum 10 years as head coach at Division I institutions; record at four-year colleges only; bowl games included; ties computed as half won, half lost. Active coaches indicated by (*). College Football Hall of Fame members indicated by (†).

BY PERCENTAGE

Coach (Alma Mater) (Colleges Coached, Tenure)	Years	Won	Lost	Tied	Pct.
Knute Rockne (Notre Dame '14)† (Notre Dame 1918-30)	13	105	12	5	.881
Frank Leahy (Notre Dame '31)† (Boston College 1939-40; Notre Dame 1941-43, 1946-53)	13	107	13	9	.864
George Woodruff (Yale 1889)† (Pennsylvania 1892-01; Illinois 1903; Carlisle 1905)	12	142	25	2	.846
Barry Switzer (Arkansas '60) (Oklahoma 1973-88)	16	157	29	4	.837
Tom Osborne (Hastings '59)† (Nebraska 1973-97)	25	255	49	3	.836
Percy Haughton (Harvard 1899)† (Cornell 1899-00; Harvard 1908-16; Columbia 1923-24)	13	96	17	6	.832
Bob Neyland (Army '16)† (Tennessee 1926-34, 1936-40, 1946-52)	21	173	31	12	.829

Coach (Alma Mater) (Colleges Coached, Tenure)	Years	Won	Lost	Tied	Pct.
Fielding Yost (West Virginia 1895)† (Ohio Wesleyan 1897; Nebraska 1898; Kansas 1899; Stanford 1900; Michigan 1901-23, 1925-26)	29	196	36	12	.828
Bud Wilkinson (Minnesota '37)† (Oklahoma 1947-63)	17	145	29	4	.826
Jock Sutherland (Pittsburgh '18)† (Lafayette 1919-23; Pittsburgh 1924-38)	20	144	28	14	.812
Bob Devaney (Alma '39)† (Wyoming 1957-61; Nebraska 1962-72)	16	136	30	7	.806
#Phillip Fulmer (Tennessee '72) (Tennessee 1992—)	11	103	25	0	.805
Frank Thomas (Notre Dame '23)† (Chattanooga 1925-28; Alabama 1931-42, 1944-46)	19	141	33	9	.795
Henry Williams (Yale 1891)† (Army 1891; Minnesota 1900-21)	23	141	34	12	.786
Gil Dobie (Minnesota '02)† (North Dakota St. 1906-07; Washington 1908-16; Navy 1917-19; Cornell 1920-35; Boston College 1936-38)	33	180	45	15	.781
Bear Bryant (Alabama '36)† (Maryland 1945; Kentucky 1946-53; Texas A&M 1954-57; Alabama 1958-82)	38	323	85	17	.780
Fred Folsom (Dartmouth 1895) (Colorado 1895-99, 1901-02; Dartmouth 1903-06; Colorado 1908-15)	19	106	28	6	.779

Coach (Alma Mater) (Colleges Coached, Tenure)	Years	Won	Lost	Tied	Pct.
Steve Spurrier (Florida '67) (Duke 1987-89; Florida 1990-01)	15	142	40	2	.777
Bo Schembechler (Miami, Ohio '51)† (Miami [Ohio] 1963-68; Michigan 1969-89)	27	234	65	8	.775
*Bobby Bowden (Samford '53)√ (Samford 1959-62; West Virginia 1970-75; Florida St. 1976—)	37	332	96	4	.773
*Joe Paterno (Brown '50) (Penn St. 1966—)	37	336	100	3	.769
Fritz Crisler (Chicago '22)† (Minnesota 1930-31; Princeton 1932-37; Michigan 1938-47)	18	116	32	9	.768
Charley Moran (Tennessee 1898) (Texas A&M 1909-14; Centre 1919-23; Bucknell 1924-26; Catawba 1930-33)	18	122	33	12	.766
Wallace Wade (Brown '17)† (Alabama 1923-30; Duke 1931-41, 1946-50)	24	171	49	10	.765
Frank Kush (Michigan St. '53)† (Arizona St. 1958-79)	22	176	54	1	.764
Dan McGugin (Michigan '04)† (Vanderbilt 1904-17, 1919-34)#	30	197	55	19	.762
Jimmy Crowley (Notre Dame '25)# (Michigan St. 1929-32; Fordham 1933-41)	13	78	21	10	.761
Andy Smith (Penn St., Pennsylvania '05)† (Pennsylvania 1909-12; Purdue 1913-15; California 1916-25)	17	116	32	13	.761
Woody Hayes (Denison '35)† (Denison 1946-48; Miami [Ohio] 1949-50; Ohio St. 1951-78)	33	238	72	10	.759
Red Blaik (Miami [Ohio] '18; Army '20)† (Dartmouth 1934-40; Army 1941-58)	25	166	48	14	.759
Darrell Royal (Oklahoma '50)† (Mississippi St. 1954-55; Washington 1956; Texas 1957-76)	23	184	60	5	.749
John McKay (Oregon '50)† (Southern California 1960-75)	16	127	40	8	.749
John Vaught (TCU '33)† (Mississippi 1947-70, 1973)	25	190	61	12	.745
Dan Devine (Minn. Duluth '48)† (Arizona St. 1955-57; Missouri 1958-70; Notre Dame 1975-80)	22	172	57	9	.742
Gus Henderson (Oberlin '12) (Southern California 1919-24; Tulsa 1925-35; Occidental 1940-42)	20	126	42	7	.740
Ara Parseghian (Miami [Ohio] '49)† (Miami [Ohio] 1951-55; Northwestern 1956-63; Notre Dame 1964-74)	24	170	58	6	.739
Elmer Layden (Notre Dame '25)# (Loras 1925-26; Duquesne 1927-33; Notre Dame 1934-40)	16	103	34	11	.733
Pop Warner (Cornell 1895)† (Georgia 1895-96; Cornell 1897-98; Carlisle 1899-03; Cornell 1904-06; Carlisle 1907-14; Pittsburgh 1915-23; Stanford 1924-32; Temple 1933-38)	44	319	106	32	.733
Howard Jones (Yale '08)† (Syracuse 1908; Yale 1909; Ohio St. 1910; Yale 1913; Iowa 1916-23; Duke 1924; Southern California 1925-40)	29	194	64	21	.733
Frank Cavanaugh (Dartmouth 1897)† (Cincinnati 1898; Holy Cross 1903-05; Dartmouth 1911-16; Boston College 1919-26; Fordham 1927-32)	24	145	48	17	.731
Jim Tatum (North Carolina '35)† (North Carolina 1942; Oklahoma 1946; Maryland 1947-55; North Carolina 1956-58)	14	100	35	7	.729
Francis Schmidt (Nebraska '14)† (Tulsa 1919-21; Arkansas 1922-28; TCU 1929-33; Ohio St. 1934-40; Idaho 1941-42)	24	158	57	11	.723
Bill Roper (Princeton '03)† (VMI 1903-04; Princeton 1906-08; Missouri 1909; Princeton 1910-11; Swarthmore 1915-16; Princeton 1919-30)	22	112	37	19	.723
R.C. Slocum (McNeese St. '67) (Texas A&M 1989-02)	14	123	47	2	.721
Doc Kennedy (Kansas & Pennsylvania '03) (Kansas 1904-10; Haskell 1911-16)	13	85	31	7	.720
Tad Jones (Yale '08)† (Syracuse 1909-10; Yale 1916, 1920-27)	11	66	24	6	.719
LaVell Edwards (Utah St. '52) (Brigham Young 1972-00)	29	257	101	3	.716
Dennis Erickson (Montana St. '69) (Idaho 1982-85; Wyoming 1986; Washington St. 1987-88; Miami [Fla.] 1989-94; Oregon St. 1999-02)	17	144	57	1	.715
Vince Dooley (Auburn '54)† (Georgia 1964-88)	25	201	77	10	.715

Coach (Alma Mater) (Colleges Coached, Tenure)	Years	Won	Lost	Tied	Pct.
Dana Bible (Carson-Newman '12)† (Mississippi Col. 1913-15; LSU 1916; Texas A&M 1917, 1919-28; Nebraska 1929-36; Texas 1937-46)	33	198	72	23	.715
Bobby Dodd (Tennessee '31)†# (Georgia Tech 1945-66)	22	165	64	8	.713
John Heisman (Brown 1890, Pennsylvania 1892)† (Oberlin 1892; Akron 1893; Oberlin 1894; Auburn 1895-99; Clemson 1900-03; Georgia Tech 1904-19; Pennsylvania 1920-22; Wash. & Jeff. 1923; Rice 1924-27)	36	185	70	17	.711
Jumbo Stiehm (Wisconsin '09) (Ripon 1910; Nebraska 1911-15; Indiana 1916-21)	12	59	23	4	.709
Red Sanders (Vanderbilt '27)† (Vanderbilt 1940-42, 1946-48; UCLA 1949-57)	15	102	41	3	.709
Pat Dye (Georgia '62) (East Caro. 1974-79; Wyoming 1980; Auburn 1981-92)	19	153	62	5	.707
Chick Meehan (Syracuse '18) (Syracuse 1920-24; New York U. 1925-31; Manhattan 1932-37)	18	115	44	14	.705
John McEwan (Army '17) (Army 1923-25; Oregon 1926-29; Holy Cross 1930-32)	10	59	23	6	.705
Bennie Owen (Kansas '00)† (Washburn 1900; Bethany [Kan.] 1901-04; Oklahoma 1905-26)	27	155	60	19	.703
Ike Armstrong (Drake '23)† (Utah 1925-49)	25	140	55	15	.702
Frank Broyles (Georgia Tech '47)† (Missouri 1957; Arkansas 1958-76)	20	149	62	6	.700
Biff Jones (Army '17)† (Army 1926-29; LSU 1932-34; Oklahoma 1935-36; Nebraska 1937-41)	14	87	33	15	.700

#Member of College Football Hall of Fame as a player. ‡Last game of 1978 season counted as full season. √Includes games forfeited, team and/or individual statistics abrogated, and coaching records changed by action of the NCAA Committee on Infractions.

Winningest All-Time Division I-A Coaches

Minimum 10 years as head coach at Division I institutions; record at four-year colleges only; bowl games included; ties computed as half won, half lost. After each coach's name is his alma mater, year graduated, total years coached, won-lost record and percentage, tenure at each college coached, and won-lost record there. Active coaches are denoted by an asterisk (*).

BY VICTORIES

(Minimum 170 Victories)

336 *Joe Paterno (Born 12-21-26 Brooklyn, N.Y.)
Brown 1951 (37: 336-100-3 .769)
Penn St. 1966-02 (336-100-3)

332 *Bobby Bowden (Born 11-8-29 Birmingham, Ala.)
Samford 1953 (√37: 332-96-4 .773)
Samford 1959-62 (31-6-0); West Virginia 1970-75 (√42-26-0); Florida St. 1976-02 (259-64-4)

323 Bear Bryant (Born 9-11-13 Moro Bottoms, Ark.; Died 1-26-83)
Alabama 1936 (38: 323-85-17 .780)
Maryland 1945 (6-2-1); Kentucky 1946-53 (60-23-5); Texas A&M 1954-57 (25-14-2); Alabama 1958-82 (232-46-9)

319 Pop Warner (Born 4-5-1871 Springville, N.Y.; Died 9-7-54)
Cornell 1895 (44: 319-106-32 .733)
Georgia 1895-96 (7-4-0); Cornell 1897-98, 1904-06 (36-13-3); Carlisle 1899-1903, 1907-14 (114-42-8); Pittsburgh 1915-23 (60-12-4); Stanford 1924-32 (71-17-8); Temple 1933-38 (31-18-9)

314 Amos Alonzo Stagg (Born 8-16-1862 West Orange, N.J.; Died 3-17-65)
Yale 1888 (57: 314-199-35 .605)
Springfield 1890-91 (10-11-1); Chicago 1892-1932 (244-111-27); Pacific (Cal.) 1933-46 (60-77-7)

257 LaVell Edwards (Born 10-11-30 Provo, Utah)
Utah St. 1952 (29: 257-101-3 .716)
Brigham Young 1972-00 (257-101-3)

255 Tom Osborne (Born 2-23-37 Hastings, Neb.)
Hastings 1959 (25: 255-49-3 .836)
Nebraska 1973-97 (255-49-3)

238 *Lou Holtz (Born 1-6-37 Follansbee, W.Va.)
Kent St. 1959 (31: 238-120-7 .662)
William & Mary 1969-71 (13-20-0); North Carolina St. 1972-75 (33-12-3); Arkansas 1977-83 (60-21-2); Minnesota 1984-85 (10-12-0); Notre Dame 1986-96 (100-30-2); South Carolina 1999-02 (22-25-0)

238 Woody Hayes (Born 2-13-14 Clifton, Ohio; Died 3-12-87)
Denison 1935 (33: 238-72-10 .759)
Denison 1946-48 (19-6-0); Miami (Ohio) 1949-50 (14-5-0); Ohio St. 1951-78 (205-61-10)

234 Bo Schembechler (Born 9-1-29 Barberton, Ohio)
Miami (Ohio) 1951 (27: 234-65-8 .775)
Miami (Ohio) 1963-68 (40-17-3); Michigan 1969-89 (194-48-5)

232 Hayden Fry (Born 2-28-29 Odessa, Texas)
       Baylor 1951 (√37: 232-178-10 .564)
       Southern Methodist 1962-72 (49-66-1); North Texas 1973-78 (√40-23-3); Iowa
       1979-98 (142-89-6)
207 Jess Neely (Born 1-4-1898 Smyrna, Tenn.; Died 4-9-83)
       Vanderbilt 1924 (40: 207-176-19 .539)
       Rhodes 1924-27 (20-17-2); Clemson 1931-39 (43-35-7); Rice 1940-66 (144-
       124-10)
203 Warren Woodson (Born 2-24-03 Fort Worth, Texas; Died 2-22-98)
       Baylor 1924 (31: 203-95-14 .673)
       Central Ark. 1935-39 (40-8-3); Hardin-Simmons 1941-42, 1946-51 (58-24-6);
       Arizona 1952-56 (26-22-2); New Mexico St. 1958-67 (63-36-3); Trinity (Tex.)
       1972-73 (16-5-0)
202 Don Nehlen (Born 1-1-36 Canton, Ohio)
       Bowling Green 1958 (30: 202-128-8 .609)
       Bowling Green 1968-76 (53-35-4); West Virginia 1980-00 (149-93-4)
201 Vince Dooley (Born 9-4-32 Mobile, Ala.)
       Auburn 1954 (25: 201-77-10 .715)
       Georgia 1964-88 (201-77-10)
201 Eddie Anderson (Born 11-13-1900 Mason City, Iowa; Died 4-26-74)
       Notre Dame 1922 (39: 201-128-15 .606)
       Loras 1922-24 (16-6-2); DePaul 1925-31 (21-22-3); Holy Cross 1933-38,
       1950-64 (129-67-8); Iowa 1939-42, 1946-49 (35-33-2)
200 Jim Sweeney (Born 9-1-29 Butte, Mont.)
       Portland 1951 (32: 200-154-4 .564)
       Montana St. 1963-67 (31-20-0); Washington St. 1968-75 (26-59-1); Fresno St.
       1976-77, 1980-96 (143-75-3)
198 Dana X. Bible (Born 10-8-1891 Jefferson City, Tenn.; Died 1-19-80)
       Carson-Newman 1912 (33: 198-72-23 .715)
       Mississippi Col. 1913-15 (12-7-2); LSU 1916 (1-0-2); Texas A&M 1917, 1919-
       28 (72-19-9); Nebraska 1929-36 (50-15-7); Texas 1937-46 (63-31-3)
197 Dan McGugin (Born 7-29-1879 Tingley, Iowa; Died 1-19-36)
       Michigan 1904 (30: 197-55-19 .762)
       Vanderbilt 1904-17, 1919-34 (197-55-19)
196 Fielding Yost (Born 4-30-1871 Fairview, W.Va.; Died 8-20-46)
       West Virginia '95 (29: 196-36-12 .828)
       Ohio Wesleyan 1897 (7-1-1); Nebraska 1898 (7-4-0); Kansas 1899 (10-0-0);
       Stanford 1900 (7-2-1); Michigan 1901-23, 1925-26 (165-29-10)
194 Howard Jones (Born 8-23-1885 Excello, Ohio; Died 7-27-41)
       Yale 1908 (29: 194-64-21 .733)
       Syracuse 1908 (6-3-1); Yale 1909, 1913 (15-2-3); Ohio St. 1910 (6-1-3); Iowa
       1916-23 (42-17-1); Duke 1924 (4-5-0); Southern California 1925-40 (121-36-13)
192 John Cooper (Born 7-2-37 Powell, Tenn.)
       Iowa St. 1962 (24: 192-84-6 .691)
       Tulsa 1977-84 (56-32-0); Arizona St. 1985-87 (25-9-2); Ohio St. 1988-00 (112-43-4)
190 John Vaught (Born 5-6-08 Olney, Texas)
       TCU 1933 (25: 190-61-12 .745)
       Mississippi 1947-70, 1973 (190-61-12)
189 George Welsh (Born 8-26-33 Coaldale, Pa.)
       Navy 1960 (28: 189-132-4 .588)
       Navy 1973-81 (55-46-1); Virginia 1982-00 (134-86-3)
185 John Heisman (Born 10-23-1869 Cleveland, Ohio; Died 10-3-36)
       Brown 1890 (36: 185-70-17 .711)
       Oberlin 1892, 1894 (11-3-1); Akron 1893 (5-2-0); Auburn 1895-99 (12-4-2);
       Clemson 1900-03 (19-3-2); Georgia Tech 1904-19 (102-29-6); Pennsylvania
       1920-22 (16-10-2); Wash. & Jeff. 1923 (6-1-1); Rice 1924-27 (14-18-3)
185 Johnny Majors (Born 5-21-35 Lynchburg, Tenn.)
       Tennessee 1957 (29: 185-137-10 .572)
       Iowa St. 1968-72 (24-30-1); Pittsburgh 1973-76, 1993-96 (45-45-1); Tennessee
       1977-92 (116-62-8)
184 Darrell Royal (Born 7-6-24 Hollis, Okla.)
       Oklahoma 1950 (23: 184-60-5 .749)
       Mississippi St. 1954-55 (12-8-0); Washington 1956 (5-5-0); Texas 1957-76
       (167-47-5)
180 Gil Dobie (Born 1-31-1879 Hastings, Minn.; Died 12-24-48)
       Minnesota 1902 (33: 180-45-15 .781)
       North Dakota St. 1906-07 (7-0-0); Washington 1908-16 (58-0-3); Navy 1917-
       19 (17-3-0); Cornell 1920-35 (82-36-7); Boston College 1936-38 (16-6-5)
180 Carl Snavely (Born 7-30-1894 Omaha, Neb.; Died 7-12-75)
       Lebanon Valley 1915 (32: 180-96-16 .644)
       Bucknell 1927-33 (42-16-8); North Carolina 1934-35, 1945-52 (59-35-5);
       Cornell 1936-44 (46-26-3); Washington (Mo.) 1953-58 (33-19-0)
179 Jerry Claiborne (Born 8-26-28 Hopkinsville, Ky.)
       Kentucky 1950 (28: 179-122-8 .592)
       Virginia Tech 1961-70 (61-39-2); Maryland 1972-81 (77-37-3); Kentucky
       1982-89 (41-46-3)
178 *Jackie Sherrill (Born 11-28-43 Duncan, Okla.)
       Alabama 1966 (25: 178-110-4 .616)
       Washington St. 1976 (3-8-0); Pittsburgh 1977-81 (50-9-1); Texas A&M 1982-
       88 (52-28-1); Mississippi St. 1991-02 (73-65-2)
178 Ben Schwartzwalder (Born 6-2-09 Point Pleasant, W.Va.; Died 4-28-93)
       West Virginia 1933 (28: 178-96-3 .648)
       Muhlenberg 1946-48 (25-5-0); Syracuse 1949-73 (153-91-3)
176 Frank Kush (Born 1-20-29 Windber, Pa.)
       Michigan St. 1953 (22: 176-54-1 .764)
       Arizona St. 1958-79 (176-54-1)
176 Don James (Born 12-31-32 Massillon, Ohio)
       Miami (Fla.) 1954 (22: 176-78-3 .691)
       Kent St. 1971-74 (25-19-1); Washington 1975-92 (151-59-2)

176 Ralph Jordan (Born 9-25-10 Selma, Ala.; Died 7-17-80)
       Auburn 1932 (√25: 176-83-6 .675)
       Auburn 1951-75 (√176-83-6)
174 Pappy Waldorf (Born 10-3-02 Clifton Springs, N.Y.; Died 8-15-81)
       Syracuse 1925 (31: 174-100-22 .625)
       Oklahoma City 1925-27 (17-11-3); Oklahoma St. 1929-33 (34-10-7); Kansas St.
       1934 (7-2-1); Northwestern 1935-46 (49-45-7); California 1947-56 (67-32-4)
173 Bob Neyland (Born 2-17-92 Greenville, Texas; Died 3-28-62)
       Army 1916 (21: 173-31-12 .829)
       Tennessee 1926-34, 1936-40, 1946-52 (173-31-12)
172 Dan Devine (Born 12-23-24 Augusta, Wis.; Died 5-9-02)
       Minn.-Duluth 1948 (22: 172-57-9 .742)
       Arizona St. 1955-57 (27-3-1); Missouri 1958-70 (92-38-7); Notre Dame 1975-
       80 (53-16-1)
171 Wallace Wade (Born 6-15-1892 Trenton, Tenn.; Died 10-7-86)
       Brown 1917 (24: 171-49-10 .765)
       Alabama 1923-30 (61-13-3); Duke 1931-41, 1946-50 (110-36-7)
170 Ara Parseghian (Born 5-21-23 Akron, Ohio)
       Miami (Ohio) 1949 (24: 170-58-6 .739)
       Miami (Ohio) 1951-55 (39-6-1); Northwestern 1956-63 (36-35-1); Notre
       Dame 1964-74 (95-17-4)
170 Grant Teaff (Born 11-12-33 Hermleigh, Texas)
       McMurry 1956 (30: 170-151-8 .529)
       McMurry 1960-65 (23-35-2); Angelo St. 1969-71 (19-11-0); Baylor 1972-92
       (128-105-6)

√Includes games forfeited, team and/or individual statistics abrogated, and coaching
records changed by action of the NCAA Committee on Infractions.

Division I-A Best Career Starts by Wins

(Head coaches with at least half their seasons at major college at the time
and minimum five years coached)

1 SEASON

Coach, Team	Season	W	L	T	Pct.
George Woodruff, Pennsylvania	1892	15	1	0	.938
Walter Camp, Yale	1888	13	0	0	1.000
Bill Battle, Tennessee	1970	11	1	0	.917
Gary Blackney, Bowling Green	1991	11	1	0	.917
*John Robinson, Southern California	1976	11	1	0	.917
Dick Crum, Miami (Ohio)	1974	10	0	1	.955
Barry Switzer, Oklahoma	1973	10	0	1	.955
Chuck Fairbanks, Oklahoma	1967	10	1	0	.909
Larry Siemering, Pacific (Cal.)	1947	10	1	0	.909
Dwight Wallace, Ball St.	1978	10	1	0	.909
Mike Archer, LSU	1987	10	1	1	.875

2 SEASONS

Coach, Team	Seasons	W	L	T	Pct.
Walter Camp, Yale	1888-89	28	1	0	.966
George Woodruff, Pennsylvania	1892-93	27	4	0	.871
Barry Switzer, Oklahoma	1973-74	21	0	1	.977
Dick Crum, Miami (Ohio)	1974-75	21	1	1	.935
Bill Battle, Tennessee	1970-71	21	3	0	.875
Gary Blackney, Bowling Green	1991-92	21	3	0	.875
Frank Leahy, Boston College	1939-40	20	2	0	.909
Ron Meyer, UNLV	1973-74	20	4	0	.833
*Fisher DeBerry, Air Force	1984-85	20	5	0	.800
Dutch Meyer, TCU	1934-35	20	5	0	.800
Herb Deromedi, Central Mich.	1978-79	19	2	1	.886
*John Robinson, Southern California	1976-77	19	5	0	.792

3 SEASONS

Coach, Team(s)	Seasons	W	L	T	Pct.
Walter Camp, Yale	1888-90	41	2	0	.953
George Woodruff, Pennsylvania	1892-94	39	4	0	.907
Barry Switzer, Oklahoma	1973-75	32	1	1	.956
Bill Battle, Tennessee	1970-72	31	5	0	.861
*John Robinson, Southern California	1976-78	31	6	0	.838
Dutch Meyer, TCU	1934-36	29	7	2	.789
Frank Leahy, Boston College, Notre Dame	1939-41	28	2	1	.919
Larry Siemering, Pacific (Cal.)	1947-49	28	2	2	.906
Bud Wilkinson, Oklahoma	1947-49	28	3	1	.891
Herb Deromedi, Central Mich.	1978-80	28	4	1	.864
Tom Osborne, Nebraska	1973-75	28	7	1	.792

4 SEASONS

Coach, Team(s)	Seasons	W	L	T	Pct.
Walter Camp, Yale	1888-91	54	2	0	.964
George Woodruff, Pennsylvania	1892-95	53	4	0	.930
*John Robinson, Southern California	1976-79	42	6	1	.867
Barry Switzer, Oklahoma	1973-76	41	3	2	.935
Bill Battle, Tennessee	1970-73	39	9	0	.813
R.C. Slocum, Texas A&M	1989-92	39	10	1	.790

Coach, Team(s)	Seasons	W	L	T	Pct.
Bud Wilkinson, Oklahoma	1947-50	38	4	1	.895
Tom Osborne, Nebraska	1973-76	37	10	2	.776
Gary Blackney, Bowling Green	1991-94	36	8	2	.804
Frank Leahy, Boston College, Notre Dame	1939-42	35	4	3	.869
Larry Siemering, Pacific (Cal.)	1947-50	35	5	3	.849
*Joe Paterno, Penn St.	1966-69	35	7	1	.826
Claude Gilbert, San Diego St.	1973-76	35	7	2	.818
Herb Deromedi, Central Mich.	1978-81	35	8	1	.807
*Fisher DeBerry, Air Force	1984-87	35	14	0	.714

5 SEASONS

Coach, Team(s)	Seasons	W	L	T	Pct.
Walter Camp, Yale, Stanford	1888-92	69	2	2	.959
George Woodruff, Pennsylvania	1892-96	67	5	0	.931
Barry Switzer, Oklahoma	1973-77	51	5	2	.896
*John Robinson, Southern California	1976-80	50	8	2	.850
R.C. Slocum, Texas A&M	1989-93	49	12	1	.798
*Lloyd Carr, Michigan	1995-99	49	13	0	.790
Henry Williams, Army, Minnesota 1891,	1900-03	47	4	6	.877
Bud Wilkinson, Oklahoma	1947-51	46	6	1	.877
Bill Battle, Tennessee	1970-74	46	12	2	.783
Tom Osborne, Nebraska	1973-77	46	13	2	.770
Claude Gilbert, San Diego St.	1973-77	45	8	2	.836

6 SEASONS

Coach, Team(s)	Seasons	W	L	T	Pct.
George Woodruff, Pennsylvania	1892-97	82	5	0	.943
Walter Camp, Yale, Stanford	1888-92, 94	75	5	2	.927
Barry Switzer, Oklahoma	1973-78	62	6	2	.900
Henry Williams, Army, Minnesota 1891,	1900-04	60	4	6	.900
*John Robinson, Southern California	1976-81	59	11	2	.833
R.C. Slocum, Texas A&M	1989-94	59	12	2	.822
Tom Osborne, Nebraska	1973-78	55	16	2	.767
Bud Wilkinson, Oklahoma	1947-52	54	7	2	.873
*Phillip Fulmer, Tennessee	1992-97	54	11	0	.841
Fielding Yost, Ohio Wesleyan, Nebraska, Kansas, Stanford, Michigan	1897-1902	53	7	2	.871
*Joe Paterno, Penn St.	1966-71	53	11	1	.823
*Jackie Sherrill, Washington St., Pittsburgh	1976-81	53	17	1	.754
Bill Battle, Tennessee	1970-75	53	17	2	.750

7 SEASONS

Coach, Team(s)	Seasons	W	L	T	Pct.
George Woodruff, Pennsylvania	1892-98	94	6	0	.940
Walter Camp, Yale, Stanford	1888-92, 94-95	79	5	3	.925
Barry Switzer, Oklahoma	1973-79	73	7	2	.902
Henry Williams, Army, Minnesota 1891,	1900-05	70	5	6	.901
R.C. Slocum, Texas A&M	1989-95	68	15	2	.812
*Phillip Fulmer, Tennessee	1992-98	67	11	0	.859
*John Robinson, Southern California	1976-82	67	14	2	.819
Tom Osborne, Nebraska	1973-79	65	18	2	.776
Fielding Yost, Ohio Wesleyan, Nebraska, Kansas, Stanford, Michigan	1897-1903	64	7	3	.897
Bud Wilkinson, Oklahoma	1947-53	63	8	3	.872
*Joe Paterno, Penn St.	1966-72	63	13	1	.825
Amos Alonzo Stagg, Springfield, Chicago	1890-96	63	31	7	.658

8 SEASONS

Coach, Team(s)	Seasons	W	L	T	Pct.
George Woodruff, Pennsylvania	1892-99	102	9	2	.912
Barry Switzer, Oklahoma	1973-80	83	9	2	.894
*Phillip Fulmer, Tennessee	1992-99	76	14	0	.844
*Joe Paterno, Penn St.	1966-73	75	13	1	.848
*John Robinson, Southern California	1976-82, 93	75	19	2	.792
Tom Osborne, Nebraska	1973-80	75	20	2	.784
Fielding Yost, Ohio Wesleyan, Nebraska, Kansas, Stanford, Michigan	1897-1904	74	7	3	.898
Henry Williams, Army, Minnesota 1891,	1900-06	74	6	6	.895
R.C. Slocum, Texas A&M	1989-96	74	21	2	.773
Amos Alonzo Stagg, Springfield, Chicago	1890-97	74	32	7	.686
Bud Wilkinson, Oklahoma	1947-54	73	8	3	.887
Frank Leahy, Boston College, Notre Dame	1939-43, 46-48	70	5	5	.882

9 SEASONS

Coach, Team(s)	Seasons	W	L	T	Pct.
George Woodruff, Pennsylvania	1892-1900	114	10	2	.913
Barry Switzer, Oklahoma	1973-81	90	13	3	.863
Fielding Yost, Ohio Wesleyan, Nebraska, Kansas, Stanford, Michigan	1897-1905	86	8	3	.902
*Joe Paterno, Penn St.	1966-74	85	15	1	.847
Bud Wilkinson, Oklahoma	1947-55	84	8	3	.900
*Phillip Fulmer, Tennessee	1992-00	84	18	0	.824
Tom Osborne, Nebraska	1973-81	84	23	2	.780

Coach, Team(s)	Seasons	W	L	T	Pct.
*John Robinson, Southern California	1976-82, 93-94	83	22	3	.782
R.C. Slocum, Texas A&M	1989-97	83	25	2	.764
Amos Alonzo Stagg, Springfield, Chicago	1890-98	83	34	7	.698
Steve Spurrier, Duke, Florida	1987-95	81	26	2	.752
Frank Leahy, Boston College, Notre Dame	1939-43, 46-49	80	5	5	.917
Bob Neyland, Tennessee	1926-34	76	7	5	.892
Henry Williams, Army, Minnesota 1891,	1900-07	76	8	7	.874
Dick Crum, Miami (Ohio), North Carolina	1974-82	76	26	2	.740
Fred Akers, Wyoming, Texas	1975-83	76	30	1	.715

10 SEASONS

Coach, Team(s)	Seasons	W	L	T	Pct.
George Woodruff, Pennsylvania	1892-1901	124	15	2	.887
Barry Switzer, Oklahoma	1973-82	98	17	3	.843
Tom Osborne, Nebraska	1973-82	96	24	2	.795
*Phillip Fulmer, Tennessee	1992-01	95	20	0	.826
Amos Alonzo Stagg, Springfield, Chicago	1890-99	95	34	9	.721
Bud Wilkinson, Oklahoma	1947-56	94	8	3	.910
*Joe Paterno, Penn St.	1966-75	94	18	1	.836
R.C. Slocum, Texas A&M	1989-98	94	28	2	.766
Steve Spurrier, Duke, Florida	1987-96	93	27	2	.770
*John Robinson, Southern California	1976-82, 93-95	92	24	4	.783
Fielding Yost, Ohio Wesleyan, Nebraska, Kansas, Stanford, Michigan	1897-1906	90	9	3	.897
Frank Leahy, Boston College, Notre Dame	1939-43, 46-50	84	9	6	.879
Dick Crum, Miami (Ohio), North Carolina	1974-83	84	30	2	.733
Dennis Erickson, Idaho, Wyoming, Washington St., Miami (Fla.)	1982-91	83	34	1	.708
Fred Akers, Wyoming, Texas	1975-84	83	34	2	.706

11 SEASONS

Coach, Team(s)	Seasons	W	L	T	Pct.
George Woodruff, Pennsylvania, Illinois....	1892-1901, 03	132	21	2	.858
Tom Osborne, Nebraska	1973-83	108	25	2	.807
Barry Switzer, Oklahoma	1973-83	106	21	3	.827
Bud Wilkinson, Oklahoma	1947-57	104	9	3	.909
*Phillip Fulmer, Tennessee	1992-02	103	25	0	.805
Steve Spurrier, Duke, Florida	1987-97	103	29	2	.776
R.C. Slocum, Texas A&M	1989-99	102	32	2	.757
Amos Alonzo Stagg, Springfield, Chicago	1890-1900	102	39	10	.709
*Joe Paterno, Penn St.	1966-76	101	23	1	.812
*John Robinson, Southern California	1976-82, 93-96	98	30	4	.758
Fielding Yost, Ohio Wesleyan, Nebraska, Kansas, Stanford, Michigan	1897-1907	95	10	3	.894
Dennis Erickson, Idaho, Wyoming, Washington St., Miami (Fla.)	1982-92	94	35	1	.727
Frank Leahy, Boston College, Notre Dame	1939-43, 46-51	91	11	7	.867
Bobby Dodd, Georgia Tech	1945-55	91	27	3	.764
Fred Akers, Wyoming, Texas	1975-85	91	38	2	.702

12 SEASONS

Coach, Team(s)	Seasons	W	L	T	Pct.
George Woodruff, Pennsylvania, Illinois, Carlisle	1892-1901, 03, 05	142	25	2	.846
Tom Osborne, Nebraska	1973-84	118	27	2	.810
Barry Switzer, Oklahoma	1973-84	115	23	4	.824
Bud Wilkinson, Oklahoma	1947-58	114	10	3	.909
Steve Spurrier, Duke, Florida	1987-98	113	31	2	.781
*Joe Paterno, Penn St.	1966-77	112	24	1	.821
R.C. Slocum, Texas A&M	1989-00	109	37	2	.743
Amos Alonzo Stagg, Springfield, Chicago	1890-1901	107	44	12	.693
*John Robinson, Southern California	1976-82, 93-97	104	35	4	.741
Dennis Erickson, Idaho, Wyoming, Washington St., Miami (Fla.)	1982-93	103	38	1	.729
Bobby Dodd, Georgia Tech	1945-56	101	28	3	.777
Fielding Yost, Ohio Wesleyan, Nebraska, Kansas, Stanford, Michigan	1897-1908	100	12	4	.879
Bob Neyland, Tennessee	1926-34, 36-38	99	12	8	.866

13 SEASONS

Coach, Team(s)	Seasons	W	L	T	Pct.
Tom Osborne, Nebraska	1973-85	127	30	2	.805
Barry Switzer, Oklahoma	1973-85	126	24	4	.831
*Joe Paterno, Penn St.	1966-78	123	25	1	.829
Steve Spurrier, Duke, Florida	1987-99	122	35	2	.774
Bud Wilkinson, Oklahoma	1947-59	121	13	3	.894
LaVell Edwards, Brigham Young	1972-84	118	37	1	.760
Amos Alonzo Stagg, Springfield, Chicago	1890-1902	118	45	12	.709
R.C. Slocum, Texas A&M	1989-01	117	41	2	.738
Dennis Erickson, Idaho, Wyoming, Washington St., Miami (Fla.)	1982-94	113	40	1	.737
Bob Neyland, Tennessee	1926-34, 36-39	109	13	8	.869
Terry Donahue, UCLA	1976-88	108	38	7	.729
Frank Leahy, Boston College, Notre Dame	1939-43, 46-53	107	13	9	.864
*John Robinson, Southern California, UNLV	1976-82, 93-97, 99	107	43	4	.708

14 SEASONS

Coach, Team(s)	Seasons	W	L	T	Pct.
Barry Switzer, Oklahoma	1973-86	137	25	4	.837
Tom Osborne, Nebraska	1973-86	137	32	2	.807
Steve Spurrier, Duke, Florida	1987-00	132	38	2	.773
*Joe Paterno, Penn St.	1966-79	131	29	1	.817
LaVell Edwards, Brigham Young	1972-85	129	40	1	.762
Amos Alonzo Stagg, Springfield, Chicago.	1890-1903	128	47	13	.715
Bud Wilkinson, Oklahoma	1947-60	124	19	4	.857
R.C. Slocum, Texas A&M	1989-02	123	47	2	.721
Dennis Erickson, Idaho, Wyoming, Washington St., Miami (Fla.), Oregon St.	1982-94, 99	120	45	1	.726
Bob Neyland, Tennessee	1926-34, 36-40	119	14	8	.872
Bo Schembechler, Miami (Ohio), Michigan	1963-76	116	28	6	.793
Pat Dye, East Caro., Wyoming, Auburn	1974-87	115	44	3	.719
*John Robinson, Southern California, UNLV	1976-82, 93-97, 99-00	115	48	4	.701
Bob Devaney, Wyoming, Nebraska	1957-70	114	28	6	.791

15 SEASONS

Coach, Team(s)	Seasons	W	L	T	Pct.
Barry Switzer, Oklahoma	1973-87	148	26	4	.843
Tom Osborne, Nebraska	1973-87	147	34	2	.809
*Joe Paterno, Penn St.	1966-80	141	31	1	.818
LaVell Edwards, Brigham Young	1972-86	137	45	1	.751
Amos Alonzo Stagg, Springfield, Chicago	1890-1904	136	48	14	.722
Dennis Erickson, Idaho, Wyoming, Washington St., Miami (Fla.), Oregon St.	1982-94, 99-00	131	46	1	.739
Bud Wilkinson, Oklahoma	1947-61	129	24	4	.834
Bob Neyland, Tennessee	1926-34, 36-40, 46	128	16	8	.868
Bob Devaney, Wyoming, Nebraska	1957-71	127	28	6	.807
Bo Schembechler, Miami (Ohio), Michigan	1963-77	126	30	6	.796
Pat Dye, East Caro., Wyoming, Auburn	1974-88	125	46	3	.727

16 SEASONS

Coach, Team(s)	Seasons	W	L	T	Pct.
Tom Osborne, Nebraska	1973-88	158	36	2	.811
Barry Switzer, Oklahoma	1973-88	157	29	4	.837
*Joe Paterno, Penn St.	1966-81	151	33	1	.819
LaVell Edwards, Brigham Young	1972-87	146	49	1	.747
Amos Alonzo Stagg, Springfield, Chicago	1890-1905	146	48	14	.736
Bud Wilkinson, Oklahoma	1947-62	137	27	4	.827
Bob Devaney, Wyoming, Nebraska	1957-72	136	30	7	.806
Bo Schembechler, Miami (Ohio), Michigan	1963-78	136	32	6	799
Dennis Erickson, Idaho, Wyoming, Washington St., Miami (Fla.), Oregon St.	1982-94, 99-01	136	52	1	.722
Pat Dye, East Caro., Wyoming, Auburn	1974-89	135	48	3	.734
Bob Neyland, Tennessee	1926-34, 36-40, 46-47	133	21	8	.846

17 SEASONS

Coach, Team(s)	Seasons	W	L	T	Pct.
Tom Osborne, Nebraska	1973-89	168	38	2	.813
*Joe Paterno, Penn St.	1966-82	162	34	1	.825
LaVell Edwards, Brigham Young	1972-88	155	53	1	.744
Amos Alonzo Stagg, Springfield, Chicago	1890-1906	150	49	15	.736
Bud Wilkinson, Oklahoma	1947-63	145	29	4	.826
Bo Schembechler, Miami (Ohio), Michigan	1963-79	144	36	6	.790
Dennis Erickson, Idaho, Wyoming, Washington St., Miami (Fla.), Oregon St.	1982-94, 99-02	144	57	1	.715
Pat Dye, East Caro., Wyoming, Auburn	1974-90	143	51	4	.732
Frank Kush, Arizona St.	1958-74	139	39	1	.779
Bob Neyland, Tennessee	1926-34, 36-40, 46-48	137	25	10	.826
Johnny Vaught, Mississippi	1947-63	137	32	9	.795
Tony Knap, Utah St., Boise St., UNLV	1963-66, 68-80	137	47	4	.739

18 SEASONS

Coach, Team(s)	Seasons	W	L	T	Pct.
Tom Osborne, Nebraska	1973-90	177	41	2	.809
*Joe Paterno, Penn St.	1966-83	170	38	2	.814
LaVell Edwards, Brigham Young	1972-89	165	56	1	.745
Bo Schembechler, Miami (Ohio), Michigan	1963-80	154	38	6	.793
Amos Alonzo Stagg, Springfield, Chicago	1890-1907	154	50	15	.737
Frank Kush, Arizona St.	1958-75	151	39	1	.793
Pat Dye, East Caro., Wyoming, Auburn	1974-91	148	57	4	.718
Bob Neyland, Tennessee	1926-34, 36-40, 46-49	144	27	11	.821
Darrell Royal, Mississippi St., Washington, Texas	1954-71	143	45	4	.755
Tony Knap, Utah St., Boise St., UNLV	1963-66, 68-81	143	53	4	.725

19 SEASONS

Coach, Team(s)	Seasons	W	L	T	Pct.
Tom Osborne, Nebraska	1973-91	186	43	3	.808
*Joe Paterno, Penn St.	1966-84	176	43	2	.801
LaVell Edwards, Brigham Young	1972-90	175	59	1	.747
Bo Schembechler, Miami (Ohio), Michigan	1963-81	163	41	6	.790
Amos Alonzo Stagg, Springfield, Chicago	1890-1908	159	50	16	.742
Bob Neyland, Tennessee	1926-34, 36-40, 46-50	155	28	11	.827
Frank Kush, Arizona St.	1958-76	155	46	1	.770
Darrell Royal, Mississippi St., Washington, Texas	1954-72	153	46	4	.764
Pat Dye, East Caro., Wyoming, Auburn	1974-92	153	62	5	.707
Pop Warner, Georgia, Cornell, Carlisle	1895-1913	152	50	10	.741

20 SEASONS

Coach, Team(s)	Seasons	W	L	T	Pct.
Tom Osborne, Nebraska	1973-92	195	46	3	.805
*Joe Paterno, Penn St.	1966-85	187	44	2	.807
LaVell Edwards, Brigham Young	1972-91	183	62	3	.744
Bo Schembechler, Miami (Ohio), Michigan	1963-82	171	45	6	.784
Bob Neyland, Tennessee	1926-34, 36-40, 46-51	165	29	11	.832
Frank Kush, Arizona St.	1958-77	164	49	1	.769
Amos Alonzo Stagg, Springfield, Chicago	1890-1909	163	51	18	.741
Darrell Royal, Mississippi St., Washington, Texas	1954-73	161	49	4	.762
Vince Dooley, Georgia	1964-83	161	60	7	.721
Johnny Vaught, Mississippi	1947-66	157	44	10	.768
Pop Warner, Georgia, Cornell, Carlisle	1895-1914	157	59	11	.716
John Cooper, Tulsa, Arizona St., Ohio St.	1977-96	157	70	6	.687

21 SEASONS

Coach, Team(s)	Seasons	W	L	T	Pct.
Tom Osborne, Nebraska	1973-93	206	47	3	.811
*Joe Paterno, Penn St.	1966-86	199	44	2	.816
LaVell Edwards, Brigham Young	1972-92	191	67	3	.738
Bo Schembechler, Miami (Ohio), Michigan	1963-83	180	48	6	.782
Bob Neyland, Tennessee	1926-34, 36-40, 46-52	173	31	12	.829
Frank Kush, Arizona St.	1958-78	173	52	1	.768
Darrell Royal, Mississippi St., Washington, Texas	1954-74	169	53	4	.757
Vince Dooley, Georgia	1964-84	168	64	8	.717
John Cooper, Tulsa, Arizona St., Ohio St.	1977-97	167	73	6	.691
Don James, Kent St., Washington	1971-91	167	75	3	.688
Amos Alonzo Stagg, Springfield, Chicago	1890-1910	165	56	18	.728
Pop Warner, Georgia, Cornell, Carlisle, Pittsburgh	1895-1915	165	59	11	.726

22 SEASONS

Coach, Team(s)	Seasons	W	L	T	Pct.
Tom Osborne, Nebraska	1973-94	219	47	3	.820
*Joe Paterno, Penn St.	1966-87	207	48	2	.809
LaVell Edwards, Brigham Young	1972-93	197	73	3	.727
Bo Schembechler, Miami (Ohio), Michigan	1963-84	186	54	6	.768
Darrell Royal, Mississippi St., Washington, Texas	1954-75	179	55	4	.761
John Cooper, Tulsa, Arizona St., Ohio St.	1977-98	178	74	6	.702
Frank Kush, Arizona St.	1958-79	176	54	1	.764
Don James, Kent St., Washington	1971-92	176	78	3	.691
Vince Dooley, Georgia	1964-85	175	67	10	.714
*Bobby Bowden, Samford, West Virginia, Florida St.	1959-62, 70-87	174	69	3	.713
Pop Warner, Georgia, Cornell, Carlisle, Pittsburgh	1895-1916	173	59	11	.735

23 SEASONS

Coach, Team(s)	Seasons	W	L	T	Pct.
Tom Osborne, Nebraska	1973-95	231	47	3	.827
*Joe Paterno, Penn St.	1966-88	212	54	2	.795
LaVell Edwards, Brigham Young	1972-94	207	76	3	.729
Bo Schembechler, Miami (Ohio), Michigan	1963-85	196	55	7	.773
*Bobby Bowden, Samford, West Virginia, Florida St.	1959-62, 70-88	185	70	3	.723
Darrell Royal, Mississippi St., Washington, Texas	1954-76	184	60	5	.749
John Cooper, Tulsa, Arizona St., Ohio St.	1977-99	184	80	6	.693
Pop Warner, Georgia, Cornell, Carlisle, Pittsburgh	1895-1917	183	59	11	.745
Vince Dooley, Georgia	1964-86	183	71	10	.712
*Lou Holtz, William & Mary, North Carolina St., Arkansas, Minnesota, Notre Dame	1969-92	182	83	6	.683

Coach, Team(s)	Seasons	W	L	T	Pct.
Bear Bryant, Maryland, Kentucky, Texas A&M, Alabama	1945-67	179	53	15	.755
Johnny Vaught, Mississippi	1947-69	178	54	12	.754

24 SEASONS

Coach, Team(s)	Seasons	W	L	T	Pct.
Tom Osborne, Nebraska	1973-96	242	49	3	.828
*Joe Paterno, Penn St.	1966-89	220	57	3	.791
LaVell Edwards, Brigham Young	1972-95	214	80	3	.726
Bo Schembechler, Miami (Ohio), Michigan	1963-86	207	57	7	.777
*Bobby Bowden, Samford, West Virginia, Florida St.	1959-62, 70-89	195	72	3	.728
*Lou Holtz, William & Mary, North Carolina St., Arkansas, Minnesota, Notre Dame	1969-93	193	84	6	.693
Vince Dooley, Georgia	1964-87	192	74	10	.714
John Cooper, Tulsa, Arizona St., Ohio St.	1977-00	192	84	6	.691
Pop Warner, Georgia, Cornell, Carlisle, Pittsburgh	1895-1918	187	60	11	.746
Johnny Vaught, Mississippi	1947-70	185	58	12	.749
Amos Alonzo Stagg, Springfield, Chicago	1890-1913	184	58	18	.742

25 SEASONS

Coach, Team(s)	Seasons	W	L	T	Pct.
Tom Osborne, Nebraska	1973-97	255	49	3	.836
*Joe Paterno, Penn St.	1966-90	229	60	3	.789
LaVell Edwards, Brigham Young	1972-96	228	81	3	.736
Bo Schembechler, Miami (Ohio), Michigan	1963-87	215	61	7	.772
*Bobby Bowden, Samford, West Virginia, Florida St.	1959-62, 70-90	205	74	3	.732
Vince Dooley, Georgia	1964-88	201	77	10	.715
*Lou Holtz, William & Mary, North Carolina St., Arkansas, Minnesota, Notre Dame	1969-94	199	89	7	.686
Bear Bryant, Maryland, Kentucky, Texas A&M, Alabama	1945-69	193	61	15	.745
Pop Warner, Georgia, Cornell, Carlisle, Pittsburgh	1895-1919	193	62	12	.745
Johnny Vaught, Mississippi	1947-70, 73	190	61	12	.745
Amos Alonzo Stagg, Springfield, Chicago	1890-1914	188	60	19	.740

26 SEASONS

Coach, Team(s)	Seasons	W	L	T	Pct.
*Joe Paterno, Penn St.	1966-91	240	62	3	.792
LaVell Edwards, Brigham Young	1972-97	234	86	3	.729
Bo Schembechler, Miami (Ohio), Michigan	1963-88	224	63	8	.773
*Bobby Bowden, Samford, West Virginia, Florida St.	1959-62, 70-91	216	76	3	.737
*Lou Holtz, William & Mary, North Carolina St., Arkansas, Minnesota, Notre Dame	1969-95	208	92	7	.689
Pop Warner, Georgia, Cornell, Carlisle, Pittsburgh	1895-1920	199	62	14	.749
Bear Bryant, Maryland, Kentucky, Texas A&M, Alabama	1945-70	199	66	16	.737
Amos Alonzo Stagg, Springfield, Chicago	1890-1915	193	62	19	.739

27 SEASONS

Coach, Team(s)	Seasons	W	L	T	Pct.
*Joe Paterno, Penn St.	1966-92	247	67	3	.784
LaVell Edwards, Brigham Young	1972-98	243	91	3	.726
Bo Schembechler, Miami (Ohio), Michigan	1963-89	234	65	8	.775
*Bobby Bowden, Samford, West Virginia, Florida St.	1959-62, 70-92	227	77	3	.744
*Lou Holtz, William & Mary, North Carolina St., Arkansas, Minnesota, Notre Dame	1969-96	216	95	7	.690
Bear Bryant, Maryland, Kentucky, Texas A&M, Alabama	1945-71	210	67	16	.744
Pop Warner, Georgia, Cornell, Carlisle, Pittsburgh	1895-1921	204	65	15	.745
Amos Alonzo Stagg, Springfield, Chicago	1890-1916	196	66	19	.731

28 SEASONS

Coach, Team(s)	Seasons	W	L	T	Pct.
*Joe Paterno, Penn St.	1966-93	257	69	3	.786
LaVell Edwards, Brigham Young	1972-99	251	95	3	.724
*Bobby Bowden, Samford, West Virginia, Florida St.	1959-62, 70-93	239	78	3	.752
Bear Bryant, Maryland, Kentucky, Texas A&M, Alabama	1945-72	220	69	16	.748
*Lou Holtz, William & Mary, North Carolina St., Arkansas, Minnesota, Notre Dame, South Carolina	1969-96, 99	216	106	7	.667
Pop Warner, Georgia, Cornell, Carlisle, Pittsburgh	1895-1922	212	67	15	.747
Amos Alonzo Stagg, Springfield, Chicago	1890-1917	199	68	20	.728
Woody Hayes, Denison, Miami (Ohio), Ohio St.	1946-73	192	60	8	.754

Coach, Team(s)	Seasons	W	L	T	Pct.
Howard Jones, Syracuse, Yale, Ohio St., Iowa, Duke, Southern California	1908-10, 13, 16-39	191	60	19	.743
Don Nehlen, Bowling Green, West Virginia	1968-76, 80-98	191	116	8	.619

29 SEASONS

Coach, Team(s)	Seasons	W	L	T	Pct.
*Joe Paterno, Penn St.	1966-94	269	69	3	.793
LaVell Edwards, Brigham Young	1972-00	257	101	3	.716
*Bobby Bowden, Samford, West Virginia, Florida St.	1959-62, 70-94	249	79	4	.756
Bear Bryant, Maryland, Kentucky, Texas A&M, Alabama	1945-73	231	70	16	.754
*Lou Holtz, William & Mary, North Carolina St., Arkansas, Minnesota, Notre Dame, South Carolina	1969-96, 99-00	224	110	7	.667
Pop Warner, Georgia, Cornell, Carlisle, Pittsburgh	1895-1923	217	71	15	.741
Woody Hayes, Denison, Miami (Ohio), Ohio St.	1946-74	202	62	8	.757
Amos Alonzo Stagg, Springfield, Chicago	1890-1918	199	74	20	.713
Fielding Yost, Ohio Wesleyan, Nebraska, Kansas, Stanford, Michigan	1897-1923, 25-26	196	36	12	.828
Don Nehlen, Bowling Green, West Virginia	1968-76, 80-99	195	123	8	.610
Howard Jones, Syracuse, Yale, Ohio St., Iowa, Duke, Southern California	1908-10, 13, 16-40	194	64	21	.733
Dan McGugin, Vanderbilt	1904-17, 19-33	191	52	19	.765

30 SEASONS

Coach, Team(s)	Seasons	W	L	T	Pct.
*Joe Paterno, Penn St.	1966-95	278	72	3	.792
*Bobby Bowden, Samford, West Virginia, Florida St.	1959-62, 70-95	259	81	4	.759
Bear Bryant, Maryland, Kentucky, Texas A&M, Alabama	1945-74	242	71	16	.760
*Lou Holtz, William & Mary, North Carolina St., Arkansas, Minnesota, Notre Dame, South Carolina	1969-96, 99-01	233	113	7	.670
Pop Warner, Georgia, Cornell, Carlisle, Pittsburgh, Stanford	1895-1924	224	72	16	.744
Woody Hayes, Denison, Miami (Ohio), Ohio St.	1946-75	213	63	8	.764
Amos Alonzo Stagg, Springfield, Chicago	1890-1919	204	76	20	.713

31 SEASONS

Coach, Team(s)	Seasons	W	L	T	Pct.
*Joe Paterno, Penn St.	1966-96	289	74	3	.794
*Bobby Bowden, Samford, West Virginia, Florida St.	1959-62, 70-96	270	82	4	.764
Bear Bryant, Maryland, Kentucky, Texas A&M, Alabama	1945-75	253	72	16	.765
*Lou Holtz, William & Mary, North Carolina St., Arkansas, Minnesota, Notre Dame, South Carolina	1969-96, 99-02	238	120	7	.662
Pop Warner, Georgia, Cornell, Carlisle, Pittsburgh, Stanford	1895-1925	231	74	16	.745
Woody Hayes, Denison, Miami (Ohio), Ohio St.	1946-76	222	65	9	.765
Amos Alonzo Stagg, Springfield, Chicago	1890-1920	207	80	20	.707
Warren Woodson, Central Ark., Hardin-Simmons, Arizona, New Mexico St., Trinity (Tex.)	1935-42, 46-56, 58-67, 72-73	203	95	14	.673
Dana X. Bible, Mississippi Col., LSU, Texas A&M, Nebraska, Texas	1913-17, 19-44	180	69	23	.704

32 SEASONS

Coach, Team(s)	Seasons	W	L	T	Pct.
*Joe Paterno, Penn St.	1966-97	298	77	3	.792
*Bobby Bowden, Samford, West Virginia, Florida St.	1959-62, 70-97	281	83	4	.769
Bear Bryant, Maryland, Kentucky, Texas A&M, Alabama	1945-76	262	75	16	.765
Pop Warner, Georgia, Cornell, Carlisle, Pittsburgh, Stanford	1895-1926	241	74	17	.752
Woody Hayes, Denison, Miami (Ohio), Ohio St.	1946-77	231	68	9	.765
Amos Alonzo Stagg, Springfield, Chicago	1890-1921	213	81	20	.710
Hayden Fry, Southern Methodist, North Texas, Iowa	1962-93	200	153	9	.565
Dana X. Bible, Mississippi Col., LSU, Texas A&M, Nebraska, Texas	1913-17, 19-45	190	70	23	.712

33 SEASONS

Coach, Team(s)	Seasons	W	L	T	Pct.
*Joe Paterno, Penn St.	1966-98	307	80	3	.791
*Bobby Bowden, Samford, West Virginia, Florida St.	1959-62, 70-98	292	85	4	.772

COACHING RECORDS

Coach, Team(s)	Seasons	W	L	T	Pct.
Bear Bryant, Maryland, Kentucky, Texas A&M, Alabama	1945-77	273	76	16	.770
Pop Warner, Georgia, Cornell, Carlisle, Pittsburgh, Stanford	1895-1927	249	76	18	.752
Woody Hayes, Denison, Miami (Ohio), Ohio St.	1946-78	238	72	10	.759
Amos Alonzo Stagg, Springfield, Chicago	1890-1922	219	82	20	.713
Hayden Fry, Southern Methodist, North Texas, Iowa	1962-94	205	158	10	.563
Dana X. Bible, Mississippi Col., LSU, Texas A&M, Nebraska, Texas	1913-17, 19-46	198	72	23	.715

34 SEASONS

Coach, Team(s)	Seasons	W	L	T	Pct.
*Joe Paterno, Penn St.	1966-99	317	83	3	.790
*Bobby Bowden, Samford, West Virginia, Florida St.	1959-62, 70-99	304	85	4	.779
Bear Bryant, Maryland, Kentucky, Texas A&M, Alabama	1945-78	284	77	16	.775
Pop Warner, Georgia, Cornell, Carlisle, Pittsburgh, Stanford	1895-1928	257	79	19	.751
Amos Alonzo Stagg, Springfield, Chicago	1890-1923	226	83	20	.717
Hayden Fry, Southern Methodist, North Texas, Iowa	1962-95	213	162	10	.566

35 SEASONS

Coach, Team(s)	Seasons	W	L	T	Pct.
*Joe Paterno, Penn St.	1966-00	322	90	3	.780
*Bobby Bowden, Samford, West Virginia, Florida St.	1959-62, 70-00	315	87	4	.781
Bear Bryant, Maryland, Kentucky, Texas A&M, Alabama	1945-79	296	77	16	.781
Pop Warner, Georgia, Cornell, Carlisle, Pittsburgh, Stanford	1895-1929	266	81	19	.753
Amos Alonzo Stagg, Springfield, Chicago	1890-1924	230	84	23	.717
Hayden Fry, Southern Methodist, North Texas, Iowa	1962-96	222	165	10	.572

36 SEASONS

Coach, Team(s)	Seasons	W	L	T	Pct.
*Joe Paterno, Penn St.	1966-01	327	96	3	.771
*Bobby Bowden, Samford, West Virginia, Florida St.	1959-62, 70-01	323	91	4	.778
Bear Bryant, Maryland, Kentucky, Texas A&M, Alabama	1945-80	306	79	16	.783
Pop Warner, Georgia, Cornell, Carlisle, Pittsburgh, Stanford	1895-1930	275	82	20	.756
Amos Alonzo Stagg, Springfield, Chicago	1890-1925	233	88	24	.710
Hayden Fry, Southern Methodist, North Texas, Iowa	1962-97	229	170	10	.572

37 SEASONS

Coach, Team(s)	Seasons	W	L	T	Pct.
*Joe Paterno, Penn St.	1996-02	336	100	3	.769
*Bobby Bowden, Samford, West Virginia, Florida St.	1959-62, 70-02	332	96	4	.773
Bear Bryant, Maryland, Kentucky, Texas A&M, Alabama	1945-81	315	81	17	.783
Pop Warner, Georgia, Cornell, Carlisle, Pittsburgh, Stanford	1895-1931	282	84	22	.755
Amos Alonzo Stagg, Springfield, Chicago	1890-1926	235	94	24	.700
Hayden Fry, Southern Methodist, North Texas, Iowa	1962-98	232	178	10	.564

38 SEASONS

Coach, Team(s)	Seasons	W	L	T	Pct.
Bear Bryant, Maryland, Kentucky, Texas A&M, Alabama	1945-82	323	85	17	.780
Pop Warner, Georgia, Cornell, Carlisle, Pittsburgh, Stanford	1895-1932	288	88	23	.751
Amos Alonzo Stagg, Springfield, Chicago	1890-1927	239	98	24	.695
Jess Neely, Rhodes, Clemson, Rice	1924-27, 31-64	203	160	19	.556

39 SEASONS

Coach, Team(s)	Seasons	W	L	T	Pct.
Pop Warner, Georgia, Cornell, Carlisle, Pittsburgh, Stanford, Temple	1895-1933	293	91	23	.748
Amos Alonzo Stagg, Springfield, Chicago	1890-1928	241	105	24	.684
Jess Neely, Rhodes, Clemson, Rice	1924-27, 31-65	205	168	19	.539
Eddie Anderson, Loras, DePaul, Holy Cross, Iowa	1922-42, 46-64	201	128	15	.606

40 SEASONS

Coach, Team(s)	Seasons	W	L	T	Pct.
Pop Warner, Georgia, Cornell, Carlisle, Pittsburgh, Stanford, Temple	1895-1934	300	92	25	.749

Coach, Team(s)	Seasons	W	L	T	Pct.
Amos Alonzo Stagg, Springfield, Chicago	1890-1929	248	108	24	.684
Jess Neely, Rhodes, Clemson, Rice	1924-27, 31-66	207	176	19	.539

41 SEASONS

Coach, Team(s)	Seasons	W	L	T	Pct.
Pop Warner, Georgia, Cornell, Carlisle, Pittsburgh, Stanford, Temple	1895-1935	307	95	25	.748
Amos Alonzo Stagg, Springfield, Chicago	1890-1930	249	113	26	.675

42 SEASONS

Coach, Team(s)	Seasons	W	L	T	Pct.
Pop Warner, Georgia, Cornell, Carlisle, Pittsburgh, Stanford, Temple	1895-1936	313	98	27	.745
Amos Alonzo Stagg, Springfield, Chicago	1890-1931	251	118	27	.668

43 SEASONS

Coach, Team(s)	Seasons	W	L	T	Pct.
Pop Warner, Georgia, Cornell, Carlisle, Pittsburgh, Stanford, Temple	1895-1937	316	100	31	.742
Amos Alonzo Stagg, Springfield, Chicago	1890-1932	254	122	28	.663

44 SEASONS

Coach, Team(s)	Seasons	W	L	T	Pct.
Pop Warner, Georgia, Cornell, Carlisle, Pittsburgh, Stanford, Temple	1895-1938	319	106	32	.733
Amos Alonzo Stagg, Springfield, Chicago, Pacific (Cal.)	1890-1933	259	127	28	.659

*Active coach.

Division I-A Best Career Starts by Percentage

(Head coaches with at least half their seasons at major college at the time and minimum five years coached)

1 SEASON

Coach, Team	Season	W	L	T	Pct.
Walter Camp, Yale	1888	13	0	0	1.000
Dan McGugin, Vanderbilt	1904	9	0	0	1.000
Bennie Oosterbaan, Michigan	1948	9	0	0	1.000
Carroll Widdoes, Ohio St.	1944	9	0	0	1.000
Galen Hall, Florida	1984	8	0	0	1.000
William Dietz, Washington St.	1915	7	0	0	1.000
John Heisman, Oberlin	1892	7	0	0	1.000
Dick Crum, Miami (Ohio)	1974	10	0	1	.955
Barry Switzer, Oklahoma	1973	10	0	1	.955
Aldo Donelli, Duquesne	1939	8	0	1	.944
Francis Schmidt, Tulsa	1919	8	0	1	.944

2 SEASONS

Coach, Team	Seasons	W	L	T	Pct.
Barry Switzer, Oklahoma	1973-74	21	0	1	977
Walter Camp, Yale	1888-89	28	1	0	.966
Francis Schmidt, Tulsa	1919-20	18	0	2	.950
John Bateman, Rutgers	1960-61	17	1	0	.944
Dan McGugin, Vanderbilt	1904-05	16	1	0	.941
Dick Crum, Miami (Ohio)	1974-75	21	1	1	.935
Galen Hall, Florida	1984-85	17	1	1	.921
Bob Neyland, Tennessee	1926-27	16	1	1	.917
Aldo Donelli, Duquesne	1939-40	15	1	1	.912
Charley Moran, Texas A&M	1909-10	15	1	1	.912

3 SEASONS

Coach, Team(s)	Seasons	W	L	T	Pct.
Barry Switzer, Oklahoma	1973-75	32	1	1	.956
Walter Camp, Yale	1888-90	41	2	0	.953
Aldo Donelli, Duquesne	1939-41	23	1	1	.940
Bob Neyland, Tennessee	1926-28	25	1	2	.929
Dan McGugin, Vanderbilt	1904-06	24	2	0	.923
Frank Leahy, Boston College, Notre Dame	1939-41	28	2	1	.919
Knute Rockne, Notre Dame	1918-20	21	1	2	.917
Elmer Henderson, Southern California	1919-21	20	2	0	.909
George Woodruff, Pennsylvania	1892-94	39	4	0	.907
Larry Siemering, Pacific (Cal.)	1947-49	28	2	2	.906

4 SEASONS

Coach, Team(s)	Seasons	W	L	T	Pct.
Gil Dobie, North Dakota St., Washington	1906-09	20	0	1	.976
Walter Camp, Yale	1888-91	54	2	0	.964
Barry Switzer, Oklahoma	1973-76	41	3	2	.935
Bob Neyland, Tennessee	1926-29	34	1	3	.934
George Woodruff, Pennsylvania	1892-95	53	4	0	.930

Coach, Team(s)	Seasons	W	L	T	Pct.
Knute Rockne, Notre Dame	1918-21	31	2	2	.914
Elmer Henderson, Southern California	1919-22	30	3	0	.909
Wallace Wade, Alabama	1923-26	34	3	2	.897
William Murray, Delaware	1940-42, 46	30	3	1	.897
Bud Wilkinson, Oklahoma	1947-50	38	4	1	.895

5 SEASONS

Coach, Team(s)	Seasons	W	L	T	Pct.
Gil Dobie, North Dakota St., Washington	1906-10	26	0	1	.981
Walter Camp, Yale, Stanford	1888-92	69	2	2	.959
George Woodruff, Pennsylvania	1892-96	67	5	0	.931
Bob Neyland, Tennessee	1926-30	43	2	3	.927
Knute Rockne, Notre Dame	1918-22	39	3	3	.900
Barry Switzer, Oklahoma	1973-77	51	5	2	.896
Elmer Henderson, Southern California	1919-23	36	5	0	.878
Bud Wilkinson, Oklahoma	1947-51	46	6	1	.877
Henry Williams, Army, Minnesota	1891, 1900-03	47	4	6	.877
Frank Leahy, Boston College, Notre Dame	1939-43	44	5	3	.875

6 SEASONS

Coach, Team(s)	Seasons	W	L	T	Pct.
Gil Dobie, North Dakota St., Washington	1906-11	33	0	1	.985
George Woodruff, Pennsylvania	1892-97	82	5	0	.943
Bob Neyland, Tennessee	1926-31	52	2	4	.931
Walter Camp, Yale, Stanford	1888-92, 94	75	5	2	.927
Knute Rockne, Notre Dame	1918-23	48	4	3	.900
Barry Switzer, Oklahoma	1973-78	62	6	2	.900
Henry Williams, Army, Minnesota	1891, 1900-04	60	4	6	.900
Frank Leahy, Boston College, Notre Dame	1939-43, 46	52	5	4	.885
Bud Wilkinson, Oklahoma	1947-52	54	7	2	.873
Fielding Yost, Ohio Wesleyan, Nebraska, Kansas, Stanford, Michigan	1897-1902	53	7	2	.871

7 SEASONS

Coach, Team(s)	Seasons	W	L	T	Pct.
Gil Dobie, North Dakota St., Washington	1906-12	39	0	1	.988
George Woodruff, Pennsylvania	1892-98	94	6	0	.940
Bob Neyland, Tennessee	1926-32	61	2	5	.934
Walter Camp, Yale, Stanford	1888-92, 94-95	79	5	3	.925
Knute Rockne, Notre Dame	1918-24	58	4	3	.915
Barry Switzer, Oklahoma	1973-79	73	7	2	.902
Henry Williams, Army, Minnesota	1891, 1900-05	70	5	6	.901
Frank Leahy, Boston College, Notre Dame	1939-43, 46-47	61	5	4	.900
Fielding Yost, Ohio Wesleyan, Nebraska, Kansas, Stanford, Michigan	1897-1903	64	7	3	.897
Bud Wilkinson, Oklahoma	1947-53	63	8	3	.872

8 SEASONS

Coach, Team(s)	Seasons	W	L	T	Pct.
Gil Dobie, North Dakota St., Washington	1906-13	46	0	1	.989
George Woodruff, Pennsylvania	1892-99	102	9	2	.912
Bob Neyland, Tennessee	1926-33	68	5	5	.904
Fielding Yost, Ohio Wesleyan, Nebraska, Kansas, Stanford, Michigan	1897-1904	74	7	3	.898
Henry Williams, Army, Minnesota	1891, 1900-06	74	6	6	.895
Barry Switzer, Oklahoma	1973-80	83	9	2	.894
Knute Rockne, Notre Dame	1918-25	65	6	4	.893
Bud Wilkinson, Oklahoma	1947-54	73	8	3	.887
Frank Leahy, Boston College, Notre Dame	1939-43, 46-48	70	5	5	.882
Percy Haughton, Cornell, Harvard	1899-1900, 08-13	66	8	3	.877

9 SEASONS

Coach, Team(s)	Seasons	W	L	T	Pct.
Gil Dobie, North Dakota St., Washington	1906-14	52	0	2	.981
Frank Leahy, Boston College, Notre Dame	1939-43, 46-49	80	5	5	.917
George Woodruff, Pennsylvania	1892-1900	114	10	2	.913
Fielding Yost, Ohio Wesleyan, Nebraska, Kansas, Stanford, Michigan	1897-1905	86	8	3	.902
Bud Wilkinson, Oklahoma	1947-55	84	8	3	.900
Knute Rockne, Notre Dame	1918-26	74	7	4	.894
Bob Neyland, Tennessee	1926-34	76	7	5	.892
Percy Haughton, Cornell, Harvard	1899-1900, 08-14	73	8	5	.878
Henry Williams, Army, Minnesota	1891, 1900-07	76	8	7	.874
Barry Switzer, Oklahoma	1973-81	90	13	3	.863

10 SEASONS

Coach, Team(s)	Seasons	W	L	T	Pct.
Gil Dobie, North Dakota St., Washington	1906-15	59	0	2	.984
Bud Wilkinson, Oklahoma	1947-56	94	8	3	.910
Fielding Yost, Ohio Wesleyan, Nebraska, Kansas, Stanford, Michigan	1897-1906	90	9	3	.897
Knute Rockne, Notre Dame	1918-27	81	8	5	.888
George Woodruff, Pennsylvania	1892-1901	124	15	2	.887

Coach, Team(s)	Seasons	W	L	T	Pct.
Percy Haughton, Cornell, Harvard	1899-1900, 08-15	81	9	5	.879
Frank Leahy, Boston College, Notre Dame	1939-43, 46-50	84	9	6	.879
Bob Neyland, Tennessee	1926-34, 36	82	9	7	.872
Henry Williams, Army, Minnesota	1891, 1900-08	79	10	8	.856
Barry Switzer, Oklahoma	1973-82	98	17	3	.843

11 SEASONS

Coach, Team(s)	Seasons	W	L	T	Pct.
Gil Dobie, North Dakota St., Washington	1906-16	65	0	3	.978
Bud Wilkinson, Oklahoma	1947-57	104	9	3	.909
Fielding Yost, Ohio Wesleyan, Nebraska, Kansas, Stanford, Michigan	1897-1907	95	10	3	.894
Frank Leahy, Boston College, Notre Dame	1939-43, 46-51	91	11	7	.867
Percy Haughton, Cornell, Harvard	1899-1900, 08-16	88	12	5	.862
Knute Rockne, Notre Dame	1918-28	86	12	5	.859
George Woodruff, Pennsylvania, Illinois	1892-1901, 03	132	21	2	.858
Henry Williams, Army, Minnesota	1891, 1900-09	85	11	8	.856
Bob Neyland, Tennessee	1926-34, 36-37	88	12	8	.852
Charley Moran, Texas A&M, Centre	1909-14, 19-23	80	14	5	.833

12 SEASONS

Coach, Team(s)	Seasons	W	L	T	Pct.
Gil Dobie, North Dakota St., Washington, Navy	1906-17	72	1	3	.967
Bud Wilkinson, Oklahoma	1947-58	114	10	3	.909
Fielding Yost, Ohio Wesleyan, Nebraska, Kansas, Stanford, Michigan	1897-1908	100	12	4	.879
Knute Rockne, Notre Dame	1918-29	95	12	5	.871
Bob Neyland, Tennessee	1926-34, 36-38	99	12	8	.866
Frank Leahy, Boston College, Notre Dame	1939-43, 46-52	98	13	8	.857
Henry Williams, Army, Minnesota	1891, 1900-10	91	12	8	.856
George Woodruff, Pennsylvania, Illinois, Carlisle	1892-1901, 03, 05	142	25	2	.846
Percy Haughton, Cornell, Harvard, Columbia	1899-1900, 08-16, 23	92	16	6	.833
Charley Moran, Texas A&M, Centre, Bucknell	1909-14, 19-24	88	16	5	.830

13 SEASONS

Coach, Team(s)	Seasons	W	L	T	Pct.
Gil Dobie, North Dakota St., Washington, Navy	1906-18	76	2	3	.957
Bud Wilkinson, Oklahoma	1947-59	121	13	3	.894
Knute Rockne, Notre Dame	1918-30	105	12	5	.881
Fielding Yost, Ohio Wesleyan, Nebraska, Kansas, Stanford, Michigan	1897-1909	106	13	4	.878
Bob Neyland, Tennessee	1926-34, 36-39	109	13	8	.869
Frank Leahy, Boston College, Notre Dame	1939-43, 46-53	107	13	9	.864
Henry Williams, Army, Minnesota	1891, 1900-11	97	12	9	.860
Percy Haughton, Cornell, Harvard, Columbia	1899-1900, 08-16, 23-24	96	17	6	.832
Barry Switzer, Oklahoma	1973-85	126	24	4	.831
*Joe Paterno, Penn St.	1966-78	123	25	1	.829

14 SEASONS

Coach, Team(s)	Seasons	W	L	T	Pct.
Gil Dobie, North Dakota St., Washington, Navy	1906-19	82	3	3	.949
Bob Neyland, Tennessee	1926-34, 36-40	119	14	8	.872
Fielding Yost, Ohio Wesleyan, Nebraska, Kansas, Stanford, Michigan	1897-1910	109	13	7	.872
Bud Wilkinson, Oklahoma	1947-60	124	19	4	.857
Henry Williams, Army, Minnesota	1891, 1900-12	101	15	9	.844
Barry Switzer, Oklahoma	1973-86	137	25	4	.837
*Joe Paterno, Penn St.	1966-79	131	29	1	.817
Fred Folsom, Colorado, Dartmouth	1895-99, 1901-06, 08-10	83	17	5	.814
Elmer Henderson, Southern California, Tulsa	1919-32	101	23	3	.807
Tom Osborne, Nebraska	1973-86	137	32	2	.807

15 SEASONS

Coach, Team(s)	Seasons	W	L	T	Pct.
Gil Dobie, North Dakota St., Washington, Navy, Cornell	1906-20	88	5	3	.932
Bob Neyland, Tennessee	1926-34, 36-40, 46	128	16	8	.868
Fielding Yost, Ohio Wesleyan, Nebraska, Kansas, Stanford, Michigan	1897-1911	114	14	9	.858
Barry Switzer, Oklahoma	1973-87	148	26	4	.843
Henry Williams, Army, Minnesota	1891, 1900-13	106	17	9	.837
Bud Wilkinson, Oklahoma	1947-61	129	24	4	.834
Fred Folsom, Colorado, Dartmouth	1895-99, 1901-06, 08-11	89	17	5	.824

Coach, Team(s)	Seasons	W	L	T	Pct.
*Joe Paterno, Penn St.	1966-80	141	31	1	.818
Elmer Henderson, Southern California, Tulsa	1919-33	107	24	3	.810
Tom Osborne, Nebraska	1973-87	147	34	2	.809

16 SEASONS

Coach, Team(s)	Seasons	W	L	T	Pct.
Gil Dobie, North Dakota St., Washington, Navy, Cornell	1906-21	96	5	3	.938
Fielding Yost, Ohio Wesleyan, Nebraska, Kansas, Stanford, Michigan	1897-1912	119	16	9	.858
Bob Neyland, Tennessee	1926-34, 36-40, 46-47	133	21	8	.846
Henry Williams, Army, Minnesota	1891, 1900-14	112	18	9	.838
Barry Switzer, Oklahoma	1973-88	157	29	4	.837
Bud Wilkinson, Oklahoma	1947-62	137	27	4	.827
*Joe Paterno, Penn St.	1966-81	151	33	1	.819
Fred Folsom, Colorado, Dartmouth	1895-99, 1901-06, 08-12	95	20	5	.813
Tom Osborne, Nebraska	1973-88	158	36	2	.811
Bob Devaney, Wyoming, Nebraska	1957-72	136	30	7	.806

17 SEASONS

Coach, Team(s)	Seasons	W	L	T	Pct.
Gil Dobie, North Dakota St., Washington, Navy, Cornell	1906-22	104	5	3	.942
Fielding Yost, Ohio Wesleyan, Nebraska, Kansas, Stanford, Michigan	1897-1913	125	17	9	.858
Henry Williams, Army, Minnesota	1891, 1900-15	118	18	10	.842
Bud Wilkinson, Oklahoma	1947-63	145	29	4	.826
Bob Neyland, Tennessee	1926-34, 36-40, 46-48	137	25	10	.826
*Joe Paterno, Penn St.	1966-82	162	34	1	.825
Tom Osborne, Nebraska	1973-89	168	38	2	.813
Fred Folsom, Colorado, Dartmouth	1895-99, 1901-06, 08-13	100	21	6	.811
Wallace Wade, Alabama, Duke	1923-39	130	29	6	.806
Red Blaik, Dartmouth, Army	1934-50	120	26	10	.801
Jock Sutherland, Lafayette, Pittsburgh	1919-35	119	25	12	.801

18 SEASONS

Coach, Team(s)	Seasons	W	L	T	Pct.
Gil Dobie, North Dakota St., Washington, Navy, Cornell	1906-23	112	5	3	.946
Fielding Yost, Ohio Wesleyan, Nebraska Kansas, Stanford, Michigan	1897-1914	131	20	9	.847
Henry Williams, Army, Minnesota	1891, 1900-16	124	19	10	.843
Bob Neyland, Tennessee	1926-34, 36-40, 46-49	144	27	11	.821
*Joe Paterno, Penn St.	1966-83	170	38	2	.814
Fred Folsom, Colorado, Dartmouth	1895-99, 1901-06, 08-14	105	22	6	.812
Tom Osborne, Nebraska	1973-90	177	41	2	.809
Frank Thomas, Chattanooga, Alabama	1925-28, 31-42, 44-45	134	29	9	.805
Wallace Wade, Alabama, Duke	1923-40	137	31	6	.805
Jock Sutherland, Lafayette, Pittsburgh	1919-36	127	26	13	.804

19 SEASONS

Coach, Team(s)	Seasons	W	L	T	Pct.
Gil Dobie, North Dakota St., Washington, Navy, Cornell	1906-24	116	9	3	.918
Henry Williams, Army, Minnesota	1891, 1900-17	128	20	10	.842
Fielding Yost, Ohio Wesleyan, Nebraska, Kansas, Stanford, Michigan	1897-1915	135	23	10	.833
Bob Neyland, Tennessee	1926-34, 36-40, 46-50	155	28	11	.827
Jock Sutherland, Lafayette, Pittsburgh	1919-37	136	26	14	.813
Wallace Wade, Alabama, Duke	1923-41	146	32	6	.810
Tom Osborne, Nebraska	1973-91	186	43	3	.808
*Joe Paterno, Penn St.	1966-84	176	43	2	.801
Frank Thomas, Chattanooga, Alabama	1925-28, 31-42, 44-46	141	33	9	.795
Bo Schembechler, Miami (Ohio), Michigan	1963-81	163	41	6	.790

20 SEASONS

Coach, Team(s)	Seasons	W	L	T	Pct.
Gil Dobie, North Dakota St., Washington, Navy, Cornell	1906-25	122	11	3	.908
Henry Williams, Army, Minnesota	1891, 1900-18	133	22	11	.834
Bob Neyland, Tennessee	1926-34, 36-40, 46-51	165	29	11	.832
Fielding Yost, Ohio Wesleyan, Nebraska, Kansas, Stanford, Michigan	1897-1916	142	25	10	.831
Jock Sutherland, Lafayette, Pittsburgh	1919-38	144	28	14	.812
*Joe Paterno, Penn St.	1966-85	187	44	2	.807

Coach, Team(s)	Seasons	W	L	T	Pct.
Tom Osborne, Nebraska	1973-92	195	46	3	.805
Wallace Wade, Alabama, Duke	1923-41, 46	150	37	6	.793
Bo Schembechler, Miami (Ohio), Michigan	1963-82	171	45	6	.784
Dan McGugin, Vanderbilt	1904-17, 19-24	131	33	12	.778

21 SEASONS

Coach, Team(s)	Seasons	W	L	T	Pct.
Gil Dobie, North Dakota St., Washington, Navy, Cornell	1906-26	128	12	4	.903
Fielding Yost, Ohio Wesleyan, Nebraska, Kansas, Stanford, Michigan	1897-1917	150	27	10	.829
Bob Neyland, Tennessee	1926-34, 36-40, 46-52	173	31	12	.829
Henry Williams, Army, Minnesota	1891, 1900-19	137	24	12	.827
*Joe Paterno, Penn St.	1966-86	199	44	2	.816
Tom Osborne, Nebraska	1973-93	206	47	3	.811
Wallace Wade, Alabama, Duke	1923-41, 46-47	154	40	8	.782
Bo Schembechler, Miami (Ohio), Michigan	1963-83	180	48	6	.782
Howard Jones, Syracuse, Yale, Ohio St., Iowa, Duke, Southern California	1908-10, 13, 16-32	147	38	10	.779
Dan McGugin, Vanderbilt	1904-17, 19-25	137	36	12	.773

22 SEASONS

Coach, Team(s)	Seasons	W	L	T	Pct.
Gil Dobie, North Dakota St., Washington, Navy, Cornell	1906-27	131	15	6	.882
Fielding Yost, Ohio Wesleyan, Nebraska, Kansas, Stanford, Michigan	1897-1918	155	27	10	.833
Tom Osborne, Nebraska	1973-94	219	47	3	.820
*Joe Paterno, Penn St.	1966-87	207	48	2	.809
Henry Williams, Army, Minnesota	1891, 1900-20	138	30	12	.800
Howard Jones, Syracuse, Yale, Ohio St., Iowa, Duke, Southern California	1908-10, 13, 16-33	157	39	11	.785
Dan McGugin, Vanderbilt	1904-17, 19-26	145	37	12	.778
Wallace Wade, Alabama, Duke	1923-41, 46-48	158	43	10	.773
Bo Schembechler, Miami (Ohio), Michigan	1963-84	186	54	6	.768
Bear Bryant, Maryland, Kentucky, Texas A&M, Alabama	1945-66	171	51	14	.767

23 SEASONS

Coach, Team(s)	Seasons	W	L	T	Pct.
Gil Dobie, North Dakota St., Washington, Navy, Cornell	1906-28	134	18	8	.863
Tom Osborne, Nebraska	1973-95	231	47	3	.827
Fielding Yost, Ohio Wesleyan, Nebraska, Kansas, Stanford, Michigan	1897-1919	158	31	10	.819
*Joe Paterno, Penn St.	1966-88	212	54	2	.795
Henry Williams, Army, Minnesota	1891, 1900-21	141	34	12	.786
Dan McGugin, Vanderbilt	1904-17, 19-27	153	38	14	.780
Bo Schembechler, Miami (Ohio), Michigan	1963-85	196	55	7	.773
Wallace Wade, Alabama, Duke	1923-41, 46-49	164	46	10	.768
Howard Jones, Syracuse, Yale, Ohio St., Iowa, Duke, Southern California	1908-10, 13, 16-34	161	45	12	.766
Bear Bryant, Maryland, Kentucky, Texas A&M, Alabama	1945-67	179	53	15	.755
Johnny Vaught, Mississippi	1947-69	178	54	12	.754

24 SEASONS

Coach, Team(s)	Seasons	W	L	T	Pct.
Gil Dobie, North Dakota St., Washington, Navy, Cornell	1906-29	140	20	8	.857
Tom Osborne, Nebraska	1973-96	242	49	3	.828
Fielding Yost, Ohio Wesleyan, Nebraska, Kansas, Stanford, Michigan	1897-1920	163	33	10	.816
*Joe Paterno, Penn St.	1966-89	220	57	3	.791
Dan McGugin, Vanderbilt	1904-17, 19-28	161	40	14	.781
Bo Schembechler, Miami (Ohio), Michigan	1963-86	207	57	7	.777
Wallace Wade, Alabama, Duke	1923-41, 46-50	171	49	10	.765
Bear Bryant, Maryland, Kentucky, Texas A&M, Alabama	1945-68	187	56	15	.754
Red Blaik, Dartmouth, Army	1934-57	158	48	13	.751
Johnny Vaught, Mississippi	1947-70	185	58	12	.749
Howard Jones, Syracuse, Yale, Ohio St., Iowa, Duke, Southern California	1908-10, 13, 16-35	166	52	12	.748

25 SEASONS

Coach, Team(s)	Seasons	W	L	T	Pct.
Gil Dobie, North Dakota St., Washington, Navy, Cornell	1906-30	146	22	8	.852
Tom Osborne, Nebraska	1973-97	255	49	3	.836
Fielding Yost, Ohio Wesleyan, Nebraska, Kansas, Stanford, Michigan	1897-1921	168	34	11	.815
*Joe Paterno, Penn St.	1966-90	229	60	3	.789
Dan McGugin, Vanderbilt	1904-17, 19-29	168	42	14	.781
Bo Schembechler, Miami (Ohio), Michigan	1963-87	215	61	7	.772

Coach, Team(s)	Seasons	W	L	T	Pct.
Red Blaik, Dartmouth, Army	1934-58	166	48	14	.759
John Heisman, Oberlin, Akron, Auburn, Clemson, Georgia Tech	1892-1916	127	37	11	.757
Howard Jones, Syracuse, Yale, Ohio St., Iowa, Duke, Southern California	1908-10, 13, 16-36	170	54	15	.755
Woody Hayes, Denison, Miami (Ohio), Ohio St.	1946-70	167	54	7	.748
Bear Bryant, Maryland, Kentucky, Texas A&M, Alabama	1945-69	193	61	15	.745

26 SEASONS

Coach, Team(s)	Seasons	W	L	T	Pct.
Gil Dobie, North Dakota St., Washington, Navy, Cornell	1906-31	153	23	8	.853
Fielding Yost, Ohio Wesleyan, Nebraska, Kansas, Stanford, Michigan	1897-1922	174	34	12	.818
*Joe Paterno, Penn St.	1966-91	240	62	3	.792
Dan McGugin, Vanderbilt	1904-17, 19-30	176	44	14	.782
Bo Schembechler, Miami (Ohio), Michigan	1963-88	224	63	8	.773
John Heisman, Oberlin, Akron, Auburn, Clemson, Georgia Tech	1892-1917	136	37	11	.769
Pop Warner, Georgia, Cornell, Carlisle, Pittsburgh	1895-1920	199	62	14	.749
Woody Hayes, Denison, Miami (Ohio), Ohio St.	1946-71	173	58	7	.742
Amos Alonzo Stagg, Springfield, Chicago	1890-1915	193	62	19	.739
*Bobby Bowden, Samford, West Virginia, Florida St.	1959-62, 70-91	216	76	3	.737

27 SEASONS

Coach, Team(s)	Seasons	W	L	T	Pct.
Gil Dobie, North Dakota St., Washington, Navy, Cornell	1906-32	158	25	9	.846
Fielding Yost, Ohio Wesleyan, Nebraska, Kansas, Stanford, Michigan	1897-1923	182	34	12	.825
*Joe Paterno, Penn St.	1966-92	247	67	3	.784
Bo Schembechler, Miami (Ohio), Michigan	1963-89	234	65	8	.775
Dan McGugin, Vanderbilt	1904-17, 19-31	181	48	14	.774
John Heisman, Oberlin, Akron, Auburn, Clemson, Georgia Tech	1892-1918	142	38	11	.772
Woody Hayes, Denison, Miami (Ohio), Ohio St.	1946-72	182	60	7	.745
Pop Warner, Georgia, Cornell, Carlisle, Pittsburgh	1895-1921	204	65	15	.745
*Bobby Bowden, Samford, West Virginia, Florida St.	1959-62, 70-92	227	77	3	.744
Bear Bryant, Maryland, Kentucky, Texas A&M, Alabama	1945-71	210	67	16	.744

28 SEASONS

Coach, Team(s)	Seasons	W	L	T	Pct.
Gil Dobie, North Dakota St., Washington, Navy, Cornell	1906-33	162	28	9	.837
Fielding Yost, Ohio Wesleyan, Nebraska, Kansas, Stanford, Michigan	1897-1923, 25	189	35	12	.826
*Joe Paterno, Penn St.	1966-93	257	69	3	.786
Dan McGugin, Vanderbilt	1904-17, 19-32	187	49	16	.774
John Heisman, Oberlin, Akron, Auburn, Clemson, Georgia Tech	1892-1919	149	41	11	.769
Woody Hayes, Denison, Miami (Ohio), Ohio St.	1946-73	192	60	8	.754
*Bobby Bowden, Samford, West Virginia, Florida St.	1959-62, 70-93	239	78	3	.752
Bear Bryant, Maryland, Kentucky, Texas A&M, Alabama	1945-72	220	69	16	.748
Pop Warner, Georgia, Cornell, Carlisle, Pittsburgh	1895-1922	212	67	15	.747
Howard Jones, Syracuse, Yale, Ohio St., Iowa, Duke, Southern California	1908-10, 13, 16-39	191	60	19	.743

29 SEASONS

Coach, Team(s)	Seasons	W	L	T	Pct.
Fielding Yost, Ohio Wesleyan, Nebraska, Kansas, Stanford, Michigan	1897-1923, 25-26	196	36	12	.828
Gil Dobie, North Dakota St., Washington, Navy, Cornell	1906-34	164	33	9	.818
*Joe Paterno, Penn St.	1966-94	269	69	3	.793
Dan McGugin, Vanderbilt	1904-17, 19-33	191	52	19	.765
John Heisman, Oberlin, Akron, Auburn, Clemson, Georgia Tech, Pennsylvania	1892-1920	155	45	11	.761
Woody Hayes, Denison, Miami (Ohio), Ohio St.	1946-74	202	62	8	.757
*Bobby Bowden, Samford, West Virginia, Florida St.	1959-62, 70-94	249	79	4	.756
Bear Bryant, Maryland, Kentucky, Texas A&M, Alabama	1945-73	231	70	16	.754

Coach, Team(s)	Seasons	W	L	T	Pct.
Pop Warner, Georgia, Cornell, Carlisle, Pittsburgh	1895-1923	217	71	15	.741
Howard Jones, Syracuse, Yale, Ohio St., Iowa, Duke, Southern California	1908-10, 13, 16-40	194	64	21	.733

30 SEASONS

Coach, Team(s)	Seasons	W	L	T	Pct.
Gil Dobie, North Dakota St., Washington, Navy, Cornell	1906-35	164	39	10	.793
*Joe Paterno, Penn St.	1966-95	278	72	3	.792
Woody Hayes, Denison, Miami (Ohio), Ohio St.	1946-75	213	63	8	.764
Dan McGugin, Vanderbilt	1904-17, 19-34	197	55	19	.762
Bear Bryant, Maryland, Kentucky, Texas A&M, Alabama	1945-74	242	71	16	.760
*Bobby Bowden, Samford, West Virginia, Florida St.	1959-62, 70-95	259	81	4	.759
John Heisman, Oberlin, Akron, Auburn, Clemson, Georgia Tech, Pennsylvania	1892-1921	159	48	13	.752
Pop Warner, Georgia, Cornell, Carlisle, Pittsburgh, Stanford	1895-1924	224	72	16	.744
Amos Alonzo Stagg, Springfield, Chicago	1890-1919	204	76	20	.713
Dana X. Bible, Mississippi Col., LSU, Texas A&M, Nebraska, Texas	1913-17, 19-43	175	67	23	.704

31 SEASONS

Coach, Team(s)	Seasons	W	L	T	Pct.
*Joe Paterno, Penn St.	1966-96	289	74	3	.794
Gil Dobie, North Dakota St., Washington, Navy, Cornell, Boston College	1906-36	170	40	12	.793
Bear Bryant, Maryland, Kentucky, Texas A&M, Alabama	1945-75	253	72	16	.765
Woody Hayes, Denison, Miami (Ohio), Ohio St.	1946-76	222	65	9	.765
*Bobby Bowden, Samford, West Virginia, Florida St.	1959-62, 70-96	270	82	4	.764
John Heisman, Oberlin, Akron, Auburn, Clemson, Georgia Tech, Pennsylvania	1892-1922	165	51	13	.749
Pop Warner, Georgia, Cornell, Carlisle, Pittsburgh, Stanford	1895-1925	231	74	16	.745
Amos Alonzo Stagg, Springfield, Chicago	1890-1920	207	80	20	.707
Dana X. Bible, Mississippi Col., LSU, Texas A&M, Nebraska, Texas	1913-17, 19-44	180	69	23	.704

32 SEASONS

Coach, Team(s)	Seasons	W	L	T	Pct.
*Joe Paterno, Penn St.	1966-97	298	77	3	.792
Gil Dobie, North Dakota St., Washington, Navy, Cornell, Boston College	1906-37	174	44	13	.781
*Bobby Bowden, Stamford, West Virginia, Florida St.	1959-62, 70-97	281	83	4	.769
Bear Bryant, Maryland, Kentucky, Texas A&M, Alabama	1945-76	262	75	16	.765
Woody Hayes, Denison, Miami (Ohio), Ohio St.	1946-77	231	68	9	.765
Pop Warner, Georgia, Cornell, Carlisle, Pittsburgh, Stanford	1895-1926	241	74	17	.752
John Heisman, Oberlin, Akron, Auburn, Clemson, Georgia Tech, Pennsylvania, Wash. & Jeff.	1892-1923	171	52	14	.751
Dana X. Bible, Mississippi Col., LSU, Texas A&M, Nebraska, Texas	1913-17, 19-45	190	70	23	.712
Amos Alonzo Stagg, Springfield, Chicago	1890-1921	213	81	20	.710

33 SEASONS

Coach, Team(s)	Seasons	W	L	T	Pct.
*Joe Paterno, Penn St.	1966-98	307	80	3	.791
Gil Dobie, North Dakota St., Washington, Navy, Cornell, Boston College	1906-38	180	45	15	.781
*Bobby Bowden, Samford, West Virginia	1959-62, 70-98	292	85	4	.772
Bear Bryant, Maryland, Kentucky, Texas A&M, Alabama	1945-77	273	76	16	.770
Woody Hayes, Denison, Miami (Ohio), Ohio St.	1946-78	238	72	10	.759
Pop Warner, Georgia, Cornell, Carlisle, Pittsburgh, Stanford	1895-1927	249	76	18	.752
John Heisman, Oberlin, Akron, Auburn, Clemson, Georgia Tech, Pennsylvania, Wash. & Jeff., Rice	1892-1924	175	56	14	.743
Dana X. Bible, Mississippi Col., LSU, Texas A&M, Nebraska, Texas	1913-17, 19-46	198	72	23	.715
Amos Alonzo Stagg, Springfield, Chicago	1890-1922	219	82	20	.713

34 SEASONS

Coach, Team(s)	Seasons	W	L	T	Pct.
*Joe Paterno, Penn St.	1966-99	317	83	3	.790

Coach, Team(s)	Seasons	W	L	T	Pct.
*Bobby Bowden, Samford, West Virginia, Florida St.	1959-62, 70-99	304	85	4	.779
Bear Bryant, Maryland, Kentucky, Texas A&M, Alabama	1945-78	284	77	16	.775
Pop Warner, Georgia, Cornell, Carlisle, Pittsburgh, Stanford	1895-1928	257	79	19	.751
John Heisman, Oberlin, Akron, Auburn, Clemson, Georgia Tech, Pennsylvania, Wash. & Jeff., Rice	1892-1925	179	60	15	.734
Amos Alonzo Stagg, Springfield, Chicago.	1890-1923	226	83	20	.717

35 SEASONS

Coach, Team(s)	Seasons	W	L	T	Pct.
*Bobby Bowden, Samford, West Virginia, Florida St.	1959-62, 70-00	315	87	4	.781
Bear Bryant, Maryland, Kentucky, Texas A&M, Alabama	1945-79	296	77	16	.781
*Joe Paterno, Penn St.	1966-00	322	90	3	.780
Pop Warner, Georgia, Cornell, Carlisle, Pittsburgh, Stanford	1895-1929	266	81	19	.753
John Heisman, Oberlin, Akron, Auburn, Clemson, Georgia Tech, Pennsylvania, Wash. & Jeff., Rice	1892-1926	183	64	16	.726
Amos Alonzo Stagg, Springfield, Chicago.	1890-1924	230	84	23	.717

36 SEASONS

Coach, Team(s)	Seasons	W	L	T	Pct.
Bear Bryant, Maryland, Kentucky, Texas A&M, Alabama	1945-80	306	79	16	.783
*Bobby Bowden, Samford, West Virginia, Florida St.	1959-62, 70-01	323	91	4	.778
*Joe Paterno, Penn St.	1966-01	327	96	3	.771
Pop Warner, Georgia, Cornell, Carlisle, Pittsburgh, Stanford	1895-1930	275	82	20	.756
John Heisman, Oberlin, Akron, Auburn, Clemson, Georgia Tech, Pennsylvania, Wash. & Jeff., Rice	1892-1927	185	70	17	.711
Amos Alonzo Stagg, Springfield, Chicago.	1890-1925	233	88	24	.710

37 SEASONS

Coach, Team(s)	Seasons	W	L	T	Pct.
Bear Bryant, Maryland, Kentucky, Texas A&M, Alabama	1945-81	315	81	17	.783
*Bobby Bowden, Samford, West Virginia, Florida St.	1959-62, 70-02	332	96	4	.773
*Joe Paterno, Penn St.	1966-02	336	100	3	.769
Pop Warner, Georgia, Cornell, Carlisle, Pittsburgh, Stanford	1895-1931	282	84	22	.755
Amos Alonzo Stagg, Springfield, Chicago.	1890-1926	235	94	24	.700
Eddie Anderson, Loras, DePaul, Holy Cross, Iowa	1922-31, 33-42, 46-62	194	117	14	.618

38 SEASONS

Coach, Team(s)	Seasons	W	L	T	Pct.
Bear Bryant, Maryland, Kentucky, Texas A&M, Alabama	1945-82	323	85	17	.780
Pop Warner, Georgia, Cornell, Carlisle, Pittsburgh, Stanford	1895-1932	288	88	23	.751
Amos Alonzo Stagg, Springfield, Chicago	1890-1927	239	98	24	.695
Eddie Anderson, Loras, DePaul, Holy Cross, Iowa	1922-31, 33-42, 46-63	196	123	15	.609

39 SEASONS

Coach, Team(s)	Seasons	W	L	T	Pct.
Pop Warner, Georgia, Cornell, Carlisle, Pittsburgh, Stanford, Temple	1895-1933	293	91	23	.748
Amos Alonzo Stagg, Springfield, Chicago	1890-1928	241	105	24	.684
Eddie Anderson, Loras, DePaul, Holy Cross, Iowa	1922-31, 33-42, 46-64	201	128	15	.606

40 SEASONS

Coach, Team(s)	Seasons	W	L	T	Pct.
Pop Warner, Georgia, Cornell, Carlisle, Pittsburgh, Stanford, Temple	1895-1934	300	92	25	.749
Amos Alonzo Stagg, Springfield, Chicago	1890-1929	248	108	24	.684

41 SEASONS

Coach, Team(s)	Seasons	W	L	T	Pct.
Pop Warner, Georgia, Cornell, Carlisle, Pittsburgh, Stanford, Temple	1895-1935	307	95	25	.748
Amos Alonzo Stagg, Springfield, Chicago	1890-1930	249	113	26	.675

42 SEASONS

Coach, Team(s)	Seasons	W	L	T	Pct.
Pop Warner, Georgia, Cornell, Carlisle, Pittsburgh, Stanford, Temple	1895-1936	313	98	27	.745
Amos Alonzo Stagg, Springfield, Chicago	1890-1931	251	118	27	.668

43 SEASONS

Coach, Team(s)	Seasons	W	L	T	Pct.
Pop Warner, Georgia, Cornell, Carlisle, Pittsburgh, Stanford, Temple	1895-1937	316	100	31	.742
Amos Alonzo Stagg, Springfield, Chicago	1890-1932	254	122	28	.663

44 SEASONS

Coach, Team(s)	Seasons	W	L	T	Pct.
Pop Warner, Georgia, Cornell, Carlisle, Pittsburgh, Stanford, Temple	1895-1938	319	106	32	.733
Amos Alonzo Stagg, Springfield, Chicago, Pacific (Cal.)	1890-1933	259	127	28	.659

*Active coach.

Coaches to Reach 100, 200 and 300 Victories

(Must have five years or 50 victories at a school that was classified as a major college at the time)

100 VICTORIES

Coach (Date Reached Milestone) (Schools Coached and Years)	WHEN MILESTONE REACHED		
	Age in Yrs.-Days	Career Game (Record)	Career Yr.-Game
FRED AKERS (9-17-88) (Wyoming 1975-76, Texas 1977-86, Purdue 1987-90)	50-184	155th (100-52-3)	14-2
WILLIAM ALEXANDER (11-18-39) (Georgia Tech 1920-44)	49-233	189th (100-74-15)	20-7
EDDIE ANDERSON (10-12-46) (Loras 1922-24, DePaul 1925-31, Holy Cross 1933-38, Iowa 1939-42, 1946-49, Holy Cross 1950-64)	45-333	160th (100-50-10)	21-4
IKE ARMSTRONG (10-17-42) (Utah 1925-49)	47-131	141st (100-30-11)	18-4
#FRANK BEAMER (11-9-96) (Murray St. 1981-86, Virginia Tech 1987—)	50-22	177th (100-73-4)	16-8
MATTY BELL (11-5-38) (Haskell 1920-21, Carroll [Wis.] 1922, TCU 1923-28, Texas A&M 1929-33, Southern Methodist 1935-41, 1945-49)	39-256	169th (100-60-9)	18-6
HUGO BEZDEK (11-22-24) (Oregon 1906, Arkansas 1908-12, Oregon 1913-17, Penn St. 1918-29, Delaware Valley 1949)	40-120	147th (100-34-13)	18-9
DANA X. BIBLE (11-21-31) (Mississippi Col. 1913-15, LSU 1916, Texas A&M 1917, 1919-28, Nebraska 1929-36, Texas 1937-46)	40-44	149th (100-31-18)	18-8

Coach (Date Reached Milestone) (Schools Coached and Years)	WHEN MILESTONE REACHED		
	Age in Yrs.-Days	Career Game (Record)	Career Yr.-Game
BERNIE BIERMAN (11-11-39) (Montana St. 1919-21, Mississippi St. 1925-26, Tulane 1927-31, Minnesota 1932-41, 1945-50)	45-245	149th (100-38-11)	18-6
BOB BLACKMAN (9-27-69) (Denver 1953-54, Dartmouth 1955-70, Illinois 1971-76, Cornell 1977-82)	51-82	147th (100-42-5)	17-1
RED BLAIK (10-23-48) (Dartmouth 1934-40, Army 1941-58)	51-249	134th (100-25-9)	15-5
#BOBBY BOWDEN (10-7-78) (Samford 1959-62, West Virginia 1970-75, Florida St. 1976—)	48-333	144th (100-44-0)	14-5
TERRY BOWDEN (12-31-96) (Salem Int'l 1983-85, Samford 1987-92, Auburn 1993-98)	40-280	147th (100-45-2)	13-12
BILLY BREWER (10-6-90) (Southeastern La. 1974-79, Louisiana Tech 1980-82, Mississippi 1983-93)	54-363	184th (100-78-6)	17-5
#MACK BROWN (10-9-99) (Appalachian St. 1983, Tulane 1985-87, North Carolina 1988-97, Texas 1998—)	48-43	180th (100-79-1)	16-7
FRANK BROYLES (11-27-69) (Missouri 1957, Arkansas 1958-76)	44-336	138th (100-36-2)	13-9
EARLE BRUCE (11-3-84) (Tampa 1972, Iowa St. 1973-78, Ohio St. 1979-87, Northern Iowa 1988, Colorado St. 1989-92)	53-240	149th (100-49-0)	13-9
BEAR BRYANT (11-7-59) (Maryland 1945, Kentucky 1946-53, Texas A&M 1954-57, Alabama 1958-82)	46-57	154th (100-44-10)	15-7
WALLY BUTTS (11-15-52) (Georgia 1939-60)	47-281	151st (100-44-7)	14-9
CHARLIE CALDWELL (10-21-50) (Williams 1928-42, Princeton 1945-56)	48-80	163rd (100-55-8)	21-4
FRANK CAMP (10-23-65) (Louisville 1946-68)	60-39	182nd (100-80-2)	20-6
JIM CARLEN (11-8-80) (West Virginia 1966-69, Texas Tech 1970-74, South Carolina 1975-81)	47-120	167th (100-61-6)	15-9
LEN CASANOVA (10-2-65) (Santa Clara 1946-49, Pittsburgh 1950, Oregon 1951-66)	59-263	192nd (100-82-10)	20-3
FRANK CAVANAUGH (10-3-25) (Cincinnati 1898, Holy Cross 1903-05, Dartmouth 1911-16, Boston College 1919-26, Fordham 1927-32)	49-158	143rd (100-32-11)	17-1
JERRY CLAIBORNE (11-6-76) (Virginia Tech 1961-70, Maryland 1972-81, Kentucky 1982-89)	48-72	158th (100-54-4)	15-9
JOHN COOPER (11-17-90) (Tulsa 1977-84, Arizona St. 1985-87, Ohio St. 1988-00)	53-137	162nd (100-57-5)	14-10
CARMEN COZZA (10-4-80) (Yale 1965-96)	50-116	138th (100-35-3)	16-3
FRITZ CRISLER (11-24-45) (Minnesota 1930-31, Princeton 1932-37, Michigan 1938-47)	46-316	138th (100-30-8)	16-10
DICK CRUM (11-15-86) (Miami [Ohio] 1974-77, North Carolina 1978-87, Kent St.1988-90)	52-200	148th (100-44-4)	13-10
JACK CURTICE (10-3-64) (West Tex. A&M 1940-41, UTEP 1946-49, Utah 1950-57, Stanford 1958-61, UC Santa Barb. 1962-69)	56-118	202nd (100-95-7)	21-1
DUFFY DAUGHERTY (9-25-71) (Michigan St. 1954-72)	56-17	164th (100-60-4)	18-3
#FISHER DeBERRY (9-6-97) (Air Force 1984—)	59-89	161st (100-60-1)	14-2
DUDLEY DeGROOT (9-17-49) (UC Santa Barb. 1926-28, San Jose St. 1932-39, Rochester 1940-43, West Virginia 1948-49, New Mexico 1950-52)	49-302	152nd (100-44-8)	17-1
HERB DEROMEDI (11-16-91) (Central Mich. 1978-93)	52-171	153rd (100-43-10)	14-11
BOB DEVANEY (11-8-69) (Wyoming 1957-61, Nebraska 1962-72)	54-209	133rd (100-28-5)	13-8
DAN DEVINE (10-12-68) (Arizona St. 1955-57, Missouri 1958-70, Notre Dame 1975-80)	43-293	139th (100-31-8)	14-4
DOUG DICKEY (11-27-77) (Tennessee 1964-69, Florida 1970-78)	45-202	156th (100-50-6)	14-10
PAUL DIETZEL (10-6-73) (LSU 1955-61, Army 1962-65, South Carolina 1966-74)	47-188	191st (100-86-5)	19-4
GIL DOBIE (10-20-22) (North Dakota St. 1906-07, Washington 1908-16, Navy 1917-19, Cornell 1920-35, Boston College 1936-38)	43-262	108th (100-5-3)	17-4
BOBBY DODD (12-1-56) (Georgia Tech 1945-66)	48-20	131st (100-28-3)	12-10
MIKE DONAHUE (9-29-23) (Auburn 1904-06, 1908-22, LSU 1923-27)	42-111	140th (100-35-5)	19-1
TERRY DONAHUE (9-10-88) (UCLA 1976-95)	44-78	143rd (100-36-7)	13-2
ALDO DONELLI (10-16-65) (Duquesne 1939-42, Boston U. 1947-56, Columbia 1957-67)	58-86	197th (100-89-8)	23-4
BILL DOOLEY (11-27-82) (North Carolina 1967-77, Virginia Tech 1978-86, Wake Forest 1987-92)	48-192	180th (100-78-2)	16-11
VINCE DOOLEY (9-24-77) (Georgia 1964-88)	45-20	149th (100-44-5)	14-3
FRED DUNLAP (10-29-83) (Lehigh 1965-75, Colgate 1976-87)	55-194	195th (100-91-4)	19-8

Tennessee Sports Information

Tennessee's Phillip Fulmer earned his 100th head coaching victory when the Volunteers won at South Carolina, 18-10, November 2, 2002.

Colorado State Sports Information

Sonny Lubick also joined the 100-win club last year when his Colorado State team upended Wyoming at home, 44-36, on October 12.

Coach (Date Reached Milestone) (Schools Coached and Years)	WHEN MILESTONE REACHED		
	Age in Yrs.-Days	Career Game (Record)	Career Yr.-Game
PAT DYE (10-4-86) (East Caro. 1974-79, Wyoming 1980, Auburn 1981-92)	46-332	142nd (100-41-1)	13-4
LLOYD EATON (10-4-69) (Alma 1949-55, Northern Mich. 1956, Wyoming 1962-70)	51-101	145th (100-40-5)	16-3
LaVELL EDWARDS (10-22-83) (Brigham Young 1972-00)	53-11	138th (100-37-1)	12-7
RAY ELIOT (10-10-59) (Illinois Col. 1933-36, Illinois 1942-59)	54-119	191st (100-79-12)	22-3
RIP ENGLE (10-21-61) (Brown 1944-49, Penn St. 1950-65)	55-209	161st (100-53-8)	18-5
DENNIS ERICKSON (10-30-93) (Idaho 1982-85, Wyoming 1986, Washington St. 1987-88, Miami [Fla.] 1989-94, Oregon St. 1999-02)	46-334	137th (100-36-1)	12-7
DON FAUROT (11-1-41) (Truman 1926-34, Missouri 1935-42, 1946-56)	39-131	171st (100-63-8)	16-6
FRED FOLSOM (11-1-13) (Colorado 1895-1902, Dartmouth 1903-06, Colorado 1908-15)	41-357	126th (100-20-6)	17-6
DANNY FORD (11-13-93) (Clemson 1978-89, Arkansas 1993-97)	45-225	139th (100-34-5)	13-9
#DENNIS FRANCHIONE (9-7-96) (Southwestern [Kan.] 1981-82, Pittsburg St. 1985-89; Southwest Tex. St. 1990-91, New Mexico 1992-97, TCU 1998-00, Alabama 2001-02, Texas A&M 2003—)	45-163	148th (100-46-2)	14-2
HAYDEN FRY (9-26-81) (Southern Methodist 1962-72, North Texas 1973-78, Iowa 1979-98)	52-185	207th (100-103-4)	20-3
#PHILLIP FULMER (11-2-2002) (Tennessee 1992—)	52-62	123rd (100-23-0)	11-8
ANDY GUSTAFSON (9-29-61) (Virginia Tech 1926-29, Miami [Fla.] 1948-63)	58-179	168th (100-64-4)	18-3
WAYNE HARDIN (10-13-79) (Navy 1959-64, Temple 1970-82)	52-204	159th (100-54-5)	16-6
JIM HARKEMA (9-16-89) (Grand Valley St. 1973-82, Eastern Mich. 1983-92)	47-83	167th (100-63-4)	17-3
DICK HARLOW (11-3-34) (Penn St. 1915-17, Colgate 1922-25, McDaniel 1926-34, Harvard 1935-42, 1945-47)	44-67	142nd (100-31-11)	16-5
HARVEY HARMAN (10-4-47) (Haverford 1922-29, Sewanee 1930, Pennsylvania 1931-37, Rutgers 1938-55)	46-334	177th (100-70-7)	22-2
#KEN HATFIELD (11-20-91) (Air Force 1979-83, Arkansas 1984-89, Clemson 1990-93, Rice 1994—)	48-174	155th (100-52-3)	13-11
WOODY HAYES (10-21-61) (Denison 1946-48, Miami [Ohio] 1949-50, Ohio St. 1951-78)	48-249	140th (100-34-6)	16-4
JOHN HEISMAN (9-27-13) (Oberlin 1892, Akron 1893, Oberlin 1894, Auburn 1895-99, Clemson 1900-03, Georgia Tech 1904-19, Pennsylvania 1920-22, Wash. & Jeff. 1923, Rice 1924-27)	43-339	142nd (100-33-9)	22-1
GUS HENDERSON (11-24-32) (Southern California 1919-24, Tulsa 1925-35, Occidental 1940-42)	43-259	126th (100-23-3)	14-8
BILL HESS (9-4-76) (Ohio 1958-77)	51-106	182nd (100-78-4)	19-1
JIM HESS (9-5-87) (Angelo St. 1974-81, Stephen F. Austin 1982-88, New Mexico St. 1990-96)	50-278	147th (100-43-4)	14-1
#LOU HOLTZ (12-31-82) (William & Mary 1969-71, North Carolina St. 1972-75, Arkansas 1977-83, Minnesota 1984-85, Notre Dame 1986-96, South Carolina 1999—)	45-359	153rd (100-48-5)	13-12
FRANK HOWARD (9-27-58) (Clemson 1940-69)	49-186	175th (100-65-10)	19-2
DON JAMES (9-15-84) (Kent St. 1971-74, Washington 1975-92)	51-258	153rd (100-52-1)	14-2
MORLEY JENNINGS (10-3-31) (Ouachita Baptist 1912-25, Baylor 1926-40)	46-253	136th (100-33-3)	20-1
HOWARD JONES (12-3-27) (Syracuse 1908, Yale 1909, Ohio St. 1910, Yale 1913, Iowa 1916-23, Duke 1924, Southern California 1925-40)	42-102	142nd (100-33-9)	16-10
LLOYD JORDAN (10-27-56) (Amherst 1932-49, Harvard 1950-56)	55-317	172nd (100-65-7)	22-4
SHUG JORDAN (10-9-65) (Auburn 1951-75)	55-14	148th (100-43-5)	15-4
FRANK KIMBROUGH (9-29-56) (Hardin-Simmons 1935-40, Baylor 1941-42, 1945-46, West Tex. A&M 1947-57)	52-97	181st (100-73-8)	20-3
TONY KNAP (10-2-76) (Utah St. 1963-66, Boise St. 1968-75, UNLV 1976-81)	61-298	135th (100-33-2)	13-4
FRANK KUSH (12-30-70) (Arizona St. 1958-79)	41-344	131st (100-30-1)	13-11
ELMER LAYDEN (10-26-40) (Loras 1925-26, Duquesne 1927-33, Notre Dame 1934-40)	37-175	143rd (100-32-11)	16-4
FRANK LEAHY (10-3-53) (Boston College 1939-40, Notre Dame 1941-53)	45-37	121st (100-13-8)	13-2
LOU LITTLE (9-26-42) (Georgetown 1924-29, Columbia 1930-56)	48-294	161st (100-49-12)	19-1
#SONNY LUBICK (10-12-2002) (Montana St. 1978-81, Colorado St. 1993—)	65-214	155th (100-55-0)	14-7

Coach (Date Reached Milestone) (Schools Coached and Years)	WHEN MILESTONE REACHED		
	Age in Yrs.-Days	Career Game (Record)	Career Yr.-Game
DICK MacPHERSON (10-28-89) .... (Massachusetts 1971-77, Syracuse 1981-90)	58-358	171st (100-68-3)	16-7
JOHNNY MAJORS (11-19-83) .... (Iowa St. 1968-72, Pittsburgh 1973-76, Tennessee 1977-92, Pittsburgh 1993-96)	48-181	185th (100-81-4)	16-10
BILL MALLORY (9-14-85)... (Miami [Ohio] 1969-73, Colorado 1974-78, Northern Ill. 1980-83, Indiana 1984-96)	50-107	164th (100-63-1)	16-1
BEN MARTIN (11-20-76) .... (Virginia 1956-57, Air Force 1958-77)	55-145	217th (100-108-9)	21-11
CHARLIE McCLENDON (11-2-74).. (LSU 1962-79)	46-222	141st (100-35-6)	13-7
DAN McGUGIN (11-15-19)... (Vanderbilt 1904-34)	40-78	132nd (100-25-7)	15-7
JOHN McKAY (1-1-73) .... (Southern California 1960-75)	49-209	139th (100-33-6)	13-12
TUSS McLAUGHRY (10-25-41) .... (Westminster [Pa.] 1916-18, 1921, Amherst 1922-25, Brown 1926-40, Dartmouth 1941-42, 1945-54)	48-109	196th (100-86-10)	23-5
CHICK MEEHAN (9-28-35) .... (Syracuse 1920-24, New York U. 1925-31, Manhattan 1932-37)	42-23	146th (100-34-12)	16-2
DUTCH MEYER (9-29-51) .... (TCU 1934-52)	53-204	182nd (100-71-11)	18-2
CHUCK MILLS (9-15-84).. (Pomona-Pitzer 1959-61, Indiana [Pa.] 1962-63, Merchant Marine 1964, Utah St. 1967-72, Wake Forest 1973-77, Southern Ore. St. 1980-88, Coast Guard 1997)	55-287	213th (100-109-4)	22-2
ODUS MITCHELL (11-25-61) .... (North Texas 1946-66)	59-116	167th (100-59-8)	16-10
AL MOLDE (10-11-86) .... (Sioux Falls 1971-72, Minn.-Morris 1973-79, Central Mo. St. 1980-82, Eastern Ill. 1983-86, Western Mich. 1987-96)	42-330	162nd (100-56-6)	16-6
CHARLEY MORAN (9-27-30) .... (Texas A&M 1909-14, Centre 1919-23, Bucknell 1924-26, Catawba 1930-33)	52-217	131st (100-24-7)	15-1
JOE MORRISON (10-29-88).. (Chattanooga 1973-79, New Mexico 1980-82, South Carolina 1983-88)	51-69	176th (100-69-7)	16-8
RAY MORRISON (10-2-37) .... (Southern Methodist 1915-16, Vanderbilt 1918, Southern Methodist 1922-34, Vanderbilt 1935-39, Temple 1940-48, Austin College 1949-52)	52-216	177th (100-54-23)	19-2
BILL MURRAY (11-22-58)... (Delaware 1940-42, 1946-50, Duke 1951-65)	50-74	149th (100-40-9)	16-10
JESS NEELY (10-19-46) .... (Rhodes 1924-27, Clemson 1931-39, Rice 1940-66)	48-288	190th (100-79-11)	20-4
DON NEHLEN (11-16-85).. (Bowling Green 1968-76, West Virginia 1980-00)	48-319	162nd (100-57-5)	15-10
BOB NEYLAND (9-29-39).. (Tennessee 1926-34, 1936-40, 1946-52)	47-224	120th (100-12-8)	13-1
BOB ODELL (9-24-77)... (Bucknell 1958-64, Pennsylvania 1965-70, Williams 1971-86)	55-203	166th (100-64-2)	20-1
JORDAN OLIVAR (10-15-60).. (Villanova 1943-48, Loyola Marymount 1949-51, Yale 1952-60)	45-258	159th (100-53-6)	18-4
TOM OSBORNE (9-24-83).. (Nebraska 1973-97)	46-211	126th (100-24-2)	11-4
BENNIE OWEN (10-4-15).. (Washburn 1900, Bethany [Kan.] 1901-04, Oklahoma 1905-26)	40-72	136th (100-28-8)	16-5
ARA PARSEGHIAN (11-26-66).. (Miami [Ohio] 1951-55, Northwestern 1956-63, Notre Dame 1964-74)	43-189	147th (100-43-4)	16-10
#PAUL PASQUALONI (11-14-98).. (Western Conn. St. 1982-86, Syracuse 1991—)	49-92	143rd (100-42-1)	13-9
#JOE PATERNO (11-6-76).. (Penn St. 1966—)	49-320	122nd (100-21-1)	11-9
MIKE PRICE (9-5-98) .... (Weber St. 1981-88, Washington St. 1989-02)	52-152	193rd (100-93-0)	18-1
TOMMY PROTHRO (9-19-70)... (Oregon St. 1955-64, UCLA 1965-70)	50-38	155th (100-50-5)	16-2
EDWARD ROBINSON (11-6-15)... (Nebraska 1896-97, Brown 1898-1901, Maine 1902, Brown 1904-07, 1910-25)	41-344	165th (100-56-9)	17-7
#JOHN ROBINSON (10-4-97) .... (Southern California 1976-82, 93-97, UNLV 1999—)	62-71	136th (100-32-4)	12-4
KNUTE ROCKNE (11-1-30).. (Notre Dame 1918-30)	42-242	117th (100-12-5)	13-5
DARRYL ROGERS (9-12-81)... (Cal St. Hayward 1965, Fresno St. 1966-72, San Jose St. 1973-75, Michigan St. 1976-79, Arizona St. 1980-84)	47-106	176th (100-70-6)	17-1
BILL ROPER (10-8-27) .... (VMI 1903-04, Princeton 1906-08, Missouri 1909, Princeton 1910-11, Swarthmore 1915-16, Princeton 1919-30)	47-47	141st (100-26-15)	19-2
DARRELL ROYAL (10-7-67) .... (Mississippi St. 1954-55, Washington 1956, Texas 1957-76)	43-93	141st (100-38-3)	14-3
RED SANDERS (11-9-57)... (Vanderbilt 1940-48, UCLA 1949-57)	52-216	144th (100-41-3)	15-8

Coach (Date Reached Milestone) (Schools Coached and Years)	WHEN MILESTONE REACHED		
	Age in Yrs.-Days	Career Game (Record)	Career Yr.-Game
PHILIP SARBOE (12-1-60) (Central Wash. 1941-42, Washington St. 1945-49, Humboldt St. 1951-65, Hawaii 1966)	48-233	160th (100-53-7)	17-11
BO SCHEMBECHLER (10-4-75) (Miami [Ohio] 1963-68, Michigan 1969-89)	46-33	130th (100-24-6)	13-4
FRANCIS SCHMIDT (11-5-32) (Tulsa 1919-21, Arkansas 1922-28, TCU 1929-33, Ohio St. 1934-40, Idaho 1941-42)	46-336	136th (100-27-9)	14-8
#HOWARD SCHNELLENBERGER (10-28-95) (Miami [Fla.] 1979-83, Louisville 1985-94, Oklahoma 1995, Fla. Atlantic 2001—)	61-226	177th (100-74-3)	16-8
BEN SCHWARTZWALDER (9-30-65) (Muhlenberg 1946-48, Syracuse 1949-73)	52-120	143rd (100-41-2)	16-2
CLARK SHAUGHNESSY (10-20-34) (Tulane 1915-20, 1922-26, Loyola [Ill.] 1927-32, Chicago 1933-39, Stanford 1940-41, Maryland 1942, Pittsburgh 1943-45, Maryland 1946, Hawaii 1965)	42-228	164th (100-50-14)	19-3
DICK SHERIDAN (10-6-90) (Furman 1978-85, North Carolina St. 1986-92)	49-58	147th (100-43-4)	13-6
#JACKIE SHERRILL (10-8-88) (Washington St. 1976, Pittsburgh 1977-81, Texas A&M 1982-88, Mississippi St. 1991—)	44-314	145th (100-43-2)	13-5
R.C. SLOCUM (10-30-99) (Texas A&M 1989-02)	54-357	132nd (100-30-2)	11-8
ANDY SMITH (11-10-23) (Pennsylvania 1909-12, Purdue 1913-15, California 1916-25)	40-71	140th (100-29-11)	15-8
CLIPPER SMITH (11-6-42) (Gonzaga 1925-28, Santa Clara 1929-35, Villanova 1936-42, San Francisco 1946, Lafayette 1949-51)	44-81	159th (100-47-12)	18-5
#JOHN L. SMITH (11-3-2001) (Idaho 1989-94; Utah St. 1995-97; Louisville 1998-02, Michigan St. 2003—)	52-363	153rd (100-53-0)	13-9
LARRY SMITH (11-10-90) (Tulane 1976-79, Arizona 1980-86, Southern California 1987-92, Missouri 1994-00)	51-59	170th (100-65-5)	15-10
CARL SNAVELY (9-30-44) (Bucknell 1927-33, North Carolina 1934-35, Cornell 1936-44, North Carolina 1945-52, Washington [Mo.] 1953-58)	50-60	152nd (100-40-12)	18-2
#BILL SNYDER (9-8-2001) (Kansas St. 1989—)	61-336	144th (100-43-1)	13-1
BRUCE SNYDER (9-13-97) (Utah St. 1976-82, California 1987-91, Arizona St. 1992-00)	57-183	192nd (100-86-6)	18-2
OSSIE SOLEM (10-24-42) (Luther 1920, Drake 1921-31, Iowa 1932-36, Syracuse 1937-45, Springfield 1946-57)	50-315	183rd (100-71-12)	23-5
STEVE SPURRIER (11-8-97) (Duke 1987-89, Florida 1990-01)	52-202	131st (100-29-2)	11-9
AMOS ALONZO STAGG (10-6-1900) (Springfield 1890-91, Chicago 1892-1932, Pacific [Cal.] 1933-46)	38-51	143rd (100-34-9)	11-6
DENNY STOLZ (9-14-85) (Alma 1965-70, Michigan St. 1973-75, Bowling Green 1977-85, San Diego St. 1986-88)	51-2	175th (100-73-2)	18-2
ABE STUBER (10-16-48) (Westminster [Mo.] 1929-31, Southeast Mo. St. 1932-44, 1946, Iowa St. 1947-52)	43-338	162nd (100-54-8)	19-5
JOCK SUTHERLAND (10-14-33) (Lafayette 1919-23, Pittsburgh 1924-38)	44-207	132nd (100-22-10)	15-4
JIM SWEENEY (9-8-84) (Montana St. 1963-67, Washington St. 1968-75, Fresno St. 1976-77, 1980-96)	55-7	206th (100-105-1)	20-2
BARRY SWITZER (9-24-83) (Oklahoma 1973-88)	45-353	122nd (100-18-4)	11-3
JIM TATUM (11-8-58) (North Carolina 1942, Oklahoma 1946, Maryland 1947-55, North Carolina 1956-58)	45-78	140th (100-33-7)	14-8
GRANT TEAFF (9-25-82) (McMurry 1960-65, Angelo St. 1969-71, Baylor 1972-92)	48-317	206th (100-101-5)	20-3
FRANK THOMAS (11-9-40) (Chattanooga 1925-28, Alabama 1931-42, 1944-46)	41-359	128th (100-21-7)	14-6
DICK TOMEY (9-4-93) (Hawaii 1977-86, Arizona 1987-00)	55-76	182nd (100-75-7)	17-1
PIE VANN (10-6-62) (Southern Miss. 1949-68)	55-14	137th (100-36-1)	14-4
JOHNNY VAUGHT (11-28-59) (Mississippi 1947-73)	51-206	135th (100-29-6)	13-10
JIM WACKER (11-14-81) (Texas Lutheran 1971-75, North Dakota St. 1976-78, Southwest Tex. St. 1979-82, TCU 1983-91, Minnesota 1992-96)	44-200	134th (100-33-1)	12-10
WALLACE WADE (10-3-36) (Alabama 1923-30, Duke 1931-41, 1946-50)	44-110	129th (100-24-5)	14-3
PAPPY WALDORF (10-27-45) (Oklahoma City 1925-27, Oklahoma St. 1929-33, Kansas St. 1934, Northwestern 1935-46, California 1947-56)	43-24	173rd (100-56-17)	20-5
POP WARNER (11-26-08) (Georgia 1895-96, Cornell 1897-98, Carlisle 1899-1903, Cornell 1904-06, Carlisle 1907-14, Pittsburgh 1915-23, Stanford 1924-32, Temple 1933-38)	37-235	145th (100-38-7)	14-11

Coach (Date Reached Milestone) (Schools Coached and Years)	Age in Yrs.-Days	Career Game (Record)	Career Yr.-Game
GEORGE WELSH (10-14-89) (Navy 1973-81, Virginia 1982-00)	56-49	188th (100-85-3)	17-7
BUD WILKINSON (11-2-57) (Oklahoma 1947-63)	41-193	111th (100-8-3)	11-6
HENRY WILLIAMS (10-2-12) (Army 1891, Minnesota 1900-21)	43-98	122nd (100-13-9)	14-4
GEORGE WOODRUFF (11-11-1898) (Pennsylvania 1892-1901, Illinois 1903, Carlisle 1905)	35-261	109th (100-9-0)	8-11
WARREN WOODSON (9-27-52) (Conway 1935-40, Hardin-Simmons 1941-51, Arizona St. 1952-56, New Mexico St. 1958-67, Trinity [Tex.] 1972-73)	49-215	141st (100-32-9)	15-2
BILL YEOMAN (9-12-77) (Houston 1962-86)	49-260	161st (100-56-5)	16-1
FIELDING YOST (11-7-08) (Ohio Wesleyan 1897, Nebraska 1898, Kansas 1899, Stanford 1900, Michigan 1901-23, 1925-26)	37-191	114th (100-10-4)	12-6
JIM YOUNG (9-10-88) (Arizona 1973-76, Purdue 1977-81, Army 1983-90)	53-142	160th (100-58-2)	15-1
JOHN YOVICSIN (11-16-68) (Gettysburg 1952-56, Harvard 1957-70)	50-131	150th (100-45-5)	17-8
JOSEPH YUKICA (11-20-82) (New Hampshire 1966-67, Boston College 1968-77, Dartmouth 1978-86)	51-177	169th (100-68-1)	17-10
ROBERT ZUPPKE (11-12-32) (Illinois 1913-41)	53-102	152nd (100-44-8)	20-9

#Active coach.

200 VICTORIES

Coach (Date Reached Milestone)	Age in Yrs.-Days	Career Game (Record)	Career Yr.-Game
Eddie Anderson (11-14-64)	64-1	342nd (200-127-15)	39-8
#Bobby Bowden (10-27-90)	60-353	279th (200-76-3)	25-7
Bear Bryant (9-10-71)	57-364	282nd (200-66-16)	27-1
Vince Dooley (11-26-88)	56-84	286th (200-76-10)	25-11
LaVell Edwards (9-24-94)	64-348	277th (200-74-3)	23-4
Hayden Fry (11-20-93)	64-265	361st (200-152-9)	32-11
Woody Hayes (11-2-74)	61-261	268th (200-60-8)	29-8
#Lou Holtz (9-9-95)	58-243	297th (200-90-7)	26-2
Jess Neely (9-26-64)	66-265	373rd (200-155-18)	38-1
Don Nehlen (11-11-00)	64-314	355th (200-127-8)	30-9
Tom Osborne (10-7-93)	56-224	249th (200-46-3)	21-5
#Joe Paterno (9-5-87)	60-258	246th (200-44-2)	22-1
Bo Schembechler (10-4-86)	57-33	262nd (200-55-7)	24-4
Jim Sweeney (11-2-96)	67-62	326th (200-158-4)	32-8
Amos Alonzo Stagg (10-11-19)	57-56	294th (200-74-20)	30-1
Pop Warner (9-24-21)	50-172	276th (200-62-14)	28-1
Warren Woodson (10-13-73)	70-231	307th (200-93-14)	31-6

#Active coach.

300 VICTORIES

Coach (Date Reached Milestone)	Age in Yrs.-Days	Career Game (Record)	Career Yr.-Game
#Joe Paterno (9-12-98)	71-266	380th (300-77-3)	32-2
#Bobby Bowden (10-23-99)	69-349	389th (300-85-4)	34-8
Bear Bryant (10-3-80)	67-22	393rd (300-77-16)	36-4
Amos Alonzo Stagg (11-6-43)	81-82	507th (300-173-34)	54-7
Pop Warner (11-24-34)	63-233	415th (300-91-24)	41-8

#Active coach.

EDDIE ROBINSON
A Coach For The Ages

Because Grambling is not a Division I-A member, most football historians agree that Grambling's Eddie Robinson not be listed in the major college coaches' section. But there is no denying that the Tigers' former head coach belongs in any mention of great collegiate coaches.

Robinson, who retired following the 1997 season, compiled one of the most impressive coaching legacies in collegiate history. He is the only college football coach with more than 400 victories (408) and he has coached in more games (588) than any other coach in the 132 years of college football.

Only the legendary Amos Alonzo Stagg had more years as a college head coach (57) than Robinson's 55 seasons at Grambling (he coached two war years at Grambling High School). Robinson began his career in 1941, at the start of World War II and continued through more than half a century of change.

Here is a breakdown of the milestone victories in his career:

Victory No.	(Date Reached Milestone)	Age in Yrs.-Days	Career Game (Record)	Career Yr.-Game
100th	(11-9-57)	38-270	146th (100-39-7)	15-6
200th	(10-16-71)	52-246	285th (200-74-11)	29-6
300th	(9-25-82)	63-225	411th (300-98-13)	40-3
400th	(10-7-95)	76-237	560th (400-145-15)	53-5

JOHN GAGLIARDI
A Coach For The Ages

John Gagliardi is probably not as well known as Eddie Robinson, but his accomplishments are no less remarkable. Both coaches are known as great teachers, men whose lives touched many young college student-athletes and molded them into responsible adults.

Gagliardi has amassed 400 collegiate victories over 54 years of coaching (400-114-11) and seems a good bet in 2003 to break Robinson's all-time collegiate record of 408 wins that he reached in 1995.

Fifty of Gagliardi's seasons have been at St. John's University in Collegeville, Minnesota. Gagliardi's biggest strength is his ability to relate to his players and get them to play hard even though they receive no scholarships based on athletics ability. In fact, his basic philosophy is boiled down to "Winning With Nos." That is:

* No spring practices;
* No scholarships;
* No compulsory weightlifting program;
* No calling him "coach"— players call him John;
* No long practices — an hour and a half or less; and
* No tackling in practice — players wear shorts or sweats.

Gagliardi began his remarkable career in 1949 at Carroll College (Montana), where he coached for four seasons before assuming the St. John's head position in 1953. He is now coaching in his seventh decade and seems fit enough to continue well into the new century. If he coaches through the 2005 season, he will tie the legendary Amos Alonzo Stagg in coaching longevity at 57 years.

His career includes 25 Minnesota Intercollegiate Athletic Conference titles and three national championships (1963, 1965 and 1976).

Here is a breakdown of the milestones in his career:

Victory No.	(Date Reached Milestone)	Age in Yrs.-Days	Career Game (Record)	Career Yr.-Game
100th	(10-9-65)	38-343	135th (100-32-3)	17-5
200th	(10-11-80)	53-345	274th (200-67-7)	32-5
300th	(10-16-93)	66-350	405th (300-95-10)	45-6
400th	(12-7-02)	76-38	524th (400-113-11)	54-13

Other Coaching Milestones

(Must have five years or 50 victories at a school that was classified as a major college at the time)

YOUNGEST COACHES TO REACH 100 VICTORIES

Coach	Age in Yrs.-Days
George Woodruff	35-261
Elmer Layden	37-175
Fielding Yost	37-191
Pop Warner	37-235
Amos Alonzo Stagg	38-51
Don Faurot	39-131
Matty Bell	39-256
Dana X. Bible	40-44
Andy Smith	40-71
Bennie Owen	40-72
Dan McGugin	40-78
Hugo Bezdek	40-120
Terry Bowden	40-280

YOUNGEST COACHES TO REACH 200 VICTORIES

Coach	Age in Yrs.-Days
Pop Warner	50-172
Vince Dooley	56-84
Tom Osborne	56-224
Bo Schembechler	57-33
Amos Alonzo Stagg	57-56
Bear Bryant	57-364
*Lou Holtz	58-243

*Active coach.

YOUNGEST COACHES TO REACH 300 VICTORIES

Coach	Age in Yrs.-Days
Pop Warner	63-233
Bear Bryant	67-22
*Bobby Bowden	69-349
*Joe Paterno	71-266
Amos Alonzo Stagg	81-82

*Active coach.

FEWEST GAMES TO REACH 100 VICTORIES

Coach	Career Game (Record at Time)
Gil Dobie	108 (100-5-3)
George Woodruff	109 (100-9-0)
Bud Wilkinson	111 (100-8-3)
Fielding Yost	114 (100-10-4)
Knute Rockne	117 (100-12-5)
Bob Neyland	120 (100-12-8)
Frank Leahy	121 (100-13-8)
*Joe Paterno	122 (100-21-1)
Barry Switzer	122 (100-18-4)
Henry Williams	122 (100-13-9)
*Phillip Fulmer	123 (100-23-0)
Fred Folsom	126 (100-20-6)
Gus Henderson	126 (100-23-3)
Tom Osborne	126 (100-24-2)
Frank Thomas	128 (100-21-7)
Wallace Wade	129 (100-24-5)
Bo Schembechler	130 (100-24-6)
Bobby Dodd	131 (100-28-3)
Steve Spurrier	131 (100-29-2)
Frank Kush	131 (100-30-1)
Charley Moran	131 (100-24-7)
Dan McGugin	132 (100-25-7)
R.C. Slocum	132 (100-30-2)
Jock Sutherland	132 (100-22-10)
Bob Devaney	133 (100-28-5)
Red Blaik	134 (100-25-9)
Jim Wacker	134 (100-33-1)
Tony Knap	135 (100-33-2)
Johnny Vaught	135 (100-29-6)
Morley Jennings	136 (100-33-3)
Bennie Owen	136 (100-28-8)
*John Robinson	136 (100-32-4)
Francis Schmidt	136 (100-27-9)
Dennis Erickson	137 (100-36-1)
Pie Vann	137 (100-36-1)
Frank Broyles	138 (100-36-2)
Carmen Cozza	138 (100-35-3)
Fritz Crisler	138 (100-30-8)
LaVell Edwards	138 (100-37-1)
Dan Devine	139 (100-31-8)
Danny Ford	139 (100-34-5)
John McKay	139 (100-33-6)

*Active coach.

FEWEST GAMES TO REACH 200 VICTORIES

Coach	Career Game (Record at Time)
*Joe Paterno	246 (200-44-2)
Tom Osborne	249 (200-46-3)
Bo Schembechler	262 (200-55-7)
Woody Hayes	268 (200-60-8)
Pop Warner	276 (200-62-14)
LaVell Edwards	277 (200-74-3)
*Bobby Bowden	279 (200-76-3)
Bear Bryant	282 (200-66-16)
Vince Dooley	286 (200-76-10)
Amos Alonzo Stagg	294 (200-74-20)

*Active coach.

FEWEST GAMES TO REACH 300 VICTORIES

Coach	Career Game (Record at Time)
*Joe Paterno	380 (300-77-3)
*Bobby Bowden	389 (300-85-4)
Bear Bryant	393 (300-77-16)
Pop Warner	415 (300-91-24)
Amos Alonzo Stagg	507 (300-173-34)

*Active coach.

All-Time Division I Coaching Longevity Records

(Minimum 10 Head-Coaching Seasons in Division I; Bowl Games Included)

MOST GAMES

Games	Coach, School(s) and Years
548	Amos Alonzo Stagg, Springfield 1890-91, Chicago 1892-1932, Pacific (Cal.) 1933-46
457	Pop Warner, Georgia 1895-96, Cornell 1897-98 and 1904-06, Carlisle 1899-1903 and 1907-14, Pittsburgh 1915-23, Stanford 1924-32, Temple 1933-38
439	*Joe Paterno, Penn St. 1966-02
432	*Bobby Bowden, Samford 1959-62, West Virginia 1970-75, Florida St. 1976-02
425	Bear Bryant, Maryland 1945, Kentucky 1946-53, Texas A&M 1954-57, Alabama 1958-82
420	Hayden Fry, Southern Methodist 1962-72, North Texas 1973-78, Iowa 1979-98
402	Jess Neely, Rhodes 1924-27, Clemson 1931-39, Rice 1940-66
368	Jim Sweeney, Montana St. 1963-67, Washington St. 1968-75, Fresno St. 1976-77 and 1980-96
365	*Lou Holtz, William & Mary 1969-71, North Carolina St. 1972-75, Arkansas 1977-83, Minnesota 1984-85, Notre Dame 1986-96, South Carolina 1999-02
361	LaVell Edwards, Brigham Young 1972-00
344	Eddie Anderson, Loras 1922-24, DePaul 1925-31, Holy Cross 1933-38 and 1950-64, Iowa 1939-42 and 1946-49
338	Don Nehlen, Bowling Green 1968-76, West Virginia 1980-00
332	Johnny Majors, Iowa St. 1968-72, Pittsburgh 1973-76 and 1993-96, Tennessee 1977-92
329	Grant Teaff, McMurry 1960-65, Angelo St. 1969-71, Baylor 1972-92
325	George Welsh, Navy 1973-81, Virginia 1982-00
320	Woody Hayes, Denison 1946-48, Miami (Ohio) 1949-50, Ohio St. 1951-78
318	Ray Morrison, Southern Methodist 1915-16 and 1922-34, Vanderbilt 1918 and 1935-39, Temple 1940-48, Austin 1949-52
312	Warren Woodson, Central Ark. 1935-39, Hardin-Simmons 1941-42 and 1946-51, Arizona 1952-56, New Mexico St. 1958-67, Trinity (Tex.) 1972-73
309	Jerry Claiborne, Virginia Tech 1961-70, Maryland 1972-81, Kentucky 1982-89
307	Tom Osborne, Nebraska 1973-97
307	Bo Schembechler, Miami (Ohio) 1963-68, Michigan 1969-89
301	Bill Mallory, Miami (Ohio) 1969-73, Colorado 1974-78, Northern Ill. 1980-83, Indiana 1984-96
299	Ossie Solem, Luther 1920, Drake 1921-31, Iowa 1932-36, Syracuse 1937-42 and 1944-45, Springfield 1946-57
296	Tuss McLaughry, Westminster (Pa.) 1916, 1918 and 1921, Amherst 1922-25, Brown 1926-40, Dartmouth 1941-54
296	Pappy Waldorf, Oklahoma City 1925-27, Oklahoma St. 1929-33, Kansas St. 1934, Northwestern 1935-46, California 1947-56
295	Frank Howard, Clemson 1940-69
293	Dana X. Bible, Mississippi Col. 1913-15, LSU 1916, Texas A&M 1917 and 1919-28, Nebraska 1929-36, Texas 1937-46
293	Bill Dooley, North Carolina 1967-77, Virginia Tech 1978-86, Wake Forest 1987-92
293	Jim Wacker, Texas Lutheran 1971-75, North Dakota St. 1976-78, Southwest Tex. St. 1979-82, TCU 1983-91, Minnesota 1992-95
292	Lou Little, Georgetown 1924-29, Columbia 1930-56
292	*Jackie Sherrill, Washington St. 1976, Pittsburgh 1977-81, Texas A&M 1982-88, Mississippi St. 1991-02
292	Carl Snavely, Bucknell 1927-33, North Carolina 1934-35 and 1945-52, Cornell 1936-44, Washington (Mo.) 1953-58
288	Vince Dooley, Georgia 1964-88
287	Bob Blackman, Denver 1953-54, Dartmouth 1955-70, Illinois 1971-76, Cornell 1977-82
282	John Cooper, Tulsa 1977-84, Arizona St. 1985-87, Ohio St. 1988-00
282	Clark Shaughnessy, Tulane 1915-20 and 1922-26, Loyola (Ill.) 1927-32, Chicago 1933-39, Stanford 1940-41, Maryland 1942 and 1946, Pittsburgh 1943-45, Hawaii 1965
279	Howard Jones, Syracuse 1908, Yale 1909 and 1913, Ohio St. 1910, Iowa 1916-23, Duke 1924, Southern California 1925-40
278	*Ken Hatfield, Air Force 1979-83, Arkansas 1984-89, Clemson 1990-93, Rice 1994-02
277	Ben Schwartzwalder, Muhlenberg 1946-48, Syracuse 1949-73
276	Larry Smith, Tulane 1976-79, Arizona 1980-86, Southern California 1987-92, Missouri 1994-00
276	Bill Yeoman, Houston 1962-86

Games	Coach, School(s) and Years
275	Dick Tomey, Hawaii 1977-86, Arizona 1986-00
272	John Heisman, Oberlin 1892 and 1894, Akron 1893, Auburn 1895-99, Clemson 1900-03, Georgia Tech 1904-19, Pennsylvania 1920-22, Wash. & Jeff. 1923, Rice 1924-27
271	Dan McGugin, Vanderbilt 1904-17 and 1919-34
271	Chuck Mills, Pomona-Pitzer 1959-61, Indiana (Pa.) 1962-63, Merchant Marine 1964, Utah St. 1967-72, Wake Forest 1973-77, Southern Ore. St. 1980-88, Coast Guard 1997
269	Don Faurot, Truman 1926-34, Missouri 1935-42 and 1946-56
265	Shug Jordan, Auburn 1951-75
263	John Vaught, Mississippi 1947-70 and 1973
260	Jack Curtice, West Tex. A&M 1940-41, UTEP 1946-49, Utah 1950-57, Stanford 1958-61, UC Santa Barb. 1962-69
260	Frank Dobson, Georgia 1909, Clemson 1910-12, Richmond 1913-17 and 1919-33, South Carolina 1918, Maryland 1935-39

*Active coach.

MOST YEARS

Years	Coach, School(s) and Years
57	Amos Alonzo Stagg, Springfield 1890-91, Chicago 1892-1932, Pacific (Cal.) 1933-46
44	Pop Warner, Georgia 1895-96, Cornell 1897-98 and 1904-06, Carlisle 1899-1903 and 1907-14, Pittsburgh 1915-23, Stanford 1924-32, Temple 1933-38
40	Jess Neely, Rhodes 1924-27, Clemson 1931-39, Rice 1940-66
39	Eddie Anderson, Loras 1922-24, DePaul 1925-31, Holy Cross 1933-38 and 1950-54, Iowa 1939-42 and 1946-49
38	Bear Bryant, Maryland 1945, Kentucky 1946-53, Texas A&M 1954-57, Alabama 1958-82
37	*Bobby Bowden, Samford 1959-62, West Virginia 1970-75, Florida St. 1976-02
37	Hayden Fry, Southern Methodist 1962-72, North Texas 1973-78, Iowa 1979-98
37	*Joe Paterno, Penn St. 1966-02
37	Ossie Solem, Luther 1920, Drake 1921-31, Iowa 1932-36, Syracuse 1937-45, Springfield 1946-57
36	John Heisman, Oberlin 1892 and 1894, Akron 1893, Auburn 1895-99, Clemson 1900-03, Georgia Tech 1904-19, Pennsylvania 1920-22, Wash. & Jeff. 1923, Rice 1924-27
34	Tuss McLaughry, Westminster (Pa.) 1916, 1918 and 1921, Amherst 1922-25, Brown 1926-40, Dartmouth 1941-54
34	Ray Morrison, Southern Methodist 1915-16 and 1922-34, Vanderbilt 1918 and 1935-39, Temple 1940-48, Austin 1949-52
33	Dana X. Bible, Mississippi Col. 1913-15, LSU 1916, Texas A&M 1917 and 1919-28, Nebraska 1929-36, Texas 1937-46
33	Gil Dobie, North Dakota St. 1906-07, Washington 1908-16, Navy 1917-19, Cornell 1920-35, Boston College 1936-38
33	Woody Hayes, Denison 1946-48, Miami (Ohio) 1949-50, Ohio St. 1951-78
33	Lou Little, Georgetown 1924-29, Columbia 1930-56
32	Clark Shaughnessy, Tulane 1915-20 and 1922-26, Loyola (Ill.) 1927-32, Chicago 1933-39, Stanford 1940-41, Maryland 1942 and 1946, Pittsburgh 1943-45, Hawaii 1965
32	Carl Snavely, Bucknell 1927-33, North Carolina 1934-35 and 1945-52, Cornell 1936-44, Washington (Mo.) 1953-58
32	William Spaulding, Western Mich. 1907-21, Minnesota 1922-24, UCLA 1925-38
32	Jim Sweeney, Montana St. 1963-67, Washington St. 1968-75, Fresno St. 1976-77 and 1980-96
31	*Lou Holtz, William & Mary 1969-71, North Carolina St. 1972-75, Arkansas 1977-83, Minnesota 1984-85, Notre Dame 1986-96, South Carolina 1999-02
31	Pappy Waldorf, Oklahoma City 1925-27, Oklahoma St. 1929-33, Kansas St. 1934, Northwestern 1935-46, California 1947-56
31	Warren Woodson, Central Ark. 1935-39, Hardin-Simmons 1941-42 and 1946-51, Arizona 1952-56, New Mexico St. 1958-67, Trinity (Tex.) 1972-73
30	Bob Blackman, Denver 1953-54, Dartmouth 1955-70, Illinois 1971-76, Cornell 1977-82
30	Frank Dobson, Georgia 1909, Clemson 1910-12, Richmond 1913-17 and 1919-33, South Carolina 1918, Maryland 1935-39
30	Harvey Harman, Haverford 1922-29, Sewanee 1930, Pennsylvania 1931-37, Rutgers 1938-55
30	Frank Howard, Clemson 1940-69
30	Dan McGugin, Vanderbilt 1904-17 and 1919-34
30	Grant Teaff, McMurry 1960-65, Angelo St. 1969-71, Baylor 1972-92

*Active coach.

MOST SCHOOLS
(Must Have Coached at Least One Division I or Major-College Team)

Schools	Coach, Schools and Years
8	John Heisman, Oberlin 1892 and 1894, Akron 1893, Auburn 1895-99, Clemson 1900-03, Georgia Tech 1904-19, Pennsylvania 1920-22, Wash. & Jeff. 1923, Rice 1924-27
8	Lou Saban, Case Reserve 1950-52, Northwestern 1955, Western Ill. 1957-59, Maryland 1966, Miami (Fla.) 1977-78, Army 1979, UCF 1983-84, Chowan 2001-02
7	*Dennis Franchione, Southwestern (Kan.) 1981-82, Pittsburg St. 1985-89, Southwest Tex. St. 1990-91, New Mexico 1992-97, TCU 1998-00, Alabama 2001-02, Texas A&M 2003

Schools	Coach, Schools and Years
7	Chuck Mills, Pomona-Pitzer 1959-61, Indiana (Pa.) 1962-63, Merchant Marine 1964, Utah St. 1967-72, Wake Forest 1973-77, Southern Ore. St. 1980-88, Coast Guard 1997
7	Darrell Mudra, Adams St. 1959-62, North Dakota St. 1963-65, Arizona 1967-68, Western Ill. 1969-73, Florida St. 1974-75, Eastern Ill. 1978-82, Northern Iowa 1983-87
7	Clark Shaughnessy, Tulane 1915-20 and 1922-26, Loyola (Ill.) 1927-32, Chicago 1933-39, Stanford 1940-41, Maryland 1942 and 1946, Pittsburgh 1943-45, Hawaii 1965
7	Clarence Spears, Dartmouth 1917-20, West Virginia 1921-24, Minnesota 1925-29, Oregon 1930-31, Wisconsin 1932-35, Toledo 1936-42, Maryland 1943-44
6	*Lou Holtz, William & Mary 1969-71, North Carolina St. 1972-75, Arkansas 1977-83, Minnesota 1984-85, Notre Dame 1986-96, South Carolina 1999-02
6	Howard Jones, Syracuse 1908, Yale 1909 and 1913, Ohio St. 1910, Iowa 1916-23, Duke 1924, Southern California 1925-40
6	Pop Warner, Georgia 1895-96, Cornell 1897-98 and 1904-06, Carlisle 1899-1903 and 1907-14, Pittsburgh 1915-23, Stanford 1924-32, Temple 1933-38
5	Matty Bell, Haskell 1920-21, Carroll (Wis.) 1922, TCU 1923-28, Texas A&M 1929-33, Southern Methodist 1935-41 and 1945-49
5	Dana X. Bible, Mississippi Col. 1913-15, LSU 1916, Texas A&M 1917 and 1919-28, Nebraska 1929-36, Texas 1937-46
5	*Watson Brown, Austin Peay 1979-80, Cincinnati 1983, Rice 1984-85, Vanderbilt 1986-90, UAB 1995-02
5	Earle Bruce, Tampa 1972, Iowa St. 1973-78, Ohio St. 1979-87, Northern Iowa 1988, Colorado St. 1989-92
5	Frank Cavanaugh, Cincinnati 1898, Holy Cross 1903-05, Dartmouth 1911-16, Boston College 1919-26, Fordham 1927-32
5	Jack Curtice, West Tex. A&M 1940-41, UTEP 1946-49, Utah 1950-57, Stanford 1958-61, UC Santa Barb. 1962-69
5	Dudley DeGroot, UC Santa Barb. 1926-28, San Jose St. 1932-39, Rochester 1940-43, West Virginia 1948-49, New Mexico 1950-52
5	Gil Dobie, North Dakota St. 1906-07, Washington 1908-16, Navy 1917-19, Cornell 1920-35, Boston College 1936-38
5	Frank Dobson, Georgia 1909, Clemson 1910-12, Richmond 1913-17 and 1919-33, South Carolina 1918, Maryland 1935-39
5	Ed Doherty, Arizona St. 1947-50, Rhode Island 1951, Arizona 1957-58, Xavier (Ohio) 1959-61, Holy Cross 1971-75
5	Red Drew, Trinity (Conn.) 1921-23, Birmingham So. 1924-27, Chattanooga 1929-30, Mississippi 1946, Alabama 1947-54
5	Dennis Erickson, Idaho 1982-85, Wyoming 1986, Washington St. 1987-88, Miami (Fla.) 1989-94, Oregon St. 1999-02
5	Stuart Holcomb, Findlay 1932-35, Muskingum 1936-40, Wash. & Jeff. 1941, Miami (Ohio) 1942-43, Purdue 1947-55
5	Al Molde, Sioux Falls 1971-72, Minn.-Morris 1973-79, Central Mo. St. 1980-82, Eastern Ill. 1983-86, Western Mich. 1987-96
5	Darryl Rogers, Cal St. Hayward 1965, Fresno St. 1966-72, San Jose St. 1973-75, Michigan St. 1976-79, Arizona St. 1980-84
5	John Rowland, Henderson St. 1925-30, Ouachita Baptist 1931, Citadel 1940-42, Oklahoma City 1946-47, George Washington 1948-51
5	Francis Schmidt, Tulsa 1919-21, Arkansas 1922-28, TCU 1929-33, Ohio St. 1934-40, Idaho 1941-42
5	Clipper Smith, Gonzaga 1925-28, Santa Clara 1929-35, Villanova 1936-42, San Francisco 1946, Lafayette 1949-51
5	Ossie Solem, Luther 1920, Drake 1921-31, Iowa 1932-36, Syracuse 1937-45, Springfield 1946-57
5	Skip Stahley, Delaware 1934, Brown 1941-43, George Washington 1946-47, Toledo 1948-49, Idaho 1954-60
5	Jim Wacker, Texas Lutheran 1971-75, North Dakota St. 1976-78, Southwest Tex. St. 1979-82, TCU 1983-91, Minnesota 1992-96
5	Pappy Waldorf, Oklahoma City 1925-27, Oklahoma St. 1929-33, Kansas St. 1934, Northwestern 1935-46, California 1947-56
5	Warren Woodson, Central Ark. 1935-39, Hardin-Simmons 1941-42, Arizona 1952-56, New Mexico St. 1958-67, Trinity (Tex.) 1972-73
5	Fielding Yost, Ohio Wesleyan 1897, Nebraska 1898, Kansas 1899, Stanford 1900, Michigan 1901-23 and 1925-26
4	Eddie Anderson, Loras 1922-24, DePaul 1925-31, Holy Cross 1933-38 and 1950-64, Iowa 1939-42 and 1946-49
4	Charles Bachman, Northwestern 1919, Kansas St. 1920-27, Florida 1928-32, Michigan St. 1933-42 and 1944-46
4	Jerry Berndt, DePauw 1979-80, Pennsylvania 1981-85, Rice 1986-88, Temple 1989-92
4	Bob Blackman, Denver 1953-54, Dartmouth 1955-70, Illinois 1971-76, Cornell 1977-82
4	*Mack Brown, Appalachian St. 1983, Tulane 1985-87, North Carolina 1988-97, Texas 1998-02
4	Bear Bryant, Maryland 1945, Kentucky 1946-53, Texas A&M 1954-57, Alabama 1958-82
4	Pete Elliott, Nebraska 1956, California 1957-59, Illinois 1960-66, Miami (Fla.) 1973-74
4	Wesley Fesler, Wesleyan (Conn.) 1941-42, Pittsburgh 1946, Ohio St. 1947-50, Minnesota 1951-53
4	Mike Gottfried, Murray St. 1978-80, Cincinnati 1981-82, Kansas 1983-85, Pittsburgh 1986-89
4	Harvey Harman, Haverford 1922-29, Sewanee 1930, Pennsylvania 1931-37, Rutgers 1938-55

Schools	Coach, Schools and Years
4	Ken Hatfield, Air Force 1979-83, Arkansas 1984-89, Clemson 1990-93, Rice 1994-02
4	*John Mackovic, Wake Forest 1978-80, Illinois 1988-91, Texas 1992-97, Arizona 2001-02
4	Bill Mallory, Miami (Ohio) 1969-73, Colorado 1974-78, Northern Ill. 1980-83, Indiana 1984-96
4	Tuss McLaughry, Westminster (Pa.) 1916, 1918 and 1921, Amherst 1922-25, Brown 1926-40, Dartmouth 1941-54
4	Joe McMullen, Stetson 1950-51, Wash. & Jeff. 1952-53, Akron 1954-60, San Jose St. 1969-70
4	Bill Meek, Kansas St. 1951-54, Houston 1955-56, Southern Methodist 1957-61, Utah 1968-73
4	Charley Moran, Texas A&M 1909-14, Centre 1919-23, Bucknell 1924-26, Catawba 1930-31
4	Ray Morrison, Southern Methodist 1915-16 and 1922-34, Vanderbilt 1918 and 1935-39, Temple 1940-48, Austin 1949-52
4	Frank Navarro, Williams 1963-67, Columbia 1968-73, Wabash 1974-77, Princeton 1978-84
4	John Pont, Miami (Ohio) 1956-62, Yale 1963-64, Indiana 1965-72, Northwestern 1973-77
4	Bill Roper, VMI 1903-04, Princeton 1906-08, 1910-11 and 1919-30, Missouri 1909, Swarthmore 1915-16
4	Philip Sarboe, Central Wash. 1941-42, Washington St. 1945-49, Humboldt St. 1951-65, Hawaii 1966
4	George Sauer, New Hampshire 1937-41, Kansas 1946-47, Navy 1948-49, Baylor 1950-55
4	Jackie Sherrill, Washington St. 1976, Pittsburgh 1977-81, Texas A&M 1982-88, Mississippi St. 1991-02
4	Steve Sloan, Vanderbilt 1973-74, Texas Tech 1975-77, Mississippi 1978-82, Duke 1983-86
4	*John L. Smith, Idaho 1989-94, Utah St. 1995-97, Louisville 1998-02, Michigan St. 2003
4	Larry Smith, Tulane 1976-79, Arizona 1980-86, Southern California 1987-92, Missouri 1994-00
4	Carl Snavely, Bucknell 1927-33, North Carolina 1934-35 and 1945-52, Cornell 1936-44, Washington (Mo.) 1953-58
4	Denny Stolz, Alma 1965-70, Michigan St. 1973-75, Bowling Green 1977-85, San Diego St. 1986-88

*Active coach.

MOST YEARS COACHED AT ONE COLLEGE
(Minimum 15 Years)

Coach, College (Years)	Years	School W-L-T	Overall W-L-T
Amos Alonzo Stagg, Chicago (1892-1932)	41	244-111-27	314-199-35
*Joe Paterno, Penn St. (1966-02)	37 #	336-100-3	336-100-3
Frank Howard, Clemson (1940-69)	30 #	165-118-12	165-118-12
Dan McGugin, Vanderbilt (1904-17, 1919-34)	30 #	197-55-19	197-55-19
LaVell Edwards, Brigham Young (1972-00)	29 #	257-101-3	257-101-3
Robert Zuppke, Illinois (1913-41)	29 #	131-81-13	131-81-13
Woody Hayes, Ohio St. (1951-78)	28	205-61-10	238-72-10
*Bobby Bowden, Florida St. (1976-02)	27	259-64-4	332-96-4
Lou Little, Columbia (1930-56)	27	110-116-10	151-128-13
Jess Neely, Rice (1940-66)	27	144-124-10	207-176-19
William Alexander, Georgia Tech (1920-44)	25 #	134-95-15	134-95-15
Ike Armstrong, Utah (1925-49)	25 #	140-55-15	140-55-15
Bear Bryant, Alabama (1958-82)	25	232-46-9	323-85-17
Vince Dooley, Georgia (1964-88)	25 #	201-77-10	201-77-10
Ralph Jordan, Auburn (1951-75)	25 #	176-83-6	176-83-6
Tom Osborne, Nebraska (1973-97)	25 #	255-49-3	255-49-3
Ben Schwartzwalder, Syracuse (1949-73)	25	153-91-3	178-96-3
John Vaught, Mississippi (1947-70, 1973)	25 #	190-61-12	190-61-12
Bill Yeoman, Houston (1962-86)	25 #	160-108-8	160-108-8
Fielding Yost, Michigan (1901-23, 1925-26)	25	165-29-10	196-36-12
Edward Robinson, Brown (1898-1901, 1904-07, 1910-25)	24	140-82-12	157-88-13
Frank Camp, Louisville (1946-68)	23 #	118-96-2	118-96-2
Wally Butts, Georgia (1939-60)	22 #	140-86-9	140-86-9
Bobby Dodd, Georgia Tech (1945-66)	22 #	165-64-8	165-64-8
Frank Kush, Arizona St. (1958-79)	22 #	176-54-1	176-54-1
Bennie Owen, Oklahoma (1905-26)	22	122-54-16	155-60-19
Henry Williams, Minnesota (1900-21)	22	140-33-11	141-34-12
Eddie Anderson, Holy Cross (1933-38, 1950-64)	21	129-67-8	201-128-15
Don Nehlen, West Virginia (1980-00)	21	149-93-4	202-128-8
Bob Neyland, Tennessee (1926-34, 1936-40, 1946-52)	21 #	173-31-12	173-31-12
Bo Schembechler, Michigan (1969-89)	21	194-48-5	234-65-8
Grant Teaff, Baylor (1972-92)	21	128-105-6	170-151-8
Terry Donahue, UCLA (1976-95)	20 #	151-74-8	151-74-8
Hayden Fry, Iowa (1979-98)	20	143-89-6	232-178-10
Bill Hess, Ohio (1958-77)	20 #	107-92-4	107-92-4
Ben Martin, Air Force (1958-77)	20	96-103-9	102-116-10
Darrell Royal, Texas (1957-76)	20	167-47-5	184-60-5
Pie Vann, Southern Miss. (1949-68)	20 #	139-59-2	139-59-2
Chris Ault, Nevada (1976-92, 1994-95)	19 #	163-63-1	163-63-1

Coach, College (Years)	Years	School W-L-T	Overall W-L-T
Frank Broyles, Arkansas (1958-76)	19	144-58-5	149-62-6
*Fisher DeBerry, Air Force (1984-02)	19 #	149-83-1	149-83-1
Robert Higgins, Penn St. (1930-48)	19	91-57-10	123-79-18
Jim Sweeney, Fresno St. (1976-77, 1980-96)	19	143-75-3	200-154-4
George Welsh, Virginia (1982-00)	19	134-86-3	189-132-4
Red Blaik, Army (1941-58)	18	121-33-10	166-48-14
Rich Brooks, Oregon (1977-94)	18 #	91-109-4	91-109-4
Ray Eliot, Illinois (1942-59)	18	83-73-11	102-82-13
Don James, Washington (1975-92)	18	151-59-2	176-78-3
Charlie McClendon, LSU (1962-79)	18 #	137-59-7	137-59-7
Jim Owens, Washington (1957-74)	18 #	99-82-6	99-82-6
Murray Warmath, Minnesota (1954-71)	18	87-78-7	97-84-10
Earle Edwards, North Carolina St. (1954-70)	17 #	77-88-8	77-88-8
Johnny Majors, Tennessee (1977-92)	17	120-69-8	185-137-10
Bud Wilkinson, Oklahoma (1947-63)	17 #	145-29-4	145-29-4
*Frank Beamer, Virginia Tech (1987-02)	16	117-69-2	159-92-4
Bob Blackman, Dartmouth (1955-70)	16	104-37-3	168-112-7
Len Casanova, Oregon (1951-66)	16	82-73-8	104-94-11
Herb Deromedi, Central Mich. (1978-93)	16 #	110-55-10	110-55-10
Gil Dobie, Cornell (1920-35)	16	82-36-7	180-45-15
Rip Engle, Penn St. (1950-65)	16	104-48-4	132-68-8
Andy Gustafson, Miami (Fla.) (1948-63)	16	93-65-3	115-78-4
John Heisman, Georgia Tech (1904-19)	16	102-29-6	185-70-17
Howard Jones, Southern California (1925-40)	16	121-36-13	194-64-21
John McKay, Southern California (1960-75)	16 #	127-40-8	127-40-8
Barry Switzer, Oklahoma (1973-88)	16 #	157-29-4	157-29-4
Wallace Wade, Duke (1931-41, 1946-50)	16	110-36-7	171-49-10
Rex Enright, South Carolina (1938-42, 1946-55)	15 #	64-69-7	64-69-7
Morley Jennings, Baylor (1926-40)	15	83-60-6	153-75-18
Ray Morrison, Southern Methodist (1915-16, 1922-34)	15	84-44-22	155-130-33
Bill Murray, Duke (1951-65)	15	83-51-9	142-67-11
Jock Sutherland, Pittsburgh (1924-38)	15	111-20-12	144-28-14
Frank Thomas, Alabama (1931-42, 1944-46)	15	115-24-7	141-33-9

*Active coach. #Never coached at any other college.

Active Coaching Longevity Records
(Minimum Five Years as a Division I-A Head Coach; Includes Bowl Games)

MOST GAMES

Games	Coach, School(s) and Years
439	Joe Paterno, Penn St., 1966-02
432	Bobby Bowden, Samford 1959-62, West Virginia 1970-75, Florida St. 1976-02
365	Lou Holtz, William & Mary 1969-71, North Carolina St. 1972-75, Arkansas 1977-83, Minnesota 1984-85, Notre Dame 1986-96, South Carolina 1999-02
293	Jackie Sherrill, Washington St. 1976, Pittsburgh 1977-81, Texas A&M 1982-88, Mississippi St. 1991-02
278	Ken Hatfield, Air Force 1979-83, Arkansas 1984-89, Clemson 1990-93, Rice 1994-02
255	Frank Beamer, Murray St. 1981-86, Virginia Tech 1987-02

MOST YEARS

Years	Coach, School(s) and Years
37	Bobby Bowden, Samford 1959-62, West Virginia 1970-75, Florida St. 1976-02
37	Joe Paterno, Penn St. 1966-02
31	Lou Holtz, William & Mary 1969-71, North Carolina St. 1972-75, Arkansas 1977-83, Minnesota 1984-85, Notre Dame 1986-96, South Carolina 1999-02
25	Jackie Sherrill, Washington St. 1976, Pittsburgh 1977-81, Texas A&M 1982-88, Mississippi St. 1991-02
24	Ken Hatfield, Air Force 1979-83, Arkansas 1984-89, Clemson 1990-93, Rice 1994-02
22	Frank Beamer, Murray St. 1981-86, Virginia Tech 1987-02
20	Dennis Franchione, Southwestern (Kan.) 1981-82, Pittsburg St. 1985-89, Southwest Tex. St. 1990-91, New Mexico 1992-97, TCU 1998-00, Alabama 2001-02, Texas A&M 2003

MOST YEARS AT CURRENT SCHOOL

Years	Coach, School and Years
37	Joe Paterno, Penn St. 1966-02
27	Bobby Bowden, Florida St. 1976-02
19	Fisher DeBerry, Air Force 1984-02

MOST SCHOOLS

Schools	Coach, Schools and Years
7	Dennis Franchione, Southwestern (Kan.) 1981-82, Pittsburg St. 1985-89, Southwest Tex. St. 1990-91, New Mexico 1992-97, TCU 1998-00, Alabama 2001-02, Texas A&M 2003
6	Lou Holtz, William & Mary 1969-71, North Carolina St. 1972-75, Arkansas 1977-83, Minnesota 1984-85, Notre Dame 1986-96, South Carolina 1999-02

COACHING RECORDS

Schools	Coach, Schools and Years
5	Watson Brown, Austin Peay 1979-80, Cincinnati 1983, Rice 1984-85, Vanderbilt 1986-90, UAB 1995-02
4	Mack Brown, Appalachian St. 1983, Tulane 1985-87, North Carolina 1988-97, Texas 1998-02
4	Ken Hatfield, Air Force 1979-83, Arkansas 1984-89, Clemson 1990-93, Rice 1994-02

Schools	Coach, Schools and Years
4	John Mackovic, Wake Forest 1978-80, Illinois 1988-91, Texas 1992-97, Arizona 2001-02
4	Jackie Sherrill, Washington St. 1976, Pittsburgh 1977-81, Texas A&M 1982-88, Mississippi St. 1991-02

Major-College Brother vs. Brother Coaching Matchups

(Thanks to Tex Noel of Bedford, Indiana)
(Each brother's victories in parentheses)

Mack Brown, Tulane (2), vs. Watson, Vanderbilt (0), 1986-87

Vince Dooley, Georgia (1), vs. Bill, North Carolina (0), 1971 Gator Bowl

Bump Elliott, Michigan (6), vs. Pete, Illinois (1), 1960-66

Howard Jones, Yale 1909 and Iowa 1922 (2), vs. Tad, Syracuse 1909 and Yale 1922 (0)

Pop Warner, Cornell (0) vs. Bill, Colgate (0) (tie), 1906

Annual Division I-A Head-Coaching Changes

Year	Changes	Teams	Pct.
1947	27	125	.216
1948	24	121	.198
1949	22	114	.193
1950	23	119	.193
1951	23	115	.200
1952	15	113	.133
1953	18	111	.162
1954	14	103	.136
1955	23	103	.223
1956	19	105	.181
1957	22	108	.204
1958	18	109	.165
1959	18	110	.164
1960	18	114	.158
1961	11	112	.098
1962	20	119	.168
1963	12	118	.102
1964	14	116	.121
1965	16	114	.140
1966	16	116	.138
1967	21	114	.184
1968	14	114	.123
1969	22	118	.186
1970	13	118	.110
1971	27	119	.227
1972	17	121	.140
1973	36	126	†.286
1974	28	128	.219
1975	18	134	.134
1976	23	137	.168
1977	27	144	.188
1978	27	139	.194
1979	26	139	.187
1980	27	139	.194
1981	17	137	.123
1982	17	97	.175
1983	22	105	.210
1984	16	105	.152
1985	15	105	.143
1986	22	105	.210
1987	24	104	.231
1988	9	104	.087
1989	19	106	.179
1990	20	106	.189
1991	16	106	.151
1992	16	107	.150
1993	15	106	.142
1994	15	107	.140
1995	21	108	.194
1996	9	111	*.081
1997	24	112	.214
1998	14	112	.125
1999	20	114	.175
2000	14	114	.123
2001	24	115	.209
2002	13	117	.111
2003	18	117	.154

*Record low. †Record high.

Records of Division I-A First-Year Head Coaches

(Coaches with no previous head-coaching experience at a four-year college.)

Year	No.	Won	Lost	Tied	Pct.	Bowl Record	Won	Lost	Tied	Pct.	Bowl Record
								Team's Previous Season Record			
1948	14	56	68	7	.454	0-1	76	52	8	.588	2-1
1949	8	26	49	3	.353	0-1	35	41	4	.463	0-0
1950	10	37	56	4	.402	0-0	49	42	6	.536	2-0
1951	13	60	67	4	.473	1-2	39	88	7	.317	1-1
1952	8	31	42	3	.428	0-0	38	40	0	.487	0-0
1953	8	29	45	5	.399	0-0	48	28	7	.620	1-2
1954	8	31	43	4	.423	0-0	40	33	7	.543	1-0
1955	9	36	50	4	.422	0-1	36	52	1	.410	0-0
1956	14	47	80	11	.380	1-0	61	68	6	.474	0-1
1957	9	32	50	6	.398	0-0	44	42	2	.511	0-0
1958	7	26	44	0	.371	0-0	37	31	2	.543	0-0
1959	8	34	43	2	.443	0-0	41	35	2	.538	0-1
1960	14	54	80	5	.406	0-0	57	78	2	.423	0-0
1961	8	26	50	0	.342	0-0	38	38	2	.500	0-0
1962	12	40	74	4	.356	2-0	52	66	2	.442	1-1
1963	8	23	49	6	.333	0-0	32	46	1	.411	0-1
1964	12	45	67	7	.408	1-1	42	71	4	.376	0-0
1965	8	28	47	2	.377	0-0	36	42	1	.462	0-0
1966	10	46	50	3	.480	0-0	38	56	5	.409	0-0
1967	18	58	114	5	.342	1-0	60	116	4	.344	0-1
1968	6	19	40	1	.325	0-0	20	38	2	.350	0-0
1969	15	49	90	1	.353	0-0	62	85	3	.423	0-1
1970	10	45	61	1	.425	1-0	46	54	0	.460	0-2
1971	12	57	72	0	.442	1-1	64	61	0	.512	0-1
1972	11	57	64	1	.471	1-0	53	64	2	.454	1-0
1973	14	84	63	8	.568	1-0	83	71	2	.538	3-0
1974	17	63	116	5	.356	1-0	78	105	1	.427	1-0
1975	10	38	72	0	.345	0-1	43	67	0	.391	0-0
1976	15	57	109	2	.345	3-1	72	91	5	.443	3-1
1977	14	55	94	5	.373	1-0	66	88	3	.430	0-2
1978	16	68	104	3	.397	0-0	77	96	3	.446	0-1
1979	11	53	66	3	.447	0-0	66	57	1	.536	2-2
1980	12	54	75	2	.420	0-0	60	68	3	.469	1-0
1981	6	25	40	0	.385	0-0	31	35	1	.470	0-1
1982	10	51	59	1	.464	0-1	58	57	2	.504	2-2
1983	12	51	82	2	.385	1-0	60	73	1	.451	1-1
1984	7	47	28	1	*.625	2-1	45	35	1	.562	3-0
1985	5	19	37	0	.339	0-0	20	32	4	.393	0-0
1986	12	53	81	0	.396	0-1	56	76	3	.426	1-1
1987	9	51	49	3	.510	1-1	52	50	1	.510	0-2
1988	4	25	20	0	.556	1-0	22	23	1	.489	1-1
1989	7	32	49	1	.396	0-2	39	43	0	.476	1-2
1990	9	46	42	2	.522	1-1	41	48	1	.461	0-1
1991	10	38	72	1	.347	1-0	46	64	2	.420	1-1
1992	4	15	20	1	.431	0-0	32	14	0	.696	1-1
1993	8	29	58	2	.337	0-1	41	51	1	.446	2-2
1994	7	30	40	2	.431	2-1	40	39	0	.506	1-0
1995	10	57	56	2	.504	1-2	45	65	3	.412	2-1
1996	6	27	42	0	.391	1-1	29	38	1	.434	0-1
1997	11	47	79	0	.373	0-1	56	70	0	.444	1-1
1998	9	44	59	0	.427	0-2	52	52	0	.500	1-2
1999	8	40	51	0	.440	1-1	34	55	0	.382	0-0
2000	8	39	54	0	.419	1-2	41	49	0	.456	0-0
2001	12	72	67	0	.518	2-2	68	68	0	.500	2-0
2002	6	27	47	0	.365	0-1	24	43	0	.358	1-0

*Record percentage for first-year coaches. 1984 coaches and their records, with bowl game indicated by an asterisk (*): Pat Jones, Oklahoma St. (*10-2-0); Galen Hall, Florida (8-0-0, took over from Charley Pell after three games); Bill Arnsparger, LSU (8-*3-1); Fisher DeBerry, Air Force (*8-4-0); Dick Anderson, Rutgers (7-3-0); Mike Sheppard, Long Beach St. (4-7-0); Ron Chismar, Wichita St. (2-9-0).

Most Victories by Division I-A First-Year Head Coaches

Coach, College, Year	W	L	T
Larry Coker, Miami (Fla.), 2001	*12	0	0
Gary Blackney, Bowling Green, 1991	*11	0	0
John Robinson, Southern California, 1976	*11	1	0
Bill Battle, Tennessee, 1970	*11	1	0
Dick Crum, Miami (Ohio), 1974	*10	0	1

Coach, College, Year	W	L	T
Barry Switzer, Oklahoma, 1973	10	0	1
John Jenkins, Houston, 1990	10	1	0
Dwight Wallace, Ball St., 1978	10	1	0
Chuck Fairbanks, Oklahoma, 1967	*10	1	0
Mike Archer, LSU, 1987	*10	1	1
Ralph Friedgen, Maryland, 2001	10	2	0
Tom Amstutz, Toledo, 2001	*10	2	0
Rick Neuheisel, Colorado, 1995	*10	2	0
Curley Hallman, Southern Miss., 1988	*10	2	0
Pat Jones, Oklahoma St., 1984	*10	2	0
Earle Bruce, Tampa, 1972	*10	2	0
Billy Kinard, Mississippi, 1971	*10	2	0

*Bowl game victory included.
Only first-year coaches to win a national championship: Bennie Oosterbaan, Michigan, 1948 (9-0-0); Larry Coker, Miami (Fla.), 2001 (12-0-0).

Division I-AA Coaching Records

Winningest Active Division I-AA Coaches

(Minimum five years as Division I-A and/or Division I-AA head coach; record at four-year colleges only.)

BY PERCENTAGE

Coach, College	Years	Won	Lost	Tied	†Pct.	#Postseason W-L-T
Mike Kelly, Dayton	22	206	41	1	.83266	13-8-0
Greg Gattuso, Duquesne	10	82	25	0	.76636	0-0-0
Al Bagnoli, Pennsylvania	21	163	51	0	.76168	7-6-0
Pete Richardson, Southern U.	15	126	47	1	.72701	0-3-0
Joe Gardi, Hofstra	13	105	42	2	.71141	4-6-0
Billy Joe, Florida A&M	29	228	94	4	.70552	3-6-0
Joe Taylor, Hampton	20	153	64	4	.70136	1-7-0
Walt Hameline, Wagner	22	157	71	2	.68696	4-2-0
Joe Walton, Robert Morris	9	61	28	1	.68333	0-0-0
Dick Biddle, Colgate	7	54	26	0	.67500	0-3-0
Alvin Wyatt, Bethune-Cookman	6	45	22	0	.67164	0-2-0
Doug Williams, Grambling	6	46	23	0	.66667	0-0-0
Mark Whipple, Massachusetts	15	110	57	0	.65868	8-3-0
Jack Siedlecki, Yale	15	88	49	2	.64029	0-1-0
Phil Estes, Brown	5	31	18	0	.63265	0-0-0
Rob Ash, Drake	23	145	85	5	.62766	0-0-0
Andy Talley, Villanova	23	152	91	2	.62449	4-7-0
Hal Mumme, Southeastern La.	12	85	53	1	.61511	2-2-0
Tim Stowers, Rhode Island	9	65	43	0	.60185	6-2-0
Tim Walsh, Portland St.	14	93	62	0	.60000	2-4-0

Coach, College	Years	Won	Lost	Tied	†Pct.	#Postseason W-L-T
Bob Benson, Georgetown	10	61	41	0	.59804	0-0-0
Jimmye Laycock, William & Mary	23	154	105	2	.59387	2-6-0
L.C. Cole, Alabama St.	7	48	33	0	.59259	0-2-0
Jim Parady, Marist	11	64	46	1	.58108	0-0-0
Jerry Moore, Appalachian St.	21	142	103	2	.57895	6-10-0
Ron Randleman, Sam Houston St.	34	205	155	6	.56831	1-3-0
Randy Ball, Southwest Mo. St.	13	84	65	1	.56333	3-4-0
Gordy Combs, Towson	11	64	50	0	.56140	0-0-0
Bob Spoo, Eastern Ill.	16	101	81	1	.55464	1-6-0
Matt Ballard, Morehead St.	15	84	68	1	.55229	0-0-0
Lee Hardman, Ark.-Pine Bluff	10	60	50	0	.54545	0-0-0
Denver Johnson, Illinois St.	6	36	30	0	.54545	0-0-0
Jerome Souers, Northern Ariz.	5	31	26	0	.54386	0-2-0
Howard Schellenberger, Fla. Atlantic	18	106	92	3	.53483	0-0-0
Jim Reid, Richmond	14	82	73	3	.52848	1-4-0
Mike Hennigan, Tennessee Tech	7	40	36	0	.52632	0-0-0
Paul Schudel, Central Conn. St.	12	67	61	4	.52273	0-2-0
Bill Thomas, Texas Southern	14	79	72	3	.52273	1-1-0
Mike Ayers, Wofford	18	101	96	2	.51256	0-2-0
Kevin Callahan, Monmouth	10	49	47	0	.51042	0-0-0
John Lyons, Dartmouth	11	54	54	1	.50000	0-0-0
Paul Hamilton, East Tenn. St.	6	33	34	0	.49254	0-0-0
Jack Cosgrove, Maine	10	56	58	0	.49123	2-2-0
Tim Murphy, Harvard	16	81	85	1	.48802	0-1-0
Kevin McGarry, San Diego	7	34	36	0	.48571	0-0-0
Mike Kramer, Montana St.	9	49	55	0	.47115	2-2-0
Fred Mariani, Iona	5	22	29	0	.43137	0-0-0
Steve Gilbert, Jacksonville	14	59	79	0	.42754	0-1-0
Dan Allen, Holy Cross	13	61	85	0	.41781	1-2-0
Tom Horne, Valparaiso	17	71	104	2	.40678	0-0-0
Jerry Graybeal, Weber St.	5	22	33	0	.40000	0-0-0
Johnny Thomas, Alcorn St.	5	20	34	0	.37037	0-0-0
Jack Crowe, Jacksonville St.	8	28	48	0	.36842	0-0-0
John Volek, Sacramento St.	8	31	57	1	.35393	0-0-0
Tim McGuire, Indiana St.	7	24	54	0	.30769	0-0-0

Less than five years as Division I-A and/or Division I-AA head coach (school followed by years in Division I-A or I-AA, includes record at all four-year colleges):

Coach, College	Years	Won	Lost	Tied	†Pct.	#Postseason W-L-T
David Bennett, Coastal Caro. (0)	7	63	17	0	.78750	4-3-0
K.C. Keeler, Delaware (1)	10	94	27	1	.77459	21-7-0
Steve Patton, Gardner-Webb (1)	11	72	44	1	.61966	0-0-0
Manny Matsakis, Southwest Tex. St. (0)	5	26	18	0	.59091	0-0-0
Robert Ford, Albany (N.Y.) (4)	34	194	137	1	.58584	1-1-0
Jerry Kill, Southern Ill. (2)	9	54	43	0	.55670	0-0-0
Al Seagraves, Elon (4)	7	38	39	0	.49351	0-0-0
Sam Kornhauser, Stony Brook (4)	19	88	94	2	.48370	0-0-0
Ken Pettiford, Savannah St. (3)	6	24	41	0	.36923	0-0-0

†Ties computed as half won and half lost. #Includes bowl and playoff games.

BY VICTORIES

(Minimum five years as Division I-A or Division I-AA head coach)

Coach, College	*Wins
Billy Joe, Florida A&M	228
Mike Kelly, Dayton	206
Ron Randleman, Sam Houston St.	205
Al Bagnoli, Pennsylvania	163
Walt Hameline, Wagner	157
Jimmye Laycock, William & Mary	154
Joe Taylor, Hampton	153
Andy Talley, Villanova	152
Rob Ash, Drake	145
Jerry Moore, Appalachian St.	142
Pete Richardson, Southern U.	126
Mark Whipple, Massachusetts	110
Howard Schellenberger, Fla. Atlantic	106
Joe Gardi, Hofstra	105
Mike Ayers, Wofford	101
Bob Spoo, Eastern Ill.	101
K.C. Keeler, Delaware	94
Tim Walsh, Portland St.	93
Jack Siedlecki, Yale	88
Hal Mumme, Southeastern La.	85

Coach, College	*Wins
Randy Ball, Southwest Mo. St.	84
Matt Ballard, Morehead St.	84
Greg Gattuso, Duquesne	82
Jim Reid, Richmond	82
Tim Murphy, Harvard	81
Bill Thomas, Texas Southern	79
Tom Horne, Valparaiso	71
Paul Schudel, Central Conn. St.	67
Tim Stowers, Rhode Island	65
Jim Parady, Marist	64
Gordy Combs, Towson	64
Dan Allen, Holy Cross	61
Bob Benson, Georgetown	61
Joe Walton, Robert Morris	61
Lee Hardman, Ark.-Pine Bluff	60
Steve Gilbert, Jacksonville	59
Jack Cosgrove, Maine	56
Dick Biddle, Colgate	54
John Lyons, Dartmouth	54
Kevin Callahan, Monmouth	49
Mike Kramer, Montana St.	49
L.C. Cole, Alabama St.	48
Doug Williams, Grambling	46
Alvin Wyatt, Bethune-Cookman	45

Bob Spoo of Eastern Illinois topped the 100-win mark in 2002, and took the Panthers to the Division I-AA playoffs for the sixth time.

Eastern Illinois Sports Information

Coach, College	*Wins
Mike Hennigan, Tennessee Tech	40
Denver Johnson, Illinois St.	36
Kevin McGarry, San Diego	34
Paul Hamilton, East Tenn. St.	33
Phil Estes, Brown	31
Jerome Souers, Northern Ariz.	31
John Volek, Sacramento St.	31
Jack Crowe, Jacksonville St.	28
Tim McGuire, Indiana St.	24
Jerry Graybeal, Weber St.	22
Fred Mariani, Iona	22
Johnny Thomas, Alcorn St.	20

*Includes bowls and playoff games.

Annual Division I-AA Head-Coaching Changes

(From the 1982 reorganization of the division for parallel comparisons)

Year	Changes	Teams	Pct.
1982	7	92	.076
1983	17	84	.202
1984	14	87	.161
1985	11	87	.126
1986	18	86	.209
1987	13	87	.149
1988	12	88	.136
1989	21	89	†.236
1990	16	89	.180
1991	6	87	*.069
1992	14	89	.157
1993	13	#115	.113
1994	17	116	.147
1995	11	119	.092
1996	11	116	.095
1997	20	118	.169
1998	14	119	.118
1999	17	122	.139
2000	24	122	.197
2001	12	123	.098
2002	14	122	.115
2003	17	122	.139

*Record low. †Record high. #Twenty-seven teams switched from Divisions II & III to I-AA.

Division I-AA Championship Coaches

All coaches who have coached teams in the Division I-AA championship playoffs since 1978 are listed here with their playoff record, alma mater and year graduated, team, year coached, opponent, and score.

Dan Allen (1-2) (Hanover '78)
Boston U. .... 93 Northern Iowa 27-21 (2 ot)
Boston U. .... 93 Idaho 14-21
Boston U. .... 94 Eastern Ky. 23-30

Pokey Allen (3-1) (Utah '65)
Boise St. .... 94 North Texas 42-20
Boise St. .... 94 Appalachian St. 17-14
Boise St. .... 94 Marshall 28-24
Boise St. .... 94 Youngstown St. 14-28

Terry Allen (6-7) (Northern Iowa '79)
Northern Iowa ...... 90 Boise St. 3-20
Northern Iowa ...... 91 Weber St. 38-21
Northern Iowa ...... 91 Marshall 13-41
Northern Iowa ...... 92 Eastern Wash. 17-14
Northern Iowa ...... 92 McNeese St. 29-7
Northern Iowa ...... 92 Youngstown St. 7-19
Northern Iowa ...... 93 Boston U. 21-27 (2 ot)
Northern Iowa ...... 94 Montana 20-23
Northern Iowa ...... 95 Murray St. 35-34
Northern Iowa ...... 95 Marshall 24-41
Northern Iowa ...... 96 Eastern Ill. 21-14
Northern Iowa ...... 96 William & Mary 38-35
Northern Iowa ...... 96 Marshall 14-31

Dave Arnold (3-0) (Drake '67)
Montana St. .... 84 Arkansas St. 31-24
Montana St. .... 84 Rhode Island 32-20
Montana St. .... 84* Louisiana Tech 19-6

Dave Arslanian (0-1) (Weber St. '72)
Weber St. .... 91 Northern Iowa 21-38

Chris Ault (9-7) (Nevada '68)
Nevada .... 78 Massachusetts 21-44
Nevada .... 79 Eastern Ky. 30-33
Nevada .... 83 Idaho St. 27-20
Nevada .... 83 North Texas 20-17 (ot)
Nevada .... 83 Southern Ill. 7-23
Nevada .... 85 Arkansas St. 24-23
Nevada .... 85 Furman 12-35
Nevada .... 86 Idaho 27-7
Nevada .... 86 Tennessee St. 33-6
Nevada .... 86 Ga. Southern 38-48
Nevada .... 90 La.-Monroe 27-14
Nevada .... 90 Furman 42-35 (3 ot)
Nevada .... 90 Boise St. 59-52 (3 ot)
Nevada .... 90 Ga. Southern 13-36
Nevada .... 91 McNeese St. 22-16
Nevada .... 91 Youngstown St. 28-30

Stephen Axman (0-1) (C.W. Post '69)
Northern Ariz. ..... 96 Furman 31-42

Randy Ball (3-4) (Truman '73)
Western Ill. .... 91 Marshall 17-20 (ot)
Western Ill. .... 96 Murray St. 6-34
Western Ill. .... 97 Jackson St. 31-24
Western Ill. .... 97 McNeese St. 12-14
Western Ill. .... 98 Montana 52-9
Western Ill. .... 98 Florida A&M 24-21
Western Ill. .... 98 Ga. Southern 14-42

Darren Barbier (0-1) (Nicholls St. '82)
Nicholls St. .... 96 Montana 3-48

Frank Beamer (0-1) (Virginia Tech '69)
Murray St. .... 86 Eastern Ill. 21-28

Todd Berry (2-2) (Tulsa '83)
Illinois St. .... 98 Northwestern St. 28-48
Illinois St. .... 99 Colgate 56-13
Illinois St. .... 99 Hofstra 37-20
Illinois St. .... 99 Ga. Southern 17-28

Dick Biddle (0-3) (Duke '71)
Colgate .... 97 Villanova 28-49
Colgate .... 98 Ga. Southern 28-49
Colgate .... 99 Illinois St. 13-56

Larry Blakeney (5-7) (Auburn '70)
Troy St. .... 93 Stephen F. Austin 42-20
Troy St. .... 93 McNeese St. 35-28
Troy St. .... 93 Marshall 21-24
Troy St. .... 94 James Madison 26-45
Troy St. .... 95 Ga. Southern 21-24
Troy St. .... 96 Florida A&M 29-25
Troy St. .... 96 Murray St. 31-3
Troy St. .... 96 Montana 7-70
Troy St. .... 98 Florida A&M 17-27
Troy St. .... 99 James Madison 27-7
Troy St. .... 99 Florida A&M 10-17
Troy St. .... 00 Appalachian St. 30-33

Terry Bowden (2-2) (West Virginia '78)
Samford .... 91 New Hampshire 29-13
Samford .... 91 James Madison 24-21
Samford .... 91 Youngstown St. 0-10
Samford .... 92 Delaware 21-56

Bill Bowes (0-2) (Penn St. '65)
New Hampshire ...... 91 Samford 13-29
New Hampshire ...... 94 Appalachian St. 10-17 (ot)

Jesse Branch (1-2) (Arkansas '64)
Southwest Mo. St. .. 89 Maine 35-8
Southwest Mo. St. .. 89 Stephen F. Austin 25-55
Southwest Mo. St. .. 90 Idaho 35-41

Billy Brewer (1-1) (Mississippi '61)
Louisiana Tech...... 82 South Carolina St. 38-3
Louisiana Tech...... 82 Delaware 0-17

Don Brown (0-1) (Norwich '77)
Northeastern .... 02 Fordham 24-29

James Carson (0-3) (Jackson St. '63)
Jackson St. .... 95 Marshall 8-38
Jackson St. .... 96 William & Mary 6-45
Jackson St. .... 97 Western Ill. 24-31

Rick Carter (0-1) (Earlham '65)
Holy Cross .... 83 Western Caro. 21-28

Marino Casem (0-1) (Xavier [La.] '56)
Alcorn St. .... 84 Louisiana Tech 21-44

Mike Cavan (1-1) (Georgia '72)
East Tenn. St. ..... 96 Villanova 35-29
East Tenn. St. ..... 96 Montana 14-44

George Chaump (4-2) (Bloomsburg '58)
Marshall .... 87 James Madison 41-12
Marshall .... 87 Weber St. 51-23
Marshall .... 87 Appalachian St. 24-10
Marshall .... 87 La.-Monroe 42-43
Marshall .... 88 North Texas 7-0
Marshall .... 88 Furman 9-13

David Clawson (1-1) (Williams '89)
Fordham .... 02 Northeastern 29-24
Fordham .... 02 Villanova 10-24

L.C. Cole (0-2) (Nebraska '80)
Tennessee St........ 98 Appalachian St. 31-45
Tennessee St........ 99 N.C. A&T 10-24

Pat Collins (4-0) (Louisiana Tech '63)
La.-Monroe .... 87 North Texas 30-9
La.-Monroe .... 87 Eastern Ky. 33-32
La.-Monroe .... 87 Northern Iowa 44-41 (ot)
La.-Monroe .... 87* Marshall 43-42

Archie Cooley Jr. (0-1) (Jackson St. '62)
Mississippi Val. ... 84 Louisiana Tech 19-66

Jack Cosgrove (2-2) (Maine '78)
Maine .... 01 McNeese St. 14-10
Maine .... 01 Northern Iowa 28-56
Maine .... 02 Appalachian St. 14-13
Maine .... 02 Ga. Southern 7-31

Bruce Craddock (0-1) (Truman '66)
Western Ill. .... 88 Western Ky. 32-35

Jim Criner (3-1) (Cal Poly Pomona '61)
Boise St. .... 80 Grambling 14-9
Boise St. .... 80* Eastern Ky. 31-29
Boise St. .... 81 Jackson St. 19-7
Boise St. .... 81 Eastern Ky. 17-23

Bill Davis (2-2) (Johnson Smith '65)
South Carolina St. .. 81 Tennessee St. 26-25
South Carolina St. .. 81 Idaho St. 12-41
South Carolina St. .. 82 Furman 17-0
South Carolina St. .. 82 Louisiana Tech 3-38

Rey Dempsey (3-0) (Geneva '58)
Southern Ill. ...... 83 Indiana St. 23-7
Southern Ill. ...... 83 Nevada 23-7
Southern Ill. ...... 83* Western Caro. 43-7

Mick Dennehy (3-4) (Montana '73)
Montana .... 96 Nicholls St. 48-3
Montana .... 96 East Tenn. St. 44-14
Montana .... 96 Troy St. 70-7
Montana .... 96 Marshall 29-49
Montana .... 97 McNeese St. 14-19
Montana .... 98 Western Ill. 9-52
Montana .... 99 Youngstown St. 27-30

Jim Dennison (0-1) (Wooster '60)
Akron .... 85 Rhode Island 27-35

Jim Donnan (15-4) (North Carolina St. '67)
Marshall .... 91 Western Ill. 20-17 (ot)
Marshall .... 91 Northern Iowa 41-13
Marshall .... 91 Eastern Ky. 14-7
Marshall .... 91 Youngstown St. 17-25
Marshall .... 92 Eastern Ky. 44-0
Marshall .... 92 Middle Tenn. 35-21
Marshall .... 92 Delaware 28-7
Marshall .... 92* Youngstown St. 31-28
Marshall .... 93 Howard 28-14
Marshall .... 93 Delaware 34-31
Marshall .... 93 Troy St. 24-21
Marshall .... 93 Youngstown St. 5-17
Marshall .... 94 Middle Tenn. 49-14
Marshall .... 94 James Madison 28-21 (ot)
Marshall .... 94 Boise St. 24-28
Marshall .... 95 Jackson St. 38-8
Marshall .... 95 Northern Iowa 41-24
Marshall .... 95 McNeese St. 25-13
Marshall .... 95 Montana 20-22

Boots Donnelly (6-7) (Middle Tenn. '65)
Middle Tenn. .... 84 Eastern Ky. 27-10
Middle Tenn. .... 84 Indiana St. 42-41 (3 ot)
Middle Tenn. .... 84 Louisiana Tech 13-21
Middle Tenn. .... 85 Ga. Southern 21-28
Middle Tenn. .... 89 Appalachian St. 24-21
Middle Tenn. .... 89 Ga. Southern 3-45
Middle Tenn. .... 90 Jackson St. 28-7
Middle Tenn. .... 90 Boise St. 13-20
Middle Tenn. .... 91 Sam Houston St. 20-19 (ot)
Middle Tenn. .... 91 Eastern Ky. 13-23
Middle Tenn. .... 92 Appalachian St. 35-10
Middle Tenn. .... 92 Marshall 21-35
Middle Tenn. .... 94 Marshall 14-49

Larry Donovan (0-1) (Nebraska '64)
Montana	82	Idaho 7-21

Fred Dunlap (1-2) (Colgate '50)
Colgate	82	Boston U. 21-7
Colgate	82	Delaware 13-20
Colgate	83	Western Caro. 23-24

Dennis Erickson (1-2) (Montana St. '70)
Idaho	82	Montana 21-7
Idaho	82	Eastern Ky. 30-38
Idaho	85	Eastern Wash. 38-42

Mark Farley (2-1) (Northern Iowa '86)
Northern Iowa	01	Eastern Ill. 49-43
Northern Iowa	01	Maine 56-28
Northern Iowa	01	Montana 0-38

Mo Forte (0-1) (Minnesota '71)
N.C. A&T	86	Ga. Southern 21-52

Joe Gardi (2-5) (Maryland '60)
Hofstra	95	Delaware 17-38
Hofstra	97	Delaware 14-24
Hofstra	99	Lehigh 27-15
Hofstra	99	Illinois St. 20-37
Hofstra	00	Furman 31-24
Hofstra	00	Ga. Southern 20-48
Hofstra	01	Lehigh 24-27 (ot)

Keith Gilbertson (2-3) (Central Wash. '71)
Idaho	86	Nevada 7-27
Idaho	87	Weber St. 30-59
Idaho	88	Montana 38-19
Idaho	88	Northwestern St. 38-30
Idaho	88	Furman 7-38

Joe Glenn (8-2) (South Dakota '71)
Montana	00	Eastern Ill. 45-13
Montana	00	Richmond 34-20
Montana	00	Appalachian St. 19-16 (ot)
Montana	00	Ga. Southern 25-27
Montana	01	Northwestern St. 28-19
Montana	01	Sam Houston St. 49-24
Montana	01	Northern Iowa 38-0
Montana	01*	Furman 13-6
Montana	02	Northwestern St. 45-14
Montana	02	McNeese St. 20-24

Sam Goodwin (3-3) (Henderson St. '66)
Northwestern St.	88	Boise St. 22-13
Northwestern St.	88	Idaho 30-38
Northwestern St.	97	Eastern Wash. 10-40
Northwestern St.	98	Illinois St. 48-28
Northwestern St.	98	Appalachian St. 31-20
Northwestern St.	98	Massachusetts 31-41

W.C. Gorden (0-9) (Tennessee St. '52)
Jackson St.	78	Florida A&M 10-15
Jackson St.	81	Boise St. 7-19
Jackson St.	82	Eastern Ill. 13-16 (ot)
Jackson St.	85	Ga. Southern 0-27
Jackson St.	86	Tennessee St. 23-32
Jackson St.	87	Arkansas St. 32-35
Jackson St.	88	Stephen F. Austin 0-24
Jackson St.	89	Montana 7-48
Jackson St.	90	Middle Tenn. 7-28

Mike Gottfried (0-1) (Morehead St. '66)
Murray St.	79	Lehigh 9-28

Lynn Graves (%3-1) (Stephen F. Austin '65)
Stephen F. Austin	89%	Grambling 59-56
Stephen F. Austin	89%	Southwest Mo. St. 55-25
Stephen F. Austin	89%	Furman 21-19
Stephen F. Austin	89%	Ga. Southern 34-37

Bob Griffin (2-3) (Southern Conn. St. '63)
Rhode Island	81	Idaho St. 0-51
Rhode Island	84	Richmond 23-17
Rhode Island	84	Montana 20-32
Rhode Island	85	Akron 35-27
Rhode Island	85	Furman 15-59

Skip Hall (2-2) (Concordia-M'head '66)
Boise St.	88	Northwestern St. 13-22
Boise St.	90	Northern Iowa 20-3
Boise St.	90	Middle Tenn. 20-13
Boise St.	90	Nevada 52-59 (3 ot)

Jack Harbaugh (6-3) (Bowling Green '61)
Western Ky.	97	Eastern Ill. 42-14
Western Ky.	97	Eastern Wash. 21-38
Western Ky.	00	Florida A&M 27-0
Western Ky.	00	Appalachian St. 14-17
Western Ky.	01	Furman 20-24
Western Ky.	02	Murray St. 59-20
Western Ky.	02	Western Ill. 31-28
Western Ky.	02	Ga. Southern 31-28
Western Ky.	02*	McNeese St. 34-14

Bill Hayes (1-2) (N.C. Central '64)
N.C. A&T	92	Citadel 0-44
N.C. A&T	99	Tennessee St. 24-10
N.C. A&T	99	Youngstown St. 3-41

Jim Hess (1-1) (Southeastern Okla. '59)
Stephen F. Austin	88	Jackson St. 24-0
Stephen F. Austin	88	Ga. Southern 6-27

Kevin Higgins (2-3) (West Chester '79)
Lehigh	98	Richmond 24-33
Lehigh	98	Massachusetts 21-27
Lehigh	99	Hofstra 15-27
Lehigh	00	Western Ill. 37-7
Lehigh	00	Delaware 22-47

Skip Holtz (1-1) (Notre Dame '86)
Connecticut	98	Hampton 42-34
Connecticut	98	Ga. Southern 30-52

Rudy Hubbard (2-0) (Ohio St. '68)
Florida A&M	78	Jackson St. 15-10
Florida A&M	78*	Massachusetts 35-28

Sonny Jackson (1-1) (Nicholls St. '63)
Nicholls St.	86	Appalachian St. 28-26
Nicholls St.	86	Ga. Southern 31-55

Billy Joe (3-6) (Villanova '63)
Florida A&M	96	Troy St. 25-29
Florida A&M	97	Ga. Southern 37-52
Florida A&M	98	Troy St. 27-17
Florida A&M	98	Western Ill. 21-24
Florida A&M	99	Appalachian St. 44-29
Florida A&M	99	Troy St. 17-10
Florida A&M	99	Youngstown St. 24-27
Florida A&M	00	Western Ky. 0-27
Florida A&M	01	Ga. Southern 35-60

Bobby Johnson (4-4) (Clemson '73)
Furman	96	Northern Ariz. 42-31
Furman	96	Marshall 0-54
Furman	99	Massachusetts 23-30 (ot)
Furman	00	Hofstra 24-31
Furman	01	Western Ky. 24-20
Furman	01	Lehigh 34-17
Furman	01	Ga. Southern 24-17
Furman	01	Montana 6-13

Paul Johnson (14-3) (Western Caro. '79)
Ga. Southern	97	Florida A&M 52-37
Ga. Southern	97	Delaware 7-16
Ga. Southern	98	Colgate 49-28
Ga. Southern	98	Connecticut 52-30
Ga. Southern	98	Western Ill. 42-14
Ga. Southern	98	Massachusetts 43-55
Ga. Southern	99	Northern Ariz. 72-29
Ga. Southern	99	Massachusetts 38-21
Ga. Southern	99	Illinois St. 28-17
Ga. Southern	99*	Youngstown St. 59-24
Ga. Southern	00	McNeese St. 42-17
Ga. Southern	00	Hofstra 48-20
Ga. Southern	00	Delaware 27-18
Ga. Southern	00*	Montana 27-25
Ga. Southern	01	Florida A&M 60-35
Ga. Southern	01	Appalachian St. 38-24
Ga. Southern	01	Furman 17-24

Cardell Jones (0-2) (Alcorn St. '65)
Alcorn St.	92	La.-Monroe 27-78
Alcorn St.	94	Youngstown St. 20-63

Bobby Keasler (8-7) (La.-Monroe '70)
McNeese St.	91	Nevada 16-22
McNeese St.	92	Idaho 23-20
McNeese St.	92	Northern Iowa 7-29
McNeese St.	93	William & Mary 34-28
McNeese St.	93	Troy St. 28-35
McNeese St.	94	Idaho 38-21
McNeese St.	94	Montana 28-30
McNeese St.	95	Idaho 33-3
McNeese St.	95	Delaware 52-18
McNeese St.	95	Marshall 13-25
McNeese St.	97	Montana 19-14
McNeese St.	97	Western Ill. 14-12
McNeese St.	97	Delaware 23-21
McNeese St.	97	Youngstown St. 9-10
McNeese St.	98	Massachusetts 19-21

Roy Kidd (16-15) (Eastern Ky. '54)
Eastern Ky.	79	Nevada 33-30
Eastern Ky.	79*	Lehigh 30-7
Eastern Ky.	80	Lehigh 23-20
Eastern Ky.	80	Boise St. 29-31
Eastern Ky.	81	Delaware 35-28
Eastern Ky.	81	Boise St. 23-17
Eastern Ky.	81	Idaho St. 23-34
Eastern Ky.	82	Idaho St. 38-30
Eastern Ky.	82	Tennessee St. 13-7
Eastern Ky.	82*	Delaware 17-14
Eastern Ky.	83	Boston U. 20-24
Eastern Ky.	84	Middle Tenn. 10-27
Eastern Ky.	86	Furman 23-10
Eastern Ky.	86	Eastern Ill. 24-22
Eastern Ky.	86	Arkansas St. 10-24
Eastern Ky.	87	Western Ky. 40-17
Eastern Ky.	87	La.-Monroe 32-33
Eastern Ky.	88	Massachusetts 28-17
Eastern Ky.	88	Western Ky. 41-24
Eastern Ky.	88	Ga. Southern 17-21
Eastern Ky.	89	Youngstown St. 24-28
Eastern Ky.	90	Furman 17-45
Eastern Ky.	91	Appalachian St. 14-3
Eastern Ky.	91	Middle Tenn. 23-13
Eastern Ky.	91	Marshall 7-14
Eastern Ky.	92	Marshall 0-44
Eastern Ky.	93	Ga. Southern 12-14
Eastern Ky.	94	Boston U. 30-23
Eastern Ky.	94	Youngstown St. 15-18
Eastern Ky.	95	Montana 0-48
Eastern Ky.	97	Western Ky. 14-42

Jim Koetter (0-1) (Idaho St. '61)
Idaho St.	83	Nevada 20-27

Dave Kragthorpe (3-0) (Utah St. '55)
Idaho St.	81	Rhode Island 51-0
Idaho St.	81	South Carolina St. 41-12
Idaho St.	81*	Eastern Ky. 34-23

Mike Kramer (2-2) (Idaho '77)
Eastern Wash.	97	Northwestern St. 40-10
Eastern Wash.	97	Western Ky. 38-21
Eastern Wash.	97	Youngstown St. 14-25
Montana St.	02	McNeese St. 14-21

Larry Lacewell (6-4) (Ark.-Monticello '59)
Arkansas St.	84	Chattanooga 37-10
Arkansas St.	84	Montana St. 14-31
Arkansas St.	85	Grambling 10-7
Arkansas St.	85	Nevada 23-24
Arkansas St.	86	Sam Houston St. 48-7
Arkansas St.	86	Delaware 55-14
Arkansas St.	86	Eastern Ky. 24-10
Arkansas St.	86	Ga. Southern 21-48
Arkansas St.	87	Jackson St. 35-32
Arkansas St.	87	Northern Iowa 28-49

Bobby Lamb (0-1) (Furman '87)
Furman	02	Villanova 38-45

Jimmye Laycock (2-6) (William & Mary '70)
William & Mary	86	Delaware 17-51
William & Mary	89	Furman 10-24
William & Mary	90	Massachusetts 38-0
William & Mary	90	UCF 38-52
William & Mary	93	McNeese St. 28-34
William & Mary	96	Jackson St. 45-6
William & Mary	96	Northern Iowa 35-38
William & Mary	01	Appalachian St. 27-40

Pete Lembo (1-1) (Georgetown '92)
Lehigh	01	Hofstra 27-24 (ot)
Lehigh	01	Furman 17-34

Tom Lichtenberg (0-1) (Louisville '62)
Maine	89	Southwest Mo. St. 35-38

Mickey Matthews (0-1) (West Tex. A&M '86)
James Madison	99	Troy St. 7-27

Gene McDowell (2-2) (Florida St. '63)
UCF	90	Youngstown St. 20-17
UCF	90	William & Mary 52-38
UCF	90	Ga. Southern 7-44
UCF	93	Youngstown St. 30-56

John Merritt (†1-2) (Kentucky St. '50)
Tennessee St.	81†	South Carolina St. 25-26 (ot)
Tennessee St.	82†	Eastern Ill. 20-19
Tennessee St.	82†	Eastern Ky. 7-13

Al Molde (1-2) (Gust. Adolphus '66)
Eastern Ill.	83	Indiana St. 13-16 (2 ot)
Eastern Ill.	86	Murray St. 28-21
Eastern Ill.	86	Eastern Ky. 22-24

Jerry Moore (6-10) (Baylor '61)
Appalachian St.	89	Middle Tenn. 21-24
Appalachian St.	91	Eastern Ky. 3-14
Appalachian St.	92	Middle Tenn. 10-35
Appalachian St.	94	New Hampshire 17-10 (ot)
Appalachian St.	94	Boise St. 14-17
Appalachian St.	95	James Madison 31-24

Appalachian St. 95   Stephen F. Austin 17-27
Appalachian St. 98   Tennessee St. 45-31
Appalachian St. 98   Northwestern St. 20-31
Appalachian St. 99   Florida A&M 29-44

Appalachian St. 00   Troy St. 33-30
Appalachian St. 00   Western Ky. 17-14
Appalachian St. 00   Montana 16-19 (ot)
Appalachian St. 01   William & Mary 40-27
Appalachian St. 01   Ga. Southern 24-38

Appalachian St. 02   Maine 13-14

Darrell Mudra (4-3) (Peru St. '51)
Eastern Ill. 82   Jackson St. 16-13 (ot)
Eastern Ill. 82   Tennessee St. 19-20
Northern Iowa 85   Eastern Wash. 17-14
Northern Iowa 85   Ga. Southern 33-40
Northern Iowa 87   Youngstown St. 31-28
Northern Iowa 87   Arkansas St. 49-28
Northern Iowa 87   La.-Monroe 41-44 (ot)

Tim Murphy (0-1) (Springfield '78)
Maine 87   Ga. Southern 28-31 (ot)

Corky Nelson (0-3) (Southwest Tex. St. '64)
North Texas 83   Nevada 17-20 (ot)
North Texas 87   La.-Monroe 9-30
North Texas 88   Marshall 0-7

Buddy Nix (0-1) (West Ala. '61)
Chattanooga 84   Arkansas St. 10-37

Houston Nutt (1-2) (Oklahoma St. '81)
Murray St. 95   Northern Iowa 34-35
Murray St. 96   Western Ill. 34-6
Murray St. 96   Troy St. 3-31

Joe Pannunzio (0-1) (Southern Colo. '82)
Murray St. 02   Western Ky. 20-59

Don Patterson (1-2) (Army '73)
Western Ill. 00   Lehigh 7-37
Western Ill. 02   Eastern Ill. 48-9
Western Ill. 02   Western Ky. 28-31

John Pearce (2-2) (Tex. A&M-Commerce '70)
Stephen F. Austin ... 93   Troy St. 20-42
Stephen F. Austin ... 95   Eastern Ill. 34-29
Stephen F. Austin ... 95   Appalachian St. 27-17
Stephen F. Austin ... 95   Montana 14-70

Bob Pickett (1-1) (Maine '59)
Massachusetts 78   Nevada 44-21
Massachusetts 78   Florida A&M 28-35

Mike Price (1-1) (Puget Sound '69)
Weber St. 87   Idaho 59-30
Weber St. 87   Marshall 23-51

Bob Pruett (4-0) (Marshall '65)
Marshall 96   Delaware 59-14
Marshall 96   Furman 54-0
Marshall 96   Northern Iowa 31-14
Marshall .... 96*   Montana 49-29

Joe Purzycki (0-1) (Delaware '71)
James Madison 87   Marshall 12-41

Dennis Raetz (1-2) (Nebraska '68)
Indiana St. 83   Eastern Ill. 16-13 (2 ot)
Indiana St. 83   Southern Ill. 7-23
Indiana St. 84   Middle Tenn. 41-42 (3 ot)

Ron Randleman (1-3) (William Penn '64)
Sam Houston St. 86   Arkansas St. 7-48
Sam Houston St. 91   Middle Tenn. 19-20 (ot)
Sam Houston St. 01   Northern Ariz. 34-31
Sam Houston St. 01   Montana 24-49

Tubby Raymond (11-11) (Michigan '50)
Delaware 81   Eastern Ky. 28-35
Delaware 82   Colgate 20-13
Delaware 82   Louisiana Tech 17-0
Delaware 82   Eastern Ky. 14-17
Delaware 86   William & Mary 51-17
Delaware 86   Arkansas St. 14-55
Delaware 88   Furman 7-34
Delaware 91   James Madison 35-42 (2 ot)
Delaware 92   Samford 56-21
Delaware 92   La.-Monroe 41-18
Delaware 92   Marshall 7-28
Delaware 93   Montana 49-48
Delaware 93   Marshall 31-34
Delaware 95   Hofstra 38-17
Delaware 95   McNeese St. 18-52
Delaware 96   Marshall 14-59
Delaware 97   Hofstra 24-14
Delaware 97   Ga. Southern 16-7
Delaware 97   McNeese St. 21-23

Delaware 00   Portland St. 49-14
Delaware 00   Lehigh 47-22
Delaware 00   Ga. Southern 18-27

Don Read (8-4) (Sacramento St. '59)
Montana 88   Idaho 19-38
Montana 89   Jackson St. 48-7
Montana 89   Eastern Ill. 25-19
Montana 89   Ga. Southern 15-45
Montana 93   Delaware 48-49
Montana 94   Northern Iowa 23-20
Montana 94   McNeese St. 30-28
Montana 94   Youngstown St. 9-28
Montana 95   Eastern Ky. 48-0
Montana 95   Ga. Southern 45-0
Montana 95   Stephen F. Austin 70-14
Montana .... 95*   Marshall 22-20

Jim Reid (1-4) (Maine '73)
Massachusetts 88   Eastern Ky. 17-28
Massachusetts 90   William & Mary 0-38
Richmond 98   Lehigh 23-24
Richmond 00   Youngstown St. 10-3
Richmond 00   Montana 20-34

Dave Roberts (2-5) (Western Caro. '68)
Western Ky. 87   Eastern Ky. 17-40
Western Ky. 88   Western Ill. 35-32
Western Ky. 88   Eastern Ky. 24-41
La.-Monroe 90   Nevada 14-27
La.-Monroe 92   Alcorn St. 78-27
La.-Monroe 92   Delaware 18-41
La.-Monroe 93   Idaho 31-34

Steve Roberts (0-1) (Ouachita Baptist '87)
Northwestern St. 01   Montana 19-28

Eddie Robinson (0-3) (Leland '41)
Grambling 80   Boise St. 9-14
Grambling 85   Arkansas St. 7-10
Grambling 89   Stephen F. Austin 56-59

Erk Russell (16-2) (Auburn '49)
Ga. Southern 85   Jackson St. 27-0
Ga. Southern 85   Middle Tenn. 28-21
Ga. Southern 85   Northern Iowa 40-33
Ga. Southern .... 85*   Furman 44-42
Ga. Southern 86   N.C. A&T 52-21
Ga. Southern 86   Nicholls St. 55-31
Ga. Southern 86   Nevada 48-38
Ga. Southern .... 86*   Arkansas St. 48-21
Ga. Southern 87   Maine 31-28 (ot)
Ga. Southern 87   Appalachian St. 0-19
Ga. Southern 88   Citadel 38-20
Ga. Southern 88   Stephen F. Austin 27-6
Ga. Southern 88   Eastern Ky. 21-17
Ga. Southern 88   Furman 12-17
Ga. Southern 89   Villanova 52-36
Ga. Southern 89   Middle Tenn. 45-3
Ga. Southern 89   Montana 45-15
Ga. Southern .... 89*   Stephen F. Austin 37-34

Jimmy Satterfield (7-3) (South Carolina '62)
Furman 86   Eastern Ky. 10-23
Furman 88   Delaware 21-7
Furman 88   Marshall 13-9
Furman 88   Idaho 38-7
Furman .... 88*   Ga. Southern 17-12
Furman 89   William & Mary 24-10
Furman 89   Youngstown St. 42-23
Furman 89   Stephen F. Austin 19-21
Furman 90   Eastern Ky. 45-17
Furman 90   Nevada 35-42 (3 ot)

Rip Scherer (2-2) (William & Mary '74)
James Madison 91   Delaware 42-35 (2 ot)
James Madison 91   Samford 21-24
James Madison 94   Troy St. 45-26
James Madison 94   Marshall 21-28 (ot)

Mike Sewak (2-1) (Virginia '81)
Ga. Southern 02   Bethune-Cookman 34-0
Ga. Southern 02   Maine 31-7
Ga. Southern 02   Western Ky. 28-31

Dal Shealy (1-2) (Carson-Newman '60)
Richmond 84   Boston U. 35-33
Richmond 84   Rhode Island 17-23
Richmond 87   Appalachian St. 3-20

Dick Sheridan (3-3) (South Carolina '64)
Furman 82   South Carolina St. 0-17
Furman 83   Boston U. 35-16
Furman 83   Western Caro. 7-14
Furman 85   Rhode Island 59-15

Furman 85   Nevada 35-12
Furman 85   Ga. Southern 42-44

Matt Simon (0-1) (Eastern N.M. '76)
North Texas 94   Boise St. 20-24

John L. Smith (3-5) (Weber St. '71)
Idaho 89   Eastern Ill. 21-38
Idaho 90   Southwest Mo. St. 41-35
Idaho 90   Ga. Southern 27-28
Idaho 92   McNeese St. 20-23
Idaho 93   La.-Monroe 34-31
Idaho 93   Boston U. 21-14
Idaho 93   Youngstown St. 16-35
Idaho 94   McNeese St. 21-38

Jerome Souers (^0-2) (Oregon '83)
Northern Ariz. .... 99^   Ga. Southern 29-72
Northern Ariz. 01   Sam Houston St. 31-34

Bob Spoo (1-6) (Purdue '60)
Eastern Ill. 89   Idaho 38-21
Eastern Ill. 89   Montana 19-25
Eastern Ill. 95   Stephen F. Austin 29-34
Eastern Ill. 96   Northern Iowa 14-21
Eastern Ill. 00   Montana 13-45
Eastern Ill. 01   Northern Iowa 43-49
Eastern Ill. 02   Western Ill. 9-48

Scott Stoker (0-1) (Northwestern St. '91)
Northwestern St. 02   Montana 14-45

Tim Stowers (6-2) (Auburn '79)
Ga. Southern 90   Citadel 31-0
Ga. Southern 90   Idaho 28-27
Ga. Southern 90   UCF 44-7
Ga. Southern .... 90*   Nevada 36-13
Ga. Southern 93   Eastern Ky. 14-12
Ga. Southern 93   Youngstown St. 14-34
Ga. Southern 95   Troy St. 24-21
Ga. Southern 95   Montana 0-45

Charlie Taaffe (1-3) (Siena '73)
Citadel 88   Ga. Southern 20-38
Citadel 90   Ga. Southern 0-31
Citadel 92   N.C. A&T 44-0
Citadel 92   Youngstown St. 17-42

Andy Talley (3-6) (Southern Conn. St. '67)
Villanova 89   Ga. Southern 36-52
Villanova 91   Youngstown St. 16-17
Villanova 92   Youngstown St. 20-23
Villanova 96   East Tenn. St. 29-35
Villanova 97   Colgate 49-28
Villanova 97   Youngstown St. 34-37
Villanova 02   Furman 45-38
Villanova 02   Fordham 24-10
Villanova 02   McNeese St. 28-39

Tommy Tate (3-3) (McNeese St. '79)
McNeese St. 00   Ga. Southern 17-42
McNeese St. 01   Maine 10-14
McNeese St. 02   Montana St. 21-14
McNeese St. 02   Montana 24-20
McNeese St. 02   Villanova 39-28
McNeese St. 02   Western Ky. 14-34

Joe Taylor (0-2) (Western Ill. '72)
Hampton 97   Youngstown St. 13-28
Hampton 98   Connecticut 34-42

Rick Taylor (1-3) (Gettysburg '64)
Boston U. 82   Colgate 7-21
Boston U. 83   Eastern Ky. 24-20
Boston U. 83   Furman 16-35
Boston U. 84   Richmond 33-35

Bill Thomas (1-1) (Tennessee St. '71)
Tennessee St. 86   Jackson St. 32-23
Tennessee St. 86   Nevada 6-33

Chris Tormey (0-1) (Idaho '78)
Idaho 95   McNeese St. 3-33

Jim Tressel (23-6) (Baldwin-Wallace '75)
Youngstown St. 87   Northern Iowa 28-31
Youngstown St. 89   Eastern Ky. 28-24
Youngstown St. 89   Furman 23-42
Youngstown St. 90   UCF 17-20
Youngstown St. 91   Villanova 17-16
Youngstown St. 91   Nevada 30-28
Youngstown St. 91   Samford 10-0
Youngstown St. ...... 91*   Marshall 25-17
Youngstown St. 92   Villanova 23-20
Youngstown St. 92   Citadel 42-17
Youngstown St. 92   Northern Iowa 19-7
Youngstown St. 92   Marshall 28-31

Youngstown St. ...... 93 UCF 56-30
Youngstown St. ...... 93 Ga. Southern 34-14
Youngstown St. ...... 93 Idaho 35-16
Youngstown St. ...... 93* Marshall 17-5
Youngstown St. ...... 94 Alcorn St. 63-20
Youngstown St. ...... 94 Eastern Ky. 18-15
Youngstown St. ...... 94 Montana 28-9
Youngstown St. ...... 94* Boise St. 28-14
Youngstown St. ...... 97 Hampton 28-13
Youngstown St. ...... 97 Villanova 37-34
Youngstown St. ...... 97 Eastern Wash. 25-14
Youngstown St. ...... 97* McNeese St. 10-9
Youngstown St. ...... 99 Montana 30-27
Youngstown St. ...... 99 N.C. A&T 41-3
Youngstown St. ...... 99 Florida A&M 27-24
Youngstown St. ...... 99 Ga. Southern 24-59
Youngstown St. ...... 00 Richmond 3-10

Tim Walsh (0-1) (UC Riverside '77)
Portland St. .... 00 Delaware 14-49

Bob Waters (3-1) (Presbyterian '60)
Western Caro. ...... 83 Colgate 24-23

Western Caro. ...... 83 Holy Cross 28-21
Western Caro. ...... 83 Furman 14-7
Western Caro. ...... 83 Southern Ill. 7-43

Mark Whipple (5-1) (Brown '79)
Massachusetts .... 98 McNeese St. 21-19
Massachusetts .... 98 Lehigh 27-21
Massachusetts .... 98 Northwestern St. 41-31
Massachusetts .... 98* Ga. Southern 55-43
Massachusetts .... 99 Furman 30-23 (ot)
Massachusetts .... 99 Ga. Southern 21-38

John Whitehead (1-2) (East Stroudsburg '50)
Lehigh .... 79 Murray St. 28-9
Lehigh .... 79 Eastern Ky. 7-30
Lehigh .... 80 Eastern Ky. 20-23

A.L. Williams (3-1) (Louisiana Tech '57)
Louisiana Tech .... 84 Mississippi Val. 66-19
Louisiana Tech .... 84 Alcorn St. 44-21
Louisiana Tech .... 84 Middle Tenn. 21-13
Louisiana Tech .... 84 Montana St. 6-19

Steve Wilson (0-1) (Howard '79)
Howard .... 93 Marshall 14-28

Alex Wood (0-1) (Iowa '79)
James Madison....... 95 Appalachian St. 24-31

Sparky Woods (2-2) (Carson-Newman '76)
Appalachian St. ..... 86 Nicholls St. 26-28
Appalachian St. ..... 87 Richmond 20-3
Appalachian St. ..... 87 Ga. Southern 19-0
Appalachian St. ..... 87 Marshall 10-24

Alvin Wyatt (0-1) (Bethune-Cookman '70)
Bethune-Cookman ... 02 Ga. Southern 0-34

Dick Zornes (1-2) (Eastern Wash. '68)
Eastern Wash. .... 85 Idaho 42-38
Eastern Wash. .... 85 Northern Iowa 14-17
Eastern Wash. .... 92 Northern Iowa 14-17

*National championship. †Tennessee State's participation vacated by action of the NCAA Committee on Infractions. %Stephen F. Austin's participation vacated by action of the NCAA Committee on Infractions. ^Northern Arizona's participation vacated by action of the NCAA Committee on Infractions.

Division II Coaching Records

Winningest Active Division II Coaches

(Minimum five years as college head coach; record at four-year colleges only.)

BY PERCENTAGE

Coach, College	Years	Won	Lost	Tied	†Pct.	#Postseason W-L-T
Bryan Collins, C.W. Post	5	46	9	0	.83636	0-1-0
Chuck Broyles, Pittsburg St.	13	131	26	2	.83019	13-10-0
Ken Sparks, Carson-Newman	23	223	53	2	.80866	13-8-0
Bill Zwaan, West Chester	6	54	14	0	.79412	5-2-0
John Luckhardt, Calif. (Pa.)	18	143	42	2	.77005	13-11-0
Brian Kelly, Grand Valley St.	12	104	34	2	.75000	7-4-0
Bob Biggs, UC Davis	10	90	30	1	.74793	11-8-0
Danny Hale, Bloomsburg	15	121	44	1	.73193	3-4-0
Peter Yetten, Bentley	15	108	40	1	.72819	0-0-0
Frank Cignetti, Indiana (Pa.)	21	176	69	1	.71748	15-13-0
Dale Lennon, North Dakota	6	48	21	0	.69565	4-1-0
Tom Sawyer, Winona St.	7	54	24	0	.69231	0-1-0
O. Kay Dalton, Northern Colo.	8	56	25	0	.69136	2-1-0
Brad Smith, Chadron St.	16	117	52	1	.69118	0-4-0
Mel Tjeerdsma, Northwest Mo. St.	19	147	65	4	.68981	11-4-0
Willie Fritz, Central Mo. St.	6	46	21	0	.68657	0-1-0
Bob Nielson, Minn. Duluth	14	100	48	1	.67450	3-4-0
Rob Smith, Western Wash.	14	95	46	1	.67254	0-1-0
Rick Comegy, Tuskegee	11	80	41	0	.66116	0-0-0
George Mihalik, Slippery Rock	15	107	54	4	.66061	3-3-0
Willard Bailey, Virginia Union	30	205	105	8	.65723	0-6-0
Duke Iverson, Western Ore.	19	120	70	3	.62953	0-3-0
Monte Cater, Shepherd	22	137	82	2	.62443	1-2-0
Jerry Vandergriff, Angelo St.	21	138	83	2	.62332	2-2-0
Jeff Zenisek, Western St.	7	43	26	1	.62143	0-0-0
Jeff Pierce, Ferris St.	8	54	34	0	.61364	3-2-0
Jerry Partridge, Mo. Western St.	7	47	30	0	.61039	0-0-0
Jim Miceli, Bryant	8	46	30	0	.60526	0-0-0
Keith Otterbein, Hillsdale	9	60	39	3	.60294	2-3-0
Pat Behrns, Neb.-Omaha	15	99	66	0	.60000	1-4-0
Tom Eckert, Northeastern St.	16	103	69	3	.59714	2-1-0
Randy Awrey, Saginaw Valley	13	81	55	1	.59489	1-3-0
Art Wilkins, American Int'l	9	58	40	0	.59184	0-0-0
Rick Rhoades, Delta St.	7	40	28	0	.58824	4-1-0
Dennis Douds, East Stroudsburg	29	170	122	3	.58136	0-0-0
John Zamberlin, Central Wash.	6	36	26	0	.58065	0-1-0
Joe Ramunno, Mesa St.	5	33	24	0	.57895	1-1-0
Steve Mullins, Arkansas Tech	6	37	27	0	.57813	0-1-0
Kermit Blount, Winston-Salem	10	59	43	3	.57619	0-0-0
Rocky Rees, Shippensburg	18	111	83	2	.57143	2-2-0
Ken Heupel, Northern St.	5	31	24	0	.56364	0-0-0
John Ware, Truman	8	49	38	0	.56322	0-0-0
Randy Hedberg, St. Cloud St.	12	62	49	2	.55752	0-0-0
John Stiegelmeier, South Dakota St.	6	35	29	0	.54688	0-0-0
Malen Luke, Clarion	15	85	71	0	.54487	2-1-0
Kevin Kiesel, Millersville	10	55	46	1	.54412	0-0-0
Randy Tribble, Harding	9	50	42	1	.54301	0-0-0
Jeff Tesch, Bemidji St.	7	40	34	0	.54054	0-0-0
Dan Simrell, Findlay	11	64	55	2	.53719	0-0-0
Frankie DeBusk, Tusculum	5	29	25	0	.53704	0-0-0

Bentley's Peter Yetten had his winning percentage climb 15 points during 2002, when the Falcons went 10-1. Among Yetten's 2002 victories was the 100th of his head coaching career.

Coach, College	Years	Won	Lost	Tied	†Pct.	#Postseason W-L-T
Bud Elliott, Eastern N.M.	35	193	169	9	.53235	0-1-0
Doug Sams, Northern Mich.	12	64	57	0	.52893	0-0-0
Richard Cavanaugh, Southern Conn. St.	18	96	86	1	.52732	0-0-0
Steve Kazor, Wayne St. (Mich.)	6	37	34	0	.52113	0-0-0
Gary Keller, Ashland	9	49	46	0	.51579	0-1-0
Tim Clifton, Mars Hill	10	54	51	0	.51429	0-0-0
Paul Sharp, Southwestern Okla.	17	87	84	1	.50872	0-0-0
Jesse Branch, Henderson St.	11	61	60	1	.50410	1-2-0
David Keeny, Kutztown	5	26	26	0	.50000	0-0-0
Pat Riepma, Northwood	10	51	51	2	.50000	1-1-0
Bob Eaton, West Liberty St.	13	65	65	1	.50000	0-0-0
Joe Polizzi, Indianapolis	9	47	49	1	.48969	0-0-0
Jim Heinitz, Augustana (S.D.)	15	75	87	1	.46319	0-2-0
Greg Lusardi, Pace	9	41	48	0	.46067	0-0-0
Bernie Anderson, Michigan Tech	16	71	87	0	.44937	0-0-0
Bill Struble, West Va. Wesleyan	20	89	110	0	.44724	0-0-0
Lou Tepper, Edinboro	8	39	49	2	.44444	0-0-0
Bill Cooke, Mo. Southern St.	9	38	50	1	.43258	0-0-0
Ralph Micheli, Minn. St. Moorhead	20	82	111	2	.42564	0-1-0
Todd Knight, Ouachita Baptist	10	41	59	2	.41176	0-1-0
Dennis Darnell, East Central	9	37	58	1	.39063	0-0-0
Tom Riva, St. Joseph's (Ind.)	6	24	40	0	.37500	0-0-0
John Johnson, Ky. Wesleyan	9	34	58	0	.36957	0-0-0
Carl Lee, West Virginia St.	7	27	48	0	.36000	0-0-0
Ralph Young, Okla. Panhandle	13	42	76	0	.35593	0-0-0
Scott Hoffman, Wayne St. (Neb.)	7	25	46	0	.35211	0-0-0
Greg Quick, Concord	10	32	63	0	.33684	0-0-0
Michael Costa, St. Augustine's	5	10	41	0	.19608	0-0-0
John Parker, Cheyney	7	9	64	0	.12329	0-0-0
Kirby Cannon, Mo.-Rolla	5	6	49	0	.10909	0-0-0

†Ties computed as half won and half lost. #Includes bowl and playoff games.

COACHING RECORDS

BY VICTORIES

(Minimum five years as college head coach)

Coach, College	*Wins
Ken Sparks, Carson-Newman	223
Willard Bailey, Virginia Union	205
Bud Elliott, Eastern N.M.	193
Frank Cignetti, Indiana (Pa.)	176
Dennis Douds, East Stroudsburg	170
Mel Tjeerdsma, Northwest Mo. St.	147
John Luckhardt, Calif. (Pa.)	143
Jerry Vandergriff, Angelo St.	138
Monte Cater, Shepherd	137
Chuck Broyles, Pittsburg St.	131
Danny Hale, Bloomsburg	121
Duke Iverson, Western Ore.	120
Brad Smith, Chadron St.	117
Rocky Rees, Shippensburg	111
Peter Yetten, Bentley	108
George Mihalik, Slippery Rock	107
Brian Kelly, Grand Valley St.	104
Tom Eckert, Northeastern St.	103
Bob Nielson, Minn. Duluth	100
Pat Behrns, Neb.-Omaha	99
Richard Cavanaugh, Southern Conn. St.	96
Rob Smith, Western Wash.	95
Bob Biggs, UC Davis	90
Bill Struble, West Va. Wesleyan	89
Paul Sharp, Southwestern Okla.	87
Malen Luke, Clarion	85
Ralph Micheli, Minn. St. Moorhead	82
Randy Awrey, Saginaw Valley	81
Rick Comegy, Tuskegee	80
Jim Heinitz, Augustana (S.D.)	75
Bernie Anderson, Michigan Tech	71
Bob Eaton, West Liberty St.	65
Doug Sams, Northern Mich.	64
Dan Simrell, Findlay	64
Randy Hedberg, St. Cloud St.	62
Jesse Branch, Henderson St.	61
Keith Otterbein, Hillsdale	60
Kermit Blount, Winston-Salem	59
Art Wilkins, American Int'l.	58
O. Kay Dalton, Northern Colo.	56
Kevin Kiesel, Millersville	55
Tim Clifton, Mars Hill	54
Jeff Pierce, Ferris St.	54
Tom Sawyer, Winona St.	54
Bill Zwaan, West Chester	54
Pat Riepma, Northwood	51
Randy Tribble, Harding	50
Gary Keller, Ashland	49
John Ware, Truman	49
Dale Lennon, North Dakota	48
Jerry Partridge, Mo. Western St.	47
Joe Polizzi, Indianapolis	47
Bryan Collins, C.W. Post	46
Willie Fritz, Central Mo. St.	46
Jim Miceli, Bryant	46
Jeff Zenisek, Western St.	43
Ralph Young, Okla. Panhandle	42
Todd Knight, Ouachita Baptist	41
Greg Lusardi, Pace	41
Rick Rhoades, Delta St.	40
Jeff Tesch, Bemidji St.	40
Lou Tepper, Edinboro	39
Bill Cooke, Mo. Southern St.	38
Dennis Darnell, East Central	37
Steve Kazor, Wayne St. (Mich.)	37
Steve Mullins, Arkansas Tech	37
John Zamberlin, Central Wash.	36
John Stiegelmeier, South Dakota St.	35
John Johnson, Ky. Wesleyan	34
Joe Ramunno, Mesa St.	33
Greg Quick, Concord	32
Ken Heupel, Northern St.	31
Frankie DeBusk, Tusculum	29
Carl Lee, West Virginia St.	27
David Keeny, Kutztown	26
Scott Hoffman, Wayne St. (Neb.)	25
Tom Riva, St. Joseph's (Ind.)	24
Michael Costa, St. Augustine's	10
John Parker, Cheyney	9
Kirby Cannon, Mo.-Rolla	6

Includes bowls and playoff games.

Division II Championship Coaches

All coaches who have coached teams in the Division II championship playoffs since 1973 are listed here with their playoff record, alma mater and year graduated, team, year coached, opponent, and score.

Phil Albert (1-3) (Arizona '66)
Towson	83	North Dakota St. 17-24
Towson	84	Norfolk St. 31-21
Towson	84	Troy St. 3-45
Towson	86	Central St. 0-31

Pokey Allen (10-5) (Utah '65)
Portland St.	87	Minn. St. Mankato 27-21
Portland St.	87	Northern Mich. 13-7
Portland St.	87	Troy St. 17-31
Portland St.	88	Bowie St. 34-17
Portland St.	88	Jacksonville St. 20-13
Portland St.	88	Tex. A&M-Kingsville 35-27
Portland St.	88	North Dakota St. 21-35
Portland St.	89	West Chester 56-50 (3 ot)
Portland St.	89	Indiana (Pa.) 0-17
Portland St.	91	Northern Colo. 28-24
Portland St.	91	Minn. St.-Mankato 37-27
Portland St.	91	Pittsburg St. 21-53
Portland St.	92	UC Davis 42-28
Portland St.	92	Tex. A&M-Kingsville 35-30
Portland St.	92	Pittsburg St. 38-41

Randy Awrey (1-3) (Northern Mich. '78)
Saginaw Valley	00	Bloomsburg 32-46
Saginaw Valley	01	Indiana (Pa.) 33-32
Saginaw Valley	01	Grand Valley St. 30-33
Saginaw Valley	02	Indiana (Pa.) 23-27

Mike Ayers (0-2) (Georgetown [Ky.] '74)
| Wofford | 90 | Mississippi Col. 19-70 |
| Wofford | 91 | Mississippi Col. 15-28 |

Bob Babich (2-2) (Tulsa '84)
North Dakota St.	97	Northwest Mo. St. 28-39
North Dakota St.	00	Northwest Mo. St. 31-17
North Dakota St.	00	Neb.-Omaha 43-21
North Dakota St.	00	Delta St. 16-34

Willard Bailey (0-6) (Norfolk St. '62)
Virginia Union	79	Delaware 28-58
Virginia Union	80	North Ala. 8-17
Virginia Union	81	Shippensburg 27-40
Virginia Union	82	North Dakota St. 20-21
Virginia Union	83	North Ala. 14-16
Norfolk St.	84	Towson 21-31

Bob Bartolomeo (0-1) (Butler '77)
| Butler | 91 | Pittsburg St. 16-26 |

Tom Beck (0-2) (Northern Ill. '61)
| Grand Valley St. | 89 | Indiana (Pa.) 24-34 |
| Grand Valley St. | 90 | Tex. A&M-Commerce 14-20 |

Pat Behrns (1-4) (Dakota St. '72)
Neb.-Omaha	96	Northwest Mo. St. 21-22
Neb.-Omaha	98	Northwest Mo. St. 14-28
Neb.-Omaha	00	Pittsburg St. 14-3
Neb.-Omaha	00	North Dakota St. 21-43
Neb.-Omaha	01	Pittsburg St. 7-20

David Bennett (4-3) (Presbyterian '84)
Catawba	99	Fort Valley St. 48-17
Catawba	99	Carson-Newman 25-28
Catawba	00	West Ga. 28-24
Catawba	00	Delta St. 14-20
Catawba	01	Central Ark. 35-34
Catawba	01	Valdosta St. 37-34 (ot)
Catawba	01	Grand Valley St. 16-34

Bob Biggs (11-8) (UC Davis '73)
UC Davis	93	Fort Hays St. 37-34
UC Davis	93	Tex. A&M-Kingsville 28-51
UC Davis	96	Tex. A&M-Kingsville 17-14
UC Davis	96	Central Okla. 26-6
UC Davis	96	Carson-Newman 26-29
UC Davis	97	Tex. A&M-Kingsville 37-34
UC Davis	97	Angelo St. 50-33
UC Davis	97	New Haven 25-27
UC Davis	98	Tex. A&M-Kingsville 21-54
UC Davis	99	Central Okla. 33-17
UC Davis	99	Northeastern St. 14-19
UC Davis	00	Chadron St. 48-10
UC Davis	00	Mesa St. 62-18
UC Davis	00	Bloomsburg 48-58
UC Davis	01	Tex. A&M-Kingsville 37-32
UC Davis	01	Tarleton St. 42-25
UC Davis	01	North Dakota 2-14
UC Davis	02	Central Wash. 24-6
UC Davis	02	Tex. A&M-Kingsville 20-27 (ot)

Bob Blasi (0-1) (Colorado St. '53)
| Northern Colo. | 80 | Eastern Ill. 14-21 |

Bill Bowes (1-2) (Penn St. '65)
New Hampshire	75	Lehigh 35-21
New Hampshire	75	Western Ky. 3-14
New Hampshire	76	Montana 16-17

Chuck Broyles (13-10) (Pittsburg St. '70)
Pittsburg St.	90	Truman 59-3
Pittsburg St.	90	Tex. A&M-Commerce 60-28
Pittsburg St.	90	North Dakota St. 29-39
Pittsburg St.	91	Butler 26-16
Pittsburg St.	91	Tex. A&M-Commerce 38-28
Pittsburg St.	91	Portland St. 53-21
Pittsburg St.	91*	Jacksonville St. 23-6
Pittsburg St.	92	North Dakota 26-21
Pittsburg St.	92	North Dakota St. 38-37 (ot)
Pittsburg St.	92	Portland St. 41-38
Pittsburg St.	92	Jacksonville St. 13-17
Pittsburg St.	93	North Dakota 14-17
Pittsburg St.	94	North Dakota St. 12-18 (3 ot)
Pittsburg St.	95	Northern Colo. 36-17
Pittsburg St.	95	North Dakota St. 9-7
Pittsburg St.	95	Tex. A&M-Kingsville 28-25 (ot)
Pittsburg St.	95	North Ala. 7-27
Pittsburg St.	96	Northern Colo. 21-24
Pittsburg St.	97	Northern Colo. 16-24
Pittsburg St.	99	Northern Colo. 31-34
Pittsburg St.	00	Neb.-Omaha 3-14
Pittsburg St.	01	Neb.-Omaha 20-7
Pittsburg St.	01	North Dakota 0-38

Sandy Buda (1-2) (Kansas '67)
Neb.-Omaha	78	Youngstown St. 14-21
Neb.-Omaha	84	Northwest Mo. St. 28-15
Neb.-Omaha	84	North Dakota St. 14-25

Bill Burgess (12-4) (Auburn '63)
Jacksonville St.	88	West Chester 63-24
Jacksonville St.	88	Portland St. 13-20
Jacksonville St.	89	Alabama A&M 33-9
Jacksonville St.	89	North Dakota St. 21-17
Jacksonville St.	89	Angelo St. 34-16
Jacksonville St.	89	Mississippi Col. 0-3
Jacksonville St.	90	North Ala. 38-14
Jacksonville St.	90	Mississippi Col. 7-14
Jacksonville St.	91	Winston-Salem 49-24
Jacksonville St.	91	Mississippi Col. 35-7
Jacksonville St.	91	Indiana (Pa.) 27-20
Jacksonville St.	91	Pittsburg St. 6-23
Jacksonville St.	92	Savannah St. 41-16
Jacksonville St.	92	North Ala. 14-12
Jacksonville St.	92	New Haven 46-35
Jacksonville St.	92*	Pittsburg St. 17-13

Bob Burt (0-1) (Cal St. Los Angeles '62)
| Cal St. Northridge | 90 | Cal Poly 7-14 |

Steve Campbell (4-0) (Troy St. '87)
Delta St.	00	Valdosta St. 49-12
Delta St.	00	Catawba 20-14
Delta St.	00	North Dakota St. 34-16
Delta St.	00*	Bloomsburg 63-34

Gene Carpenter (2-3) (Huron '63)
Millersville	88	Indiana (Pa.) 27-24
Millersville	88	North Dakota St. 26-36
Millersville	95	Ferris St. 26-36
Millersville	99	Shepherd 21-14
Millersville	99	Indiana (Pa.) 21-26

Marino Casem (0-1) (Xavier [La.] '56)
| Alcorn St. | 74 | UNLV 22-35 |

Monte Cater (1-2) (Millikin '71)
Shepherd	98	Indiana (Pa.) 9-6
Shepherd	98	Slippery Rock 20-31
Shepherd	99	Millersville 14-21

Frank Cignetti (15-13) (Indiana [Pa.] '60)
Indiana (Pa.)	87	UCF 10-12
Indiana (Pa.)	88	Millersville 24-27
Indiana (Pa.)	89	Grand Valley St. 34-24
Indiana (Pa.)	89	Portland St. 17-0
Indiana (Pa.)	89	Mississippi Col. 14-26
Indiana (Pa.)	90	Winston-Salem 48-0
Indiana (Pa.)	90	Edinboro 14-7
Indiana (Pa.)	90	Mississippi Col. 27-8

Indiana (Pa.)........... 90 North Dakota St. 11-51
Indiana (Pa.)........... 91 Virginia Union 56-7
Indiana (Pa.)........... 91 Shippensburg 52-7
Indiana (Pa.)........... 91 Jacksonville St. 20-27
Indiana (Pa.)........... 93 Ferris St. 28-21
Indiana (Pa.)........... 93 New Haven 38-35
Indiana (Pa.)........... 93 North Dakota 21-6
Indiana (Pa.)........... 93 North Ala. 34-41
Indiana (Pa.)........... 94 Grand Valley St. 35-27
Indiana (Pa.)........... 94 Ferris St. 21-17
Indiana (Pa.)........... 94 Tex. A&M-Kingsville 20-46
Indiana (Pa.)........... 96 Ferris St. 23-24
Indiana (Pa.)........... 98 Shepherd 6-9
Indiana (Pa.)........... 99 Slippery Rock 27-20 (ot)
Indiana (Pa.)........... 99 Millersville 26-21
Indiana (Pa.)........... 99 Northwest Mo. St. 12-20
Indiana (Pa.)........... 00 Northwood 0-28
Indiana (Pa.)........... 01 Saginaw Valley 32-33
Indiana (Pa.)........... 02 Saginaw Valley 27-23
Indiana (Pa.)........... 02 Grand Valley St. 21-62

Brian Collins (0-1) (St. John's [N.Y.] '87)
C.W. Post .... 02 Grand Valley St. 13-62

Clint Conque (0-1) (Nicholls St. '83)
Central Ark. .... 01 Catawaba 34-35

Bob Cortese (0-2) (Colorado '67)
Fort Hays St. .... 93 UC Davis 34-37
Fort Hays St. .... 95 Tex. A&M-Kingsville 28-59

Bruce Craddock (0-1) (Truman '66)
Truman .... 82 Jacksonville St. 21-34

Richard Cundiff (2-2) (Lincoln Memorial '73)
Tex. A&M-Kingsville 01 UC Davis 32-37
Tex. A&M-Kingsville 02 Neb.-Kearney 58-40
Tex. A&M-Kingsville 02 UC Davis 27-20 (ot)
Tex. A&M-Kingsville 02 Valdosta St. 12-21

O. Kay Dalton (2-1) (Colorado St. '54)
Northern Colo. .... 02 Central Mo. St. 49-28
Northern Colo. .... 02 Northwest Mo. St. 23-12
Northern Colo. .... 02 Grand Valley St. 7-44

Rick Daniels (0-3) (West Chester '75)
West Chester.......... 89 Portland St. 50-56 (3 ot)
West Chester.......... 92 New Haven 26-38
West Chester.......... 94 Ferris St. 40-43

Bill Davis (0-1) (Johnson Smith '65)
Savannah St. .... 92 Jacksonville St. 16-41

Rey Dempsey (0-1) (Geneva '58)
Youngstown St. ...... 74 Delaware 14-35

Jim Dennison (2-1) (Wooster '60)
Akron .... 76 UNLV 26-6
Akron .... 76 Northern Mich. 29-26
Akron .... 76 Montana St. 13-24

Dennis Douds (0-1) (Slippery Rock '63)
East Stroudsburg..... 91 Shippensburg 33-34

Fred Dunlap (0-2) (Colgate '50)
Lehigh.................... 73 Western Ky. 16-25
Lehigh.................... 75 New Hampshire 21-35

Tom Eckert (2-2) (Northeastern St. '66)
Northeastern St. ..... 99 Western Wash. 27-24 (ot)
Northeastern St. ..... 99 UC Davis 19-14
Northeastern St. ..... 99 Carson-Newman 7-42
Northeastern St. ..... 00 Mesa St. 21-40

Bud Elliott (0-1) (Baker '53)
Northwest Mo. St.... 89 Pittsburg St. 7-28

Jimmy Feix (4-2) (Western Ky. '53)
Western Ky. .... 73 Lehigh 25-16
Western Ky. .... 73 Grambling 28-20
Western Ky. .... 73 Louisiana Tech 0-34
Western Ky. .... 75 Northern Iowa 14-12
Western Ky. .... 75 New Hampshire 14-3
Western Ky. .... 75 Northern Mich. 14-16

Charlie Fisher (0-2) (Springfield '81)
West Ga. .... 95 Carson-Newman 26-37
West Ga. .... 96 Carson-Newman 7-41

Bob Foster (0-2) (UC Davis '62)
UC Davis .... 89 Angelo St. 23-28
UC Davis .... 92 Portland St. 28-42

Dennis Franchione (1-1) (Pittsburg St. '73)
Pittsburg St. .... 89 Northwest Mo. St. 28-7
Pittsburg St. .... 89 Angelo St. 21-24

Fred Freeman (0-1) (Mississippi Val. '66)
Hampton................ 85 Bloomsburg 28-38

Willie Fritz (0-1) (Pittsburg St. '83)
Central Mo. St........ 02 Northern Colo. 28-49

Jim Fuller (3-5) (Alabama '67)
Jacksonville St. .... 77 Northern Ariz. 35-0
Jacksonville St. .... 77 North Dakota St. 31-7
Jacksonville St. .... 77 Lehigh 0-33
Jacksonville St. .... 78 Delaware 27-42
Jacksonville St. .... 80 Cal Poly 0-15
Jacksonville St. .... 81 Southwest Tex. St. 22-38
Jacksonville St. .... 82 Truman 34-21
Jacksonville St. .... 82 Southwest Tex. St. 14-19

Chan Gailey (3-0) (Florida '74)
Troy St. .... 84 Central St. 31-21
Troy St. .... 84 Towson 45-3
Troy St. .... 84* North Dakota St. 18-17

Joe Glenn (10-5) (South Dakota '71)
Northern Colo. ...... 90 North Dakota St. 7-17
Northern Colo. ...... 91 Portland St. 24-28
Northern Colo. ...... 95 Pittsburg St. 17-36
Northern Colo. ...... 96 Pittsburg St. 24-21
Northern Colo. ...... 96 Northwest Mo. St. 27-26
Northern Colo. ...... 96 Clarion 19-18
Northern Colo. ...... 96* Carson-Newman 23-14
Northern Colo. ...... 97 Pittsburg St. 24-16
Northern Colo. ...... 97 Northwest Mo. St. 35-19
Northern Colo. ...... 97 Carson-Newman 30-29
Northern Colo. ...... 97* New Haven 51-0
Northern Colo. ...... 98 North Dakota 52-24
Northern Colo. ...... 98 Northwest Mo. St. 17-42
Northern Colo. ...... 99 Pittsburg St. 34-31
Northern Colo. ...... 99 Northwest Mo. St. 35-41

Ray Greene (1-1) (Akron '63)
Alabama A&M....... 79 Morgan St. 27-7
Alabama A&M....... 79 Youngstown St. 0-52

John Gregory (0-1) (Northern Iowa '61)
South Dakota St. .... 79 Youngstown St. 7-50

Herb Grenke (1-1) (Wis.-Milwaukee '63)
Northern Mich. ...... 87 Angelo St. 23-20 (ot)
Northern Mich. ...... 87 Portland St. 7-13

Wayne Grubb (4-3) (Tennessee '61)
North Ala. .... 80 Virginia Union 17-8
North Ala. .... 80 Eastern Ill. 31-56
North Ala. .... 83 Virginia Union 16-14
North Ala. .... 83 Central St. 24-27
North Ala. .... 85 Fort Valley St. 14-7
North Ala. .... 85 Bloomsburg 34-0
North Ala. .... 85 North Dakota St. 7-35

Rocky Hager (12-5) (Minot St. '74)
North Dakota St. .... 88 Augustana (S.D.) 49-7
North Dakota St. .... 88 Millersville 36-26
North Dakota St. .... 88 Sacramento St. 42-20
North Dakota St. .... 88* Portland St. 35-21
North Dakota St. .... 89 Edinboro 45-32
North Dakota St. .... 89 Jacksonville St. 17-21
North Dakota St. .... 90 Northern Colo. 17-7
North Dakota St. .... 90 Cal Poly 47-0
North Dakota St. .... 90 Pittsburg St. 39-29
North Dakota St. .... 90* Indiana (Pa.) 51-11
North Dakota St. .... 91 Minn. St. Mankato 7-27
North Dakota St. .... 92 Truman 42-7
North Dakota St. .... 93 Pittsburg St. 37-38 (ot)
North Dakota St. .... 94 Pittsburg St. 18-12 (3 ot)
North Dakota St. .... 94 North Dakota 7-14
North Dakota St. .... 95 North Dakota 41-10
North Dakota St. .... 95 Pittsburg St. 7-9

Danny Hale (3-4) (West Chester '68)
West Chester.......... 88 Jacksonville St. 24-63
Bloomsburg .... 96 Clarion 29-42
Bloomsburg .... 00 Saginaw Valley 46-32
Bloomsburg .... 00 Northwood 38-14
Bloomsburg .... 00 UC Davis 58-48
Bloomsburg .... 00 Delta St. 34-63
Bloomsburg .... 01 Grand Valley St. 14-42

Ron Harms (^12-9) (Valparaiso '59)
Tex. A&M-Kingsville .. 88 Mississippi Col. 39-15
Tex. A&M-Kingsville .. 88 Tenn.-Martin 34-0
Tex. A&M-Kingsville .. 88 Portland St. 27-35
Tex. A&M-Kingsville .. 89 Mississippi Col. 19-34
Tex. A&M-Kingsville .. 92 Western St. 22-13
Tex. A&M-Kingsville .. 92 Portland St. 30-35
Tex. A&M-Kingsville .. 93 Portland St. 50-15
Tex. A&M-Kingsville .. 93 UC Davis 51-28
Tex. A&M-Kingsville .. 93 North Ala. 25-27

Tex. A&M-Kingsville .. 94 Western St. 43-7
Tex. A&M-Kingsville .. 94 Portland St. 21-16
Tex. A&M-Kingsville .. 94 Indiana (Pa.) 46-20
Tex. A&M-Kingsville .. 94 North Ala. 10-16
Tex. A&M-Kingsville .. 95 Fort Hays St. 59-28
Tex. A&M-Kingsville .. 95 Portland St. 30-3
Tex. A&M-Kingsville .. 95 Pittsburg St. 25-28 (ot)
Tex. A&M-Kingsville .. 96^ UC Davis 14-17
Tex. A&M-Kingsville .. 97^ UC Davis 34-37
Tex. A&M-Kingsville .. 98^ UC Davis 54-21
Tex. A&M-Kingsville .. 98^ Central Okla. 24-21 (ot)
Tex. A&M-Kingsville .. 98^ Northwest Mo. St. 34-49

Joe Harper (3-1) (UCLA '59)
Cal Poly .... 78 Winston-Salem 0-17
Cal Poly .... 80 Jacksonville St. 15-0
Cal Poly .... 80 Santa Clara 38-14
Cal Poly .... 80* Eastern Ill. 21-13

Chris Hatcher (4-3) (Valdosta St. '95)
Valdosta St. .... 00 Delta St. 12-49
Valdosta St. .... 01 Fort Valley St. 40-24
Valdosta St. .... 01 Catawba 34-37 (ot)
Valdosta St. .... 02 Catawba 24-7
Valdosta St. .... 02 Carson-Newman 31-28
Valdosta St. .... 02 Tex. A&M-Kingsville 21-12
Valdosta St. .... 02 Grand Valley St. 24-31

Bill Hayes (1-2) (N.C. Central '64)
Winston-Salem........ 78 Cal Poly 17-0
Winston-Salem........ 78 Delaware 0-41
Winston-Salem........ 87 Troy St. 14-45

Jim Heinitz (0-2) (South Dakota St. '72)
Augustana (S.D.)..... 88 North Dakota St. 7-49
Augustana (S.D.)..... 89 St. Cloud St. 20-27

Chip Hester (0-1) (Guilford '92)
Catawba .... 02 Valdosta St. 7-24

Andy Hinson (0-1) (Bethune-Cookman '53)
Bethune-Cookman ... 77 UC Davis 16-34

Sonny Holland (3-0) (Montana St. '60)
Montana St. .... 76 New Hampshire 17-16
Montana St. .... 76 North Dakota St. 10-3
Montana St. .... 76* Akron 24-13

Tom Hollman (1-5) (Ohio Northern '68)
Edinboro .... 89 North Dakota St. 32-45
Edinboro .... 90 Virginia Union 38-14
Edinboro .... 90 Indiana (Pa.) 7-14
Edinboro .... 92 Ferris St. 15-19
Edinboro .... 93 New Haven 28-48
Edinboro .... 95 New Haven 12-27

Eric Holm (0-3) (Truman '81)
Truman .... 90 Pittsburg St. 3-59
Truman .... 92 North Dakota St. 7-42
Truman .... 94 North Dakota 6-18

Gary Howard (2-3) (Arkansas '64)
Central Okla. .... 96 Chadron 23-21
Central Okla. .... 96 UC Davis 6-26
Central Okla. .... 98 Chadron St. 21-19
Central Okla. .... 98 Tex. A&M-Kingsville 21-24 (ot)
Central Okla. .... 99 UC Davis 17-33

Carl Iverson (0-3) (Whitman '62)
Western St. .... 92 Tex. A&M-Kingsville 13-22
Western St. .... 94 Tex. A&M-Kingsville 7-43
Western St. .... 97 Angelo St. 12-46

Billy Joe (3-4) (Villanova '63)
Central St. .... 83 Southwest Tex. St. 24-16
Central St. .... 83 North Ala. 27-24
Central St. .... 83 North Dakota St. 21-41
Central St. .... 84 Troy St. 21-31
Central St. .... 85 South Dakota 10-13 (2 ot)
Central St. .... 86 Towson 31-0
Central St. .... 86 North Dakota St. 12-35

Gary Keller (0-1) (Bluffton '73)
Ashland .... 97 Slippery Rock 20-30

Brian Kelly (7-4) (Assumption '83)
Grand Valley St. .... 91 Tex. A&M-Commerce 15-36
Grand Valley St. .... 94 Indiana (Pa.) 27-35
Grand Valley St. .... 98 Slippery Rock 21-37
Grand Valley St. .... 01 Bloomsburg 42-14
Grand Valley St. .... 01 Saginaw Valley 33-32
Grand Valley St. .... 01 Catawba 30-14
Grand Valley St. .... 01 North Dakota 14-17
Grand Valley St. .... 02 C.W. Post 62-13
Grand Valley St. .... 02 Indiana (Pa.) 62-21
Grand Valley St. .... 02 Northern Colo. 44-7
Grand Valley St. .... 02* Valdosta St. 31-24

Roy Kidd (0-1) (Eastern Ky. '54)
Eastern Ky. 76   North Dakota St. 7-10

Jim King (1-1)
West Ala. 75   North Dakota 34-14
West Ala. 75   Northern Mich. 26-28

Tony Knap (1-4) (Idaho '39)
Boise St. 73   South Dakota 53-10
Boise St. 73   Louisiana Tech 34-38
Boise St. 74   Central Mich. 6-20
Boise St. 75   Northern Mich. 21-24
UNLV 76   Akron 6-26

Todd Knight (0-1) (Ouachita Baptist '86)
Delta St. 98   Fort Valley St. 14-21

Roy Kramer (3-0) (Maryville [Tenn.] '53)
Central Mich. 74   Boise St. 20-6
Central Mich. 74   Louisiana Tech 35-14
Central Mich. .... 74*   Delaware 54-14

Gil Krueger (4-2) (Marquette '52)
Northern Mich. 75   Boise St. 24-21
Northern Mich. 75   West Ala. 28-26
Northern Mich. ...... 75*   Western Ky. 16-14
Northern Mich. 76   Delaware 28-17
Northern Mich. 76   Akron 26-29

Northern Mich. 77   North Dakota St. 6-20

Maxie Lambright (4-1) (Southern Miss. '49)
Louisiana Tech........ 73   Western Ill. 18-13
Louisiana Tech........ 73   Boise St. 38-34
Louisiana Tech........ 73*   Western Ky. 34-0
Louisiana Tech........ 74   Western Caro. 10-7
Louisiana Tech........ 74   Central Mich. 14-35

George Landis (1-1) (Penn St. '71)
Bloomsburg 85   Hampton 38-28
Bloomsburg 85   North Ala. 0-34

Jon Lantz (0-1) (Okla. Panhandle '74)
Mo. Southern St. 93   Minn St. Mankato 13-34

Henry Lattimore (1-1) (Jackson St. '57)
N.C. Central 88   Winston-Salem 31-16
N.C. Central 88   Sacramento St. 7-56

Dale Lennon (4-1) (North Dakota '85)
North Dakota 99   Northwest Mo. St. 13-20 (ot)
North Dakota 01   Winona St. 42-28
North Dakota 01   Pittsburg St. 38-0
North Dakota 01   UC Davis 14-2
North Dakota .... 01*   Grand Valley St. 17-14

Malen Luke (2-1) (Westminster [Pa.] '76)
Clarion 96   Bloomsburg 42-29
Clarion 96   Ferris St. 23-21
Clarion 96   Northern Colo. 18-19

Bill Lynch (0-1) (Butler '77)
Butler 88   Tenn.-Martin 6-23

Dick MacPherson (0-1) (Springfield '58)
Massachusetts....... 77   Lehigh 23-30

George Mahalik (3-3) (Slippery Rock '74)
Slippery Rock 97   Ashland 30-20
Slippery Rock 97   New Haven 21-49
Slippery Rock 98   Grand Valley St. 37-21
Slippery Rock 98   Shepherd 31-20
Slippery Rock 98   Carson-Newman 21-47

Slippery Rock 99   Indiana (Pa.) 20-27 (ot)

Pat Malley (1-1) (Santa Clara '53)
Santa Clara........... 80   Northern Mich. 27-26
Santa Clara........... 80   Cal Poly 14-38

Noel Martin (1-1) (Nebraska '63)
St. Cloud St. 89   Augustana (S.D.) 27-20
St. Cloud St. 89   Mississippi Col. 24-55

Fred Martinelli (0-1) (Otterbein '51)
Ashland 86   North Dakota St. 0-50

Bob Mattos (2-1) (Sacramento St. '64)
Sacramento St. 88   UC Davis 35-14
Sacramento St. 88   N.C. Central 56-7
Sacramento St. 88   North Dakota St. 20-42

Gene McDowell (1-1) (Florida St. '65)
UCF 87   Indiana (Pa.) 12-10
UCF 87   Troy St. 10-31

Don McLeary (1-1) (Tennessee '70)
Tenn.-Martin 88   Butler 23-6
Tenn.-Martin 88   Tex. A&M-Kingsville 0-34

Terry McMillan (1-1) (Southern Miss. '69)
Mississippi Col. 91   Wofford 28-15
Mississippi Col. 91   Jacksonville St. 7-35

Ron Meyer (1-1) (Purdue '63)
UNLV 74   Alcorn St. 35-22
UNLV 74   Delaware 11-49

Darrell Morris (0-1) (Northwest Mo. St. '83)
Neb.-Kearney 02   Tex. A&M-Kingsville 40-58

Don Morton (8-3) (Augustana [Ill.] '69)
North Dakota St. 81   Puget Sound 24-10
North Dakota St. 81   Shippensburg 18-6
North Dakota St. 81   Southwest Tex. St. 13-42
North Dakota St. 82   Virginia Union 21-20
North Dakota St. 82   UC Davis 14-19

North Dakota St. 83   Towson 24-17
North Dakota St. 83   UC Davis 26-17
North Dakota St. .... 83*   Central St. 41-21
North Dakota St. 84   UC Davis 31-23
North Dakota St. 84   Neb.-Omaha 25-14

North Dakota St. 84   Troy St. 17-18

Darrell Mudra (5-2) (Peru St. '51)
Western Ill. 73   Louisiana Tech 13-18
Eastern Ill. 78   UC Davis 35-31
Eastern Ill. 78   Youngstown St. 26-22
Eastern Ill. .... 78*   Delaware 10-9
Eastern Ill. 80   Northern Colo. 21-14
Eastern Ill. 80   North Ala. 56-31
Eastern Ill. 80   Cal Poly 13-21

Steve Mullins (0-1) (Ark-Monticello '80)
Arkansas Tech 99   Carson-Newman 28-40

Hal Mumme (2-2) (Tarleton St. '75)
Valdosta St. 94   Albany St. (Ga.) 14-7
Valdosta St. 94   North Ala. 24-27 (2 ot)
Valdosta St. 96   Albany St. (Ga.) 38-28
Valdosta St. 96   Carson-Newman 19-24

Gene Murphy (0-1) (North Dakota '62)
North Dakota 79   Mississippi Col. 15-35

Bill Narduzzi (3-2) (Miami [Ohio] '59)
Youngstown St. 78   Neb.-Omaha 21-14
Youngstown St. 78   Eastern Ill. 22-26
Youngstown St. 79   South Dakota St. 50-7
Youngstown St. 79   Alabama A&M 52-0
Youngstown St. 79   Delaware 21-38

Bob Nielson (0-1) (Wartburg '82)
Minn. Duluth.......... 02   Northwest Mo. St. 41-45

John O'Hara (0-1) (Okla. Panhandle '67)
Southwest Tex. St. .. 83   Central St. 16-24

Jerry Olson (0-1) (Valley City St. '55)
North Dakota 75   West Ala. 14-34

Keith Otterbein (3-2) (Ferris St. '79)
Ferris St. 92   Edinboro 19-15
Ferris St. 92   New Haven 13-35
Ferris St. 93   Indiana (Pa.) 21-28
Ferris St. 94   West Chester 43-40
Ferris St. 94   Indiana (Pa.) 17-21

Kenny Phillips (0-1) (East Caro. '87)
Fayetteville St. 02   Carson-Newman 27-40

Jeff Pierce (3-2) (Ferris St. '79)
Ferris St. 95   Millersville 36-26
Ferris St. 95   New Haven 17-9
Ferris St. 95   North Ala. 7-45
Ferris St. 96   Indiana (Pa.) 24-23
Ferris St. 96   Clarion 21-23

Doug Porter (0-1) (Xavier [La.] '52)
Fort Valley St. 82   Southwest Tex. St. 6-27

George Pugh (0-1) (Alabama '76)
Alabama A&M 89   Jacksonville St. 9-33

Bill Rademacher (1-3) (Northern Mich. '63)
Northern Mich. 80   Santa Clara 6-27
Northern Mich. 81   Elizabeth City St. 55-6
Northern Mich. 81   Southwest Tex. St. 0-62
Northern Mich. 82   UC Davis 21-42

Vito Ragazzo (1-1) (William & Mary '51)
Shippensburg 81   Virginia Union 40-27
Shippensburg 81   North Dakota St. 6-18

Joe Ramunno (1-1) (Wyoming '84)
Mesa St. 00   Northeastern St. 40-21
Mesa St. 00   UC Davis 18-62

Tubby Raymond (7-4) (Michigan '50)
Delaware 73   Grambling 8-17
Delaware 74   Youngstown St. 35-14
Delaware 74   UNLV 49-11
Delaware 74   Central Mich. 14-54
Delaware 76   Northern Mich. 17-28

Delaware 78   Jacksonville St. 42-27
Delaware 78   Winston-Salem 41-0
Delaware 78   Eastern Ill. 9-10
Delaware 79   Virginia Union 58-28
Delaware 79   Mississippi Col. 60-10

Delaware .... 79*   Youngstown St. 38-21

Rocky Rees (1-1) (West Chester '71)
Shippensburg 91   East Stroudsburg 34-33
Shippensburg 91   Indiana (Pa.) 7-52

Rick Rhodes (4-1) (Troy St.)
Troy St. 86   Virginia Union 31-7
Troy St. 86   South Dakota 28-42
Troy St. 87   Winston-Salem 45-14
Troy St. 87   UCF 31-10
Troy St. .... 87*   Portland St. 31-17

Pete Richardson (0-3) (Dayton '68)
Winston-Salem 88   N.C. Central 16-31
Winston-Salem 90   Indiana (Pa.) 0-48
Winston-Salem 91   Jacksonville St. 24-49

Pat Riepma (1-1) (Hillsdale '83)
Northwood............. 00   Indiana (Pa.) 28-0
Northwood............. 00   Bloomsburg 14-38

Steve Roberts (0-1) (Ouachita Baptist '87)
Southern Ark. 97   Albany St. (Ga.) 6-10

Eddie Robinson (1-1) (Leland '41)
Grambling.............. 73   Delaware 17-8
Grambling.............. 73   Western Ky. 20-28

Warren Ruggerio (0-1) (Delaware '88)
Glenville St. 97   New Haven 7-47

Dan Runkle (2-3) (Illinois Col. '68)
Minn. St. Mankato .. 87   Portland St. 21-27
Minn. St. Mankato .. 91   North Dakota 27-7
Minn. St. Mankato .. 91   Portland St. 27-37
Minn. St. Mankato .. 93   Mo. Southern St. 34-13
Minn. St. Mankato .. 93   North Dakota 21-54

Joe Salem (0-2) (Minnesota '61)
South Dakota 73   Boise St. 10-53
Northern Ariz. 77   Jacksonville St. 0-35

Tom Sawyer (0-1) (Winona St. '83)
Winona St. 01   North Dakota 28-42

Kent Schoolfield (1-3) (Florida A&M '70)
Fort Valley St. 98   Delta St. 21-14
Fort Valley St. 98   Carson-Newman 31-38 (ot)
Fort Valley St. 99   Catawba 17-48
Fort Valley St. 01   Valdosta St. 24-40

Lyle Setencich (1-1) (Fresno St. '68)
Cal Poly 90   Cal St. Northridge 14-7
Cal Poly 90   North Dakota St. 0-47

Stan Sheriff (0-1) (Cal Poly '54)
Northern Iowa........ 75   Western Ky. 12-14

Sanders Shiver (0-1) (Carson-Newman '76)
Bowie St. 88   Portland St. 17-34

Ron Simonson (0-1) (Portland St. '65)
Puget Sound 81   North Dakota St. 10-24

Brad Smith (0-4) (Western Ill. '72)
Chadron St. 96   Central Okla. 21-23
Chadron St. 98   Central Okla. 19-21
Chadron St. 00   UC Davis 10-48
Chadron St. 01   Tarleton St. 24-28

Hampton Smith (1-5) (Mississippi Val. '57)
Albany St. (Ga.) 93   Hampton 7-33
Albany St. (Ga.) 94   Valdosta St. 7-14
Albany St. (Ga.) 95   North Ala. 28-38
Albany St. (Ga.) 96   Valdosta St. 28-38
Albany St. (Ga.) 97   Southern Ark. 10-6

Albany St. (Ga.) 97   Carson-Newman 22-23

Rob Smith (0-1) (Washington '81)
Western Wash. 99   Northeastern St. 24-27 (ot)

Jim Sochor (4-8) (San Fran. St. '60)
UC Davis 77   Bethune-Cookman 34-16
UC Davis 77   Lehigh 30-39
UC Davis 78   Eastern Ill. 31-35
UC Davis 82   Northern Mich. 42-21
UC Davis 82   North Dakota St. 19-14

UC Davis 82   Southwest Tex. St. 9-34
UC Davis 83   Butler 25-6
UC Davis 83   North Dakota St. 17-26
UC Davis 84   North Dakota St. 23-31
UC Davis 85   North Dakota St. 12-31

UC Davis 86   South Dakota 23-26
UC Davis 88   Sacramento St. 14-35

Earle Solomonson (6-0) (Augsburg '69)
North Dakota St. 85   UC Davis 31-12
North Dakota St. 85   South Dakota 16-7
North Dakota St. .... 85*   North Ala. 35-7
North Dakota St. 86   Ashland 50-0
North Dakota St. 86   Central St. 35-1 2
North Dakota St. .... 86*   South Dakota 27-7

Tony Sparano (4-2) (New Haven '82)
New Haven............ 95 Edinboro 27-12
New Haven............ 95 Ferris St. 9-17
New Haven............ 97 Glenville St. 47-7
New Haven............ 97 Slippery Rock 49-21
New Haven............ 97 UC Davis 27-25

New Haven............ 97 Northern Colo. 0-51

Ken Sparks (13-8) (Carson-Newman '68)
Carson-Newman..... 93 North Ala. 28-38
Carson-Newman..... 94 North Ala. 13-17
Carson-Newman..... 95 West Ga. 37-26
Carson-Newman..... 95 North Ala. 7-28
Carson-Newman..... 96 West Ga. 41-7

Carson-Newman..... 96 Valdosta St. 24-19
Carson-Newman..... 96 UC Davis 29-26
Carson-Newman..... 96 Northern Colo. 14-23
Carson-Newman..... 97 North Ala. 21-7
Carson-Newman..... 97 Albany St. (Ga.) 23-22

Carson-Newman..... 97 Northern Colo. 29-30
Carson-Newman..... 98 West Ga. 30-20
Carson-Newman..... 98 Fort Valley St. 38-31 (ot)
Carson-Newman..... 98 Slippery Rock 47-21
Carson-Newman..... 98 Northwest Mo. St. 6-24

Carson-Newman..... 99 Arkansas Tech 40-28
Carson-Newman..... 99 Catawba 28-25
Carson-Newman..... 99 Northeastern St. 42-7
Carson-Newman ..... 99* Northwest Mo. St. 52-58 (4 ot)
Carson-Newman ..... 02 Fayetteville 40-27

Carson-Newman ..... 02 Valdosta St. 28-31

Glenn Spencer (0-2) (Georgia Tech '86)
West Ga. .... 98 Carson-Newman 20-30
West Ga. .... 00 Catawba 24-28

Bill Sylvester (0-1) (Butler '50)
Butler .... 83 UC Davis 6-25

Joe Taylor (1-5) (Western Ill. '72)
Virginia Union .... 86 Troy St. 7-31
Virginia Union .... 90 Edinboro 14-38
Virginia Union .... 91 Indiana (Pa.) 7-56
Hampton................ 92 North Ala. 21-33
Hampton................ 93 Albany St. (Ga.) 33-7
Hampton................ 93 North Ala. 20-45

Clarence Thomas (0-1)
Morgan St. .... 79 Alabama A&M 7-27

Roger Thomas (4-5) (Augustana [Ill.] '69)
North Dakota .... 92 Pittsburg St. 21-26
North Dakota .... 93 Pittsburg St. 17-14
North Dakota .... 93 Minn. St. Mankato 54-21
North Dakota .... 93 Indiana (Pa.) 6-21
North Dakota .... 94 Truman 18-6

North Dakota .... 94 North Dakota St. 14-7
North Dakota .... 94 North Ala. 7-35
North Dakota .... 95 North Dakota St. 10-41
North Dakota .... 98 Northern Colo. 24-52

Vern Thomsen (0-1) (Peru St. '61)
Northwest Mo. St. .. 84 Neb.-Omaha 15-28

Mel Tjeerdsma (11-4) (Southern St. '67)
Northwest Mo. St. .. 96 Neb.-Omaha 22-21
Northwest Mo. St. .. 96 Northern Colo. 26-27
Northwest Mo. St. .. 97 North Dakota St. 39-28
Northwest Mo. St. .. 97 Northern Colo. 19-35
Northwest Mo. St. .. 98 Neb.-Omaha 28-14

Northwest Mo. St. .. 98 Northern Colo. 42-17
Northwest Mo. St. .. 98 Tex. A&M-Kingsville 49-34
Northwest Mo. St. .. 98* Carson-Newman 24-6
Northwest Mo. St. .. 99 North Dakota 20-13 (ot)
Northwest Mo. St. .. 99 Northern Colo. 41-35

Northwest Mo. St. .. 99 Indiana (Pa.) 20-12
Northwest Mo. St. .. 99* Carson-Newman 58-52 (4 ot)
Northwest Mo. St. .. 00 North Dakota St. 17-31
Northwest Mo. St. .. 02 Minn. Duluth 45-41
Northwest Mo. St. ... 02 Northern Colo. 12-23

Dave Triplett (3-2) (Iowa '72)
South Dakota .... 85 Central St. 13-10 (2 ot)
South Dakota .... 85 North Dakota St. 7-16
South Dakota .... 86 UC Davis 26-23
South Dakota .... 86 Troy St. 42-28
South Dakota .... 86 North Dakota St. 7-27

Jerry Vandergriff (3-4) (Corpus Christi '65)
Angelo St. .... 87 Northern Mich. 20-23 (ot)
Angelo St. .... 89 UC Davis 28-23
Angelo St. .... 89 Pittsburg St. 24-21
Angelo St. .... 89 Jacksonville St. 16-34
Angelo St. .... 94 Portland St. 0-29

Angelo St. .... 97 Western St. 46-12
Angelo St. .... 97 UC Davis 33-50

Eddie Vowell (2-3) (Southwestern Okla. '69)
Tex. A&M-Commerce 90 Grand Valley St. 20-14
Tex. A&M-Commerce 90 Pittsburg St. 28-60
Tex. A&M-Commerce 91 Grand Valley St. 36-15
Tex. A&M-Commerce 91 Pittsburg St. 28-38
Tex. A&M-Commerce 95 Portland St. 35-56

Jim Wacker (8-2) (Valparaiso '60)
North Dakota St. .... 76 Eastern Ky. 10-7
North Dakota St. .... 76 Montana St. 3-10
North Dakota St. .... 77 Northern Mich. 20-6
North Dakota St. .... 77 Jacksonville St. 7-31
Southwest Tex. St. .. 81 Jacksonville St. 38-22

Southwest Tex. St. .. 81 Northern Mich. 62-0
Southwest Tex. St. .. 81* North Dakota St. 42-13
Southwest Tex. St. .. 82 Fort Valley St. 27-6
Southwest Tex. St. .. 82 Jacksonville St. 19-14
Southwest Tex. St. .. 82* UC Davis 34-9

Gerald Walker (0-1) (Lincoln [Mo.] '62)
Fort Valley St. .... 85 North Ala. 7-14

Bobby Wallace (13-3) (Mississippi St. '76)
North Ala. .... 90 Jacksonville St. 14-38
North Ala. .... 92 Hampton 33-21
North Ala. .... 92 Jacksonville St. 12-14

North Ala. .... 93 Carson-Newman 38-28
North Ala. .... 93 Hampton 45-20

North Ala. .... 93 Tex. A&M-Kingsville 27-25
North Ala. .... 93* Indiana (Pa.) 41-34
North Ala. .... 94 Carson-Newman 17-13
North Ala. .... 94 Valdosta St. 27-24 (2 ot)
North Ala. .... 94 North Dakota 35-7

North Ala. .... 94* Tex. A&M-Kingsville 16-10
North Ala. .... 95 Albany St. (Ga.) 38-28
North Ala. .... 95 Carson-Newman 28-7
North Ala. .... 95 Ferris St. 45-7
North Ala. .... 95* Pittsburg St. 27-7

North Ala. .... 97 Carson-Newman 7-21

Tim Walsh (2-3) (UC Riverside '77)
Portland St. .... 93 Tex. A&M-Kingsville 15-50
Portland St. .... 94 Angelo St. 29-0
Portland St. .... 94 Tex. A&M-Kingsville 16-21
Portland St. .... 95 Tex. A&M-Commerce 56-35
Portland St. .... 95 Tex. A&M-Kingsville 3-30

Johnnie Walton (0-1) (Elizabeth City St. '69)
Elizabeth City St. ... 81 Northern Mich. 6-55

Bob Waters (0-1) (Presbyterian '60)
Western Caro. ..... 74 Louisiana Tech 7-10

Mark Whipple (3-2) (Brown '79)
New Haven............ 92 West Chester 38-26
New Haven............ 92 Ferris St. 35-13
New Haven............ 92 Jacksonville St. 35-46
New Haven............ 93 Edinboro 48-28
New Haven............ 93 Indiana (Pa.) 35-38

John Whitehead (3-0) (East Stroudsburg '50)
Lehigh.................... 77 Massachusetts 30-23
Lehigh.................... 77 UC Davis 39-30
Lehigh.................... 77* Jacksonville St. 33-0

John Williams (†7-3) (Mississippi Col. '57)
Mississippi Col. ..... 79 North Dakota 35-15
Mississippi Col. ..... 79 Delaware 10-60
Mississippi Col. ..... 88 Tex. A&M-Kingsville 15-39
Mississippi Col. ..... 89† Tex. A&M-Kingsville 34-19
Mississippi Col. ..... 89† St. Cloud St. 55-24

Mississippi Col. ..... 89† Indiana (Pa.) 26-14
Mississippi Col. ..... 89†* Jacksonville St. 3-0
Mississippi Col. ..... 90† Wofford 70-19
Mississippi Col. ..... 90† Jacksonville St. 14-7
Mississippi Col. ..... 90† Indiana (Pa.) 8-27

Todd Whitten (1-1) (Stephen F. Austin '87)
Tarleton St. .... 01 Chadron St. 28-24
Tarleton St. .... 01 UC Davis 25-42

John Zamberlin (0-1) (Pacific Lutheran '79)
Central Wash........ 02 UC Davis 6-24

*National championship. †Mississippi College's partici-
pation vacated by action of the NCAA Committee on
Infractions. ^Texas A&M-Kingsville's participation vacated
by action of the NCAA Committee on Infractions.

Division III
Coaching Records

Winningest Active Division III Coaches

(Minimum five years as college head coach; record at four-year colleges only.)

BY PERCENTAGE

Coach, College	Years	Won	Lost	Tied	†Pct.	#Postseason W-L-T
Larry Kehres, Mount Union..............	17	192	17	3	.91274	36-6-0
Joe Fincham, Wittenberg	7	73	9	0	.89024	7-5-0
Dick Farley, Williams	16	108	17	3	.85547	0-0-0
Rick Kacmarynski, Central (Iowa).....	6	57	10	0	.85075	3-4-0
Rick Willis, Wartburg	6	53	10	0	.84127	1-2-0
Chris Creighton, Wabash	6	52	10	0	.83871	2-1-0
John Gagliardi, St. John's (Minn.)	54	400	114	11	.77238	26-14-0
E.J. Mills, Amherst........................	6	37	11	0	.77083	0-0-0
Jimmie Keeling, Hardin-Simmons......	13	109	34	0	.76224	4-3-0

Coach, College	Years	Won	Lost	Tied	†Pct.	#Postseason W-L-T
Frank Girardi, Lycoming	31	232	72	5	.75890	12-10-0
Frosty Westering, Pacific Lutheran....	38	299	93	7	.75815	8-3-0
Jay Locey, Linfield	7	50	16	0	.75758	1-2-0
Jim Barnes, Augustana (Ill.)	8	61	20	0	.75309	2-2-0
Mike Welch, Ithaca.......................	9	70	26	0	.72917	4-2-0
Rich Lackner, Carnegie Mellon	17	121	46	2	.72189	0-1-0
Mike Swider, Wheaton (Ill.)	7	49	19	0	.72059	1-1-0
John Audino, Union (N.Y.)	13	94	37	0	.71756	1-1-0
Joe King, Rensselaer......................	14	93	37	2	.71212	0-2-0
Wayne Perry, Hanover	21	150	62	2	.70561	1-5-0
Lou Wacker, Emory & Henry...........	21	155	65	0	.70455	3-5-0
Doug Neibuhr, Millikin	14	96	40	1	.70438	0-3-0
Norm Eash, Ill. Wesleyan	16	105	44	1	.70333	2-2-0
Steven Mohr, Trinity (Tex.)..............	13	102	44	0	.69863	12-7-0
Mike Drass, Wesley	10	70	30	0	.69802	0-1-0
Tom Clark, Catholic	9	63	27	1	.69780	0-3-0
Bob Frey, MacMurray	8	57	25	0	.69512	0-2-0
Ron Ernst, Ripon..........................	12	79	35	0	.69298	0-0-0
Mike Maynard, Redlands	15	94	42	0	.68978	0-3-0
Steve Nelson, Curry	5	35	16	0	.68627	0-0-0
Vance Gibson, Howard Payne	11	76	35	0	.68468	0-0-0

Coach, College	Years	Won	Lost	Tied	†Pct.	#Postseason W-L-T
Rick Giancola, Montclair St.	20	139	66	2	.67633	5-6-0
Pete Fredenburg, Mary Hardin-Baylor	5	34	17	0	.66667	0-2-0
John Miech, Wis.-Stevens Point	15	99	50	2	.66225	1-2-0
Tim Keating, McDaniel	15	101	51	3	.66129	2-5-0
Greg Carlson, Whittier	18	112	57	2	.66082	
Steve Johnson, Bethel (Minn.)	14	91	49	1	.64894	0-2-0
Jeff Gabrielson, Concordia (Wis.)	13	79	44	0	.64228	0-0-0
Rocco Salomone, Brockport St.	8	52	29	1	.64024	2-3-0
Don Roney, St. Thomas (Minn.)	5	32	18	0	.64000	0-0-0
Bob Berezowitz, Wis.-Whitewater	18	116	65	4	.63784	1-3-0
Steve Briggs, Susquehanna	13	84	48	0	.63636	2-1-0
Darwin Breaux, Dickinson	10	65	37	1	.63592	0-1-0
Mike Cragg, Hobart	8	49	29	0	.62821	0-1-0
Eric Hamilton, Col. of New Jersey	27	165	99	6	.62222	3-4-0
Blair Hrovat, Allegheny	5	31	19	0	.62000	
Nick Mourouzis, DePauw	22	133	82	4	.61644	0-0-0
Brien Cullen, Worcester St.	18	107	67	0	.61494	0-0-0
Dick Maloney, Chicago	9	51	32	0	.61446	0-0-0
Bill Kavanaugh, Mass.-Dartmouth	13	78	49	0	.61417	0-1-0
Scot Dapp, Moravian	16	100	63	1	.61280	1-2-0
John O'Grady, Wis.-River Falls	14	84	54	3	.60638	1-2-0
Craig Rundle, Albion	17	97	64	1	.60185	0-1-0
Jim Scott, Aurora	17	91	60	3	.60065	0-2-0
Larry Kindbom, Washington (Mo.)	20	118	80	1	.59548	0-1-0
Mike Donnelly, Muhlenberg	6	38	26	0	.59375	1-1-0
Jim Cole, Alma	12	67	46	0	.59292	0-2-0
Jim Margraff, Johns Hopkins	13	75	52	3	.58846	0-0-0
Mike Hollway, Ohio Wesleyan	20	116	81	2	.58794	0-0-0
Dale Widolff, Occidental	21	111	81	2	.57732	1-3-0
Bob Bierie, Loras	23	133	97	5	.57660	0-0-0
Frank Hauser, Wesleyan (Conn.)	11	50	38	0	.56818	0-0-0
Dean Kreps, Hope	8	42	32	0	.56757	0-0-0
Roger Caron, Pomona-Pitzer	9	42	32	0	.56757	0-0-0
Dan MacNeill, Cortland St.	6	35	27	0	.56452	0-1-0
Peter Mazzaferro, Bridgewater St.	39	197	151	11	.56407	0-2-0
Frank Sheptock, Wilkes	7	40	31	0	.56338	0-0-0
Ed Sweeney, Mount Ida	17	95	74	3	.56105	0-2-0
Andy Frye, Centre	5	28	22	0	.56000	0-0-0
Mike DeLong, Springfield	21	114	91	2	.55556	2-3-0
Scott Boone, Randolph-Macon	6	33	27	0	.55000	0-0-0
Dennis Miller, Wis. Lutheran	15	87	74	0	.54037	0-0-0
Tom Kaczkowski, Ohio Northern	17	93	79	2	.54023	3-2-0
Mark Speckman, Willamette	5	27	23	0	.54000	0-1-0
Jay Schoenebeck, Gust. Adolphus	9	48	42	0	.53333	0-0-0
Steve Stetson, Hartwick	17	84	76	4	.52439	0-0-0
Michael Clark, Bridgewater (Va.)	8	45	41	1	.52299	4-3-0
Regis Scafe, John Carroll	9	49	45	0	.52128	3-1-0
Larry Terry, Wis.-La Crosse	7	39	36	1	.51974	0-0-0
Vince Brautigam, Dubuque	13	70	65	0	.51852	0-0-0
Steve Marino, Westfield St.	13	66	62	1	.51550	0-1-0
Barry Streeter, Gettysburg	25	127	121	5	.51186	2-1-0
Dave Davis, Ferrum	9	45	43	0	.51136	0-0-0
Ed DeGeorge, Beloit	26	123	118	1	.51033	5-0-0
Brian Keller, Neb. Wesleyan	6	31	30	0	.50820	0-1-0
John Tully, Whitworth	13	65	63	1	.50775	0-1-0
Dave Murray, Alfred	13	67	65	1	.50752	0-1-0

Coach, College	Years	Won	Lost	Tied	†Pct.	#Postseason W-L-T
Robin Cooper, North Park	13	59	58	0	.50427	0-0-0
Bill Samko, Tufts	16	67	67	1	.50000	0-0-0
John Windham, Sewanee	7	33	33	0	.50000	0-0-0
Don Morel, La Verne	8	35	36	0	.49296	0-0-0
Ed Meierkort, Wis.-Stout	10	49	51	0	.49000	0-1-0
Terry Price, Maranatha Baptist	26	120	125	1	.48984	0-0-0
Frank Miriello, Wash. & Lee	8	38	40	1	.48734	0-0-0
Jim Sypult, Methodist	11	54	57	0	.48649	0-0-0
Tim Rogers, Kalamazoo	5	22	24	0	.47826	0-0-0
Rick Candaele, Claremont-M-S	11	47	52	0	.47475	0-1-0
Theophilus Danzy, Stillman	14	64	71	3	.47464	0-0-0
Joe White, Rhodes	6	27	30	0	.47368	0-0-0
Jeff Heacock, Muskingum	22	99	114	4	.46544	0-0-0
Ken Visser, Chapman	12	50	58	0	.46330	0-0-0
Scott Squires, Cal Lutheran	7	29	34	0	.46032	0-0-0
Tom Austin, Colby	17	62	73	1	.45956	0-0-0
E.J. Sandusky, Albright	6	28	33	0	.45902	0-0-0
Jack Osberg, Augsburg	12	55	66	0	.45455	1-1-0
Carlin Carpenter, Bluffton	24	103	125	1	.45197	0-0-0
Andy Gibbons, Knox	7	30	37	0	.44776	0-0-0
Kevin Burke, Juniata	5	22	28	0	.44000	0-0-0
Mike Wallace, Wilmington (Ohio)	12	51	66	1	.43644	0-0-0
Greg Pscodna, Defiance	7	29	38	0	.43284	0-1-0
Mike Ketchum, Guilford	12	50	68	0	.42373	0-0-0
Nick Fletcher, Denison	8	33	46	0	.41772	0-0-0
Chris Smith, Grove City	19	74	104	2	.41667	0-0-0
Mike Yesalonia, Norwich	6	25	35	0	.41667	0-0-0
Phil Wilks, Maryville (Tenn.)	15	62	87	0	.41611	0-0-0
Dennis Gorsline, Martin Luther	32	117	165	1	.41519	0-0-0
Sherman Wood, Salisbury	10	41	58	1	.41500	0-1-0
Jim Lyall, Adrian	13	49	70	1	.41250	0-0-0
David Norman, Austin	9	36	52	0	.40909	0-0-0
Rich Mannello, King's (Pa.)	10	41	61	1	.40291	1-1-0
Greg Wallace, Grinnell	15	55	84	1	.39643	0-0-0
Ed Zaloom, WPI	7	26	40	0	.39394	0-0-0
Dwight Smith, MIT	15	48	77	1	.38492	0-0-0
Tim Rucks, Carthage	13	44	72	4	.38333	0-0-0
John Welty, Westminster (Mo.)	13	47	76	1	.38306	0-0-0
Jeff Hynes, Concordia (Ill.)	5	19	31	0	.38000	0-0-0
Rod Humenuik, Principia	5	14	26	0	.35000	0-0-0
Gerry Martin, Western New Eng.	12	33	71	1	.31905	0-0-0
Steve Keenum, McMurry	11	33	72	0	.31429	0-0-0
Dave Harms, Manchester	8	25	55	0	.31250	0-0-0
Mark Kreydt, Rochester	5	15	33	0	.31250	0-0-0
Paul Vosburgh, St. John Fisher	15	42	100	1	.29720	0-0-0
Jim Collins, Capital	9	26	64	0	.28889	0-0-0
Greg Polnasek, Colorado Col.	10	26	67	0	.27957	0-0-0
Mark Harriman, Bates	5	10	30	0	.25000	0-0-0
Paul Krohn, Elmhurst	10	21	71	1	.23118	0-0-0
Larry Arico, Wm. Paterson	6	13	47	0	.21667	0-0-0
Bob Thomas, Hiram	11	22	88	0	.20000	0-0-0
Dennis Czech, Macalester	5	12	48	0	.20000	0-0-0
Mike Strachan, Framingham St.	8	15	61	0	.19737	0-0-0
Mike Silecchia, Lebanon Valley	5	9	41	0	.18000	0-0-0
Peter Alvanos, Hamilton	5	6	36	0	.14286	0-0-0

†Ties computed as half won and half lost. #Includes bowl and playoff games.

BY VICTORIES

(Minimum five years as college head coach)

Coach, College	*Wins
John Gagliardi, St. John's (Minn.)	400
Frosty Westering, Pacific Lutheran	299
Frank Girardi, Lycoming	232
Peter Mazzaferro, Bridgewater St.	197
Larry Kehres, Mount Union	192
Eric Hamilton, Col. of New Jersey	165
Lou Wacker, Emory & Henry	155
Wayne Perry, Hanover	150
Rick Giancola, Montclair St.	139
Bob Bierie, Loras	133
Nick Mourouzis, DePauw	133
Barry Streeter, Gettysburg	127
Ed DeGeorge, Beloit	123
Rich Lackner, Carnegie Mellon	121
Terry Price, Maranatha Baptist	120

Coach, College	*Wins
Larry Kindbom, Washington (Mo.)	118
Dennis Gorsline, Martin Luther	117
Bob Berezowitz, Wis.-Whitewater	116
Mike Hollway, Ohio Wesleyan	116
Mike DeLong, Springfield	114
Greg Carlson, Whittier	112
Dale Widolff, Occidental	111
Jimmie Keeling, Hardin-Simmons	109
Dick Farley, Williams	108
Brien Cullen, Worcester St.	107
Norm Eash, Ill. Wesleyan	105
Carlin Carpenter, Bluffton	103
Steven Mohr, Trinity (Tex.)	102
Tim Keating, McDaniel	101
Scot Dapp, Moravian	100
Jeff Heacock, Muskingum	99
John Miech, Wis.-Stevens Point	99
Craig Rundle, Albion	97

Coach, College	*Wins
Doug Neibuhr, Millikin	96
Ed Sweeney, Mount Ida	95
John Audino, Union (N.Y.)	94
Mike Maynard, Redlands	94
Tom Kaczkowski, Ohio Northern	93
Joe King, Rensselaer	93
Steve Johnson, Bethel (Minn.)	91
Jim Scott, Aurora	91
Dennis Miller, Wis. Lutheran	87
Steve Briggs, Susquehanna	84
John O'Grady, Wis.-River Falls	84
Steve Stetson, Hartwick	84
Ron Ernst, Ripon	79
Jeff Gabrielson, Concordia (Wis.)	79
Bill Kavanaugh, Mass.-Dartmouth	78
Vance Gibson, Howard Payne	75
Jim Margraff, Johns Hopkins	75
Chris Smith, Grove City	74

Coach, College	*Wins
Joe Fincham, Wittenberg	73
Vince Brautigam, Dubuque	70
Mike Drass, Wesley	70
Mike Welch, Ithaca	70
Jim Cole, Alma	67
Dave Murray, Alfred	67
Bill Samko, Tufts	67
Steve Marino, Westfield St.	66
Darwin Breaux, Dickinson	65
John Tully, Whitworth	65
Theophilus Danzy, Stillman	64
Tom Clark, Catholic	63
Tom Austin, Colby	62
Phil Wilks, Maryville (Tenn.)	62
Jim Barnes, Augustana (Ill.)	61
Robin Cooper, North Park	59
Bob Frey, MacMurray	57
Rick Kacmarynski, Central (Iowa)	57
Jack Osberg, Augsburg	55
Greg Wallace, Grinnell	55
Jim Sypult, Methodist	54
Rick Willis, Wartburg	53
Chris Creighton, Wabash	52
Rocco Salomone, Brockport St.	52
Dick Maloney, Chicago	51
Mike Wallace, Wilmington (Ohio)	51
Frank Hauser, Wesleyan (Conn.)	50
Mike Ketchum, Guilford	50
Jay Locey, Linfield	50
Ken Visser, Chapman	50
Mike Cragg, Hobart	49
Jim Lyall, Adrian	49
Ed Meierkort, Wis.-Stout	49
Regis Scafe, John Carroll	49
Mike Swider, Wheaton (Ill.)	49
Jay Schoenebeck, Gust. Adolphus	48
Dwight Smith, MIT	48
Rick Candaele, Claremont-M-S	47
John Welty, Westminster (Mo.)	47
Michael Clark, Bridgewater (Va.)	45
Dave Davis, Ferrum	45
Tim Rucks, Carthage	44
Roger Caron, Pomona-Pitzer	42
Dean Kreps, Hope	42
Paul Vosburgh, St. John Fisher	42
Rich Mannello, King's (Pa.)	41
Sherman Wood, Salisbury	41
Frank Sheptock, Wilkes	40
Larry Terry, Wis.-La Crosse	39
Mike Donnelly, Muhlenberg	38
Frank Miriello, Wash. & Lee	38
E.J. Mills, Amherst	37
David Norman, Austin	36
Dan MacNeill, Cortland St.	35
Don Morel, La Verne	35
Steve Nelson, Curry	35
Pete Fredenburg, Mary Hardin-Baylor	34
Scott Boone, Randolph-Macon	33
Nick Fletcher, Denison	33
Steve Keenum, McMurry	33
Gerry Martin, Western New Eng.	33
John Windham, Sewanee	33
Don Roney, St. Thomas (Minn.)	32
Blair Hrovat, Allegheny	31
Brian Keller, Neb. Wesleyan	31
Andy Gibbons, Knox	30
Greg Pscodna, Defiance	29
Greg Wallace, Grinnell	
Scott Squires, Cal Lutheran	29
Andy Frye, Centre	28
E.J. Sandusky, Albright	28
Mark Speckman, Willamette	27
Joe White, Rhodes	27
Jim Collins, Capital	26
Greg Polnasek, Colorado Col.	26
Ed Zaloom, WPI	26
Dave Harms, Manchester	25
Mike Yesalonia, Norwich	25
Kevin Burke, Juniata	22
Tim Rogers, Kalamazoo	22
Bob Thomas, Hiram	22
Paul Krohn, Elmhurst	21
Jeff Hynes, Concordia (Ill.)	19
Mark Kreydt, Rochester	15
Mike Strachan, Framingham St.	15

Coach, College	*Wins
Rod Humenuik, Principia	14
Larry Arico, Wm. Paterson	13
Dennis Czech, Macalester	12
Mark Harriman, Bates	10
Mike Silecchia, Lebanon Valley	9
Peter Alvanos, Hamilton	6

*Includes bowls and playoff games.

Division III Championship Coaches

All coaches who have coached teams in the Division III championship playoffs since 1973 are listed here with their playoff record, alma mater and year graduated, team, year coached, opponent, and score.

Jay Accorsi (0-1) (Nichols '85)
Rowan 02   Brockport St. 12-15

Phil Albert (2-1) (Arizona '66)
Towson 76   C.W. Post 14-10
Towson 76   St. Lawrence 38-36
Towson 76   St. John's (Minn.) 28-31

Dom Anile (0-1) (C. W. Post '59)
C. W. Post 76   Towson 10-14

John Audino (1-3) (Notre Dame '75)
Union (N.Y.) 93   Wm. Paterson 7-17
Union (N.Y.) 95   Plymouth St. 24-7
Union (N.Y.) 95   Rowan 7-38
Union (N.Y.) 00   Widener 26-33

Don Ault (0-1) (West Liberty St. '52)
Bethany (W.Va.) 80   Widener 12-43

Al Bagnoli (7-6) (Central Conn. St. '74)
Union (N.Y.) 83   Hofstra 51-19
Union (N.Y.) 83   Salisbury 23-21
Union (N.Y.) 83   Augustana (Ill.) 17-21
Union (N.Y.) 84   Plymouth St. 26-14
Union (N.Y.) 84   Augustana (Ill.) 6-23
Union (N.Y.) 85   Ithaca 12-13
Union (N.Y.) 86   Ithaca 17-24 (ot)
Union (N.Y.) 89   Cortland St. 42-14
Union (N.Y.) 89   Montclair St. 45-6
Union (N.Y.) 89   Ferrum 37-21
Union (N.Y.) 89   Dayton 7-17
Union (N.Y.) 91   Mass.-Lowell 55-16
Union (N.Y.) 91   Ithaca 23-35

John Banaszak (3-4) (Eastern Mich. '75)
Wash. & Jeff. 99   Lycoming 14-7
Wash. & Jeff. 99   Hardin-Simmons 3-51
Wash. & Jeff. 00   Bridgewater (Va.) 42-59
Wash. & Jeff. 01   McDaniel 24-21
Wash. & Jeff. 01   Widener 30-46
Wash. & Jeff. 02   Chris. Newport 24-10
Wash. & Jeff. 02   Trinity (Tex.) 10-45

Jim Barnes (1-1) (Augustana [Ill.] '81)
Augustana (Ill.) 01   Defiance 54-14
Augustana (Ill.) 01   Mount Union 7-32

Bob Berezowitz (1-3) (Wis.-Whitewater '67)
Wis.-Whitewater..... 88   Simpson 29-27
Wis.-Whitewater..... 88   Central (Iowa) 13-16
Wis.-Whitewater..... 90   St. Thomas (Minn.) 23-24
Wis.-Whitewater..... 97   Simpson 31-34

Don Birmingham (0-2) (Westmar '62)
Dubuque 79   Ithaca 7-27
Dubuque 80   Minn.-Morris 35-41

J.R. Bishop (1-1) (Franklin '61)
Wheaton (Ill.) 95   Wittenberg 63-41
Wheaton (Ill.) 95   Mount Union 14-40

Jim Blackburn (0-1) (Virginia '71)
Randolph-Macon..... 84   Wash. & Jeff. 21-22

Bill Bless (0-1) (Indianapolis '63)
Indianapolis........... 75   Wittenberg 13-17

Jerry Boyes (2-7) (Ithaca '76)
Buffalo St. 92   Ithaca 28-26
Buffalo St. 92   Rowan 19-28
Buffalo St. 93   Rowan 6-29
Buffalo St. 94   Ithaca 7-10 (2 ot)
Buffalo St. 95   Rowan 7-46
Buffalo St. 96   Rowan 20-21
Buffalo St. 98   Springfield 38-35
Buffalo St. 98   Rowan 17-19
Buffalo St. 98   Montclair St. 34-37

Darwin Breaux (0-1) (West Chester '77)
Dickinson 94   Widener 0-14

Steve Briggs (2-1) (Springfield '84)
Susquehanna......... 91   Dickinson 21-20
Susquehanna......... 91   Lycoming 31-24
Susquehanna......... 91   Ithaca 13-49

Don Brown (1-2) (Norwich '77)
Plymouth St. 94   Merchant Marine 19-18
Plymouth St. 94   Ithaca 7-22
Plymouth St. 95   Union (N.Y.) 7-24

John Bunting (2-2) (North Carolina '72)
Rowan 91   Ithaca 10-31
Rowan 92   WPI 41-14
Rowan 92   Buffalo St. 28-19
Rowan 92   Wash. & Jeff. 13-18

Jim Butterfield (21-8) (Maine '53)
Ithaca 74   Slippery Rock 27-14
Ithaca 74   Central (Iowa) 8-10
Ithaca 75   Fort Valley St. 41-12
Ithaca 75   Widener 23-14
Ithaca 75   Wittenberg 0-28
Ithaca 78   Wittenberg 3-6
Ithaca 79   Dubuque 27-7
Ithaca 79   Carnegie Mellon 15-6
Ithaca .... 79* Wittenberg 14-10
Ithaca 80   Wagner 41-13
Ithaca 80   Minn.-Morris 36-0
Ithaca 80   Dayton 0-63
Ithaca 85   Union (N.Y.) 13-12
Ithaca 85   Montclair St. 50-28
Ithaca 85   Gettysburg 34-0
Ithaca 85   Augustana (Ill.) 7-20
Ithaca 86   Union (N.Y.) 24-17 (ot)
Ithaca 86   Montclair St. 29-15
Ithaca 86   Salisbury 40-44
Ithaca 88   Wagner 34-31 (ot)
Ithaca 88   Cortland St. 24-17
Ithaca 88   Ferrum 62-28
Ithaca .... 88* Central (Iowa) 39-24
Ithaca 90   Col. of New Jersey 14-24
Ithaca 91   Rowan 31-10
Ithaca 91   Union (N.Y.) 35-23
Ithaca 91   Susquehanna 49-13
Ithaca .... 91* Dayton 34-20
Ithaca 92   Buffalo St. 26-28

Jim Byers (0-1) (Michigan '59)
Evansville 74   Central (Iowa) 16-17

Don Canfield (0-1)
Wartburg 82   Bishop 7-32

Jerry Carle (0-1) (Northwestern '48)
Colorado Col. 75   Millsaps 21-28

Gene Carpenter (0-1) (Huron '63)
Millersville 79   Wittenberg 14-21

Rick Carter (3-1) (Earlham '65)
Dayton 78   Carnegie Mellon 21-24
Dayton 80   Baldwin-Wallace 34-0
Dayton 80   Widener 28-24
Dayton .... 80* Ithaca 63-0

John Cervino (0-1) (West Va. Wesleyan '82)
Western Conn. St. . 99   Montclair St. 24-32

Don Charlton (0-1) (Lock Haven '65)
Hiram 87   Augustana (Ill.) 0-53

Jim Christopherson (2-4) (Concordia-M'head '60)
Concordia-M'head.. 86   Wis.-Stevens Point 24-15
Concordia-M'head.. 86   Central (Iowa) 17-14
Concordia-M'head.. 86   Augustana (Ill.) 7-41
Concordia-M'head.. 88   Central (Iowa) 0-7
Concordia-M'head.. 95   Wis.-La Crosse 7-45
Concordia-M'head.. 97   Augsburg 22-34

Mike Clark (5-3) (Cincinnati '79)
Bridgewater (Va.).... 00   Wash. & Jeff. 59-42
Bridgewater (Va.).... 00   Trinity (Tex.) 41-47 (ot)
Bridgewater (Va.).... 01   Trinity (Tex.) 41-37
Bridgewater (Va.).... 01   Widener 57-32
Bridgewater (Va.).... 01   Rowan 29-24
Bridgewater (Va.).... 01   Mount Union 27-30
Bridgewater (Va.).... 02   King's (Pa.) 19-17
Bridgewater (Va.).... 02   Trinity (Tex.) 32-38

Tom Clark (0-3) (Maryland '86)
Catholic 97   Trinity (Tex.) 33-44
Catholic 98   Lycoming 14-49
Catholic 99   McDaniel 16-20

Vic Clark (0-1) (Indiana St. '71)
Thomas More 92   Emory & Henry 0-17

COACHING RECORDS

Mike Clary (0-1) (Rhodes '77)
Rhodes 88   Ferrum 10-35

Jim Cole (0-2) (Alma '74)
Alma 99   Wittenberg 19-42
Alma 02   Wheaton (Ill.) 14-42

Jay Cottone (0-1) (Norwich '71)
Plymouth St. 84   Union (N.Y.) 14-26

Michael Cragg (1-2) (Slippery Rock '81)
Hobart 00   Bridgewater St. 25-0
Hobart 00   Widener 14-40
Hobart 02   John Carroll 7-27

Chris Creighton (2-1) (Kenyon '91)
Wabash 02   MacMurray 42-7
Wabash 02   Wittenberg 25-14
Wabash 02   Mount Union 16-45

Bill Cubit (1-2) (Delaware '75)
Widener 94   Dickinson 14-0
Widener 94   Wash. & Jeff. 21-37
Widener 95   Lycoming 27-31

Scot Dapp (1-2) (West Chester '73)
Moravian 88   Widener 17-7
Moravian 88   Ferrum 28-49
Moravian 93   Wash. & Jeff. 7-27

Harper Davis (1-1) (Mississippi St. '49)
Millsaps 75   Colorado Col. 28-21
Millsaps 75   Wittenberg 22-55

Tony DeCarlo (1-2) (Kent St. '62)
John Carroll 89   Dayton 10-35
John Carroll 97   Hanover 30-20
John Carroll 97   Mount Union 7-59

Mike DeLong (2-3) (Springfield '74)
Springfield 98   Buffalo St. 35-38
Springfield 00   Montclair St. 31-29
Springfield 00   Brockport St. 13-6
Springfield 00   Widener 27-61
Springfield 02   Brockport St. 0-16

Mike Donnelly (1-1) (Ithaca '75)
Muhlenberg 02   Mass.-Dartmouth 56-6
Muhlenberg 02   John Carroll 10-21

Joe DeMelfi (0-1) (Delta St. '66)
Wilkes 93   Frostburg St. 25-26

Bob Di Spirito (0-1) (Rhode Island '53)
Slippery Rock 74   Ithaca 14-27

Mike Drass (0-1) (Mansfield '83)
Wesley 00   Trinity (Tex.) 3-21

Norm Eash (2-2) (Ill. Wesleyan '75)
Ill. Wesleyan 92   Aurora 21-12
Ill. Wesleyan 92   Mount Union 27-49
Ill. Wesleyan 96   Albion 23-20
Ill. Wesleyan 96   Mount Union 14-49

Chad Eisele (0-1) (Knox '90)
Lake Forest 02   Wartburg 0-45

Ed Farrell (0-1) (Rutgers '56)
Bridgeport 73   Juniata 14-35

Joe Fincham (7-5) (Ohio '88)
Wittenberg 98   Millikin 13-10
Wittenberg 98   Mount Union 19-21
Wittenberg 99   Alma 42-19
Wittenberg 99   Ohio Northern 24-58
Wittenberg 00   Aurora 31-20
Wittenberg 00   Hanover 32-21
Wittenberg 00   Mount Union 15-32
Wittenberg 01   Hardin-Simmons 38-35 (ot)
Wittenberg 01   Thomas More 41-0
Wittenberg 01   Mount Union 21-49
Wittenberg 02   Hanover 34-33
Wittenberg 02   Wabash 14-25

Bob Ford (1-1) (Springfield '59)
Albany (N.Y.) 77   Hampden-Sydney 51-45
Albany (N.Y.) 77   Widener 15-33

Pete Fredenburg (0-2) (Southwest Tex. St. '70)
Mary Hardin-Baylor. 01   Trinity (Tex.) 6-30
Mary Hardin-Baylor. 02   Trinity (Tex.) 38-48

Bob Frey (0-2) (Mount Union '85)
MacMurray 01   Thomas More 30-34
MacMurray 02   Wabash 7-42

Stokeley Fulton (0-1) (Hampden-Sydney '55)
Hampden-Sydney.... 77   Albany (N.Y.) 45-51

John Gagliardi (26-13) (Colorado Col. '49)
St. John's (Minn.) 76   Augustana (Ill.) 46-7
St. John's (Minn.) 76   Buena Vista 61-0
St. John's (Minn.) .... 76*   Towson 31-28
St. John's (Minn.) 77   Wabash 9-20

St. John's (Minn.) 85   Occidental 10-28
St. John's (Minn.) 87   Gust. Adolphus 7-3
St. John's (Minn.) 87   Central (Iowa) 3-13
St. John's (Minn.) 89   Simpson 42-35
St. John's (Minn.) 89   Central (Iowa) 27-24
St. John's (Minn.) 89   Dayton 0-28
St. John's (Minn.) 91   Coe 75-2
St. John's (Minn.) 91   Wis.-La Crosse 29-10
St. John's (Minn.) 91   Dayton 7-19
St. John's (Minn.) 93   Coe 32-14
St. John's (Minn.) 93   Wis.-La Crosse 47-25
St. John's (Minn.) 93   Mount Union 8-56
St. John's (Minn.) 94   La Verne 51-12
St. John's (Minn.) 94   Wartburg 42-14
St. John's (Minn.) 94   Albion 16-19
St. John's (Minn.) 96   Simpson 21-18
St. John's (Minn.) 96   Wis.-La Crosse 30-37
St. John's (Minn.) 98   Pacific Lutheran 33-20
St. John's (Minn.) 98   Wis.-Eau Claire 7-10
St. John's (Minn.) 99   Wis.-Stevens Point 23-10
St. John's (Minn.) 99   Central (Iowa) 10-9
St. John's (Minn.) 99   Pacific Lutheran 9-19
St. John's (Minn.) 00   Wis.-Stout 26-19
St. John's (Minn.) 00   Pacific Lutheran 28-21 (ot)
St. John's (Minn.) 00   Central (Iowa) 21-18
St. John's (Minn.) 00   Hardin-Simmons 38-14
St. John's (Minn.) 00   Mount Union 7-10
St. John's (Minn.) 01   St. Norbert 27-20
St. John's (Minn.) 01   Wis.-Stevens Point 9-7
St. John's (Minn.) 01   Pacific Lutheran 31-6
St. John's (Minn.) 01   Mount Union 14-35
St. John's (Minn.) 02   Redlands 31-24
St. John's (Minn.) 02   Coe 45-14
St. John's (Minn.) 02   Linfield 21-14
St. John's (Minn.) 02   Trinity (Tex.) 34-41

Gerry Gallagher (1-1) (Wm. Paterson '74)
Wm. Paterson 93   Union (N.Y.) 17-7
Wm. Paterson 93   Rowan 0-37

Joe Gardi (2-1) (Maryland '60)
Hofstra 90   Cortland St. 35-9
Hofstra 90   Col. of New Jersey 38-3
Hofstra 90   Lycoming 10-20

Rick Giancola (5-6) (Rowan '68)
Montclair St. 85   Western Conn. St. 28-0
Montclair St. 85   Ithaca 28-50
Montclair St. 86   Hofstra 24-21
Montclair St. 86   Ithaca 15-29
Montclair St. 89   Hofstra 23-6
Montclair St. 89   Union (N.Y.) 6-45
Montclair St. 99   Buffalo St. 37-34
Montclair St. 99   Western Conn. St. 32-24
Montclair St. 99   Rowan 13-42
Montclair St. 00   Springfield 29-31
Montclair St. 01   Ithaca 23-35

Steve Gilbert (0-1) (West Chester '79)
Ursinus 96   Lycoming 24-31

Frank Girardi (12-10) (West Chester '61)
Lycoming 85   Gettysburg 10-14
Lycoming 89   Dickinson 21-0
Lycoming 89   Ferrum 24-49
Lycoming 90   Carnegie Mellon 17-7
Lycoming 90   Wash. & Jeff. 24-0
Lycoming 90   Hofstra 20-10
Lycoming 90   Allegheny 14-21 (ot)
Lycoming 91   Wash. & Jeff. 18-16
Lycoming 91   Susquehanna 24-31
Lycoming 92   Wash. & Jeff. 0-33
Lycoming 95   Widener 31-27
Lycoming 95   Wash. & Jeff. 0-48
Lycoming 96   Ursinus 31-24
Lycoming 96   Albright 31-13
Lycoming 96   Rowan 14-33
Lycoming 97   McDaniel 27-13
Lycoming 97   Trinity (Tex.) 46-26
Lycoming 97   Rowan 28-20
Lycoming .... 97*   Mount Union 12-61
Lycoming 98   Catholic 49-14
Lycoming 98   Trinity (Tex.) 21-37
Lycoming 99   Wash. & Jeff. 7-14

Larry Glueck (1-1) (Villanova '63)
Fordham 87   Hofstra 41-6
Fordham 87   Wagner 0-21

Paul Guenther (1-1) (Ursinus '94)
Ursinus 99   Bridgewater St. 43-38
Ursinus 99   Rowan 0-55

Walt Hameline (4-2) (Brockport St. '75)
Wagner 82   St. Lawrence 34-43
Wagner 87   Rochester 38-14
Wagner 87   Fordham 21-0
Wagner 87   Emory & Henry 20-15
Wagner .... 87*   Dayton 19-3
Wagner 88   Ithaca 31-34 (ot)

Eric Hamilton (3-4) (Col. of New Jersey '75)
Col. of New Jersey.. 90   Ithaca 24-14
Col. of New Jersey.. 90   Hofstra 3-38
Col. of New Jersey.. 96   Coast Guard 17-16
Col. of New Jersey.. 96   Rowan 3-7
Col. of New Jersey.. 97   Cortland St. 34-30
Col. of New Jersey.. 97   Rowan 7-13
Col. of New Jersey.. 98   Rowan 2-26

Roger Harring (13-5) (Wis.-La Crosse '58)
Wis.-La Crosse 83   Occidental 43-42
Wis.-La Crosse 83   Augustana (Ill.) 15-21
Wis.-La Crosse 91   Simpson 28-13
Wis.-La Crosse 91   St. John's (Minn.) 10-29
Wis.-La Crosse 92   Redlands 47-26
Wis.-La Crosse 92   Central (Iowa) 34-9
Wis.-La Crosse 92   Mount Union 29-24
Wis.-La Crosse .... 92*   Wash. & Jeff. 16-12
Wis.-La Crosse 93   Wartburg 55-26
Wis.-La Crosse 93   St. John's (Minn.) 25-47
Wis.-La Crosse 95   Concordia-M'head 45-7
Wis.-La Crosse 95   Wis.-River Falls 28-14
Wis.-La Crosse 95   Mount Union 20-17
Wis.-La Crosse .... 95*   Rowan 36-7
Wis.-La Crosse 96   Wis.-River Falls 44-0
Wis.-La Crosse 96   St. John's (Minn.) 37-30
Wis.-La Crosse 96   Mount Union 21-39
Wis.-La Crosse 96   Central (Iowa) 17-38

Jim Hershberger (1-2) (Northern Iowa '57)
Buena Vista 76   Carroll (Wis.) 20-14 (ot)
Buena Vista 76   St. John's (Minn.) 0-61
Buena Vista 86   Central (Iowa) 0-37

Fred Hill (1-1) (Upsala '57)
Montclair St. 81   Alfred 13-12
Montclair St. 81   Widener 12-23

Rex Huigens (0-1) (La Verne '70)
La Verne 94   St. John's (Minn.) 12-51

Steve Johnson (0-2) (Bethel [Minn.] '80)
Bethel (Minn.) 00   Pacific Lutheran 13-41
Bethel (Minn.) 01   Wis.-Stevens Point 27-37

James Jones (1-1) (Bishop '49)
Bishop 82   Wartburg 32-7
Bishop 82   West Ga. 6-27

Frank Joranko (0-1) (Albion '52)
Albion 77   Minn.-Morris 10-13

Rich Kacmarynski (3-4) (Central [Iowa] '92)
Central (Iowa)......... 98   Wis.-Eau Claire 21-28
Central (Iowa)......... 99   Wis.-La Crosse 38-17
Central (Iowa)......... 99   St. John's (Minn.) 9-10
Central (Iowa)......... 00   St. Norbert 29-14
Central (Iowa)......... 00   Linfield 20-17 (ot)
Central (Iowa)......... 00   St. John's (Minn.) 18-21
Central (Iowa)......... 01   Pacific Lutheran 21-27 (ot)

Tom Kaczkowski (3-2) (Illinois '78)
Ohio Northern 99   Hanover 56-14
Ohio Northern 99   Wittenberg 58-24
Ohio Northern 99   Mount Union 31-56
Ohio Northern 00   Millikin 47-21
Ohio Northern 00   Mount Union 28-59

Bill Kavanaugh (0-1) (Stonehill '72)
Mass.-Dartmouth 02   Muhlenberg 6-56

Dennis Kayser (1-2) (Ithaca '74)
Cortland St. 88   Hofstra 32-27
Cortland St. 88   Ithaca 17-24
Cortland St. 89   Union (N.Y.) 14-42

Tim Keating (2-5) (Bethany [W.Va.] '75)
McDaniel 97   Lycoming 13-27
McDaniel 98   Trinity (Tex.) 20-30
McDaniel 99   Catholic 20-16
McDaniel 99   Trinity (Tex.) 16-20
McDaniel 00   Emory & Henry 38-14
McDaniel 00   Hardin-Simmons 10-32
McDaniel 01   Wash. & Jeff. 21-24

K.C. Keeler (21-7) (Delaware '81)

Rowan	93	Buffalo St. 29-6
Rowan	93	Wm. Paterson 37-0
Rowan	93	Wash. & Jeff. 23-16
Rowan	93	Mount Union 24-34
Rowan	95	Buffalo St. 46-7
Rowan	95	Union (N.Y.) 38-7
Rowan	95	Wash. & Jeff. 28-15
Rowan	95	Wis.-La Crosse 7-36
Rowan	96	Buffalo St. 21-20
Rowan	96	Col. of New Jersey 7-3
Rowan	96	Lycoming 33-14
Rowan	96	Mount Union 24-56
Rowan	97	Coast Guard 43-0
Rowan	97	Col. of New Jersey 13-7
Rowan	97	Lycoming 20-28
Rowan	98	Col. of New Jersey 26-2
Rowan	98	Buffalo St. 19-17
Rowan	98	Wis.-Eau Claire 22-19
Rowan	98	Mount Union 24-44
Rowan	99	Rensselaer 29-10
Rowan	99	Ursinus 55-0
Rowan	99	Montclair St. 42-13
Rowan	99	Mount Union 24-17 (ot)
Rowan	99*	Pacific Lutheran 13-42
Rowan	01	Brockport St. 40-17
Rowan	01	Western Conn. St. 43-14
Rowan	01	Ithaca 48-0
Rowan	01	Bridgewater (Va.) 24-29

Jimmie Keeling (4-3) (Howard Payne '58)

Hardin-Simmons	99	Washington (Mo.) 28-21
Hardin-Simmons	99	Wash. & Jeff. 51-3
Hardin-Simmons	99	Trinity (Tex.) 33-40
Hardin-Simmons	00	McDaniel 32-10
Hardin-Simmons	00	Trinity (Tex.) 33-30
Hardin-Simmons	00	St. John's (Minn.) 14-38
Hardin-Simmons	01	Wittenberg 35-38 (ot)

Larry Kehres (36-6) (Mount Union '71)

Mount Union	86	Dayton 42-36
Mount Union	86	Augustana (Ill.) 7-16
Mount Union	90	Allegheny 15-26
Mount Union	92	Dayton 27-10
Mount Union	92	Ill. Wesleyan 49-27
Mount Union	92	Wis.-La Crosse 24-29
Mount Union	93	Allegheny 40-7
Mount Union	93	Albion 30-16
Mount Union	93	St. John's (Minn.) 56-8
Mount Union	93*	Rowan 34-24
Mount Union	94	Allegheny 28-19
Mount Union	94	Albion 33-34
Mount Union	95	Hanover 52-18
Mount Union	95	Wheaton (Ill.) 40-14
Mount Union	95	Wis.-La Crosse 17-20
Mount Union	96	Allegheny 31-26
Mount Union	96	Ill. Wesleyan 49-14
Mount Union	96	Wis.-La Crosse 39-21
Mount Union	96*	Rowan 56-24
Mount Union	97	Allegheny 34-30
Mount Union	97	John Carroll 59-7
Mount Union	97	Simpson 54-7
Mount Union	97*	Lycoming 61-12
Mount Union	98	Albion 21-19
Mount Union	98	Wittenberg 21-19
Mount Union	98	Trinity (Tex.) 34-29
Mount Union	98*	Rowan 44-24
Mount Union	99	Augustana (Ill.) 42-33
Mount Union	99	Ohio Northern 56-31
Mount Union	99	Rowan 17-24 (ot)
Mount Union	00	Ohio Northern 59-28
Mount Union	00	Wittenberg 32-15
Mount Union	00	Widener 70-30
Mount Union	00*	St. John's (Minn.) 10-7
Mount Union	01	Augustana (Ill.) 32-7
Mount Union	01	Wittenberg 49-21
Mount Union	01	St. John's (Minn.) 35-14
Mount Union	01*	Bridgewater (Va.) 30-27
Mount Union	02	Wheaton (Ill.) 42-21
Mount Union	02	Wabash 45-16
Mount Union	02	John Carroll 57-19
Mount Union	02*	Trinity (Tex.) 48-7

Matt Kelchner (0-2) (Susquehanna '82)

Chris. Newport	01	Widener 7-56
Chris. Newport	02	Wash. & Jeff. 10-24

Mike Kelly (13-8) (Manchester '70)

Dayton	81	Augustana (Ill.) 19-7
Dayton	81	Lawrence 38-0
Dayton	81	Widener 10-17
Dayton	84	Augustana (Ill.) 13-14
Dayton	86	Mount Union 36-42
Dayton	87	Capital 52-28
Dayton	87	Augustana (Ill.) 38-36
Dayton	87	Central (Iowa) 34-0
Dayton	87	Wagner 3-19
Dayton	88	Wittenberg 28-35 (2 ot)
Dayton	89	John Carroll 35-10
Dayton	89	Millikin 28-16
Dayton	89	St. John's (Minn.) 28-0
Dayton	89*	Union (N.Y.) 17-7
Dayton	89	Augustana (Ill.) 24-14
Dayton	90	Allegheny 23-31
Dayton	91	Baldwin-Wallace 27-10
Dayton	91	Allegheny 28-25 (ot)
Dayton	91	St. John's (Minn.) 19-7
Dayton	91	Ithaca 20-34
Dayton	92	Mount Union 10-27

Larry Kindbom (0-1) (Kalamazoo '74)

Washington (Mo.)	99	Hardin-Simmons 21-28

Joe King (0-2) (Siena '70)

Rensselaer	99	Rowan 10-29
Rensselaer	01	Ithaca 10-27

Chuck Klausing (2-4) (Slippery Rock '48)

Carnegie Mellon	78	Dayton 24-21
Carnegie Mellon	78	Baldwin-Wallace 6-31
Carnegie Mellon	79	Minn.-Morris 31-25
Carnegie Mellon	79	Ithaca 6-15
Carnegie Mellon	83	Salisbury 14-16
Carnegie Mellon	85	Salisbury 22-35

Dean Kreps (0-1) (Monmouth [Ill.] '83)

Hope	00	Hanover 3-20

Mickey Kwiatkowski (0-5) (Delaware '70)

Hofstra	83	Union (N.Y.) 19-51
Hofstra	86	Montclair St. 21-24
Hofstra	87	Fordham 6-41
Hofstra	88	Cortland St. 27-32
Hofstra	89	Montclair St. 6-23

Ron Labadie (0-2) (Adrian '71)

Adrian	83	Augustana (Ill.) 21-22
Adrian	88	Augustana (Ill.) 7-25

Rich Lackner (0-1) (Carnegie Mellon '79)

Carnegie Mellon	90	Lycoming 7-17

Don LaViolette (0-1) (St. Norbert '54)

St. Norbert	89	Central (Iowa) 7-55

D.J. LeRoy (0-3) (Wis.-Eau Claire '79)

Wis.-Stevens Point	86	Concordia-M'head 15-24
Coe	91	St. John's (Minn.) 2-75
Coe	93	St. John's (Minn.) 14-32

Jay Locey (1-2) (Oregon St. '76)

Linfield	00	Central (Iowa) 17-20 (ot)
Linfield	02	Wartburg 52-15
Linfield	02	St. John's (Minn.) 14-21

Leon Lomax (0-1) (Fort Valley St. '43)

Fort Valley St.	75	Ithaca 12-41

John Luckhardt (13-11) (Purdue '67)

Wash. & Jeff.	84	Randolph-Macon 22-21
Wash. & Jeff.	84	Central (Iowa) 0-20
Wash. & Jeff.	86	Susquehanna 20-28
Wash. & Jeff.	87	Allegheny 23-17 (ot)
Wash. & Jeff.	87	Emory & Henry 16-23
Wash. & Jeff.	89	Ferrum 7-41
Wash. & Jeff.	90	Ferrum 10-7
Wash. & Jeff.	90	Lycoming 0-24
Wash. & Jeff.	91	Lycoming 16-18
Wash. & Jeff.	92	Lycoming 33-0
Wash. & Jeff.	92	Emory & Henry 51-15
Wash. & Jeff.	92	Rowan 18-13
Wash. & Jeff.	92	Wis.-La Crosse 12-16
Wash. & Jeff.	93	Moravian 27-7
Wash. & Jeff.	93	Frostburg St. 28-7
Wash. & Jeff.	93	Rowan 16-23
Wash. & Jeff.	94	Trinity (Tex.) 28-0
Wash. & Jeff.	94	Widener 37-21
Wash. & Jeff.	94	Ithaca 23-19
Wash. & Jeff.	94	Albion 15-38
Wash. & Jeff.	95	Emory & Henry 35-16
Wash. & Jeff.	95	Lycoming 48-0
Wash. & Jeff.	95	Rowan 15-28
Wash. & Jeff.	96	Albright 17-31

Dan MacNeil (0-1) (Cortland St. '79)

Cortland St.	97	Col. of New Jersey 30-34

Ron Maier (1-1) (Bentley '86)

Albright	96	Wash. & Jeff. 31-17
Albright	96	Lycoming 13-31

Mike Manley (0-1) (Anderson [Ind.] '73)

Anderson (Ind.)	93	Albion 21-41

Bill Manlove (9-5) (Temple '58)

Widener	75	Albright 14-6
Widener	75	Ithaca 14-23
Widener	77	Central (Iowa) 19-0
Widener	77	Albany (N.Y.) 33-15
Widener	77*	Wabash 39-36
Widener	79	Baldwin-Wallace 29-8
Widener	79	Wittenberg 14-17
Widener	80	Bethany (W.Va.) 43-12
Widener	80	Dayton 24-28
Widener	81	West Ga. 10-3
Widener	81	Montclair St. 23-12
Widener	81*	Dayton 17-10
Widener	82	West Ga. 24-31 (3 ot)
Widener	88	Moravian 7-17

Rich Mannello (1-1) (Springfield '83)

King's (Pa.)	02	Salisbury 28-0
King's (Pa.)	02	Bridgewater (Va.) 17-19

Steve Marino (0-1) (Westfield St. '71)

Westfield St.	01	Western Conn. St. 7-8

Dave Maurer (9-2) (Denison '54)

Wittenberg	73	San Diego 21-14
Wittenberg	73*	Juniata 41-0
Wittenberg	75	Indianapolis 17-13
Wittenberg	75	Millsaps 55-22
Wittenberg	75*	Ithaca 28-0
Wittenberg	78	Ithaca 6-3
Wittenberg	78	Minn.-Morris 35-14
Wittenberg	78	Baldwin-Wallace 10-24
Wittenberg	79	Millersville 21-14
Wittenberg	79	Widener 17-14
Wittenberg	79	Ithaca 10-14

Mike Maynard (0-3) (Ill. Wesleyan '80)

Redlands	90	Central (Iowa) 14-24
Redlands	92	Wis.-La Crosse 26-47
Redlands	02	St. John's (Minn.) 24-31

Peter Mazzaferro (0-2) (Centre '54)

Bridgewater St.	99	Ursinus 38-43
Bridgewater St.	00	Hobart 0-25

Mike McGlinchey (6-4) (Delaware '67)

Salisbury	83	Carnegie Mellon 16-14
Salisbury	83	Union (N.Y.) 21-23
Salisbury	85	Carnegie Mellon 35-22
Salisbury	85	Gettysburg 6-22
Salisbury	86	Emory & Henry 34-20
Salisbury	86	Susquehanna 31-17
Salisbury	86	Ithaca 44-40
Salisbury	86	Augustana (Ill.) 3-31
Frostburg St.	93	Wilkes 26-25
Frostburg St.	93	Wash. & Jeff. 7-28

Ed Meierkort (0-1) (Dakota Wesleyan '81)

Wis.-Stout	00	St. John's (Minn.) 19-26

John Miech (1-2) (Wis.-Stevens Point '75)

Wis.-Stevens Point	99	St. John's (Minn.) 17-38
Wis.-Stevens Point	01	Bethel (Minn.) 37-27
Wis.-Stevens Point	01	St. John's (Minn.) 7-9

Steve Miller (0-1) (Cornell College '65)

Carroll (Wis.)	76	Buena Vista 14-20 (ot)

Chuck Mills (0-1) (Illinois St. '50)

Coast Guard	79	Rowan 0-43

Steve Mohr (12-7) (Denison '76)

Trinity (Tex.)	94	Wash. & Jeff. 0-28
Trinity (Tex.)	97	Catholic 44-33
Trinity (Tex.)	97	Lycoming 26-46
Trinity (Tex.)	98	McDaniel 30-20
Trinity (Tex.)	98	Lycoming 37-21
Trinity (Tex.)	98	Mount Union 29-34
Trinity (Tex.)	99	McDaniel 20-16
Trinity (Tex.)	99	Hardin-Simmons 40-33
Trinity (Tex.)	99	Pacific Lutheran 28-49
Trinity (Tex.)	00	Wesley 21-3
Trinity (Tex.)	00	Bridgewater (Va.) 47-41 (ot)
Trinity (Tex.)	00	Hardin-Simmons
Trinity (Tex.)	01	Mary Hardin-Baylor 30-6
Trinity (Tex.)	01	Bridgewater (Va.) 37-41
Trinity (Tex.)	02	Mary Hardin-Baylor 48-38

Trinity (Tex.)............ 02   Wash. & Jeff. 45-10
Trinity (Tex.)............ 02   Bridgewater (Va.) 38-32
Trinity (Tex.)............ 02   St. John's (Minn.) 41-34
Trinity (Tex.)............ 02   Mount Union 7-48

Al Molde (2-3) (Gust. Adolphus '66)
Minn.-Morris........... 77   Albion 13-10
Minn.-Morris........... 77   Wabash 21-37
Minn.-Morris........... 78   St. Olaf 23-10
Minn.-Morris........... 78   Wittenberg 14-35
Minn.-Morris........... 79   Carnegie Mellon 25-31

Ron Murphy (1-1) (Wittenberg '60)
Wittenberg........ 88   Dayton 35-28 (2 ot)
Wittenberg........ 88   Augustana (Ill.) 14-28

Dave Murray (0-1) (Springfield '81)
Cortland St. 90   Hofstra 9-35

Walt Nadzak (1-1) (Denison '57)
Juniata 73   Bridgeport 35-14
Juniata 73   Wittenberg 0-41

Frank Navarro (2-1) (Maryland '53)
Wabash............... 77   St. John's (Minn.) 20-9
Wabash............... 77   Minn.-Morris 37-21
Wabash............... 77   Widener 36-39

Doug Neibuhr (0-3) (Millikin '75)
Wittenberg........... 95   Wheaton (Ill.) 41-63
Millikin 98   Wittenberg 10-13
Millikin 00   Ohio Northern 21-47

Ben Newcomb (0-1) (Augustana [S.D.] '57)
Augustana (Ill.)... 76   St. John's (Minn.) 7-46

Bob Nielson (3-3) (Wartburg '81)
Wartburg 93   Wis.-La Crosse 26-55
Wartburg 94   Central (Iowa) 22-21
Wartburg 94   St. John's (Minn.) 14-42
Wis.-Eau Claire 98   Central (Iowa) 28-21
Wis.-Eau Claire 98   St. John's (Minn.) 10-7
Wis.-Eau Claire 98   Rowan 19-22

Hank Norton (4-4) (Lynchburg '51)
Ferrum 87   Emory & Henry 7-49
Ferrum 88   Rhodes 35-10
Ferrum 88   Moravian 49-28
Ferrum 88   Ithaca 28-62
Ferrum 89   Wash. & Jeff. 41-7
Ferrum 89   Lycoming 49-24
Ferrum 89   Union (N.Y.) 21-37
Ferrum 90   Wash. & Jeff. 7-10

John O'Grady (1-2) (Wis.-River Falls '79)
Wis.-River Falls 95   Central (Iowa) 10-7
Wis.-River Falls 95   Wis.-La Crosse 14-28
Wis.-River Falls 96   Wis.-La Crosse 0-44

Ken O'Keefe (5-5) (John Carroll '75)
Allegheny............. 90   Mount Union 26-15
Allegheny............. 90   Dayton 31-23
Allegheny............. 90   Central (Iowa) 24-7
Allegheny............. 90*   Lycoming 21-14 (ot)
Allegheny............. 91   Albion 24-21 (ot)
Allegheny............. 91   Dayton 25-28 (ot)
Allegheny............. 93   Mount Union 7-40
Allegheny............. 94   Mount Union 19-28
Allegheny............. 96   Mount Union 26-31
Allegheny............. 97   Mount Union 30-34

Jack Osberg (1-1) (Augsburg '62)
Augsburg 97   Concordia-M'head 34-22
Augsburg 97   Simpson 21-61

Bob Packard (0-2) (Baldwin-Wallace '65)
Baldwin-Wallace 82   Augustana (Ill.) 22-28
Baldwin-Wallace 91   Dayton 10-27

Paul Pasqualoni (0-1) (Penn St. '72)
Western Conn. St. .. 85   Montclair St. 0-28

Bobby Pate (3-1) (Georgia '63)
West Ga. 81   Widener 3-10
West Ga. 82   Widener 31-24 (3 ot)
West Ga. 82   Bishop 27-6
West Ga. .... 82*   Augustana (Ill.) 14-0

Dean Paul (1-1) (Mount Union '90)
Thomas More 01   MacMurray 34-30
Thomas More 01   Wittenberg 0-41

C. Wayne Perry (1-5) (DePauw '72)
Hanover 95   Mount Union 18-52
Hanover 97   John Carroll 20-30
Hanover 99   Ohio Northern 14-56
Hanover 99   Hope 20-3
Hanover 00   Wittenberg 21-32
Hanover 02   Wittenberg 33-34

Keith Piper (0-1) (Baldwin-Wallace '48)
Denison................. 85   Mount Union 3-35

Carl Poelker (1-1) (Millikin '68)
Millikin 89   Augustana (Ill.) 21-12
Millikin 89   Dayton 16-28

Tom Porter (0-1) (St. Olaf '51)
St. Olaf 78   Minn.-Morris 10-23

John Potsklan (0-2) (Penn St. '49)
Albright.................. 75   Widener 6-14
Albright.................. 76   St. Lawrence 7-26

Charlie Pravata (0-1) (Adelphi '72)
Merchant Marine 94   Plymouth St. 18-19

Greg Pscodna (0-1) (Adrian '86)
Defiance 01   Augustana (Ill.) 14-54

Jim Purtill (0-3) (Miami [Ohio] '78)
St. Norbert 99   Augustana (Ill.) 32-39
St. Norbert 00   Central (Iowa) 14-29
St. Norbert 01   St. John's (Minn.) 20-27

Steve Raarup (0-1) (Gust. Adolphus '53)
Gust. Adolphus........ 87   St. John's (Minn.) 3-7

Erik Raeburn (1-1) (Mount Union '94)
Coe 02   Wis.-La Crosse 21-18
Coe 02   St. John's (Minn.) 14-45

Bob Reade (19-7) (Cornell College '54)
Augustana (Ill.)........ 81   Dayton 7-19
Augustana (Ill.)........ 82   Baldwin-Wallace 28-22
Augustana (Ill.)........ 82   St. Lawrence 14-0
Augustana (Ill.)........ 82   West Ga. 0-14
Augustana (Ill.)........ 83   Adrian 22-21
Augustana (Ill.)........ 83   Wis.-La Crosse 21-15
Augustana (Ill.)........ 83*   Union (N.Y.) 21-17
Augustana (Ill.)........ 84   Dayton 14-13
Augustana (Ill.)........ 84   Union (N.Y.) 23-6
Augustana (Ill.)........ 84*   Central (Iowa) 21-12
Augustana (Ill.)........ 85   Albion 26-10
Augustana (Ill.)........ 85   Mount Union 21-14
Augustana (Ill.)........ 85   Central (Iowa) 14-7
Augustana (Ill.)........ 85*   Ithaca 20-7
Augustana (Ill.)........ 86   Hope 34-10
Augustana (Ill.)........ 86   Mount Union 16-7
Augustana (Ill.)........ 86   Concordia-M'head 41-7
Augustana (Ill.)........ 86*   Salisbury 31-3
Augustana (Ill.)........ 87   Hiram 53-0
Augustana (Ill.)........ 87   Dayton 36-38
Augustana (Ill.)........ 88   Adrian 25-7
Augustana (Ill.)........ 88   Wittenberg 28-14
Augustana (Ill.)........ 88   Central (Iowa) 17-23 (2 ot)
Augustana (Ill.)........ 89   Millikin 12-21
Augustana (Ill.)........ 90   Dayton 14-24
Augustana (Ill.)........ 94   Albion 21-28

Rocky Rees (1-1) (West Chester '71)
Susquehanna.......... 86   Wash. & Jeff. 28-20
Susquehanna.......... 86   Salisbury 17-31

Ron Roberts (1-1) (Wisconsin '54)
Lawrence............... 81   Minn.-Morris 21-14 (ot)
Lawrence............... 81   Dayton 0-38

Craig Rundle (0-1) (Albion '74)
Albion 98   Mount Union 19-21

Bill Russo (0-1)
Wagner 80   Ithaca 13-41

Rocco Salomone (2-3) (Brockport St. '88)
Brockport St. 00   Springfield 6-13
Brockport St............ 01   Rowan 17-40
Brockport St............ 02   Springfield 16-0
Brockport St............ 02   Rowan 15-12
Brockport St............ 02   John Carroll 10-16 (ot)

Sam Sanders (0-1) (Buffalo '60)
Alfred 81   Montclair St. 12-13

Regis Scafe (3-1) (Case Reserve '71)
John Carroll 02   Hobart 27-7
John Carroll 02   Muhlenberg 21-10
John Carroll 02   Brockport St. 16-10 (ot)
John Carroll 02   Mount Union 19-57

Dennis Scannell (0-1) (Villanova '74)
Mass.-Lowell 91   Union (N.Y.) 16-55

Ron Schipper (16-11) (Hope '52)
Central (Iowa)......... 74   Evansville 17-16
Central (Iowa)......... 74*   Ithaca 10-8
Central (Iowa)......... 77   Widener 0-19
Central (Iowa)......... 84   Occidental 23-22
Central (Iowa)......... 84   Wash. & Jeff. 20-0
Central (Iowa)......... 84   Augustana (Ill.) 12-21
Central (Iowa)......... 85   Coe 27-7
Central (Iowa)......... 85   Occidental 71-0

Central (Iowa)........ 85   Augustana (Ill.) 7-14
Central (Iowa)........ 86   Buena Vista 37-0
Central (Iowa)........ 86   Concordia-M'head 14-17
Central (Iowa)........ 87   Menlo 37-0
Central (Iowa)........ 87   St. John's (Minn.) 13-3
Central (Iowa)........ 87   Dayton 0-34
Central (Iowa)........ 88   Concordia-M'head 7-0
Central (Iowa)........ 88   Wis.-Whitewater 16-13
Central (Iowa)........ 88   Augustana (Ill.) 23-17 (2 ot)
Central (Iowa)........ 88   Ithaca 24-39
Central (Iowa)........ 89   St. Norbert 55-7
Central (Iowa)........ 89   St. John's (Minn.) 24-27
Central (Iowa)........ 90   Redlands 24-14
Central (Iowa)........ 90   St. Thomas (Minn.) 33-32
Central (Iowa)........ 90   Allegheny 7-24
Central (Iowa)........ 92   Carleton 20-8
Central (Iowa)........ 92   Wis.-La Crosse 9-34
Central (Iowa)........ 94   Wartburg 21-22
Central (Iowa)........ 95   Wis.-River Falls 7-10

Pete Schmidt (5-4) (Alma '70)
Albion 85   Augustana (Ill.) 10-26
Albion 91   Allegheny 21-24 (ot)
Albion 93   Anderson (Ind.) 41-21
Albion 93   Mount Union 16-30
Albion 94   Augustana (Ill.) 28-21
Albion 94   Mount Union 34-33
Albion 94   St. John's (Minn.) 19-16
Albion .... 94*   Wash. & Jeff. 38-15
Albion 96   Ill. Wesleyan 20-23

Bill Schmitz (0-1) (Coast Guard '76)
Coast Guard 96   Col. of New Jersey 16-17

Tom Schmulbach (1-1) (Western Ill. '69)
Augustana (Ill.)...... 99   St. Norbert 39-32
Augustana (Ill.)...... 99   Mount Union 33-42

Jim Scott (0-2) (Luther '61)
Aurora 92   Ill. Wesleyan 12-21
Aurora 00   Wittenberg 20-31

Jack Siedlecki (0-1) (Union [N.Y.] '73)
WPI 92   Rowan 14-41

Dick Smith (1-2) (Coe '68)
Minn.-Morris........... 80   Dubuque 41-35
Minn.-Morris........... 80   Ithaca 0-36
Minn.-Morris........... 81   Lawrence 14-21 (ot)

Ray Smith (0-1) (UCLA '61)
Hope 86   Augustana (Ill.) 10-34

Ray Solari (0-1) (California '51)
Menlo 87   Central (Iowa) 0-17

Mark Speckman (0-1) (Azusa Pacific '77)
Willamette............. 99   Pacific Lutheran 24-28

Ted Stratford (1-2) (St. Lawrence '57)
St. Lawrence.......... 76   Albright 26-7
St. Lawrence.......... 76   Towson 36-38
St. Lawrence.......... 78   Baldwin-Wallace 7-71

Barry Streeter (2-1) (Lebanon Valley '71)
Gettysburg 85   Lycoming 14-10
Gettysburg 85   Salisbury 22-6
Gettysburg 85   Ithaca 0-34

Bob Sullivan (0-1) (St. John's [Minn.] '59)
Carleton 92   Central (Iowa) 8-20

Bob Surace (1-1) (Princeton '90)
Western Conn. St. . 00   Westfield St. 8-7
Western Conn. St. . 01   Rowan 14-43

Ed Sweeney (0-2) (C. W. Post '71)
Dickinson 89   Lycoming 0-21
Dickinson 91   Susquehanna 20-21

Mike Swider (1-1) (Wheaton [Ill.] '87)
Wheaton (Ill.) 02   Alma 42-14
Wheaton (Ill.) 02   Mount Union 21-42

Andy Talley (1-1) (Southern Conn. St. '67)
St. Lawrence.......... 82   Wagner 43-34
St. Lawrence.......... 82   Augustana (Ill.) 0-14

Ray Tellier (0-1) (Connecticut '73)
Rochester 82   Wagner 14-38

Larry Terry (0-1) (Wis.-La Crosse '77)
Wis.-La Crosse........ 02   Coe 18-21

Bob Thurness (0-1) (Coe '62)
Coe 85   Central (Iowa) 7-27

Lee Tressel (3-2) (Baldwin-Wallace '48)
Baldwin-Wallace..... 78   St. Lawrence 11-7
Baldwin-Wallace..... 78   Carnegie Mellon 31-6
Baldwin-Wallace..... 78*   Wittenberg 24-10

Baldwin-Wallace..... 79   Widener 8-29
Baldwin-Wallace..... 80   Dayton 0-34

John Tully (0-1) (Azusa Pacific '85)
Whitworth 01   Pacific Lutheran 26-27 (ot)

Peter Vaas (0-1) (Holy Cross '74)
Allegheny.............. 87   Wash. & Jeff. 17-23 (ot)

Andy Vinci (0-1) (Cal St. Los Angeles '63)
San Diego............. 73   Wittenberg 14-21

Ken Wable (1-1) (Muskingum '52)
Mount Union 85   Denison 35-3
Mount Union 85   Augustana (Ill.) 14-21

Lou Wacker (3-5) (Richmond '56)
Emory & Henry 86   Salisbury 20-34
Emory & Henry 87   Ferrum 49-7
Emory & Henry 87   Wash. & Jeff. 23-16
Emory & Henry 87   Wagner 15-20
Emory & Henry 92   Thomas More 17-0
Emory & Henry 92   Wash. & Jeff. 15-51
Emory & Henry 95   Wash. & Jeff. 16-35
Emory & Henry 00   McDaniel 14-38

Vic Wallace (1-1) (Cornell College '65)
St. Thomas (Minn.) .. 90   Wis.-Whitewater 24-23
St. Thomas (Minn.) .. 90   Central (Iowa) 32-33

Mike Welch (4-2) (Ithaca '73)
Ithaca 94   Buffalo St. 10-7 (2 ot)
Ithaca 94   Plymouth St. 22-7
Ithaca 94   Wash. & Jeff. 19-23
Ithaca 01   Montclair St. 35-23
Ithaca 01   Rensselaer 27-10
Ithaca 01   Rowan 0-48

Roger Welsh (0-1) (Muskingum '64)
Capital.................. 87   Dayton 28-52

Frosty Westering (8-3) (Neb.-Omaha '52)
Pacific Lutheran 98   St. John's (Minn.) 20-33
Pacific Lutheran 99   Willamette 28-24
Pacific Lutheran 99   Wartburg 49-14
Pacific Lutheran 99   St. John's (Minn.) 19-9
Pacific Lutheran 99   Trinity (Tex.) 49-28
Pacific Lutheran ...... 99*   Rowan 42-13
Pacific Lutheran 00   Bethel (Minn.) 41-13
Pacific Lutheran 00   St. John's (Minn.) 21-28 (ot)
Pacific Lutheran 01   Whitworth 27-26 (ot)
Pacific Lutheran 01   Central (Iowa) 27-21 (ot)
Pacific Lutheran 01   St. John's (Minn.) 6-31

Dale Widolff (1-3) (Indiana Central '75)
Occidental 83   Wis.-La Crosse 42-43
Occidental 84   Central (Iowa) 22-23
Occidental 85   St. John's (Minn.) 28-10
Occidental 85   Central (Iowa) 0-71

Jim Williams (2-5) (Northern Iowa '60)
Simpson 88   Wis.-Whitewater 27-29
Simpson 89   St. John's (Minn.) 35-42
Simpson 91   Wis.-La Crosse 13-28
Simpson 96   St. John's (Minn.) 18-21
Simpson 97   Wis.-Whitewater 34-31
Simpson 97   Augsburg 61-21
Simpson 97   Mount Union 7-54

Rick Willis (1-2) (Cornell '88)
Wartburg 99   Pacific Lutheran 14-49
Wartburg 02   Lake Forest 45-0
Wartburg 02   Linfield 15-52

Sherman Wood (0-1) (Salisbury '84)
Salisbury 02   King's (Pa.) 0-28

Bill Zwaan (5-2) (Delaware '79)
Widener 00   Union (N.Y.) 33-26
Widener 00   Hobart 40-14
Widener 00   Springfield 61-27
Widener 00   Mount Union 30-70
Widener 01   Chris. Newport 56-7
Widener 01   Wash. & Jeff. 46-30
Widener 01   Bridgewater (Va.) 32-57

*National championship.

Coaching Honors

Division I-A Coach-of-the-Year Award

(Selected by the American Football Coaches Association/GTE and the Football Writers Association of America)

AFCA

1935	Lynn Waldorf, Northwestern
1936	Dick Harlow, Harvard
1937	Edward Mylin, Lafayette
1938	Bill Kern, Carnegie Mellon
1939	Eddie Anderson, Iowa
1940	Clark Shaughnessy, Stanford
1941	Frank Leahy, Notre Dame
1942	Bill Alexander, Georgia Tech
1943	Amos Alonzo Stagg, Pacific (Cal.)
1944	Carroll Widdoes, Ohio St.
1945	Bo McMillin, Indiana
1946	Red Blaik, Army
1947	Fritz Crisler, Michigan
1948	Bennie Oosterbaan, Michigan
1949	Bud Wilkinson, Oklahoma
1950	Charlie Caldwell, Princeton
1951	Chuck Taylor, Stanford
1952	Biggie Munn, Michigan St.
1953	Jim Tatum, Maryland
1954	Red Sanders, UCLA
1955	Duffy Daugherty, Michigan St.
1956	Bowden Wyatt, Tennessee
1957	Woody Hayes, Ohio St.
1958	Paul Dietzel, LSU
1959	Ben Schwartzwalder, Syracuse
1960	Murray Warmath, Minnesota
1961	Bear Bryant, Alabama
1962	John McKay, Southern California
1963	Darrell Royal, Texas
1964	Frank Broyles, Arkansas, and Ara Parseghian, Notre Dame
1965	Tommy Prothro, UCLA
1966	Tom Cahill, Army
1967	John Pont, Indiana
1968	Joe Paterno, Penn St.
1969	Bo Schembechler, Michigan
1970	Charlie McClendon, LSU, and Darrell Royal, Texas
1971	Bear Bryant, Alabama
1972	John McKay, Southern California
1973	Bear Bryant, Alabama
1974	Grant Teaff, Baylor
1975	Frank Kush, Arizona St.
1976	Johnny Majors, Pittsburgh
1977	Don James, Washington
1978	Joe Paterno, Penn St.
1979	Earle Bruce, Ohio St.
1980	Vince Dooley, Georgia
1981	Danny Ford, Clemson
1982	Joe Paterno, Penn St.
1983	Ken Hatfield, Air Force
1984	LaVell Edwards, Brigham Young
1985	Fisher DeBerry, Air Force
1986	Joe Paterno, Penn St.
1987	Dick MacPherson, Syracuse
1988	Don Nehlen, West Virginia
1989	Bill McCartney, Colorado
1990	Bobby Ross, Georgia Tech
1991	Bill Lewis, East Carolina
1992	Gene Stallings, Alabama
1993	Barry Alvarez, Wisconsin
1994	Tom Osborne, Nebraska
1995	Gary Barnett, Northwestern
1996	Bruce Snyder, Arizona St.
1997	Lloyd Carr, Michigan
1998	Phillip Fulmer, Tennessee
1999	Frank Beamer, Virginia Tech
2000	Bob Stoops, Oklahoma
2001	Larry Coker, Miami (Fla.) & Ralph Friedgen, Maryland
2002	Jim Tressel, Ohio St.

FWAA

1957	Woody Hayes, Ohio St.
1958	Paul Dietzel, LSU
1959	Ben Schwartzwalder, Syracuse
1960	Murray Warmath, Minnesota
1961	Darrell Royal, Texas
1962	John McKay, Southern California
1963	Darrell Royal, Texas
1964	Ara Parseghian, Notre Dame
1965	Duffy Daugherty, Michigan St.
1966	Tom Cahill, Army
1967	John Pont, Indiana
1968	Woody Hayes, Ohio St.
1969	Bo Schembechler, Michigan
1970	Alex Agase, Northwestern
1971	Bob Devaney, Nebraska
1972	John McKay, Southern California
1973	Johnny Majors, Pittsburgh
1974	Grant Teaff, Baylor
1975	Woody Hayes, Ohio St.
1976	Johnny Majors, Pittsburgh
1977	Lou Holtz, Arkansas
1978	Joe Paterno, Penn St.
1979	Earle Bruce, Ohio St.
1980	Vince Dooley, Georgia
1981	Danny Ford, Clemson
1982	Joe Paterno, Penn St.
1983	Howard Schnellenberger, Miami (Fla.)
1984	LaVell Edwards, Brigham Young
1985	Fisher DeBerry, Air Force
1986	Joe Paterno, Penn St.
1987	Dick MacPherson, Syracuse
1988	Lou Holtz, Notre Dame
1989	Bill McCartney, Colorado
1990	Bobby Ross, Georgia Tech
1991	Don James, Washington
1992	Gene Stallings, Alabama
1993	Terry Bowden, Auburn
1994	Rich Brooks, Oregon
1995	Gary Barnett, Northwestern
1996	Bruce Snyder, Arizona St.
1997	Mike Price, Washington St.
1998	Phillip Fulmer, Tennessee
1999	Frank Beamer, Virginia Tech
2000	Bob Stoops, Oklahoma
2001	Ralph Friedgen, Maryland
2002	Jim Tressel, Ohio St.

Division I-AA Coach-of-the-Year Award

(Selected by the American Football Coaches Association/GTE)

1983	Rey Dempsey, Southern Ill.
1984	Dave Arnold, Montana St.
1985	Dick Sheridan, Furman
1986	Erk Russell, Ga. Southern
1987	Mark Duffner, Holy Cross

COACHING RECORDS

1988	Jimmy Satterfield, Furman
1989	Erk Russell, Ga. Southern
1990	Tim Stowers, Ga. Southern
1991	Mark Duffner, Holy Cross
1992	Charlie Taafe, Citadel
1993	Dan Allen, Boston U.
1994	Jim Tressel, Youngstown St.
1995	Don Read, Montana
1996	Ray Tellier, Columbia
1997	Andy Talley, Villanova
1998	Mark Whipple, Massachusetts
1999	Paul Johnson, Ga. Southern
2000	Paul Johnson, Ga. Southern
2001	Bobby Johnson, Furman
2002	Jack Harbaugh, Western Ky.

Small College Coach-of-the-Year Awards

(Selected by the American Football Coaches Association/GTE)

COLLEGE DIVISION

1960	Warren Woodson, New Mexico St.
1961	Jake Gaither, Florida A&M
1962	Bill Edwards, Wittenberg
1963	Bill Edwards, Wittenberg
1964	Clarence Stasavich, East Carolina
1965	Jack Curtice, UC Santa Barb.
1966	Dan Jessee, Trinity (Conn.)
1967	Scrappy Moore, Chattanooga
1968	Jim Root, New Hampshire
1969	Larry Naviaux, Boston U.
1970	Bennie Ellender, Arkansas St.
1971	Tubby Raymond, Delaware
1972	Tubby Raymond, Delaware
1973	Dave Maurer, Wittenberg
1974	Roy Kramer, Central Mich.
1975	Dave Maurer, Wittenberg
1976	Jim Dennison, Akron
1977	Bill Manlove, Widener
1978	Lee Tressel, Baldwin-Wallace
1979	Bill Narduzzi, Youngstown St.
1980	Rick Carter, Dayton
1981	Vito Ragazzo, Shippensburg
1982	Jim Wacker, Southwest Tex. St.

COLLEGE DIVISION I

(NCAA Division II)

1983	Don Morton, North Dakota St.
1984	Chan Gailey, Troy St.
1985	George Landis, Bloomsburg
1986	Earle Solomonson, North Dakota St.
1987	Rick Rhoades, Troy St.
1988	Rocky Hager, North Dakota St.
1989	John Williams, Mississippi Col.
1990	Rocky Hager, North Dakota St.
1991	Frank Cignetti, Indiana (Pa.)
1992	Bill Burgess, Jacksonville St.
1993	Bobby Wallace, North Ala.
1994	Bobby Wallace, North Ala.
1995	Bobby Wallace, North Ala.
1996	Joe Glenn, Northern Colo.
1997	Joe Glenn, Northern Colo.
1998	Mel Tjeerdsma, Northwest Mo. St.
1999	Mel Tjeerdsma, Northwest Mo. St.
2000	Danny Hale, Bloomsburg
2001	Dale Lennon, North Dakota
2002	Brian Kelly, Grand Valley St.

COLLEGE DIVISION II

(NCAA Division III)

1983	Bob Reade, Augustana (Ill.)
1984	Bob Reade, Augustana (Ill.)
1985	Bob Reade, Augustana (Ill.)
1986	Bob Reade, Augustana (Ill.)
1987	Walt Hameline, Wagner
1988	Jim Butterfield, Ithaca
1989	Mike Kelly, Dayton
1990	Ken O'Keefe, Allegheny
1991	Mike Kelly, Dayton
1992	John Luckhardt, Wash. & Jeff.
1993	Larry Kehres, Mount Union
1994	Pete Schmidt, Albion
1995	Roger Harring, Wis.-La Crosse
1996	Larry Kehres, Mount Union
1997	Larry Kehres, Mount Union
1998	Larry Kehres, Mount Union
1999	Frosty Westering, Pacific Lutheran
2000	Larry Kehres, Mount Union
2001	Larry Kehres, Mount Union
2002	Larry Kehres, Mount Union

Added and Discontinued Programs

Nationally Prominent Teams That Permanently Dropped Football

Listed alphabetically at right are the all-time records of teams formerly classified as major college that permanently discontinued football. Also included are those teams that, retroactively, are considered to have been major college (before the advent of official classification in 1937) by virtue of their schedules (i.e., at least half of their games versus other major-college opponents). All schools listed were considered to have been major college or classified in either Division I-A or I-AA for a minimum of 10 consecutive seasons.

Team	Inclusive Seasons	Years	Won	Lost	Tied	Pct.†
Cal St. Fullerton	1970-1992	23	107	150	3	.417
Carlisle Indian School..	1893-1917	25	167	88	13	.647
Centenary (La.)	1894-1947	36	148	100	21	.589
Creighton	1900-1942	43	183	139	27	.563
Denver	1885-1960	73	273	262	40	.510
Detroit.......................	1896-1964	64	305	200	25	.599
George Washington ...	1890-1966	58	209	240	34	.468
Gonzaga	1892-1941	39	130	99	20	.562
Haskell Institute	1896-1938	43	199	166	18	.543
Lamar........................	1951-1989	39	171	225	9	.433
Long Beach St.............	1955-1991	37	199	183	4	.521
Manhattan..................	1923-1942	20	77	75	11	.506
Marquette..................	1892-1960	68	273	220	38	.550
New York U.	1873-1952	66	201	231	32	.468
Pacific (Cal.)	1919-1995	77	346	397	23	.467
St. Louis....................	1899-1949	49	235	179	33	.563
San Francisco *1924-1951; 1959-1971		38	133	169	20	.444
Texas-Arlington............	1959-1985	27	129	150	2	.463
Wichita St..................	1897-1986	89	375	402	47	.484
Xavier (Ohio)..............	1900-1973	61	302	223	21	.572

†Ties computed as half won and half lost. *Discontinued football during 1952 after having been classified major college. Resumed at the Division II level during 1959-71, when it was discontinued again.

Added or Resumed Programs Since 1968

NCAA Member Colleges

1968 (4)
Boise St.; *Chicago; New Jersey City (dropped 2002); UNLV.

1969 (2)
*Adelphi (dropped 1972); Towson

1970 (6)
Cal St. Fullerton (dropped 1993); *Fordham; *Georgetown; Plattsburgh St. (dropped 1979); Plymouth St.; *St. Mary's (Cal.).

1971 (6)
Boston St. (dropped 1982); Dist. Columbia (dropped 1974, resumed 1978, dropped 1990); Federal City (dropped 1975); *New England Col. (dropped 1973); Rochester Tech (dropped 1978); St. Peter's (suspended after one game 1984, resumed 1985, dropped 1988, resumed 1989).

1972 (6)
Kean; *Lake Forest; Nicholls St.; Salisbury; *San Diego; Wm. Paterson.

1973 (7)
Albany St. (N.Y.); *Benedictine (Ill.); Bowie St.; James Madison; New Haven; New York Tech (dropped 1984); Seton Hall (dropped 1982).

1974 (2)
FDU-Florham; Framingham St.

1975 (2)
*Brooklyn (dropped 1991); *Canisius (dropped 2002).

1976 (1)
Oswego St. (dropped 1977).

1977 (2)
*Catholic; *Minn. St. Mankato

1978 (7)
*Buffalo; *Dist. Columbia (dropped 1990); Iona; Marist; Pace; *St. Francis (Pa.); *St. John's (N.Y.) (dropped 2002).

1979 (2)
UCF; *Duquesne.

1980 (5)
*Loras; Mass.-Lowell; *Miles (dropped 1989, resumed 1990); Ramapo (dropped 1993); *Sonoma St. (dropped 1997)

1981 (4)
Buffalo St.; Mercyhurst; *West Ga.; Western New Eng.

1982 (2)
Valdosta St.; Westfield St.

1983 (2)
*Ky. Wesleyan; Stony Brook.

1984 (3)
Fitchburg St.; *Ga. Southern; *Samford.

1985 (6)
Ferrum; MacMurray; N.Y. Maritime (dropped 1986, resumed 1987, dropped 1989); *St. Peter's (dropped 1988, resumed 1989); *Villanova; Worcester St.

1986 (4)
*UC Santa Barb. (dropped 1992); Menlo; *Quincy; Wesley.

1987 (5)
*Aurora; *Drake; Gallaudet; *N.Y. Maritime (dropped 1989); St. John Fisher.

1988 (7)
Assumption; Bentley; Mass.-Boston; Mass.-Dartmouth; *MIT (last team was in 1901); Siena; Stonehill.

1989 (4)
*Gannon; Methodist; *St. Peter's; *Southern Methodist.

1990 (3)
*Hardin-Simmons; *Miles; Thomas More.

1991 (3)
UAB; Charleston So.; Sacred Heart.

1992 (1)
*West Tex. A&M.

1993 (3)
*King's (Pa.); Monmouth; Salve Regina.

1994 (2)
Chapman; Robert Morris.

1996 (3)
Fairfield; Merrimack; Westminster (Mo.)

1997 (3)
Hartwick; *La Salle; South Fla.

1998 (1)
Jacksonville

1999 (3)
Bryant; St. Anselm; Wis. Lutheran

2000 (4)
East Tex. Baptist; Greensboro; Mary Hardin-Baylor; Shenandoah

2001 (6)
Averett; Chris. Newport; Fla. Atlantic; Rockford; Stillman; Utica

2002 (2)
Florida Int'l; * St. Augustine's (dropped 1966)

2003 (3)
*Charleston (W.Va.) (dropped 1957); Coastal Caro.; *Southeastern La. (dropped 1986)

*Previously dropped football.

Non-NCAA Senior Colleges

1968 (2)
#Mo. Southern St.; #Southwest St.

1970 (1)
#Mo. Western St.

1971 (3)
Concordia (St. Paul); #Gardner-Webb; #Grand Valley St.

1972 (5)
#Dr. Martin Luther; #Mars Hill; N'western (Minn.); Pillsbury; #Western Conn. St.

1973 (2)
#Liberty; #Mass. Maritime.

1974 (3)
#*N.M. Highlands; #Northeastern Ill. (dropped 1988); #Saginaw Valley.

1976 (2)
#Maranatha Baptist; #Mesa St.

1977 (2)
Evangel; Olivet Nazarene.

1978 (3)
*Baptist Christian (dropped 1983); *St. Ambrose; *Yankton (dropped 1984).

1979 (2)
Fort Lauderdale (dropped 1982); Lubbock Christian (dropped 1983).

1980 (1)
Mid-America Nazarene.

1983 (2)
Ga. Southwestern (dropped 1989); #Loras.

1984 (3)
St. Paul Bible; #Southwest Baptist; *Union (Ky.).

1985 (4)
*Cumberland (Ky.); *Lambuth; *Tenn. Wesleyan; #Tiffin.

1986 (4)
*#St. Francis (Ill.); Trinity Bible (N.D.); Urbana; #Wingate.

1987 (1)
#Greenville.

1988 (5)
Campbellsville; Mary; #Midwestern St.; Trinity (Ill.); *Western Mont.

1990 (3)
*Cumberland; Lindenwood; #Mt. St. Joseph (Ohio).

1991 (3)
#Clinch Valley; #Lees-McRae (dropped 1994); #*Tusculum.

1993 (6)
#Ark.-Pine Bluff; *Bethel (Tenn.); #Chowan; Malone; St. Xavier (Ill.); Sue Bennett.

1996 (1)
*McKendree

1998 (1)
#*Texas Lutheran

2000 (3)
#Mount Ida; Northern Mont. (dropped 1972); Paul Quinn (dropped 1961)

2001 (4)
Louisiana (dropped 1969); #Minn.-Crookston; Southwestern Assemblies of God; #Va.-Wise.

2002 (1):
St. Paul's (Va.)

*Previously dropped football. #Now NCAA member.

Discontinued Programs Since 1950

(Includes NCAA member colleges and non-member colleges; also colleges that closed or merged with other institutions.)

1950 (9)
Alliance; Canisius (resumed 1975; dropped 2002); Huntington; Oklahoma City; *Portland; Rio Grande; Rollins; *St. Louis; Steubenville.

1951 (38)
Arkansas Col.; Atlantic Christian; Canterbury; Catholic (resumed 1977); CCNY; Corpus Christi (resumed 1954, dropped 1967); Daniel Baker; Detroit Tech; *Duquesne (resumed 1979); East Tex. Baptist (resumed 2000); Gannon (resumed 1989); *Georgetown (resumed 1970); Glassboro St. (resumed 1964—name changed to Rowan in 1992); Hartwick; High Point; LeMoyne-Owen; Lowell Textile; Lycoming (resumed 1954); McKendree (resumed 1996); Milligan; Mt. St. Mary's (Md.); Nevada (resumed 1952); New Bedford Textile; New England Col. (resumed 1971, dropped 1973); Niagara; Northern Idaho; Panzer; St. Mary's (Cal.) (resumed 1970); St. Michael's (N.M.); Shurtleff (resumed 1953, dropped 1954); Southern Idaho; Southwestern (Tenn.) (resumed 1952—name changed to Rhodes in 1986); Tillotson; Tusculum (resumed 1991); Washington (Md.); West Va. Wesleyan (resumed 1953); William Penn (resumed 1953).

1952 (13)
Aquinas; Clarkson; Erskine; Louisville Municipal; *Loyola Marymount; Nebraska Central; Rider; Samuel Huston; *San Francisco (resumed 1959, dropped 1972); Shaw (resumed 1953, dropped 1979); St. Bonaventure; St. Martin's; Teikyo Westmar (resumed 1953).

1953 (10)
Arnold; Aurora; Bethel (Tenn.) (resumed 1993); Cedarville; Champlain; Davis & Elkins (resumed 1955, dropped 1962); Georgetown (Ky.) (resumed 1955); *New York U.; *Santa Clara (resumed 1959, dropped 1993); Union (Tenn.).

1954 (8)
Adelphi (resumed 1969, dropped 1972); Case Tech (resumed 1955); Quincy (resumed 1986); St. Francis (Pa.) (resumed 1978); St. Michael's (Vt.); Shurtleff; *Wash. & Lee (resumed 1955); York (Neb.).

1955 (2)
*Fordham (resumed 1970); St. Mary's (Minn.).

1956 (4)
Brooklyn (resumed 1975, dropped 1991); Hendrix (resumed 1957, dropped 1961); William Carey; Wisconsin Extension.

1957 (4)
Charleston (W.Va.) (resumed 2003); Lewis; Midwestern (Iowa) (resumed 1966); Stetson.

1959 (2)
Florida N&I; West Ga. (resumed 1981).

1960 (5)
Brandeis; Leland; Loras (resumed 1980); St. Ambrose (resumed 1978); Xavier (La.).

1961 (9)
*Denver; Hawaii (resumed 1962); Hendrix; Lincoln (Pa.); *Marquette; Paul Quinn; Scranton; Texas College; Tougaloo.

1962 (5)
Azusa Pacific (resumed 1965); Davis & Elkins; San Diego (resumed 1972); Southern Cal Col.; Westminster (Utah) (resumed 1965, dropped 1979).

1963 (3)
Benedictine (Ill.) (resumed 1973); *Hardin-Simmons (resumed 1990); St. Vincent (Pa.).

1964 (2)
King's (Pa.) (resumed 1993); Paine.

1965 (7)
Claflin; *Detroit; Dillard; Miss. Industrial; Morris; Philander Smith; Rust.

1966 (1)
St. Augustine's (resumed 2002).

1967 (6)
Benedict; Corpus Christi; *George Washington; Jarvis Christian; Ozarks; South Caro. Trade.

1968 (2)
Edward Waters; Frederick.

1969 (6)
Allen; Case Tech and Western Reserve merged to form Case Reserve; George Fox; Louisiana Col. (resumed 2001); UC San Diego; Wiley.

1971 (5)
Bradley; *Buffalo (resumed 1978); Hiram Scott; Lake Forest (resumed 1972); Parsons.

1972 (8)
Adelphi; UC Santa Barb. (resumed 1986, dropped 1992); Haverford; North Dak.-Ellendale; Northern Mont. (resumed 2000); Northwood (Tex.); San Francisco; Sonoma St. (resumed 1980, dropped 1997).

1973 (2)
New England Col.; N.M. Highlands (resumed 1974).

1974 (6)
Col. of Emporia; Dist. Columbia (resumed 1978, dropped 1990); Drexel; Ill.-Chicago; Samford (resumed 1984); *Xavier (Ohio).

1975 (6)
Baptist Christian (resumed 1978, dropped 1983); Bridgeport; Federal City; *Tampa; Vermont; Wis.-Milwaukee.

1976 (3)
UC Riverside; Minn. St. Mankato (resumed 1977); Northland.

1977 (4)
Cal Tech; Oswego St.; Whitman; Yankton (resumed 1978, dropped 1984).

1978 (3)
Cal St. Los Angeles; Col. of Idaho; Rochester Tech.

1979 (5)
Miles (resumed 1980, dropped 1989, resumed 1990); Mont. St.-Billings; Plattsburgh St.; Shaw; Westminster (Utah).

1980 (3)
†Gallaudet; Md.-East. Shore; U.S. Int'l.

1981 (2)
Bluefield St.; *Villanova (resumed 1985).

1982 (4)
Boston St.; Fort Lauderdale; Milton; Seton Hall.

1983 (3)
Baptist Christian; Cal Poly Pomona; Lubbock Christian.

1984 (5)
Fisk; New York Tech; St. Peter's (suspended after one game, resumed 1985, dropped 1988, resumed 1989); So. Dak.-Springfield; Yankton.

1985 (1)
Southern Colo.

1986 (4)
Drake (resumed 1987); N.Y. Maritime (resumed 1987, dropped 1989); Southeastern La. (resumed 2003); *Texas-Arlington.

1987 (4)
Bishop; *Southern Methodist (resumed 1989); Western Mont. (resumed 1988); *Wichita St.

1988 (4)
Northeastern Ill.; St. Paul's; St. Peter's (resumed 1989); Texas Lutheran (resumed 1998).

1989 (3)
Ga. Southwestern; Miles (resumed 1990); N.Y. Maritime.

1990 (2)
*Lamar; Lincoln (Mo.) (resumed 1999).

1991 (3)
Brooklyn; Tarkio; West Tex. A&M (resumed 1992).

1992 (3)
*Long Beach St.; Pacific (Ore.); St. Mary of the Plains.

1993 (5)
*Cal St. Fullerton; Cameron; Ramapo; Santa Clara; Wis.-Superior.

1994 (4)
Cal St. Hayward; Lees-McRae; Oregon Tech; Upsala.

1995 (1)
San Fran. St.

1996 (1)
*Pacific (Cal.).

1997 (2)
Cal St. Chico; Sonoma St.

1998 (2)
Boston U.; Evansville

2000 (3)
Mass.-Boston; Morningside; Swarthmore

2001 (1)
Cal St. Northridge

2002 (6)
Canisius; Fairfield; Mass.-Lowell; Morris Brown; New Jersey City; St. John's (N.Y.)

*Classified major college previous year. †Did not play a 7-game varsity schedule, 1980-86, and returned to club status in 1995.

Championship Results

Jon Frazier (21) of Western Kentucky breaks into the clear on one of his two touchdown runs in the Hilltoppers' defeat of McNeese State in the title game.

Patrick Murphy Racey/NCAA Photos

Division I-AA Championship

2002 Title Game Summary

Hilltoppers Reach Mountain Peak: Western Kentucky avenged a regular-season loss to McNeese State by defeating the Cowboys, 34-14.

Jon Frazier ran for 159 yards and two touchdowns, and Jason Michael accounted for two scores, as the Hilltoppers won their 10th consecutive game and stopped McNeese State's nine-game winning streak. Western Kentucky finished the year with a 12-3 mark, and the Cowboys ended with a 13-2 record.

Michael connected with Jeremi Johnson on a 16-yard pass to open the scoring. The Western Kentucky quarterback also scored on a 2-yard run early in the fourth quarter after McNeese State had pulled to within 24-14.

Frazier dashed for touchdowns of 55 and 14 yards. Peter Martinez added two field goals for Western Kentucky to set both school single-season (18) and career (49) records.

Brian Lowder led the Hilltoppers with 12 tackles, and Charles Thompson added 11. Karl Maslowski contributed seven stops and an interception.

Luke Lawton caught a touchdown pass from Scott Pendarvis, and John Marino booted two field goals, to account for McNeese State's scoring.

FINLEY STADIUM/DAVENPORT FIELD, CHATTANOOGA, TENNESSEE; DECEMBER 20

	Western Ky.	McNeese St.
First downs	13	26
Rushes-yards	50-195	34-137
Passing yardage	185	268
Passes (comp.-att.-int.)	6-10-0	25-48-3
Punts (no.-avg.)	6-37.3	6-35.5
Fumbles (no.-lost)	1-1	2-0
Penalties (no.-yards)	7-38	6-35
Time of possession	30:18	29:42

Western Ky.	7	10	7	10	34
McNeese St.	0	6	8	0	14

FIRST QUARTER
Western Ky.—Jeremi Johnson 16 pass from Jason Michael (Peter Martinez kick) (9:36)

SECOND QUARTER
Western Ky.—Jon Frazier 55 run (Martinez kick) (14:51)
McNeese St.—John Marino 30 field goal (7:32)
Western Ky.—Martinez 40 field goal (4:55)
McNeese St.—Marino 24 field goal (0:07)

THIRD QUARTER
Western Ky.—Frazier 14 run (Martinez kick) (11:03)
McNeese St.—Luke Lawton 15 pass from Scott Pendarvis (Jeff Hamilton pass from Pendarvis) (3:49)

FOURTH QUARTER
Western Ky.—Michael 2 run (Martinez kick) (13:49)
Western Ky.—Martinez 23 field goal (2:51)

INDIVIDUAL LEADERS
Rushing: Western Ky.—Frazier 27-159, Maurice Bradley 2-15, Casey Rooney 2-13, Johnson 5-12, Michael 11-7, Team 2-0, Shannon Hayes 1-(minus 11); McNeese St.—Marcus Trahan 12-82, B.J. Sams 5-32, Jacob Prim 8-15, Luke Lawton 4-12, Andrew Robin 1-0, Scott Pendarvis 4-(minus 4).
Passing: Western Ky.—Michael 6-10-0-185; McNeese St.—Pendarvis 21-38-1-244, Ryan Corcoran 4-9-2-24, Team 0-1-0-0.
Receiving: Western Ky.—Johnson 3-90, Frazier 1-54, Matt Rogers 1-21, Shannon Hayes 1-20; McNeese St.—Sams 7-69, Jermaine Martin 5-74, Jeff Hamilton 4-42, Lawton 3-35, Britt Brodhead 2-16, Robin 1-12, Jacob Prim 1-12, Trahan 1-5, Darren Oustalet 1-3.

NCAA I-AA Football Championship History

1978 At the 72nd NCAA Convention (January 1978) in Atlanta, Ga., the membership voted to establish the Division I-AA Football Championship and a statistics program for the division. The format for the first I-AA championship, held in Wichita Falls, Texas, was a single-elimination, four-team tournament. Florida A&M defeated Massachusetts, 35-28, in the title game. The game was televised by ABC.

1981 The championship expanded to include eight teams in a single-elimination tournament.

1982 The championship expanded to include 12 teams. Eight teams played first-round games at campus sites, and the top four teams, seeded by the Division I-AA Football Committee, received byes.

1986 The championship field expanded to its current format of 16 teams with each team playing a first-round game.

1987 Louisiana-Monroe defeated Marshall, 43-42, in the closest game in championship history.

1989 A then-record 25,725 fans watched Georgia Southern down Stephen F. Austin, 37-34, in the championship game at Allen E. Paulson Stadium in Statesboro, Ga.

1990 Georgia Southern won its fourth I-AA championship, adding to its titles in 1985, 1986 and 1989.

1991 Youngstown State won its first national championship with a 25-17 victory over Marshall. Penguin head coach Jim Tressel joined his father, Lee, as the only father-son combination to win NCAA football titles. Lee Tressel won the 1978 Division III championship at Baldwin-Wallace.

1992 A then-record crowd of 31,304 in Huntington, W.Va., saw Marshall return the favor with a 31-28 win over Youngstown State for its first I-AA title.

1993 The I-AA championship provided for a maximum field of 16 teams. Six member conferences (Big Sky, Gateway, Ohio Valley, Southern, Southland and Yankee) were granted automatic qualification for their respective winners.

Youngstown State won its second I-AA title with a 17-5 victory over Marshall before a crowd of 29,218 in Huntington, W. Va.

1994 Youngstown State won its third national title in four years with a 28-14 victory over Boise State.

1995 Montana won its first Division I-AA title before a championship record crowd of 32,106 in Huntington, W.Va.

1996 Marshall, making its fifth visit to the championship game since 1991, won its second Division I-AA title with a 49-29 victory over defending champion Montana before 30,052 in Huntington, W. Va.

1997 Youngstown State won its fourth national title in the 1990s with a 10-9 victory over McNeese State in Chattanooga, Tennessee.

1999 Georgia Southern closed out the century with another national title, posting a 59-24 victory over Youngstown State. The Eagles won their fifth title, surpassing Youngstown State's four championships and taking over the division lead in crowns.

2000 Georgia Southern rallied past Montana, 27-25, to claim back-to-back titles for the third time in its Division I-AA history.

2001 Montana won a defensive duel with Furman, 13-6, to claim its second title.

2002 Western Kentucky won its first I-AA championship with a 34-14 victory over McNeese State, which lost in the final for the second time (1997 in 10-9 loss to Youngstown State). Coach Jack Harbaugh, father of former Chicago Bears' and Indianapolis Colts' quarterback Jim Harbaugh, won his first I-AA title.

Division I-AA All-Time Championship Results

Year	Champion	Coach	Score	Runner-Up	Site	Attendance
1978	Florida A&M	Rudy Hubbard	35-28	Massachusetts	Wichita Falls, Texas	13,604
1979	Eastern Ky.	Roy Kidd	30-7	Lehigh	Orlando, Fla.	5,500
1980	Boise St.	Jim Criner	31-29	Eastern Ky.	Sacramento, Calif.	8,157
1981	Idaho St.	Dave Kragthorpe	34-23	Eastern Ky.	Wichita Falls, Texas	11,003
1982	Eastern Ky.	Roy Kidd	17-14	Delaware	Wichita Falls, Texas	11,257
1983	Southern Ill.	Rey Dempsey	43-7	Western Caro.	Charleston, S.C.	15,950
1984	Montana St.	Dave Arnold	19-6	Louisiana Tech	Charleston, S.C.	9,125
1985	Ga. Southern	Erk Russell	44-42	Furman	Tacoma, Wash.	5,306
1986	Ga. Southern	Erk Russell	48-21	Arkansas St.	Tacoma, Wash.	4,419
1987	La.-Monroe	Pat Collins	43-42	Marshall	Pocatello, Idaho	11,513
1988	Furman	Jimmy Satterfield	17-12	Ga. Southern	Pocatello, Idaho	11,500
1989	Ga. Southern	Erk Russell	37-34	*Stephen F. Austin	Statesboro, Ga.	25,725
1990	Ga. Southern	Tim Stowers	36-13	Nevada	Statesboro, Ga.	23,204
1991	Youngstown St.	Jim Tressel	25-17	Marshall	Statesboro, Ga.	12,667
1992	Marshall	Jim Donnan	31-28	Youngstown St.	Huntington, W.Va.	31,304
1993	Youngstown St.	Jim Tressel	17-5	Marshall	Huntington, W.Va.	29,218
1994	Youngstown St.	Jim Tressel	28-14	Boise St.	Huntington, W.Va.	27,674
1995	Montana	Don Read	22-20	Marshall	Huntington, W.Va.	32,106
1996	Marshall	Bob Pruett	49-29	Montana	Huntington, W.Va.	30,052
1997	Youngstown St.	Jim Tressel	10-9	McNeese St.	Chattanooga, Tenn.	14,771
1998	Massachusetts	Mark Whipple	55-43	Ga. Southern	Chattanooga, Tenn.	17,501
1999	Ga. Southern	Paul Johnson	59-24	Youngstown St.	Chattanooga, Tenn.	20,052
2000	Ga. Southern	Paul Johnson	27-25	Montana	Chattanooga, Tenn.	17,156
2001	Montana	Joe Glenn	13-6	Furman	Chattanooga, Tenn.	12,698
2002	Western Ky.	Jack Harbaugh	34-14	McNeese St.	Chattanooga, Tenn.	12,360

*Stephen F. Austin's participation in 1989 Division I-AA championship vacated.

2002 Division I-AA Championship Results

FIRST ROUND
McNeese St. 21, Montana St. 14
Montana 45, Northwestern St. 14
Villanova 45, Furman 38
Fordham 29, Northeastern 24
Ga. Southern 34, Bethune-Cookman 0
Maine 14, Appalachian St. 13
Western Ky. 59, Murray St. 20
Western Ill. 48, Eastern Ill. 9

QUARTERFINALS
McNeese St. 24, Montana 20
Villanova 24, Fordham 10
Ga. Southern 31, Maine 7
Western Ky. 31, Western Ill. 28

SEMIFINALS
McNeese St. 39, Villanova 28
Western Ky. 31, Ga. Southern 28

CHAMPIONSHIP
Western Ky. 34, McNeese St. 14

Individual Records

GAME

NET YARDS RUSHING
333—Adrian Peterson, Ga. Southern (38) vs. Massachusetts (21), 12-4-99.

RUSHES ATTEMPTED
46—Tamron Smith, Youngstown St. (10) vs. Samford (0), 12-14-91.

TOUCHDOWNS BY RUSHING
6—Sean Sanders, Weber St. (59) vs. Idaho (30), 11-28-87.

NET YARDS PASSING
517—Todd Hammel, Stephen F. Austin (59) vs. Grambling (56), 11-25-89.

PASSES ATTEMPTED
82—Steve McNair, Alcorn St. (20) vs. Youngstown St. (63), 11-25-94.

PASSES COMPLETED
52—Steve McNair, Alcorn St. (20) vs. Youngstown St. (63), 11-25-94.

PASSES INTERCEPTED
7—Jeff Gilbert, Western Caro. (7) vs. Southern Ill. (43), 12-17-83.

TOUCHDOWN PASSES
6—Mike Smith, Northern Iowa (41) vs. La.-Monroe (44), 12-12-87; Clemente Gordon, Grambling (56) vs. Stephen F. Austin (59), 11-25-89.

COMPLETION PERCENTAGE (Min. 15 Attempts)
.882—Jeff Ryan, Youngstown St. (41) vs. N.C. A&T (3), 12-4-99 (15 of 17).

NET YARDS RUSHING AND PASSING
539—Todd Hammel, Stephen F. Austin (59) vs. Grambling (56), 11-25-89 (22 rushing, 517 passing).

RUSHING AND PASSING PLAYS
91—Steve McNair, Alcorn St. (20) vs. Youngstown St. (63), 11-25-94 (9 rushing, 82 passing).

PUNTING AVERAGE (Min. 3 Punts)
54.5— Jay Heibel, Lehigh (22) vs. Delaware (47), 12-2-00 (4 for 218).

PUNTS
14—Fred McRae, Jackson St. (0) vs. Stephen F. Austin (24), 11-26-88.

RECEPTIONS
18—Brian Forster, Rhode Island (23) vs. Richmond (17), 12-1-84.

NET YARDS RECEIVING
288—Randy Moss, Marshall (59) vs. Delaware (14), 11-30-96 (8 catches).

TOUCHDOWN RECEPTIONS
4—Tony DiMaggio, Rhode Island (35) vs. Akron (27), 11-30-85; Randy Moss, Marshall (49) vs. Montana (29), 12-21-96.

INTERCEPTIONS
4—Greg Shipp, Southern Ill. (43) vs. Western Caro. (7), 12-17-83.

YARDS GAINED ON INTERCEPTION RETURNS
117—Kevin Sullivan, Massachusetts (44) vs. Nevada (21), 12-9-78.

YARDS GAINED ON PUNT RETURNS
121—Darren Sharper, William & Mary (45) vs. Jackson St. (6), 11-30-96.

YARDS GAINED ON KICKOFF RETURNS
232—Mike Cadore, Eastern Ky. (32) vs. La.-Monroe (33), 12-5-87, 6 returns, 1 for 99-yard TD.

POINTS
36—Sean Sanders, Weber St. (59) vs. Idaho (30), 11-28-87.

TOUCHDOWNS
6—Sean Sanders, Weber St. (59) vs. Idaho (30), 11-28-87.

EXTRA POINTS
10—Andy Larson, Montana (70) vs. Stephen F. Austin (14), 12-9-95.

FIELD GOALS
5—Matt Fordyce, Fordham (29) vs. Northeastern (24), 11-30-2002.

TOURNAMENT

NET YARDS RUSHING
897—Adrian Peterson, Ga. Southern, 1999 (134 vs. Northern Ariz., 333 vs. Massachusetts, 183 vs. Illinois St., 247 vs. Youngstown St.)

RUSHES ATTEMPTED
123—Ray Whalen, Nevada, 1990 (21 vs. La.-Monroe, 34 vs. Furman, 44 vs. Boise St., 24 vs. Ga. Southern).

NET YARDS PASSING
1,500—Dave Dickenson, Montana, 1995 (441 vs. Eastern Ky., 408 vs. Ga. Southern, 370 vs. Stephen F. Austin, 281 vs. Marshall).

PASSES ATTEMPTED
177—Jeff Gilbert, Western Caro., 1983 (47 vs. Colgate, 52 vs. Holy Cross, 45 vs. Furman, 33 vs. Southern Ill.); Brian Ah Yat, Montana, 1996 (48 vs. Nicholls St., 34 vs. East Tenn. St., 40 vs. Troy St., 55 vs. Marshall).

PASSES COMPLETED
122—Dave Dickenson, Montana, 1995 (31 vs. Eastern Ky., 37 vs. Ga. Southern, 25 vs. Stephen F. Austin, 29 vs. Marshall).

PASSES INTERCEPTED
11—Todd Hammel, Stephen F. Austin, 1989 (0 vs. Grambling, 4 vs. Southwest Mo. St., 2 vs. Furman, 5 vs. Ga. Southern).

TOUCHDOWN PASSES
14—Todd Hammel, Stephen F. Austin, 1989 (5 vs. Grambling, 4 vs. Southwest Mo. St., 2 vs. Furman, 3 vs. Ga. Southern).

COMPLETION PERCENTAGE (Min. 40 Completions)
.769—Giovanni Carmazzi, Hofstra, 1999, 50 of 65 (22-30 vs. Lehigh, 28-35 vs. Illinois St.)

RECEPTIONS
41—Joe Douglass, Montana, 1996 (10 vs. Nicholls St., 10 vs. East Tenn. St., 8 vs. Troy St., 13 vs. Marshall).

NET YARDS RECEIVING
636—Randy Moss, Marshall, 1996 (288 vs. Delaware, 82 vs. Furman, 46 vs. Northern Iowa, 220 vs. Montana).

TOUCHDOWN RECEPTIONS
10—Randy Moss, Marshall, 1996 (3 vs. Delaware, 2 vs. Furman, 1 vs. Northern Iowa, 4 vs. Montana).

POINTS
74—Adrian Peterson, Ga. Southern, 1999 (6 vs. Northern Ariz., 32 vs. Massachusetts, 18 vs. Illinois St., 18 vs. Youngstown St.).

TOUCHDOWNS
12—Adrian Peterson, Ga. Southern, 1999 (1 vs. Northern Ariz., 5 vs. Massachusetts, 3 vs. Illinois St., 3 vs. Youngstown St.).

LONGEST PLAYS

RUSH
90—Henry Fields, McNeese St. (38) vs. Idaho (21), 11-26-94, TD.

PASS (Including Run)
90—Paul Singer 22 pass to Derek Swanson and 68 fumble recovery advancement by Steve Williams, Western Ill. (32) vs. Western Ky. (35), 11-26-88.

FIELD GOAL
56—Tony Zendejas, Nevada (27) vs. Idaho St. (20), 11-26-83.

PUNT
88—Mike Cassidy, Rhode Island (20) vs. Montana St. (32), 12-8-84.

PUNT RETURN
86—Antonio Veals, Western Ky. (59) vs. Murray St. (20), 11-30-2002, TD.

KICKOFF RETURN
100—Chris Fontenette, McNeese St. (7) vs. Northern Iowa (29), 12-5-92, TD.

INTERCEPTION RETURN
100—Melvin Cunningham, Marshall (28) vs. James Madison (21) (ot), 12-3-94, TD; Paul Williams, Delaware (38) vs. Hofstra (17), 11-25-95, TD.

FUMBLE RETURN
95—Randy Smith, Youngstown St. (63) vs. Alcorn St. (20), 11-25-94, TD.

Team Records

GAME

FIRST DOWNS
41—Montana (45) vs. Ga. Southern (0), 12-2-95.

FIRST DOWNS BY RUSHING
26—La.-Monroe (78) vs. Alcorn St. (27), 11-28-92.

FIRST DOWNS BY PASSING
29—Alcorn St. (20) vs. Youngstown St. (63), 11-25-94.

NET YARDS RUSHING
638—Ga. Southern (59) vs. Youngstown St. (24), 12-18-99 (59 rushes).

RUSHES ATTEMPTED
81—Youngstown St. (10) vs. Samford (0), 12-14-91.

NET YARDS PASSING
537—Montana (30) vs. McNeese St. (28), 12-3-94.

PASSES ATTEMPTED
90—Rhode Island (15) vs. Furman (59), 12-7-85.

PASSES COMPLETED
52—Alcorn St. (20) vs. Youngstown St. (63), 11-25-94.

PASSES INTERCEPTED
7—Western Caro. (7) vs. Southern Ill. (43), 12-17-83; Rhode Island (15) vs. Furman (59), 12-7-85; Weber St. (23) vs. Marshall (51), 12-5-87.

COMPLETION PERCENTAGE (Min. 20 Attempts)
.850—Illinois St. (37) vs. Hofstra (20), 12-4-99 (34 of 40).

NET YARDS RUSHING AND PASSING
742—La.-Monroe (78) vs. Alcorn St. (27), 11-28-92 (502 rushing, 240 passing).

RUSHING AND PASSING PLAYS
114—Nevada (42) vs. Furman (35) (3 ot), 12-1-90 (47 rushing, 67 passing).

PUNTING AVERAGE (Min. 4 Punts)
54.5—Lehigh (22) vs. Delaware (47), 12-2-2000 (4 for 218).

PUNTS
14—Jackson St. (0) vs. Stephen F. Austin (24), 11-26-88.

PUNTS BLOCKED
2—Florida A&M (35) vs. Massachusetts (28), 12-16-78; Boise St. (14) vs. Grambling (9), 12-13-80.

YARDS GAINED ON PUNT RETURNS
128—William & Mary (45) vs. Jackson St. (6), 11-30-96.

YARDS GAINED ON KICKOFF RETURNS
232—Eastern Ky. (32) vs. La.-Monroe (33), 12-5-87.

YARDS GAINED ON INTERCEPTION RETURNS
164—Marshall (51) vs. Weber St. (23), 12-5-87.

YARDS PENALIZED
172—Tennessee St. (32) vs. Jackson St. (23), 11-29-86.

FUMBLES LOST
7—Jackson St. (8) vs. Marshall (38), 11-25-95.

POINTS
78—La.-Monroe vs. Alcorn St. (27), 11-28-92.

TOURNAMENT

FIRST DOWNS
125—Montana, 1995 (25 vs. Eastern Ky., 41 vs. Ga. Southern, 38 vs. Stephen F. Austin, 21 vs. Marshall).

NET YARDS RUSHING
2,030—Ga. Southern, 1999 (559 vs. Northern Ariz., 470 vs. Massachusetts, 363 vs. Illinois St., 638 vs. Youngstown St.).

NET YARDS PASSING
1,703—Montana, 1996 (447 vs. Nicholls St., 467 vs. East Tenn. St., 454 vs. Troy St., 335 vs. Marshall).

NET YARDS RUSHING AND PASSING
2,253—Ga. Southern, 1999 (659 vs. Northern Ariz., 500 vs. Massachusetts, 439 vs. Illinois St., 655 vs. Youngstown St.).

PASSES ATTEMPTED
197—Montana, 1996 (53 vs. Nicholls St., 44 vs. East Tenn. St., 45 vs. Troy St., 55 vs. Marshall).

PASSES COMPLETED
137—Montana, 1995 (35 vs. Eastern Ky., 42 vs. Ga. Southern, 31 vs. Stephen F. Austin, 29 vs. Marshall).

PASSES INTERCEPTED
11—Stephen F. Austin, 1989 (0 vs. Grambling, 4 vs. Southwest Mo. St., 2 vs. Furman, 5 vs. Ga. Southern).

PUNTS
29—Northern Iowa, 1992 (11 vs. Eastern Wash., 10 vs. McNeese St., 8 vs. Youngstown St.).

YARDS PENALIZED
350—Ga. Southern, 1986 (106 vs. N.C. A&T, 104 vs. Nicholls St., 75 vs. Nevada, 65 vs. Arkansas St.).

FUMBLES LOST
9—Nevada, 1983 (3 vs. Idaho St., 4 vs. North Texas, 2 vs. Southern Ill.); Youngstown St., 1991 (3 vs. Villanova, 1 vs. Nevada, 4 vs. Samford, 1 vs. Marshall); Ga. Southern, 1998 (1 vs. Colgate, 2 vs. Connecticut, 0 vs. Western Ill., 6 vs. Massachusetts).

POINTS
203—Ga. Southern, 1986 (52 vs. N.C. A&T, 55 vs. Nicholls St., 48 vs. Nevada, 48 vs. Arkansas St.).

Championship Game Records

INDIVIDUAL

NET YARDS RUSHING
247—Adrian Peterson, Ga. Southern (59) vs. Youngstown St. (24), 1999 (25 rushes).

RUSHES ATTEMPTED
35—Marcel Shipp, Massachusetts (55) vs. Ga. Southern (43), 1998 (244 yards).

TOUCHDOWNS BY RUSHING
4—John Bagwell, Furman (42) vs. Ga. Southern (44), 1985.

NET YARDS PASSING
474—Tony Peterson, Marshall (42) vs. La.-Monroe (43), 1987 (28 of 54).

PASSES ATTEMPTED
57—Kelly Bradley, Montana St. (19) vs. Louisiana Tech (6), 1984 (32 completions).

PASSES COMPLETED
36—Brian Ah Yat, Montana (29) vs. Marshall (49), 1996 (55 attempts).

PASSES HAD INTERCEPTED
7—Jeff Gilbert, Western Caro. (7) vs. Southern Ill. (43), 1983.

TOUCHDOWN PASSES
4—Tracy Ham, Ga. Southern (44) vs. Furman (42), 1985; Tony Peterson, Marshall (42) vs. La.-Monroe (43), 1987; Eric Kresser, Marshall (49) vs. Montana (29), 1996.

**COMPLETION PERCENTAGE
(Min. 8 Attempts)**
.875—Mark Brungard, Youngstown St. (17) vs. Marshall (5), 1993 (7 of 8).

NET YARDS RUSHING AND PASSING
509—Tracy Ham, Ga. Southern (44) vs. Furman (42), 1985 (90 rushing, 419 passing; 56 plays).

RUSHING AND PASSING PLAYS
67—Brian Ah Yat, Montana (29) vs. Marshall (49), 1996 (12 rush, 55 pass; 301 yards).

**PUNTING AVERAGE
(Min. 3 Punts)**
51.0—Andrew Maclay, Massachusetts (55) vs. Ga. Southern (43), 1998 (4 for 204).

PUNTS
10—Rick Titus, Delaware (14) vs. Eastern Ky. (17), 1982 (41.6 average).

RECEPTIONS
13—Joe Douglass, Montana (29) vs. Marshall (49), 1996 (117 yards).

NET YARDS RECEIVING
220—Randy Moss, Marshall (49) vs. Montana (29), 1996 (9 catches).

TOUCHDOWN RECEPTIONS
4—Randy Moss, Marshall (49) vs. Montana (29), 1996 (9 catches for 220 yards).

INTERCEPTIONS
4—Greg Shipp, Southern Ill. (43) vs. Western Caro. (7), 1983.

YARDS GAINED ON INTERCEPTION RETURNS
58—Chris Cook, Boise St. (14) vs. Youngstown St. (28), 1994 (1 interception).

YARDS GAINED ON PUNT RETURNS
99—Anthony Williams, Ga. Southern (59) vs. Youngstown St. (24), 1999 (6 returns).

YARDS GAINED ON KICKOFF RETURNS
213—Andre Coleman, Youngstown St. (24) vs. Ga. Southern (59), 1999 (9 returns).

POINTS
24—John Bagwell, Furman (42) vs. Ga. Southern (44), 1985; Randy Moss, Marshall (49) vs. Montana (29), 1996.

TOUCHDOWNS
4—John Bagwell, Furman (42) vs. Ga. Southern (44), 1985; Randy Moss, Marshall (49) vs. Montana (29), 1996.

EXTRA POINTS
8—Chris Chambers, Ga. Southern (59) vs. Youngstown St. (24), 1999.

FIELD GOALS
4—Tim Foley, Ga. Southern (48) vs. Arkansas St. (21), 1986.

LONGEST PLAYS

RUSH
73—Mark Myers, Ga. Southern (27) vs. Montana (25), 2000.

PASS COMPLETION
79—Tracy Ham to Ricky Harris, Ga. Southern (48) vs. Arkansas St. (21), 1986.

FIELD GOAL
55—David Cool, Ga. Southern (12) vs. Furman (17), 1988.

PUNT
72—Rick Titus, Delaware (14) vs. Eastern Ky. (17), 1982.

TEAM

FIRST DOWNS
31—Montana (29) vs. Marshall (49), 1996 (11 rushing, 17 passing, 3 by penalty).

FIRST DOWNS BY RUSHING
23—Ga. Southern (59) vs. Youngstown St. (24), 1999.

FIRST DOWNS BY PASSING
19—Marshall (42) vs. La.-Monroe (43), 1987.

FIRST DOWNS BY PENALTY
3—Eastern Ky. (23) vs. Idaho St. (34), 1981; Furman (42) vs. Ga. Southern (44), 1985; La.-Monroe (43) vs. Marshall (42), 1987; Montana (29) vs. Marshall (49), 1996.

NET YARDS RUSHING
638—Ga. Southern (59) vs. Youngstown St. (24), 1999 (59 rushes).

RUSHES ATTEMPTED
76—Florida A&M (35) vs. Massachusetts (28), 1978 (470 yards).

NET YARDS PASSING
474—Marshall (42) vs. La.-Monroe (43), 1987 (28 of 54).

PASSES ATTEMPTED
57—Montana St. (19) vs. Louisiana Tech (6), 1984 (32 completions).

PASSES COMPLETED
36—Montana (29) vs. Marshall (49), 1996 (55 attempts).

**COMPLETION PERCENTAGE
(Min. 10 Attempts)**
.760—Southern Ill. (43) vs. Western Caro. (7), 1983 (19 of 25).

PASSES HAD INTERCEPTED
7—Western Caro. (7) vs. Southern Ill. (43), 1983.

NET YARDS RUSHING AND PASSING
655—Ga. Southern (59) vs. Youngstown St. (24), 1999 (638 rushing, 17 passing; 63 plays).

RUSHING AND PASSING PLAYS
90—Montana (29) vs. Marshall (49), 1996 (35 rushing, 55 passing; 430 yards).

**PUNTING AVERAGE
(Min. 3 Punts)**
51.0—Massachusetts (55) vs. Ga. Southern (43), 1998 (4 for 204).

PUNTS
10—Delaware (14) vs. Eastern Ky. (17), 1982 (41.6 average).

YARDS GAINED ON PUNT RETURNS
99—Ga. Southern (59) vs. Youngstown St. (24), 1999 (7 returns).

YARDS GAINED ON KICKOFF RETURNS
229—Western Caro. (7) vs. Southern Ill. (43), 1983 (8 returns).

YARDS GAINED ON INTERCEPTION RETURNS
70—Marshall (31) vs. Youngstown St. (28), 1992 (2 interceptions).

YARDS PENALIZED
162—Idaho St. (34) vs. Eastern Ky. (23), 1981 (12 penalties).

FUMBLES
6—Ga. Southern (43) vs. Massachusetts (55), 1998 (6 lost).

FUMBLES LOST
6—Ga. Southern (43) vs. Massachusetts (55), 1998 (6 fumbles).

POINTS
59—Ga. Southern vs. Youngstown St. (24), 1999.

ATTENDANCE
32,106—Marshall University Stadium, Huntington, W.Va., 1995.

Year-by-Year Division I-AA Championship Results

Year (Number of Teams)	Coach	Record	Result
1978 (4)			
Florida A&M	Rudy Hubbard	2-0	Champion
Massachusetts	Bob Pickett	1-1	Second
Jackson St.	W.C. Gorden	0-1	Lost 1st Round
Nevada	Chris Ault	0-1	Lost 1st Round
1979 (4)			
Eastern Ky.	Roy Kidd	2-0	Champion
Lehigh	John Whitehead	1-1	Second
Murray St.	Mike Gottfried	0-1	Lost 1st Round
Nevada	Chris Ault	0-1	Lost 1st Round
1980 (4)			
Boise St.	Jim Criner	2-0	Champion
Eastern Ky.	Roy Kidd	1-1	Second
Grambling	Eddie Robinson	0-1	Lost 1st Round
Lehigh	John Whitehead	0-1	Lost 1st Round

Year (Number of Teams)	Coach	Record	Result
1981 (8)			
Idaho St.	Dave Kragthorpe	3-0	Champion
Eastern Ky.	Roy Kidd	2-1	Second
Boise St.	Jim Criner	1-1	Semifinalist
South Carolina St.	Bill Davis	1-1	Semifinalist
Delaware	Tubby Raymond	0-1	Lost 1st Round
Jackson St.	W.C. Gorden	0-1	Lost 1st Round
Rhode Island	Bob Griffin	0-1	Lost 1st Round
*Tennessee St.	John Merritt	0-1	Vacated
1982 (12)			
Eastern Ky.	Roy Kidd	3-0	Champion
Delaware	Tubby Raymond	2-1	Second
Louisiana Tech	Billy Brewer	1-1	Semifinalist
*Tennessee St.	John Merritt	1-1	Vacated
Colgate	Fred Dunlap	1-1	Quarterfinalist
Eastern Ill.	Darrell Mudra	1-1	Quarterfinalist
Idaho	Dennis Erickson	1-1	Quarterfinalist
South Carolina St.	Bill Davis	1-1	Quarterfinalist
Boston U.	Rick Taylor	0-1	Lost 1st Round
Furman	Dick Sheridan	0-1	Lost 1st Round
Jackson St.	W.C. Gorden	0-1	Lost 1st Round
Montana	Larry Donovan	0-1	Lost 1st Round
1983 (12)			
Southern Ill.	Rey Dempsey	3-0	Champion
Western Caro.	Bob Waters	3-1	Second
Furman	Dick Sheridan	1-1	Semifinalist
Nevada	Chris Ault	2-1	Semifinalist
Boston U.	Rick Taylor	1-1	Quarterfinalist
Holy Cross	Rick Carter	0-1	Quarterfinalist
Indiana St.	Dennis Raetz	1-1	Quarterfinalist
North Texas	Corky Nelson	0-1	Quarterfinalist
Colgate	Fred Dunlap	0-1	Lost 1st Round
Eastern Ill.	Al Molde	0-1	Lost 1st Round
Eastern Ky.	Roy Kidd	0-1	Lost 1st Round
Idaho St.	Jim Koetter	0-1	Lost 1st Round
1984 (12)			
Montana St.	Dave Arnold	3-0	Champion
Louisiana Tech	A.L. Williams	3-1	Second
Middle Tenn.	James Donnelly	2-1	Semifinalist
Rhode Island	Bob Griffin	1-1	Semifinalist
Alcorn St.	Marino Casem	0-1	Quarterfinalist
Arkansas St.	Larry Lacewell	1-1	Quarterfinalist
Indiana St.	Dennis Raetz	0-1	Quarterfinalist
Richmond	Dal Shealy	1-1	Quarterfinalist
Boston U.	Rick Taylor	0-1	Lost 1st Round
Eastern Ky.	Roy Kidd	0-1	Lost 1st Round
Mississippi Val.	Archie Cooley Jr.	0-1	Lost 1st Round
Chattanooga	Buddy Nix	0-1	Lost 1st Round
1985 (12)			
Ga. Southern	Erk Russell	4-0	Champion
Furman	Dick Sheridan	2-1	Second
Nevada	Chris Ault	1-1	Semifinalist
Northern Iowa	Darrell Mudra	1-1	Semifinalist
Arkansas St.	Larry Lacewell	1-1	Quarterfinalist
Eastern Wash.	Dick Zornes	1-1	Quarterfinalist
Middle Tenn.	James Donnelly	0-1	Quarterfinalist
Rhode Island	Bob Griffin	1-1	Quarterfinalist
Akron	Jim Dennison	0-1	Lost 1st Round
Grambling	Eddie Robinson	0-1	Lost 1st Round
Idaho	Dennis Erickson	0-1	Lost 1st Round
Jackson St.	W.C. Gorden	0-1	Lost 1st Round
1986 (16)			
Ga. Southern	Erk Russell	4-0	Champion
Arkansas St.	Larry Lacewell	3-1	Second
Eastern Ky.	Roy Kidd	2-1	Semifinalist
Nevada	Chris Ault	2-1	Semifinalist
Delaware	Tubby Raymond	1-1	Quarterfinalist
Eastern Ill.	Al Molde	1-1	Quarterfinalist
Nicholls St.	Sonny Jackson	1-1	Quarterfinalist
Tennessee St.	William Thomas	1-1	Quarterfinalist
Appalachian St.	Sparky Woods	0-1	Lost 1st Round
Furman	Jimmy Satterfield	0-1	Lost 1st Round
Idaho	Keith Gilbertson	0-1	Lost 1st Round
Jackson St.	W.C. Gorden	0-1	Lost 1st Round
Murray St.	Frank Beamer	0-1	Lost 1st Round
N.C. A&T	Maurice Forte	0-1	Lost 1st Round
Sam Houston St.	Ron Randleman	0-1	Lost 1st Round
William & Mary	Jimmye Laycock	0-1	Lost 1st Round
1987 (16)			
La.-Monroe	Pat Collins	4-0	Champion
Marshall	George Chaump	3-1	Second
Appalachian St.	Sparky Woods	2-1	Semifinalist

Year (Number of Teams)	Coach	Record	Result
Northern Iowa	Darrell Mudra	2-1	Semifinalist
Arkansas St.	Larry Lacewell	1-1	Quarterfinalist
Eastern Ky.	Roy Kidd	1-1	Quarterfinalist
Ga. Southern	Erk Russell	1-1	Quarterfinalist
Weber St.	Mike Price	1-1	Quarterfinalist
Idaho	Keith Gilbertson	0-1	Lost 1st Round
Jackson St.	W.C. Gorden	0-1	Lost 1st Round
James Madison	Joe Purzycki	0-1	Lost 1st Round
Maine	Tim Murphy	0-1	Lost 1st Round
North Texas	Corky Nelson	0-1	Lost 1st Round
Richmond	Dal Shealy	0-1	Lost 1st Round
Western Ky.	Dave Roberts	0-1	Lost 1st Round
Youngstown St.	Jim Tressel	0-1	Lost 1st Round
1988 (16)			
Furman	Jimmy Satterfield	4-0	Champion
Ga. Southern	Erk Russell	3-1	Second
Eastern Ky.	Roy Kidd	2-1	Semifinalist
Idaho	Keith Gilbertson	2-1	Semifinalist
Marshall	George Chaump	1-1	Quarterfinalist
Northwestern St.	Sam Goodwin	1-1	Quarterfinalist
Stephen F. Austin	Jim Hess	1-1	Quarterfinalist
Western Ky.	Dave Roberts	1-1	Quarterfinalist
Boise St.	Skip Hall	0-1	Lost 1st Round
Citadel	Charlie Taaffe	0-1	Lost 1st Round
Delaware	Tubby Raymond	0-1	Lost 1st Round
Jackson St.	W.C. Gorden	0-1	Lost 1st Round
Massachusetts	Jim Reid	0-1	Lost 1st Round
Montana	Don Read	0-1	Lost 1st Round
North Texas	Corky Nelson	0-1	Lost 1st Round
Western Ill.	Bruce Craddock	0-1	Lost 1st Round
1989 (16)			
Ga. Southern	Erk Russell	4-0	Champion
*Stephen F. Austin	Lynn Graves	3-1	Vacated
Furman	Jimmy Satterfield	2-1	Semifinalist
Montana	Don Read	2-1	Semifinalist
Eastern Ill.	Bob Spoo	1-1	Quarterfinalist
Middle Tenn.	James Donnelly	1-1	Quarterfinalist
Southwest Mo. St.	Jesse Branch	1-1	Quarterfinalist
Youngstown St.	Jim Tressel	1-1	Quarterfinalist
Appalachian St.	Jerry Moore	0-1	Lost 1st Round
Eastern Ky.	Roy Kidd	0-1	Lost 1st Round
Grambling	Eddie Robinson	0-1	Lost 1st Round
Idaho	John L. Smith	0-1	Lost 1st Round
Jackson St.	W.C. Gorden	0-1	Lost 1st Round
Maine	Tom Lichtenberg	0-1	Lost 1st Round
Villanova	Andy Talley	0-1	Lost 1st Round
William & Mary	Jimmye Laycock	0-1	Lost 1st Round
1990 (16)			
Ga. Southern	Tim Stowers	4-0	Champion
Nevada	Chris Ault	3-1	Second
Boise St.	Skip Hall	2-1	Semifinalist
UCF	Gene McDowell	2-1	Semifinalist
Furman	Jimmy Satterfield	1-1	Quarterfinalist
Idaho	John L. Smith	1-1	Quarterfinalist
Middle Tenn.	James Donnelly	1-1	Quarterfinalist
William & Mary	Jimmye Laycock	1-1	Quarterfinalist
Citadel	Charlie Taaffe	0-1	Lost 1st Round
Eastern Ky.	Roy Kidd	0-1	Lost 1st Round
Jackson St.	W.C. Gorden	0-1	Lost 1st Round
La.-Monroe	Dave Roberts	0-1	Lost 1st Round
Massachusetts	Jim Reid	0-1	Lost 1st Round
Northern Iowa	Terry Allen	0-1	Lost 1st Round
Southwest Mo. St.	Jesse Branch	0-1	Lost 1st Round
Youngstown St.	Jim Tressel	0-1	Lost 1st Round
1991 (16)			
Youngstown St.	Jim Tressel	4-0	Champion
Marshall	Jim Donnan	3-1	Second
Eastern Ky.	Roy Kidd	2-1	Semifinalist
Samford	Terry Bowden	2-1	Semifinalist
James Madison	Rip Scherer	1-1	Quarterfinalist
Middle Tenn.	James Donnelly	1-1	Quarterfinalist
Nevada	Chris Ault	1-1	Quarterfinalist
Northern Iowa	Terry Allen	1-1	Quarterfinalist
Appalachian St.	Jerry Moore	0-1	Lost 1st Round
Delaware	Tubby Raymond	0-1	Lost 1st Round
McNeese St.	Bobby Keasler	0-1	Lost 1st Round
New Hampshire	Bill Bowes	0-1	Lost 1st Round
Sam Houston St.	Ron Randleman	0-1	Lost 1st Round
Villanova	Andy Talley	0-1	Lost 1st Round
Weber St.	Dave Arslanian	0-1	Lost 1st Round
Western Ill.	Randy Ball	0-1	Lost 1st Round

1992 (16)

Year (Number of Teams)	Coach	Record	Result
Marshall	Jim Donnan	4-0	Champion
Youngstown St.	Jim Tressel	3-1	Second
Delaware	Tubby Raymond	2-1	Semifinalist
Northern Iowa	Terry Allen	2-1	Semifinalist
Citadel	Charlie Taaffe	1-1	Quarterfinalist
La.-Monroe	Dave Roberts	1-1	Quarterfinalist
McNeese St.	Bobby Keasler	1-1	Quarterfinalist
Middle Tenn.	James Donnelly	1-1	Quarterfinalist
Alcorn St.	Cardell Jones	0-1	Lost 1st Round
Appalachian St.	Jerry Moore	0-1	Lost 1st Round
Eastern Ky.	Roy Kidd	0-1	Lost 1st Round
Eastern Wash.	Dick Zornes	0-1	Lost 1st Round
Idaho	John L. Smith	0-1	Lost 1st Round
N.C. A&T	Bill Hayes	0-1	Lost 1st Round
Samford	Terry Bowden	0-1	Lost 1st Round
Villanova	Andy Talley	0-1	Lost 1st Round

1993 (16)

Team	Coach	Record	Result
Youngstown St.	Jim Tressel	4-0	Champion
Marshall	Jim Donnan	3-1	Second
Idaho	John L. Smith	2-1	Semifinalist
Troy St.	Larry Blakeney	2-1	Semifinalist
Boston U.	Dan Allen	1-1	Quarterfinalist
Delaware	Tubby Raymond	1-1	Quarterfinalist
Ga. Southern	Tim Stowers	1-1	Quarterfinalist
McNeese St.	Bobby Keasler	1-1	Quarterfinalist
UCF	Gene McDowell	0-1	Lost 1st Round
Eastern Ky.	Roy Kidd	0-1	Lost 1st Round
Howard	Steve Wilson	0-1	Lost 1st Round
La.-Monroe	Dave Roberts	0-1	Lost 1st Round
Montana	Don Read	0-1	Lost 1st Round
Northern Iowa	Terry Allen	0-1	Lost 1st Round
Stephen F. Austin	John Pearce	0-1	Lost 1st Round
William & Mary	Jimmye Laycock	0-1	Lost 1st Round

1994 (16)

Team	Coach	Record	Result
Youngstown St.	Jim Tressel	4-0	Champion
Boise St.	Pokey Allen	3-1	Second
Marshall	Jim Donnan	2-1	Semifinalist
Montana	Don Read	2-1	Semifinalist
Appalachian St.	Jerry Moore	1-1	Quarterfinalist
Eastern Ky.	Roy Kidd	1-1	Quarterfinalist
James Madison	Rip Scherer	1-1	Quarterfinalist
McNeese St.	Bobby Keasler	1-1	Quarterfinalist
Alcorn St.	Cardell Jones	0-1	Lost 1st Round
Boston U.	Dan Allen	0-1	Lost 1st Round
Idaho	John L. Smith	0-1	Lost 1st Round
Middle Tenn.	James Donnelly	0-1	Lost 1st Round
New Hampshire	Bill Bowes	0-1	Lost 1st Round
North Texas	Matt Simon	0-1	Lost 1st Round
Northern Iowa	Terry Allen	0-1	Lost 1st Round
Troy St.	Larry Blakeney	0-1	Lost 1st Round

1995 (16)

Team	Coach	Record	Result
Montana	Don Read	4-0	Champion
Marshall	Jim Donnan	3-1	Second
McNeese St.	Bobby Keasler	2-1	Semifinalist
Stephen F. Austin	John Pearce	2-1	Semifinalist
Appalachian St.	Jerry Moore	1-1	Quarterfinalist
Delaware	Tubby Raymond	1-1	Quarterfinalist
Ga. Southern	Tim Stowers	1-1	Quarterfinalist
Northern Iowa	Terry Allen	1-1	Quarterfinalist
Eastern Ill.	Bob Spoo	0-1	Lost 1st Round
Eastern Ky.	Roy Kidd	0-1	Lost 1st Round
Hofstra	Joe Gardi	0-1	Lost 1st Round
Idaho	Chris Tormey	0-1	Lost 1st Round
Jackson St.	James Carson	0-1	Lost 1st Round
James Madison	Alex Wood	0-1	Lost 1st Round
Murray St.	Houston Nutt	0-1	Lost 1st Round
Troy St.	Larry Blakeney	0-1	Lost 1st Round

1996 (16)

Team	Coach	Record	Result
Marshall	Bob Pruett	4-0	Champion
Montana	Mick Dennehy	3-1	Second
Northern Iowa	Terry Allen	2-1	Semifinalist
Troy St.	Larry Blakeney	2-1	Semifinalist
East Tenn. St.	Mike Cavan	1-1	Quarterfinalist
Furman	Bobby Johnson	1-1	Quarterfinalist
Murray St.	Houston Nutt	1-1	Quarterfinalist
William & Mary	Jimmye Laycock	1-1	Quarterfinalist
Delaware	Tubby Raymond	0-1	Lost 1st Round
Eastern Ill.	Bob Spoo	0-1	Lost 1st Round
Florida A&M	Billy Joe	0-1	Lost 1st Round
Jackson St.	James Carson	0-1	Lost 1st Round
Nicholls St.	Darren Barbier	0-1	Lost 1st Round
Northern Ariz.	Stephen Axman	0-1	Lost 1st Round
Villanova	Andy Talley	0-1	Lost 1st Round
Western Ill.	Randy Ball	0-1	Lost 1st Round

1997 (16)

Team	Coach	Record	Result
Youngstown St.	Jim Tressel	4-0	Champion
McNeese St.	Bobby Keasler	3-1	Second
Delaware	Tubby Raymond	2-1	Semifinalist
Eastern Wash.	Mike Kramer	2-1	Semifinalist
Ga. Southern	Paul Johnson	1-1	Quarterfinalist
Villanova	Andy Talley	1-1	Quarterfinalist
Western Ill.	Randy Ball	1-1	Quarterfinalist
Western Ky.	Jack Harbaugh	1-1	Quarterfinalist
Colgate	Dick Biddle	0-1	Lost 1st Round
Eastern Ky.	Roy Kidd	0-1	Lost 1st Round
Florida A&M	Billy Joe	0-1	Lost 1st Round
Hampton	Joe Taylor	0-1	Lost 1st Round
Hofstra	Joe Gardi	0-1	Lost 1st Round
Jackson St.	James Carson	0-1	Lost 1st Round
Montana	Mick Dennehy	0-1	Lost 1st Round
Northwestern St.	Sam Goodwin	0-1	Lost 1st Round

1998 (16)

Team	Coach	Record	Result
Massachusetts	Mark Whipple	4-0	Champion
Ga. Southern	Paul Johnson	3-1	Second
Northwestern St.	Sam Goodwin	2-1	Semifinalist
Western Ill.	Randy Ball	2-1	Semifinalist
Appalachian St.	Jerry Moore	1-1	Quarterfinalist
Connecticut	Skip Holtz	1-1	Quarterfinalist
Florida A&M	Billy Joe	1-1	Quarterfinalist
Lehigh	Kevin Higgins	1-1	Quarterfinalist
Colgate	Dick Biddle	0-1	Lost 1st Round
Hampton	Joe Taylor	0-1	Lost 1st Round
Illinois St.	Todd Berry	0-1	Lost 1st Round
McNeese St.	Bobby Keasler	0-1	Lost 1st Round
Montana	Mick Dennehy	0-1	Lost 1st Round
Richmond	Jim Reid	0-1	Lost 1st Round
Tennessee St.	L.C. Cole	0-1	Lost 1st Round
Troy St.	Larry Blakeney	0-1	Lost 1st Round

1999 (16)

Team	Coach	Record	Result
Ga. Southern	Paul Johnson	4-0	Champion
Youngstown St.	Jim Tressel	3-1	Second
Florida A&M	Billy Joe	2-1	Semifinalist
Illinois St.	Todd Berry	2-1	Semifinalist
Hofstra	Joe Gardi	1-1	Quarterfinalist
Massachusetts	Mark Whipple	1-1	Quarterfinalist
N.C. A&T	Bill Hayes	1-1	Quarterfinalist
Troy St.	Larry Blakeney	1-1	Quarterfinalist
Appalachian St.	Jerry Moore	0-1	Lost 1st Round
Colgate	Dick Biddle	0-1	Lost 1st Round
Furman	Bobby Johnson	0-1	Lost 1st Round
James Madison	Mickey Matthews	0-1	Lost 1st Round
Lehigh	Kevin Higgins	0-1	Lost 1st Round
Montana	Mick Dennehy	0-1	Lost 1st Round
*Northern Ariz.	Jerome Souers	0-1	Lost 1st Round
Tennessee St.	L.C. Cole	0-1	Lost 1st Round

2000 (16)

Team	Coach	Record	Result
Ga. Southern	Paul Johnson	4-0	Champion
Montana	Joe Glenn	3-1	Second
Appalachian St.	Jerry Moore	2-1	Semifinalist
Delaware	Tubby Raymond	2-1	Semifinalist
Hofstra	Joe Gardi	1-1	Quarterfinalist
Lehigh	Kevin Higgins	1-1	Quarterfinalist
Richmond	Jim Reid	1-1	Quarterfinalist
Western Ky.	Jack Harbaugh	1-1	Quarterfinalist
Eastern Ill.	Bob Spoo	0-1	Lost 1st Round
Florida A&M	Billy Joe	0-1	Lost 1st Round
Furman	Bobby Johnson	0-1	Lost 1st Round
McNeese St.	Tommy Tate	0-1	Lost 1st Round
Portland St.	Tim Walsh	0-1	Lost 1st Round
Troy St.	Larry Blakeney	0-1	Lost 1st Round
Western Ill.	Don Patterson	0-1	Lost 1st Round
Youngstown St.	Jim Tressel	0-1	Lost 1st Round

2001 (16)

Team	Coach	Record	Result
Montana	Joe Glenn	4-0	Champion
Furman	Bobby Johnson	3-1	Second
Northern Iowa	Mark Farley	2-1	Semifinalist
Ga. Southern	Paul Johnson	2-1	Semifinalist
Appalachian St.	Jerry Moore	1-1	Quarterfinalist
Lehigh	Pete Lembo	1-1	Quarterfinalist
Maine	Jack Cosgrove	1-1	Quarterfinalist
Sam Houston St.	Ron Randleman	1-1	Quarterfinalist
Eastern Ill.	Bob Spoo	0-1	Lost 1st Round
Florida A&M	Billy Joe	0-1	Lost 1st Round
Hofstra	Joe Gardi	0-1	Lost 1st Round

CHAMPIONSHIP RESULTS

Year (Number of Teams)	Coach	Record	Result
McNeese St.	Tommy Tate	0-1	Lost 1st Round
Northern Ariz.	Jerome Souers	0-1	Lost 1st Round
Northwestern St.	Steve Roberts	0-1	Lost 1st Round
Western Ky.	Jack Harbaugh	0-1	Lost 1st Round
William & Mary	Jimmye Laycock	0-1	Lost 1st Round

2002 (16)

	Coach	Record	Result
Western Ky.	Jack Harbaugh	4-0	Champion
McNeese St.	Tommy Tate	3-1	Second
Ga. Southern	Mike Sewak	2-1	Semifinalist
Villanova	Andy Talley	2-1	Semifinalist
Fordham	David Clawson	1-1	Quarterfinalist
Maine	Jack Cosgrove	1-1	Quarterfinalist
Montana	Joe Glenn	1-1	Quarterfinalist
Western Ill.	Don Patterson	1-1	Quarterfinalist
Appalachian St.	Jerry Moore	0-1	Lost 1st Round
Bethune-Cookman	Alvin Wyatt	0-1	Lost 1st Round
Eastern Ill.	Bob Spoo	0-1	Lost 1st Round
Furman	Bobby Lamb	0-1	Lost 1st Round
Montana St.	Mike Kramer	0-1	Lost 1st Round
Murray St.	Joe Pannunzio	0-1	Lost 1st Round
Northeastern	Don Brown	0-1	Lost 1st Round
Northwestern St.	Scott Stoker	0-1	Lost 1st Round

Competition in championship vacated by action of the NCAA Committee on Infractions.

Division I-AA Championship
Record of Each College by Coach

(73 Colleges; 1978-02)

	Yrs	Won	Lost	CH	2D
AKRON					
Jim Dennison (Wooster '60) 85	1	0	1	0	0
ALCORN ST.					
Marino Casem (Xavier [La.] '56) 84	1	0	1	0	0
Cardell Jones (Alcorn St. '65) 92, 94	2	0	2	0	0
TOTAL	3	0	3	0	0
APPALACHIAN ST.					
Sparky Woods (Carson-Newman '76) 86, 87	2	2	2	0	0
Jerry Moore (Baylor '61) 89, 91, 92, 94, 95, 98, 99, 00, 01, 02	10	6	10	0	0
TOTAL	12	8	12	0	0
ARKANSAS ST.					
Larry Lacewell (Ark.-Monticello '59) 84, 85, 86-2D, 87	4	6	4	0	1
BETHUNE-COOKMAN					
Alvin Wyatt (Bethune-Cookman '70) 02	1	0	1	0	0
BOISE ST.					
Jim Criner (Cal Poly Pomona '61) 80-CH, 81	2	3	1	1	0
Skip Hall (Concordia-M'head '66) 88, 90	2	2	2	0	0
Pokey Allen (Utah '65) 94-2D	1	3	1	0	1
TOTAL	5	8	4	1	1
BOSTON U.					
Rick Taylor (Gettysburg '64) 82, 83, 84	3	1	3	0	0
Dan Allen (Hanover '78) 93, 94	2	1	2	0	0
TOTAL	5	2	5	0	0
UCF					
Gene McDowell (Florida St. '63) 90, 93	2	2	2	0	0
CHATTANOOGA					
Buddy Nix (West Ala. '61) 84	1	0	1	0	0
CITADEL					
Charlie Taaffe (Siena '73) 88, 90, 92	3	1	3	0	0
COLGATE					
Fred Dunlap (Colgate '50) 82, 83	2	1	2	0	0
Dick Biddle (Duke '71) 97, 98, 99	3	0	3	0	0
TOTAL	5	1	5	0	0
DELAWARE					
Harold "Tubby" Raymond (Michigan '50) 81, 82-2D, 86, 88, 91, 92, 93, 95, 96, 97, 00	11	11	11	0	1
EAST TENN. ST.					
Mike Cavan (Georgia '72) 96	1	1	1	0	0
EASTERN ILL.					
Darrell Mudra (Peru St. '51) 82	1	1	1	0	0
Al Molde (Gust. Adolphus '66) 83, 86	2	1	2	0	0
Bob Spoo (Purdue '60) 89, 95, 96, 00, 01, 02	6	1	6	0	0
TOTAL	9	3	9	0	0
EASTERN KY.					
Roy Kidd (Eastern Ky. '54) 79-CH, 80-2D, 81-2D, 82-CH, 83, 84, 86, 87, 88, 89, 90, 91, 92, 93, 94, 95, 97	17	16	15	2	2

	Yrs	Won	Lost	CH	2D
EASTERN WASH.					
Dick Zornes (Eastern Wash. '68) 85, 92	2	1	2	0	0
Mike Kramer (Idaho '77) 97	1	2	1	0	0
TOTAL	3	3	3	0	0
FLORIDA A&M					
Rudy Hubbard (Ohio St. '68) 78-CH	1	2	0	1	0
Billy Joe (Villanova '63) 96, 97, 98, 99, 00, 01.	6	3	6	0	0
TOTAL	7	5	6	1	0
FORDHAM					
David Clawson (Williams '89) 02	1	1	1	0	0
FURMAN					
Dick Sheridan (South Carolina '64) 82, 83, 85-2D	3	3	3	0	1
Jimmy Satterfield (South Carolina '62) 86, 88-CH, 89, 90	4	7	3	1	0
Bobby Johnson (Clemson '73) 96, 99, 00, 01-2D	4	4	4	0	1
Bobby Lamb (Furman '87) 02	1	0	1	0	0
TOTAL	12	14	11	1	2
GA. SOUTHERN					
Erk Russell (Auburn '49) 85-CH, 86-CH, 87, 88-2D, 89-CH	5	16	2	3	1
Tim Stowers (Auburn '79) 90-CH, 93, 95	3	6	2	1	0
Paul Johnson (Western Caro. '74) 97, 98-2D, 99-CH, 00-CH, 01	5	14	3	2	1
Mike Sewak (Virginia '81) 02	1	2	1	0	0
TOTAL	14	38	8	6	2
GRAMBLING					
Eddie Robinson (Leland '41) 80, 85, 89	3	0	3	0	0
HOFSTRA					
Joe Gardi (Maryland '60) 95, 97, 99, 00, 01	5	2	5	0	0
HOLY CROSS					
Rick Carter (Earlham '65) 83	1	0	1	0	0
HOWARD					
Steve Wilson (Howard '79) 93	1	0	1	0	0
IDAHO					
Dennis Erickson (Montana St. '70) 82, 85	2	1	2	0	0
Keith Gilbertson (Central Wash. '71) 86, 87, 88	3	2	3	0	0
John L. Smith (Weber St. '71) 89, 90, 92, 93, 94	5	3	5	0	0
Chris Tormey (Idaho '78) 95	1	0	1	0	0
TOTAL	11	6	11	0	0
IDAHO ST.					
Dave Kragthorpe (Utah St. '55) 81-CH	1	3	0	1	0
Jim Koetter (Idaho St. '61) 83	1	0	1	0	0
TOTAL	2	3	1	1	0
ILLINOIS ST.					
Todd Berry (Tulsa '83) 99	1	2	1	0	0
INDIANA ST.					
Dennis Raetz (Nebraska '68) 83, 84	2	1	2	0	0
JACKSON ST.					
W.C. Gorden (Tennessee St. '52) 78, 81, 82, 85, 86, 87, 88, 89, 90	9	0	9	0	0
James Carson (Jackson St. '63) 95, 96, 97	3	0	3	0	0
TOTAL	12	0	12	0	0
JAMES MADISON					
Joe Purzycki (Delaware '71) 87	1	0	1	0	0
Rip Scherer (William & Mary '74) 91, 94	2	2	2	0	0
Alex Wood (Iowa '79) 95	1	0	1	0	0
Mickey Matthews (West Tex. A&M '76) 99	1	0	1	0	0
TOTAL	5	2	5	0	0
LEHIGH					
John Whitehead (East Stroudsburg '50) 79-2D, 80	2	1	2	0	1
Kevin Higgins (West Chester '77) 98, 99, 00	3	2	3	0	0
Pete Lembo (Georgetown '92) 01	1	1	1	0	0
TOTAL	6	4	6	0	1
LA.-MONROE					
Pat Collins (Louisiana Tech '63) 87-CH	1	4	0	1	0
Dave Roberts (Western Caro. '68) 90, 92, 93	3	1	3	0	0
TOTAL	4	5	3	1	0
LOUISIANA TECH					
Billy Brewer (Mississippi '61) 82	1	1	1	0	0
A.L. Williams (Louisiana Tech '57) 84-2D	1	3	1	0	1
TOTAL	2	4	2	0	1
MAINE					
Tim Murphy (Springfield '78) 87	1	0	1	0	0
Tom Lichtenberg (Louisville '62) 89	1	0	1	0	0
Jack Cosgrove (Maine '78) 01, 02	2	2	2	0	0
TOTAL	4	2	4	0	0

	Yrs	Won	Lost	CH	2D
MARSHALL					
George Chaump (Bloomsburg '58) 87-2D, 88	2	4	2	0	1
Jim Donnan (North Carolina St. '67) 91-2D, 92-CH, 93-2D, 94, 95-2D	5	15	4	1	3
Bob Pruett (Marshall '65) 96-CH	1	4	0	1	0
TOTAL	8	23	6	2	4
MASSACHUSETTS					
Bob Pickett (Maine '59) 78-2D	1	1	1	0	1
Jim Reid (Maine '73) 88, 90	2	0	2	0	0
Mark Whipple (Brown '79) 98-CH, 99	2	5	1	1	0
TOTAL	5	6	4	1	1
McNEESE ST.					
Bobby Keasler (La.-Monroe '70) 91, 92, 93, 94, 95, 97-2D, 98	7	8	7	0	1
Tommy Tate (McNeese St. '79) 00, 01, 02-2D ...	3	3	3	0	1
TOTAL	10	11	10	0	2
MIDDLE TENN.					
James "Boots" Donnelly (Middle Tenn. '65) 84, 85, 89, 90, 91, 92, 94	7	6	7	0	0
MISSISSIPPI VAL.					
Archie Cooley Jr. (Jackson St. '62) 84	1	0	1	0	0
MONTANA					
Larry Donovan (Nebraska '64) 82	1	0	1	0	0
Don Read (Sacramento St. '59) 88, 89, 93, 94, 95-CH	5	8	4	1	0
Mick Dennehy (Montana '73) 96-2D, 97, 98, 99	4	3	4	0	1
Joe Glenn (South Dakota '71) 00-2D, 01-CH, 02	3	8	2	1	1
TOTAL	13	19	11	2	2
MONTANA ST.					
Dave Arnold (Drake '67) 84-CH	1	3	0	1	0
Mike Kramer (Idaho '77) 02	1	0	1	0	0
TOTAL	2	3	1	1	0
MURRAY ST.					
Mike Gottfried (Morehead St. '66) 79	1	0	1	0	0
Frank Beamer (Virginia Tech '69) 86	1	0	1	0	0
Houston Nutt (Oklahoma St. '81) 95, 96	2	1	2	0	0
Joe Pannunzio (Southern Colo. '82) 02	1	0	1	0	0
TOTAL	5	1	5	0	0
NEVADA					
Chris Ault (Nevada '68) 78, 79, 83, 85, 86, 90-2D, 91	7	9	7	0	1
NEW HAMPSHIRE					
Bill Bowes (Penn St. '65) 91, 94	2	0	2	0	0
NICHOLLS ST.					
Sonny Jackson (Nicholls St. '63) 86	1	1	1	0	0
Darren Barbier (Nicholls St. '82) 96	1	0	1	0	0
TOTAL	2	1	2	0	0
N.C. A&T					
Maurice "Mo" Forte (Minnesota '71) 86	1	0	1	0	0
Bill Hayes (N.C. Central '64) 92, 99	2	1	2	0	0
TOTAL	3	1	3	0	0
NORTH TEXAS					
Corky Nelson (Southwest Tex. St. '64) 83, 87, 88	3	0	3	0	0
Matt Simon (Eastern N.M. '76) 94	1	0	1	0	0
TOTAL	4	0	4	0	0
NORTHEASTERN					
Don Brown (Norwich '77) 02	1	0	1	0	0
NORTHERN ARIZ. #					
Stephen Axman (C.W. Post '69) 96	1	0	1	0	0
Jerome Souers (Oregon '83) 99, 01	2	0	2	0	0
TOTAL	3	0	3	0	0
NORTHERN IOWA					
Darrell Mudra (Peru St. '51) 85, 87	2	3	2	0	0
Terry Allen (Northern Iowa '79) 90, 91, 92, 93, 94, 95, 96	7	6	7	0	0
Mark Farley (Northern Iowa '86) 01	1	2	1	0	0
TOTAL	10	11	10	0	0

	Yrs	Won	Lost	CH	2D
NORTHWESTERN ST.					
Sam Goodwin (Henderson St. '66) 88, 97, 98...	3	3	3	0	0
Steve Roberts (Ouachita Baptist '87) 01	1	0	1	0	0
Scott Stoker (Northwestern St. '91) 02	1	0	1	0	0
TOTAL	5	3	5	0	0
PORTLAND ST.					
Tim Walsh (UC Riverside '77) 00......................	1	0	1	0	0
RHODE ISLAND					
Bob Griffin (Southern Conn. St. '63) 81, 84, 85..	3	2	3	0	0
RICHMOND					
Dal Shealy (Carson-Newman '60) 84, 87	2	1	2	0	0
Jim Reid (Maine '73) 98, 00	2	1	2	0	0
TOTAL	4	2	4	0	0
SAM HOUSTON ST.					
Ron Randleman (William Penn '64) 86, 91, 01 ..	3	1	3	0	0
SAMFORD					
Terry Bowden (West Virginia '78) 91, 92	2	2	2	0	0
SOUTH CAROLINA ST.					
Bill Davis (Johnson Smith '65) 81, 82	2	2	2	0	0
SOUTHERN ILL.					
Rey Dempsey (Geneva '58) 83-CH	1	3	0	1	0
SOUTHWEST MO. ST.					
Jesse Branch (Arkansas '64) 89, 90	2	1	2	0	0
STEPHEN F. AUSTIN¢					
Jim Hess (Southeastern Okla. '59) 88...............	1	1	1	0	0
Lynn Graves (Stephen F. Austin '65) 89-2D.........	1	3	1	0	1
John Pearce (Tex. A&M-Kingsville '70) 93, 95	2	2	2	0	0
TOTAL	4	6	4	0	1
TENNESSEE ST.*					
John Merritt (Kentucky St. '50) 81, 82	2	1	2	0	0
Bill Thomas (Tennessee St. '71) 86	1	1	1	0	0
L.C. Cole (Nebraska '80) 98, 99	2	0	2	0	0
TOTAL	5	2	5	0	0
TROY ST.					
Larry Blakeney (Auburn '70) 93, 94, 95, 96, 98, 99,00	7	5	7	0	0
VILLANOVA					
Andy Talley (Southern Conn. St. '67) 89, 91, 92, 96, 97, 02	6	3	6	0	0
WEBER ST.					
Mike Price (Puget Sound '69) 87	1	1	1	0	0
Dave Arslanian (Weber St. '72) 91....................	1	0	1	0	0
TOTAL	2	1	2	0	0
WESTERN CARO.					
Bob Waters (Presbyterian '60) 83-2D................	1	3	1	0	1
WESTERN ILL.					
Bruce Craddock (Truman '66) 88......................	1	0	1	0	0
Randy Ball (Truman '73) 91, 96, 97, 98	4	3	4	0	0
Don Patterson (Army '73) 00, 02......................	2	1	2	0	0
TOTAL	7	4	7	0	0
WESTERN KY.					
Dave Roberts (Western Caro. '68) 87, 88..........	2	1	2	0	0
Jack Harbaugh (Bowling Green '61) 97, 00, 01, 02-CH..	4	6	3	1	0
TOTAL	6	7	5	1	0
WILLIAM & MARY					
Jimmye Laycock (William & Mary '70) 86, 89, 90, 93, 96, 01	6	2	6	0	0
YOUNGSTOWN ST.					
Jim Tressel (Baldwin-Wallace '75) 87, 89, 90, 91-CH, 92-2D, 93-CH, 94-CH, 97-CH, 99-2D, 00..	10	23	6	4	2

#Northern Arizona's competition in the 1999 Division I-AA championship was vacated by action of the NCAA Committee on Infractions (record was 0-1). *Tennessee State's competition in the 1981 and 1982 Division I-AA championships was vacated by action of the NCAA Committee on Infractions (record was 1-2). ¢Stephen F. Austin's competition in the 1989 Division I-AA championship was vacated by action of the NCAA Committee on Infractions (record was 3-1).

CHAMPIONSHIP RESULTS

Division I-AA Championship Team Leaders

MOST APPEARANCES

MOST VICTORIES
Ga. Southern	38
Marshall#	23
Youngstown St.	23
Montana	19
Eastern Ky.	16
Furman	14
Delaware	11
McNeese St.	11
Northern Iowa	11

MOST CONSECUTIVE APPEARANCES
10	Eastern Ky.	1986-95
10	Montana	1993-present
7	Northern Iowa	1990-96
6	Eastern Ky.	1979-84
6	Florida A&M	1996-01
6	Georgia Southern	1997-present
6	Georgia Southern	1985-90

6	Idaho	1985-90
6	Jackson St.	1985-90
6	Marshall	1991-96
6	Youngstown St.	1989-94

HIGHEST WINNING PERCENTAGE
(Min. 10 Games Played)
Ga. Southern	38-8	.826
Marshall#	23-6	.793
Youngstown St.	23-6	.793
Boise St. #	8-4	.667
Montana	19-11	.633
Arkansas St. #	6-4	.600
Massachusetts	6-4	.600
Stephen F. Austin	6-4	.600
Western Ky.	7-5	.583

#No longer a Division I-AA member.

Division I-AA Championship Attendance History

Year	Teams	G	Total Attend.	Avg. PG
1978	4	3	34,630	11,543
1979	4	3	20,300	6,767
1980	4	3	36,957	12,319
1981	8	7	81,455	11,636
1982	12	11	106,801	9,709
1983	12	11	103,631	9,421
1984	12	11	122,142	11,104
1985	12	11	86,996	7,909
1986	16	15	153,832	10,255
1987	16	15	133,956	8,930
1988	16	15	146,782	9,785
1989	16	15	145,198	9,680
1990	16	15	180,027	12,002
1991	16	15	169,605	11,307
1992	16	15	199,450	13,297
1993	16	15	178,884	11,926
1994	16	15	209,761	13,984
1995	16	15	209,367	13,958
1996	16	15	178,768	11,918
1997	16	15	152,219	10,418
1998	16	15	146,084	9,739
1999	16	15	178,742	11,916
2000	16	15	163,764	10,918
2001	16	15	166,707	11,114
2002	16	15	124,835	8,322

1978
First Round (12/9):
	Site	Attendance
Florida A&M 15, Jackson St. 10	Jackson, Miss.	7,000
Massachusetts 44, Nevada 21	Reno, Nev.	14,026

Championship (12/16):
Florida A&M 35, Massachusetts 28	Wichita Falls, Tex.	13,604

1979
First Round (12/8):
	Site	Attendance
Lehigh 28, Murray St. 9	Murray, Ky.	10,000
Eastern Ky. 33, Nevada 30 (2 ot)	Richmond, Ky.	5,100

Championship (12/15):
Eastern Ky. 30, Lehigh 7	Orlando, Fla.	5,200

1980
First Round (12/13):
	Site	Attendance
Eastern Ky. 23, Lehigh 20	Bethlehem, Pa.	11,500
Boise St. 14, Grambling 9	Boise, Id.	17,300

Championship (12/20):
Boise St. 31, Eastern Ky. 29	Sacramento, Cal.	8,157

1981
First Round (12/5):
	Site	Attendance
Eastern Ky. 35, Delaware 28	Richmond, Ky.	8,100
Boise St. 19, Jackson St. 7	Jackson, Miss.	11,500
Idaho St. 51, Rhode Island 0	Pocatello, Id.	12,153
South Carolina St. 26, Tennessee St. 25 (ot)	Orangeburg, S.C.	6,224

Semifinals (12/12):
Eastern Ky. 23, Boise St. 17	Boise, Id.	20,176
Idaho St. 41, South Carolina St. 12	Pocatello, Id.	12,300

Championship (12/19):
Idaho St. 34, Eastern Ky. 23	Wichita Falls, Tex.	11,002

1982
First Round (11/27):
	Site	Attendance
Idaho 21, Montana 7	Moscow, Id.	8,000
Eastern Ill. 16, Jackson St. 13 (ot)	Charleston, Ill.	5,000
South Carolina St. 17, Furman 0	Greenville, S.C.	13,865
Colgate 21, Boston U. 7	Hamilton, N.Y.	5,000

Quarterfinals (12/4):
Eastern Ky. 38, Idaho 30	Richmond, Ky.	10,893
Tennessee St. 20, Eastern Ill. 19	Nashville, Tenn.	8,000
Louisiana Tech 38, South Carolina St. 3	Ruston, La.	13,000
Delaware 20, Colgate 13	Newark, Del.	11,448

Semifinals (12/11):
Eastern Ky. 13, Tennessee St. 7	Richmond, Ky.	7,338
Delaware 17, Louisiana Tech 0	Ruston, La.	13,000

Championship (12/18):
Eastern Ky. 17, Delaware 14	Wichita Falls, Tex.	11,257

1983
First Round (11/27):
	Site	Attendance
Indiana St. 16, Eastern Ill. 13 (2 ot)	Terre Haute, Ind.	6,222
Nevada 27, Idaho St. 20	Pocatello, Id.	10,333
Western Caro. 24, Colgate 23	Cullowhee, N.C.	6,500
Boston U. 24, Eastern Ky. 20	Richmond, Ky.	4,800

Quarterfinals (12/3):
Southern Ill. 23, Indiana St. 7	Carbondale, Ill.	8,000
Nevada 20, North Texas 17 (ot)	Reno, Nev.	7,878
Western Caro. 28, Holy Cross 21	Worcester, Mass.	10,814
Furman 35, Boston U. 16	Greenville, S.C.	7,600

Semifinals (12/10):
Southern Ill. 23, Nevada 7	Carbondale, Ill.	12,500
Western Caro. 14, Furman 7	Greenville, S.C.	13,034

Championship (12/17):
Southern Ill. 43, Western Caro. 7	Charleston, S.C.	15,950

1984
First Round (11/24):
	Site	Attendance
Louisiana Tech 66, Mississippi Val. 19	Ruston, La.	17,500
Middle Tenn. 27, Eastern Ky. 10	Richmond, Ky.	4,800
Richmond 35, Boston U. 33	Richmond, Va.	11,236
Arkansas St. 37, Chattanooga 10	Jonesboro, Ark.	10,872

Quarterfinals (12/1):
Louisiana Tech 44, Alcorn St. 21	Jackson, Miss.	16,204
Middle Tenn. 42, Indiana St. 41 (3 ot)	Terre Haute, Ind.	6,225
Rhode Island 23, Richmond 17	Kingston, R.I.	10,446
Montana St. 31, Arkansas St. 14	Bozeman, Mont.	12,037

Semifinals (12/8):
Louisiana Tech 21, Middle Tenn. 13	Murfreesboro, Tenn.	11,000
Montana St. 32, Rhode Island 20	Bozeman, Mont.	12,697

Championship (12/15):
Montana St. 19, Louisiana Tech 6	Charleston, S.C.	9,125

1985
First Round (11/30):
	Site	Attendance
Ga. Southern 27, Jackson St. 0	Statesboro, Ga.	4,128
Eastern Wash. 42, Idaho 38	Moscow, Id.	6,500
Rhode Island 35, Akron 27	Kingston, R.I.	7,317
Arkansas St. 10, Grambling 7	Jonesboro, Ark.	5,730

Quarterfinals (12/7):
Ga. Southern 28, Middle Tenn. 21	Murfreesboro, Tenn.	9,500
Northern Iowa 17, Eastern Wash. 14	Cedar Falls, Ia.	6,220
Furman 59, Rhode Island 15	Greenville, S.C.	9,454
Nevada 24, Arkansas St. 23	Reno, Nev.	10,241

Semifinals (12/14):
Ga. Southern 40, Northern Iowa 33	Cedar Falls, Ia.	12,300
Furman 35, Nevada 12	Greenville, S.C.	10,300

Championship (12/21):
Ga. Southern 44, Furman 42	Tacoma, Wash.	5,306

1986
First Round (11/29):

	Site	Attendance
Nevada 27, Idaho 7	Reno, Nev.	13,715
Tennessee St. 32, Jackson St. 23	Jackson, Miss.	24,000
Ga. Southern 52, N.C. A&T 21	Statesboro, Ga.	7,767
Nicholls St. 28, Appalachian St. 26	Boone, N.C.	6,250
Arkansas St. 48, Sam Houston St. 7	Jonesboro, Ark.	4,500
Delaware 51, William & Mary 17	Williamsburg, Va.	6,340
Eastern Ill. 28, Murray St. 21	Charleston, Ill.	9,500
Eastern Ky. 23, Furman 10	Greenville, S.C.	8,000

Quarterfinals (12/6):

	Site	Attendance
Nevada 33, Tennessee St. 6	Reno, Nev.	13,102
Ga. Southern 55, Nicholls St. 31	Statesboro, Ga.	9,121
Arkansas St. 55, Delaware 14	Newark, Del.	12,018
Eastern Ky. 24, Eastern Ill. 22	Charleston, Ill.	9,500

Semifinals (12/13):

	Site	Attendance
Ga. Southern 48, Nevada 38	Reno. Nev.	15,100
Arkansas St. 24, Eastern Ky. 10	Jonesboro, Ark.	10,500

Championship (12/20):

	Site	Attendance
Ga. Southern 48, Arkansas St. 21	Tacoma, Wash.	4,419

1987
First Round (11/28):

	Site	Attendance
Appalachian St. 20, Richmond 3	Boone, N.C.	4,138
Ga. Southern 31, Maine 28 (ot)	Statesboro, Ga.	9,440
Weber St. 59, Idaho 30	Moscow, Id.	4,900
Marshall 41, James Madison 12	Huntington, W.Va.	15,584
La.-Monroe 30, North Texas 9	Monroe, La.	9,500
Eastern Ky. 40, Western Ky. 17	Richmond, Ky.	4,050
Northern Iowa 31, Youngstown St. 28	Cedar Falls, Ia.	3,887
Arkansas St. 35, Jackson St. 32	Jackson, Miss.	7,500

Quarterfinals (12/5):

	Site	Attendance
Appalachian St. 19, Ga. Southern 0	Boone, N.C.	9,229
Marshall 51, Weber St. 23	Huntington, W.Va.	13,197
La.-Monroe 33, Eastern Ky. 32	Monroe, La.	10,475
Northern Iowa 49, Arkansas St. 28	Cedar Falls, Ia.	6,100

Semifinals (12/12):

	Site	Attendance
Marshall 24, Appalachian St. 10	Boone, N.C.	10,000
La.-Monroe 44, Northern Iowa 41 (2ot)	Monroe, La.	14,443

Championship (12/19):

	Site	Attendance
La.-Monroe 43, Marshall 42	Pocatello, Id.	11,513

1988
First Round (11/26):

	Site	Attendance
Idaho 38, Montana 19	Moscow, Id.	5,500
Northwestern St. 22, Boise St. 13	Boise, Id.	10,537
Furman 21, Delaware 7	Greenville, S.C.	7,487
Marshall 7, North Texas 0	Huntington, W.Va.	15,086
Ga. Southern 38, Citadel 20	Statesboro, Ga.	11,011
Stephen F. Austin 24, Jackson St. 0	Nacogdoches, Tex.	5,384
Western Ky. 35, Western Ill. 32	Macomb, Ill.	6,000
Eastern Ky. 28, Massachusetts 17	Richmond, Ky.	4,600

Quarterfinals (12/3):

	Site	Attendance
Idaho 38, Northwestern St. 30	Moscow, Id.	6,800
Furman 13, Marshall 9	Huntington, W.Va.	16,820
Ga. Southern 27, Stephen F. Austin 6	Statesboro, Ga.	12,289
Eastern Ky. 41, Western Ky. 24	Richmnond, Ky.	8,100

Semifinals (12/10):

	Site	Attendance
Furman 38, Idaho 7	Greenville, S.C.	11,645
Ga. Southern 21, Eastern Ky. 17	Statesboro, Ga.	14,023

Championship (12/17):

	Site	Attendance
Furman 17, Ga. Southern 12	Pocatello, Id.	11,500

1989
First Round (11/25):

	Site	Attendance
Ga. Southern 52, Villanova 36	Statesboro, Ga.	10,161
Middle Tenn. 24, Appalachian St. 21	Murfreesboro, Tenn.	5,000
Eastern Ill. 38, Idaho 21	Moscow, Id.	6,025
Montana 48, Jackson St. 7	Missoula, Mont.	11,854
Furman 24, William & Mary 10	Greenville, S.C.	8,642
Youngstown St. 28, Eastern Ky. 24	Richmond, Ky.	3,898
Stephen F. Austin 59, Grambling 56	Nacogdoches, Tex.	7,106
Southwest Mo. St. 38, Maine 35	Springfield, Mo.	7,270

Quarterfinals (12/2):

	Site	Attendance
Ga. Southern 45, Middle Tenn. 3	Statesboro, Ga.	11,272
Montana 25, Eastern Ill. 19	Missoula, Mont.	12,285
Furman 42, Youngstown St. 23	Greenville, S.C.	8,033
Stephen F. Austin 55, Southwest Mo. St. 25	Nacogdoches, Tex.	10,491

Semifinals (12/9):

	Site	Attendance
Ga. Southern 45, Montana 15	Statesboro, Ga.	10,421
Stephen F. Austin 21, Furman 19	Greenville, S.C.	7,015

Championship (12/16):

	Site	Attendance
Ga. Southern 37, Stephen F. Austin 34	Statesboro, Ga.	25,725

1990
First Round (11/24):

	Site	Attendance
Middle Tenn. 28, Jackson St. 7	Murfreesboro, Tenn.	7,000
Boise St. 20, Northern Iowa 3	Boise, Id.	11,691
Nevada 27, La.-Monroe 14	Reno, Nev.	11,008
Furman 45, Eastern Ky. 17	Richmond, Ky.	4,528
UCF 20, Youngstown St. 17	Youngstown, Ohio	5,000
William & Mary 38, Massachusetts 0	Williamsburg, Va.	5,000

	Site	Attendance
Ga. Southern 31, Citadel 0	Statesboro, Ga.	11,881
Idaho 41, Southwest Mo. St. 35	Springfield, Mo.	8,750

Quarterfinals (12/1):

	Site	Attendance
Boise St. 20, Middle Tenn. 13	Boise, Id.	15,849
Nevada 42, Furman 35 (3 ot)	Reno, Nev.	11,519
UCF 52, William & Mary 38	Orlando, Fla.	20,067
Ga. Southern 28, Idaho 27	Statesboro, Ga.	11,571

Semifinals (12/8):

	Site	Attendance
Nevada 59, Boise St. 52 (3 ot)	Reno, Nev.	19,776
Ga. Southern 44, UCF 7	Statesboro, Ga.	13,183

Championship (12/15):

	Site	Attendance
Ga. Southern 36, Nevada 13	Statesboro, Ga.	23,204

1991
First Round (11/30):

	Site	Attendance
Nevada 22, McNeese St. 16	Reno, Nev.	15,000
Youngstown St. 17, Villanova 16	Youngstown, Ohio	9,556
James Madison 42, Delaware 35 (2 ot)	Newark, Del.	14,905
Samford 29, New Hampshire 13	Durham, N.H.	6,034
Eastern Ky. 14, Appalachian St. 3	Richmond, Ky.	2,750
Middle Tenn. 20, Sam Houston St. 19 (ot)	Murfreesboro, Tenn.	2,000
Northern Iowa 38, Weber St. 21	Cedar Falls, Ia.	8,723
Marshall 20, Western Ill. 17 (ot)	Huntington, W.Va.	16,840

Quarterfinals (12/7):

	Site	Attendance
Youngstown St. 30, Nevada 28	Reno, Nev.	13,476
Samford 24, James Madison 21	Harrisonburg, Va.	9,028
Eastern Ky. 23, Middle Tenn. 13	Richmond, Ky.	3,650
Marshall 41, Northern Iowa 13	Huntington, W.Va.	16,889

Semifinals (12/14):

	Site	Attendance
Youngstown St. 10, Samford 0	Youngstown, Ohio	17,003
Marshall 14, Eastern Ky. 7	Huntington, W.Va.	21,084

Championship (12/21):

	Site	Attendance
Youngstown St. 25, Marshall 17	Statesboro, Ga.	12,667

1992
First Round (11/28):

	Site	Attendance
La.-Monroe 78, Alcorn St. 27	Monroe, La.	14,416
Delaware 56, Samford 21	Newark, Del.	11,364
Middle Tenn. 35, Appalachian St. 10	Murfreesboro, Tenn.	4,000
Marshall 44, Eastern Ky. 0	Huntington, W.Va.	16,598
Citadel 44, N.C. A&T 0	Charleston, S.C.	12,300
Youngstown St. 23, Villanova 20	Youngstown, Ohio	9,465
Northern Iowa 17, Eastern Wash. 14	Cedar Falls, Ia.	13,149
McNeese St. 23, Idaho 20	Moscow, Id.	6,000

Quarterfinals (12/5):

	Site	Attendance
Delaware 41, La.-Monroe 18	Monroe, La.	10,172
Marshall 35, Middle Tenn. 21	Huntington, W.Va.	14,011
Youngstown St. 42, Citadel 17	Charleston, S.C.	12,300
Northern Iowa 29, McNeese St. 7	Cedar Falls, Ia.	13,375

Semifinals (12/12):

	Site	Attendance
Marshall 28, Delaware 7	Huntington, W.Va.	16,323
Youngstown St. 19, Northern Iowa 7	Cedar Falls, Ia.	14,682

Championship (12/19):

	Site	Attendance
Marshall 31, Youngstown St. 28	Huntington, W.Va.	31,304

1993
First Round (11/27):

	Site	Attendance
Ga. Southern 14, Eastern Ky. 12	Statesboro, Ga.	7,278
Youngstown St. 56, UCF 30	Youngstown, Ohio	7,408
Boston U. 27, Northern Iowa 21 (2 ot)	Boston, Mass.	6,882
Idaho 34, La.-Monroe 31	Monroe, La.	5,500
Delaware 49, Montana 48	Missoula, Mont.	11,271
Marshall 28, Howard 14	Huntington, W.Va.	13,554
McNeese St. 34, William & Mary 28	Lake Charles, La.	17,167
Troy St. 42, Stephen F. Austin 20	Troy, Ala.	4,500

Quarterfinals (12/4):

	Site	Attendance
Youngstown St. 34, Ga. Southern 14	Youngstown, Ohio	9,503
Idaho 21, Boston U. 14	Moscow, Id.	8,800
Marshall 34, Delaware 31	Huntington, W.Va.	13,687
Troy St. 35, McNeese St. 28	Lake Charles, La.	20,000

Semifinals (12/11):

	Site	Attendance
Youngstown St. 35, Idaho 16	Youngstown, Ohio	9,644
Marshall 24, Troy St. 21	Huntington, W.Va.	14,472

Championship (12/18):

	Site	Attendance
Youngstown St. 17, Marshall 5	Huntington, W.Va.	29,218

1994
First Round (11/26):

	Site	Attendance
Youngstown St. 63, Alcorn St. 20	Youngstown, Ohio	17,795
Eastern Ky. 30, Boston U. 23	Richmond, Ky.	4,111
McNeese St. 38, Idaho 17	Lake Charles, La.	16,000
Montana 23, Northern Iowa 20	Missoula, Mont.	7,958
Marshall 49, Middle Tenn. St. 14	Huntington, W.Va.	17,349
James Madison 45, Troy St. 26	Harrisonburg, Va.	5,200
Boise St. 24, North Texas 20	Boise, Id.	14,706
Appalachian St. 17, New Hampshire 10 (ot)	Durham, N.H.	7,329

Quarterfinals (12/3):

	Site	Attendance
Youngstown St. 18, Eastern Ky. 15	Youngstown, Ohio	16,023
Montana 30, McNeese St. 28	Missoula, Mont.	8,419
Marshall 28, James Madison 21 (ot)	Huntington, W.Va.	16,494
Boise St. 17, Appalachian St. 14	Boise, Id.	15,302

Semifinals (12/10):

	Site	Attendance
Youngstown St. 28, Montana 9	Youngstown, Ohio	15,333
Boise St. 28, Marshall 24	Boise, Id.	20,068

Championship (12/17):

Youngstown St. 28, Boise St. 14	Huntington, W.Va.	27,674

1995

First Round (11/25):

	Site	Attendance
McNeese St. 33, Idaho 3	Lake Charles, La.	15,736
Delaware 38, Hofstra 17	Newark, Del.	13,295
Northern Iowa 35, Murray St. 34	Murray, Ky.	7,635
Marshall 38, Jackson St. 8	Huntington, W.Va.	13,035
Appalachian St. 31, James Madison 24	Boone, N.C.	9,467
Stephen F. Austin 34, Eastern Ill. 29	Nacogdoches, Tex.	3,552
Ga. Southern 24, Troy St. 21	Troy, Ala.	6,000
Montana 48, Eastern Ky. 0	Missoula, Mont.	13,830

Quarterfinals (12/2):

McNeese St. 52, Delaware 18	Lake Charles, La.	17,239
Marshall 41, Northern Iowa 24	Huntington, W.Va.	14,472
Stephen F. Austin 27, Appalachian St. 17	Boone, N.C.	8,941
Montana 45, Ga. Southern 0	Missoula, Mont.	18,518

Semifinals (12/9):

Marshall 25, McNeese St. 13	Lake Charles, La.	18,018
Montana 70, Stephen F. Austin 14	Missoula, Mont.	18,523

Championship (12/16):

Montana 22, Marshall 20	Huntington, W.Va.	32,106

1996

First Round (11/30):

	Site	Attendance
Montana 48, Nicholls St. 3	Missoula, Mont.	13,438
East Tenn. St. 35, Villanova 29	Johnson City, Tenn.	4,939
Troy St. 29, Florida A&M 25	Troy, Ala.	10,200
Murray St. 34, Western Ill. 6	Murray, Ky.	2,753
Marshall 59, Delaware 14	Huntington, W.Va.	15,429
Furman 42, Northern Ariz. 31	Flagstaff, Ariz.	8,700
Northern Iowa 21, Eastern Ill. 14	Cedar Falls, Ia.	10,402
William & Mary 45, Jackson St. 6	Williamsburg, Va.	4,057

Quarterfinals (12/7):

Montana 44, East Tenn. St. 14	Missoula, Mont.	15,025
Troy St. 31, Murray St. 3	Troy, Ala.	6,100
Marshall 54, Furman 0	Huntington, W.Va.	14,096
Northern Iowa 38, William & Mary 35	Cedar Falls, Ia.	10,796

Semifinals (12/14):

Montana 70, Troy St. 7	Missoula, Mont.	18,367
Marshall 31, Northern Iowa 14	Huntington, W.Va.	14,414

Championship (12/21):

Marshall 49, Montana 29	Huntington, W.Va.	30,052

1997

First Round (11/29):

	Site	Attendance
Villanova 49, Colgate 28	Villanova, Pa.	8,875
Youngstown St. 28, Hampton 13	Youngstown, Ohio	12,431
Western Ky. 42, Eastern Ky. 14	Bowling Green, Ky.	9,000
Eastern Wash. 40, Northwestern St. 10	Cheney, Wash.	6,384
Delaware 24, Hofstra 14	Newark, Del.	14,075
Ga. Southern 52, Florida A&M 37	Statesboro, Ga.	10,409
McNeese St. 19, Montana 14	Lake Charles, La.	13,681
Western Ill. 31, Jackson St. 24	Macomb, Ill.	8,980

Quarterfinals (12/6):

Youngstown St. 37, Villanova 34	Villanova, Pa.	7,591
Eastern Wash. 38, Western Ky. 21	Cheney, Wash.	6,829
Delaware 16, Ga. Southern 7	Newark, Del.	11,203
McNeese St. 14, Western Ill. 12	Macomb, Ill.	5,000

Semifinals (12/13):

Youngstown St. 25, Eastern Wash. 14	Cheney, Wash.	8,529
McNeese St. 23, Delaware 21	Newark, Del.	14,461

Championship (12/20):

Youngstown St. 10, McNeese St. 9	Chattanooga, Tenn.	14,771

1998

First Round (11/28):

	Site	Attendance
Ga. Southern 49, Colgate 28	Statesboro, Ga.	7,676
Connecticut 42, Hampton 34	Storrs, Conn.	6,193
Florida A&M 27, Troy St. 17	Tallahassee, Fla.	16,509
Western Ill. 52, Montana 9	Macomb, Ill.	3,614
Lehigh 24, Richmond 23	Richmond, Va.	10,254
Massachusetts 21, McNeese St. 19	Lake Charles, La.	11,349
Appalachian St. 45, Tennessee St. 31	Boone, N.C.	3,885
Northwestern St. 48, Illinois St. 28	Natchitoches, La.	8,118

Quarterfinals (12/5):

Ga. Southern 52, Connecticut 30	Statesboro, Ga.	9,096
Western Ill. 24, Florida A&M 21 (12/4)	Macomb, Ill.	7,400
Massachusetts 27, Lehigh 21	Amherst, Mass.	12,108
Northwestern St. 31, Appalachian St. 20	Natchitoches, La.	10,817

Semifinals (12/12):

Ga. Southern 42, Western Ill. 14	Statesboro, Ga.	11,140
Massachusetts 41, Northwestern St. 31	Natchitoches, La.	10,424

Championship (12/19):

	Site	Attendance
Massachusetts 55, Ga. Southern 43	Chattanooga, Tenn.	17,501

1999

First Round (11/27):

	Site	Attendance
N.C. A&T 24, Tennessee St. 10	Nashville, Tenn.	10,736
Youngstown St. 30, Montana 27	Missoula, Mont.	17,261
Troy St. 27, James Madison 7	Troy, Ala.	17,102
Florida A&M 44, Appalachian St. 29	Boone, N.C.	6,837
Hofstra 27, Lehigh 15	Hempstead, N.Y.	6,770
Illinois St. 56, Colgate 13	Normal, Ill.	7,133
Massachusetts 30, Furman 23 (ot)	Greenville, S.C.	7,215
Ga. Southern 72, Northern Ariz. 29	Statesboro, Ga.	7,140

Quarterfinals (12/4):

Youngstown St. 41, N.C. A&T 3	Youngstown, Ohio	16,955
Illinois St. 37, Hofstra 20	Hempstead, N.Y.	5,586
Florida A&M 17, Troy St. 10	Troy, Ala.	12,689
Ga. Southern 38, Massachusetts 21	Statesboro, Ga.	13,121

Semifinals (12/11):

Youngstown St. 27, Florida A&M 24	Youngstown, Ohio	17,846
Ga. Southern 28, Illinois St. 17	Statesboro, Ga.	12,299

Championship (12/20):

Ga. Southern 59, Youngstown St. 24	Chattanooga, Tenn.	20,052

2000

First Round (11/25):

	Site	Attendance
Montana 45, Eastern Ill. 13	Missoula, Mont.	16,212
Richmond 10, Youngstown St. 3	Richmond, Va.	5,484
Western Ky. 27, Florida A&M 0	Bowling Green, Ky.	3,200
Appalachian St. 33, Troy St. 30	Troy, Ala.	17,589
Ga. Southern 42, McNeese St. 17	Statesboro, Ga.	5,350
Hofstra 31, Furman 24	Greenville, S.C.	4,214
Lehigh 37, Western Ill. 7	Macomb, Ill.	3,204
Delaware 49, Portland St. 14	Newark, Del.	12,945

Quarterfinals (12/2):

Montana 34, Richmond 20	Missoula, Mont.	17,345
Appalachian St. 17, Western Ky. 14	Boone, N.C.	5,100
Ga. Southern 48, Hofstra 20	Statesboro, Ga.	7,139
Delaware 47, Lehigh 22	Newark, Del.	16,390

Semifinals (12/9):

Montana 19, Appalachian St. 16 (ot)	Missoula, Mont.	17,401
Ga. Southern 27, Delaware 18	Newark, Del.	15,035

Championship (12/16):

Ga. Southern 27, Montana 25	Chattanooga, Tenn.	17,156

2001

First Round (12/1):

	Site	Attendance
Montana 28, Northwestern St. 19	Missoula, Mont.	17,289
Sam Houston St. 34, Northern Ariz. 31	Huntsville, Tex.	8,143
Maine 14, McNeese St. 10	Lake Charles, La.	12,450
Northern Iowa 49, Eastern Ill. 43	Charleston, Ill.	6,824
Ga. Southern 60, Florida A&M 35	Statesboro, Ga.	9,884
Appalachian St. 40, William & Mary 27	Boone, N.C.	5,279
Lehigh 27, Hofstra 24 (ot)	Bethlehem, Pa.	10,131
Furman 24, Western Ky. 20	Greenville, S.C.	6,143

Quarterfinals (12/8):

Montana 49, Sam Houston St. 24	Missoula, Mont.	18,125
Northern Iowa 56, Maine 28	Cedar Falls, Ia.	9,525
Ga. Southern 38, Appalachian St. 24	Statesboro, Ga.	9,352
Furman 34, Lehigh 17	Greenville, S.C.	10,189

Semifinals (12/15):

Montana 38, Northern Iowa 0	Missoula, Mont.	18,848
Furman 24, Ga. Southern 17	Statesboro, Ga.	11,827

Championship (12/21):

Montana 13, Furman 6	Chattanooga, Tenn.	12,698

2002

First Round (11/30):

	Site	Attendance
McNeese St. 21, Montana St. 14	Lake Charles, La.	16,211
Montana 45, Northwestern St. 14	Missoula, Mont.	15,758
Villanova 45, Furman 38	Villanova, Pa.	3,031
Fordham 29, Northeastern 24	Boston, Mass.	6,848
Ga. Southern 34, Bethune-Cookman 0	Statesboro, Ga.	7,395
Maine 14, Appalachian St. 13	Boone, N.C.	4,311
Western Ky. 59, Murray St. 20	Bowling Green, Ky.	3,300
Western Ill. 48, Eastern Ill. 9	Macomb, Ill.	2,429

Quarterfinals (12/7):

McNeese St. 24, Montana 20	Lake Charles, La.	15,758
Villanova 24, Fordham 10	Villanova, Pa.	4,351
Ga. Southern 31, Maine 7	Statesboro, Ga.	6,708
Western Ky. 31, Western Ill. 28	Macomb, Ill.	3,285

Semifinals (12/14):

McNeese St. 39, Villanova 28	Lake Charles, La.	16,517
Western Ky. 31, Ga. Southern 28	Statesboro, Ga.	6,573

Championship (12/20):

Western Ky. 34, McNeese St. 14	Chattanooga, Tenn.	12,360

Division II Championship

2002 Title Game Summary

Anes-to-Kircus Equals Title for Lakers: Curt Anes culminated the game-winning drive with his third touchdown pass of the day as Grand Valley State defeated Valdosta State, 31-24.

Valdosta State completed its rally from a 24-6 deficit when defensive end Tim Thompson recovered a fumble in the Lakers' end zone and Buster Faulkner connected with C.J. Lofton for the tying two-point conversion with 3:09 remaining in the fourth quarter.

Anes then led the Lakers 68 yards in seven plays, capped by a 10-yard pass to David Kircus for the title-winning TD with only 64 seconds to play.

Kircus was on the receiving end of each of Anes's touchdown tosses as he totaled 11 receptions for a championship-game record 270 yards. The number of total and TD catches tied the records for a championship contest.

Anes completed 23 of his 36 pass attempts for 361 yards, another division championship-game high. Terrance Banks made nine catches for 66 yards for the Lakers.

Will Rhody helped Valdosta State's cause with three field goals. Aaron Jenkins rushed for 99 yards and scored the Blazers' lone offensive touchdown.

Grand Valley State did not lose in 14 games, while Valdosta State finished the season with a 14-1 record.

Jamie Schwaberow/NCAA Photos

Grand Valley State's Terrance Banks (5) looks for running room after making one of his nine catches in the Lakers' 31-24 championship-game victory over Valdosta State.

BRALY MUNICIPAL STADIUM, FLORENCE, ALABAMA; DECEMBER 14

			Valdosta St.			Grand Valley St.
First downs			14			17
Rushes-yards			35-65			30-65
Passing yardage			181			361
Passes (comp.-att.-int.)			27-42-3			23-36-1
Punts (no.-avg.)			7-35.3			4-41.8
Fumbles (no.-lost)			3-0			2-2
Penalties (no.-yards)			1-10			6-39
Time of possession			32:35			27:25
Valdosta St.	3	3	7	11—24		
Grand Valley St.	14	3	7	7—31		

FIRST QUARTER
Valdosta St.—Will Rhody 26 field goal (6:23)
Grand Valley St.—Reggie Spearmon 9 run (Dave Hendrix kick) (5:37)
Grand Valley St.—David Kircus 54 pass from Curt Anes (Hendrix kick) (1:06)

SECOND QUARTER
Grand Valley St.—Hendrix 38 field goal (12:54)
Valdosta St.—Rhody 27 field goal (0:34)

THIRD QUARTER
Grand Valley St.—Kircus 67 pass from Anes (Hendrix kick) (12:28)
Valdosta St.—Aaron Jenkins 7 run (Rhody kick) (3:51)

FOURTH QUARTER
Valdosta St.—Rhody 43 field goal (3:30)
Valdosta St.—Tim Thompson fumble recovery in end zone (C.J. Lofton pass from Buster Faulkner) (3:09)
Grand Valley St.—Kircus 10 pass from Anes (Hendrix kick) (1:04)

INDIVIDUAL LEADERS
Rushing: Valdosta St.—Jenkins 20-99, Lee Tarpley 1-1, Tyrone Jordan 1-(minus 7), Faulkner 13-(minus 28); Grand Valley St.—Brent Lesniak 8-56, Spearmon 14-29, Terrance Banks 1-14, Team 1-(minus 1), Ryan Brady 2-(minus 15), Anes 4-(minus 18).
Passing: Valdosta St.—Faulkner 26-41-3-139, Bama Adams 1-1-0-42; Grand Valley St.—Anes 23-36-3-361.
Receiving: Valdosta St.—Reggie Mosley 9-47, C.J. Lofton 5-35, Jordan 4-57, Jenkins 4-21, Adams 3-15, Greg Lofton 2-6; Grand Valley St.—Kircus 11-270, Banks 9-66, Mike Holloway 1-12, Spearmon 1-9, Mario Locricchio 1-4.

Division II All-Time Championship Results

Year	Champion	Coach	Score	Runner-Up	Site
1973	Louisiana Tech	Maxie Lambright	34-0	Western Ky.	Sacramento, Calif.
1974	Central Mich.	Roy Kramer	54-14	Delaware	Sacramento, Calif.
1975	Northern Mich.	Gil Krueger	16-14	Western Ky.	Sacramento, Calif.
1976	Montana St.	Sonny Holland	24-13	Akron	Wichita Falls, Texas
1977	Lehigh	John Whitehead	33-0	Jacksonville St.	Wichita Falls, Texas
1978	Eastern Ill.	Darrell Mudra	10-9	Delaware	Longview, Texas
1979	Delaware	Tubby Raymond	38-21	Youngstown St.	Albuquerque, N.M.
1980	Cal Poly	Joe Harper	21-13	Eastern Ill.	Albuquerque, N.M.
1981	Southwest Tex. St.	Jim Wacker	42-13	North Dakota St.	McAllen, Texas
1982	Southwest Tex. St.	Jim Wacker	34-9	UC Davis	McAllen, Texas
1983	North Dakota St.	Don Morton	41-21	Central St.	McAllen, Texas
1984	Troy St.	Chan Gailey	18-17	North Dakota St.	McAllen, Texas
1985	North Dakota St.	Earle Solomonson	35-7	North Ala.	McAllen, Texas
1986	North Dakota St.	Earle Solomonson	27-7	South Dakota	Florence, Ala.
1987	Troy St.	Rick Rhoades	31-17	Portland St.	Florence, Ala.

Year	Champion	Coach	Score	Runner-Up	Site
1988	North Dakota St.	Rocky Hager	35-21	Portland St.	Florence, Ala.
1989	*Mississippi Col.	John Williams	3-0	Jacksonville St.	Florence, Ala.
1990	North Dakota St.	Rocky Hager	51-11	Indiana (Pa.)	Florence, Ala.
1991	Pittsburg St.	Chuck Broyles	23-6	Jacksonville St.	Florence, Ala.
1992	Jacksonville St.	Bill Burgess	17-13	Pittsburg St.	Florence, Ala.
1993	North Ala.	Bobby Wallace	41-34	Indiana (Pa.)	Florence, Ala.
1994	North Ala.	Bobby Wallace	16-10	Tex. A&M-Kingsville	Florence, Ala.
1995	North Ala.	Bobby Wallace	27-7	Pittsburg St.	Florence, Ala.
1996	Northern Colo.	Joe Glenn	23-14	Carson-Newman	Florence, Ala.
1997	Northern Colo.	Joe Glenn	51-0	New Haven	Florence, Ala.
1998	Northwest Mo. St.	Mel Tieerdsma	24-6	Carson-Newman	Florence, Ala.
1999	Northwest Mo. St.	Mel Tjeerdsma	58-52 (4 ot)	Carson-Newman	Florence, Ala.
2000	Delta St.	Steve Campbell	63-34	Bloomsburg	Florence, Ala.
2001	North Dakota	Dale Lennon	17-14	Grand Valley St.	Florence, Ala.
2002	Grand Valley St.	Brian Kelly	31-24	Valdosta St.	Florence, Ala.

*Mississippi College's participation in the 1989 Division II championship vacated by the NCAA Committee on Infractions.

Regional Championship Results

Before 1973, there was no Division II Football Championship. Instead, four regional bowl games were played in order to provide postseason action for what then were called NCAA College Division member institutions. Following are the results of those bowl games:

Year	Champion	Coach	Score	Runner-Up	Site
EAST (TANGERINE BOWL)					
1964	East Caro.	Clarence Stasavich	14-13	Massachusetts	Orlando, Fla.
1965	East Caro.	Clarence Stasavich	31-0	Maine	Orlando, Fla.
1966	Morgan St.	Earl Banks	14-6	West Chester	Orlando, Fla.
1967	Tenn.-Martin	Robert Carroll	25-8	West Chester	Orlando, Fla.
EAST (BOARDWALK BOWL)					
1968	Delaware	Tubby Raymond	31-24	Indiana (Pa.)	Atlantic City, N.J.
1969	Delaware	Tubby Raymond	31-13	N.C. Central	Atlantic City, N.J.
1970	Delaware	Tubby Raymond	38-23	Morgan St.	Atlantic City, N.J.
1971	Delaware	Tubby Raymond	72-22	C.W. Post	Atlantic City, N.J.
1972	Massachusetts	Dick MacPherson	35-14	UC Davis	Atlantic City, N.J.
MIDEAST (GRANTLAND RICE BOWL)					
1964	Middle Tenn.	Charles Murphy	20-0	Muskingum	Murfreesboro, Tenn.
1965	Ball St.	Ray Louthen	14-14	—	Murfreesboro, Tenn.
	Tennessee St.	John Merritt			
1966	Tennessee St.	John Merritt	34-7	Muskingum	Murfreesboro, Tenn.
1967	Eastern Ky.	Roy Kidd	27-13	Ball St.	Murfreesboro, Tenn.
1968	Louisiana Tech	Maxie Lambright	33-13	Akron	Murfreesboro, Tenn.
1969	East Tenn. St.	John Bell	34-14	Louisiana Tech	Baton Rouge, La.
1970	Tennessee St.	John Merritt	26-25	La.-Lafayette	Baton Rouge, La.
1971	Tennessee St.	John Merritt	26-23	McNeese St.	Baton Rouge, La.
1972	Louisiana Tech	Maxie Lambright	35-0	Tennessee Tech	Baton Rouge, La.
MIDWEST (PECAN BOWL)					
1964	Northern Iowa	Stan Sheriff	19-17	Lamar	Abilene, Texas
1965	North Dakota St.	Darrell Mudra	20-7	Grambling	Abilene, Texas
1966	North Dakota	Marv Helling	42-24	Parsons	Abilene, Texas
1967	Texas-Arlington	Burley Bearden	13-0	North Dakota St.	Abilene, Texas
1968	North Dakota St.	Ron Erhardt	23-14	Arkansas St.	Arlington, Texas
1969	Arkansas St.	Bennie Ellender	29-21	Drake	Arlington, Texas
1970	Arkansas St.	Bennie Ellender	38-21	Central Mo. St.	Arlington, Texas
MIDWEST (PIONEER BOWL)					
1971	Louisiana Tech	Maxie Lambright	14-3	Eastern Mich.	Wichita Falls, Texas
1972	Tennessee St.	John Merritt	29-7	Drake	Wichita Falls, Texas
WEST (CAMELLIA BOWL)					
1964	Montana St.	Jim Sweeney	28-7	Sacramento St.	Sacramento, Calif.
1965	Cal St. Los Angeles	Homer Beatty	18-10	UC Santa Barb.	Sacramento, Calif.
1966	San Diego St.	Don Coryell	28-7	Montana St.	Sacramento, Calif.
1967	San Diego St.	Don Coryell	27-6	San Fran. St.	Sacramento, Calif.
1968	Humboldt St.	Frank VanDeren	29-14	Fresno St.	Sacramento, Calif.
1969	North Dakota St.	Ron Erhardt	30-3	Montana	Sacramento, Calif.
1970	North Dakota St.	Ron Erhardt	31-16	Montana	Sacramento, Calif.
1971	Boise St.	Tony Knap	32-28	Cal St. Chico	Sacramento, Calif.
1972	North Dakota	Jerry Olson	38-21	Cal Poly	Sacramento, Calif.

2002 Division II Championship Results

FIRST ROUND
Valdosta St. 24, Catawba 7
Carson-Newman 40, Fayetteville St. 27
UC Davis 24, Central Wash. 6
Tex. A&M-Kingsville 58, Neb.-Kearney 40
Grand Valley St. 62, C.W. Post 13
Indiana (Pa.) 27, Saginaw Valley 23
Northwest Mo. St. 45, Minn. Duluth 41
Northern Colo. 49, Central Mo. St. 28

QUARTERFINALS
Valdosta St. 31, Carson-Newman 28
Tex. A&M-Kingsville 27, UC Davis 20 (ot)
Grand Valley St. 62, Indiana (Pa.) 21
Northern Colo. 23, Northwest Mo. St. 12

SEMIFINALS
Valdosta St. 21, Tex. A&M-Kingsville 12
Grand Valley St. 44, Northern Colo. 7

CHAMPIONSHIP
Grand Valley St. 31, Valdosta St. 24

Individual Records

GAME

NET YARDS RUSHING
379—Ronald Moore, Pittsburg St. (41) vs. Portland St. (38), 12-5-92.

RUSHES ATTEMPTED
51—Terry Morrow, Central St. (31) vs. Towson (0), 11-28-86.

TOUCHDOWNS BY RUSHING
5—Ronald Moore, Pittsburg St. (38) vs. North Dakota St. (37) (ot), 11-28-92; Ronald Moore, Pittsburg St. (41) vs. Portland St. (38), 12-5-92.

NET YARDS PASSING
497—Dusty Bonner, Valdosta St. (40) vs. Fort Valley St. (24), 11-17-2001.

PASSES ATTEMPTED
64—Kevin Daft, UC Davis (25) vs. New Haven (27), 12-6-97.

PASSES COMPLETED
43—Kevin Daft, UC Davis (25) vs. New Haven (27), 12-6-97.

PASSES HAD INTERCEPTED
6—Dennis Tomek, Western Ky. (28) vs. Grambling (20), 12-8-73.

TOUCHDOWN PASSES
6—Darren Del'Andrae, Portland St. (56) vs. West Chester (50) (3 ot), 11-18-89; J.T. O'Sullivan, UC Davis (62) vs. Mesa St. (18), 11-25-2000; Kelby Klosterman, North Dakota (42) vs. Winona St. (28), 11-17-2001; Curt Anes, Grand Valley St. (62) vs. C.W. Post (13), 11-23-2002.

COMPLETION PERCENTAGE (Min. 10 Attempts)
.909—Kevin Feeney, North Dakota St. (41) vs. North Dakota (10), 11-18-95 (10 of 11).

NET YARDS RUSHING AND PASSING
505—Kevin Daft, UC Davis (25) vs. New Haven (27), 12-6-97 (23 rushing, 482 passing).

RUSHING AND PASSING PLAYS
69—Kevin Daft, UC Davis (25) vs. New Haven (27), 12-6-97 (5 rushing, 64 passing).

PUNTING AVERAGE (Min. 3 Punts)
53.7—Chris Humes, UC Davis (23) vs. Angelo St. (28), 11-18-89 (7 for 376).

PUNTS
11—Charlie Johnson, Western Ky. (28) vs. Grambling (20), 12-8-73; Billy Becher, Northeastern St. (19) vs. UC Davis (14), 11-27-99; Jason Brown, Central Mo. St. (28) vs. Northern Colo. (49), 11-23-2002; Kenn Barnett, Valdosta St. (21) vs. Tex. A&M-Kingsville (12), 12-7-2002.

RECEPTIONS
14—Don Hutt, Boise St. (34) vs. Louisiana Tech (38), 12-8-73.

NET YARDS RECEIVING
270—David Kircus, Grand Valley St. (31) vs. Valdosta St. (24), 12-14-2002.

TOUCHDOWN RECEPTIONS
4—Steve Kreider, Lehigh (30) vs. Massachusetts (23), 11-26-77; Scott Asman, West Chester (50) vs. Portland St. (56) (3 ot), 11-18-89; Brian Penecale, West Chester (40) vs. Ferris St. (43), 11-19-94; Jesse Smith, North Dakota (42) vs. Winona St. (28), 11-17-2001; David Kircus, Grand Valley St. (62) vs. C.W. Post (13), 11-23-2002; David Kircus, Grand Valley St. (44) vs. Northern Colo. (7), 12-7-2002.

INTERCEPTIONS
4—Vince Buck, Central St. (31) vs. Towson (0), 11-28-86.

YARDS GAINED ON INTERCEPTION RETURNS
113—Darren Ryals, Millersville (27) vs. Indiana (Pa.) (24), 2 returns for 53- and 60-yard TDs, 11-19-88.

YARDS GAINED ON PUNT RETURNS
138—Rick Caswell, Western Ky. (14) vs. New Hampshire (3), 12-6-75.

YARDS GAINED ON KICKOFF RETURNS
215—Sean Smith, Bloomsburg (29) vs. Clarion (42), 11-23-96.

POINTS
32—Ronald Moore, Pittsburg St. (38) vs. North Dakota St. (37) (ot), 11-28-92; Ronald Moore, Pittsburg St. (41) vs. Portland St. (38), 12-5-92.

TOUCHDOWNS
5—Ronald Moore, Pittsburg St. (38) vs. North Dakota St. (37) (ot), 11-28-92; Ronald Moore, Pittsburg St. (41) vs. Portland St. (38), 12-5-92; Dexter Deese, Tex. A&M-Kingsville (43) vs. Western St. (7), 11-19-94.

EXTRA POINTS
9—Ashley Kay, Jacksonville St. (63) vs. West Chester (24), 11-19-88.

FIELD GOALS
4—Mario Ferretti, Northern Mich. (55) vs. Elizabeth City St. (6), 11-28-81; Ken Kubisz, North Dakota St. (26) vs. UC Davis (17), 12-3-83; Henrik Juul-Nielsen, Neb.-Kearney (40) vs. Tex. A&M-Kingsville (58), 11-23-2002.

TOURNAMENT

NET YARDS RUSHING
721—Ronald Moore, Pittsburg St., 1992 (108 vs. North Dakota, 151 vs. North Dakota St., 379 vs. Portland St., 83 vs. Jacksonville St.).

RUSHES ATTEMPTED
117—Ronald Moore, Pittsburg St., 1992 (29 vs. North Dakota, 31 vs. North Dakota St., 37 vs. Portland St., 20 vs. Jacksonville St.).

NET YARDS PASSING
1,236—Eric Miller, Bloomsburg, 2000 (316 vs. Saginaw Valley, 274 vs. Northwood, 385 vs. UC Davis, 261 vs. Delta St.)

PASSES ATTEMPTED
153—Travis Miles, Northwest Mo. St., 1999 (42 vs. North Dakota, 36 vs. Northern Colo., 30 vs. Indiana [Pa.], 45 vs. Carson-Newman).

PASSES COMPLETED
94—Chris Crawford, Portland St., 1988 (20 vs. Bowie St., 27 vs. Jacksonville St., 25 vs. Tex. A&M-Kingsville, 22 vs. North Dakota St.).

PASSES HAD INTERCEPTED
9—Dennis Tomek, Western Ky., 1973 (0 vs. Lehigh, 6 vs. Grambling, 3 vs. Louisiana Tech).

TOUCHDOWN PASSES
17—Eric Miller, Bloomsburg, 2000 (5 vs. Saginaw Valley, 4 vs. Northwood, 5 vs. UC Davis, 3 vs. Delta St.).

COMPLETION PERCENTAGE (Min. 2 Games)
.824—Mike Turk, Troy St., 1984, 14 of 17 (4-5 vs. Central St., 5-5 vs. Towson, 5-7 vs. North Dakota St.).

RECEPTIONS
34—Terrance Banks, Grand Valley St., 2002 (7 vs. C.W. Post, 7 vs. Indiana [Pa.], 11 vs. Northern Colo., 9 vs. Valdosta St.).

NET YARDS RECEIVING
544—David Kircus, Grand Valley St., 2002 (161 vs. C.W. Post, 23 vs. Indiana [Pa.], 90 vs. Northern Colo., 270 vs. Valdosta St.).

TOUCHDOWN RECEPTIONS
12—David Kircus, Grand Valley St., 2002 (4 vs. C.W. Post, 1 vs. Indiana [Pa.], 4 vs. Northern Colo., 3 vs. Valdosta St.).

POINTS
88—Ronald Moore, Pittsburg St., 1992 (18 vs. North Dakota, 32 vs. North Dakota St., 32 vs. Portland St., 6 vs. Jacksonville St.).

TOUCHDOWNS
14—Ronald Moore, Pittsburg St., 1992 (3 vs. North Dakota, 5 vs. North Dakota St., 5 vs. Portland St., 1 vs. Jacksonville St.).

LONGEST PLAYS

RUSH
98—Wesley Whiten, Tex. A&M-Kingsville (59) vs. Fort Hays St. (28), 11-18-95, TD.

PASS (Including Run)
99—Ken Suhl to Tony Willis, New Haven (35) vs. Ferris St. (13), 11-28-92, TD.

FIELD GOAL
59—Cameron Peterka, North Dakota (38) vs. Pittsburg St. (0), 11-24-2001.

PUNT
76—Chris Humes, UC Davis (23) vs. Angelo St. (28), 11-18-89.

PUNT RETURN
87—Rick Caswell, Western Ky. (14) vs. New Hampshire (3), 12-6-75, TD.

KICKOFF RETURN
100—Ken Bowles, UNLV (6) vs. Akron (26), 11-26-76, TD; Garth Mins, Neb.-Kearney (40) vs. Tex. A&M-Kingsville (58), 11-23-2002, TD.

INTERCEPTION RETURN
100—Charles Harris, Jacksonville St. (34) vs. Truman (21), 11-27-82, TD.

FUMBLE RETURN
77—Jeffrey Rodgers, Tex. A&M-Kingsville (30) vs. Portland St. (35), 11-28-92, TD.

Team Records

GAME

FIRST DOWNS
36—Delta St. (63) vs. Bloomsburg (34), 12-9-2000.

FIRST DOWNS BY RUSHING
29—Delta St. (63) vs. Bloomsburg (34), 12-9-2000.

FIRST DOWNS BY PASSING
25—UC Davis (25) vs. New Haven (27), 12-6-97.

NET YARDS RUSHING
566—Jacksonville St. (63) vs. West Chester (24), 11-19-88.

RUSHES ATTEMPTED
84—Southwest Tex. St. (34) vs. UC Davis (9), 12-11-82.

LONGEST RUSH
99—Northwood (14) vs. Bloomsburg (38), 11-25-2000 (29-yard run by Jason Martin and 70 yards after lateral by Chad Coons).

NET YARDS PASSING
497—Valdosta St. (40) vs. Fort Valley St. (24), 11-17-2001.

PASSES ATTEMPTED
64—UC Davis (25) vs. New Haven (27), 12-6-97.

PASSES COMPLETED
43—UC Davis (25) vs. New Haven (27), 12-6-97.

PASSES HAD INTERCEPTED
7—Towson (0) vs. Central St. (31), 11-28-86.

COMPLETION PERCENTAGE (Min. 10 Attempts)
.909—North Dakota St. (41) vs. North Dakota (10), 11-18-95 (10 of 11).

NET YARDS RUSHING AND PASSING
697—UC Davis (62) vs. Mesa St. (18), 11-25-2000 (261 rushing, 436 passing).

RUSHING AND PASSING PLAYS
99—Carson-Newman (52) vs. Northwest Mo. St. (58) (4 ot), 12-11-99 (77 rushing, 22 passing).

PUNTING AVERAGE (Min. 3 Punts)
53.7—UC Davis (23) vs. Angelo St. (28), 11-18-89 (7 for 376).

PUNTS
12—Delaware (8) vs. Grambling (17), 12-1-73; Western Ky. (0) vs. Louisiana Tech (34), 12-15-73; Central Mo. St. (28) vs. Northern Colo. (49), 11-23-2002.

PUNTS BLOCKED
2—Truman (21) vs. Jacksonville St. (34), 11-27-82.

YARDS GAINED ON PUNT RETURNS
140—Southwest Tex. St. (62) vs. Northern Mich. (0), 12-5-81.

YARDS GAINED ON KICKOFF RETURNS
215—Bloomsburg (29) vs. Clarion (42), 11-23-96.

YARDS GAINED ON INTERCEPTION RETURNS
131—Millersville (27) vs. Indiana (Pa.) (24), 11-19-88.

YARDS PENALIZED
185—Tex. A&M-Kingsville (30) vs. Portland St. (3), 11-25-95.

PENALTIES
18—Portland St. (16) vs. Tex. A&M-Kingsville (21), 11-26-94.

FUMBLES
10—Winston-Salem (0) vs. Delaware (41), 12-2-78.

FUMBLES LOST
7—Louisiana Tech (10) vs. Western Caro. (7), 11-30-74.

POINTS
*63—Jacksonville St. vs. West Chester (24), 11-19-88; Delta St. vs. Bloomsburg (34), 12-9-00.
*Mississippi Col. defeated Wofford, 70-19, on 11-17-90, but its participation in the championship was vacated.

TOURNAMENT

FIRST DOWNS
110—Bloomsburg, 2000 (27 vs. Saginaw Valley, 28 vs. Northwood, 34 vs. UC Davis, 21 vs. Delta St.).

NET YARDS RUSHING
1,660—North Dakota St., 1988 (474 vs. Augustana [S.D.], 434 vs. Millersville, 413 vs. Sacramento St., 339 vs. Portland St.).

NET YARDS PASSING
1,236—Bloomsburg, 2000 (316 vs. Saginaw Valley, 274 vs. Northwood, 385 vs. UC Davis, 261 vs. Delta St.).

NET YARDS RUSHING AND PASSING
2,114—Bloomsburg, 2000 (573 vs. Saginaw Valley, 487 vs. Northwood, 660 vs. UC Davis, 394 vs. Delta St.).

PASSES ATTEMPTED
156—Northwest Mo. St., 1999 (43 vs. North Dakota, 37 vs. Northern Colo., 31 vs. Indiana [Pa.], 45 vs. Carson-Newman).

PASSES COMPLETED
94—Portland St., 1988 (20 vs. Bowie St., 27 vs. Jacksonville St., 25 vs. Tex. A&M-Kingsville, 22 vs. North Dakota St.).

PASSES HAD INTERCEPTED
10—Western Ky., 1973 (0 vs. Lehigh, 6 vs. Grambling, 4 vs. Louisiana Tech).

NUMBER OF PUNTS
29—Western Ky., 1973 (6 vs. Lehigh, 11 vs. Grambling, 12 vs. Louisiana Tech).

YARDS PENALIZED
362—Carson-Newman, 1999 (102 vs. Arkansas Tech, 79 vs. Catawba, 94 vs. Northeastern St., 87 vs. Northwest Mo. St.).

FUMBLES
16—Delaware, 1978 (8 vs. Jacksonville St., 2 vs. Winston-Salem, 6 vs. Eastern Ill.).

FUMBLES LOST
12—Delaware, 1978 (6 vs. Jacksonville St., 2 vs. Winston-Salem, 4 vs. Eastern Ill.).

POINTS
199—Grand Valley St., 2002 (62 vs. C.W. Post, 62 vs. Indiana [Pa.], 44 vs. Northern Colo., 31 vs. Valdosta St.).

Championship Game Records

INDIVIDUAL

NET YARDS RUSHING
195—Billy Holmes, Northern Colo. (51) vs. New Haven (0), 1997 (30 rushes).

TOUCHDOWNS BY RUSHING
4—Dick Dunham, Central Mich. (56) vs. Delaware (14), 1974.

PASSES ATTEMPTED
45—Travis Miles, Northwest Mo. St. (58) vs. Carson-Newman (52) (4 ot), 1999 (24 completions).

PASSES COMPLETED
26—Buster Faulkner, Valdosta St. (24) vs. Grand Valley St. (31), 2002 (41 attempts).

TOUCHDOWN PASSES
5—Travis Miles, Northwest Mo. St. (58) vs. Carson-Newman (52) (4 ot), 1999.

RECEPTIONS
11—Pete Ravettine, Delaware (9) vs. Eastern Ill. (10), 1978 (156 yards); David Kircus, Grand Valley St. (31) vs. Valdosta St. (24), 2002 (270 yards).

NET YARDS RECEIVING
270—David Kircus, Grand Valley St. (31) vs. Valdosta St. (24), 2002.

TOUCHDOWN RECEPTIONS
3—J.R. Hill, Northwest Mo. St. (58) vs. Carson-Newman (52) (4 ot), 1999; David Kircus, Grand Valley St. (31) vs. Valdosta St. (24), 2002.

POINTS
24—Dick Dunham, Central Mich. (56) vs. Delaware (14), 1974.

TOUCHDOWNS
4—Dick Dunham, Central Mich. (56) vs. Delaware (14), 1974.

LONGEST PLAYS

RUSH
90—Kenyatta Jones, North Ala. (16) vs. Tex. A&M-Kingsville (10), 1994, TD.

PASS (INCLUDING RUN)
75—Chris Simdorn to T.R. McDonald, North Dakota St. (51) vs. Indiana (Pa.) (11), 1990, TD.

FIELD GOAL
50—Ted Clem, Troy St. (18) vs. North Dakota St. (17), 1984.

PUNT RETURN
86—Ques Rumph, Carson-Newman (52) vs. Northwest Mo. St. (58) (4 ot), 1999, TD.

KICKOFF RETURN
99—Ronald Moore, Pittsburg St. (13) vs. Jacksonville St. (17), 1992, TD.

INTERCEPTION RETURN
61—Vince Hyland, Delaware (38) vs. Youngstown St. (21), 1979, TD.

TEAM

FIRST DOWNS
36—Delta St. (63) vs. Bloomsburg (34), 2000 (29 rushing, 6 passing, 1 by penalty).

NET YARDS RUSHING
524—Delta St. (63) vs. Bloomsburg (34), 2000 (69 rushes).

NET YARDS PASSING
361—Grand Valley St. (31) vs. Valdosta St. (24), 2002 (23 of 36).

PASSES ATTEMPTED
45—Northwest Mo. St. (58) vs. Carson-Newman (52) (4 ot), 1999 (24 completions).

PASSES COMPLETED
27—Valdosta St. (24) vs. Grand Valley St. (31), 2002 (42 attempts).

PASSES HAD INTERCEPTED
4—Western Ky. (0) vs. La. Tech (34), 1973; Delaware (14) vs. Central Mich. (56), 1974.

YARDS PENALIZED
140—Eastern Ill. (13) vs. Cal Poly (21), 1980 (11 penalties).

FUMBLES LOST
4—Jacksonville St. (0) vs. Lehigh (33), 1977; Delaware (9) vs. Eastern Ill. (10), 1978 (6 fumbles); North Dakota St. (13) vs. Southwest Tex. St. (42), 1981 (5 fumbles); UC Davis (9) vs. Southwest Tex. St. (34), 1982 (4 fumbles).

POINTS
63—Delta St. vs. Bloomsburg (34), 2000.

POINTS, BOTH TEAMS
110—Northwest Mo. St. (58) and Carson-Newman (52) (4 ot), 1999.

Championship Game Records researched and submitted by Jeff Hodges, SID, University of North Alabama.

Year-by-Year Division II Championship Results

Year (Number of Teams)	Coach	Record	Result
1973 (8)			
Louisiana Tech	Maxie Lambright	3-0	Champion
Western Ky.	Jimmy Feix	2-1	Second
Boise St.	Tony Knap	1-1	Semifinalist
Grambling	Eddie Robinson	1-1	Semifinalist
Delaware	Tubby Raymond	0-1	Lost 1st Round
Lehigh	Fred Dunlap	0-1	Lost 1st Round
South Dakota	Joe Salem	0-1	Lost 1st Round
Western Ill.	Darrell Mudra	0-1	Lost 1st Round
1974 (8)			
Central Mich.	Roy Kramer	3-0	Champion
Delaware	Tubby Raymond	2-1	Second
Louisiana Tech	Maxie Lambright	1-1	Semifinalist
UNLV	Ron Meyer	1-1	Semifinalist
Alcorn St.	Marino Casem	0-1	Lost 1st Round
Boise St.	Tony Knap	0-1	Lost 1st Round
Western Caro.	Bob Waters	0-1	Lost 1st Round
Youngstown St.	Rey Dempsey	0-1	Lost 1st Round
1975 (8)			
Northern Mich.	Gil Krueger	3-0	Champion
Western Ky.	Jimmy Feix	2-1	Second
New Hampshire	Bill Bowes	1-1	Semifinalist
West Ala.	Jim King	1-1	Semifinalist
Boise St.	Tony Knap	0-1	Lost 1st Round
Lehigh	Fred Dunlap	0-1	Lost 1st Round
North Dakota	Jerry Olson	0-1	Lost 1st Round
Northern Iowa	Stan Sheriff	0-1	Lost 1st Round
1976 (8)			
Montana St.	Sonny Holland	3-0	Champion
Akron	Jim Dennison	2-1	Second
North Dakota St.	Jim Wacker	1-1	Semifinalist
Northern Mich.	Gil Krueger	1-1	Semifinalist
Delaware	Tubby Raymond	0-1	Lost 1st Round
Eastern Ky.	Roy Kidd	0-1	Lost 1st Round
UNLV	Tony Knap	0-1	Lost 1st Round
New Hampshire	Bill Bowes	0-1	Lost 1st Round
1977 (8)			
Lehigh	John Whitehead	3-0	Champion
Jacksonville St.	Jim Fuller	2-1	Second
UC Davis	Jim Sochor	1-1	Semifinalist
North Dakota St.	Jim Wacker	1-1	Semifinalist
Bethune-Cookman	Andy Hinson	0-1	Lost 1st Round
Massachusetts	Dick MacPherson	0-1	Lost 1st Round
Northern Ariz.	Joe Salem	0-1	Lost 1st Round
Northern Mich.	Gil Krueger	0-1	Lost 1st Round
1978 (8)			
Eastern Ill.	Darrell Mudra	3-0	Champion
Delaware	Tubby Raymond	2-1	Second
Winston-Salem	Bill Hayes	1-1	Semifinalist
Youngstown St.	Bill Narduzzi	1-1	Semifinalist
UC Davis	Jim Sochor	0-1	Lost 1st Round
Cal Poly	Joe Harper	0-1	Lost 1st Round
Jacksonville St.	Jim Fuller	0-1	Lost 1st Round
Neb.-Omaha	Sandy Buda	0-1	Lost 1st Round
1979 (8)			
Delaware	Tubby Raymond	3-0	Champion
Youngstown St.	Bill Narduzzi	2-1	Second
Alabama A&M	Ray Greene	1-1	Semifinalist
Mississippi Col.	John Williams	1-1	Semifinalist
Morgan St.	Clarence Thomas	0-1	Lost 1st Round
North Dakota	Gene Murphy	0-1	Lost 1st Round
South Dakota St.	John Gregory	0-1	Lost 1st Round
Virginia Union	Willard Bailey	0-1	Lost 1st Round
1980 (8)			
Cal Poly	Joe Harper	3-0	Champion
Eastern Ill.	Darrell Mudra	2-1	Second
North Ala.	Wayne Grubb	1-1	Semifinalist
Santa Clara	Pat Malley	1-1	Semifinalist
Jacksonville St.	Jim Fuller	0-1	Lost 1st Round
Northern Colo.	Bob Blasi	0-1	Lost 1st Round
Northern Mich.	Bill Rademacher	0-1	Lost 1st Round
Virginia Union	Willard Bailey	0-1	Lost 1st Round
1981 (8)			
Southwest Tex. St.	Jim Wacker	3-0	Champion
North Dakota St.	Don Morton	2-1	Second
Northern Mich.	Bill Rademacher	1-1	Semifinalist
Shippensburg	Vito Ragazzo	1-1	Semifinalist
Elizabeth City St.	Johnnie Walton	0-1	Lost 1st Round
Jacksonville St.	Jim Fuller	0-1	Lost 1st Round
Puget Sound	Ron Simonson	0-1	Lost 1st Round
Virginia Union	Willard Bailey	0-1	Lost 1st Round
1982 (8)			
Southwest Tex. St.	Jim Wacker	3-0	Champion
UC Davis	Jim Sochor	2-1	Second
Jacksonville St.	Jim Fuller	1-1	Semifinalist
North Dakota St.	Don Morton	1-1	Semifinalist
Fort Valley St.	Doug Porter	0-1	Lost 1st Round
Northern Mich.	Bill Rademacher	0-1	Lost 1st Round
Truman	Bruce Craddock	0-1	Lost 1st Round
Virginia Union	Willard Bailey	0-1	Lost 1st Round
1983 (8)			
North Dakota St.	Don Morton	3-0	Champion
Central St.	Billy Joe	2-1	Second
UC Davis	Jim Sochor	1-1	Semifinalist
North Ala.	Wayne Grubb	1-1	Semifinalist
Butler	Bill Sylvester	0-1	Lost 1st Round
Southwest Tex. St.	John O'Hara	0-1	Lost 1st Round
Towson	Phil Albert	0-1	Lost 1st Round
Virginia Union	Willard Bailey	0-1	Lost 1st Round
1984 (8)			
Troy St.	Chan Gailey	3-0	Champion
North Dakota St.	Don Morton	2-1	Second
Neb.-Omaha	Sandy Buda	1-1	Semifinalist
Towson	Phil Albert	1-1	Semifinalist
UC Davis	Jim Sochor	0-1	Lost 1st Round
Central St.	Billy Joe	0-1	Lost 1st Round
Norfolk St.	Willard Bailey	0-1	Lost 1st Round
Northwest Mo. St.	Vern Thomsen	0-1	Lost 1st Round
1985 (8)			
North Dakota St.	Earle Solomonson	3-0	Champion
North Ala.	Wayne Grubb	2-1	Second
Bloomsburg	George Landis	1-1	Semifinalist
South Dakota	Dave Triplett	1-1	Semifinalist
UC Davis	Jim Sochor	0-1	Lost 1st Round
Central St.	Billy Joe	0-1	Lost 1st Round
Fort Valley St.	Gerald Walker	0-1	Lost 1st Round
Hampton	Fred Freeman	0-1	Lost 1st Round
1986 (8)			
North Dakota St.	Earle Solomonson	3-0	Champion
South Dakota	Dave Triplett	2-1	Second
Central St.	Billy Joe	1-1	Semifinalist
Troy St.	Rick Rhodes	1-1	Semifinalist
Ashland	Fred Martinelli	0-1	Lost 1st Round
UC Davis	Jim Sochor	0-1	Lost 1st Round
Towson	Phil Albert	0-1	Lost 1st Round
Virginia Union	Joe Taylor	0-1	Lost 1st Round
1987 (8)			
Troy St.	Rick Rhodes	3-0	Champion
Portland St.	Pokey Allen	2-1	Second
UCF	Gene McDowell	1-1	Semifinalist
Northern Mich.	Herb Grenke	1-1	Semifinalist
Angelo St.	Jerry Vandergriff	0-1	Lost 1st Round
Indiana (Pa.)	Frank Cignetti	0-1	Lost 1st Round
Minn. St. Mankato	Dan Runkle	0-1	Lost 1st Round
Winston-Salem	Bill Hayes	0-1	Lost 1st Round
1988 (16)			
North Dakota St.	Rocky Hager	4-0	Champion
Portland St.	Pokey Allen	3-1	Second
Sacramento St.	Bob Mattos	2-1	Semifinalist
Tex. A&M-Kingsville	Ron Harms	2-1	Semifinalist
Jacksonville St.	Bill Burgess	1-1	Quarterfinalist
Millersville	Gene Carpenter	1-1	Quarterfinalist
N.C. Central	Henry Lattimore	1-1	Quarterfinalist
Tenn.-Martin	Don McLeary	1-1	Quarterfinalist
Augustana (S.D.)	Jim Heinitz	0-1	Lost 1st Round
Bowie St.	Sanders Shiver	0-1	Lost 1st Round
Butler	Bill Lynch	0-1	Lost 1st Round
UC Davis	Jim Sochor	0-1	Lost 1st Round
Indiana (Pa.)	Frank Cignetti	0-1	Lost 1st Round
Mississippi Col.	John Williams	0-1	Lost 1st Round
West Chester	Danny Hale	0-1	Lost 1st Round
Winston-Salem	Pete Richardson	0-1	Lost 1st Round
1989 (16)			
*Mississippi Col.	John Williams	4-0	Champion
Jacksonville St.	Bill Burgess	3-1	Second
Angelo St.	Jerry Vandergriff	2-1	Semifinalist
Indiana (Pa.)	Frank Cignetti	2-1	Semifinalist
North Dakota St.	Rocky Hager	1-1	Quarterfinalist

Year (Number of Teams)	Coach	Record	Result
Pittsburg St.	Dennis Franchione	1-1	Quarterfinalist
Portland St.	Pokey Allen	1-1	Quarterfinalist
St. Cloud St.	Noel Martin	1-1	Quarterfinalist
Alabama A&M	George Pugh	0-1	Lost 1st Round
Augustana (S.D.)	Jim Heinitz	0-1	Lost 1st Round
UC Davis	Bob Foster	0-1	Lost 1st Round
Edinboro	Tom Hollman	0-1	Lost 1st Round
Grand Valley St.	Tom Beck	0-1	Lost 1st Round
Northwest Mo. St.	Bud Elliott	0-1	Lost 1st Round
Tex. A&M-Kingsville	Ron Harms	0-1	Lost 1st Round
West Chester	Rick Daniels	0-1	Lost 1st Round

1990 (16)

Year (Number of Teams)	Coach	Record	Result
North Dakota St.	Rocky Hager	4-0	Champion
Indiana (Pa.)	Frank Cignetti	3-1	Second
*Mississippi Col.	John Williams	2-1	Semifinalist
Pittsburg St.	Chuck Broyles	2-1	Semifinalist
Cal Poly	Lyle Setencich	1-1	Quarterfinalist
Edinboro	Tom Hollman	1-1	Quarterfinalist
Jacksonville St.	Bill Burgess	1-1	Quarterfinalist
Tex. A&M-Commerce	Eddie Vowell	1-1	Quarterfinalist
Cal St. Northridge	Bob Burt	0-1	Lost 1st Round
Grand Valley St.	Tom Beck	0-1	Lost 1st Round
North Ala.	Bobby Wallace	0-1	Lost 1st Round
Northern Colo.	Joe Glenn	0-1	Lost 1st Round
Truman	Eric Holm	0-1	Lost 1st Round
Virginia Union	Joe Taylor	0-1	Lost 1st Round
Winston-Salem	Pete Richardson	0-1	Lost 1st Round
Wofford	Mike Ayers	0-1	Lost 1st Round

1991 (16)

Year (Number of Teams)	Coach	Record	Result
Pittsburg St.	Chuck Broyles	4-0	Champion
Jacksonville St.	Bill Burgess	3-1	Second
Indiana (Pa.)	Frank Cignetti	2-1	Semifinalist
Portland St.	Pokey Allen	2-1	Semifinalist
Minn. St. Mankato	Dan Runkle	1-1	Quarterfinalist
Mississippi Col.	Terry McMillan	1-1	Quarterfinalist
Shippensburg	Rocky Rees	1-1	Quarterfinalist
Tex. A&M-Commerce	Eddie Vowell	1-1	Quarterfinalist
Butler	Bob Bartolomeo	0-1	Lost 1st Round
East Stroudsburg	Dennis Douds	0-1	Lost 1st Round
Grand Valley St.	Brian Kelly	0-1	Lost 1st Round
North Dakota St.	Rocky Hager	0-1	Lost 1st Round
Northern Colo.	Joe Glenn	0-1	Lost 1st Round
Virginia Union	Joe Taylor	0-1	Lost 1st Round
Winston-Salem	Pete Richardson	0-1	Lost 1st Round
Wofford	Mike Ayers	0-1	Lost 1st Round

1992 (16)

Year (Number of Teams)	Coach	Record	Result
Jacksonville St.	Bill Burgess	4-0	Champion
Pittsburg St.	Chuck Broyles	3-1	Second
New Haven	Mark Whipple	2-1	Semifinalist
Portland St.	Pokey Allen	2-1	Semifinalist
Ferris St.	Keith Otterbein	1-1	Quarterfinalist
North Ala.	Bobby Wallace	1-1	Quarterfinalist
North Dakota St.	Rocky Hager	1-1	Quarterfinalist
Tex. A&M-Kingsville	Ron Harms	1-1	Quarterfinalist
UC Davis	Bob Foster	0-1	Lost 1st Round
Edinboro	Tom Hollman	0-1	Lost 1st Round
Hampton	Joe Taylor	0-1	Lost 1st Round
North Dakota	Roger Thomas	0-1	Lost 1st Round
Savannah St.	Bill Davis	0-1	Lost 1st Round
Truman	Eric Holm	0-1	Lost 1st Round
West Chester	Rick Daniels	0-1	Lost 1st Round
Western St.	Carl Iverson	0-1	Lost 1st Round

1993 (16)

Year (Number of Teams)	Coach	Record	Result
North Ala.	Bobby Wallace	4-0	Champion
Indiana (Pa.)	Frank Cignetti	3-1	Second
North Dakota	Roger Thomas	2-1	Semifinalist
Tex. A&M Kingsville	Ron Harms	2-1	Semifinalist
UC Davis	Bob Biggs	1-1	Quarterfinalist
Hampton	Joe Taylor	1-1	Quarterfinalist
Minn. St. Mankato	Dan Runkle	1-1	Quarterfinalist
New Haven	Mark Whipple	1-1	Quarterfinalist
Albany St. (Ga.)	Hampton Smith	0-1	Lost 1st Round
Carson-Newman	Ken Sparks	0-1	Lost 1st Round
Edinboro	Tom Hollman	0-1	Lost 1st Round
Ferris St.	Keith Otterbein	0-1	Lost 1st Round
Fort Hays St.	Bob Cortese	0-1	Lost 1st Round
Mo. Southern St.	Jon Lantz	0-1	Lost 1st Round
Pittsburg St.	Chuck Broyles	0-1	Lost 1st Round
Portland St.	Tim Walsh	0-1	Lost 1st Round

1994 (16)

Year (Number of Teams)	Coach	Record	Result
North Ala.	Bobby Wallace	4-0	Champion
Tex. A&M-Kingsville	Ron Harms	3-1	Second
Indiana (Pa.)	Frank Cignetti	2-1	Semifinalist
North Dakota	Roger Thomas	2-1	Semifinalist
Ferris St.	Keith Otterbein	1-1	Quarterfinalist
North Dakota St.	Rocky Hager	1-1	Quarterfinalist
Portland St.	Tim Walsh	1-1	Quarterfinalist
Valdosta St.	Hal Mumme	1-1	Quarterfinalist
Albany St. (Ga.)	Hampton Smith	0-1	Lost 1st Round
Angelo St.	Jerry Vandergriff	0-1	Lost 1st Round
Carson-Newman	Ken Sparks	0-1	Lost 1st Round
Grand Valley St.	Brian Kelly	0-1	Lost 1st Round
Pittsburg St.	Chuck Broyles	0-1	Lost 1st Round
Truman	Eric Holm	0-1	Lost 1st Round
West Chester	Rick Daniels	0-1	Lost 1st Round
Western St.	Carl Iverson	0-1	Lost 1st Round

1995 (16)

Year (Number of Teams)	Coach	Record	Result
North Ala.	Bobby Wallace	4-0	Champion
Pittsburg St.	Chuck Broyles	3-1	Second
Ferris St.	Jeff Pierce	2-1	Semifinalist
Tex. A&M-Kingsville	Ron Harms	2-1	Semifinalist
Carson-Newman	Ken Sparks	1-1	Quarterfinalist
New Haven	Tony Sparano	1-1	Quarterfinalist
North Dakota St.	Rocky Hager	1-1	Quarterfinalist
Portland St.	Tim Walsh	1-1	Quarterfinalist
Albany St. (Ga.)	Hampton Smith	0-1	Lost 1st Round
Edinboro	Tom Hollman	0-1	Lost 1st Round
Fort Hays St.	Bob Cortese	0-1	Lost 1st Round
Millersville	Gene Carpenter	0-1	Lost 1st Round
North Dakota	Roger Thomas	0-1	Lost 1st Round
Northern Colo.	Joe Glenn	0-1	Lost 1st Round
Tex. A&M-Commerce	Eddie Vowell	0-1	Lost 1st Round
West Ga.	Charlie Fisher	0-1	Lost 1st Round

1996 (16)

Year (Number of Teams)	Coach	Record	Result
Northern Colo.	Joe Glenn	4-0	Champion
Carson-Newman	Ken Sparks	3-1	Second
UC Davis	Bob Biggs	2-1	Semifinalist
Clarion	Malen Luke	2-1	Semifinalist
Central Okla.	Gary Howard	1-1	Quarterfinalist
Ferris St.	Jeff Pierce	1-1	Quarterfinalist
Northwest Mo. St.	Mel Tjeerdsma	1-1	Quarterfinalist
Valdosta St.	Hal Mumme	1-1	Quarterfinalist
Bloomsburg	Danny Hale	0-1	Lost 1st Round
Indiana (Pa.)	Frank Cignetti	0-1	Lost 1st Round
Pittsburg St.	Chuck Broyles	0-1	Lost 1st Round
Neb.-Omaha	Pat Behrns	0-1	Lost 1st Round
Albany St. (Ga.)	Hampton Smith	0-1	Lost 1st Round
West Ga.	Charlie Fisher	0-1	Lost 1st Round
Chadron St.	Brad Smith	0-1	Lost 1st Round
*Tex. A&M-Kingsville	Ron Harms	0-1	Lost 1st Round

1997 (16)

Year (Number of Teams)	Coach	Record	Result
Northern Colo.	Joe Glenn	4-0	Champion
New Haven	Tony Sparano	3-1	Second
UC Davis	Bob Biggs	2-1	Semifinalist
Carson-Newman	Ken Sparks	2-1	Semifinalist
Angelo St.	Jerry Vandergriff	1-1	Quarterfinalist
Slippery Rock	George Mahalik	1-1	Quarterfinalist
Northwest Mo. St.	Mel Tjeerdsma	1-1	Quarterfinalist
Albany St. (Ga.)	Hampton Smith	1-1	Quarterfinalist
*Tex. A&M-Kingsville	Ron Harms	0-1	Lost 1st Round
Western St.	Carl Iverson	0-1	Lost 1st Round
Glenville St.	Warren Ruggerio	0-1	Lost 1st Round
Ashland	Gary Keller	0-1	Lost 1st Round
North Dakota St.	Bob Babich	0-1	Lost 1st Round
Pittsburg St.	Chuck Broyles	0-1	Lost 1st Round
North Ala.	Bobby Wallace	0-1	Lost 1st Round
Southern Ark.	Steve Roberts	0-1	Lost 1st Round

1998 (16)

Year (Number of Teams)	Coach	Record	Result
Northwest Mo. St.	Mel Tjeerdsma	4-0	Champion
Carson-Newman	Ken Sparks	3-1	Second
Slippery Rock	George Mihalik	2-1	Semifinalist
*Tex. A&M-Kingsville	Ron Harms	2-1	Semifinalist
Central Okla.	Gary Howard	1-1	Quarterfinalist
Fort Valley St.	Kent Schoolfield	1-1	Quarterfinalist
Northern Colo.	Joe Glen	1-1	Quarterfinalist
Shepherd	Monte Cater	1-1	Quarterfinalist
UC Davis	Bob Biggs	0-1	Lost 1st Round
Chadron St.	Brad Smith	0-1	Lost 1st Round
Delta St.	Todd Knight	0-1	Lost 1st Round
Grand Valley St.	Brian Kelly	0-1	Lost 1st Round
Indiana (Pa.)	Frank Cignetti	0-1	Lost 1st Round
Neb.-Omaha	Pat Behrns	0-1	Lost 1st Round
North Dakota	Roger Thomas	0-1	Lost 1st Round
West Ga.	Glenn Spencer	0-1	Lost 1st Round

1999 (16)

Year (Number of Teams)	Coach	Record	Result
Northwest Mo. St.	Mel Tjeerdsma	4-0	Champion
Carson-Newman	Ken Sparks	3-1	Second

Year (Number of Teams)	Coach	Record	Result
Indiana (Pa.)	Frank Cignetti	2-1	Semifinalist
Northeastern St.	Tom Eckert	2-1	Semifinalist
UC Davis	Bob Biggs	1-1	Quarterfinalist
Catawba	David Bennett	1-1	Quarterfinalist
Millersville	Gene Carpenter	1-1	Quarterfinalist
Northern Colo.	Joe Glenn	1-1	Quarterfinalist
Arkansas Tech	Steve Mullins	0-1	Lost 1st Round
Central Okla.	Gary Howard	0-1	Lost 1st Round
Fort Valley St.	Kent Schoolfield	0-1	Lost 1st Round
North Dakota	Dale Lennon	0-1	Lost 1st Round
Pittsburg St.	Chuck Broyles	0-1	Lost 1st Round
Shepherd	Monte Cater	0-1	Lost 1st Round
Slippery Rock	George Mihalik	0-1	Lost 1st Round
Western Wash.	Rob Smith	0-1	Lost 1st Round

2000 (16)

Delta St.	Steve Campbell	4-0	Champion
Bloomsburg	Danny Hale	3-1	Second
UC Davis	Bob Biggs	2-1	Semifinalist
North Dakota St.	Bob Babich	2-1	Semifinalist
Catawba	David Bennett	1-1	Quarterfinalist
Mesa St.	Joe Ramunno	1-1	Quarterfinalist
Neb.-Omaha	Pat Behrns	1-1	Quarterfinalist
Northwood	Pat Riepma	1-1	Quarterfinalist
Chadron St.	Brad Smith	0-1	Lost 1st Round
Indiana (Pa.)	Frank Cignetti	0-1	Lost 1st Round
Northeastern St.	Tom Eckert	0-1	Lost 1st Round
Northwest Mo. St.	Mel Tjeersdma	0-1	Lost 1st Round
Pittsburg St.	Chuck Broyles	0-1	Lost 1st Round
Saginaw Valley	Randy Awrey	0-1	Lost 1st Round
Valdosta St.	Chris Hatcher	0-1	Lost 1st Round
West Ga.	Glenn Spencer	0-1	Lost 1st Round

2001 (16)

North Dakota	Dale Lennon	4-0	Champion
Grand Valley St.	Brian Kelly	3-1	Second
UC Davis	Bob Biggs	2-1	Semifinalist
Catawba	David Bennett	2-1	Semifinalist
Pittsburg St.	Chuck Broyles	1-1	Quarterfinalist
Saginaw Valley	Randy Awrey	1-1	Quarterfinalist
Tarleton St.	Todd Whitten	1-1	Quarterfinalist
Valdosta St.	Chris Hatcher	1-1	Quarterfinalist
Bloomsburg	Danny Hale	0-1	Lost 1st Round
Central Ark.	Clint Conque	0-1	Lost 1st Round
Chadron St.	Brad Smith	0-1	Lost 1st Round
Fort Valley St.	Kent Schoolfield	0-1	Lost 1st Round
Indiana (Pa.)	Frank Cignetti	0-1	Lost 1st Round
Neb.-Omaha	Pat Behrns	0-1	Lost 1st Round
Tex. A&M-Kingsville	Richard Cundiff	0-1	Lost 1st Round
Winona St.	Tom Sawyer	0-1	Lost 1st Round

2002 (16)

Grand Valley St.	Brian Kelly	4-0	Champion
Valdosta St.	Chris Hatcher	3-1	Second
Northern Colo.	O. Kay Dalton	2-1	Semifinalist
Tex. A&M-Kingsville	Richard Cundiff	2-1	Semifinalist
UC Davis	Bob Biggs	1-1	Quarterfinalist
Carson-Newman	Ken Sparks	1-1	Quarterfinalist
Indiana (Pa.)	Frank Cignetti	1-1	Quarterfinalist
Northwest Mo. St.	Mel Tjeersdma	1-1	Quarterfinalist
C.W. Post	Bryan Collins	0-1	Lost 1st Round
Catawba	Chip Hester	0-1	Lost 1st Round
Central Mo. St.	Willie Fritz	0-1	Lost 1st Round
Central Wash.	John Zamberlin	0-1	Lost 1st Round
Fayetteville St.	Kenny Phillips	0-1	Lost 1st Round
Minn. Duluth	Bob Nielson	0-1	Lost 1st Round
Neb.-Kearney	Darrell Morris	0-1	Lost 1st Round
Saginaw Valley	Randy Awrey	0-1	Lost 1st Round

Competition in championship vacated by action of the NCAA Committee on Infractions.

Division II Championship Record of Each College by Coach

(109 Colleges; 1973-02)

	Yrs	Won	Lost	CH	2D
AKRON					
Jim Dennison (Wooster '60) 76-2D	1	2	1	0	1
ALABAMA A&M					
Ray Green (Akron '63) 79	1	1	1	0	0
George Pugh (Alabama '76) 89	1	0	1	0	0
TOTAL	2	1	2	0	0
ALBANY ST. (GA.)					
Hampton Smith (Mississippi Val. '57) 93, 94, 95, 96, 97	5	1	5	0	0

	Yrs	Won	Lost	CH	2D
ALCORN ST.					
Marino Casem (Xavier [La.] '56) 74	1	0	1	0	0
ANGELO ST.					
Jerry Vandergriff (Tex. A&M-Corp. Chris. '65) 87, 89, 94, 97	4	3	4	0	0
ARKANSAS TECH					
Steve Mullins (Ark.-Monticello '80) 99	1	0	1	0	0
ASHLAND					
Fred Martinelli (Otterbein '51) 86	1	0	1	0	0
Gary Keller (Bluffton '73) 97	1	0	1	0	0
TOTAL	2	0	2	0	0
AUGUSTANA (S.D.)					
Jim Heinitz (South Dakota St. '72) 88, 89	2	0	2	0	0
BETHUNE-COOKMAN					
Andy Hinson (Bethune-Cookman '53) 77	1	0	1	0	0
BLOOMSBURG					
George Landis (Penn St. '71) 85	1	1	1	0	0
Danny Hale (West Chester '68) 96, 00-2D, 01	3	3	3	0	1
TOTAL	4	4	4	0	1
BOISE ST.					
Tony Knap (Idaho '39) 73, 74, 75	3	1	3	0	0
BOWIE ST.					
Sanders Shiver (Carson-Newman '76) 88	1	0	1	0	0
BUTLER					
Bill Sylvester (Butler '50) 83	1	0	1	0	0
Bill Lynch (Butler '77) 88	1	0	1	0	0
Bob Bartolomeo (Butler '77) 91	1	0	1	0	0
TOTAL	3	0	3	0	0
C.W. POST					
Bryan Collins (St. John's [N.Y.] '87) 02	1	0	1	0	0
UC DAVIS					
Jim Sochor (San Fran. St. '60) 77, 78, 82-2D, 83, 84, 85, 86, 88	8	4	8	0	1
Bob Foster (UC Davis '62) 89, 92	2	0	2	0	0
Bob Biggs (UC Davis '73) 93, 96, 97, 98, 99,00, 01, 02	8	11	8	0	0
TOTAL	18	15	18	0	1
CAL POLY					
Joe Harper (UCLA '59) 78, 80-CH	2	3	1	1	0
Lyle Setencich (Fresno St. '68) 90	1	1	1	0	0
TOTAL	3	4	2	1	0
CAL ST. NORTHRIDGE					
Bob Burt (Cal St. Los Angeles '62) 90	1	0	1	0	0
CARSON-NEWMAN					
Ken Sparks (Carson-Newman '68) 93, 94, 95, 96-2D, 97, 98-2D, 99-2D, 02	8	13	8	0	3
CATAWBA					
David Bennett (Presbyterian '84) 99, 00, 01	3	4	3	0	0
Chip Hester (Guilford '92) 02	1	0	1	0	0
TOTAL	4	4	4	0	0
CENTRAL ARK.					
Clint Conque (Nicholls St. '83)	1	0	1	0	0
UCF					
Gene McDowell (Florida St. '65) 87	1	1	1	0	0
CENTRAL MICH.					
Roy Kramer (Maryville [Tenn.] '53) 74-CH	1	3	0	1	0
CENTRAL MO. ST.					
Willie Fritz (Pittsburg St. '83) 02	1	0	1	0	0
CENTRAL OKLA.					
Gary Howard (Arkansas '64) 96, 98, 99	3	2	3	0	0
CENTRAL ST.					
Billy Joe (Villanova '63) 83-2D, 84, 85, 86	4	3	4	0	1
CENTRAL WASH.					
John Zamberlin (Pacific Lutheran '79) 02	1	0	1	0	0
CHADRON ST.					
Brad Smith (Western Ill. '72) 96, 98, 00, 01	4	0	4	0	0
CLARION					
Malen Luke (Westminster [Pa.] '76) 96	1	2	1	0	0
DELAWARE					
Harold "Tubby" Raymond (Michigan '50) 73, 74-2D, 76, 78-2D, 79-CH	5	7	4	1	2
DELTA ST.					
Todd Knight (Ouachita Baptist '86) 98	1	0	1	0	0
Steve Campbell (Troy St. '88) 00-CH	1	4	0	1	0
TOTAL	2	4	1	1	0
EAST STROUDSBURG					
Dennis Douds (Slippery Rock '63) 91	1	0	1	0	0
EASTERN ILL.					
Darrell Mudra (Peru St. '51) 78-CH, 80-2D	2	5	1	1	1

	Yrs	Won	Lost	CH	2D
EASTERN KY.					
Roy Kidd (Eastern Ky. '54) 76	1	0	1	0	0
EDINBORO					
Tom Hollman (Ohio Northern '68) 89, 90, 92, 93, 95	5	1	5	0	0
ELIZABETH CITY ST.					
Johnnie Walton (Elizabeth City St. '69) 81	1	0	1	0	0
FAYETTEVILLE ST.					
Kenny Phillips (East Caro. '87) 02	1	0	1	0	0
FERRIS ST.					
Keith Otterbein (Ferris St. '79) 92, 93, 94	3	2	3	0	0
Jeff Pierce (Ferris St. '79) 95, 96	2	3	2	0	0
TOTAL	5	5	5	0	0
FORT HAYS ST.					
Bob Cortese (Colorado '67) 93, 95	2	0	2	0	0
FORT VALLEY ST.					
Doug Porter (Xavier [La.] '52) 82	1	0	1	0	0
Gerald Walker (Lincoln [Mo.] '62) 85	1	0	1	0	0
Kent Schoolfield (Florida A&M '70) 98, 99, 01	3	1	3	0	0
TOTAL	5	1	5	0	0
GLENVILLE ST.					
Warren Ruggerio (Delaware '88) 97	1	0	1	0	0
GRAMBLING					
Eddie Robinson (Leland '41) 73	1	1	1	0	0
GRAND VALLEY ST.					
Tom Beck (Northern Ill. '61) 89, 90	2	0	2	0	0
Brian Kelly (Assumption '83) 91, 94, 98, 01-2D, 02-CH	5	7	4	1	1
TOTAL	7	7	6	1	1
HAMPTON					
Fred Freeman (Mississippi Val. '66) 85	1	0	1	0	0
Joe Taylor (Western Ill. '72) 92, 93	2	1	2	0	0
TOTAL	3	1	3	0	0
INDIANA (PA.)					
Frank Cignetti (Indiana [Pa.] '60) 87, 88, 89, 90-2D, 91, 93-2D, 94, 96, 98, 99, 00, 01, 02	13	15	13	0	2
JACKSONVILLE ST.					
Jim Fuller (Alabama '67) 77-2D, 78, 80, 81, 82	5	3	5	0	1
Bill Burgess (Auburn '63) 88, 89-2D, 90, 91-2D, 92-CH	5	12	4	1	2
TOTAL	10	15	9	1	3
LEHIGH					
Fred Dunlap (Colgate '50) 73, 75	2	0	2	0	0
John Whitehead (East Stroudsburg '50) 77-CH	1	3	0	1	0
TOTAL	3	3	2	1	0
LOUISIANA TECH					
Maxie Lambright (Southern Miss. '49) 73-CH, 74	2	4	1	1	0
MASSACHUSETTS					
Dick MacPherson (Springfield '58) 77	1	0	1	0	0
MESA ST.					
Joe Ramunno (Wyoming '85) 00	1	1	1	0	0
MILLERSVILLE					
Gene Carpenter (Huron '63) 88, 95, 99	3	2	3	0	0
MINN. DULUTH					
Bob Nielson (Wartburg '82) 02	1	0	1	0	0
MINN. ST. MANKATO					
Dan Runkle (Illinois Col. '68) 87, 91, 93	3	2	3	0	0
MISSISSIPPI COL.*					
John Williams (Mississippi Col. '57) 79, 88, 89-CH, 90	4	7	3	1	0
Terry McMillan (Southern Miss. '69) 91	1	1	1	0	0
TOTAL	5	8	4	1	0
MO. SOUTHERN ST.					
Jon Lantz (Okla. Panhandle '74) 93	1	0	1	0	0
MONTANA ST.					
Sonny Holland (Montana St. '60) 76-CH	1	3	0	1	0
MORGAN ST.					
Clarence Thomas 79	1	0	1	0	0
NEB.-KEARNEY					
Darrell Morris (Northwest Mo. St. '83) 02	1	0	1	0	0
NEB.-OMAHA					
Sandy Buda (Kansas '67) 78, 84	2	1	2	0	0
Pat Behrns (Dakota St. '72) 96, 98, 00, 01	4	1	4	0	0
TOTAL	6	2	6	0	0
UNLV					
Ron Meyer (Purdue '63) 74	1	1	1	0	0

	Yrs	Won	Lost	CH	2D
Tony Knap (Idaho '39) 76	1	0	1	0	0
TOTAL	2	1	2	0	0
NEW HAMPSHIRE					
Bill Bowes (Penn St. '65) 75, 76	2	1	2	0	0
NEW HAVEN					
Mark Whipple (Brown '79) 92, 93	2	3	2	0	0
Tony Sparano (New Haven '82) 95, 97-2D	2	4	2	0	1
TOTAL	4	7	4	0	1
NORFOLK ST.					
Willard Bailey (Norfolk St. '62) 84	1	0	1	0	0
NORTH ALA.					
Wayne Grubb (Tennessee '61) 80, 83, 85-2D	3	4	3	0	1
Bobby Wallace (Mississippi St. '76) 90, 92, 93-CH, 94-CH, 95-CH, 97	6	13	3	3	0
TOTAL	9	17	6	3	1
N.C. CENTRAL					
Henry Lattimore (Jackson St. '57) 88	1	0	1	0	0
NORTH DAKOTA					
Jerry Olson (Valley City St. '55) 75	1	0	1	0	0
Gene Murphy (North Dakota '62) 79	1	0	1	0	0
Roger Thomas (Augustana [Ill.] '69) 92, 93, 94, 95, 98	5	4	5	0	0
Dale Lennon (North Dakota '85) 99, 01-CH	2	4	1	1	0
TOTAL	9	8	8	1	0
NORTH DAKOTA ST.					
Jim Wacker (Valparaiso '60) 76, 77	2	2	2	0	0
Don Morton (Augustana [Ill.] '69) 81-2D, 82, 83-CH, 84-2D	4	8	3	1	2
Earle Solomonson (Augsburg '69) 85-CH, 86-CH	2	6	0	2	0
Rocky Hager (Minot St. '74) 88-CH, 89, 90-CH, 91, 92, 94, 95	7	12	5	2	0
Bob Babich (Tulsa '84) 97, 00	2	2	2	0	0
TOTAL	17	30	12	5	2
NORTHEASTERN ST.					
Tom Eckert (Northeastern St. '66) 99, 00	2	2	2	0	0
NORTHERN ARIZ.					
Joe Salem (Minnesota '61) 77	1	0	1	0	0
NORTHERN COLO.					
Bob Blasi (Colorado St. '53) 80	1	0	1	0	0
Joe Glenn (South Dakota '71) 90, 91, 95, 96-CH, 97-CH, 98, 99	7	10	5	2	0
O. Kay Dalton (Colorado St. '54) 02	1	2	1	0	0
TOTAL	9	12	7	2	0
NORTHERN IOWA					
Stan Sheriff (Cal Poly '54) 75	1	0	1	0	0
NORTHERN MICH.					
Gil Krueger (Marquette '52) 75-CH, 76, 77	3	4	2	1	0
Bill Rademacher (Northern Mich. '63) 80, 81, 82	3	1	3	0	0
Herb Grenke (Wis.-Milwaukee '63) 87	1	1	1	0	0
TOTAL	7	6	6	1	0
NORTHWEST MO. ST.					
Vern Thomsen (Peru St. '61) 84	1	0	1	0	0
Bud Elliott (Baker '53) 89	1	0	1	0	0
Mel Tjeerdsma (Southern St. [S.D.] '67) 96, 97, 98-CH, 99-CH, 00, 02	6	11	4	2	0
TOTAL	8	11	6	2	0
NORTHWOOD					
Pat Riepma (Hillsdale '83) 00	1	1	1	0	0
PITTSBURG ST.					
Dennis Franchione (Pittsburg St. '73) 89	1	1	1	0	0
Chuck Broyles (Pittsburg St. '70) 90, 91-CH, 92-2D, 93, 94, 95-2D, 96, 97, 99, 00, 01	11	13	10	1	2
TOTAL	12	14	11	1	2
PORTLAND ST.					
Pokey Allen (Utah '65) 87-2D, 88-2D, 89, 91, 92	5	10	5	0	2
Tim Walsh (UC Riverside '77) 93, 94, 95	3	2	3	0	0
TOTAL	8	12	8	0	2
PUGET SOUND					
Ron Simonson (Portland St. '65) 81	1	0	1	0	0
SACRAMENTO ST.					
Bob Mattos (Sacramento St. '64) 88	1	2	1	0	0
SAGINAW VALLEY					
Randy Awrey (Northern Mich. '78) 00, 01, 02	3	1	3	0	0
ST. CLOUD ST.					
Noel Martin (Nebraska '63) 89	1	1	1	0	0

	Yrs	Won	Lost	CH	2D
SANTA CLARA					
Pat Malley (Santa Clara '53) 80	1	1	1	0	0
SAVANNAH ST.					
Bill Davis (Johnson Smith '65) 92	1	0	1	0	0
SHEPHERD					
Monte Cater (Millikin '71) 98, 99	2	1	2	0	0
SHIPPENSBURG					
Vito Ragazzo (William & Mary '51) 81	1	1	1	0	0
Rocky Rees (West Chester '71) 91	1	1	1	0	0
TOTAL	2	2	2	0	0
SLIPPERY ROCK					
George Mahalik (Slippery Rock '74) 97, 98, 99.	3	3	3	0	0
SOUTH DAKOTA					
Joe Salem (Minnesota '61) 73	1	0	1	0	0
Dave Triplett (Iowa '72) 85, 86-2D	2	3	2	0	1
TOTAL	3	3	3	0	1
SOUTH DAKOTA ST.					
John Gregory (Northern Iowa '61) 79	1	0	1	0	0
SOUTHERN ARK.					
Steve Roberts (Ouachita Baptist '87) 97	1	0	1	0	0
SOUTHWEST TEX. ST.					
Jim Wacker (Valparaiso '60) 81-CH, 82-CH	2	6	0	2	0
John O'Hara (Okla. Panhandle '67) 83	1	0	1	0	0
TOTAL	3	6	1	2	0
TARLETON ST.					
Todd Whitten (Stephen F. Austin '87) 01	1	1	1	0	0
TENN.-MARTIN					
Don McLeary (Tennessee '70) 88	1	1	1	0	0
TEX. A&M-COMMERCE					
Eddie Vowell (Southwestern Okla. '69) 90, 91, 95	3	2	3	0	0
TEX. A&M-KINGSVILLE#					
Ron Harms (Valparaiso '59) 88, 89, 92, 93, 94-2D, 95, 96, 97, 98	9	12	9	0	1
Richard Cundiff (Lincoln Mem. '73) 01, 02	2	2	2	0	0
TOTAL	11	14	11	0	1
TOWSON					
Phil Albert (Arizona '66) 83, 84, 86	3	1	3	0	0
TROY ST.					
Chan Gailey (Florida '74) 84-CH	1	3	0	1	0
Rick Rhoades 86, 87-CH	2	4	1	1	0
TOTAL	3	7	1	2	0
TRUMAN					
Bruce Craddock (Truman '66) 82	1	0	1	0	0
Eric Holm (Truman '81) 90, 92, 94	3	0	3	0	0
TOTAL	4	0	4	0	0

	Yrs	Won	Lost	CH	2D
VALDOSTA ST.					
Hal Mumme (Tarleton St. '75) 94, 96	2	2	2	0	0
Chris Hatcher (Valdosta St. '95) 00, 01, 02-2D ..	3	4	3	0	1
TOTAL	5	6	5	0	1
VIRGINIA UNION					
Willard Bailey (Norfolk St. '62) 79, 80, 81, 82, 83	5	0	5	0	0
Joe Taylor (Western Ill. '72) 86, 90, 91	3	0	3	0	0
TOTAL	8	0	8	0	0
WEST ALA.					
Jim King 75	1	1	1	0	0
WEST CHESTER					
Danny Hale (West Chester '68) 88	1	0	1	0	0
Rick Daniels (West Chester '75) 89, 92, 94	3	0	3	0	0
TOTAL	4	0	4	0	0
WEST GA.					
Charlie Fisher (Springfield '81) 95, 96	2	0	2	0	0
Glenn Spencer (Georgia Tech '86) 98, 00	2	0	2	0	0
TOTAL	4	0	4	0	0
WESTERN CARO.					
Bob Waters (Presbyterian '60) 74	1	0	1	0	0
WESTERN ILL.					
Darrell Mudra (Peru St. '51) 73	1	0	1	0	0
WESTERN KY.					
Jimmy Feix (Western Ky. '53) 73-2D, 75-2D	2	4	2	0	2
WESTERN ST.					
Carl Iverson (Whitman '62) 92, 94, 97	3	0	3	0	0
WESTERN WASH.					
Rob Smith (Washington '81) 99	1	0	1	0	0
WINONA ST.					
Tom Sawyer (Winona St. '83) 01	1	0	1	0	0
WINSTON-SALEM					
Bill Hayes (N.C. Central '64) 78, 87	2	1	2	0	0
Pete Richardson (Dayton '68) 88, 90, 91	3	0	3	0	0
TOTAL	5	1	5	0	0
WOFFORD					
Mike Ayers (Georgetown [Ky.] '74) 90, 91	2	0	2	0	0
YOUNGSTOWN ST.					
Rey Dempsey (Geneva '58) 74	1	0	1	0	0
Bill Narduzzi (Miami [Ohio] '59) 78, 79-2D	2	3	2	0	1
TOTAL	3	3	3	0	1

*Mississippi College's competition in the 1989 and 1990 Division II championships was vacated by action of the NCAA Committee on Infractions (record was 6-1). #Texas A&M-Kingsville's participation in the 1996, 1997 and 1998 Division II championships was vacated by action of the NCAA Committee on Infractions (record was 2-3).

Division II Championship Team Leaders

MOST APPEARANCES
UC Davis	18
North Dakota St.	17
Indiana (Pa.)	13
Pittsburg St.	12
Jacksonville St. #	10

MOST VICTORIES
North Dakota St.	30
North Ala.	17
Jacksonville St. #	15
UC Davis	15
Indiana (Pa.)	15
Pittsburg St.	14
Tex. A&M-Kingsville	14

MOST CONSECUTIVE APPEARANCES
9	Pittsburg St.	1989-97
7	UC Davis	1996-present
7	Carson-Newman	1993-99
6	North Dakota St.	1981-86

HIGHEST WINNING PERCENTAGE
(Min. 10 Games Played)
North Dakota St.	17-6	.739
North Dakota St.	30-12	.714
Northwest Mo. St.	11-6	.647
Delaware#	7-4	.636
New Haven	7-4	.636

#No longer a Division II member.

CHAMPIONSHIP RESULTS

All-Time Results

1973 First Round: Grambling 17, Delaware 8; Western Ky. 25, Lehigh 16; Louisiana Tech 18, Western Ill. 13; Boise St. 53, South Dakota 10. **Semifinals:** Western Ky. 28, Grambling 20; Louisiana Tech 38, Boise St. 34. **Championship:** Louisiana Tech 34, Western Ky. 0.

1974 First Round: Central Mich. 20, Boise St. 6; Louisiana Tech 10, Western Caro. 7; UNLV 35, Alcorn St. 22; Delaware 35, Youngstown St. 14. **Semifinals:** Central Mich. 35, Louisiana Tech 14; Delaware 49, UNLV 11. **Championship:** Central Mich. 54, Delaware 14.

1975 First Round: Northern Mich. 24, Boise St. 21; West Ala. 34, North Dakota 14; Western Ky. 14, Northern Iowa 12; New Hampshire 35, Lehigh 21. **Semifinals:** Northern Mich. 28, West Ala. 26; Western Ky. 14, New Hampshire 3. **Championship:** Northern Mich. 16, Western Ky. 14.

1976 First Round: Akron 26, UNLV 6; Northern Mich. 28, Delaware 17; North Dakota St. 10, Eastern Ky. 7; Montana St. 17, New Hampshire 16. **Semifinals:** Akron 29, Northern Mich. 26; Montana St. 10, North Dakota St. 3. **Championship:** Montana St. 24, Akron 13.

1977 First Round: UC Davis 34, Bethune-Cookman 16; Lehigh 30, Massachusetts 23; North Dakota St. 20, Northern Mich. 6; Jacksonville St. 35, Northern Ariz. 0. **Semifinals:** Lehigh 39, UC Davis 30; Jacksonville St. 31, North Dakota St. 7. **Championship:** Lehigh 33, Jacksonville St. 0.

1978 First Round: Winston-Salem 17, Cal Poly 0; Delaware 42, Jacksonville St. 27; Youngstown St. 21, Neb.-Omaha 14; Eastern Ill. 35, UC Davis 31. **Semifinals:** Delaware 41, Winston-Salem 0; Eastern Ill. 26, Youngstown St. 22. **Championship:** Eastern Ill. 10, Delaware 9.

1979 First Round: Delaware 58, Virginia Union 28; Mississippi Col. 35, North Dakota 15; Youngstown St. 50, South Dakota St. 7; Alabama A&M 27, Morgan St. 7. **Semifinals:** Delaware 60, Mississippi Col. 10; Youngstown St. 52, Alabama A&M 0. **Championship:** Delaware 38, Youngstown St. 21.

1980 First Round: Eastern Ill. 21, Northern Colo. 14; North Ala. 17, Virginia Union 8; Santa Clara 27, Northern Mich. 26; Cal Poly 15, Jacksonville St. 0. **Semifinals:** Eastern Ill. 56, North Ala. 31; Cal Poly 38, Santa Clara 14. **Championship:** Cal Poly 21, Eastern Ill. 13.

1981 First Round: Northern Mich. 55, Elizabeth City St. 6; Southwest Tex. St. 38, Jacksonville St. 22; North Dakota St. 24, Puget Sound 10; Shippensburg 40, Virginia Union 27. **Semifinals:** Southwest Tex. St. 62, Northern Mich. 0; North Dakota St. 18, Shippensburg 6. **Championship:** Southwest Tex. St. 42, North Dakota St. 13.

1982 First Round: Southwest Tex. St. 27, Fort Valley St. 6; Jacksonville St. 34, Truman 21; North Dakota St. 21, Virginia Union 20; UC Davis 42, Northern Mich. 21. **Semifinals:** Southwest Tex. St. 19, Jacksonville St. 14; UC Davis 19, North Dakota St. 14. **Championship:** Southwest Tex. St. 34, UC Davis 9.

1983 First Round: UC Davis 25, Butler 6; North Dakota St. 24, Towson 17; North Ala. 16, Virginia Union 14; Central St. 24, Southwest Tex. St. 16. **Semifinals:** North Dakota St. 26, UC Davis 17; Central St. 27, North Ala. 24. **Championship:** North Dakota St. 41, Central St. 21.

1984 First Round: North Dakota St. 31, UC Davis 23; Neb.-Omaha 28, Northwest Mo. St. 15; Troy St. 31, Central St. 21; Towson 31, Norfolk St. 21. **Semifinals:** North Dakota St. 25, Neb.-Omaha 14; Troy St. 45, Towson 3. **Championship:** Troy St. 18, North Dakota St. 17.

1985 First Round: North Dakota St. 31, UC Davis 12; South Dakota 13, Central St. 10 (2 ot); Bloomsburg 38, Hampton 28; North Ala. 14, Fort Valley St. 7. **Semifinals:** North Dakota St. 16, South Dakota 7; North Ala. 34, Bloomsburg 0. **Championship:** North Dakota St. 35, North Ala. 7.

1986 First Round: North Dakota St. 50, Ashland 0; Central St. 31, Towson 0; Troy St. 31, Virginia Union 7; South Dakota 26, UC Davis 23. **Semifinals:** North Dakota St. 35, Central St. 12; South Dakota 42, Troy St. 28. **Championship:** North Dakota St. 27, South Dakota 7.

1987 First Round: Portland St. 27, Minn. St. Mankato 21; Northern Mich. 23, Angelo St. 20 (ot); UCF 12, Indiana (Pa.) 10; Troy St. 45, Winston-Salem 14. **Semifinals:** Portland St. 13, Northern Mich. 7; Troy St. 31, Central Fla. 10. **Championship:** Troy St. 31, Portland St. 17.

1988 First Round: North Dakota St. 49, Augustana (S.D.) 7; Millersville 27, Indiana (Pa.) 24; Sacramento St. 35, UC Davis 14; N.C. Central 31, Winston-Salem 16; Tex. A&M-Kingsville 39, Mississippi Col. 15; Tenn.-Martin 23, Butler 6; Portland St. 34, Bowie St. 17; Jacksonville St. 63, West Chester 24. **Quarterfinals:** North Dakota St. 36, Millersville 26; Sacramento St. 56, N.C. Central 7; Tex. A&M-Kingsville 34, Tenn.-Martin 0; Portland St. 20, Jacksonville St. 13. **Semifinals:** North Dakota St. 42, Sacramento St. 20; Portland St. 35, Tex. A&M-Kingsville 27. **Championship:** North Dakota St. 35, Portland St. 21.

1989 First Round: *Mississippi Col. 34, Tex. A&M-Kingsville 19; St. Cloud St. 27, Augustana (S.D.) 20; Portland St. 56, West Chester 50 (3 ot); Indiana (Pa.) 34, Grand Valley St. 24; Pittsburg St. 28, Northwest Mo. St. 7; Angelo St. 28, UC Davis 23; North Dakota St. 45, Edinboro 32; Jacksonville St. 33, Alabama A&M 9. **Quarterfinals:** *Mississippi Col. 55, St. Cloud St. 24; Indiana (Pa.) 17, Portland St. 0; Angelo St. 24, Pittsburg St. 21; Jacksonville St. 21, North Dakota St. 17. **Semifinals:** *Mississippi Col. 26, Indiana (Pa.) 14; Jacksonville St. 34, Angelo St. 16. **Championship:** *Mississippi Col. 3, Jacksonville St. 0.

**Mississippi College's participation vacated.*

1990 First Round: *Mississippi Col. 70, Wofford 19; Jacksonville St. 38, North Ala. 14; Indiana (Pa.) 48, Winston-Salem 0; Edinboro 38, Virginia Union 14; North Dakota St. 17, Northern Colo. 7; Cal Poly 14, Cal St. Northridge 7; Pittsburg St. 59, Truman 3; Tex. A&M-Commerce 20, Grand Valley St. 14. **Quarterfinals:** *Mississippi Col. 14, Jacksonville St. 7; Indiana (Pa.) 14, Edinboro 7; North Dakota St. 47, Cal Poly 0; Pittsburg St. 60, Tex. A&M-Commerce 28. **Semifinals:** Indiana (Pa.) 27, *Mississippi Col. 8; North Dakota St. 39, Pittsburg St. 29. **Championship:** North Dakota St. 51, Indiana (Pa.) 11.

**Mississippi College's participation vacated.*

1991 First Round: Pittsburg St. 26, Butler 16; Tex. A&M-Commerce 36, Grand Valley St. 15; Portland St. 28, Northern Colo. 24; Minn. St. Mankato 27, North Dakota St. 7; Jacksonville St. 49, Winston-Salem 24; Mississippi Col. 28, Wofford 15; Indiana (Pa.) 56, Virginia Union 7; Shippensburg 34, East Stroudsburg 33 (ot). **Quarterfinals:** Pittsburg St. 38, Tex. A&M-Commerce 28; Portland St. 37, Minn. St. Mankato 27; Jacksonville St. 35, Mississippi Col. 7; Indiana (Pa.) 52, Shippensburg 7. **Semifinals:** Pittsburg St. 53, Portland St. 21; Jacksonville St. 27, Indiana (Pa.) 20. **Championship:** Pittsburg St. 23, Jacksonville St. 6.

1992 First Round: Ferris St. 19, Edinboro 15; New Haven 38, West Chester 26; Jacksonville St. 41, Savannah St. 16; North Ala. 33, Hampton 21; Tex. A&M-Kingsville 22, Western St. 13; Portland St. 42, UC Davis 28; Pittsburg St. 26, North Dakota 21; North Dakota St. 42, Truman 7. **Quarterfinals:** New Haven 35, Ferris St. 13; Jacksonville St. 14, North Ala. 12; Portland St. 35, Tex. A&M-Kingsville 30; Pittsburg St. 38, North Dakota St. 37 (ot). **Semifinals:** Jacksonville St. 46, New Haven 35; Pittsburg St. 41, Portland St. 38. **Championship:** Jacksonville St. 17, Pittsburg St. 13.

1993 First Round: North Ala. 38, Carson-Newman 28; Hampton 33, Albany St. (Ga.) 7; Tex. A&M-Kingsville 50, Portland St. 15; UC Davis 37, Fort Hays St. 34; Minn. St. Mankato 34, Mo. Southern St. 13; North Dakota 17, Pittsburg St. 14; New Haven 48, Edinboro 28; Indiana (Pa.) 28, Ferris St. 21. **Quarterfinals:** North Ala. 45, Hampton 20; Tex. A&M-Kingsville 51, UC Davis 28; North Dakota 54, Minn. St. Mankato 21; Indiana (Pa.) 38, New Haven 35. **Semifinals:** North Ala. 27, Tex. A&M-Kingsville 25; Indiana (Pa.) 21, North Dakota 6. **Championship:** North Ala. 41, Indiana (Pa.) 34.

1994 First Round: Ferris St. 43, West Chester 40; Indiana (Pa.) 35, Grand Valley St. 27; Tex. A&M-Kingsville 43, Western St. 7; Portland St. 29, Angelo St. 0; North Dakota St. 18, Pittsburg St. 12 (3 ot); North Dakota 18, Truman 6; North Ala. 17, Carson-Newman 13; Valdosta St. 14, Albany St. (Ga.) 7. **Quarterfinals:** Indiana (Pa.) 21, Ferris St. 17; Tex. A&M-Kingsville 21, Portland St. 16; North Dakota 14, North Dakota St. 7; North Ala. 27, Valdosta St. 24 (2 ot). **Semifinals:** Tex. A&M-Kingsville 46, Indiana (Pa.) 20; North Ala. 35, North Dakota 7. **Championship:** North Ala. 16, Tex. A&M-Kingsville 10.

1995 First Round: Ferris St. 36, Millersville 26; New Haven 27, Edinboro 12; North Ala. 38, Albany St. (Ga.) 28; Carson-Newman 37, West Ga. 26; Pittsburg St. 36, Northern Colo. 17; North Dakota St. 41, North Dakota 10; Tex. A&M-Kingsville 59, Fort Hays St. 28; Portland St. 56, Tex. A&M-Commerce 35. **Quarterfinals:** Ferris St. 17, New Haven 9; North Ala. 28, Carson-Newman 7; Pittsburg St. 9, North Dakota St. 7; Tex. A&M-Kingsville 30, Portland St. 3. **Semifinals:** North Ala. 45, Ferris St. 7; Pittsburg St. 28, Tex. A&M-Kingsville 25 (ot). **Championship:** North Ala. 27, Pittsburg St. 7.

1996 First Round: Clarion 42, Bloomsburg 29; Ferris St. 24, Indiana (Pa.) 23; Northern Colo. 24, Pittsburg St. 21; Northwest Mo. St. 22, Neb.-Omaha 21; Valdosta St. 38, Albany St. (Ga.) 28; Carson-Newman 41, West Ga. 7; Central Okla. 23, Chadron St. 21; UC Davis 17, *Tex. A&M-Kingsville 14. **Quarterfinals:** Clarion 23, Ferris St. 21; Northern Colo. 27, Northwest Mo. St. 26; Carson-Newman 24, Valdosta St. 19; UC Davis 26, Central Okla. 7. **Semifinals:** Northern Colo. 19, Clarion 18; Carson-Newman 29, UC Davis 26. **Championship:** Northern Colo. 23, Carson-Newman 14.

**Tex. A&M-Kingsville's participation vacated.*

1997 First Round: UC Davis 37, *Tex. A&M-Kingsville 34; Angelo St. 46, Western St. 12; New Haven 47, Glenville St. 7; Slippery Rock 30, Ashland 20; Northwest Mo. St. 39, North Dakota St. 28; Northern Colo. 24, Pittsburg St. 16; Carson-Newman 21, North Ala. 7; Albany St. (Ga.) 10, Southern Ark. 6. **Quarterfinals:** UC Davis 50, Angelo St. 33; New Haven 49, Slippery Rock 21; Northern Colo. 35, Northwest Mo. St. 19; Carson-Newman 23, Albany St. (Ga.) 22. **Semifinals:** New Haven 27, UC Davis 25; Northern Colo. 30, Carson-Newman 29. **Championship:** Northern Colo. 51, New Haven 0.

**Tex. A&M-Kingsville's participation vacated.*

1998 First Round: Carson-Newman 30, West Ga. 20; Fort Valley St. 21, Delta St. 14; Slippery Rock 37, Grand Valley St. 14; Shepherd 9, Indiana (Pa.) 6; Northwest Mo. St. 28, Neb.-Omaha 14; Northern Colo. 52, North Dakota 24; Central Okla. 21, Chadron St. 19; *Tex. A&M-Kingsville 54, UC Davis 21. **Quarterfinals:** Carson-Newman 38, Fort Valley St. 31 (ot); Slippery Rock 31, Shepherd 20; Northwest Mo. St. 42, Northern Colo. 17; *Tex. A&M-Kingsville 24, Central Okla. 21 (ot). **Semifinals:** Carson-Newman 47, Slippery Rock 21; Northwest Mo. St. 49, *Tex. A&M-Kingsville 34. **Championship:** Northwest Mo. St. 24, Carson-Newman 6.

**Tex. A&M-Kingsville's participation vacated.*

1999 First Round: Carson-Newman 40, Arkansas Tech 28; Catawba 48, Fort Valley St. 17; UC Davis 33, Central Okla. 17; Northeastern St. 27, Western Wash. 24 (ot); Indiana (Pa.) 27, Slippery Rock 20 (ot); Millersville 21, Shepherd 14; Northern Colo. 34, Pittsburg St. 31; Northwest Mo. St. 20, North Dakota 13 (ot). **Quarterfinals:** Carson-Newman 28, Catawba 25; Northeastern St. 19, UC Davis 14; Indiana (Pa.) 26, Millersville 21; Northwest Mo. St. 41, Northern Colo. 35. **Semifinals:** Carson-Newman 42, Northeastern St. 7; Northwest Mo. St. 20, Indiana (Pa.) 12. **Championship:** Northwest Mo. St. 58, Carson-Newman 52 (4 ot).

2000 First Round: North Dakota St., 31, Northwest Mo. St. 17; Neb.-Omaha 14, Pittsburg St. 3; Catawba 28, West Ga. 24; Delta St. 49, Valdosta St. 12; Northwood 28, Indiana (Pa.) 0; Bloomsburg 46, Saginaw Valley 32; UC Davis 48, Chadron St. 10; Mesa St. 40, Northeastern St. 21. **Quarterfinals:** North Dakota St. 43, Neb.-Omaha 21; Delta St. 20, Catawba 14; Bloomsburg 38, Northwood 14; UC Davis 62, Mesa St. 18. **Semifinals:** Delta St. 34, North Dakota St. 16; Bloomsburg 58, UC Davis 48. **Championship:** Delta St. 63, Bloomsburg 34.

2001 First Round: North Dakota 42, Winona St. 28; Pittsburg St. 20, Neb.-Omaha 7; Tarleton St. 28, Chadron St. 24; UC Davis 37, Tex. A&M-Kingsville 32; Valdosta St. 40, Fort Valley St. 24; Catawba 35, Central Ark. 34; Grand Valley St. 42, Bloomsburg 14; Saginaw Valley 33, Indiana (Pa.) 32. **Quarterfinals:** North Dakota 38, Pittsburg St. 0; UC Davis 42, Tarleton St. 25; Catawba 37, Valdosta St. 34 (ot); Grand Valley St. 33, Saginaw Valley 30. **Semifinals:** North Dakota 14, UC Davis 2; Grand Valley St. 34, Catawba 16. **Championship:** North Dakota 17, Grand Valley St. 14.

2002 First Round: Valdosta St. 24, Catawba 7; Carson-Newman 40, Fayetteville St. 27; UC Davis 24, Central Wash. 6; Tex. A&M-Kingsville 58, Neb.-Kearney 40; Grand Valley St. 62, C.W. Post 13; Indiana (Pa.) 27, Saginaw Valley 23; Northwest Mo. St. 45, Minn. Duluth 41; Northern Colo. 49, Central Mo. St. 28. **Quarterfinals:** Valdosta St. 31, Carson-Newman 28; Tex. A&M-Kingsville 27, UC Davis 20 (ot); Grand Valley St. 62, Indiana (Pa.) 21; Northern Colo. 23, Northwest Mo. St. 12. **Semifinals:** Valdosta St. 21, Tex. A&M-Kingsville 12; Grand Valley St. 44, Northern Colo. 7. **Championship:** Grand Valley St. 31, Valdosta St. 24.

Division III Championship

2002 Title Game Summary

More for Mount Union: The pedestal on which Mount Union sits was made even higher as the Purple Raiders won their third straight championship, defeating Trinity (Texas), 48-7 in the Amos Alonzo Stagg Bowl.

Mount Union took over the all-divisions lead in NCAA football championships after capturing its seventh title, all coming since 1993. Georgia Southern has won the Division I-AA championship six times.

Dan Pugh, who was voted the game's Most Valuable Player, set Stagg Bowl records for points scored (26) and rushing attempts (49). He gained 253 yards, scored four touchdowns and added a two-point conversion.

Pugh also established new Division III tournament highs for points scored with 92 and touchdowns with 15. His 41 touchdowns on the year sets an NCAA all-divisions single-season mark, surpassing Barry Sanders' previous record of 39 in 1988 while at Oklahoma State.

Mount Union quarterback Rob Adamson completed 12 of 23 pases for 222 yards and three touchdowns. Randell Knapp had a team-high four catches for 58 yards, and both of Derrick Leach's receptions went for touchdowns.

Justin Burton finished with a team-high seven tackles and added an interception for Mount Union, while Chris Carter had six tackles and one sack.

Dan DesPlaines threw an 18-yard touchdown pass to B.J. Smith for Trinity's only score. Jeremy Boyce rushed 15 times for 93 yards for the Tigers, who suffered their first defeat after 14 victories.

The victory extended Mount Union's winning streak to 42 games after a 14-0 season. The Purple Raiders have won 96 of their last 97 games and have a .955 winning percentage (162-17-1) since 1990.

Dan Pugh (31) heads outside on one of his Stagg Bowl-record 49 rushing attempts. Pugh scored four touchdowns as Mount Union won its third consecutive championship with a 48-7 win over Trinity (Texas).

Andres Alonzo/NCAA Photos

SALEM STADIUM, SALEM, VIRGINIA; DECEMBER 21

	Mount Union	Trinity (Tex.)
First downs	27	11
Rushes-yards	59-268	29-117
Passing yardage	222	86
Passes (comp.-att.-int.)	12-23-0	9-18-1
Punts (no.-avg.)	1-22.0	5-29.4
Fumbles (no.-lost)	3-0	1-0
Penalties (no.-yards)	7-90	3-30
Time of possession	38:29	21:31
Mount Union	7 21	7 13—48
Trinity (Tex.)	0 0	7 0— 7

FIRST QUARTER
Mount Union—Dan Pugh 19 run (Chad Teague kick) (8:32)

SECOND QUARTER
Mount Union—Randell Knapp 9 pass from Rob Adamson (kick blocked) (10:27)
Mount Union—Derrick Leach 19 pass from Adamson (Pugh run) (3:13)
Mount Union—Pugh 2 run (Teague kick) (0:24)

THIRD QUARTER
Trinity (Tex.)—B.J. Smith 18 pass from Dan DesPlaines (Todd Canion kick) (7:59)
Mount Union—Pugh 1 run (Teague kick) (1:08)

FOURTH QUARTER
Mount Union—Pugh 2 run (kick failed) (12:57)
Mount Union—Leach 55 pass from Adamson (Teague kick) (10:38)

INDIVIDUAL LEADERS
Rushing: Mount Union—Pugh 49-253; Zac Bruney 4-18; Jeff Strauch 1-3; Jesse Burghardt 2-3; Rick Ciccone 1-0; Adamson 2-(minus 9); Trinity (Tex.)—Jeremy Boyce 15-93; Jason Hunt 1-24; Matt Federle 2-4; Jerheme Urban 2-0; Dan DesPlaines 9-(minus 4).
Passing: Mount Union—Adamson 12-23-0-222; Trinity (Tex.)—DesPlaines 9-18-1-86.
Receiving: Mount Union—Knapp 4-58, Josh Liddell 3-34, Leach 2-74, Nick Sirianni 2-52, Pugh 1-4; Trinity (Tex.)—Urban 3-19, Hunt 2-35, Boyce 2-5, Smith 1-18; Jacob Respondek 1-9.

Division III All-Time Championship Results

Year	Champion	Coach	Score	Runner-Up	Site
1973	Wittenberg	Dave Maurer	41-0	Juniata	Phenix City, Ala.
1974	Central (Iowa)	Ron Schipper	10-8	Ithaca	Phenix City, Ala.
1975	Wittenberg	Dave Maurer	28-0	Ithaca	Phenix City, Ala.
1976	St. John's (Minn.)	John Gagliardi	31-28	Towson	Phenix City, Ala.
1977	Widener	Bill Manlove	39-36	Wabash	Phenix City, Ala.
1978	Baldwin-Wallace	Lee Tressel	24-10	Wittenberg	Phenix City, Ala.
1979	Ithaca	Jim Butterfield	14-10	Wittenberg	Phenix City, Ala.
1980	Dayton	Rick Carter	63-0	Ithaca	Phenix City, Ala.
1981	Widener	Bill Manlove	17-10	Dayton	Phenix City, Ala.
1982	West Ga.	Bobby Pate	14-0	Augustana (Ill.)	Phenix City, Ala.
1983	Augustana (Ill.)	Bob Reade	21-17	Union (N.Y.)	Kings Island, Ohio
1984	Augustana (Ill.)	Bob Reade	21-12	Central (Iowa)	Kings Island, Ohio
1985	Augustana (Ill.)	Bob Reade	20-7	Ithaca	Phenix City, Ala.
1986	Augustana (Ill.)	Bob Reade	31-3	Salisbury	Phenix City, Ala.
1987	Wagner	Walt Hameline	19-3	Dayton	Phenix City, Ala.
1988	Ithaca	Jim Butterfield	39-24	Central (Iowa)	Phenix City, Ala.
1989	Dayton	Mike Kelly	17-7	Union (N.Y.)	Phenix City, Ala.
1990	Allegheny	Ken O'Keefe	21-14 (OT)	Lycoming	Bradenton, Fla.
1991	Ithaca	Jim Butterfield	34-20	Dayton	Bradenton, Fla.
1992	Wis.-La Crosse	Roger Harring	16-12	Wash. & Jeff.	Bradenton, Fla.

Year	Champion	Coach	Score	Runner-Up	Site
1993	Mount Union	Larry Kehres	34-24	Rowan	Salem, Va.
1994	Albion	Pete Schmidt	38-15	Wash. & Jeff.	Salem, Va.
1995	Wis.-La Crosse	Roger Harring	36-7	Rowan	Salem, Va.
1996	Mount Union	Larry Kehres	56-24	Rowan	Salem, Va.
1997	Mount Union	Larry Kehres	61-12	Lycoming	Salem, Va.
1998	Mount Union	Larry Kehres	44-24	Rowan	Salem, Va.
1999	Pacific Lutheran	Frosty Westering	42-13	Rowan	Salem, Va.
2000	Mount Union	Larry Kehres	10-7	St. John's (Minn.)	Salem, Va.
2001	Mount Union	Larry Kehres	30-27	Bridgewater (Va.)	Salem, Va.
2002	Mount Union	Larry Kehres	48-7	Trinity (Tex.)	Salem, Va.

Regional Championship Results

(Before Division III Championship)

EAST (KNUTE ROCKNE BOWL)

Year	Champion	Coach	Score	Runner-Up	Site
1969	Randolph-Macon	Ted Keller	47-28	Bridgeport	Bridgeport, Conn.
1970	Montclair St.	Clary Anderson	7-6	Hampden-Sydney	Atlantic City, N.J.
1971	Bridgeport	Ed Farrell	17-12	Hampden-Sydney	Atlantic City, N.J.
1972	Bridgeport	Ed Farrell	27-22	Slippery Rock	Atlantic City, N.J.

WEST (AMOS ALONZO STAGG BOWL)

Year	Champion	Coach	Score	Runner-Up	Site
1969	Wittenberg	Dave Maurer	27-21	William Jewell	Springfield, Ohio
1970	Capital	Gene Slaughter	34-21	Luther	Columbus, Ohio
1971	Samford*		20-10	Ohio Wesleyan	Phenix City, Ala.
1972	Heidelberg	Pete Riesen	28-16	Fort Valley St.	Phenix City, Ala.

Samford's participation in the Amos Alonzo Stagg Bowl vacated by the NCAA Committee on Infractions.

2002 Division III Championship Results

FIRST ROUND
Wheaton (Ill.) 42, Alma 14
Wittenberg 34, Hanover 33
Wabash 42, MacMurray 7
Brockport St. 16, Springfield 0
John Carroll 27, Hobart 7
Muhlenberg 56, Mass.-Dartmouth 6
Wartburg 45, Lake Forest 0
Coe 21, Wis.-La Crosse 18
St. John's (Minn.) 31, Redlands 24
King's (Pa.) 28, Salisbury 0
Wash. & Jeff. 24, Chris. Newport 10
Trinity (Tex.) 48, Mary Hardin-Baylor 38

SECOND ROUND
Mount Union 42, Wheaton (Ill.) 21
Wabash 25, Wittenberg 14
Brockport St. 15, Rowan 12
John Carroll 21, Muhlenberg 10
Linfield 52, Wartburg 15
St. John's (Minn.) 45, Coe 14
Bridgewater (Va.) 19, King's (Pa.) 17
Trinity (Tex.) 45, Wash. & Jeff. 10

QUARTERFINALS
Mount Union 45, Wabash 16
John Carroll 16, Brockport St. 10 (ot)
St. John's (Minn.) 21, Linfield 14
Trinity (Tex.) 38, Bridgewater (Va.) 32

SEMIFINALS
Mount Union 57, John Carroll 19
Trinity (Tex.) 41, St. John's (Minn.) 34

CHAMPIONSHIP
Mount Union 48, Trinity (Tex.) 7

Individual Records

GAME

NET YARDS RUSHING
389—Ricky Gales, Simpson (35) vs. St. John's (Minn.) (42), 11-18-89.

RUSHES ATTEMPTED
51—Ricky Gales, Simpson (35) vs. St. John's (Minn.) (42), 11-18-89.

TOUCHDOWNS BY RUSHING
5—Jeff Norman, St. John's (Minn.) (46) vs. Augustana (Ill.) (7), 11-20-76; Mike Coppa, Salisbury (44) vs. Ithaca (40), 12-6-86; Paul Parker, Ithaca (62) vs. Ferrum (28), 12-3-88; Kevin Hofacre, Dayton (35) vs. John Carroll (10), 11-18-89; Casey Donaldson, Wittenberg (32) vs. Hanover (21), 11-25-2000; David Russell, Linfield (52) vs. Wartburg (15), 11-30-2002; Dan Pugh, Mount Union (57) vs. John Carroll (19), 12-14-2002.

NET YARDS PASSING
584—Bill Borchert, Mount Union (52) vs. Hanover (18), 11-18-95.

PASSES ATTEMPTED
67—Vic Ameye, Widener (27) vs. Lycoming (31), 11-18-95; Terry Peebles, Hanover (18) vs. Mount Union (52), 11-18-95.

PASSES COMPLETED
42—Eric Bruns, Hanover (21) vs. Wittenberg (32), 11-25-2000.

PASSES INTERCEPTED
7—Rick Steil, Dubuque (7) vs. Ithaca (27), 11-17-79; Brian Dawson, Wash. & Jeff. (42) vs. Bridgewater (Va.) (59), 11-18-2000.

TOUCHDOWN PASSES
8—Jim Ballard, Mount Union (56) vs. St. John's (Minn.) (8), 12-4-93.

COMPLETION PERCENTAGE (Min. 10 Attempts)
.900—Robb Disbennett, Salisbury (16) vs. Carnegie Mellon (14), 11-19-83 (18 of 20).

NET YARDS RUSHING AND PASSING
595—Bill Borchert, Mount Union (52) vs. Hanover (18), 11-18-95 (11 rushing, 584 passing).

RUSHING AND PASSING PLAYS
77—Terry Peebles, Hanover (18) vs. Mount Union (52), 11-18-95 (10 rushing, 67 passing).

PUNTING AVERAGE (Min. 3 Punts)
48.6—Phil Macken, Minn.-Morris (25) vs. Carnegie Mellon (31), 11-17-79 (7 for 340).

PUNTS
14—Tim Flynn, Gettysburg (14) vs. Lycoming (10), 11-23-85.

RECEPTIONS
17—Jeff Clay, Catholic (33) vs. Trinity (Tex.) (44), 11-22-97; Adam Marino, Mount Union (70) vs. Widener (30), 12-9-2000.

NET YARDS RECEIVING
265—Todd Zufra, Mount Union (52) vs. Hanover (18), 11-18-95 (16 catches).

TOUCHDOWN RECEPTIONS
4—Kirk Liesimer, Ill. Wesleyan (27) vs. Mount Union (49), 11-28-92; Rob Atwood, Mount Union (56) vs. St. John's (Minn.) (8), 12-4-93; Mike Coleman, Widener (61) vs. Springfield (27), 12-2-2000.

INTERCEPTIONS
3—John Bertino, Ithaca (27) vs. Dubuque (7), 11-17-79; Troy Westerman, Augustana (Ill.) (23) vs. Union (N.Y.) (6), 11-24-84; Mike Gray, Augustana (Ill.) (23) vs. Union (N.Y.) (6), 11-24-84; Rich Samuelson, Union (N.Y.) (17) vs. Ithaca (24) (ot), 11-22-86; Mike Gray, Augustana (Ill.) (31) vs. Salisbury (3), 12-13-86; Tom Knapp, Ithaca (39) vs. Central (Iowa) (24), 12-10-88; Bill Luette, Rowan (37) vs. Wm. Paterson (0), 11-27-93; David Lefere, Albion (19) vs. St. John's (Minn.) (16), 12-3-94; Arnell Palmer, Rowan (28) vs. Wash. & Jeff. (15), 12-2-95; Logan Ramirez, Trinity (Tex.) (40) vs. Hardin-Simmons (33), 12-4-99; Jeff Thomas, Redlands (24) vs. St. John's (Minn.) (31), 11-23-2002.

YARDS GAINED ON INTERCEPTION RETURNS
158—Beau LaBore, St. John's (Minn.) (23) vs. Wis.-Stevens Point (10), 11-20-99 (2 interceptions).

YARDS GAINED ON PUNT RETURNS
159—Blake Elliott, St. John's (Minn.) (9) vs. Wis.-Stevens Point (7), 11-24-2001 (3 returns).

YARDS GAINED ON KICKOFF RETURNS
197—Jeremy Unertl, Wis.-La Crosse (17) vs. Central (Iowa) (38), 11-20-99 (7 returns).

POINTS
36—Mike Coppa, Salisbury (44) vs. Ithaca (40), 12-6-86.

TOUCHDOWNS
6—Mike Coppa, Salisbury (44) vs. Ithaca (40), 12-6-86.

EXTRA POINTS
10—Rodney Chenos, Mount Union (70) vs. Widener (30), 12-9-2000.

TOURNAMENT

NET YARDS RUSHING
998—Chuck Moore, Mount Union, 2001 (146 vs. Augustana [Ill.], 346 vs. Wittenberg, 233 vs. St. John's [Minn.], 273 vs. Bridgewater [Va.]).

RUSHES ATTEMPTED
155—Dan Pugh, Mount Union, 2002 (36 vs. Wheaton [Ill.], 25 vs. Wabash, 45 vs. John Carroll, 49 vs. Trinity [Tex.])

NET YARDS PASSING
1,402—Bill Borchert, Mount Union, 1997 (317 vs. Allegheny, 278 vs. John Carroll, 396 vs. Simpson, 411 vs. Lycoming).

PASSES ATTEMPTED
159—Ross Denne, St. John's (Minn.), 2002 (42 vs. Redlands, 35 vs. Coe, 39 vs. Linfield, 43 vs. Trinity [Tex.]).

PASSES COMPLETED
99—Gary Smeck, Mount Union, 1998 (30 vs. Albion, 29 vs. Wittenberg, 21 vs. Trinity [Tex.], 19 vs. Rowan).

PASSES INTERCEPTED
9—Rollie Wiebers, Buena Vista, 1976 (4 vs. Carroll [Wis.], 5 vs. St. John's [Minn.]).

TOUCHDOWN PASSES
17—Jim Ballard, Mount Union, 1993 (5 vs. Allegheny, 1 vs. Albion, 8 vs. St. John's [Minn.], 3 vs. Rowan); Bill Borchert, Mount Union, 1996 (4 vs. Allegheny, 3 vs. Ill. Wesleyan, 3 vs. Wis.-La Crosse, 7 vs. Rowan).

COMPLETION PERCENTAGE (Min. 2 Games)
.696—Gary Smeck, Mount Union, 2000, 80 of 115 (24-34 vs. Ohio Northern, 14-24 vs. Wittenberg, 23-30 vs. Widener, 19-27 vs. St. John's [Minn.]).

RECEPTIONS
41—Blake Elliott, St. John's (Minn.), 2002 (9 vs. Redlands, 8 vs. Coe, 9 vs. Linfield, 15 vs. Trinity [Tex.]).

NET YARDS RECEIVING
599—Nick Ismailoff, Ithaca, 1991 (179 vs. Rowan, 122 vs. Union [N.Y.], 105 vs. Susquehanna, 193 vs. Dayton).

TOUCHDOWN RECEPTIONS
8—Mike Coleman, Widener, 2000 (2 vs. Union [N.Y.], 0 vs. Hobart, 4 vs. Springfield, 2 vs. Mount Union).

POINTS
92—Dan Pugh, Mount Union, 2002 (24 vs. Wheaton [Ill.], 12 vs. Wabash, 30 vs. John Carroll, 26 vs. Trinity [Tex.]).

TOUCHDOWNS
15—Dan Pugh, Mount Union, 2002 (4 vs. Wheaton [Ill.], 2 vs. Wabash, 5 vs. John Carroll, 4 vs. Trinity [Tex.]).

LONGEST PLAYS

RUSH
95—Chuck Moore, Mount Union (30) vs. Bridgewater (Va.) (27), 12-15-2001, TD.

PASS (INCLUDING RUN)
96—Mark Blom to Tom McDonald, Central (Iowa) (37) vs. Buena Vista (0), 11-22-86, TD.

FIELD GOAL
52—Rod Vesling, St. Lawrence (43) vs. Wagner (34), 11-20-82.

PUNT
79—Tom Hansen, Ithaca (3) vs. Wittenberg (6), 11-18-78.

PUNT RETURN
89—Blake Elliott, St. John's (Minn.) (9) vs. Wis.-Stevens Point (7), 11-24-2001, TD.

KICKOFF RETURN
100—Tom Deery, Widener (23) vs. Montclair St. (12), 11-30-81, TD.

INTERCEPTION RETURN
100—Jay Zunic, Ithaca (31) vs. Rowan (10), 11-23-91, TD; Seth Berghoff, Pacific Lutheran (41) vs. Bethel (Minn.) (13), 11-18-2000, TD.

FUMBLE RETURN
97—Liam Stull, John Carroll (27) vs. Hobart (7), 11-23-2002, TD.

Team Records

GAME

FIRST DOWNS
40—Mount Union (52) vs. Hanover (18), 11-18-95.

FIRST DOWNS BY RUSHING
30—Central (Iowa) (71) vs. Occidental (0), 12-7-85.

FIRST DOWNS BY PASSING
34—Mount Union (52) vs. Hanover (18), 11-18-95.

NET YARDS RUSHING
530—St. John's (Minn.) (46) vs. Augustana (Ill.) (7), 11-20-76.

RUSHES ATTEMPTED
83—Baldwin-Wallace (31) vs. Carnegie Mellon (6), 11-25-78; Augustana (Ill.) (33) vs. Mount Union (42), 11-27-99.

NET YARDS PASSING
614—Mount Union (52) vs. Hanover (18), 11-18-95.

PASSES ATTEMPTED
67—Hanover (18) vs. Mount Union (52), 11-18-95; Widener (27) vs. Lycoming (31), 11-18-95.

PASSES COMPLETED
42—Hanover (21) vs. Wittenberg (32), 11-25-2000.

PASSES INTERCEPTED
9—Dubuque (7) vs. Ithaca (27), 11-17-79.

COMPLETION PERCENTAGE (Min. 10 Attempts)
.857—Salisbury (16) vs. Carnegie Mellon (14), 11-19-83 (18 of 21).

NET YARDS RUSHING AND PASSING
773—Mount Union (52) vs. Hanover (18), 11-18-95 (159 rushing, 614 passing).

RUSHING AND PASSING PLAYS
101—Union (N.Y.) (45) vs. Montclair St. (6), 11-25-89 (63 rushing, 38 passing).

PUNTING AVERAGE
48.6—Minn.-Morris (25) vs. Carnegie Mellon (31), 11-17-79 (7 for 340).

PUNTS
14—Gettysburg (14) vs. Lycoming (10), 11-23-85.

YARDS GAINED ON PUNT RETURNS
140—John Carroll (30) vs. Hanover (20), 11-22-97.

YARDS GAINED ON KICKOFF RETURNS
234—Ithaca (40) vs. Salisbury (44), 12-6-86.

YARDS GAINED ON INTERCEPTION RETURNS
176—Augustana (Ill.) (14) vs. St. Lawrence (0), 11-27-82.

YARDS PENALIZED
166—Ferrum (49) vs. Moravian (28), 11-26-88.

FUMBLES LOST
6—Albright (7) vs. St. Lawrence (26), 11-20-76; St. John's (Minn.) (7) vs. Dayton (19), 12-7-91.

POINTS
75—St. John's (Minn.) vs. Coe (2), 11-23-91.

TOURNAMENT

FIRST DOWNS
118—Trinity (Tex.), 2002 (19 vs. Mary Hardin-Baylor, 33 vs. Wash. & Jeff., 28 vs. Bridgewater [Va.], 27 vs. St. John's [Minn.], 11 vs. Mount Union).

NET YARDS RUSHING
1,377—Ithaca, 1988 (251 vs. Wagner, 293 vs. Cortland St., 425 vs. Ferrum, 408 vs. Central [Iowa]).

NET YARDS PASSING
1,445—Trinity (Tex.), 2002 (414 vs. Mary Hardin-Baylor, 293 vs. Wash. & Jeff., 481 vs. Bridgewater [Va.], 171 vs. St. John's [Minn.], 86 vs. Mount Union).

NET YARDS RUSHING AND PASSING
2,470—Mount Union, 1997 (528 vs. Allegheny, 601 vs. John Carroll, 644 vs. Simpson, 697 vs. Lycoming).

PASSES ATTEMPTED
161—St. John's (Minn.), 2002 (43 vs. Redlands, 36 vs. Coe, 39 vs. Linfield, 43 vs. Trinity [Tex.]).

PASSES COMPLETED
99—Mount Union, 1998 (30 vs. Albion, 29 vs. Wittenberg, 21 vs. Trinity [Tex.], 19 vs. Rowan).

PASSES INTERCEPTED
11—Hofstra, 1990 (5 vs. Cortland St., 3 vs. Col. of New Jersey, 3 vs. Lycoming).

PUNTS
35—St. John's (Minn.), 2000 (6 vs. Wis.-Stout, 4 vs. Pacific Lutheran, 10 vs. Central [Iowa], 6 vs. Hardin-Simmons, 9 vs. Mount Union).

YARDS PENALIZED
331—Wagner, 1987 (61 vs. Rochester, 80 vs. Fordham, 87 vs. Emory & Henry, 103 vs. Dayton).

FUMBLES LOST
10—Wittenberg, 1978 (4 vs. Ithaca, 2 vs. Minn.-Morris, 4 vs. Baldwin-Wallace); Rowan, 1995 (2 vs. Buffalo St., 4 vs. Union [N.Y.], 2 vs. Wash. & Jeff., 2 vs. Wis.-La Crosse).

POINTS
208—Mount Union, 1997 (34 vs. Allegheny, 59 vs. John Carroll, 54 vs. Simpson, 61 vs. Lycoming).

Championship Game Records

INDIVIDUAL

NET YARDS RUSHING
273—Chuck Moore, Mount Union (30) vs. Bridgewater (Va.) (27), 2001 (34 rushes).

RUSHES ATTEMPTED
49—Dan Pugh, Mount Union (48) vs. Trinity (Tex.) (7), 2002 (253 yards).

TOUCHDOWNS BY RUSHING
4—Lloyd Ball, Wittenberg (41) vs. Juniata (0), 1973; Dan Pugh, Mount Union (48) vs. Trinity (Tex.) (7), 2002.

RUSHING AVERAGE (Min. 10 Rushes)
10.8—Jyi Peterson, Rowan (24) vs. Mount Union (56), 1996 (15 for 162).

NET YARDS PASSING
505—Bill Borchert, Mount Union (56) vs. Rowan (24), 1996 (26 of 38).

PASSES ATTEMPTED
47—David Harvey, Wabash (36) vs. Widener (39), 1977 (24 completions).

PASSES COMPLETED
28—Jim Ballard, Mount Union (34) vs. Rowan (24), 1993 (45 attempts).

PASSES HAD INTERCEPTED
5—Dan Dullea, Towson (28) vs. St. John's (Minn.) (31), 1976.

TOUCHDOWN PASSES
7—Bill Borchert, Mount Union (56) vs. Rowan (24), 1996.

COMPLETION PERCENTAGE (Min. 10 Attempts)
.704—Gary Smeck, Mount Union (10) vs. St. John's (Minn.) (7), 2000 (19 of 27).

NET YARDS RUSHING AND PASSING
532—Bill Borchert, Mount Union (56) vs. Rowan (24), 1996 (27 rushing, 505 passing).

RUSHING AND PASSING PLAYS
56—David Harvey, Wabash (36) vs. Widener (39), 1977 (9 rushing, 47 passing).

PUNTS
9—By 6 players. Most recent: Charlie Carr, St. John's (Minn.) (7) vs. Mount Union (10), 2000.

PUNTING AVERAGE
46.4—Gary Sitler, Wittenberg (28) vs. Ithaca (0), 1975 (7 for 325).

RECEPTIONS
13—Taman Bryant, Rowan (13) vs. Pacific Lutheran (42), 1999 (141 yards).

NET RECEIVING YARDS
211—Kevin Knestrick, Mount Union (56) vs. Rowan (24), 1996 (7 receptions).

TOUCHDOWN RECEPTIONS
2—By 13 players. Most recent: Derrick Leach, Mount Union (48) vs. Trinity (Tex.) (7), 2002.

INTERCEPTIONS
3—Mike Gray, Augustana (Ill.) (31) vs. Salisbury (3), 1986; Tom Knapp, Ithaca (39) vs. Central (Iowa) (24), 1988.

YARDS GAINED ON INTERCEPTION RETURNS
54—Mike Gray, Augustana (Ill.) (31) vs. Salisbury (3), 1986 (3 interceptions).

PUNT RETURNS
6—Steve Warrington, Widener (39) vs. Wabash (36), 1977.

YARDS GAINED ON PUNT RETURNS
79—Tom Deery, Widener (17) vs. Dayton (10), 1981 (2 returns).

PUNT RETURN AVERAGE (Min. 3 Returns)
25.7—Dan Pugh, Mount Union (30) vs. Bridgewater (Va.) (27), 2001 (3 for 77).

KICKOFF RETURNS
7—Terry Jarvie, Ithaca (0) vs. Dayton (63), 1980.

YARDS GAINED ON KICKOFF RETURNS
145—Terrick Grace, Rowan (24) vs. Mount Union (56), 1996 (5 returns).

KICKOFF RETURN AVERAGE (Min. 2 Returns)
31.5—Chuck Moore, Mount Union (30) vs. Bridgewater (Va.) (27), 2001 (2 for 63).

POINTS
26—Dan Pugh, Mount Union (48) vs. Trinity (Tex.) (7), 2002.

TOUCHDOWNS
4—Lloyd Ball, Wittenberg (41) vs. Juniata (0), 1973; Dan Pugh, Mount Union (48) vs. Trinity (Tex.) (7), 2002.

EXTRA POINTS
8—Bill Andrea, Mount Union (56) vs. Rowan (24), 1996 (8 attempted).

EXTRA POINTS ATTEMPTED
9—Bill Andrea, Mount Union (61) vs. Lycoming (12), 1997 (7 made).

FIELD GOALS
2—Frank Markowick, Ithaca (8) vs. Central (Iowa) (10), 1974; Matt Schulte, Central (Iowa) (12) vs. Augustana (Ill.) (21), 1984; Brad Burns, Dayton (20) vs. Ithaca (34), 1991.

FIELD GOALS ATTEMPTED
3—Frank Markowick, Ithaca (8) vs. Central (Iowa) (10), 1974 (2 made); Tim Robinson, Baldwin-Wallace (24) vs. Wittenberg (10), 1978 (1 made); Scott Goodwin, Union (N.Y.) (7) vs. Dayton (17), 1989 (0 made).

LONGEST PLAYS

RUSH
95—Chuck Moore, Mount Union (30) vs. Bridgewater (Va.) (27), 2001, TD.

PASS (INCLUDING RUN)
85—Craig Kusick to Jeremy Earp, Wis.-La Crosse (36) vs. Rowan (7), 1995, TD.

PUNT RETURN
76—Tom Deery, Widener (17) vs. Dayton (10), 1981, TD.

KICKOFF RETURN
84—Mike Scott, Ithaca (39) vs. Central (Iowa) (24), 1988, TD.

INTERCEPTION RETURN
44—Jason Perkins, Mount Union (30) vs. Bridgewater (Va.) (27), 2001, TD.

FIELD GOAL
47—Mike Pignatiello, Dayton (10) vs. Widener (17), 1981.

FIELD GOAL ATTEMPTED
48—Mike Street, Central (Iowa) (10) vs. Ithaca (8), 1974.

PUNT
77—Brad Burns, Dayton (20) vs. Ithaca (34), 1991.

TEAM

FIRST DOWNS
33—Mount Union (61) vs. Lycoming (12), 1997.

FIRST DOWNS, BOTH TEAMS
48—Mount Union (30) [56] vs. Rowan (18) [24], 1996.

FIRST DOWNS BY RUSHING
21—Augustana (Ill.) (31) vs. Salisbury (3), 1986.

FIRST DOWNS BY RUSHING, BOTH TEAMS
28—Augustana (Ill.) (21) [31] vs. Salisbury (7) [3], 1986.

FIRST DOWNS BY PASSING
20—Mount Union (56) vs. Rowan (24), 1996.

FIRST DOWNS BY PASSING, BOTH TEAMS
29—Mount Union (18) [34] vs. Rowan (11) [24], 1993.

FIRST DOWNS BY PENALTY
5—Wabash (36) vs. Widener (39), 1977.

FIRST DOWNS BY PENALTY, BOTH TEAMS
5—Wabash (5) [36] vs. Widener (0) [39], 1977.

NET YARDS RUSHING
408—Ithaca (39) vs. Central (Iowa) (24), 1988.

NET YARDS RUSHING, BOTH TEAMS
464—Ithaca (408) [39] vs. Central (Iowa) (56) [24], 1988.

RUSHES ATTEMPTED
75—Augustana (Ill.) (31) vs. Salisbury (3), 1986.

RUSHES ATTEMPTED, BOTH TEAMS
113—Dayton (70) [63] vs. Ithaca (43) [0], 1980.

TOUCHDOWNS BY RUSHING
8—Dayton (63) vs. Ithaca (0), 1980.

TOUCHDOWNS BY RUSHING, BOTH TEAMS
8—Dayton (8) [63] vs. Ithaca (0) [0], 1980.

FEWEST NET YARDS RUSHING ALLOWED
Minus 63—Pacific Lutheran (42) vs. Rowan (13), 1999.

NET YARDS PASSING
505—Mount Union (56) vs. Rowan (24), 1996 (26 of 38).

NET YARDS PASSING, BOTH TEAMS
662—Mount Union (505) [56] vs. Rowan (157) [24], 1996.

PASSES ATTEMPTED
48—Wabash (36) vs. Widener (39), 1977.

PASSES ATTEMPTED, BOTH TEAMS
77—Mount Union (45) [34] vs. Rowan (32) [24], 1993.

PASSES COMPLETED
28—Mount Union (34) vs. Rowan (24), 1993.

PASSES COMPLETED, BOTH TEAMS
48—Mount Union (28) [34] vs. Rowan (20) [24], 1993.

PASSES HAD INTERCEPTED
5—Towson (28) vs. St. John's (Minn.) (31), 1976.

PASSES HAD INTERCEPTED, BOTH TEAMS
6—Towson (5) [28] vs. St. John's (Minn.) (1) [31], 1976; Salisbury (4) [3] vs. Augustana (Ill.) (2) [31], 1986; Mount Union (3) [10] vs. St. John's (Minn.) (3) [7], 2000.

TOUCHDOWN PASSES
7—Mount Union (56) vs. Rowan (24), 1996.

TOUCHDOWN PASSES, BOTH TEAMS
8—Mount Union (7) [56] vs. Rowan (1) [24], 1996; Mount Union (6) [61] vs. Lycoming (2) [12], 1997.

COMPLETION PERCENTAGE (Min. 10 Attempts)
.733—Ithaca (39) vs. Central (Iowa) (24), 1988 (11 of 15).

NET YARDS RUSHING AND PASSING
697—Mount Union (61) vs. Lycoming (12), 1997 (258 rushing, 439 passing).

NET YARDS RUSHING AND PASSING, BOTH TEAMS
1,105—Mount Union (682) [56] vs. Rowan (423) [24], 1996.

RUSHING AND PASSING PLAYS
91—Ithaca (34) vs. Dayton (20), 1991 (65 rushing, 26 passing).

RUSHING AND PASSING PLAYS, BOTH TEAMS
165—Widener (78) [39] vs. Wabash (87) [36], 1977.

PUNTING AVERAGE
47.8—Allegheny (21) vs. Lycoming (14) (ot), 1990 (5 for 239).

PUNTS
10—Lycoming (12) vs. Mount Union (61), 1997 (313 yards).

PUNT RETURN AVERAGE
39.5—Widener (17) vs. Dayton (10), 1981 (2 for 79).

YARDS GAINED ON PUNT RETURNS
104—Mount Union (30) vs. Bridgewater (Va.) (27), 2001 (4 returns).

PUNT RETURNS
7—Mount Union (10) vs. St. John's (Minn.) (7), 2000 (4 yards).

KICKOFF RETURN AVERAGE
31.7—Albion (38) vs. Wash. & Jeff. (15), 1994 (3 for 95).

YARDS GAINED ON KICKOFF RETURNS
213—Rowan (24) vs. Mount Union (56), 1996 (9 returns).

KICKOFF RETURNS
10—Ithaca (0) vs. Dayton (63), 1980 (159 yards).

YARDS GAINED ON INTERCEPTION RETURNS
89—Dayton (63) vs. Ithaca (0), 1980 (4 interceptions).

YARDS PENALIZED
113—Widener (39) vs. Wabash (36), 1977 (12 penalties).

YARDS PENALIZED, BOTH TEAMS
140—Widener (113) [39] vs. Wabash (27) [36], 1977 (15 penalties).

PENALTIES
12—Widener (39) vs. Wabash (36), 1977 (113 yards).

PENALTIES, BOTH TEAMS
15—Widener (12) [39] vs. Wabash (3) [36], 1977 (140 yards).

FUMBLES
6—Wittenberg (10) vs. Baldwin-Wallace (24), 1978 (4 lost); Dayton (10) vs. Widener (17), 1981 (3 lost); Widener (17) vs. Dayton (10), 1981 (2 lost).

FUMBLES, BOTH TEAMS
12—Dayton (6) [10] vs. Widener (6) [17], 1981 (5 lost).

FUMBLES LOST
4—Wittenberg (10) vs. Baldwin-Wallace (24), 1978 (6 fumbles); Wittenberg (10) vs. Ithaca (14), 1979 (4 fumbles).

FUMBLES LOST, BOTH TEAMS
5—Wittenberg (4) [10] vs. Ithaca (1) [14], 1979 (6 fumbles); Dayton (3) [10] vs. Widener (2) [17], 1981 (12 fumbles).

POINTS
63—Dayton vs. Ithaca (0), 1980.

POINTS, BOTH TEAMS
80—Mount Union (56) vs. Rowan (24), 1996.

TOUCHDOWNS
9—Dayton (63) vs. Ithaca (0), 1980; Mount Union (61) vs. Lycoming (12), 1997.

TOUCHDOWNS, BOTH TEAMS
11—Widener (6) [39] vs. Wabash (5) [36], 1977; Mount Union (8) [56] vs. Rowan (3) [24], 1996; Mount Union (9) [61] vs. Lycoming (2) [12], 1997.

FIELD GOALS
2—Ithaca (8) vs. Central (Iowa) (10), 1974; Central (Iowa) (12) vs. Augustana (Ill.) (21), 1984; Dayton (20) vs. Ithaca (34), 1991.

FIELD GOALS, BOTH TEAMS
3—Ithaca (2) [8] vs. Central (Iowa) (1) [10], 1974.

PUNT RETURN AVERAGE
39.5—Widener (17) vs. Dayton (10), 1981 (2 for 79).

YARDS GAINED ON PUNT RETURNS
104—Mount Union (30) vs. Bridgewater (Va.) (27), 2001 (4 returns).

PUNT RETURNS
7—Mount Union (10) vs. St. John's (Minn.) (7), 2000 (4 yards).

KICKOFF RETURN AVERAGE
31.7—Albion (38) vs. Wash. & Jeff. (15), 1994 (3 for 95).

YARDS GAINED ON KICKOFF RETURNS
213—Rowan (24) vs. Mount Union (56), 1996 (9 returns).

KICKOFF RETURNS
10—Ithaca (0) vs. Dayton (63), 1980 (159 yards).

YARDS GAINED ON INTERCEPTION RETURNS
89—Dayton (63) vs. Ithaca (0), 1980 (4 interceptions).

YARDS PENALIZED
113—Widener (39) vs. Wabash (36), 1977 (12 penalties).

YARDS PENALIZED, BOTH TEAMS
140—Widener (113) [39] vs. Wabash (27) [36], 1977 (15 penalties).

PENALTIES
12—Widener (39) vs. Wabash (36), 1977 (113 yards).

PENALTIES, BOTH TEAMS
15—Widener (12) [39] vs. Wabash (3) [36], 1977 (140 yards).

FUMBLES
6—Wittenberg (10) vs. Baldwin-Wallace (24), 1978 (4 lost); Dayton (10) vs. Widener (17), 1981 (3 lost); Widener (17) vs. Dayton (10), 1981 (2 lost).

FUMBLES, BOTH TEAMS
12—Dayton (6) [10] vs. Widener (6) [17], 1981 (5 lost).

FUMBLES LOST
4—Wittenberg (10) vs. Baldwin-Wallace (24), 1978 (6 fumbles); Wittenberg (10) vs. Ithaca (14), 1979 (4 fumbles).

FUMBLES LOST, BOTH TEAMS
5—Wittenberg (4) [10] vs. Ithaca (1) [14], 1979 (6 fumbles); Dayton (3) [10] vs. Widener (2) [17], 1981 (12 fumbles).

POINTS
63—Dayton vs. Ithaca (0), 1980.

POINTS, BOTH TEAMS
80—Mount Union (56) vs. Rowan (24), 1996.

TOUCHDOWNS
9—Dayton (63) vs. Ithaca (0), 1980; Mount Union (61) vs. Lycoming (12), 1997.

TOUCHDOWNS, BOTH TEAMS
11—Widener (6) [39] vs. Wabash (5) [36], 1977; Mount Union (8) [56] vs. Rowan (3) [24], 1996; Mount Union (9) [61] vs. Lycoming (2) [12], 1997.

FIELD GOALS
2—Ithaca (8) vs. Central (Iowa) (10), 1974; Central (Iowa) (12) vs. Augustana (Ill.) (21), 1984; Dayton (20) vs. Ithaca (34), 1991.

FIELD GOALS, BOTH TEAMS
3—Ithaca (2) [8] vs. Central (Iowa) (1) [10], 1974.

Year-by-Year Division III Championship Results

Year (Number of Teams)	Coach	Record	Result
1973 (4)			
Wittenberg	Dave Maurer	2-0	Champion
Juniata	Walt Nadzak	1-1	Second
Bridgeport	Ed Farrell	0-1	Semifinalist
San Diego	Andy Vinci	0-1	Semifinalist
1974 (4)			
Central (Iowa)	Ron Schipper	2-0	Champion
Ithaca	Jim Butterfield	1-1	Second
Evansville	Jim Byers	0-1	Semifinalist
Slippery Rock	Bob Di Spirito	0-1	Semifinalist
1975 (8)			
Wittenberg	Dave Maurer	3-0	Champion
Ithaca	Jim Butterfield	2-1	Second
Millsaps	Harper Davis	1-1	Semifinalist
Widener	Bill Manlove	1-1	Semifinalist
Albright	John Potsklan	0-1	Lost 1st Round
Colorado Col.	Jerry Carle	0-1	Lost 1st Round
Fort Valley St.	Leon Lomax	0-1	Lost 1st Round
Indianapolis	Bill Bless	0-1	Lost 1st Round
1976 (8)			
St. John's (Minn.)	John Gagliardi	3-0	Champion
Towson	Phil Albert	2-1	Second
Buena Vista	Jim Hershberger	1-1	Semifinalist
St. Lawrence	Ted Stratford	1-1	Semifinalist
Albright	John Potsklan	0-1	Lost 1st Round
Augustana (Ill.)	Ben Newcomb	0-1	Lost 1st Round
C.W. Post	Dom Anile	0-1	Lost 1st Round
Carroll (Wis.)	Steve Miller	0-1	Lost 1st Round
1977 (8)			
Widener	Bill Manlove	3-0	Champion
Wabash	Frank Navarro	2-1	Second
Albany (N.Y.)	Bob Ford	1-1	Semifinalist
Minn.-Morris	Al Molde	1-1	Semifinalist
Albion	Frank Joranko	0-1	Lost 1st Round

Year (Number of Teams)	Coach	Record	Result
Central (Iowa)	Ron Schipper	0-1	Lost 1st Round
Hampden-Sydney	Stokeley Fulton	0-1	Lost 1st Round
St. John's (Minn.)	John Gagliardi	0-1	Lost 1st Round
1978 (8)			
Baldwin-Wallace	Lee Tressel	3-0	Champion
Wittenberg	Dave Maurer	2-1	Second
Carnegie Mellon	Chuck Klausing	1-1	Semifinalist
Minn.-Morris	Al Molde	1-1	Semifinalist
Dayton	Rick Carter	0-1	Lost 1st Round
Ithaca	Jim Butterfield	0-1	Lost 1st Round
St. Lawrence	Ted Stratford	0-1	Lost 1st Round
St. Olaf	Tom Porter	0-1	Lost 1st Round
1979 (8)			
Ithaca	Jim Butterfield	3-0	Champion
Wittenberg	Dave Maurer	2-1	Second
Carnegie Mellon	Chuck Klausing	1-1	Semifinalist
Widener	Bill Manlove	1-1	Semifinalist
Baldwin-Wallace	Lee Tressel	0-1	Lost 1st Round
Dubuque	Don Birmingham	0-1	Lost 1st Round
Millersville	Gene Carpenter	0-1	Lost 1st Round
Minn.-Morris	Al Molde	0-1	Lost 1st Round
1980 (8)			
Dayton	Rick Carter	3-0	Champion
Ithaca	Jim Butterfield	2-1	Second
Minn.-Morris	Dick Smith	1-1	Semifinalist
Widener	Bill Manlove	1-1	Semifinalist
Baldwin-Wallace	Lee Tressel	0-1	Lost 1st Round
Bethany (W.Va.)	Don Ault	0-1	Lost 1st Round
Dubuque	Don Birmingham	0-1	Lost 1st Round
Wagner	Bill Russo	0-1	Lost 1st Round
1981 (8)			
Widener	Bill Manlove	3-0	Champion
Dayton	Mike Kelly	2-1	Second
Lawrence	Ron Roberts	1-1	Semifinalist
Montclair St.	Fred Hill	1-1	Semifinalist
Alfred	Sam Sanders	0-1	Lost 1st Round
Augustana (Ill.)	Bob Reade	0-1	Lost 1st Round
Minn.-Morris	Dick Smith	0-1	Lost 1st Round
West Ga.	Bobby Pate	0-1	Lost 1st Round

Year (Number of Teams)	Coach	Record	Result
1982 (8)			
West Ga.	Bobby Pate	3-0	Champion
Augustana (Ill.)	Bob Reade	2-1	Second
Bishop	James Jones	1-1	Semifinalist
St. Lawrence	Andy Talley	1-1	Semifinalist
Baldwin-Wallace	Bob Packard	0-1	Lost 1st Round
Wagner	Walt Hameline	0-1	Lost 1st Round
Wartburg	Don Canfield	0-1	Lost 1st Round
Widener	Bill Manlove	0-1	Lost 1st Round
1983 (8)			
Augustana (Ill.)	Bob Reade	3-0	Champion
Union (N.Y.)	Al Bagnoli	2-1	Second
Salisbury	Mike McGlinchey	1-1	Semifinalist
Wis.-La Crosse	Roger Harring	1-1	Semifinalist
Adrian	Ron Labadie	0-1	Lost 1st Round
Carnegie Mellon	Chuck Klausing	0-1	Lost 1st Round
Hofstra	Mickey Kwiatkowski	0-1	Lost 1st Round
Occidental	Dale Widolff	0-1	Lost 1st Round
1984 (8)			
Augustana (Ill.)	Bob Reade	3-0	Champion
Central (Iowa)	Ron Schipper	2-1	Second
Union (N.Y.)	Al Bagnoli	1-1	Semifinalist
Wash. & Jeff.	John Luckhardt	1-1	Semifinalist
Dayton	Mike Kelly	0-1	Lost 1st Round
Occidental	Dale Widolff	0-1	Lost 1st Round
Plymouth St.	Jay Cottone	0-1	Lost 1st Round
Randolph-Macon	Jim Blackburn	0-1	Lost 1st Round
1985 (16)			
Augustana (Ill.)	Bob Reade	4-0	Champion
Ithaca	Jim Butterfield	3-1	Second
Central (Iowa)	Ron Schipper	2-1	Semifinalist
Gettysburg	Barry Streeter	2-1	Semifinalist
Montclair St.	Rick Giancola	1-1	Quarterfinalist
Mount Union	Ken Wable	1-1	Quarterfinalist
Occidental	Dale Widolff	1-1	Quarterfinalist
Salisbury	Mike McGlinchey	1-1	Quarterfinalist
Albion	Pete Schmidt	0-1	Lost 1st Round
Carnegie Mellon	Chuck Klausing	0-1	Lost 1st Round
Coe	Bob Thurness	0-1	Lost 1st Round
Denison	Keith Piper	0-1	Lost 1st Round
Lycoming	Frank Girardi	0-1	Lost 1st Round
St. John's (Minn.)	John Gagliardi	0-1	Lost 1st Round
Union (N.Y.)	Al Bagnoli	0-1	Lost 1st Round
Western Conn. St.	Paul Pasqualoni	0-1	Lost 1st Round
1986 (16)			
Augustana (Ill.)	Bob Reade	4-0	Champion
Salisbury	Mike McGlinchey	3-1	Second
Concordia-M'head	Jim Christopherson	2-1	Semifinalist
Ithaca	Jim Butterfield	2-1	Semifinalist
Central (Iowa)	Ron Schipper	1-1	Quarterfinalist
Montclair St.	Rick Giancola	1-1	Quarterfinalist
Mount Union	Larry Kehres	1-1	Quarterfinalist
Susquehanna	Rocky Rees	1-1	Quarterfinalist
Buena Vista	Jim Hershberger	0-1	Lost 1st Round
Dayton	Mike Kelly	0-1	Lost 1st Round
Emory & Henry	Lou Wacker	0-1	Lost 1st Round
Hofstra	Mickey Kwiatkowski	0-1	Lost 1st Round
Hope	Ray Smith	0-1	Lost 1st Round
Union (N.Y.)	Al Bagnoli	0-1	Lost 1st Round
Wash. & Jeff.	John Luckhardt	0-1	Lost 1st Round
Wis.-Stevens Point	D. J. LeRoy	0-1	Lost 1st Round
1987 (16)			
Wagner	Walt Hameline	4-0	Champion
Dayton	Mike Kelly	3-1	Second
Central (Iowa)	Ron Schipper	2-1	Semifinalist
Emory & Henry	Lou Wacker	2-1	Semifinalist
Augustana (Ill.)	Bob Reade	1-1	Quarterfinalist
Fordham	Larry Glueck	1-1	Quarterfinalist
St. John's (Minn.)	John Gagliardi	1-1	Quarterfinalist
Wash. & Jeff.	John Luckhardt	1-1	Quarterfinalist
Allegheny	Peter Vaas	0-1	Lost 1st Round
Capital	Roger Welsh	0-1	Lost 1st Round
Ferrum	Hank Norton	0-1	Lost 1st Round
Gust. Adolphus	Steve Raarup	0-1	Lost 1st Round
Hiram	Don Charlton	0-1	Lost 1st Round
Hofstra	Mickey Kwiatkowski	0-1	Lost 1st Round
Menlo	Ray Solari	0-1	Lost 1st Round
Rochester	Ray Tellier	0-1	Lost 1st Round
1988 (16)			
Ithaca	Jim Butterfield	4-0	Champion
Central (Iowa)	Ron Schipper	3-1	Second

Year (Number of Teams)	Coach	Record	Result
Augustana (Ill.)	Bob Reade	2-1	Semifinalist
Ferrum	Hank Norton	2-1	Semifinalist
Cortland St.	Dennis Kayser	1-1	Quarterfinalist
Moravian	Scot Dapp	1-1	Quarterfinalist
Wis.-Whitewater	Bob Berezowitz	1-1	Quarterfinalist
Wittenberg	Ron Murphy	1-1	Quarterfinalist
Adrian	Ron Labadie	0-1	Lost Regionals
Concordia-M'head	Jim Christopherson	0-1	Lost Regionals
Dayton	Mike Kelly	0-1	Lost Regionals
Hofstra	Mickey Kwiatkowski	0-1	Lost Regionals
Rhodes	Mike Clary	0-1	Lost Regionals
Simpson	Jim Williams	0-1	Lost Regionals
Wagner	Walt Hameline	0-1	Lost Regionals
Widener	Bill Manlove	0-1	Lost Regionals
1989 (16)			
Dayton	Mike Kelly	4-0	Champion
Union (N.Y.)	Al Bagnoli	3-1	Second
Ferrum	Hank Norton	2-1	Semifinalist
St. John's (Minn.)	John Gagliardi	2-1	Semifinalist
Central (Iowa)	Ron Schipper	1-1	Quarterfinalist
Lycoming	Frank Girardi	1-1	Quarterfinalist
Millikin	Carl Poelker	1-1	Quarterfinalist
Montclair St.	Rick Giancola	1-1	Quarterfinalist
Augustana (Ill.)	Bob Reade	0-1	Lost Regionals
Cortland St.	Dennis Kayser	0-1	Lost Regionals
Dickinson	Ed Sweeney	0-1	Lost Regionals
Hofstra	Mickey Kwiatkowski	0-1	Lost Regionals
John Carroll	Tony DeCarlo	0-1	Lost Regionals
St. Norbert	Don LaViolette	0-1	Lost Regionals
Simpson	Jim Williams	0-1	Lost Regionals
Wash. & Jeff.	John Luckhardt	0-1	Lost Regionals
1990 (16)			
Allegheny	Ken O'Keefe	4-0	Champion
Lycoming	Frank Girardi	3-1	Second
Central (Iowa)	Ron Schipper	2-1	Semifinalist
Hofstra	Joe Gardi	2-1	Semifinalist
Dayton	Mike Kelly	1-1	Quarterfinalist
Col. of New Jersey	Eric Hamilton	1-1	Quarterfinalist
St. Thomas (Minn.)	Vic Wallace	1-1	Quarterfinalist
Wash. & Jeff.	John Luckhardt	1-1	Quarterfinalist
Augustana (Ill.)	Bob Reade	0-1	Lost Regionals
Carnegie Mellon	Rich Lackner	0-1	Lost Regionals
Cortland St.	Dave Murray	0-1	Lost Regionals
Ferrum	Hank Norton	0-1	Lost Regionals
Ithaca	Jim Butterfield	0-1	Lost Regionals
Mount Union	Larry Kehres	0-1	Lost Regionals
Redlands	Mike Maynard	0-1	Lost Regionals
Wis.-Whitewater	Bob Berezowitz	0-1	Lost Regionals
1991 (16)			
Ithaca	Jim Butterfield	4-0	Champion
Dayton	Mike Kelly	3-1	Second
St. John's (Minn.)	John Gagliardi	2-1	Semifinalist
Susquehanna	Steve Briggs	2-1	Semifinalist
Allegheny	Ken O'Keefe	1-1	Quarterfinalist
Lycoming	Frank Girardi	1-1	Quarterfinalist
Union (N.Y.)	Al Bagnoli	1-1	Quarterfinalist
Wis.-La Crosse	Roger Harring	1-1	Quarterfinalist
Albion	Pete Schmidt	0-1	Lost Regionals
Baldwin-Wallace	Bob Packard	0-1	Lost Regionals
Coe	D.J. LeRoy	0-1	Lost Regionals
Dickinson	Ed Sweeney	0-1	Lost Regionals
Mass.-Lowell	Dennis Scannell	0-1	Lost Regionals
Rowan	John Bunting	0-1	Lost Regionals
Simpson	Jim Williams	0-1	Lost Regionals
Wash. & Jeff.	John Luckhardt	0-1	Lost Regionals
1992 (16)			
Wis.-La Crosse	Roger Harring	4-0	Champion
Wash. & Jeff.	John Luckhardt	3-1	Second
Mount Union	Larry Kehres	2-1	Semifinalist
Rowan	John Bunting	2-1	Semifinalist
Buffalo St.	Jerry Boyes	1-1	Quarterfinalist
Central (Iowa)	Ron Schipper	1-1	Quarterfinalist
Emory & Henry	Lou Wacker	1-1	Quarterfinalist
Ill. Wesleyan	Norm Eash	1-1	Quarterfinalist
Aurora	Jim Scott	0-1	Lost Regionals
Carleton	Bob Sullivan	0-1	Lost Regionals
Dayton	Mike Kelly	0-1	Lost Regionals
Ithaca	Jim Butterfield	0-1	Lost Regionals
Lycoming	Frank Girardi	0-1	Lost Regionals
Redlands	Mike Maynard	0-1	Lost Regionals
Thomas More	Vic Clark	0-1	Lost Regionals
WPI	Jack Siedlecki	0-1	Lost Regionals

1993 (16)

Mount Union	Larry Kehres	4-0	Champion
Rowan	K.C. Keeler	3-1	Second
St. John's (Minn.)	John Gagliardi	2-1	Semifinalist
Wash. & Jeff.	John Luckhardt	2-1	Semifinalist
Albion	Pete Schmidt	1-1	Quarterfinalist
Frostburg St.	Mike McGlinchey	1-1	Quarterfinalist
Wm. Paterson	Gerry Gallagher	1-1	Quarterfinalist
Wis.-La Crosse	Roger Harring	1-1	Quarterfinalist
Allegheny	Ken O'Keefe	0-1	Lost Regionals
Anderson (Ind.)	Mike Manley	0-1	Lost Regionals
Buffalo St.	Jerry Boyes	0-1	Lost Regionals
Coe	D.J. LeRoy	0-1	Lost Regionals
Moravian	Scot Dapp	0-1	Lost Regionals
Union (N.Y.)	John Audino	0-1	Lost Regionals
Wartburg	Bob Nielson	0-1	Lost Regionals
Wilkes	Joe DeMelfi	0-1	Lost Regionals

1994 (16)

Albion	Pete Schmidt	4-0	Champion
Wash. & Jeff.	John Luckhardt	3-1	Second
Ithaca	Michael Welch	2-1	Semifinalist
St. John's (Minn.)	John Gagliardi	2-1	Semifinalist
Mount Union	Larry Kehres	1-1	Quarterfinalist
Plymouth St.	Don Brown	1-1	Quarterfinalist
Wartburg	Bob Nielson	1-1	Quarterfinalist
Widener	Bill Cubit	1-1	Quarterfinalist
Allegheny	Ken O'Keefe	0-1	Lost Regionals
Augustana (Ill.)	Bob Reade	0-1	Lost Regionals
Buffalo St.	Jerry Boyes	0-1	Lost Regionals
Central (Iowa)	Ron Schipper	0-1	Lost Regionals
Dickinson	Darwin Breaux	0-1	Lost Regionals
La Verne	Rex Huigens	0-1	Lost Regionals
Merchant Marine	Charlie Pravata	0-1	Lost Regionals
Trinity (Tex.)	Steven Mohr	0-1	Lost Regionals

1995 (16)

Wis.-La Crosse	Roger Harring	4-0	Champion
Rowan	K.C. Keeler	3-1	Second
Mount Union	Larry Kehres	2-1	Semifinalist
Wash. & Jeff.	John Luckhardt	2-1	Semifinalist
Lycoming	Frank Girardi	1-1	Quarterfinalist
Union (N.Y.)	John Audino	1-1	Quarterfinalist
Wheaton (Ill.)	J.R. Bishop	1-1	Quarterfinalist
Wis.-River Falls	John O'Grady	1-1	Quarterfinalist
Buffalo St.	Jerry Boyes	0-1	Lost Regionals
Central (Iowa)	Ron Schipper	0-1	Lost Regionals
Concordia-M'head	Jim Christopherson	0-1	Lost Regionals
Emory & Henry	Lou Wacker	0-1	Lost Regionals
Hanover	C. Wayne Perry	0-1	Lost Regionals
Plymouth St.	Don Brown	0-1	Lost Regionals
Widener	Bill Cubit	0-1	Lost Regionals
Wittenberg	Doug Neibuhr	0-1	Lost Regionals

1996 (16)

Mount Union	Larry Kehres	4-0	Champion
Rowan	K.C. Keeler	3-1	Second
Lycoming	Frank Girardi	2-1	Semifinalist
Wis.-LaCrosse	Roger Harring	2-1	Semifinalist
Albright	Ron Maier	1-1	Quarterfinalist
Ill. Wesleyan	Norm Eash	1-1	Quarterfinalist
Col. of New Jersey	Eric Hamilton	1-1	Quarterfinalist
St. John's (Minn.)	John Gagliardi	1-1	Quarterfinalist
Albion	Pete Schmidt	0-1	Lost Regionals
Allegheny	Ken O'Keefe	0-1	Lost Regionals
Buffalo St.	Jerry Boyes	0-1	Lost Regionals
Coast Guard	Bill Schmitz	0-1	Lost Regionals
Simpson	Jim Williams	0-1	Lost Regionals
Ursinus	Steve Gilbert	0-1	Lost Regionals
Wash. & Jeff.	John Luckhardt	0-1	Lost Regionals
Wis.-River Falls	John O'Grady	0-1	Lost Regionals

1997 (16)

Mount Union	Larry Kehres	4-0	Champion
Lycoming	Frank Girardi	3-1	Second
Rowan	K.C. Keeler	2-1	Semifinalist
Simpson	Jim Williams	2-1	Semifinalist
Augsburg	Jack Osberg	1-1	Quarterfinalist
John Carroll	Tony DeCarlo	1-1	Quarterfinalist
Col. of New Jersey	Eric Hamilton	1-1	Quarterfinalist
Trinity (Tex.)	Steven Mohr	1-1	Quarterfinalist
Allegheny	Ken O'Keefe	0-1	Lost Regionals
Catholic	Tom Clark	0-1	Lost Regionals
Coast Guard	Chuck Mills	0-1	Lost Regionals
Concordia-M'head	Jim Christopherson	0-1	Lost Regionals
Cortland St.	Dan MacNeil	0-1	Lost Regionals
Hanover	C. Wayne Perry	0-1	Lost Regionals

Year (Number of Teams)	Coach	Record	Result
McDaniel	Tim Keating	0-1	Lost Regionals
Wis.-Whitewater	Bob Berezowitz	0-1	Lost Regionals

1998 (16)

Mount Union	Larry Kehres	4-0	Champion
Rowan	K.C. Keeler	3-1	Second
Trinity (Tex.)	Steven Mohr	2-1	Semifinalist
Wis.-Eau Claire	Bob Nielson	2-1	Semifinalist
Buffalo St.	Jerry Boyes	1-1	Quarterfinalist
Lycoming	Frank Girardi	1-1	Quarterfinalist
St. John's (Minn.)	John Gagliardi	1-1	Quarterfinalist
Wittenberg	Joe Fincham	1-1	Quarterfinalist
Albion	Craig Rundle	0-1	Lost 1st Round
Catholic	Tom Clark	0-1	Lost 1st Round
Central (Iowa)	Rich Kacmarynski	0-1	Lost 1st Round
McDaniel	Tim Keating	0-1	Lost 1st Round
Millikin	Doug Neibuhr	0-1	Lost 1st Round
Col. of New Jersey	Eric Hamilton	0-1	Lost 1st Round
Pacific Lutheran	Frosty Westering	0-1	Lost 1st Round
Springfield	Mike DeLong	0-1	Lost 1st Round

1999 (28)

Pacific Lutheran	Frosty Westering	5-0	Champion
Rowan	K.C. Keeler	3-1	Second
Mount Union	Larry Kehres	2-1	Semifinalist
Trinity (Tex.)	Steven Mohr	2-1	Semifinalist
Hardin-Simmons	Jimmie Keeling	2-1	Quarterfinalist
Montclair St.	Rick Giancola	2-1	Quarterfinalist
Ohio Northern	Tom Kaczkowski	2-1	Quarterfinalist
St. John's (Minn.)	John Gagliardi	2-1	Quarterfinalist
Augustana (Ill.)	Tom Schmulbach	1-1	Lost 2nd Round
Central (Iowa)	Rich Kacmarynski	1-1	Lost 2nd Round
McDaniel	Tim Keating	1-1	Lost 2nd Round
Ursinus	Paul Guenther	1-1	Lost 2nd Round
Wartburg	Rick Willis	0-1	Lost 2nd Round
Wash. & Jeff.	John Banaszak	1-1	Lost 2nd Round
Western Conn. St.	John Cervino	0-1	Lost 2nd Round
Wittenberg	Joe Fincham	1-1	Lost 2nd Round
Alma	Jim Cole	0-1	Lost 1st Round
Bridgewater St.	Peter Mazzaferro	0-1	Lost 1st Round
Buffalo St.	Jerry Boyes	0-1	Lost 1st Round
Catholic	Tom Clark	0-1	Lost 1st Round
Hanover	Wayne Perry	0-1	Lost 1st Round
Lycoming	Frank Girardi	0-1	Lost 1st Round
Rensselaer	Joe King	0-1	Lost 1st Round
St. Norbert	Jim Purtill	0-1	Lost 1st Round
Washington (Mo.)	Larry Kindbom	0-1	Lost 1st Round
Willamette	Mark Speckman	0-1	Lost 1st Round
Wis.-La Crosse	Roger Harring	0-1	Lost 1st Round
Wis.-Stevens Point	John Miech	0-1	Lost 1st Round

2000 (28)

Mount Union	Larry Kehres	4-0	Champion
St. John's (Minn.)	John Gagliardi	4-1	Second
Hardin-Simmons	Jimmy Keeling	2-1	Semifinalist
Widener	Bill Zwann	3-1	Semifinalist
Central (Iowa)	Rich Kacmarynski	2-1	Quarterfinalist
Springfield	Mike DeLong	2-1	Quarterfinalist
Trinity (Tex.)	Steve Mohr	2-1	Quarterfinalist
Wittenberg	Joe Fincham	2-1	Quarterfinalist
Bridgewater (Va.)	Mike Clark	1-1	Lost 2nd Round
Brockport St.	Rocco Salomone	0-1	Lost 2nd Round
Hanover	Wayne Perry	1-1	Lost 2nd Round
Hobart	Michael Cragg	1-1	Lost 2nd Round
Linfield	Jay Locey	0-1	Lost 2nd Round
McDaniel	Tim Keating	1-1	Lost 2nd Round
Ohio Northern	Tom Kaczkowski	1-1	Lost 2nd Round
Pacific Lutheran	Frosty Westering	1-1	Lost 2nd Round
Aurora	Jim Scott	0-1	Lost 1st Round
Bethel (Minn.)	Steve Johnson	0-1	Lost 1st Round
Bridgewater St.	Peter Mazzaferro	0-1	Lost 1st Round
Emory & Henry	Lou Wacker	0-1	Lost 1st Round
Hope	Dean Kreps	0-1	Lost 1st Round
Millikin	Don Neibuhr	0-1	Lost 1st Round
Montclair St.	Rick Giancola	0-1	Lost 1st Round
St. Norbert	Jim Purtill	0-1	Lost 1st Round
Union (N.Y.)	John Audino	0-1	Lost 1st Round
Wash. & Jeff.	John Banaszak	0-1	Lost 1st Round
Wesley	Mike Drass	0-1	Lost 1st Round
Wis.-Stout	Ed Meierkort	0-1	Lost 1st Round

2001 (28)

Mount Union	Larry Kehres	4-0	Champion
Bridgewater (Va.)	Mike Clark	3-1	Second
Rowan	K.C. Keeler	3-1	Semifinalist
St. John's (Minn.)	John Gagliardi	3-1	Semifinalist

Year (Number of Teams)	Coach	Record	Result
Ithaca	Mike Welch	2-1	Quarterfinalist
Pacific Lutheran	Frosty Westering	2-1	Quarterfinalist
Widener	Bill Zwaan	2-1	Quarterfinalist
Wittenberg	Joe Fincham	2-1	Quarterfinalist
Augustana (Ill.)	Jim Barnes	1-1	Lost 2nd Round
Central (Iowa)	Rick Kacmarynski	0-1	Lost 2nd Round
Rensselaer	Joe King	0-1	Lost 2nd Round
Thomas More	Dean Paul	1-1	Lost 2nd Round
Trinity (Tex.)	Steven Mohr	1-1	Lost 2nd Round
Wash. & Jeff.	John Banaszak	1-1	Lost 2nd Round
Western Conn. St.	Bob Surace	1-1	Lost 2nd Round
Wis.-Stevens Point	John Miech	1-1	Lost 2nd Round
Bethel (Minn.)	Steve Johnson	0-1	Lost 1st Round
Brockport St.	Rocco Salomone	0-1	Lost 1st Round
Chris. Newport	Matt Kelchner	0-1	Lost 1st Round
Defiance	Greg Pscodna	0-1	Lost 1st Round
Hardin-Simmons	Jimmie Keeling	0-1	Lost 1st Round
MacMurray	Bob Frey	0-1	Lost 1st Round
Mary Hardin-Baylor	Peter Fredenburg	0-1	Lost 1st Round
McDaniel	Tim Keating	0-1	Lost 1st Round
Montclair St.	Rick Giancola	0-1	Lost 1st Round
St. Norbert	Jim Purtill	0-1	Lost 1st Round
Westfield St.	Steve Marino	0-1	Lost 1st Round
Whitworth	John Tully	0-1	Lost 1st Round

2002 (28)

Team	Coach	Record	Result
Mount Union	Larry Kehres	4-0	Champion
Trinity (Tex.)	Steven Mohr	4-1	Second
John Carroll	Regis Scafe	3-1	Semifinalist
St. John's (Minn.)	John Gagliardi	3-1	Semifinalist
Bridgewater (Va.)	Michael Clark	1-1	Quarterfinalist
Brockport St.	Rocco Salomone	2-1	Quarterfinalist
Linfield	Jay Locey	1-1	Quarterfinalist
Wabash	Chris Creighton	2-1	Quarterfinalist
Coe	Erik Raeburn	1-1	Lost 2nd Round
King's (Pa.)	Rich Mannello	1-1	Lost 2nd Round
Muhlenberg	Mike Donnelly	1-1	Lost 2nd Round
Rowan	Jay Accorsi	0-1	Lost 2nd Round
Wartburg	Rick Willis	1-1	Lost 2nd Round
Wash. & Jeff.	John Banaszak	1-1	Lost 2nd Round
Wheaton (Ill.)	Mike Swider	1-1	Lost 2nd Round
Wittenberg	Joe Fincham	1-1	Lost 2nd Round
Alma	Jim Cole	0-1	Lost 1st Round
Chris. Newport	Matt Kelchner	0-1	Lost 1st Round
Hanover	Wayne Perry	0-1	Lost 1st Round
Hobart	Mike Cragg	0-1	Lost 1st Round
Lake Forest	Chad Eisele	0-1	Lost 1st Round
MacMurray	Bob Frey	0-1	Lost 1st Round
Mary Hardin-Baylor	Pete Fredenburg	0-1	Lost 1st Round
Mass.-Dartmouth	Bill Kavanaugh	0-1	Lost 1st Round
Redlands	Mike Maynard	0-1	Lost 1st Round
Salisbury	Sherman Wood	0-1	Lost 1st Round
Springfield	Mike DeLong	0-1	Lost 1st Round
Wis.-La Crosse	Larry Terry	0-1	Lost 1st Round

Division III Championship Record of Each College by Coach

(120 Colleges; 1973-02)

College / Coach	Yrs	Won	Lost	CH	2D
ADRIAN					
Ron Labadie (Adrian '71) 83, 88	2	0	2	0	0
ALBANY (N.Y.)					
Bob Ford (Springfield '59) 77	1	1	1	0	0
ALBION					
Frank Joranko (Albion '52) 77	1	0	1	0	0
Pete Schmidt (Alma '70) 85, 91, 93, 94-CH, 96.	5	5	4	1	0
Craig Rundle (Albion '74) 98	1	0	1	0	0
TOTAL	7	5	6	1	0
ALBRIGHT					
John Potsklan (Penn St. '49) 75, 76	2	0	2	0	0
Ron Maier (Bentley '86) 96	1	1	1	0	0
TOTAL	3	1	3	0	0
ALFRED					
Sam Sanders (Buffalo '60) 81	1	0	1	0	0
ALLEGHENY					
Peter Vaas (Holy Cross '74) 87	1	0	1	0	0
Ken O'Keefe (John Carroll '75) 90-CH, 91, 93, 94, 96, 97	6	5	5	1	0
TOTAL	7	5	6	1	0

College / Coach	Yrs	Won	Lost	CH	2D
ALMA					
Jim Cole (Alma '74) 99, 02	2	0	2	0	0
ANDERSON (IND.)					
Mike Manley (Anderson [Ind.] '73) 93	1	0	1	0	0
AUGSBURG					
Jack Osberg (Augsburg '62) 97	1	1	1	0	0
AUGUSTANA (ILL.)					
Ben Newcomb 76	1	0	1	0	0
Bob Reade (Cornell College '54) 81, 82-2D, 83-CH, 84-CH, 85-CH, 86-CH, 87, 88, 89, 90, 94	11	19	7	4	1
Tom Schmulbach (Western Ill. '69) 99	1	1	1	0	0
Jim Barnes (Augustana [Ill.] '81) 01	1	1	1	0	0
TOTAL	14	21	10	4	1
AURORA					
Jim Scott (Luther '61) 92, 00	2	0	2	0	0
BALDWIN-WALLACE					
Lee Tressel (Baldwin-Wallace '48) 78-CH, 79, 80	3	3	2	1	0
Bob Packard (Baldwin-Wallace '65) 82, 91	2	0	2	0	0
TOTAL	5	3	4	1	0
BETHANY (W.VA.)					
Don Ault (West Liberty St. '52) 80	1	0	1	0	0
BETHEL (MINN.)					
Steve Johnson (Bethel [Minn.] '79) 00, 01	2	0	2	0	0
BISHOP					
James Jones (Bishop '49) 82	1	1	1	0	0
BRIDGEPORT					
Ed Farrell (Rutgers '56) 73	1	0	1	0	0
BRIDGEWATER ST.					
Peter Mazzaferro (Centre '54) 99, 00	2	0	2	0	0
BRIDGEWATER (VA.)					
Mike Clark (Cincinnati '77) 00, 01-2D, 02	3	5	3	0	1
BROCKPORT ST.					
Rocco Salomone (Brockport St. '88) 00, 01, 02..	3	2	3	0	0
BUENA VISTA					
Jim Hershberger (Northern Iowa '57) 76, 86	2	1	2	0	0
BUFFALO ST.					
Jerry Boyes (Ithaca '76) 92, 93, 94, 95, 96, 98, 99	7	2	7	0	0
C.W. POST					
Dom Anile (C.W. Post '59) 76	1	0	1	0	0
CAPITAL					
Roger Welsh (Muskingum '64) 87	1	0	1	0	0
CARLETON					
Bob Sullivan (St. John's [Minn.] '59) 92	1	0	1	0	0
CARNEGIE MELLON					
Chuck Klausing (Slippery Rock '48) 78, 79, 83, 85	4	2	4	0	0
Rich Lackner (Carnegie Mellon '79) 90	1	0	1	0	0
TOTAL	5	2	5	0	0
CARROLL (WIS.)					
Steve Miller (Cornell College '65) 76	1	0	1	0	0
CATHOLIC					
Tom Clark (Maryland '86) 97, 98, 99	3	0	3	0	0
CENTRAL (IOWA)					
Ron Schipper (Hope '52) 74-CH, 77, 84-2D, 85, 86, 87, 88-2D, 89, 90, 92, 94, 95	12	16	11	1	2
Rich Kacmarynski (Central [Iowa] '92) 98, 99, 00, 01	4	3	4	0	0
TOTAL	16	19	15	1	2
CHRIS. NEWPORT					
Matt Kelchner (Susquehanna '82) 01, 02	2	0	2	0	0
COAST GUARD					
Bill Schmitz (Coast Guard '76) 96	1	0	1	0	0
Chuck Mills 97	1	0	1	0	0
TOTAL	2	0	2	0	0
COE					
Bob Thurness (Coe '62) 85	1	0	1	0	0
D.J. LeRoy (Wis.-Eau Claire '79) 91, 93	2	0	2	0	0
Erik Raeburn (Mount Union '94) 02	1	1	1	0	0
TOTAL	4	1	4	0	0
COLORADO COL.					
Jerry Carle (Northwestern '48) 75	1	0	1	0	0

	Yrs	Won	Lost	CH	2D
CONCORDIA-M'HEAD					
Jim Christopherson (Concordia-M'head '60) 86, 88, 95, 97	4	2	4	0	0
CORTLAND ST.					
Dennis Kayser (Ithaca '74) 88, 89	2	1	2	0	0
Dave Murray (Springfield '81) 90	1	0	1	0	0
Dan MacNeil (Cortland St. '79) 97	1	0	1	0	0
TOTAL	4	1	4	0	0
DAYTON					
Rick Carter (Earlham '65) 78, 80-CH	2	3	1	1	0
Mike Kelly (Manchester '70) 81-2D, 84, 86, 87-2D, 88, 89-CH, 90, 91-2D, 92	9	13	8	1	3
TOTAL	11	16	9	2	3
DEFIANCE					
Greg Pscodna (Adrian '86) 01	1	0	1	0	0
DENISON					
Keith Piper (Baldwin-Wallace '48) 85	1	0	1	0	0
DICKINSON					
Ed Sweeney (C.W. Post '71) 89, 91	2	0	2	0	0
Darwin Breaux (West Chester '77) 94	1	0	1	0	0
TOTAL	3	0	3	0	0
DUBUQUE					
Don Birmingham (Westmar '62) 79, 80	2	0	2	0	0
EMORY & HENRY					
Lou Wacker (Richmond '56) 86, 87, 92, 95, 00	5	3	5	0	0
EVANSVILLE					
Jim Byers (Michigan '59) 74	1	0	1	0	0
FERRUM					
Hank Norton (Lynchburg '51) 87, 88, 89, 90	4	4	4	0	0
FORDHAM					
Larry Glueck (Villanova '63) 87	1	1	1	0	0
FORT VALLEY ST.					
Leon Lomax (Fort Valley St. '43) 75	1	0	1	0	0
FROSTBURG ST.					
Mike McGlinchey (Delaware '67) 93	1	1	1	0	0
GETTYSBURG					
Barry Streeter (Lebanon Valley '71) 85	1	2	1	0	0
GUST. ADOLPHUS					
Steve Raarup (Gust. Adolphus '53) 87	1	0	1	0	0
HAMPDEN-SYDNEY					
Stokeley Fulton (Hampden-Sydney '55) 77	1	0	1	0	0
HANOVER					
Wayne Perry (DePauw '72) 95, 97, 99, 00, 02	5	1	5	0	0
HARDIN-SIMMONS					
Jimmie Keeling (Howard Payne '58) 99, 00, 01	3	2	3	0	0
HIRAM					
Don Charlton (Lock Haven '65) 87	1	0	1	0	0
HOBART					
Michael Cragg (Slippery Rock '83) 00, 02	2	1	2	0	0
HOFSTRA					
Mickey Kwiatkowski (Delaware '70) 83, 86, 87, 88, 89	5	0	5	0	0
Joe Gardi (Maryland '60) 90	1	2	1	0	0
TOTAL	6	2	6	0	0
HOPE					
Ray Smith (UCLA '61) 86	1	0	1	0	0
Dean Kreps (Monmouth [Ill.] '84) 00	1	0	1	0	0
TOTAL	2	0	2	0	0
ILL. WESLEYAN					
Norm Eash (Ill. Wesleyan '75) 92, 96	2	2	2	0	0
INDIANAPOLIS					
Bill Bless (Indianapolis '63) 75	1	0	1	0	0
ITHACA					
Jim Butterfield (Maine '53) 74-2D, 75-2D, 78, 79-CH, 80-2D, 85-2D, 86, 88-CH, 90, 91-CH, 92	11	21	8	3	4
Michael Welch (Ithaca '73) 94, 01	2	4	2	0	0
TOTAL	13	25	10	3	4
JOHN CARROLL					
Tony DeCarlo (Kent St. '62) 89, 97	2	1	2	0	0
Regis Scafe (Case Reserve '71) 02	1	3	1	0	0
TOTAL	3	4	3	0	0
JUNIATA					
Walt Nadzak (Denison '57) 73-2D	1	1	1	0	1
KING'S (PA.)					
Rich Mannello (Springfield '83) 02	1	1	1	0	0

	Yrs	Won	Lost	CH	2D
LA VERNE					
Rex Huigens (La Verne '70) 94	1	0	1	0	0
LAKE FOREST					
Chad Eisele (Knox '90) 02	1	0	1	0	0
LAWRENCE					
Ron Roberts (Wisconsin '54) 81	1	1	1	0	0
LINFIELD					
Jay Locey (Oregon St. '77) 00, 02	2	1	2	0	0
LYCOMING					
Frank Girardi (West Chester '61) 85, 89, 90-2D, 91, 92, 95, 96, 97-2D, 98, 99	10	12	10	0	1
MacMURRAY					
Bob Frey (Mount Union '85) 01, 02	2	0	2	0	0
MARY HARDIN-BAYLOR					
Peter Fredenburg (Southwest Tex. St. '70), 01, 02	2	0	2	0	0
MASS.-DARTMOUTH					
Bill Kavanaugh (Stonehill '72) 02	1	0	1	0	0
MASS.-LOWELL					
Dennis Scannell (Villanova '74) 91	1	0	1	0	0
McDANIEL					
Tim Keating (Bethany [W.Va.] '75) 97, 98, 99, 00, 01	5	2	5	0	0
MENLO					
Ray Solari (California '51) 87	1	0	1	0	0
MERCHANT MARINE					
Charlie Pravata (Adelphi '72) 94	1	0	1	0	0
MILLERSVILLE					
Gene Carpenter (Huron '63) 79	1	0	1	0	0
MILLIKIN					
Carl Poelker (Millikin '68) 89	1	1	1	0	0
Doug Neibuhr (Millikin '75) 98, 00	2	0	2	0	0
TOTAL	3	1	3	0	0
MILLSAPS					
Harper Davis (Mississippi St. '49) 75	1	1	1	0	0
MINN.-MORRIS					
Al Molde (Gust. Adolphus '66) 77, 78, 79	3	2	3	0	0
Dick Smith (Coe '68) 80, 81	2	1	2	0	0
TOTAL	5	3	5	0	0
MONTCLAIR ST.					
Fred Hill (Upsala '57) 81	1	1	1	0	0
Rick Giancola (Rowan '68) 85, 86, 89, 99, 00, 01	6	5	6	0	0
TOTAL	7	6	7	0	0
MORAVIAN					
Scot Dapp (West Chester '73) 88, 93	2	1	2	0	0
MOUNT UNION					
Ken Wable (Muskingum '52) 85	1	1	1	0	0
Larry Kehres (Mount Union '71) 86, 90, 92, 93-CH, 94, 95, 96-CH, 97-CH, 98-CH, 99, 00-CH, 01-CH, 02-CH	13	36	6	7	0
TOTAL	14	37	7	7	0
MUHLENBERG					
Mike Donnelly (Ithaca '75) 02	1	1	1	0	0
COL. OF NEW JERSEY					
Eric Hamilton (Col. of New Jersey '75) 90, 96, 97, 98	4	3	4	0	0
OCCIDENTAL					
Dale Widolff (Indiana Central '75) 83, 84, 85	3	1	3	0	0
OHIO NORTHERN					
Tom Kaczkowski (Illinois '78) 99, 00	2	3	2	0	0
PACIFIC LUTHERAN					
Frosty Westering (Neb.-Omaha '52) 98, 99-CH, 00, 01	4	8	3	1	0
PLYMOUTH ST.					
Jay Cottone (Norwich '71) 84	1	0	1	0	0
Don Brown (Norwich '77) 94, 95	2	1	2	0	0
TOTAL	3	1	3	0	0
RANDOLPH-MACON					
Jim Blackburn (Virginia '71) 84	1	0	1	0	0
REDLANDS					
Mike Maynard (Ill. Wesleyan '80) 90, 92, 02	3	0	3	0	0
RENSSELAER					
Joe King (Siena '70) 99, 01	2	0	2	0	0
RHODES					
Mike Clary (Rhodes '77) 88	1	0	1	0	0

	Yrs	Won	Lost	CH	2D
ROCHESTER					
Ray Tellier (Connecticut '73) 87	1	0	1	0	0
ROWAN					
John Bunting (North Carolina '72) 91, 92	2	2	2	0	0
K.C. Keeler (Delaware '81) 93-2D, 95-2D, 96-2D, 97, 98-2D, 99-2D, 01	7	20	7	0	5
Jay Accorsi (Nichols '85) 02	1	0	1	0	0
TOTAL	10	22	10	0	5
ST. JOHN'S (MINN.)					
John Gagliardi (Colorado Col. '49) 76-CH, 77, 85, 87, 89, 91, 93, 94, 96, 98, 99, 00, 01, 02	14	26	13	1	1
ST. LAWRENCE					
Ted Stratford (St. Lawrence '57) 76, 78	2	1	2	0	0
Andy Talley (Southern Conn. St. '67) 82	1	1	1	0	0
TOTAL	3	2	3	0	0
ST. NORBERT					
Don LaViolette (St. Norbert '54) 89	1	0	1	0	0
Jim Purtill (Miami [Ohio] '78) 99, 00, 01	3	0	3	0	0
TOTAL	4	0	4	0	0
ST. OLAF					
Tom Porter (St. Olaf '51) 78	1	0	1	0	0
ST. THOMAS (MINN.)					
Vic Wallace (Cornell College '65) 90	1	1	1	0	0
SALISBURY					
Mike McGlinchey (Delaware '67) 83, 85, 86-2D	3	5	3	0	1
Sherman Wood (Salisbury '84) 02	1	0	1	0	0
TOTAL	4	5	4	0	1
SAN DIEGO					
Andy Vinci (Cal St. Los Angeles '63) 73	1	0	1	0	0
SIMPSON					
Jim Williams (Northern Iowa '60) 88, 89, 91, 96, 97	5	2	5	0	0
SLIPPERY ROCK					
Bob Di Spirito (Rhode Island '53) 74	1	0	1	0	0
SPRINGFIELD					
Mike DeLong (Springfield '74) 98, 00, 02	3	2	3	0	0
SUSQUEHANNA					
Rocky Rees (West Chester '71) 86	1	1	1	0	0
Steve Briggs (Springfield '84) 91	1	2	1	0	0
TOTAL	2	3	2	0	0
THOMAS MORE					
Vic Clark (Indiana St. '71) 92	1	0	1	0	0
Dean Paul (Mount Union '90) 01	1	1	1	0	0
TOTAL	2	1	2	0	0
TOWSON					
Phil Albert (Arizona '66) 76-2D	1	2	1	0	1
TRINITY (TEX.)					
Steven Mohr (Denison '76) 94, 97, 98, 99, 00, 01, 02-2D	7	12	7	0	1
UNION (N.Y.)					
Al Bagnoli (Central Conn. St. '74) 83-2D, 84, 85, 86, 89-2D, 91	6	7	6	0	2
John Audino (Notre Dame '75) 93, 95, 00	3	1	3	0	0
TOTAL	9	8	9	0	2
URSINUS					
Steve Gilbert (West Chester '79) 96	1	0	1	0	0
Paul Guenther (Ursinus '94) 99	1	1	1	0	0
TOTAL	2	1	2	0	0
WABASH					
Frank Navarro (Maryland '53) 77-2D	1	2	1	0	1
Chris Creighton (Kenyon '91) 02	1	2	1	0	0
TOTAL	2	4	2	0	1
WAGNER					
Bill Russo 80	1	0	1	0	0
Walt Hameline (Brockport St. '75) 82, 87-CH, 88	3	4	2	1	0
TOTAL	4	4	3	1	0

	Yrs	Won	Lost	CH	2D
WARTBURG					
Don Canfield 82	1	0	1	0	0
Bob Nielson (Wartburg '81) 93, 94	2	1	2	0	0
Rick Willis (Cornell College '88) 99, 02	2	1	2	0	0
TOTAL	5	2	5	0	0
WASHINGTON (MO.)					
Larry Kindbom (Kalamazoo '74) 99	1	0	1	0	0
WASH. & JEFF.					
John Luckhardt (Purdue '67) 84, 86, 87, 89, 90, 91 92-2D, 93, 94-2D, 95, 96	11	13	11	0	2
John Banaszak (Eastern Mich. '75) 99, 00, 01, 02	4	3	4	0	0
TOTAL	15	16	15	0	2
WESLEY					
Mike Drass (Mansfield '83) 00	1	0	1	0	0
WEST GA.					
Bobby Pate (Georgia '63) 81, 82-CH	2	3	1	1	0
WESTERN CONN. ST.					
Paul Pasqualoni (Penn St. '72) 85	1	0	1	0	0
John Cervino (West Va. Wesleyan '82) 99	1	0	1	0	0
Bob Surace (Princeton '90) 01	1	1	1	0	0
TOTAL	3	1	3	0	0
WESTFIELD ST.					
Steve Marino (Westfield St. '71)	1	0	1	0	0
WHEATON (ILL.)					
J.R. Bishop (Franklin '61) 95	1	1	1	0	0
Mike Swider (Wheaton [Ill.] '77) 02	1	1	1	0	0
TOTAL	2	2	2	0	0
WHITWORTH					
John Tully (Azusa Pacific '75)	1	0	1	0	0
WIDENER					
Bill Manlove (Temple '58) 75, 77-CH, 79, 80, 81-CH, 82, 88	7	9	5	2	0
Bill Cubit (Delaware '75) 94, 95	2	1	2	0	0
Bill Zwaan (Delaware '79) 00, 01	2	5	2	0	0
TOTAL	11	15	9	2	0
WILKES					
Joe DeMelfi (Delta St. '66) 93	1	0	1	0	0
WILLAMETTE					
Mark Speckman (Azusa Pacific '77) 99	1	0	1	0	0
WM. PATERSON					
Gerry Gallagher (Wm. Paterson '74) 93	1	1	1	0	0
WIS-EAU CLAIRE					
Bob Nielson (Wartburg '82) 98	1	2	1	0	0
WIS.-LA CROSSE					
Roger Harring (Wis.-La Crosse '58) 83, 91, 92-CH, 93, 95-CH, 96, 99	7	13	5	2	0
Larry Terry (Wis.-La Crosse '77) 02	1	0	1	0	0
TOTAL	8	13	6	2	0
WIS.-RIVER FALLS					
John O'Grady (Wis.-River Falls '79) 95, 96	2	1	2	0	0
WIS.-STEVENS POINT					
D. J. LeRoy (Wis.-Eau Claire '79) 86	1	0	1	0	0
John Miech (Wis.-Stevens Point '75) 99, 01	2	1	2	0	0
TOTAL	3	1	3	0	0
WIS.-STOUT					
Ed Meierkort (Dakota Wesleyan '81) 00	1	0	1	0	0
WIS.-WHITEWATER					
Bob Berezowitz (Wis.-Whitewater '67) 88, 90, 97	3	1	3	0	0
WITTENBERG					
Dave Maurer (Denison '54) 73-CH, 75-CH, 78-2D, 79-2D	4	9	2	2	2
Ron Murphy 88	1	1	1	0	0
Doug Neibuhr (Millikin '75) 95	1	0	1	0	0
Joe Fincham (Ohio '88) 98, 99, 00, 01, 02	5	7	5	0	0
TOTAL	11	17	9	2	2
WPI					
Jack Siedlecki (Union [N.Y.] '73) 92	1	0	1	0	0

Division III Championship Team Leaders

MOST APPEARANCES

Central (Iowa)	16
Wash. & Jeff.	15
Augustana (Ill.)	14
Mount Union	14
Ithaca	13
St. John's (Minn.)	13
Dayton#	11
Widener	11
Wittenberg	11
Lycoming	10
Rowan	10

MOST VICTORIES

Mount Union	37
St. John's (Minn.)	26
Ithaca	25
Rowan	22
Augustana (Ill.)	21

Central (Iowa)	19
Wittenberg	17
Dayton#	16
Wash. & Jeff.	16
Widener	15

MOST CONSECUTIVE APPEARANCES

11	Mount Union	1992-present
10	Augustana (Ill.)	1981-90
8	Wash. & Jeff.	1989-96
7	Central (Iowa)	1984-90
7	Dayton#	1986-92
6	Trinity (Tex.)	1997-present

HIGHEST WINNING PERCENTAGE
(Min. 10 Games Played)

Mount Union	37-7	.841
Pacific Lutheran	8-3	.727
Ithaca	25-10	.714
Rowan	22-10	.688
Wis.-La Crosse	13-6	.684
Augustana (Ill.)	21-10	.677
St. John's (Minn.)	26-13	.667

#No longer a Division III member.

All-Time Results

1973 Semifinals: Juniata 35, Bridgeport 14; Wittenberg 21, San Diego 14. **Championship:** Wittenberg 41, Juniata 0.

1974 Semifinals: Central (Iowa) 17, Evansville 16; Ithaca 27, Slippery Rock 14. **Championship:** Central (Iowa) 10, Ithaca 8.

1975 First Round: Widener 14, Albright 6; Ithaca 41, Fort Valley St. 12; Wittenberg 17, Indianapolis 13; Millsaps 28, Colorado Col. 21. **Semifinals:** Ithaca 23, Widener 14; Wittenberg 55, Millsaps 22. **Championship:** Wittenberg 28, Ithaca 0.

1976 First Round: St. John's (Minn.) 46, Augustana (Ill.) 7; Buena Vista 20, Carroll (Wis.) 14 (ot); St. Lawrence 26, Albright 7; Towson 14, C.W. Post 10. **Semifinals:** St. John's (Minn.) 61, Buena Vista 0; Towson 38, St. Lawrence 36. **Championship:** St. John's (Minn.) 31, Towson 28.

1977 First Round: Minn.-Morris 13, Albion 10; Wabash 20, St. John's (Minn.) 9; Widener 19, Central (Iowa) 0; Albany (N.Y.) 51, Hampden-Sydney 45. **Semifinals:** Wabash 37, Minn.-Morris 21; Widener 33, Albany (N.Y.) 15. **Championship:** Widener 39, Wabash 36.

1978 First Round: Minn.-Morris 23, St. Olaf 10; Wittenberg 6, Ithaca 3; Carnegie Mellon 24, Dayton 21; Baldwin-Wallace 71, St. Lawrence 7. **Semifinals:** Wittenberg 35, Minn.-Morris 14; Baldwin-Wallace 31, Carnegie Mellon 6. **Championship:** Baldwin-Wallace 24, Wittenberg 10.

1979 First Round: Wittenberg 21, Millersville 14; Widener 29, Baldwin-Wallace 8; Carnegie Mellon 31, Minn.-Morris 25; Ithaca 27, Dubuque 7. **Semifinals:** Wittenberg 17, Widener 14; Ithaca 15, Carnegie Mellon 6. **Championship:** Ithaca 14, Wittenberg 10.

1980 First Round: Ithaca 41, Wagner 13; Minn.-Morris 41, Dubuque 35; Dayton 34, Baldwin-Wallace 0; Widener 43, Bethany (W.Va.) 12. **Semifinals:** Ithaca 36, Minn.-Morris 0; Dayton 28, Widener 24. **Championship:** Dayton 63, Ithaca 0.

1981 First Round: Dayton 19, Augustana (Ill.) 7; Lawrence 21, Minn.-Morris 14 (ot); Montclair St. 13, Alfred 12; Widener 10, West Ga. 3. **Semifinals:** Dayton 38, Lawrence 0; Widener 23, Montclair St. 12. **Championship:** Widener 17, Dayton 10.

1982 First Round: Augustana (Ill.) 28, Baldwin-Wallace 22; St. Lawrence 43, Wagner 34; Bishop 32, Wartburg 7; West Ga. 31, Widener 24 (3 ot). **Semifinals:** Augustana (Ill.) 14, St. Lawrence 0; West Ga. 27, Bishop 6. **Championship:** West Ga. 14, Augustana (Ill.) 0.

1983 First Round: Union (N.Y.) 51, Hofstra 19; Salisbury 16, Carnegie Mellon 14; Augustana (Ill.) 22, Adrian 21; Wis.-La Crosse 43, Occidental 42. **Semi-finals:** Union (N.Y.) 23, Salisbury 21; Augustana (Ill.) 21, Wis.-La Crosse 15. **Championship:** Augustana (Ill.) 21, Union (N.Y.) 17.

1984 First Round: Union (N.Y.) 26, Plymouth St. 14; Augustana (Ill.) 14, Dayton 13; Wash. & Jeff. 22, Randolph-Macon 21; Central (Iowa) 23, Occidental 22. **Semifinals:** Augustana (Ill.) 23, Union (N.Y.) 6; Central (Iowa) 20, Wash. & Jeff. 0. **Championship:** Augustana (Ill.) 21, Central (Iowa) 12.

1985 First Round: Ithaca 13, Union (N.Y.) 12; Montclair St. 28, Western Conn. St. 0; Salisbury 35, Carnegie Mellon 22; Gettysburg 14, Lycoming 10; Augustana (Ill.) 26, Albion 10; Mount Union 35, Denison 3; Central (Iowa) 27, Coe 7; Occidental 28, St. John's (Minn.) 10. **Quarterfinals:** Ithaca 50, Montclair St. 28; Gettysburg 22, Salisbury 6; Augustana (Ill.) 21, Mount Union 14; Central (Iowa) 71, Occidental 0. **Semifinals:** Ithaca 34, Gettysburg 0; Augustana (Ill.) 14, Central (Iowa) 7. **Championship:** Augustana (Ill.) 20, Ithaca 7.

1986 First Round: Ithaca 24, Union (N.Y.) 17 (ot); Montclair St. 24, Hofstra 21; Susquehanna 28, Wash. & Jeff. 20; Salisbury 34, Emory & Henry 20; Mount Union 42, Dayton 36; Augustana (Ill.) 34, Hope 10; Central (Iowa) 37, Buena Vista 0; Concordia-M'head 24, Wis.-Stevens Point 15. **Quarterfinals:** Ithaca 29, Montclair St. 15; Salisbury 31, Susquehanna 17; Augustana (Ill.) 16, Mount Union 7; Concordia-M'head 17, Central (Iowa) 14. **Semifinals:** Salisbury 44, Ithaca 40; Augustana (Ill.) 41, Concordia-M'head 7. **Championship:** Augustana (Ill.) 31, Salisbury 3.

1987 First Round: Wagner 38, Rochester 14; Fordham 41, Hofstra 6; Wash. & Jeff. 23, Allegheny 17 (ot); Emory & Henry 49, Ferrum 7; Dayton 52, Capital 28; Augustana (Ill.) 53, Hiram 6; St. John's (Minn.) 7, Gust. Adolphus 3; Central (Iowa) 17, Menlo 0. **Quarterfinals:** Wagner 21, Fordham 0; Emory & Henry 23, Wash. & Jeff. 16; Dayton 38, Augustana (Ill.) 36; Central (Iowa) 13, St. John's (Minn.) 3. **Semifinals:** Wagner 20, Emory & Henry 15; Dayton 34, Central (Iowa) 0. **Championship:** Wagner 19, Dayton 3.

1988 Regionals: Cortland St. 32, Hofstra 27; Ithaca 34, Wagner 31 (ot); Ferrum 34, Rhodes 10; Moravian 17, Widener 7; Wittenberg 35, Dayton 28 (ot); Augustana (Ill.) 25, Adrian 7; Central (Iowa) 7, Concordia-M'head 0; Wis.-Whitewater 29, Simpson 27. **Quarterfinals:** Ithaca 24, Cortland St. 17; Ferrum 49, Moravian 28; Central (Iowa) 28, Wittenberg 14; Central (Iowa) 16, Wis.-Whitewater 13. **Semifinals:** Ithaca 62, Ferrum 28; Central (Iowa) 23, Augustana (Ill.) 17 (2 ot). **Championship:** Ithaca 39, Central (Iowa) 24.

1989 Regionals: Union (N.Y.) 42, Cortland St. 14; Montclair St. 23, Hofstra 6; Lycoming 21, Dickinson 0; Ferrum 41, Wash. & Jeff. 7; Dayton 35, John Carroll 10; Millikin 21, Augustana (Ill.) 12; Central (Iowa) 55, St. Norbert 7; St. John's (Minn.) 42, Simpson 35. **Quarterfinals:** Union (N.Y.) 45, Montclair St. 6; Ferrum 49, Lycoming 24; Dayton 28, Millikin 16; St. John's (Minn.) 27, Central (Iowa) 24. **Semifinals:** Union (N.Y.) 37, Ferrum 21; Dayton 28, St. John's (Minn.) 0. **Championship:** Dayton 17, Union (N.Y.) 7.

1990 Regionals: Hofstra 35, Cortland St. 9; Col. of New Jersey 24, Ithaca 14; Wash. & Jeff. 10, Ferrum 7; Lycoming 17, Carnegie Mellon 7; Dayton 24, Augustana (Ill.) 14; Allegheny 26, Mount Union 15; St. Thomas (Minn.) 24, Wis.-Whitewater 23; Central (Iowa) 24, Redlands 14. **Quarterfinals:** Hofstra 38, Col. of New Jersey 3; Lycoming 24, Wash. & Jeff. 0; Allegheny 31, Dayton 23; Central (Iowa) 33, St. Thomas (Minn.) 32. **Semifinals:** Lycoming 20, Hofstra 10; Allegheny 24, Central (Iowa) 7. **Championship:** Allegheny 21, Lycoming 14 (ot).

1991 Regionals: St. John's (Minn.) 75, Coe 2; Wis.-La Crosse 28, Simpson 13; Allegheny 24, Albion 21 (ot); Dayton 27, Baldwin-Wallace 10; Ithaca 31, Rowan 10; Union (N.Y.) 55, Mass.-Lowell 12; Lycoming 18, Wash. & Jeff. 16; Susquehanna 21, Dickinson 20. **Quarterfinals:** St. John's (Minn.) 29, Wis.-La Crosse 10; Dayton 28, Allegheny 25 (ot); Ithaca 35, Union (N.Y.) 23; Susquehanna 31, Lycoming 24. **Semifinals:** Dayton 19, St. John's (Minn.) 7; Ithaca 49, Susquehanna 13. **Championship:** Ithaca 34, Dayton 20.

1992 Regionals: Mount Union 27, Dayton 10; Ill. Wesleyan 21, Aurora 12; Central (Iowa) 20, Carleton 8; Wis.-La Crosse 47, Redlands 26; Emory & Henry 17, Thomas More 0; Wash. & Jeff. 33, Lycoming 0; Rowan 41, WPI 14; Buffalo St. 28, Ithaca 26. **Quarterfinals:** Mount Union 49, Ill. Wesleyan 27; Wis.-La Crosse 34, Central (Iowa) 9; Wash. & Jeff. 51, Emory & Henry 15; Rowan 28, Buffalo St. 19. **Semifinals:** Wis.-La Crosse 29, Mount Union 24; Wash. & Jeff. 18, Rowan 13. **Championship:** Wis.-La Crosse 16, Wash. & Jeff. 12.

1993 Regionals: Mount Union 40, Allegheny 7; Albion 41, Anderson (Ind.) 21; Wis.-La Crosse 55, Wartburg 21; Dayton 28, St. John's (Minn.) 32, Coe 14; Wash. & Jeff. 27, Moravian 7; Frostburg St. 26, Wilkes 25; Rowan 29, Buffalo St. 6; Wm. Paterson 17, Union (N.Y.) 7. **Quarterfinals:** Mount Union 40, Albion 16; St. John's (Minn.) 47, Wis.-La Crosse 25; Wash. & Jeff. 28, Frostburg St. 7; Rowan 37, Wm. Paterson 0. **Semifinals:** Mount Union 56, St. John's (Minn.) 8; Rowan 23, Wash. & Jeff. 16. **Championship:** Mount Union 34, Rowan 24.

1994 Regionals: Mount Union 28, Allegheny 19; Albion 28, Augustana (Ill.) 21; Wartburg 22, Central (Iowa) 21; St. John's (Minn.) 51, La Verne 12; Widener 14, Dickinson 0; Wash. & Jeff. 28, Trinity (Tex.) 0; Plymouth St. 19, Merchant Marine 18; Ithaca 10, Buffalo St. 7 (2 ot). **Quarterfinals:** Albion 34, Mount Union 33; St. John's (Minn.) 42, Wartburg 14; Wash. & Jeff. 37, Widener 21; Ithaca 22, Plymouth St. 7. **Semifinals:** Albion 19, St. John's (Minn.) 16; Wash. & Jeff. 23, Ithaca 19. **Championship:** Albion 38, Wash. & Jeff. 15.

1995 Regionals: Mount Union 52, Hanover 18; Wheaton (Ill.) 63, Wittenberg 41; Wis.-La Crosse 45, Concordia-M'head 7; Wis.-River Falls 10, Central (Iowa) 7; Wash. & Jeff. 35, Emory & Henry 16; Lycoming 31, Widener 27; Rowan 46, Buffalo St. 7; Union (N.Y.) 24, Plymouth St. 7. **Quarterfinals:** Mount Union 40, Wheaton (Ill.) 14; Wis.-La Crosse 28, Wis.-River Falls 14; Wash. & Jeff. 48, Lycoming 0; Rowan 38, Union (N.Y.) 7. **Semifinals:** Wis.-La Crosse 20, Mount Union 17; Rowan 28, Wash. & Jeff. 15. **Championship:** Wis.-La Crosse 36, Rowan 7.

1996 Regionals: Mount Union 31, Allegheny 26; Ill. Wesleyan 23, Albion 20; Wis.-La Crosse 44, Wis.-River Falls 0; St John's (Minn.) 21, Lycoming 31, Ursinus 24; Albright 31, Wash. & Jeff. 17; Rowan 21, Buffalo St. 20; Col. of New Jersey 17, Coast Guard 16. **Quarterfinals:** Mount Union 49, Ill. Wesleyan 14; Wis.-La Crosse 37, St. John's (Minn.) 30; Lycoming 31, Albright 13; Rowan 7, Col. of New Jersey 3. **Semifinals:** Mount Union 39, Wis.-La Crosse 21; Rowan 33, Lycoming 14. **Championship:** Mount Union 56, Rowan 24.

1997 First Round: Mount Union 34, Allegheny 30; John Carroll 30, Hanover 20; Simpson 34, Wis.-Whitewater 31; Augsburg 34, Concordia-M'head 22; Lycoming 27, McDaniel 13; Trinity (Tex.) 44, Catholic 33; Rowan 43, Coast Guard 0; Col. of New Jersey 34, Cortland St. 30. **Quarterfinals:** Mount Union 59, John Carroll 7; Simpson 61, Augsburg 21; Lycoming 46, Trinity (Tex.) 26; Rowan 13, Col. of New Jersey 7. **Semifinals:** Mount Union 54, Simpson 7; Lycoming 28, Rowan 20. **Championship:** Mount Union 61, Lycoming 12.

1998 First Round: Mount Union 21, Albion 19; Wittenberg 13, Millikin 10; Lycoming 49, Catholic 14; Trinity (Tex.) 30, McDaniel 20; Wis.-Eau Claire 28, Central (Iowa) 21; St. John's (Minn.) 33, Pacific Lutheran 20; Buffalo St. 38, Springfield 35; Rowan 26, Col. of New Jersey 2. **Quarterfinals:** Mount Union 21, Wittenberg 19; Trinity (Tex.) 37, Lycoming 21; Wis.-Eau Claire 10, St. John's (Minn.) 7; Rowan 19, Buffalo St. 17. **Semifinals:** Mount Union 34, Trinity (Tex.) 29; Rowan 22, Wis.-Eau Claire 19. **Championship:** Mount Union 44, Rowan 24.

1999 First Round: Augustana (Ill.) 39, St. Norbert 32; Ohio Northern 56, Hanover 14; Wittenberg 42, Alma 19; Montclair St. 37, Buffalo St. 34; Rowan 29, Rensselaer 10; Ursinus 43, Bridgewater St. 38; Pacific Lutheran 28, Willamette 24; Central (Iowa) 38, Wis.-La Crosse 17; St. John's (Minn.) 23, Wis.-Stevens Point 10; McDaniel 20, Catholic 16; Hardin-Simmons 28, Washington (Mo.) 21; Wash. & Jeff. 14, Lycoming 7. **Second Round:** Mount Union 42, Augustana (Ill.) 33; Ohio Northern 58, Wittenberg 24; Montclair St. 32, Western Conn. St. 24; Rowan 55, Ursinus 0; Pacific Lutheran 49, Wartburg 14; St. John's (Minn.) 10, Central (Iowa) 9; Trinity (Tex.) 20, McDaniel 16; Hardin-Simmons 51, Wash. & Jeff. 3. **Quarterfinals:** Mount Union 56, Ohio Northern 31; Rowan 42, Montclair St. 13; Pacific Lutheran 19, St. John's (Minn.) 9; Trinity (Tex.) 40, Hardin-Simmons 33. **Semifinals:** Rowan 24, Mount Union 17 (ot); Pacific Lutheran 49, Trinity (Tex.) 28. **Championship:** Pacific Lutheran 42, Rowan 13.

2000 First Round: Ohio Northern 47, Millikin 21; Hanover 20, Hope 3; Wittenberg 31, Aurora 20; Springfield 31, Montclair St. 29; Widener 33, Union (N.Y.) 26; Hobart 25, Bridgewater St. 0; Central (Iowa) 28, St. Norbert 14; Pacific Lutheran 41, Bethel (Minn.) 13; St. John's (Minn.), Wis.-Stout 19; McDaniel 38, Emory & Henry 14; Trinity (Tex.) 21, Wesley 3; Bridgewater (Va.) 59, Wash. & Jeff. 42. **Second Round:** Mount Union 59, Ohio Northern 28; Wittenberg 32, Hanover 21; Springfield 13, Brockport St. 6; Widener 40, Hobart 14; Central (Iowa) 20, Linfield 17 (ot); St. John's (Minn.) 28, Pacific Lutheran 21 (ot); Hardin-Simmons 32, McDaniel 10; Trinity (Tex.) 47, Bridgewater (Va.) 41 (ot). **Quarterfinals:** Mount Union 32, Wittenberg 15; Widener 61, Springfield 27; St. John's (Minn.) 21, Central (Iowa) 18; Hardin-Simmons 33, Trinity (Tex.) 30. **Semifinals:** Mount Union 70, Widener 30; St. John's (Minn.) 38, Hardin-Simmons 14. **Championship:** Mount Union 10, St. John's (Minn.) 7.

2001 First Round: Augustana (Ill.) 54, Defiance 14; Wittenberg 38, Hardin-Simmons 35 (ot); Thomas More 34, MacMurray 30; Pacific Lutheran 27, Whitworth 26 (ot); Wis.-Stevens Point 37, Bethel (Minn.) 27; St. John's (Minn.) 27, St. Norbert 20; Ithaca 35, Montclair St. 23; Rowan 40, Brockport St. 17; Western Conn. St. 8, Westfield St. 7; Trinity (Tex.) 30, Mary Hardin-Baylor 6; Wash. & Jeff. 24, McDaniel 21; Widener 56, Chris. Newport 7. **Second Round:** Mount Union 32, Augustana (Ill.) 7; Wittenberg 41, Thomas More 0; Pacific Lutheran 27, Central (Iowa) 21 (ot); St. John's (Minn.) 9, Wis.-Stevens Point 3; Ithaca 27, Rensselaer 10; Rowan 43, Western Conn. St. 14; Bridgewater (Va.) 41, Trinity (Tex.) 37; Widener 46, Wash. & Jeff. 30. **Quarterfinals:** Mount Union 49, Wittenberg 21; St. John's (Minn.) 31, Pacific Lutheran 6; Rowan 48, Ithaca 0; Bridgewater (Va.) 57, Widener 32. **Semifinals:** Mount Union 35, St. John's (Minn.) 14; Bridgewater (Va.) 29, Rowan 24. **Championship:** Mount Union 30, Bridgewater (Va.) 27.

2002 First Round: Wheaton (Ill.) 42, Alma 14; Wittenberg 34, Hanover 33; Wabash 42, MacMurray 7; Brockport St. 16, Springfield 0; John Carroll 27, Hobart 7; Muhlenberg 56, Mass.-Dartmouth 6; Wartburg 45, Lake Forest 0; Coe 21, Wis.-La Crosse 18; St. John's (Minn.) 31, Redlands 24; King's (Pa.) 28, Salisbury 0; Wash. & Jeff. 24, Chris. Newport 10; Trinity (Tex.) 48, Mary Hardin-Baylor 38. **Second Round:** Mount Union 42, Wheaton (Ill.) 21; Wabash 25, Wittenberg 14; Brockport St. 15, Rowan 12; John Carroll 21, Muhlenberg 10; Linfield 52, Wartburg 15; St. John's (Minn.) 45, Coe 14; Bridgewater (Va.) 19, King's (Pa.) 17; Trinity (Tex.) 45, Wash. & Jeff. 10. **Quarterfinals:** Mount Union 45, Wabash 16; John Carroll 16, Brockport St. 10 (ot); St. John's (Minn.) 21, Linfield 14; Trinity (Tex.) 38, Bridgewater (Va.) 32. **Semifinals:** Mount Union 57, John Carroll 19; Trinity (Tex.) 41, St. John's (Minn.) 34. **Championship:** Mount Union 48, Trinity (Tex.) 7.

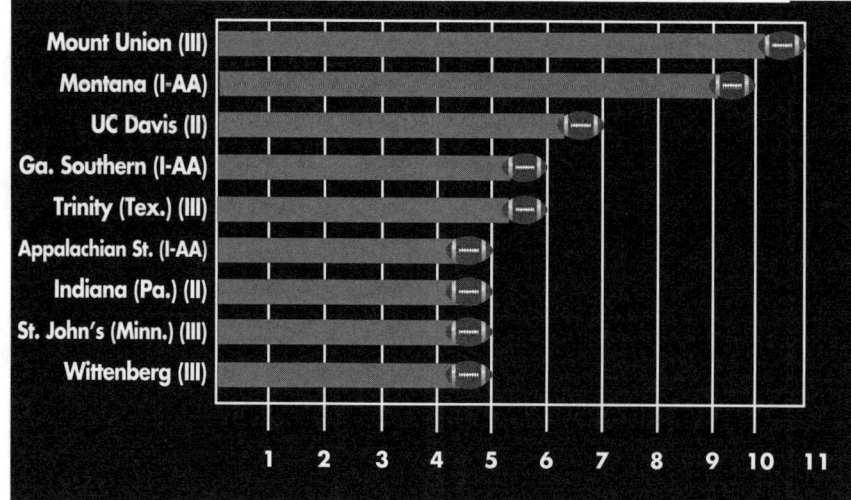

Longest Active Championship Selection Streaks

(Minimum 5 Years)

Attendance Records

All-Time College Football Attendance

(Includes all divisions and non-NCAA teams)

Year	No. Teams	G	Total Attendance	P/G Avg.	Yearly Change Total Att.	Percent
1948	685	—	19,134,159	—	—	—
1949	682	—	19,651,995	—	Up 517,836	+2.71
1950	674	—	18,961,688	—	Dn 690,307	-3.51
1951	635	—	17,480,533	—	Dn 1,481,155	-7.81
1952	625	—	17,288,062	—	Dn 192,471	-1.10
1953	618	—	16,681,731	—	Dn 606,331	-3.51
1954	614	—	17,048,603	—	Up 366,872	+2.20
1955	621	—	17,266,556	—	Up 217,953	+1.28
1956	618	—	18,031,805	—	Up 765,249	+4.43
1957	618	2,586	18,290,724	7,073	Up 258,919	+1.44
1958	618	2,673	19,280,709	7,213	Up 989,985	+5.41
1959	623	2,695	19,615,344	7,278	Up 334,635	+1.74
1960	620	2,711	20,403,409	7,526	Up 788,065	+4.02
1961	616	2,697	20,677,604	7,667	Up 274,195	+1.34
1962	610	2,679	21,227,162	7,924	Up 549,558	+2.66
1963	616	2,686	22,237,094	8,279	Up 1,009,932	+4.76
1964	622	2,745	23,354,477	8,508	Up 1,117,383	+5.02
1965	616	2,749	24,682,572	8,979	Up 1,328,095	+5.69
1966	616	2,768	25,275,899	9,131	Up 593,327	+2.40
1967	610	2,764	26,430,639	9,562	Up 1,154,740	+4.57
1968	612	2,786	27,025,846	9,701	Up 595,207	+2.25
1969	615	2,820	27,626,160	9,797	Up 600,314	+2.22
1970	617	2,895	29,465,604	10,178	Up 1,839,444	+6.66
1971	618	2,955	30,455,442	10,306	Up 989,838	+3.36
1972	620	2,997	30,828,802	10,287	Up 373,360	+1.23
1973	630	3,062	31,282,540	10,216	Up 453,738	+1.47
1974	634	3,101	31,234,855	10,073	Dn 47,685	-0.15
1975	634	3,089	31,687,847	10,258	Up 452,992	+1.45
1976	637	3,108	32,012,008	10,299	Up 324,161	+1.02
1977	638	3,145	32,905,178	10,463	Up 893,170	+2.79

Beginning in 1978, attendance includes NCAA teams only.

All-Time NCAA Attendance

Annual Total NCAA Attendance

(Includes Only NCAA Teams, All Divisions)

Year	No. Teams	G	Total Attendance	P/G Avg.	Yearly Change Total	Percent
1978	484	2,422	32,369,730	13,365	—	—
1979	478	2,381	32,874,755	13,807	Up 505,025	+1.56
1980	485	2,451	33,707,772	13,753	Up 833,017	+2.53
1981	497	2,505	34,230,471	13,665	Up 522,699	+1.55
1982	510	2,569	35,176,195	13,693	Up 945,724	+2.76
1983	505	2,557	34,817,264	13,616	Dn 358,931	-1.02
1984	501	2,542	35,211,076	*13,852	Up 393,812	+1.13
1985	509	2,599	34,951,548	13,448	Dn 259,528	-0.74
1986	510	2,605	35,030,902	13,448	Up 79,354	+0.23
1987	507	2,589	35,007,541	13,522	Dn 23,361	-0.07
1988	524	2,644	34,323,842	12,982	Dn 683,699	-1.95
1989	524	2,630	35,116,188	13,352	Up 792,346	+2.31
1990	533	2,704	35,329,946	13,066	Up 213,758	+0.61
1991	548	2,776	35,528,220	12,798	Up 198,274	+0.56
1992	552	2,824	35,225,431	12,474	Dn 302,789	-0.85
1993	560	2,888	34,870,634	12,074	Dn 354,797	-1.01
1994	568	2,907	36,459,896	12,542	Up 1,591,352	+4.56
1995	565	2,923	35,637,784	12,192	Dn 822,112	-2.25
1996	566	2,925	36,083,053	12,336	Up 445,269	+1.25
1997	581	2,998	36,857,849	12,294	Up 774,796	+2.15
1998	595	3,044	37,491,078	12,316	Up 633,229	+1.72
1999	601	3,137	39,482,657	12,586	Up 1,991,477	+5.31
2000	606	3,122	39,059,225	12,511	Dn 423,432	-1.07
2001	608	3,193	40,480,823	12,678	Up 1,421,598	+3.64
2002	*617	3,395	*44,556,215	13,124	*Up 4,075,392	*+10.07

*Record.

Annual Division I-A Attendance

Year	Teams	G	Attendance	Avg.
1976	137	796	23,917,522	30,047
1977	144	799	24,613,285	30,805
1978	139	772	25,017,915	32,407
1979	139	774	25,862,801	33,414
1980	139	776	26,499,022	34,148
1981	137	768	26,588,688	34,621
1982	97	567	24,771,855	43,689
1983	105	602	25,381,761	42,162
1984	105	606	25,783,807	42,548
1985	105	605	25,434,412	42,040
1986	105	611	25,692,095	42,049
1987	104	607	25,471,744	41,963
1988	104	605	25,079,490	41,454
1989	106	603	25,307,915	41,970
1990	106	615	25,513,098	41,485
1991	106	610	25,646,067	42,043
1992	107	617	25,402,046	41,170
1993	106	613	25,305,438	41,281
1994	107	614	25,590,190	41,678
1995	108	623	25,836,469	41,471
1996	111	644	26,620,942	41,337
1997	112	655	27,565,959	42,085
1998	112	651	27,674,217	42,510
1999	114	666	29,032,973	43,593
2000	114	661	28,839,284	43,630
2001	115	688	30,298,574	44,039
2002	117	775	*34,384,264	*44,367

*Record.

Annual Division I-AA Attendance

Year	Teams	G	Attendance	Avg.
1978	38	201	2,032,766	10,113
1979	39	211	2,073,890	9,829
1980	46	251	2,617,932	10,430
1981	50	270	2,950,156	10,927
1982	92	483	5,655,519	*11,709
1983	84	450	4,879,709	10,844
1984	87	465	5,061,480	10,885
1985	87	471	5,143,077	10,919
1986	86	456	5,044,992	11,064
1987	87	460	5,129,250	11,151
1988	88	465	4,801,637	10,326
1989	89	471	5,278,520	11,020
1990	87	473	5,328,477	11,265
1991	89	490	5,386,425	10,993
1992	88	485	5,057,955	10,429
1993	115	623	5,356,873	8,599
1994	117	643	*6,193,989	9,633
1995	119	647	5,660,329	8,749
1996	116	629	5,255,033	8,355
1997	118	642	5,212,048	8,118
1998	119	631	5,555,862	8,805
1999	122	661	5,949,345	9,001
2000	122	664	5,722,107	8,618
2001	123	649	5,375,851	8,283
2002	123	700	5,525,250	7,893

*Record.

Annual Division II Attendance

Year	Teams	G	Attendance	Avg.
1978	103	518	*2,871,683	*5,544
1979	105	526	2,775,569	5,277
1980	111	546	2,584,765	4,734
1981	121	589	2,726,537	4,629
1982	126	618	2,745,964	4,443
1983	122	611	2,705,892	4,429
1984	114	568	2,413,947	4,250
1985	114	569	2,475,325	4,350
1986	111	551	2,404,852	4,365
1987	107	541	2,424,041	4,481
1988	117	580	2,570,964	4,493
1989	116	579	2,572,496	4,428
1990	120	580	2,472,811	4,263
1991	128	622	2,490,929	4,005
1992	129	643	2,733,094	4,251
1993	142	718	2,572,053	3,582
1994	142	704	2,791,074	3,965
1995	138	705	2,459,792	3,489
1996	139	701	2,514,241	3,587
1997	142	710	2,349,442	3,309
1998	149	747	2,443,660	3,271
1999	147	749	2,504,118	3,343

Year	Teams	G	Attendance	Avg.
2000	149	739	2,512,290	3,400
2001	145	752	2,648,761	3,522
2002	149	783	2,647,038	3,381

*Record.

Annual Division III Attendance

Year	Teams	G	Attendance	Avg.
1978	204	931	*2,447,366	*2,629
1979	195	870	2,162,495	2,486
1980	189	878	2,006,053	2,285
1981	189	878	1,965,090	2,238
1982	195	901	2,002,857	2,223
1983	194	894	1,849,902	2,069
1984	195	903	1,951,842	2,162
1985	203	954	1,898,734	1,990
1986	208	987	1,888,963	1,914
1987	209	981	1,982,506	2,021
1988	215	994	1,871,751	1,883
1989	213	977	1,957,257	1,948
1990	220	1,036	2,015,560	1,946
1991	225	1,054	2,004,799	1,902
1992	228	1,079	2,032,336	1,884
1993	197	934	1,636,270	1,752
1994	202	946	1,884,643	1,992
1995	200	948	1,681,194	1,773
1996	200	951	1,692,837	1,780
1997	209	991	1,730,400	1,746
1998	215	1,015	1,817,339	1,790
1999	218	1,061	1,996,221	1,881
2000	221	1,058	1,985,544	1,877
2001	225	1,104	2,157,637	1,954
2002	228	1,137	1,999,663	1,759

*Record.

Annual Conference Attendance Leaders

(Based on per-game average; minimum 20 games)

Division I-A

Year	Conference	Teams	Attendance	P/G Avg.
1978	Big Ten	10	3,668,926	61,149
1979	Big Ten	10	3,865,170	63,363
1980	Big Ten	10	3,781,232	64,089
1981	Big Ten	10	3,818,728	63,645
1982	Big Ten	10	3,935,722	66,707
1983	Big Ten	10	3,710,931	67,471
1984	Big Ten	10	3,943,802	67,997
1985	Big Ten	10	4,015,693	66,928
1986	Big Ten	10	4,006,845	65,686
1987	Big Ten	10	3,990,524	65,418
1988	Southeastern	10	3,912,241	63,101
1989	Southeastern	10	4,123,005	65,445
1990	Southeastern	10	4,215,400	63,870
1991	Southeastern	10	4,063,190	66,610
1992	Southeastern	12	4,844,014	63,737
1993	Big Ten	11	4,320,397	63,535
1994	Big Ten	11	4,452,839	66,460
1995	Big Ten	11	4,592,499	67,537
1996	Big Ten	11	4,321,276	67,520
1997	Big Ten	11	4,744,211	67,774
1998	Southeastern	12	5,059,534	69,309
1999	Southeastern	12	5,500,664	70,521
2000	Southeastern	12	5,143,777	72,448
2001	Southeastern	12	5,554,028	73,079
2002	Southeastern	12	*6,085,156	*73,315

*Record.

Division I-AA

Year	Conference	Teams	Attendance	P/G Avg.
1978	Southwestern Athletic	5	483,159	17,895
1979	Southwestern Athletic	6	513,768	16,055
1980	Southwestern Athletic	7	611,234	16,085
1981	Southwestern Athletic	7	662,221	18,921
1982	Southwestern Athletic	7	634,505	18,129
1983	Southwestern Athletic	8	709,160	16,117
1984	Southwestern Athletic	8	702,186	17,555
1985	Southwestern Athletic	8	790,296	17,961
1986	Southwestern Athletic	8	621,584	16,357
1987	Southwestern Athletic	8	697,534	16,608
1988	Southwestern Athletic	8	541,127	14,240
1989	Southwestern Athletic	8	796,844	18,110
1990	Southwestern Athletic	7	828,169	20,704
1991	Southwestern Athletic	8	856,491	18,223
1992	Southwestern Athletic	8	873,772	20,804
1993	Southwestern Athletic	8	772,714	18,398
1994	Southwestern Athletic	8	*958,508	*23,378
1995	Southwestern Athletic	8	628,702	16,545
1996	Southwestern Athletic	8	600,798	15,405
1997	Southwestern Athletic	8	567,929	15,776
1998	Southwestern Athletic	9	516,042	13,580
1999	Southwestern Athletic	10	781,226	15,318
2000	Southwestern Athletic	10	506,076	11,502
2001	Southwestern Athletic	10	583,599	12,417
2002	Southwestern Athletic	10	459,911	10,950

*Record.

Division II

Year	Conference	Teams	Attendance	P/G Avg.
1978	Mid-Continent	6	237,458	9,133
1979	Mid-Continent	6	313,790	9,509
1980	Southern Intercollegiate	12	356,744	7,280
1981	Lone Star	8	340,876	7,575
1982	Lone Star	8	348,780	8,507
1983	Lone Star	8	296,350	7,228
1984	Central Intercollegiate	12	418,075	6,743
1985	Central Intercollegiate	12	378,160	6,099
1986	Central Intercollegiate	12	380,172	6,670
1987	Lone Star	6	208,709	6,325
1988	Central Intercollegiate	12	343,070	6,473
1989	Lone Star	8	249,570	5,942
1990	Southern Intercollegiate	9	264,741	6,967
1991	Central Intercollegiate	11	349,962	6,603
1992	Southern Intercollegiate	9	344,504	7,489
1993	Southern Intercollegiate	9	342,446	8,352
1994	Southern Intercollegiate	9	*456,289	*10,140
1995	Southern Intercollegiate	10	321,751	6,846
1996	Southern Intercollegiate	10	310,491	6,750
1997	Southern Intercollegiate	10	314,975	6,562
1998	Southern Intercollegiate	11	399,277	7,005
1999	Southern Intercollegiate	10	305,640	6,946
2000	Southern Intercollegiate	8	288,807	7,405
2001	Southern Intercollegiate	8	220,869	7,125
2002	North Central	9	307,688	5,594

*Record.

Division III

Year	Conference	Teams	Attendance	P/G Avg.
1979	Great Lakes	6	90,531	3,482
1980	Great Lakes	7	113,307	3,333
1981	Ohio Athletic	14	*196,640	2,979
1982	New Jersey State	7	98,502	2,985
1983	Heartland	7	121,825	3,384
1984	Heartland	7	107,500	2,986
1985	Ohio Athletic	9	125,074	2,719
1986	Heartland	7	91,793	2,550
1987	Heartland	6	84,815	3,029
1988	Heartland	5	82,966	2,963
1989	Old Dominion	5	70,676	2,945
1990	Old Dominion	6	86,238	2,974
1991	Old Dominion	6	101,774	3,283
1992	Old Dominion	6	100,132	3,338
1993	Old Dominion	6	96,526	3,218
1994	Old Dominion	6	111,334	*3,976
1995	Old Dominion	6	105,819	3,527
1996	Old Dominion	6	90,277	3,113
1997	Old Dominion	6	92,810	3,094
1998	Old Dominion	6	112,329	3,744
1999	Old Dominion	7	103,435	2,955
2000	Old Dominion	7	115,054	3,486
2001	Old Dominion	7	108,487	3,014
2002	Ohio Athletic	10	149,453	2,768

*Record. Note: 1978 figures not available.

ATTENDANCE RECORDS

Annual Division I-A Conference Attendance

(Since 1978)

ATLANTIC COAST CONFERENCE

Season		Teams	Games	Attendance	P/G	Change in P/G (Percent)	
1978		7	39	1,475,410	37,831	Up	3.88
1979		7	40	1,620,776	40,519	Up	7.11
1980		7	41	1,590,495	38,793	Dn	4.26
1981		7	40	1,589,152	39,729	Up	2.41
1982		7	41	1,706,451	41,621	Up	4.76
1983		8	49	2,087,800	42,608	Up	3.71
1984		8	46	1,998,274	43,441	Up	1.96
1985		8	48	2,029,574	42,283	Dn	2.67
1986		8	45	1,848,949	41,088	Dn	2.83
1987		8	47	1,970,198	41,919	Up	2.02
1988		8	47	1,911,949	40,680	Dn	2.96
1989		8	49	2,010,317	41,027	Up	0.85
1990		8	47	1,988,781	42,314	Up	3.14
1991		8	51	2,257,413	44,263	Up	4.61
1992		9	53	2,332,674	44,013	Dn	0.56
1993		9	54	2,379,045	44,056	Up	0.10
1994		9	51	2,248,700	44,092	Up	0.08
1995		9	51	2,329,868	45,684	Up	3.61
1996		9	50	2,203,849	44,077	Dn	3.52
1997		9	52	2,333,784	44,880	Up	1.82
1998		9	51	2,330,879	45,704	Up	1.84
1999		9	51	2,298,711	45,073	Dn	1.38
2000		9	54	2,653,816	49,145	Up	9.03
2001		9	56	2,784,520	49,724	Up	1.18
2002		9	58	2,957,611	50,993	Up	2.55

BIG EAST CONFERENCE

Season		Teams	Games	Attendance	P/G	Change in P/G (Percent)	
1991		8	47	1,788,611	38,056	Dn	7.00
1992		8	48	1,847,269	38,485	Up	1.13
1993		8	47	1,787,843	38,039	Dn	1.16
1994		8	46	1,902,096	41,350	Up	8.70
1995		8	44	1,679,043	38,160	Dn	7.71
1996		8	47	1,825,870	38,848	Up	1.80
1997		8	46	1,657,056	36,023	Dn	7.27
1998		8	48	1,914,957	39,895	Up	10.75
1999		8	46	1,837,478	39,945	Up	0.13
2000		8	49	2,030,230	41,433	Up	3.73
2001		8	49	1,927,280	39,332	Dn	5.07
2002		8	53	2,315,608	43,691	Up	11.08

BIG TEN CONFERENCE

Season		Teams	Games	Attendance	P/G	Change in P/G (Percent)	
1978		10	60	3,668,926	61,149	Up	2.87
1979		10	61	3,865,170	63,363	Up	3.62
1980		10	59	3,781,232	64,089	Up	1.15
1981		10	60	3,818,728	63,645	Dn	0.69
1982		10	59	3,935,722	66,707	Up	4.81
1983		10	55	3,710,931	67,471	Up	1.15
1984		10	58	3,943,802	67,997	Up	0.78
1985		10	60	4,015,693	66,928	Dn	1.57
1986		10	61	4,006,845	65,686	Dn	1.86
1987		10	61	3,990,524	65,418	Dn	0.41
1988		10	59	3,714,231	62,953	Dn	3.77
1989		10	59	3,492,647	59,197	Dn	5.97
1990		10	60	3,533,504	58,892	Dn	0.52
1991		10	61	3,674,654	60,240	Up	2.29
1992		10	60	3,600,410	60,007	Dn	0.39
1993		11	68	4,320,397	63,535	Up	5.88
1994		11	67	4,452,839	66,460	Up	4.60
1995		11	68	4,592,499	67,537	Up	1.62
1996		11	64	4,321,276	67,520	Dn	0.03
1997		11	70	4,744,211	67,774	Up	0.38
1998		11	65	4,354,383	66,991	Dn	1.16
1999		11	70	4,701,095	67,159	Up	0.25
2000		11	67	4,591,153	68,525	Up	2.03
2001		11	66	4,622,376	70,036	Up	2.21
2002		11	78	5,455,105	69,937	Dn	0.14

BIG 12 CONFERENCE

Season		Teams	Games	Attendance	P/G	Change in P/G (Percent)	
1996		12	69	3,549,474	51,442	Up	3.39
1997		12	71	3,640,692	51,277	Dn	0.32
1998		12	71	3,661,740	51,574	Up	0.58
1999		12	72	3,904,491	54,229	Up	5.15
2000		12	74	3,995,338	53,991	Dn	0.44
2001		12	76	4,215,088	55,462	Up	2.72
2002		12	79	4,358,818	55,175	Dn	0.52

CONFERENCE USA

Season		Teams	Games	Attendance	P/G	Change in P/G (Percent)	
1996		6	33	825,899	25,027	Up	12.87
1997		7	38	963,239	25,348	Up	1.28
1998		8	44	1,239,052	28,160	Up	11.09
1999		9	52	1,476,223	28,389	Up	0.81
2000		9	49	1,388,331	28,333	Dn	0.20
2001		10	53	1,432,512	27,029	Dn	4.60
2002		10	61	1,627,131	26,674	Dn	1.31

MID-AMERICAN CONFERENCE

Season		Teams	Games	Attendance	P/G	Change in P/G (Percent)	
1978		10	51	722,026	14,157	Up	14.36
1979		10	52	696,784	13,400	Dn	5.35
1980		10	51	714,415	14,008	Up	4.54
1981		10	53	804,158	15,173	Up	8.32
1982@		10	51	980,087	19,217	Up	26.65
1983		10	51	884,888	17,351	Dn	9.71
1984		10	53	918,133	17,323	Dn	0.16
1985		10	49	719,024	14,674	Dn	15.29
1986		9	47	679,866	14,465	Dn	1.42
1987		9	45	652,285	14,495	Up	0.21
1988		9	46	765,563	16,643	Up	14.82
1989		9	44	689,698	15,675	Dn	5.82
1990		9	45	744,368	16,542	Up	5.53
1991		9	45	608,485	13,522	Dn	18.26
1992		10	49	704,233	14,372	Up	5.97
1993		10	51	726,847	14,252	Dn	0.83
1994		10	51	754,296	14,790	Up	3.77
1995		10	50	748,138	14,963	Up	1.17
1996		10	50	787,035	15,741	Up	5.18
1997		12	63	1,130,939	17,951	Up	14.04
1998		12	61	1,022,567	16,763	Dn	6.62
1999		13	67	1,195,463	17,843	Up	5.32
2000		13	67	1,080,812	16,132	Dn	9.59
2001		13	66	1,171,999	17,758	Up	10.08
2002		14	81	1,420,525	17,537	Dn	1.24

@Mid-American and Missouri Valley divided between I-A and I-AA.

MOUNTAIN WEST CONFERENCE
(Members came from Western Athletic Conference)

Season		Teams	Games	Attendance	P/G	Change in P/G (Percent)	
1999		8	43	1,489,527	34,640	Up	3.12
2000		8	44	1,419,326	32,257	Dn	6.88
2001		8	45	1,432,365	31,830	Dn	1.32
2002		8	46	1,604,755	34,886	Up	9.60

PACIFIC-10 CONFERENCE

Season		Teams	Games	Attendance	P/G	Change in P/G (Percent)	
1978		10	57	2,632,755	46,189	Up	5.56
1979		10	59	2,741,656	46,469	Up	0.61
1980		10	58	2,777,146	47,882	Up	3.04
1981		10	59	2,772,237	46,987	Dn	1.87
1982		10	59	2,745,676	46,537	Dn	0.96
1983		10	58	2,740,406	47,248	Up	1.53
1984		10	63	2,976,655	47,248	No Change	
1985		10	56	2,665,356	47,596	Up	0.74
1986		10	59	2,856,910	48,422	Up	1.74
1987		10	57	2,866,723	50,293	Up	3.86
1988		10	60	3,058,637	50,977	Up	1.36
1989		10	60	3,006,176	50,103	Dn	1.71
1990		10	58	2,872,173	49,520	Dn	1.16
1991		10	59	2,851,991	48,339	Dn	2.38
1992		10	60	2,825,401	47,090	Dn	2.58
1993		10	57	2,731,361	47,919	Up	1.76
1994		10	59	2,785,373	47,210	Dn	1.48
1995		10	57	2,680,510	47,026	Dn	0.39
1996		10	58	2,761,006	47,604	Up	1.23
1997		10	60	2,891,522	48,192	Up	1.24
1998		10	60	3,024,262	50,404	Up	4.59
1999		10	59	2,857,994	48,441	Dn	3.89
2000		10	61	2,987,809	48,980	Up	1.11
2001		10	58	2,784,069	48,001	Dn	2.00
2002		10	66	3,299,852	49,998	Up	4.16

SOUTHEASTERN CONFERENCE

Season	Teams	Games	Attendance	P/G	Change in P/G (Percent)	
1978	10	61	3,464,112	56,789	Up	2.62
1979	10	59	3,376,833	57,234	Up	0.78
1980	10	66	3,951,104	59,865	Up	4.60
1981	10	61	3,846,492	63,057	Up	5.33
1982	10	66	4,206,507	63,735	Up	1.08
1983	10	65	4,214,702	64,842	Up	1.74
1984	10	63	4,007,351	63,609	Dn	1.90
1985	10	63	4,017,104	63,764	Up	0.24
1986	10	69	4,351,832	63,070	Dn	1.09
1987	10	64	4,117,046	64,329	Up	2.00
1988	10	62	3,912,241	63,101	Dn	1.91
1989	10	63	4,123,005	65,445	Up	3.71
1990	10	66	4,215,400	63,870	Dn	2.41
1991	10	61	4,063,190	66,610	Up	4.29
1992	12	76	4,844,014	63,737	Dn	4.31
1993	12	78	4,897,564	62,789	Dn	1.49
1994	12	77	4,891,615	63,527	Up	1.18
1995	12	76	4,827,834	63,524	Dn	0.01
1996	12	76	4,932,802	64,905	Up	2.17
1997	12	76	5,005,126	65,857	Up	1.47
1998	12	73	5,059,534	69,309	Up	5.24
1999	12	78	5,500,664	70,521	Up	1.75
2000	12	71	5,143,777	72,448	Up	2.73
2001	12	76	5,554,028	73,079	Up	0.87
2002	12	83	6,085,156	73,315	Up	0.32

SUN BELT

Season	Teams	Games	Attendance	P/G	Change in P/G (Percent)	
2001	7	34	454,829	13,377		
2002	7	38	498,801	13,126	Dn	1.88

WESTERN ATHLETIC CONFERENCE

Season	Teams	Games	Attendance	P/G	Change in P/G (Percent)	
1978	7	37	906,518	24,500	Dn	1.84
1979	8	47	1,349,156	28,705	Up	17.16
1980	9	51	1,354,492	26,559	Dn	5.41
1981	9	51	1,443,515	28,304	Up	6.57
1982	9	53	1,605,684	30,296	Up	7.04
1983	9	52	1,567,062	30,136	Dn	0.53
1984	9	55	1,741,793	31,669	Up	5.09
1985	9	55	1,744,123	31,711	Up	0.13
1986	9	51	1,748,857	34,291	Up	8.14
1987	9	54	1,927,572	35,696	Up	4.10
1988	9	54	1,795,735	33,254	Dn	6.84
1989	9	55	1,844,999	33,545	Up	0.88
1990	9	55	1,784,807	32,451	Dn	3.26
1991	9	55	1,883,861	34,252	Up	5.55
1992	10	60	2,111,587	35,193	Up	2.85
1993	10	61	2,109,441	34,581	Dn	1.74
1994	10	61	2,090,620	34,272	Dn	0.89
1995	10	63	1,987,860	31,553	Dn	7.93
1996	16	91	2,615,219	28,739	Dn	8.92
1997	16	92	2,758,817	29,987	Up	4.34
1998	16	91	2,594,194	28,508	Dn	4.93
1999	8	45	1,207,602	26,836	Dn	5.87
2000	9	51	1,403,284	27,515	Up	2.53
2001	10	49	1,212,887	24,753	Dn	10.04
2002	10	58	1,453,406	25,059	Up	1.24

ALL-TIME ATTENDANCE OTHER CONFERENCES
(Conferences that either discontinued or changed names)

BIG EIGHT CONFERENCE
(All members went into Big 12 Conference after 1995 season)

Season	Teams	Games	Attendance	P/G	Change in P/G (Percent)	
1978	8	48	2,549,553	53,116	Dn	1.45
1979	8	46	2,457,633	53,427	Up	0.59
1980	8	49	2,629,195	53,657	Up	0.43
1981	8	50	2,559,480	51,190	Dn	4.60
1982	8	48	2,377,389	49,529	Dn	3.24
1983	8	49	2,398,134	48,943	Dn	1.18
1984	8	45	2,247,010	49,934	Up	2.02
1985	8	54	2,504,509	46,380	Dn	7.12
1986	8	49	2,242,082	45,757	Dn	1.34
1987	8	49	2,182,199	44,535	Dn	2.67
1988	8	49	2,184,333	44,578	Up	0.10
1989	8	49	2,362,465	48,214	Up	8.16
1990	8	49	2,257,825	46,078	Dn	4.43
1991	8	49	2,308,238	47,107	Up	2.23

Season	Teams	Games	Attendance	P/G	Change in P/G (Percent)	
1992	8	47	2,247,907	47,828	Up	1.53
1993	8	48	2,126,247	44,297	Dn	7.38
1994	8	46	2,194,545	47,708	Up	7.70
1995	8	50	2,414,804	48,296	Up	1.23

BIG WEST CONFERENCE
(Discontinued sponsorship of football after 2000 season)

Season	Teams	Games	Attendance	P/G	Change in P/G (Percent)	
1988	8	38	570,533	15,014	Up	2.58
1989	8	37	528,921	14,295	Dn	4.79
1990	8	41	650,800	15,873	Up	11.04
1991	8	37	570,332	15,414	Dn	2.89
1992	7	36	515,291	14,314	Dn	7.14
1993	10	48	778,224	16,213	Up	13.27
1994	10	49	705,539	14,399	Dn	11.19
1995	10	51	793,452	15,558	Up	8.05
1996	6	34	554,684	16,314	Up	4.86
1997	6	32	584,020	18,251	Up	11.87
1998	7	37	631,791	17,075	Dn	6.44
1999	7	35	669,254	19,122	Up	11.99
2000	6	29	504,238	17,388	Dn	9.07

IVY GROUP
(Went into Division I-AA after 1981 season)

Season	Teams	Games	Attendance	P/G	Change in P/G (Percent)	
1978	8	40	547,395	13,685	Up	4.87
1979	8	40	534,597	13,365	Dn	2.34
1980	8	43	514,433	11,964	Dn	10.48
1981	8	41	564,059	13,758	Up	14.99

MISSOURI VALLEY CONFERENCE
(Conference discontinued after 1985 season)

Season	Teams	Games	Attendance	P/G	Change in P/G (Percent)	
1978	7	39	523,565	13,425	Up	5.83
1979	7	37	481,706	13,019	Dn	3.02
1980	7	35	473,462	13,527	Up	3.90
1981	8	43	575,174	13,376	Dn	1.12
1982	8	40	594,515	14,863	Up	11.12
1983	7	37	412,412	11,146	Dn	23.63
1984	7	37	427,112	11,544	Up	3.57
1985	5	26	308,137	11,851	Up	2.66

PACIFIC COAST CONFERENCE
(Became Big West Conference after 1987 season)

Season	Teams	Games	Attendance	P/G	Change in P/G (Percent)	
1978	6	29	279,772	9,647	Dn	3.81
1979	6	25	322,305	12,892	Up	33.64
1980	6	28	353,022	12,608	Dn	2.20
1981	6	27	360,005	13,334	Up	5.76
1982	7	34	487,638	14,342	Up	7.56
1983	7	35	500,380	14,297	Dn	0.31
1984	8	39	597,420	15,318	Up	5.52
1985	8	40	654,045	16,351	Up	6.74
1986	8	42	753,466	17,940	Up	9.72
1987	8	41	600,129	14,637	Dn	18.41

SOUTHERN CONFERENCE
(Went into Division I-AA after 1981 season)

Season	Teams	Games	Attendance	P/G	Change in P/G (Percent)	
1978	7	34	372,009	10,941	Up	11.20
1979	8	47	478,107	10,172	Dn	7.03
1980	8	40	484,727	12,118	Up	19.13
1981	8	42	459,576	10,942	Dn	9.70

SOUTHLAND CONFERENCE
(Went into Division I-AA after 1981 season)

Season	Teams	Games	Attendance	P/G	Change in P/G (Percent)	
1978	6	37	467,915	12,646	Dn	13.67
1979	6	31	491,917	15,868	Up	25.48
1980	6	32	452,311	14,135	Dn	10.92
1981	6	30	427,106	14,237	Up	0.72

SOUTHWEST CONFERENCE
(Discontinued after 1995 season; teams went to Big 12 and Western Athletic Conferences)

Season	Teams	Games	Attendance	P/G	Change in P/G (Percent)	
1978	9	45	2,033,212	45,182	Up	15.46
1979	9	52	2,301,148	44,253	Dn	2.06
1980	9	54	2,263,881	41,924	Dn	5.26
1981	9	54	2,232,757	41,347	Dn	1.38

ATTENDANCE RECORDS

Season	Teams	Games	Attendance	P/G	Change in P/G (Percent)
1982	9	52	2,226,009	42,808	Up 3.53
1983	9	56	2,292,540	40,938	Dn 4.37
1984	9	53	2,177,507	41,085	Up 0.36
1985	9	51	2,077,717	40,740	Dn 0.84
1986	9	53	2,006,663	37,862	Dn 7.06
1987	8	48	1,859,454	38,739	Up 2.32
1988	8	46	1,774,120	38,568	Dn 0.44
1989	9	51	1,914,608	37,541	Dn 2.66
1990	9	53	2,087,248	39,382	Up 4.90
1991	9	50	2,062,309	41,246	Up 4.73
1992	8	47	1,697,152	36,110	Dn 12.45
1993	8	45	1,587,652	35,281	Dn 2.30
1994	8	43	1,588,955	36,952	Up 4.74
1995	8	43	1,653,888	38,463	Up 4.09

Annual Division I-AA Conference Attendance

(Since 1978)

ATLANTIC 10 CONFERENCE
(Formerly Yankee Conference)

Season	Teams	Games	Attendance	P/G	Change in P/G (Percent)
1978	6	32	207,502	6,484	Dn 9.81
1979	6	29	197,293	6,803	Up 4.92
1980	6	32	211,822	6,619	Dn 2.70
1981	6	29	233,680	8,058	Up 21.74
1982	6	32	254,789	7,962	Dn 1.19
1983	6	30	218,186	7,273	Dn 8.65
1984	6	31	284,709	9,184	Up 26.28
1985	6	36	257,170	7,144	Dn 22.21
1986	8	44	486,299	11,052	Up 54.70
1987	8	43	408,170	9,492	Dn 14.12
1988	9	47	447,641	9,524	Up 0.34
1989	9	48	460,683	9,598	Up 0.78
1990	9	49	423,459	8,642	Dn 9.96
1991	9	48	431,522	8,990	Up 4.03
1992	9	53	461,366	8,705	Dn 3.17
1993	12	67	550,245	8,213	Dn 7.09
1994	12	67	630,847	9,416	Up 14.65
1995	12	66	578,742	8,769	Dn 6.87
1996	12	64	526,442	8,226	Dn 6.19
1997	12	65	486,798	7,489	Dn 8.96
1998	11	59	533,945	9,050	Up 20.84
1999	11	61	563,885	9,244	Up 2.14
2000	10	58	512,307	8,833	Dn 4.45
2001	11	57	433,699	7,609	Dn 13.86
2002	11	67	488,814	7,296	Dn 4.11

BIG SKY CONFERENCE

Season	Teams	Games	Attendance	P/G	Change in P/G (Percent)
1978	7	36	393,274	10,924	Up 4.16
1979	8	47	463,920	9,871	Dn 7.70
1980	8	45	520,250	11,561	Up 17.12
1981	8	47	538,920	11,466	Dn 0.82
1982	8	43	463,393	10,777	Dn 6.01
1983	8	44	474,167	10,777	No change
1984	8	47	475,645	10,120	Dn 6.10
1985	8	48	481,015	10,021	Dn 0.98
1986	8	46	469,368	10,204	Up 1.83
1987	9	52	537,300	10,333	Up 1.26
1988	9	50	513,467	10,269	Dn 0.62
1989	9	52	550,975	10,596	Up 3.18
1990	9	50	531,060	10,621	Up 0.24
1991	9	56	623,326	11,131	Up 4.80
1992	8	46	437,592	9,513	Dn 14.54
1993	8	48	460,613	9,596	Up 0.87
1994	8	47	530,089	11,278	Up 17.53
1995	8	46	530,022	11,522	Up 2.16
1996	8	44	360,082	8,184	Dn 28.97
1997	8	47	385,728	8,207	Up 0.03
1998	9	49	398,690	8,137	Dn 0.85
1999	9	50	492,618	9,852	Up 21.08
2000	9	51	420,423	8,244	Dn 16.32
2001	8	46	414,964	9,021	Up 9.43
2002	8	47	452,885	9,636	Up 6.82

GATEWAY FOOTBALL CONFERENCE

Season	Teams	Games	Attendance	P/G	Change in P/G (Percent)
1985	6	35	281,632	8,047	Up 8.01
1986	7	37	351,972	9,513	Up 16.03
1987	7	36	315,318	8,759	Dn 7.93
1988	7	36	332,800	9,244	Up 5.54
1989	7	40	315,633	7,891	Dn 14.64
1990	7	36	313,409	8,706	Up 10.33
1991	7	38	332,482	8,750	Up 0.51
1992	7	40	345,823	8,646	Dn 1.19
1993	7	36	285,921	7,942	Dn 8.14
1994	7	40	293,437	7,336	Dn 7.63
1995	7	41	317,344	7,740	Up 5.51
1996	6	33	294,724	8,931	Up 15.39
1997	7	41	399,221	9,737	Up 9.02
1998	7	39	366,029	9,385	Dn 3.62
1999	7	39	392,203	10,056	Up 7.15
2000	7	40	385,483	9,637	Dn 4.17
2001	8	44	436,217	9,914	Up 2.87
2002	8	49	458,622	9,360	Dn 5.59

IVY GROUP

Season	Teams	Games	Attendance	P/G	Change in P/G (Percent)
1982	8	44	602,857	13,701	Dn 0.41
1983	8	43	653,263	15,192	Up 10.88
1984	8	39	591,562	15,168	Dn 0.16
1985	8	41	562,184	13,712	Dn 9.60
1986	8	43	543,983	12,651	Dn 7.74
1987	8	42	602,480	14,345	Up 13.39
1988	8	42	513,674	12,230	Dn 14.74
1989	8	43	557,872	12,974	Up 6.08
1990	8	41	471,245	11,494	Dn 11.41
1991	8	39	466,928	11,973	Up 4.17
1992	8	40	401,980	10,050	Dn 16.06
1993	8	42	420,915	10,022	Dn 0.28
1994	8	42	445,900	10,617	Up 5.94
1995	8	42	396,539	9,441	Dn 11.08
1996	8	40	413,112	10,328	Up 9.40
1997	8	39	284,650	7,299	Dn 29.33
1998	8	40	445,801	11,145	Up 52.69
1999	8	44	516,589	11,741	Up 5.35
2000	8	40	456,317	11,408	Dn 2.84
2001	8	38	410,268	10,797	Dn 5.36
2002	8	41	387,600	9,454	Dn 12.44

METRO ATLANTIC ATHLETIC CONFERENCE

Season	Teams	Games	Attendance	P/G	Change in P/G (Percent)
1993	6	29	34,483	1,189	Up 13.02
1994	7	35	41,364	1,182	Dn 0.59
1995	8	37	51,549	1,393	Up 17.85
1996	9	41	57,742	1,408	Up 1.08
1997	9	46	69,249	1,505	Up 6.89
1998	9	44	75,134	1,708	Up 13.49
1999	9	46	96,105	2,089	Up 22.31
2000	8	39	73,227	1,878	Dn 10.10
2001	8	38	76,874	2,023	Up 7.72
2002	9	46	88,361	1,921	Dn 5.04

MID-EASTERN ATHLETIC CONFERENCE

Season	Teams	Games	Attendance	P/G	Change in P/G (Percent)
1978	4	19	141,234	7,433	Dn 2.96
1979	4	24	131,942	5,498	Dn 26.03
1980	6	29	308,530	10,639	Up 93.51
1981	6	35	357,982	10,228	Dn 3.86
1982	6	35	358,315	10,238	Up 0.10
1983	6	34	335,664	9,872	Dn 3.57
1984	5	27	209,612	7,763	Dn 21.36
1985	5	23	263,687	11,465	Up 47.69
1986	6	32	270,405	8,450	Dn 32.29
1987	6	30	354,899	11,830	Up 40.00
1988	7	39	466,030	11,948	Up 1.00
1989	7	41	521,529	12,720	Up 6.45
1990	7	36	475,909	13,220	Up 3.93
1991	7	40	578,412	14,460	Up 9.38
1992	7	38	450,962	11,867	Dn 17.93
1993	7	40	440,012	11,000	Dn 7.31
1994	7	40	556,159	13,904	Up 26.40
1995	8	37	350,770	9,480	Dn 31.82
1996	8	41	445,672	10,870	Up 14.66
1997	9	42	427,794	10,186	Dn 6.29
1998	9	41	466,929	11,389	Up 11.81
1999	9	41	479,754	11,701	Up 2.74
2000	9	40	424,796	10,620	Dn 9.24
2001	9	41	431,278	10,519	Up 0.95
2002	9	49	453,947	9,264	Dn 11.93

NORTHEAST CONFERENCE

Season	Teams	Games	Attendance	P/G	Change in P/G (Percent)
1996	5	27	40,800	1,511	Dn 10.70
1997	5	24	37,014	1,542	Up 2.05
1998	5	24	36,189	1,508	Dn 2.20
1999	8	37	70,411	1,903	Up 26.19
2000	9	47	70,750	1,505	Dn 20.91
2001	9	41	71,428	1,742	Up 15.75
2002	8	41	84,272	2,055	Up 17.97

OHIO VALLEY CONFERENCE

Season	Teams	Games	Attendance	P/G	Change in P/G (Percent)
1978	7	37	355,893	9,619	Dn 8.47
1979	7	36	349,165	9,699	Up 0.83
1980	8	45	470,001	10,444	Up 7.68
1981	9	47	428,182	9,110	Dn 12.77
1982	8	43	367,591	8,549	Dn 6.16
1983	8	44	356,124	8,094	Dn 5.32
1984	8	45	377,991	8,400	Up 3.78
1985	8	44	420,016	9,546	Up 13.64
1986	8	44	379,014	8,614	Dn 9.76
1987	7	35	277,978	7,942	Dn 7.80
1988	7	38	302,609	7,963	Up 0.26
1989	7	34	296,739	8,728	Up 9.61
1990	7	40	465,183	11,630	Up 33.25
1991	8	42	316,755	7,542	Dn 35.15
1992	9	49	395,264	8,067	Up 8.83
1993	9	49	294,714	6,015	Dn 25.44
1994	9	49	354,903	7,243	Up 20.42
1995	9	50	373,967	7,479	Up 3.26
1996	9	49	363,860	7,426	Dn 0.71
1997	8	42	265,345	6,318	Dn 14.92
1998	8	42	365,046	8,692	Up 37.58
1999	8	42	346,085	8,240	Dn 5.20
2000	8	41	308,925	7,535	Dn 8.56
2001	7	36	247,651	6,879	Dn 8.71
2002	7	38	261,071	6,870	Dn 0.13

PATRIOT LEAGUE

Season	Teams	Games	Attendance	P/G	Change in P/G (Percent)
1990	6	30	223,893	7,463	Up 3.15
1991	6	32	231,155	7,224	Dn 3.20
1992	6	31	202,187	6,522	Dn 9.72
1993	6	29	165,581	5,710	Dn 12.45
1994	6	32	198,274	6,196	Up 8.51
1995	6	29	157,625	5,435	Dn 12.28
1996	6	32	185,275	5,790	Up 6.53
1997	7	38	175,992	4,631	Dn 20.02
1998	7	40	239,275	5,982	Up 29.17
1999	7	39	194,058	4,976	Dn 16.82
2000	7	36	214,731	5,965	Up 19.88
2001	8	39	220,294	5,649	Dn 5.30
2002	8	45	234,475	5,211	Dn 7.75

PIONEER FOOTBALL LEAGUE

Season	Teams	Games	Attendance	P/G	Change in P/G (Percent)
1993	6	32	94,995	2,969	Dn 16.15
1994	6	32	129,678	4,052	Up 36.48
1995	6	32	115,148	3,598	Dn 11.20
1996	6	31	117,406	3,787	Up 5.25
1997	6	30	109,234	3,641	Dn 3.86
1998	5	27	103,882	3,847	Dn 6.65
1999	5	28	116,840	4,173	Up 8.47
2000	5	27	125,886	4,662	Up 11.72
2001	9	45	146,710	3,260	Dn 30.07
2002	9	50	166,582	3,332	Up 2.21

SOUTHERN CONFERENCE

Season	Teams	Games	Attendance	P/G	Change in P/G (Percent)
1982	8	42	451,214	10,743	Dn 1.82
1983	9	47	442,328	9,411	Dn 12.40
1984	9	49	497,040	10,144	Up 7.79
1985	9	49	501,420	10,233	Up 0.88
1986	9	47	484,589	10,310	Up 0.75
1987	8	47	516,773	10,995	Up 6.64
1988	8	43	479,649	11,155	Up 1.46
1989	8	44	495,918	11,271	Up 1.04
1990	8	44	504,248	11,415	Up 1.28
1991	8	46	574,059	12,480	Up 9.33
1992	9	55	700,613	12,738	Up 2.07
1993	9	51	617,620	12,110	Dn 4.93
1994	9	53	667,283	12,590	Up 3.96
1995	9	47	532,530	11,330	Dn 10.01
1996	9	51	578,350	11,340	Up 0.09
1997	9	52	491,680	9,455	Dn 16.62
1998	9	50	483,003	9,660	Up 2.17
1999	9	49	514,800	10,506	Up 8.76
2000	9	52	545,732	10,495	Dn 0.10
2001	9	51	496,364	9,733	Dn 7.26
2002	9	53	520,455	9,820	Up 0.89

SOUTHLAND CONFERENCE

Season	Teams	Games	Attendance	P/G	Change in P/G (Percent)
1982	6	31	438,147	14,134	Up 0.63
1983	7	35	469,010	13,400	Dn 5.19
1984	7	38	458,259	12,059	Dn 10.01
1985	7	35	408,960	11,685	Dn 3.10
1986	6	30	395,515	13,184	Up 12.83
1987	7	35	412,898	11,797	Dn 10.52
1988	7	40	441,301	11,033	Dn 6.48
1989	7	38	423,772	11,152	Up 1.08
1990	7	38	436,110	11,477	Up 2.91
1991	8	41	392,513	9,573	Dn 16.59
1992	8	45	429,971	9,555	Dn 0.19
1993	8	43	403,508	9,384	Dn 1.79
1994	7	43	435,078	10,118	Up 7.82
1995	6	33	316,426	9,589	Dn 5.23
1996	8	46	411,357	8,943	Dn 6.74
1997	8	46	388,593	8,448	Dn 5.54
1998	8	44	460,335	10,462	Up 23.84
1999	8	44	406,336	9,235	Dn 11.73
2000	8	40	399,925	9,998	Up 8.26
2001	7	36	330,689	9,186	Dn 8.12
2002	7	41	394,810	9,630	Up 4.83

SOUTHWESTERN ATHLETIC CONFERENCE

Season	Teams	Games	Attendance	P/G	Change in P/G (Percent)
1978	5	27	483,159	17,895	Dn 5.30
1979	6	32	513,768	16,055	Dn 10.28
1980	7	38	611,234	16,085	Up 0.19
1981	7	35	662,221	18,921	Up 17.63
1982	7	35	634,505	18,129	Dn 4.19
1983	8	44	709,160	16,117	Dn 11.10
1984	8	40	702,186	17,555	Up 8.92
1985	8	44	790,296	17,961	Up 2.31
1986	8	38	621,584	16,357	Dn 8.93
1987	8	42	697,534	16,608	Up 1.53
1988	8	38	541,127	14,240	Dn 14.26
1989	8	44	796,844	18,110	Up 27.18
1990	7	40	828,169	20,704	Up 14.32
1991	8	47	856,491	18,223	Dn 11.98
1992	8	42	873,772	20,804	Up 14.16
1993	8	42	772,714	18,398	Dn 11.57
1994	8	41	958,508	23,378	Up 27.07
1995	8	38	628,702	16,545	Dn 29.23
1996	8	39	600,798	15,405	Dn 6.35
1997	8	36	567,929	15,776	Up 2.41
1998	9	38	516,042	13,580	Dn 13.92
1999	10	51	781,226	15,318	Up 12.80
2000	10	44	506,076	11,502	Dn 24.91
2001	10	47	583,597	12,417	Up 7.96
2002	10	42	459,911	10,950	Dn 11.81

ALL-TIME ATTENDANCE OTHER CONFERENCES
(Conferences that either discontinued or changed names)

AMERICAN WEST CONFERENCE

Season	Teams	Games	Attendance	P/G	Change in P/G (Percent)
1994	4	20	82,986	4,149	Dn 8.77
1995	4	23	97,798	4,252	Up 2.48

COLONIAL ATHLETIC ASSOCIATION

Season	Teams	Games	Attendance	P/G	Change in P/G (Percent)
1986	5	24	241,192	10,050	Up 23.97
1987	6	29	241,831	8,339	Dn 17.02
1988	6	31	195,686	6,312	Dn 24.31
1989	5	26	196,767	7,568	Up 19.90

ATTENDANCE RECORDS

An expansion to Autzen Stadium, completed in time for the 2002 season, enabled Oregon to average more than 10,000 spectators per game than in 2001.

GULF STAR CONFERENCE
(Teams went to Southland Conference)

Season		Teams	Games	Attendance	P/G	Change in P/G (Percent)
1984	....	4	20	149,516	7,476	Dn 9.23
1985	....	4	22	166,046	7,548	Up 0.96
1986	....	5	25	211,094	8,444	Up 11.87

MID-CONTINENT CONFERENCE
(Discontinued after 1984 season; Four members went to Gateway)

Season		Teams	Games	Attendance	P/G	Change in P/G (Percent)
1981	....	3	17	140,506	8,265	Up 4.74
1982	....	4	23	191,975	8,347	Up 0.99
1983	....	4	21	167,219	7,963	Dn 4.60
1984	....	4	24	175,181	7,299	Dn 8.34

Largest Regular-Season Crowds

Largest Regular-Season Crowds*

Attendance	Date	Home Visitor
111,794	11-6-99	Michigan 37, Northwestern 3
111,575	11-20-99	Michigan 24, Ohio St. 17
111,571	11-24-01	Michigan 20, Ohio St. 26
111,542	11-2-02	Michigan 49, Michigan St. 3
111,523	9-4-99	Michigan 26, Notre Dame 22
111,514	10-21-00	Michigan 14, Michigan St. 0
111,502	10-12-02	Michigan 27, Penn St. 24 (ot)
111,496	10-26-02	Michigan 9, Iowa 34
111,491	8-31-02	Michigan 31, Washington 29
111,341	9-30-00	Michigan 13, Wisconsin 10
111,238	9-26-98	Michigan 29, Michigan St. 17
111,217	11-14-98	Michigan 27, Wisconsin 10
111,019	11-7-98	Michigan 27, Penn St. 0
111,012	9-12-98	Michigan 28, Syracuse 38
110,909	10-14-00	Michigan 58, Indiana 0
110,863	10-24-98	Michigan 21, Indiana 10
110,828	11-10-01	Michigan 31, Minnesota 10
110,803	11-11-00	Michigan 33, Penn St. 11
110,753	9-14-02	Penn St. 40, Nebraska 7
110,585	9-2-00	Michigan 42, Bowling Green 7
110,501	9-11-99	Michigan 37, Rice 3
110,468	10-2-99	Michigan 38, Purdue 12
110,450	10-13-01	Michigan 24, Purdue 10
110,438	9-19-98	Michigan 59, Eastern Mich. 20
110,412	11-16-02	Michigan 21, Wisconsin 14
110,188	10-23-99	Michigan 29, Illinois 35
109,837	9-22-01	Michigan 38, Western Mich. 21
109,778	9-9-00	Michigan 38, Rice 7
109,734	9-21-02	Michigan 10, Utah 7
109,676	9-1-01	Michigan 31, Miami (Ohio) 13
109,313	9-1-01	Penn St. 7, Miami (Fla.) 33

In the 55 seasons official national attendance records have been maintained.

2002 Top Ten Regular-Season Crowds

Attendance	Home	Visitor	Date	Site
111,542	Michigan 49	Michigan St. 3	11-2	Ann Arbor, Mich.
111,502	Michigan 27	Penn St. 24 (ot)	10-12	Ann Arbor, Mich.
111,496	Michigan 9	Iowa 34	10-26	Ann Arbor, Mich.
111,491	Michigan 31	Washington 29	8-31	Ann Arbor, Mich.
110,753	Penn St. 40	Nebraska 7	9-14	State College, Pa.
110,412	Michigan 21	Wisconsin 14	11-16	Ann Arbor, Mich.
109,734	Michigan 10	Utah 7	9-21	Ann Arbor, Mich.
108,853	Penn St. 49	Northwestern 0	10-19	State College, Pa.
108,755	Penn St. 61	Michigan St. 7	11-23	State College, Pa.
108,698	Penn St. 35	Virginia 14	11-9	State College, Pa.

Pre-1948 Regular-Season Crowds in Excess of 100,000

Attendance	Date	Site	Opponents, Score
120,000*	11-26-27	Soldier Field, Chicago	Notre Dame 7, Southern California 6
120,000*	10-13-28	Soldier Field, Chicago	Notre Dame 7, Navy 0
112,912	11-16-29	Soldier Field, Chicago	Notre Dame 13, Southern California 12
110,000*	11-27-26	Soldier Field, Chicago	Army 21, Navy 21
110,000*	11-29-30	Soldier Field, Chicago	Notre Dame 7, Army 6
104,953	12-6-47	Los Angeles	Notre Dame 38, Southern California 7

Estimated attendance; others are audited figures.

Additional Records

Highest Average Attendance Per Home Game: 111,175, Michigan, 1999 (667,049 in 6)

Highest Total Home Attendance: 857,911, Penn St., 2002 (8 games); (7-game total: 774,033, Michigan, 2002)

Highest Total Attendance, Home and Away: 1,247,707, Penn St., 2002 (13 games); (11-game total: 1,044,370, Michigan, 1997)

Highest Bowl Single-Game Attendance: 106,869, 1973 Rose Bowl (Southern California 42, Ohio St. 17)

Most Consecutive Home Sellout Crowds: 255, Nebraska (current, from Nov. 3, 1962)

Most Consecutive 100,000-Plus Crowds: 173, Michigan (current, from Nov. 8, 1975)

2002 Attendance

Division I-A

		Games	Attendance	Average	Change in Avg. from 2001
1.	Michigan	7	774,033	110,576	668
2.	Penn St.	8	857,911	107,239	-337
3.	Tennessee	7	746,936	106,705	-138
4.	Ohio St.	8	827,904	103,488	-44
5.	LSU	7	632,147	90,307	-185
6.	Georgia	7	605,640	86,520	0
7.	Florida.......................	7	596,296	85,185	-247
8.	Auburn	7	580,600	82,943	-2,506
9.	Alabama	7	579,999	82,857	545
10.	South Carolina	6	492,828	82,138	-476
11.	Florida St.	6	490,598	81,766	326
12.	Notre Dame..............	6	484,910	80,818	23
13.	Texas A&M...............	7	561,389	80,198	-2,513
14.	Texas	6	474,319	79,053	-4,009
15.	Wisconsin..................	8	624,182	78,023	25
16.	Nebraska	8	622,415	77,802	-3
17.	Clemson	7	542,675	77,525	-2,627
18.	Oklahoma	6	450,621	75,104	-280
19.	Michigan St.	8	591,539	73,942	227
20.	Washington	7	500,042	71,435	-1,034
21.	Miami (Fla.)	6	417,233	69,539	22,407
22.	Southern California	6	401,115	66,853	9,108
23.	UCLA	6	392,375	65,396	782
24.	Kentucky...................	7	449,084	64,155	675
25.	Brigham Young	6	373,055	62,176	1,726
26.	Iowa	7	432,232	61,747	-2,917
27.	Arkansas	8	486,016	60,752	47

		Games	Attendance	Average	Change in Avg. from 2001
28.	Virginia Tech	8	479,379	59,922	9,161
29.	Mississippi	7	400,520	57,217	11,477
30.	Purdue	7	395,008	56,430	-5,042
31.	Virginia	7	394,998	56,428	146
32.	Oregon	8	450,730	56,341	10,415
33.	Illinois	6	331,192	55,199	2,003
34.	Missouri	6	316,339	52,723	167
35.	West Virginia	6	314,477	52,413	4,090
36.	North Carolina	6	301,750	50,292	-2,292
37.	North Carolina St.	7	346,340	49,477	223
38.	Colorado	6	295,316	49,219	1,745
39.	Mississippi St.	6	289,748	48,291	5,940
40.	Kansas St.	8	384,654	48,082	-459
41.	Arizona St.	7	328,607	46,944	213
42.	Maryland	7	323,758	46,251	2,686
43.	Arizona	7	315,032	45,005	621
44.	Pittsburgh	7	310,971	44,424	-4,491
45.	Iowa St.	7	307,728	43,961	-1,211
46.	Oklahoma St.	7	302,669	43,238	2,879
47.	Georgia Tech	6	258,938	43,156	1,471
48.	Texas Tech	6	258,758	43,126	-2,975
49.	Air Force	7	298,993	42,713	4,275
50.	Syracuse	6	253,365	42,228	1,089
51.	Minnesota	7	292,492	41,785	-1,285
52.	Boston College	7	287,737	41,105	-1,534
53.	Fresno St.	6	234,800	39,133	-3,669
54.	Stanford	5	193,850	38,770	-12,764
55.	Hawaii	8	310,074	38,759	-409
56.	California	7	259,719	37,103	6,980
57.	Louisville	6	218,838	36,473	-3,084
58.	Oregon St.	7	255,054	36,436	24
59.	Kansas	6	216,500	36,083	-3,410
60.	Utah	5	178,419	35,684	1,614
61.	Washington St.	6	203,328	33,888	6,137
62.	Navy	6	203,210	33,868	2,373
63.	Army	6	195,636	32,606	1,558
64.	Vanderbilt	7	225,342	32,192	-1,798
65.	Colorado St.	5	152,307	30,461	2,899
66.	East Caro.	5	148,144	29,629	-7,746
67.	New Mexico	6	174,184	29,031	-1,309
68.	Memphis	6	170,362	28,394	2,948
69.	UTEP	5	141,552	28,310	-50
70.	Cincinnati	7	196,497	28,071	6,235
71.	Baylor	6	168,110	28,018	-2,583
72.	Boise St.	7	195,641	27,949	4,118
73.	Tulane	7	195,309	27,901	4,703
74.	TCU	6	166,879	27,813	-1,159
75.	Marshall	7	194,520	27,789	1,210
76.	Northwestern	6	165,574	27,596	-6,167
77.	UNLV	6	165,493	27,582	-515
78.	Indiana	6	163,038	27,173	-6,957
79.	Southern Miss	6	161,766	26,961	1,312
80.	Wake Forest	6	159,222	26,537	3,445
81.	South Fla.	6	157,824	26,304	484
82.	San Diego St.	5	126,650	25,330	7,560
83.	Toledo	6	143,791	23,965	-8,046
84.	Duke	6	139,332	23,222	3,832
85.	Wyoming	6	135,654	22,609	5,654
86.	New Mexico St.	5	110,813	22,163	3,317
87.	UCF	6	131,832	21,972	2,179
88.	Northern Ill.	6	125,715	20,953	6,349
89.	Rice	5	100,344	20,069	3,145
90.	Rutgers	6	118,910	19,818	-637
91.	Temple	7	133,536	19,077	637
92.	Tulsa	6	113,914	18,986	-523
93.	Nevada	6	113,508	18,918	1,345
94.	Western Mich.	6	113,263	18,877	-3,518
95.	Louisiana Tech	5	92,383	18,477	-1,956
96.	Southern Methodist	6	109,752	18,292	906
97.	Miami (Ohio)	5	91,425	18,285	3,588
98.	Ohio	5	90,382	18,076	-2,820
99.	Bowling Green	6	107,016	17,836	24
100.	Central Mich.	6	103,865	17,311	246
101.	Utah St.	5	84,145	16,829	-4,955
102.	UAB	6	98,682	16,447	-2,053
103.	Connecticut	6	94,843	15,807	1,271
104.	North Texas	5	76,302	15,260	-46
105.	La.-Lafayette	5	75,279	15,056	5,600
106.	Buffalo	6	83,770	13,962	1,710
107.	Troy St.	4	53,611	13,403	-3,564
108.	Houston	6	75,018	12,503	-6,954
109.	Ball St.	5	61,519	12,304	-3,697
110.	Akron	5	57,999	11,600	-1,011

Montana ranked third in 2002 home attendance in Division I-AA at picturesque Washington-Grizzly Stadium.

Montana Sports Information

		Games	Attendance	Average	Change in Avg. from 2001
111.	Middle Tenn.	5	55,816	11,163	-6,694
112.	Idaho	5	54,655	10,931	-5,299
113.	Eastern Mich.	6	64,659	10,777	-2,500
114.	Arkansas St.	7	75,114	10,731	-45
115.	San Jose St.	4	41,438	10,360	152
116.	La.-Monroe	6	50,822	8,470	806
117.	Kent St.	6	50,769	8,462	1,866

Division I-AA

		Games	Attendance	Average	Change in Avg. from 2001
1.	Jackson St.	4	94,765	23,691	-5,376
2.	Delaware	6	121,545	20,258	-246
3.	Montana	8	152,354	19,044	145
4.	Southern U.	5	91,467	18,293	-1,077
5.	Florida A&M	5	90,239	18,048	-1,040
6.	Youngstown St.	6	103,046	17,174	856
7.	N.C. A&T	5	83,988	16,798	543
8.	Harvard	5	81,997	16,399	7,639
9.	McNeese St.	8	130,575	16,322	2,042
10.	Alcorn St.	3	47,026	15,675	5,983
11.	Citadel	6	93,494	15,582	-104
12.	Pennsylvania	5	70,682	14,136	1,947
13.	Princeton	6	82,197	13,700	-720
14.	Appalachian St.	6	75,518	12,586	2,556
15.	Ga. Southern	9	110,552	12,284	-6,377
16.	Alabama St.	5	59,397	11,879	-1,855
17.	Grambling	4	44,430	11,108	-16,065
18.	Tennessee St.	5	54,872	10,974	847
19.	Furman	5	54,390	10,878	267
20.	Northern Iowa	6	64,549	10,758	-606
21.	Hampton	6	62,278	10,380	2,751
22.	Lehigh	6	61,074	10,179	-1,622
23.	James Madison	7	69,641	9,949	-391
24.	Northwestern St.	6	59,496	9,916	-1,621
25.	Bethune-Cookman	3	29,369	9,790	338
26.	Southwest Tex. St.	6	58,651	9,775	-907
27.	Fla. Atlantic	4	39,026	9,757	-3,231
28.	Montana St.	6	57,214	9,536	-1,307
29.	Jacksonville St.	5	46,457	9,291	-1,080
30.	Morris Brown	5	46,370	9,274	-285
31.	Western Ill.	7	64,723	9,246	-1,799
32.	Yale	5	45,823	9,165	-16,368
33.	Southwest Mo. St.	6	54,598	9,100	-911
34.	Illinois St.	5	45,064	9,013	913
35.	Eastern Ky.	6	53,000	8,833	-183
36.	South Carolina St.	6	50,977	8,496	-1,763
37.	William & Mary	5	42,162	8,432	1,420
38.	Wofford	5	41,953	8,391	904
39.	Prairie View	1	8,307	8,307	5,102
40.	Weber St.	5	40,374	8,075	1,527
41.	Stephen F. Austin	6	48,241	8,040	388
42.	Massachusetts	6	47,701	7,950	146
43.	Southern Ill.	7	55,400	7,914	1,737

ATTENDANCE RECORDS

	Games	Attendance	Average	Change in Avg. from 2001
44. Idaho St.	6	46,937	7,823	1,573
45. Florida Int'l	7	54,353	7,765	7,765
46. Portland St.	6	46,409	7,735	1,955
47. Western Caro.	5	38,333	7,667	801
48. Brown	4	30,163	7,541	-98
49. Western Ky.	7	51,700	7,386	-2,331
50. Sacramento St.	5	36,313	7,263	-4,228
51. Northern Ariz.	5	36,058	7,212	-389
52. Liberty	6	42,612	7,102	-229
53. Lafayette	6	42,212	7,035	2,456
54. Eastern Ill.	5	35,030	7,006	637
55. Villanova	8	54,724	6,841	-1,046
56. Norfolk St.	7	47,508	6,787	-5,191
57. Morehead St.	7	46,822	6,689	935
58. Alabama A&M	5	32,624	6,525	446
59. VMI	5	32,003	6,401	1,280
60. East Tenn. St.	6	37,960	6,327	446
61. Sam Houston St.	5	31,218	6,244	-2,959
62. Richmond	6	37,253	6,209	-3,002
63. Eastern Wash.	6	37,226	6,204	2,095
64. Cornell	6	36,615	6,103	-1,687
65. Tennessee Tech	6	36,520	6,087	-1,593
66. Mississippi Val.	5	30,295	6,059	1,832
67. Morgan St.	5	30,274	6,055	-2,865
68. Elon	5	30,269	6,054	-1,262
69. Chattanooga	6	36,252	6,042	-624
70. Southeast Mo. St.	5	30,093	6,019	-1,415
71. Cal Poly	5	29,760	5,952	-1,226
72. Samford	5	29,513	5,903	1
73. Howard	6	34,409	5,735	-1,570
74. Murray St.	6	34,000	5,667	2,770
75. Ark.-Pine Bluff	5	28,139	5,628	-1,917
76. Maine	5	27,969	5,594	1,526
77. Stony Brook	5	27,378	5,476	4,333
78. Bucknell	5	27,362	5,472	-597
79. Savannah St.	4	19,830	4,958	213
80. Texas Southern	5	23,461	4,692	-7,099
81. Northeastern	7	32,533	4,648	540
82. Colgate	6	27,633	4,606	1,731
83. Holy Cross	5	20,803	4,161	-5,418
84. Delaware St.	6	24,905	4,151	-1,598
85. Columbia	5	20,499	4,100	-773
86. Fordham	6	24,542	4,090	-661
87. Towson	6	24,514	4,086	1,001
88. Nicholls St.	5	20,172	4,034	15
89. San Diego	6	24,000	4,000	678
90. Dartmouth	5	19,624	3,925	-2,053
91. Indiana St.	5	19,542	3,908	-512
92. Austin Peay	5	18,827	3,765	180
93. Butler	5	18,013	3,603	239
94. Duquesne	6	21,495	3,583	-328
95. Tenn.-Martin	5	17,556	3,511	281
96. Southern Utah	6	19,858	3,310	-3,053
97. New Hampshire	5	16,531	3,306	-1,685
98. Hofstra	6	19,505	3,251	-912
99. Rhode Island	6	19,250	3,208	-1,315
100. Dayton	6	19,033	3,172	-548
101. Gardner-Webb	5	15,651	3,130	69
102. Marist	6	15,759	2,627	676
103. St. Mary's (Cal.)	6	15,570	2,595	845
104. Drake	4	10,257	2,564	-1,949
105. Davidson	5	12,406	2,481	-83
106. Fairfield	6	13,239	2,207	257
107. St. Peter's	4	8,611	2,153	12
108. Sacred Heart	6	12,336	2,056	-694
109. Wagner	4	7,754	1,939	-222
110. Monmouth	5	9,627	1,925	-422
111. Charleston So.	6	10,656	1,776	-334
112. Central Conn. St.	5	8,273	1,655	-380
113. Iona	5	7,976	1,595	-455
114. La Salle	6	9,434	1,572	-267
115. Jacksonville	5	7,835	1,567	581
116. Albany (N.Y.)	6	9,292	1,549	-796
117. Valparaiso	7	9,389	1,341	-584
118. Robert Morris	4	5,183	1,296	-251
119. Georgetown	5	6,335	1,267	-670
120. Canisius	4	4,047	1,012	71
121. Siena	5	4,615	923	102
122. St. John's (N.Y.)	4	3,185	796	-132
123. St. Francis (Pa.)	6	4,429	738	-63

Division II

	Games	Attendance	Average	Change in Avg. from 2001
1. Tuskegee	5	59,256	11,851	-1,106
2. North Dakota St.	6	63,721	10,620	-1,494
3. Northwest Mo. St.	7	68,895	9,842	2,534
4. Tex. A&M-Kingsville	6	57,500	9,583	-792
5. North Dakota	6	56,930	9,488	-1,029
6. UC Davis	5	45,968	9,194	1,686
7. Miles	3	21,500	7,167	-694
8. Grand Valley St.	9	61,235	6,804	1,095
9. Pittsburg St.	7	46,640	6,663	-1,192
10. Central Ark.	5	31,758	6,352	-110
11. Fort Valley St.	3	18,972	6,324	0
12. Bowie St.	5	31,584	6,317	472
13. N.C. Central	6	37,199	6,200	2,542
14. Morehouse	1	6,192	6,192	-4,131
15. Winston-Salem	5	30,798	6,160	875
16. South Dakota St.	6	35,804	5,967	-765
17. Northern Colo.	7	41,259	5,894	664
18. Livingstone	3	17,594	5,865	1,675
19. Lenoir-Rhyne	5	28,625	5,725	2,933
20. Emporia St.	5	28,497	5,699	658
21. Glenville St.	6	33,282	5,547	5,246
22. Abilene Christian	5	27,565	5,513	-1,092
23. Valdosta St.	9	48,826	5,425	-2,453
24. Angelo St.	5	26,849	5,370	-920
25. Northeastern St.	5	26,700	5,340	-200
26. Mo. Western St.	4	20,934	5,234	2,644
27. Virginia Union	3	15,602	5,201	1,812
28. Saginaw Valley	5	25,938	5,188	790
29. Neb.-Omaha	7	35,000	5,000	-1,875
30. Slippery Rock	5	24,300	4,860	105
31. Central Mo. St.	6	28,374	4,729	-2,389
32. Central Wash.	6	27,269	4,545	2,957
33. Southern Ark.	5	22,444	4,489	-79
34. Neb.-Kearney	6	26,753	4,459	1,084
35. North Ala.	5	21,376	4,275	699
36. Virginia St.	4	16,529	4,132	-997
37. Harding	6	24,640	4,107	-443
38. Northern Mich.	5	20,350	4,070	1,462
39. Mo. Southern St.	6	24,172	4,029	-1,631
40. Henderson St.	5	20,135	4,027	3,260
41. West Ga.	5	20,095	4,019	-418
42. South Dakota	6	23,666	3,944	-701
43. Ouachita Baptist	5	19,321	3,864	-616
44. Arkansas Tech	6	23,168	3,861	-1,724
45. Minn. Duluth	6	23,046	3,841	1,082
46. Midwestern St.	5	18,947	3,789	-1,111
47. West Chester	5	18,698	3,740	619
48. Shippensburg	6	22,400	3,733	-192
49. Catawba	3	11,155	3,718	7
50. West Ala.	5	18,500	3,700	767
51. Indiana (Pa.)	7	25,765	3,681	-1,895
52. Tarleton St.	6	21,700	3,617	1,016
53. Washburn	5	17,683	3,537	2,052
54. Chadron St.	5	17,605	3,521	-154
55. Benedict	3	10,515	3,505	3,505
56. Carson-Newman	8	27,507	3,438	-368
57. Johnson Smith	4	13,486	3,372	-1,001
58. Southwestern Okla.	5	16,800	3,360	-233
59. Hillsdale	5	16,708	3,342	440
60. Southeastern Okla.	6	19,850	3,308	137
61. Minn. St. Mankato	5	16,418	3,284	1,021
62. West Tex. A&M	6	19,424	3,237	-160
63. Ferris St.	5	15,786	3,157	77
64. Humboldt St.	4	12,516	3,129	448
65. Fayetteville St.	5	15,577	3,115	-1,761
66. Augustana (S.D.)	6	18,627	3,105	-897
67. Tex. A&M-Commerce	6	18,513	3,086	-1,570
68. Northwood	6	17,720	2,953	152
69. Clarion	5	14,750	2,950	-877
70. East Central	5	14,667	2,933	-617
71. Indianapolis	6	17,500	2,917	-83
72. Winona St.	4	11,532	2,883	321
73. Shepherd	5	14,081	2,816	-298
74. Truman	6	16,835	2,806	-687
75. East Stroudsburg	5	13,984	2,797	2,097
76. Mars Hill	6	16,488	2,748	470
77. Kentucky St.	5	13,720	2,744	-2,589
78. St. Cloud St.	6	16,263	2,711	-37
79. Wayne St. (Mich.)	5	13,548	2,710	596
80. Edinboro	5	13,300	2,660	-971

		Games	Attendance	Average	Change in Avg. from 2001
81.	Clark Atlanta	6	15,726	2,621	0
82.	Mansfield	5	13,095	2,619	494
83.	Ashland	5	13,050	2,610	-723
84.	Albany St. (Ga.)	5	12,834	2,567	-4,935
85.	Central Okla.	6	15,400	2,567	-493
86.	Bryant	5	12,579	2,516	-169
87.	Lane	1	2,500	2,500	-151
88.	Tusculum	5	12,225	2,445	-68
89.	Western Wash.	5	12,189	2,438	-807
90.	St. Augustine's	1	2,431	2,431	2,431
91.	C.W. Post	5	11,955	2,391	102
92.	Kutztown	6	14,097	2,350	796
93.	Western Ore.	4	9,300	2,325	-351
94.	Colorado Mines	5	11,322	2,264	1,214
95.	Eastern N.M.	5	11,285	2,257	-93
96.	West Va. Wesleyan	5	11,115	2,223	988
97.	Adams St.	5	10,879	2,176	154
98.	Lock Haven	5	10,692	2,138	44
99.	Ark.-Monticello	4	8,525	2,131	-40
100.	Fort Hays St.	5	10,576	2,115	-340
101.	Southwest Baptist	5	10,460	2,092	-582
102.	Elizabeth City St.	5	10,454	2,091	-1,654
103.	Delta St.	4	8,320	2,080	-1,211
104.	Bloomsburg	5	10,372	2,074	-1,360
105.	Cheyney	3	6,182	2,061	775
106.	Findlay	6	12,105	2,018	-347
107.	Wingate	4	7,962	1,991	-825
108.	Northern St.	6	11,891	1,982	-350
109.	Millersville	5	9,751	1,950	7
110.	Lincoln (Mo.)	7	13,400	1,914	64
111.	Presbyterian	6	11,426	1,904	387
112.	Newberry	5	9,457	1,891	-495
113.	Mercyhurst	6	10,087	1,681	-372
114.	Mo.-Rolla	6	9,850	1,642	-1,018
115.	Calif. (Pa.)	5	8,040	1,608	-243
116.	Minn. St. Moorhead	5	7,681	1,536	508
117.	N.M. Highlands	5	7,526	1,505	-293
118.	Michigan Tech	5	7,438	1,488	-233
119.	Fairmont St.	5	7,397	1,479	-677
120.	Bentley	5	7,347	1,469	346
121.	Fort Lewis	4	5,672	1,418	-140
122.	Southwest St.	5	7,049	1,410	195
123.	Gannon	5	7,000	1,400	-233
124.	Mesa St.	5	6,968	1,394	-533
125.	Concord	5	6,912	1,382	-167
126.	West Va. Tech	5	6,826	1,365	462
127.	Wayne St. (Neb.)	6	7,730	1,288	-65
128.	St. Anselm	5	5,920	1,184	-920
129.	Concordia-St. Paul	5	5,885	1,177	1,177
130.	Bemidji St.	5	5,555	1,111	-452
131.	Stonehill	6	6,466	1,078	-112
132.	Okla. Panhandle	5	5,000	1,000	0
133.	Quincy	5	4,937	987	132
134.	West Liberty St.	5	4,862	972	-1,233
135.	Assumption	6	5,649	942	-208
136.	Pace	5	4,706	941	145
137.	West Virginia St.	6	5,617	936	-532
138.	Ky. Wesleyan	6	5,400	900	-313
139.	New Haven	5	4,464	893	-1,056
140.	Western N.M.	5	4,137	827	-552
141.	Merrimack	5	3,963	793	-222
142.	St. Joseph's (Ind.)	5	3,800	760	-278
143.	Southern Conn. St.	5	3,328	666	-283
144.	American Int'l	5	3,050	610	-169
145.	Mass.-Lowell	5	2,722	544	-275
146.	Minn.-Morris	5	2,306	461	-384
147.	Minn.-Crookston	5	2,238	448	448
148.	Western St.	5	2,000	400	-1,587
149.	Tiffin	4	1,221	305	0

Division III

		Games	Attendance	Average	Change in Avg. from 2001
1.	St. John's (Minn.)	7	40,017	5,717	-957
2.	Mount Union	8	41,860	5,233	261
3.	Stillman	5	23,800	4,760	793
4.	Randolph-Macon	5	21,095	4,219	-35
5.	Baldwin-Wallace	5	20,600	4,120	-530
6.	Wabash	7	28,543	4,078	1221
7.	North Central	4	16,007	4,002	982
8.	Chris. Newport	5	19,742	3,948	-681
9.	Hampden-Sydney	5	19,384	3,877	1262
10.	Williams	4	14,494	3,624	-1952
11.	Mississippi Col.	5	17,646	3,529	-1592

		Games	Attendance	Average	Change in Avg. from 2001
12.	Hope	5	17,445	3,489	-137
13.	Amherst	4	13,826	3,457	-298
14.	Albion	5	17,195	3,439	1175
15.	Rowan	6	19,671	3,279	-242
16.	Wartburg	6	19,667	3,278	-782
17.	Wheaton (Ill.)	5	16,250	3,250	-150
18.	Cortland St.	7	22,300	3,186	1167
19.	Wis.-Whitewater	4	12,614	3,154	142
20.	Loras	5	15,395	3,079	339
21.	Wis.-Stout	5	15,253	3,051	-412
22.	Hardin-Simmons	5	15,018	3,004	-498
23.	Millikin	4	12,000	3,000	1892
24.	Trinity (Conn.)	4	11,997	2,999	-1864
25.	Wash. & Jeff.	6	17,947	2,991	-626
26.	Wis.-Eau Claire	5	14,942	2,988	138
27.	Defiance	5	14,900	2,980	-537
28.	Gust. Adolphus	4	11,712	2,928	154
29.	Anderson (Ind.)	5	14,500	2,900	1211
30.	McDaniel	5	14,325	2,865	1243
31.	Millsaps	4	11,356	2,839	-1032
32.	Grove City	4	11,300	2,825	755
33.	Howard Payne	5	13,950	2,790	15
34.	Wooster	5	13,886	2,777	256
35.	Susquehanna	5	13,700	2,740	100
36.	Bethel (Minn.)	5	13,600	2,720	-1043
37.	Col. of New Jersey	5	13,544	2,709	827
38.	Central (Iowa)	5	13,500	2,700	940
39.	Linfield	7	18,800	2,686	726
40.	St. John Fisher	5	13,389	2,678	1339
41.	Wash. & Lee	5	13,232	2,646	-860
42.	John Carroll	6	15,842	2,640	-451
43.	Tufts	4	10,500	2,625	-375
44.	Muhlenberg	7	18,168	2,595	-587
45.	Alma	6	15,539	2,590	-10
46.	Capital	5	12,899	2,580	-117
47.	Widener	5	12,800	2,560	0
48.	Pacific Lutheran	4	10,200	2,550	388
49.	Augustana (Ill.)	4	10,127	2,532	232
50.	Concordia-M'head	4	9,975	2,494	-2856
51.	Ohio Northern	5	12,277	2,455	457
52.	Juniata	4	9,750	2,438	1068
53.	Emory & Henry	5	12,100	2,420	-4040
54.	Moravian	5	12,053	2,411	-381
55.	St. Thomas (Minn.)	5	11,850	2,370	-363
56.	Otterbein	5	11,738	2,348	-599
57.	Ursinus	5	11,450	2,290	-960
58.	Whitworth	5	11,420	2,284	318
59.	St. Norbert	5	11,315	2,263	454
60.	Monmouth (Ill.)	5	11,250	2,250	550
61.	East Tex. Baptist	5	11,177	2,235	253
62.	Heidelberg	5	11,133	2,227	1639
63.	Wesleyan (Conn.)	4	8,900	2,225	-363
64.	Dickinson	5	11,100	2,220	-100
65.	Mary Hardin-Baylor	5	10,984	2,197	-92
66.	Adrian	5	10,913	2,183	493
67.	Norwich	5	10,801	2,160	-38
68.	Catholic	4	8,500	2,125	778
69.	Wilmington (Ohio)	5	10,615	2,123	-536
70.	Lebanon Valley	5	10,600	2,120	275
71.	Lycoming	5	10,519	2,104	-1623
72.	Bluffton	5	10,432	2,086	-223
73.	Westminster (Pa.)	5	10,284	2,057	0
74.	Ithaca	4	8,169	2,042	-1910
75.	Middlebury	4	7,927	1,982	50
76.	Bates	4	7,897	1,974	49
77.	Ohio Wesleyan	5	9,766	1,953	-442
78.	Coast Guard	4	7,700	1,925	17
79.	Delaware Valley	5	9,400	1,880	150
80.	Ferrum	5	9,224	1,845	-598
81.	Chapman	5	9,132	1,826	-924
82.	King's (Pa.)	7	12,700	1,814	-466
83.	Wis.-La Crosse	4	7,178	1,795	-308
84.	Wittenberg	5	8,918	1,784	-471
85.	Wis.-Stevens Point	4	7,121	1,780	-549
86.	Wis.-Platteville	5	8,894	1,779	-305
87.	Gettysburg	5	8,815	1,763	-171
88.	Texas Lutheran	5	8,668	1,734	165
89.	Allegheny	5	8,594	1,719	276
90.	Cornell College	4	6,800	1,700	-823
91.	Louisiana Col.	6	10,100	1,683	1683
92.	Muskingum	5	8,416	1,683	-361
93.	Ill. Wesleyan	5	8,400	1,680	-208
94.	Bowdoin	4	6,705	1,676	-1061
95.	Kalamazoo	5	8,361	1,672	310
96.	Montclair St.	5	8,352	1,670	-363
97.	FDU-Florham	5	8,329	1,666	-474

		Games	Attendance	Average	Change in Avg. from 2001
98.	Shenandoah	4	6,639	1,660	-885
99.	Trinity (Tex.)	8	13,250	1,656	-97
100.	Sewanee	5	8,250	1,650	-250
101.	Bridgewater (Va.)	8	13,180	1,648	-632
102.	Coe	6	9,773	1,629	-184
103.	Washington (Mo.)	6	9,754	1,626	-501
104.	Wis.-Oshkosh	5	8,072	1,614	-4
105.	Franklin	5	8,050	1,610	269
106.	Simpson	5	8,000	1,600	-2653
107.	MIT	4	6,369	1,592	520
108.	Union (N.Y.)	5	7,774	1,555	-1025
109.	Maine Maritime	5	7,637	1,527	487
110.	Redlands	5	7,602	1,520	-276
111.	Wm. Paterson	5	7,526	1,505	-383
112.	Colby	4	5,999	1,500	568
113.	Curry	5	7,334	1,467	86
114.	Hamilton	4	5,832	1,458	-403
115.	Luther	5	7,273	1,455	1227
116.	Thiel	5	7,194	1,439	145
117.	Beloit	5	7,191	1,438	62
118.	Springfield	5	7,144	1,429	203
119.	St. Olaf	4	5,696	1,424	-1476
120.	Merchant Marine	6	8,543	1,424	-711
121.	Salisbury	5	7,090	1,418	67
122.	DePauw	5	7,000	1,400	-1060
	Knox	5	7,000	1,400	-625
124.	Case Reserve	5	6,980	1,396	216
125.	Nichols	6	8,144	1,357	-111
126.	Rhodes	5	6,761	1,352	172
127.	Olivet	5	6,753	1,351	-263
128.	Brockport St.	7	9,450	1,350	-634
129.	Buena Vista	5	6,650	1,330	179
	Rose-Hulman	5	6,650	1,330	-315
131.	Frank. & Marsh.	5	6,494	1,299	443
132.	Cal Lutheran	5	6,400	1,280	295
133.	Chicago	5	6,350	1,270	-146
134.	Austin	4	5,058	1,265	47
135.	Waynesburg	4	5,050	1,263	242
136.	Mass.-Dartmouth	6	7,512	1,252	0
137.	Carthage	5	6,225	1,245	112
138.	Rensselaer	5	6,200	1,240	-837
139.	Chowan	5	6,199	1,240	-322
140.	Claremont-M-S	4	4,917	1,229	-268
141.	Frostburg St.	4	4,900	1,225	-350
	Menlo	4	4,900	1,225	71
	Willamette	4	4,900	1,225	-45
144.	Rochester	5	6,112	1,222	-931
145.	Oberlin	6	7,250	1,208	262
146.	Westminster (Mo.)	4	4,800	1,200	525
147.	Hanover	6	7,176	1,196	0
148.	Neb. Wesleyan	5	5,978	1,196	53
149.	Wesley	5	5,915	1,183	0
150.	Westfield St.	4	4,553	1,138	-847
151.	WPI	5	5,635	1,127	318
152.	Carnegie Mellon	4	4,491	1,123	-901
153.	Wilkes	6	6,700	1,117	-758
154.	Manchester	5	5,483	1,097	-443
155.	Salve Regina	4	4,368	1,092	25
156.	Centre	5	5,450	1,090	15
157.	Eastern Ore.	5	5,379	1,076	-237
158.	Worcester St.	6	6,440	1,073	-19
159.	Elmhurst	5	5,350	1,070	196
160.	Lawrence	4	4,256	1,064	57
161.	Benedictine (Ill.)	5	5,300	1,060	394
162.	Illinois Col.	6	6,350	1,058	-202
163.	Hamline	4	4,229	1,057	467

		Games	Attendance	Average	Change in Avg. from 2001
164.	Wis.-River Falls	4	4,150	1,038	-1362
165.	Occidental	5	5,163	1,033	-977
166.	St. Lawrence	4	4,070	1,018	93
167.	Western Conn. St.	4	4,068	1,017	31
168.	Puget Sound	5	5,075	1,015	-86
169.	Thomas More	5	5,048	1,010	76
170.	Greenville	5	5,000	1,000	217
171.	Western New Eng.	5	4,954	991	-1360
172.	Martin Luther	4	3,950	988	-835
173.	Johns Hopkins	6	5,900	983	-167
174.	Averett	5	4,823	965	-35
175.	Carroll (Wis.)	6	5,740	957	150
176.	Kean	6	5,675	946	-653
177.	Hiram	4	3,778	945	-1
178.	Denison	5	4,700	940	-460
179.	Maryville (Tenn.)	4	3,750	938	-163
180.	Colorado Col.	5	4,678	936	55
181.	Framingham St.	4	3,717	929	166
182.	Guilford	4	3,700	925	-42
183.	Lewis & Clark	5	4,600	920	71
184.	Augsburg	5	4,582	916	-68
185.	Lake Forest	5	4,554	911	311
186.	Earlham	5	4,536	907	-68
187.	Rockford	5	4,501	900	22
188.	Plymouth St.	4	3,559	890	-263
189.	Mass. Maritime	4	3,529	882	264
190.	Bridgewater St.	4	3,450	863	3
191.	Alfred	5	4,260	852	-1120
192.	Hartwick	5	4,226	845	-424
193.	Greensboro	5	4,190	838	-764
194.	McMurry	4	3,350	838	-196
195.	Aurora	5	4,100	820	-468
196.	Marietta	5	4,073	815	-625
197.	Mount Ida	4	3,247	812	182
198.	Methodist	5	4,052	810	-470
199.	Wis. Lutheran	6	4,769	795	278
200.	North Park	5	3,925	785	-289
201.	Bethany (W.Va.)	5	3,800	760	-921
202.	Utica	5	3,774	755	-245
203.	Buffalo St.	5	3,602	720	-223
204.	New Jersey City	4	2,848	712	-411
205.	Mt. St. Joseph	5	3,553	711	11
206.	Whittier	5	3,141	628	-388
207.	Concordia (Ill.)	4	2,500	625	-35
208.	Kenyon	5	2,948	590	-78
209.	MacMurray	5	2,900	580	10
210.	La Verne	3	1,731	577	0
211.	Eureka	5	2,769	554	-256
212.	Fitchburg St.	4	2,117	529	192
213.	Pomona-Pitzer	5	2,600	520	-161
214.	Hobart	6	3,023	504	138
215.	Gallaudet	3	1,500	500	0
	Lakeland	4	2,000	500	-325
217.	Concordia (Wis.)	5	2,300	460	-1165
218.	Carleton	6	2,750	458	-77
219.	Sul Ross St.	5	2,004	401	-599
220.	Macalester	6	2,300	383	-1077
221.	Albright	5	1,850	370	-1354
222.	Ripon	5	1,761	352	-1198
223.	Maranatha Baptist	4	1,400	350	-150
224.	Upper Iowa	4	1,366	342	-134
225.	Principia	3	750	250	0
226.	Dubuque	6	1,100	183	-1246
227.	Grinnell	5	900	180	-250
228.	Blackburn	5	550	110	-516

Divisions I-A and I-AA Conferences and Independents, and Divisions II and III Totals

	Total Teams	Games	2002 Attend.	Avg. PG	Change+ In Avg.		Change+ In Total	
1. Southeastern (I-A)	12	83	*6,085,156	*73,315	Up	236	Up	531,128
2. Big Ten (I-A)	11	78	*5,455,105	69,937	Dn	99	Up	832,729
3. Big 12 (I-A)	12	79	*4,358,818	55,175	Dn	287	Up	143,730
4. Atlantic Coast (I-A)	9	58	*2,957,611	*50,993	Up	1,269	Up	173,091
5. Pacific-10 (I-A)	10	66	*3,299,852	49,998	Up	1,997	Up	515,783
6. Big East (I-A)	8	53	*2,315,608	*43,691	Up	4,359	Up	388,328
7. Mountain West (I-A)	8	46	*1,604,755	*34,886	Up	3,056	Up	72,390
8. Div. I-A Independents#	6	33	1,078,543	32,683	Dn	330	Dn	10,878
9. Conference USA (I-A)	10	61	*1,627,131	26,674	Up	355	Up	194,619
10. Western Athletic (I-A)	10	58	1,453,406	25,059	Up	306	Up	240,519
11. Mid-American (I-A)#	14	81	*1,420,525	17,537	Dn	364	Up	149,559

	Total Teams	Games	2002 Attend.	Avg. PG	Change+ In Avg.		Change+ In Total	
12. Sun Belt (I-A)	7	38	*498,801	13,126	Dn	251	Up	43,972
13. Southwestern Athletic (I-AA)	10	42	459,911	10,950	Dn	1,467	Dn	123,688
14. Southern (I-AA)	9	53	520,455	9,820	Up	87	Up	24,091
15. Big Sky (I-AA)	8	47	452,885	9,636	Up	615	Up	37,921
16. Southland (I-AA)	7	41	394,810	9,630	Up	444	Up	64,121
17. Ivy (I-AA)	8	41	387,600	9,454	Dn	1,343	Dn	22,668
18. Gateway (I-AA)	8	49	*458,622	9,360	Dn	554	Up	22,405
19. Mid-Eastern Athletic (I-AA)	9	49	453,947	9,264	Dn	1,255	Up	22,669
20. Atlantic 10 (I-AA)	11	67	488,814	7,296	Dn	313	Up	55,115
21. Ohio Valley (I-AA)	7	38	261,071	6,870	Dn	9	Up	13,420
22. Big South (I-AA)%	3	16	88,532	5,533	Dn	478	Up	9,384
23. Div I-AA Independents#	9	48	264,936	5,520	Up	999	Dn	61,036
24. Patriot (I-AA)	8	45	234,475	5,211	Dn	438	Up	14,181
25. Pioneer Football (I-AA)	9	50	*166,582	3,332	Up	72	Up	19,872
26. Northeast (I-AA)#	8	41	*84,272	*2,055	Up	173	Up	18,416
27. Metro Atlantic (I-AA)#	9	46	88,361	1,921	Up	47	Up	5,915
Div. I-A Teams	117	734	32,155,311	43,808	—	—	—	—
Div. I-A Neutral Sites		14	839,308	59,951	—	—	—	—
Div. I-A Bowl Games$		27	1,389,645	51,468	—	—	—	—
Div. I-A Totals#	117	775	*34,384,264	*44,367	Up	299	Up	4,085,690

$Does not include Humanitarian Bowl (30,446 included in Boise St. home attendance).

	Total Teams	Games	2002 Attend.	Avg. PG	Change+ In Avg.		Change+ In Total	
Div. I-AA Teams	123	673	4,805,273	7,140	—	—	—	—
Div. I-AA Neutral Sites		26	707,617	27,216	—	—	—	—
Div. I-AA Championship Game		1	12,360	12,360	—	—	—	—
Div. I-AA Totals#	123	700	5,525,250	7,893	Dn	390	Up	149,399
Div. II Teams	149	769	2,555,133	3,323	—	—	—	—
Div. II Neutral Sites		13	82,122	6,317	—	—	—	—
Div. II Championship		1	9,783	9,783	—	—	—	—
Div. II Totals#	149	783	2,647,038	3,381	Dn	141	Dn	1,723
Div. III Teams	228	1,121	1,951,338	1,741	—	—	—	—
Div. III Neutral Sites		15	43,936	2,929	—	—	—	—
Div. III Championship		1	4,389	4,389	—	—	—	—
Div. III Totals#	228	1,137	1,999,663	1,759	Dn	195	Dn	157,974
ALL NCAA TEAMS	*617	*3,395	*44,556,215	13,124	Up	440	Up	4,055,392

#Did not have same lineup as 2001. %New conference. *Record high. +The figures used for comparison reflect changes in conference and division lineups to provide parallel, valid comparisons.

Conferences and Independents Below Division I-AA

	Total Teams	Games	2002 Attend.	Avg. PG	Change+ In Avg		Change+ In Total	
1. North Central (II)	9	55	307,688	5,594	Dn	587	Up	10,994
2. Southern Intercollegiate (II)#	9	32	161,215	5,038	Dn	2,087	Dn	59,654
3. Mid-America Intercollegiate (II)	10	57	272,340	4,778	Up	155	Up	8,845
4. Central Intercollegiate (II)#..	10	41	191,254	4,665	Up	130	Up	3,750
5. Gulf South (II)	12	64	267,108	4,174	Dn	87	Dn	1,362
6. Lone Star (II)	13	71	295,200	4,158	Dn	386	Dn	142
7. Great Lakes Intercollegiate (II)	12	68	231,465	3,404	Up	314	Up	39,913
8. Columbia Football (II)	4	19	61,274	3,225	Up	677	Up	10,322
9. South Atlantic (II)	8	42	124,845	2,973	Up	261	Up	10,943
10. Pennsylvania State (II)	14	72	205,426	2,853	Up	21	Up	1,536
11. Ohio Athletic (III)	10	54	149,453	2,768	Up	108	Up	21,766
12. Old Dominion (III)	7	36	91,191	2,533	Dn	481	Dn	17,296
13. Minnesota Intercollegiate (III)#	9	44	104,411	2,373	Dn	491	Dn	35,901
14. New England Small College (III)	10	40	94,077	2,352	Dn	565	Dn	22,591
15. Rocky Mountain (II)	9	45	99,301	2,207	Up	17	Up	8,020
16. Michigan Intercollegiate (III)#	7	37	80,975	2,189	Dn	32	Up	16,561
17. Wisconsin Intercollegiate (III)	8	36	78,224	2,173	Dn	298	Dn	10,732
18. West Virginia (II)	8	42	90,092	2,145	Up	526	Up	26,943
19. Illinois & Wisconsin (III)	8	37	78,284	2,116	Up	303	Up	3,944
20. Centennial (III)	7	38	76,252	2,007	Dn	28	Up	9,082
21. American Southwest (III)#	10	49	97,955	1,999	Dn	541	Up	14,124
22. Presidents' Athletic (III)	6	29	55,575	1,916	Dn	244	Dn	9,228
23. Middle Atlantic (III)	11	57	108,401	1,902	Dn	322	Up	11,688
24. New Jersey Athletic (III)	7	31	57,616	1,859	Dn	158	Up	3,146
25. Division II Independents#	10	52	95,327	1,833	Dn	360	Dn	3,356
26. Northwest (III)	6	30	54,995	1,833	Up	320	Up	15,648
27. North Coast (III)	10	52	92,919	1,787	Up	157	Up	11,396
28. Heartland Collegiate (III)	7	36	64,094	1,780	Up	36	Up	1,295
29. Iowa Intercollegiate (III)	10	51	89,524	1,755	Dn	288	Dn	12,612
30. Northern Sun (II)#	10	52	84,913	1,633	Dn	70	Up	20,915
31. Dixie (III)	7	34	54,869	1,614	Dn	468	Up	15,912
32. Southern Collegiate (III)	7	37	58,717	1,587	Dn	472	Dn	19,523
33. Freedom Football (III)	7	33	47,450	1,438	Dn	29	Dn	968
34. University Athletic (III)	5	25	33,687	1,347	Dn	433	Up	10,807
35. Division III Independents#	29	137	163,138	1,191	Dn	251	Up	4,481
36. Northeast-10 (II)	11	57	67,685	1,187	Dn	190	Dn	9,421
37. Midwest (III)	10	51	60,317	1,183	Dn	67	Up	325
38. New England Football (III)	13	61	70,124	1,150	Dn	27	Dn	1,658
39. Southern California (III)	6	27	28,954	1,072	Dn	220	Dn	4,645
40. Upstate Collegiate (III)	4	20	21,067	1,053	Dn	644	Dn	9,474
41. Illini-Badger (III)	8	38	26,869	707	Dn	193	Dn	10,048

#Did not have the same lineup as 2001. +The figures used for comparison reflect changes in conference and division lineups to provide parallel, valid comparisons.

Annual Team Attendance Leaders

Annual Leading Division I-A Teams in Per-Game Home Attendance

Year/Teams	G	Attendance	Avg.
1949			
Michigan	6	563,363	93,894
Ohio St.	5	382,146	76,429
Southern Methodist	8	484,000	60,500
1950			
Michigan	6	493,924	82,321
Ohio St.	5	368,021	73,604
Southern Methodist	5	309,000	61,800
1951			
Ohio St.	6	455,737	75,956
Michigan	6	445,635	74,273
Illinois	4	237,035	59,259
1952			
Ohio St.	6	453,911	75,652
Michigan	6	395,907	65,985
Texas	#5	311,160	62,232
1953			
Ohio St.	5	397,998	79,600
Southern California	6	413,617	68,936
Michigan	6	353,860	58,977
1954			
Ohio St.	6	479,840	79,973
Michigan	6	409,454	68,242
UCLA	5	318,371	63,674
1955			
Michigan	7	544,838	77,834
Ohio St.	7	493,178	70,454
Southern California	7	467,085	66,726
1956			
Ohio St.	6	494,575	82,429
Michigan	7	566,145	80,878
Minnesota	6	375,407	62,568
1957			
Michigan	6	504,954	84,159
Ohio St.	6	484,118	80,686
Minnesota	5	319,942	63,988
1958			
Ohio St.	6	499,352	82,225
Michigan	6	405,115	67,519
LSU	5	296,576	59,315
1959			
Ohio St.	6	495,536	82,589
Michigan	6	456,385	76,064
LSU	7	408,727	58,390
1960			
Ohio St.	5	413,583	82,717
Michigan St.	4	274,367	68,592
Michigan	6	374,682	62,447
1961			
Ohio St.	5	414,712	82,942
Michigan	7	514,924	73,561
LSU	6	381,409	63,651
1962			
Ohio St.	6	497,644	82,941
Michigan St.	4	272,568	68,142
LSU	6	397,701	66,284
1963			
Ohio St.	5	416,023	83,205
LSU	6	396,846	66,141
Michigan St.	5	326,597	65,319
1964			
Ohio St.	7	583,740	83,391
Michigan St.	4	284,933	71,233
Michigan	6	388,829	64,805
1965			
Ohio St.	5	416,282	83,256
Michigan	6	480,487	80,081
Michigan St.	5	346,296	69,259
1966			
Ohio St.	6	488,399	81,400
Michigan St.	6	426,750	71,125
Michigan	6	413,599	68,933
1967			
Ohio St.	5	383,502	76,700
Michigan	6	447,289	74,548
Michigan St.	6	411,916	68,653
1968			
Ohio St.	6	482,564	80,427
Southern California	5	354,945	70,989
Michigan St.	6	414,177	69,030
1969			
Ohio St.	5	431,175	86,235
Michigan	6	428,780	71,463
Michigan St.	5	352,123	70,425
1970			
Ohio St.	5	432,451	86,490
Michigan	6	476,164	79,361
Purdue	5	340,090	68,018
1971			
Ohio St.	6	506,699	84,450
Michigan	7	564,376	80,625
Wisconsin	6	408,885	68,148
1972			
Michigan	6	513,398	85,566
Ohio St.	6	509,420	84,903
Nebraska	6	456,859	76,143
1973			
Ohio St.	6	523,369	87,228
Michigan	7	595,171	85,024
Nebraska	6	456,726	76,121
1974			
Michigan	6	562,105	93,684
Ohio St.	6	525,314	87,552
Nebraska	7	534,388	76,341
1975			
Michigan	7	689,146	98,449
Ohio St.	6	527,141	87,856
Nebraska	7	533,368	76,195
1976			
Michigan	7	722,113	103,159
Ohio St.	6	526,216	87,702
Tennessee	7	564,922	80,703
1977			
Michigan	7	729,418	104,203
Ohio St.	6	525,535	87,589
Tennessee	7	582,979	83,283
1978			
Michigan	6	629,690	104,948
Ohio St.	7	614,881	87,840
Tennessee	†8	627,381	78,422
1979			
Michigan	7	730,315	104,331
Ohio St.	7	611,794	87,399
Tennessee	6	512,139	85,357
1980			
Michigan	6	625,750	104,292
Tennessee	†8	709,193	88,649
Ohio St.	7	615,476	87,925
1981			
Michigan	6	632,990	105,498
Tennessee	6	558,996	93,166
Ohio St.	6	521,760	86,960
1982			
Michigan	6	631,743	105,291
Tennessee	6	561,102	93,517
Ohio St.	7	623,152	89,022
1983			
Michigan	6	626,916	104,486
Ohio St.	6	534,110	89,018
Tennessee	†8	679,420	84,928
1984			
Michigan	7	726,734	103,819
Tennessee	7	654,602	93,515
Ohio St.	6	536,691	89,449
1985			
Michigan	6	633,530	105,588
Tennessee	7	658,690	94,099
Ohio St.	6	535,284	89,214
1986			
Michigan	6	631,261	105,210
Tennessee	7	643,317	91,902
Ohio St.	6	536,210	89,368
1987			
Michigan	7	731,281	104,469
Tennessee	‡8	705,434	88,179
Ohio St.	6	511,772	85,295
1988			
Michigan	6	628,807	104,801
Tennessee	6	551,677	91,946
Ohio St.	6	516,972	86,162
1989			
Michigan	6	632,136	105,356
Tennessee	6	563,502	93,917
Ohio St.	6	511,812	85,302
1990			
Michigan	6	627,046	104,508
Tennessee	7	666,540	95,220
Ohio St.	6	536,297	89,383
1991			
Michigan	6	632,024	105,337
Tennessee	6	578,389	96,398
Penn St.	6	575,077	95,846
1992			
Michigan	6	635,201	105,867
Tennessee	6	575,544	95,924
Penn St.	6	569,195	94,866
1993			
Michigan	7	739,620	105,660
Tennessee	7	667,280	95,326
Penn St.	6	564,190	94,032
1994			
Michigan	6	637,300	106,217
Penn St.	6	577,731	96,289
Tennessee	6	573,821	95,637
1995			
Michigan	7	726,368	103,767
Tennessee	7	662,857	94,694
Penn St.	6	561,546	93,591
1996			
Michigan	6	635,589	105,932
Tennessee	6	632,509	105,418
Penn St.	6	577,001	96,167
1997			
Tennessee	6	639,227	106,538
Michigan	7	745,139	106,448
Penn St.	6	582,517	97,086
1998			
Michigan	6	665,787	110,965
Tennessee	6	641,484	106,914
Penn St.	6	579,190	96,532
1999			
Michigan	6	667,049	*111,175
Tennessee	7	747,870	106,839
Penn St.	7	675,503	96,500
2000			
Michigan	6	664,930	110,822
Tennessee	6	645,567	107,595
Ohio St.	6	586,542	97,757
2001			
Michigan	6	659,447	109,908
Penn St.	6	645,457	107,576
Tennessee	6	641,059	106,843
2002			
Michigan	7	774,033	110,576
Penn St.	8	*857,911	107,239
Tennessee	7	746,936	106,705

*Record. #Includes neutral-site game (Oklahoma) at Dallas counted as a home game (75,500). †Includes neutral-site game at Memphis counted as a home game. Attendance: 1978 (40,879), 1980 (50,003), 1983 (20,135). ‡Includes neutral-site game at East Rutherford (54,681).

Annual Leading Division I-AA Teams in Per-Game Home Attendance

Year	Team	Avg.
1978	Southern U.	28,333
1979	Grambling	29,900
1980	Southern U.	29,708
1981	Grambling	30,835
1982	Southern U.	32,265
1983	Jackson St.	29,117
1984	Jackson St.	29,215
1985	Yale	29,347
1986	Jackson St.	25,177
1987	Jackson St.	32,734
1988	Jackson St.	26,500
1989	Jackson St.	32,269
1990	Grambling	30,152
1991	Grambling	27,181
1992	Southern U.	28,906
1993	Jackson St.	28,917
1994	Alcorn St.	26,203
1995	Jackson St.	34,849
1996	Alcorn St.	21,536
1997	Jackson St.	*38,873
1998	South Fla.	27,143
1999	Jackson St.	28,933
2000	Southern U.	27,190
2001	Jackson St.	29,067
2002	Jackson St.	23,691

*Record.

Annual Leading Division II Teams in Per-Game Home Attendance

Year	Team	Avg.
1958	Southern Miss.	11,998
1959	Southern Miss.	13,964
1960	Florida A&M	12,083
1961	Akron	12,988
1962	Mississippi Col.	13,125
1963	San Diego St.	14,200
1964	Southern U.	12,633
1965	San Diego St.	15,227
1966	San Diego St.	15,972
1967	San Diego St.	*41,030
1968	San Diego St.	36,969
1969	Grambling	27,680
1970	Tampa	24,204
1971	Grambling	29,341
1972	Grambling	22,663
1973	Morgan St.	22,371
1974	Southern U.	33,563
1975	Texas Southern	22,800
1976	Southern U.	25,864
1977	Florida A&M	21,376
1978	Delaware	18,981
1979	Delaware	19,644
1980	Alabama A&M	15,820
1981	Norfolk St.	19,750
1982	Norfolk St.	16,183
1983	Norfolk St.	15,417
1984	Norfolk St.	18,500
1985	Norfolk St.	18,430
1986	Norfolk St.	13,836
1987	North Dakota St.	14,120
1988	UCF	21,905
1989	North Dakota St.	16,833
1990	Norfolk St.	14,904
1991	Norfolk St.	16,779
1992	Norfolk St.	14,196
1993	Norfolk St.	15,346
1994	Clark Atlanta	20,223
1995	Norfolk St.	16,593
1996	Norfolk St.	15,676
1997	North Dakota St.	12,512
1998	Tuskegee	13,269
1999	Tuskegee	13,336
2000	North Dakota St.	12,723
2001	Tuskegee	12,957
2002	Tuskegee	11,851

*Record.

Annual Leading Division III Teams in Per-Game Home Attendance

Year	Team	Avg.
1974	Albany St. (Ga.)	9,380
1975	Wittenberg	7,000
1976	Morehouse	11,600
1977	Dayton	10,315
1978	Dayton	9,827
1979	UCF	11,240
1980	UCF	10,450
1981	Dayton	10,025
1982	Dayton	7,906
1983	Dayton	6,542
1984	Dayton	8,332
1985	Villanova	11,740
1986	Villanova	*11,883
1987	Trinity (Conn.)	6,254
1988	St. John's (Minn.)	5,788
1989	Dayton	5,962
1990	Dayton	6,185
1991	Dayton	7,657
1992	Dayton	6,098
1993	St. John's (Minn.)	6,655
1994	Hampden-Sydney	6,614
1995	St. John's (Minn.)	6,574
1996	St. John's (Minn.)	6,834
1997	Emory & Henry	5,853
1998	St. John's (Minn.)	6,562
1999	Mount Union	5,743
2000	Emory & Henry	6,263
2001	St. John's (Minn.)	6,674
2002	St. John's (Minn.)	5,717

*Record.

ATTENDANCE RECORDS

2002 Statistical Leaders

Scott Walstrom/Northern Illinois Media Services

Michael Turner, Northern Illinois

2002 Division I-A Individual Leaders

All-Purpose Running

Rank, Player	Pos	Cl	Gm	Rush	Rec	PR	KOR	Yards	Yds/Gm	Plays	Ydspl
1 Larry Johnson, Penn St.	TB	SR	13	2,087	349	0	219	2,655	204.23	323	8.22
2 Michael Turner, Northern Ill.	**RB**	**JR**	**12**	**1,915**	**100**	**0**	**269**	**2,284**	**190.33**	**358**	**6.38**
3 Robbie Mixon, Central Mich.	RB	SR	12	1,361	253	0	524	2,138	178.17	308	6.94
4 Jason Wright, Northwestern	WR	JR	12	1,234	266	0	513	2,013	167.75	264	7.63
5 Brock Forsey, Boise St.	RB	SR	13	1,611	282	0	234	2,127	163.62	340	6.26
6 Domanick Davis, LSU	RB	SR	13	931	130	499	560	2,120	163.08	269	7.88
7 Bobby Wade, Arizona	WR	SR	12	4	1389	224	332	1,949	162.42	127	15.35
8 Willis McGahee, Miami (Fla.)	RB	SO	13	1,753	355	0	0	2,108	162.15	309	6.82
9 Charles Pauley, San Jose St.	WR	SR	13	67	804	237	978	2,086	160.46	138	15.12
10 Derek Abney, Kentucky	WR	JR	12	5	569	544	804	1,922	160.17	109	17.63
11 Doug Gabriel, UCF	WR	SR	12	52	1237	0	632	1,921	160.08	113	17
12 Chris Brown, Colorado	RB	JR	12	1,841	40	0	0	1,881	156.75	308	6.11
13 Andre Forde, Buffalo	WR	SR	10	21	748	161	626	1,556	155.6	106	14.68
14 Quentin Griffin, Oklahoma	RB	SR	14	1,884	264	0	0	2,148	153.43	322	6.67
15 Nate Burleson, Nevada	WR	SR	12	115	1629	24	67	1,835	152.92	167	10.99
16 Marcus Merriweather, Ball St.	RB	SR	12	1,618	207	0	0	1,825	152.08	354	5.16
17 William White, Army	WR	SO	11	13	384	10	1239	1,646	149.64	89	18.49
18 Wes Welker, Texas Tech	RB	JR	14	244	1054	752	5	2,055	146.79	175	11.74
19 Terry Caulley, Connecticut	RB	FR	10	1,247	205	0	0	1,452	145.2	245	5.93
20 Derrick Hamilton, Clemson	WR	SO	13	208	602	377	696	1,883	144.85	140	13.45
21 Avon Cobourne, West Virginia	RB	SR	13	1,710	146	0	0	1,856	142.77	351	5.29
22 Steven Jackson, Oregon St.	RB	SO	13	1,690	165	0	0	1,855	142.69	336	5.52
23 Donta Greene, Toledo	WR	SR	14	18	712	443	809	1,982	141.57	134	14.79
24 J.R. Tolver, San Diego St.	WR	SR	13	40	1785	5	0	1,830	140.77	136	13.46
25 Joffrey Reynolds, Houston	RB	SR	12	1,545	135	0	0	1,680	140	335	5.01
26 Artose Pinner, Kentucky	RB	SR	12	1,414	264	0	0	1,678	139.83	320	5.24
27 Onterrio Smith, Oregon	RB	JR	10	1,141	78	0	175	1,394	139.4	264	5.28
28 Derrick Knight, Boston College	RB	JR	13	1,432	372	0	0	1,804	138.77	296	6.09
29 Darren Sproles, Kansas St.	RB	SO	13	1,465	99	154	82	1,800	138.46	265	6.79
30 Kwane Doster, Vanderbilt	TB	FR	11	798	109	0	616	1,523	138.45	196	7.77
31 Fabian Davis, Wake Forest	WR	SR	13	446	575	363	363	1,747	134.38	145	12.05
32 Joe Smith, Louisiana Tech	RB	SR	12	1,217	352	0	0	1,569	130.75	254	6.18
33 Rashaun Woods, Oklahoma St.	WR	JR	13	0	1695	0	0	1,695	130.38	107	15.84
34 Mewelde Moore, Tulane	RB	JR	13	1,138	545	0	0	1,683	129.46	340	4.95
35 LaShaun Ward, California	WR	SR	12	35	709	0	809	1,553	129.42	72	21.57
36 Dan Sheldon, Northern Ill.	WR	SO	12	135	783	477	147	1,542	128.5	82	18.8
37 Rodney Davis, Fresno St.	RB	JR	14	1,586	162	0	0	1,748	124.86	332	5.27
38 DeMarco McCleskey, Cincinnati	RB	SR	14	1,361	368	0	0	1,729	123.5	347	4.98
39 Tanardo Sharps, Temple	RB	SR	12	1,276	205	0	0	1,481	123.42	338	4.38
40 Anthony Davis, Wisconsin	RB	SO	13	1,555	48	0	0	1,603	123.31	306	5.24
41 Ime Akpan, Eastern Mich.	RB	SR	11	1,231	115	0	0	1,346	122.36	294	4.58
42 Shaud Williams, Alabama	RB	JR	13	921	228	346	91	1,586	122	196	8.09
43 Maurice Clarett, Ohio St.	RB	FR	11	1,237	104	0	0	1,341	121.91	234	5.73
44 Antoineo Harris, Illinois	RB	SR	12	1,330	129	0	0	1,459	121.58	294	4.96
45 Steve Suter, Maryland	WR	SO	14	82	303	771	546	1,702	121.57	100	17.02
46 Derrick Nix, Southern Miss.	RB	SR	11	1,194	138	0	0	1,332	121.09	232	5.74
47 Art Brown, East Caro.	RB	JR	10	1,029	181	0	0	1,210	121	240	5.04
47 David Mikell, Boise St.	RB	JR	11	606	193	0	532	1,331	121	142	9.37
49 Kerry Watkins, Georgia Tech	WR	SR	13	39	1050	0	481	1,570	120.77	103	15.24
50 Keylon Kincade, Southern Methodist	RB	JR	12	1,279	143	0	24	1,446	120.5	348	4.16
51 Charles Rogers, Michigan St.	WR	JR	12	74	1351	19	0	1,444	120.33	77	18.75
52 Joe Igber, California	RB	SR	12	1,130	309	0	0	1,439	119.92	275	5.23
53 Kassim Osgood, San Diego St.	WR	SR	13	0	1552	0	0	1,552	119.38	108	14.37
54 Bryant Jacobs, La.-Monroe	RB	SR	12	1,043	32	0	357	1,432	119.33	230	6.23
55 Wali Lundy, Virginia	RB	FR	14	826	435	0	409	1,670	119.29	271	6.16
56 DeAndrew Rubin, South Fla.	WR	SR	10	0	357	432	402	1,191	119.1	62	19.21
57 Cecil Sapp, Colorado St.	RB	SR	14	1,601	63	0	0	1,664	118.86	359	4.64
58 Kevin Curtis, Utah St.	WR	SR	11	21	1258	12	0	1,291	117.36	82	15.74
59 Howard Jackson, UTEP	RB	SO	12	844	55	0	507	1,406	117.17	205	6.86
60 Danny Smith, Arkansas St.	RB	SR	13	1,390	121	0	0	1,511	116.23	265	5.7
61 Fred Russell, Iowa	RB	JR	11	1,264	11	0	0	1,275	115.91	221	5.77
62 Dwone Hicks, Middle Tenn.	RB	SR	11	1,011	250	0	0	1,261	114.64	199	6.34
63 Kevin Walter, Eastern Mich.	WR	SR	12	0	1368	0	0	1,368	114	93	14.71
64 Blair Lewis, Idaho	RB	SR	10	930	203	0	0	1,133	113.3	198	5.72
65 James Hickenbotham, Arkansas St.	WR	SR	11	46	468	247	483	1,244	113.09	82	15.17
66 Lee Suggs, Virginia Tech	RB	SR	14	1,325	126	0	132	1,583	113.07	273	5.8
67 T.A. McLendon, North Carolina St.	RB	FR	13	1,101	354	0	0	1,455	111.92	287	5.07
68 Luke Clemens, Miami (Ohio)	RB	JR	12	1,009	334	0	0	1,343	111.92	250	5.37
69 Reggie Williams, Washington	WR	SO	13	0	1454	0	0	1,454	111.85	94	15.47
70 Bryant Johnson, Penn St.	WR	SR	13	0	917	528	0	1,445	111.15	89	16.24
71 Tab Perry, UCLA	WR	JR	12	5	698	0	626	1,329	110.75	61	21.79
72 Musa Smith, Georgia	RB	JR	13	1,324	107	0	0	1,431	110.08	275	5.2
73 Cedric Benson, Texas	RB	SO	13	1,293	119	0	0	1,412	108.62	326	4.33
74 Courtney Roby, Indiana	WR	SO	12	37	1039	0	227	1,303	108.58	72	18.1
75 Charles Frederick, Washington	WR	SO	13	11	651	146	601	1,409	108.38	96	14.68
76 Joe Alls, Bowling Green	RB	SR	10	801	125	0	157	1,083	108.3	144	7.52
77 Marque Davis, Fresno St.	WR	JR	13	18	956	0	420	1,394	107.23	86	16.21
78 Damien Dorsey, Louisville	WR	SR	12	-2	753	508	20	1,279	106.58	88	14.53

Rank, Player	Pos	Cl	Gm	Rush	Rec	PR	KOR	Yards	Yds/Gm	Plays	Ydspl
79 Alex Haynes, UCF	DB	SO	11	1,038	132	0	0	1,170	106.36	228	5.13
80 Kendrick Mosley, Western Mich.	WR	SR	9	10	507	440	0	957	106.33	68	14.07
81 Tyler Ebell, UCLA	RB	FR	13	994	72	273	43	1,382	106.31	272	5.08
82 Joshua Cribbs, Kent St.	QB	SO	10	1,057	0	0	0	1,057	105.7	137	7.72
83 Damien Rhodes, Syracuse	RB	FR	12	568	108	3	589	1,268	105.67	176	7.2
84 Aaron Leeper, Buffalo	RB	FR	12	917	132	0	218	1,267	105.58	275	4.61
85 Brandon Warfield, Utah	RB	JR	9	919	28	0	0	947	105.22	206	4.6
86 DeAngelo Williams, Memphis	RB	FR	11	684	51	0	420	1155	105	126	9.17
86 Tatum Bell, Oklahoma St.	RB	JR	11	1,096	59	0	0	1,155	105	179	6.45
88 Cedric Thompson, Idaho	WR	JR	11	19	50	245	836	1,150	104.55	76	15.13
89 James Newson, Oregon St.	WR	JR	13	22	1284	52	0	1,358	104.46	82	16.56
90 Philip Reed, Western Mich.	RB	JR	12	1,053	199	0	0	1,252	104.33	236	5.31
91 Mack Vincent, La.-Monroe	WR	JR	12	53	1198	0	0	1,251	104.25	95	13.17
92 Shaun McDonald, Arizona St.	WR	JR	14	25	1405	29	0	1,459	104.21	94	15.52
93 Taurean Henderson, Texas Tech	RB	FR	14	793	633	0	27	1,453	103.79	253	5.74
94 Terry Jackson II, Minnesota	RB	SO	13	1,318	30	0	0	1,348	103.69	245	5.5
95 Erick Franklin, Louisiana Tech	WR	JR	12	-7	356	0	887	1,236	103	69	17.91
96 Taylor Jacobs, Florida	WR	SR	11	43	1088	0	0	1,131	102.82	74	15.28
97 Chad Brinker, Ohio	RB	SR	12	1,099	115	19	-3	1,230	102.5	243	5.06
98 Roy Williams, Texas	WR	JR	12	85	1142	0	0	1,227	102.25	69	17.78
99 DonTrell Moore, New Mexico	RB	FR	13	1,134	139	0	55	1,328	102.15	271	4.9
100 Marcus Whalen, Brigham Young	RB	SO	11	918	203	0	0	1121	101.91	208	5.39

Field Goals

Min. 75 Pct. of Team's Games Played

Rank, Player	Pos	Cl	Gm	FGA	FGM	Avg	FG/Gm
1 Nick Browne, TCU	K	JR	12	30	23	0.767	1.92
2 Billy Bennett, Georgia	K	JR	14	33	26	0.788	1.86
3 Mike Nugent, Ohio St.	K	SO	14	28	25	0.893	1.79
4 Sandro Sciortino, Boston College	K	JR	13	32	23	0.719	1.77
5 Nick Novak, Maryland	K	SO	14	28	24	0.857	1.71
5 Jeff Babcock, Colorado St.	K	SO	14	32	24	0.75	1.71
7 John Anderson, Washington	K	SR	13	34	22	0.647	1.69
7 Drew Dunning, Washington St.	K	JR	13	33	22	0.667	1.69
9 Mike Barth, Arizona St.	K	SR	14	33	23	0.697	1.64
9 Asen Asparuhov, Fresno St.	K	SR	14	30	23	0.767	1.64
11 Nate Kaeding, Iowa	K	JR	13	24	21	0.875	1.62
12 Mark-Christian Jensen, California	K	SR	12	27	19	0.704	1.58
13 Dan Nystrom, Minnesota	K	SR	13	21	20	0.952	1.54
13 Jared Siegel, Oregon	K	SO	13	24	20	0.833	1.54
13 Seth Marler, Tulane	K	SR	13	33	20	0.606	1.54
16 Steve Azar, Northern Ill.	K	JR	12	25	18	0.72	1.5
17 Santiago Gramatica, South Fla.	K	SO	11	21	16	0.762	1.45
18 Dario Aguiniga, New Mexico St.	K	JR	12	23	17	0.739	1.42
18 Nick Hayes, UAB	K	SO	12	22	17	0.773	1.42
18 Kevin Miller, East Caro.	K	SR	12	22	17	0.773	1.42
18 Aaron Hunt, Clemson	K	JR	12	22	17	0.773	1.42
22 Xavier Beitia, Florida St.	PK	SO	14	28	19	0.679	1.36
22 Jonathan Ruffin, Cincinnati	K	SR	14	22	19	0.864	1.36
24 Brent Smith, Mississippi St.	K	JR	12	20	16	0.8	1.33
24 Josh Scobee, Louisiana Tech	K	JR	12	21	16	0.762	1.33
26 Matt Wisnosky, Wake Forest	P	SO	13	25	17	0.68	1.31
26 Robbie Gould, Penn St.	K	SO	13	22	17	0.773	1.31
26 Tommy Kirovski, San Diego St.	K	SR	13	27	17	0.63	1.31
26 John Corbello, LSU	K	SR	13	24	17	0.708	1.31
30 Dane Kidman, Utah St.	K	SR	11	17	14	0.824	1.27
31 Kirk Yliniemi, Oregon St.	K	JR	12	16	15	0.938	1.25
32 Curtis Head, Marshall	P	SR	13	20	16	0.8	1.23
32 Joey Ashcroft, Air Force	K	JR	13	18	16	0.889	1.23
32 Dusty Mangum, Texas	K	SO	13	26	16	0.615	1.23
32 Ryan Killeen, Southern California	K	SO	13	23	16	0.696	1.23
36 Adam Benike, Iowa St.	K	JR	14	23	17	0.739	1.21
37 Alex Walls, Tennessee	K	SR	10	17	12	0.706	1.2
38 Brent Garber, Duke	K	JR	12	25	14	0.56	1.17
38 Mike Gruzwalski, Central Mich.	K	FR	12	19	14	0.737	1.17
38 Matt Prater, UCF	K	FR	12	21	14	0.667	1.17
38 Cap Poklemba, Temple	K	SR	12	20	14	0.7	1.17
38 Jared Parseghian, Miami (Ohio)	K	SO	12	14	14	1	1.17
43 Jonathan Nichols, Mississippi	K	SO	13	20	15	0.75	1.15
43 Curt Jones, Southern Miss.	K	SR	13	26	15	0.577	1.15
45 Trey DiCarlo, Oklahoma	K	FR	14	22	16	0.727	1.14
46 Nick Calaycay, Boise St.	K	SR	10	13	11	0.846	1.1
47 Todd Pegram, Texas A&M	K	FR	11	21	12	0.571	1.09
48 Matt Payne, Brigham Young	K	SO	12	16	13	0.813	1.08
49 Nicholas Setta, Notre Dame	K	SR	13	25	14	0.56	1.08
50 Justin Ayat, Hawaii	K	SO	14	23	15	0.652	1.07
51 Luke Manget, Georgia Tech	K	SR	12	17	12	0.706	1
51 Marc Hickok, Connecticut	K	SR	12	17	12	0.706	1
51 Josh Brown, Nebraska	K	SR	14	18	14	0.778	1
51 Dustin Bell, Houston	K	SO	12	14	12	0.857	1
51 Bryan Borreson, Utah	K	FR	11	21	11	0.524	1
51 Travis Mayle, Kent St.	K	FR	12	14	12	0.857	1
51 Shaun Suisham, Bowling Green	K	JR	12	14	12	0.857	1
51 Mike Allen, Wisconsin	K	SO	12	19	12	0.632	1
51 Todd Sievers, Miami (Fla.)	K	SR	13	22	13	0.591	1
51 David Abdul, Pittsburgh	K	FR	13	20	13	0.65	1
61 Jason Robbins, Toledo	K	FR	14	16	13	0.813	0.93
61 Robert Treece, Texas Tech	K	SR	14	19	13	0.684	0.93
63 Nate Fikse, UCLA	P	SR	13	13	12	0.923	0.92
63 Nick Gilliam, San Jose St.	K	SR	13	20	12	0.6	0.92
63 Nate Smith, Louisville	K	JR	13	19	12	0.632	0.92
66 Collin Barber, Syracuse	K	SO	12	20	11	0.55	0.92
66 Thomas Olmsted, Troy St.	P	FR	12	15	11	0.733	0.92
68 Anthony Apa, Western Mich.	K	JR	9	12	8	0.667	0.89
69 David Carlton, Arkansas	K	SO	14	16	12	0.75	0.86
70 Todd James, West Virginia	K	JR	13	16	11	0.688	0.85
70 Luke Phillips, Oklahoma St.	K	JR	13	16	11	0.688	0.85
72 Brian Kelly, Middle Tenn.	K	JR	12	13	10	0.769	0.83
72 David Wasielewski, Northwestern	K	SR	12	18	10	0.556	0.83
72 Damon Fine, Nevada	K	SO	12	17	10	0.588	0.83
72 Daniel Weaver, South Carolina	K	JR	12	16	10	0.625	0.83
72 Kevin Kerr, Ohio	K	SR	12	16	10	0.625	0.83
72 David Rayner, Michigan St.	K	SO	12	16	10	0.625	0.83
78 Carter Warley, Virginia Tech	K	JR	11	15	9	0.6	0.82
78 Peter Christofilakos, Illinois	K	JR	11	12	9	0.75	0.82

Nick Browne, TCU

TCU Sports Information

Rank, Player	Pos	Cl	Gm	FGA	FGM	Avg	FG/Gm
78 Joe Rheem, Kansas St.	K	SO	11	12	9	0.75	0.82
78 Michael Sgroi, Stanford	K	FR	11	15	9	0.6	0.82
82 Pat Brougham, Colorado	K	SR	14	26	11	0.423	0.79
83 Brad DeVault, Tulsa	K	FR	9	12	7	0.583	0.78
84 Eric Neihouse, Arkansas St.	K	FR	13	22	10	0.455	0.77
84 Nicke Bazaldua, North Texas	K	FR	13	15	10	0.667	0.77
84 Berin Lacevic, Purdue	K	JR	13	19	10	0.526	0.77
87 Sean Comiskey, La.-Lafayette	K	FR	12	18	9	0.5	0.75
87 Michael Matheny, Missouri	K	JR	12	13	9	0.692	0.75
87 Stephen Gostkowski, Memphis	K	FR	12	14	9	0.643	0.75
87 Taylor Begley, Kentucky	K	FR	12	14	9	0.643	0.75
87 Dallas Pelz, Buffalo	K	JR	12	13	9	0.692	0.75
87 Mike Langford, Ball St.	K	JR	12	13	9	0.692	0.75
87 Bryan Robertson, Indiana	K	SO	12	12	9	0.75	0.75
87 Dan Orner, North Carolina	K	JR	12	14	9	0.643	0.75
95 Brennan Landry, Rice	K	FR	11	15	8	0.533	0.73
96 Trent Stephenson, Southern Methodist	K	SO	10	10	7	0.7	0.7
97 Matt Leach, Florida	P	SO	13	15	9	0.6	0.69
98 Greg Johnson, Vanderbilt	P	FR	12	13	8	0.615	0.67
98 Keith Robinson, UTEP	K	SO	12	12	8	0.667	0.67
100 Johnny Beck, Kansas	K	SO	11	17	7	0.412	0.64

Interceptions

Min. 75 Pct. of Team's Games Played

Rank, Player	Pos	Cl	Gm	Int	Yds	TDs	Int/Gm
1 Jim Leonhard, Wisconsin	DB	SO	14	11	115	0	0.79
2 Jason David, Washington St.	DB	JR	10	7	101	0	0.7
3 Gerald Jones, San Jose St.	DB	JR	12	8	116	1	0.67
3 Jason Goss, TCU	DB	SR	12	8	27	0	0.67
5 Gabe Franklin, Boise St.	DB	SO	13	8	70	0	0.62
5 Lynaris Elpheage, Tulane	DB	JR	13	8	133	1	0.62
5 Justin Miller, Clemson	DB	FR	13	8	70	0	0.62
8 Randee Drew, Northern Ill.	DB	JR	12	7	103	0	0.58
9 Vince Thompson, Northern Ill.	DB	SR	9	5	4	0	0.56
10 Bop White, Ohio	DB	SR	11	6	52	0	0.55
10 Bobby Walker, Kansas St.	DB	SR	11	6	177	3	0.55
10 J.R. Reed, South Fla.	DB	JR	11	6	34	1	0.55
13 Corey Webster, LSU	DB	JR	13	7	75	1	0.54
13 Shane Walton, Notre Dame	DB	SR	13	7	84	2	0.54
15 Von Hutchins, Mississippi	DB	JR	12	6	28	0	0.5
15 Remuise Johnson, Kansas	DB	SR	12	6	7	0	0.5
15 Roy Hopkins, Connecticut	DB	SR	12	6	28	0	0.5
15 Milt Bowen, Miami (Ohio)	DB	SR	12	6	38	0	0.5
15 Mitch Meeuwsen, Oregon St.	DB	SO	10	5	26	0	0.5
15 Mark Graham, Buffalo	DB	JR	12	6	72	0	0.5
21 Brian Mance, Clemson	DB	SR	13	6	1	0	0.46
21 Etric Pruitt, Southern Miss.	DB	JR	13	6	96	1	0.46

Rank, Player	Pos	Cl	Gm	Int	Yds	TDs	Int/Gm
21 Dakarai Pearson, Texas	DB	JR	13	6	88	0	0.46
24 Rashad Baker, Tennessee	DB	JR	11	5	0	0	0.45
24 Ron Hemingway, South Fla.	DB	JR	11	5	45	1	0.45
26 Jaxson Appel, Texas A&M	DB	FR	9	4	46	0	0.44
27 Blue Adams, Cincinnati	DB	SR	14	6	104	2	0.43
27 Derrick Strait, Oklahoma	DB	JR	14	6	175	1	0.43
27 Brandon Everage, Oklahoma	DB	JR	14	6	107	0	0.43
27 Brandon Hefflin, Toledo	DB	JR	14	6	18	0	0.43
31 Tony Carr, Western Mich.	DB	SO	12	5	30	0	0.42
31 Jemeel Powell, California	DB	SR	12	5	63	1	0.42
31 Kenneth Hilliard, TCU	DB	SR	12	5	4	0	0.42
34 Courtney Watson, Notre Dame	LB	SR	10	4	123	1	0.4
35 Matt Grier, Mississippi	DB	SR	13	5	55	1	0.38
35 Demetrius Hookfin, LSU	DB	SR	13	5	104	1	0.38
35 Terence Newman, Kansas St.	DB	SR	13	5	21	0	0.38
35 Quentin Brown, Tulane	DB	SR	13	5	48	0	0.38
35 Jonathan Burke, Arkansas St.	DB	SO	13	5	59	1	0.38
35 Steven Moore, Oregon	DB	JR	13	5	0	0	0.38
35 Keith Lewis, Oregon	DB	JR	13	5	16	0	0.38
35 Derrick Johnson, Washington	DB	SO	13	5	56	1	0.38
35 Jeremy Muyres, Georgia Tech	DB	SR	13	5	37	0	0.38
35 Chuck Allen, Arkansas St.	DB	SR	13	5	90	0	0.38
35 Don McGee, North Texas	DB	SR	13	5	109	0	0.38
46 Nashville Dyer, Kent St.	DB	SR	11	4	0	0	0.36
46 D.J. Walker, UTEP	DB	SR	11	4	39	0	0.36
46 Gerome Sapp, Notre Dame	DB	SR	11	4	17	0	0.36
46 Nathan Vasher, Texas	DB	JR	11	4	3	0	0.36
46 Wes Crawley, Air Force	DB	SR	11	4	28	0	0.36
51 Cameron Worrell, Fresno St.	DB	SR	14	5	97	1	0.36
51 Domonique Foxworth, Maryland	DB	SO	14	5	64	0	0.36
51 B.J. Tucker, Wisconsin	DB	SR	14	5	67	1	0.36
51 Garnell Wilds, Virginia Tech	DB	JR	14	5	8	0	0.36
55 Brandon Haw, Rutgers	DB	SR	12	4	17	0	0.33
55 Ben Emanuel, UCLA	DB	SO	12	4	77	1	0.33
55 James Bethea, California	DB	JR	12	4	48	0	0.33
55 Dante McKnight, Central Mich.	DB	JR	12	4	5	0	0.33
55 James King, Central Mich.	DB	SO	12	4	17	0	0.33
55 Asante Samuel, UCF	DB	SR	12	4	26	0	0.33
55 Raheem Covington, Northwestern	DB	SR	12	4	17	0	0.33
55 Thomas Wright, Michigan St.	DB	SR	12	4	91	1	0.33
55 Lawrence Richardson, Arkansas	DB	JR	12	4	25	0	0.33
55 Dunta Robinson, South Carolina	DB	JR	12	4	63	0	0.33
55 Kenoe Kauo, Nevada	FS	SO	12	4	34	1	0.33
55 Maurice Lloyd, Connecticut	LB	SO	12	4	94	0	0.33
55 Byron Jones, Texas A&M	DB	SO	12	4	117	1	0.33
55 R.J. Jones, Missouri	DB	SR	12	4	39	0	0.33
55 Chris Brown, UAB	DB	SR	12	4	-4	0	0.33
55 Josh Powell, San Jose St.	DB	SO	12	4	85	0	0.33
55 Hyrum Peters, Hawaii	DB	JR	12	4	176	3	0.33
72 Carlos Rogers, Auburn	DB	SO	13	4	48	0	0.31
72 Derrick Johnson, Texas	LB	SO	13	4	85	0	0.31
72 Fabian Washington, Nebraska	DB	FR	13	4	35	1	0.31
72 Travaris Robinson, Auburn	DB	SR	13	4	64	0	0.31
72 Charlie Peprah, Alabama	DB	FR	13	4	90	1	0.31
72 Waine Bacon, Alabama	DB	SR	13	4	32	0	0.31
72 Melvin Cook, San Jose St.	DB	JR	13	4	11	0	0.31
72 Sean Taylor, Miami (Fla.)	DB	SO	13	4	122	0	0.31
72 Jason Leach, Southern California	DB	SO	13	4	52	0	0.31
72 Lawrence Turner, Oregon St.	DB	JR	13	4	40	0	0.31
72 Ricky Manning, UCLA	DB	SR	13	4	47	1	0.31
72 Derek Pagel, Iowa	DB	SR	13	4	89	1	0.31
72 Shawn Mayer, Penn St.	S	SR	13	4	7	0	0.31
72 Bryan Scott, Penn St.	DB	SR	13	4	47	0	0.31
72 Jovon Johnson, Iowa	DB	FR	13	4	71	0	0.31
72 Jahmile Addae, West Virginia	DB	SO	13	4	14	0	0.31
72 DeAngelo Hall, Virginia Tech	DB	SO	13	4	124	1	0.31
89 Jason Harmon, Michigan St.	DB	SO	10	3	-1	0	0.3
89 Jahmal Fenner, UTEP	DB	SO	10	3	24	0	0.3
89 Victor Malone, Houston	DB	SR	10	3	62	0	0.3
89 Brandon Heaney, Brigham Young	DB	JR	10	3	6	0	0.3
93 Ken Hamlin, Arkansas	DB	JR	14	4	33	0	0.29
93 Kentrell Curry, Georgia	DB	JR	14	4	145	1	0.29
93 DeJuan Groce, Nebraska	DB	SR	14	4	26	0	0.29
93 Antonio Perkins, Oklahoma	DB	SO	14	4	111	1	0.29
93 Medford Moorer, Colorado	DB	JR	14	4	84	1	0.29
93 Kelvin Millhouse, Hawaii	DB	JR	14	4	17	0	0.29
93 Madieu Williams, Maryland	DB	JR	14	4	0	0	0.29
93 R.J. Oliver, Arizona St.	DB	SO	14	4	51	0	0.29
93 Brett Hudson, Arizona St.	DB	JR	14	4	66	0	0.29
93 Vincent Fuller, Virginia Tech	DB	SO	14	4	0	0	0.29
93 Willie Pile, Virginia Tech	DB	SR	14	4	171	1	0.29
93 Rod Johnson, North Carolina St.	DB	SR	14	4	67	0	0.29
93 Chris Gamble, Ohio St.	WR	SO	14	4	40	1	0.29

Wisconsin Sports Information

Jim Leonhard, Wisconsin

Kickoff Returns

Rank, Player	Pos	Cl	Gm	Ret	Yds	TDs	Avg	Ret/Gm
1 Charles Pauley, San Jose St.	WR	SR	13	31	978	2	31.55	2.38
2 Broderick Clark, Louisville	WR	FR	13	31	897	2	28.94	2.38
3 LaShaun Ward, California	WR	SR	12	28	809	1	28.89	2.33
4 Jason Wright, Northwestern	WR	JR	12	18	513	1	28.5	1.5
5 Nathan Jones, Rutgers	DB	JR	12	26	736	2	28.31	2.17
6 LaTarence Dunbar, TCU	WR	SR	11	18	501	1	27.83	1.64
7 Jerome Dennis, Utah St.	DB	SO	11	14	388	0	27.71	1.27
8 Vontez Duff, Notre Dame	DB	JR	13	19	526	1	27.68	1.46
9 Makonnen Fenton, Temple	RB	JR	10	14	380	1	27.14	1.4
10 Derek Abney, Kentucky	WR	JR	12	30	804	2	26.8	2.5
10 DeAndrew Rubin, South Fla.	WR	SR	10	15	402	1	26.8	1.5
12 C.J. Jones, Iowa	WR	SR	13	19	506	1	26.63	1.46
13 Jeff Backes, Northwestern	RB	FR	12	18	472	0	26.22	1.5
14 Greg Heaggans, Kansas	WR	FR	12	23	603	1	26.22	1.92
15 Randee Drew, Northern Ill.	DB	JR	12	15	392	0	26.13	1.25
16 Rod Sneed, Colorado	DB	SR	13	20	517	0	25.85	1.54
17 Kwane Doster, Vanderbilt	TB	FR	11	24	616	0	25.67	2.18
18 David Mikell, Boise St.	RB	JR	11	21	532	0	25.33	1.91
19 Lynaris Elpheage, Tulane	DB	JR	13	18	453	1	25.17	1.38
20 Tab Perry, UCLA	WR	JR	12	25	626	0	25.04	2.08
21 Steve Suter, Maryland	WR	SO	14	22	546	0	24.82	1.57
22 Fred Reid, Mississippi St.	RB	SO	12	18	441	0	24.5	1.5
23 Chris Massey, Oklahoma St.	DB	SR	13	22	534	0	24.27	1.69
24 Fred Gibson, Georgia	WR	SO	12	19	460	1	24.21	1.58
25 Matt Carter, Akron	RB	JR	10	36	867	0	24.08	3.6
26 Shirdonya Mitchell, Missouri	WR	JR	11	16	385	0	24.06	1.45
27 Wali Lundy, Virginia	RB	FR	14	17	409	0	24.06	1.21
28 Phil Braxton, West Virginia	WR	SR	13	20	481	0	24.05	1.54
29 Jason Southall, UAB	DB	JR	12	32	768	0	24	2.67
30 John Eubanks, Southern Miss.	DB	FR	12	22	526	0	23.91	1.83
31 Bryant Jacobs, La.-Monroe	RB	SR	12	15	357	0	23.8	1.25
32 Jonas Rutledge, Southern Methodist	RB	JR	12	38	901	0	23.71	3.17
33 Josh Davis, Nebraska	RB	JR	13	42	994	0	23.67	3.23
34 Corey Larkins, Tennessee	DB	SO	13	26	611	0	23.5	2
35 Domanick Davis, LSU	RB	SR	13	24	560	0	23.33	1.85
35 DeAngelo Williams, Memphis	RB	FR	11	18	420	0	23.33	1.64
37 Torrie Cox, Pittsburgh	DB	JR	13	30	690	0	23	2.31
38 Bryan Blew, Air Force	WR	SR	13	16	366	0	22.88	1.23
39 Maurice Hall, Ohio St.	RB	SO	14	19	434	0	22.84	1.36
40 Decori Birmingham, Arkansas	WR	SO	14	28	638	0	22.79	2
41 Ronnie Hardiman, Nevada	DB	JR	10	22	501	0	22.77	2.2
42 Cedric Thompson, Idaho	WR	JR	11	37	836	0	22.59	3.36
43 William White, Army	WR	SO	11	55	1239	0	22.53	5
44 Will Blackmon, Boston College	DB	FR	13	28	630	0	22.5	2.15
45 Donta Greene, Toledo	WR	SR	14	36	809	0	22.47	2.57
46 Greg Golden, North Carolina St.	RB	SO	13	16	359	0	22.44	1.23
47 Jeremy LeSueur, Michigan	DB	JR	13	26	583	0	22.42	2
48 Ran Carthon, Florida	RB	JR	13	17	380	0	22.35	1.31
49 Damarcus Fox, East Caro.	WR	SO	10	20	447	0	22.35	2
50 Dexter Wynn, Colorado St.	DB	JR	14	22	490	0	22.27	1.57
51 Freddie Keiaho, San Diego St.	RB	FR	12	15	334	0	22.27	1.25
52 Martez Johnson, Bowling Green	RB	SR	12	18	400	0	22.22	1.5
53 Erick Franklin, Louisiana Tech	WR	JR	12	40	887	0	22.18	3.33
54 Steve Gregory, Syracuse	DB	FR	11	17	376	0	22.12	1.55
55 Marque Davis, Fresno St.	WR	JR	13	19	420	0	22.11	1.46
56 Howard Jackson, UTEP	RB	SO	12	23	507	0	22.04	1.92
57 Tony Lane, Navy	RB	JR	12	22	484	0	22	1.83
58 James Hickenbotham, Arkansas St.	WR	SR	11	22	483	0	21.95	2
59 Milt Bowen, Miami (Ohio)	DB	SR	12	27	592	0	21.93	2.25
60 Hakim Hill, Arizona St.	RB	FR	14	32	701	0	21.91	2.29
61 Larry Bostic, Ball St.	RB	FR	12	22	481	0	21.86	1.83
62 Allan Amundson, Oregon	RB	SR	13	27	590	0	21.85	2.08
63 Derrick Hamilton, Clemson	WR	SO	13	32	696	0	21.75	2.46
64 Jason Geathers, Miami (Fla.)	WR	JR	13	24	521	0	21.71	1.85
65 Wallace Wright, North Carolina	WR	SO	12	29	624	0	21.52	2.42
66 Troy Mason, UNLV	WR	SR	9	13	279	0	21.46	1.44
67 Fabian Davis, Wake Forest	WR	SR	13	17	363	0	21.35	1.31
68 Richard Johnson, Virginia Tech	WR	SO	13	23	485	0	21.09	1.77
69 Lance Young, Iowa St.	WR	JR	14	28	590	0	21.07	2

Charles Pauley, San Jose State

Ron Fried

Rank, Player	Pos	Cl	Gm	Ret	Yds	TDs	Avg	Ret/Gm
70 Jason Caesar, Ohio	WR	SR	12	24	505	0	21.04	2
71 Damien Rhodes, Syracuse	RB	FR	12	28	589	0	21.04	2.33
72 Brandon Williams, Wisconsin	WR	FR	14	32	670	0	20.94	2.29
72 Arnaz Battle, Notre Dame	WR	SR	13	16	335	0	20.94	1.23
74 Jermaine Moore, San Diego St.	WR	JR	11	15	314	0	20.93	1.36
75 Kerry Watkins, Georgia Tech	WR	SR	13	23	481	0	20.91	1.77
76 Roshawn Pope, Houston	DB	FR	10	24	501	0	20.88	2.4
77 Andre Forde, Buffalo	WR	SR	10	30	626	0	20.87	3
78 P.J. Winston, New Mexico St.	WR	SR	12	21	437	0	20.81	1.75
79 Dion Byrum, Ohio	RB	FR	12	26	541	0	20.81	2.17
80 Morris Virgil, Illinois	RB	SO	10	16	332	0	20.75	1.6
81 Jason Dellaselva, Connecticut	DB	JR	12	23	477	0	20.74	1.92
82 Chris R. Roberson, Eastern Mich.	WR	SO	12	16	328	0	20.5	1.33
83 Doug Gabriel, UCF	WR	SR	12	31	632	0	20.39	2.58
84 Tyrone Roberson, Missouri	RB	SO	9	11	224	0	20.36	1.22
85 Leonard Jones, Wyoming	RB	JR	12	28	570	0	20.36	2.33
86 A.C. Carter, Indiana	DB	SR	12	36	732	0	20.33	3
87 Brandon Middleton, Houston	WR	JR	12	19	386	0	20.32	1.58
88 Ja'Mel Branch, North Texas	WR	SO	13	19	385	0	20.26	1.46
89 Jerome Janet, Tulsa	WR	FR	9	13	261	0	20.08	1.44
90 Charles Frederick, Washington	WR	SO	13	30	601	0	20.03	2.31
91 Sean White, Rice	RB	SR	10	18	359	0	19.94	1.8
92 Antonio King, Kent St.	RB	SO	12	30	598	0	19.93	2.5
93 Ryan Wells, Stanford	WR	SR	11	36	715	0	19.86	3.27
94 Roderick Hood, Auburn	DB	SR	13	21	416	0	19.81	1.62
95 Jermaine Mays, Minnesota	WR	SR	11	18	352	0	19.56	1.64
96 Bobby Wade, Arizona	WR	SR	12	17	332	0	19.53	1.42
97 Robbie Mixon, Central Mich.	RB	SR	12	27	524	0	19.41	2.25
98 Antoine Harden, Memphis	WR	JR	12	26	504	0	19.38	2.17
99 Rod Bryant, Idaho	DB	JR	12	16	307	0	19.19	1.33
100 Jaren Hayes, Michigan St.	RB	FR	12	31	585	0	18.87	2.58

Passing

Min. 75 Pct. of Team's Games Played

Rank, Player	Pos	Cl	G	Att	Cmp	Int	CPct	Yds	Yds/ Att	Yds/ Cmp	TD	Comp/ Gm
1 Kliff Kingsbury, Texas Tech..QB	QB	SR	14	712	479	13	67.28	5,017	7.05	10.47	45	34.21
2 Cody Pickett, Washington...QB	QB	JR	13	612	365	14	59.64	4,458	7.28	12.21	28	28.08
3 Byron Leftwich, Marshall .....QB	QB	SR	12	491	331	10	67.41	4,268	8.69	12.89	30	27.58
4 Timmy Chang, Hawaii........QB	QB	SO	14	624	349	22	55.93	4,474	7.17	12.82	25	24.93
5 Adam Hall, San Diego St. QB	QB	JR	11	452	272	9	60.18	3,253	7.2	11.96	17	24.73
6 Luke McCown, Louisiana Tech ....QB	QB	JR	12	505	296	19	58.61	3,539	7.01	11.96	19	24.67
7 Carson Palmer, Southern California.....................QB	QB	SR	13	489	309	10	63.19	3,942	8.06	12.76	33	23.77
8 Casey Bramlet, Wyoming ...QB	QB	JR	12	464	277	18	59.7	3,290	7.09	11.88	24	23.08
9 Zack Threadgill, Nevada ....QB	QB	SR	12	451	275	17	60.98	3,418	7.58	12.43	26	22.92
10 Ben Roethlisberger, Miami (Ohio)........................QB	QB	SO	12	428	271	11	63.32	3,238	7.57	11.95	22	22.58
11 Jose Fuentes, Utah St. ....QB	QB	SR	11	454	246	15	54.19	3,268	7.2	13.28	20	22.36
12 Ryan Schneider, UCF...........QB	QB	JR	12	430	265	16	61.63	3,770	8.77	14.23	31	22.08
13 Rex Grossman, Florida ....QB	QB	JR	13	503	287	17	57.06	3,402	6.76	11.85	22	22.08
14 Brian Lindgren, Idaho ....QB	QB	JR	11	382	240	10	62.83	2,763	7.23	11.51	19	21.82
15 Eli Manning, Mississippi .....QB	QB	JR	13	481	279	15	58	3,401	7.07	12.19	21	21.46
16 Brian Jones, Toledo ....QB	QB	SR	14	423	297	9	70.21	3,446	8.15	11.6	23	21.21
17 Scott Rislov, San Jose St. .....QB	QB	JR	13	449	275	14	61.25	3,251	7.24	11.82	22	21.15
18 Marquel Blackwell, South Fla.......................QB	QB	SR	11	403	230	3	57.07	2,590	6.43	11.26	18	20.91
19 Charlie Frye, Akron ....QB	QB	SO	12	380	250	9	65.79	2,824	7.43	11.3	15	20.83
20 Matt Schaub, Virginia.........QB	QB	JR	14	418	288	7	68.9	2,976	7.12	10.33	28	20.57
21 Jason Johnson, Arizona ......QB	QB	SR	12	410	239	13	58.29	3,327	8.11	13.92	16	19.92
22 Danny Wimprine, Memphis QB	QB	JR	12	435	235	18	54.02	2,820	6.48	12	23	19.58
23 Andrew Walter, Arizona St. QB	QB	SO	14	483	274	15	56.73	3,877	8.03	14.15	28	19.57
24 Troy Edwards, Eastern Mich. QB	QB	SR	12	410	232	18	56.59	2,762	6.74	11.91	22	19.33
25 John Navarre, Michigan .....QB	QB	JR	13	448	248	7	55.36	2,905	6.48	11.71	21	19.08
26 Brett Basanez, Northwestern QB	QB	FR	10	325	190	7	58.46	2,204	6.78	11.6	7	19
27 Kyle Boller, California.........QB	QB	SR	12	421	225	10	53.44	2,815	6.69	12.51	28	18.75
28 Philip Rivers, North Carolina St. ....QB	QB	JR	14	418	262	10	62.68	3,353	8.02	12.8	20	18.71
29 Gino Guidugli, Cincinnati ...QB	QB	SO	14	472	258	21	54.66	3,543	7.51	13.73	22	18.43
30 Dan Orlovsky, Connecticut..QB	QB	SO	12	366	221	11	60.38	2,488	6.8	11.26	19	18.42
31 Brian St.Pierre, Boston College..........................QB	QB	SR	13	407	237	17	58.23	2,983	7.33	12.59	18	18.23
31 Dave Ragone, Louisville ......QB	QB	SR	13	442	237	11	53.62	2,880	6.52	12.15	24	18.23
33 Jason Gesser, Washington St. ....QB	QB	SR	13	402	236	13	58.71	3,408	8.48	14.44	28	18.15
34 Chris Simms, Texas ....QB	QB	SR	13	396	235	12	59.34	3,207	8.1	13.65	26	18.08
35 J.P. Losman, Tulane ....QB	QB	JR	13	401	230	10	57.36	2,468	6.15	10.73	19	17.69
36 Casey Clausen, Tennessee ..QB	QB	JR	11	310	194	7	62.58	2,297	7.41	11.84	11	17.64
37 Jon Beutjer, Illinois..............QB	QB	JR	11	327	193	11	59.02	2,511	7.68	13.01	11	17.55
38 Seneca Wallace, Iowa St. ..QB	QB	SR	14	443	244	18	55.08	3,245	7.33	13.3	15	17.43
39 Josh Fields, Oklahoma St. ...QB	QB	SO	13	408	226	10	55.39	3,145	7.71	13.92	31	17.38
40 Tyler Gooch, Tulsa ....QB	QB	SO	11	348	190	8	54.6	2,100	6.03	11.05	17	17.27
41 Ken Dorsey, Miami (Fla.) ....QB	QB	SR	13	393	222	12	56.49	3,369	8.57	15.18	28	17.08
42 Randall Secky, Buffalo ....QB	QB	SO	12	421	204	13	48.46	2,015	4.79	9.88	12	17
43 Bill Whittemore, Kansas......QB	QB	JR	9	305	151	6	49.51	1,666	5.46	11.03	11	16.78
44 Josh Harris, Bowling Green QB	QB	JR	12	353	198	11	56.09	2,425	6.87	12.25	19	16.5
45 Paul Pinegar, Fresno St. ......QB	QB	FR	14	403	230	10	57.07	2,929	7.27	12.73	20	16.43
46 Brad Smith, Missouri...........QB	QB	FR	12	366	196	6	53.55	2,333	6.37	11.9	15	16.33
47 Derek Anderson, Oregon St. QB	QB	SO	13	449	211	13	46.99	3,313	7.38	15.7	25	16.23
48 A.J. Suggs, Georgia Tech ...QB	QB	JR	13	363	208	15	57.3	2,242	6.18	10.78	12	16
49 David Greene, Georgia.......QB	QB	SO	14	379	218	8	57.52	2,924	7.72	13.41	22	15.57
50 Jon VanCleave, La.-Lafayette QB	QB	JR	11	302	169	15	53.48	2,081	6.59	12.31	9	15.36
51 Jared Lorenzen, Kentucky....QB	QB	JR	12	327	183	5	55.96	2,267	6.93	12.39	24	15.25
52 Steven Jyles, La.-Monroe .....QB	QB	FR	12	368	181	9	49.18	2,318	6.3	12.81	17	15.08
53 Nate Hybl, Oklahoma........QB	QB	SR	14	363	209	8	57.58	2,538	6.99	12.14	24	14.93
54 Kevin Fant, Mississippi St. ...QB	QB	JR	11	311	163	12	52.41	1,918	6.17	11.77	10	14.82
55 Rod Rutherford, Pittsburgh ...QB	QB	JR	13	367	192	12	52.32	2,783	7.58	14.49	22	14.77
55 Kyle Orton, Purdue.............QB	QB	SO	13	317	192	9	60.57	2,257	7.12	11.76	13	14.77
57 Paul Troth, East Caro. ....QB	QB	SO	12	359	177	20	49.3	2,315	6.45	13.08	15	14.75
57 Dustin Long, Texas A&M.....QB	QB	SO	12	333	177	16	53.15	2,509	7.53	14.18	19	14.75
59 Jason Fife, Oregon.............QB	QB	JR	13	367	190	10	51.77	2,752	7.5	14.48	24	14.62
60 Derrick Vickers, Central Mich...........................QB	QB	JR	12	320	175	5	54.69	1,828	5.71	10.45	9	14.58
61 Adam Smith, Duke ....QB	QB	SO	12	308	174	9	56.49	2,031	6.59	11.67	12	14.5
62 Zack Mills, Penn St. ....QB	QB	JR	13	333	188	10	56.46	2,417	7.26	12.86	11	14.46
63 Mike McGann, Temple ....QB	QB	SO	12	353	173	22	49.01	1,994	5.65	11.53	13	14.42
64 Gibran Hamdan, Indiana ...QB	QB	SR	11	293	152	14	51.88	2,115	7.22	13.91	9	13.82
65 Asad Abdul-Khaliq, Minnesota.....................QB	QB	JR	12	314	164	11	52.23	2,184	6.96	13.32	19	13.67
66 Aaron Karas, Baylor...........QB	QB	SO	11	251	150	13	59.76	1,792	7.14	11.95	6	13.64
67 Darrell Hackney, UAB ....QB	QB	FR	11	293	149	7	50.85	1,977	6.75	13.27	14	13.55
68 Chad Munson, Western Mich............................QB	QB	JR	12	309	162	17	52.43	2,160	6.99	13.33	14	13.5
69 Bret Engemann, Brigham Young.........................QB	QB	JR	9	215	119	8	55.35	1,334	6.2	11.21	6	13.22

Rank, Player	Pos	Cl	G	Att	Cmp	Int	CPct	Yds	Yds/ Att	Yds/ Cmp	TD	Comp/ Gm
70 Brad Banks, Iowa...............QB	SR	13	294	170	5	57.82	2,573	8.75	15.14	26	13.08
71 Casey Kelly, New Mexico ..QB	JR	14	314	181	7	57.64	1,904	6.06	10.52	14	12.93
72 Willie Simmons, Clemson ...QB	JR	11	244	142	7	58.2	1,559	6.39	10.98	6	12.91
73 Troy Nunes, Syracuse.........QB	SR	9	198	115	7	58.08	1,337	6.75	11.63	8	12.78
74 Sean Stilley, TCU ....QB	SR	9	204	114	11	55.88	1,371	6.72	12.03	6	12.67
75 Jason Thomas, UNLV.........QB	SR	11	274	134	7	48.91	1,936	7.07	14.45	8	12.18
75 Nick Eddy, Houston ....QB	JR	11	265	134	18	50.57	2,054	7.75	15.33	16	12.18
77 Matt Berry, Brigham Young QB	FR	9	184	108	9	58.7	1,309	7.11	12.12	7	12
78 Andrico Hines, Middle											
Tenn. St. ....QB	JR	12	243	142	7	58.44	1,753	7.21	12.35	6	11.83
79 Kyle Matter, Stanford.........QB	FR	10	214	116	10	54.21	1,219	5.7	10.51	8	11.6
80 Scott McBrien, Maryland ....QB	JR	14	284	162	10	57.04	2,497	8.79	15.41	15	11.57
81 Andy Roesch, Ball St. ....QB	JR	10	202	113	7	55.94	1,341	6.64	11.87	15	11.3
82 Bryan Randall, Virginia Tech QB	SO	14	248	158	11	63.71	2,134	8.6	13.51	12	11.29
83 Joshua Haldi, Northern Ill. QB	SO	12	254	130	6	51.18	2,027	7.98	15.59	15	10.83
84 Carlyle Holiday, Notre											
Dame............................QB	JR	12	257	129	5	50.19	1,788	6.96	13.86	10	10.75
85 Chris Rix, Florida St. ....QB	SO	11	225	118	7	52.44	1,684	7.48	14.27	13	10.73
86 Bradlee Van Pelt,											
Colorado St. ....QB	JR	14	287	150	7	52.26	2,073	7.22	13.82	10	10.71
87 Rasheed Marshall, West											
Virginia.........................QB	SO	13	259	139	5	53.67	1,616	6.24	11.63	9	10.69
88 Craig Krenzel, Ohio St. ......QB	SR	14	249	148	7	59.44	2,110	8.47	14.26	12	10.57
89 Robert Hodge, Colorado ....QB	SR	13	258	137	9	53.1	1,609	6.24	11.74	13	10.54
90 Elliot Jacobs, Arkansas St. ..QB	SO	13	258	136	7	52.71	1,751	6.79	12.88	7	10.46
91 Hansell Bearden, Troy St. ...QB	SO	12	288	125	16	43.4	1,463	5.08	11.7	6	10.42
92 Tyler Watts, Alabama.........QB	SR	11	181	112	4	61.88	1,414	7.81	12.63	7	10.18
93 Micky D'Angelo, Southern											
Miss..............................QB	SO	12	232	122	8	52.59	1,647	7.1	13.5	7	10.17
94 Brooks Bollinger, Wisconsin QB	SR	13	245	131	4	53.47	1,758	7.18	13.42	14	10.08
95 James MacPherson, Wake											
Forest............................QB	SR	13	223	123	4	55.16	1,837	8.24	14.93	8	9.46
96 Jay Cutler, Vanderbilt ....QB	FR	11	212	103	9	48.58	1,433	6.76	13.91	10	9.36
97 Joshua Cribbs, Kent St. ....QB	SO	10	186	91	14	48.92	1,014	5.45	11.14	4	9.1
98 Zac Dahman, Army ....QB	FR	10	184	89	9	48.37	1,039	5.65	11.67	5	8.9
99 Matt Jones, Arkansas..........QB	SO	14	234	122	8	52.14	1,592	6.8	13.05	16	8.71
100 B.J. Rhode, Boise St. ....QB	SR	13	176	113	5	64.2	1,444	8.2	12.78	11	8.69

Passing Efficiency

Min. 75 Pct. of Team's Games Played, 15 Attempts Per Game

Rank, Player	Pos	Cl	G	Att	Comp	CPct	Int	IPct	Yds	Yds/Att	TD	TDpct	Rating
1 Brad Banks, Iowa...............QB	SR	13	294	170	57.82	5	1.7	2,573	8.75	26	8.84	157.1
2 Byron Leftwich, Marshall .....QB	SR	12	491	331	67.41	10	2.04	4,268	8.69	30	6.11	156.5
3 Brian Jones, Toledo ....QB	SR	14	423	297	70.21	9	2.13	3,446	8.15	23	5.44	152.3
4 Ryan Schneider, UCF...........QB	JR	12	430	265	61.63	16	3.72	3,770	8.77	31	7.21	151.6
5 Carson Palmer, Southern													
California........................QB	SR	13	489	309	63.19	10	2.04	3,942	8.06	33	6.75	149.1
6 Matt Schaub, Virginia.........QB	JR	14	418	288	68.9	7	1.67	2,976	7.12	28	6.7	147.5
7 Jason Gesser,													
Washington St. ....QB	SR	13	402	236	58.71	13	3.23	3,408	8.48	28	6.97	146.4
8 Ken Dorsey, Miami (Fla.) ....QB	SR	13	393	222	56.49	12	3.05	3,369	8.57	28	7.12	145.9
9 Kliff Kingsbury, Texas Tech...QB	SR	14	712	479	67.28	13	1.83	5,017	7.05	45	6.32	143.7
10 Bryan Randall, Virginia Tech QB	SO	14	248	158	63.71	11	4.44	2,134	8.6	12	4.84	143.1
11 Chris Simms, Texas ....QB	SR	13	396	235	59.34	12	3.03	3,207	8.1	26	6.57	143
12 Scott McBrien, Maryland ....QB	JR	14	284	162	57.04	10	3.52	2,497	8.79	15	5.28	141.3
13 Philip Rivers, North													
Carolina St....................QB	JR	14	418	262	62.68	10	2.39	3,353	8.02	20	4.78	141.1
14 Craig Krenzel, Ohio St. ......QB	SR	14	249	148	59.44	7	2.81	2,110	8.47	12	4.82	140.9
15 Josh Fields, Oklahoma St. ...QB	SO	13	408	226	55.39	10	2.45	3,145	7.71	31	7.6	140.3
16 Ben Roethlisberger,													
Miami (Ohio)..................QB	SO	12	428	271	63.32	11	2.57	3,238	7.57	22	5.14	138.7
17 Jon Beutjer, Illinois..............QB	JR	11	327	193	59.02	11	3.36	2,511	7.68	21	6.42	138
18 David Greene, Georgia......QB	SO	14	379	218	57.52	8	2.11	2,924	7.72	22	5.8	137.3
19 Andrew Walter, Arizona St. QB	SO	14	483	274	56.73	15	3.11	3,877	8.03	28	5.8	137.1
20 Charlie Frye, Akron ....QB	SO	12	380	250	65.79	9	2.37	2,824	7.43	15	3.95	136.5
21 Zack Threadgill, Nevada ....QB	SR	12	451	275	60.98	17	3.77	3,418	7.58	26	5.76	136.1
22 Tyler Watts, Alabama.........QB	SR	11	181	112	61.88	4	2.21	1,414	7.81	7	3.87	135.8
23 Jared Lorenzen, Kentucky ....QB	JR	12	327	183	55.96	5	1.53	2,267	6.93	24	7.34	135.4
24 Brian Lindgren, Idaho ....QB	JR	11	382	240	62.83	10	2.62	2,763	7.23	19	4.97	134.8
25 Nate Hybl, Oklahoma ....QB	SR	14	363	209	57.58	8	2.2	2,538	6.99	24	6.61	133.7
26 Jason Johnson, Arizona ......QB	SR	12	410	239	58.29	13	3.17	3,327	8.11	16	3.9	133
27 Joshua Haldi, Northern Ill....QB	SO	12	254	130	51.18	6	2.36	2,027	7.98	15	5.91	133
28 James MacPherson, Wake													
Forest............................QB	SR	13	223	123	55.16	4	1.79	1,837	8.24	8	3.59	132.6
29 Casey Clausen, Tennessee ..QB	JR	11	310	194	62.58	7	2.26	2,297	7.41	11	3.55	132
30 Scott Rislov, San Jose St. ....QB	JR	13	449	275	61.25	14	3.12	3,251	7.24	22	4.9	132
31 Cody Pickett, Washington...QB	JR	13	612	365	59.64	14	2.29	4,458	7.28	28	4.58	131.4
32 Jason Fife, Oregon ....QB	JR	13	367	190	51.77	10	2.72	2,752	7.5	24	6.54	130.9
33 Paul Pinegar, Fresno St. ......QB	FR	14	403	230	57.07	10	2.48	2,929	7.27	20	4.96	129.5
34 Brooks Bollinger, Wisconsin QB	SR	13	245	131	53.47	4	1.63	1,758	7.18	14	5.71	129.3
35 Andy Roesch, Ball St. ....QB	JR	10	202	113	55.94	7	3.47	1,341	6.64	15	7.43	129.3
36 Rod Rutherford, Pittsburgh ...QB	JR	13	367	192	52.32	12	3.27	2,783	7.58	22	5.99	129.3

Rank, Player	Pos	Cl	G	Att	Comp	CPct	Int	IPct	Yds	Yds/Att	TD	TDpct	Rating
37 Adam Hall, San Diego St.	QB	JR	11	452	272	60.18	9	1.99	3,253	7.2	17	3.76	129.1
38 Dan Orlovsky, Connecticut..	QB	SO	12	366	221	60.38	11	3.01	2,488	6.8	19	5.19	128.6
39 Casey Bramlet, Wyoming ...	QB	JR	12	464	277	59.7	18	3.88	3,290	7.09	24	5.17	128.6
40 Zack Mills, Penn St.	QB	JR	13	333	188	56.46	10	3	2,417	7.26	17	5.11	128.3
41 Kyle Orton, Purdue............	QB	SO	13	317	192	60.57	9	2.84	2,257	7.12	13	4.1	128.2
42 Chris Rix, Florida St.	QB	SO	11	225	118	52.44	7	3.11	1,684	7.48	13	5.78	128.2
43 Kyle Boller, California.........	QB	SR	12	421	225	53.44	10	2.38	2,815	6.69	28	6.65	126.8
44 Damon Dowdell, Michigan St.	QB	SO	11	165	92	55.76	4	2.42	1,097	6.65	10	6.06	126.8
45 Brian St.Pierre, Boston College...........................	QB	SR	13	407	237	58.23	17	4.18	2,983	7.33	18	4.42	126
46 Dustin Long, Texas A&M.....	QB	SO	12	333	177	53.15	16	4.8	2,509	7.53	19	5.71	125.7
47 Eli Manning, Mississippi	QB	JR	13	481	279	58	15	3.12	3,401	7.07	21	4.37	125.6
48 Josh Harris, Bowling Green	QB	JR	12	353	198	56.09	11	3.12	2,425	6.87	19	5.38	125.3
49 Matt Jones, Arkansas	QB	SO	14	234	122	52.14	8	3.42	1,592	6.8	16	6.84	125
50 Marquel Blackwell, South Fla.	QB	SR	11	403	230	57.07	3	0.74	2,590	6.43	18	4.47	124.3
51 Gino Guidugli, Cincinnati ...	QB	SO	14	472	258	54.66	21	4.45	3,543	7.51	22	4.66	124.2
52 Asad Abdul-Khaliq, Minnesota	QB	JR	12	314	164	52.23	11	3.5	2,184	6.96	19	6.05	123.6
53 Jose Fuentes, Utah St.	QB	SR	11	454	246	54.19	15	3.3	3,268	7.2	20	4.41	122.6
54 Luke McCown, Louisiana Tech...............	QB	JR	12	505	296	58.61	19	3.76	3,539	7.01	19	3.76	122.4
55 Timmy Chang, Hawaii........	QB	SO	14	624	349	55.93	22	3.53	4,474	7.17	25	4.01	122.3
56 John Navarre, Michigan	QB	JR	13	448	248	55.36	7	1.56	2,905	6.48	21	4.69	122.2
57 Troy Edwards, Eastern Mich.	QB	JR	12	410	232	56.59	18	4.39	2,762	6.74	22	5.37	122.1
58 Nick Eddy, Houston	QB	JR	11	265	134	50.57	18	6.79	2,054	7.75	16	6.04	122
59 Derek Anderson, Oregon St.	QB	SO	13	449	211	46.99	13	2.9	3,313	7.38	25	5.57	121.6
60 Rex Grossman, Florida	QB	JR	13	503	287	57.06	17	3.38	3,402	6.76	22	4.37	121.5
61 Andrico Hines, Middle Tenn. St.	QB	JR	12	243	142	58.44	7	2.88	1,753	7.21	6	2.47	121.4
62 Dave Ragone, Louisville	QB	SR	13	442	237	53.62	11	2.49	2,880	6.52	24	5.43	121.3
63 Matt Berry, Brigham Young	QB	FR	9	184	108	58.7	9	4.89	1,309	7.11	7	3.8	121.2
64 Troy Nunes, Syracuse.........	QB	JR	9	198	115	58.08	7	3.54	1,337	6.75	8	4.04	121.1
65 J.P. Losman, Tulane	QB	JR	13	401	230	57.36	10	2.49	2,468	6.15	19	4.74	119.7
66 Seneca Wallace, Iowa St. ..	QB	SR	14	443	244	55.08	18	4.06	3,245	7.33	15	3.39	119.7
67 Bradlee Van Pelt, Colorado St.	QB	JR	14	287	150	52.26	7	2.44	2,073	7.22	10	3.48	119.6
68 Corey Jenkins, South Carolina......................	QB	SR	12	180	100	55.56	10	5.56	1,334	7.41	7	3.89	119.5
69 Adam Smith, Duke	QB	SO	12	308	174	56.49	9	2.92	2,031	6.59	12	3.9	118.9
70 Casey Kelly, New Mexico ..	QB	JR	14	314	181	57.64	7	2.23	1,904	6.06	14	4.46	118.8
71 Darrell Hackney, UAB	QB	FR	11	293	149	50.85	7	2.39	1,977	6.75	14	4.78	118.5
72 Brett Basanez, Northwestern	QB	FR	10	325	190	58.46	7	2.15	2,204	6.78	7	2.15	118.2
73 Danny Wimprine, Memphis	QB	JR	12	435	235	54.02	18	4.14	2,820	6.48	23	5.29	117.7
74 Carlyle Holiday, Notre Dame	QB	JR	12	257	129	50.19	5	1.95	1,788	6.96	10	3.89	117.6
75 Brad Smith, Missouri...........	QB	FR	12	366	196	53.55	6	1.64	2,333	6.37	15	4.1	117.3
76 Aaron Karas, Baylor...........	QB	SO	11	251	150	59.76	13	5.18	1,792	7.14	6	2.39	117.3
77 Tyler Gooch, Tulsa	QB	SO	11	348	190	54.6	8	2.3	2,100	6.03	17	4.89	116.8
78 Micky D'Angelo, Southern Miss.	QB	SO	12	232	122	52.59	8	3.45	1,647	7.1	7	3.02	115.3
79 Robert Hodge, Colorado	QB	SR	13	258	137	53.1	9	3.49	1,609	6.24	13	5.04	115.1
80 Chad Munson, Western Mich.	QB	JR	12	309	162	52.43	17	5.5	2,160	6.99	14	4.53	115.1
81 Willie Simmons, Clemson ...	QB	JR	11	244	142	58.2	7	2.87	1,559	6.39	6	2.46	114.2
82 Rasheed Marshall, West Virginia	QB	SO	13	259	139	53.67	5	1.93	1,616	6.24	9	3.47	113.7
83 Elliot Jacobs, Arkansas St. ..	QB	SO	13	258	136	52.71	7	2.71	1,751	6.79	7	2.71	113.2
84 Gibran Hamdan, Indiana ...	QB	SR	11	293	152	51.88	14	4.78	2,115	7.22	9	3.07	113.1
85 Jason Thomas, UNLV.........	QB	SR	11	274	134	48.91	7	2.55	1,936	7.07	8	2.92	112.8
86 Steven Jyles, La.-Monroe	QB	FR	12	368	181	49.18	9	2.45	2,318	6.3	17	4.62	112.4
87 Jay Cutler, Vanderbilt	QB	FR	11	212	103	48.58	9	4.25	1,433	6.76	10	4.72	112.4
88 A.J. Suggs, Georgia Tech ...	QB	JR	13	363	208	57.3	15	4.13	2,242	6.18	12	3.31	111.8
89 Sean Stilley, TCU	QB	SR	9	204	114	55.88	11	5.39	1,371	6.72	6	2.94	111.3
90 Marcus Randall, LSU	QB	SO	12	181	87	48.07	5	2.76	1,173	6.48	7	3.87	109.7
91 Bret Engemann, Brigham Young...........................	QB	JR	9	215	119	55.35	8	3.72	1,334	6.2	6	2.79	109.2
92 Derrick Vickers, Central Mich.	QB	JR	12	320	175	54.69	5	1.56	1,828	5.71	9	2.81	108.8
93 Jon VanCleave, La.-Lafayette	QB	JR	11	316	169	53.48	15	4.75	2,081	6.59	9	2.85	108.7
94 Tommy Jones, Indiana	QB	SR	9	152	75	49.34	7	4.61	879	5.78	9	5.92	108.2
95 Kevin Fant, Mississippi St. ..	QB	JR	11	311	163	52.41	12	3.86	1,918	6.17	10	3.22	107.1
96 Paul Troth, East Caro.........	QB	SO	12	359	177	49.3	20	5.57	2,315	6.45	15	4.18	106.1
97 Kyle Matter, Stanford.........	QB	FR	10	214	116	54.21	10	4.67	1,219	5.7	8	3.74	105
98 Bill Whittemore, Kansas......	QB	JR	9	305	151	49.51	6	1.97	1,666	5.46	11	3.61	103.4
99 C.J. Stephens, North Carolina	QB	JR	10	156	80	51.28	5	3.21	921	5.9	4	2.56	102.9
100 Andrew Smith, North Texas	QB	FR	13	196	91	46.43	9	4.59	1,206	6.15	7	3.57	100.7

Points Responsible For

Rank, Player	Pos	Cl	G	Cnv	Pass TD	Pts	Tot RFr	PtsRFr/Gm
1 Kliff Kingsbury, Texas Tech	QB	SR	14	4	45	16	294	21
2 Josh Harris, Bowling Green	QB	JR	12	1	19	134	250	20.83
3 Carson Palmer, Southern California	QB	SR	13	0	33	24	222	17.08
4 Ryan Schneider, UCF	QB	JR	12	2	31	14	204	17
4 Byron Leftwich, Marshall	QB	SR	12	2	30	20	204	17
6 Josh Fields, Oklahoma St.	QB	SO	13	1	31	20	208	16
6 Kyle Boller, California	QB	SR	12	0	28	24	192	16
8 Casey Bramlet, Wyoming	QB	JR	12	4	24	36	188	15.67
9 Bill Whittemore, Kansas	QB	JR	9	2	11	70	140	15.56
10 Chance Harridge, Air Force	QB	JR	13	0	10	132	192	14.77
10 Brock Forsey, Boise St.	RB	SR	13	0	0	192	192	14.77
12 Brad Banks, Iowa	QB	SR	13	0	26	30	186	14.31
12 Cody Pickett, Washington	QB	JR	13	0	28	18	186	14.31
14 Chris Simms, Texas	QB	SR	13	0	26	24	180	13.85
15 Zack Threadgill, Nevada	QB	SR	12	1	26	6	164	13.67
16 Jason Gesser, Washington St.	QB	SR	13	1	28	2	172	13.23
16 Rod Rutherford, Pittsburgh	QB	JR	13	1	22	38	172	13.23
18 Matt Schaub, Virginia	QB	JR	14	1	28	14	184	13.14
19 Jon Beutjer, Illinois	QB	JR	11	2	21	14	144	13.09
20 Danny Wimprine, Memphis	QB	JR	12	0	23	18	156	13
21 Ken Dorsey, Miami (Fla.)	QB	SR	13	0	28	0	168	12.92
21 Willis McGahee, Miami (Fla.)	RB	SO	13	0	0	168	168	12.92
23 Philip Rivers, North Carolina St.	QB	JR	14	0	20	60	180	12.86
24 Derek Anderson, Oregon St.	QB	SO	13	1	25	14	166	12.77
25 Andrew Walter, Arizona St.	QB	SO	14	3	28	4	178	12.71
26 Marquel Blackwell, South Fla.	QB	SR	11	0	18	30	138	12.55
27 Jason Fife, Oregon	QB	JR	13	0	24	18	162	12.46
28 Brian Jones, Toledo	QB	SR	14	1	23	34	174	12.43
29 J.P. Losman, Tulane	QB	JR	13	4	19	38	160	12.31
30 Asad Abdul-Khaliq, Minnesota	QB	JR	12	1	19	30	146	12.17
31 Jared Lorenzen, Kentucky	QB	JR	12	0	24	0	144	12
32 Ben Roethlisberger, Miami (Ohio)	QB	SO	12	1	22	8	142	11.83
33 Dave Ragone, Louisville	QB	SR	13	2	24	4	152	11.69
34 Ell Roberson, Kansas St.	QB	JR	12	0	7	98	140	11.67
35 Timmy Chang, Hawaii	QB	SO	14	2	25	8	162	11.57
36 Dan Orlovsky, Connecticut	QB	SO	12	0	19	24	138	11.5
37 Craig Candeto, Navy	QB	JR	11	0	5	96	126	11.45
38 Nate Hybl, Oklahoma	QB	SR	14	3	24	10	160	11.43
39 Jose Fuentes, Utah St.	QB	SR	11	1	20	2	124	11.27
40 Rex Grossman, Florida	QB	JR	13	1	22	10	144	11.08
41 Gino Guidugli, Cincinnati	QB	SO	14	0	22	22	154	11
41 Brad Smith, Missouri	QB	FR	12	0	15	42	132	11
41 Charlie Frye, Akron	QB	SO	12	0	15	42	132	11
41 Troy Edwards, Eastern Mich.	QB	SR	12	0	22	0	132	11
45 Scott Rislov, San Jose St.	QB	JR	13	1	22	8	142	10.92
45 Eli Manning, Mississippi	QB	JR	13	2	21	12	142	10.92
47 Tyler Gooch, Tulsa	QB	SO	11	3	17	12	120	10.91
48 Larry Johnson, Penn St.	TB	SR	13	0	0	140	140	10.77
49 Luke McCown, Louisiana Tech	QB	JR	12	1	19	12	128	10.67
50 John Navarre, Michigan	QB	JR	13	0	21	12	138	10.62
51 Jay Cutler, Vanderbilt	QB	FR	11	1	10	54	116	10.55
52 Nick Eddy, Houston	QB	JR	11	1	16	16	114	10.36
52 Brian Lindgren, Idaho	QB	JR	11	0	19	0	114	10.36
54 Lee Suggs, Virginia Tech	RB	SR	14	0	0	144	144	10.29
54 David Greene, Georgia	QB	SO	14	0	22	12	144	10.29
56 Art Brown, East Caro.	RB	JR	10	0	0	102	102	10.2
57 Paul Dombrowski, New Mexico St.	QB	SO	12	2	7	76	122	10.17
58 Brooks Bollinger, Wisconsin	QB	SR	13	0	14	48	132	10.15
58 Rasheed Marshall, West Virginia	QB	SO	13	0	9	78	132	10.15
60 Jason Thomas, UNLV	QB	SR	11	2	8	58	110	10
60 Steven Jyles, La.-Monroe	QB	FR	12	0	17	18	120	10
60 Michael Turner, Northern Ill.	RB	JR	12	0	0	120	120	10
60 Seneca Wallace, Iowa St.	QB	SR	14	0	15	50	140	10
60 Dustin Long, Texas A&M	QB	SO	12	0	19	6	120	10
65 Zack Mills, Penn St.	QB	JR	13	2	17	22	128	9.85
66 Maurice Clarett, Ohio St.	RB	FR	11	0	0	108	108	9.82
67 Nick Calaycay, Boise St.	K	SR	10	0	0	96	96	9.6
67 Terry Caulley, Connecticut	RB	FR	10	0	0	96	96	9.6
67 Andy Roesch, Ball St.	QB	JR	10	0	15	6	96	9.6
70 Chris Brown, Colorado	RB	JR	12	0	0	114	114	9.5
71 Scott McBrien, Maryland	QB	JR	14	0	15	42	132	9.43
72 Billy Bennett, Georgia	K	JR	14	0	0	130	130	9.29
72 Bradlee Van Pelt, Colorado St.	QB	JR	14	2	10	66	130	9.29
74 Adam Hall, San Diego St.	QB	JR	11	0	17	0	102	9.27
74 Zack Abron, Missouri	RB	JR	11	0	0	102	102	9.27
76 Nate Kaeding, Iowa	K	JR	13	0	0	120	120	9.23
77 Darrell Hackney, UAB	QB	FR	11	1	14	14	100	9.09
78 Brian St.Pierre, Boston College	QB	SR	13	1	18	8	118	9.08
79 Matt Jones, Arkansas	QB	SO	14	0	16	30	126	9
79 Paul Pinegar, Fresno St.	QB	FR	14	0	20	6	126	9
81 Nick Novak, Maryland	K	SO	14	0	0	125	125	8.93
82 Mark-Christian Jensen, California	K	SR	12	0	0	107	107	8.92
83 Nick Browne, TCU	K	JR	12	0	0	105	105	8.75
84 Chris Rix, Florida St.	QB	SO	11	0	13	18	96	8.73
85 Drew Dunning, Washington St.	K	JR	13	0	0	113	113	8.69
86 Walter Reyes, Syracuse	RB	SO	12	0	0	104	104	8.67
86 Mike McGann, Temple	QB	SO	12	2	13	22	104	8.67
88 Mike Nugent, Ohio St.	K	SO	14	0	0	120	120	8.57
88 Casey Kelly, New Mexico	QB	JR	14	0	14	36	120	8.57
88 Jammal Lord, Nebraska	QB	JR	14	0	12	48	120	8.57
91 Luke Clemens, Miami (Ohio)	RB	JR	12	0	0	102	102	8.5
92 Mike Barth, Arizona St.	K	SR	14	0	0	118	118	8.43
92 Jeff Babcock, Colorado St.	K	SO	14	0	0	118	118	8.43
94 Jared Cribbs, Kent St.	QB	SO	10	0	4	60	84	8.4
94 Fred Ray, Ohio	QB	SR	10	0	5	54	84	8.4
96 Jared Siegel, Oregon	K	SO	13	0	0	109	109	8.38
97 Paul Troth, East Caro.	QB	SO	12	1	15	8	100	8.33
98 T.A. McLendon, North Carolina St.	RB	FR	13	0	0	108	108	8.31
98 John Anderson, Washington	K	SR	13	0	0	108	108	8.31
100 Sandro Sciortino, Boston College	K	JR	13	0	0	107	107	8.23

Punting

Min. 75 Pct. of Team's Games Played, 3.6 Punts per Game

Rank, Player	Pos	Cl	G	Pnt	Yds	Avg	Punt/Gm
1 Matt Payne, Brigham Young	K	SO	12	51	2,427	47.59	4.25
2 Mark Mariscal, Colorado	K	SR	14	67	3,186	47.55	4.79
3 Glenn Pakulak, Kentucky	P	SR	12	66	3,008	45.58	5.5
4 Andy Groom, Ohio St.	P	SR	14	60	2,697	44.95	4.29
5 Donnie Jones, LSU	P	JR	12	64	2,813	43.95	5.33
6 Greg Johnson, Vanderbilt	P	FR	12	66	2,892	43.82	5.5
7 Cody Scates, Texas A&M	P	JR	12	67	2,931	43.75	5.58
8 Dustin Colquitt, Tennessee	P	SO	13	65	2,833	43.58	5
9 Jarad Preston, East Caro.	P	SR	12	73	3,170	43.42	6.08
10 Damon Duval, Auburn	P	SR	13	54	2,344	43.41	4.15
11 Kyle Larson, Nebraska	P	JR	14	73	3,156	43.23	5.21
12 Brooks Barnard, Maryland	P	SR	13	55	2,373	43.15	3.93
13 Andy Lee, Pittsburgh	P	JR	13	73	3,147	43.11	5.62
14 Luke Donovan, Wyoming	P	JR	12	58	2,493	42.98	4.83
15 Seth Marler, Tulane	K	SR	13	72	3,090	42.92	5.54
16 Tim Parker, Arizona St.	P	JR	14	79	3,372	42.68	5.64
17 Robert Billings, Middle Tenn.	P	JR	12	61	2,599	42.61	5.08
18 Brian Lewis, Utah	P	SR	11	54	2,471	42.6	5.27
19 Brad Kadlubar, North Texas	K	SO	13	85	3,619	42.58	6.54
20 Brock Harvey, Missouri	P	SO	10	54	2,295	42.5	5.4
21 Tyeler Dean, South Carolina	P	SR	11	45	1,909	42.42	4.09
22 Cody Ridgeway, Mississippi	P	SO	13	67	2,840	42.39	5.15
23 Jonathan Kilgo, Georgia	P	SR	14	64	2,708	42.31	4.57
24 Jose Arroyo, Oregon	P	SR	13	77	3,250	42.21	5.92
25 Curtis Ansel, Kansas	P	SR	12	82	3,459	42.18	6.83
26 Jared Cook, Mississippi St.	P	SO	10	48	2,024	42.17	4.8
27 Adam Finley, Michigan	P	SO	13	69	2,909	42.16	5.31
28 Tom Malone, Southern California	P	FR	13	62	2,609	42.08	4.77
29 Brian Simnjanovski, San Diego St.	P	SR	13	60	2,524	42.07	4.62
30 Devin Sanderson, South Fla.	P	SR	11	66	2,776	42.07	6
31 Ross Stewart, UAB	P	SR	12	75	3,154	42.05	6.25
32 Nate Fikse, UCLA	P	JR	13	71	2,975	41.9	5.46
33 Mark Haulman, Southern Miss.	P	SR	13	80	3,344	41.8	6.15
34 Ryan Downes, Idaho	P	JR	12	56	2,338	41.75	4.67
35 David Rysko, Eastern Mich.	P	JR	12	64	2,660	41.56	5.33
36 Lane Bearden, Alabama	P	SR	12	50	2,074	41.48	4.17
37 Brian Huffman, Northwestern	K	SO	12	66	2,737	41.47	5.5
38 Cole Farden, Oklahoma St.	K	SO	13	57	2,358	41.37	4.38
39 John Skaggs, Navy			12	46	1,896	41.22	3.83
40 Freddie Capshaw, Miami (Fla.)	P	SR	13	53	2,182	41.17	4.08
41 Travis Brown, Kansas St.	K	SR	13	49	2,015	41.12	3.77
42 David Royer, Penn St.	P	SR	13	50	2,053	41.06	3.85
42 Kyle Basler, Washington St.	P	SO	13	50	2,053	41.06	3.85
44 Kevin Kerr, Ohio	K	SR	12	55	2,258	41.05	4.58
45 Derek Jones, Nevada	P	JR	12	63	2,579	40.94	5.25
46 Jared Fritz, Kent St.	K	SR	12	59	2,409	40.83	4.92
47 Bryce Benekos, UTEP	K	SO	12	70	2,855	40.79	5.83
48 Jason Simpson, Fresno St.	P	SR	14	74	3,007	40.64	5.29
49 Travis Hale, Rice	P	SR	11	58	2,352	40.55	5.27
50 Tyler Gaus, New Mexico	P	FR	14	79	3,202	40.53	5.64
51 Vinnie Burns, Virginia Tech	P	SO	14	64	2,591	40.48	4.57
52 Jason Daily, Michigan St.	P	JR	12	66	2,668	40.42	5.5
53 Andy Jerdon, Akron	P	JR	12	46	1,856	40.35	3.83
54 Reggie Hodges, Ball St.	P	JR	12	57	2,299	40.33	4.75
55 Mike Barr, Rutgers	P	SR	12	92	3,707	40.29	7.67
56 Carl Tobey, Oregon St.	P	JR	13	74	2,981	40.28	5.69

STATISTICAL LEADERS

Rank, Player	Pos	Cl	G	Pnt	Yds	Avg	Punt/Gm
57 Joey Huber, Colorado St.	P	SR	14	53	2,135	40.28	3.79
58 Scott McMahan, Buffalo	P	SR	12	81	3,258	40.22	6.75
59 Cort Moffitt, Tulsa	K	JR	12	75	3,016	40.21	6.25
60 Brian Bradford, Texas	P	SR	13	67	2,685	40.07	5.15
61 Preston Gruening, Minnesota	P	SR	13	57	2,282	40.04	4.38
62 Thomas Olmsted, Troy St.	P	FR	12	72	2,871	39.88	6
63 Adam Coles, Connecticut	P	JR	12	76	3,030	39.87	6.33
64 Grant Autrey, La.-Lafayette	P	SR	12	78	3,108	39.85	6.5
65 Eric Johnson, Stanford	P	JR	11	58	2,306	39.76	5.27
66 Chance Gwaltney, Florida St.	P	SR	14	72	2,862	39.75	5.14
67 Joey Biasatti, TCU	P	SR	12	77	3,060	39.74	6.42
68 Steve Mullins, Utah St.	P	SR	11	63	2,500	39.68	5.73
69 Brian Brandt, Central Mich.	P	JR	11	71	2,815	39.65	6.45
70 Tyler Fredrickson, California	P	JR	12	62	2,450	39.52	5.17
71 David Bradley, Iowa	K	SO	13	53	2,093	39.49	4.08
72 Brent Slaton, Purdue	P	JR	13	63	2,485	39.44	4.85
73 Richie Butler, Arkansas	P	SR	14	69	2,715	39.35	4.93
74 Trey McDonald, Duke	P	JR	10	49	1,923	39.24	4.9
75 Mike Shafer, Syracuse	K	SR	12	69	2,707	39.23	5.75
76 Pat Fleming, Bowling Green	P	SR	12	51	2,000	39.22	4.25
77 Joey Hildbold, Notre Dame	P	SR	13	78	3,038	38.95	6
78 Jimmy McClary, Houston	P	JR	12	62	2,411	38.89	5.17
79 Garvin Ringwelski, Temple	P	JR	11	47	1,819	38.7	4.27
80 Mike Alexander, Arkansas St.	P	SR	13	64	2,469	38.58	4.92
81 Ryan Mentzel, Southern Methodist	P	FR	12	69	2,659	38.54	5.75
82 Blake Ferguson, Oklahoma	P	SO	14	74	2,851	38.53	5.29
83 Derek McLaughlin, Washington	P	SO	12	57	2,194	38.49	4.75
84 Jimmy Erwin, Northern Ill.	P	SR	12	63	2,412	38.29	5.25
84 Gary Cook, UNLV	P	SO	12	70	2,680	38.29	5.83
86 Ryan Hamre, Indiana	P	JR	12	58	2,214	38.17	4.83
87 Michael Carr, San Jose St.	K	SR	13	57	2,174	38.14	4.38
88 Chet Ervin, Cincinnati	K	FR	14	66	2,511	38.05	4.71
89 Dustin Upton, Louisiana Tech	P	JR	12	64	2,405	37.58	5.33
90 Nate Smith, Louisville	K	JR	13	50	1,873	37.46	3.85
91 R.J. Morse, Wisconsin	P	SO	14	74	2,765	37.36	5.29
92 Austin Herbert, North Carolina St.	K	JR	14	61	2,268	37.18	4.36
93 Kevin McMyler, Boston College	P	SR	13	56	2,081	37.16	4.31
94 Wynn Kopp, Clemson	P	SR	13	63	2,340	37.14	4.85
95 Mark Fazzolari, West Virginia	P	SR	13	53	1,949	36.77	4.08
96 Chris Castelli, Army	P	SR	12	65	2,383	36.66	5.42
97 Tom Hagan, Virginia	P	FR	14	62	2,273	36.66	4.43
98 John Lafferty, North Carolina	P	JR	12	61	2,235	36.64	5.08
99 Kjell Nesen, La.-Monroe	QB	JR	10	56	2,048	36.57	5.6
100 Jeremy Parker, Baylor	K	FR	12	73	2,599	35.6	6.08

Punt Returns

Min. 75 Pct. of Team's Games Played, 1.2 Punt Returns per Game

Rank, Player	Pos	Cl	G	Ret	Yds	TD	Yds/Ret	Ret/Gm
1 Dan Sheldon, Northern Ill.	WR	SO	12	21	477	3	22.71	1.75
2 Aris Comeaux, Army	WR	SR	9	12	233	2	19.42	1.33
3 Cody Cardwell, Southern Methodist	WR	SR	12	27	467	1	17.3	2.25
4 DeJuan Groce, Nebraska	DB	SR	14	43	732	4	17.02	3.07
5 Lynaris Elpheage, Tulane	DB	JR	13	28	463	1	16.54	2.15
6 Dexter Wynn, Colorado St.	DB	JR	14	35	567	1	16.2	2.5
7 DeAngelo Hall, Virginia Tech	DB	SO	13	22	352	2	16	1.69
7 Craig Bragg, UCLA	WR	SR	13	16	256	1	16	1.23
9 Damien Dorsey, Louisville	WR	SR	12	33	508	1	15.39	2.75
10 Kendrick Mosley, Western Mich.	WR	SR	9	29	440	2	15.17	3.22
11 Derek Abney, Kentucky	WR	JR	12	36	544	4	15.11	3
12 Antonio Perkins, Oklahoma	DB	SO	14	43	647	3	15.05	3.07
13 Jeremy Bloom, Colorado	WR	FR	13	23	344	2	14.96	1.77
14 Terence Newman, Kansas St.	DB	SR	13	26	388	1	14.92	2
15 DeAndrew Rubin, South Fla.	WR	SR	10	29	432	2	14.9	2.9
16 Roscoe Parrish, Miami (Fla.)	WR	FR	13	27	392	0	14.52	2.08
17 Keenan Howry, Oregon	WR	SR	13	32	458	2	14.31	2.46
18 Donta Greene, Toledo	WR	SR	14	31	443	1	14.29	2.21
19 Nathan Vasher, Texas	DB	JR	11	26	370	1	14.23	2.36
20 Tim Gilligan, Boise St.	WR	JR	13	35	491	0	14.03	2.69
21 Bobby Wade, Arizona	WR	SR	12	16	224	0	14	1.33
22 Domanick Davis, LSU	RB	SR	13	36	499	1	13.86	2.77
23 Steve Suter, Maryland	WR	SO	14	56	771	4	13.77	4
24 Jamel Riddle, Syracuse	WR	JR	11	23	316	1	13.74	2.09
25 Marcus James, Missouri	WR	JR	11	24	327	1	13.63	2.18
26 Marvin Young, Southern Miss.	WR	SO	13	29	388	0	13.38	2.23
27 Wes Welker, Texas Tech	RB	JR	14	57	752	3	13.19	4.07
28 Reno Mahe, Brigham Young	WR	SR	12	15	196	0	13.07	1.25
29 Bryant Johnson, Penn St.	WR	SR	13	41	528	1	12.88	3.15
30 Asante Samuel, UCF	DB	JR	12	19	233	0	12.26	1.58
31 Decori Birmingham, Arkansas	WR	SO	14	28	342	0	12.21	2
32 Jemeel Powell, California	DB	SR	12	32	389	2	12.16	2.67
33 Jim Leonhard, Wisconsin	DB	SO	14	36	434	1	12.06	2.57
34 Ed Hinkel, Iowa	WR	FR	13	27	325	1	12.04	2.08
35 Jason Armstead, Mississippi	WR	SR	12	32	383	1	11.97	2.67
36 Jamal Burke, Boston College	WR	SR	13	24	286	1	11.92	1.85
37 Eugene Wilson, Illinois	DB	SR	12	23	270	1	11.74	1.92
38 Sean Schembra, Ball St.	WR	SR	12	21	246	0	11.71	1.75
39 Roderick Hood, Auburn	DB	SR	13	36	417	0	11.58	2.77
40 Leon Washington, Florida St.	RB	FR	14	34	392	0	11.53	2.43
41 Tyler Ebell, UCLA	RB	FR	13	24	273	0	11.38	1.85
42 Dwight Counter, New Mexico	WR	JR	14	31	352	1	11.35	2.21
43 Charles Pauley, San Jose St.	WR	SR	13	21	237	0	11.29	1.62
44 Morgan Scalley, Utah	RB	SO	11	24	270	0	11.25	2.18
45 Chris R. Roberson, Eastern Mich.	WR	SO	12	21	232	1	11.05	1.75
46 Heyward Skipper, Troy St.	WR	SR	12	16	176	0	11	1.33
47 Terrance Copper, East Caro.	WR	JR	12	30	328	0	10.93	2.5
48 Derrick Hamilton, Clemson	WR	SO	13	35	377	0	10.77	2.69
49 James Hickenbotham, Arkansas St.	WR	SR	11	23	247	0	10.74	2.09
50 Keiwan Ratliff, Florida	DB	JR	13	32	341	0	10.66	2.46
51 Tyrone Gifford, New Mexico St.	DB	SR	12	26	276	0	10.62	2.17
52 Terrance Davis-Bryant, Oklahoma St.	WR	SR	13	31	329	0	10.61	2.38
53 Marcus Trufant, Washington St.	CB	SR	13	38	402	0	10.58	2.92
54 Willie Quinnie, UAB	WR	SR	11	25	257	0	10.28	2.27
55 Stafford Owens, Ohio	RB	JR	12	27	271	1	10.04	2.25
56 Anthony Chambers, Purdue	WR	JR	13	28	281	1	10.04	2.15
57 Korey Banks, Mississippi St.	DB	SR	12	20	200	0	10	1.67
57 Bobby Hart, Baylor	DB	SR	12	15	150	0	10	1.25
59 Ethenic Sands, Miami (Fla.)	WR	SR	13	17	169	0	9.94	1.31
60 Kelley Rhino, Georgia Tech	DB	SR	11	45	447	0	9.93	4.09
61 Leotis Palmer, Air Force	RB	SR	13	17	167	0	9.82	1.31
62 Todd Miller, Iowa St.	WR	SO	14	37	363	2	9.81	2.64
63 Terrell Roberts, Oregon St.	DB	SR	13	18	174	0	9.67	1.38
64 Zamir Cobb, Temple	WR	SR	12	23	222	0	9.65	1.92
65 Vontez Duff, Notre Dame	DB	JR	13	40	385	1	9.63	3.08
66 Fabian Davis, Wake Forest	WR	SR	13	39	363	1	9.31	3
67 Mark Jones, Tennessee	DB	JR	13	26	240	0	9.23	2
68 Marques Hagans, Virginia	QB	FR	14	29	262	1	9.03	2.07
69 Jamal Fenner, UTEP	DB	SO	14	25	223	0	8.92	2.5
70 Daryl Lightfoot, Arizona St.	WR	SR	14	22	193	0	8.77	1.57
71 Cedric Thompson, Idaho	WR	JR	11	28	245	0	8.75	2.55
72 Ziehl Kavanaght, Michigan St.	WR	JR	11	33	287	1	8.7	3
73 Terran Williams, TCU	WR	SR	12	36	312	1	8.67	3
74 Shaud Williams, Alabama	RB	JR	13	40	346	0	8.65	3.08
75 Adam Jennings, Fresno St.	DB	FR	14	36	310	1	8.61	2.57
76 Dante McKnight, Central Mich.	DB	JR	12	18	153	0	8.5	1.5
77 Andre Forde, Buffalo	WR	SR	10	19	161	1	8.47	1.9
78 Chris Gamble, Ohio St.	WR	SO	14	35	293	0	8.37	2.5
79 Darron White, Memphis	WR	SO	12	36	301	0	8.36	3
80 Andrew Amerson, Troy St.	WR	SR	9	17	142	0	8.35	1.89
81 KeyKowa Bell, Houston	WR	SR	12	30	249	0	8.3	2.5
82 Charles Frederick, Washington	WR	SO	13	18	146	0	8.11	1.38
83 Luke Powell, Stanford	WR	JR	10	19	154	0	8.11	1.9
84 Andre George, La.-Lafayette	WR	SR	11	21	170	0	8.1	1.91
85 Michael Franklin, San Diego St.	RB	FR	12	20	159	0	7.95	1.67
86 Corey Brazil, Louisiana Tech	DB	JR	12	36	285	0	7.92	3
87 Ja'Mel Branch, North Texas	WR	SR	13	29	229	0	7.9	2.23
88 Tye Keith, Cincinnati	WR	SR	14	36	280	0	7.78	2.57
89 Aric Williams, Oregon St.	DB	SO	13	24	183	0	7.63	1.85
90 Kunle Patrick, Northwestern	WR	JR	12	19	142	0	7.47	1.58
91 Troy Mason, UNLV	WR	SR	9	18	134	0	7.44	2
92 Eddie Tillitz, Miami (Ohio)	WR	SR	12	28	206	0	7.36	2.33
93 Danny Upchurch, Minnesota	DB	FR	13	40	287	0	7.18	3.08
94 Jermaine Landrum, Tulsa	WR	SO	12	16	112	0	7	1.33
95 Lance Frazier, West Virginia	DB	JR	13	30	208	0	6.93	2.31
96 Scottie Vines, Wyoming	WR	SR	15	103	0		6.87	1.25
97 Robert Redd, Bowling Green	WR	SR	12	31	209	0	6.74	2.58
98 Kevin Ford, Rice	DB	FR	11	15	100	0	6.67	1.36
99 Greig Carlson, Southern California	WR	FR	13	27	177	0	6.56	2.08
100 Remuise Johnson, Kansas	DB	SR	12	19	124	0	6.53	1.58

Receptions Per Game

Nate Burleson, Nevada

Nevada Sports Inormation

Rank, Player	Pos	Cl	Gm	Catches	Yds	TDs	Rec/ Gm	Yds/ Catch	Yds/ Gm
1 Nate Burleson, Nevada.........	WR	SR	12	138	1,629	12	11.5	11.8	135.75
2 J.R. Tolver, San Diego St.	WR	SR	13	128	1,785	13	9.85	13.95	137.31
3 Kassim Osgood, San Diego St.	WR	SR	13	108	1,552	8	8.31	14.37	119.38
4 Rashaun Woods, Oklahoma St.	WR	JR	13	107	1,695	17	8.23	15.84	130.38
5 Kevin Walter, Eastern Mich..........	WR	SR	12	93	1,368	9	7.75	14.71	114
5 Bobby Wade, Arizona	WR	SR	12	93	1,389	8	7.75	14.94	115.75
7 Taylor Stubblefield, Purdue............	WR	SO	10	77	789	0	7.7	10.25	78.9
8 Reggie Williams, Washington	WR	SO	13	94	1,454	11	7.23	15.47	111.85
9 Taurean Henderson, Texas Tech	RB	FR	14	98	633	6	7	6.46	45.21
10 Robert Redd, Bowling Green	WR	SR	12	83	973	9	6.92	11.72	81.08
11 Justin Gage, Missouri	WR	SR	12	82	1,074	9	6.83	13.1	89.5
12 Kevin Curtis, Utah St.	WR	SR	11	74	1,258	9	6.73	17	114.36
13 Denero Marriott, Marshall............	WR	SR	13	86	993	8	6.62	11.55	76.38
14 Mack Vincent, La.-Monroe	WR	JR	12	79	1,198	7	6.58	15.16	99.83
15 Justin Colbert, Hawaii.................	WR	SR	14	92	1,302	8	6.57	14.15	93
16 Taylor Jacobs, Florida.................	WR	SR	11	71	1,088	8	6.45	15.32	98.91
17 Josh Jelmberg, Idaho	WR	SR	10	64	785	8	6.4	12.27	78.5
18 Doug Gabriel, UCF	WR	SR	12	75	1,237	11	6.25	16.49	103.08
18 Reggie Newhouse, Baylor............	WR	SR	12	75	1,140	3	6.25	15.2	95
20 Mike Williams, Southern California	WR	FR	13	81	1,265	14	6.23	15.62	97.31
21 Shaun McDonald, Arizona St.	WR	JR	14	87	1,405	13	6.21	16.15	100.36
22 Wes Welker, Texas Tech	RB	JR	14	86	1,054	7	6.14	12.26	75.29
23 Darius Watts, Marshall................	WR	JR	12	71	1,030	12	5.92	14.51	85.83
24 John Standeford, Purdue.............	WR	JR	13	75	1,307	13	5.77	17.43	100.54
24 Josh Davis, Marshall...................	WR	SO	13	75	1,191	5	5.77	15.88	91.62
26 James Newson, Oregon St.	WR	JR	13	74	1,284	12	5.69	17.35	98.77
27 Sam Aiken, North Carolina..........	WR	SR	12	68	990	4	5.67	14.56	82.5
27 Charles Rogers, Michigan St.	WR	JR	12	68	1,351	13	5.67	19.87	112.58
29 Carl Ford, Toledo.....................	WR	SR	14	79	1,062	9	5.64	13.44	75.86
30 Hugh Smith, South Fla.	WR	SR	11	62	661	5	5.64	10.66	60.09
31 Chris Norwood, Louisiana Tech.....	WR	JR	11	61	748	4	5.55	12.26	68
32 Keary Colbert, Southern California	WR	JR	13	71	1,029	5	5.46	14.49	79.15
32 Kerry Watkins, Georgia Tech........	WR	SR	13	71	1,050	5	5.46	14.79	80.77
34 Brandon Lloyd, Illinois	WR	JR	12	65	1,010	9	5.42	15.54	84.17
35 Andre Forde, Buffalo	WR	SR	10	54	748	7	5.4	13.85	74.8
36 Roy Williams, Texas.....................	WR	JR	12	64	1,142	12	5.33	17.84	95.17
37 Larry Fitzgerald, Pittsburgh	WR	FR	13	69	1,005	12	5.31	14.57	77.31
38 Carlos Perez, Florida..................	WR	JR	11	58	591	4	5.27	10.19	53.73
39 Jovon Bouknight, Wyoming..........	WR	FR	12	63	689	3	5.25	10.94	57.42
40 Braylon Edwards, Michigan	WR	SO	13	67	1035	10	5.15	15.45	79.62
41 Andrae Thurman, Arizona............	WR	JR	12	61	915	3	5.08	15	76.25
42 LaDaris Vann, Cincinnati	WR	SR	14	71	844	5	5.07	11.89	60.29
43 Billy McMullen, Virginia...............	WR	SR	14	69	894	3	4.93	12.96	63.86
44 Mickey Peters, Texas Tech............	TE	JR	13	64	749	8	4.92	11.7	57.62
44 Marque Davis, Fresno St.	WR	JR	13	64	956	7	4.92	14.94	73.54
46 Reno Mahe, Brigham Young	WR	SR	12	59	771	2	4.92	13.07	64.25
46 Courtney Roby, Indiana	WR	SO	12	59	1,039	4	4.92	17.61	86.58
48 Lane Danielsen, Iowa St.	WR	JR	13	63	1,073	3	4.85	17.03	82.54
49 Jon Schweighardt, Northwestern....	WR	SR	12	58	719	3	4.83	12.4	59.92
49 Jimmy Fryzel, UCF	WR	SR	12	58	1,126	5	4.83	19.41	93.83
51 Jerricho Cotchery, North Carolina St.	WR	JR	14	67	1,192	7	4.79	17.79	85.14
52 Billy Wingfield, Boise St.	WR	SR	13	62	1,138	7	4.77	18.35	87.54
52 Jamall Broussard, San Jose St.	WR	JR	13	62	681	5	4.77	10.98	52.38
54 Jerome Riley, Washington St.	WR	SR	12	57	939	7	4.75	16.47	78.25
54 D.J. Curry, Louisiana Tech............	WR	JR	12	57	730	3	4.75	12.81	60.83
54 Walter Young, Illinois..................	WR	SR	12	57	832	6	4.75	14.6	69.33
57 Anquan Boldin, Florida St.	WR	SR	14	65	1,011	13	4.64	15.55	72.21
58 Earvin Johnson, UNLV.................	WR	SO	11	51	793	4	4.64	15.55	72.09
59 Charles Pauley, San Jose St.	WR	SR	13	60	804	4	4.62	13.4	61.85
60 Travis Anglin, Memphis	WR	SR	12	55	740	5	4.58	13.45	61.67
61 H.B. Briscoe, New Mexico St.	WR	SR	11	50	880	5	4.55	17.6	80
61 Orlando Winston, Idaho..............	WR	JR	11	50	624	1	4.55	12.48	56.73
63 Kevin Youngblood, Clemson	WR	JR	13	59	591	2	4.54	10.02	45.46
63 Terrence Edwards, Georgia	WR	SR	13	59	1,004	11	4.54	17.02	77.23
65 Frederick Stamps, La.-Lafayette	WR	JR	12	54	1,002	8	4.5	18.56	83.5
66 Donta Greene, Toledo.................	WR	SR	14	63	712	1	4.5	11.3	50.86
67 Jonathan Makonnen, California.....	WR	JR	12	54	682	7	4.5	12.63	56.83
68 Arnaz Battle, Notre Dame............	WR	SR	13	58	786	5	4.46	13.55	60.46
69 Andre George, La.-Lafayette..........	WR	SR	11	49	531	2	4.45	10.84	48.27
70 Glenn Johnson, Indiana	WR	JR	12	53	837	5	4.42	15.79	69.75
70 Miquel Irvin, Akron	WR	JR	12	53	535	1	4.42	10.09	44.58
72 Jamaar Taylor, Texas A&M...........	WR	JR	10	44	760	3	4.4	17.27	76
73 Michael Clayton, LSU..................	WR	SO	13	57	749	5	4.38	13.14	57.62
73 Kellen Winslow, Miami (Fla.)	TE	SO	13	57	726	8	4.38	12.74	55.85
75 Michael Jenkins, Ohio St.	WR	JR	14	61	1,076	6	4.36	17.64	76.86
76 Andre Johnson, Miami (Fla.)	WR	JR	12	52	1,092	9	4.33	21	91
76 Damien Dorsey, Louisville............	WR	SR	12	52	753	7	4.33	14.48	62.75
78 Ronnie Davenport, San Diego St. ..	WR	SR	13	56	431	2	4.31	7.7	33.15
79 Chris Pittman, Colorado St.	WR	JR	14	60	807	1	4.29	13.45	57.64
80 Gary Coleman, Utah St.	WR	SR	11	47	571	3	4.27	12.15	51.91
81 Craig Bragg, UCLA.....................	WR	SO	13	55	889	8	4.23	16.16	68.38

Rank, Player	Pos	Cl	Gm	Catches	Yds	TDs	Rec/ Gm	Yds/ Catch	Yds/ Gm
81 Chris Collins, Mississippi	WR	JR	13	55	812	10	4.23	14.76	62.46
83 Chris Johnson, Southern Miss.	WR	SO	12	50	673	3	4.17	13.46	56.08
84 Devard Darling, Washington St. ...	WR	SO	13	54	800	11	4.15	14.81	61.54
85 Britton Komine, Hawaii.................	WR	SO	14	58	886	10	4.14	15.28	63.29
85 Wali Lundy, Virginia	RB	FR	14	58	435	4	4.14	7.5	31.07
87 Kendrick Mosley, Western Mich. ...	WR	SR	9	37	507	3	4.11	13.7	56.33
88 Kunle Patrick, Northwestern..........	WR	JR	12	49	558	2	4.08	11.39	46.5
88 Jeremiah Cockheran, Hawaii	WR	JR	12	49	731	5	4.08	14.92	60.92
88 Romby Bryant, Tulsa	WR	JR	12	49	593	7	4.08	12.1	49.42
88 Cody Cardwell, Southern Methodist	WR	SR	12	49	674	3	4.08	13.76	56.17
88 Robert Quiroga, Baylor	WR	JR	12	49	556	1	4.08	11.35	46.33
93 Bill Flowers, Mississippi	WR	SO	13	53	588	3	4.08	11.09	45.23
93 Bennie Joppru, Michigan	TE	SR	13	53	579	5	4.08	10.92	44.54
95 Derrick Hamilton, Clemson............	WR	SO	13	52	602	2	4	11.58	46.31
95 J.J. McKelvey, Clemson................	WR	SR	13	52	785	4	4	15.1	60.38
97 Jason Branch, Miami (Ohio)..........	WR	SR	10	40	505	7	4	12.63	50.5
98 Josh Lyman, Utah	WR	SR	11	44	590	3	4	13.41	53.64
99 Jack Whitver, Iowa St.	WR	JR	13	52	685	0	4	13.17	52.69
100 Greg Porter, Texas A&M	WR	SR	12	48	669	4	4	13.94	55.75

Total Receiving Yards

Min. 75 Pct. of Team's Games Played

Rank, Player	Pos	Cl	Gm	Catches	Yds	TDs	Rec/ Gm	Yds/ Catch	Yds/ Gm
1 J.R. Tolver, San Diego St.	WR	SR	13	128	1,785	13	9.85	13.95	137.31
2 Rashaun Woods, Oklahoma St.	WR	JR	13	107	1,695	17	8.23	15.84	130.38
3 Nate Burleson, Nevada...............	WR	SR	12	138	1,629	12	11.5	11.8	135.75
4 Kassim Osgood, San Diego St.	WR	SR	13	108	1,552	8	8.31	14.37	119.38
5 Reggie Williams, Washington	WR	SO	13	94	1,454	11	7.23	15.47	111.85
6 Shaun McDonald, Arizona St.	WR	JR	14	87	1,405	13	6.21	16.15	100.36
7 Bobby Wade, Arizona	WR	SR	12	93	1,389	8	7.75	14.94	115.75
8 Kevin Walter, Eastern Mich..........	WR	SR	12	93	1,368	9	7.75	14.71	114
9 Charles Rogers, Michigan St.	WR	JR	12	68	1,351	13	5.67	19.87	112.58
10 John Standeford, Purdue...............	WR	JR	13	75	1,307	13	5.77	17.43	100.54
11 Justin Colbert, Hawaii.................	WR	SR	14	92	1,302	8	6.57	14.15	93
12 James Newson, Oregon St.	WR	JR	13	74	1,284	12	5.69	17.35	98.77
13 Mike Williams, Southern California	WR	FR	13	81	1,265	14	6.23	15.62	97.31
14 Kevin Curtis, Utah St.	WR	SR	11	74	1,258	9	6.73	17	114.36
15 Doug Gabriel, UCF	WR	SR	12	75	1,237	11	6.25	16.49	103.08
16 Mack Vincent, La.-Monroe	WR	JR	12	79	1,198	7	6.58	15.16	99.83
17 Jerricho Cotchery, North Carolina St.	WR	JR	14	67	1,192	7	4.79	17.79	85.14
18 Josh Davis, Marshall....................	WR	SO	13	75	1,191	5	5.77	15.88	91.62
19 Roy Williams, Texas	WR	JR	12	64	1,142	12	5.33	17.84	95.17
20 Reggie Newhouse, Baylor............	WR	SR	12	75	1,140	3	6.25	15.2	95
21 Billy Wingfield, Boise St.	WR	SR	13	62	1,138	7	4.77	18.35	87.54
22 Jimmy Fryzel, UCF	WR	SR	12	58	1,126	5	4.83	19.41	93.83
23 Jon Olinger, Cincinnati	WR	SR	14	54	1,114	7	3.86	20.63	79.57
24 Andre Johnson, Miami (Fla.).........	WR	JR	12	52	1,092	9	4.33	21	91
25 Taylor Jacobs, Florida.................	WR	SR	11	71	1,088	8	6.45	15.32	98.91
26 Michael Jenkins, Ohio St.	WR	JR	14	61	1,076	6	4.36	17.64	76.86
27 Justin Gage, Missouri	WR	SR	12	82	1,039	9	6.83	13.1	89.5
28 Lane Danielson, Iowa St.	WR	JR	13	63	1,073	3	4.85	17.03	82.54
29 Carl Ford, Toledo......................	WR	SR	14	79	1,062	9	5.64	13.44	75.86
30 Wes Welker, Texas Tech	RB	JR	14	86	1,054	7	6.14	12.26	75.29
31 Kerry Watkins, Georgia Tech	WR	SR	13	71	1,050	5	5.46	14.79	80.77
32 Courtney Roby, Indiana	WR	SO	12	59	1,039	4	4.92	17.61	86.58
33 Braylon Edwards, Michigan	WR	SO	13	67	1,035	10	5.15	15.45	79.62
34 Darius Watts, Marshall...............	WR	JR	12	71	1,030	12	5.92	14.51	85.83
35 Keary Colbert, Southern California	WR	JR	13	71	1,029	5	5.46	14.49	79.15
36 Anquan Boldin, Florida St.	WR	SR	14	65	1,011	13	4.64	15.55	72.21
37 Brandon Lloyd, Illinois	WR	JR	12	65	1,010	9	5.42	15.54	84.17
38 Larry Fitzgerald, Pittsburgh	WR	FR	13	69	1,005	12	5.31	14.57	77.31
39 Terrence Edwards, Georgia	WR	SR	13	59	1,004	11	4.54	17.02	77.23
40 Frederick Stamps, La.-Lafayette	WR	JR	12	54	1,002	8	4.5	18.56	83.5
41 Denero Marriott, Marshall............	WR	SR	13	86	993	8	6.62	11.55	76.38
42 Sam Aiken, North Carolina...........	WR	SR	12	68	990	4	5.67	14.56	82.5
43 Robert Redd, Bowling Green	WR	SR	12	83	973	9	6.92	11.72	81.08
44 Maurice Brown, Iowa	WR	JR	13	48	966	11	3.69	20.13	74.31
45 Marque Davis, Fresno St.	WR	JR	13	64	956	7	4.92	14.94	73.54
46 Jerome Riley, Washington St.	WR	SR	12	57	939	7	4.75	16.47	78.25
47 Ernest Wilford, Virginia Tech.........	WR	JR	14	51	925	7	3.64	18.14	66.07
48 Bryant Johnson, Penn St.	WR	SR	13	48	917	4	3.69	19.1	70.54
49 Andrae Thurman, Arizona............	WR	JR	12	61	915	3	5.08	15	76.25
50 Billy McMullen, Virginia..............	WR	SR	14	69	894	3	4.93	12.96	63.86
51 Craig Bragg, UCLA....................	WR	SO	13	55	889	8	4.23	16.16	68.38
52 Britton Komine, Hawaii.................	WR	SO	14	58	886	10	4.14	15.28	63.29
53 H.B. Briscoe, New Mexico St.	WR	SR	11	50	880	5	4.55	17.6	80
54 LaDaris Vann, Cincinnati	WR	SR	14	71	844	5	5.07	11.89	60.29
55 Jonathon Orr, Wisconsin	WR	FR	14	47	842	8	3.36	17.91	60.14
56 Glenn Johnson, Indiana	WR	JR	12	53	837	5	4.42	15.79	69.75
57 Walter Young, Illinois..................	WR	SR	12	57	832	6	4.75	14.6	69.33
58 Chris Collins, Mississippi	WR	JR	13	55	812	10	4.23	14.76	62.46

Rank, Player	Pos	Cl	Gm	Catches	Yds	TDs	Rec/ Gm	Yds/ Catch	Yds/ Gm
59 Chris Pittman, Colorado St.	WR	JR	14	60	807	1	4.29	13.45	57.64
60 Charles Pauley, San Jose St.	WR	SR	13	60	804	4	4.62	13.4	61.85
61 Devard Darling, Washington St.	WR	SO	13	54	800	11	4.15	14.81	61.54
62 Earvin Johnson, UNLV	WR	SO	11	51	793	4	4.64	15.55	72.09
63 Taylor Stubblefield, Purdue	WR	SO	10	77	789	0	7.7	10.25	78.9
64 Arnaz Battle, Notre Dame	WR	SR	13	58	786	5	4.46	13.55	60.46
65 Josh Jelmberg, Idaho	WR	SR	10	64	785	8	6.4	12.27	78.5
65 J.J. McKelvey, Clemson	WR	SR	13	52	785	4	4	15.1	60.38
67 Keenan Howry, Oregon	WR	SR	13	40	784	5	3.08	19.6	60.31
68 Dan Sheldon, Northern Ill.	WR	SO	12	40	783	5	3.33	19.58	65.25
69 Reno Mahe, Brigham Young	WR	SR	12	59	771	2	4.92	13.07	64.25
70 Jamaar Taylor, Texas A&M	WR	JR	10	44	760	3	4.4	17.27	76
71 Fred Gibson, Georgia	WR	SO	12	43	758	4	3.58	17.63	63.17
72 Damien Dorsey, Louisville	WR	SR	12	52	753	7	4.33	14.48	62.75
73 Mickey Peters, Texas Tech	TE	JR	13	64	749	8	4.92	11.7	57.62
73 Michael Clayton, LSU	WR	SO	13	57	749	5	4.38	13.14	57.62
75 Chris Norwood, Louisiana Tech	WR	JR	11	61	748	4	5.55	12.26	68
75 Andre Forde, Buffalo	WR	SR	10	54	748	7	5.4	13.85	74.8
77 Dallas Clark, Iowa	TE	JR	13	43	742	4	3.31	17.26	57.08
78 Travis Anglin, Memphis	WR	SR	12	55	740	5	4.58	13.45	61.67
79 Jeremiah Cockheran, Hawaii	WR	JR	12	49	731	5	4.08	14.92	60.92
80 D.J. Curry, Louisiana Tech	WR	JR	12	57	730	3	4.75	12.81	60.83
81 Kellen Winslow, Miami (Fla.)	TE	SO	13	57	726	8	4.38	12.74	55.85
82 Samie Parker, Oregon	WR	JR	13	49	724	4	3.77	14.78	55.69
83 Jon Schweighardt, Northwestern	WR	SR	12	58	719	3	4.83	12.4	59.92
84 Bethel Johnson, Texas A&M	WR	SR	12	40	718	8	3.33	17.95	59.83
85 Donta Greene, Toledo	WR	SR	14	63	712	1	4.5	11.3	50.86
86 LaShaun Ward, California	WR	SR	12	39	709	9	3.25	18.18	59.08
87 Aaron Boone, Kentucky	WR	SR	12	41	706	10	3.42	17.22	58.83
88 Scottie Vines, Wyoming	WR	SR	12	46	705	9	3.83	15.33	58.75
89 Lance Young, Iowa St.	WR	JR	14	43	704	6	3.07	16.37	50.29
89 Taco Wallace, Kansas St.	WR	SR	13	39	704	5	3	18.05	54.15
91 Richard Alston, East Caro.	WR	SR	11	36	702	6	3.27	19.5	63.82
92 Joey Cuppari, Colorado St.	WR	SR	14	35	699	4	2.5	19.97	49.93
92 Mike Bush, Washington St.	WR	SR	13	49	699	6	3.77	14.27	53.77
94 Tab Perry, UCLA	WR	JR	12	35	698	1	2.92	19.94	58.17
95 Lou Fanucchi, Boise St.	WR	SR	13	38	697	5	2.92	18.34	53.62
96 Jovon Bouknight, Wyoming	WR	FR	12	63	689	3	5.25	10.94	57.42
97 Jack Whitver, Iowa St.	WR	JR	13	52	685	0	4	13.17	52.69
98 Jonathan Makonnen, California	WR	JR	12	54	682	7	4.5	12.63	56.83
99 Jamall Broussard, San Jose St.	WR	JR	13	62	681	5	4.77	10.98	52.38
100 Cody Cardwell, Southern Methodist	WR	SR	12	49	674	3	4.08	13.76	56.17
100 Brandon Middleton, Houston	WR	JR	12	28	674	6	2.33	24.07	56.17

Receiving Yards Per Game

Min. 75 Pct. of Team's Games Played

Rank, Player	Pos	Cl	Gm	Catches	Yds	TDs	Rec/ Gm	Yds/ Catch	Yds/ Gm
1 J.R. Tolver, San Diego St.	WR	SR	13	128	1,785	13	9.85	13.95	137.31
2 Nate Burleson, Nevada	WR	SR	12	138	1,629	12	11.5	11.8	135.75
3 Rashaun Woods, Oklahoma St.	WR	JR	13	107	1,695	17	8.23	15.84	130.38
4 Kassim Osgood, San Diego St.	WR	SR	13	108	1,552	8	8.31	14.37	119.38
5 Bobby Wade, Arizona	WR	SR	12	93	1,389	8	7.75	14.94	115.75
6 Kevin Curtis, Utah St.	WR	SR	11	74	1,258	9	6.73	17	114.36
7 Kevin Walter, Eastern Mich.	WR	SR	12	93	1,368	9	7.75	14.71	114
8 Charles Rogers, Michigan St.	WR	JR	12	68	1,351	13	5.67	19.87	112.58
9 Reggie Williams, Washington	WR	SO	13	94	1,454	11	7.23	15.47	111.85
10 Doug Gabriel, UCF	WR	SR	12	75	1,237	11	6.25	16.49	103.08
11 John Standeford, Purdue	WR	JR	13	75	1,307	13	5.77	17.43	100.54
12 Shaun McDonald, Arizona St.	WR	JR	14	87	1,405	13	6.21	16.15	100.36
13 Mack Vincent, La.-Monroe	WR	JR	12	79	1,198	7	6.58	15.16	99.83
14 Taylor Jacobs, Florida	WR	SR	11	71	1,088	8	6.45	15.32	98.91
15 James Newson, Oregon St.	WR	JR	13	74	1,284	12	5.69	17.35	98.77
16 Mike Williams, Southern California	WR	FR	13	81	1,265	14	6.23	15.62	97.31
17 Roy Williams, Texas	WR	JR	12	64	1,142	12	5.33	17.84	95.17
18 Reggie Newhouse, Baylor	WR	SR	12	75	1,140	3	6.25	15.2	95
19 Jimmy Fryzel, UCF	WR	SR	12	58	1,126	5	4.83	19.41	93.83
20 Justin Colbert, Hawaii	WR	SR	14	92	1,302	8	6.57	14.15	93
21 Josh Davis, Marshall	WR	SO	13	75	1,191	5	5.77	15.88	91.62
22 Andre Johnson, Miami (Fla.)	WR	JR	12	52	1,092	9	4.33	21	91
23 Justin Gage, Missouri	WR	SR	12	82	1,074	9	6.83	13.1	89.5
24 Billy Wingfield, Boise St.	WR	SR	13	62	1,138	7	4.77	18.35	87.54
25 Courtney Roby, Indiana	WR	SO	12	59	1,039	4	4.92	17.61	86.58
26 Darius Watts, Marshall	WR	JR	12	71	1,030	12	5.92	14.51	85.83
27 Jerricho Cotchery, North Carolina St.	WR	JR	14	67	1,192	7	4.79	17.79	85.14
28 Brandon Lloyd, Illinois	WR	JR	12	65	1,010	9	5.42	15.54	84.17
29 Frederick Stamps, La.-Lafayette	WR	JR	12	54	1,002	8	4.5	18.56	83.5
30 Lane Danielsen, Iowa St.	WR	JR	13	63	1,073	3	4.85	17.03	82.54
31 Sam Aiken, North Carolina	WR	SR	12	68	990	4	5.67	14.56	82.5
32 Robert Redd, Bowling Green	WR	SR	12	83	973	9	6.92	11.72	81.08
33 Kerry Watkins, Georgia Tech	WR	SR	13	71	1,050	5	5.46	14.79	80.77

Rank, Player	Pos	Cl	Gm	Catches	Yds	TDs	Rec/ Gm	Yds/ Catch	Yds/ Gm
34 H.B. Briscoe, New Mexico St.	WR	SR	11	50	880	5	4.55	17.6	80
35 Braylon Edwards, Michigan	WR	SO	13	67	1,035	10	5.15	15.45	79.62
36 Jon Olinger, Cincinnati	WR	SR	14	54	1,114	7	3.86	20.63	79.57
37 Keary Colbert, Southern California	WR	JR	13	71	1,029	5	5.46	14.49	79.15
38 Taylor Stubblefield, Purdue	WR	SO	10	77	789	0	7.7	10.25	78.9
39 Josh Jelmberg, Idaho	WR	SR	10	64	785	8	6.4	12.27	78.5
40 Jerome Riley, Washington St.	WR	SR	12	57	939	7	4.75	16.47	78.25
41 Larry Fitzgerald, Pittsburgh	WR	FR	13	69	1,005	12	5.31	14.57	77.31
42 Terrence Edwards, Georgia	WR	SR	13	59	1,004	11	4.54	17.02	77.23
43 Michael Jenkins, Ohio St.	WR	JR	14	61	1,076	6	4.36	17.64	76.86
44 Denero Marriott, Marshall	WR	SR	13	86	993	8	6.62	11.55	76.38
45 Andrae Thurman, Arizona	WR	JR	12	61	915	3	5.08	15	76.25
46 Jamaar Taylor, Texas A&M	WR	JR	10	44	760	3	4.4	17.27	76
47 Carl Ford, Toledo	WR	JR	14	79	1,062	9	5.64	13.44	75.86
48 Wes Welker, Texas Tech	RB	JR	14	86	1,054	7	6.14	12.26	75.29
49 Andre Forde, Buffalo	WR	SR	10	54	748	7	5.4	13.85	74.8
50 Maurice Brown, Iowa	WR	JR	13	48	966	11	3.69	20.13	74.31
51 Marque Davis, Fresno St.	WR	JR	13	64	956	7	4.92	14.94	73.54
52 Anquan Boldin, Florida St.	WR	SR	14	65	1,011	13	4.64	15.55	72.21
53 Earvin Johnson, UNLV	WR	SO	11	51	793	4	4.64	15.55	72.09
54 Bryant Johnson, Penn St.	WR	SR	13	48	917	4	3.69	19.1	70.54
55 Glenn Johnson, Indiana	WR	JR	12	53	837	5	4.42	15.79	69.75
56 Walter Young, Illinois	WR	SR	12	57	832	6	4.75	14.6	69.33
57 Craig Bragg, UCLA	WR	SO	13	55	889	8	4.23	16.16	68.38
58 Chris Norwood, Louisiana Tech	WR	JR	11	61	748	4	5.55	12.26	68
59 Ernest Wilford, Virginia Tech	WR	JR	14	51	925	7	3.64	18.14	66.07
60 Dan Sheldon, Northern Ill.	WR	SO	12	40	783	5	3.33	19.58	65.25
61 Reno Mahe, Brigham Young	WR	SR	12	59	771	2	4.92	13.07	64.25
62 Billy McMullen, Virginia	WR	SR	14	69	894	3	4.93	12.96	63.86
63 Richard Alston, East Caro.	WR	SR	11	36	702	6	3.27	19.5	63.82
64 Britton Komine, Hawaii	WR	SO	14	58	886	10	4.14	15.28	63.29
65 Fred Gibson, Georgia	WR	SO	12	43	758	4	3.58	17.63	63.17
66 Damien Dorsey, Louisville	WR	SR	12	52	753	7	4.33	14.48	62.75
67 Chris Collins, Mississippi	WR	JR	13	55	812	10	4.23	14.76	62.46
68 Charles Pauley, San Jose St.	WR	SR	13	60	804	4	4.62	13.4	61.85
69 Travis Anglin, Memphis	WR	SR	12	55	740	5	4.58	13.45	61.67
70 Devard Darling, Washington St.	WR	SO	13	54	800	11	4.15	14.81	61.54
71 Jeremiah Cockheran, Hawaii	WR	JR	12	49	731	5	4.08	14.92	60.92
72 D.J. Curry, Louisiana Tech	WR	JR	12	57	730	3	4.75	12.81	60.83
73 Arnaz Battle, Notre Dame	WR	SR	13	58	786	5	4.46	13.55	60.46
74 J.J. McKelvey, Clemson	WR	SR	13	52	785	4	4	15.1	60.38
75 Keenan Howry, Oregon	WR	SR	13	40	784	5	3.08	19.6	60.31
76 LaDaris Vann, Cincinnati	WR	SR	14	71	844	5	5.07	11.89	60.29
77 Jonathon Orr, Wisconsin	WR	FR	14	47	842	8	3.36	17.91	60.14
78 Hugh Smith, South Fla.	WR	SR	11	62	661	5	5.64	10.66	60.09
79 Jon Schweighardt, Northwestern	WR	SR	12	58	719	3	4.83	12.4	59.92
80 Bethel Johnson, Texas A&M	WR	SR	12	40	718	8	3.33	17.95	59.83
81 LaShaun Ward, California	WR	SR	12	39	709	9	3.25	18.18	59.08
82 Aaron Boone, Kentucky	WR	SR	12	41	706	10	3.42	17.22	58.83
83 Scottie Vines, Wyoming	WR	SR	12	46	705	9	3.83	15.33	58.75
84 Tab Perry, UCLA	WR	JR	12	35	698	1	2.92	19.94	58.17
85 Chris Pittman, Colorado St.	WR	JR	14	60	807	1	4.29	13.45	57.64
86 Mickey Peters, Texas Tech	TE	JR	13	64	749	8	4.92	11.7	57.62
86 Michael Clayton, LSU	WR	SO	13	57	749	5	4.38	13.14	57.62
88 Jovon Bouknight, Wyoming	WR	FR	12	63	689	3	5.25	10.94	57.42
89 Dallas Clark, Iowa	TE	JR	13	43	742	4	3.31	17.26	57.08
90 Willie Quinnie, UAB	WR	SR	11	36	627	6	3.27	17.42	57
91 Jamel Riddle, Syracuse	WR	JR	11	41	626	5	3.73	15.27	56.91
92 Jonathan Makonnen, California	WR	JR	12	54	682	7	4.5	12.63	56.83
93 Orlando Winston, Idaho	WR	JR	11	50	624	1	4.55	12.48	56.73
94 Kendrick Mosley, Western Mich.	WR	SR	9	37	507	3	4.11	13.7	56.33
95 Brandon Middleton, Houston	WR	JR	12	28	674	6	2.33	24.07	56.17
95 Cody Cardwell, Southern Methodist	WR	SR	12	49	674	3	4.08	13.76	56.17
97 Chris Johnson, Southern Miss.	WR	SO	12	50	673	3	4.17	13.46	56.08
98 Kellen Winslow, Miami (Fla.)	TE	SO	13	57	726	8	4.38	12.74	55.85
99 Greg Porter, Texas A&M	WR	SR	12	48	669	4	4	13.94	55.75
100 Samie Parker, Oregon	WR	JR	13	49	724	8	3.77	14.78	55.69

Rushing

Min. 75 Pct. of Team's Games Played

Rank, Player	Pos	Cl	Gm	Carries	Net	TDs	Avg	Ydspgm
1 Larry Johnson, Penn St.	TB	SR	13	271	2,087	20	7.7	160.54
2 Michael Turner, Northern Ill.	RB	JR	12	338	1,915	19	5.67	159.58
3 Chris Brown, Colorado	RB	JR	12	303	1,841	19	6.08	153.42
4 Willis McGahee, Miami (Fla.)	RB	SO	13	282	1,753	28	6.22	134.85
5 Marcus Merriweather, Ball St.	RB	SR	12	332	1,618	12	4.87	134.83
6 Quentin Griffin, Oklahoma	RB	SR	14	287	1,884	15	6.56	134.57
7 Avon Cobourne, West Virginia	RB	SR	13	335	1,710	17	5.1	131.54
8 Steven Jackson, Oregon St.	RB	SO	13	319	1,690	15	5.3	130
9 Joffrey Reynolds, Houston	RB	SR	12	316	1,545	11	4.89	128.75
10 Terry Caulley, Connecticut	RB	FR	10	220	1,247	15	5.67	124.7

Rank, Player	Pos	Cl	Gm	Carries	Net	TDs	Avg	Ydspgm
11 Brock Forsey, Boise St.	RB	SR	13	295	1,611	26	5.46	123.92
12 Anthony Davis, Wisconsin	RB	SO	13	300	1,555	13	5.18	119.62
13 Artose Pinner, Kentucky	RB	SR	12	283	1,414	13	5	117.83
14 Fred Russell, Iowa	RB	JR	11	220	1,264	9	5.75	114.91
15 Cecil Sapp, Colorado St.	RB	SR	14	347	1,601	17	4.61	114.36
16 Onterrio Smith, Oregon	RB	JR	10	244	1,141	12	4.68	114.1
17 Robbie Mixon, Central Mich.	RB	SR	12	255	1,361	9	5.34	113.42
18 Rodney Davis, Fresno St.	RB	JR	14	313	1,586	9	5.07	113.29
19 Darren Sproles, Kansas St.	RB	SO	13	237	1,465	17	6.18	112.69
20 Maurice Clarett, Ohio St.	RB	FR	11	222	1,237	16	5.57	112.45
21 Ime Akpan, Eastern Mich.	RB	SR	11	267	1,231	15	4.61	111.91
22 Antoineo Harris, Illinois	RB	SR	12	278	1,330	8	4.78	110.83
23 Derrick Knight, Boston College	RB	JR	13	259	1,432	12	5.53	110.15
24 Derrick Nix, Southern Miss.	RB	SR	11	219	1,194	11	5.45	108.55
25 Danny Smith, Arkansas St.	RB	SR	13	254	1,390	14	5.47	106.92
26 Keylon Kincade, Southern Methodist	RB	JR	12	327	1,279	7	3.91	106.58
27 Tanardo Sharps, Temple	RB	SR	12	311	1,276	8	4.1	106.33
28 Joshua Cribbs, Kent St.	QB	SO	10	137	1,057	10	7.72	105.7
29 Art Brown, East Caro.	RB	JR	10	214	1,029	14	4.81	102.9
30 Jason Wright, Northwestern	WR	JR	12	219	1,234	12	5.63	102.83
31 Brandon Warfield, Utah	RB	JR	9	201	919	9	4.57	102.11
32 Musa Smith, Georgia	RB	JR	13	260	1,324	8	5.09	101.85
33 Joe Smith, Louisiana Tech	RB	SR	12	207	1,217	16	5.88	101.42
34 Terry Jackson II, Minnesota	RB	SO	13	238	1,318	6	5.54	101.38
35 Jammal Lord, Nebraska	QB	JR	14	251	1,412	8	5.63	100.86
36 Kevin Galbreath, North Texas	RB	SR	13	272	1,298	9	4.77	99.85
37 Tatum Bell, Oklahoma St.	RB	JR	11	175	1,096	11	6.26	99.64
38 Cedric Benson, Texas	RB	SO	13	305	1,293	12	4.24	99.46
39 DeMarco McCleskey, Cincinnati	RB	SR	14	315	1,361	15	4.32	97.21
40 Lee Suggs, Virginia Tech	RB	SR	14	257	1,325	22	5.16	94.64
41 Walter Reyes, Syracuse	RB	SO	12	182	1,135	17	6.24	94.58
42 Chance Harridge, Air Force	QB	JR	13	252	1,229	22	4.88	94.54
43 Alex Haynes, UCF	DB	SO	11	204	1,038	8	5.09	94.36
44 Joe Igber, California	RB	SR	12	241	1,130	7	4.69	94.17
45 Blair Lewis, Idaho	RB	SR	10	176	930	11	5.28	93
46 Bob Hendry, Akron	RB	JR	11	208	1,021	8	4.91	92.82
47 Matt Milton, Nevada	RB	FR	12	225	1,108	9	4.92	92.33
48 Dwone Hicks, Middle Tenn.	RB	SR	11	184	1,011	11	5.49	91.91
49 Chad Brinker, Ohio	RB	SR	12	228	1,099	10	4.82	91.58
50 Philip Reed, Western Mich.	RB	JR	12	221	1,053	10	4.76	87.75
51 Mewelde Moore, Tulane	RB	JR	13	288	1,138	6	3.95	87.54
52 DonTrell Moore, New Mexico	RB	FR	13	245	1,134	13	4.63	87.23
53 Bryant Jacobs, La.-Monroe	RB	SR	12	205	1,043	7	5.09	86.92
54 Ell Roberson, Kansas St.	QB	JR	12	202	1,032	16	5.11	86
55 Joey Harris, Purdue	RB	JR	13	250	1,115	8	4.46	85.77
56 Brad Smith, Missouri	QB	FR	12	193	1,029	7	5.33	85.75
57 Chris Perry, Michigan	RB	JR	13	267	1,110	14	4.16	85.38
58 T.A. McLendon, North Carolina St.	RB	FR	13	245	1,101	18	4.49	84.69
59 Luke Clemens, Miami (Ohio)	RB	JR	12	223	1,009	16	4.52	84.08
60 Ronnie Brown, Auburn	RB	SO	12	175	1,008	13	5.76	84
61 Earnest Graham, Florida	RB	SR	13	240	1,085	11	4.52	83.46
61 Ryan Grant, Notre Dame	RB	SO	13	261	1,085	9	4.16	83.46
63 Marcus Whalen, Brigham Young	RB	SO	11	181	918	6	5.07	83.45
64 Chris Downs, Maryland	RB	SR	14	208	1,154	13	5.55	82.43
65 Alex Wade, Duke	RB	JR	12	201	979	4	4.87	81.58
66 Joe Alls, Bowling Green	RB	SR	10	122	801	4	6.57	80.1
67 Fred Talley, Arkansas	RB	SR	14	197	1,119	2	5.68	79.93
68 Eric Richardson, Tulsa	RB	JR	12	182	957	6	5.26	79.75
69 Tyler Ebell, UCLA	RB	FR	13	234	994	10	4.25	76.46
70 Aaron Leeper, Buffalo	RB	FR	12	235	917	10	3.9	76.42
71 Derek Farmer, Texas A&M	RB	SO	10	172	739	7	4.3	73.9
72 Kwane Doster, Vanderbilt	TB	FR	11	160	798	3	4.99	72.55
73 Brandon Miree, Pittsburgh	RB	JR	13	214	943	4	4.41	72.54
74 Paul Dombrowski, New Mexico St.	QB	SO	12	189	868	12	4.59	72.33
75 Domanick Davis, LSU	RB	SR	13	193	931	7	4.82	71.62
76 Shaud Williams, Alabama	RB	JR	13	130	921	5	7.08	70.85
77 Craig Candeto, Navy	QB	JR	11	177	775	16	4.38	70.45
78 Howard Jackson, UTEP	RB	SO	12	173	844	7	4.88	70.33
79 Joe Haro, UNLV	RB	SR	12	159	841	5	5.29	70.08
80 Thomas Tapeh, Minnesota	RB	JR	13	182	905	8	4.97	69.62
81 Quincy Wilson, West Virginia	RB	JR	13	140	901	6	6.44	69.31
82 Zack Abron, Missouri	RB	JR	11	176	758	15	4.31	68.91
83 Clark Green, Kansas	RB	FR	12	197	813	4	4.13	67.75
84 Kevin Jones, Virginia Tech	RB	SO	13	160	871	9	5.44	67
85 Dahrran Diedrick, Nebraska	RB	SR	14	179	931	6	5.2	66.5
86 Dawan Moss, Michigan St.	RB	SR	9	125	592	4	4.74	65.78
87 Tarence Williams, Wake Forest	RB	JR	13	186	852	5	4.58	65.54
88 Ricky Madison, TCU	RB	JR	11	155	719	3	4.64	65.36
89 Cedric Houston, Tennessee	RB	SO	12	153	779	6	5.09	64.92
90 DeWhitt Betterson, Troy St.	RB	SO	11	101	711	5	7.04	64.64
91 Jermaine Green, Washington St.	RB	JR	13	150	829	9	5.53	63.77
92 James Samuel, Utah St.	RB	JR	10	120	633	7	5.28	63.3
93 LaBarron Black, Troy St.	RB	SR	12	210	757	8	3.6	63.08
94 Sultan McCullough, Southern California	RB	SR	13	179	814	8	4.55	62.62
95 Rich Alexis, Washington	RB	JR	11	202	688	10	3.41	62.55

Rank, Player	Pos	Cl	Gm	Carries	Net	TDs	Avg	Ydspgm
96 Santonio Beard, Alabama	RB	JR	13	165	811	12	4.92	62.38
97 DeAngelo Williams, Memphis	RB	FR	11	103	684	5	6.64	62.18
98 Josh Harris, Bowling Green	QB	JR	12	186	737	20	3.96	61.42
99 Bill Whittemore, Kansas	QB	JR	9	137	549	11	4.01	61
100 Eddie Beccles, Kent St.	RB	SO	10	114	602	3	5.28	60.2

Scoring

Min. 75 Pct. of Team's Games Played

Rank, Player	Pos	Cl	Gm	TDs	OKM	OKA	FGM	FGA	Points	PTPG
1 Brock Forsey, Boise St.	RB	SR	13	32	0	0	0	0	192	14.77
2 Willis McGahee, Miami (Fla.)	RB	SO	13	28	0	0	0	0	168	12.92
3 Josh Harris, Bowling Green	QB	JR	12	22	0	0	0	0	134	11.17
4 Larry Johnson, Penn St.	TB	SR	13	23	0	0	0	0	140	10.77
5 Lee Suggs, Virginia Tech	RB	SR	14	24	0	0	0	0	144	10.29
6 Art Brown, East Caro.	RB	JR	10	17	0	0	0	0	102	10.2
7 Chance Harridge, Air Force	QB	JR	13	22	0	0	0	0	132	10.15
8 Michael Turner, Northern Ill.	RB	JR	12	20	0	0	0	0	120	10
9 Maurice Clarett, Ohio St.	RB	FR	11	18	0	0	0	0	108	9.82
10 Terry Caulley, Connecticut	RB	FR	10	16	0	0	0	0	96	9.6
10 Nick Calaycay, Boise St.	K	SR	10	0	63	66	11	13	96	9.6
12 Chris Brown, Colorado	RB	JR	12	19	0	0	0	0	114	9.5
13 Billy Bennett, Georgia	K	JR	14	0	52	52	26	33	130	9.29
14 Zack Abron, Missouri	RB	JR	11	17	0	0	0	0	102	9.27
15 Nate Kaeding, Iowa	K	JR	13	0	57	58	21	24	120	9.23
16 Nick Novak, Maryland	K	SO	14	0	53	54	24	28	125	8.93
17 Mark-Christian Jensen, California	K	SR	12	0	50	51	19	27	107	8.92
18 Nick Browne, TCU	K	JR	12	0	36	38	23	30	105	8.75
19 Craig Candeto, Navy	QB	JR	11	16	0	0	0	0	96	8.73
20 Drew Dunning, Washington St.	K	JR	13	0	47	49	22	33	113	8.69
21 Walter Reyes, Syracuse	RB	SO	12	17	0	0	0	0	104	8.67
22 Mike Nugent, Ohio St.	K	SO	14	0	45	46	25	28	120	8.57
23 Luke Clemens, Miami (Ohio)	RB	JR	12	17	0	0	0	0	102	8.5
24 Mike Barth, Arizona St.	K	SR	14	0	49	49	23	33	118	8.43
24 Jeff Babcock, Colorado St.	K	SO	14	1	40	44	24	32	118	8.43
26 Jared Siegel, Oregon	K	SO	13	0	49	50	20	24	109	8.38
27 John Anderson, Washington	K	SR	13	0	42	44	22	34	108	8.31
27 T.A. McLendon, North Carolina St.	RB	FR	13	18	0	0	0	0	108	8.31
29 Sandro Sciortino, Boston College	K	JR	13	0	38	40	23	32	107	8.23
30 Ime Akpan, Eastern Mich.	RB	SR	11	15	0	0	0	0	90	8.18
31 Joe Smith, Louisiana Tech	RB	SR	12	16	0	0	0	0	98	8.17
31 Ell Roberson, Kansas St.	QB	JR	12	16	0	0	0	0	98	8.17
33 Todd Sievers, Miami (Fla.)	K	SR	13	0	66	69	13	22	105	8.08
34 Darren Sproles, Kansas St.	RB	JR	13	17	0	0	0	0	104	8
34 Asen Asparuhov, Fresno St.	K	SR	14	0	43	43	23	30	112	8
36 Steve Azar, Northern Ill.	K	JR	12	0	41	43	18	25	95	7.92
37 Steven Jackson, Oregon St.	RB	SO	13	17	0	0	0	0	102	7.85
37 Avon Cobourne, West Virginia	RB	SR	13	17	0	0	0	0	102	7.85
37 Dan Nystrom, Minnesota	K	SR	13	0	42	42	20	21	102	7.85
37 Dusty Mangum, Texas	K	SO	13	0	54	54	16	26	102	7.85
37 Rashaun Woods, Oklahoma St.	WR	JR	13	17	0	0	0	0	102	7.85
42 Bill Whittemore, Kansas	QB	JR	9	11	0	0	0	0	70	7.78
43 Shaun Suisham, Bowling Green	K	JR	12	0	57	59	12	14	93	7.75
44 Quentin Griffin, Oklahoma	RB	SR	14	18	0	0	0	0	108	7.71
44 Xavier Beitia, Florida St.	PK	SO	14	0	51	51	19	28	108	7.71
46 Trey DiCarlo, Oklahoma	K	FR	14	0	58	62	16	22	106	7.57
47 Santiago Gramatica, South Fla.	K	SO	11	0	35	40	16	21	83	7.55
48 Kirk Yliniemi, Oregon St.	K	JR	12	0	45	46	15	16	90	7.5
48 Artose Pinner, Kentucky	RB	SR	12	15	0	0	0	0	90	7.5
50 Curtis Head, Marshall	P	SR	13	0	49	53	16	20	97	7.46
51 Aaron Hunt, Clemson	K	JR	12	0	37	38	17	22	88	7.33
52 Ryan Killeen, Southern California	K	SO	13	0	47	49	16	23	95	7.31
52 Joey Ashcroft, Air Force	K	JR	13	0	47	50	16	18	95	7.31
54 Cecil Sapp, Colorado St.	RB	SR	14	17	0	0	0	0	102	7.29
54 DeMarco McCleskey, Cincinnati	RB	SR	14	17	0	0	0	0	102	7.29
56 Joe Rheem, Kansas St.	K	SO	11	0	53	59	9	12	80	7.27
57 Jonathan Ruffin, Cincinnati	K	SR	14	0	44	46	19	22	101	7.21
58 Onterrio Smith, Oregon	RB	JR	10	12	0	0	0	0	72	7.2
58 Blair Lewis, Idaho	RB	SR	10	12	0	0	0	0	72	7.2
60 Jared Parseghian, Miami (Ohio)	K	SO	12	0	44	46	14	14	86	7.17
60 Matt Prater, UCF	K	FR	12	0	44	47	14	21	86	7.17
62 Gould, Penn St.			13	0	42	45	17	22	93	7.15
63 Justin Ayat, Hawaii	K	SO	14	0	55	56	15	23	100	7.14
64 Tatum Bell, Oklahoma St.	RB	JR	11	13	0	0	0	0	78	7.09
65 Kevin Miller, East Caro.	K	SR	12	0	34	36	17	22	85	7.08
66 Ronnie Brown, Auburn	RB	SO	12	14	0	0	0	0	84	7
66 Marcus Merriweather, Ball St.	RB	SR	12	14	0	0	0	0	84	7
68 Adam Benike, Iowa St.	K	JR	14	0	46	48	17	23	97	6.93
69 DonTrell Moore, New Mexico	RB	FR	13	15	0	0	0	0	90	6.92
70 Dario Aguiniga, New Mexico St.	K	JR	12	0	32	33	17	23	83	6.92
70 Marc Hickok, Connecticut	K	SR	12	0	47	48	12	17	83	6.92
72 Seth Marler, Tulane	K	SR	13	0	29	33	20	33	89	6.85
73 Dane Kidman, Utah St.	K	SR	11	0	33	35	14	17	75	6.82
74 Luke Phillips, Oklahoma St.	K	JR	13	0	55	56	11	16	88	6.77

Rank, Player	Pos	Cl	Gm	TDs	OKM	OKA	FGM	FGA	Points	PTPG
75 Nick Hayes, UAB	K	SO	12	0	29	29	17	22	80	6.67
76 Robert Treece, Texas Tech	K	SR	14	0	54	54	13	19	93	6.64
76 Jason Robbins, Toledo	K	FR	14	0	54	62	13	16	93	6.64
78 J.R. Tolver, San Diego St.	WR	SR	13	14	0	0	0	0	86	6.62
79 Jonathan Nichols, Mississippi	K	SO	13	0	40	40	15	20	85	6.54
79 John Corbello, LSU	K	SR	13	0	34	35	17	24	85	6.54
81 Nate Burleson, Nevada	WR	SR	12	13	0	0	0	0	78	6.5
81 Josh Scobee, Louisiana Tech	K	JR	12	0	30	35	16	21	78	6.5
81 Joffrey Reynolds, Houston	RB	SR	12	13	0	0	0	0	78	6.5
81 Jason Wright, Northwestern	WR	JR	12	13	0	0	0	0	78	6.5
81 Roy Williams, Texas	WR	JR	12	13	0	0	0	0	78	6.5
81 Charles Rogers, Michigan St.	WR	JR	12	13	0	0	0	0	78	6.5
87 Danny Smith, Arkansas St.	RB	SR	13	14	0	0	0	0	84	6.46
87 Derrick Knight, Boston College	RB	JR	13	14	0	0	0	0	84	6.46
87 Matt Wisnosky, Wake Forest	P	SO	13	0	33	36	17	25	84	6.46
87 Chris Perry, Michigan	RB	JR	13	14	0	0	0	0	84	6.46
87 Mike Williams, Southern California	WR	FR	13	14	0	0	0	0	84	6.46
92 Chris Downs, Maryland	RB	SR	14	15	0	0	0	0	90	6.43
93 Tommy Kirovski, San Diego St.	K	SR	13	0	32	35	17	27	83	6.38
94 Paul Dombrowski, New Mexico St.	QB	SO	12	12	0	0	0	0	76	6.33
95 Josh Brown, Nebraska	K	SR	14	0	46	46	14	18	88	6.29
96 Todd Pegram, Texas A&M	K	FR	11	0	32	33	12	21	68	6.18
97 Peter Christofilakos, Illinois	K	JR	11	0	40	40	9	12	67	6.09
98 Todd James, West Virginia	K	JR	13	0	46	50	11	16	79	6.08
99 Dwone Hicks, Middle Tenn.	RB	SR	11	11	0	0	0	0	66	6
99 Rasheed Marshall, West Virginia	QB	SO	13	13	0	0	0	0	78	6
99 Kejuan Jones, Oklahoma	RB	FR	14	14	0	0	0	0	84	6
99 Anthony Davis, Wisconsin	RB	SO	13	13	0	0	0	0	78	6
99 Berin Lacevic, Purdue	K	JR	13	0	48	49	10	19	78	6
99 John Standeford, Purdue	WR	JR	13	13	0	0	0	0	78	6
99 Doug Gabriel, UCF	WR	SR	12	12	0	0	0	0	72	6
99 Darius Watts, Marshall	WR	JR	12	12	0	0	0	0	72	6
99 Joshua Cribbs, Kent St.	QB	SO	10	10	0	0	0	0	60	6
99 Brandon Warfield, Utah	RB	JR	9	9	0	0	0	0	54	6
99 Derrick Nix, Southern Miss.	RB	SR	11	11	0	0	0	0	66	6
99 Nick Gilliam, San Jose St.	K	SR	13	0	42	44	12	20	78	6

Total Offense

Min. 75 Pct. of Team's Games Played

Rank, Player	Pos	Cl	Gm	Rush Gn	Loss	Net	Patt	Pyds	Pl	Tot/ yds	Yds/ pl	Yds/ gm
1 Byron Leftwich, Marshall	QB	SR	12	37 93	94	-1	491	4,268	528	4,267	8.08	355.6
2 Kliff Kingsbury, Texas Tech	QB	SR	14	102 221	335	-114	712	5,017	814	4,903	6.02	350.2
3 Cody Pickett, Washington	QB	JR	13	86 154	339	-185	612	4,458	698	4,273	6.12	328.7
4 Timmy Chang, Hawaii	QB	SO	14	39 120	137	-17	624	4,474	663	4,457	6.72	318.4
5 Ryan Schneider, UCF	QB	JR	12	37 44	133	-89	430	3,770	467	3,681	7.88	306.8
6 Luke McCown, Louisiana Tech	QB	JR	12	61 220	190	30	505	3,539	566	3,569	6.31	297.4
7 Zack Threadgill, Nevada	QB	SR	12	62 229	113	116	451	3,418	513	3,534	6.89	294.5
8 Carson Palmer, Southern California	QB	SR	13	50 105	227	-122	489	3,942	539	3,820	7.09	
9 Jose Fuentes, Utah St.	QB	SR	11	57 112	216	-104	454	3,268	511	3,164	6.19	287.6
10 Adam Hall, San Diego St.	QB	JR	11	64 128	238	-110	452	3,253	516	3,143	6.09	285.7
11 Brad Smith, Missouri	QB	FR	12	193 1179	150	1029	366	2,333	559	3,362	6.01	280.2
12 Casey Bramlet, Wyoming	QB	JR	12	101 322	287	35	464	3,290	565	3,325	5.88	277.1
13 Brian Jones, Toledo	QB	SR	14	85 558	144	414	423	3,446	508	3,860	7.6	275.7
14 Ben Roethlisberger, Miami (Ohio)	QB	SO	12	82 215	269	-54	428	3,238	510	3,184	6.24	265.3
15 Josh Harris, Bowling Green	QB	JR	12	186 862	125	737	353	2,425	539	3,162	5.87	263.5
16 Seneca Wallace, Iowa St.	QB	SR	14	123 676	239	437	443	3,245	566	3,682	6.51	263
17 Marquel Blackwell, South Fla.	QB	SR	11	89 415	113	302	403	2,590	492	2,892	5.88	262.9
18 Andrew Walter, Arizona St.	QB	SO	14	56 74	290	-216	483	3,877	539	3,661	6.79	261.5
19 Rex Grossman, Florida	QB	JR	13	58 174	239	-65	503	3,402	561	3,337	5.95	256.7
20 Ken Dorsey, Miami (Fla.)	QB	SR	13	23 45	93	-48	393	3,369	416	3,321	7.98	255.5
21 Gino Guidugli, Cincinnati	QB	SO	14	69 187	160	27	472	3,543	541	3,570	6.6	255
22 Jason Gesser, Washington St.	QB	SR	13	54 98	214	-116	402	3,408	456	3,292	7.22	253.2
23 Eli Manning, Mississippi	QB	JR	13	39 45	165	-120	481	3,401	520	3,281	6.31	252.4
24 Scott Rislov, San Jose St.	QB	JR	13	72 212	199	13	449	3,251	521	3,264	6.26	251.1
25 Philip Rivers, North Carolina St.	QB	JR	14	57 162	62	100	418	3,353	475	3,453	7.27	246.6
26 Jason Johnson, Arizona	QB	SR	12	60 36	409	-373	410	3,327	470	2,954	6.29	246.2
27 Bill Whittemore, Kansas	QB	JR	9	137 749	200	549	305	1,666	442	2,215	5.01	246.1
28 Charlie Frye, Akron	QB	SO	12	102 416	291	125	380	2,824	482	2,949	6.12	245.8
29 Rod Rutherford, Pittsburgh	QB	JR	13	182 739	341	398	367	2,783	549	3,181	5.79	244.7
30 Brian Lindgren, Idaho	QB	JR	11	47 52	149	-97	382	2,763	429	2,666	6.21	242.4
31 Dave Ragone, Louisville	QB	SR	13	131 574	326	248	442	2,880	573	3,128	5.46	240.6
32 Brian St.Pierre, Boston College	QB	SR	13	68 274	148	126	407	2,983	475	3,109	6.55	239.2
33 Danny Wimprine, Memphis	QB	JR	12	98 247	207	40	435	2,820	533	2,860	5.37	238.3
34 Chris Simms, Texas	QB	SR	13	70 123	247	-124	396	3,207	466	3,083	6.62	237.2
35 Derek Anderson, Oregon St.	QB	SO	13	45 36	267	-231	449	3,313	494	3,082	6.24	237.1
36 Josh Fields, Oklahoma St.	QB	SO	13	50 93	165	-72	408	3,145	458	3,073	6.71	236.4
37 Brad Banks, Iowa	QB	SR	13	81 519	96	423	294	2,573	375	2,996	7.99	230.5
38 Brett Basanez, Northwestern	QB	FR	10	67 235	139	96	325	2,204	392	2,300	5.87	230

Rank, Player	Pos	Cl	Gm	Rush	Gn	Loss	Net	Patt	Pyds	Pl	Tot/ yds	Yds/ pl	Yds/ gm
39 Jon Beutjer, Illinois	QB	JR	11	44	127	120	7	327	2,511	371	2,518	6.79	228.9
40 Kyle Boller, California	QB	SR	12	72	151	234	-83	421	2,815	493	2,732	5.54	227.7
41 Troy Edwards, Eastern Mich.	QB	SR	12	45	120	215	-95	410	2,762	455	2,667	5.86	222.3
42 John Navarre, Michigan	QB	JR	13	40	106	122	-16	448	2,905	488	2,889	5.92	222.2
43 Matt Schaub, Virginia	QB	JR	14	70	273	178	95	418	2,976	488	3,071	6.29	219.4
44 Ell Roberson, Kansas St.	QB	JR	12	202	1,276	244	1032	175	1,580	377	2,612	6.93	217.7
45 Jason Fife, Oregon	QB	JR	13	76	223	156	67	367	2,752	443	2,819	6.36	216.8
46 Jason Thomas, UNLV	QB	SR	11	124	619	171	448	274	1,936	398	2,384	5.99	216.7
47 Tyler Gooch, Tulsa	QB	SO	11	127	493	274	219	348	2,100	475	2,319	4.88	210.8
48 Dustin Long, Texas A&M	QB	SO	12	49	161	148	13	333	2,509	382	2,522	6.6	210.2
49 Asad Abdul-Khaliq, Minnesota	QB	JR	12	86	460	132	328	314	2,184	400	2,512	6.28	209.3
50 Casey Clausen, Tennessee	QB	JR	11	61	157	164	-7	310	2,297	371	2,290	6.17	208.2
51 Joshua Cribbs, Kent St.	QB	SO	10	137	1,189	132	1057	186	1,014	323	2,071	6.41	207.1
52 Steven Jyles, La.-Monroe	QB	FR	12	85	339	174	165	368	2,318	453	2,483	5.48	206.9
53 Bradlee Van Pelt, Colorado St.	QB	JR	14	150	940	121	819	287	2,073	437	2,892	6.62	206.6
54 David Greene, Georgia	QB	SO	14	65	154	206	-52	379	2,924	444	2,872	6.47	205.1
55 Zack Mills, Penn St.	QB	JR	13	87	342	141	201	333	2,417	420	2,618	6.23	201.4
56 Dan Orlovsky, Connecticut	QB	SO	12	50	132	218	-86	366	2,488	416	2,402	5.77	200.2
57 Paul Pinegar, Fresno St.	QB	FR	14	65	171	302	-131	403	2,929	468	2,798	5.98	199.9
58 Scott McBrien, Maryland	QB	JR	14	88	400	116	284	284	2,497	372	2,781	7.48	198.6
59 Jammal Lord, Nebraska	QB	JR	14	251	1,708	296	1412	204	1,362	455	2,774	6.1	198.1
60 J.P. Losman, Tulane	QB	JR	13	88	281	262	19	401	2,468	489	2,487	5.09	191.3
61 Bryan Randall, Virginia Tech	QB	SO	14	171	769	262	507	248	2,134	419	2,641	6.3	188.6
62 Gibran Hamdan, Indiana	QB	SR	11	55	101	153	-52	293	2,115	348	2,063	5.93	187.5
63 Andrico Hines, Middle Tenn. St.	QB	JR	12	150	645	159	486	243	1,753	393	2,239	5.7	186.6
64 Jared Lorenzen, Kentucky	QB	JR	12	60	148	199	-51	327	2,267	387	2,216	5.73	184.7
65 Jon VanCleave, La.-Lafayette	QB	JR	11	64	157	207	-50	316	2,081	380	2,031	5.34	184.6
66 Nick Eddy, Houston	QB	JR	11	37	72	111	-39	265	2,054	302	2,015	6.67	183.2
67 Paul Dombrowski, New Mexico St.	QB	SO	12	189	962	94	868	158	1,327	347	2,195	6.33	182.9
68 Mike McGann, Temple	QB	SO	12	95	371	171	200	353	1,994	448	2,194	4.9	182.8
69 Chris Rix, Florida St.	QB	SO	11	86	386	97	289	225	1,684	311	1,973	6.34	179.4
70 Darrell Hackney, UAB	QB	FR	11	85	242	258	-16	293	1,977	378	1,961	5.19	178.3
71 Nate Hybl, Oklahoma	QB	SR	14	63	136	190	-54	363	2,538	426	2,484	5.83	177.4
72 Kyle Orton, Purdue	QB	SO	13	43	140	93	47	317	2,257	360	2,304	6.4	177.2
73 Craig Krenzel, Ohio St.	QB	JR	14	125	548	180	368	249	2,110	374	2,478	6.63	177
74 Chance Harridge, Air Force	QB	JR	13	252	1,307	78	1229	144	1,062	396	2,291	5.79	176.2
75 Rasheed Marshall, West Virginia	QB	SO	13	173	833	167	666	259	1,616	432	2,282	5.28	175.5
76 Paul Troth, East Caro.	QB	SO	12	61	102	312	-210	359	2,315	420	2,105	5.01	175.4
77 A.J. Suggs, Georgia Tech	QB	JR	13	52	151	130	21	363	2,242	415	2,263	5.45	174.1
78 Brooks Bollinger, Wisconsin	QB	SR	13	160	729	263	466	245	1,758	405	2,224	5.49	171.1
79 Chad Munson, Western Mich.	QB	JR	12	34	32	152	-120	309	2,160	343	2,040	5.95	170
80 Kevin Fant, Mississippi St.	QB	JR	11	61	129	198	-69	311	1,918	372	1,849	4.97	168.1
81 Jay Cutler, Vanderbilt	QB	FR	11	123	561	168	393	212	1,433	335	1,826	5.45	166
82 Corey Jenkins, South Carolina	QB	SR	12	160	762	107	655	180	1,334	340	1,989	5.85	165.8
83 Carlyle Holiday, Notre Dame	QB	JR	12	92	432	232	200	257	1,788	349	1,988	5.7	165.7
84 Aaron Karas, Baylor	QB	SO	11	95	293	296	-3	251	1,792	346	1,789	5.17	162.6
85 Sean Stilley, TCU	QB	SR	9	65	201	115	86	204	1,371	269	1,457	5.42	161.9
86 Joshua Haldi, Northern Ill.	QB	SO	12	59	100	190	-90	254	2,027	313	1,937	6.19	161.4
87 Derrick Vickers, Central Mich.	QB	JR	12	62	190	85	105	320	1,828	382	1,933	5.06	161.1
88 Tyler Watts, Alabama	QB	SR	11	130	487	131	356	181	1,414	311	1,770	5.69	160.9
89 Larry Johnson, Penn St.	TB	SR	13	271	2,143	56	2087	0	0	271	2,087	7.7	160.5
90 Michael Turner, Northern Ill.	RB	JR	12	338	2,027	112	1915	0	0	338	1,915	5.67	159.6
91 Adam Smith, Duke	QB	SO	12	62	116	235	-119	308	2,031	370	1,912	5.17	159.3
92 Matt Jones, Arkansas	QB	SO	14	129	822	208	614	234	1,592	363	2,206	6.08	157.5
93 Randall Secky, Buffalo	QB	SO	12	59	115	268	-153	421	2,015	480	1,862	3.88	155.2
94 James MacPherson, Wake Forest	QB	SR	13	68	280	103	177	223	1,837	291	2,014	6.92	154.9
95 Chris Brown, Colorado	RB	JR	12	303	1,887	46	1841	0	0	303	1,841	6.08	153.4
96 Casey Kelly, New Mexico	QB	JR	14	116	396	171	225	314	1,904	430	2,129	4.95	152.1
97 Troy Nunes, Syracuse	QB	SR	9	51	175	151	24	198	1,337	249	1,361	5.47	151.2
98 Elliot Jacobs, Arkansas St.	QB	SO	13	82	343	150	193	258	1,751	340	1,944	5.72	149.5
99 Brandon Kirsch, Purdue	QB	FR	10	72	468	45	423	134	1,067	206	1,490	7.23	149
100 Craig Candeto, Navy	QB	JR	11	177	908	133	775	103	843	280	1,618	5.78	147.1

2002 Division I-A Team Leaders

Pass Efficiency Defense

Rank, School	G	Att	Com	Pct	Int	IPct	Yds	Yds/Att	TD	TDPct	Rating	W	L	T
1 Miami (Fla.)	13	353	163	46.18	12	3.4	1,556	4.41	8	2.27	83.91	12	1	0
2 TCU	12	406	158	38.92	22	5.42	2,105	5.18	16	3.94	84.62	10	2	0
3 Kansas St.	13	418	191	45.69	20	4.78	2,333	5.58	11	2.63	91.7	11	2	0
4 Southern Miss.	13	379	177	46.7	16	4.22	2,195	5.79	6	1.58	92.13	7	6	0
5 LSU	13	361	163	45.15	17	4.71	1,985	5.5	13	3.6	93.85	8	5	0
6 Oregon St.	13	456	222	48.68	20	4.39	2,591	5.68	10	2.19	94.89	8	5	0

Rank, School	G	Att	Com	Pct	Int	IPct	Yds	Yds/Att	TD	TDPct	Rating	W	L	T
7 Texas	13	400	192	48	22	5.5	2,147	5.37	17	4.25	96.11	11	2	0
8 Marshall	13	366	175	47.81	15	4.1	2,099	5.73	10	2.73	96.79	11	2	0
9 Oklahoma	14	432	206	47.69	24	5.56	2,594	6	13	3.01	96.96	12	2	0
10 Notre Dame	13	452	223	49.34	21	4.65	2,662	5.89	12	2.65	98.24	10	3	0
11 Tennessee	13	349	170	48.71	12	3.44	2,031	5.82	9	2.58	99.22	8	5	0
12 North Carolina St.	14	437	217	49.66	16	3.66	2,457	5.62	13	2.97	99.42	11	3	0
13 Tulane	13	436	229	52.52	22	5.05	2,494	5.72	12	2.75	99.54	8	5	0
14 Auburn	13	425	235	55.29	21	4.94	2,424	5.7	9	2.12	100.32	9	4	0
15 Pittsburgh	13	400	210	52.5	15	3.75	2,321	5.8	8	2	100.34	9	4	0
16 Alabama	13	374	185	49.47	18	4.81	2,303	6.16	11	2.94	101.31	10	3	0
17 Cincinnati	14	427	220	51.52	17	3.98	2,519	5.9	12	2.81	102.37	7	7	0
18 Connecticut	12	322	162	50.31	20	6.21	1,925	5.98	14	4.35	102.44	6	6	0
19 Southern California	13	454	226	49.78	17	3.74	2,623	5.78	16	3.52	102.47	11	2	0
20 North Texas	13	368	200	54.35	16	4.35	2,232	6.07	8	2.17	103.73	8	5	0
21 Boise St.	13	529	274	51.8	19	3.59	3,008	5.69	20	3.78	104.86	12	1	0
22 Purdue	13	419	202	48.21	15	3.58	2,613	6.24	15	3.58	105.24	7	6	0
23 Brigham Young	12	377	196	51.99	18	4.77	2,483	6.59	9	2.39	105.65	5	7	0
24 South Fla.	11	400	210	52.5	22	5.5	2,439	6.1	17	4.25	106.74	9	2	0
25 Boston College	13	373	201	53.89	15	4.02	2,237	6	12	3.22	106.85	9	4	0
26 Virginia Tech	14	443	230	51.92	24	5.42	2,991	6.75	14	3.16	108.21	10	4	0
27 Nebraska	14	459	231	50.33	13	2.83	3,014	6.57	12	2.61	108.42	7	7	0
28 Florida	13	362	185	51.1	7	1.93	2,111	5.83	14	3.87	108.98	8	5	0
29 Georgia Tech	13	440	235	53.41	11	2.5	2,874	6.53	11	2.5	111.52	7	6	0
30 Hawaii	14	495	253	51.11	18	3.64	3,168	6.4	21	4.24	111.59	10	4	0
31 Colorado	14	453	254	56.07	15	3.31	2,739	6.05	16	3.53	111.92	9	5	0
32 Ohio St.	14	546	315	57.69	18	3.3	3,404	6.23	14	2.56	111.94	14	0	0
33 Troy St.	12	328	171	52.13	9	2.74	2,059	6.28	13	3.96	112.42	4	8	0
34 Georgia	14	410	226	55.12	16	3.9	2,653	6.47	14	3.41	112.92	13	1	0
35 Louisville	13	427	205	48.01	9	2.11	2,690	6.3	21	4.92	112.93	7	6	0
36 Maryland	14	444	251	56.53	18	4.05	2,942	6.63	12	2.7	112.97	11	3	0
37 Iowa	13	535	300	56.07	20	3.74	3,554	6.64	15	2.8	113.68	11	2	0
38 Bowling Green	12	398	214	53.77	12	3.02	2,537	6.37	15	3.77	113.75	9	3	0
39 Michigan	13	440	236	53.64	16	3.64	2,919	6.63	17	3.86	114.8	10	3	0
40 Washington St.	13	535	305	57.01	17	3.18	3,318	6.2	20	3.74	115.08	10	3	0
41 Texas A&M	12	401	229	57.11	16	3.99	2,490	6.21	17	4.24	115.27	6	6	0
42 Western Mich.	12	362	195	53.87	14	3.87	2,154	5.95	21	5.8	115.29	4	8	0
43 UCLA	13	432	217	50.23	17	3.94	2,967	6.87	20	4.63	115.3	8	5	0
44 Iowa St.	14	426	242	56.81	10	2.35	2,580	6.06	16	3.76	115.37	7	7	0
45 Minnesota	13	367	203	55.31	7	1.91	2,322	6.33	12	3.27	115.42	8	5	0
46 Utah	11	378	198	52.38	12	3.17	2,500	6.61	16	4.23	115.57	5	6	0
47 West Virginia	13	416	230	55.29	19	4.57	2,777	6.68	17	4.09	115.73	9	4	0
48 Arkansas	14	483	267	55.28	19	3.93	3,283	6.8	17	3.52	116.14	9	5	0
49 Mississippi	13	349	181	51.86	18	5.16	2,435	6.98	17	4.87	116.27	7	6	0
50 Memphis	12	336	202	60.12	12	3.57	1,989	5.92	14	4.17	116.43	3	9	0
51 Penn St.	13	454	288	63.44	20	4.41	2,799	6.17	15	3.3	117.28	9	4	0
52 Air Force	13	370	210	56.76	12	3.24	2,584	6.98	10	2.7	117.9	8	5	0
53 Colorado St.	14	444	259	58.33	14	3.15	2,881	6.49	16	3.6	118.39	10	4	0
54 Arizona St.	14	487	243	49.9	22	4.52	3,420	7.02	28	5.75	118.83	8	6	0
55 Northern Ill.	12	428	243	56.78	21	4.91	3,059	7.15	17	3.97	120.13	8	4	0
56 Illinois	12	404	227	56.19	8	1.98	2,764	6.84	13	3.22	120.33	5	7	0
57 Michigan St.	12	334	165	49.4	13	3.89	2,266	6.78	22	6.59	120.34	4	8	0
58 Mississippi St.	12	282	140	49.65	14	4.96	1,847	6.55	22	7.8	120.43	3	9	0
59 UCF	12	380	216	56.84	13	3.42	2,449	6.44	19	5	120.59	7	5	0
60 Oklahoma St.	13	480	263	54.79	12	2.5	3,271	6.81	20	4.17	120.79	8	5	0
61 Florida St.	14	465	249	53.55	16	3.44	3,293	7.08	21	4.52	121.01	9	5	0
62 Clemson	13	389	233	59.9	21	5.4	2,564	6.59	20	5.14	121.44	7	6	0
63 Toledo	14	426	248	58.22	19	4.46	2,984	7	18	4.23	122.06	9	5	0
64 New Mexico	14	452	244	53.98	15	3.32	3,051	6.75	25	5.53	122.32	7	7	0
65 Wisconsin	14	432	237	54.86	22	5.09	3,139	7.27	22	5.09	122.56	8	6	0
66 Virginia	14	433	262	60.51	15	3.46	3,020	6.97	14	3.23	122.83	9	5	0
67 South Carolina	12	355	210	59.15	9	2.54	2,243	6.32	17	4.79	123.01	5	7	0
68 Kentucky	12	369	174	47.15	10	2.71	2,723	7.38	23	6.23	124.34	7	5	0
69 Fresno St.	14	460	254	55.22	19	4.13	3,432	7.46	21	4.57	124.68	9	5	0
70 Tulsa	12	342	201	58.77	13	3.8	2,429	7.1	15	4.39	125.33	1	11	0
71 Texas Tech	14	472	263	55.72	16	3.39	3,354	7.11	26	5.51	126.79	9	5	0
72 Arkansas St.	13	316	183	57.91	16	5.06	2,293	7.26	19	6.01	128.57	6	7	0
73 UAB	12	362	204	56.35	15	4.14	2,738	7.56	19	5.25	128.97	5	7	0
74 Washington	13	446	249	55.83	16	3.59	3,373	7.56	23	5.16	129.17	7	6	0
75 Arizona	12	368	214	58.15	7	1.9	2,692	7.32	15	4.08	129.29	4	8	0
76 Rutgers	12	333	171	51.35	11	3.3	2,376	7.14	25	7.51	129.5	1	11	0
77 Temple	12	356	210	58.99	11	3.09	2,488	6.99	20	5.62	130.07	4	8	0
78 California	12	435	253	58.16	15	3.45	3,346	7.69	20	4.6	131.09	7	5	0
79 Stanford	11	364	204	56.04	16	4.4	2,772	7.62	22	6.04	131.12	2	9	0
80 UNLV	12	389	219	56.3	9	2.31	2,816	7.24	22	5.66	131.14	5	7	0
81 Wake Forest	13	413	242	58.6	13	3.15	3,016	7.3	22	5.33	131.23	7	6	0
82 La.-Lafayette	12	305	159	52.13	8	2.62	2,375	7.79	18	5.9	131.74	3	9	0
83 Kent St.	12	344	209	60.76	9	2.62	2,423	7.04	18	5.23	132	3	9	0
84 Duke	12	405	245	60.49	12	2.96	3,056	7.55	18	4.44	132.62	2	10	0
85 New Mexico St.	12	339	210	61.95	7	2.06	2,412	7.12	16	4.72	133.11	7	5	0
86 San Diego St.	13	435	243	55.86	14	3.22	3,116	7.16	31	7.13	133.15	4	9	0
87 Miami (Ohio)	12	424	251	59.2	13	3.07	3,276	7.73	21	4.95	134.31	7	5	0
88 Nevada	12	358	195	54.47	9	2.51	2,899	8.1	19	5.31	135.01	5	7	0
89 Ohio	12	360	209	58.06	14	3.89	2,689	7.47	24	6.67	135.07	4	8	0
90 East Caro.	12	364	196	53.85	10	2.75	2,863	7.87	23	6.32	135.23	4	8	0

Rank, School	G	Att	Com	Pct	Int	IPct	Yds	Yds/Att	TD	TDPct	Rating	W	L	T
91 Missouri	12	426	253	59.39	12	2.82	3,391	7.96	19	4.46	135.35	5	7	0
92 Southern Methodist	12	370	200	54.05	8	2.16	2,932	7.92	22	5.95	135.96	3	9	0
93 Buffalo	12	353	204	57.79	14	3.97	2,731	7.74	23	6.52	136.36	1	11	0
94 Indiana	12	335	202	60.3	8	2.39	2,322	6.93	23	6.87	136.4	3	9	0
95 Vanderbilt	12	337	216	64.09	6	1.78	2,630	7.8	11	3.26	136.87	2	10	0
96 Utah St.	11	332	178	53.61	7	2.11	2,599	7.83	24	6.63	137.01	4	7	0
97 Ball St.	12	390	246	63.08	10	2.56	2,834	7.27	22	5.64	137.63	6	6	0
98 Rice	11	363	222	61.16	8	2.2	2,663	7.34	23	6.34	139.32	4	7	0
99 San Jose St.	13	475	275	57.89	23	4.84	3,906	8.22	32	6.74	139.52	6	7	0
100 Houston	12	394	220	55.84	10	2.54	3,232	8.2	24	6.09	139.73	5	7	0
101 Middle Tenn.	12	347	213	61.38	10	2.88	2,749	7.92	19	5.48	140.25	4	8	0
102 Oregon	13	475	272	57.26	18	3.79	3,785	7.97	35	7.37	140.97	7	6	0
103 La.-Monroe	12	355	213	60	10	2.82	2,860	8.06	22	6.2	142.49	3	9	0
104 Army	12	293	181	61.77	6	2.05	2,195	7.49	20	6.83	143.16	1	11	0
105 Akron	12	340	214	62.94	9	2.65	2,726	8.02	20	5.88	144.37	4	8	0
106 Central Mich.	12	393	249	63.36	12	3.05	3,173	8.07	23	5.85	144.43	4	8	0
107 Baylor	12	382	235	61.52	8	2.09	2,900	7.59	30	7.85	147	3	9	0
108 Wyoming	12	406	262	64.53	9	2.22	3,421	8.43	21	5.17	147.91	2	10	0
109 Kansas	12	302	167	55.3	12	3.97	2,594	8.59	27	8.94	149.01	2	10	0
110 UTEP	12	352	199	56.53	10	2.84	2,951	8.38	30	8.52	149.36	2	10	0
111 Louisiana Tech	12	383	238	62.14	5	1.31	3,173	8.28	24	6.27	149.76	4	8	0
112 Syracuse	12	384	223	58.07	10	2.6	3,645	9.49	22	5.73	151.53	4	8	0
113 Idaho	12	354	208	58.76	8	2.26	3,293	9.3	21	5.93	152	2	10	0
114 North Carolina	12	306	168	54.9	6	1.96	2,775	9.07	24	7.84	153.04	3	9	0
115 Northwestern	12	239	144	60.25	8	3.35	2,265	9.48	20	8.37	160.83	3	9	0
116 Navy	12	287	189	65.85	5	1.74	2,643	9.21	24	8.36	167.37	2	10	0
117 Eastern Mich.	12	281	179	63.7	4	1.42	2,710	9.64	28	9.96	174.75	3	9	0

Fumbles Recovered

Rank, School	No.	Rank, School	No.
1 Virginia	22	39 Tennessee	13
2 California	21	39 San Diego St.	13
2 Tulane	21	39 Rice	13
2 Wake Forest	21	39 Oregon St.	13
5 TCU	20	39 New Mexico	13
6 Southern California	19	39 Kansas St.	13
7 Arizona St.	18	39 Duke	13
7 La.-Lafayette	18	53 Boise St.	12
7 Syracuse	18	53 Washington	12
7 Pittsburgh	18	53 Utah	12
11 Arkansas St.	17	53 South Carolina	12
11 Cincinnati	17	53 Oklahoma	12
11 Arkansas	17	53 Ohio St.	12
11 Iowa St.	17	53 Notre Dame	12
11 Boston College	17	53 Missouri	12
16 Akron	16	53 Miami (Fla.)	12
16 Colorado St.	16	53 Kentucky	12
16 Florida St.	16	53 Connecticut	12
16 Navy	16	53 Buffalo	12
16 Troy St.	16	65 Arizona	11
21 Alabama	15	65 Georgia Tech	11
21 Bowling Green	15	65 Middle Tenn.	11
21 Colorado	15	65 Utah St.	11
21 North Carolina St.	15	65 Southern Miss.	11
21 West Virginia	15	65 Penn St.	11
21 Tulsa	15	65 Ohio	11
21 San Jose St.	15	65 Mississippi	11
21 Georgia	15	65 Louisiana Tech	11
29 UCF	14	65 Iowa	11
29 Minnesota	14	65 Illinois	11
29 Northwestern	14	65 East Caro.	11
29 Army	14	65 Auburn	11
29 Air Force	14	65 Ball St.	11
29 Texas A&M	14	79 UAB	10
29 South Fla.	14	79 La.-Monroe	10
29 Rutgers	14	79 New Mexico St.	10
29 North Texas	14	79 Nevada	10
29 Miami (Ohio)	14	79 Michigan	10
39 Fresno St.	13	79 Memphis	10
39 Houston	13	79 Florida	10
39 Temple	13	79 Baylor	10
39 Wyoming	13	79 Brigham Young	10
39 Wisconsin	13	88 Central Mich.	9
39 Virginia Tech	13	88 UNLV	9
39 Texas	13	88 Hawaii	9

Rank, School	No.	Rank, School	No.
88 Indiana	9	100 Maryland	8
88 Southern Methodist	9	100 LSU	8
88 Toledo	9	107 Eastern Mich.	7
88 Western Mich.	9	107 Kent St.	7
88 Stanford	9	107 Northern Ill.	7
88 Purdue	9	107 Marshall	7
88 North Carolina	9	107 Louisville	7
88 Mississippi St.	9	112 Idaho	6
88 Clemson	9	112 Oregon	6
100 UCLA	8	112 Michigan St.	6
100 Washington St.	8	115 Kansas	5
100 UTEP	8	115 Vanderbilt	5
100 Oklahoma St.	8	117 Texas Tech	3
100 Nebraska	8		

Fumbles Lost

Rank, School	Fumbles Lost	Rank, School	Fumbles Lost
1 Missouri	5	28 Wake Forest	10
2 Arkansas	6	28 Air Force	10
2 Oklahoma	6	28 South Fla.	10
2 Texas	6	28 Ohio St.	10
2 Wyoming	6	28 Minnesota	10
2 West Virginia	6	28 Michigan	10
2 Penn St.	6	28 Louisiana Tech	10
8 Boston College	7	28 Iowa St.	10
8 Buffalo	7	28 Idaho	10
8 Miami (Ohio)	7	28 Georgia Tech	10
8 Oklahoma St.	7	28 Duke	10
8 Bowling Green	7	28 Central Mich.	10
13 California	8	41 Arizona	11
13 Indiana	8	41 Cincinnati	11
13 Nevada	8	41 Kent St.	11
13 Stanford	8	41 Tulane	11
13 Southern California	8	41 Toledo	11
13 Oregon	8	41 Syracuse	11
13 Florida	8	41 Southern Methodist	11
13 Connecticut	8	41 South Carolina	11
21 Alabama	9	41 Pittsburgh	11
21 Wisconsin	9	41 Oregon St.	11
21 Michigan St.	9	41 New Mexico St.	11
21 Mississippi	9	41 Iowa	11
21 Texas A&M	9	41 Illinois	11
21 Kentucky	9	41 Florida St.	11
21 East Caro.	9	41 Colorado	11
28 Ball St.	10	56 Fresno St.	12

Fumbles Lost

Rank, School	Fumbles Lost
56 Nebraska	12
56 Eastern Mich.	12
56 Utah	12
56 Tulsa	12
56 Maryland	12
56 Miami (Fla.)	12
56 UCLA	12
64 Auburn	13
64 Western Mich.	13
64 Washington	13
64 Vanderbilt	13
64 Utah St.	13
64 Army	13
64 Northern Ill.	13
64 La.-Monroe	13
64 North Carolina St.	13
64 UNLV	13
64 Middle Tenn.	13
64 Kansas	13
64 Georgia	13
64 Baylor	13
78 Akron	14
78 Marshall	14
78 Brigham Young	14
78 Rice	14
78 Texas Tech	14
78 Virginia	14
78 TCU	14
78 Northwestern	14
86 UAB	15
86 Clemson	15

Rank, School	Fumbles Lost
86 Hawaii	15
86 Washington St.	15
86 Temple	15
86 La.-Lafayette	15
86 San Jose St.	15
86 Rutgers	15
86 Notre Dame	15
86 Colorado St.	15
86 Boise St.	15
97 UCF	16
97 North Carolina	16
97 Memphis	16
97 Mississippi St.	16
97 New Mexico	16
97 Troy St.	16
97 UTEP	16
97 Tennessee	16
97 Ohio	16
106 Arkansas St.	17
106 San Diego St.	17
106 Houston	17
106 North Texas	17
110 Kansas St.	18
110 LSU	18
110 Virginia Tech	18
113 Purdue	19
113 Southern Miss.	19
115 Arizona St.	20
115 Louisville	20
117 Navy	25

Kickoff Returns

Rank, School	G	Ret	Yds	TD	Avg	W	L	T
1 Iowa	13	37	929	2	25.11	11	2	0
2 North Carolina St.	14	37	923	3	24.95	11	3	0
3 San Jose St.	13	57	1,395	2	24.47	6	7	0
4 California	12	43	1,052	1	24.47	7	5	0
5 Clemson	13	52	1,264	1	24.31	7	6	0
6 Northwestern	12	51	1,229	1	24.1	3	9	0
7 LSU	13	38	914	0	24.05	8	5	0
8 Oregon	13	44	1,048	0	23.82	7	6	0
9 Texas	13	20	476	0	23.8	11	2	0
10 Southern Methodist	12	51	1,204	0	23.61	3	9	0
11 Kentucky	12	49	1,154	2	23.55	7	5	0
12 TCU	12	32	742	1	23.19	10	2	0
13 Boise St.	13	36	833	0	23.14	12	1	0
14 Tennessee	13	37	855	1	23.11	8	5	0
15 Notre Dame	13	38	877	1	23.08	10	3	0
16 Utah	11	26	599	0	23.04	5	6	0
17 Nevada	12	40	917	0	22.93	5	7	0
18 Colorado	14	28	641	0	22.89	9	5	0
19 Western Mich.	12	44	1,007	0	22.89	4	8	0
20 Mississippi St.	12	46	1,051	0	22.85	3	9	0
21 Akron	12	53	1,209	0	22.81	4	8	0
22 Tulane	13	41	932	1	22.73	8	5	0
23 Maryland	14	29	659	0	22.72	11	3	0
24 Kansas St.	13	21	476	1	22.67	11	2	0
25 North Texas	13	30	676	0	22.53	8	5	0
26 South Fla.	11	29	651	1	22.45	9	2	0
27 Nebraska	14	48	1,071	0	22.31	7	7	0
28 Virginia	14	49	1,083	1	22.1	9	5	0
29 Illinois	12	30	663	1	22.1	5	7	0
30 UAB	12	55	1,211	0	22.02	5	7	0
31 Louisville	13	51	1,120	2	21.96	7	6	0
32 Pittsburgh	13	40	878	0	21.95	9	4	0
33 Northern Ill.	12	42	921	1	21.93	8	4	0
34 Oregon St.	13	40	866	0	21.65	8	5	0
35 UCLA	13	46	991	0	21.54	8	5	0
36 Hawaii	14	59	1,264	0	21.42	10	4	0
37 Louisiana Tech	12	52	1,114	0	21.42	4	8	0
38 Florida St.	14	43	921	1	21.42	9	5	0
39 Idaho	12	58	1,235	0	21.29	2	10	0
40 Air Force	13	33	695	0	21.06	8	5	0
41 Brigham Young	12	36	756	0	21	5	7	0

Rank, School	G	Ret	Yds	TD	Avg	W	L	T
42 Rutgers	12	53	1,112	2	20.98	1	11	0
43 Miami (Fla.)	13	38	797	0	20.97	12	1	0
44 Missouri	12	48	1,003	0	20.9	5	7	0
45 Arkansas	14	42	872	0	20.76	9	5	0
46 Syracuse	12	54	1,118	0	20.7	4	8	0
47 Michigan	13	32	661	0	20.66	10	3	0
48 Temple	12	39	803	1	20.59	4	8	0
49 Southern Miss.	13	46	944	0	20.52	7	6	0
50 Virginia Tech	14	33	677	0	20.52	10	4	0
51 Houston	12	54	1,106	0	20.48	5	7	0
52 Vanderbilt	12	50	1,021	0	20.42	2	10	0
53 Arizona St.	12	61	1,239	0	20.31	8	6	0
54 San Diego St.	13	46	931	0	20.24	4	9	0
55 Ohio St.	14	37	747	0	20.19	14	0	0
56 Navy	12	59	1,187	0	20.12	2	10	0
57 Georgia	14	38	764	1	20.11	13	1	0
58 Memphis	12	48	964	0	20.08	3	9	0
59 West Virginia	13	41	823	0	20.07	9	4	0
60 Oklahoma	14	29	582	0	20.07	12	2	0
61 Toledo	14	60	1,198	0	19.97	9	5	0
62 Colorado St.	14	37	738	0	19.95	10	4	0
63 Bowling Green	12	41	814	0	19.85	9	3	0
64 Indiana	12	56	1,109	0	19.8	3	9	0
65 Oklahoma St.	13	41	811	0	19.78	8	5	0
66 UTEP	12	64	1,265	0	19.77	2	10	0
67 Arkansas St.	12	46	909	0	19.76	6	7	0
68 Texas A&M	12	36	711	0	19.75	6	6	0
69 Miami (Ohio)	12	47	927	0	19.72	7	5	0
70 South Carolina	12	43	844	1	19.63	5	7	0
71 Utah St.	11	52	1,019	0	19.6	4	7	0
72 New Mexico	14	41	803	0	19.59	7	7	0
73 Army	12	79	1,546	0	19.57	1	11	0
74 Ohio	12	57	1,115	0	19.56	4	8	0
75 Kansas	12	52	1,016	1	19.54	2	10	0
76 Georgia Tech	13	43	839	0	19.51	7	6	0
77 North Carolina	12	52	1,012	0	19.46	3	9	0
78 Alabama	13	29	563	0	19.41	10	3	0
79 Wyoming	12	51	988	0	19.37	2	10	0
80 Wisconsin	14	44	852	0	19.36	8	6	0
81 Tulsa	12	52	1,001	0	19.25	1	11	0
82 Boston College	13	46	883	0	19.2	9	4	0
83 Cincinnati	14	46	879	0	19.11	7	7	0
84 Connecticut	12	30	572	0	19.07	6	6	0
85 New Mexico St.	12	44	838	0	19.05	7	5	0
86 Michigan St.	12	55	1,045	0	19	4	8	0
87 Washington St.	13	42	797	1	18.98	10	3	0
88 UNLV	12	46	872	0	18.96	5	7	0
89 East Caro.	12	49	928	0	18.94	4	8	0
90 UCF	12	39	738	0	18.92	7	5	0
91 Buffalo	12	48	905	0	18.85	1	11	0
92 Rice	11	33	619	0	18.76	4	7	0
93 La.-Lafayette	12	47	880	0	18.72	3	9	0
94 Minnesota	13	39	728	0	18.67	8	5	0
95 Washington	13	39	726	0	18.62	7	6	0
96 Central Mich.	12	48	891	0	18.56	4	8	0
97 La.-Monroe	12	51	944	0	18.51	3	9	0
98 Fresno St.	14	46	850	0	18.48	9	5	0
99 Penn St.	13	26	480	0	18.46	9	4	0
100 Stanford	11	44	803	0	18.25	2	9	0
101 Mississippi	13	50	910	0	18.2	7	6	0
102 Florida	13	34	618	0	18.18	8	5	0
103 Ball St.	12	49	886	0	18.08	6	6	0
104 Texas Tech	14	51	914	1	17.92	9	5	0
105 Auburn	13	35	622	0	17.77	9	4	0
106 Iowa St.	14	51	905	0	17.75	7	7	0
107 Wake Forest	13	38	673	0	17.71	7	6	0
108 Arizona	12	34	601	0	17.68	4	8	0
109 Purdue	13	36	630	0	17.5	7	6	0
109 Southern California	13	26	455	0	17.5	11	2	0
111 Eastern Mich.	12	68	1,171	0	17.22	3	9	0
112 Kent St.	12	53	911	0	17.19	3	9	0
113 Duke	12	40	685	0	17.13	2	10	0
114 Middle Tenn.	12	40	660	0	16.5	4	8	0
115 Baylor	12	64	1,043	0	16.3	3	9	0
116 Troy St.	12	37	588	0	15.89	4	8	0
117 Marshall	13	43	676	0	15.72	11	2	0

Net Punting

Rank, School	G	Punts	Yds	Avg	Ret	Rtyd	NetAvg	W	L	T
1 Brigham Young	12	52	2,427	46.67	21	207	42.69	5	7	0
2 Colorado	14	72	3,373	46.85	37	381	41.56	9	5	0
3 Kentucky	12	71	3,143	44.27	33	296	40.1	7	5	0
4 Vanderbilt	12	67	2,892	43.16	34	295	38.76	2	10	0
5 Nebraska	14	75	3,156	42.08	31	291	38.2	7	7	0
6 South Carolina	12	53	2,181	41.15	22	158	38.17	5	7	0
7 Syracuse	12	69	2,707	39.23	32	79	38.09	4	8	0
8 Tennessee	13	68	2,883	42.4	30	294	38.07	8	5	0
9 Maryland	14	55	2,373	43.15	28	297	37.75	11	3	0
10 Oregon	13	77	3,250	42.21	43	358	37.56	7	6	0
11 UCF	12	40	1,673	41.83	20	172	37.53	7	5	0
12 LSU	13	69	2,869	41.58	35	283	37.48	8	5	0
13 Ohio St.	14	61	2,697	44.21	33	423	37.28	14	0	0
14 Ohio	12	55	2,258	41.05	27	208	37.27	4	8	0
15 North Texas	13	88	3,673	41.74	37	397	37.23	8	5	0
16 Kansas St.	13	55	2,186	39.75	27	146	37.09	11	2	0
17 Idaho	12	56	2,338	41.75	35	261	37.09	2	10	0
18 Iowa	13	53	2,093	39.49	31	134	36.96	11	2	0
19 Missouri	12	67	2,844	42.45	29	371	36.91	5	7	0
20 Michigan	13	74	3,077	41.58	41	358	36.74	10	3	0
21 Marshall	13	46	1,926	41.87	18	243	36.59	11	2	0
22 Southern California	13	65	2,632	40.49	26	258	36.52	11	2	0
23 Auburn	13	56	2,351	41.98	24	311	36.43	9	4	0
24 UCLA	13	74	3,021	40.82	32	329	36.38	8	5	0
25 Pittsburgh	13	76	3,166	41.66	39	402	36.37	9	4	0
26 South Fla.	11	76	3,043	40.04	31	290	36.22	9	2	0
27 Arizona St.	14	82	3,372	41.12	46	407	36.16	8	6	0
28 Nevada	12	64	2,579	40.3	38	266	36.14	5	7	0
29 Texas A&M	12	68	2,931	43.1	36	477	36.09	6	6	0
30 Georgia	14	64	2,708	42.31	33	400	36.06	13	1	0
31 New Mexico	14	82	3,261	39.77	37	313	35.95	7	7	0
32 Houston	12	62	2,411	38.89	30	186	35.89	5	7	0
33 Middle Tenn.	12	63	2,599	41.25	37	342	35.83	4	8	0
34 Georgia Tech	13	74	2,956	39.95	37	306	35.81	7	6	0
35 Tulane	13	74	3,106	41.97	39	461	35.74	8	5	0
36 Penn St.	13	52	2,137	41.1	28	287	35.58	9	4	0
37 Connecticut	12	79	3,064	38.78	39	264	35.44	6	6	0
38 TCU	12	80	3,098	38.73	35	265	35.41	10	2	0
39 Southern Miss.	13	81	3,354	41.41	44	487	35.4	7	6	0
40 Washington St.	13	50	2,053	41.06	19	288	35.3	10	3	0
41 Kansas	12	85	3,489	41.05	41	494	35.24	2	10	0
42 La.-Lafayette	12	78	3,108	39.85	39	360	35.23	3	9	0
43 Navy	12	48	1,896	39.5	20	206	35.21	2	10	0
44 Notre Dame	13	79	3,069	38.85	33	288	35.2	10	3	0
45 East Caro.	12	75	3,177	42.36	43	539	35.17	4	8	0
46 Oklahoma	14	78	2,919	37.42	28	186	35.04	12	2	0
47 Mississippi	13	71	2,982	42	45	501	34.94	7	6	0
48 Wake Forest	13	61	2,458	40.3	32	327	34.93	7	6	0
49 Utah	11	67	2,730	40.75	39	393	34.88	5	6	0
50 Rutgers	12	93	3,707	39.86	51	466	34.85	1	11	0
51 Alabama	13	60	2,412	40.2	40	326	34.77	10	3	0
52 Oklahoma St.	13	68	2,820	41.47	37	456	34.76	8	5	0
53 Colorado St.	14	54	2,135	39.54	20	262	34.69	10	4	0
54 Oregon St.	13	77	3,016	39.17	31	348	34.65	8	5	0
55 Southern Methodist	12	71	2,673	37.65	40	225	34.48	3	9	0
56 Eastern Mich.	12	65	2,689	41.37	38	451	34.43	3	9	0
57 Wyoming	12	60	2,493	41.55	32	428	34.42	2	10	0
58 Ball St.	12	61	2,461	40.34	32	362	34.41	6	6	0
59 Michigan St.	12	66	2,668	40.42	34	402	34.33	4	8	0
60 Texas	13	72	2,797	38.85	30	328	34.29	11	2	0
61 San Diego St.	13	65	2,549	39.22	34	325	34.22	4	9	0
62 Virginia Tech	14	66	2,592	39.27	30	338	34.15	10	4	0
63 Miami (Ohio)	12	53	2,148	40.53	31	338	34.15	7	5	0
64 San Jose St.	13	58	2,214	38.17	25	234	34.14	6	7	0
65 Iowa St.	14	71	2,793	39.34	36	370	34.13	7	7	0
66 Buffalo	12	86	3,357	39.03	48	425	34.09	1	11	0
67 Purdue	13	66	2,485	37.65	28	235	34.09	7	6	0
68 Utah St.	11	65	2,500	38.46	31	294	33.94	4	7	0
69 Hawaii	14	50	2,148	42.96	25	453	33.9	10	4	0
70 Boston College	13	56	2,081	37.16	31	190	33.77	9	4	0
71 Washington	13	58	2,210	38.1	24	253	33.74	7	6	0
72 Indiana	12	59	2,214	37.53	27	228	33.66	3	9	0
73 Wisconsin	14	77	2,780	36.1	28	194	33.58	8	6	0
74 Air Force	13	48	1,832	38.17	16	225	33.48	8	5	0
75 Kent St.	12	62	2,429	39.18	32	355	33.45	3	9	0
76 Minnesota	13	60	2,282	38.03	32	275	33.45	8	5	0
77 Miami (Fla.)	13	63	2,425	38.49	31	322	33.38	12	1	0
78 Bowling Green	12	51	2,000	39.22	19	298	33.37	9	3	0
79 Florida St.	14	76	2,932	38.58	45	399	33.33	9	5	0
80 Fresno St.	14	78	3,077	39.45	43	484	33.24	9	5	0
81 UTEP	12	75	2,903	38.71	33	422	33.08	2	10	0
82 Stanford	11	58	2,306	39.76	34	392	33	2	9	0

Rank, School	G	Punts	Yds	Avg	Ret	Rtyd	NetAvg	W	L	T
83 Louisville	13	83	3,010	36.27	32	275	32.95	7	6	0
84 Illinois	12	57	2,156	37.82	35	279	32.93	5	7	0
85 Northwestern	12	68	2,737	40.25	42	511	32.74	3	9	0
86 Arkansas	14	74	2,729	36.88	32	318	32.58	9	5	0
87 Arkansas St.	13	65	2,469	37.98	27	358	32.48	6	7	0
88 Duke	12	70	2,651	37.87	42	378	32.47	2	10	0
89 UNLV	12	70	2,680	38.29	34	411	32.41	5	7	0
90 UAB	12	79	3,167	40.09	44	630	32.11	5	7	0
91 North Carolina St.	14	61	2,268	37.18	34	311	32.08	11	3	0
92 Memphis	12	64	2,475	38.67	31	426	32.02	3	9	0
93 Texas Tech	14	49	1,867	38.1	20	303	31.92	9	5	0
94 Tulsa	12	77	3,016	39.17	45	567	31.81	1	11	0
95 New Mexico St.	12	44	1,597	36.3	17	212	31.48	7	5	0
96 Rice	11	60	2,375	39.58	34	490	31.42	4	7	0
97 Temple	12	63	2,281	36.21	33	303	31.4	4	8	0
98 North Carolina	12	68	2,451	36.04	36	317	31.38	3	9	0
99 Troy St.	12	76	2,871	37.78	39	487	31.37	4	8	0
100 Akron	12	49	1,868	38.12	30	331	31.37	4	8	0
101 Mississippi St.	12	71	2,932	41.3	45	706	31.35	3	9	0
102 Cincinnati	14	68	2,520	37.06	34	391	31.31	7	7	0
103 Arizona	12	69	2,501	36.25	38	361	31.01	4	8	0
104 Western Mich.	12	65	2,299	35.37	37	313	30.55	4	8	0
105 Louisiana Tech	12	66	2,412	36.55	35	411	30.32	4	8	0
106 Florida	13	76	2,745	36.12	36	443	30.29	8	5	0
107 Virginia	14	66	2,299	34.83	36	308	30.17	9	5	0
108 California	12	66	2,450	37.12	41	461	30.14	7	5	0
109 Toledo	14	46	1,612	35.04	22	226	30.13	9	5	0
110 Northern Ill.	12	65	2,443	37.58	33	505	29.82	8	4	0
111 Central Mich.	12	73	2,815	38.56	41	648	29.68	4	8	0
112 West Virginia	13	71	2,593	36.52	38	487	29.66	9	4	0
113 Clemson	13	65	2,340	36	41	413	29.65	7	6	0
114 La.-Monroe	12	88	3,052	34.68	50	530	28.66	3	9	0
115 Boise St.	13	36	1,254	34.83	24	247	27.97	12	1	0
116 Army	12	69	2,414	34.99	34	501	27.72	1	11	0
117 Baylor	12	86	2,991	34.78	45	706	26.57	3	9	0

Passing Offense

Rank, School	G	Att	Com	Int	Pct	Yds	YdsAtt	TD	Yds/Gm	IPct	YdCp	W	L	T
1 Texas Tech	14	770	515	15	66.88	5,444	7.07	50	388.9	1.95	10.57	9	5	0
2 Hawaii	14	731	407	26	55.68	5,406	7.4	35	386.1	3.56	13.28	10	4	0
3 Marshall	13	575	383	15	66.61	4,804	8.35	35	369.5	2.61	12.54	11	2	0
4 Washington	13	621	372	14	59.9	4,501	7.25	28	346.2	2.25	12.1	7	6	0
5 San Diego St.	13	584	352	10	60.27	4,302	7.37	24	330.9	1.71	12.22	4	9	0
6 UCF	12	442	270	17	61.09	3,837	8.68	31	319.8	3.85	14.21	7	5	0
7 Utah St.	11	487	258	16	52.98	3,388	6.96	21	308	3.29	13.13	4	7	0
8 Southern California	13	494	313	10	63.36	3,988	8.07	33	306.8	2.02	12.74	11	2	0
9 Arizona St.	14	558	306	16	54.84	4,254	7.62	31	303.9	2.87	13.9	8	6	0
10 Louisiana Tech	12	527	305	19	57.87	3,633	6.89	19	302.8	3.61	11.91	4	8	0
11 Nevada	12	477	292	17	61.22	3,556	7.45	27	296.3	3.56	12.18	5	7	0
12 Boise St.	13	390	251	8	64.36	3,808	9.76	32	292.9	2.05	15.17	12	1	0
13 Washington St.	13	458	273	14	59.61	3,805	8.31	30	292.7	3.06	13.94	10	3	0
14 Arizona	12	430	246	14	57.21	3,477	8.09	17	289.8	3.26	14.13	4	8	0
15 Idaho	12	512	302	18	58.98	3,475	6.79	23	289.6	3.52	11.51	2	10	0
16 Miami (Fla.)	13	432	241	13	55.79	3,695	8.55	32	284.2	3.01	15.33	12	1	0
17 Illinois	12	454	258	16	56.83	3,388	7.46	26	282.3	3.52	13.13	5	7	0
18 Wyoming	12	471	279	18	59.24	3,357	7.13	25	279.8	3.82	12.03	2	10	0
19 Miami (Ohio)	12	446	278	13	62.33	3,331	7.47	25	277.6	2.91	11.98	7	5	0
20 Florida	13	517	295	18	57.06	3,519	6.81	22	270.7	3.48	11.93	8	5	0
21 Texas A&M	12	425	219	19	51.53	3,216	7.57	25	268	4.47	14.68	6	6	0
22 North Carolina	12	433	237	14	54.73	3,199	7.39	21	266.6	3.23	13.5	3	9	0
23 Mississippi	13	486	283	15	58.23	3,437	7.07	21	264.4	3.09	12.14	7	6	0
24 San Jose St.	13	483	290	17	60.04	3,424	7.09	24	263.4	3.52	11.81	6	7	0
25 Oklahoma St.	13	454	243	15	53.52	3,414	7.52	32	262.6	3.3	14.05	8	5	0
25 Oregon St.	13	468	221	14	47.22	3,414	7.29	26	262.6	2.99	15.45	8	5	0
27 Brigham Young	12	501	277	21	55.29	3,129	6.25	16	260.8	4.19	11.3	5	7	0
28 Cincinnati	14	485	264	22	54.43	3,649	7.52	22	260.6	4.54	13.82	7	7	0
29 Toledo	14	443	309	9	69.75	3,611	8.15	25	257.9	2.03	11.69	9	5	0
30 Western Mich.	12	467	244	22	52.25	3,073	6.58	18	256.1	4.71	12.59	4	8	0
31 Purdue	13	452	271	15	59.96	3,324	7.35	21	255.7	3.32	12.27	7	6	0
32 South Fla.	11	427	241	5	56.44	2,772	6.49	20	252	1.17	11.5	9	2	0
33 Indiana	12	446	228	21	51.12	3,020	6.77	18	251.7	4.71	13.25	3	9	0
34 Texas	13	404	240	12	59.41	3,251	8.05	26	250.1	2.97	13.55	11	2	0
35 North Carolina St.	14	447	273	11	61.07	3,468	7.76	20	247.7	2.46	12.7	11	3	0
36 California	12	428	230	10	53.74	2,971	6.94	31	247.6	2.34	12.92	7	5	0
37 Akron	12	404	265	12	65.59	2,962	7.33	18	246.8	2.97	11.18	4	8	0
38 Eastern Mich.	12	441	248	22	56.24	2,961	6.71	23	246.8	4.99	11.94	3	9	0
39 Georgia	14	445	257	10	57.75	3,435	7.72	28	245.4	2.25	13.37	13	1	0
40 Clemson	13	462	268	13	58.01	3,157	6.83	16	242.8	2.81	11.78	7	6	0
41 Fresno St.	14	483	266	14	55.07	3,382	7	23	241.6	2.9	12.71	9	5	0
42 Memphis	12	452	241	20	53.32	2,868	6.35	24	239	4.42	11.9	3	9	0
43 Iowa St.	14	454	250	18	55.07	3,308	7.29	16	236.3	3.96	13.23	7	7	0
44 Michigan	13	472	259	7	54.87	3,026	6.41	21	232.8	1.48	11.68	10	3	0
45 Northwestern	12	451	261	14	57.87	2,784	6.17	9	232	3.1	10.67	3	9	0

Rank, School	G	Att	Com	Int	Pct	Yds	YdsAtt	TD	Yds/Gm	IPct	YdCp	W	L	T
46 Boston College	13	414	243	17	58.7	3,011	7.27	18	231.6	4.11	12.39	9	4	0
47 Baylor	12	400	224	22	56	2,778	6.95	10	231.5	5.5	12.4	3	9	0
48 Virginia	14	448	306	8	68.3	3,222	7.19	32	230.1	1.79	10.53	9	5	0
49 Bowling Green	12	398	227	11	57.04	2,758	6.93	27	229.8	2.76	12.15	9	3	0
50 UCLA	13	367	204	11	55.59	2,985	8.13	19	229.6	3	14.63	8	5	0
51 Michigan St.	12	377	208	17	55.17	2,743	7.28	24	228.6	4.51	13.19	4	8	0
52 La.-Lafayette	12	432	234	19	54.17	2,733	6.33	13	227.8	4.4	11.68	3	9	0
53 Oregon	13	412	214	11	51.94	2,959	7.18	26	227.6	2.67	13.83	7	6	0
54 Louisville	13	451	243	11	53.88	2,944	6.53	25	226.5	2.44	12.12	7	6	0
55 Connecticut	12	392	232	12	59.18	2,671	6.81	21	222.6	3.06	11.51	6	6	0
56 Houston	12	357	184	22	51.54	2,670	7.48	19	222.5	6.16	14.51	5	7	0
57 La.-Monroe	12	422	204	14	48.34	2,664	6.31	17	222	3.32	13.06	3	9	0
58 Mississippi St.	12	442	226	22	51.13	2,611	5.91	13	217.6	4.98	11.55	3	9	0
59 Pittsburgh	13	371	194	12	52.29	2,796	7.54	22	215.1	3.23	14.41	9	4	0
60 East Caro.	12	410	200	22	48.78	2,577	6.29	16	214.8	5.37	12.89	4	8	0
61 Georgia Tech	13	435	239	20	54.94	2,744	6.31	15	211.1	4.6	11.48	7	6	0
62 Florida St.	14	419	217	10	51.79	2,955	7.05	27	211.1	2.39	13.62	9	5	0
63 Iowa	13	314	182	5	57.96	2,734	8.71	27	210.3	1.59	15.02	11	2	0
64 Utah	11	381	215	13	56.43	2,291	6.01	16	208.3	3.41	10.66	5	6	0
65 Tulane	13	438	245	10	55.94	2,646	6.04	20	203.5	2.28	10.8	8	5	0
66 Missouri	12	380	204	7	53.68	2,438	6.42	17	203.2	1.84	11.95	5	7	0
67 Tennessee	13	356	218	7	61.24	2,635	7.4	14	202.7	1.97	12.09	8	5	0
68 Oklahoma	14	419	242	11	57.76	2,828	6.75	28	202	2.63	11.69	12	2	0
69 Duke	12	386	206	13	53.37	2,399	6.22	18	199.9	3.37	11.65	2	10	0
70 Kentucky	12	350	195	6	55.71	2,387	6.82	24	198.9	1.71	12.24	7	5	0
71 UNLV	12	345	169	12	48.99	2,341	6.79	14	195.1	3.48	13.85	5	7	0
72 Penn St.	13	351	198	11	56.41	2,536	7.23	17	195.1	3.13	12.81	9	4	0
73 New Mexico St.	12	276	169	6	61.23	2,337	8.47	13	194.8	2.17	13.83	7	5	0
74 Tulsa	12	403	213	10	52.85	2,321	5.76	18	193.4	2.48	10.9	1	11	0
75 Maryland	14	324	179	13	55.25	2,668	8.23	15	190.6	4.01	14.91	11	3	0
76 Kansas	12	430	200	13	46.51	2,286	5.32	13	190.5	3.02	11.43	2	10	0
77 Alabama	13	310	174	9	56.13	2,473	7.98	12	190.2	2.9	14.21	10	3	0
78 Southern Miss.	13	371	186	11	50.13	2,451	6.61	11	188.5	2.96	13.18	7	6	0
79 Syracuse	12	333	174	15	52.25	2,252	6.76	12	187.7	4.5	12.94	4	8	0
80 UAB	12	347	169	9	48.7	2,214	6.38	15	184.5	2.59	13.1	5	7	0
81 Auburn	13	299	174	10	58.19	2,390	7.99	18	183.8	3.34	13.74	9	4	0
82 Minnesota	13	333	174	11	52.25	2,384	7.16	21	183.4	3.3	13.7	8	5	0
83 Colorado St.	14	351	184	12	52.42	2,560	7.29	15	182.9	3.42	13.91	10	4	0
84 Temple	12	380	186	23	48.95	2,166	5.7	15	180.5	6.05	11.65	4	8	0
85 Army	12	377	180	21	47.75	2,149	5.7	11	179.1	5.57	11.94	1	11	0
86 UTEP	12	375	170	21	45.33	2,145	5.72	13	178.8	5.6	12.62	2	10	0
87 Ball St.	12	348	199	16	57.18	2,144	6.16	20	178.7	4.6	10.77	6	6	0
88 Stanford	11	369	190	22	51.49	1,960	5.31	14	178.2	5.96	10.32	2	9	0
89 Buffalo	12	432	209	13	48.38	2,134	4.94	13	177.8	3.01	10.21	1	11	0
90 Northern Ill.	12	265	135	7	50.94	2,105	7.94	16	175.4	2.64	15.59	8	4	0
91 Notre Dame	13	341	172	13	50.44	2,264	6.64	11	174.2	3.81	13.16	10	3	0
92 Ohio St.	14	280	173	7	61.79	2,425	8.66	14	173.2	2.5	14.02	14	0	0
93 Wake Forest	13	272	147	6	54.04	2,170	7.98	8	166.9	2.21	14.76	7	6	0
94 TCU	12	296	171	13	57.77	2,003	6.77	12	166.9	4.39	11.71	10	2	0
95 Central Mich.	12	374	194	8	51.87	1,994	5.33	10	166.2	2.14	10.28	4	8	0
96 Wisconsin	12	322	171	8	53.11	2,303	7.15	15	164.5	2.48	13.47	8	6	0
97 Rutgers	12	413	188	23	45.52	1,948	4.72	12	162.3	5.57	10.36	1	11	0
98 Southern Methodist	12	330	172	18	52.12	1,912	5.79	11	159.3	5.45	11.12	3	9	0
99 Virginia Tech	14	272	168	11	61.76	2,229	8.19	14	159.2	4.04	13.27	10	4	0
100 Kansas St.	13	223	120	6	53.81	2,066	9.26	14	158.9	2.69	17.22	11	2	0
101 Middle Tenn.	12	256	148	8	57.81	1,848	7.22	6	154	3.13	12.49	4	8	0
102 LSU	13	325	155	8	47.69	1,990	6.12	16	153.1	2.46	12.84	8	5	0
103 South Carolina	12	261	140	15	53.64	1,821	6.98	10	151.8	5.75	13.01	5	7	0
104 New Mexico	12	352	192	10	54.55	2,037	5.79	15	145.5	2.84	10.61	7	7	0
105 Arkansas St.	13	290	150	9	51.72	1,868	6.44	7	143.7	3.1	12.45	6	7	0
106 Colorado	14	316	163	12	51.58	1,984	6.28	16	141.7	3.8	12.17	9	5	0
107 Vanderbilt	12	257	128	12	49.81	1,669	6.49	10	139.1	4.67	13.04	2	10	0
108 West Virginia	13	279	148	9	53.05	1,753	6.28	11	134.8	3.23	11.84	9	4	0
109 Arkansas	14	299	148	13	49.5	1,885	6.3	18	134.6	4.35	12.74	9	5	0
110 Troy St.	12	305	132	19	43.28	1,528	5.01	6	127.3	6.23	11.58	4	8	0
111 Kent St.	12	278	137	21	49.28	1,442	5.19	6	120.2	7.55	10.53	3	9	0
112 Nebraska	14	235	105	12	44.68	1,462	6.22	12	104.4	5.11	13.92	7	7	0
113 North Texas	13	217	98	9	45.16	1,327	6.12	8	102.1	4.15	13.54	8	5	0
114 Rice	11	151	67	7	44.37	1,091	7.23	6	99.2	4.64	16.28	4	7	0
115 Navy	12	161	74	10	45.96	1,184	7.35	5	98.7	6.21	16	2	10	0
116 Air Force	13	154	67	7	43.51	1,175	7.63	12	90.4	4.55	17.54	8	5	0
117 Ohio	12	160	84	9	52.5	1,049	6.56	6	87.4	5.63	12.49	4	8	0

Pass Defense

Rank, School	G	Att	Com	Pct	Yds/Cmp	Int	IPct	Yds	Yds/Att	TD	Yds/Gm	CM	W	L	T
1 Miami (Fla.)	13	353	163	46.18	9.55	12	3.4	1,556	4.41	8	119.69	1	12	1	0
2 LSU	13	361	163	45.15	12.18	17	4.71	1,985	5.5	13	152.69	0	8	5	0
3 Mississippi St.	12	282	140	49.65	13.19	14	4.96	1,847	6.55	22	153.92	1	3	9	0
4 Tennessee	13	349	170	48.71	11.95	12	3.44	2,031	5.82	9	156.23	0	8	5	0
5 Connecticut	12	322	162	50.31	11.88	20	6.21	1,925	5.98	14	160.42	1	6	6	0
6 Marshall	13	366	175	47.81	11.99	15	4.1	2,099	5.73	10	161.46	2	11	2	0
7 Florida	13	362	185	51.1	11.41	7	1.93	2,111	5.83	14	162.38	1	8	5	0
8 Texas	13	400	192	48	11.18	22	5.5	2,147	5.37	17	165.15	2	11	2	0

Rank, School	G	Att	Com	Pct	Yds/Cmp	Int	IPct	Yds	Yds/Att	TD	Yds/Gm	CM	W	L	T
9 Memphis	12	336	202	60.12	9.85	12	3.57	1,989	5.92	14	165.75	0	3	9	0
10 Southern Miss.	13	379	177	46.7	12.4	16	4.22	2,195	5.79	6	168.85	0	7	6	0
11 Troy St.	12	328	171	52.13	12.04	9	2.74	2,059	6.28	13	171.58	1	4	8	0
12 North Texas	13	368	200	54.35	11.16	16	4.35	2,232	6.07	8	171.69	0	8	5	0
13 Boston College	13	373	201	53.89	11.13	15	4.02	2,237	6	12	172.08	0	9	4	0
14 TCU	12	406	158	38.92	13.32	22	5.42	2,105	5.18	16	175.42	2	10	2	0
15 North Carolina St.	14	437	217	49.66	11.32	16	3.66	2,457	5.62	13	175.5	1	11	3	0
16 Arkansas St.	13	316	183	57.91	12.53	16	5.06	2,293	7.26	19	176.38	0	6	7	0
17 Alabama	13	374	185	49.47	12.45	18	4.81	2,303	6.16	11	177.15	2	10	3	0
18 Pittsburgh	13	400	210	52.5	11.05	15	3.75	2,321	5.8	8	178.54	0	9	4	0
19 Minnesota	13	367	203	55.31	11.44	7	1.91	2,322	6.33	12	178.62	1	8	5	0
20 Kansas St.	13	418	191	45.69	12.21	20	4.78	2,333	5.58	11	179.46	0	11	2	0
21 Western Mich.	12	362	195	53.87	11.05	14	3.87	2,154	5.95	21	179.5	1	4	8	0
22 Cincinnati	14	427	220	51.52	11.45	17	3.98	2,519	5.9	12	179.93	0	7	7	0
23 Army	12	293	181	61.77	12.13	6	2.05	2,195	7.49	20	182.92	2	1	11	0
24 Iowa St.	14	426	242	56.81	10.66	10	2.35	2,580	6.06	16	184.29	0	7	7	0
25 Oklahoma	14	432	206	47.69	12.59	24	5.56	2,594	6	13	185.29	2	12	2	0
26 Auburn	13	425	235	55.29	10.31	21	4.94	2,424	5.7	9	186.46	0	9	4	0
27 South Carolina	12	355	210	59.15	10.68	9	2.54	2,243	6.32	17	186.92	2	5	7	0
28 Mississippi	13	349	181	51.86	13.45	18	5.16	2,435	6.98	17	187.31	2	7	6	0
29 Northwestern	12	239	144	60.25	15.73	8	3.35	2,265	9.48	20	188.75	2	3	9	0
30 Michigan St.	12	334	165	49.4	13.73	13	3.89	2,266	6.78	22	188.83	2	4	8	0
31 Georgia	14	410	226	55.12	11.74	16	3.9	2,653	6.47	14	189.5	0	13	1	0
32 Tulane	13	436	229	52.52	10.89	22	5.05	2,494	5.72	12	191.85	1	8	5	0
33 Indiana	12	335	202	60.3	11.5	8	2.39	2,322	6.93	23	193.5	0	3	9	0
34 Colorado	14	453	254	56.07	10.78	15	3.31	2,739	6.05	16	195.64	0	9	5	0
35 Clemson	13	389	233	59.9	11	21	5.4	2,564	6.59	20	197.23	0	7	6	0
36 La.-Lafayette	12	305	159	52.13	14.94	8	2.62	2,375	7.79	18	197.92	1	3	9	0
37 Rutgers	12	333	171	51.35	13.89	11	3.3	2,376	7.14	25	198	1	1	11	0
38 Air Force	13	370	210	56.76	12.3	12	3.24	2,584	6.98	10	198.77	1	8	5	0
39 Oregon St.	13	456	222	48.68	11.67	20	4.39	2,591	5.68	10	199.31	0	8	5	0
40 New Mexico St.	12	339	210	61.95	11.49	7	2.06	2,412	7.12	16	201	0	7	5	0
40 Purdue	13	419	202	48.21	12.94	15	3.58	2,613	6.24	15	201	0	7	6	0
42 Southern California	13	454	226	49.78	11.61	17	3.74	2,623	5.78	16	201.77	0	11	2	0
43 Kent St.	12	344	209	60.76	11.59	9	2.62	2,423	7.04	18	201.92	1	3	9	0
44 Tulsa	12	342	201	58.77	12.08	13	3.8	2,429	7.1	15	202.42	1	1	11	0
45 UCF	12	380	216	56.84	11.34	13	3.42	2,449	6.44	19	204.08	1	7	5	0
46 Notre Dame	13	452	223	49.34	11.94	21	4.65	2,662	5.89	12	204.77	1	10	3	0
47 Colorado St.	14	444	259	58.33	11.12	14	3.15	2,881	6.49	16	205.79	4	10	4	0
48 Brigham Young	12	377	196	51.99	12.67	18	4.77	2,483	6.59	9	206.92	3	5	7	0
49 Louisville	13	427	205	48.01	13.12	9	2.11	2,690	6.3	21	206.92	0	7	6	0
50 Temple	12	356	210	58.99	11.85	11	3.09	2,488	6.99	20	207.33	1	4	8	0
51 Texas A&M	12	401	229	57.11	10.87	16	3.99	2,490	6.21	17	207.5	2	6	6	0
52 Maryland	14	444	251	56.53	11.72	18	4.05	2,942	6.63	12	210.14	0	11	3	0
53 Bowling Green	12	398	214	53.77	11.86	12	3.02	2,537	6.37	15	211.42	0	9	3	0
54 Toledo	14	426	248	58.22	12.03	19	4.46	2,984	7	18	213.14	0	9	5	0
55 West Virginia	13	416	230	55.29	12.07	19	4.57	2,777	6.68	17	213.62	0	9	4	0
56 Virginia Tech	14	443	230	51.92	13	24	5.42	2,991	6.75	14	213.64	1	10	4	0
57 Nebraska	14	459	231	50.33	13.05	13	2.83	3,014	6.57	12	215.29	0	7	7	0
58 Penn St.	13	454	288	63.44	9.72	20	4.41	2,799	6.17	15	215.31	1	9	4	0
59 Virginia	14	433	262	60.51	11.53	15	3.46	3,020	6.97	14	215.71	0	9	5	0
60 Kansas	12	302	167	55.3	15.53	12	3.97	2,594	8.59	27	216.17	3	2	10	0
61 New Mexico	14	452	244	53.98	12.5	15	3.32	3,051	6.75	25	217.93	1	7	7	0
62 Vanderbilt	12	337	216	64.09	12.18	6	1.78	2,630	7.8	11	219.17	1	2	10	0
63 Navy	12	287	189	65.85	13.98	5	1.74	2,643	9.21	24	220.25	2	2	10	0
64 Georgia Tech	13	440	235	53.41	12.23	11	2.5	2,874	6.53	11	221.08	0	7	6	0
65 South Fla.	11	400	210	52.5	11.61	22	5.5	2,439	6.1	17	221.73	0	9	2	0
66 Ohio	12	360	209	58.06	12.87	14	3.89	2,689	7.47	24	224.08	0	4	8	0
67 Wisconsin	14	432	237	54.86	13.24	22	5.09	3,139	7.27	22	224.21	3	8	6	0
68 Arizona	12	368	214	58.15	12.58	7	1.9	2,692	7.32	15	224.33	0	4	8	0
69 Michigan	13	440	236	53.64	12.37	16	3.64	2,919	6.63	17	224.54	2	10	3	0
70 Eastern Mich.	12	281	179	63.7	15.14	4	1.42	2,710	9.64	28	225.83	1	3	9	0
71 Hawaii	14	495	253	51.11	12.52	18	3.64	3,168	6.4	21	226.29	1	10	4	0
72 Kentucky	12	369	174	47.15	15.65	10	2.71	2,723	7.38	23	226.92	0	7	5	0
73 Akron	12	340	214	62.94	12.74	9	2.65	2,726	8.02	20	227.17	0	4	8	0
74 Utah	11	378	198	52.38	12.63	12	3.17	2,500	6.61	16	227.27	1	5	6	0
75 Buffalo	12	353	204	57.79	13.39	14	3.97	2,731	7.74	23	227.58	1	1	11	0
76 UAB	12	362	204	56.35	13.42	15	4.14	2,738	7.56	19	228.17	1	5	7	0
77 UCLA	13	432	217	50.23	13.67	17	3.94	2,967	6.87	20	228.23	2	8	5	0
78 Middle Tenn.	12	347	213	61.38	12.91	10	2.88	2,749	7.92	19	229.08	2	4	8	0
79 Illinois	12	404	227	56.19	12.18	8	1.98	2,764	6.84	13	230.33	1	5	7	0
80 North Carolina	12	306	168	54.9	16.52	6	1.96	2,775	9.07	24	231.25	1	3	9	0
81 Boise St.	13	529	274	51.8	10.98	19	3.59	3,008	5.69	20	231.38	1	12	1	0
82 Wake Forest	13	413	242	58.6	12.46	13	3.15	3,016	7.3	22	232	1	7	6	0
83 Arkansas	14	483	267	55.28	12.3	19	3.93	3,283	6.8	17	234.5	0	9	5	0
84 UNLV	12	389	219	56.3	12.86	9	2.31	2,816	7.24	22	234.67	2	5	7	0
85 Florida	14	465	249	53.55	13.22	16	3.44	3,293	7.08	21	235.21	1	9	5	0
86 Ball St.	12	390	246	63.08	11.52	10	2.56	2,834	7.27	22	236.17	1	6	6	0
87 Utah St.	11	332	178	53.61	14.6	7	2.11	2,599	7.83	22	236.27	0	4	7	0
88 La.-Monroe	12	355	213	60	13.43	10	2.82	2,860	8.06	22	238.33	2	3	9	0
89 East Caro.	12	364	196	53.85	14.61	10	2.75	2,863	7.87	23	238.58	0	4	8	0
90 Texas Tech	14	472	263	55.72	12.75	16	3.39	3,354	7.11	26	239.57	0	9	5	0
91 San Diego St.	13	435	243	55.86	12.82	14	3.22	3,116	7.16	31	239.69	1	4	9	0
92 Nevada	12	358	195	54.47	14.87	9	2.51	2,899	8.1	19	241.58	1	5	7	0

Rank, School	G	Att	Com	Pct	Yds/Cmp	Int	IPct	Yds	Yds/Att	TD	Yds/Gm	CM	W	L	T
93 Baylor	12	382	235	61.52	12.34	8	2.09	2,900	7.59	30	241.67	0	3	9	0
94 Rice	11	363	222	61.16	12	8	2.2	2,663	7.34	23	242.09	0	4	7	0
95 Ohio St.	14	546	315	57.69	10.81	18	3.3	3,404	6.23	14	243.14	1	14	0	0
96 Arizona St.	14	487	243	49.9	14.07	22	4.52	3,420	7.02	28	244.29	1	8	6	0
97 Southern Methodist	12	370	200	54.05	14.66	8	2.16	2,932	7.92	22	244.33	1	3	9	0
98 Fresno St.	14	460	254	55.22	13.51	19	4.13	3,432	7.46	21	245.14	1	9	5	0
99 UTEP	12	352	199	56.53	14.83	10	2.84	2,951	8.38	30	245.92	0	2	10	0
100 Oklahoma St.	13	480	263	54.79	12.44	12	2.5	3,271	6.81	20	251.62	2	8	5	0
101 Stanford	11	364	204	56.04	13.59	16	4.4	2,772	7.62	22	252	1	2	9	0
102 Duke	12	405	245	60.49	12.47	12	2.96	3,056	7.55	18	254.67	0	2	10	0
103 Northern Ill.	12	428	243	56.78	12.59	21	4.91	3,059	7.15	17	254.92	2	8	4	0
104 Washington St.	13	535	305	57.01	10.88	17	3.18	3,318	6.2	20	255.23	1	10	3	0
105 Washington	13	446	249	55.83	13.55	16	3.59	3,373	7.56	23	259.46	0	7	6	0
106 Central Mich.	12	393	249	63.36	12.74	12	3.05	3,173	8.07	23	264.42	1	4	8	0
106 Louisiana Tech	12	383	238	62.14	13.33	5	1.31	3,173	8.28	24	264.42	1	4	8	0
108 Houston	12	394	220	55.84	14.69	10	2.54	3,232	8.2	24	269.33	0	5	7	0
109 Miami (Ohio)	12	424	251	59.2	13.05	13	3.07	3,276	7.73	21	273	0	7	5	0
110 Iowa	13	535	300	56.07	11.85	20	3.74	3,554	6.64	15	273.38	0	11	2	0
111 Idaho	12	354	208	58.76	15.83	8	2.26	3,293	9.3	21	274.42	1	2	10	0
112 California	12	435	253	58.16	13.23	15	3.45	3,346	7.69	20	278.83	3	7	5	0
113 Missouri	12	426	253	59.39	13.4	12	2.82	3,391	7.96	19	282.58	3	5	7	0
114 Wyoming	12	406	262	64.53	13.06	9	2.22	3,421	8.43	21	285.08	0	2	10	0
115 Oregon	13	475	272	57.26	13.92	18	3.79	3,785	7.97	35	291.15	1	7	6	0
116 San Jose St.	13	475	275	57.89	14.2	23	4.84	3,906	8.22	32	300.46	2	6	7	0
117 Syracuse	12	384	223	58.07	16.35	10	2.6	3,645	9.49	22	303.75	1	4	8	0

Passing Efficiency

Rank, School	G	Att	Com	Pct	Int	IPct	Yds	Yds/Att	TD	TDPct	Rating	W	L	T
1 Boise St.	13	390	251	64.36	8	2.05	3,808	9.76	32	8.21	169.39	12	1	0
2 Iowa	13	314	182	57.96	5	1.59	2,734	8.71	27	8.6	156.33	11	2	0
3 Toledo	14	443	309	69.75	9	2.03	3,611	8.15	25	5.64	152.83	9	5	0
4 Marshall	13	575	383	66.61	15	2.61	4,804	8.35	35	6.09	151.65	11	2	0
5 UCF	12	442	270	61.09	17	3.85	3,837	8.68	31	7.01	149.47	7	5	0
6 Southern California	13	494	313	63.36	10	2.02	3,988	8.07	33	6.68	149.21	11	2	0
7 Virginia	14	448	306	68.3	8	1.79	3,222	7.19	32	7.14	148.71	9	5	0
8 Kansas St.	13	223	120	53.81	6	2.69	2,066	9.26	14	6.28	146.96	11	2	0
9 Miami (Fla.)	13	432	241	55.79	13	3.01	3,695	8.55	32	7.41	146.07	12	1	0
10 Ohio St.	14	280	173	61.79	7	2.5	2,425	8.66	14	5	146.05	14	0	0
11 Washington St.	13	458	273	59.61	14	3.06	3,805	8.31	30	6.55	144.89	10	3	0
12 Texas Tech	14	770	515	66.88	15	1.95	5,444	7.07	50	6.49	143.82	9	5	0
13 New Mexico St.	12	276	169	61.23	6	2.17	2,337	8.47	13	4.71	143.52	7	5	0
14 Texas	13	404	240	59.41	12	2.97	3,251	8.05	26	6.44	142.29	11	2	0
15 Virginia Tech	14	272	168	61.76	11	4.04	2,229	8.19	14	5.15	139.53	10	4	0
16 Georgia	14	445	257	57.75	10	2.25	3,435	7.72	28	6.29	138.91	13	1	0
17 Auburn	13	299	174	58.19	10	3.34	2,390	7.99	18	6.02	138.52	9	4	0
18 Miami (Ohio)	12	446	278	62.33	13	2.91	3,331	7.47	25	5.61	137.7	7	5	0
19 North Carolina St.	14	447	273	61.07	11	2.46	3,468	7.76	20	4.47	136.11	11	3	0
20 Akron	12	404	265	65.59	12	2.97	2,962	7.33	18	4.46	135.95	4	8	0
21 Nevada	12	477	292	61.22	17	3.56	3,556	7.45	27	5.66	135.37	5	7	0
22 UCLA	13	367	204	55.59	11	3	2,985	8.13	19	5.18	135.01	8	5	0
23 Oklahoma St.	13	454	243	53.52	15	3.3	3,414	7.52	32	7.05	133.32	8	5	0
24 Tennessee	13	356	218	61.24	7	1.97	2,635	7.4	14	3.93	132.42	8	5	0
25 San Diego St.	13	584	352	60.27	10	1.71	4,302	7.37	24	4.11	132.32	4	9	0
26 Northern Ill.	12	265	135	50.94	7	2.64	2,105	7.94	16	6.04	132.27	8	4	0
27 Kentucky	12	350	195	55.71	6	1.71	2,387	6.82	24	6.86	132.19	7	5	0
28 Bowling Green	12	398	227	57.04	11	2.76	2,758	6.93	27	6.78	132.07	9	3	0
29 Arizona	12	430	246	57.21	14	3.26	3,477	8.09	17	3.95	131.66	4	8	0
30 Maryland	14	324	179	55.25	13	4.01	2,668	8.23	15	4.63	131.62	11	3	0
31 Arizona St.	14	558	306	54.84	16	2.87	4,254	7.62	31	5.56	131.44	8	6	0
32 Illinois	12	454	258	56.83	16	3.52	3,388	7.46	26	5.73	131.34	5	7	0
33 Oklahoma	14	419	242	57.76	11	2.63	2,828	6.75	28	6.68	131.3	12	2	0
34 California	12	428	230	53.74	10	2.34	2,971	6.94	31	7.24	131.24	7	5	0
35 Washington	13	621	372	59.9	14	2.25	4,501	7.25	28	4.51	131.15	7	6	0
36 Purdue	13	452	271	59.96	15	3.32	3,324	7.35	21	4.65	130.47	7	6	0
37 Alabama	13	310	174	56.13	9	2.9	2,473	7.98	12	3.87	130.08	10	3	0
38 Wyoming	12	471	279	59.24	18	3.82	3,357	7.13	25	5.31	128.94	2	10	0
39 San Jose St.	13	483	290	60.04	17	3.52	3,424	7.09	24	4.97	128.91	6	7	0
40 Pittsburgh	13	371	194	52.29	12	3.23	2,796	7.54	22	5.93	128.71	9	4	0
41 Michigan St.	12	377	208	55.17	17	4.51	2,743	7.28	24	6.37	128.31	4	8	0
42 Connecticut	12	392	232	59.18	12	3.06	2,671	6.81	21	5.36	127.99	6	6	0
43 Oregon	13	412	214	51.94	11	2.67	2,959	7.18	26	6.31	127.71	7	6	0
44 Florida St.	14	419	217	51.79	10	2.39	2,955	7.05	27	6.44	127.53	9	5	0
45 Penn St.	13	351	198	56.41	11	3.13	2,536	7.23	17	4.84	126.81	9	4	0
46 Minnesota	13	333	174	52.25	11	3.3	2,384	7.16	21	6.31	126.64	8	5	0
47 Hawaii	14	731	407	55.68	26	3.56	5,406	7.4	35	4.79	126.51	10	4	0
48 Wake Forest	13	272	147	54.04	6	2.21	2,170	7.98	8	2.94	126.31	7	6	0
49 North Carolina	12	433	237	54.73	14	3.23	3,199	7.39	21	4.85	126.3	3	9	0

Rank, School	G	Att	Com	Pct	Int	IPct	Yds	Yds/Att	TD	TDPct	Rating	W	L	T
50 Boston College	13	414	243	58.7	17	4.11	3,011	7.27	18	4.35	125.93	9	4	0
51 Mississippi	13	486	283	58.23	15	3.09	3,437	7.07	21	4.32	125.69	7	6	0
52 Texas A&M	12	425	219	51.53	19	4.47	3,216	7.57	25	5.88	125.53	6	6	0
53 Air Force	13	154	67	43.51	7	4.55	1,175	7.63	12	7.79	124.21	8	5	0
54 South Fla.	11	427	241	56.44	5	1.17	2,772	6.49	20	4.68	124.05	9	2	0
55 Fresno St.	14	483	266	55.07	14	2.9	3,382	7	23	4.76	123.83	9	5	0
56 Idaho	12	512	302	58.98	18	3.52	3,475	6.79	23	4.49	123.8	2	10	0
57 Wisconsin	14	322	171	53.11	8	2.48	2,303	7.15	15	4.66	123.58	8	6	0
58 Cincinnati	14	485	264	54.43	22	4.54	3,649	7.52	22	4.54	123.5	7	7	0
59 Louisville	13	451	243	53.88	11	2.44	2,944	6.53	25	5.54	122.15	7	6	0
60 Florida	13	517	295	57.06	18	3.48	3,519	6.81	22	4.26	121.35	8	5	0
61 Clemson	13	462	268	58.01	13	2.81	3,157	6.83	16	3.46	121.2	7	6	0
62 Colorado St.	14	351	184	52.42	12	3.42	2,560	7.29	15	4.27	120.93	10	4	0
63 Oregon St.	13	468	221	47.22	14	2.99	3,414	7.29	26	5.56	120.83	8	5	0
64 Louisiana Tech	12	527	305	57.87	19	3.61	3,633	6.89	19	3.61	120.49	4	8	0
65 Michigan	13	472	259	54.87	7	1.48	3,026	6.41	21	4.45	120.47	10	3	0
66 Iowa St.	14	454	250	55.07	18	3.96	3,308	7.29	16	3.52	120.01	7	7	0
67 Middle Tenn.	12	256	148	57.81	8	3.13	1,848	7.22	6	2.34	119.92	4	8	0
68 Eastern Mich.	12	441	248	56.24	22	4.99	2,961	6.71	23	5.22	119.83	3	9	0
69 Houston	12	357	184	51.54	22	6.16	2,670	7.48	19	5.32	119.56	5	7	0
70 TCU	12	296	171	57.77	13	4.39	2,003	6.77	12	4.05	119.24	10	2	0
71 Utah St.	11	487	258	52.98	16	3.29	3,388	6.96	21	4.31	119.1	4	7	0
72 Ball St.	12	348	199	57.18	16	4.6	2,144	6.16	20	5.75	118.72	6	6	0
73 Missouri	12	380	204	53.68	7	1.84	2,438	6.42	17	4.47	118.67	5	7	0
74 Tulane	13	438	245	55.94	10	2.28	2,646	6.04	20	4.57	117.15	8	5	0
75 Memphis	12	452	241	53.32	20	4.42	2,868	6.35	24	5.31	115.27	3	9	0
76 Duke	12	386	206	53.37	13	3.37	2,399	6.22	18	4.66	114.26	2	10	0
77 Utah	11	381	215	56.43	13	3.41	2,291	6.01	16	4.2	113.94	5	6	0
78 Arkansas	14	299	148	49.5	13	4.35	1,885	6.3	18	6.02	113.63	9	5	0
79 Colorado	14	316	163	51.58	12	3.8	1,984	6.28	16	5.06	113.45	9	5	0
80 South Carolina	12	261	140	53.64	15	5.75	1,821	6.98	10	3.83	113.36	5		0
81 UNLV	12	345	169	48.99	12	3.48	2,341	6.79	14	4.06	112.43	5	7	0
82 West Virginia	13	279	148	53.05	9	3.23	1,753	6.28	11	3.94	112.34	9	4	0
83 Syracuse	12	333	174	52.25	15	4.5	2,252	6.76	12	3.6	111.99	4	8	0
84 Indiana	12	446	228	51.12	21	4.71	3,020	6.77	18	4.04	111.88	3	9	0
85 Baylor	12	400	224	56	22	5.5	2,778	6.95	10	2.5	111.59	3	9	0
86 New Mexico	14	352	192	54.55	10	2.84	2,037	5.79	15	4.26	111.49	7	7	0
87 UAB	12	347	169	48.7	9	2.59	2,214	6.38	15	4.32	111.37	5	7	0
88 Tulsa	12	403	213	52.85	10	2.48	2,321	5.76	18	4.47	111.05	1	11	0
89 Western Mich.	12	467	244	52.25	22	4.71	3,073	6.58	18	3.85	110.77	4	8	0
90 LSU	13	325	155	47.69	8	2.46	1,990	6.12	16	4.92	110.46	8	5	0
91 Northwestern	12	451	261	57.87	14	3.1	2,784	6.17	9	2	110.13	3	9	0
92 Georgia Tech	13	435	239	54.94	20	4.6	2,744	6.31	15	3.45	110.07	7	6	0
93 Brigham Young	12	501	277	55.29	21	4.19	3,129	6.25	16	3.19	109.92	5	7	0
94 Southern Miss.	13	371	186	50.13	11	2.96	2,451	6.61	11	2.96	109.45	7	6	0
95 Notre Dame	13	341	172	50.44	13	3.81	2,264	6.64	11	3.23	109.19	10	3	0
96 Rice	11	151	67	44.37	7	4.64	1,091	7.23	6	3.97	108.93	4	7	0
97 Ohio	12	160	84	52.5	9	5.63	1,049	6.56	6	3.75	108.7	4	8	0
98 La.-Lafayette	12	432	234	54.17	19	4.4	2,733	6.33	13	3.01	108.48	3	9	0
99 La.-Monroe	12	422	204	48.34	14	3.32	2,664	6.31	17	4.03	107.99	3	9	0
100 Vanderbilt	12	257	128	49.81	12	4.67	1,669	6.49	10	3.89	107.85	2	10	0
101 Arkansas St.	13	290	150	51.72	9	3.1	1,868	6.44	7	2.41	107.57	6	7	0
102 Navy	12	161	74	45.96	10	6.21	1,184	7.35	5	3.11	105.6	2	10	0
103 East Caro.	12	410	200	48.78	22	5.37	2,577	6.29	16	3.9	103.74	4	8	0
104 Nebraska	14	235	105	44.68	12	5.11	1,462	6.22	12	5.11	103.6	7	7	0
105 Central Mich.	12	374	194	51.87	8	2.14	1,994	5.33	10	2.67	101.23	4	8	0
106 Southern Methodist	12	330	172	52.12	18	5.45	1,912	5.79	11	3.33	100.86	3	9	0
107 Mississippi St.	12	442	226	51.13	22	4.98	2,611	5.91	13	2.94	100.47	3	9	0
108 North Texas	13	217	98	45.16	9	4.15	1,327	6.12	8	3.69	100.44	8	5	0
109 Temple	12	380	186	48.95	23	6.05	2,166	5.7	15	3.95	97.7	4	8	0
110 Stanford	11	369	190	51.49	22	5.96	1,960	5.31	14	3.79	96.71	2	9	0
111 Kansas	12	430	200	46.51	13	3.02	2,286	5.32	13	3.02	95.09	2	10	0
112 Army	12	377	180	47.75	21	5.57	2,149	5.7	11	2.92	94.07	1	11	0
113 Buffalo	12	432	209	48.38	13	3.01	2,134	4.94	13	3.01	93.81	1	11	0
114 UTEP	12	375	170	45.33	21	5.6	2,145	5.72	13	3.47	93.59	2	10	0
115 Kent St.	12	278	137	49.28	21	7.55	1,442	5.19	6	2.16	84.89	3	9	0
116 Rutgers	12	413	188	45.52	23	5.57	1,948	4.72	12	2.91	83.57	1	11	0
117 Troy St.	12	305	132	43.28	19	6.23	1,528	5.01	6	1.97	79.42	4	8	0

Passes Had Intercepted

Rank, School	No.
1 Iowa	5
1 South Fla.	5
3 Kansas St.	6
3 New Mexico St.	6
3 Wake Forest	6
3 Kentucky	6
7 Michigan	7
7 Ohio St.	7
7 Air Force	7
7 Tennessee	7
7 Rice	7
7 Northern Ill.	7
7 Missouri	7
14 Boise St.	8
14 Central Mich.	8
14 LSU	8
14 Wisconsin	8
14 Virginia	8
14 Middle Tenn.	8
20 Alabama	9
20 UAB	9
20 Arkansas St.	9
20 Ohio	9
20 West Virginia	9
20 Toledo	9
20 North Texas	9
27 Auburn	10
27 Florida St.	10
27 California	10
27 Georgia	10
27 Navy	10
27 Tulsa	10
27 Tulane	10
27 Southern California	10
27 San Diego St.	10
27 New Mexico	10
37 Bowling Green	11
37 UCLA	11
37 Oklahoma	11
37 North Carolina St.	11
37 Minnesota	11
37 Louisville	11
37 Oregon	11
37 Virginia Tech	11
37 Southern Miss.	11
37 Penn St.	11
47 Akron	12
47 UNLV	12
47 Nebraska	12
47 Texas	12
47 Vanderbilt	12
47 Pittsburgh	12
47 Colorado	12
47 Connecticut	12
47 Colorado St.	12
56 Arkansas	13
56 Buffalo	13
56 Utah	13
56 TCU	13
56 Notre Dame	13
56 Miami (Fla.)	13
56 Miami (Ohio)	13
56 Maryland	13
56 Kansas	13
56 Duke	13
56 Clemson	13
67 Arizona	14
67 North Carolina	14
67 Washington	14
67 Washington St.	14
67 Oregon St.	14
67 Northwestern	14
67 La.-Monroe	14
67 Fresno St.	14
75 Marshall	15
75 Mississippi	15
75 South Carolina	15
75 Texas Tech	15
75 Syracuse	15
75 Purdue	15
75 Oklahoma St.	15
82 Arizona St.	16
82 Utah St.	16
82 Ball St.	16
82 Illinois	16
86 Boston College	17
86 UCF	17
86 San Jose St.	17
86 Nevada	17
86 Michigan St.	17
91 Florida	18
91 Idaho	18
91 Southern Methodist	18
91 Iowa St.	18
91 Wyoming	18
96 Louisiana Tech	19
96 La.-Lafayette	19
96 Texas A&M	19
96 Troy St.	19
100 Georgia Tech	20
100 Memphis	20
102 Brigham Young	21
102 Army	21
102 UTEP	21
102 Indiana	21
102 Kent St.	21
107 Baylor	22
107 Houston	22
107 Mississippi St.	22
107 Western Mich.	22
107 Stanford	22
107 Cincinnati	22
107 East Caro.	22
107 Eastern Mich.	22
115 Rutgers	23
115 Temple	23
117 Hawaii	26

Passes Intercepted

Rank, School	No.
1 Oklahoma	24
1 Virginia Tech	24
3 San Jose St.	23
4 Arizona St.	22
4 TCU	22
4 South Fla.	22
4 Texas	22
4 Wisconsin	22
4 Tulane	22
10 Auburn	21
10 Clemson	21
10 Notre Dame	21
10 Northern Ill.	21
14 Connecticut	20
14 Penn St.	20
14 Oregon St.	20
14 Iowa	20
14 Kansas St.	20
19 Arkansas	19
19 Boise St.	19
19 West Virginia	19
19 Fresno St.	19
23 Alabama	18
23 Toledo	18
23 Oregon	18
23 Ohio St.	18
23 Mississippi	18
23 Maryland	18
23 Hawaii	18
23 Brigham Young	18
31 UCLA	17
31 Cincinnati	17
31 Washington St.	17
31 Southern California	17
31 LSU	17
36 Arkansas St.	16
36 Florida St.	16
36 Southern Miss.	16
36 Texas A&M	16
36 Washington	16
36 Texas Tech	16
36 Stanford	16
36 North Carolina St.	16
36 North Texas	16
36 Michigan	16
36 Georgia	16
47 UAB	15
47 Virginia	15
47 Purdue	15
47 Pittsburgh	15
47 New Mexico	15
47 Marshall	15
47 Colorado	15
47 California	15
47 Boston College	15
56 Buffalo	14
56 Mississippi St.	14
56 Western Mich.	14
56 San Diego St.	14
56 Ohio	14
56 Colorado St.	14
62 UCF	13
62 Tulsa	13
62 Wake Forest	13
62 Miami (Ohio)	13
62 Nebraska	13
62 Michigan St.	13
68 Bowling Green	12
68 Central Mich.	12
68 Utah	12
68 Air Force	12
68 Tennessee	12
68 Oklahoma St.	12
68 Missouri	12
68 Miami (Fla.)	12
68 Memphis	12
68 Kansas	12
68 Duke	12
79 Georgia Tech	11
79 Rutgers	11
79 Temple	11
82 Ball St.	10
82 Kentucky	10
82 Iowa St.	10
82 Middle Tenn.	10
82 UTEP	10
82 Syracuse	10
82 La.-Monroe	10
82 East Caro.	10
82 Houston	10
91 Akron	9
91 Wyoming	9
91 Troy St.	9
91 South Carolina	9
91 Nevada	9
91 UNLV	9
91 Louisville	9
91 Kent St.	9
99 Baylor	8
99 Idaho	8
99 Indiana	8
99 Illinois	8
99 La.-Lafayette	8
99 Southern Methodist	8
99 Rice	8
99 Northwestern	8
107 Arizona	7
107 Florida	7
107 Minnesota	7
107 Utah St.	7
107 New Mexico St.	7
112 North Carolina	6
112 Army	6
112 Vanderbilt	6
115 Louisiana Tech	5
115 Navy	5
117 Eastern Mich.	4

Punt Returns

Rank, School	G	Ret	Yds	TD	Avg	W	L	T
1 Northern Ill.	12	26	525	4	20.19	8	4	0
2 Tulane	13	28	484	2	17.29	8	5	0
3 Southern Methodist	12	29	501	1	17.28	3	9	0
4 Arizona	12	20	332	1	16.6	4	8	0
5 Nebraska	14	51	830	6	16.27	7	7	0
6 Colorado St.	14	36	573	1	15.92	10	4	0
7 South Fla.	11	34	540	2	15.88	9	2	0
8 Kentucky	12	40	625	4	15.63	7	5	0
9 Oklahoma	14	47	730	5	15.53	12	2	0
10 Georgia	14	50	746	2	14.92	13	1	0
11 Oregon	13	36	537	2	14.92	7	6	0
12 Army	12	18	265	1	14.72	1	11	0
13 Boise St.	13	42	606	1	14.43	12	1	0
14 Toledo	14	33	466	1	14.12	9	5	0
15 Texas	13	36	507	2	14.08	11	2	0
16 Virginia Tech	14	41	572	3	13.95	10	4	0
17 LSU	13	41	569	1	13.88	8	5	0
18 Kansas St.	13	50	687	5	13.74	11	2	0
19 UCLA	13	43	589	2	13.7	8	5	0
20 Syracuse	12	31	421	2	13.58	4	8	0
21 Western Mich.	12	40	534	2	13.35	4	8	0
22 Maryland	14	58	773	4	13.33	11	3	0
23 Louisville	13	54	716	4	13.26	7	6	0
24 Miami (Fla.)	13	50	662	1	13.24	12	1	0
25 Missouri	12	27	353	1	13.07	5	7	0
26 Texas Tech	14	59	766	2	12.98	9	5	0
27 Oklahoma St.	13	43	554	1	12.88	8	5	0
28 Tulsa	12	21	269	0	12.81	1	11	0
29 California	12	36	461	3	12.81	7	5	0
30 Colorado	14	35	435	2	12.43	9	5	0
31 Penn St.	13	44	538	1	12.23	9	4	0
32 Southern Miss.	13	34	415	0	12.21	7	6	0
33 Arkansas	14	37	439	2	11.86	9	5	0
34 Illinois	12	24	284	1	11.83	5	7	0
35 Iowa	13	35	413	3	11.8	11	2	0
36 Ball St.	12	22	255	0	11.59	6	6	0

Rank, School	G	Ret	Yds	TD	Avg	W	L	T
37 East Caro.	12	34	389	1	11.44	4	8	0
38 Mississippi	13	38	431	1	11.34	7	6	0
39 Wisconsin	14	43	487	1	11.33	8	6	0
40 Washington St.	13	42	473	1	11.26	10	3	0
41 New Mexico	14	34	382	1	11.24	7	7	0
42 Utah	11	33	370	0	11.21	5	6	0
43 San Jose St.	13	24	266	0	11.08	6	7	0
44 Eastern Mich.	12	21	232	1	11.05	3	9	0
45 Auburn	13	48	530	0	11.04	9	4	0
46 Brigham Young	12	25	276	0	11.04	5	7	0
47 La.-Lafayette	12	34	371	2	10.91	3	9	0
48 Air Force	13	21	229	1	10.9	8	5	0
49 UCF	12	26	280	1	10.77	7	5	0
50 Florida St.	14	45	477	0	10.6	9	5	0
51 Iowa	14	40	423	3	10.58	7	7	0
52 San Diego St.	13	36	379	2	10.53	4	9	0
53 UAB	12	28	294	1	10.5	5	7	0
54 Florida	13	38	396	0	10.42	8	5	0
55 Clemson	13	42	437	0	10.4	7	6	0
56 Ohio	12	28	290	1	10.36	4	8	0
57 New Mexico St.	12	27	275	0	10.19	7	5	0
58 Tennessee	13	43	435	0	10.12	8	5	0
59 Georgia Tech	13	52	524	0	10.08	7	6	0
60 Idaho	12	34	341	1	10.03	2	10	0
61 Arkansas St.	13	27	267	0	9.89	6	7	0
62 Virginia	14	39	385	2	9.87	9	5	0
63 Boston College	13	35	345	1	9.86	9	4	0
64 Troy St.	12	37	364	0	9.84	4	8	0
65 Notre Dame	13	53	518	2	9.77	10	3	0
66 Mississippi St.	12	35	332	0	9.49	3	9	0
67 Michigan	13	43	398	0	9.26	10	3	0
68 Vanderbilt	12	23	212	0	9.22	2	10	0
69 Purdue	13	32	293	1	9.16	7	6	0
70 TCU	12	49	443	2	9.04	10	2	0
71 Wake Forest	13	41	370	1	9.02	7	6	0
72 Arizona St.	14	45	403	1	8.96	8	6	0
73 Fresno St.	14	40	356	2	8.9	9	5	0
74 Stanford	11	27	237	0	8.78	2	9	0
75 Kent St.	12	16	139	1	8.69	3	9	0
76 UTEP	12	30	259	0	8.63	2	10	0
77 Temple	12	30	257	0	8.57	4	8	0
78 Hawaii	14	39	334	0	8.56	10	4	0
79 Michigan St.	12	40	341	1	8.53	4	8	0
80 Louisiana Tech	12	39	327	1	8.38	4	8	0
81 North Texas	13	37	310	0	8.38	8	5	0
82 Alabama	13	45	376	1	8.36	10	3	0
83 Texas A&M	12	29	242	0	8.34	6	6	0
84 Ohio St.	14	43	358	0	8.33	14	0	0
85 North Carolina St.	14	35	290	3	8.29	11	3	0
86 Wyoming	12	16	132	1	8.25	2	10	0
87 Oregon St.	13	50	410	0	8.2	8	5	0
88 Central Mich.	12	20	163	0	8.15	4	8	0
89 Bowling Green	12	40	325	1	8.13	9	3	0
90 Houston	12	31	251	0	8.1	5	7	0
91 Baylor	12	27	216	0	8	3	9	0
92 Memphis	12	44	348	0	7.91	3	9	0
93 Utah St.	11	26	205	1	7.88	4	7	0
94 Cincinnati	14	38	298	0	7.84	7	7	0
95 Buffalo	12	26	201	1	7.73	1	11	0
95 Minnesota	13	52	402	2	7.73	8	5	0
97 Rice	11	25	189	2	7.56	4	7	0
98 Washington	13	20	148	0	7.4	7	6	0
99 Rutgers	12	33	242	1	7.33	1	11	0
100 Connecticut	12	38	275	2	7.24	6	6	0
101 Southern California	13	41	296	1	7.22	11	2	0
102 Miami (Ohio)	12	29	205	0	7.07	7	5	0
103 UNLV	12	32	226	0	7.06	5	7	0
104 Pittsburgh	13	43	303	1	7.05	9	4	0
105 West Virginia	13	34	239	0	7.03	9	4	0
106 Kansas	12	19	124	0	6.53	2	10	0
107 Indiana	12	25	163	0	6.52	3	9	0
108 Navy	12	16	101	0	6.31	2	10	0
109 Akron	12	19	117	0	6.16	4	8	0
110 Middle Tenn.	12	28	167	1	5.96	4	8	0
111 Northwestern	12	26	153	0	5.88	3	9	0
112 Duke	12	32	187	0	5.84	2	10	0
113 North Carolina	12	24	137	0	5.71	3	9	0
114 La.-Monroe	12	23	128	1	5.57	3	9	0
115 Nevada	12	27	131	0	4.85	5	7	0
116 Marshall	13	27	130	0	4.81	11	2	0
117 South Carolina	12	15	64	0	4.27	5	7	0

Rushing Offense

Rank, School	G	Rsh	Net	Avg	TD	Yds/Gm	W	L	T
1 Air Force	13	786	4,001	5.09	41	307.77	8	5	0
2 West Virginia	13	714	3,687	5.16	39	283.62	9	4	0
3 Navy	12	652	3,249	4.98	34	270.75	2	10	0
4 Nebraska	14	724	3,762	5.2	29	268.71	7	7	0
5 Kansas St.	13	655	3,433	5.24	53	264.08	11	2	0
6 Rice	11	606	2,725	4.5	24	247.73	4	7	0
7 Wake Forest	13	718	3,135	4.37	33	241.15	7	6	0
8 Ohio	12	649	2,878	4.43	30	239.83	4	8	0
9 Colorado	14	652	3,259	5	28	232.79	9	5	0
10 Penn St.	13	526	2,972	5.65	36	228.62	9	4	0
11 Bowling Green	12	500	2,629	5.26	34	219.08	9	3	0
12 Arkansas	14	643	3,065	4.77	22	218.93	9	5	0
13 Kent St.	12	485	2,579	5.32	16	214.92	3	9	0
14 New Mexico St.	12	573	2,575	4.49	25	214.58	7	5	0
15 UNLV	12	498	2,573	5.17	22	214.42	5	7	0
16 Toledo	14	590	3,000	5.08	38	214.29	9	5	0
17 Iowa	13	553	2,784	5.03	24	214.15	11	2	0
18 Alabama	13	619	2,772	4.48	29	213.23	10	3	0
19 Virginia Tech	14	659	2,974	4.51	35	212.43	10	4	0
20 Minnesota	13	586	2,727	4.65	22	209.77	8	5	0
21 Middle Tenn.	12	528	2,504	4.74	30	208.67	4	8	0
22 Boise St.	13	560	2,711	4.84	43	208.54	12	1	0
23 Central Mich.	12	556	2,473	4.45	22	206.08	4	8	0
24 Colorado St.	14	622	2,880	4.63	32	205.71	10	4	0
25 Auburn	13	563	2,648	4.7	32	203.69	9	4	0
26 TCU	12	589	2,438	4.14	23	203.17	10	2	0
27 Northern Ill.	12	541	2,409	4.45	24	200.75	8	4	0
28 Maryland	14	592	2,783	4.7	32	198.79	11	3	0
29 LSU	13	558	2,560	4.59	19	196.92	8	5	0
30 Purdue	13	582	2,555	4.39	26	196.54	7	6	0
31 Ohio St.	14	629	2,678	4.26	31	191.29	14	0	0
32 Oklahoma	14	591	2,668	4.51	33	190.57	12	2	0
33 Wisconsin	14	645	2,663	4.13	30	190.21	8	6	0
34 Syracuse	12	528	2,265	4.29	30	188.75	4	8	0
35 Florida St.	14	562	2,618	4.66	20	187	9	5	0
36 Missouri	12	494	2,204	4.46	27	183.67	5	7	0
37 Arkansas St.	13	537	2,374	4.42	25	182.62	6	7	0
38 North Texas	13	587	2,372	4.04	23	182.46	8	5	0
39 Southern Methodist	12	551	2,187	3.97	15	182.25	3	9	0
40 Miami (Fla.)	13	455	2,361	5.19	33	181.62	12	1	0
41 New Mexico	14	593	2,504	4.22	26	178.86	7	7	0
42 Troy St.	12	536	2,116	3.95	20	176.33	4	8	0
43 Vanderbilt	12	481	2,082	4.33	18	173.5	2	10	0
44 Houston	12	524	2,043	3.9	22	170.25	5	7	0
45 South Carolina	12	477	2,004	4.2	16	167	5	7	0
46 Illinois	12	461	1,968	4.27	13	164	5	7	0
47 Utah	11	442	1,803	4.08	15	163.91	5	6	0
48 Georgia Tech	13	500	2,127	4.25	20	163.62	7	6	0
49 Ball St.	12	499	1,955	3.92	15	162.92	6	6	0
50 Boston College	13	492	2,068	4.2	25	159.08	9	4	0
51 Duke	12	487	1,901	3.9	8	158.42	2	10	0
52 Akron	12	489	1,890	3.87	25	157.5	4	8	0
53 Northwestern	12	437	1,884	4.31	25	157	3	9	0
54 UTEP	12	509	1,849	3.63	13	154.08	2	10	0
55 Tennessee	13	517	1,957	3.79	19	150.54	8	5	0
56 Oregon St.	13	502	1,933	3.85	21	148.69	8	5	0
57 Kentucky	12	430	1,782	4.14	19	148.5	7	5	0
58 Oklahoma St.	13	441	1,930	4.38	24	148.46	8	5	0
59 Michigan	13	505	1,929	3.82	25	148.38	10	3	0
60 Oregon	13	476	1,893	3.98	21	145.62	7	6	0
61 Iowa St.	14	554	2,030	3.66	30	145	7	7	0
62 North Carolina St.	14	522	2,017	3.86	33	144.07	11	3	0
63 Southern Miss.	13	523	1,868	3.57	20	143.69	7	6	0
64 Pittsburgh	13	547	1,860	3.4	15	143.08	9	4	0
65 Southern California	13	515	1,852	3.6	25	142.46	11	2	0
66 Michigan St.	12	430	1,709	3.97	14	142.42	4	8	0
67 Georgia	14	536	1,954	3.65	18	139.57	13	1	0
68 Notre Dame	13	528	1,812	3.43	15	139.38	10	3	0
69 Nevada	12	420	1,654	3.94	15	137.83	5	7	0
70 Temple	12	474	1,647	3.47	11	137.25	4	8	0
71 Cincinnati	14	545	1,916	3.52	21	136.86	7	7	0
72 Connecticut	12	450	1,639	3.64	22	136.58	6	6	0
73 Florida	13	465	1,771	3.81	20	136.23	8	5	0
74 Texas	13	511	1,762	3.45	23	135.54	11	2	0
75 South Fla.	11	403	1,481	3.67	16	134.64	9	2	0
76 Stanford	11	427	1,465	3.43	12	133.18	2	9	0
77 Fresno St.	14	518	1,854	3.58	9	132.43	9	5	0
78 UAB	12	458	1,562	3.41	12	130.17	5	7	0
79 Washington St.	13	433	1,680	3.88	17	129.23	10	3	0
80 Miami (Ohio)	12	451	1,532	3.4	23	127.67	7	5	0
81 UCLA	13	519	1,658	3.19	20	127.54	8	5	0

STATISTICAL LEADERS

Rank, School	G	Rsh	Net	Avg	TD	Yds/Gm	W	L	T
82 Virginia	14	486	1,777	3.66	16	126.93	9	5	0
83 Kansas	12	472	1,515	3.21	18	126.25	2	10	0
84 Marshall	13	416	1,635	3.93	21	125.77	11	2	0
85 East Caro.	12	439	1,488	3.39	20	124	4	8	0
86 Tulsa	12	430	1,480	3.44	12	123.33	1	11	0
87 La.-Monroe	12	413	1,461	3.54	12	121.75	3	9	0
88 Brigham Young	12	420	1,453	3.46	17	121.08	5	7	0
89 Clemson	13	458	1,569	3.43	22	120.69	7	6	0
90 Army	12	428	1,445	3.38	15	120.42	1	11	0
91 Mississippi St.	12	421	1,431	3.4	10	119.25	3	9	0
92 Texas A&M	12	421	1,418	3.37	16	118.17	6	6	0
93 Indiana	12	434	1,398	3.22	12	116.5	3	9	0
94 UCF	12	361	1,396	3.87	18	116.33	7	5	0
95 Memphis	12	390	1,390	3.56	15	115.83	3	9	0
96 Louisiana Tech	12	310	1,382	4.46	18	115.17	4	8	0
97 Idaho	12	396	1,380	3.48	14	115	2	10	0
98 Eastern Mich.	12	391	1,366	3.49	15	113.83	3	9	0
99 San Jose St.	13	410	1,459	3.56	18	112.23	6	7	0
100 Hawaii	14	308	1,533	4.98	26	109.5	10	4	0
101 Tulane	13	475	1,422	2.99	14	109.38	8	5	0
102 California	12	392	1,296	3.31	14	108	7	5	0
103 Western Mich.	12	393	1,287	3.27	13	107.25	4	8	0
104 Louisville	12	453	1,390	3.07	16	106.92	7	6	0
105 Baylor	12	447	1,241	2.78	16	103.42	3	9	0
106 North Carolina	12	414	1,230	2.97	7	102.5	3	9	0
107 Wyoming	12	387	1,200	3.1	13	100	2	10	0
108 Texas Tech	14	385	1,391	3.61	15	99.36	9	5	0
109 Buffalo	12	382	1,180	3.09	13	98.33	1	11	0
110 Mississippi	13	413	1,226	2.97	20	94.31	7	6	0
111 Arizona St.	14	489	1,246	2.55	20	89	8	6	0
112 Utah St.	11	302	929	3.08	14	84.45	4	7	0
113 Washington	13	454	968	2.13	15	74.46	7	6	0
114 San Diego St.	13	370	948	2.56	9	72.92	4	9	0
115 La.-Lafayette	12	384	734	1.91	9	61.17	3	9	0
116 Rutgers	12	420	620	1.48	5	51.67	1	11	0
117 Arizona	12	360	526	1.46	7	43.83	4	8	0

Rushing Defense

Rank, School	G	Rsh	Net	Avg	TD	Yds/Gm	W	L	T
1 TCU	12	393	778	1.98	9	64.8	10	2	0
2 Kansas St.	13	446	904	2.03	7	69.5	11	2	0
3 Ohio St.	14	418	1,088	2.6	5	77.7	14	0	0
4 Alabama	13	390	1,042	2.67	10	80.2	10	3	0
5 Iowa	13	416	1,065	2.56	17	81.9	11	2	0
6 Southern California	13	388	1,081	2.79	9	83.2	11	2	0
7 South Fla.	11	420	959	2.28	8	87.2	9	2	0
8 Washington St.	13	453	1,134	2.5	11	87.2	10	3	0
9 Oregon St.	13	479	1,225	2.56	13	94.2	8	5	0
10 Notre Dame	13	439	1,238	2.82	11	95.2	10	3	0
11 Washington	13	447	1,270	2.84	16	97.7	7	6	0
12 Utah	11	391	1,153	2.95	10	104.8	5	6	0
13 Troy St.	12	456	1,263	2.77	9	105.3	4	8	0
14 Oklahoma	14	496	1,510	3.04	9	107.9	12	2	0
15 Temple	12	459	1,300	2.83	22	108.3	4	8	0
16 Boise St.	13	418	1,422	3.4	9	109.4	12	1	0
17 Louisville	13	514	1,469	2.86	15	113	7	6	0
18 Arkansas	14	504	1,590	3.15	11	113.6	9	5	0
19 California	12	456	1,368	3	15	114	7	5	0
19 Georgia	14	524	1,596	3.05	11	114	13	1	0
21 Penn St.	13	479	1,492	3.11	11	114.8	9	4	0
22 New Mexico	14	513	1,608	3.13	15	114.9	7	7	0
23 Purdue	13	452	1,510	3.34	12	116.2	7	6	0
24 Pittsburgh	13	478	1,527	3.19	17	117.5	9	4	0
25 Oregon	13	507	1,536	3.03	13	118.2	7	6	0
26 North Texas	13	502	1,546	3.08	13	118.9	8	5	0
27 Arizona St.	14	498	1,671	3.36	18	119.4	8	6	0
28 Duke	12	425	1,446	3.4	20	120.5	2	10	0
29 Virginia Tech	12	495	1,700	3.43	19	121.4	10	4	0
30 West Virginia	13	453	1,584	3.5	19	121.8	9	4	0
31 Michigan	13	465	1,601	3.44	16	123.2	10	3	0
32 North Carolina St.	14	525	1,754	3.34	13	125.3	11	3	0
33 Tennessee	13	491	1,672	3.41	12	128.6	8	5	0
34 Maryland	14	531	1,801	3.39	12	128.6	11	3	0
35 UCLA	13	476	1,684	3.54	15	129.5	8	5	0
36 Florida St.	14	497	1,831	3.68	13	130.8	9	5	0
37 Texas A&M	12	468	1,571	3.36	14	130.9	6	6	0
38 Northern Ill.	12	447	1,582	3.54	17	131.8	8	4	0
39 Stanford	11	392	1,460	3.72	18	132.7	2	9	0
40 LSU	13	464	1,743	3.76	16	134.1	8	5	0
41 Houston	12	437	1,609	3.68	20	134.1	5	7	0
42 Georgia Tech	13	486	1,750	3.6	16	134.6	7	6	0
43 Cincinnati	14	537	1,934	3.6	23	138.1	7	7	0
44 Miami (Ohio)	12	393	1,676	4.26	20	139.7	7	5	0
45 Central Mich.	12	473	1,690	3.57	22	140.8	4	8	0
46 Auburn	13	467	1,842	3.94	17	141.7	9	4	0
47 Texas	13	474	1,853	3.91	10	142.5	11	2	0
48 Rice	11	417	1,573	3.77	14	143	4	7	0
49 Nebraska	14	549	2,053	3.74	25	146.6	7	7	0
50 Oklahoma St.	13	539	1,912	3.55	25	147.1	8	5	0
51 Wisconsin	14	516	2,082	4.03	14	148.7	8	6	0
52 UCF	12	499	1,796	3.6	15	149.7	7	5	0
53 Toledo	14	502	2,108	4.2	27	150.6	9	5	0
54 Western Mich.	12	483	1,814	3.76	16	151.2	4	8	0
55 Bowling Green	12	469	1,844	3.93	23	153.7	9	3	0
55 Ohio	12	454	1,844	4.06	23	153.7	4	8	0
57 UAB	12	496	1,848	3.73	21	154	5	7	0
58 Air Force	13	509	2,022	3.97	25	155.5	8	5	0
59 Connecticut	12	459	1,868	4.07	18	155.7	6	6	0
60 Clemson	13	530	2,056	3.88	17	158.2	7	6	0
61 Wake Forest	13	498	2,057	4.13	17	158.2	7	6	0
62 UNLV	12	481	1,909	3.97	20	159.1	5	7	0
63 Southern Methodist	12	423	1,913	4.52	21	159.4	3	9	0
64 Fresno St.	14	568	2,234	3.93	23	159.6	9	5	0
65 Mississippi	13	518	2,080	4.02	18	160	7	6	0
66 New Mexico St.	12	427	1,927	4.51	26	160.6	7	5	0
67 Arizona	12	508	1,942	3.82	18	161.8	4	8	0
68 Florida	13	526	2,121	4.03	14	162.3	8	5	0
69 Baylor	12	440	1,963	4.46	31	163.6	3	9	0
70 Texas Tech	14	548	2,295	4.19	29	163.9	9	5	0
71 South Carolina	12	481	1,974	4.1	11	164.5	5	7	0
72 Arkansas	13	524	2,149	4.1	21	165.3	9	5	0
72 Miami (Fla.)	13	582	2,149	3.69	19	165.3	12	1	0
74 Akron	12	492	2,008	4.08	20	167.3	4	8	0
75 Boston College	13	550	2,176	3.96	17	167.4	9	4	0
75 Southern Miss.	13	568	2,176	3.83	13	167.4	7	6	0
77 Colorado St.	14	543	2,346	4.32	25	167.6	10	4	0
78 Missouri	12	511	2,013	3.94	22	167.8	5	7	0
79 Hawaii	14	596	2,362	3.96	24	168.7	10	4	0
80 Ball St.	12	439	2,029	4.62	21	169.1	6	6	0
81 Colorado	14	558	2,381	4.27	25	170.1	9	5	0
82 Mississippi St.	12	525	2,041	3.89	17	170.1	3	9	0
83 San Diego St.	13	568	2,225	3.92	19	171.2	4	9	0
84 Middle Tenn.	12	476	2,060	4.33	20	171.7	4	8	0
85 Syracuse	12	497	2,063	4.15	26	171.9	4	8	0
86 Marshall	13	528	2,243	4.25	29	172.5	11	2	0
87 Kentucky	12	495	2,092	4.23	13	174.3	7	5	0
88 Iowa St.	14	584	2,444	4.18	30	174.6	7	7	0
89 Louisiana Tech	12	516	2,121	4.11	30	176.8	4	8	0
90 Minnesota	13	534	2,298	4.3	28	176.8	8	5	0
91 Brigham Young	12	518	2,133	4.12	29	177.8	5	7	0
92 Nevada	12	452	2,136	4.73	25	178	5	7	0
93 Tulane	13	533	2,341	4.39	26	180.1	8	5	0
94 La.-Lafayette	12	508	2,187	4.31	26	182.3	3	9	0
95 Vanderbilt	12	491	2,239	4.56	30	186.6	2	10	0
96 Idaho	12	489	2,282	4.67	32	190.2	2	10	0
96 Illinois	12	526	2,282	4.34	23	190.2	5	7	0
98 San Jose St.	13	518	2,508	4.84	25	192.9	6	7	0
99 UTEP	12	480	2,331	4.86	33	194.3	2	10	0
100 La.-Monroe	12	504	2,348	4.66	33	195.7	3	9	0
101 Memphis	12	538	2,365	4.4	22	197.1	3	9	0
102 Navy	12	562	2,430	4.32	28	202.5	2	10	0
103 Kent St.	12	518	2,452	4.73	32	204.3	3	9	0
104 Wyoming	12	537	2,469	4.6	30	205.8	2	10	0
105 Buffalo	12	549	2,482	4.52	26	206.8	1	11	0
106 Rutgers	12	525	2,484	4.73	20	207	1	11	0
107 East Caro.	12	545	2,485	4.56	21	207.1	4	8	0
108 Virginia	14	640	2,924	4.57	25	208.9	9	5	0
109 Army	12	575	2,520	4.38	36	210	1	11	0
110 Michigan St.	12	542	2,566	4.73	26	213.8	4	8	0
111 North Carolina	12	555	2,654	4.78	32	221.2	3	9	0
112 Utah St.	11	509	2,583	5.07	30	234.8	4	7	0
113 Indiana	12	522	2,819	5.4	33	234.9	3	9	0
114 Kansas	12	533	3,075	5.77	34	256.3	2	10	0
114 Tulsa	12	537	3,075	5.73	38	256.3	1	11	0
116 Eastern Mich.	12	576	3,529	6.13	45	294.1	3	9	0
117 Northwestern	12	694	3,763	5.42	39	313.6	3	9	0

Scoring Defense

Rank, School	G	TD	Kxp	Oxp	DKx	Dox	FG	Sf	Pts	Pts/Gm	W	L	T
1 Kansas St.	13	19	17	0	1	0	7	0	154	11.8	11	2	0
2 Ohio St.	14	19	16	1	0	0	17	0	183	13.1	14	0	0
3 North Texas	13	23	19	0	0	0	11	1	192	14.8	8	5	0
4 Georgia	14	28	21	1	0	0	7	0	212	15.1	13	1	0
5 Alabama	13	24	19	3	0	0	9	2	200	15.4	10	3	0
6 Oklahoma	14	27	23	2	0	0	9	0	216	15.4	12	2	0
7 Maryland	14	25	22	0	0	0	18	1	228	16.3	11	3	0
8 Texas	13	27	20	3	0	0	8	0	212	16.3	11	2	0
9 Notre Dame	13	27	23	1	0	0	10	0	217	16.7	10	3	0
10 North Carolina St.	14	29	23	1	0	0	13	0	238	17	11	3	0
11 Penn St.	13	29	20	2	1	0	9	0	227	17.5	9	4	0
11 Tennessee	13	24	21	0	0	0	20	1	227	17.5	8	5	0
13 Auburn	13	27	27	0	0	0	14	0	231	17.8	9	4	0
14 Pittsburgh	13	27	25	0	0	0	15	0	232	17.8	9	4	0
15 LSU	13	30	27	1	0	0	9	1	238	18.3	8	5	0
15 Southern Miss.	13	23	21	2	0	0	25	0	238	18.3	7	6	0
17 Boise St.	13	31	28	1	0	0	8	0	240	18.5	12	1	0
17 Southern California	13	27	26	1	1	0	16	0	240	18.5	11	2	0
19 TCU	12	27	20	4	0	0	10	1	222	18.5	10	2	0
20 South Fla.	11	27	20	2	0	0	6	0	204	18.5	9	2	0
21 Virginia Tech	14	34	28	2	0	0	9	0	263	18.8	10	4	0
22 Miami (Fla.)	13	31	27	1	0	0	11	0	248	19.1	12	1	0
23 Boston College	13	31	29	1	0	0	12	0	253	19.5	9	4	0
24 Iowa	13	32	29	1	0	0	9	3	256	19.7	11	2	0
25 Arkansas	14	30	23	0	0	0	24	1	277	19.8	9	5	0
26 Michigan	13	34	25	2	0	0	10	1	265	20.4	10	3	0
27 Georgia Tech	13	30	27	2	0	0	18	1	267	20.5	7	6	0
27 Oregon St.	13	29	28	0	0	0	21	1	267	20.5	8	5	0
29 Utah	11	27	23	1	0	0	13	0	226	20.5	5	6	0
30 Troy St.	12	31	26	2	0	0	12	0	252	21	4	8	0
31 Florida	13	34	28	3	0	0	13	1	279	21.5	8	5	0
32 Florida St.	14	35	31	1	0	0	18	2	301	21.5	9	5	0
33 Tulane	13	35	31	1	0	0	13	0	282	21.7	8	5	0
34 South Carolina	12	31	25	2	0	0	15	1	262	21.8	5	7	0
35 Purdue	13	36	30	0	0	0	14	0	288	22.2	7	6	0
36 Connecticut	12	35	31	1	0	0	9	0	270	22.5	6	6	0
37 Washington St.	13	35	32	1	0	0	16	2	296	22.8	10	3	0
38 Wisconsin	14	37	31	3	0	0	21	0	322	23	8	6	0
39 Colorado	14	43	35	0	0	0	10	1	325	23.2	9	5	0
40 West Virginia	13	39	34	1	0	0	10	1	302	23.2	9	4	0
41 Air Force	13	36	32	1	0	0	17	1	303	23.3	8	5	0
42 Texas A&M	12	34	27	2	0	0	15	0	280	23.3	6	6	0
43 Cincinnati	14	40	33	0	0	0	18	1	329	23.5	7	7	0
44 Colorado St.	14	45	32	4	0	1	6	1	332	23.7	10	4	0
45 Nebraska	14	41	38	0	0	0	17	0	335	23.9	7	7	0
46 Marshall	13	41	33	3	0	0	10	0	315	24.2	11	2	0
47 Louisville	13	39	34	0	0	0	17	0	319	24.5	7	6	0
47 Minnesota	13	42	38	2	0	0	7	2	319	24.5	8	5	0
49 Northern Ill.	12	37	27	3	0	0	13	2	298	24.8	8	4	0
50 Virginia	14	41	32	1	0	0	22	1	348	24.9	9	5	0
51 UCLA	13	41	37	2	0	0	13	0	326	25.1	8	5	0
52 Kentucky	12	39	31	2	0	1	10	0	301	25.1	7	5	0
53 Wake Forest	13	41	35	1	0	0	14	1	327	25.2	7	6	0
54 Bowling Green	12	39	38	0	0	0	10	1	304	25.3	9	3	0
55 Mississippi	13	41	37	2	0	0	14	1	331	25.5	7	6	0
56 New Mexico	14	44	38	2	0	0	16	2	358	25.6	7	7	0
57 Illinois	12	39	33	1	0	0	12	1	307	25.6	5	7	0
58 Arizona	12	35	32	0	0	0	22	1	310	25.8	4	8	0
59 UCF	12	39	30	2	0	0	15	1	315	26.3	7	5	0
60 Washington	13	41	39	0	0	0	19	0	342	26.3	7	6	0
61 California	12	38	30	4	0	0	16	2	318	26.5	7	5	0
62 Clemson	13	42	36	1	0	0	19	1	349	26.8	7	6	0
63 Rice	11	38	32	0	0	0	12	0	296	26.9	4	7	0
64 Toledo	14	48	45	0	0	0	15	0	378	27	9	5	0
65 Fresno St.	14	47	39	1	0	0	18	1	379	27.1	9	5	0
66 Miami (Ohio)	12	42	35	0	0	0	12	1	325	27.1	7	5	0
67 Memphis	12	42	35	1	0	0	12	1	327	27.3	3	9	0
68 New Mexico St.	12	44	38	1	0	0	8	1	328	27.3	7	5	0
69 Oklahoma St.	13	47	33	3	0	0	11	1	356	27.4	8	5	0
70 Western Mich.	12	43	38	2	0	0	10	0	330	27.5	4	8	0
71 Middle Tenn.	12	43	34	3	0	0	10	2	332	27.7	4	8	0
72 Ball St.	12	45	40	1	0	0	7	0	333	27.8	6	6	0
72 Brigham Young	12	42	36	3	0	0	13	0	333	27.8	5	7	0
74 Arkansas St.	13	47	42	0	0	0	11	2	361	27.8	6	7	0
75 Hawaii	14	48	38	2	0	0	19	1	389	27.8	10	4	0
76 Oregon	13	48	42	1	0	0	10	0	362	27.8	7	6	0
77 Mississippi St.	12	44	39	1	0	0	10	2	339	28.3	3	9	0
78 Iowa St.	14	52	48	0	0	0	12	0	396	28.3	7	7	0
79 Arizona St.	14	50	43	1	0	0	20	1	407	29.1	8	6	0
80 Temple	12	46	41	1	0	0	10	1	351	29.3	4	8	0
81 Missouri	12	44	35	4	0	0	15	0	352	29.3	5	7	0

Rank, School	G	TD	Kxp	Oxp	DKx	Dox	FG	Sf	Pts	Pts/Gm	W	L	T
81 La.-Lafayette	12	46	41	1	0	0	11	0	352	29.3	3	9	0
83 Duke	12	44	39	0	0	0	16	1	353	29.4	2	10	0
84 UNLV	12	45	39	3	0	1	15	2	366	30.5	5	7	0
85 Vanderbilt	12	45	40	1	0	0	18	1	368	30.7	2	10	0
86 UAB	12	46	39	1	0	0	17	1	370	30.8	5	7	0
87 Nevada	12	49	45	1	0	0	10	0	371	30.9	5	7	0
88 Ohio	12	49	44	0	0	0	12	0	374	31.2	4	8	0
89 Texas Tech	14	59	51	2	0	0	8	3	439	31.4	9	5	0
90 Southern Methodist	12	50	46	1	0	0	10	0	378	31.5	3	9	0
91 Akron	12	48	47	0	0	0	14	1	379	31.6	4	8	0
92 San Diego St.	13	54	43	2	0	0	12	2	411	31.6	4	9	0
93 Central Mich.	12	48	44	1	0	0	16	1	384	32	4	8	0
94 Houston	12	50	45	0	0	0	16	0	393	32.8	5	7	0
95 Rutgers	12	51	44	1	0	0	13	3	397	33.1	1	11	0
96 Michigan St.	12	52	47	2	0	0	11	1	398	33.2	4	8	0
97 East Caro.	12	50	43	1	0	0	18	0	399	33.3	4	8	0
98 Syracuse	12	52	47	1	0	0	15	0	406	33.8	4	8	0
99 Stanford	11	44	40	1	0	0	23	1	377	34.3	2	9	0
100 Buffalo	12	55	51	1	0	0	11	0	416	34.7	1	11	0
101 Tulsa	12	55	50	1	1	0	11	0	417	34.8	1	11	0
102 North Carolina	12	58	53	1	0	0	6	0	421	35.1	3	9	0
103 Kent St.	12	55	48	1	0	0	14	1	424	35.3	3	9	0
104 Louisiana Tech	12	57	48	2	0	0	10	1	426	35.5	4	8	0
105 Idaho	12	54	48	4	0	0	16	0	428	35.7	2	10	0
106 San Jose St.	13	59	53	2	0	0	18	1	467	35.9	6	7	0
107 Wyoming	12	54	50	1	0	0	18	1	432	36	2	10	0
108 Navy	12	57	47	3	0	0	13	1	436	36.3	2	10	0
109 Indiana	12	58	52	0	0	0	15	0	445	37.1	3	9	0
110 La.-Monroe	12	59	51	2	0	0	14	0	451	37.6	3	9	0
111 Utah St.	11	57	51	0	0	0	13	0	432	39.3	4	7	0
112 Army	12	61	58	2	0	0	19	3	491	40.9	1	11	0
113 Northwestern	12	65	59	2	0	0	12	2	493	41.1	3	9	0
114 Baylor	12	67	58	0	0	0	12	0	496	41.3	3	9	0
115 Kansas	12	67	57	4	0	0	12	2	507	42.3	2	10	0
116 UTEP	12	70	64	0	0	0	9	0	511	42.6	2	10	0
117 Eastern Mich.	12	76	68	3	0	0	12	0	566	47.2	3	9	0

Scoring Offense

Rank, School	G	Pts	Pts/Gm	TD	Kxp	Oxp	Dkx	Dox	FG	Sf	W	L	T
1 Boise St.	13	593	45.62	79	75	0	0	0	14	1	12	1	0
2 Kansas St.	13	582	44.77	79	65	3	1	0	11	1	11	2	0
3 Bowling Green	12	490	40.83	65	60	2	0	0	12	0	9	3	0
4 Miami (Fla.)	13	527	40.54	70	66	0	0	0	13	1	12	1	0
5 Oklahoma	14	541	38.64	70	61	3	0	0	16	3	12	2	0
6 Texas Tech	14	537	38.36	71	62	5	0	0	13	0	9	5	0
7 Iowa	13	484	37.23	60	57	0	1	0	21	1	11	2	0
8 Hawaii	14	502	35.86	66	55	2	0	0	15	1	10	4	0
9 Southern California	13	465	35.77	60	54	0	0	0	17	0	11	2	0
10 California	12	427	35.58	53	50	0	0	0	19	1	7	5	0
11 Toledo	14	495	35.36	66	54	3	0	0	13	0	9	5	0
12 Marshall	13	457	35.15	59	51	2	0	0	16	0	11	2	0
13 Oklahoma St.	13	446	34.31	59	55	1	1	0	11	0	8	5	0
13 Penn St.	13	446	34.31	57	45	4	0	0	17	0	9	4	0
15 Air Force	13	440	33.85	56	50	1	0	0	16	2	8	5	0
16 Texas	13	439	33.77	56	55	0	0	0	16	0	11	2	0
17 Washington St.	13	431	33.15	52	47	1	0	0	22	2	10	3	0
18 North Carolina St.	14	460	32.86	62	52	1	0	0	10	2	11	3	0
19 UCF	12	391	32.58	50	45	2	0	0	14	0	7	5	0
20 Arizona St.	14	452	32.29	54	49	3	0	0	23	2	8	6	0
21 Maryland	14	451	32.21	54	53	0	0	0	24	1	11	3	0
22 Georgia	14	450	32.14	53	52	0	0	0	26	1	13	1	0
23 Kentucky	12	385	32.08	52	42	0	0	0	9	2	7	5	0
24 Oregon	13	417	32.08	51	49	0	0	0	20	1	7	6	0
25 Miami (Ohio)	12	384	32	49	44	2	0	0	14	0	7	5	0
26 Oregon St.	13	414	31.85	52	50	1	0	0	16	1	8	5	0
27 Northern Ill.	12	375	31.25	46	41	1	0	0	18	1	8	4	0
28 Connecticut	12	373	31.08	48	47	0	0	0	12	1	6	6	0
29 South Fla.	11	339	30.82	42	35	0	0	0	16	2	9	2	0
30 Virginia Tech	14	429	30.64	56	51	1	0	0	12	2	10	4	0
31 Washington	13	398	30.62	48	42	0	0	0	22	1	7	6	0
32 Florida St.	14	428	30.57	53	51	0	0	0	19	1	9	5	0
33 West Virginia	13	396	30.46	52	47	0	0	0	11	2	9	4	0
34 Boston College	13	392	30.15	46	40	2	0	0	24	0	9	4	0
35 TCU	12	361	30.08	41	36	3	0	0	23	2	10	2	0
36 Missouri	12	360	30	48	43	0	0	0	9	1	5	7	0
37 Colorado St.	14	418	29.86	50	40	2	0	0	24	1	10	4	0
38 Auburn	13	388	29.85	52	47	3	0	0	7	1	9	4	0
39 UCLA	13	387	29.77	46	43	0	0	1	20	3	8	5	0
40 Purdue	13	386	29.69	51	48	1	0	0	10	0	7	6	0
41 Ohio St.	14	410	29.29	48	45	0	0	0	25	1	14	0	0
42 Cincinnati	14	409	29.21	50	44	3	0	0	19	1	7	7	0
43 Minnesota	13	376	28.92	45	42	2	0	0	20	0	8	5	0

Rank, School	G	Pts	Pts/Gm	TD	Kxp	Oxp	Dkx	Dox	FG	Sf	W	L	T
43 San Jose St.	13	376	28.92	49	42	2	0	0	12	0	6	7	0
45 Syracuse	12	347	28.92	45	38	3	0	0	11	0	4	8	0
46 Iowa St.	14	404	28.86	50	46	1	0	0	18	1	7	7	0
47 Illinois	12	346	28.83	43	40	2	0	0	14	1	5	7	0
48 Louisville	13	374	28.77	48	40	3	0	0	12	2	7	6	0
49 Texas A&M	12	345	28.75	45	39	0	0	0	12	0	6	6	0
50 Virginia	14	402	28.71	53	42	3	0	0	12	0	9	5	0
51 Colorado	14	398	28.43	52	45	4	0	0	11	0	9	5	0
52 Alabama	13	367	28.23	45	39	2	0	0	18	0	10	3	0
53 East Caro.	12	335	27.92	41	34	1	0	0	17	1	4	8	0
54 Michigan	13	361	27.77	47	43	0	0	0	12	0	10	3	0
54 Tulane	13	361	27.77	43	29	6	0	0	20	1	8	5	0
56 Utah St.	11	305	27.73	38	33	1	0	0	14	0	4	7	0
57 Nevada	12	331	27.58	44	35	1	0	0	10	0	5	7	0
58 Wake Forest	13	356	27.38	44	37	2	0	0	17	0	7	6	0
59 Nebraska	14	383	27.36	48	47	0	0	0	16	0	7	7	0
60 New Mexico St.	12	327	27.25	39	32	4	0	0	17	1	7	5	0
61 Akron	12	325	27.08	44	40	0	0	0	7	0	4	8	0
62 Fresno St.	14	378	27	44	43	0	0	0	23	1	9	5	0
62 Mississippi	13	351	27	43	40	2	0	0	15	2	7	6	0
64 Houston	12	320	26.67	41	32	3	0	0	12	0	5	7	0
64 Louisiana Tech	12	320	26.67	39	30	2	1	0	16	1	4	8	0
66 Wisconsin	14	372	26.57	47	43	1	0	0	15	0	8	6	0
67 Arkansas	14	370	26.43	45	42	0	0	0	18	2	9	5	0
68 Michigan St.	12	316	26.33	41	36	1	0	0	10	1	4	8	0
69 Florida	13	336	25.85	45	33	2	0	1	9	0	8	5	0
70 Pittsburgh	13	331	25.46	41	35	1	0	0	16	0	9	4	0
71 Clemson	13	330	25.38	40	37	0	0	0	17	1	7	6	0
72 Memphis	12	303	25.25	40	32	2	0	0	9	0	3	9	0
72 Western Mich.	12	303	25.25	37	34	1	0	0	15	0	4	8	0
74 Ohio	12	299	24.92	39	31	1	0	0	10	1	4	8	0
75 LSU	13	323	24.85	39	34	2	0	0	17	0	8	5	0
76 Middle Tenn.	12	297	24.75	38	31	4	0	0	10	0	4	8	0
77 New Mexico	14	341	24.36	46	40	1	0	1	5	3	7	7	0
78 UNLV	12	292	24.33	39	33	2	0	0	7	0	5	7	0
79 Navy	12	290	24.17	39	34	0	0	0	6	2	2	10	0
80 Wyoming	12	288	24	40	24	6	0	0	4	0	2	10	0
81 Eastern Mich.	12	286	23.83	40	37	0	0	0	3	0	3	9	0
82 San Diego St.	13	309	23.77	37	32	1	0	0	17	1	4	9	0
83 Idaho	12	285	23.75	38	36	0	0	0	7	0	2	10	0
84 Ball St.	12	278	23.17	36	31	1	0	0	9	1	6	6	0
85 Rice	11	253	23	33	31	0	0	0	8	0	4	7	0
86 Tennessee	13	296	22.77	36	28	0	0	0	16	2	8	5	0
87 Brigham Young	12	272	22.67	34	27	1	0	0	13	0	5	7	0
87 Northwestern	12	272	22.67	35	30	1	0	0	10	0	3	9	0
89 Utah	11	249	22.64	31	26	1	0	0	11	1	5	6	0
90 UAB	12	268	22.33	31	29	1	0	0	17	0	5	7	0
91 Notre Dame	13	290	22.31	35	32	1	0	0	14	2	10	3	0
92 Central Mich.	12	267	22.25	33	27	0	0	0	14	0	4	8	0
93 Southern Miss.	13	282	21.69	33	31	1	0	0	15	3	7	6	0
94 Georgia Tech	13	280	21.54	35	32	1	0	0	12	0	7	6	0
95 Indiana	12	258	21.5	33	23	2	0	0	9	3	3	9	0
96 Kansas	12	248	20.67	33	23	2	0	0	7	1	2	10	0
97 Stanford	11	225	20.45	28	24	3	0	0	9	0	2	9	0
98 Temple	12	242	20.17	29	22	2	0	0	14	0	4	8	0
99 Arkansas St.	13	259	19.92	33	31	0	0	0	10	0	6	7	0
100 La.-Monroe	12	236	19.67	32	27	0	0	0	5	1	3	9	0
101 Tulsa	12	233	19.42	31	15	3	0	0	8	1	1	11	0
102 North Texas	13	249	19.15	32	25	1	0	0	10	0	8	5	0
103 Arizona	12	227	18.92	27	26	0	0	0	13	0	4	8	0
103 Mississippi St.	12	227	18.92	26	17	2	0	0	16	1	3	9	0
103 Duke	12	227	18.92	27	21	0	0	0	14	1	2	10	0
106 Army	12	226	18.83	29	25	0	0	0	9	0	1	11	0
107 South Carolina	12	225	18.75	28	25	1	0	0	10	0	5	7	0
108 North Carolina	12	223	18.58	28	26	0	0	0	9	1	3	9	0
109 Vanderbilt	12	221	18.42	28	27	1	0	0	8	0	2	10	0
110 UTEP	12	220	18.33	28	28	0	0	0	8	0	2	10	0
111 Troy St.	12	218	18.17	27	21	1	0	0	11	0	4	8	0
112 Buffalo	12	214	17.83	27	16	2	0	0	10	1	1	11	0
113 Southern Methodist	12	207	17.25	27	19	1	0	0	8	0	3	9	0
114 La.-Lafayette	12	203	16.92	25	20	1	0	0	9	2	3	9	0
115 Baylor	12	202	16.83	26	17	4	0	0	7	0	3	9	0
115 Kent St.	12	202	16.83	24	22	0	0	0	12	0	3	9	0
117 Rutgers	12	167	13.92	22	18	1	0	0	5	0	1	11	0

Total Defense

Rank, School	G	Pl	Yds	Avg	TD	Yds/Gm	W	L	T
1 TCU	12	799	2,883	3.61	27	240.25	10	2	0
2 Kansas St.	13	864	3,237	3.75	19	249	11	2	0
3 Alabama	13	764	3,345	4.38	24	257.31	10	3	0
4 Troy St.	12	784	3,322	4.24	31	276.83	4	8	0
5 Tennessee	13	840	3,703	4.41	24	284.85	8	5	0
6 Southern California	13	842	3,704	4.4	27	284.92	11	2	0
7 Miami (Fla.)	13	935	3,705	3.96	31	285	12	1	0
8 LSU	13	825	3,728	4.52	30	286.77	8	5	0
9 North Texas	13	870	3,778	4.34	23	290.62	8	5	0
10 Oklahoma	14	928	4,104	4.42	27	293.14	12	2	0
11 Oregon St.	13	935	3,816	4.08	29	293.54	8	5	0
12 Pittsburgh	13	878	3,848	4.38	27	296	9	4	0
13 Notre Dame	13	891	3,900	4.38	27	300	10	3	0
14 North Carolina St.	14	962	4,211	4.38	29	300.79	11	3	0
15 Georgia	14	934	4,249	4.55	28	303.5	13	1	0
16 Texas	13	874	4,000	4.58	27	307.69	11	2	0
17 South Fla.	11	820	3,398	4.14	27	308.91	9	2	0
18 Temple	12	815	3,788	4.65	46	315.67	4	8	0
19 Connecticut	12	781	3,793	4.86	35	316.08	6	6	0
20 Purdue	13	871	4,123	4.73	36	317.15	7	6	0
21 Cincinnati	14	964	4,453	4.62	40	318.07	7	7	0
22 Louisville	13	941	4,159	4.42	39	319.92	7	6	0
23 Ohio St.	14	964	4,492	4.66	19	320.86	14	0	0
24 Mississippi St.	12	807	3,888	4.82	44	324	3	9	0
25 Florida	13	888	4,232	4.77	34	325.54	8	5	0
26 Auburn	13	892	4,266	4.78	27	328.15	9	4	0
27 Penn St.	13	933	4,291	4.6	29	330.08	9	4	0
28 Western Mich.	12	845	3,968	4.7	43	330.67	4	8	0
29 Utah	11	769	3,653	4.75	27	332.09	5	6	0
30 New Mexico	14	965	4,659	4.83	44	332.79	7	7	0
31 Marshall	13	894	4,342	4.86	41	334	11	2	0
32 Virginia Tech	14	938	4,691	5	34	335.07	10	4	0
33 West Virginia	13	869	4,361	5.02	39	335.46	9	4	0
34 Southern Miss.	13	947	4,371	4.62	23	336.23	7	6	0
35 Texas A&M	12	869	4,061	4.67	34	338.42	6	6	0
36 Maryland	14	975	4,743	4.86	25	338.79	11	3	0
37 Boston College	13	923	4,413	4.78	31	339.46	9	4	0
38 Boise St.	13	947	4,430	4.68	31	340.77	12	1	0
39 Arkansas St.	13	840	4,442	5.29	47	341.69	6	7	0
40 Washington St.	13	988	4,452	4.51	35	342.46	10	3	0
41 Mississippi	13	867	4,515	5.21	41	347.31	7	6	0
42 Michigan	13	905	4,520	4.99	34	347.69	10	3	0
43 Arkansas	14	987	4,873	4.94	30	348.07	9	5	0
44 South Carolina	12	836	4,217	5.04	31	351.42	5	7	0
45 UCF	12	879	4,245	4.83	39	353.75	7	5	0
46 Air Force	13	879	4,606	5.24	36	354.31	8	5	0
47 Iowa	13	951	4,619	4.86	32	355.31	11	2	0
48 Clemson	13	919	4,620	5.03	42	355.38	7	6	0
48 Minnesota	13	901	4,620	5.13	42	355.38	8	5	0
50 Georgia Tech	13	926	4,624	4.99	30	355.69	7	6	0
51 Washington	13	893	4,643	5.2	41	357.15	7	6	0
52 UCLA	13	908	4,651	5.12	41	357.77	8	5	0
53 Iowa St.	14	1010	5,024	4.97	52	358.86	7	7	0
54 New Mexico St.	12	766	4,339	5.66	44	361.58	7	5	0
55 Nebraska	14	1008	5,067	5.03	41	361.93	7	7	0
56 Memphis	12	874	4,354	4.98	42	362.83	3	9	0
57 Arizona St.	14	985	5,091	5.17	50	363.64	8	6	0
58 Toledo	14	928	5,092	5.49	48	363.71	9	5	0
59 Bowling Green	12	867	4,381	5.05	39	365.08	9	3	0
60 Colorado	14	1011	5,120	5.06	43	365.71	9	5	0
61 Florida St.	14	962	5,124	5.33	35	366	9	5	0
62 Tulane	13	969	4,835	4.99	35	371.92	8	5	0
63 Wisconsin	14	948	5,221	5.51	37	372.93	8	6	0
64 Colorado St.	14	987	5,227	5.3	45	373.36	10	4	0
65 Duke	12	830	4,502	5.42	44	375.17	2	10	0
66 Ohio	12	814	4,533	5.57	49	377.75	4	8	0
67 La.-Lafayette	12	813	4,562	5.61	46	380.17	3	9	0
68 UAB	12	858	4,586	5.34	46	382.17	5	7	0
69 Brigham Young	12	895	4,616	5.16	42	384.67	5	7	0
70 Stanford	11	756	4,232	5.6	44	384.73	2	9	0
71 Rice	11	780	4,236	5.43	38	385.09	4	7	0
72 Arizona	12	876	4,634	5.29	35	386.17	4	8	0
73 Northern Ill.	12	875	4,641	5.3	37	386.75	8	4	0
74 Wake Forest	13	911	5,073	5.57	41	390.23	7	6	0
75 California	12	891	4,714	5.29	38	392.83	7	5	0
76 Army	12	868	4,715	5.43	61	392.92	1	11	0
77 UNLV	12	870	4,725	5.43	45	393.75	4	8	0
78 Akron	12	832	4,734	5.69	48	394.5	4	8	0
79 Hawaii	14	1091	5,530	5.07	48	395	10	4	0
80 Oklahoma St.	13	1019	5,183	5.09	47	398.69	8	5	0
81 Middle Tenn.	12	823	4,809	5.84	43	400.75	4	8	0

Rank, Name	G	Pl	Yds	Avg	TD	Yds/Gm	W	L	T
82 Kentucky	12	864	4,815	5.57	39	401.25	7	5	0
83 Michigan St.	12	876	4,832	5.52	52	402.67	4	8	0
84 Houston	12	831	4,841	5.83	50	403.42	5	7	0
85 Texas Tech	14	1020	5,649	5.54	59	403.5	9	5	0
86 Southern Methodist	12	793	4,845	6.11	50	403.75	3	9	0
87 Fresno St.	14	1028	5,666	5.51	47	404.71	9	5	0
88 Rutgers	12	858	4,860	5.66	51	405	1	11	0
89 Ball St.	12	829	4,863	5.87	45	405.25	6	6	0
89 Baylor	12	822	4,863	5.92	67	405.25	3	9	0
89 Central Mich.	12	866	4,863	5.62	48	405.25	4	8	0
92 Vanderbilt	12	828	4,869	5.88	45	405.75	2	10	0
93 Kent St.	12	862	4,875	5.66	55	406.25	3	9	0
94 Oregon	13	982	5,321	5.42	48	409.31	7	6	0
95 San Diego St.	13	1003	5,341	5.33	54	410.85	4	9	0
96 Miami (Ohio)	12	817	4,952	6.06	42	412.67	7	5	0
97 Nevada	12	810	5,035	6.22	49	419.58	5	7	0
98 Illinois	12	930	5,046	5.43	39	420.5	5	7	0
99 Navy	12	849	5,073	5.98	57	422.75	2	10	0
100 Virginia	14	1073	5,944	5.54	41	424.57	9	5	0
101 Indiana	12	857	5,141	6	58	428.42	3	9	0
102 La.-Monroe	12	859	5,208	6.06	59	434	3	9	0
103 Buffalo	12	902	5,213	5.78	55	434.42	1	11	0
104 UTEP	12	832	5,282	6.35	70	440.17	2	10	0
105 Louisiana Tech	12	899	5,294	5.89	57	441.17	4	8	0
106 East Caro.	12	909	5,348	5.88	50	445.67	4	8	0
107 Missouri	12	937	5,404	5.77	44	450.33	5	7	0
108 North Carolina	12	861	5,429	6.31	58	452.42	3	9	0
109 Tulsa	12	879	5,504	6.26	55	458.67	1	11	0
110 Idaho	12	843	5,575	6.61	54	464.58	2	10	0
111 Utah St.	11	841	5,182	6.16	57	471.09	4	7	0
112 Kansas	12	835	5,669	6.79	67	472.42	2	10	0
113 Syracuse	12	881	5,708	6.48	52	475.67	4	8	0
114 Wyoming	12	943	5,890	6.25	54	490.83	2	10	0
115 San Jose St.	13	993	6,414	6.46	59	493.38	6	7	0
116 Northwestern	12	933	6,028	6.46	65	502.33	3	9	0
117 Eastern Mich.	12	857	6,239	7.28	76	519.92	3	9	0

Total Offense

Rank, School	G	Pl	Yds	Avg	TD	Yds/Gm	W	L	T
1 Boise St.	13	950	6,519	6.86	79	501.46	12	1	0
2 Hawaii	14	1039	6,939	6.68	66	495.64	10	4	0
3 Marshall	13	991	6,439	6.5	59	495.31	11	2	0
4 Texas Tech	14	1155	6,835	5.92	71	488.21	9	5	0
5 Toledo	14	1033	6,611	6.4	66	472.21	9	5	0
6 Miami (Fla.)	13	887	6,056	6.83	70	465.85	12	1	0
7 Purdue	13	1034	5,879	5.69	51	452.23	7	6	0
8 Southern California	13	1009	5,840	5.79	60	449.23	11	2	0
9 Bowling Green	12	898	5,387	6	65	448.92	9	3	0
10 Illinois	12	915	5,356	5.85	43	446.33	5	7	0
11 UCF	12	803	5,233	6.52	50	436.08	7	5	0
12 Nevada	12	897	5,210	5.81	44	434.17	5	7	0
13 Iowa	13	867	5,518	6.36	60	424.46	11	2	0
14 Penn St.	13	877	5,508	6.28	57	423.69	9	4	0
15 Kansas St.	13	878	5,499	6.26	79	423	11	2	0
16 Washington St.	13	891	5,485	6.16	52	421.92	10	3	0
17 Washington	13	1075	5,469	5.09	48	420.69	7	6	0
18 West Virginia	13	993	5,440	5.48	52	418.46	9	4	0
19 Louisiana Tech	12	837	5,015	5.99	39	417.92	4	8	0
20 Oregon St.	13	970	5,347	5.51	52	411.31	8	5	0
21 Oklahoma St.	13	895	5,344	5.97	59	411.08	8	5	0
22 UNLV	12	843	4,914	5.83	39	409.5	5	7	0
23 New Mexico St.	12	849	4,912	5.79	39	409.33	7	5	0
24 Wake Forest	13	990	5,305	5.36	44	408.08	7	6	0
25 Florida	13	982	5,290	5.39	45	406.92	8	5	0
26 Miami (Ohio)	12	897	4,863	5.42	49	405.25	7	5	0
27 Idaho	12	908	4,855	5.35	38	404.58	2	10	0
28 Akron	12	893	4,852	5.43	44	404.33	4	8	0
29 San Diego St.	13	954	5,250	5.5	37	403.85	4	9	0
30 Alabama	13	929	5,245	5.65	45	403.46	10	3	0
31 Air Force	13	940	5,176	5.51	56	398.15	8	5	0
32 Florida St.	14	981	5,573	5.68	53	398.07	9	5	0
33 Cincinnati	14	1030	5,565	5.4	50	397.5	7	7	0
34 Minnesota	13	991	5,111	5.56	45	393.15	8	5	0
35 Arizona St.	14	1047	5,500	5.25	54	392.86	8	6	0
36 Houston	12	881	4,713	5.35	41	392.75	5	7	0
37 Oklahoma	14	1010	5,496	5.44	70	392.57	12	2	0
38 Utah St.	11	789	4,317	5.47	38	392.45	4	7	0
39 North Carolina St.	14	969	5,485	5.66	62	391.79	11	3	0
40 Boston College	13	906	5,079	5.61	46	390.69	9	4	0
41 Maryland	14	916	5,451	5.95	54	389.36	11	3	0
42 Northwestern	12	888	4,668	5.26	35	389	3	9	0
43 Colorado St.	14	973	5,440	5.59	50	388.57	10	4	0
44 Auburn	13	862	5,038	5.84	52	387.54	9	4	0

Rank, School	G	Pl	Yds	Avg	TD	Yds/Gm	W	L	T
45 Missouri	12	874	4,642	5.31	48	386.83	5	7	0
46 South Fla.	11	830	4,253	5.12	42	386.64	9	2	0
47 Texas A&M	12	846	4,634	5.48	45	386.17	6	6	0
48 Texas	13	915	5,013	5.48	56	385.62	11	2	0
49 Georgia	14	981	5,389	5.49	53	384.93	13	1	0
50 Brigham Young	12	921	4,582	4.98	34	381.83	5	7	0
51 Iowa St.	14	1,008	5,338	5.3	50	381.29	7	7	0
52 Michigan	13	977	4,955	5.07	47	381.15	10	3	0
53 Wyoming	12	858	4,557	5.31	40	379.75	2	10	0
54 Syracuse	12	861	4,517	5.25	45	376.42	4	8	0
55 Northern Ill.	12	806	4,514	5.6	46	376.17	8	4	0
56 San Jose St.	13	893	4,883	5.47	49	375.62	6	7	0
57 Georgia Tech	13	935	4,871	5.21	35	374.69	7	6	0
58 Colorado	14	968	5,243	5.42	52	374.5	9	5	0
59 Fresno St.	14	1,001	5,236	5.23	44	374	9	5	0
60 Oregon	13	888	4,852	5.46	51	373.23	7	6	0
61 Nebraska	14	959	5,224	5.45	48	373.14	7	7	0
62 Central Mich.	12	930	4,467	4.8	33	372.25	4	8	0
63 Utah	11	823	4,094	4.97	31	372.18	5	6	0
64 Virginia Tech	14	931	5,203	5.59	56	371.64	10	4	0
65 Michigan St.	12	807	4,452	5.52	41	371	4	8	0
66 TCU	12	885	4,441	5.02	41	370.08	10	2	0
67 Navy	12	813	4,433	5.45	39	369.42	2	10	0
68 North Carolina	12	847	4,429	5.23	28	369.08	3	9	0
69 Indiana	12	880	4,418	5.02	33	368.17	3	9	0
70 Ohio St.	14	909	5,103	5.61	48	364.5	14	0	0
71 Clemson	13	920	4,726	5.14	40	363.54	7	6	0
72 Western Mich.	12	860	4,360	5.07	37	363.33	4	8	0
73 Middle Tenn.	12	784	4,352	5.55	38	362.67	4	8	0
74 Eastern Mich.	12	832	4,327	5.2	40	360.58	3	9	0
75 Connecticut	12	842	4,310	5.12	48	359.17	6	6	0
76 Mississippi	13	899	4,663	5.19	43	358.69	7	6	0
77 Duke	12	873	4,300	4.93	27	358.33	2	10	0
78 Pittsburgh	13	918	4,656	5.07	41	358.15	9	4	0
79 UCLA	13	886	4,643	5.24	46	357.15	8	5	0
80 Virginia	14	934	4,999	5.35	53	357.07	9	5	0
81 California	12	820	4,267	5.2	53	355.58	7	5	0
82 Memphis	12	842	4,258	5.06	40	354.83	3	9	0
83 Wisconsin	14	967	4,966	5.14	47	354.71	8	6	0
84 Arkansas	14	942	4,950	5.25	45	353.57	9	5	0
85 Tennessee	13	873	4,592	5.26	36	353.23	8	5	0
86 LSU	13	883	4,550	5.15	39	350	8	5	0
87 Kentucky	12	780	4,169	5.34	52	347.42	7	5	0
88 Rice	11	757	3,816	5.04	33	346.91	4	7	0
89 La.-Monroe	12	835	4,125	4.94	32	343.75	3	9	0
90 Ball St.	12	847	4,099	4.84	36	341.58	6	6	0
90 Southern Methodist	12	881	4,099	4.65	27	341.58	3	9	0
92 East Caro.	12	849	4,065	4.79	41	338.75	4	8	0
93 Mississippi St.	12	863	4,042	4.68	26	336.83	3	9	0
94 Kent St.	12	763	4,021	5.27	24	335.08	3	9	0
95 Baylor	12	847	4,019	4.74	26	334.92	3	9	0
96 Arizona	12	790	4,003	5.07	27	333.58	4	8	0
97 Louisville	13	904	4,334	4.79	48	333.38	7	6	0
98 UTEP	12	884	3,994	4.52	28	332.83	2	10	0
99 Southern Miss.	13	894	4,319	4.83	33	332.23	7	6	0
100 Ohio	12	809	3,927	4.85	39	327.25	4	8	0
101 Arkansas St.	13	827	4,242	5.13	33	326.31	6	7	0
102 New Mexico	14	945	4,541	4.81	46	324.36	7	7	0
103 South Carolina	12	738	3,825	5.18	28	318.75	5	7	0
104 Temple	12	854	3,813	4.46	29	317.75	4	8	0
105 Kansas	12	902	3,801	4.21	33	316.75	2	10	0
105 Tulsa	12	833	3,801	4.56	31	316.75	1	11	0
107 UAB	12	805	3,776	4.69	31	314.67	5	7	0
108 Notre Dame	13	869	4,076	4.69	35	313.54	10	3	0
109 Tulane	13	913	4,068	4.46	43	312.92	8	5	0
110 Vanderbilt	12	738	3,751	5.08	28	312.58	2	10	0
111 Stanford	11	796	3,425	4.3	28	311.36	2	9	0
112 Troy St.	12	841	3,644	4.33	27	303.67	4	8	0
113 Army	12	805	3,594	4.46	29	299.5	1	11	0
114 La.-Lafayette	12	816	3,467	4.25	25	288.92	3	9	0
115 North Texas	13	804	3,699	4.6	32	284.54	8	5	0
116 Buffalo	12	814	3,314	4.07	27	276.17	1	11	0
117 Rutgers	12	833	2,568	3.08	22	214	1	11	0

Turnovers Gained

Rank, School	No.
1 Tulane	43
2 TCU	42
3 Arizona St.	40
4 San Jose St.	38
5 Virginia Tech	37
5 Virginia	37
7 Arkansas	36
7 California	36
7 Southern California	36
7 South Fla.	36
7 Oklahoma	36
12 Texas	35
12 Wisconsin	35
14 Cincinnati	34
14 Wake Forest	34
14 West Virginia	34
17 Alabama	33
17 Oregon St.	33
17 Pittsburgh	33
17 Notre Dame	33
17 Kansas St.	33
17 Arkansas St.	33
23 Auburn	32
23 Connecticut	32
23 Florida St.	32
23 Boston College	32
23 Fresno St.	32
28 Boise St.	31
28 Georgia	31
28 Iowa	31
28 North Carolina St.	31
28 Penn St.	31
33 Clemson	30
33 Colorado St.	30
33 North Texas	30
33 Ohio St.	30
33 Texas A&M	30
33 Colorado	30
39 Mississippi	29
40 Brigham Young	28
40 Washington	28
40 Tulsa	28
40 Syracuse	28
40 Northern Ill.	28
40 New Mexico	28
46 Bowling Green	27
46 UCF	27
46 Iowa St.	27
46 Toledo	27
46 Southern Miss.	27
46 San Diego St.	27
46 Miami (Ohio)	27
46 Hawaii	27
54 Buffalo	26
54 Maryland	26
54 Michigan	26
54 Air Force	26
54 La.-Lafayette	26
59 Akron	25
59 UAB	25
59 Duke	25
59 LSU	25
59 UCLA	25
59 Ohio	25
59 Stanford	25
59 Washington St.	25
59 Troy St.	25
59 Tennessee	25
59 Rutgers	25
70 Miami (Fla.)	24
70 Missouri	24
70 Utah	24
70 Oregon	24
70 Temple	24
70 Purdue	24
76 Houston	23
76 Mississippi St.	23
76 Western Mich.	23
79 Georgia Tech	22
79 Wyoming	22
79 Northwestern	22
79 Memphis	22
79 Marshall	22
79 Kentucky	22
85 Ball St.	21
85 Central Mich.	21
85 Middle Tenn.	21
85 Nebraska	21
85 Minnesota	21
85 Navy	21
85 South Carolina	21
85 Rice	21
85 East Caro.	21
94 La.-Monroe	20
94 Oklahoma St.	20
94 Army	20
97 Illinois	19
97 Texas Tech	19
97 Michigan St.	19
97 Nevada	19
101 Arizona	18
101 Utah St.	18
101 UTEP	18
101 Baylor	18
101 UNLV	18
106 Florida	17
106 Southern Methodist	17
106 New Mexico St.	17
106 Indiana	17
106 Kansas	17
111 Kent St.	16
111 Louisville	16
111 Louisiana Tech	16
114 North Carolina	15
115 Idaho	14
116 Eastern Mich.	11
116 Vanderbilt	11

Turnovers Lost

Rank, School	No.
1 Missouri	12
2 Kentucky	15
2 West Virginia	15
2 South Fla.	15
5 Iowa	16
5 Wake Forest	16
7 Michigan	17
7 New Mexico St.	17
7 Wisconsin	17
7 Oklahoma	17
7 Air Force	17
7 Penn St.	17
7 Ohio St.	17
14 Alabama	18
14 Bowling Green	18
14 California	18
14 Central Mich.	18
14 Texas	18
14 Southern California	18
20 Arkansas	19
20 Oregon	19
22 Buffalo	20
22 Connecticut	20
22 Miami (Ohio)	20
22 Toledo	20
22 Northern Ill.	20
27 Florida St.	21
27 Middle Tenn.	21
27 Tulane	21
27 Rice	21
27 Minnesota	21
32 Oklahoma St.	22
32 Virginia	22
32 Tulsa	22
35 Auburn	23
35 Tennessee	23
35 Pittsburgh	23
35 Boise St.	23
35 UCLA	23
35 Colorado	23
35 Georgia	23
35 Duke	23
43 UAB	24
43 Kansas St.	24
43 Mississippi	24
43 North Carolina St.	24
43 Wyoming	24
43 Nebraska	24
43 Boston College	24
50 Arizona	25
50 Vanderbilt	25
50 Utah	25

STATISTICAL LEADERS

Rank, School	No.
50 Oregon St.	25
50 Ohio	25
50 Nevada	25
50 UNLV	25
50 Miami (Fla.)	25
50 Maryland	25
59 Akron	26
59 Arkansas St.	26
59 New Mexico	26
59 Syracuse	26
59 South Carolina	26
59 North Texas	26
59 Ball St.	26
59 Michigan St.	26
59 Kansas	26
59 Florida	26

Rank, School	No.
59 Fresno St.	26
59 LSU	26
71 Colorado St.	27
71 Washington	27
71 TCU	27
71 San Diego St.	27
71 La.-Monroe	27
71 Illinois	27
77 Clemson	28
77 Iowa St.	28
77 Northwestern	28
77 Texas A&M	28
77 Notre Dame	28
77 Idaho	28
83 Indiana	29
83 Texas Tech	29

Rank, School	No.
83 Virginia Tech	29
83 Washington St.	29
83 Utah St.	29
83 Southern Methodist	29
83 Marshall	29
83 Louisiana Tech	29
91 Georgia Tech	30
91 Stanford	30
91 Southern Miss.	30
91 North Carolina	30
95 East Caro.	31
95 Louisville	31
97 Kent St.	32
97 San Jose St.	32
99 UCF	33
99 Cincinnati	33
101 Eastern Mich.	34

Rank, School	No.
101 Purdue	34
101 Army	34
101 La.-Lafayette	34
105 Baylor	35
105 Western Mich.	35
105 Navy	35
105 Troy St.	35
105 Brigham Young	35
110 Arizona St.	36
110 Memphis	36
112 UTEP	37
113 Mississippi St.	38
113 Rutgers	38
113 Temple	38
116 Houston	39
117 Hawaii	41

Turnover Margin

Rank, School	G	Gained Fm	Int	Tot	Lost Fm	Int	Tot	Margin/ Gm	W	L	T
1 South Fla.	11	14	22	36	10	5	15	1.91	9	2	0
2 Tulane	13	21	22	43	11	10	21	1.69	8	5	0
3 California	12	21	15	36	8	10	18	1.5	7	5	0
4 West Virginia	13	15	19	34	6	9	15	1.46	9	4	0
5 Southern California	13	19	17	36	8	10	18	1.38	11	2	0
5 Wake Forest	13	21	13	34	10	6	16	1.38	7	6	0
7 Oklahoma	14	12	24	36	6	11	17	1.36	12	2	0
8 Texas	13	13	22	35	6	12	18	1.31	11	2	0
9 Wisconsin	14	13	22	35	9	8	17	1.29	8	6	0
10 TCU	12	20	22	42	14	13	27	1.25	10	2	0
11 Arkansas	14	17	19	36	6	13	19	1.21	9	5	0
12 Alabama	13	15	18	33	9	9	18	1.15	10	3	0
12 Iowa	13	11	20	31	11	5	16	1.15	11	2	0
14 Penn St.	13	11	20	31	6	11	17	1.08	9	4	0
15 Virginia	14	22	15	37	14	8	22	1.07	9	5	0
16 Connecticut	12	12	20	32	8	12	20	1	6	6	0
16 Missouri	12	12	12	24	5	7	12	1	5	7	0
18 Ohio St.	14	12	18	30	10	7	17	0.93	14	0	0
19 Florida St.	14	16	16	32	11	10	21	0.79	9	5	0
20 Pittsburgh	13	18	15	33	11	12	23	0.77	9	4	0
21 Bowling Green	12	15	12	27	7	11	18	0.75	9	3	0
22 Auburn	13	11	21	32	13	10	23	0.69	9	4	0
22 Kansas St.	13	13	20	33	18	6	24	0.69	11	2	0
22 Air Force	13	14	12	26	10	7	17	0.69	8	5	0
22 Michigan	13	10	16	26	10	7	17	0.69	10	3	0
26 Northern Ill.	12	7	21	28	13	7	20	0.67	8	4	0
27 Boise St.	13	12	19	31	15	8	23	0.62	12	1	0
27 Oregon St.	13	13	20	33	11	14	25	0.62	8	5	0
27 Boston College	13	17	15	32	7	17	24	0.62	9	4	0
30 Kentucky	12	12	10	22	9	6	15	0.58	7	5	0
30 Miami (Ohio)	12	14	13	27	7	13	20	0.58	7	5	0
32 Georgia	14	15	16	31	13	10	23	0.57	13	1	0
32 Virginia Tech	14	13	24	37	18	11	29	0.57	10	4	0
34 Arkansas St.	13	17	16	33	17	9	26	0.54	6	7	0
35 Buffalo	12	12	14	26	7	13	20	0.5	1	11	0
35 North Carolina St.	14	15	16	31	13	11	24	0.5	11	3	0
35 Tulsa	12	15	13	28	12	10	22	0.5	1	11	0
35 Toledo	14	9	18	27	11	9	20	0.5	9	5	0
35 Colorado	14	15	15	30	11	12	23	0.5	9	5	0
40 San Jose St.	13	15	23	38	15	17	32	0.46	6	7	0
41 Fresno St.	14	13	19	32	12	14	26	0.43	9	5	0
42 Mississippi	13	11	18	29	9	15	24	0.38	7	6	0
42 Oregon	13	6	18	24	8	11	19	0.38	7	6	0
42 Notre Dame	13	12	21	33	15	13	28	0.38	10	3	0
45 North Texas	13	14	16	30	17	9	26	0.31	8	5	0
46 Arizona St.	14	18	22	40	20	16	36	0.29	8	6	0
47 Central Mich.	12	9	12	21	10	8	18	0.25	4	8	0
48 Colorado St.	14	16	14	30	15	12	27	0.21	10	4	0
49 Duke	12	13	12	25	10	13	23	0.17	2	10	0
49 Syracuse	12	18	10	28	11	15	26	0.17	4	8	0
49 Texas A&M	12	14	16	30	9	19	28	0.17	6	6	0
52 UCLA	13	8	17	25	12	11	23	0.15	8	5	0
52 Clemson	13	9	21	30	15	13	28	0.15	7	6	0
52 Tennessee	13	13	12	25	16	7	23	0.15	8	5	0
55 New Mexico	14	13	15	28	16	10	26	0.14	7	7	0
56 UAB	12	10	15	25	15	9	24	0.08	5	7	0
57 Washington	13	12	16	28	11	9	20	0.08	7	6	0
58 Cincinnati	14	17	17	34	11	22	33	0.07	7	7	0
58 Maryland	14	8	18	26	12	13	25	0.07	11	3	0
60 Middle Tenn.	12	11	10	21	13	8	21	0	4	8	0

| Rank, School | G | Gained | | | Lost | | | Margin/ | W | L | T |
		Fm	Int	Tot	Fm	Int	Tot	Gm			
60 New Mexico St.	12	10	7	17	11	6	17	0	7	5	0
60 Minnesota	13	14	7	21	10	11	21	0	8	5	0
60 Ohio	12	11	14	25	16	9	25	0	4	8	0
60 Rice	11	13	8	21	14	7	21	0	4	7	0
60 San Diego St.	13	13	14	27	17	10	27	0	4	9	0
66 Iowa St.	14	17	10	27	10	18	28	-0.07	7	7	0
67 LSU	13	8	17	25	18	8	26	-0.08	8	5	0
67 Miami (Fla.)	13	12	12	24	12	13	25	-0.08	12	1	0
69 Akron	12	16	9	25	14	12	26	-0.08	4	8	0
70 Utah	11	12	12	24	12	13	25	-0.09	5	6	0
71 Oklahoma St.	13	8	12	20	7	15	22	-0.15	8	5	0
72 Wyoming	12	13	9	22	6	18	24	-0.17	2	10	0
73 Nebraska	14	8	13	21	12	12	24	-0.21	7	7	0
74 Southern Miss.	13	11	16	27	19	11	30	-0.23	7	6	0
75 Washington St.	13	8	17	25	15	14	29	-0.31	10	3	0
76 Ball St.	12	11	10	21	10	16	26	-0.42	6	6	0
76 South Carolina	12	12	9	21	11	15	26	-0.42	5	7	0
78 Stanford	11	9	16	25	8	22	30	-0.45	2	9	0
79 UCF	12	14	13	27	16	17	33	-0.5	7	5	0
79 Northwestern	12	14	8	22	14	14	28	-0.5	3	9	0
79 Nevada	12	10	9	19	8	17	25	-0.5	5	7	0
82 Marshall	13	7	15	22	14	15	29	-0.54	11	2	0
83 Arizona	12	11	7	18	11	14	25	-0.58	4	8	0
83 La.-Monroe	12	10	10	20	13	14	27	-0.58	3	9	0
83 UNLV	12	9	9	18	13	12	25	-0.58	5	7	0
83 Michigan St.	12	6	13	19	9	17	26	-0.58	4	8	0
83 Brigham Young	12	10	18	28	14	21	35	-0.58	5	7	0
88 Georgia Tech	13	11	11	22	10	20	30	-0.62	7	6	0
89 Illinois	12	11	8	19	11	16	27	-0.67	5	7	0
89 La.-Lafayette	12	18	8	26	15	19	34	-0.67	3	9	0
91 Florida	13	10	7	17	8	18	26	-0.69	8	5	0
92 Texas Tech	14	3	16	19	14	15	29	-0.71	9	5	0
93 Kansas	12	5	12	17	13	13	26	-0.75	2	10	0
94 Purdue	13	9	15	24	19	15	34	-0.77	7	6	0
95 East Caro.	12	11	10	21	9	22	31	-0.83	4	8	0
95 Troy St.	12	16	9	25	16	19	35	-0.83	4	8	0
97 Hawaii	14	9	18	27	15	26	41	-1	10	4	0
97 Indiana	12	9	8	17	8	21	29	-1	3	9	0
97 Southern Methodist	12	9	8	17	11	18	29	-1	3	9	0
97 Utah St.	11	11	7	18	13	16	29	-1	4	7	0
97 Western Mich.	12	9	14	23	13	22	35	-1	4	8	0
102 Louisiana Tech	12	11	5	16	10	19	29	-1.08	4	8	0
102 Rutgers	12	14	11	25	15	23	38	-1.08	1	11	0
104 Louisville	13	7	9	16	20	11	31	-1.15	7	6	0
105 Idaho	12	6	8	14	10	18	28	-1.17	2	10	0
105 Memphis	12	10	12	22	16	20	36	-1.17	3	9	0
105 Navy	12	16	5	21	25	10	35	-1.17	2	10	0
105 Vanderbilt	12	5	6	11	13	12	25	-1.17	2	10	0
105 Army	12	14	6	20	13	21	34	-1.17	1	11	0
105 Temple	12	13	11	24	15	23	38	-1.17	4	8	0
111 Mississippi St.	12	9	14	23	16	22	38	-1.25	3	9	0
111 North Carolina	12	9	6	15	16	14	30	-1.25	3	9	0
113 Houston	12	13	10	23	17	22	39	-1.33	5	7	0
113 Kent St.	12	7	9	16	11	21	32	-1.33	3	9	0
115 Baylor	12	10	8	18	13	22	35	-1.42	3	9	0
116 UTEP	12	8	10	18	16	21	37	-1.58	2	10	0
117 Eastern Mich.	12	7	4	11	12	22	34	-1.92	3	9	0

2002 Division I-AA Individual Leaders

All-Purpose Running

Rank, Player	Pos	Cl	G	Rush	Rec	PR	KOR	Yds	Yds/Gm	Pl	Yds/Pl
1 Stephan Lewis, New Hampshire	RB	SR	11	1,152	419	13	645	2,229	202.64	315	7.08
2 Andre Raymond, Eastern Ill.	RB	JR	12	612	672	112	872	2,268	189	244	9.3
3 Jay Bailey, Austin Peay	RB	SR	12	1,687	85	0	381	2,153	179.42	351	6.13
4 Ari Confesor, Holy Cross	WR	JR	12	113	721	322	841	1,997	166.42	124	16.1
5 Fred Amey, Sacramento St.	WR	SO	11	31	989	278	514	1,812	164.73	117	15.49
6 Tony Tompkins, Stephen F. Austin	RB	FR	11	688	255	265	587	1,795	163.18	198	9.07
7 Gary Jones, Albany (N.Y.)	RB	JR	12	1,509	163	0	277	1,949	162.42	254	7.67
8 T.J. Stallings, Morgan St.	WR	SR	12	1,169	654	0	106	1,929	160.75	287	6.72
9 Korea McKay, Ark.-Pine Bluff	WR	JR	11	0	1,009	124	595	1,728	157.09	98	17.63
10 Justin Campbell, Butler	WR	SO	10	427	146	0	971	1,544	154.4	124	12.45
11 James Bialasik, Canisius	WR	SR	11	97	414	339	827	1,677	152.45	101	16.6
12 Javarus Dudley, Fordham	WR	JR	13	0	1,106	0	840	1,946	149.69	114	17.07
13 Willie Ponder, Southeast Mo. St.	WR	SR	12	0	1,453	25	257	1,786	148.83	102	17.51
14 Carl Morris, Harvard	WR	SR	10	19	1,288	153	14	1,474	147.4	117	12.6
15 Tramon Douglas, Grambling	WR	JR	12	0	1,704	50	0	1,754	146.17	95	18.46
16 Jermaine Pugh, Lehigh	RB	JR	12	1,339	156	257	0	1,752	146	305	5.74

Stephan Lewis, New Hampshire

New Hampshire Sports Information

STATISTICAL LEADERS

Rank, Player	Pos	Cl	G	Rush	Rec	PR	KOR	Yds	Yds/Gm	Pl	Yds/Pl
17 Robert Carr, Yale	TB	SO	10	1,083	26	0	333	1,442	144.2	256	5.63
18 Joe McCourt, Lafayette	RB	SO	12	1,393	332	0	2	1,727	143.92	355	4.86
19 Aryvia Holmes, Samford	WR	SR	10	0	1,158	250	0	1,408	140.8	100	14.08
20 Verondre Barnes, Liberty	RB	SO	11	1,304	169	0	66	1,539	139.91	242	6.36
21 Dale Jennings, Butler	RB	SR	10	973	345	0	42	1,360	136	220	6.18
22 P.J. Mays, Youngstown St.	RB	SR	11	1,284	192	0	0	1,476	134.18	266	5.55
23 Ryan Fuqua, Portland St.	RB	SO	11	1,283	179	0	0	1,462	132.91	331	4.42
24 J.R. Taylor, Eastern Ill.	RB	SR	12	1,522	69	0	0	1,591	132.58	264	6.03
25 Lee Davis, Southwest Tex. St.	RB	SR	10	788	195	0	321	1,304	130.4	206	6.33
26 Isaac Mitchell, Idaho St.	RB	JR	10	968	329	0	0	1,297	129.7	215	6.03
26 Cameron Atkinson, Princeton	RB	SR	10	1,028	112	0	157	1,297	129.7	202	6.42
28 Jon Frazier, Western Ky.	RB	SR	15	1,537	78	0	328	1,943	129.53	324	6
29 Derek Clayton, St. Peter's	RB	JR	11	1,277	134	0	0	1,411	128.27	248	5.69
30 Travis Chmelka, Columbia	WR	JR	10	12	500	225	525	1,262	126.2	98	12.88
31 Phillip Doolin, Ark.-Pine Bluff	RB	JR	11	31	1,021	0	327	1,379	125.36	69	19.99
32 Shawn Holmes, Alabama St.	WR	JR	12	16	334	534	616	1,500	125	111	13.51
33 B.J. Sams, McNeese St.	WR	JR	14	254	658	471	353	1,736	124	132	13.15
34 Ben Sanderson, Northern Iowa	WR	SR	11	4	411	418	502	1,335	121.36	96	13.91
35 Johnathan Taylor, Drake	RB	JR	11	1,072	262	0	0	1,334	121.27	219	6.09
36 Rich Musinski, William & Mary	WR	JR	11	52	1,140	127	13	1,332	121.09	79	16.86
37 Jeremy Grier, Chattanooga	WR	SO	10	5	521	0	682	1,208	120.8	78	15.49
38 Cortez Hankton, Texas Southern	WR	SR	11	51	1,270	0	0	1,321	120.09	69	19.14
39 Kirwin Watson, Fordham	RB	JR	13	1,467	94	0	0	1,561	120.08	297	5.26
40 Jesse McCoy, Wofford	RB	SR	11	1,001	122	57	139	1,319	119.91	145	9.1
41 Chas Gessner, Brown	WR	SR	10	31	1,166	0	0	1,197	119.7	121	9.89
42 Luke McArdle, Georgetown	WR	JR	11	-5	802	245	265	1,307	118.82	88	14.85
43 DaShaun Morris, Delaware St.	WR	JR	12	7	566	136	708	1,417	118.08	79	17.94
44 Chad Davis, Jacksonville	RB	FR	8	452	178	0	301	931	116.38	137	6.8
45 Mike Hilliard, Duquesne	RB	JR	12	1,310	86	0	0	1,396	116.33	318	4.39
46 Rob Milanese, Pennsylvania	WR	SR	10	48	1,112	0	0	1,160	116	94	12.34
47 R.J. Cobbs, Massachusetts	RB	FR	11	1,067	140	0	61	1,268	115.27	217	5.84
48 Levander Segars, Montana	DB	SO	14	40	628	474	465	1,607	114.79	122	13.17
49 Darrell Jones, Cal Poly	WR	SO	11	54	328	228	650	1,260	114.55	97	12.99
50 Eric Kimble, Eastern Wash.	RB	FR	11	49	851	212	147	1,259	114.45	87	14.47
51 Ryan Johnson, Montana St.	RB	SR	11	1,092	165	0	0	1,257	114.27	296	4.25
52 Tim Manning, Jackson St.	WR	JR	11	35	1,077	118	24	1,254	114	87	14.41
53 Aaron Overton, Drake	WR	SR	11	42	1,180	25	0	1,247	113.36	81	15.4
54 Adam Benge, Northern Iowa	RB	SR	11	1,133	103	0	0	1,236	112.36	285	4.34
55 Christopher Price, Marist	RB	SR	11	1,196	37	0	0	1,233	112.09	237	5.2
56 Quincy Washington, Illinois St.	RB	SR	11	1,158	71	0	0	1,229	111.73	261	4.71
56 Corey Kinsey, Southeast Mo. St.	RB	SO	11	1,067	123	0	39	1,229	111.73	249	4.94
58 Melvin Bryant, La Salle	WR	SO	11	28	492	0	701	1,221	111	71	17.2
59 Zuriel Smith, Hampton	WR	SR	12	0	773	500	57	1,330	110.83	81	16.42
60 Wendall Williams, Rhode Island	RB	JR	12	427	166	109	611	1,313	109.42	76	17.28
61 Matt Romeo, Towson	RB	JR	11	990	206	0	0	1,196	108.73	280	4.27
62 Jovan Griffith, Eastern Wash.	RB	SR	11	1,130	57	0	0	1,187	107.91	206	5.76
63 Rodney Byrnes, Harvard	WR	SO	10	211	482	0	386	1,079	107.9	112	9.63
64 Rashaud Palmer, Elon	RB	JR	11	879	46	0	256	1,181	107.36	168	7.03
65 Scooter Johnson, Citadel	QB	JR	12	23	950	118	187	1,278	106.5	92	13.89
66 Jermaine Austin, Ga. Southern	RB	FR	14	1,416	73	0	0	1,489	106.36	246	6.05
67 Jay Barnard, Dartmouth	WR	JR	10	0	899	156	0	1,055	105.5	104	10.14
68 Nehemiah Broughton, Citadel	RB	SO	12	1,038	181	0	32	1,251	104.25	244	5.13
69 Matthew Loy, Morehead St.	WR	JR	12	0	546	389	310	1,245	103.75	89	13.99
70 Jeremy Conley, Duquesne	WR	SR	12	6	1,216	0	17	1,239	103.25	75	16.52
71 Patrick Jenkins, Tennessee St.	WR	SR	12	25	272	139	797	1,233	102.75	83	14.86
72 Nick Chournos, Weber St.	RB	SO	11	874	238	0	12	1,124	102.18	201	5.59
73 Major Cole, Central Conn. St.	RB	SR	11	1,024	97	0	0	1,121	101.91	254	4.41
74 Marcus Williams, Maine	RB	SO	14	1,406	20	0	0	1,426	101.86	266	5.36
75 Casey Cramer, Dartmouth	TE	JR	10	0	1,017	0	0	1,017	101.7	72	14.13
76 Jerome Mathis, Hampton	WR	SO	12	188	615	0	417	1,220	101.67	64	19.06
77 Carlos Wright, Tennessee St.	WR	JR	10	134	236	236	410	1,016	101.6	63	16.13
78 Chaz Williams, Ga. Southern	QB	SO	14	1,422	0	0	0	1,422	101.57	290	4.9
79 Billy Blanchard, Murray St.	RB	SR	11	1,081	36	0	0	1,117	101.55	184	6.07
80 Rob Giancola, Valparaiso	WR	SO	11	0	1,103	8	0	1,111	101	52	21.37
81 Erik Lash, Bethune-Cookman	WR	SR	12	181	1,006	0	0	1,206	100.5	95	12.69
82 C.J. Hudson, Eastern Ky.	RB	SO	12	1,110	59	0	32	1,201	100.08	241	4.98
83 Garrett White, Sacramento St.	RB	SR	12	887	312	0	0	1,199	99.92	215	5.58
84 Derrick Johnese, Northwestern St.	RB	SO	13	960	87	0	250	1,297	99.77	226	5.74
85 Jay Colbert, Howard	RB	JR	11	1,001	13	69	14	1,097	99.73	202	5.43
86 Johnathan Smith, William & Mary	RB	SO	11	838	129	0	126	1,093	99.36	232	4.71
87 Luke Graham, Colgate	WR	SO	12	0	1,182	9	0	1,191	99.25	67	17.78
88 Peter Athans, Sacred Heart	DB	SR	10	0	0	323	595	988	98.8	60	16.47
89 Bear Rinehart, Furman	WR	SR	12	40	892	253	0	1,185	98.75	90	13.17
90 Anthony Owens, Norfolk St.	DB	JR	11	0	0	232	832	1,086	98.73	60	18.1
91 Joe Rackley, Brown	RB	SR	9	572	312	0	0	884	98.22	181	4.88
92 Eddie Linscomb, Southwest Mo. St.	RB	SR	9	758	74	0	48	880	97.78	180	4.89
93 Arketa Banks, Elon	WR	SR	11	120	329	78	539	1,066	96.91	64	16.66
94 Jon Turner, Jacksonville	WR	SR	10	37	890	24	17	968	96.8	68	14.24
95 Gavin Ng, San Diego	DB	JR	10	0	0	194	747	966	96.6	57	16.95
96 Nicholas Wells, Alabama A&M	WR	JR	12	0	465	409	282	1,156	96.33	72	16.06
97 Jason Mathenia, Sam Houston St.	WR	SO	11	27	749	197	85	1,058	96.18	84	12.6
98 Clint Wilson, St. Mary's (Cal.)	RB	SO	12	1,100	47	0	0	1,147	95.58	217	5.29
99 Brian Bratton, Furman	WR	SO	12	38	398	4	705	1,145	95.42	71	16.13
100 Chisom Opara, Princeton	WR	SR	9	31	772	0	48	851	94.56	64	13.3

Field Goals

Rank, Player	Pos	Cl	G	FGA	FGM	Avg	FG/Gm
1 MacKenzie Hoambrecker, Northern Iowa	K	SR	11	28	25	0.893	2.27
2 Justin Langan, Western Ill.	**K**	**SO**	**13**	**27**	**20**	**0.741**	**1.54**
3 Jesse Obert, Dayton	P	SR	12	23	17	0.739	1.42
4 Matt Fordyce, Fordham	P	SR	13	26	18	0.692	1.38
5 Chris Snyder, Montana	K	JR	14	32	19	0.594	1.36
6 Martin Brecht, Lafayette	K	SR	12	26	16	0.615	1.33
7 Stephen Carroll, Illinois St.	K	SO	10	19	13	0.684	1.3
8 Greg Kuehn, William & Mary	K	SO	11	21	14	0.667	1.27
8 Mike Cajal-Willis, Portland St.	K	SR	11	22	14	0.636	1.27
8 Vince Patrick, Texas Southern	K	JR	11	19	14	0.737	1.27
8 Jeremy Hershey, Idaho St.	K	JR	11	26	14	0.538	1.27
12 Chris Onorato, Hofstra	P	JR	12	22	15	0.682	1.25
12 Mark Wright, Appalachian St.	K	SR	12	23	15	0.652	1.25
14 Peter Martinez, Western Ky.	K	SR	15	25	18	0.72	1.2
14 Tyler Lavin, Dartmouth	K	SO	10	16	12	0.75	1.2
14 Peter Veldman, Pennsylvania	K	JR	10	15	12	0.8	1.2
17 Paul Ernster, Northern Ariz.	K	SO	11	19	13	0.684	1.18
18 Bret LeVier, Sacramento St.	K	SO	12	18	14	0.778	1.17
18 Travis Zobel, Citadel	P	JR	12	19	14	0.737	1.17
20 Andrew Harmon, Gardner-Webb	K	SR	10	17	11	0.647	1.1
20 Adam Williams, San Diego	K	JR	10	16	11	0.688	1.1
20 Tim Redican, Sacred Heart	K	SR	10	16	11	0.688	1.1
23 Navid Niakan, Cal Poly	K	SR	11	20	12	0.6	1.09
24 Burke George, James Madison	K	SO	12	21	13	0.619	1.08
24 Lane Schwarzberg, Colgate	K	SO	12	17	13	0.765	1.08
26 Scott Collins, Delaware	K	SR	12	22	12	0.545	1
26 Chris Vella, Holy Cross	K	JR	12	14	12	0.857	1
26 Chris Vought, Western Caro.	K	JR	10	17	10	0.588	1
26 Chip Walters, Samford	K	SR	11	18	11	0.611	1
26 Danny Marshall, Furman	K	JR	12	15	12	0.8	1
31 John Marino, McNeese St.	K	JR	15	23	14	0.609	0.93
32 Nate Cook, Montana St.	P	JR	13	19	12	0.632	0.92
33 Shane Laisle, Rhode Island	K	JR	12	15	11	0.733	0.92
33 Joey Hudak, Tennessee St.	K	SO	12	16	11	0.688	0.92
33 Brent Harris, Tenn.-Martin	P	SO	12	16	11	0.688	0.92
33 Adam Smith, Eastern Ky.	K	JR	12	15	11	0.733	0.92
33 Shane Andrus, Murray St.	K	JR	12	14	11	0.786	0.92
38 Connor McCormick, New Hampshire	K	FR	11	15	10	0.667	0.91
38 James Galea, St. Peter's	K	SO	11	13	10	0.769	0.91
40 Daniel Hanks, Davidson	K	SR	10	14	9	0.643	0.9
41 Miro Kesic, Northeastern	K	FR	13	17	11	0.647	0.85
42 Tellis Bolden, Hampton	P	JR	12	19	10	0.526	0.83
42 Ezequiel Arevalo, St. Mary's (Cal.)	K	SR	12	14	10	0.714	0.83
44 Robert Pate, Wagner	P	JR	11	18	9	0.5	0.82
44 Joey Price, Sam Houston St.	K	SO	11	15	9	0.6	0.82
44 Mark Myers, Fla. Atlantic	K	SO	11	12	9	0.75	0.82
47 Derek Javarone, Princeton	K	FR	10	13	8	0.615	0.8
47 Trevor MacMeekin, Cornell	K	SO	10	9	8	0.889	0.8
49 Scott Shelton, Ga. Southern	P	SR	14	17	11	0.647	0.79
50 Juan Vasquez, Florida A&M	PK	JR	12	10	9	0.9	0.75
50 Justin Deardorff, Austin Peay	K	JR	12	20	9	0.45	0.75
52 Adam James, Villanova	P	SO	15	14	11	0.786	0.73
53 Doug Kirchner, Richmond	K	SR	11	14	8	0.571	0.73
53 Stephen Coker, Stephen F. Austin	K	FR	11	15	8	0.533	0.73
53 Joseph Blanco, Mississippi Val.	K	FR	11	17	8	0.471	0.73
53 Adam Hudak, Valparaiso	K	SR	11	12	8	0.667	0.73
53 Aaron Wall, Ark.-Pine Bluff	P	SR	11	14	8	0.571	0.73
53 David McConnell, Alcorn St.	K	FR	11	16	8	0.5	0.73
53 Steven Lee, Jacksonville	K	JR	11	12	8	0.667	0.73
53 Spencer Callahan, Iona	K	JR	11	12	8	0.667	0.73
53 Chris Lundberg, Bucknell	K	SR	11	14	8	0.571	0.73
62 Mike Mellow, Maine	K	SO	14	17	10	0.588	0.71
63 Tom Gavenonis, St. John's (N.Y.)	K	SR	10	8	7	0.875	0.7
64 Tommy Hebert, Northwestern St.	K	SO	13	13	9	0.692	0.69
65 Doug White, Massachusetts	K	SR	12	10	8	0.8	0.67
65 Chris Nichols, Alabama St.			12	11	8	0.727	0.67
65 Joey Herbst, Morehead St.	K	FR	12	15	8	0.533	0.67
65 Patrick Shutters, Chattanooga	P	JR	12	10	8	0.8	0.67
65 Derek Kutz, Southeast Mo. St.	K	SO	12	14	8	0.571	0.67
70 Anthony Turowski, Elon	K	SO	11	12	7	0.583	0.64
70 Jake Stewart, Youngstown St.	K	JR	11	10	7	0.7	0.64
70 Gideon Tekola, Norfolk St.	K	SR	11	11	7	0.636	0.64
70 Brett Biggs, Marist	K	SR	11	12	7	0.583	0.64
74 Nick Rudd, Columbia	PK	SO	10	13	6	0.462	0.6
75 Mike Megyesi, Indiana St.	K	JR	12	12	7	0.583	0.58
75 Rashad Cylar, Alabama A&M	P	JR	12	13	7	0.538	0.58
75 Colby Miller, Southern U.	K	FR	12	14	7	0.5	0.58
78 Matt Taber, Butler	K	FR	9	7	5	0.714	0.56
79 Rich Heintz, Eastern Wash.	K	JR	11	9	6	0.667	0.55
79 Brian Long, Southwest Mo. St.	K	SR	11	11	6	0.545	0.55
79 Joe Johnson, Weber St.	K	FR	11	10	6	0.6	0.55

Justin Langan, Western Illinois

Rank, Player	Pos	Cl	G	FGA	FGM	Avg	FG/Gm
82 Brian Morgan, Grambling	K	SO	13	21	7	0.333	0.54
83 Matthew Douglas, Lehigh	K	JR	12	12	6	0.5	0.5
83 Michael Soto, Stony Brook	K	JR	10	7	5	0.714	0.5
83 Charles Conklin, Siena	K	SO	10	8	5	0.625	0.5
83 Ross Shmunes, Jacksonville	K	FR	10	7	5	0.714	0.5
83 Kyle McCrery, Savannah St.	K	FR	10	9	5	0.556	0.5
83 Matt Sharpe, VMI	PK	SO	12	9	6	0.667	0.5
83 Pat Simcox, N.C. A&T	PK	SO	10	12	5	0.417	0.5
83 Scott Everhart, Southern Ill.	K	SR	12	11	6	0.545	0.5
83 Stan Zylinski, Albany (N.Y.)	K	JR	12	10	6	0.6	0.5
83 Ryan Peterson, Monmouth	K	SR	10	13	5	0.385	0.5
93 Daniel King, Bethune-Cookman	K	FR	13	11	6	0.545	0.46
94 Ben Whitacre, Towson	K	SR	11	12	5	0.417	0.45
94 David Pretzer, Southern Utah	K	SR	11	12	5	0.417	0.45
94 Tyler McGlade, Drake	K	FR	11	8	5	0.625	0.45
94 Philip Gibbs, Fairfield	K	FR	11	9	5	0.556	0.45
94 Derek Pearson, Central Conn. St.	K	FR	11	6	5	0.833	0.45
99 Jon Vorosholin, Morgan St.	P	SR	12	9	5	0.556	0.42
99 Yonnick Matthews, N.C. A&T	P	JR	12	5	5	1.000	0.42

Interceptions

Rank, Player	Pos	Cl	G	Int	Yds	TD	Int/Gm
1 Rashean Mathis, Bethune-Cookman	DB	SR	13	14	455	3	1.08
2 Mark Kasmer, Dayton	DB	SR	12	11	157	2	0.92
3 Antwan Hill, Alabama St.	DB	SO	12	10	199	1	0.83
4 Corey Oaks, Robert Morris	DB	SR	10	7	130	2	0.7
4 Chris Blackshear, Central Conn. St.	DB	SO	10	7	204	1	0.7
4 Chad King, Stony Brook	DB	JR	10	7	109	1	0.7
4 Mike Devore, St. John's (N.Y.)	DB	JR	10	7	45	0	0.7
8 Ricky Brown, Florida A&M	SS	SR	12	8	38	0	0.67
9 Tyrone Parsons, Alcorn St.	DB	JR	11	7	75	0	0.64
9 Randy Caldwell, Ark.-Pine Bluff	DB	SO	11	7	62	0	0.64
9 Edmund Carazo, Towson	DB	SR	11	7	88	0	0.64
12 Rod Gulley, McNeese St.	DB	JR	15	9	160	2	0.6
13 Greg Kavulich, St. Mary's (Cal.)	DB	SO	12	7	99	0	0.58
13 Leigh Bodden, Duquesne	DB	SR	12	7	71	0	0.58
15 Quinton Freeman, Idaho St.	DB	FR	11	6	15	0	0.55
15 Cam Newton, Towson	DB	SO	11	6	101	0	0.55
15 Oliver Celestin, Texas Southern	DB	SR	11	6	135	2	0.55
15 Tyrone Walker, Ark.-Pine Bluff	DB	SO	11	6	86	1	0.55
19 Octavious Bond, Grambling	DB	JR	13	7	66	0	0.54
20 Jason Horton, N.C. A&T	DB	SR	12	6	58	0	0.5
20 Rodney Johnson, Furman	DB	SR	12	6	74	0	0.5
20 Montreal Harkley, East Tenn. St.	DB	JR	12	6	107	0	0.5
20 Denmark Reed, Grambling	DB	SR	12	6	133	1	0.5
20 Charles Byrd, Morehead St.	DB	JR	12	6	87	0	0.5
20 Lenny Williams, Southern U.	DB	JR	12	6	0	0	0.5
20 Musa Sarki, VMI	DB	JR	12	6	134	1	0.5

Rank, Player	Pos	Cl	G	Int	Yds	TD	Int/Gm
20 Lamar Ingram, Gardner-Webb	DB	SR	10	5	34	0	0.5
20 Vince Alexander, Pennsylvania	DB	SR	10	5	102	1	0.5
20 Jay McCareins, Princeton	DB	SO	10	5	33	0	0.5
30 Chris Brown, Grambling	DB	SR	13	6	148	1	0.46
31 Chris Thompson, Nicholls St.	DB	JR	11	5	77	1	0.45
31 Nick Turnbull, Florida Int'l	DB	FR	11	5	79	0	0.45
31 Markee Coleman, Jacksonville St.	DB	SR	11	5	74	1	0.45
31 Billy Parker, William & Mary	DB	JR	11	5	96	2	0.45
31 Stephen Gebernick, Northern Ariz.	DB	JR	11	5	120	2	0.45
31 David Goodloe, Portland St.	DB	SR	11	5	62	0	0.45
31 Nick Totaro, Fairfield	DB	JR	11	5	81	1	0.45
38 Cj Moore, Canisius	DB	SO	9	4	38	0	0.44
39 Vernon Smith, Montana	DB	JR	14	6	87	1	0.43
40 Mike Washington, Charleston So.	DB	SR	12	5	49	0	0.42
40 Armar Watson, Duquesne	DB	SO	12	5	95	1	0.42
40 Eddie Ravenall, N.C. A&T	DB	JR	12	5	84	0	0.42
40 Montrail Pittman, N.C. A&T	DB	SR	12	5	103	1	0.42
40 Travis Oliver, Hampton	DB	JR	12	5	48	1	0.42
40 Sunsett Graham, Eastern Ky.	DB	SR	12	5	73	0	0.42
40 Brandon Phillips, Morehead St.	CB	SR	12	5	45	0	0.42
40 Rand Williams, Southern U.	DB	SR	12	5	46	1	0.42
40 Dion Giddens, Tennessee St.	DB	JR	12	5	3	0	0.42
40 Perez Boyd, Tenn.-Martin	DB	SR	12	5	79	0	0.42
50 Thurman Roy, Prairie View	DB	SR	10	4	23	0	0.4
50 Lawerence Williams, Lehigh	DB	JR	10	4	83	1	0.4
50 Brandon Mueller, Princeton	DB	JR	10	4	21	0	0.4
50 Brian Pawlowski, Sacred Heart	DB	JR	10	4	37	0	0.4
50 Patrick McManus, Pennsylvania	DB	JR	10	4	38	0	0.4
55 Tim Banks, Georgetown	DB	SO	11	4	85	2	0.36
55 Daryl Warren, Southwest Mo. St.	DB	JR	11	4	43	0	0.36
55 Jeremy Balina, Wagner	LB	SR	11	4	64	0	0.36
55 Benny Sapp, Northern Iowa	DB	JR	11	4	42	0	0.36
55 Frank Meade, Iona	DB	SO	11	4	37	0	0.36
55 Joe Scarpelli, Fairfield	DB	SR	11	4	57	0	0.36
55 Chris Lumley, Canisius	DB	JR	11	4	34	0	0.36
55 Justin Sandy, Northern Iowa	DB	JR	11	4	26	0	0.36
55 Donnie Rose, Central Conn. St.	DB	SO	11	4	43	0	0.36
55 Tim Batts, Alcorn St.	DB	JR	11	4	9	0	0.36
55 O'Keefe Henderson, Mississippi Val.	DB	FR	11	4	102	1	0.36
55 Vaughn Jarrett, Cal Poly	DB	SR	11	4	0	0	0.36
67 Leveronte Turner, Alabama A&M	DB	FR	12	4	23	0	0.33
67 Erlin Sanders, Alabama St.	DB	SR	12	4	30	1	0.33
67 Marcus Colvin, Dayton	DB	SR	12	4	12	0	0.33
67 Keon Mainor, Morris Brown	DB	JR	12	4	46	0	0.33
67 Weston Borba, St. Mary's (Cal.)	DB	JR	12	4	167	2	0.33
67 James Thornton, Morris Brown	RB	SR	12	4	75	2	0.33
67 Aaron Furman, Dayton	DB	SR	12	4	72	2	0.33
67 Thomas Sexton, Austin Peay	DB	SR	12	4	32	0	0.33
67 Henry Freeman, Alabama A&M	DB	JR	12	4	38	0	0.33
67 Steve Costello, Massachusetts	DB	SO	12	4	86	0	0.33
67 Khalid Rice, Siena	DB	JR	9	3	0	0	0.33
67 Trent Wissner, Duquesne	LB	SR	12	4	121	1	0.33
67 Jeremy Chandler, Western Ky.	DB	JR	15	5	56	0	0.33
67 Ryan MacLean, Albany (N.Y.)	DB	SR	12	4	30	0	0.33
67 Shannon James, Massachusetts	DB	FR	12	4	12	0	0.33
67 Nick Nester, Charleston So.	—	—	12	4	46	0	0.33
67 William Haith, Liberty	DB	SR	9	3	90	1	0.33
84 Kane Ioane, Montana St.	DB	JR	13	4	10	0	0.31
84 Lee Russell, Western Ill.	LB	JR	13	4	87	2	0.31
86 Isaiah Trufant, Eastern Wash.	DB	FR	10	3	9	0	0.3
86 Jesse Mays, St. Peter's	S	JR	10	3	3	0	0.3
86 Niall Murphy, Harvard	LB	SR	10	3	0	0	0.3
86 Clayton Smith, Dartmouth	WR	SO	10	3	34	0	0.3
86 Nate Spitler, Cornell	LB	SR	10	3	13	0	0.3
86 Philip Murray, Columbia	FS	SR	10	3	39	0	0.3
86 Josh Hubbard, Gardner-Webb	DB	FR	10	3	16	0	0.3
86 Blake Neri, Sacred Heart	DB	SR	10	3	31	1	0.3
86 Marcus Haines, St. Francis (Pa.)	DB	JR	10	3	29	0	0.3
86 Fred Plaza, Pennsylvania	DB	SR	10	3	65	2	0.3
86 Jason Ching, Brown	DB	FR	10	3	14	0	0.3
86 Jimmy Landrom, St. Francis (Pa.)	DB	JR	10	3	17	0	0.3
86 Mario Williams, Gardner-Webb	DB	SO	10	3	47	1	0.3
86 Trent Findley, Tenn.-Martin	DB	SR	10	3	40	1	0.3
86 David Walker, Savannah St.	DB	JR	10	3	8	0	0.3
86 Bryan Newbrough, San Diego	RB	JR	10	3	57	0	0.3
86 Boshawn Mack, Jacksonville	DB	SR	10	3	-1	0	0.3
86 Charlton Williams, Jacksonville	DB	JR	10	3	35	0	0.3

Kickoff Returns

(Minimum: 1.2 Punt Returns per Game)

Rank, Player	Pos	Cl	G	Ret	Yds	TD	Yds/ Ret	Ret/ Gm
1 Corey Alexander, Texas Southern	DB	SO	11	19	615	1	32.37	1.73
2 Cortland Finnegan, Samford	DB	FR	11	23	741	2	32.22	2.09
3 William Sherman, Morgan St.	WR	SR	12	15	452	0	30.13	1.25
4 LeJuan Walker, Nicholls St.	DB	SO	11	18	535	0	29.72	1.64
5 DaShaun Morris, Delaware St.	WR	JR	12	25	708	3	28.32	2.08
6 D'Brian Hudgins, N.C. A&T	RB	FR	12	16	450	1	28.13	1.33
7 Chad King, Stony Brook	DB	JR	10	16	445	2	27.81	1.6
8 Anthony Owens, Norfolk St.	DB	FR	11	30	832	1	27.73	2.73
9 Andre Raymond, Eastern Ill.	RB	JR	12	32	872	1	27.25	2.67
10 Bud Pough, Citadel	WR	JR	12	18	487	1	27.06	1.5
11 Justin Campbell, Butler	WR	SO	10	37	971	1	26.24	3.7
12 Anthony Williams, Ga. Southern	WR	SR	14	18	470	1	26.11	1.29
13 Hashim Hall, Portland St.	RB	SR	11	21	543	0	25.86	1.91
14 Rodney Byrnes, Harvard	WR	SO	10	15	386	1	25.73	1.5
15 Fred Amey, Sacramento St.	WR	SO	11	20	514	0	25.7	1.82
16 Soso Dede, Indiana St.	RB	JR	12	18	459	1	25.5	1.5
17 Ari Confesor, Holy Cross	WR	JR	12	33	841	1	25.48	2.75
18 Jay Bailey, Austin Peay	RB	SR	12	15	381	0	25.4	1.25
19 Ryan MacLean, Albany (N.Y.)	DB	SR	12	16	405	0	25.31	1.33
20 Peter Green, Siena	WR	SO	9	11	278	0	25.27	1.22
21 Mike Washington, Charleston So.	DB	SR	12	33	831	1	25.18	2.75
22 Korea McKay, Ark.-Pine Bluff	WR	JR	11	24	595	0	24.79	2.18
23 Ezra Landry, Southern U.	WR	JR	12	30	743	0	24.77	2.5
24 Jimmy Landrom, St. Francis (Pa.)	DB	JR	10	15	371	1	24.73	1.5
25 Jermane Little, Appalachian St.	WR	SO	12	25	617	0	24.68	2.08
26 Jamie Scott, South Carolina St.	RB	JR	12	17	419	0	24.65	1.42
27 Levander Segars, Montana	DB	SO	14	19	465	0	24.47	1.36
27 Terrance Patrick, Hampton	WR	JR	12	19	465	2	24.47	1.58
29 James Bialasik, Canisius	WR	SR	11	34	827	1	24.32	3.09
30 Maurice Daughtry, Jacksonville St.	WR	SO	9	19	461	0	24.26	2.11
31 Truesun Thomas, Wagner	DB	SO	11	16	388	0	24.25	1.45
32 Melvin Bryant, La Salle	WR	SO	11	29	701	1	24.17	2.64
33 Javarus Dudley, Fordham	WR	JR	13	35	840	0	24	2.69
34 Stephan Lewis, New Hampshire	RB	SR	11	27	645	0	23.89	2.45
35 Kyle Ware, St. Francis (Pa.)	RB	FR	8	15	356	0	23.73	1.88
36 Xavier Godard, Western Caro.	WR	FR	11	21	498	1	23.71	1.91
37 Wendall Williams, Rhode Island	RB	JR	12	26	611	1	23.5	2.17
38 Robert Garmon, Sam Houston St.	DB	SO	11	23	540	0	23.48	2.09
39 Anthony Sullivan, Southwest Mo. St.	WR	JR	11	24	563	0	23.46	2.18
40 Kevin Solomon, VMI	SB	SR	12	32	750	0	23.44	2.67
41 Ricardo Walker, Delaware	DB	SR	11	22	514	1	23.36	2
42 Martin Gibson, Villanova	RB	FR	15	35	817	1	23.34	2.33
43 Peter Athans, Sacred Heart	DB	SR	10	26	595	0	22.88	2.6
44 Andrew Nuckolls, East Tenn. St.	WR	JR	12	28	640	0	22.86	2.33
45 Ben Sanderson, Northern Iowa	WR	SR	11	22	502	0	22.82	2
46 Michael Johnson, Jackson St.	WR	FR	11	19	427	0	22.47	1.73
47 Arketa Banks, Elon	WR	SR	11	24	539	0	22.46	2.18
48 Darrell Jones, Cal Poly	WR	SO	11	29	650	2	22.41	2.64
49 J.B. Gerald, Colgate	WR	JR	12	20	446	0	22.3	1.67
50 Richmond Sanders, Eastern Wash.	WR	FR	10	13	289	0	22.23	1.3
51 Stephen McNair, Robert Morris	WR	SO	10	13	288	0	22.15	1.3
52 Dennis Butler, Illinois St.	DB	SR	11	22	485	0	22.05	2
53 Gary Sonkur, Harvard	DB	SO	9	15	330	0	22	1.67
53 Jeremy Grier, Chattanooga	WR	SO	10	31	682	0	22	3.1
55 Gavin Ng, San Diego	DB	JR	10	34	747	0	21.97	3.4
56 Emery Beckles, Idaho St.	DB	JR	11	19	417	0	21.95	1.73
57 Jamel Oliver, Southeast Mo. St.	RB	FR	12	25	548	0	21.92	2.08
58 Courtney White, Prairie View			11	14	305	0	21.79	1.27
59 Tony Tompkins, Stephen F. Austin	RB	FR	11	27	587	0	21.74	2.45
60 John Solan, Iona	RB	FR	11	14	303	0	21.64	1.27
61 Carlos Wright, Tennessee St.	WR	JR	10	19	410	0	21.58	1.9
62 Quea Williams, Austin Peay	RB	FR	12	21	453	0	21.57	1.75
63 Reggie Gray, Western Ill.	WR	FR	13	23	492	0	21.39	1.77
64 Shawn Holmes, Alabama St.	WR	JR	12	29	616	0	21.24	2.42
65 Sean Mizzer, VMI	RB	FR	12	17	361	0	21.24	1.42
66 Linj Shell, Jacksonville	DB	SR	10	20	424	0	21.2	2
67 Chad Nice, Cornell	WR	JR	9	20	421	0	21.05	2.22
68 Quorey Payne, Southern Ill.	DB	FR	11	16	336	0	21	1.45
68 Jay McCareins, Princeton	DB	SO	10	14	294	0	21	1.4
70 Patrick Jenkins, Tennessee St.	WR	SR	12	38	797	0	20.97	3.17
71 Adrian Hall, Liberty	WR	SO	11	33	692	0	20.97	3
72 Jerome Mathis, Hampton	WR	SO	12	20	417	1	20.85	1.67
73 Kory Chapman, Jacksonville St.	RB	JR	10	19	393	0	20.68	1.9
74 Matthew Loy, Morehead St.	WR	JR	12	15	310	0	20.67	1.25
75 Tom Campion, Fairfield	RB	SO	9	17	348	0	20.47	1.89
76 E.J. Collier, Florida A&M	RB	JR	11	29	586	0	20.21	2.64
77 Travis Chmelka, Columbia	WR	JR	10	26	525	0	20.19	2.6
78 Larry Johnson, Lafayette	DB	FR	12	23	464	0	20.17	1.92
79 Lee Davis, Southwest Tex. St.	RB	SR	10	16	321	0	20.06	1.6
80 Chris Green, Dartmouth	CB	FR	10	25	500	0	20	2.5
80 Xavier Butler, Morris Brown	WR	JR	12	32	640	0	20	2.67
80 Octavious Bond, Grambling	DB	JR	13	17	340	0	20	1.31
83 Josh Smith, Southwest Tex. St.	WR	FR	11	14	279	0	19.93	1.27
84 Donnel Horton, Tennessee Tech	DB	SO	12	27	537	0	19.89	2.25
85 Keon Coleman, Howard	RB	FR	11	22	436	0	19.82	2
86 Chris Daniels, Valparaiso	RB	SO	11	44	870	0	19.77	4
87 Muhammed Kanteh, Savannah St.	WR	SO	9	14	275	0	19.64	1.56

Rank, Player	Pos	Cl	G	Ret	Yds	TD	Yds/Ret	Ret/Gm
88 Robert Carr, Yale	TB	SO	10	17	333	0	19.59	1.7
89 Brian Bratton, Furman	WR	SO	12	36	705	0	19.58	3
90 Jc Ruddy, Drake	DB	FR	9	23	448	0	19.48	2.56
91 Reggie Danage, Towson	DB	SR	10	19	370	0	19.47	1.9
92 R.J. Harvey, New Hampshire	RB	SO	10	13	250	0	19.23	1.3
93 Corey Smith, Montana St.	WR	JR	13	20	383	0	19.15	1.54
94 Anthony Johnson, St. Mary's (Cal.)	RB	SO	10	19	363	0	19.11	1.9
95 Kim Sarin, Georgetown	RB	FR	10	29	550	0	18.97	2.9
96 Travis Armitstead, Southern Utah	DB	JR	11	33	625	0	18.94	3
97 Ern Mills, Citadel	RB	SO	9	14	265	0	18.93	1.56
98 Chad Davis, Jacksonville	RB	FR	8	16	301	0	18.81	2
99 Bob Lomoriello, Monmouth	DB	SO	10	16	300	0	18.75	1.6
100 Tyronne Gross, Sacramento St.	RB	FR	10	14	260	0	18.57	1.4

Passing

Rank, Player	Pos	Cl	G	Att	Cmp	Int	CPct	Yds	Yds/Att	Yds/Cmp	TD	Comp/Gm
1 Brett Gordon, Villanova	QB	SR	15	578	385	14	66.61	4,305	7.45	11.18	36	25.67
2 Brian Mann, Dartmouth	QB	SR	10	423	253	10	59.81	2,913	6.89	11.51	19	25.3
3 Mike Mitchell, Pennsylvania	QB	SR	10	371	241	13	64.96	2,803	7.56	11.63	20	24.1
4 Kyle Slager, Brown	QB	JR	10	340	230	10	67.65	2,609	7.67	11.34	19	23
5 Josh Blankenship, Eastern Wash.	QB	SR	11	418	250	7	59.81	3,243	7.76	12.97	30	22.73
6 Tony Romo, Eastern Ill.	QB	SR	12	407	258	16	63.39	3,165	7.78	12.27	34	21.5
7 Doug Baughman, Idaho St.	QB	SR	11	394	236	11	59.9	2,936	7.45	12.44	21	21.45
8 Steve Hunsberger, Columbia	QB	JR	10	370	212	8	57.3	2,023	5.47	9.54	6	21.2
9 Robert Kent, Jackson St.	QB	JR	11	395	232	12	58.73	3,386	8.57	14.59	31	21.09
10 Bruce Eugene, Grambling	QB	SO	13	543	269	16	49.54	4,483	8.26	16.67	43	20.69
11 Jack Tomco, Southeast Mo. St.	QB	JR	12	372	242	16	65.05	3,132	8.42	12.94	29	20.17
12 Ryan Cosentino, Hofstra	QB	JR	12	415	238	11	57.35	2,608	6.28	10.96	15	19.83
13 Jeremy Martin, Gardner-Webb	QB	SR	10	327	193	4	59.02	2,166	6.62	11.22	17	19.3
14 David Macchi, Valparaiso	QB	JR	11	390	212	18	54.36	3,326	8.53	15.69	21	19.27
15 Ira Vandever, Drake	QB	SR	11	361	205	11	56.79	3,239	8.97	15.8	32	18.64
16 Ryan Leadingham, Sacramento St.	QB	SO	12	373	221	7	59.25	2,788	7.47	12.62	15	18.42
16 Marko Glavic, Lafayette	QB	JR	12	399	221	15	55.39	2,670	6.69	12.08	20	18.42
18 Kevin Eakin, Fordham	QB	JR	13	383	239	9	62.4	3,040	7.94	12.72	22	18.38
19 John Edwards, Montana	QB	SR	14	449	257	9	57.24	3,209	7.15	12.49	20	18.36
20 Dave Corley, William & Mary	QB	SR	11	329	200	9	60.79	2,672	8.12	13.36	21	18.18
21 Tate Bennett, Weber St.	QB	JR	10	311	181	11	58.2	2,228	7.16	12.31	16	18.1
22 Paul Nichols, Davidson	QB	SR	10	308	174	10	56.49	2,189	7.11	12.58	25	17.4
23 Eric Rasmussen, San Diego	QB	JR	10	279	170	1	60.93	2,473	8.86	14.55	25	17
24 Jeff Klein, Citadel	QB	JR	12	378	203	10	53.7	2,561	6.78	12.62	17	16.92
25 David Caudill, Morehead St.	QB	JR	12	362	201	18	55.52	2,979	8.23	14.82	20	16.75
26 Carey Weaver, Mississippi Val.	QB	SR	11	323	179	13	55.42	2,116	6.55	11.82	15	16.27
27 Ed Marynowitz, La Salle	QB	FR	11	369	177	14	47.97	2,339	6.34	13.21	12	16.09
28 Juston Wood, Portland St.	QB	SR	11	324	176	14	54.32	2,211	6.82	12.56	13	16
28 Tom McCune, Colgate	QB	SR	9	255	144	6	56.47	1,951	7.65	13.55	11	16
30 Brian Hall, Holy Cross	QB	SR	12	345	191	11	55.36	2,279	6.61	11.93	20	15.92
30 Niel Loebig, Duquesne	QB	SO	12	362	191	13	52.76	2,685	7.42	14.06	29	15.92
32 Mike Sturgill, Jacksonville	QB	FR	10	279	158	13	56.63	1,876	6.72	11.87	11	15.8
33 Billy Napier, Furman	QB	SR	12	276	189	8	68.48	2,475	8.97	13.1	16	15.75
34 Mike Granieri, New Hampshire	QB	SO	11	297	170	12	57.24	1,826	6.15	10.74	12	15.45
35 Neil Rose, Harvard	QB	SR	8	186	123	5	66.13	1,438	7.73	11.69	8	15.38
36 Jeff Krohn, Massachusetts	QB	JR	10	287	152	12	52.96	2,032	7.08	13.37	16	15.2
37 Joey Gibson, VMI	QB	SR	12	348	181	13	52.01	2,328	6.69	12.86	17	15.08
38 Jay Amer, Towson	QB	JR	11	299	163	10	54.52	2,214	7.4	13.58	16	14.82
39 Ryan McCann, Chattanooga	QB	SR	12	297	177	11	59.6	2,099	7.07	11.86	18	14.75
40 Clint Womack, Northern Ariz.	QB	JR	10	265	147	13	55.47	1,950	7.36	13.27	10	14.7
41 Russ Michna, Western Ill.	QB	JR	13	330	189	5	57.27	3,037	9.2	16.07	23	14.54
42 Andy Hall, Delaware	QB	FR	11	306	159	5	51.96	1,832	5.99	11.52	9	14.45
43 Donald Carrie, Alcorn St.	QB	SO	11	338	155	17	45.86	2,197	6.5	14.17	19	14.09
44 Stewart Childress, Murray St.	QB	JR	12	266	169	7	63.53	1,894	7.12	11.21	14	14.08
45 Jake Eaton, Maine	QB	SR	11	269	154	9	57.25	1,849	6.87	12.01	16	14
45 Joe Burchette, Appalachian St.	QB	SR	12	284	168	8	59.15	1,949	6.86	11.6	15	14
45 Robert Craft, Tennessee Tech	QB	SO	12	310	168	11	54.19	2,448	7.9	14.57	16	14
48 Michael White, Southwest Mo. St.	QB	JR	10	249	138	9	55.42	1,708	6.86	12.38	12	13.8
49 Casey Printers, Florida A&M	QB	SR	9	218	123	5	56.42	1,517	6.96	12.33	12	13.67
50 Mick Razzano, Cornell	QB	SR	10	275	136	7	49.45	1,548	5.63	11.38	7	13.6
51 Chad Schwenk, Lehigh	QB	JR	10	247	135	10	54.66	1,618	6.55	11.99	11	13.5
51 Jeff Mroz, Yale	QB	SO	10	244	135	6	55.33	1,731	7.09	12.82	14	13.5
53 Mike Cerchio, Fairfield	QB	SR	10	267	133	11	49.81	1,707	6.39	12.83	10	13.3
54 Joe Kroells, Sacred Heart	QB	JR	10	276	131	11	47.46	1,627	5.89	12.42	14	13.1
55 Scott Bard, Stony Brook	QB	SR	10	237	129	10	54.43	1,478	6.24	11.46	12	12.9
56 Matt Millheiser, St. John's (N.Y.)	RB	JR	10	290	128	12	44.14	1,694	5.84	13.23	16	12.8
57 Travis Lulay, Montana St.	QB	FR	13	272	157	5	57.72	2,042	7.51	13.01	14	12.08

STATISTICAL LEADERS

San Diego Sports Information

Eric Rasmussen, San Diego

Drake Sports Information

Ira Vandever, Drake

Rank, Player	Pos	Cl	G	Att	Cmp	Int	CPct	Yds	Yds/Att	Yds/Cmp	TD	Comp/Gm
58 Pat Cilento, Western Caro.	QB	SR	11	221	132	5	59.73	1,636	7.4	12.39	8	12
59 Julian Reese, Indiana St.	QB	SR	12	266	143	9	53.76	1,725	6.48	12.06	12	11.92
60 Josh Kellett, Samford	QB	SR	11	225	130	11	57.78	1,518	6.75	11.68	12	11.82
61 Ryan Roeder, Albany (N.Y.)	QB	SR	12	213	131	5	61.5	1,366	6.41	10.43	8	10.92
62 Scott Pendarvis, McNeese St.	QB	SO	15	288	163	6	56.6	2,050	7.12	12.58	11	10.87
63 Tom Petrie, Northern Iowa	QB	SO	10	210	108	8	51.43	1,363	6.49	12.62	6	10.8
64 Donald Clark, Howard	QB	SR	11	247	118	12	47.77	1,459	5.91	12.36	16	10.73
65 David Splithoff, Princeton	QB	JR	8	142	85	4	59.86	1,223	8.61	14.39	8	10.63
66 Leon McCampbell, South Carolina St.	QB	JR	12	233	127	11	54.51	1,972	8.46	15.53	15	10.58
67 Jamie Burke, Florida Int'l	QB	FR	11	195	113	11	57.95	1,652	8.47	14.62	14	10.27
68 Kevin Magee, Northwestern St.	QB	SR	13	252	133	11	52.78	1,844	7.32	13.86	13	10.23
69 Clyde Tullis, Savannah St.	QB	FR	10	266	101	17	37.97	1,233	4.64	12.21	3	10.1
70 Jatavis Sanders, East Tenn. St.	QB	SR	12	229	121	5	52.84	1,311	5.72	10.83	7	10.08
71 Quincy Richard, Southern U.	QB	JR	12	239	119	9	49.79	1,279	5.35	10.75	11	9.92
72 Michael Souza, Illinois St.	QB	JR	11	233	108	9	46.35	1,404	6.03	13	8	9.82
73 David Paulus, Georgetown	QB	SR	11	182	107	4	58.79	1,438	7.9	13.44	17	9.73
74 Todd Wenrich, Bucknell	QB	SR	10	167	95	8	56.89	1,079	6.46	11.36	8	9.5
75 Ryan Fitzpatrick, Harvard	QB	SO	10	150	94	0	62.67	1,155	7.7	12.29	8	9.4
76 Bill Rankin, Monmouth	QB	SR	10	239	93	10	38.91	1,189	4.97	12.78	6	9.3
77 Cody McCauley, Southwest Tex. St.	QB	SO	11	168	102	6	60.71	1,223	7.28	11.99	9	9.27
78 Scott Dolch, Central Conn. St.	QB	SO	10	218	92	12	42.2	1,121	5.14	12.18	3	9.2
79 Billy Brieden, Iona	QB	JR	11	227	101	18	44.49	1,387	6.11	13.73	7	9.18
80 Travis Turner, Eastern Ky.	QB	SR	11	190	100	8	52.63	1,381	7.27	13.81	9	9.09
81 Zeke Dixon, Stephen F. Austin	QB	SO	11	188	98	7	52.13	1,486	7.9	15.16	10	8.91
81 Jared Allen, Fla. Atlantic	QB	SO	11	193	98	6	50.78	1,358	7.04	13.86	7	8.91
83 Vance Smith, Sam Houston St.	QB	SR	10	178	89	7	50	1,020	5.73	11.46	7	8.9
84 Jermaine Crenshaw, Alabama St.	QB	JR	12	204	106	10	51.96	1,185	5.81	11.18	10	8.83
85 Matt LeZotte, James Madison	QB	SO	12	199	103	8	51.76	1,481	7.44	14.38	3	8.58
86 Shawn Brady, Northeastern	QB	SO	13	224	111	6	49.55	1,497	6.68	13.49	16	8.54
87 Timothy Frazier, Hampton	QB	JR	12	201	101	5	50.25	1,351	6.72	13.38	11	8.42
88 Reggie Hayes, Florida A&M	QB	SR	12	202	100	14	49.5	1,459	7.22	14.59	13	8.33
88 Gary Brashears, Alabama St.	QB	JR	12	208	100	9	48.08	1,097	5.27	10.97	12	8.33
90 Shawn Martin, Robert Morris	SE	SR	10	168	83	8	49.4	1,195	7.11	14.4	5	8.3
91 Ian Nelson, Butler	QB	SO	10	150	82	8	54.67	1,031	6.87	12.57	4	8.2
92 Jason Douglas, N.C. A&T	QB	JR	12	168	98	6	58.33	1,158	6.89	11.82	9	8.17
93 Jacob Chavan, Texas Southern	QB	FR	11	169	89	9	52.66	1,397	8.27	15.7	8	8.09
94 Dontrell Leonard, Norfolk St.	QB	JR	11	180	88	9	48.89	1,104	6.13	12.55	3	8
95 Joel Sambursky, Southern Ill.	QB	SO	12	167	92	5	55.09	1,308	7.83	14.22	10	7.67
96 Ramon Nelson, Samford	QB	SO	11	161	84	2	52.17	918	5.7	10.93	4	7.64
97 Tyler Thomas, Montana St.	QB	SR	10	160	75	4	46.88	879	5.49	11.72	9	7.5
98 Travis Tobaben, Sam Houston St.	QB	SO	11	160	80	6	50	960	6	12	1	7.27
98 Antonio Lovelady, Ark.-Pine Bluff	QB	SO	11	170	80	9	47.06	1318	7.75	16.48	11	7.27
100 Kittrell Barnes, Delaware St.	QB	SR	9	124	65	7	52.42	809	6.52	12.45	6	7.22

Passing Efficiency

Min. 75 Pct. of Team's Games Played, 15 Attempts Per Game

Rank, Player	Pos	Cl	G	Att	Comp	CPct	Int	IPct	Yds	Yds/Att	TD	TDpct	Rating
1 Eric Rasmussen, San Diego	QB	JR	10	279	170	60.93	1	0.36	2,473	8.86	25	8.96	164.2
2 Billy Napier, Furman	QB	SR	12	276	189	68.48	8	2.9	2,475	8.97	16	5.8	157.1
3 Ira Vandever, Drake	QB	SR	11	361	205	56.79	11	3.05	3,239	8.97	32	8.86	155.3
4 Russ Michna, Western Ill.	QB	JR	13	330	189	57.27	5	1.52	3,037	9.2	23	6.97	154.5
5 Jack Tomco, Southeast Mo. St.	QB	JR	12	372	242	65.05	16	4.3	3,132	8.42	29	7.8	152.9
6 David Paulus, Georgetown	QB	SR	11	182	107	58.79	4	2.2	1,438	7.9	17	9.34	151.6
7 Robert Kent, Jackson St.	QB	JR	11	395	232	58.73	12	3.04	3,386	8.57	31	7.85	150.6
8 Tony Romo, Eastern Ill.	QB	SR	12	407	258	63.39	16	3.93	3,165	7.78	34	8.35	148.4
9 Josh Blankenship, Eastern Wash.	QB	SR	11	418	250	59.81	7	1.67	3,243	7.76	30	7.18	145.3
10 David Splithoff, Princeton	QB	JR	8	142	85	59.86	4	2.82	1,223	8.61	8	5.63	145.2
11 Ryan Fitzpatrick, Harvard	QB	SO	10	150	94	62.67	0	0	1,155	7.7	8	5.33	144.9
12 Brett Gordon, Villanova	QB	SR	15	578	385	66.61	14	2.42	4,305	7.45	36	6.23	144.9
13 Kyle Slager, Brown	QB	JR	10	340	230	67.65	10	2.94	2,609	7.67	19	5.59	144.7
14 Dave Corley, William & Mary	QB	SR	11	329	200	60.79	9	2.74	2,672	8.12	21	6.38	144.6
15 Kevin Eakin, Fordham	QB	JR	13	383	239	62.4	9	2.35	3,040	7.94	22	5.74	143.3
16 Jamie Burke, Florida Int'l	QB	FR	11	195	113	57.95	11	5.64	1,652	8.47	14	7.18	141.5
17 Neil Rose, Harvard	QB	SR	8	186	123	66.13	5	2.69	1,438	7.73	8	4.3	139.9
18 Mike Mitchell, Pennsylvania	QB	SR	10	371	241	64.96	13	3.5	2,803	7.56	20	5.39	139.2
19 Bruce Eugene, Grambling	QB	SO	13	543	269	49.54	16	2.95	4,483	8.26	43	7.92	139.1

Rank, Player	Pos	Cl	G	Att	Comp	CPct	Int	IPct	Yds	Yds/Att	TD	TDpct	Rating
20 Leon McCampbell, South Carolina St.	QB	JR	12	233	127	54.51	11	4.72	1,972	8.46	15	6.44	137.4
21 Paul Nichols, Davidson	QB	SR	10	308	174	56.49	10	3.25	2,189	7.11	25	8.12	136.5
22 Stewart Childress, Murray St.	QB	JR	12	266	169	63.53	7	2.63	1,894	7.12	14	5.26	135.4
23 David Macchi, Valparaiso	QB	JR	11	390	212	54.36	18	4.62	3,326	8.53	21	5.38	134.5
24 Doug Baughman, Idaho St.	QB	SR	11	394	236	59.9	11	2.79	2,936	7.45	21	5.33	134.5
25 Niel Loebig, Duquesne	QB	SO	12	362	191	52.76	13	3.59	2,685	7.42	29	8.01	134.3
26 Travis Lulay, Montana St.	QB	FR	13	272	157	57.72	5	1.84	2,042	7.51	14	5.15	134.1
27 David Caudill, Morehead St.	QB	JR	12	362	201	55.52	18	4.97	2,979	8.23	20	5.52	132.9
28 Cody McCauley, Southwest Tex. St.	QB	SO	11	168	102	60.71	6	3.57	1,223	7.28	9	5.36	132.4
29 Ryan McCann, Chattanooga	QB	SR	12	297	177	59.6	11	3.7	2,099	7.07	18	6.06	131.6
30 Ryan Leadingham, Sacramento St.	QB	SO	12	373	221	59.25	7	1.88	2,788	7.47	15	4.02	131.6
31 Robert Craft, Tennessee Tech	QB	SO	12	310	168	54.19	11	3.55	2,448	7.9	16	5.16	130.5
32 Tom McCune, Colgate	QB	SR	9	255	144	56.47	6	2.35	1,951	7.65	11	4.31	130.3
33 Jeremy Martin, Gardner-Webb	QB	SR	10	327	193	59.02	4	1.22	2,166	6.62	17	5.2	129.4
34 Pat Cilento, Western Caro.	QB	SR	11	221	132	59.73	5	2.26	1,636	7.4	8	3.62	129.3
35 Jeff Mroz, Yale	QB	SO	10	244	135	55.33	6	2.46	1,731	7.09	14	5.74	128.9
36 Zeke Dixon, Stephen F. Austin	QB	SO	11	188	98	52.13	7	3.72	1,486	7.9	10	5.32	128.6
37 Joe Burchette, Appalachian St.	QB	SR	12	284	168	59.15	8	2.82	1,949	6.86	15	5.28	128.6
38 Casey Printers, Florida A&M	QB	SR	9	218	123	56.42	5	2.29	1,517	6.96	12	5.5	128.5
39 Tate Bennett, Weber St.	QB	JR	10	311	181	58.2	11	3.54	2,228	7.16	16	5.14	128.3
40 John Edwards, Montana	QB	SR	14	449	257	57.24	9	2	3,209	7.15	20	4.45	128
41 Jake Eaton, Maine	QB	SR	11	269	154	57.25	9	3.35	1,849	6.87	16	5.95	127.9
42 Brian Mann, Dartmouth	QB	SR	10	423	253	59.81	10	2.36	2,913	6.89	19	4.49	127.8
43 Jay Amer, Towson	QB	JR	11	299	163	54.52	10	3.34	2,214	7.4	16	5.35	127.7
44 Jacob Chavan, Texas Southern	QB	FR	11	169	89	52.66	9	5.33	1,397	8.27	8	4.73	127.1
45 Scott Pendarvis, McNeese St.	QB	SO	15	288	163	56.6	6	2.08	2,050	7.12	11	3.82	124.8
46 Shawn Brady, Northeastern	QB	SO	13	224	111	49.55	6	2.68	1,497	6.68	16	7.14	123.9
47 Brian Hall, Holy Cross	QB	SR	12	345	191	55.36	11	3.19	2,279	6.61	20	5.8	123.4
48 Ryan Roeder, Albany (N.Y.)	QB	SR	12	213	131	61.5	5	2.35	1,366	6.41	8	3.76	123.1
49 Antonio Lovelady, Ark.-Pine Bluff	QB	SO	11	170	80	47.06	9	5.29	1,318	7.75	11	6.47	122.9
50 Kevin Magee, Northwestern St.	QB	SR	13	252	133	52.78	11	4.37	1,844	7.32	13	5.16	122.5
51 Jeff Krohn, Massachusetts	QB	JR	10	287	152	52.96	12	4.18	2,032	7.08	16	5.57	122.5
52 Josh Kellett, Samford	QB	SR	11	225	130	57.78	11	4.89	1,518	6.75	12	5.33	122.3
53 Michael White, Southwest Mo. St.	QB	JR	10	249	138	55.42	9	3.61	1,708	6.86	12	4.82	121.7
54 Travis Turner, Eastern Ky.	QB	SR	11	190	100	52.63	8	4.21	1,381	7.27	9	4.74	120.9
55 Marko Glavic, Lafayette	QB	JR	12	399	221	55.39	15	3.76	2,670	6.69	20	5.01	120.6
56 Jeff Klein, Citadel	QB	SR	12	378	203	53.7	10	2.65	2,561	6.78	17	4.5	120.2
57 Clint Womack, Northern Ariz.	QB	JR	10	265	147	55.47	13	4.91	1,950	7.36	10	3.77	119.9
58 Timothy Frazier, Hampton	QB	JR	12	201	101	50.25	5	2.49	1,351	6.72	11	5.47	119.8
59 Carey Weaver, Mississippi Val.	QB	SR	11	323	179	55.42	13	4.02	2,116	6.55	15	4.64	117.7
60 Reggie Hayes, Florida A&M	QB	SR	12	202	100	49.5	14	6.93	1,459	7.22	13	6.44	117.6
61 Todd Wenrich, Bucknell	QB	SR	10	167	95	56.89	8	4.79	1,079	6.46	8	4.79	117.4
62 Joey Gibson, VMI	QB	SR	12	348	181	52.01	13	3.74	2,328	6.69	17	4.89	116.9
63 Mike Sturgill, Jacksonville	QB	FR	10	279	158	56.63	13	4.66	1,876	6.72	11	3.94	116.8
64 Ryan Cosentino, Hofstra	QB	JR	12	415	238	57.35	11	2.65	2,608	6.28	15	3.61	116.8
65 Julian Reese, Indiana St.	QB	SR	12	266	143	53.76	9	3.38	1,725	6.48	12	4.51	116.4
66 Chad Schwenk, Lehigh	QB	JR	10	247	135	54.66	10	4.05	1,618	6.55	11	4.45	116.3
67 Juston Wood, Portland St.	QB	SR	11	324	176	54.32	14	4.32	2,211	6.82	13	4.01	116.2
68 Jared Allen, Fla. Atlantic	QB	SO	11	193	98	50.78	6	3.11	1,358	7.04	7	3.63	115.6
69 Scott Bard, Stony Brook	QB	SR	10	237	129	54.43	10	4.22	1,478	6.24	12	5.06	115.1
70 Mike Granieri, New Hampshire	QB	SO	11	297	170	57.24	12	4.04	1,826	6.15	12	4.04	114.1
71 Matt LeZotte, James Madison	QB	SO	12	199	103	51.76	8	4.02	1,481	7.44	3	1.51	111.2
72 Ian Nelson, Butler	QB	SO	10	150	82	54.67	8	5.33	1,031	6.87	4	2.67	110.5
73 Shawn Martin, Robert Morris	SE	SR	10	168	83	49.4	8	4.76	1,195	7.11	5	2.98	109.5
74 Donald Clark, Howard	QB	SR	11	247	118	47.77	12	4.86	1,459	5.91	16	6.48	109.1
75 Donald Carrie, Alcorn St.	QB	SO	11	338	155	45.86	17	5.03	2,197	6.5	19	5.62	108.9
76 Andy Hall, Delaware	QB	FR	11	306	159	51.96	5	1.63	1,832	5.99	9	2.94	108.7
77 Tom Petrie, Northern Iowa	QB	SO	10	210	108	51.43	8	3.81	1,363	6.49	6	2.86	107.8
78 Mike Cerchio, Fairfield	QB	SR	10	267	133	49.81	11	4.12	1,707	6.39	10	3.75	107.6
79 Jermaine Crenshaw, Alabama St.	QB	JR	12	204	106	51.96	10	4.9	1,185	5.81	10	4.9	107.1
80 Jatavis Sanders, East Tenn. St.	QB	SR	12	229	121	52.84	5	2.18	1,311	5.72	7	3.06	106.6
81 Tyler Thomas, Montana St.	QB	SR	10	160	75	46.88	4	2.5	879	5.49	9	5.63	106.6
82 Joe Kroells, Sacred Heart	QB	JR	10	276	131	47.46	11	3.99	1,627	5.89	14	5.07	105.7
83 Ed Marynowitz, La Salle	QB	FR	11	369	177	47.97	14	3.79	2,339	6.34	12	3.25	104.4
84 Steve Hunsberger, Columbia	QB	JR	10	370	212	57.3	8	2.16	2,023	5.47	6	1.62	104.3

Rank, Player	Pos	Cl	G	Att	Comp	CPct	Int	IPct	Yds	Yds/Att	TD	TDpct	Rating
85 Vance Smith, Sam Houston St.	QB	SR	10	178	89	50	7	3.93	1,020	5.73	7	3.93	103.2
86 Matt Millheiser, St. John's (N.Y.)	RB	JR	10	290	128	44.14	12	4.14	1,694	5.84	16	5.52	103.1
87 Gary Brashears, Alabama St.	QB	JR	12	208	100	48.08	9	4.33	1,097	5.27	12	5.77	102.8
88 Quincy Richard, Southern U.	QB	JR	12	239	119	49.79	9	3.77	1,279	5.35	11	4.6	102.4
89 LaKendrick Powell, Ark.-Pine Bluff	QB	SR	11	175	77	44	8	4.57	1,072	6.13	8	4.57	101.4
90 Michael Souza, Illinois St.	QB	JR	11	233	108	46.35	9	3.86	1,404	6.03	8	3.43	100.6
91 Mick Razzano, Cornell	QB	SR	10	275	136	49.45	7	2.55	1,548	5.63	7	2.55	100
92 Anthony Mayo, Jacksonville St.	QB	SO	11	174	78	44.83	6	3.45	981	5.64	6	3.45	96.7
93 Dontrell Leonard, Norfolk St.	QB	JR	11	180	88	48.89	9	5	1,104	6.13	3	1.67	95.9
94 Chris Peterson, Cal Poly	QB	JR	11	174	76	43.68	10	5.75	1,066	6.13	5	2.87	93.1
95 Billy Brieden, Iona	QB	JR	11	227	101	44.49	18	7.93	1,387	6.11	7	3.08	90.1
96 James Condon, Liberty	QB	SR	10	154	61	39.61	10	6.49	892	5.79	6	3.9	88.1
97 Christian Karolus, Siena	QB	JR	10	164	66	40.24	7	4.27	808	4.93	6	3.66	85.2
98 Kevin Bielen, Marist	QB	SR	11	192	71	36.98	8	4.17	1,002	5.22	5	2.6	81.1
99 Bill Rankin, Monmouth	QB	SR	10	239	93	38.91	10	4.18	1,189	4.97	6	2.51	80.6
100 Scott Dolch, Central Conn. St.	QB	SO	10	218	92	42.2	12	5.5	1,121	5.14	3	1.38	78.9

Points Responsible For

Min. 75 Pct. of Team's Games Played

Rank, Player	Pos	Cl	G	Pass Cnv	TD	Pts	Tot RFr	PtsRFr/Gm
1 Bruce Eugene, Grambling	QB	SO	13	3	43	58	322	24.77
2 Ira Vandever, Drake	QB	JR	11	1	32	20	214	19.45
3 Robert Kent, Jackson St.	QB	JR	11	0	31	24	210	19.09
4 Tony Romo, Eastern Ill.	QB	SR	12	1	34	6	212	17.67
5 Josh Blankenship, Eastern Wash.	QB	SR	11	0	30	0	180	16.36
6 David Caudill, Morehead St.	OB	JR	12	2	29	66	190	15.83
6 Niel Loebig, Duquesne	QB	SO	12	2	29	12	190	15.83
8 Paul Nichols, Davidson	QB	SR	10	1	25	6	158	15.8
8 Eric Rasmussen, San Diego	QB	JR	10	1	25	6	158	15.8
10 Chaz Williams, Ga. Southern	QB	SO	14	0	9	162	216	15.43
11 Jack Tomco, Southeast Mo. St.	QB	JR	12	3	29	4	184	15.33
12 Brett Gordon, Villanova	QB	SR	15	0	36	6	222	14.8
13 Dave Corley, William & Mary	QB	SR	11	1	21	26	154	14
13 Brian Mann, Dartmouth	QB	SO	10	0	19	26	140	14
15 Kyle Slager, Brown	QB	JR	10	0	19	24	138	13.8
16 David Macchi, Valparaiso	QB	JR	11	2	21	12	142	12.91
17 Jake Eaton, Maine	QB	SR	11	1	16	42	140	12.73
18 Mike Mitchell, Pennsylvania	QB	SO	10	0	20	6	126	12.6
19 T.J. Stallings, Morgan St.	WR	SR	12	0	1	144	150	12.5
20 Russ Michna, Western Ill.	QB	JR	13	0	23	24	162	12.46
20 Kevin Eakin, Fordham	QB	JR	13	0	22	30	162	12.46
22 Allen Suber, Bethune-Cookman	QB	JR	12	2	8	94	146	12.17
22 Joey Gibson, VMI	QB	SR	12	1	17	42	146	12.17
24 John Edwards, Montana	QB	SR	14	1	20	48	170	12.14
25 Dale Jennings, Butler	RB	SR	10	0	0	120	120	12
25 Matt Millheiser, St. John's (N.Y.)	RB	JR	10	2	16	20	120	12
27 Doug Baughman, Idaho St.	QB	SR	11	2	21	0	130	11.82
28 Jeremy Martin, Gardner-Webb	QB	SR	10	2	17	10	116	11.6
29 Brian Hall, Holy Cross	QB	SR	12	0	20	18	138	11.5
29 Gary Jones, Albany (N.Y.)	RB	JR	12	0	0	138	138	11.5
31 Donald Carrie, Alcorn St.	QB	SO	11	0	19	12	126	11.45
32 Tate Bennett, Weber St.	QB	JR	10	0	18	6	114	11.4
33 Marko Glavic, Lafayette	QB	JR	12	1	20	14	136	11.33
34 Billy Napier, Furman	QB	SR	12	0	16	36	132	11
34 Jeff Klein, Citadel	QB	SR	12	2	17	26	132	11
36 Jeff Krohn, Massachusetts	QB	JR	10	0	16	6	102	10.2
37 Leon McCampbell, South Carolina St.	QB	JR	12	1	15	30	122	10.17
38 Donald Clark, Howard	QB	SR	11	1	16	12	110	10
38 Tom McCune, Colgate	QB	SR	9	0	11	24	90	10
38 Casey Printers, Florida A&M	QB	SR	9	0	12	18	90	10
38 Reggie Hayes, Florida A&M	QB	SR	12	0	13	42	120	10
42 Chris Peterson, Cal Poly	QB	JR	11	0	5	78	108	9.82
42 Carey Weaver, Mississippi Val.	QB	SR	11	0	15	18	108	9.82
44 Ryan McCann, Chattanooga	QB	SR	12	0	18	6	114	9.5
45 David Paulus, Georgetown	QB	SR	11	1	17	0	104	9.45
46 J.R. Taylor, Eastern Ill.	RB	SR	12	0	0	112	112	9.33
47 Jay Amer, Towson	QB	JR	11	0	16	6	102	9.27
48 Shawn Brady, Northeastern	QB	SO	13	0	16	24	120	9.23
49 Jeff Mroz, Yale	QB	SO	10	1	14	6	92	9.2
49 Jason Michael, Western Ky.	QB	SR	15	0	9	84	138	9.2
51 Joe Burchette, Appalachian St.	QB	SR	12	2	15	16	110	9.17
52 Robert Craft, Tennessee Tech	QB	SO	12	0	16	12	108	9
52 Ryan Cosentino, Hofstra	QB	JR	12	0	15	18	108	9
52 Tramon Douglas, Grambling	WR	JR	12	0	0	108	108	9
52 Jay Bailey, Austin Peay	RB	SR	12	0	0	108	108	9
52 Mike Cerchio, Fairfield	QB	SR	10	2	10	26	90	9
52 Joe Kroells, Sacred Heart	QB	JR	10	0	14	6	90	9
58 Justin Langan, Western Ill.	K	SO	13	0	0	116	116	8.92
59 Andy Hall, Delaware	QB	FR	11	1	9	42	98	8.91
60 Kirwin Watson, Fordham	RB	JR	13	0	0	114	114	8.77
61 Josh Kellett, Samford	QB	SR	11	2	12	20	96	8.73
61 Billy Blanchard, Murray St.	RB	SR	11	0	0	96	96	8.73
63 Jermaine Crenshaw, Alabama St.	QB	JR	12	0	10	42	102	8.5
64 MacKenzie Hoambrecker, Northern Iowa	K	SR	11	0	0	93	93	8.45
65 Scott Bard, Stony Brook	QB	SR	10	0	12	12	84	8.4
65 Trevor Johnston, St. Mary's (Cal.)	QB	FR	10	0	2	72	84	8.4
65 Lee Davis, Southwest Tex. St.	RB	SO	10	0	0	84	84	8.4
68 Jamie Burke, Florida Int'l	QB	FR	11	1	14	6	92	8.36
69 C.J. Hudson, Eastern Ky.	RB	SO	12	1	0	98	100	8.33
70 Jesse Obert, Dayton	P	SR	12	0	0	99	99	8.25
71 Chad Schwenk, Lehigh	QB	JR	10	1	11	14	82	8.2
72 Alfredo Rulliano, Marist	RB	SR	11	0	0	90	90	8.18
72 R.J. Cobbs, Massachusetts	RB	FR	11	0	0	90	90	8.18
74 Willie Ponder, Southeast Mo. St.	WR	SR	12	0	0	98	98	8.17
74 Ryan Leadingham, Sacramento St.	QB	SO	12	1	15	6	98	8.17
74 Ryan Roeder, Albany (N.Y.)	QB	SR	12	1	8	48	98	8.17
77 Ed Marynowitz, La Salle	QB	FR	11	1	12	14	88	8
77 Steve Hunsberger, Columbia	QB	JR	10	2	6	40	80	8
77 Mike Granieri, New Hampshire	QB	SO	11	2	12	12	88	8
80 Peter Veldman, Pennsylvania	K	JR	10	0	0	79	79	7.9
81 Kelly Spiker, Dayton	QB	JR	12	0	6	58	94	7.83
81 Clint Womack, Northern Ariz.	QB	JR	10	0	10	18	78	7.8
82 Isaac Mitchell, Idaho St.	RB	JR	10	0	0	78	78	7.8
82 Ryan Fitzpatrick, Harvard	QB	SO	10	0	8	30	78	7.8
85 Chris Snyder, Montana	K	JR	14	0	0	107	107	7.64
86 Juston Wood, Portland St.	QB	SR	11	0	13	6	84	7.64
86 Johnathan Taylor, Drake	RB	JR	11	0	0	84	84	7.64
88 Travis Lulay, Montana St.	QB	FR	13	1	14	12	98	7.54
88 Matt Fordyce, Fordham	P	SR	13	0	0	98	98	7.54
90 Joel Sambursky, Southern Ill.	QB	SO	12	0	10	30	90	7.5
90 Stewart Childress, Murray St.	QB	JR	12	0	14	6	90	7.5
90 Quincy Richard, Southern U.	QB	JR	12	0	11	24	90	7.5
93 Stephan Lewis, New Hampshire	RB	SR	11	0	0	82	82	7.45
94 Mike Chase, Davidson	TE	SR	10	0	0	74	74	7.4
94 Mike Sturgill, Jacksonville	QB	FR	10	1	11	6	74	7.4
94 Michael White, Southwest Mo. St.	QB	JR	10	1	12	0	74	7.4
97 Tim Gale, Northeastern	RB	SR	13	0	0	96	96	7.38
98 Kyle Painter, Liberty	QB	SO	9	0	10	6	66	7.33
99 Jayson Davis, Rhode Island	QB	FR	11	1	2	66	80	7.27
99 Antonio Lovelady, Ark.-Pine Bluff	QB	SO	11	4	11	6	80	7.27
99 Cortez Hankton, Texas Southern	WR	SR	11	0	0	80	80	7.27

Punting

Min. 75 Pct. of Team's Games Played 75, 3.6 Punts per Game

Rank, Player	Pos	Cl	G	Pnt	Yds	Avg	Punt/Gm
1 Mark Gould, Northern Ariz.	P	JR	11	62	2,987	48.18	5.64
2 Mike Scifres, Western Ill.	P	SR	13	53	2,545	48.02	4.08
3 Brent Barth, VMI	P	SR	12	64	3,032	47.38	5.33
4 Eddie Johnson, Idaho St.	**P**	**SR**	**11**	**51**	**2,357**	**46.22**	**4.64**
5 David Beckford, Alabama St.	P	SR	12	57	2,505	43.95	4.75
6 Travis Grubb, Chattanooga	P	SR	12	66	2,893	43.83	5.5
7 Derrick Frost, Northern Iowa	P	SR	11	49	2,137	43.61	4.45
8 Richie Rhodes, Jacksonville St.	P	SO	11	60	2,583	43.05	5.45
9 Aaron Bass, East Tenn. St.	P	JR	12	77	3,306	42.94	6.42
10 Travis Zobel, Citadel	P	JR	12	48	2,050	42.71	4
11 Aaron Wall, Ark.-Pine Bluff	P	SR	11	67	2,859	42.67	6.09
12 Gilbert Rocha, Cal Poly	P	JR	11	62	2,640	42.58	5.64
13 Jimmy Miner, Wofford	P	JR	12	47	1,985	42.23	3.92
14 Nathan McKinney, Appalachian St.	P	JR	12	59	2,488	42.17	4.92
15 Jeff Gomulinski, Fairfield	P	SO	11	66	2,776	42.06	6
16 Josh Polgar, New Hampshire	P	JR	11	49	2,019	41.2	4.45
17 Ryan Horvath, Drake	P	FR	11	44	1,806	41.05	4
18 Shane Laisle, Rhode Island	K	JR	12	66	2,701	40.92	5.5
19 David Paulus, Georgetown	QB	SR	11	59	2,399	40.66	5.36
20 Joe Nolan, Hofstra	P	SO	12	68	2,764	40.65	5.67
21 Cody Reeves, Sam Houston St.	WR	FR	11	65	2,629	40.45	5.91
22 David Sanger, Massachusetts	P	SR	12	68	2,750	40.44	5.67
23 Jesse Nicassio, Eastern Wash.	P	JR	11	59	2,383	40.39	5.36
24 Rob Muller, Southern Utah	QB	JR	10	48	1,938	40.38	4.8
25 Brian Bivens, Murray St.	P	JR	12	56	2,258	40.32	4.67
26 Stanton Horne, Western Caro.	P	JR	11	68	2,730	40.15	6.18
27 Nick Englehart, James Madison	P	FR	12	52	2,081	40.02	4.33
28 Brian Claybourn, Western Ky.	P	SO	15	67	2,653	39.6	4.47
29 Ryan Bleiler, Delaware	P	JR	12	64	2,525	39.45	5.33
30 Troy Maskel, Illinois St.	K	FR	11	52	2,051	39.44	4.73
31 Scott Everhart, Southern Ill.	K	SR	12	52	2,045	39.33	4.33
32 Nick Rudd, Columbia	PK	SO	10	57	2,230	39.12	5.7
33 Nate Cook, Montana St.	P	JR	13	76	2,971	39.09	5.85
34 Michael MeSi, William & Mary	P	SO	11	47	1,837	39.09	4.27
35 Andy Rosas, Fla. Atlantic	K	JR	11	70	2,734	39.06	6.36
36 Billy Pike, Albany (N.Y.)	P	SR	12	55	2,147	39.04	4.58
37 Rashad Cylar, Alabama A&M	P	JR	12	61	2,377	38.97	5.08
38 Paul Kerr, Sacramento St.	K	SO	12	47	1,831	38.96	3.92
39 Damon Miller, Florida A&M	P	—	11	61	2,357	38.64	5.55
40 Alex Ware, Dartmouth	K	SR	10	47	1,811	38.53	4.7
41 Shane Phillips, Alcorn St.	P	FR	11	74	2,851	38.53	6.73
42 Matt Fordyce, Fordham	P	SR	13	57	2,193	38.47	4.38
43 Mark Spencer, Montana	P	SR	14	68	2,614	38.44	4.86
44 Joey Spendlove, Weber St.	P	SO	11	50	1,920	38.4	4.55
45 Ben Antongiovanni, St. Mary's (Cal.)	K	JR	12	63	2,417	38.37	5.25
46 Tellis Bolden, Hampton	P	SR	12	67	2,567	38.31	5.58
47 Adam Resnick, Charleston So.	K	SO	12	45	1,724	38.31	3.75
48 Steve Bulcavage, Towson	P	JR	11	60	2,296	38.27	5.45
49 Chris Costello, Davidson	K	JR	10	48	1,835	38.23	4.8
50 J.P. Hogan, Austin Peay	P	JR	12	78	2,980	38.21	6.5
51 Dennis Wellman, Canisius	QB	FR	11	75	2,865	38.2	6.82
52 John Manly, Nicholls St.	PK	JR	11	53	2,021	38.13	4.82
53 Mike Kraft, Sacred Heart	P	SR	10	65	2,477	38.11	6.5
54 Patrick Jordan, Indiana St.	P	JR	12	57	2,169	38.05	4.75
55 Bill Ballard, Morehead St.	P	SR	12	50	1,897	37.94	4.17
56 Josh Appell, Pennsylvania	P	SO	10	51	1,933	37.9	5.1
57 Timothy Goobic, Brown	K	JR	10	50	1,887	37.74	5
58 Marvin McCurry, Southwest Tex. St.	P	SO	11	65	2,443	37.58	5.91
59 Jon Vorosholin, Morgan St.	P	SR	12	44	1,647	37.43	3.67
60 Russel Griffith, Mississippi Val.	P	—	11	63	2,357	37.41	5.73
61 Michael Schlaepfer, Robert Morris	P	FR	10	60	2,240	37.33	6
62 Mike Mellow, Maine	K	SO	14	74	2,762	37.32	5.29
63 Scott Shelton, Ga. Southern	P	SR	14	51	1,903	37.31	3.64
64 Yonnick Matthews, N.C. A&T	P	JR	12	83	3,096	37.3	6.92
65 Chris Stegall, Northwestern St.	P	FR	13	74	2,753	37.2	5.69
66 Ryan Bateman, Valparaiso	K	JR	11	48	1,770	36.88	4.36
67 Jason Cook, McNeese St.	P	FR	15	83	3,060	36.87	5.53
68 Phil Kuhl, Eastern Ky.	P	SO	12	54	1,981	36.69	4.5
69 Ty Neil, Samford	K	JR	11	55	2,017	36.67	5
70 Glenn Wilson, Texas Southern	RB	SO	11	43	1,576	36.65	3.91
71 Michael Bryson, Morris Brown	P	JR	12	45	1,649	36.64	3.75
72 Mike Davis, Lafayette	P	SO	12	52	1,904	36.62	4.33
73 Robbie Kemp, Southwest Mo. St.	P	JR	11	53	1,937	36.55	4.82
74 Anthony Turowski, Elon	K	SO	11	55	2,004	36.44	5
75 Joe Maker, Duquesne	P	JR	12	52	1,892	36.38	4.33
76 Zach Bussey, Delaware St.	K	JR	12	64	2,326	36.34	5.33
77 Chris Cummings, Tennessee Tech	K	FR	12	53	1,921	36.25	4.42
78 Brett Keener, Jacksonville	P	SR	10	63	2,283	36.24	6.3
79 Adam Kingston, Harvard	K	JR	10	54	1,955	36.2	5.4
80 Mike Kien, Central Conn. St.	P	SR	11	80	2,895	36.19	7.27

Eddie Johnson, Idaho State

Idaho State Sports Information

Rank, Player	Pos	Cl	G	Pnt	Yds	Avg	Punt/Gm
81 Brendon Biddle, Colgate	P	SR	12	61	2,207	36.18	5.08
82 Adam James, Villanova	P	SO	15	56	2,026	36.18	3.73
83 Edi Pazos, Portland St.	P	SR	11	58	2,096	36.14	5.27
84 Billy Windle, Bucknell	P	SR	11	71	2,563	36.1	6.45
85 Kosta Karapetsas, Youngstown St.	P	SR	11	67	2,416	36.06	6.09
86 Jeff Fallis, Dayton	P	SR	12	50	1,789	35.78	4.17
87 Clay Gilbert, Stephen F. Austin	P	SO	11	51	1,806	35.41	4.64
88 Vaughn Waters, Howard	WR	FR	11	51	1,805	35.39	4.64
89 Tyler Grogan, Northeastern	P	JR	13	50	1,767	35.34	3.85
90 Chris Radford, Richmond	K	JR	11	62	2,190	35.32	5.64
91 Jay Ambrosino, St. Peter's	P	SO	11	65	2,282	35.11	5.91
92 Kyle Keating, Lehigh	QB	SO	12	58	2,036	35.1	4.83
93 Tom Schofield, Eastern Ill.	K	FR	12	55	1,924	34.98	4.58
94 Bryan Tornee', Stony Brook	WR	SO	10	58	2,022	34.86	5.8
95 Davis Player, Bethune-Cookman	P	FR	13	56	1,944	34.71	4.31
96 Doug Jones, Florida Int'l	K	SO	11	58	2,013	34.71	5.27
97 Marcus Yanez, Grambling	LB	SO	13	55	1,907	34.67	4.23
98 Ryan Peterson, Monmouth	K	SR	10	64	2,219	34.67	6.4
99 Mike Baumgartel, Cornell	P	SO	10	63	2,170	34.44	6.3
100 Colby Miller, Southern U.	K	FR	12	69	2,368	34.32	5.75

Punt Returns

(Minimum: 1.2 Punt Returns per Game)

Rank, Player	Pos	Cl	G	Ret	Yds	TD	Yds/Ret	Ret/Gm
1 Zuriel Smith, Hampton	WR	SR	12	27	500	1	18.52	2.25
2 Toby Zeigler, Northwestern St.	WR	FR	13	24	392	1	16.33	1.85
3 Aryvia Holmes, Samford	WR	SR	10	16	250	0	15.63	1.6
4 Fred Akon, Mississippi Val.	WR	SR	11	16	241	1	15.06	1.45
5 Bear Rinehart, Furman	WR	SR	12	17	253	1	14.88	1.42
6 Kris Peters, Alcorn St.	WR	SR	11	16	235	1	14.69	1.45
7 Antonio Veals, Western Ky.	DB	JR	12	33	484	1	14.67	2.75
8 Corey Smith, Montana St.	WR	JR	13	25	366	1	14.64	1.92
9 Ari Confesor, Holy Cross	WR	JR	12	22	322	1	14.64	1.83
10 Emery Beckles, Idaho St.	DB	JR	11	37	526	1	14.22	3.36
11 Justin George, Southern Ill.	RB	SO	10	14	194	0	13.86	1.4
12 Dan McGrath, Fordham	DB	JR	13	48	662	2	13.79	3.69
13 Lonnie Teagle, Alcorn St.	WR	SR	11	19	262	0	13.79	1.73
14 Ryan Castellani, Wagner	DB	SR	11	36	491	1	13.64	3.27
15 Nicholas Wells, Alabama A&M	WR	JR	12	30	409	0	13.63	2.5
16 Ryan Thornton, Northern Ariz.	DB	JR	11	20	270	0	13.5	1.82
17 Darrell Jones, Cal Poly	WR	SO	11	17	228	1	13.41	1.55
18 DaVon Fowlkes, Appalachian St.	WR	SR	12	36	478	1	13.28	3
19 Brandon Martin, Butler	DB	JR	10	13	171	1	13.15	1.3
20 Linj Shell, Jacksonville	DB	SR	10	17	222	0	13.06	1.7
21 James Bialasik, Canisius	WR	SR	11	26	339	1	13.04	2.36
22 Shawn Holmes, Alabama St.	WR	JR	12	41	534	1	13.02	3.42
23 David Plaisance, Nicholls St.	RB	SO	11	17	213	1	12.53	1.55
24 Ben Winters, Dayton	WR	SR	12	19	237	0	12.47	1.58
25 Eric Kimble, Eastern Wash.	RB	FR	11	18	212	1	11.78	1.64
26 Terrence McGee, Northwestern St.	DB	SR	12	18	208	0	11.56	1.5

Rank, Player	Pos	Cl	G	Ret	Yds	TD	Yds/Ret	Ret/Gm
27 B.J. Sams, McNeese St.	WR	JR	14	41	471	2	11.49	2.93
28 Corey Alexander, Texas Southern	DB	SO	11	19	210	0	11.05	1.73
29 Leonard Goolsby, South Carolina St.	RB	JR	11	17	184	1	10.82	1.55
30 Anthony Williams, Ga. Southern	WR	SR	14	44	474	1	10.77	3.14
31 George Piggott, Grambling	DB	FR	13	34	362	0	10.65	2.62
32 Jon Ambrose, St. Peter's	DB	SR	11	21	220	1	10.48	1.91
33 Ben Sanderson, Northern Iowa	WR	SR	11	40	418	1	10.45	3.64
34 Mike Washington, Charleston So.	DB	SR	12	20	208	0	10.4	1.67
35 Matt Higgins, St. John's (N.Y.)	RB	FR	10	19	197	0	10.37	1.9
36 Levander Segars, Montana	DB	SO	14	46	474	1	10.3	3.29
37 Jermaine Pugh, Lehigh	RB	JR	12	25	257	1	10.28	2.08
37 Kevin Faulkner, Monmouth	DB	SR	10	25	257	1	10.28	2.5
39 Matthew Loy, Morehead St.	WR	JR	12	38	389	0	10.24	3.17
40 Travis Chmelka, Columbia	WR	JR	10	22	225	0	10.23	2.2
41 Peter Athans, Sacred Heart	DB	SR	10	32	323	1	10.09	3.2
42 Chad King, Stony Brook	DB	JR	10	32	317	1	9.91	3.2
43 Matt Crudo, Albany (N.Y.)	WR	SO	12	21	208	0	9.9	1.75
44 Jason Mathenia, Sam Houston St.	WR	SO	11	20	197	0	9.85	1.82
45 Bryan Hollermeier, Valparaiso	RB	SR	11	14	135	0	9.64	1.27
46 Xavier Butler, Morris Brown	WR	JR	12	20	192	0	9.6	1.67
47 William Deshazo, Morgan St.	RB	SO	12	31	296	0	9.55	2.58
48 Ralph Plumb, Yale	WR	SO	10	15	139	0	9.27	1.5
49 Gavin Ng, San Diego	DB	JR	10	21	194	1	9.24	2.1
50 Caleb Reddick, Iona	DB	SR	11	37	336	1	9.08	3.36
51 Luke McArdle, Georgetown	WR	JR	11	27	245	0	9.07	2.45
52 DaShaun Morris, Delaware St.	WR	JR	12	15	136	0	9.07	1.25
53 Todd Campbell, Chattanooga	WR	SR	12	17	152	0	8.94	1.42
54 Mike Connelly, James Madison	WR	SR	12	16	141	0	8.81	1.33
55 James Robinson, Tennessee Tech	DB	JR	12	23	200	0	8.7	1.92
56 Anthony Owens, Norfolk St.	DB	FR	11	27	232	0	8.59	2.45
57 Maurice Demps, Florida A&M	WR	SO	12	27	230	0	8.52	2.25
58 Dennis Butler, Illinois St.	DB	SR	11	31	263	0	8.48	2.82
59 Fred Amey, Sacramento St.	WR	SO	11	33	278	1	8.42	3
60 Reggie Gray, Western Ill.	WR	FR	13	19	158	2	8.32	1.46
61 Malcolm Moore, Murray St.	DB	SR	12	16	133	0	8.31	1.33
62 Tony Tompkins, Stephen F. Austin	RB	FR	11	32	265	1	8.28	2.91
63 Cecil Moore, East Tenn. St.	WR	JR	12	19	157	0	8.26	1.58
64 Sidney Haugabrook, Delaware	DB	SO	12	24	196	0	8.17	2
64 Jermaine Anderson, Citadel	WR	SO	12	18	147	0	8.17	1.5
66 Carl Morris, Harvard	WR	SR	10	19	153	0	8.05	1.9
67 Chris NesSmith, Southeast Mo. St.	WR	SO	12	22	176	1	8	1.83
67 Drew Hill, Wofford	—	—	12	16	128	0	8	1.33
69 Michael Banks, Western Caro.	WR	SR	11	21	163	0	7.76	1.91
70 Patrick Jenkins, Tennessee St.	WR	SR	12	18	139	0	7.72	1.5
71 Andy Bryant, Princeton	WR	SR	10	24	185	0	7.71	2.4
72 Maurice Daughtry, Jacksonville St.	WR	SO	9	12	92	0	7.67	1.33
73 Brandon Stanford, Lafayette	WR	FR	12	24	183	0	7.63	2
74 Chris Peters, Prairie View	KR	FR	11	17	129	0	7.59	1.55
75 Corey Oaks, Robert Morris	DB	SR	10	12	90	0	7.5	1.2
76 Jay Barnard, Dartmouth	WR	JR	10	21	156	0	7.43	2.1
77 Jason Schmidt, Dayton	WR	JR	12	21	150	0	7.14	1.75
78 Rich Musinski, William & Mary	WR	JR	11	18	127	0	7.06	1.64
79 Curtis DeLoatch, N.C. A&T	DB	JR	12	28	193	0	6.89	2.33
80 Jerald Burley, Youngstown St.	WR	SR	11	18	124	0	6.89	1.64
81 Matt O'Malley, Brown	WR	SR	10	23	158	0	6.87	2.3
82 Weston Borba, St. Mary's (Cal.)	DB	JR	12	34	233	0	6.85	2.83
83 Ezra Landry, Southern U.	WR	JR	12	24	163	0	6.79	2
84 Boyd Ouden, Richmond	WR	JR	11	20	133	0	6.65	1.82
85 Kyle Ware, St. Francis (Pa.)	RB	FR	8	11	73	0	6.64	1.38
86 Jeff Barrett, Eastern Ky.	WR	SO	12	19	126	0	6.63	1.58
87 Jason Galloway, Towson	WR	JR	11	34	225	0	6.62	3.09
88 J.B. Gerald, Colgate	WR	JR	12	25	165	0	6.6	2.08
89 Rashean Mathis, Bethune-Cookman	DB	SR	13	22	145	0	6.59	1.69
90 Travis Anderson, Gardner-Webb	WR	FR	9	14	90	0	6.43	1.56
91 Adrian Hall, Liberty	WR	SO	11	16	102	0	6.38	1.45
92 Brittney Tellis, Fla. Atlantic	WR	SO	11	20	124	0	6.2	1.82
93 Clythel Branson, Indiana St.	DB	SR	12	24	148	0	6.17	2
94 Peter Green, Siena	WR	SO	9	15	91	0	6.07	1.67
95 Vincent Bates, Cornell	DB	SR	8	16	96	0	6	2
95 Randy Vulakovich, Duquesne	WR	JR	12	49	294	0	6	4.08
97 Andre Raymond, Eastern Ill.	RB	JR	12	19	112	0	5.89	1.58
98 Randall Hardy, Davidson	WR	JR	9	19	111	0	5.84	2.11
99 Steve Shinen, Portland St.	DB	FR	11	18	98	0	5.44	1.64
100 Joe Phillips, Pennsylvania	WR	JR	10	38	199	0	5.24	3.8

Hunter Martin

Rob Milanese, Pennsylvania

Receptions Per Game

Min. 75 Pct. of Team's Games Played

Rank, Player	Pos	Cl	G	Rec	Yds	TD	Rec/Gm	Yds/Rec	Yds/Gm
1 Chas Gessner, Brown	WR	SR	10	114	1,166	11	11.4	10.23	116.6
2 Carl Morris, Harvard	WR	SR	10	90	1,288	8	9	14.31	128.8
3 Rob Milanese, Pennsylvania ...	**WR**	**SR**	**10**	**85**	**1,112**	**8**	**8.5**	**13.08**	**111.2**
4 Aryvia Holmes, Samford	WR	SR	10	84	1,158	9	8.4	13.79	115.8
5 Jay Barnard, Dartmouth	WR	JR	10	83	899	8	8.3	10.83	89.9
6 Tramon Douglas, Grambling	WR	JR	12	92	1,704	18	7.67	18.52	142
7 Willie Ponder, Southeast Mo. St.	WR	SR	12	87	1,453	15	7.25	16.7	121.08
8 Casey Cramer, Dartmouth	TE	JR	10	72	1,017	7	7.2	14.13	101.7
9 Keith Ferguson, Cornell	WR	SR	10	69	844	2	6.9	12.23	84.4
10 Chisom Opara, Princeton	WR	SR	9	57	772	3	6.33	13.54	85.78
11 Aaron Overton, Drake	WR	SR	11	68	1,180	12	6.18	17.35	107.27
12 Tim Manning, Jackson St.	WR	JR	11	66	1,077	7	6	16.32	97.91
12 Korea McKay, Ark.-Pine Bluff	WR	JR	11	66	1,009	7	6	15.29	91.73
14 Jon Turner, Jacksonville	WR	SR	10	60	890	6	6	14.83	89
15 Jeremy Conley, Duquesne	WR	SR	12	72	1,216	14	6	16.89	101.33
16 Javarus Dudley, Fordham	WR	JR	13	77	1,106	8	5.92	14.36	85.08
17 Andre Raymond, Eastern Ill.	RB	JR	12	70	672	5	5.83	9.6	56
17 Bear Rinehart, Furman	WR	SR	12	70	892	3	5.83	12.74	74.33
19 Cortez Hankton, Texas Southern	WR	SR	11	64	1,270	13	5.82	19.84	115.45
20 Michael Hayes, Southern U.	WR	SR	12	69	873	9	5.75	12.65	72.75
20 Deandre Green, Murray St.	WR	JR	12	69	1,005	6	5.75	14.57	83.75
20 Scooter Johnson, Citadel	QB	JR	12	69	950	7	5.75	13.77	79.17
23 Michael Gasperson, San Diego	WR	SO	10	57	907	10	5.7	15.91	90.7
24 Fred Amey, Sacramento St.	WR	SO	11	62	989	9	5.64	15.95	89.91
25 Andrew Turf, Fairfield	WR	SR	10	56	684	5	5.6	12.21	68.4
26 Ricky Bryant, Hofstra	WR	SR	12	67	793	4	5.58	11.84	66.08
27 Clarence Moore, Northern Ariz.	WR	JR	11	61	925	9	5.55	15.16	84.09
28 Junior Adams, Montana St.	WR	SR	12	66	983	8	5.5	14.89	81.92
29 Ralph Plumb, Yale	WR	SO	10	55	592	3	5.5	10.76	59.2
30 Charles Allen, Florida A&M.	WR	SR	12	66	872	7	5.5	13.21	72.67
31 Luke Graham, Colgate	WR	SO	12	65	1,182	7	5.42	18.18	98.5
32 Stacy Coleman, Western Ill.	WR	SR	13	70	1,103	10	5.38	15.76	84.85
33 Erik Lash, Bethune-Cookman	WR	SR	12	64	1,006	8	5.33	15.72	83.83
34 Rich Musinski, William & Mary	WR	JR	11	58	1,140	9	5.27	19.66	103.64
35 John Weyrauch, Lafayette	WR	JR	12	63	910	8	5.25	14.44	75.83
36 Zachary Van Zant, Columbia	WR	JR	10	51	592	0	5.1	11.61	59.2

Rank, Player	Pos	Cl	G	Rec	Yds	TD	Rec/ Gm	Yds/ Rec	Yds/ Gm
36 Barrett Johnson, Davidson	WR	JR	10	51	766	8	5.1	15.02	76.6
38 Chris Jones, Jackson St.	WR	SO	11	56	801	9	5.09	14.3	72.82
39 Rodney Byrnes, Harvard	WR	SO	10	50	482	2	5	9.64	48.2
40 Jamal White, Towson......................	WR	SR	11	54	892	7	4.91	16.52	81.09
40 Marlus Mays, Northern Iowa...........	WR	JR	11	54	992	5	4.91	18.37	90.18
40 David Murnane, La Salle................	QB	JR	11	54	685	1	4.91	12.69	62.27
40 Kyler Randall, Eastern Wash.	WR	JR	11	54	630	5	4.91	11.67	57.27
44 Matt May, St. John's (N.Y.)	WR	SR	10	49	833	10	4.9	17	83.3
45 Johnny Marshall, Northern Ariz.	WR	JR	9	44	581	2	4.89	13.2	64.56
46 Brian White, Villanova	WR	SR	15	72	805	8	4.8	11.18	53.67
47 Travis Chmelka, Columbia	WR	JR	10	48	500	2	4.8	10.42	50
48 Ari Confesor, Holy Cross................	WR	JR	12	57	721	9	4.75	12.65	60.08
48 Nick Eller, Eastern Ill.	TE	JR	12	57	721	7	4.75	12.65	60.08
48 Jason Jones, Chattanooga	WR	JR	12	57	815	10	4.75	14.3	67.92
51 Kevin Simmonds, Howard	WR	SR	11	52	646	9	4.73	12.42	58.73
51 Jason Mathenia, Sam Houston St.	WR	SO	11	52	749	2	4.73	14.4	68.09
51 Kris Peters, Alcorn St......................	WR	SR	11	52	756	8	4.73	14.54	68.73
54 Andrew Gonzalez, Sacred Heart.....	WR	SR	10	47	461	3	4.7	9.81	46.1
54 Erik Bolinder, Pennsylvania	WR	SR	10	47	592	3	4.7	12.6	59.2
56 O.J. Moore, Mississippi Val............	WR	SR	11	51	490	3	4.64	9.61	44.55
56 Torrey Ross, Jackson St.	WR	FR	11	51	714	6	4.64	14	64.91
56 Rob Giancola, Valparaiso..............	WR	SO	11	51	1103	11	4.64	21.63	100.27
59 Jeremy Grier, Chattanooga	WR	SO	10	46	521	4	4.6	11.33	52.1
59 Ian Malepeai, Brown	WR	SR	10	46	493	2	4.6	10.72	49.3
61 Isaac Irby, Hofstra	WR	JR	12	55	526	4	4.58	9.56	43.83
62 Jonathon Talmage, Montana	WR	FR	11	50	689	5	4.55	13.78	62.64
63 William Andrews, Gardner-Webb ...	WR	JR	10	45	685	8	4.5	15.22	68.5
63 Mike Chase, Davidson	TE	SR	10	45	645	12	4.5	14.33	64.5
63 Adam Hannula, San Diego	QB	FR	10	45	624	7	4.5	13.87	62.4
66 Zuriel Smith, Hampton	WR	SR	12	53	773	6	4.42	14.58	64.42
67 Scott Wedum, Dartmouth	RB	JR	10	44	413	3	4.4	9.39	41.3
68 William Smith, Mississippi Val.	WR	SR	11	48	725	6	4.36	15.1	65.91
69 Isaac West, Furman	WR	SO	9	39	708	7	4.33	18.15	78.67
70 Adrian Zullo, Massachusetts	WR	SR	12	52	762	9	4.33	14.65	63.5
71 Eugene Mirador, Idaho St.	WR	SR	11	47	370	0	4.27	7.87	33.64
71 Luke McArdle, Georgetown............	WR	JR	11	47	802	6	4.27	17.06	72.91
73 Shaz Brown, Villanova	WR	SR	15	64	866	6	4.27	13.53	57.73
74 Machion Sanders, Alabama St.	WR	JR	12	51	688	9	4.25	13.49	57.33
75 Thyron Anderson, Grambling...........	WR	SR	13	55	999	10	4.23	18.16	76.85
76 Phillip Doolin, Ark.-Pine Bluff...........	RB	JR	11	46	1,021	11	4.18	22.2	92.82
76 Justin Long, Delaware	WR	FR	11	46	559	4	4.18	12.15	50.82
76 Scott Peery, Weber St.	WR	JR	11	46	501	4	4.18	10.89	45.55
76 Brett Fowler, Idaho St.	QB	JR	11	46	741	6	4.18	16.11	67.36
76 Matt Giugliano, Fairfield	TE	SR	11	46	636	3	4.18	13.83	57.82
81 Jamaal Perry, Hofstra	WR	JR	12	50	540	2	4.17	10.8	45
82 Brian Ingram, Delaware	WR	FR	9	37	456	1	4.11	12.32	50.67
83 Mark Marcos, Southwest Mo. St.	WR	SR	10	41	581	2	4.1	14.17	58.1
83 Nate Lawrie, Yale.........................	TE	JR	10	41	505	4	4.1	12.32	50.5
85 Vito Golson, Illinois St.	WR	JR	11	45	740	5	4.09	16.44	67.27
85 Eric Kimble, Eastern Wash.	RB	FR	11	45	851	9	4.09	18.91	77.36
85 Jim Horan, Bucknell	WR	SR	11	45	556	4	4.09	12.36	50.55
85 C.J. Johnson, Tennessee St.	WR	JR	11	45	1,034	9	4.09	22.98	94
89 Al'Trevion Joubert, Southern U.	WR	SR	12	49	515	4	4.08	10.51	42.92
90 Michael Taylor, New Hampshire	WR	SR	11	44	624	3	4	14.18	56.73
91 Steve Porco, Fordham	WR	SO	13	52	672	5	4	12.92	51.69
92 Yardon Brantley, Duquesne	WR	JR	12	48	632	5	4	13.17	52.67
93 Marques Colston, Hofstra...............	WR	SO	12	47	614	3	3.92	13.06	51.17
93 Aaron Hill, Montana St.	WR	JR	12	47	721	9	3.92	15.34	60.08
95 Jesse Levin, Portland St.	WR	SR	11	43	625	2	3.91	14.53	56.82
95 Joe Pierce, Eastern Wash.	WR	JR	11	43	610	6	3.91	14.19	55.45
95 Michael Banks, Western Caro.	WR	SR	11	43	678	3	3.91	15.77	61.64
98 Justin DeFour, Weber St.	WR	JR	10	39	515	4	3.9	13.21	51.5
99 Pedro Garcia, VMI	WR	SR	12	46	803	7	3.83	17.46	66.92
100 Cory Mckinney, Florida Int'l............	WR	SO	11	42	890	7	3.82	21.19	80.91

Total Receiving Yards

Min. 75 Pct. of Team's Games Played

Rank, Player	Pos	Cl	G	Rec	Yds	TD	Rec/ Gm	Yds/ Rec	Yds/ Gm
1 Tramon Douglas, Grambling	WR	JR	12	92	1,704	18	7.67	18.52	142
2 Willie Ponder, Southeast Mo. St.	WR	SR	12	87	1,453	15	7.25	16.7	121.08
3 Carl Morris, Harvard...............	**WR**	**SR**	**10**	**90**	**1,288**	**8**	**9**	**14.31**	**128.8**
4 Cortez Hankton, Texas Southern	WR	SR	11	64	1,270	13	5.82	19.84	115.45
5 Jeremy Conley, Duquesne	WR	SR	12	72	1,216	14	6	16.89	101.33
6 Luke Graham, Colgate..................	WR	SO	12	65	1,182	7	5.42	18.18	98.5
7 Aaron Overton, Drake	WR	SR	11	68	1,180	12	6.18	17.35	107.27
8 Chas Gessner, Brown	WR	SR	10	114	1,166	11	11.4	10.23	116.6
9 Aryvia Holmes, Samford	WR	SR	10	84	1,158	9	8.4	13.79	115.8
10 Rich Musinski, William & Mary........	WR	JR	11	58	1,140	9	5.27	19.66	103.64
11 Rob Milanese, Pennsylvania	WR	SR	10	85	1,112	8	8.5	13.08	111.2
12 Javarus Dudley, Fordham	WR	JR	13	77	1,106	8	5.92	14.36	85.08

Carl Morris, Harvard

Harvard Sports Information

Rank, Player	Pos	Cl	G	Rec	Yds	TD	Rec/ Gm	Yds/ Rec	Yds/ Gm
13 Stacy Coleman, Western Ill.	WR	SR	13	70	1,103	10	5.38	15.76	84.85
13 Rob Giancola, Valparaiso	WR	SO	11	51	1,103	11	4.64	21.63	100.27
15 Tim Manning, Jackson St.	WR	JR	11	66	1,077	7	6	16.32	97.91
16 C.J. Johnson, Tennessee St.	WR	JR	11	45	1,034	9	4.09	22.98	94
17 Phillip Doolin, Ark.-Pine Bluff	RB	JR	11	46	1,021	11	4.18	22.2	92.82
18 Casey Cramer, Dartmouth	TE	JR	10	72	1,017	7	7.2	14.13	101.7
19 Korea McKay, Ark.-Pine Bluff	WR	JR	11	66	1,009	7	6	15.29	91.73
20 Erik Lash, Bethune-Cookman	WR	SR	12	64	1,006	8	5.33	15.72	83.83
21 Deandre Green, Murray St.	WR	JR	12	69	1,005	6	5.75	14.57	83.75
22 Thyron Anderson, Grambling	WR	SR	11	55	999	10	4.23	18.16	76.85
23 Marlus Mays, Northern Iowa	WR	JR	11	54	992	5	4.91	18.37	90.18
24 Fred Amey, Sacramento St.	WR	SO	11	62	989	9	5.64	15.95	89.91
25 Junior Adams, Montana St.	WR	SR	12	66	983	8	5.5	14.89	81.92
26 Scooter Johnson, Citadel	QB	JR	12	69	950	7	5.75	13.77	79.17
27 Clarence Moore, Northern Ariz.	WR	JR	11	61	925	9	5.55	15.16	84.09
28 John Weyrauch, Lafayette	WR	JR	12	63	910	8	5.25	14.44	75.83
29 Michael Gasperson, San Diego	WR	SO	10	57	907	10	5.7	15.91	90.7
30 Jay Barnard, Dartmouth	WR	JR	10	83	899	8	8.3	10.83	89.9
31 Jamal White, Towson	WR	SR	11	54	892	7	4.91	16.52	81.09
31 Bear Rinehart, Furman	WR	SR	12	70	892	3	5.83	12.74	74.33
33 Jon Turner, Jacksonville	WR	SR	10	60	890	6	6	14.83	89
33 Cory Mckinney, Florida Int'l.	WR	SO	11	42	890	7	3.82	21.19	80.91
35 Michael Hayes, Southern U.	WR	SR	12	69	873	9	5.75	12.65	72.75
36 Charles Allen, Florida A&M	WR	SR	12	66	872	7	5.5	13.21	72.67
37 Shaz Brown, Villanova	WR	SR	15	64	866	6	4.27	13.53	57.73
38 Eric Kimble, Eastern Wash.	RB	FR	11	45	851	9	4.09	18.91	77.36
39 Keith Ferguson, Cornell	WR	SR	10	69	844	2	6.9	12.23	84.4
40 Matt May, St. John's (N.Y.)	WR	SR	10	49	833	10	4.9	17	83.3
41 Calvin Colquitt, Grambling	WR	SO	13	42	816	4	3.23	19.43	62.77
42 Jason Jones, Chattanooga	WR	JR	12	57	815	10	4.75	14.3	67.92
43 Boyd Ouden, Richmond	WR	JR	11	36	809	7	3.27	22.47	73.55
44 Brian White, Villanova	WR	SR	15	72	805	8	4.8	11.18	53.67
45 Pedro Garcia, VMI	WR	SR	12	46	803	7	3.83	17.46	66.92
46 Luke McArdle, Georgetown	WR	JR	11	47	802	6	4.27	17.06	72.91
47 Chris Jones, Jackson St.	WR	SO	11	56	801	9	5.09	14.3	72.82
48 Ricky Bryant, Hofstra	WR	SR	12	67	793	4	5.58	11.84	66.08
49 Zuriel Smith, Hampton	WR	SR	12	53	773	6	4.42	14.58	64.42
50 Chisom Opara, Princeton	WR	SR	9	57	772	3	6.33	13.54	85.78
51 Barrett Johnson, Davidson	WR	JR	10	51	766	8	5.1	15.02	76.6
52 Adrian Zullo, Massachusetts	WR	SR	12	52	762	9	4.33	14.65	63.5
53 Derek Lee, Tennessee Tech	WR	JR	12	36	760	10	3	21.11	63.33
54 Kris Peters, Alcorn St.	WR	SR	11	52	756	8	4.73	14.54	68.73
55 Jason Mathenia, Sam Houston St.	WR	SO	11	52	749	2	4.73	14.4	68.09
56 Brett Fowler, Idaho St.	QB	JR	11	46	741	6	4.18	16.11	67.36
57 Vito Golson, Illinois St.	WR	SR	11	45	740	5	4.09	16.44	67.27
58 R.J. Luke, Western Ill.	TE	SR	13	40	725	6	3.08	18.13	55.77
58 William Smith, Mississippi Val.	WR	SR	11	48	725	6	4.36	15.1	65.91
60 Terrence Metcalf, South Carolina St.	WR	SR	12	30	724	7	2.5	24.13	60.33
61 Aaron Dunklin, Charleston So.	WR	JR	12	45	723	6	3.75	16.07	60.25
62 Aaron Hill, Montana St.	WR	JR	12	47	721	9	3.92	15.34	60.08
62 Ari Confesor, Holy Cross	WR	JR	12	57	721	9	4.75	12.65	60.08
62 Nick Eller, Eastern Ill.	TE	JR	12	57	721	7	4.75	12.65	60.08
65 Jermaine Martin, McNeese St.	WR	SR	15	43	720	2	2.87	16.74	48
66 Torrey Ross, Jackson St.	WR	FR	11	51	714	6	4.64	14	64.91
67 Jeff Seaman, Drake	TE	SR	11	36	710	8	3.27	19.72	64.55
68 Isaac West, Furman	WR	SO	9	39	708	7	4.33	18.15	78.67
69 Alan Harrison, James Madison	WR	JR	12	35	705	3	2.92	20.14	58.75
70 Brittney Tellis, Fla. Atlantic	WR	SO	11	38	702	2	3.45	18.47	63.82
71 Jonathon Talmage, Montana	WR	FR	11	50	689	5	4.55	13.78	62.64
72 Machion Sanders, Alabama St.	WR	JR	12	51	688	9	4.25	13.49	57.33
73 William Andrews, Gardner-Webb	WR	JR	10	45	685	8	4.5	15.22	68.5
73 David Murnane, La Salle	QB	JR	11	54	685	1	4.91	12.69	62.27
75 Andrew Turf, Fairfield	WR	SR	10	56	684	5	5.6	12.21	68.4
76 Cecil Moore, East Tenn. St.	WR	SR	12	44	682	7	3.67	15.5	56.83
77 Michael Banks, Western Caro.	WR	SR	11	43	678	3	3.91	15.77	61.64
78 Ralph Delsardo, Morehead St.	WR	JR	12	31	675	5	2.58	21.77	56.25
79 Andre Raymond, Eastern Ill.	RB	JR	12	70	672	5	5.83	9.6	56
79 Steve Porco, Fordham	WR	SO	13	52	672	5	4	12.92	51.69
81 B.J. Sams, McNeese St.	WR	JR	14	46	658	5	3.29	14.3	47
82 Adam Lafferty, Butler	WR	SR	10	35	657	3	3.5	18.77	65.7
83 T.J. Stallings, Morgan St.	WR	SR	12	39	654	4	3.25	16.77	54.5
84 Kevin Simmonds, Howard	WR	SR	11	52	646	9	4.73	12.42	58.73
85 Mike Chase, Davidson	TE	SR	10	45	645	12	4.5	14.33	64.5
85 Kevin Knutson, Valparaiso	WR	SO	11	38	645	7	3.45	16.97	58.64
87 Anton Thomison, Tennessee Tech	WR	JR	11	35	642	4	3.18	18.34	58.36
88 Matt Miller, Eastern Ky.	WR	FR	12	37	639	5	3.08	17.27	53.25
89 Matt Giugliano, Fairfield	TE	SR	11	46	636	3	4.18	13.83	57.82
90 Ben Winters, Dayton	WR	SR	12	28	635	5	2.33	22.68	52.92
91 Yardon Brantley, Duquesne	WR	JR	12	48	632	5	4	13.17	52.67
92 Kyler Randall, Eastern Wash.	WR	JR	11	54	630	5	4.91	11.67	57.27
93 Levander Segars, Montana	DB	SO	14	51	628	2	3.64	12.31	44.86
94 Jesse Levin, Portland St.	WR	SR	11	43	625	2	3.91	14.53	56.82
95 Michael Taylor, New Hampshire	WR	SR	11	44	624	3	4	14.18	56.73

Rank, Player	Pos	Cl	G	Rec	Yds	TD	Rec/ Gm	Yds/ Rec	Yds/ Gm
95 Adam Hannula, San Diego	QB	FR	10	45	624	7	4.5	13.87	62.4
97 Jerome Mathis, Hampton	WR	SO	12	24	615	3	2	25.63	51.25
98 Marques Colston, Hofstra	WR	SO	12	47	614	3	3.92	13.06	51.17
99 Scott Turnquist, Montana St.	WR	JR	13	36	613	2	2.77	17.03	47.15
99 Courtnee Garcia, Stephen F. Austin	WR	SR	11	36	613	1	3.27	17.03	55.73

Receiving Yards Per Game

Min. 75 Pct. of Team's Games Played

Rank, Player	Pos	Cl	G	Rec	Yds	TD	Rec/ Gm	Yds/ Rec	Yds/ Gm
1 Tramon Douglas, Grambling	WR	JR	12	92	1,704	18	7.67	18.52	142
2 Carl Morris, Harvard	WR	SR	10	90	1,288	8	9	14.31	128.8
3 Willie Ponder, Southeast Mo. St.	WR	SR	12	87	1,453	15	7.25	16.7	121.08
4 Chas Gessner, Brown	WR	SR	10	114	1,166	11	11.4	10.23	116.6
5 Aryvia Holmes, Samford	WR	SR	10	84	1,158	9	8.4	13.79	115.8
6 Cortez Hankton, Texas Southern	WR	SR	11	64	1,270	13	5.82	19.84	115.45
7 Rob Milanese, Pennsylvania	WR	SR	10	85	1,112	8	8.5	13.08	111.2
8 Aaron Overton, Drake	WR	SR	11	68	1,180	12	6.18	17.35	107.27
9 Rich Musinski, William & Mary	WR	JR	11	58	1,140	9	5.27	19.66	103.64
10 Casey Cramer, Dartmouth	TE	JR	10	72	1,017	7	7.2	14.13	101.7
11 Jeremy Conley, Duquesne	WR	SR	12	72	1,216	14	6	16.89	101.33
12 Rob Giancola, Valparaiso	WR	SO	11	51	1,103	11	4.64	21.63	100.27
13 Luke Graham, Colgate	WR	SO	12	65	1,182	7	5.42	18.18	98.5
14 Tim Manning, Jackson St.	WR	JR	11	66	1,077	7	6	16.32	97.91
15 C.J. Johnson, Tennessee St.	WR	JR	11	45	1,034	9	4.09	22.98	94
16 Phillip Doolin, Ark.-Pine Bluff	RB	JR	11	46	1,021	11	4.18	22.2	92.82
17 Korea McKay, Ark.-Pine Bluff	WR	JR	11	66	1,009	7	6	15.29	91.73
18 Michael Gasperson, San Diego	WR	SO	10	57	907	10	5.7	15.91	90.7
19 Marlus Mays, Northern Iowa	WR	JR	11	54	992	5	4.91	18.37	90.18
20 Fred Amey, Sacramento St.	WR	SO	11	62	989	9	5.64	15.95	89.91
21 Jay Barnard, Dartmouth	WR	JR	10	83	899	8	8.3	10.83	89.9
22 Jon Turner, Jacksonville	WR	SR	10	60	890	6	6	14.83	89
23 Chisom Opara, Princeton	WR	SR	9	57	772	3	6.33	13.54	85.78
24 Javarus Dudley, Fordham	WR	JR	13	77	1,106	8	5.92	14.36	85.08
25 Stacy Coleman, Western Ill.	WR	SR	13	70	1,103	10	5.38	15.76	84.85
26 Keith Ferguson, Cornell	WR	SR	10	69	844	2	6.9	12.23	84.4
27 Clarence Moore, Northern Ariz.	WR	JR	11	61	925	9	5.55	15.16	84.09
28 Erik Lash, Bethune-Cookman	WR	SR	12	64	1,006	8	5.33	15.72	83.83
29 Deandre Green, Murray St.	WR	JR	12	69	1,005	6	5.75	14.57	83.75
30 Matt May, St. John's (N.Y.)	WR	SR	10	49	833	10	4.9	17	83.3
31 Junior Adams, Montana St.	WR	SR	12	66	983	8	5.5	14.89	81.92
32 Jamal White, Towson	WR	SR	11	54	892	7	4.91	16.52	81.09
33 Cory Mckinney, Florida Int'l	WR	SO	11	42	890	7	3.82	21.19	80.91
34 Scooter Johnson, Citadel	QB	JR	12	69	950	7	5.75	13.77	79.17
35 Isaac West, Furman	WR	SO	9	39	708	7	4.33	18.15	78.67
36 Eric Kimble, Eastern Wash.	RB	FR	11	45	851	9	4.09	18.91	77.36
37 Thyron Anderson, Grambling	WR	SR	13	55	999	10	4.23	18.16	76.85
38 Barrett Johnson, Davidson	WR	JR	10	51	766	8	5.1	15.02	76.6
39 John Weyrauch, Lafayette	WR	JR	12	63	910	8	5.25	14.44	75.83
40 Bear Rinehart, Furman	WR	SR	12	70	892	3	5.83	12.74	74.33
41 Boyd Ouden, Richmond	WR	JR	11	36	809	7	3.27	22.47	73.55
42 Luke McArdle, Georgetown	WR	JR	11	47	802	6	4.27	17.06	72.91
43 Chris Jones, Jackson St.	WR	SO	11	56	801	9	5.09	14.3	72.82
44 Michael Hayes, Southern U.	WR	SR	12	69	873	9	5.75	12.65	72.75
45 Charles Allen, Florida A&M	WR	SR	12	66	872	7	5.5	13.21	72.67
46 Kris Peters, Alcorn St.	WR	SR	11	52	756	8	4.73	14.54	68.73
47 William Andrews, Gardner-Webb	WR	JR	10	45	685	8	4.5	15.22	68.5
48 Andrew Turf, Fairfield	WR	SR	10	56	684	5	5.6	12.21	68.4
49 Jason Mathenia, Sam Houston St.	WR	SO	11	52	749	2	4.73	14.4	68.09
50 Jason Jones, Chattanooga	WR	JR	12	57	815	10	4.75	14.3	67.92
51 Brett Fowler, Idaho St.	QB	JR	11	46	741	6	4.18	16.11	67.36
52 Vito Golson, Illinois St.	WR	SR	11	45	740	5	4.09	16.44	67.27
53 Pedro Garcia, VMI	WR	SR	12	46	803	7	3.83	17.46	66.92
54 Ricky Bryant, Hofstra	WR	SR	12	67	793	4	5.58	11.84	66.08
55 William Smith, Mississippi Val.	WR	SR	11	48	725	6	4.36	15.1	65.91
56 Adam Lafferty, Butler	WR	SR	10	35	657	3	3.5	18.77	65.7
57 Torrey Ross, Jackson St.	WR	FR	11	51	714	6	4.64	14	64.91
58 Johnny Marshall, Northern Ariz.	WR	JR	9	44	581	2	4.89	13.2	64.56
59 Jeff Seaman, Drake	TE	SR	11	36	710	8	3.27	19.72	64.55
60 Mike Chase, Davidson	TE	SR	10	45	645	12	4.5	14.33	64.5
61 Zuriel Smith, Hampton	WR	SR	12	53	773	6	4.42	14.58	64.42
62 Brittney Tellis, Fla. Atlantic	WR	SO	11	38	702	2	3.45	18.47	63.82
63 Adrian Zullo, Massachusetts	WR	SR	12	52	762	9	4.33	14.65	63.5
64 Derek Lee, Tennessee Tech	WR	JR	12	36	760	10	3	21.11	63.33
65 Calvin Colquitt, Grambling	WR	SO	13	42	816	4	3.23	19.43	62.77
66 Jonathon Talmage, Montana	WR	FR	11	50	689	5	4.55	13.78	62.64
67 Adam Hannula, San Diego	QB	FR	10	45	624	7	4.5	13.87	62.4
68 David Murnane, La Salle	QB	JR	11	54	685	1	4.91	12.69	62.27
69 Michael Banks, Western Caro.	WR	SR	11	43	678	3	3.91	15.77	61.64
70 Terrence Metcalf, South Carolina St.	WR	SR	12	30	724	7	2.5	24.13	60.33
71 Aaron Dunklin, Charleston So.	WR	JR	12	45	723	6	3.75	16.07	60.25
72 Aaron Hill, Montana St.	WR	JR	12	47	721	9	3.92	15.34	60.08

Rank, Player	Pos	Cl	G	Rec	Yds	TD	Rec/Gm	Yds/Rec	Yds/Gm
72 Ari Confesor, Holy Cross	WR	JR	12	57	721	9	4.75	12.65	60.08
72 Nick Eller, Eastern Ill.	TE	JR	12	57	721	7	4.75	12.65	60.08
75 Erik Bolinder, Pennsylvania	WR	SR	10	47	592	3	4.7	12.6	59.2
75 Zachary Van Zant, Columbia	WR	JR	10	51	592	0	5.1	11.61	59.2
75 Ralph Plumb, Yale	WR	SO	10	55	592	3	5.5	10.76	59.2
78 Alan Harrison, James Madison	WR	JR	12	35	705	3	2.92	20.14	58.75
79 Kevin Simmonds, Howard	WR	SR	11	52	646	9	4.73	12.42	58.73
80 Kevin Knutson, Valparaiso	WR	SO	11	38	645	7	3.45	16.97	58.64
81 Anton Thomison, Tennessee Tech	WR	JR	11	35	642	4	3.18	18.34	58.36
82 Mark Marcos, Southwest Mo. St.	WR	SR	10	41	581	2	4.1	14.17	58.1
83 Matt Giugliano, Fairfield	TE	SR	11	46	636	3	4.18	13.83	57.82
84 Shaz Brown, Villanova	WR	SR	15	64	866	6	4.27	13.53	57.73
85 Machion Sanders, Alabama St.	WR	JR	12	51	688	9	4.25	13.49	57.33
86 Kyler Randall, Eastern Wash.	WR	JR	11	54	630	5	4.91	11.67	57.27
87 Cecil Moore, East Tenn. St.	WR	SR	12	44	682	7	3.67	15.5	56.83
88 Jesse Levin, Portland St.	WR	SR	11	43	625	2	3.91	14.53	56.82
89 Michael Taylor, New Hampshire	WR	SR	11	44	624	3	4	14.18	56.73
90 B.J. Szymanski, Princeton	WR	SO	10	33	567	2	3.3	17.18	56.7
91 Ralph Delsardo, Morehead St.	WR	JR	12	31	675	5	2.58	21.77	56.25
92 Andre Raymond, Eastern Ill.	RB	JR	12	70	672	5	5.83	9.6	56
93 R.J. Luke, Western Ill.	TE	SR	13	40	725	6	3.08	18.13	55.77
94 Courtnee Garcia, Stephen F. Austin	WR	SR	11	36	613	1	3.27	17.03	55.73
95 Joe Pierce, Eastern Wash.	WR	JR	11	43	610	6	3.91	14.19	55.45
96 Jason Jones, Drake	WR	SO	11	40	607	6	3.64	15.18	55.18
97 Ron Benigno, Yale	WR	JR	9	28	491	6	3.11	17.54	54.56
98 David Kasouf, Holy Cross	WR	SR	10	35	545	1	3.5	15.57	54.5
98 T.J. Stallings, Morgan St.	WR	SR	12	39	654	4	3.25	16.77	54.5
100 Ralph Jenkins, Jacksonville St.	WR	JR	10	32	537	6	3.2	16.78	53.7

Rushing

Min. 75 Pct. of Team's Games Played

Rank, Player	Pos	Cl	G	Car	Net	TD	Avg	Yds/Gm
1 Jay Bailey, Austin Peay	RB	SR	12	319	1,687	18	5.29	140.58
2 J.R. Taylor, Eastern Ill.	**RB**	**SR**	**12**	**254**	**1,522**	**18**	**5.99**	**126.83**
3 Gary Jones, Albany (N.Y.)	RB	JR	12	231	1,509	22	6.53	125.75
4 Verondre Barnes, Liberty	RB	SO	11	221	1,304	5	5.9	118.55
5 P.J. Mays, Youngstown St.	RB	SR	11	255	1,284	11	5.04	116.73
6 Ryan Fuqua, Portland St.	RB	SO	11	305	1,283	10	4.21	116.64
7 Derek Clayton, St. Peter's	RB	JR	11	233	1,277	9	5.48	116.09
8 Joe McCourt, Lafayette	RB	SO	12	314	1,393	13	4.44	116.08
9 Kirwin Watson, Fordham	RB	JR	13	285	1,467	18	5.15	112.85
10 Jermaine Pugh, Lehigh	RB	JR	12	263	1,339	11	5.09	111.58
11 Mike Hilliard, Duquesne	RB	JR	12	303	1,310	14	4.32	109.17
12 Christopher Price, Marist	RB	SR	11	230	1,196	9	5.2	108.73
13 Robert Carr, Yale	TB	SO	10	236	1,083	10	4.59	108.3
14 Quincy Washington, Illinois St.	RB	SR	11	254	1,158	9	4.56	105.27
15 Stephan Lewis, New Hampshire	RB	SR	11	242	1,152	8	4.76	104.73
16 Adam Benge, Northern Iowa	RB	SR	11	271	1,133	6	4.18	103
17 Cameron Atkinson, Princeton	RB	SR	10	187	1,028	10	5.5	102.8
18 Jovan Griffith, Eastern Wash.	RB	SR	11	192	1,130	12	5.89	102.73
19 Jon Frazier, Western Ky.	RB	SR	15	303	1,537	12	5.07	102.47
20 Chaz Williams, Ga. Southern	QB	SO	14	290	1,422	27	4.9	101.57
21 Jermaine Austin, Ga. Southern	RB	FR	14	244	1,416	8	5.8	101.14
22 Marcus Williams, Maine	RB	SO	14	263	1,406	7	5.35	100.43
23 Ryan Johnson, Montana St.	RB	SR	11	269	1,092	7	4.06	99.27
24 Billy Blanchard, Murray St.	RB	SR	11	179	1,081	16	6.04	98.27
25 Johnathan Taylor, Drake	RB	JR	11	193	1,072	13	5.55	97.45
26 T.J. Stallings, Morgan St.	WR	SR	12	243	1,169	11	4.81	97.42
27 Dale Jennings, Butler	RB	SR	10	187	973	16	5.2	97.3
28 Corey Kinsey, Southeast Mo. St.	RB	SO	11	231	1,067	2	4.62	97
28 R.J. Cobbs, Massachusetts	RB	FR	11	192	1,067	14	5.56	97
30 Isaac Mitchell, Idaho St.	RB	JR	10	182	968	12	5.32	96.8
31 Major Cole, Central Conn. St.	RB	SR	11	244	1,024	5	4.2	93.09
32 C.J. Hudson, Eastern Ky.	RB	SO	12	230	1,110	16	4.83	92.5
33 Clint Wilson, St. Mary's (Cal.)	RB	SO	12	212	1,100	6	5.19	91.67
34 Jay Colbert, Howard	RB	JR	11	187	1,001	6	5.35	91
34 Jesse McCoy, Wofford	RB	SR	11	128	1,001	10	7.82	91
36 Matt Romeo, Towson	RB	JR	11	250	990	9	3.96	90
37 Michael Hall, St. Francis (Pa.)	RB	JR	10	189	878	6	4.65	87.8
38 Rashod Smith, Florida Int'l	RB	SO	9	131	784	9	5.98	87.11
39 Nehemiah Broughton, Citadel	RB	SO	12	224	1,038	11	4.63	86.5
40 Allen Suber, Bethune-Cookman	QB	JR	12	158	1,035	15	6.55	86.25
41 Eddie Linscomb, Southwest Mo. St.	RB	SR	9	169	758	3	4.49	84.22
42 Jason Ballard, Tennessee Tech	RB	JR	12	216	1,000	11	4.63	83.33
43 Alfredo Rulliano, Marist	RB	SR	11	175	896	6	5.12	81.45
44 Rashaud Palmer, Elon	RB	JR	11	148	879	9	5.94	79.91
45 Keith Burnell, Delaware	RB	SR	12	222	956	9	4.31	79.67
46 Nick Chournos, Weber St.	RB	SO	11	174	874	9	5.02	79.45
47 Terrell Johnson, Norfolk St.	RB	FR	11	169	872	9	5.16	79.27
48 Lee Davis, Southwest Tex. St.	RB	SR	10	173	788	12	4.55	78.8

J.R. Taylor, Eastern Illinois

Rank, Player	Pos	Cl	G	Car	Net	TD	Avg	Yds/Gm
49 Andy Hall, Delaware	QB	FR	11	153	863	7	5.64	78.45
50 Rob Terry, Iona	RB	SR	11	227	859	4	3.78	78.09
51 Ontreal Bowers, Savannah St.	RB	JR	10	216	768	7	3.56	76.8
52 Chuck Henderson, Southern Utah	QB	JR	11	218	842	7	3.86	76.55
53 Johnathan Smith, William & Mary	RB	SO	11	206	838	9	4.07	76.18
54 Garrett White, Sacramento St.	RB	SR	12	189	887	8	4.69	73.92
55 Derrick Johnese, Northwestern St.	RB	SO	13	203	960	14	4.73	73.85
56 Vick King, McNeese St.	RB	JR	15	216	1,103	9	5.11	73.53
57 Charles Anthony, Tennessee St.	RB	SO	12	150	882	10	5.88	73.5
58 Ray LaMonica, Colgate	RB	SO	12	163	877	6	5.38	73.08
59 Jerry Beard, Appalachian St.	RB	SR	12	176	876	7	4.98	73
60 Anthony Riley, Northeastern	RB	FR	13	173	940	3	5.43	72.31
61 Kelly Spiker, Dayton	QB	JR	12	172	863	9	5.02	71.92
62 Gideon Akande, Holy Cross	DB	FR	12	177	853	5	4.82	71.08
63 Rondy Rogers, Jacksonville St.	RB	SR	11	183	772	4	4.22	70.18
64 Leon McCampbell, South Carolina St.	QB	JR	12	180	841	5	4.67	70.08
65 Travis Glasford, Western Ill.	RB	FR	10	179	689	5	3.85	68.9
66 Terry Ennis, Eastern Ky.	RB	JR	12	147	825	4	5.61	68.75
67 Chris Davis, Wagner	RB	JR	11	188	740	7	3.94	67.27
68 Rian Thompson, Hampton	RB	JR	11	219	730	12	3.33	66.36
69 Attley Lawson, Western Ill.	RB	SO	12	198	795	8	4.02	66.25
70 Tim Gale, Northeastern	RB	JR	13	169	860	14	5.09	66.15
71 Tarnaka Counselor, Jackson St.	RB	SR	11	141	723	6	5.13	65.73
72 Ken Triboletti, La Salle	RB	SO	11	103	713	8	6.92	64.82
73 Kenneth Peoples, Southern U.	RB	SO	12	165	777	3	4.71	64.75
74 Joe Rackley, Brown	RB	SR	9	150	572	5	3.81	63.56
75 Hindley Brigham, Furman	RB	JR	12	129	762	5	5.91	63.5
76 Matthew Ward, St. Peter's	RB	FR	11	112	697	7	6.22	63.36
77 Chris Foster, Gardner-Webb	RB	JR	10	109	632	7	5.8	63.2
78 Raunny Rosario, Massachusetts	RB	FR	12	154	758	3	4.92	63.17
79 Keiki Misipeka, Southeast Mo. St.	RB	SR	12	140	756	13	5.4	63
80 Kenneth Villalobos, San Diego	RB	SR	10	122	628	6	5.15	62.8
81 Tony Tompkins, Stephen F. Austin	RB	FR	11	113	688	10	6.09	62.55
82 Marcus Blanks, Cornell	RB	SO	9	128	559	5	4.37	62.11
83 Jayson Davis, Rhode Island	QB	FR	11	216	679	11	3.14	61.73
84 Rondell Bradley, James Madison	RB	SO	12	183	737	6	4.03	61.42
85 Shelton Sampson, Northwestern St.	RB	SO	13	170	795	7	4.68	61.15
86 Rashard Pompey, Florida A&M	—	—	11	138	668	3	4.84	60.73
87 Manny DeShauteurs, Western Caro.	RB	JR	10	159	606	5	3.81	60.6
88 Brandon Robinson, Southern Ill.	RB	JR	12	131	727	3	5.55	60.58
89 Timothy Boutte, Texas Southern	RB	JR	11	174	664	4	3.82	60.36
90 Melvin Jones, Wofford	RB	SR	12	154	716	7	4.65	59.67
91 J.R. Waller, Montana	RB	FR	14	182	826	7	4.54	59
92 Mike Giles, Dartmouth	DB	JR	10	151	586	4	3.88	58.6
93 Josh Son, Nicholls St.	QB	JR	11	161	642	7	3.99	58.36
94 J.R. McNair, Wofford	RB	JR	12	148	700	9	4.73	58.33
95 Terry Butler, Villanova	RB	SO	15	202	868	9	4.3	57.87
96 Cliff Sachini, Dayton	RB	JR	12	134	694	8	5.18	57.83
97 Karrell Charles, Grambling	RB	JR	13	150	740	9	4.93	56.92
98 Chad Davis, Jacksonville	RB	FR	8	104	452	5	4.35	56.5
99 Bradshaw Littlejohn, Morgan St.	QB	SO	12	103	672	3	6.52	56
100 Vemba Bukula, Hofstra	DB	JR	12	131	664	3	5.07	55.33

Scoring

Min. 75 Pct. of Team's Games Played

Rank, Player	Pos	Cl	G	TD	OKM	OKA	FGM	FGA	Pts	Pts/Gm
1 T.J. Stallings, Morgan St.	WR	SR	12	23	0	0	0	0	144	12
1 Dale Jennings, Butler	RB	SR	10	20	0	0	0	0	120	12
3 Chaz Williams, Ga. Southern	QB	SO	14	27	0	0	0	0	162	11.57
4 Gary Jones, Albany (N.Y.)	RB	JR	12	23	0	0	0	0	138	11.5
5 J.R. Taylor, Eastern Ill.	RB	SR	12	18	0	0	0	0	112	9.33
6 Tramon Douglas, Grambling	WR	JR	12	18	0	0	0	0	108	9
6 Jay Bailey, Austin Peay	RB	SR	12	18	0	0	0	0	108	9
8 Justin Langan, Western Ill.	K	SO	13	0	56	58	20	27	116	8.92
9 Kirwin Watson, Fordham	RB	JR	13	19	0	0	0	0	114	8.77
10 Billy Blanchard, Murray St.	RB	SR	11	16	0	0	0	0	96	8.73
11 MacKenzie Hoambrecker, Northern Iowa	K	SR	11	0	18	19	25	28	93	8.45
12 Lee Davis, Southwest Tex. St.	RB	SR	10	14	0	0	0	0	84	8.4
13 Jesse Obert, Dayton	P	SR	12	0	48	50	17	23	99	8.25
14 Alfredo Rulliano, Marist	RB	SR	11	15	0	0	0	0	90	8.18
14 R.J. Cobbs, Massachusetts	RB	FR	11	15	0	0	0	0	90	8.18
16 C.J. Hudson, Eastern Ky.	RB	SO	12	16	0	0	0	0	98	8.17
16 Willie Ponder, Southeast Mo. St.	WR	SR	12	16	0	0	0	0	98	8.17
18 Peter Veldman, Pennsylvania	K	JR	10	0	43	43	12	15	79	7.9
19 Allen Suber, Bethune-Cookman	QB	JR	12	15	0	0	0	0	94	7.83
20 Isaac Mitchell, Idaho St.	RB	JR	10	13	0	0	0	0	78	7.8
21 Chris Snyder, Montana	K	JR	14	0	50	50	19	32	107	7.64
22 Johnathan Taylor, Drake	RB	JR	11	14	0	0	0	0	84	7.64
23 Matt Fordyce, Fordham	P	SR	13	0	44	51	18	26	98	7.54
24 Stephan Lewis, New Hampshire	RB	SR	11	13	0	0	0	0	82	7.45
25 Mike Chase, Davidson	TE	SR	10	12	0	0	0	0	74	7.4
26 Tim Gale, Northeastern	RB	JR	13	16	0	0	0	0	96	7.38

Rank, Player	Pos	Cl	G	TD	OKM	OKA	FGM	FGA	Pts	Pts/Gm
27 Cortez Hankton, Texas Southern	WR	SR	11	13	0	0	0	0	80	7.27
28 Trevor Johnston, St. Mary's (Cal.)	QB	FR	10	12	0	0	0	0	72	7.2
28 Stephen Faulk, Pennsylvania	RB	SR	10	12	0	0	0	0	72	7.2
30 Jeremy Conley, Duquesne	WR	SR	12	14	0	0	0	0	86	7.17
31 P.J. Mays, Youngstown St.	RB	SR	11	13	0	0	0	0	78	7.09
31 Aaron Overton, Drake	WR	SR	11	13	0	0	0	0	78	7.09
31 Chris Peterson, Cal Poly	QB	JR	11	13	0	0	0	0	78	7.09
31 Greg Kuehn, William & Mary	K	SO	11	0	36	39	14	21	78	7.09
31 Jovan Griffith, Eastern Wash.	RB	SR	11	13	0	0	0	0	78	7.09
31 Ryan Fuqua, Portland St.	RB	SO	11	13	0	0	0	0	78	7.09
31 Tony Tompkins, Stephen F. Austin	RB	FR	11	13	0	0	0	0	78	7.09
31 Will Bumphus, Eastern Ill.	WR	SR	11	13	0	0	0	0	78	7.09
39 Joe McCourt, Lafayette	RB	SO	12	14	0	0	0	0	84	7
39 Mike Hilliard, Duquesne	RB	JR	12	14	0	0	0	0	84	7
41 Stephen Carroll, Illinois St.	K	SO	10	0	30	30	13	19	69	6.9
42 Peter Martinez, Western Ky.	K	SR	15	0	49	50	18	25	103	6.87
43 Scott Shelton, Ga. Southern	P	SR	14	0	61	62	11	17	94	6.71
44 Adam Williams, San Diego	K	JR	10	0	34	35	11	16	67	6.7
45 Nick Palazzo, Harvard	RB	SR	9	10	0	0	0	0	60	6.67
45 Shane Andrus, Murray St.	K	JR	12	0	47	48	11	14	80	6.67
47 Jeremy Hershey, Idaho St.	K	JR	11	0	31	38	14	26	73	6.64
48 Chas Gessner, Brown	WR	SR	10	11	0	0	0	0	66	6.6
49 Martin Brecht, Lafayette	K	SR	12	0	31	34	16	26	79	6.58
50 Rian Thompson, Hampton	RB	JR	11	12	0	0	0	0	72	6.55
50 Phillip Doolin, Ark.-Pine Bluff	RB	JR	11	11	0	0	0	0	72	6.55
52 Miro Kesic, Northeastern	K	FR	13	0	52	53	11	17	85	6.54
53 Keiki Misipeka, Southeast Mo. St.	RB	JR	12	13	0	0	0	0	78	6.5
54 Derrick Johnese, Northwestern St.	RB	SO	13	14	0	0	0	0	84	6.46
55 Bret LeVier, Sacramento St.	K	SO	12	0	35	38	14	18	77	6.42
56 Daniel Hanks, Davidson	K	SR	10	0	37	39	9	14	64	6.4
57 Vince Patrick, Texas Southern	K	JR	11	0	28	32	14	19	70	6.36
58 Chris Onorato, Hofstra	P	JR	12	0	31	32	15	22	76	6.33
59 Chris Vought, Western Caro.	K	JR	10	0	33	36	10	17	63	6.3
60 John Marino, McNeese St.	K	JR	15	0	52	57	14	23	94	6.27
61 Danny Marshall, Furman	K	JR	12	0	39	42	12	15	75	6.25
62 Rashod Smith, Florida Int'l	RB	SO	9	9	0	0	0	0	56	6.22
63 Mike Cajal-Willis, Portland St.	K	SR	11	0	26	26	14	22	68	6.18
64 Tellis Bolden, Hampton	P	SR	12	0	44	48	10	19	74	6.17
65 Derek Kutz, Southeast Mo. St.	K	SO	12	0	49	51	8	14	73	6.08
65 Travis Zobel, Citadel	P	JR	12	0	31	35	14	19	73	6.08
65 Mark Wright, Appalachian St.	K	SO	12	0	28	33	15	23	73	6.08
65 Lane Schwarzberg, Colgate	K	SO	12	0	34	36	13	17	73	6.08
69 Jayson Davis, Rhode Island	QB	FR	11	11	0	0	0	0	66	6
69 Paul Ernster, Northern Ariz.	K	SO	11	0	27	29	13	19	66	6
69 Michael Gasperson, San Diego	WR	SO	10	10	0	0	0	0	60	6
69 Rob Giancola, Valparaiso	WR	SO	11	11	0	0	0	0	66	6
69 Ari Confesor, Holy Cross	WR	JR	12	12	0	0	0	0	72	6
69 Cameron Atkinson, Princeton	RB	SR	10	10	0	0	0	0	60	6
69 Robert Carr, Yale	TB	SO	10	10	0	0	0	0	60	6
69 Matt May, St. John's (N.Y.)	WR	SR	10	10	0	0	0	0	60	6
69 Nehemiah Broughton, Citadel	RB	SO	12	12	0	0	0	0	72	6
69 Erik Lash, Bethune-Cookman	WR	SR	12	12	0	0	0	0	72	6
69 Jesse McCoy, Wofford	RB	SR	11	11	0	0	0	0	66	6
69 Geno Mattioda, Dayton	RB	JR	12	12	0	0	0	0	72	6
69 David White, Morehead St.	FB	SR	12	12	0	0	0	0	72	6
82 Adam Smith, Eastern Ky.	K	JR	12	0	38	40	11	15	71	5.92
83 Adam James, Villanova	P	SO	15	0	55	59	11	14	88	5.87
84 Brian Morgan, Grambling	K	SO	13	0	55	62	7	21	76	5.85
85 Charles Anthony, Tennessee St.	RB	SO	12	11	0	0	0	0	70	5.83
86 Andrew Harmon, Gardner-Webb	K	SR	10	0	25	28	11	17	58	5.8
87 Jason Ballard, Tennessee Tech	RB	JR	12	11	0	0	0	0	68	5.67
88 Terrell Johnson, Norfolk St.	RB	FR	11	10	0	0	0	0	62	5.64
88 Rich Heintz, Eastern Wash.	K	JR	11	0	44	49	6	9	62	5.64
90 Tommy Hebert, Northwestern St.	K	SO	13	0	46	47	9	13	73	5.62
91 Aryvia Holmes, Samford	WR	SR	10	9	0	0	0	0	56	5.6
91 Jason Michael, Western Ky.	QB	SR	15	14	0	0	0	0	84	5.6
93 Scott Collins, Delaware	K	SR	12	0	31	31	12	22	67	5.58
94 Navid Niakan, Cal Poly	K	SR	11	0	25	29	12	20	61	5.55
95 Garrett White, Sacramento St.	RB	SR	12	11	0	0	0	0	66	5.5
95 Jermaine Pugh, Lehigh	RB	JR	12	11	0	0	0	0	66	5.5
95 Tim Redican, Sacred Heart	K	SR	10	0	22	25	11	16	55	5.5
95 David Caudill, Morehead St.	QB	JR	12	11	0	0	0	0	66	5.5
99 Derek Clayton, St. Peter's	RB	JR	11	10	0	0	0	0	60	5.45
99 Matt Romeo, Towson	RB	JR	11	10	0	0	0	0	60	5.45
99 George Scott, Wagner	RB	SR	11	10	0	0	0	0	60	5.45
99 Christopher Price, Marist	RB	SR	11	10	0	0	0	0	60	5.45
99 Johnathan Smith, William & Mary	RB	SO	11	10	0	0	0	0	60	5.45
99 Nick Chournos, Weber St.	RB	SO	11	10	0	0	0	0	60	5.45
99 Eric Kimble, Eastern Wash.	RB	FR	11	10	0	0	0	0	60	5.45
99 Fred Amey, Sacramento St.	WR	SO	11	10	0	0	0	0	60	5.45

Total Offense

Min. 75 Pct. of Team's Games Played

Rank, Player	Pos	Cl	G	Rush Gn	Loss	Net	Patt	Pyds	Pl	Tot	Yds/ Pl	Yds/ Gm
1 Bruce Eugene, Grambling.....QB		SO	13	137 723	188	535	543	4,483	680	5018	7.38	386
2 Ira Vandever, Drake.............QB		SR	11	127 646	231	415	361	3,239	488	3654	7.49	332.2
3 Brian Mann, Dartmouth ....QB		SR	10	118 565	172	393	423	2,913	541	3306	6.11	330.6
4 Robert Kent, Jackson St. ......QB		JR	11	118 450	271	179	395	3,386	513	3565	6.95	324.1
5 David Macchi, Valparaiso ....QB		JR	11	132 479	256	223	390	3,326	522	3549	6.8	322.6
6 David Caudill, Morehead St. OB		JR	12	162 733	200	533	362	2,979	524	3512	6.7	292.7
7 Josh Blankenship, Eastern Wash...................QB		SR	11	41 80	176	-96	418	3,243	459	3147	6.86	286.1
8 Brett Gordon, Villanova ....QB		SR	15	87 148	298	-150	578	4,305	665	4155	6.25	277
9 Doug Baughman, Idaho St. .QB		SR	11	69 198	126	72	394	2,936	463	3008	6.5	273.5
10 Mike Mitchell, Pennsylvania ..QB		SR	10	41 65	139	-74	371	2,803	412	2729	6.62	272.9
11 Tony Romo, Eastern Ill. ....QB		SR	12	35 72	88	-16	407	3,165	442	3149	7.12	262.4
12 Kyle Slager, Brown ....QB		JR	10	57 133	160	-27	340	2,609	397	2582	6.5	258.2
13 Jack Tomco, Southeast Mo. St.QB		JR	12	24 29	91	-62	372	3,132	396	3070	7.75	255.8
14 Jeremy Martin, Gardner-Webb.............................QB		SR	10	114 464	103	361	327	2,166	441	2527	5.73	252.7
15 Dave Corley, William & Mary..............................QB		SR	11	106 403	301	102	329	2,672	435	2774	6.38	252.2
16 Tom McCune, Colgate ....QB		SR	9	91 466	155	311	255	1,951	346	2262	6.54	251.3
17 Andy Hall, Delaware ....QB		FR	11	153 956	93	863	306	1,832	459	2695	5.87	245
18 Eric Rasmussen, San Diego...QB		JR	10	66 200	227	-27	279	2,473	345	2446	7.09	244.6
19 Russ Michna, Western Ill. .....QB		JR	13	81 312	182	130	330	3,037	411	3167	7.71	243.6
20 John Edwards, Montana ....QB		SR	14	119 361	257	104	449	3,209	568	3313	5.83	236.6
21 Ryan Leadingham, Sacramento St. ....QB		SO	12	80 282	254	28	373	2,788	453	2816	6.22	234.7
22 Leon McCampbell, South Carolina St. ....QB		JR	12	180 961	120	841	233	1,972	413	2813	6.81	234.4
23 Marko Glavic, Lafayette ....QB		JR	12	87 243	123	120	399	2,670	486	2790	5.74	232.5
24 Kevin Eakin, Fordham ....QB		JR	13	66 141	198	-57	383	3,040	449	2983	6.64	229.5
25 Paul Nichols, Davidson.........QB		SR	10	50 167	102	65	308	2,189	358	2254	6.3	225.4
26 Ryan Cosentino, Hofstra ....QB		JR	12	79 290	220	70	415	2,608	494	2678	5.42	223.2
27 Tate Bennett, Weber St. ......QB		JR	10	46 122	143	-21	311	2,228	357	2207	6.18	220.7
28 Steve Hunsberger, Columbia QB		JR	10	136 440	274	166	370	2,023	506	2189	4.33	218.9
29 Brian Hall, Holy Cross.........QB		JR	12	129 505	169	336	345	2,279	474	2615	5.52	217.9
30 Joey Gibson, VMI.................QB		SR	12	107 426	157	269	348	2,328	455	2597	5.71	216.4
31 Niel Loebig, Duquesne ....QB		SO	12	39 59	166	-107	362	2,685	401	2578	6.43	214.8
32 Jeff Klein, Citadel ....QB		SR	12	41 79	74	5	378	2,561	419	2566	6.12	213.8
33 Billy Napier, Furman ....QB		SR	12	79 198	171	27	276	2,475	355	2502	7.05	208.5
34 Carey Weaver, Mississippi Val. ....QB		SR	11	156 599	440	159	323	2,116	479	2275	4.75	206.8
35 Juston Wood, Portland St. ...QB		SR	11	63 237	218	19	324	2,211	387	2230	5.76	202.7
36 Jake Eaton, Maine ....OB		SR	11	112 499	172	327	269	1,849	381	2176	5.71	197.8
37 Robert Craft, Tennessee Tech..QB		SO	12	52 79	165	-86	310	2,448	362	2362	6.52	196.8
38 Jay Amer, Towson................QB		JR	11	64 164	219	-55	299	2,214	363	2159	5.95	196.3
39 Jeff Krohn, Massachusetts .....QB		JR	10	42 84	160	-76	287	2,032	329	1956	5.95	195.6
40 Ed Marynowitz, La Salle.......QB		FR	11	92 139	330	-191	369	2,339	461	2148	4.66	195.3
41 Allen Suber, Bethune-Cookman........................QB		JR	12	158 1227	192	1035	164	1,307	322	2342	7.27	195.2
42 Neil Rose, Harvard ....QB		SR	8	42 130	17	113	186	1,438	228	1551	6.8	193.9
43 Donald Carrie, Alcorn St. .....QB		SO	11	54 167	242	-75	338	2,197	392	2122	5.41	192.9
44 Mike Sturgill, Jacksonville......QB		FR	10	65 197	189	8	279	1,876	344	1884	5.48	188.4
45 Julian Reese, Indiana St.......QB		SR	12	176 780	247	533	266	1,725	442	2258	5.11	188.2
46 Mike Cerchio, Fairfield........QB		SR	10	109 450	305	145	267	1,707	376	1852	4.93	185.2
47 Clint Womack, Northern Ariz.QB		JR	10	83 171	280	-109	265	1,950	348	1841	5.29	184.1
48 Mike Granieri, New Hampshire ....QB		SO	11	147 471	285	186	297	1,826	444	2012	4.53	182.9
49 Matt Millheiser, St. John's (N.Y.).................RB		JR	10	118 350	243	107	290	1,694	408	1801	4.41	180.1
50 Ryan McCann, Chattanooga QB		SR	12	62 193	137	56	297	2,099	359	2155	6	179.6
51 Kelly Spiker, Dayton ....QB		JR	12	172 1054	191	863	136	1,240	308	2103	6.83	175.3
52 Chaz Williams, Ga. Southern QB		SO	14	290 1538	116	1422	100	1,022	390	2444	6.27	174.6
53 David Splithoff, Princeton......QB		JR	8	90 302	130	172	142	1,223	232	1395	6.01	174.4
54 Travis Lulay, Montana St. ....QB		FR	13	88 358	177	181	272	2,042	360	2223	6.18	171
55 Reggie Hayes, Florida A&M.QB		SR	12	149 729	139	590	202	1,459	351	2049	5.84	170.8
56 Pat Cilento, Western Caro. ..QB		SR	11	81 351	124	227	221	1,636	302	1863	6.16	169.4
57 Stewart Childress, Murray St.QB		JR	12	48 209	76	133	266	1,894	314	2027	6.46	168.9
58 Tom Petrie, Northern Iowa ....QB		SO	10	88 435	113	322	210	1,363	298	1685	5.65	168.5
59 Ryan Fitzpatrick, Harvard ....QB		SO	10	115 598	75	523	150	1,155	265	1678	6.33	167.8
60 Jeff Mroz, Yale ....QB		SO	10	36 66	120	-54	244	1,731	280	1677	5.99	167.7
61 Mick Razzano, Cornell.........QB		SR	10	93 284	176	108	275	1,548	368	1656	4.5	165.6
62 Casey Printers, Florida A&M.QB		SR	9	72 192	229	-37	218	1,517	290	1480	5.1	164.4
63 Michael White, Southwest Mo. St. ....QB		JR	10	47 107	180	-73	249	1,708	296	1635	5.52	163.5
64 Joe Burchette, Appalachian St.QB		SR	12	64 159	157	2	284	1,949	348	1951	5.61	162.6
65 Chad Schwenk, Lehigh.........QB		JR	10	46 123	133	-10	247	1,618	293	1608	5.49	160.8
66 Joe Kroells, Sacred Heart......QB		JR	10	69 162	204	-42	276	1,627	345	1585	4.59	158.5
67 Jason Michael, Western Ky...QB		SR	15	170 772	130	642	165	1,661	335	2303	6.87	153.5
68 Bradshaw Littlejohn, Morgan St. ....QB		SO	12	103 772	100	672	134	1,128	237	1800	7.59	150
69 Scott Bard, Stony Brook........QB		SR	10	79 203	182	21	237	1,478	316	1499	4.74	149.9
70 Joel Sambursky, Southern Ill. .QB		SO	12	138 653	166	487	167	1,308	305	1795	5.89	149.6

Rank, Player	Pos	Cl	G	Rush	Gn	Loss	Net	Patt	Pyds	Pl	Tot	Yds/Pl	Yds/Gm
71 Michael Souza, Illinois St.	QB	JR	11	88	363	139	224	233	1,404	321	1628	5.07	148
72 Josh Kellett, Samford	QB	SR	11	44	178	107	71	225	1,518	269	1589	5.91	144.5
73 Chris Peterson, Cal Poly	QB	JR	11	151	675	168	507	174	1,066	325	1573	4.84	143
74 Chuck Henderson, Southern Utah	QB	JR	11	218	1014	172	842	89	729	307	1571	5.12	142.8
75 Travis Turner, Eastern Ky.	QB	SR	11	75	322	137	185	190	1,381	265	1566	5.91	142.4
76 Kevin Magee, Northwestern St.	QB	SR	13	61	161	163	-2	252	1,844	313	1842	5.88	141.7
77 Jay Bailey, Austin Peay	RB	SR	12	319	1759	72	1687	0	0	319	1687	5.29	140.6
78 David Paulus, Georgetown	QB	SR	11	51	232	135	97	182	1,438	233	1535	6.59	139.5
79 Donald Clark, Howard	QB	SR	11	83	274	225	49	247	1,459	330	1508	4.57	137.1
80 Jermaine Crenshaw, Alabama St.	QB	JR	12	82	523	83	440	204	1,185	286	1625	5.68	135.4
80 Ryan Roeder, Albany (N.Y.)	QB	SR	12	97	420	161	259	213	1,366	310	1625	5.24	135.4
82 Scott Pendarvis, McNeese St.	QB	SO	15	65	132	197	-65	288	2,050	353	1985	5.62	132.3
83 Jatavis Sanders, East Tenn. St.	QB	SR	12	134	525	250	275	229	1,311	363	1586	4.37	132.2
84 Matt LeZotte, James Madison	QB	SO	12	69	257	159	98	199	1,481	268	1579	5.89	131.6
85 Ian Nelson, Butler	QB	SO	10	72	362	85	277	150	1,031	222	1308	5.89	130.8
86 Zeke Dixon, Stephen F. Austin	QB	SO	11	23	25	88	-63	188	1,486	211	1423	6.74	129.4
87 Jayson Davis, Rhode Island	QB	FR	11	216	949	270	679	129	734	345	1413	4.1	128.5
88 Jacob Chavan, Texas Southern	QB	FR	11	26	88	80	8	169	1,397	195	1405	7.21	127.7
89 Bill Rankin, Monmouth	QB	SR	10	68	236	149	87	239	1,189	307	1276	4.16	127.6
90 D'Arcy Wills, Richmond	QB	SR	11	102	466	127	339	138	1,058	240	1397	5.82	127
91 J.R. Taylor, Eastern Ill.	RB	SR	12	254	1567	45	1522	0	0	254	1522	5.99	126.8
92 Gary Jones, Albany (N.Y.)	RB	JR	12	231	1557	48	1509	0	0	231	1509	6.53	125.8
93 Quincy Richard, Southern U.	QB	JR	12	95	390	173	217	239	1,279	334	1496	4.48	124.7
94 Jamie Burke, Florida Int'l	QB	FR	11	41	15	302	-287	195	1,652	236	1365	5.78	124.1
95 Shawn Brady, Northeastern	QB	SO	13	73	226	114	112	224	1,497	297	1609	5.42	123.8
96 Verondre Barnes, Liberty	RB	SO	11	221	1364	60	1304	2	35	223	1339	6	121.7
97 Timothy Frazier, Hampton	QB	JR	12	50	169	66	103	201	1,351	251	1454	5.79	121.2
98 Cody McCauley, Southwest Tex. St.	QB	SO	11	83	295	216	79	168	1,223	251	1302	5.19	118.4
99 Clyde Tullis, Savannah St.	QB	FR	10	87	215	267	-52	266	1,233	353	1181	3.35	118.1
100 Billy Brieden, Iona	QB	JR	11	77	172	273	-101	227	1,387	304	1286	4.23	116.9

2002 Division I-AA Team Leaders

Pass Efficiency Defense

Rank, School	G	Att	Com	Pct	Int	IPct	Yds	Yds/Att	TD	TDPct	Rating	W	L	T
1 Sacred Heart	10	252	87	34.52	19	7.54	1,091	4.33	4	1.59	61.03	7	3	0
2 Duquesne	12	256	104	40.63	25	9.77	1,140	4.45	5	1.95	64.92	11	1	0
3 Bethune-Cookman	13	298	120	40.27	21	7.05	1,652	5.54	7	2.35	80.52	11	2	0
4 St. Francis (Pa.)	10	220	92	41.82	11	5	1,077	4.9	6	2.73	81.92	2	8	0
5 Morehead St.	12	314	146	46.5	20	6.37	1,651	5.26	6	1.91	84.23	9	3	0
6 Robert Morris	10	164	69	42.07	13	7.93	909	5.54	6	3.66	84.88	3	7	0
7 Wagner	11	207	102	49.28	12	5.8	1,075	5.19	5	2.42	89.3	7	4	0
8 Dayton	12	434	203	46.77	28	6.45	2,617	6.03	8	1.84	90.63	11	1	0
9 Maine	14	333	153	45.95	20	6.01	1,854	5.57	11	3.3	91.56	11	3	0
10 Stephen F. Austin	11	273	132	48.35	12	4.4	1,584	5.8	5	1.83	94.39	6	5	0
11 Ga. Southern	14	385	180	46.75	15	3.9	2,154	5.59	10	2.6	94.58	11	3	0
12 Stony Brook	10	268	142	52.99	12	4.48	1,390	5.19	6	2.24	95	8	2	0
13 Mississippi Val.	11	324	154	47.53	18	5.56	1,833	5.66	12	3.7	96.13	5	6	0
14 Siena	10	263	129	49.05	12	4.56	1,378	5.24	10	3.8	96.43	3	7	0
15 Lehigh	12	338	166	49.11	12	3.55	1,903	5.63	8	2.37	97.1	8	4	0
16 McNeese St.	15	398	168	42.21	20	5.03	2,491	6.26	15	3.77	97.16	13	2	0
17 Villanova	15	400	206	51.5	15	3.75	2,276	5.69	8	2	98.4	11	4	0
18 Pennsylvania	10	388	215	55.41	20	5.15	2,198	5.66	7	1.8	98.63	9	1	0
19 Marist	11	299	116	38.8	15	5.02	1,868	6.25	16	5.35	98.9	7	4	0
20 Jackson St.	11	368	169	45.92	15	4.08	2,132	5.79	14	3.8	98.97	7	4	0
21 Fairfield	11	299	124	41.47	16	5.35	1,846	6.17	15	5.02	99.21	5	6	0
22 Alabama A&M	12	409	187	45.72	17	4.16	2,461	6.02	15	3.67	100.03	8	4	0
23 South Carolina St.	12	278	130	46.76	17	6.12	1,763	6.34	11	3.96	100.9	7	5	0
24 Howard	11	285	126	44.21	15	5.26	1,854	6.51	11	3.86	101.05	6	5	0
25 Princeton	10	374	199	53.21	16	4.28	2,063	5.52	12	3.21	101.57	6	4	0
26 Alabama St.	12	425	189	44.47	20	4.71	2,790	6.56	15	3.53	101.88	6	6	0
27 Nicholls St.	11	284	153	53.87	12	4.23	1,694	5.96	6	2.11	102.53	7	4	0
28 N.C. A&T	12	344	166	48.26	27	7.85	2,271	6.6	16	4.65	103.41	4	8	0
29 Monmouth	10	252	121	48.02	6	2.38	1,509	5.99	8	3.17	104.01	2	8	0
30 East Tenn. St.	12	295	151	51.19	14	4.75	1,875	6.36	8	2.71	104.05	4	8	0
31 Florida Int'l	11	221	123	55.66	10	4.52	1,287	5.82	6	2.71	104.53	5	6	0
32 Grambling	13	405	184	45.43	24	5.93	2,571	6.35	22	5.43	104.8	11	2	0
33 Western Ky.	15	348	174	50	20	5.75	2,404	6.91	10	2.87	106.02	12	3	0
34 Hampton	12	356	171	48.03	12	3.37	2,294	6.44	12	3.37	106.51	7	5	0
35 Youngstown St.	11	280	153	54.64	9	3.21	1,650	5.89	8	2.86	107.1	7	4	0
36 Massachusetts	12	398	210	52.76	20	5.03	2,503	6.29	14	3.52	107.18	8	4	0
37 Western Ill.	13	373	187	50.13	15	4.02	2,383	6.39	13	3.49	107.22	11	2	0

Rank, School	G	Att	Com	Pct	Int	IPct	Yds	Yds/Att	TD	TDPct	Rating	W	L	T
38 Southern U.	12	355	161	45.35	14	3.94	2,166	6.1	20	5.63	107.36	6	6	0
39 Northeastern	13	401	205	51.12	16	3.99	2,529	6.31	14	3.49	107.62	10	3	0
40 Alcorn St.	11	365	159	43.56	17	4.66	2,415	6.62	21	5.75	108.85	6	5	0
41 Montana St.	13	413	209	50.61	9	2.18	2,540	6.15	14	3.39	109.09	7	6	0
42 Texas Southern	11	350	156	44.57	19	5.43	2,317	6.62	21	6	109.15	4	7	0
43 Towson	11	375	191	50.93	18	4.8	2,451	6.54	15	4	109.4	6	5	0
44 Florida A&M	12	302	140	46.36	16	5.3	1,827	6.05	21	6.95	109.57	7	5	0
45 Fordham	13	398	225	56.53	15	3.77	2,443	6.14	11	2.76	109.64	10	3	0
46 Eastern Ky.	12	309	138	44.66	12	3.88	2,131	6.9	14	4.53	109.81	8	4	0
47 Gardner-Webb	10	211	110	52.13	16	7.58	1,488	7.05	9	4.27	110.25	9	1	0
48 William & Mary	11	292	140	47.95	15	5.14	1,779	6.09	19	6.51	110.28	6	5	0
49 Idaho St.	11	355	180	50.7	16	4.51	2,316	6.52	15	4.23	110.43	8	3	0
50 Charleston So.	12	338	172	50.89	16	4.73	2,117	6.26	17	5.03	110.64	4	8	0
51 Furman	12	297	176	59.26	17	5.72	1,829	6.16	10	3.37	110.69	8	4	0
52 St. John's (N.Y.)	10	233	103	44.21	13	5.58	1,656	7.11	13	5.58	111.15	2	8	0
53 Northern Iowa	11	304	153	50.33	13	4.28	1,997	6.57	14	4.61	112.13	5	6	0
54 Central Conn. St.	11	317	173	54.57	17	5.36	1,987	6.27	15	4.73	112.14	5	6	0
55 St. Peter's	11	286	138	48.25	15	5.24	1,888	6.6	17	5.94	112.88	6	5	0
56 New Hampshire	11	264	145	54.92	10	3.79	1,601	6.06	12	4.55	113.27	3	8	0
57 Hofstra	12	261	139	53.26	7	2.68	1,573	6.03	12	4.6	113.73	6	6	0
58 Iona	11	286	156	54.55	9	3.15	1,780	6.22	12	4.2	114.33	5	6	0
59 Appalachian St.	12	279	137	49.1	12	4.3	1,896	6.8	15	5.38	115.32	8	4	0
60 Wofford	12	286	174	60.84	11	3.85	1,734	6.06	10	3.5	115.57	9	3	0
61 Montana	14	460	248	53.91	16	3.48	3,209	6.98	16	3.48	117.02	11	3	0
62 Ark.-Pine Bluff	11	368	169	45.92	16	4.35	2,385	6.48	29	7.88	117.65	3	8	0
63 Savannah St.	10	250	129	51.6	10	4	1,775	7.1	12	4.8	119.08	1	9	0
64 Albany (N.Y.)	12	364	185	50.82	11	3.02	2,403	6.6	21	5.77	119.25	8	4	0
65 Canisius	11	250	127	50.8	11	4.4	1,798	7.19	13	5.2	119.57	2	9	0
66 Lafayette	12	378	203	53.7	11	2.91	2,561	6.78	17	4.5	119.63	7	5	0
67 Northwestern St.	13	346	185	53.47	9	2.6	2,304	6.66	17	4.91	120.45	9	4	0
68 Delaware St.	12	338	188	55.62	12	3.55	2,228	6.59	17	5.03	120.47	4	8	0
69 Delaware	12	370	206	55.68	9	2.43	2,558	6.91	14	3.78	121.4	6	6	0
70 Norfolk St.	11	315	153	48.57	13	4.13	2,230	7.08	21	6.67	121.81	5	6	0
71 Austin Peay	12	372	201	54.03	16	4.3	2,581	6.94	22	5.91	123.19	7	5	0
72 Richmond	11	264	151	57.2	14	5.3	1,977	7.49	11	4.17	123.25	4	7	0
73 Morris Brown	12	325	160	49.23	15	4.62	2,359	7.26	22	6.77	123.28	1	11	0
74 Colgate	12	432	250	57.87	14	3.24	3,160	7.31	14	3.24	123.56	9	3	0
75 Eastern Wash.	11	336	189	56.25	10	2.98	2,229	6.63	18	5.36	123.75	6	5	0
76 Western Caro.	11	307	159	51.79	8	2.61	2,237	7.29	15	4.89	123.92	5	6	0
77 Bucknell	11	315	174	55.24	8	2.54	1,958	6.22	21	6.67	124.33	2	9	0
78 St. Mary's (Cal.)	12	334	188	56.29	21	6.29	2,506	7.5	18	5.39	124.53	6	6	0
79 La Salle	11	241	119	49.38	6	2.49	1,776	7.37	14	5.81	125.49	7	5	0
80 Murray St.	12	340	205	60.29	13	3.82	2,281	6.71	17	5	125.51	7	5	0
81 Southwest Mo. St.	11	259	155	59.85	11	4.25	1,821	7.03	12	4.63	125.65	4	7	0
82 Davidson	10	328	184	56.1	9	2.74	2,271	6.92	17	5.18	125.88	7	3	0
83 Northern Ariz.	11	385	210	54.55	15	3.9	2,816	7.31	21	5.45	126.15	6	5	0
84 Yale	10	306	178	58.17	5	1.63	2,149	7.02	12	3.92	126.87	6	4	0
85 Cal Poly	11	265	141	53.21	11	4.15	2,201	8.31	10	3.77	127.12	3	8	0
86 Liberty	11	317	185	58.36	9	2.84	2,263	7.14	14	4.42	127.26	2	9	0
87 Morgan St.	12	301	147	48.84	7	2.33	2,278	7.57	18	5.98	127.46	7	5	0
88 Harvard	10	342	183	53.51	11	3.22	2,416	7.06	22	6.43	127.64	7	3	0
89 Jacksonville St.	11	261	138	52.87	12	4.6	2,045	7.84	15	5.75	128.49	5	6	0
90 Sam Houston St.	11	255	152	59.61	9	3.53	1,723	6.76	15	5.88	128.71	4	7	0
91 Tennessee St.	12	348	183	52.59	11	3.16	2,583	7.42	22	6.32	129.49	2	10	0
92 James Madison	12	318	196	61.64	9	2.83	2,072	6.52	19	5.97	130.39	5	7	0
93 Portland St.	11	387	243	62.79	11	2.84	2,694	6.96	18	4.65	130.94	6	5	0
94 Illinois St.	11	252	133	52.78	4	1.59	1,827	7.25	16	6.35	131.48	6	5	0
95 VMI	12	338	187	55.33	12	3.55	2,567	7.59	21	6.21	132.5	6	6	0
96 Southeast Mo. St.	12	370	220	59.46	13	3.51	2,803	7.58	20	5.41	133.95	8	4	0
97 Southern Ill.	12	324	176	54.32	12	3.7	2,502	7.72	22	6.79	134.17	4	8	0
98 Tenn.-Martin	12	329	197	59.88	12	3.65	2,377	7.22	21	6.38	134.36	2	10	0
99 Southwest Tex. St.	11	221	131	59.28	11	4.98	1,901	8.6	9	4.07	135.04	4	7	0
100 Brown	10	327	200	61.16	9	2.75	2,348	7.18	19	5.81	135.19	2	8	0
101 Columbia	10	320	198	61.88	7	2.19	2,352	7.35	16	5	135.77	1	9	0
102 Fla. Atlantic	11	252	143	56.75	6	2.38	1,919	7.62	16	6.35	136.86	2	9	0
103 Weber St.	11	313	182	58.15	7	2.24	2,482	7.93	16	5.11	137.11	3	8	0
104 Indiana St.	12	252	153	60.71	9	3.57	1,854	7.36	17	6.75	137.62	5	7	0
105 Tennessee Tech	12	329	198	60.18	10	3.04	2,529	7.69	19	5.78	137.75	5	7	0
106 Prairie View	11	296	153	51.69	9	3.04	2,313	7.81	24	8.11	138.01	1	10	0
107 Sacramento St.	12	414	254	61.35	10	2.42	3,138	7.58	24	5.8	139.37	5	7	0
108 Georgetown	11	354	211	59.6	12	3.39	2,794	7.89	22	6.21	139.63	5	6	0
109 Chattanooga	12	340	202	59.41	5	1.47	2,512	7.39	23	6.76	140.84	2	10	0
110 Jacksonville	10	275	148	53.82	10	3.64	2,216	8.06	23	8.36	141.82	3	7	0
111 Cornell	10	309	203	65.7	9	2.91	2,387	7.72	16	5.18	141.85	4	6	0
112 Eastern Ill.	12	362	202	55.8	9	2.49	3,002	8.29	24	6.63	142.37	8	4	0
113 Citadel	12	276	165	59.78	10	3.62	2,362	8.56	15	5.43	142.38	3	9	0
114 San Diego	10	290	168	57.93	13	4.48	2,408	8.3	22	7.59	143.72	5	5	0
115 Drake	10	326	187	57.36	7	2.15	2,756	8.45	20	6.13	144.36	5	5	0
116 Southern Utah	11	259	150	57.92	4	1.54	2,026	7.82	19	7.34	144.73	1	10	0
117 Holy Cross	12	272	167	61.4	6	2.21	2,207	8.11	19	6.99	148.2	4	8	0
118 Dartmouth	10	341	222	65.1	7	2.05	2,752	8.07	21	6.16	149.11	3	7	0
119 Butler	10	302	175	57.95	10	3.31	2,704	8.95	22	7.28	150.53	4	6	0
120 Samford	11	274	163	59.49	11	4.01	2,476	9.04	21	7.66	152.67	4	7	0
121 Elon	11	292	165	56.51	10	3.42	2,655	9.09	27	9.25	156.54	4	7	0
122 Rhode Island	12	334	214	64.07	8	2.4	2,972	8.9	25	7.49	158.76	3	9	0
123 Valparaiso	11	277	153	55.23	4	1.44	2,673	9.65	31	11.19	170.3	1	10	0

Fumbles Recovered

Rank, School	No.
1 Hampton	21
2 Florida Int'l	20
2 Northeastern	20
4 East Tenn. St.	19
4 Morris Brown	19
6 Austin Peay	18
6 Montana	18
6 Florida A&M	18
6 Bethune-Cookman	18
6 Southern Ill.	18
6 Richmond	18
6 Northwestern St.	18
6 N.C. A&T	18
14 Marist	17
14 Massachusetts	17
14 Wagner	17
14 Western Ill.	17
14 Western Caro.	17
14 Southwest Tex. St.	17
14 Portland St.	17
14 McNeese St.	17
22 Alabama A&M	16
22 Alabama St.	16
22 Central Conn. St.	16
22 Canisius	16
22 Ark.-Pine Bluff	16
22 Elon	16
22 Stony Brook	16
22 Savannah St.	16
22 Liberty	16
22 Delaware St.	16
22 Alcorn St.	16
33 Colgate	15
33 Duquesne	15
33 South Carolina St.	15
33 Southern Utah	15
33 Youngstown St.	15
33 Western Ky.	15
33 Southern U.	15
33 Morgan St.	15
33 Maine	15
33 Holy Cross	15
33 Eastern Ill.	15
33 Davidson	15
45 Brown	14
45 Butler	14
45 Siena	14
45 Sam Houston St.	14
45 St. Peter's	14
45 St. Francis (Pa.)	14
45 Prairie View	14
45 Murray St.	14
45 Morehead St.	14
45 Monmouth	14
45 Lafayette	14
45 La Salle	14
45 Villanova	14
45 Fairfield	14
45 Sacramento St.	14
60 Cal Poly	13
60 Indiana St.	13
60 Fla. Atlantic	13
60 Furman	13
60 Iona	13
60 Jacksonville St.	13
60 Texas Southern	13
60 Pennsylvania	13
60 Norfolk St.	13
60 Nicholls St.	13
60 Jackson St.	13
71 Albany (N.Y.)	12
71 Charleston So.	12
71 Grambling	12
71 Rhode Island	12
71 VMI	12
71 Tennessee St.	12
71 Samford	12
71 St. John's (N.Y.)	12
71 Sacred Heart	12
71 Jacksonville	12
71 Mississippi Val.	12
82 Citadel	11
82 Tenn.-Martin	11
82 Gardner-Webb	11
82 Chattanooga	11
82 Columbia	11
82 Montana St.	11
82 Southwest Mo. St.	11
82 Tennessee Tech	11
82 Lehigh	11
91 Bucknell	10
91 Eastern Wash.	10
91 William & Mary	10
91 Southeast Mo. St.	10
91 Illinois St.	10
91 Howard	10
91 Hofstra	10
91 Harvard	10
91 Fordham	10
91 Delaware	10
101 Dartmouth	9
101 Eastern Ky.	9
101 Wofford	9
101 Stephen F. Austin	9
101 St. Mary's (Cal.)	9
101 Northern Iowa	9
101 New Hampshire	9
101 James Madison	9
101 Dayton	9
110 Appalachian St.	8
110 Cornell	8
110 Northern Ariz.	8
110 Yale	8
110 Weber St	8
110 Towson	8
110 Drake	8
110 Ga. Southern	8
118 Robert Morris	7
118 San Diego	7
120 Georgetown	6
120 Princeton	6
122 Idaho St.	5
123 Valparaiso	4

Fumbles Lost

Rank, School	No.
1 Montana	5
2 Brown	6
2 Wagner	6
2 Yale	6
5 Butler	7
5 Ark.-Pine Bluff	7
5 Drake	7
5 VMI	7
5 Towson	7
5 Harvard	7
11 Austin Peay	8
11 Southeast Mo. St.	8
11 Cal Poly	8
11 Fordham	8
11 Western Caro.	8
11 Bethune-Cookman	8
17 Appalachian St.	9
17 Eastern Ky.	9
17 Fairfield	9
17 Gardner-Webb	9
17 William & Mary	9
17 San Diego	9
17 Massachusetts	9
17 Eastern Wash.	9
17 Davidson	9
26 Alabama A&M	10
26 Colgate	10
26 Holy Cross	10
26 Siena	10
26 Stephen F. Austin	10
26 Northern Ariz.	10
26 Murray St.	10
26 Illinois St.	10
26 Hampton	10
26 Dayton	10
26 Columbia	10
37 Canisius	11
37 Central Conn. St.	11
37 Chattanooga	11
37 Tennessee Tech	11
37 Southwest Tex. St.	11
37 Southwest Mo. St.	11
37 Princeton	11
37 Hofstra	11
45 Dartmouth	12
45 Northeastern	12
45 East Tenn. St.	12
45 Tennessee St.	12
45 Western Ky.	12
45 St. Peter's	12
45 Sam Houston St.	12
45 Portland St.	12
53 Alcorn St.	13
53 Jacksonville	13
53 Lehigh	13
53 Marist	13
53 Morris Brown	13
53 Valparaiso	13
53 Tenn.-Martin	13
53 Pennsylvania	13
53 N.C. A&T	13
53 Norfolk St.	13
53 Nicholls St.	13
53 Monmouth	13
53 Liberty	13
53 Lafayette	13
53 Eastern Ill.	13
53 Charleston So.	13
53 Duquesne	13
53 Cornell	13
71 Sacramento St.	14
71 Western Ill.	14
71 Villanova	14
71 Texas Southern	14
71 Stony Brook	14
71 Southern Ill.	14
71 St. John's (N.Y.)	14
71 St. Francis (Pa.)	14
71 Richmond	14
71 Morgan St.	14
71 Jacksonville St.	14
71 Idaho St.	14
71 Furman	14
71 Florida Int'l	14
85 Alabama St.	15
85 Howard	15
85 Bucknell	15
85 Delaware	15
85 Georgetown	15
85 Youngstown St.	15
85 Weber St.	15
85 Southern Utah	15
85 Southern U.	15
85 Samford	15
85 Northwestern St.	15
85 Montana St.	15
85 La Salle	15
98 Citadel	16
98 Ga. Southern	16
98 Wofford	16
98 New Hampshire	16
98 Robert Morris	16
98 Northern Iowa	16
98 McNeese St.	16
98 Maine	16
106 Delaware St.	17
106 Grambling	17
106 Indiana St.	17
109 Fla. Atlantic	18
109 Iona	18
109 Sacred Heart	18
109 Savannah St.	18
109 James Madison	18
114 Albany (N.Y.)	19
114 Mississippi Val.	19
114 Elon	19
114 South Carolina St.	19
118 Florida A&M	20
118 St. Mary's (Cal.)	20
120 Prairie View	21
121 Morehead St.	22
122 Jackson St.	23
122 Rhode Island	23

Kickoff Returns

Rank, School	G	Ret	Yds	TD	Avg	W	L	T
1 Portland St.	11	36	908	0	25.22	6	5	0
2 Montana	14	44	1,089	2	24.75	11	3	0
3 Stony Brook	10	30	729	3	24.3	8	2	0
4 Norfolk St.	11	45	1,073	1	23.84	5	6	0
5 Sacred Heart	10	34	810	0	23.82	7	3	0
6 Samford	11	59	1,403	2	23.78	4	7	0
7 Nicholls St.	11	37	874	0	23.62	7	4	0
8 Canisius	11	51	1,191	1	23.35	2	9	0
9 Yale	10	29	660	1	22.76	6	4	0
10 Southern Ill.	12	34	773	1	22.74	4	8	0
11 Alabama St.	12	49	1,102	0	22.49	6	6	0
12 Hampton	12	44	980	3	22.27	7	5	0
13 Butler	10	52	1,155	1	22.21	4	6	0
14 McNeese St.	15	51	1,130	0	22.16	13	2	0
15 Colgate	12	36	796	0	22.11	9	3	0
16 Southern U.	12	46	1,017	0	22.11	6	6	0
17 Morgan St.	12	45	985	0	21.89	7	5	0
18 VMI	12	61	1,328	0	21.77	6	6	0
19 St. Francis (Pa.)	10	43	932	1	21.67	2	8	0
20 San Diego	10	47	1,010	0	21.49	5	5	0
21 Ark.-Pine Bluff	11	58	1,242	0	21.41	3	8	0
22 Southeast Mo. St.	12	50	1,070	0	21.4	8	4	0
23 Northeastern	13	35	748	1	21.37	10	3	0
24 Ga. Southern	14	29	619	1	21.34	11	3	0
25 Eastern Ill.	12	57	1,212	1	21.26	8	4	0
26 N.C. A&T	12	48	1,020	1	21.25	4	8	0
27 Texas Southern	11	49	1,040	1	21.22	4	7	0
28 Sacramento St.	12	55	1,159	0	21.07	5	7	0
29 Appalachian St.	12	41	863	0	21.05	8	4	0

Rank, School	G	Ret	Yds	TD	Avg	W	L	T
30 Tennessee St.	12	67	1,408	0	21.01	2	10	0
31 Wagner	11	28	588	0	21	7	4	0
32 Sam Houston St.	11	42	879	0	20.93	4	7	0
33 Austin Peay	12	48	1,002	0	20.88	7	5	0
34 Lehigh	12	38	785	0	20.66	8	4	0
35 Southwest Tex. St.	11	38	784	0	20.63	4	7	0
36 Harvard	10	42	866	1	20.62	7	3	0
37 Holy Cross	12	52	1,070	0	20.58	4	8	0
38 Fordham	13	48	987	0	20.56	10	3	0
39 Chattanooga	12	56	1,150	0	20.54	2	10	0
40 Citadel	12	56	1,148	2	20.5	3	9	0
41 Siena	10	38	778	0	20.47	3	7	0
42 Villanova	15	59	1,206	1	20.44	11	4	0
43 Davidson	10	35	714	1	20.4	7	3	0
44 Jacksonville St.	11	50	1,017	0	20.34	5	6	0
45 Georgetown	11	51	1,037	1	20.33	5	6	0
46 Albany (N.Y.)	12	39	790	0	20.26	8	4	0
47 Morehead St.	12	35	708	0	20.23	9	3	0
48 Northern Ariz.	11	33	667	0	20.21	6	5	0
49 Western Caro.	11	46	927	1	20.15	5	6	0
50 William & Mary	11	41	826	0	20.15	6	5	0
51 Idaho St.	11	27	543	0	20.11	8	3	0
52 Hofstra	12	34	679	0	19.97	6	6	0
53 East Tenn. St.	12	47	933	0	19.85	4	8	0
54 Western Ill.	13	32	633	0	19.78	11	2	0
55 Indiana St.	12	34	669	1	19.68	5	7	0
56 New Hampshire	11	53	1,041	0	19.64	3	8	0
57 Dayton	12	26	508	0	19.54	11	1	0
58 Stephen F. Austin	11	38	742	0	19.53	6	5	0
59 Towson	11	45	878	0	19.51	6	5	0
60 Delaware St.	12	50	975	3	19.5	4	8	0
60 Mississippi Val.	11	40	780	1	19.5	5	6	0
62 Southwest Mo. St.	11	41	791	0	19.29	4	7	0
63 Furman	12	43	829	0	19.28	8	4	0
64 Western Ky.	15	41	789	0	19.24	12	3	0
65 Florida Int'l	11	32	613	0	19.16	5	6	0
66 South Carolina St.	12	40	766	0	19.15	7	5	0
67 Elon	11	52	990	0	19.04	4	7	0
68 Northern Iowa	11	30	571	0	19.03	5	6	0
69 Illinois St.	11	39	738	0	18.92	6	5	0
70 Valparaiso	11	61	1,154	0	18.92	1	10	0
71 Montana St.	13	37	698	0	18.86	7	6	0
72 Cornell	10	40	753	0	18.83	4	6	0
73 Monmouth	10	37	695	0	18.78	2	8	0
74 Youngstown St.	11	27	507	0	18.78	7	4	0
75 Charleston So.	12	58	1,085	1	18.71	4	8	0
76 La Salle	11	62	1,154	1	18.61	2	9	0
77 Grambling	13	59	1,098	0	18.61	11	2	0
78 Northwestern St.	13	47	872	0	18.55	9	4	0
79 Jackson St.	11	46	853	0	18.54	7	4	0
80 Alabama A&M	12	39	719	0	18.44	8	4	0
81 Jacksonville	10	53	976	0	18.42	3	7	0
82 Weber St.	11	43	786	1	18.28	3	8	0
83 Liberty	11	52	941	0	18.1	2	9	0
84 Dartmouth	10	49	885	0	18.06	3	7	0
85 Tennessee Tech	12	52	930	0	17.88	5	7	0
86 Cal Poly	11	43	767	2	17.84	3	8	0
87 St. Mary's (Cal.)	12	39	695	0	17.82	6	6	0
88 Florida A&M	12	49	872	0	17.8	7	5	0
89 Princeton	10	36	640	0	17.78	6	4	0
90 Bethune-Cookman	13	42	745	0	17.74	11	2	0
91 Columbia	10	45	798	0	17.73	1	9	0
91 Southern Utah	11	60	1,064	1	17.73	1	10	0
93 Murray St.	12	47	831	0	17.68	7	5	0
94 Iona	11	44	771	0	17.52	5	6	0
95 Brown	10	46	806	0	17.52	2	8	0
96 Drake	10	62	1,080	0	17.42	5	5	0
97 Eastern Wash.	11	38	661	0	17.39	6	5	0
98 Delaware	12	43	747	1	17.37	6	6	0
99 Rhode Island	12	58	1,001	1	17.26	3	9	0
100 Savannah St.	10	53	907	0	17.11	1	9	0
101 Bucknell	11	39	665	0	17.05	2	9	0
102 Howard	11	46	784	0	17.04	6	5	0
103 Lafayette	12	47	801	0	17.04	7	5	0
104 Fla. Atlantic	11	54	918	0	17	2	9	0
105 Marist	11	46	769	0	16.72	7	4	0
106 Tenn.-Martin	12	55	914	0	16.62	2	10	0
107 Maine	14	43	709	0	16.49	11	3	0
108 Eastern Ky.	12	37	608	0	16.43	8	4	0
109 Fairfield	11	45	733	0	16.29	5	6	0
110 Gardner-Webb	10	35	563	0	16.09	9	1	0
110 Wofford	12	35	563	0	16.09	9	3	0
112 Morris Brown	12	61	976	0	16	1	11	0
112 Robert Morris	10	36	576	0	16	3	7	0
114 Prairie View	11	60	959	0	15.98	1	10	0
115 St. John's (N.Y.)	10	51	815	0	15.98	2	8	0
116 Duquesne	12	23	367	0	15.96	11	1	0
117 Massachusetts	12	44	690	0	15.68	8	4	0
118 Central Conn. St.	11	40	621	0	15.53	5	6	0
119 Richmond	11	35	543	0	15.51	4	7	0
120 James Madison	12	37	566	0	15.3	5	7	0
121 St. Peter's	11	36	528	0	14.67	6	5	0
122 Alcorn St.	11	47	681	0	14.49	6	5	0
123 Pennsylvania	10	27	389	0	14.41	9	1	0

Net Punting

Rank, School	G	Punts	Yds	Avg	Ret	Rtyd	NetAvg	W	L	T
1 Idaho St.	11	52	2,377	45.71	19	156	42.71	8	3	0
2 Western Ill.	13	56	2,632	47	23	284	41.93	11	2	0
3 Appalachian St.	12	59	2,488	42.17	22	115	40.22	8	4	0
4 Wofford	12	47	1,985	42.23	18	148	39.09	9	3	0
5 Alabama St.	12	58	2,514	43.34	26	256	38.93	6	6	0
6 Northern Ariz.	11	66	3,044	46.12	38	512	38.36	6	5	0
7 Rhode Island	12	68	2,744	40.35	37	204	37.35	3	9	0
8 VMI	12	66	3,032	45.94	41	567	37.35	6	6	0
9 Delaware	12	65	2,541	39.09	32	134	37.03	6	6	0
10 Illinois St.	11	57	2,259	39.63	27	156	36.89	6	5	0
11 Southern Ill.	12	53	2,053	38.74	20	101	36.83	4	8	0
12 Jacksonville St.	11	62	2,595	41.85	36	317	36.74	5	6	0
13 Citadel	12	53	2,159	40.74	22	220	36.58	3	9	0
14 Northern Iowa	11	53	2,194	41.4	24	259	36.51	5	6	0
15 William & Mary	11	48	1,839	38.31	17	89	36.46	6	5	0
16 Nicholls St.	11	55	2,095	38.09	28	93	36.4	7	4	0
17 Maine	14	74	2,762	37.32	31	81	36.23	11	3	0
18 Southern Utah	11	57	2,268	39.79	27	209	36.12	1	10	0
19 Fordham	13	57	2,193	38.47	28	154	35.77	10	3	0
20 Hofstra	12	71	2,764	38.93	27	226	35.75	6	6	0
21 Hampton	12	67	2,567	38.31	31	181	35.61	7	5	0
22 Cal Poly	11	66	2,653	40.2	34	303	35.61	3	8	0
23 Chattanooga	12	69	2,893	41.93	42	438	35.58	2	10	0
24 Massachusetts	12	70	2,750	39.29	20	268	35.46	8	4	0
25 Sam Houston St.	11	68	2,642	38.85	25	233	35.43	4	7	0
26 Alcorn St.	11	75	2,878	38.37	29	226	35.36	6	5	0
27 East Tenn. St.	12	79	3,319	42.01	44	535	35.24	4	8	0
28 Ga. Southern	14	51	1,903	37.31	18	111	35.14	11	3	0
29 Furman	12	46	1,709	37.15	19	96	35.07	8	4	0

Rank, School	G	Punts	Yds	Avg	Ret	Rtyd	NetAvg	W	L	T
30 New Hampshire	11	56	2,127	37.98	28	166	35.02	3	8	0
31 San Diego	10	43	1,616	37.58	20	114	34.93	5	5	0
32 Towson	11	62	2,323	37.47	29	169	34.74	6	5	0
33 Western Caro.	11	69	2,730	39.57	36	348	34.52	5	6	0
34 Western Ky.	15	68	2,663	39.16	33	318	34.49	12	3	0
35 Eastern Wash.	11	60	2,383	39.72	33	318	34.42	6	5	0
36 Montana	14	69	2,651	38.42	38	288	34.25	11	3	0
37 Dayton	12	56	2,018	36.04	43	107	34.13	11	1	0
37 Drake	10	48	1,863	38.81	21	225	34.13	5	5	0
39 Alabama A&M	12	80	3,033	37.91	35	304	34.11	8	4	0
40 Murray St.	12	57	2,258	39.61	16	314	34.11	7	5	0
41 Georgetown	11	70	2,724	38.91	35	338	34.09	5	6	0
42 James Madison	12	66	2,485	37.65	22	237	34.06	5	7	0
43 Columbia	10	58	2,230	38.45	32	255	34.05	1	9	0
44 St. Mary's (Cal.)	12	65	2,417	37.18	23	205	34.03	6	6	0
45 Morgan St.	12	44	1,647	37.43	17	152	33.98	7	5	0
46 Montana St.	13	77	2,971	38.58	37	359	33.92	7	6	0
47 Eastern Ky.	12	55	2,019	36.71	26	154	33.91	8	4	0
48 McNeese St.	15	84	3,078	36.64	44	234	33.86	13	2	0
49 Sacred Heart	10	67	2,524	37.67	39	257	33.84	7	3	0
50 Elon	11	56	2,016	36	28	124	33.79	4	7	0
51 Southwest Tex. St.	11	65	2,443	37.58	22	248	33.77	4	7	0
52 South Carolina St.	12	57	2,164	37.96	30	265	33.32	7	5	0
53 Florida Int'l	11	58	2,013	34.71	19	87	33.21	5	6	0
54 Lafayette	12	52	1,904	36.62	33	181	33.13	7	5	0
55 Austin Peay	12	80	2,980	37.25	46	334	33.08	7	5	0
56 Dartmouth	10	49	1,811	36.96	29	209	32.69	3	7	0
57 Northeastern	13	77	2,783	36.14	35	269	32.65	10	3	0
58 N.C. A&T	12	86	3,120	36.28	35	314	32.63	4	8	0
59 Monmouth	10	65	2,219	34.14	19	106	32.51	2	8	0
60 Delaware St.	12	66	2,326	35.24	27	191	32.35	4	8	0
61 Davidson	10	52	1,848	35.54	27	166	32.35	7	3	0
62 Canisius	11	79	2,896	36.66	42	344	32.3	2	9	0
63 Pennsylvania	10	53	1,933	36.47	23	230	32.13	9	1	0
64 Central Conn. St.	11	82	2,929	35.72	46	316	31.87	5	6	0
65 Gardner-Webb	10	36	1,380	38.33	21	233	31.86	9	1	0
66 Weber St.	11	52	1,920	36.92	33	273	31.67	3	8	0
67 Sacramento St.	12	66	2,415	36.59	34	328	31.62	5	7	0
68 Albany (N.Y.)	12	63	2,303	36.56	27	315	31.56	8	4	0
69 Fairfield	11	69	2,777	40.25	47	604	31.49	5	6	0
70 Portland St.	11	60	2,142	35.7	27	255	31.45	6	5	0
71 Brown	10	50	1,887	37.74	29	316	31.42	2	8	0
72 Valparaiso	11	52	1,865	35.87	25	232	31.4	1	10	0
73 Richmond	11	63	2,207	35.03	33	233	31.33	4	7	0
74 Cornell	10	64	2,170	33.91	35	165	31.33	4	6	0
75 Charleston So.	12	68	2,454	36.09	33	327	31.28	4	8	0
76 Wagner	11	60	1,981	33.02	29	105	31.27	7	4	0
77 Samford	11	56	2,052	36.64	30	303	31.23	4	7	0
78 Colgate	12	62	2,207	35.6	29	283	31.03	9	3	0
79 Southeast Mo. St.	12	40	1,385	34.63	19	147	30.95	8	4	0
80 Morehead St.	12	53	1,901	35.87	31	268	30.81	9	3	0
81 Fla. Atlantic	11	81	2,959	36.53	43	473	30.69	2	9	0
82 Stony Brook	10	62	2,028	32.71	25	133	30.56	8	2	0
83 Southwest Mo. St.	11	56	1,937	34.59	26	227	30.54	4	7	0
84 Stephen F. Austin	11	55	1,901	34.56	24	227	30.44	6	5	0
85 Tennessee St.	12	66	2,214	33.55	30	216	30.27	2	10	0
86 Morris Brown	12	89	3,164	35.55	51	471	30.26	1	11	0
87 Liberty	11	55	1,929	35.07	27	267	30.22	2	9	0
88 La Salle	11	71	2,445	34.44	30	313	30.03	2	9	0
89 Florida A&M	12	74	2,634	35.59	35	415	29.99	7	5	0
90 Princeton	10	47	1,544	32.85	17	136	29.96	6	4	0
91 Lehigh	12	59	2,036	34.51	23	279	29.78	8	4	0
92 Northwestern St.	13	77	2,755	35.78	36	473	29.64	9	4	0
93 Texas Southern	11	65	2,299	35.37	35	380	29.52	4	7	0
94 Butler	10	56	1,837	32.8	29	185	29.5	4	6	0
95 Eastern Ill.	12	57	1,926	33.79	24	248	29.44	8	4	0
96 Yale	10	55	1,720	31.27	21	118	29.13	6	4	0
97 Mississippi Val.	11	74	2,557	34.55	32	409	29.03	5	6	0
98 Youngstown St.	11	68	2,416	35.53	39	444	29	7	4	0
99 Holy Cross	12	53	1,778	33.55	23	244	28.94	4	8	0
100 St. Peter's	11	67	2,310	34.48	35	374	28.9	6	5	0
101 Howard	11	59	2,013	34.12	22	319	28.71	6	5	0
102 St. John's (N.Y.)	10	70	2,349	33.56	41	346	28.61	2	8	0
103 Bethune-Cookman	13	65	2,066	31.78	26	209	28.57	11	2	0
104 St. Francis (Pa.)	10	74	2,401	32.45	31	288	28.55	2	8	0
105 Indiana St.	12	68	2,355	34.63	36	414	28.54	5	7	0
106 Duquesne	12	58	1,953	33.67	27	299	28.52	11	1	0
107 Marist	11	70	2,221	31.73	37	239	28.31	7	4	0
108 Grambling	13	57	1,948	34.18	31	344	28.14	11	2	0
109 Tennessee Tech	12	56	1,921	34.3	30	346	28.13	5	7	0
110 Bucknell	11	74	2,603	35.18	52	524	28.09	2	9	0
111 Southern U.	12	70	2,368	33.83	38	414	27.91	6	6	0
112 Ark.-Pine Bluff	11	73	2,859	39.16	50	834	27.74	3	8	0
113 Prairie View	11	71	2,334	32.87	29	370	27.66	1	10	0

Rank, School	G	Punts	Yds	Avg	Ret	Rtyd	NetAvg	W	L	T
114 Siena	10	75	2,492	33.23	52	427	27.53	3	7	0
115 Jacksonville	10	67	2,283	34.07	33	454	27.3	3	7	0
116 Villanova	15	61	2,064	33.84	34	432	26.75	11	4	0
117 Harvard	10	55	1,955	35.55	34	487	26.69	7	3	0
118 Robert Morris	10	61	2,251	36.9	37	631	26.56	3	7	0
119 Jackson St.	11	42	1,347	32.07	18	235	26.48	7	4	0
120 Iona	11	63	1,979	31.41	24	333	26.13	5	6	0
121 Norfolk St.	11	79	2,364	29.92	39	320	25.87	5	6	0
122 Tenn.-Martin	12	70	2,206	31.51	34	417	25.56	2	10	0
123 Savannah St.	10	70	2,151	30.73	41	478	23.9	1	9	0

Passing Offense

Rank, School	G	Att	Com	Int	Pct	Yds	YdsAtt	TD	Yds/Gm	IPct	YdCp	W	L	T
1 Grambling	13	574	277	18	48.26	4,689	8.17	45	360.7	3.14	16.93	11	2	0
2 Jackson St.	11	426	244	14	57.28	3,519	8.26	31	319.9	3.29	14.42	7	4	0
3 Eastern Wash.	11	444	267	7	60.14	3,493	7.87	33	317.5	1.58	13.08	6	5	0
4 Valparaiso	11	412	221	19	53.64	3,465	8.41	24	315	4.61	15.68	1	10	0
5 Drake	10	380	214	15	56.32	3,360	8.84	32	305.5	3.95	15.7	5	5	0
6 Brown	10	421	274	16	65.08	2,963	7.04	21	296.3	3.8	10.81	2	8	0
7 Pennsylvania	10	384	250	13	65.1	2,962	7.71	23	296.2	3.39	11.85	9	1	0
8 Dartmouth	10	426	255	10	59.86	2,931	6.88	19	293.1	2.35	11.49	3	7	0
9 Villanova	15	587	388	14	66.1	4,303	7.33	36	286.9	2.39	11.09	11	4	0
10 Southeast Mo. St.	12	413	264	18	63.92	3,442	8.33	34	286.8	4.36	13.04	8	4	0
11 Idaho St.	11	414	248	12	59.9	3,074	7.43	22	279.5	2.9	12.4	8	3	0
12 San Diego	10	319	195	4	61.13	2,781	8.72	26	278.1	1.25	14.26	5	5	0
13 Eastern Ill.	12	423	263	17	62.17	3,213	7.6	34	267.8	4.02	12.22	8	4	0
14 Harvard	10	337	218	5	64.69	2,627	7.8	17	262.7	1.48	12.05	7	3	0
15 Ark.-Pine Bluff	11	408	177	21	43.38	2,857	7	23	259.7	5.15	16.14	3	8	0
16 Weber St.	11	399	225	15	56.39	2,781	6.97	20	252.8	3.76	12.36	3	8	0
17 Sacramento St.	12	388	230	7	59.28	3,019	7.78	18	251.6	1.8	13.13	5	7	0
18 Florida A&M	12	425	224	19	52.71	3,009	7.08	25	250.8	4.47	13.43	7	5	0
19 Morehead St.	12	370	204	19	55.14	2,994	8.09	20	249.5	5.14	14.68	9	3	0
20 William & Mary	11	343	207	9	60.35	2,741	7.99	24	249.2	2.62	13.24	6	5	0
21 Duquesne	12	399	210	14	52.63	2,947	7.39	30	245.6	3.51	14.03	11	1	0
22 Montana	14	480	273	10	56.88	3,438	7.16	23	245.6	2.08	12.59	11	3	0
23 Fordham	13	411	253	9	61.56	3,188	7.76	23	245.2	2.19	12.6	10	3	0
24 Tennessee Tech	12	364	197	14	54.12	2,923	8.03	22	243.6	3.85	14.84	5	7	0
25 Western Caro.	11	370	201	13	54.32	2,679	7.24	13	243.5	3.51	13.33	5	6	0
26 Western Ill.	13	345	196	5	56.81	3,159	9.16	23	243	1.45	16.12	11	2	0
27 Davidson	10	337	187	12	55.49	2,337	6.93	27	233.7	3.56	12.5	7	3	0
28 Columbia	10	411	237	10	57.66	2,298	5.59	7	229.8	2.43	9.7	1	9	0
29 Southern U.	12	482	242	17	50.21	2,748	5.7	20	229	3.53	11.36	6	6	0
30 Hofstra	12	442	249	13	56.33	2,743	6.21	17	228.6	2.94	11.02	6	6	0
31 Tennessee St.	12	357	170	22	47.62	2,727	7.64	19	227.3	6.16	16.04	2	10	0
32 La Salle	11	404	194	16	48.02	2,498	6.18	12	227.1	3.96	12.88	2	9	0
33 Montana St.	13	438	234	9	53.42	2,943	6.72	23	226.4	2.05	12.58	7	6	0
34 Texas Southern	11	331	168	21	50.76	2,471	7.47	19	224.6	6.34	14.71	4	7	0
35 Lafayette	12	403	222	15	55.09	2,679	6.65	20	223.3	3.72	12.07	7	5	0
36 Gardner-Webb	10	338	201	4	59.47	2,220	6.57	17	222	1.18	11.04	9	1	0
37 Samford	11	389	215	13	55.27	2,439	6.27	16	221.7	3.34	11.34	4	7	0
38 Stephen F. Austin	11	309	175	13	56.63	2,430	7.86	15	220.9	4.21	13.89	6	5	0
39 Chattanooga	12	392	227	14	57.91	2,645	6.75	22	220.4	3.57	11.65	2	10	0
40 Citadel	12	391	208	12	53.2	2,638	6.75	18	219.8	3.07	12.68	3	9	0
41 Furman	12	301	201	9	66.78	2,619	8.7	18	218.3	2.99	13.03	8	4	0
42 Princeton	10	296	161	11	54.39	2,172	7.34	12	217.2	3.72	13.49	6	4	0
43 Northern Ariz.	11	324	181	17	55.86	2,379	7.34	13	216.3	5.25	13.14	6	5	0
44 Towson	11	322	171	11	53.11	2,366	7.35	17	215.1	3.42	13.84	6	5	0
45 Colgate	12	321	184	8	57.32	2,580	8.04	12	215	2.49	14.02	9	3	0
46 Mississippi Val.	11	378	204	14	53.97	2,356	6.23	16	214.2	3.7	11.55	5	6	0
47 Alcorn St.	11	359	161	17	44.85	2,259	6.29	20	205.4	4.74	14.03	6	5	0
48 Jacksonville	10	305	172	13	56.39	2,050	6.72	11	205	4.26	11.92	3	7	0
49 VMI	12	360	187	14	51.94	2,457	6.83	17	204.8	3.89	13.14	6	6	0
50 Massachusetts	12	360	189	17	52.5	2,447	6.8	19	203.9	4.72	12.95	8	4	0
51 Yale	10	270	153	6	56.67	2,014	7.46	17	201.4	2.22	13.16	6	4	0
52 Alabama St.	12	437	215	21	49.2	2,414	5.52	24	201.2	4.81	11.23	6	6	0
53 Northern Iowa	11	335	169	18	50.45	2,207	6.59	11	200.6	5.37	13.06	5	6	0
53 Portland St.	11	329	177	14	53.8	2,207	6.71	13	200.6	4.26	12.47	6	5	0
55 Florida Int'l	11	271	149	14	54.98	2,191	8.08	20	199.2	5.17	14.7	5	6	0
56 Holy Cross	12	367	197	14	53.68	2,381	6.49	21	198.4	3.81	12.09	4	8	0
57 Fairfield	11	356	178	17	50	2,139	6.01	11	194.5	4.78	12.02	5	6	0
58 Sam Houston St.	11	358	182	13	50.84	2,138	5.97	10	194.4	3.63	11.75	4	7	0
59 Butler	10	267	141	16	52.81	1,935	7.25	11	193.5	5.99	13.72	4	6	0
60 Lehigh	12	360	193	14	53.61	2,300	6.39	16	191.7	3.89	11.92	8	4	0
61 Charleston So.	12	380	190	21	50	2,273	5.98	15	189.4	5.53	11.96	4	8	0
62 Illinois St.	11	338	165	12	48.82	2,050	6.07	11	186.4	3.55	12.42	6	5	0
63 Northwestern St.	13	335	176	13	52.54	2,416	7.21	17	185.8	3.88	13.73	9	4	0
64 Robert Morris	10	272	138	13	50.74	1,855	6.82	8	185.5	4.78	13.44	3	7	0
65 Southwest Mo. St.	11	305	166	11	54.43	2,035	6.67	14	185	3.61	12.26	4	7	0
66 Georgetown	11	290	153	8	52.76	2,019	6.96	18	183.5	2.76	13.2	5	6	0
67 N.C. A&T	12	368	189	12	51.36	2,175	5.91	15	181.3	3.26	11.51	4	8	0
68 Appalachian St.	12	342	192	11	56.14	2,169	6.34	16	180.8	3.22	11.3	8	4	0
69 South Carolina St.	12	249	135	14	54.22	2,116	8.5	16	176.3	5.62	15.67	7	5	0
70 Bethune-Cookman	13	310	159	17	51.29	2,287	7.38	13	175.9	5.48	14.38	11	2	0

Rank, School	G	Att	Com	Int	Pct	Yds	YdsAtt	TD	Yds/Gm	IPct	YdCp	W	L	T
71 McNeese St.	15	373	207	11	55.5	2,629	7.05	16	175.3	2.95	12.7	13	2	0
72 Hampton	12	298	150	9	50.34	2,070	6.95	14	172.5	3.02	13.8	7	5	0
73 Cal Poly	11	310	145	16	46.77	1,892	6.1	8	172	5.16	13.05	3	8	0
74 Delaware	12	328	170	6	51.83	2,063	6.29	10	171.9	1.83	12.14	6	6	0
75 Cornell	10	307	148	11	48.21	1,710	5.57	7	171	3.58	11.55	4	6	0
76 Bucknell	11	314	178	20	56.69	1,880	5.99	10	170.9	6.37	10.56	2	9	0
77 St. John's (N.Y.)	10	294	130	12	44.22	1,705	5.8	16	170.5	4.08	13.12	2	8	0
78 Morgan St.	12	274	118	12	43.07	2,040	7.45	18	170	4.38	17.29	7	5	0
79 New Hampshire	11	310	176	14	56.77	1,856	5.99	12	168.7	4.52	10.55	3	8	0
80 Liberty	11	277	122	15	44.04	1,837	6.63	19	167	5.42	15.06	2	9	0
81 Sacred Heart	10	280	135	11	48.21	1,643	5.87	14	164.3	3.93	12.17	7	3	0
82 James Madison	12	249	126	15	50.6	1,962	7.88	7	163.5	6.02	15.57	5	7	0
83 Murray St.	12	276	174	7	63.04	1,950	7.07	15	162.5	2.54	11.21	7	5	0
84 Stony Brook	10	260	140	10	53.85	1,587	6.1	12	158.7	3.85	11.34	8	2	0
85 Maine	14	348	185	11	53.16	2,214	6.36	22	158.1	3.16	11.97	11	3	0
86 Fla. Atlantic	11	254	122	8	48.03	1,711	6.74	10	155.5	3.15	14.02	2	9	0
87 Eastern Ky.	12	238	129	11	54.2	1,808	7.6	11	150.7	4.62	14.02	8	4	0
88 Morris Brown	12	361	148	18	41	1,794	4.97	8	149.5	4.99	12.12	1	11	0
89 Howard	11	295	136	15	46.1	1,644	5.57	18	149.5	5.08	12.09	6	5	0
90 Austin Peay	12	315	156	10	49.52	1,793	5.69	9	149.4	3.17	11.49	7	5	0
91 Indiana St.	12	278	147	11	52.88	1,754	6.31	12	146.2	3.96	11.93	5	7	0
92 Norfolk St.	11	284	134	12	47.18	1,550	5.46	5	140.9	4.23	11.57	5	6	0
93 Savannah St.	10	277	107	18	38.63	1,336	4.82	4	133.6	6.5	12.49	1	9	0
94 Richmond	11	193	86	10	44.56	1,466	7.6	10	133.3	5.18	17.05	4	7	0
95 Northeastern	13	267	131	8	49.06	1,712	6.41	18	131.7	3	13.07	10	3	0
96 Iona	11	242	105	21	43.39	1,446	5.98	7	131.5	8.68	13.77	5	6	0
97 Prairie View	11	293	123	17	41.98	1,444	4.93	8	131.3	5.8	11.74	1	10	0
98 Jacksonville St.	11	273	120	11	43.96	1,423	5.21	11	129.4	4.03	11.86	5	6	0
99 Delaware St.	12	233	115	15	49.36	1,550	6.65	13	129.2	6.44	13.48	4	8	0
100 Wagner	11	219	112	13	51.14	1,420	6.48	6	129.1	5.94	12.68	7	4	0
101 Monmouth	10	245	96	10	39.18	1,260	5.14	7	126	4.08	13.13	2	8	0
102 Tenn.-Martin	12	204	99	12	48.53	1,456	7.14	5	121.3	5.88	14.71	2	10	0
103 Dayton	12	163	79	4	48.47	1,454	8.92	7	121.2	2.45	18.41	11	1	0
104 East Tenn. St.	12	258	128	10	49.61	1,450	5.62	9	120.8	3.88	11.33	4	8	0
105 Southwest Tex. St.	11	187	109	8	58.29	1,313	7.02	9	119.4	4.28	12.05	4	7	0
106 Albany (N.Y.)	12	231	140	6	60.61	1,429	6.19	8	119.1	2.6	10.21	8	4	0
107 Alabama A&M	12	274	100	20	36.5	1,423	5.19	9	118.6	7.3	14.23	8	4	0
108 Southern Ill.	12	184	98	5	53.26	1,419	7.71	14	118.3	2.72	14.48	4	8	0
109 Central Conn. St.	11	264	113	15	42.8	1,292	4.89	6	117.5	5.68	11.43	5	6	0
110 Youngstown St.	11	178	88	6	49.44	1,280	7.19	7	116.4	3.37	14.55	7	4	0
111 Western Ky.	15	168	101	6	60.12	1,686	10.04	9	112.4	3.57	16.69	12	3	0
112 Canisius	11	282	104	27	36.88	1,190	4.22	6	108.2	9.57	11.44	2	9	0
113 St. Francis (Pa.)	10	249	86	18	34.54	1,068	4.29	3	106.8	7.23	12.42	2	8	0
114 Marist	11	230	82	10	35.65	1,123	4.88	5	102.1	4.35	13.7	7	4	0
115 Southern Utah	11	153	58	14	37.91	1,006	6.58	4	91.5	9.15	17.34	1	10	0
116 Siena	10	171	70	8	40.94	850	4.97	6	85	4.68	12.14	3	7	0
117 Ga. Southern	14	122	54	4	44.26	1,168	9.57	3	83.4	3.28	21.63	11	3	0
118 St. Mary's (Cal.)	12	138	70	6	50.72	977	7.08	7	81.4	4.35	13.96	6	6	0
119 Rhode Island	12	155	66	7	42.58	830	5.35	2	69.2	4.52	12.58	3	9	0
120 Elon	11	124	53	12	42.74	744	6	6	67.6	9.68	14.04	4	7	0
121 St. Peter's	11	193	77	14	39.9	715	3.7	5	65	7.25	9.29	6	5	0
122 Nicholls St.	11	79	36	7	45.57	680	8.61	3	61.8	8.86	18.89	7	4	0
123 Wofford	12	108	55	3	50.93	681	6.31	3	56.8	2.78	12.38	9	3	0

Pass Defense

Rank, School	G	Att	Com	Pct	Yds/Cmp	Int	IPct	Yds	Yds/Att	TD	Yds/Gm	CM	W	L	T
1 Robert Morris	10	164	69	42.07	13.17	13	7.93	909	5.54	6	90.9	1	3	7	0
2 Duquesne	12	256	104	40.63	10.96	25	9.77	1,140	4.45	5	95	0	11	1	0
3 Wagner	11	207	102	49.28	10.54	12	5.8	1,075	5.19	5	97.73	0	7	4	0
4 St. Francis (Pa.)	10	220	92	41.82	11.71	11	5	1,077	4.9	6	107.7	1	2	8	0
5 Sacred Heart	10	252	87	34.52	12.54	19	7.54	1,091	4.33	4	109.1	0	7	3	0
6 Florida Int'l	11	221	123	55.66	10.46	10	4.52	1,287	5.82	6	117	0	5	6	0
7 Bethune-Cookman	13	298	120	40.27	13.77	21	7.05	1,652	5.54	7	127.08	1	11	2	0
8 Hofstra	12	261	139	53.26	11.32	7	2.68	1,573	6.03	12	131.08	2	6	6	0
9 Maine	14	333	153	45.95	12.12	20	6.01	1,854	5.57	11	132.43	0	11	3	0
10 Morehead St.	12	314	146	46.5	11.31	20	6.37	1,651	5.26	1	137.58	1	9	3	0
11 Siena	10	263	129	49.05	10.68	12	4.56	1,378	5.24	10	137.8	1	3	7	0
12 Stony Brook	10	268	142	52.99	9.79	12	4.48	1,390	5.19	6	139	0	8	2	0
13 Stephen F. Austin	11	273	132	48.35	12	12	4.4	1,584	5.8	5	144	0	6	5	0
14 Wofford	12	286	174	60.84	9.97	11	3.85	1,734	6.06	10	144.5	2	9	3	0
15 New Hampshire	11	264	145	54.92	11.04	10	3.79	1,601	6.06	12	145.55	0	3	8	0
16 South Carolina St.	12	278	130	46.76	13.56	17	6.12	1,763	6.34	11	146.92	0	7	5	0
17 Gardner-Webb	10	211	110	52.13	13.53	16	7.58	1,488	7.05	9	148.8	0	9	1	0
18 Youngstown St.	11	280	153	54.64	10.78	9	3.21	1,650	5.89	8	150	1	7	4	0
19 Monmouth	10	252	121	48.02	12.47	6	2.38	1,509	5.99	8	150.9	2	2	8	0
20 Villanova	15	400	206	51.5	11.05	15	3.75	2,276	5.69	8	151.73	1	11	4	0
21 Florida A&M	12	302	140	46.36	13.05	16	5.3	1,827	6.05	21	152.25	0	7	5	0
22 Furman	12	297	176	59.26	10.39	17	5.72	1,829	6.16	10	152.42	0	8	4	0
23 Ga. Southern	14	385	180	46.75	11.97	15	3.9	2,154	5.59	10	153.86	1	11	3	0
24 Nicholls St.	11	284	153	53.87	11.07	12	4.23	1,694	5.96	6	154	0	7	4	0
25 Indiana St.	12	252	153	60.71	12.12	9	3.57	1,854	7.36	17	154.5	0	5	7	0
26 East Tenn. St.	12	295	151	51.19	12.42	14	4.75	1,875	6.36	8	156.25	1	4	8	0

Rank, School	G	Att	Com	Pct	Yds/Cmp	Int	IPct	Yds	Yds/Att	TD	Yds/Gm	CM	W	L	T
27 Sam Houston St.	11	255	152	59.61	11.34	9	3.53	1,723	6.76	15	156.64	0	4	7	0
28 Appalachian St.	12	279	137	49.1	13.84	12	4.3	1,896	6.8	15	158	1	8	4	0
29 Lehigh	12	338	166	49.11	11.46	12	3.55	1,903	5.63	8	158.58	0	8	4	0
30 Western Ky.	15	348	174	50	13.82	20	5.75	2,404	6.91	10	160.27	1	12	3	0
31 La Salle	11	241	119	49.38	14.92	6	2.49	1,776	7.37	14	161.45	1	2	9	0
32 William & Mary	11	292	140	47.95	12.71	15	5.14	1,779	6.09	19	161.73	1	6	5	0
33 Iona	11	286	156	54.55	11.41	9	3.15	1,780	6.22	12	161.82	2	5	6	0
34 Canisius	11	250	127	50.8	14.16	11	4.4	1,798	7.19	13	163.45	0	2	9	0
35 Southwest Mo. St.	11	259	155	59.85	11.75	11	4.25	1,821	7.03	12	165.55	1	4	7	0
36 St. John's (N.Y.)	10	233	103	44.21	16.08	13	5.58	1,656	7.11	13	165.6	2	2	8	0
37 McNeese St.	15	398	168	42.21	14.83	20	5.03	2,491	6.26	15	166.07	0	13	2	0
38 Illinois St.	11	252	133	52.78	13.74	4	1.59	1,827	7.25	16	166.09	0	6	5	0
39 Mississippi Val.	11	324	154	47.53	11.9	18	5.56	1,833	5.66	12	166.64	4	5	6	0
40 Fairfield	11	299	124	41.47	14.89	16	5.35	1,846	6.17	15	167.82	1	5	6	0
41 Howard	11	285	126	44.21	14.71	15	5.26	1,854	6.51	11	168.55	1	6	5	0
42 Marist	11	299	116	38.8	16.1	15	5.02	1,868	6.25	16	169.82	2	7	4	0
43 St. Peter's	11	286	138	48.25	13.68	15	5.24	1,888	6.6	17	171.64	2	6	5	0
44 James Madison	12	318	196	61.64	10.57	9	2.83	2,072	6.52	19	172.67	0	5	7	0
45 Southwest Tex. St.	11	221	131	59.28	14.51	11	4.98	1,901	8.6	9	172.82	0	4	7	0
46 Fla. Atlantic	11	252	143	56.75	13.42	6	2.38	1,919	7.62	16	174.45	1	2	9	0
47 Charleston So.	12	338	172	50.89	12.31	16	4.73	2,117	6.26	17	176.42	3	4	8	0
48 Northwestern St.	13	346	185	53.47	12.45	9	2.6	2,304	6.66	17	177.23	1	9	4	0
49 Savannah St.	10	250	129	51.6	13.76	10	4	1,775	7.1	12	177.5	1	1	9	0
50 Eastern Ky.	12	309	138	44.66	15.44	12	3.88	2,131	6.9	14	177.58	0	8	4	0
51 Bucknell	11	315	174	55.24	11.25	8	2.54	1,958	6.22	21	178	0	2	9	0
52 Richmond	11	264	151	57.2	13.09	14	5.3	1,977	7.49	11	179.73	0	4	7	0
53 Southern U.	12	355	161	45.35	13.45	14	3.94	2,166	6.1	20	180.5	0	6	6	0
54 Central Conn. St.	11	317	173	54.57	11.49	17	5.36	1,987	6.27	15	180.64	1	5	6	0
55 Northern Iowa	11	304	153	50.33	13.05	13	4.28	1,997	6.57	14	181.55	0	5	6	0
56 Western Ill.	13	373	187	50.13	12.74	15	4.02	2,383	6.39	13	183.31	0	11	2	0
57 Holy Cross	12	272	167	61.4	13.22	6	2.21	2,207	8.11	19	183.92	0	4	8	0
58 Southern Utah	12	259	150	57.92	13.51	4	1.54	2,026	7.82	19	184.18	1	1	10	0
59 Delaware St.	12	338	188	55.62	11.85	12	3.55	2,228	6.59	17	185.67	2	4	8	0
60 Jacksonville St.	11	261	138	52.87	14.82	12	4.6	2,045	7.84	15	185.91	1	5	6	0
61 Fordham	13	398	225	56.53	10.86	15	3.77	2,443	6.14	11	187.92	0	10	3	0
62 N.C. A&T	12	344	166	48.26	13.68	27	7.85	2,271	6.6	16	189.25	0	4	8	0
63 Morgan St.	12	301	147	48.84	15.5	7	2.33	2,278	7.57	18	189.83	4	7	5	0
64 Murray St.	12	340	205	60.29	11.13	13	3.82	2,281	6.71	17	190.08	0	7	5	0
65 Hampton	12	356	171	48.03	13.42	12	3.37	2,294	6.44	12	191.17	3	7	5	0
66 Jackson St.	11	368	169	45.92	12.62	15	4.08	2,132	5.79	14	193.82	1	7	4	0
67 Northeastern	12	401	205	51.12	12.34	16	3.99	2,529	6.31	14	194.54	1	10	3	0
68 Montana St.	13	413	209	50.61	12.15	9	2.18	2,540	6.15	14	195.38	0	7	6	0
69 Morris Brown	12	325	160	49.23	14.74	15	4.62	2,359	7.26	22	196.58	1	1	11	0
70 Citadel	12	276	165	59.78	14.32	10	3.62	2,362	8.56	15	196.83	0	3	9	0
71 Grambling	13	405	184	45.43	13.97	24	5.93	2,571	6.35	22	197.77	1	11	2	0
72 Tenn.-Martin	12	329	197	59.88	12.07	12	3.65	2,377	7.22	21	198.08	1	2	10	0
73 Cal Poly	11	265	141	53.21	15.61	11	4.15	2,201	8.31	10	200.09	1	3	8	0
74 Albany (N.Y.)	12	364	185	50.82	12.99	11	3.02	2,403	6.6	21	200.25	1	8	4	0
75 Eastern Wash.	11	336	189	56.25	11.79	10	2.98	2,229	6.63	18	202.64	0	6	5	0
76 Norfolk St.	11	315	153	48.57	14.58	13	4.13	2,230	7.08	21	202.73	1	5	6	0
77 Western Caro.	11	307	159	51.79	14.07	8	2.61	2,237	7.29	15	203.36	0	5	6	0
78 Alabama A&M	12	409	187	45.72	13.16	17	4.16	2,461	6.02	15	205.08	1	8	4	0
79 Liberty	11	317	185	58.36	12.23	9	2.84	2,263	7.14	14	205.73	6	2	9	0
80 Princeton	10	374	199	53.21	10.37	16	4.28	2,063	5.52	12	206.3	2	6	4	0
81 Southern Ill.	12	324	176	54.32	14.22	12	3.7	2,502	7.72	22	208.5	0	4	8	0
82 Massachusetts	12	398	210	52.76	11.92	20	5.03	2,503	6.29	14	208.58	0	8	4	0
83 St. Mary's (Cal.)	12	334	188	56.29	13.33	21	6.29	2,506	7.5	18	208.83	0	6	6	0
84 Chattanooga	12	340	202	59.41	12.44	5	1.47	2,512	7.39	20	209.33	1	2	10	0
85 Prairie View	11	296	153	51.69	15.12	9	3.04	2,313	7.81	24	210.27	2	1	10	0
86 Idaho St.	11	355	180	50.7	12.87	16	4.51	2,316	6.52	15	210.55	0	8	3	0
87 Texas Southern	11	350	156	44.57	14.85	19	5.43	2,317	6.62	21	210.64	1	4	7	0
88 Tennessee Tech	12	329	198	60.18	12.77	10	3.04	2,529	7.69	19	210.75	2	5	7	0
89 Delaware	12	370	206	55.68	12.42	9	2.43	2,558	6.91	14	213.17	1	6	6	0
90 Lafayette	12	378	203	53.7	12.62	11	2.91	2,561	6.78	17	213.42	0	7	5	0
91 VMI	12	338	187	55.33	13.73	12	3.55	2,567	7.59	21	213.92	1	6	6	0
92 Yale	10	306	178	58.17	12.07	5	1.63	2,149	7.02	12	214.9	0	6	4	0
93 Austin Peay	12	372	201	54.03	12.84	16	4.3	2,581	6.94	22	215.08	1	7	5	0
94 Tennessee St.	12	348	183	52.59	14.11	11	3.16	2,583	7.42	22	215.25	0	2	10	0
95 Ark.-Pine Bluff	11	368	169	45.92	14.11	16	4.35	2,385	6.48	29	216.82	1	3	8	0
96 Dayton	12	434	203	46.77	12.89	28	6.45	2,617	6.03	8	218.08	0	11	1	0
97 Alcorn St.	11	365	159	43.56	15.19	17	4.66	2,415	6.62	21	219.55	1	6	5	0
98 Pennsylvania	10	388	215	55.41	10.22	20	5.15	2,198	5.66	7	219.8	0	9	1	0
99 Jacksonville	10	275	148	53.82	14.97	10	3.64	2,216	8.06	23	221.6	2	3	7	0
100 Towson	11	375	191	50.93	12.83	18	4.8	2,451	6.54	15	222.82	1	6	5	0
101 Samford	11	274	163	59.49	15.19	11	4.01	2,476	9.04	21	225.09	0	4	7	0
102 Weber St.	11	313	182	58.15	13.64	7	2.24	2,482	7.93	16	225.64	1	3	8	0
103 Davidson	10	328	184	56.1	12.34	9	2.74	2,271	6.92	17	227.1	0	7	3	0
104 Montana	14	460	248	53.91	12.94	16	3.48	3,209	6.98	16	229.21	0	11	3	0
105 Alabama St.	12	425	189	44.47	14.76	20	4.71	2,790	6.56	15	232.5	3	6	6	0
106 Southeast Mo. St.	12	370	220	59.46	12.74	13	3.51	2,803	7.58	20	233.58	1	8	4	0
107 Brown	10	327	200	61.16	11.74	9	2.75	2,348	7.18	19	234.8	2	2	8	0
108 Columbia	10	320	198	61.88	11.88	7	2.19	2,352	7.35	16	235.2	1	1	9	0
109 Cornell	10	309	203	65.7	11.76	9	2.91	2,387	7.72	16	238.7	1	4	6	0

Rank, School	G	Att	Com	Pct	Yds/Cmp	Int	IPct	Yds	Yds/Att	TD	Yds/Gm	CM	W	L	T
110 San Diego	10	290	168	57.93	14.33	13	4.48	2,408	8.3	22	240.8	2	5	5	0
111 Elon	11	292	165	56.51	16.09	10	3.42	2,655	9.09	27	241.36	2	4	7	0
112 Harvard	10	342	183	53.51	13.2	11	3.22	2,416	7.06	22	241.6	0	7	3	0
113 Valparaiso	11	277	153	55.23	17.47	4	1.44	2,673	9.65	31	243	2	1	10	0
114 Portland St.	11	387	243	62.79	11.09	11	2.84	2,694	6.96	18	244.91	1	6	5	0
115 Rhode Island	12	334	214	64.07	13.89	8	2.4	2,972	8.9	25	247.67	1	3	9	0
116 Eastern Ill.	12	362	202	55.8	14.86	9	2.49	3,002	8.29	24	250.17	3	8	4	0
117 Drake	10	326	187	57.36	14.74	7	2.15	2,756	8.45	20	250.55	0	5	5	0
118 Georgetown	11	354	211	59.6	13.24	12	3.39	2,794	7.89	22	254	0	5	6	0
119 Northern Ariz.	11	385	210	54.55	13.41	15	3.9	2,816	7.31	21	256	0	6	5	0
120 Sacramento St.	12	414	254	61.35	12.35	10	2.42	3,138	7.58	24	261.5	2	5	7	0
121 Colgate	12	432	250	57.87	12.64	14	3.24	3,160	7.31	14	263.33	1	9	3	0
122 Butler	10	302	175	57.95	15.45	10	3.31	2,704	8.95	22	270.4	0	4	6	0
123 Dartmouth	10	341	222	65.1	12.4	7	2.05	2,752	8.07	21	275.2	0	3	7	0

Passing Efficiency

Rank, School	G	Att	Com	Pct	Int	IPct	Yds	Yds/Att	TD	TDPct	Rating	W	L	T
1 San Diego	10	319	195	61.13	4	1.25	2,781	8.72	26	8.15	158.72	5	5	0
2 Western Ky.	15	168	101	60.12	6	3.57	1,686	10.04	9	5.36	154.94	12	3	0
3 Furman	12	301	201	66.78	9	2.99	2,619	8.7	18	5.98	153.64	8	4	0
4 Western Ill.	13	345	196	56.81	5	1.45	3,159	9.16	23	6.67	152.82	11	2	0
5 Southeast Mo. St.	12	413	264	63.92	18	4.36	3,442	8.33	34	8.23	152.36	8	4	0
6 Drake	10	380	214	56.32	15	3.95	3,360	8.84	32	8.42	150.47	5	5	0
7 Eastern Wash.	11	444	267	60.14	7	1.58	3,493	7.87	33	7.43	147.56	6	5	0
8 Eastern Ill.	12	423	263	62.17	17	4.02	3,213	7.6	34	8.04	144.49	8	4	0
9 Jackson St.	11	426	244	57.28	14	3.29	3,519	8.26	31	7.28	144.13	7	4	0
10 Harvard	10	337	218	64.69	5	1.48	2,627	7.8	17	5.04	143.86	7	3	0
11 William & Mary	11	343	207	60.35	9	2.62	2,741	7.99	22	6.41	143.34	6	5	0
12 Villanova	15	587	388	66.1	14	2.39	4,303	7.33	36	6.13	143.14	11	4	0
13 Pennsylvania	10	384	250	65.1	13	3.39	2,962	7.71	23	5.99	142.89	9	1	0
14 Ga. Southern	14	122	54	44.26	4	3.28	1,168	9.57	9	7.38	142.51	11	3	0
15 Fordham	13	411	253	61.56	9	2.19	3,188	7.76	23	5.6	140.84	10	3	0
16 Southern Ill.	12	184	98	53.26	5	2.72	1,419	7.71	14	7.61	137.75	4	8	0
17 Florida Int'l	11	271	149	54.98	14	5.17	2,191	8.08	20	7.38	136.94	5	6	0
18 Grambling	13	574	277	48.26	18	3.14	4,689	8.17	45	7.84	136.52	11	2	0
19 Sacramento St.	12	388	230	59.28	7	1.8	3,019	7.78	18	4.64	136.36	5	7	0
20 Yale	10	270	153	56.67	6	2.22	2,014	7.46	17	6.3	135.69	6	4	0
21 South Carolina St.	12	249	135	54.22	14	5.62	2,116	8.5	16	6.43	135.54	7	5	0
22 Murray St.	12	276	174	63.04	7	2.54	1,950	7.07	15	5.43	135.21	7	5	0
23 Valparaiso	11	412	221	53.64	19	4.61	3,465	8.41	24	5.83	134.25	1	10	0
24 Idaho St.	11	414	248	59.9	12	2.9	3,074	7.43	22	5.31	134.01	8	3	0
25 Tennessee Tech	12	364	197	54.12	14	3.85	2,923	8.03	22	6.04	133.81	5	7	0
26 Brown	10	421	274	65.08	16	3.8	2,963	7.04	21	4.99	133.08	2	8	0
27 Davidson	10	337	187	55.49	12	3.56	2,337	6.93	27	8.01	133.07	7	3	0
28 Dayton	12	163	79	48.47	4	2.45	1,454	8.92	7	4.29	132.69	11	1	0
29 Duquesne	12	399	210	52.63	14	3.51	2,947	7.39	30	7.52	132.44	11	1	0
30 Colgate	12	321	184	57.32	8	2.49	2,580	8.04	12	3.74	132.17	9	3	0
31 Morehead St.	12	370	204	55.14	19	5.14	2,994	8.09	20	5.41	130.64	9	3	0
32 Stephen F. Austin	11	309	175	56.63	13	4.21	2,430	7.86	15	4.85	130.26	6	5	0
33 Gardner-Webb	10	338	201	59.47	4	1.18	2,220	6.57	17	5.03	128.9	9	3	0
34 Montana	14	480	273	56.88	10	2.08	3,438	7.16	23	4.79	128.71	11	3	0
35 Dartmouth	10	426	255	59.86	10	2.35	2,931	6.88	19	4.46	127.72	3	7	0
36 Georgetown	11	290	153	52.76	8	2.76	2,019	6.96	18	6.21	126.25	5	6	0
37 Chattanooga	12	392	227	57.91	14	3.57	2,645	6.75	22	5.61	125.96	2	10	0
38 Towson	11	322	171	53.11	11	3.42	2,366	7.35	17	5.28	125.41	6	5	0
39 Southwest Tex. St.	11	187	109	58.29	8	4.28	1,313	7.02	9	4.81	124.61	4	7	0
40 Eastern Ky.	12	238	129	54.2	11	4.62	1,808	7.6	11	4.62	124.02	8	4	0
41 Weber St.	11	399	225	56.39	15	3.76	2,781	6.97	20	5.01	123.97	3	8	0
42 Montana St.	13	438	234	53.42	9	2.05	2,943	6.72	23	5.25	123.06	7	6	0
43 McNeese St.	15	373	207	55.5	11	2.95	2,629	7.05	16	4.29	122.96	13	2	0
44 Florida A&M	12	425	224	52.71	19	4.47	3,009	7.08	25	5.88	122.64	7	5	0
45 Northwestern St.	13	335	176	52.54	13	3.88	2,416	7.21	17	5.07	122.07	9	4	0
46 Princeton	10	296	161	54.39	11	3.72	2,172	7.34	12	4.05	121.98	6	4	0
47 Maine	14	348	185	53.16	11	3.16	2,214	6.36	22	6.32	121.18	11	3	0
48 Northern Ariz.	11	324	181	55.86	17	5.25	2,379	7.34	13	4.01	120.32	6	5	0
49 Lafayette	12	403	222	55.09	15	3.72	2,679	6.65	20	4.96	119.87	7	5	0
50 Texas Southern	11	331	168	50.76	21	6.34	2,471	7.47	19	5.74	119.76	4	7	0
51 Western Caro.	11	370	201	54.32	13	3.51	2,679	7.24	13	3.51	119.69	5	6	0
52 Holy Cross	12	367	197	53.68	14	3.81	2,381	6.49	21	5.72	119.45	4	8	0
53 Northeastern	13	267	131	49.06	8	3	1,712	6.41	18	6.74	119.22	10	3	0
54 Citadel	12	391	208	53.2	12	3.07	2,638	6.75	18	4.6	118.93	3	7	0
55 Albany (N.Y.)	12	231	140	60.61	6	2.6	1,429	6.19	8	3.46	118.8	8	4	0
56 Morgan St.	12	274	118	43.07	12	4.38	2,040	7.45	18	6.57	118.56	7	5	0
57 Appalachian St.	12	342	192	56.14	11	3.22	2,169	6.34	16	4.68	118.38	8	4	0
58 Southwest Mo. St.	11	305	166	54.43	11	3.61	2,035	6.67	14	4.59	118.38	4	7	0
59 St. Mary's (Cal.)	12	138	70	50.72	6	4.35	977	7.08	7	5.07	118.21	6	6	0
60 Hampton	12	298	150	50.34	9	3.02	2,070	6.95	14	4.7	118.11	7	5	0
61 Massachusetts	12	360	189	52.5	17	4.72	2,447	6.8	19	5.28	117.57	8	4	0

Rank, School	G	Att	Com	Pct	Int	IPct	Yds	Yds/Att	TD	TDPct	Rating	W	L	T
62 VMI	12	360	187	51.94	14	3.89	2,457	6.83	17	4.72	117.04	6	6	0
63 Tennessee St.	12	357	170	47.62	22	6.16	2,727	7.64	19	5.32	117	2	10	0
64 Jacksonville	10	305	172	56.39	13	4.26	2,050	6.72	11	3.61	116.24	3	7	0
65 Bethune-Cookman	13	310	159	51.29	17	5.48	2,287	7.38	13	4.19	116.14	11	2	0
66 Youngstown St.	11	178	88	49.44	6	3.37	1,280	7.19	7	3.93	116.04	7	4	0
67 Lehigh	12	360	193	53.61	14	3.89	2,300	6.39	18	5	115.99	8	4	0
68 Butler	10	267	141	52.81	16	5.99	1,935	7.25	11	4.12	115.29	4	6	0
69 Hofstra	12	442	249	56.33	13	2.94	2,743	6.21	17	3.85	115.24	6	6	0
70 Richmond	11	193	86	44.56	10	5.18	1,466	7.6	10	5.18	115.14	4	7	0
71 Samford	11	389	215	55.27	13	3.34	2,439	6.27	16	4.11	114.86	4	7	0
72 Portland St.	11	329	177	53.8	14	4.26	2,207	6.71	13	3.95	114.68	6	5	0
73 James Madison	12	249	126	50.6	15	6.02	1,962	7.88	7	2.81	114.02	5	7	0
74 Mississippi Val.	11	378	204	53.97	14	3.7	2,356	6.23	16	4.23	112.92	5	6	0
75 Nicholls St.	11	79	36	45.57	7	8.86	680	8.61	3	3.8	112.71	7	4	0
76 Stony Brook	10	260	140	53.85	10	3.85	1,587	6.1	12	4.62	112.61	8	2	0
77 Indiana St.	12	278	147	52.88	11	3.96	1,754	6.31	12	4.32	112.23	5	7	0
78 Liberty	11	277	122	44.04	15	5.42	1,837	6.63	19	6.86	111.51	2	9	0
79 Fla. Atlantic	11	254	122	48.03	8	3.15	1,711	6.74	10	3.94	111.28	2	9	0
80 Delaware	12	328	170	51.83	6	1.83	2,063	6.29	10	3.05	111.04	6	6	0
81 New Hampshire	11	310	176	56.77	14	4.52	1,856	5.99	12	3.87	110.83	3	8	0
82 Delaware St.	12	233	115	49.36	15	6.44	1,550	6.65	13	5.58	110.82	4	8	0
83 Ark.-Pine Bluff	11	408	177	43.38	21	5.15	2,857	7	23	5.64	110.53	3	8	0
84 Robert Morris	10	272	138	50.74	13	4.78	1,855	6.82	8	2.94	108.13	3	7	0
85 N.C. A&T	12	368	189	51.36	12	3.26	2,175	5.91	15	4.08	107.98	4	8	0
86 Wofford	12	108	55	50.93	3	2.78	681	6.31	3	2.78	107.48	9	3	0
87 Alcorn St.	11	359	161	44.85	17	4.74	2,259	6.29	20	5.57	106.57	6	5	0
88 Sacred Heart	10	280	135	48.21	11	3.93	1,643	5.87	14	5	106.13	7	3	0
89 Northern Iowa	11	335	169	50.45	18	5.37	2,207	6.59	11	3.28	105.83	5	6	0
90 Columbia	10	411	237	57.66	10	2.43	2,298	5.59	7	1.7	105.42	1	9	0
91 Tenn.-Martin	12	204	99	48.53	12	5.88	1,456	7.14	5	2.45	104.78	2	10	0
92 Bucknell	11	314	178	56.69	20	6.37	1,880	5.99	10	3.18	104.76	2	9	0
93 Southern U.	12	482	242	50.21	17	3.53	2,748	5.7	20	4.15	104.73	6	6	0
94 Alabama St.	12	437	215	49.2	21	4.81	2,414	5.52	24	5.49	104.11	6	6	0
95 Illinois St.	11	338	165	48.82	12	3.55	2,050	6.07	11	3.25	103.39	6	5	0
96 Sam Houston St.	11	358	182	50.84	13	3.63	2,138	5.97	10	2.79	102.92	4	7	0
97 Howard	11	295	136	46.1	15	5.08	1,644	5.57	18	6.1	102.88	6	5	0
98 Wagner	11	219	112	51.14	13	5.94	1,420	6.48	6	2.74	102.73	7	4	0
99 St. John's (N.Y.)	10	294	130	44.22	12	4.08	1,705	5.8	16	5.44	102.71	2	8	0
100 Charleston So.	12	380	190	50	21	5.53	2,273	5.98	15	3.95	102.22	4	8	0
101 La Salle	11	404	194	48.02	16	3.96	2,498	6.18	12	2.97	101.82	2	9	0
102 Fairfield	11	356	178	50	17	4.78	2,139	6.01	11	3.09	101.12	5	6	0
103 East Tenn. St.	12	258	128	49.61	10	3.88	1,450	5.62	9	3.49	100.57	4	8	0
104 Austin Peay	12	315	156	49.52	10	3.17	1,793	5.69	9	2.86	100.39	7	5	0
105 Cal Poly	11	310	145	46.77	16	5.16	1,892	6.1	8	2.58	96.26	3	8	0
106 Cornell	10	307	148	48.21	11	3.58	1,710	5.57	7	2.28	95.35	4	6	0
107 Jacksonville St.	11	273	120	43.96	11	4.03	1,423	5.21	11	4.03	93.02	5	6	0
108 Norfolk St.	11	284	134	47.18	12	4.23	1,550	5.46	5	1.76	90.4	5	6	0
109 Elon	11	124	53	42.74	12	9.68	744	6	6	4.84	89.71	4	7	0
110 Iona	11	242	105	43.39	21	8.68	1,446	5.98	7	2.89	85.78	5	6	0
111 Siena	10	171	70	40.94	8	4.68	850	4.97	6	3.51	84.88	3	7	0
112 Monmouth	10	245	96	39.18	10	4.08	1,260	5.14	7	2.86	83.67	2	8	0
113 Southern Utah	11	153	58	37.91	14	9.15	1,006	6.58	4	2.61	83.46	1	10	0
114 Rhode Island	12	155	66	42.58	7	4.52	830	5.35	2	1.29	82.81	3	9	0
115 Prairie View	11	293	123	41.98	17	5.8	1,444	4.93	8	2.73	80.8	1	10	0
116 Morris Brown	12	361	148	41	18	4.99	1,794	4.97	8	2.22	80.08	1	11	0
117 Central Conn. St.	11	264	113	42.8	15	5.68	1,292	4.89	6	2.27	80.05	5	6	0
118 Alabama A&M	12	274	100	36.5	20	7.3	1,423	5.19	9	3.28	76.37	8	4	0
119 Marist	11	230	82	35.65	10	4.35	1,123	4.88	5	2.17	75.19	7	4	0
120 Savannah St.	10	277	107	38.63	18	6.5	1,336	4.82	4	1.44	70.88	1	9	0
121 St. Peter's	11	193	77	39.9	14	7.25	715	3.7	5	2.59	65.06	6	5	0
122 Canisius	11	282	104	36.88	27	9.57	1,190	4.22	6	2.13	60.22	2	9	0
123 St. Francis (Pa.)	10	249	86	34.54	18	7.23	1,068	4.29	3	1.2	60.05	2	8	0

Passes Had Intercepted

Rank, School	No.	Rank, School	No.	Rank, School	No.	Rank, School	No.
1 Wofford	3	9 Western Ky.	6	26 William & Mary	9	40 Sacred Heart	11
2 Dayton	4	15 Sacramento St.	7	26 Hampton	9	40 Princeton	11
2 Ga. Southern	4	15 Rhode Island	7	26 Montana St.	9	40 McNeese St.	11
2 San Diego	4	15 Nicholls St.	7	26 Furman	9	40 Maine	11
2 Gardner-Webb	4	15 Eastern Wash.	7	31 Austin Peay	10	40 Jacksonville St.	11
6 Harvard	5	15 Murray St.	7	31 Stony Brook	10	40 Indiana St.	11
6 Western Ill.	5	20 Colgate	8	31 Richmond	10	40 Eastern Ky.	11
6 Southern Ill.	5	20 Fla. Atlantic	8	31 Montana	10	40 Cornell	11
9 Albany (N.Y.)	6	20 Georgetown	8	31 Monmouth	10	51 Citadel	12
9 St. Mary's (Cal.)	6	20 Southwest Tex. St.	8	31 Marist	10	51 Norfolk St.	12
9 Delaware	6	20 Siena	8	31 Columbia	10	51 Elon	12
9 Youngstown St.	6	20 Northeastern	8	31 East Tenn. St.	10	51 Tenn.-Martin	12
9 Yale	6	26 Fordham	9	31 Dartmouth	10	51 St. John's (N.Y.)	12
				40 Appalachian St.	11	51 N.C. A&T	12
				40 Towson	11	51 Morgan St.	12
				40 Southwest Mo. St.	11	51 Idaho St.	12
						51 Illinois St.	12

Rank, School	No.
51 Davidson	12
61 Hofstra	13
61 Stephen F. Austin	13
61 Western Caro.	13
61 Wagner	13
61 Samford	13
61 Jacksonville	13
61 Northwestern St.	13
61 Robert Morris	13
61 Sam Houston St.	13
61 Pennsylvania	13
71 Duquesne	14
71 Holy Cross	14
71 VMI	14
71 Villanova	14
71 Chattanooga	14
71 Tennessee Tech	14
71 Southern Utah	14
71 South Carolina St.	14
71 St. Peter's	14
71 Portland St.	14
71 New Hampshire	14
71 Mississippi Val.	14
71 Lehigh	14
71 Jackson St.	14
71 Florida Int'l	14
86 Central Conn. St.	15
86 Drake	15
86 Weber St.	15
86 James Madison	15
86 Liberty	15
86 Lafayette	15
86 Delaware St.	15
86 Howard	15
94 Brown	16
94 Butler	16
94 Cal Poly	16
94 La Salle	16
98 Alcorn St.	17
98 Bethune-Cookman	17
98 Massachusetts	17
98 Northern Ariz.	17
98 Prairie View	17
98 Fairfield	17
98 Southern U.	17
98 Eastern Ill.	17
106 Grambling	18
106 St. Francis (Pa.)	18
106 Savannah St.	18
106 Southeast Mo. St.	18
106 Northern Iowa	18
106 Morris Brown	18
112 Florida A&M	19
112 Valparaiso	19
112 Morehead St.	19
115 Alabama A&M	20
115 Bucknell	20
117 Alabama St.	21
117 Ark.-Pine Bluff	21
117 Texas Southern	21
117 Iona	21
117 Charleston So.	21
122 Tennessee St.	22
123 Canisius	27
82 Sacramento St.	10
92 Brown	9
92 Delaware	9
92 Prairie View	9
92 Northwestern St.	9
92 Montana St.	9
92 Liberty	9
92 James Madison	9
92 Iona	9
92 Indiana St.	9
92 Eastern Ill.	9
92 Cornell	9
92 Youngstown St.	9
92 Sam Houston St.	9
92 Davidson	9
106 Bucknell	8
106 Rhode Island	8
106 Western Caro.	8
109 Columbia	7
109 Weber St.	7
109 Dartmouth	7
109 Morgan St.	7
109 Hofstra	7
109 Drake	7
115 Fla. Atlantic	6
115 Monmouth	6
115 La Salle	6
115 Holy Cross	6
119 Chattanooga	5
119 Yale	5
121 Illinois St.	4
121 Valparaiso	4
121 Southern Utah	4

Passes Intercepted

Rank, School	No.
1 Dayton	28
2 N.C. A&T	27
3 Duquesne	25
4 Grambling	24
5 Bethune-Cookman	21
5 St. Mary's (Cal.)	21
7 Alabama St.	20
7 Maine	20
7 Massachusetts	20
7 McNeese St.	20
7 Western Ky.	20
7 Pennsylvania	20
7 Morehead St.	20
14 Sacred Heart	19
14 Texas Southern	19
16 Mississippi Val.	18
16 Towson	18
18 Alabama A&M	17
18 South Carolina St.	17
18 Furman	17
18 Alcorn St.	17
18 Central Conn. St.	17
23 Austin Peay	16
23 Florida A&M	16
23 Ark.-Pine Bluff	16
23 Gardner-Webb	16
23 Princeton	16
23 Northeastern	16
23 Montana	16
23 Idaho St.	16
23 Fairfield	16
23 Charleston So.	16
33 Fordham	15
33 Villanova	15
33 William & Mary	15
33 Western Ill.	15
33 St. Peter's	15
33 Northern Ariz.	15
33 Morris Brown	15
33 Marist	15
33 Howard	15
33 Jackson St.	15
33 Ga. Southern	15
44 Colgate	14
44 Southern U.	14
44 Richmond	14
44 East Tenn. St.	14
48 Murray St.	13
48 St. John's (N.Y.)	13
48 Southeast Mo. St.	13
48 San Diego	13
48 Robert Morris	13
48 Norfolk St.	13
48 Northern Iowa	13
55 Appalachian St.	12
55 Wagner	12
55 VMI	12
55 Tenn.-Martin	12
55 Stony Brook	12
55 Stephen F. Austin	12
55 Southern Ill.	12
55 Siena	12
55 Delaware St.	12
55 Jacksonville St.	12
55 Nicholls St.	12
55 Lehigh	12
55 Hampton	12
55 Georgetown	12
55 Eastern Ky.	12
70 Albany (N.Y.)	11
70 Wofford	11
70 Tennessee St.	11
70 Southwest Tex. St.	11
70 Southwest Mo. St.	11
70 Samford	11
70 St. Francis (Pa.)	11
70 Portland St.	11
70 Lafayette	11
70 Harvard	11
70 Cal Poly	11
70 Canisius	11
82 Butler	10
82 Elon	10
82 Tennessee Tech	10
82 Savannah St.	10
82 Eastern Wash.	10
82 New Hampshire	10
82 Jacksonville	10
82 Florida Int'l	10
82 Citadel	10

Punt Returns

Rank, School	G	Ret	Yds	TD	Avg	W	L	T
1 Hampton	12	35	622	3	17.77	7	5	0
2 Holy Cross	12	27	415	2	15.37	4	8	0
3 Southern Ill.	12	27	400	2	14.81	4	8	0
4 Alcorn St.	11	36	530	1	14.72	6	5	0
5 Northwestern St.	13	44	634	1	14.41	9	4	0
6 Furman	12	18	257	1	14.28	8	4	0
7 Alabama A&M	12	43	607	1	14.12	6	5	0
8 Rhode Island	12	15	210	1	14	3	9	0
9 Montana St.	13	30	418	1	13.93	7	6	0
10 Appalachian St.	12	40	557	1	13.93	8	4	0
11 Fordham	13	53	734	2	13.85	10	3	0
12 Jacksonville	10	26	356	2	13.69	7	4	0
13 Samford	11	29	395	1	13.62	4	7	0
14 Alabama St.	12	44	591	1	13.43	6	6	0
15 Mississippi Val.	11	23	304	1	13.22	5	6	0
16 Wagner	11	39	515	1	13.21	7	4	0
17 Cal Poly	11	20	264	1	13.2	3	8	0
18 Tennessee St.	12	30	395	2	13.17	2	10	0
19 Idaho St.	11	48	630	2	13.13	8	3	0
20 Western Ky.	15	47	609	1	12.96	12	3	0
21 Northern Ariz.	11	27	338	0	12.52	6	5	0
22 Canisius	11	28	350	1	12.5	2	9	0
23 Nicholls St.	11	28	345	3	12.32	7	4	0
24 Ark.-Pine Bluff	11	16	197	0	12.31	3	8	0
25 McNeese St.	15	50	599	2	11.98	13	2	0
26 Columbia	10	25	280	0	11.2	1	9	0
27 Charleston So.	12	24	267	1	11.13	4	8	0
28 Southern Utah	11	17	189	0	11.12	1	10	0
29 Ga. Southern	11	48	530	1	11.04	11	3	0
30 Montana	14	56	616	3	11	11	3	0
30 Valparaiso	11	25	275	1	11	1	10	0
32 Lehigh	12	38	412	2	10.84	8	4	0
33 Morehead St.	12	49	529	2	10.8	9	3	0
34 Florida Int'l	11	22	230	0	10.45	5	6	0
34 Northern Iowa	11	44	460	2	10.45	5	6	0
36 Eastern Wash.	11	32	332	1	10.38	6	5	0
37 Sacred Heart	10	37	383	2	10.35	7	3	0
38 Southwest Mo. St.	11	25	258	1	10.32	4	7	0
39 East Tenn. St.	12	22	227	0	10.32	4	8	0
40 Richmond	11	33	335	0	10.15	4	7	0
41 Butler	10	22	222	1	10.09	4	6	0
42 St. Peter's	11	27	271	1	10.04	6	5	0
43 Iona	11	41	411	2	10.02	5	6	0
44 Gardner-Webb	10	15	149	1	9.93	9	1	0
45 Morgan St.	12	32	317	0	9.91	7	5	0
46 Central Conn. St.	11	16	156	1	9.75	5	6	0
46 Delaware	12	24	234	0	9.75	4	8	0
48 South Carolina St.	12	30	289	1	9.63	7	5	0
49 Dayton	12	47	452	1	9.62	11	1	0
50 Texas Southern	11	28	269	0	9.61	4	7	0
51 Robert Morris	10	31	297	2	9.58	3	7	0
52 Southeast Mo. St.	12	26	249	0	9.58	8	4	0
53 Monmouth	10	30	287	1	9.57	2	8	0
54 Stony Brook	10	34	324	1	9.53	8	2	0
55 Sam Houston St.	11	23	216	1	9.39	4	7	0
56 Georgetown	11	29	268	0	9.24	5	6	0
57 Lafayette	12	26	240	1	9.23	7	5	0
58 Norfolk St.	11	29	266	0	9.17	5	6	0
59 Southwest Tex. St.	11	21	190	1	9.05	4	7	0
60 Grambling	13	51	456	0	8.94	11	2	0
61 Howard	11	23	203	3	8.83	6	5	0

Rank, School	G	Ret	Yds	TD	Avg	W	L	T
62 Western Ill.	13	36	316	4	8.78	11	2	0
63 Tennessee Tech	12	24	210	0	8.75	5	7	0
64 Citadel	12	31	270	0	8.71	3	9	0
65 Morris Brown	12	23	200	0	8.7	1	11	0
66 Stephen F. Austin	11	37	320	2	8.65	6	5	0
67 Sacramento St.	12	38	325	1	8.55	5	7	0
68 San Diego	10	25	212	1	8.48	5	5	0
69 Dartmouth	10	22	186	1	8.45	3	7	0
70 Wofford	12	30	253	0	8.43	9	3	0
71 Delaware	12	36	302	0	8.39	6	6	0
72 Youngstown St.	11	25	207	0	8.28	7	4	0
73 Eastern Ky.	12	35	284	1	8.11	8	4	0
74 Murray St.	12	18	144	0	8	7	5	0
74 St. John's (N.Y.)	10	32	256	0	8	2	8	0
76 Illinois St.	11	34	269	0	7.91	6	5	0
77 Jackson St.	11	23	180	0	7.83	7	4	0
78 Albany (N.Y.)	12	35	272	0	7.77	8	4	0
79 Harvard	10	20	155	0	7.75	7	3	0
80 Tenn.-Martin	12	16	123	0	7.69	2	10	0
81 Princeton	10	27	207	0	7.67	6	4	0
81 Chattanooga	12	30	230	1	7.67	2	10	0
83 Florida A&M	12	38	290	0	7.63	7	5	0
84 Weber St.	11	24	182	1	7.58	3	8	0
85 N.C. A&T	12	37	275	0	7.43	4	8	0
86 Bethune-Cookman	13	28	203	0	7.25	11	2	0
87 Western Caro.	11	27	194	0	7.19	5	6	0
88 Southern U.	12	25	179	0	7.16	6	6	0
89 Cornell	10	26	184	0	7.08	4	6	0
90 James Madison	12	32	225	0	7.03	5	7	0
91 St. Mary's (Cal.)	12	35	246	0	7.03	6	6	0
92 Massachusetts	12	31	216	0	6.97	8	4	0
93 Colgate	12	29	202	1	6.97	9	3	0
94 Siena	10	25	174	0	6.96	3	7	0
95 La Salle	11	20	139	0	6.95	2	9	0
96 Northeastern	13	33	229	0	6.94	10	3	0
97 Austin Peay	12	49	338	0	6.9	7	5	0
98 Yale	10	28	193	0	6.89	6	4	0
99 Brown	10	23	158	0	6.87	2	8	0
100 William & Mary	11	22	151	0	6.86	6	5	0
101 Prairie View	11	24	164	0	6.83	1	10	0
102 Towson	11	36	243	0	6.75	6	5	0
103 Hofstra	12	33	221	0	6.7	6	6	0
104 VMI	12	21	139	0	6.62	6	6	0
105 Fla. Atlantic	11	28	181	1	6.46	2	9	0
106 Bucknell	11	33	206	0	6.24	2	9	0
107 Duquesne	12	55	342	0	6.22	11	1	0
108 Indiana St.	12	24	148	0	6.17	5	7	0
109 Portland St.	11	26	154	0	5.92	6	5	0
110 Liberty	11	21	123	0	5.86	2	9	0
111 Maine	14	37	215	0	5.81	11	3	0
112 Fairfield	11	26	151	0	5.81	5	6	0
113 Jacksonville St.	11	32	182	0	5.69	5	6	0
114 Eastern Ill.	12	22	125	0	5.68	8	4	0
115 Davidson	10	20	111	0	5.55	7	3	0
116 Pennsylvania	10	41	215	0	5.24	9	1	0
117 Villanova	15	29	152	0	5.24	11	4	0
118 Marist	11	44	222	0	5.05	7	4	0
119 Elon	11	16	78	0	4.88	4	7	0
120 Drake	10	23	110	0	4.78	5	5	0
121 Savannah St.	10	18	81	0	4.5	1	9	0
122 St. Francis (Pa.)	10	35	156	0	4.46	2	8	0
123 New Hampshire	11	18	76	0	4.22	3	8	0

Rushing Offense

Rank, School	G	Rsh	Net	Avg	TD	Yds/Gm	W	L	T
1 Ga. Southern	14	859	5,407	6.29	54	386.21	11	3	0
2 Wofford	12	752	4,106	5.46	39	342.17	9	3	0
3 Southern Ill.	12	613	3,308	5.4	36	275.67	4	8	0
4 St. Mary's (Cal.)	12	659	3,168	4.81	32	264	6	6	0
5 Dayton	12	637	3,058	4.8	39	254.83	11	1	0
6 Western Ky.	15	828	3,793	4.58	41	252.87	12	3	0
7 Albany (N.Y.)	12	589	3,028	5.14	39	252.33	8	4	0
8 Nicholls St.	11	561	2,749	4.9	33	249.91	7	4	0
9 St. Peter's	11	523	2,686	5.14	22	244.18	6	5	0
10 Rhode Island	12	624	2,904	4.65	17	242	3	9	0
11 Murray St.	12	557	2,849	5.11	35	237.42	7	5	0
12 Bethune-Cookman	13	564	3,009	5.34	36	231.46	11	2	0
13 Eastern Ky.	12	597	2,769	4.64	33	230.75	8	4	0
14 Marist	11	559	2,524	4.52	29	229.45	7	4	0
15 Elon	11	594	2,454	4.13	25	223.09	4	7	0
16 Southern Utah	11	599	2,385	3.98	22	216.82	1	10	0
17 Morgan St.	12	529	2,535	4.79	28	211.25	7	5	0

Rank, School	G	Rsh	Net	Avg	TD	Yds/Gm	W	L	T
18 McNeese St.	15	714	3,108	4.35	38	207.2	13	2	0
19 Northeastern	13	617	2,691	4.36	27	207	10	3	0
20 Delaware	12	535	2,475	4.63	23	206.25	6	6	0
21 Richmond	11	555	2,185	3.94	16	198.64	4	7	0
22 Youngstown St.	11	519	2,169	4.18	19	197.18	7	4	0
23 Furman	12	541	2,347	4.34	29	195.58	8	4	0
24 South Carolina St.	12	499	2,335	4.68	27	194.58	7	5	0
25 Gardner-Webb	10	401	1,929	4.81	16	192.9	9	1	0
26 Hampton	12	595	2,230	3.75	31	185.83	7	5	0
27 Eastern Ill.	12	465	2,218	4.77	25	184.83	8	4	0
28 Liberty	11	426	2,019	4.74	9	183.55	2	9	0
29 Northwestern St.	13	573	2,367	4.13	27	182.08	9	4	0
30 Maine	14	588	2,488	4.23	20	177.71	11	3	0
31 Colgate	12	503	2,130	4.23	24	177.5	9	3	0
32 Morehead St.	12	519	2,114	4.07	22	176.17	9	3	0
33 Austin Peay	12	488	2,088	4.28	26	174	7	5	0
34 Butler	10	400	1,738	4.35	26	173.8	4	6	0
35 Appalachian St.	12	484	2,010	4.15	18	167.5	8	4	0
36 Howard	11	486	1,840	3.79	14	167.27	6	5	0
37 Stephen F. Austin	11	405	1,833	4.53	26	166.64	6	5	0
38 Massachusetts	12	477	1,993	4.18	22	166.08	8	4	0
39 Jackson St.	11	443	1,821	4.11	16	165.55	7	4	0
40 Yale	10	416	1,651	3.97	16	165.1	6	4	0
41 Jacksonville St.	11	486	1,805	3.71	14	164.09	5	6	0
42 Harvard	10	421	1,640	3.9	20	164	7	3	0
42 Illinois St.	11	448	1,804	4.03	19	164	6	5	0
44 James Madison	12	553	1,961	3.55	14	163.42	5	7	0
45 VMI	12	509	1,946	3.82	23	162.17	6	6	0
46 Northern Iowa	11	471	1,779	3.78	9	161.73	5	6	0
47 Duquesne	12	506	1,931	3.82	23	160.92	11	1	0
48 Southeast Mo. St.	12	473	1,926	4.07	19	160.5	8	4	0
49 Southwest Tex. St.	11	469	1,764	3.76	18	160.36	4	7	0
50 Lehigh	12	505	1,923	3.81	20	160.25	8	4	0
51 Towson	11	506	1,754	3.47	19	159.45	6	5	0
52 Tennessee Tech	12	431	1,899	4.41	23	158.25	5	7	0
53 New Hampshire	11	487	1,718	3.53	11	156.18	3	8	0
54 Sacramento St.	12	516	1,874	3.63	20	156.17	5	7	0
55 Drake	10	384	1,710	4.45	17	155.45	5	5	0
56 Princeton	10	429	1,552	3.62	17	155.2	6	4	0
57 Delaware St.	12	549	1,853	3.38	12	154.42	4	8	0
58 Western Ill.	13	574	1,990	3.47	27	153.08	11	2	0
59 Citadel	12	468	1,829	3.91	15	152.42	3	9	0
60 Alabama A&M	12	477	1,823	3.82	20	151.92	8	4	0
61 Lafayette	12	502	1,805	3.6	16	150.42	7	5	0
62 Tenn.-Martin	12	555	1,770	3.19	16	147.5	2	10	0
63 Portland St.	11	434	1,593	3.67	13	144.82	6	5	0
64 Indiana St.	12	470	1,735	3.69	17	144.58	5	7	0
65 Wagner	11	490	1,576	3.22	19	143.27	7	4	0
66 Cal Poly	11	428	1,541	3.6	18	140.09	3	8	0
67 Fordham	13	452	1,807	4	26	139	10	3	0
68 Stony Brook	10	375	1,381	3.68	13	138.1	8	2	0
69 Tennessee St.	12	438	1,638	3.74	18	136.5	2	10	0
70 Holy Cross	12	426	1,635	3.84	13	136.25	4	8	0
71 Southwest Mo. St.	11	426	1,488	3.49	14	135.27	4	7	0
72 William & Mary	11	425	1,487	3.5	17	135.18	6	5	0
73 Alabama St.	12	449	1,609	3.58	15	134.08	6	6	0
74 Southern U.	12	450	1,607	3.57	16	133.92	6	6	0
75 Florida A&M	12	486	1,599	3.29	17	133.25	7	5	0
76 Idaho St.	11	375	1,460	3.89	17	132.73	8	3	0
77 Eastern Wash.	11	322	1,430	4.44	16	130	6	5	0
78 San Diego	10	365	1,294	3.55	11	129.4	5	5	0
79 Montana	14	517	1,793	3.47	24	128.07	11	3	0
80 Western Caro.	11	396	1,396	3.53	21	126.91	5	6	0
81 Davidson	10	364	1,269	3.49	11	126.9	7	3	0
82 Hofstra	12	393	1,519	3.87	13	126.58	6	6	0
83 Central Conn. St.	11	462	1,386	3	8	126	5	6	0
84 Cornell	10	379	1,255	3.31	13	125.5	4	6	0
85 Norfolk St.	11	460	1,376	2.99	21	125.09	5	6	0
86 Texas Southern	11	436	1,365	3.13	15	124.09	4	7	0
87 Dartmouth	10	341	1,235	3.62	11	123.5	3	7	0
88 Bucknell	11	437	1,355	3.1	10	123.18	2	9	0
89 Villanova	15	529	1,843	3.48	23	122.87	11	4	0
90 East Tenn. St.	12	488	1,450	2.97	9	120.83	4	8	0
91 Alcorn St.	11	418	1,329	3.18	15	120.82	6	5	0
92 N.C. A&T	12	405	1,439	3.55	15	119.92	4	8	0
93 Morris Brown	12	441	1,432	3.25	17	119.33	1	11	0
94 Grambling	13	395	1,528	3.87	20	117.54	11	2	0
95 Pennsylvania	10	365	1,122	3.07	19	112.2	9	1	0
96 St. Francis (Pa.)	10	423	1,118	2.64	8	111.8	2	8	0
97 Siena	10	443	1,108	2.5	8	110.8	3	7	0
98 Samford	11	349	1,205	3.45	16	109.55	4	7	0
99 Montana St.	13	436	1,399	3.21	10	107.62	7	6	0
100 Canisius	11	438	1,170	2.67	7	106.36	2	9	0
101 Weber St.	11	351	1,166	3.32	13	106	3	8	0

Rank, School	G	Rsh	Net	Avg	TD	Yds/Gm	W	L	T
102 Florida Int'l	11	361	1,164	3.22	14	105.82	5	6	0
103 Iona	11	472	1,116	2.36	10	101.45	5	6	0
104 Sacred Heart	10	363	978	2.69	8	97.8	7	3	0
105 Northern Ariz.	11	400	1,070	2.68	11	97.27	6	5	0
106 Fairfield	11	458	1,052	2.3	15	95.64	5	6	0
107 Monmouth	10	379	941	2.48	8	94.1	2	8	0
108 Mississippi Val.	11	389	1,030	2.65	9	93.64	5	6	0
109 Jacksonville	10	353	935	2.65	9	93.5	3	7	0
110 Sam Houston St.	11	369	1,019	2.76	12	92.64	4	7	0
111 Savannah St.	10	409	921	2.25	8	92.1	1	9	0
112 Columbia	10	346	917	2.65	13	91.7	1	9	0
113 Charleston So.	12	387	1,067	2.76	9	88.92	4	8	0
114 Brown	10	316	889	2.81	11	88.9	2	8	0
115 Chattanooga	12	371	1,058	2.85	7	88.17	2	10	0
116 Prairie View	11	426	924	2.17	8	84	1	10	0
117 Valparaiso	11	370	923	2.49	10	83.91	1	10	0
118 Ark.-Pine Bluff	11	357	890	2.49	12	80.91	3	8	0
119 La Salle	11	293	882	3.01	13	80.18	2	9	0
120 St. John's (N.Y.)	10	326	760	2.33	7	76	2	8	0
121 Georgetown	11	346	814	2.35	5	74	5	6	0
122 Fla. Atlantic	11	424	764	1.8	9	69.45	2	9	0
123 Robert Morris	10	367	620	1.69	6	62	3	7	0

Rushing Defense

Rank, School	G	Rsh	Net	Avg	TD	Yds/Gm	W	L	T
1 Pennsylvania	10	301	558	1.85	7	55.8	9	1	0
2 Dayton	12	380	813	2.14	7	67.8	11	1	0
3 Marist	11	372	863	2.32	13	78.5	7	4	0
4 Alabama A&M	12	432	1,005	2.33	10	83.8	8	4	0
5 Albany (N.Y.)	12	399	1,114	2.79	9	92.8	8	4	0
6 Duquesne	12	468	1,116	2.38	6	93	11	1	0
7 Alabama St.	12	414	1,135	2.74	19	94.6	6	6	0
8 Sacred Heart	10	426	972	2.28	9	97.2	7	3	0
9 Colgate	12	428	1,191	2.78	11	99.3	9	3	0
10 Bucknell	11	418	1,093	2.61	8	99.4	2	9	0
11 Northwestern St.	13	471	1,292	2.74	15	99.4	9	4	0
12 Eastern Ky.	12	432	1,198	2.77	13	99.8	8	4	0
13 Montana	14	516	1,410	2.73	14	100.7	11	3	0
14 Wagner	11	421	1,117	2.65	8	101.5	7	4	0
15 Northern Ariz.	11	417	1,137	2.73	13	103.4	6	5	0
16 Northeastern	13	494	1,344	2.72	9	103.4	10	3	0
17 Iona	11	440	1,167	2.65	18	106.1	5	6	0
18 St. Peter's	11	414	1,169	2.82	8	106.3	6	5	0
19 Jackson St.	11	354	1,195	3.38	15	108.6	7	4	0
20 Montana St.	13	490	1,459	2.98	19	112.2	7	6	0
21 McNeese St.	15	548	1,691	3.09	18	112.7	13	2	0
22 Princeton	10	342	1,130	3.3	17	113	6	4	0
23 Harvard	10	357	1,142	3.2	7	114.2	7	3	0
24 Yale	10	375	1,151	3.07	11	115.1	6	4	0
25 Texas Southern	11	448	1,278	2.85	13	116.2	4	7	0
26 Stony Brook	10	425	1,180	2.78	6	118	8	2	0
27 Western Ky.	15	560	1,784	3.19	20	118.9	12	3	0
28 Lehigh	12	480	1,438	3	18	119.8	8	4	0
29 Grambling	13	474	1,577	3.33	23	121.3	11	2	0
30 Towson	11	363	1,344	3.7	15	122.2	6	5	0
31 Norfolk St.	11	393	1,370	3.49	16	124.5	5	6	0
32 Wofford	12	466	1,511	3.24	12	125.9	9	3	0
33 Monmouth	10	403	1,260	3.13	12	126	2	8	0
34 Siena	10	373	1,267	3.4	11	126.7	3	7	0
35 Fordham	13	518	1,654	3.19	16	127.2	10	3	0
36 Alcorn St.	11	432	1,408	3.26	13	128	6	5	0
37 Mississippi Val.	11	431	1,412	3.28	19	128.4	5	6	0
38 Youngstown St.	11	451	1,414	3.14	10	128.5	7	4	0
39 Villanova	15	596	1,959	3.29	23	130.6	11	4	0
40 Hampton	12	527	1,606	3.05	21	133.8	7	5	0
41 Maine	14	575	1,893	3.29	14	135.2	11	3	0
42 Davidson	10	394	1,367	3.47	13	136.7	7	3	0
43 Massachusetts	12	518	1,644	3.17	15	137	8	4	0
44 Morehead St.	12	444	1,660	3.74	20	138.3	9	3	0
45 Lafayette	12	460	1,667	3.62	17	138.9	7	5	0
46 Delaware	12	506	1,668	3.3	11	139	6	6	0
47 Fairfield	11	411	1,542	3.75	15	140.2	5	6	0
48 Weber St.	11	420	1,548	3.69	15	140.7	3	8	0

Rank, Name	G	Rsh	Net	Avg	TD	Yds/Gm	W	L	T
49 Ga. Southern	14	526	1,972	3.75	13	140.9	11	3	0
50 Idaho St.	11	413	1,552	3.76	7	141.1	8	3	0
51 Richmond	11	459	1,566	3.41	11	142.4	4	7	0
52 St. Mary's (Cal.)	12	493	1,712	3.47	13	142.7	6	6	0
53 St. Francis (Pa.)	10	403	1,431	3.55	17	143.1	2	8	0
54 South Carolina St.	12	561	1,737	3.1	15	144.8	7	5	0
55 Georgetown	11	458	1,615	3.53	26	146.8	5	6	0
56 James Madison	12	500	1,769	3.54	11	147.4	5	7	0
57 Bethune-Cookman	13	531	1,932	3.64	14	148.6	11	2	0
58 Delaware St.	12	468	1,808	3.86	21	150.7	4	8	0
59 Tennessee Tech	12	476	1,810	3.8	18	150.8	5	7	0
60 Portland St.	11	421	1,678	3.99	9	152.5	6	5	0
61 Southeast Mo. St.	12	451	1,844	4.09	26	153.7	8	4	0
62 Western Ill.	13	542	2,001	3.69	17	153.9	11	2	0
63 Sacramento St.	12	446	1,854	4.16	22	154.5	5	7	0
64 Eastern Ill.	12	470	1,855	3.95	25	154.6	8	4	0
65 Eastern Wash.	11	465	1,703	3.66	14	154.8	6	5	0
66 Elon	11	417	1,725	4.14	20	156.8	4	7	0
67 Prairie View	11	389	1,751	4.5	23	159.2	1	10	0
68 Nicholls St.	11	423	1,766	4.17	16	160.5	7	4	0
69 Southern U.	12	494	1,957	3.96	13	163.1	6	6	0
70 Stephen F. Austin	11	490	1,802	3.68	20	163.8	6	5	0
71 San Diego	10	393	1,669	4.25	15	166.9	5	5	0
72 Northern Iowa	11	460	1,856	4.03	20	168.7	5	6	0
73 Robert Morris	10	455	1,707	3.75	17	170.7	3	7	0
74 Charleston So.	12	522	2,056	3.94	17	171.3	4	8	0
75 Central Conn. St.	11	418	1,898	4.54	17	172.5	5	6	0
76 Dartmouth	10	390	1,736	4.45	18	173.6	3	7	0
77 Cornell	10	437	1,742	3.99	22	174.2	4	6	0
78 Appalachian St.	12	519	2,093	4.03	17	174.4	8	4	0
79 Howard	11	456	1,934	4.24	20	175.8	6	5	0
80 Brown	10	386	1,760	4.56	16	176	2	8	0
81 Columbia	10	423	1,769	4.18	19	176.9	1	9	0
82 Southwest Mo. St.	11	523	1,947	3.72	20	177	4	7	0
83 Savannah St.	10	424	1,771	4.18	27	177.1	1	9	0
84 Florida A&M	12	471	2,139	4.54	15	178.3	7	5	0
85 N.C. A&T	12	581	2,170	3.73	17	180.8	4	8	0
86 Furman	12	464	2,181	4.7	22	181.8	8	4	0
87 Murray St.	12	450	2,191	4.87	25	182.6	7	5	0
88 Ark.-Pine Bluff	11	443	2,012	4.54	15	182.9	3	8	0
89 Indiana St.	12	593	2,209	3.73	18	184.1	5	7	0
90 Austin Peay	12	497	2,229	4.48	21	185.8	7	5	0
91 Rhode Island	12	513	2,239	4.36	26	186.6	3	9	0
92 Fla. Atlantic	11	498	2,098	4.21	24	190.7	2	9	0
93 Hofstra	12	573	2,293	4	19	191.1	6	6	0
94 Holy Cross	12	559	2,300	4.11	27	191.7	4	8	0
95 William & Mary	11	472	2,118	4.49	16	192.5	6	5	0
96 East Tenn. St.	12	536	2,311	4.31	28	192.6	4	8	0
97 Gardner-Webb	10	418	1,936	4.63	18	193.6	9	1	0
98 Illinois St.	11	513	2,130	4.15	14	193.6	6	5	0
99 Jacksonville	10	417	1,938	4.65	16	193.8	3	7	0
100 Southwest Tex. St.	11	485	2,132	4.4	27	193.8	4	7	0
101 Samford	11	488	2,145	4.4	25	195	4	7	0
102 Southern Ill.	12	512	2,369	4.63	28	197.4	4	8	0
103 Cal Poly	11	502	2,172	4.33	21	197.5	3	8	0
104 Tennessee St.	12	524	2,376	4.53	30	198	2	10	0
105 Jacksonville St.	11	443	2,200	4.97	20	200	5	6	0
106 Sam Houston St.	11	509	2,244	4.41	22	204	4	7	0
107 Citadel	12	549	2,457	4.48	30	204.8	3	9	0
108 Morgan St.	12	558	2,495	4.47	29	207.9	7	5	0
109 St. John's (N.Y.)	10	511	2,084	4.08	22	208.4	2	8	0
110 Valparaiso	11	476	2,341	4.92	34	212.8	1	10	0
111 Florida Int'l	11	546	2,353	4.31	21	213.9	5	6	0
112 Tenn.-Martin	12	491	2,587	5.27	37	215.6	2	10	0
113 Butler	10	430	2,187	5.09	29	218.7	4	6	0
114 Chattanooga	12	571	2,625	4.6	22	218.8	2	10	0
115 Southern Utah	11	437	2,434	5.57	38	221.3	1	10	0
116 Western Caro.	11	546	2,442	4.47	22	222	5	6	0
117 Morris Brown	12	538	2,772	5.15	36	231	1	11	0
118 Drake	10	488	2,556	5.24	36	232.4	5	5	0
119 VMI	12	509	2,814	5.53	31	234.5	6	6	0
120 Liberty	12	510	2,756	5.4	31	250.5	2	9	0
121 Canisius	11	530	2,835	5.35	32	257.7	2	9	0
122 New Hampshire	11	527	2,929	5.56	29	266.3	3	8	0
123 La Salle	11	608	2,989	4.92	38	271.7	2	9	0

Scoring Defense

Rank, School	G	TD	Kxp	Oxp	DKx	Dox	FG	Sf	Pts	Pts/Gm	W	L	T
1 Duquesne	12	13	11	1	0	0	8	0	115	9.6	11	1	0
2 Dayton	12	15	13	0	0	0	5	0	118	9.8	11	1	0
3 Stony Brook	10	15	13	0	0	0	5	0	118	11.8	8	2	0
4 Wagner	11	16	16	0	0	0	6	2	134	12.2	7	4	0
5 Sacred Heart	10	15	15	0	0	0	8	0	129	12.9	7	3	0
6 Pennsylvania	10	17	16	0	0	0	4	1	132	13.2	9	1	0
7 Ga. Southern	14	24	18	2	0	0	8	0	190	13.6	11	3	0
8 Bethune-Cookman	13	26	16	2	0	0	8	0	200	15.4	11	2	0
9 Maine	14	27	24	0	0	0	10	0	216	15.4	11	3	0
10 Northeastern	13	24	20	1	0	0	14	0	208	16	10	3	0
11 Western Ky.	15	32	28	1	0	0	8	0	246	16.4	12	3	0
12 Wofford	12	24	19	2	0	0	10	0	197	16.4	9	3	0
13 Idaho St.	11	24	23	0	0	0	7	0	188	17.1	8	3	0
14 Fordham	13	27	24	0	0	0	13	0	225	17.3	10	3	0
15 South Carolina St.	12	26	22	0	2	0	10	0	212	17.7	7	5	0
16 Monmouth	10	22	16	2	0	0	7	2	177	17.7	2	8	0
17 Nicholls St.	11	25	18	0	0	0	9	0	195	17.7	7	4	0
18 Colgate	12	27	22	1	0	0	10	0	216	18	9	3	0
18 Lehigh	12	27	24	0	0	0	10	0	216	18	8	4	0
20 Alabama A&M	12	29	15	3	0	0	6	2	217	18.1	8	4	0
21 Morehead St.	12	30	21	1	0	0	5	0	218	18.2	9	3	0
22 McNeese St.	15	35	30	0	0	0	11	0	273	18.2	13	2	0
23 Youngstown St.	11	22	19	1	0	0	16	0	201	18.3	7	4	0
24 Eastern Ky.	12	29	22	2	0	0	6	1	220	18.3	8	4	0
25 Richmond	11	24	22	0	0	0	12	0	202	18.4	4	7	0
26 Villanova	15	35	28	1	0	0	12	1	278	18.5	11	4	0
27 Western Ill.	13	31	23	1	0	0	8	3	241	18.5	11	2	0
28 Montana	14	33	28	2	0	0	10	0	260	18.6	11	3	0
29 Yale	10	24	21	0	0	0	7	1	188	18.8	6	4	0
30 St. Peter's	11	27	17	3	2	0	6	0	207	18.8	6	5	0
31 Delaware	12	27	21	1	0	0	14	0	227	18.9	6	6	0
32 Siena	10	24	19	1	0	0	9	1	194	19.4	3	7	0
33 Gardner-Webb	10	28	23	0	0	0	3	2	204	20.4	9	1	0
34 Albany (N.Y.)	12	33	30	1	0	0	5	0	245	20.4	8	4	0
35 Florida Int'l	11	30	25	0	0	0	7	1	228	20.7	5	6	0
36 Hampton	12	34	23	3	0	0	5	1	250	20.8	7	5	0
36 Massachusetts	12	34	31	0	0	0	5	0	250	20.8	8	4	0
38 Marist	11	30	19	2	0	0	9	0	230	20.9	7	4	0
39 Furman	12	35	34	0	0	1	3	0	255	21.3	8	4	0
39 Hofstra	12	33	27	2	0	0	8	1	255	21.3	6	6	0
41 Montana St.	13	34	30	0	0	0	16	0	282	21.7	7	6	0
42 Northwestern St.	13	39	33	1	0	0	4	1	283	21.8	9	4	0
43 Iona	11	33	19	3	0	0	6	1	243	22.1	5	6	0
44 St. Mary's (Cal.)	12	34	30	0	0	0	11	0	267	22.3	6	6	0
45 Portland St.	11	30	27	1	0	0	12	0	245	22.3	6	5	0
45 Stephen F. Austin	11	30	28	1	0	0	11	1	245	22.3	6	5	0
45 Towson	11	31	27	1	0	0	10	0	245	22.3	6	5	0
48 Lafayette	12	36	30	0	0	0	8	0	270	22.5	7	5	0
49 N.C. A&T	12	36	23	1	0	0	10	0	271	22.6	4	8	0
50 James Madison	12	34	31	0	0	0	11	2	272	22.7	5	7	0
51 Davidson	10	31	23	0	0	0	6	0	227	22.7	7	3	0
51 Robert Morris	10	29	20	1	0	0	9	2	227	22.7	3	7	0
53 Illinois St.	11	31	26	0	0	Dox	12	1	250	22.7	6	5	0
54 Appalachian St.	12	36	24	3	0	0	9	0	273	22.8	8	4	0
55 Central Conn. St.	11	33	30	1	0	0	7	0	251	22.8	5	6	0
56 St. Francis (Pa.)	10	30	27	1	1	0	6	0	229	22.9	2	8	0
57 Alabama St.	12	36	22	4	0	0	10	0	276	23	6	6	0
57 Harvard	10	31	20	0	0	0	8	0	230	23	7	3	0
59 Bucknell	11	34	27	0	0	0	7	1	254	23.1	2	9	0
60 Princeton	10	31	21	4	0	0	5	3	236	23.6	6	4	0
61 Mississippi Val.	11	34	16	7	1	0	8	0	260	23.6	5	6	0
62 East Tenn. St.	12	38	27	1	0	0	9	1	286	23.8	4	8	0
63 Fairfield	11	37	27	1	0	0	5	0	266	24.2	5	6	0
64 Jackson St.	11	34	30	2	0	0	9	1	267	24.3	7	4	0
65 Southern U.	12	38	21	4	0	0	13	0	296	24.7	6	6	0
66 Texas Southern	11	37	31	1	0	0	6	1	275	25	4	7	0
67 Eastern Wash.	11	35	30	0	0	0	12	0	276	25.1	6	5	0
68 Alcorn St.	11	39	24	3	0	0	5	2	283	25.7	6	5	0
69 Northern Ariz.	11	36	33	0	0	0	11	1	284	25.8	6	5	0
69 William & Mary	11	36	31	1	0	0	11	1	284	25.8	6	5	0
71 Howard	11	38	30	3	0	0	6	2	286	26	6	5	0
71 Northern Iowa	11	37	37	0	0	0	9	0	286	26	5	6	0
71 Norfolk St.	11	40	28	2	0	0	4	1	286	26	5	6	0
74 Delaware St.	12	42	31	2	0	0	8	1	313	26.1	4	8	0
75 Southwest Tex. St.	11	38	33	0	0	0	9	1	290	26.4	4	7	0
76 Indiana St.	12	40	37	0	0	0	13	1	318	26.5	5	7	0
77 Florida A&M	12	44	31	3	0	0	6	0	319	26.6	7	5	0
78 Southwest Mo. St.	11	36	29	1	0	0	15	1	294	26.7	4	7	0
78 Western Caro.	11	38	37	0	0	0	9	1	294	26.7	5	6	0
80 Jacksonville St.	11	39	28	2	0	0	10	1	298	27.1	5	6	0
81 Charleston So.	12	40	28	3	0	0	17	1	327	27.3	4	8	0

Rank, School	G	TD	Kxp	Oxp	DKx	Dox	FG	Sf	Pts	Pts/Gm	W	L	T
82 Grambling	13	51	26	5	0	0	3	2	355	27.3	11	2	0
83 Cal Poly	11	37	28	1	0	0	16	1	302	27.5	3	8	0
84 Austin Peay	12	44	38	1	0	0	9	1	333	27.8	7	5	0
84 Tennessee Tech	12	41	34	3	0	0	15	1	333	27.8	5	7	0
86 Brown	10	36	28	2	0	0	10	0	278	27.8	2	8	0
87 Weber St.	11	36	31	2	0	0	18	2	309	28.1	3	8	0
88 Citadel	12	47	36	1	0	0	6	0	338	28.2	3	9	0
89 Sam Houston St.	11	42	34	1	0	0	7	2	313	28.5	4	7	0
90 Holy Cross	12	48	42	0	0	0	4	1	344	28.7	4	8	0
91 Morgan St.	12	49	32	5	0	0	3	0	345	28.8	7	5	0
92 Southeast Mo. St.	12	47	36	2	0	0	9	0	349	29.1	8	4	0
93 Cornell	10	40	36	2	0	0	4	0	292	29.2	4	6	0
94 Murray St.	12	46	37	4	0	0	10	0	351	29.3	7	5	0
95 Columbia	10	37	34	1	0	0	11	2	295	29.5	1	9	0
95 Dartmouth	10	40	32	0	0	0	7	1	295	29.5	3	7	0
97 Canisius	11	45	43	1	0	0	4	1	329	29.9	2	9	0
98 Southern Ill.	12	51	48	0	0	0	2	0	360	30	4	8	0
99 St. John's (N.Y.)	10	40	34	2	0	0	10	0	308	30.8	2	8	0
100 Fla. Atlantic	11	44	34	1	0	0	11	3	339	30.8	2	9	0
101 San Diego	10	41	33	2	0	0	8	1	309	30.9	5	5	0
102 Georgetown	11	48	39	0	0	0	6	0	345	31.4	5	6	0
102 New Hampshire	11	43	42	0	0	0	15	0	345	31.4	3	8	0
104 Jacksonville	10	42	29	2	0	0	9	1	314	31.4	3	7	0
105 Chattanooga	12	49	43	2	0	0	12	0	377	31.4	2	10	0
106 Sacramento St.	12	49	41	3	0	0	13	0	380	31.7	5	7	0
107 Elon	11	48	40	2	0	0	6	1	352	32	4	7	0
108 Rhode Island	12	53	45	1	0	0	8	0	389	32.4	3	9	0
109 Liberty	11	48	39	3	0	0	9	2	364	33.1	2	9	0
110 Ark.-Pine Bluff	11	49	33	3	1	0	11	0	368	33.5	3	8	0
111 Tennessee St.	12	56	45	4	0	0	4	1	403	33.6	2	10	0
112 Savannah St.	10	48	27	4	0	0	4	3	341	34.1	1	9	0
113 Eastern Ill.	12	56	43	4	0	0	9	0	414	34.5	8	4	0
114 VMI	12	55	50	1	0	0	11	0	415	34.6	6	6	0
115 Samford	11	49	44	1	0	0	13	3	385	35	4	7	0
116 La Salle	11	54	45	1	1	0	5	0	388	35.3	2	9	0
117 Morris Brown	12	59	40	6	0	0	7	2	431	35.9	1	11	0
118 Butler	10	52	41	0	0	0	7	0	374	37.4	4	6	0
119 Prairie View	11	56	42	2	0	0	9	2	413	37.5	1	10	0
120 Tenn.-Martin	12	64	52	2	0	0	5	2	459	38.3	2	10	0
121 Southern Utah	11	59	53	1	0	0	6	0	427	38.8	1	10	0
122 Drake	10	57	48	2	0	0	11	1	429	39	5	5	0
123 Valparaiso	11	70	59	2	0	0	5	0	498	45.3	1	10	0

Scoring Offense

Rank, School	G	Pts	Pts/Gm	TD	Kxp	Oxp	Dkx	Dox	FG	Sf	W	L	T
1 Grambling	13	506	38.92	70	55	4	0	0	7	1	11	2	0
2 Pennsylvania	10	363	36.3	46	46	0	0	0	13	1	9	1	0
3 Western Ill.	13	470	36.15	58	56	0	0	0	20	3	11	2	0
4 Eastern Ill.	12	424	35.33	61	39	4	0	0	3	1	8	4	0
5 Dayton	12	423	35.25	53	48	3	0	0	17	0	11	1	0
6 Ga. Southern	14	493	35.21	66	62	0	0	0	11	1	11	3	0
7 Southeast Mo. St.	12	416	34.67	56	50	3	0	0	8	0	8	4	0
8 Southern Ill.	12	414	34.5	56	47	2	0	0	9	0	4	8	0
9 Hampton	12	405	33.75	54	45	2	0	0	10	1	7	5	0
10 Eastern Wash.	11	365	33.18	50	45	0	0	0	6	1	6	5	0
11 Duquesne	12	397	33.08	56	45	2	0	0	4	0	11	1	0
12 Drake	10	355	35.5	49	44	1	0	0	5	0	5	5	0
13 Fordham	13	418	32.15	53	44	0	0	0	18	1	10	3	0
14 Davidson	10	320	32	42	37	1	0	0	9	1	7	3	0
15 Eastern Ky.	12	383	31.92	49	40	5	0	0	11	3	8	4	0
16 McNeese St.	15	478	31.87	62	52	3	0	0	14	3	13	2	0
17 Murray St.	12	382	31.83	50	47	0	0	0	11	1	7	5	0
18 Montana	14	441	31.5	55	50	2	0	0	19	0	11	3	0
19 Bethune-Cookman	13	407	31.31	56	41	2	0	0	6	4	11	2	0
20 Northeastern	13	403	31	53	52	0	0	0	11	0	10	3	0
21 Furman	12	365	30.42	48	39	1	0	0	12	0	8	4	0
22 Morgan St.	12	364	30.33	50	29	9	0	0	5	1	7	5	0
23 Idaho St.	11	331	30.09	42	31	2	0	0	14	1	8	3	0
24 Jackson St.	11	330	30	47	32	1	0	0	4	1	7	4	0
25 Villanova	15	448	29.87	60	55	0	0	0	11	0	11	4	0
26 Albany (N.Y.)	12	357	29.75	49	41	1	0	0	6	1	8	4	0
27 San Diego	10	297	29.7	38	34	1	0	0	11	0	5	5	0
28 William & Mary	11	326	29.64	41	36	1	0	0	14	0	6	5	0
29 Butler	10	294	29.4	40	31	3	0	0	5	1	4	6	0
30 Stephen F. Austin	11	322	29.27	43	37	0	0	0	9	0	6	5	0
31 Morehead St.	12	347	28.92	47	35	2	0	0	8	1	9	3	0
32 Western Ky.	15	432	28.8	54	52	0	0	0	18	1	12	3	0
33 Texas Southern	11	314	28.55	40	28	2	0	0	14	0	4	7	0
34 Alabama St.	12	337	28.08	46	35	1	0	0	8	0	6	6	0
35 Gardner-Webb	10	278	27.8	35	26	3	0	0	12	0	9	1	0
36 Northwestern St.	13	359	27.62	47	46	0	0	0	9	2	9	4	0
37 Tennessee Tech	12	328	27.33	45	34	2	0	0	6	1	5	7	0
38 Massachusetts	12	327	27.25	44	39	0	0	0	8	0	8	4	0

Rank, School	G	Pts	Pts/Gm	TD	Kxp	Oxp	Dkx	Dox	FG	Sf	W	L	T
39 Sacramento St.	12	325	27.08	41	35	1	0	0	14	0	5	7	0
40 Florida A&M	12	321	26.75	43	34	1	0	0	9	0	7	5	0
40 South Carolina St.	12	321	26.75	48	22	3	0	0	1	1	7	5	0
42 Harvard	10	267	26.7	38	31	0	0	0	2	1	7	3	0
43 Lehigh	12	319	26.58	43	35	1	0	0	8	0	8	4	0
44 St. Mary's (Cal.)	12	318	26.5	42	32	1	0	0	10	1	6	6	0
45 Appalachian St.	12	314	26.17	38	29	3	0	1	15	2	8	4	0
45 VMI	12	314	26.17	42	37	1	0	0	7	1	6	6	0
47 Samford	11	285	25.91	36	24	5	0	0	11	1	4	7	0
47 Towson	11	285	25.91	39	36	0	0	0	5	0	6	5	0
49 Nicholls St.	11	283	25.73	40	37	0	0	0	2	0	7	4	0
50 Yale	10	257	25.7	35	33	1	0	0	4	0	6	4	0
51 Tennessee St.	12	308	25.67	40	31	2	0	0	11	0	2	10	0
52 Marist	11	282	25.64	37	33	2	1	0	7	0	7	4	0
52 Ark.-Pine Bluff	11	282	25.64	37	24	6	0	0	8	0	3	8	0
54 Alcorn St.	11	280	25.45	38	26	0	0	0	8	1	6	5	0
55 Citadel	12	305	25.42	38	31	2	0	0	14	0	3	9	0
56 Western Caro.	11	279	25.36	36	33	0	0	0	10	0	5	6	0
57 Lafayette	12	303	25.25	37	31	1	0	0	16	0	7	5	0
58 Colgate	12	301	25.08	38	34	0	0	0	13	0	9	3	0
59 Wofford	12	298	24.83	42	26	2	0	0	4	2	9	3	0
60 Dartmouth	10	247	24.7	31	19	1	0	0	12	2	3	7	0
61 Maine	14	343	24.5	45	41	1	0	0	10	0	11	3	0
62 Holy Cross	12	293	24.42	37	25	1	0	0	14	1	4	8	0
63 Valparaiso	11	268	24.36	35	27	2	0	0	9	0	1	10	0
64 Delaware	12	291	24.25	36	31	3	0	0	12	1	6	6	0
65 Weber St.	11	266	24.18	36	32	0	0	0	6	0	3	8	0
66 Sacred Heart	10	241	24.1	29	22	2	0	0	11	4	7	3	0
67 Austin Peay	12	287	23.92	38	32	0	0	0	9	0	7	5	0
68 N.C. A&T	12	281	23.42	37	25	2	0	0	10	0	4	8	0
69 Southern U.	12	279	23.25	38	22	2	0	0	7	2	6	6	0
70 Stony Brook	10	232	23.2	31	29	0	0	0	5	1	8	2	0
71 Southwest Mo. St.	11	255	23.18	33	28	1	0	0	9	0	4	7	0
72 Montana St.	13	298	22.92	37	32	1	0	0	14	0	7	6	0
73 Northern Ariz.	11	252	22.91	31	27	0	0	0	13	0	6	5	0
74 Illinois St.	11	249	22.64	30	30	0	0	0	13	0	6	5	0
74 Elon	11	249	22.64	33	26	1	0	0	7	1	4	7	0
76 Princeton	10	226	22.6	29	26	1	0	0	8	0	6	4	0
77 Hofstra	12	270	22.5	32	31	0	0	0	15	1	6	6	0
78 Cal Poly	11	247	22.45	30	25	1	0	0	12	2	3	8	0
79 Brown	10	222	22.2	32	27	0	0	0	1	0	2	8	0
80 Howard	11	243	22.09	35	20	4	0	0	1	1	6	5	0
81 Florida Int'l	11	241	21.91	34	24	1	0	0	3	1	5	6	0
81 Mississippi Val.	11	241	21.91	31	24	0	0	0	9	2	5	6	0
83 Alabama A&M	12	261	21.75	34	16	8	1	0	7	1	8	4	0
84 Portland St.	11	236	21.45	28	26	0	0	0	14	0	6	5	0
85 St. Peter's	11	234	21.27	30	24	0	0	0	10	0	6	5	0
86 Wagner	11	232	21.09	29	29	0	0	0	9	1	7	4	0
87 Liberty	11	230	20.91	31	30	1	0	0	4	0	2	9	0
88 Jacksonville St.	11	229	20.82	29	20	2	0	0	9	2	5	6	0
89 Northern Iowa	11	227	20.64	22	18	0	0	0	25	1	5	6	0
90 Youngstown St.	11	215	19.55	28	26	0	0	0	7	0	7	4	0
91 Chattanooga	12	232	19.33	30	28	0	0	0	8	0	2	10	0
92 Southwest Tex. St.	11	211	19.18	30	28	0	0	0	1	0	4	7	0
93 Fairfield	11	210	19.09	28	21	3	0	0	5	0	5	6	0
94 Norfolk St.	11	209	19	27	20	2	1	0	7	0	5	6	0
95 Indiana St.	12	226	18.83	30	21	1	0	0	7	1	5	7	0
96 Morris Brown	12	225	18.75	32	19	3	0	0	2	1	1	11	0
97 Jacksonville	10	185	18.5	24	20	1	1	0	5	1	3	7	0
98 St. John's (N.Y.)	10	184	18.4	24	15	2	0	0	7	0	2	8	0
99 Southern Utah	11	202	18.36	27	15	4	0	0	5	1	1	10	0
100 La Salle	11	200	18.18	27	20	1	2	0	4	0	2	9	0
101 Delaware St.	12	218	18.17	30	16	4	0	0	4	1	4	8	0
102 New Hampshire	11	199	18.09	24	19	2	0	0	10	1	3	8	0
102 Richmond	11	199	18.09	26	19	0	0	0	8	0	4	7	0
104 Sam Houston St.	11	197	17.91	25	20	0	0	0	9	0	4	7	0
105 Georgetown	11	190	17.27	26	18	1	0	0	4	1	5	6	0
106 Cornell	10	169	16.9	21	17	0	0	0	8	1	4	6	0
107 James Madison	12	196	16.33	23	17	1	0	0	13	0	5	7	0
108 Columbia	10	161	16.1	20	15	3	0	0	6	1	1	9	0
109 Fla. Atlantic	11	176	16	22	17	0	0	0	9	0	2	9	0
110 Charleston So.	12	189	15.75	26	17	0	0	0	4	2	4	8	0
111 Rhode Island	12	187	15.58	21	20	1	0	0	11	3	3	9	0
112 Tenn.-Martin	12	186	15.5	22	13	4	0	0	11	0	2	10	0
113 Bucknell	11	163	14.82	20	19	0	0	0	8	0	2	9	0
114 Iona	11	156	14.18	19	16	0	1	0	8	0	5	6	0
115 East Tenn. St.	12	167	13.92	21	20	0	0	0	7	0	4	8	0
116 Robert Morris	10	128	12.8	18	13	1	0	0	1	1	3	7	0
117 Central Conn. St.	11	139	12.64	17	11	1	0	0	8	0	5	6	0
118 Monmouth	10	115	11.5	14	10	0	0	0	7	0	2	8	0
119 Siena	10	112	11.2	14	11	1	0	0	5	0	3	7	0
120 Prairie View	11	123	11.18	17	5	4	0	0	2	1	1	10	0
121 Savannah St.	10	106	10.6	14	5	0	1	0	5	0	1	9	0
122 Canisius	11	113	10.27	15	8	2	0	0	3	1	2	9	0
123 St. Francis (Pa.)	10	101	10.1	14	11	0	0	0	2	0	2	8	0

STATISTICAL LEADERS

Total Defense

Rank, School	G	Pl	Yds	Avg	TD	Yds/Gm	W	L	T
1 Duquesne	12	724	2,256	3.12	13	188	11	1	0
2 Wagner	11	628	2,192	3.49	16	199.27	7	4	0
3 Sacred Heart	10	678	2,063	3.04	15	206.3	7	3	0
4 Marist	11	671	2,731	4.07	30	248.27	7	4	0
5 St. Francis (Pa.)	10	623	2,508	4.03	30	250.8	2	8	0
6 Stony Brook	10	693	2,570	3.71	15	257	8	2	0
7 Robert Morris	10	619	2,616	4.23	29	261.6	3	7	0
8 Siena	10	636	2,645	4.16	24	264.5	3	7	0
9 Maine	14	908	3,747	4.13	27	267.64	11	3	0
10 Iona	11	726	2,947	4.06	33	267.91	5	6	0
11 Wofford	12	752	3,245	4.32	24	270.42	9	3	0
12 Pennsylvania	10	689	2,756	4	17	275.6	9	1	0
13 Bethune-Cookman	13	829	3,584	4.32	26	275.69	11	2	0
14 Morehead St.	12	758	3,311	4.37	30	275.92	9	3	0
15 Northwestern St.	13	817	3,596	4.4	39	276.62	9	4	0
16 Monmouth	10	655	2,769	4.23	22	276.9	2	8	0
17 Bucknell	11	733	3,051	4.16	34	277.36	2	9	0
18 Eastern Ky.	12	741	3,329	4.49	29	277.42	8	4	0
19 St. Peter's	11	700	3,057	4.37	27	277.91	6	5	0
20 Lehigh	12	818	3,341	4.08	27	278.42	8	4	0
21 Youngstown St.	11	731	3,064	4.19	22	278.55	7	4	0
22 McNeese St.	15	946	4,182	4.42	35	278.8	13	2	0
23 Western Ky.	15	908	4,188	4.61	32	279.2	12	3	0
24 Villanova	15	996	4,235	4.25	35	282.33	11	4	0
25 Dayton	12	814	3,430	4.21	15	285.83	11	1	0
26 Alabama A&M	12	841	3,466	4.12	29	288.83	8	4	0
27 South Carolina St.	12	839	3,500	4.17	26	291.67	7	5	0
28 Albany (N.Y.)	12	763	3,517	4.61	33	293.08	8	4	0
29 Ga. Southern	14	911	4,126	4.53	24	294.71	11	3	0
30 Mississippi Val.	11	755	3,245	4.3	34	295	5	6	0
31 Northeastern	13	895	3,873	4.33	24	297.92	10	3	0
32 Jackson St.	11	722	3,327	4.61	34	302.45	7	4	0
33 Montana St.	13	903	3,999	4.43	34	307.62	7	6	0
34 Stephen F. Austin	11	763	3,386	4.44	30	307.82	6	5	0
35 Fairfield	11	710	3,388	4.77	37	308	5	6	0
36 Nicholls St.	11	707	3,460	4.89	25	314.55	7	4	0
37 Fordham	13	916	4,097	4.47	27	315.15	10	3	0
38 Grambling	13	879	4,148	4.72	51	319.08	11	2	0
39 Princeton	10	716	3,193	4.46	31	319.3	6	4	0
40 James Madison	12	818	3,841	4.7	34	320.08	5	7	0
41 Richmond	11	723	3,543	4.9	24	322.09	4	7	0
42 Hofstra	12	834	3,866	4.64	33	322.17	6	6	0
43 Hampton	12	883	3,900	4.42	34	325	7	5	0
44 Texas Southern	11	798	3,595	4.51	37	326.82	4	7	0
45 Alabama St.	12	839	3,925	4.68	36	327.08	6	6	0
46 Norfolk St.	11	708	3,600	5.08	40	327.27	5	6	0
47 Montana	14	976	4,619	4.73	33	329.93	11	3	0
48 Yale	10	681	3,300	4.85	24	330	6	4	0
49 Florida A&M	12	773	3,966	5.13	44	330.5	7	5	0
50 Florida Int'l	11	767	3,640	4.75	30	330.91	5	6	0
51 Appalachian St.	12	798	3,989	5	36	332.42	8	4	0
52 Furman	12	761	4,010	5.27	35	334.17	8	4	0
53 Delaware St.	12	806	4,036	5.01	42	336.33	4	8	0
54 Western Ill.	13	915	4,384	4.79	31	337.23	11	2	0
55 Indiana St.	12	845	4,063	4.81	40	338.58	5	7	0
56 Gardner-Webb	10	629	3,424	5.44	28	342.4	9	1	0
57 Southwest Mo. St.	11	782	3,768	4.82	36	342.55	4	7	0
58 Southern U.	12	849	4,123	4.86	38	343.58	6	6	0
59 Howard	11	741	3,788	5.11	38	344.36	6	5	0
60 Towson	11	738	3,795	5.14	31	345	6	5	0
61 Massachusetts	12	916	4,147	4.53	34	345.58	8	4	0
62 Alcorn St.	11	797	3,823	4.8	39	347.55	6	5	0
63 Charleston So.	12	860	4,173	4.85	40	347.75	4	8	0
64 East Tenn. St.	12	831	4,186	5.04	38	348.83	4	8	0
65 Northern Iowa	11	764	3,853	5.04	37	350.27	5	6	0
66 St. Mary's (Cal.)	12	827	4,218	5.1	34	351.5	6	6	0
67 Idaho St.	11	768	3,868	5.04	24	351.64	8	3	0
68 Delaware	12	876	4,226	4.82	27	352.17	6	6	0
69 Lafayette	12	838	4,228	5.05	36	352.33	7	5	0
70 Central Conn. St.	11	735	3,885	5.29	33	353.18	5	6	0
71 William & Mary	11	764	3,897	5.1	36	354.27	6	5	0
72 Savannah St.	10	674	3,546	5.26	48	354.6	1	9	0
73 Harvard	10	699	3,558	5.09	31	355.8	7	3	0
74 Eastern Wash.	11	801	3,932	4.91	35	357.45	6	5	0
75 Northern Ariz.	11	802	3,953	4.93	36	359.36	6	5	0
76 Illinois St.	11	765	3,957	5.17	31	359.73	6	5	0
77 Sam Houston St.	11	764	3,967	5.19	42	360.64	4	7	0
78 Tennessee Tech	12	805	4,339	5.39	41	361.58	5	7	0
79 Colgate	12	860	4,351	5.06	27	362.58	9	3	0
80 Davidson	10	722	3,638	5.04	31	363.8	7	3	0
81 Fla. Atlantic	11	750	4,017	5.36	44	365.18	2	9	0
82 Weber St.	11	733	4,030	5.5	36	366.36	3	8	0
83 Southwest Tex. St.	11	706	4,033	5.71	38	366.64	4	7	0
84 Prairie View	11	685	4,064	5.93	56	369.45	1	10	0
85 N.C. A&T	12	925	4,441	4.8	36	370.08	4	8	0
86 Murray St.	12	790	4,472	5.66	46	372.67	7	5	0
87 St. John's (N.Y.)	10	744	3,740	5.03	40	374	2	8	0
88 Holy Cross	12	831	4,507	5.42	48	375.58	4	8	0
89 Jacksonville St.	11	704	4,245	6.03	39	385.91	5	6	0
90 Southeast Mo. St.	12	821	4,647	5.66	47	387.25	8	4	0
91 Portland St.	11	808	4,372	5.41	30	397.45	6	5	0
92 Cal Poly	11	767	4,373	5.7	37	397.55	3	8	0
93 Morgan St.	12	859	4,773	5.56	49	397.75	7	5	0
94 Elon	11	709	4,380	6.18	48	398.18	4	7	0
95 Ark.-Pine Bluff	11	811	4,397	5.42	49	399.73	3	8	0
96 Georgetown	11	812	4,409	5.43	48	400.82	5	6	0
97 Austin Peay	12	869	4,810	5.54	49	400.83	7	5	0
98 Citadel	12	825	4,819	5.84	47	401.58	3	9	0
99 Eastern Ill.	12	832	4,857	5.84	56	404.75	8	4	0
100 Southern Utah	11	696	4,460	6.41	59	405.45	1	10	0
101 Southern Ill.	12	836	4,871	5.83	51	405.92	4	8	0
102 San Diego	10	683	4,077	5.97	41	407.7	5	5	0
103 Brown	10	713	4,108	5.76	36	410.8	2	8	0
104 New Hampshire	11	791	4,530	5.73	43	411.82	3	8	0
105 Columbia	10	743	4,121	5.55	37	412.1	1	9	0
106 Cornell	10	746	4,129	5.53	40	412.9	4	6	0
107 Tennessee St.	12	872	4,959	5.69	56	413.25	2	10	0
108 Tenn.-Martin	12	820	4,964	6.05	64	413.67	2	10	0
109 Jacksonville	10	692	4,154	6	42	415.4	3	7	0
110 Sacramento St.	12	860	4,992	5.8	54	416	5	7	0
111 Samford	11	762	4,621	6.06	49	420.09	4	7	0
112 Canisius	11	780	4,633	5.94	45	421.18	2	9	0
113 Western Caro.	11	853	4,679	5.49	38	425.36	5	6	0
114 Morris Brown	12	863	5,131	5.95	59	427.58	1	11	0
115 Chattanooga	12	911	5,137	5.64	49	428.08	2	10	0
116 La Salle	11	849	4,765	5.61	54	433.18	2	9	0
117 Rhode Island	12	847	5,211	6.15	53	434.25	3	9	0
118 VMI	12	847	5,381	6.35	55	448.42	6	6	0
119 Dartmouth	10	731	4,488	6.14	40	448.8	3	7	0
120 Valparaiso	11	753	5,014	6.66	70	455.82	1	10	0
121 Liberty	11	827	5,019	6.07	48	456.27	2	9	0
122 Drake	10	814	5,312	6.53	57	482.91	5	5	0
123 Butler	10	732	4,891	6.68	52	489.1	4	6	0

Total Offense

Rank, School	G	Pl	Yds	Avg	TD	Yds/Gm	W	L	T
1 Jackson St.	11	869	5,340	6.14	47	485.45	7	4	0
2 Grambling	13	969	6,217	6.42	70	478.23	11	2	0
3 Ga. Southern	14	981	6,575	6.7	66	469.64	11	3	0
4 Drake	10	764	5,070	6.64	49	460.91	5	5	0
5 Eastern Ill.	12	888	5,431	6.12	61	452.58	8	4	0
6 Eastern Wash.	11	766	4,923	6.43	50	447.55	6	5	0
7 Southeast Mo. St.	12	886	5,368	6.06	56	447.33	8	4	0
8 Harvard	10	758	4,267	5.63	38	426.7	7	3	0
9 Morehead St.	12	889	5,108	5.75	47	425.67	9	3	0
10 Dartmouth	10	767	4,166	5.43	31	416.6	3	7	0
11 Gardner-Webb	10	739	4,149	5.61	35	414.9	9	1	0
12 Furman	12	842	4,966	5.9	48	413.83	8	4	0
13 Idaho St.	11	789	4,534	5.75	42	412.18	8	3	0
14 Villanova	15	1116	6,146	5.51	60	409.73	11	4	0
15 Pennsylvania	10	749	4,084	5.45	46	408.4	9	1	0
16 Sacramento St.	12	904	4,893	5.41	41	407.75	5	7	0
17 San Diego	10	684	4,075	5.96	38	407.5	5	5	0
18 Bethune-Cookman	13	874	5,296	6.06	56	407.38	11	2	0
19 Duquesne	12	905	4,878	5.39	46	406.5	11	1	0
20 Tennessee Tech	12	795	4,822	6.07	45	401.83	5	7	0
21 Murray St.	12	833	4,799	5.76	50	399.92	7	5	0
22 Wofford	12	860	4,787	5.57	42	398.92	9	3	0
23 Valparaiso	11	782	4,388	5.61	35	398.91	1	10	0
24 Western Ill.	13	919	5,149	5.6	58	396.08	11	2	0
25 Southern Ill.	12	797	4,727	5.93	56	393.92	4	8	0
26 Colgate	12	824	4,710	5.72	38	392.5	9	3	0
27 Stephen F. Austin	11	714	4,263	5.97	42	387.55	6	5	0
28 Brown	10	737	3,852	5.23	32	385.2	2	8	0
29 William & Mary	11	768	4,228	5.51	41	384.36	6	5	0
30 Fordham	13	863	4,995	5.79	53	384.23	10	3	0
31 Florida A&M	12	911	4,608	5.06	43	384	7	5	0
32 McNeese St.	15	1087	5,737	5.28	62	382.47	13	2	0
33 Eastern Ky.	12	835	4,577	5.48	49	381.42	8	4	0
34 Morgan St.	12	803	4,575	5.7	50	381.25	7	5	0
35 Delaware	12	863	4,538	5.26	36	378.17	6	6	0
36 Dayton	12	800	4,512	5.64	53	376	11	1	0

Rank, School	G	Pl	Yds	Avg	TD	Yds/Gm	W	L	T
37 Towson	11	828	4,120	4.98	39	374.55	6	5	0
38 Lafayette	12	905	4,484	4.95	37	373.67	7	5	0
39 Montana	14	997	5,231	5.25	55	373.64	11	3	0
40 Princeton	10	725	3,724	5.14	29	372.4	6	4	0
41 Citadel	12	859	4,467	5.2	38	372.25	3	9	0
42 Albany (N.Y.)	12	820	4,457	5.44	49	371.42	8	4	0
43 South Carolina St.	12	748	4,451	5.95	48	370.92	7	5	0
44 Western Caro.	11	766	4,075	5.32	36	370.45	5	6	0
45 Massachusetts	12	837	4,440	5.3	44	370	8	4	0
46 Northwestern St.	13	908	4,783	5.27	47	367.92	9	4	0
47 Butler	10	667	3,673	5.51	46	367.3	4	6	0
48 VMI	12	869	4,403	5.07	42	366.92	6	6	0
49 Yale	10	686	3,665	5.34	35	366.5	6	4	0
50 Western Ky.	15	996	5,479	5.5	54	365.27	12	3	0
51 Tennessee St.	12	795	4,365	5.49	40	363.75	2	10	0
52 Southern U.	12	932	4,355	4.67	38	362.92	6	6	0
53 Northern Iowa	11	806	3,986	4.95	22	362.36	5	6	0
54 Davidson	10	701	3,606	5.14	42	360.6	7	3	0
55 Weber St.	11	750	3,947	5.26	36	358.82	3	8	0
56 Hampton	12	893	4,300	4.82	54	358.33	7	5	0
57 Hofstra	12	835	4,262	5.1	32	355.17	6	6	0
58 Lehigh	12	865	4,223	4.88	43	351.92	8	4	0
59 Liberty	11	703	3,856	5.49	31	350.55	2	9	0
60 Illinois St.	11	786	3,854	4.9	30	350.36	6	5	0
61 Texas Southern	11	767	3,836	5	40	348.73	4	7	0
62 Appalachian St.	12	826	4,179	5.06	38	348.25	8	4	0
63 Portland St.	11	763	3,800	4.98	28	345.45	6	5	0
64 St. Mary's (Cal.)	12	797	4,145	5.2	42	345.42	6	6	0
65 Ark.-Pine Bluff	11	765	3,747	4.9	37	340.64	3	8	0
66 Northeastern	13	884	4,403	4.98	53	338.69	10	3	0
67 Maine	14	936	4,702	5.02	45	335.86	11	3	0
68 Alabama St.	12	886	4,023	4.54	46	335.25	6	6	0
69 Holy Cross	12	793	4,016	5.06	37	334.67	4	8	0
70 Montana St.	13	874	4,342	4.97	37	334	7	6	0
71 Richmond	11	748	3,651	4.88	26	331.91	4	7	0
72 Marist	11	789	3,647	4.62	37	331.55	7	4	0
73 Samford	11	738	3,644	4.94	36	331.27	4	7	0
74 James Madison	12	802	3,923	4.89	23	326.92	5	7	0
75 Alcorn St.	11	777	3,588	4.62	38	326.18	6	5	0
76 New Hampshire	11	797	3,574	4.48	24	324.91	3	8	0
77 Austin Peay	12	803	3,881	4.83	38	323.42	7	5	0
78 Columbia	10	757	3,215	4.25	20	321.5	1	9	0
79 Southwest Mo. St.	11	731	3,523	4.82	33	320.27	4	7	0
80 Howard	11	781	3,484	4.46	35	316.73	6	5	0
81 Northern Ariz.	11	724	3,449	4.76	31	313.55	6	5	0
81 Youngstown St.	11	697	3,449	4.95	28	313.55	7	4	0
83 Cal Poly	11	738	3,433	4.65	30	312.09	3	8	0
84 Nicholls St.	11	640	3,429	5.36	40	311.73	7	4	0
85 Rhode Island	12	779	3,734	4.79	21	311.17	3	9	0
86 St. Peter's	11	716	3,401	4.75	30	309.18	6	5	0
87 Chattanooga	12	763	3,703	4.85	30	308.58	2	10	0
88 Southern Utah	11	752	3,391	4.51	27	308.27	1	10	0
89 Mississippi Val.	11	767	3,386	4.41	31	307.82	5	6	0
90 La Salle	11	697	3,380	4.85	27	307.27	2	9	0
91 Florida Int'l	11	632	3,355	5.31	34	305	5	6	0
92 N.C. A&T	12	773	3,614	4.68	37	301.17	4	8	0
93 Jacksonville	10	658	2,985	4.54	24	298.5	3	7	0
94 Stony Brook	10	635	2,968	4.67	31	296.8	8	2	0
95 Cornell	10	686	2,965	4.32	21	296.5	4	6	0
96 Bucknell	11	751	3,235	4.31	20	294.09	2	9	0
97 Jacksonville St.	11	759	3,228	4.25	29	293.45	5	6	0
98 Indiana St.	12	748	3,489	4.66	30	290.75	5	7	0
99 Elon	11	718	3,198	4.45	33	290.73	4	7	0
100 Fairfield	11	814	3,191	3.92	28	290.09	5	6	0
101 Sam Houston St.	11	727	3,157	4.34	25	287	4	7	0
102 Delaware St.	12	782	3,403	4.35	30	283.58	4	8	0
103 Southwest Tex. St.	11	656	3,077	4.69	30	279.73	4	7	0
104 Charleston So.	12	767	3,340	4.35	26	278.33	4	8	0
105 Wagner	11	709	2,996	4.23	29	272.36	7	4	0
106 Alabama A&M	12	751	3,246	4.32	34	270.5	8	4	0
107 Morris Brown	12	802	3,226	4.02	32	268.83	1	11	0
107 Tenn.-Martin	12	759	3,226	4.25	22	268.83	2	10	0
109 Norfolk St.	11	744	2,926	3.93	27	266	5	6	0
110 Sacred Heart	10	643	2,621	4.08	29	262.1	7	3	0
111 Georgetown	11	636	2,833	4.45	26	257.55	5	6	0
112 Robert Morris	10	639	2,475	3.87	18	247.5	3	7	0
113 St. John's (N.Y.)	10	620	2,465	3.98	24	246.5	2	8	0
114 Central Conn. St.	11	726	2,678	3.69	17	243.45	5	6	0
115 East Tenn. St.	12	746	2,900	3.89	21	241.67	4	8	0
116 Iona	11	714	2,562	3.59	19	232.91	5	6	0
117 Savannah St.	10	686	2,257	3.29	14	225.7	1	9	0
118 Fla. Atlantic	11	678	2,475	3.65	22	225	2	9	0
119 Monmouth	10	624	2,201	3.53	14	220.1	2	8	0
120 St. Francis (Pa.)	10	672	2,186	3.25	14	218.6	2	8	0

Rank, School	G	Pl	Yds	Avg	TD	Yds/Gm	W	L	T
121 Prairie View	11	719	2,368	3.29	17	215.27	1	10	0
122 Canisius	11	720	2,360	3.28	15	214.55	2	9	0
123 Siena	10	614	1,958	3.19	14	195.8	3	7	0

Turnovers Gained

Rank, School	No.	Rank, School	No.
1 N.C. A&T	45	56 St. Francis (Pa.)	25
2 Duquesne	40	56 Howard	25
3 Bethune-Cookman	39	56 Jacksonville St.	25
4 Dayton	37	66 Butler	24
4 McNeese St.	37	66 Youngstown St.	24
4 Massachusetts	37	66 VMI	24
7 Alabama St.	36	66 Eastern Ill.	24
7 Northeastern	36	66 Davidson	24
7 Grambling	36	66 Sacramento St.	24
10 Maine	35	66 Cal Poly	24
10 Western Ky.	35	73 Albany (N.Y.)	23
12 Austin Peay	34	73 Brown	23
12 Florida A&M	34	73 Lehigh	23
12 Montana	34	73 Northern Ariz.	23
12 Morehead St.	34	73 Tenn.-Martin	23
12 Morris Brown	34	73 Tennessee St.	23
17 Alabama A&M	33	73 Southeast Mo. St.	23
17 Central Conn. St.	33	73 Samford	23
17 East Tenn. St.	33	73 Sam Houston St.	23
17 Pennsylvania	33	73 Prairie View	23
17 Hampton	33	73 Ga. Southern	23
17 Alcorn St.	33	84 Indiana St.	22
23 Marist	32	84 Southwest Mo. St.	22
23 Western Ill.	32	84 Jacksonville	22
23 Ark.-Pine Bluff	32	84 Princeton	22
23 Texas Southern	32	84 Northern Iowa	22
23 Richmond	32	84 Morgan St.	22
23 South Carolina St.	32	84 Iona	22
29 Sacred Heart	31	91 Citadel	21
30 Fairfield	30	91 Eastern Ky.	21
30 Southern Ill.	30	91 Tennessee Tech	21
30 Mississippi Val.	30	91 Stephen F. Austin	21
30 Furman	30	91 Idaho St.	21
30 Portland Int'l	30	91 Holy Cross	21
30 St. Mary's (Cal.)	30	91 Harvard	21
36 Colgate	29	98 Appalachian St.	20
36 St. Peter's	29	98 Monmouth	20
36 Southern U.	29	98 Montana St.	20
36 Wagner	29	98 Robert Morris	20
36 Villanova	29	98 San Diego	20
41 Charleston So.	28	98 Wofford	20
41 Delaware St.	28	98 Rhode Island	20
41 Stony Brook	28	98 La Salle	20
41 Southwest Tex. St.	28	98 Eastern Wash.	20
41 Portland St.	28	107 Delaware	19
41 Jackson St.	28	107 Fla. Atlantic	19
47 Canisius	27	107 Southern Utah	19
47 Northwestern St.	27	107 New Hampshire	19
47 Gardner-Webb	27	111 Bucknell	18
47 Murray St.	27	111 James Madison	18
51 Norfolk St.	26	111 Georgetown	18
51 Towson	26	111 Columbia	18
51 Elon	26	115 Cornell	17
51 Siena	26	115 Hofstra	17
51 Savannah St.	26	117 Dartmouth	16
56 Fordham	25	117 Chattanooga	16
56 William & Mary	25	119 Drake	15
56 Western Caro.	25	119 Weber St.	15
56 St. John's (N.Y.)	25	121 Illinois St.	14
56 Nicholls St.	25	122 Yale	13
56 Liberty	25	123 Valparaiso	8
56 Lafayette	25		

Turnovers Lost

Rank, School	No.	Rank, School	No.
1 Harvard	12	8 Murray St.	17
1 Yale	12	10 Austin Peay	18
3 San Diego	13	10 Siena	18
3 Gardner-Webb	13	10 Western Ky.	18
5 Dayton	14	10 William & Mary	18
6 Montana	15	10 Towson	18
7 Eastern Wash.	16	10 Colgate	18
8 Fordham	17	16 Hampton	19

Rank, School	No.
16 Wofford	19
16 Western Ill.	19
16 Wagner	19
16 Southwest Tex. St.	19
16 Southern Ill.	19
22 Appalachian St.	20
22 Ga. Southern	20
22 Columbia	20
22 Eastern Ky.	20
22 Northeastern	20
22 Nicholls St.	20
28 Sacramento St.	21
28 VMI	21
28 Youngstown St.	21
28 Western Caro.	21
28 Delaware	21
28 Davidson	21
34 Brown	22
34 Southwest Mo. St.	22
34 Princeton	22
34 Illinois St.	22
34 East Tenn. St.	22
34 Dartmouth	22
34 Drake	22
41 Butler	23
41 Furman	23
41 Georgetown	23

Rank, School	No.
41 Marist	23
41 Stephen F. Austin	23
41 Monmouth	23
47 Cal Poly	24
47 Cornell	24
47 Hofstra	24
47 Montana St.	24
47 Holy Cross	24
47 Stony Brook	24
47 Richmond	24
54 Albany (N.Y.)	25
54 Bethune-Cookman	25
54 N.C. A&T	25
54 Chattanooga	25
54 Tenn.-Martin	25
54 Tennessee Tech	25
54 Sam Houston St.	25
54 Norfolk St.	25
54 Jacksonville St.	25
63 Central Conn. St.	26
63 Southeast Mo. St.	26
63 St. Peter's	26
63 St. Mary's (Cal.)	26
63 St. John's (N.Y.)	26
63 Portland St.	26
63 Pennsylvania	26
63 Morgan St.	26

Rank, School	No.
63 Massachusetts	26
63 Jacksonville	26
63 Idaho St.	26
63 Fla. Atlantic	26
63 Fairfield	26
76 Duquesne	27
76 Maine	27
76 Lehigh	27
76 Northern Ariz.	27
76 McNeese St.	27
81 Citadel	28
81 Florida Int'l	28
81 Indiana St.	28
81 Northwestern St.	28
81 Samford	28
81 Villanova	28
81 Ark.-Pine Bluff	28
81 Lafayette	28
81 Liberty	28
90 Robert Morris	29
90 Sacred Heart	29
90 Southern Utah	29
93 Alabama A&M	30
93 Alcorn St.	30
93 Eastern Ill.	30
93 Weber St.	30
93 Rhode Island	30

Rank, School	No.
93 New Hampshire	30
93 Howard	30
100 La Salle	31
100 Morris Brown	31
100 Elon	31
103 Delaware St.	32
103 Southern U.	32
103 Valparaiso	32
103 St. Francis (Pa.)	32
107 James Madison	33
107 Mississippi Val.	33
107 South Carolina St.	33
110 Charleston So.	34
110 Northern Iowa	34
110 Tennessee St.	34
113 Bucknell	35
113 Texas Southern	35
113 Grambling	35
116 Alabama St.	36
116 Savannah St.	36
118 Jackson St.	37
119 Canisius	38
119 Prairie View	38
121 Florida A&M	39
121 Iona	39
123 Morehead St.	41

Turnover Margin

Rank, School	G	Gained Fm	Gained Int	Tot	Lost Fm	Lost Int	Tot	Margin/ Gm	W	L	T
1 Dayton	12	9	28	37	10	4	14	1.92	11	1	0
2 N.C. A&T	12	18	27	45	13	12	25	1.67	4	8	0
3 Gardner-Webb	10	11	16	27	9	4	13	1.4	9	1	0
4 Montana	14	18	16	34	5	10	15	1.36	11	3	0
5 Austin Peay	12	18	16	34	8	10	18	1.33	7	5	0
6 Northeastern	13	20	16	36	12	8	20	1.23	10	3	0
7 Hampton	12	21	12	33	10	9	19	1.17	7	5	0
8 Western Ky.	15	15	20	35	12	6	18	1.13	12	3	0
9 Duquesne	12	15	25	40	13	14	27	1.08	11	1	0
10 Bethune-Cookman	13	18	21	39	8	17	25	1.08	11	2	0
11 Western Ill.	13	17	15	32	14	5	19	1	11	2	0
12 Colgate	12	15	14	29	10	8	18	0.92	9	3	0
12 Southern Ill.	12	18	12	30	14	5	19	0.92	4	8	0
12 Massachusetts	12	17	20	37	9	17	26	0.92	8	4	0
12 East Tenn. St.	12	19	14	33	12	10	22	0.92	4	8	0
16 Wagner	11	17	12	29	6	13	19	0.91	7	4	0
17 Harvard	10	10	11	21	7	5	12	0.9	7	3	0
18 Murray St.	12	14	13	27	10	7	17	0.83	7	5	0
19 Marist	11	17	15	32	13	10	23	0.82	7	4	0
19 Southwest Tex. St.	11	17	11	28	11	8	19	0.82	4	7	0
21 Siena	10	14	12	26	10	8	18	0.8	3	7	0
22 Richmond	11	18	14	32	14	10	24	0.73	4	7	0
22 Towson	11	8	18	26	7	11	18	0.73	6	5	0
24 Pennsylvania	10	13	20	33	13	13	26	0.7	9	1	0
24 San Diego	10	7	13	20	9	4	13	0.7	5	5	0
26 McNeese St.	15	17	20	37	16	11	27	0.67	13	2	0
27 Central Conn. St.	11	16	17	33	11	15	26	0.64	5	6	0
27 William & Mary	11	10	15	25	9	9	18	0.64	6	5	0
29 Fordham	13	10	15	25	8	9	17	0.62	10	3	0
30 Furman	12	13	17	30	14	9	23	0.58	8	4	0
31 Maine	14	15	20	35	16	11	27	0.57	11	3	0
32 Nicholls St.	11	13	12	25	13	7	20	0.45	7	4	0
33 Stony Brook	10	16	12	28	14	10	24	0.4	8	2	0
34 Eastern Wash.	11	10	10	20	9	7	16	0.36	6	5	0
34 Fairfield	11	14	16	30	9	17	26	0.36	5	6	0
34 Ark.-Pine Bluff	11	16	16	32	7	21	28	0.36	3	8	0
34 Western Caro.	11	17	8	25	8	13	21	0.36	5	6	0
38 St. Mary's (Cal.)	12	9	21	30	20	6	26	0.33	6	6	0
39 Davidson	10	15	9	24	9	12	21	0.3	7	3	0
40 Alcorn St.	11	16	17	33	13	17	30	0.27	6	5	0
40 St. Peter's	11	14	15	29	12	14	26	0.27	6	5	0
40 Youngstown St.	11	15	9	24	15	6	21	0.27	7	4	0
43 Alabama A&M	12	16	17	33	10	20	30	0.25	8	4	0
43 Sacramento St.	12	14	10	24	14	7	21	0.25	5	7	0
43 Morris Brown	12	19	15	34	13	18	31	0.25	1	11	0
43 VMI	12	12	12	24	7	14	21	0.25	6	6	0
47 Ga. Southern	14	8	15	23	16	4	20	0.21	11	3	0

Rank, School	G	Gained			Lost			Margin/Gm	W	L	T
		Fm	Int	Tot	Fm	Int	Tot				
48 Sacred Heart	10	12	19	31	18	11	29	0.2	7	3	0
49 Florida Int'l	11	20	10	30	14	14	28	0.18	5	6	0
49 Portland St.	11	17	11	28	12	14	26	0.18	6	5	0
51 Brown	10	14	9	23	6	16	22	0.1	2	8	0
51 Butler	10	14	10	24	7	16	23	0.1	4	6	0
51 Yale	10	8	5	13	6	6	12	0.1	6	4	0
54 Norfolk St.	11	13	13	26	13	12	25	0.09	5	6	0
55 Eastern Ky.	12	9	12	21	9	11	20	0.08	8	4	0
55 Wofford	12	9	11	20	16	3	19	0.08	9	3	0
57 Grambling	13	12	24	36	17	18	35	0.08	11	2	0
58 Villanova	15	14	15	29	14	14	28	0.07	11	4	0
59 Alabama St.	12	16	20	36	15	21	36	0	6	6	0
59 Southwest Mo. St.	11	11	11	22	11	11	22	0	4	7	0
59 Princeton	10	6	16	22	11	11	22	0	6	4	0
59 Jacksonville St.	11	13	12	25	14	11	25	0	5	6	0
59 Appalachian St.	12	8	12	20	9	11	20	0	8	4	0
59 Cal Poly	11	13	11	24	8	16	24	0	3	8	0
65 Northwestern St.	13	18	9	27	15	13	28	-0.08	9	4	0
66 South Carolina St.	12	15	17	32	19	14	33	-0.08	7	5	0
67 St. John's (N.Y.)	10	12	13	25	14	12	26	-0.1	2	8	0
68 Albany (N.Y.)	12	12	11	23	19	6	25	-0.17	8	4	0
68 Tenn.-Martin	12	11	12	23	13	12	25	-0.17	2	10	0
68 Delaware	12	10	9	19	15	6	21	-0.17	6	6	0
71 Sam Houston St.	11	14	9	23	12	13	25	-0.18	4	7	0
71 Stephen F. Austin	11	9	12	21	10	13	23	-0.18	6	5	0
73 Columbia	10	11	7	18	10	10	20	-0.2	1	9	0
74 Holy Cross	12	15	6	21	10	14	24	-0.25	4	8	0
74 Lafayette	12	14	11	25	13	15	28	-0.25	7	5	0
74 Southern U.	12	15	14	29	15	17	32	-0.25	6	6	0
74 Southeast Mo. St.	12	10	13	23	8	18	26	-0.25	8	4	0
78 Liberty	11	16	9	25	13	15	28	-0.27	2	9	0
78 Mississippi Val.	11	12	18	30	19	14	33	-0.27	5	6	0
78 Texas Southern	11	13	19	32	14	21	35	-0.27	4	7	0
81 Monmouth	10	14	6	20	13	10	23	-0.3	2	8	0
82 Montana St.	13	11	9	20	15	9	24	-0.31	7	6	0
83 Delaware St.	12	16	12	28	17	15	32	-0.33	4	8	0
83 Lehigh	12	11	12	23	13	14	27	-0.33	8	4	0
83 Morgan St.	12	15	7	22	14	12	26	-0.33	7	5	0
83 Tennessee Tech	12	11	10	21	11	14	25	-0.33	5	7	0
87 Northern Ariz.	11	8	15	23	10	17	27	-0.36	6	5	0
88 Jacksonville	10	12	10	22	13	13	26	-0.4	3	7	0
89 Florida A&M	12	18	16	34	20	19	39	-0.42	7	5	0
90 Georgetown	11	6	12	18	15	8	23	-0.45	5	6	0
90 Samford	11	12	11	23	15	13	28	-0.45	4	7	0
90 Howard	11	10	15	25	15	15	30	-0.45	6	5	0
90 Elon	11	16	10	26	19	12	31	-0.45	4	7	0
90 Idaho St.	11	5	16	21	14	12	26	-0.45	8	3	0
95 Charleston So.	12	12	16	28	13	21	34	-0.5	4	8	0
95 Indiana St.	12	13	9	22	17	11	28	-0.5	5	7	0
95 Eastern Ill.	12	15	9	24	13	17	30	-0.5	8	4	0
98 Citadel	12	11	10	21	16	12	28	-0.58	3	9	0
98 Hofstra	12	10	7	17	11	13	24	-0.58	6	6	0
98 Morehead St.	12	14	20	34	22	19	41	-0.58	9	3	0
101 Dartmouth	10	9	7	16	12	10	22	-0.6	3	7	0
102 Drake	10	8	7	15	7	15	22	-0.64	5	5	0
102 Fla. Atlantic	11	13	6	19	18	8	26	-0.64	2	9	0
104 Cornell	10	8	9	17	13	11	24	-0.7	4	6	0
104 St. Francis (Pa.)	10	14	11	25	14	18	32	-0.7	2	8	0
106 Illinois St.	11	10	4	14	10	12	22	-0.73	6	5	0
107 Chattanooga	12	11	5	16	11	14	25	-0.75	2	10	0
108 Jackson St.	11	13	15	28	23	14	37	-0.82	7	4	0
109 Rhode Island	12	12	8	20	23	7	30	-0.83	3	9	0
110 Robert Morris	10	7	13	20	16	13	29	-0.9	3	7	0
111 Southern Utah	11	15	4	19	15	14	29	-0.91	1	10	0
112 Tennessee St.	12	12	11	23	12	22	34	-0.92	2	10	0
113 Canisius	11	16	11	27	11	27	38	-1	2	9	0
113 La Salle	11	14	6	20	15	16	31	-1	2	9	0
113 Savannah St.	10	16	10	26	18	18	36	-1	1	9	0
113 New Hampshire	11	9	10	19	16	14	30	-1	3	8	0
117 Northern Iowa	11	9	13	22	16	18	34	-1.09	5	6	0
118 James Madison	12	9	9	18	18	15	33	-1.25	5	7	0
119 Prairie View	11	14	9	23	21	17	38	-1.36	1	10	0
119 Weber St.	11	8	7	15	15	15	30	-1.36	3	8	0
121 Bucknell	11	10	8	18	15	20	35	-1.55	2	9	0
121 Iona	11	13	9	22	18	21	39	-1.55	5	6	0
123 Valparaiso	11	4	4	8	13	19	32	-2.18	1	10	0

Southern Connecticut State Sports Information

Darrin Davis, Southern Connecticut State

2002 Division II Individual Leaders

Rushing

Minimum 100 Yards Per Game

Rank, Name, Team	Cl	Pos	G	Rush	Rush Yds	Rush TD	YPG
1 Ian Smart, C.W. Post	Sr.	RB	12	287	2,023	30	168.6
2 LeVar Ammons, Quincy	So.	RB	10	249	1,650	13	165.0
3 Darrin Davis, Southern Conn. St.	**Sr.**	**RB**	**11**	**327**	**1,620**	**15**	**147.3**
4 Mike Miller, Neb.-Kearney	So.	RB	11	333	1,600	13	145.5
5 Robert Campbell, Findlay	Jr.	RB	11	341	1,575	16	143.2
6 Mike Eckmeyer, West Chester	Jr.	RB	11	295	1,539	14	139.9
7 Paris Moore, Minn.-Morris	Sr.	RB	11	292	1,449	13	131.7
8 Duriel Cobb, West Va. Wesleyan	Sr.	RB	11	265	1,440	10	130.9
9 Joe Johnson, Michigan Tech	Jr.	RB	10	274	1,278	9	127.8
10 Duron Croson, Fort Valley St.	Jr.	RB	11	252	1,384	18	125.8
11 Gerome Castleberry, East Central	Sr.	RB	11	317	1,379	7	125.4
12 John Kuhn, Shippensburg	So.	RB	11	243	1,368	16	124.4
13 Kevin Clive, Hillsdale	Sr.	RB	11	276	1,350	15	122.7
14 Craig Duppong, Wayne St. (Mich.)	Jr.	RB	11	219	1,315	12	119.5
15 Tyler Paul, Emporia St.	Jr.	RB	12	305	1,434	11	119.5
16 Corwin Elliott, Ark.-Monticello	Sr.	RB	10	274	1,192	7	119.2
17 Alonzo Roebuck, Edinboro	Sr.	RB	10	243	1,177	13	117.7
18 Garrion Corbin, Tiffin	Fr.	RB	10	188	1,160	16	116.0
19 Matt Massari, UC Davis	So.	RB	11	210	1,274	11	115.8
20 Larry Williams, Tex. A&M-Kingsville	Jr.	-	13	240	1,496	18	115.1
21 Kegan Coleman, Central Mo. St.	So.	RB	12	262	1,379	22	114.9
22 Reginald Spearmon, Grand Valley St.	Sr.	RB	14	291	1,500	21	107.1
23 Cortlandt Florence, Tuskegee	Jr.	RB	11	225	1,162	12	105.6
24 Codolyous Wilson, Lincoln (Mo.)	So.	RB	10	230	1,055	12	105.5
25 Nate Campbell, Western St. (Colo.)	Sr.	DB	11	240	1,142	7	103.8
26 Darmel Whitfield, Gannon	So.	QB	10	227	1,032	11	103.2
27 Tarik Abdullah, Central Okla.	Jr.	RB	10	168	1,030	14	103.0
28 Derek Fudge, Ferris St.	Jr.	RB	10	233	1,016	10	101.6
29 Montoya Brown, Ouachita Baptist	Jr.	RB	10	212	1,012	10	101.2
30 Chris Washington, Concordia-St. Paul	Jr.	RB	11	214	1,106	12	100.5
31 Ricky Covington, Winston-Salem	Fr.	RB	10	231	1,005	6	100.5
32 Chad Coons, Northwood	Fr.	-	11	117	955	13	86.8
33 Keath Bartynski, Saginaw Valley	Sr.	RB	10	129	856	8	85.6
34 DeAngelo Bridgers, Fayetteville St.	Sr.	RB	12	207	963	11	80.3
35 J.R. McCoy, Ashland	Sr.	RB	11	258	800	6	72.7

Passing Efficiency

Minimum 130.0 Rating
Minimum 15 Attempts Per Game

Rank, Name, Team	Cl	Pos	G	Pass Att	Comp	Int	Pass Yds	Pass TD	Pass Eff
1 Curt Anes, Grand Valley St.	Sr.	QB	14	414	278	6	3,692	47	176.6
2 Brian Eyerman, Indiana (Pa.)	Sr.	QB	12	290	173	7	2,724	36	174.7
3 Ricky Fritz, Minn.-Duluth	Sr.	QB	12	287	160	13	2,760	34	166.6
4 Ryan Flanigan, UC Davis	Jr.	QB	12	253	166	10	2,397	20	163.4
5 Zak Hill, Central Wash.	Jr.	QB	9	308	209	7	2,694	22	160.4
6 Keith Heckendorf, St. Cloud St.	Jr.	QB	11	349	203	12	2,817	37	154.1
7 Bruce Carpenter, Winona St.	Sr.	QB	12	335	177	8	2,933	32	153.1
8 Matt Lafleur, Saginaw Valley	Sr.	QB	12	273	168	5	2,243	20	151.1
9 Buster Faulkner, Valdosta St.	So.	QB	15	502	326	17	3,821	41	149.1
10 James McNear, Concordia-St. Paul	Fr.	QB	10	271	155	7	2,264	20	146.6
11 Chad Friehauf, Colorado Mines	So.	QB	11	281	174	7	2,220	21	145.8
12 Dennis Gile, Central Mo. St.	Jr.	QB	12	265	145	11	2,270	22	145.8
13 Josh Shimek, Western Wash.	Jr.	QB	9	172	109	5	1,327	12	145.4
14 Abel Gonzalez, Tex. A&M-Kingsville	Sr.	QB	13	218	123	7	1,834	16	144.9
15 Andrew Webb, Fort Lewis	Jr.	QB	11	529	317	13	4,109	37	143.3
16 Chase Sugarek, Tarleton St.	Sr.	QB	11	278	176	7	2,232	13	141.1
17 Phillip Boggs, Midwestern St.	Jr.	QB	11	232	134	5	1,763	16	140.0
18 Andrew Herrmann, Bloomsburg	Sr.	QB	10	231	124	14	1,975	18	139.1
19 Freddie Langston, Harding	Sr.	QB	10	301	177	8	2,275	20	138.9
20 Pat Korth, Neb.-Kearney	Jr.	QB	11	314	170	10	2,689	17	137.6
21 Bill Skelton, Hillsdale	Jr.	QB	11	278	173	5	1,942	17	137.5
22 Will Hall, North Ala.	Jr.	QB	10	321	204	12	2,635	12	137.4
23 Chris Cormier, West Va. Wesleyan	Jr.	QB	11	237	122	9	1,982	16	136.4
24 Zak Clark, Central Ark.	Jr.	QB	11	427	263	13	3,157	24	136.2
25 Jason Smith, Bemidji St.	So.	QB	11	288	155	10	2,153	23	136.0
26 John McMenamin, Northwest Mo. St.	Sr.	QB	13	491	296	12	3,583	28	135.5
27 John Esquivel, Southern Conn. St.	Sr.	QB	11	348	188	8	2,582	25	135.5
28 Erick Johnson, Central Okla.	Jr.	QB	11	242	132	11	2,218	9	134.7
29 Marc Eddy, Bentley	So.	QB	11	306	164	12	2,365	22	134.4
30 Josh McGee, Winston-Salem	So.	QB	10	222	137	5	1,554	12	133.8
31 Colby Freeman, Abilene Christian	Jr.	QB	10	250	138	10	2,093	12	133.4
32 Jake Parten, Northern St.	Sr.	QB	11	314	162	16	2,465	24	132.6
33 Brett Gilliland, West Ala.	Jr.	QB	11	451	280	10	3,213	20	132.1

Rank, Name, Team	Cl	Pos	G	Pass Att	Comp	Int	Pass Yds	Pass TD	Pass Eff
34 Drew Beard, Southeastern Okla.	So.	QB	10	202	101	9	1,675	13	132.0
35 Eric Smith, West Va. Tech	Fr.	QB	11	333	173	16	2,662	22	131.3

Receptions Per Game

Min. 5.0 Receptions Per Game

Rank, Name, Team	Cl	Pos	G	Rec	Rec Yds	Rec TD	Rec PG
1 Andrew Blakley, Truman	Sr.	WR	11	96	965	6	8.7
Gerald Gales, West Ala.	Jr.	WR	11	96	994	4	8.7
3 Chris Brewer, Fort Lewis	So.	WR	11	85	1,274	18	7.7
Marc Green, Southwest Baptist	Jr.	WR	11	85	1,014	4	7.7
5 Jamal Allen, Fort Lewis	Sr.	WR	11	80	939	5	7.3
6 Brian Potucek, Central Wash.	So.	WR	12	86	1,265	11	7.2
7 Terrance Banks, Grand Valley St.	Sr.	WR	14	98	1,170	6	7.0
Josh Davis, South Dakota St.	Fr.	WR	10	70	732	6	7.0
Garvin Graves, Calif. (Pa.)	Fr.	-	10	70	870	6	7.0
10 Brandon Munson, Northern Mich.	Sr.	WR	11	76	950	6	6.9
11 Michael Hull, Ashland	So.	WR	11	72	823	3	6.5
Kory Wright, Concord	Jr.	TE	11	72	892	4	6.5
13 Jamaica Rector, Northwest Mo. St.	So.	WR	12	78	1,242	6	6.5
14 Michael Wahlstrom, Chadron St.	Jr.	WR	10	64	801	7	6.4
15 Antonio Carter, Glenville St.	So.	WR	11	70	956	8	6.4
Jesse Smith, North Dakota	Sr.	WR	11	70	1,011	6	6.4
17 Willie Lane, East Central	So.	WR	11	69	645	5	6.3
Ben Nelson, St. Cloud St.	Sr.	WR	11	69	1,072	23	6.3
19 Jeff Cupe, Southern Conn. St.	Sr.	WR	11	67	1,051	13	6.1
Ryshaune Ward, Concord	Sr.	WR	11	67	1,214	11	6.1
21 Louis Datil, Southern Conn. St.	Jr.	WR	10	60	931	5	6.0
22 Nikolas Lewis, Southern Ark.	So.	WR	11	65	1,239	14	5.9
23 Chris Bryant, Kentucky St.	Fr.	WR	9	53	625	4	5.9
Greg Dykstra, Western Wash.	Sr.	WR	9	53	777	9	5.9
25 Pat Rouzard, Northern Mich.	Fr.	-	11	64	622	2	5.8
Ryan Welle, Bemidji St.	Sr.	WR	11	64	989	10	5.8
27 Brandon Free, Winston-Salem	So.	WR	10	58	692	8	5.8
28 Detronn Harris, West Ga.	Sr.	-	11	63	944	5	5.7
Gordon Miles, Kentucky St.	So.	WR	11	63	649	4	5.7
30 Brad Satran, Western Ore.	Jr.	WR	10	56	873	6	5.6
31 Keith Lessner, American Int'l	Sr.	WR	11	61	1,076	7	5.5
Joseph Mapson, Concordia-St. Paul	Sr.	WR	11	61	908	11	5.5
Ryan McKavish, Slippery Rock	Sr.	WR	11	61	1,030	6	5.5
Will Moody, Tarleton St.	Jr.	WR	11	61	759	7	5.5
35 Zac Jones, Chadron St.	Sr.	WR	10	55	587	5	5.5
David Kircus, Grand Valley St.	Sr.	WR	14	77	1,341	35	5.5
Michael Oliva, UC Davis	Sr.	WR	12	66	1,091	11	5.5

Receiving Yards Per Game

Min. 85 Yards Per Game

Rank, Name, Team	Cl	Pos	G	Rec	Yds Rec	TD Rec	YD PG
1 Chris Brewer, Fort Lewis	So.	WR	11	85	1,274	18	115.8
2 Nikolas Lewis, Southern Ark.	So.	WR	11	65	1,239	14	112.6
3 Nate Washington, Tiffin	So.	WR	10	53	1,120	11	112.0
4 Ryshaune Ward, Concord	Sr.	WR	11	67	1,214	11	110.4
5 Kyle Henderson, West Ala.	Sr.	WR	11	58	1,190	14	108.2
6 Rocco Forgione, Bloomsburg	Sr.	WR	10	54	1,075	12	107.5
7 Brian Potucek, Central Wash.	So.	WR	12	86	1,265	11	105.4
8 Richard Ross, Neb.-Kearney	Fr.	WR	11	56	1,142	10	103.8
9 Craig Brown, Johnson Smith	Sr.	WR	9	46	933	10	103.7
10 Jamaica Rector, Northwest Mo. St.	So.	WR	12	78	1,242	6	103.5
11 Dee Dee Carter, Central Okla.	Jr.	WR	11	49	1,093	5	99.4
12 Keith Lessner, American Int'l	Sr.	WR	11	61	1,076	7	97.8
13 Ben Nelson, St. Cloud St.	Sr.	WR	11	69	1,072	23	97.5
14 Tim Battaglia, Minn.-Duluth	Jr.	WR	12	55	1,166	19	97.2
15 David Kircus, Grand Valley St.	Sr.	WR	14	77	1,341	35	95.8
16 Jeff Cupe, Southern Conn. St.	Sr.	WR	11	67	1,051	13	95.5
17 Brian Sump, Colorado Mines	Sr.	WR	9	46	849	7	94.3
18 Ryan McKavish, Slippery Rock	Sr.	WR	11	61	1,030	6	93.6
19 Louis Datil, Southern Conn. St.	Jr.	WR	10	60	931	5	93.1
20 Marc Green, Southwest Baptist	Jr.	WR	11	85	1,014	4	92.2
21 Jesse Smith, North Dakota	Sr.	WR	11	70	1,011	6	91.9
22 Chris Samp, Winona St.	Jr.	WR	12	56	1,099	11	91.6
23 Michael Oliva, UC Davis	Sr.	WR	12	66	1,091	11	90.9
24 Gerald Gales, West Ala.	Jr.	WR	11	96	994	4	90.4
25 Ryan Welle, Bemidji St.	Sr.	WR	11	64	989	10	89.9
26 Marvin Brown, Ark.-Monticello	Sr.	WR	8	43	707	5	88.4

Chris Brewer, Fort Lewis

Rank, Name, Team	Cl	Pos	G	Rec Rec	Yds Rec	TD Rec	YD PG
27 Shaun Fonoimoana, Minn. St. Mankato	Fr.	-	10	42	879	7	87.9
28 Andrew Blakley, Truman	Sr.	WR	11	96	965	6	87.7
29 Brad Satran, Western Ore.	Jr.	WR	10	56	873	6	87.3
30 Todd Devoe, Central Mo. St.	Sr.	WR	12	58	1,045	12	87.1
31 Garvin Graves, Calif. (Pa.)	Fr.	-	10	70	870	6	87.0
32 Antonio Carter, Glenville St.	So.	WR	11	70	956	8	86.9
33 Brandon Munson, Northern Mich.	Sr.	WR	11	76	950	6	86.4
34 Greg Dykstra, Western Wash.	Sr.	WR	9	53	777	9	86.3
Reggie Mosley, Valdosta St.	Sr.	WR	15	79	1,295	15	86.3

Interceptions

Min. 0.5 Interceptions Per Game

Rank, Name, Team	Cl	Pos	G	Int	Int Ret Yds	Int PG
1 Nicholas Murray, Johnson Smith	Jr.	DB	10	10	97	1.0
2 Rico Cody, Fort Valley St.	Sr.	DB	11	10	73	0.9
3 Jon Arnold, Calif. (Pa.)	Jr.	DB	11	9	48	0.8
Ryan Bowers, Presbyterian	Sr.	DB	11	9	43	0.8
5 Jamel Jackson, Catawba	Jr.	DB	9	7	130	0.8
6 Brent Grimes, Shippensburg	Fr.	DB	11	8	43	0.7
Mike Mayer, West Virginia St.	Jr.	DB	11	8	132	0.7
Grant Newton, Colorado Mines	So.	DB	11	8	122	0.7
9 Nick Beisker, East Stroudsburg	Jr.	-	10	7	114	0.7
10 Levi Neville, Pittsburg St.	Jr.	DB	9	6	88	0.7
11 Pete Mendez, Kutztown	Sr.	DB	11	7	154	0.6
Michael Stotz, Augustana (S.D.)	So.	DB	11	7	80	0.6
13 Michael Demasi, St. Anselm	So.	DB	10	6	13	0.6
Daniel Henderson, Ark.-Monticello	Jr.	DB	10	6	76	0.6
Marvin Jackson, Chadron St.	Jr.	DB	10	6	99	0.6
Matt Meadows, Shepherd	Jr.	DB	10	6	81	0.6
Sean Murray, Virginia St.	Fr.	-	10	6	66	0.6
Isaac Weaver, Fairmont St.	So.	DB	10	6	86	0.6
George Williams, Mars Hill	Sr.	DB	10	6	36	0.6
20 Ryan Prochnow, Saginaw Valley	Fr.	K	12	7	116	0.6

Rank, Name, Team	Cl	Pos	G	Int	Int Ret Yds	Int PG
21 Michael Glover, East Stroudsburg	Jr.	-	9	5	48	0.6
Mitch May, Hillsdale	Fr.	DB	9	5	56	0.6
23 James Dell, Concordia-St. Paul	Jr.	DB	11	6	-1	0.5
Jeff Molesso, Bentley	Fr.	DB	11	6	60	0.5
Ulexis Williams, Southwest Baptist	So.	DB	11	6	56	0.5

Punt Returns

Min. 10.5 Yards Per Return
Minimum 1.2 Returns Per Game

Rank, Name, Team	Cl	Pos	G	Punt Ret	Punt Ret Yds	Avg
1 Kevin Curtin, Winona St.	Jr.	RB	12	19	430	22.6
2 Donald Amaker, Tusculum	Jr.	DB	9	16	273	17.1
3 Mike Olsonowski, Minn.-Crookston	Sr.	WR	10	13	215	16.5
4 Keith Green, Benedict	Jr.	RB	11	17	281	16.5
5 Andre Freeman, Fort Hays St.	Fr.	-	11	16	263	16.4
6 Joseph Mapson, Concordia-St. Paul	Sr.	WR	11	24	394	16.4
7 Alfonso Pugh, Truman	Sr.	WR	11	19	310	16.3
8 Cordell Roane, Virginia Union	Fr.	-	10	26	420	16.2
9 Terry Meng, Presbyterian	Jr.	WR	11	22	355	16.1
10 Robert Carey, Lock Haven	Jr.	DB	11	19	300	15.8
11 Dustin Dudinski, Shepherd	So.	WR	10	18	281	15.6
12 Ryan Russell, West Liberty St.	Fr.	-	11	14	204	14.6
13 Jamaica Rector, Northwest Mo. St.	So.	WR	12	36	514	14.3
14 Tiago Collins, Harding	Fr.	-	10	17	234	13.8
15 Craig Brown, Johnson Smith	Sr.	WR	9	11	151	13.7
16 Chase Pratt, Southwestern Okla.	So.	-	11	21	287	13.7
17 Jeremy Craighead, Western St. (Colo.)	Jr.	WR	11	30	408	13.6
18 Eric Mickelson, St. Cloud St.	Jr.	DB	11	37	500	13.5
19 Nate Thomas, Central Mo. St.	Sr.	WR	12	26	349	13.4
20 Nikolas Lewis, Southern Ark.	So.	WR	11	14	179	12.8
21 Dexter Daniels, Southeastern Okla.	So.	DB	10	21	263	12.5
22 Ivan McCrae, Western Ore.	Jr.	RB	9	19	236	12.4
23 Mitch Barry, Chadron St.	So.	DB	10	22	272	12.4
24 Michael Bryant, Bowie St.	Sr.	WR	11	24	295	12.3
25 Terry Jefferson, Midwestern St.	Fr.	-	11	30	366	12.2
26 Scott Mackey, Grand Valley St.	So.	DB	14	24	291	12.1
27 Rober' Freeman, Clark Atlanta	Fr.	-	9	13	155	11.9
28 Kevin Brown, South Dakota St.	Jr.	DB	10	17	200	11.8
29 Ben Culver, Clarion	So.	WR	11	33	386	11.7
30 Deacon Burns, Northern St.	Fr.	RB	11	32	372	11.6
31 Charlie Rollins, Miles	Fr.	-	11	26	288	11.1
32 Keith Lessner, American Int'l	Sr.	WR	11	16	175	10.9
33 Ike Guobodia, C.W. Post	So.	WR	11	23	250	10.9
34 Gerald Gales, West Ala.	Jr.	WR	11	27	289	10.7
35 Louis Datil, Southern Conn. St.	Jr.	WR	10	18	191	10.6

Kickoff Returns

Min. 24.0 Yards Per Return
Minimum 1.2 Returns Per Game

Rank, Name, Team	Cl	Pos	G	KO Ret	KO Ret Yds	Avg
1 Rj Abercrombie, Calif. (Pa.)	Jr.	DB	11	14	493	35.2
2 Daray Sims, Abilene Christian	Fr.	-	10	15	520	34.7
3 Jonny Chan, Colorado Mines	So.	WR	10	19	603	31.7
4 Toby Roy-Oden, Mass.-Lowell	Sr.	RB	11	29	868	29.9
5 Garth Mins, Neb.-Kearney	So.	WR	11	20	588	29.4
6 Jeffrey Stanton, Tuskegee	Sr.	DB	11	17	492	28.9
7 Martin Hicks, Winston-Salem	Fr.	RB	9	15	433	28.9
8 Kevin Brown, South Dakota St.	Jr.	DB	10	18	511	28.4
9 Ryan Bowers, Presbyterian	Sr.	DB	11	19	529	27.8
10 Charlie Rollins, Miles	Fr.	-	11	16	444	27.8
11 Germaine Johnson, Fairmont St.	Sr.	WR	10	19	516	27.2
12 Morris White, Northwest Mo. St.	So.	WR	13	16	434	27.1
13 Torrince Ruth, Concord	Fr.	RB	10	13	351	27.0
14 Nick Kurtz, Bloomsburg	So.	WR	10	23	616	26.8
15 Detronn Harris, West Ga.	Sr.	-	11	17	455	26.8
16 Marvin Jackson, Chadron St.	Jr.	DB	10	15	399	26.6
17 Shane Carter, Minn. St. Moorhead	Sr.	RB	10	23	607	26.4
18 Nick Davis, Tex. A&M-Kingsville	Sr.	-	13	23	606	26.3
19 Donald Amaker, Tusculum	Jr.	DB	9	14	363	25.9
20 Dustin Dudinski, Shepherd	So.	WR	10	16	410	25.6
21 Altrikii Brown, Central Ark.	Sr.	RB	9	15	384	25.6
22 Ryan Johnson, Emporia St.	Jr.	WR	12	35	891	25.5
23 Tremain Forrest, Midwestern St.	Fr.	-	9	11	280	25.5
24 James Fuller, Benedict	So.	WR	10	15	380	25.3
25 J.R. Thomas, Indiana (Pa.)	Sr.	WR	13	16	404	25.3
26 Dontreal Williams, Albany St. (Ga.)	So.	WR	11	27	677	25.1
27 Patrick Wilson, North Ala.	Fr.	WR	9	17	426	25.1
28 Chris Gruse, Northwood	Fr.	-	11	19	475	25.0

Rank, Name, Team	Cl	Pos	G	KO Ret	KO Ret Yds	Avg
29 Michael Bryant, Bowie St.	Sr.	WR	11	14	349	24.9
30 Mike Yanocha, East Stroudsburg	So.	-	10	19	467	24.6
31 Kevin Clive, Hillsdale	Sr.	RB	11	22	535	24.3
32 Christopher Winford, Lenoir-Rhyne	Fr.	RB	9	21	510	24.3
33 Steve Hinson, Eastern N.M.	So.	QB	11	30	727	24.2
34 Tony Goodman, Southwestern Okla.	Sr.	-	11	14	338	24.1

Punting

Min. 39.0 Yards Per Punt
Minimum 3.6 Punts Per Game

Rank, Name, Team	Cl	Pos	G	Punts	Punt Yds	Avg
1 Michael Koenen, Western Wash.	So.	K	9	43	1,910	44.4
2 Sean McNicholas, Edinboro	Sr.	K	11	58	2,566	44.2
3 Eric Roth, Washburn	Sr.	P	11	53	2,252	42.5
4 Jeff Williams, Adams St.	Fr.	P	11	65	2,751	42.3
5 Daniel de la Corte, Fort Lewis	So.	P	11	53	2,218	41.8
6 Ryan Wettstein, Northern Mich.	Jr.	P	11	60	2,506	41.8
7 Josh Hodsdon, Colorado Mines	Sr.	K	11	43	1,779	41.4
8 Chris Shibel, UC Davis	So.	P	12	55	2,271	41.3
9 Josh Raphael, Concordia-St. Paul	Fr.	P	11	50	2,051	41.0
10 Travis Gumbs, Tuskegee	So.	K	11	56	2,294	41.0
11 Jarrod Edelen, South Dakota	Sr.	K	11	63	2,578	40.9
12 Chris Miller, Tex. A&M-Commerce	So.	P	11	56	2,288	40.9
13 Tommy Edwards, Arkansas Tech	Jr.	DL	11	73	2,982	40.8
14 Kevin Ruch, Neb.-Omaha	Sr.	P	11	48	1,960	40.8
15 John Newberry, Central Ark.	Jr.	P	11	43	1,750	40.7
16 Richard Straup, Wingate	Sr.	K	11	56	2,260	40.4
17 Lucas Taroli, Western Ore.	Jr.	P	9	49	1,977	40.3
18 Ben Thoma, West Ala.	Jr.	P	11	58	2,336	40.3
19 Bryan Poole, Southwestern Okla.	So.	-	11	49	1,973	40.3
20 Chris Evatt, Tarleton St.	Sr.	P	10	49	1,971	40.2
21 Jesse Ramirez, East Central	Fr.	-	11	48	1,930	40.2
22 John Bonicelli, North Dakota St.	Jr.	P	10	55	2,193	39.9
23 Jamie VanDenElzen, Minn. St. Mankato	Fr.	QB	11	62	2,469	39.8
24 Ryan Prochnow, Saginaw Valley	Fr.	-	12	49	1,943	39.7
25 Victor Sauceda, Tex. A&M-Kingsville	Sr.	-	13	62	2,448	39.5
26 Jason Brown, Central Mo. St.	Jr.	P	11	44	1,736	39.5
27 Jason Langland, South Dakota St.	Sr.	P	10	45	1,774	39.4
28 Joel Mathews, Northwest Mo. St.	So.	P	13	59	2,321	39.3
29 Travis Snyder, Western St. (Colo.)	So.	K	11	56	2,197	39.2
30 Pete Sterbick, Augustana (S.D.)	Sr.	WR	11	62	2,429	39.2
31 Mike Halberg, Slippery Rock	Sr.	P	11	60	2,340	39.0

Field Goals Per Game

Min. 0.7 Field Goals Made Per Game

Rank, Name, Team	Cl	Pos	G	FG	FGA	FG PG
1 Henrik Juul-Nielsen, Neb.-Kearney	Sr.	K	11	20	24	1.8
2 Andrew Keippela, Western Ore.	So.	K	9	14	23	1.6
3 J.W. Boren, Tarleton St.	Sr.	K	11	17	25	1.5
4 Austin Wellock, Ashland	Fr.	K	11	15	19	1.4
5 Keith Witt, South Dakota St.	Fr.	-	10	13	25	1.3
6 Cody Finney, East Central	Sr.	P	11	14	20	1.3
Jeff Glas, North Dakota	So.	K	11	14	22	1.3
Alan Rohrbaugh, Catawba	Jr.	K	11	14	18	1.3
9 Mike Swim, Northern Colo.	Fr.	K	14	17	28	1.2
10 Eben Nelson, Abilene Christian	Fr.	-	10	12	18	1.2
11 Daniel Chappell, Pittsburg St.	Sr.	K	11	13	15	1.2
Coy Nance, Harding	Jr.	K	11	13	19	1.2
13 Scott Lambert, Kentucky St.	Jr.	P	10	11	20	1.1
14 Adam Brinkman, Augustana (S.D.)	Jr.	K	11	12	17	1.1
Kyle Marotz, Northern Mich.	Fr.	K	11	12	16	1.1
16 Richard Hammond, Tex. A&M-Kingsville	Fr.	-	13	14	23	1.1
Eddie Ibarra, Northwest Mo. St.	Sr.	K	13	14	26	1.1
18 Will Rhody, Valdosta St.	So.	K	15	16	24	1.1
19 Cody Butler, South Dakota	So.	K	11	11	18	1.0
Chad Gerlach, Minn.-Duluth	Jr.	P	12	12	16	1.0
Michael Koenen, Western Wash.	So.	K	9	9	15	1.0
Anthony May, Adams St.	Jr.	K	11	11	16	1.0
Nick Parker, Indianapolis	Fr.	K	11	11	16	1.0
John Raptis, Lenoir-Rhyne	Fr.	K	8	8	11	1.0
Vinny Repucci, Mercyhurst	Sr.	K	11	11	19	1.0
Randy Weston, Tex. A&M-Commerce	Sr.	K	10	10	14	1.0
27 Justin Gray, Emporia St.	So.	K	12	11	25	0.9
Eric Houle, Saginaw Valley	Jr.	K	12	11	15	0.9
29 Daniel Breech, West Va. Wesleyan	Fr.	K	11	10	14	0.9
Geoff Heyl, Edinboro	Sr.	K	11	10	18	0.9
Bryan Poole, Southwestern Okla.	So.	-	11	10	20	0.9

Rank, Name, Team	Cl	Pos	G	FG	FGA	FG PG
Troy Severson, Neb.-Omaha	Sr.	K	11	10	21	0.9
Ben Thoma, West Ala.	Jr.	P	11	10	17	0.9
34 Jerry Holstrom, Midwestern St.	Jr.	K	10	9	15	0.9

Rank, Name, Team	Cl	Pos	G	FG	FGA	FG PG
Ben Sandrock, Tiffin	Fr.	K	10	9	13	0.9
Bryan Walker, Delta St.	Fr.	-	10	9	14	0.9

All-Purpose Running

Min. 130.0 Yards Per Game

Rank, Name, Team	Cl	Pos	G	Rush Yds	Punt Rec Yds	Ret Yds	KO Ret Yds	Int Ret Yds	YDS	YPG
1 Kevin Clive, Hillsdale	Sr.	RB	11	1,350	208	0	535	0	2,093	190.3
2 LeVar Ammons, Quincy	So.	RB	10	1,650	227	0	0	0	1,877	187.7
3 Kevin Curtin, Winona St.	**Jr.**	**RB**	**12**	**1,059**	**157**	**430**	**595**	**0**	**2,241**	**186.8**
4 Ian Smart, C.W. Post	Sr.	RB	12	2,023	55	0	90	0	2,168	180.7
5 Craig Duppong, Wayne St. (Mich.)	Jr.	RB	11	1,315	135	0	425	0	1,875	170.5
6 Gerald Gales, West Ala.	Jr.	WR	11	28	994	289	442	0	1,753	159.4
7 Michael Hamm, Tiffin	So.	WR	10	-5	326	184	1,073	0	1,578	157.8
8 Robert Campbell, Findlay	Jr.	RB	11	1,575	142	0	0	0	1,717	156.1
9 Mike Hinshaw, Western Ore.	Jr.	WR	10	10	841	0	705	0	1,556	155.6
10 Mike Miller, Neb.-Kearney	So.	RB	11	1,600	106	0	0	0	1,706	155.1
11 Shane Carter, Minn. St. Moorhead	Sr.	RB	10	810	132	0	607	0	1,549	154.9
12 Keith Lessner, American Int'l	Sr.	WR	11	30	1,076	175	420	0	1,701	154.6
13 Mike Eckmeyer, West Chester	Jr.	RB	11	1,539	112	0	35	0	1,686	153.3
14 Duriel Cobb, West Va. Wesleyan	Sr.	RB	11	1,440	236	0	0	0	1,676	152.4
15 Jamaica Rector, Northwest Mo. St.	Sr.	WR	12	54	1,242	514	18	0	1,828	152.3
16 Ken Sather, Southwest St.	Sr.	RB	11	993	333	-2	338	0	1,662	151.1
17 Gerome Castleberry, East Central	Sr.	RB	11	1,379	277	0	0	0	1,656	150.5
18 Darrin Davis, Southern Conn. St.	Sr.	RB	11	1,620	32	0	0	0	1,652	150.2
19 Ryan Johnson, Emporia St.	Sr.	WR	12	33	846	0	891	0	1,770	147.5
20 Paris Moore, Minn.-Morris	Sr.	RB	11	1,449	168	0	0	0	1,617	147.0
21 Kegan Coleman, Central Mo. St.	So.	RB	12	1,379	147	32	205	0	1,763	146.9
22 Joseph Mapson, Concordia-St. Paul	Sr.	WR	11	18	908	394	283	0	1,603	145.7
23 Codolyous Wilson, Lincoln (Mo.)	So.	RB	10	1,055	38	118	243	0	1,454	145.4
24 Craig Brown, Johnson Smith	Sr.	WR	9	3	933	151	144	73	1,304	144.9
25 Brian Sump, Colorado Mines	Sr.	WR	9	12	849	157	284	0	1,302	144.7
26 Joe Johnson, Michigan Tech	Jr.	RB	10	1,278	152	0	0	0	1,430	143.0
27 Chris Brewer, Fort Lewis	So.	WR	11	13	1,274	0	279	4	1,570	142.7
28 Deacon Burns, Northern St.	Fr.	RB	11	589	192	372	416	0	1,569	142.6
29 Derek Fudge, Ferris St.	Jr.	RB	10	1,016	386	0	18	0	1,420	142.0
30 Alonzo Roebuck, Edinboro	Sr.	RB	10	1,177	113	0	129	0	1,419	141.9
31 Matt Massari, UC Davis	So.	RB	11	1,274	280	0	0	0	1,554	141.3
32 Aaron Jenkins, Valdosta St.	Jr.	RB	14	1,304	355	0	313	0	1,972	140.9
33 Corwin Elliott, Ark.-Monticello	Sr.	RB	10	1,192	90	0	121	0	1,403	140.3
34 Toby Roy-Oden, Mass.-Lowell	Sr.	RB	11	629	45	0	868	0	1,542	140.2
35 Olan Coleman, Tarleton St.	Sr.	RB	11	883	368	23	261	0	1,535	139.5

Kevin Curtin, Winona State

Winona State Sports Information

Total Tackles

Min. 10 Total Tackles Per Game

Rank, Name, Team	Cl	Pos	G	Solo Tack	Asst Tack	TT	TPG
1 Dan Holland, Mansfield	Jr.	LB	10	85	56	141	14.1
2 Justin Valentine, West Virginia St.	Sr.	LB	11	52	89	141	12.8
3 Rob North, Hillsdale	Jr.	LB	11	66	73	139	12.6
4 Deric Sieck, Winona St.	Jr.	LB	12	88	63	151	12.6
5 John Grant, Morehouse	Sr.	-	10	80	45	125	12.5
Brian Holliday, Fayetteville St.	Sr.	LB	12	45	105	150	12.5
7 Josh Ison, Fairmont St.	Sr.	LB	10	75	43	118	11.8
Jason Ocean, Livingstone	Jr.	LB	10	45	73	118	11.8
9 Joe Corcoran, Washburn	So.	DB	11	60	65	125	11.4
Kwame Ferguson, East Central	Jr.	LB	11	57	68	125	11.4
11 James Williamson, Angelo St.	So.	LB	10	51	62	113	11.3
12 Kevin Myers, Ferris St.	So.	LB	10	60	51	111	11.1
Reggie Williams, Tex. A&M-Commerce	Sr.	LB	10	28	83	111	11.1
14 Alan Houston, Henderson St.	Sr.	LB	11	61	61	122	11.1
15 Derrik Metz, Lock Haven	Jr.	LB	11	78	40	118	10.7
16 Jon Aamot, Bemidji St.	Jr.	LB	11	61	54	115	10.5
17 Matt Carter, Mars Hill	Sr.	LB	11	58	56	114	10.4
18 Adam Long, Wayne St. (Neb.)	So.	LB	11	47	66	113	10.3
19 Timothy King, Cheyney	So.	RB	11	69	43	112	10.2
Doug McDaniel, West Liberty St.	Fr.	-	11	49	63	112	10.2
21 Mark Dircksen, Tiffin	Jr.	LB	10	61	40	101	10.1
Ryan Marsh, Michigan Tech	Sr.	DB	10	53	48	101	10.1
23 Nate Becker, Minn.-Morris	Jr.	DB	11	41	70	111	10.1
Brian Davis, Southern Ark.	Jr.	DB	11	63	48	111	10.1
Michael Sims, West Ala.	Sr.	DB	11	52	59	111	10.1

Rank, Name, Team	Cl	Pos	G	Solo Tack	Asst Tack	TT	TPG
Daryl Wilson, Concord	Fr.	LB	11	68	43	111	10.1
27 Andrew Bonk, Michigan Tech	Fr.	DB	10	43	57	100	10.0
Ryan Burpo, Mo. Southern St.	Jr.	DB	11	50	60	110	10.0
Darryl Gallegos, Fort Lewis	Fr.	LB	11	48	62	110	10.0
Courtney Johnson, Fairmont St.	Sr.	LB	10	63	37	100	10.0
Kelly King, West Va. Tech	Fr.	-	11	63	47	110	10.0
Daniel Leger, Colorado Mines	So.	DB	11	55	55	110	10.0
Bobby Petras, Tiffin	Sr.	DB	10	71	29	100	10.0
Nick Starcevic, Minn.-Crookston	Fr.	LB	11	50	60	110	10.0

Pass Sacks

Min. 0.5 Sacks Per Game

Rank, Name, Team	Cl	Pos	G	Solo Sack	Asst Sack	Sack Yds	Tot Sack	Sacks PG
1 Bill Teerlinck, Chadron St.	Sr.	DB	10	11	3	87	12.5	1.3
2 Bill Kavanaugh, Bentley	Jr.	DL	11	9	9	69	13.5	1.2
Ted Krautmann, Bentley	Fr.	-	11	11	5	94	13.5	1.2
4 Damian Walker, Bowie St.	Sr.	DL	11	12	1	81	12.5	1.1
5 Tommy Edwards, Arkansas Tech	Jr.	DL	11	12	0	84	12.0	1.1
6 Jermaine Burney, Southern Conn. St.	Sr.	DL	11	8	6	91	11.0	1.0
Anthony Koon, Fort Valley St.	Sr.	DL	11	10	2	75	11.0	1.0
Bo Moore, Ferris St.	Sr.	DL	10	10	0	73	10.0	1.0
Jason Ocean, Livingstone	Jr.	LB	10	9	2	73	10.0	1.0
Dewayne Wilson, Virginia St.	Fr.	-	10	10	0	79	10.0	1.0
11 Shawn Morgan, Fayetteville St.	Sr.	DB	12	8	7	94	11.5	1.0

STATISTICAL LEADERS

Tommy Edwards, Arkansas Tech

Arkansas Tech Sports Information

Rank, Name, Team	Cl	Pos	G	FF	FFPG
12 Nick Beisker, East Stroudsburg	Jr.	-	10	4	0.40
Kevin Clement, Hillsdale	So.	DL	10	4	0.40
Dav Gohagon, American Int'l	Fr.	-	10	4	0.40
15 Cody Cramer, Findlay	Jr.	LB	11	4	0.36
Tommy Edwards, Arkansas Tech	Jr.	DL	11	4	0.36
Darryl Gallegos, Fort Lewis	Fr.	-	11	4	0.36
Alvin Mask, Wayne St. (Mich.)	Jr.	DB	11	4	0.36
Derek Thomas, Tarleton St.	Jr.	LB	11	4	0.36
20 Andre Cannon, N.C. Central	Fr.	-	9	3	0.33
Gabe Florio, Colorado Mines	So.	DB	9	3	0.33
Lucas Garcia, Western Ore.	So.	DL	9	3	0.33
Matt Horgan, St. Anselm	Jr.	LB	9	3	0.33
Dontaye McCoy, Emporia St.	Sr.	DB	12	4	0.33
Lann Olson, Western Wash.	Jr.	LB	9	3	0.33
Mike Saunds, Pace	Sr.	LB	9	3	0.33
Daniel Stuckey, Wayne St. (Mich.)	Sr.	LB	9	3	0.33
Andrew Westfall, Ouachita Baptist	So.	LB	9	3	0.33
Eric Williams, C.W. Post	Fr.	-	12	4	0.33
30 Neal Wood, Indiana (Pa.)	So.	LB	13	4	0.31
31 Tony Black, Ky. Wesleyan	Sr.	DL	10	3	0.30
Ty Breitlow, Winona St.	Jr.	DL	10	3	0.30
Virgil Burton, Virginia Union	Fr.	-	10	3	0.30
Corey Ellis, Virginia Union	Jr.	DL	10	3	0.30
Rashad Gibbs, Elizabeth City St.	So.	DL	10	3	0.30
Chamel Hampton, Mansfield	Sr.	LB	10	3	0.30
Brian Holshek, Pace	Jr.	DB	10	3	0.30
Darren Johnson, Angelo St.	Jr.	DB	10	3	0.30
Jayson Jones, East Central	Fr.	-	10	3	0.30
Mike Macek, Wayne St. (Mich.)	Jr.	LB	10	3	0.30
Luke Piepkow, Ferris St.	Jr.	LB	10	3	0.30
Chris Ramsey, Fort Hays St.	Fr.	-	10	3	0.30
Bill Teerlinck, Chadron St.	Sr.	DB	10	3	0.30
Matt Wayne, Winona St.	Jr.	DL	10	3	0.30
Jabari Weatherspoon, Clarion	Fr.	-	10	3	0.30
Bo Williams, West Ga.	Sr.	-	10	3	0.30
Ivory Witherspoon, Virginia St.	Sr.	-	10	3	0.30

Rank, Name, Team	Cl	Pos	G	Solo Tack	Asst Tack	TT	TPG
12 Andrew Tippins, Minn. St. Mankato	Sr.	DL	11	9	3	69	10.5	1.0
13 Jason Feasel, Ferris St.	Sr.	DL	10	9	1	65	9.5	1.0
Lance Flagg, St. Anselm	Sr.	DL	10	9	1	61	9.5	1.0
15 Lance Gibson, Central Wash.	Sr.	DL	12	10	2	81	11.0	0.9
16 Troy Bowers, Clarion	Fr.	-	11	8	4	77	10.0	0.9
17 Philip Mabion, Emporia St.	Jr.	DL	12	9	3	77	10.5	0.9
18 Jamie Doyle, Harding	Sr.	DL	11	9	1	74	9.5	0.9
Reccardo Moore, Mars Hill	Sr.	DL	11	9	1	68	9.5	0.9
20 Dave Armstrong, Bloomsburg	Sr.	DL	10	6	5	47	8.5	0.9
21 Jackson Harris, Findlay	Jr.	DL	11	8	2	59	9.0	0.8
Tom Strickland, Bentley	Sr.	OL	11	8	2	52	9.0	0.8
Ben Wellington, Bryant	Sr.	DL	11	8	2	76	9.0	0.8
24 Jayme Jackson, Abilene Christian	Fr.	-	8	6	1	43	6.5	0.8
25 Alfred Dubose, Virginia Union	Sr.	LB	10	7	2	44	8.0	0.8
26 Joe Kay, C.W. Post	Fr.	-	12	7	5	47	9.5	0.8
Peter Lazare, C.W. Post	Fr.	-	12	7	5	94	9.5	0.8
28 George Allen, Gannon	Sr.	LB	9	7	0	60	7.0	0.8
Joe Fermano, Merrimack	So.	DL	9	6	2	36	7.0	0.8
Jake Walker, West Chester	Jr.	DL	9	7	0	46	7.0	0.8
31 Kevin Mohr, Tarleton St.	Sr.	DL	11	7	3	55	8.5	0.8
32 William Moody, Carson-Newman	Jr.	LB	13	8	4	95	10.0	0.8
33 Dewayne Smith, Valdosta St.	Sr.	DL	15	10	3	82	11.5	0.8
34 Andrew Battle, Indiana (Pa.)	Jr.	DL	12	9	0	35	9.0	0.8
Casey Haldeman, Chadron St.	So.	DL	10	6	3	48	7.5	0.8
Adam Hyrb, Angelo St.	Jr.	DL	10	7	1	44	7.5	0.8
Elias Shehadeh, Pace	Fr.	-	10	6	3	56	7.5	0.8

Forced Fumbles

Min. 0.25 Per Game

Rank, Name, Team	Cl	Pos	G	FF	FFPG
1 Al Sullivan, Midwestern St.	Jr.	LB	11	7	0.64
2 Michael Hicks, West Virginia St.	Jr.	DB	10	6	0.60
3 James Ward, St. Anselm	Jr.	LB	10	5	0.50
James Williamson, Angelo St.	So.	LB	10	5	0.50
5 Nick Davis, Tex. A&M-Kingsville	Sr.	-	13	6	0.46
6 Charles Alston, Bowie St.	Sr.	DL	11	5	0.45
Jason Carson, Northern St.	Jr.	LB	11	5	0.45
8 Joe Fermano, Merrimack	So.	DL	9	4	0.44
Keenan Washington, Southern Ark.	So.	LB	9	4	0.44
Rob White, Western Wash.	So.	DB	9	4	0.44
11 Adam Skinner, Minn. Duluth	Fr.	LB	12	5	0.42

Tackles for Loss

Min. 1.1 Per Game

Rank, Name, Team	Cl	Pos	G	STFL	ATFL	Tackle Yds	TTFL	TFLPG
1 Jason Ocean, Livingstone	Jr.	LB	10	23	14	143	30.0	3.0
2 George Allen, Gannon	Sr	IB	9	22	0	95	22.0	2.4
3 Lance Flagg, St. Anselm	Sr.	DL	10	22	4	93	24.0	2.4
4 Shawn Morgan, Fayetteville St.	Sr.	DB	12	20	16	139	28.0	2.3
5 Anthony Koon, Fort Valley St.	Sr.	DL	11	25	0	117	25.0	2.3
6 Tommy Edwards, Arkansas Tech	**Jr.**	**DL**	**11**	**23**	**2**	**130**	**24.0**	**2.2**
7 Troy Bowers, Clarion	Fr.	-	11	20	7	109	23.5	2.1
8 Damian Walker, Bowie St.	Sr.	DL	11	22	2	119	23.0	2.1
9 Alfred Dubose, Virginia Union	Sr.	LB	10	19	3	89	20.5	2.1
10 Bill Gassen, South Dakota	Sr.	DL	11	18	9	78	22.5	2.0
11 Dewayne Smith, Valdosta St.	Sr.	DL	15	25	8	127	29.0	1.9
12 Charles Alston, Bowie St.	Sr.	DL	11	19	3	80	20.5	1.9
13 Jermaine Burney, Southern Conn. St.	Sr.	DL	11	19	2	103	20.0	1.8
14 Owen Rhodes, Jr., Gannon	Jr.	LB	10	18	0	54	18.0	1.8
Dewayne Wilson, Virginia St.	Fr.	-	10	18	0	117	18.0	1.8
16 Philip Mabion, Emporia St.	Jr.	DL	12	20	2	97	21.0	1.8
Elias Shehadeh, Pace	Fr.	-	10	17	1	72	17.5	1.8
18 Bill Kavanaugh, Bentley	Jr.	DL	11	12	14	95	19.0	1.7
19 Rashad Gibbs, Elizabeth City St.	So.	DL	10	15	4	66	17.0	1.7
20 Atcheson Conway, Bowie St.	So.	LB	11	17	3	57	18.5	1.7
Brian Doyle, Concordia-St. Paul	Fr.	-	11	17	3	73	18.5	1.7
Ben Wellington, Bryant	Sr.	DL	11	18	1	108	18.5	1.7
23 Tim Bliefnick, Quincy	So.	LB	15	15	0	43	15.0	1.7
Joe Fermano, Merrimack	So.	DL	9	14	2	53	15.0	1.7
Lance Gibson, Central Wash.	Sr.	DL	12	18	4	104	20.0	1.7
26 Sheldon Connor, N.C. Central	So.	DL	10	14	5	54	16.5	1.7
Jamin Phipps, Angelo St.	Jr.	LB	10	16	1	33	16.5	1.7
RaShawn Spencer, Elizabeth City St.	Sr.	DL	10	15	3	52	16.5	1.7
29 Keyonta Marshall, Grand Valley St.	So.	DL	14	22	2	92	23.0	1.6
30 Brian Gordon, Assumption	So.	DL	11	15	6	76	18.0	1.6
Ted Krautmann, Bentley	Fr.	-	11	14	8	105	18.0	1.6
Derek Thomas, Tarleton St.	Jr.	LB	11	17	2	67	18.0	1.6
33 Davylyn Nelson, Tex. A&M-Kingsville	Sr.	-	13	19	4	72	21.0	1.6
34 Bill Teerlinck, Chadron St.	Sr.	DB	10	13	6	95	16.0	1.6
35 Floyd Black, Harding	Sr.	DL	11	16	3	72	17.5	1.6
Sam Fakunle, North Ala.	Sr.	DL	11	15	5	75	17.5	1.6

Total Offense

Min. 215 Yards Per Game

Rank, Name, Team	Cl	Pos	G	Plays	YDS	YPG
1 Andrew Webb, Fort Lewis	Jr.	QB	11	613	4,245	385.9
2 Dusty Burk, Truman	Sr.	QB	11	551	3,441	312.8
3 Josh Chapman, Mo. Southern St.	Sr.	QB	11	519	3,408	309.8
4 Zak Hill, Central Wash.	Jr.	QB	9	339	2,692	299.1
5 Brett Gilliland, West Ala.	Jr.	QB	11	575	3,213	292.1
6 Zak Clark, Central Ark.	Jr.	QB	11	467	3,186	289.6
7 Darmel Whitfield, Gannon	So.	QB	10	509	2,802	280.2
8 Tom Guy, American Int'l	Jr.	QB	11	509	3,030	275.5
9 James McNear, Concordia-St. Paul	Fr.	QB	10	379	2,752	275.2
10 Curt Anes, Grand Valley St.	Sr.	QB	14	457	3,821	272.9
11 Keith Heckendorf, St. Cloud St.	Jr.	QB	11	427	2,944	267.6
12 Kyle Swenor, Northern Mich.	Jr.	QB	11	550	2,943	267.5
13 Jeremy Palm, East Stroudsburg	Fr.	-	9	342	2,381	264.6
14 John McMenamin, Northwest Mo. St.	Sr.	QB	13	525	3,423	263.3
15 Will Hall, North Ala.	Jr.	QB	10	427	2,613	261.3
16 Eric Smith, West Va. Tech	Fr.	-	11	427	2,872	261.1
17 Nick Higgs, N.M. Highlands	Jr.	QB	10	453	2,576	257.6
18 Dan Fjeldheim, South Dakota St.	Sr.	QB	10	434	2,562	256.2
19 Ricky Fritz, Minn. Duluth	Sr.	QB	12	361	3,055	254.6
20 Josh Aliveto, Concord	Jr.	QB	10	439	2,539	253.9
21 Shawn Johnson, Kentucky St.	Fr.	QB	9	479	2,271	252.3
22 Joey Conrad, Glenville St.	Fr.	QB	10	435	2,523	252.3
23 Bruce Carpenter, Winona St.	Sr.	QB	12	388	3,004	250.3
24 Shane Desherlia, Quincy	Sr.	QB	11	505	2,752	250.2
25 Pat Korth, Neb.-Kearney	Jr.	QB	11	387	2,713	246.6
26 Drew Beard, Southeastern Okla.	So.	QB	10	373	2,433	243.3
27 Shawn Eisenreich, Chadron St.	So.	QB	10	409	2,395	239.5
28 Ryan Harpold, Tiffin	So.	QB	10	335	2,391	239.1
29 Tom Marsan, Ferris St.	So.	QB	10	446	2,388	238.8
30 Travis Motley, Mansfield	Jr.	QB	10	431	2,365	236.5
31 John Esquivel, Southern Conn. St.	Sr.	QB	11	408	2,594	235.8
32 Jake Parten, Northern St.	Sr.	QB	11	394	2,588	235.3
33 Tim Hicks, West Liberty St.	Fr.	-	11	364	2,585	235.0
34 Buster Faulkner, Valdosta St.	So.	QB	15	610	3,508	233.9
35 Dustin Hickel, Washburn	So.	QB	11	418	2,571	233.7

Passes Defended

Min. 1.25 Passes Defended Per Game

Rank, Name, Team	Cl	Pos	G	PBU	Int	TPD	PDPG
1 Kevin Brown, South Dakota St.	Jr.	DB	10	19	3	22	2.2
2 Nicholas Murray, Johnson Smith	Jr.	DB	10	10	10	20	2.0
3 Ryan Bowers, Presbyterian	Sr.	DB	11	12	9	21	1.9
4 George Williams, Mars Hill	Sr.	DB	10	13	6	19	1.9
5 James Dell, Concordia-St. Paul	Jr.	DB	11	14	6	20	1.8
Drayton Florence, Tuskegee	Sr.	DB	11	15	5	20	1.8
Grant Newton, Colorado Mines	So.	DB	11	12	8	20	1.8
8 John English, Neb.-Kearney	Sr.	DB	10	14	4	18	1.8
9 Michael Glover, East Stroudsburg	Jr.	-	9	11	5	16	1.8
10 Anthony Floyd, Fort Valley St.	Sr.	DB	11	14	5	19	1.7
11 Terran Edwards, Virginia Union	Fr.	-	9	12	3	15	1.7
12 Jon Arnold, Calif. (Pa.)	Jr.	DB	11	9	9	18	1.6
Rico Cody, Fort Valley St.	Sr.	DB	11	8	10	18	1.6
14 Matt Meadows, Shepherd	Jr.	DB	10	10	6	16	1.6
Omar Philmore, Virginia St.	Jr.	-	10	15	1	16	1.6
Kevin Scott, Gannon	Fr.	DB	10	12	4	16	1.6
17 Levi Neville, Pittsburg St.	Jr.	DB	9	8	6	14	1.6
18 Aaron Jackson, St. Joseph's (Ind.)	So.	DB	10	13	2	15	1.5
Pat Reiman, Mesa St.	Jr.	DB	10	13	2	15	1.5
20 Myron Hargon, Clarion	Fr.	-	11	13	3	16	1.5
Pete Mendez, Kutztown	Sr.	DB	11	9	7	16	1.5
Darold Smith, Washburn	Jr.	DB	11	12	4	16	1.5
Frank Walker, Tuskegee	Sr.	DB	11	13	3	16	1.5
24 Ricardo Colclough, Tusculum	Jr.	DB	9	9	4	13	1.4
25 Marvin Jackson, Chadron St.	Jr.	DB	10	8	6	14	1.4
Casey Kannel, Minn. St. Moorhead	Fr.	-	10	10	4	14	1.4
Eddie Moton, Tex. A&M-Kingsville	Fr.	-	10	9	5	14	1.4
Sean Wade, Virginia St.	Fr.	-	10	8	6	14	1.4
Brandon White, Virginia Union	Fr.	-	10	10	4	14	1.4
30 Franklin Rhames, Livingstone	Sr.	DB	8	8	3	11	1.4
31 Ant Anderson, West Va. Tech	Fr.	-	11	14	1	15	1.4
Nick Bushere, Western St. (Colo.)	So.	DB	11	14	1	15	1.4
Eric Mickelson, St. Cloud St.	Jr.	DB	11	15	0	15	1.4
Greg Rush, Tusculum	Sr.	DB	11	13	2	15	1.4
Michael Stotz, Augustana (S.D.)	So.	DB	11	8	7	15	1.4

Scoring

Min. 8.0 Points Per Game

Rank, Name, Team	Cl	Pos	G	TDs	PAT	2PT	FG	Def Pts	Pts	PPG
1 David Kircus, Grand Valley St.	Sr.	WR	14	35	0	1	0	0	212	15.1
2 Ian Smart, C.W. Post	Sr.	RB	12	30	0	0	0	0	180	15.0
3 Ben Nelson, St. Cloud St.	Sr.	WR	11	23	0	0	0	0	138	12.5
4 Kegan Coleman, Central Mo. St.	So.	RB	12	24	0	0	0	0	144	12.0
5 DeMarcus Blount, North Ala.	Fr.	RB	11	20	0	0	0	0	120	10.9
6 Chris Brewer, Fort Lewis	So.	WR	11	19	0	0	0	0	114	10.4
7 Reginald Spearmon, Grand Valley St.	Sr.	RB	14	24	0	0	0	0	144	10.3
8 Garrion Corbin, Tiffin	Fr.	RB	10	17	0	0	0	0	102	10.2
9 Duron Croson, Fort Valley St.	Jr.	RB	11	18	0	0	0	0	108	9.8
Will Johnson, Central Wash.	So.	RB	11	18	0	0	0	0	108	9.8
11 Brad Duerr, Minn. St. Moorhead	Sr.	QB	10	16	0	1	0	0	98	9.8
12 Tim Battaglia, Minn. Duluth	Jr.	WR	12	19	0	0	0	0	114	9.5
13 Blake Christensen, Henderson St.	So.	QB	11	17	0	1	0	0	104	9.5
14 Kevin Clive, Hillsdale	Jr.	RB	11	17	0	0	0	0	102	9.3
15 John Kuhn, Shippensburg	So.	RB	11	16	0	1	0	0	98	8.9
16 Henrik Juul-Nielsen, Neb.-Kearney		K	11	0	37	0	20	0	97	8.8
17 Robert Campbell, Findlay	Jr.	RB	11	16	0	0	0	0	96	8.7
Darrin Evans, Southern Conn. St.	Sr.	RB	11	16	0	0	0	0	96	8.7
19 Robert Lolohea, Harding	Sr.	RB	9	13	0	0	0	0	78	8.7
Neal Philpot, Pittsburg St.	So.	QB	9	13	0	0	0	0	78	8.7
21 Tarik Abdullah, Central Okla.	Jr.	RB	10	14	0	0	0	0	84	8.4
22 Mike Eckmeyer, West Chester	Jr.	RB	11	15	0	1	0	0	92	8.4
23 Larry Williams, Tex. A&M-Kingsville	Jr.	-	13	18	0	0	0	0	108	8.3
24 J.W. Boren, Tarleton St.	Sr.	K	11	0	39	0	17	0	90	8.2
Daniel Chappell, Pittsburg St.	Sr.	K	11	0	51	0	13	0	90	8.2
Dallas Mall, Bentley	So.	WR	11	14	0	3	0	0	90	8.2
27 Craig Brown, Johnson Smith	Sr.	WR	9	12	0	0	0	0	72	8.0
Chad Gerlach, Minn. Duluth	Jr.	P	12	0	60	0	12	0	96	8.0
Carmelo Ocasio, Indiana (Pa.)	Sr.	WR	12	16	0	0	0	0	96	8.0

Solo Tackles

Min. 4.5 Solo Tackles Per Game

Rank, Name, Team	Cl	Pos	G	Solo Tack	STPG
1 Dan Holland, Mansfield	Jr.	LB	10	85	8.5
2 John Grant, Morehouse	Sr.	-	10	80	8.0
3 Josh Ison, Fairmont St.	Sr.	LB	10	75	7.5
4 Deric Sieck, Winona St.	Jr.	LB	12	88	7.3
5 Bobby Petras, Tiffin	Sr.	DB	10	71	7.1
6 Derrik Metz, Lock Haven	Jr.	LB	11	78	7.1

Mansfield Sports Information

Dan Holland, Mansfield

Rank, Name, Team	Cl	Pos	G	Solo Tack	STPG
7 Ty Touchstone, Eastern N.M.	So.	DB	11	72	6.5
8 Jon Horn, Northwood	Fr.	-	11	70	6.4
9 Courtney Johnson, Fairmont St.	Sr.	LB	10	63	6.3
10 Timothy King, Cheyney	So.	RB	11	69	6.3
11 Khalid Abdullah, Mars Hill	Sr.	LB	11	68	6.2
Daryl Wilson, Concord	Fr.	LB	11	68	6.2
13 Mark Dircksen, Tiffin	Jr.	LB	10	61	6.1
14 Kevin Myers, Ferris St.	So.	LB	10	60	6.0
Rob North, Hillsdale	Jr.	LB	11	66	6.0
Jared Ziemke, Minn. St. Mankato	Jr.	DB	11	66	6.0
17 Forrest Jackson, West Ga.	Sr.	-	11	65	5.9
Joseph Killins, Miles	Sr.	-	11	65	5.9
19 James Perkins, St. Joseph's (Ind.)	Sr.	DB	11	64	5.8
20 Brian Davis, Southern Ark.	Jr.	DB	11	63	5.7
Kelly King, West Va. Tech	Fr.	-	11	63	5.7
22 Karl Pfistner, Mass.-Lowell	So.	DB	11	62	5.6
23 Drew Spencer, Tiffin	Jr.	DB	10	56	5.6
24 Jon Aamot, Bemidji St.	Jr.	LB	11	61	5.5
Alan Houston, Henderson St.	Sr.	LB	11	61	5.5
Jon Nalewak, Lock Haven	So.	LB	11	61	5.5
27 Tycen Brock, Ky. Wesleyan	So.	DB	11	60	5.5
Joe Corcoran, Washburn	So.	DB	11	60	5.5
29 Keenan Washington, Southern Ark.	So.	LB	9	49	5.4
30 Tommy Edwards, Arkansas Tech	Jr.	DL	11	59	5.4
31 Shawn Butler, Bloomsburg	Jr.	LB	10	53	5.3
Ryan Jarois, Michigan Tech	Sr.	DB	10	53	5.3
Matt Natle, American Int'l	Fr.	-	10	53	5.3
34 Robert Carey, Lock Haven	Jr.	DB	11	58	5.3
Matt Carter, Mars Hill	Sr.	LB	11	58	5.3
Atcheson Conway, Bowie St.	So.	LB	11	58	5.3
Robert Hinton, Glenville St.	Jr.	LB	11	58	5.3
Toby Stepsis, Ashland	Sr.	DB	11	58	5.3
Mike Swaro, Western St. (Colo.)	So.	LB	11	58	5.3
Chaun Thompson, West Tex. A&M	Sr.	-	11	58	5.3

2002 Division II Team Leaders

Total Offense

Min. 390 Yards Per Game

Rank, School	G	Plays	YDS	YPG
1 Carson-Newman	13	806	6,472	497.8
2 Grand Valley St.	14	1,032	6,841	488.6
3 Fort Lewis	11	813	5,135	466.8
4 Central Wash.	12	886	5,583	465.3
5 Saginaw Valley	12	790	5,475	456.3
6 Southern Conn. St.	11	861	4,946	449.6
7 Concordia-St. Paul	11	738	4,926	447.8
8 Minn. Duluth	12	837	5,355	446.3
9 Central Ark.	11	787	4,905	445.9
10 St. Cloud St.	11	797	4,858	441.6
11 Mo. Southern St.	11	819	4,844	440.4
12 Quincy	11	859	4,806	436.9
13 Western Wash.	9	717	3,911	434.6
14 Gannon	10	808	4,325	432.5
15 Winona St.	12	808	5,178	431.5
16 Neb.-Kearney	11	790	4,703	427.5
17 Northwood	11	772	4,692	426.5
18 UC Davis	12	839	5,112	426.0
19 Tiffin	10	697	4,256	425.6
20 Truman	11	793	4,613	419.4
21 West Va. Wesleyan	11	773	4,588	417.1
22 Southern Ark.	11	770	4,571	415.5
23 Tusculum	11	800	4,547	413.4
24 North Ala.	11	795	4,545	413.2
25 West Liberty St.	11	771	4,516	410.5
26 Central Mo. St.	12	738	4,909	409.1
27 Chadron St.	10	763	4,073	407.3
28 Eastern N.M.	11	759	4,457	405.2
29 Findlay	11	833	4,454	404.9
30 Northern St.	11	803	4,416	401.5
31 West Va. Tech	11	792	4,395	399.5
32 Valdosta St.	15	1,095	5,978	398.5
33 Minn. St. Moorhead	10	765	3,960	396.0
34 Tarleton St.	11	700	4,341	394.6
35 Bentley	11	821	4,327	393.4

Rushing Offense

Min. 200 Yards Per Game

Rank, School	G	Rush	Rush Yds	YPG
1 Carson-Newman	13	636	4,503	346.4
2 Northwood	11	621	3,274	297.6
3 Eastern N.M.	11	602	3,188	289.8
4 Henderson St.	11	620	3,152	286.5
5 Clarion	11	590	3,003	273.0
6 Minn. St. Moorhead	10	570	2,665	266.5
7 C.W. Post	12	563	3,187	265.6
8 Gannon	10	519	2,532	253.2
9 Pittsburg St.	11	550	2,734	248.5
10 Quincy	11	524	2,709	246.3
11 Bryant	11	589	2,670	242.7
12 Southern Ark.	11	530	2,574	234.0
13 Mesa St.	11	562	2,541	231.0
14 Fort Valley St.	11	569	2,490	226.4
15 Shippensburg	11	564	2,482	225.6
16 St. Joseph's (Ind.)	11	504	2,461	223.7
17 West Va. Wesleyan	11	503	2,431	221.0
18 Findlay	11	526	2,407	218.8
19 Tex. A&M-Kingsville	13	556	2,783	214.1
20 Delta St.	11	523	2,304	209.5
21 Emporia St.	12	561	2,513	209.4
22 Fort Hays St.	11	520	2,287	207.9
23 Shepherd	10	417	2,078	207.8
24 Neb.-Omaha	11	553	2,285	207.7
25 Southeastern Okla.	10	465	2,060	206.0
26 Grand Valley St.	14	587	2,862	204.4
27 Michigan Tech	10	451	2,043	204.3
28 Stonehill	11	514	2,223	202.1
29 Southern Conn. St.	11	500	2,203	200.3
30 Tiffin	10	387	1,833	183.3
31 Lincoln (Mo.)	11	462	1,866	169.6
32 Saginaw Valley	12	439	2,016	168.0
33 Wayne St. (Mich.)	11	407	1,807	164.3
34 Hillsdale	11	426	1,729	157.2
35 Miles	11	449	1,727	157.0

Rushing Defense

Maximum 125.0 Yards Per Game

Rank, School	G	Opp Rush	Opp Yds Rush	YPG
1 C.W. Post	12	380	525	43.8
2 Valdosta St.	15	458	832	55.5
3 St. Cloud St.	11	296	707	64.3
4 Fort Valley St.	11	360	821	74.6
5 Central Wash.	12	387	954	79.5
6 Chadron St.	10	375	826	82.6
7 Bowie St.	11	419	922	83.8
8 N.C. Central	10	356	862	86.2
9 Northern Colo.	14	473	1,207	86.2
10 Albany St. (Ga.)	11	459	959	87.2
11 Elizabeth City St.	10	382	872	87.2
12 Fayetteville St.	12	504	1,094	91.2
13 Pittsburg St.	11	365	1,009	91.7
14 UC Davis	12	395	1,104	92.0
15 North Dakota	11	359	1,013	92.1
16 Mars Hill	11	386	1,014	92.2
17 Minn. Duluth	12	414	1,107	92.3
18 Merrimack	10	385	932	93.2
19 Neb.-Kearney	11	367	1,031	93.7
20 Gannon	10	374	946	94.6
21 Augustana (S.D.)	11	371	1,050	95.5
22 Virginia St.	10	344	958	95.8
23 Livingstone	10	362	961	96.1
24 Bentley	11	399	1,067	97.0
25 Northwest Mo. St.	13	463	1,283	98.7
26 Southeastern Okla.	10	326	994	99.4
27 Carson-Newman	13	476	1,325	101.9
28 Shippensburg	11	369	1,126	102.4
29 Tex. A&M-Kingsville	13	456	1,340	103.1
30 Emporia St.	12	426	1,245	103.8
31 Grand Valley St.	14	502	1,461	104.4
32 West Va. Wesleyan	11	375	1,183	107.5
33 Virginia Union	10	378	1,101	110.1
34 Adams St.	11	442	1,222	111.1
35 Tusculum	11	465	1,258	114.4

Passing Offense

Minimum 240.0 Yards Per Game

Rank, School	G	Pass Att	Comp	Int	Pass Yds	YPG
1 Fort Lewis	11	532	317	13	4,109	373.5
2 Central Wash.	12	451	290	9	3,782	315.2
3 Central Ark.	11	468	287	13	3,416	310.5
4 West Ala.	11	474	293	10	3,385	307.7
5 Western Wash.	9	376	222	9	2,747	305.2
6 Colorado Mines	11	396	244	14	3,195	290.5
7 Saginaw Valley	12	351	216	10	3,459	288.3
8 Tusculum	11	458	275	10	3,170	288.2
9 Northwest Mo. St.	13	504	302	14	3,696	284.3
10 Grand Valley St.	14	445	301	6	3,979	284.2
11 Valdosta St.	15	547	355	19	4,162	277.5
12 American Int'l.	11	421	220	9	3,036	276.0
13 North Ala.	11	373	231	17	2,984	271.3
14 Concord	11	459	238	23	2,969	269.9
15 St. Cloud St.	11	361	210	12	2,968	269.8
16 West Va. Tech	11	397	196	19	2,956	268.7
17 South Dakota St.	10	375	237	9	2,663	266.3
18 Concordia-St. Paul	11	312	183	9	2,889	262.6
19 Northern Mich.	11	464	269	21	2,839	258.1
20 Neb.-Kearney	11	324	175	10	2,837	257.9
21 Ky. Wesleyan	11	507	223	34	2,814	255.8
22 Lenoir-Rhyne	10	368	216	17	2,546	254.6
23 Chadron St.	10	379	210	11	2,536	253.6
24 Truman	11	399	245	15	2,786	253.3
25 Winona St.	12	358	191	9	3,028	252.3
26 Minn. Duluth	12	316	178	15	3,025	252.1
27 Southern Conn. St.	11	361	197	8	2,743	249.4
28 Glenville St.	11	446	230	23	2,721	247.4
29 UC Davis	12	320	204	13	2,964	247.0
30 Mo. Southern St.	11	379	216	13	2,711	246.5
31 Mass.-Lowell	11	437	237	24	2,678	243.5
32 Ferris St.	10	398	204	16	2,429	242.9
33 Tiffin	10	310	162	13	2,423	242.3
34 East Stroudsburg	10	352	167	11	2,421	242.1
35 N.M. Highlands	10	353	157	16	2,401	240.1

Pass Efficiency Defense

Maximum 105.0 Pass Efficiency Rating

Rank, School	G	Opp Pass	Opp Cpl Pass	Opp Int	Opp Pass Yds	Opp Pass TDs	Pass Eff
1 Tuskegee	11	279	108	16	1,349	12	82.0
2 Calif. (Pa.)	11	291	120	16	1,532	8	83.5
3 Albany St. (Ga.)	11	338	155	22	1,769	8	84.6
4 Presbyterian	11	357	171	22	1,916	7	87.1
5 Fayetteville St.	12	324	145	17	1,745	8	87.6
6 C.W. Post	12	437	206	19	2,061	15	89.4
7 Bentley	11	342	157	19	1,838	11	90.6
8 Fort Valley St.	11	306	133	22	1,861	11	92.0
9 Tarleton St.	11	289	139	15	1,553	9	93.1
10 Grand Valley St.	14	455	226	22	2,458	12	94.1
11 Pittsburg St.	11	349	187	24	1,903	9	94.1
12 Northern Colo.	14	472	244	24	2,348	16	94.5
13 Virginia Union	10	254	105	15	1,442	14	95.4
14 Tusculum	11	311	149	16	1,747	10	95.4
15 Mars Hill	11	347	153	19	2,082	13	95.9
16 Northwest Mo. St.	13	430	205	20	2,475	13	96.7
17 Chadron St.	10	299	152	16	1,586	11	96.8
18 Bloomsburg	10	312	138	13	1,758	15	99.1
19 Miles	11	336	146	15	1,959	17	100.2
20 Southwestern Okla.	11	292	125	13	1,796	13	100.3
21 Valdosta St.	15	526	264	26	3,227	14	100.6
22 Tex. A&M-Kingsville	13	358	168	16	2,253	11	101.0
23 Elizabeth City St.	10	268	121	17	1,566	16	101.2
24 Ferris St.	10	291	154	17	1,610	12	101.3
25 Harding	11	309	151	13	1,797	12	102.1
26 Lock Haven	11	291	138	17	1,799	13	102.4
27 Bowie St.	11	241	123	16	1,513	9	102.8
28 Southwest Baptist	11	301	145	18	1,766	16	103.0
29 Indiana (Pa.)	13	338	179	23	2,014	14	103.1
30 Lincoln (Mo.)	11	243	108	15	1,628	11	103.3
31 Slippery Rock	11	276	136	17	1,755	11	103.5
32 Kutztown	11	286	153	22	1,680	14	103.6
33 Shepherd	10	314	151	15	1,958	13	104.6
34 Saginaw Valley	12	396	211	22	2,436	13	104.7
35 Virginia St.	10	267	138	14	1,744	7	104.7

Turnover Margin

Minimum 0.75 Per Game

Rank, School	G	Fumbles Gained	Opp Int	Turn Gain	Fumbles Lost	Int	Turn Lost	Margin	Avg
1 Southwestern Okla.	11	14	13	27	6	3	9	18	1.6
2 St. Anselm	10	16	14	30	7	7	14	16	1.6
3 East Stroudsburg	10	15	18	33	7	11	18	15	1.5
C.W. Post	12	19	19	38	14	6	20	18	1.5
5 Central Ark.	11	14	22	36	7	13	20	16	1.5
Tarleton St.	11	19	15	34	11	7	18	16	1.5
7 Virginia St.	10	16	14	30	7	9	16	14	1.4
8 Catawba	11	13	15	28	5	8	13	15	1.4
9 Saginaw Valley	12	15	22	37	12	10	22	15	1.3
10 Bentley	11	14	19	33	7	13	20	13	1.2
Midwestern St.	11	21	6	27	8	6	14	13	1.2
12 Ouachita Baptist	10	14	12	26	4	11	15	11	1.1
13 Albany St. (Ga.)	11	0	22	22	0	10	10	12	1.1
14 Northern Colo.	14	16	24	40	13	13	26	14	1.0
Mo. Western St.	11	13	17	30	8	11	19	11	1.0
Mars Hill	11	17	19	36	13	12	25	11	1.0
South Dakota St.	10	11	14	25	6	9	15	10	1.0
18 Indiana (Pa.)	13	19	23	42	20	10	30	12	0.9
19 St. Cloud St.	11	11	20	31	9	12	21	10	0.9
20 Virginia Union	10	19	15	34	14	11	25	9	0.9
Chadron St.	10	16	16	32	12	11	23	9	0.9
22 Winona St.	12	16	15	31	12	9	21	10	0.8
23 Findlay	11	17	13	30	9	12	21	9	0.8
24 Grand Valley St.	14	13	22	35	18	6	24	11	0.8
25 Fort Valley St.	11	12	22	34	16	10	26	8	0.7
Lock Haven	11	16	17	33	7	18	25	8	0.7
Hillsdale	11	13	11	24	11	5	16	8	0.7
28 Johnson Smith	10	24	13	37	16	14	30	7	0.7
Merrimack	10	16	13	29	15	7	22	7	0.7
Winston-Salem	10	16	10	26	13	6	19	7	0.7
31 West Ala.	11	17	13	30	13	10	23	7	0.6
Pittsburg St.	11	6	24	30	13	10	23	7	0.6
Tusculum	11	15	16	31	14	10	24	7	0.6
Shippensburg	11	15	13	28	8	13	21	7	0.6
35 Valdosta St.	15	19	26	45	17	19	36	9	0.6

Kickoff Returns

Rank, School	KO Ret	KO Ret Yds	Kick Ret TDs	Avg
1 Truman	32	834	2	26.06
2 Winston-Salem	26	663	1	25.50
3 Concordia-St. Paul	37	920	0	24.86
4 Presbyterian	27	668	0	24.74
5 Tuskegee	34	838	2	24.65
6 Emporia St.	39	940	0	24.10
7 Mo. Western St.	24	578	0	24.08
8 Neb.-Kearney	33	790	2	23.94
9 Abilene Christian	37	881	0	23.81
10 South Dakota St.	37	877	1	23.70
11 Northwest Mo. St.	35	826	1	23.60
12 Fort Valley St.	42	987	2	23.50
13 Mass.-Lowell	55	1,291	2	23.47
14 Slippery Rock	26	607	0	23.35
15 East Stroudsburg	32	747	2	23.34
16 Tusculum	32	745	0	23.28
17 Carson-Newman	39	907	1	23.26
18 Miles	38	878	1	23.11
19 Bloomsburg	35	806	1	23.03
20 Southern Ark.	35	798	0	22.80
21 Indianapolis	35	796	0	22.74
22 Colorado Mines	46	1,041	2	22.63
23 Virginia Union	30	678	0	22.60
24 Adams St.	40	896	0	22.40
25 Tex. A&M-Kingsville	33	739	0	22.39
26 Fort Hays St.	55	1,231	1	22.38
27 West Virginia St.	58	1,289	0	22.22
28 Harding	42	932	0	22.19
29 Western Ore.	49	1,087	0	22.18
30 Minn. St. Moorhead	42	928	0	22.10
31 Bowie St.	33	724	0	21.94
32 Humboldt St.	54	1,168	0	21.63
33 Winona St.	37	796	1	21.51
34 Minn. Duluth	42	902	1	21.48
35 Calif. (Pa.)	41	873	1	21.29

STATISTICAL LEADERS

Punt Returns

Rank, School	Punt Ret	Punt Ret Yds	Punt Ret TDs	Avg
1 Winona St.	23	458	3	19.91
2 Fort Hays St.	17	306	1	18.00
3 Truman	29	490	2	16.90
4 Lock Haven	23	384	3	16.70
5 Tusculum	35	575	4	16.43
6 Minn.-Crookston	14	219	0	15.64
7 Adams St.	23	358	1	15.57
8 Virginia Union	35	504	2	14.40
9 Central Mo. St.	33	472	3	14.30
10 Bloomsburg	27	385	2	14.26
11 Colorado Mines	21	288	1	13.71
12 Lenoir-Rhyne	28	383	1	13.68
13 Concordia-St. Paul	31	422	2	13.61
14 Western St. (Colo.)	34	448	2	13.18
15 St. Cloud St.	43	558	1	12.98
16 Northwest Mo. St.	48	618	2	12.88
17 Eastern N.M.	33	419	0	12.70
18 Mars Hill	38	479	3	12.61
19 Southwestern Okla.	28	352	1	12.57
20 Northern St.	35	438	0	12.51
21 Midwestern St.	33	411	0	12.45
22 Quincy	17	211	1	12.41
23 Western Wash.	15	184	1	12.27
24 Shepherd	26	315	0	12.12
25 Findlay	30	362	2	12.07
26 North Dakota	39	470	4	12.05
27 Presbyterian	35	419	1	11.97
28 Tarleton St.	34	405	3	11.91
29 Western Ore.	26	302	1	11.62
30 Central Wash.	39	450	2	11.54
31 Clarion	38	437	1	11.50
32 West Liberty St.	19	216	0	11.37
33 Southeastern Okla.	25	284	0	11.36
34 Bowie St.	42	464	2	11.05

Net Punting

Rank, School	Opp Punt Yds	Punt Ret Yds	Punts	Net Yds
1 Central Wash.	1,757	114	40	41.08
2 Western Wash.	2,217	283	50	38.68
3 Northern Mich.	2,506	195	60	38.52
4 South Dakota	2,578	211	63	37.57
5 Edinboro	2,617	306	62	37.27
6 Northwest Mo. St.	2,321	86	60	37.25
7 Neb.-Omaha	1,960	173	48	37.23
8 Washburn	2,287	277	54	37.22
9 Western St. (Colo.)	2,276	119	58	37.19
10 Fort Lewis	2,293	232	56	36.80
11 Colorado Mines	1,779	182	44	36.30
12 Tuskegee	2,294	200	58	36.10
13 Stonehill	2,154	103	57	35.98
14 Truman	1,838	89	49	35.69
15 Tex. A&M-Commerce	2,353	292	58	35.53
16 East Central	1,957	216	49	35.53
17 Northwood	1,021	63	27	35.48
18 Arkansas Tech	3,080	386	76	35.45
19 Tex. A&M-Kingsville	2,448	185	64	35.36
20 Western Ore.	1,977	248	49	35.29
21 Mo. Western St.	2,445	196	64	35.14
22 Wingate	2,260	295	56	35.09
23 Abilene Christian	1,847	58	51	35.08
24 Pittsburg St.	1,600	92	43	35.07
25 UC Davis	2,271	344	55	35.04
26 Clarion	2,326	233	60	34.88
27 Tarleton St.	1,971	263	49	34.86
28 Indianapolis	1,734	134	46	34.78
29 Hillsdale	2,011	240	51	34.73
30 Catawba	2,330	250	60	34.67
31 Saginaw Valley	2,044	244	52	34.62
32 Harding	2,197	121	60	34.60
33 West Virginia St.	2,078	141	56	34.59
34 Concordia-St. Paul	2,089	327	51	34.55
35 Central Ark.	1,802	282	44	34.55

Total Defense

Maximum 300.0 Yards Per Game

Rank, School	G	Plays	YDS	YPG
1 C.W. Post	12	817	2,586	215.5
2 Bowie St.	11	660	2,435	221.4
3 Fayetteville St.	12	828	2,839	236.6
4 Chadron St.	10	674	2,412	241.2
5 Elizabeth City St.	10	650	2,438	243.8
6 Fort Valley St.	11	666	2,682	243.8
7 Albany St. (Ga.)	11	797	2,728	248.0
8 Northern Colo.	14	945	3,555	253.9
9 Virginia Union	10	632	2,543	254.3
10 Merrimack	10	649	2,608	260.8
11 N.C. Central	10	613	2,624	262.4
12 Bentley	11	741	2,905	264.1
13 Pittsburg St.	11	714	2,912	264.7
14 Calif. (Pa.)	11	694	2,966	269.6
15 Virginia St.	10	611	2,702	270.2
16 Valdosta St.	15	984	4,059	270.6
17 Tarleton St.	11	735	2,983	271.2
18 Tusculum	11	776	3,005	273.2
19 North Dakota	11	663	3,034	275.8
20 Tex. A&M-Kingsville	13	814	3,593	276.4
21 Tuskegee	11	730	3,077	279.7
22 Grand Valley St.	14	957	3,919	279.9
23 Central Wash.	12	753	3,365	280.4
24 Southeastern Okla.	10	573	2,811	281.1
25 Mars Hill	11	733	3,096	281.5
26 Slippery Rock	11	725	3,111	282.8
27 Shippensburg	11	645	3,117	283.4
28 Livingstone	10	651	2,850	285.0
29 Gannon	10	627	2,876	287.6
30 Northwest Mo. St.	13	893	3,758	289.1
31 Adams St.	11	729	3,195	290.5
32 Presbyterian	11	741	3,213	292.1
33 Mansfield	10	659	2,925	292.5
34 Bloomsburg	10	700	2,939	293.9
35 Neb.-Kearney	11	722	3,236	294.2

Scoring Offense

Minimum 30.0 Points Per Game

Rank, School	G	TDs	PAT	2PT	Def Pts	FG	Saf	Pts	PPG
1 Grand Valley St.	14	90	74	4	0	10	1	654	46.7
2 Minn. Duluth	12	72	60	3	1	13	0	539	44.9
3 Carson-Newman	13	80	66	2	0	5	1	567	43.6
4 Saginaw Valley	12	63	58	3	0	11	2	479	39.9
5 Winona St.	12	64	53	1	0	10	1	471	39.3
6 Central Mo. St.	12	64	58	1	0	5	0	459	38.3
7 St. Cloud St.	11	55	41	5	0	9	3	414	37.6
8 Central Ark.	11	56	43	3	0	9	0	412	37.5
9 Pittsburg St.	11	52	51	1	0	13	2	408	37.1
10 Fort Lewis	11	56	43	3	0	7	0	406	36.9
11 Central Wash.	12	61	51	0	0	7	2	442	36.8
12 Tarleton St.	11	49	39	2	0	17	7	402	36.5
13 Concordia-St. Paul	11	54	42	3	2	4	0	388	35.3
14 Southern Ark.	11	51	37	1	0	9	0	372	33.8
15 Chadron St.	10	45	36	1	0	8	2	336	33.6
16 Valdosta St.	15	65	58	1	0	16	1	500	33.3
17 Colorado Mines	11	50	43	2	0	6	0	365	33.2
18 Indiana (Pa.)	13	60	50	0	0	7	0	431	33.2
19 Truman	11	50	43	1	0	6	0	363	33.0
20 C.W. Post	12	57	44	1	0	2	0	394	32.8
21 Southern Conn. St.	11	52	39	1	0	2	1	361	32.8
22 Western Wash.	9	37	34	2	0	9	2	291	32.3
23 Minn. St. Moorhead	10	45	40	1	0	3	0	321	32.1
24 Northwood	11	49	39	0	0	6	0	350	31.8
25 Neb.-Kearney	11	42	37	0	0	20	0	349	31.7
26 Bentley	11	49	30	6	0	2	2	346	31.5
27 Eastern N.M.	11	48	35	1	0	4	1	339	30.8
28 Tex. A&M-Kingsville	13	52	42	0	0	14	2	400	30.8
29 North Ala.	11	45	40	1	0	8	1	339	30.8
30 UC Davis	12	50	45	0	0	7	1	368	30.7
31 Northwest Mo. St.	13	51	42	2	0	14	1	396	30.5
32 Harding	11	42	34	2	0	13	2	333	30.3
33 West Va. Tech	11	47	38	1	0	3	0	331	30.1
34 Bloomsburg	10	41	34	1	0	6	0	300	30.0

Scoring Defense

Maximum 20.0 Points Per Game

Rank, School	G	TDs	Opp XP	2PT	Opp DXP	Opp FGM	Opp Saf	Pts	Avg
1 Morehouse	11	15	18	0	0	5	0	123	11.2
2 C.W. Post	12	20	11	3	0	5	1	154	12.8
3 Bentley	11	21	12	1	0	1	1	145	13.2
4 Virginia St.	10	18	14	0	0	5	1	139	13.9
5 Presbyterian	11	19	15	1	0	7	1	154	14.0
6 Bowie St.	11	20	17	1	0	5	1	156	14.2
7 Northwest Mo. St.	13	23	16	1	0	10	2	190	14.6
8 Albany St. (Ga.)	11	21	15	3	0	5	1	164	14.9
9 Fayetteville St.	12	25	14	1	1	4	0	180	15.0
Tusculum	11	22	16	1	0	5	0	165	15.0
11 Merrimack	10	21	17	2	0	1	1	152	15.2
12 Valdosta St.	15	29	20	3	0	12	0	236	15.7
13 Tuskegee	11	20	13	1	0	11	3	174	15.8
14 Central Mo. St.	12	25	20	1	0	6	0	190	15.8
15 Chadron St.	10	20	14	2	0	7	0	159	15.9
16 Pittsburg St.	11	23	16	1	0	7	0	177	16.1
17 Grand Valley St.	14	29	21	2	0	10	1	231	16.5
18 Fort Valley St.	11	23	17	1	0	8	1	183	16.6
Slippery Rock	11	25	22	0	0	3	1	183	16.6
20 Tex. A&M-Kingsville	13	27	23	1	0	10	0	217	16.7
21 Mo. Western St.	11	23	18	1	0	8	1	184	16.7
22 Northern Colo.	14	30	24	1	0	10	0	236	16.9
23 Virginia Union	10	24	16	1	1	2	0	170	17.0
24 Central Wash.	12	29	23	1	0	3	0	208	17.3
25 Mars Hill	11	26	16	2	0	5	0	191	17.4
26 Tarleton St.	11	24	13	3	0	9	1	192	17.5
27 Shepherd	10	24	19	1	0	3	1	176	17.6
28 St. Cloud St.	11	26	20	1	0	6	0	196	17.8
29 Minn. Duluth	12	31	18	0	0	4	0	216	18.0
30 N.C. Central	10	23	14	1	0	7	3	181	18.1
31 Benedict	11	33	5	0	0	0	0	203	18.5
32 East Stroudsburg	10	26	20	0	0	3	0	185	18.5
Emporia St.	12	28	22	0	0	10	1	222	18.5
34 UC Davis	12	31	25	0	0	4	0	223	18.6
35 Saginaw Valley	12	27	24	1	0	12	0	224	18.7

2002 Division III Individual Leaders

Rushing

Rank, Name, Team	Cl	Pos	G	Rush	Rush Yds	Rush TD	YPG
1 Aaron Stepka, Colby	So.	RB	8	293	1,370	11	171.3
2 David McNeal, Merchant Marine	Jr.	RB	11	338	1,860	17	169.1
3 Randal Baker, Carthage	Sr.	RB	10	286	1,680	16	168.0
4 Dan Pugh, Mount Union	Sr.	RB	14	384	2,300	35	164.3
5 Luke Hagel, Ripon	Sr.	RB	10	265	1,616	19	161.6
6 Tony Sutton, Wooster	So.	RB	9	215	1,418	15	157.6
7 Sean Atkins, Bates	Sr.	RB	7	228	1,069	11	152.7
8 Raphael Zammit, Curry	Jr.	RB	10	240	1,479	18	147.9
9 Richard Jackson, King's (Pa.)	So.	RB	12	369	1,731	13	144.3
10 Fletcher Ladd, Amherst	Jr.	RB	8	236	1,148	6	143.5
11 Fredrick Jackson, Coe	Sr.	RB	12	299	1,702	24	141.8
12 David Russell, Linfield	Sr.	RB	11	250	1,541	29	140.1
13 Justin Berrens, Lawrence	Jr.	RB	10	288	1,396	6	139.6
14 Geary Pryor, Aurora	Jr.	RB	8	176	1,095	15	136.9
15 Dontrell Harriel, Greenville	Jr.	RB	10	296	1,336	7	133.6
16 Kevin Bostelman, Adrian	Sr.	RB	10	257	1,311	14	131.1
17 Scott Froelich, Westminster (Pa.)	So.	RB	10	298	1,305	8	130.5
18 Ryan Gocong, Claremont-M-S	Sr.	RB	9	233	1,172	11	130.2
19 Mike Johnson, Bethel (Minn.)	Sr.	RB	10	293	1,257	14	125.7
20 Chris Morris, Wabash	Jr.	RB	12	263	1,497	19	124.8
21 Gary Sheffield, Ursinus	Jr.	RB	10	241	1,245	8	124.5
22 Drew Ecklund, Willamette	Sr.	RB	10	150	1,240	10	124.0
23 Preston Roberts, WPI	Jr.	RB	10	232	1,232	13	123.2
24 Andy Traetow, Gust. Adolphus	Sr.	RB	10	211	1,230	10	123.0
25 Brandon Mcdowell, Case Reserve	Jr.	RB	8	182	978	10	122.3
26 Joey Nichols, Wash. & Jeff.	Sr.	RB	12	336	1,460	12	121.7
27 Will Anderson, Bethany (W.Va.)	Sr.	RB	10	216	1,186	10	118.6
28 Craig Moshier, Juniata	Jr.	RB	10	222	1,177	15	117.7
29 Matt Bernardo, Muhlenberg	Jr.	RB	12	288	1,393	17	116.1
30 Jeremy Boyce, Trinity (Tex.)	Sr.	RB	13	229	1,500	13	115.4
31 Adam Webster, Brockport St.	Jr.	RB	13	344	1,473	7	113.3
32 Chris Sullivan, Wash. & Lee	Sr.	RB	10	294	1,123	10	112.3
33 Ed Cracchiolo, FDU-Florham	Sr.	RB	10	244	1,118	10	111.8
34 Jeremy Brown, Loras	Jr.	RB	10	237	1,117	11	111.7
35 Jared Morris, Lycoming	Sr.	RB	9	159	1,005	11	111.7
36 John Peterlik, Wis.-River Falls	So.	LB	10	188	1,114	11	111.4
37 Zach Weber, Ohio Northern	So.	RB	10	198	1,106	6	110.6
38 Dustin Johnson, Salisbury	Fr.	QB	11	201	1,203	11	109.4
39 Chad Wurth, Wis.-Whitewater	Jr.	RB	10	259	1,093	6	109.3
40 Bill Lazzaro, Middlebury	Sr.	RB	8	175	870	7	108.8
41 Greg Wood, Worcester St.	Jr.	RB	11	161	1,189	25	108.1
42 Trevor Cooper, Muskingum	So.	DB	10	230	1,052	9	105.2
43 Eddie Sulton'El, Norwich	Jr.	RB	9	205	939	7	104.3
44 Fred Edwards, Wesley	Sr.	RB	10	244	1,042	11	104.2
45 Gary Tope, Heidelberg	Jr.	RB	10	245	1,039	7	103.9
46 Brad Hodapp, Wartburg	Jr.	RB	12	184	1,246	14	103.8
47 Damien Brown, Olivet	Fr.	RB	7	106	724	5	103.4
48 Marcus Howard, Rockford	Jr.	RB	10	204	1,034	11	103.4
Cedric Simmons, Concordia (Wis.)	So.	RB	10	125	1,034	10	103.4
50 Matt Munson, Macalester	Jr.	RB	9	197	916	8	101.8

STATISTICAL LEADERS

Passing Efficiency

Minimum 15 Attempts Per Game

Rank, Name, Team	Cl	Pos	G	Pass Att	Comp	Int	Pass Yds	Pass TD	Pass Eff
1 Roy Hampton, Trinity (Tex.)	Jr.	QB	14	397	260	6	4,095	43	184.9
2 Rob Adamson, Mount Union	Sr.	QB	11	231	139	9	2,424	30	183.4
3 Eli Grant, Case Reserve	Jr.	QB	10	345	220	7	3,265	33	170.8
4 Matt Trickey, Ripon	So.	QB	10	217	126	13	2,228	23	167.3
5 Mike Donnenwerth, Simpson	Jr.	QB	10	258	158	5	2,318	22	161.0
6 Joel Steele, Anderson (Ind.)	Jr.	QB	10	362	228	11	3,125	33	159.5
7 Nick Ambrasas, St. Thomas (Minn.)	Sr.	QB	10	277	175	10	2,576	21	159.1
8 Dan Cole, Rensselaer	Jr.	QB	10	331	204	8	2,861	29	158.3
9 Greg Cornett, Wittenberg	Sr.	QB	12	283	178	8	2,464	21	154.9
10 Daniel Pincelli, Hartwick	Sr.	QB	10	361	198	14	3,208	36	154.6
11 Dan Larlham, Baldwin-Wallace	Jr.	QB	10	216	141	10	1,873	16	153.3
12 Bryan Gnyp, Kalamazoo	Jr.	QB	10	337	210	16	2,867	28	151.7
13 Sean Smith, Gust. Adolphus	Jr.	QB	10	272	181	8	2,143	20	151.1
14 Adam King, Howard Payne	So.	QB	10	379	245	13	3,177	26	150.8
15 Michael Scipione, Western Conn. St.	Sr.	QB	10	268	142	11	2,326	26	149.7
16 Robert Jenkins, Bridgewater (Va.)	Sr.	QB	12	251	134	14	2,341	22	149.5
17 Dustin Proctor, Hardin-Simmons	Sr.	QB	10	295	186	13	2,429	23	149.1
18 Ross Denne, St. John's (Minn.)	Sr.	QB	13	358	213	14	2,964	29	148.0
19 Tyler Matthews, Linfield	Jr.	QB	11	258	155	7	2,236	16	147.9
20 Kyle Daniels, Aurora	So.	QB	9	140	79	8	1,264	11	146.8
21 Tom Arth, John Carroll	Sr.	QB	11	346	207	6	2,671	26	146.0
22 Phil Mann, Lycoming	So.	QB	7	134	80	5	1,100	9	143.4
23 Tony Racioppi, Rowan	Sr.	QB	11	344	195	16	2,930	25	142.9
24 Mike Warker, Widener	Sr.	QB	10	296	152	15	2,616	24	142.2
25 Scott Biglin, Whitworth	Sr.	QB	10	272	164	10	2,143	19	142.2
26 Ryan Hartman, St. Norbert	Jr.	QB	10	291	178	9	2,153	22	142.1
27 Cody Fredenburg, Mary Hardin-Baylor	Jr.	QB	11	168	91	7	1,562	9	141.6
28 Donnell Brown, Millikin	Jr.	QB	10	203	108	5	1,627	16	141.6
29 Rob Purlee, Monmouth (Ill.)	Jr.	QB	10	279	152	14	2,443	19	140.5
30 Jake Knott, Wabash	Sr.	QB	13	408	232	12	2,954	35	140.1
31 Jeff Spraggins, Wooster	Sr.	QB	10	199	100	10	1,609	19	139.6
32 Craig Swanson, Hobart	Jr.	QB	10	290	170	10	2,209	21	139.6
33 Chad Bradley, Wheaton (Ill.)	Jr.	QB	10	278	171	11	2,253	15	139.5
34 Bob Schurtz, Col. of New Jersey	Jr.	QB	9	214	125	6	1,689	13	139.1
35 Joe Reardon, Williams	Jr.	QB	8	243	149	9	1,790	17	138.9
36 Tyvun Green, Stillman	So.	QB	10	345	169	13	2,682	33	138.3
37 J.J. Tutwiler, Cortland St.	Jr.	QB	11	274	163	6	2,105	15	137.7
38 Brett Dietz, Hanover	Jr.	QB	11	365	219	15	2,632	28	137.7
39 Brian Senske, St. Olaf	Jr.	QB	10	292	172	10	2,292	17	137.2
40 Jeff Dumm, Waynesburg	So.	QB	9	347	211	14	2,493	22	134.0
41 Corey Minnfield, Defiance	So.	QB	9	258	153	10	1,861	17	133.9
42 Marsh Mosley, Amherst	So.	QB	7	130	74	8	945	11	133.6
43 Luke Knuppenbur, Concordia (Wis.)	So.	QB	10	152	87	4	872	15	132.7
44 Nate Skelton, Beloit	Fr.	QB	10	228	118	8	1,837	14	132.7
45 Steve Slowke, Alma	Sr.	QB	10	340	210	14	2,354	21	132.1
46 Mike Erwin, Knox	Sr.	QB	10	323	173	8	2,372	21	131.7
47 Mike Bowman, Susquehanna	Sr.	QB	10	296	165	9	2,212	17	131.4
48 Justin Jones, Muhlenberg	Sr.	QB	12	274	153	12	2,042	18	131.4
49 Jake Olsen, Wartburg	Sr.	QB	12	248	137	15	1,962	16	130.9
50 Scott Krause, Wis.-Stevens Point	Jr.	QB	10	269	143	8	2,001	17	130.6

Blake Elliott, St. John's (Minnesota)

Receptions Per Game

Rank, Name, Team	Cl	Pos	G	Rec	Rec Yds	Rec TD	Rec PG
1 Luis Uresti, Sul Ross St.	Sr.	WR	9	87	1,082	4	9.7
2 Conrad Singh, Hampden-Sydney	Jr.	WR	10	86	831	5	8.6
3 Blake Elliott, St. John's (Minn.)	**Jr.**	**WR**	**14**	**120**	**1,484**	**22**	**8.6**
4 Jim Raptis, Chicago	Jr.	WR	9	77	983	4	8.6
5 Dwayne Tawney, Whitworth	Jr.	WR	10	83	1,226	8	8.3
6 Mark Boehms, Alma	Sr.	WR	11	91	1,116	11	8.3
7 Walter Hays, Howard Payne	Jr.	WR	10	80	1,110	14	8.0
8 Jeffrey Jourdan, Hanover	Sr.	WR	11	87	1,133	14	7.9
9 Lewis Howes, Principia	So.	WR	9	71	1,218	10	7.9
10 Justin Salton, Frank. & Marsh.	Sr.	WR	10	77	1,078	11	7.7
David Vance, Anderson (Ind.)	So.	WR	10	77	1,022	10	7.7
Eric White, Ill. Wesleyan	So.	WR	10	77	1,064	8	7.7
13 Ryan Soule, Hartwick	Sr.	WR	10	76	1,550	20	7.6
14 Ryan Friend, Williams	Sr.	WR	8	60	766	8	7.5
T.J. Thayer, Kalamazoo	Sr.	WR	10	75	1,085	9	7.5
16 Mark Bartosic, Susquehanna	Jr.	WR	10	74	1,202	14	7.4
Greg Fleming, Otterbein	Sr.	TE	10	74	854	7	7.4
18 Frankie Bass, St. Olaf	So.	WR	10	73	1,109	9	7.3
19 Matt Kent, Wis.-Platteville	Jr.	WR	9	65	1,139	13	7.2
20 Nick Cushman, Albright	So.	WR	10	72	774	6	7.2
21 Chris Glowacki, Ursinus	Sr.	WR	10	71	940	5	7.1
Zach Mendence, Maryville (Tenn.)	Sr.	WR	10	71	947	4	7.1

Rank, Name, Team	Cl	Pos	G	Rec	Rec Yds	Rec TD	Rec PG
Tom Neagle, Knox	Jr.	WR	10	71	991	16	7.1
24 Brad Duesing, Washington (Mo.)	Fr.	WR	10	69	1,073	11	6.9
25 Shawn Brown, Principia	Jr.	DB	9	62	794	9	6.9
26 Juan Quesada, Elmhurst	Jr.	QB	10	67	715	5	6.7
27 Tivo Gonzalez, Sul Ross St.	Sr.	TE	9	60	540	6	6.7
28 Matt Yvon, Westfield St.	Jr.	WR	11	73	993	12	6.6
29 Flynn Cochran, Rensselaer	Jr.	QB	10	66	968	5	6.6
30 Dustin Devening, Illinois Col.	Jr.	WR	10	64	655	3	6.4
Dan Ryan, DePauw	Sr.	WR	10	64	941	15	6.4
32 Jason Hunt, Trinity (Tex.)	Sr.	WR	15	95	1,348	8	6.3
33 Rob Kief, Rose-Hulman	Sr.	WR	10	63	626	1	6.3
34 Nick Bublavi, Catholic	So.	WR	10	62	1,206	14	6.2
Marshall Haggard, Randolph-Macon	Sr.	WR	10	62	569	4	6.2
36 Evan Cochran, Rensselaer	Sr.	WR	10	61	950	15	6.1
David Kallevig, Case Reserve	So.	WR	10	61	1,039	12	6.1
Jesse Von Behren, Simpson	Sr.	WR	10	61	1,079	13	6.1
39 Josh Espinosa, Buena Vista	Sr.	WR	10	60	964	10	6.0
Andy Mamula, Franklin	Sr.	WR	10	60	723	9	6.0
41 Jason Cellura, Case Reserve	Fr.	QB	10	59	831	9	5.9
42 Yarzwe Slowon, Augsburg	Jr.	WR	9	53	726	6	5.9
43 Denny Smith, Middlebury	Sr.	WR	8	47	717	7	5.9
44 Matt Ditch, Cornell College	Jr.	WR	10	58	907	9	5.8
David Strong, Randolph-Macon	Sr.	RB	10	58	478	0	5.8
46 Andy Graham, Kalamazoo	Sr.	WR	8	46	593	10	5.8
47 Rich Gear, Delaware Valley	Sr.	WR	10	57	973	11	5.7
Adam Johnson, Macalester	Sr.	WR	10	57	733	4	5.7
Eric Magrini, Montclair St.	Sr.	WR	10	57	798	5	5.7
50 Matt Rizzo, Wis.-La Crosse	Sr.	WR	11	62	650	5	5.6

Receiving Yards Per Game

Rank, Name, Team	Cl	Pos	G	Rec	Rec Yds	Rec TD	RecYD PG
1 Ryan Soule, Hartwick	Sr.	WR	10	76	1,550	20	155.0
2 Lewis Howes, Principia	So.	WR	9	71	1,218	10	135.3
3 Matt Kent, Wis.-Platteville	Jr.	WR	9	65	1,139	13	126.6
4 Dwayne Tawney, Whitworth	Jr.	WR	10	83	1,226	4	122.6
5 Nick Bublavi, Catholic	So.	WR	10	62	1,206	14	120.6
6 Luis Uresti, Sul Ross St.	Sr.	WR	9	87	1,082	4	120.2
7 Mark Bartosic, Susquehanna	Jr.	WR	10	74	1,202	14	120.2
8 Pat Moffett, Wesleyan (Conn.)	Jr.	WR	8	39	900	7	112.5
9 Walter Hays, Howard Payne	Jr.	WR	10	80	1,110	14	111.0
10 Frankie Bass, St. Olaf	So.	WR	10	73	1,109	9	110.9
11 Jim Raptis, Chicago	Jr.	WR	9	77	983	4	109.2
12 T.J. Thayer, Kalamazoo	Sr.	WR	10	75	1,085	9	108.5
13 Jesse Von Behren, Simpson	Sr.	WR	10	61	1,079	13	107.9
14 Justin Salton, Frank. & Marsh.	Sr.	WR	10	77	1,078	11	107.8
15 Brad Duesing, Washington (Mo.)	Fr.	WR	10	69	1,073	11	107.3
16 Eric White, Ill. Wesleyan	So.	WR	10	77	1,064	8	106.4
17 Blake Elliott, St. John's (Minn.)	Jr.	WR	14	120	1,484	22	106.0
18 Kyle Brown, Pacific Lutheran	Sr.	WR	9	49	950	10	105.6
19 David Kallevig, Case Reserve	So.	WR	10	61	1,039	12	103.9
20 Jeffrey Jourdan, Hanover	Sr.	WR	11	87	1,133	14	103.0
21 David Vance, Anderson (Ind.)	So.	WR	10	77	1,022	10	102.2
22 Mark Boehms, Alma	Jr.	WR	11	91	1,116	11	101.5
23 Tom Neagle, Knox	Jr.	WR	10	71	991	16	99.1
24 Brad Musso, Wheaton (Ill.)	So.	WR	12	62	1,189	11	99.1
25 Rich Gear, Delaware Valley	Sr.	WR	10	57	973	11	97.3
26 Flynn Cochran, Rensselaer	Jr.	QB	10	66	968	5	96.8
27 Josh Espinosa, Buena Vista	Sr.	WR	10	60	964	10	96.4
28 Ryan Friend, Williams	Sr.	WR	8	60	766	8	95.8
29 Evan Cochran, Rensselaer	Sr.	WR	10	61	950	15	95.0
30 Zach Mendence, Maryville (Tenn.)	Sr.	WR	10	71	947	4	94.7
31 Tyreak Saviour, Widener	So.	WR	9	39	851	9	94.6
32 Dan Ryan, DePauw	Sr.	WR	10	64	941	15	94.1
33 Chris Glowacki, Ursinus	Sr.	WR	10	71	940	5	94.0
34 Matt Ditch, Cornell College	Jr.	WR	10	58	907	9	90.7
35 Matt Yvon, Westfield St.	Jr.	WR	11	73	993	12	90.3
36 Drenzo Payne, Stillman	Sr.	WR	8	39	720	6	90.0
37 Jason Hunt, Trinity (Tex.)	Sr.	WR	15	95	1,348	8	89.9
38 Denny Smith, Middlebury	Sr.	WR	8	47	717	7	89.6
39 Shawn Brown, Principia	Jr.	DB	9	62	794	9	88.2
40 Brian Ferris, Rochester	Jr.	WR	10	53	882	11	88.2
41 Dan Suozzi, Hobart	So.	WR	8	44	703	4	87.9
42 Tim Carlock, FDU-Florham	Sr.	WR	10	37	862	7	86.2
43 Joe Gargione, Col. of New Jersey	Sr.	WR	9	49	772	6	85.8
44 Zach Michael, Lawrence	Sr.	WR	10	52	855	8	85.5
45 Greg Fleming, Otterbein	Sr.	TE	10	74	854	7	85.4
46 Jerheme Urban, Trinity (Tex.)	Sr.	WR	15	75	1,274	17	84.9
47 Jason Cellura, Case Reserve	Fr.	QB	10	59	831	9	83.1
Conrad Singh, Hampden-Sydney	Jr.	WR	10	86	831	5	83.1
49 Tim Roehrig, Ripon	Jr.	WR	10	33	829	14	82.9
50 Andrew Hilliard, St. Thomas (Minn.)	Sr.	WR	9	49	739	4	82.1

Interceptions

Rank, Name, Team	Cl	Pos	G	Int	Int Ret Yds	Int PG
1 Jeff Thomas, Redlands	Sr.	DB	10	13	127	1.3
2 James Patrick, Stillman	Sr.	DB	10	11	146	1.1
3 David Simpson, Alma	Sr.	DB	11	12	134	1.1
4 Kyle Hausler, Capital	Fr.	DB	10	10	158	1.0
5 Alex Hansen, Hardin-Simmons	So.	DB	10	9	108	0.9
6 Jeff French, Maranatha Baptist	Jr.	LB	9	8	159	0.9
7 Jeremy Carroll, Amherst	Sr.	DB	8	7	112	0.9
Josh Vickerman, Concordia-M'head	Sr.	DB	8	7	-43	0.9
Evan Zupancic, Tufts	Sr.	DB	8	7	57	0.9
10 B.J. Edwards, Manchester	Jr.	DB	10	8	35	0.8
Kory Schramm, Hartwick	Sr.	DB	10	8	115	0.8
Robert Spiegel, Benedictine (Ill.)	Sr.	DB	10	8	55	0.8
13 Mike Linhardt, Westminster (Mo.)	Sr.	DB	9	7	179	0.8
14 Eric Kluft, Hanover	Jr.	DB	11	8	118	0.7
15 Jeremy Goltz, St. John's (Minn.)	Jr.	DB	14	10	117	0.7
Jason Pflipsen, St. John's (Minn.)	Sr.	DB	14	10	66	0.7
17 Paul Evans, Juniata	Sr.	DB	10	7	69	0.7
Chris Fredrick, Concordia (Wis.)	Jr.	DL	10	7	35	0.7
Jon Klosner, Utica	So.	DB	10	7	106	0.7
Matt Louis, Muskingum	Sr.	DB	10	7	53	0.7
Greg Lowder, Illinois Col.	Jr.	DB	10	7	40	0.7
Marshall Mullenbach, Macalester	Sr.	DB	10	7	85	0.7
23 Marcus Boards, Willamette	Jr.	DB	9	6	89	0.7
Lewis Howes, Principia	So.	WR	9	6	79	0.7
25 Drew Holman, Lake Forest	Jr.	DB	11	7	52	0.6
Nate Pogue, Moravian	Jr.	DB	11	7	86	0.6
27 Nate Harrell, Chicago	Jr.	DB	8	5	8	0.6
28 Mike Capotosto, Springfield	Sr.	DB	10	6	57	0.6
Mike Defilippi, Rensselaer	Jr.	DB	10	6	32	0.6
Seth Kopf, Knox	Jr.	DB	10	6	34	0.6
Travis LeRoy, Ripon	Sr.	DB	10	6	38	0.6
Gifford Louden, Rhodes	Fr.	DB	10	6	33	0.6
Andy Matzke, Augsburg	So.	DB	10	6	68	0.6
Jarald Ridley, Manchester	Jr.	DB	10	6	101	0.6
Jason Salman, Thiel	Jr.	DB	10	6	95	0.6
Chris Scott, Hampden-Sydney	Sr.	DB	10	6	187	0.6
Brian Sparby, Luther	Sr.	DB	10	6	32	0.6
38 Justin Conyers, Westminster (Mo.)	Jr.	WR	7	4	69	0.6
39 Fulton Bell III, Wis.-Whitewater	So.	DB	9	5	18	0.6
Vinny Fazio, Claremont-M-S	Jr.	LB	9	5	95	0.6
41 Kelvin Bellamy, Rowan	Fr.	DB	11	6	103	0.5
Eric Hillison, Linfield	So.	DB	11	6	15	0.5
Phil Marr, Linfield	Sr.	DB	11	6	54	0.5
Anthony Matthews, Chris. Newport	Jr.	DB	11	6	49	0.5
45 David Aird, Austin	Jr.	DB	10	5	27	0.5
Bobby Akers, Randolph-Macon	Sr.	DB	10	5	90	0.5
Trey Bates, McMurry	So.	DB	10	5	71	0.5
Devin Brewer, Beloit	Jr.	WR	10	5	8	0.5
Justin Brown, La Verne	Jr.	DB	8	4	0	0.5
Jack Byers, Albright	Jr.	DB	10	5	18	0.5
Casey Cronin, Benedictine (Ill.)	Sr.	DB	10	5	73	0.5
Kennard Davis, Thiel	So.	DB	10	5	110	0.5
Shawn Defoor, Stillman	Sr.	DB	10	5	54	0.5
J.J. Edwards, Guilford	Sr.	DB	8	4	8	0.5
Scott Farley, Williams	Sr.	DB	8	4	29	0.5
David Garcia, Texas Lutheran	Fr.	DB	10	5	17	0.5
Joe Getz, Muhlenberg	Jr.	DB	12	6	71	0.5
Adrian Gongora, Eureka	Jr.	DB	10	5	19	0.5
Mervin Harrison, Howard Payne	Jr.	DB	10	5	36	0.5
B.J. Harvey, Illinois Col.	Jr.	DB	10	5	32	0.5
Scott Heighland, Defiance	Jr.	DB	10	5	0	0.5
Gene Iannuzzi, Grove City	So.	DB	10	5	62	0.5
Brandon Irwin, Colby	Sr.	WR	8	4	65	0.5
Kevin Kaplan, Ill. Wesleyan	Sr.	DB	10	5	14	0.5
Kevin Keen, Knox	Sr.	DB	10	5	62	0.5
Cody Kelley, Wartburg	Jr.	DB	12	6	129	0.5
Justin Kelly, Catholic	Jr.	DB	10	5	9	0.5
Greg Koch, Baldwin-Wallace	Jr.	DB	10	5	70	0.5
James Kostack, Wesley	Jr.	DB	10	5	17	0.5
Stephen Latimer, Western Conn. St.	Sr.	DB	10	5	124	0.5
Matt Lavalle, Mass.-Dartmouth	Fr.	DB	12	6	1	0.5
Conor Lefere, Kalamazoo	Jr.	DB	10	5	49	0.5
Michael Litrenta, Concordia (Wis.)	So.	DB	10	5	42	0.5
Nick Loafman, Albion	Sr.	LB	10	5	56	0.5
Sherod Long, Guilford	Sr.	DB	10	5	105	0.5
Ryan McCarty, Ohio Wesleyan	Fr.	DB	10	5	23	0.5
Ryan Mcmillen, Carnegie Mellon	Sr.	DB	8	4	107	0.5
Eric Moe, Wis.-Stout	Sr.	DB	10	5	56	0.5

STATISTICAL LEADERS

Rank, Name, Team	Cl	Pos	G	Int	Int Ret Yds	Int PG
Eric Pickett, Merchant Marine	Sr.	DB	10	5	41	0.5
Andy Ransick, Mt. St. Joseph	So.	DB	8	4	16	0.5
Shaun Ritchie, Coe	Sr.	DB	12	6	46	0.5
Aaron Rose, Denison	So.	DB	10	5	38	0.5
Craig Schuette, Middlebury	Sr.	DB	8	4	77	0.5
Mike Simpson, Wesley	Sr.	DB	10	5	36	0.5
Matt Stahley, DePauw	Sr.	DB	10	5	23	0.5
Josh Thomas, Upper Iowa	Fr.	DB	10	5	86	0.5
Anthony Tomaino, Hartwick	So.	DB	10	5	104	0.5
Kyle Westphal, Simpson	So.	DB	10	5	77	0.5
Gilead Ziemba, WPI	So.	DB	10	5	44	0.5

Punt Returns

Minimum 1.2 Returns Per Game

Rank, Name, Team	Cl	Pos	G	Punt Ret	Punt Ret Yds	Avg
1 Chad Strehlo, Hamline	Sr.	DB	9	11	192	17.5
2 Justin Alsterlund, Eastern Ore.	Fr.	WR	10	16	278	17.4
3 Matt Tosh, Ithaca	So.	DB	10	14	238	17.0
4 Tommy O'Connor, Waynesburg	Sr.	DB	9	29	483	16.7
5 Jay Morris, Cal Lutheran	Jr.	DB	9	20	320	16.0
6 Eric Schroeder, Martin Luther	Sr.	DB	9	25	396	15.8
7 Nate Ness, Maranatha Baptist	Fr.	DB	8	21	329	15.7
8 Blair Lemons, Rockford	Jr.	QB	9	19	289	15.2
9 Justin McHugh, Alma	So.	DB	10	16	243	15.2
10 Kevin Kaplan, Ill. Wesleyan	Sr.	DB	10	16	241	15.1
11 Joe Masciopinto, St. Norbert	Jr.	DB	10	30	451	15.0
12 B.J. Harvey, Illinois Col.	Jr.	DB	10	14	210	15.0
13 Antonio Wilkerson, Methodist	Sr.	WR	9	18	269	14.9
14 Gerald Dias, St. John Fisher	Sr.	DB	10	20	294	14.7
15 Ryan Soule, Hartwick	Sr.	WR	10	16	234	14.6
16 Brad Hodapp, Wartburg	Jr.	RB	12	15	215	14.3
17 Jason Wagstaff, Amherst	So.	WR	8	15	212	14.1
18 Jason Hunt, Trinity (Tex.)	Sr.	WR	15	32	452	14.1
19 Dan Holz, Wis.-Platteville	So.	WR	9	14	191	13.6
20 Shaun Rochon, Mary Hardin-Baylor	So.	WR	11	34	458	13.5
21 Anthony Devonish, Averett	Fr.	WR	9	15	201	13.4
22 Derek Sikora, Wis.-Eau Claire	So.	DB	10	12	159	13.3
23 Mario Martinez Jr., Texas Lutheran	So.	WR	10	16	208	13.0
24 Anthony Smith, Nichols	Fr.	RB	9	19	246	12.9
25 Adam Auvenshine, Albion	Sr.	WR	10	16	206	12.9
26 Josh Espinosa, Buena Vista	Sr.	WR	10	18	231	12.8
27 Nathan Davis, Chris. Newport	Fr.	WR	10	14	179	12.8
28 Michael Drach, Wheaton (Ill.)	Jr.	DB	11	27	339	12.6
29 Robert Clark, Concordia-M'head	Jr.	RB	10	26	321	12.3
30 Ben Dorsey, Wis.-La Crosse	So.	RB	11	25	307	12.3
31 Jeff Lerner, John Carroll	Sr.	WR	14	24	292	12.2
32 Mike Postell, Kean	Fr.	DB	9	12	145	12.1
33 Joseph Lemberg, Hardin-Simmons	Jr.	WR	10	13	155	11.9
34 Dustan Christian, Anderson (Ind.)	Jr.	DB	9	11	131	11.9
35 Nick Hajjar, Wooster	Sr.	DB	10	37	439	11.9
36 Jeffrey Welch, Ithaca	So.	WR	10	16	186	11.6
37 Jordan Sinz, Wis.-Stout	So.	DB	9	11	127	11.5
38 Matt Dean, St. Olaf	So.	WR	10	17	195	11.5
39 Josh Addis, Ill. Wesleyan	Jr.	DB	10	14	159	11.4
Rusty Midlam, Ohio Northern	Fr.	DB	10	14	159	11.4
41 Aaron Krepps, Wash. & Jeff.	Fr.	WR	12	28	317	11.3
42 John Kilde, Bethel (Minn.)	Jr.	RB	10	13	147	11.3
43 Kyle Snell, Whitworth	Jr.	DB	9	12	134	11.2
44 Jeremy Lynch, Brockport St.	Sr.	DB	13	41	454	11.1
45 Jason Cavell, Mount Union	So.	WR	13	32	352	11.0
James Mann, Wilmington (Ohio)	Sr.	DB	9	13	143	11.0
47 Jason Scheerer, Albright	Sr.	WR	9	21	230	11.0
48 Josh Bronaugh, Wabash	Jr.	WR	13	26	281	10.8
49 Dennis Freeman, Ferrum	Sr.	DB	9	13	140	10.8
50 Sebastian Singleton, Benedictine (Ill.)	Jr.	WR	10	12	129	10.8
Dale Williams, Sewanee	So.	WR	10	12	129	10.8

Kickoff Returns

Minimum 1.2 Returns Per Game

Rank, Name, Team	Cl	Pos	G	KO Ret	KO Ret Yds	Avg
1 Roger Snyder, Wash. & Jeff.	Sr.	DB	12	19	616	32.4
2 Andrew Garrod, Carnegie Mellon	Sr.	RB	9	12	371	30.9
3 Ryan Hoag, Gust. Adolphus	Sr.	WR	10	13	396	30.5
4 Josh Bronaugh, Wabash	Jr.	WR	13	21	636	30.3
5 Collin West, Ripon	Fr.	RB	10	19	567	29.8
6 Ryan Schneider, St. Norbert	So.	WR	10	24	709	29.5
7 Clint Pace, Hardin-Simmons	So.	WR	9	13	379	29.2
8 B.J. Harvey, Illinois Col.	Jr.	DB	10	20	583	29.2
9 John Kilde, Bethel (Minn.)	Jr.	RB	10	32	931	29.1
10 Shaun Rochon, Mary Hardin-Baylor	So.	WR	11	17	493	29.0
11 Rico Gardner, Howard Payne	Sr.	RB	10	14	392	28.0
12 Cory Flisakowski, Wis.-Stevens Point	So.	RB	8	14	390	27.9
13 Chris Nappi, Union (N.Y.)	So.	RB	10	17	469	27.6
14 Antonio Wilkerson, Methodist	Sr.	WR	9	12	329	27.4
15 Adrian Gongora, Eureka	Sr.	DB	10	13	349	26.8
16 Ely Santos, Centre	Sr.	WR	10	20	534	26.7
17 Antonio Nash, Susquehanna	Sr.	DB	10	17	453	26.6
18 Jonathan Samples, Pomona-Pitzer	Jr.	RB	6	12	313	26.1
19 Chris Gillette, Shenandoah	Fr.	DB	10	13	338	26.0
20 Ben Earls, Austin	So.	RB	10	24	617	25.7
21 Anthony Smith, Nichols	Fr.	RB	9	15	383	25.5
22 Jerheme Urban, Trinity (Tex.)	Sr.	WR	15	24	611	25.5
23 Dan DeCosta, Salve Regina	So.	RB	9	14	356	25.4
24 Robert Coleman, Westminster (Mo.)	So.	RB	9	14	355	25.4
25 Jason Gendron, Defiance	Fr.	RB	10	25	627	25.1
26 Shawn Brown, Principia	Jr.	DB	9	13	324	24.9
27 Greg Wood, Worcester St.	Jr.	RB	11	17	423	24.9
28 Nathan Smith, Gettysburg	Fr.	DB	10	21	522	24.9
29 Bradley Parker, Thomas More	Fr.	WR	10	16	397	24.8
30 Mike Labarbera, Wis.-Eau Claire	Jr.	DB	10	14	347	24.8
31 Scott Peterson, Pacific Lutheran	Fr.	RB	7	13	322	24.8
32 John Conroy, Kean	So.	WR	10	19	467	24.6
33 Travis Neet, Occidental	Jr.	DB	9	11	270	24.5
34 Dominic DiDomenico, Middlebury	Fr.	RB	8	11	269	24.5
35 Ryan Troge, Wis. Lutheran	Jr.	WR	10	19	464	24.4
36 Titan Mann, Menlo	Jr.	WR	10	12	292	24.3
37 Rob Patchett, Bowdoin	So.	RB	7	14	340	24.3
38 Jeff Lerner, John Carroll	Sr.	WR	14	23	558	24.3
39 Zach Mendence, Maryville (Tenn.)	Sr.	WR	10	38	921	24.2
40 Mike Postell, Kean	Fr.	DB	9	18	436	24.2
41 Jed Warsager, Moravian	Jr.	WR	11	23	556	24.2
42 Andy Kocoloski, Albion	Jr.	RB	10	15	362	24.1
43 Tim Herrod, Earlham	So.	DB	9	14	336	24.0
44 Josh Addis, Ill. Wesleyan	Jr.	DB	10	21	503	24.0
45 Owen Jarrette, Principia	Jr.	DB	9	25	598	23.9
46 Sean Smith, Bridgewater (Va.)	So.	DB	12	16	380	23.8
47 Tim Roehrig, Ripon	Jr.	WR	10	13	308	23.7
48 Tom Gipson, St. Lawrence	Fr.	RB	9	20	473	23.7
49 Nick Kilton, Wis.-Oshkosh	Fr.	DB	10	27	637	23.6
50 Rex Gray, Central (Iowa)	Jr.	WR	10	22	518	23.5

Punting

Minimum 3.6 Punts Per Game

Rank, Name, Team	Cl	Pos	G	Punts	Punt Yds	Avg
1 Scott Verhalen, East Tex. Baptist	Jr.	P	10	39	1,687	43.3
2 Cory Ohnesorge, Occidental	Fr.	K	9	39	1,647	42.2
3 Sean Lipscomb, Redlands	Sr.	P	10	45	1,877	41.7
4 Dusty Lehr, Juniata	Sr.	P	10	48	1,922	40.0
5 Philip Stuebs, Martin Luther	Jr.	WR	8	34	1,358	39.9

East Texas Baptist Sports Information

Scott Verhalen, East Texas Baptist

Rank, Name, Team	Cl	Pos	G	Punts	Punt Yds	Avg
6 Brian Loper, Howard Payne	So.	P	10	43	1,710	39.8
7 Mike Donnenwerth, Simpson	Jr.	QB	10	59	2,327	39.4
8 Andy English, Rhodes	Sr.	DL	10	52	2,050	39.4
9 Aaron Polack, Allegheny	Jr.	K	9	50	1,958	39.2
10 Arty Alvarez, Cal Lutheran	Fr.	P	9	44	1,714	39.0
11 Chris Tedeschi, Waynesburg	So.	P	9	58	2,259	38.9
12 Scott Farley, Williams	Sr.	DB	8	31	1,204	38.8
13 Laird Stabler, Carnegie Mellon	So.	P	10	43	1,670	38.8
14 John McLain, Moravian	Jr.	P	11	54	2,097	38.8
15 John Jennings, Centre	Jr.	K	10	49	1,894	38.7
16 Nick Schlieman, Augsburg	Fr.	TE	10	56	2,156	38.5
17 Curt Miller, Carroll (Wis.)	Sr.	QB	10	58	2,231	38.5
18 Adam Hicks, Capital	Sr.	K	10	64	2,458	38.4
19 Chris Arp, Mary Hardin-Baylor	So.	K	11	48	1,843	38.4
20 Doug Loomis, Maryville (Tenn.)	Sr.	P	10	60	2,303	38.4
21 Brian Bicher, Ithaca	Sr.	P	10	46	1,763	38.3
22 Nick Frade, Rowan	Sr.	K	11	44	1,684	38.3
23 Jonathan Mizglewski, Col. of New Jersey	Jr.	P	9	41	1,563	38.1
24 Dan Ries, Earlham	So.	RB	10	52	1,981	38.1
25 Mike Titzel, Grove City	Jr.	K	10	53	2,012	38.0
26 John Wheaton, Frostburg St.	Fr.	P	11	61	2,314	37.9
27 Christian Janney, Widener	Sr.	P	10	50	1,896	37.9
28 Marc Menchetti, Brockport St.	So.	K	13	65	2,458	37.8
29 Zack Krelle, Claremont-M-S	Sr.	K	9	50	1,884	37.7
30 Denny Smith, Middlebury	Sr.	WR	8	45	1,693	37.6
31 Paul Alejo, Whitworth	Sr.	P	10	43	1,615	37.6
32 Seth Brody, Bethany (W.Va.)	Sr.	P	10	46	1,721	37.4
33 Roberto Pino, Loras	Sr.	P	10	54	2,019	37.4
34 Christian Adams, Guilford	So.	K	10	59	2,204	37.4
35 Bryan Morris, Wis.-La Crosse	Sr.	K	11	69	2,575	37.3
36 David Samsal, Bluffton	So.	K	10	42	1,563	37.2
37 Craig Janney, Chowan	Jr.	K	10	60	2,232	37.2
38 Rick Nistler, Salisbury	So.	P	11	44	1,631	37.1
39 Brad Burright, Eastern Ore.	Fr.	P	10	49	1,816	37.1
40 Pat Dunne, Lake Forest	Sr.	K	11	70	2,593	37.0
41 Tim Goodridge, Norwich	So.	P	9	49	1,813	37.0
42 Maupin J.R., Whittier	Sr.	RB	9	41	1,514	36.9
43 Kyle Haug, Wis.-Whitewater	Jr.	P	10	60	2,214	36.9
44 Matt Rear, Dubuque	So.	QB	10	84	3,099	36.9
45 Geoff Bough, Amherst	Sr.	P	8	43	1,586	36.9
46 Ryan Hartschuh, Wooster	Sr.	P	10	47	1,730	36.8
47 Clay Brocious, Thiel	So.	P	10	52	1,914	36.8
48 Willie Thompson, Illinois Col.	So.	DL	10	54	1,977	36.6
49 Dillon Maney, Wis.-Stevens Point	Sr.	DB	10	64	2,342	36.6
50 Brett Dietz, Hanover	Jr.	QB	11	42	1,536	36.6

Field Goals Per Game

Rank, Name, Team	Cl	Pos	G	FG	FGA	FG PG
1 Ben Lambert, Washington (Mo.)	So.	K	10	15	21	1.5
2 Alex Espinoza, Cal Lutheran	Jr.	K	9	13	19	1.4
3 Christopher Reed, Muhlenberg	**Sr.**	**K**	**12**	**16**	**21**	**1.3**
4 Pat Dunne, Lake Forest	Sr.	K	11	14	22	1.3
5 Andy Cline, Albion	So.	K	10	12	15	1.2
Brian Klesath, Ill. Wesleyan	Jr.	K	10	12	17	1.2
Nicholas Zilich, Centre	Sr.	K	10	12	20	1.2
8 Jason Borchardt, Wis.-Platteville	So.	K	9	10	11	1.1
Michael Morzenti, Chicago	Fr.	K	9	10	12	1.1
10 Cliff Eisenhut, Union (N.Y.)	So.	K	10	11	14	1.1
Scott VanAlst, St. John Fisher	Jr.	K	10	11	12	1.1
Steve Willever, Oberlin	So.	K	10	11	14	1.1
Chad Wurth, Wis.-Whitewater	Jr.	RB	10	11	17	1.1
14 Andrew Beals, Millikin	Jr.	K	10	10	14	1.0
David Bodner, Amherst	So.	K	8	8	14	1.0
Brian Cence, Waynesburg	Jr.	WR	9	9	15	1.0
Scott Elzey, Muskingum	Jr.	P	10	10	12	1.0

Christopher Reed, Muhlenberg

Muhlenberg Sports Information

Rank, Name, Team	Cl	Pos	G	FG	FGA	FG PG
Sean Lipscomb, Redlands	Sr.	P	10	10	18	1.0
George Oostmeyer, Cortland St.	Sr.	K	11	11	20	1.0
Marcellus Rolle, Tufts	Jr.	K	7	7	12	1.0
21 Jordan Maus, Wartburg	So.	DB	12	11	16	0.9
Luke Ravenstahl, Wash. & Jeff.	Sr.	K	12	11	17	0.9
23 Nick Frade, Rowan	Sr.	K	11	10	16	0.9
Will McLaughlin, Wilkes	Sr.	K	11	10	17	0.9
Matt Piccirilli, Alma	Sr.	K	11	10	16	0.9
26 Dusty Bigham, Hardin-Simmons	Sr.	K	10	9	12	0.9
Dusty Lehr, Juniata	Sr.	P	10	9	13	0.9
Odell McGinty, Mary Hardin-Baylor	Jr.	K	10	9	11	0.9
Greg Switaj, Springfield	Jr.	K	10	9	10	0.9
Ben Tuck, Sewanee	Sr.	K	10	9	11	0.9
31 Todd Canion, Trinity (Tex.)	So.	K	15	13	16	0.9
32 Mike Laney, Brockport St.	Jr.	K	13	11	15	0.8
33 Brian West, Mass.-Dartmouth	Sr.	K	12	10	20	0.8
34 Joel Aromi, Concordia (Ill.)	Sr.	K	10	8	14	0.8
Bobby Corn, Ferrum	So.	K	10	8	13	0.8
Andy English, Rhodes	Sr.	DL	10	8	15	0.8
Chris Griffin, St. Norbert	Jr.	K	10	8	13	0.8
David King, Kean	Fr.	K	10	8	9	0.8
Dan Liebmann, Concordia (Wis.)	So.	K	10	8	12	0.8
Bill Lovendale, Curry	Sr.	LB	10	8	12	0.8
Chris Smolyn, Johns Hopkins	Jr.	P	10	8	10	0.8
42 Nate Strohl, Moravian	Fr.	K	11	8	11	0.7
43 Chad Teague, Mount Union	So.	K	14	10	14	0.7
44 Drew McMaster, Howard Payne	Jr.	K	10	7	9	0.7
John Ostrom, Texas Lutheran	Sr.	K	10	7	11	0.7
David Ping, Randolph-Macon	So.	K	10	7	10	0.7
Josh Simpson, Westminster (Pa.)	So.	K	10	7	8	0.7
Matt Verenini, Rensselaer	Jr.	K	10	7	9	0.7
49 Erik Hedval, Merchant Marine	Sr.	K	11	7	11	0.6
50 Eric Nielsen, Pomona-Pitzer	Sr.	K	8	5	9	0.6

STATISTICAL LEADERS

Coe Sports Information

Fredrick Jackson, Coe

All-Purpose Running

Rank, Name, Team	Cl	Pos	G	Rush Yds	Rec Yds	Punt Ret Yds	KO Ret Yds	Int Ret Yds	YDS	YPG
1 Dan Pugh, Mount Union	Sr.	RB	14	2,300	382	0	507	0	3,189	227.8
2 Ryan Soule, Hartwick	Sr.	WR	10	0	1,550	234	419	0	2,203	220.3
3 Fredrick Jackson, Coe	**Sr.**	**RB**	**12**	**1,702**	**234**	**260**	**346**	**0**	**2,542**	**211.8**
4 Zach Mendence, Maryville (Tenn.)	Sr.	WR	10	8	947	140	921	0	2,016	201.6
5 Brandon Mcdowell, Case Reserve	Jr.	RB	8	978	543	0	55	0	1,576	197.0
6 Greg Wood, Worcester St.	Jr.	RB	11	1,189	349	158	423	0	2,119	192.6
7 Raphael Zammit, Curry	Jr.	RB	10	1,479	156	14	232	0	1,881	188.1
8 David McNeal, Merchant Marine	Jr.	RB	11	1,860	207	0	0	0	2,067	187.9
9 Pete Henning, Lebanon Valley	Jr.	RB	10	770	352	147	604	0	1,873	187.3
10 Rico Gardner, Howard Payne	Sr.	RB	10	844	601	0	392	0	1,837	183.7
11 Matt Bernardo, Muhlenberg	Jr.	RB	12	1,393	340	0	440	0	2,173	181.1
12 Shaun Rochon, Mary Hardin-Baylor	So.	WR	11	236	779	458	493	0	1,966	178.7
13 Blake Elliott, St. John's (Minn.)	Jr.	WR	14	72	1,484	385	520	0	2,461	175.8
14 Tony Sutton, Wooster	So.	RB	9	1,418	110	0	50	0	1,578	175.3
15 Chris Sullivan, Wash. & Lee	Sr.	RB	10	1,123	223	88	319	0	1,753	175.3
16 Aaron Stepka, Colby	So.	RB	8	1,370	21	0	0	0	1,391	173.9
17 Josh Espinosa, Buena Vista	Sr.	WR	10	0	964	231	533	0	1,728	172.8
18 Randal Baker, Carthage	Sr.	RB	10	1,680	46	0	0	0	1,726	172.6
19 Andy Traetow, Gust. Adolphus	Sr.	RB	10	1,230	216	0	278	0	1,724	172.4
20 Zach Weber, Ohio Northern	So.	RB	10	1,106	224	33	360	0	1,723	172.3
21 Drew Ecklund, Willamette	Sr.	RB	10	1,240	142	0	339	0	1,721	172.1
22 T.J. Thayer, Kalamazoo	Sr.	WR	10	16	1,085	142	445	0	1,688	168.8
23 Luke Hagel, Ripon	Sr.	RB	10	1,616	69	0	0	0	1,685	168.5
24 Robert Clark, Concordia-M'head	Jr.	RB	10	726	254	321	358	0	1,659	165.9
25 Craig Moshier, Juniata	Jr.	RB	10	1,177	324	0	151	0	1,652	165.2
26 Will Anderson, Bethany (W.Va.)	Sr.	RB	10	1,186	398	8	53	0	1,645	164.5
27 Kevin Bostelman, Adrian	Sr.	RB	10	1,311	204	0	124	0	1,639	163.9
28 Frankie Bass, St. Olaf	So.	WR	10	12	1,109	92	411	0	1,624	162.4
29 Nick Bublavi, Catholic	So.	WR	10	5	1,206	95	305	0	1,611	161.1
30 Shawn Brown, Principia	Jr.	DB	9	182	794	145	324	2	1,447	160.8
31 Jovan Johnson, Bluffton	Jr.	RB	10	627	588	70	294	0	1,579	157.9
32 Jonathan Samples, Pomona-Pitzer	Jr.	RB	6	575	58	0	313	0	946	157.7
33 Mario Martinez Jr., Texas Lutheran	So.	WR	10	87	437	208	840	0	1,572	157.2
34 Robert Coleman, Westminster (Mo.)	So.	RB	9	595	441	13	355	0	1,404	156.0
Lewis Howes, Principia	So.	WR	9	0	1,218	0	107	79	1,404	156.0
36 Sean Atkins, Bates	Sr.	RB	7	1,069	16	0	0	0	1,085	155.0
37 Scott Froelich, Westminster (Pa.)	So.	RB	10	1,305	244	0	0	0	1,549	154.9
38 Anthony Smith, Nichols	Fr.	RB	9	685	76	246	383	0	1,390	154.4
39 Justin Berrens, Lawrence	Jr.	RB	10	1,396	0	0	141	0	1,537	153.7
40 David Russell, Linfield	Sr.	RB	11	1,541	123	0	10	0	1,674	152.2
41 Mike Johnson, Bethel (Minn.)	Sr.	RB	10	1,257	53	0	209	0	1,519	151.9
42 Cedric Simmons, Concordia (Wis.)	So.	RB	10	1,034	381	103	0	0	1,518	151.8
43 Pat Moffett, Wesleyan (Conn.)	Jr.	WR	8	0	900	28	279	0	1,207	150.9
44 Mike Jefferson, Luther	Jr.	RB	10	749	48	0	691	0	1,488	148.8
45 Calvin Hatfield, Kenyon	So.	RB	10	709	146	13	569	37	1,474	147.4
46 Brad Hodapp, Wartburg	Jr.	RB	12	1,246	52	215	248	0	1,761	146.8
47 Eddie Sulton'El, Norwich	Jr.	RB	9	939	184	0	190	0	1,313	145.9
48 Fletcher Ladd, Amherst	Sr.	RB	8	1,148	18	0	0	0	1,166	145.8
49 Jason Meyers, St. John Fisher	Jr.	RB	10	1,005	452	0	0	0	1,457	145.7
50 Richard Jackson, King's (Pa.)	So.	RB	12	1,731	15	0	0	0	1,746	145.5

Total Tackles

Rank, Name, Team	Cl	Pos	G	Solo Tack	Asst Tack	TT	TPG
1 Donnie Hohman, Chapman	Sr.	DL	10	77	95	172	17.2
2 Chet Knake, Cornell College	Sr.	LB	10	60	88	148	14.8
3 Casey McConnell, Kenyon	So.	LB	10	78	65	143	14.3
4 Mike Hanna, Olivet	Jr.	LB	9	81	43	124	13.8
5 Jon Foss, Bethel (Minn.)	Sr.	DL	10	51	77	128	12.8
6 Quincy Francis, Wesleyan (Conn.)	So.	LB	8	68	34	102	12.8
7 Mike Davis, Heidelberg	Jr.	LB	10	92	35	127	12.7
8 Danny Hernandez, MacMurray	Sr.	LB	11	33	106	139	12.6
9 Bryan Madden, Mississippi Col.	Sr.	LB	9	29	81	110	12.2
10 Bobby Hawley, Principia	Sr.	LB	9	41	67	108	12.0
Nick Loafman, Albion	Sr.	LB	10	53	67	120	12.0
12 Nate Enciso, Puget Sound	Jr.	LB	9	55	51	106	11.8
13 Dirk Erickson, Gust. Adolphus	Sr.	LB	10	46	71	117	11.7
14 Chris Stokes, Lewis & Clark	So.	LB	9	39	66	105	11.7
15 Brad Maguth, Hiram	Sr.	LB	10	45	71	116	11.6
Chris Sommers, Bluffton	Jr.	LB	10	41	75	116	11.6
Ron Swearingin, Capital	Sr.	LB	10	60	56	116	11.6
18 Charles Adams, Western New Eng.	Sr.	LB	8	47	45	92	11.5
19 Matt O'Bryant, Millsaps	Sr.	LB	9	51	50	101	11.2
20 Anthony Venturino, Utica	Jr.	LB	10	53	59	112	11.2
21 Chris Dembosz, Elmhurst	Jr.	RB	10	62	49	111	11.1
Joe Kostiha, Beloit	Sr.	LB	10	32	79	111	11.1
Dan Lombreglia, Union (N.Y.)	Jr.	LB	10	59	52	111	11.1

Rank, Name, Team	Cl	Pos	G	Solo Tack	Asst Tack	TT	TPG
24 Billy Chrisovergis, Ohio Wesleyan	Jr.	LB	10	61	48	109	10.9
Chris Dewey, Norwich	Sr.	LB	10	56	53	109	10.9
26 Prince Bussie, Dubuque	Fr.	DB	10	79	29	108	10.8
Jon Craig, Ursinus	Sr.	LB	10	67	41	108	10.8
28 Chris Horsey, Wesley	So.	LB	9	49	48	97	10.8
29 Clint Rider, Franklin	Jr.	DB	10	59	48	107	10.7
30 Kelvin Fuller, Ferrum	Sr.	LB	9	40	56	96	10.7
Byron Hook, Upper Iowa	So.	DB	9	41	55	96	10.7
32 Chris Cubero, John Carroll	Sr.	LB	14	77	72	149	10.6
33 Brandon Brown, Howard Payne	Sr.	LB	10	43	63	106	10.6
Andrew Erby, Delaware Valley	So.	LB	10	56	50	106	10.6
Jason Shaw, Marietta	Jr.	LB	10	37	69	106	10.6
36 Jesse Hoffman, St. Lawrence	Sr.	LB	9	58	37	95	10.6
Colin MacNeil, Occidental	Fr.	LB	9	56	39	95	10.6
38 Casey Urlacher, Lake Forest	Sr.	LB	11	55	61	116	10.5
39 Peter Thomas, Juniata	Fr.	LB	10	48	57	105	10.5
40 Jason Bogan, Aurora	Jr.	LB	9	57	37	94	10.4
Jon Ingram, Aurora	Sr.	LB	9	59	35	94	10.4
Ben Krasnoff, Wash. & Lee	Jr.	LB	9	48	46	94	10.4
43 Kris Hueber, Manchester	So.	LB	10	61	43	104	10.4
44 Jermaine Taylor, Bridgewater (Va.)	Jr.	LB	12	57	67	124	10.3
45 John Kaiser, St. Thomas (Minn.)	Jr.	LB	10	50	53	103	10.3
Jacob Knighton, Concordia (Wis.)	Jr.	LB	10	62	41	103	10.3
Nick Kraemer, Macalester	Sr.	LB	10	54	49	103	10.3
48 Mike Dempsey, Beloit	Jr.	DB	9	59	33	92	10.2
49 Mike Dempsey, Beloit	Jr.	LB	10	35	67	102	10.2
David Suitor, Otterbein	Sr.	LB	10	47	55	102	10.2

Pass Sacks

Rank, Name, Team	Cl	Pos	G	Solo Sack	Asst Sack	Sack Yds	Tot Sack	Sacks PG
1 Jon Foss, Bethel (Minn.)	Sr.	DL	10	15	2	90	16.0	1.6
2 Andrew Porter, Macalester	Sr.	DL	10	13	4	91	15.0	1.5
3 Steve Wilson, King's (Pa.)	Sr.	DL	12	15	4	159	17.0	1.4
4 Sean O'Leary, St. Thomas (Minn.)	Sr.	DL	9	10	3	67	11.5	1.3
5 Mike Condello, Brockport St.	Sr.	DL	13	15	3	105	16.5	1.3
6 James McKenney, Concordia (Wis.)	Jr.	DL	8	9	2	33	10.0	1.3
7 Chris Keene, King's (Pa.)	Sr.	DL	12	13	3	118	14.5	1.2
8 Jermaine Blakely, Stillman	Sr.	DL	10	12	0	113	12.0	1.2
Fred Taber, Juniata	Sr.	DL	10	11	2	108	12.0	1.2
10 Nick Dunn, Cal Lutheran	Sr.	DL	9	10	1	74	10.5	1.2
11 Ryan Killian, Widener	Sr.	DL	10	10	3	100	11.5	1.2
Dave Pisanick, Allegheny	Jr.	DL	10	10	3	60	11.5	1.2
Brandon Tisdale, Wilmington (Ohio)	So.	DL	10	11	1	90	11.5	1.2
14 Dwayne Robinson, Springfield	Jr.	DB	9	8	4	77	10.0	1.1
15 Brenden Givan, Stillman	Sr.	LB	10	11	0	70	11.0	1.1
Nate Matlock, Willamette	So.	DL	10	11	0	71	11.0	1.1
Walt Wagner, Merchant Marine	Sr.	DL	10	9	4	88	11.0	1.1
18 John Cloutier, Westfield St.	Sr.	DL	11	11	2	76	12.0	1.1
Gerrit Tosh, Rowan	Sr.	DL	11	11	2	113	12.0	1.1
20 Casey Carlson, Pacific Lutheran	Jr.	LB	9	9	1	73	9.5	1.1
21 Travis Little, Ohio Wesleyan	Jr.	DL	10	10	1	68	10.5	1.1
22 Robert Branch, Stillman	So.	DL	10	10	0	48	10.0	1.0
Beck Daniel, Gettysburg	Sr.	DL	10	8	4	58	10.0	1.0
Jeff Horton, Wis.-River Falls	Sr.	DL	10	9	2	53	10.0	1.0
Paul Jacobson, Concordia (Wis.)	Sr.	LB	10	9	2	42	10.0	1.0
Pat McAtee, Mt. St. Joseph	Jr.	DL	9	9	0	68	9.0	1.0
Kevin Yurkewich, MIT	Fr.	DL	7	6	2	71	7.0	1.0
28 Kyle Franklin, Merchant Marine	Jr.	DL	11	8	5	81	10.5	1.0
29 Ray Hartmann, Carthage	Sr.	DL	10	9	1	58	9.5	1.0
Ryan Kalcich, Lakeland	Sr.	DL	10	8	3	56	9.5	1.0
Tommy Knapp, Hartwick	Sr.	DL	10	6	7	51	9.5	1.0
Nick Reynolds, Kean	Sr.	DL	10	7	5	61	9.5	1.0
33 James Aimonetti, Principia	Jr.	DL	9	6	5	51	8.5	0.9
34 Ryan Bailey, Bridgewater (Va.)	Jr.	DL	12	10	2	78	11.0	0.9
35 Andrew Ackerman, Mt. St. Joseph	Fr.	LB	10	8	2	74	9.0	0.9
Chris Gallino, Frank. & Marsh.	Sr.	DL	10	8	2	77	9.0	0.9
Greg Liggens, Wilmington (Ohio)	Sr.	DL	10	8	2	60	9.0	0.9
Bernie Luna, Sul Ross St.	Sr.	DL	10	8	2	70	9.0	0.9
Lucas Robinson, Lebanon Valley	So.	OL	10	8	2	74	9.0	0.9
Patrick Ryan, Benedictine (Ill.)	So.	DL	10	9	0	53	9.0	0.9
Steve Varrasse, Widener	Sr.	LB	10	8	2	59	9.0	0.9
42 Chet King, Col. of New Jersey	Sr.	DL	9	6	4	59	8.0	0.9
Jed Mooney, Millsaps	Sr.	DL	9	7	2	45	8.0	0.9
Michael Sykes, Col. of New Jersey	Jr.	LB	9	7	2	61	8.0	0.9
Tim Williams, Augustana (Ill.)	Sr.	DL	9	8	0	43	8.0	0.9
46 George O'Brien, Frostburg St.	Sr.	DL	11	8	3	0	9.5	0.9
47 Jeremy Hood, St. John's (Minn.)	Jr.	DL	14	10	4	78	12.0	0.9
48 Dan Luce, St. John Fisher	So.	DL	10	8	1	50	8.5	0.9
Brian Park, Capital	Sr.	DL	10	8	1	54	8.5	0.9
Mike Rasmussen, Central (Iowa)	Jr.	DL	10	7	3	65	8.5	0.9

Forced Fumbles

Rank, Name, Team	Cl	Pos	G	FF	FFPG
1 Brian Cook, Johns Hopkins	Fr.	DL	10	5	0.50
Casey McConnell, Kenyon	So.	LB	10	5	0.50
3 John Cupples, Moravian	Sr.	LB	11	5	0.45
4 Jarrod LaRoche, Olivet	Fr.	LB	9	4	0.44
Dan Rosen, Maine Maritime	Fr.	LB	9	4	0.44
Matt Scaravaglione, Col. of New Jersey	Sr.	LB	9	4	0.44
Nick Tigue, Averett	Jr.	DL	9	4	0.44
8 Justin Tevis, Claremont-M-S	So.	DB	7	3	0.43
9 Michael Doleman, Shenandoah	Jr.	DL	10	4	0.40
Terrence Norve, Curry	Sr.	LB	10	4	0.40
Nick Rice, Thomas More	Sr.	LB	10	4	0.40
Mike Simpson, Wesley	Sr.	DB	10	4	0.40
Jason Stouffer, Juniata	Sr.	LB	10	4	0.40
Tim Swan, Rose-Hulman	Sr.	RB	10	4	0.40
Josh Vogel, Ohio Northern	Sr.	DL	10	4	0.40
16 Darren Bragg, Montclair St.	Jr.	DL	8	3	0.38
Donald Carter, Lebanon Valley	Jr.	DL	8	3	0.38
Jamie Creed, Trinity (Conn.)	Jr.	DL	8	3	0.38
Richard Decembrele, Middlebury	So.	LB	8	3	0.38
Dan McNamara, Amherst	Jr.	LB	8	3	0.38
21 Vince Cowlishaw, Moravian	Sr.	LB	11	4	0.36
Chris Lentz, Frostburg St.	Fr.	LB	11	4	0.36
David Simpson, Alma	Sr.	DB	11	4	0.36
24 Jason Bogan, Aurora	Sr.	LB	9	3	0.33
Kyle Crager, Mississippi Col.	Jr.	LB	9	3	0.33

Jon Foss, Bethel (Minnesota)

Rank, Name, Team	Cl	Pos	G	FF	FFPG
Nick Dunn, Cal Lutheran	Sr.	DL	9	3	0.33
Marvin Nash, Austin	Sr.	LB	9	3	0.33
Brian Person, Guilford	Jr.	DL	9	3	0.33
Brandon Schweinler, Aurora	Sr.	LB	9	3	0.33
Tim Tanous, Occidental	Fr.	LB	9	3	0.33
Andrew Wild, Carleton	Jr.	LB	9	3	0.33
32 Mcpatrick Coyne, John Carroll	So.	DL	13	4	0.31
Blair Hammer, Wabash	Jr.	DL	13	4	0.31
Chad Springer, Wabash	Sr.	DB	13	4	0.31
35 Tom Bernard, Rensselaer	Jr.	LB	10	3	0.30
Tim Booth, Hobart	Sr.	LB	10	3	0.30
Sam Cammarata, Denison	Jr.	DB	10	3	0.30
Matt Capone, Frank. & Marsh.	So.	DL	10	3	0.30
Matt Colatrgulio, Rose-Hulman	Jr.	DB	10	3	0.30
Dan Derksen, Kalamazoo	Sr.	LB	10	3	0.30
Troy Ebensberger, Texas Lutheran	Fr.	DL	10	3	0.30
Justin Fletcher, Springfield	So.	LB	10	3	0.30
Jack Fugate, Adrian	Jr.	DL	10	3	0.30
Matt Komar, Allegheny	Jr.	DB	10	3	0.30
Cliff Mason, Gettysburg	Sr.	LB	10	3	0.30
Jonathan Mitchem, Case Reserve	Sr.	DB	10	3	0.30
Joseph Orlandini, Case Reserve	Sr.	DB	10	3	0.30
Nick Reynolds, Kean	Sr.	DL	10	3	0.30
Nick Sabean, Delaware Valley	Jr.	LB	10	3	0.30
Mike Saddy, Wis.-Whitewater	Sr.	DL	10	3	0.30
Mike Salmons, Thomas More	Sr.	DL	10	3	0.30
Justin Schneider, Wis.-Oshkosh	Sr.	LB	10	3	0.30
Rick Schontz, Baldwin-Wallace	Jr.	DL	10	3	0.30
Derek Sikora, Wis.-Eau Claire	So.	DB	10	3	0.30
Mark Smith, Alfred	So.	DB	10	3	0.30
Joe Sollitt, Concordia (Ill.)	Fr.	LB	10	3	0.30
Shane Steele, Grinnell	Jr.	LB	10	3	0.30
Kevin Turner, Mississippi Col.	Sr.	DL	10	3	0.30
Jeremy Vanisacker, Kalamazoo	So.	LB	10	3	0.30
Tyler Vargo, Thiel	Sr.	DB	10	3	0.30
Ricky Vesce, Wm. Paterson	So.	DL	10	3	0.30
Andy Wagenbach, Illinois Col.	So.	DL	10	3	0.30
Greg Washington, East Tex. Baptist	So.	LB	10	3	0.30
Daryl Whitley, Kean	So.	LB	10	3	0.30

Tackles for Loss

Rank, Name, Team	Cl	Pos	G	Tackle STFL	ATFL	Yds	TTFL	TFLPG
1 Patrick Ryan, Benedictine (Ill.)	So.	DL	10	33	0	138	33.0	3.3
2 Steve Wilson, King's (Pa.)	Sr.	DL	12	38	2	229	39.0	3.3
3 Brian Robitialle, Curry	So.	LB	10	30	1	101	30.5	3.1
4 Sean O'Leary, St. Thomas (Minn.)	Sr.	DL	9	21	5	98	23.5	2.6
5 Robert Branch, Stillman	So.	DL	10	26	0	114	26.0	2.6
John Longo, Cortland St.	Sr.	DL	10	23	6	107	26.0	2.6
7 Jed Mooney, Millsaps	Sr.	DL	9	19	8	90	23.0	2.6
Vince King, Wartburg	Jr.	DL	12	25	8	114	29.0	2.4
9 Kyle Franklin, Merchant Marine	Jr.	DL	11	26	1	115	26.5	2.4
10 Jon Foss, Bethel (Minn.)	Sr.	DL	10	19	10	124	24.0	2.4
Andrew Porter, Macalester	Sr.	DL	10	20	8	111	24.0	2.4

STATISTICAL LEADERS

Rank, Name, Team	Cl	Pos	G	STFL	ATFL	Tackle Yds	TTFL	TFLPG
Fred Taber, Juniata	Sr.	DL	10	24	0	132	24.0	2.4
13 Matt O'Bryant, Millsaps	Sr.	LB	9	17	9	94	21.5	2.4
14 Chris Keene, King's (Pa.)	Sr.	DL	12	27	3	166	28.5	2.4
15 Gerrit Tosh, Rowan	Sr.	DL	11	25	2	171	26.0	2.4
16 Ryan Killian, Widener	Sr.	DL	10	23	0	118	23.0	2.3
Brandon Tisdale, Wilmington (Ohio)	So.	DL	10	23	0	116	23.0	2.3
18 Andy Gerhardstein, Aurora	Sr.	DL	9	20	0	70	20.0	2.2
19 Mike Condello, Brockport St.	Sr.	DL	13	28	0	134	28.0	2.2
20 Jamal Leggett, Methodist	Sr.	DL	9	19	0	77	19.0	2.1
21 Anthony Balthazor, Knox	Sr.	LB	10	20	2	59	21.0	2.1
22 Andrew Deming, Salisbury	Fr.	DL	11	23	0	83	23.0	2.1
23 Dan Luce, St. John Fisher	So.	DL	10	20	1	80	20.5	2.1
Chris Staley, Beloit	Jr.	DL	10	20	1	97	20.5	2.1
Anthony Venturino, Utica	Jr.	LB	10	18	5	65	20.5	2.1
26 Tom Blackledge, Moravian	Sr.	DL	11	18	9	66	22.5	2.0
27 Michael Sykes, Col. of New Jersey	Jr.	LB	9	18	0	85	18.0	2.0
28 John Cloutier, Westfield St.	Sr.	DL	11	19	4	95	21.0	1.9
29 Jermaine Blakely, Stillman	Sr.	DL	10	19	0	154	19.0	1.9
Chris Gallino, Frank. & Marsh.	Sr.	DL	10	19	0	94	19.0	1.9
Lucas Robinson, Lebanon Valley	So.	OL	10	19	0	95	19.0	1.9
Mike Simpson, Wesley	Sr.	DB	10	19	0	65	19.0	1.9
Willie Thompson, Illinois Col.	So.	DL	10	17	4	84	19.0	1.9
34 Pat McAtee, Mt. St. Joseph	Jr.	DL	9	14	6	99	17.0	1.9
35 Dave Pisanick, Allegheny	Jr.	DL	10	15	7	86	18.5	1.9
36 Matt Campbell, Mount Union	Sr.	DL	14	24	3	100	25.5	1.8
37 Brenden Givan, Stillman	Sr.	LB	10	18	0	97	18.0	1.8
Matt Lerner, Monmouth (Ill.)	Sr.	DL	10	16	4	65	18.0	1.8
Nick Reynolds, Kean	Sr.	DL	10	11	14	95	18.0	1.8
Walt Wagner, Merchant Marine	Sr.	DL	10	18	0	103	18.0	1.8
41 Rich Converse, St. John Fisher	Sr.	LB	9	16	0	50	16.0	1.8
Chris Roantree, Lycoming	Sr.	DL	9	16	0	54	16.0	1.8
Brandon Schweinler, Aurora	Sr.	LB	9	16	0	122	16.0	1.8
Johnny Williams, Occidental	Jr.	DL	9	16	0	54	16.0	1.8
45 Wesley Connors, Williams	So.	LB	8	14	0	58	14.0	1.8
Chris Cubero, John Carroll	Sr.	LB	14	24	1	72	24.5	1.8
Jim Lackmeyer, Wittenberg	So.	DL	12	16	10	77	21.0	1.8
48 Casey Carlson, Pacific Lutheran	Jr.	LB	9	13	5	91	15.5	1.7
Nick Dunn, Cal Lutheran	Sr.	DL	9	15	1	89	15.5	1.7
Marvin Nash, Austin	Jr.	LB	9	15	1	55	15.5	1.7

Total Offense

Rank, Name, Team	Cl	Pos	G	Plays	YDS	YPG
1 Adam King, Howard Payne	So.	QB	10	505	3,613	361.3
2 Tom Stetzer, Wis.-Platteville	Jr.	QB	9	553	3,136	348.4
3 Eli Grant, Case Reserve	Jr.	QB	10	406	3,192	319.2
4 Dan Cole, Rensselaer	Jr.	QB	10	438	3,173	317.3
5 Roy Hampton, Trinity (Tex.)	Jr.	QB	14	464	4,418	315.6
6 Joel Steele, Anderson (Ind.)	Jr.	QB	10	396	3,062	306.2
7 Daniel Pincelli, Hartwick	Sr.	QB	10	405	3,050	305.0
8 Bryan Gnyp, Kalamazoo	Jr.	QB	10	412	2,990	299.0
9 Grant Burrough, Frostburg St.	Jr.	QB	11	504	3,243	294.8
10 Steve Slowke, Alma	Sr.	QB	10	468	2,925	292.5
11 Jeff Dumm, Waynesburg	So.	QB	9	433	2,629	292.1
12 Daniel Swanstrom, Rhodes	So.	QB	10	543	2,905	290.5
13 Josh Dunn, Chicago	Sr.	QB	9	426	2,602	289.1
14 Chris Girbes-Pierce, Principia	Jr.	QB	9	404	2,589	287.7
15 Trent Thompson, Lewis & Clark	Jr.	QB	9	404	2,555	283.9
16 Brent Luebke, Lakeland	Jr.	QB	8	399	2,270	283.8
17 Dustin Proctor, Hardin-Simmons	Sr.	QB	10	398	2,822	282.2
18 Tony Racioppi, Rowan	Jr.	QB	11	415	3,057	277.9
19 Scott Kello, Sul Ross St.	Jr.	QB	10	591	2,717	271.7
20 Tyvun Green, Stillman	So.	QB	10	384	2,697	269.7
21 Andy Yoder, DePauw	Jr.	QB	9	412	2,427	269.7
22 Jerremy Neibert, Franklin	Jr.	QB	9	413	2,386	265.1
23 Mike Warker, Widener	Sr.	QB	10	373	2,624	262.4
24 Jared Tharpe, Rose-Hulman	Sr.	QB	10	506	2,612	261.2
25 Greg Troutman, Juniata	So.	QB	9	464	2,344	260.4
26 Clay Groefsema, Redlands	Sr.	QB	10	432	2,558	255.8
27 Chris Marshall, Westminster (Mo.)	Sr.	QB	9	345	2,281	253.4
28 Brett Dietz, Hanover	Sr.	QB	11	419	2,782	252.9
29 Nick Ambrasas, St. Thomas (Minn.)	Sr.	QB	10	327	2,478	247.8
30 Jake Knott, Wabash	Sr.	QB	13	506	3,215	247.3
31 Josh Akin, Ill. Wesleyan	Sr.	QB	10	442	2,465	246.5
32 Jeremy Lacaria, Bethany (W.Va.)	Jr.	QB	10	479	2,455	245.5
33 Scott Biglin, Whitworth	Sr.	QB	10	372	2,432	243.2
34 Bill Sutton, Catholic	Sr.	QB	10	377	2,430	243.0
35 Matt Makaryk, Wis.-La Crosse	Sr.	QB	11	424	2,661	241.9
36 Nathan Szep, Washington (Mo.)	Fr.	QB	10	370	2,411	241.1

Rank, Name, Team	Cl	Pos	G	Plays	YDS	YPG
37 Mark Mejia, Whittier	Sr.	QB	9	420	2,154	239.3
38 Michael Scipione, Western Conn. St.	Sr.	QB	10	330	2,392	239.2
39 Dylan Kruse, Menlo	Jr.	QB	10	412	2,384	238.4
40 Tom Arth, John Carroll	Sr.	QB	11	437	2,609	237.2
41 Dan Larlham, Baldwin-Wallace	Jr.	QB	10	336	2,366	236.6
42 Brian Behrendt, Centre	So.	QB	10	425	2,348	234.8
43 Rob Purlee, Monmouth (Ill.)	Jr.	QB	10	323	2,333	233.3
44 John Port, Albright	So.	QB	10	442	2,330	233.0
45 Mike Erwin, Knox	Sr.	QB	10	365	2,308	230.8
46 Kirk Holtgrewe, Sewanee	Sr.	QB	10	508	2,297	229.7
47 Tyler PaoPao, Occidental	Sr.	QB	9	369	2,066	229.6
48 Ross Denne, St. John's (Minn.)	Sr.	QB	13	411	2,982	229.4
49 Mac Russell, Hampden-Sydney	Sr.	QB	10	416	2,292	229.2
50 Scott Krause, Wis.-Stevens Point	Jr.	QB	10	372	2,288	228.8

Passes Defended

Rank, Name, Team	Cl	Pos	G	PBU	Int	TPD	PDPG
1 James Patrick, Stillman	Jr.	DB	10	20	11	31	3.1
2 Chris Fredrick, Concordia (Wis.)	Sr.	DL	10	18	7	25	2.5
Lorenzo Morgan, Mary Hardin-Baylor	Sr.	DB	10	25	0	25	2.5
Jim Schueller, Grinnell	Sr.	DB	10	21	4	25	2.5
5 Kyle Westphal, Simpson	So.	DB	10	19	5	24	2.4
6 Evan Zupancic, Tufts	Sr.	DB	8	12	7	19	2.4
7 B.J. Edwards, Manchester	Sr.	DB	10	14	8	22	2.2
8 Josh Vickerman, Concordia-M'head	Sr.	DB	8	10	7	17	2.1
9 Kyle Hausler, Capital	Fr.	DB	10	11	10	21	2.1
Travis LeRoy, Ripon	Sr.	DB	10	15	6	21	2.1
11 B.J. Harvey, Illinois Col.	Jr.	DB	10	15	5	20	2.0
Tommy O'Connor, Waynesburg	Sr.	DB	9	14	4	18	2.0
Eric Pickett, Merchant Marine	Sr.	DB	10	15	5	20	2.0
Nate Pogue, Moravian	Jr.	DB	11	15	7	22	2.0
15 Michael Litrenta, Concordia (Wis.)	So.	DB	10	14	5	19	1.9
Eric Moe, Wis.-Stout	Sr.	DB	10	14	5	19	1.9
Kory Schramm, Hartwick	Sr.	DB	10	11	8	19	1.9
Robert Spiegel, Benedictine (Ill.)	Sr.	DB	10	11	8	19	1.9
19 DeShaun Warren, Olivet	So.	DB	8	12	3	15	1.9
20 Devin Brewer, Beloit	Jr.	WR	10	13	5	18	1.8
Kevin Kaplan, Ill. Wesleyan	Sr.	DB	10	13	5	18	1.8
James Kostack, Wesley	Jr.	DB	10	13	5	18	1.8
Marshall Mullenbach, Macalester	Sr.	DB	10	11	7	18	1.8
Taylor Whaley, Rhodes	So.	DB	10	15	3	18	1.8
25 Travis Neet, Occidental	Jr.	DB	9	12	4	16	1.8
Joel Schwartz, Martin Luther	Jr.	DB	9	14	2	16	1.8
27 Scott Farley, Williams	Sr.	DB	8	10	4	14	1.8
28 David Simpson, Alma	Sr.	DB	11	7	12	19	1.7
29 Antonio Harrison, Grinnell	So.	DB	10	15	2	17	1.7
Greg Lowder, Illinois Col.	Jr.	DB	10	10	7	17	1.7
31 Jarrod Pence, Moravian	Sr.	DB	11	15	3	18	1.6
32 Matt Glasz, Trinity (Conn.)	Jr.	DB	8	12	1	13	1.6
Brandon Irwin, Colby	Jr.	WR	8	9	4	13	1.6
34 Mike DeFilippi, Rensselaer	Jr.	DB	10	10	6	16	1.6
Alex Hansen, Hardin-Simmons	So.	DB	10	7	9	16	1.6
Matt Louis, Muskingum	Sr.	DB	10	9	7	16	1.6
Brett Munn, Marietta	So.	WR	10	14	2	16	1.6
Matt Stahley, DePauw	Sr.	DB	10	11	5	16	1.6
Jeff Thomas, Redlands	Sr.	DB	10	3	13	16	1.6
Anthony Tomaino, Hartwick	So.	DB	10	11	5	16	1.6
Gareth Watts, Curry	Sr.	WR	10	14	2	16	1.6
42 Cody Kelley, Wartburg	Sr.	DB	12	13	6	19	1.6
43 Justin Conyers, Westminster (Mo.)	Jr.	WR	7	7	4	11	1.6
44 Quinton Bolden, Howard Payne	Fr.	DB	9	12	2	14	1.6
Mike Linhardt, Westminster (Mo.)	Sr.	DB	9	7	7	14	1.6
Caleb Nerstad, Claremont-M-S	Sr.	DB	9	13	1	14	1.6
47 Phil Marr, Linfield	Sr.	DB	11	11	6	17	1.6
48 Trey Bates, McMurry	So.	DB	10	10	5	15	1.5
David Blackburn, DePauw	Jr.	DB	10	13	2	15	1.5
Justin Brown, La Verne	Sr.	DB	8	8	4	12	1.5
Joe Camacho, Manchester	Sr.	DB	10	11	4	15	1.5
Matt Dean, St. Olaf	So.	WR	10	12	3	15	1.5
Johnny Kelly, Williams	Sr.	DB	8	10	2	12	1.5
Jon Klosner, Utica	So.	DB	10	8	7	15	1.5
Andy Matzke, Augsburg	So.	DB	10	9	6	15	1.5
Cameron McCambridge, St. John's (Minn.)	Jr.	LB	14	19	2	21	1.5
John Panikiewsky, Moravian	Jr.	DB	10	11	4	15	1.5
Jason Pflipsen, St. John's (Minn.)	Jr.	DB	14	11	10	21	1.5
Anthony Verdina, Loras	Sr.	DB	10	12	3	15	1.5
Shawn Wildt, Wheaton (Ill.)	Sr.	DB	12	15	3	18	1.5

Scoring

Rank, Name, Team	Cl	Pos	G	TDs	PAT	2PT	FG	Def Pts	Pts	PPG
1 Dan Pugh, Mount Union	Sr.	RB	14	41	0	1	0	0	248	17.7
2 David Russell, Linfield	Sr.	RB	11	30	0	0	0	0	180	16.4
3 Fredrick Jackson, Coe	Sr.	RB	12	29	0	0	0	0	174	14.5
4 Greg Wood, Worcester St.	Jr.	RB	11	26	0	1	0	0	158	14.4
5 Ryan Soule, Hartwick	Sr.	WR	10	22	0	0	0	0	132	13.2
6 Rico Gardner, Howard Payne	Sr.	RB	10	21	0	0	0	0	126	12.6
7 Luke Hagel, Ripon	Sr.	RB	10	20	0	0	0	0	120	12.0
8 Blake Elliott, St. John's (Minn.)	Jr.	WR	14	27	0	0	0	0	162	11.6
9 Raphael Zammit, Curry	Jr.	RB	10	19	0	0	0	0	114	11.4
10 Geary Pryor, Aurora		RB	8	15	0	0	0	0	90	11.3
11 Matt Bernardo, Muhlenberg	Jr.	RB	12	22	0	0	0	0	132	11.0
Cedric Simmons, Concordia (Wis.)	So.	RB	10	18	0	1	0	0	110	11.0
13 Tony Sutton, Wooster	So.	RB	9	16	0	0	0	0	96	10.7
Tremayne Willie, Westminster (Mo.)	Fr.	RB	9	16	0	0	0	0	96	10.7
Kyle Zick, Augustana (Ill.)	Jr.	RB	9	16	0	0	0	0	96	10.7
16 Brandon Mcdowell, Case Reserve	Jr.	RB	8	14	0	0	0	0	84	10.5
17 Jason Meyers, St. John Fisher	Jr.	RB	10	17	0	1	0	0	104	10.4
Craig Moshier, Juniata	Jr.	RB	10	17	0	1	0	0	104	10.4
19 Evan Cochran, Rensselaer	Sr.	WR	10	17	0	0	0	0	102	10.2
20 Chris Morris, Wabash	Jr.	RB	12	20	0	0	0	0	120	10.0
Tom Neagle, Knox	Jr.	WR	10	16	0	2	0	0	100	10.0
22 David McNeal, Merchant Marine	Jr.	RB	11	18	0	0	0	0	108	9.8
23 Randal Baker, Carthage	Sr.	RB	10	16	0	1	0	0	98	9.8
24 Kevin Bostelman, Adrian	Sr.	RB	10	16	0	0	0	0	96	9.6
Jason Eck, Susquehanna	So.	RB	10	16	0	0	0	0	96	9.6
26 Chad Wurth, Wis.-Whitewater	Jr.	RB	10	6	24	1	11	0	95	9.5
27 Sean Atkins, Bates	Sr.	RB	7	11	0	0	0	0	66	9.4
28 Aaron Binger, Pacific Lutheran	Jr.	RB	7	10	0	2	0	0	64	9.1
29 Will Anderson, Bethany (W.Va.)	Sr.	RB	10	15	0	0	0	0	90	9.0
Kent Crowley, St. John's (Minn.)	Sr.	RB	14	21	0	0	0	0	126	9.0
Dan Price, Wheaton (Ill.)	Jr.	RB	12	18	0	0	0	0	108	9.0
Dan Ryan, DePauw	Sr.	RB	10	15	0	0	0	0	90	9.0
33 Matt Kent, Wis.-Platteville	Jr.	WR	9	13	0	1	0	0	80	8.9
34 Ty Godinho, Hobart	So.	RB	10	14	0	1	0	0	86	8.6
35 Mark Anders, Baldwin-Wallace	Jr.	RB	10	14	0	0	0	0	84	8.4
Mark Bartosic, Susquehanna	Jr.	WR	10	14	0	0	0	0	84	8.4
Nick Bublavi, Catholic	So.	WR	10	14	0	0	0	0	84	8.4
Walter Hays, Howard Payne	Jr.	WR	10	14	0	0	0	0	84	8.4
Mike Johnson, Bethel (Minn.)	Sr.	RB	10	14	0	0	0	0	84	8.4
Mike Kenders, Millikin	So.	RB	10	14	0	0	0	0	84	8.4
Tim Roehrig, Ripon	Jr.	WR	10	14	0	0	0	0	84	8.4
Jesse Von Behren, Simpson	Sr.	WR	10	14	0	0	0	0	84	8.4
43 Aaron Stepka, Colby	So.	RB	8	11	0	0	0	0	66	8.3
44 Jeffrey Jourdan, Hanover	Sr.	WR	11	15	0	0	0	0	90	8.2
45 Christopher Reed, Muhlenberg	Sr.	K	12	0	49	0	16	0	97	8.1
46 Todd Canion, Trinity (Tex.)	So.	K	15	0	82	0	13	0	121	8.1
47 Eduardo Borrego, Occidental	Jr.	WR	9	12	0	0	0	0	72	8.0
Shawn Brown, Principia	Jr.	DB	9	12	0	0	0	0	72	8.0
Jared Morris, Lycoming	Sr.	RB	9	12	0	0	0	0	72	8.0
Adam Wallace, Grinnell	Sr.	RB	10	13	0	1	0	0	80	8.0

Solo Tackles

Rank, Name, Team	Cl	Pos	G	Solo Tack	STPG
1 Mike Davis, Heidelberg	Jr.	LB	10	92	9.2
2 Mike Hanna, Olivet	**Sr.**	**LB**	**9**	**81**	**9.0**
3 Quincy Francis, Wesleyan (Conn.)	So.	LB	8	68	8.5
4 Prince Bussie, Dubuque	Fr.	DB	10	79	7.9
5 Casey McConnell, Kenyon	So.	LB	10	78	7.8
6 Donnie Hohman, Chapman	Sr.	DL	10	77	7.7
7 Nick Wehrheim, Lebanon Valley	So.	DB	10	68	6.8
8 Nicholas Brokke, Carleton	Fr.	DB	10	67	6.7
Jon Craig, Ursinus	Sr.	LB	10	67	6.7
10 Jon Ingram, Aurora	Sr.	LB	9	59	6.6
Drew Sparn, Puget Sound	So.	DB	9	59	6.6
12 Mike Gancarz, Albright	Sr.	LB	10	65	6.5
13 Jesse Hoffman, St. Lawrence	Sr.	LB	9	58	6.4
14 Matt DeNardo, FDU-Florham	Jr.	DB	10	64	6.4
Brian Downs, Centre	So.	LB	10	64	6.4
Michael Irvin, Buena Vista	So.	LB	10	64	6.4
Brian Robitialle, Curry	So.	LB	10	64	6.4
18 Jason Bogan, Aurora	Sr.	LB	9	57	6.3
Mitch Repka, Wis.-Platteville	Jr.	LB	9	57	6.3
20 Colin MacNeil, Occidental	Fr.	LB	9	56	6.2
21 Chris Dembosz, Elmhurst	Jr.	RB	10	62	6.2
Jacob Knighton, Concordia (Wis.)	Jr.	LB	10	62	6.2
Chad Thomas, St. Olaf	Sr.	OL	10	62	6.2
24 Eric Eickhorst, FDU-Florham	Sr.	DB	9	55	6.1
Nate Enciso, Puget Sound	Jr.	LB	9	55	6.1
26 Nick Carlson, Wis.-Oshkosh	Sr.	DB	10	61	6.1

Mike Hanna (tackling quarterback), Olivet

Olivet Sports Information

Rank, Name, Team	Cl	Pos	G	Solo Tack	STPG
Billy Chrisovergis, Ohio Wesleyan	Jr.	LB	10	61	6.1
Kris Hueber, Manchester	So.	LB	10	61	6.1
29 Chet Knake, Cornell College	Sr.	LB	10	60	6.0
Tom Moran, Wesleyan (Conn.)	Sr.	DL	8	48	6.0
John Ortega, Centre	Jr.	DB	9	54	6.0
Brandon Schweinler, Aurora	Sr.	LB	9	54	6.0
Derek Sikora, Wis.-Eau Claire	So.	DB	10	60	6.0
Ron Swearingin, Capital	Jr.	LB	10	60	6.0
35 Dan Lombreglia, Union (N.Y.)	Jr.	LB	10	59	5.9
Clint Rider, Franklin	Jr.	DB	10	59	5.9
Jamie Spielman, Wis.-Stout	Sr.	LB	10	59	5.9
38 Charles Adams, Western New Eng.	Sr.	LB	8	47	5.9
39 Jason Leshikar, Trinity (Tex.)	Sr.	LB	15	87	5.8
Kevin Rooker, Wooster	Sr.	DB	10	58	5.8
Mike Simpson, Wesley	Sr.	DB	10	58	5.8
42 Sean Ross, Waynesburg	Jr.	LB	9	52	5.8
43 Antonio Nash, Susquehanna	Sr.	DB	10	57	5.7
44 Mark Darling, Mass. Maritime	Sr.	DB	9	51	5.7
Matt O'Bryant, Millsaps	Sr.	LB	9	51	5.7
Andy Peterson, Maranatha Baptist	Sr.	LB	9	51	5.7
47 Tim Boothroyd, Plymouth St.	Sr.	LB	10	56	5.6
Chris Dewey, Norwich	Sr.	LB	10	56	5.6
Andrew Erby, Delaware Valley	So.	LB	10	56	5.6
Nick Haffele, Wis.-Stevens Point	Jr.	LB	10	56	5.6

2002 Division III Team Leaders

Total Offense

Rank, School	G	Plays	YDS	YPG
1 Trinity (Tex.)	15	983	7,766	517.7
2 Case Reserve	10	738	5,073	507.3
3 Mount Union	14	973	6,975	498.2
4 Wheaton (Ill.)	12	999	5,839	486.6
5 Hanover	11	845	5,195	472.3
6 Linfield	11	828	5,149	468.1
7 St. John's (Minn.)	14	1,093	6,525	466.1
8 Westminster (Mo.)	9	699	4,170	463.3
9 Stillman	10	723	4,600	460.0
10 Willamette	10	699	4,595	459.5
11 Hardin-Simmons	10	710	4,594	459.4
12 Anderson (Ind.)	10	753	4,507	450.7
13 Howard Payne	10	702	4,487	448.7
14 Wittenberg	12	813	5,368	447.3
15 Ripon	10	697	4,446	444.6
16 St. Thomas (Minn.)	10	696	4,445	444.5
17 Bridgewater (Va.)	12	818	5,331	444.3

Rank, School	G	Plays	YDS	YPG
18 Rensselaer	10	689	4,362	436.2
19 Aurora	9	676	3,909	434.3
20 Alma	11	801	4,762	432.9
21 Frostburg St.	11	868	4,757	432.5
22 Rowan	11	778	4,728	429.8
23 Concordia (Wis.)	10	667	4,272	427.2
24 Chicago	9	702	3,833	425.9
25 Hartwick	10	693	4,241	424.1
26 Williams	8	615	3,371	421.4
27 Kalamazoo	10	699	4,203	420.3
28 Baldwin-Wallace	10	672	4,193	419.3
29 Augustana (Ill.)	9	664	3,764	418.2
30 Mary Hardin-Baylor	11	752	4,584	416.7
31 Worcester St.	11	770	4,572	415.6
32 Springfield	10	648	4,139	413.9
33 Beloit	10	772	4,133	413.3
34 Juniata	10	817	4,091	409.1
Millikin	10	677	4,091	409.1
36 Wabash	13	950	5,288	406.8
37 Coe	12	868	4,865	405.4
38 Lakeland	10	720	4,054	405.4
39 Pacific Lutheran	9	607	3,640	404.4
40 Wartburg	12	819	4,839	403.3
41 Widener	10	693	3,996	399.6
42 Bethany (W.Va.)	10	766	3,987	398.7
43 Western Conn. St.	10	681	3,982	398.2
44 Wis.-Platteville	9	682	3,583	398.1
45 Wis.-Stout	10	806	3,978	397.8
46 Wooster	10	687	3,975	397.5
47 St. Norbert	10	734	3,967	396.7
48 Hampden-Sydney	10	761	3,946	394.6
49 St. John Fisher	10	732	3,933	393.3
50 Olivet	9	654	3,535	392.8

Rushing Offense

Rank, School	G	Rush	Rush Yds	YPG
1 Springfield	10	583	3,567	356.7
2 Willamette	10	561	3,500	350.0
3 Concordia (Wis.)	10	493	3,228	322.8
4 Salisbury	11	595	3,450	313.6
5 Augustana (Ill.)	9	535	2,709	301.0
6 Olivet	9	554	2,682	298.0
7 Aurora	9	493	2,352	261.3
8 Mount Union	14	651	3,650	260.7
9 Carnegie Mellon	10	600	2,592	259.2
10 Carthage	10	521	2,460	246.0
11 Wilkes	11	584	2,668	242.5
12 Linfield	11	530	2,625	238.6
13 Wartburg	12	563	2,863	238.6
14 Wooster	10	483	2,357	235.7
15 Mary Hardin-Baylor	11	543	2,579	234.5
16 Wis.-River Falls	10	563	2,343	234.3
17 Worcester St.	11	466	2,541	231.0
18 Gettysburg	10	486	2,305	230.5
19 Ohio Wesleyan	10	499	2,274	227.4
20 Bridgewater (Va.)	12	522	2,718	226.5
21 Coe	12	572	2,717	226.4
22 Wis.-Stout	10	530	2,248	224.8
23 Wheaton (Ill.)	12	603	2,696	224.7
24 Baldwin-Wallace	10	444	2,231	223.1
25 Millikin	10	452	2,228	222.8
26 Westminster (Mo.)	9	414	1,999	222.1
27 Wittenberg	12	487	2,643	220.3
28 Chapman	10	421	2,191	219.1
29 Beloit	10	516	2,163	216.3
30 Thomas More	10	450	2,155	215.5
31 McDaniel	11	522	2,349	213.5
32 Maine Maritime	9	480	1,907	211.9
33 King's (Pa.)	12	628	2,537	211.4
34 Ripon	10	462	2,098	209.8
35 Lycoming	9	389	1,882	209.1
36 Claremont-M-S	9	451	1,880	208.9
37 Millsaps	9	469	1,878	208.7
38 Concordia-M'head	10	526	2,085	208.5
39 Trinity (Tex.)	15	530	3,114	207.6
40 Austin	10	469	2,057	205.7
41 Chris. Newport	11	544	2,240	203.6
42 Central (Iowa)	10	481	1,964	196.4
43 Amherst	8	379	1,543	192.9
44 Cornell College	10	451	1,923	192.3
45 Dickinson	10	465	1,919	191.9
46 Martin Luther	9	410	1,727	191.9

Rank, School	G	Rush	Rush Yds	YPG
47 Ohio Northern	10	435	1,909	190.9
48 Merchant Marine	11	499	2,081	189.2
49 Shenandoah	10	523	1,884	188.4
50 Methodist	10	419	1,880	188.0

Rushing Defense

Rank, School	G	Opp Rush	Opp Rush Yds	YPG
1 Wis.-Stout	10	302	500	50.0
2 Westfield St.	11	394	701	63.7
3 Thomas More	10	309	678	67.8
4 Trinity (Conn.)	8	280	552	69.0
5 Mary Hardin-Baylor	11	308	800	72.7
6 Widener	10	386	734	73.4
7 Wartburg	12	410	881	73.4
8 Wabash	13	432	984	75.7
9 Concordia (Wis.)	10	347	777	77.7
10 McDaniel	11	375	875	79.5
11 King's (Pa.)	12	445	955	79.6
12 DePauw	10	341	803	80.3
13 Martin Luther	9	328	730	81.1
14 Lake Forest	11	414	931	84.6
15 Millsaps	9	291	763	84.8
16 Wittenberg	12	413	1,027	85.6
17 Augustana (Ill.)	9	309	793	88.1
18 Wheaton (Ill.)	12	383	1,061	88.4
19 Maranatha Baptist	9	311	832	92.4
20 Moravian	11	400	1,033	93.9
21 Wilkes	11	343	1,042	94.7
22 Ithaca	10	358	949	94.9
23 Westminster (Mo.)	9	286	856	95.1
24 Johns Hopkins	11	380	1,052	95.6
25 Baldwin-Wallace	10	358	965	96.5
26 Cortland St.	11	406	1,070	97.3
27 Salisbury	11	409	1,081	98.3
28 Central (Iowa)	10	409	988	98.8
29 Stillman	10	346	999	99.9
30 Concordia-M'head	10	362	1,019	101.9
31 Olivet	9	272	918	102.0
32 Hartwick	10	385	1,027	102.7
33 Wis.-Eau Claire	10	374	1,029	102.9
34 Knox	10	335	1,039	103.9
35 Capital	10	353	1,049	104.9
36 Alma	11	419	1,160	105.5
37 Brockport St.	13	503	1,373	105.6
38 Hampden-Sydney	10	369	1,057	105.7
39 Lycoming	9	332	953	105.9
40 Ohio Northern	10	415	1,061	106.1
41 Hobart	10	353	1,089	108.9
42 Bridgewater (Va.)	12	443	1,321	110.1
43 Randolph-Macon	10	356	1,103	110.3
44 St. Norbert	10	392	1,104	110.4
45 Hanover	11	403	1,223	111.2
46 Mt. St. Joseph	10	351	1,115	111.5
47 Colby	8	291	893	111.6
48 Carnegie Mellon	10	355	1,119	111.9
49 Howard Payne	10	344	1,121	112.1
50 Curry	10	399	1,132	113.2

Passing Offense

Rank, School	G	Pass Att	Comp	Int	Pass Yds	YPG
1 Case Reserve	10	391	244	10	3,706	370.6
2 Hanover	11	510	300	19	3,764	342.2
3 Hartwick	10	371	201	15	3,286	328.6
4 Wis.-Platteville	9	462	238	17	2,957	328.6
5 Anderson (Ind.)	10	387	242	14	3,237	323.7
6 Howard Payne	10	401	250	15	3,194	319.4
7 Trinity (Tex.)	15	453	295	8	4,652	310.1
8 Lakeland	10	423	257	12	3,065	306.5
9 Rensselaer	10	347	211	9	3,036	303.6
10 Chicago	9	391	211	14	2,728	303.1
11 Sul Ross St.	10	599	358	24	3,031	303.1
12 Kalamazoo	10	354	220	18	2,983	298.3
13 Principia	9	352	184	18	2,657	295.2
14 St. John's (Minn.)	14	525	313	22	4,130	295.0
15 Hardin-Simmons	10	347	210	15	2,930	293.0
16 Waynesburg	9	353	214	15	2,555	283.9
17 St. Thomas (Minn.)	10	304	188	12	2,796	279.6
18 Rowan	11	369	204	18	3,070	279.1

Rank, School	G	Pass Att	Comp	Int	Pass Yds	YPG
19 Frostburg St.	11	427	233	17	3,044	276.7
20 Franklin	10	424	247	18	2,762	276.2
21 Widener	10	305	158	15	2,740	274.0
22 Stillman	10	360	173	16	2,739	273.9
23 Catholic	10	379	183	18	2,704	270.4
24 DePauw	10	381	231	15	2,683	268.3
25 Rhodes	10	428	221	6	2,667	266.7
26 Wheaton (Ill.)	12	396	239	17	3,143	261.9
27 Washington (Mo.)	10	378	216	23	2,605	260.5
28 Redlands	10	383	201	13	2,592	259.2
29 Menlo	10	409	221	16	2,589	258.9
30 Alma	11	412	254	19	2,844	258.5
31 Centre	10	370	216	13	2,547	254.7
32 Williams	8	285	169	13	2,029	253.6
33 St. Olaf	10	305	177	10	2,505	250.5
34 Albright	10	374	215	15	2,485	248.5
35 Monmouth (Ill.)	10	288	155	15	2,473	247.3
36 Illinois Col.	10	395	214	13	2,439	243.9
37 Knox	10	332	178	8	2,437	243.7
38 Western Conn. St.	10	280	146	13	2,419	241.9
39 Westminster (Mo.)	9	285	159	10	2,171	241.2
40 Wabash	13	440	249	15	3,107	239.0
41 Mount Union	14	322	199	11	3,325	237.5
42 Montclair St.	10	335	165	11	2,369	236.9
43 Maryville (Tenn.)	10	364	194	20	2,366	236.6
44 John Carroll	14	442	250	12	3,304	236.0
45 Simpson	10	260	159	5	2,350	235.0
46 Ripon	10	235	134	13	2,348	234.8
47 Lewis & Clark	9	293	155	16	2,108	234.2
48 Wis.-La Crosse	11	368	178	13	2,569	233.5
49 St. Norbert	10	318	192	11	2,326	232.6
50 Bethany (W.Va.)	10	365	192	13	2,318	231.8

Turnover Margin

Rank, School	G	Fumbles Gained	Int	Turn Gain	Fumbles Lost	Int	Opp Turn Lost	Margin	Avg
1 Mass.-Dartmouth	12	25	28	53	16	5	21	32	2.7
2 Muhlenberg	12	22	23	45	5	12	17	28	2.3
3 Capital	10	11	27	38	6	13	19	19	1.9
4 Linfield	11	16	20	36	8	8	16	20	1.8
5 Westfield St.	11	25	19	44	14	11	25	19	1.7
6 Juniata	10	15	16	31	4	10	14	17	1.7
7 Shenandoah	10	22	14	36	15	5	20	16	1.6
8 Wabash	13	18	25	43	8	15	23	20	1.5
9 Middlebury	8	10	17	27	6	9	15	12	1.5
Tufts	8	11	22	33	8	13	21	12	1.5
Wis.-Whitewater	10	16	10	26	5	6	11	15	1.5
Simpson	10	9	17	26	6	5	11	15	1.5
13 MacMurray	11	11	23	34	8	10	18	16	1.5
14 St. Olaf	10	14	19	33	9	10	19	14	1.4
15 Cortland St.	11	14	16	30	7	8	15	15	1.4
16 Redlands	10	11	25	36	10	13	23	13	1.3
Western Conn. St.	10	21	15	36	10	13	23	13	1.3
18 Chris. Newport	11	9	17	26	6	6	12	14	1.3
19 Augustana (Ill.)	9	10	16	26	9	6	15	11	1.2
20 Rhodes	10	15	14	29	11	6	17	12	1.2
21 Lake Forest	11	15	24	39	9	17	26	13	1.2
22 Bridgewater (Va.)	12	21	22	43	15	14	29	14	1.2
23 Amherst	8	10	15	25	5	11	16	9	1.1
24 Hartwick	10	16	22	38	12	15	27	11	1.1
Macalester	10	13	22	35	6	18	24	11	1.1
Mississippi Col.	10	19	22	41	15	15	30	11	1.1
Willamette	10	14	21	35	16	8	24	11	1.1
Concordia (Wis.)	10	7	19	26	10	5	15	11	1.1
29 Albion	10	18	18	36	11	15	26	10	1.0
John Carroll	14	18	23	41	15	12	27	14	1.0
Rensselaer	10	12	15	27	8	9	17	10	1.0
Concordia-M'head	10	15	16	31	12	9	21	10	1.0
33 Allegheny	10	10	14	24	7	8	15	9	0.9
Austin	10	22	15	37	13	15	28	9	0.9
Springfield	10	14	21	35	24	2	26	9	0.9
Knox	10	7	23	30	13	8	21	9	0.9
37 St. John's (Minn.)	14	17	32	49	15	22	37	12	0.9
38 Beloit	10	9	18	27	9	10	19	8	0.8
Rockford	10	7	14	21	3	10	13	8	0.8
St. Norbert	10	11	18	29	10	11	21	8	0.8
Wis.-River Falls	10	18	15	33	16	9	25	8	0.8
Howard Payne	10	8	19	27	4	15	19	8	0.8
Whitworth	10	7	17	24	6	10	16	8	0.8
44 Lycoming	9	6	17	23	4	12	16	7	0.8
45 King's (Pa.)	12	14	24	38	16	13	29	9	0.8
46 Worcester St.	11	18	14	32	13	11	24	8	0.7

Rank, School	G	Fumbles Gained	Int	Turn Gain	Fumbles Lost	Int	Opp Turn Lost	Margin	Avg
Hanover	11	8	21	29	2	19	21	8	0.7
48 Hobart	10	15	12	27	10	10	20	7	0.7
Ill. Wesleyan	10	6	15	21	5	9	14	7	0.7
Manchester	10	12	22	34	8	19	27	7	0.7

Pass Efficiency Defense

Rank, School	G	Opp Pass Att	Opp Pass Cpl	Int	Opp Pass Yds	Opp Pass TDs	Pass Eff
1 Brockport St.	13	325	123	27	1,587	9	71.4
2 Westfield St.	11	274	113	19	1,231	6	72.3
3 Ferrum	10	203	76	13	944	6	73.4
4 Nichols	9	207	74	11	939	8	76.0
5 Mass.-Dartmouth	12	288	136	28	1,534	5	78.2
6 MacMurray	11	279	132	23	1,369	6	79.1
7 Merchant Marine	11	309	132	14	1,438	6	79.2
8 Concordia (Wis.)	10	260	114	19	1,169	10	79.7
9 Tufts	8	223	102	22	1,206	6	80.3
10 Central (Iowa)	10	253	109	13	1,231	6	81.5
11 Rowan	11	384	169	22	1,940	8	81.9
12 Wartburg	12	314	132	15	1,619	6	82.1
13 Hartwick	10	289	119	22	1,534	12	84.2
14 Springfield	10	261	127	21	1,356	8	86.3
15 Stillman	10	287	112	23	1,593	15	86.9
16 Claremont-M-S	9	300	114	13	1,625	11	86.9
17 Lycoming	9	231	93	17	1,259	11	87.0
18 Mount Union	14	362	165	14	1,657	12	87.2
19 Greensboro	10	183	77	5	910	5	87.2
20 St. John's (Minn.)	14	448	216	32	2,512	9	87.7
21 Linfield	11	301	138	20	1,647	9	88.4
22 Augustana (Ill.)	9	223	102	16	1,205	8	88.6
23 Maranatha Baptist	9	273	114	16	1,523	10	89.0
24 King's (Pa.)	12	321	138	24	1,879	12	89.5
25 Wittenberg	12	402	196	19	1,988	12	90.7
26 Averett	9	150	60	4	766	6	90.8
27 Muhlenberg	12	339	160	23	1,809	13	91.1
28 McDaniel	11	344	151	12	1,831	11	91.2
29 Baldwin-Wallace	10	293	147	19	1,671	6	91.9
30 Amherst	8	210	115	15	1,103	5	92.5
31 Lake Forest	11	406	210	24	2,088	12	92.9
32 Williams	8	197	84	11	1,047	6	92.9
33 Benedictine (Ill.)	10	260	125	18	1,399	11	93.4
34 Shenandoah	10	193	85	14	1,038	11	93.5
35 Wabash	13	449	218	25	2,309	18	93.8
36 Wheaton (Ill.)	12	371	179	12	1,859	12	94.5
37 Bates	8	193	89	13	1,212	6	95.7
38 Mississippi Col.	10	287	135	22	1,714	12	95.7
39 Westminster (Mo.)	9	247	107	18	1,500	12	95.8
40 Coe	12	382	176	13	2,079	14	97.1
41 Knox	10	350	161	23	2,092	15	97.2
42 John Carroll	14	376	191	23	2,092	14	97.6
43 Chris. Newport	11	254	119	17	1,507	11	97.6
44 Simpson	10	284	123	17	1,776	12	97.8
45 Worcester St.	11	254	113	14	1,409	14	98.3
46 Wash. & Jeff.	12	318	149	19	1,756	17	98.9
47 Mary Hardin-Baylor	11	381	180	20	2,193	16	99.0
48 Fitchburg St.	9	190	90	9	1,150	6	99.2
49 Wesley	10	236	129	16	1,300	9	100.0
50 Wis.-Stout	10	314	142	15	1,896	13	100.1

Kickoff Returns

Rank, School	KO Ret	KO Ret Yds	Kick Ret TDs	Avg
1 Wabash	35	961	2	27.46
2 Mount Union	34	895	2	26.32
3 Muhlenberg	31	784	1	25.29
4 St. Norbert	35	877	2	25.06
5 Bethel (Minn.)	46	1,109	1	24.11
6 Ripon	38	916	1	24.11
7 Brockport St.	29	682	1	23.52
8 Wash. & Jeff.	44	1,033	1	23.48
9 Westminster (Mo.)	30	702	0	23.40
10 Chris. Newport	31	717	2	23.13
11 Coe	35	809	1	23.11
12 King's (Pa.)	24	553	1	23.04
13 Alfred	40	907	0	22.68
14 Principia	45	1,014	2	22.53
15 Pacific Lutheran	30	674	0	22.47
16 Central (Iowa)	25	559	0	22.36
17 Middlebury	22	490	0	22.27

Rank, School	KO KO Ret	Kick Ret Yds	Ret TDs	Avg
18 Mary Hardin-Baylor	32	708	1	22.13
19 Defiance	39	862	0	22.10
20 Eastern Ore.	52	1,144	0	22.00
21 Colby	21	458	0	21.81
22 Trinity (Tex.)	49	1,066	2	21.76
23 Shenandoah	34	739	0	21.74
24 Kean	47	1,021	1	21.72
25 Benedictine (Ill.)	45	975	0	21.67
Monmouth (Ill.)	42	910	0	21.67
27 Salve Regina	47	1,014	0	21.57
28 John Carroll	41	883	1	21.54
29 Ill. Wesleyan	40	851	0	21.28
30 Albion	36	765	1	21.25
31 Hanover	37	782	0	21.14
32 Col. of New Jersey	34	717	1	21.09
33 Hardin-Simmons	36	756	0	21.00
34 Ohio Northern	41	858	0	20.93
35 Ithaca	34	711	1	20.91
36 Wis.-Oshkosh	39	813	1	20.85
37 DePauw	37	770	1	20.81
38 Lewis & Clark	36	748	1	20.78
39 Austin	42	867	2	20.64
40 Allegheny	35	722	1	20.63
41 Moravian	37	763	1	20.62
42 Bluffton	34	701	1	20.62
43 Menlo	41	845	0	20.61
44 Concordia (Wis.)	23	474	0	20.61
45 Centre	44	903	1	20.52
46 Linfield	25	513	0	20.52
47 Illinois Col.	55	1,128	0	20.51
48 Gust. Adolphus	38	777	0	20.45
Martin Luther	38	777	0	20.45
50 Bridgewater (Va.)	34	694	0	20.41

Punt Returns

Rank, School	Punt Ret	Punt Ret Yds	Punt Ret TDs	Avg
1 Whittier	12	244	0	20.33
2 Waynesburg	29	538	1	18.55
3 Cal Lutheran	23	360	0	15.65
4 St. Norbert	35	544	2	15.54
5 Martin Luther	32	478	1	14.94
6 Eastern Ore.	23	340	1	14.78
7 Rockford	26	368	2	14.15
8 Amherst	15	212	1	14.13
Ithaca	30	424	0	14.13
10 Alma	29	399	1	13.76
11 Albion	18	245	1	13.61
12 Illinois Col.	25	337	2	13.48
Wis.-Platteville	25	337	2	13.48
14 MIT	10	134	1	13.40
15 Trinity (Tex.)	40	533	3	13.33
16 North Park	7	92	0	13.14
17 Coe	39	512	2	13.13
18 St. Olaf	22	287	1	13.05
19 Hamline	25	324	2	12.96
20 Ill. Wesleyan	32	413	2	12.91
21 St. John Fisher	33	421	1	12.76
22 Greenville	11	135	1	12.27
23 Wittenberg	41	495	3	12.07
24 Buena Vista	26	313	0	12.04
25 Concordia-M'head	31	373	1	12.03
26 Carnegie Mellon	22	264	0	12.00
Wis. Lutheran	8	96	0	12.00
28 Wooster	37	439	1	11.86
29 Maranatha Baptist	36	423	1	11.75
30 Muhlenberg	37	434	2	11.73
31 Texas Lutheran	18	211	1	11.72
32 Sewanee	23	269	3	11.70
33 Bridgewater (Va.)	36	419	0	11.64
34 Mary Hardin-Baylor	52	595	5	11.44
35 Hartwick	38	434	3	11.42
36 Methodist	23	261	0	11.35
37 Western New Eng.	29	329	0	11.34
38 MacMurray	32	363	1	11.34
39 Allegheny	15	170	0	11.33
40 Kean	23	260	1	11.30
41 Mount Union	52	586	1	11.27
42 Alfred	23	257	0	11.17
43 Chris. Newport	34	376	0	11.06

Rank, School	Punt Ret	Punt Ret Yds	Punt Ret TDs	Avg
44 Occidental	30	331	0	11.03
45 Bluffton	14	153	0	10.93
46 Wis.-La Crosse	34	371	2	10.91
47 Wilmington (Ohio)	27	294	1	10.89
48 Brockport St.	44	478	2	10.86
49 St. John's (Minn.)	48	520	2	10.83
50 Wesley	28	302	2	10.79

Net Punting

Rank, School	Punt Yds	Opp Punt Ret Yds	Punts	Net Yds
1 East Tex. Baptist	1,690	146	40	38.60
2 Occidental	2,021	102	50	38.38
3 Linfield	1,634	134	40	37.50
4 Simpson	2,361	115	61	36.82
5 Redlands	2,012	175	50	36.74
6 Ithaca	1,804	47	48	36.60
7 Williams	1,301	57	34	36.59
8 Pacific Lutheran	1,080	60	28	36.43
9 Mary Hardin-Baylor	1,886	109	49	36.27
10 Carnegie Mellon	1,670	119	43	36.07
11 Howard Payne	1,710	126	44	36.00
12 Middlebury	1,816	69	49	35.65
13 Martin Luther	1,702	98	45	35.64
14 Baldwin-Wallace	1,386	115	36	35.31
15 Brockport St.	2,548	163	68	35.07
16 Col. of New Jersey	1,624	89	44	34.89
17 Whitworth	1,615	118	43	34.81
18 Hanover	1,680	65	47	34.36
19 Earlham	2,322	130	64	34.25
20 Moravian	2,097	199	56	33.89
21 Claremont-M-S	1,884	192	50	33.84
22 Waynesburg	2,276	213	61	33.82
23 Chicago	1,101	55	31	33.74
24 Benedictine (Ill.)	1,929	110	54	33.69
25 Bridgewater (Va.)	1,610	133	44	33.57
26 Wilkes	1,899	90	54	33.50
27 Mass.-Dartmouth	1,706	99	48	33.48
28 Anderson (Ind.)	1,740	234	45	33.47
29 Alma	1,581	76	45	33.44
30 Bluffton	1,563	160	42	33.40
31 St. Norbert	1,491	93	42	33.29
32 Wis.-Stout	1,903	143	53	33.21
33 Capital	2,458	333	64	33.20
34 Centre	1,924	233	51	33.16
35 Rowan	1,885	129	53	33.13
36 Hobart	2,027	150	57	32.93
37 John Carroll	2,298	132	66	32.82
38 Lycoming	1,274	34	38	32.63
39 Hampden-Sydney	1,462	160	40	32.55
40 Trinity (Conn.)	1,299	97	37	32.49
41 Frostburg St.	2,314	337	61	32.41
42 Mississippi Col.	2,397	228	67	32.37
43 Wis.-La Crosse	2,603	312	71	32.27
44 Albright	2,074	172	59	32.24
45 Lake Forest	2,593	305	71	32.23
46 Wooster	1,730	153	49	32.18
47 Muskingum	2,478	292	68	32.15
48 Greenville	2,599	131	77	32.05
49 Marietta	2,217	203	63	31.97
50 Muhlenberg	1,906	84	57	31.96

Total Defense

Rank, School	G	Plays	YDS	YPG
1 Westfield St.	11	668	1,932	175.6
2 Concordia (Wis.)	10	607	1,946	194.6
3 Wartburg	12	724	2,500	208.3
4 Trinity (Conn.)	8	516	1,760	220.0
5 Central (Iowa)	10	662	2,219	221.9
6 Augustana (Ill.)	9	532	1,998	222.0
7 Brockport St.	13	828	2,960	227.7
8 King's (Pa.)	12	766	2,834	236.2
9 Mount Union	14	882	3,325	237.5
10 Wis.-Stout	10	616	2,396	239.6
11 Wheaton (Ill.)	12	754	2,920	243.3
12 Mass.-Dartmouth	12	730	2,942	245.2
13 Lycoming	9	563	2,212	245.8
14 McDaniel	11	719	2,706	246.0

Rank, School	G	Plays	YDS	YPG
15 Nichols	9	597	2,215	246.1
16 Ferrum	10	631	2,478	247.8
17 Aurora	9	546	2,256	250.7
18 Wittenberg	12	815	3,015	251.3
19 Merchant Marine	11	761	2,771	251.9
20 Wabash	13	881	3,293	253.3
21 Salisbury	11	686	2,788	253.5
22 Springfield	10	640	2,535	253.5
Williams	8	500	2,028	253.5
24 Wesley	10	653	2,540	254.0
25 Hartwick	10	674	2,561	256.1
26 MacMurray	11	722	2,846	258.7
27 Stillman	10	633	2,592	259.2
28 Colby	8	462	2,078	259.8
29 Maranatha Baptist	9	584	2,355	261.7
30 Westminster (Mo.)	9	533	2,356	261.8
31 Baldwin-Wallace	10	651	2,636	263.6
32 Concordia-M'head	10	666	2,659	265.9
33 Muhlenberg	12	801	3,197	266.4
34 Widener	10	716	2,675	267.5
35 Linfield	11	679	2,944	267.6
36 John Carroll	14	936	3,769	269.2
37 Chris. Newport	11	693	2,990	271.8
38 Mary Hardin-Baylor	11	689	2,993	272.1
39 Lake Forest	11	820	3,019	274.5
40 Worcester St.	11	763	3,026	275.1
41 Greensboro	10	669	2,782	278.2
42 Tufts	8	569	2,249	281.1
43 Millsaps	9	562	2,566	285.1
44 Montclair St.	10	664	2,873	287.3
45 Cortland St.	11	726	3,172	288.4
46 Wash. & Jeff.	12	768	3,462	288.5
47 Coe	12	825	3,471	289.3
48 Millikin	10	657	2,895	289.5
49 Thomas More	10	646	2,896	289.6
50 Ithaca	10	672	2,916	291.6

Scoring Offense

Rank, School	G	TDs	PAT	2PT	Def Pts	FG	Saf	Pts	PPG
1 Mount Union	14	89	77	5	0	11	0	654	46.7
2 Wittenberg	12	75	63	1	0	6	0	533	44.4
3 Trinity (Tex.)	15	90	84	0	0	13	1	665	44.3
4 Hanover	11	68	55	2	0	5	0	482	43.8
Linfield	11	67	52	5	0	6	0	482	43.8
6 St. Norbert	10	58	50	0	0	8	1	424	42.4
7 Wheaton (Ill.)	12	70	53	4	0	5	0	496	41.3
8 Mary Hardin-Baylor	11	60	54	0	1	10	0	446	40.5
9 Augustana (Ill.)	9	47	40	1	0	8	0	348	38.7
10 Hartwick	10	55	42	0	0	4	1	386	38.6
11 Bridgewater (Va.)	12	64	52	1	0	7	1	461	38.4
12 Baldwin-Wallace	10	54	43	1	0	4	0	381	38.1
Millikin	10	50	45	1	1	10	0	381	38.1
14 Howard Payne	10	52	43	1	0	7	0	378	37.8
15 Wabash	13	67	49	4	0	10	1	491	37.8
16 St. John's (Minn.)	14	75	65	1	0	3	0	526	37.6
17 Willamette	10	52	40	3	0	5	1	375	37.5
18 Stillman	10	53	43	0	0	4	0	373	37.3
19 Case Reserve	10	51	44	2	0	5	1	371	37.1
20 Springfield	10	49	40	2	0	9	0	365	36.5
21 Ripon	10	51	33	2	1	6	0	363	36.3
22 Hardin-Simmons	10	48	43	1	0	9	1	362	36.2
23 Widener	10	51	37	2	0	4	1	361	36.1
24 Rensselaer	10	49	39	3	0	7	0	360	36.0
25 Muhlenberg	12	55	49	0	0	16	1	429	35.8
26 Concordia (Wis.)	10	47	42	1	0	8	0	352	35.2
27 Westminster (Mo.)	9	46	23	7	0	1	0	316	35.1
28 Alma	11	49	48	0	1	10	2	378	34.4
29 Aurora	9	44	27	1	0	5	0	308	34.2
30 John Carroll	14	66	51	1	0	9	0	476	34.0
31 Rowan	11	50	37	3	0	10	0	373	33.9
32 Western Conn. St.	10	46	39	2	0	5	1	336	33.6
33 Kalamazoo	10	47	36	1	0	5	0	335	33.5
34 Anderson (Ind.)	10	46	31	2	0	6	2	333	33.3

Rank, School	G	TDs	PAT	2PT	Def Pts	FG	Saf	Pts	PPG
35 Lycoming	9	42	34	3	0	2	0	298	33.1
36 Williams	8	36	30	1	0	4	1	262	32.8
37 Hampden-Sydney	10	44	35	4	0	6	1	327	32.7
38 St. Thomas (Minn.)	10	46	41	0	0	3	0	326	32.6
39 Wartburg	12	52	43	1	0	11	0	390	32.5
40 Wooster	10	44	39	2	0	5	0	322	32.2
41 Frostburg St.	11	48	42	1	0	6	1	352	32.0
Worcester St.	11	51	36	1	0	2	1	352	32.0
43 Concordia-M'head	10	44	37	1	0	5	0	318	31.8
44 Pacific Lutheran	9	40	30	5	0	2	0	286	31.8
45 St. Olaf	10	45	31	3	0	2	1	315	31.5
46 Principia	9	40	23	4	0	4	0	283	31.4
47 Ill. Wesleyan	10	40	35	1	0	12	0	313	31.3
48 Juniata	10	41	30	2	0	9	1	309	30.9
49 DePauw	10	44	35	1	0	2	0	307	30.7
50 Coe	12	54	44	0	0	0	0	368	30.7

Scoring Defense

Rank, School	G	TDs	Opp XP	2PT	Opp DXP	Opp FGM	Opp Saf	Pts	Avg
1 Brockport St.	13	15	10	2	0	6	0	122	9.4
2 Central (Iowa)	10	13	12	0	0	3	0	99	9.9
3 Westfield St.	11	15	9	1	0	5	0	116	10.5
4 Concordia (Wis.)	10	14	12	0	0	4	0	108	10.8
5 McDaniel	11	16	13	0	0	4	0	121	11.0
6 Mass.-Dartmouth	12	18	15	0	0	3	1	134	11.2
7 King's (Pa.)	12	20	14	0	0	1	1	139	11.6
8 MacMurray	11	18	9	0	0	5	0	132	12.0
Wartburg	12	19	16	1	0	4	0	144	12.0
10 Rowan	11	19	12	1	0	2	0	134	12.2
11 Mount Union	14	24	15	3	0	5	0	180	12.9
12 Baldwin-Wallace	10	19	12	2	0	1	1	135	13.5
13 Muhlenberg	12	22	15	2	0	4	0	163	13.6
Wittenberg	12	22	14	1	0	5	0	163	13.6
15 Bridgewater (Va.)	12	22	12	2	0	4	2	164	13.7
16 Ithaca	10	17	7	2	0	8	0	137	13.7
17 Trinity (Conn.)	8	15	11	0	0	3	0	110	13.8
18 Linfield	11	22	17	2	0	0	0	153	13.9
19 Coe	12	24	13	1	0	3	1	170	14.2
20 John Carroll	14	26	23	1	0	6	0	199	14.2
21 Nichols	9	19	14	0	0	1	0	131	14.6
Maranatha Baptist	9	18	14	0	0	3	0	131	14.6
23 Augustana (Ill.)	9	17	16	1	0	4	0	132	14.7
Lycoming	9	18	9	0	0	5	0	132	14.7
25 Cortland St.	11	22	14	0	0	4	2	162	14.7
26 Worcester St.	11	24	13	0	0	2	0	163	14.8
27 Colby	8	16	12	0	0	4	0	120	15.0
28 Wabash	13	26	21	2	0	6	0	199	15.3
29 Amherst	8	17	16	0	0	2	0	124	15.5
30 Wis.-Stout	10	21	15	2	0	4	0	157	15.7
31 Chris. Newport	11	23	16	1	1	5	0	173	15.7
32 Lake Forest	11	23	16	2	1	5	0	175	15.9
33 Hobart	10	23	15	1	0	2	0	161	16.1
34 Tufts	8	17	11	0	0	4	1	129	16.1
35 Johns Hopkins	11	23	20	1	0	6	0	178	16.2
36 Williams	8	18	13	0	0	3	0	130	16.3
37 Salisbury	11	25	13	1	0	4	1	179	16.3
38 Wheaton (Ill.)	12	27	20	3	1	2	0	196	16.3
39 Moravian	11	24	15	2	0	5	0	180	16.4
Mary Hardin-Baylor	11	24	15	2	0	5	1	180	16.4
41 Hartwick	10	23	13	2	0	3	0	164	16.4
42 Wesley	10	22	16	0	0	5	1	165	16.5
43 Rockford	10	23	12	4	0	3	0	167	16.7
44 Thomas More	10	23	17	1	0	4	0	169	16.9
45 Greensboro	10	23	12	3	0	4	1	170	17.0
46 Randolph-Macon	10	23	15	1	0	5	1	172	17.2
47 Middlebury	8	18	15	0	0	5	0	138	17.3
48 Wooster	10	24	14	3	0	5	0	173	17.3
49 St. John's (Minn.)	14	33	24	3	0	5	0	243	17.4
50 Springfield	10	24	17	0	0	4	1	175	17.5

STATISTICAL LEADERS

Longest Division III Plays of 2002

Rushing

Player, Team (Opponent)	Yards
Abe Bascon, Framingham St. (Mass. Maritime)	95
Mike Johnson, Bethel (Minn.) (Concordia-M'head)	93
Jason Meyers, St. John Fisher (Mass. Maritime)	92
Justin Peterson, Willamette (Southern Ore.)	90
Todd Sabean, Monmouth (Ill.) (Eureka)	89
Shaun Rochon, Mary Hardin-Baylor (Austin)	85
Jeff Wakefield, Western Conn. St. (Merchant Marine)	80
Jimmy Kinch, Ohio Wesleyan (Kenyon)	80
Mike Moran, Defiance (Mt. St. Joseph)	80
Chris Morris, Wabash (Hiram)	80

Passing

Passer-Receiver, Team (Opponent)	Yards
Clay Groefsema-Shawn Watson, Redlands (Whittier)	99
Scott Kello-Luis Uresti, Sul Ross St. (Hardin-Simmons)	98
Rob Adamson-Derrick Leach, Mount Union (Marietta)	94
Ben Stevens-Jared Rance, Coe (Luther)	92
Scott Kello-Luis Uresti, Sul Ross St. (Howard Payne)	91
Scott Krause-Ross Adamczak, Wis.-Stevens Point (Wis.-Platteville)	90
Dustin Proctor-Kirk Brennan, Hardin-Simmons (East Tex. Baptist)	90
Brennan Carney, Wesleyan (Conn.) (Trinity [Conn.])	90
Ryan Squatrito-Zach Lewis, Oberlin (Hiram)	86
Rob Adamson-Jason Candle, Mount Union (Capital)	84

Interceptions

Player, Team (Opponent)	Yards
David Thompson, Earlham (Manchester)	96
Seth Berghoff, Pacific Lutheran (Linfield)	96
Brian Pierce, Bethel (Minn.) (Carleton)	95
Milo Austin, Salisbury (Col. of New Jersey)	90

Punt Returns

Player, Team (Opponent)	Yards
Chris McKinney, Guilford (Catholic)	86
Seth Berghoff, Pacific Lutheran (Puget Sound)	85
Kaveh Conaway, Chris. Newport (Greensboro)	85
French Pope, McDaniel (Dickinson)	82
Dustin Winkler, Defiance (Mt. St. Joseph)	82
Chris McKinney, Guilford (Methodist)	80

Kickoff Returns

Player, Team (Opponent)	Yards
Gino Gosciaco, Menlo (La Verne)	100
Shaun Rochon, Mary Hardin-Baylor (Hardin-Simmons)	98
Chuck Moore, Mount Union (Wilmington [Ohio])	94
Jabori Jackson, East Tex. Baptist (Southwestern Assemblies of God)	93
Hayd Mathis, Rhodes (DePauw)	93
Phil Brietchaft, Wis.-Platteville (Wis.-Oshkosh)	93
Tom DeLuca, Baldwin-Wallace (Otterbein)	90

Punts

Player, Team (Opponent)	Yards
Scott Verhalen, East Tex. Baptist (Howard Payne)	82
John Jennings, Centre (Maryville [Tenn.])	78
Kevin Vermeersch, Alma (Gannon)	75
Dusty Lehr, Juniata (Susquehanna)	72
Craig Wirt, Colorado Col. (Washington [Mo.])	71
Patrick Howell, Kenyon (Allegheny)	70
Charlie Carr, St. John's (Minn.) (St. Thomas [Minn.])	70

Division III Individual Single-Game Highs of 2002

Total Offensive Yards

Rank, Name, Team	Cl	Pos	vs. Opponent	Game Date	Tot Off
1 Dustin Proctor, Hardin-Simmons	Sr.	QB	Howard Payne	10/12/2002	584
2 Roy Hampton, Trinity (Tex.)	Jr.	QB	Bridgewater (Va.)	12/07/2002	513
3 Brent Luebke, Lakeland	Jr.	QB	Carthage	09/14/2002	505
4 Daniel Swanstrom, Rhodes	So.	QB	Sewanee	10/19/2002	488
5 Eli Grant, Case Reserve	Jr.	QB	Washington (Mo.)	10/26/2002	486
6 Jared Tharpe, Rose-Hulman	Sr.	QB	Washington (Mo.)	09/28/2002	470
Michael Robinson, Benedictine (Ill.)	Sr.	QB	North Central	09/14/2002	470
8 Eric Wiebers, Buena Vista	So.	QB	Dubuque	11/09/2002	468
9 Clay Groefsema, Redlands	Sr.	QB	Willamette	09/07/2002	467
10 Bryan Gnyp, Kalamazoo	Jr.	QB	Hope	10/05/2002	464
11 Grant Burrough, Frostburg St.	Jr.	QB	Waynesburg	11/09/2002	458
12 J.J. Tutwiler, Cortland St.	Jr.	QB	Col. of New Jersey	09/14/2002	456
13 Scott Kello, Sul Ross St.	Jr.	QB	Louisiana Col.	09/21/2002	453
14 Trent Thompson, Lewis & Clark	Jr.	QB	Occidental	09/21/2002	450
15 Josh Dunn, Chicago	Sr.	QB	Case Reserve	11/16/2002	449
Dominic Demma, Elmhurst	So.	QB	Chicago	09/28/2002	449
17 Jeremy Lacaria, Bethany (W.Va.)	Sr.	QB	Wooster	09/21/2002	442
18 Josh Dunn, Chicago	Sr.	QB	Elmhurst	09/21/2002	440
19 Tom Stetzer, Wis.-Platteville	Jr.	QB	Hope	09/21/2002	434
20 Joel Steele, Anderson (Ind.)	Jr.	QB	Capital	09/07/2002	433
21 Tom Stetzer, Wis.-Platteville	Jr.	QB	Wis.-River Falls	11/16/2002	430
22 Nels Fredrickson, Wis.-Eau Claire	So.	QB	Wis.-Whitewater	11/02/2002	426
Scott Kello, Sul Ross St.	Jr.	QB	Howard Payne	10/05/2002	426
Tom Stetzer, Wis.-Platteville	Jr.	QB	Wis.-Stout	10/05/2002	426
Jason Desotell, Adrian	Sr.	-	Albion	09/02/2002	426

Rushing Yards

Rank, Name, Team	Cl	Pos	vs. Opponent	Game Date	Rush Yds
1 Tony Sutton, Wooster	So.	RB	Ohio Wesleyan	10/05/2002	313
2 Sean Atkins, Bates	Sr.	RB	Bowdoin	11/02/2002	298
3 Randal Baker, Carthage	Sr.	RB	North Park	11/16/2002	296
4 Justin Frisk, Thomas More	Jr.	RB	Chapman	10/26/2002	280
5 Luke Hagel, Ripon	Sr.	RB	Lawrence	11/09/2002	277
6 Geary Pryor, Aurora	Jr.	RB	Benedictine (Ill.)	10/05/2002	276
7 Sean Atkins, Bates	Sr.	RB	Hamilton	11/09/2002	275
8 Les Simon, Redlands	Jr.	RB	Claremont-M-S	11/16/2002	263
9 Tony Sutton, Wooster	So.	RB	Case Reserve	09/28/2002	261
10 Randal Baker, Carthage	Sr.	RB	Benedictine (Ill.)	09/21/2002	255
11 Dan Pugh, Mount Union	Sr.	RB	John Carroll	12/14/2002	254
12 Dan Pugh, Mount Union	Sr.	RB	Trinity (Tex.)	12/21/2002	253
13 Ryan Gocong, Claremont-M-S	Sr.	RB	Redlands	11/16/2002	252
Andy Traetow, Gust. Adolphus	Sr.	RB	Hamline	10/26/2002	252
15 Brett Trichilo, Wilkes	So.	RB	Albright	10/19/2002	248
16 Rufus Wilkins, Thomas More	Fr.	RB	Shenandoah	09/21/2002	245
Fred Edwards, Wesley	Sr.	RB	Rowan	09/13/2002	245
Fred Edwards, Wesley	Sr.	RB	Rowan	09/13/2002	245
19 John Sanders, Chapman	Sr.	RB	Thomas More	10/26/2002	244
20 Trevor Cooper, Muskingum	So.	DB	Wilmington (Ohio)	10/12/2002	243
Jake Barkley, St. Thomas (Minn.)	Sr.	RB	Bethel (Minn.)	09/14/2002	243
Fredrick Jackson, Coe	Sr.	RB	Eureka	09/14/2002	243
23 Trevor Cooper, Muskingum	So.	DB	Otterbein	10/19/2002	242
24 Chris Ross, Ill. Wesleyan	Sr.	RB	North Central	10/19/2002	238
Geary Pryor, Aurora	Jr.	RB	Concordia (Ill.)	10/12/2002	238
Gary Sheffield, Ursinus	Jr.	RB	Mount Ida	10/05/2002	238
Randal Baker, Carthage	Sr.	RB	Adrian	09/28/2002	238

Passing Yards

Rank, Name, Team	Cl	Pos	vs. Opponent	Game Date	Pass Yds
1 Eli Grant, Case Reserve	Jr.	QB	Washington (Mo.)	10/26/2002	492
2 Daniel Pincelli, Hartwick	Sr.	QB	Rensselaer	10/26/2002	483
3 Roy Hampton, Trinity (Tex.)	Jr.	QB	Bridgewater (Va.)	12/07/2002	481
4 Dustin Proctor, Hardin-Simmons	Sr.	QB	Howard Payne	10/12/2002	472
5 Clay Groefsema, Redlands	Jr.	QB	Willamette	09/07/2002	467
6 Dominic Demma, Elmhurst	So.	QB	Chicago	09/21/2002	455
7 Grant Burrough, Frostburg St.	Jr.	QB	Waynesburg	11/09/2002	452
8 Scott Kello, Sul Ross St.	Jr.	QB	Louisiana Col.	09/21/2002	449
9 Phil Butler, Hope	Jr.	QB	Wis.-Platteville	09/21/2002	441
10 Josh Dunn, Chicago	Sr.	QB	Elmhurst	09/21/2002	440
Joel Steele, Anderson (Ind.)	Jr.	QB	Capital	09/07/2002	440
12 Bryan Gnyp, Kalamazoo	Jr.	QB	Hope	10/05/2002	437
Scott Kello, Sul Ross St.	Jr.	QB	Howard Payne	10/05/2002	437
14 Eli Grant, Case Reserve	Jr.	QB	Chicago	11/16/2002	436
15 Brent Luebke, Lakeland	Jr.	QB	Carthage	09/14/2002	432
16 Josh Dunn, Chicago	Sr.	QB	Case Reserve	11/16/2002	431
Eric Wiebers, Buena Vista	So.	QB	Dubuque	11/09/2002	431
18 Daniel Pincelli, Hartwick	Sr.	QB	Union (N.Y.)	11/02/2002	429
19 Tom Stetzer, Wis.-Platteville	Jr.	QB	Hope	09/21/2002	427
20 Tom Stetzer, Wis.-Platteville	Jr.	QB	Wis.-River Falls	11/16/2002	426

Pass Completions

Rank, Name, Team	Cl	Pos	vs. Opponent	Game Date	Pass Comp
1 Scott Kello, Sul Ross St.	Jr.	QB	Howard Payne	10/05/2002	51
2 Scott Kello, Sul Ross St.	Jr.	QB	Texas Lutheran	11/16/2002	45
3 Scott Kello, Sul Ross St.	Jr.	QB	Louisiana Col.	09/21/2002	44
4 Joel Steele, Anderson (Ind.)	Jr.	QB	Capital	09/07/2002	41
5 Brett Dietz, Hanover	Jr.	QB	Wittenberg	11/23/2002	37
Nick Wara, Wis.-Oshkosh	So.	QB	Wis.-Whitewater	11/16/2002	37
7 Eli Grant, Case Reserve	Jr.	QB	Washington (Mo.)	10/26/2002	36
8 Grant Burrough, Frostburg St.	Jr.	QB	Waynesburg	11/09/2002	35
Grant Burrough, Frostburg St.	Jr.	QB	Catholic	10/19/2002	35
Adam King, Howard Payne	So.	QB	Sul Ross St.	10/05/2002	35
Jared Tharpe, Rose-Hulman	Sr.	QB	Washington (Mo.)	09/28/2002	35
Andy Yoder, DePauw	Jr.	QB	Hanover	09/21/2002	35
13 Justin Papania, Marietta	So.	QB	Muskingum	11/15/2002	34
Greg Troutman, Juniata	So.	QB	Moravian	10/12/2002	34
Phil Butler, Hope	Jr.	QB	Wis.-Platteville	09/21/2002	34
Dave Fransen, Augsburg	Sr.	QB	St. Olaf	09/21/2002	34
Tom Stetzer, Wis.-Platteville	Jr.	QB	Hope	09/21/2002	34
Daniel Swanstrom, Rhodes	So.	QB	Centre	09/21/2002	34
19 Greg Cornett, Wittenberg	Sr.	QB	Wabash	10/12/2002	33
20 Jeff Dumm, Waynesburg	So.	QB	Westminster (Pa.)	11/16/2002	32
Randy Borgardt, Wis.-Whitewater	Sr.	QB	Wis.-Eau Claire	11/02/2002	32
Dominic Demma, Elmhurst	So.	QB	Chicago	09/21/2002	32
Scott Kello, Sul Ross St.	Jr.	QB	Mississippi Col.	09/14/2002	32
24 Josh Dunn, Chicago	Sr.	QB	Case Reserve	11/16/2002	31
Geoff Zentz, Franklin	Fr.	QB	Anderson (Ind.)	11/09/2002	31
Clay Groefsema, Redlands	Sr.	QB	Occidental	10/12/2002	31
Corey Minnfield, Defiance	Sr.	QB	Hanover	10/12/2002	31
Nathan Szep, Washington (Mo.)	Fr.	QB	Rhodes	10/05/2002	31
Greg Troutman, Juniata	So.	QB	Wilkes	09/28/2002	31
Jeremy Lacaria, Bethany (W.Va.)	Sr.	QB	Wooster	09/21/2002	31
Scott Kello, Sul Ross St.	Jr.	QB	Western N.M.	09/14/2002	31

Receptions

Rank, Name, Team	Cl	Pos	vs. Opponent	Game Date	Rec
1 Luis Uresti, Sul Ross St.	Sr.	WR	Louisiana Col.	09/21/2002	19
2 Lewis Howes, Principia	So.	WR	Martin Luther	10/12/2002	18
3 Jim Raptis, Chicago	Jr.	WR	Elmhurst	09/21/2002	17
4 Rob Kief, Rose-Hulman	Sr.	WR	Centre	11/16/2002	16
5 Mark Bartosic, Susquehanna	Jr.	WR	Widener	10/12/2002	15
Craig Moshier, Juniata	Jr.	RB	Moravian	10/12/2002	15
Jason Cellura, Case Reserve	Fr.	QB	Kalamazoo	10/05/2002	15
Luis Uresti, Sul Ross St.	Sr.	WR	Howard Payne	10/05/2002	15
Mike DeMarteleire, Widener	Sr.	WR	Moravian	09/28/2002	15
10 T.J. Thayer, Kalamazoo	Sr.	WR	Alma	11/02/2002	14
Frankie Bass, St. Olaf	So.	WR	Bethel (Minn.)	10/12/2002	14
12 Jim Raptis, Chicago	Jr.	WR	Case Reserve	11/16/2002	13
Bobby Hughes, Concordia (Ill.)	Sr.	WR	Greenville	10/26/2002	13
Matt Kent, Wis.-Platteville	Jr.	WR	Wis.-Whitewater	10/19/2002	13
Blake Elliott, St. John's (Minn.)	Jr.	WR	St. Olaf	09/28/2002	13
Ryan Friend, Williams	Sr.	WR	Bowdoin	09/21/2002	13

Rank, Name, Team	Cl	Pos	vs. Opponent	Game Date	Rec
Juan Quesada, Elmhurst	Jr.	QB	Chicago	09/21/2002	13
Greg Fleming, Otterbein	Sr.	TE	Waynesburg	09/14/2002	13
Dwayne Tawney, Whitworth	Jr.	WR	Bethel (Minn.)	09/07/2002	13
20 Steve Wagner, Wis.-Oshkosh	Sr.	WR	Wis.-Whitewater	11/16/2002	12
Jeffrey Jourdan, Hanover	Sr.	WR	Bluffton	10/19/2002	12
Tom Neagle, Knox	Jr.	WR	St. Norbert	09/28/2002	12
Tres Poyner, Howard Payne	Fr.	-	East Tex. Baptist	09/28/2002	12
Justin Salton, Frank. & Marsh.	Sr.	WR	Muhlenberg	09/28/2002	12
Mike Fitzgerald, Lake Forest	Sr.	WR	Beloit	09/21/2002	12
Jamarcus Shephard, DePauw	So.	WR	Hanover	09/21/2002	12
Brandon Tugmon, Manchester	Fr.	WR	Alma	09/21/2002	12
Todd Fry, Wash. & Jeff.	Sr.	WR	Allegheny	09/14/2002	12
Luis Uresti, Sul Ross St.	Sr.	WR	Western N.M.	09/14/2002	12

Receiving Yards

Rank, Name, Team	Cl	Pos	vs. Opponent	Game Date	Rec Yds
1 Lewis Howes, Principia	So.	WR	Martin Luther	10/12/2002	418
2 Matt Kent, Wis.-Platteville	Jr.	WR	Wis.-Whitewater	10/19/2002	288
3 Luis Uresti, Sul Ross St.	Sr.	WR	Howard Payne	10/05/2002	271
4 Jim Raptis, Chicago	Jr.	WR	Elmhurst	09/21/2002	270
5 Mark Bartosic, Susquehanna	Jr.	WR	Widener	10/12/2002	261
6 Nick Bodeman, Lewis & Clark	Fr.	WR	Occidental	09/21/2002	258
7 Pat Moffett, Wesleyan (Conn.)	Jr.	WR	Colby	10/05/2002	256
8 Luis Uresti, Sul Ross St.	Sr.	WR	Louisiana Col.	09/21/2002	252
9 Greg Fleming, Otterbein	Sr.	TE	Wilmington (Ohio)	09/28/2002	235
10 Ryan Soule, Hartwick	Sr.	WR	Union (N.Y.)	11/02/2002	234
11 Rich Gear, Delaware Valley	Sr.	WR	Albright	09/14/2002	220
12 Brad Duesing, Washington (Mo.)	Fr.	WR	Rhodes	10/05/2002	217
13 Ryan Soule, Hartwick	Sr.	WR	Rensselaer	10/26/2002	210
14 Nathan Gaskill, Monmouth (Ill.)	Jr.	WR	St. Norbert	09/21/2002	209
15 Jeff Moyer, Hartwick	Jr.	WR	Rensselaer	10/26/2002	208
16 Noah Fehrenbach, St. John Fisher	Fr.	WR	Ithaca	09/28/2002	207
17 Jamarcus Shephard, DePauw	So.	WR	Trinity (Tex.)	09/28/2002	206
18 Jim Raptis, Chicago	Jr.	WR	Case Reserve	11/16/2002	203
19 Sebastian Singleton, Benedictine (Ill.)	Jr.	WR	North Central	09/14/2002	202
20 Dan Ryks, Hamline	So.	WR	St. Olaf	10/19/2002	201
Rich Gear, Delaware Valley	Sr.	WR	King's (Pa.)	09/21/2002	201

All-Purpose Yards

Rank, Name, Team	Cl	Pos	vs. Opponent	Game Date	All-Purp Yds
1 Lewis Howes, Principia	So.	WR	Martin Luther	10/12/2002	418
2 Fredrick Jackson, Coe	Sr.	RB	Luther	11/09/2002	299
3 Tony Sutton, Wooster	So.	RB	Bethany (W.Va.)	09/21/2002	298
4 Trevor Cooper, Muskingum	So.	DB	Otterbein	10/19/2002	293
Raphael Zammit, Curry	Jr.	RB	Nichols	10/19/2002	293
6 Dan Pugh, Mount Union	Sr.	RB	John Carroll	12/14/2002	292
7 Matt Kent, Wis.-Platteville	Jr.	WR	Wis.-Whitewater	10/19/2002	291
8 Fredrick Jackson, Coe	Sr.	RB	Dubuque	10/12/2002	279
9 Jason Hunt, Trinity (Tex.)	Sr.	WR	Rhodes	11/02/2002	274
10 Jeremy Brown, Loras	Jr.	RB	Buena Vista	10/12/2002	272
11 Tony Sutton, Wooster	So.	RB	Case Reserve	09/28/2002	264
12 Josh Espinosa, Buena Vista	Sr.	WR	Simpson	09/21/2002	263
13 Cory Flisakowski, Wis.-Stevens Point	So.	RB	Wis.-La Crosse	10/05/2002	262
14 Fredrick Jackson, Coe	Sr.	RB	Cornell	11/02/2002	260
15 Pat Moffett, Wesleyan (Conn.)	Jr.	WR	Middlebury	09/21/2002	258
16 Dan Pugh, Mount Union	Sr.	RB	Trinity (Tex.)	12/21/2002	257
John Sanders, Chapman	Sr.	RB	Thomas More	10/26/2002	257
Brad Hodapp, Wartburg	Sr.	RB	Loras	10/05/2002	257
19 Pat Moffett, Wesleyan (Conn.)	Jr.	WR	Colby	10/05/2002	256
20 Trevor Cooper, Muskingum	So.	DB	Wilmington (Ohio)	10/12/2002	248

Division III Team Single-Game Highs of 2002

Points

Rank, Name	vs. Opponent	Game Date	Points
1 Wittenberg	Kenyon	11/09/2002	79
2 Wittenberg	Hiram	10/19/2002	77
3 John Carroll	Otterbein	11/09/2002	73

Rank, Name	vs. Opponent	Game Date	Points
4 Millikin	North Park	11/02/2002	72
5 Wash. & Jeff.	Apprentice	11/02/2002	71
6 Howard Payne	Sul Ross St.	10/05/2002	70
7 Hartwick	Curry	11/23/2002	69
Simpson	Loras	11/02/2002	69
Mary Hardin-Baylor	Louisiana Col.	10/05/2002	69
Springfield	Salve Regina	09/06/2002	69
11 Wheaton (Ill.)	North Park	11/09/2002	68
Muhlenberg	Frank. & Marsh.	09/28/2002	68
13 Aurora	Concordia (Ill.)	10/12/2002	67
14 Trinity (Tex.)	Pomona-Pitzer	09/21/2002	66
15 Augustana (Ill.)	North Central	10/05/2002	65
Millikin	Anderson (Ind.)	09/28/2002	65
17 Springfield	Coast Guard	09/28/2002	64
18 Concordia-M'head	St. Thomas (Minn.)	11/08/2002	63
St. Norbert	Carroll (Wis.)	10/19/2002	63
Wash. & Jeff.	Ursinus	09/07/2002	63
21 Mount Union	Wilmington (Ohio)	11/16/2002	62
22 Mount Union	Heidelberg	10/12/2002	61
23 St. Norbert	Illinois Col.	10/05/2002	60
Anderson (Ind.)	Concordia (Ill.)	09/21/2002	60
25 Trinity (Tex.)	Rhodes	11/02/2002	59
John Carroll	Heidelberg	10/26/2002	59
Rhodes	Colorado Col.	10/26/2002	59
Alma	Hope	10/05/2002	59
St. John's (Minn.)	St. Olaf	09/28/2002	59
Linfield	Redlands	09/14/2002	59

Total Offensive Yards

Rank, Name	vs. Opponent	Game Date	Tot Off
1 Case Reserve	Denison	09/14/2002	766
2 Linfield	Redlands	09/14/2002	725
3 Ripon	Lawrence	11/09/2002	709
St. John's (Minn.)	St. Thomas (Minn.)	11/02/2002	709
5 Springfield	Union (N.Y.)	11/16/2002	688
6 Chicago	Case Reserve	11/16/2002	685
7 Augustana (Ill.)	Elmhurst	11/02/2002	652
Trinity (Tex.)	Centre	10/26/2002	652
9 Trinity (Tex.)	Wash. & Jeff.	11/30/2002	648
10 Hardin-Simmons	Howard Payne	10/12/2002	641
11 Trinity (Tex.)	Rose-Hulman	10/05/2002	638
St. John's (Minn.)	St. Olaf	09/28/2002	638
13 Mount Union	Marietta	11/02/2002	637
14 St. Thomas (Minn.)	Augsburg	10/26/2002	634
Stillman	Lincoln (Mo.)	10/12/2002	634
Frostburg St.	Apprentice	09/14/2002	634
17 Aurora	Benedictine (Ill.)	10/05/2002	626
18 Wheaton (Ill.)	North Park	11/09/2002	625
19 Anderson (Ind.)	Concordia (Ill.)	09/21/2002	619
20 Cortland St.	Col. of New Jersey	09/14/2002	614
21 Trinity (Tex.)	Bridgewater (Va.)	12/07/2002	613
22 Pacific Lutheran	Azusa Pacific	09/14/2002	612
23 Willamette	Redlands	09/07/2002	610
24 Simpson	Loras	11/02/2002	609
25 Alma	Albion	10/19/2002	608

Rushing Yards

Rank, Name	vs. Opponent	Game Date	Rush Yds
1 Aurora	Benedictine (Ill.)	10/05/2002	603
2 Springfield	Union (N.Y.)	11/16/2002	586
3 Springfield	Salve Regina	09/06/2002	553
4 Coe	Eureka	09/14/2002	500
5 Earlham	Kenyon	10/05/2002	487
6 Augustana (Ill.)	Elmhurst	11/02/2002	478
7 Salisbury	Methodist	09/21/2002	477
8 Coe	Eureka	09/14/2002	472
9 Wheaton (Ill.)	North Park	11/09/2002	465
10 Austin	McMurry	09/28/2002	457
11 Salisbury	Apprentice	10/26/2002	455
12 Wartburg	Buena Vista	11/16/2002	437
13 Wittenberg	Kenyon	11/09/2002	434
Augustana (Ill.)	North Central	10/05/2002	434
15 Olivet	Wis. Lutheran	11/16/2002	431

Passing Yards

Rank, Name	vs. Opponent	Game Date	Pass Yds
1 Case Reserve	Washington (Mo.)	10/26/2002	492
2 Case Reserve	Chicago	11/16/2002	487
3 Hartwick	Rensselaer	10/26/2002	483
4 Trinity (Tex.)	Bridgewater (Va.)	12/07/2002	481
5 Case Reserve	Denison	09/14/2002	473
6 Hardin-Simmons	Howard Payne	10/12/2002	472
7 St. Thomas (Minn.)	Augsburg	10/26/2002	467
Sul Ross St.	Louisiana Col.	09/21/2002	467
Redlands	Willamette	09/07/2002	467
10 Elmhurst	Chicago	09/21/2002	455
11 Frostburg St.	Waynesburg	11/09/2002	452
12 Trinity (Tex.)	Rhodes	11/02/2002	447
13 St. John's (Minn.)	St. Thomas (Minn.)	11/02/2002	445
14 Defiance	Hanover	10/12/2002	444
15 Chicago	Case Reserve	11/16/2002	441
Sul Ross St.	Howard Payne	10/05/2002	441
17 Chicago	Elmhurst	09/21/2002	440
Anderson (Ind.)	Capital	09/07/2002	440
19 St. Thomas (Minn.)	St. Olaf	10/05/2002	439
St. Thomas (Minn.)	St. Olaf	10/05/2002	439
21 Kalamazoo	Hope	10/05/2002	437
22 Buena Vista	Dubuque	11/09/2002	431
23 Wis.-Platteville	Hope	09/21/2002	427
24 Wis.-Platteville	Wis.-River Falls	11/16/2002	426
St. John's (Minn.)	St. Olaf	09/28/2002	426

Conference Standings and Champions

2002 Conference Standings

(Full-season records include postseason play; ties in standings broken by full-season records unless otherwise noted.)

Division I-A

ATLANTIC COAST CONFERENCE

Team	Conference W	L	Pct.	Full Season W	L	Pct.
Florida St.	7	1	.875	9	5	.643
Maryland	6	2	.750	11	3	.786
Virginia	6	2	.750	9	5	.643
North Carolina St.	5	3	.625	11	3	.786
Georgia Tech	4	4	.500	7	6	.538
Clemson	4	4	.500	7	6	.538
Wake Forest	3	5	.375	7	6	.538
North Carolina	1	7	.125	3	9	.250
Duke	0	8	.000	2	10	.167

Bowl Games (4-3): Clemson (0-1, lost to Texas Tech, 55-15, in Tangerine Bowl); Virginia (1-0, beat West Virginia, 48-22, in Continental Tire Bowl); Wake Forest (1-0, beat Oregon, 38-17, in Seattle Bowl); Georgia Tech (0-1, lost to Fresno St., 30-21, in Silicon Valley Bowl); Maryland (1-0, beat Tennessee, 30-3, in Peach Bowl); North Carolina St. (1-0, beat Notre Dame, 28-6, in Gator Bowl); Florida St. (0-1, lost to Georgia, 26-13, in Sugar Bowl)

BIG EAST CONFERENCE

Team	Conference W	L	Pct.	Full Season W	L	Pct.
Miami (Fla.)	7	0	1.000	12	1	.923
West Virginia	6	1	.857	9	4	.692
Pittsburgh	5	2	.714	9	4	.692
Virginia Tech	3	4	.429	10	4	.714
Boston College	3	4	.429	9	4	.692
Temple	2	5	.286	4	8	.333
Syracuse	2	5	.286	4	8	.333
Rutgers	0	7	.000	1	11	.083

Bowl Games (3-2): Miami (Fla.) (0-1, lost to Ohio St., 31-24 [2 ot], in Fiesta Bowl); West Virginia (0-1, lost to Virginia, 48-22, in Continental Tire Bowl); Pittsburgh (1-0, beat Oregon St., 38-13, in Insight Bowl); Virginia Tech (1-0, beat Air Force, 20-13, in San Francisco Bowl); Boston College (1-0, beat Toledo, 51-25, in Motor City Bowl)

BIG TEN CONFERENCE

Team	Conference W	L	Pct.	Full Season W	L	Pct.
Ohio St.	8	0	1.000	14	0	1.000
Iowa	8	0	1.000	11	2	.846
Michigan	6	2	.750	10	3	.769
Penn St.	5	3	.625	9	4	.692
Purdue	4	4	.500	7	6	.538
Illinois	4	4	.500	5	7	.417
Minnesota	3	5	.375	8	5	.615
Wisconsin	2	6	.250	8	6	.333
Michigan St.	2	6	.250	4	8	.333
Northwestern	1	7	.125	3	9	.250
Indiana	1	7	.125	3	9	.250

Bowl Games (5-2): Ohio St. (1-0, beat Miami [Fla.], 31-24 [2 ot], in Fiesta Bowl); Iowa (0-1, lost to Southern California, 38-17, in Orange Bowl); Michigan (1-0, beat Florida, 38-30, in Outback Bowl); Penn St. (0-1, lost to Auburn, 13-9, in Capital One Bowl); Purdue (1-0, beat Washington, 34-24, in Sun Bowl); Minnesota (1-0, beat Arkansas, 29-14, in Music City Bowl); Wisconsin (1-0, beat Colorado, 31-28 [ot], in Alamo Bowl)

BIG 12 CONFERENCE

Team	Conference W	L	Pct.	Full Season W	L	Pct.
North						
Colorado	7	2	.778	9	5	.643
Kansas St.	6	2	.750	11	2	.846
Iowa St.	4	4	.500	7	7	.500
Nebraska	3	5	.375	7	7	.500
Missouri	2	6	.250	5	7	.417
Kansas	0	8	.000	2	10	.167
South						
Oklahoma	7	2	.778	12	2	.857
Texas	6	2	.750	11	2	.846
Texas Tech	5	3	.625	9	5	.643
Oklahoma St.	5	3	.625	8	5	.615
Texas A&M	3	5	.375	6	6	.500
Baylor	1	7	.125	3	9	.250

Big 12 Championship Game: Oklahoma 29, Colorado 7, on December 7, at Houston, Texas.

Bowl Games (5-3): Colorado (0-1, lost to Wisconsin, 31-28 [ot], in Alamo Bowl); Kansas St. (1-0, beat Arizona St., 34-27, in Holiday Bowl; Iowa St. (0-1, lost to Boise St., 34-16, in Humanitarian Bowl); Nebraska (0-1, lost to Mississippi, 27-23, in Independence Bowl); Oklahoma (1-0, beat Washington St., 34-14, in Rose Bowl); Texas (1-0, beat LSU, 35-20, in Cotton Bowl); Texas Tech (1-0, beat Clemson, 55-15, in Tangerine Bowl); Oklahoma St. (1-0, beat Southern Miss., 33-23, in Houston Bowl)

CONFERENCE USA

Team	Conference W	L	Pct.	Full Season W	L	Pct.
TCU	6	2	.750	10	2	.833
Cincinnati	6	2	.750	7	7	.500
Southern Miss.	5	3	.625	7	6	.538
Louisville	5	3	.625	7	6	.538
Tulane	4	4	.500	8	5	.615
UAB	4	4	.500	5	7	.417
East Caro.	4	4	.500	4	8	.333
Houston	3	5	.375	5	7	.417
Memphis	2	6	.250	3	9	.250
Army	1	7	.125	1	11	.083

Bowl Games (2-3): TCU (1-0, beat Colorado St., 17-3, in Liberty Bowl); Cincinnati (0-1, lost to North Texas, 24-19, in New Orleans Bowl); Southern Miss. (0-1, lost to Oklahoma St., 33-23, in Houston Bowl); Tulane (1-0, beat Hawaii, 36-28, in Hawaii Bowl); Louisville (0-1, lost to Marshall, 38-15, in GMAC Bowl)

MID-AMERICAN CONFERENCE

Team	Conference W	L	Pct.	Full Season W	L	Pct.
East						
Marshall	7	1	.875	11	2	.846
UCF	6	2	.750	7	5	.583
Miami (Ohio)	5	3	.625	7	5	.583
Ohio	4	4	.500	4	8	.333
Akron	3	5	.375	4	8	.333
Kent St.	1	7	.125	3	9	.250
Buffalo	0	8	.000	1	11	.083
West						
Toledo	7	1	.875	9	5	.643
Northern Ill.	7	1	.875	8	4	.667
Bowling Green	6	2	.750	9	3	.750
Ball St.	4	4	.500	6	6	.500
Western Mich.	3	5	.375	4	8	.333
Central Mich.	2	6	.250	4	8	.333
Eastern Mich.	1	7	.125	3	9	.250

MAC Championship Game: Marshall 49, Toledo 45, on December 7, at Huntington, West Virginia.

Bowl Games (1-1): Marshall (1-0, beat Louisville, 38-15, in GMAC Bowl); Toledo (0-1, lost to Boston College, 51-25, in Motor City Bowl)

MOUNTAIN WEST CONFERENCE

Team	Conference W	L	Pct.	Full Season W	L	Pct.
Colorado St.	6	1	.857	10	4	.714
New Mexico	5	2	.714	7	7	.500
Air Force	4	3	.571	8	5	.615
San Diego St.	4	3	.571	4	9	.308
Utah	3	4	.429	5	6	.455
UNLV	3	4	.429	5	7	.417
Brigham Young	2	5	.286	5	7	.417
Wyoming	1	6	.143	2	10	.167

Bowl Games (0-3): Colorado St. (0-1, lost to TCU, 17-3, in Liberty Bowl); New Mexico (0-1, lost to UCLA, 27-13, in Las Vegas Bowl); Air Force (0-1, lost to Virginia Tech, 20-13, in San Francisco Bowl)

PACIFIC-10 CONFERENCE

Team	Conference W	L	Pct.	Full Season W	L	Pct.
Southern Calif.	7	1	.875	11	2	.846
Washington St.	7	1	.875	10	3	.769
Arizona St.	3	5	.625	8	6	.571
UCLA	4	4	.500	8	5	.615
Oregon St.	4	4	.500	8	5	.615
California	4	4	.500	7	5	.583
Washington	4	4	.500	7	6	.538
Oregon	3	5	.375	7	6	.538
Arizona	1	7	.125	4	8	.333
Stanford	1	7	.125	2	9	.182

Bowl Games (2-5): Southern California (1-0, beat Iowa, 38-17, in Orange Bowl); Washington St. (0-1, lost to Oklahoma, 34-14, in Rose Bowl); Arizona St. (0-1, lost to Kansas St., 34-27, in Holiday Bowl); UCLA (1-0, beat New Mexico, 27-13, in Las Vegas Bowl); Oregon St. (0-1, lost to Pittsburgh, 38-13, in Insight Bowl); Washington (0-1, lost to Purdue, 34-24, in Sun Bowl); Oregon (0-1, lost to Wake Forest, 38-17, in Seattle Bowl)

SOUTHEASTERN CONFERENCE

Team	Conference W	L	Pct.	Full Season W	L	Pct.
East						
Georgia	7	1	.875	13	1	.929
Florida	6	2	.750	8	5	.615
Tennessee	5	3	.625	8	5	.615
South Carolina	3	5	.375	5	7	.417
Vanderbilt	0	8	.000	2	10	.167
Kentucky#	3	5	.375	7	5	.583
West						
Arkansas	5	3	.625	9	5	.643
Auburn	5	3	.625	9	4	.692
LSU	5	3	.625	8	5	.615
Mississippi	3	5	.375	7	6	.538
Mississippi St.	0	8	.000	3	9	.250
Alabama#	6	2	.750	10	3	.769

#Ineligible for conference title.

SEC Championship Game: Georgia 30, Arkansas 3, on December 7, at Atlanta, Georgia.

Bowl Games (3-4): Georgia (1-0, beat Florida St., 26-13, in Sugar Bowl); Florida (0-1, lost to Michigan, 38-30, in Outback Bowl); Tennessee (0-1, lost to Maryland, 30-3, in Peach Bowl); Auburn (1-0, beat Penn St., 13-9, in Capital One Bowl); LSU (0-1, lost to Texas, 35-20, in Cotton Bowl); Arkansas (0-1, lost to Minnesota, 29-14, in Music City Bowl); Mississippi (1-0, beat Nebraska, 27-23, in Independence Bowl)

SUN BELT CONFERENCE

Team	Conference W	L	Pct.	Full Season W	L	Pct.
North Texas	6	0	1.000	8	5	.615
New Mexico St.	5	1	.833	7	5	.583
Arkansas St.	3	3	.500	6	7	.462
Middle Tenn.	2	4	.333	4	8	.333
La.-Lafayette	2	4	.333	3	9	.250
La.-Monroe	2	4	.333	3	9	.250
Idaho	1	5	.167	2	10	.167

Bowl Game (1-0): North Texas (1-0, beat Cincinnati, 24-19, in New Orleans Bowl)

WESTERN ATHLETIC CONFERENCE

Team	Conference W	L	Pct.	Full Season W	L	Pct.
Boise St.	8	0	1.000	12	1	.923
Hawaii	7	1	.875	10	4	.714
Fresno St.	6	2	.750	9	5	.643
San Jose St.	4	4	.500	6	7	.462
Nevada	4	4	.500	5	7	.417
Rice	3	5	.375	4	7	.364
Louisiana Tech	3	5	.375	4	8	.333
Southern Methodist	3	5	.375	3	9	.250
UTEP	1	7	.125	2	10	.167
Tulsa	1	7	.125	1	11	.083

Bowl Games (2-1): Boise St. (1-0, beat Iowa St., 34-16, in Humanitarian Bowl); Hawaii (0-1, lost to Tulane, 36-28, in Hawaii Bowl); Fresno St. (1-0, beat Georgia Tech, 30-21, in Silicon Valley Bowl)

INDEPENDENTS

Team	Full Season W	L	Pct.
South Fla.	9	2	.818
Notre Dame	10	3	.769
Connecticut	6	6	.500
Utah St.	4	7	.364
Troy St.	4	8	.333
Navy	2	10	.167

Bowl Game (0-1): Notre Dame (0-1, lost to North Carolina St., 28-6, in Gator Bowl)

Major-College Alignment History

(Originally called major-college, now Division I-A)

Team	Years Major
Air Force	1957-present
Akron	1987-present
Alabama	1937-present
UAB	1996-present
Alcorn St.	1977
Appalachian St.	1974-81
Arizona	1939-40, 46-present
Arizona St.	1946-48, 50-54, 56-present
Arkansas	1937-40, 46-present
Arkansas St.	1975-81, 92-present
Army	1937-40, 46-present
Auburn	1937-40, 46-present
Ball St.	1975-81, 83-present
Baylor	1937-40, 46-present
Boise St.	1996-present
Boston College	1939-40, 46-present
Boston U.	1939-40, 47-65
Bowling Green	1961-81, 83-present
Brigham Young	1938-40, 46-present
Brown	1937-40, 46-81
Bucknell	1938-40, 46-47
Buffalo	1962-70, 99-present
California	1937-40, 46-present
Cal St. Fullerton	1976-92
Carnegie Tech	1937-40
Case Reserve	1948
Centenary	1938-47
UCF	1996-present
Central Mich.	1975-present
Chattanooga	1946-48, 50, 77-81
Chicago	1937-39
Cincinnati	1946, 48-81, 83-present
Citadel	1939, 46-52, 59-81
Clemson	1937-40, 46-present
Colgate	1937-40, 46-81
Colorado	1937-40, 46-present
Colorado Col.	1946-47
Colorado St.	1940, 46-present
Columbia	1938-40, 46-81
Connecticut	2002-present
Cornell	1937-40, 46-81
Creighton	1939-42
Dartmouth	1937-40, 46-81
Davidson	1937-40, 46-53, 67-76
Dayton	1956-76
Denver	1940-60
Detroit	1939-64
Drake	1939-40, 46-58, 73-80
Duke	1937-40, 46-present
Duquesne	1937-40, 47-50
East Caro.	1966-present
East Tenn. St.	1978-81
Eastern Mich.	1976-81, 83-present
Florida	1937-40, 46-present
Florida St.	1955-present
Fordham	1937-40, 46-54
Fresno St.	1973-present
Furman	1946-53, 55-57, 65, 73-81
Georgetown	1937-40, 46-50
George Washington	1939-66
Georgia	1937-40, 46-present
Georgia Tech	1937-40, 46-present
Gonzaga	1938-41
Grambling	1977
Hardin-Simmons	1946-48, 50-62
Harvard	1937-40, 46-81

Team	Years Major
Haskell	1937-38
Hawaii	1974-present
Holy Cross	1938-40, 46-81
Houston	1949-present
Idaho	1938-40, 46-67, 69-77, 97-present
Illinois	1937-40, 46-present
Illinois St.	1976-81
Indiana	1937-40, 46-present
Indiana St.	1976-81
Iowa	1937-40, 46-present
Iowa St.	1937-40, 46-present
Jackson St.	1977
Kansas	1937-40, 46-present
Kansas St.	1937-40, 46-present
Kent St.	1962-81, 83-present
Kentucky	1937, 40-present
Lafayette	1938-40, 46-50
Lamar	1974-81
Lehigh	1938-40, 46-47
Long Beach St.	1973-91
La.-Lafayette	1974-present
La.-Monroe	1975-81, 94-present
LSU	1937-40, 46-present
Louisiana Tech	1975-81, 89-present
Louisville	1951, 62-present
Loyola Marymount	1950-51
Loyola (Ill.)	1940
Manhattan	1937-42
Marquette	1937-60
Marshall	1962-81, 98-present
Maryland	1937, 40, 46-present
McNeese St.	1975-81
Memphis	1960-present
Merchant Marine	1946-47
Miami (Fla.)	1946-present
Miami (Ohio)	1948-49, 61-81, 83-present
Michigan	1937-40, 46-present
Michigan St.	1937-40, 46-present
Middle Tenn.	1999-present
Minnesota	1937-40, 46-present
Mississippi	1937-40, 46-present
Mississippi St.	1937-40, 46-present
Missouri	1937-40, 46-present
Montana	1939-40, 46-62
Montana St.	1946-48
Navy	1937-40, 46-present
Nebraska	1937-40, 46-present
UNLV	1978-present
Nevada	1946-50, 92-present
New Hampshire	1940
New Mexico	1940, 46-present
New Mexico St.	1946-47, 52-53, 59-present
New York U.	1937-48, 51-52
North Carolina	1937-40, 46-present
North Carolina St.	1940, 46-present
North Texas	1957-81, 95-present
Northern Ariz.	1946-47
Northern Colo.	1946-47
Northern Ill.	1969-81, 83-present
Northwestern	1937-40, 46-present
Northwestern St.	1976-77
Notre Dame	1937-40, 46-present
Ohio	1948, 61-81, 83-present
Ohio St.	1937-40, 46-present
Oklahoma	1937-40, 46-present
Oklahoma St.	1939-40, 46-present

Team	Years Major
Oregon	1937-40, 46-present
Oregon St.	1937-40, 46-present
Pacific (Cal.)	1950-60, 62-63, 66, 69-95
Pennsylvania	1937-40, 46-81
Penn St.	1938-40, 46-present
Pittsburgh	1937-40, 46-present
Portland	1946-48
Princeton	1937-40, 46-81
Purdue	1937-40, 46-present
Rice	1937-40, 46-present
Richmond	1940, 46-81
Rutgers	1946-present
St. Louis	1940-49
St. Mary's (Cal.)	1937-40, 46-50
San Diego St.	1969-present
San Francisco	1940-51
San Jose St.	1939-40, 50-present
Santa Clara	1937-42, 46-52
Sewanee	1937
South Carolina	1939-40, 46-present
South Fla.	2001-present
Southern California	1937-40, 46-present
Southern Ill.	1973-81
Southern Methodist	1937-40, 46-86, 89-present
Southern Miss.	1960, 63-present
Southern U.	1977
Stanford	1937-40, 46-present
Syracuse	1937-40, 46-present
Tampa	1973-74
Temple	1938-40, 46-53, 71-present
Tennessee	1937-40, 46-present
Tennessee St.	1977-80
Texas	1937-40, 46-present
Texas-Arlington	1972-81
Texas A&M	1937-40, 46-present
TCU	1937-40, 46-present
UTEP	1940, 46-present
Texas Southern	1977
Texas Tech	1937-40, 46-present
Toledo	1962-present
Trinity (Tex.)	1960
Troy St.	2002-present
Tulane	1937-40, 46-present
Tulsa	1937-40, 46-present
UCLA	1937-40, 46-present
Utah	1938-40, 46-present
Utah St.	1939-40, 46-present
Vanderbilt	1937-40, 46-present
Villanova	1939-40, 46-80
Virginia	1940, 46-present
VMI	1939-40, 46-81
Virginia Tech	1940, 46-present
Wake Forest	1939-40, 46-present
Washington	1937-40, 46-present
Wash. & Lee	1940, 46-53
Washington (Mo.)	1937-40
Washington St.	1937-40, 46-present
West Tex. A&M	1946-47, 51-53, 58-80
West Virginia	1939-40, 46-present
Western Caro.	1977-81
Western Mich.	1962-present
Wichita St.	1946-86
William & Mary	1940, 46-81
Wisconsin	1937-40, 46-present
Wyoming	1940, 46-present
Xavier (Ohio)	1960-73
Yale	1937-40, 46-81

Division I-AA

ATLANTIC 10 CONFERENCE

Team	Conference			Full Season		
	W	L	Pct.	W	L	Pct.
Northeastern	7	2	.778	10	3	.769
Maine	7	2	.778	11	3	.786
Villanova	6	3	.667	11	4	.733
Massachusetts	6	3	.667	8	4	.667
William & Mary	5	4	.556	6	5	.545
Delaware	4	5	.444	6	6	.500
Hofstra	4	5	.444	6	6	.500
Richmond	4	5	.444	4	7	.364
James Madison	3	6	.333	5	7	.417
New Hampshire	2	7	.222	3	8	.273
Rhode Island	1	8	.111	3	9	.250

NCAA Division I-AA Playoffs (3-3): Maine (1-1, beat Appalachian St., 14-13, in first round; lost to Ga. Southern, 31-7, in quarterfinals); Villanova (2-1, beat Furman, 45-38, in first round; beat Fordham, 24-10, in quarterfinals; lost to McNeese St., 39-28, in semifinals); Northeastern (0-1, lost to Fordham, 29-24, in first round)

BIG SKY CONFERENCE

Team	Conference			Full Season		
	W	L	Pct.	W	L	Pct.
Montana	5	2	.714	11	3	.786
Idaho St.	5	2	.714	8	3	.727
Montana St.	5	2	.714	7	6	.538
Portland St.	3	4	.429	6	5	.545
Northern Ariz.	3	4	.429	6	5	.545
Eastern Wash.	3	4	.429	6	5	.545
Sacramento St.	3	4	.429	5	7	.417
Weber St.	1	6	.143	3	8	.273

NCAA Division I-AA Playoffs (1-2): Montana (1-1, beat Northwestern St., 45-14, in first round; lost to McNeese St., 24-20, in quarterfinals); Montana St. (0-1, lost to McNeese St., 21-14, in first round)

BIG SOUTH CONFERENCE

Team	Conference			Full Season		
	W	L	Pct.	W	L	Pct.
Gardner-Webb	3	0	1.000	9	1	.900
Elon	2	1	.667	4	7	.364
Liberty	1	2	.333	2	9	.182
Charleston So.	0	3	.000	4	8	.333

GATEWAY ATHLETIC CONFERENCE

Team	Conference			Full Season		
	W	L	Pct.	W	L	Pct.
Western Ill.	6	1	.857	11	2	.846
Western Ky.	6	1	.857	12	3	.800
Youngstown St.	4	3	.571	7	4	.636
Illinois St.	4	3	.571	6	5	.545
Indiana St.	3	4	.429	5	7	.417
Nothern Iowa	2	5	.286	5	6	.455
Southern Ill.	2	5	.286	4	8	.333
Southwest Mo. St.	1	6	.143	4	7	.364

NCAA Division I-AA Playoffs (5-1): Western Ill. (1-1, beat Eastern Ill., 48-9, in first round; lost to Western Ky., 31-28, in quarterfinals); Western Ky. (4-0, beat Murray St., 59-20, in first round; beat Western Ill., 31-28, in quarterfinals; beat Ga. Southern, 31-28, in semifinals; beat McNeese St., 34-14, in championship)

IVY GROUP

Team	Conference			Full Season		
	W	L	Pct.	W	L	Pct.
Pennsylvania	7	0	1.000	9	1	.900
Harvard	6	1	.857	7	3	.700
Princeton	4	3	.571	6	4	.600
Yale	4	3	.571	6	4	.600
Cornell	3	4	.429	4	6	.400
Dartmouth	2	5	.286	3	7	.300
Brown	2	5	.286	2	8	.200
Columbia	0	7	.000	1	9	.100

METRO ATLANTIC ATHLETIC CONFERENCE

Team	Conference			Full Season		
	W	L	Pct.	W	L	Pct.
Duquesne#	8	0	1.000	11	1	.917
Fairfield	5	3	.625	5	6	.455
St. Peter's	5	3	.625	6	5	.545
Marist	5	3	.625	7	4	.636
Iona	4	4	.500	5	6	.455
Siena	3	5	.375	3	7	.300
St. John's (N.Y.)	2	6	.250	2	8	.200
Canisius	2	6	.250	2	9	.182
La Salle	2	6	.250	2	9	.182

#Overall record includes the ECAC Bowl, in which Albany (N.Y.) defeated Duquesne, 24-0, on November 23 in Albany, New York.

MID-EASTERN ATHLETIC CONFERENCE

Team	Conference			Full Season		
	W	L	Pct.	W	L	Pct.
Bethune-Cookman	7	1	.875	11	2	.846
Florida A&M	5	3	.625	7	5	.583
Hampton	5	3	.625	7	5	.583
Morgan St.	5	3	.625	7	5	.583
South Carolina St.	4	4	.500	7	5	.583
Howard	4	4	.500	6	5	.545
Norfolk St.	2	6	.250	5	6	.455
Delaware St.	2	6	.250	4	8	.333
N.C. A&T	2	6	.250	4	8	.333

NCAA Division I-AA Playoffs (0-1): Bethune-Cookman (0-1, lost to Ga. Southern, 34-0, in first round)

NORTHEAST CONFERENCE

Team	Conference			Full Season		
	W	L	Pct.	W	L	Pct.
Albany (N.Y.)#	6	1	.857	8	4	.667
Stony Brook	5	2	.714	8	2	.800
Sacred Heart	5	2	.714	7	3	.700
Wagner	4	3	.571	7	4	.636
Central Conn. St.	3	4	.429	5	6	.455
Robert Morris	2	5	.286	3	7	.300
Monmouth	2	5	.286	2	8	.200
St. Francis (Pa.)	1	6	.143	2	8	.200

#Overall record includes ECAC Bowl, in which Albany (N.Y.) defeated Duquesne, 24-0, on November 23 in Albany, New York.

OHIO VALLEY CONFERENCE

Team	Conference			Full Season		
	W	L	Pct.	W	L	Pct.
Eastern Ill.	5	1	.833	8	4	.667
Murray St.	5	1	.833	7	5	.583
Southeast Mo. St.	4	2	.667	8	4	.667
Eastern Ky.	4	2	.667	8	4	.667
Tennessee Tech	2	4	.333	5	7	.417
Tennessee St.	1	5	.167	2	10	.167
Tenn.-Martin	0	6	.000	2	10	.167

NCAA Division I-AA Playoffs (0-2): Eastern Ill.(0-1, lost to Western Ill., 48-9, in first round); Murray St. (0-1, lost to Western Ky., 59-20, in first round)

PATRIOT LEAGUE

Team	Conference			Full Season		
	W	L	Pct.	W	L	Pct.
Fordham	6	1	.857	10	3	.769
Colgate	6	1	.857	9	3	.750
Lafayette	5	2	.714	7	5	.583
Lehigh	4	3	.571	8	4	.667
Towson	3	4	.429	6	5	.545
Georgetown	2	5	.286	5	6	.455
Holy Cross	2	5	.286	4	8	.333
Bucknell	0	7	.000	2	9	.182

NCAA Division I-AA Playoffs (1-1): Fordham (1-1, beat Northeastern, 29-24, in first round; lost to Villanova, 24-10, in quarterfinals)

PIONEER FOOTBALL LEAGUE

Team	Conference			Full Season		
	W	L	Pct.	W	L	Pct.
North Division						
Dayton	4	0	1.000	11	1	.917
San Diego	3	1	.750	5	5	.500
Butler	2	2	.500	4	6	.400
Drake	1	3	.250	5	6	.455
Valparaiso	0	4	.000	1	10	.091
South Division						
Morehead St.	3	0	1.000	9	3	.750
Davidson	2	1	.667	7	3	.700
Austin Peay	1	2	.333	7	5	.583
Jacksonville	0	3	.000	3	7	.300

PFL Championship Game: Dayton 28, Morehead St. 0, on November 23, at Morehead, Kentucky.

SOUTHERN CONFERENCE

Team	Conference			Full Season		
	W	L	Pct.	W	L	Pct.
Ga. Southern	7	1	.875	11	3	.786
Wofford	6	2	.750	9	3	.750
Furman	6	2	.750	8	4	.667
Appalachian St.	6	2	.750	8	4	.667
VMI	3	5	.375	6	6	.500
Western Caro.	3	5	.375	5	6	.455
East Tenn. St.	2	6	.250	4	8	.333
Chattanooga	2	6	.250	2	10	.167
Citadel	1	7	.125	3	9	.250

NCAA Division I-AA Playoffs (2-3): Ga. Southern (2-1, beat Bethune-Cookman, 34-0, in first round; beat Maine, 31-7, in quarterfinals; lost to Western Ky., 31-28, in semifinals); Appalachian St. (0-1, lost to Maine, 14-13, in first round); Furman (0-1, lost to Villanova, 45-38, in first round)

SOUTHLAND FOOTBALL LEAGUE

Team	Conference			Full Season		
	W	L	Pct.	W	L	Pct.
McNeese St.	6	0	1.000	13	2	.867
Northwestern St.	4	2	.667	9	4	.692
Nicholls St.	3	3	.500	7	4	.636
Stephen F. Austin	3	3	.500	6	5	.545
Jacksonville St.	2	4	.333	5	6	.455
Sam Houston St.	2	4	.333	4	7	.364
Southwest Tex. St.	1	5	.167	4	7	.364

NCAA Division I-AA Playoffs (3-2): McNeese St. (3-1, beat Montana St., 21-14, in first round; beat Montana, 24-20, in quarterfinals; beat Villanova, 39-28, in semifinals; lost to Western Ky., 34-14, in championship); Northwestern St. (0-1, lost to Montana, 45-14, in first round)

SOUTHWESTERN ATHLETIC CONFERENCE

Team	Conference			Full Season		
	W	L	Pct.	W	L	Pct.
Eastern Division						
Alabama A&M	6	1	.857	8	4	.667
Jackson St.	5	2	.714	7	4	.636
Alcorn St.	3	4	.429	5	6	.545
Mississippi Val.	3	4	.429	5	6	.455
Alabama St.	2	5	.286	6	6	.500
Western Division						
Grambling	6	1	.857	11	2	.846
Southern U.	5	2	.714	6	6	.500
Texas Southern	3	4	.429	4	7	.364
Ark.-Pine Bluff	2	5	.286	3	8	.273
Prairie View	0	7	.000	1	10	.091

SWAC Championship Game: Grambling 31, Alabama A&M 19, on December 14, at Birmingham, Alabama.

INDEPENDENTS

Team	Full Season		
	W	L	Pct.
St. Mary's (Cal.)	6	6	.500
Florida Int'l	5	6	.455
Samford	4	7	.364
Cal Poly	3	8	.273
Fla. Atlantic	2	9	.182
Savannah St.	1	9	.100
Southern Utah	1	10	.091
Morris Brown	1	11	.083

Division II

CENTRAL INTERCOLLEGIATE ATHLETIC ASSOCIATION*

Team	Conference			Full Season		
	W	L	Pct.	W	L	Pct.
East Division						
Bowie St.#	5	2	.714	6	5	.545
Virginia St.	5	2	.714	7	3	.700

Team	Conference			Full Season		
	W	L	Pct.	W	L	Pct.
Virginia Union	4	3	.571	6	4	.600
Elizabeth City St.	2	5	.286	2	8	.200
West Division						
Fayetteville St.#	7	0	1.000	10	2	.833
Winston-Salem	4	3	.571	4	6	.400
N.C. Central	2	5	.286	4	6	.400
Livingstone	2	5	.286	3	7	.300
Johnson C. Smith	1	7	.125	2	8	.200
St. Augustine's	0	7	.000	1	9	.100

NCAA Division II Playoffs (0-1): Fayetteville St. (0-1, lost to Carson-Newman, 40-27, in first round)

#Overall record includes CIAA Championship game, in which Fayetteville St. defeated Bowie St., 17-14, on November 16 at Winston-Salem, North Carolina. The Pioneer Bowl matching teams from the CIAA and the SIAC was cancelled.

GREAT LAKES INTERCOLLEGIATE ATHLETIC CONFERENCE

Team	Conference			Full Season		
	W	L	Pct.	W	L	Pct.
Grand Valley St.	9	0	1.000	14	0	1.000
Saginaw Valley	8	2	.800	9	3	.750
Findlay	8	2	.800	9	2	.818
Northwood	7	3	.700	7	4	.636
Northern Mich.	6	4	.600	6	5	.545
Ferris St.	4	5	.444	5	5	.500
Indianapolis	4	6	.400	5	6	.455
Hillsdale	4	6	.400	4	7	.364
Michigan Tech	3	7	.300	3	7	.300
Wayne St. (Mich.)	3	7	.300	3	8	.273
Ashland	2	8	.200	2	9	.182
Mercyhurst	1	9	.100	2	9	.182

NCAA Division II Playoffs (4-1): Grand Valley St. (4-0, beat C.W. Post, 62-13, in first round; beat Indiana [Pa.], 62-21, in quarterfinals; beat Northern Colo., 44-7, in semifinals; beat Valdosta St., 31-24, in championship); Saginaw Valley (0-1, lost to Indiana [Pa.], 27-23, in first round)

GREAT NORTHWEST ATHLETIC CONFERENCE

Team	Conference			Full Season		
	W	L	Pct.	W	L	Pct.
Central Wash.	3	0	1.000	11	1	.917
Western Wash.	2	1	.667	6	4	.600
Western Ore.	1	2	.333	5	5	.500
Humboldt St.	0	3	.000	1	10	.091

NCAA Division II Playoffs (0-1): Central Wash. (0-1, lost to UC Davis, 24-6, in first round)

GULF SOUTH CONFERENCE

Team	Conference			Full Season		
	W	L	Pct.	W	L	Pct.
Valdosta St.	9	0	1.000	14	1	.933
Harding	7	2	.778	9	2	.818
Central Ark.	6	3	.667	8	3	.727
Southern Ark.	6	3	.667	7	4	.636
Ouachita Baptist	5	4	.556	5	5	.500
Henderson St.	5	4	.556	5	6	.455
Delta St.	4	5	.444	4	7	.364
West Ala.	3	6	.333	5	6	.455
North Ala.	3	6	.333	4	7	.364
Arkansas Tech	3	6	.333	4	7	.364
Ark.-Monticello	2	7	.222	2	8	.200
West Ga.	1	8	.111	3	8	.273

NCAA Division II Playoffs (3-1): Valdosta St. (3-1, beat Catawba, 24-7, in first round; beat Carson-Newman, 31-28, in quarterfinals; beat Tex. A&M-Kingsville, 21-12, in semifinals; lost to Grand Valley St., 31-24, in championship)

LONE STAR CONFERENCE

Team	Conference			Full Season		
	W	L	Pct.	W	L	Pct.
North Division						
Tarleton St.	4	1	.800	9	2	.818
Southeastern Okla.	3	2	.600	7	3	.700
Southwestern Okla.	3	2	.600	7	4	.636
Central Okla.	2	3	.400	5	6	.455
Northeastern St.	2	3	.400	4	7	.364
East Central	1	4	.200	3	8	.273

Team	Conference			Full Season		
	W	L	Pct.	W	L	Pct.
South Division						
Tex. A&M-Kingsville	5	1	.833	10	3	.769
Abilene Christian	5	1	.833	6	4	.600
Eastern N.M.	4	2	.667	8	3	.727
Midwestern St.	4	2	.667	7	4	.636
Angelo St.	2	4	.333	2	8	.200
Tex. A&M-Commerce	1	5	.167	2	8	.200
West Tex. A&M	0	6	.000	0	11	.000

NCAA Division II Playoffs (2-1): Tex. A&M-Kingsville (2-1, beat Neb.-Kearney, 58-40, in first round; beat UC Davis, 27-20 [ot], in quarterfinals; lost to Valdosta St., 21-12, in semifinals)

MID-AMERICAN INTERCOLLEGIATE ATHLETICS ASSOCIATION

Team	Conference			Full Season		
	W	L	Pct.	W	L	Pct.
Northwest Mo. St.	9	0	1.000	12	1	.923
Central Mo. St.	8	1	.889	10	2	.833
Emporia St.#	6	3	.667	9	3	.750
Pittsburg St.	6	3	.667	8	3	.727
Mo. Western St.	4	5	.444	6	5	.545
Truman	4	5	.444	6	5	.545
Mo. Southern St.	3	6	.333	5	6	.455
Washburn	3	6	.333	3	8	.273
Southwest Baptist	2	7	.222	3	8	.273
Mo.-Rolla	0	9	.000	0	11	.000

NCAA Division II Playoffs (1-2): Northwest Mo. St. (1-1, beat Minn. Duluth, 45-41, in first round; lost to Northern Colo., 23-12, in quarterfinals); Central Mo. St. (0-1, lost to Northern Colo., 49-28, in first round)

#Overall record includes Mineral Water Bowl, in which Emporia St. defeated Winona St., 34-27 [ot], on December 7 at Excelsior Springs, Missouri.

NORTH CENTRAL INTERCOLLEGIATE ATHLETIC CONFERENCE

Team	Conference			Full Season		
	W	L	Pct.	W	L	Pct.
Northern Colo.	8	0	1.000	12	2	.857
St. Cloud St.	6	2	.750	9	2	.818
Neb.-Omaha	5	3	.625	6	5	.545
Augustana (S.D.)	4	4	.500	7	4	.636
South Dakota St.	4	4	.500	6	4	.600
North Dakota	3	5	.375	5	6	.455
Minn. St. Mankato	3	5	.375	4	7	.364
South Dakota	2	6	.250	3	8	.273
North Dakota St.	1	7	.125	2	8	.200

NCAA Division II Playoffs (2-1): Northern Colo. (2-1, beat Central Mo. St., 49-28, in first round; beat Northwest Mo. St., 23-12, in quarterfinals; lost to Grand Valley St., 44-7, in semifinals)

NORTHEAST-10 CONFERENCE

Team	Conference			Full Season		
	W	L	Pct.	W	L	Pct.
C.W. Post	10	0	1.000	11	1	.917
Bentley	9	1	.900	10	1	.909
Southern Conn. St.	7	3	.700	8	3	.727
Merrimack	6	4	.600	6	4	.600
St. Anselm	5	5	.500	5	5	.500
Bryant	5	5	.500	5	6	.455
American Int'l	5	5	.500	5	6	.455
Pace	3	7	.300	3	7	.300
Mass.-Lowell	3	7	.300	3	8	.273
Stonehill	1	9	.100	2	9	.182
Assumption	1	9	.100	2	9	.182

NCAA Division II Playoffs (0-1): C.W. Post (0-1, lost to Grand Valley St., 62-13, in first round)

NORTHERN SUN INTERCOLLEGIATE ATHLETIC CONFERENCE

Team	Conference			Full Season		
	W	L	Pct.	W	L	Pct.
Minn. Duluth	9	0	1.000	11	1	.917
Winona St.#	8	1	.889	8	4	.667
Concordia-St. Paul	7	2	.778	9	2	.818
Bemidji St.	6	3	.667	6	5	.545
Minn. St. Moorhead	4	5	.444	5	5	.500
Northern St.	4	5	.444	4	7	.364
Southwest St.	3	6	.333	4	7	.364
Wayne St. (Neb.)	3	6	.333	3	8	.273
Minn.-Crookston	1	8	.111	1	10	.091
Minn. Morris	0	9	.000	0	11	.000

NCAA Division II Playoffs (0-1): Minn. Duluth (0-1, lost to Northwest Mo. St., 45-41, in first round)

#Overall record includes Mineral Water Bowl, in which Emporia St. defeated Winona St., 34-27 [ot], on December 7 at Excelsior Springs, Missouri.

PENNSYLVANIA STATE ATHLETIC CONFERENCE

Team	Conference			Full Season		
	W	L	Pct.	W	L	Pct.
Western Division						
Indiana (Pa.)#	8	0	1.000	11	2	.846
Slippery Rock	5	3	.625	7	4	.636
Shippensburg	6	4	.600	6	5	.545
East Stroudsburg	7	1	.875	8	2	.800
Clarion	6	3	.667	7	4	.636
Edinboro	2	6	.250	5	6	.455
California (Pa.)	3	5	.375	6	5	.545
Lock Haven	4	6	.400	4	7	.364
Eastern Division						
Bloomsburg*	5	1	.833	8	2	.800
East Stroudsburg*	5	1	.833	8	2	.800
West Chester	3	3	.500	3	7	.300
Millersville	3	3	.500	3	7	.300
Kutztown	2	4	.333	4	7	.364
Mansfield	2	4	.333	3	7	.300
Cheyney	0	6	.000	0	11	.000

*#Western Division champion. *Eastern Division co-champions.*

NCAA Division II Playoffs (1-1): Indiana (Pa.) (1-1, beat Saginaw Valley, 27-23, in first round; lost to Grand Valley St., 62-21, in quarterfinals)

ROCKY MOUNTAIN ATHLETIC CONFERENCE

Team	Conference			Full Season		
	W	L	Pct.	W	L	Pct.
Neb.-Kearney	7	1	.875	9	2	.818
Chadron St.	7	1	.875	8	2	.800
Mesa St.	5	3	.625	5	6	.455
Colorado Mines	4	4	.500	7	4	.636
Western St.	4	4	.500	5	6	.455
Adams St.	4	4	.500	5	6	.455
Fort Hays St.	3	5	.375	5	6	.455
Fort Lewis	2	6	.250	3	8	.273
N.M. Highlands	0	8	.000	0	10	.000

NCAA Division II Playoffs (0-1): Neb.-Kearney (0-1, lost to Tex. A&M-Kingsville, 58-40, in first round)

SOUTH ATLANTIC CONFERENCE

Team	Conference			Full Season		
	W	L	Pct.	W	L	Pct.
Carson-Newman	7	0	1.000	12	1	.923
Catawba	6	1	.857	8	3	.727
Presbyterian	5	2	.714	8	3	.727
Mars Hill	4	3	.571	7	4	.636
Tusculum	3	4	.429	7	4	.636
Wingate	2	5	.286	5	6	.455
Lenoir-Rhyne	1	6	.143	3	7	.300
Newberry	0	7	.000	1	10	.091

NCAA Division II Playoffs (1-2): Carson-Newman (1-1, beat Fayetteville St., 40-27, in first round; lost to Valdosta St., 31-28, in quarterfinals); Catawba (0-1, lost to Valdosta St., 24-7, in first round)

SOUTHERN INTERCOLLEGIATE ATHLETIC CONFERENCE

Team	Conference			Full Season		
	W	L	Pct.	W	L	Pct.
Tuskegee	7	1	.875	10	1	.909
Fort Valley St.	6	2	.750	7	4	.636
Albany St. (Ga.)	6	2	.750	7	4	.636
Miles	5	3	.625	6	5	.545
Morehouse	5	3	.625	5	5	.500
Lane	3	5	.375	4	7	.364
Kentucky St.	2	6	.250	3	8	.273
Benedict	2	6	.250	2	9	.182
Clark Atlanta	1	7	.125	2	9	.182

The Pioneer Bowl matching teams from the SIAC and the CIAA was cancelled.

WEST VIRGINIA INTERCOLLEGIATE ATHLETIC CONFERENCE

Team	Conference			Full Season		
	W	L	Pct.	W	L	Pct.
West Va. Wesleyan	6	1	.857	7	4	.636
Shepherd	5	2	.714	7	3	.700
West Va. Tech	5	2	.714	6	5	.545
West Liberty St.	5	2	.714	6	5	.545
Glenville St.	3	4	.429	4	7	.364
Fairmont St.	2	5	.286	3	7	.300
Concord	2	5	.286	3	7	.300
West Virginia St.	0	7	.000	1	10	.091

INDEPENDENTS

Team	Full Season		
	W	L	Pct.
UC Davis	9	3	.750
Gannon	5	5	.500
New Haven	4	6	.400
Lincoln (Mo.)	4	7	.364
Quincy	4	7	.364
St. Joseph's (Ind.)	4	7	.364
North Greenville	3	6	.333
Western N.M.	2	7	.222
Tiffin	2	8	.200
Panhandle St.	2	9	.182
Ky. Wesleyan	1	10	.091

NCAA Division II Playoffs (1-1): UC Davis (1-1, beat Central Wash., 24-6, in first round; lost to Tex. A&M-Kingsville, 27-20 [ot], in quarterfinals)

Division III

AMERICA SOUTHWEST CONFERENCE

Team	Conference			Full Season		
	W	L	Pct.	W	L	Pct.
Mary Hardin-Baylor	9	0	1.000	10	1	.909
Howard Payne	8	1	.889	9	1	.900
Hardin-Simmons	7	2	.778	8	2	.800
East Tex. Baptist	6	3	.667	6	4	.600
Austin	4	5	.444	4	6	.400
Mississippi Col.	4	5	.444	4	6	.400
Louisiana Col.	3	6	.333	4	6	.400
Sul Ross St.	2	7	.222	2	8	.200
Texas Lutheran	2	7	.222	2	8	.200
McMurry	0	9	.000	0	10	.000

Division III Playoffs (0-1): Mary Hardin-Baylor (0-1, lost to Trinity [Tex.], 48-38, in first round)

ATLANTIC CENTRAL FOOTBALL CONFERENCE

Team	Conference			Full Season		
	W	L	Pct.	W	L	Pct.
Frostburg St.	3	0	1.000	6	5	.545
Salisbury	2	1	.667	9	2	.818
Wesley	1	2	.333	5	5	.500
Newport News	0	3	.000	5	5	.500

ECAC Southwest Championship: Johns Hopkins 24, Frostburg St. 21, on November 23, at Cumberland, Maryland.

NCAA Division III Playoffs (0-1): Salisbury (0-1, lost to King's [Pa.], 28-0, in first round)

CENTENNIAL CONFERENCE

Team	Conference			Full Season		
	W	L	Pct.	W	L	Pct.
Muhlenberg*	5	1	.833	10	2	.833
Johns Hopkins*	5	1	.833	9	2	.818
McDaniel*	5	1	.833	9	2	.818
Dickinson	3	3	.500	5	5	.500
Frank. & Marsh.	2	4	.333	4	6	.400
Gettysburg	1	5	.167	4	6	.400
Ursinus	0	6	.000	2	8	.200
*Tri-champions.						

ECAC Southeast Championship: McDaniel 21, Moravian 7, on November 23, at Westminster, Maryland.

ECAC Southwest Championship: Johns Hopkins 24, Frostburg St. 21, on November 23, at Cumberland, Maryland.

NCAA Division III Playoffs (1-1): Muhlenberg (1-1, beat Mass.-Dartmouth, 56-6, in first round; lost to John Carroll, 21-10, in second round)

DIXIE CONFERENCE

Team	Conference			Full Season		
	W	L	Pct.	W	L	Pct.
Chris. Newport	5	1	.833	6	5	.545
Ferrum	5	1	.833	5	5	.500
Shenandoah	4	2	.667	5	5	.500
Greensboro	4	2	.667	4	6	.400
Methodist	2	4	.333	3	7	.300
Averett	1	5	.167	2	7	.222
Chowan	0	6	.000	0	10	.000

NCAA Division III Playoffs (0-1): Chris. Newport (0-1, lost to Wash. & Jeff., 24-10, in first round)

EMPIRE 8 CONFERENCE

Team	Conference			Full Season		
	W	L	Pct.	W	L	Pct.
Ithaca	4	0	1.000	7	3	.700
Hartwick	3	1	.750	8	2	.800
St. John Fisher	2	2	.500	6	4	.600
Alfred	1	3	.250	4	6	.400
Utica	0	4	.000	1	9	.100

ECAC North Atlantic Championship: Hartwick 69, Curry 14, on November 23, at Oneonta, New York.

FREEDOM FOOTBALL CONFERENCE

Team	Conference			Full Season		
	W	L	Pct.	W	L	Pct.
Springfield	6	0	1.000	8	2	.800
Merchant Marine	5	1	.833	8	3	.727
Western Conn. St.	4	2	.667	7	3	.700
WPI	3	3	.500	4	6	.400
Norwich	2	4	.333	4	6	.400
Coast Guard	1	5	.167	2	7	.222
Plymouth St.	0	6	.000	0	10	.000

ECAC South Atlantic Championship: Wilkes 33, Merchant Marine 7, on November 23, at King's Point, New York.

NCAA Division III Playoffs (0-1): Springfield (0-1, lost to Brockport St., 16-0, in first round)

HEARTLAND COLLEGIATE ATHLETIC CONFERENCE

Team	Conference			Full Season		
	W	L	Pct.	W	L	Pct.
Hanover	6	0	1.000	10	1	.909
Anderson	5	1	.833	7	3	.700
Mt. St. Joseph	4	2	.667	5	5	.500
Manchester	2	4	.333	3	7	.300
Franklin	2	4	.333	2	8	.200
Bluffton	1	5	.167	3	7	.300
Defiance	1	5	.167	3	7	.300

NCAA Division III Playoffs (0-1): Hanover (0-1, lost to Wittenberg, 34-33, in first round)

ILLINI-BADGER CONFERENCE

Team	Conference			Full Season		
	W	L	Pct.	W	L	Pct.
MacMurray	7	0	1.000	10	1	.909
Concordia (Wis.)	6	1	.857	8	2	.800
Aurora	5	2	.714	5	4	.556
Lakeland	4	3	.571	6	4	.600
Benedictine (Ill.)	3	4	.429	4	6	.400
Eureka	2	5	.286	2	8	.200
Greenville	1	6	.143	1	9	.100
Concordia (Ill.)	0	7	.000	0	10	.000

NCAA Division III Playoffs (0-1): MacMurray (0-1, lost to Wabash, 42-7, in first round)

COLLEGE CONFERENCE OF ILLINOIS AND WISCONSIN

Team	Conference			Full Season		
	W	L	Pct.	W	L	Pct.
Wheaton (Ill.)	7	0	1.000	10	2	.833
Augustana (Ill.)	6	1	.857	7	2	.778
Millikin	5	2	.714	7	3	.700
North Central	4	3	.571	6	4	.600
Ill. Wesleyan	3	4	.429	6	4	.600
Carthage	3	4	.429	4	6	.400
Elmhurst	1	6	.143	3	7	.300
North Park	0	7	.000	1	9	.100

NCAA Division III Playoffs (1-1): Wheaton (Ill.) (1-1, beat Alma, 42-14, in first round; lost to Mount Union, 42-21, in second round)

IOWA INTERCOLLEGIATE ATHLETIC CONFERENCE

Team	Conference			Full Season		
	W	L	Pct.	W	L	Pct.
Coe	8	1	.889	10	2	.833
Wartburg	8	1	.889	10	2	.833
Central (Iowa)	8	1	.889	8	2	.800
Simpson	6	3	.667	6	4	.600
Loras	4	5	.444	5	5	.500
Luther	3	6	.333	4	6	.400
Cornell College	3	6	.333	4	6	.400
Buena Vista	3	6	.333	3	7	.300
Upper Iowa	2	7	.222	2	8	.200
Dubuque	0	9	.000	1	9	.100

NCAA Division III Playoffs (2-2): Coe (1-1, beat Wis.-La Crosse, 21-18, in first round; lost to St. John's [Minn.], 45-14, in second round); Wartburg (1-1, beat Lake Forest, 45-0, in first round; lost to Linfield, 52-15, in second round)

MICHIGAN INTERCOLLEGIATE ATHLETIC CONFERENCE

Team	Conference			Full Season		
	W	L	Pct.	W	L	Pct.
Alma	6	0	1.000	9	2	.818
Adrian	4	2	.667	7	3	.700
Hope	4	2	.667	5	5	.500
Olivet	3	3	.500	5	4	.556
Albion	3	3	.500	5	5	.500
Kalamazoo	1	5	.167	4	6	.400
Wis. Lutheran	0	6	.000	3	7	.300

NCAA Division III Playoffs (0-1): Alma (0-1, lost to Wheaton [Ill.], 42-14, in first round)

MIDDLE ATLANTIC CONFERENCE

Team	Conference			Full Season		
	W	L	Pct.	W	L	Pct.
Widener	8	1	.889	9	1	.900
King's (Pa.)	8	1	.889	9	3	.750
Moravian	7	2	.778	7	4	.636
Lycoming	6	3	.667	6	3	.667
Wilkes	5	4	.556	7	4	.636
Susquehanna	5	4	.556	5	5	.500
Juniata	4	5	.444	4	6	.400
Albright	2	6	.250	2	8	.200
FDU-Florham	2	7	.222	2	8	.200
Delaware Valley	1	8	.111	2	8	.200
Lebanon Valley	1	8	.111	1	9	.100

ECAC South Atlantic Championship: Wilkes 33, Merchant Marine 7, on November 23, at King's Point, New York.

ECAC Southeast Championship: McDaniel 21, Moravian 7, on November 23, at Westminster, Maryland.

NCAA Division III Playoffs (1-1): King's (Pa.) (1-1, beat Salisbury, 28-0, in first round; lost to Bridgewater [Va.], 19-17, in second round)

MIDWEST COLLEGIATE ATHLETIC CONFERENCE

Team	Conference			Full Season		
	W	L	Pct.	W	L	Pct.
St. Norbert	8	1	.889	9	1	.900
Lake Forest	8	1	.889	9	2	.818
Ripon	7	2	.778	7	3	.700
Beloit	5	4	.556	6	4	.600
Knox	5	4	.556	6	4	.600
Monmouth (Ill.)	5	4	.556	5	5	.500
Grinnell	4	5	.444	4	6	.400
Illinois Col.	2	7	.222	3	7	.300
Carroll (Wis.)	1	8	.111	1	9	.100
Lawrence	0	9	.000	0	10	.000

NCAA Division III Playoffs (0-1): Lake Forest (0-1, lost to Wartburg, 45-0, in first round)

MINNESOTA INTERCOLLEGIATE ATHLETIC CONFERENCE

Team	Conference			Full Season		
	W	L	Pct.	W	L	Pct.
St. John's (Minn.)	8	0	1.000	12	2	.857
Concordia-M'head..	7	1	.875	7	3	.700
Gust. Adolphus	5	3	.625	6	4	.600
Bethel (Minn.)	5	3	.625	5	5	.500
St. Thomas (Minn.) .	5	3	.625	5	5	.500
St. Olaf	3	5	.375	5	5	.500
Hamline	2	6	.250	3	7	.300
Augsburg	1	7	.125	2	8	.200
Carleton	0	8	.000	0	10	.000

NCAA Division III Playoffs (3-1): St. John's (Minn.) (3-1, beat Redlands, 31-24, in first round; beat Coe, 45-14, in second round; beat Linfield, 21-14, in quarterfinals; lost to Trinity [Tex.], 41-34, in semifinals)

NEW ENGLAND FOOTBALL CONFERENCE

Team	Conference			Full Season		
	W	L	Pct.	W	L	Pct.
Bogan Division						
Westfield St.	6	0	1.000	8	3	.727
Worcester St.	5	1	.833	9	2	.818
Fitchburg St.	4	2	.667	5	4	.556
Bridgewater St.	3	3	.500	4	5	.444
Framingham St.	1	5	.167	1	8	.111
Maine Maritime	1	5	.167	1	8	.111
Mass. Maritime	1	5	.167	1	8	.111
Boyd Division						
Mass.-Dartmouth	5	0	1.000	11	1	.917
Curry	3	2	.600	7	3	.700
Nichols	3	2	.600	5	4	.556
MIT	2	3	.400	4	5	.444
Salve Regina	2	3	.400	2	7	.222
Western New Eng.	0	5	.000	1	8	.111

NEFC Championship Game: Mass.-Dartmouth 16, Westfield St. 0, on November 16, at Worcester, Massachusetts.

ECAC Northwest Championship: Cortland St. 30, Westfield St. 7, on November 23, at Cortland, New York.

ECAC North Atlantic Championship: Hartwick 69, Curry 14, on November 23, at Oneonta, New York.

ECAC Northeast Championship: Rensselaer 55, Worcester St. 29, on November 23, at Worcester, Massachusetts.

NCAA Division III Playoffs (0-1): Mass.-Dartmouth (0-1, lost to Muhlenberg, 56-6, in first round)

NEW ENGLAND SMALL COLLEGE ATHLETIC FOOTBALL CONFERENCE#

Team				Full Season		
	W	L	Pct.	W	L	Pct.
Trinity (Conn.)	7	1	.875	7	1	.875
Williams	7	1	.875	7	1	.875
Amherst	6	2	.750	6	2	.750
Wesleyan	5	3	.625	5	3	.625
Colby	4	4	.500	4	4	.500
Middlebury	4	4	.500	4	4	.500
Bates	3	5	.375	3	5	.375
Tufts	3	5	.375	3	5	.375
Bowdoin	1	7	.125	1	7	.125
Hamilton	0	8	.000	0	8	.000

NEW JERSEY ATHLETIC CONFERENCE

Team	Conference			Full Season		
	W	L	Pct.	W	L	Pct.
Rowan	6	0	1.000	10	1	.909
Cortland St.	4	2	.667	9	2	.818
Coll. of New Jersey.	4	2	.667	6	3	.667
Montclair St.	4	2	.667	5	5	.500
Kean	2	4	.333	4	6	.400
New Jersey City	1	5	.167	1	8	.111
Wm. Paterson	0	6	.000	1	9	.100

ECAC Northwest Championship: Cortland St. 30, Westfield St. 7, on November 23, at Cortland, New York.

NCAA Division III Playoffs (0-1): Rowan (0-1, lost to Brockport St., 15-12, in second round)

NORTH COAST ATHLETIC CONFERENCE

Team	Conference			Full Season		
	W	L	Pct.	W	L	Pct.
Wabash	7	0	1.000	12	1	.923
Wittenberg	6	1	.857	10	2	.833
Wooster	5	2	.714	8	2	.800
Allegheny	4	3	.571	5	5	.500
Earlham	4	3	.571	4	6	.400
Ohio Wesleyan	3	4	.429	5	5	.500
Oberlin	3	4	.429	3	7	.300
Denison	2	5	.286	2	8	.200
Kenyon	1	6	.143	1	9	.100
Hiram	0	7	.000	0	10	.000

NCAA Division III Playoffs (3-2): Wabash (2-1, beat MacMurray, 42-7, in first round; beat Wittenberg, 25-14, in second round; lost to Mount Union, 45-16, in quarterfinals); Wittenberg (1-1, beat Hanover, 34-33, in first round; lost to Wabash, 25-14, in second round)

NORTHWEST CONFERENCE

Team	Conference			Full Season		
	W	L	Pct.	W	L	Pct.
Linfield	5	0	1.000	10	1	.909
Whitworth	3	2	.600	7	3	.700
Willamette	3	2	.600	6	4	.600
Pacific Lutheran	3	2	.600	5	4	.556
Lewis & Clark	1	4	.200	3	6	.333
Puget Sound	0	5	.000	1	8	.111

NCAA Division III Playoffs (1-1): Linfield (1-1, beat Wartburg, 52-15, in second round; lost to St. John's [Minn.], 21-14, in quarterfinals)

OHIO ATHLETIC CONFERENCE

Team	Conference			Full Season		
	W	L	Pct.	W	L	Pct.
Mount Union	9	0	1.000	14	0	1.000
John Carroll	8	1	.889	12	2	.857
Baldwin-Wallace	7	2	.778	8	2	.800
Capital	6	3	.667	6	4	.600
Ohio Northern	5	4	.556	5	5	.500
Muskingum	3	6	.333	3	7	.300
Marietta	2	7	.222	3	7	.300
Wilmington (Ohio) ..	2	7	.222	3	7	.300
Heidelberg	2	7	.222	2	8	.200
Otterbein	1	8	.111	2	8	.200

NCAA Division III Playoffs (7-1): Mount Union (4-0, beat Wheaton [Ill.], 42-21, in second round; beat Wabash, 45-16, in quarterfinals; beat John Carroll, 57-19, in semifinals; beat Trinity [Tex.], 48-7, in championship); John Carroll (3-1, beat Hobart, 27-7, in first round; beat Muhlenberg, 21-10, in second round; beat Brockport St., 16-10 [ot], in quarterfinals; lost to Mount Union, 57-19, in semifinals)

OLD DOMINION ATHLETIC CONFERENCE

Team	Conference			Full Season		
	W	L	Pct.	W	L	Pct.
Bridgewater (Va.)....	6	0	1.000	11	1	.917
Hampden-Sydney ...	5	1	.833	8	2	.800
Randolph-Macon.....	3	3	.500	6	4	.600
Wash. & Lee	3	3	.500	5	5	.500
Catholic	2	4	.333	4	6	.400
Emory & Henry	2	4	.333	4	6	.400
Guilford	0	6	.000	3	7	.300

NCAA Division III Playoffs (1-1): Bridgewater (Va.) (1-1, beat King's [Pa.], 19-17, in second round; lost to Trinity [Tex.], 38-32, in quarterfinals)

PRESIDENTS' ATHLETIC CONFERENCE

Team	Conference			Full Season		
	W	L	Pct.	W	L	Pct.
Wash. & Jeff.	5	0	1.000	9	3	.750
Westminster (Pa.)....	4	1	.800	6	4	.600
Waynesburg	2	3	.400	5	4	.556
Thiel	2	3	.400	3	7	.300
Bethany (W.Va.)	1	4	.200	3	7	.300
Grove City	1	4	.200	3	7	.300

NCAA Division III Playoffs (1-1): Wash. & Jeff. (1-1, beat Chris. Newport, 24-10, in first round; lost to Trinity [Tex.], 45-10, in second round)

SOUTHERN CALIFORNIA INTERCOLLEGIATE ATHLETIC CONFERENCE

Team	Conference			Full Season		
	W	L	Pct.	W	L	Pct.
Redlands	5	0	1.000	7	3	.700
Claremont-M-S	4	1	.800	7	2	.778
Cal Lutheran	3	2	.600	4	5	.444
Occidental	1	4	.200	5	4	.556
La Verne	1	4	.200	3	5	.375
Whittier	1	4	.200	1	8	.111

NCAA Division III Playoffs (0-1): Redlands (0-1, lost to St. John's [Minn.], 31-24, in first round)

SOUTHERN COLLEGIATE ATHLETIC CONFERENCE

Team	Conference			Full Season		
	W	L	Pct.	W	L	Pct.
Trinity (Tex.)	6	0	1.000	14	1	.933
DePauw	5	1	.833	7	3	.700
Sewanee	4	2	.667	5	5	.500
Centre	2	4	.333	6	4	.600
Rose-Hulman	2	4	.333	3	7	.300
Rhodes	1	5	.167	4	6	.400
Millsaps	1	5	.167	3	6	.333

NCAA Division III Playoffs (4-1): Trinity (Tex.) (4-1, beat Mary-Hardin Baylor, 48-38, in first round; beat Wash. & Jeff., 45-10, in second round; beat Bridgewater [Va.], 38-32, in quarterfinals; beat St. John's [Minn.], 41-34, in semifinals; lost to Mount Union, 48-7, in championship)

UNIVERSITY ATHLETIC ASSOCIATION

Team	Conference			Full Season		
	W	L	Pct.	W	L	Pct.
Washington (Mo.)...	4	0	1.000	6	4	.600
Case Reserve	2	2	.500	6	4	.600
Chicago	2	2	.500	4	5	.444
Carnegie Mellon	1	3	.250	5	5	.500
Rochester*	1	3	.250	2	8	.200

*Also member of Upstate Collegiate Athletic Conference.

UPSTATE COLLEGIATE ATHLETIC CONFERENCE

Team	Conference			Full Season		
	W	L	Pct.	W	L	Pct.
Hobart	4	0	1.000	8	2	.800
Union (N.Y.)	3	1	.750	5	5	.500
Rensselaer	2	2	.500	8	2	.800
Rochester*	1	3	.250	2	8	.200
St. Lawrence	0	4	.000	0	10	.000

*Also member of University Athletic Association.

ECAC Northeast Championship: Rensselaer 55, Worcester St. 29, on November 23, at Worcester, Massachusetts.

NCAA Division III Playoffs (0-1): Hobart (0-1, lost to John Carroll, 27-7, in first round)

WISCONSIN INTERCOLLEGIATE ATHLETIC CONFERENCE

Team	Conference			Full Season		
	W	L	Pct.	W	L	Pct.
Wis.-La Crosse	6	1	.857	7	4	.636
Wis.-Eau Claire	5	2	.714	8	2	.800
Wis.-Stout	4	3	.571	7	3	.700
Wis.-Stevens Point...	4	3	.571	6	4	.600
Wis.-Whitewater	4	3	.571	5	5	.500
Wis.-Oshkosh	2	5	.286	4	6	.400
Wis.-River Falls	2	5	.286	3	7	.300
Wis.-Platteville	1	6	.143	2	7	.222

NCAA Division III Playoffs (0-1): Wis.-La Crosse (0-1, lost to Coe, 21-18, in first round)

INDEPENDENTS

Team	Full Season		
	W	L	Pct.
Westminster (Mo.)	7	2	.778
Brockport St.	10	3	.769
Thomas More	7	3	.700
Maranatha Baptist	6	3	.667
Martin Luther	6	3	.667
Principia	5	4	.556
Macalester	5	5	.500

Team	Full Season W	L	Pct.
Menlo	5	5	.500
Pomona-Pitzer	4	4	.500
Rockford	4	6	.400
Chapman	3	7	.300
Mount Ida	2	7	.222
Colorado College	1	8	.111

Team	Full Season W	L	Pct.
Blackburn	1	9	.100
Buffalo St.	1	9	.100
Eastern Ore.	1	9	.100
Gallaudet	0	5	.000
Maryville (Tenn.)	0	10	.000

NCAA Division III Playoffs (2-1): Brockport St. (2-1, beat Springfield, 16-0, in first round; beat Rowan, 15-12, in second round; lost to John Carroll, 16-10 [ot], in quarterfinals)

All-Time Conference Champions

Division I-A

ATLANTIC COAST CONFERENCE

Founded: In 1953 when charter members all left the Southern Conference to form the ACC. **Charter members** (7): Clemson, Duke, Maryland, North Carolina, North Carolina St., South Carolina and Wake Forest. **Admitted later** (3): Virginia (1953), Georgia Tech (1978) and Florida St. (1992). **Withdrew later** (1): South Carolina (1971). **Current members** (9): Clemson, Duke, Florida St., Georgia Tech, Maryland, North Carolina, North Carolina St., Virginia and Wake Forest.

Year	Champion (Record)
1953	Duke (4-0) & Maryland (3-0)
1954	Duke (4-0)
1955	Maryland (4-0) & Duke (4-0)
1956	Clemson (4-0-1)
1957	North Carolina St. (5-0-1)
1958	Clemson (5-1)
1959	Clemson (6-1)
1960	Duke (5-1)
1961	Duke (5-1)
1962	Duke (6-0)
1963	North Carolina (6-1) & North Carolina St. (6-1)
1964	North Carolina St. (5-2)
1965	Clemson (5-2) & North Carolina St. (5-2)
1966	Clemson (6-1)
1967	Clemson (6-0)
1968	North Carolina St. (6-1)
1969	South Carolina (6-0)
1970	Wake Forest (5-1)
1971	North Carolina (6-0)
1972	North Carolina (6-0)
1973	North Carolina St. (6-0)
1974	Maryland (6-0)
1975	Maryland (5-0)
1976	Maryland (5-0)
1977	North Carolina (5-0-1)
1978	Clemson (6-0)
1979	North Carolina St. (5-1)
1980	North Carolina (6-0)
1981	Clemson (6-0)
1982	Clemson (6-0)
1983	Maryland (5-0)
1984	Maryland (5-0)
1985	Maryland (6-0)
1986	Clemson (5-1-1)
1987	Clemson (6-1)
1988	Clemson (6-1)
1989	Virginia (6-1) & Duke (6-1)
1990	Georgia Tech (6-0-1)
1991	Clemson (6-0-1)
1992	Florida St. (8-0)
1993	Florida St. (8-0)
1994	Florida St. (8-0)
1995	Virginia (7-1) & Florida St. (7-1)
1996	Florida St. (8-0)
1997	Florida St. (8-0)
1998	Florida St. (7-1) & Georgia Tech (7-1)
1999	Florida St. (8-0)
2000	Florida St. (8-0)
2001	Maryland (7-1)
2002	Florida St. (7-1)

BIG EAST CONFERENCE

Founded: In 1991 when eight charter members all went from independent status to form the Big East. **Charter members** (8): Boston College, Miami (Fla.), Pittsburgh, Rutgers (football only), Syracuse, Temple (football only), Virginia Tech (football only) and West Virginia (football only). **Current members** (8): Boston College, Miami (Fla.), Pittsburgh, Rutgers (now full conference member), Syracuse, Temple, Virginia Tech (now full conference member) and West Virginia (now full conference member). **Note:** In 1991 and 1992, the team ranked highest in the USA Today/CNN coaches poll was declared champion. Beginning in 1993, the champion was decided by a seven-game round-robin schedule.

Year	Champion (Record)
1991	Miami (Fla.) (2-0, No. 1) & Syracuse (5-0, No. 16)
1992	Miami (Fla.) (4-0, No. 1)
1993	West Virginia (7-0)
1994	Miami (Fla.) (7-0)
1995	Virginia Tech (6-1) & Miami (Fla.) (6-1)
1996	Virginia Tech (6-1), Miami (Fla.) (6-1) & Syracuse (6-1)
1997	Syracuse (6-1)
1998	Syracuse (6-1)
1999	Virginia Tech (7-0)
2000	Miami (Fla.) (7-0)
2001	Miami (Fla.) (7-0)
2002	Miami (Fla.) (7-0)

BIG TEN CONFERENCE

Founded: In 1895 as the Intercollegiate Conference of Faculty Representatives, better known as the Western Conference. **Charter members** (7): Chicago, Illinois, Michigan, Minnesota, Northwestern, Purdue and Wisconsin. **Admitted later** (5): Indiana (1899), Iowa (1899), Ohio St. (1912), Michigan St. (1950) and Penn St. (1993). **Withdrew later** (2): Michigan (1907, rejoined in 1917) and Chicago (1940). **Note:** Iowa belonged to both the Missouri Valley and Western Conferences from 1907 to 1910. Unofficially called the Big Ten from 1912 until after 1939, then Big Nine from 1940 until Michigan St. began conference play in 1953. Formally renamed **Big Ten** in 1984. **Current members** (11): Illinois, Indiana, Iowa, Michigan, Michigan St., Minnesota, Northwestern, Ohio St., Penn St., Purdue and Wisconsin.

Year	Champion (Record)
1896	Wisconsin (2-0-1)
1897	Wisconsin (3-0)
1898	Michigan (3-0)
1899	Chicago (4-0)
1900	Iowa (3-0-1) & Minnesota (3-0-1)
1901	Michigan (4-0) & Wisconsin (2-0)
1902	Michigan (5-0)
1903	Michigan (3-0-1), Minnesota (3-0-1) & Northwestern (1-0-2)
1904	Minnesota (3-0) & Michigan (2-0)
1905	Chicago (7-0)
1906	Wisconsin (3-0), Minnesota (2-0) & Michigan (1-0)
1907	Chicago (4-0)
1908	Chicago (5-0)
1909	Minnesota (3-0)
1910	Illinois (4-0) & Minnesota (2-0)
1911	Minnesota (3-0-1)
1912	Wisconsin (6-0)

Year	Champion (Record)
1913	Chicago (7-0)
1914	Illinois (6-0)
1915	Minnesota (3-0-1) & Illinois (3-0-2)
1916	Ohio St. (4-0)
1917	Ohio St. (4-0)
1918	Illinois (4-0), Michigan (2-0) & Purdue (1-0)
1919	Illinois (6-1)
1920	Ohio St. (5-0)
1921	Iowa (5-0)
1922	Iowa (5-0) & Michigan (4-0)
1923	Illinois (5-0) & Michigan (4-0)
1924	Chicago (3-0-3)
1925	Michigan (5-1)
1926	Michigan (5-0) & Northwestern (5-0)
1927	Illinois (5-0)
1928	Illinois (4-1)
1929	Purdue (5-0)
1930	Michigan (5-0) & Northwestern (5-0)
1931	Purdue (5-1), Michigan (5-1) & Northwestern (5-1)
1932	Michigan (6-0)
1933	Michigan (5-0-1)
1934	Minnesota (5-0)
1935	Minnesota (5-0) & Ohio St. (5-0)
1936	Northwestern (6-0)
1937	Minnesota (5-0)
1938	Minnesota (4-1)
1939	Ohio St. (5-1)
1940	Minnesota (6-0)
1941	Minnesota (5-0)
1942	Ohio St. (5-1)
1943	Purdue (6-0) & Michigan (6-0)
1944	Ohio St. (6-0)
1945	Indiana (5-0-1)
1946	Illinois (6-1)
1947	Michigan (6-0)
1948	Michigan (6-0)
1949	Ohio St. (4-1-1) & Michigan (4-1-1)
1950	Michigan (4-1-1)
1951	Illinois (5-0-1)
1952	Wisconsin (4-1-1) & Purdue (4-1-1)
1953	Michigan St. (5-1) & Illinois (5-1)
1954	Ohio St. (7-0)
1955	Ohio St. (6-0)
1956	Iowa (5-1)
1957	Ohio St. (7-0)
1958	Iowa (5-1)
1959	Wisconsin (5-2)
1960	Minnesota (5-1) & Iowa (5-1)
1961	Ohio St. (6-0)
1962	Wisconsin (6-1)
1963	Illinois (5-1-1)
1964	Michigan (6-1)
1965	Michigan St. (7-0)
1966	Michigan St. (7-0)
1967	Indiana (6-1), Purdue (6-1) & Minnesota (6-1)
1968	Ohio St. (7-0)
1969	Ohio St. (6-1) & Michigan (6-1)
1970	Ohio St. (7-0)
1971	Michigan (8-0)
1972	Ohio St. (8-0) & Michigan (7-1)
1973	Ohio St. (7-0-1) & Michigan (7-0-1)
1974	Ohio St. (7-1) & Michigan (7-1)
1975	Ohio St. (8-0)
1976	Michigan (7-1) & Ohio St. (7-1)
1977	Michigan (7-1) & Ohio St. (7-1)

Year	Champion (Record)
1978	Michigan (7-1) & Michigan St. (7-1)
1979	Ohio St. (8-0)
1980	Michigan (8-0)
1981	Iowa (6-2) & Ohio St. (6-2)
1982	Michigan (8-1)
1983	Illinois (9-0)
1984	Ohio St. (7-2)
1985	Iowa (7-1)
1986	Michigan (7-1) & Ohio St. (7-1)
1987	Michigan St. (7-0-1)
1988	Michigan (7-0-1)
1989	Michigan (8-0)
1990	Iowa (6-2), Michigan (6-2), Michigan St. (6-2) & Illinois (6-2)
1991	Michigan (8-0)
1992	Michigan (6-0-2)
1993	Ohio St. (6-1-1) & Wisconsin (6-1-1)
1994	Penn St. (8-0)
1995	Northwestern (8-0)
1996	Ohio St. (7-1) & Northwestern (7-1)
1997	Michigan (8-0)
1998	Ohio St. (7-1), Wisconsin (7-1) & Michigan (7-1)
1999	Wisconsin (7-1)
2000	Michigan (6-2), Northwestern (6-2) & Purdue (6-2)
2001	Illinois (7-1)
2002	Iowa (8-0) & Ohio St. (8-0)

BIG 12 CONFERENCE

Founded: In 1996 when 12 charter members combined eight members of Big Eight Conference with four former Southwest Conference members. **Charter members (12):** Baylor, Colorado, Iowa St., Kansas, Kansas St., Missouri, Nebraska, Oklahoma, Oklahoma St., Texas, Texas A&M and Texas Tech. **Current members (12):** Baylor, Colorado, Iowa St., Kansas, Kansas St., Missouri, Nebraska, Oklahoma, Oklahoma St., Texas, Texas A&M and Texas Tech.

Year	Champion (Record)
1996	Texas (6-2)
1997	Nebraska (8-0)
1998	Texas A&M (7-1)
1999	Nebraska (7-1)
2000	Oklahoma (8-0)
2001	Colorado (7-1)
2002	Oklahoma (6-2)

In 1996, the Big 12 began a championship game to determine the league's representative in the BCS bowls. Following are the results of the North Division Champion (N) vs. the South Division Champion (S):

1996	Texas (S) 37, Nebraska (N) 27
1997	Nebraska (N) 54, Texas A&M (S) 15
1998	Texas A&M (S) 36, Kansas St. (N) 33 (2 ot)
1999	Nebraska (N) 22, Texas (S) 6
2000	Oklahoma (S) 27, Kansas St. (N) 24
2001	Colorado (N) 39, Texas (S) 37
2002	Oklahoma (S) 29, Colorado (N) 7

CONFERENCE USA

Founded: In 1996 when five charter members went from independent status and one former Southwest Conference member combined to form Conference USA. **Charter members (6):** Cincinnati, Houston, Louisville, Memphis, Southern Miss. and Tulane. **Admitted later (5):** East Caro. (1997), Army (1998), UAB (1999), TCU (2001) and South Fla. (2003). **Current members (11):** UAB, Army, Cincinnati, East Caro., Houston, Louisville, Memphis, South Fla., Southern Miss., TCU and Tulane.

Year	Champion (Record)
1996	Houston (4-1) & Southern Miss. (4-1)
1997	Southern Miss. (6-0)
1998	Tulane (6-0)
1999	Southern Miss. (6-0)
2000	Louisville (6-1)
2001	Louisville (6-1)
2002	Cincinnati (6-2) & TCU (6-2)

MID-AMERICAN ATHLETIC CONFERENCE

Founded: In 1946. **Charter members (6):** Butler, Cincinnati, Miami (Ohio), Ohio, Western Mich. and Western Reserve (now Case Reserve). **Admitted later (12):** Kent St. (1951), Toledo (1951), Bowling Green (1952), Marshall (1954 and 1997), Central Mich. (1972), Eastern Mich. (1972), Ball St. (1973), Northern Ill. (1973 and 1997), Akron (1992) Buffalo (1999) and UCF (2002). **Withdrew later (5):** Butler (1950), Cincinnati (1953), Case Reserve (1955), Marshall (1969) and Northern Ill. (1986). **Current members (14):** Akron, Ball St., Bowling Green, Buffalo, UCF, Central Mich., Eastern Mich., Kent St., Marshall, Miami (Ohio), Northern Ill., Ohio, Toledo and Western Mich.

Year	Champion (Record)
1947	Cincinnati (3-1)
1948	Miami (Ohio) (4-0)
1949	Cincinnati (4-0)
1950	Miami (Ohio) (4-0)
1951	Cincinnati (3-0)
1952	Cincinnati (3-0)
1953	Ohio (5-0-1)
1954	Miami (Ohio) (4-0)
1955	Miami (Ohio) (5-0)
1956	Bowling Green (5-0-1)
1957	Miami (Ohio) (5-0)
1958	Miami (Ohio) (5-0)
1959	Bowling Green (6-0)
1960	Ohio (6-0)
1961	Bowling Green (5-1)
1962	Bowling Green (5-0-1)
1963	Ohio (5-1)
1964	Bowling Green (5-1)
1965	Bowling Green (5-1) & Miami (Ohio) (5-1)
1966	Miami (Ohio) (5-1) & Western Mich. (5-1)
1967	Toledo (5-1) & Ohio (5-1)
1968	Ohio (6-0)
1969	Toledo (5-0)
1970	Toledo (5-0)
1971	Toledo (5-0)
1972	Kent St. (4-1)
1973	Miami (Ohio) (5-0)
1974	Miami (Ohio) (5-0)
1975	Miami (Ohio) (6-0)
1976	Ball St. (4-1)
1977	Miami (Ohio) (5-0)
1978	Ball St. (8-0)
1979	Central Mich. (8-0-1)
1980	Central Mich. (7-2)
1981	Toledo (8-1)
1982	Bowling Green (7-2)
1983	Northern Ill. (8-1)
1984	Toledo (7-1-1)
1985	Bowling Green (9-0)
1986	Miami (Ohio) (6-2)
1987	Eastern Mich. (7-1)
1988	Western Mich. (7-1)
1989	Ball St. (6-1-1)
1990	Central Mich. (7-1)
1991	Bowling Green (8-0)
1992	Bowling Green (8-0)
1993	Ball St. (7-0-1)
1994	Central Mich. (8-1)
1995	Toledo (7-0-1)
1996	Ball St. (7-1)
1997	Marshall (7-1)
1998	Marshall (7-1)
1999	Marshall (8-0)
2000	Marshall (5-3)
2001	Toledo (4-1)
2002	Marshall (7-1)

Since 1997, the MAC has conducted a championship game between the East and West division champion to determine a league champion. Following are the results of the East Division champion (E) vs. the West Division champion (W):

1997	Marshall (E) 34, Toledo (W) 14
1998	Marshall (E) 23, Toledo (W) 17
1999	Marshall (E) 34, Western Mich. (W) 30
2000	Marshall (E) 19, Western Mich. (W) 14
2001	Toledo (W) 41, Marshall (E) 36
2002	Marshall (E) 49, Toledo (W) 45

MOUNTAIN WEST CONFERENCE

Founded: In 1999. **Charter members (8):** Air Force, Brigham Young, Colorado St., UNLV, New Mexico, San Diego St., Utah and Wyoming. All left the Western Athletic Conference after two years of 16-team league. **Current Members (8):** Air Force, Brigham Young, Colorado St., UNLV, New Mexico, San Diego St., Utah and Wyoming.

Year	Champion (Record)
1999	Brigham Young (5-2), Colorado St. (5-2) & Utah (5-2)
2000	Colorado St. (6-1)
2001	Brigham Young (7-0)
2002	Colorado St. (6-1)

PACIFIC-10 CONFERENCE

Founded: In 1915 as the **Pacific Coast Conference** by group of four charter members. **Charter members (4):** California, Oregon, Oregon St. and Washington.

Admitted later (6): Washington St. (1917), Stanford (1918), Idaho (1922), Southern California (1922), Montana (1924) and UCLA (1928). **Withdrew later (2):** Montana (1950) and Idaho (1958).

The Pacific Coast Conference dissolved in 1959 and the Athletic Association of Western Universities was founded with five charter members. **Charter members (5):** California, Southern California, Stanford, UCLA and Washington. **Admitted later (5):** Washington St. (1962), Oregon (1964), Oregon St. (1964), Arizona (1978) and Arizona St. (1978). Conference renamed **Pacific-8** in 1968 and **Pacific-10** in 1978. **Current members (10):** Arizona, Arizona St., California, Oregon, Oregon St., Southern California, Stanford, UCLA, Washington and Washington St.

Year	Champion (Record)
1916	Washington (3-0-1)
1917	Washington (3-0)
1918	California (3-0)
1919	Oregon (2-1) & Washington (2-1)
1920	California (3-0)
1921	California (5-0)
1922	California (3-0)
1923	California (5-0)
1924	Stanford (3-0-1)
1925	Washington (5-0)
1926	Stanford (4-0)
1927	Southern California (4-0-1) & Stanford (4-0-1)
1928	Southern California (4-0-1)
1929	Southern California (6-1)
1930	Washington St. (6-0)
1931	Southern California (7-0)
1932	Southern California (6-0)
1933	Oregon (4-1) & Stanford (4-1)
1934	Stanford (5-0)
1935	California (4-1), Stanford (4-1) & UCLA (4-1)
1936	Washington (6-0-1)
1937	California (6-0-1)
1938	Southern California (6-1) & California (6-1)
1939	Southern California (5-0-2) & UCLA (5-0-3)
1940	Stanford (7-0)
1941	Oregon St. (7-2)
1942	UCLA (6-1)
1943	Southern California (4-0)
1944	Southern California (3-0-2)
1945	Southern California (6-0)
1946	UCLA (7-0)
1947	Southern California (6-0)
1948	California (6-0) & Oregon (6-0)
1949	California (7-0)
1950	California (5-0-1)
1951	Stanford (6-1)
1952	Southern California (6-0)
1953	UCLA (6-1)
1954	UCLA (6-0)
1955	UCLA (6-0)
1956	Oregon St. (6-1-1)
1957	Oregon (6-2) & Oregon St. (6-2)
1958	California (6-1)
1959	Washington (3-1), Southern California (3-1) & UCLA (3-1)
1960	Washington (4-0)
1961	UCLA (3-1)
1962	Southern California (4-0)
1963	Washington (4-1)
1964	Oregon St. (3-1) & Southern California (3-1)
1965	UCLA (4-0)
1966	Southern California (4-1)
1967	Southern California (6-1)
1968	Southern California (6-0)
1969	Southern California (6-0)
1970	Stanford (6-1)
1971	Stanford (6-1)
1972	Southern California (7-0)
1973	Southern California (6-0)
1974	Southern California (6-0-1)
1975	UCLA (6-1) & California (6-1)
1976	Southern California (7-0)
1977	Washington (6-1)
1978	Southern California (6-1)
1979	Southern California (6-0-1)
1980	Washington (6-1)
1981	Washington (6-2)
1982	UCLA (5-1-1)
1983	UCLA (6-1-1)
1984	Southern California (7-1)
1985	UCLA (6-2)
1986	Arizona St. (5-1-1)
1987	Southern California (7-1) & UCLA (7-1)
1988	Southern California (8-0)
1989	Southern California (6-0-1)
1990	Washington (7-1)

Year	Champion (Record)
1991	Washington (8-0)
1992	Stanford (6-2) & Washington (6-2)
1993	UCLA (6-2), Arizona (6-2) & Southern California (6-2)
1994	Oregon (7-1)
1995	Southern California (6-1-1) & Washington (6-1-1)
1996	Arizona St. (8-0)
1997	Washington St. (7-1) & UCLA (7-1)
1998	UCLA (8-0)
1999	Stanford (7-1)
2000	Oregon (7-1), Oregon St. (7-1) & Washington (7-1)
2001	Oregon (7-1)
2002	Southern California (7-1) & Washington St. (7-1)

SOUTHEASTERN CONFERENCE

Founded: In 1933 when charter members all left the **Southern Conference** to become the SEC. **Charter members** (13): Alabama, Auburn, Florida, Georgia, Georgia Tech, Kentucky, LSU, Mississippi, Mississippi St., Sewanee, Tennessee, Tulane and Vanderbilt. **Admitted later** (2): Arkansas (1992) and South Carolina (1992). **Withdrew later** (3): Sewanee (1940), Georgia Tech (1964) and Tulane (1966). **Current members** (12): Alabama, Arkansas, Auburn, Florida, Georgia, Kentucky, LSU, Mississippi, Mississippi St., South Carolina, Tennessee and Vanderbilt.

Year	Champion (Record)
1933	Alabama (5-0-1)
1934	Tulane (8-0) & Alabama (7-0)
1935	LSU (5-0)
1936	LSU (6-0)
1937	Alabama (6-0)
1938	Tennessee (7-0)
1939	Tennessee (6-0), Georgia Tech (6-0) & Tulane (5-0)
1940	Tennessee (5-0)
1941	Mississippi St. (4-0-1)
1942	Georgia (6-1)
1943	Georgia Tech (4-0)
1944	Georgia Tech (4-0)
1945	Alabama (6-0)
1946	Georgia (5-0) & Tennessee (5-0)
1947	Mississippi (6-1)
1948	Georgia (6-0)
1949	Tulane (5-1)
1950	Kentucky (5-1)
1951	Georgia Tech (7-0) & Tennessee (5-0)
1952	Georgia (6-0)
1953	Alabama (4-0-3)
1954	Mississippi (5-1)
1955	Mississippi (5-1)
1956	Tennessee (6-0)
1957	Auburn (7-0)
1958	LSU (6-0)
1959	Georgia (7-0)
1960	Mississippi (5-0-1)
1961	Alabama (7-0) & LSU (6-0)
1962	Mississippi (6-0)
1963	Mississippi (5-0-1)
1964	Alabama (8-0)
1965	Alabama (6-1-1)
1966	Alabama (6-0) & Georgia (6-0)
1967	Tennessee (6-0)
1968	Georgia (5-0-1)
1969	Tennessee (5-1)
1970	LSU (5-0)
1971	Alabama (7-0)
1972	Alabama (7-1)
1973	Alabama (8-0)
1974	Alabama (6-0)
1975	Alabama (6-0)
1976	Georgia (5-1) & Kentucky (5-1)
1977	Alabama (7-0) & Kentucky (6-0)
1978	Alabama (6-0)
1979	Alabama (6-0)
1980	Georgia (6-0)
1981	Georgia (6-0) & Alabama (6-0)
1982	Georgia (6-0)
1983	Auburn (6-0)
1984	Florida (5-0-1)#
1985	Tennessee (5-1)*
1986	LSU (5-1)
1987	Auburn (5-0-1)
1988	Auburn (6-1) & LSU (6-1)
1989	Alabama (6-1), Tennessee (6-1) & Auburn (6-1)
1990	Tennessee (5-1-1)*
1991	Florida (7-0)
1992	Alabama (8-0)
1993	Florida (7-1)*
1994	Florida (7-1)

Year	Champion (Record)
1995	Florida (8-0)
1996	Florida (8-0)
1997	Tennessee (7-1)
1998	Tennessee (8-0)
1999	Florida (7-1) & Alabama (7-1)
2000	Florida (7-1)
2001	LSU (6-3)
2002	Georgia (7-1)

#Title vacated. *Ineligible for title (probation): Florida (5-1) in 1985, Florida (6-1) in 1990 and Auburn (8-0) in 1993.

Since 1992, the SEC has conducted a championship game to determine the league's representative in the BCS bowls. Following are the results year-by-year of the Western Division champion (W) vs. the Eastern Division champion (E):

1992	Alabama (W) 28, Florida (E) 21
1993	Florida (E) 28, Alabama (W) 13
1994	Florida (E) 24, Alabama (W) 23
1995	Florida (E) 34, Arkansas (W) 3
1996	Florida (E) 45, Alabama (W) 30
1997	Tennessee (E) 30, Auburn (W) 29
1998	Tennessee (E) 24, Mississippi St. (W) 14
1999	Alabama (W) 34, Florida (E) 7
2000	Florida (E) 28, Auburn (W) 6
2001	LSU (W) 31, Tennessee (E) 20
2002	Georgia (E) 30, Arkansas (W) 3

SUN BELT CONFERENCE

Founded: In 2001 when four former members of the Big West Conference combined with three former Division I-A independents. **Charter members (7):** Arkansas St. (from Big West), Idaho (from Big West), La.-Lafayette (independent), La.-Monroe (independent), Middle Tenn. (independent), New Mexico St. (from Big West), North Texas (from Big West). **Admitted later (1):** Utah St. (from independent, 2003). **Current members (8):** Arkansas St., Idaho, La.-Lafayette, La.-Monroe, Middle Tenn., New Mexico St., North Texas and Utah St.

Year	Champion (Record)
2001	North Texas (5-1) & Middle Tenn. (5-1)
2002	North Texas (6-0)

WESTERN ATHLETIC CONFERENCE

Founded: In 1962 when charter members left the Skyline and Border Conferences to form the WAC. In 1996, three former Southwest Conference members joined two former Big West members and one former independent team to form a 16-team league, the largest conference alignment ever in Division I-A. The league was divided into Mountain and Pacific divisions. In 1999, eight members split off to form the Mountain West Conference. **Charter members** (6): Arizona (from Border), Arizona St. (from Border), Brigham Young (from Skyline), New Mexico (from Skyline), Utah (from Skyline) and Wyoming (from Skyline). **Admitted later** (15): Colorado St. (1968), UTEP (1968), San Diego St. (1978), Hawaii (1979), Air Force (1980), Fresno St. (1992), UNLV (1996), Rice (1996), San Jose St. (1996), Southern Methodist (1996), TCU (1996), Tulsa (1996), Nevada (2000), Boise St. (2001) and Louisiana Tech (2001). **Withdrew later** (11): Arizona (1978), Arizona St. (1978), Air Force (1999), Brigham Young (1999), Colorado St. (1999), UNLV (1999), New Mexico (1999), San Diego St. (1999), Utah (1999), Wyoming (1999) and TCU (2000). **Current members** (10): Boise St., Fresno St., Hawaii, Louisiana Tech, Nevada, Rice, San Jose St., Southern Methodist, UTEP and Tulsa.

Year	Champion (Record)
1962	New Mexico (2-1-1)
1963	New Mexico (3-1)
1964	Arizona (3-1), Utah (3-1) & New Mexico (3-1)
1965	Brigham Young (4-1)
1966	Wyoming (5-0)
1967	Wyoming (5-0)
1968	Wyoming (6-1)
1969	Arizona St. (6-1)
1970	Arizona St. (7-0)
1971	Arizona St. (7-0)
1972	Arizona St. (5-1)
1973	Arizona (6-1) & Arizona St. (6-1)
1974	Brigham Young (6-0-1)
1975	Arizona St. (7-0)
1976	Brigham Young (6-1) & Wyoming (6-1)
1977	Arizona St. (6-1) & Brigham Young (6-1)
1978	Brigham Young (5-1)

Year	Champion (Record)
1979	Brigham Young (7-0)
1980	Brigham Young (6-1)
1981	Brigham Young (7-1)
1982	Brigham Young (7-0)
1983	Brigham Young (7-0)
1984	Brigham Young (8-0)
1985	Air Force (7-1) & Brigham Young (7-1)
1986	San Diego St. (7-1)
1987	Wyoming (8-0)
1988	Wyoming (8-0)
1989	Brigham Young (7-1)
1990	Brigham Young (7-1)
1991	Brigham Young (7-0-1)
1992	Hawaii (6-2), Fresno St. (6-2) & Brigham Young (6-2)
1993	Wyoming (6-2), Fresno St. (6-2) & Brigham Young (6-2)
1994	Colorado St. (7-1)
1995	Colorado St. (6-2), Air Force (6-2), Utah (6-2) & Brigham Young (6-2)
1996	Brigham Young (8-0)
1997	Colorado St. (7-1)
1998	Air Force (7-1)
1999	Fresno St. (5-2), Hawaii (5-2) & TCU (5-2)
2000	TCU (7-1) & UTEP (7-1)
2001	Louisiana Tech (7-1)
2002	Boise St. (8-0)

From 1996-98, the WAC conducted a championship game to determine the league's representative in the BCS bowls. Following are the results of the Mountain Division Champion (M) vs. the Pacific Division Champion (P):

1996	Brigham Young (M) 28, Wyoming (P) 25
1997	Colorado St. (P) 41, New Mexico (M) 13
1998	Air Force (M) 20, Brigham Young (P) 13

Division I-AA

ATLANTIC 10 CONFERENCE

Founded: In 1947 as the Yankee Conference by six institutions from the old New England College Conference. **Charter members** (6): Connecticut, Maine, Massachusetts, New Hampshire, Rhode Island and Vermont. **Admitted later** (9): Boston U. (1971), Holy Cross (1971), Delaware (1983), Richmond (1984), Villanova (1985), James Madison (1993), Northeastern (1993) William & Mary (1993) and Hofstra (2001). **Withdrew later** (4): Holy Cross (1972), Vermont (1974, dropped football), Boston U. (1997, dropped football) and Connecticut (2000). **Current members** (11): Delaware, Hofstra, James Madison, Maine, Massachusetts, New Hampshire, Northeastern, Rhode Island, Richmond, Villanova and William & Mary.

Year	Champion (Record)
1947	New Hampshire (4-0)
1948	New Hampshire (3-1)
1949	Connecticut (2-0-1) & Maine (2-0-1)
1950	New Hampshire (4-0)
1951	Maine (3-0-1)
1952	Connecticut (3-1), Maine (3-1) & Rhode Island (3-1)
1953	New Hampshire (3-1) & Rhode Island (3-1)
1954	New Hampshire (4-0)
1955	Rhode Island (4-0-1)
1956	Connecticut (3-0-1)
1957	Connecticut (3-0-1) & Rhode Island (3-0-1)
1958	Connecticut (4-0)
1959	Connecticut (4-0)
1960	Connecticut (3-1)
1961	Maine (5-0)
1962	New Hampshire (4-0-1)
1963	Massachusetts (5-0)
1964	Massachusetts (5-0)
1965	Maine (5-0)
1966	Massachusetts (5-0)
1967	Massachusetts (5-0)
1968	Connecticut (4-1) & New Hampshire (4-1)
1969	Massachusetts (5-0)
1970	Connecticut (4-0-1)
1971	Connecticut (3-1-1) & Massachusetts (3-1-1)
1972	Massachusetts (5-0)
1973	Connecticut (5-0-1)
1974	Maine (4-2) & Massachusetts (4-2)
1975	New Hampshire (5-0)
1976	New Hampshire (4-1)
1977	Massachusetts (5-0)
1978	Massachusetts (5-0)*
1979	Massachusetts (4-1)

Year	Champion (Record)
1980	Boston U. (5-0)
1981	Rhode Island (4-1) & Massachusetts (4-1)
1982	Boston U. (3-2)*, Connecticut (3-2), Maine (3-2) and Massachusetts (3-2)
1983	Boston U. (4-1)* & Connecticut (4-1)
1984	Boston U. (4-1)* & Rhode Island (4-1)*
1985	Rhode Island (5-0)*
1986	Connecticut (5-2), Delaware (5-2)* & Massachusetts (5-2)
1987	Maine (6-1)* & Richmond (6-1)*
1988	Delaware (6-2)* & Massachusetts (6-2)*
1989	Connecticut (6-2), Maine (6-2)* & Villanova (6-2)*
1990	Massachusetts (7-1)*
1991	Delaware (7-1)* & Villanova (7-1)*
1992	Delaware (7-1)*
1993	Boston U. (9-0)*
1994	New Hampshire (8-0)*
1995	Delaware (8-0)*
1996	William & Mary (7-1)*
1997	Villanova (8-0)*
1998	Richmond (7-1)*
1999	James Madison (7-1)* & Massachusetts (7-1)*
2000	Delaware (7-1)* & Richmond (7-1)*
2001	Hofstra (7-2)*, Maine (7-2)*, Villanova (7-2) & William & Mary (7-2)*
2002	Maine (7-2)* & Northeastern (7-2)*

*Participated in NCAA Division I-AA Championship.

BIG SKY CONFERENCE

Founded: In 1963 when six charter members—Gonzaga, Idaho, Idaho St., Montana, Montana St. and Weber St.—banded together to form the Big Sky. **Admitted later** (7): Boise St. (1970), Northern Ariz. (1970), Nevada (1979, replacing charter member Gonzaga), Eastern Wash. (1987), Cal St. Northridge (1996), Sacramento St. (1996) and Portland St. (1996). **Withdrew later** (5): Gonzaga (1979), Nevada (1992), Boise St. (1996) Idaho (1996) and Cal St. Northridge (2001). **Current members** (8): Eastern Wash., Idaho St., Montana, Montana St., Northern Ariz., Portland St., Sacramento St. and Weber St.

Year	Champion (Record)
1963	Idaho St. (3-1)
1964	Montana St. (3-0)
1965	Idaho (3-1) & Weber St. (3-1)
1966	Montana St. (4-0)
1967	Montana St. (4-0)
1968	Idaho (3-1), Montana St. (3-1) & Weber St. (3-1)
1969	Montana (4-0)#
1970	Montana (5-0)
1971	Idaho (4-1)
1972	Montana St. (5-1)
1973	Boise St. (6-0)#
1974	Boise St. (6-0)#
1975	Boise St. (5-0-1)#
1976	Montana St. (6-0)#
1977	Boise St. (6-0)
1978	Northern Ariz. (6-0)
1979	Montana St. (6-1)
1980	Boise St. (6-1)
1981	Idaho St. (6-1)*
1982	Montana (5-2)*
1983	Nevada (6-1)*
1984	Montana St. (6-1)*
1985	Idaho (6-1)*
1986	Nevada (7-0)*
1987	Idaho (7-1)*
1988	Idaho (7-1)*
1989	Idaho (8-0)*
1990	Nevada (7-1)*
1991	Nevada (8-0)*
1992	Eastern Wash. (6-1)* & Idaho (6-1)*
1993	Montana (7-0)*
1994	Boise St. (6-1)*
1995	Montana (6-1)*
1996	Montana (7-0)*
1997	Eastern Wash. (7-1)*
1998	Montana (6-2)*
1999	Montana (7-1)*
2000	Montana (8-0)*
2001	Montana (7-0)*
2002	Idaho St. (5-2), Montana (5-2)* & Montana St. (5-2)*

#Participated in NCAA Division II Championship.
*Participated in NCAA Division I-AA Championship.

BIG SOUTH CONFERENCE

Founded: In 1983 as an all-sports conference. Football was added as the conference's 18th championship sport in 2002. Three former Division I-AA independents and one school moving from Division II joined to play football. **Charter members** (4): Charleston So., Elon, Gardner-Webb (from Division II) and Liberty. **Admitted later (2):** Coastal Caro. (restarted program, 2003) and VMI (from Southern Conference, 2003). **Current members** (6): Charleston So., Coastal Caro., Elon, Gardner-Webb, Liberty and VMI.

Year	Champion (Record)
2002	Gardner-Webb (3-0)

GATEWAY FOOTBALL CONFERENCE

Founded: In 1982 as a women's athletics organization by 10 Midwestern universities. Six members started as a football conference in 1985. **Charter members** (6): (Football) Eastern Ill., Illinois St., Northern Iowa, Southern Ill., Southwest Mo. St. and Western Ill. Four members—Eastern Ill., Northern Iowa, Southwest Mo. St. and Western Ill.—were members of the Mid-Continent Conference for football. **Admitted later** (3): Indiana St. (1986), Youngstown St. (1997) and Western Ky. (2001). **Withdrew later** (1): Eastern Ill. (1996). **Current members** (8): Illinois St., Indiana St., Northern Iowa, Southern Ill., Southwest Mo. St., Western Ill., Western Ky. and Youngstown St.

Year	Champion (Record)
1985	Northern Iowa (5-0)*
1986	Eastern Ill. (5-1)*
1987	Northern Iowa (6-0)*
1988	Western Ill. (6-0)*
1989	Southwest Mo. St. (5-1)*
1990	Northern Iowa (5-1)*
1991	Northern Iowa (5-1)*
1992	Northern Iowa (5-1)*
1993	Northern Iowa (5-1)*
1994	Northern Iowa (6-0)*
1995	Eastern Ill. (5-1)* & Northern Iowa (5-1)*
1996	Northern Iowa (5-0)*
1997	Western Ill. (6-0)*
1998	Western Ill. (5-1)*
1999	Illinois St. (6-0)*
2000	Western Ill. (5-1)*
2001	Northern Iowa (6-1)*
2002	Western Ill. (6-1)* & Western Ky. (6-1)*

*Participated in NCAA Division I-AA Championship.

IVY GROUP

Founded: In 1956 by a group of eight charter members. **Charter members** (8): Brown, Columbia, Cornell, Dartmouth, Harvard, Pennsylvania, Princeton and Yale. **Current members** (8): Brown, Columbia, Cornell, Dartmouth, Harvard, Pennsylvania, Princeton and Yale.

Year	Champion (Record)
1956	Yale (7-0)
1957	Princeton (6-1)
1958	Dartmouth (6-1)
1959	Pennsylvania (6-1)
1960	Yale (7-0)
1961	Columbia (6-1) & Harvard (6-1)
1962	Dartmouth (7-0)
1963	Dartmouth (5-2) & Princeton (5-2)
1964	Princeton (7-0)
1965	Dartmouth (7-0)
1966	Dartmouth (6-1), Harvard (6-1) & Princeton (6-1)
1967	Yale (7-0)
1968	Harvard (6-0-1) & Yale (6-0-1)
1969	Dartmouth (6-1), Yale (6-1) & Princeton (6-1)
1970	Dartmouth (7-0)
1971	Cornell (6-1) & Dartmouth (6-1)
1972	Dartmouth (5-1-1)
1973	Dartmouth (6-1)
1974	Harvard (6-1) & Yale (6-1)
1975	Harvard (6-1)
1976	Brown (6-1) & Yale (6-1)
1977	Yale (6-1)
1978	Dartmouth (6-1)
1979	Yale (6-1)
1980	Yale (6-1)
1981	Yale (6-1) & Dartmouth (6-1)
1982	Harvard (5-2), Pennsylvania (5-2) & Dartmouth (5-2)
1983	Harvard (5-1-1) & Pennsylvania (5-1-1)

Year	Champion (Record)
1984	Pennsylvania (7-0)
1985	Pennsylvania (6-1)
1986	Pennsylvania (7-0)
1987	Harvard (6-1)
1988	Pennsylvania (6-1) & Cornell (6-1)
1989	Princeton (6-1) & Yale (6-1)
1990	Cornell (6-1) & Dartmouth (6-1)
1991	Dartmouth (6-0-1)
1992	Dartmouth (6-1) & Princeton (6-1)
1993	Pennsylvania (7-0)
1994	Pennsylvania (7-0)
1995	Princeton (5-1-1)
1996	Dartmouth (7-0)
1997	Harvard (7-0)
1998	Pennsylvania (6-1)
1999	Brown (6-1) & Yale (6-1)
2000	Pennsylvania (6-1)
2001	Harvard (7-0)
2002	Pennsylvania (7-0)

METRO ATLANTIC ATHLETIC CONFERENCE

Founded: In 1980 by six charter members — Army, Fairfield, Fordham, Iona, Manhattan and St. Peter's. Competition followed one year in men's cross country and men's soccer. Canisius and Siena both joined the conference in 1989. Football was added in 1993, with Georgetown and St. John's (N.Y.) as associate members of the conference. **Charter members (6):** Canisius, Georgetown, Iona, St. John's (N.Y.), St. Peter's and Siena. **Admitted later (4):** Duquesne (as associate member in 1994), Marist (1994), Fairfield (1996) and La Salle (as associate member in 1999). **Withdrew later (2):** St. John's (N.Y.) (1998) and Georgetown (1999). **Readmitted (1):** St. John's (N.Y.) (2002). **Current members (9):** Canisius, Duquesne, Fairfield, Iona, La Salle, Marist, St. John's (N.Y.), St. Peter's and Siena.

Year	Champion (Record)
1993	Iona (5-0)
1994	Marist (6-1) & St. John's (N.Y.) (6-1)
1995	Duquesne (7-0)
1996	Duquesne (8-0)
1997	Georgetown (7-0)
1998	Fairfield (6-1) & Georgetown (6-1)
1999	Duquesne (7-0)
2000	Duquesne (7-0)
2001	Duquesne (6-0)
2002	Duquesne (8-0)

MID-EASTERN ATHLETIC CONFERENCE

Founded: In 1970 with first playing season in 1971 by six charter members. **Charter members** (6): Delaware St., Howard, Morgan St., N.C. A&T and South Carolina St. **Admitted later** (5): Bethune-Cookman (1979), Florida A&M (1979), Hampton (1996), Norfolk St. (1997) and Savannah St. (2001). **Withdrew later** (3): Morgan St. (1979), N.C. Central (1979) and Florida A&M (1984). **Readmitted** (2): Morgan St. (1984) and Florida A&M (1986). **Current members** (10): Bethune-Cookman, Delaware St., Florida A&M, Hampton, Howard, Morgan St., Norfolk St., N.C. A&T, Savannah St. and South Carolina St.

Year	Champion (Record)
1971	Morgan St. (5-0-1)
1972	N.C. Central (5-1)
1973	N.C. Central (5-1)
1974	South Carolina St. (5-1)
1975	South Carolina St. (5-1)
1976	South Carolina St. (5-1)
1977	South Carolina St. (6-0)
1978	South Carolina St. (5-0-1)
1979	Morgan St. (5-0)#
1980	South Carolina St. (5-0)
1981	South Carolina St. (5-0)*
1982	South Carolina St. (4-1)*
1983	South Carolina St. (5-0)
1984	Bethune-Cookman (4-0)
1985	Delaware St. (4-0)
1986	N.C. A&T (4-1)*
1987	Howard (5-0)
1988	Bethune-Cookman (4-2), Florida A&M (4-2) & Delaware St. (4-2)
1989	Delaware St. (5-1)

Year	Champion (Record)
1990	Florida A&M (6-0)
1991	N.C. A&T (5-1)√
1992	N.C. A&T (5-1)*
1993	Howard (6-0)*
1994	South Carolina St. (6-0)√
1995	Florida A&M (6-0)√
1996	Florida A&M (7-0)*
1997	Hampton (7-0)*
1998	Florida A&M (7-1)* & Hampton (7-1)*
1999	N.C. A&T (8-0)*
2000	Florida A&M (7-1)*
2001	Florida A&M (7-1)*
2002	Bethune-Cookman (7-1)*

#*Participated in NCAA Division II Championship.*
**Participated in NCAA Division I-AA Championship.*
√*Participated in Division I-AA Heritage Bowl.*

NORTHEAST CONFERENCE

Founded: In 1996 when five charter members all went from independent status to form the Northeast Conference. **Charter members** (5): Central Conn. St., Monmouth, Robert Morris, St. Francis (Pa.) and Wagner. **Admitted later** (4): Sacred Heart (1998), Albany (N.Y.) (1999), Stony Brook (1999) and St. John's (N.Y.) (2000). **Withdrew later (1):** St. John's (N.Y.) (2002). **Current members** (8): Albany (N.Y.), Central Conn. St., Monmouth, Robert Morris, Sacred Heart, St. Francis (Pa.), Stony Brook and Wagner.

Year	Champion (Record)
1996	Robert Morris (3-1) & Monmouth (3-1)
1997	Robert Morris (4-0)
1998	Monmouth (4-1) & Robert Morris (4-1)
1999	Robert Morris (7-0)
2000	Robert Morris (8-0)
2001	Sacred Heart (8-0)
2002	Albany (N.Y.) (6-1)

OHIO VALLEY CONFERENCE

Founded: In 1948 by six charter members, five of which withdrew from the Kentucky Intercollegiate Athletic Conference (Eastern Ky., Louisville, Morehead St., Murray St. and Western Ky.), plus Evansville. **Charter members** (6): Eastern Ky., Evansville, Louisville, Morehead St., Murray St. and Western Ky. **Admitted later** (11): Marshall (1949), Tennessee Tech (1949), Middle Tenn. (1952), East Tenn. St (1957), Austin Peay (1962), Akron (1979), Youngstown St. (1980), Tennessee St. (1988), Southeast Mo. St. (1991), Tenn.-Martin (1992) and Eastern Ill. (1996). **Readmitted** (1): Western Ky. (1999). **Withdrew later** (10): Louisville (1949), Evansville (1952), Marshall (1952), East Tenn. St. (1979), Western Ky. (1982), Akron (1987), Youngstown St. (1988), Morehead St. (1996), Austin Peay (1997), Middle Tenn. (1998) and Western Ky. (2000). **Current members** (7): Eastern Ill., Eastern Ky., Murray St., Southeast Mo. St., Tenn.-Martin, Tennessee St. and Tennessee Tech.

Team	Champion (Record)
1948	Murray St. (3-1)
1949	Evansville (3-1)
1950	Murray St. (5-0-1)
1951	Murray St. (5-0-1)
1952	Tennessee St. (4-1) & Western Ky. (4-1)
1953	Tennessee Tech (5-0)
1954	Eastern Ky. (5-0)
1955	Tennessee Tech (5-0)
1956	Middle Tenn. (5-0)
1957	Middle Tenn. (5-0)
1958	Middle Tenn. (5-1) & Tennessee Tech (5-1)
1959	Middle Tenn. (5-0-1) & Tennessee Tech (5-0-1)
1960	Tennessee Tech (6-0)
1961	Tennessee Tech (6-0)
1962	East Tenn. St. (4-2)
1963	Western Ky. (7-0)
1964	Middle Tenn. (6-1)#
1965	Middle Tenn. (7-0)
1966	Morehead St. (6-1)
1967	Eastern Ky. (5-0-2)#
1968	Eastern Ky. (7-0)
1969	East Tenn. St. (6-0-1)#
1970	Western Ky. (5-1-1)
1971	Western Ky. (5-2)
1972	Tennessee Tech (7-0)#
1973	Western Ky. (7-0)#
1974	Eastern Ky. (5-1)
1975	Tennessee Tech (6-1) & Western Ky. (6-1)#
1976	Eastern Ky. (6-1)#
1977	Austin Peay (6-1)
1978	Western Ky. (6-0)

Team	Champion (Record)
1979	Murray St. (6-0)*
1980	Western Ky. (6-1)
1981	Eastern Ky. (8-0)*
1982	Eastern Ky. (7-0)*
1983	Eastern Ky. (6-1)*
1984	Eastern Ky. (6-1)*
1985	Middle Tenn. (7-0)*
1986	Murray St. (5-2)
1987	Eastern Ky. (5-1)* & Youngstown St. (5-1)
1988	Eastern Ky. (6-0)*
1989	Middle Tenn. (6-0)*
1990	Eastern Ky. (5-1)* & Middle Tenn. (5-1)*
1991	Eastern Ky. (7-0)*
1992	Middle Tenn. (8-0)*
1993	Eastern Ky. (8-0)*
1994	Eastern Ky. (8-0)*
1995	Murray St. (8-0)*
1996	Murray St. (8-0)*
1997	Eastern Ky. (7-0)*
1998	Tennessee St. (6-1)*
1999	Tennessee St. (7-0)*
2000	Western Ky. (7-0)*
2001	Eastern Ill. (6-0)*
2002	Eastern Ill. (5-1)* & Murray St. (5-1)*

#*Participated in NCAA Division II Championship.*
**Participated in NCAA Division I-AA Championship.*

PATRIOT LEAGUE

Founded: In 1984 originally as the Colonial League with six charter members. **Charter members** (6): Bucknell, Colgate, Davidson, Holy Cross, Lafayette and Lehigh. **Admitted later** (3): Fordham (1990), Towson (1997) and Georgetown (2001). **Withdrew later** (1): Davidson (1989). **Current members** (8): Bucknell, Colgate, Fordham, Georgetown, Holy Cross, Lafayette, Lehigh and Towson.

Year	Champion (Record)
1986	Holy Cross (4-0)
1987	Holy Cross (4-0)
1988	Lafayette (5-0)
1989	Holy Cross (4-0)
1990	Holy Cross (5-0)
1991	Holy Cross (5-0)
1992	Lafayette (5-0)
1993	Lehigh (4-1)
1994	Lafayette (5-0)
1995	Lehigh (5-0)
1996	Bucknell (4-1)
1997	Colgate (6-0)*
1998	Lehigh (6-0)*
1999	Colgate (5-1)* & Lehigh (5-1)*
2000	Lehigh (6-0)*
2001	Lehigh (7-0)*
2002	Colgate (6-1) & Fordham (6-1)*

**Participated in NCAA Division I-AA Championship.*

PIONEER FOOTBALL LEAGUE

Founded: Started in 1993 with Division I-AA charter members Butler, Dayton, Drake, Evansville, San Diego and Valparaiso. **Admitted later** (4): Austin Peay (2001), Davidson (2001), Jacksonville (2001) and Morehead St. (2001). **Withdrew later** (1): Evansville (1997, dropped football). **Current members** (9): Austin Peay, Butler, Davidson, Dayton, Drake, Jacksonville, Morehead St., San Diego and Valparaiso.

Year	Champion (Record)
1993	Dayton (5-0)
1994	Butler (4-1) & Dayton (4-1)
1995	Drake (5-0)
1996	Dayton (5-0)
1997	Dayton (5-0)
1998	Drake (4-0)
1999	Dayton (4-0)
2000	Dayton (3-1), Drake (3-1) & Valparaiso (3-1)
2001	Dayton (4-0)
2002	Dayton (4-0)

Since 2001, the PDL has conducted a championship game between the North and South division champion to determine a league champion. Following are the results of the North Division champion (N) vs. the South Division champion (S):
2001 Dayton (N) 46, Jacksonville (S) 14
2002 Dayton (N) 28, Morehead St. (S) 0

SOUTHERN CONFERENCE

Founded: In 1921 by 14 institutions to form the Southern Intercollegiate Conference. Roots for the conference can actually be traced back to 1894 when several football-playing schools formed a confederation known as the Southeastern Intercollegiate Athletic Association. **Charter members** (14): Alabama, Auburn, Clemson, Georgia, Georgia Tech, Kentucky, Maryland, Mississippi St., North Carolina, North Carolina St., Tennessee, Virginia, Virginia Tech and Wash. & Lee. **Admitted later** (17): Florida (1922), LSU (1922), Mississippi (1922), South Carolina (1922), Tulane (1922), Vanderbilt (1922), VMI (1924), Citadel (1936), Furman (1936), West Virginia (1951), Appalachian St. (1971), Marshall (1976), Chattanooga (1976), Western Caro. (1976), East Tenn. St. (1978), Ga. Southern (1992) and Wofford (1997). **Withdrew later:** Since 1922, membership has changed drastically, with a total of 39 schools having been affiliated with the league, including 11 of the 12 schools currently comprising the Southeastern Conference and eight of the nine schools currently comprising the Atlantic Coast Conference. **Current members** (8): Appalachian St., Chattanooga, Citadel, East Tenn. St., Furman, Ga. Southern, Western Caro. and Wofford.

Year	Champion (Record√)
1922	Georgia Tech
1923	Vanderbilt
1924	Alabama
1925	Alabama
1926	Alabama
1927	Georgia Tech
1928	Georgia Tech
1929	Tulane
1930	Alabama & Tulane
1931	Tulane
1932	Auburn & Tennessee
1933	Duke (4-0)
1934	Wash. & Lee (4-0)
1935	Duke (5-0)
1936	Duke (7-0)
1937	Maryland (2-0)
1938	Duke (5-0)
1939	Clemson (4-0)
1940	Clemson (4-0)
1941	Duke (5-0)
1942	William & Mary (4-0)
1943	Duke (4-0)
1944	Duke (4-0)
1945	Duke (4-0)
1946	North Carolina (4-0-1)
1947	William & Mary (7-1)
1948	Clemson (5-0)
1949	North Carolina (5-0)
1950	Wash. & Lee (6-0)
1951	Maryland (5-0) & VMI (5-0)
1952	Duke (5-0)
1953	West Virginia (4-0)
1954	West Virginia (3-0)
1955	West Virginia (4-0)
1956	West Virginia (5-0)
1957	VMI (6-0)
1958	West Virginia (4-0)
1959	VMI (6-0-1)
1960	VMI (4-1)
1961	Citadel (5-1)
1962	VMI (6-0)
1963	Virginia Tech (5-0)
1964	West Virginia (5-0)
1965	West Virginia (4-0)
1966	East Caro. (4-1-1) & William & Mary (4-1-1)
1967	West Virginia (4-0-1)
1968	Richmond (6-0)
1969	Davidson (5-1) & Richmond (5-1)
1970	William & Mary (3-1)
1971	Richmond (5-1)
1972	East Caro. (7-0)
1973	East Caro. (7-0)
1974	VMI (5-1)
1975	Richmond (5-1)
1976	East Caro. (4-1)
1977	Chattanooga (4-1) & VMI (4-1)
1978	Chattanooga (4-1) & Furman (4-1)
1979	Chattanooga (5-1)
1980	Furman (7-0)
1981	Furman (5-2)
1982	Furman (6-1)*
1983	Furman (6-0-1)*
1984	Chattanooga (5-1)*
1985	Furman (6-0)*
1986	Appalachian St. (6-0-1)*
1987	Appalachian St. (6-0)*
1988	Furman (6-1)* & Marshall (6-1)*
1989	Furman (7-0)*
1990	Furman (6-1)*
1991	Appalachian St. (6-1)*

Year	Champion (Record√)
1992	Citadel (6-1)*
1993	Ga. Southern (7-1)*
1994	Marshall (7-1)*
1995	Appalachian St. (8-0)*
1996	Marshall (8-0)*
1997	Ga. Southern (7-1)*
1998	Ga. Southern (8-0)*
1999	Appalachian St. (7-1)*, Furman (7-1)* & Ga. Southern (7-1)*
2000	Ga. Southern (7-1)*
2001	Furman (7-1)* & Ga. Southern (7-1)*
2002	Ga. Southern (7-1)*

Participated in NCAA Division I-AA Championship. √No records available until 1933.

SOUTHLAND CONFERENCE

Founded: In 1963 by a group of five institutions. **Charter members** (5): Abilene Christian, Arkansas St., Lamar, Texas-Arlington and Trinity (Tex.). **Admitted later** (12): La.-Lafayette (1971), Louisiana Tech (1971), La.-Monroe (1972), McNeese St. (1972), North Texas (1982), Northwestern St. (1987), Sam Houston St. (1987), Southwest Tex. St. (1987), Stephen F. Austin (1987), Nicholls St. (1992), Jacksonville St. (1996) and Troy St. (1996). **Withdrew later** (10): Trinity (Tex.) (1972), Abilene Christian (1973), La.-Lafayette (1982), Texas-Arlington (1986, dropped football), Arkansas St. (1987), Lamar (1987), Louisiana Tech (1987), North Texas (1995), La.-Monroe (1996) and Troy St. (2000). **Current members** (7): Jacksonville St., McNeese St., Nicholls St., Northwestern St., Sam Houston St., Southwest Tex. St. and Stephen F. Austin.

Year	Champion (Record)
1964	Lamar (3-0-1)
1965	Lamar (3-1)
1966	Texas-Arlington (3-1)
1967	Texas-Arlington (4-0)
1968	Arkansas St. (3-0-1)
1969	Arkansas St. (4-0)
1970	Arkansas St. (4-0)
1971	Louisiana Tech (4-1)
1972	Louisiana Tech (5-0)
1973	Louisiana Tech (5-0)
1974	Louisiana Tech (5-0)
1975	Arkansas St. (5-0)
1976	La.-Lafayette (4-1) & McNeese St. (4-1)
1977	Louisiana Tech (4-0-1)
1978	Louisiana Tech (4-1)
1979	McNeese St. (5-0)
1980	McNeese St. (5-0)
1981	Texas-Arlington (4-1)
1982	Louisiana Tech (5-0)*
1983	La.-Monroe (5-1) & North Texas (5-1)*
1984	Louisiana Tech (5-1)*
1985	Arkansas St. (5-1)*
1986	Arkansas St. (5-0)*
1987	La.-Monroe (6-0)*
1988	Northwestern St. (6-0)*
1989	Stephen F. Austin (5-0-1)*
1990	La.-Monroe (5-1)*
1991	McNeese St. (4-1-2)*
1992	La.-Monroe (7-0)*
1993	McNeese St. (7-0)*
1994	North Texas (5-0-1)*
1995	McNeese St. (5-0)*
1996	Troy St. (5-1)*
1997	McNeese St. (6-1)* & Northwestern St. (6-1)*
1998	Northwestern St. (6-1)*
1999	Stephen F. Austin (6-1) & Troy St. (6-1)*
2000	Troy St. (6-1)*
2001	McNeese St. (5-1)* & Sam Houston St. (5-1)*
2002	McNeese St. (6-0)*

Participated in NCAA Division I-AA Championship.

SOUTHWESTERN ATHLETIC CONFERENCE

Founded: In 1920 by a group of six institutions. **Charter members** (6): Bishop, Paul Quinn, Prairie View, Sam Houston College, Texas College and Wiley. **Admitted later** (11): Langston (1931), Southern U. (1934), Arkansas AM&N (1936), Texas Southern (1954), Grambling (1958), Jackson St. (1958), Alcorn St. (1962), Mississippi Val. (1968), Alabama St. (1982), Ark.-Pine Bluff (1998), Alabama A&M (1999) and Morris Brown (2001). **Withdrew later** (9): Paul Quinn (1929), Bishop (1956), Langston (1957), Sam Houston College (1959), Texas College (1961), Wiley (1968), Arkansas AM&N (1970), Prairie View (1990, dropped program, readmitted 1991) and Morris Brown (2002). **Current members**

(10): Alabama A&M, Alabama St., Alcorn St., Ark.-Pine Bluff, Grambling, Jackson St., Mississippi Val., Prairie View, Southern U. and Texas Southern.

Year	Champion (Record√)
1921	Wiley
1922	Paul Quinn
1923	Wiley
1924	Paul Quinn
1925	Bishop
1926	Sam Houston College
1927	Wiley
1928	Wiley
1929	Wiley
1930	Wiley
1931	Prairie View
1932	Wiley
1933	Langston & Prairie View
1934	Texas College
1935	Texas College
1936	Texas College & Langston
1937	Southern U. & Langston
1938	Southern U. & Langston
1939	Langston
1940	Southern U. & Langston
1941	No champion
1942	Texas College
1943	No champion
1944	Langston (5-1), Texas College (5-1) & Wiley (5-1)
1945	Wiley (6-0)
1946	Southern U. (5-1)
1947	Southern U. (7-0)
1948	Southern U. (7-0)
1949	Langston (6-0-1) & Southern U. (6-0-1)
1950	Southern U. (7-0)
1951	Prairie View (6-1)
1952	Prairie View (6-0)
1953	Prairie View (6-0)
1954	Prairie View (6-0)
1955	Southern U. (6-1)
1956	Langston (5-1) & Texas Southern (5-1)
1957	Wiley (6-0)
1958	Prairie View (5-0)
1959	Southern U. (7-0)
1960	Grambling (6-1), Prairie View (6-1) & Southern U. (6-1)
1961	Jackson St. (6-1)
1962	Jackson St. (6-1)
1963	Prairie View (7-0)
1964	Prairie View (7-0)
1965	Grambling (6-1)
1966	Arkansas AM&N (4-2-1), Grambling (4-2-1), Southern U. (4-2-1) & Texas Southern (4-2-1)
1967	Grambling (6-1)
1968	Alcorn St. (6-1), Grambling (6-1) & Texas Southern (6-1)
1969	Alcorn St. (6-0-1)
1970	Alcorn St. (6-0)
1971	Grambling (5-1)
1972	Grambling (5-1) & Jackson St. (5-1)
1973	Grambling (5-1) & Jackson St. (5-1)
1974	Alcorn St. (5-1) & Grambling (5-1)
1975	Grambling (4-2) & Southern U. (4-2)
1976	Alcorn St. (5-1)
1977	Grambling (6-0)
1978	Grambling (5-0-1)
1979	Alcorn St. (5-1) & Grambling (5-1)
1980	Grambling (5-1)* & Jackson St. (5-1)
1981	Jackson St. (5-1)*
1982	Jackson St. (5-0)*
1983	Grambling (6-0-1)
1984	Alcorn St. (7-0)*
1985	Grambling (6-1)* & Jackson St. (6-1)*
1986	Jackson St. (7-0)*
1987	Jackson St. (7-0)*
1988	Jackson St. (7-0)*
1989	Jackson St. (7-0)*
1990	Jackson St. (5-1)*
1991	Alabama St. (6-0-1)#
1992	Alcorn St. (7-0)*
1993	Southern U. (7-0)#
1994	Alcorn St. (6-1)* & Grambling (6-1)#
1995	Jackson St. (7-0)#
1996	Jackson St. (6-1)*
1997	Southern U. (8-0)#
1998	Southern U. (8-0)#
1999	Southern U. (9-0)#
2000	Grambling (6-1)
2001	Grambling (6-1)
2002	Grambling (6-1)

*√No records available until 1944. *Participated in NCAA Division I-AA Championship. #Participated in Division I-AA Heritage Bowl.*

Division II

(Information prior to 1997 researched and submitted by Jeff Hodges, SID, University of North Alabama.)

CENTRAL INTERCOLLEGIATE ATHLETIC ASSOCIATION

Year	Champion
1970	Virginia St.
1971	Elizabeth City St.
1972	Virginia St.
1973	Virginia Union
1974	Norfolk St.
1975	Norfolk St.
1976	Norfolk St.
1977	Winston-Salem
1978	Winston-Salem
1979	Virginia Union
1980	N.C. Central
1981	Virginia Union
1982	Virginia Union
1983	Virginia Union
1984	Norfolk St.
1985	Hampton
1986	Virginia Union
1987	Winston-Salem
1988	Winston-Salem
1989	Bowie St.
1990	Winston-Salem
1991	Winston-Salem
1992	Hampton
1993	Hampton
1994	Hampton
1995	Virginia St.
1996	Virginia St.
1997	Livingstone, Virginia St. & Virginia Union
1998	Livingstone & Winston-Salem
1999	Winston-Salem
2000	Winston-Salem
2001	Virginia Union
2002	Fayetteville St.

GREAT LAKES INTERCOLLEGIATE ATHLETIC CONFERENCE

Year	Champion
1973	Northwood
1974	Ferris St. & Northwood
1975	Wayne St. (Mich.)
1976	Northwood
1977	Grand Valley St.
1978	Grand Valley St.
1979	Saginaw Valley
1980	Hillsdale
1981	Grand Valley St.
1982	Hillsdale
1983	Saginaw Valley
1984	Saginaw Valley
1985	Hillsdale
1986	Hillsdale
1987	Northern Mich.
1988	Hillsdale
1989	Grand Valley St.
1999	Ferris St. & Northwood
2000	Northwood & Saginaw Valley
2001	Grand Valley St.
2002	Grand Valley St.

GREAT NORTHWEST ATHLETIC CONFERENCE

(Formerly Columbia Football Association)

Year	Champion
1999	Western Wash.
2000	Central Wash. & Western Wash.
2001	Western Wash.
2002	Central Wash.

GULF SOUTH CONFERENCE

Year	Champion
1972	Northwestern St.
1973	Troy St.
1974	Jacksonville St.
1975	Nicholls St.

Year	Champion
1976	Troy St.
1977	Jacksonville St.
1978	Jacksonville St.
1979	Mississippi Col.
1980	North Ala.
1981	Jacksonville St.
1982	Jacksonville St.
1983	North Ala.
1984	Troy St.
1985	North Ala.
1986	Troy St.
1987	Troy St.
1988	Tenn.-Martin, Jacksonville St. & Mississippi Col.
1989	Jacksonville St.
1990	Mississippi Col.
1991	Jacksonville St.
1992	Jacksonville St.
1993	North Ala.
1994	North Ala.
1995	North Ala.
1996	Valdosta St.
1997	Southern Ark. & West Ga.
1998	Delta St. & West Ga.
1999	Arkansas Tech
2000	Delta St., Valdosta St. & West Ga.
2001	Valdosta St.
2002	Valdosta St.

LONE STAR CONFERENCE

Year	Champion
1933	Tex. A&M-Commerce
1934	Tex. A&M-Commerce
1935	Tex. A&M-Commerce, North Texas & Stephen F. Austin
1937	Tex. A&M-Commerce
1938	Tex. A&M-Commerce
1939	North Texas
1940	North Texas
1941	North Texas
1942	Tex. A&M-Commerce
1943-45	None
1946	North Texas
1947	North Texas
1948	Southwest Tex. St.
1949	Tex. A&M-Commerce
1950	Sul Ross St.
1951	Tex. A&M-Commerce
1952	Tex. A&M-Commerce
1953	Tex. A&M-Commerce
1954	Tex. A&M-Commerce & Southwest Tex. St.
1955	Tex. A&M-Commerce, Sam Houston St. & Southwest Tex. St.
1956	Sam Houston St.
1957	Tex. A&M-Commerce & Lamar
1958	Tex. A&M-Commerce
1959	Tex. A&M-Kingsville
1960	Tex. A&M-Kingsville
1961	Sam Houston St.
1962	Tex. A&M-Kingsville
1963	Southwest Tex. St.
1964	Sam Houston St.
1965	Sul Ross St.
1966	Tex. A&M-Commerce
1967	Tex. A&M-Kingsville
1968	Tex. A&M-Kingsville
1969	Tex. A&M-Kingsville & Tex. A&M-Commerce
1970	Tex. A&M-Kingsville
1971	Howard Payne
1972	Tex. A&M-Commerce
1973	Abilene Christian
1974	Tex. A&M-Kingsville
1975	Tex. A&M-Kingsville
1976	Tex. A&M-Kingsville
1977	Tex. A&M-Kingsville & Abilene Christian
1978	Angelo St.
1979	Tex. A&M-Kingsville
1980	Southwest Tex. St.
1981	Southwest Tex. St.
1982	Southwest Tex. St.
1983	Tex. A&M-Commerce & Southwest Tex. St.
1984	Angelo St.
1985	Tex. A&M-Kingsville
1986	West Tex. A&M
1987	Tex. A&M-Kingsville & Angelo St.
1988	Tex. A&M-Kingsville
1989	Tex. A&M-Kingsville
1990	Tex. A&M-Commerce
1991	Eastern N.M.
1992	Tex. A&M-Kingsville
1993	Tex. A&M-Kingsville
1994	Tex. A&M-Kingsville
1995	Tex. A&M-Kingsville
1996	Tex. A&M-Kingsville
1997	Tex. A&M-Kingsville
1998	Central Okla.
1999	Central Okla., Northeastern St. & Southeastern St.
2000	Northeastern St.
2001	Tarleton St. & Tex. A&M-Kingsville
2002	Tex. A&M-Kingsville

MID-AMERICA INTERCOLLEGIATE ATHLETICS ASSOCIATION

(Formerly Missouri Intercollegiate Athletic Association)

Year	Champion
1924	Truman
1925	Northwest Mo. St.
1926	Central Mo. St.
1927	Truman
1928	Truman & Southwest Mo. St.
1929	Truman
1930	Truman
1931	Northwest Mo. St.
1932	Truman
1933	Truman
1934	Truman
1935	Truman
1936	Truman
1937	Southeast Mo. St.
1938	Northwest Mo. St.
1939	Northwest Mo. St.
1940	Southwest Mo. St.
1941	Northwest Mo. St. & Mo.-Rolla
1942	Northwest Mo. St. & Southeast Mo. St.
1943-45	None
1946	Southeast Mo. St.
1947	Mo.-Rolla
1948	Northwest Mo. St. Southwest Mo. St.
1949	Mo.-Rolla
1950	Mo.-Rolla
1951	Truman Southwest Mo. St.
1952	Northwest Mo. St. Truman
1953	Truman
1954	Truman
1955	Southeast Mo. St.
1956	Central Mo. St. Mo.-Rolla
1957	Southeast Mo. St.
1958	Southeast Mo. St.
1959	Southeast Mo. St.
1960	Truman
1961	Truman
1962	Southeast Mo. St.
1963	Southwest Mo. St.
1964	Truman
1965	Truman
1966	Southwest Mo. St.
1967	Southeast Mo. St.
1968	Southeast Mo. St.
1969	Truman & Southeast Mo. St.
1970	Central Mo. St. & Truman
1971	Truman
1972	Lincoln (Mo.) & Truman
1973	Southeast Mo. St.
1974	Northwest Mo. St.
1975	Southeast Mo. St.
1976	Truman & Southeast Mo. St.
1977	Mo.-Rolla & Southeast Mo. St.
1978	Southwest Mo. St.
1979	Northwest Mo. St.
1980	Mo.-Rolla
1981	Truman
1982	Truman
1983	Central Mo. St. & Mo.-Rolla
1984	Northwest Mo. St.
1985	Truman
1986	Central Mo. St.
1987	Central Mo. St. & Southeast Mo. St.
1988	Central Mo. St., Truman & Southeast Mo. St.
1989	Pittsburg St.
1990	Pittsburg St.
1991	Pittsburg St.
1992	Pittsburg St.
1993	Mo. Southern St.
1994	Pittsburg St.
1995	Pittsburg St.
1996	Northwest Mo. St. & Pittsburg St.
1997	Northwest Mo. St.
1998	Northwest Mo. St.
1999	Northwest Mo. St.
2000	Northwest Mo. St.
2001	Pittsburg St.
2002	Northwest Mo. St.

NORTH CENTRAL CONFERENCE

Year	Champion
1922	South Dakota St.
1923	Morningside
1924	South Dakota St.
1925	North Dakota St. & Creighton
1926	South Dakota St.
1927	South Dakota & Creighton
1928	North Dakota
1929	North Dakota
1930	North Dakota
1931	North Dakota
1932	North Dakota St.
1933	South Dakota St.
1934	North Dakota
1935	North Dakota St.
1936	North Dakota
1937	North Dakota
1938	South Dakota
1939	North Dakota, South Dakota St. & South Dakota
1940	Northern Iowa
1941	Northern Iowa
1942	Northern Iowa & Augustana (S.D.)
1943-45	None
1946	Northern Iowa
1947	Northern Iowa & South Dakota
1948	Northern Iowa
1949	Northern Iowa & South Dakota St.
1950	South Dakota St.
1951	South Dakota
1952	Northern Iowa
1953	South Dakota St.
1954	Morningside & South Dakota St.
1955	South Dakota St.
1956	Morningside
1957	South Dakota St.
1958	North Dakota
1959	Augustana (S.D.)
1960	Northern Iowa
1961	Northern Iowa & South Dakota St.
1962	Northern Iowa & South Dakota St.
1963	South Dakota St.
1964	North Dakota St., Northern Iowa & North Dakota
1965	North Dakota St. & North Dakota
1966	North Dakota St. & North Dakota
1967	North Dakota St.
1968	North Dakota St.
1969	North Dakota St.
1970	North Dakota St.
1971	North Dakota
1972	North Dakota St., North Dakota & South Dakota
1973	North Dakota St. & South Dakota
1974	North Dakota St., North Dakota & South Dakota
1975	North Dakota
1976	North Dakota St.
1977	North Dakota St.
1978	South Dakota
1979	North Dakota
1980	Northern Colo.
1981	North Dakota St.
1982	North Dakota St.
1983	North Dakota St. & Neb.-Omaha
1984	North Dakota St. & Neb.-Omaha
1985	North Dakota St.
1986	North Dakota St.
1987	Minn. St. Mankato
1988	North Dakota St.
1989	St. Cloud St.
1990	North Dakota St.
1991	North Dakota St.
1992	North Dakota St.
1993	North Dakota & Minn. St. Mankato
1994	North Dakota St. & North Dakota
1995	North Dakota
1996	Neb.-Omaha
1997	Northern Colo.
1998	Neb.-Omaha & Northern Colo.
1999	Northern Colo. & North Dakota
2000	Neb.-Omaha
2001	North Dakota
2002	Northern Colo.

NORTHEAST-10 CONFERENCE

Year	Champion
2001	C.W. Post
2002	C.W. Post

NORTHERN SUN INTERCOLLEGIATE ATHLETIC CONFERENCE

(Northern Intercollegiate Athletic Conference from 1932-92)

Year	Champion
1932	Minn. St. Mankato, Minn. St. Moorhead, St. Cloud St. & Minn. Duluth
1933	St. Cloud St.
1934	Minn. Duluth
1935	Minn. St. Mankato & Minn. St. Moorhead
1936	St. Cloud St.
1937	Minn. Duluth
1938	Minn. St. Mankato & Minn. Duluth
1939	Winona St.
1940	St. Cloud St.
1941	St. Cloud St.
1942	Minn. St. Mankato & St. Cloud St.
1943-45	None
1946	Minn. St. Mankato & Minn. Duluth
1947	Bemidji St. & Winona St.
1948	Minn. St. Mankato, St. Cloud St & Minn. Duluth
1949	Minn. St. Mankato
1950	Bemidji St. & Minn. St. Mankato
1951	St. Cloud St.
1952	Minn. St. Moorhead & St. Cloud St.
1953	St. Cloud St.
1954	St. Cloud St.
1955	St. Cloud St.
1956	Winona St.
1957	Bemidji St. & Winona St.
1958	Minn. St. Mankato
1959	Bemidji St., Minn. St. Mankato & Michigan Tech
1960	Minn. St. Mankato
1961	Minn. St. Mankato
1962	Winona St.
1963	Michigan Tech
1964	Winona St.
1965	Michigan Tech
1966	Minn. St. Moorhead
1967	St. Cloud St.
1968	Minn. St. Mankato & Winona St.
1969	Michigan Tech
1970	Michigan Tech, St. Cloud St. & Minn.-Morris
1971	Minn. St. Moorhead
1972	Michigan Tech
1973	Minn. St. Moorhead
1974	Michigan Tech
1975	Minn.-Morris
1976	Minn.-Morris
1977	Minn.-Morris
1978	Minn.-Morris
1979	Minn. St. Moorhead & Minn. Duluth
1980	Minn. Duluth
1981	Minn. St. Moorhead
1982	Minn. St. Moorhead
1983	Winona St.
1984	Minn. St. Moorhead & Minn.-Morris
1985	Minn. Duluth
1986	Minn.-Morris
1987	Minn.-Morris
1988	Minn. St. Moorhead
1989	Minn. St. Moorhead
1990	Minn. Duluth, Southwest St. & Northern St.
1991	Minn. St. Moorhead
1992	Northern St.
1993	Winona St.
1994	Winona St.
1995	Minn. Duluth & Minn. St. Moorhead
1996	Minn. Duluth
1997	Winona St.
1998	Winona St.
1999	Northern St.
2000	Winona St.
2001	Winona St.
2002	Minn. Duluth

PENNSYLVANIA STATE ATHLETIC CONFERENCE

Year	Champion
1934	Indiana (Pa.)
1935	Shippensburg
1936	Lock Haven
1937	Lock Haven
1938	Mansfield

Year	Champion
1939	Slippery Rock
1940	Indiana (Pa.) & Millersville
1941	Millersville
1942	East Stroudsburg
1943-45	None
1946	Calif. (Pa.)
1947	Mansfield
1948	Bloomsburg
1949	Bloomsburg
1950	West Chester
1951	Bloomsburg
1952	West Chester
1953	West Chester
1954	East Stroudsburg, Bloomsburg & West Chester
1955	Bloomsburg
1956	West Chester
1957	Lock Haven
1958	Calif. (Pa.)
1959	West Chester
1960	West Chester
1961	West Chester
1962	Slippery Rock
1963	West Chester
1964	East Stroudsburg
1965	East Stroudsburg
1966	Clarion
1967	West Chester
1968	East Stroudsburg
1969	West Chester
1970	Edinboro
1971	West Chester
1972	Slippery Rock
1973	Slippery Rock
1974	Slippery Rock
1975	East Stroudsburg
1976	East Stroudsburg
1977	Clarion
1978	East Stroudsburg
1979	Lock Haven
1980	Clarion
1981	Shippensburg
1982	East Stroudsburg
1983	Clarion
1984	Calif. (Pa.)
1985	Bloomsburg
1986	Indiana (Pa.)
1987	Indiana (Pa.)
1988	Millersville (East) Shippensburg (West)
1989	West Chester & Millersville (East) Edinboro (West)
1990	Millersville (East) Indiana (Pa.) (West)
1991	East Stroudsburg (East) Indiana (Pa.) (West)
1992	West Chester (East) Indiana (Pa.) (West)
1993	Millersville (East) Indiana (Pa.) (West)
1994	Bloomsburg & West Chester (East) Indiana (Pa.) (West)
1995	Millersville & Bloomsburg (East) Edinboro (West)
1996	Bloomsburg (East) Clarion (West)
1997	Bloomsburg (East) Slippery Rock (West)
1998	Millersville (East) Slippery Rock (West)
1999	West Chester (East) Slippery Rock (West)
2000	Bloomsburg (East) Clarion, Indiana (Pa.) & Slippery Rock (West)
2001	Bloomsburg (East) Indiana (Pa.) (West)
2002	Bloomsburg & East Stroudsburg (East) Indiana (Pa.) (West)

ROCKY MOUNTAIN ATHLETIC CONFERENCE

Year	Champion
1972	Adams St.
1973	Western St.
1974	Western St.
1975	Western St.
1976	Western St.
1977	Western St.
1978	Western St.
1979	Western St.
1980	Southern Colo. & Adams St.

Year	Champion
1981	N.M. Highlands
1982	Mesa St.
1983	Mesa St.
1984	Fort Lewis
1985	Mesa St.
1986	Mesa St.
1987	Mesa St.
1988	Mesa St.
1989	Adams St.
1990	Mesa St.
1991	Western St.
1992	Western St.
1993	Fort Hays St.
1994	Western St.
1995	Fort Hays St. & Western St.
1996	Chadron St.
1997	Western St.
1998	Chadron St. & Western St.
1999	Chadron St. & N.M. Highlands
2000	Mesa St.
2001	Chadron St.
2002	Chadron St. & Neb.-Kearney

SOUTH ATLANTIC CONFERENCE

Year	Champion
1975	Lenoir-Rhyne
1976	Elon
1977	Elon
1978	Elon & Presbyterian
1979	Presbyterian
1980	Elon & Mars Hill
1981	Elon
1982	Carson-Newman
1983	Carson-Newman
1984	Carson-Newman
1985	Mars Hill
1986	Carson-Newman
1987	Gardner-Webb
1988	Carson-Newman, Catawba & Lenoir-Rhyne
1989	Carson-Newman
1990	Carson-Newman
1991	Carson-Newman
1992	Gardner-Webb
1993	Carson-Newman
1994	Carson-Newman & Lenoir-Rhyne
1995	Carson-Newman
1996	Carson-Newman & Catawba
1997	Carson-Newman
1998	Carson-Newman
1999	Carson-Newman
2000	Catawba
2001	Catawba
2002	Carson-Newman

SOUTHERN INTERCOLLEGIATE ATHLETIC CONFERENCE

(SIAC was split into Divisions A and B from 1966-69, reorganized into Divisions II and III from 1970-77 and became a Division II-only conference in 1978)

Year	Champion
1913	Fisk
1914	Talladega
1915	Fisk
1916	Morehouse
1917	Tuskegee
1918	Talladega
1919	Fisk
1920	Morehouse
1921	Morehouse
1922	Morehouse
1923	Fisk & Morehouse
1924	Tuskegee
1925	Tuskegee
1926	Tuskegee
1927	Tuskegee
1928	Clark Atlanta & Tuskegee
1929	Tuskegee
1930	Tuskegee
1931	Tuskegee
1932	Tuskegee
1933	Tuskegee
1934	Morris Brown
1935	Alabama St.
1936	Tuskegee
1937	Florida A&M
1938	Florida A&M
1939	Alabama St.
1940	Morris Brown

Year	Champion
1941	Morris Brown
1942	Florida A&M
1943	Florida A&M
1944	Tuskegee
1945	Florida A&M
1946	Florida A&M
1947	Florida A&M
1948	Florida A&M
1949	Florida A&M
1950	Florida A&M
1951	Morris Brown
1952	Florida A&M
1953	Florida A&M
1954	Florida A&M
1955	Florida A&M
1956	Florida A&M
1957	Florida A&M
1958	Florida A&M
1959	Florida A&M
1960	Florida A&M
1961	Florida A&M
1962	Alabama A&M
1963	Florida A&M
1964	Florida A&M
1965	Florida A&M
1966	Alabama A&M (A) Alabama St. (B)
1967	Florida A&M (A) Tuskegee (B)
1968	Florida A&M (A) Tuskegee (B)
1969	Florida A&M (A) Tuskegee (B)
1970	Tuskegee (II) Fort Valley St. (III)
1971	Alabama A&M (II) Fort Valley St. (III)
1972	Alabama A&M (II) Fort Valley St. (III)
1973	Bethune-Cookman (II) Fisk (III)
1974	Tuskegee (II) Clark Atlanta (III)
1975	Bethune-Cookman (II) Fisk (III)
1976	Bethune-Cookman (II) Fort Valley St. (III)
1977	Florida A&M (II) Clark Atlanta & Miles (III)
1978	Florida A&M
1979	Alabama A&M
1980	Alabama A&M
1981	Alabama A&M
1982	Fort Valley St.
1983	Fort Valley St.
1984	Albany St. (Ga.)
1985	Albany St. (Ga.) & Fort Valley St.
1986	Albany St. (Ga.)
1987	Alabama A&M & Tuskegee
1988	Albany St. (Ga.)
1989	Alabama A&M
1990	Alabama A&M
1991	Alabama A&M, Clark Atlanta, Morehouse, Fort Valley St. & Tuskegee
1992	Fort Valley St.
1993	Albany St. (Ga.)
1994	Albany St. (Ga.)
1995	Albany St. (Ga.)
1996	Albany St. (Ga.)
1997	Albany St. (Ga.)
1998	Tuskegee
1999	Fort Valley St. & Tuskegee
2000	Tuskegee
2001	Fort Valley St., Morehouse & Tuskegee
2002	Tuskegee

WEST VIRGINIA INTERCOLLEGIATE ATHLETIC CONFERENCE

Year	Champion
1993	Glenville St.
1994	Glenville St. & Shepherd
1995	West Va. Wesleyan & Glenville St.
1996	Glenville St. & Fairmont St.
1997	Shepherd & Glenville St.
1998	Shepherd
1999	Shepherd
2000	Fairmont St. & West Liberty St.
2001	Glenville St.
2002	West Va. Wesleyan

Division III

AMERICAN SOUTHWEST CONFERENCE

Year	Champion
1976	Trinity (Tex.)
1977	Tarleton St.
1978	Tarleton St.
1979	Austin
1980	McMurry
1981	Austin & Sul Ross St.
1982	Sul Ross St.
1983	McMurry & Sul Ross St.
1984	Austin
1985	Austin & Sul Ross St.
1986	Tarleton St.
1987	Tarleton St.
1988	Austin
1989	Howard Payne & Tarleton St.
1990	Tarleton St.
1991	Midwestern St.
1992	Howard Payne
1993	Hardin-Simmons
1994	Hardin-Simmons, Howard Payne & Midwestern St.
1995	Hardin-Simmons & Howard Payne
1996	Hardin-Simmons & Sul Ross St.
1997	Mississippi Col.
1998	Hardin-Simmons
1999	Hardin-Simmons
2000	Hardin-Simmons
2001	Hardin-Simmons
2002	Mary Hardin-Baylor

ATLANTIC CENTRAL FOOTBALL CONFERENCE

Year	Champion
1999	Frostburg St. (5-1)
2000	Wesley (6-0)
2001	Wesley (3-0)
2002	Frostburg St. (3-0)

CENTENNIAL CONFERENCE

Year	Champion
1983	Gettysburg (5-2), Muhlenberg (5-2) & Swarthmore (5-2)
1984	Gettysburg (6-1) & Swarthmore (6-1)
1985	Gettysburg (6-0-1)
1986	Frank. & Marsh. (6-1) and Muhlenberg (6-1)
1987	Frank. & Marsh. (7-0)
1988	Dickinson (6-1) and Frank. & Marsh. (6-1)
1989	Dickinson (7-0)
1990	Dickinson (5-1-1)
1991	Dickinson (7-0)
1992	Dickinson (5-1-1)
1993	Dickinson (5-2) and Frank. & Marsh. (5-2)
1994	Dickinson (7-0)
1995	Frank. & Marsh. (6-1)
1996	Ursinus (7-0)
1997	McDaniel (7-0)
1998	McDaniel (7-0)
1999	McDaniel (7-0)
2000	McDaniel (6-0)
2001	McDaniel* (5-1) & Muhlenberg (5-1)
2002	Johns Hopkins, McDaniel (5-1) & Muhlenberg* (5-1)

*Received conference's automatic bid to the Division III playoffs.

EMPIRE 8 CONFERENCE

Year	Champion
2002	Ithaca (4-0)

FREEDOM FOOTBALL CONFERENCE

Year	Champion
1992	WPI (5-0)
1993	WPI (5-0)
1994	Merchant Marine (5-0) & Plymouth St. (6-0)
1995	Plymouth St. (7-0)
1996	Coast Guard (5-1) & Springfield (5-1)
1997	Coast Guard (6-0)
1998	Springfield (6-0)
1999	Western Conn. St. (6-0)
2000	Springfield (6-0)
2001	Plymouth St. (5-1) & Western Conn. St.* (5-1)
2002	Springfield (6-0)

*Received conference's automatic bid to the Division III playoffs.

HEARTLAND COLLEGIATE ATHLETIC CONFERENCE

Year	Champion
1989	Hanover (7-0)
1990	DePauw (7-0)
1991	Wabash (5-1)
1992	Wabash (5-0-1)
1993	Anderson (Ind.) (6-0)
1994	Hanover (5-1) & Wabash (5-1)
1995	Hanover (6-0)
1996	DePauw (6-0)
1997	Hanover (6-0)
1998	Wabash (7-0)
1999	Hanover (7-0)
2000	Bluffton (5-1) & Hanover* (5-1)
2001	Anderson (Ind.) (5-1) & Defiance* (5-1)
2002	Hanover (6-0)

*Received conference's automatic bid to the Division III playoffs.
Note: Known as the Indiana Collegiate Athletic Conference prior to 1998.

ILLINI-BADGER CONFERENCE

Year	Champion
1996	Lakeland (5-0)
1997	Lakeland (5-0)
1998	Aurora (7-0)
1999	Aurora (7-0)
2000	Aurora (7-0)
2001	MacMurray (7-0)
2002	MacMurray (7-0)

COLLEGE CONFERENCE OF ILLINOIS AND WISCONSIN

Year	Champion
1946	North Central (7-1)
1947	North Central (5-1)
1948	Ill. Wesleyan (5-0)
1949	Augustana (Ill.) (5-0)
1950	Wheaton (Ill.) (5-0)
1951	Ill. Wesleyan (5-0)
1952	Lake Forest & Millikin (3-0-1)
1953	Wheaton (Ill.) (4-0)
1954	Millikin & Wheaton (Ill.) (5-1)
1955	Wheaton (Ill.) (5-0-1)
1956	Wheaton (Ill.) (7-0)
1957	Lake Forest & Wheaton (Ill.) (6-1)
1958	Wheaton (Ill.) (7-0)
1959	Wheaton (Ill.) (6-0-1)
1960	North Central (4-1)
1961	Millikin (6-0)
1962	Carthage (7-0)
1963	Carthage (4-1-1)
1964	Ill. Wesleyan (5-0-1)
1965	Ill. Wesleyan (6-0)
1966	Augustana (Ill.) (5-1)
1967	Carthage (6-0)
1968	Augustana (Ill.) (6-1)
1969	Carthage (7-0)
1970	Carthage (7-0-1)
1971	Carthage (8-0)
1972	Carthage (7-1)
1973	Carthage (8-0)
1974	Ill. Wesleyan & Millikin (7-1)
1975	Augustana (Ill.) (6-2)
1976	Carroll (Wis.) (7-0-1)
1977	Ill. Wesleyan & Millikin (6-2)
1978	Elmhurst & Millikin (7-1)
1979	Millikin (7-1)
1980	Elmhurst & Ill. Wesleyan (6-2)
1981	Augustana (Ill.) (8-0)
1982	Augustana (Ill.) (8-0)
1983	Augustana (Ill.) (8-0)
1984	Augustana (Ill.) (8-0)
1985	Augustana (Ill.) (8-0)
1986	Augustana (Ill.) (7-0-1)
1987	Augustana (Ill.) (8-0)
1988	Augustana (Ill.) & Carroll (Wis.) (7-1)
1989	Millikin (8-0)
1990	Augustana (Ill.) & Millikin (7-1)

Year	Champion
1991	Augustana (Ill.) (7-1)
1992	Ill. Wesleyan (7-0)
1993	Augustana (Ill.) (7-0)
1994	Augustana (Ill.) & Ill. Wesleyan (6-1)
1995	Wheaton (Ill.) (7-0)
1996	Ill. Wesleyan (7-0)
1997	Augustana (Ill.) (6-1)
1998	Millikin (6-1)
1999	Augustana (Ill.) (6-1)
2000	Ill. Wesleyan, Millikin* & Wheaton (Ill.) (6-1)
2001	Augustana (Ill.)* & Ill. Wesleyan (6-1)
2002	Wheaton (Ill.) (7-0)

*Received conference's automatic bid to the Division III playoffs.

Note: Known as College Conference of Illinois prior to 1967.

IOWA INTERCOLLEGIATE ATHLETIC CONFERENCE

Year	Champion
1923	Simpson
1924	Simpson
1925	Simpson & Upper Iowa
1926	Parsons
1927	Iowa St. Teachers
1928	Iowa St. Teachers
1929	Iowa Wesleyan
1930	Iowa Wesleyan
1931	Simpson & William Penn
1932	Luther
1933	Simpson
1934	Simpson
1935	Luther
1936	Parsons
1937	Upper Iowa
1938	Luther
1939	Central (Iowa) & Upper Iowa
1940	Dubuque
1941	Luther
1942	Dubuque
1943	No champion
1944	No champion
1945	Central (Iowa)
1946	Central (Iowa) & Upper Iowa
1947	Upper Iowa
1948	Dubuque
1949	Simpson
1950	St. Ambrose
1951	St. Ambrose
1952	Buena Vista
1953	Iowa Wesleyan
1954	Luther
1955	Parsons
1956	Central (Iowa)
1957	Luther
1958	Wartburg
1959	Wartburg
1960	Luther & Parsons
1961	Parsons
1962	Parsons
1963	Luther
1964	Central (Iowa) & Upper Iowa
1965	Central (Iowa)
1966	Central (Iowa)
1967	Central (Iowa)
1968	Wartburg
1969	Simpson
1970	Luther
1971	Luther
1972	Buena Vista & William Penn
1973	Buena Vista
1974	Central (Iowa)
1975	William Penn
1976	William Penn
1977	Central (Iowa)
1978	Buena Vista, Central (Iowa), Dubuque & Luther
1979	Dubuque
1980	Dubuque
1981	Central (Iowa)
1982	Wartburg
1983	Central (Iowa) & Wartburg
1984	Central (Iowa)
1985	Central (Iowa)
1986	Central (Iowa)
1987	Central (Iowa)
1988	Simpson
1989	Central (Iowa)
1990	Central (Iowa)

Year	Champion
1991	Simpson
1992	Central (Iowa)
1993	Wartburg
1994	Central (Iowa)
1995	Central (Iowa)
1996	Simpson
1997	Simpson
1998	Central (Iowa)
1999	Wartburg
2000	Central (Iowa)
2001	Central (Iowa)
2002	Central (Iowa), Coe* & Wartburg

*Received conference's automatic bid to the Division III playoffs.

MICHIGAN INTERCOLLEGIATE ATHLETIC ASSOCIATION

Year	Champion
1894	Albion (3-0)
1895	Olivet (3-0)
1896	Eastern Mich. (1-0)
1897	Kalamazoo (5-0)
	Kalamazoo (5-0)
	Kalamazoo (4-1-1)
1900	Albion (5-0-1)
1901	Olivet (7-0)
1902	Alma (4-1)
1903	Albion (4-1) & Michigan St. (4-1)
1904	Albion (5-0)
1905	Michigan St. (5-0)
1906	Olivet (4-0-1)
1907	Olivet (5-1)
1908	Albion (3-0-2)
1909	Olivet (4-0)
1910	Alma (1-0)
1911	Adrian (3-0) & Olivet (4-0)
1912	Alma (3-0)
1913	Olivet (3-1)
1914	Hillsdale (3-1) & Olivet (3-1)
1915	Albion (4-0-1) & Alma (1-0-2)
1916	Kalamazoo (4-0)
1917	Alma (4-0)
1919	Kalamazoo (3-0)
1920	Albion (4-0)
1922	Albion (4-0-1)
1923	Alma (5-0)
1924	Hillsdale (5-0)
1925	Eastern Mich. (5-0)
1926	Alma (4-0)
1927	Alma (5-0)
1928	Albion (5-0)
1929	Alma (5-0)
1930	Alma (4-1) & Kalamazoo (4-1)
1931	Hillsdale (3-0-2)
1932	Hillsdale (4-0)
1933	Hillsdale (4-0)
1934	Hope (2-1-1) & Kalamazoo (2-1-1)
1935	Alma (4-0)
1936	Kalamazoo (7-0-1)
1937	Kalamazoo (4-0)
1938	Hillsdale (4-0)
1939	Albion (6-0)
1940	Albion (5-0)
1941	Alma (4-0-1)
1942	Alma (4-0)
1946	Hillsdale (4-1) & Kalamazoo (4-1)
1947	Hillsdale (3-2) & Kalamazoo (3-2)
1948	Alma (5-0)
1949	Hillsdale (5-0)
1950	Alma (4-1)
1951	Alma (4-1) & Hope (4-1)
1952	Albion (5-0)
1953	Hope (5-0-1)
1954	Hillsdale (6-0)
1955	Hillsdale (6-0)
1956	Hillsdale (6-0)
1957	Hillsdale (6-0)
1958	Albion (5-1), Hillsdale (5-1) & Hope (5-1)
1959	Hillsdale (6-0)
1961	Albion (5-0)
1962	Kalamazoo (5-0)
1963	Hope (4-1) & Kalamazoo (4-1)
1964	Albion (5-0)
1965	Albion (5-0)
1966	Albion (4-1)
1967	Alma (5-0)
1968	Alma (5-0)
1969	Albion (5-0)
1970	Adrian (4-1) & Alma (4-1)

Year	Champion
1971	Adrian (4-1) & Alma (4-1)
1972	Adrian (4-1) & Alma (4-1)
1973	Hope (5-0)
1974	Olivet (5-0)
1975	Hope (4-0-1)
1976	Albion (5-0)
1977	Albion (5-0)
1978	Hope (5-0)
1979	Hope (4-0-1)
1980	Adrian (5-0)
1981	Hope (5-0)
1982	Hope (5-0)
1983	Adrian (5-0)
1984	Hope (5-0)
1985	Albion (4-0-1)
1986	Hope (4-0-1)
1987	Hope (5-0)
1988	Adrian (4-1) & Alma (4-1)
1989	Adrian (4-1) & Albion (4-1)
1990	Albion (4-0-1)
1991	Albion (5-0)
1992	Albion (5-0)
1993	Albion (5-0)
1994	Albion (5-0)
1995	Albion (5-0)
1996	Albion (5-0)
1997	Adrian (4-1) & Hope (4-1)
1998	Albion (6-0)
1999	Albion (5-1), Alma (5-1)* & Hope (5-1)
2000	Hope (5-0)
2001	Albion (5-0)
2002	Alma (6-0)

*Received conference's automatic bid to the Division III playoffs.

No title competition in 1918, 1943, 1944, or 1945. No title in 1921 due to an eligibility controversy. 1960 title declared vacant by MIAA Governing Board. In 1991, Olivet forfeited its co-championship with Albion for using an ineligible player.

MIDDLE ATLANTIC CORPORATION

Year	Champion
1958	Juniata (North), Widener (South)
1959	Juniata (North), Johns Hopkins (South)
1960	Albright & Wagner (North), Johns Hopkins (South)
1961	Susquehanna (North), Lebanon Valley (South)
1962	Susquehanna (North), Drexel & McDaniel (South)
1963	McDaniel (South)
1964	Frank. & Marsh. (South)
1965	Swarthmore (South)
1966	Swarthmore (South)
1967	Juniata, Wagner & Wilkes (North), Johns Hopkins (South)
1968	Albright & Wilkes (North), Frank. & Marsh., Johns Hopkins (South)
1969	Wilkes (North), Johns Hopkins, Lebanon Valley & Ursinus (South)
1970	Susquehanna (North), Moravian (South)
1971	Upsala (North), Frank. & Marsh. (South)
1972	Albright (North), Frank. & Marsh. (South)
1973	Juniata (North), Frank. & Marsh. (South)
1974	Wilkes (North), Frank. & Marsh. (South)
1975	Albright (North), Widener (South)
1976	Albright (North), Frank. & Marsh. (South)
1977	Albright (North), Widener (South)
1978	Lycoming (North), Widener (South)
1979	Lycoming (North), Widener (South)
1980	Delaware Valley (North), Widener (South)
1981	Delaware Valley & Juniata (North), Widener (South)
1982	Delaware Valley & Lycoming (North), Swarthmore & Widener (South)
1983	Susquehanna (7-0-1)
1984	Widener (7-1)
1985	Lycoming (9-0)
1986	Susquehanna (9-0)
1987	Susquehanna (7-2) & Widener (7-2)
1988	Moravian (7-1) & Widener (7-1)
1989	Lycoming (7-1) & Susquehanna (7-1)
1990	Lycoming (8-0)
1991	Lycoming (8-0)
1992	Lycoming (7-0-1)
1993	Wilkes (9-0)
1994	Widener (9-0)
1995	Widener (8-2)
1996	Lycoming (8-0)
1997	Albright (8-0) & Lycoming (9-0)

Year	Champion
1998	Lycoming (9-0)
1999	Lycoming (9-0)
2000	Widener (9-0)
2001	Widener (10-0)
2002	King's (Pa.) (8-1)* & Widener (8-1)

*Received conference's automatic bid to the Division III playoffs.

MIDWEST CONFERENCE

Year	Champion
1922	Coe, Lawrence & Millikin
1923	Beloit & Carleton
1924	Cornell College, Knox & Lawrence
1925	Beloit, Carleton, Cornell College & Monmouth (Ill.)
1926	Carleton
1927	Cornell College
1928	Coe & Hamline
1929	Coe, Lawrence & Ripon
1930	Coe
1931	Carleton, Monmouth (Ill.) & Ripon
1932	Carleton, Monmouth (Ill.) & Ripon
1933	Coe
1934	Coe and Monmouth (Ill.)
1935	Ripon
1936	Carleton & Coe
1937	Cornell College
1938	Lawrence
1939	Knox, Ripon
1940	Beloit
1941	Ripon
1942	Lawrence
1946	Lawrence
1947	Lawrence
1948	Ripon
1949	Lawrence
1950	Coe, Knox & Ripon
1951	Lawrence
1952	Coe
1953	St. Olaf
1954	Carleton
1955	Coe
1956	Carleton, Knox & St. Olaf
1957	Ripon
1958	Coe
1959	Coe
1960	St. Olaf
1961	Cornell College, Grinnell & St. Olaf
1962	Grinnell
1963	Ripon
1964	Coe, Cornell College & Ripon
1965	Ripon
1966	Lawrence, Ripon & St. Olaf
1967	Lawrence
1968	Ripon
1969	St. Olaf
1970	St. Olaf
1971	Monmouth (Ill.) & St. Olaf
1972	Monmouth (Ill.)
1973	Coe
1974	Coe
1975	Lawrence
1976	Cornell College, Knox & Monmouth (Ill.)
1977	Ripon
1978	Cornell College & Ripon
1979	Lawrence
1980	Cornell College & Lawrence
1981	Lawrence
1982	Ripon
1983	Lake Forest (Cornell College)
1984	Cornell College (Lake Forest)
1985	Coe (St. Norbert)
1986	Lawrence (Coe)
1987	St. Norbert (Monmouth [Ill.])
1988	St. Norbert (Monmouth [Ill.])
1989	St. Norbert (Monmouth [Ill.])
1990	Coe (Beloit)
1991	Coe (Beloit)
1992	Cornell College (Beloit)
1993	Coe (Carroll [Wis.])
1994	Coe (Beloit)
1995	Cornell College (Ripon)
1996	Ripon (Cornell College)
1997	Carroll (Wis.) (Ripon)
1998	Grinnell
1999	St. Norbert
2000	St. Norbert

Year	Champion
2001	Ripon & St. Norbert*
2002	Lake Forest* & St. Norbert

*Received conference's automatic bid to the Division III playoffs.
Notes: Known as the Midwest Collegiate Athletic Conference from 1922-93.
Conference champion determined by championship game from 1983-97; runner-up shown in parentheses.

MINNESOTA INTERCOLLEGIATE ATHLETIC CONFERENCE

Year	Champion
1920	Hamline
1921	Hamline
1922	St. Olaf & St. Thomas (Minn.)
1923	St. Olaf
1924	Carleton
1925	Macalester (3-0)
1926	Gust. Adolphus
1927	Gust. Adolphus
1928	Augsburg & St. Mary's (Minn.)
1929	St. Thomas (Minn.)
1930	St. Olaf & St. Thomas (Minn.)
1931	Concordia-M'head
1932	St. John's (Minn.)
1933	Gust. Adolphus
1934	Concordia-M'head
1935	Gust. Adolphus, St. John's (Minn.) & St. Olaf
1936	Gust. Adolphus & St. John's (Minn.)
1937	Gust. Adolphus
1938	St. John's (Minn.)
1939	St. Thomas (Minn.)
1940	Gust. Adolphus
1941	St. Thomas (Minn.)
1942	Concordia-M'head & St. Thomas (Minn.)
1943	No Champion
1944	No Champion
1945	Gust. Adolphus
1946	Gust. Adolphus
1947	Macalester & St. Thomas (Minn.)
1948	St. Thomas (Minn.)
1949	St. Thomas (Minn.)
1950	Gust. Adolphus
1951	Gust. Adolphus
1952	Concordia-M'head & Gust. Adolphus
1953	Gust. Adolphus & St. John's (Minn.)
1954	Gust. Adolphus
1955	Gust. Adolphus
1956	St. Thomas (Minn.)
1957	Concordia-M'head
1958	Gust. Adolphus
1959	Gust. Adolphus
1960	Minn. Duluth
1961	Minn. Duluth
1962	St. John's (Minn.)
1963	St. John's (Minn.)
1964	Concordia-M'head
1965	St. John's (Minn.)
1966	Hamline
1967	Gust. Adolphus
1968	Gust. Adolphus
1969	Concordia-M'head
1970	Concordia-M'head
1971	Gust. Adolphus & St. John's (Minn.)
1972	Gust. Adolphus
1973	Minn. Duluth & St. Thomas (Minn.)
1974	Concordia-M'head & St. John's (Minn.)
1975	St. John's (Minn.)
1976	St. John's (Minn.)
1977	St. John's (Minn.)
1978	Concordia-M'head & St. Olaf
1979	Concordia-M'head, St. John's (Minn.), St. Olaf & St. Thomas (Minn.)
1980	Concordia-M'head
1981	Concordia-M'head
1982	St. John's (Minn.)
1983	St. Thomas (Minn.)
1984	Hamline
1985	St. John's (Minn.)
1986	Concordia-M'head
1987	Gust. Adolphus
1988	Concordia-M'head & Hamline
1989	St. John's (Minn.)
1990	Concordia-M'head & St. Thomas (Minn.)
1991	St. John's (Minn.)
1992	Carleton
1993	St. John's (Minn.)

Year	Champion
1994	St. John's (Minn.)
1995	Concordia-M'head & St. John's (Minn.)
1996	St. John's (Minn.)
1997	Augsburg
1998	St. John's (Minn.)
1999	St. John's (Minn.)
2000	Bethel
2001	Bethel & St. John's (Minn.)*
2002	St. John's (Minn.)

*Received conference's automatic bid to the Division III playoffs.

NEW ENGLAND FOOTBALL CONFERENCE

Year	Champion
1965	Maine Maritime
1966	Bridgewater St.
1967	Maine Maritime
1968	Maine Maritime
1969	Bridgewater St.
1970	Curry
1971	Curry
1972	Maine Maritime
1973	Nichols
1974	Boston St. & Nichols
1975	Nichols
1976	Nichols
1977	Mass. Maritime
1978	Boston St. & Nichols
1979	New Haven
1980	Maine Maritime
1981	Plymouth St.
1982	Plymouth St.
1983	Mass. Maritime & Plymouth St.
1984	Plymouth St.
1985	Plymouth St. & Western Conn. St.
1986	Plymouth St.
1987	Plymouth St.
1988	Plymouth St.
1989	Bridgewater St.
1990	Plymouth St.
1991	Mass.-Lowell
1992	Bridgewater St.
1993	Maine Maritime
1994	Maine Maritime & Mass.-Dartmouth
1995	Worcester St.
1996	Worcester St.
1997	Bridgewater St. & Worcester St.
1998	Salve Regina (Blue Division), Bridgewater St. (Red Division)
1999	Salve Regina (Blue), Bridgewater St.* (Red)
2000	Nichols & Salve Regina (Blue), Bridgewater St. (Red)
2001	Westfield St. (Bogan Division), Nichols (Boyd Division)
2002	Westfield St. (Bogan), Mass.-Dartmouth (Boyd)

*Received conference's automatic bid to the Division III playoffs.
In 2000, the New England Football Conference began a championship game to determine the league's automatic qualifier to the Division III playoffs. Following are the results of the game between the division champions:

2000	Bridgewater St. 27, Salve Regina 24
2001	Westfield St. 12, Nichols 0
2002	Mass.-Dartmouth 16, Westfield St. 0

NEW ENGLAND SMALL COLLEGE ATHLETIC CONFERENCE

Year	Champion
2000	Amherst, Colby & Middlebury
2001	Williams
2002	Trinity (Conn.) & Williams

The NESCAC did not crown a champion prior to 2000.

NEW JERSEY ATHLETIC CONFERENCE

Year	Champion
1969	Montclair St. (3-0)
1970	Montclair St. (3-0)
1971	Montclair St. (3-0)
1972	Montclair St. (3-1)*, New Jersey City (4-1) & Rowan (4-1)
1973	Montclair St. (4-0)
1974	Rowan (4-0-1)
1975	Rowan (5-0)

Year	Champion
1976	Rowan (4-1)
1977	Rowan (5-0)
1978	Montclair St. (5-0)
1979	Montclair St. (4-0-1)
1980	Col. of New Jersey (6-0)
1981	Montclair St. (6-0)
1982	Montclair St. (6-0)
1983	Montclair St., Col. of New Jersey and Rowan (5-1)
1984	Montclair St. (6-0)
1985	Montclair St. (6-0)
1986	Montclair St. (6-0)
1987	Kean (5-1)
1988	Col. of New Jersey (5-1)
1989	Montclair St. (5-0-1)
1990	Col. of New Jersey (5-1)
1991	Rowan (5-1)
1992	Rowan (6-0)
1993	Rowan (5-0)
1994	Kean & Col. of New Jersey (3-1-1)
1995	Rowan (5-0)
1996	Col. of New Jersey (5-0)
1997	Rowan (5-0)
1998	Col. of New Jersey (5-0)
1999	Montclair St. (5-0)
2000	Montclair St. (6-0)
2001	Rowan (5-1)
2002	Rowan (6-0)

*Could not reschedule one conference game.

Known as the New Jersey State Athletic Conference from 1969-84. In 1985, the New Jersey State Athletic Conference, a men's conference, merged with the Jersey Athletic Conference, a women's conference, to form the New Jersey Athletic Conference.

NORTH COAST ATHLETIC CONFERENCE

Year	Champion
1984	Case Reserve
1985	Denison
1986	Denison
1987	Allegheny
1988	Allegheny
1989	Kenyon & Ohio Wesleyan
1990	Allegheny
1991	Allegheny
1992	Wittenberg
1993	Allegheny
1994	Allegheny
1995	Wittenberg
1996	Allegheny
1997	Allegheny, Wittenberg & Wooster
1998	Wittenberg
1999	Wittenberg
2000	Wittenberg
2001	Wittenberg
2002	Wabash

NORTHWEST CONFERENCE

Year	Champion
1926	Col. of Idaho
1927	Col. of Idaho
1928	Whitman
1929	Willamette
1930	Whitman
1931	Whitman
1932	Puget Sound
1933	Puget Sound
1934	Willamette
1935	Willamette
1936	Willamette
1937	Willamette
1938	Pacific (Ore.) & Willamette
1939	Pacific (Ore.)
1940	Willamette
1941	Willamette
1942	Willamette
1943	No Football
1944	No Football
1945	No Football
1946	Willamette
1947	Willamette
1948	Col. of Idaho
1949	Lewis & Clark, Pacific (Ore.)
1950	Lewis & Clark
1951	Lewis & Clark, Pacific (Ore.)
1952	Col. of Idaho & Pacific (Ore.)
1953	Col. of Idaho

Year	Champion
1954	Col. of Idaho, Lewis & Clark, Willamette
1955	Col. of Idaho, Lewis & Clark
1956	Linfield
1957	Linfield
1958	Willamette
1959	Willamette
1960	Willamette
1961	Linfield
1962	Linfield
1963	Lewis & Clark
1964	Linfield
1965	Linfield
1966	Lewis & Clark
1967	Lewis & Clark, Willamette
1968	Willamette
1969	Lewis & Clark, Linfield, Pacific Lutheran & Whitman
1970	Linfield
1971	Linfield, Pacific Lutheran & Willamette
1972	Linfield
1973	Pacific Lutheran
1974	Linfield
1975	Linfield, Pacific Lutheran & Whitworth
1976	Linfield
1977	Linfield
1978	Linfield
1979	Pacific Lutheran
1980	Linfield
1981	Pacific Lutheran
1982	Linfield
1983	Pacific Lutheran
1984	Linfield
1996	Willamette
1997	Willamette
1998	Pacific Lutheran
1999	Willamette
2000	Linfield
2001	Linfield, Pacific Lutheran & Whitworth
2002	Linfield

Note: Conference did not sponsor football from 1985-95.

OHIO ATHLETIC CONFERENCE

Year	Champion
1979	Denison (Red Division), Wittenberg* (Blue Division)
1980	Baldwin-Wallace* (Red Division), Wittenberg (Blue Division)
1981	Baldwin-Wallace (Red Division), Wittenberg* (Blue Division)
1982	Baldwin-Wallace* (Red Division), Ohio Northern (Blue Division)
1983	Baldwin-Wallace* (Red Division), Wittenberg (Blue Division)
1984	Baldwin-Wallace (8-0)
1985	Mount Union (8-0)
1986	Mount Union (8-0)
1987	Capital (6-1-1)
1988	Baldwin-Wallace (7-1) & Wittenberg (7-1)
1989	John Carroll (7-1)
1990	Mount Union (9-0)
1991	Baldwin-Wallace (9-0)
1992	Mount Union (9-0)
1993	Mount Union (9-0)
1994	Baldwin-Wallace (8-1), John Carroll (8-1) & Mount Union (8-1)
1995	Mount Union (9-0)
1996	Mount Union (9-0)
1997	Mount Union (9-0)
1998	Mount Union (9-0)
1999	Mount Union (9-0)
2000	Mount Union (9-0)
2001	Mount Union (9-0)
2002	Mount Union (9-0)

*Defeated other division champion to win conference title.

OLD DOMINION ATHLETIC CONFERENCE

Year	Champion
1976	Randolph-Macon (3-1)
1977	Hampden-Sydney (4-0)
1978	Randolph-Macon (4-0)
1979	Randolph-Macon (4-0)
1980	Bridgewater (Va.) (4-1)
1981	Wash. & Lee (4-1)
1982	Hampden-Sydney (4-1)
1983	Hampden-Sydney (5-1)
1984	Randolph-Macon (5-0)

Year	Champion
1985	Emory & Henry (4-1), Randolph-Macon (4-1), Wash. & Lee (4-1)
1986	Emory & Henry (5-0)
1987	Hampden-Sydney (4-1)
1988	Emory & Henry (4-0)
1989	Randolph-Macon (3-1)
1990	Emory & Henry (4-0)
1991	Guilford (4-1)
1992	Emory & Henry (5-0)
1993	Randolph-Macon (5-0)
1994	Emory & Henry (4-1)
1995	Emory & Henry (5-0)
1996	Emory & Henry (4-1)
1997	Emory & Henry (4-1), Guilford (4-1) & Randolph-Macon (4-1)
1998	Emory & Henry (5-0)
1999	Catholic (6-0)
2000	Emory & Henry (5-1)
2001	Bridgewater (Va.) (6-0)
2002	Bridgewater (Va.) (6-0)

PRESIDENTS' ATHLETIC CONFERENCE

Year	Champion
1979	Carnegie Mellon (7-0)
1980	Bethany (W.Va.) (7-0)
1981	Carnegie Mellon (6-0-1)
1982	Hiram (6-1)
1983	Carnegie Mellon (7-0)
1984	Wash. & Jeff. (6-0)
1985	Carnegie Mellon (6-0)
1986	Wash. & Jeff. (6-0)
1987	Wash. & Jeff. (6-0)
1988	Wash. & Jeff. (6-0)
1989	Carnegie Mellon (4-1) and Wash. & Jeff. (4-1)
1990	Wash. & Jeff. (4-0)
1991	Wash. & Jeff. (4-0)
1992	Wash. & Jeff. (4-0)
1993	Wash. & Jeff. (4-0)
1994	Wash. & Jeff. (4-0)
1995	Wash. & Jeff. (4-0)
1996	Wash. & Jeff. (5-0)
1997	Grove City (5-0)
1998	Grove City (3-1), Wash. & Jeff. (3-1) & Waynesburg (3-1)
1999	Wash. & Jeff. (4-0)
2000	Wash. & Jeff. (4-0)
2001	Wash. & Jeff. (4-0)
2002	Wash. & Jeff. (5-0)

SOUTHERN CALIFORNIA INTERCOLLEGIATE ATHLETIC CONFERENCE

Previous members: UCLA (then known as Southern Branch of the University of California), San Diego St. (then known as San Diego State Teachers College), UC Santa Barbara (then known as Santa Barbara State Teachers College), Pomona, Pomona-Claremont and Claremont-Mudd. Current members are: Caltech, Cal Lutheran, Claremont-Mudd-Scripps, La Verne, Occidental, Pomona-Pitzer, Redlands and Whittier.

Year	Champion
1921	Whittier
1922	Pomona
1923	Caltech & Pomona
1924	Pomona
1925	Occidental
1926	Pomona
1927	Pomona & UCLA
1928	Occidental
1929	Occidental
1930	Caltech
1931	Caltech
1932	Whittier
1933	Redlands
1934	Whittier
1935	Whittier
1936	San Diego St.
1937	San Diego St.
1938	Pomona
1939	Whittier
1940	Redlands
1941	Whittier
1942	Pomona
1943	No competition
1944	No competition
1945	Redlands
1946	Redlands
1947	Redlands
1948	Occidental
1949	Whittier

Year	Champion
1950	Pomona-Claremont, Redlands & Whittier
1951	Occidental
1952	Whittier
1953	Pomona-Claremont
1954	Pomona-Claremont
1955	Pomona-Claremont
1956	Redlands
1957	Whittier
1958	Whittier
1959	Whittier
1960	Occidental, Redlands & Whittier
1961	Whittier
1962	Whittier
1963	Whittier
1964	Whittier
1965	Occidental
1966	Redlands
1967	Whittier
1968	Whittier
1969	Whittier
1970	Claremont-Mudd/Redlands
1971	Occidental
1972	Whittier
1973	Redlands
1974	Redlands
1975	La Verne/Redlands
1976	Redlands
1977	Redlands
1978	Redlands
1979	Claremont-Mudd-Scripps
1980	Redlands
1981	Whittier
1982	La Verne
1983	Occidental
1984	Occidental
1985	Occidental
1986	Claremont-Mudd-Scripps
1987	Claremont-Mudd-Scripps & Occidental
1988	Occidental
1989	Occidental
1990	Redlands
1991	Redlands
1992	Redlands
1993	La Verne
1994	La Verne
1995	La Verne
1996	Redlands
1997	Cal Lutheran, Redlands & Whittier
1998	Whittier
1999	Redlands
2000	Redlands
2001	Occidental
2002	Redlands

SOUTHERN COLLEGIATE ATHLETIC CONFERENCE

Year	Champion
1962	Wash. & Lee
1963	Sewanee
1964	Sewanee & Washington (Mo.)
1965	Sewanee
1966	Washington (Mo.)
1967	Sewanee
1968	Centre & Rhodes
1969	Centre
1970	Rhodes & Washington (Mo.)
1971	Centre & Rhodes
1972	Centre
1973	Rhodes
1974	Rose-Hulman
1975	Rose-Hulman & Sewanee
1976	Sewanee
1977	Rhodes
1978	Rhodes & Sewanee
1979	Sewanee, Rhodes & Rose-Hulman
1980	Centre
1981	Rose-Hulman
1982	Sewanee
1983	Centre & Rose-Hulman
1984	Centre
1985	Centre & Rhodes
1986	Rose-Hulman
1987	Rhodes
1988	Rose-Hulman
1989	Centre

Year	Champion
1990	Centre & Sewanee
1991	Millsaps
1992	Sewanee
1993	Trinity (Tex.)
1994	Trinity (Tex.)
1995	Centre, Rhodes & Trinity (Tex.)
1996	Millsaps & Trinity (Tex.)
1997	Trinity (Tex.)
1998	Trinity (Tex.)
1999	Trinity (Tex.)
2000	DePauw, Sewanee & Trinity (Tex.)*
2001	Trinity (Tex.)
2002	Trinity (Tex.)

*Received conference's automatic bid to the Division III playoffs.
Note: Known as the College Athletic Conference from 1962-90.

UNIVERSITY ATHLETIC ASSOCIATION

Year	Champion
1990	Carnegie Mellon (4-0)
1991	Carnegie Mellon (4-0)
1992	Rochester (4-0)
1993	Carnegie Mellon (4-0)
1994	Carnegie Mellon (3-1) & Washington (Mo.) (3-1)
1995	Carnegie Mellon (3-1) & Washington (Mo.) (3-1)
1996	Carnegie Mellon (3-1), Case Reserve (3-1) & Washington (Mo.) (3-1)
1997	Carnegie Mellon (4-0)
1998	Chicago (4-0)
1999	Washington (Mo.) (4-0)
2000	Chicago (4-0)
2001	Washington (Mo.) (4-0)
2002	Washington (Mo.) (4-0)

UPSTATE COLLEGIATE ATHLETIC ASSOCIATION

Year	Champion
1995	Union (N.Y.)
1996	Union (N.Y.)
1997	Rensselaer
1998	Rensselaer
1999	Rensselaer
2000	Hobart, Rochester & Union (N.Y.)
2001	Rensselaer
2002	Hobart

USA SOUTH ATHLETIC CONFERENCE

Year	Champion
2000	No champion named
2001	Chris. Newport* & Ferrum (5-1)
2002	Chris. Newport* & Ferrum (5-1)

*Received conference's automatic bid to the Division III playoffs.

WISCONSIN INTERCOLLEGIATE ATHLETIC CONFERENCE

Year	Champion
1913	Wis.-Superior & Wis.-Whitewater
1914	Wis.-Whitewater
1915	Wis.-River Falls
1916	Wis.-River Falls
1917	Wis.-La Crosse
1918	No Conference Play
1919	Wis.-La Crosse
1920	Wis.-Oshkosh
1921	Wis.-Stout
1922	Wis.-Eau Claire & Wis.-Whitewater
1923	Wis.-Oshkosh
1924	Wis.-River Falls
1925	Wis.-River Falls
1926	Wis.-River Falls
1927	Wis.-La Crosse
1928	Wis.-Oshkosh, Wis.-Stevens Point & Wis.-Superior
1929	Wis.-Milwaukee
1930	Wis.-Milwaukee
1931	Wis.-Milwaukee
1932	Wis.-Whitewater

Year	Champion
1933	Wis.-La Crosse, Wis.-River Falls & Wis.-Stevens Point
1934	Wis.-La Crosse & Wis.-Stevens Point
1935	Wis.-Oshkosh & Wis.-Superior
1936	Wis.-Stevens Point & Wis.-Superior
1937	Wis.-Superior & Wis.-Whitewater
1938	Wis.-Milwaukee, Wis.-Platteville & Wis.-River Falls
1939	Wis.-La Crosse & Wis.-Milwaukee
1940	Wis.-La Crosse & Wis.-Whitewater
1941	Wis.-La Crosse, Wis.-Platteville, Wis.-Stout & Wis.-Whitewater
1942	Wis.-La Crosse, Wis.-Milwaukee & Wis.-Platteville
1943	No Conference Play (WWII)
1944	No Conference Play (WWII)
1945	No Conference Play
1946	Wis.-Milwaukee, Wis.-Stevens Point & Wis.-Superior
1947	Wis.-Milwaukee & Wis.-River Falls
1948	Wis.-Eau Claire
1949	Wis.-La Crosse, Wis.-Stevens Point & Wis.-Stout
1950	Wis.-La Crosse & Wis.-Whitewater
1951	Wis.-La Crosse
1952	Wis.-La Crosse & Wis.-Platteville
1953	Wis.-La Crosse & Wis.-Platteville
1954	Wis.-La Crosse
1955	Wis.-Stevens Point
1956	Wis.-Eau Claire & Wis.-Platteville
1957	Wis.-Platteville
1958	Wis.-River Falls
1959	Wis.-Whitewater
1960	Wis.-Whitewater
1961	Wis.-Stevens Point
1962	Wis.-Whitewater
1963	Wis.-Eau Claire
1964	Wis.-Eau Claire
1965	Wis.-Stout
1966	Wis.-Whitewater (8-0)
1967	Wis.-Whitewater (7-1)
1968	Wis.-Oshkosh & Wis.-Platteville (7-1)
1969	Wis.-Platteville & Wis.-Whitewater (7-1)
1970	Wis.-Platteville (8-0)
1971	Wis.-La Crosse & Wis.-Platteville (7-1)
1972	Wis.-Oshkosh (8-0)
1973	Wis.-La Crosse (7-1)
1974	Wis.-La Crosse, Wis.-Platteville & Wis.-Whitewater (7-1)
1975	Wis.-La Crosse, Wis.-River Falls & Wis.-Whitewater (7-1)
1976	Wis.-Oshkosh, Wis.-Platteville & Wis.-River Falls (6-2)
1977	Wis.-Stevens Point (7-0-1)
1978	Wis.-La Crosse & Wis.-Whitewater (7-1)
1979	Wis.-River Falls (7-1)
1980	Wis.-La Crosse, Wis.-Platteville, Wis.-River Falls & Wis.-Whitewater (6-2)
1981	Wis.-Eau Claire (8-0)
1982	Wis.-La Crosse (7-1)
1983	Wis.-Eau Claire (7-1)
1984	Wis.-River Falls & Wis.-Whitewater (7-1)
1985	Wis.-River Falls (6-1-1)
1986	Wis.-La Crosse, Wis.-River Falls & Wis.-Stevens Point (7-1)
1987	Wis.-River Falls & Wis.-Whitewater (6-2)
1988	Wis.-Whitewater (7-1)
1989	Wis.-La Crosse (7-1)
1990	Wis.-Whitewater (8-0)
1991	Wis.-La Crosse (7-1)
1992	Wis.-La Crosse (6-0-1)
1993	Wis.-La Crosse (7-0)
1994	Wis.-Whitewater (6-1)
1995	Wis.-La Crosse (7-0)
1996	Wis.-La Crosse (7-0)
1997	Wis.-Whitewater (7-0)
1998	Wis.-Eau Claire, Wis.-River Falls, Wis.-Stevens Point & Wis.-Whitewater (5-2)
1999	Wis.-La Crosse* & Wis.-Stevens Point (6-1)
2000	Wis.-Stout (7-0)
2001	Wis.-Eau Claire & Wis.-Stevens Point* (5-2)
2002	Wis.-La Crosse (6-1)

*Received conference's automatic bid to the Division III playoffs.

Discontinued Conferences

Division I-A

BIG EIGHT CONFERENCE

Founded: Originally founded in 1907 as the Missouri Valley Intercollegiate Athletic Association. Charter members were Iowa, Kansas, Missouri, Nebraska and Washington (Mo.). Six schools were admitted later: Drake (1908), Iowa St. (1908), Kansas St. (1913), Grinnell (1919), Oklahoma (1920) and Oklahoma St. (1925). Iowa withdrew in 1911. The Big Six Conference was founded in 1928 when charter members left the MVIAA. Iowa St., Kansas, Kansas St., Missouri, Nebraska and Oklahoma were joined by Colorado (1948) (known as Big Seven) and Oklahoma St. (1958) (known as Big Eight until 1996). All eight members of Big Eight joined four former Southwest Conference members (Baylor, Texas, Texas A&M and Texas Tech) to form Big 12 Conference in 1996.

Year	Champion (Record)
1907	Iowa (1-0) & Nebraska (1-0)
1908	Kansas (4-0)
1909	Missouri (4-0-1)
1910	Nebraska (2-0)
1911	Iowa St. (2-0-1) & Nebraska (2-0-1)
1912	Iowa St. (2-0) & Nebraska (2-0)
1913	Missouri (4-0) & Nebraska (3-0)
1914	Nebraska (3-0)
1915	Nebraska (4-0)
1916	Nebraska (3-1)
1917	Nebraska (2-0)
1918	No Champion—War
1919	Missouri (4-0-1)
1920	Oklahoma (4-0-1)
1921	Nebraska (3-0)
1922	Nebraska (5-0)
1923	Nebraska (3-0-2)
1924	Missouri (5-1)
1925	Missouri (5-1)
1926	Oklahoma St. (3-0-1)
1927	Missouri (5-1)
1928	Nebraska (4-0)
1929	Nebraska (3-0-2)
1930	Kansas (4-1)
1931	Nebraska (5-0)
1932	Nebraska (5-0)
1933	Nebraska (5-0)
1934	Kansas St. (5-0)
1935	Nebraska (4-0-1)
1936	Nebraska (5-0)
1937	Nebraska (3-0-2)
1938	Oklahoma (5-0)
1939	Missouri (5-0)
1940	Nebraska (5-0)
1941	Missouri (5-0)
1942	Missouri (4-0-1)
1943	Oklahoma (5-0)
1944	Oklahoma (4-0-1)
1945	Missouri (5-0)
1946	Oklahoma (4-1) & Kansas (4-1)
1947	Kansas (4-0-1) & Oklahoma (4-0-1)
1948	Oklahoma (5-0)
1949	Oklahoma (5-0)
1950	Oklahoma (6-0)
1951	Oklahoma (6-0)
1952	Oklahoma (5-0-1)
1953	Oklahoma (6-0)
1954	Oklahoma (6-0)
1955	Oklahoma (6-0)
1956	Oklahoma (6-0)
1957	Oklahoma (6-0)
1958	Oklahoma (6-0)
1959	Oklahoma (5-1)
1960	Missouri (7-0)
1961	Colorado (7-0)
1962	Oklahoma (7-0)
1963	Nebraska (7-0)
1964	Nebraska (6-1)
1965	Nebraska (7-0)
1966	Nebraska (6-1)
1967	Oklahoma (7-0)
1968	Kansas (6-1) & Oklahoma (6-1)
1969	Missouri (6-1) & Nebraska (6-1)
1970	Nebraska (7-0)
1971	Nebraska (7-0)
1972	Nebraska (5-1-1)*
1973	Oklahoma (7-0)
1974	Oklahoma (7-0)
1975	Nebraska (6-1) & Oklahoma (6-1)
1976	Colorado (5-2), Oklahoma (5-2) & Oklahoma St. (5-2)
1977	Oklahoma (7-0)
1978	Nebraska (6-1) & Oklahoma (6-1)
1979	Oklahoma (7-0)
1980	Oklahoma (7-0)
1981	Nebraska (7-0)
1982	Nebraska (7-0)
1983	Nebraska (7-0)
1984	Oklahoma (6-1) & Nebraska (6-1)
1985	Oklahoma (7-0)
1986	Oklahoma (7-0)
1987	Oklahoma (7-0)
1988	Nebraska (7-0)
1989	Colorado (7-0)
1990	Colorado (7-0)
1991	Colorado (6-0-1) & Nebraska (6-0-1)
1992	Nebraska (6-1)
1993	Nebraska (7-0)
1994	Nebraska (7-0)
1995	Nebraska (7-0)

*Oklahoma (5-1-1) forfeited title.

BIG WEST CONFERENCE

Founded: In 1969 as the Pacific Coast Athletic Association. Charter members were UC Santa Barb., Cal St. Los Angeles, Fresno St., Long Beach St., Pacific (Cal.), San Diego St. and San Jose St. Twelve schools were admitted later: Cal St. Fullerton (1974), Utah St. (1977), UNLV (1982), New Mexico St. (1983), Nevada (1992), Arkansas St. (1993, readmitted 1998), La.-Lafayette (1993), Louisiana Tech (1993), Northern Ill. (1993), Boise St. (1996), Idaho (1996) and North Texas (1996). The following schools withdrew, in chronological order: UC Santa Barb. (1972), Cal St. Los Angeles (1974), San Diego St. (1976), Fresno St. (1991), Long Beach St. (1991, dropped football), Cal St. Fullerton (1992, dropped football), Arkansas St. (1996, readmitted 1998), La.-Lafayette (1996), Louisiana Tech (1996), UNLV (1996), Northern Ill. (1996), Pacific (Cal.) (1996, dropped football) and San Jose St. (1996). The conference was renamed the Big West Conference in 1988. In 2001, Arkansas St., Idaho, New Mexico St. and North Texas will join La.-Lafayette, La.-Monroe and Middle Tenn. for the inaugural season of football in the Sun Belt Conference. Boise St. will become a member of the Western Athletic Conference and Utah St. will compete as a Division I-A independent.

Year	Champion (Record)
1969	San Diego St. (6-0)
1970	Long Beach St. (5-1) & San Diego St. (5-1)
1971	Long Beach St. (5-1)
1972	San Diego St. (4-0)
1973	San Diego St. (3-0-1)
1974	San Diego St. (4-0)
1975	San Jose St. (5-0)
1976	San Jose St. (4-0)
1977	Fresno St. (4-0)
1978	San Jose St. (4-1) & Utah St. (4-1)
1979	Utah St. (5-0)
1980	Long Beach St. (5-0)
1981	San Jose St. (5-0)
1982	Fresno St. (6-0)
1983	Cal St. Fullerton (5-1)
1984	Cal St. Fullerton (6-1)#
1985	Fresno St. (7-0)
1986	San Jose St. (7-0)
1987	San Jose St. (7-0)
1988	Fresno St. (7-0)
1989	Fresno St. (7-0)
1990	San Jose St. (7-0)
1991	Fresno St. (6-1) & San Jose St. (6-1)
1992	Nevada (5-1)
1993	La.-Lafayette (5-1) & Utah St. (5-1)
1994	La.-Lafayette (5-1), Nevada (5-1) & UNLV (5-1)
1995	Nevada (6-0)
1996	Nevada (4-1) & Utah St. (4-1)
1997	Utah St. (4-1) & Nevada (4-1)
1998	Idaho (4-1)
1999	Boise St. (5-1)
2000	Boise St. (5-0)

#UNLV forfeited title.

BORDER INTERCOLLEGIATE ATHLETIC ASSOCIATION

Founded: In 1931 as Border Intercollegiate Athletic Association. Charters members were Arizona, Arizona St. Teachers' (Flagstaff) (now Northern Ariz.), Arizona St. Teachers' (Tempe) (now Arizona St.), New Mexico and New Mexico A&M (now New Mexico St.). Texas Tech admitted in 1932, Texas Mines (now UTEP) admitted in 1935, and Hardin-Simmons and West Texas St. Teachers' (now West Tex. A&M) in 1941.

Year	Champion (Record)
1931	Arizona St. (3-1)
1932	Texas Tech (2-0)*
1933	Texas Tech (1-0)*
1934	Texas Tech (1-0)*
1935	Arizona (4-0)
1936	Arizona (3-0-1)
1937	Texas Tech (3-0)
1938	New Mexico St. (4-1)** New Mexico (4-2)**
1939	Arizona St. (4-0)
1940	Arizona St. (3-0-1)
1941	Arizona (5-0)
1942	Hardin-Simmons (3-0-1) Texas Tech (3-0-1)
1943	No full conference program
1944	Texas Tech (2-0)
1945	Arizona (1-0)
1946	Hardin-Simmons (6-0)
1947	Texas Tech (4-0)

*Texas Tech has been listed by some as conference champion for the years 1932, 1933 and 1934, but conference rules forbade an official conference championship. This was due to the fact that the conference covered such a large area that games between all members were not practical.

**Texas Tech won its two conference games in 1938 but did not win the official championship since it did not meet the conference three-game requirement. Its victory over New Mexico did not count toward the championship, permitting New Mexico to share championship honors with New Mexico St.

MISSOURI VALLEY CONFERENCE

Founded: Originally founded as the Missouri Valley Intercollegiate Athletic Association. Several charter members left in 1928 to form the Big Six Conference, which became the Big Eight later. But Drake, Grinnell, Oklahoma A&M (now Oklahoma St.) and Washington (Mo.) continued the MVIAA. Creighton joined in 1928, Butler in 1932, Tulsa and Washburn in 1935, St. Louis in 1937, Wichita St. in 1947, Bradley and Detroit in 1949, Houston in 1951, Cincinnati and North Texas in 1957, Louisville in 1964, Memphis in 1968, and West Tex. A&M in 1972.

Year	Champion
1928	Drake
1929	Drake
1930	Drake & Oklahoma St.
1931	Drake
1932	Oklahoma St.
1933	Drake & Oklahoma St.
1934	Washington (Mo.)
1935	Washington (Mo.) & Tulsa
1936	Tulsa & Creighton
1937	Tulsa
1938	Tulsa
1939	Washington (Mo.)
1940	Tulsa
1941	Tulsa
1942	Tulsa
1943	Tulsa
1944	Oklahoma St.
1945	Oklahoma St.
1946	Tulsa
1947	Tulsa
1948	Oklahoma St.
1949	Detroit

Year	Champion
1950	Tulsa
1951	Tulsa
1952	Houston
1953	Oklahoma St. & Detroit
1954	Wichita St.
1955	Wichita St. & Detroit
1956	Houston
1957	Houston
1958	North Texas
1959	North Texas & Houston
1960	Wichita St.
1961	Wichita St.
1962	Tulsa
1963	Cincinnati & Wichita St.
1964	Cincinnati
1965	Tulsa
1966	North Texas & Tulsa
1967	North Texas
1968	Memphis
1969	Memphis
1970	Louisville
1971	Memphis
1972	Louisville, West Tex. A&M & Drake
1973	North Texas
1974	Tulsa
1975	Tulsa
1976	Tulsa & New Mexico St.
1977	West Tex. A&M
1978	New Mexico St.
1979	West Tex. A&M
1980	Tulsa
1981	Drake & Tulsa
1982	Tulsa
1983	Tulsa
1984	Tulsa
1985	Tulsa

OLD ROCKY MOUNTAIN CONFERENCE
(Mountain States Athletic Conference and Big Seven Conference)

Founded: This conference predates every conference except the Big Ten and consisted of Brigham Young (1922), Colorado (1900), Colorado Agricultural College (now Colorado St.) (1900), Colorado St. College (1900), Denver (1900), Utah (1902), Utah St. (1902) and Wyoming (1905). Before 1938, these schools were part of the Rocky Mountain Conference, other members of which, at that time, were Colorado College, Colorado Mines, Greeley St. Teachers' (now Northern Colo.), Montana St. (1917) and Western St. Teachers' (now Western St.) (1925). A split took place in 1938, when the Mountain States Athletic Conference or "Big Seven" was formed. The name Rocky Mountain Conference was retained by the last six schools after 1938. Some members went into the Western Athletic Conference when the RMC was dissolved in 1962.

Year	Champion
1900	Colorado College
1901	Colorado
1902	Colorado
1903	Colorado
1904	Colorado Mines
1905	Colorado Mines
1906	Colorado Mines
1907	Colorado Mines
1908	Denver
1909	Denver
1910	Colorado
1911	Colorado
1912	Colorado Mines
1913	Colorado
1914	Colorado Mines
1915	Colorado Aggies
1916	Colorado Aggies
1917	Denver
1918	Colorado Mines
1919	Colorado Aggies
1920	Colorado Aggies
1921	Utah St.
1922	Utah
1923	Colorado
1924	Colorado
1925	Colorado Aggies
1926	Utah
1927	Colorado Aggies
1928	Utah
1929	Utah
1930	Utah

Year	Champion
1931	Utah
1932	Utah
1933	Utah, Denver* & Colorado St.*
1934	Colorado, Northern Colo. & Colorado St.*
1935	Colorado & Utah St.*
1936	Utah St.
1937	Colorado
1938	Utah (4-0-2)
1939	Colorado (5-1-0)
1940	Utah (5-1-0)
1941	Utah (4-0-2)
1942	Colorado & Utah (5-1-0)
1943	Colorado (2-0-0)
1944	Colorado (2-0-0)
1945	Denver (4-1-0)
1946	Utah St. & Denver (4-1-1)
1947	Utah (6-0-0)
1948	Utah
1949	Wyoming
1950	Wyoming
1951	Utah
1952	Utah
1953	Utah
1954	Denver
1955	Colorado St.
1956	Wyoming
1957	Utah
1958	Wyoming
1959	Wyoming
1960	Wyoming & Utah St.
1961	Wyoming & Utah St.

*In final ratings, according to conference rules, tie games were not counted in awarding championships. Thus, teams marked with * shared the championship because one or more ties were not counted in their conference records.

SOUTHLAND CONFERENCE
(I-A only 1975-79, now I-AA conference)

SOUTHWEST CONFERENCE

Founded: In 1914 as the Southwest Athletic Conference with charter members Arkansas, Baylor, Oklahoma, Oklahoma St., Rice, Southwestern (Tex.), Texas and Texas A&M. Five teams were added: Southern Methodist (1918), Phillips (1920), TCU (1923), Texas Tech (1960) and Houston (1976). Five withdrew: Southwestern (Texas) (1917), Oklahoma (1920), Phillips (1921), Oklahoma St. (1925) and Arkansas (1992). Of the eight members in the final (1995) season, four (Baylor, Texas, Texas A&M and Texas Tech) joined with eight members of the Big Eight Conference to form the Big 12 Conference in 1996. The other members in 1996: Houston (to Conference USA), Rice (to Western Athletic Conference), Southern Methodist (to Western Athletic Conference) and TCU (to Western Athletic Conference).

Year	Champion (Record)
1914	No champion
1915	Oklahoma (3-0)*
1916	No champion
1917	Texas A&M (2-0)
1918	No champion
1919	Texas A&M (4-0)
1920	Texas (5-0)
1921	Texas A&M (3-0-2)
1922	Baylor (5-0)
1923	Southern Methodist (5-0)
1924	Baylor (4-0-1)
1925	Texas A&M (4-1)
1926	Southern Methodist (5-0)
1927	Texas A&M (4-0-1)
1928	Texas (5-1)
1929	TCU (4-0-1)
1930	Texas (4-1)
1931	Southern Methodist (5-0-1)
1932	TCU (6-0)
1933	No champion*
1934	Rice (5-1)
1935	Southern Methodist (6-0)
1936	Arkansas (5-1)
1937	Rice (4-1-1)
1938	TCU (6-0)
1939	Texas A&M (6-0)
1940	Texas A&M (5-1)
1941	Texas A&M (5-1)
1942	Texas (5-1)
1943	Texas (5-0)
1944	TCU (3-1-1)
1945	Texas (5-1)
1946	Rice (5-1) & Arkansas (5-1)

Year	Champion (Record)
1947	Southern Methodist (5-0-1)
1948	Southern Methodist (5-0-1)
1949	Rice (6-0)
1950	Texas (6-0)
1951	TCU (5-1)
1952	Texas (6-0)
1953	Rice (5-1) & Texas (5-1)
1954	Arkansas (5-1)
1955	TCU (5-1)
1956	Texas A&M (6-0)
1957	Rice (5-1)
1958	TCU (5-1)
1959	Texas (5-1), TCU (5-1) & Arkansas (5-1)
1960	Arkansas (6-1)
1961	Texas (6-1) & Arkansas (6-1)
1962	Texas (6-0-1)
1963	Texas (7-0)
1964	Arkansas (7-0)
1965	Arkansas (7-0)
1966	Southern Methodist (6-1)
1967	Texas A&M (6-1)
1968	Texas (6-1) & Arkansas (6-1)
1969	Texas (7-0)
1970	Texas (7-0)
1971	Texas (6-1)
1972	Texas (7-0)
1973	Texas (7-0)
1974	Baylor (6-1)
1975	Arkansas (6-1), Texas A&M (6-1) & Texas (6-1)
1976	Houston (7-1) & Texas Tech (7-1)
1977	Texas (8-0)
1978	Houston (7-1)
1979	Houston (7-1) & Arkansas (7-1)
1980	Baylor (8-0)
1981	Southern Methodist (7-1)¢
1982	Southern Methodist (7-0-1)
1983	Texas (8-0)
1984	Southern Methodist (6-2) & Houston (6-2)
1985	Texas A&M (7-1)
1986	Texas A&M (7-1)
1987	Texas A&M (6-1)
1988	Arkansas (7-0)
1989	Arkansas (7-1)
1990	Texas (8-0)
1991	Texas A&M (8-0)
1992	Texas A&M (7-0)
1993	Texas A&M (7-0)
1994	Baylor (4-3), Rice (4-3), Texas (4-3), TCU (4-3) & Texas Tech (4-3)*
1995	Texas (7-0)

*Forfeited title: Baylor (3-0) in 1915, Arkansas (4-1) in 1933 and Texas A&M (6-0-1) in 1994 on probation. ¢Southern Methodist on probation; did not forfeit championship.

Division I-AA

AMERICAN WEST CONFERENCE

Founded: Started Division I-AA play in 1993 with charter members Cal St. Northridge, Cal St. Sacramento and Southern Utah. Other members were UC Davis and Cal Poly (both Division II members at the time). Cal Poly became a Division I-AA member in 1994, and UC Davis withdrew in 1994. Last-year members were Cal Poly (became independent), Cal St. Northridge (to Big Sky Conference), Cal St. Sacramento (to Big Sky Conference) and Southern Utah (became independent).

Year	Champion (Record)
1993	Southern Utah (3-1) & UC Davis (3-1)#
1994	Cal Poly (3-0)
1995	Sacramento St. (3-0)

Division II

EASTERN COLLEGIATE FOOTBALL CONFERENCE

Year	Champion
1993	Bentley
1994	Bentley
1995	Stonehill
1996	Salve Regina
1997	Albany (N.Y.)
1998	Albany (N.Y.)
1999	American Int'l
2000	American Int'l

MIDWEST INTERCOLLEGIATE FOOTBALL CONFERENCE

Year	Champion
1990	Grand Valley St.
1991	Butler
1992	Ferris St., Butler, Grand Valley St. & Hillsdale
1993	Ferris St.
1994	Ferris St.
1995	Ferris St.
1996	Ferris St.
1997	Grand Valley St. & Ashland
1998	Grand Valley St.

NORTHERN CALIFORNIA ATHLETIC CONFERENCE

(Far Western Football Conference from 1929-81)

Year	Champion (Record)
1925	St. Mary's (Cal.)
1926	St. Mary's (Cal.)
1927	St. Mary's (Cal.)
1928	St. Mary's (Cal.)
1929	UC Davis
1930	Fresno St.
1931	None
1932	Nevada & San Jose St.
1933	Nevada
1934	Fresno St. & San Jose St.
1935	Fresno St.
1936	Pacific (Cal.)
1937	Fresno St.
1938	Pacific (Cal.)
1939	Nevada
1940	Pacific (Cal.)
1941	Pacific (Cal.)
1942	Pacific (Cal.)
1943-46	None
1947	UC Davis Southern Ore.
1948	Cal St. Chico & Southern Ore.
1949	UC Davis

Year	Champion (Record)
1950	San Fran. St.
1951	UC Davis
1952	Humboldt St.
1953	Cal St. Chico
1954	San Fran. St.
1955	Cal St. Chico
1956	UC Davis, Humboldt St. & San Fran. St.
1957	San Fran. St.
1958	San Fran. St.
1959	San Fran. St.
1960	Humboldt St.
1961	Humboldt St. & San Fran. St.
1962	San Fran. St.
1963	UC Davis, San Fran. St. & Humboldt St.
1964	Sacramento St.
1965	San Fran. St.
1966	Sacramento St.
1967	San Fran. St.
1968	Humboldt St.
1969	Cal St. Hayward
1970	Cal St. Chico
1971	UC Davis & Cal St. Chico
1972	UC Davis
1973	UC Davis & Cal St. Chico
1974	UC Davis
1975	UC Davis
1976	UC Davis
1977	UC Davis
1978	UC Davis
1979	UC Davis
1980	UC Davis
1981	UC Davis & Cal St. Hayward
1982	UC Davis
1983	UC Davis
1984	UC Davis
1985	UC Davis
1986	UC Davis
1987	UC Davis
1988	UC Davis
1989	UC Davis
1990	UC Davis
1991	Sonoma St.

Year	Champion (Record)
1992	UC Davis
1993	Cal St. Chico
1994	Humboldt St. & Cal St. Chico
1995	Humboldt St.
1996	Cal St. Chico

Division III

ASSOCIATION OF MIDEAST COLLEGES

Members (4): Thomas More, Bluffton, Wilmington [Ohio] and Mt. St. Joseph

Year	Champion
1991	Thomas More (3-0)
1992	Thomas More (3-0)
1993	Thomas More (3-0)
1994	Bluffton, Thomas More (2-1)
1995	Thomas More (3-0)

INDEPENDENT COLLEGE ATHLETIC CONFERENCE

Year	Champion
1970-73	Champion unknown
1974	Ithaca
1975	Ithaca
1976	Alfred
1977	Champion unknown
1978	Ithaca
1979	Ithaca
1980	Ithaca
1981	Alfred
1982	St. Lawrence
1983	St. Lawrence
1984	Ithaca
1985	Ithaca
1986	Ithaca
1987	Ithaca

2002 Results

2002 Results for

2002 Results for All Divisions

Listed alphabetically in this section are 2002 results for all football-playing NCAA member institutions. The division designation for each school is indicated to the right of the school location.

The coach listed is for the 2002 season for historical purposes.

Key: ■ –home game, *–neutral site.

ABILENE CHRISTIAN
Abilene, TX 79699 II

Coach: Gary Gaines, Angelo St. 1971
2002 RESULTS (6-4)
17	Central Ark. ■	31
17	UC Davis	34
9	Tarleton St.	12
20	Eastern N.M.	19
22	Central Okla. ■	20
30	Angelo St. ■	29
21	Midwestern St.	20
47	Tex. A&M-Commerce ■	6
16	Tex. A&M-Kingsville	22
35	West Tex. A&M ■	31

Nickname: Wildcats
Colors: Purple & White
Stadium: Shotwell
   Capacity: 15,000; Year Built: 1959
AD: Jared Mosley
SID: Lance Fleming

ADAMS ST.
Alamosa, CO 81102 II

Coach: Wayne McGinn, Adams St. 1981
2002 RESULTS (5-6)
23	Western N.M. ■	28
28	Okla. Panhandle	3
6	Montana St.	31
37	Fort Lewis	30
30	Fort Hays St. ■	6
13	Neb.-Kearney ■	17
38	N.M. Highlands	31
28	Mesa St.	35
24	Western St. (Colo.) ■	20
18	Colorado Mines ■	29
0	Chadron St.	24

Nickname: Grizzlies
Colors: Green & White
Stadium: Rex Field
   Capacity: 2,800; Year Built: 1949
AD: Jeff Geiser
SID: Chris Day

ADRIAN
Adrian, MI 49221 III

Coach: Jim Lyall, Michigan 1974
2002 RESULTS (6-4)
34	Heidelberg	31
14	Defiance	17
24	Franklin ■	14
28	Carthage	24
56	Wis. Lutheran ■	26
27	Hope ■	26
10	Olivet ■	23
31	Albion	21
16	Alma ■	27
24	Kalamazoo	31

Nickname: Bulldogs
Colors: Gold & Black
Stadium: Maple

   Capacity: 5,000; Year Built: 1960
AD: C. Henry Mensing
SID: Darcy Gifford

AIR FORCE
USAF Academy, CO 80840-5001 ....I-A

Coach: Fisher DeBerry, Wofford 1960
2002 RESULTS (8-5)
52	Northwestern ■	3
38	New Mexico ■	31
23	California	21
30	Utah	26
48	Navy ■	7
52	Brigham Young ■	9
14	Notre Dame ■	21
26	Wyoming	34
12	Colorado St. ■	31
49	Army	30
49	UNLV	32
34	San Diego St. ■	38
13	Virginia Tech (San Francisco Bowl)*	20

Nickname: Falcons
Colors: Blue & Silver
Stadium: Falcon
   Capacity: 52,480; Year Built: 1962
AD: Randall Spetman
SID: Troy Garnhart

AKRON
Akron, OH 44325 ....I-A

Coach: Lee Owens, Bluffton 1977
2002 RESULTS (4-8)
21	Iowa	57
14	Maryland	44
17	Central Mich. ■	24
29	Virginia	48
31	Miami (Ohio) ■	48
34	Eastern Mich.	42
49	Liberty ■	21
17	UCF	28
34	Marshall ■	20
10	Ohio	27
21	Buffalo ■	10
48	Kent St.	10

Nickname: Zips
Colors: Blue & Gold
Stadium: Rubber Bowl
   Capacity: 35,202; Year Built: 1940
AD: Michael J. Thomas
SID: Shawn Nestor

ALABAMA
Tuscaloosa, AL 35487 ....I-A

Coach: Dennis Franchione, Pittsburg St. 1973
2002 RESULTS (10-3)
39	Middle Tenn. ■	34
27	Oklahoma	37
33	North Texas ■	7
20	Southern Miss. ■	7
30	Arkansas	12
25	Georgia ■	27
42	Mississippi ■	7
34	Tennessee	14
30	Vanderbilt	8
28	Mississippi St. ■	14
31	LSU	0
7	Auburn ■	17
21	Hawaii	16

Nickname: Crimson Tide
Colors: Crimson & White
Stadium: Bryant-Denny
   Capacity: 83,818; Year Built: 1929

AD: Mal Moore
SID: Larry White

ALABAMA A&M
Normal, AL 35762 ....I-AA

Coach: Anthony Jones, Illinois St. 1980
2002 RESULTS (8-4)
17	Jacksonville St.	20
13	Grambling ■	23
15	Prairie View ■	12
21	Texas Southern	14
27	Southern U. *	11
25	Tennessee St. ■	21
24	Mississippi Val. ■	13
23	Alabama St. *	20
11	Jackson St.	13
27	Alcorn St. ■	20
39	Ark.-Pine Bluff	19
19	Grambling *	31

Nickname: Bulldogs
Colors: Maroon & White
Stadium: Louis Crews Stadium
   Capacity: 21,000; Year Built: 1996
AD: James A. Martin Sr.
SID: Walter G. Bishop, III

ALABAMA ST.
Montgomery, AL 36101-0271 ....I-AA

Coach: L.C. Cole, Nebraska 1980
2002 RESULTS (6-6)
27	Miles *	6
41	Chattanooga ■	23
43	Texas Southern ■	32
26	Ark.-Pine Bluff ■	32
37	Alcorn St.	48
40	Morris Brown ■	7
24	Jackson St. *	20
20	Alabama A&M *	23
21	Grambling	34
10	Mississippi Val. ■	13
28	Savannah St.	13
20	Tuskegee ■	25

Nickname: Hornets
Colors: Black & Gold
Stadium: Cramton
   Capacity: 24,600; Year Built: 1922
AD: Robert Spivery
SID: Ronnie Johnson

UAB
Birmingham, AL 35294-0110 ....I-A

Coach: Watson Brown, Vanderbilt 1973
2002 RESULTS (5-7)
3	Florida	51
27	Troy St. ■	26
20	Pittsburgh ■	26
0	La.-Lafayette	34
31	Memphis ■	17
51	Houston ■	34
14	Tulane	35
29	Army	26
13	Southern Miss. ■	20
36	East Caro. ■	29
21	Louisville	41
23	Cincinnati	31

Nickname: Blazers
Colors: Forest Green & Old Gold
Stadium: Legion Field
   Capacity: 83,091; Year Built: 1927
AD: Watson Brown
SID: Norm Reilly

ALBANY ST. (GA.)
Albany, GA 31705 II

Coach: James White, Albany St. (Ga.) 1990
2002 RESULTS (7-4)

0	Valdosta St. ■	26
19	Miles ■	25
29	West Ga. ■	32
49	Lane ■	0
36	Savannah St. *	14
40	Tuskegee	20
27	Kentucky St.	30
33	Clark Atlanta ■	0
34	Benedict	2
22	Morehouse *	8
31	Fort Valley St. *	7

Nickname: Golden Rams
Colors: Blue & Gold
Stadium: Hugh Mills Memorial
  Capacity: 11,000; Year Built: 1957
AD: John I. Davis
SID: Edythe Y. Bradley

ALBANY (N.Y.)
Albany, NY 12222 .... I-AA

Coach: Bob Ford, Springfield 1959
2002 RESULTS (8-4)

7	Montana	45
21	Central Conn. St. ■	12
38	Sacred Heart	17
20	Stony Brook	24
35	Wagner ■	14
42	Drake	49
44	Canisius ■	14
49	St. Francis (Pa.) ■	21
32	Robert Morris	7
26	Florida Int'l	35
19	Monmouth ■	7
24	Duquesne ■	0

Nickname: Great Danes
Colors: Purple & Gold
Stadium: University Field
  Capacity: 10,000; Year Built: 1967
AD: Lee McElroy
SID: Brian DePasquale

ALBION
Albion, MI 49224 III

Coach: Craig Rundle, Albion 1974
2002 RESULTS (5-5)

7	Wittenberg	44
0	Tri-State	38
51	Buffalo St. ■	7
16	Ohio Wesleyan ■	0
17	Olivet ■	14
27	Wis. Lutheran	10
31	Alma ■	52
21	Kalamazoo	20
21	Adrian ■	31
21	Hope	24

Nickname: Britons
Colors: Purple & Gold
Stadium: Sprankle-Sprandel
  Capacity: 4,244; Year Built: 1976
AD: Peter M. Hart
SID: Bobby Lee

ALBRIGHT
Reading, PA 19612-5234 III

Coach: E.J. Sandusky, Penn St. 1992
2002 RESULTS (2-8)

52	Delaware Valley ■	14
21	Juniata	48

31	Dickinson ■	38
35	Susquehanna	40
48	Lebanon Valley ■	7
22	Wilkes ■	26
12	Lycoming	35
7	Moravian	28
7	King's (Pa.) ■	35
12	Widener	13

Nickname: Lions
Colors: Red & White
Stadium: Eugene L. Shirk
  Capacity: 7,000; Year Built: 1925
AD: Sally Stetler
SID: Jeff Feiler

ALCORN ST.
Alcorn State, MS 39096-7500 .... I-AA

Coach: Johnny Thomas, Alcorn St. 1978
2002 RESULTS (6-5)

34	Ark.-Pine Bluff ■	24
35	Grambling	41
27	Hampton	23
48	Alabama St. ■	37
10	Fort Valley St. ■	7
33	Prairie View	13
25	Samford	34
22	Southern U.	20
6	Mississippi Val.	23
20	Alabama A&M	27
20	Jackson St.	34

Nickname: Braves
Colors: Purple & Gold
Stadium: Jack Spinks
  Capacity: 25,000; Year Built: 1992
AD: Robert Raines
SID: Peter Forest

ALFRED
Alfred, NY 14802 III

Coach: David Murray, Springfield 1981
2002 RESULTS (4-6)

26	St. John Fisher ■	34
11	Ithaca ■	33
16	St. Lawrence	13
3	Waynesburg ■	39
20	Union (N.Y.)	12
27	Hartwick	38
10	Utica ■	0
19	Hobart	25
7	Grove City	12
22	Thiel ■	14

Nickname: Saxons
Colors: Purple & Gold
Stadium: Merrill Field
  Capacity: 5,000; Year Built: 1926
AD: James M. Moretti
SID: Mark Whitehouse

ALLEGHENY
Meadville, PA 16335 III

Coach: Mark Matlak, Allegheny 1978
2002 RESULTS (5-5)

2	Baldwin-Wallace ■	22
28	Wash. & Jeff. ■	25
13	Westminster (Pa.)	24
14	Wabash ■	24
56	Hiram ■	0
7	Wooster ■	21
50	Denison	16
3	Wittenberg	49
28	Earlham ■	7
30	Ohio Wesleyan	16

Nickname: Gators
Colors: Blue & Gold
Stadium: Robertson Field

Capacity: 3,500; Year Built: 1948
AD: Larry Lee
SID: Ken Baker

ALMA
Alma, MI 48801 III

Coach: Jim Cole, Alma 1974
2002 RESULTS (9-2)

6	Gust. Adolphus	35
23	Wheaton (Ill.) ■	16
52	Manchester	18
49	Defiance ■	7
59	Hope ■	13
21	Olivet ■	14
52	Albion	31
41	Wis. Lutheran ■	3
34	Kalamazoo ■	20
27	Adrian	16
14	Wheaton (Ill.) ■	42

Nickname: Scots
Colors: Maroon & Cream
Stadium: Bahlke Field
  Capacity: 4,000; Year Built: 1986
AD: James Cole
SID: Dave Girrard

AMERICAN INT'L
Springfield, MA 01109-3189 II

Coach: Art Wilkins, Bucknell 1972
2002 RESULTS (5-6)

20	Stonehill	15
13	Massachusetts	42
37	St. Anselm ■	26
8	Bentley ■	26
8	Merrimack	18
9	Assumption	10
14	Southern Conn. St.	42
20	C.W. Post ■	27
34	Pace ■	7
40	Bryant	33
41	Mass.-Lowell ■	16

Nickname: Yellow Jackets
Colors: Gold, White & Black
Stadium: J. H. Miller Field
  Capacity: 5,000; Year Built: 1964
AD: Robert E. Burke
SID: George Sylvester

AMHERST
Amherst, MA 01002 III

Coach: E.J. Mills, Dayton 1988
2002 RESULTS (6-2)

19	Bates ■	0
42	Bowdoin	20
17	Middlebury	10
14	Colby ■	0
13	Wesleyan (Conn.)	14
27	Tufts ■	24
14	Trinity (Conn.)	21
45	Williams	35

Nickname: Lord Jeffs
Colors: Purple & White
Stadium: Pratt Field
  Capacity: 8,000; Year Built: 1891
AD: Peter J. Gooding
SID: Kevin Graber

ANDERSON (IND.)
Anderson, IN 46012-3495 III

Coach: Steve Barrows, Ohio 1984
2002 RESULTS (7-3)

25	Capital	24

30	Taylor (Ind.) ■	31
60	Concordia (Ill.)	7
7	Millikin ■	65
32	Defiance	24
41	Bluffton ■	17
23	Hanover	41
46	Mt. St. Joseph ■	15
34	Franklin	17
35	Manchester ■	12

Nickname: Ravens
Colors: Orange & Black
Stadium: Macholtz
  Capacity: 4,200
AD: A. Barrett Bates
SID: Justin Bates

ANGELO ST.
San Angelo, TX 76909 II

Coach: Jerry Vandergriff, Tex. A&M-Corp. Chris 1964
2002 RESULTS (2-8)

0	Tarleton St. ■	38
20	Southeastern Okla. ■	26
24	Southwestern Okla.	31
19	West Tex. A&M	0
14	Eastern N.M.	23
29	Abilene Christian	30
21	East Central	34
6	Midwestern St. ■	38
17	Tex. A&M-Commerce ■	16
14	Tex. A&M-Kingsville ■	37

Nickname: Rams
Colors: Blue & Gold
Stadium: San Angelo
  Capacity: 17,500; Year Built: 1962
AD: Jerry Vandergriff
SID: M.L. Stark Hinkle

APPALACHIAN ST.
Boone, NC 28608 ....I-AA

Coach: Jerry Moore, Baylor 1961
2002 RESULTS (8-4)

17	Marshall	50
36	Eastern Ky. ■	28
29	Liberty	22
37	Citadel ■	28
29	East Tenn. St.	10
16	Furman ■	15
20	Ga. Southern	36
19	Wofford ■	26
20	Chattanooga	17
54	VMI ■	13
24	Western Caro.	14
13	Maine ■	14

Nickname: Mountaineers
Colors: Black & Gold
Stadium: Kidd Brewer
  Capacity: 16,650; Year Built: 1962
AD: Roachel Laney
SID: Kelby Siler

ARIZONA
Tucson, AZ 85721-0096 ....I-A

Coach: John Mackovic, Wake Forest 1965
2002 RESULTS (4-8)

37	Northern Ariz. ■	3
23	Utah ■	17
10	Wisconsin	31
14	North Texas ■	9
14	Oregon ■	31
28	Washington	32
6	Stanford	16
13	Washington St. ■	21
3	Oregon St.	38
7	UCLA ■	37
52	California	41
20	Arizona St. ■	34

Nickname: Wildcats
Colors: Cardinal & Navy
Stadium: Arizona
  Capacity: 56,500; Year Built: 1928
AD: Jim Livengood
SID: Tom Duddleston Jr.

ARIZONA ST.
Tempe, AZ 85287-2505 ....I-A

Coach: Dirk Koetter, Idaho St. 1981
2002 RESULTS (8-6)

10	Nebraska	48
38	Eastern Wash. ■	2
46	UCF ■	13
39	San Diego St.	28
65	Stanford ■	24
35	North Carolina ■	38
13	Oregon St.	9
45	Oregon	42
27	Washington ■	16
22	Washington St.	44
38	California	55
13	Southern California	34
34	Arizona	20
27	Kansas St. (Holiday Bowl)*	34

Nickname: Sun Devils
Colors: Maroon & Gold
Stadium: Sun Devil
  Capacity: 73,379; Year Built: 1959
AD: Eugene Smith
SID: Mark Brand

ARKANSAS
Fayetteville, AR 72701 ....I-A

Coach: Houston Nutt, Oklahoma St. 1981
2002 RESULTS (9-5)

41	Boise St. ■	14
42	South Fla. ■	3
12	Alabama ■	30
38	Tennessee	41
38	Auburn ■	17
17	Kentucky ■	29
48	Mississippi ■	28
23	Troy St. ■	0
23	South Carolina	0
24	La.-Lafayette ■	17
26	Mississippi St.	19
21	LSU ■	20
3	Georgia *	30
14	Minnesota (Music City Bowl) *	29

Nickname: Razorbacks
Colors: Cardinal & White
Stadium: Razorback
  Capacity: 72,000; Year Built: 1938
AD: J. Frank Broyles
SID: Kevin Trainor

ARKANSAS ST.
State University, AR 72467 ....I-A

Coach: Steve Roberts, Ouachita Baptist 1987
2002 RESULTS (6-7)

7	Virginia Tech	63
14	San Jose St. *	33
21	Tulsa ■	19
7	Illinois	59
33	La.-Monroe	21
30	Tenn.-Martin ■	10
13	Middle Tenn. ■	7
17	Mississippi	52
10	North Texas ■	13
21	New Mexico St. ■	26
38	Southern Utah ■	16

10	La.-Lafayette	13
38	Idaho	29

Nickname: Indians
Colors: Scarlet & Black
Stadium: Indian
  Capacity: 30,708; Year Built: 1974
AD: Dean Lee
SID: Gina Bowman

ARKANSAS TECH
Russellville, AR 72801-2222 II

Coach: Steve Mullins, Ark.-Monticello 1980
2002 RESULTS (4-7)

7	Northeastern St. ■	9
24	Central Okla. ■	17
3	Ouachita Baptist	35
14	Harding ■	32
12	Henderson St.	18
24	Delta St. ■	17
14	North Ala.	49
14	West Ga. ■	12
25	West Ala. ■	0
24	Valdosta St.	31
0	Central Ark.	33

Nickname: Wonder Boys
Colors: Green & Gold
Stadium: Buerkle Field
  Capacity: 6,000
AD: Joe Foley
SID: Larry Smith

ARK.-MONTICELLO
Monticello, AR 71656-3596 II

Coach: Gregg Ricono, Tarkio 1986
2002 RESULTS (2-8)

41	Southeast Mo. St.	42
27	West Ala.	23
30	North Ala.	14
21	Central Ark. ■	42
17	Valdosta St.	45
21	Ouachita Baptist ■	23
27	Harding	40
0	Southern Ark.	48
7	Henderson St. ■	35
0	Delta St.	40

Nickname: Boll Weevils
Colors: Kelly Green & White
Stadium: Cotton Boll
  Capacity: 4,500; Year Built: 1934
AD: Alvy Early
SID: Chris Pluto

ARK.-PINE BLUFF
Pine Bluff, AR 71601 ....I-AA

Coach: Lee Hardman, Ark.-Pine Bluff 1972
2002 RESULTS (3-8)

24	Alcorn St.	34
36	Mississippi Val.	30
13	Southern U. ■	14
32	Alabama St.	26
44	Kentucky St. *	47
20	Texas Southern	42
15	Grambling *	54
0	Jackson St. ■	42
44	Prairie View ■	0
37	Lane ■	40
19	Alabama A&M ■	39

Nickname: Golden Lions
Colors: Black & Gold
Stadium: Golden Lion Stadium
  Capacity: 13,000; Year Built: 1999
AD: Craig Curry
SID: Carl Whimper

ARMY
West Point, NY 10996-2101 ....I–A

Coach: Todd Berry, Tulsa 1983
2002 RESULTS (1-11)
21	Holy Cross ■	30
0	Rutgers	44
14	Louisville ■	45
6	Southern Miss. ■	27
24	East Caro. ■	59
27	TCU ■	46
42	Houston ■	56
26	UAB ■	29
30	Air Force ■	49
14	Tulane	10
10	Memphis	38
12	Navy *	58

Nickname: Black Knights/Cadets
Colors: Black, Gold & Gray
Stadium: Michie
    Capacity: 40,000; Year Built: 1924
AD: Richard I. Greenspan
SID: Bob Beretta

ASHLAND
Ashland, OH 44805 II

Coach: Gary Keller, Bluffton 1973
2002 RESULTS (2-9)
23	Michigan Tech ■	30
26	Edinboro	29
7	Northwood ■	32
7	Hillsdale	37
20	Saginaw Valley ■	52
25	Wayne St. (Mich.)	20
27	Mercyhurst	20
14	Northern Mich.	24
20	Findlay ■	25
14	Indianapolis	35
8	Ferris St.	30

Nickname: Eagles
Colors: Purple & Gold
Stadium: Community
    Capacity: 5,700; Year Built: 1963
AD: Bill Goldring
SID: Al King

ASSUMPTION
Worcester, MA 01609 II

Coach: Sean Mahoney, Worcester St. 1996
2002 RESULTS (2-9)
0	C.W. Post	54
12	Southern Conn. St. ■	40
7	Merrimack ■	28
28	Bryant	43
13	St. Anselm ■	38
10	American Int'l ■	9
7	Stonehill	41
0	Pace	13
6	Bentley	37
14	Mass.-Lowell ■	37
23	Mount Ida ■	6

Nickname: Greyhounds
Colors: Royal Blue & White
Stadium: Rocheleau Field
    Capacity: 1,200; Year Built: 1961
AD: Rita M. Castagna
SID: Steve Morris

AUBURN
Auburn , AL 36849-5113 ....I–A

Coach: Tommy Tuberville, Southern Ark. 1976
2002 RESULTS (9-4)
17	Southern California	24
56	Western Caro. ■	0
31	Vanderbilt	6
42	Mississippi St.	14
37	Syracuse ■	34
17	Arkansas ■	38
23	Florida	30
31	LSU ■	7
31	Mississippi	24
52	La.-Monroe ■	14
21	Georgia ■	24
17	Alabama	7
13	Penn St. (Capital One Bowl) *	9

Nickname: Tigers
Colors: Burnt Orange & Navy Blue
Stadium: Jordan-Hare
    Capacity: 86,063; Year Built: 1939
AD: David E. Housel
SID: Meredith Jenkins

AUGSBURG
Minneapolis, MN 55454 III

Coach: Jack Osberg, Augsburg 1962
2002 RESULTS (2-8)
44	Dakota St. ■	14
13	Wis.-Eau Claire ■	37
21	St. Olaf	23
14	Gust. Adolphus ■	41
49	Carleton	6
13	Concordia-M'head	38
7	St. John's (Minn.) ■	35
6	St. Thomas (Minn.)	49
22	Bethel (Minn.) ■	29
13	Hamline *	21

Nickname: Auggies
Colors: Maroon & Gray
Stadium: Edor Nelson Field
    Capacity: 2,000; Year Built: 1984
AD: Paul Grauer
SID: Don Stoner

AUGUSTANA (ILL.)
Rock Island, IL 61201-2296.........................III

Coach: Jim Barnes, Augustana (Ill.) 1981
2002 RESULTS (7-2)
17	Wis.-Stevens Point	20
34	Central (Iowa) ■	14
65	North Central	0
27	Ill. Wesleyan ■	10
58	North Park	8
41	Millikin ■	14
58	Elmhurst ■	0
34	Carthage	28
14	Wheaton (Ill.)	38

Nickname: Vikings
Colors: Gold & Blue
Stadium: Ericson Field
    Capacity: 3,200; Year Built: 1938
AD: Gregory D. Wallace
SID: Dave Wrath

AUGUSTANA (S.D.)
Sioux Falls, SD 57197 II

Coach: Jim Heinitz, South Dakota St. 1972
2002 RESULTS (7-4)
14	Northern St. ■	6
29	Southwest St.	23
7	Minn. St. Mankato ■	0
23	North Dakota St.	6
7	St. Cloud St. ■	45
10	South Dakota	16
39	South Dakota St.	33
7	Northern Colo. ■	31
30	Lincoln (Mo.)	6
38	North Dakota ■	31
16	Neb.-Omaha	21

Nickname: Vikings
Colors: Navy & Yellow
Stadium: Howard Wood
    Capacity: 10,000; Year Built: 1957
AD: Bill Gross
SID: Karen Madsen

AURORA
Aurora, IL 60506...III

Coach: Jim Scott, Luther 1960
2002 RESULTS (5-4)
13	Trinity Int'l ■	35
13	Millikin	54
10	Concordia (Wis.) ■	20
51	Benedictine (Ill.) ■	18
67	Concordia (Ill.)	21
66	Eureka ■	7
23	Lakeland ■	13
18	MacMurray	19
47	Greenville	0

Nickname: Spartans
Colors: Royal Blue & White
Stadium: Aurora Field
    Capacity: 1,750
AD: Mark Walsh
SID: Brian Kipley

AUSTIN
Sherman, TX 75090-4440.........................III

Coach: David Norman, Austin 1983
2002 RESULTS (4-6)
0	Trinity (Tex.)	49
3	Mary Hardin-Baylor	44
38	McMurry ■	7
14	East Tex. Baptist	19
24	Texas Lutheran	21
34	Louisiana Col. ■	27
27	Mississippi Col.	23
0	Howard Payne ■	20
9	Sul Ross St.	25
24	Hardin-Simmons ■	42

Nickname: Kangaroos
Colors: Crimson & Gold
Stadium: Jerry Apple
    Capacity: 2,500; Year Built: 2000
AD: Timothy P. Millerick
SID: Chuck Sadowski

RESULTS

AUSTIN PEAY
Clarksville, TN 37044-4576 ....I–AA

Coach: Bill Schmitz, Coast Guard 1976
2002 RESULTS (7-5)
17	Cumberland (Tenn.) ■	16
45	Campbellsville	36
13	Centre ■	20
0	Dayton ■	42
20	Jacksonville	16
3	Troy St.	41
40	Butler	23
23	Ky. Wesleyan ■	21
25	Morehead St. ■	45
45	St. Joseph's (Ind.)	0
28	Davidson ■	49
28	Valparaiso	24

Nickname: Governors
Colors: Red & White
Stadium: Governors
  Capacity: 10,000; Year Built: 1946
AD: Dave Loos
SID: Brad Kirtley

AVERETT
Danville, VA 24541 III

Coach: Mike Dunlevy, Otterbein 1987
2002 RESULTS (2-7)
43	Gallaudet ■	0
14	Apprentice ■	20
10	Gettysburg	45
10	Ferrum ■	17
0	Methodist	43
14	Greensboro ■	24
13	Shenandoah	31
0	Chris. Newport	27
27	Chowan ■	0

Nickname: Cougars
Colors: Navy & Gold
Stadium: Hawkins Bradley
  Capacity: 5,000
AD: Vesa Hiltunen
SID: Sam Ferguson

BALDWIN-WALLACE
Berea, OH 44017 III

Coach: John Snell, Baldwin-Wallace 1987
2002 RESULTS (8-2)
22	Allegheny	2
21	Mount Union ■	28
47	Heidelberg	6
13	John Carroll	20
48	Ohio Northern ■	41
47	Wilmington (Ohio)	7
49	Muskingum ■	10
38	Capital ■	7
40	Marietta	14
56	Otterbein ■	0

Nickname: Yellow Jackets
Colors: Brown & Gold
Stadium: George Finnie
  Capacity: 8,100; Year Built: 1971
AD: Stephen Bankson
SID: Kevin Ruple

BALL ST.
Muncie, IN 47306 ....I–A

Coach: Bill Lynch, Butler 1977
2002 RESULTS (6-6)
6	Missouri	41
23	Indiana St. ■	21
7	Clemson	30
24	Connecticut	21
29	Northern Ill. ■	41
17	Toledo	37
42	Eastern Mich. ■	17
20	Bowling Green	38
17	Western Mich. ■	7
38	Central Mich.	21
41	Buffalo ■	21
14	Marshall	38

Nickname: Cardinals
Colors: Cardinal & White
Stadium: Ball State
  Capacity: 22,500; Year Built: 1967
AD: Lawrence R. Cunningham
SID: Joe Hernandez

BATES
Lewiston, ME 04240 III

Coach: Mark Harriman, Springfield 1980
2002 RESULTS (3-5)
0	Amherst	19
0	Tufts	27
0	Williams ■	24
17	Wesleyan (Conn.) ■	20
7	Middlebury	28
19	Colby ■	14
48	Bowdoin	28
37	Hamilton ■	0

Nickname: Bobcats
Colors: Garnet
Stadium: Garcelon Field
  Capacity: 3,000; Year Built: 1900
AD: Suzanne R. Coffey
SID: John Jordan

BAYLOR
Waco, TX 76798-7096 ....I–A

Coach: Kevin Steele, Tennessee 1981
2002 RESULTS (3-9)
22	California	70
50	Samford ■	12
0	New Mexico	23
37	Tulsa ■	25
35	Kansas ■	32
0	Texas A&M ■	41
0	Colorado	34
10	Kansas St. ■	44
11	Texas Tech	62
0	Texas	41
9	Oklahoma ■	49
28	Oklahoma St.	63

Nickname: Bears
Colors: Green & Gold
Stadium: Floyd Casey
  Capacity: 50,000; Year Built: 1950
AD: Thomas I. Stanton
SID: Scott Stricklin

BELOIT
Beloit, WI 53511-5595 III

Coach: Ed DeGeorge, Colorado Col. 1964
2002 RESULTS (6-4)
19	Macalester	14
32	St. Norbert	51
23	Lake Forest	24
44	Monmouth (Ill.) ■	28
27	Lawrence	14
39	Carroll (Wis.) ■	18
32	Grinnell ■	19
16	Knox	41
23	Ripon	34
41	Illinois Col. ■	14

Nickname: Buccaneers
Colors: Navy Blue & Gold
Stadium: Strong
  Capacity: 3,500; Year Built: 1934
AD: Edward J. DeGeorge
SID: Keith E. Domke

BEMIDJI ST.
Bemidji, MN 56601-2699 II

Coach: Jeff Tesch, Minn. St. Moorhead 1978
2002 RESULTS (6-5)
23	Minn. St. Mankato	45
28	Minot St. ■	35
23	Winona St.	25
38	Wayne St. (Neb.) ■	2
28	Northern St.	21
14	Concordia-St. Paul	38
37	Southwest St. ■	0
35	Minn. St. Moorhead	28
25	Minn. Duluth	52
38	Minn.-Morris ■	13
21	Minn.-Crookston	7

Nickname: Beavers
Colors: Kelly Green & White
Stadium: BSU
  Capacity: 4,000; Year Built: 1937
AD: Rick Goeb
SID: Andy Bartlett

BENEDICT
Columbia, SC 29204 II

Coach: Willie Felder
2002 RESULTS (2-9)
26	Lane	30
7	South Carolina St. ■	52
0	Tuskegee	7
14	Morehouse ■	23
27	Miles	28
27	Clark Atlanta ■	25
0	Fort Valley St.	15
26	Kentucky St.	21
2	Albany St. (Ga.) ■	34
27	Stillman	34
0	Edward Waters ■	6

Nickname: Tigers
Colors: Purple & Gold
AD: Willie Washington
SID: Frankie Jackson

BENEDICTINE (ILL.)
Lisle, IL 60532-0900 III

Coach: Jeff Hand, Clarion 1992
2002 RESULTS (4-6)
19	Elmhurst	22
32	North Central ■	21
20	Carthage ■	49
27	Greenville ■	21
18	Aurora	51
22	Eureka ■	3
12	MacMurray	28
3	Concordia (Wis.)	42
32	Concordia (Ill.) ■	13
13	Lakeland	27

Nickname: Eagles
Colors: Red & White
Stadium: Alumni Field
  Capacity: 2,500; Year Built: 1910
AD: Lynn O'Linski
SID: Jill Redmond

BENTLEY

Waltham, MA 02154-4705 II

Coach: Peter Yetten, Boston U. 1970
2002 RESULTS (10-1)
28	St. Anselm	0
16	Merrimack	6
34	Southern Conn. St. ■	27
26	American Int'l	8
34	Mass.-Lowell	9
44	Bryant ■	22
33	Pace ■	13
35	Plymouth St.	7
37	Assumption ■	6
18	C.W. Post	21
41	Stonehill	26

Nickname: Falcons
Colors: Blue & Gold
Stadium: Bentley College
  Capacity: 3,200; Year Built: 1990
AD: Robert De Felice
SID: Dick Lipe

BETHANY (W.VA.)

Bethany, WV 26032-0417 III

Coach: Chris Snyder, Randolph-Macon 1989
2002 RESULTS (3-7)
9	Carnegie Mellon ■	31
55	Kenyon ■	7
28	Wooster	38
20	Grove City ■	28
21	Waynesburg	42
20	Westminster (Pa.)	23
28	Wash. & Jeff. ■	37
31	Thiel ■	9
34	Apprentice	7
17	McDaniel ■	28

Nickname: Bison
Colors: Kelly Green & White
Stadium: Bethany Field
  Capacity: 1,000; Year Built: 1938
AD: Janice L. Forsty
SID: Brian Rose

BETHEL (MINN.)

St. Paul, MN 55112-6999 III

Coach: Steve Johnson, Bethel (Minn.) 1979
2002 RESULTS (5-5)
26	Whitworth	27
25	St. Thomas (Minn.)	49
14	Concordia-M'head ■	35
41	Hamline ■	7
0	Wis.-Eau Claire ■	40
36	St. Olaf ■	32
41	Gust. Adolphus	20
41	Carleton ■	0
29	Augsburg	22
26	St. John's (Minn.) *	31

Nickname: Royals
Colors: Blue & Gold
Stadium: Royal
  Capacity: 3,500; Year Built: 1996
AD: David A. Klostreich
SID: Greg Peterson

BETHUNE-COOKMAN

Daytona Beach, FL 32114-3099 ....I–AA

Coach: Alvin Wyatt Sr., Bethune-Cookman 1970
2002 RESULTS (11-2)
41	Savannah St. *	9
30	Fla. Atlantic	17

42	Morris Brown	7
31	Florida Int'l *	0
49	Norfolk St. ■	7
41	Morgan St.	27
49	Delaware St. ■	7
21	South Carolina St.	6
13	N.C. A&T	12
7	Hampton	37
46	Howard ■ *	27
37	Florida A&M *	10
0	Ga. Southern	34

Nickname: Wildcats
Colors: Maroon & Gold
Stadium: Municipal
  Capacity: 10,000
AD: Lynn W. Thompson
SID: Charles D. Jackson

BLACKBURN

Carlinville, IL 62626 III

Coach: Skip Mathieson, DePauw 1957
2002 RESULTS (1-9)
0	Illinois Col.	40
7	Crown ■	10
13	Martin Luther	14
30	Principia	52
20	Westminster (Mo.) ■	40
0	Maranatha Baptist	32
3	Northwestern (Minn.) ■	51
14	Rockford ■	26
46	Trinity Bible (N.D.) *	8
0	MacMurray	35

Nickname: Battlin' Beavers
Colors: Scarlet & Black
Stadium: Blackburn College
  Capacity: 1,500; Year Built: 1989
AD: Joe Ramsey
SID: Mary McNeely

BLOOMSBURG

Bloomsburg, PA 17815 II

Coach: Danny Hale, West Chester 1968
2002 RESULTS (8-2)
18	Indiana (Pa.)	37
27	Shippensburg	26
47	Lock Haven ■	23
38	Slippery Rock ■	14
13	East Stroudsburg ■	16
49	Millersville	26
31	Kutztown	21
37	Cheyney ■	12
23	West Chester ■	10
17	Mansfield	6

Nickname: Huskies
Colors: Maroon & Gold
Stadium: Redman
  Capacity: 5,000; Year Built: 1974
AD: Mary Gardner
SID: Tom McGuire

BLUFFTON

Bluffton, OH 45817-1196 III

Coach: Carlin Carpenter, Defiance 1964
2002 RESULTS (3-7)
27	Marietta	28
45	Hiram ■	0
6	Thiel	37
31	Urbana ■	14
17	Anderson (Ind.)	41
21	Hanover	47
35	Mt. St. Joseph	37
34	Franklin ■	21
6	Manchester	18
6	Defiance ■	29

Nickname: Beavers
Colors: Royal Purple & White
Stadium: Salzman
  Capacity: 3,000; Year Built: 1993
AD: Carlin B. Carpenter
SID: Tim Stried

BOISE ST.

Boise, ID 83725-1020 ....I–A

Coach: Dan Hawkins, UC Davis 1984
2002 RESULTS (12-1)
38	Idaho ■	21
14	Arkansas	41
35	Wyoming	13
63	Utah St. ■	38
58	Hawaii ■	31
52	Tulsa	24
67	Fresno St. ■	21
45	San Jose St.	8
58	UTEP	3
49	Rice ■	7
36	Louisiana Tech ■	10
44	Nevada	7
34	Iowa St. (Humanitarian Bowl) ■	16

Nickname: Broncos
Colors: Orange & Blue
Stadium: Bronco
  Capacity: 30,000; Year Built: 1970
AD: Gene Bleymaier
SID: Max Corbet

BOSTON COLLEGE

Chestnut Hill, MA 02467-3861 ....I–A

Coach: Tom O'Brien, Navy 1971
2002 RESULTS (9-4)
24	Connecticut ■	16
34	Stanford ■	27
6	Miami (Fla.)	38
43	Central Mich. ■	0
23	Virginia Tech ■	28
46	Navy ■	21
16	Pittsburgh	19
14	Notre Dame	7
14	West Virginia	24
41	Syracuse ■	20
36	Temple	14
44	Rutgers ■	14
51	Toledo (Motor City Bowl)*	25

Nickname: Eagles
Colors: Maroon & Gold
Stadium: Alumni
  Capacity: 44,500; Year Built: 1957
AD: Gene De Filippo
SID: Chris Cameron

BOWDOIN

Brunswick, ME 04011 III

Coach: Dave Caputi, Middlebury 1981
2002 RESULTS (1-7)
7	Williams	38
20	Amherst ■	42
13	Tufts ■	44
28	Hamilton	14
14	Trinity (Conn.) ■	35
3	Wesleyan (Conn.)	17
28	Bates ■	48
27	Colby	32

Nickname: Polar Bears
Colors: White
Stadium: Whittier Field
  Capacity: 6,000; Year Built: 1896
AD: Jeffrey H. Ward
SID: Jac Coyne

RESULTS

BOWIE ST.
Bowie, MD 20715-9465 II

Coach: Henry Frazier III, Bowie St. 1993
2002 RESULTS (6-5)
34	West Virginia St.	7
7	Johnson Smith ■	6
12	Winston-Salem ■	24
34	St. Augustine's *	2
17	Morehouse	24
19	Virginia Union ■	8
0	Hampton	49
21	Elizabeth City St. ■	0
7	Fayetteville St.	13
10	Virginia St. ■ *	6
14	Fayetteville St. *	17

Nickname: Bulldogs
Colors: Black & Gold
Stadium: Bulldog
    Capacity: 6,000; Year Built: 1992
AD: Charles Davis
SID: TBA

BOWLING GREEN
Bowling Green, OH 43403 ....I–A

Coach: Urban Meyer, Cincinnati 1986
2002 RESULTS (9-3)
41	Tennessee Tech ■	7
51	Missouri ■	28
39	Kansas	16
72	Ohio ■	21
45	Central Mich.	35
48	Western Mich. ■	45
38	Ball St. ■	20
45	Kent St.	14
17	Northern Ill.	26
7	South Fla.	29
63	Eastern Mich. ■	21
24	Toledo	42

Nickname: Falcons
Colors: Orange & Brown
Stadium: Doyt Perry
    Capacity: 30,599; Year Built: 1966
AD: Paul Krebs
SID: J.D. Campbell

BRIDGEWATER (VA.)
Bridgewater, VA 22812-1599 III

Coach: Michael Clark, Cincinnati 1980
2002 RESULTS (11-1)
23	McDaniel	20
48	Shenandoah ■	6
42	Maryville (Tenn.) ■	0
25	Chris. Newport ■	6
38	Hampden-Sydney ■	7
56	Guilford	7
48	Emory & Henry ■	18
44	Wash. & Lee ■	14
52	Randolph-Macon	18
34	Catholic	13
19	King's (Pa.) ■	17
32	Trinity (Tex.) ■	38

Nickname: Eagles
Colors: Cardinal & Vegas Gold
Stadium: Jopson Field
    Capacity: 3,500; Year Built: 1971
AD: Curtis L. Kendall
SID: Steve Cox

BRIDGEWATER ST.
Bridgewater, MA 02325-9998 III

Coach: Peter Mazzaferro, Centre 1954
2002 RESULTS (4-5)
14	Nichols	31
14	Mass.-Dartmouth ■	31
48	Framingham St.	27
13	Fitchburg St. ■	23
21	Maine Maritime	3
10	Westfield St. ■	28
27	Salve Regina	23
0	Worcester St. ■	18
48	Mass. Maritime	18

Nickname: Bears
Colors: Crimson & White
Stadium: Ed Swenson Field
    Capacity: 2,000; Year Built: 1974
AD: John C. Harper
SID: Michael Holbrook

BRIGHAM YOUNG
Provo, UT 84602.............................I–A

Coach: Gary Crowton, Brigham Young 1983
2002 RESULTS (5-7)
42	Syracuse ■	21
35	Hawaii ■	32
28	Nevada	31
19	Georgia Tech	28
35	Utah St.	34
9	Air Force	52
3	UNLV ■	24
10	Colorado St.	37
34	San Diego St. ■	10
35	Wyoming	31
16	New Mexico ■	20
6	Utah	13

Nickname: Cougars
Colors: Blue, White & Tan
Stadium: LaVell Edwards
    Capacity: 64,045; Year Built: 1964
AD: Q. Val Hale
SID: Jeff Reynolds

BROCKPORT ST.
Brockport, NY 14420-2989..........................III

Coach: Rocco Salomone, Brockport St. 1988
2002 RESULTS (10-3)
12	Cortland St.	21
25	New Jersey City	7
35	Utica	0
31	Frostburg St.	25
38	Buffalo St. ■	0
41	St. John Fisher ■	14
21	Ithaca ■	0
17	Thiel ■	0
7	TCNJ	21
17	Wesley	6
16	Springfield ■	0
15	Rowan	12
10	John Carroll ■	16

Nickname: Golden Eagles
Colors: Green & Gold
Stadium: Special Olympics
    Capacity: 10,000; Year Built: 1979
AD: Linda J. Case
SID: Eric McDowell

BROWN
Providence, RI 02912............................I–AA

Coach: Phil Estes, New Hampshire 1981
2002 RESULTS (2-8)
42	Towson	56
24	Harvard ■	26
28	Rhode Island	00
17	Fordham	24
14	Princeton	16
7	Cornell ■	10
7	Pennsylvania	31
27	Yale ■	31
21	Dartmouth	18
35	Columbia ■	28

Nickname: Bears
Colors: Brown, Red & White
Stadium: Brown
    Capacity: 20,000; Year Built: 1925
AD: David T. Roach
SID: Christopher Humm

BRYANT
Smithfield, RI 02917-1284 II

Coach: Jim Miceli, Southern Conn. St. 1979
2002 RESULTS (5-6)
0	Rhode Island	28
21	Southern Conn. St.	37
3	C.W. Post ■	14
26	Pace ■	0
43	Assumption ■	28
22	Bentley	44
25	St. Anselm ■	13
12	Mass.-Lowell	6
9	Stonehill	8
33	American Int'l ■	40
14	Merrimack ■	20

Nickname: Bulldogs
Colors: Black, Gold & White
Stadium: Bulldog
    Capacity: 4,400; Year Built: 1999
AD: Dan Gavitt
SID: Chuck Sullivan

BUCKNELL
Lewisburg, PA 17837.............................I–AA

Coach: Dave Kotulski, New Mexico St. 1974
2002 RESULTS (2-9)
14	Duquesne	35
22	St. Mary's (Cal.)	23
14	Cornell ■	3
27	Delaware St. ■	13
10	Colgate	13
14	Towson	20
31	Georgetown	32
21	Holy Cross	38
3	Lafayette ■	19
0	Lehigh	24
7	Fordham ■	34

Nickname: Bison
Colors: Orange & Blue
Stadium: Christy Mathewson
    Capacity: 13,100; Year Built: 1924
AD: John P. Hardt
SID: Jon Terry

BUENA VISTA
Storm Lake, IA 50588-9990 III

Coach: Steve Osterberger, Drake 1990
2002 RESULTS (3-7)
24	Southwest St. ■	41
17	Simpson	20
25	Cornell College	35
19	Luther ■	9
19	Loras	35
38	Upper Iowa ■	13
5	Coe	40
14	Central (Iowa) ■	28
28	Dubuque	20
3	Wartburg ■	58

Nickname: Beavers
Colors: Blue & Gold
Stadium: J. Leslie Rollins
    Capacity: 3,500; Year Built: 1980
AD: Jan Travis
SID: Paul Misner

BUFFALO
Buffalo, NY 14260.....................................I–A

Coach: Jim Hofher, Cornell 1979
2002 RESULTS (1-11)
26	Lehigh ■	37
34	Rutgers	11
3	Connecticut ■	24
17	Minnesota	41
32	Ohio	34
17	Western Mich. ■	31
21	Marshall	66
0	Miami (Ohio) ■	49
12	Kent St. ■	16
21	UCF ■	45
10	Akron	21
21	Ball St.	41

Nickname: Bulls
Colors: Royal Blue & White
Stadium: UB Stadium
    Capacity: 31,000; Year Built: 1993
AD: William J. Maher
SID: Paul Vecchio

BUFFALO ST.
Buffalo, NY 14222-1095 III

Coach: Bob Swank, Widener 1990
2002 RESULTS (1-9)
12	Robert Morris	41
19	Mansfield ■	20
7	Albion	51
0	Cortland St. ■	28
0	Brockport St.	38
7	Rowan ■	28
21	Montclair St. ■	14
18	Case Reserve	23
7	Ithaca	39
3	Wash. & Jeff. ■	7

Nickname: Bengals
Colors: Orange & Black
Stadium: Coyer Field
    Capacity: 3,000; Year Built: 1964
AD: Jerry S. Boyes
SID: Jeff Ventura

BUTLER
Indianapolis, IN 46208-3485 ....I–AA

Coach: Kit Cartwright, Bowling Green 1976
2002 RESULTS (4-6)
54	Tiffin ■	31
0	Florida Int'l	42

43	Wis.-Stevens Point ■	29
20	Morehead St.	53
0	Dayton	41
23	Austin Peay ■	40
26	San Diego ■	35
48	Drake ■	44
52	Valparaiso	22
28	Quincy	37

Nickname: Bulldogs
Colors: Blue & White
Stadium: Butler Bowl
    Capacity: 19,000; Year Built: 1927
AD: John C. Parry
SID: Jim McGrath

C.W. POST
Brookville, NY 11548 II

Coach: Bryan Collins, St. John's (N.Y.) 1987
2002 RESULTS (11-1)
54	Assumption ■	0
14	Bryant	3
57	Mass.-Lowell ■	21
42	St. Anselm	0
43	Stonehill ■	0
20	New Haven	0
34	Merrimack	6
27	American Int'l	20
34	Southern Conn. St. ■	8
21	Bentley ■	18
35	Pace	16
13	Grand Valley St.	62

Nickname: Pioneers
Colors: Green & Gold
Stadium: Hickox Field
    Capacity: 5,000; Year Built: 1966
AD: Vincent Salamone
SID: Brad Sullivan

CALIFORNIA
Berkeley, CA 94720...............................I–A

Coach: Jeff Tedford, Fresno St. 1983
2002 RESULTS (7-5)
70	Baylor	22
34	New Mexico St. ■	13
46	Michigan St.	22
21	Air Force ■	23
38	Washington St. ■	48
34	Washington	27
28	Southern California	30
17	UCLA ■	12
13	Oregon St.	24
55	Arizona St.	38
41	Arizona ■	52
30	Stanford ■	7

Nickname: Golden Bears
Colors: Blue & Gold
Stadium: Memorial
    Capacity: 73,347; Year Built: 1923
AD: Stephen Gladstone
SID: Herb Benenson

UC DAVIS
Davis, CA 95616-8674 II

Coach: Bob Biggs, UC Davis 1973
2002 RESULTS (9-3)
17	Grand Valley St.	24
34	Abilene Christian ■	17
35	North Dakota St. ■	20
64	Western Ore.	20
38	Sacramento St. ■	21
49	Humboldt St. ■	14
28	Cal Poly	14
31	St. Mary's (Cal.) ■	28
14	Central Wash.	38

14	Western Wash.	7
24	Central Wash.	6
20	Tex. A&M-Kingsville	27

Nickname: Aggies
Colors: Yale Blue & Gold
Stadium: Toomey Field
    Capacity: 10,111; Year Built: 1949
AD: Greg Warzecka
SID: Mike Robles

CALIF. (PA.)
California, PA 15419 II

Coach: John Luckhardt, Purdue 1968
2002 RESULTS (6-5)
45	Geneva	0
14	Fairmont St.	6
24	West Va. Wesleyan ■	17
51	Cheyney	7
16	Slippery Rock	41
34	Lock Haven ■	19
9	Indiana (Pa.)	20
17	Mansfield ■	9
6	Clarion	31
22	Edinboro ■	38
7	Shippensburg ■	40

Nickname: Vulcans
Colors: Red & Black
Stadium: Adamson
    Capacity: 5,000; Year Built: 1970
AD: Thomas G. Pucci
SID: David W. Smith

CAL LUTHERAN
Thousand Oaks, CA 91360-2787...............III

Coach: Scott Squires, Pacific Lutheran 1988
2002 RESULTS (4-5)
32	Muhlenberg	40
10	Azusa Pacific ■	43
30	La Verne ■	6
17	Menlo ■	22
40	Chapman ■	28
12	Redlands	31
17	Claremont-M-S	28
6	Occidental ■	0
37	Whittier	19

Nickname: Kingsmen
Colors: Purple & Gold
Stadium: Mt. Clef
    Capacity: 2,000; Year Built: 1962
AD: Bruce Bryde
SID: Scott Flanders

CAL POLY
San Luis Obispo, CA 93407...................I–AA

Coach: Rich Ellerson, Hawaii 1976
2002 RESULTS (3-8)
16	Toledo	44
24	Northern Ariz. ■	31
34	Kent St.	37
17	Sacramento St.	27
26	Northern Iowa ■	29
27	Southern Utah	21
17	St. Mary's (Cal.)	35
14	UC Davis ■	28
30	Humboldt St. ■	0
14	Idaho St.	24
28	Weber St. ■	26

Nickname: Mustangs
Colors: Green & Gold
Stadium: Mustang
    Capacity: 8,500; Year Built: 1935
AD: John F. Mc Cutcheon
SID: Eric Burdick

CANISIUS
Buffalo, NY 14208-1098 ....I–AA

Coach: Ed Argast, Colgate 1978
2002 RESULTS (2-9)
14	St. John's (N.Y.)	17
0	Marist	28
11	Siena ■	18
3	St. Peter's ■	35
14	Iona	13
30	La Salle ■	27
14	Albany (N.Y.)	44
14	Fairfield ■	21
6	Dayton	42
0	Duquesne ■	42
7	Stony Brook	42

Nickname: Golden Griffins
Colors: Blue & Gold
Stadium: Demske Sports Complex
  Capacity: 1,000; Year Built: 1989
AD: Timothy J. Dillon
SID: Marc Gignac
Note: Discontinued football program following 2002 season.

CAPITAL
Columbus, OH 43209-2394 III

Coach: Jim Collins, Wittenberg 1987
2002 RESULTS (6-4)
24	Anderson (Ind.) ■	25
35	Otterbein ■	3
47	Ohio Northern ■	12
35	Marietta	0
27	Wilmington (Ohio)	7
52	Heidelberg	13
22	Mount Union ■	38
7	Baldwin-Wallace	38
35	Muskingum ■	27
6	John Carroll	16

Nickname: Crusaders
Colors: Purple & White
Stadium: Bernlohr
  Capacity: 3,000; Year Built: 2001
AD: Roger Welsh
SID: Leonard Reich

CARLETON
Northfield, MN 55057 III

Coach: Chris Brann, West Va. Wesleyan 1991
2002 RESULTS (0-10)
6	Dana ■	28
0	St. Olaf ■	49
14	Gust. Adolphus	48
7	Concordia-M'head	51
6	Augsburg ■	49
7	St. John's (Minn.)	49
7	St. Thomas (Minn.) ■	41
0	Bethel (Minn.)	41
14	Hamline ■	24
16	Macalester ■	33

Nickname: Knights
Colors: Maize & Blue
Stadium: Laird
  Capacity: 7,500; Year Built: 1926
AD: Leon Lunder
SID: Eric Sieger

CARNEGIE MELLON
Pittsburgh, PA 15213-3890 III

Coach: Rich Lackner, Carnegie Mellon 1979
2002 RESULTS (5-5)
31	Bethany (W.Va.) ■	9
9	Grove City	6
14	Randolph-Macon	17
7	Johns Hopkins	28
21	Frank. & Marsh. ■	0
35	Case Reserve	42
27	Rose-Hulman	17
27	Chicago ■	10
17	Washington (Mo.)	31
35	Rochester ■	39

Nickname: Tartans
Colors: Cardinal, White & Grey
Stadium: Gesling
  Capacity: 3,500; Year Built: 1990
AD: John H. Harvey
SID: Bethany J. McClam

CARROLL (WIS.)
Waukesha, WI 53186-5593 III

Coach: Jeff Voris, DePauw 1989
2002 RESULTS (1-9)
14	St. Olaf ■	57
7	Knox	38
27	Illinois Col. ■	30
45	Lawrence ■	14
7	Ripon	56
18	Beloit	39
14	St. Norbert ■	63
0	Lake Forest ■	18
24	Monmouth (Ill.)	35
14	Grinnell ■	21

Nickname: Pioneers
Colors: Orange & White
Stadium: Van Male Field
  Capacity: 4,200; Year Built: 1976
AD: Kris Jacobsen
SID: Rick Mobley

CARSON-NEWMAN
Jefferson City, TN 37760 II

Coach: Ken Sparks, Carson-Newman 1968
2002 RESULTS (12-1)
47	Winston-Salem ■	35
44	Guilford ■	0
36	New Haven	31
55	Western Ore. ■	20
45	Mars Hill ■	0
60	Newberry ■	36
47	Presbyterian	14
48	Tusculum ■	23
48	Lenoir-Rhyne	7
34	Catawba	9
35	Wingate ■	10
40	Fayetteville St. ■	27
28	Valdosta St.	31

Nickname: Eagles
Colors: Orange & Blue
Stadium: Burke-Tarr
  Capacity: 5,000; Year Built: 1966
AD: David W. Barger
SID: Marlin Curnutt

CARTHAGE
Kenosha, WI 53140 III

Coach: Tim Rucks, Carthage 1983
2002 RESULTS (4-6)
34	Lakeland	37
49	Benedictine (Ill.)	20
24	Adrian ■	28
12	Millikin	21
43	Elmhurst ■	7
6	Wheaton (Ill.)	36
19	North Central	22
21	Ill. Wesleyan ■	20
28	Augustana (Ill.) ■	34
52	North Park	22

Nickname: Redmen
Colors: Red, White & Black
Stadium: Art Keller Field
  Capacity: 1,800; Year Built: 1965
AD: Robert R. Bonn
SID: Steve Marovich

CASE RESERVE
Cleveland, OH 44106 III

Coach: Joe Perella, John Carroll 1963
2002 RESULTS (6-4)
42	Denison	13
37	Oberlin ■	11
22	Wooster	27
44	Kalamazoo	47
42	Maryville (Tenn.) ■	13
42	Carnegie Mellon ■	35
42	Washington (Mo.)	49
23	Buffalo St. ■	18
38	Rochester	29
39	Chicago ■	49

Nickname: Spartans
Colors: Blue, Gray & White
Stadium: E.L. Finnigan Field
  Capacity: 3,000; Year Built: 1968
AD: David M. Hutter
SID: Creg Jantz

CATAWBA
Salisbury, NC 28144-2488 II

Coach: Chip Hester, Guilford 1992
2002 RESULTS (8-3)
30	Livingstone	22
26	Indiana (Pa.)	27
27	Fayetteville St. ■	14
27	Presbyterian ■	14
22	Mars Hill	6
41	Wingate ■	7
45	Newberry	26
29	Tusculum	17
9	Carson-Newman ■	34
37	Lenoir-Rhyne	17
7	Valdosta St.	24

Nickname: Indians
Colors: Blue & White
Stadium: Shuford
  Capacity: 4,000; Year Built: 1926
AD: Dennis Davidson
SID: Jim Lewis

CATHOLIC
Washington, DC 20064..........................III

Coach: Tom Mulholland, Catholic 1992
2002 RESULTS (4-6)
7	John Carroll	56
6	Frank. & Marsh.	13
18	Randolph-Macon	26
26	La Salle ■	15
39	Wash. & Lee ■	20
41	Frostburg St. ■	35
20	Hampden-Sydney	30
47	Emory & Henry	48
28	Guilford	26
13	Bridgewater (Va.) ■	34

Nickname: Cardinals
Colors: Cardinal Red & Black
Stadium: Dufour Field
Capacity: 3,500; Year Built: 1985
AD: Robert J. Talbot
SID: Chris Panter

CENTRAL (IOWA)
Pella, IA 50219..........................III

Coach: Rich Kacmarynski, Central (Iowa) 1992
2002 RESULTS (8-2)
14	Augustana (Ill.)	34
17	Loras ■	7
50	Upper Iowa	0
21	Coe ■	20
21	Simpson ■	7
37	Dubuque	0
0	Wartburg ■	14
28	Buena Vista	14
48	Cornell College ■	0
33	Luther	3

Nickname: Dutch
Colors: Red & White
Stadium: Kuyper
Capacity: 5,000; Year Built: 1977
AD: Al Dorenkamp
SID: Larry Happel

CENTRAL ARK.
Conway, AR 72035-0001..........................II

Coach: Clint Conque, Nicholls St. 1983
2002 RESULTS (8-3)
31	Abilene Christian	17
47	Charleston (W.Va.) ■	0
68	Henderson St.	21
30	Ouachita Baptist ■	14
42	Ark.-Monticello	21
21	Southern Ark.	38
11	Valdosta St. ■	35
33	North Ala. ■	47
49	West Ga.	33
47	West Ala.	7
33	Arkansas Tech ■	0

Nickname: Bears
Colors: Purple & Gray
Stadium: Estes
Capacity: 8,500; Year Built: 1939
AD:
SID: Steve East

CENTRAL CONN. ST.
New Britain, CT 06050-4010..............I-AA

Coach: Paul Schudel, Miami (Ohio) 1966
2002 RESULTS (5-6)
3	Maine *	52
3	Massachusetts	52
12	Albany (N.Y.)	21
0	Robert Morris	14
16	St. John's (N.Y.) ■	8
30	Gannon ■	27
28	St. Francis (Pa.) ■	10
10	Monmouth	9
3	Sacred Heart	17
10	Stony Brook ■	24
24	Wagner ■	17

Nickname: Blue Devils
Colors: Blue & White
Stadium: Arute Field
Capacity: 2,500
AD: Charles Jones Jr.
SID: Thomas Pincince

UCF
Orlando, FL 32816-3555..........................I-A

Coach: Mike Kruczek, Boston College 1976
2002 RESULTS (7-5)
24	Penn St.	27
13	Arizona St.	46
21	Marshall	26
48	Liberty ■	17
31	Western Mich.	27
24	Toledo	27
28	Akron ■	17
35	Syracuse ■	38
45	Buffalo	21
32	Kent St. ■	6
48	Miami (Ohio)	31
42	Ohio ■	32

Nickname: Golden Knights
Colors: Black & Gold
Stadium: Florida Citrus
Capacity: 70,188; Year Built: 1936
AD: Steve Orsini
SID: John Marini

CENTRAL MICH.
Mount Pleasant, MI 48859-0001..............I-A

Coach: Mike DeBord, Manchester 1978
2002 RESULTS (4-8)
34	Sam Houston St. ■	10
32	Wyoming ■	20
24	Akron	17
29	Indiana	39
0	Boston College	43
35	Bowling Green ■	45
0	Northern Ill.	49
18	Marshall ■	23
47	Eastern Mich.	21
17	Toledo	44
21	Ball St. ■	38
10	Western Mich. ■	35

Nickname: Chippewas
Colors: Maroon & Gold
Stadium: Kelly-Shorts
Capacity: 30,199; Year Built: 1972
AD: Herbert W. Deromedi
SID: Fred Stabley Jr.

CENTRAL MO. ST.
Warrensburg, MO 64093..........................II

Coach: Willie Fritz, Pittsburg St. 1983
2002 RESULTS (10-2)
63	Lincoln (Mo.)	7
72	Sterling (Kan.) ■	12
21	Mo. Western St.	14
41	Emporia St. ■	13
55	Mo.-Rolla ■	14
35	Southwest Baptist	6
55	Washburn	21
42	Mo. Southern St. ■	21
7	Northwest Mo. St.	10
17	Truman ■	3

23	Pittsburg St.	20
28	Northern Colo.	49

Nickname: Mules
Colors: Cardinal & Black
Stadium: Audrey J. Walton
Capacity: 10,000; Year Built: 1995
AD: Jerry M. Hughes
SID: Joe Moore

CENTRAL OKLA.
Edmond, OK 73034..........................II

Coach: Gary Howard, Arkansas 1964
2002 RESULTS (5-6)
16	Western Wash. ■	24
17	Arkansas Tech	24
34	West Tex. A&M	14
19	Tex. A&M-Commerce	16
21	Southwestern Okla.	24
20	Abilene Christian	22
22	East Central ■	10
56	Bacone ■	21
6	Southeastern Okla. ■	7
58	Northeastern St.	48
27	Tarleton St. ■	34

Nickname: Bronchos
Colors: Bronze & Blue
Stadium: Wantland
Capacity: 10,000; Year Built: 1965
AD: John E. Wagnon
SID: Mike Kirk

CENTRAL WASH.
Ellensburg, WA 98926..........................II

Coach: John Zamberlin, Pacific Lutheran 1979
2002 RESULTS (11-1)
75	Fort Lewis ■	41
43	North Dakota	7
26	Carroll (Mont.)	8
30	St. Mary's (Cal.) ■	20
21	New Haven	13
31	Montana St.	16
56	Western N.M.	10
35	Western Wash. ■	28
40	Western Ore. ■	13
41	Humboldt St.	14
38	UC Davis ■	14
6	UC Davis ■	24

Nickname: Wildcats
Colors: Crimson & Black
Stadium: Tomlinson
Capacity: 4,000; Year Built: 1941
AD: Jack Bishop
SID: Jonathan Gordon

CENTRE
Danville, KY 40422-1394..........................III

Coach: Andy Frye, Muskingum 1981
2002 RESULTS (6-4)
38	Kenyon ■	15
20	Austin Peay	13
28	Rhodes	7
19	Wash. & Lee ■	13
21	Sewanee ■	23
7	Millsaps	14
33	Maryville (Tenn.)	7
23	Trinity (Tex.) ■	55
17	DePauw	38
30	Rose-Hulman	29

Nickname: Colonels
Colors: Gold & White
Stadium: Farris
Capacity: 2,500; Year Built: 1925
AD: Brian E. Chafin
SID: Ed Rall

RESULTS

CHADRON ST.

Chadron, NE 69337-2690 II

Coach: Brad Smith, Western Ill. 1971
2002 RESULTS (8-2)
15	Wis.-River Falls ■	7
15	South Dakota St	28
52	Fort Hays St.	23
35	Colorado Mines	21
54	Fort Lewis ■	28
31	Mesa St.	30
0	Neb.-Kearney ■	12
48	Western St. (Colo.) ■	10
62	N.M. Highlands	0
24	Adams St. ■	0

Nickname: Eagles
Colors: Cardinal & White
Stadium: Elliott Field
  Capacity: 4,000; Year Built: 1930
AD: Bradley Roy Smith
SID: Con Marshall

CHAPMAN

Orange, CA 92866 III

Coach: Ken Visser, Occidental 1968
2002 RESULTS (3-7)
27	Whittier	7
10	Pacific Lutheran ■	35
9	Redlands	34
21	Willamette ■	52
41	Lewis & Clark	40
28	Cal Lutheran	40
48	Thomas More ■	43
7	Azusa Pacific ■	48
21	La Verne ■	29
22	Menlo	44

Nickname: Panthers
Colors: Cardinal & Gray
Stadium: Chapman
  Capacity: 3,000
AD: David Currey
SID: Doug Aiken

CHARLESTON (W.VA.)

Charleston, WV 25304 II

Coach: Mike Springston, West Va. Tech 1982
Restarted football program (dropped 1957) in 2003

CHARLESTON SO.

Charleston, SC 29423-8087 ....I-AA

Coach: David Dowd, Guilford 1976
2002 RESULTS (4-8)
24	VMI ■	27
9	North Greenville ■	0
6	Presbyterian	26
10	West Virginia St. ■	3
28	West Liberty St.	26
21	Savannah St.	3
17	Liberty	31
21	Jacksonville ■	24
6	South Fla.	56
15	Gardner-Webb ■	57
13	Elon ■	21
19	Citadel	53

Nickname: Buccaneers
Colors: Blue & Gold

Stadium: CSU Stadium
  Capacity: 4,000; Year Built: 1970
AD: Hank Small
SID: David Shelton

CHATTANOOGA

Chattanooga, TN 37403-2598 ....I-AA

Coach: Donnie Kirkpatrick, Lenoir-Rhyne 1982
2002 RESULTS (2-10)
7	West Virginia	56
23	Alabama St. ■	41
3	Tennessee Tech	13
24	Gardner-Webb ■	26
10	Ga. Southern ■	38
21	Wofford	27
31	VMI ■	35
28	Western Caro.	45
17	Appalachian St. ■	20
34	Citadel	31
27	East Tenn. St. ■	10
7	Furman	35

Nickname: Mocs
Colors: Navy Blue & Gold
Stadium: Finley
  Capacity: 20,668; Year Built: 1997
AD: Steve Sloan
SID: Jeff Romero

CHEYNEY

Cheyney, PA 19319-0200 II

Coach: John Parker, Mo. Valley 1986
2002 RESULTS (0-11)
19	West Va. Tech	56
0	West Virginia St. ■	24
19	West Liberty St.	65
7	Calif. (Pa.) ■	51
0	Lock Haven	34
7	East Stroudsburg	48
0	West Chester ■	56
12	Bloomsburg	37
17	Mansfield ■	49
13	Kutztown	37
0	Millersville ■	49

Nickname: Wolves
Colors: Blue & White
Stadium: O'Shield-Stevenson
  Capacity: 3,500
AD: Eve Atkinson
SID: Lenn Margolis

CHICAGO

Chicago, IL 60637 III

Coach: Dick Maloney, Mass.-Boston 1974
2002 RESULTS (4-5)
33	North Park ■	9
46	Elmhurst	40
16	Ill. Wesleyan ■	34
12	DePauw ■	28
22	Pomona-Pitzer	27
17	Washington (Mo.) ■	38
42	Rochester	7
10	Carnegie Mellon	27
49	Case Reserve	39

Nickname: Maroons
Colors: Maroon & White
Stadium: Stagg Field
  Capacity: 1,500; Year Built: 1969
AD: Thomas Weingartner
SID: Dave Hilbert

CHOWAN

Murfreesboro, NC 27855 III

Coach: Lou Saban, Baldwin-Wallace 1948
2002 RESULTS (0-10)
14	Randolph-Macon ■	17
16	Greensboro	20
0	Ferrum	9
22	Apprentice	29
7	Salisbury	35
3	Chris. Newport	35
7	Shenandoah ■	28
0	Methodist ■	32
0	Wesley ■	42
0	Averett	27

Nickname: Braves
Colors: Columbia Blue & White
Stadium: James G. Garrison
  Capacity: 3,500
AD: Debra P. Warren
SID: Thomas Gardner

CHRIS. NEWPORT

Newport News, VA 23606-2998 III

Coach: Matt Kelchner, Susquehanna 1982
2002 RESULTS (6-5)
13	Salisbury	20
21	Randolph-Macon ■	19
7	Rowan ■	34
6	Bridgewater (Va.)	25
15	Shenandoah	19
27	Greensboro ■	13
35	Chowan	3
20	Methodist	9
27	Averett ■	0
35	Ferrum ■	7
10	Wash. & Jeff.	24

Nickname: Captains
Colors: Blue & Silver
Stadium: POMOCO Stadium
  Capacity: 3,100; Year Built: 2001
AD: C.J. Woollum
SID: Francis Tommasino

CINCINNATI

Cincinnati, OH 45221-0021 ....I-A

Coach: Rick Minter, Henderson St. 1977
2002 RESULTS (7-7)
36	TCU ■	29
32	West Virginia ■	35
19	Ohio St. ■	23
35	Temple	22
26	Miami (Ohio) ■	31
17	Tulane	35
14	Southern Miss.	23
48	Memphis ■	10
24	Louisville	14
47	Houston ■	14
19	Hawaii	20
31	UAB ■	23
42	East Caro.	26
19	North Texas (New Orleans Bowl)*	24

Nickname: Bearcats
Colors: Red & Black
Stadium: Nippert
  Capacity: 35,000; Year Built: 1916
AD: Robert G. Goin
SID: Tom Hathaway

CITADEL

Charleston, SC 29409-6150 ....I–AA

Coach: Ellis Johnson, Citadel 1975

2002 RESULTS (3-9)

10	LSU	35
24	Delaware ■	20
34	Western Caro. ■	37
28	Appalachian St.	37
30	Wyoming	34
26	East Tenn. St. ■	7
10	Furman	37
24	Ga. Southern ■	28
14	Wofford	27
31	Chattanooga ■	34
21	VMI *	23
53	Charleston So. ■	19

Nickname: Bulldogs
Colors: Blue & White
Stadium: Johnson Hagood
  Capacity: 21,000; Year Built: 1948
AD: Les Robinson
SID: Mike Hayden

CLAREMONT-M-S

Claremont, CA 91711-6400 III

Coach: Rick Candaele, Albertson 1969

2002 RESULTS (7-2)

14	Grinnell	13
30	Puget Sound ■	20
34	La Verne ■	17
42	Colorado Col.	21
35	Whittier ■	14
39	Occidental	30
28	Cal Lutheran ■	17
7	Pomona-Pitzer	12
29	Redlands	39

Nickname: Stags
Colors: Maroon, Gold & White
Stadium: Zinda Field
  Capacity: 3,000; Year Built: 1955
AD: Michael L. Sutton
SID: Kelly Beck

CLARION

Clarion, PA 16214 II

Coach: Malen Luke, Westminster (Pa.) 1976

2002 RESULTS (7-4)

14	Youngstown St.	27
24	Millersville	3
59	Glenville St. ■	38
31	Kutztown	7
14	Indiana (Pa.)	28
34	West Chester ■	28
24	Edinboro	18
19	Shippensburg ■	20
31	Calif. (Pa.) ■	6
34	Lock Haven	31
14	Slippery Rock	21

Nickname: Golden Eagles
Colors: Blue & Gold
Stadium: Memorial Field
  Capacity: 5,000; Year Built: 1965
AD: Robert Carlson
SID: Rich Herman

CLARK ATLANTA

Atlanta, GA 30314 II

Coach: Curtis Crockett, Clark Atlanta 1964

2002 RESULTS (2-9)

0	Tuskegee ■	28
14	Lincoln (Mo.) *	12
14	Miles ■	7
7	Morris Brown ■	44
20	Fort Valley St. ■	28
17	Lane	19
25	Benedict ■	27
0	Albany St. (Ga.)	33
7	Morehouse	40
3	Texas Southern	26
6	Kentucky St.	30

Nickname: Panthers
Colors: Red, Black & Grey
Stadium: Panther's
  Capacity: 6,000; Year Built: 1995
AD: Brenda Edmond
SID: Charles Ward

CLEMSON

Clemson, SC 29634 ....I–A

Coach: Tommy Bowden, West Virginia 1977

2002 RESULTS (7-6)

28	Georgia	31
33	Louisiana Tech ■	13
24	Georgia Tech ■	19
30	Ball St. ■	7
31	Florida St.	48
17	Virginia	22
31	Wake Forest ■	23
6	North Carolina St. ■	38
34	Duke	31
42	North Carolina	12
12	Maryland ■	30
27	South Carolina ■	20
15	Texas Tech (Tangerine Bowl)*	55

Nickname: Tigers
Colors: Orange & Purple
Stadium: Memorial
  Capacity: 81,473; Year Built: 1942
AD: Terry Don Phillips
SID: Tim Bourret

COAST GUARD

New London, CT 06320-4195 III

Coach: Bill George, Ithaca 1980

2002 RESULTS (2-7)

27	Mass. Maritime ■	0
12	Rensselaer ■	34
14	Springfield	64
17	Norwich	24
14	Western Conn. St. ■	38
12	Union (N.Y.)	17
34	Plymouth St. ■	33
14	WPI	40
6	Merchant Marine	31

Nickname: Bears
Colors: Blue & White
Stadium: Cadet Memorial Field
  Capacity: 4,500; Year Built: 1932
AD: Raymond Cieplik
SID: Jason Southard

COASTAL CAROLINA

Conway, SC 29528-6054 ....I–AA

Coach: David Bennett, Presbyterian 1984
First year of varsity football in 2003

COE

Cedar Rapids, IA 52402-5092 III

Coach: Erik Raeburn, Mount Union 1994

2002 RESULTS (10-2)

50	Eureka	0
28	Upper Iowa ■	6
42	Simpson ■	13
20	Central (Iowa)	21
48	Dubuque ■	0
21	Wartburg	13
40	Buena Vista ■	5
35	Cornell College	19
21	Luther ■	10
28	Loras	20
21	Wis.-La Crosse ■	18
14	St. John's (Minn.)	45

Nickname: Kohawks
Colors: Crimson & Gold
Stadium: Clark
  Capacity: 2,000; Year Built: 1989
AD: John Chandler
SID: Bryan Boettcher

COLBY

Waterville, ME 04901-8849 III

Coach: Tom Austin, Maine 1963

2002 RESULTS (4-4)

10	Trinity (Conn.)	17
14	Middlebury ■	17
27	Wesleyan (Conn.) ■	19
0	Amherst	14
29	Hamilton ■	7
14	Bates	19
9	Tufts	0
32	Bowdoin ■	27

Nickname: Mules
Colors: Blue & Gray
Stadium: Seaverns
  Capacity: 3,000; Year Built: 1948
AD: Marcella K. Zalot
SID: Bill Sodoma

COLGATE

Hamilton, NY 13346-1304 ....I–AA

Coach: Dick Biddle, Duke 1971

2002 RESULTS (9-3)

0	Villanova ■	20
31	Fordham	40
30	Dartmouth ■	26
38	Columbia ■	6
13	Bucknell	10
10	Princeton	14
42	Cornell	13
9	Towson	7
31	Lafayette ■	24
28	Lehigh	14
44	Georgetown ■	22
25	Holy Cross ■	20

Nickname: Raiders
Colors: Maroon, Gray & White
Stadium: Andy Kerr
  Capacity: 10,221; Year Built: 1937
AD: To be named
SID: Bob Cornell

COLORADO

Boulder, CO 80309 ....I–A

Coach: Gary Barnett, Missouri 1969

2002 RESULTS (9-5)

14	Colorado St. *	19
34	San Diego St. ■	14
3	Southern California ■	40
31	UCLA	17
35	Kansas St. ■	31
53	Kansas	29
34	Baylor ■	0
37	Texas Tech ■	13
11	Oklahoma	27
42	Missouri	35
41	Iowa St. ■	27

RESULTS

28	Nebraska	13
7	Oklahoma *	29
28	Wisconsin (Alamo Bowl)*	31

Nickname: Buffaloes
Colors: Silver, Gold & Black
Stadium: Folsom
  Capacity: 53,750; Year Built: 1924
AD: Richard A. Tharp
SID: David Plati

COLORADO COL.
Colorado Springs, CO 80903 III

Coach: Greg Polnasek, Wis.-Eau Claire 1979
2002 RESULTS (1-8)

14	Cornell College ■	41
20	North Central	35
14	Macalester	24
13	Lewis & Clark ■	39
21	Claremont-M-S ■	42
0	Rhodes	59
24	Occidental	35
30	Haskell ■	0
21	Lakeland ■	33

Nickname: Tigers
Colors: Black & Gold
Stadium: Washburn Field
  Capacity: 2,000; Year Built: 1898
AD: Joel Nielsen
SID: Dave Moross

COLORADO MINES
Golden, CO 80401 II

Coach: Bob Stitt, Doane 1986
2002 RESULTS (7-4)

14	Okla. Panhandle	0
49	South Dak. Tech ■	7
34	Western N.M.	10
21	Chadron St. ■	35
42	Fort Hays St. ■	27
14	Neb.-Kearney	58
30	Fort Lewis	33
55	N.M. Highlands ■	24
30	Mesa St. ■	35
29	Adams St.	18
47	Western St. (Colo.)	37

Nickname: Orediggers
Colors: Silver & Blue
Stadium: Brooks Field
  Capacity: 5,000; Year Built: 1922
AD: Marvin L. Kay
SID: Gregory Murphy

COLORADO ST.
Fort Collins, CO 80523-6011 ....I-A

Coach: Sonny Lubick, Western Mont. 1960
2002 RESULTS (10-4)

35	Virginia	29
19	Colorado *	14
19	UCLA	30
36	Louisville ■	33
32	Nevada	28
30	Fresno St.	32
44	Wyoming ■	36
28	Utah	20
37	Brigham Young ■	10
31	Air Force	12
49	San Diego St.	21
22	New Mexico ■	14

33	UNLV ■	36
3	TCU (Liberty Bowl)*	17

Nickname: Rams
Colors: Green & Gold
Stadium: Hughes
  Capacity: 30,000; Year Built: 1968
AD: Jeffrey A. Hathaway
SID: Gary Ozzello

COLUMBIA
New York, NY 10027 ....I-AA

Coach: Ray Tellier, Connecticut 1973
2002 RESULTS (1-9)

13	Fordham ■	11
6	Colgate	38
32	Princeton ■	35
21	Lafayette ■	28
10	Pennsylvania	44
23	Dartmouth ■	24
7	Yale	35
7	Harvard	28
14	Cornell ■	17
28	Brown	35

Nickname: Lions
Colors: Columbia Blue & White
Stadium: Lawrence A. Wien
  Capacity: 17,000; Year Built: 1984
AD: John A. Reeves
SID: Patricia A. Malizia

CONCORD
Athens, WV 24712 II

Coach: Ollie Pottmeyer, Glenville St. 1964
2002 RESULTS (3-8)

20	Pikeville ■	23
32	Union (Ky.)	29
20	Lenoir-Rhyne	30
31	Wingate ■	36
0	West Liberty St. ■	48
12	Glenville St. ■	34
21	West Va. Wesleyan	55
44	West Virginia St.	14
14	Fairmont St. ■	13
20	West Va. Tech	63
14	Shepherd	60

Nickname: Mountain Lions
Colors: Maroon & Gray
Stadium: Callahan
  Capacity: 5,000
AD: Steven Lee
SID: Ron Macosko

CONCORDIA (ILL.)
River Forest, IL 60305-1499 III

Coach: Brian Baker-Watson, Benedictine (Ill.) 1990
2002 RESULTS (0-10)

10	Lake Forest	52
6	St. Xavier	79
7	Anderson (Ind.) ■	60
7	MacMurray	55
3	Concordia (Wis.)	64
21	Aurora ■	67
19	Lakeland ■	51
20	Greenville	41
13	Benedictine (Ill.)	32
13	Eureka ■	33

Nickname: Cougars

Colors: Maroon & Gold
Stadium: Concordia
  Capacity: 1,500; Year Built: 2000
AD: Janet L. Fisher
SID: Jim Egan

CONCORDIA (WIS.)
Mequon, WI 53097-2402 III

Coach: Jeffrey Gabrielsen, Ripon 1980
2002 RESULTS (8-2)

42	Ripon	19
25	Wis.-Oshkosh ■	35
24	Wis. Lutheran	7
20	Aurora	10
64	Concordia (Ill.) ■	3
29	Lakeland	7
62	Greenville	9
42	Benedictine (Ill.) ■	3
35	Eureka	7
9	MacMurray ■	14

Nickname: Falcons
Colors: Royal Blue & White
Stadium: Century
  Capacity: 2,500
AD: Robert, M Barnhill
SID: Rick Riehl

CONCORDIA-M'HEAD
Moorhead, MN 56562-3597 III

Coach: Terry Horan, Concordia-M'head 1989
2002 RESULTS (7-3)

17	Minn. St. Moorhead	41
20	Gust. Adolphus ■	14
35	Bethel (Minn.)	14
51	Carleton ■	7
40	Hamline	7
38	Augsburg ■	13
21	Wis.-Stout	27
9	St. John's (Minn.) ■	34
24	St. Olaf	14
63	St. Thomas (Minn.) *	21

Nickname: Cobbers
Colors: Maroon & Gold
Stadium: Jake Christiansen
  Capacity: 7,500; Year Built: 1966
AD: Armin Pipho
SID: Jim Cella

CONCORDIA-ST. PAUL
St. Paul, MN 55104 II

Coach: Shannon Currier, Hamline 1994
2002 RESULTS (9-2)

44	Concordia (Neb.)	26
26	Wis.-River Falls ■	21
35	Minn. St. Moorhead	28
24	Northern St.	21
63	Minn.-Morris ■	0
38	Bemidji St. ■	14
12	Minn.-Duluth	36
38	Wayne St. (Neb.) ■	17
12	Winona St.	55
48	Minn.-Crookston ■	7
48	Southwest St. *	13

Nickname: Golden Bears
Colors: Navy & Vegas Gold
AD: David Herbster
SID: Jen Foley

CONNECTICUT

Storrs, CT 06269 ....I–A

Coach: Randy Edsall, Syracuse 1980
2002 RESULTS (6-6)
16	Boston College	24
14	Georgia Tech ■	31
24	Buffalo	3
37	Ohio ■	19
21	Ball St. ■	24
14	Miami (Fla.)	48
24	Temple ■	38
24	Vanderbilt	28
61	Fla. Atlantic ■	14
63	Kent St. ■	21
38	Navy	0
37	Iowa St.	20

Nickname: Huskies, UConn
Colors: National Flag Blue & White
Stadium: Rentschler Field
   Capacity: 40,000; Year Built: 2003
AD: To be named
SID: Leigh Torbin

CORNELL

Ithaca, NY 14853 ....I–AA

Coach: Tim Pendergast, Cortland St. 1980
2002 RESULTS (4-6)
3	Bucknell	14
23	Yale ■	50
34	Towson ■	31
23	Harvard	52
13	Colgate ■	42
10	Brown	7
25	Princeton ■	32
21	Dartmouth ■	19
17	Columbia	14
0	Pennsylvania ■	31

Nickname: Big Red
Colors: Carnelian Red & White
Stadium: Schoellkopf
   Capacity: 25,597; Year Built: 1915
AD: J. Andrew Noel
SID: Laura L. Stange

CORNELL COLLEGE

Mt. Vernon, IA 52314-1098 III

Coach: Ray Reasland, Buena Vista 1979
2002 RESULTS (4-6)
41	Colorado Col.	14
14	Wartburg	31
35	Buena Vista ■	25
26	Simpson	38
33	Luther	28
23	Loras ■	42
28	Upper Iowa	35
19	Coe ■	35
0	Central (Iowa)	48
50	Dubuque ■	13

Nickname: Rams
Colors: Purple & White
Stadium: Ash Park Field
   Capacity: 2,500; Year Built: 1922
AD: Tina Hill
SID: Darren Miller

CORTLAND ST.

Cortland, NY 13045 III

Coach: Dan MacNeill, Cortland St. 1979
2002 RESULTS (9-2)
21	Brockport St. ■	12
38	TCNJ ■	41

35	Kean ■	14
28	Buffalo St.	0
20	Montclair St.	16
27	New Jersey City	6
21	Rowan	42
32	Wm. Paterson ■	0
58	Utica ■	12
16	Ithaca ■	12
30	Westfield St. ■	7

Nickname: Red Dragons
Colors: Red & White
Stadium: Cortland Stadium Complex
   Capacity: 6,500; Year Built: 2002
AD: Joan Sitterly
SID: Fran Elia

CURRY

Milton, MA 02186 III

Coach: Steve Nelson, North Dakota St. 1974
2002 RESULTS (7-3)
35	Framingham St.	6
38	Fitchburg St. ■	20
38	Maine Maritime ■	7
10	Mass.-Dartmouth	40
31	MIT	8
20	Salve Regina ■	21
24	Nichols ■	14
27	Western New Eng.	9
13	Westfield St. ■	12
14	Hartwick	69

Nickname: Colonels
Colors: Purple & White
Stadium: D. Forbes Will Field
   Capacity: 1,500
AD: Steve Nelson
SID: Ken Golner

DARTMOUTH

Hanover, NH 03755 ....I–AA

Coach: John Lyons, Pennsylvania 1974
2002 RESULTS (3-7)
26	Colgate	30
26	New Hampshire ■	29
14	Pennsylvania	49
20	Yale ■	17
44	Holy Cross ■	36
24	Columbia	23
26	Harvard ■	31
19	Cornell	21
18	Brown ■	21
30	Princeton	38

Nickname: Big Green
Colors: Green & White
Stadium: Memorial Field
   Capacity: 20,416; Year Built: 1923
AD: Jo Ann Harper
SID: Kathy Slattery

DAVIDSON

Davidson, NC 28036 ....I–AA

Coach: Mike Toop, Merchant Marine 1977
2002 RESULTS (7-3)
16	VMI	41
28	Jacksonville ■	10
34	Newberry	7
44	Emory & Henry ■	7
7	Morehead St.	39
21	Georgetown ■	25
49	Valparaiso	32
31	Wesley ■	0
41	Hampden-Sydney	38
49	Austin Peay	28

Nickname: Wildcats
Colors: Red & Black

Stadium: Smith Field at Richardson Stadium
   Capacity: 4,000; Year Built: 1924
AD: James E. Murphy III
SID: Rick Bender

DAYTON

Dayton, OH 45469 ....I–AA

Coach: Mike Kelly, Manchester 1970
2002 RESULTS (11-1)
39	St. Francis (Pa.)	0
24	Robert Morris ■	10
42	Austin Peay	0
28	Duquesne ■	35
41	Butler ■	0
52	Valparaiso	3
35	Drake ■	7
35	Tiffin	20
42	Canisius ■	6
30	Morehead St. ■	20
27	San Diego	17
28	Morehead St.	0

Nickname: Flyers
Colors: Red & Blue
Stadium: Welcome
   Capacity: 11,000; Year Built: 1949
AD: Ted Kissell
SID: Doug Hauschild

DePAUW

Greencastle, IN 46135 III

Coach: Nick Mourouzis, Miami (Ohio) 1959
2002 RESULTS (7-3)
34	Rhodes	25
28	Hope ■	21
21	Hanover ■	31
33	Trinity (Tex.) ■	42
28	Chicago	12
47	Sewanee ■	28
28	Millsaps	7
38	Centre	17
43	Rose-Hulman ■	14
7	Wabash	35

Nickname: Tigers
Colors: Old Gold & Black
Stadium: Blackstock
   Capacity: 4,000; Year Built: 1941
AD: Page Cotton Jr.
SID: Bill Wagner

DEFIANCE

Defiance, OH 43512 III

Coach: Greg Pscodna, Adrian 1986
2002 RESULTS (3-7)
22	Olivet ■	30
17	Adrian	14
37	Grove City ■	14
7	Alma	49
24	Anderson (Ind.) ■	32
35	Hanover	57
8	Mt. St. Joseph ■	21
23	Franklin	24
14	Manchester ■	18
29	Bluffton	6

Nickname: Yellow Jackets
Colors: Purple & Gold
Stadium: Justin F. Coressel
   Capacity: 4,176; Year Built: 1994
AD: Dick Kaiser
SID: To be named

DELAWARE
Newark, DE 19716 ....I–AA

Coach: K.C. Keeler, Delaware 1981
2002 RESULTS (6-6)
22	Ga. Southern ■	19
13	Richmond	15
20	Citadel	24
31	West Chester ■	10
42	William & Mary	45
27	Northeastern	10
23	James Madison ■	10
14	Rhode Island	17
21	New Hampshire ■	9
7	Massachusetts	17
37	Maine	13
34	Villanova ■	38

Nickname: Fightin' Blue Hens
Colors: Blue & Gold
Stadium: Delaware
   Capacity: 22,000; Year Built: 1952
AD: Edgar N. Johnson
SID: Scott Selheimer

DELAWARE ST.
Dover, DE 19901 ....I–AA

Coach: Ben Blacknall, N.C. A&T 1973
2002 RESULTS (4-8)
16	Morris Brown	10
41	Savannah St. ■	9
14	Northwestern St. ■	34
18	Florida A&M ■	20
13	Bucknell	27
13	Hampton ■	44
7	Bethune-Cookman	49
28	Morgan St.	35
27	South Carolina St. ■	21
7	N.C. A&T ■	34
20	Norfolk St.	23
14	Howard	7

Nickname: Hornets
Colors: Red & Columbia Blue
Stadium: Alumni Field
   Capacity: 5,000; Year Built: 1957
AD: Hallie Gregory
SID: Dennis Jones

DELAWARE VALLEY
Doylestown, PA 18901-2699 III

Coach: G.A. Mangus, Florida 1992
2002 RESULTS (2-8)
0	Lycoming ■	54
14	Albright	52
14	King's (Pa.) ■	50
28	Susquehanna ■	49
28	New Jersey City	0
24	Wilkes	38
13	Moravian ■	33
14	Widener ■	44
26	Lebanon Valley	33
35	FDU-Florham	29

Nickname: Aggies
Colors: Green & Gold
Stadium: James Work
   Capacity: 4,000; Year Built: 1978
AD: Frank Wolfgang
SID: Matthew Levy

DELTA ST.
Cloveland, MS 38733 II

Coach: Steve Campbell, Troy St. 1987
2002 RESULTS (4-7)
7	Northwestern St.	35
26	Mississippi Val.	28
0	Valdosta St.	42
24	West Ala. ■	30
27	West Ga. ■	21
17	Arkansas Tech	24
10	Southern Ark.	30
44	Henderson St. ■	14
49	Harding	25
25	Ouachita Baptist	35
40	Ark.-Monticello ■	0

Nickname: Statesmen
Colors: Forest Green & White
Stadium: Travis E. Parker Field
   Capacity: 8,000; Year Built: 1970
AD: James H. Jordan
SID: Fred Sington

DENISON
Granville, OH 43023 III

Coach: Nick Fletcher, Johns Hopkins 1976
2002 RESULTS (2-8)
7	Waynesburg ■	28
13	Case Reserve ■	42
20	Ohio Wesleyan	38
7	Wittenberg	53
41	Kenyon ■	7
0	Earlham	35
16	Allegheny ■	50
14	Hiram	0
7	Wooster ■	56
22	Oberlin	30

Nickname: Big Red
Colors: Red & White
Stadium: Deeds Field
   Capacity: 5,000; Year Built: 1922
AD: Larry Scheiderer
SID: Craig Hicks

DICKINSON
Carlisle, PA 17013 III

Coach: Darwin Breaux, West Chester 1977
2002 RESULTS (5-5)
9	Juniata ■	26
3	Hobart	27
21	Muhlenberg ■	28
38	Albright	31
14	Frank. & Marsh. ■	7

0	McDaniel	23
21	Kean ■	14
10	Johns Hopkins	17
17	Gettysburg ■	14
14	Ursinus	6

Nickname: Red Devils
Colors: Red & White
Stadium: Biddle Field
   Capacity: 2,577; Year Built: 1909
AD: Leslie J. Poolman
SID: Charlie McGuire

DRAKE
Des Moines, IA 50311-4505 ....I–AA

Coach: Rob Ash, Cornell College 1973
2002 RESULTS (5-6)
7	Western Ill.	64
14	Truman ■	38
28	Mo.-Rolla	25
35	Wis.-La Crosse ■	17
45	Quincy	28
52	Valparaiso ■	35
49	Albany (N.Y.) ■	42
7	Dayton	35
44	Butler	48
46	San Diego ■	51
28	St. Mary's (Cal.)	46

Nickname: Bulldogs
Colors: Blue & White
Stadium: Drake
   Capacity: 18,000; Year Built: 1925
AD: Dave Blank
SID: Mike Mahon

DUBUQUE
Dubuque, IA 52001 III

Coach: Vince Brautigam, Iowa Wesleyan 1988
2002 RESULTS (1-9)
36	Martin Luther ■	24
10	Luther ■	38
0	Loras	34
12	Upper Iowa ■	22
0	Coe	48
0	Central (Iowa) ■	37
6	Simpson ■	35
7	Wartburg	40
20	Buena Vista ■	28
13	Cornell College	50

Nickname: Spartans
Colors: Blue & White
Stadium: Chalmers Field
   Capacity: 2,800; Year Built: 1942
AD: Dan Runkle
SID: Jason Hughes

DUKE
Durham, NC 27708-0555 ....I–A

Coach: Carl Franks, Duke 1983
2002 RESULTS (2-10)
23	East Caro. ■	16
3	Louisville ■	40
21	Northwestern	26
17	Florida St.	48
43	Navy	17
22	Virginia ■	27
10	Wake Forest	36
22	North Carolina St.	24
12	Maryland ■	45
31	Clemson ■	34
2	Georgia Tech	17
21	North Carolina ■	23

Nickname: Blue Devils
Colors: Royal Blue & White
Stadium: Wallace Wade
    Capacity: 33,941; Year Built: 1929
AD: Joe Alleva
SID: Jon Jackson

DUQUESNE
Pittsburgh, PA 15282 ....I–AA

Coach: Greg Gattuso, Penn St. 1983
2002 RESULTS (11-1)
35	Bucknell ■	14
17	Siena ■	7
36	Marist ■	0
35	Dayton	28
23	Lafayette ■	22
14	St. Peter's	3
63	St. John's (N.Y.) ■	7
46	La Salle	0
59	Iona ■	10
42	Canisius	0
27	Fairfield ■	0
0	Albany (N.Y.)	24

Nickname: Dukes
Colors: Red & Blue
Stadium: Arthur J. Rooney Field
    Capacity: 4,500; Year Built: 1993
AD: Brian Colleary
SID: Dave Saba

EARLHAM
Richmond, IN 47374 III

Coach: Frank Carr, Albion 1978
2002 RESULTS (4-6)
0	Rose-Hulman	23
7	Manchester	17
7	Wabash ■	44
49	Kenyon	19
14	Ohio Wesleyan ■	21
35	Denison ■	0
20	Wooster	49
28	Oberlin ■	21
7	Allegheny	28
28	Hiram ■	3

Nickname: Quakers
Colors: Maroon & White
Stadium: M.O. Ross Field
    Capacity: 1,500; Year Built: 1975
AD: Frank Carr
SID: Jon Mires

EAST CARO.
Greenville, NC 27858-4353 ....I–A

Coach: Steve Logan, Tulsa 1975
2002 RESULTS (4-8)
16	Duke	23
22	Wake Forest	27
24	Tulane ■	20
17	West Virginia	37
59	Army ■	24
30	South Fla. ■	46
20	Louisville	44
54	Houston	48
29	UAB	36
31	TCU ■	28
7	Southern Miss.	24
26	Cincinnati ■	42

Nickname: Pirates
Colors: Purple & Gold
Stadium: Dowdy-Ficklen
    Capacity: 43,000; Year Built: 1963
AD: Mike Hamrick
SID: Craig Wells

EAST CENTRAL
Ada, OK 74820..II

Coach: Dennis Darnell, Southwest Mo. St. 1967
2002 RESULTS (3-8)
14	Southwest Mo. St.	26
23	Harding	34
9	Emporia St. ■	17
21	Tex. A&M-Commerce	7
29	Eastern N.M.	35
26	Tarleton St.	35
17	Southwestern Okla. ■	31
10	Central Okla.	22
34	Angelo St. ■	21
17	Southeastern Okla.	20
42	Northeastern St. ■	12

Nickname: Tigers
Colors: Orange & Black
Stadium: Norris Field
    Capacity: 5,000
AD: Tim Green
SID: Zac Underwood

EAST STROUDSBURG
East Stroudsburg, PA 18301........................II

Coach: Dennis Douds, Slippery Rock 1963
2002 RESULTS (8-2)
31	Mansfield ■	14
28	Glenville St.	33
35	Shepherd ■	23
30	Edinboro ■	24
16	Bloomsburg	13
48	Cheyney ■	7
14	West Chester	17
37	Millersville ■	26
23	Shippensburg	21
34	Kutztown ■	7

Nickname: Warriors
Colors: Red & Black
Stadium: Eiler-Martin
    Capacity: 6,000; Year Built: 1969
AD: Joy M. Richman
SID: Chris Myers

EAST TENN. ST.
Johnson City, TN 37614.........................I–AA

Coach: Paul Hamilton, Appalachian St. 1981
2002 RESULTS (4-8)
0	North Carolina St.	34
20	Mars Hill ■	10
10	Gardner-Webb	13
35	VMI ■	21
27	Western Caro.	7
10	Appalachian St. ■	29
7	Citadel	26
31	Elon ■	15
0	Furman ■	25
7	Ga. Southern	40
10	Wofford ■	39
10	Chattanooga	27

Nickname: Buccaneers
Colors: Navey Blue & Old Gold
Stadium: Memorial Center
    Capacity: 13,000; Year Built: 1977
AD: Dave Mullins
SID: Michael White

EAST TEX. BAPTIST
Marshall, TX 75670-1498 III

Coach: Ralph Harris, Sul Ross St. 1969
2002 RESULTS (6-4)
20	Southeastern Okla.	34
31	McMurry ■	21
10	Howard Payne	14
19	Austin ■	14
31	Sul Ross St. ■	0
28	Texas Lutheran	21
22	Hardin-Simmons ■	43
28	Louisiana Col.	13
22	Mary Hardin-Baylor ■	23
16	Mississippi Col.	9

Nickname: Tigers
Colors: Blue & Gold
Stadium: Ornelas Stadium
    Capacity: 2,200; Year Built: 2000
AD: Kent Reeves
SID: David Weaver

EASTERN ILL.
Charleston, IL 61920-3099 ....I–AA

Coach: Bob Spoo, Purdue 1960
2002 RESULTS (8-4)
36	Hawaii	61
13	Kansas St.	63
26	Indiana St. ■	19
45	Illinois St. ■	10
35	Tennessee Tech	28
25	Eastern Ky. ■	24
44	Southeast Mo. St.	27
54	Tennessee Tech	48
55	Tenn.-Martin ■	43
47	Fla. Atlantic ■	6
35	Murray St.	37
9	Western Ill.	48

Nickname: Panthers
Colors: Blue & Gray
Stadium: O'Brien
    Capacity: 10,000; Year Built: 1970
AD: Richard A. Mc Duffie
SID: Dave Kidwell

RESULTS

662

2002 RESULTS

EASTERN KY.
Richmond, KY 40475-3101 ....I–AA

Coach: Roy Kidd, Eastern Ky. 1955
2002 RESULTS (8-4)
10	Oregon St.	49
35	Slippery Rock ■	11
28	Appalachian St.	36
22	Fla. Atlantic ■	6
55	Glenville St. ■	0
58	Tenn.-Martin ■	3
24	Eastern Ill.	25
31	Murray St. ■	7
19	Tennessee Tech	0
35	Liberty	28
21	Southeast Mo. St. ■	35
45	Tennessee St.	20

Nickname: Colonels
Colors: Maroon & White
Stadium: Roy Kidd
    Capacity: 20,000; Year Built: 1969
AD: Jack Lengyel
SID: Karl Park

EASTERN MICH.
Ypsilanti, MI 48197 ....I–A

Coach: Jeff Woodruff, Kent St. 1979
2002 RESULTS (3-9)
7	Michigan St.	56
13	Toledo ■	65
35	Southeast Mo. St. ■	32
3	Maryland	45
48	Southern Ill. ■	45
42	Akron ■	34
27	Ohio	55
17	Ball St.	42
21	Central Mich. ■	47
31	Western Mich.	33
21	Northern Ill. ■	49
21	Bowling Green	63

Nickname: Eagles
Colors: Green & White
Stadium: Rynearson
    Capacity: 30,200; Year Built: 1969
AD: David L. Diles
SID: Jim Streeter

EASTERN N.M.
Portales, NM 88130..................................II

Coach: Bud Elliott, Baker (Kan.) 1953
2002 RESULTS (8-3)
27	Western N.M. ■	20
70	N.M. Highlands	28
46	Northeastern St. ■	14
35	East Central	29
19	Abilene Christian ■	20
23	Angelo St.	14
14	Midwestern St. ■	28
27	Tex. A&M-Commerce	17
37	Tex. A&M-Kingsville ■	34
27	West Tex. A&M	16
14	Southwestern Okla.	25

Nickname: Greyhounds
Colors: Green & Silver
Stadium: Greyhound
    Capacity: 6,100; Year Built: 1969
AD: Michael Maguire
SID: Robert McKinney

EASTERN ORE.
La Grande, OR 97850-2899 III

Coach: Jim Fenwick, Wichita St. 1974
2002 RESULTS (1-9)
21	Western Mont. ■	24
7	Weber St.	56
7	Wis.-Whitewater ■	9
26	Montana Tech	48
17	Pacific Lutheran	24
14	Linfield ■	51
13	Carroll (Mont.) ■	44
3	Whitworth	28
46	Puget Sound ■	28
19	Southern Ore.	44

Nickname: Mountaineers
Colors: Navy Blue & Vegas Gold
Stadium: Community
    Capacity: 3,000; Year Built: 1982
AD: Rob Cashell
SID: Sam Ghrist

EASTERN WASH.
Cheney, WA 99004 ....I–AA

Coach: Paul Wulff, Washington St. 1990
2002 RESULTS (6-5)
2	Arizona St.	38
50	Montana Tech ■	6
55	Western Ore. ■	20
49	Southern Utah	14
14	Idaho St. ■	21
31	Portland St.	34
41	Northern Ariz. ■	29
41	Sacramento St. ■	48
38	Weber St.	20
14	Montana ■	25
30	Montana	21

Nickname: Eagles
Colors: Red & White
Stadium: Woodward
    Capacity: 6,000; Year Built: 1967
AD: Scott Barnes
SID: Dave Cook

EDINBORO
Edinboro, PA 16444-0001 II

Coach: Lou Tepper, Rutgers 1967
2002 RESULTS (5-6)
17	Gannon	7
29	Ashland ■	26
35	Tiffin	21
24	East Stroudsburg	30
7	Shippensburg	41
35	Indiana (Pa.) ■	54
18	Clarion ■	24
3	Slippery Rock	7
10	Kutztown	14
38	Calif. (Pa.) ■	22
37	Lock Haven ■	14

Nickname: Fighting Scots
Colors: Red & White
Stadium: Sox Harrison
    Capacity: 5,000; Year Built: 1965
AD: Bruce R. Baumgartner
SID: Bob Shreve

ELIZABETH CITY ST.
Elizabeth City, NC 27909 II

Coach: John Wright, Virginia Union 1971
2002 RESULTS (2-8)
13	Kutztown	34
0	Virginia Union ■	29
0	Fayetteville St. *	16
3	N.C. Central	13
6	Johnson Smith ■	30
17	Virginia St. ■	21
0	Bowie St.	21
14	Livingstone	32
12	St. Augustine's ■	6
15	Winston-Salem	14

Nickname: Vikings
Colors: Royal Blue & White
Stadium: Roebuck Stadium
    Capacity: 6,500; Year Built: 1983
AD: Edward Mc Lean
SID: April J. Emory

ELMHURST
Elmhurst, IL 60126-3296 III

Coach: Paul Krohn, Minn. St. Mankato 1976
2002 RESULTS (3-7)
22	Benedictine (Ill.) ■	19
40	Chicago ■	46
30	Rockford	7
7	Wheaton (Ill.)	62
7	Carthage	43
14	Millikin ■	37
42	North Park ■	28
0	Augustana (Ill.)	58
29	Ill. Wesleyan	57
13	North Central	20

Nickname: Bluejays
Colors: Blue & White
Stadium: Langhorst
    Capacity: 2,500; Year Built: 1920
AD: Christopher Ragsdale
SID: Kevin Juday

ELON
Elon, NC 27244-2010 ....I–AA

Coach: Al Seagraves, Shippensburg 1975
2002 RESULTS (4-7)
23	Florida Int'l ■	22
7	Furman	57
38	Johnson Smith ■	14
20	N.C. A&T	34
20	Northwestern St.	47
27	Gardner-Webb ■	38
15	East Tenn. St.	31
13	Hofstra ■	27
56	Liberty ■	35
21	Charleston So.	13
9	Wofford ■	34

Nickname: Phoenix
Colors: Maroon & Gold
Stadium: Rhodes Stadium
    Capacity: 11,250; Year Built: 2001
AD: Alan J. White
SID: Matt Eviston

EMORY & HENRY
Emory, VA 24327-0947 III

Coach: Lou Wacker, Richmond 1958
2002 RESULTS (4-6)
15	Methodist ■	25
13	Ferrum	10
7	Davidson	44
25	Sewanee ■	24
13	Hampden-Sydney	24
13	Randolph-Macon ■	17
18	Bridgewater (Va.)	48
48	Catholic ■	47
9	Wash. & Lee	22
10	Guilford ■	0

Nickname: Wasps
Colors: Blue & Gold

Stadium: Fullerton Field
  Capacity: 5,500; Year Built: 1926
AD: Fred Selfe
SID: Nathan Graybeal

EMPORIA ST.
Emporia, KS 66801-5087 II

Coach: David Wiemers, Washburn 1989
2002 RESULTS (9-3)
38	Fort Hays St. ■	7
17	East Central	9
34	Truman ■	17
13	Central Mo. St.	41
21	Mo. Western St.	14
13	Pittsburg St. ■	3
40	Mo.-Rolla	7
21	Southwest Baptist ■	13
21	Washburn	34
47	Mo. Southern St.	16
5	Northwest Mo. St. ■	34
34	Winona St. *	27

Nickname: Hornets
Colors: Old Gold & Black
Stadium: Welch Stadium
  Capacity: 7,000; Year Built: 1937
AD: Kent Weiser
SID: Donald Weast

EUREKA
Eureka, IL 61530-1500 III

Coach: Darrell Crouch, Illinois St. 1987
2002 RESULTS (2-8)
12	Knox	49
0	Coe ■	50
8	North Park	27
0	Lakeland ■	35
22	Greenville ■	16
3	Benedictine (Ill.)	22
7	Aurora	66
0	MacMurray ■	7
7	Concordia (Wis.) ■	35
33	Concordia (Ill.)	13

Nickname: Red Devils
Colors: Maroon & Gold
Stadium: McKinzie
  Capacity: 2,000; Year Built: 1913
AD: Joe Barth
SID: Shelly Lindsey

FAIRFIELD
Fairfield, CT 06430-5195 ....I–AA

Coach: Joe Bernard, Moravian 1980
2002 RESULTS (5-6)
20	Fairmont St. ■	24
25	La Salle	14
3	Georgetown	21
6	Fordham ■	51
29	Marist	33
15	Iona ■	12
20	Siena	36
21	Canisius ■	14
27	St. Peter's ■	13
44	St. John's (N.Y.) ■	21
0	Duquesne	27

Nickname: Stags
Colors: Red & White
Stadium: Alumni
  Capacity: 3,000
AD: To be named
SID: Jack Jones
Note: Discontinued football program following 2002 season.

FDU-FLORHAM
Madison, NJ 07940 III

Coach: Rich Mosca, West Liberty St. 1972
2002 RESULTS (2-8)
14	Moravian	21
13	Juniata	30
34	Lebanon Valley ■	14
26	Wilkes ■	28
34	Lycoming	28
23	Susquehanna	48
0	King's (Pa.) ■	21
7	Widener	53
20	Ursinus	56
29	Delaware Valley ■	35

Nickname: Devils
Colors: Cardinal and Navy
Stadium: Robert T. Shields
  Capacity: 4,000; Year Built: 1973
AD: William T. Klika
SID: W. Scott Giglio

FAIRMONT ST.
Fairmont, WV 26554 II

Coach: Rusty Elliott, Fairmont St. 1979
2002 RESULTS (3-7)
24	Fairfield	20
6	Calif. (Pa.) ■	14
0	Slippery Rock	45
23	Glenville St.	49
7	Shepherd	27
14	West Liberty St. ■	22
7	West Va. Wesleyan ■	28
13	Concord	14
40	West Virginia St. ■	20
20	West Va. Tech ■	17

Nickname: Falcons
Colors: Maroon , White & Fairmont Gold
Stadium: Duvall-Rosier Field
  Capacity: 5,000; Year Built: 1929
AD: David W. Cooper
SID: Jim Brinkman

FAYETTEVILLE ST.
Fayetteville, NC 28301-4298 II

Coach: Kenny Phillips, East Caro. 1985
2002 RESULTS (10-2)
62	St. Augustine's ■	13
16	Elizabeth City St. *	0
14	Catawba	27
42	Livingstone ■	12
30	Winston-Salem	26
21	N.C. Central ■	7
20	Virginia St. ■	10
30	Johnson Smith	6
13	Bowie St. ■	7
28	Virginia Union	18
17	Bowie St. *	14
27	Carson-Newman	40

Nickname: Broncos
Colors: Royal Blue & Lilly White
Stadium: Jeralds Ath. Complex
  Capacity: 6,100; Year Built: 1940
AD: William Carver
SID: Marion Crowe Jr.

FERRIS ST.
Big Rapids, MI 49307-2295 II

Coach: Jeff Pierce, Ferris St. 1979
2002 RESULTS (5-5)
33	Hillsdale ■	21
3	Northern Mich.	17
21	Wayne St. (Mich.) ■	36
24	Northwood	41
21	Michigan Tech ■	14
19	Mercyhurst	13
24	Saginaw Valley ■	3
21	Findlay	28
30	Ashland	8
14	Indianapolis	17

Nickname: Bulldogs
Colors: Crimson & Gold
Stadium: Top Taggart Field
  Capacity: 6,200; Year Built: 1957
AD: Tom Kirinovic
SID: Joe Gorby

FERRUM
Ferrum, VA 24088 III

Coach: Dave Davis, Elon 1971
2002 RESULTS (5-5)
16	Wesley	40
10	Emory & Henry ■	13
9	Chowan ■	0
21	Shenandoah ■	14
17	Averett	10
14	Guilford ■	24
23	Methodist	20
25	Greensboro	13
13	Salisbury ■	30
7	Chris. Newport	35

Nickname: Panthers
Colors: Black & Gold
Stadium: Adams
  Capacity: 5,500; Year Built: 1970
AD: T. Michael Kinder
SID: Gary Holden

FINDLAY
Findlay, OH 45840 II

Coach: Dan Simrell, Toledo 1966
2002 RESULTS (9-2)
37	Indiana (Pa.) ■	34
33	Wayne St. (Mich.) ■	21
18	Northwood	17
42	Michigan Tech ■	23
36	Mercyhurst	3
7	Saginaw Valley ■	69
14	Indianapolis ■	10
25	Ashland	20
28	Ferris St. ■	21
35	Hillsdale	14
19	Grand Valley St.	63

Nickname: Oilers
Colors: Orange & Black
Stadium: Donnell
  Capacity: 7,500
AD: Steven Rackley
SID: To be named

FITCHBURG ST.
Fitchburg, MA 01420-2697 III

Coach: Patrick Haverty, Worcester St. 1991
2002 RESULTS (5-4)
7	Mass.-Dartmouth ■	27
20	Curry	38
7	Westfield St. ■	19
23	Bridgewater St.	13
26	Western New Eng.	25
21	Maine Maritime ■	13
32	Mass. Maritime	0
34	Framingham St. ■	28
19	Worcester St.	42

Nickname: Falcons
Colors: Green, Gold & White
Stadium: Robert Elliot

Capacity: 1,000; Year Built: 1984
AD: Sue E. Lauder
SID: Rusty Eggen

FLORIDA

Gainesville, FL 32611 ....I–A

Coach: Ron Zook, Miami (Ohio) 1976

2002 RESULTS (8-5)

51	UAB ■	3
16	Miami (Fla.) ■	41
34	Ohio ■	6
30	Tennessee	13
41	Kentucky ■	34
14	Mississippi	17
7	LSU ■	36
30	Auburn ■	23
20	Georgia *	13
21	Vanderbilt	17
28	South Carolina ■	7
14	Florida St.	31
30	Michigan (Outback Bowl)*	38

Nickname: Gators
Colors: Orange & Blue
Stadium: Florida Field
  Capacity: 83,000; Year Built: 1929
AD: Jeremy Foley
SID: Steve McClain

FLORIDA A&M

Tallahassee, FL 32307...........................I–AA

Coach: Billy Joe, Villanova 1963

2002 RESULTS (7-5)

17	Miami (Fla.)	63
64	Morris Brown ■	6
34	Morgan St. *	16
20	Delaware St.	18
37	Tennessee St. *	24
13	South Carolina St. ■	31
24	Howard ■	28
36	N.C. A&T ■	28
34	Norfolk St.	31
25	Hampton ■	13
7	Troy St. *	24
10	Bethune-Cookman *	37

Nickname: Rattlers
Colors: Orange & Green
Stadium: Bragg Memorial
  Capacity: 25,500; Year Built: 1957
AD: To be named
SID: Alvin Hollins

FLA. ATLANTIC

Boca Raton, FL 33431-0991 ....I–AA

Coach: Howard Schnellenberger, Kentucky 1956

2002 RESULTS (2-9)

10	South Fla.	51
17	Bethune-Cookman ■	30
13	James Madison	16
6	Eastern Ky.	22
22	Nicholls St.	33
17	Youngstown St. ■	24
6	Troy St.	21
14	Connecticut	61
34	Morris Brown ■	13
6	Eastern Ill.	47
31	Florida Int'l ■	21

Nickname: Owls
Colors: Blue, Red & Grey
Stadium: Lockhart Stadium
  Capacity: 20,460; Year Built: 1998
AD: Dick Young
SID: Katrina McCormack

FLORIDA INT'L

Miami, FL 33199 ....I–AA

Coach: Don Strock, Virginia Tech 1973

2002 RESULTS (5-6)

27	St. Peter's ■	3
22	Elon	23
42	Butler ■	0
0	Bethune-Cookman *	31
27	Georgetown ■	2
7	Western Ky.	56
7	Maine ■	33
39	Jacksonville ■	6
35	Albany (N.Y.) ■	26
21	Fla. Atlantic	31
14	Gardner-Webb ■	17

Nickname: Golden Panthers
Colors: Blue & Gold
Stadium: FIU Stadium
  Capacity: 12,673; Year Built: 1995
AD: Rick Mello
SID: Rich Kelch

FLORIDA ST.

Tallahassee, FL 32306 ....I–A

Coach: Bobby Bowden, Samford 1953

2002 RESULTS (9-5)

38	Iowa St. *	31
40	Virginia ■	19
37	Maryland	10
48	Duke ■	17
20	Louisville	26
48	Clemson ■	31
27	Miami (Fla.)	28
24	Notre Dame ■	34
34	Wake Forest	21
21	Georgia Tech	13
40	North Carolina ■	14
7	North Carolina St.	17
31	Florida ■	14
13	Georgia (Sugar Bowl)*	26

Nickname: Seminoles
Colors: Garnet & Gold
Stadium: Doak S. Campbell
  Capacity: 82,000; Year Built: 1950
AD: David R. Hart Jr.
SID: Rob Wilson

FORDHAM

Bronx, NY 10458-5155 ....I–AA

Coach: Dave Clawson, Williams 1989

2002 RESULTS (10-3)

43	St. Peter's ■	0
40	Colgate ■	31
11	Columbia	13
51	Fairfield	6
41	Georgetown	10
24	Brown ■	17
33	Lafayette ■	26
23	Lehigh ■	26
37	Holy Cross	27
42	Towson ■	14
34	Bucknell	7
29	Northeastern	24
10	Villanova	24

Nickname: Rams
Colors: Maroon & White
Stadium: Jack Coffey Field
  Capacity: 7,000; Year Built: 1930
AD: Francis X. Mc Laughlin
SID: Joe DiBari

FORT HAYS ST.

Hays, KS 67601 II

Coach: Tim O'Connor, Boise St. 1992

2002 RESULTS (5-6)

7	Emporia St.	38
37	Washburn ■	29
23	Chadron St. ■	52
6	Adams St.	30
27	Colorado Mines	42
58	Fort Lewis ■	27
49	Okla. Panhandle	32
20	Mesa St. ■	16
29	Neb.-Kearney	46
7	Western St. (Colo.)	34
37	N.M. Highlands ■	27

Nickname: Tigers
Colors: Black & Gold
Stadium: Lewis Field
  Capacity: 6,362; Year Built: 1936
AD: Thomas E. Spicer
SID: Jason McCullough

FORT LEWIS

Durango, CO 81301-3999 II

Coach: Todd Throckmorton, Mo. Western St. 1987

2002 RESULTS (3-8)

41	Central Wash.	75
14	Western Wash.	52
30	Adams St. ■	37
24	Western St. (Colo.) ■	49
28	Chadron St.	54
27	Fort Hays St.	58
33	Colorado Mines ■	30
25	Neb.-Kearney ■	47
67	Western N.M.	66
62	N.M. Highlands	40
55	Mesa St.	58

Nickname: Skyhawks
Colors: Navy Blue, Light Blue & Gold
Stadium: Ray Dennison Memorial
  Capacity: 4,000; Year Built: 1958
AD: David L. Preszler
SID: Sarah Meier

FORT VALLEY ST.

Fort Valley, GA 31030 II

Coach: John Morgan, Bowie St. 1993

2002 RESULTS (7-4)

23	Morehouse *	0
6	Valdosta St.	32
53	Lane	8
45	Kentucky St. ■	33
28	Clark Atlanta	20
7	Alcorn St.	10
21	Miles	9
15	Benedict ■	0
23	Tuskegee ■	34
25	Savannah St.	6
7	Albany St. (Ga.) *	31

Nickname: Wildcats
Colors: Royal Blue & Old Gold
Stadium: Wildcat
  Capacity: 7,500; Year Built: 1957
AD: Gwendolyn Reeves
SID: Russell Boone Jr.

FRAMINGHAM ST.
Framingham, MA 01701-9101...................III

Coach: Michael Strachan, Swedish Sports Institute 1990
2002 RESULTS (1-8)
27	Bridgewater St. ■	48
6	Curry ■	35
14	Fitchburg St.	34
7	Maine Maritime ■	39
13	MIT	23
31	Mass. Maritime	14
0	Western New Eng. ■	21
0	Westfield St.	42
0	Worcester St.	50

Nickname: Rams
Colors: Black & Gold
Stadium: Maple Street Field
Capacity: 1,500
AD: Thomas M. Kelley
SID: Peter Desmarais

FRANKLIN
Franklin, IN 46131 III

Coach: Bill Unsworth, Franklin 1971
2002 RESULTS (2-8)
21	Millikin ■	54
14	Adrian	24
27	North Central ■	44
13	Mt. St. Joseph ■	28
20	Thomas More	28
31	Manchester	25
24	Defiance ■	23
21	Bluffton	34
17	Anderson (Ind.) ■	34
12	Hanover	57

Nickname: Grizzlies
Colors: Navy Blue & Old Gold
Stadium: Faught
Capacity: 2,000; Year Built: 1998
AD: Kerry N. Prather
SID: Kevin Elixman

FRANK. & MARSH.
Lancaster, PA 17604-3003...........................III

Coach: Tom Gilburg, Syracuse 1961
2002 RESULTS (4-6)
13	Oberlin	6
13	Catholic ■	6
34	Ursinus ■	10
22	Muhlenberg	68
0	Carnegie Mellon	21
7	Dickinson	14
21	Hobart ■	35
6	McDaniel ■	10
21	Johns Hopkins ■	40
20	Gettysburg	14

Nickname: Diplomats
Colors: Blue & White
Stadium: Sponaugle-Williamson
Capacity: 4,000; Year Built: 1920
AD: Robert D. Bunnell
SID: Edward Haas

FRESNO ST.
Fresno, CA 93740-0048 ....I–A

Coach: Pat Hill, UC Riverside 1973
2002 RESULTS (9-5)
21	Wisconsin	23
16	San Diego St. ■	14
24	Oregon	28
19	Oregon St.	59
31	Rice ■	28
32	Colorado St. ■	30
30	Southern Methodist ■	7
21	Boise St.	67
21	Hawaii ■	31
31	Tulsa ■	12
38	Nevada ■	30
19	San Jose St.	16
45	Louisiana Tech	13
30	Georgia Tech (Silicon Valley Bowl)*	21

Nickname: Bulldogs
Colors: Bulldog Red & Blue
Stadium: Bulldog
Capacity: 41,031; Year Built: 1980
AD: Scott Johnson
SID: Steve Weakland

FROSTBURG ST.
Frostburg, MD 21532-1099 III

Coach: Rubin Stevenson, Salisbury 1987
2002 RESULTS (6-5)
42	Apprentice ■	6
27	Montclair St.	30
25	Brockport St. ■	31
48	Oberlin	14
37	Wesley ■	18
35	Catholic	41
35	Ursinus ■	14
24	Westminster (Pa.) *	17
21	Waynesburg	24
37	Salisbury *	7
21	Johns Hopkins *	24

Nickname: Bobcats
Colors: Red, White & Black
Stadium: Bobcat
Capacity: 5,000; Year Built: 1974
AD: Ralph Brewer
SID: Chris Starke

FURMAN
Greenville, SC 29613 ....I–AA

Coach: Bobby Lamb, Furman 1987
2002 RESULTS (8-4)
18	Vanderbilt	49
57	Elon ■	7
17	Richmond	7
55	VMI	28
24	Western Caro. ■	23
15	Appalachian St.	16
37	Citadel ■	10
25	East Tenn. St.	0
21	Ga. Southern ■	42
23	Wofford	21
35	Chattanooga ■	7
38	Villanova	45

Nickname: Paladins
Colors: Purple & White
Stadium: Paladin
Capacity: 16,000; Year Built: 1981
AD: Gary Clark
SID: Hunter Reid

GANNON
Erie, PA 16541-0001 II

Coach: Bill Elias, Massachusetts 1977
2002 RESULTS (5-5)
7	Edinboro ■	17
36	Wingate	26
14	Slippery Rock ■	17
41	St. Joseph's (Ind.)	17
35	West Virginia St.	21
27	Central Conn. St.	30
48	Tiffin ■	49
14	Virginia Union	32
49	Robert Morris ■	21
21	Walsh ■	17

Nickname: Golden Knights
Colors: Maroon & Gold
Stadium: Gannon University Field
Capacity: 2,500; Year Built: 2001
AD: Dick Sukitsch
SID: Dan Teliski

GARDNER-WEBB
Boiling Springs, NC 28017 II

Coach: Steve Patton, Furman 1977
2002 RESULTS (9-1)
28	Morgan St. ■	24
0	Ga. Southern	56
13	East Tenn. St. ■	10
26	Chattanooga	24
31	Liberty	21
38	Elon ■	27
17	Florida Int'l	14
24	Tenn.-Martin ■	0
57	Charleston So.	15
44	Savannah St. ■	13

Nickname: Runnin' Bulldogs
Colors: Scarlet, White & Black
Stadium: Spangler
Capacity: 5,000; Year Built: 1969
AD: Chuck Burch
SID: Marc Rabb

GEORGETOWN
Washington, DC 20057-1121 ....I–AA

Coach: Bob Benson, Vermont 1986
2002 RESULTS (5-6)
0	Lehigh	69
13	Holy Cross ■	41
21	Fairfield ■	3
2	Florida Int'l	27
10	Fordham	41
25	Davidson	21
17	Lafayette	35
32	Bucknell ■	31
24	Marist ■	17
22	Colgate	44
24	Towson	16

Nickname: Hoyas
Colors: Blue & Gray
Stadium: Harbin Field
Capacity: 2,400; Year Built: 1979
AD: Joseph C. Lang
SID: Kevin Rieder

GEORGIA
Athens, GA 30602-1661 ....I–A

Coach: Mark Richt, Miami (Fla.) 1982
2002 RESULTS (13-1)
31	Clemson ■	28
13	South Carolina	7
45	Northwestern St. ■	7
41	New Mexico St. ■	10
27	Alabama	25
18	Tennessee ■	13
48	Vanderbilt ■	17
52	Kentucky	24
13	Florida *	20
31	Mississippi ■	17
24	Auburn	21
51	Georgia Tech ■	7
30	Arkansas *	3
26	Florida St. (Sugar Bowl)*	13

Nickname: Bulldogs
Colors: Red & Black
Stadium: Sanford

Capacity: 92,020; Year Built: 1929
AD: Vincent J. Dooley
SID: Claude Felton

GA. SOUTHERN
Statesboro, GA 30460-8086 ....I–AA

Coach: Mike Sewak, Virginia 1901
2002 RESULTS (11-3)

19	Delaware	22
56	Gardner-Webb ■	0
7	Wofford ■	14
38	Chattanooga	10
52	VMI ■	7
41	Western Caro.	24
36	Appalachian St. ■	20
28	Citadel	24
40	East Tenn. St. ■	7
42	Furman	21
41	Jacksonville St. ■	3
34	Bethune-Cookman ■	0
31	Maine ■	7
28	Western Ky. ■	31

Nickname: Eagles
Colors: Blue & White
Stadium: Allen E. Paulson
  Capacity: 18,000; Year Built: 1984
AD: Samuel Q. Baker
SID: Tom McClellan

GEORGIA TECH
Atlanta, GA 30332-0455 ....I–A

Coach: Chan Gailey, Florida 1974
2002 RESULTS (7-6)

45	Vanderbilt	3
31	Connecticut	14
19	Clemson	24
28	Brigham Young ■	19
21	North Carolina	13
21	Wake Forest ■	24
10	Maryland	34
23	Virginia ■	15
24	North Carolina St.	17
13	Florida St. ■	21
17	Duke ■	2
7	Georgia	51
21	Fresno St. (Silicon Valley Bowl)*	30

Nickname: Yellow Jackets
Colors: Old Gold, White, Navy Blue
Stadium: Bobby Dodd Stadium/Grant Field
  Capacity: 55,000; Year Built: 1913
AD: David T. Braine
SID: Allison George

GETTYSBURG
Gettysburg, PA 17325-1668 III

Coach: Barry Streeter, Lebanon Valley 1971
2002 RESULTS (4-6)

31	Lebanon Valley	10
22	Hampden-Sydney ■	37
6	McDaniel	28
45	Averett ■	10
21	Johns Hopkins	23
29	Ursinus ■	27
0	Muhlenberg	41
49	St. Lawrence ■	21
14	Dickinson	17
14	Frank. & Marsh. ■	20

Nickname: Bullets
Colors: Orange & Blue
Stadium: Musselman
  Capacity: 6,176; Year Built: 1965
AD: David Wright
SID: Matt Daskivich

GLENVILLE ST.
Glenville, WV 26351 II

Coach: Paul Shaffner, Ithaca 1982
2002 RESULTS (4-7)

7	West Chester ■	48
33	East Stroudsburg ■	28
38	Clarion	59
0	Eastern Ky.	55
49	Fairmont St. ■	23
34	Concord	12
28	West Va. Tech ■	42
21	Shepherd	35
35	West Virginia St. ■	27
7	West Liberty St.	19
7	West Va. Wesleyan	14

Nickname: Pioneers
Colors: Royal Blue & White
Stadium: Morris
  Capacity: 5,000; Year Built: 1977
AD: Greg Bamberger
SID: Dwaine Osborne

GRAMBLING
Grambling, LA 71245 ....I–AA

Coach: Doug Williams, Grambling 1978
2002 RESULTS (11-2)

20	McNeese St.	52
41	Alcorn St. ■	35
23	Alabama A&M	13
49	Tennessee St. *	14
37	Langston	30
35	Prairie View *	13
54	Ark.-Pine Bluff *	15
52	Jackson St. ■	31
42	Texas Southern	28
34	Alabama St. ■	21
64	Morris Brown	36
24	Southern U. *	48
31	Alabama A&M *	19

Nickname: Tigers
Colors: Black & Gold
Stadium: Robinson
  Capacity: 19,600; Year Built: 1983
AD: Albert Dennis
SID: Stanley O. Lewis

GRAND VALLEY ST.
Allendale, MI 49401 II

Coach: Brian Kelly, Assumption 1983
2002 RESULTS (14-0)

24	UC Davis ■	17
49	Wayne St. (Mich.)	14
44	Hillsdale ■	19
56	Michigan Tech	14
51	Northern Mich.	14
23	Saginaw Valley	18
33	Northwood ■	14
62	Mercyhurst	24
50	Indianapolis ■	13
63	Findlay ■	19
62	C.W. Post ■	13
62	Indiana (Pa.) ■	21
44	Northern Colo. ■	7
31	Valdosta St. *	24

Nickname: Lakers
Colors: Blue, Black & White
Stadium: Arend D. Lubbers
  Capacity: 6,344; Year Built: 1979
AD: Tim W. Selgo
SID: Tim Nott

GREENSBORO
Greensboro, NC 27401-1875 II

Coach: Neal Mitchell, Washington (Mo.) 1992
2002 RESULTS (4-6)

7	Apprentice	14
20	Chowan ■	16
18	Salisbury	23
7	Guilford	21
13	Chris. Newport	27
24	Shenandoah ■	21
24	Averett	14
13	Ferrum ■	25
13	Methodist ■	3
0	Wash. & Lee ■	6

Nickname: The Pride
Colors: Green, White & Silver
Stadium: Jamieson
  Capacity: 10,000
AD: Kim A. Strable
SID: Bob Lowe

GREENVILLE
Greenville, IL 62246 III

Coach: Scotty Kessler, Pacific Lutheran 1981
2002 RESULTS (1-9)

0	Mo. Southern St.	63
7	Westminster (Mo.) ■	20
21	Bethel (Tenn.) ■	45
21	Benedictine (Ill.) ■	27
16	Eureka	22
21	MacMurray ■	47
9	Concordia (Wis.)	62
41	Concordia (Ill.) ■	20
7	Lakeland	39
0	Aurora ■	47

Nickname: Panthers
Colors: Orange & Black
Stadium: Francis Field
  Capacity: 2,000; Year Built: 1987
AD: Doug Faulkner
SID: B.J. Schneck

GRINNELL
Grinnell, IA 50112 III

Coach: Greg Wallace, Missouri Valley 1970
2002 RESULTS (4-6)

13	Claremont-M-S ■	14
15	Lake Forest	26
22	Ripon ■	43
26	Illinois Col.	22
21	Knox ■	20
20	Monmouth (Ill.)	37
19	Beloit	32
34	Lawrence ■	30
19	St. Norbert ■	37
21	Carroll (Wis.)	14

Nickname: Pioneers
Colors: Scarlet & Black
Stadium: Rosenbloom
  Capacity: 1,750; Year Built: 1911
AD: Diane (Dee) Fairchild
SID: Andy Holmes

GROVE CITY
Grove City, PA 16127-2104 III

Coach: Chris Smith, Grove City 1972
2002 RESULTS (3-7)

30	Hiram	7
6	Carnegie Mellon ■	9

14	Defiance	37
28	Bethany (W.Va.)	20
3	Thiel ■	23
7	Wash. & Jeff.	34
24	Waynesburg	30
7	Westminster (Pa.) ■	19
12	Alfred ■	7
17	Merchant Marine	35

Nickname: Wolverines
Colors: Crimson and White
Stadium: Robert E. Thorn Field
   Capacity: 3,500; Year Built: 1981
AD: Donald L. Lyle
SID: R.A. Briggs

GUILFORD
Greensboro, NC 27410-4173...................III

Coach: Mike Ketchum, Guilford 1978
2002 RESULTS (3-7)

0	Carson-Newman	44
41	Methodist	18
30	Wash. & Lee ■	31
0	Hampden-Sydney	38
21	Greensboro ■	7
24	Ferrum	14
7	Bridgewater (Va.) ■	56
14	Randolph-Macon	21
26	Catholic ■	28
0	Emory & Henry	10

Nickname: Quakers
Colors: Crimson & Gray
Stadium: Armfield Athletic
   Capacity: 3,500; Year Built: 1960
AD: Marion Kirby
SID: Dave Walters

GUST. ADOLPHUS
St. Peter, MN 56082-1498 III

Coach: Jay Schoenebeck, Gust. Adolphus 1980
2002 RESULTS (6-4)

35	Alma ■	6
14	Concordia-M'head	20
48	Carleton ■	14
41	Augsburg	14
7	St. John's (Minn.) ■	20
25	St. Thomas (Minn.)	24
20	Bethel (Minn.) ■	41
42	Hamline	23
24	St. Olaf *	23
14	Azusa Pacific	20

Nickname: Golden Gusties
Colors: Black & Gold
Stadium: Hollingsworth Field
   Capacity: 4,000; Year Built: 1929
AD: Alan Molde
SID: Tim Kennedy

HAMILTON
Clinton, NY 13323 III

Coach: Peter Alvanos, Drexel 1988
2002 RESULTS (0-8)

0	Tufts	20
10	Wesleyan (Conn.)	37
0	Trinity (Conn.) ■	39
14	Bowdoin ■	28
7	Colby	29
6	Williams ■	31
21	Middlebury ■	41
0	Bates	37

Nickname: Continentals
Colors: Buff & Blue
Stadium: Steuben Field
   Capacity: 2,500

AD: Thomas Murphy/David Thompson
SID: Stephen Jaynes

HAMLINE
St. Paul, MN 55104 III

Coach: Donovan Larson, Hamline 1969
2002 RESULTS (3-7)

7	Northwestern (Minn.)	35
0	St. John's (Minn.)	56
7	St. Thomas (Minn.) ■	41
7	Bethel (Minn.)	41
7	Concordia-M'head ■	40
29	Macalester ■	13
12	St. Olaf	48
23	Gust. Adolphus ■	42
24	Carleton	14
21	Augsburg *	13

Nickname: Pipers
Colors: Red & Grey
Stadium: Norton Stadium
   Capacity: 2,000; Year Built: 1921
AD: Dan O'Brien
SID: Troy Mallat

HAMPDEN-SYDNEY
Hampden-Sydney, VA 23943 III

Coach: Marty Favret, Catholic 1984
2002 RESULTS (8-2)

51	Sewanee	17
37	Gettysburg	22
38	Guilford ■	0
7	Bridgewater (Va.)	38
24	Emory & Henry ■	13
44	Wash. & Lee	13
30	Catholic ■	20
38	Davidson ■	41
7	Randolph-Macon ■	0
51	Maryville (Tenn.)	23

Nickname: Tigers
Colors: Garnet & Gray
Stadium: Hundley
   Capacity: 2,400; Year Built: 1964
AD: Joseph E. Bush
SID: Donnie Turlington

HAMPTON
Hampton, VA 23668 ....I-AA

Coach: Joe Taylor, Western Ill. 1972
2002 RESULTS (7-5)

31	James Madison	28
26	Southwest Mo. St. ■	28
51	Howard ■	2
23	Alcorn St. ■	27
44	Delaware St.	13
49	Bowie St. ■	0
31	Norfolk St. ■	14
41	South Carolina St.	47
13	Florida A&M	25
37	Bethune-Cookman ■	7
17	N.C. A&T ■	7
42	Morgan St.	52

Nickname: Pirates
Colors: Royal Blue & White
Stadium: Armstrong Field
   Capacity: 17,000; Year Built: 1928
AD: Malcolm Avery
SID: Jamar Ross

HANOVER
Hanover, IN 47243-0108 III

Coach: C. Wayne Perry, DePauw 1972

2002 RESULTS (10-1)

47	Urbana ■	14
36	Thomas More ■	3
31	DePauw ■	21
49	Manchester ■	7
57	Defiance ■	35
47	Bluffton	21
41	Anderson (Ind.) ■	23
35	Wash. & Jeff.	14
49	Mt. St. Joseph	14
57	Franklin ■	12
33	Wittenberg ■	34

Nickname: Panthers
Colors: Red & Blue
Stadium: L. S. Ayres Field
   Capacity: 4,000; Year Built: 1973
AD: Lynn Hall
SID: Carter Cloyd

HARDIN-SIMMONS
Abilene, TX 79698 III

Coach: Jimmie Keeling, Howard Payne 1958
2002 RESULTS (8-2)

42	Menlo ■	34
56	Texas Lutheran ■	7
38	Louisiana Col.	24
32	Mississippi Col. ■	21
48	Howard Payne	51
31	Sul Ross St. ■	6
43	East Tex. Baptist	22
16	Mary Hardin-Baylor	35
14	McMurry ■	6
42	Austin	24

Nickname: Cowboys
Colors: Purple & Gold
Stadium: Shelton
   Capacity: 4,000; Year Built: 1993
AD: John Neese
SID: Chad Grubbs

HARDING
Searcy, AR 72149-0001 II

Coach: Randy Tribble, Harding 1977
2002 RESULTS (9-2)

23	Mo.-Rolla ■	15
34	East Central ■	23
45	North Ala.	38
32	Arkansas Tech	14
38	West Ala. ■	10
13	West Ga.	0
8	Henderson St.	29
40	Ark.-Monticello ■	27
25	Delta St. ■	49
33	Southern Ark.	13
42	Ouachita Baptist ■	30

Nickname: Bisons
Colors: Black & Gold
Stadium: First Security
   Capacity: 5,000; Year Built: 1999
AD: Greg Harnden
SID: Scott Goode

HARTWICK
Oneonta, NY 13820-4020 III

Coach: Mark Carr, New Hampshire 1990
2002 RESULTS (8-2)

21	King's (Pa.)	13
18	Ithaca	19
27	Utica ■	12
31	St. John Fisher	27
38	Alfred ■	27
34	Mount Ida	6
38	Rensselaer	39
42	Union (N.Y.) ■	0
68	St. Lawrence ■	7
69	Curry ■	14

Nickname: Hawks
Colors: Royal Blue & White
Stadium: All-Weather Field
  Capacity: 1,200; Year Built: 1985
AD: Kenneth Kutler
SID: Mike Chilson

HARVARD
Boston, MA 02163-1012 ....I–AA

Coach: Tim Murphy, Springfield 1978
2002 RESULTS (7-3)
28	Holy Cross ■	23
26	Brown	24
35	Lehigh	36
52	Cornell	23
14	Northeastern ■	17
24	Princeton	17
31	Dartmouth	26
28	Columbia ■	7
9	Pennsylvania	44
20	Yale ■	13

Nickname: Crimson
Colors: Crimson, Black & White
Stadium: Harvard
  Capacity: 30,898; Year Built: 1903
AD: Robert L. Scalise
SID: John Veneziano

HAWAII
Honolulu, HI 96822-2370 ....I–A

Coach: June Jones, Portland St. 1977
2002 RESULTS (10-4)
61	Eastern Ill. ■	36
32	Brigham Young	35
31	UTEP	6
42	Southern Methodist ■	10
31	Boise St.	58
59	Nevada	34
37	Tulsa ■	14
31	Fresno St.	21
40	San Jose St. ■	31
33	Rice	28
20	Cincinnati ■	19
16	Alabama ■	21
41	San Diego St. ■	40
28	Tulane (Hawaii Bowl)*	36

Nickname: Rainbow Warriors
Colors: Green, Black, Silver & White
Stadium: Aloha
  Capacity: 50,000; Year Built: 1975
AD: Herman R. Frazier
SID: Lois Manin

HEIDELBERG
Tiffin, OH 44883-2462 III

Coach: John Cervino
2002 RESULTS (2-8)
31	Adrian ■	34
0	Muskingum	19
6	Baldwin-Wallace ■	47
38	Marietta	27
0	Mount Union	61
13	Capital ■	52
21	John Carroll	59
33	Otterbein	14
28	Wilmington (Ohio)	35
0	Ohio Northern ■	28

Nickname: Berg
Colors: Red, Orange & Black
Stadium: Frost-Kalnow
  Capacity: 7,500; Year Built: 1941
AD: Jerry McDonald
SID: Aaron Chimenti

HENDERSON ST.
Arkadelphia, AR 71999-0001 II

Coach: Jesse Branch, Arkansas 1964
2002 RESULTS (5-6)
7	Northwestern Okla.	56
7	Stephen F. Austin	55
21	Central Ark. ■	68
3	West Ga.	44
18	Arkansas Tech ■	12
30	West Ala.	27
29	Harding ■	8
14	Delta St.	44
14	Ouachita Baptist ■	28
35	Ark.-Monticello	7
38	Southern Ark. ■	27

Nickname: Reddies
Colors: Red & Gray
Stadium: Carpenter-Haygood
  Capacity: 9,600; Year Built: 1968
AD: Sam Goodwin
SID: Matthew Bonnette

HILLSDALE
Hillsdale, MI 49242-1298 II

Coach: Dave Dye, Baldwin-Wallace 1967
2002 RESULTS (4-7)
21	Ferris St.	33
17	Indianapolis ■	24
37	Ashland ■	7
19	Grand Valley St.	44
23	Northern Mich.	26
40	Wayne St. (Mich.) ■	34
34	Northwood	41
31	Michigan Tech ■	7
20	Saginaw Valley	48
14	Findlay ■	35
56	Mercyhurst	7

Nickname: Chargers
Colors: Royal Blue & White
Stadium: Frank "Muddy" Waters Field
  Capacity: 8,500; Year Built: 1982
AD: Michael J. Kovalchik
SID: Dennis Worden

HIRAM
Hiram, OH 44234-0067 III

Coach: Bob Thomas, Hiram 1979
2002 RESULTS (0-10)
7	Grove City ■	30
0	Bluffton	45
0	Mt. St. Joseph	51
14	Oberlin	35
0	Allegheny	56
0	Wittenberg ■	77
10	Kenyon	22
0	Denison ■	14
7	Wabash ■	54
3	Earlham	28

Nickname: Terriers
Colors: Blue and Red
Stadium: Charles Henry Field
  Capacity: 2,000; Year Built: 1961
AD: Thomas E. Mulligan
SID: Jason Tirotta

HOBART
Geneva, NY 14456 III

Coach: Mike Cragg, Slippery Rock
2002 RESULTS (8-2)
27	Dickinson ■	3
14	Union (N.Y.)	6

44	St. Lawrence ■	14
59	Rochester	21
35	Frank. & Marsh.	21
25	Alfred	19
17	Ithaca ■	6
14	St. John Fisher	17
34	Rensselaer ■	27
7	John Carroll ■	27

Nickname: Statesmen
Colors: Royal Purple and Orange
Stadium: Boswell Field
  Capacity: 4,500; Year Built: 1975
AD: Michael J. Hanna
SID: Kenneth DeBolt

HOFSTRA
Hempstead, NY 11549 ....I–AA

Coach: Joe Gardi, Maryland 1960
2002 RESULTS (6-6)
0	Montana ■	21
37	Rhode Island ■	19
52	New Hampshire	28
21	James Madison ■	24
17	Northeastern	28
7	Villanova	35
3	William & Mary ■	16
17	Maine	24
27	Elon	13
26	Richmond ■	16
31	Massachusetts	28
32	Liberty ■	3

Nickname: Pride
Colors: Gold, White and Blue
Stadium: James M. Shuart Stadium
  Capacity: 15,000; Year Built: 1963
AD: Harry H. Royle
SID: Jim Sheehan

HOLY CROSS
Worcester, MA 01610-2395 ....I–AA

Coach: Dan Allen, Hanover 1978
2002 RESULTS (4-8)
30	Army	21
41	Georgetown	13
23	Harvard	28
10	Towson ■	42
19	Yale	28
24	St. Mary's (Cal.) ■	22
36	Dartmouth	44
12	Lehigh	21
38	Bucknell ■	21
27	Fordham ■	37
13	Lafayette	42
20	Colgate	25

Nickname: Crusaders
Colors: Royal Purple
Stadium: Fitton Field
  Capacity: 23,500; Year Built: 1924
AD: Richard M. Regan Jr.
SID: Larry Napolitano

HOPE
Holland, MI 49422-9000 III

Coach: Dean Kreps, Monmouth 1983
2002 RESULTS (5-5)
9	Wooster ■	14
21	DePauw	28
32	Wis.-Platteville	20
30	Wheaton (Ill.) ■	49
13	Alma	59
42	Kalamazoo	41
26	Adrian	27
41	Wis. Lutheran	27
30	Olivet ■	28
24	Albion ■	21

Nickname: Flying Dutchmen
Colors: Blue & Orange
Stadium: Holland Municipal
   Capacity: 5,322; Year Built: 1979
AD: Raymond E. Smith
SID: Tom Renner

HOUSTON
Houston, TX 77204 ....I-A

Coach: Dana Dimel, Kansas St. 1986
2002 RESULTS (5-7)
24	Rice	10
13	Tulane ■	34
36	La.-Lafayette ■	17
11	Texas	41
17	TCU	34
34	UAB	51
56	Army ■	42
26	Memphis	21
48	East Caro. ■	54
14	Cincinnati	47
14	South Fla. ■	32
27	Louisville ■	10

Nickname: Cougars
Colors: Scarlet & White with Navy Trim
Stadium: John O'Quinn/Robertson
   Capacity: 32,000; Year Built: 1942
AD: Dave Maggard
SID: Chris Burkhalter

HOWARD
Washington, DC 20059.........................I-AA

Coach: Ray Petty, Elon 1979
2002 RESULTS (6-5)
34	Texas Southern ■	31
2	Hampton	51
12	Maine ■	42
49	Morris Brown	15
28	Florida A&M	24
20	Morgan St. ■	38
20	N.C. A&T ■	16
21	Norfolk St. ■	0
23	South Carolina St.	9
27	Bethune-Cookman	46
7	Delaware St. ■	14

Nickname: Bison
Colors: Blue, White & Red
Stadium: Greene
   Capacity: 7,500; Year Built: 1986
AD: Sondra Norrell-Thomas
SID: Edward Hill

HOWARD PAYNE
Brownwood, TX 76801 III

Coach: Vance Gibson, Austin 1975
2002 RESULTS (9-1)
17	Southern Nazarene	7
50	Mississippi Col. ■	0
14	East Tex. Baptist ■	10
70	Sul Ross St.	33
51	Hardin-Simmons ■	48
17	Mary Hardin-Baylor	42
44	McMurry ■	17
20	Austin	0
49	Texas Lutheran ■	10
46	Louisiana Col.	38

Nickname: Yellow Jackets
Colors: Gold & Blue
Stadium: Gordon Wood
   Capacity: 7,600; Year Built: 1962
AD: Vance Gibson
SID: Nadir Dalleh

HUMBOLDT ST.
Arcata, CA 95521-8299 II

Coach: Doug Adkins, Central Wash. 1970
2002 RESULTS (1-10)
17	Southern Ore.	27
42	Willamette ■	28
10	Southern Ore. ■	20
7	St. Mary's (Cal.) ■	36
22	Azusa Pacific	35
14	UC Davis	49
7	Western Wash.	27
14	Central Wash. ■	41
0	Cal Poly	30
14	Western Ore.	41
35	Sacramento St.	42

Nickname: Lumberjacks
Colors: Green & Gold
Stadium: Redwood Bowl
   Capacity: 7,000; Year Built: 1946
AD: Dan Collen
SID: Dan Pambianco

IDAHO
Moscow, ID 83843-2302 ....I-A

Coach: Tom Cable, Idaho 1986
2002 RESULTS (2-10)
21	Boise St.	38
14	Washington St.	49
21	Oregon	58
48	San Diego St. ■	38
27	Washington	41
31	Montana ■	38
14	La.-Monroe	34
21	Middle Tenn. ■	18
28	La.-Lafayette	31
0	North Texas	10
29	Arkansas St. ■	38
31	New Mexico St. ■	35

Nickname: Vandals
Colors: Silver & Gold
Stadium: Kibbie Dome
   Capacity: 16,000; Year Built: 1975
AD: Mike R. Bohn
SID: Becky Paull

IDAHO ST.
Pocatello, ID 83209 ....I-AA

Coach: Larry Lewis, Boise St. 1981
2002 RESULTS (8-3)
48	Western Mont. ■	7
33	Utah St.	38
9	Montana	13
32	Sacramento St. ■	24
21	Eastern Wash.	14
18	Montana St. ■	14
34	Weber St. ■	0
24	Portland St.	27
46	Northern Ariz. ■	20
24	Cal Poly ■	14
42	Southern Utah	17

Nickname: Bengals
Colors: Orange & Black
Stadium: Holt Arena
   Capacity: 12,000; Year Built: 1970
AD: Howard L. Gauthier
SID: Frank Mercogliano

ILLINOIS
Champaign, IL 61820 ....I-A

Coach: Ron Turner, Pacific (Cal.) 1977
2002 RESULTS (5-7)
20	Missouri *	33
20	Southern Miss.	23
59	Arkansas St. ■	7
35	San Jose St. ■	38
28	Michigan ■	45
10	Minnesota	31
38	Purdue ■	31
45	Indiana ■	14
7	Penn St.	18
37	Wisconsin	20
16	Ohio St. ■	23
31	Northwestern	24

Nickname: Fighting Illini
Colors: Orange & Blue
Stadium: Memorial
   Capacity: 70,904; Year Built: 1923
AD: Ronald E. Guenther
SID: Kent Brown

ILLINOIS COL.
Jacksonville, IL 62650-2299 III

Coach: Aaron Keen, Illinois Col.
2002 RESULTS (3-7)
40	Blackburn ■	0
21	Lawrence ■	17
30	Carroll (Wis.)	27
22	Grinnell ■	26
9	St. Norbert	60
13	Ripon ■	32
20	Lake Forest	32
7	Monmouth (Ill.) ■	28
14	Knox	28
14	Beloit	41

Nickname: Blueboys
Colors: Blue & White
Stadium: England Field
   Capacity: 2,500; Year Built: 1960
AD: Gale F. Vaughn
SID: James T. Murphy

ILLINOIS ST.
Normal, IL 61790-2660 ....I-AA

Coach: Denver Johnson, Tulsa 1981
2002 RESULTS (6-5)
10	Purdue	51
55	Quincy ■	10
24	Murray St. ■	23
10	Eastern Ill.	45
30	Southwest Mo. St. ■	20
17	Western Ill.	22
35	Southern Ill. ■	14
31	Northern Iowa	20
0	Western Ky.	9
17	Youngstown St. ■	24
20	Indiana St.	12

Nickname: Redbirds
Colors: Red & White
Stadium: Hancock
   Capacity: 15,000; Year Built: 1967
AD: Perk Weisenburger
SID: Todd Kober

RESULTS

ILL. WESLEYAN
Bloomington, IL 61702-2900 III

Coach: Norm Eash, Ill. Wesleyan 1975
2002 RESULTS (6-4)
31	Washington (Mo.) ■	24
34	Chicago ■	16
49	North Park ■	9
10	Augustana (Ill.)	27
33	North Central ■	24
21	Wheaton (Ill.) ■	35
20	Carthage	21
57	Elmhurst ■	29
23	Millikin	27
35	Wis.-La Crosse	31

Nickname: Titans
Colors: Green & White
Stadium: Wesleyan
  Capacity: 3,500; Year Built: 1893
AD: Dennis Bridges
SID: Stew Salowitz

INDIANA
Bloomington, IN 47408-1590 ....I–A

Coach: Gerry DiNardo, Notre Dame 1975
2002 RESULTS (3-9)
25	William & Mary ■	17
13	Utah	40
17	Kentucky	27
39	Central Mich. ■	29
17	Ohio St.	45
32	Wisconsin ■	29
8	Iowa ■	24
14	Illinois	45
37	Northwestern ■	41
21	Michigan St. ■	56
25	Penn St. ■	58
10	Purdue	34

Nickname: Hoosiers
Colors: Cream & Crimson
Stadium: Memorial
  Capacity: 52,354; Year Built: 1960
AD: J. Terry Clapacs
SID: Jeff Fanter

INDIANA (PA.)
Indiana, PA 15705-1077 II

Coach: Frank Cignetti, Indiana (Pa.) 1960
2002 RESULTS (11-2)
34	Findlay	37
37	Bloomsburg ■	18
27	Catawba ■	26
42	New Haven ■	6
43	Millersville	16
28	Clarion ■	14
54	Edinboro	35
20	Calif. (Pa.) ■	9
31	Lock Haven ■	14
33	Shippensburg	10
34	Slippery Rock	28
27	Saginaw Valley ■	23
21	Grand Valley St.	62

Nickname: Indians
Colors: Crimson & Gray
Stadium: Miller
  Capacity: 6,500; Year Built: 1962
AD: Frank J. Condino
SID: Mike Hoffman

INDIANA ST.
Terre Haute, IN 47809 ....I–AA

Coach: Tim McGuire, Nebraska 1975
2002 RESULTS (5-7)
17	Western Mich.	48
14	Cumberland (Tenn.) ■	10
21	Ball St.	23
19	Eastern Ill.	26
34	Murray St. ■	31
16	Youngstown St.	31
23	Southwest Mo. St. ■	20
21	Western Ill.	52
7	Western Ky.	24
21	Northern Iowa ■	19
21	Southern Ill.	14
12	Illinois St. ■	20

Nickname: Sycamores
Colors: Blue & White
Stadium: Memorial
  Capacity: 12,764; Year Built: 1970
AD: Andrea Myers
SID: Kent Johnson

INDIANAPOLIS
Indianapolis, IN 46227-3697 II

Coach: Joe Polizzi, Hillsdale 1976
2002 RESULTS (5-6)
41	St. Joseph's (Ind.) ■	3
24	Hillsdale	17
24	Michigan Tech	32
10	Northern Mich. ■	24
24	Saginaw Valley	63
38	Northwood ■	40
10	Findlay	14
40	Mercyhurst ■	16
35	Ashland ■	14
13	Grand Valley St.	50
17	Ferris St. ■	14

Nickname: Greyhounds
Colors: Crimson & Grey
Stadium: Key
  Capacity: 5,500; Year Built: 1971
AD: David J. Huffman
SID: Joe Gentry

IONA
New Rochelle, NY 10801 ....I–AA

Coach: Fred Mariani, St. Joseph's (Ind.) 1974
2002 RESULTS (5-6)
14	Siena ■	7
0	Wagner	34
20	St. John's (N.Y.)	6
23	Montclair St. ■	19
13	Canisius ■	14
12	Fairfield	15
30	La Salle ■	23
17	Marist	14
10	Duquesne	59
14	St. Peter's ■	22
3	Sacred Heart	30

Nickname: Gaels
Colors: Maroon & Gold
Stadium: Mazzella Field
  Capacity: 2,440; Year Built: 1989
AD: Shawn Brennan
SID: Mike Laprey

IOWA
Iowa City, IA 52242 ....I–A

Coach: Kirk Ferentz, Connecticut 1978
2002 RESULTS (11-2)
57	Akron ■	21
29	Miami (Ohio)	24
31	Iowa St. ■	36
48	Utah St. ■	7
42	Penn St.	35
31	Purdue ■	28
44	Michigan St. ■	16
24	Indiana	8
34	Michigan	9
20	Wisconsin ■	3
62	Northwestern ■	10
45	Minnesota	21
17	Southern California (Orange Bowl)*	38

Nickname: Hawkeyes
Colors: Old Gold & Black
Stadium: Kinnick
  Capacity: 70,397; Year Built: 1929
AD: Robert A. Bowlsby
SID: Phil Haddy

IOWA ST.
Ames, IA 50011 ....I–A

Coach: Dan McCarney, Iowa 1975
2002 RESULTS (7-7)
31	Florida St. *	38
45	Kansas ■	3
58	Tennessee Tech ■	6
36	Iowa	31
42	Troy St. ■	12
36	Nebraska ■	14
31	Texas Tech ■	17
3	Oklahoma	49
10	Texas	21
42	Missouri ■	35
7	Kansas St.	58
27	Colorado	41
20	Connecticut ■	37
16	Boise St. (Humanitarian Bowl)	34

Nickname: Cyclones
Colors: Cardinal & Gold
Stadium: Jack Trice
  Capacity: 45,814; Year Built: 1975
AD: Bruce Van De Velde
SID: Tom Kroeschell

ITHACA
Ithaca, NY 14850 III

Coach: Michael Welch, Ithaca 1973
2002 RESULTS (7-3)
33	Alfred	11
19	Hartwick ■	18
30	St. John Fisher	20
44	Springfield ■	20
34	St. Lawrence ■	7
0	Brockport St.	21
13	Utica	0
6	Hobart	17
39	Buffalo St. ■	7
12	Cortland St.	16

Nickname: Bombers
Colors: Blue & Gold
Stadium: Butterfield
  Capacity: 5,000; Year Built: 1958
AD: Kristen Ford
SID: Mike Warwick

JACKSON ST.

Jackson, MS 39217 ....I–AA

Coach: Robert Hughes, Jackson St. 1967
2002 RESULTS (7-4)

7	Southern Miss.	55
36	N.C. A&T	42
31	Tennessee St. *	28
36	Southern U.	14
36	Mississippi Val. ■	12
20	Alabama St. *	24
31	Grambling	52
42	Ark.-Pine Bluff	0
13	Alabama A&M ■	11
44	Prairie View ■	9
34	Alcorn St. ■	20

Nickname: Tigers
Colors: Blue & White
Stadium: Mississippi Memorial
   Capacity: 62,512; Year Built: 1949
AD: Roy E. Culberson
SID: Deidre Bell Jones

JACKSONVILLE

Jacksonville, FL 32211-3394..................I–AA

Coach: Steve Gilbert, West Chester 1979
2002 RESULTS (3-7)

37	Lenoir-Rhyne ■	27
10	Davidson	28
7	Presbyterian ■	14
16	Austin Peay ■	20
20	San Diego	44
14	Morehead St.	48
24	Charleston So.	21
6	Florida Int'l	39
44	Edward Waters ■	31
7	Wagner ■	42

Nickname: Dolphins
Colors: Green & White
Stadium: Milne Field
   Capacity: 5,000; Year Built: 1997
AD: Thomas M. Seitz/Hugh Durham
SID: Jamie Zeitz

JACKSONVILLE ST.

Jacksonville, AL 36265-1602.................I–AA

Coach: Jack Crowe, UAB 1970
2002 RESULTS (5-6)

20	Alabama A&M ■	17
13	Mississippi St.	51
6	Nicholls St.	14
35	Tennessee Tech	29
37	Samford ■	23
28	Sam Houston St. ■	22
20	McNeese St.	28
28	Stephen F. Austin ■	36
20	Southwest Tex. St.	27
19	Northwestern St. ■	10
3	Ga. Southern	41

Nickname: Gamecocks
Colors: Red & White
Stadium: Paul Snow
   Capacity: 15,000; Year Built: 1947
AD: Thomas M. Seitz
SID: Greg Seitz

JAMES MADISON

Harrisonburg, VA 22807.......................I–AA

Coach: Mickey Matthews, West Tex. A&M 1976
2002 RESULTS (5-7)

28	Hampton ■	31
20	New Hampshire ■	14
16	Fla. Atlantic ■	13
24	Hofstra	21
26	Villanova ■	30
6	Maine ■	17
10	Delaware	23
0	Richmond	26
7	Massachusetts ■	14
15	Rhode Island	11
34	William & Mary ■	31
10	Northeastern	41

Nickname: Dukes
Colors: Purple & Gold
Stadium: Bridgeforth
   Capacity: 14,000; Year Built: 1974
AD: Jeffrey T. Bourne
SID: Gary Michael

JOHN CARROLL

University Hgts., OH 44118-4581 III

Coach: Regis Scafe, Case Reserve 1971
2002 RESULTS (12-2)

56	Catholic ■	7
40	Wilmington (Ohio) ■	0
33	Ohio Northern	7
20	Baldwin-Wallace ■	13
46	Marietta ■	0
16	Mount Union	35
59	Heidelberg ■	21
34	Muskingum	26
73	Otterbein	0
16	Capital ■	6
27	Hobart	7
21	Muhlenberg	10
16	Brockport St. *	10
19	Mount Union	57

Nickname: Blue Streaks
Colors: Blue & Gold
Stadium: Don Shula Stadium at Wasmer Field
   Capacity: 5,000; Year Built: 2003
AD: Anthony J. De Carlo
SID: Chris Wenzler

JOHNS HOPKINS

Baltimore, MD 21218-2684 III

Coach: Jim Margraff, Johns Hopkins 1982
2002 RESULTS (9-2)

21	Wash. & Lee	14
28	Carnegie Mellon ■	7
23	Gettysburg ■	21
27	Ursinus	9
10	Muhlenberg ■	23
12	Randolph-Macon	17
17	Dickinson ■	10
40	Frank. & Marsh.	21
27	McDaniel ■	7
24	Frostburg St. *	21
41	Rochester ■	28

Nickname: Blue Jays
Colors: Columbia Blue & Black
Stadium: Homewood Field
   Capacity: 8,500; Year Built: 1906
AD: Thomas P. Calder
SID: Ernie Larossa

JOHNSON SMITH

Charlotte, NC 28216 II

Coach: Timothy Harkness, Johnson Smith 1977
2002 RESULTS (2-8)

0	Wingate ■	24
6	Bowie St.	7
19	Virginia St.	23
14	Elon	38
30	Elizabeth City St.	6
27	Virginia Union ■	35
19	Livingstone	37
6	Fayetteville St. ■	30
0	Winston-Salem ■	49
29	N.C. Central	14

Nickname: Golden Bulls
Colors: Gold & Blue
Stadium: Memorial
   Capacity: 26,000; Year Built: 1990
AD: Henry White
SID: Kristene Brathwaite

JUNIATA

Huntingdon, PA 16652 III

Coach: Kevin Burke, Gettysburg 1990
2002 RESULTS (5-5)

26	Dickinson	9
30	FDU-Florham	13
48	Albright ■	21
34	Wilkes	26
20	King's (Pa.) ■	26
23	Moravian	39
54	Lebanon Valley ■	23
17	Susquehanna	45
33	Widener ■	68
24	Lycoming	55

Nickname: Eagles
Colors: Yale Blue & Old Gold
Stadium: Chuck Knox
   Capacity: 3,000; Year Built: 1988
AD: Lawrence R. Bock
SID: Joel Cookson

KALAMAZOO

Kalamazoo, MI 49006-3295......................III

Coach: Tim Rogers, Beloit 1988
2002 RESULTS (5-5)

20	Wabash	27
53	Kenyon	6
27	Mt. St. Joseph ■	13
47	Case Reserve ■	44
41	Hope	42
34	Olivet ■	49
20	Albion ■	21
20	Alma	34
42	Wis. Lutheran	7
31	Adrian ■	24

Nickname: Hornets
Colors: Orange & Black
Stadium: Angell Field
   Capacity: 3,000; Year Built: 1946
AD: Robert L. Kent
SID: Steve Wideen

KANSAS

Lawrence, KS 66045-8881 ....I–A

Coach: Mark Mangino, Youngstown St. 1987
2002 RESULTS (2-10)

3	Iowa St.	45
20	UNLV	31
44	Southwest Mo. St. ■	24
16	Bowling Green ■	39
43	Tulsa	33
32	Baylor	35
29	Colorado ■	53
22	Texas A&M ■	47
12	Missouri	36
0	Kansas St. ■	64
7	Nebraska	45
20	Oklahoma St. ■	55

Nickname: Jayhawks
Colors: Crimson & Blue
Stadium: Memorial
   Capacity: 50,250; Year Built: 1921
AD: Lew Perkins
SID: Janay Leddy

KANSAS ST.

Manhattan, KS 66502-3355 ....I–A

Coach: Bill Snyder, William Jewell 1962

2002 RESULTS (11-2)

48	Western Ky. ■	3
68	La.-Monroe ■	0
63	Eastern Ill. ■	13
27	Southern California ■	20
31	Colorado	35
44	Oklahoma St. ■	9
14	Texas ■	17
44	Baylor	10
64	Kansas	0
58	Iowa St. ■	7
49	Nebraska ■	13
38	Missouri	0
34	Arizona St. (Holiday Bowl)*	27

Nickname: Wildcats
Colors: Purple & White
Stadium: KSU Stadium
  Capacity: 50,000; Year Built: 1968
AD: Tim Weiser
SID: To be named

KEAN

Union, NJ 07083 III

Coach: Joe Loth, Otterbein 1990

2002 RESULTS (4-6)

14	Cortland St.	35
24	Shenandoah ■	16
7	Wesley ■	21
35	Wm. Paterson	7
7	Montclair St. ■	42
19	New Jersey City ■	6
14	Dickinson	21
10	Rowan ■	41
27	Western Conn. St. ■	24
14	TCNJ	55

Nickname: Cougars
Colors: Blue & Silver
Stadium: Kean Alumni
  Capacity: 2,750; Year Built: 1998
AD: Glenn Hedden
SID: Jack McKiernan

KENT ST.

Kent, OH 44242-0001 ....I–A

Coach: Dean Pees, Bowling Green 1971

2002 RESULTS (3-9)

34	New Hampshire ■	7
17	Ohio St.	51
37	Cal Poly ■	34
20	Miami (Ohio)	27
6	Northern Ill.	13
21	Marshall ■	42
0	Ohio ■	50
16	Buffalo	12
14	Bowling Green ■	45
21	Connecticut	63
6	UCF	32
10	Akron ■	48

Nickname: Golden Flashes
Colors: Navy Blue & Gold
Stadium: Dix
  Capacity: 29,287; Year Built: 1969
AD: Laing E. Kennedy
SID: Will Roleson

KENTUCKY

Lexington, KY 40506-0033 ....I–A

Coach: Guy Morriss, TCU 1973

2002 RESULTS (7-5)

22	Louisville	17
77	UTEP ■	17
27	Indiana ■	17
44	Middle Tenn. ■	22
34	Florida	41
12	South Carolina ■	16
29	Arkansas	17
24	Georgia ■	52
45	Mississippi St.	24
30	LSU ■	33
41	Vanderbilt ■	21
0	Tennessee	24

Nickname: Wildcats
Colors: Blue & White
Stadium: Commonwealth
  Capacity: 67,606; Year Built: 1973
AD: Mitch S. Barnhart
SID: Tony Neely

KENTUCKY ST.

Frankfort, KY 40601 II

Coach: Donald Smith, Western Ky. 1992

2002 RESULTS (3-8)

0	Western Ky.	49
15	Morehead St.	20
33	Fort Valley St.	45
47	Ark.-Pine Bluff *	44
16	Morehouse *	45
29	Lane ■	35
30	Albany St. (Ga.) ■	27
21	Benedict ■	26
17	Miles	39
26	Tuskegee ■	28
30	Clark Atlanta ■	6

Nickname: Thorobreds
Colors: Green & Gold
Stadium: Alumni Field
  Capacity: 6,000; Year Built: 1978
AD: Derrick Ramsey
SID: Ron Braden

KY. WESLEYAN

Owensboro, KY 42302-1039 II

Coach: John Johnson, Northern Mich. 1984

2002 RESULTS (1-10)

0	Southern Ill.	78
7	Southwest Baptist	35
14	Tenn.-Martin	42
12	Lincoln (Mo.) ■	24
21	St. Joseph's (Ind.) ■	27
13	Union (Ky.)	26
21	Austin Peay ■	23
46	North Greenville	56
40	Quincy ■	43
17	Cumberland (Ky.) ■	42
37	Bethel (Tenn.) ■	17

Nickname: Panthers
Colors: Purple & White
Stadium: Kentucky Wesleyan
  Capacity: 1,200; Year Built: 2003
AD: Larry E. Moore
SID: Roy Pickerill

KENYON

Gambier, OH 43022-9223 III

Coach: Vince Arduini, Norwich 1977

2002 RESULTS (1-9)

15	Centre	38
7	Bethany (W.Va.)	55
6	Kalamazoo	53
0	Wabash ■	58
19	Earlham ■	49
7	Denison	41
17	Oberlin ■	56
22	Hiram ■	10
3	Ohio Wesleyan	42
0	Wittenberg	79

Nickname: Lords
Colors: Purple & White
Stadium: McBride Field
  Capacity: 2,500; Year Built: 1962
AD: Peter Smith
SID: Marty Fuller

KING'S (PA.)

Wilkes-Barre, PA 18711-0801 III

Coach: Richard Mannello, Springfield 1983

2002 RESULTS (9-3)

13	Hartwick ■	21
33	Moravian ■	0
50	Delaware Valley	14
10	Lycoming ■	24
26	Juniata	20
24	Widener ■	6
21	FDU-Florham	0
22	Susquehanna ■	21
35	Albright	7
34	Wilkes ■	7
28	Salisbury ■	0
17	Bridgewater (Va.)	19

Nickname: Monarchs
Colors: Red & Gold
Stadium: Robert L. Betzler Fields
  Capacity: 3,000; Year Built: 1993
AD: Tom Baker
SID: Bob Ziadie

KNOX

Galesburg, IL 61401-4999 III

Coach: Andy Gibbons, Culver-Stockton 1990

2002 RESULTS (6-4)

49	Eureka ■	12
38	Carroll (Wis.) ■	7
19	Lawrence	0
29	St. Norbert ■	47
20	Grinnell	21
35	Lake Forest ■	30
7	Ripon	35
41	Beloit ■	16
28	Illinois Col.	14
23	Monmouth (Ill.)	27

Nickname: Prairie Fire
Colors: Purple & Gold
Stadium: Knox Bowl
  Capacity: 6,000; Year Built: 1968
AD: Dan Calandro
SID: Kevin Walden

KUTZTOWN
Kutztown, PA 19530-0721 II

Coach: David Keeny, Kutztown 1983
2002 RESULTS (4-7)
34	Elizabeth City St. ■	13
14	Lock Haven	21
14	Shippensburg ■	31
7	Clarion ■	31
24	West Chester	31
32	Mansfield ■	22
21	Bloomsburg ■	31
9	Millersville	10
14	Edinboro	10
37	Cheyney ■	13
7	East Stroudsburg	34

Nickname: Golden Bears
Colors: Maroon & Gold
Stadium: University Field
  Capacity: 5,600; Year Built: 1987
AD: Clark Yeager
SID: Josh Leiboff

LA SALLE
Philadelphia, PA 19141-1199 ....I–AA

Coach: Archie Stalcup, Rowan 1967
2002 RESULTS (2-9)
7	Wagner ■	42
14	Fairfield ■	25
2	St. Peter's	55
28	Siena ■	21
15	Catholic	26
27	Canisius	30
23	Iona	30
0	Duquesne ■	46
16	St. Francis (Pa.) ■	23
23	Marist ■	49
45	St. John's (N.Y.)	41

Nickname: Explorers
Colors: Blue & Gold
Stadium: McCarthy
  Capacity: 7,500; Year Built: 1936
AD: Thomas M. Brennan
SID: Kale Beers

LA VERNE
La Verne, CA 91750-4443..........................III

Coach: Don Morel, La Verne 1987
2002 RESULTS (3-5)
17	Pomona-Pitzer ■	16
8	San Diego	39
17	Claremont-M-S	34
6	Cal Lutheran	30
0	Redlands ■	24
12	Whittier	33
29	Chapman	21
24	Occidental ■	22

Nickname: Leopards, Leos
Colors: Orange & Green
Stadium: Ortmayer
  Capacity: 1,500; Year Built: 1991
AD: Jimmy M. Paschal
SID: Will Darity

LAFAYETTE
Easton, PA 18042..................................I–AA

Coach: Frank Tavani, Lebanon Valley 1975
2002 RESULTS (7-5)
30	Monmouth ■	29
23	Towson ■	7
21	Pennsylvania ■	52
19	Princeton	34
22	Duquesne	23
28	Columbia	21
35	Georgetown ■	17
26	Fordham	33
24	Colgate	31
19	Bucknell	3
42	Holy Cross ■	13
14	Lehigh ■	7

Nickname: Leopards
Colors: Maroon & White
Stadium: Fisher Field
  Capacity: 13,750; Year Built: 1926
AD: Jeff Cohen/Bruce McCutcheon
SID: Scott D. Morse

LAKE FOREST
Lake Forest, IL 60045 III

Coach: Chad Eisele, Knox
2002 RESULTS (9-2)
52	Concordia (Ill.) ■	10
26	Grinnell ■	15
24	Beloit	23
20	Ripon ■	18
27	Monmouth (Ill.)	3
30	Knox	35
32	Illinois Col. ■	20
18	Carroll (Wis.)	0
27	Lawrence ■	6
17	St. Norbert	0
0	Wartburg	45

Nickname: Foresters
Colors: Red & Black
Stadium: Farwell Field
  Capacity: 2,000
AD: Jackie A. Slaats
SID: Mike Wajerski

LAKELAND
Sheboygan, WI 53082-0359 III

Coach: Jeff Hynes, Concordia (Wis.) 1992
2002 RESULTS (6-4)
37	Carthage ■	34
14	Wis.-Oshkosh	33
35	Eureka	0
6	MacMurray	16
7	Concordia (Wis.) ■	29
51	Concordia (Ill.)	19
13	Aurora	23
39	Greenville ■	7
27	Benedictine (Ill.) ■	13
33	Colorado Col.	21

Nickname: Muskies
Colors: Navy & Gold
Stadium: Taylor Field
  Capacity: 1,500; Year Built: 1958
AD: Jane Bouche/Jane Bouche
SID: John Weber

LANE
Jackson, TN 38301-4598 II

Coach: Miles Brandon, Ohio 1987
2002 RESULTS (4-7)
30	Benedict ■	26
8	Fort Valley St. ■	53
20	Stillman	34
0	Albany St. (Ga.)	49
19	Clark Atlanta ■	17
35	Kentucky St.	29
32	Miles ■	34
16	Morehouse	19
0	Tuskegee	11
6	Lincoln (Mo.)	23
40	Ark.-Pine Bluff	37

Nickname: Dragons
Colors: Cardinal Red & Royal Blue
Stadium: Rothrock
  Capacity: 3,500; Year Built: 1930
AD: J.L. Perry
SID: Anthony Sawyer

LAWRENCE
Appleton, WI 54912-0599 III

Coach: Dave Brown, Coe 1985
2002 RESULTS (0-10)
23	Wis. Lutheran	45
17	Illinois Col.	21
0	Knox	19
14	Carroll (Wis.)	45
14	Beloit ■	27
0	St. Norbert	55
14	Monmouth (Ill.) ■	42
30	Grinnell	34
6	Lake Forest	27
35	Ripon ■	58

Nickname: Vikings
Colors: Blue & White
Stadium: Banta Bowl
  Capacity: 5,255; Year Built: 1965
AD: Kimberly N. Tatro
SID: Joe Vanden Acker

LEBANON VALLEY
Annville, PA 17003-1400..........................III

Coach: Mike Silecchia, Mansfield 1978
2002 RESULTS (1-9)
10	Gettysburg ■	31
6	Lycoming ■	24
21	Widener	49
14	FDU-Florham	34
21	Moravian	41
7	Albright	48
23	Juniata	54
33	Delaware Valley ■	26
6	Wilkes	44
28	Susquehanna ■	33

Nickname: Flying Dutchmen
Colors: Blue, White & Red
Stadium: Arnold Field
  Capacity: 2,500; Year Built: 1969
AD: Kathleen Tierney
SID: Gregg Matalas

LEHIGH
Bethlehem, PA 18015-3089 ....I–AA

Coach: Pete Lembo, Georgetown 1992
2002 RESULTS (8-4)
37	Buffalo	26
69	Georgetown ■	0
31	Princeton ■	24
21	Pennsylvania	24
36	Harvard ■	35
19	Towson	23
14	Yale ■	7
21	Holy Cross	12
26	Fordham	23
14	Colgate ■	28
24	Bucknell ■	0
7	Lafayette	14

Nickname: Mountain Hawks
Colors: Brown & White
Stadium: Goodman
  Capacity: 16,000; Year Built: 1988
AD: Joseph D. Sterrett
SID: Jeff Touriul

RESULTS

LENOIR-RHYNE
Hickory, NC 28603 II

Coach: Wayne Hicks, Jacksonville St. 1984
2002 RESULTS (3-7)
27	Jacksonville	37
35	West Va. Wesleyan	17
30	Concord ■	20
35	Newberry ■	7
26	Wingate ■	35
21	Mars Hill	23
3	Presbyterian	14
7	Carson-Newman ■	48
22	Tusculum	58
17	Catawba ■	37

Nickname: Bears
Colors: Red (PMS 201) & Black
Stadium: Moretz
   Capacity: 8,500; Year Built: 1923
AD: Neill McGeachy
SID: John Karrs

LEWIS & CLARK
Portland, OR 97219-7899 III

Coach: Mike Fanger, Lewis & Clark 1992
2002 RESULTS (3-6)
20	Occidental	21
28	Puget Sound	13
39	Colorado Col.	13
40	Chapman ■	41
34	Macalester ■	0
18	Pacific Lutheran ■	45
0	Linfield ■	49
14	Willamette	21
7	Whitworth ■	35

Nickname: Pioneers
Colors: Orange & Black
Stadium: Griswold
   Capacity: 3,600; Year Built: 1953
AD: Steve Wallo
SID: Kerry Kemper

LIBERTY
Lynchburg, VA 24502-2269 ....I-AA

Coach: Ken Karcher, Tulane 1986
2002 RESULTS (2-9)
3	Western Caro. ■	23
35	West Liberty St. ■	6
22	Appalachian St. ■	29
17	UCF	48
21	Gardner-Webb ■	31
21	Akron	49
31	Charleston So. ■	17
14	VMI	38
28	Eastern Ky. ■	35
35	Elon	56
3	Hofstra	32

Nickname: Flames
Colors: Red, White & Blue
Stadium: Williams
   Capacity: 12,000; Year Built: 1989
AD: Kim Graham
SID: Todd Wetmore

LINCOLN (MO.)
Jefferson City, MO 65102-0029.................II

Coach: Fred Manuel, Oregon 1973
2002 RESULTS (4-7)
7	Central Mo. St. ■	63
12	Clark Atlanta *	14
17	St. Joseph's (Ind.) ■	24

24	Ky. Wesleyan	12
34	Okla. Panhandle ■	6
20	Tuskegee	46
14	Stillman ■	58
3	Northwestern Okla. ■	57
34	Langston *	13
6	Augustana (S.D.) ■	30
23	Lane ■	6

Nickname: Blue Tigers
Colors: Navy Blue & White
Stadium: Dwight T. Reed Stadium
   Capacity: 5,600; Year Built: 1972
AD: Patric Simon
SID: David Klopfer

LINFIELD
McMinnville, OR 97128-6894....................III

Coach: Jay Locey, Oregon St. 1978
2002 RESULTS (10-1)
59	Redlands	21
42	Southern Ore. ■	35
35	Pacific Lutheran	21
57	Puget Sound ■	0
51	Eastern Ore.	14
56	Menlo ■	6
49	Lewis & Clark	0
35	Whitworth ■	0
32	Willamette ■	20
52	Wartburg ■	15
14	St. John's (Minn.) ■	21

Nickname: Wildcats
Colors: Purple & Red
Stadium: Maxwell Field/Memorial Stadium
   Capacity: 2,250; Year Built: 1945
AD: Scott Carnahan
SID: Kelly Bird

LIVINGSTONE
Salisbury, NC 28144 II

Coach: George Johnson, Jr., Alabama A&M 1974
2002 RESULTS (3-7)
22	Catawba ■	30
6	Stillman	32
13	Virginia Union *	32
12	Fayetteville St.	42
14	Virginia St.	28
6	Winston-Salem	23
37	Johnson Smith ■	19
32	Elizabeth City St. ■	14
10	N.C. Central	14
12	St. Augustine's *	7

Nickname: Blue Bears
Colors: Columbia Blue & Black
Stadium: Alumni Memorial
   Capacity: 6,000; Year Built: 1960
AD: Clifton Huff
SID: Adrian Ferguson

LOCK HAVEN
Lock Haven, PA 17745 II

Coach: Mark Luther, Penn St. 1992
2002 RESULTS (4-7)
0	Northeastern	48
21	Kutztown ■	14
23	Bloomsburg	47
33	Mansfield	30
34	Cheyney ■	0
19	Calif. (Pa.)	34
26	Shippensburg ■	13
14	Indiana (Pa.)	31
7	Slippery Rock ■	14
31	Clarion	34
14	Edinboro	37

Nickname: Bald Eagles
Colors: Crimson & White
Stadium: Hubert Jack
   Capacity: 3,000; Year Built: 1975
AD: Sharon E. Taylor
SID: Danielle Barney

LORAS
Dubuque, IA 52004-0178 III

Coach: Bob Bierie, Loras 1965
2002 RESULTS (5-5)
40	Monmouth (Ill.) ■	23
7	Central (Iowa)	17
34	Dubuque ■	0
3	Wartburg	34
35	Buena Vista ■	19
42	Cornell College	23
13	Luther ■	23
48	Simpson	69
17	Upper Iowa	14
20	Coe ■	28

Nickname: Duhawks
Colors: Purple & Gold
Stadium: Rock Bowl
   Capacity: 3,000; Year Built: 1945
AD: Greg Capell
SID: Dave Beyer

LA.-LAFAYETTE
Lafayette, LA 70506 ....I-A

Coach: Rickey Bustle, Clemson 1976
2002 RESULTS (3-9)
7	Texas A&M	31
11	Minnesota ■	35
17	Houston	36
34	UAB ■	0
0	LSU	48
28	New Mexico St.	31
35	Middle Tenn.	48
0	North Texas ■	27
31	Idaho ■	28
13	Arkansas St. ■	10
17	Arkansas	24
10	La.-Monroe	34

Nickname: Ragin' Cajuns
Colors: Vermilion & White
Stadium: Cajun Field
   Capacity: 31,000; Year Built: 1971
AD: Nelson Schexnayder Jr.
SID: Daryl Cetnar

LA.-MONROE
Monroe, LA 71209-3000........................I-A

Coach: Bobby Keasler, La.-Monroe 1970
2002 RESULTS (3-9)
3	Mississippi	31
0	Kansas St.	68
19	McNeese St. ■	24
21	Arkansas St. ■	33
9	Tulane ■	52
34	Idaho ■	14
21	New Mexico St.	34
51	Utah St. ■	48
2	North Texas	41
14	Auburn	52
28	Middle Tenn.	44
34	La.-Lafayette ■	10

Nickname: Indians
Colors: Maroon & Gold
Stadium: Malone
   Capacity: 30,427; Year Built: 1978
AD: Bruce Hanks
SID: Hank Largin

LOUISIANA COL.
Pineville, LA 71360-0001 III

Coach: Marty Secord, Austin 1984
2002 RESULTS (4-6)

49	Belhaven ■	21
44	Sul Ross St.	36
24	Hardin-Simmons ■	38
12	Mary Hardin-Baylor	69
29	McMurry ■	14
27	Austin	34
22	Texas Lutheran ■	6
13	East Tex. Baptist ■	28
10	Mississippi Col.	15
38	Howard Payne ■	46

Nickname: Wildcats
Colors: Orange & Blue
Stadium: D.C. Bates
  Capacity: 7,500; Year Built: 2000
AD: Sheila Johnson
SID: To be named

LSU
Baton Rouge, LA 70803 ....I-A

Coach: Nick Saban, Kent St. 1973
2002 RESULTS (8-5)

8	Virginia Tech	26
35	Citadel ■	10
33	Miami (Ohio) ■	7
31	Mississippi St. ■	13
48	La.-Lafayette ■	0
36	Florida	7
38	South Carolina ■	14
7	Auburn	31
33	Kentucky	30
0	Alabama ■	31
14	Mississippi	13
20	Arkansas	21
20	Texas (Cotton Bowl)*	35

Nickname: Fighting Tigers
Colors: Purple & Gold
Stadium: Tiger
  Capacity: 91,600; Year Built: 1924
AD: Skip Bertman
SID: Michael Bonnette

LOUISIANA TECH
Ruston, LA 71272.......................................I-A

Coach: Jack Bicknell III, Boston College 1984
2002 RESULTS (4-8)

39	Oklahoma St. *	36
13	Clemson	33
53	Tulsa ■	9
17	Penn St.	49
3	Texas A&M	31
20	Rice	37
34	Southern Methodist	37
50	Nevada ■	47
30	San Jose St.	42
10	Boise St.	36
38	UTEP *	24
13	Fresno St. ■	45

Nickname: Bulldogs
Colors: Red & Blue
Stadium: Joe Aillet
  Capacity: 30,600; Year Built: 1968
AD: Jim M. Oakes
SID: Malcolm Butler

LOUISVILLE
Louisville, KY 40292 ....I-A

Coach: John L. Smith, Weber St. 1971
2002 RESULTS (7-6)

17	Kentucky ■	22
40	Duke	3
33	Colorado St.	36
45	Army	14
26	Florida St. ■	20
38	Memphis	32
31	TCU ■	45
44	East Caro. ■	20
14	Cincinnati ■	24
20	Southern Miss.	17
41	UAB ■	21
10	Houston	27
15	Marshall (GMAC Bowl)*	38

Nickname: Cardinals
Colors: Red, Black & White
Stadium: Papa John's Cardinal
  Capacity: 42,000; Year Built: 1998
AD: Thomas M. Jurich
SID: Andy Knapick

LUTHER
Decorah, IA 52101-1045..........................III

Coach: Kevin Johnson, Tex.-Pan American 1986
2002 RESULTS (4-6)

40	Minn.-Morris ■	20
38	Dubuque	10
0	Wartburg ■	41
9	Buena Vista	19
28	Cornell College ■	33
14	Simpson	38
23	Loras	13
33	Upper Iowa ■	14
10	Coe	21
3	Central (Iowa) ■	33

Nickname: Norse
Colors: Blue & White
Stadium: Carlson
  Capacity: 5,000; Year Built: 1966
AD: Joe Thompson
SID: Dave Blanchard

LYCOMING
Williamsport, PA 17701-5192....................III

Coach: Frank Girardi, West Chester 1961
2002 RESULTS (6-3)

54	Delaware Valley	0
24	Lebanon Valley	6
50	Susquehanna ■	3
24	King's (Pa.)	10
14	Widener	20
28	FDU-Florham ■	34
35	Albright ■	12
14	Wilkes ■	23
55	Juniata ■	24

Nickname: Warriors
Colors: Blue & Gold
Stadium: Person Field
  Capacity: 2,500; Year Built: 1962
AD: Frank L. Girardi
SID: Robb Dietrich

MACALESTER
St. Paul, MN 55105 III

Coach: Dennis Czech, Macalester 1983
2002 RESULTS (5-5)

14	Beloit ■	19
51	Trinity Bible (N.D.) ■	6
40	Principia ■	37
24	Colorado Col. ■	14
26	Martin Luther ■	13
13	Hamline	29
0	Lewis & Clark	34
6	St. Olaf ■	34
24	Rockford *	25
33	Carleton	16

Nickname: Scots
Colors: Orange & Blue
Stadium: Macalester
  Capacity: 4,000; Year Built: 1965
AD: Irvin Cross
SID: Andy Johnson

MacMURRAY
Jacksonville, IL 62650-2590 III

Coach: Bob Frey, Mount Union 1985
2002 RESULTS (10-1)

44	Manchester ■	7
16	Washington (Mo.) ■	10
55	Concordia (Ill.) ■	7
16	Lakeland ■	6
47	Greenville	21
28	Benedictine (Ill.) ■	12
7	Eureka	0
19	Aurora ■	18
14	Concordia (Wis.)	9
35	Blackburn	0
7	Wabash	42

Nickname: Highlanders
Colors: Scarlet & Navy
Stadium: MacMurray Field
  Capacity: 5,000; Year Built: 1984
AD: Robert E. Gay
SID: Andy Danner

MAINE
Orono, ME 04469-5747 ....I-AA

Coach: Jack Cosgrove, Maine 1978
2002 RESULTS (11-3)

52	Central Conn. St. *	3
27	William & Mary ■	14
21	Villanova	14
42	Howard	12
31	Rhode Island ■	14
17	James Madison ■	6
10	Massachusetts	20
33	Florida Int'l	7
24	Hofstra ■	17
13	Delaware ■	37
21	Richmond	14
31	New Hampshire ■	14
14	Appalachian St.	13
7	Ga. Southern	31

Nickname: Black Bears
Colors: Blue & White
Stadium: Morse Field at Alfond Stadium
  Capacity: 10,000; Year Built: 1998
AD: Paul Bubb
SID: Pete Lefresne

MAINE MARITIME

Castine, ME 04421 III

Coach: Christopher McKenney, Springfield 1984

2002 RESULTS (1-8)

29	Mount Ida ■	30
7	Curry	38
13	Mass. Maritime ■	15
0	Nichols	48
3	Bridgewater St. ■	21
13	Fitchburg St.	21
19	Worcester St. ■	27
8	Westfield St. ■	34
39	Framingham St.	7

Nickname: Mariners
Colors: Royal Blue & Gold
Stadium: Ritchie
  Capacity: 3,500; Year Built: 1965
AD: William J. Mottola/William J. Mottola
SID: Katrina Dagan

MANCHESTER

North Manchester, IN 46962 III

Coach: Dave Harms, Drake 1970

2002 RESULTS (3-7)

7	MacMurray	44
17	Earlham ■	7
18	Alma ■	52
3	Olivet	35
7	Hanover ■	49
17	Mt. St. Joseph	23
25	Franklin ■	31
18	Defiance	14
18	Bluffton ■	6
12	Anderson (Ind.)	35

Nickname: Spartans
Colors: Black & Gold
Stadium: Burt Memorial
  Capacity: 4,500
AD: Tom Jarman
SID: Doug Shoemaker

MANSFIELD

Mansfield, PA 16933 II

Coach: Chris Woods, Davidson 1991

2002 RESULTS (3-7)

14	East Stroudsburg ■	31
20	Buffalo St.	19
21	Westminster (Pa.) ■	24
30	Lock Haven ■	33
12	Millersville ■	6
22	Kutztown	32
9	Calif. (Pa.)	17
49	Cheyney	17
6	Bloomsburg ■	17
7	West Chester	9

Nickname: Mountaineers
Colors: Red & Black
Stadium: Van Norman Field
  Capacity: 4,000; Year Built: 1964
AD: Roger N. Maisner
SID: Steve McCloskey

MARANATHA BAPTIST

Watertown, WI 53094-0000 III

Coach: Terry Price, Pillsbury 1971

2002 RESULTS (6-3)

13	Martin Luther	41
3	Northwestern (Minn.) ■	28
22	Crown	13
10	Westminster (Mo.) ■	0

64	Trinity Bible (N.D.)	12
32	Blackburn ■	0
24	Rockford	7
28	Principia	21
7	Northwestern (Minn.) *	9

Nickname: Crusaders
Colors: Navy Blue & Gold
Stadium: Maranatha
  Capacity: 3,000
AD: Terry Price
SID: Greg Wright

MARIETTA

Marietta, OH 45750...............................III

Coach: Gene Epley, Indiana (Pa.) 1965

2002 RESULTS (3-7)

28	Bluffton ■	27
27	Otterbein	34
0	Capital ■	35
27	Heidelberg ■	38
0	John Carroll	46
10	Ohio Northern	42
32	Wilmington (Ohio) ■	31
10	Mount Union	56
14	Baldwin-Wallace ■	40
31	Muskingum	25

Nickname: Pioneers
Colors: Navy Blue & White
Stadium: Don Drumm Field
  Capacity: 7,000; Year Built: 1935
AD: Debora Lazorik
SID: To be named

MARIST

Poughkeepsie, NY 12601-1387...............I–AA

Coach: Jim Parady, Maine 1983

2002 RESULTS (7-4)

38	Sacred Heart ■	27
28	Canisius ■	0
0	Duquesne	36
31	Wagner ■	16
33	Fairfield ■	29
28	St. John's (N.Y.) ■	22
24	St. Peter's	36
14	Iona ■	17
17	Georgetown	24
49	La Salle	23
20	Siena	0

Nickname: Red Foxes
Colors: Red & White
Stadium: Leonidoff Field
  Capacity: 2,500; Year Built: 1972
AD: Timothy S. Murray
SID: Chris O'Connor

MARS HILL

Mars Hill, NC 28754 II

Coach: Tim Clifton, Mercer 1976

2002 RESULTS (7-4)

41	Va.-Wise ■	6
10	East Tenn. St.	20
56	St. Augustine's ■	0
39	Edward Waters	27
0	Carson-Newman	45
6	Catawba ■	22
23	Lenoir-Rhyne	21
30	Wingate	24
0	Presbyterian ■	12
58	Newberry	14
6	Tusculum ■	0

Nickname: Lions
Colors: Royal Blue & Gold
Stadium: Meares

Capacity: 5,000; Year Built: 1965
AD: David Riggins
SID: Rick Baker

MARSHALL

Huntington, WV 25755 ....I–A

Coach: Bob Pruett, Marshall 1965

2002 RESULTS (11-2)

50	Appalachian St. ■	17
21	Virginia Tech	47
26	UCF ■	21
42	Kent St.	21
66	Buffalo ■	21
24	Troy St. ■	7
23	Central Mich.	18
20	Akron	34
36	Miami (Ohio) ■	34
24	Ohio	21
38	Ball St. ■	14
49	Toledo ■	45
38	Louisville (GMAC Bowl)*	15

Nickname: Thundering Herd
Colors: Green & White
Stadium: Marshall University
  Capacity: 38,019; Year Built: 1991
AD: Bob Marcum
SID: Ricky Hazel

MARTIN LUTHER

New Ulm, MN 56073-3965 III

Coach: Dennis Gorsline, Northern Mich. 1965

2002 RESULTS (6-3)

41	Maranatha Baptist ■	13
24	Dubuque	36
14	Blackburn ■	13
7	Northwestern (Minn.) ■	48
13	Macalester	26
42	Principia	35
21	Crown ■	0
59	Trinity Bible (N.D.)	6
32	Westminster (Mo.) *	28

Nickname: Knights
Colors: Black, Red & White
Stadium: MLC Bowl
  Capacity: 1,500; Year Built: 1974
AD: James M. Unke
SID: Jeremy Belter

MARY HARDIN-BAYLOR

Belton, TX 76513...............................III

Coach: Pete Fredenburg, Southwest Tex. St. 1970

2002 RESULTS (10-1)

42	Willamette ■	26
44	Austin ■	3
24	Texas Lutheran	5
69	Louisiana Col. ■	12
39	Mississippi Col.	24
42	Howard Payne ■	17
31	Sul Ross St.	0
35	Hardin-Simmons ■	16
23	East Tex. Baptist	22
59	McMurry	7
38	Trinity (Tex.)	48

Nickname: Crusaders
Colors: Purple, Gold & White
Stadium: Tiger Field
  Capacity: 7,000; Year Built: 1996
AD: Ben Shipp
SID: Jon Wallin

MARYLAND
College Park, MD 20742...........................I–A

Coach: Ralph Friedgen, Maryland 1969
2002 RESULTS (11-3)
0	Notre Dame *	22
44	Akron ■	14
10	Florida St. ■	37
45	Eastern Mich. ■	3
37	Wofford ■	8
48	West Virginia	17
34	Georgia Tech ■	10
45	Duke	12
59	North Carolina	7
24	North Carolina St. ■	21
30	Clemson	12
13	Virginia	48
32	Wake Forest ■	14
30	Tennessee (Peach Bowl)*	3

Nickname: Terps
Colors: Red, White, Black & Gold
Stadium: Byrd
 Capacity: 48,055; Year Built: 1950
AD: Deborah A. Yow
SID: Dave Haglund

MARYVILLE (TENN.)
Maryville, TN 37804-5907 III

Coach: Phil Wilks, Marshall 1970
2002 RESULTS (0-10)
38	Westminster (Mo.)	41
21	Rhodes ■	46
0	Bridgewater (Va.)	42
19	Sewanee	27
21	Millsaps ■	34
13	Case Reserve	42
7	Centre ■	33
28	Bethel (Tenn.)	33
7	Thomas More	56
23	Hampden-Sydney ■	51

Nickname: Scots
Colors: Orange & Garnet
Stadium: Lloyd Thorton
 Capacity: 2,500; Year Built: 1993
AD: Randall D. Lambert
SID: Eric Etchison

MASSACHUSETTS
Amherst, MA 01003 ....I–AA

Coach: Mark Whipple, Brown 1979
2002 RESULTS (8-4)
52	Central Conn. St. ■	3
42	American Int'l ■	13
17	Northeastern	42
24	North Carolina St.	56
34	Richmond	13
20	Maine ■	10
17	Villanova ■	16
14	James Madison	7
17	Delaware ■	7
14	New Hampshire	31
28	Hofstra ■	31
48	Rhode Island	21

Nickname: Minutemen
Colors: Maroon & White
Stadium: Warren P. McGuirk Alumni Stadium
 Capacity: 17,000; Year Built: 1965
AD: Ian McCaw
SID: Charles Bare

MASS.-DARTMOUTH
North Dartmouth, MA 02747-2300 III

Coach: Bill Kavanaugh, Stonehill 1972
2002 RESULTS (11-1)
27	Fitchburg St.	7
44	Plymouth St. ■	14
31	Bridgewater St.	14
40	Curry ■	10
44	Utica ■	0
7	Nichols ■	0
36	MIT	26
37	Western New Eng.	3
27	Mass. Maritime ■	6
38	Salve Regina	0
16	Westfield St. *	0
6	Muhlenberg	56

Nickname: Corsairs
Colors: Blue, White & Gold
Stadium: Corsair
 Capacity: 1,850
AD: Robert W. Mullen
SID: Bill Gathright

MIT
Cambridge, MA 02139-7404 III

Coach: Dwight Smith, Bates 1975
2002 RESULTS (4-5)
7	WPI	25
23	Framingham St. ■	13
23	Mass. Maritime	14
6	Worcester St.	35
8	Curry ■	31
10	Western New Eng.	0
26	Mass.-Dartmouth	36
7	Nichols	22
16	Salve Regina ■	8

Nickname: Engineers
Colors: Cardinal & Gray
Stadium: Steinbrenner
 Capacity: 1,600; Year Built: 1980
AD: Candace L. Royer
SID: Roger F. Crosley

MASS. MARITIME
Buzzards Bay, MA 02532...........................III

Coach: Joe Domingos, Bridgewater St. 1966
2002 RESULTS (1-8)
0	Coast Guard	27
14	MIT ■	23
15	Maine Maritime	13
14	Framingham St. ■	31
0	Westfield St.	54
6	Worcester St. ■	41
0	Fitchburg St.	32
6	Mass.-Dartmouth	27
18	Bridgewater St. ■	48

Nickname: Buccaneers
Colors: Blue & Gold
Stadium: Commander Ellis
 Capacity: 3,000; Year Built: 1972
AD: Robert Corradi/Robert Corradi
SID: Leroy Thompson

MASS.-LOWELL
Lowell, MA 01854 II

Coach: Wally Dembowski, Holy Cross 1988
2002 RESULTS (3-8)
7	Pace	33
41	St. Anselm ■	27
21	C.W. Post	57
25	Southern Conn. St.	29
9	Bentley ■	34
35	Stonehill ■	14
21	New Haven	69
6	Bryant ■	12
14	Merrimack ■	28
37	Assumption	14
16	American Int'l	41

Nickname: River Hawks
Colors: Red, White & Royal Blue
Stadium: Cushing Field
 Capacity: 1,500; Year Built: 2000
AD: Dana K. Skinner
SID: Chris O'Donnell

Note: Discontinued football program following 2002 season.

McDANIEL
Westminster, MD 21157-4390 III

Coach: Tim Keating, Bethany (W.Va.) 1975
2002 RESULTS (9-2)
34	Wm. Paterson	0
20	Bridgewater (Va.) ■	23
27	Susquehanna	7
28	Gettysburg ■	6
37	Ursinus	14
35	Muhlenberg ■	14
23	Dickinson ■	0
10	Frank. & Marsh.	6
28	Bethany (W.Va.)	17
7	Johns Hopkins	27
21	Moravian	7

Nickname: Green Terror
Colors: Green & Gold
Stadium: Scott S. Bair
 Capacity: 4,000; Year Built: 1981
AD: James M. Smith
SID: Stephen Peed

McMURRY
Abilene, TX 79697 III

Coach: Steve Keenum, McMurry 1980
2002 RESULTS (0-10)
13	Menlo	24
21	East Tex. Baptist	31
7	Austin	38
20	Texas Lutheran ■	21
14	Louisiana Col.	29
22	Mississippi Col. ■	25
17	Howard Payne	44
14	Sul Ross St. ■	17
6	Hardin-Simmons	14
7	Mary Hardin-Baylor ■	59

Nickname: Indians
Colors: Maroon & White
Stadium: Indian
 Capacity: 4,500; Year Built: 1937
AD: Steve Keenum
SID: Patrick Stewart

McNEESE ST.
Lake Charles, LA 70609 ....I–AA

Coach: Tommy Tate, McNeese St. 1979
2002 RESULTS (13-2)
52	Grambling ■	20
28	Youngstown St.	13
24	La.-Monroe	19
38	Western Ky. ■	13
14	Nebraska	38
28	Jacksonville St. ■	20
47	Sam Houston St.	10
42	Stephen F. Austin	13
47	Southwest Tex. St. ■	7
27	Northwestern St.	3
33	Nicholls St. ■	21
21	Montana St. ■	14
24	Montana ■	20
39	Villanova ■	28
14	Western Ky. *	34

Nickname: Cowboys
Colors: Blue & Gold
Stadium: Cowboy
   Capacity: 17,410; Year Built: 1965
AD: Sonny Watkins
SID: Louis Bonnette

MEMPHIS
Memphis, TN 38152-3370 ....I–A

Coach: Tommy West, Tennessee 1975
2002 RESULTS (3-9)
52	Murray St. ■	6
16	Mississippi	38
14	Southern Miss.	33
38	Tulane ■	10
17	UAB	31
32	Louisville ■	38
17	Mississippi St. ■	29
10	Cincinnati	48
21	Houston ■	26
28	South Fla.	31
38	Army ■	10
20	TCU	27

Nickname: Tigers
Colors: Blue & Gray
Stadium: Liberty Bowl
   Capacity: 62,380; Year Built: 1965
AD: R.C. Johnson
SID: Bob Winn

MENLO
Atherton, CA 94027-4185 III

Coach: Mark Kaanapu, Pacific (Ore.) 1990
2002 RESULTS (5-5)
24	McMurry ■	13
34	Hardin-Simmons	42
7	Whitworth ■	30
30	Willamette	52
34	Whittier ■	6
22	Cal Lutheran	17
6	Linfield	56
20	Puget Sound	21
32	Pacific Lutheran *	29
44	Chapman ■	22

Nickname: Oaks
Colors: Navy Blue & White
Stadium: Connor Field
   Capacity: 1,000; Year Built: 1972
AD: Keith Larsen
SID: Nicholas Enriquez

MERCHANT MARINE
Kings Point, NY 11024-1699 III

Coach: Charlie Pravata, Adelphi 1972
2002 RESULTS (8-3)
3	Muhlenberg	54
26	Norwich	21
13	Springfield ■	26
27	TCNJ ■	10
20	WPI	3
28	Plymouth St. ■	14
24	St. Lawrence	0
20	Western Conn. St.	17
35	Grove City ■	17
31	Coast Guard ■	6
7	Wilkes ■	33

Nickname: Mariners
Colors: Blue & Gray
Stadium: Capt. Tomb Field
   Capacity: 5,840; Year Built: 1945
AD: Susan Petersen-Lubow
SID: Kim McNulty

MERCYHURST
Erie, PA 16546 II

Coach: Tim McNulty, Mansfield 1991
2002 RESULTS (2-9)
16	West Va. Wesleyan ■	13
7	Northern Mich.	37
7	Saginaw Valley	51
17	Northwood ■	14
3	Findlay ■	36
20	Ashland	27
13	Ferris St. ■	19
16	Indianapolis	40
24	Grand Valley St. ■	62
29	Wayne St. (Mich.)	33
7	Hillsdale ■	56

Nickname: Lakers
Colors: Blue & Green
Stadium: Louis J. Tullio Field
   Capacity: 2,300; Year Built: 1996
AD: Peter J. Russo
SID: John Leisering

MERRIMACK
North Andover, MA 01845..........................II

Coach: Thomas Caito, Boston U. 1960
2002 RESULTS (6-4)
6	Bentley ■	16
28	Assumption	7
17	Stonehill	14
18	American Int'l ■	8
3	Southern Conn. St.	17
6	C.W. Post ■	34
7	St. Anselm	21
28	Mass.-Lowell	14
24	Pace ■	7
20	Bryant ■	14

Nickname: Warriors
Colors: Navy Blue & Gold
Stadium: Merrimack
   Capacity: 2,000
AD: Chris Serino
SID: Tom O'Brien

MESA ST.
Grand Junction, CO 81501 II

Coach: Joe Ramunno, Wyoming 1984
2002 RESULTS (5-6)
19	Western Ore. ■	22
0	Southern Utah	7
7	North Dakota	66
62	N.M. Highlands	14
30	Western St. (Colo.)	10
30	Chadron St. ■	31
35	Adams St. ■	28
16	Fort Hays St.	20
35	Colorado Mines	30
13	Neb.-Kearney ■	20
58	Fort Lewis ■	55

Nickname: Mavericks
Colors: Maroon, Gold & White
Stadium: Stocker
   Capacity: 8,000; Year Built: 1949
AD: Clarence Ross
SID: Tish Elliott

METHODIST
Fayetteville, NC 28311-1420 III

Coach: Jim Sypult, West Virginia 1967
2002 RESULTS (3-7)
25	Emory & Henry	15
18	Guilford ■	41
20	Salisbury ■	45
14	Apprentice	34
43	Averett ■	0
20	Ferrum ■	23
9	Chris. Newport ■	20
32	Chowan	0
3	Greensboro	13
12	Shenandoah	20

Nickname: Monarchs
Colors: Green & Gold
Stadium: Monarch Field
   Capacity: 1,500; Year Built: 1989
AD: Bob McEvoy
SID: Lee Glenn

MIAMI (FLA.)
Coral Gables, FL 33146 ....I–A

Coach: Larry Coker, Northeastern St. 1970
2002 RESULTS (12-1)
63	Florida A&M ■	17
41	Florida	16
44	Temple	21
38	Boston College ■	6
48	Connecticut	14
28	Florida St. ■	27
40	West Virginia	23
42	Rutgers	17
26	Tennessee	3
28	Pittsburgh ■	21
49	Syracuse	7
56	Virginia Tech ■	45
24	Ohio St. (Fiesta Bowl) *	31

Nickname: Hurricanes
Colors: Orange, Green & White
Stadium: Orange Bowl
   Capacity: 72,319; Year Built: 1935
AD: Paul Dee
SID: Doug Walker

MIAMI (OHIO)
Oxford, OH 45056 ....I–A

Coach: Terry Hoeppner, Franklin 1969
2002 RESULTS (7-5)
27	North Carolina	21
24	Iowa ■	29
7	LSU	33
27	Kent St. ■	20
48	Akron	31
31	Cincinnati	26
41	Northern Ill. ■	48
49	Buffalo	0
27	Toledo	13
38	Ohio ■	20
34	Marshall	36
31	UCF ■	48

Nickname: RedHawks
Colors: Red & White
Stadium: Fred C. Yager
   Capacity: 30,012; Year Built: 1983
AD: Steve Snyder
SID: Mike Harris

MICHIGAN
Ann Arbor, MI 48109-2201 ....I–A

Coach: Lloyd Carr, Northern Mich. 1968
2002 RESULTS (10-3)
31	Washington ■	29
35	Western Mich. ■	12
23	Notre Dame	25
10	Utah ■	7
45	Illinois	28
27	Penn St. ■	24
23	Purdue	21
9	Iowa ■	34
49	Michigan St. ■	3
41	Minnesota	24
21	Wisconsin ■	14
9	Ohio St.	14
38	Florida (Outback Bowl)*	30

Nickname: Wolverines
Colors: Maize & Blue
Stadium: Michigan
   Capacity: 107,501; Year Built: 1927
AD: William C. Martin
SID: David Ablauf

MICHIGAN ST.
East Lansing, MI 48824-1025 ....I–A

Coach: Bobby Williams, Purdue 1982
2002 RESULTS (4-8)
56	Eastern Mich. ■	7
27	Rice ■	10
22	California ■	46
17	Notre Dame ■	21
39	Northwestern ■	24
16	Iowa	44
7	Minnesota ■	28
24	Wisconsin ■	42
3	Michigan	49
56	Indiana	21
42	Purdue ■	45
7	Penn St.	61

Nickname: Spartans
Colors: Green & White
Stadium: Spartan
   Capacity: 72,027; Year Built: 1957
AD: Ronald H. Mason
SID: John Lewandowski

MICHIGAN TECH
Houghton, MI 49931-1295 II

Coach: Bernie Anderson, Northern Mich. 1978
2002 RESULTS (3-7)
30	Ashland	23
21	Saginaw Valley	35
32	Indianapolis ■	24
23	Findlay	42
14	Grand Valley St. ■	56
14	Ferris St.	21
31	Wayne St. (Mich.) ■	34
7	Hillsdale	31
34	Northern Mich. ■	13
23	Northwood ■	33

Nickname: Huskies
Colors: Silver, Gold & Black
Stadium: Sherman Field
   Capacity: 3,000; Year Built: 1954
AD: Rick Yeo
SID: Dave Fischer

MIDDLE TENN.
Murfreesboro, TN 37132 ....I–A

Coach: Andy McCollum, Austin Peay 1981
2002 RESULTS (4-8)
34	Alabama	39
3	Tennessee	26
22	Kentucky	44
14	Southeast Mo. St. ■	24
7	Arkansas St.	13
21	Vanderbilt	20
48	La.-Lafayette ■	35
18	Idaho	21
21	New Mexico St.	24
44	La.-Monroe ■	28
20	North Texas ■	30
45	Utah St.	28

Nickname: Blue Raiders
Colors: Royal Blue & White
Stadium: Johnny "Red" Floyd
   Capacity: 30,788; Year Built: 1933
AD: James Donnelly
SID: Mark Owens

MIDDLEBURY
Middlebury, VT 05753 III

Coach: Bob Ritter, Middlebury 1982
2002 RESULTS (4-4)
21	Wesleyan (Conn.) ■	24
17	Colby	14
10	Amherst ■	17
24	Williams	27
28	Bates ■	7
20	Trinity (Conn.)	22
41	Hamilton	21
31	Tufts ■	6

Nickname: Panthers
Colors: Blue & White
Stadium: Alumni
   Capacity: 3,500; Year Built: 1991
AD: Russell Reilly
SID: Brad Nadeau

MIDWESTERN ST.
Wichita Falls, TX 76308-2099 II

Coach: Bill Maskill, Western Ky. 1970
2002 RESULTS (7-4)
35	Southern Ark. ■	26
23	Sam Houston St.	26
23	Neb.-Omaha	45
6	Southwestern Okla. ■	0
40	Northeastern St.	30
6	Tex. A&M-Kingsville	9
54	West Tex. A&M ■	14
28	Eastern N.M.	14
20	Abilene Christian ■	21
38	Angelo St.	6
56	Tex. A&M-Commerce ■	20

Nickname: Indians
Colors: Maroon and Gold
Stadium: Memorial Stadium
   Capacity: 14,500; Year Built: 1976
AD: Jeff Ray
SID: Andy Austin

MILES
Birmingham, AL 35208 II

Coach: Wade Streeter, Southern U. 1990
2002 RESULTS (6-5)
6	Alabama St. *	27
25	Albany St. (Ga.)	19
7	Clark Atlanta	14
16	Tuskegee	26
28	Benedict ■	27
35	Stillman *	20
9	Fort Valley St. ■	21
34	Lane	32
39	Kentucky St. ■	17
21	Southern U.	28
19	Morehouse ■	10

Nickname: Golden Bears
Colors: Purple & Gold
Stadium: Alumni
   Capacity: 5,000; Year Built: 2000
AD: Augustus James
SID: Takia J. Hudson

MILLERSVILLE
Millersville, PA 17551-0302 II

Coach: Kevin Kiesel, Gettysburg 1981
2002 RESULTS (3-7)
3	Rowan	17
3	Clarion ■	24
16	Indiana (Pa.) ■	43
6	Mansfield	12
26	Bloomsburg ■	49
9	Slippery Rock	33
10	Kutztown ■	9
26	East Stroudsburg	37
31	West Chester ■	24
49	Cheyney	0

Nickname: Marauders
Colors: Black & Gold
Stadium: Biemesderfer
   Capacity: 6,500; Year Built: 1970
AD: Daniel N. Audette
SID: Greg Wright

MILLIKIN
Decatur, IL 62522-2084 III

Coach: Doug Neibuhr, Millikin 1974
2002 RESULTS (7-3)
54	Franklin	21
54	Aurora ■	13
65	Anderson (Ind.)	7
21	Carthage	12
20	Wheaton (Ill.) ■	39
37	Elmhurst	14
14	Augustana (Ill.)	41
72	North Park ■	0
17	North Central	24
27	Ill. Wesleyan ■	23

Nickname: Big Blue
Colors: Royal Blue & White
Stadium: Frank M. Lindsay Field
  Capacity: 4,000; Year Built: 1987
AD: Doug Neibuhr
SID: Julie Farr

MILLSAPS
Jackson, MS 39210 III

Coach: Bob Tyler, Mississippi 1954
2002 RESULTS (3-6)
16	Mississippi Col. *	14
6	Wis.-Stout ■	30
34	Maryville (Tenn.)	21
14	Centre ■	7
28	Rose-Hulman	35
7	DePauw ■	28
7	Sewanee	17
24	Rhodes	28
6	Trinity (Tex.) ■	38

Nickname: Majors
Colors: Purple & White
Stadium: Alumni Field
  Capacity: 5,000; Year Built: 1920
AD: Ron Jurney
SID: Jeff Mitchell

MINNESOTA
Minneapolis, MN 55455 ....I–A

Coach: Glen Mason, Ohio St. 1972
2002 RESULTS (8-5)
42	Southwest Tex. St. ■	0
35	La.-Lafayette	11
31	Toledo ■	21
41	Buffalo ■	17
15	Purdue	28
31	Illinois ■	10
45	Northwestern ■	42
28	Michigan St.	7
3	Ohio St.	34
24	Michigan ■	41
21	Iowa ■	45
31	Wisconsin	49
29	Arkansas (Music City Bowl)*	14

Nickname: Golden Gophers
Colors: Maroon & Gold
Stadium: Metrodome
  Capacity: 64,172; Year Built: 1982
AD: Joel Maturi
SID: Shane Sandersfeld

MINN. ST. MOORHEAD
Moorhead, MN 56563-2996 II

Coach: Ralph Micheli, Macalester 1970
2002 RESULTS (5-5)
41	Concordia-M'head ■	17
28	Concordia-St. Paul ■	35
10	Winona St.	37
49	Minn.-Crookston ■	21
27	Minn.-Duluth ■	53
19	Wayne St. (Neb.)	16
28	Bemidji St. ■	35
35	Minn.-Morris	13
35	Southwest St.	42
49	Northern St.	35

Nickname: Dragons
Colors: Scarlet & White
Stadium: Alex Nemzek
  Capacity: 5,000; Year Built: 1960
AD: Katy Wilson
SID: Larry Scott

MINN. ST. MANKATO
Mankato, MN 56001 II

Coach: Clarence Holley, Arkansas Tech 1985
2002 RESULTS (4-7)
45	Bemidji St. ■	23
9	Minn. Duluth	44
31	Northwest Mo. St. ■	42
0	Augustana (S.D.)	7
14	Northern Colo.	27
15	Neb.-Omaha ■	21
20	North Dakota St.	37
41	St. Cloud St. ■	40
36	North Dakota	35
23	South Dakota	17
13	South Dakota St. ■	39

Nickname: Mavericks
Colors: Purple & Gold
Stadium: Blakeslee Stadium
  Capacity: 7,500; Year Built: 1962
AD: Kevin Buisman
SID: Paul Allan

MINN.-CROOKSTON
Crookston, MN 56716-5001 II

Coach: Shannon Stassen, Valley City St. 1987
2002 RESULTS (1-10)
0	North Dakota	57
20	Mayville St.	27
21	Southwest St. ■	28
14	Minn.-Duluth	76
21	Minn. St. Moorhead	49
10	Wayne St. (Neb.) ■	17
7	Winona St.	55
46	Minn.-Morris ■	13
31	Northern St. ■	49
7	Concordia-St. Paul	48
7	Bemidji St. ■	21

Nickname: Golden Eagle
Colors: Maroon & Gold
Stadium: Ed Widseth Field
  Capacity: 3,000; Year Built: 1966
AD: Lon Boike
SID: Nick Kornder

MINN. DULUTH
Duluth, MN 55812-2496 II

Coach: Bob Nielson, Wartburg 1982
2002 RESULTS (11-1)
44	Minn. St.-Mankato ■	9
23	South Dakota	21
44	Minn.-Morris	6
76	Minn.-Crookston ■	14
38	Southwest St.	7
53	Minn. St. Moorhead	27
36	Concordia-St. Paul ■	12
48	Northern St.	22
52	Bemidji St. ■	25
42	Wayne St. (Neb.) ■	3
42	Winona St. ■	25
41	Northwest Mo. St.	45

Nickname: Bulldogs
Colors: Maroon & Gold
Stadium: Griggs Field
  Capacity: 4,000; Year Built: 1966
AD: Robert Corran
SID: Bob Nygaard

MINN.-MORRIS
Morris, MN 56267 II

Coach: Ken Crandall, Fort Hays St. 1990
2002 RESULTS (0-11)
16	Valley City St. ■	25
20	Luther	40
6	Minn.-Duluth ■	44
24	Southwest St.	43
0	Concordia-St. Paul	63
14	Winona St. ■	52
7	Northern St. ■	38
13	Minn.-Crookston	46
13	Minn. St. Moorhead ■	35
13	Bemidji St.	38
14	Wayne St. (Neb.)	35

Nickname: Cougars
Colors: Maroon & Gold
Stadium: UMM Field
  Capacity: 5,000
AD: Mark Fohl
SID: Brian Curtis

MISSISSIPPI
University, MS 38677 ....I–A

Coach: David Cutcliffe, Alabama 1976
2002 RESULTS (7-6)
31	La.-Monroe ■	3
38	Memphis ■	16
28	Texas Tech	42
45	Vanderbilt ■	38
17	Florida ■	14
52	Arkansas St. ■	17
7	Alabama	42
28	Arkansas	48
24	Auburn ■	31
17	Georgia	31
13	LSU	14
24	Mississippi St. ■	12
27	Nebraska (Independence Bowl)*	23

Nickname: Rebels
Colors: Red & Blue
Stadium: Vaught-Hemingway
  Capacity: 60,580; Year Built: 1915
AD: Pete Boone
SID: Langston Rogers

MISSISSIPPI COL.
Clinton, MS 39058 III

Coach: Johnny Mills, Mississippi Col. 1973
2002 RESULTS (4-6)
14	Millsaps *	16
0	Howard Payne	50
34	Sul Ross St. ■	21
21	Hardin-Simmons	32
24	Mary Hardin-Baylor ■	39
25	McMurry	22
23	Austin ■	27
36	Texas Lutheran	16
15	Louisiana Col. ■	10
9	East Tex. Baptist ■	16

Nickname: Choctaws
Colors: Blue & Gold
Stadium: Robinson-Hale
  Capacity: 8,500; Year Built: 1985
AD: Mike Jones
SID: Chris Brooks

MISSISSIPPI ST.
Mississippi State, MS 39762-5509 ....I-A

Coach: Jackie Sherrill, Alabama 1966
2002 RESULTS (3-9)
13	Oregon	36
51	Jacksonville St. ■	13
14	Auburn ■	42
13	LSU	31
10	South Carolina	34
11	Troy St. ■	8
29	Memphis	17
24	Kentucky ■	45
14	Alabama	28
17	Tennessee ■	35
19	Arkansas ■	26
12	Mississippi	24

Nickname: Bulldogs
Colors: Maroon & White
Stadium: Davis Wade Stadium at Scott Field
   Capacity: 55,082; Year Built: 1914
AD: Larry Templeton
SID: Mike Nemeth

MISSISSIPPI VAL.
Itta Bena, MS 38941-1400 ....I-AA

Coach: Willie Totten, Mississippi Val. 1987
2002 RESULTS (5-6)
30	Ark.-Pine Bluff ■	36
28	Delta St. ■	26
7	Sam Houston St.	45
12	Jackson St.	36
52	Paul Quinn ■	16
16	Southern U.	19
13	Alabama A&M	24
21	Texas Southern	34
26	Prairie View ■	8
23	Alcorn St. ■	6
13	Alabama St.	10

Nickname: Delta Devils
Colors: Forest Green & White
Stadium: Rice-Totten
   Capacity: 10,500; Year Built: 1958
AD: Lonza C. Hardy
SID: Marlon Reed

MISSOURI
Columbia, MO 65211-1050 ....I-A

Coach: Gary Pinkel, Kent St. 1975
2002 RESULTS (5-7)
33	Illinois *	20
41	Ball St. ■	6
28	Bowling Green	51
44	Troy St. ■	7
24	Oklahoma ■	31
13	Nebraska	24
38	Texas Tech	52
36	Kansas ■	12
35	Iowa St.	42
35	Colorado ■	42
33	Texas A&M	27
0	Kansas St.	38

Nickname: Tigers
Colors: Old Gold & Black
Stadium: Memorial/Faurot Field
   Capacity: 68,349; Year Built: 1926
AD: Michael F. Alden
SID: Chad Moller

MO.-ROLLA
Rolla, MO 65401 II

Coach: Kirby Cannon, Southwest Mo. St. 1980
2002 RESULTS (0-11)
15	Harding	23
25	Drake ■	28
9	Northwest Mo. St.	34
28	Truman ■	57
14	Central Mo. St.	55
9	Mo. Western St. ■	29
7	Emporia St. ■	40
14	Pittsburg St.	48
7	Southwest Baptist	17
0	Washburn ■	49
25	Mo. Southern St. ■	49

Nickname: Miners
Colors: Silver & Gold
Stadium: Allgood-Bailey
   Capacity: 8,000; Year Built: 1967
AD: Mark Mullin
SID: John Kean

MO. SOUTHERN ST.
Joplin, MO 64801-1595 II

Coach: Bill Cooke, Fort Lewis 1973
2002 RESULTS (5-6)
63	Greenville ■	0
38	Northeastern St.	7
40	Southwest Baptist ■	25
52	Washburn ■	28
12	Pittsburg St.	50
3	Northwest Mo. St.	47
14	Truman	28
21	Central Mo. St.	42
7	Mo. Western St. ■	28
16	Emporia St.	47
49	Mo.-Rolla	25

Nickname: Lions
Colors: Green & Gold
Stadium: Fred G. Hughes
   Capacity: 7,000; Year Built: 1975
AD: Sallie Beard
SID: Joe Moore

MO. WESTERN ST.
St. Joseph, MO 64507 II

Coach: Jerry Partridge, Mo. Western St. 1985
2002 RESULTS (6-5)
31	Winona St. ■	30
10	South Dakota	3
14	Central Mo. St. ■	21
21	Pittsburg St.	25
14	Emporia St. ■	21
29	Mo.-Rolla	9
28	Southwest Baptist ■	0
34	Washburn	28
28	Mo. Southern St.	7
10	Northwest Mo. St. ■	13
23	Truman	27

Nickname: Griffons
Colors: Black & Gold
Stadium: Spratt
   Capacity: 6,000; Year Built: 1979
AD: Mark Linder
SID: Brett King

MONMOUTH
West Long Branch, NJ 07764 ....I-AA

Coach: Kevin Callahan, Rochester 1977
2002 RESULTS (2-8)
29	Lafayette	30
13	Sacred Heart ■	32
20	Morgan St.	35
10	Robert Morris ■	15
14	Stony Brook ■	9
9	Central Conn. St. ■	10
6	Wagner	7
0	Towson ■	20
7	St. Francis (Pa.) ■	0
7	Albany (N.Y.)	19

Nickname: Hawks
Colors: Royal Blue & White
Stadium: Kessler Field
   Capacity: 4,600; Year Built: 1993
AD: Marilyn A. McNeil
SID: Thomas Dick

MONMOUTH (ILL.)
Monmouth, IL 61462-1998 III

Coach: Steve Bell, Bemidji St. 1991
2002 RESULTS (5-5)
23	Loras	40
7	Ripon	41
21	St. Norbert ■	28
28	Beloit	44
3	Lake Forest ■	27
37	Grinnell ■	20
42	Lawrence	14
28	Illinois Col.	7
35	Carroll (Wis.) ■	24
27	Knox ■	23

Nickname: Fighting Scots
Colors: Red & White
Stadium: Bobby Woll Field
   Capacity: 3,000; Year Built: 1981
AD: Terry L. Glasgow
SID: Barry McNamara/Dan Nolan

MONTANA
Missoula, MT 59812-1291 ....I-AA

Coach: Joe Glenn, South Dakota 1971
2002 RESULTS (11-3)
21	Hofstra	0
45	Albany (N.Y.) ■	7
31	Northern Colo. *	14
13	Idaho St. ■	9
38	Idaho	31
39	Weber St.	7
68	Southern Utah ■	45
24	Portland St.	21
38	Northern Ariz. ■	24
31	Sacramento St. ■	24
21	Eastern Wash.	30
7	Montana St. ■	10
45	Northwestern St. ■	14
20	McNeese St.	24

Nickname: Grizzlies
Colors: Copper, Silver & Gold
Stadium: Washington-Grizzly
   Capacity: 18,845; Year Built: 1986
AD: Wayne Hogan
SID: Dave Guffey

RESULTS

MONTANA ST.
Bozeman, MT 59717-3380 ....I–AA

Coach: Mike Kramer, Idaho 1977
2002 RESULTS (7-6)
27	St. Mary's (Cal.) ■	24
13	Stephen F. Austin	30
31	Adams St. ■	6
28	Washington St.	45
16	Central Wash. ■	31
14	Idaho St.	18
44	Weber St. ■	10
17	Northern Ariz.	20
31	Sacramento St.	30
25	Eastern Wash. ■	14
28	Portland St. ■	26
10	Montana	7
14	McNeese St.	21

Nickname: Bobcats
Colors: Blue & Gold
Stadium: Bobcat Stadium
  Capacity: 13,500; Year Built: 1973
AD: Peter Fields
SID: Bill Lamberty

MONTCLAIR ST.
Upper Montclair, NJ 07043 III

Coach: Rick Giancola, Rowan 1968
2002 RESULTS (5-5)
19	Iona	23
7	Wilkes	31
30	Frostburg St. ■	27
16	Cortland St. ■	20
42	Kean	7
35	Wm. Paterson ■	0
14	Buffalo St.	21
40	TCNJ ■	7
20	New Jersey City	8
12	Rowan ■	48

Nickname: Red Hawks
Colors: Scarlet & White
Stadium: Sprague
  Capacity: 6,000; Year Built: 1934
AD: Holly P. Gera
SID: Mike Scala

MORAVIAN
Bethlehem, PA 18018-6650 III

Coach: Scot Dapp, West Chester 1973
2002 RESULTS (7-4)
21	FDU-Florham ■	14
0	King's (Pa.)	33
20	Widener ■	27
41	Lebanon Valley	21
39	Juniata ■	23
33	Delaware Valley	13
22	Wilkes	7
28	Albright ■	7
23	Susquehanna	6
0	Muhlenberg ■	8
7	McDaniel	21

Nickname: Greyhounds
Colors: Blue & Grey
Stadium: Steel Field
  Capacity: 2,200; Year Built: 1932
AD: Paul R. Moyer
SID: Mark Fleming

MOREHEAD ST.
Morehead, KY 40351-1689 ....I–AA

Coach: Matt Ballard, Gardner-Webb 1979
2002 RESULTS (9-3)
31	Cumberland (Ky.) ■	0
27	Valparaiso	17
20	Kentucky St. ■	15
0	Tusculum	42
53	Butler ■	20
39	Davidson	7
40	St. Joseph's (Ind.) ■	7
48	Jacksonville ■	14
45	Austin Peay	25
24	Tiffin ■	13
20	Dayton	30
0	Dayton ■	28

Nickname: Eagles
Colors: Blue & Gold
Stadium: Jayne
  Capacity: 10,000; Year Built: 1964
AD: Chip Smith
SID: Randy Stacy

MOREHOUSE
Atlanta, GA 30314 II

Coach: Willard Scissum, Alabama A&M 1994
2002 RESULTS (6-5)
0	Fort Valley St. *	23
19	N.C. Central ■	3
17	Tusculum ■	24
23	Benedict	14
24	Bowie St. ■	17
45	Kentucky St. *	16
14	Tuskegee *	19
19	Lane ■	16
40	Clark Atlanta	7
8	Albany St. (Ga.) *	22
10	Miles	19

Nickname: Tigers
Colors: Maroon & White
Stadium: B.T. Harvey
  Capacity: 9,850; Year Built: 1983
AD: Andre' Pattillo
SID: Yusuf Davis

MORGAN ST.
Baltimore, MD 21251 ....I–AA

Coach: Stanley Mitchell, Morgan St. 1976
2002 RESULTS (7-5)
24	Gardner-Webb	28
28	Towson	49
16	Florida A&M *	34
35	Monmouth ■	20
27	Bethune-Cookman ■	41
30	N.C. A&T	13
38	Howard	20
35	Delaware St. ■	28
42	Morris Brown ■	41
14	Norfolk St.	17
23	South Carolina St.	12
52	Hampton ■	42

Nickname: Bears
Colors: Blue & Orange
Stadium: Hughes
  Capacity: 10,000; Year Built: 1934
AD: David Y. Thomas
SID: Joe McIver

MORRIS BROWN
Atlanta, GA 30314.................................I–AA

Coach: Soloman Brannan, Morris Brown 1964
2002 RESULTS (1-11)
10	Delaware St. ■	16
6	Florida A&M	64
7	Bethune-Cookman ■	42
44	Clark Atlanta	7
15	Howard ■	49
7	Alabama St. *	40
20	Savannah St. *	21
7	Samford ■	20
41	Morgan St.	42
13	Fla. Atlantic	34
36	Grambling ■	64
19	Norfolk St.	32

Nickname: Wolverines
Colors: Purple & Black
Stadium: Alonzo F. Herndon
  Capacity: 18,000; Year Built: 1996
AD: Russell Ellington
SID: To be named
Note: Discontinued NCAA membership following 2002 season.

MOUNT IDA
Newton Centre, MA 02459-3323................III

Coach: Edward Sweeney, C.W. Post 1971
2002 RESULTS (2-7)
32	Western New Eng. ■	14
30	Maine Maritime	29
14	Stonehill	45
24	Ursinus ■	27
6	Utica	22
6	Hartwick ■	34
6	St. John Fisher	55
6	Assumption	23
14	Norwich ■	21

Nickname: Mustangs
Colors: Green & White
AD: Jacqueline Palmer
SID: To be named

MT. ST. JOSEPH
Cincinnati, OH 45233-1672 III

Coach: Rod Huber, Cincinnati 1989
2002 RESULTS (5-5)
20	Wilmington (Ohio) ■	45
51	Hiram	0
13	Kalamazoo	27
28	Franklin	13
23	Manchester ■	17
21	Defiance	8
37	Bluffton ■	35
15	Anderson (Ind.)	46
14	Hanover ■	49
7	Thomas More	30

Nickname: Lions
Colors: Blue & Gold
Stadium: Mariemont High School
  Capacity: 2,300; Year Built: 2000
AD: Steven F. Radcliffe
SID: Dane Neumeister

MOUNT UNION
Alliance, OH 44601 III

Coach: Larry Kehres, Mount Union 1971
2002 RESULTS (14-0)
44	Wis.-Whitewater	21
28	Baldwin-Wallace	21
49	Muskingum ■	3
55	Otterbein	0
61	Heidelberg ■	0
35	John Carroll ■	16
38	Capital	22
56	Marietta ■	10
34	Ohio Northern	24
62	Wilmington (Ohio) ■	0
42	Wheaton (Ill.) ■	21
45	Wabash ■	16
57	John Carroll ■	19
48	Trinity (Tex.) *	7

Nickname: Purple Raiders
Colors: Purple & White
Stadium: Mount Union
   Capacity: 5,800; Year Built: 1915
AD: Larry Kehres
SID: Michael De Matteis

MUHLENBERG
Allentown, PA 18104-5586 III

Coach: Mike Donnelly, Ithaca 1975
2002 RESULTS (10-2)
40	Cal Lutheran ■	32
28	Dickinson	21
68	Frank. & Marsh. ■	22
14	McDaniel	35
23	Johns Hopkins	10
41	Gettysburg ■	0
43	Ursinus	0
44	Union (N.Y.) ■	13
8	Moravian	0
56	Mass.-Dartmouth ■	6
10	John Carroll ■	21
54	Merchant Marine ■	3

Nickname: Mules
Colors: Cardinal & Grey
Stadium: Scotty Wood
   Capacity: 3,000; Year Built: 1998
AD: To be named
SID: Mike Falk

MURRAY ST.
Murray, KY 42071-3318 ....I–AA

Coach: Joe Pannunzio, Southern Colo. 1982
2002 RESULTS (7-5)
6	Memphis	52
42	Southern Ill. ■	24
23	Illinois St.	24
31	Indiana St.	34
31	Tennessee Tech ■	14
7	Eastern Ky.	31
38	Southeast Mo. St. ■	31
54	Samford ■	17
51	Tennessee St. ■	27
42	Tenn.-Martin	3
37	Eastern Ill. ■	35
20	Western Ky.	59

Nickname: Racers
Colors: Navy & Gold
Stadium: Stewart
   Capacity: 16,800; Year Built: 1973
AD: E.W. Dennison
SID: Steve Parker

MUSKINGUM
New Concord, OH 43762 III

Coach: Jeff Heacock, Muskingum 1976
2002 RESULTS (3-7)
6	Thomas More ■	25
19	Heidelberg ■	0
3	Mount Union	49
7	Ohio Northern	35
21	Wilmington (Ohio) ■	13
34	Otterbein	21
10	Baldwin-Wallace	49
26	John Carroll ■	34
27	Capital	35
25	Marietta ■	31

Nickname: Fighting Muskies
Colors: Black & Magenta
Stadium: Mc Conagha
   Capacity: 5,000; Year Built: 1925
AD: Larry Shank
SID: Tom Caudill

NAVY
Annapolis, MD 21402-5000 ....I–A

Coach: Paul Johnson, Western Caro. 1979
2002 RESULTS (2-10)
38	Southern Methodist	7
19	North Carolina St. ■	65
40	Northwestern ■	49
17	Duke ■	43
7	Air Force	48
10	Rice ■	17
21	Boston College	46
30	Tulane	51
23	Notre Dame *	30
0	Connecticut ■	38
27	Wake Forest	30
58	Army *	12

Nickname: Midshipmen
Colors: Navy Blue & Gold
Stadium: Navy-Marine Corps Mem.
   Capacity: 34,000; Year Built: 1959
AD: Chet Gladchuck
SID: Scott Strasemeier

NEBRASKA
Lincoln, NE 68588 ....I–A

Coach: Frank Solich, Nebraska 1966
2002 RESULTS (7-7)
48	Arizona St. ■	10
31	Troy St. ■	16
44	Utah St. ■	13
7	Penn St.	40
14	Iowa St.	36
38	McNeese St. ■	14
24	Missouri ■	13
21	Oklahoma St.	24
38	Texas A&M	31
24	Texas	27
45	Kansas ■	7
13	Kansas St.	49
13	Colorado	28
23	Mississippi (Independence Bowl)*	27

Nickname: Cornhuskers, Huskers
Colors: Scarlet & Cream
Stadium: Memorial
   Capacity: 73,918; Year Built: 1923
AD: Steven C. Pederson
SID: Chris Anderson

NEB. WESLEYAN
Lincoln, NE 68504-2796 III

Coach: Brian Keller, Neb. Wesleyan 1983
2002 RESULTS (6-4)
25	Upper Iowa ■	7
17	Midland Lutheran ■	7
23	Dana	17
31	Northwestern (Iowa) ■	35
25	Dakota Wesleyan	21
16	Doane ■	20
40	Hastings	38
20	Concordia (Neb.) ■	27
14	Sioux Falls	24
44	Peru St.	18

Nickname: Prairie Wolves
Colors: Gold, Brown & Black
Stadium: Abel
   Capacity: 2,000; Year Built: 1986
AD: Ira Zeff
SID: Karl Skinner

NEB.-KEARNEY
Kearney, NE 68849 II

Coach: Darrell Morris, Northwest Mo. St. 1983
2002 RESULTS (9-2)
35	Neb.-Omaha ■	17
29	Wayne St. (Neb.) ■	3
3	Western St. (Colo.) ■	20
42	N.M. Highlands ■	14
17	Adams St.	13
58	Colorado Mines ■	14
12	Chadron St.	0
47	Fort Lewis	25
46	Fort Hays St. ■	29
20	Mesa St.	13
40	Tex. A&M-Kingsville ■	58

Nickname: Antelopes, Lopers
Colors: Royal Blue & Light Old Gold
Stadium: Foster Field
   Capacity: 5,100; Year Built: 1929
AD: Jon McBride
SID: Peter Yazvac

NEB.-OMAHA
Omaha, NE 68182 II

Coach: Pat Behrns, Dakota St. 1972
2002 RESULTS (6-5)
17	Neb.-Kearney ■	35
10	Northwest Mo. St.	23
45	Midwestern St. ■	23
21	South Dakota St.	38
17	South Dakota ■	10
23	Northern Colo. ■	30
21	Minn. St.-Mankato	15
20	North Dakota	17
19	St. Cloud St.	47
49	North Dakota St. ■	42
21	Augustana (S.D.) ■	16

Nickname: Mavericks
Colors: Black & Crimson
Stadium: Al F. Caniglia Field
   Capacity: 9,500; Year Built: 1949
AD: Robert Danenhauer
SID: Gary Anderson

684

2002 RESULTS

NEVADA
Reno, NV 89557 ....I–A

Coach: Chris Tormey, Idaho 1978
2002 RESULTS (5-7)
7	Washington St. *	31
31	Brigham Young ■	28
31	Rice ■	21
28	Colorado St. ■	32
17	UNLV	21
34	Hawaii	59
52	San Jose St. ■	24
47	Louisiana Tech	50
24	Southern Methodist	6
23	UTEP ■	17
30	Fresno St.	38
7	Boise St. ■	44

Nickname: Wolf Pack
Colors: Silver & Blue
Stadium: Mackay
  Capacity: 31,545; Year Built: 1967
AD: Chris Ault
SID: Jamie Klund

UNLV
Las Vegas, NV 89154 ....I–A

Coach: John Robinson, Oregon 1958
2002 RESULTS (5-7)
7	Wisconsin ■	27
31	Kansas ■	20
17	Oregon St.	47
21	Toledo	38
21	Nevada ■	17
16	New Mexico ■	25
24	Brigham Young	3
21	San Diego St.	31
49	Wyoming ■	48
17	Utah	28
32	Air Force ■	49
36	Colorado St.	33

Nickname: Runnin' Rebels
Colors: Scarlet & Gray
Stadium: Sam Boyd
  Capacity: 36,800; Year Built: 1971
AD: John Robinson
SID: Mark Wallington

NEW HAMPSHIRE
Durham, NH 03824 ....I–AA

Coach: Sean McDonnell, New Hampshire 1978
2002 RESULTS (3-8)
7	Kent St.	34
14	James Madison	20
28	Hofstra ■	52
3	Villanova	45
29	Dartmouth	26
20	Richmond ■	19
27	William & Mary ■	34
9	Delaware	21
31	Massachusetts ■	14
17	Northeastern ■	49
14	Maine	31

Nickname: Wildcats
Colors: Blue & White
Stadium: Cowell
  Capacity: 6,500; Year Built: 1936
AD: Marty Scarano
SID: Scott Stapin

NEW HAVEN
West Haven, CT 06516-1999 II

Coach: Darren Rizzi, Rhode Island 1992
2002 RESULTS (4-6)
28	West Chester	19
31	Carson-Newman ■	36
6	Indiana (Pa.)	42
13	Central Wash.	21
37	Tiffin	34
0	C.W. Post ■	20
69	Mass.-Lowell ■	21
47	Western Wash.	21
7	St. Cloud St.	51
7	Northern Colo. ■	18

Nickname: Chargers
Colors: Blue & Gold
Stadium: Robert B. Dodds
  Capacity: 3,500
AD: Deborah Chin
SID: Jason Sullivan

NEW JERSEY CITY
Jersey City, NJ 07305-1597 III

Coach: Arnold Jeter, Kent St. 1961
2002 RESULTS (1-8)
7	Brockport St. ■	25
3	Western Conn. St.	31
7	Rowan	29
0	Delaware Valley ■	28
6	Cortland St. ■	27
6	Kean	19
7	TCNJ	42
8	Montclair St. ■	20
28	Wm. Paterson	19

Nickname: Gothic Knights
Colors: Green & Gold
Stadium: Thomas Gerrity Athletic Complex
  Capacity: 3,000; Year Built: 1986
AD: Lawrence R. Schiner
SID: Ira Thor
Note: Discontinued football program following 2002 season.

TCNJ
Ewing, NJ 08628-0718 III

Coach: Eric Hamilton, Col. of New Jersey 1975
2002 RESULTS (6-3)
42	Norwich ■	10
41	Cortland St.	38
10	Merchant Marine	27
25	Rowan ■	30
24	Wm. Paterson ■	23
42	New Jersey City ■	7
7	Montclair St.	40
21	Brockport St.	7
55	Kean ■	14

Nickname: Lions
Colors: Blue & Gold
Stadium: Lions' Stadium
  Capacity: 6,000; Year Built: 1984
AD: Kevin A. McHugh
SID: Ann King

NEW MEXICO
Albuquerque, NM 87131 ....I–A

Coach: Rocky Long, New Mexico 1974
2002 RESULTS (7-7)
14	North Carolina St.	34
38	Weber St. ■	24
31	Air Force	38
23	Baylor ■	0
13	New Mexico St.	24
0	Texas Tech ■	49
25	UNLV	16
44	Utah St.	45
42	Utah ■	35
15	San Diego St. ■	8
20	Brigham Young	16
14	Colorado St.	22
49	Wyoming ■	20
13	UCLA (Las Vegas Bowl)*	27

Nickname: Lobos
Colors: Cherry & Silver
Stadium: University
  Capacity: 37,370; Year Built: 1960
AD: Rudy Davalos
SID: Greg Remington

N.M. HIGHLANDS
Las Vegas, NM 87701 II

Coach: Greg Critchette, Adams St. 1992
2002 RESULTS (0-10)
7	Tarleton St.	53
28	Eastern N.M. ■	70
14	Mesa St. ■	62
14	Neb.-Kearney	42
31	Adams St. ■	38
21	Western St. (Colo.)	52
24	Colorado Mines	55
0	Chadron St. ■	62
40	Fort Lewis ■	62
27	Fort Hays St.	37

Nickname: Cowboys
Colors: Purple & White
Stadium: Perkins Stadium
  Capacity: 5,000; Year Built: 1930
AD: Dennis Francois
SID: Tim Gotto

NEW MEXICO ST.
Las Cruces, NM 88003 ....I–A

Coach: Tony Samuel, Nebraska 1977
2002 RESULTS (7-5)
24	South Carolina	34
13	California	34
24	New Mexico ■	13
10	Georgia	41
49	UTEP ■	14
31	La.-Lafayette ■	28
34	La.-Monroe ■	21
26	Arkansas St.	21
24	Middle Tenn. ■	21
30	Utah St.	32
27	North Texas	38
35	Idaho	31

Nickname: Aggies
Colors: Crimson & White
Stadium: Aggie Memorial
  Capacity: 30,343; Year Built: 1978
AD: Brian Faison
SID: Heath Nielsen

NEWBERRY
Newberry, SC 29108..II

Coach: Mike Taylor, Newberry 1976
2002 RESULTS (1-10)
0	Wofford	48
35	North Greenville	7
7	Davidson ■	34
7	Stillman ■	30
7	Lenoir-Rhyne	35
36	Carson-Newman	60
7	Tusculum ■	24
26	Catawba ■	45
0	Wingate..	33
14	Mars Hill ■	58
10	Presbyterian	14

Nickname: Indians
Colors: Scarlet & Gray
Stadium: Setzler Field
  Capacity: 4,000; Year Built: 1930
AD: Andy Carter
SID: Ryan Rose

NICHOLLS ST.
Thibodaux, LA 70310 ....I-AA

Coach: Daryl Daye, LSU 1985
2002 RESULTS (7-4)
63	West Va. Tech ■	6
0	North Texas..................................	23
45	Samford	17
14	Jacksonville St. ■	6
21	Southern U.	13
33	Fla. Atlantic ■.............................	22
14	Stephen F. Austin ■.......................	17
24	Southwest Tex. St.	21
14	Northwestern St. ■.........................	21
34	Sam Houston St.	16
21	McNeese St...................................	33

Nickname: Colonels
Colors: Red & Gray
Stadium: John L. Guidry
  Capacity: 12,800; Year Built: 1972
AD: Robert J. Bernardi
SID: Bobby Galinsky

NICHOLS
Dudley, MA 01571-5000...........................III

Coach: William Carven, Nichols 1994
2002 RESULTS (5-4)
12	Worcester St. ■	19
31	Bridgewater St. ■	14
13	Westfield St..................................	40
27	Salve Regina ■	14
48	Maine Maritime ■	0
0	Mass.-Dartmouth	7
14	Curry	24
22	MIT ■	7
48	Western New Eng. ■.......................	6

Nickname: Bison
Colors: Green & White
Stadium: Bison Bowl
  Capacity: 3,000; Year Built: 1961
AD: Charlyn Robert
SID: Mike Serijan

NORFOLK ST.
Norfolk, VA 23504.............................I-AA

Coach: Maurice Forte, Minnesota 1969
2002 RESULTS (5-6)
31	Virginia St. ■................................	21
35	Savannah St. ■	6
7	Bethune-Cookman	49
10	N.C. A&T......................................	36

9	South Carolina St. ■	35
14	Hampton	31
31	Florida A&M ■..............................	34
0	Howard..	21
17	Morgan St. ■................................	14
23	Delaware St. ■..............................	20
32	Morris Brown	19

Nickname: Spartans
Colors: Green & Gold
Stadium: Price
  Capacity: 27,700; Year Built: 1997
AD: Orby Moss Jr.
SID: Glen Mason

NORTH ALA.
Florence, AL 35632-0001 II

Coach: Mark Hudspeth, Delta St. 1992
2002 RESULTS (4-7)
21	Samford	24
24	Lambuth	17
38	Harding ■	45
14	Ark.-Monticello	30
33	Southern Ark. ■	43
24	Ouachita Baptist	38
49	Arkansas Tech ■	14
47	Central Ark. ■...............................	33
28	Valdosta St. ■	45
36	West Ga. ■	26
24	West Ala.......................................	31

Nickname: Lions
Colors: Purple & Gold
Stadium: Braly
  Capacity: 14,215; Year Built: 1940
AD: Joel Erdmann
SID: Jeff Hodges

NORTH CAROLINA
Chapel Hill, NC 27515 ....I-A

Coach: John Bunting, North Carolina 1972
2002 RESULTS (3-9)
21	Miami (Ohio) ■	27
30	Syracuse	22
21	Texas ■..	52
13	Georgia Tech ■	21
38	Arizona St.....................................	35
17	North Carolina St. ■......................	34
27	Virginia	37
0	Wake Forest	31
7	Maryland ■	59
12	Clemson ■	42
14	Florida St.....................................	40
23	Duke	21

Nickname: Tar Heels
Colors: Carolina Blue & White
Stadium: Kenan Memorial
  Capacity: 60,000; Year Built: 1927
AD: Richard Baddour
SID: Steve Kirschner

N.C. A&T
Greensboro, NC 27411 ....I-AA

Coach: Bill Hayes, N.C. Central 1965
2002 RESULTS (4-8)
30	N.C. Central *	33
42	Jackson St. ■................................	36
20	Portland St...................................	23
34	Elon ■..	20
36	Norfolk St. ■	10
13	Morgan St.	30
28	Florida A&M.................................	36
16	Howard..	20
12	Bethune-Cookman ■	13
34	Delaware St.	7
7	Hampton	17
9	South Carolina St. ■	26

Nickname: Aggies
Colors: Blue & Gold
Stadium: Aggie
  Capacity: 23,000; Year Built: 1981
AD: Charles Davis
SID: Donal O. Ware

N.C. CENTRAL
Durham, NC 27707 II

Coach: Rudy Abrams, Livingstone 1964
2002 RESULTS (4-6)
33	N.C. A&T *	30
3	Morehouse	19
7	Virginia St. ■................................	22
13	Elizabeth City St. ■........................	3
28	St. Augustine's *	0
7	Fayetteville St.	21
12	Winston-Salem ■	23
7	Virginia Union ■............................	24
14	Livingstone	10
14	Johnson Smith ■	29

Nickname: Eagles
Colors: Maroon & Gray
Stadium: O'Kelly-Riddick
  Capacity: 10,000; Year Built: 1975
AD: William Hayes
SID: Kyle Serba

NORTH CAROLINA ST.
Raleigh, NC 27695-7001........................I-A

Coach: Chuck Amato, North Carolina St. 1969
2002 RESULTS (11-3)
34	New Mexico ■................................	14
34	East Tenn. St. ■	0
65	Navy	19
32	Wake Forest ■	13
51	Texas Tech	48
56	Massachusetts ■	24
34	North Carolina	17
24	Duke	22
38	Clemson	6
17	Georgia Tech ■	24
21	Maryland	24
9	Virginia	14
17	Florida St. ■..................................	7
28	Notre Dame (Gator Bowl)*	6

Nickname: Wolfpack
Colors: Red & White
Stadium: Carter-Finley
  Capacity: 51,500; Year Built: 1966
AD: Lee G. Fowler
SID: Annabelle Vaughan

NORTH CENTRAL
Naperville, IL 60566-7063 III

Coach: John Thorne, Ill. Wesleyan 1969
2002 RESULTS (6-4)
0	Augustana (Ill.) ■	65
21	Benedictine (Ill.)..........................	32
22	Carthage ■	19
35	Colorado Col. ■	20
20	Elmhurst.......................................	13
44	Franklin	27
24	Ill. Wesleyan...............................	33
24	Millikin ■	17
28	North Park	14
7	Wheaton (Ill.)..............................	41

Nickname: Cardinals
Colors: Cardinal & White
Stadium: Cardinal Stadium
  Capacity: 5,500; Year Built: 1999
AD: Walter J. Johnson
SID: Kevin Juday

NORTH DAKOTA
Grand Forks, ND 58202 II

Coach: Dale Lennon, North Dakota 1985
2002 RESULTS (5-6)

57	Minn.-Crookston ■	0
7	Central Wash. ■	43
66	Mesa St. ■	7
12	Northern Colo.	28
21	South Dakota St.	13
12	North Dakota St.	6
17	St. Cloud St. ■	20
17	Neb.-Omaha	20
35	Minn. St.-Mankato ■	36
31	Augustana (S.D.)	38
20	South Dakota ■	0

Nickname: Fighting Sioux
Colors: Green & White
Stadium: Alerus Center
    Capacity: 13,500; Year Built: 2001
AD: Roger Thomas
SID: Mitchell Wigness

NORTH DAKOTA ST.
Fargo, ND 58105-5600 II

Coach: Bob Babich, Tulsa 1984
2002 RESULTS (2-8)

34	Winona St. ■	23
7	UC Davis	35
6	Augustana (S.D.) ■	23
37	South Dakota	40
6	North Dakota ■	12
37	Minn. St.-Mankato ■	20
20	South Dakota St.	25
7	Northern Colo. ■	29
42	Neb.-Omaha	49
7	St. Cloud St. ■	31

Nickname: Bison
Colors: Yellow & Green
Stadium: Fargodome
    Capacity: 18,700; Year Built: 1992
AD: Gene Taylor
SID: George Ellis

NORTH GREENVILLE
Tigerville, SC 29688 II

Coach: Brian Smith, North Greenville
2002 RESULTS (4-6)

0	Tusculum	44
0	Charleston So.	9
7	Newberry ■	35
0	Wingate ■	19
0	Presbyterian	58
42	St. Paul	12
46	Allen ■	6
56	Ky. Wesleyan ■	46
30	Va.-Wise	34
47	Allen	27

Nickname: Mounties
Colors: Scarlet & Black
AD: Jan McDonald
SID: To be named

NORTH PARK
Chicago, IL 60625-4895 III

Coach: Robin Cooper, Ill. Wesleyan 1975
2002 RESULTS (1-9)

9	Chicago	33
27	Eureka ■	8
7	Wis. Lutheran	34
9	Ill. Wesleyan	49
14	North Central ■	28

8	Augustana (Ill.) ■	58
28	Elmhurst	42
0	Millikin	72
12	Wheaton (Ill.) ■	68
22	Carthage ■	52

Nickname: Vikings
Colors: Blue & Gold
Stadium: Hedstrand Field
    Capacity: 2,500; Year Built: 1955
AD: Jack Surridge
SID: Chris Nelson

NORTH TEXAS
Denton, TX 76203-6737 ....I-A

Coach: Darrell Dickey, Kansas St. 1984
2002 RESULTS (8-5)

0	Texas	27
23	Nicholls St. ■	0
7	Alabama	33
10	TCU	16
9	Arizona	14
17	South Fla. ■	24
13	Arkansas St.	10
27	La.-Lafayette	0
41	La.-Monroe ■	2
10	Idaho ■	0
38	New Mexico St. ■	27
30	Middle Tenn.	20
24	Cincinnati (New Orleans Bowl)*	19

Nickname: Mean Green
Colors: Green & White
Stadium: Fouts Field
    Capacity: 30,500; Year Built: 1952
AD: Rick Villarreal
SID: Eric Capper

NORTHEASTERN
Boston, MA 02115-5096 ....I-AA

Coach: Don Brown, Norwich 1977
2002 RESULTS (10-3)

48	Lock Haven ■	0
31	Ohio	0
42	Massachusetts ■	17
28	Hofstra ■	17
10	Delaware	27
38	Rhode Island ■	13
17	Harvard	14
13	William & Mary	30
24	Richmond	21
38	Villanova ■	13
49	New Hampshire	17
41	James Madison ■	10
24	Fordham ■	29

Nickname: Huskies
Colors: Red & Black
Stadium: Parsons Field
    Capacity: 7,000; Year Built: 1933
AD: David O'Brien
SID: Adam Polgreen

NORTHEASTERN ST.
Tahlequah, OK 74464-2399 II

Coach: Tom Eckert, Northeastern St. 1966
2002 RESULTS (4-7)

34	Bacone	24
9	Arkansas Tech	7
7	Mo. Southern St. ■	38
14	Eastern N.M.	46
30	Midwestern St. ■	40
30	Southeastern Okla.	27
10	Tex. A&M-Kingsville ■	13
29	Tarleton St. ■	28
10	Southwestern Okla.	13
48	Central Okla. ■	58
12	East Central	42

Nickname: Redmen
Colors: Green & White
Stadium: Doc Wadley Stadium
    Capacity: 12,000; Year Built: 1964
AD: Eddie Griffin
SID: Adria Lynch

NORTHERN ARIZ.
Flagstaff, AZ 86011-5400 ....I-AA

Coach: Jerome Souers, Oregon 1983
2002 RESULTS (6-5)

3	Arizona	37
31	Cal Poly	24
40	Sam Houston St. ■	14
14	Portland St. ■	10
26	Weber St. ■	21
21	Sacramento St. ■	24
29	Eastern Wash.	41
20	Montana St. ■	17
24	Montana	38
20	Idaho St.	46
24	St. Mary's (Cal.)	12

Nickname: Lumberjacks
Colors: Blue & Gold
Stadium: Walkup Skydome
    Capacity: 15,300; Year Built: 1977
AD: Steven P. Holton
SID: Steven Shaff

NORTHERN COLO.
Greeley, CO 80639 II

Coach: Kay Dalton, Colorado St. 1954
2002 RESULTS (12-2)

31	Western St. (Colo.) ■	0
14	Montana *	31
28	North Dakota ■	12
27	Minn. St.-Mankato ■	14
30	Neb.-Omaha	23
27	St. Cloud St.	24
27	South Dakota ■	10
31	Augustana (S.D.)	7
29	North Dakota St.	7
28	South Dakota St.	17
18	New Haven	7
49	Central Mo. St. ■	28
23	Northwest Mo. St.	12
7	Grand Valley St.	44

Nickname: Bears
Colors: Blue & Gold
Stadium: Nottingham Field
    Capacity: 7,000; Year Built: 1995
AD: James E. Fallis
SID: Colin McDonough

NORTHERN ILL.
De Kalb, IL 60115-2854 ....I-A

Coach: Joe Novak, Miami (Ohio) 1967
2002 RESULTS (8-4)

42	Wake Forest ■	41
6	South Fla.	37
21	Wisconsin	24
26	Western Ill. ■	29
13	Kent St. ■	6
41	Ball St.	29
48	Miami (Ohio)	41
49	Central Mich. ■	0
24	Western Mich.	20
26	Bowling Green	17
49	Eastern Mich.	21
30	Toledo ■	33

Nickname: Huskies
Colors: Cardinal & Black
Stadium: Huskie
    Capacity: 31,000; Year Built: 1965

AD: Cary Groth
SID: Mike Korcek

NORTHERN IOWA
Cedar Falls, IA 50614 ....I–AA

Coach: Mark Farley, Northern Iowa 1986
2002 RESULTS (5-6)
34	Wayne St. (Mich.) ■	0
10	Oklahoma St.	45
31	Stephen F. Austin ■	24
29	Cal Poly	26
12	Western Ky. ■	31
13	Southern Ill.	42
22	Youngstown St.	7
20	Illinois St. ■	31
19	Indiana St.	21
12	Western Ill. ■	35
25	Southwest Mo. St. ■	24

Nickname: Panthers
Colors: Purple & Old Gold
Stadium: U.N.I.-Dome
  Capacity: 16,324; Year Built: 1976
AD: Rick Hartzell
SID: Nancy Justis

NORTHERN MICH.
Marquette, MI 49855-5391 II

Coach: Doug Sams, Oregon St. 1978
2002 RESULTS (6-5)
17	St. Cloud St.	45
37	Mercyhurst ■	7
17	Ferris St. ■	3
24	Indianapolis	10
26	Hillsdale ■	23
14	Grand Valley St.	51
24	Ashland ■	14
49	Wayne St. (Mich.)	46
13	Michigan Tech	34
24	Saginaw Valley ■	28
42	Northwood	64

Nickname: Wildcats
Colors: Old Gold & Olive Green
Stadium: Superior Dome
  Capacity: 8,000; Year Built: 1991
AD: Ken Godfrey
SID: David Faiella

NORTHERN ST.
Aberdeen, SD 57401 II

Coach: Ken Heupel, Northern St. 1983
2002 RESULTS (4-7)
6	Augustana (S.D.)	14
15	St. Cloud St. ■	47
28	Wayne St. (Neb.)	20
21	Concordia-St. Paul ■	24
21	Bemidji St.	28
38	Southwest St. ■	28
38	Minn.-Morris	7
22	Minn.-Duluth	48
49	Minn.-Crookston	31
35	Winona St. ■	42
35	Minn. St. Moorhead ■	49

Nickname: Wolves
Colors: Maroon & Gold
Stadium: Swisher
  Capacity: 6,000; Year Built: 1975
AD: Robert A. Olson
SID: Mike Lefler

NORTHWEST MO. ST.
Maryville, MO 64468-6001 II

Coach: Mel Tjeerdsma, Southern St. (S.D.) 1967
2002 RESULTS (12-1)
23	Neb.-Omaha ■	10
42	Minn. St.-Mankato	31
34	Mo.-Rolla	9
28	Southwest Baptist	7
48	Washburn	13
47	Mo. Southern St. ■	3
29	Pittsburg St. *	7
31	Truman	24
10	Central Mo. St. ■	7
13	Mo. Western St.	10
34	Emporia St.	5
45	Minn.-Duluth ■	41
12	Northern Colo. ■	23

Nickname: Bearcats
Colors: Green & White
Stadium: Rickenbrode
  Capacity: 7,500; Year Built: 1917
AD: Bob Boerigter
SID: Andy Seeley

NORTHWESTERN
Evanston, IL 60208 ....I–A

Coach: Randy Walker, Miami (Ohio) 1976
2002 RESULTS (3-9)
3	Air Force	52
24	TCU ■	48
26	Duke ■	21
49	Navy	40
24	Michigan St.	39
16	Ohio St. ■	27
42	Minnesota	45
0	Penn St.	49
13	Purdue ■	42
41	Indiana ■	37
10	Iowa	62
24	Illinois ■	31

Nickname: Wildcats
Colors: Purple & White
Stadium: Ryan Field
  Capacity: 47,130; Year Built: 1997
AD: Mark H. Murphy
SID: Mike Wolf

NORTHWESTERN ST.
Natchitoches, LA 71497-0003 ....I–AA

Coach: Scott Stoker, Northwestern St. 1991
2002 RESULTS (9-4)
35	Delta St. ■	7
30	Southern U. ■	20
34	Delaware St.	14
7	Georgia	45
47	Elon ■	20
40	Southwest Tex. St. ■	27
38	Southwestern Okla. ■	0
21	Nicholls St.	14
38	Sam Houston St. ■	10
10	Jacksonville St.	19
3	McNeese St. ■	27
42	Stephen F. Austin	35
14	Montana	45

Nickname: Demons
Colors: Purple, White & Orange
Stadium: Turpin
  Capacity: 15,971; Year Built: 1976

AD: Gregory S. Burke
SID: Doug Ireland

NORTHWOOD
Midland, MI 48640-2398 II

Coach: Pat Riepma, Hillsdale 1983
2002 RESULTS (7-4)
13	Saginaw Valley *	47
32	Ashland	7
17	Findlay ■	18
14	Mercyhurst	17
41	Ferris St. ■	24
40	Indianapolis	38
41	Hillsdale ■	34
14	Grand Valley St.	33
41	Wayne St. (Mich.) ■	27
33	Michigan Tech	23
64	Northern Mich. ■	42

Nickname: Timberwolves
Colors: Columbia Blue & White
Stadium: Hantz Stadium
  Capacity: 3,000; Year Built: 2001
AD: Pat Riepma
SID: Ryan Thompson

NORWICH
Northfield, VT 05663 III

Coach: Mike Yesalonia, Norwich 1982
2002 RESULTS (4-6)
10	TCNJ	42
21	Merchant Marine ■	26
19	St. John Fisher ■	36
14	Plymouth St.	0
24	Coast Guard ■	17
17	WPI ■	34
35	St. Lawrence	27
21	Mount Ida	14
24	Springfield ■	41
21	Western Conn. St.	31

Nickname: Cadets
Colors: Maroon & Gold
Stadium: Sabine Field
  Capacity: 5,000; Year Built: 1921
AD: Anthony A. Mariano
SID: Dave Caspole

NOTRE DAME
Notre Dame, IN 46556 ....I–A

Coach: Tyrone Willingham, Michigan St. 1977
2002 RESULTS (10-3)
22	Maryland *	0
24	Purdue ■	17
25	Michigan ■	23
21	Michigan St.	17
31	Stanford ■	7
14	Pittsburgh ■	6
21	Air Force	14
34	Florida St.	24
7	Boston College ■	14
30	Navy *	23
42	Rutgers ■	0
13	Southern California	44
6	North Carolina St. (Gator Bowl)*	28

Nickname: Fighting Irish
Colors: Blue & Gold
Stadium: Notre Dame
  Capacity: 80,795; Year Built: 1930
AD: Kevin White
SID: John Heisler

RESULTS

OBERLIN
Oberlin, OH 44074..............................III

Coach: Jeff Ramsey,
2002 RESULTS (3-7)
6	Frank. & Marsh. ■	.13
11	Case Reserve	.37
35	Hiram ■	.14
14	Frostburg St. ■	.48
10	Wooster	.49
56	Kenyon	.17
6	Wabash ■	.51
21	Earlham	.28
13	Ohio Wesleyan ■	.14
30	Denison ■	.22

Nickname: Yeomen
Colors: Crimson & Gold
Stadium: Dill Field
  Capacity: 3,500; Year Built: 1925
AD: Vin Lananna
SID: Jeff Miller

OCCIDENTAL
Los Angeles, CA 90041.............................III

Coach: Dale Widolff, Indianapolis 1975
2002 RESULTS (5-4)
21	Lewis & Clark ■	.20
29	Whittier ■	.20
38	Puget Sound	.20
35	Redlands	.42
24	Pomona-Pitzer ■	.21
30	Claremont-M-S ■	.39
35	Colorado Col. ■	.24
0	Cal Lutheran	.6
22	La Verne	.24

Nickname: Tigers
Colors: Orange & Black
Stadium: Patterson Field
  Capacity: 3,000; Year Built: 1900
AD: Dixon Farmer
SID: Andrew Holmes

OHIO
Athens, OH 45701 ....I–A

Coach: Brian Knorr, Air Force 1986
2002 RESULTS (4-8)
14	Pittsburgh	.27
0	Northeastern ■	.31
6	Florida	.34
19	Connecticut	.37
34	Buffalo ■	.32
21	Bowling Green	.72
55	Eastern Mich. ■	.27
50	Kent St.	.0
20	Miami (Ohio)	.38
27	Akron	.10
21	Marshall ■	.24
32	UCF	.42

Nickname: Bobcats
Colors: Hunter Green & White
Stadium: Peden
  Capacity: 24,000; Year Built: 1929
AD: Thomas C. Boeh
SID: Jim Stephan

OHIO NORTHERN
Ada, OH 45810 III

Coach: Tom Kaczkowski, Illinois 1978
2002 RESULTS (5-5)
17	Wis.-Stevens Point ■	.31
12	Capital	.47
7	John Carroll ■	.33
35	Muskingum ■	.7
41	Baldwin-Wallace	.48
42	Marietta ■	.10
28	Otterbein	.7
31	Wilmington (Ohio)	.0
24	Mount Union ■	.34
28	Heidelberg ■	.0

Nickname: Polar Bears
Colors: Burnt Orange & Black
Stadium: Ada Memorial
  Capacity: 4,000; Year Built: 1948
AD: Thomas E. Simmons
SID: Tim Glon

OHIO ST.
Columbus, OH 43210 ....I–A

Coach: Jim Tressel, Baldwin-Wallace 1975
2002 RESULTS (14-0)
45	Texas Tech ■	.21
51	Kent St. ■	.17
25	Washington St. ■	.7
23	Cincinnati	.19
45	Indiana ■	.17
27	Northwestern	.16
50	San Jose St. ■	.7
19	Wisconsin	.14
13	Penn St. ■	.7
34	Minnesota ■	.3
10	Purdue	.6
23	Illinois	.16
14	Michigan ■	.9
31	Miami (Fla.) (Fiesta Bowl)*	.24

Nickname: Buckeyes
Colors: Scarlet & Gray
Stadium: Ohio
  Capacity: 101,568; Year Built: 1922
AD: Ferdinand A. Geiger
SID: Steve Snapp

OHIO WESLEYAN
Delaware, OH 43015 III

Coach: Mike Hollway, Michigan 1974
2002 RESULTS (5-5)
25	Olivet ■	.21
38	Denison ■	.20
0	Albion ■	.16
14	Wooster ■	.37
21	Earlham	.14
7	Wabash	.27
17	Wittenberg ■	.58
42	Kenyon ■	.3
14	Oberlin	.13
16	Allegheny ■	.30

Nickname: Battling Bishops
Colors: Red & Black
Stadium: Selby Field
  Capacity: 9,600; Year Built: 1929
AD: John A. Martin
SID: Mark Beckenbach

OKLAHOMA
Norman, OK 73019 ....I–A

Coach: Bob Stoops, Iowa 1983
2002 RESULTS (12-2)
37	Tulsa	.0
37	Alabama ■	.27
68	UTEP ■	.0
31	South Fla. ■	.14
31	Missouri	.24
35	Texas *	.24
49	Iowa St. ■	.3
27	Colorado ■	.11
26	Texas A&M	.30

49	Baylor	.9
60	Texas Tech ■	.15
28	Oklahoma St.	.38
29	Colorado *	.7
34	Washington St. (Rose Bowl)*	.14

Nickname: Sooners
Colors: Crimson & Cream
Stadium: Memorial
  Capacity: 72,765; Year Built: 1923
AD: Joseph R. Castiglione
SID: Kenny Mossman

OKLA. PANHANDLE
Goodwell, OK 73939.................................II

Coach: Ryan Held, Nebraska 1997
2002 RESULTS (2-9)
0	Colorado Mines ■	.14
3	Adams St. ■	.28
0	Southwestern Okla.	.15
19	Peru St. ■	.15
6	Lincoln (Mo.)	.34
14	Bacone	.18
13	Western St. (Colo.)	.58
32	Fort Hays St. ■	.49
46	Southwestern Aly God ■	.14
6	Northwestern Okla.	.45
6	Southern Nazarene	.7

Nickname: Aggies
Colors: Navy & Red
Stadium: Carl Wooten
  Capacity: 5,000
AD: Wayne Stewart
SID: Jason Cronin

OKLAHOMA ST.
Stillwater, OK 74078-5070.......................I–A

Coach: Les Miles, Michigan 1976
2002 RESULTS (8-5)
36	Louisiana Tech *	.39
45	Northern Iowa ■	.10
24	UCLA ■	.38
52	Southern Methodist ■	.16
15	Texas	.17
9	Kansas St.	.44
24	Nebraska ■	.21
28	Texas A&M ■	.23
24	Texas Tech	.49
55	Kansas	.20
63	Baylor ■	.28
38	Oklahoma ■	.28
33	Southern Miss. (Houston Bowl)*	.23

Nickname: Cowboys
Colors: Orange & Black
Stadium: Lewis
  Capacity: 48,000; Year Built: 1920
AD: Terry Don Phillips/Harry Birdwell
SID: Steve Buzzard

OLIVET
Olivet, MI 49076......................................III

Coach: Irv Sigler, Olivet 1965
2002 RESULTS (5-4)
30	Defiance	.22
21	Ohio Wesleyan ■	.25
35	Manchester ■	.3
14	Albion	.17
14	Alma ■	.21
49	Kalamazoo	.34
23	Adrian ■	.10
28	Hope	.30
43	Wis. Lutheran ■	.29

Nickname: Comets
Colors: Crimson & White
Stadium: Griswold Field

Capacity: 3,500; Year Built: 1972
AD: Thomas Shaw
SID: Geoffrey Henson

OREGON
Eugene, OR 97401 ....I–A

Coach: Mike Bellotti, UC Davis 1973
2002 RESULTS (7-6)
36	Mississippi St. ■	13
28	Fresno St. ■	24
58	Idaho ■	21
41	Portland St. ■	0
31	Arizona	14
31	UCLA	30
42	Arizona St.	45
33	Southern California ■	44
41	Stanford ■	14
21	Washington St.	32
14	Washington ■	42
24	Oregon St.	45
17	Wake Forest (Seattle Bowl)*	38

Nickname: Ducks
Colors: Green & Yellow
Stadium: Autzen
  Capacity: 54,000; Year Built: 1967
AD: William Moos
SID: David Williford

OREGON ST.
Corvallis, OR 97331 ....I–A

Coach: Dennis Erickson, Montana St. 1969
2002 RESULTS (8-5)
49	Eastern Ky. ■	10
35	Temple ■	3
47	UNLV ■	17
59	Fresno St. ■	19
0	Southern California	22
35	UCLA ■	43
9	Arizona St.	13
24	California ■	13
38	Arizona ■	3
29	Washington	41
31	Stanford	21
45	Oregon ■	24
13	Pittsburgh (Insight Bowl)*	38

Nickname: Beavers
Colors: Orange & Black
Stadium: Reser
  Capacity: 35,362; Year Built: 1953
AD: Mitch S. Barnhart/Robert J De Carolis
SID: Hal Cowan

OTTERBEIN
Westerville, OH 43081-2006.....................III

Coach: Paul Alt, Wittenberg 1971
2002 RESULTS (2-8)
33	Waynesburg	13
34	Marietta ■	27
14	Wilmington (Ohio)	32
0	Mount Union ■	55
3	Capital	35
21	Muskingum ■	34
7	Ohio Northern ■	28
14	Heidelberg	33
0	John Carroll ■	73
0	Baldwin-Wallace	56

Nickname: Cardinals
Colors: Tan & Cardinal
Stadium: Memorial
  Capacity: 4,000; Year Built: 1946
AD: Richard E. Reynolds
SID: Ed Syguda

OUACHITA BAPTIST
Arkadelphia, AR 71998-0001 II

Coach: Todd Knight, Ouachita Baptist 1986
2002 RESULTS (5-5)
17	Southeastern Okla.	20
35	Arkansas Tech ■	3
14	Central Ark.	30
10	Valdosta St. ■	51
38	North Ala. ■	24
23	Ark.-Monticello	21
47	Southern Ark. ■	50
28	Henderson St.	14
35	Delta St. ■	25
30	Harding	42

Nickname: Tigers
Colors: Purple & Gold
Stadium: A.U. Williams Field
  Capacity: 5,200
AD: David R. Sharp
SID: Chris Babb

PACE
Pleasantville, NY 10570-2799.....................II

Coach: Greg Lusardi, Slippery Rock 1975
2002 RESULTS (3-7)
33	Mass.-Lowell ■	7
20	Stonehill ■	14
0	Bryant	26
14	Southern Conn. St. ■	46
0	St. Anselm	31
13	Bentley	33
13	Assumption ■	0
7	American Int'l	34
7	Merrimack	24
16	C.W. Post ■	35

Nickname: Setters
Colors: Navy & Gold
Stadium: Finnerty Field
  Capacity: 1,500; Year Built: 1969
AD: Joseph F. O'Donnell
SID: Brian Mundy

PACIFIC LUTHERAN
Tacoma, WA 98447-0003 III

Coach: Frosty Westering, Neb.-Omaha 1952
2002 RESULTS (5-4)
42	Azusa Pacific ■	44
35	Chapman	10
21	Linfield ■	35
24	Eastern Ore. ■	17
21	Whitworth	7
45	Lewis & Clark	18
23	Willamette ■	30
29	Menlo *	32
46	Puget Sound	0

Nickname: Lutes
Colors: Black & Gold
Stadium: Sparks
  Capacity: 4,500
AD: Paul Hoseth
SID: Nick Dawson

PENNSYLVANIA
Philadelphia, PA 19104-6322 ....I–AA

Coach: Al Bagnoli, Central Conn. St. 1975
2002 RESULTS (9-1)
52	Lafayette	21
24	Lehigh ■	21
49	Dartmouth ■	14
3	Villanova	17
44	Columbia ■	10
41	Yale	20
31	Brown ■	7
44	Princeton	13
44	Harvard ■	9
31	Cornell	0

Nickname: Quakers
Colors: Red & Blue
Stadium: Franklin Field
  Capacity: 53,000; Year Built: 1895
AD: Steve Bilsky
SID: Rich Schepis

PENN ST.
University Park, PA 16802 ....I–A

Coach: Joe Paterno, Brown 1950
2002 RESULTS (9-4)
27	UCF ■	24
40	Nebraska ■	7
49	Louisiana Tech ■	17
35	Iowa ■	42
34	Wisconsin	31
24	Michigan	27
49	Northwestern ■	0
7	Ohio St.	13
18	Illinois ■	7
35	Virginia ■	14
58	Indiana	25
61	Michigan St. ■	7
9	Auburn (Capital One Bowl)*	13

Nickname: Nittany Lions
Colors: Blue & White
Stadium: Beaver
  Capacity: 107,282; Year Built: 1960
AD: Timothy M. Curley
SID: Jeff Nelson

PITTSBURG ST.
Pittsburg, KS 66762...................................II

Coach: Chuck Broyles, Pittsburg St. 1970
2002 RESULTS (8-3)
48	Langston	0
63	Bacone ■	3
47	Washburn	14
25	Mo. Western St. ■	21
50	Mo. Southern St. ■	12
3	Emporia St.	13
7	Northwest Mo. St. *	29
48	Mo.-Rolla ■	14
49	Truman	35
48	Southwest Baptist ■	13
20	Central Mo. St. ■	23

Nickname: Gorillas
Colors: Crimson & Gold
Stadium: Carnie Smith
  Capacity: 8,343; Year Built: 1924
AD: Charles Broyles
SID: Dan Wilkes

PITTSBURGH
Pittsburgh, PA 15260...............................I–A

Coach: Walt Harris, Pacific (Cal.) 1968
2002 RESULTS (9-4)
27	Ohio ■	14
12	Texas A&M ■	14
26	UAB	20
23	Rutgers ■	3
37	Toledo ■	19
48	Syracuse	24
6	Notre Dame	14
19	Boston College ■	16
28	Virginia Tech	21
29	Temple ■	22
21	Miami (Fla.)	28

17 West Virginia ■ 24
38 Oregon St. (Insight Bowl)* 13
Nickname: Panthers
Colors: Gold & Blue
Stadium: Heinz Field
  Capacity: 65,000; Year Built: 2001
AD: Marc Boehm
SID: E. J. Borghetti

PLYMOUTH ST.
Plymouth, NH 03264-1595 III

Coach: Paul Castonia, Trinity (Conn.) 1986
2002 RESULTS (0-10)
14 Mass.-Dartmouth 44
20 Wm. Paterson 30
0   Norwich ■ 14
19 Western Conn. St. ■ 47
14 Merchant Marine 28
0   Springfield 41
7   Bentley ■ 35
33 Coast Guard 34
0   Southern Conn. St. 49
13 WPI ■ 23
Nickname: Panthers
Colors: Green & White
Stadium: Currier Memorial Field
  Capacity: 1,000; Year Built: 1970
AD: John P. Clark
SID: Kent Cherrington

POMONA-PITZER
Claremont, CA 91711-6346 III

Coach: Roger Caron, Harvard 1985
2002 RESULTS (4-4)
16 La Verne 17
14 Trinity (Tex.) 66
27 Rhodes 24
0   Redlands ■ 37
27 Chicago ■ 22
21 Occidental 24
14 Whittier ■ 12
12 Claremont-M-S ■ 7
Nickname: Sagehens
Colors: Blue, Orange & White
Stadium: Merritt Field
  Capacity: 2,000; Year Built: 1991
AD: Charles Katsiaficas
SID: Ryan Witt

PORTLAND ST.
Portland, OR 97207-0751 ....I-AA

Coach: Tim Walsh, UC Riverside 1977
2002 RESULTS (6-5)
31 Stephen F. Austin ■ 23
23 N.C. A&T ■ 20
0   Oregon 41
10 Northern Ariz. 14
16 Southwest Tex. St. ■ 0
34 Eastern Wash. ■ 31
34 Sacramento St. 20
21 Montana ■ 24
27 Idaho St. ■ 24
14 Weber St. 20
26 Montana St. 28
Nickname: Vikings
Colors: Forest Green & White
Stadium: PGE Park
  Capacity: 20,000; Year Built: 1928
AD: Tom Burman
SID: Mike Lund

PRAIRIE VIEW
Prairie View, TX 77446 ....I-AA

Coach: Larry Dorsey, Tennessee St. 1976
2002 RESULTS (1-10)
14 Texas Southern * 44
8   Tennessee St. 41
0   Tex. A&M-Kingsville 65
12 Alabama A&M 15
13 Grambling * 35
13 Alcorn St. ■ 33
22 Paul Quinn ■ 20
24 Southern U. * 46
8   Mississippi Val. 26
0   Ark.-Pine Bluff 44
9   Jackson St. 44
Nickname: Panthers
Colors: Purple & Gold
Stadium: Blackshear
  Capacity: 6,000; Year Built: 1960
AD: Charles McClelland
SID: Harlan S. Robinson

PRESBYTERIAN
Clinton, SC 29325-2998 II

Coach: Tommy Spangler, Georgia 1983
2002 RESULTS (8-3)
35 West Ga. 37
26 Charleston So. ■ 6
14 Jacksonville 7
58 North Greenville ■ 0
14 Catawba 27
24 Tusculum 7
14 Carson-Newman ■ 47
14 Lenoir-Rhyne ■ 3
12 Mars Hill 0
26 Wingate ■ 10
14 Newberry ■ 10
Nickname: Blue Hose
Colors: Garnet & Blue
Stadium: Bailey Memorial
  Capacity: 6,500; Year Built: 2002
AD: Valerie Sheley
SID: Al Ansley

PRINCETON
Princeton, NJ 08544 ....I-AA

Coach: Roger Hughes, Doane 1982
2002 RESULTS (6-4)
24 Lehigh 31
34 Lafayette ■ 19
35 Columbia 32
14 Colgate 10
16 Brown ■ 14
17 Harvard ■ 24
32 Cornell 25
13 Pennsylvania ■ 44
3   Yale 7
38 Dartmouth ■ 30
Nickname: Tigers
Colors: Orange & Black
Stadium: Princeton
  Capacity: 27,800; Year Built: 1998
AD: Gary D. Walters
SID: Thomas Milajecki

PRINCIPIA
Elsah, IL 62028-9799 III

Coach: Michael Barthelmess, Principia 1983
2002 RESULTS (5-4)
29 Crown 0
24 Haskell 6
37 Macalester 40
52 Blackburn ■ 30
26 Rockford 17
35 Martin Luther ■ 42
32 Westminster (Mo.) 48
21 Maranatha Baptist ■ 28
27 Crown * 26
Nickname: Panthers
Colors: Gold & Blue
Stadium: Clark Field
  Capacity: 1,000; Year Built: 1937
AD: Lenore Suarez
SID: Mary Ann Sprague

PUGET SOUND
Tacoma, WA 98416 III

Coach: Philip Willenbrock, Gettysburg 1989
2002 RESULTS (1-8)
20 Claremont-M-S 30
13 Lewis & Clark 28
20 Occidental ■ 38
0   Linfield 57
24 Willamette 63
14 Whitworth ■ 38
21 Menlo ■ 20
28 Eastern Ore. 46
0   Pacific Lutheran ■ 46
Nickname: Loggers
Colors: Maroon & White
Stadium: Baker
  Capacity: 6,000; Year Built: 1964
AD: Richard P. Ulrich
SID: Robin Hamilton

PURDUE
West Lafayette, IN 47907-1031 ....I-A

Coach: Joe Tiller, Montana St. 1965
2002 RESULTS (7-6)
51 Illinois St. ■ 10
17 Notre Dame 24
28 Western Mich. ■ 24
21 Wake Forest ■ 24
28 Minnesota ■ 15
28 Iowa 31
31 Illinois 38
21 Michigan ■ 23
42 Northwestern 13
6   Ohio St. ■ 10
45 Michigan St. 42
34 Indiana ■ 10
34 Washington (Sun Bowl)* 24
Nickname: Boilermakers
Colors: Old Gold & Black
Stadium: Ross-Ade
  Capacity: 62,500; Year Built: 1924
AD: Morgan J. Burke
SID: Tom Schott

QUINCY
Quincy, IL 62301-2699 II

Coach: Bill Terlisner, Quincy 1991
2002 RESULTS (4-7)

20	McKendree ■	55
10	Illinois St.	55
14	Truman	69
20	Bacone	21
28	Drake ■	45
21	St. Francis (Ind.)	77
21	St. Joseph's (Ind.)	14
54	Culver-Stockton ■	31
43	Ky. Wesleyan	40
37	Butler ■	28
44	Tiffin ■	47

Nickname: Hawks
Colors: Brown, White & Gold
Stadium: QU
　Capacity: 2,500; Year Built: 1938
AD: Patrick Atwell
SID: Ryan Dowd

RANDOLPH-MACON
Ashland, VA 23005 III

Coach: Scott Boone, Wabash 1981
2002 RESULTS (6-4)

17	Chowan	14
19	Chris. Newport	21
17	Carnegie Mellon ■	14
26	Catholic ■	18
3	Wash. & Lee	7
17	Emory & Henry	13
17	Johns Hopkins ■	12
21	Guilford ■	14
18	Bridgewater (Va.) ■	52
0	Hampden-Sydney	7

Nickname: Yellow Jackets
Colors: Lemon & Black
Stadium: Day Field
　Capacity: 5,000; Year Built: 1953
AD: Kevin Eastman
SID: Ann Schlottman

REDLANDS
Redlands, CA 92373-0999 III

Coach: Mike Maynard, Ill. Wesleyan 1981
2002 RESULTS (7-3)

28	Willamette	52
21	Linfield ■	59
34	Chapman ■	9
37	Pomona-Pitzer	0
42	Occidental ■	35
24	La Verne	0
31	Cal Lutheran ■	12
21	Whittier	0
39	Claremont-M-S ■	29
24	St. John's (Minn.)	31

Nickname: Bulldogs
Colors: Maroon & Gray
Stadium: Ted Runner
　Capacity: 7,000; Year Built: 1968
AD: Jeffrey Martinez
SID: Rachel Johnson

RENSSELAER
Troy, NY 12180-3590 III

Coach: Joe King, Siena 1970
2002 RESULTS (8-2)

47	Utica ■	0
34	Coast Guard	12
33	WPI ■	13
31	Rochester	19
14	Union (N.Y.)	32
39	Hartwick	38
31	St. John Fisher ■	25
49	St. Lawrence ■	7
27	Hobart	34
55	Worcester St.	29

Nickname: Engineers
Colors: Cherry & White
Stadium: '86 Field
　Capacity: 3,000; Year Built: 1912
AD: Ken Ralph
SID: Kevin Beattie

RHODE ISLAND
Kingston, RI 02881-1303 ....I–AA

Coach: Tim Stowers, Auburn 1980
2002 RESULTS (3-9)

28	Bryant ■	0
19	Hofstra	37
17	Syracuse	63
14	Maine	31
38	Brown ■	28
13	Northeastern	38
17	Delaware ■	14
0	Richmond	26
11	James Madison ■	15
6	William & Mary	44
3	Villanova	45
21	Massachusetts ■	48

Nickname: Rams
Colors: Light & Dark Blue & White
Stadium: Meade Stadium
　Capacity: 6,470; Year Built: 1928
AD: Ronald J. Petro
SID: Mike Ballweg

RHODES
Memphis, TN 38112-1690 III

Coach: Joe White, Springfield 1984
2002 RESULTS (4-6)

25	DePauw ■	34
46	Maryville (Tenn.)	21
7	Centre ■	28
24	Pomona-Pitzer	27
34	Washington (Mo.) ■	27
28	Rose-Hulman	35
31	Sewanee	36
59	Colorado Col. ■	0
14	Trinity (Tex.)	59
28	Millsaps ■	24

Nickname: Lynx
Colors: Red, Black & White
Stadium: Fargason Field
　Capacity: 3,300
AD: Mike Clary
SID: Matt Dean

RICE
Houston, TX 77251-1892 ....I–A

Coach: Ken Hatfield, Arkansas 1965
2002 RESULTS (4-7)

10	Houston ■	24
10	Michigan St.	27
21	Nevada	31
28	Fresno St. ■	31
37	Louisiana Tech ■	20
17	Navy	10
35	UTEP	38
27	Southern Methodist ■	15
33	Tulsa	18
7	Boise St.	49
28	Hawaii ■	33

Nickname: Owls
Colors: Blue & Gray
Stadium: Rice
　Capacity: 70,000; Year Built: 1950
AD: John R. May
SID: Bill Cousins

RICHMOND
Richmond, VA 23173-1903 ....I–AA

Coach: Jim Reid, Maine 1973
2002 RESULTS (4-7)

7	Temple	34
15	Delaware ■	13
7	Furman ■	17
13	Massachusetts ■	34
19	New Hampshire	20
26	James Madison ■	0
26	Rhode Island	0
21	Northeastern ■	24
16	Hofstra	26
14	Maine ■	21
35	William & Mary	13

Nickname: Spiders
Colors: Red & Blue
Stadium: Richmond
　Capacity: 21,319; Year Built: 1929
AD: Jim Miller
SID: Simon Gray

RIPON
Ripon, WI 54971 III

Coach: Ron Ernst, Neb. Wesleyan 1980
2002 RESULTS (7-3)

19	Concordia (Wis.) ■	42
41	Monmouth (Ill.) ■	7
43	Grinnell	22
18	Lake Forest	20
56	Carroll (Wis.) ■	7
32	Illinois Col.	13
35	Knox ■	7
27	St. Norbert	48
34	Beloit ■	23
58	Lawrence	35

Nickname: Red Hawks
Colors: Red & White
Stadium: Ingalls Field
　Capacity: 2,500; Year Built: 1888
AD: Robert G. Gillespie
SID: Ron Ernst

ROBERT MORRIS
Moon Township, PA 15108-1189 ....I–AA

Coach: Joe Walton, Pittsburgh 1957
2002 RESULTS (3-7)

41	Buffalo St. ■	12
10	Dayton	24
14	Central Conn. St. ■	0
15	Monmouth ■	10
0	Sacred Heart	34
0	Wagner	29
21	Gannon	49
7	Albany (N.Y.) ■	32
13	Stony Brook	23
7	St. Francis (Pa.)	14

Nickname: Colonials
Colors: Blue & White
Stadium: Moon
　Capacity: 7,000; Year Built: 1950
AD: Susan Hofacre
SID: Jim Duzyk

ROCHESTER
Rochester, NY 14627-0296 III

Coach: Mark Kreydt, Rochester 1988
2002 RESULTS (2-8)
20	St. John Fisher	38
28	Johns Hopkins	41
51	St. Lawrence	7
19	Rensselaer ■	31
21	Hobart ■	59
21	Union (N.Y.) ■	31
7	Chicago	42
14	Washington (Mo.) ■	28
29	Case Reserve ■	38
39	Carnegie Mellon	35

Nickname: Yellowjackets
Colors: Yellow & Blue
Stadium: Fauver
    Capacity: 5,000; Year Built: 1930
AD: George VanderZwaag
SID: Dennis O'Donnell

ROCKFORD
Rockford, IL 61108-2393 III

Coach: Vic Clark, Indiana St. 1971
2002 RESULTS (4-6)
62	Trinity Bible (N.D.)	0
14	Wis. Lutheran ■	21
9	Northwestern (Minn.)	19
7	Elmhurst ■	30
17	Principia ■	26
7	Westminster (Mo.)	9
7	Maranatha Baptist ■	24
26	Blackburn	14
25	Macalester *	24
51	Crown ■	0

Nickname: Regents
Colors: Purple, White & Black
Stadium: Sam Greeley Field
    Capacity: 1,000; Year Built: 2001
AD: Kristyn King
SID: Dave Beyer

ROSE-HULMAN
Terre Haute, IN 47803 III

Coach: Russ Mollet, Southwest Mo. St. 1975
2002 RESULTS (3-7)
23	Earlham ■	0
12	Sewanee	19
0	Wheaton (Ill.)	49
19	Washington (Mo.)	24
15	Trinity (Tex.)	50
35	Rhodes ■	28
35	Millsaps ■	28
17	Carnegie Mellon ■	27
14	DePauw	43
29	Centre ■	30

Nickname: Fightin' Engineers
Colors: Old Rose & White
Stadium: Phil Brown Field
    Capacity: 2,500
AD: Greg Ruark
SID: Kevin Lanke

ROWAN
Glassboro, NJ 08028-1701 III

Coach: Jay Accorsi, Nichols 1985
2002 RESULTS (10-1)
17	Millersville ■	3
22	Wesley ■	20
34	Chris. Newport	7
29	New Jersey City ■	7

30	TCNJ	25
28	Buffalo St.	7
42	Cortland St. ■	21
41	Kean	10
70	Wm. Paterson ■	7
48	Montclair St.	12
12	Brockport St. ■	15

Nickname: Profs
Colors: Brown & Gold
Stadium: John Page Field
    Capacity: 5,000
AD: Joy L. Reighn
SID: Sheila Stevenson

RUTGERS
Piscataway, NJ 08854-8053 ....I-A

Coach: Greg Schiano, Bucknell 1988
2002 RESULTS (1-11)
19	Villanova ■	37
11	Buffalo ■	34
44	Army ■	0
3	Pittsburgh	23
14	Tennessee	35
0	West Virginia	40
14	Virginia Tech	35
14	Syracuse	45
17	Miami (Fla.) ■	42
17	Temple ■	20
0	Notre Dame	42
14	Boston College	44

Nickname: Scarlet Knights
Colors: Scarlet
Stadium: Rutgers
    Capacity: 41,500; Year Built: 1994
AD: Robert E. Mulcahy
SID: John Wooding

SACRAMENTO ST.
Sacramento, CA 95819 ....I-AA

Coach: John Volek, UC Riverside 1968
2002 RESULTS (5-7)
12	UTEP	42
12	St. Mary's (Cal.)	20
27	Cal Poly ■	17
24	Idaho St.	32
21	UC Davis	38
24	Northern Ariz.	21
20	Portland St. ■	34
48	Eastern Wash.	41
30	Montana St. ■	31
24	Montana	31
41	Weber St. ■	38
42	Humboldt St. ■	35

Nickname: Hornets
Colors: Green & Gold
Stadium: Hornet Field
    Capacity: 21,195; Year Built: 1964
AD: Terry Wanless
SID: Brian Berger

SACRED HEART
Fairfield, CT 06432-1000 ....I-AA

Coach: Bill Lacey, Villanova 1994
2002 RESULTS (7-3)
27	Marist	38
32	Monmouth	13
17	Albany (N.Y.) ■	38
28	St. Francis (Pa.)	0
34	Robert Morris ■	0
14	Stony Brook	24
17	Central Conn. St. ■	3
10	Wagner ■	7
32	Siena ■	3
30	Iona ■	3

Nickname: Pioneers
Colors: Scarlet & White
Stadium: Campus Field
    Capacity: 4,000; Year Built: 1993
AD: C. Donald Cook
SID: Gene Gumbs

SAGINAW VALLEY
University Center, MI 48710-0001 II

Coach: Randy Awrey, Northern Mich. 1978
2002 RESULTS (9-3)
47	Northwood *	13
35	Michigan Tech ■	21
51	Mercyhurst ■	7
52	Ashland	20
63	Indianapolis ■	24
69	Findlay	7
18	Grand Valley St. ■	23
3	Ferris St.	24
48	Hillsdale ■	20
28	Northern Mich.	24
42	Wayne St. (Mich.)	14
23	Indiana (Pa.)	27

Nickname: Cardinals
Colors: Red, White & Blue
Stadium: Harvey R. Wickes
    Capacity: 4,028; Year Built: 1975
AD: Griz Zimmermann
SID: Jason Yaman

ST. ANSELM
Manchester, NH 03102-1310 II

Coach: Geoff Harlan, Middlebury 1985
2002 RESULTS (5-5)
0	Bentley ■	28
27	Mass.-Lowell	41
26	American Int'l	37
0	C.W. Post ■	42
38	Assumption	13
31	Pace ■	0
13	Bryant	25
21	Merrimack ■	7
33	Stonehill	14
36	Southern Conn. St. ■	18

Nickname: Hawks
Colors: Blue & White
Stadium: Grappone
    Capacity: 4,500; Year Built: 1999
AD: Edward Cannon
SID: Kurt Svoboda

ST. AUGUSTINE'S
Raleigh, NC 27610 II

Coach: Michael Costa, Norfolk St. 1971
2002 RESULTS (0-8)
7	Edward Waters	18
13	Fayetteville St.	62
0	Mars Hill	56
2	Bowie St. *	34
0	Virginia St.	52
0	N.C. Central *	28
6	Elizabeth City St.	12
7	Livingstone *	12

Nickname: Falcons
Colors: Blue & White
AD: George Williams
SID: Oralia N. Washington

ST. CLOUD ST.
St. Cloud, MN 56301-4498 II

Coach: Randy Hedberg, Minot St. 1977
2002 RESULTS (9-2)
45	Northern Mich. ■	17
47	Northern St.	15
36	South Dakota ■	15
28	South Dakota St. ■	24
45	Augustana (S.D.)	7
24	Northern Colo. ■	27
20	North Dakota	17
40	Minn. St.-Mankato	41
47	Neb.-Omaha ■	19
51	New Haven ■	7
31	North Dakota St.	7

Nickname: Huskies
Colors: Cardinal Red & Black
Stadium: Selke Field
   Capacity: 4,000; Year Built: 1937
AD: Morris Kurtz
SID: Anne Abicht

ST. FRANCIS (PA.)
Loretto, PA 15940-0600 ....I–AA

Coach: Dave Opfar, Penn St. 1983
2002 RESULTS (2-8)
0	Dayton ■	39
19	St. Peter's ■	24
0	Sacred Heart ■	28
14	Stony Brook ■	24
10	Central Conn. St.	28
0	Wagner ■	7
21	Albany (N.Y.)	49
23	La Salle	16
0	Monmouth	7
14	Robert Morris ■	7

Nickname: Red Flash
Colors: Red & White
Stadium: Pine Bowl
   Capacity: 1,500; Year Built: 1979
AD: Jeffrey M. Eisen
SID: Pat Farabaugh

ST. JOHN FISHER
Rochester, NY 14618 III

Coach: Paul Vosburgh, William Penn 1975
2002 RESULTS (6-4)
34	Alfred	26
38	Rochester ■	20
36	Norwich	19
20	Ithaca ■	30
27	Hartwick	31
14	Brockport St.	41
55	Mount Ida ■	6
25	Rensselaer	31
17	Hobart ■	14
34	Utica	13

Nickname: Cardinals
Colors: Cardinal & Gold
Stadium: Growney
   Capacity: 2,100
AD: Bob Ward
SID: Norm Kieffer

ST. JOHN'S (MINN.)
Collegeville, MN 56321 III

Coach: John Gagliardi, Colorado Col. 1949
2002 RESULTS (12-2)
21	Wis.-Eau Claire ■	28
56	Hamline ■	0
42	Wis.-Whitewater ■	18
59	St. Olaf ■	20
20	Gust. Adolphus	7
49	Carleton ■	7
35	Augsburg	7
34	Concordia-M'head	9
48	St. Thomas (Minn.) ■	28
31	Bethel (Minn.) *	26
31	Redlands ■	24
45	Coe ■	14
21	Linfield	14
34	Trinity (Tex.)	41

Nickname: Johnnies
Colors: Cardinal & Blue
Stadium: Clemens
   Capacity: 5,500; Year Built: 1908
AD: Jim E. Smith
SID: Michael Hemmesch

ST. JOHN'S (N.Y.)
Jamaica, NY 11439 ....I–AA

Coach: Bob Ricca, C.W. Post 1969
2002 RESULTS (2-8)
17	Canisius ■	14
9	Stony Brook	34
6	Iona ■	20
8	Central Conn. St.	16
22	Marist	28
7	Duquesne	63
34	St. Peter's ■	24
19	Siena	24
21	Fairfield	44
41	La Salle ■	45

Nickname: Red Storm
Colors: Red & White
Stadium: Memorial Field
   Capacity: 3,000; Year Built: 1961
AD: David Wegrzyn
SID: Dominic Scianna
Note: Discontinued football program following 2002 season.

ST. JOSEPH'S (IND.)
Rensselaer, IN 47978 II

Coach: Tom Riva, Albion 1990
2002 RESULTS (4-7)
3	Indianapolis	41
28	St. Francis (Ill.) ■	27
24	Lincoln (Mo.)	17
17	Gannon ■	41
54	Valparaiso	43
27	Ky. Wesleyan ■	21
7	Morehead St.	40
14	Quincy ■	21
7	South Dakota	42
0	Austin Peay ■	45
20	Georgetown (Ky.)	54

Nickname: Pumas
Colors: Cardinal & Purple
Stadium: Alumni Field
   Capacity: 4,000; Year Built: 1947
AD: Bill Massoels
SID: Clark Teuscher

ST. LAWRENCE
Canton, NY 13617 III

Coach: Chris Phelps, St. Lawrence 1991
2002 RESULTS (0-10)
13	Union (N.Y.)	44
13	Alfred ■	16
7	Rochester ■	51
14	Hobart	44
7	Ithaca	34
0	Merchant Marine ■	24
27	Norwich ■	35

21	Gettysburg	49
7	Rensselaer	49
7	Hartwick	68

Nickname: Saints
Colors: Scarlet & Brown
Stadium: Leckonby
   Capacity: 3,000; Year Built: 2000
AD: Margaret F. Strait
SID: Ken Baker

ST. MARY'S (CAL.)
Moraga, CA 94575 ....I–AA

Coach: Mike Landis, Randolph-Macon 1986
2002 RESULTS (6-6)
24	Montana ■	27
20	Sacramento St. ■	12
23	Bucknell ■	22
20	Central Wash.	30
28	Western Wash. ■	31
36	Humboldt St.	7
22	Holy Cross	24
35	Cal Poly ■	17
24	Southern Utah	14
28	UC Davis	31
46	Drake ■	28
12	Northern Ariz. ■	24

Nickname: Gaels
Colors: Navy Blue & Red
Stadium: St. Mary's
   Capacity: 5,500; Year Built: 1972
AD: Carl Clapp
SID: Rich Davi

ST. NORBERT
DePere, WI 54115 III

Coach: Jim Purtill, Miami (Ohio) 1978
2002 RESULTS (9-1)
35	St. Thomas (Minn.)	31
51	Beloit ■	32
28	Monmouth (Ill.)	21
47	Knox	29
60	Illinois Col. ■	9
55	Lawrence ■	0
63	Carroll (Wis.)	14
48	Ripon ■	27
37	Grinnell	19
0	Lake Forest ■	17

Nickname: Green Knights
Colors: Dartmouth Green & Old Gold
Stadium: Minahan
   Capacity: 3,100; Year Built: 1937
AD: Donald Maslinski
SID: Dan Lukes

ST. OLAF
Northfield, MN 55057-1098 III

Coach: Chris Meidt, Bethel (Minn.) 1992
2002 RESULTS (5-5)
57	Carroll (Wis.)	14
49	Carleton	0
23	Augsburg ■	21
20	St. John's (Minn.)	59
15	St. Thomas (Minn.) ■	35
32	Bethel (Minn.)	36
48	Hamline ■	12
34	Macalester	6
14	Concordia-M'head ■	24
23	Gust. Adolphus *	24

Nickname: Oles
Colors: Black & Old Gold
Stadium: Manitou Field
   Capacity: 5,000; Year Built: 1930
AD: Cindy Book
SID: Le Ann Finger

ST. PETER'S
Jersey City, NJ 07306 ....I-AA

Coach: Rob Stern
2002 RESULTS (6-5)
3	Florida Int'l	27
0	Fordham	43
24	St. Francis (Pa.)	19
55	La Salle ■	2
35	Canisius	3
19	Siena ■	0
3	Duquesne ■	14
36	Marist ■	24
24	St. John's (N.Y.)	34
13	Fairfield	27
22	Iona ■	14

Nickname: Peacocks
Colors: Blue & White
Stadium: Cochrane
 Capacity: 4,000; Year Built: 1990
AD: William A. Stein
SID: Tim Camp

ST. THOMAS (MINN.)
St. Paul, MN 55105 III

Coach: Don Roney, St. Thomas (Minn.) 1983
2002 RESULTS (5-5)
31	St. Norbert ■	35
49	Bethel (Minn.) ■	25
41	Hamline	7
7	Wis.-Stout ■	28
35	St. Olaf	15
24	Gust. Adolphus ■	25
41	Carleton	7
49	Augsburg ■	6
28	St. John's (Minn.)	48
21	Concordia-M'head *	63

Nickname: Tommies
Colors: Purple & Grey
Stadium: O'Shaughnessy
 Capacity: 5,025; Year Built: 1948
AD: Stephen J. Fritz
SID: Gene McGivern

SALISBURY
Salisbury, MD 21801-6860.........................III

Coach: Sherman Wood, Salisbury 1984
2002 RESULTS (9-2)
20	Chris. Newport ■	13
55	Wm. Paterson ■	18
45	Methodist	20
23	Greensboro ■	18
41	Gallaudet	12
35	Chowan ■	7
31	Apprentice *	6
22	Wesley ■	19
30	Ferrum	13
7	Frostburg St. *	37
0	King's (Pa.)	28

Nickname: Sea Gulls
Colors: Maroon & Gold
Stadium: Sea Gull
 Capacity: 2,500; Year Built: 1980
AD: Michael Vienna
SID: G. Paul Ohanian

SALVE REGINA
Newport, RI 02840-4192.........................III

Coach: Art Bell, Rhode Island 1985
2002 RESULTS (2-7)
0	Springfield	69
12	Western Conn. St. ■	42

6	Worcester St. ■	35
14	Nichols	27
20	Western New Eng. ■	14
21	Curry	20
23	Bridgewater St. ■	27
8	MIT	16
0	Mass.-Dartmouth	38

Nickname: Seahawks
Colors: Blue, Green & White
Stadium: Toppa Field
 Capacity: 1,500; Year Built: 1966
AD: Del Malloy
SID: Ed Habershaw

SAM HOUSTON ST.
Huntsville, TX 77340 ....I-AA

Coach: Ron Randleman, William Penn 1964
2002 RESULTS (4-7)
10	Central Mich.	34
26	Midwestern St. ■	23
14	Northern Ariz.	40
45	Mississippi Val. ■	7
13	Western Ill.	41
22	Jacksonville St.	28
10	Stephen F. Austin	7
10	McNeese St. ■	47
10	Northwestern St.	38
16	Nicholls St. ■	34
21	Southwest Tex. St. ■	14

Nickname: Bearkats
Colors: Orange & White
Stadium: Elliott T. Bowers
 Capacity: 14,000; Year Built: 1986
AD: Bobby Williams
SID: Paul Ridings Jr.

SAMFORD
Birmingham, AL 35229 ....I-AA

Coach: Bill Gray, Mississippi Col. 1983
2002 RESULTS (4-7)
24	North Ala. ■	21
12	Baylor	50
17	Nicholls St. ■	45
41	Tenn.-Martin ■	10
23	Jacksonville St.	37
34	Alcorn St. ■	25
20	Morris Brown	7
17	Murray St.	54
44	Tennessee Tech ■	51
24	Southeast Mo. St.	48
29	Youngstown St.	37

Nickname: Bulldogs
Colors: Red & Blue
Stadium: Seibert
 Capacity: 6,700; Year Built: 1960
AD: Bob Roller
SID: Kerwin Lonzo

SAN DIEGO
San Diego, CA 92110-2492 ....I-AA

Coach: Kevin McGarry, San Diego 1979
2002 RESULTS (5-5)
25	Azusa Pacific	41
39	La Verne ■	8
14	Yale	49
44	Jacksonville ■	20
3	Western Ore. ■	34
35	Butler	26
59	Valparaiso ■	27
51	Drake	46
10	Southern Ore. ■	31
17	Dayton ■	27

Nickname: Toreros
Colors: Columbia Blue, Navy & White

Stadium: USD Torero Stadium
 Capacity: 7,000; Year Built: 1955
AD: Thomas Iannacone
SID: Ted Gosen

SAN DIEGO ST.
San Diego, CA 92182 ....I-A

Coach: Tom Craft, San Diego St. 1977
2002 RESULTS (4-9)
14	Fresno St.	16
14	Colorado	34
28	Arizona St. ■	39
38	Idaho	48
7	UCLA ■	43
36	Utah ■	17
24	Wyoming	20
31	UNLV ■	21
10	Brigham Young	34
8	New Mexico	15
21	Colorado St. ■	49
38	Air Force	34
40	Hawaii	41

Nickname: Aztecs
Colors: Scarlet & Black
Stadium: Qualcomm
 Capacity: 54,000; Year Built: 1967
AD: Ellene Gibbs
SID: Kevin Klintworth

SAN JOSE ST.
San Jose, CA 95192 ....I-A

Coach: Fitz Hill, Ouachita Baptist 1987
2002 RESULTS (6-7)
33	Arkansas St. *	14
10	Washington	34
26	Stanford	63
38	Illinois	35
58	UTEP ■	24
34	Southern Methodist	23
7	Ohio St.	50
24	Nevada	52
8	Boise St. ■	45
31	Hawaii	40
42	Louisiana Tech ■	30
49	Tulsa	38
16	Fresno St. ■	19

Nickname: Spartans
Colors: Gold, White & Blue
Stadium: Spartan
 Capacity: 28,067; Year Built: 1933
AD: Charles Bell
SID: Lawrence Fan

SAVANNAH ST.
Savannah, GA 31404 ....I-AA

Coach: Kenneth Pettiford, Tennessee St. 1974
2002 RESULTS (1-9)
9	Bethune-Cookman *	41
9	Delaware St.	41
6	Norfolk St.	35
12	South Carolina St. ■	50
14	Albany St. (Ga.) *	36
3	Charleston So. ■	21
21	Morris Brown *	20
6	Fort Valley St. ■	25
13	Gardner-Webb	44
13	Alabama St. ■	28

Nickname: Tigers
Colors: Reflex Blue & Orange
Stadium: Ted Wright
 Capacity: 7,500; Year Built: 1967
AD: Henry Hank Ford
SID: Lee Grant Pearson

SEWANEE
Sewanee, TN 37383-1000 III

Coach: John Windham, Vanderbilt 1986
2002 RESULTS (5-5)

17	Hampden-Sydney ∎	51
19	Rose-Hulman ∎	12
24	Emory & Henry	25
27	Maryville (Tenn.) ∎	19
23	Centre	21
28	DePauw	47
36	Rhodes ∎	31
14	Wash. & Lee	26
17	Millsaps ∎	7
14	Trinity (Tex.)	55

Nickname: Tigers
Colors: Purple & White
Stadium: McGee Field
 Capacity: 1,500; Year Built: 1935
AD: Mark Webb
SID: Larry Dagenhart

SHENANDOAH
Winchester, VA 22601 III

Coach: Paul Barnes, James Madison 1984
2002 RESULTS (5-5)

16	Kean	24
6	Bridgewater (Va.)	48
7	Thomas More ∎	26
14	Ferrum	21
19	Chris. Newport ∎	15
21	Greensboro	24
28	Chowan	7
31	Averett ∎	13
28	Utica	20
20	Methodist ∎	12

Nickname: Hornets
Colors: Red, White & Midnight Blue
Stadium: Shentel Stadium
 Capacity: 2,000; Year Built: 2001
AD: John Hill
SID: Scott Musa

SHEPHERD
Shepherdstown, WV 25443-3210..............II

Coach: Monte Cater, Millikin 1971
2002 RESULTS (7-3)

17	Shippensburg	10
26	Virginia Union ∎	9
23	East Stroudsburg	35
14	West Va. Tech	33
27	Fairmont St. ∎	7
40	West Virginia St.	0
35	Glenville St. ∎	21
26	West Liberty St.	23
14	West Va. Wesleyan ∎	24
60	Concord ∎	14

Nickname: Rams
Colors: Blue & Gold
Stadium: Ram
 Capacity: 5,000; Year Built: 1959
AD: Monte Cater
SID: Chip Ransom

SHIPPENSBURG
Shippensburg, PA 17257 II

Coach: Rocky Rees, West Chester 1971
2002 RESULTS (6-5)

10	Shepherd ∎	17
26	Bloomsburg ∎	27
31	Kutztown	14
41	West Chester	27

41	Edinboro ∎	7
13	Slippery Rock ∎	7
13	Lock Haven	26
20	Clarion	19
10	Indiana (Pa.) ∎	33
21	East Stroudsburg ∎	23
40	Calif. (Pa.)	7

Nickname: Red Raiders
Colors: Red & Blue
Stadium: Grove
 Capacity: 7,700; Year Built: 1972
AD: Roberta Page
SID: John R. Alosi

SIENA
Loudonville, NY 12211-1462 ....I–AA

Coach: Jay Bateman, Randolph-Macon 1994
2002 RESULTS (3-7)

7	Iona	14
7	Duquesne ∎	17
18	Canisius	11
21	La Salle	28
0	St. Peter's	19
36	Fairfield ∎	20
0	Stony Brook ∎	14
20	St. John's (N.Y.) ∎	19
3	Sacred Heart	32
0	Marist ∎	20

Nickname: Saints
Colors: Green & Gold
Stadium: Heritage Park
 Capacity: 5,500
AD: John M. D'Argenio
SID: Jason Rich

SIMPSON
Indianola, IA 50125 III

Coach: Robert Pratt, Aquinas 1983
2002 RESULTS (6-4)

14	Washington (Mo.)	16
20	Buena Vista ∎	17
13	Coe	42
38	Cornell College ∎	26
20	Central (Iowa)	21
38	Luther ∎	14
35	Dubuque	6
69	Loras ∎	48
17	Wartburg	33
45	Upper Iowa ∎	32

Nickname: Storm
Colors: Red & Gold
Stadium: Bill Buxton
 Capacity: 5,000; Year Built: 1990
AD: John Sirianni
SID: Matthew F. Turk

SLIPPERY ROCK
Slippery Rock, PA 16057 II

Coach: George Mihalik, Slippery Rock 1974
2002 RESULTS (7-4)

11	Eastern Ky.	35
17	Gannon	14
45	Fairmont St. ∎	0
14	Bloomsburg	38
41	Calif. (Pa.) ∎	16
7	Shippensburg	13
33	Millersville ∎	9
7	Edinboro ∎	3
14	Lock Haven	7
28	Indiana (Pa.) ∎	34
21	Clarion	14

Nickname: The Rock
Colors: Green & White
Stadium: N. Kerr Thompson

Capacity: 10,000; Year Built: 1974
AD: Paul A. Lueken
SID: Bob McComas

SOUTH CAROLINA
Columbia, SC 29208 ....I–A

Coach: Lou Holtz, Kent St. 1959
2002 RESULTS (5-7)

34	New Mexico St. ∎	24
21	Virginia	34
7	Georgia ∎	13
42	Temple ∎	21
20	Vanderbilt	14
34	Mississippi St. ∎	10
16	Kentucky	12
14	LSU	38
10	Tennessee ∎	18
0	Arkansas ∎	23
7	Florida	28
20	Clemson	27

Nickname: Gamecocks
Colors: Garnet & Black
Stadium: Williams-Brice
 Capacity: 80,250; Year Built: 1934
AD: Michael McGee
SID: Kerry Tharp

SOUTH CAROLINA ST.
Orangeburg, SC 29117-0001 ....I–AA

Coach: Oliver Pough, South Carolina St. 1992
2002 RESULTS (7-5)

52	Benedict	7
50	Savannah St.	12
31	Florida A&M	13
35	Norfolk St.	9
6	Bethune-Cookman ∎	21
47	Hampton	41
21	Delaware St.	27
9	Howard ∎	23
12	Morgan St. ∎	23
26	N.C. A&T	9
6	Wofford	7
26	Tennessee St. ∎	20

Nickname: Bulldogs
Colors: Garnet & Blue
Stadium: Dawson Bulldog
 Capacity: 22,000; Year Built: 1955
AD: Timothy J. Autry Jr.
SID: Bill Hamilton

SOUTH DAKOTA
Vermillion, SD 57069-2390 II

Coach: John Austin, South Dakota 1980
2002 RESULTS (3-8)

3	Mo. Western St. ∎	10
21	Minn.-Duluth ∎	23
15	St. Cloud St.	36
10	Neb.-Omaha	17
40	North Dakota St. ∎	37
16	Augustana (S.D.) ∎	10
10	Northern Colo.	27
42	St. Joseph's (Ind.) ∎	7
20	South Dakota St.	27
17	Minn. St.-Mankato ∎	23
0	North Dakota	20

Nickname: Coyotes
Colors: Vermillion & White
Stadium: DakotaDome
 Capacity: 10,000; Year Built: 1979
AD: Kelly J. Higgins
SID: Dan Genzler

RESULTS

SOUTH DAKOTA ST.
Brookings, SD 57007 II

Coach: John Stiegelmeier, South Dakota St. 1979
2002 RESULTS (6-4)
28 Chadron St. ■ 15
38 Neb.-Omaha 21
24 St. Cloud St. ■ 20
13 North Dakota ■ 21
23 Western Wash. ■ 19
33 Augustana (S.D.) 39
25 North Dakota St. ■ 20
27 South Dakota ■ 20
17 Northern Colo. 28
39 Minn. St.-Mankato 13

Nickname: Jackrabbits
Colors: Yellow & Blue
Stadium: Coughlin-Alumni
  Capacity: 16,000; Year Built: 1962
AD: Fred M. Oien
SID: Ron Lenz

SOUTH FLA.
Tampa, FL 33620.....................................I–A

Coach: Jim Leavitt, Missouri 1978
2002 RESULTS (9-2)
51 Fla. Atlantic ■ 10
37 Northern Ill. ■ 6
24 North Texas 17
16 Southern Miss. ■ 13
46 East Caro. 30
56 Charleston So. ■ 6
31 Memphis ■ 28
29 Bowling Green ■ 7
32 Houston 14
3   Arkansas 42
14 Oklahoma 31

Nickname: Bulls
Colors: Green & Gold
Stadium: Raymond James
  Capacity: 41,441; Year Built: 1998
AD: Lee Roy Selmon
SID: John Gerdes

SOUTHEAST MO. ST.
Cape Girardeau, MO 63701-4799 ....I–AA

Coach: Tim Billings, Southeastern Okla. 1979
2002 RESULTS (8-4)
42 Ark.-Monticello ■ 41
21 Southern Ill. 14
32 Eastern Mich. 35
21 Southwest Mo. St. 28
24 Middle Tenn. 14
49 Tennessee St. ■ 25
50 Tenn.-Martin 35
27 Eastern Ill. ■ 44
31 Murray St. 38
36 Tennessee Tech ■ 30
35 Eastern Ky. 21
48 Samford ■ 24

Nickname: Indians
Colors: Red & White
Stadium: Houck
  Capacity: 10,000; Year Built: 1930
AD: Donald L. Kaverman
SID: Ron Hines

SOUTHEASTERN LA.
Hammond, LA 70402 ....I–AA

Coach: Hal Mumme, Tarleton St. 1975
Restarted football program (dropped 1985) in 2003

SOUTHEASTERN OKLA.
Durant, OK 74701-0609 II

Coach: Keith Baxter, Northwestern Okla. 1985
2002 RESULTS (7-3)
20 Ouachita Baptist ■ 17
34 East Tex. Baptist ■ 20
26 Angelo St. 20
43 West Tex. A&M ■ 7
3   Tex. A&M-Commerce 23
27 Northeastern St. ■ 30
31 Tarleton St. 62
36 Southwestern Okla. ■ 13
7   Central Okla. 6
20 East Central ■ 17

Nickname: Savages
Colors: Blue & Gold
Stadium: Paul Laird Field
  Capacity: 4,000; Year Built: 1935
AD: Donald A. Parham
SID: Dave Wester

SOUTHERN ARK.
Magnolia, AR 71754-0000.........................II

Coach: Steve Quinn, Ouachita Baptist 1985
2002 RESULTS (7-4)
26 Midwestern St. 35
27 Tex. A&M-Commerce 23
42 West Ga. ■ 21
28 Valdosta St. 31
43 North Ala. 33
38 Central Ark. ■ 21
30 Delta St. 10
50 Ouachita Baptist 47
48 Ark.-Monticello ■ 0
13 Harding ■ 33
27 Henderson St. 38

Nickname: Muleriders
Colors: Royal Blue & Old Gold
Stadium: Wilkins
  Capacity: 6,000; Year Built: 1949
AD: Jay Adcox
SID: Houston Taylor

SOUTHERN CALIFORNIA
Los Angeles, CA 90089-0602.................I–A

Coach: Pete Carroll, Pacific (Cal.) 1973
2002 RESULTS (11-2)
24 Auburn ■ 17
40 Colorado 3
20 Kansas St. 27
22 Oregon St. ■ 0
27 Washington St. 30
30 California 28
41 Washington ■ 21
44 Oregon 33
49 Stanford 17
34 Arizona St. ■ 13
52 UCLA 21

44 Notre Dame ■ 13
38 Iowa (Orange Bowl)* 17
Nickname: Trojans
Colors: Cardinal & Gold
Stadium: L.A. Coliseum
  Capacity: 92,000; Year Built: 1923
AD: Michael Garrett
SID: Tim Tessalone

SOUTHERN CONN. ST.
New Haven, CT 06515 II

Coach: Richard Cavanaugh, American Int'l 1976
2002 RESULTS (8-3)
37 Bryant ■ 21
40 Assumption 12
27 Bentley 34
29 Mass.-Lowell ■ 25
46 Pace 14
17 Merrimack ■ 3
42 American Int'l ■ 14
48 Stonehill ■ 27
8   C.W. Post 34
49 Plymouth St. ■ 0
18 St. Anselm 36

Nickname: Owls
Colors: Blue & White
Stadium: Jess Dow Field
  Capacity: 6,000; Year Built: 1988
AD: Darryl D. Rogers
SID: Richard Leddy

SOUTHERN ILL.
Carbondale, IL 62901-6620 ....I–AA

Coach: Jerry Kill, Southwestern (Kan.) 1982
2002 RESULTS (4-8)
78 Ky. Wesleyan ■ 0
14 Southeast Mo. St. ■ 21
24 Murray St. 42
45 Eastern Mich. 48
54 Western Ill. ■ 52
42 Northern Iowa ■ 13
14 Illinois St. 35
28 Southwest Mo. St. 38
14 Indiana St. ■ 21
16 Western Ky. ■ 48
76 West Va. Tech ■ 21
9   Youngstown St. 21

Nickname: Salukis
Colors: Maroon & White
Stadium: McAndrew
  Capacity: 17,324; Year Built: 1975
AD: Paul Kowalczyk
SID: Tom Weber

SOUTHERN METHODIST
Dallas, TX 75275 ....I–A

Coach: Phil Bennett, Texas A&M 1978
2002 RESULTS (3-9)
7   Navy ■ 38
14 Texas Tech ■ 24
6   TCU 17
16 Oklahoma St. 52
10 Hawaii 42
23 San Jose St. ■ 34
7   Fresno St. 30

37	Louisiana Tech ■	34
15	Rice	27
6	Nevada ■	24
42	UTEP	35
24	Tulsa ■	21

Nickname: Mustangs
Colors: Red & Blue
Stadium: Gerald J. Ford
  Capacity: 32,000; Year Built: 2000
AD: W. James Copeland Jr.
SID: Chris Walker

SOUTHERN MISS.
Hattiesburg, MS 39402 ....I-A

Coach: Jeff Bower, Southern Miss. 1975
2002 RESULTS (7-6)
55	Jackson St. ■	7
23	Illinois ■	20
33	Memphis ■	14
7	Alabama	20
27	Army	6
13	South Fla.	16
23	Cincinnati ■	14
7	TCU	37
20	UAB	13
17	Louisville ■	20
10	Tulane	31
24	East Caro. ■	7
23	Oklahoma St. (Houston Bowl)*	33

Nickname: Golden Eagles
Colors: Black & Gold
Stadium: M. M. Roberts
  Capacity: 33,000; Year Built: 1938
AD: Richard C. Giannini
SID: Mike Montoro

SOUTHERN U.
Baton Rouge, LA 70813 ....I-AA

Coach: Pete Richardson, Dayton 1968
2002 RESULTS (6-6)
19	Tulane	37
20	Northwestern St.	30
14	Ark.-Pine Bluff	13
14	Jackson St. ■	36
13	Nicholls St. ■	21
11	Alabama A&M *	27
19	Mississippi Val. ■	16
46	Prairie View *	24
20	Alcorn St. ■	22
28	Miles ■	21
27	Texas Southern ■	25
48	Grambling *	24

Nickname: Jaguars
Colors: Columbia Blue & Gold
Stadium: A.W. Mumford
  Capacity: 24,800; Year Built: 1928
AD: Floyd Kerr
SID: Kevin Manns

SOUTHERN UTAH
Cedar City, UT 84720 ....I-AA

Coach: C. Gregory Ray, Emory & Henry 1986
2002 RESULTS (1-10)
7	Mesa St. ■	0
15	Troy St.	40
14	Eastern Wash. ■	49
19	Southwest Tex. St.	49
6	Stephen F. Austin	52
21	Cal Poly ■	27
45	Montana	68
14	St. Mary's (Cal.) ■	24
16	Arkansas St.	38
28	Western Ill. ■	38
17	Idaho St. ■	42

Nickname: Thunderbirds
Colors: Scarlet & White
Stadium: Eccles Coliseum
  Capacity: 8,500; Year Built: 1967
AD: Thomas Douple
SID: Neil Gardner

SOUTHWEST BAPTIST
Bolivar, MO 65613 II

Coach: Ray Richards, Northern Mich. 1981
2002 RESULTS (3-8)
18	Tenn.-Martin	19
35	Ky. Wesleyan ■	7
25	Mo. Southern St.	40
7	Northwest Mo. St. ■	28
32	Truman	44
6	Central Mo. St. ■	35
0	Mo. Western St.	28
13	Emporia St.	21
17	Mo.-Rolla ■	7
13	Pittsburg St.	48
26	Washburn ■	20

Nickname: Bearcats
Colors: Purple & White
Stadium: Plaster
  Capacity: 3,000; Year Built: 1986
AD: Jim Middleton
SID: Joey Roberts

SOUTHWEST MO. ST.
Springfield, MO 65804..........................I-AA

Coach: Randy Ball, Truman 1973
2002 RESULTS (4-7)
26	East Central ■	14
28	Hampton	26
24	Kansas	44
28	Southeast Mo. St. ■	21
17	Youngstown St. ■	24
20	Illinois St.	30
20	Indiana St.	23
7	Western Ky. ■	31
38	Southern Ill. ■	28
23	Western Ill. ■	28
24	Northern Iowa	25

Nickname: Bears
Colors: Maroon & White
Stadium: Plaster Field
  Capacity: 16,300; Year Built: 1941
AD: Bill Rowe Jr.
SID: Mark Stillwell

SOUTHWEST MINN. ST.
Marshall, MN 56258 II

Coach: Curt Strasheim, Minn. St. Mankato 1984
2002 RESULTS (4-7)
41	Buena Vista	24
23	Augustana (S.D.) ■	29
28	Minn.-Crookston	21
43	Minn.-Morris ■	0
7	Minn.-Duluth ■	38
28	Northern St.	38
0	Bemidji St.	37
14	Winona St. ■	45
13	Wayne St. (Neb.)	16
42	Minn. St. Moorhead ■	35
13	Concordia-St. Paul *	48

Nickname: Mustangs
Colors: Brown & Gold
Stadium: Mattke Field
  Capacity: 5,000; Year Built: 1971
AD: Lloyd "Butch" Raymond
SID: Kelly Loft

SOUTHWEST TEX. ST.
San Marcos, TX 78666-4615 ....I-AA

Coach: Bob DeBesse, Southwest Tex. St. 1982
2002 RESULTS (4-7)
0	Minnesota	42
28	Tex. A&M-Kingsville ■	21
17	Texas Southern	10
49	Southern Utah ■	19
0	Portland St.	16
27	Northwestern St.	40
21	Nicholls St. ■	24
27	Jacksonville St. ■	20
7	McNeese St.	47
21	Stephen F. Austin ■	30
14	Sam Houston St.	21

Nickname: Bobcats
Colors: Maroon & Gold
Stadium: Bobcat
  Capacity: 15,218; Year Built: 1981
AD: Greg LaFleur
SID: Tony Brubaker

SOUTHWESTERN OKLA.
Weatherford, OK 73096 II

Coach: Paul Sharp, Ouachita Baptist 1974
2002 RESULTS (7-4)
39	West Tex. A&M	21
15	Okla. Panhandle ■	0
0	Midwestern St.	6
31	Angelo St. ■	24
24	Central Okla.	21
31	East Central	17
0	Northwestern St.	38
13	Southeastern Okla.	36
13	Northeastern St. ■	10
30	Tarleton St.	33
25	Eastern N.M. ■	14

Nickname: Bulldogs
Colors: Navy Blue & White
Stadium: Milam
  Capacity: 9,000; Year Built: 1932
AD: Cecil Perkins
SID: Michael J. Bond

SPRINGFIELD
Springfield, MA 01109-3797 III

Coach: Michael DeLong, Springfield 1974
2002 RESULTS (8-2)
69	Salve Regina ■	0
26	Merchant Marine	13
64	Coast Guard ■	14
20	Ithaca	44
18	Western Conn. St. ■	15
41	Plymouth St. ■	0
31	WPI	22
41	Norwich	24
55	Union (N.Y.) ■	27
0	Brockport St.	16

Nickname: The Pride
Colors: Maroon & White
Stadium: Benedum Field
  Capacity: 2,500; Year Built: 1971
AD: Cathie Schweitzer
SID: John White

STANFORD
Stanford, CA 94305-2060.........................I-A

Coach: Buddy Teevens, Dartmouth 1979
2002 RESULTS (2-9)
| 27 | Boston College | 34 |
| 63 | San Jose St. ■ | 26 |

24	Arizona St.	.65
7	Notre Dame	.31
11	Washington St. ■	.36
16	Arizona ■	..6
18	UCLA	.28
14	Oregon	.41
17	Southern California ■	.49
21	Oregon St. ■	.31
7	California	.30

Nickname: Cardinal
Colors: Cardinal & White
Stadium: Stanford
  Capacity: 85,500; Year Built: 1921
AD: Edward Leland
SID: Gary Migdol

STEPHEN F. AUSTIN
Nacogdoches, TX 75962 ....I–AA

Coach: Mike Santiago, Southern Utah 1977
2002 RESULTS (6-5)

23	Portland St.	.31
30	Montana St. ■	.13
55	Henderson St. ■	.7
24	Northern Iowa	.31
52	Southern Utah ■	..6
17	Nicholls St.	.14
7	Sam Houston St. ■	.10
36	Jacksonville St.	.28
13	McNeese St. ■	.42
30	Southwest Tex. St.	.21
35	Northwestern St. ■	.42

Nickname: Lumberjacks
Colors: Purple & White
Stadium: Homer Bryce
  Capacity: 14,575; Year Built: 1973
AD: Steve Mc Carty
SID: Rob Meyers

STILLMAN
Tuscaloosa, AL 35403 III

Coach: Theophilus Danzy, Tennessee St. 1958
2002 RESULTS (8-2)

49	Allen ■	.7
33	West Ala. ■	.45
32	Livingstone ■	..6
34	Lane	.20
30	Newberry	.7
20	Miles *	.35
58	Lincoln (Mo.)	.14
35	Texas Southern ■	.28
48	Edward Waters	.14
34	Benedict ■	.27

Nickname: Tigers
Colors: Navy Blue & Old Gold
Stadium: Stillman
  Capacity: 9,000; Year Built: 1999
AD: Richard Cosby
SID: Wesley Peterson

STONEHILL
Easton, MA 02357 II

Coach: Rich Beal, Wesleyan (Conn.) 1985
2002 RESULTS (2-9)

15	American Int'l ■	.20
14	Pace	.20
45	Mount Ida ■	.14
14	Merrimack ■	.17
0	C.W. Post	.43
14	Mass.-Lowell	.35
41	Assumption ■	.7
27	Southern Conn. St.	.48

8	Bryant ■	.9
14	St. Anselm ■	.33
26	Bentley	.41

Nickname: Chieftains
Colors: Purple & White
Stadium: Chieftain
  Capacity: 2,000; Year Built: 1980
AD: Paula Sullivan
SID: Jim Seavey

STONY BROOK
Stony Brook, NY 11794 ....I–AA

Coach: Sam Kornhauser, Missouri Valley 1971
2002 RESULTS (8-2)

34	St. John's (N.Y.) ■	.9
14	Wagner	.17
24	Albany (N.Y.) ■	.20
24	St. Francis (Pa.)	.14
9	Monmouth	.14
24	Sacred Heart ■	.14
14	Siena	.0
24	Central Conn. St.	.10
23	Robert Morris ■	.13
42	Canisius ■	.7

Nickname: Seawolves
Colors: Scarlet & Gray
AD: Sandra R. Weeden
SID: Rob Emmerich

SUL ROSS ST.
Alpine, TX 79832 III

Coach: Jack Waggoner, Sul Ross St. 1962
2002 RESULTS (2-8)

23	Western N.M.	.45
36	Louisiana Col. ■	.44
21	Mississippi Col.	.34
33	Howard Payne ■	.70
0	East Tex. Baptist	.31
6	Hardin-Simmons	.31
0	Mary Hardin-Baylor ■	.31
17	McMurry	.14
25	Austin	.9
21	Texas Lutheran ■	.24

Nickname: Lobos
Colors: Scarlet & Gray
Stadium: Jackson Field
  Capacity: 2,500
AD: Kay Whitley
SID: Steve Lang

SUSQUEHANNA
Selinsgrove, PA 17870-1025......................III

Coach: Steve Briggs, Springfield 1984
2002 RESULTS (5-5)

7	McDaniel ■	.27
3	Lycoming	.50
49	Delaware Valley	.28
40	Albright ■	.35
35	Widener	.52
48	FDU-Florham ■	.23
45	Juniata ■	.17
21	King's (Pa.)	.22
6	Moravian	.23
33	Lebanon Valley	.28

Nickname: Crusaders
Colors: Orange & Maroon
Stadium: Lopardo Stadium
  Capacity: 3,500; Year Built: 2000
AD: Pamela Samuelson
SID: Jim Miller

SYRACUSE
Syracuse, NY 13244...............................I–A

Coach: Paul Pasqualoni, Penn St. 1972
2002 RESULTS (4-8)

21	Brigham Young	.42
22	North Carolina	.30
63	Rhode Island ■	.17
34	Auburn	.37
24	Pittsburgh ■	.48
16	Temple	.17
7	West Virginia	.34
45	Rutgers ■	.14
38	UCF	.35
50	Virginia Tech ■	.42
20	Boston College	.41
7	Miami (Fla.)	.49

Nickname: Orangemen
Colors: Orange
Stadium: Carrier Dome
  Capacity: 49,550; Year Built: 1980
AD: John J. Crouthamel
SID: Sue Cornelius Edson

TARLETON ST.
Stephenville, TX 76401 II

Coach: Todd Whitten, Stephen F. Austin 1987
2002 RESULTS (9-2)

62	Southwestern Aly God ■	.0
53	N.M. Highlands ■	.7
38	Angelo St.	.0
12	Abilene Christian ■	.9
3	Tex. A&M-Kingsville	.16
35	East Central ■	.26
62	Southeastern Okla.	.31
28	Northeastern St.	.29
42	West Tex. A&M	.17
33	Southwestern Okla. ■	.30
34	Central Okla.	.27

Nickname: Texans
Colors: Purple & White
Stadium: Memorial
  Capacity: 7,000; Year Built: 1976
AD: Lonn Reisman
SID: Stan Wagnon

TEMPLE
Philadelphia, PA 19122........................I–A

Coach: Bobby Wallace, Mississippi St. 1976
2002 RESULTS (4-8)

34	Richmond ■	.7
3	Oregon St. ■	.35
21	Miami (Fla.) ■	.44
21	South Carolina	.42
22	Cincinnati ■	.35
17	Syracuse ■	.16
38	Connecticut	.24
10	Virginia Tech	.20
20	West Virginia ■	.46
22	Pittsburgh	.29
20	Rutgers	.17
14	Boston College ■	.36

Nickname: Owls
Colors: Cherry & White
Stadium: Veterans
  Capacity: 66,592; Year Built: 1971
AD: William Bradshaw
SID: Kevin Lorincz

TENNESSEE
Knoxville, TN 37996 ....I–A

Coach: Phillip Fulmer, Tennessee 1972
2002 RESULTS (8-5)

47	Wyoming *	7
26	Middle Tenn. ■	3
13	Florida ■	30
35	Rutgers ■	14
41	Arkansas ■	38
13	Georgia	18
14	Alabama ■	34
18	South Carolina ■	10
3	Miami (Fla.) ■	26
35	Mississippi St.	17
24	Vanderbilt	0
24	Kentucky ■	0
3	Maryland (Peach Bowl) *	30

Nickname: Volunteers
Colors: Orange & White
Stadium: Neyland
    Capacity: 104,079; Year Built: 1921
AD: Douglas A. Dickey
SID: Bud Ford

TENNESSEE ST.
Nashville, TN 37209-1561 ....I–AA

Coach: James Reese, Tennessee St. 1991
2002 RESULTS (2-10)

41	Prairie View ■	8
28	Jackson St. *	31
14	Grambling *	49
24	Florida A&M *	37
25	Southeast Mo. St.	49
21	Alabama A&M	25
26	Tenn.-Martin	8
48	Eastern Ill. ■	54
27	Murray St.	51
14	Tennessee Tech ■	20
20	Eastern Ky. ■	45
20	South Carolina St.	26

Nickname: Tigers
Colors: Blue & White
Stadium: The Coliseum
    Capacity: 67,500; Year Built: 1999
AD: Teresa Phillips
SID: Lee Wilmot

TENNESSEE TECH
Cookeville, TN 38505-0001 ....I–AA

Coach: Mike Hennigan, Tennessee Tech 1973
2002 RESULTS (5-7)

7	Bowling Green	41
6	Iowa St.	58
13	Chattanooga ■	3
62	Valparaiso ■	10
29	Jacksonville St. ■	35
28	Eastern Ill. ■	35
14	Murray St.	31
0	Eastern Ky. ■	19
30	Southeast Mo. St.	36
51	Samford	44
20	Tennessee St.	14
68	Tenn.-Martin ■	7

Nickname: Golden Eagles
Colors: Purple & Gold
Stadium: Tucker
    Capacity: 16,500; Year Built: 1966
AD: David Larimore
SID: Rob Schabert

TENN.-MARTIN
Martin, TN 38238-5021 ....I–AA

Coach: Sam McCorkle, West Ala. 1973
2002 RESULTS (2-10)

19	Southwest Baptist ■	18
6	Tusculum ■	33
42	Ky. Wesleyan ■	14
10	Samford ■	41
10	Arkansas St.	30
3	Eastern Ky.	58
35	Southeast Mo. St. ■	50
8	Tennessee St.	26
0	Gardner-Webb	24
43	Eastern Ill.	55
3	Murray St. ■	42
7	Tennessee Tech	68

Nickname: Skyhawks
Colors: Orange, White & Royal Blue
Stadium: Skyhawk
    Capacity: 7,500; Year Built: 1964
AD: Phil Dane
SID: Joe Lofaro

TEXAS
Austin, TX 78712 ....I–A

Coach: Mack Brown, Florida St. 1974
2002 RESULTS (11-2)

27	North Texas ■	0
52	North Carolina	21
41	Houston ■	11
49	Tulane ■	0
17	Oklahoma St. ■	15
24	Oklahoma *	35
17	Kansas St.	14
21	Iowa St. ■	10
27	Nebraska	24
41	Baylor ■	0
38	Texas Tech	42
50	Texas A&M ■	20
35	LSU (Cotton Bowl)*	20

Nickname: Longhorns
Colors: Burnt Orange & White
Stadium: Royal-Texas Memorial
    Capacity: 80,082; Year Built: 1924
AD: DeLoss Dodds
SID: John Bianco

TEXAS A&M
College Station, TX 77843-1228 ....I–A

Coach: R.C. Slocum, McNeese St. 1967
2002 RESULTS (6-6)

31	La.-Lafayette ■	7
14	Pittsburgh ■	12
3	Virginia Tech ■	13
31	Louisiana Tech ■	3
47	Texas Tech ■	48
41	Baylor	0
47	Kansas	22
31	Nebraska ■	38
23	Oklahoma St.	28
30	Oklahoma ■	26
27	Missouri ■	33
20	Texas	50

Nickname: Aggies
Colors: Maroon & White
Stadium: Kyle Field
    Capacity: 82,600; Year Built: 1927
AD: C. William Byrne Jr.
SID: Alan Cannon

TEX. A&M-COMMERCE
Commerce, TX 75429-3011 II

Coach: Eddie Brister, Austin 1972
2002 RESULTS (2-8)

23	Southern Ark. ■	27
7	East Central ■	21
16	Central Okla.	19
23	Southeastern Okla. ■	3
15	Tex. A&M-Kingsville ■	37
18	West Tex. A&M	17
17	Eastern N.M. ■	27
6	Abilene Christian	47
16	Angelo St. ■	17
20	Midwestern St.	56

Nickname: Lions
Colors: Blue & Gold
Stadium: Memorial
    Capacity: 10,000; Year Built: 1950
AD: Paul D. Peak
SID: Bill Powers

TEX. A&M-KINGSVILLE
Kingsville, TX 78363 II

Coach: Richard Cundiff, Lincoln Mem. 1973
2002 RESULTS (10-3)

21	Southwest Tex. St.	28
65	Prairie View ■	0
16	Tarleton St. ■.	3
9	Midwestern St. ■	6
37	Tex. A&M-Commerce	15
13	Northeastern St.	10
49	West Tex. A&M ■	7
34	Eastern N.M.	37
22	Abilene Christian ■	16
37	Angelo St.	14
58	Neb.-Kearney ■	40
27	UC Davis ■	20
12	Valdosta St.	21

Nickname: Javelinas
Colors: Blue & Gold
Stadium: Javelina
    Capacity: 15,000; Year Built: 1950
AD: Jill Willson
SID: Craig Merriman

TCU
Fort Worth, TX 76129-0001 ....I–A

Coach: Gary Patterson, Kansas St. 1983
2002 RESULTS (10-2)

29	Cincinnati	36
48	Northwestern	24
17	Southern Methodist ■	6
16	North Texas ■	10
34	Houston ■	17
46	Army	27
45	Louisville	31
37	Southern Miss. ■	7
17	Tulane ■	10
28	East Caro.	31
27	Memphis ■	20
17	Colorado St. (Liberty Bowl)*	3

Nickname: Horned Frogs
Colors: Purple & White
Stadium: Amon G. Carter
    Capacity: 44,008; Year Built: 1929
AD: Eric C. Hyman
SID: Steve Fink

TEXAS LUTHERAN
Seguin, TX 78155-5999............................III

Coach: Tom Mueller, Concordia (Neb.) 1968
2002 RESULTS (2-8)
14	Trinity (Tex.) ■	42
7	Hardin-Simmons	56
5	Mary Hardin-Baylor ■	24
21	McMurry	20
21	Austin ■	24
21	East Tex. Baptist ■	28
6	Louisiana Col.	22
16	Mississippi Col. ■	36
10	Howard Payne	49
24	Sul Ross St.	21

Nickname: Bulldogs
Colors: Black & Gold
Stadium: Matador
  Capacity: 9,000; Year Built: 1959
AD: Bill Miller
SID: Tim Clark

TEXAS SOUTHERN
Houston, TX 77004............................I–AA

Coach: William "Bill" Thomas, Tennessee St. 1971
2002 RESULTS (4-7)
44	Prairie View *	14
31	Howard	34
32	Alabama St.	43
10	Southwest Tex. St.	17
14	Alabama A&M ■	21
42	Ark.-Pine Bluff ■	20
28	Stillman	35
34	Mississippi Val. ■	21
28	Grambling ■	42
26	Clark Atlanta ■	3
25	Southern U.	27

Nickname: Tigers
Colors: Maroon & Gray
Stadium: Robertson
  Capacity: 33,000; Year Built: 1965
AD: Alois Blackwell
SID: Irvin Hall

TEXAS TECH
Lubbock, TX 79409-3021 ....I–A

Coach: Mike Leach, Brigham Young 1983
2002 RESULTS (9-5)
21	Ohio St.	45
24	Southern Methodist	14
42	Mississippi ■	28
48	North Carolina St. ■	51
49	New Mexico	0
48	Texas A&M	47
17	Iowa St.	31
52	Missouri ■	38
13	Colorado	37
62	Baylor ■	11
49	Oklahoma St. ■	24
42	Texas ■	38
15	Oklahoma	60
55	Clemson (Tangerine Bowl)*	15

Nickname: Red Raiders
Colors: Scarlet & Black
Stadium: Jones SBC Stadium
  Capacity: 53,000; Year Built: 1947
AD: Gerald L. Myers
SID: Chris Cook

UTEP
El Paso, TX 79968......................................I–A

Coach: Gary Nord, Louisville 1979
2002 RESULTS (2-10)
42	Sacramento St. ■	12
17	Kentucky	77
6	Hawaii ■	31
24	San Jose St.	58
38	Rice ■	35
0	Tulsa	20
3	Boise St. ■	58
17	Nevada	23
35	Southern Methodist ■	42
24	Louisiana Tech *	38
0	Oklahoma	68
14	New Mexico St.	49

Nickname: Miners
Colors: Dark Blue, Orange & Silver
Stadium: Sun Bowl
  Capacity: 51,500; Year Built: 1963
AD: Bob Stull
SID: Jeff Darby

THIEL
Greenville, PA 16125 III

Coach: Jack Leipheimer, Thiel 1974
2002 RESULTS (3-7)
9	Malone	13
26	Geneva	41
37	Bluffton ■	6
17	Wash. & Jeff. ■	21
23	Grove City	3
21	Waynesburg	13
10	Westminster (Pa.) ■	13
9	Bethany (W.Va.)	31
0	Brockport St.	17
14	Alfred	22

Nickname: Tomcats
Colors: Navy Blue & Old Gold
Stadium: Alumni
  Capacity: 1,400; Year Built: 2001
AD: Gloria Pacsi/Joe Schaly
SID: Kevin M. Fenstermacher

THOMAS MORE
Crestview Hills, KY 41017-3495................III

Coach: Dean Paul, Mount Union 1990
2002 RESULTS (7-3)
25	Muskingum	6
3	Hanover	36
26	Shenandoah	7
6	Wittenberg ■	31
28	Franklin ■	20
14	Malone ■	7
43	Chapman	48
56	Maryville (Tenn.) ■	7
24	Westminster (Pa.)	0
30	Mt. St. Joseph ■	7

Nickname: Saints
Colors: Royal Blue, White & Silver
Stadium: Thomas More Stadium
  Capacity: 3,000; Year Built: 1999
AD: Terry Connor
SID: Jason Eichelberger

TIFFIN
Tiffin, OH 44883-2161................................II

Coach: Nathan Cole, Tiffin 1995
2002 RESULTS (2-8)
31	Butler	54
31	St. Francis (Ind.) ■	41
21	Edinboro	35
23	West Va. Wesleyan	48
34	New Haven ■	37
49	Gannon	48
20	Dayton ■	35
13	Morehead St.	24
26	Geneva	35
47	Quincy	44

Nickname: Dragons
Colors: Green & Gold
Stadium: Frost-Kalnow
  Capacity: 4,500
AD: Ian S. Day
SID: Shane O'Donnell

TOLEDO
Toledo, OH 43606 ....I–A

Coach: Tom Amstutz, Toledo 1977
2002 RESULTS (9-5)
44	Cal Poly ■	16
65	Eastern Mich.	13
21	Minnesota	31
38	UNLV ■	21
19	Pittsburgh	37
37	Ball St. ■	17
27	UCF	24
13	Miami (Ohio) ■	27
44	Central Mich. ■	17
42	Western Mich.	21
33	Northern Ill.	30
42	Bowling Green ■	24
45	Marshall	49
25	Boston College (Motor City Bowl)*	51

Nickname: Rockets
Colors: Blue & Gold
Stadium: Glass Bowl
  Capacity: 26,248; Year Built: 1937
AD: Michael E. O'Brien
SID: Paul Helgren

TOWSON
Towson, MD 21252-0001 ....I–AA

Coach: Gordy Combs, Towson 1972
2002 RESULTS (6-5)
49	Morgan St. ■	28
7	Lafayette	23
56	Brown ■	42
42	Holy Cross	10
31	Cornell	34
23	Lehigh ■	19
20	Bucknell ■	14
7	Colgate ■	9
20	Monmouth	0
14	Fordham	42
16	Georgetown ■	24

Nickname: Tigers
Colors: Gold, White & Black
Stadium: Towson University Stadium
  Capacity: 11,198; Year Built: 2002
AD: R. Wayne Edwards
SID: Peter Schlehr

TRINITY (CONN.)
Hartford, CT 06106 III

Coach: Chuck Priore, Albany (N.Y.) 1982
2002 RESULTS (7-1)
17	Colby ■	10
13	Williams	30
39	Hamilton	0
13	Tufts ■	12
35	Bowdoin	14
22	Middlebury ■	20
21	Amherst ■	14
26	Wesleyan (Conn.)	10

Nickname: Bantams
Colors: Blue & Gold
Stadium: Jessee Field
  Capacity: 7,000; Year Built: 1900
AD: Richard J. Hazelton
SID: Dave Kingsley

TRINITY (TEX.)
San Antonio, TX 78212-7200 III

Coach: Steven Mohr, Denison 1976
2002 RESULTS (14-1)
49	Austin ■	0
42	Texas Lutheran	14
66	Pomona-Pitzer ■	14
42	DePauw	33
50	Rose-Hulman ■	15
30	Washington (Mo.)	0
55	Centre	23
59	Rhodes ■	14
55	Sewanee ■	14
38	Millsaps	6
48	Mary Hardin-Baylor ■	38
45	Wash. & Jeff. ■	10
38	Bridgewater (Va.)	32
41	St. John's (Minn.) ■	34
7	Mount Union *	48

Nickname: Tigers
Colors: Maroon & White
Stadium: E.M. Stevens
  Capacity: 3,500; Year Built: 1972
AD: Robert C. King
SID: Justin Parker

TROY ST.
Troy, AL 36082...I–A

Coach: Larry Blakeney, Auburn 1970
2002 RESULTS (4-8)
16	Nebraska	31
26	UAB	27
40	Southern Utah ■	15
12	Iowa St.	42
7	Missouri	44
41	Austin Peay ■	3
8	Mississippi St.	11
7	Marshall	24
21	Fla. Atlantic ■	6
0	Arkansas	23
24	Florida A&M *	7
16	Utah St. ■	19

Nickname: Trojans
Colors: Cardinal & Black
Stadium: Memorial
  Capacity: 30,000; Year Built: 1950
AD: Johnny Williams
SID: Tom Strother

TRUMAN
Kirksville, MO 63501-4221 II

Coach: John Ware, Drake 1981
2002 RESULTS (6-5)
38	Drake	14
69	Quincy ■	14
17	Emporia St.	34
57	Mo.-Rolla	28
44	Southwest Baptist ■	32
21	Washburn ■	26
28	Mo. Southern St.	14
24	Northwest Mo. St. ■	31
35	Pittsburg St. ■	49
3	Central Mo. St.	17
27	Mo. Western St. ■	23

Nickname: Bulldogs
Colors: Purple & White
Stadium: Stokes
  Capacity: 4,000; Year Built: 1962
AD: Jerry Wollmering
SID: Melissa Ware

TUFTS
Medford, MA 02155 III

Coach: Bill Samko, Connecticut 1973
2002 RESULTS (3-5)
20	Hamilton ■	0
27	Bates ■	0
44	Bowdoin	13
12	Trinity (Conn.)	13
28	Williams ■	36
24	Amherst	27
0	Colby ■	9
6	Middlebury	31

Nickname: Jumbos
Colors: Brown & Blue
Stadium: Ellis Oval
  Capacity: 6,000; Year Built: 1923
AD: Bill Gehling
SID: Paul Sweeney

TULANE
New Orleans, LA 70118-0000 ....I–A

Coach: Chris Scelfo, La.-Monroe 1985
2002 RESULTS (8-5)
35	UAB ■	14
10	Army ■	14
35	Cincinnati ■	17
20	East Caro.	24
34	Houston	13
10	Memphis	38
51	Navy ■	30
52	La.-Monroe	9
37	Southern U. ■	19
31	Southern Miss. ■	10
10	TCU	17
0	Texas ■	49
36	Hawaii (Hawaii Bowl)*	28

Nickname: Green Wave
Colors: Olive Green & Sky Blue
Stadium: Superdome
  Capacity: 69,767; Year Built: 1975
AD: Rick Dickson
SID: Donna Turner

TULSA
Tulsa, OK 74104-3189 ....I–A

Coach: Keith Burns, Arkansas 1984
2002 RESULTS (1-11)
0	Oklahoma ■	37
19	Arkansas St.	21
9	Louisiana Tech	53
25	Baylor	37
33	Kansas ■	43
24	Boise St. ■	52
14	Hawaii	37
20	UTEP ■	0
18	Rice ■	33
12	Fresno St.	31
38	San Jose St. ■	49
21	Southern Methodist	24

Nickname: Golden Hurricane
Colors: Old Gold, Royal Blue, Crimson
Stadium: Skelly
  Capacity: 40,385; Year Built: 1930
AD: Judy MacLeod
SID: Don Tomkalski

TUSCULUM
Greeneville, TN 37743 II

Coach: Frankie DeBusk, Furman 1991
2002 RESULTS (7-4)
44	North Greenville ■	0
33	Tenn.-Martin	6
24	Morehouse	17
42	Morehead St. ■	0
49	Wingate	6
7	Presbyterian ■	24
24	Newberry	7
23	Carson-Newman	48
17	Catawba	29
58	Lenoir-Rhyne ■	22
0	Mars Hill	6

Nickname: Pioneers
Colors: Black & Orange
Stadium: Pioneer Field
  Capacity: 3,500; Year Built: 1991
AD: Ed Hoffmeyer
SID: Dom Donnelly

TUSKEGEE
Tuskegee, AL 36088 II

Coach: Rick Comegy, Millersville 1976
2002 RESULTS (10-1)
28	Clark Atlanta	0
36	Winston-Salem	15
7	Benedict ■	0
26	Miles ■	16
46	Lincoln (Mo.) ■	20
20	Albany St. (Ga.) ■	40
19	Morehouse *	14
34	Fort Valley St.	23
11	Lane ■	0
28	Kentucky St.	26
25	Alabama St.	20

Nickname: Golden Tigers
Colors: Crimson & Old Gold
Stadium: Abbott Stadium
  Capacity: 10,000; Year Built: 1925
AD: Rick Comegy
SID: Arnold Houston

UCLA

Los Angeles, CA 90095-1405 ....I–A

Coach: Bob Toledo, San Francisco 1968
2002 RESULTS (8-5)
30	Colorado St. ■	.19
38	Oklahoma St	.24
17	Colorado ■	.31
43	San Diego St. ■	.7
43	Oregon St.	.35
30	Oregon ■	.31
12	California	.17
28	Stanford ■	.18
34	Washington	.24
37	Arizona	.7
21	Southern California ■	.52
27	Washington St. ■	.48
27	New Mexico (Las Vegas Bowl)*	.13

Nickname: Bruins
Colors: Blue & Gold
Stadium: Rose Bowl
  Capacity: 91,500; Year Built: 1922
AD: Daniel G. Guerrero
SID: Marc Dellins

UNION (N.Y.)

Schenectady, NY 12308 III

Coach: John Audino, Notre Dame 1975
2002 RESULTS (5-5)
44	St. Lawrence ■	.13
20	WPI	.7
6	Hobart ■	.14
12	Alfred ■	.20
32	Rensselaer ■	.14
31	Rochester	.21
17	Coast Guard ■	.12
0	Hartwick	.42
13	Muhlenberg	.44
27	Springfield	.55

Nickname: Dutchmen
Colors: Garnet
Stadium: Frank Bailey Field
  Capacity: 2,000; Year Built: 1981
AD: Val Belmonte
SID: George Cuttita

UPPER IOWA

Fayette, IA 52142-1857 III

Coach: Craig Johnston, Coe 1989
2002 RESULTS (2-8)
7	Neb. Wesleyan	.25
6	Coe	.28
0	Central (Iowa) ■	.50
22	Dubuque	.12
7	Wartburg ■	.42
13	Buena Vista	.38
35	Cornell College ■	.28
14	Luther	.33
14	Loras ■	.17
32	Simpson	.45

Nickname: Peacocks
Colors: Columbia Blue & White
Stadium: Eischeid
  Capacity: 3,500; Year Built: 1993
AD: Gil Cloud
SID: Brian Thiessen

URSINUS

Collegeville, PA 19426-1000 III

Coach: Peter Gallagher, West Va. Wesleyan 1993
2002 RESULTS (2-8)
20	Wash. & Jeff.	.63
10	Frank. & Marsh.	.34

14	McDaniel ■	.37
27	Mount Ida	.24
9	Johns Hopkins ■	.27
27	Gettysburg	.29
14	Frostburg St.	.35
0	Muhlenberg ■	.43
56	FDU-Florham ■	.20
6	Dickinson ■	.14

Nickname: Bears
Colors: Red, Old Gold & Black
Stadium: Patterson Field
  Capacity: 2,500; Year Built: 1923
AD: Brian Thomas
SID: Bill Stiles

UTAH

Salt Lake City, UT 84112-9008 ....I–A

Coach: Ron McBride, San Jose St. 1963
2002 RESULTS (5-6)
23	Utah St.	.3
40	Indiana ■	.13
17	Arizona	.23
7	Michigan	.10
26	Air Force ■	.30
17	San Diego St.	.36
20	Colorado St.	.28
35	New Mexico	.42
28	UNLV ■	.17
23	Wyoming	.18
13	Brigham Young ■	.6

Nickname: Utes
Colors: Crimson & White
Stadium: Rice-Eccles
  Capacity: 45,017; Year Built: 1927
AD: Christopher Hill
SID: Liz Abel

UTAH ST.

Logan, UT 84322-7400 ....I–A

Coach: Mick Dennehy, Montana 1973
2002 RESULTS (4-7)
3	Utah	.23
13	Nebraska	.44
38	Idaho St. ■	.33
7	Iowa	.48
38	Boise St.	.63
34	Brigham Young ■	.35
45	New Mexico ■	.44
48	La.-Monroe	.51
32	New Mexico St. ■	.30
19	Troy St.	.16
28	Middle Tenn.	.45

Nickname: Aggies
Colors: Navy Blue & White
Stadium: E.L. Romney
  Capacity: 30,257; Year Built: 1968
AD: Rance Pugmire
SID: Mike Strauss

UTICA

Utica, NY 13502-4892 III

Coach: Mike Kemp, Notre Dame 1975
2002 RESULTS (1-9)
0	Rensselaer	.47
0	Brockport St. ■	.35
12	Hartwick	.27
0	Mass.-Dartmouth	.44
22	Mount Ida	.6
0	Alfred	.10
0	Ithaca ■	.13
12	Cortland St.	.58
20	Shenandoah	.28
13	St. John Fisher ■	.34

Nickname: Pioneers
Colors: Navy Blue & Burnt Orange

Stadium: Charles A. Gaetano
  Capacity: 1,200; Year Built: 2001
AD: James A. Spartano
SID: Ryan Hyland

VALDOSTA ST.

Valdosta, GA 31698 II

Coach: Chris Hatcher, Valdosta St. 1995
2002 RESULTS (14-1)
26	Albany St. (Ga.)	.0
32	Fort Valley St. ■	.6
42	Delta St. ■	.0
31	Southern Ark. ■	.28
51	Ouachita Baptist	.10
45	Ark.-Monticello ■	.17
35	Central Ark.	.11
43	West Ala. ■	.31
45	North Ala.	.28
31	Arkansas Tech ■	.24
19	West Ga.	.3
24	Catawba ■	.7
31	Carson-Newman ■	.28
21	Tex. A&M-Kingsville ■	.12
24	Grand Valley St. *	.31

Nickname: Blazers
Colors: Red & Black
Stadium: Cleveland Field
  Capacity: 11,500; Year Built: 1922
AD: Herb F. Reinhard III
SID: Steve Roberts

VALPARAISO

Valparaiso, IN 46383-6493 ....I–AA

Coach: Tom Horne, Wis.-La Crosse 1976
2002 RESULTS (1-10)
17	Morehead St. ■	.27
28	Campbellsville ■	.57
10	Tennessee Tech	.62
43	St. Joseph's (Ind.)	.54
35	Drake	.52
3	Dayton ■	.52
32	Davidson ■	.49
27	San Diego	.59
22	Butler ■	.52
24	Austin Peay ■	.28
27	Lindenwood ■	.6

Nickname: Crusaders
Colors: Brown & Gold
Stadium: Brown Field
  Capacity: 5,000; Year Built: 1947
AD: William L. Steinbrecher
SID: Bill Rogers

VANDERBILT

Nashville, TN 37212 ....I–A

Coach: Bobby Johnson, Clemson 1973
2002 RESULTS (2-10)
3	Georgia Tech	.45
6	Auburn	.31
38	Mississippi	.45
14	South Carolina ■	.20
20	Middle Tenn. ■	.21
17	Georgia	.48
28	Connecticut ■	.24
8	Alabama ■	.30
17	Florida ■	.21
21	Kentucky	.41
0	Tennessee ■	.24
49	Furman ■	.18

Nickname: Commodores
Colors: Black & Gold
Stadium: Vanderbilt Stadium
  Capacity: 41,600; Year Built: 1981
AD: Todd Turner
SID: Rod Williamson

VILLANOVA
Villanova, PA 19085-1674.....................I–AA

Coach: Andy Talley, Southern Conn. St. 1967
2002 RESULTS (11-4)
37	Rutgers	19
20	Colgate	0
14	Maine ■	21
45	New Hampshire ■	3
30	James Madison ■	26
35	Hofstra ■	7
17	Pennsylvania ■	3
16	Massachusetts	17
41	William & Mary ■	20
13	Northeastern	38
45	Rhode Island ■	3
38	Delaware	34
45	Furman ■	38
24	Fordham ■	10
28	McNeese St.	39

Nickname: Wildcats
Colors: Blue & White
Stadium: Villanova
    Capacity: 12,000; Year Built: 1927
AD: Vincent Nicastro
SID: Dean Kenefick

VIRGINIA
Charlottesville, VA 22904-4821 ....I–A

Coach: Al Groh, Virginia 1967
2002 RESULTS (9-5)
29	Colorado St. ■	35
19	Florida St.	40
34	South Carolina ■	21
48	Akron ■	29
38	Wake Forest	34
27	Duke	22
22	Clemson ■	17
37	North Carolina ■	27
15	Georgia Tech	23
14	Penn St.	35
14	North Carolina St. ■	9
48	Maryland ■	13
9	Virginia Tech	21
48	West Virginia (Continental Tire Bowl)*	22

Nickname: Cavaliers
Colors: Orange & Blue
Stadium: Smith/Harrison/Scott
    Capacity: 61,500; Year Built: 1931
AD: Craig K. Littlepage
SID: Michael Colley

VMI
Lexington, VA 24450-0304 ....I–AA

Coach: Cal McCombs, Citadel 1967
2002 RESULTS (6-6)
27	Charleston So.	24
41	Davidson ■	16
31	William & Mary	62
21	East Tenn. St.	35
7	Ga. Southern	52
27	Wofford ■	16
35	Chattanooga	31
38	Liberty	14
13	Appalachian St.	54
23	Citadel *	21
28	Furman ■	55
23	Western Caro. ■	35

Nickname: Keydets
Colors: Red, White, Yellow
Stadium: Alumni Field
    Capacity: 10,000; Year Built: 1962
AD: Donald T. White
SID: Wade Branner

VIRGINIA ST.
Petersburg, VA 23806-0001 II

Coach: Andrew Faison, Virginia St. 1981
2002 RESULTS (7-3)
21	Norfolk St.	31
23	Johnson Smith ■	19
22	N.C. Central	7
52	St. Augustine's ■	0
28	Livingstone	14
21	Elizabeth City St.	17
10	Fayetteville St.	20
12	Winston-Salem ■	7
21	Virginia Union	14
6	Bowie St.	10

Nickname: Trojans
Colors: Orange & Navy Blue
Stadium: Rogers
    Capacity: 13,500; Year Built: 1950
AD: Derek Carter
SID: Paul T. Williams

VIRGINIA TECH
Blacksburg, VA 24061 ....I–A

Coach: Frank Beamer, Virginia Tech 1969
2002 RESULTS (10-4)
63	Arkansas St. ■	7
26	LSU ■	8
47	Marshall ■	21
13	Texas A&M	3
30	Western Mich.	0
28	Boston College	23
35	Rutgers ■	14
20	Temple ■	10
21	Pittsburgh ■	28
42	Syracuse	50
18	West Virginia ■	21
21	Virginia ■	9
45	Miami (Fla.)	56
20	Air Force (San Francisco Bowl)*	13

Nickname: Hokies
Colors: Burnt Orange & Maroon
Stadium: Lane
    Capacity: 65,115; Year Built: 1965
AD: James C. Weaver
SID: Dave Smith

VIRGINIA UNION
Richmond, VA 23220-1790 II

Coach: Willard Bailey, Norfolk St. 1968
2002 RESULTS (6-4)
29	Elizabeth City St.	0
9	Shepherd	26
32	Livingstone *	13
18	Winston-Salem	15
8	Bowie St.	19
35	Johnson Smith	27
32	Gannon ■	14
24	N.C. Central	7
14	Virginia St. ■	21
18	Fayetteville St. ■	28

Nickname: Panthers
Colors: Steel & Maroon
Stadium: Hovey Field
    Capacity: 10,000
AD: Michael Bailey
SID: Jerry Scarboroug

WABASH
Crawfordsville, IN 47933............................III

Coach: Chris Creighton, Kenyon 1999
2002 RESULTS (12-1)
27	Kalamazoo ■	20
44	Earlham	7
58	Kenyon	0
24	Allegheny ■	14
46	Wittenberg	43
27	Ohio Wesleyan ■	7
51	Oberlin	6
42	Wooster ■	22
54	Hiram	7
35	DePauw ■	7
42	MacMurray ■	7
25	Wittenberg ■	14
16	Mount Union	45

Nickname: Little Giants
Colors: Scarlet
Stadium: Hollett Little Giant
    Capacity: 5,000; Year Built: 1967
AD: Vernon H. Mummert
SID: Brent Harris

WAGNER
Staten Island, NY 10301-4495 ....I–AA

Coach: Walt Hameline, Brockport St. 1975
2002 RESULTS (7-4)
42	La Salle	7
34	Iona	0
17	Stony Brook ■	14
16	Marist	31
14	Albany (N.Y.)	35
29	Robert Morris ■	0
7	St. Francis (Pa.)	0
7	Monmouth ■	6
7	Sacred Heart	10
17	Central Conn. St.	24
42	Jacksonville	7

Nickname: Seahawks
Colors: Green & White
Stadium: Wagner College Stadium
    Capacity: 3,300; Year Built: 1997
AD: Walt Hameline
SID: Bob Balut

WAKE FOREST
Winston-Salem, NC 27109.....................I–A

Coach: Jim Grobe, Virginia 1975
2002 RESULTS (7-6)
41	Northern Ill.	42
27	East Caro. ■	22
13	North Carolina St.	32
24	Purdue	21
34	Virginia ■	38
24	Georgia Tech	21
36	Duke ■	10
23	Clemson	31
31	North Carolina ■	0
21	Florida St. ■	34
30	Navy ■	27
14	Maryland	32
38	Oregon (Seattle Bowl)*	17

Nickname: Demon Deacons
Colors: Old Gold & Black
Stadium: Groves
    Capacity: 31,500; Year Built: 1968
AD: Ronald D. Wellman
SID: Joanna Sparkman

RESULTS

WARTBURG
Waverly, IA 50677-1003 III

Coach: Rick Willis, Cornell College 1988
2002 RESULTS (10-2)

24	Wis.-Oshkosh	20
31	Cornell College ■	14
41	Luther	0
34	Loras ■	3
42	Upper Iowa	7
13	Coe ■	21
14	Central (Iowa)	0
40	Dubuque ■	7
33	Simpson ■	17
58	Buena Vista	3
45	Lake Forest ■	0
15	Linfield	52

Nickname: Knights
Colors: Orange & Black
Stadium: Walston-Hoover
  Capacity: 4,000; Year Built: 2001
AD: Gary Grace
SID: Mark Adkins

WASHBURN
Topeka, KS 66621 II

Coach: Craig Schurig, Colorado Mines 1987
2002 RESULTS (3-8)

17	Wis.-La Crosse ■	31
29	Fort Hays St.	37
14	Pittsburg St. ■	47
28	Mo. Southern St.	52
13	Northwest Mo. St. ■	48
26	Truman	21
21	Central Mo. St.	55
28	Mo. Western St. ■	34
34	Emporia St. ■	21
49	Mo.-Rolla	0
20	Southwest Baptist	26

Nickname: Ichabods
Colors: Yale Blue & White
Stadium: Yager Stadium at Moore Bowl
  Capacity: 7,200; Year Built: 1928
AD: Loren Ferre'
SID: Gene Cassell

WASHINGTON
Seattle, WA 98195 ....I-A

Coach: Keith Gilbertson, Central Wash. 1971
2002 RESULTS (7-6)

29	Michigan	31
34	San Jose St. ■	10
38	Wyoming ■	7
41	Idaho ■	27
27	California ■	34
32	Arizona ■	28
21	Southern California	41
16	Arizona St.	27
24	UCLA ■	34
41	Oregon St. ■	29
42	Oregon	14
29	Washington St.	26
24	Purdue (Sun Bowl)*	34

Nickname: Huskies
Colors: Purple & Gold
Stadium: Husky
  Capacity: 72,500; Year Built: 1920
AD: Barbara A. Hedges
SID: Jim Daves

WASH. & JEFF.
Washington, PA 15301-4801 III

Coach: Mike Sirianni, Mount Union 1993
2002 RESULTS (9-3)

63	Ursinus ■	20
25	Allegheny	28
21	Thiel	17
29	Westminster (Pa.) ■	21
34	Grove City	7
37	Bethany (W.Va.)	28
28	Waynesburg ■	21
14	Hanover	35
71	Apprentice ■	15
7	Buffalo St.	3
24	Chris. Newport ■	10
10	Trinity (Tex.)	45

Nickname: Presidents
Colors: Red & Black
Stadium: Cameron Stadium
  Capacity: 3,500; Year Built: 1958
AD: Rick Creehan
SID: Scott McGuinness

WASH. & LEE
Lexington, VA 24450 III

Coach: Frank Miriello, East Stroudsburg 1967
2002 RESULTS (5-5)

14	Johns Hopkins ■	21
31	Guilford	30
13	Centre	19
7	Randolph-Macon ■	3
20	Catholic	39
13	Hampden-Sydney ■	44
26	Sewanee ■	14
14	Bridgewater (Va.)	44
22	Emory & Henry ■	9
6	Greensboro	0

Nickname: Generals
Colors: Royal Blue & White
Stadium: Wilson Field
  Capacity: 7,000; Year Built: 1930
AD: Michael F. Walsh
SID: Brian Laubscher

WASHINGTON (MO.)
St. Louis, MO 63130-4899 III

Coach: Larry Kindbom, Kalamazoo 1974
2002 RESULTS (6-4)

16	Simpson ■	14
10	MacMurray ■	16
24	Ill. Wesleyan ■	31
24	Rose-Hulman ■	19
27	Rhodes	34
0	Trinity (Tex.) ■	30
38	Chicago	17
49	Case Reserve ■	42
28	Rochester	14
31	Carnegie Mellon ■	17

Nickname: Bears
Colors: Red & Green
Stadium: Francis Field
  Capacity: 3,300; Year Built: 1904
AD: John M. Schael
SID: Chris Mitchell

WASHINGTON ST.
Pullman, WA 99164-1602 ....I-A

Coach: Mike Price, Puget Sound 1969
2002 RESULTS (10-3)

31	Nevada *	7
49	Idaho ■	14
7	Ohio St.	25
45	Montana St. ■	28
48	California	38
30	Southern California ■	27
36	Stanford	11
21	Arizona	13
44	Arizona St. ■	22
32	Oregon ■	21
26	Washington ■	29
48	UCLA	27
14	Oklahoma (Rose Bowl)*	34

Nickname: Cougars
Colors: Crimson & Gray
Stadium: Clarence D. Martin
  Capacity: 37,600; Year Built: 1972
AD: James Sterk
SID: Rod Commons

WAYNE ST. (MICH.)
Detroit, MI 48202-3489 II

Coach: Steve Kazor, Westminster (Utah) 1972
2002 RESULTS (3-8)

0	Northern Iowa	34
21	Findlay	33
14	Grand Valley St. ■	49
36	Ferris St.	21
20	Ashland ■	25
34	Hillsdale	40
34	Michigan Tech	31
46	Northern Mich. ■	49
27	Northwood	41
33	Mercyhurst ■	29
14	Saginaw Valley ■	42

Nickname: Warriors
Colors: Green & Gold
Stadium: Wayne State
  Capacity: 6,000; Year Built: 1968
AD: Robert Fournier
SID: Jeff Weiss

WAYNE ST. (NEB.)
Wayne, NE 68787-1172 II

Coach: Scott Hoffman, Nebraska 1978
2002 RESULTS (3-8)

21	Morningside ■	24
3	Neb.-Kearney	29
20	Northern St. ■	28
2	Bemidji St.	38
17	Winona St.	55
17	Minn.-Crookston	10
16	Minn. St. Moorhead ■	19
17	Concordia-St. Paul	38
16	Southwest St.	13
3	Minn.-Duluth	42
35	Minn.-Morris ■	14

Nickname: Wildcats
Colors: Black & Gold
Stadium: Memorial
  Capacity: 3,500; Year Built: 1931
AD: Todd Barry
SID: Jeremy Phillips

WAYNESBURG
Waynesburg, PA 15370 III

Coach: Jeff Hand, Clarion 1992
2002 RESULTS (5-4)
28	Denison	7
13	Otterbein ■	33
39	Alfred	3
42	Bethany (W.Va.) ■	21
13	Thiel	21
30	Grove City ■	24
21	Wash. & Jeff.	28
24	Frostburg St. ■	21
29	Westminster (Pa.)	33

Nickname: Yellow Jackets
Colors: Orange & Black
Stadium: John F. Wiley
  Capacity: 4,000; Year Built: 1999
AD: Rudy Marisa
SID: Justin Zackal

WEBER ST.
Ogden, UT 84408-2701 ....I-AA

Coach: Jerry Graybeal, Eastern Wash. 1981
2002 RESULTS (3-8)
24	New Mexico	38
44	Western St. (Colo.) ■	0
56	Eastern Ore. ■	7
21	Northern Ariz.	26
7	Montana ■	39
10	Montana St.	44
0	Idaho St.	34
20	Eastern Wash. ■	38
20	Portland St. ■	14
38	Sacramento St.	41
26	Cal Poly	28

Nickname: Wildcats
Colors: Royal Purple & White
Stadium: Stewart
  Capacity: 17,500; Year Built: 1966
AD: John W. Johnson
SID: Brad Larsen

WESLEY
Dover, DE 19901-3875 III

Coach: Mike Drass, Mansfield
2002 RESULTS (5-5)
40	Ferrum ■	16
20	Rowan	22
21	Kean	7
22	Allen ■	13
18	Frostburg St.	37
35	Apprentice ■	0
0	Davidson	31
19	Salisbury	22
42	Chowan	0
6	Brockport St. ■	17

Nickname: Wolverines
Colors: Navy Blue & White
Stadium: Wolverine Stadium
  Capacity: 2,500; Year Built: 1989
AD: Michele Stabley
SID: Steve Azzanesi

WESLEYAN (CONN.)
Middletown, CT 06459............................III

Coach: Frank Hauser, Wesleyan (Conn.) 1979
2002 RESULTS (5-3)
24	Middlebury	21
37	Hamilton ■	10
19	Colby	27
20	Bates	17
14	Amherst ■	13
17	Bowdoin ■	3
7	Williams	41
10	Trinity (Conn.) ■	26

Nickname: Cardinals
Colors: Red & Black
Stadium: Andrus Field
  Capacity: 5,000; Year Built: 1881
AD: John Biddiscombe
SID: Brian Katten

WEST ALA.
Livingston, AL 35470 II

Coach: Randy Pippin, Tennessee Tech 1985
2002 RESULTS (5-6)
41	Belhaven	14
45	Stillman	33
23	Ark.-Monticello ■	27
30	Delta St.	24
10	Harding	38
27	Henderson St. ■	30
35	West Ga. ■	32
31	Valdosta St.	43
0	Arkansas Tech	25
7	Central Ark. ■	47
31	North Ala. ■	24

Nickname: Tigers
Colors: Red, White & Black
Stadium: Tiger
  Capacity: 7,000; Year Built: 1952
AD: Curtis Outlaw
SID: Jason Hughes

WEST CHESTER
West Chester, PA 19383 II

Coach: Rick Daniels, West Chester 1975
2002 RESULTS (5-6)
19	New Haven ■	28
48	Glenville St.	7
10	Delaware	31
27	Shippensburg ■	41
31	Kutztown ■	24
28	Clarion	34
56	Cheyney	0
17	East Stroudsburg ■	14
10	Bloomsburg	23
24	Millersville	31
9	Mansfield ■	7

Nickname: Golden Rams
Colors: Purple & Gold
Stadium: Farrell
  Capacity: 7,500; Year Built: 1970
AD: Edward Matejkovic
SID: Tom DiCamillo

WEST GA.
Carrollton, GA 30118 II

Coach: Gary Otten, Alabama 1988
2002 RESULTS (3-8)
37	Presbyterian ■	35
32	Albany St. (Ga.)	29
21	Southern Ark.	42
44	Henderson St. ■	3
21	Delta St.	27
0	Harding ■	13
32	West Ala.	35
12	Arkansas Tech	14
33	Central Ark. ■	49
26	North Ala.	36
3	Valdosta St. ■	19

Nickname: Braves
Colors: Blue & Red

Stadium: Grisham
  Capacity: 6,500; Year Built: 1966
AD: Edward G. Murphy
SID: Mitch Gray

WEST LIBERTY ST.
West Liberty, WV 26074 II

Coach: Bob Eaton, Glenville St. 1978
2002 RESULTS (6-5)
6	Liberty	35
6	Walsh	27
65	Cheyney ■	19
26	Charleston So. ■	28
48	Concord	0
47	West Va. Wesleyan ■	37
22	Fairmont St.	14
28	West Va. Tech	38
23	Shepherd ■	26
19	Glenville St. ■	7
27	West Virginia St.	3

Nickname: Hilltoppers
Colors: Gold & Black
Stadium: Russek Field
  Capacity: 4,000; Year Built: 1960
AD: James W. Watson
SID: Lynn Ullom

WEST TEX. A&M
Canyon, TX 79016-0999 II

Coach: Ronnie Jones, Northwestern Okla. 1978
2002 RESULTS (0-11)
21	Southwestern Okla. ■	39
0	Northwestern Okla.	43
14	Central Okla.	34
7	Southeastern Okla.	43
0	Angelo St. ■	19
14	Midwestern St.	54
17	Tex. A&M-Commerce ■	18
7	Tex. A&M-Kingsville	49
17	Tarleton St. ■	42
16	Eastern N.M. ■	27
31	Abilene Christian	35

Nickname: Buffaloes
Colors: Maroon & White
Stadium: Kimbrough
  Capacity: 20,000; Year Built: 1959
AD: Ed Harris
SID: Phil Woodall

WEST VIRGINIA
Morgantown, WV 26507 ....I-A

Coach: Rich Rodriguez, West Virginia 1986
2002 RESULTS (9-4)
56	Chattanooga ■	7
17	Wisconsin	34
35	Cincinnati	32
37	East Caro. ■	17
17	Maryland ■	48
40	Rutgers	0
34	Syracuse ■	7
23	Miami (Fla.) ■	40
46	Temple	20
24	Boston College ■	14
21	Virginia Tech	18
24	Pittsburgh	17
22	Virginia (Continental Tire Bowl)*	48

Nickname: Mountaineers
Colors: Old Gold & Blue
Stadium: Mountaineer Field
  Capacity: 63,500; Year Built: 1980
AD: Ed Pastilong
SID: Shelly Poe

WEST VIRGINIA ST.

Institute, WV 25112-1000 II

Coach: Carl Lee, Marshall 1983
2002 RESULTS (1-10)

7	Bowie St. ■	34
24	Cheyney	0
3	Charleston So.	10
21	Gannon ■	35
22	West Va. Wesleyan ■	34
14	West Va. Tech	35
0	Shepherd ■	40
14	Concord ■	44
27	Glenville St.	35
20	Fairmont St.	40
3	West Liberty St. ■	27

Nickname: Yellow Jackets
Colors: Old Gold & Black
Stadium: Lakin Field
  Capacity: 5,000
AD: S. Bryce Casto
SID: Sean McAndrews

WEST VA. TECH

Montgomery, WV 25136 II

Coach: Mike Springston, West Va. Tech 1982
2002 RESULTS (6-5)

6	Nicholls St.	63
56	Cheyney ■	19
3	Western Caro.	47
21	Southern Ill.	76
33	Shepherd ■	14
35	West Virginia St. ■	14
42	Glenville St.	28
38	West Liberty St. ■	28
17	West Va. Wesleyan	28
63	Concord ■	20
17	Fairmont St.	20

Nickname: Golden Bears
Colors: Blue & Gold
Stadium: Martin Field
  Capacity: 2,500
AD: Michael Springston
SID: Russ Melvin Jr.

WEST VA. WESLEYAN

Buckhannon, WV 26201 II

Coach: Bill Struble, West Va. Wesleyan 1976
2002 RESULTS (7-4)

13	Mercyhurst	16
17	Lenoir-Rhyne ■	35
17	Calif. (Pa.)	24
48	Tiffin ■	23
34	West Virginia St.	22
37	West Liberty St.	47
55	Concord ■	21
28	Fairmont St.	7
28	West Va. Tech ■	17
24	Shepherd	14
14	Glenville St. ■	7

Nickname: Bobcats
Colors: Orange & Black
Stadium: Cebe Ross Field
  Capacity: 3,500
AD: George A. Klebez
SID: Andrea Wesp

WESTERN CARO.

Cullowhee, NC 28723...........................I-AA

Coach: Kent Briggs, Western Caro. 1979
2002 RESULTS (5-6)

23	Liberty	3
0	Auburn	56

47	West Va. Tech ■	3
37	Citadel	34
7	East Tenn. St. ■	27
23	Furman	24
24	Ga. Southern ■	41
24	Wofford	31
45	Chattanooga ■	28
35	VMI	23
14	Appalachian St. ■	24

Nickname: Catamounts
Colors: Purple & Gold
Stadium: E.J. Whitmire Stadium/Bob Waters Field
  Capacity: 13,742; Year Built: 1974
AD: Jeff Compher
SID: Mike Cawood

WESTERN CONN. ST.

Danbury, CT 06810...........................III

Coach: John Burrell, Middlebury 1990
2002 RESULTS (7-3)

42	Salve Regina	12
31	New Jersey City ■	3
34	Wm. Paterson	27
47	Plymouth St.	19
15	Springfield	18
38	Coast Guard	14
17	Merchant Marine ■	20
57	WPI ■	19
24	Kean	27
31	Norwich ■	21

Nickname: Colonials
Colors: Dark Blue, Metallic Copper & White
Stadium: Midtown Campus Field
  Capacity: 2,800
AD: Edward Farrington
SID: Scott Ames

WESTERN ILL.

Macomb, IL 61455 ....I-AA

Coach: Don Patterson, Army 1973
2002 RESULTS (11-2)

64	Drake ■	7
14	Western Ky.	0
29	Northern Ill.	26
41	Sam Houston St. ■	13
52	Southern Ill.	54
22	Illinois St.	17
52	Indiana St. ■	21
19	Youngstown St. ■	0
28	Southwest Mo. St.	23
35	Northern Iowa	12
38	Southern Utah	28
48	Eastern Ill. ■	9
28	Western Ky. ■	31

Nickname: Leathernecks
Colors: Purple & Gold
Stadium: Hanson Field
  Capacity: 15,000; Year Built: 1948
AD: Tim Van Alstine
SID: Jason Kaufman

WESTERN KY.

Bowling Green, KY 42101-3576 ....I-AA

Coach: Jack Harbaugh, Bowling Green 1961
2002 RESULTS (12-3)

3	Kansas St.	48
49	Kentucky ■	0
0	Western Ill. ■	14
13	Youngstown St. ■	7
13	McNeese St.	38
31	Northern Iowa	12
56	Florida Int'l ■	7
31	Southwest Mo. St.	7
24	Indiana St. ■	7
9	Illinois St. ■	0

48	Southern Ill.	16
59	Murray St. ■	20
31	Western Ill.	28
31	Ga. Southern	28
34	McNeese St. *	14

Nickname: Hilltoppers
Colors: Red & White
Stadium: L.T. Smith
  Capacity: 17,500; Year Built: 1968
AD: Camden Wood Selig
SID: Brian Fremund

WESTERN MICH.

Kalamazoo, MI 49008 ....I-A

Coach: Gary Darnell, Oklahoma St. 1970
2002 RESULTS (4-8)

48	Indiana St. ■	17
12	Michigan	35
24	Purdue	28
0	Virginia Tech ■	30
31	Buffalo	17
27	UCF ■	31
45	Bowling Green	48
20	Northern Ill. ■	24
7	Ball St.	17
33	Eastern Mich. ■	31
21	Toledo ■	42
35	Central Mich.	10

Nickname: Broncos
Colors: Brown & Gold
Stadium: Waldo
  Capacity: 30,200; Year Built: 1939
AD: Kathy Beauregard
SID: Daniel Jankowski

WESTERN NEW ENG.

Springfield, MA 01119 III

Coach: Gerry Martin, Connecticut 1979
2002 RESULTS (1-8)

14	Mount Ida	32
0	Westfield St. *	30
25	Fitchburg St. ■	26
14	Salve Regina	20
0	MIT ■	10
21	Framingham St.	0
3	Mass.-Dartmouth ■	37
9	Curry ■	27
6	Nichols	48

Nickname: Golden Bears
Colors: Royal Blue & Gold
Stadium: Golden Bear Stadium
  Capacity: 1,500; Year Built: 2002
AD: Michael Theulen
SID: Ken Cerino

WESTERN N.M.

Silver City, NM 88061 II

Coach: Charley Wade, Southwest Mo. St. 1963
2002 RESULTS (2-7)

28	Adams St.	23
20	Eastern N.M.	27
45	Sul Ross St. ■	23
10	Colorado Mines ■	34
10	Northwestern Okla.	55
13	Western Wash.	62
10	Central Wash. ■	36
17	Western Ore.	36
66	Fort Lewis ■	67

Nickname: Mustangs
Colors: Purple & Gold
Stadium: Ben Altamirano Field
  Capacity: 3,000; Year Built: 2001
AD: Scott Woodard
SID: Kent Beatty

WESTERN ORE.
Monmouth, OR 97361-1394.........................II

Coach: Duke Iverson, Whitman 1962
2002 RESULTS (5-5)
22	Mesa St.	19
20	Eastern Wash.	55
20	Carson-Newman	55
20	UC Davis ■	64
34	San Diego	3
36	Western N.M. ■	17
13	Central Wash.	40
34	Southern Ore.	20
17	Western Wash. ■	20
41	Humboldt St. ■	14

Nickname: Wolves
Colors: Crimson Red & White
Stadium: McArthur Field
  Capacity: 3,000
AD: Jon Carey
SID: Russ Blunck

WESTERN ST. (COLO.)
Gunnison, CO 81231 II

Coach: Jeff Zenisek, Central Wash. 1982
2002 RESULTS (5-6)
0	Northern Colo.	31
0	Weber St.	44
20	Neb.-Kearney	3
49	Fort Lewis	24
10	Mesa St. ■	30
58	Okla. Panhandle ■	13
52	N.M. Highlands ■	21
10	Chadron St.	48
20	Adams St.	24
34	Fort Hays St. ■	7
37	Colorado Mines ■	47

Nickname: Mountaineers
Colors: Crimson & Slate
Stadium: Mountaineer Bowl
  Capacity: 4,000; Year Built: 1950
AD: Greg Waggoner
SID: Bobby Heiken

WESTERN WASH.
Bellingham, WA 98225..............................II

Coach: Rob Smith, Washington 1981
2002 RESULTS (6-4)
24	Central Okla.	16
52	Fort Lewis ■	14
31	St. Mary's (Cal.)	28
62	Western N.M. ■	13
19	South Dakota St.	23
28	Central Wash.	35
27	Humboldt St. ■	7
21	New Haven ■	47
20	Western Ore.	17
7	UC Davis ■	14

Nickname: Vikings
Colors: Blue, Silver & White
Stadium: Bellingham Civic
  Capacity: 4,200; Year Built: 1961
AD: Lynda Goodrich
SID: Paul Madison

WESTFIELD ST.
Westfield, MA 01086-1630.........................III

Coach: Steve Marino, Westfield St. 1971
2002 RESULTS (8-3)
30	Western New Eng. *	0
40	Nichols ■	13

19	Fitchburg St.	7
17	Worcester St. ■	13
54	Mass. Maritime ■	0
28	Bridgewater St.	10
42	Framingham St. ■	0
34	Maine Maritime ■	8
12	Curry	13
0	Mass.-Dartmouth *	16
7	Cortland St.	30

Nickname: Owls
Colors: Blue & White
Stadium: Alumni Field
  Capacity: 4,800; Year Built: 1982
AD: Kenneth Magarian
SID: Mickey Curtis

WESTMINSTER (MO.)
Fulton, MO 65251-1299............................III

Coach: John Welty, Benedictine (Ill.) 1977
2002 RESULTS (7-2)
41	Maryville (Tenn.) ■	38
20	Greenville	7
81	Trinity Bible (N.D.) ■	12
0	Maranatha Baptist	10
40	Blackburn	20
9	Rockford ■	7
48	Principia ■	32
49	Crown	27
28	Martin Luther *	32

Nickname: Blue Jays
Colors: Blue & White
Stadium: Priest Field
  Capacity: 1,500; Year Built: 1906
AD: Terry Logue
SID: To be named

WESTMINSTER (PA.)
New Wilmington, PA 16172.........................II

Coach: Jerry Schmitt, Westminster (Pa.) 1983
2002 RESULTS (6-4)
26	Walsh ■	28
24	Mansfield	21
24	Allegheny ■	13
21	Wash. & Jeff.	29
23	Bethany (W.Va.) ■	20
13	Thiel	10
19	Grove City	7
17	Frostburg St. *	24
0	Thomas More	24
33	Waynesburg ■	29

Nickname: Titans
Colors: Navy Blue & White
Stadium: Harold Burry
  Capacity: 4,500; Year Built: 1950
AD: James E. Dafler
SID: Joe Onderko

WHEATON (ILL.)
Wheaton, IL 60187-5593 III

Coach: Mike Swider, Wheaton (Ill.) 1977
2002 RESULTS (10-2)
16	Alma	23
49	Rose-Hulman ■	0
49	Hope	30
62	Elmhurst ■	7
39	Millikin	20
36	Carthage ■	6
35	Ill. Wesleyan	21
41	North Central ■	7
68	North Park	12
38	Augustana (Ill.) ■	14
42	Alma	14
21	Mount Union	42

Nickname: Thunder
Colors: Orange & Blue
Stadium: McCully Field
  Capacity: 5,000; Year Built: 1956
AD: Tony Ladd
SID: Brett Marhanka

WHITTIER
Whittier, CA 90608-0634.........................III

Coach: Bob Owens, La Verne 1971
2002 RESULTS (1-8)
7	Chapman ■	27
6	Azusa Pacific ■	34
20	Occidental	29
6	Menlo	34
14	Claremont-M-S	35
12	Pomona-Pitzer	14
33	La Verne ■	12
0	Redlands ■	21
19	Cal Lutheran ■	37

Nickname: Poets
Colors: Purple & Gold
Stadium: Memorial
  Capacity: 7,000
AD: Wendell P. Jack
SID: Rock Carter

WHITWORTH
Spokane, WA 99251-2501 III

Coach: John Tully, Azusa Pacific 1975
2002 RESULTS (7-3)
27	Bethel (Minn.) ■	26
35	Montana Tech ■	14
30	Menlo	7
28	Western Mont.	31
44	Willamette ■	31
7	Pacific Lutheran ■	21
38	Puget Sound	14
28	Eastern Ore. ■	3
0	Linfield	35
35	Lewis & Clark	7

Nickname: Pirates
Colors: Crimson & Black
Stadium: Pine Bowl
  Capacity: 2,200
AD: Scott Mc Quilkin
SID: Steve Flegel

WIDENER
Chester, PA 19013-5792 III

Coach: Bill Zwann, Delaware 1979
2002 RESULTS (9-1)
29	Wilkes	17
49	Lebanon Valley ■	21
27	Moravian	21
20	Lycoming ■	14
52	Susquehanna ■	35
6	King's (Pa.)	24
44	Delaware Valley	14
53	FDU-Florham ■	7
68	Juniata	33
13	Albright ■	12

Nickname: Pioneers
Colors: Widener Blue & Gold
Stadium: Leslie Quick Jr.
  Capacity: 4,000; Year Built: 1994
AD: William A. Zwaan
SID: Susan Fumagalli

WILKES
Wilkes-Barre, PA 18766..........III

Coach: Frank Sheptock, Bloomsburg 1986
2002 RESULTS (7-4)
31	Montclair St. ■	7
17	Widener ■	29
26	Juniata ■	34
28	FDU-Florham	26
38	Delaware Valley ■	24
26	Albright	22
7	Moravian ■	22
23	Lycoming	14
44	Lebanon Valley ■	6
7	King's (Pa.)	34
33	Merchant Marine ■	7

Nickname: Colonels
Colors: Navy & Gold
Stadium: Ralston Field
Capacity: 4,000; Year Built: 1965
AD: Addy Malatesta
SID: John Seitzinger

WILLAMETTE
Salem, OR 97301-3931 III

Coach: Mark Speckman, Azusa Pacific 1977
2002 RESULTS (6-4)
52	Redlands ■	28
26	Mary Hardin-Baylor	42
28	Humboldt St.	42
52	Menlo ■	30
52	Chapman	21
31	Whitworth	44
63	Puget Sound ■	24
30	Pacific Lutheran	23
21	Lewis & Clark ■	14
20	Linfield	32

Nickname: Bearcats
Colors: Cardinal & Old Gold
Stadium: McCulloch
Capacity: 2,400; Year Built: 1950
AD: Mark Majeski
SID: Cliff Voliva

WILLIAM & MARY
Williamsburg, VA 23187 ....I-AA

Coach: Jimmye Laycock, William & Mary 1970
2002 RESULTS (6-5)
17	Indiana	25
14	Maine	27
62	VMI ■	31
45	Delaware ■	42
16	Hofstra	3
34	New Hampshire	27
30	Northeastern ■	13
20	Villanova	41
44	Rhode Island ■	6
31	James Madison	34
13	Richmond ■	35

Nickname: Tribe
Colors: Green, Gold, Silver
Stadium: Walter Zable
Capacity: 13,279; Year Built: 1935
AD: Edward C. Driscoll Jr.
SID: Pete Clawson

WM. PATERSON
Wayne, NJ 07470-2152 III

Coach: Larry Arico, Lehigh 1992
2002 RESULTS (1-9)
30	Plymouth St. ■	20
27	Western Conn. St. ■	34
7	Kean ■	35
18	Salisbury ■	55
23	TCNJ	24
0	Montclair St.	35
0	Cortland St.	32
7	Rowan	70
19	New Jersey City ■	28
0	McDaniel ■	34

Nickname: Pioneers
Colors: Orange & Black
Stadium: Wightman Field
Capacity: 2,000
AD: Sabrina Grant
SID: Brian Falzarano

WILLIAMS
Williamstown, MA 01267 III

Coach: Dick Farley, Boston U. 1968
2002 RESULTS (7-1)
38	Bowdoin ■	7
30	Trinity (Conn.) ■	13
24	Bates	0
27	Middlebury ■	24
36	Tufts	28
31	Hamilton	6
41	Wesleyan (Conn.) ■	7
35	Amherst	45

Nickname: Ephs
Colors: Purple & Gold
Stadium: Weston Field
Capacity: 10,000; Year Built: 1875
AD: Harry Sheehy
SID: Dick Quinn

WILMINGTON (OHIO)
Wilmington, OH 45177 III

Coach: Mike Wallace, Bowling Green 1968
2002 RESULTS (3-7)
45	Mt. St. Joseph	20
0	John Carroll	40
32	Otterbein ■	14
7	Capital ■	27
13	Muskingum	21
7	Baldwin-Wallace ■	47
31	Marietta	32
0	Ohio Northern ■	31
35	Heidelberg ■	28
0	Mount Union	62

Nickname: Quakers
Colors: Green & White
Stadium: Williams
Capacity: 3,250; Year Built: 1983
AD: Terry A. Rupert
SID: Marty Fuller

WINGATE
Wingate, NC 28174 II

Coach: Joe Reich, Gettysburg 1988
2002 RESULTS (5-6)
24	Johnson Smith	0
26	Gannon ■	36
19	North Greenville	0
36	Concord	31
6	Tusculum ■	49
35	Lenoir-Rhyne	26
7	Catawba	41
24	Mars Hill ■	30
33	Newberry ■	0
10	Presbyterian	26
10	Carson-Newman	35

Nickname: Bulldogs
Colors: Navy Blue & Old Gold
Stadium: Irwin Belk
Capacity: 3,000; Year Built: 1998

AD: Steve Poston
SID: David Sherwood

WINONA ST.
Winona, MN 55987-5838 II

Coach: Tom Sawyer, Winona St. 1983
2002 RESULTS (8-4)
30	Mo. Western St.	31
23	North Dakota St.	34
25	Bemidji St. ■	23
37	Minn. St. Moorhead ■	10
55	Wayne St. (Neb.)	17
52	Minn.-Morris	14
55	Minn.-Crookston ■	7
45	Southwest St.	14
55	Concordia-St. Paul ■	12
42	Northern St.	35
25	Minn.-Duluth	42
27	Emporia St. *	34

Nickname: Warriors
Colors: Purple & White
Stadium: Maxwell
Capacity: 3,500
AD: Larry Holstad
SID: Michael R. Herzberg

WINSTON-SALEM
Winston-Salem, NC 27110 II

Coach: Kermit Blount, Winston-Salem 1980
2002 RESULTS (4-6)
35	Carson-Newman	47
15	Tuskegee ■	36
24	Bowie St.	12
15	Virginia Union ■	18
26	Fayetteville St. ■	30
23	Livingstone ■	6
23	N.C. Central	12
7	Virginia St.	12
49	Johnson Smith	0
14	Elizabeth City St. ■	15

Nickname: Rams
Colors: Scarlet & White
Stadium: Bowman-Gray
Capacity: 18,000; Year Built: 1940
AD: Percy Caldwell
SID: Chris Zona

WISCONSIN
Madison, WI 53711 ....I-A

Coach: Barry Alvarez, Nebraska 1969
2002 RESULTS (8-6)
23	Fresno St. ■	21
27	UNLV	7
34	West Virginia ■	17
24	Northern Ill. ■	21
31	Arizona ■	10
31	Penn St. ■	34
29	Indiana	32
14	Ohio St. ■	19
42	Michigan St.	24
3	Iowa	20
20	Illinois ■	37
14	Michigan	21
49	Minnesota ■	31
31	Colorado (Alamo Bowl)*	28

Nickname: Badgers
Colors: Cardinal & White
Stadium: Camp Randall
Capacity: 76,634; Year Built: 1917
AD: Pat Richter
SID: Justin Doherty

WIS. LUTHERAN
Milwaukee, WI 53226 III

Coach: Dennis Miller, St. Cloud St. 1977
2002 RESULTS (3-7)

45	Lawrence ■	23
21	Rockford	14
7	Concordia (Wis.) ■	24
34	North Park ■	7
26	Adrian	56
10	Albion ■	27
3	Alma	41
27	Hope ■	41
7	Kalamazoo ■	42
29	Olivet	43

Nickname: Warriors
Colors: Forest Green & White
Stadium: Wisconsin Lutheran HS
   Capacity: 1,800; Year Built: 1996
AD: Edward Noon
SID: Cheryl Pasbrig

WIS.-EAU CLAIRE
Eau Claire, WI 54702-4004 III

Coach: Todd Hoffner, Valley City St. 1989
2002 RESULTS (8-2)

28	St. John's (Minn.) ■	21
14	Wis.-Stout	39
12	Wis.-Oshkosh ■	10
40	Bethel (Minn.)	0
34	Wis.-River Falls ■	12
42	Wis.-Platteville	35
30	Wis.-Whitewater ■	23
9	Wis.-La Crosse	26
21	Wis.-Stevens Point ■	16
37	Augsburg	13

Nickname: Blugolds
Colors: Navy Blue & Old Gold
Stadium: Carson Park
   Capacity: 6,500
AD: Tim Petermann
SID: Tim Petermann

WIS.-LA CROSSE
La Crosse, WI 54601 III

Coach: Larry Terry, Wis.-La Crosse 1977
2002 RESULTS (7-4)

31	Washburn	17
31	Ill. Wesleyan ■	35
17	Drake	35
31	Wis.-Stevens Point	25
35	Wis.-Platteville ■	28
34	Wis.-Oshkosh	26
20	Wis.-Whitewater	23
29	Wis.-River Falls ■	16
26	Wis.-Eau Claire ■	9
28	Wis.-Stout	27
18	Coe	21

Nickname: Eagles
Colors: Maroon & Gray
Stadium: Veterans Memorial
   Capacity: 4,349; Year Built: 1924
AD: Joe Baker
SID: David Johnson

WIS.-OSHKOSH
Oshkosh, WI 54901-8617 III

Coach: Phil Meyer, Illinois St. 1979
2002 RESULTS (4-6)

20	Wartburg ■	24
35	Concordia (Wis.)	25

33	Lakeland ■	14
10	Wis.-Eau Claire	12
3	Wis.-Stout	24
26	Wis.-La Crosse ■	34
10	Wis.-Stevens Point	12
35	Wis.-Platteville ■	31
12	Wis.-River Falls ■	13
21	Wis.-Whitewater ■	20

Nickname: Titans
Colors: Black, Gold & White
Stadium: Titan
   Capacity: 9,800; Year Built: 1970
AD: Allen F. Ackerman
SID: Kennan Timm

WIS.-PLATTEVILLE
Platteville, WI 53818-3099 III

Coach: Mike Emendorfer, William Penn 1986
2002 RESULTS (2-7)

17	Olivet Nazarene	6
20	Hope ■	32
34	Wis.-Stout ■	31
28	Wis.-La Crosse	35
33	Wis.-Whitewater ■	36
35	Wis.-Eau Claire ■	42
31	Wis.-Oshkosh	35
28	Wis.-Stevens Point	34
29	Wis.-River Falls ■	34

Nickname: Pioneers
Colors: Blue & Orange
Stadium: Ralph E. Davis Pioneer
   Capacity: 10,000; Year Built: 1972
AD: Mark Molesworth
SID: Paul Erickson

WIS.-RIVER FALLS
River Falls, WI 54022 III

Coach: John O'Grady, Wis.-River Falls 1979
2002 RESULTS (3-7)

7	Chadron St.	15
21	Concordia-St. Paul	26
23	St. Ambrose	14
14	Wis.-Whitewater ■	35
12	Wis.-Eau Claire	34
27	Wis.-Stevens Point ■	38
7	Wis.-Stout ■	21
16	Wis.-La Crosse	29
13	Wis.-Oshkosh ■	12
34	Wis.-Platteville	29

Nickname: Falcons
Colors: Red & White
Stadium: Ramer Field
   Capacity: 4,800; Year Built: 1966
AD: Rick Bowen
SID: Jim Thies

WIS.-STEVENS POINT
Stevens Point, WI 54481 III

Coach: John Miech, Wis.-Stevens Point 1975
2002 RESULTS (6-4)

20	Augustana (Ill.) ■	17
29	Butler	43
25	Wis.-La Crosse ■	31
17	Wis.-Whitewater	14
38	Wis.-River Falls	27
12	Wis.-Oshkosh ■	10
13	Wis.-Stout	37
34	Wis.-Platteville ■	21
16	Wis.-Eau Claire	21
31	Ohio Northern	17

Nickname: Pointers
Colors: Purple & Gold
Stadium: Goerke Field

   Capacity: 4,000; Year Built: 1932
AD: Frank O'Brien
SID: Jim Strick

WIS.-STOUT
Menomonie, WI 54751-0790 III

Coach: Ed Meierkort, Dakota Wesleyan 1981
2002 RESULTS (7-3)

30	Millsaps	6
39	Wis.-Eau Claire ■	14
28	St. Thomas (Minn.)	7
31	Wis.-Platteville	34
24	Wis.-Oshkosh ■	3
27	Concordia-M'head ■	21
21	Wis.-River Falls	7
37	Wis.-Stevens Point ■	13
21	Wis.-Whitewater	24
27	Wis.-La Crosse ■	28

Nickname: Blue Devils
Colors: Navy & White
Stadium: Don & Nona Williams Stadium
   Capacity: 4,500; Year Built: 2001
AD: Steve Terry
SID: Layne Pitt

WIS.-WHITEWATER
Whitewater, WI 53190...............................III

Coach: Bob Berezowitz, Wis.-Whitewater 1967
2002 RESULTS (5-5)

21	Mount Union ■	44
9	Eastern Ore.	7
18	St. John's (Minn.)	42
35	Wis.-River Falls	14
14	Wis.-Stevens Point ■	17
36	Wis.-Platteville	33
23	Wis.-La Crosse ■	20
23	Wis.-Eau Claire	30
24	Wis.-Stout ■	21
20	Wis.-Oshkosh	21

Nickname: Warhawks
Colors: Purple & White
Stadium: Warhawk
   Capacity: 11,000; Year Built: 1970
AD: Shawn Eichorst
SID: Tom Fick

WITTENBERG
Springfield, OH 45504 III

Coach: Joe Fincham, Ohio 1988
2002 RESULTS (10-2)

44	Albion ■	7
37	Urbana ■	10
31	Thomas More	6
53	Denison	7
43	Wabash ■	46
77	Hiram	0
58	Ohio Wesleyan	17
49	Allegheny ■	3
79	Kenyon ■	0
14	Wooster	9
34	Hanover	33
14	Wabash	25

Nickname: Tigers
Colors: Red & White
Stadium: Edwards-Maurer
   Capacity: 3,000; Year Built: 1994
AD: Garnett Purnell
SID: Ryan Maurer

WOFFORD
Spartanburg, SC 29303-3663 ....I–AA

Coach: Mike Ayers, Georgetown (Ky.) 1974
2002 RESULTS (9-3)
48	Newberry ■	0
7	South Carolina St.	6
14	Ga. Southern	7
8	Maryland	37
27	Chattanooga ■	21
16	VMI	27
31	Western Caro. ■	24
26	Appalachian St.	19
27	Citadel ■	14
39	East Tenn. St.	10
21	Furman ■	23
34	Elon	9

Nickname: Terriers
Colors: Old Gold & Black
Stadium: Gibbs
  Capacity: 13,000; Year Built: 1996
AD: Richard Johnson
SID: Mark Cohen

WOOSTER
Wooster, OH 44691 III

Coach: Mike Schmitz, Bowling Green 1974
2002 RESULTS (8-2)
14	Hope	9
38	Bethany (W.Va.) ■	28
27	Case Reserve ■	22
37	Ohio Wesleyan	14
49	Oberlin ■	10
21	Allegheny	7
49	Earlham ■	20
22	Wabash	42
56	Denison	7
9	Wittenberg ■	14

Nickname: Fighting Scots
Colors: Black & Old Gold
Stadium: John P. Papp
  Capacity: 4,500; Year Built: 1915
AD: Robert Malekoff
SID: Hugh Howard

WPI
Worcester, MA 01609.........................III

Coach: Ed Zaloom, Cortland St. 1975
2002 RESULTS (4-6)
25	MIT ■	7
23	Worcester St.	41
7	Union (N.Y.) ■	20
13	Rensselaer	33

3	Merchant Marine ■	20
34	Norwich	17
22	Springfield ■	31
19	Western Conn. St.	57
40	Coast Guard ■	14
23	Plymouth St.	13

Nickname: Engineers
Colors: Crimson & Gray
Stadium: Alumni Field
  Capacity: 2,800; Year Built: 1916
AD: Dana Harmon
SID: Steve Raczynski

WORCESTER ST.
Worcester, MA 01602-2597 III

Coach: Brien Cullen, Worcester St. 1977
2002 RESULTS (9-2)
19	Nichols	12
41	WPI ■	23
35	Salve Regina	6
35	MIT ■	6
13	Westfield St.	17
50	Framingham St. ■	0
41	Mass. Maritime	6
27	Maine Maritime	19
18	Bridgewater St.	0
42	Fitchburg St. ■	19
29	Rensselaer ■	55

Nickname: Lancers
Colors: Royal Blue & Gold
Stadium: John Coughlin Memorial
  Capacity: 2,500; Year Built: 1976
AD: Susan E. Chapman
SID: Paul Brown

WYOMING
Laramie, WY 82071 ....I–A

Coach: Vic Koenning, Kansas St. 1982
2002 RESULTS (2-10)
7	Tennessee *	47
20	Central Mich.	32
13	Boise St. ■	35
7	Washington	38
34	Citadel ■	30
36	Colorado St.	44
20	San Diego St. ■	24
34	Air Force ■	26
48	UNLV	49
31	Brigham Young	35
18	Utah ■	23
20	New Mexico	49

Nickname: Cowboys
Colors: Brown & Wyoming Prairie Gold
Stadium: War Memorial
  Capacity: 33,500; Year Built: 1950

AD: Lee Moon
SID: Kevin McKinney

YALE
New Haven, CT 06520-8216 ....I–AA

Coach: Jack Siedlecki, Union (N.Y.) 1974
2002 RESULTS (6-4)
49	San Diego ■	14
50	Cornell	23
28	Holy Cross ■	19
17	Dartmouth	20
7	Lehigh	14
20	Pennsylvania ■	41
35	Columbia ■	7
31	Brown	27
7	Princeton ■	3
13	Harvard	20

Nickname: Elis, Bulldogs
Colors: Yale Blue & White
Stadium: Yale Bowl
  Capacity: 60,000; Year Built: 1914
AD: Thomas A. Beckett
SID: Steve Conn

YOUNGSTOWN ST.
Youngstown, OH 44555-0001 ....I–AA

Coach: Jon Heacock, Muskingum 1983
2002 RESULTS (7-4)
27	Clarion ■	14
13	McNeese St. ■	28
7	Western Ky.	13
24	Southwest Mo. St.	17
31	Indiana St. ■	16
24	Fla. Atlantic	17
7	Northern Iowa ■	22
0	Western Ill.	19
21	Southern Ill. ■	9
24	Illinois St.	17
37	Samford ■	29

Nickname: Penguins
Colors: Red & White
Stadium: Arnold D. Stambaugh
  Capacity: 20,630; Year Built: 1982
AD: Ron Strollo
SID: Trevor Parks